BY THE SAME AUTHOR

The Penguin Encyclopedia of Popular Music

Wishing on the Moon:
The Life and Times of Billie Holiday

Donald Clarke

The Rise and Fall of Popular Music

VIKING

VIKING

Published by the Penguin Group
Penguin Books Ltd, 27 Wrights Lane, London W8 5TZ, England
Penguin Books USA Inc., 375 Hudson Street, New York, New York 10014, USA
Penguin Books Australia Ltd, Ringwood, Victoria, Australia
Penguin Books Canada Ltd, 10 Alcorn Avenue, Toronto, Ontario, Canada M4V 3B2
Penguin Books (NZ) Ltd, 182–190 Wairau Road, Auckland 10, New Zealand

Penguin Books Ltd, Registered Offices: Harmondsworth, Middlesex, England

First published 1995
1 3 5 7 9 10 8 6 4 2
First edition

Filmset by Datix International Limited, Bungay, Suffolk
Printed in England by Clays Ltd, St Ives plc
Set in 11.5/14 pt Monophoto Garamond

A CIP catalogue record for this book is available from the British Library

ISBN 0–670–83244–8

In memory of

MARTHA JEAN CHATTERTON

A beautiful girl who loved to dance,
she married Dad even though he couldn't.

Contents

Preface

During the 1980s, while I was working for five years on *The Penguin Encyclopedia of Popular Music*, my friends and acquaintances assumed, according to what they knew about music or about me, that I was working on a book either about pop music or about jazz. The word 'popular' had long since been appropriated by the post-Beatles industry that separates adolescents from their pocket money; the first time I heard the term 'pop music' was from the lips of the wonderful Welsh headmistress of a high school in south London in early 1974, and her pronunciation of the phrase left no doubt about what she thought of it.

Opera houses and symphony orchestras are subsidized, and very few classical composers ever make a living solely from their music. But there are no subsidies in popular music; if you want to play jazz piano, rock drums or country guitar, or write hit songs or sing on Broadway or form a pop group, you do not give up your day job until you can make a living at it. Popular music includes all the genres; we could also call it commercial music.

Popular music as a commercial enterprise got under way in Britain in the eighteenth century, when for the first time music publishers sprang up who published nothing but new songs, hoping that people who had heard the songs in the pleasure gardens or music halls would then buy the sheet music. It is now an international business worth many billions of dollars a year, and the number of carriers, from 'personal stereos' and piped-in music in restaurants to booming rock in shops that sell jeans, is such that the stuff is inescapable. Yet there is growing evidence that most of it could disappear overnight and nobody would miss it.

Listening to music on the radio was fun in the 1940s in the USA;

by 1953 it was not much fun any more; in the late 1950s for a while it seemed to be fun again, but nowadays serious music fans – the kind who buy records regularly and hang on to them for decades, building up large collections – no longer bother to listen to the radio much. This is because what most people think of as popular music is dominated by technology and chosen for us by lawyers and accountants who seem to be tone-deaf. The music business has always chased fads and has always been dominated by greed, but nowadays, like the US government, it is out of control and would appear to be heading for the wall. This downward spiral is assisted by the media. The reporting of the rest of the news, including most of the arts news, may seem to have some connection with the real world, but when it comes to popular music, even the so-called quality newspapers devote pages to meaningless fads that follow one another with dizzying speed. Take grunge, for example: grunge is pop-rock played by groups in Seattle, Washington, who dress in rags, hence the name; young people have been enjoying dressing in what look like rags and old bedspreads for decades, yet grunge is all the rage as this is being written. By the time this book is published grunge will probably be forgotten, but a fashion parade has taken the place of musical values.

I have written a survey of the history of popular music because music has always been the most important thing in the world to me; and because the time seemed right for such a survey. Most popular music has always been second-rate or worse, but I listen to recordings of it that have been made over a period of nearly seventy years, made for commercial reasons, speculatively, just like that eighteenth-century English sheet music. It will always be true that the best stuff lasts, but it does seem as though the music industry of today cranks out a higher percentage of inferior product than ever before.

Each nation has popular music of its own; I make no apology for concentrating here on the English-speaking world, and especially the USA, because that is where the economic power of the music business has been developed, until it now sells us an ocean of factory-made music that sounds cheap, yet has to sell in the millions before it breaks even. Today's multi-national record labels are so desperate that they will soon be trying to sell you their latest boondoggles whether you live in Australia, Argentina or Azerbaydzhanskaya.

The British pop music press insists that each new pop/rock act is going to sweep the world and become the new Beatles. From 1984 to 1993, to name just the ones who were cursed with the endorsement of Morrissey, formerly of The Smiths, there were James, The Woodentops, Shop Assistants, Easterhouse, Raymonde, Bradford, The Sundays, Phranc, Suede and Gallon Drunk. None have stayed the course. I don't run out and buy any of this stuff because I know that if the music is any good it will find me, rather than me having to risk my money on something that will almost certainly disappoint.

On the other hand, there may be cause for hope: this book has been underway in fits and jerks since 1987, and the music business is always restless, as though something good has to happen sooner or later. The latest news from the USA in 1994 was that there has been a demographic upturn; the number of young people is apparently growing again, and if this baby-boom will probably not equal that of the 1950s, at least the customers will be there, and maybe some of them will have some taste. And speaking of grunge, just when the fuss over it seemed to be on the wane, the startling international wave of grief at Kurt Cobain's suicide last spring revealed that some people admired his lyrics as much as his dress sense. This is a good sign, and my spies in the USA tell me that some of the acts coming along there are putting across some interesting things in the lyrical line. I will not name any of the up-and-comers I am mildly curious about, for fear that my imprimatur will be a curse; but I am going to keep listening.

The first people I have to thank are the authors of all the books on my shelves in which I have gleefully wallowed, in some cases for decades; they have guided and informed me. (There is a bibliography at the back of this book which will be useful as a guide to further reading.)

Chris Parker first commissioned the present volume, when he was editor of the music book list at another publisher; then Jon Riley at Viking took it on. Clare Alexander, Judith Flanders, Andrew Cameron and many others at Viking have been extraordinarily helpful and supportive, as always. Cal Morgan at St Martin's Press in New York liked the concept of the book so much that at first he wanted it to be *longer*, which was impossible. Chris, Jon and Cal made valuable suggestions and criticisms; then when it came to obtaining permissions to print the song lyrics, Jerry Leiber and Mike Stoller did the same. (None of the other publishers cared what we said, as long as we paid them.) David Duguid read the manuscript for Viking and did his usual wonderful job of querying this and that. Meanwhile, Max Harrison, one of the best writers and most rigorous critics of jazz and classical music I know of, had agreed to read the first draft of the manuscript, even though he doesn't really agree with one of its premises, that jazz has been, for most of its history, commercial music. Max gave that first draft a line-by-line going over; and with all this help, a publishable book seems to have resulted.

A reader at a certain publisher in New York also read the manuscript, and pronounced me an amateur, a nobody, a bad writer, an anti-Semite and a gay-basher, and complained that I loathed Elvis Presley. I was buying Presley records before he was born, but I am grateful to him, too, for reminding me that whether you like the book or not, I alone am responsible.

September 1994
Norfolk, England

Acknowledgements

The publishers would like to express their thanks to the music publishers who have given their permission to reprint the following lyrics:

'Some of These Days' (Brooks): by permission of Francis Day and Hunter Ltd, London WC2H 0EA, and J. Albert & Son Pty Ltd. Copyright © 1910, Will Rossiter Pub. Co., USA.

'After You've Gone' (Layton and Creamer): by permission of Francis Day and Hunter Ltd, London WC2H 0EA, and Hal Leonard Corporation. Copyright © 1918 (renewed) Edwin Morris & Company, a division of MPL Communications, Inc. All rights reserved.

'I Get a Kick Out of You' (Porter), 'I Wish I Were In Love Again' (Hart), 'Settin' the Woods on Fire' (Rose), 'Stormy Monday Blues' (Walker), 'Blue Monday' (Domino and Bartholomew), 'Desperadoes Waiting for a Train' (Clark), 'Express Yourself' (Wright): by permission of International Music Publications Limited. Copyright © Warner Chappell Music Ltd, London W1Y 3FA.

'Cool Drink of Water Blues' (Johnson): by permission of Peermusic (UK) Ltd, London WC1. Copyright © 1929 Peer International Corporation, USA.

'I Won't be Home No More' (Hank Williams, Sr): copyright © 1952 (renewed) Hiriam Music & Acuff-Rose Music, Inc. All rights on behalf of Hiriam Music administered by Rightsong Music, Inc. All rights reserved. Used by permission.

'Low Down Blues' (Hank Williams, Sr): by permission of Acuff-Rose Music, Inc. Copyright © 1954, renewed 1982. All rights reserved.

'It Wasn't God Who Made Honky Tonk Angels' (Miller): by permission of Peermusic (UK) Ltd, London WC1. Copyright © 1952 Peer International Corporation, USA.

'Well, You Needn't' (Monk): by permission of Mautoglade Music Ltd. Copyright © 1961 Regent Music Corporation.

'Long Tall Sally' (Johnson, Blackwell and Penniman): by permission of Peermusic (UK) Ltd, London WC1. Copyright © 1956 Venice Music Inc., USA.

'Tutti Frutti' (Penniman, La Bostrie and Lubin): by permission of Music Sales Ltd. Copyright © 1955 Venice Music Inc., USA. ATV Music for the UK, Eire, British Commonwealth (excluding Canada and Australasia) and the Continent of Europe. All rights reserved. International copyright secured.

'Summertime Blues' (Capehart and Cochran): by permission of Campbell Connelly & Co. Ltd and International Music Publications Ltd.

'Shake, Rattle and Roll' (Calhoun): by permission of Campbell Connelly & Co. Ltd and International Music Publications Ltd. Copyright © Warner Chappell Music Ltd, London W1Y 3FA.

'Movie Magg' (Perkins), 'Blue Suede Shoes' (Perkins), 'Honey Don't' (Perkins): by kind permission of Carlin Music Corporation, UK administrator.

'Yakety Yak' (Jerry Leiber and Mike Stoller): by kind permission of Carlin Music Corporation, UK administrator, and Warner Chappell Music, Inc. Copyright © 1958 (renewed) Jerry Leiber Music, Mike Stoller Music, and Chappell & Co. All rights reserved. Used by permission.

'Too Much Monkey Business' (Berry): by permission of Mautoglade Music Ltd. Copyright © 1956 Arc Music Corp.

'Firewater' (Hancock): copyright © 1991 Rainlight Music (ASCAP)/administered by Bug Music. All rights reserved. Used by permission.

'Senor *Aka* Tales of Yankee Power' (Dylan): copyright © 1978 by Special Rider Music (ASCAP). Used by permission.

Untitled (2 Live Crew): by permission of MCA Music Limited.

Every effort has been made to contact all copyright holders. The publishers will be pleased to make good in future editions any errors or omissions brought to our attention.

1

The Origins of Popular Music

Once upon a time there were only two kinds of music in Europe: religious music and secular music.

The earliest polyphonic music, from around 900 AD, was probably inspired by the music of Byzantium and the Middle East. Polyphonic folk-singing survives today in eastern Europe, but the music of the church was of great importance, for it encouraged technical development: in the early sixteenth century two organs were installed in the two apses of St Mark's Cathedral in Venice, which led to the use of separate choruses of singers, and increasing harmonic experimentation by the composers. As well as music for the Mass, written by some of the greatest composers in history, we have less formal music such as carols, mostly written for religious festivals. The word comes from the medieval French *carole*, a round dance; many early Christmas carols are still familiar to us today.

In the Middle Ages much secular music was dance music, which was played at court and in the halls of the aristocracy. The best tunes were also popular in the street; a good tune would soon have words fitted to it, and a clever rhyme or broadside would find a tune. A common store of tunes and ideas crossed back and forth across class barriers, and there was little distinction between 'popular' and 'serious' music.

In all times and places there was also folksong, invented and performed by the less privileged classes: lullabies, love songs, work songs, story songs and so on. By the fourteenth century the ballad (from the Latin *ballare*, 'to dance') had become a narrative solo song, often of unknown origin. The minstrel was originally an itinerant singer of such songs. They were usually story songs, but some were written in praise of powerful patrons, a practice carried on today in African music.

For over four hundred years, until the introduction in the mid nineteenth century of penny newspapers and affordable books, the English-speaking masses received much of their education and entertainment from street literature. One of the earliest surviving broadsides, from 1423, was about St Christopher and was illustrated by a woodcut. The broadside was so called because it consisted of a broad piece of paper printed on one side only, often with a combination of verse, prose and an illustration. (The broadsheet was a large piece of paper printed on both sides, which could be folded several times to make a pamphlet; hence today's 'broadsheet' newspaper.)

An uncut and unstitched pamphlet was known as a chapbook, or cheap book (perhaps from the Anglo-Saxon *ceap*, meaning 'trade'), and was sold by pedlars of needles, buttons and other household goods. The pamphlets preserved the romantic and traditional stories which were ignored by publishing in the days when books were only for the rich. A properly finished pamphlet, far too expensive for the common people, became one of the main forums for political discussion, especially in the eighteenth century.

News of royal proclamations, grisly crimes and gossip were circulated by the broadside; those who could not read could hear others read them, and the pedlars who sold them would cry them aloud in the streets. The battle of Flodden in 1513, when a Scottish king was killed, was described by John Skelton in a broadside, which included a woodcut; a fragment of this was discovered in the late nineteenth century in the binding of a book which had been sent to London generations before for repair. It is the earliest-known example of English journalism. Street literature was of enormous importance because of the influence it had on the masses, but it is usually ignored by historians in favour of the legitimate press. What concerns us here, however, is the broadside ballad.

Broadside verses were not printed with music; the pedlars would sing the songs as they hawked them, and it was assumed that the customer in the street would know a tune that would fit, or make one up. If notation was included, it was a meaningless decoration intended to impress the customer, who could not read music anyway. All broadsides were supposed to be registered with the authorities; about three thousand ballads were so recorded between 1557 and

1709, but several times that number were probably printed illegally. The broadside ballads recycled folksongs which were already well known, and carried on the minstrel tradition. But the genre was also a kind of musical journalism, for it contained social and political satire, well disguised in the days when one could lose one's head for offending the powerful.

Familiar nursery rhymes began in this way. Zealots wrote and rewrote verses for political and religious reasons, so that none of the historical sources can be pinned down conclusively. Jack Sprat and his wife may have been Charles I and his French queen Henrietta: she was fond of the spoils of war (the fat), while Charles dissolved Parliament because it would not grant supplies for his Spanish war, thus 'licking the platter clean'. In a rhyme from the seventeenth century 'Mary, Mary, quite contrary' has 'silver bells and cockle shells and pretty maids all in a row' in her garden. This is said to be either about Ann, Lady Roos, an heiress who taunted her husband with 'cuckolds all in a row', or about Mary, Queen of Scots, a brave and headstrong woman whose four ladies-in-waiting, all also called Mary, were the pretty maids. Both Protestants and Catholics claim it as a lament for their respective religions at the time of 'Bloody Mary', eldest daughter of Henry VIII, who caused much blood to be shed in the name of God.

'Hey Diddle Diddle' is said to have been a jolly description of the court of Elizabeth I, Henry's other daughter: the cat who loved to dance to the fiddle was the 'Virgin Queen' herself; the plate was the young man who brought Elizabeth her dinner, and the spoon the girl who tasted it, in case it was poisoned; the cow jumping over the moon referred to the entertainments that were organized at court; and the lap-dog who found it all so funny was one of the Queen's would-be suitors. But the rhyme is also said to be about Catherine of Aragon ('Catherine la Fidèle'), Henry's long-suffering first wife and Mary's mother.

Best of all is the story of Little Jack Horner. The name Jack was commonly used of a knave or a rogue, and there were already stories about finding things in pies. In 1539 Richard Whiting was abbot of Glastonbury Cathedral, a wealthy establishment, and to keep the peace he allegedly sent Henry VIII a pie containing the deeds to several manor houses. On the way to London, Whiting's steward, called Horner, pulled out a plum – the deed to the manor of Mells. Whatever the details, Horner testified against Whiting at a trial, helping Henry to grab all the property, and the Horners still lived at Mells four hundred years later. The manor may also be 'The House That Jack Built'.

The printers and pedlars of broadsides had a thriving industry, but a modern English-language music business waited until the language itself was established. English had been made up of Angle, Saxon, German and other elements; its development was both sidetracked and influenced by the Norman victory of William the Conqueror in 1066, after which the affairs of the government were conducted in French, while Latin remained the language of international business. Then an English composer became one of the greatest of his time, a profound influence on Renaissance music: Italians wrote of the 'new art which originated with the English under the leadership of Dunstable'. Among other things, John Dunstable introduced the declamatory motet, in which the rhythm of the music is determined by the rhythm of the words. Unfortunately, much of his music was lost in the wars of the period.

The earliest English song extant is the round 'Summer is icumen in' (*c*. 1280). Not until 1363 was Parliament opened with a speech in the vernacular, and not until 1530 was a book of songs in English published, *Twenty Songs*. It included compositions by William Cornyshe, who had been master of the boys in the Chapel Royal of Henry VIII, and John Taverner. Henry's dissolution of the Catholic Church in England encouraged religious music in English; it was very different from the broadside ballads of the people, but the strands of English music then began slowly to come together.

Nearly all of Shakespeare's plays used music and dancing; Elizabethan England was a place where musical instruments were available in shops, in case a passing customer wanted to strike up a tune; and the 'Virgin Queen' herself enjoyed secular music. From 1592 to 1594, when the theatres were closed because of the plague, the players took the plays to the Continent, songs and all. The music of William Byrd and John Dowland was popular in the most complete sense of the word. Dowland, in particular, also a great lutenist in an age that loved the lute, was famous in many countries. His tunes were played by people who had never heard of him and assumed they were folksongs. In 1602 a German visitor to Blackfriars wrote about the excellent music that was played for an hour before a play began, and impresario John Banister produced public concerts in London a hundred years before they became common in Vienna.

As the sophistication of the musical craft developed through the Renaissance, the secular dance rhythms were used in instrumental suites, and opera came into being, eventually becoming opulent entertainment for the upper classes. The early operas were modelled after what Greek theatrical music was thought to have been, and included dances. Monteverdi's *Orfeo*, first performed in 1607 at Mantua, is considered to be the first fully developed opera, astonishing with its fulsome and varied sound (a full choir of trombones, for example), but it was still tied to the conventions of court entertainment; his *L'incoronazione di Poppea* (Venice, 1642) was on a much larger scale, and may have been designed for people who bought tickets.

Instrumental suites and opera overtures evolved until in the eighteenth century symphonies and string quartets were written, while the technique of the virtuoso soloist was celebrated in the concerto. When these forms emerged during the glorious flowering of Viennese music, they were based on sonata form, the rules governing their composition corresponding to what was regarded as the logical orderliness of philosophy and the arts in classical Greece: hence 'classical' music. The masterpieces created for the concert hall and the opera house were great in number and are still loved around the world, but popular music in the sense of the term as we use it today then had to be invented, at least for English-speaking people. Other nations stayed closer in many ways to their musical traditions: in Italy the best tunes from the operas were whistled by barrow boys in the street, while German composers never hesitated to use folk tunes in their compositions, or wrote tunes which sounded as though they had always existed. The great nineteenth-century *Lieder* of Schubert, Schumann, Brahms, Mahler, Wolf and others carried more 'cultural' value than art song in English-speaking countries: they were much more accessible and more widely popular.

It was no doubt England's already highly developed class-consciousness that led to a greater gulf between serious and popular music. England was called 'the land without music', which seems absurd; yet it is true that the greatest 'English' composers of the eighteenth century were German immigrants, George Frideric Handel and Johann Christian Bach, and the audience for their music became more and more upper class. The English had beheaded Charles I in 1649, which shocked the world; they told themselves that they did it in order to restore the historical purity of their politics, but they were slowly finding political freedom. As they were unwilling to allow Italian popes and French kings to tell them what to do, so their composers did not seem to care much for strict Continental rules governing composition. When the rules began to be broken in the twentieth century, English composers of formal music again attracted worldwide attention; but in the eighteenth and nineteenth centuries English-speaking upper-class audiences listened to foreign music, while increasing economic freedom allowed the lower orders to do as they wished. The emerging middle classes conquered India, for example, by accident, beginning with a few trading posts; and they invented popular music.

The popular song may be defined as a song written for a single voice or a small vocal group, accompanied by a single chord-playing instrument or a small ensemble, usually first performed in some sort of public entertainment and afterwards published in the form of sheet music (or mechanically reproduced in the twentieth century); it is written for profit, for amateur listeners and performers. What we call popular music (or commercial music) began in the eighteenth century in the pleasure gardens in what are now the suburbs of London. But the seeds of it can certainly be found earlier, and one nominee for first popular songwriter is Henry Purcell.

Any country that could produce a Purcell was most emphatically not a 'land without music', but in his short life he wrote only one full-blown operatic masterpiece, *Dido and Aeneas* (1689). Its songs were sold in sheet music in the theatre between the acts. Most of his theatrical work was incidental music, ideally suited to commercial exploitation in the form of excerpts. For example, 'What Shall I Do to Show' was written (with words by Thomas Betterton) for the 'semi-opera' *The History of Dioclesian* (1690):

> What shall I do to show how much I love her?
> How many millions of sighs will suffice?
> That which wins others' hearts never can move her,
> Those common methods of love she'll despise.

It has a memorable and wistful tune, it is singable and its subject is still the songwriters' favourite: love, preferably unrequited. It would be surprising if this song had not been sung in many a drawing room to simple accompaniment, and perhaps by frustrated swains in their baths. It is as good a candidate as any for the title of first popular song.

Not that songwriters made any money from the sale of their music. Publishing of all kinds had been state monopolies, granted to favourite individuals, since the earliest printing in England, partly for reasons of censorship. Early publishers began as printers, and copyright law evolved as courts had to adjudicate between them. They squabbled among themselves for the right to exploit the authors, who usually received nothing at all, except perhaps a flat fee for the first sale of their work. Composers of hit songs depended upon this success to generate more work; producers of musical entertainments had occasional benefit nights, so that the composers could feed their families, and most of them died poor, no matter how successful their music. The most popular composers were the most frequently robbed. The publishers John May and John Hedgebutt blithely explained to Henry Purcell, when they published the complete music and libretto of *The Indian Queen* (1695):

Indeed we well know your innate modesty to be such, as not to be easily prevail'd upon to set anything in print, much less to Patronise your own works . . . But in regard that any one might print an imperfect copy of these admirable songs, or publish them in the nature of a Common Ballad, we were so much the more emboldened to make this attempt, even without acquainting you of our Design.

In other words, we will steal from you more elegantly than the others. This was not against the law, and there was nothing composers could do about it.

Music publishing had begun in Venice in 1501. One of the first modern English music publishers was John Playford, born in Norwich in 1623, son of a bookseller. Norwich had always been an important centre of English music; it was home of one of the oldest guilds of professional musicians, and Playford was probably also influenced by the music at Norwich Cathedral. He was apprenticed to a bookseller in London, and got into trouble with the Puritans for publishing a pamphlet on the death of Charles I. But he soon concentrated on music, and his collections of old tunes were best-sellers. *The English Dancing Master, or Plain and Easy Rules for the Dancing of Country Dances, with the Tune to Each Dance* was initially aimed at the social pretensions of Playford's customers, but went through eighteen editions between 1649 and 1728. Having expanded to a collection of nine hundred tunes in three volumes, it was known as *The Dancing Master* and was used in the American colonies, where the dancing would have been influenced by the fiddle and banjo playing of black slaves: thus Playford must have had a more or less direct effect on American music.

Playford's son sold the business in the early years of the eighteenth century, at the very time when there was a rising demand for sheet music of the latest theatre songs to be printed overnight. Music publishing was ready for the pleasure gardens, where the commercial possibilities of popular music were first fully exploited. In the seventeenth century Londoners such as Samuel Pepys and John Evelyn wrote in their diaries that they enjoyed admission to privately owned gardens; these gardens increased in number and in size, many of them beginning as spas. London had numerous springs, where the water was said to be good for this or that ailment or condition, and entertainment sprang up to keep the customers happy. Sadler's Wells, which became one of the most famous small opera houses in the world, began as a spa; a pub called the London Spa only a few hundred yards away marks the site of another.

It is curious that England thinks of itself as a law-abiding country: it has been so only for relatively short periods in the present century. Getting to and from the pleasure gardens could be dangerous, for foot-pads and thugs were common, and only the rich had carriages. On one occasion in 1757 the management of Sadler's Wells advertised that a horse patrol would be provided by Mr Fielding (a blind magistrate and relative of the novelist Henry Fielding) to protect the gentry; the next year armed patrols were stationed between Grosvenor Square and the Wells. Link-boys were employed to light the way home for revellers on foot, and the theatre management often announced at the foot of their playbills whether or not there would be moonlight on the night, allowing visitors to get home more safely.

Nevertheless, the spas and gardens were enormously popular. There were spas at Islington, Clerkenwell, Tunbridge Wells and many other places, and music was offered as early as 1697 in Lambeth and 1701 in Hampstead. John Evelyn had written about the 'pretty contrived plantation' of the New Spring Gardens at Vauxhall, near Lambeth Palace, in 1661. Vauxhall's spring was not of much account; it became the most important of the pleasure gardens because it was one of the biggest, and also the boskiest.

In most of the gardens promenades and pathways were arranged on a simple grid pattern. The grid at Ranelagh in Chelsea was merely a setting for a rotunda or 'Amphitheatrical Building' by the architect William Jones, where the fashionable walked endlessly around in a circle: 'Nobody goes anywhere else,' wrote Horace Walpole in 1742, and Mozart performed there as a child in 1764. But Vauxhall also had thickly wooded areas with larks and nightingales ('feathered minstrels'), where the illusion of Arcadia could be complete, and where no doubt many pairs of lovers sported over the decades. There was then only one bridge over the Thames, and a rehearsal of Handel's *Music for the Royal Fireworks* at Vauxhall in 1749 caused a massive traffic jam.

Jonathan Tyers had leased Vauxhall in 1728. He was only twenty-one years old; not much is known of his background, but he had money to invest. When he reopened the garden in 1732, it had a concert hall, an organ and a famous statue of Handel by Louis François Roubiliac (which is remarkably informal for the period and is now in London's Victoria and Albert Museum). William Hogarth is thought to have persuaded Tyers to decorate the supper-boxes around the Grove with large paintings by members of his academy;

this was priceless publicity, and provided a captive audience for Hogarth and his followers.

In 1758 Tyers purchased the gardens outright, and built an 'orchestra' (hall) in the Gothic style. The orchestra was the last substantial addition to the gardens, though Robert Adam wrote that Tyers had talked about commissioning a Temple of Venus. Tyers had already enlarged his orchestra (that is, the band), and hired Thomas Augustine Arne to write music for it.

While the Purcell song quoted above is not especially florid, in general the ornate Italian model strongly influenced songwriting, until Arne. A talented musical journeyman, he wrote 'Rule, Britannia' to words by James Thomson for the finale of a masque called *Alfred* (1740); his London-style instrumental pieces are still found in compilations of baroque music, and are full of good tunes. His songs were particularly innovative. Anyone who could pay the price of admission could get in at Vauxhall, and Arne had to write songs for a classless audience; they had to make their impression on the musically sophisticated and the ignorant alike at the first hearing. Often drawing on rural imagery of stylized shepherds importuning resistant maidens, the songs were tonal and diatonic, and relied mostly on common chords; they were strophic in structure, so that listeners heard recurring melodic fragments. (In other words, they were repetitious.) The excellent seventh edition of *Baker's Biographical Dictionary of Musicians* (edited by Nicolas Slonimsky) does not mention Arne's tenure at Vauxhall. Modern critics of classical music may not think much of Arne's songs, but in the function he was performing he was a predecessor of Irving Berlin.

Arne's wife Cecilia was one of many popular London singers of the day to perform at Vauxhall. According to Charles Dibdin, in his five-volume *A Complete History of the London Stage* (1800), 'Mrs Arne was deliciously captivating. She knew nothing in singing or in nature but sweetness and simplicity.' Another popular vocalist was Joe Vernon, who 'had no voice ... It is impossible to imagine that he could have arrived to any degree of reputation had he not been favoured by nature with strong conception, quick sensibility, and a correct taste.' That is still a good description of a pop singer.

Dibdin would have known what he was talking about: in his long career as actor, vocalist, playwright and impresario he worked on the Continent and even in the Orient as well as England, and wrote about nine hundred songs, of which as many as two hundred were known all over the English-speaking world. (The most successful were about the hard lot of the sailor, such as 'Poor Jack'.) Since there were no composer's royalties, if it had not been for a benefit dinner in 1810 and later a government pension, Dibdin might have starved to death. Yet thousands of popular songs were published in the second half of the eighteenth century, and sheet music sales supported several publishers. (Bookseller George Walker opened a music shop in London in the 1790s, advertising 'half-price' sheet music: he used tinted paper, claimed higher production costs and printed a price on the music which was twice the half-price.)

Also important were songs from ballad and comic operas, which bore little resemblance to opera of the Italian kind. The earliest and best example is *The Beggar's Opera*, with libretto by John Gay and music by Johann Christoph Pepusch (born in Berlin), first performed in 1728. This dispensed with recitative and used spoken dialogue, for which the beggar apologizes at the outset: 'I hope I may be forgiven, that I have not made my Opera throughout unnatural, like those in vogue.' Pepusch's music borrowed some of the tunes from already familiar street ballads, and also included Purcell's 'What Shall I Do', quoted above. The characters were not the usual operatic noblemen and pretty peasant girls, but pickpockets, prostitutes and lawyers, no doubt resembling some members of the audiences in the pleasure gardens. *The Beggar's Opera* spawned many imitations and was a spectacular success in all the principal towns in England. Dibdin quotes Jonathan Swift's praise: it had 'not wit, nor humour, but something better than either'.

At Vauxhall, along with the promenading and the enjoyment of the fresh air, there were daily concerts which started in the afternoon and continued until nine o'clock. Another important venue was Marylebone Gardens, which offered music from 1732; the garden began with the bowling green of the Rose Tavern, then a popular gambling spot. (Macheath, the thug in *The Begger's Opera*, said of the Rose: 'There will be deep play to-night and consequently money may be picked up on the road. Meet me there and I'll give you the hint who's worth setting.') James Hook, a young organist, began playing at Marylebone in 1769.

Like Playford, Hook was born in Norwich; a child prodigy, he earned his living as a musician from the age of eleven. He was lured away from Marylebone to become music director at Vauxhall in 1774. Hook's songs were similar to Arne's, but assimilated even more successfully all the elements that made up the London style: influences from the Italian through Purcell and Handel to the various ballad styles of the day resulted in graceful and technically admirable melodies; furthermore, the characters in the songs often resembled real people, as opposed to the stock shepherds. 'The Tear', one of Hook's biggest hits, was about a woman whose loved one had gone away to war.

Hook played an organ concerto every evening, and a strolling wind band perambulated after the main concert. At a celebration of the birthday of the Prince of Wales in 1799, 20,000 lanterns were lit and 1,200 chickens and 1,680 bottles of port were consumed. But soon times were changing: the entertainment at Vauxhall in 1816 included a tightrope act, and Hook retired in 1820, having written perhaps 2,000 songs, as well as much other music. Complete comic operas were presented at Vauxhall from 1830 to 1832, but the management lowered the admission price in 1833, and attracted 27,000 people on the first night.

Vauxhall remained the most important of the pleasure gardens as long as they lasted, but finally closed in 1859. It has long since disappeared into the sprawl of Greater London, and is now only a name on a railway station. (When the first station was built there, it became one of the most famous in the world, so that a word for railway station in Russian is a cognate of 'vauxhall'.) Lesser gardens survived into the 1880s, by which time the music was moving indoors, to the music halls. The pleasure gardens presented music for nearly 200 years altogether, and without a single amplifier.

In the American colonies the trial of John Peter Zenger in New York in 1735 was concerned with ballads. Zenger, who printed one of the city's two newspapers, published ballads about the election of opposition candidates, which were enjoyed in the local taverns, and the city government had him thrown into jail for libel. The court contended that it should decide on the libel, restricting the jury to the fact of publication, but Zenger's lawyer, Andrew Hamilton, successfully argued that the jury should determine whether or not the ballads were libellous. It decided they were not, and the principle of freedom of the press was established in America.

Of the forty most popular songs printed in the USA in the 1790s (the list, compiled by Charles Hamm, appears in his *Yesterdays: Popular Song in America*), no fewer than ten were written by James Hook.

The infant United States of America was a frontier in more senses than one. America's taste in music, drama and literature initially reflected the divisive War of Independence the new nation had gone through, the hardships endured and the homesickness of a people who were nearly all immigrants. Of that early top forty, only five songs were written by composers living in the USA. A difference was apparent between the most successful imports and the rest of an English composer's output: English songs covered the gamut of styles – humorous, sentimental, salacious and so on – but those most popular in America were the tear-jerkers. At the top was 'The Galley Slave' by William Reeve; the one anonymous song on the list was 'Since Then I'm Doomed'; Hook's 'The Tear' made the list (as did 'A Prey to Tender Anguish' by Haydn, whose chamber music was popular in colonial America).

A popular subject of early American musical entertainment on the stage was the Swiss patriot William Tell. *The Patriot, or Liberty Asserted* (1794) and its successor, *The Archers* (1796), were written by William Dunlap, who was born in New Jersey. The music for *The Archers* was by Benjamin Carr, an English immigrant; his 'The Little Sailor Boy' (another song about loss) was a success in the 1790s. Carr also played 'Yankee Doodle' in a concert in New York in 1794, the year it was first printed in America. This was a traditional tune with different verses in several languages; among the contributors to the American words was a British Army surgeon stationed near Albany, New York, in 1758.

American music was inevitably dominated for some time by composers and musicians who had emigrated from England. They were all necessarily versatile, playing several instruments and being able to turn a hand to any type of entertainment; they were also mostly second-rate, otherwise they would not have left the musical capital of the English-speaking world to try their luck on a frontier. But Francis Hopkinson was born in Philadelphia. A lawyer and a judge, a signer of the Declaration of Independence and the first Secretary of the Navy, he was the first American to write secular songs for voice and harpsichord. His 'My Days Have Been So Wondrous Free', often cited as the first American secular song, was one of his earliest but was discovered only after his death; he had not included it in his first printed book of songs, published in 1788. He also wrote what is described as the first American grand opera, *America Independent, or The Temple of Minerva* (1781), a pastiche of tunes from the London stage, with his own words.

The importance of the colonial music master cannot be overestimated. One famous full-time professional, William Billings, had only one eye, a short leg and was deformed by a broken shoulder, but he had a fine voice and thought everyone should sing for the joy of it. His *The New England Psalm-singer* (1770) was the first book of songs by a native-born American. Billings wrote in a joyous style, believing his work to be 'twenty times more powerful than the old slow tunes'. One of his best known was 'Chester (Let Tyrants Shake Their Iron Rods)' (1788), a marching song. He never made much money, however, for his songs were pirated, and he spent much of his time convincing people that he was the author of his own work. Oliver Shaw, who went blind after a series of accidents, was born in Massachusetts. He wrote 'Mary's Tears' (1812) and 'There's Nothing True But Heaven' (1829), both of which were enormously popular. Shaw was more typical than Billings of early American composers, being convinced that good music could be written only in emulation of the great European composers of the period.

John Hill Hewitt, the son of James Hewitt, wrote one of the first songs to be generally regarded as truly American, 'The Minstrel's Return'd from the War' (1825). It resembled his father's 'The Wounded Hussar' (on the top forty in 1800), and was the biggest American hit until the songs of Stephen Foster. The song is about a soldier who returns from battle, pledging to his sweetheart that the bugle will not part them again; but it does, and he dies on the batttlefield. The piano accompaniment suggests a march and trumpet fan-fares in its introduction. There were still five editions in print in 1870.

Many of Hewitt's other songs were successful; he was among the earliest professional American songwriters in the modern sense, in that he wrote skilfully simple songs which followed trends, specifically for the American market. In the early 1830s his songs reflected the contemporary popularity of Italian opera (Rossini's *Barber of Seville* was first performed in New York in 1825). Later in the decade, singing families from Austria and Switzerland toured the USA, and Hewitt wrote mountain songs; 'The Alpine Horn' (1843) included a yodel. 'Mary, Now the Sea Divides Us' (1840), written to words by J. T. S. Sullivan, was described as a 'Southern refrain'; according to Hamm, 'its pentatonic character' suggests 'that it may have been adapted from a tune in the Scotch-Irish-English oral tradition', already well established in the USA and the most important strain in what would become country music in the next century. Hewitt wrote 'answer' songs: 'The Fallen Oak' (1841) was inspired by Henry Russell's 'Woodman, Spare That Tree', and 'I Would Not Die at All' parodied Foster's 'I Would Not Die in Spring Time'.

Henry Russell was born and died in England, but had much of his success as a songwriter and performer in America. He had a pleasant voice, and Hewitt admired the way he made the most of a limited range; most of his songs used only five notes or so. They were a great influence on parlour singing, often appealing to nostalgia and using the word 'old', as in 'The Old Arm Chair' (1840). Like Dibdin at the height of his fame, Russell was a solo recital artist; 'Woodman, Spare That Tree' (1837) was his first and biggest hit. A setting of a poem by George Pope Morris, it was inspired by a true story: Morris and Russell were visiting in upstate New York and saw a giant oak being saved by a present to the woodcutter of a $10 gold piece. In later years Russell's favourite anecdote told of a 'snowy-bearded gentleman' who, after a performance of the song, leapt up from his seat to demand, 'Mr Russell, in the name of Heaven, tell me, was the tree spared?' Receiving an answer in the affirmative, the old fellow sat down in relief, saying, 'Thank God! Thank God! I breathe again!'

Irish emigration to the USA had an important impact long before the potato famine. Of around thirty thousand settlers in 1817, two-thirds were from the British Isles, and most of these were Irish. Their songs were already popular, and had been sung in America before 1790. Ten volumes of *Irish Melodies* published in Dublin between 1808 and 1834 included some of the most popular songs of the entire century, adapted with new texts by Thomas Moore (1779–1852); they owed much to an earlier collection of wordless tunes from the same publisher. Some of Moore's poems and his adaptations, which he sang himself in public, are still sung today: two of the best known are '('Tis) the Last Rose of Summer' (using a tune called 'The Groves of Blarney', also heard in Friedrich von Flotow's opera *Martha*, and set for piano by Beethoven and Mendelssohn), and 'Believe Me, If All These Endearing Young Charms' (sung to the tune of 'My Lodging is on the Cold Ground'). They appeared in a more modern hit parade: they were hits on Victor records, by Elizabeth Wheeler in 1909 and John McCormack in 1911.

'Yankee Doodle' had been meant by the British at the time of the War of Independence and earlier to satirize the supposedly rough and credulous colonials, who cheerfully turned the tables and adopted it as their own first patriotic song. During the War of 1812 theatre managers and song publishers were quick to capitalize on a new surge of nationalism. 'To Anacreon in Heaven' was an old drinking song, the tune of which had been used dozens of times, for example for 'Adams and Liberty' in 1798, one of the earliest native American hits. A Baltimore lawyer and poet, Francis Scott Key, adopted the tune in 1805 for verses about the struggle against the Barbary pirates, in which he first used the phrase 'star-spangled banner'. He made use of the tune and the phrase again in 1814, during the British bombardment of Baltimore's defences, creating what became the American national anthem.

The Anacreontic Society of London was a drinking club, and the original lyrics of the song urged the members to 'entwine the myrtle of Venus with Bacchus's vine'. Perhaps the tune had long been a popular drinking song because of the comic effect created by drunks trying to sing the unsingable. Key's setting is a poor piece of lyric writing, for the stresses of the music fall on the wrong syllables, making it even harder to sing; all the same, it was chosen as America's national anthem in 1931 over 'America the Beautiful'. This is a poem by Katherine Lee Bates written at Pike's Peak in Colorado in 1893, set to a hymn tune by Samuel Augustus Ward: it is singable, it celebrates beauty and it proposes love of country without hatred of somebody else's. When the Americans chose a British drinking song with words that don't fit, the British got the last laugh after all.

The War of 1812, as Americans called it, was only a sideshow of the Napoleonic Wars in Europe, and its last battle was fought in New Orleans on 8 January 1815: the news of the Treaty of Ghent of 24 December 1814 could not reach the USA in only two weeks. Two thousand Kentucky riflemen, in response to a call from Andrew Jackson, arrived in New Orleans a few days before the battle and soundly defeated some fifteen thousand of the best-trained troops in the world. A fiddle tune, 'Eighth of January', celebrated the victory; with words collected by folklorist Jimmy Driftwood, this became 'The Battle of New Orleans', a huge hit in 1959. 'My Country, 'tis of Thee' was written by Samuel Francis Smith, a Harvard-trained clergyman, in 1831; he used the tune of the British anthem 'God Save the Queen', though he is said to have been unaware of that.

A rude patriotism continued to play a large part in the nature of American entertainment and in the treatment of visiting performers: theatre audiences would often demand to hear 'Yankee Doodle', especially if the visitors were British. This combination of chauvinism and anti-élitism led to the Astor Place Riot in 1849 in New York, in which twenty-two people were killed. The conflict was between the supporters of an American and a British Shakespearian actor (the British thespian was seen to represent an aristocratic élitism), but the riot was a turning point in more ways than one. Public entertainment began to separate into several genres, each with its own audience, moving away from the pastiches of songs and melodrama which had been common until then; and art in America began to develop into highbrow and lowbrow, absurd terms from nineteenth-century anthropology. This anti-élitism has had a more ominous cultural effect in more recent times.

Yet there still was not the gulf between classical and popular music that there is today. The French-born conductor Louis Jullien was promoted by P. T. Barnum in America; a showman, he used a baton 6 feet long, wore white gloves and kept a plush chair on the podium, into which he sank, exhausted, at the end of his labours. But he was a thoughtful musician, who wrote an opera as well as dance music, and conducted both music by contemporary American composers and movements from Beethoven's symphonies.

Americans have often held contradictory attitudes. While foreigners were despised for patronizing America, foreign music was seen as somehow superior, a result of the attitude towards class inherited from Britain. Americans learned their music from their own singing masters, and American hymnals began to take on a native flavour in the late seventeenth century. But neither churches nor publishers would have admitted it, and publishers continued to look down on popular songs as the 'trash' of the 'common people'. This high regard for foreign material, however, did not extend to paying royalties on it. During the nineteenth century performing rights societies were formed in Europe, but American publishers refused to entertain such notions. They helped themselves to European music, which was therefore cheaper, and for much of the nineteenth century got away with charging twice as much for it because it was perceived to be better. This did nothing to inspire American composers of formal music. More to the point, it was an early indication of the myopia of which the musical establishment has always been capable: today's record companies and broadcasters, stumbling over themselves to milk last year's fashions, are merely an echo of their ancestors.

The operas of Rossini, Bellini and other Italian composers were immensely popular all over the world. Lorenzo Da Ponte, who had written the librettos for several of Mozart's operas, was a celebrated resident of New York City in his old age. It was thanks partly to his influence that Rossini's *Barber of Seville* was mounted there in 1825, only seven years after its Italian première, at a time when most of Beethoven's music had not been heard in America. The orchestra of twenty-four musicians was said to be the largest yet to have appeared in an American theatre. But English-speaking people still resisted opera in a foreign language, turning to English-language versions and substituting dialogue for recitative. The tunes were pirated for completely new songs, such as 'I'll Pray for Thee' (from Donizetti's *Lucia di Lammermoor*) and 'Over the Summer Sea' ('La donna è mobile' from Verdi's *Rigoletto*). Not all the Italian operas were written by Italians: *The Bohemian Girl*, by the Irishman Michael William Balfe with a libretto by Alfred Bunn, was premièred in 1843 in London, and in New York the next year, and became the most successful production on the English-speaking musical stage until the operettas of Gilbert and Sullivan. It included 'I Dreamt That I Dwelt in Marble Halls' and 'Then You'll Remember Me', two huge hits. Opera became an upper-class preserve, but not before it had had its influence: the Italian trick of holding back the accompaniment on a climactic vocal note is still heard in pop today.

The biggest success of the century was 'Home, Sweet Home', written by the Englishman Henry Bishop, with words by the American John Howard Payne, which was first performed in the opera *Clari, or The Maid of Milan* in London in 1823. It was the favourite song of both sides during the American Civil War, and there were six hit records of it between 1891 and 1915. Critics never liked it, but of its type it was a perfect marriage of words and music, so that many people have thought it was written by Stephen Foster, the first great American songwriter, and an important contributor to the first fully American genre: minstrelsy.

2

Minstrelsy, and the War between the States

Americans of African descent began making their mark very early in the nation's cultural history. There was a black playhouse in New York City in the 1820s: the African Grove Theatre presented its own versions of hit shows, such as Pierce Egan's *Tom and Jerry, or Life in London* (1823), establishing the comic convention of the city slicker and his visiting country cousin. *The Drama of King Shotaway* was probably the first play by a black playwright to be mounted in America. The theatre's director, Henry Brown, may have based the drama of a slave insurrection in the island of St Vincent on personal experience: he had emigrated from there.

The idea was to present entertainment for blacks who wished to join the white mainstream of society, but audiences of the time were unruly anyway, and white hoodlums liked to go to the Grove to disrupt proceedings. The theatre also became a tourist attraction. Its stars included James Hewlett and Ira Aldridge, both of whom toured as far as England. Aldridge played Othello to Edmund Kean's Iago; he performed Shakespeare in Russia, and died in 1864 while on tour in Poland. Regarded as one of the great actors of his day, he had also performed the first American 'slave song' that we know of: 'Opossum up a Gum Tree'.

Free blacks such as the bugle player and bandleader Francis (Frank) Johnson, born in the West Indies, made much history. Johnson was the first American black to publish music (1818), to give formal band concerts, to tour the USA and to appear in integrated concerts with white musicians. In 1824, when the French General Lafayette toured the USA to wild acclaim, Johnson was engaged for the Lafayette Ball in Philadelphia and played his 'Lafayette March', which obtained its share of publicity. He seems to have been the first American musician of any race to tour abroad, taking a band to London in 1837, the year Victoria came to the throne; she gave him a silver trumpet. On his return he introduced the promenade concert to the USA.

There were many other black bandleaders, who were often popular with the upper classes for parties and dances, and indeed talented black musicians in every category. Yet most of these were pursuing success in the American musical world by playing the styles and genres that were already popular in that world. Despite (or perhaps because of) the severe handicap of slavery, it was the music of the slaves that made the first of many profoundly important black contributions to the American mainstream.

The tradition of 'blacking up' goes back at least as far as Ben Jonson's masque for James I's Danish queen, who expressed a desire to wear black make-up with a dazzling white costume. Set-pieces requiring the performer to black up with burnt cork became a staple in America: the *New York Journal* referred to a 'Negro dance, in character' seen on stage in 1767. But the minstrel show suddenly appeared in the 1840s, and was the first entirely American musical form to become internationally popular.

Minstrelsy saw the introduction of patterns still extant in American culture. First, minstrelsy was essentially black music, while the most successful acts were white, so that songs and dances of black origin were imitated by white performers and then taken up by black performers, who thus to some extent ended up imitating themselves. Secondly, more than a few people wondered how a nation could be free which allowed the institution of slavery; but as the nation became more wealthy, it also became more powerful. As the trauma of the Revolutionary War receded, as the young nation won the War of 1812 against the British (but were soundly beaten by the Canadians when they attempted to 'liberate' that country) and as the slaughter of the American aboriginal tribes provided yet another manifestation of racism, Americans established a pattern of resisting the loss of their innocence. The affectionate, patronizing vision of plantation life conveyed by minstrelsy was similar to the simplistic and idealized depiction of family life in the television sitcoms of a hundred years later.

The phenomenon of black culture was widely and often sympathetically discussed. Blacks sang the watered-down songs of minstrelsy, as well as their own, and critics noticed the difference: there was a flavour of sadness in their own songs that was absent from the 'Ethiopian' songs that were all the rage. There is a famous quotation from *Knickerbocker Magazine* (1845) on the subject of Negro poets:

Let one of them, in the swamps of Carolina, compose a new song, and it no sooner reaches the ear of a white amateur, than it is written down, amended (that is, almost spoilt), printed, and then put upon a course of rapid dissemination, to cease only with the utmost bounds of Anglo-Saxondom, perhaps with the world. Meanwhile, the poor author digs away with his hoe, utterly ignorant of his greatness.

There were a few black minstrels, even in the early years, especially in New Orleans, where Signor Cornmeali (Mr Cornmeal, real name unknown) began as a street trader singing 'Ethiopian' songs, went on the stage and influenced white performers. William Henry Lane, known as Master Juba, was probably the only black to tour with early white companies; in England in 1849 he was praised by Charles Dickens. He was born in Rhode Island, but began entertaining in New York City, playing the banjo and the tambourine as well as dancing; he had learned some of his jigs from his desperately poor Irish neighbours, who lived on pennies they earned dancing in pubs, but then made them his own. Both blacks and whites copied his dancing. He won a grand contest (promoted by P. T. Barnum) in 1844, and historians of dance consider him to be the virtual inventor of black dancing, including tap-dancing, as we have known it ever since. He died in England; none of his fame extended to allowing numbers of blacks to make a good living with their own talent. The majority of minstrels were always white.

Much of minstrelsy's material was copied from the songs and dances of slavery and many minstrels visited plantations in search of ideas. In 1829 Thomas Dartmouth 'Daddy' Rice struck it rich with his 'Jim Crow' song and dance, copied from a crippled stable-hand named Jim who worked for a white Crow family. He 'jumped' his

'Jim Crow' between the acts of whatever shows he could get billed on, but the jump was mostly a shuffle, and the tune was borrowed from an Irish jig. 'Jim Crow' later became the stock plantation slave, while 'Zip Coon', first a song by George Washington Dixon, became the city dandy: the 'Tom and Jerry' routine reduced to racist farce.

The earliest full-length minstrel shows were organized by quartets. The Virginia Minstrels first met to rehearse in a rooming house in New York early in 1843, during an economic depression which resulted in one of the worst seasons in theatrical history. Daniel Emmett Decatur was a printer who played banjo and fiddle, working with a circus during the summer, and then began writing songs: 'Old Dan Tucker', 'Turkey in the Straw' (which used part of 'Zip Coon') and 'I Wish I Was in Dixie's Land', written for Bryant's Minstrels in 1859, were all his (but like many songwriters, he died poor). Billy Whitlock, also a printer, had learned to play banjo from Jim Sweeney, a virtuoso who is credited with adding the fifth 'thumb' string to the instrument. Dick Pelham and Frank Brower were both dancers and singers; Brower also played the bones, a set of 12-inch-long dried horse bones which were clacked together to make a rhythm instrument. Brower became one of the best vocalists in minstrelsy.

Black-face performers had been known as 'Ethiopian delineators'. The word 'minstrel' had applied to any professional entertainer since the twelfth century in Europe, but the Virginia Minstrels, who toured for only a few months before breaking up, tied the word for ever to black-face. Immediately successful, they played at record-breaking engagements in New York and Boston, and sailed for England in April. The English already loved black-face entertainment; Sweeney was touring Britain playing the banjo, and the Virginia Minstrels were a hit, but box office receipts mysteriously evaporated, so they could not support themselves and broke up.

The equally famous Christy Minstrels were formed in 1844 by Edwin P. Christy, who wrote 'Goodnight Ladies' and other songs. Born in Philadelphia, he studied black rhythms in Congo Square in New Orleans, where he was a factory foreman. First he toured as one of many imitators of Daddy Rice; he formed a group in Buffalo, New York, and borrowed the name of the Virginia Minstrels for a while, but he always billed his group as the 'oldest' and the 'first'. When he was ready, he booked a theatre in New York in 1846, and developed a family show which ran for over 2,700 performances; he also toured England. He committed suicide by jumping out of a hotel window in New York City, depressed by the outbreak of the Civil War.

The first minstrel companies made history and permanently changed show business by inventing 'black' entertainment for families, and by creating a show rather than just a series of comic turns and dances. The shows were in three parts. For the songs and jokes in the first part the performers stood in a semicircle; the comic endmen 'Tambo' and 'Bones' were distinguished by their tambourine and bone clackers, with which they would register noisy approval of a joke. (This was a signal that the audience too was supposed to laugh, a precursor of canned laughter on radio and television.) An interlocutor or master of ceremonies presided in the centre and represented the boss, so that when Tambo or Bones made a joke at his expense, there was an extra dimension to the glee. Another principal was a singer of sentimental ballads. The similar but less formal second part was made up of a string of speciality acts and novelties, called the olio. This term was already in use in white show business and survived in later vaudeville; it is probably from the Spanish *olla*, meaning 'pot-pourri'. Last came a walk-around finale, with dances, which became more and more of a spectacle.

The 'Ethiopian' dances (for example, breakdowns, double-shuffles and heel-and-toe) and instrumentation (especially the banjo) were more or less authentic, and profoundly influential. The ancestors of the banjo are thought to have been the stringed instruments of the Wolof, of what are now Senegal and Gambia in west Africa, and may be as ancient as Mesopotamia. Minstrel banjo players included Sweeney, Tom Briggs (who joined Christy's Minstrels and published *Briggs' Banjo Instructor*) and Frank Converse, who preserved the first piece he had heard played by a black musician. All of them freely admitted that they had learned from blacks, and the music they played included accents and additive rhythms that came partly from the playing style and were not obvious from the notation, like African drumming in the past and ragtime in the future.

A later element in the show was the cakewalk, in which members of the audience were invited to invent the most ridiculous strutting march, for which the prize was a cake. Interestingly, Master Juba reversed the procedure, in that some of his dances are said to have resembled Irish jigs. But minstrelsy was laden with ironies: the supposed ability of the blacks to invent outlandish dances (though it was whites who were doing most of the dancing) turned the word 'jig' into an offensive euphemism.

As the spectacle in the last act became more elaborate, playlets were mounted that included lampoons of current events and spoofs of popular plays. In one version of *Uncle Tom's Cabin* Uncle Tom was not sold down the river, Simon Legree did not appear and the author's subtitle 'Life among the Lowly' became a song called 'Life among the Happy'.

Some of minstrelsy's songs were sympathetic, such as 'The Negro Boy' ('I Sold a Guiltless Negro Boy') and 'A Negro Song' (or 'The Negro's Humanity'); the latter's words were adapted from an African song which had been transcribed by trader Mungo Park in the eighteenth century. But in general the genre had little room for abolitionist sentiment, and became more overtly racist after the Civil War: the image of the 'darky' as a comic buffoon insulated whites from the reality of free black Americans, and survived in films and television until well into the 1950s. (The 'blaxploitation' films of the 1960s, such as *Shaft*, were a profitable novelty only until blacks tired of constantly seeing themselves portrayed as violent gangsters and pimps in flashy clothes.) Minstrelsy's jokes seem to have been among the oldest in show business, some with double meanings: 'Why am I like a young widow?' a white comedian in burnt cork would ask. 'Because I do not stay long in black.'

Many 'Negro' songs were published. One of the best was 'Yellow Rose of Texas', about a 'darky' longing for his girlfriend. First published in 1858, it became a Civil War campfire song and remained popular for decades. But after the Civil War it was no longer possible to pretend that everything was all right down on the plantation. Charles A. White, whose minstrel songs were his most famous, had a big hit in 1874 with 'The Old Home Ain't What It Used To Be', known to have been sung in the North by black minstrels.

The first successful black songwriter in America was James Bland, whose father found a government job in Washington, DC, just after the war, when the capital was full of ex-slaves. Bland's songs reflect the pentatonic scales of black folk music. His best known are 'Oh Dem Golden Slippers' and 'Carry Me Back to Old Virginny' (and he is still the only black to have written a State Song). Among his more than seven hundred songs are celebrations of the end of slavery: 'De Slavery Chains am Broke at Last', 'Keep Dem Golden Gates Wide Open', 'In the Morning by the Bright Light'. He went to England in 1880 with the Haverly Colored Minstrels and organized his own troupe there; he performed for the British royal family, and also became very popular in Germany.

For decades minstrelsy was a staple of white show business, a simple format for entertainment in the days when all entertainment was necessarily live, and audiences may have been easier to please. In Philadelphia, Carncross and Dixey's Minstrels enjoyed the unique feat of prospering for forty years as a permanent organization in its own theatre. The interlocutor was J. L. Carncross, whose light tenor voice was at its best in plaintive ballads, while E. F. Dixey was the bone man, on the right-hand end of the semi-circle. He played solos on his clackers – his big finale was an imitation of a horse race – and he was also a singer. Hughey Dougherty, with the tambourine at the other end, rasped and cackled his way through comic songs, and had one of the biggest personal followings of anyone in minstrelsy.

In the same town, another famous Tambo was Lew Simmons, who owned a baseball team. (There was little money in sandlot baseball, so he sold it to Cornelius McGillicudy, who changed his name to Connie Mack and made millions with the Philadelphia Athletics.) Simmons was killed by a beer truck, which might have amused him; he himself liked a drink, and was said to be able to see the humour in almost any situation. Billy Sweatnum was the interlocutor and a man named Slocum the bone end in Simmons and Slocum's Minstrels. Charlie Reynolds was a comic who could not sing or dance and was in fact tone-deaf; he would bring down the house by making a shambles of his own act. Jimmy Mackin and Francis Wilson were a touring song and dance team who had a 'rivals' act, both after the same girl. Wilson helped found Actor's Equity in 1919.

During the long decline of minstrelsy, as with the decline of many genres, it slowly exploded into the grandiose: some of the troupes had more than a hundred members. Female impersonations and ever fancier spectacles were included in the shows; among the stock characters were uppity blacks and northern carpet-baggers. Soon minstrelsy and ragtime combined in the 'coon songs' and 'coon shouting' of early vaudeville, and by the early 1880s a minstrel show was becoming effectively a black-face variety show. Lew Dockstader's Minstrels still performed, and George M. Cohan was a partner in a minstrel show, as late as 1908. A white blacked-up minstrel show was popular on British television until well into the 1960s.

To add to all the ironies, black as well as white performers were required to 'black up'. Minstrel shows were popular among ordinary blacks, though conditions were terrible for black performers and a full-time first-class black minstrel troupe, Brooker and Clayton's Georgia Minstrels, was not organized until 1865. Furthermore, the black companies that were formed were mostly owned and managed by white businessmen. But minstrelsy established a demand for black performers, and the origins of black as well as white vaudeville are to be found in it.

We may see black-face minstrelsy as racist nowadays, but America's insistence on its innocence has often been convincing, at least in cultural terms. Of the songs to come out of minstrelsy, those of Stephen Foster survived the crude crucible of racist comedy and made him easily the most successful nineteenth-century composer of popular songs.

Stephen Collins Foster was born in Pittsburgh on the Fourth of July in 1826, the fiftieth anniversary of the signing of the Declaration of Independence. He managed to die an alcoholic and in poverty in 1864, having sold the rights to some of his most popular songs, but he was one of the first American songwriters to sign contracts for royalties and to support himself as a full-time songwriter (others were also publishers, performers or teachers). Above all, he was the first indubitably American composer whose songs are still sung more than a century after his death.

Foster was of Irish descent, and was steeped in music from childhood. He was educated in good private schools and then worked in his brother's mercantile business, but he never strayed far from music. His first published song was 'Open Thy Lattice, Love' (1844);

his early songs were simple, romantic and mediocre, based on the models of Arne and the later example of Bishop, whose songs (except for 'Home, Sweet Home') were already being forgotten.

Foster must have been familiar with slave music from childhood, but it was not until around 1845, through singing and playing them with friends, that he wrote some minstrel songs. 'Lou'siana Belle' was published in 1847, 'Away Down South', 'Uncle Ned' and 'Oh! Susanna' in 1848. The last especially was sung by minstrel companies all over the country, and became a favourite during the California gold rush, but Foster had sold it outright; only in 1849 did he sign contracts with two publishers and become a full-time songwriter. Eight more minstrel songs were published in 1850, including 'Gwine to Run All Night' (also known as 'Camptown Racetrack'); fifteen more in 1852 show him at his peak, among them 'Old Folks At Home' (or 'Way Down Upon the Swanee River'), 'My Old Kentucky Home', 'Massa's in the Cold Ground' and 'Old Dog Tray'.

He wrote a few more minstrel songs, and other fine period songs based on Italian, German and Irish models. His most famous later songs are 'Jeanie With the Light Brown Hair' (1854), which could not have been written without the influence of Thomas Moore, yet is immediately and convincingly Foster, and 'Beautiful Dreamer', which has a fine Italianate melody and was written in the last months of his life. He had a streak of melancholy, and his songs are often nostalgic for a remembered past that is happier than the flawed present. But the minstrel songs written around 1850 made him famous.

It is not true, as nineteenth-century biographers claimed, that Foster had visited 'negro camp meetings' or that he imitated 'the melodic forms and tonal characteristics of the songs of the colored slaves'. He did not need to steal his material, having a natural sympathy for it, and his best songs can stand on their own considerable merits. The melodies have proved to be deathless. More interestingly, every one of the minstrel songs has a chorus, to be sung in three- and four-part harmony, making them more complete and satisfying compositions, while none of his earlier songs have choruses at all. 'Oh! Susanna' is simply a delightful nonsense song, and is not obviously a 'Plantation Melody', as some of the later songs were called. Although many of these were written in dialect, which was later rejected for reasons of taste, they were a considerable advance on the songs of the period.

Nostalgia for a half-remembered past was not just a propensity of Foster's, but the most popular sentiment of the time; homesickness is another familiar emotion. 'Massa's in the Cold Ground' may seem to be a clear attempt to sentimentalize slavery, but many slaves must have loved their masters, on whom they depended for everything. 'Uncle Ned' emerges through the dialect as a kindly human being who was loved; in 'Nelly Was a Lady' (1850) the black man mourns the death of his own wife. The slaves experience, in all these songs, ordinary human feelings; they are people as real as the characters in Shakespeare. And because they were good songs, they must have had a consciousness-raising effect, intended or not.

Slavery made a mockery of the Declaration of Independence, and the issue came to centre on the right of individual states to practise slavery as opposed to the right of the federal government to contain it. Finally it had to be settled. Before 1860 the typical American popular song was a sentimental ballad, expressing the virtues of homeliness, fidelity and so forth. This type of song made a big comeback in the 1880s, but in the meantime, the Civil War of 1861–5, or the War between the States, brought about the end of the nation's adolescence, and should have ended its innocence. Americans were not – could not be – as free as they thought they were; questions sometimes arise which have to be resolved. So it was with the contradiction of states' rights versus federalism in the USA. Brother fought brother in one of the bloodiest wars in history; more than 630,000 died, more Americans than were killed in all other wars from the French and Indian to the Korean.

The Civil War produced a greater number of songs than any other war in American history. Many soldiers carried songbooks; one early book contained songs that were already popular, such as Foster's songs, 'Yankee Doodle', 'Annie Laurie' (from Moore's collection) and 'Pop Goes the Weasel' (a traditional English tune with words from 1858 about a London hatter pawning, or 'popping', his weasel, the tool of his trade). Both sides sang many of the same songs, since both included semi-literate recruits from the same tradition. On the evening before the Battle of Murfreesboro rival army bands, camped within earshot, took turns playing their patriotic songs, then joined together to play 'Home, Sweet Home'. The next day they slaughtered each other.

A camp-meeting song called 'Brother, Will You Meet Us?', to a tune believed to be by William Steffe of North Carolina, had new words bestowed on it by soldiers who sang it as they marched to the front in 1861: 'John Brown's body lies a-mouldering in the grave / but his soul goes marching on' honoured a radical who had been hanged in 1859 after an unsuccessful raid on the government arsenal at Harper's Ferry, intended to arm a slave revolt. Julia Ward Howe heard it and wrote new words: 'Mine eyes have seen the glory of the coming of the Lord / And His truth goes marching on . . .' 'The Battle Hymn of the Republic', published in 1862, is as well known to Americans as their national anthem. 'Tenting on the Old Camp Ground', by Walter Kittredge, was almost as popular.

Songs by George Frederick Root included 'Battle Cry of Freedom'; it was later said of Root that he ought to have been made a general. John Hill Hewitt wrote new patriotic words to his own big hit 'The Minstrel's Return'd from the War'. Among his many other songs were 'The Picket Guard', a setting of a poem that had been published in *Harper's Weekly* and told of the night a picket had been shot; since he was only an enlisted man, the official report was 'All quiet along the Potomac tonight'. James Sloane Gibbons wrote a poem called 'We are Coming, Father Abra'am' in response to Lincoln's call for volunteers. This was set to music by Luther O. Emerson and was a great commercial success, but more people sang it than volunteered: Lincoln resorted to the nation's first conscription in 1863, and riots ensued in many cities.

Dan Emmett's 'Dixie' was first sung in the South in 1860, and became wildly popular, with somewhat more bellicose words than the original; one southern commentator wrote that 'we shall be fortunate if it does not impose its very name on our country'. There was a legend of a kindly slave-owner called Dixey, and Dixey's Land was heaven for a slave; surveyors named Mason and Dixon had settled a boundary dispute between Maryland and Pennsylvania, and the 'Mason-Dixon line' thus separated the slave states from the North. But there had also been a ten-dollar note printed by a New

Orleans bank with the word 'dix' on it – French for 'ten' – which may have been the origin of Dixie-land.

The South's favourite songs included 'Aura Lee or The Maid with the Golden Hair', by W. W. Fosdick and George R. Poulton, which later became (with different words) 'Army Blue', a traditional West Point song. 'Maryland! My Maryland!' had words by James Ryder Randall and was sung to the tune of the German 'O Tannenbaum, O Tannenbaum'; it was to become a favourite of dixieland jazz bands. The Confederacy's unofficial national anthem was 'Bonnie Blue Flag', written by Harry B. Macarthy to a traditional tune, 'The Irish Jaunting Car'. Macarthy was an Englishman who left the South when the tide of battle turned.

Many tunes were borrowed more than once. 'Bonnie Blue Flag' was used by Septimus Winner for the satirical 'He's Gone to the Arms of Abraham', while the Irish tune 'The Wearing of the Green' was used for another setting of the poem 'We are Coming, Father Abra'am', and also for 'Wearing of the Gray!' in the South. 'Lorena', a song about parted lovers that was written by brothers called Webster and first published in 1857 in Chicago, was a huge hit in the South. As the slaughter dragged on with no end in sight, southern songs became ever more sentimental and tragic. Music published in the South used cheap inks and poor paper; the weak industrial base that defeated the South encompassed publishing and paper-making.

In the end the federal republic survived, at the expense of a purer political freedom which, paradoxically, had meant enslavement for many: of nearly 4.5 million Americans of African descent in 1860, fewer than 0.5 million had been free. The great southern families with their enormous plantations were the closest thing America had to an aristocracy, and the War between the States destroyed their way of life. Some said that the Civil War was an unnecessary tragedy, because slavery was becoming an economic anachronism and could not have survived much longer anyway, but that notion has been refuted by today's economists. Not only was slavery profitable, but it was cheap labour that had made the comfort of the southern aristocracy possible. That aristocracy would never have given up its primacy easily, and the aftermath of the war was very badly handled.

Americans had slaughtered each other to get rid of slavery, but clung to their innocence; they did not want to admit that slavery had been a mistake in the first place.

3

The Rise of Vaudeville and Tin Pan Alley

In order to preserve the Union, Abraham Lincoln said, he might have freed some of the slaves, or none of them; he ended by freeing them all. While the Russians had freed their serfs first, Americans were much quicker at killing their emancipator, their greatest president, whom they now needed more than ever. As with a later assassination of a lesser president, the nation was a very long time in recovering from it. The worst legacy of the war was the institutionalization of racism in its hopelessly unsuccessful aftermath.

The slave-owners had not argued that some people are born to serve others; that would have been too obvious a contradiction of the American idea. Very suddenly, as cotton became a vital crop in the 1830s, the South had taken the position that blacks were subhuman, capable only of being owned. During the reconstruction period following the Civil War much of this naked racism might have been attenuated – at first there were black congressmen from southern states – but a corrupt Congress soon sold the South to carpetbaggers, crooked politicians whose allegiance was so portable that it would fit into a holdall made of a piece of carpet, and later to the South's self-interested factions, whose cynicism became typical of the rest of the country. Poor whites were pitted against poor blacks, so that a new aristocracy of dishonesty could stay in control. And the result of Lincoln's Emancipation Proclamation was a *de facto* slavery of 'free' citizens who had no rights, while Washington became the centre of an orgy of corruption which has not been exceeded since.

Many of the popular tavern ditties of the period could not be printed in Douglas Gilbert's *Lost Chords: The Diverting Story of*

American Popular Music in 1942, yet, as Gilbert pointed out, none of them approaches the scurrility of the political songs. During the presidential race of 1868 a campaign song for Seymour, who was running against General Ulysses S. Grant, contained the paean 'Here's to the man that pulled the trigger / That killed the old cuss that freed the nigger.'

Singer Pauline Markham, a burlesque queen, took a more direct role in the profligacy of the period. She was hired by people with financial and political interests to sleep with the Hon. Robert K. Scott of Ohio, who signed a great many spurious convertible bonds, his reward being (apart from Markham) the carpet-bag governorship of South Carolina.

Among the era's larger-than-life citizens was Jim Fisk, a sort of Robin Hood who supplied coal, food and rent money to the needy, and who sent a trainload of supplies when the Chicago fire of 1871 made thousands homeless. He was also a famous crook: with Jay Gould he created a gold panic which ruined hundreds of people in 1869. For a time he led President Grant (not a crook, but not too bright either) by the nose. Fisk was murdered by a pimp who had tried and failed to blackmail him, with the cooperation of Fisk's brassy mistress, Josie Mansfield, using letters Fisk had written to her. Fisk left the courtroom in tears at the sound of Mansfield's perjury, he so loved the faithless hussy. Ed Stokes shot him a few hours later, and the letters, it turned out, were so innocent they could have been read to a child. Fisk was buried in Brattleboro, Vermont, whose citizens gave $25,000 for a monument of Italian marble.

Henry Ward Beecher was the most famous preacher and pseudo-moralist of the age, yet he also had an eye for the ladies. In 1875 he was sued by a parishioner, Theodore Tilton, accused of adultery with Tilton's wife. The jury could not agree, but Beecher was probably guilty, and none of it would have come to light except for the hypocrisy of the principals. Beecher and his sister Harriet Beecher Stowe, who wrote *Uncle Tom's Cabin*, condemned leading feminists of the period as flaming harlots. One of them, Victoria Woodhull, took no nonsense from anyone; she began by hinting in *The New York Times* that she knew of prominent people who preached against free love, but practised it in private. When they did not ameliorate their attacks on her, Woodhull blew the whistle on the lot of them, and Tilton had to bring suit.

Songs were sung about all these people, such as 'Jim Fisk, or He Never Went Back on the Poor'. Beecher never lived down the comedy; a song of thirty-two lines took a swipe at Woodhull ('sour grapes') and ended:

> They say he is nearly sixty-five
> By the time he is ninety, he'll contrive
> To set our country all alive
> With little sons of Beecher'os.

The public scandals and relaxed moral atmosphere that followed the Civil War led to a new frankness, along with the cynicism. Large taverns with music and prostitutes, called 'free-and-easies', often appeared on the outskirts of market towns to catch the farmers on their way home with money in their pockets. Among drinking songs, 'Little Brown Jug' was popular in the 1860s:

> My wife and I live all alone
> In a little log hut we call our own
> She loves gin and I love rum
> I tell you what we've lots of fun!
>
> If I had a cow that gave such milk
> I'd dress her in the finest silk.
> Feed her on the choicest hay
> And milk her forty times a day.

Story songs were sung, many of them salacious. The mother-in-law became fair game, and was combined with a political gibe in the chorus 'I'd rather be sent off to jail or to Congress / Than live all my life with my mother-in-law'. 'Captain Jinks of the Horse Marines' was written in 1868 by William Horace Lingard (words by T. Maclagan) for the British Lingard Comedy Company at a theatre in New York; it was sung by a chorus of girls in military costume (and generations later by children in primary schools, who adored it). Another song was a parody of it, describing what the marine's wife got up to when he was not at home. Still another song sent up 'Home, Sweet Home':

> When relations come to visit you,
>   There's no place like home.
> They bring all their trunks and they stick like glue,
>   There's no place like home.
> When you've got to give up the best room you've got
> And go and sleep on a rough old cot
> With your brother-in-law who is always half-shot –
>   There's no place like home.

The 1860s and 1870s were marked by the attitude of the free-and-easies: the crooks and the politicians were getting theirs, so everyone else might as well have a good time. No major songwriting talent of Stephen Foster's stature emerged until the 1890s, but the American music business went from strength to strength as trends developed which would become the business we know in more modern times.

The post-war music business was confused, to say the least. The industry believed that the enormous amount of sheet music sold during the war in both North and South had been a patriotic fluke, and that sheet music was for 'the rich and aristocratic', as in Europe, where it was twice as expensive. (This argument, incidentally, was used against any proposal to improve copyright law.) Cheap paperback songbooks were sold, like dime novels, which contained the words to songs but not the music; it was widely believed that the best vernacular music was borrowed from older and 'better' composers. In fact, music teachers all over the USA were doing a good job, and standards were going up. More and more pianos were being bought, and in 1872–3 Steinway paid the great Russian virtuoso Anton Rubinstein $40,000 to do a nationwide tour, not only promoting Steinway pianos, but showing Americans what piano music could sound like. Educated songwriters were emerging to write vernacular songs, the very individuals who, the musical snobs thought, would write high-class art songs. 'When You and I Were Young, Maggie' was written in 1866 by James Austin Butterfield, setting a poem by George W. Johnson, a teacher, for his sweetheart (who died the year they were married). It was just one of the many songs that sold in the same sort of numbers as the wartime hits (and good enough to be revived in a musical film in 1944). The mainstream music publishers failed to take advantage of songs that struck a common chord in millions of people, leaving them to new independent firms.

While 'Home, Sweet Home' and other songs of the earlier nineteenth century may sound old-fashioned to our ears, after the Civil War more songs began to be written which survive today. The American popular song (as opposed to story songs or novelties) had developed a formula. By the 1870s a piece of sheet music usually had a piano introduction of four or eight bars; this was followed by two to four verses, sung to a melody of sixteen bars, which was divided into four phrases of four bars each and conformed to a pattern such as AABC, ABAC or AABA. The chorus or refrain was most often arranged for four voices and was derived from parts of the verse, acting as a commentary or emphasis on it. In its simplicity and directness it will be seen that this form is directly descended from the repeated strophes of the English songs of the eighteenth century.

Septimus Winner was one of the most successful of the era and three of his songs (each very different) are still familiar: 'Listen to the Mockingbird', 'Whispering Hope' and 'Where, Oh Where Has My Little Dog Gone', the last foreshadowing a flood of songs in 3/4 time at the turn of the century. He had also been one of the first to arrange traditional black melodies, such as 'Heaven's a Long Way Off'.

'I'll Take You Home Again, Kathleen' was written in 1875 by Thomas Paine Westendorf, who worked as a teacher in schools for juvenile offenders. It was purchased outright by the John Church Company, and at first printed in their house journal. It made its own great reputation at a time when the marketing of songs was not highly developed, and the company paid Westendorf a mere $50 a month for years. Thomas Edison loved it so much that he requested it be sung at his funeral and sent Westendorf a cheque for $250 in appreciation. Westendorf wrote more songs, but 'Kathleen' was the only one on which the copyright was worth renewing when the time came.

Perhaps the only song from the period that was nearly as successful was 'Silver Threads Among the Gold' (1872) by Hart Pease Danks, who, unlike Westendorf, made a living from his songs; the words were by Eben Rexford, who had published them in a farm magazine.

Danks's other songs included 'Roses Underneath the Snow' and 'Don't Be Angry with Me, Darling'. 'Darling' was his wife, who left him; and Danks died a lonely and angry man. But 'Silver Threads Among the Gold' had sold two million copies by 1900, and another million in 1907, when it was revived. There were several hit recordings of it, among them one in 1904 by Richard Jose, who had first made it popular by singing it in minstrel shows, and another in 1912 by John McCormack.

Alongside all the scurrility and sentimentality of the years after the Civil War white gospel music grew in strength, and had an importance which is almost forgotten today. The respectable Protestant churches – for example, the Methodist and Congregationalist – printed their own hymnals (with words but without music, for most of the nineteenth century), and the churches had tried to control music publishing, especially religious music, since early colonial times, excluding popular 'trash'. But from earliest times singing masters had also combined secular and religious values, knowing that ordinary people loved to sing.

Shape-note music, also called fa-sol-la, was a simplified method of notation which made it possible to teach part-singing to large groups of people: each part was on a single line, and notes of various shapes were used to denote pitch, rather than a five-line stave. It was also called brush arbour music, from the practice of clearing a small area and building an arbour for an outdoor religious meeting, or 'Sacred Harp' music, from the most famous songbook in the style, compiled in 1844. Another book, *Harmonia Sacra* (1851), had been inspired by a similar simplified notation, and was called 'Hominy Soaker' by the less reverent.

The evangelical movement had got under way near a settlement on the Green River in Logan County, Kentucky, called Rogues Harbor, a haven for runaway slaves, thieves and border settlers. A self-educated minister named James McGready won over souls with his fervent brand of Calvinist Presbyterianism, urging a 'new birth' to escape the wrath of Jehovah. By 1800 McGready's followers were so numerous that they held huge outdoor meetings that went on for days, and 'camp meeting' was an accurate description. Fundamentalist evangelism became a growing phenomenon, and whenever there was an economic recession, the evangelists' business improved: before the days of the welfare state and the Social Security Act, the helpless working class would turn to religion in despair. After gold was discovered in California in 1848, more than $800 million was added to the nation's wealth, leading to speculation and then the failure of nearly thirteen thousand businesses in 1857–8: the twelfth business depression since 1790 started yet another religious revival.

Lowell Mason was musically precocious as a child, and compiled a book of psalm tunes which he reharmonized himself: *The Boston Handel and Haydn Society Collection of Church Music* (1822) was the beginning of a family publishing empire which eventually became part of Oliver Ditson in Boston. Mason had a particular interest in teaching music to children, instinctively understanding that it is easier to learn in childhood, which was then a revolutionary notion. Among Mason's over eighty collections were more than a thousand original tunes and nearly five hundred reharmonizations and arrangements, including 'From Greenland's Icy Mountains', 'Nearer, My God, to Thee', 'Joy to the World', 'Blest Be the Tie That Binds' and 'When I Survey the Wondrous Cross'.

Dwight Moody came from poverty to be a great evangelist and a good businessman. Working in a shoe store in Chicago, he saved $7,000 in five years, partly by lending money out at interest rates of up to 17 per cent a day; he also earned a handsome income by collecting overdue accounts after the depression of 1857. He was never ordained and was known as 'Crazy' Moody because of his gospel fervour, but he dressed and behaved like a businessman, which made it easier to save souls as well as bodies. He formed a non-denominational fundamentalist church for slum dwellers and a Sunday school for their children, which might have been the only school some of them ever saw; he was also president of the YMCA, and when the Chicago fire of 1871 destroyed it all, he raised the money to rebuild it. Moody had also erected prayer tents and nursed the wounded behind the lines during the Civil War; later he toured and preached in England. He returned to the USA in 1875, when the corruption at the highest levels of President Grant's administration had become public knowledge. Businessmen like J. P. Morgan and Cornelius Vanderbilt in New York, John Wanamaker in Philadelphia and Cyrus McCormick and George Armour in Chicago were only too happy to help save souls, to demonstrate the Christian side of American business.

Moody had taken vocalist Ira David Sankey with him to England, and their partnership lasted until Moody retired in 1892. Sankey also trained enormous choirs for Moody's huge new tabernacles. Moody had written: 'If you have singing that will reach the heart, it will fill the church every time.' In Brooklyn, New York, extra trolley-car tracks had to be laid to transport all the people who wanted to hear Sankey sing songs like 'Sweet Bye and Bye', 'Go Tell It to Jesus', 'Hold the Fort' and 'Where is My Wandering Boy Tonight?' He was a genuinely popular vocalist, and those who came to hear him stayed to hear Moody preach.

Fanny Crosby, who was called the Queen of Gospel Music, wrote 'Saved By Grace' and many others. Adam Geibel, like Crosby, had been blinded in childhood; he wrote 'Gathering Sea Shells from the Sea Shore' in ten minutes, and it became widely popular. (Geibel also wrote pop hits, such as the coon song 'Kentucky Babe'.) Will Lamartine also wrote both pop and gospel; Moody told W. L. Thompson that he would rather have written 'Softly and Tenderly Jesus is Calling' than have done all the good works in his life. Some of these songs were as popular in the 1890s as any secular hit.

William Ashley Sunday played baseball for the Chicago Whitestockings, later known as the White Sox. As Billy Sunday he became the most famous evangelist of all, named in 1914 as one of America's top ten favourite great men. His musical associate for twenty years was Homer Alvan 'Rody' Rodeheaver, a trombone-playing choir-leader, composer and publisher. Sunday and many others, such as Sam Jones (who was a leading figure in the Lake Chautauqua evangelist movement in western New York state, and whose favourite song was the comic plantation song 'De Brewer's Big Hosses Cain't Run Over Me'), were leaders of the temperance movement, which led to the Prohibition amendment to the Constitution in 1919, one of the biggest disasters Americans ever perpetrated on themselves: it promoted alcohol abuse rather than preventing it, and created a permanent second government of organized crime.

Rodeheaver was the first gospel artist to go into the recording studio, and formed Rainbow Records, the first label of its kind. He lived until 1955; his privately owned publishing empire was estimated to have sold more than a million copies of gospel sheet music and hymnals that year. But about seventy years earlier, when costs were lower and profits higher, Biglow and Main had sold eighteen million copies in one year. Popular-style gospel music had influenced the more mainstream churches, and all this had given birth to a thriving publishing industry that made many fortunes, and also had a deep effect on American music: its joyous, optimistic songs in the vernacular style had been the most important musical experience of many Americans. In the twentieth century, vaudeville, records and radio have made music of all kinds accessible to everyone; white gospel music is still a thriving genre, but despite fine songs such as Stuart Hamblen's 'It is No Secret', and singers such as the popular bass-baritone George Beverley Shea, it has long since ceased to have musical influence.

Black gospel, however, is another story. For the purposes of this chapter it is only necessary to mention the black college students at Fisk University in Nashville (just one of whom had not been a slave), who were trained by the school's treasurer, a young white man named George White. Fisk had been founded by the American Missionary Association in 1866. A collection of black spirituals, *Slave Songs of the United States*, was first published in 1867, but it remained obscure and was not recognized as a landmark until 1929; White was probably unaware of it. The school was in financial trouble, so White took his students on the road. Younger students replaced older ones as they left the group; they sang pop songs, such as those by Foster, and also spirituals which they remembered from their own experience. Their name was changed to the Jubilee Singers, and they performed at Henry Ward Beecher's Plymouth Church in New York City (where the press, which hated Beecher, called them 'Beecher's Nigger Minstrels').

The public didn't know what to make of them at first. For one thing, many northerners outside big cities were used to black-face entertainers, and had hardly seen real black people. (Minstrelsy had had a similar problem: sheet music was often published with pictures of composers and performers without the burnt cork, so that the public would know that they were not really black.) Enter bandleader

and cornettist Patrick Gilmore, who had started a series of International Peace Festivals in Boston after the Civil War; in a new
venue that could hold fifty thousand people he directed an orchestra
of a thousand and a chorus of ten thousand. In 1872 the eighteen-day
festival had to be underwritten by the publisher Oliver Ditson; the
support of President Grant led to visits from some of the best
military bands in the world, and Johann Strauss came to conduct his
'Blue Danube' waltz. The Jubilee Singers were a tremendous hit, and
Jubilee Songs as Sung by the Jubilee Singers was published by Biglow and
Main. Over a hundred of the songs, among them 'Swing Low, Sweet
Chariot', 'Go Down, Moses' and 'Steal Away to Jesus', were transcribed and arranged by T. F. Seward, who also became the group's
music director. On European tours they earned $175,000 for their
school in six years, and the 'slave songs' entered the world's musical
vocabulary for good. In the next century the passionate style of the
black pentecostal churches would have an even greater impact.

In the secular world of the 1880s the post-war binge of permissive-
ness turned into a hangover. The decade was anything but dull. The
West was being won, native Americans effectively exterminated and
the railways built, while settlers still found cheap homestead land; the
Brooklyn Bridge was opened and the building of the Statue of
Liberty began. New immigrants were mostly Scandinavians and
Germans, who did not immediately contribute to popular song, and
Jews, who would make their spectacular mark in the second generation. Perhaps the Civil War was far enough in the past for regret to
have crept into the lingering hatred between North and South;
whatever the reason, there was a rebirth of nostalgia, which spilled
over into the maudlin. Songs like 'The Old Slave's Dream' – evidence
of nostalgia for slavery – were sung in white parlours.

At a time when childbirth was far more risky than it is today,
many unbearably sentimental songs created a genre that W. S.
Gilbert called 'shabby genteel'. One Harry Kennedy published 'A
Flower from My Angel Mother's Grave', 'A Little Faded Rosebud in
Our Bible' and 'Cradle's Empty, Baby's Gone', among others. Temper-
ance songs were common: 'Father, Come Home' was written in 1864
by Henry Clay Work, but became popular much later. Work's Civil
War songs had included 'Kingdom's Coming', an anti-slavery song,

and 'Marching Through Georgia'; his other best-known song is 'Grandfather's Clock' (1875), in which the music in the accompaniment pauses on an abrupt quaver as the clock stops at the moment of the old man's death.

'Ten Nights in a Barroom', by Timothy Arthur, is a tear-jerker about a little girl who is sent to the tavern to bring Father home to see his dying little boy, whose last words are 'I want to kiss Papa goodnight'. Kennedy's 'Cradle's Empty, Baby's Gone' was parodied as 'Bottle's Empty, Daddy's Tight'. It is to be wondered if temperance people knew a parody when they heard one; some of these songs might be amusing in retrospect, except that they eventually encouraged the disaster of Prohibition. 'The Old Man's Drunk Again' began 'You've no doubt heard the song / Called Father dear come home', and included the lines 'How the old man used to smile / And cause his family pain'. (To 'smile' was a period euphemism for having a taste.)

Not all the songs were dreary. 'Fizz, Fizz, Glorious Fizz' was intended to be funny and there were many 'girly' songs celebrating permissiveness, which after all could never recede entirely: 'My Gal in Kalamazoo', 'Up at Jones' Wood', 'The Dance at Battery Park' were about the good times boys and girls could have. 'Flirting on Our Block' made great use of the word 'it', as in 'all the girls will "do it"', when flirting on our block'. 'It' soon became one of the most suggestive words in the language.

And some songs celebrated America's polyglot population: 'Finnegan's Wake' was already popular, and there were numerous Irish songs, others in German dialect, still others about the Jews. Harry Thompson's 'Let Us Go to the Sheeny Wedding', far from casting a slur, took note of the Jews' ability to have a good time. Frank Bush was a Yiddish comedian who sang his own songs, such as 'Sheenies in the Sand', a parody of Harrigan and Hart's 'Babies on Our Block', about Jews relaxing on Coney Island.

A traditional English tune called 'Willikens and His Dinah', well known in New England in the 1840s, had become 'Sweet Betsy from Pike' when it was sung by miners in the California gold rush, and was first published in 1853. (Stephen Foster used the tune for 'The Great Baby Show, or The Abolition Show' during the 1856 presidential campaign; and the miners also sang a parody of 'Camptown Racetrack' called 'Sacramento'.) One of the biggest hits of the 1880s, as the decade started to recover from its binge of self-pity, was '(Oh My Darling) Clementine', by Percy Montrose, with which America began to celebrate its own past: 'Clementine', a humorous song about a 'miner 49-er' and his daughter, became a huge hit, and in future years it was forgotten that the song had been written thirty years after the gold rush.

In the decades preceding the 'gay nineties', among the most popular acts in the country was Harrigan and Hart in New York City. Edward 'Ned' Harrigan was born in a neighbourhood which included, census records showed, nearly 1,500 people, of whom only 10 were native-born Americans. He wandered, worked on the West Coast waterfront and made his way east on the stage: in 1870 he played an Irishman to Sam Rickey's coon in a comedy duo that was a success in Chicago. Rickey's swelled head took him off on his own, but Harrigan had met Tony Hart (Anthony J. Cannon, born in an Irish slum in Massachusetts) while singing in a minstrel show in Chicago, and they later dominated the New York stage. Harrigan wrote the material, and the music director of the Theatre Comique variety house, David Braham (born in London), wrote the music. The sketches, with songs and ethnic characters, eventually stretched to an evening's entertainment: *The Mulligan Guard's Ball* in 1879 ran for one hundred performances. The sketches were about urban life; the ethnic identities were stereotyped, but affectionate, about basically good people. A collection of nearly a hundred of their songs was published in 1883. Harrigan and Braham wrote together for a decade after Hart left in 1885, though their work always had less appeal outside New York.

Minstrel troupes were still going strong, most of them touring, but minstrelsy as a genre was running out of steam in the 1880s, becoming a black-face variety show. With the taverns and local 'opera houses' available as venues for touring talent, and with the railways making it possible for the talent to go anywhere, a variety show circuit began to develop all over the USA. *Chanson du vau de Vire* originated in a valley in Calvados, France, which was famous for its satirical songs in the fifteenth century, and the corruption 'vau de ville' was used of any light entertainment; the American music hall tradition came to be called vaudeville. There was a Vaudeville Theatre in San Antonio, Texas, in 1882; John W. Ransone, whose speciality was the Dutch comic in dialect, is thought to have been the first to use the word generically.

Tony Pastor (born Antonio Pastore) preferred the term 'variety'. He had worked in minstrelsy, and became one of the fathers of vaudeville, opening his Opera House in the Bowery in 1865. He hired the country's most popular entertainers, but also kept an eye out for talented newcomers (not only the stars of the future, but cheaper). At first he offered prizes – a half-barrel of flour, half a ton of coal, dress patterns – to get respectable women to come to the variety theatre, which then had something of the reputation of the free-and-easies; he insisted that his acts keep their material wholesome, so that families could come without fear of being offended. Pastor opened his second theatre in 1875, as variety was replacing minstrelsy as the most important American format for entertainment. A former free-and-easy was converted by women's haberdashers Koster and Bial into a glorified concert salon, and suddenly after 1887 New York was full of variety theatres. In early 1893 F. F. Proctor put on continuous vaudeville (that is, without intervals or starting times) in a converted church, using the slogan 'After breakfast go to Proctor's; after Proctor's go to bed'. Pastor resisted all-day programming for years, but they were all overtaken by a pair of New Englanders.

B. F. (Benjamin Franklin) Keith, like Pastor, was a censor, keeping the acts suitable for families with the help of his wife. Performers were not allowed to use such phrases as 'by heck' or 'son of a gun'. He began in the circus, but during the seasonal lull one year he operated a dime-show featuring freaks, and business was so good he never went back to the tents. He opened a theatre in Boston and hired a seventeen-year-old circus animal keeper as a boy of all work. E. F. (Edward Franklin) Albee soon proposed a pirated production of *The Mikado*; a huge success, it went on the road and paid for Boston's Bijou Theatre, a 'Temple of the Arts' and first of about seven hundred Keith–Albee theatres. In 1885 they were the first to offer continuous vaudeville from ten in the morning until almost midnight.

Keith died in 1914, several years after handing over operations to Albee, who had begun by stealing Gilbert and Sullivan and never stopped stealing. The restrictive practices and blacklisting he perfected included a covert agreement with Martin Beck's Orpheum circuit, from Chicago to the Pacific, and made him the most hated man in show business. Beck had moved his Orpheum headquarters to New York in 1905; he built the Palace Theatre there, with Albee's permission, and it became the one place every vaudevillian wanted to play. But Albee secretly bought up 51 per cent of the Orpheum circuit and forced Beck to hand over the Palace, whereupon Albee made it a 'cut house': anyone working in the one place where everybody wanted to perform had to take a 25 per cent cut. During a recession there would be several times as many vaudevillians out of work as there were treading the boards, but Albee would not give up his stranglehold on national variety. The only time he was ever investigated by the federal government he lied his head off and got away with it. The pride and joy of this greedy hypocrite, who was worth $25 million when he died, was the traditional $1,000 death benefit paid by the National Vaudeville Artists union. The corpse had usually paid in twice what it got out.

The established theatrical traditional of burlesque came to accommodate the more racy fare, and eventually included strippers. A town's burlesque house might be in a seedier neighbourhood, but while the vaudeville palace put on a more respectable face, it was still regarded with a jaundiced eye by respectable citizens, and the local law kept an eye on it all.

Despite the success of all-black musical shows on Broadway, black artists were restricted to the bottom of the vaudeville hierarchy. The Theatre Owners Booking Association (TOBA), in the South and the Midwest, was formed in 1920 with an investment of $300 from each theatre operator (black or white). The circuit of thirty to forty-five theatres paid $1,200 a week for a black vaudeville troupe, so that after deductions an average weekly pay was about $20 a person. TOBA was also known as Tough On Black Asses.

The most dazzling vaudeville shows were produced by Florenz Ziegfeld, Jr. After making a start at the Chicago World's Fair in 1893, he realized that his French-born showgirl wife, Anna Held, and in particular her legs, were an instant public attraction. She was famous for bathing in milk, and sometimes receiving the press while doing so; her songs, such as 'Won't You Come and Play Wiz Me?', were meant to suggest Continental naughtiness. By 1906 Ziegfeld was 'glorifying the American girl', using costumes and lighting to give the impression of lots of flesh. The quality of it all was high, though, and from 1907 the annual *Ziegfeld Follies* set the standard and broke box office records. It comprised a succession of skits, dancing and songs, often topical; in 1907 Salome's 'Dance of the Seven Veils' was parodied, when singer Mary Garden was titillating audiences with it in Richard Strauss's version at the Metropolitan Opera House.

The New York run of each edition of the *Follies* was followed by a tour; then, after a summer vacation in Paris, Ziegfeld and Held returned to New York with new songs and skits. Ziegfeld deserves to be remembered for the stars and songs he presented: Eddie Cantor, Fanny Brice, Bert Williams, Ruth Etting, Helen Morgan, Marilyn Miller and many more of the best of the era. Ziegfeld was paid the compliment of having quality imitators, such as *George White's Scandals* and *Earl Carroll's Vanities*. He also produced other shows, among them Jerome Kern's *Show Boat*. After his death the Shubert brothers bought the name and produced some more *Follies*, the last in 1940, but the era was over. (The three-hour-long film *The Great Ziegfeld*, of 1936, was described by Graham Greene as 'This huge inflated gas-blown object . . .')

For decades vaudeville presented everything from singing and dancing to juggling and trained dogs. In each town touring performers had their favourite boarding houses that took in theatrical folk; many a child working in a family hotel eventually trod the boards, having first learned a few turns from the show business fraternity. Sophie Tucker's autobiography *Some of These Days* (1945) is excellent on the tribulations of the artist. She was responsible for her own transport, lodging, costumes, songs, arrangements and so forth; she collected her wages from the theatre manager, who decided where on the bill she would appear, and she paid a commission to her booking agent. (Under certain circumstances Albee could require an extra stagehand to travel with the star, who had to pay his wages.) It was sheer talent rather than hype or television exposure that got a performer to the top. The ultimate goal was the 'legitimate' theatre, on Broadway, where there were few jugglers to be seen.

The biggest stars of vaudeville included Norah Bayes, whose real name was Dora Goldberg. With the second of five husbands she wrote 'Shine On Harvest Moon', which they performed together in Ziegfeld's *Follies of 1908* and later that year in a Ziegfeld show called *Miss Innocence*. A plump and not very pretty black-face singer was stealing the show every night with 'Moving Day in Jungle Town', so Bayes had her fired, and that was the end of Sophie Tucker's first Broadway appearance (though she outlasted them all). Eva Tanguay, known as the 'I Don't Care' girl after her hit song of 1905, was a top performer for many years. But the first and greatest female singing star of vaudeville was Lillian Russell, discovered and named by Pastor (her real name was Helen Louise Leonard). She began singing concert ballads and became a comic opera star; according to the *New York Mirror*, she looked like 'Venus after her bath'. During her long career she played the dairymaid in Gilbert and Sullivan's *Patience*, and wore the snug-fitting clothes of young boys or sailors on stage; her speciality was spectacular hats. In later years, as her weight increased, she won a court case versus a producer when she refused to appear in tights.

The lingering prejudice against British performers was finally overcome, partly by the excellent music hall songs they brought with them. Felix McGlennon's hits included 'And Her Golden Hair Was Hanging Down Her Back' (which he had written, but Monroe Rosenfeld copyrighted in the USA), as well as 'Tell Me, Pretty Maiden' and the rest of the score of the long-running show *Florodora*. Vesta Tilley made an international hit of McGlennon's 'Daughters'. A male impersonator, Tilley was also famous for 'Birmingham Bertie' and others; in the USA her cross-dressing was considered daring. The legendary Marie Lloyd and her sister Alice Lloyd did well in the USA, but Alice was hampered by the risqué nature of some of her material. Albert Chevalier, a singing Cockney comedian in pearly costume, wrote his own songs, including 'The Old Kent Road' and 'My Old Dutch', about his wife. Chevalier was one of the highest-paid Britons to work in the USA, but Harry Lauder, the Scottish dialect singer, was among the biggest vaudeville stars of all, making $4,000 a week.

The most popular radio and screen comedy acts of the twentieth century, such as the Three Stooges, Jack Benny, W. C. Fields (who began as a juggler), Abbott and Costello, George Burns and Gracie Allen, served their time on the vaudeville stage; Phil Silvers (TV's Sergeant Bilko), Ed Wynne and many more came from the burlesque end of the spectrum. In the late 1920s vaudeville began to succumb to the competition of radio and films, and was finished off by the Depression; it was said to have died at the Palace in 1932 (though the Keith circuit was briefly revived in the early 1950s for nostalgia buffs). In 1928 there were just four theatres in the country that still presented live variety only (no films). The avaricious Albee did not even see the end coming, and was bamboozled out of his empire by a coalition, one of whose members was Joseph P. Kennedy, a financial genius, father of a future president and just as greedy as Albee. Kennedy made several million dollars out of the deal, which included RCA Photophone – an acknowledgement that talking pictures were coming – and swallowed the original Keith–Albee circuit into a merger that became RKO Pictures. Variety survived, of course, on television: Ed Sullivan's show, presented on Sunday evenings in the 1950s and 1960s by a Broadway columnist, was nothing more than weekly vaudeville, complete with the occasional dog act.

Songwriters and music publishers kept an eye on up-and-coming talent in vaudeville. It soon became apparent that the best way to make a song a hit was to get someone good to sing it. The apotheosis of this was Al Jolson, the greatest star of vaudeville's golden age, neither the first nor the last artist to be offered a songwriting credit (and hence part of the royalties) if he would sing the song. He was listed as co-writer of 'The Anniversary Song', 'Avalon', 'Back in Your Own Back Yard', 'Me and My Shadow', 'There's a Rainbow 'Round My Shoulder' and many more, but may not have written anything at all.

New York has been described as the capital of a country that does not exist. Certainly if you are not from New York, you might be from Kenosha, from Oz or from Mars, but to a New Yorker you are from out of town. During its golden age New York was the melting-pot, bubbling with all the energy and emerging talent that that implies. Music publishing was centred in New York from the 1890s; songwriting had become almost a factory process, and soon the factory had a home: the songwriting of our century began in Tin Pan Alley.

Frank Harding was one of the first song publishers to commercialize the industry. He inherited a small printing firm in the theatre district from his father, who had worked in minstrelsy; he played poker with songwriters, from whom he bought songs, sometimes getting six for $25. In the 1880s, instead of paying performers to sing his songs, he charged them for the privilege of having their pictures printed on the sheet music, and gave them free copies that they could hand out; the back covers were filled with advertising by tradesmen. One of the songs was 'December and May', with words by E. B. Marks, a travelling salesman who learned the business from Harding and sold the sheet music as a sideline on his travels. Marks became a giant of Tin Pan Alley, eventually buying out Harding.

In 1881 the music publishing company of T. B. Harms opened in New York, and in 1906 it was taken over by employees Max Dreyfus and the young composer Jerome Kern when Harms died. Kern had begun with Harms as a song plugger, and Dreyfus had one of the best noses for talent ever seen: he published Paul Dresser's 'On the Banks of the Wabash', Lawlor and Blake's 'The Sidewalks of New York', George Evans's 'In the Good Old Summer Time' and Hughie Cannon's 'Bill Bailey, Won't You Please Come Home', and over the years he discovered Rudolf Friml, George Gershwin, Vincent Youmans and Richard Rodgers.

Willis Woodward began in 1884, soon luring Dresser from Harms. M. Witmark and Sons opened in 1886: teenaged Julius Witmark, a performer in minstrelsy, had accepted credit for a song called 'Always Take Mother's Advice' from Woodward, on condition that he perform it regularly, but then never collected much in the way of royalties. With his brothers, using their father's name because they were all under age, he started a music publishing company that eventually put Woodward out of business. The Witmarks became the most powerful publishers of all, and turned out to be no different from the others: Charles K. Harris formed his own company in 1892 because he had received a royalty cheque for 85 cents from the Witmarks. Julius offered Harris $10,000 for outright ownership of another Harris song, but Harris turned publisher himself, and was soon making $25,000 a month from 'After the Ball'. Leo Feist was provided with his first hit in 1884 by Monroe Rosenfeld, when he lifted the English hit 'And Her Golden Hair Was Hanging Down Her Back'. Feist was one of the industry's best self-publicists: 'You can't go wrong with any Leo Feist song.' He was among the first to go over to full-colour covers on popular songs, and was later particularly good at choosing songs to sell in chain stores, such as Woolworth's.

Chicago, Cincinnati, Baltimore and Philadelphia had been centres of music publishing. Oliver Ditson in Boston, for example, had long been a highly respected house, formed in 1835, and had one of the biggest catalogues. But Ditson published all kinds of music, as well as thousands of popular songs, and did not risk any money on anything untried. The new New York firms (like the eighteenth-century publishers in London) published nothing but popular songs, and were willing to gamble on hunches at a time when the only place most Americans heard new songs was on the vaudeville stage.

Furthermore, in the 1890s a more modern American national consciousness was being created: the nation threw its weight about, taking over the former Spanish colonies of Cuba and the Philippines. There was a serious economic recession and there was labour strife, but in 1901 the government decreed an eight-hour working day for federal employees. Most Americans felt that everything was all right, and were optimistic about the future. Songs, along with other cultural phenomena, were becoming of national rather than regional interest. The nation had been knit together by railways and the telegraph, and the national postal service was so good that anybody could buy any song: indeed, Gottschalk's piano pieces, mentioned in the next chapter, had sold all over the country for 25 cents plus a penny postage in the 1850s. Baseball's annual World Series began in 1903, and the first American cinema was opened in McKeesport, Pennsylvania, in 1905, when two entrepreneurs remodelled a disused shop to resemble a theatre and showed a continuous twenty-minute programme all day long; they called it a Nickelodeon because it cost a nickel (5 cents) to get in. In two years there were five thousand of them all over the country.

Music publishers (and, later, record companies) have always been good at shooting themselves in the foot, but in the 1890s even they had to acknowledge that there was big money to be made in the songs of the 'common people'. Between 1890 and 1909 the wholesale value of sheet music printed in the USA (and reported to the government) more than tripled. By 1900 New York was the centre of vaudeville, with the most famous theatres and the most powerful booking agents; soon it was almost impossible for a song to become a hit unless it was published in New York first. Harris's 'After the Ball', one of the era's earliest and greatest successes, was also one of the last to be first published outside New York, and when Harris formed his own publishing company, he moved it to the Big Apple.

The publishers were located mainly in the heart of the theatre district, around Union Square on 14th Street, and then they followed the theatres uptown. Witmark led the move to 28th Street between Broadway and Sixth Avenue, which soon became a warren of small rooms, each with a piano. During the summer the windows were open, cacophony spilling out, and by 1900 the street was allegedly dubbed Tin Pan Alley by Rosenfeld.

Monroe Rosenfeld was a colourful hack with taste, a magpie when it came to tunes, a gambler, womanizer, columnist and editor; he published an article praising Scott Joplin's music in 1903. He had worked for the *New York Herald* in the 1880s, when it published pop songs as a circulation gimmick. His forte was sentimental ballads, such as 'With All Her Faults I Love Her Still' (1888). An example of what Marks called Rosenfeld's 'melodic kleptomania' was his hit 'Johnny Get Your Gun' (1886), itself later quoted by George M. Cohan in 'Over There'. One story is that after hearing Harry Von Tilzer's prepared piano (with paper strips woven through the wires), Rosenfeld titled the article on which he was working 'Tin Pan Alley'.

Charles K. Harris was more successful as a publisher than a songwriter, though his 'After the Ball' was so popular that it inaugurated the era. Nobody liked it at first, but he bribed a variety artist in Milwaukee to sing it and published it there. Most of his songs were based on events he overheard or read about: 'After the Ball' tells of a man at a dance who sees his sweetheart kissing another man; he walks out, but never gets over it, and finds out years later that the other man was her brother. His other biggest hit, 'Hello Central, Give Me Heaven' (1901), began with a news item about a child whose mother had died and who tried to phone her.

Among the other successes of the era were Albert Von Tilzer (born Albert Gumm), who wrote 'Take Me Out to the Ball Game', 'Put Your Arms Around Me, Honey' and 'I'll Be With You in Apple Blossom Time', and his brother Harry, who wrote 'Wait Till the Sun Shines, Nellie', 'A Bird in a Gilded Cage', 'I Want a Girl Just Like the Girl That Married Dear Old Dad'. (They took their mother's maiden name of Tilzer and added the 'Von'.) Kerry Mills wrote 'At a Georgia Camp Meeting', 'Red Wing (an Indian Fantasy)', 'Meet Me in St Louis, Louis'. Paul Dresser had begun as a black-face end-man; his many songs included 'My Gal Sal' and 'On the Banks of the Wabash', for which his brother, novelist Theodore Dreiser, wrote the words to the chorus.

It will be immediately obvious that we have entered a new era of popular songwriting. Plenty of sentiment and nostalgia is distributed among these titles, but the craft of writing a song with staying power had reached a new peak. We will look at the effect of the invention of sound recording in a later chapter, but meanwhile it is worth noting that there were no fewer than thirty-nine hit recordings between 1893 and 1943 of the twelve Tin Pan Alley songs mentioned above since 'After the Ball'. 'At a Georgia Camp Meeting' became a dixieland jazz favourite (at least seven recordings of it were listed in the British Music Master record catalogue in 1988); there was an instrumental Swing Era recording of 'Red Wing', a fine tune and a modern one, in the sense that it is superbly adaptable. In fact, these songs and others like them have been used throughout the twentieth century, in films, cartoons, plays and so on, to evoke what we like to think of as a happier time, when everyone believed in progress and race riots and world wars had not yet happened.

The overtly maudlin song was still around: Dresser's earlier efforts had included 'The Letter That Never Came' and 'The Pardon Came Too Late', while 'My Gal Sal' and 'In the Shade of the Old Apple Tree' (by Harry H. Williams and Egbert Van Alstyne, 1905) were about graves. But most of the songs that have survived from the period are of more general appeal and usually good-time songs. 'Down By the Old Mill Stream' and 'Sweet Adeline' became the quintessential barber-shop harmony songs. Among the many songs in 3/4 time were 'In the Good Old Summer Time', 'I Wonder Who's Kissing Her Now', 'The Band Played On', 'You Tell Me Your Dream' and 'When You Were Sweet Sixteen'; 'Meet Me Tonight in Dreamland' and 'Let Me Call You Sweetheart' (1909–10), both by Leo Friedman and Beth Slater Whitson, sold millions of copies of sheet music. Songs specifically about New York included Percy Gaunt's 'The Bowery', already a hit in 1892, and 'Sidewalks of New York' (1894), which commemorates a time when children could play in the side-streets of the world's biggest cities.

Harry Dacre was an English songwriter and performer who came to New York in the 1890s, bringing his bicycle. To his surprise, the customs people exacted a toll on it. 'Lucky for you it wasn't built for two,' a friend remarked. And the result was 'Daisy Bell', also known as 'Daisy, Daisy' or 'Bicycle Built for Two'. No publisher in America wanted the song, so Dacre gave it to Kate Lawrence, a British music hall artist on her way back to London; from there it swept the world.

Another song with a similar history is 'Ta-ra-ra-boom-de-ay'. Nobody knew where it came from – it was apparently heard in Babe Conners's brothel in St Louis in the late 1880s, where Mama Lou played the piano and sang. With cleaned-up (but not very good) lyrics, it was a flop when published in New York in 1891 by Henry J. Sayers, who admitted that he had not written it. Then Lottie Collins sang it in London. In 1892 the *New York Herald* correspondent wrote that the refrain had become 'a hideous nightmare' and had even been blurted out by an actor on stage in Oscar Wilde's *Lady Windermere's Fan*, convulsing the audience. The song shows how words, phrases and tunes from this era entered the common consciousness: sixty years later an English newspaper article about top people having to rent jewellery for Elizabeth II's coronation carried the headline 'Tiara Boom Today'.

Semi-art songs, aimed at the parlours of the genteel, included 'Oh Promise Me' (1889) by Reginald De Koven, a darling of Chicago's musical snobs; all his other attempts at high-class parlour art were failures. 'Mother Machree' (1910) and 'When Irish Eyes are Smiling' (1913) can still reduce the sort of Irish-American who has never set foot in Ireland to sentimental blubber; they were written by Ernest R. Ball, who was born in Cleveland, Ohio. This genre produced almost the only big hits of the period not published in New York: Carrie Jacobs Bond set up in Chicago when Tin Pan Alley rejected her. To support herself and her child after her husband died, she designed and hand-painted the covers of her sheet music and plugged her songs in recitals. 'Just a-Wearyin' for You' (1901), 'I Love You Truly' (1906) and 'A Perfect Day' (1910) were her best known.

Sheet music sales achieved an all-time high in 1910, led by 'Let Me Call You Sweetheart' and 'Down By the Old Mill Stream', at a time when every respectable parlour in the country had a piano. We regard these songs as corny now; we know some of the choruses, but many of them were story songs and are not complete without introductions and verses. On recent recordings of some of them William Bolcom plays a vigorously sympathetic piano accompaniment, while the talent of his wife, mezzo-soprano Joan Morris, would have made her a worldwide star in the golden afternoon of the Edwardian era. The worth of the songs is clear: they were written for an audience that had more time to listen, an audience whose ears had not been dulled by constant Muzak. They are the peak of the songwriting that began in the English pleasure gardens, artless art songs for the English-speaking masses. That we have lost the ability to appreciate the songs our ancestors loved suggests we may have lost even more.

But already hits of a new type were arriving. They came from the second American genre, after minstrelsy, to be created largely by black Americans and to become internationally popular: ragtime.

4

The Ragtime Era and the Coon Shouters

The history of modern popular music may be seen as the repeated rescuing of a moribund scene by the music of African-Americans. Stephen Foster's songs were a brilliant oasis in a desert in the mid nineteenth century. Not only were his minstrel songs sympathetic, but they had some of the feeling of the Negro church in them. He died after emancipation but before the end of the Civil War, and the black influence in mainstream songwriting temporarily disappeared with him.

When British art critic Giles Auty visited the Soviet Union in 1988, a Russian painter said to him, 'We are told that we have this thing called freedom now, but nobody knows what it is.' Auty pointed out that the rapid re-establishment of a genuine Russian identity in art would have a welcome effect on stale western criticism and the sale-room mentality, but also that it would take many years of *perestroika* before the artists found out what they wanted to do. The newly freed American slaves were in the same position after 1865, which is partly why popular music in the second half of the nineteenth century was dominated by good-time jingles and maudlin songs like 'Cradle's Empty, Baby's Gone'.

In the almost thirty years between 1885 and the First World War the modern American popular song began to emerge. The rhythms of minstrelsy continued to percolate into the mainstream; the cake-walk demanded something that the waltzes, polkas and marches of European music simply could not supply. The trauma of the Civil War was slowly left behind as the South was ignored and the North became richer and more powerful. A new American identity generated songs which could not have been written anywhere else. Many of the ex-slaves and their families drifted across the country, establishing themselves in their own neighbourhoods in most northern towns of any size. Coon songs came out of minstrelsy, and were already established in vaudeville, when all this culminated in ragtime.

Ragtime used a march-type (oompah) bass line, but set syncopated melodies against it. It swept the world between 1897 and 1920. In retrospect, ragtime is widely regarded as a solo piano music, but that was only its most highly developed and most enduring manifestation. Ragtime songs, music for small groups and brass bands and ragtime waltzes were all important, as was banjo music: ragtime may have begun with attempts to imitate the banjo on the keyboard.

The concert pianist and composer Louis Moreau Gottschalk was born in New Orleans. He studied music privately in Europe, and was praised by Berlioz and Liszt; he could be described as America's Liszt, for ladies swooned at his recitals. Like Edwin Christy, he was influenced by the dancing at Congo Square. Instead of playing florid keyboard imitations of Wagnerian operas, he used Creole and Afro-Hispanic idioms. His piano pieces, such as 'Bamboula', 'The Banjo' and 'La Bananier', and his more ambitious works might have made him America's Glinka (the great Russian nationalist) had he not died (of either yellow fever or peritonitis) while on tour in Rio de Janeiro, where a trunkful of his music, probably including operas, was lost.

He had left San Francisco suddenly on a night boat in 1865. He had taken two young ladies for a late-night carriage ride, one of whom happened to be from a prominent family. The incident was exaggerated by an enemy, who was also angry because Gottschalk preferred the Chickering piano (competition between Steinway and Chickering was intense). Gottschalk was a sensualist, and also capable of sentimentality. His biggest hit, 'The Last Hope', was written in 1850 for a Cuban fan who claimed she would expire if he did not do something about her passion; along with 'The Dying Poet', it was later a staple of cinema pianists accompanying death scenes. ('The Last Hope' also became a Protestant hymn called 'Mercy'.)

As well as Gottschalk's 'The Banjo', there was a piano piece called 'Imitation of the Banjo' (1854), by one W. K. Batchelder, which was dedicated to Christy's banjoist Thomas Briggs. If the 'banjar' is thought to have come directly from Africa, African music also features the additive rhythms that became a principal feature of ragtime. While European music has often been polyrhythmic as well as polyphonic (as for example in Italian and English madrigals), it divides its rhythms by means of bar lines. The African was unrestricted by sheet music, and loved to add rhythms in a different way. Western musicologists discovered that a chorus of several percussion instruments in an African piece, if notated in the style of western orchestral music, would have bar lines that do not coincide vertically, as they would in a European manuscript. In their dancing, in minstrelsy and then in ragtime, black Americans were insisting on setting European-style music free by refusing to be restricted to a ground beat. The dancing in Congo Square was described as in 'ragged' time in 1886; in 1888 a banjo player in Nebraska wrote to a music magazine requesting music in 'broken time' like the 'ear-players' played, but none had been printed yet.

The Chicago World's Fair of 1893, also called the World's Columbian Exposition, was a watershed in national American culture. Chicago then had more railways going in and out of it than any other city in the country, and the fair attracted tourists from all over the world; every American performer wanted to play there. One of the stars of the show was John Hutchinson, of the Hutchinson Family, thirteen brothers and sisters who had known national fame since beginning as a quartet in the 1840s. Their harmony was so close and accurate that the individual voices could not be heard. They sang in England in 1846, and in the White House for Lincoln in 1862. They hated slavery, and preferred smaller venues where they might find sympathetic audiences for abolitionist songs. During the Civil War they sang Root's 'Battle Cry of Freedom' and Kittredge's 'Tenting on the Old Camp Ground'; later they sang the spirituals of Fisk's Jubilee Singers, taking them to white audiences who might not otherwise have heard them. By 1893 the Hutchinsons' stardom was over, having spawned uncounted imitators, but John was one of the grand old men of American popular music.

Florenz Ziegfeld, a prominent local music teacher, was music director at the 1893 Fair, and sent his son to Europe to hire exciting talent. Florenz Ziegfeld, Jr, did not do that very well, but made some money by exhibiting the World's Strongest Man in Chicago (with flesh-coloured tights) and never looked back. The Fair attracted itinerant pianists, who were already playing ragtime.

Ragtime seemed to emerge in the Midwest, chiefly in Chicago, St Louis and Louisville, Kentucky; but, like jazz later, it probably grew up in many places at once, and certainly spread rapidly. The first compositions that were labelled as ragtime were published in 1896: songs called 'My Coal Black Lady', by W. H. Krell, and 'All Coons Look Alike to Me', by Ernest Hogan; the latter included optional 'Negro "Rag" Accompaniment'. In 1897 the first tunes calling themselves rags, Krell's 'Mississippi Rag' and Tom Turpin's 'Harlem Rag', appeared, the first recordings were made, on the banjo by Vess L. Ossman, who became an international celebrity, and by the Metropolitan Band, and pianist-composer Ben Harney published his *Rag-time Instructor*.

Between two and three thousand instrumental rags and a similar number of ragtime songs were published, as well as about one hundred ragtime waltzes. Most of the songs are forgotten now, but the instrumental rags remain the essence of ragtime today, and the best-known composer of these was Scott Joplin.

Born in Texarkana, Arkansas, as a young man Joplin played cornet in the Queen City Negro Band of Sedalia, Missouri, in the 1890s; he probably played at the Chicago World's Fair. He sold his first compositions ('Please Say You Will' and 'Picture of Her Face') in 1895 and his first rags in 1899. 'Original Rags' was sold outright to a publisher in Kansas City, but 'Maple Leaf Rag' was published in Sedalia by John Stark, with whom Joplin made a royalty agreement. It was the biggest ragtime hit of all: on the strength of it Stark moved his business to St Louis and then to New York. By 1915 Stark had published an orchestral folio, *Standard High-class Rags*, which became known as the 'Red Back Book' because of its binding.

Joplin wrote about fifty piano rags of his own, as well as collaborations (such as 'Sunflower Slow Drag', with Scott Hayden). He wrote the best ragtime waltzes, for example, 'Bethena' and 'Pleasant Moments'. Joplin and Stark tried to establish the classic rag in the face of a national obsession with ragtime as 'rinky-tink' party music; it became the fashion in Joplin's lifetime to play rags at breakneck speed, partly because of coin-operated player pianos in penny arcades, which were speeded up to make money faster, like some jukeboxes in more modern times. This was despite the fact that some of Joplin's pieces were printed with the admonition 'Ragtime should never be played fast'.

Joplin knew minstrelsy and vaudeville, having worked in both; he was exposed to opera by the conductor of the St Louis Choral Symphony Society, who played some of Wagner's *Tannhäuser* for him; he may have heard the great piano virtuoso Ignacy Paderewski and he probably met Harry Lawrence Freeman, the first black American to compose operas. In Joplin's time educational opportunities for blacks were few, and there were not many who had the chance to study music formally. The diminished-seventh chords which Joplin often used are found in abundance in barber-shop-quartet singing, and there is a considerable body of evidence to suggest that that style was also developed by black Americans: the well-known vaudevillian Billy McClain recalled that in the 1880s 'about every four dark faces you met was a quartet'.

Joplin aimed to create a body of serious American music in the ragtime style, but even if the form could have borne the weight of Joplin's ambition for it, he was doomed to disappointment. He worked on ballets and operas, but had little success; he died in a mental hospital in 1917. His opera *Treemonisha* was produced in Atlanta, Georgia, in 1973, and a recording was made; it received a special Pulitzer Prize in 1976. That the Pulitzer committee gave this bouncy pastiche a prize it would not give to Duke Ellington while he was alive is unfortunate, but Joplin's picture on a US postage stamp in 1983 was appropriate: his rags will live for ever.

Other rag composers whose work is often considered equal and sometimes superior to Joplin's include Tom Turpin, James Scott, Eubie Blake and Luckey Roberts, all of whom were black, and white composers Joseph Lamb (a close friend of Joplin, for whom he played part of *Treemonisha* in 1908), George Botsford, Charles L. Johnson and Percy Wenrich. Artie Matthews wrote fine rags, worked for Stark as an arranger and was later one of the first to publish songs with the word 'blues' in the title; his 'Weary Blues' became a jazz classic. Women also wrote fine rags, the most prolific being May Aufderheide and Irene Giblin, both white. Prominent banjo players apart from Ossman included Fred Van Eps, father of jazz guitarist George Van Eps.

When Douglas Gilbert published *Lost Chords*, a history of American popular music, in 1942, he thought that Ben Harney was the greatest of ragtime artists, and possibly the inventor of the genre. In fact, it was Harney who brought ragtime to New York, where he was billed at Tony Pastor's theatre as the 'Inventor of Ragtime', in the same year he published his instruction book. He wrote the hit songs 'You've Been a Good Old Wagon but You've Done Broke Down' and 'Mr Johnson, Turn Me Loose' (1895–6). The former especially has survived, possibly in variants: the Bessie Smith song of that title (recorded in 1925) is credited to John Henry, a pseudonym of Perry Bradford, and its ownership has changed hands since then. (At the turn of the century 'Mr Johnson' was black argot for a policeman.) It is not clear from most books on the subject whether or not Harney was black; Eubie Blake stated most definitely that he was. In any case, we cannot tell from the sheet music how he played his own songs: it was edited by somebody else, and the notation is old-fashioned.

It was not so much the rhythmic pattern of ragtime in each bar which distinguished it from other musics, but the fact that it was tied across to the next bar, and that the next note of the melody (in the treble clef) was not supposed to be struck on the first beat of the second bar: this is what made the melody syncopated. By this definition, as far as popular songs were concerned, a great many ragtime songs (including Harney's) were not ragtime at all, but, as with 'jazz' and 'rock' in the future, the term 'ragtime' was widely appropriated. Classical instrumental and operatic pieces were 'ragged' (played in a syncopated way). It seemed that almost any uptempo song could be called ragtime: so Irving Berlin became the most famous ragtime composer of all, thanks to 'Alexander's Ragtime Band' (1911), though Berlin is said to have confessed that he did not know what ragtime was.

Mama Lou (mentioned in the last chapter) was playing and singing 'There'll Be a Hot Time in the Old Town Tonight' and 'Who Stole the Lock on the Henhouse Door', as well as 'Ta-ra-ra-boom-de-ay', in St Louis. (The first of these, with cleaned-up lyrics, became a marching song in the Spanish-American War.) Two enormously popular songs forever described as ragtime, despite their lack of technical qualifications, are 'Hello! Ma Baby' (1899), by Joseph E. Howard, and 'Bill Bailey, Won't You Please Come Home' (1902), by Hughie Cannon. These and many others, however, were also coon songs, the black-face vaudeville genre which was already established when ragtime came along. It was the combination of ragtime and coon songs (probably the same thing to the public of the 1890s) that led to the mainstream pop songs of the next century.

One of the first coon hits was 'New Coon in Town' (1883) by J. S. Putnam. The singers were called coon shouters, and included May Irwin, who was famous for the 'Bully Song' and Harney's 'Mr Johnson, Turn Me Loose'. The biggest coon hit was Ernest Hogan's 'All Coons Look Alike to Me' (1896), about a woman rejecting her lover for another man with more money. While a great many writers of coon songs and other hits of the era were Irish, Hogan was black. His real name was Reuben Crowder, and he began his show business career as a child in *Uncle Tom's Cabin* in 1876. (The play was first staged in 1852, before the book was published, but it was well over twenty years before a producer had enough nerve to use 'real Negroes'.)

Not only did 'coon' soon become an obnoxious epithet, but Hogan's title became an obnoxious catch-phrase; Hogan is said to have regretted his greatest success. In the original version of the 'Bully Song' Mama Lou herself sang 'I'm a Tennessee nigger and I don't allow / No red-eyed river roustabout with me to raise a row'. Ethnic stereotypes of all kinds were taken for granted by a polyglot nation that still attracted millions of immigrants each year, and the institutionalization of racism was less complete in the North than in the South. Later in the twentieth century ethnic humour would be one of the casualties of racism.

Other performers who were described as ragtime singers or coon shouters were Dolly Connolly, Billy Murray, Bert Williams, Sophie Tucker and Al Jolson, all very different. Connolly was married to rag composer Percy Wenrich; her hit records in 1911–12 included 'Waiting for the Robert E. Lee' (by Lewis F. Muir). The southern or 'Dixie-land' flavour of such songs helped them into the ragtime category. Billy Murray was one of the best-known stars in the history of recording; his 'The Grand Old Rag' (1906, by George M. Cohan, and soon retitled 'You're a Grand Old Flag') was said to be the biggest hit in Victor's first decade.

Bert Williams was born in the West Indies and became the first and most successful black performer in vaudeville and then on Broadway, with his partner George Walker; in 1903 they were the stars of the first full-length musical show to be written and performed by blacks on Broadway, *In Dahomey*. Williams had a streak of melancholy; W. C. Fields described him as 'the funniest man I ever saw, and the saddest man I ever knew'. In his personal life he had middle-class tastes and aspirations, but he had to wear black-face during his entire career as a singer, dancer and comedian. Later, when he became a star of the *Ziegfeld Follies*, he had to be defended against the racism of fellow performers by the producer. On one occasion, when Williams and his wife went to visit the Ziegfelds at home, a doorman refused to admit them until Ziegfeld threatened to move out of the building. Williams made two short silent films, which had to be withdrawn; racist reaction was violent when they were shown, though he was an accepted star on the stage. His most famous number was 'Nobody', a sort of half-sung, half-spoken bit of pathos which he recorded twice (reworked by Ry Cooder on his *Jazz* album in 1978). He made dozens of hit recordings from 1902, and was immortalized by Duke Ellington in 'A Portrait of Bert Williams' in 1940.

Sophie Tucker was billed as a coon shouter early in her long career, but made no black-face appearances after 1911, by which time she was a top performer. She sang 'I'm the Last of the Red Hot Mamas' in a film in 1929, and that became her billing. Always plump and not very pretty, she astonished audiences with her costumes and her powerful stage presence, and a repertory much of which could not be broadcast. Born in 1884 somewhere between Russia and Poland, where her family escaped from tsarist pogroms, she later played the wife of the American ambassador to the Soviet Union in a Broadway musical. At her first Royal Command Performance in London in 1934 she greeted King George V with 'Hiya, King!' She was still performing three years before she died in 1966. Her best-known songs were 'Some of These Days' written by Shelton Brooks, who also wrote 'Darktown Strutters' Ball', about Chicago's State Street when the black culture scene was located near the Loop, and 'My Yiddishe Mama', by Jack Yellen and Lew Pollack, who also wrote 'Cheatin' on Me', later a hit for Jimmie Lunceford. (Yellen co-wrote 'Ain't She Sweet?' and 'Happy Days Are Here Again'.) 'My Yiddishe Mama' was recorded in 1928, in English on one side and Yiddish on the other, and sold a million copies.

Al Jolson billed himself as 'The World's Greatest Entertainer', not without justification: he was the biggest star vaudeville ever had. Born Asa Yoelson in Russia in 1886, he was an inspiration to many later artists, such as Bing Crosby, not for his style (he milked black-face for sentimentality decades after everyone else had dropped it), but for his professionalism and dedication to pleasing his audience. His catch-phrase, 'You ain't heard nothin' yet!', was first used when he followed Caruso at a benefit in 1918.

We have already seen that Jolson was the best example of a successful artist who was given co-writing credit from Tin Pan Alley in return for singing a song. Tucker was first to sing 'When the Red Red Robin Goes Bob Bob Bobbin' Along', but it was identified with Jolson. He made the first talking film, *The Jazz Singer*, in 1927. (He was no jazz singer, and the film, though a sensation, was only partly a 'talkie'.) He sang George Gershwin's 'Swanee', 'My Mammy', by Sam Lewis, Joe Young and Walter Donaldson, and 'Sonny Boy' in black-face and white gloves, and typically on one knee. 'Sonny Boy' was written by one of the most successful songwriting teams of all time, DeSylva, Brown and Henderson, as a joke. When they sent it to Jolson, to their astonishment he liked it, and sang it along with 'There's a Rainbow 'Round My Shoulder' in the 1928 film *The Singing Fool*.

Of Jolson's eighty-five hit records between 1912 and 1930, twenty-three are calculated to have been the equivalent of number one hits (most of them in the acoustic era, long before pop charts). Many were probably considered ragtime songs, such as 'California, Here I Come', 'Swanee' and 'Toot Toot Tootsie (Goo'bye)', as well as 'You Made Me Love You (I Didn't Want to Do It)' and 'April Showers'.

'Hello Central, Give Me No Man's Land' was a First World War success in 1918; Jolson sang it in the show *Sinbad*, which made him Broadway's biggest star, along with 'Rock-a-bye Your Baby With a Dixie Melody'. The next year, after the war, Irving Berlin's 'I've Got My Captain Working for Me Now' was topical. 'My Mammy' was introduced in vaudeville by William Frawley (who became famous decades later as Fred Mertz in *I Love Lucy* on television); Jolson added it to *Sinbad* after the show's New York opening.

Jolson turned producer in 1944, and sang on the soundtrack of *The Jolson Story* (1946) and *Jolson Sings Again* (1949). Since handsome Larry Parks played him on screen, teenaged girls bought Jolson's records. Jolson entertained troops in Japan and Korea a month before he died in 1950.

Ragtime also led to novelty piano music: Felix Arndt's 'Nola' and Gus Chandler's 'Canadian Capers' were hits in 1915; 'Kitten on the Keys' and 'Nickel in the Slot' were played by composer Zez Confrey at the same concert as Gershwin's *Rhapsody in Blue* in 1924. Novelty piano pieces, based on ragtime but exploiting the idiomatic possibilities of the keyboard, became a minor industry. Confrey's 'Stumbling' used rhythmic patterns of three over a basic beat of four, foreshadowing Gershwin's 'Fascinatin' Rhythm', while Gershwin himself wrote 'Rialto Ripples' in 1917. Rube Bloom's piano pieces were a prelude to his first-class popular songs, such as 'Fools Rush In' and 'Day In, Day Out'; Nacio Herb Brown's 'The Doll Dance' has never been out of print; his 'When Buddha Smiles' was a hit during the Swing Era, and he also went on to be a successful songwriter. The novelty genre died with the 1920s, but not before having its influence.

The overall effect of ragtime on popular music was permanent, and classic ragtime has never really gone away for long. It was part of the revival of early jazz which began in the late 1930s, and in 1947 bands led by Bunk Johnson and Mutt Carey recorded selections from Stark's 'Red Back Book'. *They All Played Ragtime* by Rudi Blesh and Harriet Janis was seminal in 1950, though it has since been superseded by better books. Ragtime was kept alive in the 1950s by studio musicians Dick Hyman (as Knuckles O'Toole) and Lou Busch (as Joe 'Fingers' Carr), and the novelty aspect was milked by Fritz Schulz-Reichel in Germany ('Crazy Otto') and in the USA by

Johnny Maddox (a staff musician at Dot Records, whose recording of a 'Crazy Otto' medley was a huge pop hit in 1955). Whereas many of the players of ragtime had cause to complain about the state of the piano in the average tavern, in the 1950s it was sometimes deliberately made to sound tinny, often by sticking thumbtacks on the hammers. Winifred Atwell in the UK made 'the other piano' part of her act.

Max Morath, William Bolcom, Joshua Rifkin, Gunther Schuller and André Previn have all played ragtime properly in recent decades. Rifkin's three Nonesuch albums made the USA pop album chart in 1974, after the soundtrack of the film *The Sting* (1973) gave ragtime its biggest boost in fifty years. It was Schuller who conducted the 1973 performance of *Treemonisha* and made an album of arrangements from the 'Red Back Book'.

The fact that a ragtimer's left hand rarely indulged in syncopation is perhaps less important than the fact that it sometimes did, as in the third strain of Joplin's 'The Cascades'. Ragtime pianists, like the banjo players in minstrelsy, played things that were not on the page. They took part in 'cutting' contests (where they tried to outplay each other), ranging from tavern entertainments to spectacular events, for example at Tammany Hall in New York in 1900 (sponsored by *Police Gazette* magazine) and at the St Louis World's Fair in 1904. Some of the contestants in these affairs must have been presented with unfamiliar music to play, and many of them must have been capable of faking it, or improvising. Edward A. Berlin thinks that virtually every ragtime pianist was expected to improvise. There are also 'variation' rags, such as Tom Turpin's 'Harlem Rag' (the first rag by a black musician to be published, in 1897), and 'Lion Tamer Rag' (1913), by the mysterious Mark Janza, of whom nothing is known. We have to wonder whether these were written-down improvisations.

Some of the rag composers did not approve of improvisation. Artie Matthews wrote 'Don't Fake' on some of his, and Joplin was explicit: '"Joplin ragtime" is destroyed by careless or imperfect rendering . . . [It is] harmonized with the supposition that each note will be played as it is written, as it takes this and also the proper time divisions to complete the sense intended.'

But the valuable tension with European rules was well advanced in

American black music. Controversial in its day, and seen as a racial threat by some, ragtime encouraged the posing of questions about what American music was and could be. It had made another contribution even as the first rags were being published: ragtime was one of the final ingredients in jazz. Many early jazzmen thought of themselves as ragtimers, and equated the term with improvisation.

While popular musics since the eighteenth century had been written down, with jazz the role of performer as composer was rediscovered. But it would not have developed in the way it did without another invention, already decades old when jazz began: recorded sound.

Thomas A. Edison invented his phonograph in 1877, and before 1900 there was a thriving worldwide record industry. (The greed and constant litigation characteristic of the industry were also present from the beginning.) The 'phonograph parlour' was the beginning of the penny arcade, and the ancestor of today's amusement parlours with their computerized games, while many of the songs mentioned in this chapter and in the last one made million-selling hit records during the acoustic era. Then the invention of electric recording in 1925, along with broadcasting, changed everything again: singers like Bing Crosby and Louis Armstrong did not have to be shouters, like the singers of the coon-song era, but could use the microphone to sing apparently to each individual in the audience or listening at home; this in turn influenced the way composers wrote their songs.

The performing styles of earlier times can only be approximately re-created; thanks to recording, we are more influenced musically by our immediate ancestors than ever before. Yet paradoxically, the worldwide availability of the latest trends also means that the pace of change has been accelerated. The access of African-Americans, hillbillies and other minorities to the recording studio means that never again can the music of the 'common people' be ignored. To use an appropriately modern metaphor, sound recording meant that popular music became a whole new ball game.

5

The Early Years of Jazz

Jazz has been described as the first American art form. It is character-ized by self-expression; the performer is both composer and trouba-dour. Jazz belonged to its performers, and could be developed as their abilities and needs demanded.

The word was also spelled 'jass'. Some think it came from the French *jaser* (to converse, perhaps indiscreetly); attempts to trace the word back to Africa have been inconclusive. It was used in print as early as 1909 in reference to dancing, and in 1913 about US Army musicians who were 'trained on ragtime and "jazz"' (*Oxford English Dictionary*). Clarence Williams claimed to be first to use the word on sheet music around 1915, when he described 'Brown Skin, Who You For?' as 'Jazz Song': 'I don't exactly remember where the words came from, but I heard a lady say it to me when we were playin' some music. "Oh, jazz me, baby," she said.' It certainly had sexual connotations: American slang for the male seminal emission is 'jism' or 'jizz'. Song titles such as 'Jazz Me Blues', 'Jazzin' Babies Blues' were common. The word has been used of any jazz-influenced popular music, from the time of Paul Whiteman, 'King of Jazz', to the 'jazz rock' or 'jazz funk' of recent times, and today has so many connotations that many young musicians will not use it.

The purest origins of jazz are lost in ancient history, but more scholarship is now being done than ever before. We are too much the prisoners of our received knowledge; we are taught that Columbus discovered America, and we get the impression that he discovered that the world is round. But some people believe that the Irish visited North America even before the Vikings, and many educated people knew that the world was round before 1492. There was trade between Africans and South-east Asia as early as 1000 AD, which is thought to be how xylophone-like instruments got to Africa. We are taught that polyphonic music was invented in Europe, but the musical development that took place then was inspired by musics from other places. The moresca, an African fertility dance performed with small bells on the costumes, spread to Europe, where its rhythm is found in Monteverdi's *Orfeo*. Shakespeare referred to 'a Morris for May Day' in *As You Like It*, and the morris dance was revived in England around 1900, probably because the English thought they invented it. Similarly, jazz was not a discovery, but a rediscovery of musical values which in some parts of the world had never been lost.

Samuel A. Floyd, Jr, editor of Chicago's *Black Music Research Journal*, has defined black music as 'that which reflects and expresses essentials of the Afro-American experience in the United States'. To a great extent the mainstream music business had co-opted minstrelsy and ragtime, making fads of these musics with no respect for their black input. But in the case of jazz, helped by recordings and broadcasting, the beauty, honesty and joy in the music belonged to its creators. Airchecks (off-the-air recordings) from the 1930s and 1940s are always of interest since we can hear jazz musicians trying and sometimes failing to get their message across; even the classic Benny Goodman band of the late 1930s, a precise and well-drilled outfit, sounded somehow more exciting on the bandstand than it did in the studio, because it was communicating to a human audience rather than recording a commercial product. And the jam sessions and cutting contests, which have now disappeared, were never as successful as money-spinning enterprises as they were in their original late-night informal atmosphere, where the competition and invention were untrammelled. It is thanks to this aspect of direct communication between musicians and their listeners that jazz conquered the world, and remains at the root of twentieth-century popular music.

Jazz has evolved, as any art form must, encountering resistance at every step of the way. But it is not true that it was not taken seriously in the USA; perceptive writing on the subject began there in the 1920s. Conspiracy theories about the suppression of jazz were once spread by the American far left, which tried to co-opt jazz (as it did folk music) as a music of the oppressed for political reasons, following a decision by the Communist Internationale to define jazz

as a proletarian music in 1928. It was already too late for that
nonsense, and in any case the so-called socialist countries then
disapproved of jazz for decades on the grounds that it was an
example of western decadence. Great black jazz men and women did
not receive the recognition or the money they deserved because of
racism, but by the time the music reached Chicago white businessmen
were recording the musicians and singers and hiring them to perform
for enthusiastic white audiences. The Melrose brothers, Walter and
Lester, ran a music store in Chicago and were involved in jazz and
blues in that city at an early stage; they became powerful music
publishers as a result, and copyrighted many of the early compositions. The Lincoln Gardens, where King Oliver's Creole Jazz Band
played in the early 1920s, was visited by the best white dance band
musicians, who knew where the good music was, while white kids
(Chicago jazzmen of the next generation) sat on the kerb outside
because they were too young to get in. When we were growing up,
we Americans were taught that Europeans appreciated our music
more than we did, while we took it for granted; Europeans were first
to compile discographies. We could take it for granted because it was
so popular in America.

It is true that the white entrepreneurs often tried to water down
the music, yet it survived and remained honest, becoming popular
and influential around the world. But it is also true that most
Americans hear little or no jazz today, because broadcasting and
major record labels in the USA have been turned over entirely to
accountants, who are interested only in easy money.

There have been countless fine white jazz musicians, but the great
innovators (advancing the music's stylistic frontier) were almost all
black, a situation that may now be becoming an historical one: jazz,
or 'improvised music', or just 'the music', now has so many streams
that it has become a repertory music and a viable international genre.
Yet for me at least, in the 1990s the essence of it still comes from
African-Americans.

Jazz quickly spread all over America, but New Orleans was the
most important incubator because of its location. Ragtime and the
call-and-response pattern of work songs were vital ingredients.
African-Americans had retained an astonishing amount of their Afri-

can heritage for generations, mainly because slaves had not been allowed to take part in American culture. But Louisiana slave-owners, who were French-speaking Catholics rather than Anglo-Saxon Protestants, did not try to forbid slaves to play music and dance as strictly as owners in other areas did. New Orleans was a seaport, so that influences came in from the Caribbean, and it had an easier racial atmosphere than the rest of the South, at least until the First World War. And while every town in the USA had a brass band, New Orleans had them in every neighbourhood.

It has long since become a cliché that jazz bands played hymns for funerals on the way to the graveyard, and on the way back celebrated the life of the departed, with tunes such as 'Oh, Didn't He Ramble' and 'When the Saints Go Marching In'. Just as important was the New Orleans 'second line'. The mourners were joined by anybody who happened to be nearby; they followed the band down the road, marching and dancing along and enjoying the music. The second line is still important in New Orleans clubs today, as the dancers and ringside fans have been important in the whole history of the music: the communication extends beyond mere entertainment.

The blues (like the other American rural music, now called country music) began as a folk music, but jazz was never folk music. From the beginning there was a formal content. New Orleans clarinettist Paul 'Polo' Barnes said to British journalist Max Jones in 1973, 'You see, in ragtime music they had books and . . . you just had to read that music, and when you read it you were reading another man's idea . . . We played ragtime, but we couldn't read. And we played a different ragtime from those reading musicians who actually played it. We put our own version in there.' But Barnes also said that Buddy Bolden, one of the first jazzmen, played 'the way he feel the music go. So traditional jazz is really that: you play your feelings.' There was also a difference between the better-off Creoles and the 'uptown' blacks who had recently been slaves. Clarinettist Albert Nicholas was a Creole, from a musical family, and there were musical instruments at home; he knew Louis Armstrong when they were children, but Louis came from a much harder background. The Creole and uptown players 'all played together in the brass bands . . . Those were mixed bands, Creole and uptown. In a brass band they were solid.' But the

Creoles also had their own dance bands, 'and your uptown . . . sounded a little different, more gut-bucket'. The musical influence was two-way: the self-taught musician wanted to learn to play 'straight', while musicians in marching and concert bands were proud of their ability to read and to play either straight or 'ragtime', using crying tones, slurred notes and so forth. The early jazz standard 'Fidgety Feet' was a syncopated march.

Alderman Joseph Story set aside a neighbourhood for brothels and gambling in 1897, known as the District, or Storyville; but at the beginning of the First World War Storyville was closed by order of the US Navy. While pianists found their work in bars and brothels, and bands played mostly at picnics, funerals and in the street, musicians also worked in dance halls and on riverboats. The closure of Storyville accelerated travel to the West Coast and especially up the Mississippi to Chicago, and thence to New York City. There is nothing intrinsically wrong with the 'up the river from New Orleans' version of jazz history, as long as it is understood that jazz was being played all over the country. New Orleans was where many of the best musicians came from, and they followed the work.

The most famous riverboat bandleader was Fate Marable, born in Kentucky. He played piano and calliope, and first worked on a boat at the age of seventeen with a white violinist (Emil Flindt, who wrote 'The Waltz You Saved for Me'). Marable, who was not a jazzman, formed his own band in 1917 and worked for the Streckfus line out of St Louis until 1940. He made only one recording, in 1924, which is said to be terrible. But no leader ever hired more talent: the list of sidemen who played with Marable begins with Henry 'Red' Allen, Louis Armstrong, Jimmy Blanton and Earl Bostic and continues through the alphabet. Young people who heard the music up and down the river were impressed; pianist Jess Stacy remembered hearing a Marable band with Armstrong, Baby Dodds and Johnny Dodds.

Pianist and vocalist Tony Jackson, who wrote 'Pretty Baby', and cornettist and bandleader Charles 'Buddy' Bolden probably formed links between ragtime and jazz; neither ever recorded. Bolden was renowned for his tone and his strength – it was said he could be heard clear across Lake Pontchartrain – but he was committed to a hospital in 1907 and never emerged again. Cornettist Freddie Keppard took his Original Creole Orchestra to California in 1914 and caused a sensation, playing a new ragtime music called 'jass', a 'white-tie, all-musical act, with neither blackface minstrel clowning, nor even verbal comedy', according to Rudi Blesh. Keppard's band appeared in Chicago in 1915, as did Tom Brown's Band from Dixieland, called a jazz band at a time when any new, lively dance music was already known as jazz. There is a story that the local musicians' union, which resented the competition of out-of-town outfits like Brown's, spread the word that it was nothing but a 'jazz' band, and that this backfired and helped Brown's business. Keppard was allegedly offered a chance to record for Victor late in 1916, but turned it down, afraid that other people would steal his material; he recorded only once as a leader, in Chicago in 1926. The excellent trumpeter Doc Cheatham said Keppard sounded like 'a military trumpeter playing jazz'.

Early jazz history was confused by the fact that the first jazz recordings were made by the Original Dixieland Jazz Band, a white band from New Orleans that won great acclaim at Reisenweber's Restaurant in New York. Cornettist Nick LaRocca, clarinettist Larry Shields, trombonist Eddie Edwards, drummer Tony Sbarbaro and pianist Henry Ragas recorded Keppard's 'Livery Stable Blues' early in 1917 for Victor; they also recorded for Columbia and made obsolescent vertical-cut records for Aeolian Vocalion the same year, but most of their recordings were for Victor. They later caused the same sensation in London, with a slightly different personnel. The recordings were regarded as novelties, and did much to establish the public's view of jazz as a noisy party music. LaRocca copyrighted 'Tiger Rag' (their biggest hit), 'Fidgety Feet' and other New Orleans classics, and in an interview with Leonard Feather in 1936 claimed that white musicians had invented jazz and taught it to the blacks. By then the whole world knew better than that.

Spikes' Seven Pods of Pepper, with Edward 'Kid' Ory on trombone and cornet player Thomas 'Papa Mutt' Carey, recorded in Los Angeles in 1922, but the New Orleans style was best captured by King Oliver's Creole Jazz Band in 1923. More than two dozen sides were made in Chicago and Richmond, Indiana, on the Gennett, Paramount, Okeh and Columbia labels by a New Orleans line-up.

The front line of the band included Oliver on lead cornet, Louis

Armstrong on second cornet, Johnny Dodds on clarinet and Honoré Dutrey on trombone; Lillian Hardin played piano, Bill Johnson, Arthur 'Bud' Scott or Johnny St Cyr banjo and Warren 'Baby' Dodds drums. Stump Evans on C-melody saxophone or Charlie Jackson on bass saxophone were added on some tracks. The cornets carried the melody, the clarinet added a filigree commentary on it and the trombone played a bass line or 'tailgate' style (so called because in New Orleans the trombonist sat on the tailgate of the wagon so as not to knock anyone's hat off with his slide). In fact, this was collective improvisation, with everybody listening to everybody else: an improvised counterpoint. The acoustic recording process restricted Baby Dodds to using woodblocks instead of his drum kit, but the records still sound surprisingly good, and they preserved the style in the nick of time. The band swings madly or lopes easily, sometimes seeming to do both at once.

'Dipper Mouth Blues' and 'High Society Rag' sold well enough to have been national hits, had charts existed at the time. Oliver would allow only a bucket of sugared water on the bandstand for refreshment, hence 'Dipper Mouth Blues' (which became 'Sugar Foot Stomp' a few years later). In 'High Society Rag' the harmony between Johnny Dodds's clarinet and the leader's cornet is exquisitely beautiful, harmony in jazz always being coloured by the personal sound of each musician; and Dodds gives us the famous solo on this tune that was originated by Alphonse Picou. In performance and on record Oliver and Armstrong astonished everyone by playing breaks together in harmony that were apparently improvised; years later Armstrong revealed that Oliver would show him the fingering secretly just before each break.

The concatenation of historical events often poses mysteries. Why did recorded sound come along just in time to capture a great American musician like Oliver, one of the fathers of popular music? Or perhaps there is an illusion here, created by recorded sound itself. We will never know what Frank Johnson's music sounded like (mentioned in chapter 2), because he lived before the phonograph; but, according to contemporary newspaper accounts, his bugle, in a piece called 'Philadelphia Fireman's Quadrille' of around 1840, could be heard to cry 'Fire! Fire!' Joe 'King' Oliver succeeded Bolden as the leading cornettist in New Orleans, and the vocal-like colour that emerged from his horn was one of the things that made it so deeply moving. His playing was marked by subtlety, unlike that of the 'ragtimers' or of contemporary white musicians, and its dignified melancholy reminds us of the importance of the blues in jazz. Oliver was the principal influence on Louis Armstrong, and the way he growled through his cornet was immediately influential: trumpeter Bill Coleman heard a musician called Nassau doing it in Cincinnati in 1923; Bubber Miley did it in the Duke Ellington band a few years later, and it became an element in that band's sound, and hence in all of jazz.

Oliver played in Chicago and on the West Coast, and then returned to Chicago, where he led the band at the Lincoln Gardens that made the classic recordings. He recorded two duets with Jelly Roll Morton in 1924, which are not considered very successful; from 1926 to 1928 he recorded around forty sides (including alternative takes) with the Dixie Syncopators, a band whose personnel often changed. The line-up included Ory on trombone, Buster Bailey, Omer Simeon and Albert Nicholas on reeds, Luis Russell on piano and Lawson Buford on tuba. By now the original style was already mutating: more of the music was arranged and there was more solo space and less counterpoint. In my opinion Dixie Syncopator recordings such as 'Farewell Blues', 'Every Tub', 'Willie the Weeper' and 'Someday Sweetheart' are among the most heartbreakingly beautiful ever made, in any genre, by anybody.

In 1927 Oliver moved to New York, and his career began to decline. His music was already being regarded as old-fashioned; he made many fine recordings for Victor from 1929 to 1931, but could not play on them all because his teeth were going bad. His nephew Dave Nelson played trumpet on some of them, and many other good sidemen were included. Oliver later ran a fruit stall and worked in a pool room, while collectors were already paying good prices for second-hand copies of his records; if he had lived a little longer he would have been lionized by the revivalists who re-created the New Orleans style just before the Second World War.

The Red Onion Jazz Babies, a pick-up group put together for recordings only, recorded in 1924. It included reedmen Bailey and

Sidney Bechet, and vocals by Alberta Hunter; the recordings are probably the best example we have of how the bands played in the bars and dance halls of New Orleans. In 1923 Clarence Williams's Blue Five made similar classics with his wife Eva Taylor singing, Armstrong, Bechet, Charlie Irvis on trombone and Williams instead of Lil Hardin on piano.

Clarence Williams was part Creole Negro and part Choctaw Indian; he grew up in a hotel in Louisiana and ran away from home to join a minstrel show. Inspired by Tony Jackson, he ran a cabaret in New Orleans in 1913, began writing songs and formed a publishing company. He went to Chicago and then New York, where he was the first New Orleans musician to influence others there, and the first publisher to help black musicians. He organized and participated in countless recording sessions, helping the careers of scores of black jazzmen and blues singers. He wrote words and/or music for 'Baby Won't You Please Come Home', 'Royal Garden Blues' and other jazz classics.

As Ben Harney claimed to have invented ragtime for commercial reasons, so Jelly Roll Morton claimed to have invented jazz in 1902 (he gave various dates), but with somewhat more justification: a comparison of his recording of Joplin's 'Original Rags' (made in 1939) with Joplin's sheet music provides a good illustration of the difference between the genres. Anybody can practise for years and learn to play Scott Joplin well, but nobody else sounded like Jelly Roll. He must have been one of the first to play the new style.

He was born Ferdinand Joseph Lemott in New Orleans in 1890, but he always gave a birthdate of 1885 to add weight to his claim to have invented jazz. His Creole family (of Haitian descent) had never been slaves; his godmother disowned him when she discovered he was playing piano in brothels. One of the most flamboyant characters in the history of jazz (not to say big-mouthed – the urbane Duke Ellington despised him), he got by as an entertainer, a pimp, a gambler and a pool shark. He recorded piano solos and with small bands during the acoustic era; his several sides with the white New Orleans Rhythm Kings in Chicago in 1923 were probably made at the first interracial recording session. The piano solos include the first recording of 'King Porter Stomp', still a hit twenty years later in the Swing Era. Tracks such as 'New Orleans Joys' (also known as 'New Orleans Blues'), 'Tia Juana' and 'Mamanita' are the first to show what he called his 'Spanish tinge': a habanera rhythm, which is ingrained in New Orleans music, and played over a rock-steady beat results in a tension still to be heard in New Orleans rhythm and blues decades later.

From 1926 to 1930 Morton made nearly ninety sides (including alternative takes) with a studio group of varying personnel, called Jelly Roll Morton and his Red Hot Peppers. He was not only a fine pianist but an incomparable composer and arranger in his neo-New Orleans style; as well as occasional corny humour, virtually all of these recordings present much finely judged and beautiful music. 'Black Bottom Stomp', 'Original Jelly Roll Blues' and 'Grandpa's Spells' are all from 1927 and all with Ory; 'Wolverine Blues' was made the next year with Johnny Dodds. One high point was a 1928 session that produced 'Boogaboo', 'Georgia Swing' and others, including a trio 'Shreveport Stomp', with Simeon's beautiful, liquid clarinet and Tommy Benford on drums, and a quartet 'Mournful Serenade', with Simeon, Benford and Geechie Fields on trombone. During the Peppers period Morton, like Oliver, moved to New York and began to decline. He recorded again in 1939: a dozen fine piano solos including his version of Joplin's 'Original Rags'. Among his best-known recordings are those made for Alan Lomax at the Library of Congress; his playing, singing and talking are a priceless source of information about early jazz.

Sidney Bechet was a New Orleans clarinettist of unsurpassed lyricism, and had a famous wide vibrato. His recording career was peripatetic – he had a volatile temperament and never stayed long in one place – but he was nevertheless influential. He played with Freddie Keppard as a child and later with Clarence Williams, plugging songs. He went to New York, where in 1919 he joined the Southern Syncopated Orchestra, led by Will Marion Cook, and travelled with it to Europe. Swiss conductor Ernest Ansermet heard this band and wrote: 'I wish to declaim the name of this artist of genius, because for my part, I will never forget it: it is Sidney Bechet . . . who is so happy that you like what he does, but does not know how to speak of his art, save to say that he is following his "own way" . . . perhaps

the great road that the whole world will be swept along tomorrow.'
Bechet bought a straight soprano saxophone in London and thence-
forth concentrated on that difficult instrument, the only jazzman to
do so until Steve Lacy and John Coltrane, decades later; he continued
to play clarinet, especially on recordings.

Bechet performed with Williams in 1923, Armstrong in 1924 and
briefly with Duke Ellington in 1925 in New York; he gave lessons to
young Johnny Hodges, and played with Oliver in 1926. He led the
New Orleans Feetwarmers with trumpeter Tommy Ladnier and
recorded for Victor in 1932, but times were so bad that he and
Ladnier ran a tailor's shop. He recorded with various small groups
for Victor until 1941 and for Blue Note in 1939; the Port of Harlem
Jazzmen session included 'Summertime' and 'Blues for Tommy'. He
moved to France in 1949, where he became a national hero. His most
famous tunes were 'Les Oignons', recorded in France in 1949 with
bandleader and clarinettist Claude Luter, and 'Petite Fleur', which
was an international pop hit for a British trad band in 1959.

The musician who set the music world on its ear as the first and
greatest soloist in recorded jazz, later becoming one of the best-
known and best-loved entertainers in the world, was Louis Armstrong
(known as Dippermouth, then Satchelmouth, then Satchmo, but
always Pops). He came from utter poverty in New Orleans. Early in
1913 Armstrong was sent to the Home for Colored Waifs after firing
a pistol in the air on the previous Fourth of July; there he learned to
play the cornet. He played in Marable's riverboat band, and back
in New Orleans replaced Oliver in Kid Ory's band. Oliver sent for
him and in mid-1922 he went to Chicago to play second cornet in
Oliver's band.

Louis gave different versions of his arrival in Chicago: there was
no one to meet him, and he took a cab to the Lincoln Gardens,
where Oliver was playing; or Oliver had tipped off a porter, who
took Louis to the right place. It seems to be agreed that he was a
'hick' when he got off the train, and looked it. Having been a
hungry child, he loved to eat; he was overweight and all his clothes
were too small. Furthermore, he was in awe of Oliver, and lacked
self-confidence; but he was always a first-rate musician. Oliver's band
did not need two cornets. The music it played was beautiful, but

stylized, and Louis stayed in the background because that is what the music demanded. When he can be heard on the recordings of the Creole Jazz Band, it is clear that he is already doing something that the others are not: he is swinging more freely. The earliest jazz musicians were still ragtimers, inventing a style that came out of the brass band tradition, while the three most important and influential of the New Orleans natives, Morton, Bechet and Armstrong, were deeply familiar with the blues, and with the music of the brothels and dance halls. They took jazz to its first peak of creative freedom.

Lil Hardin, the band's pianist, became Armstrong's second wife. She was a formally trained musician from Memphis, Tennessee, and urged Louis to think of himself as a soloist. He left Oliver in 1924, and was hired to play third trumpet by Fletcher Henderson, who remembered him from a 1922 tour to New Orleans with Ethel Waters. Henderson's orchestra was then becoming a hot dance band in New York, and Louis set it alight. He was still a hick, wearing high-button shoes, and he reported later that the drummer Kaiser Marshall said to him at a rehearsal, 'Man, you come up here with them policeman shoes on?' On one occasion when he played something too loud, he had his own opportunity to make the band laugh: upon being reminded that the marking in the music was 'pp', he is supposed to have said, 'Oh, I thought that meant "pound plenty"!' But nobody laughed at his solos, which were revelatory: music in New York was transformed. Henderson's men drank too much, and sometimes played sloppily, Louis later said. After a year he left.

He returned to Chicago and worked with Lil in her band, but in November 1925 he began making his famous Hot Five and Hot Seven recordings with studio groups, using the new electrical process. It is hard for us now to imagine how these records must have astonished musicians hearing them for the first time.

The Hot Five included Ory, Johnny Dodds, Johnny St Cyr on banjo and Lil on piano. They made thirty-three sides in about two years. Maturing as an artist and leaving behind the collective improvisation of the New Orleans style, Louis began doing it all himself: with complete mastery he demonstrated all the self-expression possible in jazz at the time. His tone was clear, accurate and beautiful; he was the first to improvise freely in the lower registers of the instrument;

his technical skill allowed him to place notes as he wished, bending a note or placing emphasis within it, and playing around the beat. Swing was part of the essence of jazz from the beginning, but Louis fully understood the importance of playing free from the ground beat. He could swing the entire group himself. As an improvising melodist, he went further than anyone in recomposing a song. He did not invent the stop-time chorus (in which the band just marks the time each one or two bars, leaving the soloist to do as he wishes), but he was the first to take complete advantage of that freedom. His solos were perfectly constructed, yet obviously improvised in their ebullience. He sang the same way: he seemed to have invented scat singing (wordless, improvised, swinging nonsense syllables) since he did that too with such abandon. Among the Hot Five's best recordings were 'Cornet Chop Suey' (whose roots lay in the virtuoso solos that were always a part of brass band music), 'Heebie Jeebies' (for the scat singing) and 'Hotter Than That' (for a fine series of solo choruses).

During the Hot Five series he changed permanently from cornet to the brighter trumpet. For the Hot Seven recordings Pete Briggs (tuba) and Baby Dodds (drums) were added and John Thomas replaced Ory on trombone. 'Wild Man Blues', 'Gully Low Blues' and 'Potato Head Blues' are mostly solos, the last famous for its stop-time chorus. The members of the Hot Seven were drawn from Carroll Dickerson's Savoyagers, who recorded 'Savoyagers' Stomp'; 'Chicago Breakdown' was made by Louis Armstrong and his Stompers, a group that worked in a Chicago café: these ten- or eleven-piece bands included Earl Hines on piano.

The Savoy Ballroom Five made eighteen sides in 1928, with no New Orleans players, except Louis and Zutty Singleton on drums, but with Hines, one of the few musicians Armstrong ever worked with who was his equal. Recording director Tommy Rockwell had learned how to use electrical recording, holding Singleton's snare drum above the microphone as he played brushes on the opening bars of 'Muggles'. 'West End Blues' is famous for its perfect architecture and contains the basic elements which would identify some of the best popular music for decades: a well-known introduction, in the nature of an announcement (actually based on phrases Louis had invented while accompanying blues singers), followed by the statement of the theme by the leader and a series of solos, backed harmonically by other members of the band, among them Louis's heartfelt scat singing, seemingly improvised. A classic duet with Hines, 'Weather Bird', shows two very great musicians near their peak.

From 1928 Armstrong fronted larger bands, directed by others, at first the excellent Luis Russell. In his prime at the end of the silent film era he was a top cabaret and theatre entertainer, singing as much as playing and seen as a star by audiences who often cared little about jazz itself. Armstrong frequently played more than a hundred consecutive high notes at the end of hackneyed show-stoppers such as 'Shine' or 'Tiger Rag'; but he always made beautiful recordings. An early example of Lionel Hampton's vibraphone may be heard on 'Memories of You' (1930); in 1931 the hits included a classic version of 'Stardust', as well as 'All of Me', and 'The Peanut Vendor'. 'Body and Soul' (1932) shows Armstrong's beautiful muted trumpet to advantage, while 'Rockin' Chair' was a vocal duet with the song's composer, Hoagy Carmichael. All these were made for Okeh and then Columbia, and are thus the property of Sony today; among his recordings for Victor in late 1932 and 1933 are medleys on an early attempt at a long-playing record. In 1935 he signed with Jack Kapp's new Decca label, with which he stayed for twenty years. On Decca he recorded with the Mills Brothers, Bing Crosby and Ella Fitzgerald; towards the end of that period he was often accompanied by Gordon Jenkins and his studio orchestra.

Armstrong always suffered from insecurity due to racism and the extreme poverty of his youth. He was managed at first by Rockwell, and then by Johnny Collins, a small-time gangster. Sometimes booked 365 nights a year, and never having acquired a proper embouchure, he developed a chronic lip problem. In 1933 he went to Europe, where he was idolized and had a rest. Not content with stealing from Armstrong, Collins abandoned him in London without his passport. Louis had not forgotten Oliver's advice, to find himself a white man who would put his hand on his shoulder and say, 'This is my nigger.' He put his affairs in the hands of Joe Glaser, a playboy who then became a successful booking agent. Glaser was a ruthless businessman, but he understood the value of the property he controlled, and even travelled with the band in the early years. Armstrong began appearing in better films, for example, *Pennies from Heaven* (1936); he made more than fifty altogether, and finally had financial security.

Armstrong's big bands were sometimes not very good, for their only purpose was to back him, and there is some evidence that he did not want to compete with musicians who might be his equal. Jazz fans were disappointed by his emphasis on entertainment, but Louis was grateful to his public and always gave full measure. In a famous remark he said that his favourite band was Guy Lombardo's, his point being that Lombardo's 'sweet' band was reliable and musically impeccable. Armstrong's pop records are charming. As a soloist he continued to innovate long after 1930, too good a musician to stop creating; a 1938 broadcast aircheck with Fats Waller, Bud Freeman, Al Casey, Jack Teagarden and Willmore 'Slick' Jones (Waller's drummer at the time) is priceless for Louis's singing of the introduction to 'Jeepers Creepers' alone.

At the end of the Swing Era in the late 1940s Armstrong gave up the big band and thereafter toured with a small group. We will come back to Louis later, but it is worth noting here that many Americans, on reading his obituaries in 1971, were surprised to discover that he had been one of the most influential musicians of the twentieth century.

Swing can be said to begin with Armstrong. None had such complete mastery as he of the manipulation of time in performance, according to the performer's skill, personality and mood, and the nature of the song or tune. Many other factors might enter the equation, such as how long it had been since the last square meal, or the last fight with the spouse. By the time the Swing or Big Band Era began in 1935 the word 'swing' was in common use; earlier musicians had spoken of 'getting off' or 'taking a Boston', and a swinging ensemble was 'in the groove'. Sometimes it happened, sometimes not: the band had to be in the mood. There are stories about Armstrong or Waller being asked what swing was, and replying, 'If you don't know what it is, don't mess with it', or 'If you gotta ask, you'll never know.' A medium tempo that is easy to dance to is best for swinging, *pace* the popular conception of loud, fast 'killer dillers'.

Blacks were said to have 'natural rhythm', but the truth is more interesting than such racial stereotyping might suggest. To begin with, as we have seen, African-Americans had maintained the aspect of music as a means of social intercourse as well as of self-expression from Africa, aspects that had been played down in European music. Mozart, Beethoven and Chopin were great improvisers, unlike today's concert pianists. Classical music can swing, if everybody is in the groove, but nothing has put more people off classical music than second-rate performances, and a great performance is a matter of genius interpreting the written notes: nowadays there is often not much spontaneity.

Secondly, blacks in America had less to lose from self-expression, while hundreds of years of European Protestantism on top of three thousand years of Aristotelian consciousness had left whites somewhat restrained. Slaves in America were often not allowed to learn to read; dependent upon the spoken word for communication, they were forced to live in the present, which is where you have to be to manipulate time, while whites, on the other hand, felt guilty about the past or anxious about the future. Finally, as we have seen, rhythm is at the centre of African music (and not melody, as in European music). The performer who is swinging is commenting on the beat, which is somewhere else; swing is thus a polyrhythmic phenomenon. One way to describe jazz is to say that in the performer's improvisations the rhythmic element works additional magic on the melodic and the harmonic.

Soon enough, arrangers and composers would learn to write music that would swing, if the right people were playing it and everybody was in the mood. A good comparison is provided by Fletcher Henderson's two recordings of the Fats Waller tune 'Stealin' Apples'. The first, delightful version was made in March 1936, at a session when 'Blue Lou', 'Christopher Columbus' and 'Grand Terrace Swing' were also recorded. The second, eighteen months later, was made by a band with almost completely different personnel, and in a series of sessions that included mostly pop ballads (among them a version of Joyce Kilmer's sentimental poem 'Trees'). The second version is workmanlike, but the band's heart is not in it, and Henderson's piano introduction is unusually stiff even for him.

A more modern example is found in two recordings of Thelonious Monk's 'Hackensack', made in London in 1971. In the second Monk re-enters in the wrong place after Art Blakey's drum solo, intentionally or not, and stays there. The result is recognizably Monk's tune, but sounds like something that could have been invented by a cocktail pianist.

White musicians learned quickly. Jews and Italians were especially prominent among white jazz musicians of the 1920s, while in Britain a considerable number of jazz musicians have been Scottish. Benny Carter, whose European band of the 1930s included Scots, said it was because 'wherever they are, there's happiness'. Before long many white musicians were influencing blacks, and combining technical skill, good tone and harmonic adventurousness. Many years later cornettist Rex Stewart spoke in an interview about the first time he heard Bix Beiderbecke.

Bix, for Pete's sake. You know, I worshipped Louis at that time, tried to walk like him, talk like him, even dress like him. He was God to me, and to all the other cats too. Then, all of a sudden, comes this white boy from out west, playin' stuff all his own. Didn't sound like Louis or anybody else. But just so pretty. And all that *tone* he got. Knocked us all out.

Doc Cheatham put it this way: 'All trumpet players had been playing alike when Bix came along and opened the gate.' Leon Bix Beiderbecke became a distorted legend after his death from alcoholism; a book and a film were loosely based on the life of the 'young man with a horn'. Born in Davenport, Iowa, he began learning piano at the age of three. His brother brought home records such as the Original Dixieland Jazz Band's 'Tiger Rag'; Bix slowed down the turntable so that he could pick out the cornet part on the piano, and soon took up the cornet. He performed in Chicago and on Lake Michigan excursion boats as a teenager, and joined a band called the Wolverines in 1923. He made his first recordings the following year and became the earliest white jazz musician to have a considerable influence on everybody else.

He continued studying piano, and was the first important jazzman to be inspired by contemporary classical music. But in later life he hated to perform as a pianist in public. In the modern harmonies of impressionist composers he heard the same freedom as in jazz, but he would have needed more formal training and more personal discipline than he possessed to develop this. Yet what he did was miraculous. It was with Bix's solos, and the more fully realized composition of Duke Ellington, that jazz began to absorb other influences and put them to work in the late 1920s.

Bix's technique was unorthodox and he never learned to read music well, but his intonation was perfect. He had a faultness ear, a gorgeous tone and so perfect an attack that contemporaries said each note sounded like a chime struck by a mallet. Although he knew little about the blues, he was a lyrical, linear soloist. Unlike Armstrong, he avoided bravura; he experimented harmonically from the start, but, like Armstrong, was a natural melodist. He was among the first to play solo for thirty-two bars using logically compatible phrases, recomposing as he went along rather than improvising close to the melody, and building on phrases he had just invented in a previous bar. James Lincoln Collier described 'a humility in his playing, a humbleness toward his art. Always he is saying, I do not wish to intrude, but let me show you this marvel. And marvels they were.'

The Wolverines were not a great band and their recordings were acoustic; Bix's sound has been likened to piercing a curtain of fudge. Yet in good modern transfers the records are not all that bad. On Hoagy Carmichael's recommendation the band played at Indiana University, and it became a sensation on campuses. Bix was hired by bandleader Jean Goldkette, and spent the peak of his career with Paul Whiteman; these were the best white bands of the period. Whiteman was one of the biggest recording stars of the century and his band was admired by everybody in show business, yet even there Bix's marvels stood out.

The story that Bix was frustrated by his position in that band is not true. He was at the top of his trade and knew it, and Whiteman kept a chair open for him until the end. Bix's problem was his alcoholism (he had his first breakdown with delirium tremens in 1929), together with his German Protestant background. He sent copies of his records to his family, but they did not even open the parcels. (The same thing happened decades later to Ornette Coleman.)

Bix earned the respect and admiration of his peers, and increasingly of the public, but he never had confidence in himself or in the value of his work.

Beiderbecke's best recordings were made with small groups from 1927, led by reedman Frankie Trumbauer, which often included Eddie Lang, Jimmy Dorsey and Adrian Rollini on bass saxophone. The most famous are 'I'm Comin' Virginia' and 'Singin' the Blues'; the latter especially was memorized and played by white and black bands. Bix's impressionistic compositions include 'In the Dark', 'Candlelight', 'Flashes' and 'In a Mist', the last of which he recorded as a piano solo.

His admiration of Armstrong was mutual. Louis allegedly lent Bix his horn so that he could sit in, a thing he rarely, if ever, did for anyone else. Bix influenced Red Nichols and Bobby Hackett, who influenced Roy Eldridge and Miles Davis respectively; Eldridge was in turn the greatest influence on Dizzy Gillespie. There are links between Bix's advanced harmonic thinking and that of Charlie Parker, but the beauty of his tone and his phrasing can stand alone. Carmichael's songs 'Stardust' and 'Skylark' may have been based on Bix's solos; Carmichael carried Bix's mouthpiece in his pocket for the rest of his life.

Other young white players, particularly in Chicago, imitated their black heroes: Oliver, Armstrong and clarinettists Baby Dodds and Jimmie Noone. The late show at the Lincoln Gardens would be attended by the musicians whose own gigs had finished; the teenagers sat on the pavement outside. Bud Freeman wrote many years later that the bouncer at the door would say, 'Well, it looks like the little white boys is out here to get their music lessons.' The white boys soon invented a free-wheeling small-group Chicago style, with solos between orchestral, ragtime-like ensemble passages; there was usually an 'explosion' of sound at a climax just before the repetition of the melody, and a 'clambake' ride-out at the end. With a band of soloists, collective improvisation as it had been practised in New Orleans receded into the past.

The Chicagoans include the Austin High Gang, so called because some attended Austin High School: Frank Teschemacher on reeds, guitarist Dick McPartland, trumpeter Jimmy McPartland and Bud

Freeman on tenor saxophone. Other Chicagoans were singer and kazoo player Red McKenzie, pianist Joe Sullivan, banjoist and guitarist Eddie Condon, Gene Krupa and Benny Goodman. The style may be heard on recordings as early as 1927 by McKenzie and Condon's Chicagoans. Also usually counted as Chicagoans are clarinettist Pee Wee Russell, trumpeters Wingy Manone and Muggsy Spanier and a third Melrose brother, Frank, a pianist who recorded with Manone and Freeman, among others.

The Friar's Society Orchestra became the New Orleans Rhythm Kings and began recording in 1922. This white group included cornet player Paul Mares, clarinettist Leon Roppolo (whose name is often wrongly spelled Rappolo), reedman Eddie Miller (later with Bob Crosby's band), trombonist George Brunis and drummer Ben Pollack (later an important bandleader).

Pee Wee Russell and Bud Freeman were as innovative on their instruments as Beiderbecke on his, playing pretty, thoughtful and original solos while eschewing bravura. Freeman was the first tenor saxophonist to take a fundamentally different direction from Coleman Hawkins, while Russell was an original to the end of his life. Their 'sweet' jazz may have stemmed from the use of the microphone in that they did not have to play loud to be heard in their small groups; their ability to construct solos was always underrated. Freeman's recording sessions with his Summa Cum Laude Orchestra (an octet, with Russell, Max Kaminsky and Eddie Condon) in 1939 probably represent the high point of the Chicago style, especially Freeman's *tour de force* in 'The Eel'. Muggsy Spanier's Ragtime Band (also an octet, one of whose members was George Brunis, not a great trombonist but a fine accompanist in this style) made sixteen sides the same year, playing with integrity the tunes they had all loved in their youth, including 'Livery Stable Blues', and Spanier's 'Relaxin' at the Touro', a souvenir of his stay in a New Orleans hospital. But that was the end of the era. In later years many of these musicians were submerged by their dixieland identities, making a living playing for middle-aged businessmen in cocktail lounges. Even when record companies in the LP era occasionally wanted them, it was only to re-record the dixieland chestnuts.

In the mid-1920s on the East Coast cornettist Red Nichols and trombonist Miff Mole came from Paul Whiteman's band to play in each other's small groups, under such names as the Charleston Stompers, Red and Miff's Stompers, Miff Mole and his Molers, Red Nichols and his Five Pennies and so on. Their playing was less rowdy than the Chicagoans, and has been described as a New York style. Nichols was inspired by Beiderbecke, but was thought by some to play and compose in an innovative open-chord way of his own. Mole was one of the first to liberate the trombone from the New Orleans tailgate style. Nichols and Mole split up in 1928 and Nichols's influence was short-lived; in later years he was popular with tourists visiting Las Vegas.

Eddie Lang was born Salvatore Massaro, the son of a banjo- and guitar-maker in south Philadelphia. He invented jazz guitar playing, playing rhythm and solos in an advanced style: he played four-to-the-bar rhythm, often with a newly created chord on each stroke. His solo work sparkled with innovation, and he acquired a deep and genuine feeling for the blues. On some of his duets with black guitarist Lonnie Johnson he was billed as Blind Willie Dunn. He was Bing Crosby's favourite accompanist, and his unexpected early death (from an embolism while having his tonsils out) was as great a loss as that of Bix.

Jack Teagarden came from Texas. He began learning trombone as a child, and developed a method of playing all the notes without the long positions, using his lips rather than the slide. He had perfect pitch and read music well from an early age. He could play as fast as a valve-trombone player, and made the difficult sound easy; he combined his technical proficiency with a deep southern understanding of the blues, so that his rapid execution did not contradict the impression he gave of being completely relaxed. He sang the same way, in a warm baritone drawl. When he reached New York in 1927, he was fully-fledged and caused a sensation. He ended Mole's brief dominance of eastern trombone playing and quickly became close friends with Coleman Hawkins and trombonist Jimmy Harrison, both of whom were in Henderson's band. It is interesting to speculate how different Teagarden's career would have been if he had not been white: would he have joined Henderson? He played on more than a hundred recordings in 1929, but none at all in 1932. In

1933 he signed a five-year contract with Paul Whiteman, and his talent was largely hidden, except in his freelance work. He led a big band in 1938–9 but went broke, and the rest of his recording career was peripatetic. He never played or sang a note that was not instantly recognizable.

Meanwhile, on the East Coast, Eubie Blake, Luckey Roberts, Willie 'the Lion' Smith, James P. Johnson and others had been playing stride piano, a two-fisted style built on ragtime that emphasized a strong beat with tenths in the bass. Territory bands played all over the country, and larger dance bands were learning to swing. The Swing Era itself was not far off.

6

Broadway and the Golden Age of Songwriting

If the great songs of the first Tin Pan Alley period (*c.* 1900–10) represent the peak of the popular songwriting that began in the English pleasure gardens of the eighteenth century, they also represent the end of it. These were parlour songs, to be played and sung at home as well as in public music halls. They consisted of any number of verses that told a story, and a chorus that summed up the story, or commented on it, and with which everybody was supposed to sing along.

Typical of these songs was 'Waltz Me Around Again, Willie' (1906), by Will Cobb and Ren Shields:

> Willie Fitzgibbons who used to sell ribbons,
> And stood up all day on his feet,
> Grew very spooney on Madeline Mooney,
> Who'd rather be dancing than eat.
> Each evening she'd tag him, to some dance hall drag him,
> And when the band started to play,
> She'd up like a silly and grab tired Willie,
> Steer him on the floor and she'd say:
>
> > 'Waltz me around again, Willie,
> > Around, around, around;
> > The music is dreamy, it's peaches and creamy,
> > Oh! don't let my feet touch the ground.
> > I feel just like a ship on an ocean of joy,
> > I just want to holler out loud "Ship Ahoy!"
> > Oh! waltz me around again, Willie,
> > Around, around, around.'

In another verse we learn that Willie De Vere is a dry-goods cashier who sits all day; his doctor tells him to get more exercise, so Willie Fitzgibbons hands him over to Madeline. This story-song construction survives in children's songs, campfire songs and folksongs; but the coon song, inspired by minstrelsy and ragtime, began to demonstrate its rhythmic freedom in its construction, adopting the rhythms as well as the words of the idiomatic slang of the street.

Shelton Brooks's 'Some of These Days', like 'Waltz Me Around Again, Willie', is from 1906, but it is deeply influenced by the earlier coon songs. It has rather ordinary verses, about two sweethearts in a country town who, 'the neighbors say, lived happily the whole day long, until one day he told her he must go away'; later it has a happy ending. But the verse has been ignored (as in Jimmy Rushing's driving recording from the mid-1950s, backed by a Buck Clayton big band), because in the meantime the chorus became an anthem of the new century:

> Some of these days, you'll miss me honey,
> Some of these days, you'll feel so lonely.
> You'll miss my hugging, you'll miss my kissing,
> You'll miss me honey, when you're away . . .

The words look a bit flat on the page, but this is a new kind of combination of words and melody. Although it is still about disappointed love, it is a warning, not a lament, conveying the sort of bravery that people have to find in their everyday lives, and a pride that is dented but not daunted.

Another, later pop song (from 1918) is 'After You've Gone', by the black songwriters Turner Layton and Henry Creamer:

> Now listen honey while I say
> How can you tell me that you're going away?
> Don't say that we must part,
> Don't break my achin' heart.
>
> You know I love you true for many years,
> Love you night and day,
> How can you leave me? Can't you see my tears?
> So listen while I say:

> After you've gone and left me cryin',
> After you've gone – there's no denyin' –
> You'll feel blue, you'll feel sad,
> You'll miss the dearest pal you ever had.
> There'll come a time, now don't forget it,
> There'll come a time when you'll regret it,
> Some day when you grow lonely
> Your heart will break like mine
> And you'll want me only,
> After you've gone, after you've gone away.

Creamer and Layton also wrote songs for musical shows. Layton teamed up with Clarence Johnstone when they both worked for W. C. Handy in 1923, and the following year worked in London. As Layton and Johnstone, with just a piano and a repertory of over a thousand songs, they were one of the most successful acts in British variety until 1935, when Johnstone was named co-respondent in a scandalous divorce suit. Creamer, from Virginia, also co-wrote 'Dear Old Southland', 'Way Down Yonder in New Orleans' and 'If I Could Be With You One Hour Tonight', more songs which move further away from the barroom atmosphere of the coon song, but are filled with American demotic speech, and certainly have nothing of the parlour sweetness of the 'Sweet Sixteen' genre.

Creamer and Layton's 'After You've Gone' is an advance on 'Some of These Days', and an even better example of the new age of songwriting. The verse is more powerful and sophisticated, and less sentimental, but again it was the chorus that became famous. In 1937 Lionel Hampton skipped the verse and sang an affecting straight version of the chorus (backed by Art Rollini's tenor saxophone) before jazzing up the tune at double time, as if to say, 'Take that, baby!' But it is Bessie Smith's 1927 recording that is truly outstanding. In the chorus it seems that 'Some day when you grow lonely' is not going to fit, but she phrases it across the bar lines, and by contrast makes the single syllables in the next phrase, 'Your heart will break like mine', land like hammer blows. She also sings the verse, and her treatment of words like 'heart' and 'tears' is one of the keys to the interpretation of twentieth-century songs. Paradoxically, it was the ordinariness of powerfully rhyming phrases, married to a memorable tune, that lent the song to imaginative interpretation.

Although there may be several verses or stanzas in a modern song, it is all of a piece. An individual song may be technically divisible into sections such as introduction, verse, chorus, release or bridge and so forth, but modern songs are more integrated. Perhaps partly because of the explosion of a national entertainment business, a nationwide audience now had songs that referred more directly to the emotions, rather than telling a story. A new phenomenon was the frequency with which a song came to be identified with a certain artist (as 'Some of These Days' with Sophie Tucker), so that the interpretation could be almost as important as the song itself.

An increasingly sophisticated audience for these new songs was not foreseen, but as happens again and again in popular music, that part of the audience that delights in something new can drag along the rest. On the other hand, the new popular song was partly a triumph of the masses over the 'Sunday-school circuit', as Keith and Albee's national network was called. The success of variety in the late 1880s depended upon keeping it respectable, but the stars of the early twentieth century were such big attractions that they could give the audience a slice of real life. Instead of complaining that she was 'Only a Bird in a Gilded Cage', Eva Tanguay assured fans that 'It's All been Done Before, But Not the Way I Do It'. When Tucker sang 'You're gonna miss me, honey', what the errant male was 'gonna miss' was not the sight of her looking sweet upon the seat of a bicycle built for two.

A song tended to have a short introduction which was certainly sung on stage, but was later frequently dropped as gramophone records (with their limited playing time) took over from sheet music. From the ordinary listener's point of view, this was a vestigial verse, setting the scene for the chorus, which now has several stanzas and tells the story, but the introduction was often musically important. Everybody knows the tune of 'Love Me or Leave Me' (1928), by Gus Kahn and Walter Donaldson; the hit recording by Ruth Etting includes the introduction, making the subsequent drop of nearly an octave between the words 'or' and 'leave' far more dramatic, as well as lending it musical sense. Billie Holiday in her 1941 recording also sings the introduction, but then ignores the drop in the first line of the chorus, improvises across it and restores it in the next line, 'You won't believe me': it is even more dramatic because we've had to wait for it.

Rodgers and Hammerstein's 'Hello Young Lovers' (from *The King and I*, 1951) needs its lovely introduction to justify its syrupy quality (and is a good example of a true show song, which doesn't work so well outside its intended context). Hoagy Carmichael's 'Stardust' has a beautiful introduction, which was omitted on all those smoochy dance band versions that were hits around 1940 (especially those of Glenn Miller and Artie Shaw). When Nat 'King' Cole restored it on an album track in 1957, the delightful shock took a 45 EP high in the *Billboard* singles chart, while Frank Sinatra is said to have recorded a version using just the introduction.

In *American Popular Song: The Great Innovators 1900–1950* Alec Wilder states that the introduction to 'Stardust' was added only when the words were written by Mitchell Parish, but I don't know if that is true. The song was published in 1929; the first big hit recording, by Isham Jones with no words, was in 1930, but the uptempo instrumental recording made by the Chocolate Dandies, led by Don Redman, already used the introduction in 1928. But of course many songs have been written with no introduction at all: 'I Concentrate on You', 'Begin the Beguine', 'In the Still of the Night' and 'I've Got You Under My Skin', all by Cole Porter, are such consummate syntheses of words and music that they need no preface.

The terminology of songwriting is sometimes used confusingly by the authorities themselves. Although thousands of the new songs were in a thirty-two-bar AABA format, they were freely constructed in many ways, according to the genius of the songwriter, who, after all, was combining words and music in a way that had not been done by earlier craftsmen. A song may or may not be divisible into these parts. For dramatic purposes a song often requires a bridge or release, separating the statement of the drama (corresponding to the old verse) from its resolution or commentary (the chorus). The bridge sometimes presents the composer or the arranger, and some-times the singer, with an interesting problem; and a classic treatment of a bridge may become part of the song as we know it.

The verse came to be called the introduction to the chorus; and to make things thoroughly complicated, the labels on old 78s often carried the legend 'With Vocal Chorus' or 'Vocal Refrain'. (In poetry and in medieval and Renaissance music a refrain was a short chorus of one or two lines at the end of a verse or a stanza, so familiar that the audience was presumed to know it.) Jazz musicians use the word 'chorus' to mean a complete statement of the tune (without the introduction, typically thirty-two bars), as in 'Take another chorus.'

Songwriting in its golden age (*c.* 1914–50) provided an astonishing variety of masterpieces that are popular around the world. They are often sorted into categories of theatre, film and pop. The work of some of the composers for the musical stage is consistently ranked among the greatest songwriting of all, and inspired the best of the rest, setting a standard to aim at.

It is sometimes said that the reason for this is the greater pressure involved in writing a song that fits into a plot, but the plots of Broadway musicals were often little more than fluff, and too many fine songs have long outlasted their original settings. A more likely reason is that composers for the stage were literate and thoughtful artists, working in a genre with a long and honourable history, and were willing to have their tunes compared with those of Puccini or Verdi. Jerome Kern, perhaps the most important innovator of all, was influenced by operetta (born as he was in 1885), yet invented something new.

As with the invention of the popular song in the eighteenth century, however, modern writing for the musical stage happened the way it did and where it did, among the English-speaking peoples, because it had to fill a gap. Opera was big business in New York and Chicago in the nineteenth century, and a great many provincial towns had their local 'opera' houses (actually the local vaudeville palace). Once again foreign music became the preserve of the upper classes, while the *hoi polloi* was left to amuse itself. However tuneful (and indeed popular) the works of the great opera composers might be, America needed its own genre of musical drama.

The first performance on the American musical stage may have been in 1732, in Charleston, South Carolina. A masque by Francis Hopkinson called *The Temple of Minerva* was performed as part of a concert in Philadelphia in 1781, presented by the French minister in honour of George Washington. There may have been an opera called *The Blockheads, or The Fortunate Contractor*, published in 1782, said to be a burlesque of *The Blockade of Boston*, which had been written and mounted by the British General Burgoyne himself while he occupied that city. But little survives of these early productions.

By the 1820s and 1830s comedies and operettas (usually with foreign settings) were contributing to a slowly simmering stew, but these were pastiches, and the music often had nothing to do with the action. The genre did not discover any native composers or a style of its own until the next century.

To the various strands of ballad opera and light *opéra bouffe* (such as Lingard presented) was added *The Black Crook* in 1866, which was a step forward principally because it made so much money (though not for Thomas Baker, who wrote original music for it – the Copyright Act of 1856 had secured performing rights in copyrighted drama for the owners, but not for authors). The phenomenon was an accident: several theatres had burned down in New York, with the result that an imported French ballet company had no stage, so they joined a heavily written melodrama based on Carl Maria von Weber's romantic opera *Der Freischütz* (1821), creating a musical show full of grand spectacle. The theatre chosen was owned by British-born actress Laura Keene, the first woman theatrical manager in the USA. Her first success as star and producer was *Our American Cousin*, in which she was playing the night Abraham Lincoln was shot.

The Black Crook was another pastiche; the songs were changed regularly throughout the show's run, and none was a big hit. But the girls were good dancers. They were tall, and their costumes were padded in appropriate places to cater for the tastes of the time; they wore pink tights, but word spread (not discouraged by the management) that they were showing a great deal more flesh than was usual, and *The Black Crook* was supposed to be a saucy evening. The one song that remained as long as the show lasted was 'You Naughty, Naughty Men', which was not Baker's, but imported from England. It listed many of the faults of the male sex, only to conclude: 'But with all your faults we clearly / Love you wicked fellows dearly . . .'

The show's combination of girls, costumes, dancing and expensive sets led to a run of 475 performances, outstanding for the time. One of the succeeding 'burlettas' was *Lydia Thompson's British Blondes*, starring Pauline Markham (mentioned in chapter 3); but for many years, nothing much happened on the American musical stage of other than historical interest. Blondes and 'leg shows' became a staple, and the idea was to throw some songs and dances together and have a good time. *The Black Crook* was such a legend that it was revived a dozen times, until it was well and truly out of date.

The songs of Arthur Sullivan had some popularity in the USA, and the English operettas of Gilbert and Sullivan soon followed. Composer Sir Arthur Seymour Sullivan and journalist Sir William Schwenck Gilbert collaborated on thirteen brilliant comic operettas which are still performed today, and both became very rich. Sullivan felt guilty about not pursuing more 'serious' composition; no one set English lyrics better than he did, but no less an authority than Queen Victoria told him he was wasting his time.

The first American performance of *HMS Pinafore* took place in Boston in November 1878, and in January it swept New York; by May it had played in twelve houses (up to three at once), sometimes with all-black and all-children casts. The absurd story sent up the Admiralty, as in Sir Joseph's patter song 'When I Was a Boy', as well as the romantic fiction that a well-born lady could fall in love with a simple sailor (who in the end turns out to be a runaway aristocrat). So loose were the copyright laws of the time, so successful the show and so terrible some of the American productions that in one edition Buttercup was played by a 7-foot tall female impersonator. Gilbert and Sullivan went across the Atlantic to produce *Pirates of Penzance* themselves at the end of the same year. 'With Cat-like Tread', the song of its delightful stage policemen, was a success all over America, with new lyrics, as 'Hail, Hail, the Gang's All Here'. Major-General Stanley's patter song was 'I am the very model / Of a modern Major-General.' Perhaps their best-known work is *The Mikado* (1885), which has a pseudo-Japanese setting and sends up bureaucracy; Poo-Bah resembles a certain type of British civil servant as much as a Japanese one (the portrait still rings true a century later), while 'A Wandering Minstrel', 'The Flowers That Bloom in the Spring' and 'Willow,

Tit-willow' are still familiar, even to people who do not know where they came from.

These shows had plots, set-pieces, comedy and exotic settings in foreign places and earlier times, with sets and costumes to match; Sullivan's orchestrations were as good as his tunes, and all these parts added up to a whole that was like an opera rather than a pastiche, yet they were written in English, intended to be amusing and not too demanding for a middle-class audience. They helped establish an appetite for operetta in the USA. Franz Lehár was born in what was then Hungary; *The Merry Widow* was first produced in Vienna in 1905. Some of his shows were not produced in the USA at all, and he remained an operetta composer, famous for his waltzes. Others such as Victor Herbert, Rudolf Friml and Sigmund Romberg composed songs that transcended the genre to become American standards. The operetta form was stilted by later standards, but a model which could be modernized.

Born in Dublin, Herbert was an accomplished cellist and composer. He wrote about forty musical shows, of which the best known are *Babes in Toyland* (1903; filmed in 1934 with Laurel and Hardy); *Mlle Modiste* (1906; filmed in 1930), including 'Kiss Me Again'; *Naughty Marietta* (1910; the 1935 film made stars of the romantic duo Nelson Eddy and Jeanette MacDonald), with 'Ah! Sweet Mystery of Life'; and *Orange Blossoms* (1922), with 'A Kiss in the Dark'.

Friml was born in Prague. Among his biggest hits were *Rose Marie* (1924), whose book and lyrics were written by Otto Harbach and Oscar Hammerstein II; its enduring tunes are the title song and 'Indian Love Call'. It was filmed in 1936 with Allan Jones and also starred Eddy and MacDonald, as did the film of *The Firefly* in 1937. *The Vagabond King* was filmed as late as 1956, with Kathryn Grayson.

Romberg was born in Hungary. His *Maytime* was a hit in 1917, but the Shubert brothers apparently refused to take him seriously for a long time. (Sam, Lee and J. J., or Jake, Shubert were all born in the 1870s, sons of a pedlar who had fled tsarist pogroms; from 1900 they were the most influential theatre-owners in New York. Sam was killed in a train crash in 1905; Lee remained the best-known Shubert, but Jake's love for operetta was important.) Romberg's songs were dropped into various shows over the years, and *Blossom Time* did well in 1921, but it was *The Student Prince* (1924; filmed in 1954 with Mario Lanza) and *The Desert Song* (1926; filmed three times, in 1929, 1943 and 1953) which established Romberg. He wrote about fifty shows, and songs that became standards include 'Lover, Come Back to Me', 'Softly, as in a Morning Sunrise', 'When I Grow Too Old to Dream' and 'Close as Pages in a Book'.

No survey would be complete without George M. Cohan, a huge figure on Broadway but a unique one, who does not fit into any category. An all-round talent who came from a vaudeville family to be a singer, dancer, actor, composer, lyricist, director and producer, he had written 150 sketches by the time he was twenty-one. He wrote the most successful of all American First World War songs, 'Over There', for which he received the Congressional Medal of Honor, and was associated with about thirty-five plays, musicals and straight drama, as writer or producer. His shows always had strong story lines and his dialogue contained plenty of demotic speech, making his characters credible; some of the same critics who complained that most Broadway productions were stilted and unbelievable also did not like Cohan's use of slang. *Little Johnny Jones* (1904) included 'Yankee Doodle Boy' ('I'm a Yankee Doodle Dandy . . .') and 'Give My Regards to Broadway'. Several of his songs were big hits, among them 'Mary's a Grand Old Name', 'You're a Grand Old Flag' and 'Harrigan'. (Cohan had attended a funeral at which a folded flag was stroked sentimentally by a Civil War veteran, saying, 'You're a grand old rag.' Cohan changed the title of the song at the request of veterans' groups.) He was seen as the first to break away from the operetta style, but his dynamic, tub-thumping Americanism had no sequel. Cohan's *Little Nellie Kelly* (1922) was revived in 1940 as a film for Judy Garland. James Cagney won an Oscar portraying Cohan in the film biography *Yankee Doodle Dandy* in 1942, and Joel Grey played him in the 1968 Broadway musical *George M!* (*Little Johnny Jones* was revived in 1984, starring Donny Osmond, but closed after one performance.)

While Cohan was in his prime, black Americans were already making a contribution to the stage that was to be far more influential in the end. By 1900 Harlem was already becoming the biggest black city on earth. It had been a middle-class self-contained community, in which tenement blocks were built to attract commuters from downtown; when the speculating builders were in danger of going out of business, racial prejudice did not keep them from renting to blacks. Before long the concentration of talent was so great that it exploded into the Harlem Renaissance of poetry and literature, an African-American influence in all the arts.

James Reese Europe was a bandleader and organizer of concerts and musical clubs. Born in Alabama, he went to New York in 1905 and formed an association with the dance team of Vernon and Irene Castle, who were all the rage on the Broadway stage just before the First World War. During the war he led a US Army band and in 1918 took Paris by storm. His music was called jazz, which it was not; but he encouraged techniques of brass playing, for example, which he thought were racial characteristics, and then found that he had to rehearse his men to keep them from adding more to the music than he wanted. Widely admired in the black community, he would have had an even greater influence had he not been stabbed to death by a crazy musician in Boston.

Will Marion Cook was a formally trained composer, conductor and violinist who had studied with Antonín Dvořák. His musical shows included *Clorindy or The Origin of the Cakewalk* (1898), *In Dahomey* (1903), starring Bert Williams and George Walker, and *In Darkeydom* (1914), which used Europe's band and the lyrics of the black poet Paul Lawrence Dunbar. *In Dahomey*, about the 'back to Africa' movement, was the first black show to open on Broadway itself; its long run in London was followed by a national American tour. It was the first part of a trilogy in which blacks commented on their own condition as Americans; the other two shows were *Abyssinia* (1907) and *Bandana Land* (1909), which also starred Williams and Walker. Cook's best-known composition is 'I'm Coming Virginia'. Will Vodery led a band at a theatre roof garden in 1915, worked as an arranger for the Ziegfeld Follies for twenty years and was the first black to work as a music director for a film company (Fox, in the early 1930s). Cook and Vodery gave informal advice on harmony and composition to Duke Ellington.

The first black musical to be a big hit was *Shuffle Along*, in 1921.

Two black vaudeville teams met in Philadelphia and created a libretto; they hired Eubie Blake and Noble Sissle to write the music, which was arranged by Vodery. The show featured Hall Johnson, who played violin in Europe's band and formed the Hall Johnson Choir in 1925; dancer Josephine Baker, who later went to Paris and became a European superstar; and Florence Mills, Harlem's biggest star. Mills's early sudden death was marked by a huge funeral, and she was immortalized in Duke Ellington's composition 'Black Beauty', as well as in the English composer Constant Lambert's 'Elegiac Blues'. It was Mills who sang the show's biggest hit, 'I'm Just Wild About Harry'; other songs included 'Love Will Find a Way' and 'Bandana Days'. Launched on a shoestring, tried out in one-night stands in Philadelphia and New Jersey and using costumes left over from a flop of 1919, *Shuffle Along* ran for more than five hundred performances, and visited a theatre in Chicago's Loop. Blake and Sissle's later shows, among them *Chocolate Dandies* (1924), were less well received, but both had long careers. Blake also wrote 'Memories of You' and 'You Were Meant for Me'. Sissle, who had worked for Europe, became a successful bandleader.

James P. Johnson's music for *Runnin' Wild* (1923) included 'Charleston', which launched one of the most famous dance fads of the century. *Blackbirds of 1928* had an all-white score by Jimmy McHugh and Dorothy Fields, and starred Adelaide Hall and Bill 'Bojangles' Robinson. Among its songs were 'I Can't Give You Anything But Love' and the hot rhythmic numbers 'Diga Diga Doo', 'Bandana Babies' and 'Doin' the New Low-down', all recorded by Duke Ellington on Victor; Don Redman made two recordings of 'Doin' the New Low-down', on one of which Robinson's tap-dancing may be heard. Harlem's greatest dancer, Robinson later taught Shirley Temple and danced with her on screen, and was commemorated in another Duke Ellington composition, 'Bojangles (A Portrait of Bill Robinson)'.

Hot Chocolates (1929) had begun as a floor show at Connie's Inn, written by Andy Razaf and Fats Waller, who had contributed to the less popular *Keep Shufflin'* the year before. On Broadway Louis Armstrong played in the pit band and came on stage for a solo. 'Ain't Misbehavin'' became one of Armstrong's and Waller's biggest hits, and the show ran for six months.

We will come back to some of these names. There were a score of other black shows in the 1920s, for example, *Plantation Review*, which included Mills, Vodery and Shelton Brooks. Elements of racism were evident in two kinds of reviews: white critics often compared black shows not with white shows, but with their own patronizing view of what a black show should be like; blacks sometimes criticized the shows for being too white. But the music and the dancing in all of them brought the flavour of jazz to Broadway: the tap-dancing, soft shoe, buck-and-wing and other routines put paid to the cakewalk once and for all, and were immediately influential on the part of Broadway that was further downtown. Florenz Ziegfeld knew a good thing when he saw it, and bought 'Ballin' the Jack' from a Harlem show to use in his own *Follies* in 1913; the next year there was a hit recording of it, and the tune was revived many times.

By then, the second generation of Tin Pan Alley songwriters was creating an American musical theatre. It was a phenomenon second in importance only to jazz itself in establishing the commercial dominance of American popular music in the twentieth century. Jerome Kern, Irving Berlin, George Gershwin, Vincent Youmans, Cole Porter, Richard Rodgers and others broke the mould of operetta and turned the 'musical comedy' into something as American as baseball. Hundreds of the songs have been so popular for so long that they gave rise to the genre of 'the standard'. Those named above are the most important creators of the American musical stage. Of these Berlin and Porter were the only ones who wrote both words and music, and Porter was the only one who was not born poor, and almost the only one who was not Jewish.

The nineteenth-century persecution of the Jews in eastern Europe was a turning point in world history in more ways than one. The plight of the Jews in the Russian Empire was so severe that the era saw the beginning of much modern history, including Zionism; but for our purposes the important thing was the emigration. The natural increase of the Jewish population was lost to Europe when large numbers of Jews settled in America: in the period of 1881–92 19,000 Jews a year went to the USA; in 1892–1903 the average number rose to 37,000 a year, and in 1903–14 to 76,000. The newcomers were huddled and crowded into poor neighbourhoods and sweatshops, but not for long. They organized themselves within a couple of generations, and New York became the largest Jewish city on earth. Apart from all their other accomplishments, succeeding generations of these new Americans yielded a considerable number of great entertainers (we have already met Al Jolson, Sophie Tucker and the Shuberts), and perhaps most of the best songwriters in the history of American songs.

Oscar Hammerstein II and others have recalled the occasion when Jerome Kern was thinking of writing a musical version of a popular novel by Donn Byrne, *Messer Marco Polo*. It was a book by an Irishman set in China about an Italian. 'What kind of music are you going to write?' someone asked. 'Don't worry,' said Kern. 'It'll be good Jewish music.'

Jerome David Kern was born and died in New York City. *Clorindy, or The Origin of the Cakewalk* (1898) had been 'the first Negro operetta in the new syncopated style'; six years later its white producer, Edward Everett Rice, gave Kern his first theatrical assignment: writing additional songs for a show called *Mr Wix of Wickham*. The teenage Kern was a song plugger in Wanamaker's department store and wanted to move. Ernest Ball advised him to go not to Witmark, Ball's publisher at the time, but to T. B. Harms, on the grounds that Witmark was a large house, where a young composer would get lost in the shuffle, whereas Harms was not doing too well.

Perhaps Ball had spotted the great Max Dreyfus, at Harms, as the giant he would become. It was Dreyfus who sent Kern to work in London in 1905. In early 1906, at the age of twenty-one, Kern had twelve songs performed in five theatres, his patrons including some of the most powerful producers in the business, such as Charles Frohman. Kern's first hit, 'How'd You Like To Spoon With Me?', was turned down by Frohman's New York manager in 1905, but was accepted by the Shuberts, and later by Frohman himself in London. Frohman was an American whose interest in British hit shows was entirely practical: it was in London at this time that some of the most innovative work was being done in turning the operetta into the modern musical show.

In November 1899 *Florodora*, with music mostly by Leslie Stuart and lyrics by Stuart and three other writers, had opened in London, where it had 455 performances; it opened in November 1900 in New York and, unusually for the time, ran even longer in the USA, for over 500 performances, thanks to its hit song 'Tell Me Pretty Maiden', which was performed by pairs of parasol-twirling girls and straw-hatted boys. It was the first musical show to be recorded by its original cast, on 7-inch Berliner 78s in England in 1900; an American recording of 'Maiden' by the 'Florodora Girls' was a huge hit in 1901. Clearly inspired by minstrelsy in its rhythms and its near-jazz tunes, it was itself profoundly influential on American composers. It is no coincidence that *In Dahomey* was a hit in London in 1903; without the complicated feelings of the Americans towards blacks, British showgoers may have been able to embrace it more wholeheart-edly. In the exciting English musical atmosphere, Kern's collaborating lyricists included George Grossmith (performer, author and later a renowned producer, whose father had been a famous leading man in Gilbert and Sullivan shows) and P. G. Wodehouse (one of the great humorists, and prose stylists, of the century).

Kern married an English girl and returned to New York in 1910. Dreyfus continued to find him writing assignments: about a hundred Kern songs were interpolated into various Broadway shows, while Wodehouse continued to be one of his collaborators; Kern's own first show was *The Red Petticoat* in 1912. He wrote several songs for a show imported from England, *The Girl from Utah* (1914), among them 'They Didn't Believe Me' (lyrics by Herbert Reynolds), generally considered to be his first masterpiece. However successful the songs of Victor Herbert or George M. Cohan, they soon became period pieces, but 'They Didn't Believe Me' was different: having no clichéd elements, but a key change and other innovations in construction, it was naturally shapely and made most Tin Pan Alley hits sound like jingles. It was like an art song, yet singable and memorable, the aim of the popular songwriter since the time of Thomas Arne.

Kern was a craftsman, trying to write something of which he could be proud, as well as making money. He was also the first great genius of the genre, and popular music could never be the same again. He wrote or substantially contributed to thirty-seven Broadway shows, for example *Sally* (1920), whose lyrics by Buddy DeSylva included 'Look for the Silver Lining', a distinctive song with a hymn-like quality, and *Sunny* (1925), with Harbach and Hammerstein. One of its songs, 'Who?', is unusual in that the first note is held for two and a quarter bars ('Who . . . stole my heart away?'); it was used in several films, and recorded by Tommy Dorsey (1937), among others.

In 1927, though, Kern made yet another advance on the Broadway musical. The songs had been the main element, closely followed by the dancing and the sets, while the plots were usually insignificant. *Show Boat*, however, was based on a novel by Edna Ferber, with a believable plot and characters. It contained such songs (with lyrics by Hammerstein) as 'Bill', 'Make Believe', 'Why Do I Love You?', 'Ol' Man River' and 'Can't Help Lovin' Dat Man'. It was the first great American musical show; it was filmed in 1929 and 1936, and a new full-length recording of it in 1988 restored the original orchestration by Robert Russell Bennett. (Bennett deserves to be better known. A composer hired by Dreyfus and put in charge of arranging the firm's theatre music, he worked on so many hit shows that he helped shape the very sound of Broadway, from *Show Boat* and the biggest hits of Rodgers and Hammerstein to Lerner and Loewe's *My Fair Lady*.)

What Kern wrote in *Show Boat* was perhaps the best of all operettas; his finest songs were still to come. *Roberta* (1933), with lyrics by Harbach, did not get good reviews; one critic wrote: 'There's no tune you can whistle when you leave the theatre.' This was the show that contained 'Smoke Gets in Your Eyes', 'The Touch of Your Hand' and 'Yesterdays'. Kern's writing had moved well beyond the simplicity required in the English pleasure gardens, but the public is often underestimated. Like many composers for the stage, Kern tried to insist on the restriction of his music from broadcasting for six months, but he changed his mind when the plugging of 'Smoke Gets in Your Eyes' made a hit out of the show. The film version in 1935 added 'Lovely to Look At' and 'I Won't Dance'; it was filmed again in 1952 as *Lovely to Look At*.

Kern wrote songs for several original films, among them *Swing Time* (1936), with Fred Astaire and Ginger Rogers, which included 'The Way You Look Tonight', 'Pick Yourself Up' and 'A Fine Romance' (lyrics by Dorothy Fields), as well as the instrumental 'Waltz in Swingtime'. Other Kern film songs are 'The Last Time I

Saw Paris' (lyrics by Hammerstein) for *Lady Be Good* (1941, adapted from the 1924 Gershwin show) and 'Long Ago and Far Away' for *Cover Girl* (1944, lyrics by Ira Gershwin).

New harmonic devices and suggestions of additional harmonic resources led to the adoption of the modern Broadway show song as a vehicle for the interpretation of jazz musicians. Kern's 'The Way You Look Tonight' and 'A Fine Romance' were among Billie Holiday's most beautiful recordings, and Charles Mingus interpolated 'All the Things You Are' with a Rachmaninov prelude to make the dramatic 'All the Things You C Sharp' in 1955. Indeed, such outstanding songwriters as Johnny Green ('Body and Soul'), Arthur Schwartz ('Dancing in the Dark', 'You and the Night and the Music') and Harry Warren (film hits without number) considered 'All the Things You Are', from the show *Very Warm for May* (1939), to be one of the greatest songs ever written. Not only does it change key, but its unexpected notes suggest more key changes all the way through. Even Kern was afraid that its construction would be too much for the public, but it was one of his biggest hits.

Kern's work appeared to reflect the times he lived in, yet turned out to be timeless: 'All in Fun' (also from *Very Warm for May*) seemed to hark back to the more happy-go-lucky songs Kern was writing around the time of the First World War, but the bitter-sweet harmony made it sound more modern. And this was years after George Gershwin claimed to be imitating Kern, and the schoolboy Richard Rodgers had spent all his pocket money at matinées, seeing Kern shows over and over again.

Kern died suddenly, in the street in 1945, without any identification in his pockets; it was some hours before the world knew what it had lost. He left no autobiography and no revealing interviews, deepening the mystery of where such mastery of craft came from.

George Gershwin, still one of the world's most popular composers more than fifty years after his death, was an excellent pianist. Influenced by jazz, he was one of the few great songwriters who sought out black entertainers and musicians to listen to for pleasure. He was taking American music into unexplored areas when he died because of a brain tumour in 1937.

The family acquired a piano when George was twelve; having

shown little interest in music, he surprised everyone by quickly becoming proficient. His first hit song was an untypical potboiler: 'Swanee', as we have seen, was picked up by Al Jolson in 1919; it sold a million copies of sheet music and two million records by various artists. Gershwin wrote for *George White's Scandals* for several years, collaborating with DeSylva and others, but more and more with his brother Ira (who, until he proved himself, worked under the name Arthur Francis). Ira became one of the finest American lyricists. Their first show together was *Lady Be Good* (1924), with Fred and Adele Astaire, which offered 'Fascinatin' Rhythm', the title song 'Oh, Lady Be Good!' and, originally, 'The Man I Love' (which, dropped from three shows, still became a standard).

Songs for other shows included 'That Certain Feeling', 'Someone to Watch Over Me', 'How Long Has This Been Going On?', ''S Wonderful', and 'Liza'. *Girl Crazy* (1930) was very rich: 'Bidin' My Time', 'But Not For Me', 'Embraceable You' and 'I Got Rhythm', from the chords of which more jazz tunes have been derived than perhaps any other. *Strike Up the Band* in 1927 failed in its Philadelphia try-out, despite the title song and 'I've Got a Crush On You'. It had an excellent book by George S. Kaufman, one of Broadway's most acerbic wits, but its anti-war, anti-government message was too strong. It was watered down in 1930 on Broadway and had a six-month run.

Gershwin's film work included two Fred Astaire pictures: *A Damsel in Distress* and *Shall We Dance?* (both 1937), which yielded 'A Foggy Day', 'Nice Work If You Can Get It', 'Shall We Dance?', 'They Can't Take That Away From Me' and 'Let's Call the Whole Thing Off'. The film *Goldwyn Follies* in 1938 contained 'Love Walked In' and 'Love is Here to Stay'.

His more ambitious compositions had begun in 1924. Already famous, he was commissioned by Paul Whiteman to write *Rhapsody in Blue* for piano and jazz band, for a concert at the Aeolian Hall to celebrate American music. The concert began with 'Livery Stable Blues', introduced apologetically by Whiteman 'as an example of the depraved past from which modern jazz has risen', according to Olin Downes in *The New York Times*. He added: 'The apology is herewith indignantly rejected, for this is a gorgeous piece of impudence, much better . . . than other and more polite compositions that came later.' Downes was not a jazz critic, but he was sensibly unimpressed by what he had heard of its co-option.

The concert continued with piano novelties by Zez Confrey, taken for jazz by the audience, and a large helping of Whiteman's dance band music. The second half opened with Herbert's specially commissioned *Suite of Serenades*, hastily put together from the scraps that any composer has in his trunk. It was followed by Edward MacDowell's 'To a Wild Rose' (1896), Friml's 'Chansonette' (later popular as 'Donkey Serenade') and more; members of the audience were looking at their watches as the penultimate piece on the programme began.

Herbert had helped Gershwin with the piece, advising a longer piano introduction to the main themes to add to its drama. *Rhapsody in Blue* caused a sensation. It was apparently Ross Gorman's idea to play the clarinet introduction as a glissando, instead of seventeen separately tongued notes, and this was enough to stop the audience leaving. At the end they must have left feeling as though they had heard an entire evening of the best in modern American music (despite the concert's closing piece, one of Elgar's *Pomp and Circumstance* marches). The *Rhapsody* is still one of the most popular of American compositions; it seemed to have come from nowhere, but it had been preceded by Gershwin's own 'Blue Monday' / '135th Street' (1922) to say nothing of Milhaud's ballet *Le boeuf sur le toit* (1919). Yet *Rhapsody in Blue* was and is problematical. There is such a thing as a jazz composer, but a jazz composer is a jazz musician first, and Gershwin was not. The piece is diffuse and structurally weak, and too much of a piano showcase. Nevertheless, it has some unforgettable melodies, and one would like to have heard that first performance, with Gershwin's improvisation (the piano part was not fully written out) and Gorman's free, mocking interpretation of the clarinet part. Various arrangements were made, all by Whiteman's arranger, Ferde Grofé; the one that is usually heard is the grandest, but Grofé's original, played in 1924, is among the best.

Gershwin's piano roll recordings include an arrangement for solo piano of the *Rhapsody*. Whiteman's band at the Aeolian Hall (in Grofé's first arrangement) had twenty-two players, but *Rhapsody in Blue* is usually played by a symphony orchestra. One of the more interesting recordings of the *Rhapsody* was made by RCA's artists and repertoire (A&R) executive Hugo Winterhalter in the early 1950s, with the excellent Byron Janis at the piano, a performance which tried to get away from the symphonic feeling and to make the piece swing. Critics such as Max Harrison in England campaigned for years for a more sensible treatment; finally Michael Tilson Thomas recorded the original version, using Gershwin's suitably edited piano roll, and was followed by Simon Rattle and others.

Gershwin continued to compose piano preludes and pieces for orchestra, as well as the great songs. He orchestrated the Concerto in F for piano and orchestra himself in 1925; it is better realized in its structure than the *Rhapsody*, and it too contains good tunes, especially in the bluesy slow movement. The delightful *An American in Paris* was recorded in 1928 by Nat Shilkret, with the original French taxi horns and Gershwin playing celesta, and was used in a film of the same title in 1951. (The film spoiled the music: Gershwin may not have pandered to the public, but Hollywood almost always did.)

It was Gershwin's masterpiece, *Porgy and Bess*, which suffered most from tampering, so that it did not emerge as the first successful American opera until the 1970s. DuBose Heyward's novel, inspired by a crippled beggar called Samuel Smalls, or 'Goat Sammy', had been successfully dramatized by his wife, Dorothy, who changed the completely downbeat ending to one offering an open-ended sort of hope, as Porgy sets off for New York in his goat-cart to look for Bess; the new ending was used in Gershwin's version. Gershwin spent some time with Heyward in Charleston's Cabbage Row slum and on Folly Beach off the Carolina coast, resting and relaxing as well as soaking up the Gullah dialect of the local black population. Heyward and Gershwin worked together by post, and brought Ira in to help with the lyrics. It was an unusually harmonious collaboration for a musical show.

The first run of the piece lost money in 1935–6, partly because of the public's confusion over what it expected from Gershwin. In 1918 Otto Kahn, then chairman of the Metropolitan Opera, had proposed the idea of an American opera to Jerome Kern, Irving Berlin and Gershwin; Berlin knew he was not qualified, while Kern hinted that Gershwin was a likely candidate. But when Gershwin got around to it, the Metropolitan Opera was not interested, the USA had no equivalent of European comic opera or folk opera venues and Broadway was not ready to have its horizons extended.

John W. 'Bubbles' Sublett (of the black vaudeville team Buck and Bubbles) played Sportin' Life, a flashy drug pedlar, in the first production; he was troublesome in rehearsal, but brilliant on stage. A revised version in 1942 ran longer than any revival had up to then. Sportin' Life had allegedly been written with Cab Calloway in mind, who played it in performances in the 1950s; a film was made in 1959 with Sammy Davis, Jr, as Sportin' Life. The songs, including 'Summertime', 'I Loves You, Porgy', 'I Got Plenty o' Nuttin'' and 'Bess, You is My Woman Now', had long since become standards by the time the original score was restored, as orchestrated by Gershwin and with recitatives instead of spoken dialogue. A concert version conducted by Lorin Maazel in 1975 and a production conducted by John DeMain in Houston, Texas, in 1976 were recorded; Edward Greenfield, writing in *Gramophone* magazine, compared *Porgy* to Alban Berg's *Wozzeck* and Benjamin Britten's *Peter Grimes* as a great modern portrait of human nature. The Glyndebourne Festival's production in England in 1986 was a triumph; it was recorded in 1989, conducted by Simon Rattle, with Willard White and Cynthia Haymon in the title roles and Damon Evans as Sportin' Life.

'The rest of us were songwriters,' said Irving Berlin. 'George was a composer.' If the greatest twentieth-century songs have not only been memorable and singable, but have also lent themselves to interpretation by the greatest of jazzmen, then Gershwin's songs alone would have earned him immortality; but *Porgy and Bess* has revealed him as a great 'serious' composer as well. This late recognition is better than none: he was not yet thirty-nine when he died, and his is among the greatest unfinished careers in music.

Vincent Youmans was another composer who had a relatively short career. He was a poor businessman and hopeless as his own producer; he changed lyricists for each of his twelve shows, some of which were failures; he published only ninety-three songs, yet a handful of them are standards. *No, No, Nannette* (1925) was a smash hit, perhaps the quintessential 1920s show; Irving Caesar and Otto Harbach wrote the lyrics of 'Tea for Two' and 'I Want to be Happy'.

Oh, Please (1926) was a flop though it included 'I Know That You Know', with Harbach. *Hit the Deck* (1927), another success, contained 'Sometimes I'm Happy' and 'Hallelujah' (written as a march while Youmans was in the navy), with lyrics by Caesar. *Great Day!* (1929) was again a disaster, but yielded 'Without a Song' and 'More Than You Know', with lyrics by Billy Rose. *Smiles* (1930) offered 'Time on My Hands', with Harold Adamson and Mack Gordon, but lost money in spite of being produced by Ziegfeld. Youmans went to Hollywood, where his only successful picture was *Flying Down to Rio* in 1933, the first film to team Astaire with Ginger Rogers; it included the title song, 'The Carioca' and 'Orchids in the Moonlight'. He went bankrupt and fell ill with tuberculosis. 'Tea for Two' is one of *Variety*'s top hundred Tin Pan Alley songs, and it rivals Gershwin's 'I Got Rhythm' as the tune that most inspired the era's jazz musicians; Fats Waller may have found 'Honeysuckle Rose' in it.

Another mysterious talent, an enigma in every way, is the songwriter whom every other composer in the business has admired: Irving Berlin. He was born Israel Baline in Russia, and his family settled in New York in the 1890s. He worked as a singing waiter and then a song plugger. His name was changed by a printer's error on his first published song, 'Marie from Sunny Italy'.

Many of the great songwriters of the golden age of Broadway and Tin Pan Alley had studied music formally and were familiar with classical music. They were influenced by ragtime, then jazz; they influenced jazzmen in turn, writing songs which were worthwhile vehicles for new interpretations and improvisation. Most of them could read music and play the piano well. (Kern and Friml, also a good pianist, were sometimes mildly annoyed when not asked to play at a party, because Gershwin, the best pianist, was willing to play all evening.) Irving Berlin did not have any of these qualifications; he is unique. He had no formal studies and never learned to read or write music well, but hired an arranger to write down his songs and to harmonize them. He did not like jazz or 'swing bands', and he had a piano built with a lever to shift the keyboard so that he could play in more than one key. A devoted family man who valued his privacy, he did not go to many parties.

Berlin should have been a hack; his only object was to have a hit, and his measure of a song's quality was whether it made money. Another unusual thing about Berlin's songs is that they leave no fingerprints. It is possible – we think – to tell a Kern song or a Gershwin song, but each Berlin song seems to have come out of nowhere. Yet Berlin not only wrote good songs, he did so in every category. There could be said to be broadly three types of songs from this era – show songs, film songs and pop hits – but Berlin was actually a master of four types, for he began with a knack for writing unusually catchy, cheerful Tin Pan Alley songs which were hits well before the First World War, and when Tin Pan Alley became more sophisticated, his skill became more than a knack. Berlin favoured sentimentality, and his lyrics are not as witty as Lorenz Hart's or Cole Porter's, and never cynical at all; he wrote some that are almost corny, and a few tub-thumpers. Yet he somehow held it all in check, rarely going over the top, creating a great many unpretentious songs which are still memorable.

Furthermore, the arranging and harmonizing of his songs for publication, under his close supervision, never failed to impress other composers. Although he could not do it himself, he seemed to know more about harmony instinctively than others did after years of study. If the harmony that he hired displeased him, he would pester his assistant until he got what he wanted, and his taste was invariably impeccable. His work had such variety in it and was of such high quality that he was regarded by his peers as representing American popular music all by himself.

Berlin sang his own songs on Broadway in 1910, and was already world-famous before the First World War for 'Alexander's Ragtime Band'. In 1909 he had gone to work as a song plugger and lyric writer for Ted Snyder. When 'Alexander' had sold two million copies of sheet music by the end of 1911, Snyder's manager, Henry Waterson, formed the firm of Waterson, Berlin and Snyder, which provided Berlin with his transposing piano. His first helper was Max Winslow, who offered tips as Berlin picked out his tunes. Winslow was also a superb vocal coach, and helped many female variety artists develop their musical personalities, as well as make hits of Berlin's songs; he became known as 'the man who discovered Irving Berlin', and his girl singers were known as 'Winslow's singles'. When Berlin complained about the royalties Waterson paid, Winslow suggested they start their own firm, whereupon Berlin's royalties tripled.

When he was drafted, the newspaper headline was 'Army Takes Berlin'. He organized a soldier revue in 1918, *Yip Yip Yaphank*, which included the hit 'Oh! How I Hate to Get Up in the Morning' and another song that even he thought was over the top: he put it aside, but gave it to Kate Smith in 1938, and 'God Bless America' became a second national anthem. Smith was a popular soprano on radio, and later on television; her recording of 'God Bless America' was a hit in 1939, and again in 1940 and 1942. 'God Bless America' was written by an immigrant who came from utter poverty and who had much reason to love America; he gave away all the royalties.

Among Berlin's other early hits were 'Everybody's Doing It (Now)' (1911), sung by Eddie Cantor (another singing waiter who became one of America's most popular entertainers), 'When the Midnight Choo Choo Leaves for Alabam', 'I Want to Go Back to Michigan', 'Play a Simple Melody' (which contains its own counter-melody) and many other charmers which ought to be revived more often. In 1912 Berlin had married Dorothy Goetz (sister of songwriter-producer Ray Goetz, who wrote 'For Me and My Gal'). After she died of typhus a few months later, he wrote 'When I Lost You', his first tender, sentimental ballad.

Berlin had initially used collaborators, but soon wrote his own words. 'A Pretty Girl is Like a Melody' came in 1919, 'All Alone' in 1924. He began buying back the rights to his earlier work and eventually owned virtually all his own songs. He built his own theatre, the Music Box, and presented revues there in the 1920s. Berlin married Ellin MacKay, against the wishes of her wealthy Catholic father, and during the difficult courtship he wrote 'What'll I Do?' He gave her the royalties to 'Always' (1925) as a wedding present. The press chased the couple across the Atlantic and back. MacKay later lost money in the stock market, and found that his son-in-law was richer than he was.

Berlin's songs were not usually natural material for jazzmen, but some were so good they could not be left out: 'Blue Skies' (1927) was later recorded by Benny Goodman in a Fletcher Henderson arrangement; 'Marie' (1929) became one of the biggest hits of the Swing Era for Tommy Dorsey; in 1949 Count Basie made a delightful recording of 'Cheek to Cheek' (1935), probably arranged by Don Redman. 'How Deep Is the Ocean?', a ballad, was later recorded by Coleman Hawkins, Erroll Garner, Charlie Parker and many other jazzmen, and 'Say It Isn't So' was almost as successful.

On the other hand, Berlin's 'Easter Parade' was instantly old-fashioned, yet an unforgettable hit, a perfect example of how he could celebrate the American appetite for nostalgia and sentimentality. The tune sounds as though it has always existed, and its marriage of words and melody keeps it on the safe side of pure corn. It was first heard in *As Thousands Cheer* in 1933, then in 1948 was the title song of a film with Berlin's music starring Fred Astaire and Judy Garland.

Berlin's other film work included two other Astaire pictures, *Top Hat* (1935), with 'Cheek to Cheek' and 'Top Hat, White Tie and Tails' and *Follow the Fleet* (1936), with 'Let's Face the Music and Dance'. *On the Avenue*, starring Dick Powell (1937), included 'You're Laughing at Me' and 'I've Got My Love to Keep Me Warm'; Fats Waller had a hilarious hit with the former, and the latter, in an instrumental recording of 1948 by Les Brown, was regarded as the last number one hit of the Swing Era. *Holiday Inn* (1942) contained 'Happy Holiday', 'Be Careful, It's My Heart' and 'White Christmas', which was voted best film song at the Academy Awards that year; Berlin presented his Oscar to himself, saying, 'This goes to a nice guy; I've known him all my life.' (Crosby's record of 'White Christmas' sold millions every year for decades, and the various recordings of it were said to have sold more than 225 million by 1976.)

Jerome Kern had been hired to write a show to be put on in 1946; when he died, producers Rodgers and Hammerstein hired Berlin instead. The show, *Annie Get Your Gun*, had more hits than any other in history, and presents almost a cross-section of Berlin's work: 'They Say It's Wonderful' and 'I Got the Sun in the Morning' would have been quite suitable for the pop charts at that time; 'Doin' What Comes Natur'ly' is an attempt at a hillbilly feeling; 'The Girl That I Marry' is a sentimental song in 3/4 time, harking back to the turn of the century; and 'There's No Business Like Show Business', which has belonged ever since to Ethel Merman, the show's star, is a tub-thumper like Cohan's 'Give My Regards to Broadway'.

All these represent only the highlights of Berlin's accomplishment. He controlled his own material, to the extent that he would not allow Alec Wilder to quote from it in his *American Popular Song*, and he always refused permission for a dramatized biography on stage or screen. He died, over one hundred years old, as this book was being written, our last link with Tin Pan Alley before the First World War.

Cole Porter was a late starter, and his well-to-do family did not approve of his chosen vocation even after he reached the top of it. He studied law, but dabbled in music; he went to France and served in the French army during the First World War. In 1919 he married a wealthy woman and settled in Paris, where he was at the centre of one of the richest club scenes the world has ever seen. He became a close friend of the legendary hostess Bricktop, a red-haired American black woman whose real name was Ada Beatrice Queen Victoria Louise Virginia Smith. She went to France in 1924, and her club, Chez Bricktop in Rue Pigalle, was frequented by the Prince of Wales, Ernest Hemingway and John Steinbeck, among others. Porter wrote 'Miss Otis Regrets' for Bricktop and for his friend Monty Woolley, who sang it in a film.

Porter's first hit came in 1929 with 'I'm in Love Again', written in 1924. His shows began with *Paris* in 1928, with 'Let's Do It' (saucy lyrics were later added by Noël Coward). *Fifty Million Frenchmen* (1929) included 'You Do Something to Me' and *Wake Up and Dream* (1929) yielded 'What is This Thing Called Love?' He returned to the USA in the early 1930s. A horse fell on him in 1937, shattering both his legs; the sophisticated world-traveller was a semi-invalid for the rest of his life, and constantly underwent surgery in attempts to save his legs. His right leg was amputated in 1958, after which he became even more reclusive, but his work was complete by then.

Some of his songs were suggested by events or by others' remarks, such as 'It's De-lovely' (a sunrise in Rio), or written for vocalists of limited range, such as 'Miss Otis Regrets', and 'Night and Day' (for Fred Astaire). 'Don't Fence Me In' was written as a send-up, but became the best Hollywood cowboy song of all, thanks to his lyrics.

Kern was the godfather of the modern musical show; Berlin wrote both tunes and lyrics; Gershwin was a great composer whose life was tragically short. Porter's tunes alone would have put him in this company, but the literary sophistication of his lyrics, worn lightly, made him a Rodgers and Hart all by himself. There are differences: Hart was unlucky in love, and his lyrics are often bitter-sweet, while Porter's words can fairly be said to represent the essence of the 1930s. Yet no one has surpassed Porter in making great songs of popular speech. A great many songs today are based on clichés, but Porter could write 'Don't Fence Me In', 'Night and Day', 'I Get a Kick Out of You', 'Just One of Those Things', 'I've Got You Under My Skin', 'In the Still of the Night' and many more, and over fifty years later the clichés may as well have been invented by the songwriter himself, so completely do they belong to him. Here is one of the best examples in all music of a tune and the vernacular combining, complete with an introduction and internal rhymes in the stanzas:

> My story is much too sad to be told,
> But practically everything leaves me totally cold.
> The only exception I know is the case
>   When I'm out on a quiet spree,
>   Fighting vainly the old ennui,
>   And I suddenly turn and see
> Your fabulous face.
>
>   I get no kick from champagne;
>   Mere alcohol doesn't thrill me at all.
>   So tell me why should it be true
>   That I get a kick out of you.
>
>   Some get a kick from cocaine;
>   I'm sure that if I took even one sniff,
>   That would bore me terrifically stiff,
>   But I get a kick out of you.
>
> I get a kick every time I see you
>   Standing there before me,
> I get a kick though it's clear to me
>   You obviously don't adore me.
>
>   I get no kick in a plane.
>   Flying too high with some guy in the sky

Is my idea of nothing to do,
Yet I get a kick out of you.

Among Porter's shows and songs are *The New Yorkers* (1930), including 'Love for Sale', whose sympathetically adult lyrics were often banned from the airwaves, and *The Gay Divorce* (1932), including 'Night and Day'; it was filmed as *The Gay Divorcée* in 1934. *Anything Goes* (1934) contained the title song, 'I Get a Kick Out of You', 'All Through the Night' and 'You're the Top', and is one of the richest scores of the decade and the most typical 1930s musical. The show was being rehearsed with a libretto by Guy Bolton and P. G. Wodehouse, but the plot, about a shipwreck, had to be abandoned when a cruise liner caught fire off the New Jersey coast, killing 125 people. Bolton and Wodehouse were not available, so the producer introduced director Howard Lindsay and press agent Russel Crouse, whose new book for the show was the first from one of Broadway's most successful writing partnerships. Porter's recording of 'You're the Top', accompanying himself on the piano, was a top ten hit; two lines in the song had to be changed ('I shouldn't care for those nights in the air / That the fair Mrs Lindbergh goes through') when the Lindbergh baby was kidnapped and murdered.

Jubilee (1935) offered 'Just One of Those Things' and 'Begin the Beguine', and the film *Born to Dance* (1936) 'Easy to Love' and 'I Get a Kick Out of You'; 'In the Still of the Night' came from *Rosalie* (1937). *Leave It to Me* (1938) was the show in which Sophie Tucker played the wife of the ambassador to the Soviet Union, and sang 'Most Gentlemen Don't Like Love (They just like to kick it around)'. The score also included the dramatic 'Get Out of Town', but the show was stolen by Mary Martin, making her Broadway début. She sang 'My Heart Belongs to Daddy' while sitting on a trunk at a Siberian railway station, slowly doffing her garments while rhyming 'Daddy' with 'caddie' and 'finnan haddie'. Alec Wilder thinks that the quality of Porter's work declined because of his agonizing physical condition, and certainly the later songs are not on the whole so fine, but perhaps only compared with the best of Porter. His last show was *Silk Stockings* in 1955.

Other Porter film projects were *Broadway Melody of 1940*, which contained 'I Concentrate On You' and reintroduced 'Begin the Beguine' after Artie Shaw's legendary hit record. *Something to Shout About* in 1943 had 'You'd Be So Nice to Come Home To'. *High Society* (1956) had a cast of such glittering stars as Frank Sinatra, Louis Armstrong, Bing Crosby and Grace Kelly, but the quality of the songs had definitely deteriorated: 'Well, Did You Evah!' was resuscitated from the 1939 show *Du Barry Was a Lady* (which also offered 'Do I Love You?' and was filmed in 1943); 'Now You Has Jazz' was simply silly, and the syrupy Crosby and Kelly duet 'True Love' made a Porter song a pop hit just as Elvis Presley was turning the world upside down. The film *Les Girls* (1957) was a disappointment. *Night and Day* (1946), a film biography of Porter starring Cary Grant, was so bad that Porter roared with laughter at it.

Anyone who has recognized the names of these songs will recognize them as being among the greatest of the century. Any younger readers whose musical experience has been too anaemic should get to know them. They have never been far away, but today's songs are so thin, and popular music has developed into such a rich repertory, that most of them are revived again and again. Mick Hucknall of the British pop group Simply Red sings Porter's 'Ev'ry Time We Say Goodbye', while the Irish cabaret artist Mary Coughlan has revived 'The Laziest Girl in Town'. The songs of that era will keep coming back: the great lyricists grew up before television and even before radio, so their speech had not been debased by advertising jingles and third-rate entertainment.

The songwriters who as a team were the equal of Cole Porter were composer Richard Rodgers and lyricist Lorenz Hart. Rodgers wrote his first song at the age of eleven, and saw Kern's *Very Good Eddie* at fourteen; he later said, 'Life began for me at 2.30', curtain time for Saturday matinées. In 1918 the punctual, well-groomed Rodgers met the bohemian Hart, who was adapting and translating German and Viennese operettas for the Shubert brothers; his adaptation of Ferenc Molnar's novel and play *Liliom* was a success, but Hart, on salary, received little credit. Rodgers and Hart's first hit came when 'Manhattan' was put into *The Garrick Gaieties* in 1925, along with 'Mountain Greenery'. They were signed up by a publisher and with five shows running in 1926 were suddenly each making

$1,000 a week. Rodgers used unusual chords, and would write a thirty-two-bar verse with a sixteen-bar chorus instead of the other way round; it was hard to get Hart to work, but then he quickly wrote love songs with wit.

Some of the songs from the shows of 1926 to 1930 were 'The Blue Room', 'My Heart Stood Still', 'You Took Advantage of Me', 'With a Song in My Heart', 'Ten Cents a Dance' and 'Dancing on the Ceiling'. *Jumbo* (1935) was produced by showman Billy Rose in the Hippodrome, a big old venue that was near the end of its life and had begun by sheltering circuses; the show had so many animals in it that Actor's Equity classed it as a circus. It also had Paul Whiteman's band, Jimmy Durante and three classic songs: 'Little Girl Blue', 'The Most Beautiful Girl in the World' and 'My Romance'. *Jumbo* cost so much to put on that it lost half its investment; the 1962 film (Doris Day's last musical) was also a disaster.

On Your Toes (1936) gave us 'There's a Small Hotel'; *Babes in Arms* (1937) had 'Where or When', 'The Lady Is a Tramp', 'My Funny Valentine' and 'I Wish I Were In Love Again', one of the best-known Hart lyrics:

> When love congeals
> It soon reveals
> The faint aroma of performing seals
> The double-crossing of a pair of heels
> I wish I were in love again.

A lesser songwriter might not have bothered with the fourth line, which adds to the wit and suspends the whole verse in mid-air, allowing the last line a bit more punch when it comes.

Pal Joey (1940) included 'I Could Write a Book' and 'Bewitched, Bothered and Bewildered'; the film version in 1957, with Frank Sinatra, added 'The Lady Is a Tramp'. Rodgers and Hart's film work in the early 1930s was less successful, except for *Love Me Tonight* (1932), with Maurice Chevalier, which contained 'Mimi' and 'Isn't It Romantic?' This was one of the first truly innovative musical films, directed by Rouben Mamoulian; in the opening sequence 'Isn't It Romantic?' was so tied to the action on screen that Hart had to rewrite the lyrics for the song's publication. (The song also became the title song of another film in 1948.) 'Blue Moon' never made it into a play or a film, but still became a classic.

Hart was small of stature, an alcoholic and unlucky in love; he died of pneumonia a few weeks after attending the première of Rodgers and Hammerstein's *Oklahoma!* in 1943. Like Hart, Oscar Hammerstein II had attended Columbia University before turning to the theatre; he wrote and acted in Columbia varsity shows and began as a stage manager for his impresario grandfather (hence 'II'; his father William managed one of Oscar I's theatres). He had written with Friml, Romberg, Youmans, Gershwin, Harbach, Herbert Stothart, Arthur Schwartz and Harold Arlen. Unlike Hart, he was always asleep by midnight, but had to work hard on his lyrics; like Hart, he achieved apparent spontaneity in his words, and was floundering in the early 1940s.

Rodgers and Hart's are the greater songs; Hart was one of the finest of all lyricists writing in English in the twentieth century, while Hammerstein was basically an operetta lover with a sentimental streak. But Rodgers and Hammerstein's shows marked an advance on Kern in musical theatre. For *Oklahoma!* the book as well as the lyrics were written by Hammerstein (based on the play *Green Grow the Lilacs* by Lynn Riggs), and the songs propelled the action rather than distracting the audience from a soon to be forgotten plot: with 'Oh, What a Beautiful Morning', 'People Will Say We're In Love' and 'Surrey With the Fringe On Top', it was one of the biggest Broadway hits of all time. *Carousel* (1945, ironically based on *Liliom*) included 'If I Loved You' and 'You'll Never Walk Alone'. *South Pacific* (1949) was, in my opinion, easily Rodgers and Hammerstein's best show, and another smash to match *Oklahoma!* Based on stories by James A. Michener, it offered 'Some Enchanted Evening', 'Bali Ha'i', 'Younger Than Springtime' and 'I'm In Love With a Wonderful Guy'. *The King and I* (1951, based on *Anna and the King of Siam*, by Margaret Landon) contained 'Hello Young Lovers', which has a particularly fine introduction, and 'I Have Dreamed'. In total there were over 6,300 performances of these four shows in their original productions and all were filmed. (Yul Brynner was successful for the rest of his life as the King of Siam.)

Leslie Stuart's *Florodora* was the first show to be recorded by its original cast (1900), but *Oklahoma!* was the first to be a modern hit; it was in the top five on the first *Billboard* album chart in March 1945. *South Pacific* had one of Robert Russell Bennett's most incisive orchestrations; its original cast album, which was available on all three speeds, entered the *Billboard* album chart in May 1949 and stayed there for over 400 weeks, making it one of the biggest hits of all time. Neither the 1958 film soundtrack nor a 1986 London recording, with the opera singers Kiri Te Kanawa and José Carreras, can begin to compete with it.

Rodgers and Hammerstein also wrote for the film *State Fair* in 1945 (including 'It Might As Well Be Spring'), formed a production company that mounted Berlin's *Annie Get Your Gun*, and also wrote the shows *Allegro* in 1947 ('The Gentleman Is a Dope'), *Me and Juliet* in 1953, *Pipe Dream* in 1955 and *Flower Drum Song* in 1958 ('I Enjoy Being a Girl'). Rodgers used a tune from his television music *Victory at Sea* for 'No Other Love' (in *Me and Juliet*); the song was a hit for Perry Como. Hammerstein adapted Bizet's *Carmen* as *Carmen Jones* in 1943, and it was filmed in 1954.

Some of their later shows were not as well received as the early ones, though *Me and Juliet*, for example, ran for a year and turned a profit. Critics usually blamed their disappointment on Hammerstein's plots. The sentimentality of their work together, as well as Hammerstein's affinity for operetta, reached an apotheosis with *The Sound of Music* in 1959, which became one of the most successful musical films of all time in 1965. Hammerstein died of cancer, and Rodgers began to lose his touch in a modern era. He wrote his own lyrics for *No Strings* in 1962, a hit because of a good story about interracial love, but thereafter his career declined. He had outlived his greatest partners and the golden age of Broadway.

Alec Wilder's book *American Popular Song* is recommended to readers interested in pursuing this subject. He wrote some fine songs himself, such as 'While We're Young', 'I'll Be Around', 'It's So Peaceful in the Country', 'Who Can I Turn To'. He makes a superb case for his favourite, Harold Arlen, as an example of 'this "don't-worry-about-the-mud-on-your-shoes" attitude'. Arlen wrote 'I Gotta Right to Sing the Blues', 'I've Got the World on a String', 'It's Only a Paper Moon', 'Blues in the Night', 'That Old Black Magic', 'One for My Baby' and many more, some of the best with lyrics by Johnny Mercer, a master of demotic speech.

While Broadway was providing some of the century's greatest songs, there were exciting things happening in the rest of the country. We must now examine the rest of the immensely rich popular music scene of the 1920s and 1930s, of which the American musical show was only the most glittering ingredient.

7

The Jazz Age, the Great Depression and New Markets: Race and Hillbilly Music

A San Francisco bandleader, Art Hickman, and his pianist-arranger Ferde Grofé are generally given credit for inventing the type of dance band which dominated popular music for half a century. Around the time of the First World War they were among the first to write separate music for the reed and brass sections, combining the higher and lower instruments in each section into choirs, but for dancing rather than listening, as in John Philip Sousa's concert band. Hickman seems to have been the first to hire three saxophones, enabling him to write richer harmonies. He also wrote songs, among them 'Rose Room', published in 1917. It is surely no coincidence that 'Rose Room' is the sort of tune that lends itself to an interesting arrangement, and was recorded by Benny Goodman's sextet nearly twenty-five years later; or that Duke Ellington's 'In a Mellotone' (1940) is a countermelody to it.

Hickman suffered from ill health and died relatively young in 1930, but by then bands all over the USA were playing his kind of music: black and white, hot and 'sweet' (or 'strict tempo', as it is called in Britain). Paul Whiteman's was by far the most successful. Whiteman was a good businessman and a great talent scout; we shall come back to him during the Big Band Era. He was called the 'King of Jazz' because Johann Strauss II had been the 'Waltz King' and Sousa had been the 'March King', and because publicists have tiny minds; Whiteman never took it seriously. But any sort of lively dance music was heard as 'jazz' by the public. The less strict moral atmosphere of the 1920s, in which young women went out dancing with their young men friends without supervision (and smoked cigarettes, and bobbed their hair!) carried the same association: hence the 'jazz age'.

The bands outside the biggest cities, indeed almost any bands outside New York, came to be called territory bands. Among the excellent black groups were Troy Floyd's eleven-piece band at the Plaza Hotel in San Antonio, Texas, with such sidemen as Herschel Evans (later with Count Basie); Alphonso Trent led a band in Dallas which included violinist Stuff Smith, trumpeter Harry Edison (later with Basie) and reedmen James Jeter and Hayes Pillars (who later co-led a popular dance band in St Louis for a decade). The white Coon–Sanders Orchestra, also known as the Kansas City Night Hawks owing to their late-night broadcasts, was led by drummer Carleton Coon and pianist-arranger Joe Sanders, who was nicknamed the Old Lefthander from his days as a baseball pitcher. Both were also singers and composers. In the earliest days of radio the Night Hawks was one of the bands that sold more records as a result of the novelty of broadcasting. The band's national fame ended when Coon died suddenly because of complications following an abscessed tooth; but Sanders remained a popular leader in the Chicago area (where my parents were among the young people who would travel 60 or 70 miles to dance to his music).

Another white band was the California Ramblers, who made an uncountable number of recordings between 1921 and 1937 with constantly changing personnel and under many different names. Trumpeters Henry 'Hot Lips' Levine (later on the NBC staff) and Red Nichols, Tommy and Jimmy Dorsey, bass saxophonist Adrian Rollini and, as vocalists, songwriter Sammy Fain and early country star Vernon Dalhart may be heard on some of these recordings.

Somewhat smaller bands were Roy Johnson and his Happy Pals, which included Jack Teagarden at one time, as did Peck's Bad Boys in Texas (led by the pianist Peck Kelley), and the Blue Devils, led by bassist Walter Page, which melded into the larger band of Bennie Moten. Paul Howard's Quality Serenaders, on the West Coast, included Lionel Hampton and Lawrence Brown, the great trombonist who later spent decades in Duke Ellington's band. Typical of the territory bands was that of the Midwesterner Slatz Randall, who worked and recorded in Minneapolis for a decade after 1929, making a dozen jazz-influenced pop records, such as the slightly saucy 'Bessie Couldn't Help It'; the latter was recorded by Hoagy Carmichael, Louis Armstrong and many others, but Randall's is the most fun. The Benson Orchestra of Chicago was led by Edgar A. Benson, and included Frankie Trumbauer. Erskine Tate's Vendome Orchestra, a Chicago institution, employed many famous jazzmen over the years. It recorded with Freddy Keppard in 1923 and Louis Armstrong three years later, and Tate remained one of Chicago's leading music teachers throughout the 1950s and 1960s.

Among the most successful and prolifically recorded territory bands was Bennie Moten's black band, whose classic 'South' was an acoustic hit in 1925; both the electrical remake in 1929 and its reissue in 1944 were hits. As in the ragtime era, there were a great many musicians and hundreds of bands whose contribution is now lost. Most of the bands never recorded; some remained local in more or less steady hotel or restaurant jobs, while others toured. The musical ferment was intense.

Youngsters often started out in dime-a-dance halls, where the band played one chorus of each tune: that was your 10-cent dance. In the Red Mill on North Main Street in Los Angeles, where trumpeter Buck Clayton played in the late 1920s, the band played only half the chorus of a tune on Saturday nights, speeding up the dance hall's take, much as jukeboxes were speeded up a few years later. Such bands played stock arrangements, provided by the publishers of the tunes. One of the best arrangers was Archie Bleyer, who became better known decades later through his studio and television work and as a label boss. Stock arrangements were usually not very challenging, but Clayton, who was still a teenager in the late 1920s and later became a fine arranger himself, wrote in his autobiography: 'One of my biggest troubles with the stock arrangements that we were playing were the famous Archie Bleyer arrangements ... I could see then that I had a hell of a lot to learn. "Business in F" and "Business in Q" were two particular stocks that used to hang me every night.'

The people who danced to all these bands became the equivalent of the New Orleans 'second line' as popular music changed. Dance band music was already well established by 1920, and was the biggest single category in popular music for decades after the adoption of electrical recording in 1925, for several reasons. The dancing in Broadway shows, and later in films, was incomparably better than it had been in earlier times. The girls in the back row of the chorus had studied ballet, and were better dancers than the star performers of the nineteenth century. American popular music was now a national rather than a regional affair; not only were records sold for dancing at home, but dance music was broadcast live on the radio every evening. Radio was conservative during what came to be called prime time, but later in the evening remote broadcasts from ballrooms caused the folks at home to roll up the rugs.

There was a tremendous upsurge in the popularity of ballroom dancing itself, fuelled by the success on Broadway of Vernon and Irene Castle. Vernon Blythe, an English magician, met Irene Foote in an American show in 1911; their performance in *Watch Your Step* in 1914 made them world-famous. They hired black bandleader James Reese Europe to provide their music, started a chain of dancing schools and invented the ubiquitous foxtrot (which anybody could do), as well as the turkey trot, the bunny-hug, the Castle rock and many more, and were also behind the tango craze which swept the country. Vernon joined a British flying squad in France during the First World War; he taught flying in the USA and was killed in an accident in 1918. A film of their lives made in 1939 starred (who else?) Fred Astaire and Ginger Rogers.

The scores of popular dance bands included that of Vincent Lopez, who made the first live band broadcast on radio in 1921; Wayne King, a new 'Waltz King', whose broadcasts from a Chicago ballroom were sponsored by a cosmetics company, and whose music appealed to an ageing audience (which used more and more cosmetics); and Fred Waring, who forsook mainstream 'hot' dance music and played sweeter and stricter music as time went on, subsiding into a glee club style. Live broadcasts brought fans to the ballrooms, but Waring was suspicious of recording, thinking that it must be bad for live music: he had big hits on Victor until early 1933, and then did not record at all for a decade. A radio show that paid Waring $12,500 a week became a target for pirates, who recorded Waring off the radio and sold the recordings to other stations; in 1936 Waring won one of the first lawsuits against bootleg records. Ted Lewis was a popular entertainer and second-rate clarinettist whose catch-phrase was 'Is everybody happy?'; his show band often included hot soloists on recordings, such as Fats Waller. Isham Jones made a renowned recording of 'Stardust', the third most often recorded song of the century (after 'Silent Night' and 'St Louis Blues'), establishing it as a romantic ballad; previous recordings had been at a bouncy mid-tempo, which is what Hoagy Carmichael intended.

We have met Carmichael before as a close friend of Beider-becke; he was among America's best-loved songwriters. One of his first tunes was called 'Freewheeling'; Bix changed it to 'Riverboat Shuffle', and it became a jazz classic. 'Stardust' had fifteen hit recordings from 1930 to 1943, and several more in later years. Carmichael appeared as himself in a few films, playing piano and singing and acting in his inimitable laconic drawl. He was also a recording artist, and in 1957 made a delightful album of his own songs, backed by all-star jazzmen.

Bix played on some of Carmichael's recordings, playing a fine solo on 'Riverboat', and on the high-spirited novelty 'Barnacle Bill the Sailor' (written with Carson Robison, a maverick who became known for his activities in country music). 'Barnacle Bill' is famous for one of Joe Venuti's pranks: the trio in the vocal refrain consisted of Carmichael, Robison and Venuti, who could not resist singing, 'Barnacle Bill the shithead!'

Carmichael was from Bloomington, Indiana, and many of his songs served to match his laid-back Midwestern personality. One of the most quintessentially American composers, he and his career were inseparable from the jazz age. He wrote words and music for 'Rockin' Chair', 'Memphis in June' and 'New Orleans', but he usually worked with lyricists: Mitchell Parish wrote the words of 'Stardust' and 'One Morning in May', Stuart Gorrell 'Georgia on My Mind', Sidney Arodin '(Up a) Lazy River', Ned Washington 'The Nearness of You', Paul Francis Webster 'Lamplighter's Serenade' and Johnny Mercer 'Lazybones', 'Skylark' and 'In the Cool, Cool, Cool of the Evening' (the last of which won an Oscar in 1951).

After the Swing Era began in 1935, the music was more jazz-oriented, but most of the public just wanted to dance, and the sheer number of bands was astonishing. Composer-arrangers Will Hudson and Eddie DeLange together led a well-known outfit in the late 1930s; among their vocalists was Georgia Gibbs. Horace Heidt's sidemen included Frank DeVol on reeds (later a studio arranger and conductor), Frankie Carle on piano (who later led his own sweet band) and Alvino Rey on electric guitar, which was unusual at the time. (Rey also formed his own band, taking DeVol and the King Sisters vocal quartet with him.) Lobo, a trained dog, took part in Heidt's act, and a later gimmick was giving away money on the radio, until that was outlawed as a lottery; he then held regional talent contests on local radio and early television.

Sammy Kaye and Kay Kyser were among the most successful leaders. ('Swing and Sway with Sammy Kaye' was changed by another bandleader to 'Swing and Sweat with Charlie Barnet'.) Kaye also invented an element of participation in that members of the audience were invited to lead the band, which survived well into the television era. Kyser's gimmick was the College of Musical Knowledge, a sort of quiz. Both bands used the corny device of singing the song title at the beginning of the arrangement. Neither was taken seriously by jazz-oriented critics, but both served up superbly reliable dance music, choosing the best tunes, playing them at the most appropriate tempos and pacing their sets extremely well. They had scores of hit records: Kyser's novelty 'Woody Woodpecker' drove the country crazy in 1948.

Guy Lombardo formed his Royal Canadians in the early 1920s in Canada, and it first recorded in 1924. Lombardo was a violinist turned front man (and later became a well-known speedboat racer); his brothers Lebert played trumpet, Victor baritone saxophone, while Carmen led the reed section and vocal trio, sang solo and wrote some fine songs, including 'Coquette', 'Boo Hoo' (covered by Count Basie and Jimmy Rushing, albeit with some reluctance), 'A Sailboat in the Moonlight and You' (covered by Billie Holiday) and 'Sweethearts on Parade' (of which Armstrong made a beautiful recording in 1930). A sister, Rose Marie Lombardo, was a vocalist; later the band's very popular singer was Kenny Gardner. The band featured a muted trumpet section and quavering reeds and played in strict tempo, and was regarded as a joke by jazz fans, who perhaps were not listening closely enough: the band often seemed to float over the beat, and was a hip 1920s dance band that never changed. The inclusion of some of its early recordings in Brian Rust's *Jazz Records 1897–1942* is evidence that it once played hot. Its music was good enough to make it the third-biggest act on records of the entire period 1890–1954, after Bing Crosby and Paul Whiteman, as well as Armstrong's favourite.

Paul Whiteman may not have been the 'King of Jazz', but he was the king of show business. Bandmaster of a fifty-seven-piece outfit in the US Navy during the First World War, he formed his first group in 1919, adopting Hickman's style as well as Grofé as pianist and arranger. Whiteman's bands were twice as big as those of his competitors; he presented a kind of 'symphonic jazz' which was pretentious even then. But as a dance band it was a harbinger of the Swing Era to come and has long been underrated. Whiteman's vocalists at various times included Morton Downey and Mildred Bailey. Downey was one of the first band singers; some thought Whiteman was mad to hire a singer, but as usual he was merely ahead of the field.

Grofé's arrangements for Whiteman, which initially jazzed the classics, attracted a Victor recording contract. The first disc was a 12-inch 78 of 'Avalon' (the tune taken from a Puccini opera) backed with 'Dance of the Hours' (by Ponchielli). The first hit was the two-sided 'Whispering' / 'The Japanese Sandman' in 1920; each side reached number one and the record sold over two million copies. 'Wang Wang Blues' was another hit, initially released under trumpeter Henry Busse's name. Busse was a German immigrant who later led his own band; 'Hot Lips', recorded with Whiteman in 1922, became his nickname and his theme, and his solo on 'When Day is Done' started a vogue for 'sweet jazz'.

Like Glenn Miller twenty years later, Whiteman saw off a previous era in popular music while summing it up and giving the public a little bit of everything: he recorded 'Last Night on the Back Porch' with a barber-shop quartet, led by Len Murray, in 1923; he not only jazzed the classics, but commissioned new music from George Gershwin, black composer William Grant Still and others, and his orchestra often worked as a pit band on Broadway. His number one hit 'Three O'Clock in the Morning' in 1923 sold 3.5 million copies of the song and led to a contract with Leo Feist as staff writer: this was a euphemism for song plugger and a form of bribe, giving Whiteman access to many of the best pop songs of the day. Whiteman made one of the first musical talking films, *King of Jazz*, in 1930, which contains perhaps ten minutes of worthwhile music. But he helped educate the public to listen to jazz-oriented music as well as dance to it.

Whiteman's vocal trio, the Rhythm Boys, comprised Al Rinker (Mildred Bailey's brother), Harry Barris and Bing Crosby. They had started out in vaudeville, and were lucky to land a spot with Whiteman when they were still very young. Crosby's first solo hit with Whiteman was 'Muddy Water' in 1927, and he recorded two songs from *Show Boat* the next year: 'Ol' Man River' and 'Make Believe' were among his early successes.

The Rhythm Boys left Whiteman in 1930 to work with Gus Arnheim's band at the Coconut Grove in Los Angeles. 'Them There Eyes', with the trio, was a hit that year, and Crosby's first solo hit with Arnheim was 'I Surrender, Dear' (co-written by Barris), which so impressed a CBS executive that Crosby was offered a radio show of his own. Harry Lillis Crosby, nicknamed after a cartoon character with big ears, became the top recording artist of the entire first half of the century, and by a very wide margin; he sold hundreds of millions of records (with over 350 hit titles) and starred in more than fifty films. His fame and worldwide popularity were such that during the Second World War German soldiers called him 'Der Bingle'.

Gus Arnheim wrote 'Sweet and Lovely', a beautiful song and a number one hit in 1931; he employed Woody Herman, who later made a memorable recording of it. Lombardo, Crosby and several others also had hits with 'Sweet and Lovely', and Herman's tenor saxophonist Flip Phillips made a beautiful version in 1944.

At the Coconut Grove Crosby always had a bunch of friends in his dressing room, a card game under way and a radio, so they could listen to Arnheim's two-hour broadcasts. Crosby would dash upstairs to do his bit, and on one occasion ended by saying to a nationwide audience, 'Deal me in, boys; I'll be right down.' He loved cronies, cards, alcohol and women, but, under the influence of his mother and given the example of his unsuccessful father, he realized that he was going to make big money and could not be sure how long the success was going to last: he became a very wealthy businessman, while the success lasted all his life.

Rudy Vallee was one of the biggest stars of the 1920s, and also one of the most generous people in the business. The quintessential collegiate singer of the acoustic era, he crooned through a megaphone, and he later said that as soon as he heard Crosby, he knew his style had been superseded. (He also wrote, in an introduction to Louis Armstrong's autobiography *Swing That Music* (1936), that Crosby and all the other pop singers of the day could not have helped being influenced by Armstrong's singing.) Vallee played drums and reeds, then began singing through a megaphone of his own design, just as his hit records were played through a horn (fifteen of them in 1929 alone, when most record players were still acoustic). He was one of the first to understand the commercial importance of broadcasting, and was famous for his greeting, 'Heigh-ho, everybody!' He later became a well-known comic actor, generally playing stuffed-shirt types in films, and in 1961 starred on Broadway in *How to Succeed in Business Without Really Trying*.

Crosby acknowledged his debt to Pops. By 1930 Armstrong was recording the best pop songs of the day and showing everyone how they could be interpreted with loving care by a superior stylist – in short, what good songs they were. He brought good songs to jazz and vice versa, determining the direction of jazz and pop for decades; his 'Stardust' was no less influential than Isham Jones's record.

Crosby had worked in the same band as Bix and many other first-rate jazzmen; his personal accompanist was the great guitarist Eddie Lang. Crosby's voice was a pleasant baritone – it sounded, Crosby said, like someone hollering down a rain barrel – a voice that everybody could identify with. His earliest records sound dated now, more because of the arrangements than his singing; he seems to be less at ease than at his peak in the 1940s, but he is indubitably *there*, and you can understand every word. Along with Armstrong, he was one of the first to appreciate the importance of the microphone: he sang easily, intimately and without strain, phrasing almost conversationally, as though singing personally to each listener. From jazz, perhaps, Crosby had learned the value of direct communication.

Although never a jazz singer, together with Armstrong he virtually invented modern pop singing.

Crosby recorded for Brunswick until 1934, then followed Jack Kapp to the new Decca label, where he stayed for twenty years, despite attempts to lure him elsewhere. He recorded duets with Armstrong, Jolson, Bob Hope, Mel Tormé, Jane Wyman, Connee Boswell, Peggy Lee, Judy Garland, his first wife, Dixie Lee, his son Gary and others. He was backed on records by Victor Young's orchestra, the Les Paul Trio and the bands of Waring, Lombardo, Eddie Condon, Louis Jordan, Xavier Cugat, Jimmy Dorsey, his brother Bob Crosby and many more. More than twenty of his hits, including 'Don't Fence Me In', were performed with the Andrews Sisters. He had the pick of the best songs of his era, many of which were written by Irving Berlin, but he also ranged back and forth through the history of popular song, from Brahms's 'Lullaby' through 'Mary's a Grand Old Name' (1906) and 'MacNamara's Band' (1917) to 'Swinging on a Star', by Jimmy Van Heusen and Johnny Burke, from the film *Going My Way*; both Crosby and the song won Oscars in 1944. (Young Andy was one of the Williams Brothers backing him on the record, and the song was included in children's music books.) Crosby also recorded several of the best country songs of the 1940s.

His only rival as a male pop singer in the early years was Russ Colombo, who also sang with Arnheim's band; he was credited as co-author of 'Prisoner of Love', and sang Arnheim's 'Sweet and Lovely'. Colombo died in an accident with a desk ornament, a duelling pistol that turned out to be loaded.

A popular female singer in the late 1920s was Helen Kane, the 'boop-boop-a-doop' girl, whose tunes included her theme, 'I Wanna be Loved by You', and the slightly suggestive 'Is There Anything Wrong in That?' Her little-girl voice inspired Betty Boop, the cartoon character. Kane sued the creators of Betty, but it was established that 'booping' had earlier been practised by a black singer, Baby Esther. Kane's flapper persona was soon *passé*, but her tiny voice was revived by Wee Bonnie Baker on her 1939 hit, and Kane herself was dubbed by Debbie Reynolds in a 1950 film, *Three Little Words*. (Betty Boop's sensational curves ran foul of the censors after about a hundred cartoons, but she did a cameo in *Who Framed Roger Rabbit?* in 1988.)

Many fine female singers were admired by jazzmen. Mildred Bailey was married to vibraphonist Red Norvo; in the 1930s they led a band together and were known as Mr and Mrs Swing. Connee Boswell, who was born in New Orleans, had a successful career as leader and arranger of a vocal trio with her sisters before going solo. A victim of polio, she worked in a wheelchair; she said she learned breath control by listening to Caruso records.

Ethel Waters was well known as a vocalist before Louis Armstrong. The English writer Charles Fox has described her as the first important jazz singer, because of the way she told a story; she began by singing popular blues, and could transform a pop song more subtly than Bessie Smith, displaying, as Fox says, 'a remarkably expressive voice, a keen understanding of how language should come across in song, and a rhythmic flexibility very rare at that time'. She became the biggest black star on Broadway after Bert Williams. *As Thousands Cheer* (1933) at Irving Berlin's Music Box had a book by Moss Hart and was a barbed political satire, full of laughs; Waters sang 'Supper Time' (an anti-lynching song), 'Harlem on My Mind' and the sizzling 'Heat Wave'. (Marilyn Miller and Clifton Webb sang 'Easter Parade' in *As Thousands Cheer*, stepping out of a sepia photograph, as from a rotogravure newspaper section.)

Vocal groups, popular in the acoustic era, now sold records with more modern harmony. The Boswell Sisters paved the way for the Andrews Sisters, three girls from Minneapolis whose success began with 'Bei mir bist du schön' in 1938 and whose close harmony is still redolent of nostalgia for millions. (Bette Midler revived their 'Boogie Woogie Bugle Boy' over thirty years later.) They too recorded with many other Decca artists, among them Lombardo, Les Paul, Danny Kaye and Carmen Miranda, as well as Crosby. Patti Andrews had solo hits, Patti and Maxene starred in *Over There* on Broadway in 1974 and Maxene released a new album in 1985. The King Sisters had an unusually rich harmonic style, being a quartet: Alyce, Donna, Louise and Yvonne Driggs sang with Horace Heidt, then with Alvino Rey (Louise's husband), and had a television series in the 1960s.

Male vocal groups included the Mills Brothers and the Ink Spots, both black, and enormously successful. The Ink Spots were a quartet; the voice of its lead singer, Bill Kenny, on 'If I Didn't Care' (1939) and 'To Each His Own' (1946) is unforgettable. Even more popular were the Mills Brothers, Herbert, Harry, Donald and John, the last of whom accompanied the group on his guitar. (When John died in 1935, he was replaced by their father.) They had hits from 1931 ('Tiger Rag') until the end of the 1960s; 'Paper Doll' (1943) sold over six million copies.

An influential genre was the torch song; nearly all the hit records in this style occur after 1926, because it requires an intimacy that was impossible without the microphone. Broadway stars Ruth Etting, Libby Holman, Fanny Brice and Helen Morgan were famous for songs of regretful, passionate love; in some cases their personal lives reflected their stage personae. These four had over eighty hit records, but Etting was by far the most prolific. She was picked out of a chorus line in 1922 by her manager and first husband, mobster Moe 'the Gimp' Snyder, and was best known for 'Love Me or Leave Me' and 'Ten Cents a Dance' (which she sang in Rodgers and Hart's show *Simple Simon* in 1930). Moe shot her piano player, but he recovered, and married her; in spite of all the drama in her life, she had a long and happy retirement. She was played by Doris Day in the film biography *Love Me or Leave Me* (1955), and Jimmy Cagney was Moe.

Fanny Brice was also married to a mobster, gambler Nicky Arnstein; her most famous song was 'My Man', a French import which she sang for Ziegfeld in 1920 and in a film in 1929. She also did comedy and dialect songs, and was the popular brat Baby Snooks on the radio in the late 1940s. Barbra Streisand played Brice in *Funny Girl* on Broadway in 1964 and in the film in 1968. Libby Holman was well known for sultry renditions of 'Moanin' Low' (by Ralph Rainger and Howard Dietz) and 'Body and Soul' (in the show *Three's a Crowd*, 1930). She married tobacco heir Zachary Smith Reynolds; when he was murdered a year later, she was accused but cleared, though her career never recovered. Helen Morgan sang in the Kern shows *Showboat* and *Sweet Adeline*; *The Helen Morgan Story* was made for TV in the 1950s with Polly Bergen, who made fine albums of torch songs for CBS, but the 1957 cinema version unaccountably replaced Bergen with an actress whose singing voice had to be dubbed.

In the Great Depression the record business almost disappeared, because music could be heard free on the radio, but popular music, along with the cinema, became an important avenue of escapism. Curiously, the calamity of the Depression inspired only one memorable song, 'Brother, Can You Spare a Dime?', by Jay Gorney and Yip Harburg. 'Hallelujah, I'm a Bum' is sometimes quoted as a Depression song; actually there were two songs of that title: Harry Kirby McClintock based his on the hymn 'Revive Us Again', while Rodgers and Hart wrote theirs for a film of the same name. But neither was really a Depression song. Hart wrote: 'Why work away for wealth / When you can travel for your health?' This philosophy had little appeal in 1933.

But even the Depression could not alter the fact that new markets had been discovered. Tin Pan Alley and Broadway were oriented towards New York, while many Americans had their own indigenous musics which meant much to them. The great country music producer Art Satherley, born in England, loved American rural, or folk, music, and regarded all of it as country music, whether white or black; but according to the institutionalized racism of the era, it had to be divided into 'race' and 'hillbilly' music.

Cornettist, songwriter, bandleader and publisher William Christopher Handy had become a powerful figure in the music business, having discovered or written such imperishable songs as 'St Louis Blues', 'Beale Street Blues', 'Yellow Dog Blues', 'Memphis Blues' and 'Loveless Love' (also known as 'Careless Love'). 'St Louis Blues', which has a habanera 'Spanish tinge' in the middle section, is one of the biggest hits of the century and was first recorded in 1916. 'Memphis Blues' was originally a campaign song for Mr Edward H. Crump, a Memphis political leader. Handy's songs were not really blues, according to a strict musical definition which has lost some ground in recent years. Blues was a folk music that had evolved among ex-slaves in the nineteenth century from their work songs. Although the blues was and is an important element in jazz, jazz was never a folk music, while blues relied on unsophisticated but subtle and direct communication.

The classic blues is a twelve-bar verse, three lines of four bars each; the lyric consists of couplets, with the first line repeated once. (Leonard Bernstein, in one of his recorded lectures, used Shakespeare couplets as blues.) Each line of text takes about two and a half bars; the rest of each four-bar segment is improvised fill, sometimes vocal, but usually provided by the singer's own guitar or piano. The blues goes against European musical practice, and was therefore frowned upon by educated people both black and white; it uniquely combined major and minor modes. 'Blue notes', which cannot be played on the piano, are now thought to have stemmed more or less directly from African music. Classic blues lyrics came from a storehouse of images, words and phrases, including the argot that American blacks had used to express themselves safely since the earliest days of slavery. The verses and the musical accompaniment are like two voices: the accompaniment is a commentary on the story being told, and the result is a polyrhythmic, almost poly-emotional music. The blues is not a vehicle for self-pity, contrary to the commonplace orthodoxy, but a passionate, intensely rhythmic way of keeping the spirit *up*, by commenting on problems of life and love with lyrics full of irony and earthy imagery: defeating the enemy by confronting him. Blues is, above all, a music of great human bravery.

The commercial market for blues, like that for jazz, was discovered by the record business in time to capture many classic performers. Perry Bradford, an early entrepreneur in black music, placed two of his songs with Fred Hagar, music director of Okeh Records; 'That Thing Called Love' and 'You Can't Keep a Good Man Down', both published by the Pace and Handy Music Company, were recorded by Mamie Smith. To this day we cannot be sure whether the backing group was black or white. The record sold well enough to call for another recording session, this time with a black group dubbed the Jazz Hounds. Bradford's 'Crazy Blues' (not a real blues, but a pop song) was recorded in August 1920. To everyone's surprise it was a sensation, and yet another genre of black music began to enrich the mainstream of American music. Obviously the discovery was waiting to happen; as early as 1920 Jerome Kern wrote songs with 'blues' in the title. More importantly, over five thousand genuine blues records were made before the Second World War.

Among the female blues singers were Trixie Smith (quickly signed by Harry Pace, who left W. C. Handy to form Black Swan, the first black-owned record label, for which Fletcher Henderson handled the musical side), Clara Smith, Alberta Hunter, Lucille Hegamin, Victoria Spivey, Edith Wilson and Sippie Wallace, most of whom were all-round performers who included blues numbers in their acts. The two most authentic were undoubtedly Gertrude 'Ma' Rainey and her protégée Bessie Smith, called the Mother and the Empress of the Blues respectively. (None of the Smiths was related.)

Ma Rainey and Bessie Smith seemed larger than life, having powerful voices, powerful appetites and a reluctance to take any nonsense from anybody. Ma was perhaps the purer blues singer; her biggest hit was 'See See Rider' in 1925, with Louis Armstrong and Henderson. But of all the blues singers Bessie Smith was the one who had most influence on jazz musicians. Like Ma Rainey, she had developed a method of singing each song around centre tones, perhaps in order to project her voice more easily to the back of a room; but she would also choose to sing a song in an unusual key, and her artistry in bending and stretching notes with her beautiful, powerful contralto to accommodate her own interpretation was unsurpassed: she could make a trite pop song into a blues masterpiece. Her biggest hit was her first, 'Downhearted Blues', in 1923, written by Alberta Hunter and Lovie Austin; others were 'Empty Bed Blues' in 1928 (it covered two sides of a 78, which at that time was very unusual) and 'After You've Gone', two W. C. Handy songs.

To accept the obvious orthodoxy that the music of Jelly Roll Morton, King Oliver and Bessie Smith was regarded as old-fashioned by 1930 is to ignore what might have been. What would have happened to American music if the phonograph had captured the cornet playing of Frank Johnson in 1845, or if James P. Johnson had been commissioned to write for Paul Whiteman's concert in 1924 instead of George Gershwin? Who knows how many records Morton, Oliver and Smith might have sold if the bottom had not dropped out of the record business between 1929 and 1932? As it was, Bessie earned as much as $3,000 a recording session, and in 1929 appeared in a short film, *St Louis Blues*, with the Hall Johnson Choir and a band led by James P. Johnson. But she had her last national hit the same year, 'Nobody Knows You when You're Down and Out', with Clarence Williams on piano. After 1931 there was no recording session until her last, in 1933, for which she was paid $50 for each of four sides, and her sales did not even justify that. She spent the rest of her life touring, and died of horrific injuries following a car crash, not knowing that she would influence singers who were not yet born.

The new market for race music led to a scramble to record black artists in the 1920s, not that many of them were 'signed up' in the modern sense: their records are still selling, but few of them received any royalties. Blind Lemon Jefferson, a street singer and guitarist who recorded prolifically, is thought to have been the first to record the slide guitar style (in 1926), in which the guitar is fretted with a knife-blade, steel tube, bottleneck (hence 'bottleneck' style) or some other such tool; this became an important voice in the blues. Jefferson was only in his thirties when he froze to death in a Chicago snow storm. Guitarist and vocalist Big Bill Broonzy was an early urban blues artist, so active in the Chicago area, both as soloist and sideman, that he was one of the most widely recorded and best-selling black artists of the era. Broonzy again was more than a blues singer; when asked if he sang folksongs, he replied that he had never heard a horse sing them.

The alcoholic Leroy Carr, in Indianapolis, Indiana, accompanied himself on the piano, which was unusual for a male blues singer. His smoother, more urban style, along with such songs as 'How Long Blues' and 'In the Evening when the Sun Goes Down', was to be of formative influence on the next generation. He made his classic records with Scrapper Blackwell, a guitarist who also sang and played piano. Another piano-playing bluesman was Memphis Slim (Peter Chatman), who wrote 'Alberta' (a Broonzy speciality), 'The Comeback' and 'Every Day (I Have the Blues)', made famous in 1955 by Count Basie and Joe Williams.

A genre of blues piano playing began in the lumber camps of the South: the barrelhouse piano style was so called because the room with the piano usually had a bar consisting of a barrel of whisky resting on two planks. These pianists taught themselves to play at the level required in such places; the pianism was less sophisticated than that of the ragtime-based stride pianists of the East Coast. They played a rolling rhythm in the left hand (eight notes to the bar) so that they could reach for a drink or a sandwich with the right hand.

As their music reached places like Chicago it came to be called boogie-woogie, and it was a fad in the 1940s during the Swing Era.

The blues was already becoming urbanized, for the First World War had stimulated black emigration to northern cities. But up until the next war the greatest male blues singers were still to be found in rural areas, where they were often recorded on portable disc-cutting equipment. It is significant that nearly all of them accompanied themselves on the guitar. The black woman was not a threat to white male supremacy; she often worked indoors, and if she became a singer, she was accompanied by a pianist. The black male was not a threat either, if he could be kept itinerant, preferably illiterate and utterly poor, so he had to carry his music around with him. The history of the blues provides more evidence of the fractured family lives of black Americans, the result of which is that today black children are still far more likely than white ones to come from a broken home.

The more delicate and lyrical Piedmont blues tradition of the South-east was represented by musicians like Blind Boy Fuller, Pink Anderson and Floyd Council (the last two of whom had a rock group named after them) and harmonica player Sonny Terry and Brownie McGhee. Terry and McGhee were taken up by white liberals as a popular concert act, whereupon they lost their edge.

Like Blind Lemon Jefferson, Lightnin' Hopkins, Texas Alexander and Mance Lipscomb all came from Texas. Lipscomb did not record at all until 1961, when he was discovered by Chris Strachwitz of Arhoolie Records; another all-rounder, he played excellent ragtime, pop songs and children's songs on his guitar. Mississippi John Hurt, who herded cows in Avalon, Mississippi, was another versatile artist. After being discovered by Tommy Rockwell, he recorded in Memphis and New York in 1928, but was then washed away by the Depression; he was rediscovered by Tom Hoskins in 1963, his sly charm and unique guitar playing completely intact.

The purest, most powerful – indeed, harrowing – blues of all came from the Mississippi delta. Eddie 'Son' House, Nehemiah 'Skip' James and Bukka White lived long enough to be rediscovered; Charley Patton, Robert Johnson, Tommy Johnson, Ishman Bracey, Peetie Wheatstraw and many others survive only on old recordings.

(Bracey had left the blues to become a clergyman.) Wheatstraw was known as 'the Devil's son-in-law'. Charley Patton regarded himself as an entertainer, and played an exceptionally interesting ragtime-based guitar; he was related to the Chatmon family of well-known Mississippi blues artists.

Booker T. Washington 'Bukka' White recorded for Victor in 1930, worked as a boxer and a baseball player and then made two sides for Vocalion in 1937: 'Pinebluff, Arkansas' and 'Shake 'Em On Down', the latter a blues classic which had many variants. He was sentenced to Parchman State Farm in Mississippi for assault, where he was recorded by John Lomax for the Library of Congress in 1939. After his release he made twelve sides in 1940 with Washboard Sam (Robert Brown) for Okeh and Vocalion, including 'Parchman Farm Blues', 'Where Can I Change My Clothes?' and 'District Attorney Blues'. The controlled passion of his rough-edged voice and his rhythmically inexorable guitar created some of the most beautiful and powerfully emotional music in the genre. The end of the classic blues era was already near; but White was rediscovered in 1963 by Ed Denson and guitarist John Fahey with much of his power still intact.

As these musicians were more or less self-taught, they invented their own ways of playing what they wanted, and each of the best was inspiring in his own way. Skip James's intensely lyrical style was said to have influenced Robert Johnson; he made twenty-six sides for Paramount in 1931, for which he was paid $40. Son House also served time at Parchman State Farm; he made eight or nine sides for Paramount in 1930 and test pressings for ARC (who decided on Patton instead), and recorded for the Library of Congress in 1941–2. Both House and James were rediscovered in time to perform at folk festivals and to make more recordings; both had tunes covered by rock groups.

Tommy Johnson's classic 'Cool Drink of Water Blues' begins with the famous line 'I asked her for water / She gave me gasoline', and his 'Canned Heat Blues' gave the white blues band of the 1960s its name. ('Canned heat' was used in cooking stoves; the best-known brand name was Sterno. It could be dissolved and used as a poisonous beverage by alcoholics.) Bracey was something of a Johnson sidekick; he played at almost exactly the same recording dates, and recorded a water and gasoline lyric the day after Tommy did. Johnson made few recordings, but through his unique guitar playing he was one of the most influential of all, along with Robert Johnson (to whom he was not related).

Tommy's brother Ledell, who taught him some guitar, said that Tommy had acquired his final polish by selling his soul to the devil. Son House said the same thing about Robert Johnson, who was not at first thought to be a particularly good player, but disappeared for a while, and then turned up much improved. In the hands of the greatest masters, the blues guitar sang with intensity, and Robert Johnson was a complete master. 'Hellhound on My Trail' and 'Me and the Devil Blues' are perhaps his most apposite titles. In a San Antonio hotel room in 1936 and in the back room of a Dallas office building in 1937 he made a total of forty-one sides for ARC labels (including alternative takes). Only 'Terraplane Blues' was anything like a hit in the restricted race market of the time, but 'I Believe I'll Dust My Broom' was adapted by Elmore James and became a post-war anthem of electric blues, while 'Terraplane', 'Love in Vain', 'Stop Breakin' Down' and 'Crossroads' were covered by rock groups in the 1960s. (The crossroads was where you went at midnight to do a deal with the devil.) Johnson's death was violent and said to involve a woman; his acolyte Johnny Shines had heard that 'it was something to do with the black arts'. It is now suggested that Robert Johnson was a far more 'sophisticated' performer than was hitherto thought, which makes his legacy all the more interesting. Meticulous research on his life has not been published yet because his killer is still alive.

John Hammond tried to find Johnson for his 1938 'From Spirituals to Swing' concert, but for once Hammond was too late. Hammond was the legendary producer of generations of great artists: coming from a wealthy family, he was financially independent enough to be able to work freelance during the Depression. He recorded Fletcher Henderson; he produced Billie Holiday's first recording session and Bessie Smith's last, both in 1933; he was an early champion of Benny Goodman, Count Basie, Charlie Christian and many other jazz greats; later he was director of popular music at Vanguard (1950s), which resulted in excellent jazz and folk albums, and helped to discover Bob

Dylan and Bruce Springsteen. The concerts he produced in 1938–9 represented a turning point in American popular culture.

The concert on 23 December 1938 at Carnegie Hall began with boogie-woogie pianists Pete Johnson, Albert Ammons and Meade 'Lux' Lewis, imported from the Midwest (where Ammons and Lewis had made a living washing cars and driving taxis in Chicago). This touched off the fad for boogie-woogie mentioned earlier, and inspired the young German immigrant Alfred Lion to form his Blue Note label. Big Bill Broonzy sang about having a dream in which he had a chat with President Roosevelt. Sister Rosetta Tharpe had hardly sung anywhere other than in church, but demonstrated the connection between the music of the black churches and the passion of the blues; she soon became a leading attraction with the Lucky Millinder band in Harlem. Ruby Walker Smith sang the blues (she was thought to be Bessie's niece, but Hammond said not). Other performers included Sidney Bechet, Tommy Ladnier and James P. Johnson, and the concert ended with the full Basie band; it was well received by the critics, and sophisticated fans found out where their favourite music had come from. Hammond was a man of strong views, some of them strange: he wrote in his autobiography that he thought Duke Ellington had compromised his music for success in a world dominated by whites; but he also admitted that his opinion of Ellington's music might tell the reader as much about John Hammond as about Ellington. In any case, few people have done as much for American music.

John Lomax, who began collecting songs as a child, later published such books as *Cowboy Songs and Other Frontier Ballads* (1910). He worked as a banker, but when jobs for bankers grew scarce during the Depression, he became a full-time folklorist: with the help of his son Alan, he made thousands of 78s using portable recording equipment provided by the Library of Congress. He recorded Leadbelly and Bukka White, among many others, and Alan made the Jelly Roll Morton sessions mentioned earlier. In Stovall, Mississippi, in 1941–2, McKinley Morganfield recorded for the Library of Congress; he soon went to Chicago, where he became the most important of post-war bluesmen, Muddy Waters.

There were other entrepreneurs, and other musics were being

discovered. The blues, a black country music, did not depend upon a slick formula, a New York publisher or a big vaudeville name to perform it. It came unbidden out of the hearts of its practitioners, as did white country music, which also began to enter the mainstream of popular music in the acoustic era; both would revitalize jaded pop scenes in decades to come. How the music business regarded country music has been summed up by Nolan Porterfield in his biography of Jimmie Rodgers (1979): 'a sort of backward, ugly, show-biz step-child that refused to go to school and learn from its betters but could not be locked up in the back room'.

Old-time fiddlers Eck Robertson and Henry Gilliand had recorded for Victor in New York in 1922, but the record was not then released. The country market was discovered by Ralph Sylvester Peer. After working for his father, who sold sewing machines, Columbia phonographs and records, he worked for Columbia, then for Fred Hagar at Okeh. Early in 1923 he recorded harmonica player Henry Whittier, but thought nothing of it. He was sent to Atlanta in June, where furniture dealer Polk Brockman wanted to record Fiddlin' John Carson: 'The Little Old Log Cabin in the Lane' backed with 'The Old Hen Cackled and the Rooster's Going to Crow' did not even get an Okeh release number, but when the first pressing sold out, Peer paid more attention, and became the most important talent scout in a new industry, again and again in the right place at the right time. (Before it became a fiddle tune, 'The Little Old Log Cabin in the Lane' was a parlour song, written by Will Shakespeare Hays in 1871; opera star Alma Gluck had recorded it for Victor.)

Peer discovered Ernest Van 'Pop' Stoneman, whose epic 'The Titanic' was one of the first big country hits in 1925 (and whose family are still folk and country artists today); and the same year he recorded a string band called Al Hopkins and the Hill Billies. They were the first country artists to make Washington, DC, their home base, broadcasting from there; they were also among the first to record in New York, the first to make a short film (for Warner Brothers), the first to play for a president (Coolidge) and the first to use a piano and a Hawaiian guitar. Hopkins told Peer he could call them anything he wanted, since they were 'nothing but a bunch of hillbillies anyway'. Peer liked that name, but the band was not sure until Pop Stoneman approved it.

In the second quarter of the eighteenth century, poorer British settlers had begun moving into the western parts of the colonies. They could not compete with plantation-owners, who had plenty of cheap black slave labour, and they wanted more freedom. They were escaping taxation on their farm produce by a Tory government in London which, unaware of the enormous potential of its most valuable colonies, persistently tried to placate English merchants. A hundred years earlier the Ulster rebels who had been cleared from land in northern Ireland were replaced by hard-working Scottish lowland people who were loyal to James I (who was James VI of Scotland). A good number of them were weavers, and produced cloth that competed with that of English factories, so eventually they too were driven off their land. Many of them went to Penn's Woods – Pennsylvania – where in 1750 the Cumberland Gap to the Appalachian Mountains was discovered; this barrier to the West encompassed the smaller Cumberland, Blue Ridge and Allegheny mountain ranges. As Pennsylvania began to fill up, the Cumberland Gap represented a gateway to cheap land in West Virginia and Kentucky (much of it purchased from Cherokee Indians by Daniel Boone and his business partners). Scots, Irish and runaway slaves (both black and white) poured into the mountains and beyond, bringing with them fiddles, lutes and other instruments, and their songs, ballads and attitudes, many traceable to Elizabethan England – and probably a few copies of John Playford's *Dancing Master*. It was their music that Peer discovered.

String bands consisted of fiddles, guitars, a string bass and often a banjo and/or a mandolin (the most recent addition to the lute family). The music, which had been spreading across the USA for generations, was variously described by record companies and catalogues as old-time music, mountain music, 'familiar tunes' and so on, until Peer's 'hillbilly' stuck.

The most successful string band was Gid Tanner and his Skillet Lickers, who began recording in 1926. James Gideon Tanner was a champion fiddler; George Riley Puckett, blind from childhood, was a vocalist and one of the most influential guitarists; Frank Walker, then an A & R man at Columbia, put them together with fiddler Clayton 'Pappy' McMichen and others to form the group. Puckett's baritone sold the recordings, and he also recorded as a soloist. McMichen was influenced by jazz and resented being called a hillbilly, while Tanner was strictly old-time. Perhaps because of the tension caused by these various strands, their music was hotter and more influential than the others. Comedy recordings were made, beginning with 'A Corn Likker Still in Georgia'; 'Turkey in the Straw' and 'John Henry' were hits in 1926–7. A hillbilly-style pop song, 'Down Yonder', had been published in 1921 and interpolated into the Broadway show *Tip-top*. Popular recordings of it included one by a barber-shop quartet; when the Skillet Lickers recorded it in 1934, it became one of the biggest country hits of the decade.

Another important string band was the North Carolina Ramblers, led by Charlie Poole, a banjo picker who had developed a unique three-fingered style as a result of a boyhood injury to his right hand. Their 'Don't Let Your Deal Go Down' (1925) sold 100,000 copies and remained a country standard.

There were also black string bands, which played much the same kind of music, but rarely recorded. A great many guitar pickers, fiddlers and singers had jammed with blacks. Mandolin player Bill Monroe, guitarist Sam McGee and banjo player Dock Boggs, three of the best in the business, are among those who admitted their debt to black music, while Ma Rainey often had requests for 'Heart Made of Stone', an Appalachian lament. Blues singer Yank Rachell, born in 1910 in Tennessee, also played guitar, harmonica and violin; when he was eight years old, he traded a pig for a mandolin, which added a unique rural flavour to his recording sessions, among them one with the original Sonny Boy Williamson on Bluebird (1938), and to Rachell's own more recent albums, such as *Mandolin Blues* (acoustic) and *Chicago Style* (electric) on Delmark. Brownie McGhee remembered 'jookin'', or country quilting parties, and Bill Broonzy recalled 'two-way' picnics, at which blacks and whites swapped songs. Black guitar player Leslie Riddles accompanied A. P. Carter on song-collecting trips, and had a direct effect on Maybelle Carter's famous guitar style. Jimmie Tarlton, who performed in a well-known South Carolina duo with Tom Darby, said that he picked up bottleneck guitar from a black musician when he was ten years old, which would have been many years before Blind Lemon Jefferson recorded in that style. The great black Swing Era composer Edgar Sampson plays a violin solo on a recording of 'Hot-tempered Blues', by Charlie Johnson's Paradise Ten, the house band at Smalls' Paradise in Harlem in 1928: loaded with double stops, it could have been played by Gid Tanner. Johnson's competition at the Cotton Club was Duke Ellington, who in 1936 recorded 'Lazy Man's Shuffle' (by 'Rex Stewart and his 52nd Street Stompers'). It includes Brick Fleagle (or possibly Ceele Burke) on what sounds like a Hawaiian guitar, which soon became country music's steel guitar. We will never know to what extent the colour bar in broadcasting and in the marketing of records prevented more fusions of black and white musics, but the degree of two-way influence has always been remarkable.

After Ralph Peer left Okeh, he offered to record for Victor in exchange for the song copyrights. He recorded Ishman Bracey and Tommy Johnson in Memphis in 1928, but before that, he went to Bristol, Tennessee, in 1927, because it seemed like a good location, near the Tennessee–Virginia border. There he recorded Stoneman and others, and advertised for players in local newspapers. In August he recorded a vocal and instrumental trio, the Carter Family, and a railway worker named Jimmie Rodgers: having recorded the first string band, he now found the rest of country music.

Jimmie Rodgers, also known as the Singing Brakeman and the Blue Yodeller, pulled together many strands to form the basis of mainstream country music, and became its first legend, recording 110 sides in less than five years, the last just two days before he died of tuberculosis. He had learned his music from hoboes and railway workers, black and white; he combined yodelling with the twelve-bar blues; the first of his thirteen 'blue yodels', 'T for Texas', sold a million copies and has been covered many times. Some of the blue yodels were simply numbered; others also had titles, such as 'Blue Yodel No. 4 (California Blues)'. When 'Blue Yodel No. 9' was recorded in Hollywood in 1930, Louis Armstrong was among the sidemen; Louis plays beautifully, but with unusual caution, as though he was not sure what was going to happen next: Rodgers's time was quirky. His nasal tenor voice and Mississippi drawl, and his transparent informality and good humour, brought sympathy to hoboes and hillbillies everywhere. As Nolan Porterfield put it, Rodgers 'couldn't read a note, keep time, play the "right" chords or write lyrics that fit. All he could do was reach the hearts of millions of people around the world, and lift them up. They listened, and understood.'

Rodgers often recorded solo, but also with what amounted to a dixieland band, and he was one of the first to use a Hawaiian guitar. The guitar had been introduced to Hawaii by Spanish and Portuguese cowboys in the mid nineteenth century; the Hawaiians began playing it horizontally, in the lap, with the strings raised, and in the slide style, without frets. They invented 'slack' tuning (called *ki ho alu*), or open-chord tuning. Joseph Kekeku was the first to fret the Hawaiian guitar with a comb instead of his fingers; King Bennie Nawahi played jazz and blues as well as hulas; Hawaiian guitar became a fad in vaudeville, and was even occasionally inserted into a Broadway show. Rodgers recorded with a Hollywood group called Lani McIntire's Harmony Hawaiians, and with Joe Kaipo, a genuine Hawaiian guitarist (who claimed that his father was mayor of Honolulu). When the Hawaiian guitar was later electrified, it became the steel guitar as we have known it in country music ever since.

In May 1928 Rodgers's fourth record was released ('Blue Yodel No. 2' and 'Brakeman's Blues') and by midsummer his royalties were averaging more than $1,000 a month, at that time a fortune for a peripatetic railway worker. Rodgers helped Victor's profits to return almost to where they had been before radio had bitten deeply into the record business, and Peer was making so much money that he had to start new corporations to put it in.

A song called 'The One Rose (That's Left in My Heart)', written by McIntire, was Rodgers's closest brush with pop fame. Peer did not issue it within the agreed year, so McIntire placed the song elsewhere; Bing Crosby and bandleaders Larry Clinton and Art Kassel all had national hits with it in 1937, while Rodgers's version, released several years after his death, looked like a cover. Among his other backing musicians were Pappy McMichen, who had left Tanner and was leading the first of several groups he called the Georgia Wildcats; he co-wrote 'Peach Pickin' Time Down in Georgia'.

Rodgers's most important collaborator was his sister-in-law, Elsie McWilliams, who could read and write music and play the piano. Rodgers would worry a tune until it sounded as he wanted it to, 'wrong' chords and all; Elsie could help him polish it. The songs she had a hand in were the most completely composed, and set the style of his career: for example, 'Never No Mo' Blues', 'You and Me and My Old Guitar' and 'Daddy and Home'. They wrote 'Everybody Does It in Hawaii', on the recording of which Joe Kaipo played the Hawaiian guitar in 1929. It may have been Peer, seeking more royalties for his artist as well as for his own publishing company, who was behind King Oliver's instrumental version the next year, with Roy Smeck on Hawaiian-style guitar. Rodgers's repertory included sentimental songs ('My Old Pal', 'My Little Lady'), songs about tragedy and death ('T B Blues', 'Hobo Bill's Last Ride') and hard times ('Waitin' for a Train' and many of the blue yodels), and they displayed bravado and *double entendre* ('Pistol Packin' Papa', 'Mean Mama Blues'). 'Muleskinner Blues', 'In the Jailhouse Now' and others have been covered many times; 'Miss the Mississippi and You' was a country hit in 1981.

Rodgers was a happy-go-lucky man who enjoyed his stardom. He counted among his friends crooner Gene Austin, whose record of 'My Blue Heaven' was among the biggest hits of the 1920s (and was not in fact topped until Crosby's 'White Christmas'). Rodgers considered Austin a rival: although his live gigs were mostly in the South and often in tent shows, he thought of himself as an all-round entertainer. He probably sold about twelve million records during his lifetime, which was phenomenal for the Depression. (In later years many a country boy remembered being sent to the general store for 'a pound of butter, a slab of bacon and the latest Jimmie Rodgers record'.) Gene Autry, Ernest Tubb and Hank Snow were just three of the giants in country music who began by imitating Rodgers, and nobody knows how many boys born in the 1930s were named after him.

Equally important was the other discovery Peer made in Bristol, Tennessee: the Carter Family. A. P. (Alvin Pleasant) Carter sang bass or baritone harmony in an improvisatory way, coming in wherever he felt like it; he played some fiddle and collected mountain ballads. His wife, Sara, sang lead and Maybelle (Sara's cousin, who was married to A. P.'s brother Ezra) sang harmony. Both women played autoharp and guitar; Sara's autoharp became a component of the traditional style, while Maybelle played melody on the guitar's bass strings and harmony on the treble – the influential 'Carter style' – and she also played blues licks and occasionally even steel guitar. Their songs, many of ancient lineage, are still sung by folk groups today: 'Wabash Cannon Ball' was a hit for Roy Acuff (and 'I'm Thinking Tonight of My Blue Eyes' was adapted for his 'Great Speckled Bird'); 'I Never Will Marry' was later recorded by the Weavers, 'Wildwood Flower' by Joan Baez, 'Jimmy Brown the Newsboy' by Flatt and Scruggs and 'Hello Stranger' by Emmylou Harris. 'Keep on the Sunny Side', a 1906 pop song, became their theme. 'Worried Man Blues', 'Will the Circle be Unbroken?' and many more became standards as Carter Family songs.

Peer preferred the sound of Sara's voice, while the beautiful harmony of the two women was more in evidence on their recordings for Decca and ARC labels after 1935 and Columbia in 1940; in 1941 the trio returned to Victor and brought their total to as many as three hundred sides. After 1938 the Carters broadcast on Mexican radio, as Rodgers had done earlier. (When broadcasting frequencies were assigned by international agreement, the Mexicans were left out, and so did as they pleased; one of their 100,000-watt transmitters was heard in Canada and Hawaii. Furthermore, Peer had musical interests in Mexico as early as 1930.)

A. P. and Sara were divorced, but continued to work together until 1943; by then their children Joe and Jannette were performing, as well as Maybelle's daughters Anita, June and Helen. After 1943 Maybelle and her daughters formed a group and in 1948 joined the *Grand Ole Opry*. Maybelle became the much loved First Lady of Country Music. She and Ezra had faith in Johnny Cash, whom they helped through a troubled time, and June became his second wife. Maybelle gave Chet Atkins one of his first jobs, influenced the piano style of Floyd Cramer (who later played on Elvis Presley's 'Heartbreak Hotel') and taught her granddaughter Carlene Carter to play guitar (June's daughter by her first husband, Carl Smith). Anita had solo hits until 1971.

Another Carter family began recording in 1936. D. P. 'Dad' Carter met his wife Carrie in singing school; having nine children, Carter formed a group to help make ends meet. He sang baritone, Ernest 'Jim' Carter bass, Rose soprano and Anna alto. They began broadcasting in Lubbock, Texas, as the Carter Quartet, and within a year had moved to KBAP in Forth Worth, one of the most powerful stations in Texas. They took the name of the Chuck Wagon Gang, a western band which had left the station, and sang gospel songs on the radio five days a week for fifteen years. Dad played mandolin on a few of their earliest recordings; thereafter Jim's acoustic guitar was their only accompaniment until 1954, when personnel changes began and a discreet electric guitar was played by Anna's husband. They recorded over four hundred sides; their recording of 'Church in the Wildwood', made in 1936, four years after that of the more famous Carter Family, is even more beautiful. No one knows how many records the Chuck Wagon Gang sold: country gospel music was not important to the compilers of charts, but poor people bought records by all these artists, and those of the Chuck Wagon Gang sold by the carload at revival meetings.

The broadcasting of country music began early. The first of the long-lasting radio shows was the *Chicago Barn Dance* in 1924, which soon became the *National Barn Dance*, on WLS, whose call letters stood for 'World's Largest Store': the station was owned by Sears and Roebuck, whose mail order catalogue was kept next to the bible by many rural families. The show's most famous stars over the years included Gene Autry, Bob Atcher, Red Foley, Lulu Belle and Scotty, Rex Allen, comics Homer and Jethro and bandleader Pee Wee King. The programme transferred to WGN in 1960 (after WLS had become the Midwest's biggest pop station), where it continued until 1970. Its original announcer was George D. Hay, voted most popular announcer by *Radio Digest* magazine.

Hay went to a new station, WSM in Nashville, Tennessee, in 1925. A broadcast in November featuring 85-year-old fiddler Uncle Jimmy Thompson was so successful that the WSM *Barn Dance* began in December with Hay (soon dubbed 'the solemn old judge', though he was just thirty) as MC. In 1927 the show was preceded by a classical concert whose programme included a train composition; conductor Walter Damrosch was patronizing about 'realism' in music on a programme which consisted mainly of grand opera: Hay came on the air promising the 'realest realism' on the 'Grand Ole Opry', and from that time the renamed show opened with a train tune, 'Pan-American Blues', played on the harmonica by Deford Bailey.

For years Hay would allow only string bands, with no drums or horns. The house band was Dr Humphrey Bate and his Possum Hunters. Bate, a physician, played Sousa marches along with country music, and enjoyed classical music as well; he had learned some of his songs as a boy from an ex-slave, and he accepted his hillbilly image with reluctance. (His daughter, Alcyone Bate, still played piano on the programme fifty years later.) Other *Opry* stars included banjo player and comic Uncle Dave Macon, who had turned professional when a pompous local farmer asked him to play at a party: he demanded $15 and to his surprise the farmer agreed. Kirk and Sam McGee played in Macon's Fruit Jar Drinkers; Sam was one of the best guitarists ever to pick up the instrument, and among the first to play breaks and runs in the black style. The McGee brothers had learned their music from black railway workers who hung around the family's general store in Tennessee. But the only black to appear on the *Opry* for years was Deford Bailey, who was the *Opry*'s mascot, and knew it.

Singer and mandolin player Bill Monroe and his guitarist brother Charlie worked with their brother Birch (on fiddle) from 1929 to 1934, then as a duo until 1938. After they split up, Charlie led his successful Kentucky Pardners, and Bill took his Blue Grass Boys to the *Opry* in 1939. His classic line-up in the mid-1940s included Chubby Wise on fiddle, Howard Watts (better known as Cedric Rainwater) on bass, Lester Flatt on guitar and Earl Scruggs playing a five-string banjo in the three-fingered Appalachian style; Flatt and Scruggs left to form their own band in 1948. Bill Monroe is one of the best mandolin players of all time. His string band music came to be called bluegrass; while it was quickly regarded as old-fashioned, it was rediscovered by a new generation and became a staple of folk festivals, as well as a permanent ingredient of country music.

WWHA's *Jamboree* (Wheeling, West Virginia) and the *National Barn Dance* moved on to a national radio network in 1933, the *Opry* in

1939. The *Opry* had a live audience which outgrew the WSM studios, and in 1943 it took over the local Ryman Auditorium, a country music mecca. There were many regional shows; the *Louisiana Hayride* on KWKH Shreveport began in 1948 and became a stepping-stone to the *Opry*.

Among the early country stars had been Vernon Dalhart, who sold millions of records on thirty labels under many pseudonyms; 'The Prisoner's Song' (1925) was one of the biggest hits of all time. But he was a light opera singer whose country material comprised mournful story songs; his work perhaps lacked the sincerity which is the essence of country music.

Ralph Peer had not only discovered the real stuff, but he also saw the value of copyrights and urged his artists to come up with original material. He saw too that it would be foolish to cheat them, and shared the royalties from the beginning. (But Russell Sanjek writes that it was Victor, protective of its reputation for paying its artists better than any other label, who required Peer to pay them $25 a side, as well as a royalty.) Peer was a good businessman. He formed Southern Music and sold it to Victor, the idea being that Victor would pass song copyrights his way in return, but all he got, apart from country music, was scraps (some of them rather fine, such as Hoagy Carmichael's 'Lazy Bones' and Don Redman's 'Cherry'). Victor employees, in particular A&R man Eli Oberstein, sent copyrights elsewhere because they were jealous.

Peer had recruited Oberstein from Okeh and installed him at Victor to keep an eye on his interests, but they became enemies; Oberstein was underpaid by Victor, whose largesse did not extend to staff members, and Peer was making so much money he had to try to hide it from them. Having taken over Victor, RCA then acquired an interest in RKO Pictures in 1932, and RCA boss David Sarnoff realized that he was likely to get into anti-trust trouble, since Victor owned song copyrights and RKO licensed them for film soundtracks, so he sold Southern Music back to Peer, which also resolved the squabbling. Peer also became an expert on international copyright law.

Arthur Edward Satherley, born in Bristol, England, went to the USA in 1913 and worked in a factory in Wisconsin that made cabinets for Edison's phonographs. After working as a promoter for Ma Rainey's and Blind Lemon Jefferson's recordings on Paramount, he became a producer at ARC. Unlike Peer, he loved the music he recorded and promoted; although he regarded both white and black rural musics as equally valuable, he ended up recording mostly whites. Before he retired in 1952 he had helped the careers of Lefty Frizzell, Carl Smith, Marty Robbins and many others. During the classic era he recorded the Chuck Wagon Gang, Gene Autry, Bob Wills, Roy Acuff and Molly O'Day (Acuff's female equivalent, who left music for religion in the late 1940s, but not before influencing people like Wilma Lee Cooper and Kitty Wells). O'Day was the first to record Hank Williams's religious songs, such as 'When God Comes and Gathers His Jewels'.

Singer and bandleader Roy Claxton Acuff, Satherley's favourite, became the grand old man of country music with a traditional style that never changed. He grew up on a tenant farm in the Smoky Mountains; he attended a New York Yankees summer camp, but sunstroke put an end to his athletic hopes. He first broadcast in 1933, first recorded in 1936 and first appeared on the *Opry* in 1937. He played the fiddle, though not often enough, for he lacked confidence. His band, the Smoky Mountain Boys, included string bass, five-string banjo, rhythm guitar, mandolin, accordion and harmonica, but its distinctive sound was contributed by the dobro.

The National Musical Instrument Company in California marketed a guitar with a metal body and three vibrating plates of metal behind the strings for mechanical amplification. Three of the Dopyera brothers, John (who had begun as a violin maker), Ed and Rudy, left National and formed their own company, which built an instrument with only one larger plate: this sounded less tinny and created a larger sound. They may have changed the spelling of their name at that stage, for it is often written as 'Dopera'. They began competing with National in the mid-1920s, and in 1934 the two companies merged.

The National guitar continued to be used by many bluesmen, but it was the dobro that began to help define the sound of country music. 'Dobro' stood for Dopyera brothers, but it is also a Slavic word meaning 'good'; the company's slogan was 'Dobro means good

in any language'. Roy Acuff's first dobro player was James Clell
Summey (who was later, with Pee Wee King, among the first to play
steel guitar on the *Opry*, and still later famous as the comedian Cousin
Jody); from 1938 it was Beecher 'Pete' Kirby (who also played banjo
and sang high harmony, and later became the comedian Bashful
Brother Oswald). Acuff and his band captured the 'high lonesome'
sound of mountain music, to which the dobro contributed a passionate yet mellow weight.

With his transparent sincerity (he sometimes wept at his own
performance) Acuff became the *Opry*'s greatest star and established
the vocalist at the centre of country music. Two of his biggest hits
came from his first recording session. 'Wabash Cannon Ball' is a train
song, but in the American 'Big Rock Candy Mountain' tradition: the
train will take the hobo to the promised land. 'The Great Speckled
Bird' is based on Jeremiah 12:9, and is still sung in southern
churches. With Fred Rose he formed the Acuff–Rose publishing
company in Nashville in 1943, and became wealthy; his other hits
included 'Freight Train Blues', 'Fireball Mail', 'Pins and Needles',
'Wreck on the Highway', 'Low and Lonely' and 'Night Train to
Memphis'. He continued to be successful throughout the 1940s, and
in the late 1950s he and Rose formed the Hickory label.

Both country music and blues were used to sell products on the
radio, especially flour, for many Americans still baked their own
bread and biscuits. The black harmonica player Aleck Ford (also
known as Rice Miller, and who later borrowed the name of Chicago
legend Sonny Boy Williamson) was heard along with others on *King
Biscuit Time* in the early 1940s. Ten years before that, fiddler Bob
Wills was selling on the radio; with his Texas Playboys, he was the
father of the dominant genre in the South-west, western swing.

The fiddle, the instrument of frontier America, was played everywhere, by blacks and whites. Eileen Southern, in her book *The Music
of Black Americans*, notes that eighteenth-century advertising of slaves
for sale or runaway slaves often pointed out that they were musicians,
usually fiddlers: 'RUN AWAY . . . a Negro Man named Derby, about
25 years of age, a slim black fellow, and plays on the Fiddle with his
Left Hand, which he took with him' (*Virginia Gazette*, 1772). The
fiddle remained a favourite instrument of early black jazzmen in New

Orleans, but became less common in later jazz, despite the success of Stuff Smith and his Onyx Club Boys, Eddie South (Chicago's 'Dark Angel' of the violin), Ray Nance (with Duke Ellington) and a few others. This was probably due to its lack of volume in the context of a jazz band, but the fiddle has held its own in country music to this day.

James Robert Wills came from a poor white family of Texas farmers, most of whom seem to have been fiddlers. He picked cotton as a boy alongside blacks, hearing the blues played on whatever instruments were available, and grew up without any prejudices against any kind of music. He recorded duets with guitarist Herman Arnspiger in 1929, but they were not released. He won a fiddle contest in 1930 and was already the best-known fiddler in Texas when he led a quartet on the radio called the Aladdin Laddies, for the Aladdin Mantle Lamp Company. In 1931 he went to work for Wilbert Lee 'Pappy' O'Daniel, president of the Burrus Mills and Elevator Company, on Fort Worth's KFJZ.

O'Daniel did not like their music until he realized how popular they were, whereupon he bought them a car, appeared on their show and helped himself to songwriting credits. Vocalist Milton Brown sang on some Victor records as the Light Crust Doughboys. They worked in the mill during the day, but O'Daniel tried to keep them from playing at dances in the evenings, where they made more money. Brown left and formed his Musical Brownies, which were successful until he was killed in a car crash in 1936; Wills hired Tommy Duncan to replace him, and the group played at dances occasionally, but Wills mostly knuckled under to O'Daniel until he was fired for drinking, whereupon half the band left with him.

O'Daniel sued the band for advertising themselves as 'Formerly the Light Crust Doughboys', his object being to destroy them, but the Texas Supreme Court threw the case out; he tried to get the band fired from their radio spot in Tulsa. He left Burrus Mills in 1935. (The band maintained he was fired for falsifying expenses, having paid the band very little and put the rest in his pocket.) O'Daniel started making his own Hillbilly flour and formed a band called the Hillbilly Boys; in spite of his crankiness, his folksy image and his promises to help poor people later got him elected governor of

Texas; in a special election in 1941 he beat Lyndon Johnson to the US Senate, being the bigger crook.

Wills called his new band the Texas Playboys. They broadcast from Waco, then went to KVOO in Tulsa, where Bob or his brother Johnnie Lee Wills broadcast for General Mills five days a week for twenty-three years. (The new Light Crust Doughboys in Fort Worth, with changing line-ups, broadcast well into the television era.) Wills bought prime mid-day radio time and sold it to a sponsor himself; he talked a miller into making Play Boy flour and collected a royalty on every barrel. In 1935 the band was playing to packed dance halls and private parties six nights a week, and began recording. Among its members were Duncan (vocals), Al Stricklin (piano), William E. 'Smokey' Dacus (drums), Arnspiger and C. G. 'Sleepy' Johnson (guitars), Jesse Ashlock (second fiddle) and Leon McAuliffe (steel guitar). McAuliffe had been poached from the new Doughboys; his 'Steel Guitar Rag', recorded with Wills in 1936, was influential, as was his own 'Panhandle Rag' of 1949.

The Texas Playboys played jazz, blues, rags and stomps as well as ballads and sentimental songs. Satherley, a traditionalist, did not know what to make of them at first. He told Wills that he did not want any horns, but Wills said that he would have horns or Bob Wills would not make any recordings. Wills's patented holler ('Ah-haaa!') erupted whenever the band was playing particularly hot; he would shout, 'Take it away, Leon!', just as he did at dances. Satherley got used to it all.

Duncan was a good country crooner; on the marvellous informal Tiffany transcriptions he sometimes chuckles at Wills muttering in his ear while he sings. Wills sang on tunes like 'Corrine, Corrina' and added banter to McAuliffe's vocal on 'That's What I Like About the South'. The rhythm section played in a relentless two-beat style, which dancers in the South-west liked. Charles R. Townsend's biography of Wills, *San Antonio Rose*, is full of anecdotes backed up by scholarship: a farmer who had hired Wills to play for a dance would push all the furniture to one side and roll up the rugs, as friends and neighbours arrived from miles around. The band was the most popular in a five-state area, and soon broke attendance records; Wills was generous, always paying his men well above scale.

As a bandleader Wills had one of the most valuable skills of all: watching his audience and calling just the right mixture of tunes. Once he almost got it wrong. At a dance at the University of Oklahoma, about which he had doubts to begin with, he was determined to concentrate on his big-band material, because he thought that was what the kids would want. They didn't seem to respond much at first, but then the president of the student union approached the bandstand to ask Wills politely if he had brought his fiddle, and in the end the usual good time was had by all.

Wills and his men did not regard their music as country music, and sometimes got down off the bandstand to remonstrate with ringsiders on this point. McAuliffe said years later that they gleaned none of their inspiration from other country artists, but listened to Glenn Miller, Benny Goodman and Bob Crosby. (The two-beat dixieland feel of Crosby's band was perhaps closest to the style of the Texas Playboys.) They were not prejudiced against hillbilly tunes, however, and recorded Jimmie Rodgers songs and numerous others that keep turning up: 'Sittin' on Top of the World' (sung by Wills) bears more than a passing resemblance to the tune of that name recorded twenty years later by Howlin' Wolf (though the composer credits are different).

Many regarded the band as a jazz band. Benny Strickler had played trumpet with Joe Venuti and turned down an offer from Artie Shaw to join Wills. Wills hired him on sight and then asked what instrument he played, saying later, 'I could tell by looking at him he was a good musician.' Clarinettist Woody Wood had played with Red Nichols; Alex Brashear had played trumpet with Jack Teagarden; Tubby Lewis's fine hot trumpet was heard on Wills's big-band number 'Big Beaver'. There is no doubt that Wills's music was a fusion which deserved wider acclaim; today it is stranger than it should be to hear the trombone playing the syrupy waltz 'Mexicali Rose', with Wills's fiddle playing harmony.

Wills wrote a great many songs, including 'My Shoes Keep Walking Back to You', a huge hit for Ray Price in 1957, but one of his tunes became an American classic, better known than all the rest put together. Wills had recorded an instrumental version of 'San Antonio Rose' in 1938 which did well; Venuti was among those who admired the tune and thought that more might be made of it. Irving Berlin's company offered to publish it if words were added, so Wills and a couple of others cobbled together some good lyrics. But the publishers altered the song, making it more orthodox and clearly not understanding what they were doing. Wills insisted that they publish the original version, which they now called 'New San Antonio Rose', and Wills recorded it with Duncan singing, at the same session as 'Big Beaver' in 1940; the eighteen-piece band was larger than Miller or Goodman had used on their biggest hits. In 1944 during the musicians' union strike against the record companies, just as *Billboard* began printing its first country music chart, 'New San Antonio Rose' became the first of eighteen consecutive top five hits for Wills. But before that, in 1941, Bing Crosby's recording of the song sold a million copies. (It was backed with Floyd Tillman's 'It Makes No Difference Now', another country classic; both sides used brother Bob Crosby's band, the one the Wills crew most admired.)

Among other western swing bandleaders were Hank Penny, who took up the style in Atlanta, was also recorded by Satherley and was described by one writer in the 1980s as 'the original Outlaw'; and Spade Cooley, who spent many years in prison for murdering his wife. In the 1950s Hank Thompson and Buck Owens kept the flame burning with fairly large bands. Asleep at the Wheel, formed in the 1960s and led by Ray Benson, released one of its best albums in 1988, *Western Standard Time*.

Bob Wills had made western films from 1940 to 1942 with several of his sidemen, combining music and horses. He may not have considered himself a hillbilly, but for a time he could not resist the lure of Hollywood, which brings us to the era of country and western music.

Satherley had also recorded Gene Autry, who had begun by imitating Jimmie Rodgers. By the mid-1930s Autry's records were selling well, including 'That Silver-haired Daddy of Mine' (co-written and first recorded as a duet with Jimmy Long). Gene Autry guitars were advertised in mail-order catalogues; 'The Death of Mother Jones', a labour-movement song, was available on seven labels in various catalogues from the ARC conglomerate (the Sears label was called Conqueror). Then came Hollywood.

The cowboy movie had been a staple of the silent screen, but had fallen on hard times with the invention of talkies; meanwhile, many films had to be made to fill the second half of the double features (hence 'B' pictures). Ken Maynard was the first 'singing cowboy', in 1930; then in 1934 producer Nat Levine hired Autry, who was no actor, to make films appealing to the people who bought his records. (The owner of Republic Pictures, and Levine's boss, was the head of ARC, Herbert Yates.) Autry's first effort was a cowboy-cum-sci-fi serial in twelve parts called *The Phantom Empire*. He sang 'Silver-haired Daddy' in eight episodes, and went on to make over a hundred films for the Republic and Monogram studios; his comic associates were Smiley Burnette, then Pat Buttram. Champion, Autry's horse, became famous, and his visit to Dublin in 1939 allegedly brought a million people into the streets. Autry's songs became more western-flavoured – for example 'South of the Border' and '(I've Got Spurs That) Jingle Jangle Jingle' – and country artists began to wear phoney cowboy clothes that became more and more vulgar (famously provided by Nudies of Hollywood). The cowboy pictures had interesting aspects, including a broad populist appeal; the bad guys (with the black hats) were frequently lawyers or bankers with pencil moustaches. The kids who flocked to the cinema, black and white, were infected with country music. Otis Blackwell, who later wrote some of Elvis Presley's biggest hits, remembered his own reaction as a child: 'Hot Dog! Now we got us a singin' cowboy!'

Jimmy Wakely and Johnny Bond were among those who went to Hollywood as members of Autry's entourage, and the West Coast country music scene grew in strength. Other singing cowboys were Rex Allen, Tex Ritter and Roy Rogers, who became King of the Cowboys while Autry was flying in Burma during the Second World War.

Rogers, born Leonard Slye, grew up on a farm; his father made guitars and mandolins. As Dick Weston he formed the Pioneer Trio, which appeared in Autry's sci-fi serial, then changed its name to the Sons of the Pioneers. He stayed in the Pioneers until he became a star: he made over ninety films with his palomino horse Trigger, the first being *Under Western Skies* (1938); among the films was a fairly realistic portrayal of the Pony Express. His wife, Dale Evans, who had sung with dance bands, joined Rogers in *The Cowboy and the Señorita* in 1944. Both Rogers and Autry became staples on Saturday morning television in the 1950s; both invested wisely and became very rich.

The Sons of the Pioneers had a successful career of their own. The classic line-up included original members Tim Spencer and Bob Nolan, Lloyd Perryman, who replaced Rogers, and Hugh Farr and Karl Farr, who had worked as cowboys. (When Spencer had left briefly in 1937, he was replaced by Pat Brady, who became Rogers's comic sidekick in his films.) Their close harmony was gentler and sweeter than that of the bluegrass groups; they appeared in *Rhythm on the Range* in 1936 with Bing Crosby, and in many other films. (*Rhythm on the Range* contained Johnny Mercer's 'I'm an Old Cowhand'.) Rogers and the Sons of the Pioneers were the first to perform Cole Porter's 'Don't Fence Me In', apparently both in a film of that name and in *Hollywood Canteen* in 1944, where the reprise was sung by the Andrews Sisters. (The studio recording by Crosby and the Andrews Sisters was a number one hit that year.) In Walt Disney's cartoon compilation *Melody Time* (1948) the Pioneers sang 'Pecos Bill' with Rogers, a hit on the other side of 'Blue Shadows on the Trail'. Nolan and Spencer were fine songwriters, and together they wrote 'Blue Prairie'. Nolan's 'Tumbling Tumbleweeds' was a hit for Autry, the Pioneers and Crosby, and 'Cool Water' was a hit for the Pioneers (1941) and Vaughn Monroe (1949). Spencer wrote 'The Timber Trail', 'Cowboy Camp Meetin'', 'The Everlasting Hills of Oklahoma' and 'Careless Kisses' (a hit for Eddy Howard in 1948). There were no fewer than six hit recordings of Spencer's 'Roomful of Roses' in 1949, and it was revived by Mickey Gilley in 1974.

By the late 1940s the blues and hillbilly genres discovered in the mid-1920s had grown up, and the lines around the edges of all genres were becoming blurred; the Second World War effectively broke in half the history of the century's popular music. For the story of the dominant pre-war and wartime style, we have to go back to the 1920s, when the Big Band Era began.

8

Big Band Jazz

'The world's most glamorous atmosphere. Why, it is just like the Arabian Nights!' said Duke Ellington, the first time he saw Harlem.

There was music in every neighbourhood, just as in New Orleans; even the poorest family had a 'moth-box' (a piano – you could buy one for $100 on a time-payment plan), and keyboard ticklers were employed in every tavern. The East Coast stride piano style was based on ragtime, with complete freedom in the right hand, and the left paying harmonic tribute as it strode along, tenths in the bass being common when a strong beat was wanted. But the great artists of classic stride could also play the melody in the bass, while improvising beautiful ornamentation with the right hand: the artist was a Chopin or a Liszt, and the rediscovery of the tradition of the recitalist as improviser was complete.

Charles Luckyeth 'Luckey' Roberts was drawn to Harlem by 1910, along with many other talented and ambitious blacks. In 1913 he published 'Junk Man Rag' and 'Pork and Beans'; he saw more than a dozen of his musical comedies produced, and part of one of his tunes, 'Ripples on the Nile', was slowed down and became Glenn Miller's 'Moonlight Cocktail' in 1942. Roberts fronted a Harlem club for many years, and was a society bandleader; a favourite of President Roosevelt and the Duke of Windsor, he advised the Duke on his collection of hot records. He was an extraordinary pianist who played the instrument like an orchestra; sadly he recorded very little.

Willie 'the Lion' Smith was born William Henry Joseph Bonaparte Bertholoff Smith, and had an outsized personality to match his name. Like the ragtime 'perfessers' who preceded him, he was a dapper dresser; he would stride into a club growling a warning: 'The Lion is here.' Like Jelly Roll Morton, he was fond of bragging and could

back up everything he said. His compositions include 'Contrary
Motion', 'Rippling Waters', 'Echo of Spring', 'Portrait of the Duke'
and 'The Stuff is Here (and It's Mellow)' (the latter, written with
Clarence Williams and Walter Bishop, was recorded by Cleo Brown,
who sang and played piano on Chicago radio and recorded for Decca
in the 1930s). Like Roberts, Smith played distinctive harmonies and
arabesques, and had a pop song recorded by Glenn Miller, 'Sweeter
than the Sweetest'. One explanation of his nickname put it down to
his bravery during the First World War, but he said that James P.
called him 'the Lion' because of his spunk. 'The Lion named him
The Brute. Later we gave Fats Waller the name Filthy. The three of
us, The Lion, The Brute and Filthy, and a guy called Lippy used to
run all over town playing piano.'

Jelly Roll Morton is thought to have visited New York as early as
1911. It is delicious to speculate that his New Orleans freedom might
have had an influence like that of Louis Armstrong more than a
decade later, but, on the contrary, it is said that Morton's ego took a
beating from the skills of the New York pianists. The best piano
players on the East Coast sooner or later went to New York; Luckey
Roberts was from Philadelphia, Eubie Blake from Baltimore and
James P. Johnson from New Jersey. Earlier New York ticklers, such
as the legendary John 'Jack the Bear' Wilson (fl. 1900, and another
subject of an Ellington portrait), are lost to history; so too are
Raymond 'Lippy' Boyette and his contemporaries Stephen Henderson
(known as 'the Beetle'), Corky Williams (whose speciality was playing
and singing salacious material, such as 'The Boy in the Boat', which
became Waller's 'Squeeze Me'). Willie Gant and Cliff Jackson, however, became recording artists and bandleaders.

The 1920s was the era of the rent party: for an entrance fee which
helped pay the rent, food, drink and dancing were available, as well
as first-class piano playing. Such parties were later celebrated in
Waller's hit 'The Joint is Jumping'. Lippy was said to be able to ring
anybody's doorbell in the middle of the night, saying, 'It's Lippy,
and I've got James P. with me', and gain immediate entrance.

James Price Johnson was the undisputed king of the stride piano
style, with his walking bass and his incredible right hand: his 'Carolina
Shout' was the number all the others had to be able to play. He was

taught by Roberts, and in turn taught Fats Waller. His numerous other tunes include 'Snowy Morning', 'Keep off the Grass' and 'Charleston' (from the show *Runnin' Wild*), which became the biggest dance fad of the Jazz Age. With Waller he was one of the composers of the show *Keep Shufflin'*. ('Charleston' and a great many other piano classics, such as Morton's 'King Porter', were originally created for cotillions, dances which were unofficial contests for showing off and more or less direct descendants of cakewalk exhibitions.)

Johnson's ambitions as a 'serious' composer were as doomed as Joplin's. Some of his music was performed, but the white musical establishment of the time would not reply to his letters. Fragments of his symphonies and other music are still studied by scholars, among them the *Negro Rhapsody*, or *Yamekraw*, inspired by the Negroes who spoke the Gullah dialect from the south-east coastal area Gershwin visited when writing *Porgy and Bess*.

The Lion and the Brute recorded much more than Luckey Roberts; the Lion played on Mamie Smith's 'Crazy Blues' in 1920, and on hit records in a trio with organist Milt Herth and drummer-vocalist O'Neill Spencer in 1938. But Filthy outdid them all: Fats Waller became one of America's best-loved entertainers.

Waller flashed through popular music like a shooting star, but another Harlem piano player became a bandleader, and so had more direct influence. Nothing like as good a pianist as the others, Fletcher Henderson, nicknamed Smack, nevertheless became one of the most important innovators. Born into a middle-class family in Georgia, he played piano from the age of six. He went to New York to do post-graduate work in chemistry, but there were not many jobs for black chemists; he played for Pace–Handy Music and became recording director for Harry Pace's Black Swan label; he accompanied blues singers and led a band on tour with Ethel Waters (who advised him to listen to James P. Johnson's piano rolls). He was elected leader of a band that was resident at the Club Alabam in 1923 and moved to the Roseland Ballroom in 1924. It included Coleman Hawkins and arranger Don Redman on reeds, trumpeter Joe Smith and renowned trombonist Charlie Green (known as Big Green or Long Boy). The band played pop tunes, novelties and pseudo-blues at first, but jazz was in the air. Although Louis Armstrong stayed only a year, his effect was incalculable; New Orleans clarinettist Buster Bailey played intermittently in the band.

Ross Gorman, Paul Whiteman's former clarinettist, led a pit band for *Earl Carroll's Vanities of 1925*, and recorded one of the tunes from the revue with a sixteen-piece band. 'Rhythm of the Day' was prophetic, a simple tune with interesting chord changes in an uncluttered arrangement that gave solo space to Red Nichols and Miff Mole. Despite a dixielandish ride-out, it was a remarkably forward-sounding hint of what was to come.

After Armstrong, Henderson's band was further influenced by the white band of Jean Goldkette. Born in France, Goldkette went to the USA in 1911. He could have been a concert pianist, but formed a dance band in 1924 and hired such arrangers as Russ Morgan and Bill Challis, and sidemen Bix Beiderbecke, Tommy and Jimmy Dorsey, Frankie Trumbauer, Eddie Lang and Joe Venuti; he took over Detroit's Graystone Ballroom when it could not meet his payroll. His band was smaller and more flexible than Paul Whiteman's, and soon became famous. Long after a meeting in October 1926 at the Roseland Ballroom, cornettist Rex Stewart, who was with Henderson at the time, wrote about 'this Johnny-come-lately white band from out in the sticks ... We simply could not compete ... Their arrangements were too imaginative and their rhythm too strong ... Jean Goldkette's orchestra was, without question, the greatest in the world.'

The arrangements that Stewart admired were those of Bill Challis, who came from the same coal-mining country as the Dorsey brothers, where there was a strong brass band tradition, as there still is today in the coal-mining parts of Britain. Challis was virtually self-taught, and first worked for a local bandleader called Guy Hall (who wrote 'Johnson Rag', a typically simple and attractive Swing Era riff). Challis's arrangements are full of witty little surprises that still delight today, nearly seventy years later. But Eddie King, A & R man at Victor, did not like the arrangements and would not let the Goldkette band record them. The band was expensive to operate and it was a struggle to get enough bookings; on top of everything else, violinist and arranger Eddy Sheasby, a volatile drunk, disappeared one day, taking all the band's scores with him, including Challis's. So despite having hit records, Goldkette disbanded in 1927 to concentrate on management, but not before his band had cut the Henderson outfit. Challis had already been hired by Paul Whiteman; Beiderbecke and Trumbauer joined a new band led by Adrian Rollini that played the sort of music they liked. But that band went broke, and they too ended up with Whiteman; thus the legend grew that a band that played pure jazz could not make money.

The Casa Loma band, originally one of Goldkette's groups, was formed around 1929. Saxophonist Glen Gray was elected leader when the band became a corporation; other key members were guitarist-arranger Gene Gifford, clarinettist Clarence Hutchinrider and trumpeter Sonny Dunham. It recorded prolifically and was very popular. Some writers have ignored this band, perhaps because it was white and because it played sweet – ballads such as 'For You' and 'It's the Talk of the Town' were sung by Kenny Sargent. But such recordings as 'I Got Rhythm' and Gifford's 'Casa Loma Stomp' (both 1933) prove that the band could play as hot as any. Gifford was an influential arranger, and in its twenty-year history the band included plenty of first-rate sidemen; its early popularity on college campuses whetted the nation's appetite for swing.

The conservatory-trained Don Redman could play any reed instrument, and wrote virtually all Henderson's arrangements until 1927. He refined the Hickman–Grofé concept of the dance band, no doubt under the influence of Challis, dividing brass and reed sections and having saxophones doubling clarinets and trombones playing against trumpets. He played voices against each other in call-and-response patterns; he wrote music for sections as though they were improvising in unison, while leaving space for hot soloists, behind whom sections often played riffs. While the white music business could not accommodate the real stuff, Redman continued to develop big-band jazz, as Henderson's men began to swing.

This was an even more impressive achievement than it sounds. Armstrong had changed the rhythmic nature of jazz, effectively breaking up each bar into smaller pieces in order to put rhythmic emphasis wherever he wished. This not only left behind the collectively improvised counterpoint, but brought about a new counterpoint between the soloist and the rhythm section. Instead of a 2/4 beat, as in New Orleans jazz and ragtime piano, there was now a 4/4 beat, though it was some years before the change was completely reflected in rhythm-section playing. The stride pianists had also been working in this direction, setting the bass free from the 2/4 of ragtime piano. Redman's scores (or 'charts') had to incorporate these rhythmic advances so that entire sections could play in unison.

Coleman Hawkins (also known as Hawk or Bean) began playing louder, with a stiff reed, to be heard over the band. He rescued the tenor saxophone from its role as a tubby comedian, abolishing the slap-tongue technique, and finally, inspired by the young pianist Art Tatum, began to improvise on the tune's chord structure: he single-handedly established the tenor saxophone as a primary instrument in jazz.

By the late 1920s Fletcher Henderson's band was known to musicians and in Harlem to be the hottest in the land. To list some of the players who passed through is to list the best: trumpeters Tommy Ladnier, Bobby Stark, Henry 'Red' Allen, Joe Smith and Charles Melvin 'Cootie' Williams, cornettist Rex Stewart, trombonists Benny Morton, Jimmy Harrison, Claude Jones, J. C. Higginbotham and Dicky Wells and drummer Kaiser Marshall. In 1927 Waller sold Henderson tunes, probably including 'Whiteman Stomp', 'St Louis Stomp' and 'Variety Stomp'; he allegedly asked for a bag of hamburgers as payment, but Henderson insisted on paying him $10 a tune. He played on one Henderson recording session, including a solo on 'Whiteman Stomp'.

Despite the lack of firm leadership and money (tracks labelled as by 'The Dixie Stompers' seem to have been recorded acoustically, or at least on inferior equipment, as late as 1927), musicians stayed because the music was so good: 'St Louis Shuffle', 'The Stampede', 'Tozo', 'Henderson Stomp', 'Hop Off' and scores more represent a treasure-house of jazz, to say nothing of earlier (mostly acoustic) recordings with Louis Armstrong. To point out just one nugget: on 'The Stampede' (1926) Joe Smith plays a lovely solo, pretty and perfectly constructed; after a bridge, Rex Stewart comes up and pushes the beat with his ferocity, tearing the notes off the page with a terminal vibrato at the end of each phrase: they are two first-class jazzmen, each doing it differently.

Redman left Henderson in 1927, having been hired by Goldkette as music director of a black Detroit band, McKinney's Cotton Pickers. It was fronted by former circus drummer William McKinney, and became the best of the territory bands as Redman refined his skills. When McKinney went out front to stay, he was replaced on drums by Cuba Austin. The band's discographies were long confused, because Goldkette paid Redman to rehearse some of his white bands as well, and because business in Detroit was so good that the band was not allowed to go to New York in 1929 to record, whereupon Redman recorded there with a group of Henderson's sidemen. To complicate matters still further, a Redman Chocolate Dandies date in 1928 was essentially played by the Cotton Pickers.

Under Redman the Cotton Pickers became a more modern jazz-oriented dance band, performing in a smoother but still swinging style. He added a fourth man to the reed section, making possible harmonies in that section so that to modern ears, the Cotton Pickers' records have dated less than those of most of the bands of the late 1920s. The band's number one hit (and its theme) was 'If I Could Be With You One Hour Tonight', with a vocal by reedman George 'Fathead' Thomas and an alto solo by Benny Carter; another big hit was 'Milenberg Joys', credited to Walter Melrose, Jelly Roll Morton and Leon Roppolo, whose clarinet solo from the New Orleans Rhythm Kings' recording (which included Morton) was transcribed and harmonized in Redman's arrangement.

Redman recorded his own pretty tune, 'Cherry', twice in 1928, once with the Cotton Pickers (sung by Jean Napier), and once with a pick-up group including the Dorseys and Jack Teagarden (no vocal). (The Cotton Pickers recorded for Victor, which is how 'Cherry' landed in Ralph Peer's portfolio.) Redman recorded in Chicago with Louis Armstrong's Savoy Ballroom Five, a date that included two of his own tunes. At his Chocolate Dandies date in 1928 he made one of the first recordings of Hoagy Carmichael's 'Stardust', a bouncy, medium uptempo version with a fine guitar solo by Lonnie Johnson. (Johnson recorded as a soloist with Louis Armstrong and Duke Ellington and in duets with Eddie Lang. He also made a great many blues records and had an R&B hit, 'Confused', in 1950; when criticized in later years for not playing a purer style, he complained about fans 'trying to shove a crutch under my ass'.)

At the 1929 recording session at which he used members of Henderson's band, Redman sang in his own slyly intimate, half-conversational and charming style on 'Miss Hannah', 'The Way I Feel Today' (delicately accompanied by Waller), 'Wherever There's a Will, Baby' (which has a fine Hawkins solo) and his own 'Gee Baby, Ain't I Good to You?'

In 1931, armed with management and recording contracts, Redman took over the Collegians; led by Horace Henderson, Fletcher's brother, the band had included Benny Carter and Rex Stewart in its day. Horace was at least as talented as his more famous brother, but made only a few recordings under his own name; Redman kept him on as pianist and arranger for a couple of years, after which he worked with Fletcher. Of about 120 arrangements recorded by Fletcher from March 1931 until 1939, many are uncredited, while others are by Edgar Sampson, Russ Morgan, Will Hudson or Dick Vance; but of those for which information is available in discographies, Fletcher and Horace apparently did about the same number – 28 or 30 – and Horace was the composer of tunes that are often credited to Fletcher.

Redman's first recordings in 1931 were credited to 'Harlan Lattimore and his Connie's Inn Orchestra'; Lattimore was a pleasant pop singer whose straight vocals were sometimes contrasted with Redman's patter and comedy, as on 'I Heard'. In 1932 the fourteen-piece band included Langston Curl (from the Cotton Pickers), Shirley Clay, Sidney De Paris and later Harold 'Shorty' Baker on trumpets; Claude Jones, Benny Morton and Quentin Jackson on trombones; Ed Inge in the reed section and always Bob Ysaguirre on tuba, then string bass, and Manzie Johnson on drums; Horace Henderson was pianist and arranger until he was replaced in 1933 by Don Kirkpatrick. Redman first recorded his theme, 'Chant of the Weed', in 1931; the modern-sounding arrangement proves that there is no such thing as a wrong note, using all the notes in a whole-tone scale. Redman recorded it again in 1940, and still later arranged it for a Duke Ellington album.

Redman was the first black bandleader to have his own radio show. He was an excellent teacher, and his arrangements were well known among musicians for their difficult passages, for example the reed chorus in 'Tea for Two' (which pitted Lattimore's straight vocal against the furiously swinging band) and trombone chorus in 'I Got Rhythm'. 'Nagasaki' was also a brilliant piece of swing, but Redman's band never played so fast for speed's sake that it sounded uncomfortable. He invented the 'swing choir', in which the band chanted a hip paraphrase of the words to a song while a soloist played the melody, as on 'Exactly Like You' and 'Sunny Side of the Street' (1937). The device was copied by others, for example by Tommy Dorsey on 'Marie', one of the biggest hits of the whole era (which Dorsey had got from the obscure Sunset Royals).

Redman recorded for Brunswick, then ARC labels, and by the time he transferred to Bluebird and Victor in 1938 it was a smoother swing band. 'Sweet Leilani' used the swing choir device, 'I Got Ya' had a Redman vocal ('Youse is in mine power!') and 'Rip Van Winkle', a hip rewrite of the legend, was sung by Bootsie Garrison.

Tired of the grind and not achieving the fame he deserved, Redman disbanded the group in 1940; he fronted Jay McShann's band in 1942, and in 1946 took a band to Europe (including saxophonist Don Byas), which was credited with introducing post-war jazz there. Among his freelance work was the lovely 'Just an Old Manuscript' for Count Basie in 1949. His recordings and broadcasts were an inspiration to young Canadians Gil Evans and Robert Farnon; he showed Farnon how to lay out a score, and Farnon became one of the most influential arrangers in the business. In 1951 he became music director for Pearl Bailey, who had a hit with 'Takes Two to Tango' in 1952. In 1954 he played a policeman in Harold Arlen's show *House of Flowers*; in 1957 he made two albums of big-band sides, some with Hawkins. He was a delightful man, whose personality is evident on the recordings and in the few short films he made, as well as an important innovator of popular music.

In 1928 Fletcher Henderson had suffered head injuries in a car crash; he had always been lackadaisical, and now became even less willing to take care of business. The band broke up in 1929, after a date to play a show produced by Vincent Youmans. Originally called *Horse Shoes, Great Day!* was modelled on *Show Boat,* and required a black band; Duke Ellington had turned the job down. When Youmans's white conductor began firing Henderson's men one at a time and he did nothing about it, that was the last straw for many of them. But Henderson formed another band, with Hawkins, Harrison and sometimes Morton, and the parade of talent continued: this is when Red Allen, Claude Jones, J. C. Higginbotham and others joined. He lost the Roseland Ballroom booking to the more responsible Claude Hopkins. The band's business was as unreliable as ever, but money meant little: racial equality was not on offer, and one could live very well on a musician's salary during the Depression.

Henderson recorded for Victor in 1932 (including vocals with Harlan Lattimore). He lost a gig at the Cotton Club to Irving Mills's Blue Rhythm Band and a European tour to Cab Calloway. At a Victor recording session in 1934 three of the four arrangements were by Russ Morgan or Will Hudson; Morgan was recording director at ARC, and Henderson may have hoped to curry favour, but it didn't work. Coleman Hawkins gave up and left for Europe, succeeded by Chu Berry, Lester Young and then Ben Webster: thus Henderson managed to employ, however briefly, all four of the greatest tenor saxophonists in pre-war jazz. And it was in 1934 that Henderson, in spite of everything, hit his own stride. His band was never the same after Redman left, for it lost the consistency that had made it a legend; having let alto saxophonist and arranger Benny Carter go, and possibly also feeling the heat of competition from his brother Horace, he took on more of the arranging himself. He further refined the style that Redman had developed to make a smoother music that was specifically for dancing, but still jazz-oriented, and allowed plenty of space for soloists. 'Sugar Foot Stomp' (from Oliver's 'Dipper Mouth Blues') and Jelly Roll Morton's 'King Porter Stomp', which had been Henderson staples for years, continued to be polished. Henderson began recording for the new Decca label, which was signing up all the best black bands, and 'Down South Camp Meeting', 'Wrappin' It Up' and Horace's 'Big John Special' (a tribute to John Reda, the boss at Big John's in Harlem, a favourite hang-out for musicians) were added to the store. His band broke up again and he made no recordings at all in 1935, but that was the year that lightning struck. He sold these charts to Benny Goodman, who had hits with all of them, and it was Fletcher Henderson's 1934 style that touched off the Big Band, or Swing Era.

Henderson formed a new band and made more good recordings: as Dicky Wells later wrote, 'You just had to play the notes and the arrangement was swinging.' Waller's 'Stealin' Apples', Horace's arrangement of Edgar Sampson's 'Blue Lou', 'Christopher Columbus' (a hit, based on riffs by Chu Berry and others) and Louis Prima's 'Sing, Sing, Sing (with a Swing)' were all recorded in 1936, and were also recorded by Goodman. Henderson continued to write for Goodman, for whom he arranged Youmans's 'Sometimes I'm Happy' and 'I Want to be Happy' and Berlin's 'Blue Skies'. He joined Goodman's sextet as pianist in 1939 and in 1941 formed another band with Goodman's help, but that was almost his last spark as a leader. He led a band at the Club DeLisa in Chicago in 1947, where Sonny Blount (whose real name was Sun Ra) was influenced; he led a sextet in 1950, but later that year had a stroke and never played again. The album *Tribute to Fletcher Henderson* (1957) was a joyous, swinging alumni success, unlike most all-star performances. It captured the joy in the music that Henderson played for a decade before the music business co-opted what came to be called swing, and white bands made most of the money.

It is a truism, to which I wholeheartedly subscribe, that the black bands played the best music during the Swing Era. Once jazz and the big dance band had come together in the late 1920s both black and white bands were charting the course; but the white-dominated music business could not tolerate pure jazz except in the 'race music' category, so it was the black bands and their sidemen who continued to provide the innovation.

One of the most commercially successful of all the black leaders was vocalist Cab Calloway, the exuberant, scat-singing, zoot-suited 'Highness of Hi-de-ho'. He attended law school, but left to pursue a career as a musician and toured with his sister's band. Blanche Calloway was a star in the late 1920s; a fine singer who hired good musicians, she was soon eclipsed by Cab's fame and passed over by booking agents who wanted him. Ironically, others traded on the name after Cab became famous – their brother Elmer did not play or sing, but fronted a band for a promoter, and there was Jean and/or Ruth Calloway, who was not even related – while Blanche went bankrupt.

Cab fronted a band called the Missourians, then in 1929 appeared in *Connie's Hot Chocolates* and led the Alabamians at Harlem's Savoy Ballroom. After returning to the Missourians, he changed its name to Cab Calloway and his Orchestra and followed Duke Ellington into the Cotton Club, where he became famous, as Ellington had, through live broadcasts. (On their first hit recording, 'St Louis Blues', Calloway's men were billed as the Jungle Band.) The band made several films, and signed with Victor in 1933. The pianist was Benny Payne, who later accompanied Billy Daniels and recorded duets with Fats Waller; other members were such stars as tenor saxophonists Ben Webster and Chu Berry, trumpeter Shad Collins, bass player Milt Hinton (who has probably played on more recordings than anyone else alive) and Dizzy Gillespie (1939–41).

Cab's act was full of physical energy, and his long black hair flew; he made 'hi-de-ho' a national catch-phrase. He was an underrated ballad singer, as 'You are the One in My Heart' shows. He had a top ten hit in 1942 with 'Blues in the Night', and the band of the early 1940s was his best. It played arrangements by Buster Harding, who later wrote for Count Basie's 1947 band, and it also had tremendous *esprit de corps*. As one of the highest-earning leaders for nearly two decades, he could and did pay his men well. Furthermore, he gave them credit, saying to George T. Simon, 'I'm up front there doing my act, but it's the guys themselves who are making this band what it is.' The early 1940s band would have made more recordings but for the musicians' union strike, of which more later; but this was the band that was seen and heard in the film *Stormy Weather* (1943), and the one admired by musicians. Its rhythm section played slightly behind the beat in a way that left no doubt that there was plenty of power in reserve.

When the Big Band Era was over, Calloway led a sextet (1948), and occasionally formed a bigger band for tours and special engagements. His personality was already permanently established in American popular culture, but he never stopped making new fans:

among his albums in the microgroove era were *The Hi-de-ho Man* (RCA, 1958), recorded with an excellent big band including Hinton, trumpeter Joe Wilder, trombonist Urbie Green and drummer J. C. Heard. He appeared in the film biography of W. C. Handy, *St Louis Blues*, in 1958, and starred as Horace Vandergelder opposite Pearl Bailey in an all-black version of *Hello, Dolly!* in New York in 1967. (His daughter Chris played Minnie Fay.) He published an autobiography, *Of Minnie the Moocher and Me*, in 1976. He sang 'Minnie' in the film *The Blues Brothers* (1980) and appeared in the show *Bubbling Brown Sugar* and was portrayed by Larry Marshall in the film *The Cotton Club* (1984), which featured 'Minnie', 'Lady with the Fan' and 'Jitterbug', all Calloway compositions. He made a television film *The Cotton Club Comes to the Ritz* (broadcast in the UK in 1985), in which he sang 'Blues in the Night'. His revue *Cotton Club Revisited* toured North America that year with Chris, who has had a recording career of her own. Calloway's influence has been incalculable, reaching up to new jive-jump bands in the 1980s and such pop stars as Joe Jackson.

Chick Webb was a hunch-backed drummer whose band clobbered Goodman's in a famous battle a few months before Webb's death; twenty thousand people were allegedly turned away from the Savoy Ballroom that night. Krupa, then the most famous drummer, said that he had never been beaten by anybody stronger, but Webb was killed by tuberculosis of the spine just as recording engineers were learning how to record him. Webb's arranger, Edgar Sampson, who also played violin and reeds, wrote some of the biggest hits of the era: 'Stompin' at the Savoy', 'Don't Be That Way', 'Blue Minor', 'If Dreams Come True', 'Blue Lou' and 'Lullaby in Rhythm'. Webb also discovered Ella Fitzgerald when she was only sixteen and adopted her (she was an orphan); 'A-tisket, A-tasket', with Ella and Louis Jordan on tenor saxophone, was a big hit in 1938.

The Mills Blue Rhythm Band, a black band run by white music publisher Irving Mills, made many fine recordings with sidemen such as Red Allen and J. C. Higginbotham. It was taken over by its frontman Lucky Millinder, who went bankrupt in 1939 but formed a new band in 1940 which became one of the most popular in Harlem.

Millinder employed early modern jazzmen, among them Freddie Webster and Dizzy Gillespie (trumpets), Lucky Thompson and Lockjaw Davis (reeds) and Sir Charles Thompson and Bill Doggett (piano). Vocalists were Sister Rosetta Tharpe, who also played electric guitar ('Shout, Sister Shout!' / 'I Want a Tall, Skinny Papa', 1942), and Wynonie Harris ('Who Threw the Whiskey in the Well?', 1945). Millinder's band shrank as the Big Band Era came to an end and in the early 1950s was effectively a jump band on the King label (which also recorded rhythm and blues hits with Harris). A good anthology of Millinder's work would illustrate the change from big-band jazz to rhythm and blues that took place in those years.

Trumpeter Erskine Hawkins joined a band at Alabama State Teachers College in 1935, came to New York the next year as its leader and from 1936 to 1948 had hits on Bluebird and Victor. His first, 'Until the Real Thing Comes Along', featured vocalist Billy Daniels (who later became famous for his delivery of 'That Old Black Magic'). The band's biggest hits were 'Tuxedo Junction', its own composition, on which the fine muted trumpet of Dud Bascomb may be heard, the bluesy 'After Hours', with its composer Avery Parrish on piano, and 'Tippin' In', also a bluesy instrumental.

Pianist Claude Hopkins led a band that accompanied Josephine Baker in Europe in the 1920s. By the early 1930s, when it played at Roseland for three years, it was a very popular band noted for its use of cup mutes and soft rhythm. Hits included 'Margie' (1934), with falsetto singer Orlando Robertson. Among its various sidemen were lead trumpeter Russell 'Pops' Smith (from Fletcher Henderson's band, where his brother Joe was a star), the superb New Orleans clarinettist Edmond Hall and trumpeter Jabbo Smith. Hopkins continued to play fine piano into the 1970s.

Jimmie Lunceford formed a school dance band with Jimmy Crawford on drums; they soon picked up alto saxophonist Willie Smith from Fisk University, where Lunceford had studied. After a few years it became a well-drilled show band that was enormously popular with white and black dancers alike. Other members were vocalist-trombonist Trummy Young and tenor saxophonist Joe Thomas (not to be confused with trumpeter Joe Thomas, who played in Henderson's and many other bands). Lunceford's biggest hit was 'Rhythm is

Our Business' in 1935. The vocal groups included Young, Smith, Thomas, trumpeter and arranger Sy Oliver and trumpeter Eddie Tompkins, but the whole band could sing like a glee club. They would imitate Paul Whiteman and Guy Lombardo; Tompkins would copy Louis Armstrong; the trumpet section would throw its horns in the air and catch them in unison. Some other bands looked down on Lunceford's 'trained monkeys', but they could play as well as they could clown. Will Hudson's 'Jazznocracy' and 'White Heat' were popular, if regarded as second-rate by Crawford. In Sy Oliver's arrangements, for example 'Ain't She Sweet' and 'Cheatin' on Me' (with vocal trio) and 'Well, All Right Then' (in which the whole band sings) a vocal trio and a rhythm section are in 2/4 while the rest of the band is in 4/4. They are irresistible, and prove that a 2/4 beat does not have to be lumpy. Oliver and Young were responsible for 'T'ain't What You Do (It's the Way That You Do It)', a Swing Era anthem; trombonist and guitarist Eddie Durham also wrote arrangements for Lunceford. At the time there were several hit versions of Will Hudson's 'Organ Grinder's Swing', an irritating pop song, but Oliver's arrangement for Lunceford was an outstanding piece of orchestral writing, full of contrasts and instrumental timbres.

Despite 'For Dancers Only' and 'Blues in the Night', the band's popularity in ballrooms was not well illustrated by its recordings. The grinding life of one-night performances began to take its toll, and Lunceford died suddenly. (Trummy Young always believed that he was poisoned by a bigoted restaurant manager after insisting that the band be fed.)

The Savoy Sultans, led by reedman Al Cooper, was the house band at the famous ballroom; although it was only an octet, visiting bands were not immune from a thrashing. Drummer Razz Mitchell used a riveted Chinese sizzle cymbal; Rudy Williams was a fine alto saxophonist; Sam Massenberg played trumpet; bass player Grachan Moncur II was the father of modern trombonist Grachan Moncur III. The band's name was carried on in the late 1940s by drummer Panama Francis, who had worked with Millinder opposite the Sultans; in 1976 he formed another band under the venerable name, and it has made some delightful albums.

Earl 'Fatha' Hines, one of the best pianists in jazz, was a prominent bandleader from 1928 until 1947. He had developed a 'trumpet' style, playing an octave higher in the right hand so as to be heard over an ensemble; in the late 1920s his left-hand style was more advanced than that of the great New York stride pianists. He made himself famous before 1930, playing and recording first with Louis Armstrong and then at Chicago's Apex Club with the unusual small band of clarinettist Jimmie Noone (1928), which had two reed players but no brass; his solo recordings in 1928–9 include eight for QRS (Quality Reigns Supreme, the piano-roll company, which also made gramophone records).

In 1928 Hines led a ten-piece group which grew to a full 'big band' while broadcasting from Chicago Grand Terrace Ballroom in the 1930s. His contract with the ballroom made him a prisoner of gangsters, and, as he put it, 'I couldn't afford to buy stars, so I had to find them.' He hired excellent men, among them trumpeters Shirley Clay, Freddie Webster and Walter Fuller, Trummy Young (before he joined Lunceford) and saxophonist-arranger Albert 'Budd' Johnson. Popular vocalist Herb Jeffries joined him in 1934 (and was later with Duke Ellington). Hines bought arrangements from Horace Henderson, Jimmy Mundy, Eddie Durham, multi-instrumentalist Edgar 'Puddinghead' Battle and Johnson. Budd Johnson wrote for many bands – notably those of Hines, Billy Eckstine, Dizzy Gillespie, Woody Herman and Boyd Raeburn – at the time in the 1940s when they employed most of the best young players, both black and white, of what would become bop, and then 'modern jazz'. Johnson's contribution to music is enormous. After disbanding his orchestra, possibly to get away from Chicago's gangsters, Hines formed another on the West Coast in 1940. In that decade, given his need to recruit youngsters, his band was inevitably an incubator for new stars: Gillespie, Charlie Parker, Wardell Gray, trombonist Bennie Green and vocalists Billy Eckstine and Sarah Vaughan.

In 1947 he gave up, along with many other leaders, and worked with Louis Armstrong's All Stars for a couple of years; he was gradually reduced to playing dixieland in West Coast clubs, but came to the fore again after performing at the Little Theatre in New York in 1963. Thereafter he toured the world, both with small groups (often including Johnson) and as a soloist. He made a great many albums in his last two decades (about twenty of them solo), every one of which is a monument to the sheer joy of music-making: again and again, as on 'Tea for Two' (produced in London in 1965 by Alan Bates) and 'C-jam Blues' (from a three-disc collection of Ellington songs made from 1971 to 1975), he walks a tightrope without falling off, the wit and beauty in the music always triumphing over technique for its own sake.

Hines's big band was regarded as a territory band in the mid-1930s, as was Benny Moten's; it played a style then called western swing by New York musicians, who admired it. Kansas City was a hothouse of jazz and blues which exploded at the height of the Swing Era. Corrupt local Democratic party boss Tom Pendergast ran the town until 1938, when he was indicted for tax fraud, and neither Prohibition nor its repeal, nor indeed the Depression, made much difference in Kansas City: the town was wide open and twenty or thirty clubs were doing business (while Pendergast went to bed at nine). Musicians did not get paid much, but they played all night. The Kansas City style that emerged was a blues-based, riffing style, at once looser and tighter than mainstream swing.

Bennie Moten's group, based in Kansas City, was the most prolifi-cally recorded of all the territory bands – it made about a hundred sides for Victor between 1923 and 1932. When Moten died (having his tonsils out), pianist Bill Basie took over remnants of it. Basie, from New Jersey, had toured with vaudeville acts, at the instigation of Fats Waller. Having been stranded in Kansas City, he joined bass player Walter Page's Blue Devils, which also included trumpeter Oran 'Hot Lips' Page, arranger and alto saxophonist Henry 'Buster' Smith and jazz and blues vocalist Jimmy Rushing. Basie joined Moten on piano, so that Moten (also a pianist) had more time for administration; he was featured on Moten's 'Prince of Wails' in 1932.

In 1936 Basie was leading a nine-piece group at the Reno Club in Kansas City; record producer John Hammond heard a broadcast on a car radio in Chicago, and told booking agent Willard Alexander about it. Basie hired more men and went to Chicago, but had signed a bad recording contract with Decca. Meanwhile, in October Ham-mond took a Basie group into a small studio in Chicago and recorded one of the most astonishing sessions of that decade, or any other.

The quintet – Basie, Page, drummer Jo Jones, tenor saxophonist Lester Young and trumpeter Carl 'Tatti' Smith – was billed as Jones–Smith Incorporated. They recorded 'Shoe-shine Boy' and 'Lady Be Good'; Rushing was added on 'Evenin'' and 'Boogie Woogie'. It was Young's first recording session, and he never played better in his life.

Lester Young began performing in his family's band. Inspired by the pretty sound and thoughtful craftsmanship of Frankie Trumbauer on C-melody saxophone, Young's style was lyrical and linear; he said that in a ballad he liked to keep the words of the song in mind. He had a unique tone without much vibrato, and played at the high end of the instrument's range, sometimes sounding almost like an alto instead of a tenor. His swing was incomparable, and he became one of the most influential musicians of the century.

In fact, the white Chicagoan Bud Freeman had already presented a lighter alternative to the big-toned, chromatic Coleman Hawkins style of tenor saxophone which was then dominant. But during the Swing Era Freeman led his own smaller groups or was a sideman in such bands as Tommy Dorsey's or Benny Goodman's, which were commercially oriented, however strong the jazz content. Lester Young came to fame in Basie's band, which made less money than those of Dorsey or Goodman, but was a much better place for a genius like Young to make his mark. It is true that Young was a greater musician than Freeman; nevertheless, in popular music it has also been true, at least since 1935, that the further you are from the mainstream, the more likely you are to be allowed to develop your full potential. In 1941–2 Young led a renowned band on the West Coast with his drummer brother, Lee, but it never recorded. (Lee Young played in film studios and with Nat 'King' Cole, among others; from the early 1960s he worked for Vee Jay, Motown and other record labels.)

Lester Young was a gentle, humorous, private man; he spoke an argot of his own, some phrases of which entered the language (such as 'I've got eyes', signifying approval); it was he who gave everybody nicknames, including Sweets for trumpeter Harry Edison, and Lady Day for Billie Holiday. An unlikely soldier, born in Mississippi, Young was frightened of racism; after he was drafted the Army put him in a stockade in Georgia, which didn't do him any good. When he came out he found that half the tenor players sounded like Lester Young, but the orthodox canard that he was no longer himself is not true: he knew what he was doing on his horn until the end.

Walter Page was called Big Four. 'He started that "Strolling" or "Walking" bass, going way up and then coming right on down. He did it on four strings, but other bass players couldn't get that high so they started making a five-string bass,' said Edison. Jo Jones was the best and fastest drummer of the Swing Era, but also the smoothest. He was not necessarily the first to keep time on the top cymbal, but did so with such finesse and consummate swing that he permanently altered the course of jazz, partly by setting the rest of the drum kit free to be used as a musical instrument rather than a device for constant timekeeping, as Krupa was doing at the time.

Buster Smith, an important influence on Young and on Charlie Parker, did not want to leave Kansas City (and was still performing in Dallas, Texas, in 1988). Hot Lips Page had been lured away by Joe Glaser, who hoped to make another Louis Armstrong of him; he led a good band from 1938 to 1940 and sang on Artie Shaw's hit version of 'Blues in the Night'. So Basie had not only to add men to make his octet a big band, but also to replace some of them, as well as putting up with John Hammond's meddling. When his band reached New York, it did not make an immediate impact; some of the men did not read music well, and they had trouble playing in tune because they were too poor to buy good instruments. (Don Kirkpatrick wrote arrangements for the band; tenor saxophonist Herschel Evans would tear up his part if it had too many sharps and flats in it.) But they began recording for Decca in early 1937 and soon blew open New York's Famous Door, a long, narrow room which must hardly have been able to contain the band's sound.

The playing of pianist Earl Hines and Basie's rhythm section has been said to 'swing like a (well-oiled) machine', but machines do not swing; the phenomenon is in fact indescribable. No one had ever heard anything like the classic Basie band, which soon included rhythm guitarist Freddie Green. (Young trombonist Dennis Wilson said of Green, nearly fifty years later, 'It's as though they said in the Bible, "Let there be Time", and Freddie started playing.') This was a rhythm section that played music as it swung, Green strumming chords and Page always walking in the direction of the tune.

Buck Clayton played lovely and distinctive open and muted trumpet for decades. Herschel Evans played fine tenor in the style of Hawkins; Basie encouraged an opposition with Young that was like 'Ham 'n' Eggs', as one of the band's instrumentals was called. At his peak Dicky Wells's trombone playing was second only to Teagarden's, reminding us of Whitney Balliet's description of jazz as 'the sound of surprise'. (He made some of his best recordings in Paris with Django Reinhardt in 1937 before joining Basie.) Jack Washington played baritone saxophone, Earle Warren alto; among the trumpeters were Edison, Ed Lewis and Shad Collins; at one point the trombones included Benny Morton as well as Wells and Dan Minor.

The life of guitarist, trombonist and arranger Eddie Durham, one of the most productive in popular music, was celebrated by New York's WKCR radio with a marathon sixty-nine-hour broadcast on his 79th birthday, comprising interviews, lectures and music. He wrote for Lunceford, then Basie; Wells said, 'Basie and Ed would lock up in a room with a little jug, and Basie would play the ideas, Ed would voice them.' It was probably Durham and Buster Smith who created 'One O'Clock Jump', a head arrangement first called 'Blue Balls': a player would think of a good riff and start riding it; other members of the section would play along; somebody in another section would create a piece of harmony, or an opposing or answering riff, and a new tune was born. 'One O'Clock Jump' was one of the era's biggest hits. Durham wrote or co-wrote 'Out the Window', 'Time Out', 'John's Idea' (for Hammond) and 'Swinging the Blues'; 'Topsy' (with Edgar Battle) was revived in 1957 for a pop hit by drummer Cozy Cole; 'Good Morning Blues' and 'Sent For You Yesterday and Here You Come Today' were written with Basie and Rushing. (He wrote the 1941 hit 'I Don't Want to Set the World on Fire' for Bon Bon, a black sweet pop singer with the white dance band of Russian-born violinist Jan Savitt.) Durham was music director of the International Sweethearts of Rhythm, a very good all-girl band that was formed in an orphanage and ran away; he later worked for R&B singer Wynonie Harris, and was still working in the 1980s. An early master of the electric guitar, he may be heard on an enchanting Lester Young small-group date for Commodore in 1938 (as the Kansas City Six); Young plays lovely clarinet as well as tenor, along with Clayton, Green, Page and Jones.

'Basie never did play much with his left hand, so Freddie [Green] substituted for it,' said Clayton. Basie led the band from the keyboard with an economy that became famous, saying more with one note than others did with several. The band's Decca recordings, other than those named above, included 'Jumpin' at the Woodside' (written by Basie) and 'Texas Shuffle' and 'Doggin' Around' (by Evans); 'Blue and Sentimental' featured Evans, while 'Roseland Shuffle', 'Honeysuckle Rose', 'Every Tub' and 'Cherokee' (a two-sided 78) and many others featured Young. Rushing sang 'Pennies from Heaven', and the wonderful Helen Humes 'Dark Rapture', 'Blame It on My Last Affair' and 'My Heart Belongs to Daddy'. Billie Holiday sang with the band in 1937, but could not record with it for contractual reasons (one of the great missed opportunities of the era); 'They Can't Take That Away From Me' is a famous broadcast aircheck. Among Basie's recordings for CBS labels from 1939 to 1946 are 'Taxi War Dance', 'Lester Leaps In', 'Dickie's Dream' (written by Young for Wells) and 'Ham 'n' Eggs'. He also played with the Benny Goodman Sextet in 1940 and on many other small-group recording sessions.

Basie recorded for Victor from 1947 to 1950, as the Swing Era was winding down. He had a number one novelty hit in 1947, the most popular of several versions of 'Open the Door, Richard' (with a 'vocal' by Edison), so untypical it is never included in compilation albums; today it is strange to hear Jones's smooth high-hat on what is basically a piece of R&B jive. The band's original stars were mostly gone (though Green stayed until the end); the trumpets included Edison, and such fine players as Clark Terry, Joe Newman and Emmett Berry, and the reed section Buddy Tate, Paul Gonsalves and Lucky Thompson. The excellent fare is well represented by such songs as 'Cheek to Cheek', Redman's 'Just an Old Manuscript' and a lovely, affectionate updating of Moten's 'South'.

Basie was the most famous but far from the only graduate of Kansas City. Harlan Leonard and his Kansas City Skyrockets was a twelve-piece band, many of whose members had split from Moten in

1931; Leonard had led Moten's reed section. Thamon Hayes played trombone, Ed Lewis trumpet and Jesse Stone piano. The band was initially successful, and in 1934 went to Chicago, where it was run out of town by James Petrillo's musicians' union. Hayes quit in disgust to run a music store in Kansas City, but Leonard re-formed the band as Harlan Leonard and his Rockets, briefly employed Charlie Parker (who could not turn up on time) and made sixteen sides for Bluebird in 1940, playing arrangements by Stone, Durham, Buster Smith, Tadd Dameron and Rozelle Claxton. Tenor saxophonist Henry Bridges had received an offer from Benny Goodman when he was drafted, and Fred Beckett was an advanced trombonist who died of tuberculosis contracted in the army.

Reedman Andy Kirk took over Terrence Holder's Dark Clouds of Joy in Dallas in 1929 and settled in Kansas City. Pianist-arranger Mary Lou Williams joined in 1931, and with popular singer Pha Terrell the band had big hits from 1936 to 1938, among them 'Until the Real Thing Comes Along'. Kirk carried on until 1948. Williams was a great talent whose compositions included 'Walkin' and Swingin'' for Kirk, 'Roll 'Em' for Benny Goodman and 'Trumpet No End' for Duke Ellington. Her friendships with Thelonious Monk and others made her a guru for the bop movement, and late in life she bravely played in a duo with the avant-gardist Cecil Taylor.

Pianist and band leader Jay 'Hootie' McShann in later years became a vocalist as well. Charlie Parker, trumpeter Buddy Anderson, bass player Gene Ramey and drummer Gus Johnson were members of his Kansas City band; his singers were Walter Brown (with whom he wrote 'Confessin' the Blues', which became a standard) and Al Hibbler ('Get Me on Your Mind'). Ramey and Johnson worked with Basie in 1952–3 and again with McShann in the 1970s. McShann, who was still playing fine piano, was the subject of a film, *Hootie's Blues*, in 1978, and recorded occasionally in the 1980s. Pianist and singer Julia Lee, another Kansas City artist, worked with Walter Page and Jay McShann, but mostly as a soloist. A daughter of Missouri, she performed at an inaugural party for Harry Truman. She was best known for songs of a risqué nature (for example 'King Size Papa' and 'I Didn't Like It the First Time'), though they do not show her talent to best advantage.

McShann's recordings have always been of special interest to jazz fans because of Parker. Kansas City bands made a contribution to American music that can stand by itself, but their rhythmic freedom and blues feeling, together with outstanding soloists like Lester Young and Parker, had a direct effect on modern jazz and hence are still influential today.

Benny Carter is one of the grandfathers of popular music. As an alto saxophonist, he was one of the most influential, but he also recorded on trumpet, trombone, tenor saxophone, clarinet and piano. He played with Webb, Henderson, the Cotton Pickers, Ellington and others, and by the age of twenty-one was already a well-known composer-arranger. His trademark of writing reed choruses along the chords of a tune perhaps represents the essence of this kind of music. The most famous of many Carter tunes is 'When Lights are Low'. In the late 1930s he was a staff arranger at the BBC, and led a ten-piece band in Europe which contained musicians of nine nationalities, among them two Englishmen.

Having often led his own bands in the 1940s, Carter then spent twenty-five years in film studios, where he wrote film and television scores and helped to desegregate the film industry; there were two albums written for Count Basie in 1960–61, and his own *Further Definitions* (1961), in which four saxophones together with a rhythm section provide more rich beauty than many a bigger group. This famous album re-created Carter recordings made in Europe in 1937, and was itself re-created on a CD in 1988 and at the Chicago Jazz Festival in 1989. He was still writing and playing in 1993. Listening to Benny Carter's beautiful music, one wonders again why this sort of music, so central to our popular culture, is today rarely heard on the radio.

Of all the bands that entertained crowds during the Swing Era, Duke Ellington's was one of the few that had already become well known in the late 1920s, and the only one that carried on with its leader's musical identity intact into the 1970s.

Ellington's father was a butler at the White House, and a blueprint maker for the US Navy. Duke acquired his nickname as a teenager from his elegant dress and demeanour; his parents and his middle-class upbringing gave him confidence and a knowledge of his own worth which never left him. But he was black, and made his living playing jazz, and was among the first great black musicians to become weary of the term. He was not the first to say, 'There are only two kinds of music: good and bad', though from him the aphorism had a special poignance. He was a pianist, bandleader, arranger and composer, but essentially unclassifiable, because he was all of these things at once; one of the greatest American musicians of the century, he ruled a band of unruly geniuses until he died.

He had a piano teacher called Miss Clinkscales, but was largely self-taught. A talented artist, he had won an NAACP poster-design contest and left high school to start a sign-painting business, but found that piano playing drew the girls. He performed locally, attracting more work than he could handle himself. He went to New York in March 1923 and did not find work, but returned in September with a band called the Washingtonians, led by Elmer Snowden and including trumpeter Arthur Whetsol, saxophonist Otto 'Toby' Hardwicke and drummer Sonny Greer. Vocalist Ada Smith (later famous as Bricktop) recommended them for a job at Barron's Exclusive Club, their first important engagement; then they played for four years at the Hollywood Inn (renamed the Kentucky Club after a fire).

Elmer Snowden was an indefatigable musical businessman. He made countless delightful recordings under various names (the Jungle Town Stompers, the Musical Stevedores, etc.) and at one point got into trouble with the musicians' union because he was running so many bands. Ellington became leader of the Washingtonians when Snowden left in 1925 (possibly because Greer didn't want to be leader). At the beginning of this period it was just another dance band; at the end it was Ellington's, playing his music. Whetsol left to study medicine and was replaced by Bubber Miley; Fred Guy played banjo; Charlie Irvis, who played a growling trombone, was replaced by Joe 'Tricky Sam' Nanton, and they were joined for a brief period by the profoundly influential Sidney Bechet. Duke wrote music for the revue *Chocolate Kiddies*, which toured Europe with Sam Wooding, but it is not clear whether Ellington's music was used. Ellington's band went to the Cotton Club when King Oliver turned down the job because it did not pay enough, performing there from December 1927 until February 1931, except during a few short tours. The band made a short film, *Black and Tan Fantasy*, in 1929 in New York, and became famous through broadcasts from the Cotton Club.

Sam Wooding, a success in Europe who toured as far as Russia, had also turned down the Cotton Club job because he thought that $1,100 a week was an insulting offer. He soon returned to Europe, where (he told journalist Chip Deffaa in 1985) audiences liked a hot black band better than they liked Paul Whiteman's style. Wooding's men were proud of the fact that they could double on bassoons, oboes, French horns and so forth; and anyway, as Rae Harrison, the beautiful vocalist who became Mrs Wooding, said to Deffaa, 'Why would they want to go back to Harlem, where they've been all their lives?' But Ellington had nowhere better to go, and probably appreciated the importance of the radio wire. Among the men Wooding valued most highly in his band was reedman Garvin Bushell, who said many years later that if they had understood the impact that radio was having, they would have *paid* $1,100 a week to play at the Cotton Club.

Charlie Johnson, a pianist from Philadelphia, went to Harlem after working in Atlantic City; he was a surrogate father for Wooding, and helped him to focus on music. He led his Paradise Ten at Smalls' Paradise for more than a decade, and was another leader who smarted because of Ellington's radio success. Johnson's band made lovely records for Victor in the late 1920s, such as 'Hot Tempered Blues', 'You Ain't the One' and 'Boy in the Boat', and his band did not get a chance to play live on the radio. But lightning occasionally strikes in the right place: Ellington wrote and arranged music for the Cotton Club's floor shows, and began to create a unique body of composition; when Wooding returned from Europe for good during the Depression, there were no recording contracts to be had, while Ellington was already justly famous.

Many of the Harlem clubs became legendary. Smalls' Paradise admitted blacks, if they could afford it; waiters danced the Charleston while balancing trays, and owner Ed Smalls encouraged the band to park their cars in front on quiet nights to make the place look busy. Connie's Inn, owned by George and Connie Immerman, was where Fats Waller began as a delivery boy (with bottles of bootleg alcohol hidden about his already large person) and where Waller's shows

Keep Shufflin' and *Hot Chocolates* were later first produced. But the most famous spot was the Cotton Club, built in 1918 at the corner of Lenox and 142nd Street, which had a theatre on the ground floor and a dance hall upstairs. Boxer Jack Johnson changed it into the Club Deluxe, then bootlegger Owney Madden turned it into the Cotton Club, an outlet for his beer that offered entertainment for white downtowners. The cream of society went there, including Mayor Jimmy Walker and Lady Mountbatten (who dubbed it 'The Aristocrat of Harlem'). It moved downtown to Broadway and 48th in 1936, but by then the Harlem Renaissance was over, having been based on a shaky foundation of white patronage fuelled by Prohibition, which ended in 1933.

During the Cotton Club's heyday much of the music for its revues was written by Jimmy McHugh and Dorothy Fields (daughter of vaudeville comedian Lew Fields), then by Harold Arlen and Ted Koehler. McHugh had written 'When My Sugar Walks Down the Street' with Gene Austin, who had a big hit with it in 1925; publisher Irving Mills was also credited as co-author. McHugh and Fields wrote songs for shows and revues, such as 'Diga Diga Doo', 'Bandana Babies', 'Harlem River Quiver', 'Doin' the New Low-down', 'Harle-mania', 'Doin' the Frog', 'Hot Feet', 'I Must Have That Man', 'Exactly Like You', 'I Can't Give You Anything But Love' and 'On the Sunny Side of the Street' (though the last two tunes may have been bought from Fats Waller). Many of these were recorded by Ellington, and some by Don Redman as well. In Ellington's arrangement of 'Diga Diga Doo' clarinets whistle through the trees like banshees, while his introduction to 'Bandana Babies' features Wellman Braud's bass prominently and has a vocal by Irving Mills and Ozie Ware. McHugh and Fields went to Hollywood and wrote 'Don't Blame Me', 'I'm in the Mood for Love' and others for films. (Both worked with many others; Fields's important partnership with Cy Coleman in the 1960s yielded the show *Sweet Charity*.)

Harold Arlen was mentioned earlier as Alec Wilder's favourite songwriter, and a distinctively American one. He fell in love with jazz, and played piano in cafés at the age of fifteen; he published songs in 1928 (his 'Album of My Dreams' was recorded by Rudy Vallee), but did not intend to write for a living. While working as a rehearsal pianist for Vincent Youmans, he invented an introductory vamp and was advised by Will Marion Cook to publish it before somebody stole it: it became his first big hit, 'Get Happy', with words by Koehler.

Arlen and Koehler were hired to write for the Cotton Club when McHugh and Fields were busy on Broadway: from 1931 to 1934 they wrote 'Between the Devil and the Deep Blue Sea', 'Kickin' the Gong Around' (a drug song, which was recorded by Louis Armstrong, among others) and 'Minnie the Moocher's Wedding Day' (all of which were recorded by Cab Calloway), 'Stormy Weather' (always associated with Ethel Waters, but also an instrumental hit for Ellington in 1933 and a sensation for Ivie Anderson with him in England that year), 'As Long As I Live' (introduced by Lena Horne at the age of sixteen), 'I Gotta Right to Sing the Blues' (recorded memorably by Jack Teagarden), 'It's Only a Paper Moon' and 'Let's Fall In Love'. Arlen's career was a long one: with Yip Harburg he wrote the songs for the film *The Wizard of Oz* in 1939, and 'The Man That Got Away' in 1954 (from *A Star is Born*), for Judy Garland. His Broadway shows included *Bloomer Girl* (1944, with Harburg), *St Louis Woman* (1946, an all-black show, with Johnny Mercer), *House of Flowers* (1954, with Truman Capote) and *Jamaica* (1957, with Harburg).

Ellington's band could play as hot as any other black outfit, but he was thus influenced by first-class show music almost from the beginning. His natural talent for tone colours contributed a sensual beauty to his music that was and is unique. His first recordings had been made in November 1924; in the Cotton Club period recordings were issued on many labels and under many names: the Washingtonians, the Ten Black Berries, the Jungle Band, the Harlem Footwarmers, the Whoopee Makers, Duke Ellington and his Orchestra or his Cotton Club Orchestra and so on. All the early records have ended up in the vaults of MCA, CBS or Victor, and all are fascinating: almost from the beginning he had the confidence to break the rules, to do as he wished just to see what it would sound like.

The New Orleans bass player Wellman Braud, who had played with Oliver, first recorded with Ellington in October 1927, and shortly after recruited his home-town friend, clarinettist Barney Bigard. Bigard later wrote that at first he found some of the chords he heard behind him strange, but soon realized that Ellington knew exactly what he was doing. Legend has it that European critics, especially Constant Lambert in the UK, were the first to compare Ellington's tone colours to those of Delius and Debussy; in fact (as James Lincoln Collier has pointed out), Robert Donaldson Darrell, later a distinguished classical critic, was the first to do so in *Disques*, an American magazine, in June 1932. Darrell had reviewed 'East St Louis Toodle-oo' in the *Phonograph Monthly Review* in June 1927, and 'Black and Tan Fantasy' in July, not knowing it was the same band under another name. Between November 1926 and April 1930 'East St Louis Toodle-oo' was recorded eight times on six labels (not counting alternative takes) as the young composer experimented.

Other classics of the era included 'Birmingham Breakdown', 'Jubilee Stomp' and 'Flaming Youth'; such titles as 'Jungle Blues', 'Jungle Nights in Harlem' and 'Jungle Jamboree' reveal the flavour of the club, where the musicians were black and the patrons white. Nanton and Miley used a growling 'yow-yow' instrumental device (in Miley's case inspired by King Oliver), which later had to be learned by Miley's replacements, Cootie Williams and then Ray Nance. Nanton stayed with Ellington from 1926 until his death; Miley was an unreliable alcoholic, but his influence from 1924 to 1929 was profound: the main ideas for 'East St Louis', 'Black and Tan Fantasy', among others, were Miley's, and Ellington later wrote that 'that was when we decided to forget about the sweet stuff'.

'Rockin' in Rhythm' (1930) became the band's theme (replacing 'East St Louis'); years later they still played 'The Mooche', 'Black Beauty' (for Florence Mills, the first of many portraits) and 'Creole Love Call'. Adelaide Hall had improvised a wordless obbligato off-stage during a performance of 'Creole Love Call' while standing near an open mike; she was overheard by Ellington, who then included her in a 1927 recording. In Europe Hall had worked in the show *Chocolate Kiddies*, 'with Josephine Baker at one end of the line and me at the other'. Hall was famous for her rendition of 'I Can't Give You Anything But Love'. She went back and forth to Europe before settling in England, where she had a radio show with bandleader Joe

Loss and was seen and heard in Alexander Korda's film *The Thief of Bagdad* (1940). She was still working (and receiving excellent reviews) at the end of the 1980s.

On Ellington's recording of 'Jungle Nights in Harlem' in 1930 the reed section consisted of Barney Bigard, Harry Carney and Johnny Hodges, though it seemed to be much bigger; the Victor recording, with the acoustic bass prominent, sounds astonishingly up to date today. In 'Mood Indigo' (1930) the classic tune is blended by Nanton, Bigard and Whetsol, showing the formidable skill of the arranger. Ellington had begun writing for specific players, and was an infallible judge of what each could do. In 1930 the band included Whetsol, Cootie Williams and Freddy Jenkins (trumpets), Nanton (trombone) and Juan Tizol (valve trombone), Hodges, Carney and Bigard (reeds), Guy (banjo, later guitar), Wellman Braud (bass) and Greer (drums). All were virtuosos, and most of them played intermittently with the band for decades.

If we had to name a sound that was the most important element of all in the band, it would have to be that of Harry Carney. When he joined (with his mother's permission) at the age of seventeen, he played clarinet and alto saxophone, but he soon changed to baritone, and remained the anchor of the band in more ways than one for nearly half a century. He was perhaps Ellington's closest friend; in later years they often drove together from gig to gig in Carney's Cadillac. Carney did for the baritone saxophone what Coleman Hawkins did for the tenor. His modesty and gentleness of spirit were always evident; at his appearance in a master class at the University of Wisconsin in 1973 he looked as though he still could not believe his good fortune in receiving so much affection from the public.

Johnny Hodges (also known as Rabbit or Jeep) had taken lessons from Sidney Bechet; he occasionally played soprano saxophone until 1940, but his main instrument was the alto. He joined Ellington in 1928 and stayed for life, except for the years 1951–5 when he led a successful smaller band of his own. He was the most widely admired alto saxophonist until Charlie Parker, and even after that, nobody could play a ballad like Hodges (Parker called him the Lily Pons of the instrument, and meant it as a compliment), and his hot playing in the Cotton Club period already revealed an unmistakable voice. He put on a veneer of gruffness, but, according to Bigard, was actually shy, and quite a prankster if you got to know him.

Irving Mills managed Ellington's band and published the music, sometimes writing lyrics and often taking credit as co-composer; some recordings were even issued under the name Mills' Ten Black Berries. Mills and his older brother Jack, who had been a song plugger for Waterson, Berlin and Snyder, had formed Mills Music in 1919. Irving, the 'outside' man, bought songs from people at recording sessions for 'three for a dollar' labels which they supervised. Their house group was the Hotsy Totsy Boys: Irving Mills, Mills Music's manager Jimmy McHugh, Sammy Fain (later a very famous songwriter) and Gene Austin. Later the Hotsy Totsy Gang, Goody's Goodtimers and other recording groups included Dick McPartland and the Dorsey brothers, and sometimes Irving (using pseudonyms) sang; we have seen that the black Mills Blue Rhythm Band became the Lucky Millinder band. The purpose of all this was to plug the songs.

Irving's most valuable discovery was Ellington. He helped the band get the job at the Cotton Club and landed the first good recording dates, as well as work in the film *Check and Double Check* with the enormously popular radio comedy stars Amos'n'Andy (1930). He also arranged the band's first trip to Europe in 1933. After leaving the Cotton Club (where it was replaced by Cab Calloway), the band was provided by Mills with Pullman cars when it travelled: unlike many black bands on the road, Ellington's and later Calloway's never worried about where to sleep.

Ellington understood better than most leaders the importance of recording, and of recorded balance. To this day Ellington's early records sound better than those of most of the others; he knew what he was doing in the studio. The band was first called Duke Ellington and his Famous Orchestra at a session for Brunswick in early 1931, when 'Creole Rhapsody' was recorded on a two-sided 10-inch 78; it was recorded again in June for Victor on a two-sided 12-inch record, Ellington's first attempts to exceed the limitations of the medium. In February 1932 trombonist Lawrence Brown and singer Ivie Anderson made their first recordings with the band, among them 'It Don't Mean a Thing if It Ain't Got That Swing', which helped to name the era.

The band recorded medleys on long-playing records for Victor the same month. In this early attempt to achieve longer playing time the relatively primitive 78 was simply slowed to 33⅓ rpm; it failed because the technology of the time was inadequate. But for some reason two microphones were used to cut different masters of the same take: these were combined to make very good stereo recordings more than fifty years later, on the album *Reflections in Ellington* (issued on the Everymans label in the USA in 1985). Hardwicke came back in 1932, after working for Bricktop in Paris; Darrell tried to interview Ellington that year, hoping to write a book about him, but he was already evasive about himself and his work. It was as well that he was on his guard; serious critics would take him almost too seriously.

The orthodoxy that the years from 1940 to 1942 represent Ellington's greatest period is difficult to refute, but there is a large number of masterly miniatures from every decade. The best big-band pieces were tone poems – integrated compositions for a group of specific virtuosos – and no one did this better than Ellington. His recordings in the 1930s included uptempo showpieces such as 'Stompy Jones', 'Jive Stomp', 'Merry-go-round', 'Showboat Shuffle' (with a paddle-wheel effect in the brass section), and also smoochy ballads and mood tunes: 'Prelude to a Kiss', 'Sophisticated Lady', '(There is) No Greater Love', 'Caravan' (written by Tizól), 'Azure' and 'The Gal From Joe's'.

'Solitude' (1934) had a solo by Carney, 'Clarinet Lament' (1936) featured Bigard, and on the other side was 'Echoes of Harlem', featuring Cootie Williams, 'Caravan' in 1937 was followed later in the year by 'Dusk on the Desert', also with Tizol's name on it, which has Ellington's percussion contribution, using a cardboard box. There were many, many more. To describe just one of these treasures: 'In a Jam' contains the simplest of brass riffs, a string of outstanding solos, a muted Nanton delicately traced by Bigard's clarinet, a dialogue between Hodges and Williams, an early guest appearance by Ben Webster and a ride-out by Rex Stewart.

Ivie Anderson, one of the best female singers of the era, with excellent diction and a warm vocal colour, joined Ellington in 1931.

Her numerous sides, many of them hits, include 'Truckin'', 'I'm Satisfied', 'Isn't Love the Strangest Thing?', 'There's a Lull in My Life' and 'If You Were in My Place (What Would You Do?)'. She sang 'All God's Chillun Got Rhythm' with the band in a Marx brothers film, and they recorded it twice.

'Diminuendo in Blue' and 'Crescendo in Blue', recorded on a two-sided 78 in 1937, was a composition that the band could not then play properly, especially with respect to intonation, according to Gunther Schuller in his *The Swing Era* (1989). It had been preceded by 'Reminiscin' in Tempo' in 1935, written on tour after Ellington's mother died. Schuller's essay on this is exemplary. Spread over four sides, the piece is still only about thirteen minutes long, a composition specifically for Ellington's musicians, but without much improvisation or even swing. In its skilful integration of its themes and episodes, Ellington probably never exceeded it. It is true that some of his more ambitious later 'extended' compositions are unsuccessful, or, to put it another way, that the best ones are literally suites, or strings of miniatures. But he did what he did so beautifully that it is impossible to complain that he did not have the formal training necessary to write symphonies and operas. As it was, while he was making the hit parade, he was also transcending it.

His treatments of others' tunes include a lovely 1933 version of the 1905 chestnut 'In the Shade of the Old Apple Tree', with a muted solo by Jenkins, and 'Rose of the Rio Grande' (1938), which featured Lawrence Brown and Ivie Anderson. (Brown had to play that solo for many years.) Ellington's own 'Pussy Willow' became a staple and 'I'm Checkin' Out Goombye' is the only recorded example of the jive repartee that Anderson and Greer developed in the live act; 'The Sergeant was Shy' and 'Tooting through the Roof' were all made in 1939. In the 1930s Ellington had recorded mostly for Brunswick, but the 1938–9 sides often appeared on Columbia; at his last session there in early 1940 he recorded remakes of 'Stormy Weather', 'Solitude' and 'Mood Indigo', with Anderson vocals, and a new instrumental, 'Sophisticated Lady'.

Irving Mills and Jack Kapp must have been equally energetic entrepreneurs, unwilling to take advice. Russell Sanjek reports that in 1935 Mills offered to take over the recording of all dance music for

Decca, and lectured Kapp and his staff on his expertise, where-upon Kapp directed that no talent connected with Mills was to be used. Mills's opinion of himself was justified, however, for in the mid-1930s he was the only contractor of recording artists in the business. In early 1937 he launched the 75-cent Master label and the 35-cent Variety label, distributed by Yates's ARC, and was successful for a while; among Ellington's hits were a remake of 'Caravan' with 'Azure' on the other side. But Mills failed to form an overseas affiliation, and soon turned back to selling his product to ARC labels.

Meanwhile, Wellman Braud had left Ellington, and from 1936 to 1938 the band had two bass players. In late 1939 Ellington discovered Jimmy Blanton playing a three-stringed instrument in a St Louis hotel, and advanced him the money for a four-stringed model. In the short time before he died of tuberculosis, Blanton revolutionized bass playing, not just with his unique time, but playing melody and harmony as well. Bigard had doubled on tenor saxophone, and Ellington had no star tenor player until Ben Webster became a full-time member. Arranger, composer and pianist Billy Strayhorn became more than Ellington's collaborator: in later years they worked to-gether so closely that sometimes they could not remember who had written what (or so they said).

In 1939 the agreement with Mills was severed. Ellington had done well out of it, charging a great many living expenses to Mills which would otherwise have come out of his own pocket. As James Lincoln Collier has pointed out, Ellington was not the type to be much interested in saving anything, but only in living well. There was pressure from the black press, where Adam Clayton Powell accused Ellington of being a 'musical sharecropper', but it is hard to believe, as Collier does, that Ellington, always his own man, would have let this affect him very much. But Mills was always busy trying to build an empire, and still selling Ellington's recordings to what were now CBS labels, and Ellington decided to move to RCA Victor.

Ellington's first session for Victor since 1934 was recorded in March 1940, and it was immediately obvious that a new page in Ellington's book had been turned; the quality of the music reached a new peak. 'Ko-Ko', from Ellington's uncompleted score for a stage work, came to be a jazz classic; its unforgettable opening bars were underpinned by an urgently mysterious one-note motif from Carney's baritone. 'Jack the Bear' was notable for Blanton's amazing ability to make the whole band sound like it was dancing on tip-toe; the furiously swinging 'Cotton Tail' included a controlled explosion from Webster. 'Harlem Air Shaft' had more ideas in it than most bandleaders had in a year, as did 'Sepia Panorama'. Strayhorn's 'Take the "A" Train' became the band's theme. Non-Ellington hits with pop songs were 'You, You Darlin'' and 'Flamingo' (vocals by Herb Jeffries) and 'At a Dixie Roadside Diner' (with Anderson). The hit 'I Got It Bad and That Ain't Good', sung by Anderson, came from Ellington's Los Angeles revue *Jump for Joy* which was ahead of its time. (Not even Los Angeles could take 'I've Got a Passport from Georgia (and I'm going to the USA)', and it was removed.)

There are too many great records to list here, but a few are 'Bojangles (a Portrait of Bill Robinson)' 'A Portrait of Bert Williams', 'Me and You' (with Anderson), 'In a Mellotone', 'C-jam Blues', the erotic 'Warm Valley' and the lovely 'Across the Track Blues' and four duets by Ellington and Blanton. Strayhorn wrote 'The Flaming Sword', 'After All', 'Chelsea Bridge', 'Raincheck' and 'Johnny Come Lately', as well as transmuting the 1927 pop song 'Chloe' into Ellingtonia, with an elegant Nanton 'jungle' introduction. Tizol wrote 'Bakiff' and the instant classic 'Perdido', a riff which summed up jazz composition for a whole generation. Ellington may have been having problems with royalties or income taxes at this time; at any rate, his son Mercer, who was already credited with 'Things Ain't What They Used To Be', was now listed as composer of 'Jumpin' Punkins', 'John Hardy's Wife' and the tragic 'Blue Serge'. The band was recorded live on 7 November 1940 at the Crystal Ballroom in Fargo, North Dakota, where fans took disc-cutting equipment to a dance: the result includes a Webster essay on 'Star Dust', never recorded commercially; perhaps it was suggested by Coleman Hawkins's 'Body and Soul' of the previous year.

Cootie Williams had left in 1940 to join Benny Goodman, with Ellington's blessing: Goodman could pay more, and Williams disliked the lackadaisical attitudes of Ellington's men and preferred playing with Goodman's Sextet. He later described this period as the happiest of his life, but the music business was shocked: bandleader Raymond Scott wrote 'When Cootie Left the Duke'. Williams's multi-talented replacement was Ray Nance, who also played violin (as on 'C-jam Blues') and sang delightful novelty vocals. Late in 1941 Alvin 'Junior' Raglin replaced Blanton, who was dying.

Small groups from the band had begun to record as early as 1930, soon under the nominal leadership of Barney Bigard (and his Jazzopators), Cootie Williams (and his Rug Cutters), Rex Stewart (and his Fifty-second Street Stompers) and Johnny Hodges (and his Orchestra); Ellington was usually at the piano, though Strayhorn began playing on some tracks in 1939. Rex Stewart also recorded in Paris in 1939, with his Feetwarmers: Bigard, Billy Taylor on bass and Django Reinhardt on guitar; on later issues of these tracks the group was called Rex Stewart's Big Four. Among Stewart's Ellingtonians, which recorded in 1940, were several non-Ellingtonians, for example Billy Kyle or Jimmy Jones on piano; the records were issued in a limited edition for a private jazz record club (but reissued on Fantasy's OJC label in 1985). Cootie Williams's Gotham Stompers, which recorded in New York in 1937, included Bigard, Hodges, Taylor and Carney, with such non-Ellingtonians as Tommy Fulford on piano and Chick Webb on drums. Rex Stewart and his Big Eight and Billy Taylor and his Big Eight also recorded for Keynote in 1944, and Hodges and Carney did some particularly tasty moonlighting.

Wherever any of these people played during this era they brought a flavour of Ellingtonia with them; but the cream of the Ellington small-group sessions took place in 1940–41 for Victor. Bigard, Stewart and Hodges each recorded eight tracks, as, for example, 'Johnny Hodges and Orchestra (an Ellington Unit)'. Williams, Nance, Brown, Webster and Tizol played on various recordings; common to all were Ellington (or Strayhorn), Carney, Blanton and Greer. The men were all at the peak of their powers; they had no axes to grind, no reputations to make, no trails to blaze. They played music of a quality which cannot be surpassed, because it is unique. Bigard wrote 'Ready Eddy' for his boss, whose '"C" Blues' soon became 'C-jam Blues'; 'Charlie the Chulo' was a perfect uptempo showcase for Bigard's enormous skill. From the Stewart session, 'Subtle Slough'

later became 'Just Squeeze Me (But Don't Tease Me)', with words by
Lee Gaines. Stewart growled like a fey lion on the charming 'Menelik
(the Lion of Judah)' and Carney played a few bars of alto saxophone
on 'My Sunday Gal'; 'Poor Bubber' was a salute to Miley, and
'Mobile Bay' to Cootie Williams. But if I had to choose, perhaps the
most beautiful of all these recordings are those featuring Hodges:
'Things Ain't What They Used To Be' was that unforgettable tune's
début; 'That's the Blues, Old Man' was the first appearance of a riff
that became, a decade later, the climax of the R&B classic 'Night
Train'; 'Passion Flower' was an early example of the way Strayhorn's
lyricism and Hodges's unique ballad style – erotic, but always elegant,
almost understated – complemented each other. On 'Squaty Roo'
(another of Hodges's nicknames) the flawless, pulsating time of the
performance almost sums up (if anything could) the contribution
Blanton made to all these tracks, and indeed to the whole era. In the
early days Sonny Greer had been as much showman as timekeeper;
he never played better than he did with Blanton.

Billboard began printing its 'Harlem Hit Parade', the first black
chart, in 1942. The following were number one: 'Never No Lament'
(with a new title, 'Don't Get Around Much Any More', and soon to
have words); 'Concerto for Cootie', a three-minute concerto for
Williams, which had become 'Do Nothin' Till You Hear From Me';
'Sentimental Lady', with 'A Slip of the Lip (Might Sink a Ship)' on
the other side (a wartime novelty with a hip vocal by Nance: 'It's so
bodacious / To be loquacious'); and the dramatic, driving 'Main
Stem'. During the recording ban of 1943–4 earlier recordings reached
the charts, including 'Going out the Back Way', from Hodges's 1941
date.

Ivie Anderson had to stop singing with the band because of the
asthma that eventually caused her early death. She was replaced by
Joya Sherrill, a better than average pop singer whose Ellington
tracks would make a fine album by themselves: after the ban 'I'm
Beginning to See the Light' (with lyrics by Don George) was
followed by 'I Didn't Know About You', the non-Ellington '(All of a
Sudden) My Heart Sings' (with a simple but spell-binding Strayhorn
arrangement), 'Everything But You', 'Tell Ya What I'm Gonna Do'
and 'Come To Baby, Do'. The Victor output up to 1946 included

vocals by Ray Nance and Al Hibbler (who replaced Jeffries) and a series of remakes (for example, 'Black Beauty' and 'Caravan'). On a remake of 'It Don't Mean a Thing' Sherrill, Kay Davis and Marie Ellington (no relation) introduced the tune as a round.

There was always much beauty and joy, but the burst of creativity that had marked the early years of the decade seemed to be over. Barney Bigard, who left the band in mid-1942, said later to British journalist Max Jones: 'after the original band began to break up, Duke's orchestra was never the same. Never. Cootie Williams left, other people left, and later Tricky Sam took sick and died . . . he had to get different people and change the music.' This is certainly true as far as it goes, but for the genuine Ellington fan, the band always sounded unique: if he wrote specifically for his own musicians, of course he wrote differently as the band changed. Yet it never sounded like anyone's music but his.

At his first Carnegie Hall concert early in 1943 Ellington introduced his fifty-minute composition *Black, Brown and Beige: Tone Parallel to the American Negro*. Excerpts were recorded by Victor; the complete concert was issued on Prestige after decades, and the piece has had several more recordings by other hands. The lovely 'Carnegie Blues' (recorded in 1945) and the beautiful hymn 'Come Sunday' were taken from it. The Carnegie Hall concert was an annual event for several years: Ellington's new works included *Blutopia* (1944); the twelve-minute *New World a-Comin'* (inspired by a Roi Ottley novel) and *The Perfume Suite* (both 1945). ('Dancers in Love', a delightful duet for piano and bass, was also the subject of a George Pal 'Puppetoon' semi-animated short film.) *Deep South Suite* (1946) comprised four parts: the first was 'Magnolias Just Dripping with Molasses' and the last the train anthem 'Happy-go-lucky Local'. The latter's big tune was the same riff heard earlier from Hodges's small group, later used without credit by Jimmy Forrest as 'Night Train'.

Ellington's musical show *Beggar's Holiday* in 1946 was an updating of the *Beggar's Opera* (in which Macheath is recast as a gangster) with lyrics by John Latouche. (Latouche also wrote the Vernon Duke show *Cabin in the Sky* in 1940 – the Ellington band appeared in the film version in 1943 – and the George Moore opera *Ballad of Baby Doe* in 1956.) *Beggar's Holiday* ran for just fourteen weeks. In his exhaustive *American Musical Theatre* Gerald Bordman says it failed because 'Latouche's sting and Ellington's intimacy [were] lost in the cavernous auditorium of the large, inconvenient Broadway theatre'. But its producer, John Houseman, had another explanation. On arriving at the scene, he wrote many years later, he found that Latouche

had been working on several other projects during the summer. He had written a number of lyrics but only the roughest draft of our first act and almost nothing of the second. Ellington, teeming with tunes and mood pieces, still had not faced the necessity of writing a musical score . . . [The producers on the spot] were not only inexperienced and inefficient – they were desperately short of money. Finally, owing to the Duke's enormous list of future commitments, we had no leeway at all but must start rehearsals within four weeks or not at all.

Houseman and Nicholas Ray tried to put the production together during the day, and at night worked on the script. The racially mixed cast was chosen for acting ability; as a result, Broadway star Alfred Drake fell in love with a black police chief's daughter in 1947. Libby Holman and Zero Mostel were also in the cast. (The sets, by Oliver Smith, were used a few years later almost without change for Leonard Bernstein's *West Side Story*.) During rehearsals, whenever they needed a bit of music, Strayhorn

would run up to the Duke's apartment and fish out of a drawer, crammed with unperformed music, whatever tune seemed to fit the scene. Some were wonderful, and with Latouche's lyrics, remained for years in the repertory of Lena Horne and other well-known singers. But this did not make up for the absence of a score and a book.

Since it was constantly running out of money, the production had to pay for the sets at the last minute and have them built with thirty hours of 'golden time'. (Expensive overtime is the common lot of those putting on a show that has been inadequately prepared and financed.) The dress rehearsal could not be completed and the last twenty minutes of the opening night in New Haven (under the title *Twilight Alley*) had to be improvised. The show was still a mess when it got to New York; Broadway genius George Abbott was hired to replace Houseman, but it did not help, and Houseman blamed himself, for agreeing to go into rehearsal with a show that was not ready. Houseman described Ellington as 'one of the world's great spellbinders', but if *Beggar's Holiday* was typical of his working methods, in that it relied too much on spellbinding, this would go some way to explain his shortcomings as a composer in larger forms.

The band's immediate post-war period, when there were six trumpets, and Oscar Pettiford on bass, was one of the most poorly documented. But more and more material comes to light: a wealth of broadcasts was made in 1945–6 for the US Treasury to sell bonds; another transcription series (1946–7) includes Strayhorn's works for Hodges's sensuous alto saxophone, 'Violet Blue' and 'A Flower is a Lovesome Thing' (later entitled 'Passion'), as well as Ellington's 'Sono' (a feature for Carney) and a version of 'Happy-go-lucky Local'.

Webster, Hardwicke, Stewart and Tizol had left, and Nanton had died in 1946. There were some hard years ahead for the Ellington ensemble, though Duke was finally recognized as the great American artist he was. Meanwhile, the rest of the Swing Era represents a highwater mark in the quality of popular music.

9

The Swing Era Begins

From 1935 until after the Second World War a jazz-oriented style was at the centre of popular music for the first time (and the last, so far), as opposed to merely giving it backbone. The white bands made the most money, but they had taken up the music because they loved it; they were fully aware of the debt they owed to the black innovators and they made plenty of their own contributions, resulting in popular music whose quality will be rediscovered as long as people play records.

A few white bands had been playing jazz-flavoured music and doing good business for some years, among them the Casa Loma. Roger Wolfe Kahn was the son of a millionaire; his band, which was resident at the Biltmore Hotel in New York, included such sidemen as Miff Mole, Jack Teagarden, Artie Shaw and others, but Kahn later turned to a sweet style. Chicago drummer Ben Pollack followed on from Goldkette and Kahn, employing Benny Goodman, arranger-trombonist Glenn Miller, Harry James and Teagarden, who was recruited by arranger Gil Rodin. Pollack's band was highly rated, but its recordings do not reflect its best work, because Pollack always had his eye on what he thought was the main chance; after struggling for years he sidetracked himself at exactly the time the Swing Era was about to happen. Promoting a vocalist who later became his wife, he neglected the band, which left him and hired Bob Crosby (Bing's brother) as frontman.

A big band might have three trumpets, two trombones, three or four reeds, and four rhythm instruments (piano, guitar, bass and drums): from twelve to sixteen or eighteen players, as well as singers. Henderson and Redman used banjo and brass bass (tuba) at first, but the increasing pressure of the tendency to play in 4/4 rather than 2/4 in rhythm sections accelerated the change to guitar and string bass. Gunther Schuller thinks this process may have been impeded because the tuba was easier to record than a string bass; 4/4 would have been twice as much work for a tuba player, and probably impossible at a quick tempo. But leaders who were arrangers, or who bought good arrangements, were innovating in a search for new voicings. Duke Ellington was the first to feature the string bass on recordings in the late 1920s (probably by shoving it closer to the microphone), yet more evidence of his expertise as a recording artist. When the Goldkette band went east in the mid-1920s it had two trumpets and Bix on cornet; other bands had been getting by with two trumpets, but added another to be up to date. Ellington's and Redman's bands first had three trombones in the early 1930s; Ellington had two bass players in the late 1930s, six trumpets in 1946, and always insisted that all his reed players double on clarinet.

As we have already seen, the arrangers were of the greatest importance, and we will meet many more of them in the following pages. Judging from the recorded evidence, it is easy to jump to the conclusion that it was largely the black jazzmen and arrangers who knew that allowing the music to swing was the same thing as allowing it to breathe (a lesson often forgotten in today's pop music). The recordings from the late 1920s and early 1930s by many prominent white leaders, such as Ted Weems, Irving Aaronson and Gus Arnheim, now sound excessively busy and relentlessly cute. And it is true that the (largely white) music business had concluded that 'hot' music would not sell, and that imaginative arrangers ran into trouble with producers and A & R men. Yet this conclusion must be treated with some caution. The white arrangers Gene Gifford, Gil Rodin, Deane Kincaide and Bill Challis were gifted indeed, and when Don Redman enlarged the reed section of McKinney's Cotton Pickers, he probably did it so that he could write a richer sound like that being made by the Whiteman band. One of the best of all, bandleader, composer and reedman Benny Carter, said to Gene Lees, 'Bill Challis was my *idol.*'

Challis had been influenced by Bix Beiderbecke, whose inventive phrasing, beautiful tone and advanced harmonic thinking were followed by first Goldkette and then Whiteman's band. Bix and

Trumbauer's classic 'Singin' the Blues' had been a Challis chart, as was Whiteman's little masterpiece 'San', which was recorded in 1928 by a smallish group of ten men, including Bix, Trumbauer, Jimmy Dorsey and Challis on piano. Whiteman's 'symphonic jazz' may or may not have been ponderous, but the dance band charts were excellent. Violinist Matty Malneck, pianist Tom Satterfield and others wrote good arrangements for Whiteman, but Challis's still astonish with their freshness.

Challis's arrangement of Rodgers and Hart's 'The Blue Room' was played by a big radio band, perhaps that of Nat Shilkret around 1930, and recorded by a smaller group in 1986 on the album *Bill Challis's The Goldkette Project* (on the Circle label). It illustrates Challis's witty originality: after the introduction (itself unusually fine for the period), the reed section states the tune, with a rhythmic break of four notes by the brass section after sixteen bars, and again at the end. The first break consists of four notes, in two identical units of two notes each. A less imaginative arranger might simply have repeated this pattern at the end of the second phrase, but instead Challis wrote a group of four descending notes. The effect can still raise a chuckle sixty years later.

In 1929 *Melody Maker* in Britain devoted eleven pages to an analysis of Challis's arrangement of 'Sweet Sue', composed the year before by Victor Young and Will Harris, but the paper attributed it wrongly to Ferde Grofé (as 'Singin' the Blues' was long attributed to Fud Livingston). Maceo Pinkard's 'Sugar' and Willard Robison's ''Tain't So, Honey, 'Tain't So', both recorded by Whiteman in 1928, were Challis's arrangements, the first done originally for Goldkette, then expanded for twenty-four men (including four violins). Both are miles ahead of most of the popular music of the period, and are full of fascinating chords which still sound adventurous today, yet exactly right. The Whiteman band's excellent playing of these charts and the fine recording produced by Victor make it clear why Whiteman and Challis continued to influence other musicians for many years.

The section leaders in the bands were important. They rehearsed attack and phrasing, and often helped to bring along good players who were not good readers: thus Hymie Shertzer and Art Rollini taught Vido Musso, the tenor saxophone star in the classic Benny Goodman band. (Musso said it was not the notes that bothered him but the 'resters'. Henderson's wife had helped with the music copying, and her writing could be difficult to decipher.) In the Count Basie band, Lester Young was a much better reader than Herschel Evans. Section leaders such as George Dorman 'Scoops' Carry (with Earl Hines, 1940–47), Langston Curl (with Don Redman, 1927–37) and Hilton Jefferson (who played with Claude Hopkins, Chick Webb, Henderson, Carter and Ellington) were admired by musicians, if less well known to the public. They were often not soloists, though they could hold their own when necessary; Wendell Culley, who played the famous solo on 'Li'l Darlin'' in 1957, was Basie's lead trumpet for years.

It was clarinettist Benny Goodman who was in the right place at the right time, and became the King of Swing. Born in a Chicago slum to an immigrant family, he studied music at Hull House, a charitable institution; he first performed in public at the age of twelve, and was playing good jazz while still in short trousers. He played other reed instruments as well as clarinet, and even trumpet on records in the 1920s; after leaving Pollack in 1929, he became one of the busiest freelance musicians in the business. Often working with John Hammond, he played on Bessie Smith's last recording session and led the studio band on Billie Holiday's first session, both in 1933.

Goodman's successful recordings include Holiday's 'Riffin' the Scotch', 'Ol' Pappy' (with Mildred Bailey and Coleman Hawkins) and 'I Ain't Lazy, I'm Just Dreamin'' (with Teagarden); 'Moon Glow', by a nine-piece group with Teddy Wilson on piano, appeared more than two years before the famous Goodman Quartet version; Waller and Razaf's 'Ain't-cha Glad?', backed with 'I Gotta Right to Sing the Blues' (by Arlen and Koehler), which had vocals and trombone by Jack Teagarden, was a two-sided hit at the lowest point of the Depression, when Goodman had not recorded as a leader for two years. He had played on scores of recordings backing singers, and with the Hotsy Totsy Band (Irving Mills's ongoing project, and one of the many names used by the Pollack gang as freelances), among many others. But there was not much money in records in those days, and anyway Goodman's name on records by studio pick-up groups was not satisfactory.

He formed his own band for an appearance at Billy Rose's Music Hall. Benny Goodman and his (Music Hall) Orchestra, as it was billed at first, did five successful recording sessions for Columbia, the last two in early 1935. He changed to Victor in April, and had hits with 'Japanese Sandman', from his first Victor session, and, at the end of the year, Henderson's arrangements of 'Sometimes I'm Happy' and 'King Porter' back to back, the latter with a famous trumpet solo by Bunny Berigan. Notwithstanding the importance of Henderson's arrangements, historians have also pointed out the contribution of Spud Murphy, who probably wrote as much for Goodman as Henderson did. Murphy played with Ross Gorman in 1928, and also wrote for the Casa Loma band; his 'Get Happy', for Goodman, is especially well remembered for the way in which it turns the jolly tune into a prototypical romp for swing band.

Goodman's band appeared on the *Let's Dance* radio show from late 1934 until May 1935, a three-hour dance programme shared with Xavier Cugat and the sweet band of Kel Murray. The show's radio theme was 'Let's Dance', based on 'Invitation to the Dance', by Carl Maria von Weber, though Goodman used Gordon Jenkins's 'Goodbye' as both opening and closing theme on tour. The programme was broadcast live and was received on the West Coast during prime time, earlier than it was heard in the east. When it embarked on a nationwide tour in May 1935, the band did not do very good business at first; at the Elitch Gardens in Denver, according to pianist Jess Stacy, 'everybody was across town listening to Kay Kyser'. But when the band reached California in August, they found an audience of eager young dancers. It is clear in retrospect that the Swing Era had been waiting to happen, but it was Goodman and his band that touched it off. His ten hits in 1934 doubled to twenty in 1935, and he credited his success to the fact that there were a large number of dancers who were not being well served.

In November 1935 an octet from the band made four sides in Chicago as Gene Krupa and his Chicagoans. Goodman's brother Harry was replaced on bass by the sixteen-year-old Israel Crosby (who later played for a decade with Ahmad Jamal's trio, then George

Shearing); 'Blues of Israel' is particularly fine. In February of the next year they did it again, as Gene Krupa's Swing Band, this time with Roy Eldridge replacing Nate Kazebier on trumpet, Chu Berry replacing Dick Clark on tenor and singer Helen Ward (on two tracks) instead of trombonist Joe Harris. The appeal of Ward is not obvious in retrospect, but she was very popular; to her credit she disliked 'Goody Goody', and was surprised when it became one of the full band's biggest hits in 1936.

Harry Goodman was a merely competent bass player, and Krupa's drumming was very much in the Chicago mould, with dixielandish accents. It always comes as a shock all these years later to hear the lumpy 2/4 beat on 'Down South Camp Meeting', from August 1936. (Stacy said years later, 'you can't ask all drummers to keep good time'.) The band was precise, and the reed section sounded pretty; but it was often no more than pretty, and on some of the records moos monotonously behind vocalists, the way the pedal steel guitar is often used in country music today. Despite having four reeds (as well as Goodman himself), the section had nothing like the character of that of Whiteman's band, not to mention many a black band. Perhaps the formal training of the white musicians prevented them from contributing more in terms of individual tone production, but the smoothness was probably what Goodman wanted.

Arguments still arise among critics and musicians about whether Goodman had a good enough ear to imagine a richer sound or, later, to play more modern jazz, but he was too good a musician not to be able to play anything he wanted. The truth is that he was a strange man, haunted by the poverty of his childhood; having accomplished what he had, he saw little need to change the formula, especially since his audience was getting older when the Swing Era was over, and simply did not wish for a more modern sound. The sidemen and arrangers who wanted to play more modern music were younger than Goodman, and he may have been jealous. In later life he let slip a belief that he had to have his men angry with him in order to be an effective bandleader, which would go some way towards explaining his infamous rudeness; and it may be postulated that tension is necessary in any performance art. He was also torn between popular and classical music, and adopted a different embouchure to play the latter; playing modern jazz would have exacerbated this physical confusion. On top of all that, from the time of his greatest success he was nearly always in pain from a back problem.

Certainly it was the precision and the reliability of his band (perhaps ensured by his hard discipline) that made it a success, as well as its swing, which is more evident on airchecks than on the studio recordings. He led the reed section on alto saxophone on 'Riffin' at the Ritz', one of the band's better studio tracks. The 1936 version of 'Bugle Call Rag' is hard to resist: at the beginning, when the band is stating the riff, one thinks of how many times one has heard it, but in less than three minutes the string of hot solos has worked its magic again. 'He Ain't Got Rhythm' has an irresistible guest vocal by Jimmy Rushing, and 'I Want to be Happy' has just the right chirpy tempo. In the end, one feels that white pop should always be this good. In any case, in 1935 Henderson made no records, Count Basie was still unknown, and the recordings and broadcasts of black bands were simply not promoted and marketed as the white ones were. Good as it was, Whiteman's classic band had broken up in 1930, being too big for the Depression era, and Pollack was busy courting his future wife. So it was Goodman's band that suddenly defined the centre of the era's pop music.

In mid-1935 the first recording session of the Benny Goodman Trio, with Krupa and Teddy Wilson, yielded 'Body and Soul' and 'After You've Gone' back to back; Lionel Hampton was added in August 1936, and the quartet's first recording was 'Moon Glow'. Edgar Sampson's arrangement of 'Stompin' at the Savoy', written for Chick Webb, was a hit for the band in 1936 and even more popular for the quartet in 1937. Goodman got away with a mixed-race group by presenting it during the band's intermission, like a vaudeville act; Stacy was the band's regular pianist. But the excellent chamber music of the trio and quartet, together with the intelligent, witty and swinging interplay between Goodman, Wilson and Hampton, was commercially successful, proving that the public was willing to listen to good music during the Swing Era.

There were several hit recordings of 'Christopher Columbus' in 1936, including those of Goodman and Henderson, and the smaller groups of Andy Kirk, Teddy Wilson and Fats Waller (with Andy

Razaf's words and Waller's saucy interjections: 'Since the crew was makin' merry . . . Merry got up and went home!'). Among Goodman's hits in 1937 were 'Goodnight, My Love' and 'This Year's Kisses', both with black singers, Ella Fitzgerald and Jimmy Rushing respectively. Goodman's rudeness to Helen Ward had resulted in Martha Tilton's taking over as vocalist, and her successes included 'I Let a Song Go out of My Heart' and 'And the Angels Sing', the latter with trumpeter Ziggy Elman's famous 'Hebrew dance party' gimmick: originally an instrumental written by Elman called 'Fralich in Swing', recorded by Elman with members of Goodman's band, the hit had words by Johnny Mercer.

Many bands were playing 'Sing, Sing, Sing (With a Swing)', a tune by trumpeter and bandleader Louis Prima. In 1936 the Goodman band began to interpolate its arrangement (by yet another black arranger, Jimmy Mundy, who had written for Earl Hines) with 'Christopher Columbus', and the new arrangement was recorded in 1937; more than 8.5 minutes long, it was issued on two-sided 12-inch and (edited) 10-inch 78s. It became a symbol of the Swing Era, but the studio recording has lost much of its charm today, despite good playing by the band and solos by Goodman, Harry James and Musso; the long passages of Krupa's tom-toms no longer appeal.

Goodman had played at a jazz concert at the Congress Hotel in Chicago on a Sunday afternoon, and in any ballroom there could be as many people listening as dancing. The first jazz concert at Carnegie Hall was dreamed up by the agency who were promoting the *Camel Caravan*, Goodman's radio programme, sponsored by the cigarette company. According to Irving Kolodin, when Goodman was asked how long an intermission he wanted, he replied, 'I dunno. How much does Toscanini have?'

The band that played at the concert included Hymie Shertzer (alto saxophone), George Koenig, Irving 'Babe' Russin and Art Rollini (tenor saxophones), Harry James, Ziggy Elman and Gordon Griffin (trumpets), Vernon Brown and Red Ballard (trombones), Allan Reuss (guitar), Stacy (piano), Harry Goodman (bass) and Krupa (drums); Wilson and Hampton played in the quartet. James, Krupa, Wilson and Hampton all soon left to lead their own bands, bringing to an end the most famous Goodman line-up. The concert was a celebration of the arrival of jazz as the nation's most popular music, and afterwards many of the men headed for Harlem, where Basie and Webb were battling at the Savoy. The concert offered a jam session and a set-piece billed as 'Twenty Years of Jazz', both with guests, neither of which was particularly successful. There were two Tilton vocals, selections by the trio and the quartet, three Henderson arrangements, Sampson's 'Don't Be That Way', Basie's 'One O'Clock Jump', Mundy's 'Swingtime in the Rockies' and 'Life Goes to a Party', credited to Goodman and James and suggested by a *Life* magazine photo spread on the Goodman phenomenon. The event was recorded on acetates, using a single microphone; an album was released in 1950 and was a surprise hit after the Swing Era was over.

'Sing, Sing, Sing' at Carnegie Hall was not only much better than the studio version, but contained the best item of the concert: an unscheduled piano solo by Stacy, which in 1950 turned out to be just as beautiful as everyone remembered it. In an interview with Whitney Balliet many years later (from which I have quoted above), Stacy said that Goodman usually hogged the solo space, and that he did not know why he had got the green light, unless Goodman had liked what he had been doing behind Goodman's solo. Stacy's solo was built on the tune's A-minor chord, and shows the influence of Edward MacDowell and Claude Debussy; it provided a marvellous balance for the bombastic arrangement which inspired it. It now makes us marvel at how many beautiful solos by uncounted musicians were never recorded at all: it is a high point of the whole era.

It became even more clear in 1952 that the classic Goodman band played better live than in the studio. A two-LP set of airchecks clumsily called *1937/38 Jazz Concert Number Two*, one of the first issues of its kind and a number one album in *Billboard*, demonstrated that the band got as big a kick out of the dancers as the dancers got out of the band. It was the New Orleans 'second line' effect again.

Goodman moved to the revived Columbia label in 1939 and continued to produce a steady stream of hits for another decade. Dave Tough, without doubt the best white drummer of the era, replaced Krupa and was a great improvement. Vocalist Helen Forrest wrote in her autobiography that Goodman was the rudest man she had ever met, and Stacy (a modest man) was still amused decades later that Goodman had fired the estimable Jimmy Rowles in order to re-hire Stacy in 1942. Goodman fired people for undiscernible reasons, as if he needed to remind everybody who was boss.

But he was a great talent scout. It was the young pianist Mel Powell (today a classical composer in the school of Milton Babbitt and Elliott Carter) who arranged 'String of Pearls' and 'Jersey Bounce' for a two-sided hit in 1942, as well as 'Mission to Moscow' in 1943. Eddie Sauter, who had worked for Red Norvo and Charlie Barnet, wrote 'Superman', 'Benny Rides Again', 'Clarinet à la King' and others, which were popular with jazz fans, musicians and critics, but less so with the public (though Sauter's arrangement of 'Intermezzo', a film theme, was a hit in 1941). Sauter's arrangements are regarded by many as a peak in the Goodman discography, yet Goodman often watered them down and seemed to be reluctant to play them or record them. He openly admired Mel Powell and treated him as an equal, partly because Powell would not have taken any nonsense from him, but Powell's better arrangements too were not welcomed without reluctance. And Goodman was not necessarily wrong from his point of view: some of the younger musicians in Goodman's pick-up bands in later years learned to admire Henderson's arrangements when they had been drilled to play them properly. The problem of art versus commerce is endemic in popular music, and it was Goodman's formula that kept the band working.

Henderson continued to arrange for Goodman in the 1940s, and Don Kirkpatrick arranged 'Idaho', with a vocal by Dick Haymes; other vocals were 'Darn That Dream' (Mildred Bailey), 'There'll be Some Changes Made' (Louise Tobin), 'Somebody Else is Taking My Place' (Peggy Lee) and 'Taking a Chance on Love' (Forrest). Goodman also deserved the credit he always got for hiring black musicians. The Benny Goodman Sextet recordings from 1939 to 1941 are probably the best he ever made, with Charlie Christian on electric guitar, Cootie Williams on trumpet and guests such as Count Basie; titles include 'Breakfast Feud', 'Benny's Bugle', 'Shivers', 'On the Alamo' and 'AC-DC Current'. The band's (and the sextet's) tenor saxophone soloist in 1940–41 was the excellent Georgie Auld, who later led his own bands (and played on the soundtrack of Martin Scorsese's period film *New York, New York* in 1977). On one sextet rehearsal session, unreleased for decades, Lester Young was present, together with Christian, Basie and Basie's rhythm section, an all-black group except for Goodman. With tape recording still a few years in the future, Columbia was recording everything on transcription discs, which years later yielded the warm-up sessions 'Blues in B' and 'Waitin' for Benny', both with Christian. Mundy was credited (with Goodman and Christian) on 'Good Enough to Keep', whose title was changed to 'Air Mail Special'. The band's drummers during the Columbia period included Nick Fatool as well as Dave Tough.

Goodman himself sang on 'Gotta be This or That' (1945) and 'Oh, Baby' (on two sides of a 12-inch 78 in 1946). He moved to Capitol in 1947; 'Moon-faced, Starry-eyed' had a vocal by Johnny Mercer, 'On a Slow Boat to China' had Al Hendrickson and 'It Isn't Fair' pianist and singer Buddy Greco, later a solo cabaret star.

On Capitol Goodman tried to play more modern music. In 1948 he hired Stan Hasselgard, an excellent young Swedish clarinet player – the only time he ever featured another clarinettist – but Hasselgard was killed in a car crash the same year. He also hired Wardell Gray, a superb tenor saxophonist who won much acclaim before he was murdered in Las Vegas, probably in a drug deal that went wrong. In 1949 Goodman employed Arturo O'Farrill, a young arranger from Cuba. (It was Goodman who nicknamed him Chico; he seemed to make a habit of not remembering people's names.) But Goodman did not like bop and soon gave up any willingness to play it. In 1950 he returned to Columbia, and a sextet version of the Louis Prima tune 'Oh, Babe!' was a hit, with Teddy Wilson, Terry Gibbs on vibraphone and a vocal duet by Nancy Reed and Jimmy Ricks (of the doo-wop group the Ravens).

In 1953 Goodman re-formed his classic band for an expensive tour with Louis Armstrong's All Stars that turned into a famous disaster. He managed to insult Armstrong at the beginning; then he was appalled at the vaudeville aspects of Louis's act, in which the over-weight Velma Middleton did the splits, a contradiction of everything Goodman stood for. His insecurities caught up with him and he had a nervous breakdown. The glory years were over and he knew it; he retired to become an elder statesman of popular music, still adored by his fans, playing his classic hits over and over again. In *The Benny Goodman Story* (1955) the otherwise lovable Steve Allen played Goodman; he was not an actor, and was lumbered with the usual awful Hollywood film biography script. Goodman played at the Brussels World's Fair in 1958 and in the Soviet Union in 1962, and offended everyone connected with both tours. (The Russian one is recalled in a hilarious series of articles by bass player Bill Crow, published in lyricist and journalist Gene Lees's *Jazzletter* in 1986.) The original quartet re-formed to make the album *Together Again!* on RCA, a critical and popular success, in 1964. Goodman's niche in music is secure; at the time of writing more than eighty albums and compilations of his old airchecks are listed in the USA Schwann catalogue.

Other white jazz-oriented bandleaders were waiting in the wings in the mid-1930s, with some acclaim already under their belts. The Dorsey Brothers Orchestra had hit records every year from 1928 to 1935 except one; the band included trumpeter Manny Klein (born in 1908), who was later one of the most sought-after studio musicians in the business. The Dorseys split acrimoniously, but both became very popular leaders. Artie Shaw, like Goodman an excellent and busy freelance clarinettist, was soon almost as well known, and Charlie Barnet was also an experienced leader when he hit the charts in 1936. Isham Jones's band became a cooperative in 1937, and leader Woody Herman took it on to greater things. Many white sidemen led their own bands, of whom the best known were Harry James, Gene Krupa and Bunny Berigan.

There were also a great many sweet bands, which were not all completely corny. Jan Savitt's was rather good, and the leader could play a fiddle which was both sweet and swinging. The band of society pianist Eddy Duchin got up a creditable bounce on 'Old Man Mose', sung by Patricia Norman, which was one of the biggest Duchin hits (partly because when she sang the word 'bucket' in the reprise, some listeners thought she had substituted an 'f' for a 'b'). Pianist Frankie Carle wrote 'Sunrise Serenade' and used it as a theme, but the huge hit recordings of it were by the Casa Loma band and Glenn Miller. Another Carle success was 'Oh! What It Seemed To Be', which he also wrote; his vocalist was his daughter, Marjorie Hughes.

He was too good a keyboard player to be offensively rococo; today's marvellous pianist, leader and composer Joanne Brackeen admits that she started by copying Carle off her parents' records.

One of the best of the sweet bands was that of saxophonist Hal Kemp, who was killed in a car crash in 1940. The arrangements were by John Scott Trotter. The band's singer, Robert 'Skinnay' Ennis, had a breathy, half-whispered vocal style on 'When I'm with You' and 'This Year's Kisses', and was later famous for 'Got a Date with an Angel'. Reedman Saxie Dowell did novelty vocals, and later had a charming radio D J show in Chicago. Ennis later led his own band, playing arrangements by Claude Thornhill and Gil Evans.

Harry James was a superb trumpet player, who began playing at the age of nine in his father's circus band, and was evidently one of the best-liked men in the business. His post-Goodman success was slow in coming, but he finally did well and continued to draw large audiences in places like Las Vegas until he died. His dance band music was not particularly jazz-oriented, though his first hit was a cover of 'One O'Clock Jump' (reissued in 1943 during a recording ban as 'Two O'Clock Jump'), and 'Strictly Instrumental' (written by Edgar Battle, among others) was an attractive chart from the Lunceford book. James's band was good enough in 1950 to be raided by Duke Ellington, and he later employed Buddy Rich on drums. His theme was 'Ciribiribin', in 3/4 time (published in Italy in 1898), and another hit was the trumpet virtuoso's 'Flight of the Bumble Bee'; his 'Sleepy Lagoon' was adapted from the 'valse serenade' of English composer Eric Coates.

Most of James's big hits were vocals. He hired the very young Frank Sinatra, who was soon stolen by Tommy Dorsey, and then Dick Haymes, a good singer in the same mould; Helen Ward and Helen Forrest recorded with James, and Kitty Kallen joined him around 1944. Forrest's hits were 'I Don't Want to Walk Without You' and 'I've Heard That Song Before'; James was listed as a co-writer on Duke Ellington's 'I'm Beginning to See the Light', which, sung by Kallen, was a number one hit in the white chart in 1945.

Gene Krupa's success as a bandleader was also slow at first, but was then enhanced by the great black trumpeter Roy Eldridge (thus linking two generations of jazzmen) and the young vocalist Anita

O'Day, first of a new generation of hip white jazz singers. 'Let Me Off Uptown' was their duet; Eldridge sang on 'Knock Me a Kiss'. Tenor saxophonist Charlie Ventura was another of Krupa's stars. Krupa became a better drummer as time went on, having already raised the profile of the timekeeper to that of pop star. He served some time in jail on a charge of possessing marijuana, but was widely believed to have been framed: a devout Catholic, he refused to pay off crooked policemen. He led small groups well into the 1960s.

The big band fronted by Bob Crosby, the famous crooner's brother, was an unusual one. After leaving Ben Pollack, arranger and reedman Gil Rodin organized the band as a cooperative; it hired Crosby, who was not a bad singer and got better. The band included Deane Kincaide (reedman and arranger), Yank Lawson (trumpet), Eddie Miller (tenor saxophone – he had a lovely, light tone like that of Bud Freeman and Lester Young), Matty Matlock (clarinet and arranger), Bob Haggart (bass), Nappy Lamare (guitar) and Ray Bauduc (drums). Among those who passed through were pianists Bob Zurke, Joe Sullivan and Jess Stacy, clarinettist Irving Fazola and trumpeters Muggsy Spanier and Billy Butterfield. Many of the band's founder members were from New Orleans; they played an unusual big-band dixieland style, and the Bob Cats octet played the real stuff. The band's hits included the vocals 'In a Little Gypsy Tea Room' (1935, with Frank Tennille, father of Toni Tennille, of the 1970s duo Captain and Tennille), 'Whispers in the Dark' (1937, with Kay Weber) and 'Day In, Day Out' (1939, with Helen Ward). On 'Big Noise from Winnetka', a famous novelty duo by Haggart and Bauduc, Haggart whistles through his teeth while Bauduc uses his sticks on the bass's strings. One of the band's best-known records was the 12-inch 78 'South Rampart Street Parade' / 'Dogtown Blues', written by Lawson and Haggart, who formed the Lawson–Haggart Jazz Band in the early 1950s. (It became the World's Greatest Jazz Band after appearing at the annual Colorado Jazz Party and continued making albums well into the 1970s, when there were also frequent Crosby reunions.)

The band of Mal Hallett, a New England violinist and leader, was admired by many others. His earlier groups employed Krupa, Jack Teagarden, Frankie Carle, tenor saxophonist Toots Mondello (later with Goodman) and Jack Jenney, a first-class trombonist and also a legendary prankster. Jenney's own big band of 1938–40 failed, but he played the trombone solo on the famous Artie Shaw hit version of 'Stardust'.

Bunny Berigan was probably the greatest white trumpet player of the whole era; he may be heard on Goodman and Tommy Dorsey records, and led his own bands. He also played on two RCA Victor All-star sessions. A hit version of 'Honeysuckle Rose', backed with 'Blues' (1937), was played by a quintet: Berigan, Tommy Dorsey, Fats Waller, Dick McDonough (guitar) and George Wettling (drums). 'Blue Lou' and 'The Blues' (1939) were by a big band. Berigan's unforgettable hit was 'I Can't Get Started', which he recorded twice. Artie Shaw plays clarinet on the earlier version; the more famous one, with Berigan's vocal and lengthy introduction, was issued on both 12-inch and (edited) 10-inch 78s. In retrospect, the 1938–40 band suffers from having recorded too many second-rate pop songs, while Berigan, an alcoholic, was eventually unable to play his own famous solos. Louis Armstrong is said to have refused to record 'I Can't Get Started', saying, 'That's Bunny's tune.'

Jimmy Dorsey led a band similar to that of Harry James in that it was a good mainstream dance band. He had been a superb alto player on many fine jazz records; when Tommy walked out in 1935, most of the members of the Dorsey Brothers Orchestra stayed with Jimmy, who became one of Jack Kapp's greatest successes on Decca. The band's very good and extremely popular vocalists were Bob Eberly and Helen O'Connell; Kitty Kallen sang with it in the early 1940s before she joined Harry James. Sidemen included Ray McKinley on drums, 'Tootie' Camarata on trumpet, Freddie Slack on piano and Herbie Haymer on tenor saxophone. But, as with James, his biggest hits almost all featured the singers: 'The Breeze and I' (from the Spanish song 'Andalucia' by Ernesto Lecuona), 'Maria Elena' (a Mexican song), 'Blue Champagne', 'High on a Windy Hill', 'I Hear a Rhapsody' and many others were by Eberly; 'Green Eyes' (from Cuba), 'Amapola' (a Spanish song) and 'Tangerine' (from the film *The Fleet's In*) were all duets by Eberly and O'Connell. The band's last big hit was 'Besame Mucho' (from Mexico), a duet by Eberly and Kallen. Like most leaders on Decca, Dorsey also recorded with Bing Crosby and the Andrews Sisters. He is rated as the seventeenth best-selling recording artist up to 1954, but brother Tommy was number four.

Tommy Dorsey was a volatile businessman, as well as a fine musician. He took over Joe Haymes's band in 1935 and won enormous acclaim, despite a high turnover in personnel. Like Goodman, he was not an easy man to work for, but at the time it seemed as though his band could do more things better than most others. He was a first-rate trombonist, though he knew he was outclassed by the likes of Teagarden. His strength lay in his beautiful legato playing on ballads, as on his theme 'I'm Getting Sentimental Over You' (which had already been recorded twice, and was a hit for the brothers' band in 1934). At the RCA Victor All-star date in 1939 Dorsey had to be coaxed to play 'The Blues' with Teagarden present; the enchanting solution was a Dorsey legato statement of the theme surrounded by Teagarden's obbligato.

Tommy's was a great dance band: on a two-CD collection of all of Frank Sinatra's recordings with the 1940 band, it is astonishing to hear how the band could swing at very slow tempos. Among the musicians passing through were Berigan, Bud Freeman and Skeets Herfurt on reeds and Dave Tough and Buddy Rich on drums; in 1938–9 the trumpet section had George 'Pee Wee' Erwin, Yank Lawson and Lee Castle, all of them fine players. The first big hits included 'The Music Goes Round and Round', with Edythe Wright, an inane novelty from 52nd Street that swept the USA. The very pleasant and easy-phrasing Jack Leonard, one of several boy singers, has since been underrated, followed as he was by Frank Sinatra.

On tour Dorsey played opposite a cooperative band called the Sunset Royals, who were fronted by various people, including trombonist Moran 'Doc' Wheeler (who later became an MC at the Apollo Theatre and an R & B-gospel DJ in New York City). Cat Anderson, who later became Duke Ellington's high-note specialist, joined in 1938. The band did one recording session in 1941 as Doc Wheeler and his Sunset Orchestra; but before that, in a theatre in Philadelphia, according to an item in *Metronome* magazine, the band had given Tommy Dorsey a going-over. Dorsey acquired his arrangement of Irving Berlin's 'Marie' from the Royals, and made it one of the biggest and best hits of the Swing Era, early in 1937: Leonard sings a strong straight line while the band chants a paraphrase of the lyrics, the most successful application of Don Redman's swing choir idea, and it has a superb trumpet solo by Berigan. It continued to sell for years, and reached the charts several times. On the other side was Dorsey's arrangement of 'Song of India', borrowed from Rimsky-Korsakov, also featuring Berigan.

Arranger Larry Clinton contributed 'The Dipsy Doodle' in 1937; he also wrote 'Satan Takes a Holiday', and soon led his own popular band. 'Boogie Woogie', Dorsey's most famous instrumental, was based on Pinetop Smith's piano solo of 1928. Dorsey's vocal group was the Pied Pipers, which had begun as an octet and slimmed to a quartet when hired by Dorsey; it contained the excellent Jo Stafford (who later married Paul Weston, one of Dorsey's arrangers). She sang solo on 'Manhattan Serenade' in 1942 and 'You Took My Love' the next year. Sinatra's hits with Dorsey began in 1940 with 'Polka Dots and Moonbeams' (by Johnny Burke and Jimmy Van Heusen, who became specialists at writing for Sinatra); other Sinatra hits, such as 'I'll Never Smile Again' and 'There are Such Things', all had him backed by the Pied Pipers.

From Lunceford Dorsey hired arranger Sy Oliver, whose hits included 'Yes, Indeed!' (vocal duet by Stafford and Oliver), 'Well, Git It!' (featuring Ziggy Elman), 'On the Sunny Side of the Street' (a hip swing choir style vocal by the Sentimentalists, successors of the Pied Pipers) and 'Opus No. 1', a typical Swing Era riff. By the time of the last two, in 1945, the Dorsey band had incorporated strings, an expensive and unnecessary development; the Swing Era had begun to ripen.

Artie Shaw, like Goodman, was a first-rate clarinettist and a busy freelance when he formed his own band in 1936, with vocalist Helen Forrest, arranger Jerry Gray and Tony Pastor and Georgie Auld on tenor saxophones; George Wettling and then Buddy Rich played drums. Shaw was an intelligent man who hated the music business and left it several times; in 1954 (to Goodman's horror) he put his horn down and never touched it again. Of over fifty big hits up to 1946, the most famous was a sleeper. Pastor was also a novelty vocalist who later led his own band; he sang on a joky Shaw version of 'Indian Love Call' in 1938. But disc jockeys turned the record over to discover Gray's arrangement of Cole Porter's 'Begin the Beguine', later voted the third-favourite record of all time by the jockeys in a *Billboard* poll. From the same session, Shaw's composition 'Back Bay Shuffle' was another success, and Billie Holiday recorded her only track with the band, 'Any Old Time'; Shaw's self-composed theme 'Nightmare', from the next session, was another hit.

Shaw shocked the business by walking away at the height of this first success in late 1939, only to return from a holiday in Mexico and form a new band with another outstanding hit: 'Frenesi', a Mexican song, was arranged by William Grant Still for flute, oboe, French horn and strings, as well as the fifteen-piece conventional band. It was even bigger than 'Beguine' and another top DJ favourite. Another hit by Shaw's second band was his own somewhat pretentious 'Concerto for Clarinet', issued on two sides of a 12-inch 78. Several bands, including those of Goodman, Tommy Dorsey and Glenn Miller, had huge hits with 'Star Dust' during this period, but Shaw's became the DJs' all-time favourite record (complete with slushy strings). Lena Horne made two sides with the band in 1941; vocalists Forrest, Kallen and Georgia Gibbs also worked with it.

Many of the white swing bands followed Goodman's lead in having small groups within them, such as Tommy Dorsey's Clambake Seven. Shaw's Gramercy Five was among the most interesting. The original cast made eight sides in 1940, with Billy Butterfield on trumpet, Johnny Guarnieri on harpsichord, Al Hendrickson on electric guitar, Jud DeNaut on bass and Nick Fatool on drums. 'Summit Ridge Drive' was a top ten hit. In 1945 six more bop-flavoured sides were made, with Roy Eldridge on trumpet, Dodo Marmarosa on piano, Barney Kessel on guitar, Morris Rayman and Lou Fromm on bass and drums. Shaw's ambitions for his music exceeded his ability; he was not the composer-arranger he wanted to be, and his irascibility got in his way. He later became a novelist and a theatrical producer, among other things; his autobiography *The Trouble with Cinderella* was almost a good book, but contained too much self-pity. He fronted big bands a couple of times in later years, but did not play.

Charlie Barnet came from a wealthy family and in 1929 was leading a combo on cruise liners at the age of sixteen; he led several bands before forming an excellent jazz-oriented outfit. He was a good soloist on all the saxophones, specializing on tenor at first, but later on alto and soprano, because, he said, there were too many better tenor players around. He also occasionally sang, especially in the early years. 'The most enjoyable, in terms of *fun* fun, plus one of the greatest bands I ever worked with was Charlie Barnet,' said Buddy DeFranco (quoted by Ira Gitler in *Swing to Bop*). When interviewing a musician, the story goes, Barnet would ask him if he drank. If he replied in the negative, he was either lying or was the kind of man who never took a drink; in either case, he didn't get the job. Barnet enjoyed life, and so did the people who worked for him.

Of all the white bandleaders of the Swing Era, it was Barnet who most openly admired the black bands, and whose talent and leadership paid them the finest tribute: many of Barnet's recordings are still among the most delightful of the era. He covered several Ellington compositions, notably 'The Gal from Joe's' and 'Rockin' in Rhythm'; 'Charleston Alley' was arranged by Horace Henderson; 'Southern Fried' was co-written by Harlan Leonard; 'Jump Session' was recorded by several bands, including Don Redman's, and 'Flyin' Home' was the famous Lionel Hampton screamer.

But the band (chiefly Barnet, under the pseudonym Dale Bennett) also produced fine originals. Among the best from 1939 to 1941 were 'The Duke's Idea' / 'The Count's Idea'; a month later 'The Wrong Idea', in which the band imitated the sweet bands of the time, was backed by 'The Right Idea', one of the best. 'Leapin' at the Lincoln' was a head arrangement on Gershwin's 'Lady Be Good'; 'Afternoon of a Moax' was also called 'Shake, Rattle 'n Roll' ('moax' was a southern term for a square); 'Wild Mab of the Fish Pond' was for guitarist Bus Etri, whose nickname was Wild Mab: one night after a hotel gig some of his colleagues put him in the hotel's fountain. (Barnet's nickname later became Mad Mab. Etri and trumpeter Lloyd Hundling were killed in a car crash in 1941, a personal blow to Barnet, who could not bear to hire another guitarist for months.) Ray Noble's 'Cherokee' was arranged by trumpeter Billy May; it was Barnet's biggest hit and became his theme, which is no doubt partly why the tune (with its wide-open chords, like 'I Got Rhythm') became a favourite vehicle for modern jazzmen.

The band contained no world-famous soloists during its classic period, but always good sidemen, such as May and Bobby Burnet on trumpets, and reedman-arranger Lloyd 'Skippy' Martin, who also played clarinet (for instance on 'Leapin' at the Lincoln'). The Barnet band represented a peak in the quality of mainstream popular music that has not been exceeded, demonstrating for all time that a high average level of musicianship was more important than stars. All these arrangements were extremely well played, and never fail to swing. Again and again there are felicitous touches on the recordings, for example the tasty Ellingtonian harmony of the trumpets at the end of 'Rockin' in Rhythm'. In Barnet's saxophone solo after the false ending on 'Leapin' at the Lincoln' he starts so high that he sounds like Martin coming back on clarinet, then drops several octaves in four or five notes. Or *is* it Martin coming back on clarinet? – it is done so seamlessly that it is impossible to tell. The swinging out-chorus written by May quotes Gershwin.

When playing 'Cherokee' in concert, the band improvised at some length; a sort of part two was recorded as 'Redskin Rhumba' (and there was also 'Comanche War Dance'). 'Pompton Turnpike' was written by Dick Rogers and trombonist-bandleader Will Osborne. Barnet led the band on soprano saxophone on this blues-flavoured instrumental; it celebrated Route 23 in New Jersey, the Newark–Pompton Turnpike, where the Meadowbrook was located, one of the most popular dance halls of the era. As with the other bands, many of Barnet's hits were by the vocalists. Mary Ann McCall sang 'Between 18th and 19th on Chestnut Street' (also by Rogers and Osborne) and 'Six Lessons from Madame La Zonga' (but was a better singer later, with Woody Herman). 'I Hear a Rhapsody' was sung by Bob Carroll.

'Blue Juice' may have been named after the band's bus; 'The Bar is Now Open' was another Horace Henderson tune. In October 1939 when the Palomar Ballroom in Los Angeles burned to the ground, the band lost almost everything, but Barnet's priorities were always in the right place: according to George T. Simon his comment was, 'Hell, it's better than being in Poland, with bombs dropping on your head.' Count Basie and Benny Carter lent arrangements, and one of the first new Barnet charts was called 'Are We Burnt Up?' Over the years Barnet employed more black artists than any other white leader, and without any fanfare, or even thinking about it. The only question was, 'How well does the guy play?' He simply did not bother to perform in places where there was going to be difficulty with an integrated band. As early as 1936 he hired trumpeter Frankie Newton and bass player John Kirby; among those who passed through were Benny Carter, Rex Stewart, Charlie Shavers, Trummy Young, Roy Eldridge, Clark Terry and Willie Smith, and vocalists Bunny Briggs (who later sang Ellington's *Sacred Music*) and the wonderful Lena Horne. Her lovely version of 'You're My Thrill' in 1941 featured Barnet on soprano saxophone. In 1965 she wrote: 'as far as color was concerned, it just never came up . . . I just felt safe with him.'

Barnet moved from Bluebird to Decca in 1943, and as the Second World War no doubt disrupted his line-up, the number of Barnet hits declined; but 'Skyliner' in 1945 became one of his most famous instrumentals (another 'Dale Bennett' chart), and 'Cement Mixer (Put-ti, Put-ti)' was one of several hit versions of Slim Gaillard's novelty. He later made innovative records for Capitol, using arrangers such as Johnny Richards, Neal Hefti, Kai Winding, Gil Fuller and Tiny Kahn. His autobiography *Those Swinging Years* (1984, written with Stanley Dance) is full of candour and enjoyable anecdotes, and provides trenchant commentary on the reasons for the withering of the Big Band Era.

Trombonist Wilber Schwichtenberg had played with Red Nichols and Ray Noble; he changed his name to Will Bradley when he formed a band in 1940 (co-led by drummer Ray McKinley, who had worked for the Dorsey brothers). One of its first recordings was 'Beat Me Daddy, Eight to the Bar', a two-sided hit at the height of the boogie-woogie fad, soon followed by 'Down the Road a Piece', a trio record, both with Freddie Slack on piano. Later came 'Scrub Me Mama, with A Boogie Beat', and more. It was a good, slick band; the hits included 'Celery Stalks at Midnight', yet another Swing Era riff; a copy of that record was memorably smashed by morons in the film *The Blackboard Jungle* (1955).

Given the quality of Barnet's music, and the stiff competition from the likes of Goodman and Dorsey, the phenomenon of trombonist-arranger Glenn Miller needs some explaining. Miller was far and away the most successful leader of the entire era. His time at the top was short, because he died in the English Channel on his way to entertain troops in newly liberated France, but he still managed to become the seventh best-selling recording artist of the whole period 1892–1954: with more than seventy top ten hits between July 1939 and September 1943, his success will probably never be equalled. Yet he was a tense individual who dealt in formulas, and seemed to avoid allowing his band to swing. (Tenor saxophonist Al Klink said years later, 'We were too scared to swing.') Miller did not acquire a first-rate rhythm section until he led an Army Air Force band. Many years later Billy May, who left Barnet to join Miller because the money was better, told George T. Simon, 'The only man I ever knew him to be envious of was Kay Kyser, because he was the only bandleader making more money than Glenn was.' After the war May joked in a letter to Klink: 'Adolph Hitler is alive and playing Fender bass with Glenn Miller in Argentina.'

Born in Iowa (like Bix), Miller was not a great soloist, and some say he would have given up all his success to be a top-class jazzman. He appeared to have difficulty in expressing himself emotionally, and his employees often did not know whether he liked their work or not. Yet (like Goodman) he was capable of unexpected kindness, and he kept an eye on the ticket prices at the ballrooms and theatres, refusing to allow his young fans to be ripped off. When Barnet fronted Miller's band while Miller was ill, he would have done it for nothing, but Miller insisted on paying him generously. (When Barnet did a similar favour for Goodman, the latter gave him a cigarette lighter with an engraved inscription that had been altered; somebody else had given Goodman the lighter, and furthermore, said Barnet, it didn't work.)

Miller played trombone and wrote arrangements for Ben Pollack (1924–8) and Red Nichols (1929–30). The Charleston Chasers, a Columbia pick-up group, was basically Red Nichols's outfit from 1925 to 1929; for its last recording session in 1931 an eleven-piece band was directed by Benny Goodman, including Miller, Gene

Krupa and Charlie and Jack Teagarden, and Miller wrote some special lyrics for one of Teagarden's several recordings of 'Basin Street Blues'. Goodman and Miller also played together in the pit bands for Gershwin shows. Miller added business management to his tasks while working with Smith Ballew (1932–4). Ballew, a handsome pop singer, led a successful band, employing a good deal of first-rate talent, and had several big hits on various ARC labels from 1929 to 1931; on recordings his band was often the Pollack gang, moonlighting again. (Ballew later went to Hollywood, and the rumour persists that Ballew's voice was dubbed when a studio tried to make a singing cowboy out of John Wayne.) In 1934–5 Miller worked for the Dorsey Brothers Orchestra, where his accomplishments included writing and singing some amusing novelty lyrics on 'Annie's Cousin Fanny'.

The excellent British songwriter and bandleader Ray Noble, whose records sold well in the USA, decided to move there. The musicians' union would not allow him to use his own band, so he brought vocalist Al Bowlly and one or two others, and hired Miller to assemble an American band. Noble had big hits in America every year between 1931 and 1949, except for a couple of years during the war; Miller helped him from 1935 to 1937, when Miller formed his own first band.

Noble's lovely recording of his own song, 'The Very Thought of You', was an international hit in 1934 and featured Bowlly. (Born in what is now Maputo in Mozambique of Greek and Lebanese parents, Bowlly soon returned to London, where he was killed, not by the famous German bomb that hit the Café De Paris in March 1941, killing West Indian bandleader Ken 'Snakehips' Johnson along with many others, but by another bomb a few weeks later.) Noble's HMV discs made in England were admired by producers and recording engineers in the USA for their excellent sound. The secret turned out to be that the band was recorded in a sizeable room at some distance from the microphone, rather than in the typically cramped studios of US companies, some of which were left over from the acoustic era.

Miller had a hit with 'Solo Hop' in 1935, using some of Noble's men. His own first band went broke, but late in 1938 he was recording for Bluebird with a new band, using his pretty 'sound' (a clarinet lead over the reed section) and the familiar 'oo-wah' of the muted brass. He was a huge hit at the Glen Island Casino in New Rochelle, New York, a popular ballroom where leaders played for less money because of the room's radio wire. Miller's long-time associate Chummy MacGregor was not a very good pianist; Herman 'Trigger' Alpert was a good bass player, but the various occupants of the band's drum chair never added up to much. Klink was an excellent saxophonist, but Miller's favourite (and the band's star) was Gordon 'Tex' Beneke, a vocalist whose distinctive Texas drawl was invaluable on many of the hits. Beneke was not as good a saxophonist as Klink, yet Miller featured him instead. Miller was the sort of businessman who thought that talent ran in families: Ray Eberle was nothing like as good a singer as his brother Bob Eberly, while Marion Hutton (younger sister of singer and film star Betty Hutton, the 'blonde bombshell') often had trouble singing in tune. The band's vocal group was the Modernaires. On the band's broadcasts Miller's medley theme was 'something old, something new, something borrowed, something blue'.

Miller's first big hit was his theme, 'Moonlight Serenade', originally called 'Now I Lay Me Down to Weep', a simple, saccharine tune played at a dirge-like tempo, and loaded with the clarinet lead. The uptempo numbers were often absurdly clunky records: 'Runnin' Wild' was first played by Art Hickman (and was sung by Marilyn Monroe in the film *Some Like It Hot* in 1959); Miller's 'Anvil Chorus' was a two-sided 78 based on the tune from Verdi's *Il Trovatore*: both were stinkers. Another 1939 hit was 'Little Brown Jug', a pleasant arrangement (by Bill Finegan) given a lumpy recorded performance. (It is moved to 1944 in the 1954 film biography, because the poverty of the script needed to make a gimmick of it.) A great many of the Miller hits are unremarkable renditions of popular songs of the day, such as 'Wishing Will Make It So', 'Stairway to the Stars', 'Fools Rush In' and the inevitable 'Star Dust'.

So why the enormous success? Why was one of the great peaks in popular music dominated by Glenn Miller? Why do millions of people still love his music, and why are more compilations of his recordings available today than almost anyone else's?

To begin with, despite the importance of the phenomenon of swing in music, it does not matter at all to many people, and in 1939 its lesson had definitely not been mastered by all the musicians. To put it another way, a lot of people still clapped on one and three, and things are not much different fifty years later. Barnet was certain, on the basis of personal experience, that most people cannot tell good playing from bad, let alone what swing is. Also, Miller had decided not to compete directly with Goodman, Dorsey or Barnet, but to build an essentially sweet dance band that could also be defined as a 'swing band', so that he topped polls in both categories. There was an integrity to the sweetness, and the band was superbly reliable. Miller was a stickler for dynamics in performance, for example ('Observe the markings!' he would remind the musicians), so that the kids always got the sound they expected, and many of them bought a new Miller record, whatever it was. The arrangements too were reliable, often predictable but sometimes outstanding. And, finally, the choice of material was nothing less than brilliant from a commercial point of view. Miller's achievement was to sum up popular music, as Whiteman had done earlier: each sounded to his contemporaries as if he were at the centre of it. 'Little Brown Jug' was a very old and familiar tune, and 'American Patrol', while it seems like a wartime novelty now, was in fact a march first published in 1885, and was probably vaguely familiar to Miller's audience. (The hit recording is considerably less disappointing than that of 'Little Brown Jug'.) 'Moon Love' was adapted from Tchaikovsky's Fifth Symphony. In 'Yes, My Darling Daughter', adapted by Jack Lawrence from a Ukrainian folksong, Hutton asks the leading questions and the band chants the title's answer. 'Ida (Sweet as Apple Cider)' had already been made famous by Eddie Cantor, among others, and sounded like a quintessentially American song. (In Britain cider is an alcoholic drink, but in the USA it is just apple juice.) Billy May wrote an arrangement of 'Ida' that set Beneke's vocal against that of the band, but Miller would not use it: the swing choir was not part of his formula.

There were film songs ('Over the Rainbow', 'When You Wish Upon a Star'), radio themes ('You and I', a number one hit, was the *Maxwell House Coffee-time* theme, written by Meredith Willson) and sweet Latin songs ('Adios', 'Perfidia', 'Say "Si Si"'); many tunes were forever associated with Miller because of the sweet innocence of their lyrics, for example 'Elmer's Tune' and 'Moonlight Cocktail' (written by stride pianist Luckey Roberts). Several other bands and recording artists with undoubted musical skills, from Guy Lombardo and Lawrence Welk to James Last and Barry Manilow, have been excoriated by critics for their perceived shortcomings, but to know your market as well as Miller did is an impressive accomplishment.

As in most of the other white bands, riffs were borrowed from black ones, such as Erskine Hawkins's 'Tuxedo Junction' (which is not a bad record, and a head arrangement, very different from Hawkins's own), and one of the biggest hits of the century, 'In the Mood'. A riff is a repeated rhythmic figure that suggests interesting harmonic ideas to the soloists. Among the most charming riffs are the simplest, such as Leonard and Barnet's 'Southern Fried', mentioned above. Most of the Swing Era tunes celebrating dance halls and hotel ballrooms are little more than riffs: 'Stomping at the Savoy', 'Jumping at the Woodside', 'Riffing at the Ritz' and so forth.

'In the Mood' had appeared on several earlier recordings, such as Wingy Manone's 'Tar Paper Stomp' (1930) and Horace Henderson's arrangement 'Hot and Anxious', which was recorded by Fletcher Henderson and Don Redman (at very different tempos: Henderson's is slower, Redman's hotter). The venerable British journalist C. H. Rolph was certain that he heard the riff played by a cinema orchestra before 1920. Edgar Hayes was a black pianist and bandleader whose saxophonist Joe Garland wrote an entire arrangement consisting of nothing but the riff, naming it 'In the Mood'; it appeared in 1938 on the other side of Hayes's record of 'Star Dust' (which would have made the black chart, had there been one at the time). Barnet turned it down, but Miller recorded it within a few months. If you are going to exercise a riff for most of the length of a 78 rpm side, you have to make it swing; otherwise a riff like 'In the Mood', which carries repetition to an extreme, soon becomes irritating. Among the differences between the two recordings was the fact that Hayes's drummer was the young Kenny Clarke. Despite Clyde Hurley's trumpet solo, and the famous 'chase' sequence between Klink and Beneke on tenor, Miller's version sounds like a bright-eyed and energetic imitation of swing. There are much better Miller recordings that are rarely heard – 'Sliphorn Jive', written by Eddie Durham, comes to mind – but you can hardly buy a Miller compilation without 'In the Mood' on it.

It is too bad that Miller's records are not better ones, yet a few of them hold up as well as almost any from the period. 'Chattanooga Choo Choo' and '(I've Got a Gal in) Kalamazoo' were both written by Mack Gordon and Harry Warren for the Miller films *Orchestra Wives* and *Sun Valley Serenade*. Miller saw to it that the story line incorporated the band, rather than a mere appearance by it, making them better than average films of their kind. 'Choo Choo' was the first record to be formally certified a million-seller, serving notice to the business that the Depression was over at last; RCA invented the gold record gimmick for Miller. 'Don't Sit under the Apple Tree (with Anybody Else but Me)', written in 1942 by Lew Brown, Charlie Tobias and Sam H. Stept, is the sort of song which seems always to have existed until somebody plucked it out of the air, almost a good pop song of the nineteenth century. These three continued selling for years; all were jolly arrangements, well played and with a full complement of vocalists, and all were about travel and parting, the admixture of trains and place names helping to cheer up the nation during a world war: they were good pop records, and they still are.

On the other side of 'Moonlight Serenade' was Frankie Carle's 'Sunrise Serenade', also a slow, smoochy instrumental and a top ten hit, but a much better tune, a pretty arrangement and taken at a slightly faster tempo. 'Song of the Volga Boatmen' (cleverly arranged by Finegan) and 'String of Pearls' (Jerry Gray) are unique. All three of these very different sides are among Miller's best recordings; the tempos are just right and the rhythm section plays slightly behind the beat, rather than on top of it. 'String of Pearls' included solos by Beneke, Klink and Ernie Caceres, and a cornet solo by Bobby Hackett. (Critics were irritated that Miller hired the great cornettist to play guitar, but he admired Hackett, and hired him on guitar initially because he was having lip trouble at the time.)

Miller joined the United States Army Air Force as a captain and rose to major. When he was sent to England to entertain troops, the BBC wanted him to play everything at the same volume, to make it easier to broadcast, so he broadcast on the Armed Services Network instead. Robert Farnon led a Canadian band, and George Melachrino a British one. There are those who say that Farnon's was the best, but Miller had finally put together a good rhythm section: Alpert on bass, Ray McKinley on drums and Mel Powell on piano. Miller's contribution to morale was enormous, and he insisted on putting on extra shows wherever the crush was too great to allow everyone in. From the early days he had ensured that broadcasts were recorded; the USAAF band issued no recordings at the time, but Miller broadcasts have been endlessly recycled ever since. When he was lost on his way to France, flying in terrible winter weather in a small plane with no de-icing equipment, he was forty years old. His was one of the most successful sounds in the history of pop.

Klink said, 'Miller should have lived and the music should have died.' Miller ghost bands have continued touring, with the co-operation of the estate; they were seen on UK television on the fortieth anniversary of D-Day. The best of these in musical terms was Tex Beneke and the Glenn Miller Orchestra led by Beneke until 1947, when he fell out with the estate, perhaps because he did not want to stick to the Miller formula for ever. (The estate got even by seeing to it that he was not even mentioned in the film biography of 1954.)

One of Beneke's most interesting sides was 'Lavender Coffin', about the last wishes of a gambler, which he sang accompanied by a vocal group; the arrangement was a clever one, its laid-back jive and hand-claps on the beat reminiscent of 'Volga Boatman'. Interestingly, it was a cover of a rhythm and blues tune, written by Shirley Albert, which was a top ten hit in the black chart by Boston saxophonist Paul 'Fat Man' Robinson in 1949; other recordings of it were made by Lionel Hampton and Joe Thomas, the former vocalist and reedman with Lunceford. Cover versions of rhythm and blues songs would soon become more numerous; new independent labels and other changes in the business were making sure that popular music was mutating by 1949, whether the Miller estate liked it or not.

10

Small-group Jazz, the Jukebox and the New Independent Labels

You can still start arguments by postulating that big-band jazz was not jazz at all. This is nonsense, but the small groups of the Swing Era made a very special contribution, providing more room for hot solos and using simpler arrangements, often made up on the bandstand or in the studio. The greater freedom available to small groups allowed a different kind of innovation, the hallmark of jazz since its beginning. In the small-group recordings of the Swing Era may be heard the seeds of the music of the future, both in the rhythm and blues and the modern jazz directions.

In the mid-1930s several factors combined to create the new jukebox industry, which had an incalculable effect on popular music.

Edison's phonograph had been fitted with a coin slot and four listening tubes by Louis Glass and placed in a saloon in San Francisco in 1889. In 1891 the Louisiana Phonograph Company claimed that one of its machines, costing about $200, had grossed $1,000 in two months. In 1906 the Gabel Automatic Entertainer was the first machine to play a series of gramophone discs, using a spring-loaded hand-wound motor and a 40-inch acoustic horn. There were huge, heavy, brilliantly engineered non-electric machines that played several cylinders in rotation; one handle wound the motor and changed the cylinder and the needle. But the phonograph parlour was replaced by player pianos.

Despite the fact that there had never been any adequate protection for the authors and composers of songs, and that in practice such protection could only be acquired through their publishers, Theodore Roosevelt (the 'trust buster') was outraged that the Music Publishers

Association (MPA) and Aeolian had agreed a royalty of 10 per cent on piano rolls. A revised Copyright Act for popular music in 1909 required a royalty of 2 cents and compulsory licensing of all reproductions, whether piano rolls or sound recordings, and for all publishers, not just those in the MPA. This was said to be the first time in history that the government intervened directly between supplier and user of a product.

Aeolian's Aeriola player piano had been introduced in 1895; in 1898 Wurlitzer built the first coin-operated player piano. By 1910 these had overtaken nickel-in-the-slot record players. In 1916 the 'word-roll' added the words to the songs, printed on the margin of the roll: the words were not covered by the 1909 act, a good excuse to set royalties on such rolls much higher than 2 cents.

The best player pianos, such as the Ampico, reproduced music more or less accurately, and recordings were made by great pianists such as Rachmaninov and Busoni. But the vast majority of piano rolls and players were mechanical in the extreme, and no expression of any kind was available. George Gershwin and a good number of others first heard popular music on the pianola in the corner candy store; many a jazz pianist began by slowing down the piano roll and placing fingers on the keys as they were mechanically depressed. Between 1895 and the early 1920s over two million player pianos were sold; in 1921, of 341,652 pianos of all types, nearly two-thirds were player pianos. But the business failed during the Depression, and by then the radio and electric recording were beginning to have their effect. (In the 1990s the Yamaha Disklavier is operated by 'a full library of pre-recorded discs . . . from classical to contemporary'. So you can still buy a piano that plays itself if you want to.)

In 1927 several firms built electrically operated record-playing machines; it was obvious that simply playing the records in rotation was not good enough, and selection mechanisms were developed. The Automatic Music Instrument Company (AMI) marketed the first electrically amplified, multi-selection device.

Homer Capehart worked for a company that made various coin-operated machines; he bought the rights to a record changer called the Simplex, and was fired for doing so. He formed his own company and made a splash at the Chicago Radio Show in 1928, attracting almost as much attention as the first public demonstration of television. The Capehart was not the first integrally designed automatic-changer for the home; Victor had marketed an Orthophonic acoustic player with an electrically operated changer, but it had problems. For one thing, discs in those days were not of uniform size, and did not always have lead-in grooves and a final groove spiral for tripping the mechanism. Capehart was fired again, this time from his own company, but a few years later the Capehart became the most impressive machine on the market. Its elaborate record changer played both sides of a stack of intermixed 10-inch and 12-inch records, and the machine had good sound for the period; it was slowly improved. Coleman Hawkins owned one in the late 1940s that cost $1,000, but most Americans never saw one. The price put it out of reach.

Meanwhile, Capehart took his Simplex to Wurlitzer, whose sales of pipe organs and player pianos were falling, and became the company's vice-president and sales manager. The Simplex played only one side of each record, but was robust and reliable. Prohibition had been repealed, so a great many new taverns opened up, and most of them wanted mechanical music. In 1933 there were about 25,000 jukeboxes in operation in the USA, of which only 266 were Wurlitzer's; in 1935 there were 100,000, and in 1936 Wurlitzer alone shipped nearly 45,000 machines. It remained the leader of the industry for more than a decade.

The term 'jukebox' did not become common until the mid-1930s. It probably comes from the Gullah 'juke' or 'joog', meaning 'disorderly' or 'wicked' and perhaps ultimately from the Wolof 'dzug', to live wickedly. The *Oxford English Dictionary* quotes a scholarly American source from 1941: to 'jouk' was to dance; to 'go joukin'' was to go pub-crawling. The term 'juke joint' was certainly current; blues singer Walter Roland recorded 'Jookit Jookit' for Vocalion in 1933. (A character in Tennessee Williams's *Orpheus Descending* of 1958 says 'I'd like to go out jooking with you tonight.')

Wurlitzer's Model 24 was the first to offer twenty-four selections instead of twelve or sixteen. Capehart sold the machines to independent jukebox operators, rather than directly to the taverns and restaurant owners, thus ensuring that the machines were regularly serviced and the records changed. He built up such an effective distribution system that by the time he left Wurlitzer his own Packard company could not compete with it. (After the Second World War he left the business, serving three terms in the US Senate from Indiana.)

Canadian-born David Rockola had a perfect name for the jukebox industry; his pinball-machine business went broke in 1930, but he bought the patents of the old Gabel company and, with the help of his creditors, Rock-Ola competed with Seeburg (formed in 1907 as a piano company by a Swedish immigrant) for second place in the USA jukebox business behind Wurlitzer. In 1948 Seeburg's engineer M. W. Kenney developed the first machine to offer a hundred selections – it held fifty 78s, of which either side could be selected – and the Selectomatic mechanism became nearly ubiquitous. Of all these, only Rock-Ola was still making jukeboxes in the early 1980s. Seeburg had got into anti-trust trouble, and when Wurlitzer left the jukebox business in 1974, the company destroyed all its files and spare parts. Most of the principals are now dead, so the definitive history of the industry will probably never be written.

Jukebox cabinets became an extravaganza of light and moulded plastic in the late 1930s. Wurlitzer's Model 24 had been the first to use illuminated plastics in its design; after wartime shutdown designer Paul Fuller produced the most famous jukebox of all, the Model 1015, of which Wurlitzer shipped over 56,000. Nils Miller at Seeburg was another influential designer. Paradoxically, these masterpieces of kitsch are rare and valuable today because they were too well built to wear out; Wurlitzer accepted trade-ins of any make, and then destroyed them.

Early in the Depression the record companies were not slow to understand the importance of the jukebox business. In many parts of the country hillbillies and blacks were more likely to hear their own recording artists on a jukebox than on the radio; people who could not afford to buy a radio could sip a beer and listen to music played by other people's coins in the jukebox. The jukebox used up so many records that it rescued the record industry from the Depression, and retail sales began to improve as people liked the records they heard on jukeboxes, at a time when recorded music on the radio was not yet omnipresent. Small-group jazz was ideal: small-group recordings were cheaper to make than big-band ones, especially if the musicians were black.

Coleman Hawkins and Henry 'Red' Allen co-led three sessions in 1933 that resulted in ten lovely sides aimed at this market. Allen's first recordings in 1929 were credited to Henry Allen, Jr, and his Orchestra, because his father was a prominent New Orleans bandleader. The trumpeter worked for Fletcher Henderson and many other leaders, and was unfairly but widely regarded as an Armstrong imitator for many years; in fact, he was always his own man, and in the mid-1950s, on reunion sessions with Hawkins, sounded as much like Miles Davis as he did like Armstrong. He was also a vocalist of great charm, and the ten 1933 sides capture an era that is gone for ever. Made quickly and cheaply for budget labels like Perfect and Banner, and with whichever sidemen they could pick up (such as Russell Procope, Dicky Wells, Benny Morton and Horace Henderson on some tracks), the recordings are mostly of Tin Pan Alley songs that white artists had turned down.

The most successful small group of all, both on the jukeboxes and in the charts, was led by the pianist who was nicknamed Filthy by his friends in Harlem. Thomas Wright 'Fats' Waller played the piano by ear as a child, slowing down a piano roll to learn 'Carolina Shout'. He then enlisted James P. Johnson as his teacher, who also became something of a substitute father. Waller's father was a lay preacher who could not control his wayward son; they did not get along, and Fats probably never got over the loss of his mother when he was a teenager. He developed an enormous appetite for food, drink, women and song that he could never restrain, and an outsized talent to match.

As a teenager playing the organ in a Harlem cinema he gave some lessons to a boy from Red Bank named William Basie. Later he studied formally himself, knowing that he had to discipline his talent. He made piano rolls, and his first (acoustic) gramophone sides were piano solos, 'Muscle Shoals Blues' and 'Birmingham Blues' (1922). He also accompanied blues singers such as Caroline Johnson ('Ain't Got Nobody to Grind My Coffee'), Alberta Hunter ('You Can't Do What My Last Man Did') and Sara Martin. Having written 'Squeeze

Me' with Clarence Williams, he accompanied Clarence and Sara in duets ('Squabbling Blues', 'I'm Certainly Gonna See About That').

He worked in Chicago in 1925, jamming with Louis Armstrong and Earl Hines, and playing solo piano at a hotel; he told a story about being kidnapped to play at a birthday party for Al Capone, who stuffed hundred-dollar bills in his pocket. In November 1926 he began recording for Ralph Peer on the pipe organ in a disused church in Camden, New Jersey; Handy's 'St Louis Blues' and Waller's own 'Lenox Avenue Stomp' were good enough to get him invited back. Early in 1927 he recorded a series of improvisations with titles like 'Soothin' Syrup Stomp' and 'Sloppy Water Blues'; counting alternative takes, there were fifteen tracks. Let loose with feet as well as hands on what he called the instrument of his heart, he was already a giant talent; the sheer beauty and obvious joy in music-making on the unusual instrument is unlike anything else ever recorded. In May he recorded 'Sugar', a Tin Pan Alley hit that has had many recordings, Handy's 'Beale Street Blues' and 'I'm Goin' to See My Ma', credited on record labels to one C. Todd: all three were recorded both as organ solos and on organ with vocals by Alberta Hunter. 'I'm Goin' to See My Ma (and try to find my pa)' is a sort of happy tear-jerker: you can see Alberta there on the railway platform, at the height of the Jazz Age and just before the Great Depression, perhaps with a cardboard suitcase tied up with clothes-line, happy to be going home, the place where they have to let you in.

Further sessions in 1927 yielded more organ solos, notably a beautiful 'I Ain't Got Nobody', as well as a few piano solos and some organ sides with a combo. In 1928 Waller played 'Beale Street Blues' on the organ at Carnegie Hall (with Handy's blessing), and played piano with an orchestra in a performance of James P. Johnson's *Yamekraw*. (Johnson was not allowed the night off from conducting *Keep Shufflin'*.)

In 1929 came Fats Waller and his Buddies. In *We Called It Music* Eddie Condon tells the story of being detailed to get Fats to the recording session in New York on the first day of March. Condon got him out of bed, fortified with liquid ham'n'eggs and into a taxi, where he wrote the quintet numbers 'The Minor Drag' and 'Harlem Fuss', the titles of which were reversed on the record: 'Harlem Fuss' is a slow drag, while 'The Minor Drag' is a romp. At the same session he recorded piano solos 'Numb Fumblin'' and 'Handful of Keys'. Among other solo piano recordings is 'Ain't Misbehavin'', which he had written for *Hot Chocolates* that year; Waller's recording, and those by Louis Armstrong, bandleader Leo Reisman, Gene Austin, Ruth Etting and Bill Robinson with Irving Mills, were all hits. Another solo was 'Valentine Stomp', a tribute to Hazel Valentine, who ran a Harlem good-time house called the Daisy Chain where Fats liked to hang out. (It was later also celebrated in Count Basie's 'Swingin' at the Daisy Chain'.)

At the end of the year there were more Buddies sessions, this time with a bigger band, including Condon, Red Allen and Jack Teagarden, and singers. 'Looking Good But Feelin' Bad' and 'I Need Someone Like You', both Waller songs, are sung by a male quartet, while 'Ridin' But Walkin'' and 'Won't You Get Up Off It, Please?' were instrumentals and 'When I'm Alone' (not a Waller song) had a pop vocal by one Orlando Robinson. Still another session the same month, by 'Jimmie Johnson and his Orchestra', featured two songs by J. C. (Jimmie) Johnson (another pianist, who probably used his initials so as not to be confused with James P.): 'You've Got to be Modernistic' and 'You Don't Understand' were sung by a male trio (the latter a sweet ballad also recorded by Bessie Smith). In the band were King Oliver, Dave Nelson and both James P. and Waller on pianos.

In the same year crooner Gene Austin bailed Waller out of jail. According to Maurice Waller, the judge was angry because Waller persistently fell behind with his alimony payments, and Waller was let off because Austin told the judge that Waller was needed at a recording session that afternoon, and that if he was not there, it would put several men out of work. So Waller went along to the session, where he and Austin (himself a southerner) were dismayed to find that the other musicians would not play with 'Austin's nigger', who had to be put at the other end of the studio behind a screen, and with a separate microphone. The song recorded was Waller's 'Your Fate is in My Hands', with words by Billy Rose.

The record dates dried up as the Depression began to bite. There were two piano duets with Bennie Payne on Victor in 1930, and two pianos solos on Columbia in 1931, on which he sang, accompanied by himself, his own songs 'I'm Crazy 'Bout My Baby (and My Baby's Crazy 'Bout Me)' (words by Alex Hill) and 'Draggin' My Poor Heart Around', revealing a charming high baritone. The Lion claimed credit for getting Fats to sing, but his writing partner Andy Razaf said that when they went the rounds of publishers hawking their songs, Fats's singing would sell them better than his own. (Andreamenentania Paul Razafinkeriefo was descended from the royal family of Madagascar.)

Tunes poured out of Waller, but he was profligate in more ways than one, and often sold songs outright when he needed money; the suspicion persists that he sold famous tunes to Jimmy McHugh. Publishers frequently paid an advance to acquire a song, but would then forget to pay royalties; Waller and Razaf got their own back by selling the same lead sheet to several different publishers, sometimes all in the same building on the same day. They wrote scores of songs that were never even published, but their best known, apart from 'Ain't Misbehavin'', include: '(What Did I Do to be So) Black and Blue', an affecting song that takes a swipe at racism, also used in *Hot Chocolates* and superbly recorded by Louis Armstrong; 'Honeysuckle Rose', from the same year (1929), which seems to have been a variation on 'Tea for Two' (he interpolated them on a piano solo in 1937); 'Blue, Turning Grey Over You', 'Keepin' Out of Mischief Now' and 'Ain't-cha Glad?' Razaf wrote words for tunes by many other composers.

Waller also wrote 'I've Got a Feeling I'm Falling' with Rose, and recorded it with the Rhythmakers and vocalist Billy Banks (who had a talent for happy scat and recorded under a great many names with a different line-up each time). Waller recorded with Don Redman's studio groups, Red McKenzie and Ted Lewis; a recording with one of Jack Teagarden's studio bands is notable for the repartee between Teagarden and Waller on 'You Rascal You' and 'That's What I Like About You'. He played the organ for a popular late-night radio programme in Cincinnati (and in the morning the cleaner had to remove several empty gin bottles).

In 1934, as the new jukebox industry was beginning to take off and the record business struggled out of the Depression, Victor

invited him back, to record with a combo as Fats Waller and his
Rhythm, and jukebox as well as jazz history was made. The group
included guitarist Al Casey (a teenager when Waller hired him), Gene
'Honey Bear' Sedric on reeds (one of Sam Wooding's favourite
players in his European band), Bill Coleman and then Herman
Autrey on trumpet, Charles Turner or (later) Cedric Wallace on bass
and Slick Jones, Yank Porter or Harry Dial on drums. They were an
instant success.

The songs from Broadway shows that we now regard as standards
were not often pop hits at the time, but for the first few years
Waller's hits came from some of the era's best Tin Pan Alley hacks.
Among Waller's 1934 sessions were James P. Johnson's charming 'A
Porter's Love Song to a Chambermaid' (words by Razaf) and 'I Wish
I Were Twins', by Edgar DeLange (of Hudson and DeLange), with
words by Frank Loesser, one of the great lyricists; 'Two Sleepy
People', written by Loesser and Hoagy Carmichael, was a number one
hit for Waller in 1938. Loesser wrote dummy tunes for his own lyrics
until his own 'Praise the Lord and Pass the Ammunition' was a huge
wartime hit; from then on he wrote both words and music, creating
such songs as 'Baby It's Cold Outside' and 'On a Slow Boat to China'.
His masterpiece, the show *Guys and Dolls* (1950), which included 'If I
Were a Bell', was followed by *The Most Happy Fella* (1956) and *How
To Succeed in Business Without Really Trying* (1961).

Also from 1934 came Waller and Razaf's 'How Can You Face Me',
together with the pop songs 'Then I'll Be Tired of You', 'Don't Let
It Bother You', 'Sweetie Pie' and 'Believe It, Beloved'. Like Billie
Holiday, Waller recorded tunes that were new at the time; nobody
knew whether they would be hits or not, and some survived only
because he recorded them, such as 'Dream Man (Let Me Dream
Some More)' and 'Do Me a Favor (Marry Me)'. Among the writers
were J. C. Johnson, who wrote 'Believe It, Beloved', as well as
Bessie Smith's 'Empty Bed Blues' and 'Dusky Stevedore' (recorded
by Frankie Trumbauer with Bix and many others). Mack Gordon
wrote 'Don't Let It Bother You' (suitable for the recovery period:
'Take it on the chin / Give a little grin / Everything will be okay!').
Arthur Schwartz and Yip Harburg wrote 'Then I'll Be Tired of
You'; Schwartz wrote 'Got a Bran' New Suit' and many more

with lyricist Howard Dietz. Dietz also wrote with Kern, Gershwin, Vernon Duke and Sammy Fain; Harburg wrote 'April in Paris' with Vernon Duke and, with Harold Arlen, 'It's Only a Paper Moon', 'Happiness is Just a Thing Called Joe' and the songs for *The Wizard of Oz*.

Nobody did more than Fats Waller, except Louis Armstrong himself, to bring jazz to popular music. If he liked a song, he could do it more or less straight, but he often kidded a song unmercifully, improvising his own additions to the lyrics as well as vocal ejaculations during instrumental breaks and bridges. Often he would blurt out (sometimes salacious) tag-lines at the end, such as 'No, Lady, we can't haul your ashes for twenty-five cents. That'd be bad business.' 'I'm Gonna Sit Right Down and Write Myself a Letter', a sweet love song by Fred Ahlert and Joe Young, was played straight. 'Truckin'' was written for a Cotton Club revue by Rube Bloom and Ted Koehler; it became a dance fad (a sequel was 'Let's Get Drunk and Truck', by Tampa Red in 1936). 'All My Life' was a pretty ballad by Sidney Mitchell and Sammy Stept that had several hit recordings, including one by Teddy Wilson with Ella Fitzgerald. 'A Little Bit Independent' was by Edgar Leslie and Joe Burke. As is often true of the pop charts, the best records were not usually the biggest hits, but the Waller number one 'It's a Sin to Tell a Lie' (by Billy Mayhew) is an exception: an uptempo romp, it suited the full Waller treatment: 'Get on out there and tell your lie,' he demands of Sedric before his clarinet solo, and ends with one of his favourite tags, 'What'd I say?!'

Waller was his own worst enemy, so profligate that he was always in need of money. The jukebox operators naturally preferred to buy cheaper records, and in 1939 Victor transferred Waller to its cheaper Bluebird label, the better to compete with Kapp's Decca label for the mechanical business. For whatever reason, towards the end of his career some of the songs were so bad that not even he could save them: 'Little Curly Hair in a High Chair', 'My Mommie Sent Me to the Store', 'Abercrombie Had a Zombie'. But the jazz content was nearly always present, and there are an extraordinary number of gems: definitive versions of delightful songs like 'Lulu's Back in Town' (by Al Dubin and Harry Warren), 'Rosetta' (by Earl Hines, on which Fats plays celesta), 'I Believe in Miracles' (organ), 'What's the Reason I'm Not Pleasin' You?', 'There'll be Some Changes Made', 'I Used to Love You (But It's All Over Now)', 'I'll Dance at Your Wedding' (with the tag 'Go on, get married again') and 'The Curse of an Aching Heart' ('Bump, bump, bump, bump! That's the curse back at ya!'). The mixture of jazz, jive and beauty is unique. 'Your Feet's Too Big', a charming non-love song with the tag 'One never knows, do one?', was a hit in 1939, followed by 'Your Socks Don't Match' and 'Hold Tight (I Want Some Sea Food, Mama)'. (Few knew that the last celebrated cunnilingus.)

The canard is heard that Waller's sidemen were somehow second-rate; certainly his group did not survive the loss of one of the most ebullient musical personalities of the century, but again and again on the recordings his men played exquisitely apposite solos. Waller himself is still admired, for example by Cecil Taylor 'for the depth of his notes'. There were more piano solos, among them 'Clothes Line Ballet', 'Alligator Crawl', 'African Ripples', Duke Ellington's 'Ring Dem Bells' and 'Carolina Shout'.

Waller visited Europe twice; in London in 1938 he recorded pipe organ solos and with such sidemen as trombonist George Chisholm and drummer Edmundo Ros (later the leader of a popular Latin-American band). On a 1939 trip he recorded again on pipe organ and also the *London Suite*, a set of six impressions borrowing themes here and there from some of his other tunes. In Paris he played the organ at the Cathedral of Notre-Dame, an experience at the 'God box' that he regarded as one of the great honours of his life.

He led a big band on one tour. He also recorded with a protégée, pianist and vocalist Una Mae Carlisle, who sang straight to Waller's clowning on 'I Can't Give You Anything But Love' (1939). He made recordings both solo and with his combo for Muzak (the recordings were unreleased for years) and on V-discs for the armed services, including 'The Reefer Song' ('I dreamed about a reefer five feet long . . .'). At his own Carnegie Hall concert in January 1942 he was almost too drunk to play the second half. In December of 1943 his body gave up the struggle, and he died of pneumonia on a train between engagements. He was only thirty-nine.

Following Victor's jukebox success with Waller's records, John Hammond talked Brunswick into a series of small-group sides led by pianist Teddy Wilson, who acted as a contractor, hiring whichever musicians happened to be in town for each date. Wilson, who was from a middle-class background, left college to become a full-time musician; his first recordings as a soloist in 1934 were rejected by Columbia, who did not appreciate his understated elegance, a stylistic influence for generations. From July 1935 to 1942, however, he made nearly three hundred sides for Brunswick, many featuring vocalists such as Ella Fitzgerald, Lena Horne and, above all, Billie Holiday. None of the participants received any royalties, but the records were so popular that the following year Brunswick began recording Holiday under her own name. From late 1937 Wilson was often replaced on Holiday's records by Claude Thornhill, Eddie Heywood and others, but her sessions did not stray far from Wilson's original conception.

Billie Holiday was born Elinore Harris in Philadelphia; neither her mother nor her maternal grandmother had been married, so the surname had passed down on the female side for three generations. Her father, Clarence Holiday, played guitar with Fletcher Henderson and Don Redman. She had a turbulent early life, in many ways the opposite of that of the urbane, well-educated Wilson, but, like him, she had an innate dignity that never left her, and she was a very great jazz musician. When she was young, her voice was pretty and sweet, but it already had the unique vocal colour that was all that remained when she died; if the essence of singing popular songs is to interpret them, she was one of the greatest pop singers who ever lived. She was certainly the essence of languor, always singing behind the beat; she brought high spirits, a laid-back sexiness or deep sadness to her work, depending on the song, but always showed a yearning wistfulness.

Her first recordings were sides with a Benny Goodman studio group in 1933. When she sang on Wilson's first session, she was just twenty, and he was twenty-two: 'Miss Brown to You' and 'What a Little Moonlight Can Do' became classics. Holiday's soul-mate was Lester Young. It is said that they were never lovers, but his solos with her vocals on tracks like 'A Sailboat in the Moonlight', 'On the Sentimental Side', 'Back in Your Own Back Yard' and 'When a Woman Loves a Man' (all 1937) were the musical equivalent of making love. He named her Lady Day, and called her mother the Duchess; she named him Prez, thinking that along with a Duke, an Earl, a Count and a King of Swing there ought to be a President.

Holiday recorded for Milt Gabler's Commodore label, and then for Decca, which backed her with strings: like many jazz artists of that era, she hankered after legitimacy, in the belief that string arrangements bestowed a cachet. In the 1950s she recorded for Verve and CBS (strings conducted by Ray Ellis), and toured Europe; her excellent accompanists included Bobby Tucker, Jimmy Rowles and Mal Waldron. Her career went slowly downhill; she was famous for being a heroin addict, but it was alcohol that killed her, in 1959. Even her later performances were extraordinarily moving. On a famous Timex TV jazz programme in 1957 she sang her own 'Fine and Mellow', and Young was there too; they had not long to live, and little to say to each other, except through their music.

There are too many masterpieces among Wilson's sides to describe them all, but among the highlights is a Chicago session of May 1936, which featured the bass player Israel Crosby, still a teenager, notably on the dramatic 'Blues in C Sharp Minor'; 'Warmin' Up' is a high-spirited tribute to the small-group jazz style just before modern jazz began to evolve. An unusual West Coast date in September 1937, with Wilson, Red Norvo on xylophone, John Simmons on bass and Harry James on trumpet, yielded intimate treatments of Waller's 'Honeysuckle Rose' and 'Ain't Misbehavin''. 'Just a Mood', which stretched to two sides of a 10-inch 78, was an unusually beautiful original.

The success of Wilson's contractor method of making records may have inspired Victor to hire Lionel Hampton to do the same thing in 1937. In his youth Hampton played snare drum in a drum and bugle corps and became a newsboy in Chicago so he could beat the drum in a band sponsored by the *Chicago Defender*. Somewhere along the way he also became familiar with the marimba, and soon hit the road as a drummer; he first recorded in 1929 with Paul Johnson's Quality Serenaders. As a member of Les Hite's band when it backed Louis Armstrong in a Los Angeles club Hampton played Louis's solo from 'Song of the Islands' on orchestral bells, and when the band backed Louis on his recording of 'Memories of You',

Hampton was encouraged to become the first jazzman to record playing the vibraphone. Gladys, his ambitious soon-to-be wife, prompted him to concentrate on it. A few years later he was leading a band at the Paradise Club, and among the musicians sitting in were Benny Goodman, Gene Krupa and Wilson. The Goodman quartet first recorded in August 1936, and both Wilson and Hampton became famous.

Hampton was more of a showman than Wilson, and moved from chair to chair on various sides. Most of his nearly a hundred small-group items were instrumental, except where he himself sang, as on the charming 'I'm Confessin' (That I Love You)' (the original issue of which was backed with 'Drum Stomp', based on 'Crazy Rhythm', with Hamp on drums) and 'On the Sunny Side of the Street'. One of his best-known records, the latter featured Johnny Hodges, and was backed with an uptempo romp on Vincent Youmans's 'I Know That You Know'. From the same date as 'Drum Stomp' came 'Piano Stomp' (based on 'Shine'), and Hampton also played piano on 'Twelfth Street Rag' (1939) at what seemed like an incredibly fast tempo, yet it was not too fast for his fleet two-fingered style. He played the right-hand piano part on 'Wizzin' the Wizz' while Clyde Hart played the left-hand part, and drums on 'Big Jam in the Wigwam' while Cozy Cole concentrated on the tom-toms.

Among the musicians at a session in September 1939 were Benny Carter, Coleman Hawkins, Chu Berry and Ben Webster, as well as the young Dizzy Gillespie, and Charlie Christian in the rhythm section; that date included 'Hot Mallets' and Carter's 'When Lights are Low'. The parade of sidemen used on the Wilson and Hampton records names most of the stars of the bands of Ellington, Basie, Calloway and Goodman. Pianist Jess Stacy was an asset at the first few Hampton sessions, and Hampton used no fewer than eleven of the best drummers of the era, not counting himself. The rhythm section on 'Jack the Bellboy' and 'Central Avenue Breakdown', made in Hollywood in 1940, was the Nat Cole Trio. 'Bellboy' has at least three hands on the keyboard.

As Stanley Dance pointed out in his notes for an RCA set of the complete Hampton sessions, one of the joys of the recordings is the chance to hear musicians who were not recorded often enough.

Dance singles out pianist Marlowe Morris, who was influenced by Art Tatum. Hampton's showmanship was always evident, and as his series wore on, along with all the beautiful jazz there was much joyful jive, with some forward-sounding harmonies and more than a hint of the West Coast rhythm and blues that would soon be under way. Listen, for example, to '(Latch on to Some) Dough-rey-mi', written by Southern, Cole and Hampton, and sung by the 'Hampton Rhythm Boys'. The interaction of Cole's piano and Hampton's vibraphone on this track occasionally predicts the sound of the George Shearing Quintet, which would be enormously popular a decade later. Another interesting thing about the whole series is the guitar players, from the quiet competence of Goodman's sideman Allen Reuss to Danny Barker, Charlie Christian, Al Casey, Freddie Green, Ernest Ashley, Teddy Bunn, Irving Ashby and Cole's Oscar Moore, several of whom played electric instruments.

The Nat Cole Trio used an uncommon instrumentation: piano, guitar and bass. The drummer didn't show up for their first gig, and they decided they didn't need one. Cole later became one of the most popular vocalists in the world, and deservedly so, but the trio's records did well on the jukeboxes, and it is too easily forgotten that his modern-sounding Hines-inspired keyboard was very influential, on such different musicians as Oscar Peterson and Bill Evans.

Hampton formed a big band which began recording for Decca in late 1941, and led it well into the 1950s. It was a crowd-pleaser – critics often ridiculed its theatrical aspect – but among its stars was young tenor saxophonist Illinois Jacquet. (Critics overlooked his skill as a ballad player for years because it didn't fit their thesis of Jacquet as a honker; he began recording as a leader in 1945, and in 1988 led a big band at jazz festivals.) Hampton was still a sure bet in the late 1980s if you wanted to have a good time; his ability to swing and to inspire younger musicians has had an incalculable effect.

An unusual and successful sextet was that of bass player John Kirby, the 'biggest little band in the land'. The group began to come together as 52nd Street in New York became a meeting place for jazz fans. On their first hit record (as the Claude Thornhill Orchestra in 1937) they backed Maxine Sullivan singing 'Loch Lomond'; that band included Thornhill (piano and arranger), Frankie Newton (trumpet), Pete Brown (alto saxophone), Babe Russin (tenor saxophone), Buster Bailey (clarinet), Kirby (double bass) and O'Neill Spencer (drums). They were Buster Bailey and his Rhythm Busters with slightly different personnel, then John Kirby and his Onyx Club Boys with the classic line-up, and later John Kirby and his Orchestra: Kirby, Spencer, Bailey, Charlie Shavers (trumpet), Russell Procope (alto saxophone) and Billy Kyle (piano). Shavers's composition 'Undecided' was a hit in 1939; Shavers was almost as highly regarded as Roy Eldridge then, and also wrote 'Pastel Blue'; most of the Kirby group's arrangements were his.

Kirby and Sullivan were married, and the band became one of the most successful black groups in the country, performing at high-class hotel dates and on a radio show called *Flow Gently Sweet Rhythm*, on which Sullivan sang folksongs such as 'If I Had a Ribbon Bow' and 'Molly Malone' (recorded under her name for a different label). The group also appeared on *Duffy's Tavern* and the *Chamber Music Society of Lower Basin Street*, a popular pseudo-jazz radio spot directed by NBC staffer Henry 'Hot Lips' Levine; it featured Dinah Shore, and had guests like Sidney Bechet and Jelly Roll Morton. All this was extraordinary exposure for a black band, and a tribute to its musical qualities. It was a quiet chamber group (Shavers usually played with a mute) and the arrangements, though tricky and highly stylized, were studded with lively solos. Its similarity to Wilson's stemmed from its elegance and the presence of Billy Kyle, who worked with Louis Armstrong's All Stars from 1953. Anybody who played with that group in its later years was taken for granted, but Kyle had already been an influential and underrated stylist for many years by then. His technique was the equal of Wilson's, but he had a brighter and more rhythmic side, perhaps influenced by Earl Hines. As J. R. Taylor put it in a sleeve-note for the Smithsonian Institution: 'Kyle's rising tremolo lunge behind Bailey [in 'Sweet Georgia Brown'] is probably unique in jazz accompaniment before Cecil Taylor.'

Kirby and Sullivan were divorced, the war wrecked the band's line-up and the post-war world was not interested: the group's big success lasted only a couple of years, and its style had no sequel. This was partly for the same reason that such excellent musicians as

Shavers, Billy Butterfield, Roy Eldridge, Rex Stewart and Red Allen were, in general, not as highly rewarded as they should have been. After the war there was an absurd critical division into 'dixieland' and 'modern' camps, so that the great mainstream graduates of the Swing Era got lost in the shuffle, a loss which record companies and broadcasters did nothing to prevent.

Procope, of course, subsequently played for twenty-eight years with Duke Ellington; Shavers played in the interracial studio band of Raymond Scott (later music director on the radio and television chart show *Your Hit Parade*, whose vocalist, Dorothy Collins, he married). Scott's arrangements, for example, 'In an Eighteenth Century Dining Room' and 'Dinner Music for a Pack of Hungry Cannibals', were slick and intricate, like Kirby's, but had little jazz content. Shavers remained popular among those with long memories. On a tour in England in 1969, according to Digby Fairweather, he was playing brilliantly, and was delighted to find electrical sockets in hotel bathrooms marked 'For Shavers Only'. He said, 'Wait till Eldridge sees this!'

52nd Street, New York, became a place where the amount of good music to be heard was almost unbelievable. One of the first big acts on the Street, just as Prohibition was repealed in 1933, was scat singer Leo Watson and his Five Spirits of Rhythm, a group which used a suitcase as a drum and played with whisk brooms and three tipples (novelty guitars that sounded like ukuleles). Brass players Joe Riley and Eddie Farley used a novelty tune in their act on the Street; 'The Music Goes Round and Round (and It Comes Out Here)' suddenly became a huge fluke hit, and the Riley–Farley Orchestra had one of the money-making versions. Violinist Stuff Smith and his Onyx Club Boys, with Jonah Jones on trumpet and Cozy Cole on drums, made a name on the Street in 1936 with 'I'se a Muggin'' and 'You'se a Viper' (with a vocal by Jones). The Kirby Sextet too started on the Street. By the early 1940s Art Tatum, Billie Holiday, Coleman Hawkins, Fats Waller and many more might virtually all be heard playing on the Street at once. The Street was mostly a venue for small groups, but Count Basie's band first made it big there in 1937 at the Famous Door (whose name derived from an old door it had which was covered with autographs). Other clubs, mostly in what were called 'English basements' under brownstone houses, included the Hickory House, the Yacht Club, Kelly's Stable and the Three Deuces. The Street was so successful that musicians starting a club where they could meet were soon pushed out of their own place by the tourists and fans. Today the brownstones have been replaced by steel and glass buildings occupied by banks.

Independent labels were being formed for the specific purpose of recording small-group jazz; the first one in the USA was Commodore. Milt Gabler began selling records in his father's radio shop in New York in 1926; the Commodore Music Shop became a hang-out for fans and musicians, and the records soon replaced the radio parts. Gabler was responsible for several firsts: his was probably the first record shop to have browsing bins arranged by artist, and he was the first to reissue classic discs. He began by custom-ordering pressings of out-of-print records, because he knew he could sell three hundred copies of, say, 'Pinetop's Boogie Woogie', even if it took a couple of years. But in the case of that title Vocalion decided that if Gabler wanted to buy so many copies of it, they would press a few extra and sell them to his competitors. So Gabler formed the first record club, the United Hot Clubs of America. He also hired jazz clubs on Sunday afternoons offering free jam sessions to music fans. (When other clubs copied Gabler, they charged admission, but still did not pay the musicians.)

The world's first specialized jazz record label was Swing in France, which began because not enough jazz records were available there. The first release in 1937 was the legendary Benny Carter session. 'Honeysuckle Rose' and 'Crazy Rhythm' were played by a line-up that Carter has re-created several times: himself and Alix Combelle on alto saxophones and Coleman Hawkins and André Ekyan on tenor; the rhythm section included Django Reinhardt on guitar, Stéphane Grappelly on piano, Eugène D'Hellemes on bass and Tommy Benford on drums. In January 1938 Gabler's first recording session was with Eddie Condon and his Windy City Seven: Pee Wee Russell, Bud Freeman, Bobby Hackett, drummer George Wettling, bassist Artie Bernstein and Jess Stacy (whose hands were still sore the day after Benny Goodman's Carnegie Hall concert). The hornmen were all among the finest musicians of their generation, but still underrated by the general public because they were not recorded often enough or properly promoted by the music industry, interested then as now primarily in a fast buck. Gabler was also the first to list the complete personnel on the record label.

In April 1939 Columbia lent Billie Holiday to Commodore because they did not want to issue 'Strange Fruit', a song by poet Lewis Allen about lynching, which Billie had made up her mind to record. An early protest recording, its tragic power is undiminished today. The backing band, with which Billie was appearing at Café Society, was led by trumpeter Frankie Newton, who had left the Kirby Sextet just as it went on to its great success (he and Kirby were rivals for the affection of Maxine Sullivan). Café Society, a club started by a shoe salesman named Barney Josephson, with some help and advice from John Hammond and others, was a place which practised discrimination only in favour of good music, and was popular for a decade. One of the other sides made that day was 'Fine and Mellow', which Gabler titled and helped to write; it was intended to be similar to 'Billie's Blues', which Holiday had recorded in 1936 at her first session as a leader. When Decca Records rang to inquire about the new song, Gabler knew that it must be getting jukebox plays, and he quickly registered its composition in Holiday's name before any covers were made.

From 1941 Gabler also worked for Decca; but he kept Commodore going into the 1950s. The complete Commodore reissue programme embarked upon by Mosaic Records of Stamford, Connecticut, in 1988, which fills dozens of LPs in three massive sets, is full of priceless material, the peak of which (for me, anyway) is the previously mentioned Kansas City Six session of September 1938, with Lester Young playing gorgeous clarinet (on a metal instrument), Buck Clayton on trumpet, Eddie Durham on electric guitar and Basie's rhythm section of Freddie Green, Walter Page and Jo Jones. Not to mention fourteen solos by Willie 'the Lion' Smith, Coleman Hawkins sides, clarinet quartet recordings by Edmond Hall and Pee Wee Russell, and too much more to list here.

When Harry Lim emigrated to the USA from Batavia (now Djakarta) in Indonesia in 1939, he was already a jazz fan. He began producing jam sessions and from 1943 produced records for Eric

Bernay's Keynote, until then a left-wing folk label which had recorded the Almanac Singers. One of the first jazz dates at Keynote was also the first solo session by Dinah Washington, a unique and still influential vocalist who had been discovered and re-named by Lionel Hampton. (Her real name was Ruth Lee Jones.) Leonard Feather produced the date and wrote most of the material; 'Salty Papa' and 'Evil Gal Blues' were hits in the black chart. The group from Hampton's band included Texas tenor saxophonist Arnett Cobb (making his recording début) and pianist Milt Buckner (later more famous as an organist, who had invented the 'locked hands' chordal keyboard style that was soon done to death by a generation of keyboard players). Hampton came along to help out, playing drums on one of the four sides recorded and piano on another. The best-known (and best-selling) Lim productions were those by Lester Young at a session of four tunes, made the day before the Dinah Washington date, in a quartet with Johnny Guarnieri, Slam Stewart and Sid Catlett. It was bettered only by four more tracks three months later, this time 12-inch 78s by a quintet with Basie and his rhythm section. The one track of which an alternative take was not made is 'Lester Leaps In' – it was perfect in one take.

In less than four years Lim made well over three hundred sides. His main aim was to indulge himself (though it earned him everlasting gratitude from jazz fans) by recording people who did not get many chances to record, such as trumpeter Joe Thomas, Chicago guitarist George Barnes, Milt Hinton, Willie Smith, Babe Russin, Manny Klein, tenor saxophonist Herbie Haymer and several members of the Woody Herman herd, including trombonist Bill Harris and bass player Chubby Jackson; also Red Norvo, trumpeters Jonah Jones and Roy Eldridge, Gene Sedric, Red Rodney . . . and too many more to list.

Of the several fine Coleman Hawkins dates, the most fascinating is the one with the Sax Ensemble of May 1944, at which 12-inch 78s were made. The group comprised Catlett (drums), Guarnieri (piano), Al Lucas (double bass), Tab Smith (alto saxophone and arranger – he had worked for Basie and Millinder, among others), Hawkins and Don Byas (tenor saxophones) and Harry Carney (baritone saxophone). The septet sounds like a much larger group, thanks to Smith's arrangements and the sound of four great reedmen playing together. To pick out just one track: 'On the Sunny Side of the Street' begins with a Smith solo (very different from that of Johnny Hodges on the classic recording of the same tune made by Lionel Hampton several years earlier) and ends with a dazzling Smith cadenza, which is several seconds longer on the second take and perfectly realized.

Keynote went out with a bang: two trio sessions by the young pianist Lennie Tristano, the last produced by Feather. Tristano's advanced harmonic ideas were enormously influential, but he concentrated on teaching rather than performing, and recorded all too little; the Keynote sessions yielded tracks that were not released for decades. Lim lost control (to Mercury Records) of recordings he had made using much of his own money; he later worked at the Liberty Music Shop (which, like Commodore, had its own label for a while) and, in its heyday from 1956 to 1973, for Sam Goody's record shop, where he was renowned as the world's most knowledgeable record-shop assistant. In 1972 he formed the Famous Door label and was one of those responsible for discovering Scott Hamilton, today's enormously popular Swing Era style tenor saxophonist.

Other independent jazz labels of the period included HRS (Hot Record Society), Solo Art (which recorded, among others, Chicago's Jimmy Yancey, one of the most distinctive of boogie-woogie piano players, with the accent on the blues rather than the boogie), Bob Thiele's Signature label and, the most famous of all, Blue Note. Thiele worked as an announcer on jazz radio shows in 1936, was a bandleader, editor and publisher of *Jazz Magazine*, and formed Signature in 1939, when he was still a teenager. He was among the first to record pianist Erroll Garner, and made small-group dates by Coleman Hawkins, Lester Young, Lockjaw Davis and Julian Dash. Some of the Hawkins and Young sides were 12-inch masters; it was typical of these small labels to attempt to give the artists room to blow, even though 12-inch records were less commercially viable. It was a Signature recording of Davis's 'Lockjaw' that gave him his nickname. Dash had played with Erskine Hawkins, and his tracks for Signature, with Kyle on piano, are fascinating examples of what was intended to get on Harlem jukeboxes in 1950; the smoochy 'My Silent Love' is drenched in echo.

Thiele also recorded four sessions in 1944–5 by Flip Phillips, tenor saxophone star of Woody Herman's band, with other Hermanites in the backing groups. Three sessions with Anita O'Day in 1947–8 paid a dividend: the novelty 'Hi Ho Trailus Boot Whip', arranged by Sy Oliver, was a pop hit.

Blue Note, the best-known of these labels, was formed by German immigrant Alfred Lion in 1939 to record the boogie-woogie pianos of Meade 'Lux' Lewis and Albert Ammons. The Port of Harlem Jazzmen included Ammons, then Lewis, Frankie Newton and, on some tracks, Sidney Bechet, whose 'Summertime' was an instant classic. Lion was joined by his fellow Berliner and childhood friend, Frank Wolff. In 1941 they recorded Edmond Hall's quartet: Hall, Lewis (celesta – they recorded him on harpsichord the same year), Israel Crosby (bass) and Charlie Christian (acoustic guitar). Its 'Profoundly Blue' was a classic. Blue Note too made 12-inch sides. They often recorded at night, which was far more convenient for the musicians, and provided food and drink for them. The unusual attention to the artists' welfare and the distinctive label artwork (overseen by Wolff) heralded the beginning of an illustrious chapter in the record business. The label specialized in 'swingtets' led by tenor saxophonists John Hardee and Ike Quebec, whose 'Blue Harlem' (1944) was another jukebox hit. Quebec joined the staff, and it was due partly to his influence that Blue Note was the first to record Thelonious Monk as a leader, in 1947.

But that is getting ahead of our story. Blue Note was only one of the mostly independent labels documenting the changes in popular music in the 1940s, a decade that needs close attention.

11

The 1940s: War and Other Calamities

The war years are remembered both in Britain and in the USA as an egalitarian time. In Britain food rationing and fairer distribution brought about the best diet some of the population had ever seen, and illnesses such as rickets, caused by poor nutrition, began to disappear. In the USA country boy and city slicker alike served in the armed forces; dance bands and black artists like Fats Waller and Art Tatum made V-discs for the GIs' jukeboxes; and all were exposed to each other's cultures *en masse* for the first time.

The combination of world war and music business shenanigans caused profound changes in music itself. The history of the music business is studded with instances of panic, doomsaying and dramatic events, and the participants themselves – be they music publisher, president of the American Society of Composers, Authors and Publishers (ASCAP) or a lawyer working for BMI – were often outsized personalities. In the late 1920s, for example, it was thought that Tin Pan Alley was moving to Hollywood, and that if the film producers took over completely, it would be the end of ASCAP. The constant buying and selling of music publishing houses was often due to jockeying for power in the industry, which began to worry about how charges would be made for television music years before most people had ever seen a television set. Solutions usually failed to foresee new problems, and some of the disputes directly affected the nature of the music. The decade of the 1940s, while dominated by the war, provided two cases in which self-interested organizations forced changes which had totally unexpected results and were not welcomed by those whose interests were supposedly being served: the ASCAP strike against broadcasters and the musicians' union strikes against the record companies.

ASCAP was the first and is still the largest of the American performing rights societies, which collect and distribute royalties to members from the use of their music. In 1915 ASCAP won a lawsuit against a restaurant in New York City in which Victor Herbert's music was played by a small orchestra. The decision of the United States Supreme Court was that, whether or not use of the music helped the restaurant to make a profit, 'the purpose of employing [the music] is profit, and that is enough'. This allowed ASCAP to insist on licensing fees from vaudeville managers, record companies and then broadcasters. ASCAP grew from 182 members in 1914 to more than 33,000 by the early 1980s. It is affiliated with societies in 40 other countries and runs such annual awards as the Nathan Burkan Memorial Competition for law students' essays on copyright law (started in 1938, in honour of a man who began as Witmark's lawyer) and the ASCAP–Deems Taylor Awards for writing on music (started in 1968).

For years, ASCAP was seen as just another self-serving attempt to create a monopoly in an industry that was full of them. The Board of Music Trade had been formed in 1855 to fix sheet music prices and to fight music teachers, who were middlemen, selling music to their pupils. The National Association of Music Teachers was formed in 1857. Later there were the Music Publishers Protective Association (MPPA), the Vaudeville Managers Protective Association and so on. At one point in the early history of ASCAP the MPPA collected but did not distribute millions of dollars in royalties, cash that ASCAP was supposed to pay to its members in order to justify itself. These organizations constantly squabbled with one another, especially as changes occurred in the music business; publishers joined and left them according to where they saw their best interests.

ASCAP was inevitably dominated by publishers. At one point the classification scheme according to annual turnover included an AAA category of only one publisher, E. B. Harms, who therefore raked off the fattest payments. Songwriters were not even allowed to join unless they had had several hits, and they relied on their publishers to share out the money fairly, which often did not happen. In 1932 ASCAP's operating expenses soaked up 32 cents of every dollar taken in. Its public image was so poor that it considered hiring a public relations firm, but instead it made a deal agreeing low rates with radio stations owned by newspapers, in order to be treated more kindly by those papers.

ASCAP's first agreement with the National Association of Broadcasters (NAB) was made in 1932. During the Depression sheet music sales and record sales decreased and vaudeville was dying; by then it was obvious that radio was the most important source of commercial entertainment in America, while a move to amend copyright law to free music from licence fees had been defeated in Congress. By the 1932 agreement ASCAP was entitled to fees of 3 per cent of 'time sales' (advertising income) rising to 5 per cent in 1935, with a smaller fixed fee for 'sustaining' (non-profit) programmes. Many broadcasters regarded the 1932 agreement as a sell-out, and network affiliates wanted networks to be responsible for the fees for network programmes. There was always plenty of ferment among publishers. Warner had acquired several important publishing houses and held out for a larger slice of the ASCAP pie: for the first half of 1935 the public did not hear any music on the radio by Romberg, Herbert, Gershwin and Rodgers or from Warner's many musical films; more ominously, the public did not appear to notice.

Warner tried to buy the Mutual Broadcasting System, but was rejected in 1936. Broadcasters and others had looked in vain for sources of non-ASCAP music. Schemes to compete with radio, using a signal riding piggy-back on the electricity supply, had been proposed as early as 1922. Muzak was formed in 1934, but the Society of European Stage Authors and Composers (SESAC) won a court case against a hotel in 1936 which helped to thwart Muzak's plans, and in 1938 Muzak finally failed to receive permission from the Federal Communications Commission to compete with the networks.

With cable television ubiquitous today in the USA, it would seem that this ruling has been undone, but meanwhile Muzak turned to supplying special music services for offices and factories, which became ubiquitous even sooner. This has profoundly cheapened and degraded music; no matter whether such services are operated by Muzak or one of its competitors, no matter what the quality of any individual service, the force-feeding of music is ultimately bad for it. In the 1930s Muzak had an agreement with ASCAP, but also relied upon Associated Music Publishers (AMP), which was made up of about 150 small US publishers and some European ones and effectively a holding company for non-ASCAP music. (Muzak's transcribed-music library service used an AMP label.)

In October 1939 Sydney Kaye, a member of CBS's law firm, proposed that broadcasters set up their own licensing agency, relying on SESAC, AMP and other sources, and luring some established composers away from ASCAP with promises of fairer treatment: they would be allowed to retain all non-broadcasting rights, such as publishing and stage performance. Broadcast Music Incorporated (BMI), was chartered, using funds pledged by broadcasters in expectation of an ASCAP strike against them. Many broadcasters saw BMI as yet another monopoly, but it was clear that they were not going to get away with paying nothing, and they soon fell into line. Furthermore, ASCAP was over-confident and insensitive: in two states where laws instigated by broadcasters prohibited ASCAP from interstate commerce, ASCAP offered a per-piece agreement to broadcasters, rather than a licence fee; broadcasters in other states had wanted this for years, and angrily signed with BMI. When its new demand was presented, just before the deadline of 1 April 1940 for the start of BMI's operations, ASCAP did not bother to invite the NAB's agent, Neville Miller, and the meeting ended with harsh words between CBS executives and Oscar Hammerstein II. The new demand was for 3 per cent of income for smaller stations, rising to 7.5 per cent for regional and national chains, as well as sustaining fees. ASCAP's strike against the broadcasters began at the end of 1940.

Kaye's vision of the future of radio was as great as that of Sarnoff and Paley; he already knew the power of it. In 1938 only 368 tunes received more than 47 per cent of the airplay; by September 1940 BMI was providing 14 printed popular songs a week. In 1939, it was later revealed, 13 ASCAP publishers had dominated *Your Hit Parade*, the nation's top chart showcase, collecting 60 per cent of the money paid to ASCAP's 165 members. It was clear that radio helped make hits and could dictate its own terms, and also that the terms being offered were fair. BMI signed M. M. Cole of Chicago, a leading publisher of hillbilly songs; E. B. Marks moved to BMI and Ralph Peer formed a BMI company; new firms such as Acuff–Rose joined BMI. The eccentric and musically conservative tobacco magnate who was behind *Your Hit Parade* would probably have preferred to go back to ASCAP's music of the 1910 era, but reluctantly agreed to broadcast only songs available to radio. During the strike no composition published by a member of ASCAP could be broadcast, except on independent stations that broadcast little live music anyway. In 1940 ASCAP members had sold about 300,000 pieces of sheet music a week, but this dropped to 120,000 a month.

A great deal of music that was out of copyright was performed, from Stephen Foster's songs to 'Tchaikovsky's Piano Concerto in B Flat', an extremely successful classical rip-off by Freddy Martin that was number one for eight weeks that year, with ASCAP making not a penny. The Russian folksong 'Song of the Volga Boatmen' was a big hit for Glenn Miller in early 1941, followed by 'Perfidia', a Latin tune published by Ralph Peer. Peer had scooped up Mexican and South American music, but ASCAP had refused to handle the new companies in which Peer had holdings because they were privately owned for profit (as though ASCAP members were not interested in money). ASCAP now went south of the border, in search of music with which to head off BMI, only to find that Peer had already got the best. 'The Peanut Vendor' had come from a Cuban revue, and was a success in the USA in 1930; it later became part of Peer International, and in 1941 the reissue of Louis Armstrong's delightful 1931 version was another hit. Bandleaders and composers were not fools; Charlie Barnet's 'Redskin Rhumba', for example, recorded in October 1940, was registered with a BMI company, so that it could be played on the radio, and was a hit the same year. It was at this time that Bing Crosby had hits with 'Brahms' Lullaby' and with Floyd Tillman's 'It Makes No Difference Now', a country hit published by Peer. The awful truth began to dawn: the world could get along without ASCAP music.

Various suits had been pending in federal courts against nearly all the principals, and the courts had to arbitrate, bringing order into the marketplace. The networks' creeping monopoly in the increasingly profitable industry was dealt with: General Electric and Westinghouse had disposed of their stock in RCA in 1931, and NBC stations were handed to Sarnoff (while in 1932–3 stations reluctantly began to allow prices to be mentioned in advertising). RCA/NBC had to sell off the Blue Network, which became the American Broadcasting Company. The networks were requested to divest themselves of their booking agencies; CBS's Columbia Concerts Corporation, for classical music, in which Paley still had an interest, was sold to Arthur Judson, while its pop talent agency was sold to the Chicago-based Music Corporation of America. Payment for music at source was required of the networks, removing a headache for the affiliates; all music users were offered the choice of a blanket licence, per-use fees or per-programme fees. ASCAP was barred from exclusive rights to members' work, freeing them for direct licensing, and the self-perpetuating board of directors was abolished by giving members a right to vote for it. Discrimination among similar types of user was banned.

BMI's contract of April 1941 charged a flat fee of 1.5 per cent of income to the networks, while the pressure on ASCAP was mounting: publishing houses were losing money, and Hollywood music was being kept in the can. Walt Disney, for example, anxious to get the songs from *Dumbo* on the air, instructed Irving Berlin Inc. to license them either through BMI or without charge, otherwise Disney would start his own BMI company. In July 1941 ASCAP offered the networks a licence fee of 2.75 per cent of income, considerably less than the 5 per cent they had been collecting. Many smaller broadcasters were opposed to any settlement with ASCAP, but the networks and ASCAP knew that lack of a settlement would lead to the collapse of ASCAP, chaos and anti-trust suits against the networks, so the deal was made.

Broadcasting was booming, and there was plenty of money for all. ASCAP, divested of its internal squabbling and corruption, became more prosperous than ever, and more or less respectable at last. But the formation of BMI had results reaching far beyond competition in the field. BMI's future was not at all secure at first. It soon offered advances to songwriters on getting a song recorded, and doubled the royalty rate from 1 penny per performance to 2 but it also raised the rate paid to publishers to 4 cents, naïvely expecting publishers to share the pay-out fairly with writers. Meanwhile ASCAP's distribution system had been revised and was now fairer to writers, so mainstream songwriters continued to join ASCAP – except for authors of black and hillbilly music, who could now receive advances and royalties from BMI that they had never had from ASCAP. Furthermore, after the war government restrictions on new radio stations were lifted, and by 1950 there were 1,517 independent stations compared with 627 network affiliates; half of the independents served single-station local markets, and courted them with more country music and rhythm and blues than the networks did. The outcome of all this was that BMI members were publishing a good deal of black and hillbilly music, and BMI unwittingly fed and watered the seedbed from which rock'n'roll would grow.

Only two years after BMI was formed *Billboard* began printing the first black chart (the 'Harlem Hit Parade'), and two years later, in 1944, it printed the first country chart ('Most Played Juke Box Folk Records'). Minority musics were becoming more profitable, and the major record labels, having cut back recording of minority musics during the Depression, now fell behind in serving these newly lucrative markets. Dozens of now legendary rhythm and blues labels were soon formed, all of this signalling the beginning of the end of the domination of New York and Tin Pan Alley. In retrospect, the rise of rhythm and blues, crossover hits, rockabilly and so forth was inevitable.

None of this is to be regretted now; those of us who grew up after 1940 would hardly wish to trade the delicious shock of Amos Milburn's 'Let Me Go Home, Whiskey', or Carl Perkins's 'Blue Suede Shoes', for ASCAP's continuing restriction of the music market to the products of Tin Pan Alley. Given the pop charts of the early 1950s, many listeners were bound to notice that more interesting things were happening elsewhere, and again we find apparently unconnected events combining.

BMI affiliated with overseas societies, and from 1944 included the

American Composer Alliance: Roy Harris, Walter Piston, Elliott Carter, Charles Ives and others became BMI composers. BMI has sponsored awards to student composers since 1951; its Musical Theatre Workshop (begun in 1959) and more recent Alternative Chorus Workshop have their best works presented annually to audiences of agents, publishers, producers and record company executives. BMI has long since become respectable, and in any case the competition of minority musics by itself could not have brought Tin Pan Alley and the Swing Era crashing down. There were many other factors, but among the most foolish were the musicians' union strikes.

James Caesar Petrillo was a pianist and bandleader in Chicago; his girl vocalist at one point was Frances Octavia Smith, later known as Dale Evans. Petrillo was already active in the Chicago local of the musicians' union in 1934 when it kicked the Kansas City band led by Harlan Leonard and Thamon Hayes out of town, whereupon Hayes, disgusted, quit the road, and Leonard had to start again. Petrillo, a combative little man who is said to have refused to shake hands for fear of germs, ranted against 'canned music' at the 1937 convention of the American Federation of Musicians (AFM), and was elected leader of the national AFM in 1940.

Record labels bore the legend 'unlicensed for public broadcasting', which was widely ignored. A suit had been brought by RCA, and Supreme Court Judge Learned Hand ruled in 1940 that copyright was not infringed by the playing of a record on the radio. The decision was wrong and unfair, and a contradiction of the decision which had legitimized ASCAP in 1915, but Petrillo and the record companies were also shortsighted: broadcasting helped to sell records. It seems incredible now that the rivalry between records and radio had lasted for more than a decade, when the two industries were so important to each other, but it must be remembered that Martin Block's *Make Believe Ballroom*, the first noteworthy DJ format, only got started at WNEW in New York City in 1935. On the other hand, Milt Gabler was in no doubt about the value of radio: as a record retailer and at Block's suggestion, he was happy to sell the station not only Commodore records but also all the new releases from the other labels. In every industry it is often the people who do the business who make the best decisions, and in the music business,

until more recent times anyway, they were often people who liked
music. It is the power-brokers at the top who most often get it
wrong.

Petrillo commissioned bandleader Ben Selvin, who was already
experienced in both recording and radio and had been a Muzak
executive, to determine whether recordings were putting musicians
out of live work. Selvin reported to an AFM convention in 1941
that record labels paid millions of dollars annually to musicians, and
that union action was not the answer to problems caused by the
mechanization of music. He received a standing ovation, but while
the membership, and especially the bandleaders, agreed with Selvin,
Petrillo demanded that record companies refuse to allow records to
be played on the radio and jukeboxes, though they had already tried
that. Then, on 1 August 1942, he ordered musicians to stop
recording.

This had several effects. Studio time was booked solid in the
weeks leading up to the strike, as artists tried to get their work
recorded before the drought began; this should have been evidence
enough that the strike was a mistake, but too often unions forget that
their members are likely to know which side of the bread is buttered.
It is impossible to know to what extent minority musics were given
another boost; presumably there were blacks and hillbillies who did
not belong to the union and did as they pleased during the strike.
Old recordings were reissued: Dorsey, Miller and Ellington all had
hits with sides recorded as early as 1938, some of them entering the
charts for the second time. Frank Sinatra's 'All or Nothing at All',
made with Harry James in 1939 and unnoticed at the time, reached
number one in June 1943, while Bing Crosby's 'Sweet and Lovely', a
hit in 1931, was again in the charts in 1944. But worst of all from the
point of view of jazz and big-band fans, to say nothing of musicians,
the era of the pop singer began.

The vocalists with the bands, such as Sinatra, Dick Haymes and
Perry Como, and Kitty Kallen, Rosemary Clooney, Peggy Lee, Kay
Starr, Georgia Gibbs, Margaret Whiting and Jo Stafford, had been
becoming popular anyway, and they began their rise to domination
in the post-war years. They were more logical heart-throbs for fans
who bought records. In theory, anybody could sing, while it took

many years to learn how to play a saxophone or a trumpet to professional standard. The words to the songs were important to the fans, who had been brought up on a steady diet of romantic love in songs and films, and were only too willing to imagine singing to each other. This theory of the 'singer as amateur' was carried to absurdity by the musicians' union, which did not allow vocalists to join.

Singers recorded a cappella during the strike: Haymes had eight hits backed by the Song Spinners, and Sinatra had seven with the Bobby Tucker Singers, with no instrumentalists at all. (The Song Spinners had a number one wartime hit of their own: 'Comin' in on a Wing and a Prayer'.) In mid-1943 Bing Crosby's recordings of two songs from *Oklahoma!* with Trudy Erwin and the Sportsmen Glee Club were highly successful, while the biggest hit of the decade was the Mills Brothers' 'Paper Doll', which had no backing group. At a time when the demand for union musicians was greater than ever before because so many of them were being drafted, Petrillo helped the record business to discover that it could manage without them: singers were cheaper to record (later with studio musicians on salary) than name bands. Booking agents got the same message, as for various reasons big-band venues were already closing during the war.

The record labels eventually had to cave in: Decca signed with the union in September 1943, Capitol a month later, RCA and Columbia in November 1944. The War Labor Board had instructed Petrillo to lift his recording ban; Edward Wallerstein at Columbia wrote a bitter letter to Judge Vinson of the Office of Economic Stabilization, which ended:

The economic pressures on us are such that we can wait no longer and must now either sign or go out of business. Since no action has been taken by the government, we have today entered into an agreement with Mr Petrillo's union which will include provision for payments by us directly to the Union, the principle which we have resisted for more than 27 months, which we contested before government bureaus for sixteen months and which, although successful in our contests, we are finally accepting because of the government's unwillingness or incapacity to enforce its orders.

Just in case he had not done enough damage, when disc jockeys were

becoming ubiquitous and the record business was booming, Petrillo
called a second recording ban in 1948, by which time many bands
had folded. The result of the strikes was not more money for the
musicians making the records, who had lost income through not
being able to record during the strikes, but a tax on records which
swelled the union's coffers; some of it was used to pay for free
concerts. The best musicians thus subsidized the rest, and, according
to a War Labor Board report, two-thirds of the union's rank and file
did not depend on music for a full-time living anyway.

Petrillo was almost as well known in his day as John L. Lewis, the
beetle-browed leader of the USA miners' union. To be absolutely
fair, he had to get something right occasionally: Charlie Barnet wrote
that when a Las Vegas club-owner wanted him to play in a car park,
Petrillo wired him: 'Special scale for bands playing in a parking lot:
leader $50,000.00, sidemen $1,500.00.' 'We never played in the parking lot,' recalled Barnet. In Chicago Petrillo had made the first
agreement with a radio station and kept the peace between musicians
and hotels and theatres. Nevertheless, Petrillo's Chicago local was
violent and segregated – the city had been a centre of recording of
black music until a strike in the mid-1930s priced it out of the market
for a decade – and the damage Petrillo ultimately did to the big bands
was immense. Bass player Red Callender is scathing about the musicians' union in his autobiography *Unfinished Dream* (1985): it was not
the national union that integrated white and black locals, but musicians themselves, who also had to sue the union to get their money
out of Petrillo's trust funds.

In the meantime, bands that had been going through an interesting
formative evolution had not visited the recording studios, and much
documentation of the music was lost, except for a few broadcast
airchecks. Furthermore, during this period the public heard very little
of the new music, which might have prepared listeners for the
changes to come, changes which were out of the hands of the puny
power-brokers.

The Second World War was the end of an era for all sorts of
political, social and economic reasons, and the Big Band Era may
have been coming to a close anyway. Bandleader Alvino Rey is one of
those who reflected years later that the bands had neglected the

dancers, who had made Goodman such a big success in 1935, by concentrating on flag-wavers and slow smoochers (with heart-throb vocalists) and offering little in between. Artie Shaw, Tommy Dorsey, Gene Krupa, Harry James and others hired string sections, a move which led nowhere in musical terms (partly because there were few arrangers who knew what to do with violins). But the immediate effects on music of the war were obvious. For one thing, country music became a big business.

In 1945 two soldiers in Europe wrote to Bob Wills to say that upon clearing out some 'Jerries' during house-to-house fighting, they had found some old records, one of which was Wills's 'San Antonio Rose'. (A quarter of a century later Apollo 12 astronauts broadcast the song to countless millions around the world, in an impromptu version from outer space.) The band of the early 1940s had been Wills's best, and the Tiffany Music transcriptions (220 selections made for radio stations in 1945–7) are probably the best Wills collection; he continued having hits until 1950, but with smaller and smaller groups. Decca made a new recording of 'San Antonio Rose' for jukeboxes in 1955, but it was not a patch on the original. Spade Cooley's big band filled California dance halls during the war, and he had a huge hit with 'Shame on You' in 1945 (vocal by Tex Williams). But the days of the big band were numbered.

Wills broke up his band in late 1942, when he was drafted into the US Army at the age of almost thirty-eight, not knowing that nothing would ever be the same again. After being discharged in July 1943 he formed the biggest band he ever had – twenty-two musicians and two vocalists – but it did not record, and lasted for only six months. Times had changed: musicians were in short supply, the Depression was over at last and money was more important than loyalty. It was the same story for all the other leaders.

Country music had always been essentially a small-group music. In the late 1940s the singing cowboy Roy Rogers seemed more typical of country music than he was, with such tunes as 'Chickashay Gal' and 'Blue Shadows on the Trail'. His films, with Republic's sunset-like colour process, are still redolent of nostalgia for millions of middle-aged men, especially the ones made with the Sons of the Pioneers. But more authentic country was also booming. Capitol

Records, formed in Hollywood in 1942, was successful with Tex Ritter, and hired West Coast country D J, bandleader and radio show host Cliffie Stone to build its country list; he signed Tex Williams, Jimmy Wakely, Tennessee Ernie Ford and Merle Travis; Williams's 'Smoke! Smoke! Smoke That Cigarette' (1947) was said to be the label's first million-seller. In 1949 the name of the *Billboard* country chart was changed from 'Folk Music' to 'Country and Western', after long agitation from those who disliked the 'hillbilly' appellation, especially in the West Coast scene that Hollywood had helped to create. Bing Crosby's hits with country songs encouraged more to break through to the pop chart in the form of 'covers', and in a survey immediately after the war Roy Acuff beat Frank Sinatra as the GI's favourite singer. Canadian-born Hank Snow, after many years of trying, achieved lasting stardom in 1950 with 'I'm Movin' On'.

But country music, though it was becoming big business, was kept in a commercial ghetto. The dominant Swing Era style had been a jazz-oriented one, and jazz itself, in a most dramatic development, moved away from mainstream public popularity to become 'modern jazz'.

In 1939, as politicians in Europe prepared to conduct their diplomacy by other means, Coleman Hawkins returned to the USA and formed an octet. In October he recorded 'Body and Soul', and reclaimed his title as the boss of the tenor saxophone. This technically interesting song was written by Johnny Green, an arranger, conductor and composer of film scores; he wrote few songs, but they are of very high quality, and include 'Out of Nowhere' and 'I Cover the Waterfront', also popular among jazz musicians. 'Body and Soul' was described by Alec Wilder as not only innovatory but strange, having 'one of the widest ranges and one of the most complex releases and verses'. It is another example of a high-class work of art that was accepted by the public without a murmur. Virtually a solo with rhythm section, Hawkins's recording was good for romantic dancing and a big hit, but it is also an enduring jazz milestone. His harmonic commentary on the song becomes a lovely series of arpeggios; his controlled passion from the urgency of getting it all in imparts a forward motion, as does the way he divided the beat into unequal parts. Most jazz musicians did this, but Hawk imbued it with further urgency by 'swallowing' the second part of the beat until it almost disappeared.

Hawkins was apparently influenced by the pianist Art Tatum, whose technical wizardry was unique. Born virtually blind, Tatum began to perform as a teenager, accompanied Adelaide Hall and made his first recordings in 1932. He made commercially-oriented records exclusively for Decca well into the 1940s; in 1934 he formed a trio with Slam Stewart on bass and Tiny Grimes (later replaced by Everett Barksdale) on guitar. Incredibly, he was not recorded at all for two years in the late 1940s, but later made solo and small-group albums for Norman Granz. His quartet album with Ben Webster, Red Callender and drummer Bill Douglass, made weeks before he died of uraemia, is one of the most beautiful ever made, though the sets with Buddy DeFranco, Roy Eldridge and Benny Carter are equally valuable.

Tatum acknowledged his debt to Fats Waller, but it was Waller who announced in a club with Tatum present, 'Ladies and gentlemen, I play piano, but tonight, God is in the house.' Tatum was not a composer (except in the sense that every great jazz musician is a composer); he embroidered standards. Using rich rhythmic and harmonic improvisation, he would paint himself into a corner, then miraculously escape, forcing his ideas to work after all. This was over the heads of some listeners, who complained that he played too many notes – which is one reason why his trio recordings were more commercialized than his solos would have been. After-hours recordings made on portable equipment by jazz buff Jerry Newman in 1940–41 show him in a relaxed mood, playing around the dud keys on a battered piano and quoting anything he liked while he did it.

Among Tatum's fans were Rachmaninov and Vladimir Horowitz; Oscar Peterson has a photograph of himself with Horowitz and Tatum. Contrary to popular belief, Tatum was probably not a primary influence on Peterson, though they were friends. Peterson was afraid to play in front of him, but one night, playing in a club, he heard Tatum's voice from the audience: 'Lighten up, Oscar Peterson.' It is doubtful if Tatum could have been a primary influence on anybody, since he would be impossible to copy or imitate, but his complete freedom to do as he pleased, and his insistence on doing so, was of the greatest importance.

The small-group sessions described in the last chapter document some of the changes in music, and a clue can also be heard in the soundtrack of the 1943 film *Stormy Weather*, mentioned earlier. This all-black musical was almost the only one of its kind; the stars, who included Fats Waller, Lena Horne, Bill 'Bojangles' Robinson and Cab Calloway's band, played successful and glamorous characters as well as the downtrodden, albeit restricted to roles as entertainers. In the scene in which Bojangles dances to the music of a combo, although the men are dressed in rags and it takes place on a riverboat, the music is anything but backward-looking: the rhythm section is dominated by bassist Mitt Hinton, who plays the most ecstatically solid accompaniment, and the oompah two-beat style of New Orleans is abolished by the supreme court of music.

The unique harmonic richness of Duke Ellington's music must have been an influence on younger musicians. The success of Ellington's sensational bass player Jimmy Blanton in making the instrument an equal voice in the band was paralleled by that of young drummers like Kenny Clarke and Max Roach (who replaced Clarke in Hawkins's combo in 1943). Clarke became famous for 'dropping bombs' – putting bass drum accents wherever the music seemed to demand them – later explaining (not altogether convincingly) that his foot got tired. This further liberated the drum kit from timekeeping, and the bass player, who had to take over some of that role, often played on the beat instead of slightly behind it as during the Swing Era, again injecting more urgency and forward motion into the music.

Another new voice was that of the guitarist Charlie Christian, who was born in Texas and played in Oklahoma as a teenager. He brought a blues feeling to a new solo instrument, the electric guitar. He was not the first to play it, but the first to invent a vocabulary for it, using the sustained notes of equal value possible with amplification. His swing and his ear for harmony were impeccable, though his lines were full of rhythmic figures which might have become monotonous. But he did not live long enough to develop further, dying young, like Blanton, of tuberculosis. He has been an influence on every jazz guitarist since.

Minton's Playhouse was a Harlem club run by Henry Minton, a former saxophonist; in 1941 he hired manager Teddy Hill, another saxophonist, who had fronted an excellent band in 1936–7. Monday night was Celebrity Night, and not only visiting celebrities but young turks jammed there, playing free or for tips, and the local musicians' unions often turned a blind eye. Clarke, Christian, a strange young pianist called Thelonious Monk and a confident young trumpeter, John Birks 'Dizzy' Gillespie, were among the regulars at Minton's. But Monk and Clarke were the only ones who *worked* there; the others were hanging out. When Gillespie was working on 52nd Street with Benny Carter, Monroe's Uptown House was more convenient after hours; the musicians did not make any money there either, but both Minton and Clark Monroe made plenty of food available.

Milt Hinton lived across the street from Minton's. He described how 'so many kids from downtown, kids that couldn't blow, would come in and they would interrupt'.

So Diz told me on the roof one night at the Cotton Club, 'Now look, when we go down to the jam session, we're gonna say we're gonna play 'I Got Rhythm', but we're gonna use these changes. Instead of using the B-flat and the D-flat, we're gonna use B-flat, D-flat, G-flat or F and we change.' We would do these things on the roof and then we'd go down to Minton's, and all these kids would be up there. 'What're y'all gonna play?' We'd say, 'I Got Rhythm', and we'd start out with this new set of changes ... and eventually they would put their horns away, and we could go on and blow in peace and get our little exercise.

This accelerated what they were doing, according to Gillespie: 'playing, seriously, creating a new dialogue among ourselves, blending our ideas into a new style of music. You only have so many notes, and what makes a style is how you get from one note to the next.'

Another important double bass player was Oscar Pettiford, who had come from the Midwest; he played melody bass like Jimmy Blanton, but he had been influenced by Charlie Christian, a guitarist. At Minton's, Monk and Dizzy would be showing each other things on the keyboard, exploring chords and inventing a new way of playing. Unfortunately, there are no commercial recordings document-ing the crucial period 1943–4 because of the musicians' union strikes.

Gillespie was greatly inspired by the extremely fluent Roy Eldridge, whom he had replaced in Hill's band in 1937. Gillespie wrote: 'Roy used to come by Minton's. "Look, you're supposed to be the greatest trumpet player in the world," Monk used to tell him, "but that's the best." And he'd point at me . . . Monk'll tell you the truth, whatever he thinks about it. He's not diplomatic at all.'

As a member of Cab Calloway's band (1939–41) Gillespie had written tunes like 'Pickin' the Cabbage'; he was already nicknamed Dizzy. His facility on the trumpet was similar to that of Tatum at the keyboard: he could do anything, and he was ready to do it. He worked with Benny Carter, Charlie Barnet and Earl Hines; he also began writing big-band arrangements, and he had become friends with Charlie Parker.

Parker, an alto saxophonist, had been a heroin addict since he was a teenager in Kansas City and was unreliable, which is why he was not recorded on Keynote by Harry Lim, who admired him. Lim's operation was based on efficient use of studio time, and Parker might not show up; he had been fired by Harlan Leonard and went in and out of Jay McShann's band. In 1978 James Lincoln Collier, in his mostly useful history of jazz *The Making of Jazz* (1978), speculated that the reason Parker died young, while Gillespie lived twice as long, was that Parker had less character. This is ridiculous. Gillespie and Parker were both black, both the same age, both from poor families and both brilliant musicians, but Gillespie's stern, loving father was around until he was ten years old, while Parker was spoiled by his mother, and his father, like many other African-Ameri-cans, had to be a travelling man, for practical purposes no father at all. The importance of the presence of both parents in the family has been too well established to be thrown away so easily.

As for Gillespie, he had not acquired his nickname for nothing. He was fired from Calloway's band for throwing a spitball, and had been guilty of too many pranks to be believed when he professed his innocence (though it seems to have been Jonah Jones who was guilty); afterwards he nicked Calloway with the knife he carried at the time. A good marriage no doubt helped Gillespie to survive, and what made this possible, again, was his earlier experience of a stable family life.

Parker tried to play in Kansas City clubs as a teenager, but was not ready. Having been treated with derision, he went away and practised until he could modulate from any key to any other key, perhaps, it has been suggested, because he did not know that he did not need to know that much to play in a band. He was nicknamed Bird after Yardbird, meaning chicken, one of his favourite foods. (Dizzy called him Yard.) On his first visit to New York in 1939 he washed dishes in a club while Art Tatum was playing out front; soon after, while playing 'Cherokee' at a gig, he began to improvise on the higher intervals of the chords, instead of the lower. This required new harmonic resolutions, and was in effect a new tune: he was playing the music he had already heard in his head.

Parker recorded with McShann's band in 1940–41. He played tenor in the Earl Hines band, which also included Gillespie and Billy Eckstine, for decades one of America's favourite vocalists. Eckstine left to form his own band, with Parker, Gillespie and Sarah Vaughan. Again, there were no studio sets by these epochal outfits, but recordings made in a hotel room in 1943 captured Parker on tenor and Gillespie and Eckstine on trumpets, just as the new music was being born.

Dan Morgenstern, in his notes for the complete Commodore recordings, describes one of the recording sessions as 'prototypical mature swing at its finest hour – just before bebop would change things forever'. He is referring to a 1944 date led by drummer Big Sid Catlett, with John Simmons on bass, Ben Webster on tenor saxophone and the interesting Marlowe Morris on piano; any of these men could have played with anybody at the time. Morgenstern is, of course, quite correct; all the same, the changes were already in the air (even at Commodore, which recorded a good deal of what most people thought was dixieland, though it was essentially the Chicago style of the Austin High School Gang). It is easy to make too much of a distinction between 'modern jazz' and the Swing Era, as though we still have a hangover of the awful and ridiculous war of words that went on at the time between the 'mouldy figs' (those who thought that the original New Orleans style, and its Chicago offshoot, were the only true jazz) and the beboppers. The evolution was under way.

The Benny Goodman Sextet sides of 1939–40 (with Christian) already show a tightness and a forward energy, and Georgie Auld on tenor saxophone an insouciance, which was a portent. The Flip Phillips sessions recorded in 1944–5 by Bob Thiele, using white sidemen from Woody Herman's band, were an example of music which is already modern, in comparison with any similar session of only a few years earlier, in the smoothness of the rhythm section, the stylishness of the riffs and other essential features. But it is true that it was in 1943–4 that the most dramatic turning point seems to have been reached, by the young black musicians who were ready to take things another step further – at precisely the time when the music was not being recorded.

The new music came to be called bop, short for bebop or rebop, onomatopoeic in origin from the music itself. The musicians used altered chords and wider intervals, and insisted on choosing a wider range of notes, a process that had been going on in classical music for centuries. Syncopation seemed to disappear altogether in the new, smoother rhythm section, but there were new accents within bars and even between notes, together with phrases of unusual lengths, so that even the rhythmic nature of jazz changed: an intense and technically brilliant music was created, full of pride, sardonic wit and fierce joy. The scene was accompanied by attitudes and language incomprehensible to outsiders; some of this had been pioneered by Lester Young, an influence in more ways than one, but the zany wit of Gillespie was also important.

Tempos were often furiously fast or very slow, but even when the tempo was slow the soloist might play fast, using what sounded to the swing fan like machine-gun runs of semiquavers. At the time the big bands were playing fewer tunes for dancers, and bop was not for dancers either. (Gillespie protested that he could dance to bop, and we do not doubt it, but most people did not.)

All the independent record labels of the early years of the industry – Paramount, Gennett, Okeh and Black Swan, for instance – had long since disappeared or been swallowed up. The 1940s was the second era (and not the last) in which independent labels were formed to serve an industry whose largest companies were geared towards serving the majority. It is remarkable that so many record labels were formed during the war.

Capitol, the first big label to be located on the West Coast, was formed in 1942 by record retailer Glenn Wallach and songwriters Buddy DeSylva and Johnny Mercer. That year it had a hit with 'Cow Cow Boogie', by Freddie Slack and his band and with a vocal by Ella Mae Morse. (Pianist and vocalist Cow Cow Davenport eventually got some money for his tune.) Capitol quickly became the most innovative company in the industry. The sound of the recordings made in Hollywood in 1945 by Coleman Hawkins, for example, was outstanding for the period; Capitol was the first to record everything on tape, the first to give free records to disc jockeys (not an unmixed blessing, in retrospect) and later the first to issue records at all three speeds.

Even more impressive was the number of labels formed expressly to serve the black community. Apollo was formed in the same year as Capitol in Harlem by Ike and Bess Berman to record black gospel music, and soon diversified into jazz and rhythm and blues. (John Chilton, however, writes that Apollo was formed by Teddy Gottlieb and Hi Siegel from their Rainbow Music Store.) Savoy was formed in Newark, New Jersey, by Herman Lubinsky, another record retailer. National was formed by A. B. Green in Manhattan in 1944, and its A & R director was Herb Abramson (soon to be a co-founder of Atlantic). Syd Nathan left the department store business to form King in Cincinnati in 1945. DeLuxe was formed around 1944 in Linden, New Jersey, by Jules Braun and his brothers; Fred Mendelsohn formed Regent in 1947, Deluxe was sold to King and the Brauns and Mendelsohn formed Regal in 1949. (Mendelsohn formed Herald in 1952, and ended up succeeding Lubinsky at Savoy.) On the West Coast, Specialty was formed in 1944 by Art Rupe, Black and White in 1945 by Paul and Lillian Reiner, Modern by Jules and Saul Bihari (soon to include subsidiaries Kent, Crown and Flair). At about the same time Leo, Edward and Ida Mesner formed Philo, which changed its name to Aladdin in 1946. In 1946–7 Phil and Leonard Chess formed Aristocrat in Chicago, and it became Chess in 1949–50.

Mercury had been formed in Chicago in 1945–6, and ten years later it had the first rhythm and blues hit to reach number one on the national pop chart: 'The Great Pretender' by the Platters. Don Robey formed Peacock in Houston, Texas, in 1949, which was perhaps the first black-owned label since Black Swan, and more 'indie' labels followed in the early 1950s. But another remarkable thing about the independent labels listed in the last paragraph is that they were all formed by Jews, who in those days did not find it easy to make their way in mainstream business in the USA. (It was in 1947 that Laura Z. Hobson's best-selling novel about genteel American anti-semitism, *Gentleman's Agreement*, was filmed; unfortunately it was a dull movie.) The Jews who formed the classic indies in the 1940s lived and worked in black neighbourhoods, and knew and understood the music better than anyone at a larger company could (with the possible exception of Jack Kapp at Decca, who recorded much minority music). If they had not taken the risks and done the work, the Lester Youngs on Aladdin and other priceless jazz, to say nothing of scores of wonderful rhythm and blues hits, would not exist. And these independents were the first to record bop.

Hawkins encouraged the boppers, employing them on recordings. Jazz historians have decided that the first bop recordings were made at a Hawkins session in February 1944 for Apollo, by a twelve-piece group which included Max Roach on drums, Oscar Pettiford on bass and Dizzy Gillespie in the trumpet section, as well as Don Byas in the reeds. (One of the most interesting transitional figures, who was at home in any decade's style, Byas spent his later life in Europe.) At a quartet date on another label in October Hawkins used Thelonious Monk; it was Monk's first recording session. A year later, on Savoy, Parker made his first recordings as a leader, with Miles Davis and Gillespie on trumpet (Gillespie played piano on some tracks), Roach on drums and Curley Russell on bass. The cats were well and truly out of the bag.

Cab Calloway called it 'Chinese music'. Boppers often flattened the fifth note of a chord, inventing short routes between keys; Eddie Condon said, 'We don't flatten our fifths, we drink 'em.' But Stravinsky had used flattened fifths in 1910, and Earl Hines, Bubber Miley and others in the 1920s. Bop was very obviously a black music, and the USA was not ready for black pride just yet. There were white boppers in black combos, for example trumpeter Red Rodney and pianists Al Haig, George Wallington and Joe Albany; but pressure on leaders to practise Crow Jim (the reverse of American racism, dubbed 'Jim Crow' from the early minstrel act) soon sent them into obscurity. (Some made comebacks as bop became repertory music in the 1970s.) It is said that bop left jazz in a shambles, but that is nonsense: the jazz content of pop music was decreasing anyway, and bop was not a revolution, but a further flowering of an art form already decades old, leading towards the emancipation of black music from ballrooms and taverns by making demands on the listeners. Bop was a natural musical evolution, though there must also have been a feeling on the part of the young players that they were taking their music back.

Bop was great fun for anyone prepared to listen, and the records are still selling today. The music business, however, mishandled it. The sudden success of Benny Goodman, then Tommy Dorsey and the others had come as a surprise to the industry in the mid-1930s, but those leaders were already insiders and good businessmen. The boppers were musicians (mostly black) who needed the patronage of the American music business, from the major labels to the disc jockeys, and they did not get it. The major label that recorded the most bop was young and feisty Capitol (run by musicians). Gillespie formed the Dee-Gee label in 1951 and went broke, but the recordings he made hold up better than most of the pop music of the period. The music business (including broadcasters) co-opts and tries to control (or ignore) whatever it does not understand, as it did with rock'n'roll ten years later.

The first frenetic flowering of bop was temporary; the 'hot modern' music soon began to cool off, leading to several styles – modern jazz, cool jazz, hard bop and so on – as the classic New Orleans style had immediately begun to evolve two generations earlier. In the meantime black popular music already had two tributaries. If bop can be seen as the art music of the black American audience of, say, 1949, in that year the name for its pop music was officially changed: Jerry Wexler, then a reporter at *Billboard*, convinced them to change the name of the 'Race Records' charts to 'Rhythm and Blues'.

For the black audience there was so much new music to listen to that the ferment crossed over to some extent. Some of Lionel

Hampton's big-band hits, with their strong backbeat, were not far removed from the R&B hits of later years, and in 1946 'Hey! Ba-ba-re-bop' parleyed its bop-derived nonsense lyrics to the number one spot on the black chart for sixteen weeks. Helen Humes (whose beautiful ballad with Basie a half-dozen years before had been 'Blame It On My Last Affair') had a big hit in 1945 with 'Be Baba Leba' on the new Philo label, backed by a Bill Doggett octet, and followed up in 1950 with the salacious 'Million Dollar Secret', which was recorded live with drummer Roy Milton's band in August. In November of that year she was backed in her live act by another jump band led by Dexter Gordon. A jump band was a small group that combined the beat and the drive of the big jazz band with the repetitious chorus associated with the blues, in effect making something new out of the Swing Era's predilection for riffs. Herb Morand was the trumpeter and manager of the Harlem Hamfats, one of the first jump bands, which began recording in Chicago in 1936; a 'hamfat' was a musician newly arrived from the South who used fat to grease the valves in his horn, and such a group purposely retained the flavour of the South in their sound.

Far more successful than the Hamfats was Louis Jordan, who had worked in Chick Webb's band, occasionally singing as well as playing alto saxophone. In 1938 he formed his Tympany Five (actually larger than a quintet); his showmanship brought him to the fore, and he had nearly fifty top ten hits in the black charts in less than ten years, about twenty of which crossed over to the heretofore lily-white pop chart. 'Caledonia' was covered by Woody Herman in 1945 (and his 'Inflation Blues' by B. B. King in 1983); his version of Jack McVea's novelty 'Open the Door, Richard' (1947) was one of the most popular. His skill as a leader and his innovatory vocal style not only made wonderful good-time music, but also may be seen in retrospect as an early example of a new black consciousness. The attitudes expressed in his vocals on many titles, such as 'That Chick's Too Young To Fry', 'Jack, You're Dead', 'I Know What You're Puttin' Down' and 'Ain't Nobody Here But Us Chickens', were redolent of a southern heritage, as well as of the rich humour and *joie de vivre* of the increasingly large urban black population.

Joe Liggins was a pianist, vocalist and bandleader whose goal was to create a big-band sound with a smaller combo; his own 'The Honeydripper' was number one for eighteen weeks in the black chart in 1945, and was followed by a string of hits up to 1951; his younger brother, guitarist Jimmy, was also in the charts from 1948. Lucky Millinder's band shrank until by the early 1950s it was essentially a jump band. Drummer and pianist Tiny Bradshaw had formed his own band in 1934, and finally had chart success from 1950 to 1953; among Bradshaw's tenor saxophones were Red Prysock and Sil Austin. The saxophone was the most important sound in the jump band era, and has retained an important role in R & B and rock'n'roll to this day.

Guitarist, vocalist and composer of novelty hits Slim Gaillard wrote 'Flat Foot Floogie', which was a hit in 1938 for Slim and Slam, Gaillard's duo with bass player Slam Stewart; several cover versions were also hits, notably that of Benny Goodman. Gaillard was a success in clubs on the West Coast during and after the war, and claimed years later that one of his fans had been film star Ronald Reagan; having invented a hip 'vout oreenie' language, he compiled a dictionary of it. In 1945 he recorded 'Floogie' again in Hollywood, with a small group including Charlie Parker, Dizzy Gillespie and tenor saxophonist Jack McVea. One of the other tracks was a bit of laid-back jive called 'Slim's Jam': the men come in one at a time; Gillespie is in a hurry to get to another session; Parker borrows a reed from McVea, who knocks on the door as he enters, saying, 'Open the door, Richard!'

This was a reference to a comedy routine by Dusty Fletcher, one of the biggest stars in black variety: the comic arrives home late and somewhat the worse for wear and finds himself without a key; he cannot raise Richard, his flatmate, to open the door, because Richard is busy doing something he is loath to interrupt. McVea subsequently composed a riff and turned 'Open the Door, Richard!' into a jump band set-piece which swept the USA in seven hit versions in 1947, among them those of Basie, Jordan, Fletcher and McVea. The novelty became so obsessive that a radio station in New York finally banned the tune, as well as the DJs' Richard jokes.

Most of the small-group sessions recorded in the 1940s seem to have been saxophone-led, and the music is extraordinarily rich: there was a spectrum from pure jazz at one end to good-time exhibitionism at the other. The 'swingtets' from Blue Note, led by Ike Quebec and John Hardee, were beautiful recordings aimed at jukeboxes, as were Bob Thiele's Signature discs.

Earl Bostic played alto saxophone; his compositions for big bands include Gene Krupa's 1941 hit 'Let Me Off Uptown' and he then had his own success in the late 1940s and early 1950s. Bostic had recorded some superb solos as a sideman at Commodore in 1945. He was also highly regarded as a technician and, in fact, had the reputation of sacrificing tone for technique. (Art Blakey later remarked that if John Coltrane had worked for Bostic, he must have learned a great deal: 'Nobody knew more about the saxophone than Bostic . . . and that includes Bird.') Bostic was among the first to employ Coltrane, as well as Benny Golson and Stanley Turrentine, and later wrote albums for Ella Fitzgerald and others.

Big Jay McNeely was the foremost practitioner of the acrobatic, honking R&B saxophone; his biggest hit was 'Deacon's Hop' in 1949, but he remained a legend in clubs well into the 1980s. Illinois Jacquet began with Lionel Hampton's big band, but recorded with his 'Black Velvet' combo for RCA; his main success was 'Port of Rico' on Mercury in 1952 (with Count Basie on organ). Arnett Cobb was another Texas tenor saxophonist whose ability to please a crowd obscured his excellent ballad playing. Johnny Hodges, who never honked, left Duke Ellington in 1951 and for five years led his own smaller group. His was certainly a jazz-oriented band, but his 'Castle Rock' was a hit in 1951, a good year for alto saxophones: Bostic's 'Flamingo' and Tab Smith's 'Because of You' were also hits. Jimmy Forrest was an underrated tenor saxophonist whose jump combo had a great success in 1952 with 'Night Train', actually an Ellington riff, which then became required learning for every embryo high-school rock band in the country.

The valedictory hit of the jump band era came in 1956, in time to let a whole new generation in on the secret: Bill Doggett's 'Honky Tonk' was number one for thirteen weeks in the black chart, and stuck at number two (for three weeks) on the national pop chart. Doggett, born in 1916, had played piano in many a big band when he formed a combo in 1952 and recorded this two-part instrumental with Clifford Scott on tenor and Billy Butler on guitar. Its inexorable rocking lope made it one of the biggest hits the King label ever had.

Electric guitars and pure blues became increasingly stronger in the commercial market. Composer, bass player, guitarist, vocalist and ex-boxer Willie Dixon formed the Five Breezes and recorded for Blue-bird in 1940, then with the Four Jumps of Jive on Mercury and the Big Three Trio on Columbia. He did not have a hit of his own until 1955, but meanwhile became Leonard Chess's right-hand man in the studio, as Chicago developed a blues scene of extraordinary power, headed by Muddy Waters, who brought the country blues to town. Muddy's first hit in the black chart was '(I Feel Like) Going Home' in 1948 on Aristocrat. John Lee 'Sonny Boy' Williamson, born in Tennessee, paved the way for a whole generation of Chicago blues harmonica players and had a high entry in the black chart with 'Shake the Boogie' in 1947, the year before he was murdered. Guitarist and harmonica player Aleck Ford (also known as Rice Miller) had already worked as Sonny Boy Williamson in the early 1940s on the radio; now he adopted the name permanently, and, apart from having hits of his own, played on Elmore James's 'Dust My Broom' (on the tiny Mississippi Trumpet label) in 1952, which represents another direct link from the delta to the south side of Chicago. Chester Burnette acquired the apt stage name of Howlin' Wolf; his hits in the black chart began in 1951 with 'Moanin' at Midnight'. Riley 'Blues Boy' King recorded for Nashville's Bullet label in 1949; his 'Three O'Clock Blues' was enormously popular in 1951.

Vocal groups were coming up and inventing a whole new tradition of unaccompanied doo-wop, named after the 'doo-wah' vocal device commonly used in backing harmony. As their grandfathers had sung in barber-shops, so the young groups in the post-war years sang on street corners to get the girls; they rehearsed in hallways and alleys where they liked the echo, and they made uncounted numbers of obscure records on obscure labels. There were bird groups (the Crows, Penguins, Flamingoes) and car groups (the Cadillacs, the Lincolns, the Coup De Villes, the V-eights); there were Velvetones in New York and Chicago, the Vibranairs in Baltimore and the Vibranaires in Asbury Park. The Ravens reached the black chart in 1948 with 'Write Me a Letter' on National, the Robins in 1950 with 'If It's So, Baby' and the Dominoes, with Billy Ward and Clyde McPhatter, in 1951 with 'Sixty-minute Man', which was number one in the black chart for fourteen weeks. Italian-Americans also loved the tradition, and vocal groups both black and white became ubiquitous.

All this was in addition to solo singing, which ranged from beautiful barroom crooning to shouting Kansas City blues: Ray Charles was in Seattle imitating Nat Cole in the late 1940s; Kansas City's singing bartender Big Joe Turner had his first hit, 'My Gal's a Jockey', on National in 1946; pianist and vocalist Amos Milburn's long run of big R&B hits began in 1948. Pianist, singer and songwriter Ivory Joe Hunter had his first hit in 1945 with Johnny Moore's Three Blazers. He was later backed on records by members of Duke Ellington's band, and his singing of his songs, for example, 'I Almost Lost My Mind' and 'Since I Met You Baby', achieved such crossover success that he was welcomed on the *Grand Ole Opry* before he died in 1974. Guitarist Johnny Moore's trio had years of popularity from 1946, with vocalist Charles Brown, who sang as a soloist on 'Get Yourself Another Fool' on Aladdin in 1949 (and toured as far as Scotland in 1990). Roy Brown's 'Good Rockin' Tonight' appeared in 1948 on Deluxe, and Ruth Brown's 'So Long' in 1949 on Atlantic. Black pop retained its emphasis on honest entertainment and could always be danced to, but white pop was flying around in smaller and smaller circles until it almost disappeared.

During and after the war much good music was still being played by big bands, among the best being that of clarinettist and vocalist Woody Herman, who started in show business at the age of six. He formed a band in 1933, but it failed. He worked for Gus Arnheim and then Isham Jones; when Jones retired, the band became a cooperative and each member owned shares. 'The Band That Played the Blues' had an integrity of its own from 1937 on the Decca label. 'At the Woodchopper's Ball' was a hit, 'Blues in the Night' was sung by Herman and the band's theme, 'Blue Flame', was named after a locker-room prank involving the lighting of naturally produced methane gas with a match.

As the original members left the band, a process accelerated by conscription, Herman bought their shares until he owned it. During the musicians' strike 'Woodchopper's Ball' was reissued and was again successful. Decca was one of the first major labels to settle with the musicians' union, but of twenty-four Herman titles recorded in 1944, only four were released. Meanwhile, the band that began recording for Columbia was entirely transformed. Bass player Chubby Jackson and pianist-arranger Ralph Burns had joined in 1943 (both from Charlie Barnet), and Jackson helped recruit most of the rest. Guitarist Billy Bauer had replaced the last remaining member of the old band; other key members were drummer Dave Tough (soon replaced by stand-in Buddy Rich, then Don Lamond), trumpeter-arranger Neal Hefti, tenor saxophonist Flip Phillips, trumpeter Pete Candoli and trombonist Bill Harris. Vocalist Frances Wayne's hits with the band included 'Saturday Night is the Loneliest Night of the Week' (on Decca), 'Happiness is Just a Thing Called Joe' and 'Gee, It's Good to Hold You' (Columbia); Herman sang on the frenetic 'Caldonia'. But it was on the instrumentals that this band romped, stomped, swung and screamed, without ever going over the top: 'Apple Honey', 'Northwest Passage', 'The Good Earth', 'Your Father's Mustache', 'Blowin' Up a Storm', 'Sidewalks of Cuba' and the more relaxed 'Goosey Gander' represented a new generation of young white jazz musicians who had done all their homework and knew how to share the joy with the listener. Burns's 'Bijou (Rhumba à la Jazz)' featured Harris, who wrote the beautiful 'Everywhere' (arranged by Hefti). Margie Hyams played vibraphone, but was replaced by Red Norvo, precipitating a new, modern edition of the Woodchoppers, the band within a band: the nonet – which included Herman on alto as well as clarinet, Jimmy Rowles on piano and the bright new trumpet star Sonny Berman – recorded 'Steps', 'Igor', 'Four Men on a Horse' and similar unique soundscapes. As early as mid-1944 Candoli's sixteen-year-old brother Conte played in the band during his summer holidays from high school. The band gave a famous concert at Carnegie Hall in 1946.

Pianist Claude Thornhill had arranged and recorded 'Loch Lomond' with vocalist Maxine Sullivan in 1937; Thornhill's theme was his own composition, the impressionistic 'Snowfall'. Among the musicians he hired were trumpeter Conrad Gozzo (later one of the most sought-after studio musicians), Irving Fazola and Lee Konitz on reeds and trumpeter Red Rodney, a young bopper who also recorded with Charlie Parker. In the 1940s Thornhill's innovative arrangements (many by the young Gil Evans) caught the ears of musicians and they were influential for decades. The quirky 'Portrait of a Guinea Farm' (1941) had a six-strong reed section; a choir of clarinets played a tune that could have been a Russian dance by Rimsky-Korsakov. The band's hits in the late 1940s included 'A Sunday Kind of Love', a good pop song with a vocal by Fran Warren, who in 1947 also recorded a sung version of 'Early Autumn' (written the year before by Ralph Burns as one of the four parts of 'Summer Sequence' for Woody Herman). In the same year the band recorded Parker's 'Thrivin' on a Riff', 'Donna Lee', 'Yardbird Suite' and 'Robbins' Nest' (a tribute to a DJ which became a sort of jazz classic, written by Sir Charles Thompson and Illinois Jacquet), as well as experimenting with such fare as 'La Paloma' (a Spanish song first published in the USA in 1877) and 'Warsaw Concerto' (an effective British film theme by Richard Addinsell), and such standard dance band material as 'Polka Dots and Moonbeams'. By this time Thornhill was using two French horns, a tuba and occasionally a bass clarinet, and also a crooning vocal group called the Snowflakes. Much post-war jazz, especially of the 'cool school', was influenced by Thornhill's willingness to experiment with textures and harmonies, all the while running what appeared to be a successful sweet band.

Pianist, arranger and composer Stan Kenton made his début with his own band in 1941. He presented, successively, three of the era's best girl singers in Anita O'Day ('And Her Tears Flowed Like Wine', 1944), June Christy ('Tampico', 1945) and, in the early 1950s, Chris Connor; his sidemen in 1944 included Stan Getz and in the late 1940s Kai Winding (trombone), Vido Musso (tenor saxophone), Art Pepper and Bud Shank (alto saxophones), Maynard Ferguson and Shorty Rogers (trumpets) and Shelly Manne (drums), and in the early 1950s Lee Konitz (alto saxophone): most of the best white musicians in West Coast jazz. Apart from twenty or so pop hits, such instrumental tracks as 'Eager Beaver' and a frenetic 'Peanut Vendor' were highly rated. Kenton later turned to pretentious original music beloved of high-school bandmasters, and was prone to utter futile disparaging remarks about country music ('a national disgrace') and the Beatles ('children's music'). In the 1940s his music was seen both as good pop and as good jazz, and indeed, a complete set on four Mosaic CDs of the arrangements of Bill Holman and Bill Russo (1950–63) reveals much beauty and fine playing, an admonishment to those of us who may have given up on Kenton too easily. But he insisted that his music be given parity with European classical music, which led to Kenton's most infamous album: Wagner played by a huge jazz orchestra. Self-conscious art and commerce do not mix well; Kenton was a good bandleader and talent scout, but not himself a particularly inspired composer, arranger or pianist.

Saxophonist Boyd Raeburn led a sweet band when he left college, but in New York in 1944 built a band full of young boppers; he could not record during the strike and henceforth recorded only for tiny labels. He became renowned for hiring such talented musicians as Sonny Berman, Al Cohn, Oscar Pettiford, pianist Dodo Marmarosa and clarinettist Buddy DeFranco. Dizzy Gillespie, Budd Johnson and Tadd Dameron all wrote for the band.

And there were up-to-date black big bands trying to play bop, though it is questionable whether a big band can play bop at all, just as Luis Russell could not play in the New Orleans style with a largish band twenty years earlier. Nevertheless, Billy Eckstine had one of the biggest, deepest and smoothest voices of all time, and with Budd Johnson had encouraged Earl Hines to hire progressive young musicians; in 1944 he and Johnson formed a band which until 1947 employed trumpeters Gillespie, Miles Davis, Fats Navarro and Kenny Dorham; Parker, Gene Ammons, Dexter Gordon and Lucky Thompson on reeds; and Art Blakey on drums. It played arrangements by Dameron, Johnson and Eckstine and vocalists Sarah Vaughan and Lena Horne. The band made few recordings, and its only hits were vocals by Eckstine, who sensibly made a career as a solo singer; his lovely work for MGM includes duets with Vaughan.

Dizzy Gillespie, a composer as well as the most influential trumpeter after Armstrong, an engaging vocalist and a great showman, led exciting big bands between 1946 and 1949, recording for

Musicraft, RCA and Capitol. If the line-up of sidemen was not quite as stellar as that of the earlier Eckstine band, it was more than adequate; among the reedmen alone at various times were Budd Johnson, Cecil Payne, Jimmy Heath, John Coltrane, James Moody and Paul Gonsalves. The arrangements by Johnson, John Lewis, Tadd Dameron, Gil Fuller, George Russell and others were influential as well as interesting. Cuban-born conga drummer and vocalist Chano Pozo, according to Gillespie, could play in one rhythm, sing in another and dance in a third, all at the same time. When they both worked for Cab Calloway, Gillespie had shared lodgings with Cuban trumpeter Mario Bauza (later Machito's music director), who introduced him to Latin music; Afro-Cuban jazz has been an enduring element to this day. Machito (Frank Raul Grillo) led one of the most popular Latin bands, whose music was often jazz-flavoured, and recorded with Parker, among others. Pozo was something of a roughneck, and was shot to death in a Harlem bar, but he wrote 'Tin Tin Deo' with Fuller and 'Manteca' and 'Cubana Be, Cubana Bop' with Gillespie and Russell, and played on Gillespie's recordings of the last two. In spite of everything, however, the band was not a great commercial success. And anyway, the big bands were about to disappear from mainstream popular music.

As a result of the wartime rationing of fuel, tyres and batteries, and the conversion of car factories to war production, it was increasingly hard for the dancers to get to the ballrooms and dance halls where the bands played. Furthermore, many young people had other things on their minds, such as letters from the local draft board. A stiff wartime entertainment tax made life more difficult for ballroom operators and booking agents, and it was not lifted until well into the 1950s, long after most of the clubs and dance halls had closed. All of these problems were obviously experienced in Britain as well.

Despite the popularity of the bands, and the image we all have of Glenn Miller playing for large numbers of service men and women, the primary purpose of going to war was not to entertain: there was not that much work for musicians on the military bases, where many of the dancers had gone. Even making recordings was difficult during the war (when Petrillo was not trying to prevent it) because of a shortage of the main ingredients of 78s. (Capitol signed a young and not very good bandleader because his father owned a warehouse full of shellac.) The labels also bought old records and ground them up to make new ones; quality fell as virgin shellac was mixed with the recycled material. After the war the decline of the Big Band Era was hastened by social, economic and demographic factors.

Films made in the late 1980s, such as *Who Framed Roger Rabbit?* and *Good Morning, Babylon*, featured the famous Los Angeles 'red car'; in the beautiful Californian climate a great deal of dancing took place in outdoor pavilions, and before the war young people used one of the best public transport systems in the world to get there; they could take a trolley-car clear across Los Angeles for 5 cents. The red cars (the Southern Pacific Railroad) and the yellow cars (a smaller system, the Los Angeles Railway Company) together operated over 1,000 miles of track. A great many towns had similar networks knitting together suburbs and amusement parks, a good number of which had dance pavilions. They in turn gave employment to many a local musician, as well as to touring name bands.

In 1936 National City Lines had been created by a cartel including Standard Oil, Phillips Petroleum, Goodyear Tire and Rubber and General Motors, for the purpose of buying up streetcar lines and making bus routes out of them. Those who thought this should be prevented by introducing subsidies for public transport were labelled 'Reds' by newspapers like the *Los Angeles Times*, whose reactionary owner, Harry Chandler, sat on the board of directors of Standard of California and had interests in road construction. An affiliate of National City Lines began taking the red cars out of service and tearing up the track, and after the war most of the damage had been done: few young people in the late 1940s could afford to buy cars, so the decline of public transport was another nail in the coffin of live music. Today Los Angeles has one of the world's few twenty-four-hour traffic jams, and is thinking about how to get rid of the internal combustion engine.

The country filled up with ex-soldiers who set about starting families at the time of the rise of television. It was easier to stay at home and watch TV than it was to go out, and the end of the ballrooms also saw the decline of the cinema. This was the beginning of the 'baby boom': an interesting corollary is that the preceding generation of teenaged girls was relatively small; readers of a certain age will remember that the difficulty of obtaining a babysitter was a stock joke in television sitcoms of the 1950s.

Add to all these problems the fact that after the war it was simply uneconomic to run a big band. Before the war Bob Wills could make good money playing at dance halls full of people who had paid only 75 cents to get in; but afterwards the cost of keeping a band together was much higher, while the takings were lower, since there were fewer dance halls and fewer dancers. In January 1947 the big bands of Woody Herman, Harry James, Benny Goodman, Les Brown, Tommy Dorsey, Benny Carter and Jack Teagarden, as well as the all-girl band of glamorous Ina Ray Hutton, folded. Some of these re-formed from time to time, especially Herman's, but that month was seen by the music business as terminal.

From 1939 clarinettist and arranger Les Brown had led a popular band, which had two number one hits: 'Sentimental Journey' in 1945, with a vocal by Doris Day, and 'I've Got My Love to Keep Me Warm', which was recorded in 1946; during Petrillo's second strike against the record companies it reached the top of the charts at the end of 1948. Everybody knew it was the last number one instrumental of the Swing Era. It had been a heady time, when popular music was good and good music was popular, but it was over.

12

The Early 1950s: Frustration and Confusion

After the Second World War the twentieth century seemed to be the American century. The only nation to come out of the war healthier than when it went in was the USA; the Marshall Plan helped rebuild Europe, while at home the Depression was over, and a great many ex-soldiers were taking advantage of the GI Bill to acquire further education, an opportunity that had mostly been denied their parents. During the war the income of the average white family had doubled, but the income of the average black family had tripled; industry was working flat out to supply consumers (a new buzz-word) with everything they wanted, and the perfect society seemed to be just around the corner. Could we not invent anything we needed?

There were unseen difficulties ahead, but the biggest problem facing the record business as the decade turned appeared to be technological confusion. The invention of microgroove records started the battle of the speeds, which meant dislocation in the industry and headaches for retailers. Mainstream popular music itself in the post-war years became anodyne, as though the hole at the centre of it previously occupied by the big bands could be filled only with marshmallow.

The phenomenon of what is still called light music in Britain and soon came to be called mood music by many, was an interesting one; it briefly had a new life thanks largely to the long-playing record. A good number of recordings of 'light classical' music and orchestral arrangements of popular material had always been used for what was later called easy listening. Victor's director of light music, Nathaniel Shilkret, had over fifty hit records from 1924 to 1932, and during the

1930s and 1940s Al Goodman and André Kostelanetz were tremendously popular on radio and on records that stayed in print for years, accumulating comfortable sales. Violinist and bandleader Leo Reisman not only accompanied Fred Astaire (and composer Harold Arlen singing his own 'Stormy Weather'), but had over seventy hits between 1925 and 1940. Arthur Fiedler became conductor of the Boston Pops in 1930, and stayed until he died in 1979. In 1943 studio conductor David Rose had a hit with 'Holiday for Strings'; in 1949 ace studio conductor Lennie Hayton was successful with Richard Rodgers's ballet 'Slaughter on Tenth Avenue'.

In the early 1950s the studio bandleaders and A&R men, some of them veterans of the Swing Era, were arrangers, composers and conductors: for example, Gordon Jenkins at Decca, Hugo Winterhalter and German-born Henri Rene at RCA, Percy Faith, Paul Weston and Mitch Miller at Columbia, Les Baxter at Capitol and Richard Hayman and David Carroll at Mercury. Trumpet player turned conductor Monty Kelly had a hit in 1953 with 'Tropicana'. The composers of such instrumental pieces were journeymen who turned their hands to many things; 'Tropicana' and 'Life in New York' were written by Bernie Wayne, who also wrote 'Vanessa' (an instrumental hit for Winterhalter), 'Laughing on the Outside (Crying on the Inside)', which had popular recordings in 1946 and 1953, and 'Blue Velvet', a hit for Tony Bennett in 1951 and a much bigger success for Bobby Vinton a dozen years later. Leroy Anderson was a choir director and organist who also played bass in symphony orchestras, and began arranging for the Boston Pops in 1935; his own record of 'Syncopated Clock' was a hit in 1951, and his 'Blue Tango' was in the charts for thirty-eight weeks that year. Most of these people backed vocalists on countless hit recordings, for example, Kostelanetz on Perry Como's number one 'Prisoner of Love' (1946).

Some of the arranger-conductor hits had vocals, sung by studio soloists or a chorus, but the 'popular instrumental' briefly became a genre of its own. Les Baxter was an all-rounder who later wrote scores for some of Roger Corman's horror films; his 'April in Portugal' was a hit in 1953, while Richard Hayman's 'Ruby', on which he played harmonica, reached number three that year; the tune was the theme from the film *Ruby Gentry*. Mitch Miller turned out jolly novelties like 'Oriental Polka', which usually did not reach the charts. The soundtrack title theme from the Italian film *Anna* was a hit in 1953, sung by Silvana Mangano, while Weston made an attractive dance band arrangement of it. Percy Faith was among the most successful in this class, recording over eighty profitable albums and two big hit singles: 'Delicado' (1952), a Brazilian pop song, was played by Stan Freeman on an amplified harpsichord; 'Song from "Moulin Rouge" (Where is Your Heart)' (1953), a film theme, was sung by Felicia Sanders in a brilliant arrangement. (Faith's jolly version of Hugo Alfven's 'Swedish Rhapsody', which was on the other side, also charted.)

The hits of the few dance bands that were still around, mostly playing at college proms, fell into the popular instrumental category. Pianist and arranger Ralph Flanagan was encouraged by booking agents to form a band on the Glenn Miller model; he was successful in 1952 with 'Hot Toddy' on RCA. Trumpeter Ray Anthony on Capitol had an attractive recording of 'Dancing in the Dark' and trumpeter Ralph Marterie reached high in the chart with Ellington's 'Caravan' on Mercury in 1953. 'Skokiaan' was a South African novelty named after a Zulu drink; the Bulawayo Sweet Rhythm Boys had their own hit (on London), while Anthony, Marterie and Johnny Hodges all made recordings of it. Trombonist Buddy Morrow (whose real name was Moe Zudekoff) had played with such bands as Artie Shaw's and Tommy Dorsey's; in 1952 he had a big-band hit with a cover of Jimmy Forrest's 'Night Train', but it did not appear in the *Billboard* chart (probably because by that time everybody was embarrassed, knowing that the riff properly belonged to Ellington). There was not enough work to keep a large number of dance bands in business, yet the remarkable thing about all these records was the playing of the rhythm sections, which was infinitely better than that of the average white rhythm section of earlier decades. Marterie's 'Caravan', though it was inferior to Ellington's recordings of his own tune, was a jumping disc: it introduced a new generation to the name of Ellington, and (like Marterie's pop hit 'Pretend' of the same year) it featured an electric guitar, still unusual at the time.

Most of this music, however, does not hold up very well. The wordless chorus (a common gimmick) on Baxter's 'April in

Portugal' has been known to induce nausea. In any case, the 'popular instrumental', and light music in general, was soon subsumed in Muzak, the name of the largest purveyor of wired music which became a generic term for the slush that came at you out of the walls and ceilings of airports, supermarkets and waiting rooms. Most of this superfluous and gratuitous music was third-rate; it helped to kill off, or at least drive underground, the American market for light music, because it devalued music in general (yet if you asked for it to be turned off, you heard, 'Whatsamatter? Don't you like music?'). There was less wallpaper music in Britain, which is partly why light music still has a considerable audience there. English essayist and novelist J. B. Priestley wrote:

Austere musicians dismiss this flimsy tinkling too easily; so-called light music has its own values, not really belonging to music at all . . . it acts as a series of vials, often charmingly shaped and coloured, for the distillations of memory. The first few bars of it remove the stopper; we find ourselves reliving, not remembering but magically reliving, some exact moments of our past.

That it came to be called mood music was largely due to the Englishman George Melachrino, whose series of such albums as *Music for Dining*, *Music for Reading*, *Music for Daydreaming* led to ribald suggestions for the next title. (In fact, one of them was called *Music for Two People Alone*.) Melachrino's handling of a chamber-sized string orchestra was adventurous compared with the sound cranked out by the Italian-born violinist Annunzio Paolo Mantovani. In the late 1930s Mantovani led the potted-palm sort of hotel combo, and parleyed it into what sounded like thousands of fiddles; he had over fifty hit albums from 1953, helped by UK Decca's excellent sound.

There is nothing intrinsically wrong with an arrangement of a good tune for a full-sized orchestra; the Canadian-born Percy Faith, the former Tommy Dorsey arranger Paul Weston and another Canadian, Robert Farnon, who had played trumpet in Faith's Canadian radio orchestra, were very good at it, and were at their best on albums.

Farnon has worked in England since the Second World War. His albums were used by teachers of arranging as examples of how this sort of thing should be done, and he has probably carried out more film and studio work than anyone else in the business. Weston's album *Caribbean Cruise* was wonderfully tasteful, for listening or dancing to, and his albums *Mood for Twelve* and *Solo Mood* featured solos by jazzmen such as guitarist George Van Eps. (Bobby Hackett played lovely solos on mood music albums conducted by comedian Jackie Gleason.) Weston's earlier albums on Capitol, some of them remade later in stereo, included such elegant innovations that you did not notice them: if he wanted to use violins along with brass and reeds, instead of amplifying the violins he would have everyone else playing softly, or with mutes. This sounded better than most people's efforts in that mode.

Faith had played piano in silent cinemas and might have been a concert pianist, but his hands were injured in a fire. In the USA after 1940 he continued in radio work, apparently recording for Eli Oberstein's Varsity label in the mid-1940s and for RCA in 1949, before moving to Columbia in 1950. His best work dates from the early 1950s, and on albums, which will probably never be reissued (not by Sony, anyway) because they are not stereo. The voicings in his arrangements were unique and immediately recognizable; his use of woodwind was particularly distinctive. He had a predilection for Latin rhythms, perhaps, he once said, because he came from a cold climate; albums such as *Carnival Rhythms* must have used most of the best Latin percussionists in New York. *American Waltzes, Continental Music* and *Romantic Music* belong to an era when what was thought to be sophistication could still carry an aura of innocence. And as for the rhythm sections, I would still like to know the name of Faith's studio bass player, who was always nicely behind the beat on the ballads.

Faith's series of 78s for RCA had included 'Deep Purple', Charles Trenet's 'Beyond the Sea' and the title track of one of the first RCA 12-inch pop LPs, *Soft Lights and Sweet Music*. The cover photograph was a close-up of a woman in evening dress, wearing a veil and with her eyes closed, and a man – dancing? embracing? dreaming? In 1977 when the ten tracks were reissued by Pickwick, the garish and instantly dated cover photograph pictured a fireplace and a bimbo with a skimpy dress and come-hither lipstick. A good deal had changed in less than thirty years.

Faith started the fad for instrumental albums of music from Broadway shows with *Kismet* in 1954. The tunes had been taken from the works of the Russian composer Alexander Borodin, and lent themselves to Faith's concert treatment. That the trend later became hackneyed (with umpteen versions of *My Fair Lady* and *The Sound of Music*) was not Faith's fault. He also wrote film scores that were invariably better than the films, notably *The Oscar* (1966), which yielded a good pop song, 'Maybe September'. In 1960 he had a third number one single, and received a Grammy for the syrupy 'Theme from a Summer Place', slop which limped along with a slow kling-kling-kling piano. Ironically, this was a cliché from rock'n'roll, which by then had helped Muzak relegate light music in America to the status of a bad joke. (That piano style was called claw music by studio musicians, who hated it; it was sent up unmercifully by Stan Freberg on one of his comedy records.)

Somewhere along the way Faith moved to the West Coast, and the sound of his albums was coarsened; they were recorded too close to the microphone to make them more 'hi-fi'. (R. D. Darrell complained about this in a review of Faith's album of songs from *Subways are for Sleeping*, a Jule Stein show that opened in late 1961 and lost money.) Faith later recorded an album of Beatles songs, and another called *Black Magic Woman*; even these reached the chart, for the remaining customers for string orchestras were grateful for small favours.

Easy listening on long-playing records, however appealing some of them were, could not represent the best of a nation's popular culture anyway, and the music business would have been in a state of disarray even without the 'battle of the speeds'. For a generation the centre of popular music had been the big jazz-oriented dance band, and suddenly it was gone.

Country music was seemingly always about to make a break-through. The prudish dominance of the *Grand Ole Opry* was worn away, and adult themes were approached. Floyd Tillman's 'Slippin' Around' was a number one pop hit in 1949, in a duet by Jimmy Wakely and Margaret Whiting, showing that the pop chart could handle adultery without the world coming to an end; but Tillman's own version was confined to the country chart. Webb Pierce's 'There Stands the Glass' and Kitty Wells's 'It Wasn't God Who Made Honky Tonk Angels', which treated alcoholism and sexism as something more than jokes, were just around the corner.

The honky-tonk style was considered disreputable, especially on the *Grand Ole Opry*, but it could not long be avoided; its greatest practitioner and one of the all-time great artists in American popular music was Hank Williams. He was born in utter poverty and suffered pain all his life, perhaps from an undiagnosed case of spina bifida, and was killed by the effects of alcohol and pills at the age of twenty-nine. Country music has often ignored fashion and the delicate feelings of the bourgeoisie in order to portray the real world; the fact is that a great many Americans lived from pay-cheque to pay-cheque, and spent much time drowning their sorrows or trying to enjoy themselves in the sort of taverns ('blood buckets') where Williams had served his apprenticeship. He knew these people's hopes, dreams and fears, and wrote their songs for them; he was among the greatest of folk poets.

In 1946 Williams took his religious songs to Fred Rose in Nashville, who recorded them and leased them to a Sterling label. Louis B. Mayer, head of MGM film studios, had intended to start a record company around 1940, but the musicians' strike and the war intervened; a Lion label was briefly formed to exploit new songs, but after the war MGM's parent company, Leow's, hired Frank Walker to run a new MGM label. Walker had helped keep Columbia Records afloat in the mid-1920s by signing Bessie Smith; now Rose brought him Hank Williams. He had a few hits in the country chart in 1947–8, but his recording of 'Lovesick Blues' (ironically a song older than he was) was a number one country hit for sixteen weeks in 1949. Although he was already an alcoholic, known to be unreliable and represented a style the country establishment did not like, he nevertheless had to be invited to the *Opry*, where he was a sensation. He had less than four years to live.

Fred Rose was a pop music veteran who had briefly played piano with Paul Whiteman and written or co-written such tunes as 'Deep Henderson' (recorded by both King Oliver and the Coon–Sanders Night Hawks) and others for Sophie Tucker, then Gene Autry ('Be Honest With Me', which was nominated for an Oscar in 1941) and

Roy Acuff. Thus he got into country music by accident, and formed Acuff–Rose in 1942. Williams was never known to read anything but comic books and the country charts in the trade papers; he sometimes bought lyrics from others, and always had a pocketful of scraps of paper on which he jotted down ideas. Rose helped him to polish his songs, and could probably have grabbed credit for them, yet his name appears on only a few.

Williams's songs reached the pop chart in cover versions by Frankie Laine, Tony Bennett, Guy Mitchell, Jo Stafford and Rosemary Clooney, among others; they were big hits, mostly on Columbia, where Mitch Miller knew a good song when he heard one. But Williams himself never made the pop charts, despite thirty-six top tens in the country chart in nine years, several of them after his death. One of his early teachers had been a black street singer called Tee-Tot (Rufe Payne); he was also influenced by Roy Acuff, and mainstream America was not ready for a deep southern accent.

He may have been too dangerous in the era of *The Man in the Gray Flannel Suit*. His recordings and, more especially, his legendary live performances had an insouciant swagger, almost an improvisatory quality, and a natural sexuality which presaged that of Elvis Presley. He insisted on using his excellent stage band, the Drifting Cowboys, on his recordings, and always gave them plenty of solo space; there were no drums, and none was needed. His own recording of 'Hey, Good Lookin'' for example, is much better than the pop duet by Laine and Stafford, which is too frenetically jolly. Williams sets a tempo which is just right, jaunty but not expecting too much: there may be grief tomorrow, but we can have a good time tonight if we want to. 'I Won't Be Home No More' shows how a lover's complaint became a swinging piece of bravado:

> You're just in time to be too late.
> I tried to, but I couldn't wait,
> and now I've got another date,
> so I won't be home no more.
>   I stood around a month or two,
>   And waited for your call,
>   Now I'm too busy pitchin' woo,
>   So come around next Fall.

There are more verses, in which none of the perfectly simple phrases is repeated: 'You're just in time to change your tune / Go tell your troubles to the moon' is a new way to rhyme those time-honoured Tin Pan Alley words. Fiddler Jerry Rivers and steel guitarist Don Helms seem to float over the beat, while Williams sings each group of four syllables as though they were triplets, his carelessness matching that of the spurned lover: 'Be on your way / That's all she wrote' may have more than one meaning. There is a 'Well, I'll be damned' feeling about the whole thing.

Williams also recorded quasi-religious or philosophical monologues under the name of Luke the Drifter, and recorded a few duets with his troublesome first wife, Audrey, who thought she could sing. Compilations of Williams's tracks have often selected poor songs, among them the maudlin 'My Son Calls Another Man Daddy', and not enough of the country blues:

> I went to the doctor / he took one look,
> Said 'The trouble with you / ain't in my book.
> I tell ya what it is, but / it ain' good news:
> You got an awful bad case / o' them low down blues.'

The set of the complete singles issued in 1991 still does not include 'Low Down Blues' (which was probably a demo tape with backing later dubbed), but it is an astonishing set and a cornerstone of post-war popular music. The average level of quality of both songs and performances puts Williams on a plateau where only a handful belong; his ability to communicate directly to his listener places his work beyond any consolation of genre, and has influenced generations of songwriters and vocalists. But we were not supposed to have the low-down blues in America in the early 1950s; most Americans who had enjoyed some of his songs as recorded by mainstream pop artists never heard his hillbilly accent (neither the first nor the last example of classism in the business). Nevertheless, country music provided a great many hit records and songs in the post-war years that are still selling and still being covered. As we have seen, Jimmie Rodgers and Roy Acuff had made the male vocalist the biggest star in country music, and Hank Williams was the greatest of all, but there were many more.

Ernest Tubb was nicknamed the Texas Troubadour; he was

inspired by Rodgers and encouraged by his widow, who gave him one of Jimmie's guitars. His first hit was with his own 'Walking the Floor Over You' in 1942, and when the *Billboard* country chart began in 1944, he filled it with mostly top ten hits all the way through the 1950s, and continued to appear in the chart several times a year in the next decade. He was also famous for Ernest Tubb's Record Shop in Nashville, and for a late-night radio show on WSM, where a talented newcomer might get a boost. Webb Pierce, from Louisiana, brought the honky-tonk style to Nashville for good when he joined the *Opry* in 1955. His three successive number one country hits in 1952 began with 'Back Street Affair', another classic song about adultery (called 'cheatin' songs' in the trade). Pierce had a strong voice, piercing yet rough-edged, and used the steel guitar so effectively that he did more to establish it than almost anybody else.

After attending Princeton and other universities, Texan Hank Thompson formed the Brazos Valley Boys, which had hits from 1948. His somewhat larger band helped keep the feeling of western swing alive with country hits throughout the 1950s, including 'The Wild Side of Life' (1952). Lefty Frizzell (from 1950), Carl Smith (from 1951) and Ray Price (from 1952) were among those with great songs that entered the national consciousness; not even people who hated country music could avoid hearing the biggest hits accidentally, on a jukebox or while cruising the dial on the radio.

Brother acts were also important. The male duet tradition was probably established by the Blue Sky Boys as much as anyone. Bill and Earl Bolick, from South Carolina, used the 'high lonesome' harmony of bluegrass music and traditional instruments; they left music in 1951 partly because they would not add an electric guitar to their act. The Delmore Brothers, Alton and Rabon, from Alabama, recorded for twenty years from 1931, and had a direct effect on the rockabillies of the 1950s with their black-influenced ragtime-like style; Alton is said to have written over a thousand songs, many still in the repertory of country artists today. The Louvin Brothers, actually Charlie and Ira Loudermilk, from North Carolina, began recording in 1949; their 'I Don't Believe You've Met My Baby' (1956) is an example of the portrayal of emotional pain that country music dealt with honestly and, contrary to the belief of those who do not understand country music, with pathos but without sentimentality. Johnnie and Jack were from Tennessee, but were not brothers: Johnny Wright married Kitty Wells in 1938, and Jack Anglin was killed in a car crash in 1963 (on his way to a memorial service for Patsy Cline). Their hits began in 1951 with one of their most successful, 'Poison Love'.

Women were not big stars in country music, despite the influence of Molly O'Day and Rose Maddox (of the Maddox Brothers and Sister Rose from 1947 to 1959, later a soloist). Then Kitty Wells came along. Born Muriel Ellen Deason in Nashville, her stage name was chosen by her husband. She recorded for RCA from 1949, and in 1952, almost apologetically, with a deep country vibrato and a southern accent you could cut with a knife, she established the role of women in country music, talking back to Hank Thompson:

> As I sit here tonight, the juke box playing
> The tune about the wild side of life,
> As I listen to the words you are singing,
> It brings memories of when I was a trusting wife.
>
> It wasn't God who made honky tonk angels,
> As you said in the words to your song.
> Too many times married men think they're still single.
> That has caused many a good girl to go wrong.
>
> It's a shame that all the blame is on us women.
> It's not true that only you men feel the same.
> From the start 'most every heart that's been broken
> Was because there was a man to blame.

And that is the whole song, written by one J. D. Miller. The record is less than two and a half minutes long. With a simple, memorable tune and three very plain verses (albeit with internal rhymes in the last), and years before the advent of fashionable feminism, Wells did not find it necessary to feel sorry for all those heartbroken men crying in their beer. And the next year she gently sassed Webb Pierce, with 'Paying For That Back Street Affair'. She is still the Queen of Country Music, having paved the way for such no-nonsense stars as Loretta Lynn and Tammy Wynette. And she did not rely on answer songs by any means: 'Makin' Believe' in 1955 was one of her own heartachers.

The decade was a golden age for country. While the hits of the white pop singers in the early 1950s were slick and studio-bound, it is significant that many of the country stars recorded with their own backing groups, just as the vocalists of the Swing Era had done; like them, they knew who their audience was, because they saw the faces around the bandstand night after night. Decca and Columbia reported that nearly half their sales of singles were rooted in country music, yet still restricted to a ghetto. Eddy Arnold had nearly seventy top ten hits in the *Billboard* country chart in ten years after 1945, but only two of them were allowed in the pop chart. Pee Wee King's 'Slow Poke' (1952) was one of the few country records (as opposed to covers) to be allowed to cross over. The songs and their attitudes proved far more influential than they were thought to be at the time.

In 1947 the Liberian government commissioned *Liberian Suite* from Duke Ellington; including Al Hibbler's vocal on 'I Like the Sunrise' and five instrumental dances, it was one of the first pieces recorded under Ellington's new contract with Columbia Records. *The Tattooed Bride* (1948), thought by some to be among the best of his longer works, and *Harlem* (1950), commissioned by the NBC Symphony Orchestra, were both later recorded, along with such singles as 'Brown Penny', 'Stomp, Look and Listen', 'Boogie Bop Blues' and many other Ducal delights.

Also in 1947, Woody Herman re-formed his band. The Second Herd, as it came to be called, played arrangements by Ralph Burns, Neal Hefti, Al Cohn, Jimmy Giuffre, Shorty Rogers and John LaPorta, and was as musically exciting as the first. In its first year it recorded a fourth part of Burns's 'Summer Sequence', more than a year after the first three parts; 'Keen and Peachy' was a collaboration by Rogers and Burns. The band's most famous recording was 'Four Brothers', written by Giuffre. Its spirited pastel harmony was played by a reed section of Herbie Steward on alto, Stan Getz and Zoot Sims on tenors and Serge Chaloff on baritone. It was the sound of modern jazz, played by young white musicians thoroughly familiar with the harmonic freedom of bop, and that reed section was the only one as famous among jazz fans as Ellington's.

Count Basie disbanded in 1950, led a small group with Wardell Gray and clarinettist Buddy DeFranco, but started all over again in 1952: having been invited to record for Norman Granz, he led a big band for the rest of his life. But neither Ellington, Herman nor Basie had any hits in the national pop chart in 1950. So what were the number one hits of that year?

The record business was booming in the late 1940s; all Petrillo achieved with his second strike was the establishment of a trustee to oversee the payment of record royalties. In 1947 the US industry exceeded its peak of twenty-five years earlier. But the industry, then as now, was dominated by conservative people; the frenetic recording that took place before the 1948 strike resulted in a backlog of material that the public did not particularly want.

The National Association of Disk Jockeys had been created in 1947 by a press agent, partly in order to plug a film, *Something in the Wind*, about a radio station. The disc jockey, however, was now an important figure. Capitol was the first label to send free records to DJs; the others soon fell into line, and it was understood that the DJ of the period had better judgement than the record labels about what the public wanted. Hence the black jump band of Louis Jordan began doing better on the radio and in the charts, and independent labels got a fairer share of the action. Frankie Laine, already a cabaret veteran of some years, finally struck it big on Chicago's new and energetic Mercury label, with 'That's My Desire'. The DJs were credited with putting an end to weekly radio shows by Bing Crosby, Frank Sinatra and Dinah Shore: why should fans tune in to a weekly show when they could hear their favourites just by leaving the radio on? To get a picture of the trend, here first are the number one *Billboard* hits of 1940:

Artie Shaw	'Frenesi'	RCA Victor
Bing Crosby	'Only Forever'	Decca
Tommy Dorsey, Frank Sinatra		
and the Pied Pipers	'I'll Never Smile Again'	RCA Victor
Glenn Miller	'The Woodpecker Song'	Bluebird (RCA)
Glenn Miller	'Tuxedo Junction'	Bluebird (RCA)
Glenn Miller	'In the Mood'	Bluebird (RCA)

| Frankie Masters | 'Scatter-brain' | Vocalion (Decca) |
| Shep Fields | 'South of the Border' | Bluebird (RCA) |

There are no black artists, no country songs, and only two labels are represented. Shep Fields and Frankie Masters were leaders of sweet bands, now forgotten. 'The Woodpecker Song' was an Italian song with new English words, sung by Marion Hutton (not the same as 'The Woody Woodpecker Song', from the cartoon character, which was later a huge novelty hit). 'Only Forever' was a romantic pop song with a weak middle eight, and was revived by Count Basie and Joe Williams in the mid-1950s. Of these eight titles, four are pop classics (all on RCA) and have been continuously available ever since. Compare the *Billboard* 1940 list with that of 1947:

Vaughn Monroe	'Ballerina'	RCA Victor
Francis Craig	'Near You'	Bullet
Tex Williams	'Smoke! Smoke! Smoke That Cigarette'	Capitol
The Harmonicats	'Peg o' My Heart'	Vitacoustic
Perry Como	'Chi-baba, Chi-baba (My Bambino Go to Sleep)'	RCA Victor
Art Lund	'Mam'selle'	MGM
Ted Weems	'Heartaches'	RCA Victor
Freddy Martin	'Managua, Nicaragua'	RCA Victor
Count Basie	'Open the Door, Richard!'	RCA Victor
Nat Cole Trio	'(I Love You) for Sentimental Reasons'	Capitol
Sammy Kaye	'The Old Lamp-lighter'	RCA Victor

When the figures were in, 1947 was overall a landmark year, but not so hot for the major labels. There are more number one hits, reflecting more releases, a shorter average time at the top and the DJs' ability to tickle the public's fancy with something new. 'Near You', co-written and recorded in Nashville by hotel bandleader Francis Craig, was the biggest hit of the year; another top one was 'Peg o' My Heart', a 1913 song and the first release on Vitacoustic (the harmonica group soon changed to Mercury). Another number one was on the new independent, MGM. Neither Columbia nor

Decca had any number ones. Capitol had two, one of which was a country novelty and the other by Nat Cole, the first black artist to achieve wide fame; only his title on this list might be granted 'pop classic' status. Notice that the low-priced labels, Bluebird and Vocalion, are gone: there was no margin in cheaper records. RCA again had six number ones, but two were flukes: Basie's novelty made it for one week only, and 'Heartaches', by Ted Weems, with Elmo Tanner whistling, was a reissue from 1931. Altogether there are seven male vocals, not counting the jive on the Basie record, including Billy Williams (with Kaye) and Stuart Wade (with Martin), but the other five vocalists are stars, not band singers.

The major labels were troubled by these changes, and they reacted by spending too much money on too many releases, chasing hits without knowing what they were doing. Eli Oberstein had been fired from RCA in 1938, but reinstated in 1945; now he was made a scapegoat and bounced again. In the mid-1930s, when he was doing a good job at Victor, Oberstein had been paid about $6,000 a year; in 1947 Mannie Sachs was poached from Columbia to take over pop recording at RCA at a salary somewhere between $50,000 and $75,000 a year. Sachs said that he consulted his ten-year-old niece when deciding which songs to record; this was thought to be a joke at the time, but in retrospect it is not funny.

Here are the *Billboard* number one hits from 1950:

Patti Page	'Tennessee Waltz'	Mercury
Phil Harris	'The Thing'	RCA Victor
Sammy Kaye	'Harbor Lights'	RCA Victor
Gordon Jenkins and the Weavers	'Goodnight Irene'	Decca
Nat Cole	'Mona Lisa'	Capitol
Anton Karas	'Third Man Theme'	London
Eileen Barton	'If I Knew You Were Comin' I'd've Baked a Cake'	National
Teresa Brewer	'Music! Music! Music!'	London
Red Foley	'Chattanoogie Shoe Shine Boy'	Decca
Ames Brothers	'Rag Mop'	Coral (Decca)
Andrews Sisters	'I Can Dream, Can't I'	Decca

The 1950 list is even more various, a complete jumble. Nat Cole is now no longer leading the trio. There are two titles that were perceived as country or 'folk' and another that should have been. Seven labels are represented. There is only one dance band, and few of the other hits could be danced to. The Phil Harris record illustrates a remarkable (and ominous) trend: many of the hits of the new decade would fall into *Billboard*'s 'novelty' category.

Harris was a good entertainer who deserved his success; among his hits in the 1940s had been 'The Preacher and the Bear' and 'Woodman, Spare That Tree', both revived from the acoustic era. Anton Karas wrote the music and played the zither in the soundtrack of the famous Carol Reed film. 'Rag Mop', also regarded as a novelty, had a strong beat and nonsense words; later it was speculated that 'Rag Mop' had been the first rock'n'roll record, which was not far wrong: hit versions of it included one by its co-author, Johnnie Lee Wills, on Bullet. 'Rag Mop' was a country stomp, no different from 'Osage Stomp', recorded by Bob Wills in 1935, with Johnnie Lee on banjo. The big hit version of 'Rag Mop' was less appropriate: the Ames Brothers were a smooth vocal group.

'Tennessee Waltz' is a good country song, written by Redd Stewart and Pee Wee King in 1948 and a hit in the country chart that year. Page's record was at number one for thirteen weeks and sold six million copies. It provides an early example of multi-tracking, and that gimmick, associated in the public mind with new technology, may have helped establish the 45 rpm format, though the 78 sounded exactly the same. (Mercury had been one of the first to market 45s.) Red Foley began on the WLS *National Barn Dance* in 1930; from the first *Billboard* country chart in 1944 until 1956 he had over fifty top ten hits, 'Chattanoogie Shoe Shine Boy' being another country stomp, and Foley's biggest crossover hit. But the most interesting hit of 1950, and also the biggest, was a sleeper. An urban folk scene had created itself, apparently, with no commercial possibilities at all; then along came 'Goodnight Irene', by the Weavers.

This scene had been nurtured by the American liberal left for many years. Josh White was a black folk and blues singer and guitarist; as a child he was the eyes for street singers such as Blind Blake and Blind Lemon Jefferson, but his literacy and ambition took him to the smart

Café Society Downtown in New York, whereupon he was dismissed by purists. He was also well known for his left-wing politics. Huddie Ledbetter, better known as Leadbelly, was less lucky. He was jailed twice for murder, but was discovered by John and Alan Lomax and sang his way out of jail for the second time in 1934. He worked for the Lomaxes and made his way to New York, where he was taken up by café society in an early example of radical chic, but he was less able to take advantage of it than Josh White. The modern era of folk music in the USA began with the meeting in New York of Leadbelly's country folk-blues, the itinerant dust-bowl troubadour Woody Guthrie and the incipient urban folk of Pete Seeger.

Guthrie was born in Oklahoma and became a legend in his own time. Entirely self-taught, he roamed the country, having seen his father go bankrupt, his sister killed in a coal-oil stove explosion and his mother committed to a mental institution. He worked briefly with his cousin Jack Guthrie, who had country hits on Capitol ('Oklahoma Hills' was number one while Jack was serving in the South Pacific in 1945). Woody's songs include 'This Land Is Your Land' (written as a riposte to Irving Berlin's 'God Bless America'), 'Pastures of Plenty', 'This Train Is Bound for Glory', 'Roll On, Columbia', 'So Long, It's Been Good to Know Ya' and nearly a thousand more. A true folk artist, he would put new words to an old tune as necessary, and was opposed to copyright restrictions on any songs, including his own.

Guthrie's guitar bore the legend 'This machine kills fascists.' His politics were unreservedly left and he wrote for communist news-papers, yet in the far-off days of 1940 he was hired to write songs for the Bonneville Power Administration, a little populism being allowed in the Roosevelt years. He joined the US Merchant Marine and survived torpedo attacks with another folk singer, Cisco Houston; from the mid-1950s Guthrie was seriously ill with Hunt-ington's chorea, an inherited disease of the nervous system.

Pete Seeger's father was musicologist Charles Louis Seeger, who told him that a folksong in a book is like a photograph of a bird in flight; his stepmother was composer Ruth Crawford Seeger, whose string quartet (1931) is an American masterpiece, and who was later an editor of songbooks. His half-sister and half-brother are Peggy and Mike Seeger, also prominent folk musicians; Peggy married the British singer and songwriter Ewan MacColl. Pete tried journalism and painting before he realized he could not really do anything but play the banjo; he designed his own five-string instrument, wrote a manual on how to play it and became a sort of Johnny Appleseed of music. He was described as America's tuning fork.

Seeger had admired a mimeographed collection of Guthrie's songs, and when they met, they formed the Almanac Singers in 1940, with playwright Lee Hays, actor Millard Lampell and others. The group was managed for a while by the William Morris Agency; during the time of the Popular Front it was not a sin to sing union songs, but the FBI took an interest anyway. They sang at radical meetings, sometimes narrowly escaping violence. Seeger came from a privileged background, but saw injustice all around him and had only one way to fight it. He was a member of the Communist Party, and sang for them because they were idealists, the hardest-working and most honest people in sight at a time when the world seemed to be going crazy. His politics were naïve, but his admiration was for the rank and file, not the party bosses, who suddenly did not want anti-fascist songs during the Hitler–Stalin pact.

Seeger's ancestors had fought for American freedom in the eighteenth century, and he was not the only premature anti-fascist in 1940. (The phrase 'premature anti-fascist', by the way, was actually invented by the anti-communist brigade.) The FBI went to RCA and asked them what the Almanac label was (actually Keynote recordings): RCA told the FBI to read *Variety* and *Billboard*. The Almanac era ended when Seeger went into the US Army and Guthrie went to sea.

In 1948 Seeger formed the Weavers, a quartet with voice student Ronnie Gilbert, reedy tenor Fred Hellerman and Hays, who could sing a sepulchral bass and had a nice line of gentle comedy. When they began an engagement at the Village Vanguard, poet Carl Sandburg saw them and was quoted in the papers: 'When I hear America singing, the Weavers are there.' Gordon Jenkins decided to record them at Decca, against the wishes of Dave Kapp. Their first recording was 'Tzena Tzena Tzena', a 1941 Palestinian (then Israeli) song sung in Hebrew; this attracted some interest, so they did it again in

English, this time with Jenkins's orchestral arrangement. 'Tzena' reached number two in the pop chart; DJs turned it over to find Leadbelly's 'Goodnight Irene' on the other side, which quickly became number one. The two-sided hit sold two million copies and inspired an answer song: 'Say Goodnight to the Guy, Irene'.

'Tzena' was great fun, while Jenkins's arrangement for 'Irene' began with a solo violin, like front-porch music. The Weavers were a welcome new sound in 1950, and had no competition. Was it folk? Country music? It didn't matter; it was American, straight off the prairie. Their close harmony was redolent of the Sons of the Pioneers, for kids who liked cowboy movies. 'Goodnight Irene' was a song that deserved its success, though it came too late for Leadbelly to enjoy it. They had a few more hits, but then somebody remembered they were lefties. They vanished from the airwaves, and the Decca contract ran out. Hays later said, 'First we took a sabbatical. Then we took a mondical and a tuesdical.'

A New Year's Eve concert at Carnegie Hall was recorded by Vanguard at the end of 1955, and the group sold albums on that label. Also in 1955, Seeger refused to answer questions from Congress that should have been unconstitutional to begin with; he was indicted for contempt and when the case was finally rejected in 1962, the court went out of its way to insult him. The informer Harvey Matusow had testified that three of the Weavers were party members (one had 'quit'), but later admitted that he had made it all up, and was sentenced to five years' imprisonment for perjury. Meanwhile the drunks and crooks on the House Un-American Activities Committee (one of whom was misappropriating taxpayers' money while chasing communists) had stored up trouble for their own country: a generation of kids that had loved the Weavers was not best pleased when it discovered, many years later, why they had suddenly disappeared.

What else was popular in 1950? 'Music! Music! Music!' was the first of Teresa Brewer's many successes. You either hate her squeaky but accurate voice or love it, but she was an irrepressible entertainer; some of her later hits were produced by Bob Thiele, who became her husband. The song is nothing but a jingle (written by Stephan Weiss and Bernie Baum), the middle eight of which is borrowed from a

Hungarian dance; the lyrics reminded us that a nickelodeon was also a jukebox ('Put another nickel in / In the nickelodeon . . .').

'If I Knew You Were Comin' I'd've Baked a Cake', written by Bob Merrill, is another jingle, like 'Rinso White! Rinso White!', which was a soap advertisement meant to sound like a bird-call; there were also 'Be Happy, Go Lucky!' and 'Brush Your Teeth with Colgate!' Radio had been abandoned to jingles, and the pop records of the early 1950s were made to fit between them. Wage and price controls had been abolished in 1946 in the USA; this was certainly preferable to the maintenance of rationing which went on for years in Britain, but it resulted in post-war inflation. Record prices went up; if you didn't have much money to buy records, and a new record player for the plastic discs, you had to get most of your music from the radio. And if you listened to the radio, the centre of popular music in the USA seemed to be slick studio productions that were indistinguishable from the jingles, and were themselves increasingly strident.

The orthodox view is that sales of albums finally became more important than singles in the late 1960s; in fact, much spurious orthodoxy was later dictated by demographics, or by who was buying the greatest number of records. It is evident in retrospect that the new technology of the long-playing record had an effect on the pop chart and on radio broadcasting right from the beginning. The most interesting music was being made for albums, but album tracks were as rare on post-war radio as live music. Things were better for those who lived in big cities with numerous radio stations, but only the most powerful AM stations could be clearly received 70 miles from, say, Chicago, which made them the most profitable stations – that is, the ones with the most jingles. In 1950 the few FM stations were all in big cities, and FM was difficult to receive at any distance. For a large number of listeners America was a musical wasteland: radio had succeeded in creating the illusion that popular music was boring.

It was the era of the white pop singer, who no longer travelled with a band playing one-nighters around the country, but worked mostly in studios of one kind or another, or in high-priced big-city clubs, so that most people never saw the stars in person. It must be said that many of them were fine musicians, whose roots lay in the Swing Era; without doubt the greatest of them was Frank Sinatra.

Sinatra was hired in 1939 by Harry James, who had just formed his own band; his very first notice (in *Metronome*) commended his 'easy phrasing'. After only a few months Sinatra was hired away by Tommy Dorsey, and became a bobby-socks idol well before his solo career began. When he appeared at the Paramount theatre with Benny Goodman, the band played after the film, and Goodman said simply, 'And now, Frank Sinatra.' Goodman had experienced his own stardom, but was astonished by a wall of screaming; he blurted out, 'What the fuck is *that*?' Some of the girls were paid to scream (as perhaps their grandmothers had been paid to swoon for Paderewski in the 1880s), but even more screamed for nothing, and modern pop hysteria was born.

Sinatra had improved on Bing Crosby. His baritone was even more personable and certainly more vulnerable, and, like a jazz singer, he made each song his own by phrasing it as he felt the words, often across the bar lines. Crosby had been a boyfriend; Sinatra clearly wanted to be a lover. Musicians and critics knew that he was a very good singer, yet by 1952 his career was in decline. The pop music business had fallen on hard times; the golden age of songwriting seemed to be over, and anyway the radio wanted only jingles; the boss was now the studio A&R-man rather than a bandleader who confronted a live audience nearly every day. What in the world was 'The Dum-dot Song', which Sinatra recorded in 1947? Should Sinatra have been covering 'Goodnight Irene' and 'Chattanoogie Shoe Shine Boy' in 1950? The idea was not to present the vocalist at his best, but to share in the success of somebody else's hit. Sinatra was also singing the top spot on radio's *Your Hit Parade*, which required him to imitate Woody Woodpecker for weeks on end in 1948.

Often a compulsively generous man, Sinatra has helped a great many people anonymously over the years, and has been willing to give praise where it is due. In *Ebony* magazine he described Billie Holiday as a profound influence; he said he learned about phrasing and breath control from Dorsey, and he even commended his rivals, including Tony Bennett, and said that Vic Damone had 'the best pipes in the business'. In 1945 he had recorded with the Charioteers, a black gospel group, and conducted an instrumental album of music by Alec Wilder; he admired the music, and hoped that his name would help to sell it. The same year he made a short film and a record called 'The House I Live In', pleas for racial tolerance. But he had a quick temper, a thin skin and a tempestuous private life, inevitably conducted in public. He divorced Nancy in 1950 (after eleven years) and married Ava Gardner in 1951. 'I'm a Fool to Want You', made that year, was honest and heartfelt pop singing at its best (but it was backed with 'Mama Will Bark', a novelty duet with Dagmar, an 'actress' famous for her mammary measurement).

Sinatra had been one of the biggest stars in show business for a decade, and the knives were sharpening. His television and radio appearances were flops, and he was not being offered good film parts. On top of everything else, his publicity agent and close friend George Evans died suddenly in 1950, at the age of forty-eight, and Mannie Sachs, another close friend, left Columbia to go to RCA, and Sinatra's booking agency dropped him. It did not occur to the tabloid mentality of the newspaper columnists and fanzines that the pain in Sinatra's private life might in the end make him an even better interpreter of good songs.

In 1953 he landed the part of Maggio in *From Here to Eternity*, for which he won an Oscar; he also signed a new contract with Capitol Records, which required Sinatra to pay for all his own arrangements. His first Capitol recording session was with his long-time arranger Axel Stordahl, but the next was with Nelson Riddle. 'I've Got the World on a String' from that session was a good song from 1932, by Ted Koehler and Harold Arlen, and in the summer of 1953 Sinatra's recording of it seemed to inaugurate a new era in pop: as the record came over the air on the radio, the singer was clearly a man who really *did* have the world on a string, in spite of everything.

The lush, string-laden sound of Stordahl and the rustle of spring provided by large numbers of woodwinds had lent themselves to many fine Sinatra records; when he left Columbia, Sinatra owed the label money, but before long his hits of the 1940s, still selling, were paying him royalties. In any case, the sound had been traded for the architecture of Riddle, who knew that a song tells a story, and that the arrangement has to lead up to it, with a beginning, a middle and an end. His unique touches, such as using a bass clarinet or a bass trombone as a springboard for a rhythmic phrase, made Riddle the most sought-after arranger of this kind of music, and his work in this area has dated less than almost anyone else's. Sinatra worked with Riddle on *In the Wee Small Hours*, one of the first concept albums, but also recorded with Gordon Jenkins and Billy May, and later Sy Oliver and Quincy Jones. He made recordings for grown-ups, who bought albums, and his status as the best male interpreter of America's best songs was never again in doubt. Of nineteen Capitol albums from 1954 to 1962, most reached the top five on the *Billboard* album chart; he then started his own Reprise label, and had several hit albums a year throughout the 1960s.

Nat Cole formed his King Cole Trio in 1937. He later became one of the most popular vocalists of the century, and easily the most successful black entertainer of the post-war decades. Much as the public loved his voice, and still loves it, his singing has been underrated by critics; he swings without anybody noticing. But he was even more influential as a pianist, and at first was reluctant to sing. In mid-1944 his own composition, 'Straighten Up and Fly Right', was a top ten hit, and his third number one (without the trio) was 'Mona Lisa', an Oscar-winning film song and also one of the most typical of a new era, in that it was very romantic but not very easy to dance to. Cole's phrasing and the unique beauty of his voice kept him in the charts until he died of lung cancer in 1965, and his albums are still selling.

Tony Bennett had landed a Columbia contract; 'Boulevard of Broken Dreams' revived a good song from 1933, by Al Dubin and Harry Warren, and the record was highly rated by critics, but no hit. At what would have been his last recording session he was backed by Percy Faith on 'Because of You' (from 1940, by Arthur Hammerstein and Dudley Wilkinson), which was number one for ten weeks in 1951; then he did it again the same year with Hank Williams's 'Cold, Cold Heart'. Bennett too was a singer's singer, highly rated by songwriters, musicians and critics alike, and soon sold albums.

Perry Como sang with Ted Weems from 1936 to 1942, then signed with RCA as a soloist, and his total number of hits up to 1955 was second only to Bing Crosby's. His hits included some junk, such as 'N'yot N'yow (the Pussycat Song)' and 'Hoop-de-doo' (between 1947 and that vintage year of 1950), but his transparent sincerity and his respect for a song lent him a winning way with a ballad. He was probably underrated by critics: being laid back is a sneaky way of swinging. One of his hits was 'Don't Let the Stars Get in Your Eyes' (1954), a country song that crossed over; the arrangement worked hard while Como made it sound easy. He was immensely popular on television for decades; Val Doonican copied his style in the UK.

Eddie Fisher, a strong boyish tenor, was the teenagers' heart-throb in the early 1950s. His romance and marriage to Debbie Reynolds did his career no harm, but leaving her later for Elizabeth Taylor did. His RCA recordings, backed by Hugo Winterhalter, were good studio productions and were better than some of the jingles on the radio, but Fisher was nothing like the musician Sinatra or Bennett was. Frankie Laine was regarded as an emotional 'belter' in the context of the early 1950s rather than a crooner; his first hit, 'That's My Desire' (1947), was well deserved, reviving a good song from 1931, but his belting was often deployed on novelties that quickly dated, such as 'Mule Train', 'Cry of the Wild Goose' and 'Jezebel'. Johnnie Ray had a huge hit with 'Cry' backed with his own 'The Little White Cloud That Cried'; he too was an emotional performer and a heart-throb. Guy Mitchell's first hit was 'My Heart Cries for You' (1950), which had been turned down by Sinatra; it was adapted from an eighteenth-century French song by Percy Faith. Mitch Miller, however, backed Mitchell on his hits, including 'The Roving Kind', 'Sparrow in the Tree Top', 'My Truly, Truly Fair' and 'Pittsburgh Pennsylvania', all of which show Miller's distinctive instrumental jolliness (whooping French horns). Nobody was better than Miller at competing with radio jingles.

Who do we regard today as the best male pop singers of the era? The way the singles compare with the albums in the *Billboard* charts provides a clue. Between 1950 and 1955 inclusive, Sinatra had seven hit singles (coming out of a bad period), Nat Cole twenty-one, Tony Bennett eleven, Perry Como twenty-five, Eddie Fisher thirty, Frankie

Laine twenty, Johnnie Ray ten and Guy Mitchell nine. Let us look at best-selling albums: by 1985 Sinatra had sixty-nine hit albums and Nat Cole thirty (not counting albums by the trio, and bearing in mind that he died in the mid-1960s). Tony Bennett had twenty-four hit albums, Perry Como thirty (not counting his perennial Christmas entries), Eddie Fisher nine, Frankie Laine six, Johnnie Ray two and Guy Mitchell none. Sinatra and Bennett were still making albums in the 1980s, and a point to note about albums is that they stayed in print longer and were reissued, like 78s in the old days.

As a measure of artistry, even in the heyday of the pop singer, the singles chart had ceased to matter as an indicator of quality as soon as grown-ups could buy albums.

If anything, there were even more girl singers making hits in the early 1950s, but a direct comparison with the males is difficult. To begin with, the list of hits for each female artist is shorter on average, suggesting that they received less promotion from their record companies and/or less attention from the D Js; or perhaps they simply made fewer records. On the whole, the women were more diffident about success, or less able to chase it for personal reasons: Jo Stafford, Rosemary Clooney and Joni James each retired from the music scene, for various reasons, while Peggy Lee seems to have left it and come back as she pleased. As in the case of the males, however, most had made their start during the Big Band Era.

One of the best, and best loved, was Jo Stafford, a founder member of the Pied Pipers, a vocal octet which became a quartet when it joined Tommy Dorsey in 1940. The group left Dorsey in 1942 and Stafford began a solo career in 1944, having sung lead and solo with Dorsey often enough to become known as 'GI Jo', a favourite of the soldiers fighting overseas. She had a faultless ear (almost perfect pitch), and in many ways was a quintessentially American singer: apart from her warm, distinctive tonal colour (incredibly, some critics called her 'cold'), she had a folksinger's vibrato.

Taking into account jukebox plays, radio plays and other listings, she had about seventy-five hits. Most of these were on Capitol in the 1940s; in 1950 she went with Paul Weston to Columbia, where she had several of the biggest hits of the era: 'You Belong to Me' was written by Redd Stewart, Pee Wee King and Chilton Price; 'Make Love to Me!' was based on 'Tin Roof Blues', an old jazz standard. With a good beat but without stylistic flourishes, Stafford invariably suggested swing in her music. Her last hit singles were in 1956–7. Tired of the grind, she had stopped appearing in public, and then entered a long and happy California retirement.

With Weston, by then her husband, she created Jonathan and Darlene Edwards, a comedy duo in which she sang slightly off pitch (harder than it sounds). Jonathan and Darlene achieved separate identities of their own. Jonathan claimed that he played stride piano better than Fats Waller, to which Darlene replied 'Actually, 5/4 gives you an extra stride.' The jokes convulsed musicians: drummer Jack Sperling had to be replaced on a session because he could not stop laughing.

Peggy Lee joined Benny Goodman when she was twenty-one. The first hit typical of her style was 'Why Don't You Do Right?' (1943). She left Goodman, married guitarist Dave Barbour and retired, but she could not stay away. She and Barbour wrote 'Mañana (is Soon Enough for Me)', a huge hit on Capitol in 1948. (The song has been accused in retrospect of belittling Hispanics, but this is nonsense: white America in those years could have used the advice to slow down and enjoy life; people who make such charges are themselves patronizing.) Lee went to Decca, and her material improved: her first big success there, in 1952, was something that Capitol had not wanted to record, Gordon Jenkins's arrangement of Rodgers and Hart's 'Lover'; the surrealistically, almost frenetically, swirling orchestra was a perfect setting for Lee's deceptively laconic interpretation. In the mid-1950s she went back to Capitol as an album-seller: her first hit album on that label, *The Man I Love* in 1957, was conducted by Sinatra. Her top ten cover of Little Willie John's 'Fever' (1958) was disappointing only for those who loved the R & B original. 'Is That All There Is' (1969) was more suitable: written by Jerry Leiber and Mike Stoller, by then famous for rock'n'roll songs, it was an example of the less well-known side of their talent, and a vehicle for her combination of resignation and sly humour.

Rosemary Clooney had begun in a duo with her sister Betty and the Tony Pastor band in the 1940s, then signed with Columbia, where her first smash hit was 'Come on-a My House' in 1951. A greater contrast to Peggy Lee could not be imagined: in lines like 'I'm gonna give-a you a pomegranate!' the sexuality was joyously raucous. The recording was perhaps the first to feature Stan Freeman's amplified harpsichord (used the next year on Percy Faith's instrumental 'Delicado' and on two more Clooney records, 'Botch-a-me', from an Italian film, and 'Too Old to Cut the Mustard', a duet with Marlene Dietrich). 'Come on-a My House' had been written by playwright William Saroyan and his cousin Ross Bagdasarian in 1939 and used in an off-Broadway play in 1950; its Armenian flavour was probably taken for an Italian one by most Americans at the time. (Bagdasarian later became David Seville, creator of the Chipmunks in the late 1950s.)

Joni James started out as Joan Babbo, a dancer from Chicago; she had more than a dozen hits on MGM (1952–4) with orchestral backing by Lew Douglas. 'Why Don't You Believe Me?', 'Have You Heard?' and 'Is It Any Wonder?' were all questions suited to her wistful little-girl style. The most ambitious was 'Almost Always', which had a sort of soft rhumba beat. All four of these titles had co-writers in common; it looks, in retrospect, like a clever put-up job, and the hits still reek of nostalgia for anyone who went to junior high school sock hops in those years.

Ella Mae Morse sang with Jimmy Dorsey in 1939, and had a big hit on Capitol with pianist Freddie Slack's band in 1942, 'Cow Cow Boogie'; under her own name her hits in the following decade included 'The Blacksmith Blues' (1952), which required somebody in Nelson Riddle's band to play an anvil. Georgia Gibbs had a number one on Mercury in 1952 with 'Kiss of Fire', another tango adaptation ('El choclo'); she had a second chart career a few years later. Kay Starr had been a superior big-band singer, but her hit singles were multi-tracked material, such as 'Bonaparte's Retreat' (1950) and 'Wheel of Fortune' (1952); she came back on RCA in 1955 with 'Rock and Roll Waltz', an unlovely combination of 3/4 time and kling-kling-kling piano which was number one for six weeks.

Stan Kenton's female singers, Anita O'Day, June Christy and Chris Connor, were much too good for the singles charts. Jeri Southern was a pianist and singer in an intimate cabaret style, which is to say too good an interpreter for the hit parade. (She was more popular in Britain, which did not even have charts then.) On the whole the female singers were badly mishandled by the music business of the period. Kay Starr did some attractive album work, and her 1953 duet with herself on 'Side By Side' was a treat, but 'Wheel of Fortune' was not much of a song, and was over so fast it could hardly be called an arrangement (another excellent example of something designed to fit between two jingles). Ella Mae Morse probably had more talent than we knew at the time: Capitol's A & R man Voyle Gilmore had her singing junk like 'Seventeen' and 'Razzle Dazzle', while Dave Cavanaugh was braver, with 'Greyhound' and 'Jump Back Honey'. Her version of 'Smack Dab in the Middle', however, a song which became something of a jazz standard in other hands, had a lame white-bread vocal-group backing. The white R & B of which she may have been capable never really got out of the studio.

The nadir of the whole business was plumbed in 1953. Displaying attractive vocal colour, a professional attitude and not much in the way of style, Patti Page (Clara Ann Fowler, from Oklahoma) had over eighty chart hits in the twenty years following 1948, with everything from country songs to show tunes: 'Tennessee Waltz' was a record breaker, 'I Went to Your Wedding' was another big hit and in 1953 'The Doggie in the Window' was number one in the USA for eight weeks. It would be unfair to call this a nursery rhyme; it was childish rather than childlike. Nobody knows how many music fans stopped listening to the radio after hearing 'Doggie in the Window' too many times. And who wrote 'Doggie in the Window'? Bob Merrill, the same fellow who wrote 'If I Knew You Were Comin' I'd've Baked a Cake'.

The chart album history for the women singers is similar to that of the men. The best stylists, O'Day, Christy, Connor and Lee, have been selling albums to the *cognoscenti* for decades; Stafford and Weston have leased or purchased their material from CBS so they could reissue it on their own Corinthian label, since the fans are still out there; Southern's work has been mostly out of print for years. Clooney made admirable albums, including duets with Bing Crosby; after resolving problems in her personal life, she came back to record for Concord Jazz in the 1980s, her tasteful singing of standards backed by good jazzmen. In a touring Christmas show in December 1990, with her vocalist daughter-in-law, many children and the Minnesota Orchestra (formerly the Minneapolis Symphony), Clooney had more stage presence than everyone else in the room put together. Doris Day, one of the biggest cinema box office successes of the century, had talent that shone through the dross, but her advice was poor; some of the records and most of the films have dated badly. Georgia Gibbs, Patti Page, Joni James and others, for all their successful singles, never did anything much in the grown-up market.

There were occasional pearls among the muck. The experienced Kitty Kallen had a lovely number one (for nine weeks) in 1954 with 'Little Things Mean a Lot', and Dean Martin, who had the virtue of not taking himself too seriously, did some charming work: 'Money Burns a Hole in My Pocket' was an unpretentious film song, on the other side of which was 'Sway' (a Mexican song called 'Quien Sera'); both did well in 1954. And his 'Memories are Made of This' the next year, with gentle, appropriate vocal backing by Terry Gilkyson's Easy Riders, was a more appealing than usual number one (for six weeks). None of these recordings was overproduced. Martin had more hit singles during the following decade, but eventually seemed to parody himself.

In the early 1950s the major labels sometimes shipped 100,000 copies of a new record by an unknown artist on a 100 per cent return basis, hoping for lightning to strike. This was later described by a Capitol executive as 'throwing a lot of shit at the wall to see if anything sticks'. They put their big stars on television, but these were just radio shows with pictures, and did not necessarily help to sell records. Sachs at RCA offered his big stars very expensive contracts, luring Dinah Shore back from Columbia in 1950; she was a success with a television variety show, but no longer a big pop star.

Before leaving one of the most dismal periods in the history of popular music, one more phenomenon deserves mention. Lester Polfus, the 'Wizard of Waukesha', was born in that suburb of Milwaukee in 1916 and changed his name to Les Paul. Inspired by Gene Autry, he taught himself to be one of the best guitar players that ever lived, having begun as a teenager on the radio. He could and did play everything from country music to jazz, and probably did not see much difference, concentrating as he did on musicianship. He made himself an electric guitar as early as 1929, by fixing a ceramic record-player cartridge under the strings in order to play through the amplifier and speaker. Later it took him a dozen years to convince Gibson to market his solid-body guitar, whereupon in the dozen years after 1954 the 'Les Paul model' became one of the most famous instruments ever made.

He recorded with Art Tatum around 1944, and was the best guitarist Tatum ever played with. On Decca he accompanied Bing Crosby and the Andrews Sisters with his own trio. In 1949 he married country singer Colleen Summer, who changed her name to Mary Ford; meanwhile, he had been one of the first to experiment with tape recording and multi-tracking: his solo hits on Capitol included 'Brazil' (1948), on which he played six parts. His hits in a duo with Ford began in 1950, and they had an average of four or five a year for most of the decade. After hearing Anita O'Day singing 'Vaya Con Dios' on the radio, they recorded it as a B side and persuaded D Js to turn the record over: 'Vaya Con Dios' was number one for eleven weeks. A song by Larry Russell, Inez James and Buddy Pepper, the title literally means 'Go with God' (more idiomatically, 'May God be with you'). Les Paul and Mary Ford's Mexican-flavoured waltz treatment at just the right tempo was a hit for so long that you grew tired of it, but it holds up better today than almost anything else of the period.

In any case, the applecart was about to be kicked over. In the same year as 'Doggie in the Window' and 'Vaya Con Dios', a truck driver made a custom recording in Memphis for his mother. Before discussing Elvis, we will examine the other things that were going on in the early 1950s. For it was as true then as it is now that there was a large amount of good music being made.

13

Music for Grown-ups

From the early 1950s the popular music business was fragmented in a new way. Rhythm and blues, country music and modern jazz were never in the minority so far as musical values were concerned; they were large and profitable markets, and with more lasting worth than hit pop singles. Yet the hits appeared to most people to represent the centre of the business, which was dislocated. At a time when technology and increasing prosperity should have made things easier, it became more difficult for the so-called minority musics to recruit new fans, and for hard-core fans to find something to listen to.

Of course, the music business as a whole continued to think of ways of cheating itself. Neal Hefti recorded a successful arrangement called 'Coral Reef' (on the Coral label) in 1951 which sold about 400,000 copies (though Hefti's publicity described it as a million-seller). Hefti later said:

You heard it all over. Disc jockeys used it for themes . . . Billy May was asking for it; Ralph Flanagan asked for it, Ralph Marterie: some of the bands that were sprouting up in those days, they wanted it. And we all thought, 'If you play "Coral Reef", I'll play, whatever.' And we could, sort of, maybe, between the four of us, instigate some interest in bands.

But the publisher, Jack Bregman, would not print it, not even an onion skin (a kind of cheap lead-sheet for information purposes only). Hefti had to print his own onion skin so that he could pass out copies, and after that he started keeping his own copyrights.

Then the union decided it did not like touring bands, after decades in which bands had toured the country and only fifteen years after Benny Goodman had touched off the Swing Era itself on a tour. Local 802 (the New York City branch of the AFM) made a rule that only local bands could play at the Paramount, which touring big bands had made into a shrine. And when DJs wanted to interview Hefti, he could be fined $500 by the union if he did it on a station that did not employ any musicians. 'And so the jockeys would get very salty and say, "Well, my God, Patti Page was here last week, and she couldn't have been nicer." So when I added all this up, I wasn't making any money, got two little kids, I decided to forget about it, very frankly.' And of course Patti Page did not have to belong to the AFM. So another good band bit the dust, and the music industry thus shot off the fragmented parts of itself.

One of the most evident genres throughout the 1950s was the first instance of revivalism, which several decades later has innumerable forms. In 1939 Muggsy Spanier's Ragtime Band had made sixteen sides which represented a tribute to the music that these Chicagoans had grown up with and loved. The New Orleans and Chicago styles had never really gone away, but there had been a quietly simmering attitude during the Swing Era that the only true jazz was the earliest kind, and in 1939 a self-conscious revival got under way, almost unnoticed at the time. In San Francisco Lu Watters began a residency at the Dawn Club with his Yerba Buena Jazz Band, the line-up of which was identical to that of the King Oliver band of 1923: two cornets (Watters and Bob Scobey), trombone (Turk Murphy), piano (Wally Rose), clarinet, drums, tuba (which the acoustic Oliver recordings did not allow) and banjo and vocalist (Clancy Hayes). Revivalism simmered for a while, then exploded into a vicious war of words among jazz fans and journalists at the advent of bop, which gave the traditionalists apoplexy. The word 'ragtime' had finally been dropped, and the music of the revival, along with the remnants of Chicago style, began to be called dixieland jazz, and the word 'jazz' began to lose its usefulness.

Spanier, trumpeter Wild Bill Davison and others recorded for Commodore in the mid-1940s in New York, where they worked in clubs like Nick's and Jimmy Ryan's; Eddie Condon was a spark-plug to the end of his days. Their music, unfairly or not, came to be heard as dixieland by the American public; they had been struggling to make a living in music all their lives, and were slowly relegated to the sidelines. Any recording with clarinettist Pee Wee Russell had at least that to recommend it; he recorded four titles at a quartet date for Commodore which are priceless, and towards the end of his life had opportunities to work in less tradition-bound surroundings.

Some of the dixie was dire. The Firehouse Five Plus Two were a group of amateurs led by trombonist Ward Kimball, who worked during the day at the Disney studios; they started recording in 1949, and their music was never intended to be anything but a jolly noise. The Dukes of Dixieland also began playing in 1949. A second-rate band formed by the New Orleans Assunto family, it achieved its greatest fame by making some of the first stereo recordings in excellent sound in the late 1950s. Trombonist Wilbur De Paris and his brother Sidney also recorded for Commodore, and later for Atlantic; Wilbur was the leader, and his imagination was stuck in the 1920s; the band had a certain following mainly because of Sidney, who did not say much but was a fine trumpet player.

There was nothing defensive at all about the albums made by Paul Wesley 'Doc' Evans, a cornet player from Minnesota, who was extremely well recorded on the Audiophile label; they are pretty, affectionate and cherishable. They often included pianist John 'Knocky' Parker, who had begun in western swing. The Rampart Street Paraders, Hollywood studio musicians, made albums for Columbia: clarinettist Matty Matlock, trumpeter Clyde Hurley and tenor saxophonist Eddie Miller, all of whom had once played for Ben Pollack. Their albums were loose and lovely: they were playing for anyone who wanted to listen, and had no axe to grind, but although the music was essentially Chicago style, it was heard as dixieland – hence Rampart Street Paraders, a name which helped to sell the albums.

Cornettist Bobby Hackett was a musicians' musician. Neither he nor Jack Teagarden was recorded often enough, but they made an album together for Capitol called *Coast Concert!* in the mid-1950s which was absolute magic; as if to thumb their noses at those who would pigeon-hole good music, they used banjo and tuba on one track, guitar and string bass on the next. Drummer Nick Fatool, who had worked with Shaw and Goodman, played with both the Rampart Street Paraders and Hackett and Teagarden. Don Ewell, a swinging pianist who loved to play Jelly Roll Morton and Fats Waller tunes, made a delightful two-piano album with Willie 'the Lion' Smith. Joe

Sullivan and Ralph Sutton were fine traditional pianists, Sutton two-fisted and Sullivan more of a composer. Trumpeter Al Hirt and clarinettist Pete Fountain were very good white New Orleans musicians who did well in the marketplace. Hirt in particular was a fine technician, but he stuck to the safe route of entertaining tourists, and is said to have presented young Wynton Marsalis with his first trumpet.

Watters's band broke up in the early 1950s, and Turk Murphy led a revival band for the rest of his life. He always used banjo and brass bass, but was not out to score any points: privately also admiring more modern music, he played the music he loved best well enough to make many fans happy. Bob Scobey changed from cornet to trumpet, and his Frisco Band entertained crowds in the 1950s with a sort of 'let's pretend, turn of the century, good old days' saloon music. The genial but powerful baritone of Clancy Hayes was ideal on tunes like 'Silver Dollar' (1950, Clarke Van Ness and Jack Palmer), 'Ace in the Hole' (not the Cole Porter song, but another item by James Dempsey and George Mitchell), Irving Berlin's revived 'I Want to Go Back to Michigan' and a very good version of Ma Rainey's 'See See Rider'. (Hayes was also a songwriter, and his 'Huggin' and Chalkin'' was a number one hit by Hoagy Carmichael in 1946.)

Back in the mainstream music business, Woody Herman made a long series of live recordings in various locations in 1948, which were issued years later on 'nostalgia' labels. It was more than a year before Herman's Second Herd recorded again in the studio, and for a new label, Capitol; a year after that, the personnel had almost completely changed. Not only was the band business a rocky one, but the Second Herd was full of drug addicts, which disgusted Herman and was too much trouble. Baritone saxophonist Serge Chaloff was a superb musician, but wrecked his health on heroin; he was also a proselytizer, and set up shop behind a curtain in the back of the band's bus to sell drugs to the others.

Herman continued leading big bands almost until the end of his life. He was a great talent scout, hiring many a fine young musician, and a natural editor; he would touch up an arrangement while the band tried it out until it was just right. Some of the men in the

Second Herd thought he was old-fashioned, but when he played a solo on a Gerry Mulligan arrangement, Mulligan said that Herman's solo was the only one that had anything to do with the music. Somewhere along the way a manager disappeared with money that had been withheld from the band's salaries to pay income taxes; Herman was left holding the bill and never caught up. He was a forgiving man, generous in spirit and loved by everyone who knew him. He died owing the government a large amount of money, which, as someone said, was either a tragedy or a masterpiece of forward planning.

At the other end of the absurd controversy over what was jazz and what was not was Thelonious Monk. By the late 1940s, after much furious activity, there were often clichés in bop, but never in Monk's music: it displayed only daring, boldness and the unexpected. Monk has long been described as a great composer, yet all he did was write beautifully organized and truly original themes. His idiosyncratic rhythm and harmony have meant that very few musicians have been able to improvise on them properly. Monk's keyboard style was technically unorthodox, and some said he could not play very well, but, as Paul Bacon wrote in a record review in 1948, 'his style and approach cost him 50 per cent of his technique. He relies so much on absolute musical reflex that Horowitz's technique might get in the way.' Monk was sitting with several other men in a car in which drugs were discovered; he was arrested and (like Billie Holiday) lost his cabaret card, so that he could not play in clubs in New York. He remained almost unknown to the general public.

In 1948 Miles Davis had put together an unusual nine-piece band, which contained a French horn and a tuba. It gave one performance and recorded for Capitol; the studio tracks have been almost continuously in print on an album called *Birth of the Cool*. The style required a high degree of musicianship, and was highly arranged by Mulligan, Gil Evans, John Lewis and Johnny Carisi; the sound was an outgrowth of Evans's and Mulligan's work for the Claude Thornhill band, and set the tone for what came to be called cool jazz. Many of the players and arrangers in Herman's Second Herd were leading lights in what became West Coast jazz, often considered much the same thing. The Gerry Mulligan Quartet, with handsome young Chet Baker on trumpet and, unusually, with no piano, began recording in California in 1952. When Mulligan received a ninety-day jail sentence for a drug-related offence and Baker went off on his own, his quartet had the excellent Russ Freeman on piano, and Baker began to sing, in a little-boy voice with minimal vibrato – cool, like his trumpet playing. The girls liked it (the ones who listened to jazz) but the critics did not.

West Coast jazz, largely a media invention which had the important side-effect of ignoring its black participants, had plenty of fans at the time, but jazz critics (most of whom are really only commentators) had doubts about it, because it was not pretentious or dramatic; what it was about was beauty. Perhaps there was something in the Californian climate that contributed to the laid-back quality of much of the music. It swung and it was often lovely, but the frenetic quality of bop was largely gone, which may be why the white brand was more popular with the public: they did not have to listen as hard. Yet Baker's playing and singing on 'My Buddy' (1922, Gus Kahn and Walter Donaldson), for example, has just as much integrity now as it did then; his notes were always chosen in the service of beauty. Mulligan has constantly been a spark-plug (the Eddie Condon of modern jazz), ready to jam at any time, and writing many a fine tune. Freeman retired from the road, but years later provided an interesting comment:

three or four times in my life, while playing, I have suddenly become disembodied – in the sense that I seem to be . . . watching myself play . . . you're just creating music and it's like pouring water out of a pitcher . . . That's what you're after, that high. There are a lot of layers, though, that go with it. It's a zig-zag existence and it's one of the reasons I stopped . . . It became very painful to go through those periods where you get on a bandstand and you try something and it's not happening.

Freeman's retirement was our loss for, as Mulligan told him, he was a composer: such well-known Baker tunes as 'Bea's Flat', 'Fan Tan' and 'Summer Sketch' were his. Jazz groups did not make much money recording for small labels and had no hope of jukebox hits;

they had to make a living on the road, just as the big bands had a generation earlier. This was no doubt good for the music, but it was a hard life, and by this time the heroin plague had hit jazz.

Black and white musicians on both coasts were playing contemporary music which was beautiful, important and is still selling. Yet they were treated like dirt by the music business. Coleman Hawkins had had a middle-class upbringing, or at least a secure one, by American black standards; when he was still a teenager, touring with Mamie Smith in 1922, a theatre manager absconded with box office receipts and for the first time in his life he was hungry. He later had a reputation for being fussy about money, no doubt because he never forgot that early lesson. The risks were there for everybody touring in vaudeville and in music, in every decade. But the risks were always worse for blacks, and as bad as ever in the early 1950s for those who were playing some of the best music.

It is difficult to say to what extent the heroin plague was the result of organized crime's finding a new source of income and a new supply of victims in Harlem. Charlie Parker had become addicted to heroin as a teenager in Kansas City, and some people (such as trumpeter Red Rodney) were imitating their idol, though he did everything possible to warn them off it: 'Any musician who says he is playing better on tea, the needle, or when he is juiced, is a plain, straight liar.' Parker did a remarkable job of keeping his own habit under control for a long time, but in his later years even he was affected by his own dissipation. Gerry Mulligan and Miles Davis had enough sense not to become involved at the time; Parker took heroin in front of Mulligan on one occasion: 'And he did it in the most horrendous way possible, with blood all over the place – it was just dreadful. So he made his point . . .' Yet both Davis and Mulligan later became addicted.

It was Parker who said to Davis, 'You better watch out. There's a little white cat out on the West Coast who's gonna eat you up.' Freeman claims that in the early 1950s almost all the jazz musicians were addicted, which would mean, among other things, that most of them managed to kick the habit; he also says that Baker became an addict after most others had given it up. In San Francisco in 1968 five drug addicts beat up Baker so badly that he had to have his mouth rebuilt, and did not play for two years. But Baker never gave up drugs.

Contrary to popular belief, Baker was not at first influenced by Miles Davis. Yet it is more than a coincidence that they both made a speciality of 'My Funny Valentine', emphasizing the minor-key aspects of the tune and making it into a 'feel sorry for yourself' anthem. They contributed to the invention of a new intimate and lyrical trumpet style, different from the shouting brass instrument that it often was (though the intimate side was part of the art of Roy Eldridge, Harry Edison, Gillespie and many others, to say nothing of Oliver, Bix and Rex Stewart, who all played cornet). Joe Goldberg has mentioned the 'feminine principle' of 'Attis–Adonis' adumbrated by literary critic Edmund Wilson when writing about his friend F. Scott Fitzgerald, an alcoholic who died relatively young: 'the fair youth, untimely slain, who is ritually bewailed by women, then resuscitates . . . when his legend has become full-fledged and beyond his own power to shatter it'. Only 'such a poet', not necessarily effeminate, but capable of 'a kind of feminine ventriloquism', can 'represent life's renewal'. Baker, like Bix, was supposed to die young, and for some fans he did. Drugs cost him time, money, favour in the music business and ultimately his life, when he fell out of a hotel-room window in Amsterdam in 1988; but he had played beautifully most of the time.

The death in 1947 of Woody Herman's trumpeter Sonny Berman was one of the first drug-related deaths. (In Berman's case we again meet the Jewish influence in jazz: fans have even been advised to listen to a good cantor, and then listen once more to his recorded solos.) Vocalist David Allyn sang with Jack Teagarden, becoming moderately famous (and highly regarded among musicians) while still a teenager; his introduction to drugs came through morphine, which he took after being wounded during the war, and later it wrecked his career. The trombonist Earl Swope was an athlete; in every town he went to he would find the local gym and work out. But then he became addicted. Pianist Joe Albany suffered from poor health for many years; trumpeter Fats Navarro died of tuberculosis, but his heroin addiction could not have done him any good. (Navarro had replaced Gillespie in Eckstine's band, recorded once with Benny

Goodman and had pieces written for him by Tadd Dameron, an important arranger. Navarro's playing was sculptural, perfectly under control yet magnificently impetuous.) Chaloff, Dameron, Ike Quebec and John Coltrane were all at one time narcotics addicts who later died of cancer: no one knows how much drugs predispose the victim to an early death. Parker, Billie Holiday and pianist Sonny Clarke are among those who damaged their health by attempting to wean themselves off drugs with alcohol.

It was not as if the life was not dangerous enough. Another great unfinished career was that of Navarro's disciple, Clifford Brown (known as Brownie), a clean-living man who was already becoming much better known than most jazz musicians when, like Frank Teschemacher, Bessie Smith, Chu Berry and many others, he was killed in a car crash. The excellent pianist and composer Richie Powell, Bud's younger brother, and Powell's wife were killed in the same crash that took Brownie; Doug Watkins, one of the finest bass players of the post-war decades, also died in a crash, and his contribution is now almost forgotten. An excellent black pianist who died in 1984 had contracted Aids from a needle. Why have so many chosen to add to the dangers of the road?

Red Rodney was one of those in the Herman band who did not succumb to the allure of drugs, but later, with Parker, 'standing next to that giant every day, I probably said to myself, "I wonder if I jumped over . . ."'

The issue of the effect of drugs on music has not often been discussed. Ira Gitler bravely approached it in his *Jazz Masters of the '40s* (1966), then in his oral history collection *Swing to Bop* (1985). In the earlier book he wrote: 'In spite (or because?) of [heroin] a great music was made.' Some critics questioned that, but he confesses in the later book that he would take out the question mark. The music would not have been what it was without everything that went into it; and it was hard enough being different. There is a story about a bunch of musicians on the road who got lost, driving around in Shaker Heights, the affluent Cleveland suburb, in the middle of the night. They gawked at the big moonlit houses of the relatively rich, until somebody said, 'Yeah, but what do they know? What do they know about Charlie Parker, about Dizzy Gillespie?' And everybody laughed. In fact, some of the residents of Shaker Heights must have had their stashes of Parker records, but drugs were part of what enabled musicians to say, 'We know; they don't.'

If it is dangerous to 'operate heavy machinery' under the influence of an intoxicating substance, then it is not possible to be a better musician, from a mechanical standpoint, while stoned. Music depends above all on execution, the ability to play. But a professional musician's muscles are highly trained, and the conception, the ideas, are also important. Drugs seemed to facilitate concentration, to the extent that they shut out noise and worries and allowed the musician to get on with the work. Mulligan said that for years he could write for eighteen hours at a stretch.

Gitler quoted Red Rodney: 'I think that a lot of the *good* things in the music were because of drug use. The tempos where guys really played on them . . . The tunes with the great changes in it . . . When a guy is loaded and at peace, he . . . could tune out the honking of the world. And, "Hey man, I just figured this out," and we'd try it that night, and it was great.' Charlie Rouse: 'When you're improvising, when you're playing jazz, you play what you hear. So the rhythm or whatever is behind you, you hear something, and you go ahead and make it. And you may do it when you wouldn't do it sober.' Dexter Gordon: 'I think it can arouse you; it makes you concentrate very well.' But Gordon goes on to define the concentration more specifically: 'It really activates the mind to secure money and to find connections . . . and play your games, do your little movements and all that shit.' And avoid getting arrested. David Allyn: 'You're also blocking a lot of other things out, too, like real feelings. You're numb. A goddam wall.' Rodney: 'a lot of sad things happened from the drugs, and showed in the music . . . Hostility, pettiness, a lot of us became thieves, even though we didn't want to . . . being ashamed that people we liked knew we were hooked.'

Mulligan revealed that he had avoided having relationships with women who wanted to get married; marriage at his age would have been a mistake, but he was avoiding stability: 'I think I managed to not be an adult in just about every imaginable area.' Art Pepper said that he started on drugs because he was lonely. His first wife stopped travelling with him on the road, and he felt horribly guilty if he had anything to do with another woman, and in the morality of the early 1950s he could not deal with that. And some people just have personalities that are prone to addiction.

Many musicians were surprisingly rigid in their attitudes: Herman's men, for example, thought he was corny, which angered Mulligan; it was all right to play like Bird on alto, but not on tenor; Ellington's band was trite, Basie's was the one. White musicians thought they could fight the Crow Jim attitude by aping the habits of black addicts. For blacks, being stoned, especially in such an illegal, exotic and dangerous way, helped in coping with racism, allowing the metaphorical genuflection to white society to be made with some other part of the mind, so that the profound insult could be ignored and only the music mattered.

In any case, and despite everything, contemporary jazz recordings were being made during the 1950s which forty years later are selling much better than Patti Page. Commodore, Keynote and Blue Note were followed by other new labels in the post-war years. Recordings were now made on master tape and released on long-playing records, and more records were being sold to a grown-up audience. On the West Coast, Ross Russell had formed Dial in 1946, Lester Koenig formed Good Time Jazz to record the revivalists and between 1949 and 1952 Koenig started Contemporary, Saul Zaentz formed Fantasy and Richard Bock formed Pacific Jazz. In the east Bob Weinstock started Prestige in 1949, while Orrin Keepnews and Bill Grauer formed Riverside in 1953. Keepnews later formed Milestone and Landmark.

Norman Granz, who worked as a film editor, began producing jazz concerts at the Los Angeles Philharmonic Auditorium in 1944. (The first concert was a benefit for twenty-one Chicanos who were arrested during the 'Zoot Suit Riots', convicted of murder and sent to San Quentin.) When he took Jazz at the Philharmonic (JATP) on tour, he refused to accept an engagement unless the audience was integrated, and it became an institution. He recorded the concerts from the beginning, leasing the first volume (which helped to make a jazz standard of 'How High the Moon') to Moses Asch. This was a hit (but meanwhile Asch went broke, and later formed the Folkways label). In 1947 Granz formed Clef, which was distributed by Mercury, then Norgran, and Verve in 1956. He made more jazz available in public and on record than any other individual. He sold Verve to MGM in 1961, but retained some of his masters and stayed on for a while as an adviser; then he started all over again in the 1970s with Pablo. Today almost all these legendary independent jazz labels belong to the Fantasy group in Berkeley, California, making it easily the most valuable vault of American music still owned by Americans.

A West Coast pianist and composer, Dave Brubeck (who had studied with Darius Milhaud), began recording for Fantasy, first with larger groups, then in a quartet featuring the alto saxophone of Paul Desmond. The quartet was well received on college campuses, Brubeck said, because he had played for free in high schools, and when those kids later went to college, Brubeck was the only jazz musician they had heard of. Brubeck signed with Columbia in 1954, and the quartet had far more commercial success than any other jazz group of the era. From 1956 the tasteful Joe Morello played drums.

It is hard to fault Brubeck's success. A version of 'Stardust' on Fantasy wonderfully explores the spirit of the tune, and a 1954 Columbia album called *Jazz: Red Hot and Cool*, recorded live at a club in New York and designed as part of a cosmetics promotion, had a horrible title and cover, but good music, in particular the wistful original 'Audrey'. Brubeck's tunes 'In Your Own Sweet Way' and 'The Duke' were not to be sneered at. Yet for some his music was cerebral at the expense of emotional content. The tremendous popularity of the gimmicky *Time Out*, a number two album in 1960 on which each track has a different time signature, at a time when Charles Mingus was hitting his stride on the same label but had nothing like Brubeck's sales, raises the irrefutable point that a great many black artists deserved the kind of acclaim that Brubeck had. But that was not his fault; he maintained a higher profile for jazz than it would have had otherwise, the way Paul Whiteman had done thirty years earlier, and many a fan must have gone on to stronger stuff. Besides, one could always listen to Desmond, whose playing was never other than beautiful, and often witty with it. (His memoirs, to be called 'How Many of You are There in the Quartet?', remained unfinished.)

The white cool jazz West Coast phenomenon was neither as

revolutionary as its fans thought nor as reactionary as its critics claimed. Parker and Gillespie had come to California bringing the latest thing, but there was not a large audience for it; yet as soon as Ross Russell had formed his Dial label he began recording Charlie Parker, who thus made some of his best recordings on the West Coast. Jimmy Giuffre's 'Four Brothers' was recorded by Woody Herman's band in 1947 for Columbia, at the same session as the fourth part of Ralph Burns's 'Summer Sequence', which was recorded again at the end of the following year for Capitol as 'Early Autumn'. The sound of both the 'Four Brothers' reed section and Stan Getz's solo on 'Early Autumn' (recorded in Los Angeles) were very influential; but equally influential were the New York recordings of the Miles Davis 'Birth of the Cool' sessions (with Mulligan's 'Godchild' and 'Jeru') and of the arrangements of Tadd Dameron. The Davis nonet sessions were a commercial failure at the time – the name 'Birth of the Cool' was applied to them in retrospect; they were arrangements, with seamlessly interwoven solos. Dameron had failed music at school, but was later described as 'the Romanticist of the whole movement'; tracks on Blue Note long marketed as Fats Navarro's were actually Dameron's, and such tunes as his 'Good Bait' and 'Our Delight' became jazz standards.

The West Coast cool jazz movement focused on arrangements for combos, performed by first-class white jazzmen who played lovely solos on them. Howard Rumsey, a pianist, drummer and bass player who had been a founder member of Stan Kenton's band in 1942, began presenting live music at a club called the Lighthouse in Hermosa Beach, California, in 1949. In 1951 he formed the Lighthouse All Stars, who recorded for Contemporary (with a Lighthouse logo at first), and the famous Sunday sessions started: the house band, augmented with various guests, played from two in the afternoon until two the next morning. Musicians and fans remembered the hard work and the great music for the rest of their lives; the music would sometimes begin for people in their bathing-suits who had wandered in off the street, and who would still be there twelve hours later. It was here that many of the West Coast luminaries jammed and formed their friendships and recording groups. Drummer Shelly Manne seemed to play on nearly all the recordings. Shelly

Manne and his Friends, a trio, had Leroy Vinnegar on bass and talented Hollywood wunderkind André Previn on piano. The trio's second album for Contemporary was a jazz treatment of the songs from *My Fair Lady* in 1956; being reasonably successful, it started a fad for such albums (though it did not make the lower reaches of the pop album chart until Previn did it again under his own name, for Columbia in 1964). Reedmen Jimmy Giuffre, Art Pepper, Lennie Niehaus, Bob Cooper, Bob Morgan, Bud Shank, Bill Perkins, Buddy Collette and Frank Morgan, trombonist Frank Rosolino, pianist and arranger Marty Paich and trumpeters Maynard Ferguson and Shorty Rogers, among many others, played at the Lighthouse and made albums in each other's groups and as leaders; visitors included Max Roach, Wardell Gray, Conte Candoli, Miles Davis and pianist Hampton Hawes. Most of the regulars were veterans of Kenton's line-ups, especially his Innovations in Modern Music Orchestra of 1950, but Kenton himself became less and less influential as his ideas became more grandiose.

Composer Giuffre led combos; his fetching, rhythmic tone poem 'The Train and the River' was filmed for television's *The Sound of Jazz* in 1957 and at the Newport Jazz Festival the following year (as *Jazz on a Summer's Day*, released 1960). Paich became a studio arranger, best known for albums with singer Mel Tormé. Canadian-born Maynard Ferguson was a high-note specialist and a brass technician who has led bands almost continuously, and at the time of writing seems to have come through a phase of playing jazz-rock fusion.

One of the most successful and prolific of these men was Shorty Rogers, who came from the East Coast. He was a professional musician at the age of eighteen; after military service he joined Woody Herman's band, and stayed behind when it left Hollywood in 1946. He was playing in baritone saxophonist Butch Stone's band when Herman formed the 'Four Brothers' band in 1947, wiping out Stone's band by hiring most of its members. By this time Rogers had matured as a soloist and a composer; he wrote or co-wrote 'Keen and Peachy', 'Lemon Drop', 'Keeper of the Flame' and others for Herman, and scored part of a Charlie Parker solo for the reed section on a Herman track called 'I've Got News For You'. He left Herman in late

1948 to join Kenton, and did his best to help the Innovations band swing. (It was a losing battle: there were forty musicians, including strings.) In 1951 Rogers led his first recording session with an octet: Pepper, Giuffre, Manne, John Graas (French horn), Gene Englund (tuba), Don Bagley (bass) and Hawes (piano). A series of 10-inch and 12-inch LPs on Capitol, Pacific Jazz, Atlantic and RCA followed, on which the groups ranged from a quintet and octet to a big band.

The first track recorded, Rogers's 'Popo', is a memorably rhythmic riff; Art Pepper's alto on 'Over the Rainbow' was recorded at the same date. The music was not particularly 'cool', containing plenty of high-spirited soloing, and (at the first session especially) spontaneous vocal sounds of encouragement from various sidemen. At the time the music sounded distinctly hot, yet boppish; for 'modern jazz', it had a considerable success. A quintet date in 1955 included 'Martians Go Home', which is nearly eight minutes long: a low-key Rogers composition, it features muted trumpet and Giuffre playing cha-lumeau (low-register) clarinet throughout; the excellent young Pete Jolly plays piano and Curtis Counce bass. There was plenty of solo space for everyone (especially Giuffre) and duet passages for the two horns; the whole thing is delicately punctuated by Manne, who at one point tuned his snare upwards while playing a soft roll (presum-ably with one hand). It was the nearest thing to a hit for a jazz record, and must have sold quite a few copies as an Atlantic 45 EP. Among the big-band tracks were a tribute to Basie album and four tunes written by Leith Stevens for the Marlon Brando film *The Wild One* (not the soundtrack recordings, which were played by an octet and released on Decca). In a repeat on 'Infinity Promenade' Ferguson plays a trumpet part an octave higher than the first time round, which was a pleasant shock at the time, but soon became a cliché.

Not all of the music was equally successful. From the first session, Giuffre's 'Four Mothers' is a riff that quickly becomes irritating and is repeated too often: unison riffs were one of the things that many people did not like about modern jazz. The pastel harmonies could become a kind of hip mood music, if played at similar tempos and without any hot solos, as reedman Dave Pell proved: he formed an octet out of the Les Brown band in 1955 and was frank about playing mortgage-paying music.

Rogers's experience as a composer and arranger soon earned him a good living in the studios. Indeed, nearly all these people recorded prolifically on film soundtracks. Bob Cooper played all the reeds, including cor anglais and oboe; he married Kenton's singer June Christy and was also busy in the studios. Bill Perkins was an engineer for World Pacific (as Pacific Jazz was called after it was sold to Liberty Records) and later in the studios. Years later Lennie Niehaus often worked with director Clint Eastwood; Niehaus and Bud Shank did their best work in the early 1950s, and then decided to make a living instead. Shank played on albums with Brazilian guitarist Laurindo Almeida in 1954, the first influence of bossa nova on the US scene; his later pop-song album *Michelle*, with Chet Baker on flugelhorn, made the *Billboard* chart.

Art Pepper played on many fine albums and always had as many fans as any jazzman, but he paid for his drug addiction with frequent arrests, and only survived as long as he did by spending several years of his life in the restrictive routine of the Synanon Foundation. His autobiography *Straight Life*, written with his wife Laurie and published in 1979, is a harrowing book. His best-known album is *Art Pepper Meets the Rhythm Section*, made in 1957 for Contemporary: he was strung out at the time and had not played for weeks, but it was a successful session. (The 'Rhythm Section' was that of the Miles Davis Quintet.)

The tragedy of West Coast jazz was that it was dominated by white musicians to the extent that those excellent black musicians who stayed there were almost ignored. The jazz scene in California was never big, perhaps because the climate keeps people outdoors rather than in clubs and concert halls. Even so, people who were never jazz fans heard of Brubeck, Chet Baker and Gerry Mulligan, maybe even Shorty Rogers. Tenor saxophonist Teddy Edwards went to the West Coast from Mississippi as a young man and made a series of albums on Pacific Jazz, Contemporary and Prestige, but the albums are underrated and most people have never heard of him.

Eric Dolphy and Charles Mingus were two West Coast musicians of great influence who went east to make their reputations; Dexter Gordon went to Europe. There were other black musicians on the West Coast who never achieved the reputations they deserved. Alto saxophonist Sonny Criss was born in Tennessee, and spent some of the 1960s in Europe; he recorded for Imperial in the 1950s (with West Coast drummer Lawrence Marable) and on Prestige in the 1960s. Curtis Amy, who was born in 1929 in Houston, played tenor, soprano and flute; he went to Los Angeles in 1955 and recorded for Pacific Jazz, and later played on pop and rock albums.

Born in Los Angeles, the son of a doctor, Dexter Gordon was one of the first modernists on tenor saxophone. When Coleman Hawkins listed his favourite tenor saxophonists, he included Gordon, a teenager at the time, who was playing in Lionel Hampton's band. He also played with Louis Armstrong, and in the renowned Billy Eckstine band in 1945, then recorded for Dial: in 1947 'The Chase' (with Wardell Gray) and 'The Duel' (with Teddy Edwards), both two-sided 10-inch 78s, were among Dial's best-sellers. An eighteen-minute live version of 'The Hunt' with Gray was recorded the same year by Ralph Bass at the Elks Club in Los Angeles. Gordon recorded for several labels, such as Blue Note, but lived in Europe from 1962 until 1976, and only occasionally visited the USA; he made many albums in Paris and Copenhagen, with associates such as Kenny Drew and Spanish-born Tete Montoliu on piano. Having been addicted to various substances all his life, his health was poor in later years, but he left a great many recordings of his unique tone and endless ideas: while listening, one feels, at least until the record is over, that it will never be necessary to listen to another tenor, so strong, delightful and deceptively laconic is his musical personality. Producer Michael Cuscuna lured him back to the USA for recording dates in his later career. He was nominated for an Academy Award for his portrayal of a character based on Bud Powell in the film *Round Midnight* (1986, directed by Bertrand Tavernier); like many another American actor, he was effectively playing himself.

Howard McGhee, from Tulsa, Oklahoma, became one of the most highly regarded bop trumpeters and worked for Hampton, Andy Kirk, Charlie Barnet and Georgie Auld. He was a member of Coleman Hawkins's small group when it recorded its famous Hollywood sessions in 1945, and made his first recording as a leader that year on Modern, with Mingus on bass. A 1946 Dial date became McGhee's when Charlie Parker was too messed up to play. McGhee recorded in Copenhagen in 1979 with Teddy Edwards.

Hampton Hawes was based all his life in Los Angeles; good-looking enough to be a movie star, he was an excellent modern keyboard player of the Bud Powell school. He was also a drug addict. His most famous recordings are on Contemporary: three trio sets made in 1955 and the *All Night Session* (1956), with Jim Hall (guitar), Red Mitchell (bass) and Bruz Freeman (drums), three more albums of bop classics and standards laid down with unflagging joyous energy, the sixteen selections issued with no editing of any kind. He also made a trio album with Mingus and Dannie Richmond in 1957. He was sentenced to ten years in prison in 1958 for possession of narcotics (as opposed to Mulligan's ninety days a few years earlier – did it make a difference that Mulligan was white?), but was released in 1964 after he wrote a personal letter to President Kennedy (after which everybody else in the jail was writing to Washington).

Carl Perkins, from Indianapolis, became an unusual and influential keyboard stylist. He too was a drug addict; his left hand was deformed by polio, which perhaps led to his adopting a more bluesy style than Hawes, for example. He played with R & B bands; as a leader he made trio tracks for Savoy (1949), DooTone (1956) and Pacific Jazz (1957, with guitar and bass, but no drums). He worked as a sideman with Harold Land and Art Pepper, among others. Perkins was a founder member of the Max Roach and Clifford Brown Quintet, but did not stay with it long; he is best known for his membership of the Curtis Counce Quintet. His tune 'Grooveyard', recorded with Land in 1958, became something of a standard.

Bass player and leader Curtis Counce was originally from Kansas City. After working for a few months with Shorty Rogers, he formed a quintet which recorded four albums (1956–8), all with Frank Butler on drums (once described by Jo Jones as the best drummer in the world) and Harold Land on tenor. Three albums on Contemporary had Carl Perkins on piano: his introduction and accompaniment of Jack Sheldon on 'I Can't Get Started' display bluesy harmonic ideas, which are other-worldly yet exactly right. On the last album (for DooTone) Elmo Hope replaced Perkins. The trumpet players were Jack Sheldon and Rolf Erickson (both white) and Gerald Wilson.

Wilson has rarely performed as a soloist, but has repeatedly (and against the odds) formed big bands on the West Coast, for which he writes and in which all the best musicians want to play. Sheldon (born in 1931 in Florida) has also been a singer, actor and comedian. Erickson (born in 1927 in Sweden) has been a highly regarded modernist since moving to the USA in 1947, was frequently heard at the Lighthouse and played in many of the remaining big bands, such as those of Goodman, Herman and Ellington.

Tenor saxophonist Harold Land said many years later, 'We were making progress in Los Angeles, even if nobody was aware of it. There wasn't much money, but we were having a lot of beautiful musical moments.' This survey of West Coast jazz may as well end with a remarkable Land album: if the best post-war jazz required unison playing of searing and exciting precision by musicians who could also tear the notes off the page in their solos, and furious swinging on original compositions of great quality, then *The Fox* should have been continuously in print and achieving considerable sales over the years. But it was extremely well recorded in 1959 in Los Angeles for the obscure Hifijazz label, and disappeared for a decade until it was reissued by Contemporary. It had Butler on drums, Elmo Hope on piano, Herbie Lewis on bass and the mysterious Dupree Bolton on trumpet. Bolton played on *The Fox* and on Curtis Amy's *Katanga!* in 1963 (the title track of which he wrote) and on almost nothing else; he was a trumpeter who should have entered the polls of history with Navarro and Brownie. Elmo Hope was an excellent player from New York, a childhood friend of Bud Powell; his *Elmo Hope Trio* was also made for Hifijazz and later reissued on Contemporary. He made other albums for Blue Note, Prestige, Riverside and other labels, but never achieved the fame he deserved.

One of the few groups that made it back and forth across the USA, and among the best jazz bands of all time for its integration of intelligence and musical powers, was the Max Roach Quintet. Roach was one of the finest drummers in the new music, destined to be one of those who demonstrated that the best jazz drummers are percussionists and all-round musicians, not just time-keepers. He grew up in New York, but in 1953 he worked for six months in the Lighthouse All Stars, proof enough that this was a straight-ahead blowing outfit rather than a laid-back bunch of beach boys. Promoter Gene Norman offered Roach a concert tour if he would form a band, and Roach offered Clifford Brown a job as co-leader. Brown had been out of action for a year after a car crash in 1950, but then recorded with Tadd Dameron. He was recommended by Charlie Parker for a band that Art Blakey was forming, which recorded in 1954, and it was from this group that Roach plucked him.

Tenor saxophonist Sonny Stitt was hired, but shortly after Teddy Edwards took his place. (Stitt changed back to alto after Charlie Parker died, and was probably more at home on that instrument.) Carl Perkins played piano and George Bledsoe bass. One of their early gigs was recorded by Norman. Before their first studio session Edwards was replaced by 25-year-old Harold Land, and bass player George Morrow joined. Land was a close friend of Eric Dolphy; Roach and Brownie had heard about the all-day jamming sessions at young Dolphy's house, dropped by to listen and hired both Land and Morrow. Richie Powell had wanted to be a drummer, but took Roach's advice and changed to piano; when he replaced Perkins, the classic edition of the quintet was in place. Land's big tenor sound was a perfect foil for Brownie's trumpet. Brownie also recorded for Pacific Jazz with a septet of West Coasters and for Emarcy, Mercury's jazz subsidiary, as the Max Roach–Clifford Brown Quintet made its first recordings for Emarcy: he made seven recording dates in less than two weeks in mid-1954, and in September there was another Gene Norman concert recording.

Then the quintet went back east, where it recorded again for Emarcy. In November 1955 Land was called back to Los Angeles because of illness in the family. His place was taken by Sonny Rollins, who was almost the same age, but already a giant. He had been influenced by Stitt, then by Dexter Gordon. He began recording in 1948, and by 1955 his powers were such that, like Coleman Hawkins, he almost never had to repeat himself; each time he played a tune it was as if for the first time, and he was never at a loss for ideas. The band was even stronger, but lasted for less than a year: in

June 1956 Brownie, Powell and Powell's wife skidded off the Pennsylvania Turnpike and were killed.

The Roach–Brown Quintet, and, for that matter, Curtis Counce's group and the Harold Land band that recorded *The Fox*, all with the same instrumentation, were fine examples of what came to be called post-bop or hard bop. Roach–Brown played standards beloved of the boppers, such as 'I'll Remember April' and 'What is This Thing Called Love', and originals like Dameron's 'The Scene is Clean', and Powell's 'Time' (on which he played celesta) and 'Gertrude's Bounce'. (Powell too had been on the way to becoming a major talent.) But the arrangements never depended on riffs or endless unison playing; they were themselves compositions, tone poems, exquisitely well performed by men who breathed together. In reaction perhaps to cool jazz, it was aggressive music with muscular joy, never frenetic for its own sake, and black music had taken a step beyond bop. Roach carried on for a while; Brownie was succeeded by Kenny Dorham, then by talented newcomer Booker Little. But the grief of the jazz world at the loss of Brownie was nearly unbearable.

In 1948–9 the Jazz at the Philharmonic tours included new young stars as well as familiar faces. Ella Fitzgerald, who also became a Granz recording artist, joined in 1949. Granz began recording Oscar Peterson in New York in 1950. He had played on the radio and recorded for RCA in Canada before Granz persuaded him to move south; he became an extremely popular jazz musician because of his powerful swing and outstanding technique. He mostly led trios, first with Ray Brown on bass and guitarist Irving Ashby, then Barney Kessel, then Herb Ellis; in 1958 he replaced the guitar with drummer Ed Thigpen.

Peterson has been controversial, paradoxically because he is not controversial. His two-handed style is muscular and inventive, but not formally innovative, though he has brought a very high degree of formal excellence to his playing: he has been described as the Liszt of jazz piano. His knowledge of music and his technique are so facile that at his best the phrasing and ornamentation become part of the music. Some have said that he does not swing. This foolish canard is based partly on what is perceived as his 'whiteness': his father worked all his life as a railway porter, and his very talented older sister Daisy worked as a domestic; but he did not come from a tenement slum in Harlem. Apparently being black in a white society is not handicap enough; you have to be seen to suffer, which Peterson simply refused to do. He was recorded too much by Granz; so many albums could not all be first-rate. Some of the finest were made at the London House in Chicago with the original trio, but among the best of all, including his only solo albums, were those made for MPS in Germany in the 1960s, when Granz was between labels.

When Count Basie led a small group in 1950, it contained Wardell Gray and clarinettist Buddy DeFranco. In 1953–4 DeFranco toured with an excellent quartet in which Sonny Clark played piano. Granz recorded it, but the clarinet had been considered unfashionable since the end of the Swing Era. Perhaps it was viewed as an instrument of the New Orleans style, while after its domination by Benny Goodman and Artie Shaw during the Swing Era, suddenly there were a great many very fine tenor saxophonists; perhaps the fingering of the clarinet's registers, which are divided into twelve rather than octaves, like the saxophone, make it more difficult to play fluently. At any rate, DeFranco did it, but was underrated then and has been since.

Meanwhile, Basie was invited to record for Granz in 1952, so he re-formed a big band and led it for the rest of his life. The emphasis in the new band was on arrangements rather than soloists; the early Granz albums were called 'dance dates'. But the Kansas City feeling was still there, and as the decade wore on it remained a superb ensemble, worthy of comparison on its own terms with the band of the late 1930s. Arrangers included Neal Hefti ('Sure Thing', 'Two Franks') and the 'two Franks' themselves: Frank Wess wrote 'Basie Goes Wess' and Frank Foster wrote 'Shiny Stockings' and 'Blues Backstage', among many others. A third reedman-arranger, Ernie Wilkins, wrote 'Blues Done Come Back' and 'Sixteen Men Swinging'. Marshall Royal also played reeds, as did the 'Vice Prez', Paul Quinichette; Joe Newman and Thad Jones played trumpet.

Vocalist Joe Williams joined in 1954. He had served a long Chicago apprenticeship, during which he was discriminated against by black bandleaders for being too dark; he was a star with Basie until 1960 and was then a successful, musically intelligent cabaret artist. He was typed as a blues singer for many years because of the album *Count Basie Swings – Joe Williams Sings* (1955), a pop masterpiece mostly arranged by Foster. At an all-time low point in the history of chart hits matched only by the 1980s, at least Memphis Slim's 'Every Day' was something of a hit in the black chart. (Williams had had a hit with the same song, backed by the King Kolax band, in 1952.) The album also offered Williams's own 'My Baby Upsets Me', songs by Leroy Carr and Percy Mayfield, and Sammy Cahn's pop hit 'Teach Me Tonight', turned by Williams into an imperishable erotic plea.

At the end of the decade Basie recorded for the new Roulette label: in 1957 Neal Hefti wrote *The Atomic Mr Basie*, which included 'Li'l Darlin'', an object lesson in how to swing at a slow tempo, with its famous muted trumpet solo by Wendell Culley. Among Benny Carter's compositions for the band were *Kansas City Suite* and *The Legend* (1960–61), perhaps the band's last masterpieces. Basie continued touring the world and recorded with Frank Sinatra, Tony Bennett, Teresa Brewer, Billy Eckstine and many others. In its later years the band recorded a good deal of junk and sounded like a Las Vegas show band, but Basie remained a legend until the end; he also made small-group sets for Granz's Pablo label.

Duke Ellington's band went through some rough patches. Under contract to Columbia (1947–52) the new decade's line-up varied, and included trumpeters Nance, Harold 'Shorty' Baker, Cat Anderson, Clark Terry and Willie Cook, trombonists Lawrence Brown, Wilbur DeParis, Claude Jones, Quentin 'Butter' Jackson and Tyree Glenn and reedmen Hodges, Carney and, from 1944 to 1949, Al Sears, who had star roles in the Carnegie Hall concerts. Sears remained in the shadow of Ben Webster, but was quite capable of holding his own. Valuable new recruits were Jimmy Hamilton and Russell Procope on reeds, especially clarinets; and Paul Gonsalves joined in 1950, but Johnny Hodges, Lawrence Brown and Sonny Greer all left at once in 1951. Ellington pulled the 'Great James Robbery', taking drummer Louie Bellson, the returning Tizol and ex-Lunceford alto saxophonist Willie Smith from Harry James's band. (James is said to have asked, 'Can I come too?') Guitarist Fred Guy left in 1949 (after which Duke did without a guitar), and the bass players were Oscar Pettiford, Junior Raglin and then Wendell Marshall.

The decline in the quality of Ellington's output is only relative. More personnel changes than at any other time in the band's history must have been dispiriting; times were hard for bands and from the late 1940s the band lost money and was kept going by Ellington's royalties. The patchy output on CBS, though it is essential for any Ellington fan and has a unique flavour of the period, includes over seventy attempts at pop hits: junk like 'Cowboy Rhumba' (with a vocal by Woody Herman), but also 'Brown Penny', 'Maybe I Should Change My Ways' (from *Beggar's Holiday*), Nance's hip vocal on 'You're Just an Old Antidisestablishmentarianismist' (lyric by Don George), 'Stomp, Look and Listen', 'Boogie Bop Blues', 'Lady of the Lavender Mist', 'Fancy Dan', 'Air Conditioned Jungle', 'VIP's Boogie' (featuring Carney), a famous remake of 'Do Nothin' Till You Hear From Me' (by Al Hibbler) and much more, with contributions from Strayhorn, and 'The Hawk Talks', by Bellson.

As with other artists, albums had become more important in Ellington's work than singles. *Masterpieces by Ellington* (1950) was quite a tribute, a 12-inch LP at a time when most pop LPs were 10-inch albums; on it were extended versions of classics, as well as *The Tattooed Bride*; *Ellington Uptown* (1951) included *A Tone Parallel to Harlem*, and became a best-seller at a hi-fi show because of Bellson's 'Skin Deep', but a six-minute version of 'The Mooche' was better, because of Bellson's rolling, inexorable beat and the clarinets: Procope's melody in the low register, Hamilton's obbligato in an echo chamber.

Among the other projects in the late 1940s and early 1950s were recordings on Musicraft (from late 1946, between Victor and Columbia contracts), a short-lived Sunrise label (1947) and Mercer Records, run by Mercer Ellington and Leonard Feather, with backing from Duke and Strayhorn in 1950–51. The recording quality was not high, and they were probably using inferior studios during a time of technological change; in fact, Mercer foundered partly because of the battle of the speeds. The full band did not violate the CBS contract, but various Ellingtonians contributed: for example, Pettiford plays cello on 'Perdido' and Ellington and Strayhorn play piano duets. Willie Smith, Tizol and Bellson (freshly rustled from the James corral) all played on a driving sextet recording of 'Caravan', which may have inspired Ralph Marterie's hit single two years later.

Duke recorded for Capitol from 1953 to 1955, a musically disappointing period, though as usual there was interesting material; some of the recordings unreleased at the time were better than those that were issued. Dave Dexter, Ellington's producer at Capitol, wrote that Ellington badly wanted hit records; 'Satin Doll' and 'Boo-dah' went into the top thirty, but '12th Street Mambo' disappeared without trace. It was a low point: jazz had apparently moved on, but critics should have known better than to count Ellington out, for he had done it all already. As Miles Davis later said: 'all the musicians should get together one certain day and get down on their knees and thank Duke'.

Johnny Hodges had returned by early 1956 and the band made two albums for the new Bethlehem label in Chicago: *Historically Speaking – The Duke* introduced a set of remakes with a laconically witty version of 'East St Louis' (but 'Ko-ko' was a disaster); the other album included covers of 'Laura', 'Summertime' and other standards, together with 'Frustration', a feature for Carney, and a rocking seven-minute 'The Blues'. Then came Newport.

The Newport Jazz Festival had been inaugurated in 1954 by pianist and club-owner George Wein, with the support of the wealthy Lorrilard family. Ellington played there in July 1956 with the same forces as he had used in the Bethlehem studio: Cook, Nance, Terry and Anderson (trumpets); Jackson, John Sanders and Britt Woodman (trombones); Carney, Hodges, Procope, Hamilton and Gonsalves (reeds); Jimmy Woode (bass) and Sam Woodyard (drums). The band came on last, after people had started leaving. Duke grumbled, 'What are we, the animal act, the acrobats?' Ellington and Strayhorn had written a three-part *Newport Jazz Festival Suite*; and Duke had pulled out 'Diminuendo and Crescendo in Blue', the two-part arrangement from twenty years earlier, for which Woodyard set up a rocking beat (egged on by ringside fan Jo Jones). The original point of the piece, its dynamics, was lost at Newport; the band was in the mood to wail, but Stanley Dance has reminded us that what happened next was not a first: at Birdland as early as 1951 Paul Gonsalves had played a bridge between the two parts. At Newport the bridge turned out to be twenty-seven choruses long: the audience was standing and cheering, and there is a famous photograph of a blonde dancing in the aisle. The concert made headlines, the Columbia LP made the *Billboard* pop album chart and Duke made the cover of *Time* magazine. Some Ellingtonians regarded Gonsalves's pyrotechnics as a disgrace, and the original point of the piece – its dynamics – had been completely lost, but a commercial breakthrough had been made (on an album, not a single) and Ellington's status as elder statesman was never again in doubt.

Ellington wrote film scores and made cameo appearances in films, wrote music for a Canadian production of *Timon of Athens* and a show called *My People* on the centenary of the Emancipation Proclamation in 1963 (with sections called 'King Fit the Battle of Alabam', and 'What Colour is Virtue?'). Among the albums, *Such Sweet Thunder* (1957) was good music and the lovely mood set *Ellington Indigos* (1959) was also recorded for Columbia. The enchanting *Queen's Suite* in 1959 was for Elizabeth II: one copy was made for her, and no other copy was issued until after Ellington's death. (It was not played in public until Bob Wilber's re-creation in 1989.)

Suite Thursday, recorded in 1960, is now only available on a CD with Strayhorn's and Ellington's triflings with Grieg and Tchaikovsky, but is a good example of an Ellington suite (nominally based on the book by John Steinbeck). The colours and themes of the four parts hang together beautifully, and the way the band plays it makes a very exciting seventeen minutes or so: young musicians to be should be trying to play this music this well.

Money Jungle (1962), a trio set with Charles Mingus and Max Roach, brought drama and power from each player unlike anything any of them did in other company. *Duke Ellington Meets Coleman Hawkins* and *Duke Ellington and John Coltrane*, gorgeous small-group sets, were recorded in the same year. World tours resulted in *The Far East Suite* (1966), one of Ellington's best, and the *Latin American Suite* (1969). A tribute to Strayhorn, in 1967, . . . *And His Mother Called Him Bill*, consisted entirely of his tunes, including his last, 'Blood Count', which was sent from the hospital where he was dying of cancer.

The band accompanied Ella Fitzgerald on her two-disc sets of Ellington songs, as well as on the two-disc *On the Cote D'Azur*. Among the albums on Frank Sinatra's Reprise label (1962–5) were

Concert in the Virgin Islands and *Afro-bossa*, as well as one with Sinatra. *This One's for Blanton!* (1972) comprises duets with bass player Ray Brown, remakes of the famous 1940 duets for Norman Granz's Pablo label. The *Seventieth Birthday Concert* opened with a riotous version of 'Rockin' in Rhythm', once again the band's theme.

The late triumph *New Orleans Suite* (1970) had five parts interleaved with portraits of Mahalia Jackson, Louis Armstrong (with Cootie Williams), Wellman Braud (with Joe Benjamin on bass) and Sidney Bechet. Ellington had tried to persuade Hodges to polish his soprano saxophone, but he died days before the session, and the tribute to Bechet was made by Gonsalves on tenor. The suite's opening 'Blues for New Orleans' featured Wild Bill Davis on organ, but the organ effect in Jackson's portrait was made by three clarinets, tenor saxophone and flute – a tone-painter's palette unique in popular music.

André Previn, an accomplished and highly rated musician in several genres, often and crossly denies making this remark: 'Stan Kenton can stand in front of a thousand fiddles and a thousand brass and make a dramatic gesture, and every studio arranger can nod his head and say, "Oh yes, that's done like this." But Duke merely lifts his finger, three horns make a sound, and I don't know what it is.' Yet the substance of the remark had been true as early as the Cotton Club period. In 1965 the Advisory Board of the Pulitzer Prize Committee rejected a unanimous recommendation of its music jury that Ellington be awarded a special citation; his best music was behind him, but that is when prizes are often awarded. He received honorary degrees and a medal from Lyndon Johnson, and Richard Nixon played 'Happy Birthday' on the piano for him.

His 'Sacred Concerts', which started in San Francisco in 1965, were important to him but unfortunately they are not very good. Always urbane and witty, Ellington was also a private man, vain and superstitious: *Music is My Mistress* in 1973 was not an autobiography. He sometimes did not write his music down, let alone his life, and did not even leave a will; but he left recordings, which are still being issued, often produced by Mercer and Stanley Dance. James Lincoln Collier's biography of 1987 examined the band and its members as a composing machine, comparing Ellington to a master chef, who 'plans the menus, trains the assistants, supervises them, tastes everything, adjusts the spices . . . and in the end we credit him with the result'.

Ellington came back to the fore in the 1950s and died famous, but meanwhile, in New York, other younger black musicians were finding their way. The decade of the 1950s was not kind to them, yet they too made recordings that we still listen to forty years later.

Thelonious Monk did not record at all in 1949 or 1950, but Blue Note recorded him again in 1952 and 1953, despite the fact that he did not sell. His associates included alto saxophonists Sahib Shihab (a modest man and an underrated musician) and Lou Donaldson, trumpeter Kenny Dorham and tenor saxophonist Lucky Thompson. Prestige took over in late 1952 and Riverside in mid-1955; in 1962, after European tours and several appearances at Newport, he finally signed a major label contract with Columbia, so that there were albums every year from 1952 to 1968. (At Newport in 1963 Pee Wee Russell played on two tracks.) No doubt in 1968, when Clive Davis was in charge at Columbia, Monk did not sell as well as the now forgotten rock band Electric Flag, and there were no recordings at all in the USA during the last dozen years of Monk's life. The rumour persists that Columbia wanted him to record Beatles tunes; if it is not true, it may as well be.

There is no public record of any violence or serious drug problem in Monk's life; indeed, he seems to have been a gentle man. Yet he frightened club-owners and others with his personal act. He wore goofy caps, and he would get up from the piano and do a little dance when the pulse of the music was not quite right, trying to show his musicians what he wanted. Dizzy Gillespie got away with bizarre humour and even made capital out of it, but Monk was a more private man, who probably wanted to be valued more for his music than for his sense of humour. There was never enough work, and while Dizzy the clown became a much loved figure, Monk the mild eccentric was widely ignored.

His solo recording sessions began with a 1954 date on the French Swing label (later on Vogue), and he recorded Ellington tunes for Riverside the next year; there were also *Thelonious Himself* and *Thelonious Monk Alone in San Francisco* on Riverside. He later made *Solo Monk* for Columbia, and decorated the quartet albums with solo tracks. He would play 'Just a Gigolo' or 'Dinah' or 'Lulu's Back in Town', or a ballad like 'I Love You', just because he liked the song, and the accents were entirely his; a note anywhere in a phrase, or in the rhythmic left hand in a bouncy number like 'Dinah', might seem to come late, yet when it arrives, it is exactly on schedule, and the tune becomes a Monk tune.

The trick was to get other people to play his themes properly. One of his most interesting failures is *Monk's Music* (1957), with a septet: trumpeter Ray Copeland (a highly regarded New York bandleader, arranger and lead player who later toured Europe with Monk), Gigi Gryce (alto saxophone), Coleman Hawkins and John Coltrane (tenors), Wilbur Ware (bass) and Art Blakey (drums). An informal yet structured outing on five Monk tunes (Hawk tries to enter in the wrong place at one point), it was not exceeded in its irresistible way until Monk's tours of Europe in the 1960s, which were widely broadcast and recorded. The opener was a statement of 'Abide With Me', less than a minute long and played only by the horns; the simple, homely hymn was written in 1861 by William Henry Monk (no relation as far as we know).

Other tenor saxophonists who worked for Monk over the years included Chicago's Johnny Griffin, who was not very good at playing Monk's music, Sonny Rollins and Coltrane. Monk first recorded with Charlie Rouse in 1959 on the album *5 by Monk by 5* (on which Thad Jones's perceptive trumpet may be heard on two tracks), and Rouse stayed with him through all the Columbia quartet albums. So afraid of Monk were many of the critics and even some of the musicians that it was whispered that Rouse was lucky to have the job, that he was somehow not a very good musician and was stuck with playing Monk's music because Monk could not get anybody else to do it. That all this was balderdash is proved by later Rouse albums, such as the quintets *The Upper Manhattan Jazz Society* (1981) and *Social Call* (1984), with trumpeters Benny Bailey and Red Rodney respectively; the former has Keith Copeland, Ray's son, on drums.

Monk's music will never be easy to play well, but it now represents a set of post-bop anthems which younger musicians have to approach sooner or later whether they like it or not. 'Epistrophy' and ''Round Midnight' were recorded, in 1942 and 1944, by Cootie Williams's

band. The former was brought to Williams by drummer Kenny
Clarke, though he did not play on the recording, which was called
'Fly Right' and was not released at the time; ''Round Midnight' had
Bud Powell on piano in the band's rhythm section. Soprano saxophonist Steve Lacy, who had begun by playing dixieland and then worked
with Cecil Taylor, joined Monk in 1960. He made it his business to
play Monk's tunes almost exclusively for some time, until he had
learned as much from them as he could for the time being, whereupon
he was qualified to become one of the most interesting and widely
recorded avant-gardists of succeeding years.

It has since become more common for younger musicians to tackle
Monk's tunes, as shown by Anthony Braxton's *Six Monk's Composition*
(1987) and Paul Motian's *Monk in Motian* (1988). Braxton, the Chicago
composer and alto saxophonist, usually plays only his own music; his
album is for a quartet, with Mal Waldron on piano, Buell Neidlinger
on bass and Bill Osbourne on drums. Motian is a poet of the drum
kit, and his album is mostly a duet, with Bill Frisell on guitar,
though tenor saxophonist Dewey Redman and pianist Geri Allen are
added on some tracks. Frisell's electric guitar is an acquired taste, for
the notes lack any attack whatever, and sound like they are being
played backwards on a tape recorder. Both albums are brave attempts
by highly qualified people to pay tribute to one of their great and still
underrated inspirations. Young Marcus Roberts tackles a solo, 'Blue
Monk', on *The Truth is Spoken Here* (1988): he sounds rhythmically
unsure here and there, as though he has not decided whether to play
it in the style of Fats Waller or to attempt Monk's unique accents,
but he makes something of his own out of it while paying his dues,
and he knows that Monk's tunes will remain a challenge.

Words have been written for Monk's tunes and recorded by his
friend Carmen McRae (1988). After Monk's death the right to put
words to the tunes was sold to Ben Sidran, but now others are
allowed to write words by giving the songs new titles, so that 'Well,
You Needn't' becomes 'It's Over Now'. Chicagoan Mike Ferro's
words are as sassy as the tune:

> You're bending my ear?
> Well, you needn't.

You're calling me 'Dear'?
    Well, you needn't.
You're acting sincere?
    Well, you needn't.
It's over now! It's over now!

Monk's sound was recorded for the last time during one of the Giants of Jazz's tours of Europe, when he played with Gillespie, Sonny Stitt, trombonist Kai Winding, bass player Al McKibbon and drummer Art Blakey. Black Lion's Alan Bates recorded twenty-six trio and solo tracks (including alternative takes) in London in 1971 during the tour. (The complete set is available on Mosaic, along with the 1954 Paris set.) On the charming, informal 'Chordially' Monk is just trying out the piano at Chappell Studios. McKibbon and Blakey were old associates, who first recorded with Monk as a team at a Blue Note session in 1953. A good example of the mystery of what swings and what does not, mentioned earlier, occurs on a take of 'Hackensack': after Blakey's drum solo near the end, Monk enters in the wrong place, and stays there, eschewing his usual built-in swing. He was quite capable of doing that on purpose: in Mexico City in 1971 he played 'I Love You' in a bawdy-house piano style, saying afterwards that the audience didn't know what the song was anyway; and at the Black Lion session there had been some badinage about somebody having played some wrong notes on stage.

Another pianist and composer who had even worse luck was Herbie Nichols. In 1944 he wrote the first-ever article about Thelonious Monk. Later he said, 'It seems like you either have to be an Uncle Tom or a drug addict to make it in jazz, and I'm not either one.' He spent most of his professional career playing in dixieland bands. There were five Blue Note record dates in 1955 and a less successful Bethlehem album in 1957, all trio tracks; his 10-inch Blue Note LPs sold even less well than Monk's earlier ones. But his tunes, like Monk's, are unique. On 'Double Exposure', 'Cro-magnon Nights', 'The Gig', 'Shuffle Montgomery', 'Chit Chatting' and many other carefully titled keyboard tone poems on Blue Note he was accompanied by McKibbon or Teddy Kotick on bass and Blakey or Roach on drums. Nichols died of leukaemia in 1963; all his Blue

Note recordings have been collected on a three-CD set issued by Mosaic.

Bud Powell was probably the most influential pianist in early modern jazz; he had incredibly fleet improvisational skills and an equally incredible ear for harmony. The musical universe was as real for Powell as the 'real' universe; he heard music even when there was no keyboard available. An early promoter of Monk's music, he played his tunes very well and recorded them, and was harmonically influenced by Monk. Like other pianists, he regarded Art Tatum as God. Ira Gitler recounts the story of how one night at Birdland in 1950 Powell told Tatum that he had made mistakes when playing a piece by Chopin. 'Tatum saltily responded with, "You're just a right-hand piano player. You've got no left hand. Look, I've got a rhythm section in my left hand." The next night Bud played "Sometimes I'm Happy" entirely with his left hand at a furious tempo and drew Tatum's praise . . . Bud's jubilation knew no bounds that evening.' There is no doubt that, in using his left hand for harmonic punctuation and inspiring less talented imitators, Powell (and bop piano in general) created a gulf for the ordinary listener between the New York stride style and later development. The exploitation of the keyboard, with its tremendous harmonic possibilities, was perhaps the single greatest innovation in modern jazz. Pianist Billy Taylor told Gitler that using a different part of the keyboard in order to get out of the way of the bass player was part of the experimentation which amounted to a sort of 'pre-bop' period from around 1936; Basie may have been an early exponent. Powell's first influence was probably Billy Kyle, but in his right hand he was finally inspired more by a saxophonist, Charlie Parker, than by any other pianist.

Tales of Powell's live gigs are legion: for example, he played twenty or twenty-five choruses of Monk's '52nd Street Theme' at a blistering tempo at the Three Deuces in mid-1947. But his recordings were sporadic and variable in quality; his most important are probably those made for Blue Note in a quintet (1949) and trio (1949, 1951, 1953, 1957 and 1958).

Powell was apparently badly beaten over the head by policemen in Philadelphia in 1945, and during the next decade had five sojourns in mental institutions, where he was given shock treatments which damaged his memory. In 1951–2 he was subjected to eleven months of this, and allowed to play the piano once a week. In 1959 he took up permanent residence in Paris, where he joined drummer Kenny Clarke and bass player Pierre Michelot to make one of history's great rhythm sections; it often backed such visitors as Dexter Gordon, on *Our Man in Paris* (1963). He returned to New York in 1964 for treatment of suspected tuberculosis, and never made it back to Paris. He was the principal inspiration for the character played by Dexter Gordon in the film *Round Midnight*.

The main line in piano jazz stretches from Tatum to Powell, but Erroll Garner has to be in here somewhere. He was the kind of musician like Fats Waller and Louis Armstrong, whose work was widely loved by people who did not know anything or care about jazz itself. Unable to read music, he improvised unique and richly beautiful tone poems at the keyboard, for all the world like a modern black Chopin. The poetry of his early *Overture to Dawn* sessions, privately (and poorly) recorded in 1944, was probably never exceeded even by Garner. His extremely famous trio album *Concert by the Sea* (1955) and several other sets reached the *Billboard* album chart. Among his many compositions was 'Misty', one of the most widely performed tunes of all time.

Dave Brubeck and Lennie Tristano were both white and of approximately the same age, and both are seen as cerebral modernists, but there the resemblance ends: Brubeck has been among the most popular and successful jazzmen of the century, while Tristano purposely remained obscure, and in the end was more influential. Born during a measles epidemic, he was blind by the time he was eleven years old. Woody Herman's bass player Chubby Jackson, who seems to have been a great talent scout, persuaded Tristano to go to New York.

Tristano could allegedly play anything Tatum could play, only faster. (This, of course, would have required skill, but not invention.) He disliked performing in public and did not record very much, and preferred to play his own music. Nevertheless, he became a cult figure among musicians and hard-core modern fans. He made his most important impact as a teacher; his students included bass players Arnold Fishkin and Peter Ind, pianist Sal Mosca, guitarist Billy

Bauer, alto saxophonist Lee Konitz and tenor saxophonists Warne Marsh and Ted Brown.

These reedmen were all born in 1927. Konitz, a well-known and highly regarded musician, is usually lumped with the West Coast cool jazz school; Marsh, for all his hard work and quite a few beautiful records, remained obscure until his death in 1987; and Brown, who has been even more obscure, performed and recorded with the British-born pianist Ronnie Ball in the mid-1950s, and made one album under his own name on Vanguard in 1955. Exactly thirty years later came his quartet album *Ted Brown in Good Company*, followed by the trio set *Free Spirit* in 1987, both for the Dutch Criss Cross label. The latter, on which Hod O'Brien plays piano and Jacques Schols bass, is one of the finest albums of that or any decade. (Konitz, Marsh and Brown may all be heard on Jimmy Giuffre's lovely *Lee Konitz Meets Jimmy Giuffre*, made in 1959 for Verve with five reeds and rhythm, though Marsh and Brown do not play any solos.)

During Capitol's brief flirtation with modern jazz in the late 1940s a Tristano sextet was recorded in New York in 1949; Tristano, guitarist Billy Bauer, Konitz, Marsh, Fishkin and drummer Harold Granowsky. Five of the tracks recorded were quite advanced enough for the period, but then for 'Intuition' and 'Digression' Tristano merely provided a harmonically free piano part and instructed his men to play along as they pleased, with no cues whatsoever, foreshadowing so-called free jazz by many years. Capitol was furious and refused to pay Tristano's session fee until the musicians' union intervened. Tristano, along with Tatum and Ellington, was among the greatest harmonists in jazz; his object seemed to be to retain a link with the past while forging a future, as Bix Beiderbecke had done, by restricting himself to the chord sequences of a small number of old pop songs. Tristano has been compared to Bach in the harmonic and contrapuntal tension he achieved. He insisted that a drummer, for example, play with an unadorned beat, responding instead to Tristano's subtle deviations of pulse. His music is as hard to play as Monk's, if not harder.

Another influential pianist in the music of the 1950s was Horace Silver. Two 10-inch LPs by the Horace Silver Quintet, in which Art Blakey played drums, were combined in the 12-inch *Horace Silver and the Jazz Messengers*; it includes 'Doodlin'' (soon covered by Ray Charles) and 'The Preacher'. It was the music of Silver and Blakey that was first called hard bop; Silver's came to be called funk, a post-bop style with a rhythm and blues feeling. (The word 'funk' originally referred to strong smells – there was a club in New Orleans called the Funky Butt – and meant 'low-down' or 'gutbucket' in music. In recent times it has been misused, and means nothing in today's post-jazz world.)

Blakey had earlier used the name Jazz Messengers for a big-band recording, and retained it. Between them, Art Blakey's Jazz Messengers and Silver's various quintets employed on their albums, mostly on Blue Note, virtually all the best young black musicians to come forward in the ensuing decades, far too many to list here. (I recommend *The Penguin Encyclopedia of Popular Music*: follow the cross-references and use the index.) It was the sound of these albums that defined the Blue Note ethos for countless fans across two decades; among Silver's best-known tunes was 'Señor Blues'. Others built on his foundation: trumpeter Lee Morgan (who was murdered by a jealous girlfriend) wrote 'The Sidewinder', and keyboard player Herbie Hancock wrote 'Maiden Voyage' before turning to more lucrative pop-rock-funk-jazz in the 1970s. Blakey employed everyone from Morgan to Wynton Marsalis, Branford Marsalis, Terence Blanchard and Donald Harrison, four of today's most successful young post-bop revivalists.

At an opposite pole from the funk of the Jazz Messengers was the Modern Jazz Quartet, formed in 1952: John Lewis (pianist and composer), Milt Jackson (vibraphone), Percy Heath (double bass) and Kenny Clarke (drums); when Clarke moved to Paris in 1955, he was replaced by Connie Kay. Having no horns at all and usually dressing in evening wear, the quartet was unique, elegant and very popular. Lewis has also been active in film music and 'third-stream' attempts to blend jazz and 'serious' music, along with Gunther Schuller and others, which, however worthy, never seemed to set the world on fire. Jackson's nickname is Bags: there have been many recordings of 'Bags' Groove', but none more deceptively powerful than the one on *The Modern Jazz Quartet* (1957, Atlantic). That it sneaks up on you to knock your socks off is a result of dynamics as

well as the ideas in the solos, for the tempo never changes. All the
players have also had their separate careers; Jackson perhaps plays
with more evident soul on his many other albums, such as *Bags and
Trane*, recorded with John Coltrane. Dynamics is the strong suit of
Connie Kay, whose precision and good taste are reminiscent of
Brubeck's drummer Joe Morello; Kay played on a great many
rhythm and blues hits as the house drummer at Atlantic and, later, on
several Van Morrison albums. Percy Heath's family moved from
North Carolina to Philadelphia, where his younger brothers, reedman
Jimmy and drummer Albert 'Tootie' Heath, were at the centre of a
thriving scene that encompassed composer-reedman Benny Golson,
whose 'Stablemates' became a jazz standard, and Coltrane.

The countless 'blowing sessions' recorded by the East Coast jazz
labels in the 1950s and early 1960s took the place of the jam sessions
and cutting contests of earlier times, which were dying out for
various reasons: the musicians' union disapproved of 'sitting in', and
anyway there were fewer places in which to do it. The blowing
sessions were often informal, and little rehearsal time was allowed
because of the low-budget nature of the whole operation; they gave
the soloists room to stretch and to work out new ideas. Many of
them have by now been reissued and recycled several times, so that
an Elmo Hope date called *Informal Jazz* (1956, Prestige) became *Two
Tenors*, a Coltrane album with Hank Mobley; a Kenny Dorham date
became a Coltrane album, Mal Waldron albums became Eric Dolphy
albums and so forth. But none of the jazz labels was making much
money. One reason most of Herbie Nichols's tracks were not released
at the time was that Blue Note was caught between the large number
of 10-inch LPs in its catalogue and the new demand by retailers for
12-inch LPs; a large label could shrug off this sort of problem, but
it was a major stumbling block for an independent. The frequency of
recording dates, however, was a godsend to the musicians, who
could often get an advance against the next one when they were short
of cash.

Miles Davis came from a middle-class family (his father was a
dentist). Having begun playing trumpet at the age of thirteen, he
soon proved to be something of a prodigy; he went to New York to
study at the Juilliard School, but hung out on 52nd Street instead.

He was later a drug addict for four years, but by 1954 had stopped thanks to his own effort, aided by his pride in himself and his disgust at what he had become. He was outspoken and could be hard to get along with. His ability to give up heroin had banished fear: 'Some people accuse me of being mean and racist because I don't bow and scrape. When they look in my eyes and don't see fear they know it's a draw.'

George Russell, three years older than Davis, had been asked by Charlie Parker to play drums in his group, but was hospitalized because of his weak lungs; he spent the time thinking about music theory, partly inspired by Davis's remark to the effect that he wanted to be able to play a wider choice of notes. Russell's *The Lydian Chromatic Concept of Tonal Organization in Improvisation* was published in 1953. Russell's own record dates between 1956 and 1962 on RCA, Decca and Riverside were not more frequent partly because his music required rehearsal; he was inventing a style in which the ancient modes were combined with chromaticism, so that instead of using a key signature, which limits the musician's choice to the notes in the chords, the tonal centre of the music is its centre of gravity, and the soloist can select a much wider variety of notes. Russell spent the next fifteen years in Scandinavia, because in Europe there were still radio orchestras, and broadcasting took its responsibility to the arts more seriously. Meanwhile, Davis, once free of drugs, began to discover his own centre.

He had always been an individual stylist, and did not attempt to play in the fleet and quicksilvery way of bop trumpet soloists for long; his studio recordings in the early 1950s were few. In early 1953 he recorded for Prestige in a sextet including two reeds: Sonny Rollins, and Charlie Parker, also playing tenor (under the name Charlie Chan, because he was contracted to Granz). In April 1954 there was a sextet session for which Davis had asked tenor saxophonist Lucky Thompson to write some tunes, as Bob Weinstock at Prestige could not afford studio time for workouts; yet in the end the date's importance was indeed worked out in the studio. Thompson has not recorded since the mid-1970s, which is unlucky for his many fans; on this occasion he stayed up all night writing, but to no avail: the tunes did not work. So Davis took over, and discovered his talent for setting moods. 'Blue 'n' Boogie' and 'Walkin'', were his first masterpieces. Of the first, Ian Carr wrote in his biography of Davis:

After an eight-bar horn introduction over offbeats, the theme of 'Walkin'' is played twice. This theme, with its use of flattened fifths, and its stark call-and-response pattern, is highly evocative – a distilled essence of the traditional and the post-bop blues. The atmosphere and sense of drama are heightened by the sonorities of trumpet, trombone [J. J. Johnson] and tenor all in unison, and their beautifully poised timing . . . an elastic, laid-back, lazy feel on a knife-edge of balance. Kenny Clarke's immensely sensitive and subtle use of the high-hat cymbal which he opens and closes to point up the rhythms of the theme, also intensifies the drama.

Thompson, perhaps partly out of the frustration he must have felt, produced some of the best playing of his career. The truth is that Davis had never really been a bopper. At this time he also began using the cup mute, which is restrictive and difficult to play in tune. Davis's forte was (and remained, despite the changing nature of his backing material in later years) the economical, intimate and voice-like choice of notes, which tug at both heart and intellect.

   In June he recorded with a quintet that consisted of Rollins and the same rhythm section as in April: Horace Silver, Percy Heath and Clarke. The session included two of Rollins's tunes, 'Oleo' and 'Airegin' ('Nigeria' spelled backwards), which Davis continued to use for some years. It was on 'Oleo' that Davis first recorded with the metallic harmon mute, adapted by having its stem removed, and in effect amplified, played very close to the microphone. Its full, breathy lower register and thin, shrill higher notes could be contrasted with each other, and completed the development of one of the most important sounds of the 1950s. Weinstock had now turned over all his recording to engineer Rudy Van Gelder, in whose studio in New Jersey most of the best East Coast jazz records were made, and made so well that nearly forty years later they still sound fresh as paint.

   At the end of 1954 Weinstock arranged an all-star date which included Monk. Davis admired Monk but the great man was too idiosyncratic for a Davis recording session; yet jazz has always required musicians to communicate with each other, and even from this session there emerged some fascinating toing and froing. In March of 1955 Charlie Parker died, and, as Carr points out, the feeling everyone had had that an era was coming to an end was confirmed.

In July 1955 Davis played at the second Newport Jazz Festival, and was offered a Columbia recording contract with an advance. By this time, after some variable recordings, he had assembled a quintet that Weinstock compared with Louis Armstrong's Hot Five of 1925 in its importance. The drummer was Philly Joe Jones, Red Garland played piano and Paul Chambers double bass; Davis wanted Sonny Rollins, who was unavailable, and the others recommended John Coltrane. This group was important in a different way from that of Armstrong: the greatness of the Hot Five had stemmed almost entirely from Louis, whereas the Miles Davis Quintet of 1956 was one of the most seminal in a market that had more talent than it could support. Despite this it was criticized, not so much by the public as by the critics, who always like to tell their favourites what to do: Philly Joe was too loud, Coltrane's solos went on too long and so forth. But Davis knew what he wanted. Of Philly Joe he said, 'He could turn up with one arm and in his BVDs [underwear] as long as he plays what I want.' Coltrane had toured with Johnny Hodges and Earl Bostic, and had been developing for years in blowing sessions; Ira Gitler invented the phrase 'sheets of sound' to describe the way in which Coltrane, in his controlled urgency, tried to play all the notes in a chord at once.

Davis was still under contract to Prestige, but Weinstock knew that he could not afford to hang on to the phenomenon that the Miles Davis Quintet was becoming, so a deal was made: as long as Davis fulfilled his contract, he could sign with Columbia, take the advance and even record for the other label, as long as no records were released until the Prestige contract was fulfilled. The Five albums made for Prestige, *Miles* (late 1955) and *Steamin'*, *Workin'*, *Cookin'* and *Relaxin' with the Miles Davis Quintet* (all 1956), far from representing too much recording activity in too short a time, showed a progressive strengthening of skills.

'*Round about Midnight* was released in 1958 on Columbia, and Davis began recording with arranger-composer Gil Evans, which resulted in *Miles Ahead*, *Porgy and Bess*, *Sketches of Spain* and *Directions*. There was also a Carnegie Hall concert and a television film with Evans and Davis. Evans was the arranger who came closest to creating a viable third stream, but there was not enough money in the music to pursue it until it bore fruit in the form of more commercial success. And that sort of success was not forthcoming: the music was much too good for what American broadcasting had become by then.

Gary McFarland, who died when a prankster slipped liquid methadone into a drink, and Oliver Nelson, whose album *Blues and the Abstract Truth* (1961) on Impulse was a milestone in the genre, were talented individuals who were lost too soon, though Nelson's later albums consistently missed the mark. George Russell had to go to Europe to make a living, and trumpeter and arranger Johnny Carisi had so little work as a recording artist over the years that his name remained all but unknown.

An album by Carisi in 1956 scheduled for an RCA Jazz Workshop series was not issued; alto saxophonist and leader Hal McKusick recorded tracks by Gil Evans and George Russell which made it on to an album in that series; trombonist and arranger Rod Levitt remained obscure despite RCA albums in the mid-1960s. Mike Zwerin arranged the music of Kurt Weill for the Sextet of Orchestra USA and conducted it on RCA in 1966. (Zwerin had played in Davis's group in 1949, but missed out on the recording sessions, and now writes for the *International Herald Tribune*.) Gerry Mulligan worked with big bands and orchestras over the years, but never for any length of time. The problem in modern jazz was the same as that at the end of a big-band era: it was economically impossible to keep a large performing group together, and repertory groups (such as European broadcasting supported, even in eastern Europe) simply did not exist in the USA.

Of all these, Evans was the most successful. He and Carisi had both contributed to the *Birth of the Cool* sessions, and before that to Claude Thornhill's band. Evans issued no work under his own name until *Gil Evans and Ten* was recorded on Prestige in 1957. Then his albums *New Bottle, Old Wine* (1958) and *Great Jazz Standards*

(1959) on World Pacific, together with the albums with Davis during the same period, announced a major 'new' talent and at least the possibility of a new genre.

Davis's *Porgy and Bess* was the most exciting treatment of Gershwin's music since the opera's première; *Sketches of Spain* included Evans's impressionistic arrangement of Rodrigo's *Concierto de Aranjuez* and an excerpt from Manuel de Falla's ballet *El amor brujo*. The sessions for *Sketches of Spain* were lavish and expensive for the time. George Avakian had produced Davis's first orchestral album, *Miles Ahead*, before retiring, but it was producer Teo Macero, a musician himself with a degree from the Juilliard School, who not only understood and worked with the dichotomy of commerce versus art in the record industry, but had the backing of Goddard Lieberson, then the president of Columbia and one of the most civilized people ever to hold such a post. One problem had been to convince the big band that it could play 'sloppy': most of the musicians had experience of jazz, but they had to be convinced that what was required was not the usual precision of a 'legit' session. The album also required months of editing.

Some of Davis's tracks were recorded with a band led by Michel Legrand in 1958, but another Legrand album from the year before, sometimes included in Davis's discographies, was made in Paris with trumpet solos by Fernand Verstraete. Miles had been in Paris in late 1957, though, recording soundtrack music for *L'ascenseur pour l'échafaud*, with Pierre Michelot, Kenny Clarke, Barney Wilen on tenor and René Urtreger on piano. This was episodic, like most soundtrack music, but its ethereal moodiness was a clue to what was coming next.

At the beginning of Davis's first great period, all of his sidemen were drug addicts, but he was never judgemental, saying that when they got tired of the conflict between the habit and the music, they would stop if they could. (Similarly, Duke Ellington's attitude towards his unruly band was that they were grown men and would sooner or later have to look after themselves.) Coltrane had been fired by Johnny Hodges because he was an addict, whereupon he had played in a succession of rhythm and blues bands. He left Davis suddenly in November 1956.

The story persists that when Davis was forming his quintet in 1955, Rollins had made himself scarce so that Coltrane would get the chance; but Rollins was also dealing with a drug problem. In 1956–7 recording sessions and broadcasts occasionally included Rollins instead of Coltrane. Coltrane joined Thelonious Monk at the Five Spot in New York. The association did not last long – it coincided with one of the periods during which Monk did not record much – but Monk taught Coltrane his difficult music and harmony as well, and encouraged him to take long solos, searching until he found what he wanted to play. And it was in 1957 that *Monk's Music* was made, the septet album with Coltrane and Coleman Hawkins. Art Blakey later reported:

Hawk was having trouble reading [the music], so he asked Monk to explain it to both Trane and himself. Monk said to Hawk, 'You're the great Coleman Hawkins, right? You're the guy who invented the tenor saxophone, right?' Hawk agreed. Then Monk said to Trane, 'You're the great John Coltrane, right?' Trane blushed and mumbled . . . Then Monk said to both of them, 'You both play tenor saxophone, right?' They nodded. 'Well, the music is on the horn. Between the two of you, you should be able to find it.'

It was hard to get Monk to say much, while Blakey loved to talk; he may have embroidered this. At any rate, Coltrane had become much better known while playing with Davis, and his membership of Monk's group caused a stir. Ray Copeland recalled the 1957 recording session in which he took part:

We were sitting near the rhythm section while the leader was taking a long piano solo. It was almost time for Coltrane's solo, and as I turned to look at him I noticed that he was nodding out, holding his horn in his lap. Before I could do anything, the leader happened to look up from the piano, saw Trane's condition, and screamed, 'Coltrane . . . *Coltrane!*' What happened next was so amazing I'll never forget it as long as I live. Trane was suddenly on his feet, playing in perfect cadence and following the piano solo as if nothing had happened. He played a pretty good solo, and when he was finished he sat down and went back to nodding out.

Copeland does not name the recording session, but on *Monk's Music,* on 'Well, You Needn't', you can hear Monk, at the end of his solo, shout 'Coltrane . . . *Coltrane!*' while Blakey's drum roll is announcing a new soloist. In J. C. Thomas's biography of Coltrane, *Chasin' the Trane*, he writes that it was in the spring of 1957 that Coltrane overcame his drug addiction; *Monk's Music* was made in June. After a period of not working much Coltrane decided, just as Davis had thought he would, that his habit was getting in the way of his music. He shut himself in a room in his mother's house and fasted for several days, and never touched drugs again. And soon Miles Davis called and said, 'I want you back.'

Milestones in 1958 was a sextet album, on which Cannonball Adderley was added on alto saxophone. (Miles also played on an Adderley album on Blue Note.) Julian Adderley had led a combo with his brother Nat on cornet, but he knew how valuable his experience with Miles was, for Davis was bridging the gap between funk and third-stream music. When Adderley went back to leading, he contributed to the stock of funk in the land, and his single 'Mercy, Mercy, Mercy' (written by pianist Joe Zawinul) almost reached the top ten of the *Billboard* pop chart. One of the things Miles liked about Adderley was that he never touched drugs; yet the big man, whose nickname was originally Cannibal, from his love of food as a teenager, died after a heart attack at the peak of his success.

Davis liked to use words like 'nigger', but in fact he has always hired the people he wanted without regard to race; in the late 1950s he began using pianist Bill Evans. If Oscar Peterson was the Liszt of jazz, Bill Evans was its Chopin: he thought about getting vibrato from the piano, knowing it to be impossible, because that approach to the keyboard somehow helped to give him the results he wanted; and his economy of notes was also to Davis's liking. In 1959 came the album *Kind of Blue*, a tremendous influence on the following decade, made with Coltrane, Adderley, Chambers, drummer Jimmy Cobb and pianist Evans (who was replaced by Wynton Kelly on one track). On *Kind of Blue* Davis broke through to an entirely modal way of playing. There were no standards, but five originals of pure atmosphere, drenched with Davis's plaintive economical sadness, yet intellectually powerful, and pure jazz. Evans was listed as the arranger and all the tunes as Davis's but it is thought that Evans was the author of 'Flamenco Sketches' and 'Blue in Green'.

In 1959 Coltrane had his own breakthrough. He had signed a one-year contract with Atlantic, with an option for another year. In April he recorded a version of his own tune, 'Giant Steps', which did not satisfy him, so the next month he did it again, with Paul Chambers on bass, Tommy Flanagan on piano and Art Taylor on drums, and the Atlantic album *John Coltrane: Giant Steps* was released in 1960. The mature Coltrane, one of the half-dozen most influential jazz musicians of all time, had arrived, riding an uptempo burst of joy, playing plenty of notes, but not one too many.

Meanwhile, Sonny Rollins, who was three years younger than Coltrane but better known, perhaps because he was less introspective and had more confidence, had solved his drug problem, and made a trio album, with Ray Brown on bass and Shelly Manne on drums, on the West Coast in March 1957: *Way Out West* has been a classic ever since. The lead track is Johnny Mercer's 'I'm an Old Cowhand'. (It was said to be Rollins's idea to have himself photographed in the desert for the album cover with cowboy hat and tenor saxophone instead of a six-gun; he later said he was embarrassed by it.) The album was recorded by Roy DuNann at Lester Koenig's Contemporary studio, and they were just as good at it as Rudy Van Gelder: decades later it sounds like it was recorded yesterday, and the CD edition, with four very different alternative takes, is one of the best buys in the jazz market.

Great black music was once again receiving public attention, and the next decade held more surprises. But one more giant remains to be announced in this chapter. Charles Mingus was the volatile master of the string bass, capable of playing it like a guitar; he had physical power as well as that of a composer. He was born on an army base in Arizona; he died in Mexico of a muscular wasting disease, having been in many ways an eternal exile. His ancestry included Swedish, Afro-American, American Indian and probably Scottish blood. Mingus was unaware of racism until a certain age, and it shocked him profoundly, but he turned it like everything else into an ingredient in his music. He heard Ellington on the radio; his stepmother would allow only religious music in the home, but took him to the Holiness

Church, where the 'moaning and riffs . . . between the preacher and the audience' were perhaps his most basic influence.

As a teenager he studied trombone and cello, then was steered towards playing bass in a school band (which also included Dexter Gordon). His excellent pitch and poor teaching meant that he began as a slow reader, but eventually he found better teachers, among them Red Callender, for decades one of the busiest freelance musicians on the West Coast, whom he replaced in Lee Young's band. He played with Louis Armstrong's band in 1943 and performed widely. He recorded with Illinois Jacquet, Dinah Washington and Ivie Anderson, as well as making obscure sides of his own, one of which (in 1946 for the Excelsior label) was the first appearance of a theme called 'Weird Nightmare'. While he was with Lionel Hampton (1947–8), the band made a recording on Decca called 'Mingus Fingers'. He then gave up and worked in a post office until he was hired to play in Red Norvo's trio, along with Tal Farlow on guitar.

A combination of racism and union rules meant that Mingus would have had to be replaced for a television broadcast in 1951, so he left, wanting anyway to move to New York. He joined his idol Ellington in early 1953, but after a short time his temperament caused a violent clash with Juan Tizol, and Ellington said, 'Charles, I've never fired anybody, so you're going to have to leave.'

Mingus and Max Roach formed Debut Records in 1952, and were thus among the first black jazzmen to try to maintain control of their own product. They recorded the first sessions under their own names, with reedmen Teo Macero, Sam Most and John LaPorta, trumpeters Thad Jones and Kenny Dorham and pianist-composer Paul Bley. There was also a Miles Davis session in 1955, with Mingus, vibraphonist Teddy Charles, trombonist Britt Woodman (Mingus's Los Angeles classmate and a future sideman with both Mingus and Ellington) and Coltrane's future drummer Elvin Jones, brother of Thad (and pianist Hank, all from Detroit).

Another Debut project included four trombonists, and resulted in the success of Jay and Kai, the quintet led by trombonists J. J. Johnson, the first bop trombonist, who played difficult runs with such ease that some thought he must have been playing a valve trombone, and Danish-born Kai Winding. Mingus performed on their first two albums, on Savoy and Blue Note in 1954, and in 1955 they began recording for Columbia, achieving a much higher profile than Mingus ever did.

The most famous Debut release was the first: the recording of the Massey Hall concert, made in Toronto in 1953, with Mingus, Roach, Bud Powell, Dizzy Gillespie and Charlie Parker, and an album of trio selections without the horns. The sound was not as bad as we had been led to believe; apparently it was Mingus's ego that prompted him to overdub his bass part later. The set remains one of the most renowned documents in jazz history.

In early 1955 a reunion was arranged at Birdland for Parker, Bud Powell, Mingus, Art Blakey and Kenny Dorham. They were unable to work together. Powell had to be helped from the stand, incapable; Parker stood at the microphone calling 'Bud Powell! Bud Powell!' over and over. Mingus announced, 'Ladies and gentlemen, please don't associate me with any of this. This is not jazz. These are sick people.' Years afterwards he revealed that later that night Thelonious Monk had said to Bird and Bud, 'I told you guys to act crazy, but I didn't tell you to fall in love with the act. You're really crazy now.' Parker had only a week or so to live, but life and music carry on: Miles Davis would form his quintet the same year, and Mingus's apprenticeship was almost over.

Mingus also recorded as a leader for Period and Savoy, sometimes with LaPorta and Macero. Mingus and Roach could not afford to turn down other work; the only artist Debut signed to an exclusive contract was Thad Jones, for a year, and then Mingus used his own artist as 'Oliver King' on Savoy. Debut suffered, like all small labels, from poor distribution and cash-flow problems, despite the faithful Celia, Mingus's first wife, who did most of the work. Items were later leased to Fantasy, including live performances recorded at the Café Bohemia in late December 1955, on which Mingus combined a Kern standard with a Rachmaninov prelude to make 'All the Things You C Sharp'. Debut closed down in 1957.

While running his Jazz Workshop in the early 1950s in New York, Mingus had learned by trial and error how he wanted his own music played. He recalled that he himself had joined the others in complaining when Teddy Charles left a few bars empty for blowing: 'Man, are you crazy? Write it out!' But he soon realized that no combination of writing it down and leaving spaces for blowing would give him the results he wanted. For much of his career he went through sidemen very quickly, because his patented method was too tough for them: he would proceed with no music at all, teaching it to the men a bar at a time on the piano, leaving it up to them to play his music their way. Although Mingus's personality was very different from Duke Ellington's, his working method was similar. Barney Bigard told Max Jones that Ellington would often not even give the music to his men on paper, but play it for them on the piano; and if he left a blank space, you were supposed to play his music your way. Mingus chose people who he knew could play his music, but he was much less of a diplomat, so it was harder work getting it out of them. His music, like Ellington's, did not sound like anyone else's. He also pointed the way towards greater freedom: out of necessity, he wrote mostly for smaller groups than Ellington, he gave his people more freedom and simultaneously demanded it from them. His bass playing was ferocious; he would bend a pitch not only by stopping a string but by pulling it out of true, as T-Bone Walker did on the blues guitar. And he would not hesitate to shout or sing a snatch of blues himself, encouraging another man's solo. He found resources inside himself, and his men had to do the same.

Early in 1956 he recorded his first typical work, the tone poem 'Pithecanthropus Erectus', for Atlantic, with J. R. Monterose on tenor saxophone, Jackie McLean on alto, Mal Waldron on piano and Willie Jones on drums. It depicted the emergence and grandiose follies of early man in less than eleven minutes; the moaning, inexorable passion of it was vintage Mingus. By now he had a set of tricks in his bag, suggested by tunes like 'Minor Intrusion' and 'Thrice upon a Theme'. Two other tracks on *Pithecanthropus* were 'Profile of Jackie' and 'Love Chant', which is almost fifteen minutes long and does not hold up as well as the title track; it is marred by somebody apparently playing a tambourine almost all the way through.

A year later, by the time of his next Atlantic album, he had discovered Dannie Richmond, a budding young saxophonist who changed to drums at Mingus's suggestion, and was his faithful musical colleague until the end. He played music on the drums to

Mingus's satisfaction, as well as keeping time and pushing the beat as required, adding immeasurably to the Mingus magic. The album, *The Clown*, is spoiled by a recitation on the title track: the combination of poetry and jazz was a fad at the time (another example is 'Scenes in the City', recorded for Bethlehem). Words meant a lot to Mingus; his autobiography, *Beneath the Underdog*, which amounted to a trunkful of manuscript, was savagely edited down to a book in 1971. But the combination of music and recitation works only for a live audience, when it works at all: few want to listen to it on a record.

In July there was the Hampton Hawes trio album (Jubilee) and a quintet album for trombonist Jimmy Knepper (Debut). Later that summer came Mingus's first complete success: *Tijuana Moods* is a thirty-five-minute tone poem in five parts, suggested by a visit to the Mexican border town. It was recorded basically by a sextet, including Clarence Shaw on trumpet, Knepper on trombone and Shafi Hadi (Curtis Porter) on alto, but it sounds bigger, thanks to the best recorded sound Mingus had yet received (good stereo in 1957), to the castanets, extra percussion and voices on some tracks and, mainly, to the complete success of the music. Martin Williams wrote for the album's sleeve-note about two aspects of Mingus's work:

The first is the full texture he achieves with a small group with no feeling of contrivance ... Even with one horn in solo, there is a denseness to the performance, a feeling of total movement that is always integrated. The second is the naturalness with which shifts of dominant rhythm and of tempo usually happen without the feeling of a stilted effort at 'effect'. Almost everything comes because it enables the music and the musicians to say something they have to say.

With the variable luck Mingus always had, *Tijuana Moods* was not released for six years.

In the autumn of 1957 Mingus made two albums for Bethlehem, one of which, *East Coasting*, keeps up the momentum; but they did not sell as well as expected. In 1958 he discovered pianist Horace Parlan, alto saxophonist John Handy and tenor saxophonist Booker Ervin; just when he seemed to have got a hot group together as well as his music, he learned that RCA was not going to bring out *Tijuana Moods*, Bethlehem was not going to record him any more and the William Morris Agency was going to drop him; and on top of all that, the long-suffering Celia left him. He tried to find relief for his frustrations at Bellevue, New York's mental hospital; he went there voluntarily, but bureaucrats locked him up. Critic and record producer Nat Hentoff had to help secure his release. Mingus later said that he had got himself locked up on purpose in order to get out of a personal management contract; his contact with people who were genuinely in mental trouble seems to have concentrated his energies.

Early in 1959 a live concert recording was made at the Nonagan Art Gallery, including 'Nostalgia in Times Square', written for the film *Shadows* (directed by John Cassavetes). In February came *Blues and Roots*, an epochal Atlantic album whose highlight was 'Wednesday Night Prayer Meeting'. This tune, which was something of a hit, was played by other bands and issued in two parts on a single. But the album was not released for more than a year, because Atlantic was then still a smallish label. Mingus in the meantime made two masterpieces for Columbia, *Mingus Ah Um* and *Mingus Dynasty*.

The first is recorded by an octet – Hadi, Handy and Ervin (reeds), Parlan (piano) and Knepper and Willie Dennis (trombones), but again it sounds like a much bigger group. Among the Mingus classics were 'Better Git It in Your Soul' and 'Goodbye Pork Pie Hat'; 'Jelly Roll' is a salute to that master, while 'Fables of Faubus' seems just a sardonic tune with a sarcastic title. *Mingus Dynasty* used a slightly larger group, and included 'Gunslinging Bird', of which the full title (in Mingus's afterthought) was 'If Bird came back as a gunslinger there'd be a whole lot of dead copycats'. (The band knew it as 'Gunslinger'.) There were also 'Open Letter to Duke' and Ellington's 'Mood Indigo'.

In May 1960 he recorded an ambitious and interesting album for Mercury, first called *Pre-Bird* and now once more available under that title. Ten musicians play on some tracks and twenty-five on others. 'Weird Nightmare' receives another outing: it is the same tune as 'Pipe Dream' (1946), 'Smooch' (1953, recorded by Miles Davis) and 'Vasserlean' (1960). 'Nightmare' and 'Eclipse' had vocals by Lorraine Cousins; Mingus said he had written the latter for Billie Holiday, but was afraid to give it to her. 'Half-mast Inhibition' was conducted by Gunther Schuller (as the original sleeve-note pointed out, a good

Mingus title: Half-masked inhibition? Half-past intermission?). The smaller group performed 'Prayer for Passive Resistance', another Mingus standard, and such furious interpolations as 'Take the "A" Train' with 'Exactly Like You' and 'Do Nothing Till You Hear From Me' with 'I Let a Song Go Out of My Heart'. *Pre-Bird* was Mingus's first attempt at a summary: some of the material was nearly twenty years old. He felt until the end of his life that what he was doing was all of a piece, but his chaotic way of working, usually caused by his shortage of cash, was exacerbated by his temperament (and vice versa), and was to bring about some disasters in the next decade.

In July a Mingus set was recorded live at a jazz festival at Antibes; Bud Powell, a guest, plays a furious solo on 'I'll Remember April'. The other tunes recorded were played by Mingus, Richmond, Eric Dolphy (alto saxophone and bass clarinet), Booker Ervin (tenor saxophone) and Ted Curson (trumpet). *Tijuana Moods* had no tenor saxophone; *Mingus Ah Um* had no trumpet; now Mingus had moved further into his vision, and missed out the piano. Mingus's studio dates are wonderful, but the driving, passionate personality of the composer came out even better in an informal setting. 'Wednesday Night Prayer Meeting', 'Better Get Hit in Your Soul' and 'Prayer for Passive Resistance' were full of the feeling of the Holiness Church; among the new tunes were 'What Love?' and 'Folk Forms 1': in the latter the musicians talked to each other on their instruments.

Ted Curson later led a band with Bill Barron, a tenor saxophonist from Philadelphia whose sound was like that of Coltrane; according to Curson, he had developed it 'when John Coltrane was still playing alto'. From the late 1960s Curson lived in Europe and was the first foreign musician to receive a grant from the Finnish government. Booker Ervin and Eric Dolphy were outstandingly gifted reedmen; both died because of kidney problems, Dolphy's exacerbated by undiagnosed diabetes.

Ervin and Dolphy complemented each other wonderfully, and were among Mingus's greatest discoveries. Ervin (and trumpeter Booker Little) are often lost in the shuffle when considering jazzmen of this era who died young, because Dolphy's in particular is another of the unfinished careers in music. Dolphy played all the reed instruments, including flute, but mostly alto saxophone, and was one of the first to take up the bass clarinet, played now by David Murray, Chico Freeman and others. He began in a quintet with drummer Chico Hamilton (a Mingus classmate), which unusually contained a cellist, Fred Katz. When he joined Mingus, he was mature and played with a hard-won voice-like tonal purity and a rich harmonic imagination, influenced by bird-calls, marching bands and much else. He went on to make albums of his own and with Mal Waldron on Prestige, and on Blue Note, before his death while on tour in Europe. Dolphy foreshadowed free jazz, yet his playing was not as far 'out' as it sounded; he purposely stuck to chord structures, but sounded as though he did not. He said that the notes he chose were technically acceptable in the orthodox sense, yet he seemed to lurch into another universe and back again, lending his swing sometimes to a wild and wonderful wackiness, particularly at faster tempos. He was a much bigger influence than many a musician with a longer career.

In October Mingus recorded for Archie Bleyer's Candid label, a short-lived subsidiary of Cadence, at Nola Studios in New York, where a successful attempt was made to create an informal club-type atmosphere. The recordings were produced by Nat Hentoff. The first album from these sessions had just Mingus, Richmond, Dolphy and Curson.

One of the quartet's tunes is called 'All the Things You Could be by Now if Sigmund Freud's Wife was Your Mother'. Dolphy and Curson were both soon to leave Mingus; on a more integrated and even more exciting performance of 'Folk Forms No. 1' than the one played at Antibes, they carry on an impassioned conversation while Mingus and Richmond lay out entirely, but they never drop the driving beat for an instant; in 'What Love?', Mingus and Dolphy talk things over. 'Original Faubus Fables' restores the lyrics Columbia would not allow and is dedicated to 'the first, or second or third, all-American heel, Orville Faubus' (governor of Arkansas, who ran a chicken restaurant and whose hobby was waving an axe-handle at black children). The lyrics not only introduce the superior, dramatic rhythm of the tune, but the vocal interjections and the informal setting allow its sardonicism full rein.

The whole set represents one of the high points in post-war jazz. It

is driven and dominated by Mingus and his bass with such power
and tone that, on the evidence, there is no reason for anyone to play a
solid-body electric bass, ever – except that playing bass like Mingus
must be much harder work. Another track by the quartet, later issued
on another album, was a marvellous version of 'Stormy Weather'.
The second Mingus–Candid session featured the short-lived Newport
Rebels and Jazz Artists Guild, with elder statesman Roy Eldridge,
who said to Mingus, 'I wanted to find out what bag you're in. Now I
know you're in the right bag.'

   There were more triumphs and tragedies for Mingus, but as the
1960s began jazz seemed to be in good shape: Miles Davis, Mingus
and Coltrane were hitting their stride, and Ornette Coleman was
upsetting everybody. A few jazz records were selling tens of thousands, at a time when six thousand was a good average sale. But
demographic and other changes were about to turn the whole business
upside down: millions of kids who had never heard any jazz were
about to wreak revenge on a business that had fed them pap ever
since they could sit up and listen. The tragedy of rock'n'roll is that it
was forced to become more than music.

14

Rock'n'roll; or, Black Music to the Rescue (Again)

Jazz and blues, or black urban music and black country music, were treated as separate, if related, genres in earlier decades; the saying was that the blues was not jazz, but jazz had the blues in it. But that had altered by the 1950s. While jazz effectively became the art music of the urban black (and some whites), the strands of black pop had come together. The blues had come to town, and rhythm and blues was big business.

Historically, black recording artists had often been given Tin Pan Alley tunes that white artists had already turned down. When Red Allen and Coleman Hawkins together led small-group dates in 1933, of eleven titles from three of the sessions, nine were pop songs of the day, only two of which had any currency: 'The Day You Came Along' was recorded by Bing Crosby and 'You're Gonna Lose Your Gal' by the Casa Loma band. All had probably been shoved at the record producer by song pluggers; 'Shadows on the Swanee', 'My Galveston Gal' and the rest have not been heard of since.

Some of the Tin Pan Alley and Broadway songs were so good that jazzmen improvised lovingly on them. 'How High the Moon' became a bop standard, and countless riffs were composed on its chords. As late as 1960 Mingus did something interesting with 'Girl of My Dreams', a waltz from 1927. Plenty of black tunes were big hits for white bands. The success blacks and whites had with each other's tunes and arrangements was not a fair trade-off, but black bands were never going to get the best jobs anyway, and there was money in black tunes that were hits. Joe Garland was no doubt happy to have 'In the Mood' recorded note for note by Glenn Miller.

By the early 1950s, however, everything had changed. Blacks were doing their own thing in a new era, for labels created especially to sell to the black market; and good white songs were becoming scarce. The Berlins, Gershwins and the rest had died or retired, and the classic songs they had written could not be imitated. What with Hitler, atomic bombs and a new Cold War mentality, perhaps something had been lost which made it impossible to accept songs in the style of a more innocent era. In any case, other changes in the music business meant that new, younger composers did not get a chance to build on what Kern's generation had done. The ballads still played by jazzmen were now standards, the airwaves were filled with jingles and the Broadway musical was beginning to disappear.

In the 1949–50 season the new shows included Rodgers and Hammerstein's *The King and I*, Irving Berlin's *Call Me Madam* and Frank Loesser's *Guys and Dolls*. (The latter included 'If I Were a Bell', soon to be played by the Miles Davis Quintet.) But in 1950–51 only nine new productions were offered, the lowest number since well back in the nineteenth century. Some were revivals, like *Pal Joey* from 1940, and two were Yiddish-American shows which in earlier times would not have found room on Broadway. All the new shows of that season lost money, including *Top Banana*, with lyrics by Johnny Mercer (and starring Phil Silvers), and Lerner and Loewe's *Paint Your Wagon*. Musical shows were increasingly expensive to mount, while television and other social changes meant there were smaller audiences on the Great White Way, as Broadway used to be known. The hit shows of the 1950s, such as *The Pajama Game* (1954) and *Damn Yankees* (1955), both by Richard Adler and Jerry Ross, occasionally produced above-average pop songs, for example, 'Hey There' and 'Whatever Lola Wants', but not of the quality of earlier decades. *West Side Story* (music by Leonard Bernstein and lyrics by Stephen Sondheim) and *The Music Man* (Meredith Willson) were both huge hits in 1957, and great in contrast, the one about racial strife in New York, the other, through rose-tinted glasses, about a small town. *Gypsy* (1959) was probably a masterpiece in every respect: it was Ethel Merman's last big role, it effortlessly revived all the 'shtick' of Broadway tradition, and the songs were by Jule Styne and Stephen Sondheim. But among the most interesting events on Broadway in the 1950s were Bernstein's failure *Candide* (1956, lyrics by Lillian Hellman) and the emergence of Sondheim as a major talent.

Broadway shows were not what they used to be and were trying to become something else; no longer would they provide a central strand of America's pop culture. Nowadays the only shows certain to be profitable, indeed to set records for making money, are those of Britain's Andrew Lloyd Webber; even his third marriage in early 1991 got columns of space in British newspapers. Yet Lloyd Webber's music is perfect FM fodder, of no lasting value at all, in my opinion. Stephen Sondheim is acknowledged to be the most important composer for the stage today, even by the same critics who find something wrong with every show. All the same, even his *Into the Woods*, which received better reviews from the British critics than any of his previous works, lasted only five months in London. The musical theatre, once at the centre of popular music, is now well outside it.

It is impossible to say how much was lost on account of the low standards of American broadcasting. Harold Arlen's *House of Flowers* and many another show may simply have been too good to survive at a time when people went to a Broadway show despite the increasing price of the tickets only because their neighbours had seen it. Cabaret singers such as Bobby Short, Mabel Mercer and Blossom Dearie have had a huge repertory of songs that were almost totally unknown to the general public, raising the question of whether that sort of songwriting disappeared or is living in the garden shed on reduced rations. The big bands and the late-night live radio broadcasts that once promoted such songs no longer exist. It is tantalizing to imagine television's having taken over the function of the Broadway musical, but it was not to be. It did not take television long to descend from the live drama of the 1950s to the banality of today's assembly-line mini-series; there is no original music drama on television. Polly Bergen was a good actress as well as a good singer, but there was no place for her to work; similarly, Maureen McGovern has an excellent voice, a musical intelligence and is a first-class modern actress, but the genre in which she would have been a star has disappeared.

Music on television's variety shows was almost exclusively ASCAP music, partly because there were few black faces to be seen, and radio DJ shows reflected this at first. But as the name of the *Billboard* 'race' chart was changed to rhythm and blues in 1949, a revolution was already brewing.

We have seen that Woody Herman had covered Louis Jordan's 'Caldonia' in 1945, that one of the biggest hits of 1950 was an inappropriate version of a country stomp, 'Rag Mop', and that Buddy Morrow covered the jump band hits of Jimmy Forrest. Along the way an historic court case settled the question of whether musical arrangements could be copyrighted, and the answer was that they could not. 'A Little Bird Told Me', a song by Harvey O. Brooks, was recorded by Paula Watson on a Supreme label. Decca copied not only the arrangement but also the vocal style to the last inflection, and had a big hit in 1948 by Evelyn Knight (whose other most successful hit, the same year, was 'Powder Your Face With Sunshine', a Lombardo song). Supreme sued, and lost. The Watson original sold well, but she had only one more minor hit, and there was now nothing to keep anybody from copying another's hit right down to the backbeat.

By 1954 there were at least 4 radio stations in New York aimed at the black market exclusively, and over 250 stations around the country. The number of black DJs had increased from only a few to over 700, and they were joined by a handful of hip whites, such as Art Leboe in Los Angeles, Dewey Phillips in Memphis, Gene Nobles and John Richborough in Nashville, Zenas Sears in Atlanta, Bob Smith (known as Wolfman Jack) in Shreveport, Ken 'the Cat' Elliott in New Orleans and Alan Freed in Cleveland. Several elements were at work: television forced non-network radio to turn to specialized programming to find an audience, while many sponsors found television too expensive, and could still reach large numbers of black families, who had fewer television sets than whites, and perhaps found it hard to relate to white sitcoms. But even with regard to black pop, the famous DJs were white: they were the ones that had the effect on the white market. And even today the black market is simply not valued in the marketplace.

In 1953 $15 million worth of R&B records were sold, more than the entire record industry's sales of fifteen years earlier. Ruth Brown's contract was so valuable to Atlantic that it was renewed with an advance of $100,000: having been recommended to Atlantic by Duke Ellington, she had twenty-one top ten hits in the black chart from 1949 to 1960, five of which reached number one, and was the only female star under contract at Atlantic until LaVern Baker, whose first hit was in 1955. The Clovers, a vocal quartet and guitarist, also on Atlantic, had fifteen top ten black hits in four years; one of them reportedly sold two million copies (probably 'Fool, Fool, Fool', which was number one for six weeks in 1951).

Most new releases by the major labels never broke even, for they had to sell 40,000 copies to do so in 1953. The independent labels selling R & B, however, had lower costs and their own distribution, and new releases by artists like Amos Milburn on Aladdin and Little Esther (Phillips) on Savoy regularly sold 150,000 copies, and sometimes much more than that. A Texas-born pianist and barroom crooner, Milburn had nineteen top ten black hits (1948–54); his first, 'Chicken Shack Boogie', was number one for five weeks. Esther Mae Jones, also from Texas, was barely fourteen years old when her 'Double Crossing Blues' was number one in the black chart for nine weeks in early 1950. (Her career was interrupted by drug problems but she came back in 1962 as Esther Phillips.)

The major labels formed subsidiaries for R & B – Decca had Coral, and later Brunswick, while Columbia revived Okeh – but the product was too slick, and the independent producers of R & B had the D Js in their employ, while the big companies were making a late start in black radio. In order to do more business they began to cream it off the top, covering R & B hits with white artists.

The Orioles, a seminal black doo-wop quartet (plus a guitarist) from Baltimore, had black hits almost every year from 1948. Their 'Crying in the Chapel' (on Jubilee, 1953) was a number one black hit, but there were cover versions by Ella Fitzgerald, country singers Darrell Glenn and Rex Allen, former Benny Goodman vocalist Art Lund and (the biggest hit, on RCA) June Valli.

White vocal groups were big business in the early 1950s. The Ames Brothers were a quartet, with a sweet, pretty sound, led by Ed, who is still a popular balladeer today. But the other groups all used the same conventional white harmony, and after decades of beautiful black, country and folk vocal groups, most white pop groups of the early 1950s sounded like they were working too hard. The Four Lads were from Toronto; their voices blended well, but like most white vocal groups they sounded overwrought. They began by backing Johnnie Ray on 'Cry' in 1951. (Significantly, it was released on Okeh: Ray had help and encouragement from LaVern Baker and her manager, and his emotional delivery was seen as appealing to black audiences.) Like Ray, the Four Lads then transferred to the parent Columbia label, where their hits included 'Moments to Remember' (1955), a perennial college prom song for decades, 'No, Not Much' (1956), a good pop song by the same writers, Robert Allen and Ray Stillman, and 'Standing on the Corner (Watching All the Girls Go By)', which at least was supposed to be sung by a group. (It came from the Frank Loesser show *Most Happy Fella*.) The Four Lads had hits throughout the 1950s, according to *Billboard*, but I don't remember any of them.

The Four Aces, from Pennsylvania, were worse. Their biggest hit was 'Love is a Many-splendored Thing', a soupy film song in 1955, and the way they belted out the word 'luuuuuve' with their patented slow shuffle beat made you want to cry with boredom. There were also the Four Coins, the Four Esquires and so forth; the sound of the Hilltoppers on Dot was not too obnoxious (and included Billy Vaughan, who became the label's music director and house band-leader). The Four Freshmen and the Hi-lo's were good singers who used adventurous harmonies and arrangements, and sold mostly albums. Few white groups had learned anything from the essential sweetness of the doo-wop tradition.

The Crew-cuts were the worst of all, another quartet from Toronto, where they had all been choirboys. Their first hit on Mercury in 1954 was a white novelty, 'Crazy 'Bout Ya Baby'. Meanwhile, a black Bronx group called the Chords, on the Cat label, had covered Patti Page's hit 'Cross Over the Bridge', basically a country song; the B side was 'Sh-boom', their own rhythm novelty with a fast shuffle beat. DJs turned it over and made it number two in the black chart. The Crew-cuts, however, had already copied it: their 'Sh-boom' was a number one novelty hit for nine weeks in the pop chart, and is still described as the first rock'n'roll record, which it certainly was not. Their next and lesser hit, 'Oop-shoop', was written to cash in on the success of 'Sh-boom'. In 1955 a Los Angeles group, the Penguins, had a number one black hit on DooTone with a pretty doo-wop ballad written by the group's bass, Curtis Williams, called 'Earth Angel (Will You Be Mine)'; the Crew-cuts' version was a national number three. Gene and Eunice had a rhythm hit with 'Ko Ko Mo' in 1955, originally on Combo, soon picked up by Aladdin; there were several white covers, and the Crew-cuts' was beaten in the charts by that of Perry Como.

Georgia Gibbs, who recorded on Mercury, the same label as the Crew-cuts, was born Fredda Gibbons in 1920 and was a band singer of many years' experience, having worked with Hudson and DeLange, Frankie Trumbauer and Artie Shaw. She had a unique vocal colour, always an advantage in a pop singer, and could set up a rocking beat. In short, she was not as offensive as the Crew-cuts, and might have deserved something better than to go down in history as a rip-off artist. She had one of the hit versions of 'If I Knew You Were Comin' I'd've Baked a Cake' in 1950 and a huge hit in 1952 with an Argentine tango retitled 'Kiss of Fire'. (Mike Stoller: 'I frankly believe that a lot of those songs were bullshit and funny at the same time because they were so terrible.') 'Seven Lonely Days' was a good rhythm tune in 1953, a cover of a country hit by Bonnie Lou on King. In 1955 LaVern Baker had a top five black hit on Atlantic with 'Tweedle-dee'; Gibbs's version reached number two in the national pop chart. (There is a story that Baker and Gibbs, both on tour, met in an airport, and Baker asked, 'Did you buy flight insurance on *me*?')

In 1954 Hank Ballard and the Midnighters had an R & B hit called 'Work With Me Annie', which stayed at number one for seven weeks; the composer credit included Ballard, Johnny Otis and Etta James. The hit was slightly suggestive, in that the work assignment in question was meant to be horizontal. It was covered by James, who was only seventeen in February 1955 when her answer version, 'The Wallflower', was a black number one for four weeks, and this became the most flagrant swindle of all: Georgia Gibbs's 'Dance With Me Henry (Wallflower)' was a pop number one for three weeks. The Midnighters had already followed up with 'Annie Had a Baby' and 'Annie's Aunt Fannie', but Mercury passed on those.

The kids who cared about music and who knew that what they

heard on the radio were cover versions were curious about the originals. In fact, stations in the South that catered for blacks were aware that 20 or 30 per cent of their listeners were white youngsters, who had already discovered that black was best, and that most of the covers were very poor compared with the real thing: the Crew-cuts' 'Sh-boom' was an irritating novelty; in the Chords' original the rhythm was the whole point, yet the singing was sweeter. LaVern Baker's 'Tweedle-dee' reached the top fifteen in the pop chart and her 'Jim Dandy' (1956) was a number one black hit and a top twenty pop hit. The white covers of these artists cheated them of greater success, and in any case was a mistake on the part of the major labels.

Despite the success of Nat 'King' Cole, Billy Eckstine, Ella Fitz-gerald and a few other black artists in the white market, there was an unthinking knee-jerk racism working in the music business. Eckstine had been the first black man to appear on the cover of *Life* magazine, which dubbed him 'the Sepia Sinatra'. He was seen to some extent as aping the dominant white pop style of the late 1940s, as though blacks should not be singing the best love songs for their own sake, which rankled Eckstine. Black pop's rhythm tunes were clearly gaining in popularity, and were thought to be more acceptable in their sterilized white versions, but the large minority of young white people who were listening to black radio and to the original black hits were ultimately the taste-makers, the most influential segment of music fans, and they were not fooled by any of this. They lost respect for the music business and for business in general, disgusted by the mindless greed for short-term profits, while the music business had no idea what was going on.

By 1955 the Platters, a black vocal quintet from Los Angeles, had already had their own national hits. Buck Ram had worked as an arranger for Mills Music and had managed the Three Suns, a sweet white vocal and instrumental trio who had hits in the 1940s; he then turned to black music. He managed the Penguins and saw their big hit ripped off; he wrote 'Only You' for the Platters, and it was recorded by a quintet for Federal, which did not want to issue it. Having made a personnel change and added the beautiful Zola Taylor, he took a sextet to Mercury and remade 'Only You', which reached the top five, followed by 'The Great Pretender', a national number one for two weeks. The next year 'My Prayer' (a revival of a French and English song recorded by Glenn Miller in 1939) was number one for five weeks. Furthermore, the Platters had staying power; they had hits every year until 1967, including two more number ones in 1958: 'Twilight Time', a lovely song written in 1944 by Ram and the Three Suns, and 'Smoke Gets in Your Eyes'.

Another factor in the burgeoning success of R&B was that the live shows on tour were cheaper to produce than those of big-name white acts. Promoters in the South and the Midwest found that they could get two top R&B acts for the cost of a white one, while the audience for R&B shows was already integrated and sharply increasing. After some years as a classical and record-request DJ, Cleveland's Alan Freed began playing R&B at the suggestion of a sponsor, a record-shop owner who saw the white kids buying the records. In March 1952 a dance at the Cleveland Arena offered Charles Brown, the Dominoes with Clyde McPhatter (one of the most influential of lead vocalists), the Orioles, the Moonglows and the jump bands of Tiny Grimes and Jimmy Forrest. Seventeen thousand fans of Freed's *Rock'n'roll House Party* radio show bought tickets (according to Russell Sanjek). Unfortunately, the Arena held only ten thousand people, and Freed almost went to jail after the resulting mêlée, and before everybody realized that the whole thing had been an accident: the huge ticket sales had been unexpected. Freed later packed dance halls with such shows, and the audiences were never less than one-third white.

Freed was not the first white DJ to play R&B from choice; that may have been Art Leboe in Los Angeles, who made his station the most popular in the Hispanic community. But Freed knew a good thing when he saw it, and borrowed the term 'rock'n'roll' to describe it. To call it rhythm and blues would have been to point out that white people were listening to black music, and few people knew that rockin' and rollin' was a black euphemism for sexual intercourse. In any case, the term was not new: the Boswell Sisters had recorded a film song called 'Rock and Roll' in 1934, and there were many more song titles and lyrics that used the phrase.

It is possible to excuse various music business practices over the years on the grounds that that was the way it was, and it was not up to individual promoters or record industry moguls to try to change things. But there can be only one reason why the Chords, Penguins, Clovers and the rest did not do better in the lily-white pop chart; why Baker's own 'Tweedle-dee' was not as widely played on the air as Gibbs's version; why 'Dance With Me Henry' had to have its lyrics cleaned up. But the white man's racist fear, not only of the black man's supposed sexual prowess but of the power of sex itself, could not keep down the pressure that had built up by the mid-1950s. Black pop records could no longer be confined to 'race', 'sepia', 'ebony' or R & B charts. White pop was boring and black pop was not, and the floodgates soon opened.

Chuck Berry had grown up in St Louis, where he played guitar and led a trio including pianist Johnnie Johnson, whose importance has long been overlooked: Berry's songs and his guitar style were influenced by Johnson's keyboard, which gave them an unusual sound. Berry took a demo tape to Chicago, where Muddy Waters introduced him to Leonard Chess; one of the tunes on the tape was an adaptation of 'Ida Red', a country stomp recorded, for example, by Bob Wills in 1938. Its name was changed to 'Maybellene' and Berry recorded it in May 1955, with Johnson on piano, Willie Dixon on bass and Jasper Thomas on drums; Alan Freed promoted the song and took a co-writing credit; it entered both charts in August, and was number one for eleven weeks in the black chart, reaching the top five in the white. A fast, swinging blues about cars and a girl, it inaugurated a new era. That month, with a few other kids, I was on my way across country (in a 1951 V-8 Ford, in fact) for a week of camping out, the car radio blasting out 'Maybellene' ('Nothin' outrunnin' my V-8 Ford'), and none of our lives was ever the same again. On the other side was 'Wee Wee Hours', a slow, midnight blues with fine piano playing from Johnson, which also changed a few heads. Berry's singing, his guitar and his lyrics still perhaps represent the essence of rock'n'roll. With his songs the genre became fully the music of a younger generation: 'School Day (Ring! Ring! Goes the Bell)' added high school to the list of teenage obsessions, while 'Rock and Roll Music', 'Sweet Little Sixteen' and 'Johnny B. Goode' all became anthems.

His 'Brown-eyed Handsome Man' and 'Too Much Monkey Business' never reached the white chart, nor did Bo Diddley's 'Bo Diddley', 'I'm a Man' or 'Diddley Daddy', but by now more and more kids were checking out the black charts. Diddley was another transplanted Chicagoan; his records (on Checker, a Chess sister label) were weird, mysterious and slightly scary, known for the bags of echo on the guitar and his 'shave-and-a-haircut, six bits' beat. He has been copied by rockers ever since, but only had one top twenty pop hit: 'Say Man' (1959), listed by *Billboard* as a novelty.

The same year Chuck Berry broke through, New Orleans also got into the act. Lew Chudd had been the producer of the *Let's Dance* radio show that helped Benny Goodman to fame in 1935. In 1947 he formed Imperial Records to record top ten hits in Spanish-language covers for that market in the South-west, and used the profits to expand into square-dance records, kiddie records, country music and R & B. Slim Whitman was a country success on Imperial, and his 'Indian Love Call' was a huge hit; he played in London in 1952 and for years was a bigger star in the UK than in the USA.

Chudd's R & B talent scout and producer was a New Orleans trumpeter and bandleader, Dave Bartholomew, who as a freelance produced Lloyd Price's 'Lawdy Miss Clawdy' for Specialty and Shirley and Lee's 'I'm Gone' for Aladdin (both hits in 1952), as well as his own 'Country Boy' (1949, DeLuxe). He recorded other R & B songs in leftover studio time: 'Preachin' and Teachin'' (Ace, 1952), like 'Country Boy', used the excellent session drummer Earl Palmer; 'Who Drank My Beer While I Was in the Rear' that year was on Imperial. But Bartholomew had more success producing others, such as Fats Domino.

Pianist and singer Domino was born in New Orleans; his first language was French. The New Orleans piano style can be traced directly from Jelly Roll Morton through Joseph Louis 'Red' Cayou (born around 1905) and Isadore 'Tuts' Washington (born in 1907, finally recorded in 1983), through Professor Longhair (Roy Byrd), who worked for Bartholomew in 1949, to Fats Domino, Huey Smith, Allen Toussaint and Mac Rebennack (Dr John, the Night Tripper). Professor Longhair's imposition of fast triplets on a syncopated rhumba beat is directly descended from Jelly Roll's 'Spanish tinge'.

Domino was compared to Fats Waller by the bone-headed musical press when he later had a hit with 'What's the Reason I'm Not Pleasin' You'; he was not a stylist of the calibre of Waller or Jelly Roll, but he did what he did extremely well. His warm personality transcended any question of race, and the music had a lilt, as well as a beat, that could only have come from New Orleans. Domino's smoky, laid-back voice, with just a trace of a French accent, together with the songs and Bartholomew's band, made history.

His first recording session yielded 'Hey La Bas', a coming together of strands of New Orleans history, including voodoo and French and Catholic influences. 'The Fat Man', a cleaned-up drug song recorded the same day, was his first R & B hit. His fifth release, 'Every Night About This Time', was a hit the same year; it incorporated the keyboard triplet which became a trademark, and may have been influenced by Little Willie Littlefield as well as Longhair. (Blues pianist Littlefield had a hit with 'It's Midnight' on Modern in 1949.) Domino's R & B hits 'Goin' Home' (1952) and 'Goin' to the River' (1953) were as good as national top thirty hits, they sold so well and got so much airplay, but they were not allowed on the white chart.

Randy Wood operated an appliance repair shop in Nashville in 1946, and dabbled in radio. He bought several thousand remaindered R & B records and sold them over the radio at six for a dollar; with some of the profits he formed Dot Records in 1950. He produced country records, but the demand for R & B was such that he began covering the songs with a squeaky-clean college student named Pat Boone, who was twenty years old when he had his first hit in 1955 with 'Two Hearts', an R & B hit by the Charms. Boone's second hit was a national number one version of Fats Domino's 'Ain't That a Shame' the same year, which helped pull Domino's own record out of the R & B ghetto into the pop top ten.

Domino's seventeenth and eighteenth top ten R & B hits were back to back, 'Bo Weevil' and 'Don't Blame It On Me'. In the first, an irresistibly rocking folksong, the melody is played tremolo by guitarist Ernest McLean, who floats over the backbeat, making the whole thing a timeless country stomp. 'Bo Weevil' reached number thirty-five in the pop charts, while the slick cover with much less style by squeaky Teresa Brewer entered the top twenty. The other side of Domino's record, 'Don't Blame It On Me', was not covered and didn't make the pop chart, but kids discovered it: the playing of Clarence Ford (alto), Herb Hardesty, Buddy Hagans and Lee Allen (tenors), McLean (guitar), Frank Fields (bass) and Cornelius Coleman (drums) sounded so good on jukeboxes after so many years of pap that we couldn't believe our luck.

In the same year, 1956, Domino's 'I'm In Love Again' was a number three national hit. Altogether he had over sixty Hot 100 *Billboard* entries in less than ten years. The New Orleans backbeat was rock solid, yet is like a happy afterthought compared with the noisy banging on today's pop records, and the riffing saxophones and Domino's laid-back style combine to make these some of the best party records of all time.

Also in 1956, and in New Orleans, the totally impossible, irrational and outrageous became reality; the inmates left the asylum, never to be recaptured, with a cry of WOMP-BOMP-A-LOO-MOMP ALOP-BOMP-BOMP! Little Richard was bisexual, he wore make-up, he was a tornado on stage and he passionately shouted dirty songs in a sanctified style, screams and all:

> Long Tall Sally she's
> Built for speed
> She got everything
> That Uncle John needs . . .

In two minutes Richard Wayne Penniman used as much energy as an all-night party.

He came from a large, poor family in Macon, Georgia. He was influenced by Billy Wright, who wore loud clothes, curled his hair and performed a gospel-shouting R&B style, and was encouraged to play piano by Esquerita (who was also known as Eskew Reeder, SQ Reeder, the Magnificent Malucci and so on, and later imitated Richard, recording in New Orleans in the mid-1960s). Little Richard recorded for RCA with Wright's band in 1951 and 1952 after winning a talent contest; DJ Zenas Sears helped make the deal and the sides were recorded at WGST in Atlanta: 'Every Hour' was a local hit, but Richard's persona was not yet let loose. He recorded for

Peacock in 1953 in Houston, at the second of the two sessions using Johnny Otis's band. But he was washing dishes in an Atlanta bus station when stardom beckoned. He had sent a demonstration tape to Specialty in Hollywood.

Art Rupe dispatched his assistant, Bumps Blackwell, to New Orleans to make records; and Cosimo Matassa's J and M Studio was primitive by today's standards, or even by major-label standards of the time: Blackwell placed his microphones by trial and error, going back and forth into the next room to listen to a two-track Ampex tape recorder on headphones; the bass player was on the other side of the room and the drummer was outside the door. But both Richard and Fats Domino made their classic hits at Cosimo's.

The band on Richard's first sessions, like Domino's band, included New Orleans' best: Melvin Dowden (piano), Justin Adams (guitar), Lee Allen (tenor saxophone), Alvin 'Red' Tyler (baritone saxophone), Frank Fields (double bass) and Earl Palmer (drums); Huey Smith was present part of the time and probably played some piano, and Richard himself played on 'Tutti Frutti', an outrageous song from the club scene. Blackwell heard him playing around with it during a lunch break – the nearby premises had a piano, and Richard could not resist showing off. Dorothy La Bostrie was asked to clean up the lyrics: 'Tutti Frutti, good booty / if it don't fit, don't force it / You can grease it, make it easy' became 'Tutti Frutti, awrootie / I got a gal, named Sue / She knows just what to do', which at least left something to the imagination.

'Tutti Frutti' reached number two in the R&B chart and the top twenty of the pop chart, and – incredibly – Pat Boone's cover went higher than Little Richard's. (Bible student Boone later claimed he had not known what the song was about.) This was a bit like June Allyson having a hit with 'Jazz Me Blues', and it was the end of the cover era: white kids were by now sorting each other out according to who bought 'Baboon' and who bought Richard. Later the same year Richard tried to record 'Long Tall Sally' as fast as possible so that Boone would not be able to sing it; they both had hits with it, but this time Richard's record went higher than Boone's, and the rest of Boone's hits were mostly Hollywood ballads. A new kind of cover era immediately began: Blackwell and John Marascalco wrote 'Rip It

Up' and 'Ready Teddy', a two-sided hit for Richard; both were covered by Elvis Presley and Bill Haley, but more appropriately and out of admiration for the songs: ripping it off was out, but ripping it up was definitely in.

Some of Richard's records were too frenetic to dance to. The master of 'Keep a Knockin'' was only fifty-seven seconds long, and a single was made of it by means of repetition. Others were better: 'Lucille' is one of the finest, inexorable at exactly the right tempo, while 'Send Me Some Lovin'' and 'Can't Believe You Wanna Leave' are actually slow. One of Richard's biggest contributions was his personality. His live act was like nothing anyone had ever seen. He wore his hair in a huge pompadour with marcelled waves on top; he wore the loudest clothes in the business and cosmetics to match. At the beginning of a set his band never knew what direction he would come from. When producer H. B. Barnum first saw Richard, Barnum was about fourteen years old, and playing saxophone with touring R & B shows:

He'd just burst onto the stage from anywhere, and you wouldn't be able to hear anything but the roar of the audience ... We might vamp that first number for four to five minutes before he even got to the piano. He'd be on the stage, he'd be off the stage, he'd be jumping and yelling, screaming, whipping the audience on ... Then when he finally did hit the piano and just went into di-di-di-di-di-di-di-di, you know, well nobody can do that as fast as Richard. It just took everybody by surprise ... That's the first time I ever saw spotlights and flicker lights used at a concert show. It had all been used in show business, but he brought it into *our* world.

At the end of a set Richard was covered with sweat, and it was not long before girls started throwing their underwear on to the stage.

For the second time New Orleans permanently altered the course of the world's popular music. Huey 'Piano' Smith had a hit in 1957 with 'Rockin' Pneumonia and the Boogie Woogie Flu', and the next year with 'Don't You Just Know It'. He had played piano on Bartholomew's wonderful 'I Hear You Knockin'', an R & B classic by Smiley Lewis which had not made the pop charts in 1955 (but was covered in a dull but successful version on Dot by actress Gale

Storm). Smith's band, the Clowns, included lead singer Bobby Marchan, as well as Red Tyler and Lee Allen. Another seminal figure was pianist and bandleader Paul Gayten, whose R&B hits in 1949–50 included 'I'll Never be Free' (with vocalist Annie Laurie), and who wrote 'For You My Love', on which he backed Larry Darnell for a number one. (The song was also a hit duet by Nat Cole and Nellie Lutcher.) Later he backed Clarence Henry on 'Ain't Got No Home' (1956), which became a pop hit, and took a co-writing credit for the amusing 'Troubles, Troubles' on the reverse side. Gayten's own instrumental jukebox hits, such as 'Nervous Boogie' in 1957, were tossed off during leftover studio time, like some of Bartholomew's. Tenor saxophonist Lee Allen wrote his 1958 hit 'Walkin' with Mr Lee' while working as Gayten's sideman.

But while rhythm and blues was breaking through to the pop charts and washing away the cover merchants, rock'n'roll was also coming from another direction. Among those white kids listening to R&B in the early 1950s were the hillbilly cats who invented rockabilly; in fact, it was at first called 'cat music'.

For decades the excellent playing of a great many instrumentalists in country music had been directly influenced by black music. There was the lingering effect of the country jazz, or western swing, of Bob Wills, and the important folk poems of Hank Williams, with their swaggering beat and their true-to-life concerns. 'Country boogie' had been gaining ground. The Delmore Brothers had recorded 'Hillbilly Boogie' as early as 1945, and then 'Freight Train Boogie', 'Blues Stay Away From Me' and 'Pan American Boogie' were hits. Jack Guthrie, Woody's cousin, had a hit with 'Oakie Boogie' in 1947, and Hawkshaw Hawkins's 'Dog House Boogie' and guitarist Arthur Smith's 'Guitar Boogie' were successful in 1948.

'Guitar Boogie' may have been recorded much earlier, in 1945, on a Super Disc label; an instrumental, it was played by a string band, with a gently amplified guitar and no drums. It continued selling for years. The chart hit, perhaps a new recording, was on MGM, and it was issued on that label in England. It had a 4/4 feeling but with a backbeat. (Compare it with the other side of the British 78, for example, called 'Bebop Rag': despite the title, its two-beat style is corny.) Tennessee Ernie Ford's 'Shotgun Boogie' was a big country hit in 1950; Webb Pierce's band had hit after hit from 1952 with a honky-tonk backbeat. Meanwhile, Bill Haley and his Saddlemen, billed as the Cowboy Jive Band, mixed yodels, polkas and western swing.

Haley was born in Michigan and grew up in Pennsylvania; he began as a yodelling cowboy on radio. His Downhomers first recorded in 1944, and his various groups included the Four Aces of Western Swing. He started covering R & B hits like Jackie Brenston's 1951 'Rocket "88"', which sold fairly well, then 'Rock the Joint', a 1949 hit by Jimmy Preston, which sold even better. The country covers were not selling at all, so he threw caution to the wind: he changed the name of the Saddlemen to Bill Haley and his Comets and recorded his own 'Crazy Man Crazy' for the tiny Essex label (whose most popular star was the mood music conductor Monty Kelly, whose 'Tropicana' was the label's biggest hit). Haley suddenly reached the pop top fifteen in 1953. The tune was just a stomp, like 'Rag Mop', with words that were not up to much, but seemed at the time to borrow from jazz: 'Man, that music's gone, gone!' This already sounded trite then, but Haley's 'jive' slang was as much a part of the act as the relentlessly slapped string bass. The hit was covered on Mercury by dance band leader Ralph Marterie, who, with his bigger name (and vocal by the Smarty-aires), almost caught Haley in the charts with his own tune.

After a couple of similar, lesser hits on Essex, Haley moved to Decca, where he was produced by Milt Gabler. Haley could not read music, according to Gabler, so he had to hum the riffs to him: 'It was like recording a barbershop quartet or the Mills Brothers, you have to woodshed it and learn it by rote. They'd work out the harmony among themselves.' Gabler had recorded not only Louis Jordan, but the jump band of Buddy Johnson, with vocalist Arthur Prysock. Johnson's drummer, and also Lionel Hampton's, had to be kept from playing too loud for the recording technology of the time, Gabler said, but Haley's band was recorded in a disused ballroom, which had a high ceiling, curtains hanging from the balcony and a live wooden floor. This acoustic, together with up-to-date recording equipment, allowed Haley's drummer to play his tinny rim-shot backbeat as loudly as possible, and the steel player to bang his bar on the strings until sparks flew. Gabler put reverb on the master tape and overdubbed Haley's weak voice.

'Rock Around the Clock' was a Tin Pan Alley rhythm novelty, and similar tunes and lyrics had been around for years. It barely made the top twenty-five. But the next hit, still in 1954, reached the top ten. It was a cover of 'Shake, Rattle and Roll', a number one R & B tune by Big Joe Turner, originally a singing bartender from the roaring days of Kansas City. By the mid-1950s Turner was a seasoned blues shouter; after his R & B hit 'Chains of Love' (1951) on a Freedom label, Turner moved to Atlantic and had big hits in the black chart every year until 1958. He was too big, too old, too black and too powerful to become a pop star, but hits like 'Corrine Corrina' and 'Lipstick Powder and Paint' (both 1956) made him a more deserving father of rock'n'roll than most. 'Shake, Rattle and Roll', with its three-chord tune and the lines 'Get out in that kitchen / And rattle those pots and pans!' was an archetypal rock'n'roll song.

Then came the film *The Blackboard Jungle*, released in 1955, starring Glenn Ford and a very young Sidney Poitier. Gabler makes the point that film soundtracks were usually 'pinched' at the top and bottom of the frequency range, to save the ears of the people in the front rows from the noise of the huge speakers and amplifiers used in big cinemas; but *The Blackboard Jungle* soundtrack was processed wide open. It was a realistic film (for the time) about a rough high school ('juvenile delinquency' had been a media theme for years), and its music director was said to be the publisher of 'Rock Around the Clock'. Haley's record dominated the soundtrack and shot to number one more than a year after it was first released, and also reached number three in the R & B chart.

Haley had sixty USA chart hits in seven years, but 'Rock Around the Clock' was his only number one. It might be named by many as the first number one rock'n'roll record, and therein lies part of the music's tragedy. Bill Haley did for rock'n'roll what the Original Dixieland Jazz Band did for jazz in 1917, establishing it in the public mind as a noisy party music, but the ODJB was at least an innovation at the time. Haley was an unlikely pop star, a chubby married man and almost thirty years old when he came to the fore; he was far more popular in the UK, where he had no competition, than in the USA. By all accounts he was a pleasant man, modest and grateful for his success. It is a pity that the music was so bad. It was worse than bad; it was a major environmental hazard. The bass *had* to be slapped all the way through every record, and the drums *had* to be tinny and loud, and nobody showed any understanding of time. The closest to musical excitement the Comets ever came was 'Rudy's Rock', an instrumental in which Rudy Pompilli plays a decent jump band saxophone style; it moves at a faster tempo than the band's usual clock-ticking, so the rhythm section may have had to concentrate on what it was doing. Haley and his group starred in several rock'n'roll films of the period, such as *Rock Around the Clock* in 1956 (the song was endlessly recycled). The films were mostly dreadful, but this particular Freed epic had at least the virtue of integrating the music, featuring the Platters as well as Haley. Haley was soon reduced to a nostalgia act, eclipsed by more talented hillbillies.

Sun Records, in Memphis, Tennessee, would have more influence on popular music in the 1950s than all the major labels put together. Radio engineer Sam Phillips formed the Memphis Recording Service in 1950, and taped a session with jazz pianist Phineas Newborn for RPM/Modern. He soon launched a Phillips label, with local DJ Dewey Phillips (no relation). The idea was to record local black R&B talent, but masters continued to be leased to other labels. B. B. King worked at the local black radio station, and his hits on RPM began appearing in 1951, some of them recorded in the Sun studio.

Guitarist and bandleader Ike Turner was a talent scout for RPM/ Modern, and saw to it that B. B. King remained an RPM artist, but some of the other records were leased to Chess in Chicago. Howlin' Wolf (Chester Burnett) became an R&B legend. He had a double-sided hit, 'Moanin' at Midnight' / 'How Many More Years', in 1951, the same year Turner scored a massive number one under the name of his saxophonist and vocalist: Jackie Brenston and his Delta Cats were Ike Turner's Kings of Rhythm. 'Rocket "88"' is often described as the first rock'n'roll record; it sounds tame today, but its four-wheeled subject-matter beat Chuck Berry by four years.

Rosco Gordon had a top ten hit on RPM, then a number one in 1952 that had been leased to Chess. RPM/Modern decided that they had Gordon under contract and successfully got 'Booted' back from

Chess. Walter Horton, Earl Hooker, Bobby Bland and Joe Hill Louis were other blues artists who recorded for Phillips, but this was almost too much success. Some of them moved to Chicago. James Mattis and Bill Fitzgerald formed the Duke label in Memphis in April 1952 and leased some tracks from Phillips, but sold Duke to Peacock in Houston only a few months later; Duke squabbled with RPM/Modern over Gordon, and in December Lester Bihari, of the entrepreneurial family that had founded RPM/Modern and Flair, came to Memphis to form the Meteor label. With all this activity the obvious thing for Phillips to do was form another label, and the first Sun records were released in March 1952.

Sun limped for a while because Phillips was still leasing masters to others, but in 1953 it made a distribution deal with Nashville's Jim Bulleit, who had sold his Bullet label and now operated Delta and J-B Records; Sam Phillips's brother Judd came in, bringing his promotion experience. The new label's first success was 'Bear Cat', by Rufus Thomas, Jr, an answer song to Big Mama Thornton's 'Hound Dog' on Peacock, using the same melody. (Don Robey's Lion Music sued and won.) 'Feelin' Good' and 'Mystery Train' by Little Junior (Parker) and his Blue Flames were hits, and Billy 'the Kid' Emerson and Little Milton were doing well.

Phillips was also recording country music: the Ripley Cotton Choppers, Earl Peterson ('Michigan's Singing Cowboy' doing 'Boogie Blues'), Doug Poindexter and his Starlite Wranglers, Malcolm Yelvington and his Star Rhythm Boys (who performed a hillbilly version of 'Drinkin' Wine Spodee-o-dee', which had been the first big R & B hit for the Atlantic label in 1949, by Stick McGhee). And there was Hardrock Gunter. Sidney Louie Gunter may have been the first rockabilly; he growled 'We're gonna rock'n'roll' on 'Gonna Dance All Night' on the Bama label in 1950, and recorded for Bullet, Decca, MGM, King and his own labels, but without much luck. A new version of 'Gonna Dance All Night' came out on Sun 201 in 1954, but it was too late: Sun 209 was Elvis Presley's first record.

Phillips knew there was a bread-and-butter country market out there, and he was doing well with R & B, but his secretary, Marion Keisker, remembered his saying that if he could find a white boy who could sing like a black he would make a million dollars: all the musical fusions in the world would not do any good if the talent could not appear on network television or reach the pop chart. When Judd Phillips was peddling the records out of his car in the early days, 'even then it occurred to me that people were really digging the music that was on our R&B records ... But there was so much prejudice and division that they couldn't idolize the artist that was delivering the song.' Marion remembered the truck driver who had come in one day in 1953 to make a record for his mother's birthday, and suggested getting him in to see what he could do.

In July 1954 bass player Bill Black and guitarist Scotty Moore, who had already played on Sun sessions, got together with the nineteen-year-old truck driver in the studio. It was apparent from the beginning that Elvis Presley had no idea who he was or what he wanted to do. An only child, he had been haunted all his life by a twin who had died at birth; his father was a lazy failure and his mother a doting monster. He had certainly heard spirited singing in church and was steeped in country music; B. B. King said he had seen the kid hanging around the black part of town, but in any case Elvis heard black music on the radio. He played with a guitar and had the makings of a good voice; in fact, he had an enormous natural talent, and the flowing juices of any horny nineteen-year-old, but no confidence to go with it. His life was to be the tragedy of a born loser, yet he became a cultural artefact.

They tried ballads, because Elvis basically wanted to be Dean Martin, but none worked. 'Casual Love Affair' was a tune written and given to Phillips by an inmate at the Tennessee state prison, and years later a version of 'Harbor Lights', such as you might hear in any threadbare small-town supper club, was discovered in Sun's vault. Then, as with Little Richard in New Orleans the following year, the magic happened during a break, fooling around with 'That's All Right (Mama)', a blues by Arthur Crudup. There were no drums, but it didn't matter; the bass was slapped, but with style and urgency, and country jive finally became the fusion known as rockabilly. Bill Monroe's 'Blue Moon of Kentucky' was worked over until it too became something new. A white kid could sing the blues, and a bluegrass tune could yield rockabilly heat.

As soon as the record was played on local radio a few days later, orders for seven thousand copies came in. Elvis was interviewed on the radio, and the name of his high school established that he was white. But the legendary success did not happen overnight. Marty Robbins covered 'That's All Right' on Columbia, adding a fiddle, and the Presley record was the nearest thing to a national hit that Phillips had had since Junior Parker's 'Feelin' Good', but the market was confused: pop stations thought the record was so country that it should not be played after 5 a.m., while country stations did not know what to make of it either. Elvis was a flop on the *Grand Ole Opry*, who told him to go back to driving a truck, but found a regular spot on the *Louisiana Hayride*, and played at county fairs and dance halls for anybody who would have him.

Sun persisted in releasing a country song and a black song back to back: the only way to crack the market was to take it head-on. 'I Don't Care if the Sun Don't Shine', written in 1949 by Mack David and recorded by Presley's idol, Dean Martin, became a country boogie, backed with 'Good Rockin' Tonight', a Wynonie Harris R&B hit in 1948. 'You're a Heartbreaker' was a bore, backed with 'Milkcow Blues Boogie', credited to Kokomo Arnold and complete with some badly dated jive; this was Presley's worst record on Sun. With the fourth single the recording quality improved: 'I'm Left, You're Right, She's Gone' was a good country song with a beat, and a kid named Jimmie Lott on drums; 'Baby Let's Play House' on the flip had been an R&B hit in 1955 on Excello, the only hit Arthur Gunter ever had (not Hardrock Gunter, as Albert Goldman reported). This side of the record did not need the drums; the primitive plea was right up Presley's alley and his first national hit, top five in the country chart. The fifth and last Sun release was 'I Forgot to Remember to Forget' backed with Junior Parker's 'Mystery Train'. The former was a number one country hit for five weeks in 1955, and in November Presley's contract and Sun masters were purchased by RCA.

The effect that Presley had on women did not go unnoticed in the music industry. The fact that he looked and dressed like white trash went with his excess of hormones: like Hank Williams a few years earlier, he had only to twitch a leg to make all the females scream. He enjoyed himself on stage; for the first and last time in his life he did as he pleased, and the girls loved it. He was managed at first by Scotty Moore, then by Memphis D J Bob Neal, and they were all snookered by 'Colonel' Tom Parker, who also snookered his business partner at the time, country star Hank Snow. Parker was a carnival huckster who had managed Eddy Arnold for a while, but Arnold probably had too much self-respect to be handled for long by such a man. Phillips offered Presley's contract to Nashville producer Owen Bradley, who turned it down; Columbia's Mitch Miller made an inquiry, but would not pay the price, allegedly $20,000 and going up. Snow had alerted the industry to the new sensation, and RCA executive Steve Sholes was instrumental in the final gamble. Parker secured Presley for RCA for $35,000, of which $5,000 went to Presley for unpaid royalties on the Sun records, and which he spent on a Cadillac. This was a large amount of money for an artist who was still a cult, but Phillips knew he could not promote Presley properly, and had more rockabillies waiting in the wings.

Presley's first RCA recording session, in Nashville in January 1956, yielded covers of Ray Charles's 'I Got a Woman', a big R&B hit a year earlier, and 'Money Honey', by the Drifters with Clyde McPhatter, which had been at number one for eleven weeks in 1953. Presley's young voice sounded strained on country ballads: 'I'm Counting On You' is a decent song by proven hit-writer Don Robertson, but the dreadful 'I Was the One' was chosen as the B side of 'Heartbreak Hotel'.

The sound quality of that first session was not good, and 'Heartbreak Hotel' is the worst of them all. Chet Atkins played rhythm guitar and Floyd Cramer was added on piano, together with an entirely unnecessary vocal trio led by Gordon Stoker, lead singer of the Jordanaires, a gospel quartet. Scotty Moore's guitar sounds exceptionally, irritatingly tinny, Cramer is too prominent and the whole track sounds like it was made underwater in a breadbox. It was a disgraceful recording for 1956, but a good song for Presley. Written by Mae Axton and Tommy Durden, it was inspired by a newspaper account of a suicide note saying, 'I walk a lonely street'. Despite its shortcomings, 'Heartbreak Hotel' reached all three *Billboard* charts in March. It was number one for eight weeks in the pop chart and for seventeen weeks in the country chart, and a number three R & B hit.

Think of it: one of the biggest, most famous hits of all time, recorded in January and in the charts less than forty-five days later. And this was already well into the age of tape recording, overdubbing, reverberation and all the rest. Why does it take months to make a pop record nowadays? Is it that today's record producers are muscle-bound with their technology? If only the studio had been up to the job: one cannot help wondering what these records would sound like if one could go back to the master tapes and tinker with them. (RCA's release of 'I'm Left, You're Right, She's Gone' revealed it as one of the cleanest records Sun ever made, while an English LP reissue in the 1970s was dreadful.)

More recording dates in New York, in late January and early February, were the most successful of Presley's entire career. With better sound and adding only Shorty Long on piano to Scotty, Bill and D. J. Fontana, the eight sides were a permanent statement of what rock'n'roll is supposed to be, and represent the last time that Elvis Presley's inherent talent was let loose in front of a microphone. Presley was hitting the big time, recording in New York rather than in some provincial hole in the wall, and he gave it everything the natural optimism of youth can offer. He and the group pushed the beat on every track, generating tremendous excitement; Fontana seemed the ideally functional rock'n'roll drummer and Scotty's guitar solos became unpretentious templates for the new genre. 'I'm Gonna Sit Right Down and Cry Over You' and 'One-sided Love Affair' were good rhythm tunes; Little Richard's 'Tutti Frutti', Lloyd Price's 'Lawdy Miss Clawdy' and Joe Turner's 'Shake, Rattle and Roll' were already rock'n'roll classics, and Carl Perkins's 'Blue Suede Shoes' was a brand new one; 'So Glad You're Mine' and 'My Baby Left Me' were both by Crudup. Presley was different: his R & B covers, from July 1954 to February 1956, are equal to the originals, and even better in the case of one or two of Crudup's songs. Arthur 'Big Boy' Crudup made nearly eighty sides from 1943 to 1954, almost all for RCA; 'Goin' Back to Georgia' (1952) is particularly fine, but some of them sound as though there should have been another take, while there was not much money for studio time in major-label

R&B. Crudup never received a penny from his Presley covers, by the way, any of which had soon sold more copies than all Crudup's records put together.

But it was already over. In April, back in Nashville, he recorded 'I Want You, I Need You, I Love You', an incredibly dreary rockaballad and his second number one hit (with 'My Baby Left Me' on the flip side, one of the two or three best records he ever made). They couldn't find decent songs for Presley because they were not looking. We were lucky with 'Heartbreak Hotel'; Axton and Durden were experienced songwriters, but even so Presley got a co-writing credit. 'I Want You, I Need You, I Love You' was written by hacks and published by Elvis Presley Music. 'My Baby Left Me' is mysteriously listed as published by Elvis Presley Music, which did not exist when Crudup had his R&B hit in 1946. Parker knew he was sitting on a gold mine, and became an archetype of everything that has gone wrong with pop music in the decades since then. He milked Presley's career in order to live in a Las Vegas hotel, gambling at Presley's expense for the rest of his life; he started by gambling away the music, and Presley let him do it.

In July 1956 'Hound Dog' and 'Don't Be Cruel' were recorded, Presley's back-to-back third and fourth number ones. 'Hound Dog' had been an R&B hit in 1953 for Big Mama Thornton, credited to Jerry Leiber and Mike Stoller, soon experienced writers of pop hits; Johnny Otis claimed to have had something to do with writing 'Hound Dog' as well. Leiber and Stoller achieved their greatest fame writing for Presley ('Jailhouse Rock', 'Loving You', 'Bossa Nova Baby' and others). 'Don't Be Cruel' was by Otis Blackwell, a black New York songwriter who had sold it the previous Christmas Eve with a bag of others for $25 each. Both songs were ruined by the incessant caterwauling of the Jordanaires, who added hand-clapping on 'Hound Dog', which, in the hands of Presley and his managers, ominously became a novelty.

From then on the songs were pop songs, and almost from the beginning Presley seems to have copied the demo records he was given, such as 'Heartbreak Hotel' (sung by Glen Reeves) and 'Don't Be Cruel' (Blackwell). Leiber said, 'If Jeff Barry was the singer on the demo, Elvis would imitate Jeff Barry.' Presley was willing to work hard and would sing all night; but except for low-down dirty country blues, the boy had no style of his own. He could wiggle an audience of girls into a frenzy, but had no idea what to do with a slow blues, which 'Hound Dog' should have been. It is said that during his first Las Vegas gig, which was a flop, he heard a black vocal group doing a frenetic version of 'Hound Dog', which he simply imitated. By the time he copied 'One Night' in 1958, which should have been his type of song, something was missing: it was a tantalizing moment for those of us who hoped for a return to the truth, but perhaps he had already had too many cheeseburgers. 'One Night' by Dave Bartholomew and Pearl King, an R&B hit for Smiley Lewis in 1956, was now published by Elvis Presley Music; the lyrics were cleaned up for Presley, just as lyrics had been cleaned up for Georgia Gibbs a few years earlier.

Blackwell wrote 'All Shook Up' for Presley, who was credited as co-writer on that as well as on 'Don't Be Cruel', and later 'Return to Sender'. Meanwhile, Scotty Moore and Bill Black had left in 1957, because Elvis was making millions and they were still on $100 a week. Doc Pomus and Mort Shuman wrote '(Marie's the Name) His Latest Flame', 'Little Sister', 'A Mess of Blues', 'Suspicion' and others, all published by Presley. Leiber and Stoller and Pomus and Shuman were hardened professionals who at least did not have to give up a writing credit, but if Presley published the song and recorded it, he was paid twice every time a record was sold; and if he got a co-writing credit, he was paid three times, and so was Parker, who had set it all up. Hence the dire quality of most of Presley's later material, and the dire future of pop music. (To be fair, Presley disowned his songwriting credits, admitting he'd never written anything.)

A few of these were fine pop records, especially, for example, the two-sided hit 'Little Sister' / 'His Latest Flame'. Presley's voice matured and became a beautiful one, and he acquired an easiness which the best pop singers had had ever since Bing Crosby. He continued to be influential, in the same way as Crosby had been, but he had abdicated, and was no more the 'King of Rock'n'roll' than Paul Whiteman was the 'King of Jazz': rock'n'roll was supposed to wash away the Crosbys. He became the God of show business because he had been a nobody who had come from nowhere to accomplish the important thing that he did in two or three years, and the illusion that people with talent are Just Like Us was becoming the guiding principle of show business.

He had been controversial at first because he was sexy, 'ruining the morals of our youth' and all that, but he confused everyone, for off-stage he was polite and soft-spoken and worshipped his mother. He ended up singing for blue-rinsed matrons in Las Vegas. Those of us who were interested in a fence-flattening fusion like rock'n'roll had known the worst since Presley's first appearance on Ed Sullivan's show. The Sunday evening vaudeville hour was the biggest thing on the air; in September 1956 came the first Presley appearance on the show, and we all metaphorically flipped a coin when we tuned in. We had listened to the ballads alternating with the rock'n'roll, some of them excruciating, and we knew that Elvis was going to be a movie star, and that he was going to sing the title song from his first film. We held our breaths, and we lost the toss. 'Love Me Tender' turned out to be 'Aura Lee', the Civil War campfire ballad, conveniently out of copyright, with new words; claiming 'words and music by Elvis Presley and Vera Matson', it was published by Elvis Presley Music.

He made over 30 films, each one worse than the last, full of songs like the one about how to do the hula in a sports car. During his lifetime he had 146 Hot 100 hits and 75 chart albums (including most of the wretched film soundtracks), but the good recordings he made after the first 19 months might fill up a compact disc. His number one hits in 1960–61 were 'It's Now or Never', adapted from 'O Sole Mio', 'Are You Lonesome To-night?', a 3/4 time porch-ballad from 1927, and 'Surrender', adapted from 'Come Back to Sorrento'. From 1962 to 1969 he had no number ones at all. His status as an icon carried a once great record label for twenty years; he should have had as much power over pop music as anyone who ever lived, but he blew it. There were no worthwhile interviews with Presley because Tom Parker would have charged a fortune for the privilege. Parker saw to it that Presley paid the maximum in income taxes and never toured overseas, because Parker was an illegal immigrant (from Holland) and didn't want the government snooping around. He was divested of his interests in Presley in 1983, long after it was too late.

Presley's recording of Paul Anka's 'My Way' was a hit after he died; the tragedy was that he had done almost nothing his way.

Carl Perkins, also from a poor family, had formed a band with his brothers to help make ends meet. They played country songs and jump tunes, and Carl started writing his own songs, in the style that did not yet have a name. He picked cotton during the day and his wife took in laundry. When they heard Presley's 'Blue Moon of Kentucky' on the radio, the brothers went to Memphis and camped on Sam Phillips's doorstep; having signed a contract and added drummer W. S. Holland, they made their first recording, 'Movie Magg', a two-beat bit of country fatalism about a boy who is taking his girl out on horseback. He might also want to get up to something else; he knows her father is keeping an eye on her, and that all this might lead to a lifetime of obligations, but he doesn't mind:

> That double-barrel behind the door
> Lordy, waits for me I know,
> So climb up on ol' Becky's back
> And let's ride to the picture show.

The second release was happy rockabilly jive, 'Gone, Gone, Gone', and a month after Presley had left for RCA 'Blue Suede Shoes' was recorded. In February 1956 it was number one on the country jukebox chart for two weeks, after which it was knocked out of the top spot by 'Heartbreak Hotel'. In March Perkins's record reached number two in both the pop and R & B jukebox charts, being kept from the top by Presley, and was number two or three in the 'best seller' charts in all three categories. The song had been suggested by a remark overheard at a dance; but a hillbilly singing about his shoes was widely regarded as a novelty, because middle-class Americans do not know who is in their midst.

A poor man has nothing to look forward to but a lifetime of working for somebody else; this, above all, was what the great majority of southern blacks and whites had in common. On his way out to 'Rip It Up', Little Richard announced:

> Well, it's Saturday night and I just got paid,
> Spend all my money, don't try to save.

Hank Williams, out on the town with his best girl, had told her:

> You clap hands and I'll start bowin',
> We'll do all the law's allowin',
> Tomorrow I'll be right back plowin',
> Settin' the woods on fire!

Carl Perkins allegedly worked in a bakery, as well as picking cotton. In a bakery in the 1950s the hours were long, the pay was low, the work was hard and it was *hot*. In the car factory, on some summer nights, they had to send you home, it was so hot; you could not even light a cigarette, because the sweat ran down the Lucky Strike and soaked it before you could get the match to it. But if you came from a poor family, or if you were poorly educated, and above all if you were black, you were going to sweat in that bakery or on that assembly line from pay-cheque to pay-cheque, since that was what your father did, and his father before him. This sort of fatalism on the part of the people who do most of the work is exactly what the American economy has always depended upon. The hillbilly cat with the new shoes is just going out to rip it up on a Saturday night, and if he has squeezed a few bucks out of his pay-cheque for some fashionable footwear, he will have just that much more fun. He knows that on Monday he is going to pick that cotton, or punch that time-clock, and he knows that the shoes will be worn out in a few months and thrown away. But that does not bother him either; he can't afford to think too far ahead. It is not surprising how many early rock'n'roll songs are about working for a living.

T-Bone Walker sang in 1947, 'The eagle flies on Friday / And Saturday I go out to play.' US military parlance was 'the eagle shits on Friday' (payday). In 'Blue Monday' Fats Domino sang:

> On Monday my head is bad.
> But it's worth it,
> For the times that I've had.

Chuck Berry made us feel guilty every time we bought a buck's worth:

> Workin' in a filling station,
> Too many tasks: wipe the windows,
> Check the tires, check the oil,
> Dollar gas! Ahhhh!
> Too much monkey business!

Carl Perkins's hillbilly goes out to party:

> Well, you can knock me down, step in my face;
> Slander my name all over the place.
> Do any thing that you wanna do,
> But uh, uh, buddy, lay offa my shoes!

The way Presley sang 'Blue Suede Shoes', he was daring you to step on them, so he could try to punch you out. Perkins, by contrast, is almost saying please. He doesn't want any fuss; he is tickled with his new shoes, and all he asks is, please don't step on 'em. But if you step on 'em by mistake, let alone on purpose, you *might* get into trouble. 'Blue Suede Shoes' is what rock'n'roll (or rhythm and blues) is supposed to be: instant folk music for the working class. It sounds as though it has been made up on the spot, rather than calculated to sell a million; and it is also full of joy, because you can dance your feet off to it.

The other side of 'Blue Suede Shoes' was 'Honey Don't', too strange in 1956, too country, and without the novelty aspect of the shoes. 'How come you say you will when you won't' seemed like a powerful, swinging line, but when you played that side at a party, the other kids didn't want to know. In another era, just a few years later, the Beatles covered it.

Johnny Cash was another of Phillips's discoveries. His first recording on Sun and his first country hit was 'Cry! Cry! Cry!', with the Tennessee Two (Luther Perkins on guitar and Marshall Grant on bass). 'I Walk the Line' (1956) was his first country number one and his first pop chart entry. He wrote those two, as well as 'Train of Love' and others. His songs were similar to each other but his words were as simple and memorable as those of Hank Williams and his voice was both yearning and sepulchral; rhythmically the records had that rockabilly inevitability about them. 'Ballad of a Teenage Queen' was overproduced, but 'Guess Things Happen That Way' was better;

both were written by 'Cowboy' Jack Clement, a maverick producer who cut his teeth at Sun. Cash became renowned, but stayed in the country camp; he had sixty-nine hits in the *Billboard* country chart up to 1970, but only forty-five in the pop chart.

The last Sun superstar was Jerry Lee Lewis, whose cousins include country singer Mickey Gilley, television evangelist Jimmy Swaggart and Myra Gale Brown, his third wife, whom he married when she was thirteen, and evidently without quite divorcing his previous wife. Jerry Lee was shy at first, but on tour Perkins and Cash told him to make a fuss, so he began kicking over the piano stool, revealing a compulsive and frenetic pianist and performer. After that he always wanted to close the show, but on another tour, with Chuck Berry, he was forced to open it, so he set fire to the piano as he left the stage, saying, 'I'd like to see any son of a bitch try to follow *that*.'

Lewis's first hit was 'Whole Lot of Shakin' Goin' On' in 1957, closely followed by 'Great Balls of Fire' and 'Breathless', both written by Otis Blackwell. These were big pop and R & B hits, and the first two were number one country hits: they were pretty noisy and not very good to dance to, but exciting novelties. The flip side of the second, a cover of Hank Williams's 'You Win Again', also reached the country top five. His 'pumping piano' was simplistic and dominated by right-hand glissandos, though effective in its context.

In 1958 when he went to England on tour, he took young Myra with him and introduced her to the British tabloid newspapers. The British have some of the worst newspapers in the English-speaking world; they sell millions of copies daily to the kind of people who like to spy on the neighbours from behind the curtains, pretending that the Presleys, Perkinses and Lewises are not the direct descendants of British white trash. Lewis was crucified by the press, the nonsense spread to the USA and Lewis never had another top ten pop hit. He remained a compelling performer, and made a strong comeback in the country charts from 1968, with songs like 'What's Made Milwaukee Famous (Made a Loser out of Me)' and 'She Even Woke Me Up to Say Goodbye'. He was nicknamed the Killer, not necessarily because some of his wives died young; Myra lasted longer than most and wrote a book about it. Like Presley and some of the others,

Lewis was a gun freak, and once shot his bass player. Myra's father was a bass player.

Roy Orbison's recordings for Sun included his 'Ooby Dooby', a minor hit. His soaring voice on 'Only the Lonely' and 'Oh! Pretty Woman' and aching ballads like 'It's Over' were influential in the next decade on another label, Monument. Pianist, singer and songwriter Charlie Rich, a sideman at Sun, became a country star from 1968 on other labels and was known as the Silver Fox. Doug Poindexter, Malcolm Yelvington, Warren Smith, Charlie Feathers and other Sun artists were good rockabillies, but never broke into the national charts. Dorsey and Johnny Burnette were just about the only local rockabillies who never recorded for Sun.

Phillips carried on into the 1960s, but by then his era was over. His credit was always good in the record industry and he could have had a bigger label, but he never wanted to order pressings too far ahead; he became famous without risking too much. 'Until rock'n'roll came along,' he said, talking about genres, 'the worst discrimination in America was in music . . . I just hope I played some part in breaking that segregation down in some way.'

Meanwhile, other labels were scrambling to catch up with what Sun had discovered. Capitol's Gene Vincent and his Blue Caps had a top ten hit with 'Be-bop-a-lula' in 1956, which seemed an archetypal bit of rockabilly. The new West Coast Liberty label discovered Eddie Cochran, whose first hit was 'Sittin' in the Balcony', a sweet tune about going to the cinema with his girlfriend. It was also a hit on an obscure Colonial label for Johnny Dee; this was the song's composer, John D. Loudermilk, a singer-songwriter who later found his own following.

Cochran's next two hits were his own songs. 'Summertime Blues', a top ten hit in 1958, was perfect teen fodder, the story of a kid who can't go out because he has to work late:

> I called my congressman,
> And he said, quote:
> 'I'd like to help ya, Son, but
> You're too young to vote.'

This was followed by 'C'mon Everybody', about a boy who is rolling up the rugs for a party because his parents aren't home. Cochran was a good guitar player and an innovator in the studio who knew exactly what he was doing; and the session drummer on his best records was Earl Palmer. (When rock'n'roll spread through the industry, many of the best session musicians were black, including pianist Ernie Freeman and tenor saxophonist Plas Johnson, who first played Henry Mancini's *Pink Panther* theme.)

At Art Rupe's Specialty label the bread-and-butter acts were black gospel groups. One of the most successful was the Soul Stirrers, who had been around for a while: they had once recorded for Lew Chudd. Their new lead singer, Sam Cooke, had a gorgeous voice and a big following among young female gospel fans. Rupe knew that gospel fans disapproved of their heroes recording secular material, so when he caught Bumps Blackwell recording Cooke on a song called 'You Send Me', he told them to keep the tape in lieu of royalties and get out. Blackwell took the tape to Bob Keene, who put it out on his own Keen label and had one of the biggest hits of the year – number one in both the pop and R&B charts in 1957. The dreary song was a vehicle for Sam's melisma, the gospel-derived technique of wordless improvisation on the melody; his uncanny voice was one of the most beautiful in pop. He was signed by RCA, where he was over-produced; like many black entertainers, Cooke had different acts for black and white audiences.

Johnny Otis, a musical all-rounder, was born in California, where his Greek parents (named Veliotes) ran a grocery store. He grew up in a black neighbourhood and never considered himself anything but black. He helped to invent rhythm and blues; at his shows in the Watts area of Los Angeles Hispanics were among the most enthusiastic fans. On his other label, Del-Fi, Bob Keene recorded Richard Valenzuela, renamed Ritchie Valens, whose 'Donna' was a number two hit in 1958. It was not much of a song, but good for slow dancing, no doubt born out of long experience of playing for teen dances. It was backed by 'La Bamba', a pan-Latin folksong sung in Spanish, with a guitar riff that generated excitement, and became a legend. (Keene later recorded more of what came to be called Tex-Mex groups, including the Bobby Fuller Four, whose 'I Fought the Law' was a hit in 1966.)

Norman Petty was a musician from Clovis, New Mexico, across the border from Texas, where he had a small recording studio. His trio had a couple of minor hits in the mid-1950s (among them Ellington's 'Mood Indigo', with Norman on organ, his wife on piano and a guitarist). He used the money to improve his studio, and began recording local rockabillies. Buddy Knox had written 'Party Doll' as early as 1948, and was leading a trio called the Rhythm Orchids, with Jimmy Bowen on bass. 'Party Doll' was released with Bowen's 'I'm Sticking With You' on Knox's Triple-D label, using a cardboard box as a drum because Petty did not know how to record drums. It aroused national interest and was picked up by Roulette, who separated the tracks and had two million-sellers in 1957. (Bowen later became one of the most successful producers of country music.)

Roulette had been formed in New York in 1956 by George Goldner and Morris Levy. Goldner, who had started out in black doo-wop, had a hit on his Rama label in 1954 with 'Gee', by the Crows. On the Gee label he had an international million-seller, 'Why Do Fools Fall in Love', by Frankie Lymon and the Teenagers. The thirteen-year-old Lymon sang himself into history: bouncy, beautiful and heartfelt, replete with doo-wop trimming and a rocking saxophone solo, the record almost justifies all the sins committed in the teen-love genre since.

In the meantime, back in Clovis, Petty was recording Buddy Holly, from Lubbock, Texas. Holly had signed with Decca Records and recorded in Nashville in early 1956 when he was only nineteen; his group included guitarist Sonny Curtis and drummer Jerry Allison, and among the sides was an early version of 'That'll Be the Day'. In 1957 he formed a new group, the Crickets, and began experimenting with Petty. Together they taught themselves how to do what they wanted to do in the studio, such as recording drums. Roulette turned the records down; Bob Thiele signed them to separate Decca subsidiaries as Holly and as the Crickets. 'That'll Be the Day', early but fully-fledged rock'n'roll, was number one in August 1957; 'Peggy Sue' and 'Oh, Boy!' reached the top ten; 'Early in the Morning', written by Bobby Darin, was not with the Crickets, but had Sam 'the Man' Taylor on tenor saxophone; 'It's So Easy' and 'Every Day' did not enter the chart.

Holly's career was not moving fast enough to suit him; he split from the Crickets and from Petty. His last recordings, in New York, included a Paul Anka song, 'It Doesn't Matter Any More', made with strings. Like Cochran, Holly was an innovator in the studio, though some of his songs amount to little more than cowboy jingles; he had a good voice, but his hiccupping vocal style was an acquired taste. Like many of the others, he was more popular at the time in Britain.

In 1957 a new phenomenon appeared in the record shops: advance orders for a record that nobody had yet heard. Archie Bleyer, author of those remarkable stock arrangements in the late 1920s, became prominent as music director for radio and television personality Arthur Godfrey, and in 1953 formed his own Cadence label, which had high production standards and good technology. He had hits by the Chordettes ('Mr Sandman') and Julius LaRosa from Godfrey's television show, by pianist Roger Williams and singer Andy Williams, and also his own instrumental hits, such as 'Hernando's Hideaway'. Then he signed the Everly Brothers, Don and Phil, whose parents had played and sung on the radio. (Ike Everly had inspired many a guitar player.)

However the excitement over their first Cadence release was generated, it was not misplaced: distributors and jukebox operators were besieged with orders for 'Bye Bye Love', a song by Felice and Boudleaux Bryant, who had been writing country hits since 1949; its rockabilly beat (provided by acoustic guitars and bass, no drums) and the brothers' traditional country harmony was irresistible. The Everlys' first album contained two big hits, but their second, *Songs Our Daddy Taught Us*, was a beautiful compilation of their roots, folksongs and old country songs, including Gene Autry's 'That Silver-haired Daddy of Mine'. They had a total of thirty-eight Hot 100 *Billboard* hits before they split up in 1968.

There were a great many miscellaneous hit records, or one-hit wonders, that gave the quick pleasure of a novelty, yet seemed to be more than that. Cadence had one in 1958 with Link Wray; for the menacing instrumental 'Rumble', holes were poked with a pencil in the speaker fed by the electric guitar's amplifier, giving the music (and the listener) a buzz. (In the 1950s a rumble was a gang fight.)

The fuzz-tone became every electric guitar's accessory, and was done to death in the next twenty years. The slightly uptempo flip, 'The Swag', was also a good instrumental; Wray made a few albums over the years which became cult items.

A Texas DJ, J. P. 'Jape' Richardson, chuckled and nonsensed his way through 'Chantilly Lace' on Mercury as the Big Bopper in 1958. There was Sanford Clark's laid-back rockabilly 'The Fool' in 1956, with Al Casey on guitar (not the same Al Casey who played with Fats Waller). Jim Lowe's 'The Green Door' was a hit the same year. (Was the mysterious door the back entrance to the local hot-spot, or to the musicians' union?) Doo-wop continued to produce lovely records which did not appear in the chart, and a few that did: the Dell-Vikings' 'Come Go with Me' (1957) and 'Get a Job' by the Silhouettes (1958). The latter, which included rhythmic doo-wop nonsense syllables, was about a kid whose parents are nagging him to get a job.

Parents did not like rock'n'roll, of course, whatever it was called. Elvis Presley 78s were given away free at a Texas petrol station, so that customers could smash them. ASCAP did not like it because many of the hits were BMI publications (though 'Rock Around the Clock', the most notorious hit of all, associated with riots in cinemas, was an ASCAP song). When BMI added an annual R&B award to its pop and country awards in 1957, an NBC executive huffily declared that this was bad public relations in view of the anti-R&B attitude in some quarters; the obvious response, that NBC's subsidiary RCA should divest itself of Elvis Presley, was met with silence.

Frank Sinatra had long complained that Mitch Miller at Columbia had forced him to perform sub-standard material, and sent a telegram to a congressional subcommittee investigating the networks in 1956. It turned out that of all the songs Miller had recorded during his sensationally successful period at Columbia, 95 per cent were ASCAP songs. Of the fifty-seven tracks Sinatra had recorded, only five were BMI songs, and two of those were published by Sinatra's own BMI company. Furthermore, it was revealed, the sweet ballad that had done the most for Sinatra's comeback, 'Young at Heart' (on Capitol, 1954), was a BMI song.

Much of the music business hated rock'n'roll, even as it scrambled to take it over and reap the profits. Yet at the time rock'n'roll suddenly seemed to be dead almost as soon as it had been born. In March 1956, while on the road promoting 'Blue Suede Shoes', Carl Perkins was badly injured in a car crash. Little Richard's lifestyle and his sincere religious feelings were in conflict; in 1957, on tour in Australia, he suddenly quit, which cost him a good deal of money in cancelled dates. Presley was selling out, and was drafted in 1958; Jerry Lee Lewis's career had gone on hold; in February 1959 a plane crash took Buddy Holly, Ritchie Valens and the Big Bopper. That year Chuck Berry opened a club in St Louis, and was arrested for taking a fourteen-year-old hatcheck girl (who already had a criminal record for prostitution) across a state line for immoral purposes. In 1960 a car crash in England killed Eddie Cochran and badly injured Gene Vincent, who, already unstable, soon became an alcoholic. It was 1964 before Sam Cooke was murdered; but the great white hopes of rock'n'roll and a couple of the black ones were out of action. Some came back, and of course Elvis and Tom Parker got richer, but one way or another, none of these careers ever recovered its momentum. The music appeared to have been strangled in its cradle, yet it was too late: the rock generation had already been born.

15

The Abdication of a Generation

We have moved in less than half a lifetime from a scene in which live music was still ubiquitous to a time when *Top of the Pops*, the major British television pop show, celebrates not music, but children prancing in funny clothes; while a factory-made tape unreels in the background, they do not even pretend they can play or sing. On the USA's MTV the music no longer competes with the jingles, but has become the advertising. In the later 1950s the confusion and hypocrisy in the music business seemed to grow. This was an illusion – the business had always been stupid and greedy – but new factors causing the illusion were ever increasing amounts of money and runaway technology.

In about 1953 I attended a stage show at a theatre in Chicago. I forget whether the main attraction was Patti Page or Kay Starr, but I was startled to hear not a multi-tracked voice, but just a singer: it had not occurred to me when I was a child that the studio trick I heard on the radio could not then be reproduced on stage. A quarter of a century later, in London, I saw Joan Armatrading in concert at the Hammersmith Odeon, and was impressed that the slightest shimmer of echo on a single cymbal sound could be reproduced accurately, just as it was on the album. Armatrading's songs and her honest delivery of them were a welcome oasis in the popular music of the late 1970s, but she was reproducing her album on stage: impressive technically, but why not just stay at home and listen to the record? Tenor saxophonist Stan Getz told the story of a performance at which the electricity failed, whereupon he rediscovered the pleasure of making entirely acoustic music. Afterwards, a young fan came up to him and gushed about his tone, which was flattering at first, until Getz realized that what had astonished the fan was the sound of the reed instrument, without microphone or amplification. The young fan had never heard it before.

Technology and money have reigned supreme for so long that the manufacture, marketing and distribution of the product has long since become more important than its content, while an uncountable number of tiny record labels around the world who care about music cannot get their records into the shops or on the air. The confusion of values in the music business and the beginning of the complete abandonment of musical considerations are illustrated by the appearances of Elvis Presley on television variety shows in 1956.

In 1984 RCA issued a five-record set called *Elvis 50th Anniversary*, collecting together tracks from the Sun vault (including the infamous, dismal 'Harbor Lights'), live performances from the Mississippi-Alabama State Fair and Dairy Show in September 1956, and informal tracks made while filming a TV show in June 1968. For years these last had been rumoured to be the most exciting recordings Presley had made since early 1956, but they are a terrible let-down. To our purpose, however, are the appearances on the *Dorsey Brothers Stage Show* and the Milton Berle, Steve Allen and Ed Sullivan programmes, between early 1956 and early 1957. Berle's Tuesday night comedy and variety show was the hottest thing on US television in 1948, but it was limping in the ratings by 1956. It was Presley's appearance on Steve Allen's show on a Sunday evening in July that reduced Sullivan's ratings, and led to three Sullivan spots. Tommy and Jimmy Dorsey were two of the best white musicians in popular music. They had each led one of the most popular bands of the Swing Era, and worked together on a film biography in 1947; then Jimmy joined Tommy's band, and their television variety show in 1954 (a summer substitute for the Jackie Gleason show) was so successful that it was given its own spot, and continued until Tommy died in November 1956.

The Dorseys, their sidemen, music directors and arrangers must have been among the most experienced of studio players; they probably considered themselves jazzmen, or at least jazz-oriented musicians. Yet they threw away Elvis Presley. I was there watching, nearly thirty-five years ago; something was wrong, but I was too young to know what it was. In retrospect, it is obvious. I had listened to country music, to rhythm and blues and to Tommy Dorsey; Elvis Presley was exciting, but it was not as if he had come from Mars. These would-be jazzmen, their music directors and arrangers, however, apparently had no idea what was going on. Presley came on and did his thing, just as he did at a great many country fairs, while the band sat on its hands as though none of them had ever heard of the blues.

It doesn't matter whether you regard Elvis Presley plonked in front of the Dorsey band as a weed in a flower-bed or a pearl in a pigsty – it is the deliberate abdication of everyone involved that is interesting. On the six appearances with the Dorseys' band, it plays the same brief, corny fanfare it must have played for every performer, then sits quietly for Presley, and at the end of each song plays a single, blaring brass chord, perhaps to let us know the song has ended. Thirty-three tracks were recorded on the total of twelve television spots, including several of 'Heartbreak Hotel'. (One or two of these are better than the commercial record; they take the tune at a slightly slower tempo and have no piano, and Scotty Moore's guitar is either less tinny or absent.) But the first version, from March 1956, is the only one of these thirty-three opportunities on which television tried to do anything with the new show business sensation.

There is an appropriate introduction from the brass section; the band's drummer starts out playing the backbeat too softly, and thereafter overdoes it; there are brass punctuations at the end of each phrase in the chorus, where Scotty Moore's guitar usually clangs. At the end of the first verse and as the next one begins, the reed section rises with a smooth moan out of the background, sliding downwards in a glissando at the end of the verse to meet the beat, and it sounds like they are trying to do something appropriate with this music. But then in the middle of the simple arrangement there is a trumpet solo, not particularly thoughtful to start with and soon dissolving in confusion, as though the trumpeter suddenly woke up and did not know where he was; after that Presley screws up the beat and the whole thing turns into a shambles. Presley's amateurish guitar strumming is occasionally heard throughout.

This was the same kid who, years later, put on professional shows in Las Vegas, and some of his television tracks are already better than the studio tracks: the showman was there somewhere. Was there no money for a rehearsal for this band, whose co-leaders had already been showbusiness legends for the best part of thirty years? And on the other thirty-two television tracks there is nothing except, towards the end of the sequence, the familiar banality of the Jordanaires. No wonder Presley let Tom Parker tell him what to do; nobody else was doing it.

We know that Jimmie Rodgers and Louis Armstrong made a lovely recording together in 1929. On the Tiffany transcriptions made by Bob Wills's band in 1946, there is nothing bashful or inappropriate about hot solos from Fred Kelso's piano, or from Alex Brashear's muted trumpet, sometimes behind Tommy Duncan's vocals: they fit right in with the fiddle and the electric guitar. T-Bone Walker, the most influential of all guitarists and blues singers, made 144 tracks between 1940 and 1954, and many of them feature felicitous touches of reed writing, and saxophone and trumpet solos. Buddy Morrow's big-band R & B covers in 1952 were full of the right spirit. Why could the Dorseys not do it?

I do not believe that there was nobody in New York in 1956 who knew what was going on. I think they did not *want* to know. If Elvis Presley became the God of show business basically because all the white trash in the country could identify with him, the other side of the coin is that the music industry abandoned the Presleys to the Tom Parkers by pretending that white trash had no business being anything but a fluke, a novelty. The same white liberals who had made a fuss over Leadbelly in café society could not credit a Mississippi redneck singing the blues. New York studio musicians who were spending their working lives playing a jazz-oriented style were good readers of music, but not so good at reading the writing on the wall; and the power-brokers in the music industry were so helpless that they could not even find the wall.

There was a time when the music business, when it had to present a novelty act or cover a country song, would at least go through the motions of pretending that everybody was working in the same industry. But there had been a complete change in the way it all worked since the music publishers gambled on the songs, promising to make this or that their number one plug if so-and-so would record it. By the early 1950s the record labels' artist and repertory executives did the choosing, and by the late 1950s it was the disc jockeys.

Among the industry giants who abdicated at the threat of rock-'n'roll was Mitch Miller, the most successful A & R man in the history of the record business. Miller was only about six years younger than Tommy Dorsey. He began his career as a virtuoso on the oboe and the cor anglais and toured with an orchestra accompanying George Gershwin on piano; it was conducted on various occasions by Joe Reisman or Charles Previn (André's father). He played with the Budapest String Quartet, and with such conductors as Fritz Reiner and Sir Thomas Beecham; he was hand-picked by Leopold Stokowski for recording sessions in 1947, and may be heard on classic versions of Sibelius's 'Swan of Tuonela' and Dvořák's Symphony 'From the New World', which contain two of the most famous cor anglais solos in music. In short, before he became a record company executive, he was an accomplished musician and recording artist.

In the late 1940s he was involved with the Little Golden Records for children; they were unbreakable plastic 78s to begin with and sold millions of copies. He was asked by John Hammond to produce some classical recording sessions for Keynote, which was taken over by Mercury, where Miller helped with the first multi-tracked recordings, as well as developing the careers of Vic Damone and Frankie Laine, who later followed him to Columbia. He played on and helped to produce the album *Charlie Parker with Strings*. When interviewer Ted Fox asked Miller in 1985 if it had not been a big change moving from classical to pop, Miller replied that he was always surprised when asked that:

I never compartmentalised it in my own mind. And the same rules apply ... taste, musicianship, get the best out of the artist. Many times the artist doesn't know what his best characteristics are, and you're there to remind them. You can't put in what isn't there, but you can remind them of what they have and they're not using.

Alec Wilder, Goddard Lieberson and Miller had all been classmates at the Eastman School. When Mannie Sachs left Columbia to go to RCA, Lieberson, a composer, Renaissance man and CBS employee since before the war, hired Miller to replace him. Columbia's hit rate shot up by 60 per cent or more, and the label dominated popular music in the USA for the rest of the decade. Miller reported to Jimmy Conkling, who at thirty-five was the youngest major-label chief in the industry until he was succeeded in 1956 by Lieberson. (Conkling had come from Capitol, and went on to Warner Brothers.) They all believed that the label was there to have hits and to make money, but also to preserve the best of popular culture, so that, for example, Columbia recorded Duke Ellington during one of the least commercial periods of that great career.

During the 1950s Miller selected or passed on most of the company's singles output, overseeing more than seventy-five hit singles in the pop charts, of which at least a third reached the top ten – a much higher percentage of hits to releases than any other label could boast. At first, nobody could cover a hit faster than Miller, such as 'Tzena Tzena Tzena', with a chorus, under his own name, and 'Goodnight Irene', with Sinatra (both 1950). But he soon made his own hits for others to chase. Sinatra refused to record the pseudo-folksongs that Miller was bringing in, so he gave them to a singer named Al Cernick, who became Guy Mitchell, and they were all huge hits. It was Miller who first made pop hits out of Hank Williams's songs, and the themes from *Bridge on the River Kwai* and *High Noon*. The lyrics of the latter were rewritten at Miller's insistence.

All A&R men were pestered by songwriters, but Miller had his pick of the songs and got his way because he was so successful, and when he made a deal, he kept his word. It was Miller's idea to change around Percy Faith's arrangement of 'On the Street Where You Live' for Vic Damone, so that it began with the bridge – 'Oh, that towering feeling . . .' – making the record a grabber, and a top five hit.

George Avakian discovered Johnny Mathis, who was young and derivative. His first records flopped, but Miller waited until the right songs came along: 'Wonderful! Wonderful!', 'It's Not for Me to Say', 'Chances Are' and 'The Twelfth of Never' (all 1957) made a star of Mathis. (The second and third of these were written by Stillman and Allen, who had written hits for the Four Lads; the fourth was an adaptation of a folksong.)

During Miller's time countless classic country hits were made, by

Carl Smith, Ray Price, Lefty Frizzell, Marty Robbins and many others. These were honest recordings, not overproduced, though it was Art Satherley and Don Law who were in charge of country music. It was under Miller that more country songs crossed over, such as 'Just Walkin' in the Rain', by Johnnie Ray. In 1956 Miller came as close to rockabilly as he ever did, with 'Singing the Blues', a huge hit which was the best and most popular of Guy Mitchell's career. Robbins had an equally big country hit with that song, whereupon Robbins crossed over with his next, 'A White Sport Coat'. Mahalia Jackson recorded classic gospel music on Columbia from the early 1950s; Miller gave gospel songs to Rosemary Clooney and Johnnie Ray.

Miller had too much power and not enough taste. We do not know how much he had to do with the *Charlie Parker with Strings* album back at Mercury, but arranger Jimmy Carroll's charts were worse than unimaginative; he had no idea what to do with strings. Miller was as responsible as anyone for turning pop music into jingles. He had a penchant for unusual sounds, and it was probably his idea to amplify a harpsichord for Faith's 'Delicado' and for Clooney's biggest hits. One of his bad ideas was putting bagpipes on a recording by Dinah Shore; DJs took the record off and broke it on the air. Some of his material was overproduced: the relentless snare drum on his 'Yellow Rose of Texas' (1955) was a natural target for satirist Stan Freberg, but the snare came back on Johnny Horton's 'Battle of New Orleans' in 1959.

Still, live pop music seemed to be dead by Miller's time and, as jingles went, Miller's jolly records had more personality than most. His own instrumental 'Oriental Polka' was a wacky twittering tune for woodwind doubled by a marimba. Percy Faith's 'Funny Fellow' was a slowish, cock-eyed samba, which had a cheerful, noisy rhythm section and a piccolo carrying the tune, to test the speaker on your 'hi-fi' record player; in the middle of the arrangement the band laid out and the tune was carried by a solo bassoon, and the band's 'funny fellow' made you chuckle. On the other side of the record was 'Amorada', a Latin frenzy, on which Artie Ryerson played an electric guitar solo that most of today's rockers could not even attempt.

None of these reached the chart; perhaps they were too much better than the jingles, but they were what Miller called 'turntable hits': you enjoy it, but you don't go out to buy it. They were all musical fun.

A typical Miller coup was 'Let Me Go, Lover'. The producer of CBS TV's *Studio One*, a top-rated drama showcase, needed a song, so Miller dusted off a temperance plea called 'Let Me Go, Devil', which had flopped on another label, and had new lyrics written. A slow country waltz, the song was just right, because it did not get in the way of the play's action. He used an unknown girl singer, since he did not want a star's distraction either: 21-year-old Joan Weber's record was number one for four weeks at the end of 1955. But Weber never had another hit.

It was no secret that Miller was not crazy about rock'n'roll, but neither did he join in the pulpit crusade against it, declaring that there was no such thing as an 'immoral' music. But he also did not like the way the music business was changing, and was unwilling to do what you had to do in the later 1950s to get your records played on the radio. In those days Columbia kept its hands clean. At first it did not own a music publishing company, so that Miller could not have cut a DJ in on a song if he had wanted to; and the company would not buy radio spots, which should have been perfectly legal, except that CBS was also a radio network, and afraid of an anti-trust suit. Record labels and promotion men have always paid to get records played; part of the problem was that many DJs were not paid much in the way of a salary, but they played Columbia records because they liked them. When the business began to get dirtier and the money got bigger, fewer Columbia singles were heard on the radio. Miller was always working hard, making a hundred decisions a day, flying back and forth between coasts and selling truckloads of product. He was also an opinionated man, whose tough attitude was justified by his track record, and he occasionally stepped on toes; but why should he bribe DJs?

The most important change in the business was demographic. The largest group of young Americans in history would also have more spending money in its pockets than any earlier American generation, and already in the 1950s they were spending it on rock'n'roll records. Soon some of them were even going out on the road and playing the stuff, generating more easy money, and by then it was not just kids who were buying rock'n'roll records. At the first annual Pop Music Disk Jockey Festival in March 1958 Miller complained in a famous speech called 'The Great Abdication':

You carefully built yourselves into the monarchs of radio and abdicated your programming to the corner record shop, to the eight to 14-year-olds, to the preshave crowds that make up 12 per cent of the country's population and zero per cent of its buying power. It must be more than a coincidence that single record buying went into a decline at the very time the number of stations that programme Top 40 climbed to a new high.

But the coincidence was that grown-ups were using their purchasing power to buy LPs, not singles. Two years earlier RCA had released an unprecedented six singles at once by Elvis Presley (they even had sequential catalogue numbers), as well as 'Heartbreak Hotel', making Presley's Sun material and some of his February 1956 classics available nationwide. The singles were selling twelve thousand copies a day, representing two-thirds of RCA's singles sales, and for the first time the company had to use outside pressing facilities. If rock'n'roll fans had zero buying power, who was buying all those records? Presley's first album broke sales records set by Mario Lanza's *The Student Prince* and the soundtrack from *The Glenn Miller Story*.

Nevertheless, the issue concerned not solely Elvis Presley. A lot of pop music was junk and everybody knew it. Miller's main point was that adults had more buying power than their children, the albums they bought moved fewer units but made up 65 per cent of the record industry's volume and a much higher portion of its profits, and the adults were listening to less and less radio. The convention gave Miller its only ovation, but the Storz broadcasting chain, which was sponsoring the convention, banned Columbia records.

Miller didn't care. Power had long since gone to his head. He had talked Lieberson into putting him in charge of albums as well as singles, and one of the first things he did was fire Paul Weston in California, who had been making beautiful albums for grown-ups for a decade. (Weston was immediately snapped up by a television network.) Les and Larry Elgart co-led a polite dance band on Columbia; according to one story, Larry said to drummer Karl Kiffe, 'When the band starts to swing, I want you to play the ride cymbal', and Kiffe replied, 'When the band starts to swing, will you please raise your hand?' Miller suggested that trombonist Ray Conniff should rearrange his old Artie Shaw material to include male and female choruses. These records amounted to superior Muzak, but never mind; grown-ups could dance to them, and they made pots of money. It was Miller's idea to do the first greatest hits album, by Mathis, which cost the company nothing and sold in the millions. A few months after that DJ convention, in July 1958, *Sing Along with Mitch* was the number one album in the USA for eight weeks. Fourteen later male chorus singalong albums, helped by Miller's television show, reached the top ten albums; twenty-two million were sold, and people stopped buying them only because there were so many of them in the shops that they could not remember which ones they already had.

But it was Miller and his generation who had abdicated. He cannot be blamed for not wanting to get his hands dirty, and he must have thought, as many people did, that rock'n'roll and an increasingly cutthroat music business were passing fads. But the singalong albums are of no importance to the history of music. It is interesting to speculate about what would have happened if Miller had put up the $20,000 that Sam Phillips was asking for Presley in 1955; Presley probably would have ended up in Las Vegas anyway, but at least Miller might have been a match for Tom Parker. But Presley went to RCA, as did Leiber and Stoller, in 1958. All the offices at RCA were identical cubicles; Jerry Leiber could not find his. They told Ted Fox:

By the time you filled out a requisition for something, the idea was stale . . . We produced seven records in the first four months we were there, and had six Picks of the Week in *Cashbox* . . . But they never sold any of those records. Meanwhile we made one record for Atlantic during that period and it was a smash . . . The records were being sold by people who sold refrigerators.

Maybe RCA did not want to bribe DJs either, but, on the other hand, post-war RCA never had a hand at the helm as firm as Miller's. That once great label was coasting, and never recovered; and meanwhile broadcasting was going down the drain.

Robert 'Todd' Storz bought a radio station in Omaha, Nebraska, for $60,000 in 1949; in 1953 he added a station in New Orleans. Most radio stations were soon relying on music, news and jingles, and Storz's new Mid-Continent Broadcasting Corporation was no exception. Storz had grown up listening to *Your Hit Parade*, which simply performed the top ten hits live each week. (The music publishers had never liked it, because the constant plugging of hits kept new songs from getting exposure.) Storz was not going to allow DJs or anybody else to deflect him from his purpose of making money; at the same time, neither was he the type to pay DJs enough money to keep them straight: Miller thought that Storz's DJs were among those on the take, whether Storz knew it or not. The twenty-four-hour format of hits Storz invented, varied with a few white covers of R&B or country hit songs, did not require any talent or musical knowledge, and therefore demanded of a DJ only the ability to cut a ribbon at a new supermarket. In 1956 Storz's corporation sold $3.5 million worth of advertising, and his method was being copied by others, including the Plough group, which bought Chicago's WLS and turned it into the most popular station in the Midwest. In 1957 Storz sold the Omaha station to William F. Buckley, America's leading conservative pundit, for $800,000; Buckley, of course, preserved the deadening format. (In America, 'conservative' rhymes with 'easy money'.)

Somewhere along the way Storz and his programme manager were having a beer in a nearby tavern when they noticed that the other patrons kept playing a small number of hit tunes over and over again on the jukebox, and not only that, but the barmaids or waitresses would then use some of their tip money to play the same tunes. The 'hit parade' formula was tightened up still further, and the Top 40 programming format was born. By the late 1950s a Plough station had a playlist of only one hundred records, concentrating on forty of them and playing them so as to vary the tempo to keep listeners from falling asleep. This meant that whatever was already a hit got constant airplay. It meant that novelties, such as David Seville's 'Witch Doctor' and Sheb Wooley's 'Flying Purple People Eater', which sold quickly anyway, oozed up the charts like castor oil through a pig. And it meant that country music was confined even more to its ghetto, that black hits had less chance of getting wider exposure and that jazz, folk music, Sinatra albums, polka bands and all the rest might as well not even exist. Storz and his imitators sold American airwaves for cash, and nobody cared.

The better music is, the more dangerous it seems. Millions of Americans grumbled that the Swing Era was over, but they did nothing to make it possible for big bands to survive in the 1950s, while every country in Europe still has radio big bands today (though how much longer the BBC's will last is a moot point). It is tempting to suggest that Americans are afraid of swing, in the broadest sense of the term. We have seen that for most of the nineteenth century American songs were regarded by the biggest publishers as not worth publishing, while European music was 'good' music. The fact that American publishers did not pay royalties on European music until 1891, so that there was several hundred per cent profit on each piece of sheet music, was, of course, irrelevant.

In 1899 the *Musical Courier* complained, 'A wave of vulgar, filthy and suggestive music has inundated the land. Nothing but ragtime prevails, and the cakewalk with its obscene posturings, its lewd gestures ... our children ... are continually exposed to ... this vulgarising music.' The owner of the magazine also hated Victor Herbert, to the point where Herbert finally sued him for libel, and won. Coincidentally, Witmark, Herbert's publisher and also the biggest publisher of ragtime songs, had long refused to buy advertising in the *Musical Courier*. Naturally there was no connection.

It was black bandleader James Reese Europe's advice to dancer Vernon Castle to make his moves to the backbeat, in the style of black music, which led to the two-step, the foxtrot and the fad for dancing that swept the country before 1920 and was regarded as corrupting the morals of youth. Come to think of it, while in minstrelsy the blacks remained comic darkies, and were therefore not threatening, from ragtime to rock'n'roll it was music with a black element that was found most objectionable. In mid-1956 local members of the White Citizens Council beat up Nat Cole at a concert in Birmingham, Alabama, in front of an all-white audience, because they disliked 'nigger music', at a time when Elvis Presley was selling more records in black neighbourhoods than Cole.

There is no such thing as a dangerous music; Americans just like being paranoid. Speaking of paranoia, many people wondered why Presley's local draft board, made up like all draft boards of solid, respectable citizens, happened to choose him to drive tanks in Germany. And why was the pilot of the chartered plane carrying Holly, who was not qualified to fly on instruments, not informed that only a few thousand yards from the airfield the weather was turning very bad? And when Chuck Berry's first trial had been thrown out as blatantly racist, would the law not have earned more respect, in the case of a violation of the outmoded Mann Act, which was widely regarded as a joke anyway, by dismissing it? But there was another trial, just to make sure that Berry was sent to prison. We did not have to be paranoid; the decision-makers were probably only stupid, but, one way or another, it seemed as if they really were after us.

Since any business can be manipulated, rock'n'roll was soon taken over by banal (but less dangerous) teen-love songs, or by jingles with a pseudo rock'n'roll beat. Typical of early rock acts were Johnny and the Hurricanes, an organ-led trio whose hit 'Red River Rock' was a nervously fast shuffle on 'Red River Valley', a folksong dating from 1896 and itself based on earlier songs. Somehow it was copyrighted in 1959 as a new song (by a BMI company, let us admit), and was followed by rock versions of the bugle call 'Reveille', 'Blue Tail Fly' and others. Then there was 'The Happy Organ', by Dave 'Baby' Cortez, which was number one for seven weeks in 1959. This was the kind of trash that was being played by hopefuls in a great many bars across the USA, while the nation's best white musicians, and some of the black ones, made a living in the studios, their names unknown to the public. No wonder many of them hated rock'n'roll.

Rock'n'roll may have been taken over, but the charts were not. What were some of the other number one hits of the era? In 1958: 'It's Only Make Believe', a country ballad by Conway Twitty; 'Tom Dooley', a slicked-up folksong by the Kingston Trio; 'It's All in the

Game', a ballad by Tommy Edwards, whose Tin Pan Alley words were set to a melody composed in 1912 by General Charles Gates Dawes, later vice-president of the United States (how respectable can you get?); 'Volare', by Domenico Modugno, an Italian cabaret song; 'All I Have to Do is Dream', another country ballad, by the Everly Brothers; 'Twilight Time', from 1944, by the Platters. In 1959: 'Mack the Knife', sung in his new Sinatra style by Bobby Darin; 'The Three Bells', a French folksong sung by the Browns, a country trio; 'The Battle of New Orleans', by Johnny Horton, and 'El Paso', by Marty Robbins, a pair of country story songs; 'Smoke Gets in Your Eyes', by the Platters, from 1933, one of Jerome Kern's greatest songs (which rock writer Dave Marsh thinks was a 'Tin Pan Alley trifle').

All these were number one, along with some Chipmunk novelties and a sprinkling of rock'n'roll. (Presley's 1924 front-porch ballad, 'Are You Lonesome To-night?', doesn't count as rock'n'roll either.) Top 40 radio saw to it that a hit stayed a hit, because it was all you heard, which is why 'Volare' nearly drove us nuts. So what was the music business afraid of? The truth is that America was floundering; the most powerful nation in the history of the world was frightened of that responsibility, because there were no cultural or political values at the top. Hence the paranoia about rock'n'roll, among other things, even as the USA was selling its own popular culture down the river.

'It was general knowledge in the industry in 1955 that payola flourished,' wrote Russell Sanjek, a retired BMI executive. He meant specifically the bribing of DJs to play records, but, of course, bribery had been endemic in the music industry from the beginning, and for that matter can be found in any industry in any country. (The Soviet economy depended on it until not even bribery could keep it going.)

Perhaps payola began with short-changing the creator. In Britain for generations composers depended for their living upon selling music outright and then writing and selling new music; they offered whatever inducements they could to get it performed. When top bananas from Al Jolson to Elvis Presley sang a song in exchange for a co-writing credit, they were demanding payola. The term itself was invented (like much other entertainment terminology) by *Variety*,

which in 1938 carried the headline 'Plug Payola Purplexed': maybe
that was the case of the two West Coast bandleaders who were listed
as co-writers of a song neither of them had yet seen. In 1953 *Time*
carried a story about 'cut-ins' (performance shares of a song) and 'hot
stoves' (outright bribery).

'Videola' was already a less well-known aspect of the business.
Guests on quiz and variety shows were introduced with a drum roll
or a simple fanfare, until television producers realized that if they
could lock up the copyrights on recognizable pieces of music, they
could make a good deal of extra money. It is an irony that the corny
and inappropriate fanfare with which Elvis Presley was greeted on
the Dorsey Brothers' programme may have been worth a fat weekly
sum to whoever owned it. By 1958 $6 million was being paid
annually by ASCAP just for theme songs and background music,
chosen not by the public but by television producers.

It was no accident that the theme tunes of radio soap operas,
usually played in the studio by an organist, used music that was out
of copyright: the big tune from Tchaikovsky's Sixth Symphony for
Road of Life, the old Italian pop song 'Funiculi Funicula' for *Lorenzo
Jones* and so on. *The FBI in Peace and War* used the march from
Prokofiev's *Love for Three Oranges*. (Whether or not royalties were
paid on that, the interesting question here is did J. Edgar Hoover
know that the FBI was being promoted by a Soviet composer?)

But radio themes soon disappeared. In 1954 there was panic in the
radio industry when advertising investment suddenly fell. Daytime
radio drama is still a strong and very special genre in Britain, thanks
to the BBC, but it died decades ago in the USA, where the mass
audience, having turned to television, used radio only as aural
wallpaper while they worked, or in their cars, and minority audiences
of any kind did not matter.

Top DJs in big cities earned as much as $35,000 a year, a lot
of money in the mid-1950s. Men like Bill Randle in Cleveland
and Howard Miller in Chicago had recognizable personalities, but
most DJs were staff announcers with a talent for talking about
anything that came into their heads, and as long as they didn't stop
talking between records, it was assumed that they had some taste in
music. They had long been courted by special interests with drinks,

meals and complimentary adverts in trade magazines. But in the mid-1950s the stakes went up; radio drama had been heard mainly on the networks, and the sudden death of it made many more poorly paid local DJs available to circling record industry promo sharks. With Top 40 radio, Storz, whether his DJs were on the take or not, had helped create a situation in which they were worth bribing.

Martin Block, who had pioneered the DJ format in 1935, retired in 1960; he was frank, describing the $10 that came with a new record as the equivalent of a head waiter's tip for a good table in a nightclub. Alan Freed never denied accepting gifts, but denied taking them in advance: 'If I've helped somebody, I'll accept a nice gift, but I wouldn't take a dime to plug a record . . . I'd be giving up control of my program.' Besides, it was Freed who had discovered the popularity of R&B among white kids and popularized the term 'rock'n'roll' when it was a daring thing to do and before there was much money in it, and who almost went to jail when early rock concerts turned into mini-riots. Later he bragged that he could name rooms in his house after record companies; he said that Atlantic had paid for his swimming pool, but also that when Atlantic reminded him of the pool because they wanted a favour, he told them that when they sent him some records he liked, he would play them. He was believed when he said that he had never played a record that he didn't like, and the truth seemed to be that payola was not against the law anyway. But Freed's flamboyance and lack of political awareness made him the most prominent victim of the payola 'scandal'.

Howard Miller said he could name people who took money, or paid it, but that it would be unfair to put a few on the rack for a practice that was so widespread. Willie Dixon, a power in Chicago R&B at Chess Records, was open in his autobiography *I Am the Blues* (written with Don Snowden, 1989). It was necessary to give free records to jukebox operators and to distributors; they were supposed to be promotional copies, but everybody knew they were sold. Furthermore:

no disc jockey was going to play your record then without you paying him and that was the truth . . . They would play 'em two weeks, three times a day and that was it unless you came up with more money.

Some of the disc jockeys would play all of one company's records and there wasn't a whole lot of radio stations like there are now.

Joe Smith began as a DJ at Yale. In the 1950s he wanted to play Nat Cole records.

Frankly, I didn't understand Elvis Presley. I had no background to understand Elvis Presley. But I could instantly sense the impact the guy was having, so I figured I'd better play his records. [The decision to play rock'n'roll was made easier as time went on.] The record companies . . . took care of you, you never picked up a tab anywhere. Some guys gave you $100 or $200 a month.

Some years after Freed was ruined, Smith became president of Capitol Records, but he still finds time to write letters. Gene Lees is a former editor of *down beat* and contributed to *Stereo Review* and *High Fidelity* for many years. A successful lyricist, he has published English words to music by bossa nova composers, Charles Aznavour, pianist Bill Evans and others. Since launching his own monthly *Jazzletter* in 1981 he has regularly chastised the music business. Smith wrote to him in January 1989 to say that he had never heard of him: 'Just who are you and what credentials do you possess to wrap up this industry with that kind of rhetoric? . . . When lessons in honesty, ethics and principle are given, I wouldn't be looking to enroll in your class.' Smith had no doubt been careful to pay taxes on the money he took.

In 1959 it was big news that television quiz shows such as *Twenty One*, *The $64,000 Question* and *The $64,000 Challenge* were rigged, often at the request of the sponsors, in order to keep the most popular contestants on week after week. Congressional Representative Oren Harris of Arkansas, chairman of a Special Subcommittee on Legislative Oversight, decided to dig deeper, hoping to find more scandal to keep the subcommittee in the public eye. This was good for votes: the House Un-American Activities Committee, populated by alcoholics and bounders, had kept themselves in office for many years by getting some of the most valuable people in the State Department sacked, and by encouraging blacklists in the entertainment industry. That blacklists themselves were against the law was not important; and as for the name of Harris's subcommittee, if it is not against the law to bribe a D J, that must be a Legislative Oversight, or a job for the boys.

Burton Lane, president of the American Guild of Authors and Composers, wrote to the chairman of the Federal Communications Commission (FCC), urging it to require owners of broadcasting licences to divest themselves of conflicting business interests, such as music publishing companies. Payola was only a symptom of the disease, wrote Lane, which was 'the involvement of the entire broadcasting industry, networks and local stations, in a deliberate and successful distortion of music programming for their own financial gain'. This was fine as far as it went, but Congress was not going to do much about the state of broadcasting; there was more publicity in going after D Js. And Lane did not mention videola, because that put money in his members' pockets.

After a riot at a concert in Boston in 1958, Freed was indicted on a charge of inciting to destroy public property, which was later dropped. Some stations banned rock'n'roll. Freed moved from the most popular station in New York, the independent WINS, to an ABC affiliate, where he had an evening show, but he was already being eclipsed in the fame stakes: on television Freed had to make do with a local independent station, because ABC-TV already had Dick Clark.

Clark had begun as a newsreader at WFIL in Philadelphia at the age of twenty-three; he replaced Bob Horn (who'd been fired for being convicted of drunken driving) on the station's *Philadelphia Bandstand* in 1956. The show had kids dancing, guest artists miming their records and not much talk. It was broadcast five days a week after school, rather than in more expensive prime time, and teenagers rushed home to watch it. Clark's low-key, squeaky-clean personality helped make it a success. In 1957 it was networked for ninety minutes a day as *American Bandstand*, and by 1959 it was shown on over one hundred affiliates and had twenty million fans, or 60 per cent of the audience. Imitations of the show included Chicago's *Bandstand Matinee*, and the dancing kids on the show themselves became mini-stars.

Clark used local television time, before the network part of the show, to test new records, and once played the wrong version of

'Tequila' for weeks before his studio audience let him know. On network time he nearly always played records that were already hits, but the record companies and distributors pushed him as the most influential DJ in the country. They must have done this hoping for favours, so it was a sort of pre-payola. By 1959 Clark had investments in the music business, of which he divested himself on ABC's advice.

Despite occasional reactions against rock'n'roll, Top 40 continued to grow. National advertisers took over the printing of tip sheets, which were plug sheets for new records, and were displayed in record shops. Record companies stepped up releases to around a hundred a week, so that more records had less chance of being heard, thus raising the stakes still further. On the first day of 1959 the CBS radio network cut back programming again, leaving affiliates with twenty more hours a week to fill with music. The Federal Communications Commission and the Federal Trade Commission both started investigations, but they were not investigating the basic causes of the degradation of American radio broadcasting. Soon Representative Emanuel Celler was gunning for BMI, seeing public unrest about 'dirty songs' as a ticket to a seat in the Senate. It was clear that complainants were often connected with ASCAP, using unease about rock'n'roll as a stick with which to beat BMI; but if it was a conflict of interest that some broadcasters had holdings in BMI, ASCAP itself had brought this about in the first place with its strike against the broadcasters in 1940.

The hearings revealed the usual special pleading and hypocrisy. One witness stated that a record company had paid to have its recording of a Tchaikovsky symphony favoured over another, whereupon it was observed that the committee was interested only in corruption as it applied to 'bad' music. Burton Lane ranted about BMI's influence, but had to admit that ownership of radio stations by such members of his organization as Bing Crosby, Frank Sinatra and Pat Boone might also represent a conflict of interest. ASCAP's general counsel Herman Finkelstein stated that the 'artificial ratings' for BMI songs would be substantially reduced if Congress acted, claiming that ASCAP hits were successful on 'sheer merit'; but he also did not know how top ten tunes were chosen, so he could not be

more specific. (*Variety*'s headline was 'Put Up or Shut Up'.) Sydney
Kaye of BMI refuted much of this: the percentage of BMI records
in broadcaster–DJ charts was lower than that in retail record sales,
and the performance rate of BMI music had been lower in 1958 than
in 1957. Kaye also brought up the subject of videola, pointing out
that a snatch of an old song accompanying the closing of a door in a
melodrama brought in just as much money as if an artist sang the
whole song on a musical programme; and it was noted that in 1957
more than 42 per cent of all ASCAP's payments came from television
networks. Kaye said that if BMI was held in greater esteem by
broadcasters than ASCAP, it was because BMI did not habitually
vilify them.

Celler proposed a bill which would have prohibited DJs' interviews with recording artists from leading to a playing of the artist's
new record, or a 'Salute to ASCAP' on Ed Sullivan's show from
involving appearances by member songwriters whose songs would
then be used. It would have required radio stations to buy all their
records, playing free ones only if it was announced on the air that
they were free. This was silly, because of the way the economics of
the industry had changed. When so much airtime had to be filled
with recorded music, buying new releases would have cost stations
thousands of dollars a year, which the smaller ones could not afford,
and would have made it even harder for an independent label or a
new artist to be heard at all.

Dick Clark and Alan Freed were heard in closed as well as open
session. Clark's lawyers testified that he had earned $500,000 in
twenty-seven months from music publishing, record pressing and
distribution and talent management, but that he had disposed of
these interests. Freed said that he had been paid $40,000 a year by
WABC-AM, but that he had paid $30,000 of it back to the station
in exchange for advertising of his rock'n'roll concerts. Representative
John Moss said that Freed was 'one of the few completely truthful
men we've had before us'. Three hundred and thirty-five DJs admitted
having received $263,245 for being 'consultants' in recent years. The
sheer abundance of product had taken the control of hit-making
away from song pluggers and publishers and given it to radio; a
station or a DJ in a major market might receive one thousand LPs

and five thousand singles in a year, which would give rise to payola, because there was no way twenty thousand or so tracks could each get an equal hearing.

The result was an amendment to the Communications Act of 1934 outlawing play-for-pay, but committee lawyer Bernard Schwartz had wanted a more wide-ranging investigation. He wrote in the *New York Post* that improprieties other than those of DJs remained buried in Harris's subcommittee's files: 'Those fully aware of the material involved know we are really deceiving ourselves to believe that the Congressmen carried out anything like the really thorough investigation of the federal agencies that is so urgently needed.' To make sure Schwartz remained an obscure voice, he was fired in early 1959.

In the middle of the unsuccessful war on rock'n'roll came news of the international popularity of it. In the Soviet Union rock'n'roll records were being bootlegged on exposed X-ray film, while other bootlegs on 7-inch 78s made from short-wave broadcasts were being sold by the GUM department store in Moscow. As far as anyone knew, there was no related bribing of DJs in the Soviet Union.

Freed had earlier suffered severe internal injuries in a car crash. He was a heavy drinker; his son said years later that he had never seen him drunk, but Freed was not supposed to drink at all. He was an enthusiastic man who enjoyed life; in refusing throughout his career to play white covers of black hits he had made enemies, and it seemed he could not stay out of trouble. He was fired from WABC in late 1959 for refusing to sign an affidavit to the effect that he had never accepted payola; his combination of honesty and naïvety resulted in twenty-six charges of commercial bribery. He escaped with fines and a suspended jail sentence, but his career was over and his health was failing; he died a broken man in 1965, facing charges of income tax evasion. *Cashbox* wrote that 'he suffered the most . . . for alleged wrongs that had become a way of life for many others', and which for the most part were not against the law when he committed them; but the hypocrites had got their scapegoat.

Both Freed and Clark did their bit to break down racism. Clark's dance party programme integrated a live network show in 1957, allowing black teenaged couples to join the whites without any fanfare, not knowing if they would get away with it. He later said that the first time he talked to a black kid on the air he was frightened to death, but there was not one single complaining letter out of fifteen thousand a week. (To put this in context, it was not until well into the 1960s that Duke Ellington's granddaughter became the first black in a mixed group of professional dancers on television.)

Clark was seen by some as a goody-goody who was let off lightly while Freed was ruined, but Clark was simply better at public relations. He told the hearings that he felt as though he had been convicted of something before he had even testified, and years later was still bitter, describing politicians as pimps. In an interview with *Rolling Stone* in 1989 he observed that the whole thing had been about headlines: congressmen left the hearings early to make the evening television news. One was a drunk who did not even know who Clark was; the most insulting interrogating lawyer would afterwards ask Clark for an autograph and to pose for a snapshot. The government finally sent Clark back to work with a pat on the head, but they had broken into his home and tapped his phone: he was twenty-seven years old and he was shocked. It is worth remembering that those were the Eisenhower years, before assassinations, Vietnam, Watergate; most people still hoped that the government was on the up and up, but Clark learned early that the lawyers in Congress are worse than the rest. According to *Rolling Stone*, he is even more scathing off the record; what he learned from the payola hearings was 'Protect your ass at all times.'

So far as his image is concerned, he also points out that his suit-and-tie style deflected criticism of rock'n'roll, and that most of the people who have been elected to the Rock and Roll Hall of Fame made their television débuts on *American Bandstand*. He had all the wild ones on his programme that parents hated most, such as Little Richard and Jerry Lee Lewis, though not Elvis. (It was a low-budget show, and Tom Parker would not allow his boy to appear for a low fee, while others who demanded big money from Perry Como and Ed Sullivan did *American Bandstand* for scale.) When Hank Ballard didn't turn up to record 'The Twist', Clark gave the job to a former chicken-plucker named Ernest Evans, and Clark's wife changed his name to Chubby Checker. There was also Clark's

Caravan of Stars: an integrated group of big-name entertainers toured the USA, including the Deep South, on a bus for sixty or ninety days.

All Clark did was 'stock the store with what the public wanted', but inevitably, given the association with Philadelphia, where so much cheap pop came from, he was linked with music as poor as anything before or since. About a recording artist such as Fabian, Clark observes that he was a sign of the times; the fans went for his looks, not his singing. The uncomfortable question remains: did Alan Freed play Fabian's records?

One of the first teen-pop stars was Ricky Nelson. Bandleader Ozzie Nelson had married his vocalist, Harriet Hilliard, and, with their sons David and Ricky, their *Ozzie and Harriet* was a top-rated sitcom on radio and then television, and is still typical of American television in its idealization of family life (not necessarily intended as a put-down). The first hit was part of a plot: Elvis Presley was big, and Ricky wanted to impress a girlfriend. 'A Teen-ager's Romance' (on Verve) was pretty lame, but it was a hit, and it is interesting that he covered a Fats Domino hit on the flip side rather than imitating Presley: 'I'm Walkin'' also entered the chart, around Ricky's seventeenth birthday in May 1957. Having plugged his first record on a top-rated national showcase, he was snapped up by Imperial, Domino's label, where he stayed well into the 1960s. He improved as a vocalist; produced by Jimmy Haskell with Ozzie meddling, he achieved several gold records in a row, and they were not bad pop records. The best of his later work falls into the country rock category; his Stone Canyon Band in 1969 used excellent sidemen, such as James Burton. He had many fans when he was killed in a plane crash in 1985.

In July of 1957 Canadian Paul Anka, almost a year older than Nelson, reached number one with 'Diana'. A successful songwriter as well as a vocalist, Anka turned out to have staying power, and had over fifty hits in the *Billboard* chart in the 1970s. He had his own television show in 1973 and was long popular in Las Vegas. His best-known accomplishment is the English lyric he wrote to a French song, 'Comme d'habitude', which became 'My Way' and was sung by Frank Sinatra in 1967. It is hard to argue with success, but 'Diana' was trash, a brash bellowing of a teenage heartache, to say nothing of the banal harshness of the sound of the record. Any girl responding to 'Put Your Head on My Shoulder' (1959) must have used earplugs as a precaution. He had nothing to do with rock'n'roll and everything to do with parting teens from their money.

But much worse was to come. Frankie Avalon, born Francis Avallone in Philadelphia, was more than a year younger than Nelson; he played trumpet as a child on radio and television with Paul Whiteman. He was seventeen when he reached the top ten with 'Dede Dinah' in 1958, and he then had twenty-four hits up to 1962, of which the only one I remember is 'Venus', an inescapable number one for five weeks in 1959. He sounded like a kid who had been inveigled into singing at a high-school dance, having no idea that he was making a fool of himself; in only six years we had come from 'Doggie in the Window' to 'Venus'. It mattered to me, deeply mattered, that he could not sing at all; already a lifelong music fan, the same age as Avalon, I could not figure out where this junk was coming from, and I was ashamed for my generation. Then came Fabian, also from Philadelphia, who was barely fifteen in early 1959, when he had the first of ten hits in two years. These two oafs were the real beginning of what is remembered as the 'teen idol' era.

They were both on the same label, Chancellor, which was formed in 1958 by Peter de Angelis. The promoter was Bob Marcucci, who was consultant to the well-made film *The Idolmaker* (1980), based on the period. The promoter in the film is a frustrated performer and songwriter himself, and makes a star out of a nasty Italian-American kid he knows from local cabaret; the payola is graphically illustrated. The promoter (played well by Ray Sharkey) is betrayed by his star, and sets out to find another good-looking boy (a waiter in the film) who has no experience or discernible talent, but whom he can mould. Most of the music in the film is infinitely better than the Philadelphia hits of 1958 to 1960; written by Jeff Barry and sung by Jessie Frederick (dubbing for actor Paul Land), the cabaret rock gives no idea at all of the awfulness of the stuff of the period. At the end the film asks whether the waiter has any real talent, but we already know the answer. The period was sent up by Stan Freberg, whose character

Clyde Ankle is discovered on his front porch. I quote from memory:

> 'Hey, kid, ya wanna be a star?'
> 'Who, me? But I can't sing.'
> 'Believe me, kid, that don't matter . . .'

The Cameo and Parkway labels were formed by songwriters Karl Mann and Bernie Lowe; they issued recordings by Charlie Gracie, also from Philadelphia, a good guitarist with a rockabilly vocal style who had only three hits, all in 1957, including 'Butterfly'. Bobby Rydell (born Ridarelli, in Philadelphia) had played drums in 1956 in a group with Avalon, but was a much better singer. His forgettable material did not keep him from having thirty chart hits from 1959 to 1965. Parkway was also Chubby Checker's label. Freddy Cannon (born Picariello, in Massachusetts) had a hit on the Swan label in 1959, 'Tallahassee Lassie', which was written by his mother; Dickie Doo and the Don'ts (Philadelphia) also recorded 'Click-clack' and 'Nee Nee Na Na Na Na Nu Nu' on Swan. In case teenagers did not have enough trouble with puppy love and pimples, the death song arrived and became a genre all its own; the Los Angeles Demon label offered Jody Reynolds on 'Endless Sleep', a top five hit.

Not all the hits were totally devoid of merit, and some had interesting aspects. Jimmy Clanton, from Louisiana, recorded 'Just a Dream', a rockaballad, in New Orleans, with a band that included Huey Smith on piano, Earl King on guitar and Lee Allen on tenor saxophone. But his later hits included 'Venus in Blue Jeans', written by Neil Sedaka. Bobby Vee came to fame because he knew the words to Buddy Holly's songs; his newly formed band replaced Holly in Fargo, North Dakota, when Holly did not make the gig. Among Vee's hits were 'Take Good Care of My Baby', 'Run to Him', 'The Night Has a Thousand Eyes' and 'Rubber Ball', the last co-written with Gene Pitney, whose biggest hit was 'It Hurts To Be In Love'. Then there was Mouseketeer Annette Funicello, who recorded for Disney. Avalon and Funicello were still making beach party movies as late as 1965, but nobody will admit to having seen them.

Most of this material either had an irritatingly monotonous shuffle beat or was saccharine, banal and obvious in its sentiment, or both.

As a body of songs it is beneath consideration and has nothing to do with R&B or rock'n'roll. Yet some of it is now regarded as classic early rock in some quarters, principally because no distinction is made between nostalgia and art. Around 1957 composer Virgil Thomson, one of the most highly respected music critics in American history, spoke at New York's Yale Club:

[A] society must have some vulgarity if it is to have vigor and energy. As for Presley . . . he has never missed an engagement, or given a bad show, and that is the mark of a responsible workman. Twenty years ago, Frank Sinatra created a scandal as Presley does today. Frank Sinatra was at the time a first-class artist-workman and so is Presley.

Rock'n'roll was not the problem. The taste-makers of earlier times were musicians (mainly bandleaders), then the DJs, who played records because they liked them. By 1960 they had abdicated, broadcasting had sold its soul and there was a youth market, encouraged to think that people with talent were kids just like them. What we now call pop music (defined as what we hear on the radio, and including a large amount of 'rock') was invented in the late 1950s in an artistic and commercial vacuum. Layers of this lucrative, faddish rubbish have been accumulating for over thirty years.

16

A Last Gasp of Innocence

As the first wave of rock'n'roll performers was devastated by accidents, racist arrests and other disasters, sales of singles seemed to be falling. Paul Ackerman, music editor of *Billboard*, said that at the end of 1959 only 20 per cent of the dollar volume of the record industry was in singles, and 80 per cent in albums. It must be remembered, too, that singles were not loss leaders for albums in those days; most album artists no longer expected to have hit singles. Presley was in the army and Chuck Berry almost absent from the top forty; when the likes of Fabian had seven hits in 1959, adults had probably stopped buying singles altogether.

But the pop revolution was only taking a breather. During this transitional period people emerged who were at least able to impose a personal stamp and in some cases even integrity on their work. The writing and production of Jerry Leiber and Mike Stoller, the hit factory at Motown in Detroit and the songs of the Brill Building era appealed to the first generation of rock'n'roll fans without excessively pandering to it.

Leiber and Stoller were both from the East Coast, but met in Los Angeles as teenagers. They were enchanted by black culture, including jazz and R&B, and began writing songs for R&B acts, having been helped into the industry by Johnny Otis. Their first hit was 'Hard Times', sung by Charles Brown in 1952, and the same year they wrote 'Kansas City' for Little Willie Littlefield. It was Stoller's idea to write a blues with a melody, rather than use the familiar blues changes. They were working with Ralph Bass, who had taken his Federal label to King in 1951. Bass had produced records by Charlie Parker, Charles Mingus and others, but had most success in R&B; he was described by Peter Guralnick as a 'flamboyant, white jive-talking hepcat'. Bass had been responsible for 'Open the Door, Richard' (1947) and several of the biggest R&B hits of 1950 by Little Esther, among others, 'Sixty-minute Man' by the Dominoes (1951) and 'Work With Me Annie' by the Midnighters (1954); later he discovered James Brown, and worked at Chess in Chicago. He changed the title of 'Kansas City' to 'K. C. Lovin'', but revived with its original title in 1959 by Wilbert Harrison on the tiny Fury label it was a number one pop hit and became a rock classic.

Big Mama Thornton's 'Hound Dog' was the first record Leiber and Stoller produced themselves. They took over the session because their work had sometimes been misrepresented, and on this one they knew how they wanted the drums to sound; Otis was supposed to produce it, but they wanted him on drums. They formed their own Spark label and worked with the Robins, who had had an R&B hit on Savoy as early as 1950. Produced by Leiber and Stoller, the Robins had success on the West Coast with 'Framed' and 'Riot in Cell Block Number Nine', helped by Lester Sill, said to be the world's greatest record salesman; in a record shop he would pull some sand out of his pocket, throw it on the floor and do a sand dance to the record. Sill was the promo man for Modern Records, and had introduced Leiber and Stoller to the Bihari brothers at Modern, to the Messners at Aladdin, to Gene Norman, who ran jazz and blues concerts, and to Bass.

Spark did not have national distribution, but 'Smokey Joe's Café' was picked up by Atlantic for their subsidiary Atco label, became an R&B hit in 1955 and crossed over to pop. The Robins' management was not satisfied with the new arrangements, so Leiber and Stoller formed a hand-picked group called the Coasters, whom they later described as a bunch of comedians. They did what they did with no thought of making history, but above all because it was fun. And the original Coasters – lead singer Carl Gardner and bass Bobby Nunn from the Robins, tenor Leon Hughes and baritone Billy Guy – had as much fun as they did.

The first big hit in May 1957 was a two-sided one: 'Young Blood' reached the top ten, but the flip side rose even higher: 'Searchin'' was an unusual Coasters hit, in that it was done quickly at the end of a recording session, just to make four sides. Most of their recordings should have sounded overproduced, but somehow did not: they were meticulously spliced together from many takes to make a fast, aural cartoon strip. (Leiber and Stoller compared them to little radio plays.) They did as much as anything in the period to transcend race. The funniest and biggest hit was 'Yakety Yak' (1958), about nagging parents and a sassy kid. The father is played by Will 'Dub' Jones's deep voice:

> Don't you give me no dirty looks!
> Your father's hip, he knows what cooks!
> Just tell your hoodlum friends outside
> You ain't got time to take a ride!
> YAKETY YAK!
> Don't talk back!

In 'Charlie Brown' a high-school boy shoots craps in the boys' gym, smokes in the auditorium and complains 'Why is everybody always pickin' on me?' 'Along Came Jones' was about a cowboy movie hero coming to the rescue. Leiber and Stoller said to Ted Fox, 'What could be funnier than a bunch of black cats doing a send-up of a bunch of white cowboys? . . . The most fun we ever had . . . was with the Coasters. We'd be falling on the floor – all of us – staggering around the room holding our bellies because we were laughing so hard.'

After writing hits for Presley, Leiber and Stoller were hired by Jerry Wexler at Atlantic as independent producers, the first such arrangement in the record business. The Drifters had had a string of top ten R & B hits with lead singer Clyde McPhatter, who began a solo career in 1955; the story is that the Drifters had gone cold, but after all those hits, maybe they just wanted more of the money. They had some success in 1956–7, then were re-formed by their manager George Treadwell, who owned the name and distributed the cash. New lead singers included Johnny Moore, Bobby Hendricks and bass-baritone Ben E. King (also a songwriter), who sang the lead on 'There Goes My Baby' in 1959.

Leiber and Stoller produced 'There Goes My Baby', which they wrote under the pseudonym Elmo Glick, along with King and Lover Patterson, and Treadwell took some credit as well. (That kind of payola was still not against the law, and never will be.) 'There Goes My Baby' was the first R & B record to have strings: Stoller invented a line on the piano that needed unison violins and cellos. The beat was a Brazilian *baion*, which Leiber and Stoller had been fond of since 'Anna' in 1953, and thereafter influenced pop music for several years; and timpani were played out of tune by an R & B drummer. It was an experimental date since the planned material had not worked out, and the group seemed to be singing in a different key from the backing; Leiber described the result as sounding like a radio bringing in two different stations at once. Wexler thought it was so bad that he threw a tuna fish sandwich at the wall. But Tommy Dowd, Atlantic's brilliant engineer, tinkered with it, and it became the Drifters' first crossover top ten pop hit, and launched the new, better-known Drifters.

King had started with the Moonglows, and joined the Five Crowns in 1957, who became the new Drifters in 1958; he left the Drifters to pursue a solo career because he was being paid practically nothing. Leiber and Stoller helped him with his 'Stand By Me', a pop hit (and a hit again over twenty-five years later, when it was used in a film of the same title). It was during this period that Leiber and Stoller spent some time at RCA, gave Phil Spector work as a favour to Lester Sill and also helped the Brill Building songwriters with their hits. They would demand rewrites as necessary for the sake of the finished product: Doc Pomus rewrote part of 'Save the Last Dance for Me', the Drifters' first number one pop hit, and Carole King part of 'Up on the Roof', her Drifters hit of 1963.

Leiber and Stoller left Atlantic, had hits on United Artists and then decided to do it themselves, but records on their Daisy and Tiger labels disappeared without trace because they were released during the period of John F. Kennedy's assassination. They formed Red Bird Records in 1964 with George Goldner, and delegated much of the production to George 'Shadow' Morton (another legend of the period). They had hit after hit with girl groups, starting with a spectacular number one, 'Chapel of Love' by the Dixie Cups (written by Jeff Barry, Ellie Greenwich and Phil Spector). The black female trio from New Orleans had five hits in two years, the most interesting being the last, 'Iko Iko', which had a simple call-and-response pattern and a percussive backing, like an African children's song. The Shangri-las, two sets of sisters from a high school in Queens, New York, had eleven hits in three years, including the death song 'Leader of the Pack'. This playlet about a biker boyfriend who gets killed (motorcycle noises and a crash are heard on the record) had an answer song, 'Leader of the Laundromat' by the Detergents (on Roulette, in which Goldner no doubt still had an interest).

Leiber and Stoller grew bored with Red Bird and sold it to Goldner for a dollar. They were already bored with Elvis Presley. They admired his voice and his knowledge of R & B and country music, but they had to shut themselves up in a room to write the songs for the film *Jailhouse Rock* in one afternoon, and after that the films got even worse, so that it was no longer any *fun*. In 1962 they wrote 'I'm a Woman' for Peggy Lee, and later 'Is That All There Is?' (inspired by the Thomas Mann novella *Disillusionment*) which was arranged by Randy Newman, then unknown. Johnny Mercer said to Leiber, 'Kid, you finally wrote a good song.' They had started out with profound admiration for writers like Gershwin and Cole Porter, but thought all the standards had been written. While writing songs for Peggy Lee was not as much easy fun as writing jokes for the Coasters, it may have been more gratifying.

Already famous, and having written perhaps fifty pop hits, in the last twenty-five years Leiber and Stoller have applied their theatrical sense and expanded musical vocabulary to new genres. 'Is That All There Is?' and 'Longings for a Simpler Time' were intended for an experimental play in the 1960s; 'Humphrey Bogart', a send-up of cinema idolatry, and 'I Ain't Here', about a black domestic servant working in a white middle-class home, were both meant for another production in the 1970s. 'Tango', about a murder, was 'provoked' by an obituary for actor Ramon Navarro. 'I've Got Them Feelin' Too Good Today Blues', they said, was 'as simple and straightforward a song of joy as Jerry Leiber is capable of writing'. These and others were recorded by pianist William Bolcom and mezzo-soprano Joan Morris for an album called *Other Songs by Leiber and Stoller* (1978). Bolcom and Morris have made albums of the works of Rodgers and Hart, Gershwin, Berlin and others, as well as collections of hit songs from Edwardian vaudeville and the golden age of Tin Pan Alley –

pretty good company for the men who wrote 'Hound Dog', but of course there was not as much money in it. Most of their erstwhile fans probably thought they had retired.

Phil Spector, Neil Diamond, Neil Sedaka, Barry Mann and Cynthia Weil, Gerry Goffin and Carole King and Jeff Barry and Ellie Greenwich were all born between 1939 and 1942, mostly in New York, and all except Spector became songwriters in the neighbour-hood of the Brill Building, at 1619 Broadway in Manhattan, which had been part of the heart of Tin Pan Alley (Fats Waller once had an office there) and became the generic name of an era of pop. It began across the street, where Aldon Music was located. Aldon consisted of Al Nevins and Don Kirshner: Nevins was an experienced older man, originally one of the Three Suns, and Kirshner, not much older than the writers he hired, had the key to the youth market of the period. Most of these writers have also made records: Diamond had thirty-six hits in the *Billboard* pop chart (1966–83); Sedaka, who also plays piano, had thirteen top forty hits (1959–63); Carole King made albums of her own songs.

The time when teenagers, especially girls, went to the record shop and bought the latest record by Perry Como, Frankie Laine or Eddie Fisher, whatever it was and whoever had written the song, was over. Record buyers in the early 1960s became aware of the songwriters and producers (though it was not until the 1970s that *Billboard*, always a few years behind, began to include this information on its charts). The Brill Building era was the beginning of a new singer-songwriter genre, in itself a good thing.

Sedaka (with Howard Greenfield, another successful writer) wrote 'Stupid Cupid' for Connie Francis, a 1958 hit whose irritation quotient was exceeded by 'Lipstick on Your Collar' the next year (by Edna Lewis and George Goehring). Francis has to be mentioned here somewhere, for she had over fifty *Billboard* Hot 100 entries in ten years and represented a transition from the period of early 1950s jingle-pop, with a foot in each camp: her hits were either junk like those named above, or revivals of chestnuts like 'Who's Sorry Now' (1923) and 'Among My Souvenirs' (1928). Her backing groups usually sounded like slick aspirants for a Las Vegas cabaret spot.

Sedaka himself was not much of an improvement. He wrote 'Oh!

Carol' about King (who wrote 'Oh! Neil', which flopped), as well as 'Breaking Up Is Hard To Do'. Neil Diamond was a notch above this, writing 'Sunday and Me' for Jay and the Americans, and later 'I'm a Believer' for the Monkees; he had a duet hit with Barbra Streisand in 1978 with 'You Don't Bring Me Flowers'. He wrote songs for a film of *Jonathan Livingston Seagull* (1973), one of the wettest cultural artefacts of the most self-indulgent period in American history, and for his own remake of *The Jazz Singer* (1980) which was widely panned, but both albums sold very well. Sedaka and Diamond are staples now in the MOR market (which means 'Middle of the Road').

Kirshner was a personal friend of Steve Lawrence and Eydie Gormé, who increasingly appealed to the middle-aged audience both as a duo and separately, and who were hip enough to sing a good song no matter where it came from. Hence Barry Mann (with Hank Hunter) wrote 'Footsteps' for Lawrence, Mann and Weil wrote 'Blame It on the Bossa Nova' for Gormé; Goffin and King wrote 'Go Away, Little Girl', a hit for Lawrence which has been revived several times since, and 'I Want to Stay Here', a duet hit. The successes of the Brill Building era ranged from Jeff Barry's death song 'Tell Laura I Love Her' (for Ray Peterson in 1960) to Mann and Weil's 'You've Lost That Lovin' Feelin'' (for the Righteous Brothers, Bill Medley and Bobby Hatfield, the inventors of blue-eyed soul, in 1964) and Barry, Greenwich and Spector's 'River Deep – Mountain High' (for Ike and Tina Turner, in 1966). Ray Peterson's second and last top ten single, 'Corinna, Corinna' (also 1960), was produced by Phil Spector, because Leiber and Stoller were busy, and the Hatfield and Turner tracks were Spector's as well. Those six years represent the rise and fall of Spector, who was the other producer, with Leiber and Stoller, of the girl groups, a genre all by itself.

Spector began in high school in Los Angeles with the Teddy Bears, writing and singing in a trio. 'To Know Him, Is To Love Him', an extremely slow, mournful song suggested by the inscription on his father's tombstone, became a huge pop hit in 1958. He worked with Lester Sill and Lee Hazlewood in Phoenix. Hazlewood was another successful producer of the period who, with session guitarist Al Casey, began experimenting with studio techniques; they were the ones who recorded Sanford Clark's 'The Fool', leasing it to Dot. They formed the Jamie label and developed minimalist guitarist Duane Eddy, who obligingly played melodies (such as they were) on the bass strings while the sound was drenched in echo; the biggest of twenty Eddy hits was 'Rebel Rouser'. The production gimmicks that Hazlewood was developing were useful to Spector when he went east to work with Leiber and Stoller. Among other things, he wrote Ben E. King's hit 'Spanish Harlem' with Leiber, but he walked out on his contract with them, using as an excuse the fact that he had been a minor when he signed it.

Spector then formed the Philles label with Sill, for which Johnny Mathis's manager Helen Noga put up the money. The first release was 'There's No Other (Like My Baby)' by the Crystals, a female vocal quintet from Brooklyn, which reached the top twenty. At the same time Spector had taken an A&R job at Liberty; after learning that Liberty was going to record Gene Pitney's 'He's a Rebel' with Vikki Carr, he beat them into the shops with the Crystals, and the sixth release on Philles reached number one. Of the first twenty Philles numbers, at least fifteen were hits, which would have been an astonishing achievement in any decade; Spector bought out his partners and was a millionaire at the age of twenty-one.

Part of his success was due to his instinct that the day of the girl groups had arrived, and part to his production style. Some of the Crystals' recordings ('He's a Rebel' among them) were not by the Crystals at all; Bob B. Soxx and the Blue Jeans had Darlene Love singing lead, who was also a solo artist and lead singer on some of the Crystals' recordings. The Ronettes were a trio who had worked professionally since junior high school, and sang back-up for Spector. He fell in love with Veronica Bennett, the lead singer, and did his best to make a star out of her. Eight of the Ronettes' records made the Hot 100, but only 'Be My Baby' the top twenty. (He was married to Ronnie from 1966 to 1975.)

Spector overproduced on purpose. 'Uptown', written by Mann and Weil, had an interesting theme: a boy who might be black works downtown in a menial job, but he is nothing there; when he goes uptown, where the real people live, to visit his girlfriend, she makes him feel important. Kirshner didn't like it, but the Crystals took it into the top fifteen; the backing consisted of strings, a strummed mandolin, castanets, flamenco guitar, a feisty bass part and sandpaper blocks. Few noticed that it had no drums. But it was with Barry, Greenwich and Spector's songs 'Da Doo Ron Ron (When He Walked Me Home)' followed by 'Then He Kissed Me' that Spector's 'wall of sound' was perfected. He jammed a studio so full of instruments and musicians that there was nowhere to move; he wanted to record everything in one take, reserving overdubs for repeating sounds, just to make them bigger. He did plenty of that; in those days overdubs created a good deal of tape hiss, but that could be covered up with echo. The result, combined with the songs, made a complete melodrama in less than three minutes. The sound grabbed the listener; it was compelling as it came out of the era's tiny transistor radios, but it was not a good model and has dated badly. The engineer and the producer traditionally tried to make the best recording they could, so that a great many records made over sixty years ago can still sound good today, but Spector's records still sound like they are trying to come out of a tiny, tinny speaker. You feel instant nostalgia for the period if you are the right age, but the music does not breathe, and becomes claustrophobic.

Carole King and Gerry Goffin's 'The Loco-motion' was a hit for Little Eva (Boyd), their babysitter; they were amused by a dance she did while they were playing the piano at home. It hit the charts the day after Eva's seventeenth birthday. Goffin and King were probably the most talented of the Brill Building crowd. Aldon's house label was Dimension, and 'Loco-motion' appeared on that label, as did King and Goffin's 'Chains' by the Cookies (which was soon covered by the Beatles).

One of their best was 'Will You Love Me Tomorrow' (1960) for the Shirelles. A daring song for the time, it addressed a real problem, as opposed to puppy love: the girl wants to give her boyfriend what he wants, but will he still be around after she has lost her 'reputation'? The Shirelles were a black quartet, and almost the only girl group of the era not created by either Leiber and Stoller or Phil Spector (although Leiber and Stoller produced some of their records). Their manager, Florence Greenberg, issued 'I Met Him On a Sunday', which they had written themselves, on her tiny Tiara label; having been picked up by Decca, it was a minor hit in 1958, the beginning of the girl group genre. Greenberg formed the Scepter label and the group had twenty-five more hits, including 'Dedicated to the One I Love' (which was written by Lowman Pauling of the '5' Royales – though Ralph Bass was also credited – and revived a few years later by the Mamas and the Papas) and 'Baby It's You', by Mack David and Burt Bacharach (also covered by the Beatles).

Bacharach soon teamed with Mack's brother, Hal David. They wrote a great many songs for Dionne Warwick, who was also a Scepter artist and had thirty-eight hits on that label, beginning in 1962 with Bacharach and David's 'Don't Make Me Over'. Bacharach and David are often included in the Brill Building set, but they outlived it; some of their songs became cabaret classics and used a wider musical vocabulary than that to which pop was already restricting itself. Many of the records of the era, in fact, written by and aimed exclusively at young people (Goffin and King had married at nineteen and were writing from personal experience), have a sameness and a lack of adventure about them – they often suggest the shuffle beat that seemed to be the arranger's favourite in those years, and in any case the cluttered production tends to preclude any chance of swing. In Spector's production of Darlene Love's '(Today I Met) the Boy I'm Gonna Marry', written by Ellie Greenwich and Tony Powers, and a top forty hit in 1963, a glockenspiel delicately accompanies the vocal; Spector, who had begun his career as a teenager himself (and perhaps remained one), understood the lies that kids allowed themselves to believe. But the songs are sometimes better than the records. Goffin and King went on to write '(You Make Me Feel Like) a Natural Woman' for Aretha Franklin, one of the classics of the soul era, which was already under way.

Mann and Weil's 'You've Lost That Lovin' Feelin'' (1964), recorded by the Righteous Brothers, presaged the soul era. Although Hatfield and Medley were white boys, they had the right feeling; the record was number one for two weeks, and almost reached the top of the black chart as well. Their versions of 'Just Once in My Life', 'Unchained Melody' and 'Ebb Tide', full of soul even in Spector's production, also did well in both charts. They left Spector, saying that they wanted more control over their own work, and never did as well again.

Meanwhile, the experienced Ike Turner had met Annie Mae Bullock, married her in 1958 and developed the Ike and Tina Turner Revue around her. Their black hits began to cross over, and Spector produced them on 'River Deep – Mountain High', which he co-wrote with Barry and Greenwich. Perhaps the song and its title were too obscure for the pop market; perhaps Spector had made many enemies. It was claimed that the record was too black for white radio and too white for black radio. It stalled at number eighty-eight in the pop chart, and Spector, resentful and increasingly reclusive, effectively retired, and has since been only intermittently active.

In the spring of 1963, after sweeping the BMI awards, Nevins and Kirshner sold Aldon Music to Columbia Pictures–Screen Gems, and Kirshner took over Colpix Records. Mini-eras in pop were ending almost as soon as they began, while Kirshner began his descent into complete banality. If it was not true in the late 1950s that the people who were buying rock'n'roll records had zero per cent of the nation's buying power, it was true by the late 1960s that Kirshner and others were selling comic-strip records to pre-teen children by groups that did not even exist. Jeff Barry thought of the songs they were all writing in the early 1960s as 'ear candy'; he took his craftsmanship to Kirshner's Hollywood bubble-gum empire, and wrote 'Sugar, Sugar' for the Archies, who were cartoon characters. In 1969 it was the fastest-selling single in RCA's history.

Barry Mann was disappointed by the fate of 'Only in America', which he had written for the Drifters: 'Only in America, land of opportunity, do they save the seat in the back of the bus just for me.' Jerry Wexler made him rewrite it to the effect that only in America can anybody become president. The Drifters recorded it, but R & B DJs would not play it. It was finally a hit for Jay and the Americans, a white group.

Gerry Goffin thought that 'Go Away Little Girl', originally written for Bobby Vee, 'should have died in the closet . . . I was never happy with the song, but I am happy with the money I received on it.' Early on he asked himself, 'Am I going to have to write this shit until I'm thirty-two?' But by the time he was thirty-two the era was over, and they had all moved on to other things. As with Leiber and Stoller, Goffin's later work included biting lyrics and adult emotions; if America had had anything like the thriving Broadway stage it had once had, some of these people might have continued to be the voices of their generation, as both they and their contemporaries matured. Carole King's style as pianist and vocalist was an acquired taste, but there was no denying the wide popularity of her songs, and the singer-songwriter genre remained important for a decade. In the meantime, other things were happening, in England, in Newport, once again in Memphis and, most immediately, in Detroit.

No one could have predicted that an unskilled car-factory worker one generation removed from the cotton fields would be one of the most successful black businessmen in American history; nor that black music would invent its own brand of pop, immeasurably popular with the white audience, and still loved by it decades later. Berry Gordy left school at the age of sixteen to become a professional boxer, after working out with a Golden Gloves winner named Jackie Wilson, but his light weight kept him from being a contender. He later worked in his father's printing and plastering businesses, and frequented Detroit clubs at night. He had a jazz record shop in 1953 but went broke because Detroiters did not want jazz, but rhythm and blues; so in 1955 Gordy joined a Ford assembly line for $86.40 a week. And he began writing songs.

When Clyde McPhatter left Billy Ward's Dominoes to join the Drifters in 1953, he was replaced by Jackie Wilson. Gordy's old sparring partner became a soloist in 1957 and had hits with three Gordy songs: 'Reet Petite', 'That Is Why (I Love You So)' and 'I'll Be Satisfied'. Gordy was still an inexperienced writer, but Wilson's genuinely warm personality, his crowd-pleasing act and, above all, his big, beautiful and supple voice made him a star. 'Reet Petite' is not much of a song, and the big-band backing on the record has dated, but the joy in Wilson's glorious voice is unforgettable.

Wilson was a hard worker, and after suffering a massive heart attack on stage he remained in a coma for eight years before he died; 'Reet Petite' was reissued for a number one hit in Britain in 1986. As Nelson George points out in his history of the Motown

sound, *Where Did Our Love Go?* (1985), the records included elements
both lyrical and musical which would later become part of the
hallmark Motown sound, for example, the use of the tambourine
on the drum beat. George notes that 'the lyric of "That Is Why" is
full of specifics about relationships, something Gordy would later
preach'.

But as any writer will tell you, having a few hits does not
bring in vast amounts of money. With the help of his second wife,
Raynoma Liles, who had been a musical child prodigy, Gordy went
into production; their Rayber Voices were available for backing.
Detroit vocalist Mary Johnson's 'Come to Me' was Berry Gordy's
first release, on Tamla 101. It was picked up by the United Artists
label in early 1959, and reached the top thirty of the pop chart, and
the top ten of the R&B chart; among other Gordy and Johnson
records were 'You Got What It Takes' and 'I Love the Way You
Love' (1959–60). According to George, however, Gordy's income
was $27.70 a week in 1959, taking into account $1,000 for 'Lonely
Teardrops', one of Wilson's biggest hits.

Gordy's big hit songs were earning him a fraction of what he
earned on a Ford assembly line; that is what the music business is still
like, the business that Gene Lees scolds and Joe Smith defends. Billy
Davis and Berry's sister Gwen Gordy had started the Anna label,
named for another sister, which was distributed by Chess in Chicago;
'Money (That's What I Want)', by Barrett Strong, became their
biggest hit, and they kept more of the profits, because the song was
co-written by Gordy and the record produced by him as well. The
next step was clear: forming Motown.

The first release from Tamla-Motown in mid-1959 was 'Way Over
There', by Smokey Robinson and the Miracles; Amos Milburn,
Mabel John (sister of R&B Star Little Willie John) and Singing
Sammy Ward generated cash with regional hits; in 1960 the Miracles'
'Shop Around' was number one in the R&B chart and two in the
pop chart, and the company never looked back, becoming the success
story of the new decade: it had 110 singles in the pop top ten
between 1961 and 1971. Gordy's accomplishment was to become
more successful than Mitch Miller in the previous decade, and there
are more areas of comparison than just record sales. Gordy's hand

was as firm on the tiller as Miller's had ever been, and on the till; he had learned from his father the importance of hard work and attention to the bottom line. Berry Gordy, Sr, had come from a family of rural entrepreneurs who were too good for Georgia, where clever blacks often came to a violent end. When he first arrived in Detroit in the 1920s, he bought a house which soon had to be condemned, but that was the last time anybody ever cheated him. Diana Ross, Marvin Gaye, Smokey Robinson and Stevie Wonder had a hit in 1979 with 'Pops, We Love You (a Tribute to Father)', on Gordy Sr's ninetieth birthday.

The new record company became a family operation; Pops gave good advice, selected close friends were allowed in the door, and the boss made the rules. None of the Motown hits of the 1960s was certified gold, because not even the Record Industry Association of America was allowed to see the books. No talent manager would have accepted the contractual conditions that Motown artists did; it is true that the staff and the artists were paid salaries even when they were not working, but some of the artists continued being paid a salary when their records were selling in the millions.

Harvey Fuqua had formed the Moonglows in Cleveland in 1951; as vocalist, writer and producer he had been responsible for many a hit when he came to Detroit, bringing young Marvin Gaye with him. Like all small labels, Fuqua's faced the problem of how to pay for more pressings of a hit when the money came in so slowly from the distributors. Fuqua married Gwen Gordy and Gaye married Anna; they all joined the family firm, while another sister worked in the billing department.

A & R director was William 'Mickey' Stevenson, who had earlier failed to get the local black bourgeoisie to invest in a black Motor-town record company. He knew that the product had to be polished to be successful, and that jazz musicians were more skilful than bluesmen. Local musicians became Motown staff members and worked for less than scale on the promise (hardly kept) that they would be able to make jazz recordings as well. Barney Ales, vice-president in charge of distribution, was the only white person on the staff. He knew distributors all over the Midwest and how to deal with them; he and Gordy were close friends, and if some of the distributors thought at first that the company was run by whites, that was good for business.

Gordy had met seventeen-year-old Smokey Robinson in 1957 and changed the name of his group from the Matadors to the Miracles. The first recording by Smokey and the Miracles was 'Got a Job' (an answer to the Silhouettes' 1958 hit 'Get a Job'), which Gordy had placed on the End label. Smokey, a bookish boy, had been writing poems and songs for years, and his love songs made him the favourite poet of a whole generation of Americans; the Miracles had nearly fifty Hot 100 pop hits in fifteen years. The Temptations, originally called the Primes, with such sensational co-lead singers as Eddie Kendricks and David Ruffin (whose brother Jimmy also had soul hits), remain perhaps the best-loved male vocal group of their generation, and had over fifty hits between 1964 and 1986. The Supremes, first called the Primettes, came from a Detroit housing project to become the most famous girl group of all: both with and without Diana Ross, they had forty-five hits from 1962 to 1976 (including those with the Four Tops or the Temptations); of seventeen top ten hits between 1964 and 1969, eleven reached number one. The Four Tops were formed in Detroit in 1954 as the Four Aims. Levi Stubbs, Renaldo 'Obie' Benson, Lawrence Payton and Abdul 'Duke' Fakir refused to be typecast, leaving Motown and later returning. Basically a first-class cabaret act, they had forty-four pop hits before 1983 and are still performing today in their original line-up.

Martha Reeves was a secretary at Motown; already an experienced singer, she sang in the backing group on Marvin Gaye's recordings, then formed a trio, Martha and the Vandellas, which had twenty-three hits on the Gordy label in eight years. Their 'Dancing in the Street' was number two in 1964, the year of the riots in America's ghettos; nothing more or less than a joyous pop anthem, it was suspected by American puritans of being an incitement to insurrection. The favourite Motown star of all may be Mary Wells, said to be the first to record on Motown, whose thirteen hits in four years included 'My Guy', written and produced by Smokey Robinson. Unable to take Gordy's patronizing attitude, she left in 1964 and had hits on several other labels. Gladys Knight and the Pips, a family group from Atlanta, first recorded for Brunswick when Gladys was fourteen; by the mid-1980s they had had over forty hits, mostly on Gordy's Soul label, among them their majestic 'I Heard It Through the Grapevine' (1967).

The Jackson Five were a male quintet managed by their father, and began in Gary, Indiana, in 1967, when the youngest, Michael, was only nine. It may have been Gladys Knight who recommended them to Motown, but Gordy gave the credit to Diana Ross. They were one of the biggest acts in show business during the 1970s, and their first four singles in 1969–70 all reached number one. After leaving Motown for Epic in 1976, they had to call themselves the Jacksons, because Gordy had tied up the name. Little Stevie Wonder, born blind in Detroit, signed with Tamla-Motown when he was ten; he played harmonica, sang back-up and was the office prankster, but he was learning all the time. His hits began in 1963 and had totalled over ninety by 1993; he is still with the firm. And there were hits by Junior Walker and the All Stars, the Marvelettes, the Velvelettes, the Contours, the Isley Brothers, Brenda Holloway and others.

Eddie Holland looked like becoming another Sam Cooke; his 'Jamie' was a top ten R & B hit and reached the top thirty in the pop chart in 1962. But he hated performing, and started writing and producing with his brother Brian and Lamont Dozier. The legend 'Holland–Dozier–Holland' appeared under the title on scores of Motown records, including seventeen hits in a row for the Supremes. They fought with Gordy for royalties and left on bad terms; the husband and wife team of (Nickolas) Ashford and (Valerie) Simpson took up some of the slack, writing duet hits for Marvin Gaye and Tammi Terrell, and for Diana Ross when she began her solo career.

The Motown show had soon gone on the road, promoting the records but also generating income which helped make up for late payments from distributors. Strict conditions of behaviour were laid down and an eye was kept on expenses; the acts were taught manners, deportment and stagecraft by Maxine Powell, who ran a Detroit finishing school, and Cholly Atkins, a legendary Broadway choreographer who was teaching nearly every act that appeared at the Apollo: he knew that Motown was a black-owned company and wanted to see it grow.

There were tragedies along the way. Drummer Benny Benjamin

and especially bass player James 'Jamie' Jamerson created some of
the most influential pop sounds of the decade, but both had fatal
weaknesses for alcohol. Florence Ballard, co-founder and original
lead singer of the Supremes, was squeezed out when she resented
Gordy's grooming of Diana Ross for greater stardom; her solo career
failed and she died of drug abuse. But the greatest tragedy was that
of Marvin Gaye.

Stevie Wonder and Gaye were the only Motown artists to get their
own way in the Gordy empire. When Wonder turned twenty-one the
company owed him a lot of money, and it became apparent how
much he had learned over the years: he was the master of increasingly
sophisticated studio techniques. (Whether this is a good thing is
debatable: in 1988 one of Wonder's concerts had to be postponed
when somebody swiped his Synclavier discs containing backing
tracks.) He soon dictated his terms to Berry Gordy, who would have
been a fool not to accept them.

Gaye had duet hits with Tammi Terrell, among others; a beautiful
girl with a wonderful voice, she died of a brain tumour in 1970 in her
early twenties. After this shattering blow Gaye wanted to make
concept albums, both brooding and personal and also containing
social statements: *What's Going On* (1971) reached number six in the
Billboard album chart (and three of its singles were hits) and *Let's Get
It On* (1973) reached number two. But Gaye lacked self-confidence;
he was dominated by his father, a fundamentalist clergyman and a
transvestite. One of Gaye's wives was Janis Hunter, Slim Gaillard's
daughter; Slim recalled Marvin's father coming downstairs in the
middle of the night 'wearing a dress, with lipstick on, and carrying
one of those little dogs. It was a real strange house to be in.'
Marvin's life ended when his father shot him in 1984.

The production on the classic Motown hits is very tight and busy,
designed like Phil Spector's to sound good on a car radio or a
teenager's radio; yet they are not as claustrophobic. In the days of
eight-track rather than twenty-four-track recording, Motown pioneered then difficult recording techniques which were soon widely
used, such as 'punching', whereby a vocal or a saxophone solo could
be brought up or down or covered by a new take. In the early days
the easiest way to do this was to cut the tape, so two tapes were made

of everything, for safety. The resulting hits are a goldmine – good songs, good singing and slick production that never loses that R & B feeling in the beat. The connection with Detroit clubs and Detroit housing projects is always evident; the people who made these records could never forget where they came from. It is often hard to tell how good the hits sound when they are remastered; a compact disc available in Europe called *Motown's Greatest Artists: The Most-played Oldies on America's Jukeboxes* has the virtue of beginning with Gladys Knight and the Pips' 'I Heard It Through the Grapevine' (written by Norman Whitfield and Barrett Strong) and ending with Marvin Gaye's even bigger hit on the same tune (later used to sell raisins). But some of the tracks are better in the mono mode, which in turn sounds like an entirely different mix. Some fans say nothing is as good as the original 45 singles.

Gordy moved his empire to Los Angeles in 1971, and his dabbling in films was less than successful. The company grossed $40 million in 1973, but by then the glory years were over. Gordy signed a distribution deal with MCA in 1988, effectively giving up control; but nothing lasts for ever. Stevie Wonder, Diana Ross and Michael Jackson, among the biggest stars in show business, all started out in the Motown stable, and the empire of the one-time Ford worker was the only American pop enterprise that probably did not even notice the British Invasion.

17

The 1960s: A Folk Boom, a British Invasion, the Soul Years and the Legacy of an Era

Like everything else in post-war Britain, popular music was controlled by an ineffective establishment. Rationing of consumer goods went on for many years after the Second World War, as the British desperately tried to be polite to one another rather than allowing the market to do its work. This contributed to a continuing British drabness while the Germans and the Japanese were well on the way to recovery.

Which musics would make money in Britain was decided by this establishment through the BBC; as a result, popular music was a mixture inherited from the British variety tradition of music hall.

Pianist Winifred Atwell, whose cheerful keyboard hits from 1952 included 'Britannia Rag', 'Coronation Rag', 'Let's Have a Party' and 'Let's Have Another Party', was perhaps typical of this. Venezuelan-born drummer Edmundo Ros had recorded on drums with Fats Waller in London in 1938; his Latin dance band, said to be one of Princess Margaret's favourites, had a hit in the USA in 1950 with 'The Wedding Samba'. In 1952 Vera Lynn, the most popular British vocalist during the war, reached number one in the USA with her British top ten hit 'Auf Wiederseh'n'. Arranger-conductor Frank Chacksfield's lush instrumentals 'Limelight' and 'Ebb Tide' were hits in 1953, and David Whitfield's operatic voice reached the USA top ten with 'Cara Mia' in 1954, backed by Mantovani. All of these were on the London label in America, aided by excellent sound, but in general British pop music was not exported; Alma Cogan had her own UK television show, but she is remembered as much for her gowns as for her voice. American stars like Johnnie Ray, Rosemary Clooney, Frankie Laine, Perry Como and the rest were so popular in Britain that it was noteworthy when British vocalist Dickie Valentine sold out the London Palladium.

The big band of trombonist Ted Heath, formed in 1944 and one of the best of the post-war era, at various times boasted such fine musicians as drummer Jack Parnell, trombonist Don Lusher, trumpeter Kenny Baker and tenor saxophonist Ronnie Scott. Valentine was the band's vocalist, and later a solo success: among his biggest hits was a cover of Frankie Avalon's 'Venus'. Heath's band had a few hit singles in the early 1950s, but in general the Big Band Era was over in Britain as it was in the USA.

British jazz fans had a hard time of it, because until 1956 the British musicians' union would not allow American musicians to perform in Britain unless there was a reciprocal opportunity in the USA for British musicians. Visiting American stars might have made news and generated enthusiasm for the music in general; homegrown British jazz musicians did not have much work anyway, and wanted to see their heroes in action and perhaps get a chance to play with them. But when Charlie Parker, Coleman Hawkins and others toured Europe, they could not work in Britain, for the government let the unions call the shots. It was only in instrumental music that this discrimination was practised; as in the USA during the musicians' union strikes, pop singers came and went freely.

As rhythm and blues began to have its influence in the USA, it was not heard on the radio in Britain, and few American blacks toured there at first, except for a small number of bluesmen who were seen as folk artists. The British Isles are rich in folk heritages, but unlike the rural musics of America, British folk forms never became urbanized and commercial. This is part of the reason why American country music has always had as big a following in Britain as the indigenous folk music, if not bigger. While Americans sold their popular culture down the river, Britain stood at the opposite extreme: if there was any hint of payola on the BBC, the artist and the song publisher would be banned for a year. But musical conservatism caused pressure to build up. British kids were fascinated by rock'n'roll, but they had to hear it on Radio Luxembourg or on pirate radio.

In the early 1960s the BBC offered the Home Service (chat, public service and cosiness), the Light Programme (entertainment) and the Third Programme, which was not just classical music, like Radio 3 today: it was the BBC's finest hour, a showcase of all aspects of European high culture, a sort of university of the air. The widest knowledge of American trends was found in seaports such as Liverpool, where merchant seamen often brought home records that were not played on the BBC, or in London, where a few shops had imported records.

Then on Easter Sunday in 1964 Radio Caroline opened up. *Caroline* (named after President Kennedy's daughter by its operator, Ronan O'Rahilly) and her sister ship, *Mi Amigo*, were anchored in the Channel at opposite ends of Britain, and had an audience of twenty-two million on Sunday mornings. 'They took the music that only London hipsters were listening to,' remembered one old fan, 'all those rare, imported records, and put them where spotty little bozos like me could have their minds twisted.'

The Marine Offences Bill of 1967 made advertising on pirate radio illegal, but by then BBC Radio had transformed itself into Radio 1 for pop-rock, 2 mainly for chat and drama, 3 for classical and 4 for news and chat, some drama and very little music. (There are now also thirty-nine local BBC stations in England, which play some music, and then Radio 5, which at this writing is floundering.) Caroline's more popular DJs found work on the BBC; Caroline reopened in 1973 and limped along until 1989, but its work had been done. Meanwhile it is hard for an American who grew up within range of Dick Biondi on Chicago's WLS to imagine how frustrating radio was to a British kid in the early 1960s, and this goes some way towards explaining the hysteria that eventually occurred.

Jazz in Britain was based on the style of the Swing Era until a New Orleans revival began during the Second World War; George Webb's Dixielanders trained trumpeter Humphrey Lyttelton, who later went more modern. In the 1950s the revival was watered down (as in America) to become 'trad', which had a considerable following. Lyttelton's musical integrity, gigs and recordings with visiting Americans such as Buck Clayton and Buddy Tate have ensured his influence; his only hit single, 'Bad Penny Blues' (1956), however, is inane, repetitious and unrepresentative of his work. Knowing how popular trad was in Britain in those years, one is surprised to learn that there were so few hit singles. It remained a cult until around 1960; American-born film director Richard Lester later became famous directing the Beatles, but his first feature was *It's Trad, Dad!* in 1961. The Temperance Seven had a number one hit that year with 'You're Driving Me Crazy' from 1930 (their trombone player was John R. T. Davies, also a transfer engineer who has been responsible for an uncounted number of excellent transfers to modern master tape of old 78s). Trumpeter Kenny Ball and his Jazzmen had fourteen hits from 1961, perhaps because he led one of the worst trad bands; 'Midnight in Moscow', a Russian tune, was also a success in the USA. Trombonist Chris Barber and his Jazz Band had a big transatlantic hit with 'Petite Fleur', written by Sidney Bechet in 1952, a pretty record, mostly a solo by clarinettist Monty Sunshine, who seemed to imitate Bechet's vibrato but actually sounded more like Boyd Senter, an American dance band leader of the 1920s.

Trad never became a force in British pop, but soon gave rise to another genre that did. Anthony Donegan, from Glasgow, changed his name to Lonnie in homage to bluesman Lonnie Johnson; he played guitar or banjo in trad bands, and began appearing on stage between sets playing what came to be called skiffle. The cheap Spanish guitar, the washboard and the bass made out of a tea-chest and a broom-handle created a do-it-yourself movement, causing countless British schoolboys to take up the guitar.

The word 'skiffle' had already been used in the USA to describe music played by those who were too poor to buy musical instruments and used washboards, jugs and so on instead; 'Hometown Skiffle' (on Paramount, 1929), one of the first samplers, included the Hokum Boys and Blind Lemon Jefferson. Like rock'n'roll in the USA, skiffle was a novelty at first, but it is impossible to underestimate its importance. As one British writer put it, 'A strange bedlam was taking over which had nothing to do with anything we had previously known.' This would not be a bad description of the impact of rock'n'roll in the USA. One of the skiffle hits was a portent of things to come: both Donegan and the Vipers Skiffle Group had hits with 'Don't You Rock Me Daddy-o', written by members of the Vipers, some of whom later turned to electric guitars and became the Shadows, the best-known British rock band of the early 1960s.

Another skiffle hit, with an indefinably sweet sound, was 'Freight Train', by the Charles McDevitt Skiffle Group and singer Nancy Whiskey. It reached the UK top five in 1957 on the Oriole label, an independent soon purchased by CBS to form the basis of CBS UK, and also entered the top forty in the USA. The song had been written by Elizabeth Cotton as a child; Libba was a protégée of the Seeger family. But Donegan was the first and most successful skiffler; in early 1956 his 'Rock Island Line' beat Elvis Presley's 'Heartbreak Hotel' to the British charts by several months. The popular British jazz singer Beryl Bryden played washboard on that record.

Skiffle was easy to satirize. 'Rock Island Line' was also a hit in the USA, where it was sent up by Stan Freberg; in the UK Jim Dale recorded 'Piccadilly Line'. The genre plundered the American folk-songs of Woody Guthrie and Leadbelly, some of which had anteced-ents in Britain to begin with. Donegan's over thirty UK hits included 'Lost John', 'Stewball', 'Cumberland Gap' and 'Grand Coolie Dam', but also his own quintessentially British 'My Old Man's a Dustman' (or 'garbageman', as we said in the USA), and the 1924 hit 'Does Your Chewing Gum Lose Its Flavour on the Bedpost Overnight'. Donegan was another beneficiary of Decca/London's excellent sound, which all through the 1950s was a light-year ahead of RCA's. When he recorded the music hall material, he was accused by folk purists of selling out.

'Freight Train' had been introduced to Britain by Peggy Seeger, whose husband, Ewan MacColl, was born James Miller, of Scottish parents, in the English town of Salford, and grew up there at a time when the social attitude of 'us and them' was the only realistic one to take. He learned proletarian songs from his parents, and took the name of an obscure Scottish poet. In those days what is still called the working class in Britain was inclined to try to better itself; MacColl spent much time reading in public libraries, joined the Communist Party and spent the rest of his life making a case for the proletariat. With his first wife, Joan Littlewood, he formed a theatre workshop in London in 1945, and became a highly regarded play-wright. He later turned to folk music with Seeger, his third wife; he wrote some fine songs, among them 'Dirty Old Town', based on his memories of Salford, which was covered by Rod Stewart, and 'The First Time Ever I Saw Your Face', a love song for Seeger, which was a number one hit in the USA for Roberta Flack in 1972 and has become a cabaret standard (partly because it was included in Clint Eastwood's film *Play Misty for Me*). Through all his various activities and workshops, including documentaries on radio about the working class and its music, MacColl had become one of the most important British 'folkies'.

MacColl and Seeger were delighted with skiffle. Young people making their own music could be influenced by the songs of their ancestors, and indeed a folk revival seemed to be happening, in the USA as well as in the UK. Alan Lomax, son of the pioneering folklorist John Lomax, lived in Britain during the 1950s, and gave some encouragement. Ramblin' Jack Elliott, a singing cowboy from Brooklyn and Woody Guthrie acolyte, spent most of the 1950s in Europe, especially England, where his guitar playing influenced folk music. And in the 1950s some Americans still followed the peripatetic fortunes of the Weavers.

Children always love folksongs, which are easy to remember, easy to sing and seem to be about things that matter. Such musicians as Pete Seeger, Burl Ives, Oscar Brand, Ed McCurdy and Win Stracke ('Chicago's Minstrel') often worked for and with children. Some of these artists were not taken in by the cranks in the American Communist Party: Ives testified before the House Un-American Activities Committee about the party's attempts to co-opt folk music for its own ends; Canadian-born Brand refused to testify and was not subpoenaed. MacColl was chairman of the Pete Seeger Committee in London in 1961 during the period when Seeger was being persecuted. It is a nasty paradox for those who love both music and freedom that while the USSR devoted resources to researching and preserving its multitude of folk styles before they disappeared, the Library of Congress's archive needed private donations, and Pete Seeger, collecting songs around the world, was blacklisted.

Folkish sounds had occasionally been heard in US pop during the

1950s. Harry Belafonte's cabaret-style calypso was very successful; his 1956 album, which was number one for thirty-one weeks, included 'Banana Boat (Day-o)', of which there were half a dozen hit versions. Since an increasing number of people from the Caribbean were settling in Britain, and especially London, real calypso could be heard there. One of the most attractive US hits of the period was 'Summertime, Summertime', by the Jamies, a quartet led by Tom Janison, who wrote the song; its combination of bounce and almost medieval harmony made the top forty twice. Around 1960 *Continental Café* on Chicago's Channel 9 regularly presented international folk dancers and singers, among them the young Judy Collins.

Folk music goes in and out of fashion; by the late 1980s it was in fashion once again, included in 'roots' music. When folk music is not in fashion, it is always there on obscure labels in specialist shops for those who want it, and those who do not want it are people who have no souls. In October 1990 on a BBC TV programme about MacColl, a year after his death, Peggy Seeger, accompanied by her own autoharp and a discreet background guitar, sang 'Thoughts of Time': it was one of the most frankly and directly beautiful musical moments I have ever seen on television.

The folk act that made the biggest stir in the late 1950s was the Kingston Trio, three Californian boys who deflected the left-wing taint attached in America to folksingers by wearing matching short-sleeved shirts and short haircuts. Their whole act was so slick that purists dismissed them, but their intent was honest enough; their first and biggest hit, in 1958, was a real folk-song, 'Tom Dooley', about a man who was hanged for murder in 1866. When Dave Guard, who wrote 'Scotch and Soda', later a cabaret staple, left the group and formed the Whiskey Hill Singers with Judy Henske, he was replaced by John Stewart, still a highly regarded singer-songwriter today. The Kingston Trio eventually had six alumni, seventeen Hot 100 singles and over thirty albums. They inspired the Brothers Four, the Highwaymen and other such groups, including perhaps the Limeliters: Glen Yarbrough, Lou Gottlieb and Alex Hassilev were good singers with an amusing cabaret act who had only one minor hit single, but ten chart albums in four years from 1961. Clearly there was a market hungry for folk, even if it was urban folk.

In 1959 the Kingston Trio were booked for the first Newport Folk Festival, where they were outclassed by the likes of Pete Seeger, Earl Scruggs, Sonny Terry and Brownie McGhee, John Jacob Niles, Jean Ritchie, Brand and McCurdy. Niles, one of the patriarchs of folk music, presented old songs in a formal style rather than as early hillbilly music. Jean Ritchie was born in a Kentucky family of fourteen. Her parents collected songs, and were visited by English folklorist Cecil Sharpe in 1922, five years before Jean was born; in the 1930s the family was recorded by John and Alan Lomax. Later Jean was on the board of directors of the original Newport Folk Festival.

The sensation at Newport in 1959 and 1960, however, must have been Joan Baez, whose first albums on Vanguard, made in 1960–61, reached high in the *Billboard* chart, and were followed by live concert sets which did even better. Born in 1941, Baez was a revelation for her own generation, playing acoustic guitar and in a silvery soprano singing straight unfussy versions of Child ballads (collected by Francis James Child in the nineteenth century) and similar material, such as the Scottish border song 'Mary Hamilton' and 'House Carpenter' (from the 'daemon lover' genre). 'Wildwood Flower' was a Carter Family song, the melody of which Woody Guthrie had used for his 'Reuben James' (about a disaster at sea). Baez's contemporaries also knew that the compilers of blacklists had had their day: she sang Guthrie's 'Pretty Boy Floyd', and Malvina Reynolds's 'What Have They Done to the Rain?' Thus in popular music the new decade began with chart success for Motown on the one hand, as black pop was coming of age, and folk music which was not preserved in aspic on the other.

After fighting for democracy during the war, Seeger had started People's Songs, Inc., to publish songs, which was taken seriously by the FBI. In May 1947 the United States Army's *Weekly Domestic Intelligence Summary* listed PSI as a communist front. In September its tiny staff was joined by Irwin Silber, a left-wing college kid who was sounder on radical theory than on compassion. When Leadbelly died in 1949 he was on welfare, but Silber complained about Seeger misusing Leadbelly's music when the Weavers had their hit with 'Goodnight Irene' in 1950; Leadbelly's widow was taking in laundry, and no doubt did not misuse the money. The American far left had long been dominated by people like Silber. With the Communist Party marginalized, its membership and its ties with the unions shrinking, Seeger drifted away, hoping that the fundamental democracy implicit in folk music would seep through to the people. This did not prevent him from being victimized by paranoia on both left and right; while he was building a house with his own hands during this period, living through the first winter in New York State without any heat and feeding his family on beans, his former comrades and others kept a rumour going that he had a lavish estate on the Hudson. But his aim was to get America singing, and during the 1950s he flitted from one meeting hall or college campus to another, often coming and going before the local patriots could organize themselves to keep him out. Whatever his views on communism, his musical instinct was correct: when the Weavers sang 'Rock Island Line', the Senate Internal Security Subcommittee investigated them for sedition; when Lonnie Donegan had a hit with the same song a few years later, the only result was a Freberg send-up. The USA had survived the internal communist menace, and also a tendency towards Stalinist show trials.

The songbook *Sing Out!* was edited by Silber from 1951 to 1967. When Seeger visited England in 1961, he was impressed with the number of topical songs being written; he went home and formed *Broadside*. By then the coffee houses of New York City were hothouses of folk-oriented singer-songwriters: Jack Elliott, Phil Ochs, Eric Andersen, David Blue, Dave Van Ronk, Tim Hardin, Eric Von Schmidt and Bob Dylan were soon joined by Tom Paxton, Tom Rush, Arlo Guthrie, John Prine, Steve Goodman, Loudon Wainwright, Canadians Buffy Sainte-Marie, Ian and Sylvia and scores more, many of whom had songs published in *Sing Out!* or *Broadside*. The greatest of all these was Dylan, who was introduced by Joan Baez at the Newport Folk Festival in 1963.

Like almost everyone else of his generation, Dylan had grown up cut off from the pre-war history of popular music, listening to Little Richard and Buddy Holly; maybe he really did play piano with Bobby Vee. He certainly valued Hank Williams and Woody Guthrie; he made his way to New York and joined the folk boom while still a teenager. The only category he could fit into was the category of people who come from nowhere; his home town of Hibbing, Minnesota, had no 'other' side of the tracks. The mainstream music business that had tried to ignore Elvis Presley meant nothing to him at first; he went to the East Coast because that was where Woody Guthrie was.

Some people thought that Dylan had the solution to the banal hypocrisy of the post-war era. He had a relatively small number of fans; of about thirty albums in the twenty-five years from 1962, only two were certified as million-sellers. But crazies picked through his garbage, urban terrorists named themselves after a phrase in a Dylan lyric, college professors lectured on Dylan's words, and they all missed the point. One of Dylan's intellectual predecessors was a radical union leader early in the century, Eugene V. Debs, who told a cheering crowd of railway workers that if they needed him to lead them into the promised land, somebody else would lead them right back out again. Dylan never intended to tell anyone what to think; the only thing he understood was that there is nothing to be understood, that there are no rules and no answers except those that come from within us as individuals. That is what freedom ultimately means; but this was not convenient for a generation who became consumers in the end, like every generation, and wanted their politics off the shelf, like breakfast food.

Dylan was ignored by Folkways, Vanguard and Elektra, the primary folk labels of the early 1960s, but was signed to Columbia by John Hammond. His first album in early 1962 was a straight folk album, described by a Columbia record salesman as a 'piece of shit'. (It should have included 'Talking John Birch Society Blues', but Columbia would not allow it.) The second album, *The Freewheelin' Bob Dylan*, consisted almost entirely of originals: 'Blowin' in the Wind', 'A Hard Rain's a-Gonna Fall' and a few others made him a 'protest singer', though in retrospect were merely pithy observations. Everybody was writing anti-war songs, like Dylan's 'Masters of War', or 'Talkin' World War III Blues'. 'The answer, my friend, is blowin' in the wind,' Dylan wrote, and it still is. He changed nothing, but never said he would.

Dylan did what Cole Porter had done in a very different decade, and for a very different audience. He combined cadences and catch-phrases from everyday speech in such a way that they re-entered the language, but instead of promoting escapism into a world of pent-houses and evening clothes, Dylan offered solace to a generation living on a moral desolation row. We had grown up in an era when many of America's friends were butchers, all breeding chickens which would come home to roost, from Trujillo, Batista and Samoza in our own back yard to generals and potentates in the Middle East and Asia; the threat of nuclear war was becoming tiresome and the Cold War merely good for business. We were tired of it, but could only keep on keepin' on, in spite of the blood on the tracks.

Dylan continued to accompany himself on harmonica and acoustic guitar. His third and fourth albums contained much rich material, and then *Bringing It All Back Home* (1965) included a whole side that seemed to top off Dylan's acoustic era: 'Mr Tambourine Man', 'Gates of Eden', 'It's Alright, Ma (I'm Only Bleeding)' and 'It's All Over Now, Baby Blue' were all masterpieces. But on side one of the album he was backed by an electric rock band. Rock'n'roll came of age with Dylan, just as its element of folk music had been revived.

At a Newport Folk Festival in that period the Paul Butterfield Blues Band was loud and electric, and nobody was bothered, because few in the audience knew anything about the blues anyway. But when Dylan's electric set began, fans as well as the Seegers and the MacColls were outraged, perhaps because they knew that their time was over. Their best songs would live, but their politics had been rendered absurd by history; we may not be able to keep our politicians under control, but we don't have to work on Maggie's farm if we don't want to. Irritated by criticism of his new music, Dylan said, 'Folk music is a bunch of fat people.' Some of the controversy was caused by the endemic problem of electric rock that it is nearly always unnecessarily loud; but for better or worse, among the influences on Dylan were skifflers from Liverpool who spearheaded the British Invasion of 1964.

The Quarrymen, one of countless British schoolboy groups in-spired by skiffle and/or rock'n'roll, was formed in Liverpool in 1956 by John Lennon, who named it after his school. Lennon sang and played rhythm guitar; Paul McCartney on rhythm guitar and George

Harrison on lead were added in 1957. In 1958 Lennon's close friend from art school joined; Stuart Sutcliffe could not play at first, but he had money from the sale of a painting which he was willing to spend on a bass guitar. As they evolved from skiffle to rock'n'roll, the group's name changed to Johnny and the Moondogs; for the next incarnation Sutcliffe suggested Beetles, after Buddy Holly's Crickets, and Lennon's predilection for puns finally made them the Beatles. Their first regular drummer was Pete Best, whose broody good looks made him a heart-throb among Liverpool fans.

Like many overnight sensations they served a long apprenticeship, playing in tough seaside clubs in Hamburg, Germany, for prostitutes, drunks and slumming tourists while honing their stagecraft. Like a good number of show business folk, they took amphetamines and other drugs to keep going; the squeaky-clean Beatles of a few years later had little to do with the rough-and-ready English rock'n'roll band that played covers of American hits. They also began writing songs of their own.

In between their Hamburg tours they played hundreds of gigs at the Cavern Club in Liverpool, thereby building up a substantial local following. They had recorded in Germany (produced by bandleader Bert Kaempfert), backing UK pop singer Tony Sheridan on a few tracks which did nothing, but their fans in Liverpool began asking for the imported record. Brian Epstein, manager of the record department of his parents' furniture emporium, was intrigued to learn that they were a local band. He was a middle-class Jewish boy and an unhappy homosexual (at a time when it was still illegal in Britain to be a practising homosexual) and he preferred classical music, but he literally fell in love with the Beatles, and became their manager. The orthodoxy is that Epstein was a poor businessman, but that can only be said with hindsight; nobody predicted the extent of Beatlemania, and, as Lennon put it after Epstein's death from an accidental drug overdose, they never would have made it without him.

Sutcliffe was not a good musician and did not get along with McCartney, who wanted to play bass. He left in 1961 to settle in Hamburg with his German girlfriend, photographer Astrid Kirchherr; he died of a brain tumour, possibly caused by a vicious kick in the head from a hooligan after a 1961 gig in England. Kirchherr had influenced the group's sartorial style, including their haircuts, which though seen as traditional English 'pudding bowl' cuts, were modelled on what upper-class German boys had worn for decades. Kirchherr's photographs represent the beginning of the importance of visual style, which would carry more weight in pop than the music. Her then boyfriend, Klaus Voorman, was also impressed by the group, and became an influential designer of record covers. Epstein forced the boys to sharpen up their act, nagging them about deportment and reliability, and building their image on what Kirchherr had started; then he began trying to get them a recording contract. Decca, among others, turned them down, a mistake that lives in history. Then came an audition with George Martin.

Martin deservedly became one of the most famous producers in history, and was known as the fifth Beatle. He had attended the Guildhall School of Music and worked in the BBC music library before joining Parlophone as an assistant. Parlophone had been an internationally famous record label; in the 1920s it issued records by pianist Claudio Arrau, for example, and was the main British source of jazz records in its Parlophone Rhythm Style series (which included issues of Louis Armstrong's Hot Five). But by the 1960s it had become EMI's repository for material that did not belong anywhere else. Martin produced a Scottish dance band led by Jimmy Shand, and the hit novelty 'Experiments with Mice' (1956) by Johnny Dankworth, in which the British saxophonist led a group playing 'Three Blind Mice' in the styles of Glenn Miller, Stan Kenton and others. Martin made comedy records by Peter Ustinov and Peter Sellers, as well as skiffle hits.

The Beatles recorded 'Love Me Do' at an audition, and Martin, seeing something in their raw energy, advised Epstein that Pete Best was not good enough. Best seemed to be the odd man out anyway, unimpressed as he was by Kirchherr's ideas, so the group recruited Richard Starkey, alias Ringo Starr, from Rory Storm and the Hurricanes, another Liverpool group which had shared the Hamburg gigs. A recording of 'Love Me Do' by the new quartet reached the top twenty of the British charts in October 1962. 'Please Please Me', number two early the next year, was followed by three number ones;

the Beatles could not go anywhere in public without being mobbed, and popular music would never be the same again: rock'n'roll began to change to rock, which was no longer a fad, and in the decade of the 1960s the music business was altered beyond recognition.

Philip Norman, in his *Shout! The True Story of The Beatles* (1981), described what Kirchherr had captured in her photographs as their 'would-be toughness and undisguisable, all-protecting innocence'. For all Lennon's cynicism, a blanket of self-protection that came from his background as an orphan, and for all the high-jinks they had got up to in Hamburg's Reeperbahn, they were still Liverpool lads who could not believe their luck. They were greater than the sum of their parts; Lennon and McCartney wrote the songs, Lennon's acerbity balancing McCartney's tendency to sweetness, and their native cheekiness was a sort of genuine bravado.

The music of the British Invasion represented a climax of a decade of pop jingles. It was British variety influenced by the first wave of rock'n'roll, which was already over in the USA. The Beatles did it better than anyone else, and should have been the end of it, instead of inspiring generations of imitators. As long as the baby boom lasted, there was an inexhaustible supply of children who wanted either to be pop stars or to worship pop stars, so the business accommodated itself to raking in increasing amounts of money, and there was no reason to change anything, except that more accountants were required. Meanwhile, Bing Crosby, American cinema and Broadway songs had invaded and conquered Britain for decades, so now the British reversed the flow for a time.

'Love Me Do' was a sort of bouncy white blues which had the virtue of simplicity, and there was something pleasant about their essentially folkish harmony. 'She Loves You' was unremarkable, its 'Yeah, yeah yeah' chorus typical of the trashiness of pop. 'I Want To Hold Your Hand' was worse: one of the most irritating aspects of pop was the growing tendency not to bother writing a song at all; and the seven notes on the word 'hand' was a good example of the use of a cheap white imitation of melisma to disguise the paucity of the lyrics. This was a warning of the triumph of style over substance that was already taking place in pop, but in the Beatles' case better work was to come. They were tempted to follow Ringo around with pencil and paper because of the way he talked: 'That was a hard day's night,' he said after one gig, which gave them the name of a song and of their first film.

Capitol Records had been sold to EMI in 1955 for £3 million. Joseph Lockwood was criticized for paying so much, but by the end of the decade the label of Frank Sinatra, Nat 'King' Cole, the Kingston Trio and others was said to be worth £85 million. The UK came up with rock'n'roll stars such as Tommy Hicks (renamed Tommy Steele) who were pale imitations of the US product, until they found Cliff Richard, who in thirty years has had only nineteen hit singles in the USA, but a hundred in the UK. (Steele, not so incidentally, became an all-round entertainer in the end, in the music hall rather than the Presley tradition.) *Billboard* published an annual list of the world's best-selling artists based on charts in thirty-four countries, and suddenly in 1963 the top four were Cliff Richard, Elvis Presley, the Shadows (Cliff's backing band) and Frank Ifield, an Australian-born pop singer who specialized in old songs. All except Presley shared the same label (EMI-Columbia), producer (Norrie Paramor), manager and agent. Number seven on the list were the Beatles, also EMI artists, who the following year went to the top. Capitol in the USA passed on all of them, quite understandably; neither Richard nor Ifield became superstars in the USA, while the Ventures, a guitar band from Seattle, were already the homegrown equivalent of the Shadows. And who could have expected four kids from Liverpool to become the biggest act of the decade?

Frank Ifield's 'I Remember You' (a top ten hit by Jimmy Dorsey in 1944) was a top five US hit in 1963 on Vee-Jay, the black-owned Chicago label which also picked up the Beatles. After Motown in Detroit and Duke/Peacock in Houston (which remained strictly R & B and gospel), Vee-Jay was the most important black-owned label in the USA. It had been formed in 1953 by Vivian Carter Bracken and James Bracken, who were joined by Vivian's brother Calvin Carter. Their biggest act was the guitarist and singer Jimmy Reed, who also wrote songs and played a harmonica fixed on a wire bracket around his neck, as street singers had done and as Dylan did later. Reed's blues had a sweetness that took the edge off the usual Chicago passion; he began crossing over to the pop chart in 1957. Soul balladeer Jerry Butler had fourteen Vee-Jay hits between 1960 and 1966, nearly all of which dented the white chart; the Spaniels, the Dells and the El Dorados were vocal groups who crossed over. Frankie Valli was lead singer and Bob Gaudio (formerly of the Royal Teens) keyboard player and tunesmith in the Four Seasons, a white group which had three number ones in the pop chart in 1962 and 1963 on Vee-Jay before moving to Philips. There were many more Vee-Jay hits by Dee Clark, Rosco Gordon, John Lee Hooker and others; Gene Chandler's 'Duke of Earl' was a number one in both the white and black charts in 1962.

Ifield's hit came from left field to make a little money for Vee-Jay in 1963, more than a year after it had been more successful in England. The label had also taken a chance on 'Please Please Me' and 'From Me to You' back to back, the Beatles' second and third UK hits from early 1963, but they made no mark in the USA at first. Vee-Jay lost interest, and 'She Loves You' came out on Swan in the USA; 'Twist and Shout' / 'There's a Place' and 'Love Me Do' / 'P.S. I Love You' were issued in the USA on a Tollie label. But Capitol was prodded into action by their head office in London. As the Beatles flew to New York in January 1964 with an appearance on Ed Sullivan's show lined up, 'I Want To Hold Your Hand' backed with 'I Saw Her Standing There' was screaming up the USA pop chart, narrowly beating the Swan and Vee-Jay singles to the top. Vee-Jay had released the first Beatles album in the USA in July 1963, and it suddenly reached only number two in February 1964, because a Capitol album was already at number one: hip fans sought out the imported Parlophone editions, because they had seven songs on each side instead of six, owing to different methods of calculating song royalties on albums. Adding further to the confusion, two of the Tollie tracks appeared on the first pressing of the Vee-Jay album, and had to be changed in later editions. And this success was the beginning of the end for Vee-Jay.

Having suddenly to buy truckloads of pressings of Beatles records meant that Vee-Jay was short of cash, because distributors sat for up to ninety days on money needed to pay for new pressings. But that was not the whole story; a label that had already achieved so much in a decade should have been in a better position. When Vee-Jay collapsed in 1965, there were recriminations about financial dishonesty, but the truth was probably more prosaic. Nelson George quotes an anonymous participant at a Vee-Jay party for a dozen Chicago DJs that took place in Las Vegas in the early 1960s: they were asked what they wanted, and they did not want free poker chips; they wanted women, so the company flew a dozen tall blondes from Oslo across the North Pole for the weekend, spending a good deal of money that would have come in handy a couple of years later. Vee-Jay might have been as big as Motown, but it did not have Berry Gordy watching the bottom line.

John Fitzgerald Kennedy was murdered in November 1963; in early 1964 the Beatles helped cheer up the nation. Music lovers had to withhold judgement until hearing the records: the screaming on Sullivan's show in February was insane. If you went to the shopping mall to buy a Beatles album and they were sold out, you could buy the Dave Clark Five instead; this was another EMI act on which Capitol had passed, a beat group formed in London to benefit a football club. All they could do was thump, but they sold records.

Between 1963 and 1965, the height of the British Invasion (so dubbed by *Billboard*), fifteen EMI acts reached the chart in the USA, only six of which eventually appeared on Capitol. Capitol mopped up what was left of Vee-Jay and rode the gravy train for a few years: Nat Cole, whose Capitol albums are also still selling decades later, telephoned one day to be greeted by a cheerful 'Capitol Records, Home of the Beatles!' After the Fab Four broke up in 1970 Capitol found itself with a rack-jobbing distributorship, a mail-order record club and a bloated staff of hangers-on and their girlfriends, all losing money. The once great label formed by Johnny Mercer and his friends was managed no better than Vee-Jay.

Years later Bob Dylan (in Anthony Scaduto's 1971 biography) remembered driving across country in 1964 with the Beatles all over the radio dial. 'Their chords were outrageous, just outrageous, and their harmonies made it all valid. You could only do that with other musicians ... I knew they were pointing the direction where music had to go.' They were certainly pointing the direction in which rock would go, and gave Dylan the excuse to do it his way.

Another result of British interest in American roots music was a blues boom. Guitarist and vocalist Alexis Korner and banjoist turned harmonica player Cyril Davies had been members of Chris Barber's Jazz Band, which they left in 1961 to form Blues Incorporated. Despite visits from such bluesmen as Big Bill Broonzy, playing the blues was not an economic proposition. Caught between British imitation rock'n'roll and trad jazz, Korner and Davies played once a week or so in any club that would have them, ending up at the Marquee in London's Wardour Street.

Davies left in 1962 to form his own All Stars, taking over Screaming Lord Sutch's Savages, in which Nicky Hopkins played piano. When Davies died of leukaemia, vocalist Long John Baldry stepped in and formed the Hoochie Koochie Men, which included vocalist Rod Stewart. Baldry and Stewart went to Brian Auger's Steampacket, an interesting group that did not succeed; Baldry took over Bluesology, whose keyboard player was Reg Dwight (who later became Elton John). David Sutch was a rocker who never had much commercial success; he imitated Screaming Jay Hawkins and Jack the Ripper on stage, and now stands for Parliament for the Raving Monster Loony Party. Hopkins played piano with most of the rock greats, while Baldry eventually took his big voice to ballads, where he won some acclaim.

The British blues boom was destined to be eclipsed by rock when Mick Jagger and Keith Richards met on a train. They had been close friends when they were small, and they recognized each other and found something new in common: Jagger had been sending away to the USA for Chess albums, and had a bunch of them under his arm. They began to get together for private jams with Dick Taylor, who later formed the Pretty Things, a band which 'resembled nothing so much as *Spitting Image* puppets of the early Rolling Stones', according to English writer Charles Shaar Murray. When Jagger and Richards went to a gig at the Marquee, they heard a guest who sounded like Elmore James on slide guitar: Brian Jones. After adding older men Bill Wyman on bass and Charlie Watts on drums, they began performing.

'Can you imagine a British-composed R&B song? It just wouldn't make it,' said Jagger in 1963, before somebody told him how much money the Beatles were making with their own songs. Jagger was

right; British R & B was and is a contradiction in terms. The first
Stones album included songs by Rufus Thomas, Willie Dixon, Chuck
Berry, Slim Harpo and even Motown artists (Holland–Dozier–
Holland). They had their first UK chart entry in mid-1963; an
American edition of their first album reached number eleven in the
Billboard album chart in 1964, but many Americans could not figure
out why they should listen to white English kids singing Chuck
Berry when they already had Chuck Berry records. Giorgio
Gomelsky, manager of London's Crawdaddy Club, was the first
manager of the Stones; the bluesmen visiting London used to get
together at his home. He recalled, in Dixon's autobiography:

I'll never forget – it was an afternoon about four o'clock in March of
1964 or something. There was Howlin' Wolf, Sonny Boy [Williamson]
and Willie Dixon, the three of them sitting on this sofa . . . Willie was
just singing and tapping on the back of the chair and Sonny Boy would
play the harmonica and they would do new songs . . . These three grand
viziers were sitting on this thing and there's like Jimmy Page, Eric
Clapton and everybody sitting at their feet . . . I remember '300 Pounds
of Joy', 'Little Red Rooster', 'You Shook Me' . . . We'd heard them
really fresh, before anybody had made a record of them.

In fact, a song called 'Little Red Rooster' had been an R & B hit by
someone called Margie Day in 1951, and Wolf had already recorded
it. 'Little Red Rooster' was the first number one UK hit for the
Stones, in November 1964. But songs like that, when performed by
blacks for blacks in Chicago, were celebrations of the joy of sexuality;
sung by spotty ex-schoolboys, they conjured up only sweaty palms.
Whether that is fair or not is beside the point; there are social and
economic as well as rhythmic reasons for this. Songs such as Muddy
Waters's 'Rock Me' are pleas for comfort, for sanctuary in a cruel
world. When they were taken over by the rock generation, they came
to be about the domination of women, leading to the heavy metal
threat to 'nail your ass to the floor'.

On the one hand, the Stones were one of the few groups who gave
proper credit and paid royalties to the composer. As Jagger put in his
letter to *Melody Maker* in 1964, 'These legendary characters wouldn't
mean a light commercially today if groups were not going round

Britain doing their numbers.' In the early 1960s the US music industry was not admitting Willie Dixon to any Hall of Fame. On the other hand, the Stones were being promoted as opposite numbers to the Beatles: the Mop Tops were cute (however outrageous their behaviour behind closed doors); the Stones were arrested for urinating in public in 1965 and they refused to wave bye-bye with the other stars at the end of a television pop show. The dirtier and more surly the Stones were, the better. The credit 'Nanker Phelge' began to appear on their songs; a 'nankie', said Brian Jones, is a little man who thinks he represents authority; but it is an appropriate rock joke that 'nanker' rhymes with 'wanker', British slang for one whose greatest skill is for the solitary vice.

In any case, once the Stones were convinced they could write songs, 'Stupid Girl' may have been about a female who subscribed to social shibboleths which seemed to be going out of date, whether we liked it or not; 'Mother's Little Helper' was about the drugs house-wives took to get them through the day, while the press screamed about marijuana; 'Sittin' on the Fence' was about bitter-sweet reluc-tance to join a new generation of baby-boomers, helping the economy by tying themselves up in knots with mortgages and a new generation of babies. 'I Can't Get No Satisfaction' was their first number one in the USA in 1965. Jagger couldn't swing, and his execrable accent and phrasing should have been a drawback, but his narcissistic image was useful, and the band could swing. Watts was a jazz drummer who played well behind the beat, Richards and Jones were very good musicians indeed, and the band set Jagger off perfectly. Later, after Jones had left, Jagger seemed to be the nominal leader, but their manager Andrew Loog Oldham recalled years later:

Mick may have thought he was running the show, but Keith was always in charge of the music. When I was remastering one of the tracks for CD I came across something I had not noticed at the time. There was a song where the key was easy for Keith's voice, but had caused Mick trouble and he could hardly sing it.

I said to Keith: 'Did you pick the key for that song?' And he just looked at me and smiled.

In 1964 the Stones paid their respects in Chicago, where they made the EP *4 × 5* at the Chess studios; but they had eschewed the purism of the blues and soon garnered the title 'The World's Greatest Rock and Roll Band', and deserved it. The decade of the 1960s cannot be understood without their albums *Beggar's Banquet* (1968) and *Let It Bleed* (1969); the horrors of assassinations and war in Vietnam told us all too much about our 'Sympathy for the Devil'.

After the Beatles and the Stones, the two most successful British groups were the Who and the Kinks; both remained bigger in the UK but had cult followings in the USA. Pete Townshend's 'My Generation' (for the Who) typified the blatant self-indulgence of the era; their act made a fetish out of smashing their instruments, and they graduated to the grandiose 'rock opera' (*Tommy*). Drummer Keith Moon died in 1978 of an overdose of a drug he was taking to combat his alcoholism, and the survivors later realized they should have quit.

The Kinks' first hit was 'You Really Got Me' (1964), which resembled the Dave Clark Five's thumpers, but Ray Davies went on to create English music of his own. Even more than the Beatles' work, his was in the music hall tradition, and also grieved for a disappearing England. The caustic weariness of his 'Tired of Waiting for You' (1965) was followed by social commentary in 'Dedicated Follower of Fashion' and 'A Well Respected Man', and vignettes such as 'Sunny Afternoon' and 'Waterloo Sunset'. Davies was too bright to turn to drugs like others of the era, and understood the nature of the music business. (He went to the House of Lords to get himself out of a terrible management contract.) His concept albums in the 1970s were among the least grandiose of that genre, and the Kinks outlasted everybody except the Stones.

The British Invasion carried with it harmless pop and measures of fraud. The Small Faces had a fresh sound, and recorded on Andrew Loog Oldham's Immediate label: in 1969 they re-formed as the Faces, from which Rod Stewart emerged to become a generation's favourite Jack the Lad. The first three singles by Gerry and the Pacemakers, another Liverpool group produced by Martin, made history by all being number one UK hits. Billy J. Kramer's success was due to Martin's production and songs lent by the Beatles. Peter and Gordon were a preppy duo; Gordon Waller later imitated Elvis in *Joseph and His Amazing Technicolor Dreamcoat*, and Peter Asher became a prominent record producer. Some groups were successful in the USA because they were British, and remained virtually unknown at home, but the Strangeloves, Myles, Gyles and Nyles, pulled off the best joke: putting on accents and pretending to be British by way of Australia, they had hits in the mid-1960s, but they were actually American music insiders Bob Feldman, Jerry Goldstein and Richard Gottehrer.

The Strangeloves supported the Beach Boys on tour, who were in on the joke. The Beach Boys were an American act whose popularity was unaffected by the British; Brian, Dennis and Carl Wilson and cousins Mike Love and Al Jardine had over fifty hit singles from 1962. They stole some of their tunes from Chuck Berry, but their harmony was different; their clean-cut sound owed much to decades of pop from Glenn Miller's Modernaires to the Four Freshmen and the Hi-lo's. Dennis was full of alcohol when he drowned in 1983, while Brian, the most talented of the group, had addled his brain with drugs; yet what could be more innocent than their concern with surfing, cars and pretty girls? The apparent divorce of their hedonism from its consequences is a paradigm of their Californian lotus-land, and of rock itself.

There are many reasons why the 1960s still look like a golden age compared with the following decades. It had already been several years since the successful use of obviously black material by Elvis Presley, and the explosion of Chuck Berry, Fats Domino and Little Richard into the pop chart; the girl groups were mostly black, and the Motown hit factory's formula clearly appealed equally to black and white fans. Furthermore, the civil rights era was well under way: Americans were making a collective decision that second-class citizenship for a large minority was no longer acceptable, if only because they did not want to see southern police chiefs using dogs and fire-hoses against black schoolchildren on television. Between 30 November 1963 and 23 January 1965 there was no R&B chart in *Billboard*: for the first time in the history of popular music black and white fans were following the same music to such an extent that separate charts did not seem to be necessary, because rhythm and blues had triumphed in the form of soul music.

Ray Charles had left the Atlantic label for ABC-Paramount, where he made an unprecedented deal for a black entertainer, retaining

ownership of his own recordings. His version of Hoagy Carmichael's lovely 'Georgia on My Mind' was a huge hit in both charts.
He had already had a hit with Hank Snow's 'I'm Movin' On' on
Atlantic in 1959; for ABC he made two albums of country songs,
and his version of Don Gibson's 'I Can't Stop Loving You' was even
bigger than 'Georgia'.

Charles was born in Georgia but soon moved to Florida, where he
went blind as a child. He performed in the mid-1940s in Florida,
playing piano with a white country band, among others, and then
went as far away as he could within the USA, to Seattle, Washington.
There he led a trio in a style similar to that of Nat Cole, and had hits
including 'Baby Let Me Hold Your Hand' in the style of the West
Coast R&B crooner Charles Brown. On his very first recordings,
made at the age of seventeen on a friend's wire recorder in Florida,
although he was using the Nat Cole and Charles Brown trio style, his
honest moaning was that of a seasoned sufferer. (His mother had
recently died and he was extremely poor.) In 1951 he went on the
road with guitarist and vocalist Lowell Fulson, filling the shoes of
Lloyd Glenn, one of the most successful pianists in R&B. Jack
Lauderdale's West Coast Swing Time R&B label was going out of
business, and Atlantic snapped up Ray Charles.

The guitar turned out to be of the greatest importance – indeed it
has been played to death by countless white soundalike 'guitar
heroes' in the last twenty years. Aaron Thibeaux 'T-Bone' Walker
was the prime mover behind rock guitar, sharing the same teacher
and influences as Charlie Christian and doing for the instrument in
R&B what Christian did for it in jazz: he brought his intimate
baritone and his guitar playing to a huge number of tracks, nearly all
of which were blues but usually had a jazz-flavoured backing that
reveals much about the origins of R&B, and which must have been a
big influence on the young Ray Charles. The slide guitar of Elmore
James and his somewhat rougher country blues style derived from
Robert Johnson. The four Kings, B. B., Albert, Earl and Freddie, all
unrelated, all played guitar and had black hits. Riley 'Blues Boy'
King is the first of these in more ways than one, having become one
of the world's best-loved entertainers after decades of working the
chitlin' circuit, without changing himself or his act.

An extremely rich stew of rhythm and blues had been bubbling in the early 1950s. Ray Charles arranged and played piano on Guitar Slim's 'The Things That I Used to Do', a number one black hit for fourteen weeks in early 1954. (He was the best known of several entertainers to use the name Guitar Slim and one of the first to use a long lead on his electric guitar, so he could move around the stage.) Ray Charles then brought to black pop one of its most important ingredients: the music of the black church. In the late 1950s he finally crossed over to the white chart, but by then he was already a national institution; one of Bill Cosby's comedy routines had Columbus sailing to America so he could discover Ray Charles.

At his first Atlantic recording session Charles allegedly wanted to stick to his Brown-style crooning, but the label soon helped him change his mind. Tired of using pick-up musicians, he was now successful enough to form his own band. His first Atlantic hit was 'It Should've Been Me', a ghetto comedy which owed something to Louis Jordan and was the sort of thing which probably influenced Leiber and Stoller's work with the Coasters. In later hits he became completely himself, bringing the passion of religion to the aches and pains of the secular world, and even using the melodies of gospel music: 'Talkin' 'Bout Jesus' became 'Talkin' 'Bout You'; Clara Ward's 'This Little Light of Mine' became 'This Little Girl of Mine'; 'How Jesus Died' became 'Lonely Avenue'; and 'I've Got a Savior' became 'I Got a Woman', his first number one in the black chart, which shortly after was covered by Elvis Presley, who brought rockabilly urgency to it. Charles added a preaching, commentating female trio to his act, the Raelettes (sometimes spelled Raylettes), and there was even a touch of feminism: black women are not famous for taking a lot of nonsense, and the Raelettes carried 'What Kind of Man are You?' by themselves. Later, on Percy Mayfield's 'Hit the Road, Jack', Charles adds a man's patronizing puzzlement to the Raelettes' lead: 'Well, I guess if you say so / I'll have to pack my bags and go / ... You can't *mean* it!'

Religious blacks were scandalized when one of their stars changed to secular music. Popular as Sam Cooke had been with the Soul Stirrers, he was booed when he turned up at a gospel meeting after having pop hits. Of Ray Charles, Big Bill Broonzy said, 'He's mixing the blues with the spirituals. I know that's wrong ... He should be singing in a church.' The relationship between the blues and the church was already well known to aficionados, and the gospel recordings of Blind Willie Johnson (1927–30) and Rev. Gary Davis (from 1935) were highly prized. Black gospel music, though a thriving market, was not widely known in the white community; nevertheless, such fine singers as Claude Jeter (with the Swan Silvertones) and Archie Brownlee (with the Five Blind Boys) had a profound indirect influence on popular music.

In the early 1950s Mahalia Jackson, an artist of the stature of Bessie Smith who refused to record secular material, became known throughout the white community. While Ray Charles was still registering only in the black chart, Little Richard's sanctified screaming and Sam Cooke's beautiful gospel melisma reached the white charts. The Staple Singers' gospel recordings for Vee-Jay in the 1950s included 'This Could be the Last Time', later covered by the Rolling Stones, with the lyrics adapted. Charles's first top ten hit in the white chart, and one of his last singles on Atlantic, was 'What'd I Say', which came as a considerable revelation in 1959 because of its driving passion and call-and-response moaning.

His 1961 album with members of the Basie band was called *Genius + Soul = Jazz*. The word 'soul' was already in wide use in black culture: soul food, soul music; one of Charles Mingus's best-known tunes is 'Better Git It in Your Soul'. The addition of the feeling of the church to R & B was immediately called soul. As the soul is the essence of a human being, so soul in music, like swing, is self-expression.

The gift of soul to America at last began to bear fruit during the civil rights era, which unexpectedly, perhaps, seemed to begin with Louis Armstrong. Louis had given up leading big bands after a sensationally successful Town Hall concert in New York in 1947 by a small integrated band including Jack Teagarden, Bobby Hackett, Peanuts Hucko (clarinet), Dick Cary (piano), Bob Haggart (bass) and Sid Catlett (drums). He toured for the rest of his life with his All Stars. In 1955 a European tour was so successful (more so than an East–West summit in Switzerland at the same time) that it made headlines all over the world; an album of live recordings was issued as *Ambassador Satch*, on which Edmond Hall plays clarinet and Trummy Young trombone. The State Department then decided to sponsor tours by one of America's most popular exports.

Louis was never noted for racial controversy; some regarded him as an Uncle Tom, but others knew better: as Billie Holiday put it, 'Pops toms from the heart.' Music transcended race. But in May 1957 the United States Supreme Court struck down the pernicious 'separate but equal' doctrine that had ensured second-rate educational facilities for black children, ruling that the states must end segregation in the schools; on 3 September at Little Rock, Arkansas, the state's National Guard was used to prevent black students from entering Central High School; and on the 18th, in Grand Forks, North Dakota, Armstrong was watching live coverage on television as a howling mob of white trash confronted a handful of frightened black children. A local reporter got the scoop of his life when a furious Armstrong told him that the President had 'no guts', allowing a 'plowboy' like Governor Orville Faubus to run the country, and that 'the way they are treating my people in the South, the government can go to hell'. America's best-loved entertainer had made headlines in spite of himself. Two days later a federal court ordered Faubus to stop using the National Guard to defy the law, and on 23 September Eisenhower sent federal troops to Little Rock to prevent mob rule. After nearly a century of *de facto* second-class citizenship for blacks, the civil rights era was under way.

The Interstate Commerce Commission ordered the desegregation of bus and rail terminals. A new Civil Rights Bill was to be introduced by the Kennedy administration when he was murdered (and one of my co-workers in the car factory muttered, 'It's about time somebody got that nigger-lover'). A few days later the *Billboard* R&B chart was abolished. Up to that date both black and white acts such as Garnet Mimms and the Enchanters, Jackie Wilson, the Chiffons, Mary Wells, Leslie Gore, Jimmy Gilmer and the Fireballs had had hits riding high in both the black and white pop charts. But the Beatles and the rest of the British Invasion dominated the pop chart from early 1964; the *Billboard* R&B chart reappeared a year later, and no Beatles record ever appeared in it, despite their love for black pop. It was not until August 1969, when classic soul had peaked, that the name of the chart was changed to 'Best Selling Soul Singles'.

James Brown was unique, as important a progenitor of soul as Ray Charles. He came from poverty and prison for teenage offences to put together a soul revue made up of elements of gospel, black vaudeville and the influence of R & B pioneers such as Jordan (who thought of himself first and last as an entertainer). Singer, songwriter, producer and bandleader James Brown maintained absolute control over every aspect of his show, riding his band so hard that they would leave him, forcing him to re-form more than once; also the best in the business, they were called the Famous Flames, and later the JBs. He was known as the Godfather of Soul, Mr Dynamite and the Hardest-working Man in Show Business. His first hit, 'Please, Please, Please' (on Federal), was nothing but a passionately incantatory plea: Syd Nathan at King did not understand it, but Ralph Bass talked him into it, and it was a top five in the black chart in 1956. Brown's next hit, 'Try Me' (1958), crossed over to the pop chart.

Again and again Brown was ahead of the label. When King would not record his dance hit '(Do the) Mashed Potatoes', he recorded it in Florida under his drummer's name (Nat Kendricks and the Swans, with vocal shouts by Miami DJ 'King' Coleman), and it was a 1960 hit on both charts. When King didn't think a live album would be worth doing, Brown paid for the recording himself, and had a number two hit in the *Billboard* pop album chart in mid-1963 with *Live at the Apollo*, still regarded as one of the most exciting live albums ever made. In twenty years he had nearly one hundred hits in the pop chart, and well over one hundred in the black. Not only were 'Papa's Got a Brand New Bag' (1965) and 'Say It Loud – I'm Black and Proud' (1968) number one black hits and top tens in the white chart, but their titles entered the language. His hits slowed down when he was eclipsed by mechanical disco music and hip-hop, both of which owed nearly everything to him.

Clyde McPhatter was essentially a soul singer; with the various editions of the Drifters, the voice of Ben E. King and all its other assets, and the perfection of its sound, thanks to engineer Tommy Dowd, and its backbeat, thanks to arranger Jesse Stone, Atlantic might have been the most important soul factory all by itself. When Mercury covered LaVern Baker's 'Tweedle-dee' with Georgia Gibbs, they hired the musicians who had played on the Baker record and they wanted Dowd as well, but he would not take the job. And the importance of Stone cannot be overestimated.

Stone's territory band, the Blues Serenaders, recorded for Okeh in 1927, and 'Starvation Blues' is described thus by Gunther Schuller in his *Early Jazz*:

In fact, in 1927 jazz could as yet offer very little that matched the depth of feeling that Stone's orchestra purveyed ... This expressivity was achieved in terms of (or perhaps despite) written-out arrangements, and very advanced, sophisticated ones at that. For Jesse Stone was a well-trained musician, a composer and arranger.

Stone played piano for George E. Lee (Julia's bandleader brother), and for that band wrote 'Paseo Strut', of which a lovely recording was made in Kansas City in 1929. He wrote arrangements for the Kansas City Skyrockets in 1934, and later for Jimmie Lunceford, Harlan Leonard and Earl Hines. Then he replaced Eddie Durham as music director of the International Sweethearts of Rhythm, a very good all-girl mixed-race band that had run away from an orphanage. (It played for big crowds and appeared in films during the 1940s, but never had a good recording contract.) Stone's compositions included 'Idaho' for one of Roy Rogers's films, a hit for the bands of Alvino Rey and Benny Goodman, and 'Sorghum Switch' for Doc Wheeler, covered for a hit by Jimmy Dorsey (both 1942); retitled 'Cole Slaw', the latter was a hit for saxophonists Frank Culley and Louis Jordan in 1949.

In 1950 Stone experimented at Atlantic, working on Ruth Brown's recordings, and rehearsing and recording the vocal groups. He was not the only arranger at Atlantic, but the most important. When the Chords brought in 'Sh-boom', Stone recorded it for Atlantic's subsidiary Cat, and was thus responsible for one of the first big hits of the rock'n'roll era (albeit in the nasty copycat version by the Crew-cuts). He arranged 'Chains of Love' and 'Shake, Rattle and Roll' (taking composer credit as Charles Calhoun) for Joe Turner and wrote 'Money Honey', the first recording by the Drifters and their first big hit; it was number one in the black chart for eleven weeks in 1953, and later covered by Elvis Presley. Stone was one of those who helped persuade Ray Charles to let his hair down when he came to Atlantic. He took a break in 1954 to be A & R director at Lamp, an East Coast subsidiary of Aladdin which failed, but one of its groups, the Cookies, became Ray Charles's Raelettes.

It was at Atlantic that Stone had an unsung influence on the music of ensuing decades. Atlantic's recordings were more polished than those of other R & B labels, as though they were intended to be hits, rather than just slung into the market to see what happened; yet they also swung, because people like Stone brought the skills and values of decades of black music with them.

As the golden age of soul approached, Atlantic received a massive boost from a historical accident. Satellite Records was formed in 1960 in Memphis, Tennessee, by Jim Stewart and his sister, Estelle Axton, to record local talent. A local white R & B group called the Royal Spades became the house band, and had a national hit with 'Last Night' on Satellite, but shortly after the name of the label was changed to Stax, because there was already a Satellite label on the West Coast. In the band were guitarist Steve Cropper and bass player Donald 'Duck' Dunn; it soon mutated into Booker T. and the MGs (for 'Memphis Group'), which had Booker T. Jones on keyboards and Al Jackson on drums. The Memphis Horns originally included Charles 'Packy' Axton on tenor saxophone, Don Nix on baritone and Wayne Jackson on trumpet. Thus a bunch of country boys, both white and black, working for an amateur record company, laid down their own tracks as well as backing some of the most beautiful black voices of the decade, and together polished one of the great facets of American music at a time when they could not eat together at a local lunch counter.

Fame Studios was started in Muscle Shoals, a town built on reclaimed land across the river from Florence, Alabama, with producers Rick Hall and Billy Sherrill (who was later a leading producer in Nashville country music). Bellboy Arthur Alexander wrote songs and worked with Hall, and Fame leased his hits to Dot: 'Anna (Go to Him)' was a top ten black hit in 1962, and was covered by the Beatles. Otis Redding was the greatest Stax discovery; he died in a plane crash just as he was hitting the big time, but had about thirty hit singles in six years. Stax had made a distribution agreement with

Atlantic, and that label's Jerry Wexler sent Aretha Franklin, Wilson Pickett, Solomon Burke, Don Covay, Ben E. King, Joe Tex and others to Memphis and/or Alabama to record.

With the success of Redding, Jerry Wexler assigned Sam and Dave to Stax; Isaac Hayes and David Porter wrote songs for them. Wexler dispatched Tommy Dowd to Memphis to bring Stax's technology into the modern era, and Stax and Atlantic began copying each other. The Memphis black and white soul fusion, Wexler saw, was something that no money could buy, yet his influence inevitably helped to ruin it, by changing it. There would always have been a danger that Atlantic's polish would be overdone (and in fact the label soon turned to slickly produced white pop), but Memphis had been a return to head arrangements and to a house rhythm section. The amateurish management and racially charged atmosphere was available for classic recording until Stax made the mistake of asking itself how it had done what it did in the first place: personalities intruded and the magic was lost. But not right away.

Wilson Pickett, who was not an easy man to get along with, went to Stax after two flop singles to record with Booker T. and the MGs. This resulted in 'In the Midnight Hour' (co-written with Steve Cropper) and '634–5789' (by Cropper and Eddie Floyd), Pickett's first two black-chart number ones, in 1966. After three sessions at Stax Pickett never came back and neither did Wexler; but Pickett recorded at Fame.

Aretha Franklin was the daughter of the Rev. C. L. Franklin, a famous gospel artist; she sang in his Detroit Baptist church and was contracted to Columbia between 1961 and 1966, when she made worthy recordings which didn't sell, and then changed to Atlantic. She made only one recording session in Muscle Shoals. Alcohol was flowing and hostility broke out between her husband and one of the locals, but 'I Never Loved a Man (the Way I Loved You)' was recorded, and a start made at the flip side, 'Do Right Woman – Do Right Man'; this was a mess that nobody liked, a demonstration tape with Dan Penn's voice on it. The first became a pop top ten and was number one in the black chart for seven weeks in 1967; the second was turned into another soul classic at Atlantic, with Aretha's piano and her sisters singing back-up. Wexler and Hall had quarrelled, so

Wexler hired Oldham and others to come to New York to work on a King Curtis album and, without telling Hall, also used them on the rest of Aretha's first Atlantic album, named after the first hit. It was number three in the *Billboard* album chart, and included her first number one pop hit, which was also number one (for eight weeks) in the black chart: she made Otis Redding's 'Respect' for ever her own. Nobody who listened to the radio at all could be ignorant of soul, once the Queen arrived; but Wexler had soon broken with everybody.

By this time psychedelia and the drug culture were well under way. In New York the Velvet Underground, including vocalist-songwriter Lou Reed, made albums of understated songs about heroin and masochism which recorded the underbelly of urban culture without celebrating it: their feeling of doom was real, not schoolboy self-indulgence. Their influence did not become evident until after they had split up. To some extent it was pressure from the counterculture that stopped Lyndon Johnson from running again in 1968, and it was a victory of sorts when Chicago policemen stupidly rioted outside the Democratic national convention that year, for Mayor Richard J. Daley was several decades out of touch. The Grateful Dead, Jefferson Airplane and others were basically very loud West Coast folk bands. The Beatles and George Martin had produced their music hall masterpiece, *Sgt Pepper's Lonely Hearts Club Band*, and at the end of that year the Rolling Stones, who were hopelessly unsuited to psyche-delia, released *Their Satanic Majesties Request*, a failure, and then went on to do their best work. Jim Morrison ('Death and my cock are the world') and the Doors had seven top ten albums from 1967 to 1971. The Woodstock Festival in August 1969 was a sodden disaster in a muddy field, but felt like the triumph of peace. Black San Francisco DJ and sometime producer Sylvester Stewart, as Sly Stone, put together Sly and the Family Stone, an integrated 'psychedelic soul' outfit, which experimentally pulled together several of the era's strands to make joyous music that made dancing shoes twitch.

Janis Joplin, from Port Arthur, Texas, seemed to have an exciting voice for a white girl because she was willing to throw it away for the sake of a good time tonight, and forget tomorrow. She was an unhappy, insecure girl who took to drugs and alcohol; appearing at a

Stax/Volt Christmas party at the end of 1968, she strolled on after her band had spent fifteen minutes setting up, carrying her bottle of Southern Comfort, and could not understand why people started to leave; they had watched some of the classiest professional acts in the business, including all the Stax stars and Mr James Brown himself, acts that prided themselves on their professionalism and their respect for their audience. They were insulted by Janis Joplin.

The black guitarist Jimi Hendrix had been fired from job after job on the R&B circuit. He was unpunctual, he wore funny clothes that looked like they had been slept in, and indulged in his own funny business on the stand, distracting the audience from the attraction, whether it was a nobody MC like 'Gorgeous' George Odell or a star like Little Richard. Black entertainers who had worked themselves out of poverty by putting on a professional show did not need a weird black hippie like Hendrix to spoil it; he would not have lasted five minutes with James Brown. Nevertheless, let it be said that 'I Don't Know What You've Got (But It's Got Me)', a Don Covay song recorded by Little Richard in 1965 with Hendrix on guitar, is described by Peter Guralnick as 'the Mount Rushmore of Soul'.

In any case, Hendrix was nothing like as confused as Joplin. He knew exactly what he was doing; it was just that his guitar was everything, and the rest didn't matter. He had absorbed the Delta blues, the R&B of the chitlin' circuit and the lessons of soul. He became the complete master of the electric guitar at a time when its technology was still relatively primitive, and he knew his jazz too: when he went to 'swinging' London to set it on its ear, he carried with him his favourite album by Roland Kirk, a blind saxophonist who could play three horns at once. Joplin was a mess, the Beatles were prisoners of their own fame and some of the biggest white pop stars of the era were vain monsters. But Hendrix was the best musician of them all, and the only black to become a superstar on the same level as the rest. He returned to the USA a conquering hero.

The Jimi Hendrix Experience, a trio, included Mitch Mitchell on drums and Noel Redding on bass, both of whom were basically jazz-oriented English musicians. They had hit singles in England and the USA and made hit albums, but Hendrix was hassled by money problems (because of a contract he had signed in New York with a music business shark named Ed Chalpin), by racial politics (certain people thought he should be using black sidemen) and by his own propensity for hedonism. But he was composing unique material, with lyrics as allusive as Dylan's, and there were signs that he was pulling his act together: Hendrix might have made a fusion of black and white musics to be getting on with.

The legendary decade of the 1960s really began only in 1964, when the Beatles swept the USA, or perhaps even later, when the hippie phenomenon was celebrated in *Time* magazine, at about the time Hendrix returned to the USA. By then the psychedelic influence in design (posters, record albums, clothes) seemed ubiquitous, and use of marijuana was becoming common among middle-class youth. And there was the foolish disaster of the war in Vietnam to protest about. Only a bit more than two years had passed between the first Monterey Pop Festival, where the Hendrix Experience made its US début, and Woodstock, which in retrospect was the beginning of the end. But it all seemed to have happened rather suddenly, and it did seem like the counterculture was taking over.

It has become commonplace to speak of the 1960s as being dominated by the narcissism of the baby boom, but the fact that that generation had enough leisure and prosperity to allow introspection was not in itself a bad thing; in fact, it is a necessary (if not sufficient) condition for the creation of art. Furthermore, that generation had to make its own popular culture, including its music, out of the influences that it found available, and unlike previous generations, it had been largely cut off from many of its own cultural roots, yet it was a large enough generation to sustain some artists of integrity. It is clear with hindsight that it was the singer-songwriters, the troubadours, rather than the pop groups and rock bands, who recorded the 1960s with humour and style.

The most important trend in the broader popular music of the last two decades has been that rock'n'roll and its best songwriting have gone back to the prairies and the gin mills whence they came. Country music, with its strings and choirs, was overproduced during the 1960s, and came to be called 'countrypolitan', leading to the reaction described in Jan Reid's book *The Improbable Rise of Redneck Rock* (1974). But this is not so surprising. The folk-rock and country-rock of the fab decade, with elements of the singer-songwriter phenomenon mixed in, soon retired from the charts, but the best rock was always a fusion of several genres.

It was not necessary to pay much attention to pop in the 1960s unless you were a card-carrying member of the counterculture; if any of it was any good, it would be around long enough to seep into the consciousness. We knew from the history of popular music that if we liked something that turned out to be a cover, the original would be worth investigating: many people had discovered black music through white covers in the 1950s, and, similarly, some discovered Bob Dylan through the Byrds and Peter, Paul and Mary. Meanwhile, we danced with each other's wives, for example in a basement joint in Kenosha called Mr Z's. (We were so much older then; we're younger than that now.) We heard numerous touring rock'n'roll bands in the period when the music was coming to be called rock; those of us in back-waters like Kenosha didn't mind that we had never heard of any of the bands, and anyhow some of them were pretty good. One of them was probably the Hawks.

They were a quintet of Canadians, except for the drummer, who was from Arkansas. They were called the Hawks because they had started out backing an Arkansas rockabilly called Ronnie Hawkins. Then they backed blues singer John Hammond, son of Columbia's A & R man, and, in 1966, Dylan, on a controversial tour. After much screaming and cat-calling from outraged folkies, for example at the Albert Hall in London, guitarist Robbie Robertson later said, 'We'd go back to the hotel room, listen to a tape of the show and think, shit, that's not so bad. Why is everybody so upset?' The folkies did not know that rock'n'roll *is* folk music. Maybe they should have danced at Mr Z's with other people's wives.

When the Hawks wanted a new name, they chose the Band, because that was what they had always called the group. They made the famous bootleg 'basement tapes' with Dylan near Woodstock, New York, later released commercially; their own first album, released in 1968, was called *Big Pink*, after the house with the famous basement. They had learned how to do what they did by playing in bars, back rooms and dance halls back and forth across North America, so that shortly after they began making their own albums they were described as the only band that could have warmed up the crowd for Abraham Lincoln. They played 'Long Black Veil', a country hit in 1959 which had been covered by Joan Baez, and which sounds like a copyrighted folksong. They sang Dylan songs and songs co-written with Dylan, such as 'Tears of Rage' and 'This Wheel's on Fire', as well as Robertson's 'The Weight', 'Up on Cripple Creek' and 'The Night They Drove Old Dixie Down' (which was a hit for Baez, who would have done better in the late 1960s if she could have found more good songs). They quit, after sixteen years on the road, so as not to end up parodying themselves. On Thanksgiving Day in 1976 the Band had a party in San Francisco, with an audience and many musical guests, which was recorded and made into the film *The Last Waltz*.

Another good band was Little Feat, whose albums *Dixie Chicken* and *Feats Don't Fail Me Now* carried the same fusion of rock'n'roll, country, blues and folk, and the singing and slide guitar of Lowell George, who was to die of a drug-related heart attack in 1979. Essentially, the Hawks and Little Feat were two of the best and most successful bar bands, of which there were plenty, especially in the South-west, just as in the 1920s, when they were called territory bands. In the 1960s, Doug Sahm (born in San Antonio in 1941) had a few hits with a Tex-Mex flavour as the Sir Douglas Quintet (either muscling in on or sending up the British Invasion); his later career has marked the tip of a valuable sub-genre called swamp rock. In Tulsa, Oklahoma, Rockin' Jimmy and the Brothers of the Night made two albums in the early 1980s and then gave up, because vocalist and songwriter Jimmy Byfield did not want to go on the road: a rocker who actually walked away from fame. But the albums are great fun.

The Byrds, whose pretty harmony came by way of bluegrass, and Gram Parsons, who had various groups, are credited with inventing country rock. Parsons was a member of the Byrds when they recorded their album *Sweetheart of the Rodeo* (1968), which is regarded as a rock classic and a signpost to the fusion, but true rock'n'roll already had a good deal of country in it. Ex-Byrd Chris Hillman and Parsons formed the Flying Burrito Brothers, who were less self-consciously pop: *Burrito Deluxe* (1970) was a better classic in its own quiet way, some tracks using an accordion for a touch of Tex-Mex. Parsons was not yet twenty-seven when he died of the effects of too much drink and drugs in a motel in California, in 1973; meanwhile, Hillman and Parsons had discovered Emmylou Harris, a would-be folksinger who made one terrible album in 1969.

Having found her true musical nature singing harmony with Parsons, she became the Queen of Country Rock and easily one of the most valuable American recording artists of the era. Her proper début album *Pieces of the Sky* (1975) included 'From Boulder to Birmingham', her tribute to Parsons; before long she had formed her aptly named Hot Band, with such good musicians as the British-born guitarist Albert Lee, multi-instrumentalist Ricky Skaggs, soon a country star himself, and James Burton, sometime sideman with Rick Nelson and Presley and one of the best American guitarists of all. Although she seems basically to be a country artist, every Harris album reaches high in the pop chart; she writes songs herself, but has enough taste and good sense to draw her material from wherever she likes – R & B, classic country, even Hollywood – making it all her own. Each track is respectably skilful in production terms, yet the band sounds like a bunch of friends having a good time. Her guest appearance in the film *The Last Waltz*, singing Robertson's 'Evange-line', was one of its high points.

Kitty Wells had staked out territory in the country market that would for ever belong to the women. Patsy Cline, Loretta Lynn, Tammy Wynette and several more have been highly regarded; even if the production of some of their albums had been too smooth in Nashville's countrypolitan era, their professionalism, good songs, down-home values and no-nonsense attitudes defined them as people who could be trusted. There are too many fine songs and songwriters to list here, but Harlan Howard's hits, for example, many for girl singers, include 'Pick Me Up on Your Way Down', 'Heartaches by the Number', 'Too Many Rivers', 'I Fall to Pieces', 'Busted' (for Ray Charles); the total is said to include sixty number ones in a chart where success still meant something besides money. Dolly Parton came from a television and recording partnership with country star Porter Wagoner to be one of the greatest of all. Her own excellent songs, such as 'Coat of Many Colors' and 'Jolene', show a degree of integrity that so many women in music have known how to retain; she branched out into the cinema and the chat-show circuit and now seems to have left songwriting, but not before she reminded us how important good songs are.

Linda Ronstadt, originally in a folk-rock group called the Stone Poneys, came to be widely popular in the 1970s. Her albums, produced by Peter Asher, were too slick, and when she tried to do Frank Sinatra's type of songs, she was utterly unable to phrase them as required. But there was no doubting her lovely voice and her skill with more suitable material. Harris, Parton and Ronstadt made an album called *Trio* in 1987 which in several ways capped all their careers: singing solo and in various combinations, they demonstrated many of the strengths always to be found in American music, especially beauty.

Bonnie Raitt, daughter of John Raitt (Broadway star of *Carousel* in 1945, *The Pajama Game* in 1954 and others), was a good guitarist with a distinctive voice and emotionally mature beyond her years. She performed a selection of material that could have been called white blues or country rock, but added up to what rock'n'roll should always have been. Most of her albums made the pop chart without setting any sales records; in the mid-to-late 1980s a couple of them suffered from the endemic pop problem of overproduction, ridiculously stiff rhythm sections and bad songs. She came back in 1990 with *Nick of Time*, which won four Grammys and single-handedly almost restored some honour to the whole idea of music awards. Guitarist and singer Ry Cooder was a well-known sideman on many record dates, including some with the Rolling Stones. He began making a series of albums celebrating the whole history of American post-war pop, from R&B and rock'n'roll to Tex-Mex and much else; although they are still selling, he was never rewarded in chart terms, and latterly concentrated on atmospheric film music. (But in the 1990s he branched out even further, making duet albums with 'world music' guitarists such as the Indian Vishwa Mohan Bhatt and the West African bluesman Ali Farka Toure, and gathered kudos all over again.)

Singer-songwriters contributed a viable commercial genre for a while, and among the best of the confessionalist type was James Taylor, who came through much self-indulgence and a marriage to Carly Simon, which was destructive to both their careers, to retain a

large following. Two confessing narcissists in one household may
have been too many, but Simon herself, from the publishing family
of Simon and Schuster, was a valuable commentator. Her best-known
song was 'You're So Vain', which might have been about any of the
world's most visible boyfriends, but was mainly a flash of insight
into her own generation. Jackson Browne, despite the critical wise-
guy label of 'chilled white whine', has done some good work. Carole
King's *Tapestry* in 1971 matched *Sgt Pepper* in the US charts.

Joni Mitchell was a Canadian whose singing, writing, guitar playing, painting and photography were all of a piece. She examined
herself and her emotions with the detachment of an artist, and wrote
such songs as 'Big Yellow Taxi', 'Both Sides Now' and 'The Circle
Game', which were unusual in her generation (but not in her genre)
in that they were good enough to be widely covered.

One of the greatest of all was Van Morrison, from Northern
Ireland, an unlikely pop star who hates the music business and rarely
gives interviews. His father's record collection included Hank Williams and Leadbelly; he began in a pop group called Them, made one
solo album in 1967, which he later disowned, then threw the dice.
Stranded in New York when his producer Bert Berns died of a heart
attack, he signed a solo deal and made *Astral Weeks* in forty-eight
hours, embarking on a career that combined the blues, biographical
yearning and Celtic mysticism. He became a giant, one of the few
troubadours to compare with Bob Dylan.

Many of these people have done their best work. Several of
Mitchell's last albums have suffered from the studio-bound production of her husband; some people complain that Van the Man is
repeating himself. Some of the chroniclers of their times did not
survive: Phil Ochs was a powerful songwriter whose work was tied
up with his politics, and killed himself when it was evident that
music could not change the world. David Blue died of a heart attack
while jogging. Tim Hardin died of drugs, his own haunting version
of his folk-blues 'If I Were a Carpenter' showing up any number of
polished hit covers. The much loved Jim Croce ('I'll Have to Say I
Love You in a Song') was killed in a car crash.

But there are dozens, probably hundreds more still at it: Jack
Elliott, Loudon Wainwright, John D. Loudermilk, Tom Paxton

(whose other love is baseball), John Prine, Janis Ian, Laura Nyro, John Stewart, Ian Tyson, to name just a few. Mitch Miller made a wisecrack about Nyro, talking about the music of the era: 'Where is Laura Nyro now?' But she had left music for a few years, which was her business, and when she came back, the commercial success of the genre had peaked. Those who were enchanted by her albums still are; her delivery of her songs may have been highly wrought, but they were good enough to be covered by the likes of Ronstadt, Aretha Franklin, Thelma Houston, Frank Sinatra and Barbra Streisand, as well as pop groups.

John Stewart left the Cumberland Three to join the Kingston Trio, unable to turn down such a lucrative offer, but knowing that he could not bring politics to their act; he later worked for Bobby Kennedy, who had a tin ear but understood the importance of music, and (some feel) may have been our greatest political loss in a bloody decade. Ian Tyson was successful with his then wife Sylvia Fricker in the Canadian folk duo in the 1960s, and is now a rancher; both Stewart and Tyson are still writing good songs.

Some of the Byrds stayed in country rock or went back to the neo-bluegrass they started out with: there are all kinds of lovely records on tiny labels by people like Chris Hillman, groups called Old and in the Way and others who never found it necessary to pretend to be progressive. Buffalo Springfield was a pop band, for whom Steven Stills wrote 'For What It's Worth (Stop, Hey, What's That Sound)' after a police riot in Los Angeles; the song was a hit in 1967 and remains a potent artefact. Crosby (from the Byrds), Stills and Young (from Buffalo Springfield) and Nash (from the British group the Hollies) formed a vocal supergroup; they sang pretty, but reunions didn't work. Canadian-born Young carried on; over twenty albums of varying quality have now been in the chart. His earliest ones, with a group of friends called Crazy Horse, are essential, and another in 1990 was a reunion with them; rock critics gave it high marks with obvious feelings of relief.

In England such folk-rock bands as Steeleye Span, Pentangle and Fairport Convention mutated into new groups, or have reunions. The number of good musicians who have passed through them and sing and play together in various combinations is very high: any gig with Ashley Hutchings, Martin Carthy, John Kirkpatrick, Bert Jansch, John Renbourn, Dave Swarbrick or Ralph McTell must be worth attending, while singer, songwriter and guitarist Richard Thompson was described as England's best-kept secret. Among the younger generation of eclectic folk-popsters, the Pogues are always interesting. The Men They Couldn't Hang was a British folk-rock band that has already gone: their label, MCA, released the single the boys wanted to put out, but did not bother to promote it. Why did they sign them in the first place? And since the market is already there, why cannot broadcasters make more room for it at the expense of pre-teen music? The way the business makes its decisions remains a mystery.

There were occasionally new singer-songwriters, of whom one of the best was Joan Armatrading, who released her first solo album in 1975. Her love songs were literate, and had the detachment that is necessary for a useful appraisal of anything, qualities which seem to be lacking in later, younger confessors.

There can be no doubt that today many of the best troubadours and balladeers come from the prairies, a psychological and metaphysical area the geographical centre of which is Texas. Jerry Jeff Walker is a folkie turned country rocker who had a couple of chart entries decades ago and has long been an adopted Texan. His music, like all the music in this genre, is full of smiles; he introduced a live album by saying 'Howdy, buckaroos', both sending up and celebrating himself, his music and his audience. His generous CD selection of his own songs, *Gypsy Songman* (1987), is a joy: no intrusive production, just guitars, fiddles, love songs, story songs and jump tunes.

J. J.'s earlier album tracks include 'Standing at the Big Hotel', and one of his Hot 100 entries was called 'L.A. Freeway'. Among the joys of country rock is that the songs are real songs, worth covering; consequently it is again fun and rewarding to look at the name of the composer under the name of the song on the label: 'Standing at the Big Hotel' is by Butch Hancock, and 'L.A. Freeway' is by Guy Clark.

Hancock's first set, around 1978, was a solo effort called *West Texas Waltzes and Dust Blown Tractor Tunes*, and obviously influenced by Bob Dylan. His words are worth listening to, like Dylan's, but this is shit-kicking music, in the best sense: his family have survived farming in that tough country for decades, and no Hancock needs a major-label deal to make music. He has more energy, more positive directness and more humour in his music than Dylan. *Firewater Seeks Its Own Level* (1981) was recorded live in the Alamo Lounge in Austin, with Butch, a bass, an electric guitar and a fiddle: no drums, no production to speak of (no room behind the bar), just a great deal of fun. A. P. Carter's gospel blues 'There's No Hiding Place Down Here' swings like anything and has hot solos, and the title song is one of Butch's best:

> You got drunk last night
> You say you seen the Devil?
> Don't you know firewater
> Seeks its own level?

The verses are too long to quote here, but they excoriate the self-pity of the loved and lost, with rough humour and sympathy. The song's structure, interestingly, seems to recover and turn on its head those Tin Pan Alley story songs of around 1910, but it is done artlessly, adding the swing and vernacular values that that genre lacked; and the long verses are not one word too long.

Guy Clark's songs have been covered by David Allan Coe (a jailbird whose own 'Would You Lay With Me in a Field of Stone' and 'Take This Job and Shove It' are classics in the genre), as well as by Walker, Skaggs, Johnny Cash, Bobby Bare and others. Some of his songs are the ones against which all others should be measured: like all good songs, they are for people who have to try to live in the real world. 'L.A. Freeway' is for anybody who wonders what he or she is doing stuck in a traffic jam; 'Home Grown Tomatoes' should make you want to go out and plant some seeds; 'Texas 1947' is about the day the steam locomotive was replaced by the diesel-electric: a small, dusty town turns out to watch the silver Streamliner go by, and it doesn't even stop, but nothing will ever be the same again. 'Desperadoes Waiting for a Train' is about a bunch of old men playing dominoes, beer stains on their shirts, waiting for death, one of whom is the singer's father: 'I mean, he's one of the heroes of this country / What's he doin' dressed up like some old man?' If 'Virginia's Reel' and 'New Cut Road' don't make you feel good, if 'Fool in the

Mirror' doesn't make you laugh, you may as well lie down; you must be dead.

There is Willie Nelson, godfather of all the redneck rockers, whose 'Hello Walls' and 'Night Life' became country classics in the 1960s, by Faron Young and Ray Price respectively. His annual outdoor Fourth of July party, held near Austin for eight years during the 1970s, pushed along the movement. He began to become a star after years of doing it his way, and his old labels had to scrabble in their vaults, so that in 1976 he had eight singles in the country chart on three labels. RCA released an album called *Wanted: The Outlaws* that year, with tracks by Nelson, Tompall Glaser, Jesse Colter and Colter's husband, Waylon Jennings (perhaps the original outlaw, who had played bass for Buddy Holly, and just missed going along on Holly's last ride); it was the first country album to sell a million copies. Willie and Waylon made three albums of duets and became the biggest-grossing country act in the USA. In 1983, with Merle Haggard, Nelson recorded Townes Van Zandt's 'Poncho and Lefty', because he knew his friend Townes was a great songwriter who needed the money: it was a number one hit. He has recorded Irving Berlin and Hoagy Carmichael, and he has everybody foxed: my mother bought his records, and she would not have been caught dead listening to country music twenty-five years ago. I saw Willie on PBS a few years ago, and he was not even singing, just picking: there were three guitars, a bass and a fiddle, the same instrumentation as the pre-war Django Reinhardt Quintet of the Hot Club of France, and the music made you feel good in the same way.

Richard Dobson's albums on his own label are showcases for his songs. His *Save the World* in 1982 offered mostly songs about work, including 'The Ballad of Robin Wintersmith', which was covered by Nanci Griffith, who calls it his 'lifestyle justification song'. Based on a true story, it is about a young man who jumps over cars on a motorcycle, and gets killed. Dobson understands why he does it: we each have to do whatever we can do for a living. Terry Allen is a sculptor and an art teacher; his two-disc *Lubbock (On Everything)* is a funny, moving memoir, with much in it to touch the heart of any baby-boomer, such as 'The Pink and Black Song', an affectionate send-up of the late 1950s. Allen thought he had left Lubbock, but producer Lloyd Maines convinced him he did not have to stay away; his *Smoking the Dummy* truly smokes. When it comes to rock, Dobson's backing on *Save the World* and Allen's Panhandle Mystery Band are the best there is. Joe Ely made a reputation in his native Texas, and has since struggled with MCA to make the music he wants to make, but he is pulling it off. A tiny English label has collected together all Ely's covers of Hancock's songs on one LP.

And they keep coming out of the woods: Jimmie Dale Gilmore (erstwhile sidekick of Hancock and Ely – Richard Dobson's first CD was a set of Gilmore's songs in 1993), Lyle Lovett, Darden Smith, Wes McGhee (from Texas by way of London), Steven Fromholz, David Halley (from the Lubbock axis), Robert Earl Keen, Steve Earle (with the accent on rock, but his 'Hillbilly Highway' is as country as they come). They are not all from Texas, they are not all hillbillies and they are not all men: there is Griffith, k. d. lang, K. T. Oslin, Kathy Mattea, Reba McIntyre, the Forester Sisters; from Ireland, Mary Coughlan; from Canada, Mary Margaret O'Hara and the French-Canadian McGarrigle Sisters. Some of them are not so young, because by the time you and I have heard of them they already know a lot of songs and how to put them across. Such is the legacy of the legendary decade: good songs, good friends and good times, if you know where to look. Some of the older songwriters, storytellers and country rockers had chart success once upon a while ago, but most of them have long since retired to their valuable subculture; Jerry Jeff is fond of saying to his audiences that the music business is so awful he is glad he is not part of it, a rueful joke on more than one level. For there is another legacy of the 1960s.

At the end of the decade it had all gone wrong. Stax changed hands, and Jim Stewart found to his surprise that Atlantic owned its classic soul hits. In April 1968 Martin Luther King was murdered in Memphis; the mood in black neighbourhoods all over the USA was immediately hostile, and the staff at Stax could not even go to work. In August 1968, just a year after Otis Redding's joyous party in Atlanta for all his friends at the convention for the National Association of Radio and Television Announcers, the thirteenth annual convention in Miami was haunted by gun-toting scum who wanted something for nothing: an effigy of Wexler was hanged, New Orleans

R & B entrepreneur Marshall Sehorn was pistol-whipped in a toilet and Phil Walden, a champion of black music, was frightened out of it entirely and switched to white rock.

Brian Jones had become a victim of alcohol, drugs and his own lack of confidence; eased out of the Rolling Stones, he drowned in his swimming pool in July 1969. In December the Stones put on a free concert at a disused racetrack in California, and Altamont was a shambles, just a few months after Woodstock: a young black man (stupidly waving a pistol) was kicked and stabbed to death by some hell's angels, who had been hired as security. The Beatles could not stand each other any more and broke up in April of 1970. Hendrix accidentally killed himself with a cocktail of alcohol and drugs in September and Joplin did the same thing in October. (Her version of Kris Kristofferson's lovely 'Me and Bobby McGee', probably the best record she ever made, became her only number one single, indeed her only top forty hit: 'Freedom's just another word / For nothing more to lose'.) Jim Morrison, self-appointed poet of the counterculture and the original monster of narcissism, died from the effects of drugs in July of 1971. Sly Stone, who had as much influence as any of them, slid away in a haze of drugs and unreliability.

Rock'n'roll had seemed to be over in 1960. A decade or so later rock should have been mercifully allowed to retire to the roadhouses of Austin and Lubbock. But by then there was far too much invested in it; the younger generations knew nothing else, and neither did the greedy music business. The pop charts of the last two decades have been dominated by the toys of technology and the sound of money talking.

18

The Heat Death of Pop Music

In 1955, just before Elvis Presley appeared on network television, I was fifteen years old. Five years later, in 1960, there were almost half a million more fifteen-year-olds in the USA than in 1955; between 1960 and 1965 the increase in that age group was well over 700,000, and in another five years it increased by over half a million again. By then the rate of increase in fifteen-year-olds was slowing down, but this already represented a phenomenal rise in the number of young Americans.

All those new citizens needed baby clothes and housing; then more primary schools had to be built, and later more college professors were needed, and all the while there were more cars on the road, still more houses in the suburbs and, finally – the ultimate shrine to western civilization – the shopping mall. America's post-war economy is a progress of the demographic bulge through it. All this economic activity meant more tax money for politicians to spend, but the individuals who comprise that demographic bulge will soon start reaching retirement age, and as they each expect to receive hundreds of dollars a month in Social Security whether they need it or not, the fall in the relative number of people paying the bills may result in economic disaster, and even growing social unrest.

Meanwhile, the American economy has had a free ride for over forty years, and has turned into a simple computer, with only one instruction: make a profit. The car factory in which I worked years ago has been closed and torn down, because it is easier to make a profit selling Japanese or German cars than it is to do the necessary investment and development to keep the domestic industry going. The nation which once thought of itself as the most competitive in the world has forgotten how to do it in less than a lifetime.

Of those thousands of jobs lost in my home town, many were jobs for African-Americans. America may or may not still have a racial problem, but it certainly has something new to the USA: a highly visible and apparently intractable class problem. The reason there is a black urban underclass – or, to put it another way, the reason the black middle class has not grown fast enough – is because there are not enough decent jobs to get people out of the ghettos. The economic machine is not necessarily racist, but it is stupidly blind. If you have money, it will sell you a piece of the action, but there is no money in black neighbourhoods, so they crumble: $50 million could be found to make a flop movie called *Harlem Nights*, but nobody can borrow money to fix up Harlem, and New York City has no money because Washington is a leech that sucks it away. And if you add the white people who are losing hope, the underclass is massive: unlike earlier generations of Americans, today we fear that our children and grandchildren are never going to have it so good; but the white underclass does not tug at the racial conscience, so we do not read much about it in the newspapers.

Nelson George, in *The Death of Rhythm and Blues*, complained that there are no longer any black-owned record shops in black neighbourhoods. The fact is that there are no longer any mom'n'pop record shops in white neighbourhoods either. Thirty years ago in my home town of perhaps 65,000 people, there were three full-service record shops, where you could buy any kind of music you wanted; now there are none. The only decent record shops are in big cities, and the reason is that the record companies and their distributors could no longer be bothered to sell small numbers of records directly to smaller shops, which then had to pay a commission to middlemen for their stock, and went broke.

The effect on the music business of the increasing stupidity of the economic machine does not end there. In 1947 the American record industry finally matched its previous best year (1921); the 1947 sales were matched again in 1955, and four years after that they had doubled. The plastic long-playing record made it possible for shops to stock a greater selection and for people to have larger record collections at home (because LPs took up so much less room than 78s), at the same time as growing prosperity made it possible for people to buy more records. But something has gone wrong. In 1975 John D. Glover of the Cambridge Research Institute said that in 1963 61 per cent of long-playing records did not make a profit; in 1965 an LP broke even at about 7,800 copies, while in 1975 the break-even point for an album was a massive 61,000 copies, and 77 per cent of releases lost money. And that trend has continued.

Just as it is easier to sell Japanese or German cars than to build American ones that people will buy, so it is easier to sell a million copies of one album than to sell 100,000 copies each of ten albums. (That is why all the shopping-mall record shops are the same.) Today the major labels still throw a lot of shit at the wall to see what sticks, but it is much more expensive to operate that way than it was thirty-five years ago. If you guarantee Michael Jackson, Prince, Madonna and whoever millions of dollars for each album, you are taking a very foolish risk.

Today's pop-rock is a paradigm of a society that has no values; it is ubiquitous even though the record companies admit that most of it loses money. Perhaps the problem begins with the fact that nowadays we have less input into our own popular culture. For example, nearly all of it comes to us electronically, whereas years ago we bought tickets: in 1942–3, 80 per cent of the hit songs were from films or Broadway shows; that figure had fallen to 40 per cent by 1950, and has dropped to zero today. Television helped to kill Broadway and musical films, and has not replaced them; on TV we are given endless footage of Californians getting in and out of their cars, but no original music of any kind.

The demographic bulge allowed a marketing style that is now in the process of collapsing. The power of the song pluggers of old passed to the A & R men; when there was a great deal more money involved than ever before, the A & R men were reduced to functionaries, and the power passed again, this time to label bosses who were no longer musicians. The deal-makers have now retained the power for a quarter of a century; the major record companies of today are riding an expensive tiger, and they do not know how to get off.

Suppose for a moment that rock'n'roll had never happened. Suppose American radio had been successful (as the BBC was for a few years) in suppressing it. Suppose nobody had ever paid Tom Parker's price for Elvis Presley, so that he remained a regional phenomenon, and then went back to driving a truck. Suppose that the Beatles had never been signed by George Martin, and remained a short-lived Liverpool cult, and that in 1970 all we heard on the radio was the style of Glenn Miller and Tommy Dorsey, but played absurdly loud by synthesizers. That is what we have got now: rock'n'roll, the urban folk music of the working class, has been around for over forty years (if you count its hillbilly and rhythm and blues antecedents), and it is as inflated and worn out as minstrelsy was a century ago. The economic machine unwittingly created by the counterculture sees to it that pop-rock is aimed at each generation of new customers, yet each year not only is it of less musical value, but the market gets smaller, so it is not selling very well these days. You need not take my word for that. Here is Maurice Oberstein, chairman of Polygram UK, interviewed on television in 1991: 'By and large we have been starved of the hit records turning into hit artists turning into album performance that we can sell. I think as a result we have fewer new artist development [*sic*] . . . We don't have any new artists delivering big new albums.' Oberstein was explaining why Polygram is repackaging Eric Clapton, Jimi Hendrix and the rest on CD, having discovered that the baby-boomers are still the biggest market. Other labels are doing the same thing. And why do CDs cost so much? Jon Webster, managing director of Virgin Records UK, complained to Sean O'Hagen in *The Times* that the record industry's expenses include 'launching a new act. We're in a fashion business. Ninety per cent of what we release loses money; that has to be recouped somewhere.' Every time we buy a record we are subsidizing trash that nobody wants; that has always been the case, but today it is absurdly expensive trash.

The twin problems, fuelling each other, have been overuse of technology and the sound of money shouting. It is hard to deal with them separately, but let us begin with the studio toys. The possibilities of the tape recorder used in the creation of the multi-tracked recordings of Patti Page and Les Paul of the early 1950s, and carried on by Phil Spector and others, were adopted and developed by producers on both sides of the Atlantic, and the monster began to devour the shop.

Joe Meek in England performed miracles in a hole in the wall above a shop in north London; John Leyton's 'Johnny Remember Me' was a UK number one in 1961: Meek had created a pop artefact by twiddling knobs, using compression, echo and overdubbing; he was accused of manufacturing a pop star from a non-singer, which was of course correct. One of Meek's biggest hits was 'Telstar' (1962), an instrumental by the Tornados, his house band. The overdriven sound was the first transatlantic number one, the first USA number one by a UK rock act and is still the only British instrumental to have reached number one in the USA. One of the Tornados described 'Telstar' as 'crap', but kids liked the gimmicky sound, and Meek made major-label producers in the UK look rather sad, because all they could do with their more elaborate studios was imitate each other imitating American pop hits.

Meek became a legend, yet you will find few who will claim that the records are anything but junk: they are quite remarkably bad. His echoing productions of singers who sounded like you or me in the bathtub had an element of sadness in their badness, a hint of doom, as though lamenting their own ignorant boredom. Meek became paranoid about his techniques being copied. As the Beatles and their imitators brought about a new era, in which such producers as George Martin learned to use their equipment to its limits, the likes of Spector and Meek with their claustrophobic production were superseded: Spector retired in 1965, and Meek committed suicide in early 1967, on the anniversary of Buddy Holly's death. They were not the last pop people to take themselves too seriously.

Leiber and Stoller had already been aware that they were making records rather than recording music, but they were smart enough and talented enough to keep that fact in perspective. Suddenly there was so much money in it that the trend became the manufacture of pop artefacts instead of the recording of musical events. The stars would then tour fewer but larger venues to promote the records, rather than making records for fans they had already gained by touring.

The Beatles became so popular that they stopped touring; their work had got so highly polished that there was nothing more to be done with the jingle format. Their hits were witty, slick and catchy little jewels of pop; Maureen McGovern sings some of their love songs along with those of Cole Porter. In the same month as Meek shot himself, 'Penny Lane' and 'Strawberry Fields Forever' came out back to back, surreal (or psychedelic) snapshots respectively of Paul McCartney's and John Lennon's Liverpool childhoods: masterpieces of pop production, they revealed Meek's stuff to be the junk it was. They had been intended for a new album which was taking so long that they were issued as a single; four months later *Sgt Pepper's Lonely Hearts Club Band* was released. It was the number one album in the USA for fifteen weeks and stayed in the UK charts for nearly three years.

As a carefully assembled concept album, *Sgt Pepper* was an expensive production; it was the first Beatles album released in identical editions in both the USA and the UK, and cost $1 more in the USA than most pop albums. In the future a great many rock-pop albums would be expensive productions, taking many months and hundreds of thousands of dollars to produce, and the Beatles were blamed. But they had made eight albums in about four years, including *Sgt Pepper*. In 1989 Kate Bush, Tears for Fears and Blue Nile released new albums which had taken a total of fourteen years to produce: these were reviewed variously as 'drifting piece of atmospheric waffle ... woefully studio-bound extravaganza ... moody sonic ramble ... serves in the end as an example of what an exhausted and exhausting business mainstream pop-rock albums have become'. Today it is the record companies who invest huge amounts of money in grandiosity; let us not blame the Beatles any more than we blame Leiber and Stoller.

In those far-off years *Sgt Pepper* was a complete success on its own terms, the apotheosis of pop. 'When I'm Sixty-four' was nothing more or less than pure music hall, and a better indicator of the Beatles' roots than the rock'n'roll of Chuck Berry or Elvis Presley. McCartney's earlier 'Yesterday' was evidence of the skilful tunesmithing that would make McCartney one of the richest men in the world, and it has been covered hundreds of times. Yet in general the new pop songs of the 1960s would not stand on their own, for the Beatles had accomplished something else. The trade of the professional songwriter began to wither, because each new pop group was required to write its own material. Thousands of tenth-rate songs were published, while the craft of interpretation of good songs fell by the wayside; and the customers had been plugged into their radios and televisions for so long, and had heard so little live music, that they did not know that anything was being destroyed. Music became a throw-away commodity, hence the word 'bubble gum' was used to describe the worst of it. The fans bought records, not music; and the experience was not a musical one, but had become a social one.

Oblivious in their complete economic power and ignorant of other kinds of music, the new generation mistook the smooth efficiency of modern record production for art itself, and the new pop began to be called 'progressive rock'. Pink Floyd, Moody Blues, Genesis, King Crimson, Emerson, Lake and Palmer, Yes and many more groups composed meandering, pretentious and pseudo-philosophical music to get stoned by, which had nothing progressive about it at all, but a touch of doom left over from the Meek influence. The adoption by the Moody Blues of the Mellotron, an early synthesizer, so that they could tour without the big orchestra their ponderous stuff called for, was another sign of things to come. Today's rock critics poke fun at it, but in many cases they are the people who were buying these records when they were a little younger, and they are still looking for something progressive in a music scene that becomes less progressive each year.

The blues were not neglected, however. The legend 'BIRD LIVES' was chalked on walls in New York after Charlie Parker died; but 'CLAPTON IS GOD' was chalked in London when Eric Clapton was barely out of short trousers. A very good young guitarist who wanted to play the blues, he left the successful Yardbirds because they were turning from R&B to pop; he played with John Mayall's Bluesbreakers and then formed Cream, with Jack Bruce on bass and Ginger Baker on drums. The lyrics of Pete Brown were important on their hit singles, but in concert their improvisation was thought to be meaningful because it was very loud (hence the label 'power trio'). It is easy to make fun of progressive rock, but an even greater tragedy was the attempt to force the blues to carry the weight of pop's white-bread narcissism. Cream covered Skip James's 'I'm So Glad' and Robert Johnson's 'Crossroads'; the trio was commercially successful, but soon disbanded, perhaps because Clapton knew perfectly well that their self-indulgence was about as far from Robert Johnson's sort of authority as you could get.

After some vicissitudes, Clapton embarked on a long series of studio albums that continues today. He is still a very good guitar player; he fills the Albert Hall for a series of concerts early each year, and six nights in 1987 became twenty-four in 1991. This is in spite of the fact that he has little more to say than many another good guitar player; the critics have been disappointed in virtually every album since 1970.

Jeff Beck, Robert Fripp and Jimmy Page are three more English musicians who became famous guitar heroes. Beck has never made an album or led a band that has fulfilled the promise he seemed to hold out. Fripp, a technician, came from King Crimson to combine his guitar with electronics, and has become a darling of pop-rock's avant-garde. Jimmy Page was a member of Led Zeppelin, one of the most successful bands of all time.

Like the American West Coast hippie bands, Led Zeppelin were loud folkies, and had their own distinctive sound. They were less pretentious than some of the other progressives, and they were carefully recorded as four individuals: of its kind, the production of their records is still to be admired, and, remastered by Page, is impressive today on CD. Their music had space in it, and they resorted occasionally to acoustic instruments. But their sound was more original than their material, and their best-known anthem, 'Stairway to Heaven', has to be likened to the Moodys' 'Nights in White Satin', in that its primary function today is one of nostalgia. After decades of classic black rhythm and blues and soul music, the riff that imitators have started out with more often than any other is Page's riff from 'Stairway to Heaven'. But Led Zeppelin's worst legacy was not their fault. Their imitators invented heavy metal.

Out of the post-war boredom with Joni James's records and lookalike Levittowns inhabited by GI Bill graduates came the black motorcycle jacket and the image of Marlon Brando in *The Wild One* (1954) who, when asked what he was rebelling against, replied 'Whataya got?' Each generation has thought that it invented sex, iconoclasm and much else, but the larger generation of the 1960s could get away with more; and there was the notion that rock'n'roll was somehow dangerous. Today there are a great many parents who were themselves rock fans. You would think that the notion of dangerous music would have withered, but in the meantime rebellion has become a market: in the middle of the Vietnam War, which was, after all, something worth protesting against, was there not a book called *Revolution for the Hell of It?* So in 1968 a band called Steppen-wolf, named after a novel by Hermann Hesse which few had read, had a hit called 'Born To Be Wild', a biker's anthem, which included the words 'heavy metal thunder', taken from a William Burroughs novel.

Heavy metal is the ultimate in phoney rebellion, the logical and boring exaggeration of rock'n'roll as the music to make our parents angry, just as a logical and boring heat death of the universe may be the ultimate result of the original Big Bang. Heavy metal combines blues-based rock with the portentous doom of progressive pop; it is the loudest music of all; it uses the imagery of vaguely Viking mythical heroes, like the trashy children's cartoon 'He-man': the artwork heroes ripple with muscles, while heavy metal's guitar heroes are often skinny weeds. Or the HM bands promote images of devil worship, suicide and even Nazism, showing a paucity of any values at all. Yet heavy metal's largely working-class audience is curiously well behaved; the male fans at the concert-as-ritual are succoured by the phallic symbolism of the guitar hero, the females content to play their supportive roles, and all go back to work on Monday morning feeling as though they have rebelled. The cost of their cheap rebellion is that when they are older, they will find that their hearing has been damaged.

Vanilla Fudge's gimmick in the USA in the 1960s was playing pop covers very slowly, for listeners who were stoned. Deep Purple began as British Fudge imitators; Grand Funk and Mountain carried on in the USA; Britain's Black Sabbath started the sword-and-sorcery nonsense, and Charles Shaar Murray points out that if the Sabs had not been so loud that they took your head off, it would have been obvious that they were not very good. Some of these ponderous giants made so much money that they stopped playing or went into tax exile, hence the New Wave of British Heavy Metal: Def Leppard, Iron Maiden, Whitesnake, Saxon. 'Heavy metal is the basic rock and roll message,' said John Swenson of *Rock World*. 'The least sophisti-cated kid can get as much out of it as its dedicated followers.' There is no arguing with that.

David Bowie seemed to have more substance than most in the 1970s. He began as David Jones, and wanted terribly to be a star. With his finger on the pulse of the times he changed images, from Ziggy Stardust to Plastic Soul to the dissolution of the Thin White Duke and beyond, mourning lost innocence as he searched for himself, as he knew his generation was searching. His lyrics were allusive and full of the grief of the search. He was intelligent enough to know how perfectly his unbridled ambition and his chameleon act fitted the decade. He ran out of images and faded back into combo rock'n'roll, but with less good songs; in 1993 the latest news was that he had found a new image again.

And there have been groups without number coming and going on both sides of the Atlantic, in a spectrum from bubble gum for the kiddies through ear candy for grown-ups to arty stuff for the critics. As the Beatles grew up, then broke up, the music business was handed a formula on a plate, and used it to rope in each new generation of pre-teen children, while slightly older teenagers were only too happy to become recording artists. Acts which did not exist had hits like 'Yummy Yummy Yummy I've Got Love In My Tummy', vehicles for hack songwriters; as the customers grew older, they were herded into the corral by pop-rock groups who wrote their own material and were more pretentious, but still just looking for a piece of the action, each hoping they did not sound too much like all the others.

Pop-rock acts appeared on the chat shows, such as those hosted by Terry Wogan in the UK, watched mostly by housewives, and Johnny Carson in the USA, unassailable in his polished cynicism. The kids who buy pop records do not watch the chat shows, but the pop group is given the slot because the press agents and the television producers do not know what they are doing. The Wogans and the Carsons do not even talk to the popsters; there may be a musical guest on the sofa, but the guest talks and then sits while Richard Marx, say, does the musical slot. Marx has a slick band, an expensive hairdo, a polished act and no soul; his song is instantly forgettable.

The lead singer of the Del Fuegos sounds like a tired mixture of Mick Jagger, Bob Dylan and Randy Newman. Fairground Attraction's song is not even finished. *Each line* is not finished: the gimmick is that each line runs out of energy, the words trailing off, the rhythm section stumbling. But the rhythm sections often sound amateurish. One of the Cure's videos in early 1991 seemed to portray a bunch of kids noodling, or improvising, in the basement, which is appropriate. In today's entertainment business we can all be stars, because the stars are just like us; and the Cure were made by their videos, not their music.

During the 1970s it was already obvious that the original thrill that was rock'n'roll had become a middle-class marketplace, as many of the heroes of the 1960s become tax exiles and Elvis Presley killed himself with pills. A few teenagers in flared trousers were still furtively getting stoned, but the counterculture was dead. The answer to the problem of the death of rock'n'roll, since the younger generations knew nothing else, was more of it. Rock split into the rock generation's answer to Mantovani on the one hand and punk rock on the other.

Punk was supposed to make rock'n'roll dangerous again, but the danger had been an illusion, and the pathetic fallacy of punk was another. The difference was that the punks bragged about not being able to play or sing, and spat on their audience, and the audience cooperated by spitting back. (If any punk rocker had tried spitting on Jerry Lee Lewis, he would have found out what danger was.) Acts in New York clubs such as Richard Hell and the Voidoids wore torn clothes and safety-pins through their skin, and made a ranting anarchic style of noise. English entrepreneur Malcolm McLaren, working in New York, knew a good thing when he saw it, and never made any bones about *The Great Rock'n'roll Swindle*, as the 1978 film was called. Back in London, McLaren ran a boutique, and recruited the Sex Pistols from among his customers; the most famous and typical of the punks, their music was an indescribable noise of buzz-saw guitar whine and tuneless screaming. Punk became a do-it-yourself era, and entire reference books have been compiled of terrible, amateurish pop singles made in garages with a shelf life of two weeks. Virtually the only band to survive from punk with any reputation is the Clash, and nobody calls their music punk today. David Johansen of the New York Dolls, who later changed his name to Buster Poindexter and invented a cabaret act, said of his earlier career: 'I was basically just doing a rock-oriented or a teen-oriented show – you know, for rebels without a clue.'

In the pop charts punk disappeared into New Wave, followed by the New Romantics. Pop songs by Boy George in the UK, Blondie in the USA and countless more were slick, harmless and slightly cynical, but less portentous. Boy George was frank about dressing up and wearing make-up because it was fun; not much portent there. The songs were forgettable, but by now the pop charts were ignored by serious music fans anyway.

We could always go to the disco. *Discothèque* is French for 'record library'. Already in the 1960s American towns had discos, bars where scantily clad women danced in cages to the jukebox. Workers, white collar and blue, would stop on their way home to sip a beer without blinking, so as not to miss anything: the working-class dancer was often a single mother, with no other way of making a living, but she might get into the spirit of the thing and flash a bit of something naughty. The dancers were also called go-go dancers, because several French clubs and American imitations called themselves 'Whiskey à gogo' (from the French title of the 1949 Ealing comedy *Whiskey Galore*).

In larger cities the gay male subculture picked up on the disco. Banned from the semi-literate suburban family rooms where popular culture is legitimized, a subculture embraces the absurd, which then emerges to become the norm, and suburbia does not even know that it has been sent up; you cannot make fun of a society which has no taste. Young urban blacks also adopted the disco as a place to dress up and show off, playing records being a cheaper way to run a club than hiring live music. And the machinery began to take over completely.

Dr Robert A. Moog had built the first synthesizer in 1964; he combined a PhD in engineering with experience as a composer of jingles. Sly Stone had been the first to use a drum machine, on a 1971 number one US hit, 'Family Affair'. The Family Stone was racially, sexually and stylistically integrated, and played a fusion of pop, soul and rock that was unique; Larry Graham's popping electric bass was one of the most important elements. The drum machine was first used in the family room's electric organ, in case somebody wanted to play a rhumba, a cha-cha or a little bebop. But Sly's followers were mere imitators; the music of the disco came initially from black pop, and Sly's music was a natural source for copycats, as was James Brown's.

Music business insiders had their ears to the ground. Shirley Pixley Goodman was half of Shirley and Lee, whose huge R&B hits included 'Let the Good Times Roll' (1956); her disco hit was produced by Sylvia (Vanderpool) Robinson, who as half of Mickey and Sylvia had the wonderful 'Love is Strange' the same year. Soon 'bpm' numbers (beats per minute) were printed on record labels, to make it easier for the disco DJ to segue from one disc to the next, and the formula of pop-rock pabulum was complete: soon we had everything from Mozart to Beatles tunes set to the mechanical thump. Larry Graham became a crooner, and his bass was replaced in the pop chart by a computer chip.

Thus good party music became godfather to a formula that did more to wreck pop music than any other, because the market for it had more to do with dressing up than with music. And the pop video was coming along, which meant that the stars could make films of themselves having fun, and sell the films at a profit too. Chic was a disco band that could play, including Nile Rodgers, who soon became a producer of plastic music; Giorgio Moroder, with a studio full of toys in Munich, took it all international. In 1977, with the film *Saturday Night Fever*, it became a larger bubble that soon burst, but whose effects are with us still.

In 1979 came this first crash in the pop-rock market. Rock's original customers were growing up and the size of each following generation was shrinking. Disco albums, such as the soundtracks from *Saturday Night Fever*, *Grease* and *Sgt Pepper's Lonely Hearts Club Band* (nothing to do with the Beatles), had been overshipped by the record companies and came back by the truckload. Nevertheless, what is now called dance music is made by computers. A late 1980s manifestation was house, named after a club in Chicago; acid house was another spiral further into computer sampling of other people's music. But the twanging synthesizers and thumping machines all have one thing in common: they do not and cannot swing, so that generations of popsters making music by imitating metronomes do not know what swing is, and often cannot play at all. Once again we have recording engineers who cannot record real drums.

The label 'dance music' implies that previous generations did not dance to music made by humans; but there are amusing aspects. Today's dance hits are made by independent one-off technocrats rather than by pop stars, and are throw-away items, like the good old singles of yore: buy one, enjoy it for a while, then buy another. This confounds the major labels, who need a marketing strategy before they can sell anything. The phenomenon of dance music that sounds like a malfunctioning compact disc player is laden with irony. Since it is all on tape tracks generated by machines, it is a simple matter to remix it, taking the fans' money several times, or to issue several versions until one finally becomes a hit.

Another side of the rise of technology is that in pop-rock the visual record of the act, the video, is more important than ever. Paula Abdul is not a singer but an ex-cheerleader and a choreographer of video dancing. Of her latest album, Tony Parsons wrote in the *Daily Telegraph*: '*Spellbound* is slightly less spontaneous than a pocket calculator . . . Her dance tracks consist of boil-in-the-bag funk and her sexy stuff has fewer erogenous zones than Barbie's boyfriend.' But the fans who buy the records visualize her dancing while they listen. The kids who danced on television's *Bandstand Matinee* thirty-some years ago and the girls who danced in the cage at Freddy's Bar in Kenosha in the next decade are now the stars, and the streets of Los Angeles are full of hopefuls.

The epitome of all this in the 1980s was the success of producers Mike Stock, Matt Aitken and Pete Waterman, who perfected knob-twisting, switch-flipping and button-punching until their bank managers were very happy. They were responsible for thirty or forty hit singles in the UK; they told *Time* magazine that they have 'pretty much a hard and fast rule that no one we work with is over 25': they thus ensure that should they run across anyone with talent, he or she will not have had much time to hone it. Stock–Aitken–Waterman's ménage included Bananarama, three pretty girls; Mel and Kim, two pretty girls; and Kylie Minogue, one pretty girl. I am sure someone called Sonia was not unattractive; Jason Donovan and Rick Astley were pretty boys. None of these people had any discernible talent. Minogue and Donovan were the teenage stars of an Australian soap opera; an Australian commentator put Minogue's appeal down to her 'blinding ordinariness'; a British critic whose job required him to attend her live concert described her as a 'prancing dancing antiseptic swab'. The funniest artefact was Astley's version of 'When I Fall In Love' in 1987. Not only was he covering a classic Nat Cole hit from exactly thirty years earlier, but the producers programmed their computers to imitate Gordon Jenkins's arrangement. The result was so bad it helped the reissued original into the UK charts.

Critics pretended not to take the likes of Stock–Aitken–Waterman seriously, but why not? They were only doing what Joe Meek did, and somebody wrote a whole book about him; in the next century we may be expected to read a book about the technocrats of the 1980s. But actually by this time something is beginning to trouble the critics. They might like to try to ignore the kiddie pop, but anything taking itself seriously is given a good deal of space in the so-called quality newspapers.

In Britain in September 1990 a new Broadcasting Act empowered the government to award three new national radio services to the highest bidders, stipulating only that one should be other than a pop station and one should be for talk. Richard Findlay, managing director of Radio Forth Ltd (one of the hopefuls, to be sure), wrote to *The Times* to complain:

There is a potent and vociferous lobby at work attempting to prove that rock music is not pop music and that . . . rock music consortia should be allowed to bid [along with pop consortia]. Needless to say, it is likely that such groups would outbid groups seeking to establish a classical-music station.

In the same issue of *The Times* a letter was printed from Robert Plant and Phil Collins, also complaining:

It is a fact that the majority of records, tapes and compact discs sold in the UK are sold to rock music fans . . . Rock music has become an essential part of contemporary culture . . . There is, however, no national radio station that caters for the musical tastes of this large percentage of our population. A pop station, based around top 40 singles, does not reflect the depth and quality of a vigorous popular art that supports this multi-million pound industry in which Britain enjoys world leadership.

The pop-rock industry's greatest talent is for begging questions. Are they saying that the people who do not listen to 'rock' are uncultured, or not contemporary? If rock is separate from pop, then let us add up pop, classical, jazz, country and everything else and see if rock still sells the majority of records. Is Michael Jackson rock or pop? How many top forty singles have Plant and Collins sold?

Phil Collins, the drummer with Genesis, has become a big-time rock crooner, helped by the image of the 'nice guy next door'. As Led Zeppelin's vocalist, Plant is one of the giants of the pop-rock of the last twenty-five years. His four solo albums spent a total of forty weeks in the UK charts in the 1980s, three of them making the top ten. Collins had fourteen hit singles in the UK during the 1980s (seven in the top five) and four hit albums (only one of which did not reach number one – it was number two) in the UK album chart for a total of 592 weeks. This is not counting their MOR success in the USA, nor the chart success of Genesis and Led Zeppelin. What are these people moaning about? The truth is that the only distinction between pop and rock is that the popsters are out to be stars and to make money, while the rockers take themselves more seriously and pretend they care less about the loot. Rockists would maintain that their music has progressed since 1956, but there is so little musical difference between rock and pop that many of the artists would be impossible to place in one camp or the other.

As for the words of the songs, we have come from the folk poetry of Hank Williams, Carl Perkins and Bob Dylan to empty posturing; the rockists are no more literate than the popsters. Take U2, an Irish group who began composing their own material because they could not perform anybody else's, and who were suddenly found to be relevant in the wasteland of the late 1980s. In the *Daily Telegraph* film critic Iain Johnstone reviewed their film *Rattle and Hum*, which is so lame it does not bother to tell you which member of U2 is which:

The Edge, I think, says: 'There are people who say you shouldn't mix music and politics but I think that's bullshit.' And we wait, open-mouthed, for him to expand on this sententious theory; but answer comes there none. Accordingly, names like Bishop Tutu and Martin Luther King are taken down from the shelves like proprietary brands and lobbed into their songs, like supermarket shopping thrown into a basket . . . Bono, I think, tells us that he is upset about the Enniskillen bombing [an IRA outrage]. He begins the song, 'I can't believe the news today . . .', but then his well-intentioned sentiments are drowned by the backing. Compared to John Lennon's threnody on the death of Tara Browne – 'I read the news today, oh boy' – there is no comparison.

David Sinclair in *The Times* described the soundtrack album as 'a brilliant patchwork . . . which found the hottest rock'n'roll band in the world on a belated quest to acquire some roots'. The hottest rock'n'roll band in the world is only now looking for some roots, and the track singled out for praise is the one featuring guest B. B. King, and this is in a round-up of the year's best albums.

Bruce Springsteen was basically a folkie whose concerts were incredibly popular because he had working-class sincerity. His song 'The River' is about a young couple in an industrial town who were married too young; their lives are over, and all they can do is sit by the river and watch it go by. This song is about the first half of my life, and it should reduce me to a puddle of self-pity, but it doesn't, because it's not a very good song. His solo acoustic album, *Nebraska*, was a relative failure, but the critics were too embarrassed to point out that stripped-down Springsteen is unfinished: the songs have not got the bumps ironed out of them, the words do not fit the tunes. It was Springsteen who said that 'Chuck [Berry] played in a lot of strange keys, like B-flat and E-flat'. (I always wondered what was so weird about Beethoven's 'Eroica'.) But Springsteen, like Elton John, scooped up fans who had no other home. Charles Shaar Murray notes that Springsteen's concerts were better value than his records: he was, after all, only a white boy playing R&B; in person he acknowledges his debt to the golden oldies, and with a good live band he is at least a showman.

Then there is Prince, who has been described as a toothpick in a purple doily. His obsession with sex is partly the obsession of each new generation and partly narcissism. There is no doubt about the professionalism of his act (he paid his dues in Minneapolis clubs), but there is nothing new in his music. He must be a serious artist, because he never laughs or smiles, never gives interviews and goes everywhere with bodyguards. Sting also never smiles. His hit single 'If You Love Somebody Set Them Free' was a perfect farrago of me-too noise, the almost drowned-out sentiment being today's excuse for a love song: 'I'll have sex with you, but don't expect me to hang around.' George Michael was a big hit in a pop duo called Wham! and made all the money he wanted, then gave interviews about being a serious artist; the name of his latest album was *Listen Without Prejudice*. Madonna is not a singer or a dancer or a songwriter, but a 'performance artist' who knows how to get the media to manipulate themselves. In 1991 she told Robert Sandall of *The Times*: 'My musical career was an accident. I got a record deal in 1982 and just veered off that way. But the more I did it, the less interested I became in being superficial.' I suspect that the pop-rock critics despise her, but it takes somebody like Michael Ignatieff, not a music critic at all, to blow the whistle:

Last week, in an amazing abdication of editorial responsibility, the BBC's usually excellent arts programme, *Omnibus*, allowed [Madonna] to go on . . . and on . . . about 'her work'. Her work? You mean the bits where she writhes on satin sheets, miming self-abuse, while two Egyptian-style hermaphrodites sporting huge strap-on conical breasts give her a helping hand? Surely some mistake. But no. The usual po-faced 'cultural critics' were rounded up . . . The weird thing about modern celebrity is that mediocrity does not give itself away when magnified to planetary dimensions . . . When planetary marketing takes over, some smooth intellectual sucker can always be found to tell you it is Culture, with a capital C.

These artists do not give concerts; they put on 'shows'. The stadium act is said to be an important phenomenon – music as spectacle. But if an act has big enough hits, it will sell enough tickets to fill a stadium, and if the show has lasers, smoke machines, costumes and choreography, this will distract from the fact that in most cases there is nothing compelling about the music. The huge audience, waving its arms in the air in unison like a giant beetle on its back, is celebrating itself at a social event.

The rock critics write reviews and articles in the papers which are supposed to make us run out and buy records. With all the records coming out, they wouldn't waste space on stuff they don't like, would they? Here is Simon Reynolds in the *Observer* on Suicide, the 'two-man performance art group': 'brutally simple use of the synthesizer and the drum machine . . . critically reviled and ignored . . . strict adherence to the fundamental precepts of minimalism and monotony . . . too much even for the punk crowd. After recording two excellent albums in the Seventies . . .' You can read the whole article over and over, but you keep missing something. Here is Sinclair in *The Times* on a trio with the enchanting name of Rapeman: 'Albini favours a thin, scratchy guitar sound, massively overcranked to deliver squalls of feedback at the drop of a hat . . . Solos . . . unfold like so much sonic splatter . . . Albini's singing [is] a rabidly incoherent, hysterical shriek that brings a number of the songs to the verge of self-destruction.' Yet it displays 'a high degree of individual musicianship . . . and the scalpel-sharp sense of purpose to which it is harnessed'. To be fair, the most serious rock acts (which do not include Phil Collins and Robert Plant) are trying to make their comment on the nasty world we live in, but the only vocabulary they have is the same one Elvis Presley used, and it will not do the job, so they trash it, and become part of the problem.

John Peel is a British DJ who made his name presenting bizarre popsters, few of whom became as famous as Peel. In his review of an appearance in London of an American group called Pussy Galore, which plays 'deeply confrontational music', six paragraphs read like an amusing send-up of the pop-rock concert scene and of irritating noise. But then he assures us that, although our initial impression would have been 'of undisciplined uproar and unreasonable aggression',

a more informed listen would have revealed highly structured pieces of some complexity, through which wildly distorted quotes were whipped as though carried in the teeth of some mephitic gale . . .

Pussy Galore played a vicious street brawl of a set, leaving the impression that the band pursue a musical scorched-earth policy in the hope that the traditions on which they base their impressive music can never be used again.

If flower power manifestly failed to solve our problems, we can turn to feedback. (Bass player and producer Bill Laswell: 'I never need songs ... The most interesting thing in the last 50 years is noise – the sound of technology.') The frustration of these people is understandable, but it is unclear why anyone should listen to their music.

Closing his review, Peel makes a gratuitous remark (typical of a British critic) about the 'clodhoppery that infests most of American music'. Meanwhile, not only are the clodhoppers and shit-kickers in America making some of the best music, but their fans, far from being rock critics and DJs, are people who have the same old trouble making a living as Carl Perkins had when he worked in a bakery. 'I think a lot of the stuff I'm playing now is crap,' Peel said recently. He is suffering from syndromes that can be overcome with liberal doses of happy music; he ought to try some British clodhoppers, like the Famous Potatoes, an octet of melodeon, accordion, trombone, clarinet, fiddle and rhythm, who first called themselves the Folk Pistols, and who, instead of destroying their roots, play them all. They had made six albums by 1992, but most of them are already out of print, partly because people like Peel make a career of not having a good time.

He could take a cue from Wolfman Jack, one of the great DJs of early rock'n'roll, who played a lovely cameo role in the film *American Graffiti* (1973), which was set in 1962. (It is curious how much nostalgia there is among baby-boomers for the period just before they became a counterculture.) In 1989 the Wolf was working on Nashville Network Radio via satellite, and he told a Florida news-paper that he plays a lot of country music these days. 'It's old-fashioned rock'n'roll, man.'

Mojo Nixon is an American who has coined the terms 'Stingism' and 'Stingology' to describe the phenomenon of the rock person as Serious Artist: 'Sting? *George Michael*? Are these people *kidding*?' Nixon calls himself a punk rocker, but he is using the term in its original meaning of garage music: he is a rock'n'roller who knows that the music is supposed to be *fun*.

Most of today's pop-rock is not fun; it is tired and boring and its energy is forced. But the difficulty in being a pop-rock critic nowadays is relieved occasionally; it's OK to denigrate something that is going to sell millions anyway. Here is Sinclair on Phil Collins's album . . . *But Seriously*: 'Like those Woolworth's paintings of little urchin girls with pearly tears on their cheeks it is of course all superficial tat, airbrushed without guile to mass market perfection.' But you cannot do this too often. Elsewhere Sinclair, reviewing Rick Astley's live act, thinks that he 'demonstrated the timeless ability to carry a good tune, irrespective of style'. Unless it's Nat Cole's style. Robert Sandall seemed to praise a new album in early 1990 by Robert Plant: '*Manic Nirvana* does sound in many respects like the best album Led Zeppelin never made, as, in fact, it was supposed to . . . The interesting point . . . is that Plant hasn't merely set out to recapitulate himself.' And again we've missed something.

The critics on the daily national papers in Britain are paid well for pretending that the fodder of the consumer culture is worth writing about, and it is not easy to write about something that basically is not very interesting. David Cheal in the *Telegraph* reviewed a gig by a band called the Dream Academy. The sound, lights and visual effects were fine, he wrote.

So why was this such a disappointing experience? Some blame could be attributed to lead singer Nick Lairds-Clowes, whose rock-star demeanour seemed at odds with the intimacy of this cosy auditorium. The show was badly paced; often there was an unsettling silence between the end of the applause and the beginning of the next song (though the exceptionally polite audience could be held partly responsible for this).

Then there is the band's dearth of first-class material.

The critic is watching a group which has no stagecraft, doesn't know how to work an audience, doesn't know what kind of room it is in and has made three albums yet cannot fill up a live gig with worthwhile material. It is true that British audiences are sometimes too polite, but why is Cheal so polite?

Attempts at live performance by such non-acts as Minogue, Bananarama and the Pet Shop Boys bring out the best in the critics; they have to depict a disaster as they have seen it, and they enjoy it. These performers have to depend on their backing tapes, and sometimes they don't work. The Pet Shop Boys' tape accidentally included their vocals, so at their live début they stood on stage with nothing to do. In mid-1991 Betty Boo, voted most promising newcomer by the British pop industry a few months earlier, was pretending to sing on stage when she dropped her prop microphone. There are groups called Pop Will Eat Itself, and the Scene That Celebrates Itself. Perhaps the whole point is that it is all meaningless.

Bandleader Bon Jovi treads a careful and cynical path between very loud music that is just melodic enough to be pop and not quite loud enough to be head-banging music. Steve Turner describes the familiar ritual of a pop concert, and concludes: 'Bon Jovi music can only really work for you if you believe the Bon Jovi myth. If you don't believe, you are left with the sound of one man worshipping himself in the mirror of an audience and an audience worshipping itself in the mirror of a man.' Bon Jovi also provides us with an example of the nature of today's record business. His series of theatre concerts on the West Coast in early 1990 was compared with that of Steve Lawrence and Eydie Gormé. Steve and Eydie attracted about the same number of customers and grossed roughly the same amount of money, but Bon Jovi is promoting the new album, whereas Steve and Eydie do not bother making records at all, because they will not be played on the radio or available in the shops.

Then there is Jonathan King, sometime pop star, producer turned self-appointed critic. 'Jump Up and Down and Wave Your Knickers In the Air' was one of his in the early 1970s. More recently, he presented a series of travelogues on television called *Entertainment USA*, each segment of which included a music slot as inappropriate as those on the Johnny Carson show. When he visited New Orleans, we got a pop video featuring a skinny young woman who had nothing to do with New Orleans and whose raucous female Mick Jagger imitation was filmed close-up with a fish-eye lens so that she appeared to fellate a bulbous microphone, itself unnecessary with today's technology. Jonathan King would be of no importance, except that when showing us New Orleans on prime-time television, he could have offered us the R & B dynasty represented by the Neville Brothers, or legendary pianist Tuts Washington, or Ellis Marsalis, pianist father of the talented clan. He could have pulled off a coup by presenting Harry Connick, Jr, then on the brink of stardom. Instead he showed us a pop video, and this brings us to the problem that is even bigger than the technology of pop-rock. The music business has been chasing money for many years; the problem is that the true cost (as economists call it) includes the cost of not doing business some other way. But the deal-makers took over twenty-five years ago.

Clive Davis, a lawyer, became head of CBS's Columbia Records in 1967. That year at the Monterey Pop Festival he was surrounded by West Coast rock groups who already had followings, though many of them had no recording contracts. Discovering an unserved market, Davis signed everybody in sight. After a decade of rock'n'roll the major labels were still undecided about it, but as the rest of the nation was losing its soul to the marketplace, Davis tied Columbia to a phenomenon that corporations did not even understand.

Davis bought Big Brother and the Holding Company (with Janis Joplin) from tiny Mainstream Records; other acts he got for less. He signed Electric Flag and Moby Grape (where are they now?), Blood, Sweat and Tears (successful after one-time rock superstar Al Kooper was replaced by vocalist David Clayton-Thomas) and Chicago (originally Chicago Transit Authority), the last two of which sold records because rock was already becoming easy-listening music. Davis signed baby acts (those without previous contracts) for nothing; if they made money he reaped the credit. Santana, and later Billy Joel and Earth, Wind and Fire, were profitable. John Hammond brought Bruce Springsteen to Columbia, but Bruce took so long to become a superstar that Davis got the credit.

By around 1970 Simon and Garfunkel had split up; Andy Williams and Johnny Cash no longer had television shows and their sales began to drop. Davis had run out of baby acts, so he raided other companies, and Columbia became the house of deals. He grabbed Pink Floyd (from Capitol) and signed Neil Diamond for what seemed like a large amount of money, but everything turned out all right. In 1971 Davis was made president of a reconstituted CBS Records

Group, which included all the labels and their overseas offices. Columbia was doing very little in the black music market; it invested money in what was left of Stax, and lost it. Davis became involved with black record producers Kenny Gamble and Leon Huff and their label, and once again he was lucky: in less than a year Philadelphia International had crossover success with the O'Jays, Harold Melvin and the Blue Notes (including Teddy Pendergrass) and others.

The lush, overproduced sound of Philadelphia International was one of the things that was happening to black pop. Worse than that, however, Gamble and Huff did not like Columbia's promotion and were allowed to handle their own, and they were into payola. Davis had also made a promotion deal with Kal Rudman, a talented tip-sheet operator who took payola: Rudman had a real skill for picking hits, and took money for records he liked (why not?). There was now even more money involved. Davis, full of himself, liked big money, the power and stardom that could be found in an industry where flash counted for more than talent. He charged a bar-mitzvah party to a false account. He hired an assistant, David Wynshaw, who had gangster friends and who cheated Columbia with phoney invoices. One of Wynshaw's friends was caught with a roomful of heroin; Gamble was later fined for payola; it had all begun to stink, and Davis was fired in 1973. Everyone was shocked, because even if Davis had been careless with money, he was one of the most successful record men in sight; but CBS was always a conservative company, and Davis's luck had run out. (Charges were brought against Davis and later dropped, which is common in the record industry when firing somebody. The same thing had happened to Eli Oberstein decades earlier.)

Jann Wenner had also discovered a market when he launched *Rolling Stone* magazine after the 1967 Monterey Pop Festival. *Rolling Stone* became the voice of the counterculture, another example of how middle class it was. Wenner never pretended to be anything but a commercial operation. There were not many bad record reviews, because advertising was important. The connection with Davis lies in the contradiction that while CBS, one of the country's biggest corporations, had pushed rock records by advertising in *Rolling Stone* that it was on the side of the Revolution, it bounced Davis at the first sign of getting its fingers burnt.

The counterculture never knew that it was a middle-class phenomenon, though Davis at Columbia Records in New York wearing Nehru jackets should have been a give-away. As Louis Menand wrote in the *New Republic* in 1991, the American middle class is too insecure to resist a new self-concept when one is offered.

The difficulties begin with the word 'counterculture' itself ... For during those years the counterculture *was* culture ... It had all the attributes of a typical mass culture episode: it was a lifestyle that could be practiced on weekends; it came into fashion when the media discovered it and went out of fashion when the media lost interest; and it was, from the beginning, thoroughly commercialized. Its failure to grasp this last fact about itself is the essence of its sentimentalism.

Bob Dylan knew that nothing had changed. On *Street Legal* (1978), his last album before he turned to religion, he asked:

> Can you tell me where we're headin'?
> Lincoln County Road, or Armageddon?
> Seems like I've been down this way before.
> Is there any truth in that, Señor?

The counterculture, as consumers, became the willing partners of big business. But Clive Davis had done nothing good for Columbia. He brought the label back to the top of the marketplace, but on a much less sound basis. The ever larger amounts of money involved resulted in the major labels being forced to try to buy success, and he helped destroy the tradition that a recording artist should have some kind of following before a contract was offered. What happened to Columbia Records was what was happening to the country: the deal, the quick profit, the clever scam that impressed one's rivals was more important than the product.

Davis's ultimate successor, in 1975, was Walter Yetnikoff, another New York lawyer. He bragged that he was tone-deaf; one of his girlfriends told Frederick Dannen (author of *Hit Men*, 1990) that Yetnikoff could not tell one piece of music from another. Yetnikoff was the boss when the disco boom collapsed in 1979. One of the worst deals he presided over was the acquisition of Paul McCartney. Columbia not only paid $20 million, but gave McCartney the priceless Frank Loesser publishing catalogue, and did not even get in return any of McCartney's backlist. (Much of the profit in a big star comes from steady sales of old hits.) McCartney's next few albums did not do that well; Columbia lost money on McCartney, and will continue losing money as long as Loesser's *Guys and Dolls* keeps making it. Yetnikoff had bought the Loesser property in the first place, and promised the estate that it would be the jewel in the crown of CBS Songs; Mitch Miller's comment was, 'If I were a Columbia stockholder, I would sue for dilution of its assets.'

WEA (Warner–Elektra–Atlantic, including Reprise) is a much better-run company. It was WEA and its predecessor companies who gave Ry Cooder a contract at a time when he had not made a single album of his own, and who have issued albums of integrity by Emmylou Harris and many others. This was possible because WEA was the artist-oriented company that Columbia used to be, with bosses for each label who were allowed to make their own decisions. Yet WEA too got sucked into the table-pounding ego-ridden style of management: Yetnikoff took James Taylor from WEA (just as Taylor was passing his commercial peak); from Columbia WEA took Paul Simon, who wanted to leave anyway, and it was some years before WEA began to get its money back with Simon's *Graceland*. Mo Ostin at WEA renewed Rod Stewart's contract for an absurd $2 million each for ten albums, believing that Stewart's manager was talking to Yetnikoff. Compare the cost of Rod Stewart's contract with the $425,000 for each Neil Diamond album, which seemed so high in 1970. How long could this hyperinflation go on?

After the disco crash of 1979 Columbia came back on the strength of only two albums: Michael Jackson's *Thriller* and Bruce Springsteen's *Born in the USA*. But its erratic performance contributed to a climate in which one of the crown jewels of the record industry was soon sold overseas. The oldest record company in the world had become a liability.

The Network, the system of independent promo men of which Kal Rudman had been one of the midwives, had begun to take over. The major labels farmed out their promotion work so that the payola was kept at arm's length, and a handful of gangster types controlled what records were played on the most important stations in America. In 1985 the US record industry grossed $4.5 billion (maximum) and made pre-tax profits (maximum) of $200 million. That is only about 2.5 per cent return (pre-tax) on an investment, but there is more: they were also spending (minimum) $60 million, or 30 per cent of their pre-tax profits, on promotion, some of which, everybody knew, was kicked back to corporate vice-presidents.

In December 1989 Joseph Isgro, a record promoter and leading member of the Network, was indicted on fifty-one counts of racketeering and conspiracy to defraud and to distribute cocaine. In March 1990 the American press reported with a straight face that Columbia had been revived, thanks to Yetnikoff's appointment of failed 1960s popster Tony Mottola to head the domestic label. Mottola hired three more executives away from Arista, Atlantic and Polygram, which made five high-powered big shots to revive the label, set to have a good year thanks mainly to a bubble-gum act, New Kids on the Block. The label of Bessie Smith, Robert Johnson, most of the best of Fletcher Henderson, Duke Ellington, Billie Holiday, Tony Bennett, Johnny Mathis, *South Pacific* and much else is now over one hundred years old, and wastes so much money that it has to rely on bubble gum to stay afloat. Sony, the new owners, finally dismissed Yetnikoff in early 1991, reportedly with a $25,000,000 handshake.

As Frederick Dannen points out in his book *Hit Men*, if the pioneers of rock'n'roll, such as George Goldner and Morris Levy, were all crooks, at least they did not pay out tens of millions of dollars in bribery. It took New York lawyers to do that. All the promotion money goes to sell singles, which do not even make money nowadays; what the industry is after is a hit single to sell an album, where there is more profit. The Top 40 format is now called CHR, Contemporary Hit Records: it can't be called Top 40 any more because some of the radio stations don't even have forty records on the playlist. And who was the top-selling artist in the pop album charts of 1991, according to *Billboard*? Country singer Garth Brooks, whose label did not even bother to promote his singles in the pop market.

After 1975 sales of pop singles fell by 50 per cent in ten years, both in the USA and in the UK. Twang-thump 'dance music' on 12-inch singles survives, but in early 1993 Sony and EMI in Britain announced that they were going to stop making singles almost entirely. The pop single is as dead as an Edison cylinder, because there are a great many toys to distract kids today, such as computer games, and anyway there are fewer kids to buy records than there were twenty-five years ago.

In the 1950s radio abandoned the adult audience, which had more purchasing power and bought albums rather than singles, which meant more profit for the record companies. You could argue that this was a smart thing to do at the time, because the youth market was increasing, but there is no evidence that broadcasters were studying demographics; and in the 1970s they did it again as the baby boom passed its peak.

In October 1965 the Federal Communications Commission ordered broadcasters to stop duplicating their AM and FM transmissions, and around that time manufacturers of radios were required to include FM as well as AM bands. In the early 1970s FM discovered new prosperity when Tom Donahue, a California DJ, pioneered a policy of playing longer, more interesting album tracks with less talk and no commercial jingles, taking the counterculture away from AM radio. But by the end of the 1970s, as the pop chart was taken over by overproduced AOR (Adult or Album Oriented Rock), electro-pop and bubble gum for all ages, FM broadcasters discovered that they could make money faster by playing CHR on FM: by this time the number of fifteen-year-olds in the country was declining and the number of thirty-year-olds increasing. Once again the broadcasters and their advertisers had abandoned a sizeable percentage of listeners with purchasing power, but this time it was a growing rather than a shrinking group. AM stations were given over to talk and pop music continued to decline in quality.

Not making easy money the way it used to, and having to find the money for the bribery somewhere, the industry now wants a tax on blank tape. *The Times* reported in a subhead: 'Home taping costs European music companies about £10 million a year.' The testifying witness in the text turns out to be the record companies' trade body, the International Federation of Phonogram Producers. It is not the little independent record labels who want the tax. They know perfectly well that people tape each other's records for the same reasons they used to swap them and borrow them, and that more fans for more music will result, if the music is any good.

Meanwhile, Clive Davis landed at Arista, where he was successful with Barry Manilow and Melissa Manchester, not Monterey-type acts, but MOR or AOR (which also means 'All Over the Road'). Davis has been compared to Mitch Miller, who snorts with derision:

A record executive must be a nurturer, in the mold of Conkling and Lieberson, and not take credit that rightfully belongs to his staff ... There's guys in the field who brought the stuff to [Davis], and the rest were all deals ... I could take a list of people who were promoted with four-color posters as the second coming of the Lord who couldn't ad lib a burp after a radish dinner.

Miller thought it was ironic that Manchester and Manilow were his kind of artists, but more typical of the industry was an album by British rocker Roy Hill in 1978. There are demonstration tapes by Roy Hill that sound good enough to release: tough, spare, inexorable urban laments full of sexual and social grief. But the album Davis released was a party record and grossly overproduced by Gus Dudgeon, a flavour of the month in the late 1970s. It went well over budget, sank without a trace and Hill never made another. The way the major labels do business almost guarantees that records will be overproduced. Less and less has been done in-house since the 1960s, since the lawyers don't know anything about records anyway; they call in experts who have had a couple of hits and who behave like children in a toyshop. B. B. King gave one of the best live shows ever seen at the Hammersmith Odeon in October 1977, but his album at the time had twelve dull soundalike songs by two writers nobody had ever heard of: the music business had succeeded in making B. B. King boring.

More recently, the English rocker Graham Parker complained, 'I don't *want* my cymbal to sound like a refrigerator falling on to a pile of glass.' Tom Waits, the Californian chronicler of the seamy side, said, 'If I want a sound, I usually feel better if I've chased it and killed it, skinned it and cooked it.' Steve Earle would sound less rockist if his production was not so claustrophobically amplified and had more space in it. The Forester Sisters, a quartet from Georgia, sang beautifully and their songs were mostly good ones, but their albums had a tad too much sheen. Country rocker T. Graham Brown's act was praised in *Country Music People*, but the magazine was a bit reserved about the albums: sure enough, Brown's touring band had been replaced by bags of studio production, including loud, stiff, unswinging rock drums.

The paucity of good music in the mainstream marketplace and the domination of technology mean that the record producers have become stars. Jazz trumpeter Wynton Marsalis unwittingly provides a good story; he used as a guest on an album the elderly New Orleans guitarist Danny Barker, and was impressed because Barker did not wear headphones in the studio. It is hard to believe that Marsalis does not know that the best records of the century have been made with the headphones on the engineers. Musicians cannot listen to each other sitting in cork-lined cubicles wearing headphones; one hopes that Marsalis's drummer does not need a click track to tell him where the beat is. Bob Dylan comments in the notes to *Biograph*, a retrospective collection, about the simple way he used to make records; he should take a cue from the fact that the reviews of his new albums jabber more about his production than about his songs.

By the time Manilow and Manchester had faded, Davis had discovered Whitney Houston. Somebody had to find this beautiful girl with a beautiful voice from a whole family of beautiful voices: Cissy Houston is her mother; Dee Dee and Dionne Warwick are her cousins; she calls Aretha Franklin Auntie Ree. Knowing from personal experience how precarious employment in the record business can be, Davis signed Houston to a personal contract, so that if he gets fired again, he can take her with him. She has had huge hit albums and singles, and Davis has done it again; but the only memorable song Houston has recorded is 'The Star Spangled Banner'. Her hit material consists of non-songs written in the studio by hacks and producers, and laden with that sterile sheen that makes good wallpaper for the ears. The girl is still young, but nobody knows whether she can sing a good song or not.

In a pub recently I heard a cassette playing which was so typical of today's pop-rock that I asked to see it. It was a compilation called *Soft Metal*, with several pop-rock acts of which the only one I remember is Saxon. What was typical about it was skill combined with empty content. The rock beat had nothing to do with any of the roots of country music, rhythm and blues or rock'n'roll. The songs were sung well enough, for all the tools in the modern pop vocalist's kit had been adequately mastered: the gospel melisma, the country catch in the voice, the blues inflections. All the bits copied from all the musics had been liquidized and squirted into a dozen moulds of utterly uninspired songs, adding up to rock as elevator music. First the deal-makers in fast food took the malt powder out and made the milkshake; then in the music business they took the soul out and made pop-rock.

It is no surprise that when *Billboard* introduced a more accurate method of counting sales in May 1991, using the bar codes on the packaging and including more supermarket racks, country music received a big boost up the album-chart ladder at the expense of pop-rock; country music has been unfairly neglected by the industry for decades. But there is another parallel music industry which still cannot be counted, because the records are not found in the racks at all. A large number of small independent labels put out everything from Cajun swamp rock to avant-garde jazz for knowledgeable hard-core music fans; a small army of them spends a lot of money on their favourite sounds, of which most people remain totally unaware. In this market will be found much of the best music of today. Nowadays a great many records are sold through the post; the music magazines are full of advertisements for this service. Who counts the records that are sold through the post because they cannot be found in the shopping-mall record shops, which are little more than racks? When we read in the papers that jazz, for example, amounts to only 1 or 2 per cent of the market, we know the figures are distorted by the domination of the major labels, and we have their word for it that most of their stuff doesn't sell any more.

And that is almost the end of the history of popular music, because the best of it nowadays remains a secret.

19

Black Music: Everybody's Still Doing It

'Trouble is, he can't play it straight.' So said Charles Mingus about Ornette Coleman. Mingus had been regarded as avant-garde in his own time, and should have known better. In fact, he later assessed the situation more carefully: 'I'm not saying everybody's going to have to play like Coleman. But they're going to have to stop playing like Bird.'

Nearly fifty years after the advent of bop it is now revival music, and some youngsters are playing it without the fire of the generation of the 1940s, so that some of it sounds like wine-bar Muzak. In the 1940s bop was controversial; similarly, thirty years after the advent of free jazz one could wonder what all that fuss was about. Ornette Coleman's earliest tracks are simply and perfectly beautiful, especially to anyone who listens to contemporary classical music, to say nothing of horror-film soundtracks, where Hollywood hacks have used 'weird' sounds since the beginning of talkies.

I have defined popular music as commercial music, but what we used to call jazz has effectively become art music, confusing my definition. You will find records by Anthony Braxton, Bill Dixon and George Russell in the jazz section of the record catalogue, but all three are academics, like most classical composers. There is not much room for art in a music industry dominated by greed, but it is no coincidence that as the mainstream music industry has concentrated on making deals, music that can be described as contemporary has had to find a specialist audience.

It may be argued that the best music has often had a small audience. The court composers of the Renaissance who developed the classical forms which later flourished in Vienna were working for a musically educated aristocracy, which did not admit riff-raff to its music rooms. San Marco in Venice, the church for which Andrea and Giovanni Gabrieli, uncle and nephew, composed their innovative music in the sixteenth and seventeenth centuries, held 420 people comfortably, which was exactly the size of the Venetian government; there is no evidence that anyone else ever heard it. Opera was originally created for an audience that represented a small proportion of the total population of Italy around 1600. And it is fair to point out that some people want to leave the theatre whistling the tunes – or, to put it another way, Schoenberg never wrote a comic opera. (Actually, he did, *Von Heute auf Morgen* in 1928, but Schoenberg was not a funny man.) We will wait a long time for a laugh from Andrew Lloyd Webber, whose music is popular (that is, makes money) but is derivative and second-rate.

Irving Berlin said that popular music is popular because lots of people like it. But Berlin would not sanction much interpretation of his songs, and Jerome Kern's estate did not like Dizzy Gillespie's first recordings with strings (1946), which were not issued for many years (despite some extraordinary trumpet playing), nor the Platters' version of 'Smoke Gets in Your Eyes' (1958) until they realized how much money they would get from a number one hit.

The anti-modernists among us will turn Berlin round and say that some contemporary music is not very popular because not many people like it, but that argument will not wash with me. Grandma Clarke's idea of culture was a cracked 12-inch 78 of Madame Schumann-Heink singing 'Stille Nacht', but that did not stop me from embarking on a lifelong voyage of discovery. We do not know how popular Ornette Coleman, Cecil Taylor, Roscoe Mitchell or Braxton or the others might be, because we do not hear them on the radio, nor can we buy their records in the shopping-mall record outlets. Listeners who allow music to be pigeon-holed for them are effectively shutting their ear-holes. There are many instances of the public's adopting new music more enthusiastically than the critics. ASCAP used to complain with regard to BMI that if you restrict the public's listening, the public will quite happily settle for whatever it gets. This, of course, ignored the monopoly that ASCAP and Tin

Pan Alley had operated for many years, but the statement is true enough as far as it goes. Anthony Braxton has made albums of standards and of Monk's tunes, but you will not find them in the shopping-mall racks any more than you will find his spikier stuff.

It is also fair to add that the music of such avant-garde rock groups as Suicide, Rapeman and Pussy Galore is not meant to be easy-listening music, and is also not heard on the radio. But their thrashing is the sound of desperation, without any leavening of beauty. Most contemporary music still makes its point using acoustic instruments, and the musicians still listen to each other without the help of thousands of watts.

In any case, jazz has not been allowed near the centre of the marketplace for decades. That is partly why several of the best-known young (mostly white) saxophonists of today, although they play the same instruments as Johnny Hodges, Lester Young and Ben Webster played, all sound like they are playing for television commercials. Their carefully neutral tone is like the cooked milk you get for your tea or instant coffee in British restaurants, and the shopping-mall chord changes of their jazz present a big problem. It must be admitted that the modal method offers a cop-out opportunity, like having to use only the white keys on the piano. Some of today's jazz is wrapped in cellophane, like one of those big Easter baskets full of cheap chocolate and fake grass.

In fact, the word 'jazz' does not mean much any more, so the real stuff we now call improvised music, and even that label is not good enough; some modern music is entirely improvised, and some not very much at all. Jesse Stone told Frank Driggs that he wrote out the solos for his Blues Serenaders on 'Starvation Blues' in 1927. And despite all the efforts to create a third-stream music over the years, jazz and classical (contemporary) music have been cuddling together over in the corner while nobody was watching.

As we saw in an earlier chapter, pianist and composer Lennie Tristano was a retiring sort, whose teaching points were adventurous harmony and complex inner rhythms. Among his pupils were saxophonists Lee Konitz, Warne Marsh and Ted Brown, of whom Konitz is the best known. Having studied with Tristano, he was one of the few alto saxophonists who was not overwhelmed by Charlie Parker.

Warne Marsh died in 1987, still in obscurity; he made twenty or so albums, most of them on tiny labels. *All Music* (1977) is probably one of the best: touring with Supersax, a band that played transcriptions of Charlie Parker solos, he made an album in Chicago because Chuck Nessa offered him the chance. His tone was unique, and his approach to tonality and his slightly quirky time (a matter of personal accents) made him a more interesting player than most, for those who cared to listen. Ted Brown recorded with Marsh and British-born pianist Ronnie Ball in the 1950s, but made only one album as a leader, in 1956, and did not make another for twenty-nine years. I found Brown's trio set *Free Spirit* (1987), his second album for the Dutch Criss Cross label, not on the radio, not in the media, not in a record shop, but in a friend's basement. For me it was one of the discoveries of a decade: Jacques Scholes on bass provides a strong walking beat from which the piano and the saxophone can launch themselves; Hod O'Brien's agreeable, swinging piano would alone be worth the price of the album, and Brown's tone is the kind of sound your best friend would make if he or she could play saxophone. The whole thing is so mellow and so beautiful that it is astonishing to realize that Brown had not made any albums for three decades.

These people play standards: *Free Spirit* includes 'Body and Soul', 'Darn That Dream' and 'Lover Come Back to Me'. They play jazz classics, like Lester Young's 'Lester Leaps In' and Charlie Parker's 'Relaxin' at Camarillo', and their own tunes, such as Brown's 'Smog Eyes' and Marsh's sardonically titled 'Background Music', all of which are more or less based on the same chord structures that were used by the composers of the standards. And where else is there to go? If you want something a little more adventurous, there is the bold humour and unique tone of Von Freeman, and the 'metallic cocaine bebop' of Fred Anderson, both black Chicagoans, both available (though you have to try hard to buy good records) and neither particularly hard to take for tender ears. Or you can listen to somebody who has taken a leap and invented his own music, as Louis Armstrong, Coleman Hawkins, Lester Young and Charlie Parker did in the past.

Enter Ornette Coleman, and free jazz. Alto saxophonist and composer Coleman played in a school marching band with reedmen

Prince Lasha and Dewey Redman, and drummer (and trumpeter) Charles Moffett. At sixteen he changed from alto to tenor for a while, inspired by local tenor saxophonist Red Connors. He had never listened to R&B as a boy, but played in R&B bands to make a living, sometimes getting fired because he was trying to find his own way; he settled in Los Angeles, working in day jobs while studying theory. He did not find sympathetic collaborators until he had been playing for a decade. He worked with trumpeter Bobby Bradford, drummer Ed Blackwell and pianist and composer Paul Bley in the mid-1950s, and then he began intensive private sessions with trumpeter Don Cherry, drummer Billy Higgins and bass player Charlie Haden, the group that became the Ornette Coleman Quartet.

After being introduced by bass player Red Mitchell to Lester Koenig, head of the Contemporary label, Coleman made his first album in early 1958, *Something Else!!!*, with a quintet that included Cherry and Higgins. *Tomorrow is the Question!* in early 1959 included Cherry, Shelly Manne and Mitchell. Mitchell then introduced Coleman to third-streamers John Lewis and Gunther Schuller, who helped him get to a summer jazz school at Lenox, Massachusetts, and a gig at the Five Spot in New York in November. He had signed with Atlantic, and made seven albums' worth of tracks between May 1959 and March 1961 (there was still unissued material, and a six-CD set of the complete Atlantic recordings is available in 1994). He played at the Newport and Monterey jazz festivals, and a recording of a Town Hall concert in late 1962 was issued on ESP, but he did not record again in the studio until mid-1965. He was composing and studying trumpet and violin, but he was also disgusted that Dave Brubeck's quartet could get much more money: Coleman demanded similar fees, and did not get any work. He was criticized for this, but he had a right to price his own work, and he has been a good deal more influential than Brubeck ever was.

Coleman's appearance in New York was a great shock, much more sudden than bop had been. During the acoustic era a tin-eared A&R man at Victor would not record Bill Challis's arrangements for Jean Goldkette, and did not like Bix Beiderbecke's 'wrong' notes; in the late 1940s the boppers ran into the same problem, and in 1960 it was Coleman's turn. For a while he was famous, as fame in jazz goes, though controversy does not pay the rent. He played a white plastic alto saxophone, because he liked the sound of it, and Cherry played a pocket trumpet. The instruments looked like toys, which gave the critics something else to complain about (but perhaps led to the Coleman title 'Joy of a Toy'). Some people thought Coleman was a charlatan, but Leonard Bernstein was a fan, while George Russell, who had written a textbook on the use of modes, knew exactly what was happening: 'Ornette seems to depend on the overall tonality of the song as a point of departure for melody ... This approach liberates the improvisor to play his own song, really, without having to meet the deadline of any particular chord.' I do not know what Coleman's theory of 'harmelodics' means, but it doesn't matter; to the ordinary listener the music is aharmonic.

Writing about music is not as secure as working in the car factory, and certainly does not pay as well, but it has one big advantage. There was no music in the car factory, whereas while writing this I am listening to *The Art of Improvisation*, a 1970 compilation of unissued Coleman tracks from a decade earlier. 'The Fifth of Beethoven', for example, with Cherry, Haden and Blackwell, is enormous fun; it is a bright, funny, uptempo piece on which Coleman's alto sound reminds me of Eric Dolphy (who also came out of intensive private jams in Los Angeles). The influence of Charlie Parker is there, and also of Thelonious Monk, in that Coleman is first and last a composer whose time is unique – like Monk's, a matter of phrasing and accents. As I listen, I hear Blackwell's tom-toms in a duet with Coleman, and just as I am chuckling at that, I notice that Haden's driving bass on the other channel is doubling the alto's phrases, and while my attention is away, Blackwell is up to something else. The music has the cry of the blues in it, and we are reminded once again that the blues was never a dead end in the black community in the way that rock has become a blind alley for the white. The best black music always has the blues in it.

It was called free jazz, and some people still call it that, but it is certainly hard to see now why it was controversial, or why it has not made more money for Coleman, especially since some of the shopping-mall Muzak rockers of today are trying feebly to imitate it. It was, of course, not free at all, not as free as those experimental tracks Tristano made in 1949, with Marsh and Konitz. Coleman's Atlantic album of late 1960, *Free Jazz*, was played by a double quartet of Coleman, Cherry, Haden and Blackwell, and Eric Dolphy, Freddie Hubbard, Higgins and the brilliant young bass player Scott La Faro (who was killed in a car crash). The album is generally regarded as a noble failure, though Max Harrison, in his brilliant collection *A Jazz Retrospect* (1976), describes it as a perfectly coherent whole, its shape arising out of its language. In any case, this was not completely free either.

There is completely free music. The British guitarist Derek Bailey is an exponent of it and has written a book about it. But music seems to need a leadership factor, however much the leader may rely upon or allow a supporting cast to do its own thing. This is not to denigrate Bailey or saxophonist Evan Parker or any of the free players; many of them are loaded with talent. They know that improvisation is of enormous importance to music, and always has been; and improvisation is one of the things missing from today's rock and pop; the Grateful Dead have been improvising since the 1960s and still have an enormous following for their live gigs. It is not the public that is afraid of improvisation, but the record companies and the broadcasters. Yet the freest experiments have the smallest audience of all, for the same reasons that spaceships do not carry passengers: the air is too thin and the risk too great.

Ornette Coleman's many projects have included the *Chappaqua Suite* (1965), written for a quartet and a studio band, and *Skies of America* (1972), for the quartet and the London Symphony Orchestra. Coleman's work at the rehearsals and recording sessions earned him a standing ovation from the LSO, but the project must have been a commercial disaster. *Dancing in Your Head* (1973) was for sextet, two guitars and musicians in Joujouka, Morocco. In the late 1970s he formed Prime Time, whose electric sound was influenced by rock. Critics seem to have been disappointed with whatever he has done since the early 1960s; he seems not to be providing the leadership factor he began with. He has not been as influential as he was in those first few years, but then we do not know what he might have done had he been able to do whatever he liked. He set us all on our ears with a new kind of fire and beauty three decades ago, and

Harrison believes that Coleman was the single most revolutionary musician in the history of jazz: while Louis Armstrong and Charlie Parker accelerated development, Coleman opened doors.

Cecil Taylor, who has almost become celebrated, is one of the best-known international performers in this music, and has many recordings under his belt. He first recorded in 1956, with Steve Lacy on soprano and Buell Neidlinger on bass (both of whom were white and had started in dixieland) and Dennis Charles on drums. From his playing of standards, it was already obvious that Taylor was singing in his own language. A fascinating if unsuccessful session for United Artists in 1959 included John Coltrane (and is now marketed under his name); the trumpet player was Kenny Dorham, a fine bop musician who was already aware of Taylor's reputation and did not like it. (Taylor had wanted Ted Curson for the date.) Taylor soon decided to play only his own music, developing his unique keyboard sound into a musical world of tough, dancing beauty.

He and Neidlinger led sessions on Candid in 1960–61, which were not issued in full until a Mosaic box in 1989. In the early 1960s he was involved in a jazz composers' collective in New York that failed. His Blue Note recordings, *Unit Structures* and *Conquistador* (1966), were breakthroughs, his first commercial recordings for five years.

Like all the best musicians, Taylor understood and valued tradition without being bound to it and without showing any self-conscious need to be avant-garde. He has been described as using the piano as '88 tuned drums', yet again and again his sidemen and collaborators, such as Neidlinger, who once shared a flat with him and watched him practise, speak of the importance of singing and dancing in Taylor's music. We are reminded again of Dizzy Gillespie's complaining that he could dance to bop: why couldn't others?

Whitney Balliet compared Ornette Coleman with Cecil Taylor:

Taylor and Ornette Coleman are the nominal heads of the jazz avant-garde, but they are very different. Coleman refuses to record or play in public unless he is paid handsomely. Taylor until recent years often played for pennies – when he was asked to play at all. Coleman's music is accessible, but he is loath to share it; Taylor's music is difficult, and he is delighted to share it ... The American aesthetic landscape is littered with idiosyncratic marvels – Walt Whitman, Charles Ives, D. W. Griffith, Duke Ellington, Jackson Pollock – and Taylor belongs with them.

But so does Coleman. Balliet warns us that Taylor's music is difficult, but he was writing about an audience that had just listened to Oscar Peterson, and walked out in droves on Taylor. It is a weird concert or festival that plans juxtapositions like that. Contemporary improvised music is sometimes loud; so are symphonies, and, like the symphonies, improvised music does not need electronics. It sometimes has everyone playing at once; so did New Orleans jazz. It is often passionate, even angry, but it is equally often about tonal beauty. The screaming avant-garde electric rock group seems to attack its roots; contemporary improvised music celebrates them, but it is tough music for people who know that music is important.

The young Miles Davis had evolved an economic style that did not require him to compete in a front line with the fiery likes of Charlie Parker; his limitations became his starting point. There had always been some danger in bop of using too many notes, which might get in the way of the rhythm; in earlier styles of jazz each note was an essential part of the story, while in bop the overall feeling of the solo and the ensemble made the individual notes less important. Bop was bound to cool off, and Davis had always been a lyricist. Over the years since 1960 the modal style of composition has sometimes produced players who sound like they are taking it easy, but Davis's combination of soul, economy and lyricism and the weight of each note made him a complete master of the style. His effect on the free movement has probably been underrated. His development was always in the direction of a stripped-down music without any unnecessary adornments (showing the influence of Monk), so that he helped to create the new freedom to use structure and harmony as tools in the musician's kit along with melody and rhythm.

By 1965 his quintet included Wayne Shorter on tenor; Ron Carter's acoustic bass and cello had been influential on Prestige albums with Eric Dolphy and pianist-composer Mal Waldron; pianist Herbie Hancock and drummer Tony Williams rounded out one of the most important rhythm sections of the 1960s. They would all go on to become inspirational leaders and producers in their turn. Davis's

group still played standards on the bandstand, and was more adventurous in the studio; *Live at the Plugged Nickel* was made in the Chicago
club in 1965, but not released in the USA until 1976: Shorter in
particular might have been even more influential at the time if this set
had been released earlier. Their studio album *Nefertiti* (1967) was the
last album Davis made without electric instruments.

Davis's music became more controversial and left some jazz fans
behind, but commercially he was the most successful jazz musician
since Brubeck. Every album he ever made is still selling, and eight of
them made *Billboard*'s list of the top two hundred best-selling albums
during the 1960s, four in the top hundred. Yet throughout his career
he battled to squeeze out of record companies, booking agents and
promoters the money to maintain the lifestyle to which he felt he was
entitled. Monk had lost his cabaret card and was unable to work in
jazz venues in New York; Mingus struggled through the 1960s; it is
clear that very few of the best American musicians of the past thirty
years have received sufficient support from the music industry to be
able to do whatever they may have liked to do, in terms of writing,
recording and touring with larger groups, for example. Mingus
especially saw himself as a composer, his work all of a piece, yet his
gigantic *Epitaph* was not put together and recorded by a twenty-nine-
piece group directed by Gunther Schuller until 1989, a decade after
his death. But he had written an appropriate chant for the black
community, which adds to the flavour of his *Cumbia and Jazz Fusion*
(1977):

> Who said mama's little baby likes shortnin' bread?
> Who said mama's little baby likes shortnin', shortnin' bread?
> That's some lie some *white* man upped an' said!
> Mama's little baby likes *truffles*!
> Mama's little baby likes *caviar*!

As drummer Dannie Richmond joins in, the chant is 'Diamonds!
Diamonds in the nose! Diamonds in the toes! Diamonds all *over*
mama's little baby!' And 'Schools! So our kids won't be raised to act
like no fools!' But America still has not heard the message.

Cannonball Adderley was the only jazz musician to rival Davis as a
commercial success, but he was not progressing musically. Without a

doubt the single most influential jazz musician of the decade, spawn-
ing legions of imitators as Armstrong, Young, Hawkins, Gillespie
and Parker had done before him, was John Coltrane, who sought
overtly spiritual values through his music – indeed, sought to go
beyond music with his horn – and almost single-handedly made it hip
to buy jazz records in an era dominated by rock.

In 1950, playing alto in Dizzy Gillespie's big band, Coltrane had
been introduced to Islam by Yusef Lateef. He later studied the
cabbala and Sufism, the mystical branches of Judaism and Islam
respectively. Coltrane had discovered the soprano saxophone in 1959;
in 1960 he first played it on a one-off album for Atlantic called *The
Avant Garde*, for which he borrowed sidemen from Coleman, and
also first recorded Rodgers and Hammerstein's 'My Favorite Things'
on Atlantic. His ballad 'Naima' was named after his first wife, and
remained one of his own favourite tunes. He had always played long
solos, as though unable to get it all in; the ballads and modal tunes
began to set a pattern of an almost hypnotic function of music-
making. Just before his death he was experimenting with the Varitone
electronic device, which would have allowed him to play a duet with
himself in octaves.

In 1961 he was the first artist signed to the Impulse label, a new
jazz division of ABC-Paramount. *Africa/Brass*, on which he was
backed by a large ensemble (including four French horns), offers
hints of African rhythms and Indian ragas, as well as 'Greensleeves'.
It was produced by Creed Taylor, but Bob Thiele then joined
Impulse; Coltrane had found a label that helped make him the
highest-paid black jazzman after Davis, and a producer who would
let him record as much as he wanted.

His epochal quartet included Jimmy Garrison on bass, Elvin
Jones, a furiously polyrhythmic powerhouse of a drummer, and
McCoy Tyner on piano, a still underrated player whose function was
often to pour oil on turbulent waters. Among the albums in 1962 was
Ballads. Coltrane's essential modesty came to the fore on the date for
Duke Ellington and John Coltrane (on various tracks of which Duke and
Trane swap sidemen); he had to be assured that one take was good
enough. With all his passion and religious intensity, Coltrane was
also always a lyricist, and named Stan Getz as one of his favourite

saxophonists. In 1963 *John Coltrane with Johnny Hartman* featured a Chicago vocalist with a deep, beautiful voice whose career needed help at the time.

The quartet recorded *A Love Supreme* in 1964, perhaps Coltrane's most famous album and certainly one of his most fully realized: he said that the four-part composition came to him all at once. His albums sold twenty-five to fifty thousand copies, which was very good for jazz, but *A Love Supreme* made it to six figures. As Bob Thiele remarked, you did not hear Coltrane's music on the radio, but he discovered that college students and young musicians were buying it. *Ascension* (June 1965) was more ambitious: a single piece covers an entire album played by eleven instruments (including five reeds: Coltrane, Pharoah Sanders and Archie Shepp on tenors, John Tchicai and Marion Brown on altos). 'Vigil' and 'Welcome' were recorded by the quartet the same day, and in October 'Kulu se Mama' completed an album of that title, a strongly rhythmic African-influenced piece for octet inspired by a poem by Juno Lewis. The five-part *Meditations* was recorded twice: once with the quartet in September 1965, and again by a sextet a few weeks later, adding Sanders and drummer Rashied Ali.

Coltrane's soprano was compared to the sound of Indian and African oboe-like instruments (today all his imitators play soprano, and they mostly all sound the same). He closely questioned Ravi Shankar, the genius of the sitar, about Indian music (and named one of his sons after him). He was inspired by his friend the Nigerian drummer Babatunde Olatunji, whose albums had been released on Columbia, but they never recorded together. He took to using two basses, because the sound reminded him of African water drums. He always valued Elvin Jones (despite Jones's volatile personality and voracious appetites) for his polyrhythmic abilities, but even Jones was not enough; Jones left after Coltrane began using two drummers. Tyner had already left, both because he wanted to pursue his own musical ideas and because Coltrane had added his second wife, Alice, on piano. (After his death she released Coltrane recordings with herself dubbed on harp, which was widely regarded as a questionable move.)

Coltrane was never afraid to use a certain coarseness of tone, or a squeak or an overblown note, yet none of it was ever gratuitous. The hypnotic qualities in some of his music worked perfectly, rather than sounding like hippie repetition celebrating the stoned state, of which there was plenty in that decade. Coltrane's music, sometimes incorporating chanting, and often atonal passages next to tonal ones, was a broad church. Artie Shaw was an admirer. Coltrane had fans who were jazz enthusiasts and others who were hippies, and he also had fans who were essentially religious people, for whom Coltrane's spiritual side was an open book. Shankar liked Coltrane's music, but was also troubled by it, for the passion in the music was troubled passion: Coltrane was a gentle, modest man who put everything he had into his vision of a world conquered by a love which transcended race, religion or nationality. Perhaps he knew that his was an unearthly vision, and that he did not have long to describe it.

After Eric Dolphy died, his parents gave his bass clarinet and his flute to Coltrane, who played them both. *Expression* was made in early 1967, by the quartet plus Sanders, and the music has been reduced to an emotional essence: on 'To Be' Coltrane on flute and Sanders on piccolo accompany each other, and on the rest of the album Coltrane plays tenor. Much of the music is relatively quiet and reflective, yet there is none of the tension-and-release structure normally associated with jazz: the emotional intensity is complete, unrelieved and harrowing. He died of cancer in July of that year. It would be interesting to know how sales of, say, *A Love Supreme* over twenty-five years compare with the total sales of, say, *In-a-gadda-da-vida*, by Iron Butterfly, a piece of hippie junk that was number four not long after Coltrane's death.

There are those who regret that so many tenor saxophonists have sounded like Coltrane since he died, but that is not Coltrane's fault. All the best have had large numbers of imitators. Those influenced by Ornette Coleman do not get many chances to be heard; there have been fewer places for young saxophonists to play in recent decades, and fewer chances for them to hear each other.

Pharoah Sanders formed a band that contained pianist-composer Lonnie Liston Smith and Leon Thomas, a vocalist who had sung with Count Basie and whose bag of tricks in the late 1960s included an evocative yodelling technique learned from central African music. Archie Shepp was a failed guru in that decade, a sort of safe shadow

of Albert Ayler. He also recorded for Impulse. His style was described
as darkly operatic, but he changed it too often and lost the thread,
the theory becoming as important as the music. In 1991 Shepp
seemed to have mellowed – among the songs played at a gig in
London were Ellington ballads – yet still produced a unique sound
on his horn.

Miles Davis turned to electric music in 1969 and sold records to
the more stylish rock fans; from *In a Silent Way* and *Bitches Brew*
onwards he lost old fans and made new ones. His sidemen from that
period, electric pianists Chick Corea and Joe Zawinul, Wayne
Shorter, guitarist John McLaughlin and others, formed electric
fusion bands, such as Weather Report and Return to Forever. Electric bass player Jaco Pastorius brought considerable artistry to this
music, and was destitute when he died in 1987, not yet thirty-six
years old, manic depressive and alcoholic; the music seemed to have
run out of steam as well. Its most ardent fans would have to admit
that the quality of the noodling was variable; other fusions were
going on which were not self-consciously forced, and did not need
electricity.

All these fusions, forced and unforced, are a clue to the reason why
there has been no single influential figure in recent years such as
Armstrong, Parker, Coleman or Coltrane. Contemporary music has
become an international and collectivist endeavour, and a post-
modernist one in that all music is now repertory music. Such a
multiplicity of styles is played everywhere that there may never again
be domination by a single individual. This is a serious inconvenience
to those young artists who need somebody to copy as they start out,
and this may be another reason why Coltrane has been so imitated:
there has not been anyone so powerful since.

Albert Ayler might have been similarly influential, but he did not
live long enough. The tenor saxophonist burst upon the public
apparently using the honks and squawks of the early Jazz at the
Philharmonic concerts, but had more than that in mind; he was
searching even more aggressively than Coleman or Coltrane for
spiritual and musical freedom. John Litweiler wrote about two
simultaneous solos on 'Green Dolphin Street' on one of Ayler's first
albums, a tape made for Danish radio in early 1963:

One solo is inside, in observance of the bland harmonic structure (he pays dogged attention to turnbacks, chorus outline, alarming turns of phrases from free motions to inside tonality), and the other solo is outside by way of his sound (alternately gigantic, braying, slurring, or else whiny and querulous) and his occasional phrasing (fast, arhythmic, spiraling upward like fireworks from which smaller explosions shoot off). There's no doubt that in these performances Ayler's music is in great crisis; 'Summertime' . . . accepts the crisis, balancing the standard setting against his ideas of sound and his drifting sense of tonality to result in a long, tragic masterpiece.

Ayler came from a middle-class background, but knew the cry of the church, and had spent two summers as a young man touring in R&B with Little Walter and his Jukes. Then he seemed to take apart the history of jazz in order to reinvent it. Soon, like Taylor, he began playing only his own music (he made eight recordings of 'Ghosts'). Musicians like drummer Sunny Murray and bass player Henry Grimes were already playing free, but under Ayler's influence they gained in authority. Murray, for example, was not a loud drummer and never used a fancy kit, yet completely liberated percussion by means of delicacy and dynamics. Ayler puzzled or irritated many; Alan Bates recorded him for an appearance on a BBC jazz programme in 1966, but the BBC wiped the tape. He changed direction, changed to alto (losing some weight in his music) and dabbled in Mexican and folk musics, and in 1968 even tried rock on an album called *New Grass*. Some thought he was in decline, distracted by the powerful effect the psychedelic counterculture was having at the time, but Ayler, like Coltrane, was searching for something beyond music. He may have been recovering his sense of purpose in 1970, but his body was found in the East River, his death never explained. His music ultimately included everything, and for all the shortness of his career, he has been more influential than most.

African drummer Olatunji and John Coltrane had begun to form a centre for the creation of African-American music, but it was never fully realized. Musicians began to see that there was not enough room in the American commercial market for everyone, and that they had no choice but to take matters into their own hands. Trumpeter, composer and academic Bill Dixon was behind the 'October Revolution', a series of concerts at New York's Cellar Café in 1964, the same year in which lawyer Bernard Stollman formed ESP Records, an almost underground label that recorded Ayler, Milford Graves and others (as well as the Fugs and other New York City exotica). Dixon was a charter member of the Jazz Composers Guild, with Shepp, Cecil Taylor, Carla Bley, Paul Bley, Mike Mantler, Sun Ra, alto saxophonist John Tchicai, trombonist Roswell Rudd and others; they gave concerts in late 1964. Then Shepp signed a contract with Impulse, foolishly regarded as a sell-out by some of the others, and, according to Valerie Wilmer, bandleader Sun Ra professed himself superstitious: like a sailor, he did not like having a woman on board. The Guild failed, but led to the creation of the Jazz Composer's Orchestra Association (JCOA), formed by Carla Bley and Mantler. The first fruit was a two-disc set of Mantler's thickly textured music for a large orchestra called simply *JCOA* (1968), with such soloists as Taylor, Pharoah Sanders, Don Cherry, Roswell Rudd, guitarist Larry Coryell, tenor saxophonist Gato Barbieri and bass player Steve Swallow. Further albums by Carla Bley, Charlie Haden, soprano saxophonist Steve Lacy and others were released. Carla Bley became the leader of one of the few avant-garde big bands, directly competing with Ra for the audience: in music there is no more place for misogyny than for racism. In 1970 the Jazz and People's Movement interrupted taping of the chat shows of Merv Griffin, Johnny Carson and Dick Cavett (thus hitting all three television networks), and the result of this attention-seeking device was an appearance on Ed Sullivan's show by an all-star band including Roland Kirk.

The Archie Shepp–Bill Dixon Quartet and the New York Contemporary Five, for which Dixon wrote, never had enough work. It was clear that the music had to be taken back to the community from which it came, so that the community could demand support for it. There was always an enthusiastic response to open rehearsals and so forth, especially from young people, but there was never going to be enough commercial sponsorship. Dixon taught art history for a living; a University of the Streets was formed by Puerto Ricans in 1967 and Dixon helped form the Free Conservatory of the University of the Streets the following year, leading an orchestral rehearsal which helped to clinch one of the first federal grants for such a project. Percussionist Milford Graves was also an activist in this field, and among other, similar projects was Graves's Storefront Museum, a warehouse converted into a community project in Queens. In Harlem writer Leroi Jones (who later became Amiri Baraka) had formed the Black Arts group, which presented music in the street. The Jazzmobile was a bandstand on a truck that in 1964 began to take music from neighbourhood to neighbourhood. Encouraged by the Harlem Community Council and originally sponsored by Coca-Cola and Ballentine beer, it took the music to several New York boroughs, often presenting it to black youngsters who had never heard it before. People emerged from their houses out of curiosity and always responded positively.

Despite all this activity, the omens were never good. The artists who recorded for ESP were irritated that it did not result in more income for them, but if the music is not widely heard and the records widely distributed, there is never going to be any money in a record label. When Roland Kirk asked Ed Sullivan in 1970, several years after John Coltrane's death, why he had never had Coltrane on his programme, the most famous presenter of American talent asked, 'Does John Coltrane have any records out?' An important source for recordings of contemporary music, the New Music Distribution Service, originally connected with the JCOA, lasted until 1990 before going under.

The Black Artists Group was formed in St Louis, Strata in Detroit; but easily the most important of the collectives was the Association for the Advancement of Creative Musicians in Chicago.

Chicago has always been a centre of musical activity. In the 1920s the scene of the thriving black culture was virtually next to the Loop (the downtown area defined by the tracks of the elevated trains). The recording of black music in Chicago was hurt by one of Petrillo's early strikes, but nothing can keep Chicago down for long. In the late 1940s and 1950s pianist and composer Andrew Hill, saxophonists Eddie Johnson and Von Freeman, multi-instrumentalist Hal Russell and many others played in Chicago clubs, and bigger names from New York also visited. Pianist Ahmad Jamal formed a trio and became a national figure, and an influence on Miles Davis.

The importance of Captain Walter Dyett cannot be overestimated.

He began on violin, and played banjo and guitar in Erskine Tate's Vendome Theater Orchestra; he conducted an all-black US Army band, and in 1931 became bandmaster at Wendell Phillips High School, the name of which was changed to DuSable High School in 1936. According to Dempsey Travis, Dyett 'could hear a mosquito urinate on a bale of cotton'. He directed five high-school bands and the annual *Hi-jinks* show, which raised money to buy instruments (since the Board of Education would not buy them), as well as an alumni band which played in local clubs, at annual entertainments for Shriners conventions and so forth. He taught Bo Diddley violin. His students over the years included pianists Nat Cole, Dorothy Donegan and John Young, trombonists Bennie Green and Julian Priester, bass players Fred Hopkins and Richard Davis (who said, 'Maybe you weren't afraid of the cops, but you were afraid of Captain Dyett'), drummers Wilbur Campbell and Bruz Freeman, vocalist Dinah Washington, reedmen Gene 'Jug' Ammons (son of boogie-woogie pianist Albert), Eddie Harris, John Gilmore, Clifford Jordan, Johnny Griffin and Von Freeman, and guitarist George Freeman. (The three Freemans are brothers.) Some of them went straight off to work with Lionel Hampton or Count Basie. The names of teachers are usually obscure, but they are of the highest importance, and Captain Dyett was one of the greatest of all.

Sonny Blount, a young pianist and composer from Birmingham, Alabama, worked for Fletcher Henderson at Chicago's Club DeLisa in 1946–7; before long he was reincarnated as a messenger from the planet Venus called Sun Ra, whose influence and example have been priceless. 'Who knows the history of a prophet?' wrote J. B. Figi in a sleeve-note in 1967, for a reissue of Ra's first album:

July 12, 1956. Charlie Parker was but fifteen months dead. John Coltrane was barely beginning to tug ears as a sideman. No-one expected the still-distant messianic coming of Ornette Coleman. The musician usually credited with being the first of the current avant-garde to make his statement, Cecil Taylor, was gingerly putting together his first pieces, and would have to wait two months for his first recording date . . . On that day, [the Transition label] was busy elsewhere, having come to Chicago to summon to a recording studio Sun Ra and his frankly far-out rehearsal band . . . 'Music rushing forth like a fiery law,' Sun Ra promises in a poem, and delivers. The band moves like a big loose threshing machine through a field of heavy, sun-swollen grain. This mystic band of Chicagoans, driven by donkey-engine rhythms, roars, stomps, chugs along full of its own purpose, sounding like a Midwestern riff-jump band and a wig band at one and the same time, solos jumping out of the whole with spontaneity, yet spare and telling.

That first album, *Sun Song*, is now available on CD, and sounds as though it ought to have been a *Billboard* best-seller in 1957. It is impossible now to understand how those donkey-engine rhythms, like Chicago itself chunky and swinging at the same time, could ever have been called 'far out'.

The band left town in 1960 for a gig in Montreal: the club-owner seems to have been expecting a rock band, and the gig was not a success. They drifted to New York, and maintained a worldwide hand-to-mouth existence, staying together because nobody else can do what they do, and because big bands are important. Countless records with little in the way of documentation were issued on their own Saturn label, and finally in the 1980s the market and the listeners' ears began to catch up. Ra's music had soon admitted more abstract sounds, and later electronics, but never any effects for their own sake; the band's Buck Rogers costumes acquired an African flavour. The act included powerful percussion pieces, in which everybody in the band contributed to a multi-rhythmic sound that could make the building jump; musical melodramas with reedmen chasing each other around the stage, always with beautifully clear individual tone and never dropping a beat or a note; and a cappella chants ('Space is the place!') that could make a mob follow them into the nearest teleport chamber. Suddenly they might break into their version of a fifty-year-old arrangement by Henderson, or Ellington or Lunceford. Long before he died in 1992, Ra did not sound so weird any more; and the band's earlier works are being reissued on the Evidence label.

But back in Chicago, Sun Ra's departure had left a hole in the musical scene. Pianist and composer Muhal Richard Abrams formed his Experimental Band to encourage creative collaboration between composers and improvisers: 'Now I can take eight measures and play a concert,' he later said to John Litweiler. After several years of

Abram's inspiring tuition the cooperative became official in May 1965 with the formation of the Association for the Advancement of Creative Musicians (AACM), when thirty or so founders gathered at the home of trumpeter Phil Cohran.

Cohran ran an Afro-arts Ensemble, which included drummer Robert Crowder. Thurman Barker is a percussionist whose career as a composer and recording artist had to fight with steady demand for his skills: he had regular employment at Chicago's Schubert Theater for a dozen years, and only released his own first album, *Voyage*, in 1984. Fred Anderson, a distinctive tenor saxophonist and composer, ran a tavern, practising in the back when business was slow. Anthony Braxton, an extremely bright, witty and serious composer, reedman and leader, has since become one of the leading international concert artists in contemporary music, working as a teacher to pay the bills. Reedman Henry Threadgill, bass player Fred Hopkins and percussionist Steve McCall formed Air, which became well known on the concert circuit and made several fine albums, but never had enough full-time work.

McCall was replaced by Pheeroan akLaff when New Air was formed in 1983, and at about that time Threadgill also began putting together his Sextet (actually a septet, counting the leader); after three albums on the New York label About Time, Threadgill signed to Novus, a subsidiary of RCA/BMG, and the spelling changed to Sextett; they had released three more albums by 1990. Threadgill's tunes were structured tone poems, not at all 'atonal', but also used gospel voicings and collective improvisation. Like all the best music, they were unclassifiable and immediately unique, and the reeds, trumpet, trombone, bass, cello and two percussionists played them with the spirit of neighbourhood street music. In the 1990s Threadgill's new group was Very Very Circus, a septet containing two electric guitars and two tubas.

The purpose of the AACM was to seek employment among themselves instead of waiting for somebody to hire them. They began with concerts and open rehearsals of free jazz, original compositions only, and composers wrote for anyone who wanted to play. Perhaps it was the flavour of Chicago, laid back yet positive, that made it work. The AACM has remained one of the most popular

and fertile collectives ever organized, despite the fact that, for example, a series of ten concerts celebrating its twentieth anniversary in
1985 had to be run on a shoestring. The collective itself has never
had any money, concentrating as it does on presenting Chicago's
music to Chicago's neighbourhoods.

The best-known and most successful progeny of the AACM has
been the Art Ensemble of Chicago. The original members, also
founder members of the AACM, were bass player Malachi Favors,
trumpeter Lester Bowie and reedmen Joseph Jarman and Roscoe
Mitchell; Jarman had led an informal group with Barker and others.
Iowa-born Chuck Nessa, who worked in the Jazz Record Mart for
peanuts in exchange for the opportunity to produce some records,
recorded Abrams, Jarman and Mitchell for Delmark, then formed his
own eponymous label and recorded the nucleus of what was to
become the Art Ensemble.

Three albums made in 1967–8, released under the names of Bowie,
Jarman and Mitchell, included trio, quartet and solo items. *Old/
Quartet*, with Philip Wilson (who shortly after joined the Paul Butterfield Blues Band in order to make a living), was their basement
tapes; a good introduction to their casual brilliance, it reaches out to
nourish its roots in the street. Once again Chicago was a world-
beater in music, but this time fewer were listening. Born and raised
only 65 miles away, I did not hear of the AACM until it had been
under way for several years, and this was at a time when there were
more radio stations and the record industry was moving four or five
times as much product as twenty-five years earlier.

Mitchell's *Congliptuous* was recorded by a quartet of Bowie, Mitchell, Favors and Robert Crowder; the other side of the record contained
three solos, for Favor's bass, Mitchell's alto and Bowie's trumpet.
After being asked by the journalist Dave Flexenbergstein (of *Jism*
magazine), 'Is jazz, as we know it, dead, yet?', Bowie plays a seven-
minute solo, built on what sounds like a marching-band fragment,
stopping halfway through to ask Flexenbergstein to please remove
his hat. Having established himself with his slurs and burnished tone
as the Cootie Williams of the avant-garde, he answers at the end,
'Well, that, I guess, that all depends on, uh, how much you *know*.'

Pianist Christopher Gaddy and cellist and bass player Charles Clark were immensely gifted, and seemingly had brilliant futures; they both died at the age of twenty-four. They had both played on Jarman's Delmark album *Song For*; Gaddy died in 1968; Jarman recorded 'Song for Christopher' on his *As if It Were the Seasons*, on which Clark played; then Clark died in April of 1969 of a brain haemorrhage. These tragedies may have concentrated the minds of the group: Mitchell, Jarman, Bowie and Favors left for France (instead of New York, marking a change in the history and economics of modern music), became the Art Ensemble of Chicago and, from June, made about a dozen albums in less than two years, including studio sets, live concert performances and a soundtrack for the film *Les Stances à Sophie*, featuring Mrs Bowie, Fontella Bass, one of the best voices in the black chart in the mid-1960s. ('Rescue Me' had been a number one, on Checker.)

The soundtrack and the tone poem *People in Sorrow* were recorded in Boulogne for Pathé and issued in the USA on Nessa. Jean-Luc Young and Jean Georgakarakos had formed a chain of record shops in France; they also formed *Actuel*, a trendy paper, and, in 1967, the Byg label, for which they leased the American Savoy catalogue and made over sixty albums of new free jazz, much of it by Chicago artists. They went broke in 1975, mainly because of spending too much money on one of the biggest festivals Europe ever saw. There were accusations of carelessness with their properties, and at one point they dumped carloads of LPs in America, getting into trouble with the American owners of some of the material. Jean Karakos, as he is now known, formed Celluloid in 1976 in New York, and several offshoots, still serving experimental music. Young formed Charly in Paris in 1974 and moved it to London the next year. Charly reissues rockabilly, country and R&B and has a delightful catalogue; its managing director, Joop Visser, started Affinity in 1976 for jazz reissues, including most of the Byg recordings.

Byg recorded several of the Art Ensemble's classics. *Message from Our Folks* offered Charlie Parker's 'Dexterity', the percussion feature 'Rock On' and the moving, hypnotic avant-garde revival meeting of 'Old-time Religion', as well as the tone poem 'Brain for the Seine'. *There's a Jackson in Your House* was a wacky, swinging statement of fact: there had been a Jackson in the house for decades, and it was long past time that Robert Crumb's nervously sweating comic-book Whiteman (no relation to Paul) joined the parade.

By early 1971 they had recruited percussionist Famoudou Don Moye; in 1972 their performance at the Ann Arbor (Michigan) Blues Festival was recorded; that album and a 1973 studio set, both produced by Michael Cuscuna, were released on Atlantic. More albums were issued on Freedom, Prestige and other labels; they ended up on Manfred Eicher's high-class ECM label in the late 1970s, and recorded the mature classics *Nice Guys*, *Full Force* and *Urban Bushmen*.

Nessa was twenty-two years old in the mid-1960s. At first, he said, 'I honestly had no idea what they were doing . . . I had to figure out how this music worked and whether it was bullshit or not . . . The thing that was obvious to me was that they knew what they were doing musically. I was lost but they had such confidence in their presentation that I was drawn to it.'

[Roscoe's] idea was for each to make his own music but to have stuff happening on different levels that meshed into a full sound, where each player would play at a different tempo (say) to create a kaleidoscopic effect . . . On *Old/Quartet* there is a piece where you have really soft drum patterns with brushes, and the bass playing a fast running line, with the saxophone and the trumpet each sounding like they are playing a different kind of music. The overall effect of the tension and release of this music is wonderful, and is really hard to sustain. I think this was the greatest creative music band that I've ever heard. They were incredibly consistent; it takes intensive rehearsal to sustain that kind of music, and keep a flow going in it.

Not long after being interviewed at length in Canada's venerable *Coda* jazz magazine, in 1993 Nessa issued a limited-edition five-CD set of everything in his vaults by these men, one of the releases of the decade. Working most of his life as a record distributor, he has never made a profit from his tiny record label and never will, but the twenty or so albums he made in Chicago over a period of twenty-five years are pearls without price.

The Art Ensemble that went to Paris was not Roscoe's group but a collective, and the music changed; some pieces were more Roscoe's and some Jarman's. Their 'Great Black Music' did not just practise collective improvisation, but swelled and roared with the sheer joy of it. Experiments with bassoon and bass saxophone had generated a desire for an infinite number of textures and timbres; everybody played 'little instruments', an uncountable collection of tuned and untuned percussion and horns from cowbells and woodblocks to whistles, steerhorns, bicycle horns and garbage-can lids. Yet the music is never cluttered, each timbre surprises in exactly the right place and the whole contains the entire history of black music and the black experience. A theatrical element – warpaint, costumes and mime – probably inspired by Jarman, enlivened the act and helped maintain the connection with community roots. Its absence took little away from the recordings, however; the music works without a video.

That the great Chicago tenor saxophonist Von Freeman is not a household name is partly because he preferred to play at the Enterprise Lounge on the South Side rather than chase precarious fame in less friendly environments. He tossed off two albums for Nessa in one day in 1975, and anyone who owns them knows that he belongs up there with Dexter, Rollins and Coltrane. He was no doubt available to the younger generation for moral support; his son Chico Freeman was a member of the AACM in the early 1970s and became a prolific recording artist. Chico is a master of the reeds, including the bass clarinet; his touring groups and albums have employed such musicians as bass players Cecil McBee and drummers Elvin Jones, Jack DeJohnette and Fred Waits. Chico is a composer, but not an innovator, and his music ought to work fine on the radio. You will not hear it on the radio, though, and the last time I talked to him he was selling computers on the side.

Anthony Braxton plays the music of Monk and has made albums of standards; he writes books about his own music, but his books make it look more difficult than it is. His quartet – Mark Dresser on bass, Gerry Hemingway on percussion and Marilyn Crispell on piano – set London on its ear in 1985, but Braxton does not make a living composing and playing. Since the Art Ensemble does not tour as much as it used to, Lester Bowie has been leading a crowd-pleasing brass ensemble. Roscoe Mitchell is, in my opinion, one of today's greatest composers, whether he is warming up his alto saxophone until it says, 'OK, you can play me now', or demonstrating all the timbres of which sixteen brass and woodwind instruments are capable, as in 'L-R-G', with only three musicians, or conducting 'The Maze', for eight percussionists, shot through with light, space and texture. But few have even heard of Roscoe.

How the obscure pianist and composer Joel Futterman survives is anybody's guess. He spent two years with the AACM, and released two or three albums on his own label from 1979. The loss of his frequent collaborator, the great alto saxophonist Jimmy Lyons, to cancer in 1986, was a terrible blow. His original, percussive and tough-minded solo pieces and his trio and quartet work with Jarman, Lyons, bass player Richard Davis and others deserve much wider exposure and are now available on CD (on Ear-Rational and Bellaphon, two more of the world's smaller labels).

Whitney Balliet might describe Futterman's music as difficult. If you want sheer obvious fun from the so-called avant-garde, you could have tried the white Chicagoan Hal Russell and his NRG Ensemble. Born in Detroit, Russell worked in Chicago most of his life, performing with such visiting firemen as Ellington, Miles, Rollins and Coltrane. He played drums at Newport with the free-jazz trio of saxophonist Joe Daley in 1963, began leading his own groups in the early 1970s and only discovered that the reeds were his true love around 1977. He led four younger men in a repertory of a couple of hundred original tunes whose stomping vigour and zany humour had to be heard to be believed. They made their first album in 1982; there were only two personnel changes in over a decade.

On their albums the quintet plays two trumpets, two basses, several reeds, drums, vibraphone, electric guitar, didgeridoos and anything else they fancy. After hearing them at the Moers Festival in June 1990 (their first trip to Europe), Steve Lake wrote in the *Wire*: 'Tales of neglect are the stuff of jazz, but I've rarely encountered a case as extreme as this one . . . Trust me, one of the hottest, hippest, wittiest bands on the globe.' Russell also made a duet album, *Eftsoons*, with reedman Mars Williams, who had been an early member of the NRG and re-joined in the late 1980s, and a solo album (with a lot of overdubbing), *Hal's Bells*. Only five NRG albums were released (on Nessa, Chief, Principally Jazz and ECM). Russell had once issued a cassette called *Don't Wait Too Long or I Could be Dead*; he died in 1992 at the age of sixty-six: the music business had waited too long. Three of the younger men were not even full-time musicians: drummer Steve Hunt works in the family clothing firm, and one of the others restores houses. Such is the best of the music business; but the NRG Ensemble intends to carry on.

This chapter should be several times as long. I have not said anything about Julius Hemphill, Frank Lowe, Charles Tyler, Hamiet Bluiett, John Stevens, Leo Smith, Rory Stuart, Edward Wilkerson, Jr, John Carter, Sunny Murray, David Murray, Ronald Shannon Jackson, Charles Brackeen, Joe Locke, Phil Markowitz, Slava Ganelin, Ran Blake, Paul Bley, Kenny Wheeler or Randy Weston. Youngish people who carry on the traditions and may or may not do something original someday are Jason Rebello, Tommy Smith, Andy Sheppard, Courtney Pine, Marcus Roberts, Roy Hargrove, Christopher Hollyday, Terence Blanchard, Donald Harrison and a bunch of Marsalises. These people are white, black, American, British, Russian. (The Norwegian Jan Garbarek, born in 1947, plays folk styles on the saxophones, and may be one of the most influential musicians in the world today, for better or worse.) They are revivalists and avant-gardists. Not enough of them are women, but Joanne Brackeen, Geri Allen and Marilyn Crispell, more or less in that order of 'accessibility', are pianist-composers worth any music lover's time. Bass player Richard Davis plays with post-bop revivalists and then turns in the wittiest, most zinging and precise avant-garde playing (with Futterman, for example) you have ever heard. Meanwhile, so many people are still sounding like John Coltrane, who has been gone over twenty-five years, that Scott Hamilton feels free to play in the fifty-year-old Ben Webster style, and gets better and better at it. Soprano saxophonist and clarinettist Bob Wilber, who studied as a teenager with Sidney Bechet, has recreated Benny Goodman and Duke Ellington sessions, and performed as a guest on an album of Bill Challis's arrangements recorded in 1986. Not only is improvised music alive and well, but revivalism has never been in better hands.

Guitarist George Benson, pianist Herbie Hancock and others have left jazz for high-class pop or for rock fusion, sometimes coming back again. Producer and arranger Quincy Jones seems to have disappeared entirely into slick studio pop. Miles Davis played his spare phrases over disco-flavoured backing tracks in the 1980s; you could hear more Miles by listening to his old recordings. Trumpeter Donald Byrd left for academia and formed a band of students called the Blackbyrds to play what amounted to disco, but at least they were flesh-and-blood musicians instead of computers. We can call it selling out, but they call it paying the rent. Arthur Blythe, a reedman, seems to change styles with every album; as he put it, 'I don't want to make records for posterity. I want to make records for prosperity.' Benson has a family to raise, and points out that when he recorded jazz, most of the record-buying public never heard it.

Yet a former car dealer has built a big catalogue on California's Concord Jazz label, recording mainstream jazz for an audience which has been starved of it for generations, while the major labels waste so much money chasing bubble-gum blockbusters that they cannot afford to bother with the audiences that are there. And yuppies fill their shelves full of immaculately recorded note-spinning 'New Age' dinner party music, the contemporary equivalent of Mantovani's strings. They are probably searching for chamber jazz, but they never learned how to listen. They should buy records by Stan Getz, Paul Bley, Bill Evans, Ted Brown, but the jazz bins in the shopping-mall record shops are full of the new mood music.

Will Ackerman ran a construction company and also played the guitar. When he released *In Search of the Turtle's Navel* in 1976 for a few fans, naming the Wyndham Hill label after his company, he effectively launched New Age, and had sales of $20 million in 1984. The artwork on the New Age records resembles that of ECM, the European label for improvised music formed by Manfred Eicher in 1970. Guitarist John Abercrombie made nine ECM albums between 1974 and 1981, and there are so many albums on that label by several people that some of them inevitably amount to note-spinning. Keith Jarrett spins out his notes across entire albums, moaning along with it, and sells many records, while the British pianist and composer Keith Tippett remains virtually unknown.

Pure New Age, sometimes confused by marketing people and by

magazine critics with jazz, perhaps began with the recordings of John Fahey and Leo Kottke on acoustic guitar in the 1960s. It is sometimes called new acoustic, and indeed often sounds folkish. The *Los Angeles Free Press* wrote of the album *Timeless* (1974) by keyboard player Jan Hammer and drummer Jack DeJohnette: 'You lie back, close your eyes and journey-soft ...' If we have loud narcissism in pop-rock, New Age is contemplative narcissism. The new mood music is impeccably played and recorded, but my old Percy Faith records have more musical content and less pretence. The acoustic piano album *Pianissimo* (1990, on Private Music) composed and played by Suzanne Ciani is also immaculately recorded, but her piano style on her soundalike tunes sounds to me like Carole King with a muscular spasm.

Many jazz musicians are still noodling. Chick Corea strolls on-stage with so many electronic keyboards around his neck it is a wonder the clatter does not drown out the music, but in 1991 an album was issued in five or six formats, including videodisc. Reedman Steve Coleman and others are playing something called M-base, combining elements of rock with jazz. What I have heard of it sounds rockist to me, but at least it is not background music. Maybe something will come of the various fusions some day; after all, most of Gunther Schuller's third-stream music over the decades has not been recorded and much of it has not even been played. If contemporary musicians sign conventional deals with major labels, tin-eared lawyers and producers try to tell them what to play; perhaps it is just as well that nearly all their best work is on dinky labels that the shops do not stock, many of them live recordings from European festivals such as Moers, Willisau and Zurich.

I began by describing the popular songs of the eighteenth century as strophic – that is, repetitious, so that the audience hears the melodic fragments over and over. It is clear that the most profitable popular music has been repetitious in nature, and that the golden age of American songwriting and the Swing Era itself were accidents of history, perhaps never to be repeated. Popular music since the invention of electrical recording has developed a spectrum that now includes kiddie music at one end and at the other music which is, to quote the title of Wilmer's book, *As Serious as Your Life*. But the word 'serious' in this context does not mean without joy. Our greatest artists do not strike poses for the media; the media do not pay much attention to them anyway. So why is it that everybody's doing it? If you have to ask, you are not listening. As for me, new records by Braxton, Mitchell and the others come out faster than I can afford to buy them, so as a music lover, I am happy.

But what about black pop?

In his book *The Death of Rhythm and Blues* Nelson George points out that forty years ago black communities had their own restaurants, hotels, baseball teams and so forth. Then came improvements in civil rights. The best black players were hired by major-league baseball and the black leagues went out of business, and where are the black owners and managers in the major leagues? Similarly, when blacks could use white restaurants and hotels, their own smaller businesses went broke: thrown into the same economic meat-grinder as the rest of us but with less money in their pockets and fewer jobs, they can now vote, but their neighbourhoods have crumbled. What remained of R & B was prettified, overproduced and burdened with technology, like white pop. Bedroom crooners and often beautiful 'sweet soul' voices were heard, but for the most part, unless you were Lionel Richie, the business did not want to know about black music. And meanwhile music education in the schools disintegrated. American taxpayers will vote against anything that costs money if they get a chance, so forget frills, like libraries. Forget music. The schools in some American states almost closed in the late 1970s because there was not enough money to keep the doors open; at the same time a new generation of black kids were inventing rap.

You can draw a parallel between black music and the American economy as a whole. The tiny middle class are the composers and performers celebrated around the world: Roscoe Mitchell, Leo Smith, Braxton and the rest, relatively poor as they are. The working class is really nowhere: if all an aspiring young black musician wants to do is play in the Hollywood studios or in a symphony orchestra, there are not enough jobs.

And there is the underclass, which could not even afford to go to discos, and had no musical training whatever. But they had turntables and a few records. So they invented their own mixes, by switching back and forth between two copies of the same record, such as James Brown's 'Get on the Good Foot', the harder, funkier music that disco had come from. Using microphones, they chanted over their music, as in Jamaican dub, in which the D J chants over an instrumental reggae track (one of the first in the new rap genre was Jamaican-born Kool Herc of the South Bronx). The inventiveness of the street dancers was soon called breaking, or break dancing. The amateur D Js would break into a street-lamp for electricity in the middle of the afternoon, and by two or three the next morning there would be hundreds of kids hanging out, watching the dancers, enjoying the sounds.

The fad was called hip-hop, from a Lovebug Starsky record: 'To the hip, hop, hippedy-hop.' Then it came to be called rap, itself originally from black slang, a trendy 1960s word for conversation. The chanting was supposed to be improvised, and the whole thing remained a cult for a while, until it crossed over into the commercial music business. Fifteen years later the fad is still with us.

'Rapper's Delight' by the Sugar Hill Gang (producer Sylvia Vanderpool again, seizing the opportunity as she had done in the early days of disco) was a freak hit in 1979. 'The Breaks' in 1980 on Mercury was regarded as a novelty. Afrika Bambaataa and his Soul Sonic Force were big in 1982; James Brown himself may be heard in a duet on 'Unity' (1984). Grandmaster Flash (Joseph Sadler) was one of the first to use 'montage' on records, adding sound effects and making rhythmic fills by 'scratching' the stylus back and forth in the groove. (He made a video with director Spike Lee.) Finally, Run DMC, a trio from Queens, had the genre's first million-selling album in 1986, *Raising Hell*. Using a drum machine and scratching on a double-deck turntable, the trio filled Madison Square Garden and were seen as controversial, but stronger stuff was on the way.

Many people hate rap. Considered purely as music, it is the ultimate reduction of pop to absurdity. Charles Shaar Murray claims that rap was the most exciting thing to happen in pop in the 1980s, but that's not saying much. There are, however, interesting things to be said about it, not least that it made its own way with little help from the mainstream music business. Originally it was improvised, and may have had some value as street poetry; the rappers prize words and are more literate in their own way than your average pop star: where words are found there must be a message. But the uncomfortable fact is that rap was born of musical starvation. In the late 1980s the great jazz percussionist and composer Max Roach received a foundation grant, and was widely interviewed in American newspapers. One of the subjects he spoke about was music education. No matter how poor they were, no matter what kinds of backgrounds they came from, Roach's generation, including Charlie Parker and Dizzy Gillespie, had been able to get real musical tuition, on real musical instruments, in the schools. But that had changed. 'If you don't like rap,' Roach pointed out to the American people, 'you're getting what you paid for.'

But each generation has to make its own noise, invent its own genre; and what we paid for, or did not pay for, is rap. 'The Message' (1982), by Grandmaster Flash and the Furious Five, had more meaningful words than most pop songs of that period; it is about the neighbourhood and its 'junkies in the alley / with a baseball bat'. The rap groups did the best they could to communicate with America about the conditions to which they were confined, and to which their brothers and sisters are still confined. The message, however, has already been ignored.

Boo-yah TRIBE are 'Six Bad Brothas' of Samoan extraction from the Carson district of Los Angeles; 'Boo-yah' is derived from the sound of a sawn-off shotgun. Their track 'Once Upon a Drive By' tells of teenagers killing each other from the car window while driving by; 'Rated R' is about how to use the word 'motherfucker' fifty times in one song. NWA ('Niggers with Attitude'), from California, were the first successful rap group to come from outside New York; their album was called *Straight Outta Compton*. They too celebrate the world of drive-by killings and robbery with violence; one of their tracks urges listeners to kill and fuck the police. Public Enemy's second album, *It Takes a Nation of Millions to Hold Us Back*, reached the top twenty in Britain. The group's 'minister of propaganda', Richard Griffin, alias Professor Griff, said in an interview, 'The Jews are evil. And we can prove this.' 2 Live Crew rap about bitches, dicks, cunts and pussies: 'Forget the salad, just eat my meat', 'I can't be pussywhipped by a dick-sucker', and so on.

Of course, this stuff has its defenders among today's college professors and literary critics – drama critic Kenneth Tynan thought that the Beatles' *Sgt Pepper* was a turning point in western civilization – but they miss the point. As David Toop noted in England, 'the concoction appealed to intellectuals, who saw rap as the supreme expression of post-modernism, creative retro, television inspired blip culture and goodness knows what else'. The *New Republic* remarked that the rock critics 'are regularly laughable in their nervous translations of the primal and the obscene into the polysyllabic prettifications of their trade'.

The magazine quoted Jon Pareles on the subject of rap: 'Rappers live by their wit – their ability to rhyme, their speed of articulation – and by their ability to create outsized personas with words.' But not even a *New York Times* critic can justify rap by himself, so Pareles called in Professor Henry Louis Gates, of Duke University, who has become a prominent black critic by embracing the intellectual contrick of structuralism, or deconstructuralism, or post-structuralism, or whatever it is called this week. What 2 Live Crew do, Professor Gates says, is 'take the white Western culture's worst fear of black men and make a game of it'. But the fear is 2 Live Crew's fear of women in general, and black women in particular. It does not scare me, it disgusts me, and I do not think it is a game.

Gates soon got his own space in *The New York Times* in which he carried on the literary criticism: to understand 2 Live Crew we must become 'literate in the vernacular traditions of African Americans'. We are now so anti-élitist that we invent crackpot critical theory to justify anything as art. The *New Republic* again:

There are mistakes of which only professors are capable, and this is one of them . . . When you promote 'Suck my dick, bitch, and make it puke' into a 'vernacular tradition', you wound your culture. You teach that the culture need aspire to nothing high, because the low *is* the high; and that your culture – in this instance, the culture of Duke Ellington and Ralph Ellison – need look no further than the street . . . The truth about the street, of course, is that it is the scene of the greatest catastrophe to have befallen black America since slavery.

And so we get to the point. Rap is an illustration not just of what pop music has come to, but of what a nation has come to. We have known for years that American black males suffer more strokes and heart attacks than American white males. Murder is the leading cause of death among young black males in Washington, DC; the life expectancy of a male in Harlem is shorter than that of a male in Bangladesh. An American secretary of health has warned that 'the young black American male is a species in danger'. The rappers see Jews only as their local shopkeepers and landlords; nobody has ever taught them that for generations Jews were the best friends blacks had in America, because they knew what it was like to be slaves thousands of years before the first African was taken to the New World. Nobody has ever taught them that Jews as businessmen (and musicians) did more for black music in this century than any other non-black group. Nobody has ever taught them that men and women are supposed to console each other. No doubt some of them have never heard of Duke Ellington, and even more have never heard of Ralph Ellison. Nobody has ever taught them anything because they have no schools to speak of. All they have is the label 'underclass', which means 'garbage'. Naturally they are angry.

NWA's Easy-E sings:

> Do I look like a motherfucking role model?
> To a kid looking up to me
> Life ain't nothing but bitches and money.

The rest of us may appear to behave ourselves, but there is little evidence that we care about anything more than Easy-E does. All the rapper knows is what he sees, and he does not see a society which is interested in any kind of justice, to say nothing of the quality of its music. He may appear to be a creep, an idiot, a moron, but he is more honest than we are: he knows that he has no control over his life, while we pretend that we have control over ours. His anger is what we have paid for, or the result of what we have not paid for; and his warning has been wasted, for rap has been processed by the music industry.

There is already, of course, white rap. Every black genre has been imitated so far, and not even rap could escape. The Beastie Boys were among the first off the mark, three middle-class boys whose parents are music business veterans; four million copies of their first album were sold. Their second received rave reviews in 'quality' newspapers: the one by David Sinclair in *The Times* was headed 'Rude, lewd and shamelessly funny': '*Paul's Boutique* is strewn with foul language and lewd innuendo; it shamelessly glorifies all manner of deviant, violent and criminal behaviour and it unequivocally condones recreational drug-dabbling. It is also very funny . . . Brooklyn's Beastie Boys have recaptured the essence of rock as the perfect adolescent vehicle for the flaunting of outrage.' If some of our children are murdering each other, they are just reviving the whiskered old essence of rock'n'roll, invented by the media in the first place. This is so funny I am holding my sides.

There must also be rap that is completely innocuous, which happens as soon as a genre starts making money. Some thought that Run DMC were funny in the beginning, but, having been knocked from the commercial top of the genre by newer acts, they were unintentionally amusing when they appeared on a British music magazine programme in early 1991, obviously puzzled and uncertain, these big black kids from one of the toughest neighbourhoods on earth. So what were they doing about competition from the likes of Vanilla Ice? They were in England to 'sample' Manchester bands for sounds to use in their act. (That is one way to get out of Queens; the last I heard the police in Manchester still did not carry guns.) Vanilla Ice is, inevitably, white, and has impressive cheekbones; he was described by one critic as 'all mouth and trousers', but his backing tracks are very slick. M. C. Hammer is black; his 'We've Got the Power' was used in 1991 in Britain as psych-up music for people selling time-share schemes.

A few of these youngsters who grew up in the street are making money from hit records, but there are many more still in the street, still angry and still shedding each other's blood. And as rap is legitimized and joins the mainstream, it is clear that it now bears the burden of being a phoncy sign of hope. As fast as its obscene cry was mistaken for mere outrageousness, it has become one of the commodities which substitute for social and economic stability, no more useful than any other and less useful than most, because if it is not angry, it has no substance. Lloyd Bradley in *Q* got it right, reviewing

Public Enemy's *Fear of a Black Planet*: 'the music is only a back-ground for the most singleminded attack on the state of modern urban America heard on record'. Evidently that group had not been bought off yet.

Of course, some older musicians must try to make sense of rap. A year or so after his remarks on the state of the music education in America, Max Roach told Chris Parker in England that he was working with the Fab Five, and quoted them:

'The political system in the inner cities has taken out all the cultural enrichment courses, no music, no rhetoric, visuals, dance – so we created something . . . no one gave us anything, it's pure.' So they came up with a way of dealing with this world of sound and rhetoric, which is rhyme and visual, graffiti and dance . . . total theatre. So I became interested from that aspect, but I have to have it explained by them.

Conventional methods of making music have 'just about been used up. So if you don't want to repeat, you have to deal with this world out there that's blessed us with electronics,' says Mr Roach. Thanks, but when all the drummers have been replaced by computers, I will stay indoors and listen to my Max Roach records.

In late 1990 a piece called *Long Tongues: A Saxophone Opera*, by composer and saxophonist Julius Hemphill, was seen at the Apollo Theatre. The interlocutor was once master of ceremonies at a Washington club, and is now a street sweeper. He shows a rap duo through black history since the 1940s: the end of the Swing Era, the beginning of rhythm and blues and bop, later modern jazz and several styles of dancing. In the end the rappers trade licks with a saxophonist. I would rather see Julius Hemphill's opera than watch Michael Jackson's movie again. *Moonwalker* had no story to speak of, but lots of high-tech sci-fi fireworks, to make the children happy, and good dancing. There was a wonderfully designed scene that looked like a black club of the 1940s, and in the background a suggestion of a piano and a saxophonist. Was there a piano in the soundtrack? Any reeds at all? No: just the usual pop-rock, all at the same volume and tempo. Jackson appears to be a sort of superhero in the film; he could have made himself a real hero, by exposing all our children to his rich cultural heritage, but he threw away that opportunity and opted for flash. I wonder how much his multi-talented producer Quincy Jones had to do with it, but I am reminded of James Blood Ulmer, on his album *America – Do You Remember the Love?* 'I belong to the USA / I don't know if I want to stay.'

Having raped black music, today we have world music, in which there are many lovely things. The Cajun music of French-speaking white swamp dwellers in Louisiana, and zydeco, the black variant, are happy and unpretentious folk-dance musics, which may properly belong to folk roots rather than to world music. Klezmer is being rediscovered, a sort of Yiddish dance music that has things in common with jazz, from the Odessa of eighty years ago. The multi-part harmony of a Bulgarian women's choir is already familiar to anyone who has heard Janáček's *Glagolitic Mass*. Africans play music resembling the blues on folk instruments, their time as subtle and beautiful as that of Robert Johnson or Charley Patton. Forty years ago the janitor at my primary school played Japanese 78s for us which he had brought back from there after the war; they sounded infinitely strange and interesting. I do not know whether they represented traditional music or the Japanese pop of the period, but I do know that today the Japanese play the most banal pop-rock in the world, adopting our poverty-stricken values with perfect unselfconsciousness.

The performers of the music of the so-called Third World know that they will not be allowed into our marketplace until they have already been influenced by western pop-rock, and in any case their own pop music has already been so influenced. The songs of Thomas Mapfumo, in modern Zimbabwe, for example, although they still sound like they ought to be played on the thumb piano, are played on the electric guitar, and all at the same tempo. White and black South Africans formed Juluka (which means 'sweat' or 'work') which performed beautiful folkish songs full of poetry and African harmony, but that era is over; and Johnny Clegg has since formed Savuka ('we have awakened'), which is 'dance music', still African-flavoured, but electric and with the usual thumping beat. Raï is the music of the north African Muslim working class; it is already electric, and tacky nightclubs are similar the world over. We have not heard much lately about fado, a sort of Portuguese blues; perhaps the artists refused to be plugged in. Jamaican reggae has already had its superhero, Bob Marley, who was admitted to the pantheon by the sentimentality of the counterculture; but the biggest Jamaican influence is the dub aspect of rap.

We can hope for a liberating influence on our pop music from the Third World, but we will force our trendy values on music from anywhere. Novelist Sousa Jamba, writing for the *Spectator*, hoped 'that the "world music" frenzy will not be ephemeral, like most things in Western culture'. He walked into a London record shop to hear his mother tongue booming at him.

The Kafala Brothers, two Angolan singers . . . made me proud to be an Angolan: the lullabies were the best I ever heard; and the words to the songs were first-class poetry . . . But I fumed when I read the English translation of the songs that came with the cassette. It read like the work of a semi-literate party hack with an edict that he should give a political twist to every line. One song, for instance, concerns a man returning to his village and finding his relatives maimed. No reason for their injuries is given. The song's translation says that the injured are 'victims of the traitors to the nation and the lackeys of apartheid'.

A girl called Yarima from a Stone Age tribe in the Amazon rainforest married an American, and went with him to live in televisionland. 'I did not know what music was. My people have no musical instruments. All is chanting. When I first heard your music I hated it. Then I started snapping my fingers and tapping my toes. Madonna has a good voice and I like the way Michael Jackson moves.' Never mind that the word 'chant' means 'song'; so much for music. We cultists who have money in our pockets can celebrate six centuries of music on records, but our own best musicians and composers live on hand-outs. Our republic has failed; our Caesars have feet of clay; the barbarians are inside the gates. We have seen the enemy; he is in the mirror.

Afterword

What can be done about what most people think of as popular music?

Britain still has better record shops than American towns. Norwich, in the English county of Norfolk, has three or four record shops that are better than any between Chicago and Milwaukee, a distance of around 100 miles; the Norwich City Council area has a population of about 124,000. The tiniest village shop may not have much stock, but the salesperson there will know how to order any record you want (from a middleman, at full price).

The number of recordings available commercially in Britain is much smaller than in the USA, yet the shops have better selections: this is partly because Britain has better broadcasting, by a wide margin, than the USA. Britain's first national commercial radio station is a classical one, because the government awarded the franchise with some care; launched while this book was being written, it is already commercially successful. Margaret Thatcher, however, arranged for commercial television to be sold to the highest bidder before she left office, and was then astonished at the unfair results of the auction: there are signs that Britain is only a decade or two behind the USA in trashing itself.

The real problem began in the USA, and it is not too late for the Federal Communications Commission to wake up. The experience of the last twenty years shows that the USA needs regulation. The deregulation of the Savings and Loans led to the biggest financial disaster in American history; long after the deregulation of the airlines it still cost $700 to fly from Milwaukee to New York and back in December 1990, while some of the oldest airlines in the world have gone bust. Similarly, the playing of non-stop pop videos is nothing but free advertising for the record companies; if the government is going to regulate anything at all, America's MTV channel ought to be seen as violating existing law. If Americans can chop up the world's best telephone service into fifty small bits and require car manufacturers to obtain an overall mileage from their products, they can do anything.

Radio stations relying on recorded music should be required to do their own programming, rather than subscribing to a factory-compiled tape which is identical in every urban area. Mass-produced pap is bad enough in a supermarket; and, for that matter, it is not too late to ban wired music in public places, if music is thought to be of any value: it is an irony typical of our times that although the stuff must make a profit, *nobody would miss it*. A law prohibiting any radio station from playing any track more than once a day (or even better, once a *week*) would still allow any station to play all the hits, but would require somebody somewhere to think about which records to play for the rest of the time. Such rules might result in jobs in radio for people who actually like music.

Needle time could be made more expensive by raising the royalty on the records played after a certain number of hours a day, forcing stations to think about what kind of music they want to pay for; or the additional expense could be avoided by allowing a balance with live music: the practical difficulties broadcasters will foresee would quickly be overcome with the pressure of necessity, putting today's technology to some good use for a change. The need for live entertainment would soon result in a wider variety of it; broadcasters would learn to choose a good polka band over a mediocre teen-pop outfit, and, for that matter, a great many university music departments have excellent ensembles of various kinds. Why should there be relatively more live music in British broadcasting, with fewer stations and a fraction of the population, than there is in America? The performers would have to learn how to play for a live audience, and as listeners discover what live music sounds like, they might demand records that sound like music.

Small specialist and local stations could be exempt from some of this, and if Congress or the FCC will not act, state legislatures could do something. None of these measures would amount to discrimination against any musical genre, but another result would be the redundance of pro-censorship groups, such as the American Parents Music Resource Center, who will accomplish nothing anyway because they attack symptoms instead of problems. Successful pressure on behalf of a wider range of musics would swamp much of the childish dirtiness to which the censors object.

But the Davises and the Yetnikoffs are in charge of American business, and legislatures are full of lawyers who make too many laws and too few examples. Our only hope is that the pop-rock business goes smash, so that we can start all over again. Maybe it is only a matter of time; Michael Jackson's latest album has sold fifteen million copies at the time of writing, and apparently has not made enough money for Sony. Any industry that does business that way will go to the wall sooner or later.

Bibliography

Here is a listing by author or editor of many of the best books I have been using. I have not named editions, since they vary from one country to another, many of my copies are old and some of the books are out of print. There are also entries under the headings Biography, Discography and Reference.

ALLEN, Walter C.
Hendersonia (1973; self-published)
Allen, who died in 1974, was a doyen of the small army of researchers into early jazz. His book about Fletcher Henderson is a history of the band, almost day by day, and includes a complete discography. Hard going for the uninitiated but indispensable for the dedicated fan, it is the fruit of the sort of meticulous scholarship that only a fan could produce.

BALLIET, Whitney
American Musicians: 56 Portraits in Jazz (1986)
American Singers: 27 Portraits in Song (1988)
Barney, Bradley and Max: 16 Portraits in Jazz (1989)
Balliet is jazz correspondent of the *New Yorker*, and these are the latest collections of his journalism. Barney, Bradley and Max ran the most famous clubs in New York.

BIOGRAPHY
Biographies of individual musicians and pop stars are uncountable, but here are some of my favourites. (*See also* ALLEN, CHILTON, LEES, MURRAY, SHAW and WRIGHT.)

Bix: Man and Legend, by Richard M. Sudhalter and Philip R. Evans (1974), was the first great jazz biography, and new ones can still be measured against it: Hoagy Carmichael, Paul Whiteman, Bill Challis and the whole cast are discussed in great detail. Also recommendable are *Mingus* by Brian Priestley (1982), *Miles Davis* by Ian Carr (1982), *Forces in Motion* by Graham Lock (1988; interviews and notes on Anthony Braxton's 1985 tour of England), *Swing, Swing, Swing: The Life and Times of Benny Goodman* by Ross Firestone (1993) and *Wishing on the Moon: The Life and Times of Billie Holiday* by Donald Clarke (1994). There is no definitive book on Duke Ellington, and perhaps cannot be, but a recent one that bodes well for the future is *Ellington: The Early Years* by Mark Tucker; Tucker's *Duke Ellington Reader* and *A Lester Young Reader*, edited by Lewis Porter (1991), are excellent compilations.

Autobiographies are usually 'as told to' books. Some of the best of these are mentioned in the text.

Biographies of pop people tend to be disappointing, such as the several fat books about Bob Dylan, perhaps because the whole point of his work is that we are supposed to be living our own lives, not reading about him. (*See* MURRAY for Jimi Hendrix.) The best books about pop and rock tell us as much about the times as the lives, for example, Jon Savage's *England's Dreaming: Sex Pistols and Punk Rock* and Chris Heath's *Pet Shop Boys, Literally*. Significantly, both these are too long, telling us more than we need to know.

In country music, Nolan Porterfield's *Jimmie Rodgers* (1979) and Charles R. Townsend's *San Antonio Rose: The Life and Music of Bob Wills* (1976) are excellent, and Roger M. Williams's *Sing a Sad Song: The Life of Hank Williams* (1970) is also good; all have discographies.

BORDMAN, Gerald
American Musical Theatre: A Chronicle (1978; rev. 1986)
This describes year by year all the musical shows that opened on the New York stage from 1866 (*The Black Crook*) to 1984–5, with enough style to make the book a time-eater: once you open it, a couple of hours will go by.

Bordman's other books include a biography of Kern (1980); in this connection Andrew Lamb's *Jerome Kern in Edwardian London* also must be mentioned (ISAM monograph no. 22). The Institute for Study in American Music, Conservatory of Music, Brooklyn College of the City University of New York, has published about thirty monographs, all worthwhile (*see* SANJEK), and needs support.

BROVEN, John
Rhythm and Blues in New Orleans (1977)
South to Louisiana: The Music of the Cajun Bayous (1987)
The first of these was originally called *Walking to New Orleans*. The books combine passionate advocacy with good writing and an almost off-hand ability to set everything in its time and place.

CHAPPLE, Steve, and Reebee GAROFALO
Rock'n'roll is Here to Pay (1977)
A useful book about the development of the modern music business, though the last chapter predicts some sort of flower-power utopia.

CHILTON, John
Who's Who of Jazz (1985)
Sidney Bechet: The Wizard of Jazz (1987)
The Song of the Hawk: Life and Recordings of Coleman Hawkins (1990)
English trumpeter and bandleader Chilton is a very good researcher. *Who's Who of Jazz*, first published in 1972, is subtitled 'Storyville to Swing Street'. An A–Z of jazz people born before 1920 who did most of their work in the USA, it is a specialists' lodestar of accuracy.

Biographies of Louis Armstrong (1971, with Max Jones) and Billie Holiday (*Billie's Blues*, 1975, surveying only her musical career from 1933) were trail-blazers; monographs on McKinney's Cotton Pickers (1978) and the Jenkins' Orphanage (*A Jazz Nursery*, 1980) are each one of a kind; *Stomp Off, Let's Go* (1983), about the Bob Crosby band, is fun (though it apparently had no editor and looks like an explosion in a print shop). With his biographies of Bechet, Hawkins and recently Louis Jordan, Chilton reached a new height: the combination of the cantankerous and the lyrical that was Bechet and the very private Hawkins will probably never be better captured, and all the recordings are expertly dealt with.

COOK, Richard, and Brian MORTON
The Penguin Guide to Jazz (1992)
The first print-run of this book was too short, because bookshops refused to order enough copies; sales are brisk, and no wonder. Virtually every jazz artist is found here in A–Z format and nearly all their currently available releases are intelligently commented upon, so that if you are interested in an artist, you can decide which records to take a chance on. The coverage is international, and sensibly ignores the fact that many discs nowadays are imports in various countries. There are almost 1,200 pages and an index for finding side men and women. This book is indispensable.

DANCE, Stanley
The World of Duke Ellington (1970)
The World of Swing (1974)
The World of Earl Hines (1977)
The World of Count Basie (1980)
'As told to . . .'
Night People by Dicky Wells (1971)
Duke Ellington in Person by Mercer Ellington (1978)
Those Swinging Years by Charlie Barnet (1984)
The British-born Stanley Dance, long resident in California, once had a letter printed in a British jazz journal in which he angrily refused to understand why so many jazz records have been bootlegged over the years, despite the way the owners of the masters sat on them, or occasionally issued a few tracks as though they were a dog's dinner. He is an opinionated man and no doubt a 'mouldy fig', but a valuable journalist. Most of the books are oral histories, revealed by Dance's power of observation and editorial skill to be perhaps the most important genre of all. *The World of Swing*, for example, covers over forty musicians and singers, mostly interviewed, from the world-famous to the more obscure but still influential. It is a myth that jazz musicians are inarticulate. Dance lets the feeling of what the music is all about come through the personalities.

DANNEN, Frederick
Hit Men (1990)
The damning book we were all recommending to each other, and well written too. The subtitle, 'Power Brokers and Fast Money inside the Music Business', says it all. The paperback edition is updated.

DEFAA, Chip
Voices of the Jazz Age (1990)
Swing Legacy (1991)
Eight vintage profiles and twenty somewhat later ones. The first contains a good article about Bix, and the interview with Sam Wooding not long before he died is good stuff taken down in the nick of time.

DISCOGRAPHY
A thriving industry. (*See also* ALLEN, COOK and MORTON, HARRISON, KINKLE and WHITBURN.)

RUST, Brian. *Jazz Records 1897–1942* (n.d.). Now published by Storyville Publications (*see* WRIGHT), these two fat volumes are the basis of jazz discography, and have been used for many years by fans, collectors, researchers and authors of sleeve-notes, who sometimes even acknowledge it. Rust's *The Victor Master Book*, vol. 2 (self-published) was a fascinating one-off, listing Victor records made from 1925 to 1936 by master number (with indexes for artists and song titles). There never was a volume 1. A new edition of Rust's two volumes on American dance bands is being prepared.

DIXON, Robert M. W., and John GODRICH. *Blues and Gospel Records 1902–1943* (1982). Another classic from Storyville.

LEADBITTER, Mike, and Neil SLAVEN. *Blues Records 1943 to 1970*, vol. 1. An update of an earlier classic including R&B, published by Paul Pelletier's Record Information Services in 1987. It is touch and go as to whether volume 2 will ever appear; Leadbitter died in 1974 and Pelletier has done his best, but some of the other people involved are evidently not reliable.

BRUYNINCKX, W. A complete jazz discography printed in Belgium, divided into categories of traditional, swing, modern, progressive, modern big band and vocalists. It comprises a total of thirty-five paperback volumes.

HOUNSOME, Terry. *Rock Record* (1991). Began as the limited edition *Rockmaster* in 1978. This edition (which could be the sixth, depending on how you count them) lists all the albums by 10,000 rock bands and artists, with personnel, labels and numbers of editions in various countries. A new edition has just come out in 1994. His Record Researcher Publications also issues *Single File*, which lists over 100,000 British singles.

FLANAGAN, Bill
Written in my Soul (1987)
Interviews with 'rock' songwriters (including Carl Perkins and Willie Dixon). Elvis Costello: 'I can't actually play any musical instrument properly. I can't read music. And here's the *New York Times* calling me the new George Gershwin . . . It was embarrassing to watch these people fall into the trap of their own critical conceits.'

FOX, Ted
Showtime at the Apollo (1985)
In the Groove (1986)
The first covers fifty years of the great Harlem venue, while the second contains interviews with a dozen record producers, from John Hammond and Milt Gabler to Nile Rodgers.

GARFIELD, Simon
Expensive Habits (1986)
Subtitled 'The Dark Side of the Music Business', stories from the British pop industry about how easy it is to get cheated. Of Gilbert O'Sullivan's hit albums in the early 1970s, *Back to Front* was number one and grossed £1,700,000, of which he received only £60,000. He had to go to court to get more royalties and control of his own copyrights.

GELATT, Roland
The Fabulous Phonograph 1877–1977 (rev. 1977)
Still a good survey, updated from the 1955 edition.

GEORGE, Nelson
Where Did Our Love Go? (1985)
The Death of Rhythm and Blues (1988)
The first tells the history of the Motown label. The second study asks how black music can retain its identity in a white-dominated music industry, inevitably touching on the perilous position of black culture in a society whose engine is white-bread economics.

GILBERT, Douglas
Lost Chords (1942; repr. 1970)
'The Diverting Story of American Popular Music', a period survey of songs and business up to the 1930s. The last chapter is titled 'Juke Box, Jazz, Swing, and Boogie-woogie' to make the book look up to date, but says little about any of these, sticking to Tin Pan Alley.

GILLETT, Charlie
The Sound of the City (1970; rev. 1983)
Somewhat breathless 'Rise of Rock and Roll' story by a British DJ and label boss who knows his stuff, written around the records themselves and not neglecting byways such as swamp rock.

GITLER, Ira
Jazz Masters of the '40s (1966)
Swing to Bop (1985)
The first is one of a series, of which the others (*Jazz Masters of the '20s* by Richard Hadlock, *'30s* by Rex Stewart, etc.) are also worthwhile. The more recent book is 'an oral history of the transition in jazz in the 1940s' in the musicians' own words, and priceless.

GOLDBERG, Isaac
Tin Pan Alley (1930)
A period piece on the heyday, with an introduction by Gershwin.

GORDON, Robert
Jazz West Coast: The Los Angeles Jazz Scene of the 1950s (1986)
The largely white cool jazz scene was commercially successful (as post-war jazz went), but suffered from critical snobbery in a sort of

reverse racism. This survey is full of good sense and especially useful now that many of the records are being reissued on CD. *West Coast Jazz* by Ted Gioia (1992) looks pretty good too.

GURALNICK, Peter
Feel Like Going Home: Portraits in Blues and Rock'n'roll (1971)
Lost Highway: Journeys and Arrivals of American Musicians (1979)
Sweet Soul Music: Rhythm and Blues and the Southern Dream of Freedom (1986)
Two volumes of affectionate, well-written portraits, and a definitive history of soul music. His latest book is about Robert Johnson, but will be superseded when controversial research may be published.

HAASE, John Edward (ed.)
Ragtime (1985)
A marvellous survey of every aspect – waltzes, the banjo, women in ragtime, everything you can think of – in nineteen chapters. Contributors include Max Morath and Edward A. Berlin (whose own 1980 book is very good), and there are interviews with Gunther Schuller and Rudi Blesh.

HAMM, Charles
Yesterdays: Popular Song in America (1979)
The best survey I know, it begins in England and sticks to songs, and is well illustrated. Weakest in the last couple of chapters, because the rock era's songs lend themselves less well to serious treatment.

HANNUSCH, Jeff
I Hear You Knockin' (1985)
'The Sound of New Orleans Rhythm and Blues', in the form of profiles of over thirty musicians and producers. The best sort of fan's book, to put alongside Broven.

HARRISON, Max
A Jazz Retrospect (1976; new edn 1991)
A collection of first-class jazz journalism, the kind that never goes out of date. Harrison was one of the first to describe Ellington

accurately as a miniaturist. He also wrote the jazz entry in *The New Grove Dictionary of Music and Musicians*, and he writes about classical music too; a collection of that would also be worth having.

HARRISON, Max with Charles Fox and Eric Thacker
The Essential Jazz Records, vol. 1: *Ragtime to Swing* (1984)
Thematically arranged by decades and styles, it provides commentary on a great many of the most valuable recordings. LP issues are listed, but that does not matter; original recording dates and complete personnel are given, so you can know what you are getting in today's CD editions. The point is that the commentary is illuminating, and so stylish that it can be enjoyed for its own sake; it is even fun to read about music you have already been listening to for years. A neat hardback published by Mansell in Britain, this is the sort of book that will become a legend without selling many copies.

HIRSHEY, Gerry
Nowhere to Run: The Story of Soul Music (1984)
Well written, full of interviews and love of the subject, to go on the shelf next to Guralnick.

HOSKYNS, Barney
Say It One Time for the Brokenhearted (1987)
Subtitled 'The Country Side of Southern Soul', this is an eye-opener of a book, about the influence of country and soul on each other. His list of forty masterpieces of country soul ought to be bootlegged if necessary on CD.

JONES, Max
Talking Jazz (1987)
A valuable collection by one of the best British music journalists, introduced by Jones and intelligently edited, often from interviews over a period of years. His piece on Billie Holiday alone is worth the price.

KINKLE, Roger D.
The Complete Encyclopedia of Popular Music and Jazz 1900–1950 (1974)
Compiled by a dealer and auctioneer in old records, these four fat
hardback volumes have now been out of print for a while. Two
volumes are an A–Z of recording artists (many mainstream people
with no entries in other books) and two are lists and indexes: one
lists musical shows and films, representative hit songs and records
year by year; also listed (by catalogue number, which sounds boring
until you learn how to wallow in it) are all releases on several
important labels from the mid-1920s to the early 1940s. Incredibly
accurate, Kinkle's work was computer typeset in the USA twenty
years ago, and after many years of using it I finally found one
mistake: he got Judy Garland's death date wrong by six months.

LAX, Roger, and Frederick SMITH
The Great Song Thesaurus (1984)
Lists songs with dates and information about each, and is divided
into several sections (British, American, Indexes, etc.). Goes back
much further than Shapiro, but accepts stories as fact, such as that
Mother Goose was an American.

LEES, Gene
Singers and the Song (1987)
Meet Me at Jim and Andy's: Jazz Musicians and Their World (1988)
Oscar Peterson: The Will to Swing (1988)
Inventing Champagne: The Worlds of Lerner and Loewe (1990)
Journalist, editor, lyricist and sometime vocalist, Gene Lees always
writes well, but when he writes about something he loves, magic
happens. The first two of these books collect pieces from his unique
monthly *Jazzletter*, launched ten years ago. His biographies of Peter-
son and Lerner and Loewe are useful, but an 'as told to' book, Henry
Mancini's *Did They Mention the Music?* (1989), is less good; apparently
Mancini is too private a man for an autobiography.

LITWEILER, John
The Freedom Principle: Jazz after 1958 (1985)
A first-class book on the subject by an important Chicago journal-

ist. You know it is good because it sends you straight to the record shelf for a listen. His new book about Ornette Coleman will be worth a look.

LYTTELTON, Humphrey
Best of Jazz: Basin Street to Harlem (1978)
Enter the Giants (1981)
Trumpeter, bandleader and a famous voice on British radio through his jazz record programme, Lyttelton is also a good writer. His article on Basie trombonist Dicky Wells, for example, should send you to the records to hear what he is talking about.

MALONE, Bill C.
Country Music USA (1968; rev. 1985)
Impossible to imagine a better survey of the subject: fat, authoritative, a good read, a good index.

MARSH, Dave
The Heart of Rock and Soul: The 1,001 Greatest Singles Ever Made (1989)
You can argue with Marsh, founder of Detroit's *Creem* magazine in 1969, about his choices, but not about his love of the music. Relive the days when it was fun to buy singles, and be reminded why.

MATTFELD, Julius
Variety Music Cavalcade (1959; rev. 1962)
Subtitled 'Musical-historical Review 1620–1961', this was a terrific idea spoiled by its lack of proper indexes. A list of hit songs for each year is accompanied by contemporary news: with 'Shake, Rattle and Roll' in 1954 came the US Senate's censure of Joe McCarthy, the first news of a link between cigarettes and lung cancer and the coining by *McCall's*, a women's magazine, of the word 'togetherness'; the fiction best-seller, Lloyd Douglas's *The Robe*, was held over from the year before. But the index lists only the songs.

MURRAY, Charles Shaar
Crosstown Traffic: Jimi Hendrix and Post-war Pop (1989)
Shots from the Hip (1991)

Murray is the brightest and most amusing of rock critics. The American Lester Bangs had an enchantingly surreal style, but was a believer in rock myths and did not convince me. You have to love the music to be a critic, and I know some who have gone off it, but Murray (who is British) will never have to give up on it, because he has no illusions about it, or about anything else: he seems to have the sense to find most things funny. His biography of Hendrix is a model of its kind, ranging more widely and intelligently than most rock biographies; his collection of journalism from 1972 to the present will remain valuable. You can *trust* this man (even if he does like rap).

RAMSEY, Frederick, Jr, and Charles Edward SMITH (eds)
Jazzmen (1939; repr. 1985 with introduction by Nat Hentoff)
A collection of fifteen pieces by such authors as Wilder Hobson and Otis Ferguson, two of the earliest American jazz journalists. Hentoff's generation was inspired by it, and it is still recommendable.

READ, Oliver, and Walter L. WELCH
From Tinfoil to Stereo (1959; rev. 1976)
Written by enthusiasts, wordy and even repetitious but 'unput-downable', this classic came from an obscure publisher in Indianapolis. Still the best account of the evolution of sound recording, by the time it was updated and republished copies of the original edition were changing hands for up to $200. Interesting illustrations too, as well as several indexes.

REFERENCE
A–Z books of rock, pop, country music and so on have too many words and not enough entries, rarely an index and usually an unacceptable number of factual errors. *The Penguin Encyclopedia of Popular Music*, edited by Donald Clarke (1989), was the first single-volume reference book to cover all the genres; I name my own work because it is still the best value, with more than three thousand entries (including entries for genres, and listing albums for most artists) and a very good index. Its nearest competition was compiled by rockers who have Buck Clayton playing saxophone instead of trumpet, and have no index at all.

In jazz, however, there are irreplaceable books for specialists. John Chilton's *Who's Who of Jazz* is mentioned above, Leonard Feather's venerable three volumes of *The Encyclopedia of Jazz* (1960, 1966 and 1976) are valuable for the large number of more obscure entries, and a new project is on the way. *Jazz: The Essential Companion*, by Ian Carr, Digby Fairweather and Brian Priestley, is a well-written and useful A–Z. *Blues Who's Who* by Sheldon Harris (1979) is also indispensable. (*See also* KINKLE; for A–Z books of songs, *see* LAX and SMITH, and SHAPIRO.)

REID, Jan
The Improbable Rise of Redneck Rock (1974)
The story of how country music was reborn in Texas when Nashville got too slick while remaining intolerant. Incredible that this book does not have an index.

RUSSELL, Ross
Jazz Style in Kansas City and the Southwest (1971)
A good survey. Russell was the founder of Dial Records, recorded Charlie Parker and was Parker's manager for two years; he also wrote *Bird Lives!* (1973), the first and still the fullest Parker biography, but all the books about him seem to be flawed by bad memories and wishful thinking on the part of the witnesses, as though Parker were a mirror in which people saw what they wanted to see.

SANJEK, Russell
American Popular Music and Its Business (1988)
Sanjek was a BMI executive who spent his retirement completing this massive three-volume work, which began as an ISAM monograph. The volumes are titled 'The Beginning to 1790', '1790 to 1909' and '1900 to 1984', and have nearly 1,500 pages as well as indexes and bibliographies. When I obtained my copies, I stopped everything and wallowed in them for weeks, and still consult them as often as any books on my shelves. Statistics, squabbles, technology and takeovers are all here; since Sanjek's death his son has done an abridged single-volume edition.

SCHULLER, Gunther
Early Jazz: Its Roots and Musical Development (1968)
The Swing Era (1989)
There is not really a recommendable single-volume history of jazz;
you need to read several books, of which these should be the first.
Recognized as a gem of good sense and scholarship on publication,
Early Jazz is also immensely readable, and the recent volume is just
as good.

SHAPIRO, Harry
Waiting for the Man (1988)
'The Story of Drugs and Popular Music' is more than that, going
back to the medicine shows seen in so many old Westerns, which
were peddling nothing but dope; it comes up through the Harrison
Narcotics Act of 1914 and the problems of Keith Richards and the
Allman Brothers Band to the substitute addiction to scientology,
giving a list of victims.

SHAPIRO, Nat, and Nat HENTOFF
Hear Me Talkin' to Ya (1955)
One of the first oral histories of jazz, compiled from interviews,
letters, magazine articles and so on. A classic and still fascinating.

SHAW, Arnold
52nd St: The Street of Jazz (1971)
Honkers and Shouters: The Golden Years of Rhythm and Blues (c. 1974)
The Rockin' 50s (c. 1974)
Black Popular Music in America (1986)
The Jazz Age: Popular Music in the 1920s (1987)
Shaw joined Leeds Music (which later became MCA) in 1945; a
songwriter, publicist, record producer and college professor, he won
ASCAP's Deems Taylor Award a couple of times. He also wrote
biographies of Frank Sinatra (1968) and Harry Belafonte, among
other things. The first three listed here are the best. *52nd St* was
originally called *The Street That Never Slept*, and is good on the clubs
and their influence on music. The next two are insider's books, full
of vitality, detail (for example, on the origins of the classic R & B

labels) and, especially *Honkers*, valuable interviews with such people as Ralph Bass and Art Rupe. Shaw's later books are surveys and appear hurried; they are cramped and hard to read and have the occasional minor error.

SMITH, Joe
Off the Record (1988)
In this book, record-company executive Joe Smith combines arrogance and ignorance. His book is a disgrace (and from a Warner Communications Company). Not only is there no index, you have to make your own table of contents: over two hundred short interviews are put together in no particular order. The interviews themselves do not look like interviews at all, and many of them are worthless. There are so many that there are nuggets to be found, however, and the book goes on the shelf next to Fox and Flanagan. Smith is like a cook in a bad restaurant, not knowing that the job could just as well be done properly.

SOUTHERN, Eileen
The Music of Black Americans (1971; rev. 1983)
A masterpiece of scholarship by a Harvard professor of music and Afro-American studies, it covers every aspect of black musical achievement in the USA beginning in the early seventeenth century, and provides plenty of social context as well. Indispensable.

SPELLMAN, A. B.
Black Music: Four Lives (1966)
Originally called *Four Lives in the Bebop Business*, a classic on the music of its period in the form of profiles of Cecil Taylor, Ornette Coleman, Herbie Nichols and Jackie McLean. It also paints a depressing picture of what it is like to be a black artist trying to make a living as an original, competing with your own dead predecessors, who themselves struggled all their lives.

TOSCHES, Nick
Country: Living Legends and Dying Metaphors in America's Biggest Music (1977)
Unsung Heroes of Rock'n'roll (1984)

Country gives the lie to the Nashville image of country music as upright and puritanical: not just gossip, but songs, personalities, forgotten roots and the darker side of the history. The second book is useful fun on the most influential popular music of the late 1940s and early 1950s; not all the heroes are entirely unsung, but most people have never heard of Hardrock Gunter or Jesse Stone. His book on Jerry Lee Lewis, *Hellfire*, is useful. His recent book on Dean Martin had bad reviews because, although unauthorized, it apparently puts words into Martin's mouth.

TRAVIS, Dempsey J.
An Autobiography of Black Jazz (1983)
An affectionate memoir of Chicago's musical history, using a great many interviews and illustrations. Travis became a pianist like his father, and at the age of sixteen in the mid-1930s was the youngest bandleader registered with the musicians' union. A good read.

VAN DER MERWE, Peter
Origins of the Popular Style: The Antecedents of Twentieth-century Popular Music (1989)
A scholarly book and a delight, tracing influences around the world and down through a thousand years. European folk music, for example – hence much American country music – probably comes originally from the Middle East, not medieval or Renaissance Europe.

WARD, Ed, Geoffrey STOKES and Ken TUCKER
Rock of Ages: The Rolling Stone History of Rock and Roll (1986)
A readable history by three journalists, one each for the 1950s, 1960s and 1970s. Like most rock books, it assumes that nothing much happened before 1956; it is not true, for instance, that Stephen Foster never received any royalties. But when it gets to the meat, there are insights, such as Stokes on why Bob Dylan did not sell records to blacks: 'Though Dick Gregory might joke about finally getting served at a Woolworth's lunch counter only to find out that the food was lousy, the subversive sentiment underlying the joke would remain buried.'

WHITBURN, Joel
Top Pop Singles 1955–1986
Top Pop Albums 1955–1985
Top R&B Singles 1942–1988
Top Country Singles 1944–1988
Pop Memories 1890–1954
Whitburn's Record Research, Inc., began reprinting the *Billboard* charts in the early 1970s, producing expensive books for D Js and cultists which turned out to have a wider appeal. The latest editions do much more than this, providing blurbs on the artists and much else; they are still expensive but unusually well made for a good deal of use. *Top Pop Singles* has recently been updated and a new edition of *Albums* is coming. There is an annual *Music and Video Yearbook* update; the spiral-bound *Daily No. 1 Hits* tells you what was number one in the USA each day from 1 January 1940.

The most remarkable is *Pop Memories*, which goes far beyond *Billboard*, researching hobbyist columns, sheet music sales, record company lists, radio plays and so on to create charts going right back to the beginning, the only source for the hits of the acoustic era (though I would like to know more about just how the calculations were made). The earliest *Billboard* charts had only fifteen or twenty places, but *Pop Memories* effectively creates a longer list, giving a better view of many artists. By including jukebox sales the book makes it clear that somebody made money from Billie Holiday's recordings of 1935 to 1942, for example, even if she did not.

WILDER, Alec
American Popular Song: The Great Innovators 1900–1950 (1972)
A gentle, loving, intelligent masterpiece: an appreciation of the best songs and composers of our century by a man who was one of them, but too modest to include any of his own. Of perhaps 300,000 songs, Wilder examined about 17,000 and mentions or quotes the music of around 800 of the best. More valuable for those who read music, but there are insights for everybody who loves songs.

WILMER, Val
As Serious as Your Life: The Story of the New Jazz (1977)
A detailed survey, full of interviews, about how hard it is to make
a living at it, it also affirms that the music is an important part of the
community; by a British woman who earned the trust of that
community.

WRIGHT, Laurie
Mr Jelly Lord (1980)
'King' Oliver (1987)
'Fats' in Fact (1992)
Like Walter Allen's *Hendersonia*, these are documentary histories of
the artists' activities with discographies and illustrations. *'King' Oliver*
is an update of an earlier book by Allen and Brian Rust. Wright is
publisher and editor of *Storyville* magazine, and also publishes Tom
Lord's *Clarence Williams* (which documents the activities of one of the
busiest people who ever worked in black music), Rust and Dixon and
Godrich (*see* DISCOGRAPHY).

Index

Guide to
Modern World
Literature

Guide to
Modern World
Literature

MARTIN
SEYMOUR-SMITH

'Real literature can be created only by madmen, hermits, heretics, dreamers, rebels, and sceptics, not by diligent and trustworthy functionaries'.

—Evgeny Zamyatin

Wolfe Publishing Limited
10 Earlham Street   London WC2

Printed in Great Britain by Morrison and Gibb Ltd, London and Edinburgh

TO THE MEMORY OF MY FATHER
and
TO MY MOTHER

When Scaliger, whole years of labour past,
Beheld his Lexicon complete at last,
And weary of his task, with wond'ring eyes,
Saw from words pil'd on words a fabric rise,
He curs'd the industry, inertly strong,
In creeping toil that could persist so long,
And if, enrag'd he cried, heav'n meant to shed
Its keenest vengeance on the guilty head,
The drudgery of words the damn'd would know,
Doom'd to write lexicons in endless woe.

(From Dr. Johnson's Latin poem 'Know Yourself',
written after revising and enlarging his lexicon, or
dictionary; translated into English by Arthur Murphy,
in his *Life*, 1772.)

Contents

Introduction

I

The scope of this book extends to writers, of all nationalities, who survived 31 December 1899. In certain instances (e.g. Hopkins, Mallarmé) I have had, for obvious reasons, to discuss writers who died before that; but I have strictly limited these. I have given an account of the major literary movements of the past century and a half; the names of these will be found in the index. The system of putting 'q.v.' after names of literary movements, authors, and titles of books, is intended to be a practical aid to the reader: if he turns to the index he will find the main entry he requires in **bold** type. This should make cross-reference quick and simple. Such philosophers and concepts (e.g. Bergson, *Künstlerschuld*) as are not dealt with at length in the body of the text are discussed or explained in this introduction.

Complete accuracy in a comprehensive work such as this is, alas, impossible: errors of dating are repeated from reference-book to reference-book; it is frequently impossible to check the dates of first publication of books without seeing the original editions. . . . I have made every effort to give correct information (e.g. my dates of birth for Tennessee Williams and E. Lasker-Schüler differ from most authorities, but are right). I shall be glad to correct any errors, with acknowledgements, in future editions.

The dates given for dramatic works are of publication, not first production.

Dates after individual books are of earliest publication, wherever or in whatever form this took place.

The list of abbreviations consists mainly of books in which translations into English of works by writers (other than British and American) discussed in the text are conveniently available. It is hoped it will be useful; but it is not a bibliography, and makes no pretence to completeness. Fortunately more and more such collections are being published each year; all libraries and book-shops in large cities stock them. Not all books listed are currently in print.

Unsigned translations are by me.

The emphasis, since in the interests of space I have had to place emphases, is on the more universal areas of interest and language-knowledge (English, German, French, Spanish, Russian, Italian); and on the earlier rather than the later part of the period, which may less surely be assessed. But I have discussed some authors I believe to be neglected or misunderstood or underrated (e.g. George Moore, Céline, Ford) at length; and one great literature that is neglected, at least in Great Britain, the Japanese, has received a fuller treatment.

II

All Western literature has developed, with of course some national exceptions and variations, to a consistent pattern. In the succeeding very brief sketch I have kept definitions as broad as possible: our understanding of literature does not benefit from attempts to narrow down the meanings of terms too precisely —and the terms themselves lose their value.

By the mid-century *realism*, particularly in the novel, was well established. Realism, of course, is an essential part of any work of art or literature: in its broadest sense it simply means verisimilitude to actuality. But this leaves entirely open the question of how the artist or author regards actuality—as an outward or an inward phenomenon, or both, or whatever. Nineteenth-century realism, the literary method out of which modern literature developed, does, even though it remains one of the broadest of all literary concepts, have a less vague connotation.

First, realism is essentially a part of romanticism—however much it may sometimes look like a reaction against it, and however certainly the romantic movement may have seemed, in the positivist Fifties, to have collapsed. We are still, of course, living in a romantic period—nor, indeed, can there ever be any return to the limitations and artificialities of classicism.

Realism has no significant relationship to the literary classicism of antiquity or to the neo-classicism of the eighteenth century. It originates in the age-old tendency towards accuracy of representation (usually manifesting itself as an anti- or non-classical depiction of plebeian life—Cervantes, Jonson, Shakespeare, Smollett—or as regionalism), and in philosophical realism and all proto-pragmatic and proto-utilitarian inclinations. Nineteenth-century realism, at various times and in various writers, exhibited the following characteristics: objectivity (in the sense of concentration on facts rather than on interpretations of them); lucidity (rather than style or rhetoric); 'ordinary' or 'commonplace' experience; a search for immediate, verifiable, relativistic truth; secularism; emphasis on the psychological motivations of the characters, often at the expense of 'plot'. In general the good realist authors (for example, George Eliot, Howells, Henry James) had good or even idealistic intentions towards their audience; but they refused to uplift their hearts, thus raising false hopes. A few realists (to some extent Flaubert; certainly Maupassant) had rather more aggressive intentions towards the bourgeois. But the milieu chosen was emphatically middle-class.

In certain countries (notably France) realism turned into *naturalism*. This term is frequently used, particularly by journalists and reviewers of plays (but also by critics who should know better) as a synonym for realism. This is misleading. Naturalism is a more precise term than realism: a narrowing-down of it. (Zola's programme—described in the account of him—is entirely naturalist; his practice, of course, is not.) Naturalist fiction is guided, or thinks it is guided, by the principles of scientific determinism. This arose largely from 'Darwinism', a movement or climate of thought that has less connection with Charles Darwin, from whom it derives its name, than might seem apparent. Darwin had in fact given a new and viable interpretation of the theory of transformism; according to 'Darwinism' he invented and 'proved' it. Actually it went back, as a theory, to at least 550 B.C. The naturalists extracted from Darwinism the notion of man-as-animal, of his life as a bloody struggle (they could have found this more definitely and confidently stated in Hobbes' *Leviathan*, as distinct from hypothetically in Darwin; but Darwin seemed *scientifically* respectable)—'the strongest, the swiftest and the cunningest live to fight another day', said T. H. Huxley. The lives of the poor, to the depiction of which the naturalists turned, gave ample justification for such a view. However, in practice the best naturalists (e.g. Zola, Dreiser) have transcended their deterministic programmes. Zola is as romantic as he is naturalistic, and Dreiser is massively puzzled as well as sentimental; both are naturalists, it is true; but both gain their ultimate effects from their power of psychological penetration.

The so-called *neo-romanticism*, and then *decadence*, that manifested itself in nearly all the Western literatures between about 1885 and 1905 was not as remote from either realism or naturalism as it may have seemed at the time.

All great literary movements eventually deteriorate: into preciosity, over-aestheticism, over-self-consciousness, trivial scholarship, cultivation of debility and whatever society may at the time determine as perverse behaviour. . . . The decadent movement (it is more of a tendency) at the end of the nineteenth century is sometimes called *fin de siècle*, a term I have occasionally employed. It is as much a development, or etiolation, of *Parnassianism* and *symbolism* (both these terms are discussed in the section on French literature) as a reaction against positivism and naturalism. Symbolism had contained the religious impulses inherent in human beings, never completely submergeable, during the realist-naturalist period. The decadent writers—they range from the only partly decadent, like Verlaine, to the wholly decadent, like Dowson—were nearly all 'religious' (if only in the sense that they embraced 'Satanism' or aspects of it and died incense-sniffing Catholics); but they viewed civilization as in decay rather than growth: they worshipped entropy, degeneration, disorder; they transformed the romantic cult of the individual into the romantic-decadent cult of the self (narcissism)—hence their interest in or cultivation of homosexuality. They made a cult of the erotic and hurled themselves into hopeless loves. They worshipped the urban and the ugliness it offered—but in a deliberately perverse spirit.

The foregoing are the chief characteristics of decadence in general; no single writer manifests all of them—except, possibly, some entirely trivial one. In its least extreme form this neo-romantic spirit began to pervade the works of realists and naturalists—for example, Zola's novels are increasingly full of symbols.

In the course of literary history movements (or tendencies) provoke reactions to themselves; but these reactions usually absorb the essences, the genuine discoveries, of the movements that have engendered them. To give an over-simple illustration: romanticism at its best contains the essence of classicism. The best neo-romantic writers had learned the important lessons of realism. And it was essentially from neo-romanticism that modernism arose.

Expressionism, which I have fully described in the section on German literature, was a specifically German movement. However, literary modernism can most usefully be described as expressionism: every modern movement after symbolism (which was in any case nineteenth-century in origin) may conveniently be described as a version of expressionism.

Modernism, which often arouses great hostility, has a number of character-istics (the writer who combines every one of them in his work is likely to be a charlatan). Realism remains committed—more or less subtly—to a *mimetic* theory: literature is an imitation, a photograph, of life. Modernism (in the sense used in this book) is non- or anti-mimetic. In its extremest form, modern-ism may resolutely omit what is 'essential' in societal, communal or simply representational terms. On the other hand, it will stress precisely what is 'unessential' in such terms. This amounts to an emphasis on inner life, and therefore on the life of the individual. Causality, carefully observed in the nineteenth century, may be deliberately deleted. This does not mean, of course, that it is rejected. It means that it is not an essential part of what the modernist writer is trying to say.

An even more important aspect of modernist writing—and one which puzzles many of its readers, for whom 'time' remains, consciously, a means of manipulating reality into acceptable forms—is its jettisoning of conventional chronology. I have explained this at some length in my treatment of the French *nouveau roman* (q.v.).

It is here that the French philosopher, Henri Bergson, is relevant. Bergson did not 'discover' either unconventional time or *stream-of-consciousness*; but his philosophy reflected much contemporary thinking. Bergson is part of the neo-romantic reaction against positivism; he also complements the phenomenology of the German philosopher Husserl (discussed with the French *nouveau roman*) inasmuch as he concentrates upon the concrete rather than the abstract (Husserl was not himself at all interested in this problem; but the effect of his work has been to draw attention to perceptual actualities). It is in a sense appropriate that Bergson, although not an imaginative writer, should have received the Nobel Prize for Literature (1928): his influence on literature has been wide and deep. He demanded a return to the 'immediate data of consciousness', and he believed that this could be grasped by means of what he called 'intuition'. Like a number of modern novelists he saw character not as 'personality' but as a process of ceaseless becoming.

The actual term *stream-of-consciousness* originated with Henry James' brother William James; stream-of-consciousness fiction tends to lay emphasis on pre-verbal types of experience; by implication, therefore, this type of fiction regards internal experience as more 'important' than external. (However, stream-of-consciousness can be used simply as an extension of realist technique: the fact that mental minutiae are recorded is not in itself guarantee of a phenomenological approach.) Bergson's attitude was similar: for him consciousness was *duration* (*la durée*); intellect conceptualizes this flow into something static; intuition *thinks in duration*. Sartre has summarized Bergson's position well: 'on going into the past an event does not cease to be; it merely ceases to act and remains "in its place" at its date for eternity. In this way being has been restored to the past, and it is very well done; we even affirm that duration is a multiplicity of interpenetration and that the past is continually organized with the present'.

Bergson is important above all for his anti-intellectuality and his continual suggestion of new ways of seeing ourselves in the world. 'There is one reality, at least', he wrote, 'which we all seize from within, by intuition and not by simple analysis. It is our own personality in its flowing through time—our self which endures'.

III

I have referred throughout to a number of concepts, and used certain terms, which require initial definition.

I have categorized some writers as *naïve* and others as *sentimentive*. This requires explanation. In 1795 Goethe's friend and contemporary, the German poet, dramatist and critic Friedrich Schiller published his essay *On Naïve and Sentimentive Poetry* (*Über naive und sentimentalische Dichtung*)—I have followed the sensible practice of translating 'sentimentalische' as 'sentimentive'. 'Naïve' is misleading, too, but 'simple' does not help; 'sentimentive' is less hopelessly misleading, if only because less familiar, than 'sentimental'. This great essay has not had, in the English-speaking world, the recognition that it deserves. However, the question of Schiller's exact intentions, and of its significance in its time, is not relevant here. What I have done is to borrow Schiller's terms and to simplify them for the purposes of this book. For, even in my modified and restricted usage, they convey indispensable information that is not contained in the more familiar romantic-classical opposition.

For Schiller the naïve poet is one who is in perfect harmony with nature—with, indeed, the universe; his personality cannot be found in his poetry. He may even seem 'repulsive', 'callous', 'invisible'. The sentimentive poet, on the other hand, has lost his contact with and even his faith in nature, for which he yearns. Naïve poetry (Schiller says) is characteristic of the ancients: an immediate, inspired, detailed representation of the sensuous surface of life. In sentimentive poetry the author is everywhere present; he is self-conscious. The object does 'not possess him utterly'.

On Naïve and Sentimentive Poetry was originally prompted by the example of Goethe, whom Schiller saw, as he saw Shakespeare, as a serene and naïve poet born out of his time. It was Goethe, too, who made the most profound comment on the essay: '. . . he plagued himself with the design of perfectly separating sentimentive from naïve poetry. . . . As if . . . sentimentive poetry could exist at all without the naïve ground in which . . . it has its root'.

Schiller was contrasting the objective (naïve) poetry written in the early (progressive) stages of a culture, and the subjective (self-conscious, sentimentive) poetry written in its decline. Goethe, again, summed the matter up: 'All eras in a state of decline and dissolution are subjective . . . all progressive eras have an objective tendency'. Thus, in the poetry of Shakespeare there is a centrifugal tendency (called 'healthy' by Goethe), an inwards-outwards movement; in most of the poetry of Schiller's contemporaries, and more of that of our century, there is a centripetal tendency, an outwards-inwards movement.

Now Schiller wished to justify his own kind of (sentimentive) poetry in the light of what he felt to be Goethe's naïve poetry. As I have remarked, his precise concerns and (in particular) his programme need not—in this context—be ours.

Here I mean by the naïve writer the writer whose inspiration is above all drawn from his unsophisticated, uncomplicated, *direct* view of the universe. His view is uncluttered by intellectualization. The naïve writers of the nineteenth and twentieth centuries have been poor thinkers—this is a point of which I have made a good deal. Hardy, Dreiser and Sherwood Anderson (for example) were all writers of great power—but poor thinkers. (True, Anderson was something of a sage: but sages are not thinkers.) The naïve writer does not proceed by thought. The phenomenon can still only be explained by recourse to Schiller's distinction. And even where a writer—Pablo Neruda, pioneer explorer of the unconscious, comes immediately to mind—neither wants or tries to 'think', Schiller's essay immediately enriches our understanding.

I mean by the sentimentive writer—but always bearing in mind Goethe's stipulation that no work that has not roots in the naïve has any creative status—the writer who is sophisticated, trained in thinking, self-conscious. Thomas Mann is perhaps the prime example in the twentieth century.

Of course there is no such thing as a purely naïve writer—any more than there can be a purely sentimentive writer. But this applies to the romantic-classical opposition as well. Schiller's distinction is essential; and very important for our time. It reveals not only how the naïve writer can wreck and corrupt his work and himself by betraying his impulses, but also how sentimentive writing is becoming increasingly sterile as it draws cunningly away from the naïve; it reveals, too, the terrible predicament of the sophisticated creative writer in this second half of our century. It is towards the truly mysterious—and yet authentic—that the creative writer must now aim. This is why much of the newest poetry and fiction is coming from Latin America: an exotic and largely unexplored region of the world that well matches our own even more exotic, even less explored regions. Recourse to the purely surreal can lead to nothing better than the raw material of the dream—which, as it comes into consciousness, is censored, screened. What is needed—we have had it in Rilke, Vallejo and some others—is the *real dream*: the meaning of the dream in terms of *its own original, unknown, mysterious, day-haunting images*—not in those of (say) a psychoanalytical interpretation. This truth contains, absorbs and accepts death.

The problem is one of control as well as of inspiration: what kind of control must the writer exercise over his immediate impulses to return to this naïve realm? Here the animal cunning of sentimentive writers such as Vallejo or Rilke can be useful. One thinks in this connection of the cunning art of the 'primitive' man who hunts, for food, animals he loves: this is nearer to the required sentimentive than is the cleverness of the regular academic critic—for all the ancient wisdom that is locked up—one might say fossilized—inside the notions with which he plays.

*

Another concept that I have used freely is what I have christened *Künstlerschuld*: 'artist-guilt'. Increasingly in this century poets and writers (Rilke, Mann and Broch are examples) have been beset by the fear that literature fulfils no useful, but only a selfish function. The writers who feel this particular kind of anguish have been or are almost invariably dedicated to literature to the exclusion of everything else (Broch is an exception). The question is, of course, as old as Plato (this was how Aristotle and others understood Plato); but for some writers of the past hundred or so years it has become crucial. Broch tried not to be a writer. At one point Rilke wanted to be a country doctor. Laura Riding has repudiated poetry. Mann portrayed the writer as a sick Faustus. . . .

This is of course a relevant theme in an age of 'committed literature' and *socialist realism* (this is discussed fully in the section devoted to Russian literature; it must, of course, be distinguished from mere *social realism*, which means no more than it implies). The naïve writer has no doubts: Neruda, the most substantial living naïve poet, has no difficulty in reconciling his poetry with what he calls his communism. But the more sentimentive the writer the more wracked he is by doubts. . . .

*

I have very often spoken of *midcult* and *middlebrow*. This is a dangerous but essential concept in an age that is desperate to reject the wildness of the imagination by absorbing it (hence literary prizes, government-sponsored culture-feasts, and so on). One of the chief features of the truly middlebrow literature is that, however 'tragic' or 'modern' it may seem, it consists of material manipulated to satisfy the *conscious* desires of a pseudo-cultured (some would simply say cultured) audience: an audience that still thinks of the world-as-it-is as essentially the best; an audience of individuals who, in varying degrees, reject their endogenous suffering ('decent', externally prompted grief is allowed: in midcult novels relatives die young, girls get raped or crippled, babies are murdered by 'beasts' and/or so on, and it is 'very sad'): that suffering they experience as a result of their failure to attain authenticity. Middlebrow literature is, in Sartre's existentialist sense, *slimy, viscous*: it helps us to remain *filthy swine (salauds)*. Some middlebrow literature is apparently *avant garde*; at its worst it may not even be intended for reading, but simply for display (hence the phrase 'coffee-table book'). The great midcult successes are seldom, probably never, planned. They arise from the innate vulgarity and ignorance or (usually) pretentiousness of their progenitors.

Of course few works are entirely middlebrow; equally, some works are merely tainted with middlebrowism in one or another aspect. Some of the characteristics of the kind of midcult literature with which I have been concerned here (where this has not been taken seriously by critics regarded as serious I have happily ignored it), though they never co-exist all together, are: 'uncanniness', 'weirdness', 'occultness'; 'profundity' in the sense that dictionaries of 'great ideas that have changed the world' are profound; fashionableness—whether in the matter of being sexy or using 'dirty' language or whatever; slickness of technique; pseudo-complexity, conferring upon the reader the sense that he is reading a 'difficult' (and therefore 'worthwhile', 'deep') book; potential for discussion at lounge-, drawing-room-, or pub-level (or in the foyers of theatres); liability to excite certain reviewers.

*

The useful term *objective correlative* was first used by the American painter Washington Allston in 1850; T. S. Eliot revived it in 1919. It has been much criticized as putting either too much or too little emphasis on the objectivity of works of literature. . . . I am not concerned with this: here I mean by it simply: *objective equation for personal emotion*. If the writer, in expressing a personal emotion about having killed his wife, composes a work about a toad eating dry, red eggs, then that situation is the *objective correlative* for his emotion at killing his wife. I imply absolutely nothing more by my use of the term: it is purely descriptive.

*

For a truly viable (non-commercial) theatre to exist there has to be a truly viable audience. This certainly exists—or existed until a few years ago—in Belgium. The theatre of today is largely in the hands of the directors (hence the term, used pejoratively by me, *director's theatre*), who do not work in true conjunction with the authors of plays, but rather as more or less commercial *entrepreneurs*, 'realists' who manipulate such dramatic texts as they decide to exploit to meet the needs of their (alas, mostly middlebrow) audiences. The genuine dramatist has to survive this and to assert himself. All he has on his side is the spirit of the genuine theatre—but this, fortunately, survives along with (and often in the purveyors of) the commercial theatre. There are two tests of a genuine dramatist: his work must be playable on the stage, in some form, at any time during or after his lifetime; and it must stand the test of reading as well as viewing. Perhaps there are a score of twentieth-century dramatists who will fulfil these requirements. I have discussed these and a number of other interesting ones. But it must be remembered that this is a guide to literature and not to the entertainment industry or the history of intelligently motivated socio-anthropological phenomena.

IV

Finally, many people have helped me in many ways with the writing of this book. None is of course in any way whatever responsible for any of the opinions expressed in it, or for any errors. The following have given me aid, of kinds too various to mention, that I found invaluable:— of my colleagues on the English Faculty at the University of Wisconsin-Parkside, where I am currently spending a happy and instructive year as Visiting Professor: James and Angelica Dean, Andrew Maclean, James Mehoke; my family, which has worked harder than I have—and suffered much: my wife, my daughters Miranda Britt and Charlotte Seymour-Smith, my son-in-law Colin Britt (in particular), who made things memorably cheerful at a time when they were difficult; Ivar Ivask, for generously overlooking some of the material—and correcting me on a number of points; Toby Zucker, for help with the German section; S. K. Pearce, my bank manager, without whose practical understanding and help I could not have proceeded; and B. H. Bal, George Barker, Robert Bly, Edward Charlesworth, Sally Chilver, Tony Gottlieb, Robert Graves, Fujio Hashima, Wing-Commander Vernon 'Coils' Pocock, James Reeves, C. H. Sisson, Hilary Spurling, Anthony Thwaite, David Wright. I should also like to thank the printers, who have performed a difficult task (and not the first one composed by me) with exemplary intelligence and fortitude. My greatest debt is expressed in my dedication; the greatest sorrow of my life in its first part. Libraries have as always been helpful and courteous beyond the line of duty: The London Library; the East Sussex County Library, both at Bexhill-on-Sea and at Lewes; and the Library at the University of Wisconsin-Parkside.

The University of Wisconsin-Parkside,   18 April 1972
Kenosha, Wisconsin, U.S.A.

Abbreviations

AD: *Absurd Drama*, P. Meyer, 1965
ad.: adapted
add.: with additional matter
AL: *Albanian Literature*, S. E. Mann, 1955
AMEP: *Anthology of Modern Estonian Poetry*, W. K. Matthews, 1955
AMHP: *Anthology of Modern Hebrew Poetry*, A. Birman, 1968
AMYP: *Anthology of Modern Yugoslav Poetry*, J. Lavrin, 1963
ANZP: *Anthology of New Zealand Poetry*, V. O'Sullivan, 1970
AP: *Africa in Prose*, O. R. Dathorne and W. Feuser, 1969
ARL: *Anthology of Russian Literature in the Soviet Period*, B. G. Guerney, 1960
ASP: Apollinaire: *Selected Poems*, O. Bernard, 1965
AU: *Agenda*, Vol. 8, No. 2, Ungaretti Special Issue, Spring 1970
AW: *Australian Writing Today*, C. Higham, 1968
AWT: *African Writing Today*, E. Mphahlele, 1967
BAP: Bella Akmadulina: *Fever and Other Poems*, G. Dutton and I. Mezhakov-
  Koriakin, 1970
BAV: *Book of Australian Verse*, J. Wright, 1956
BEJD: Josef Brodsky: *Elegy for John Donne and Other Poems*, N. Bethell, 1967
BISS: *Penguin Book of Italian Short Stories*, G. Waldman, 1969
BP: Bert Brecht: *Plays*, 2 vols, J. Willett and E. Bentley, 1960–2
BRV: *Book of Russian Verse*, C. M. Bowra, 1943
BRV2: *Second Book of Russian Verse*, C. M. Bowra, 1948
BSP: André Breton: *Selected Poems*, K. White, 1969
CCD: *Chief Contemporary Dramatists*, 3 vols, T. H. Dickinson, 1915–30
CFP: *Contemporary French Poetry*, A. Aspel and D. Justice, 1965
CGP: *Contemporary German Poetry*, J. Bithell, 1909
CGPD: *Contemporary German Poetry*, B. Deutsch and A. Yarinolinsky, 1923
CIP: *Contemporary Italian Poetry*, C. L. Golino, 1962
CIV: *Contemporary Italian Verse*, G. Singh, 1968
CLP: *Century of Latvian Poetry*, W. K. Matthews, 1957
CP: Anton Chekhov, *Plays*, 1959
CRP: *Anthology of Contemporary Rumanian Poetry*, R. MacGregor-Hastie, 1969
CTP: Albert Camus: *Caligula and Three Other Plays*, S. Gilbert, 1958
CV: *Caribbean Verse*, O. R. Dathorne, 1967

CWT: *Canadian Writing Today*, M. Richler, 1970

DFP: Friedrich Dürrenmatt: *Four Plays*, G. Nellhaus et al, 1964

ed.: edited by

ESW: Paul Eluard: *Selected Writings*, L. Alexander, 1951

FBS: Marcel Raymond: *From Baudelaire to Surrealism*, 1950

FCP: *Five Centuries of Polish Poetry*, J. Peterkiewicz, Burns Singer and J. Stallworthy, 1970

FGP: *Four Greek Poets*, E. Keeley and P. Sherrard, 1966

FMR: *From the Modern Repertoire*, 3 vols, E. Bentley, 1949–56

FTP: Max Frisch: *Three Plays*, M. Bullock, 1962

FTS: Frank Wedekind: *Five Tragedies of Sex*, B. Fawcett and S. Spender, 1952

FWT: *French Writing Today*, S. W. Taylor, 1968

GED: *Anthology of German Expressionist Drama*, W. H. Sokel, 1963

GMS: *Plays of Gregorio Martínez Sierra*, H. Granville-Barker and J. G. Underhill, 1923

GSP: Michel de Ghelderode: *Seven Plays*, G. Hauger and G. Hopkins, 1960

GSS: *German Short Stories*, R. Newnham, 1964

GWT: *German Writing Today*, C. Middleton, 1967

HE: *Heart of Europe*, T. Mann and H. Kesten, 1943

HW: René Char: *Hypnos Waking*, J. Matthews, 1956

HWL: Joseph Reményi, *Hungarian Writers as Literature*, 1964

IMPL: *Introduction to Modern Polish Literature*, A. Gillon and L. Krzyzanowski, 1964

IMSL: *Introduction to Modern Spanish Literature*, K. Schwartz, 1968

IN: P. J. Jouve: *An Idiom of Night*, K. Bosley, 1968

IP4: Eugene Ionesco: *4 Plays*, D. Watson, 1958

IQ: *Italian Quartet*, R. Fulton, 1966

ISS: *Italian Short Stories*, R. Trevelyan, 1965

IWT: *Italian Writing Today*, R. Trevelyan, 1967

JDP: Max Jacob: *Drawings and Poems*, S. J. Collier, 1951

JLME: Y. Okazakix: *Japanese Literature in the Meiji Era*, V. H. Vigliemo, 1955

LAP: *Anthology of Latin-American Poetry*, D. Fitts, 1942

LTT: Federico García Lorca: *Three Tragedies*, J. Graham-Luján and R. L. O'Connell, 1961

LWLF: *An Anthology of Byelorussian Poetry from 1928 until the Present Day*, 1971

LWT: *Latin-American Writing Today*, J. M. Cohen, 1967

MAP: *Modern African Prose*, R. Rive, 1964

MBL: *Introduction to Modern Bulgarian Literature*, N. Kirilov and F. Kirk, 1969

MBSP: V. Mayakovsky: *The Bedbug and Selected Poetry*, P. Blake, 1961

MEP: *Modern European Poetry*, W. Barnstone, 1966

MFC: *Four Modern French Comedies*, A. Bermel, 1960

MGL: *Introduction to Modern Greek Literature*, M. P. Gianos, 1969

MGP: *Modern German Poetry*, M. Hamburger and C. Middleton, 1962
MHP: *Mayakovsky and his Poetry*, H. Marshall, 1965
MJL: *Modern Japanese Literature*, D. Keene, 1956
MJS: *Modern Japanese Stories*, I. Morris, 1961
MPA: *Modern Poetry from Africa*, G. Moore and U. Beier, 1963
MRD: *Masterpieces of Russian Drama*, 1933
MRP: *Modern Russian Poetry*, V. Markov and M. Sparks, 1966
MSP: Oscar Venceslas de Lubicz Milosz: *14 Poems*, K. Rexroth, 1952
MST: *Modern Spanish Theatre*, M. Benedikt and G. E. Wellwarth, 1968
MSW: Henri Michaux: *Selected Writings*, R. Ellmann, 1968
MT: *Modern Theatre*, 6 vols, E. Bentley, 1955–60
NVSP: *Selected Poems of Neruda and Vallejo*, R. Bly, 1970
NWC: *New Writing in Czechoslovakia*, G. Theiner, 1969
NWP: *New Writing from the Philippines*, L. Caspar, 1966
NWSD: *The New Wave Spanish Drama*, G. E. Wellwarth, 1970
NWY: *New Writing in Yugoslavia*, B. Johnson, 1970
OBCV: *The Oxford Book of Canadian Verse*, A. J. M. Smith, 1960
PAWT: *African Writing Today*, E. Mphahlele, 1967
PBFV3, PBFV4: *Penguin Book of French Verse 3, 4*, A. Hartley, 1957, 1959
PBGV: *Penguin Book of Greek Verse*, C. Trypanis, 1971
PC: Anton Chekhov: *Plays*, E. Fen, 1959
PGV: *Penguin Book of German Verse*, L. Forster, 1957
PI: *Poem Itself*, S. Burnshaw, 1960
PIV: *Penguin Book of Italian Verse*, G. Kay, 1965
PJV: *Penguin Book of Japanese Verse*, G. Bownas and A. Thwaite, 1964
PKM: Kai Munk: *Five Plays*, R. P. Keigwin, 1953
PLAV: *Penguin Book of Latin-American Verse*, E. Caracciolo-Trejo, 1971
PLJ: *Poetry of Living Japan*, D. J. Enright and T. Ninomiya, 1957
PP: Alfred French: *The Poets of Prague*, 1969
PPPP: *Post-War Polish Poetry*, C. Milosz, 1965
PRP: Robert Pinget: *Plays*, 2 vols, S. Beckett, B. Bray, 1965–7
PRV: *Penguin Book of Russian Verse*, D. Obolensky, 1965
ps.: pseudonym of
PSAV: *Penguin Book of South-African Verse*, J. Cope and U. Krige, 1968
PSV: *Penguin Book of Spanish Verse*, J. M. Cohen, 1956
pt.: part
PTP: Luigi Pirandello: *Three Plays*, A. Livingstone, 1923
PWT: *Polish Writing Today*, C. Wieniewska, 1967
rev.: revised
RP: *Russian Poetry 1917–55*, J. Lindsay, 1956
RSP: Pierre Reverdy: *Poems*, A. Greet, 1968

SAWT: *South-African Writing Today*, N. Gordimer and L. Abraham, 1967
SCO: *Swan, Cygnets and Owl*, M. E. Johnson, 1956
sel.: selected by
SL: *Soviet Literature, an Anthology*, G. Reavey and M. Slonim, 1933
SP: Bert Brecht: *Seven Plays*, E. Bentley, 1961
SSP: *Six Soviet Plays*, E. Lyons, 1934
SSW: Jules Supervielle: *Selected Writings*, 1967
TC: Anton Chekhov: *The Tales*, 13 vols, C. Garnett, 1916–22
TCG: *Penguin Book of Twentieth Century German Verse*, P. Bridgwater, 1963
TCGV: *Twentieth Century German Verse*, H. Salinger, 1952
TCSP: *20th Century Scandinavian Poetry*, M. S. Allwood, 1950
TGBP: *Two Great Belgian Plays about Love*, 1966
TMCP: *Three Modern Czech Poets*, E. Osers and G. Theiner, 1971
TMP: *Twenty-five Modern Plays*, S. F. Tucker, 1931
TNM: *Two Novels of Mexico*, L. B. Simpson, 1964
TT: *Tellers of Tales*, W. S. Maugham, 1939
tr.: translated by
UP: *Ukranian Poets*, W. Kirkconnell and C. H. Andrusyshen, 1963
VA: Andrey Voznesensky: *Antiworlds*, P. Blake and M. Hayward, 1967
VCW: Paul Valéry: *Collected Works*, J. Matthews, 1962
VSW: Paul Valéry: *Selected Writings*, 1950
VTT: Paul Éluard: *Thorns of Thunder*, G. Reavey, S. Beckett, 1936
WNC: *Writers in the New Cuba*, J. M. Cohen, 1967
ZS: Nikolay Zabolotsky: *Scrolls*, D. Weissbert, 1970

African and Caribbean Literature

I

The emergence of a people, oppressed for centuries, into articulate awareness of their insulted and traumatic history is a matter of concern to everyone. The literature of Black Africa is, of course, only one aspect of this confused but increasingly evident emergence. But its intrinsic literary importance has—with every justification—been somewhat exaggerated. Such works (I take a random example) as the Ethiopian SAHLE SELLASIE's (1936) *Shinega's Village: Scenes of Ethiopian Life* (1964; tr. W. Leslau, 1970), the first work written in Chaha—a hitherto unwritten Ethiopian dialect which Sellasie used an Arabic script to transcribe—are immensely important in sociological and historical terms. So is his *The Afersata* (1969), written in English, describing how a remote Ethiopian community with no police force investigate an outbreak of arson by their age-old 'Afersata' method. But neither is a work of great literary importance. Even the more famous African writers, such as Senghor (q.v.), may have had exaggerated claims made for them. These writers will be important figures in the history of the literature now emerging; but the intrinsic importance of their work—as literature—will surely be seen to be smaller than is now apparent. I mean that no indisputably major poets or novelists, with the possible or probable exceptions of those I have chosen—out of a hundred or so—to discuss here, have yet emerged. I have quoted the South African writer Ezekiel Mphahlele's (q.v.) reasons for his holding of a similar view in the section dealing with black South African writing, which should be read in conjunction with this.

The tensions in black literature are acute. What black man, who is also a writer, is to assert that it is more important for him to function independently—as a writer must—when he and his fellows' freedom seems to be threatened and insulted? Good writing has arisen from such tensions; interesting writing has arisen from them; as yet unquestioned masterpieces have not. The only possible exception is Césaire's *Return to My Native Land* (q.v.).

Yet two strands are already clearly discernible in the black literature of the world: one is 'committed' to negritude (q.v.), or something akin to it or developed from it (at the most extreme, 'black power'); the other is less easily definable, but it leaves writers freer. Its spokesmen (the South African Ezekiel Mphahlele, q.v., is one of them) are often accused, by adherents of negritude, of such crimes as 'colonialism, neo-colonialism and imperialism'. But this is an attack by political upon literary animals; it also represents a misunderstanding of the nature of literature. It may be that, in the wider context, the activists are correct; it may be that they are wrong. In the context of literature they are missing the point. Literature is made not with ideas but with imagination; and despite the arguments of committed writers, the imagination is autonomous, and owes no allegiance to dogma. Writers in favour of Marxist commitment call this view 'mystical'. But it is not mystical: it merely acknowledges a mystery.

However, this is the situation at present. But such writers as Mphahlele and Soyinka (qq.v.)—who has pointed out that tigers do not need to advertise their tigritude—readily acknowledge that negritude was a 'necessary phase'.

Although the concept of negritude was fully developed in Paris during the Thirties by such poets as Senghor (q.v.), it originated in the Caribbean. In the French islands the Africans were as violently alienated from their original nature as any black men anywhere: displaced, separated from their immediate families, forced into the Roman Catholicism of their masters, they either developed secret systems such as Voodoo (in Haiti)—a distorted means of asserting their essential Africanity—or they tried to become, by imitation, the very thing that oppressed them. The French were always glad to bestow upon a 'good', Catholic, educated, 'civilized' black the ultimate honour: to be a black Frenchman. But this system of 'assimilation', still practised by the Portuguese in their colonies, does not allow for French (or Portuguese) black men. . . . Thus, the 'good' black slaves of the French were told of their 'Gallic' ancestry. Assimilation is based on the anthropologically erroneous assumption (convenient to master-races engaged in economic exploitation, and therefore primarily a Victorian notion) that the concept of evolution can be applied to the human species. The insult contained in such an attitude—'you are a primitive non-European, a version of my unperfected self'—is both loveless and humanly wounding. Only now are we beginning to realize that so-called 'primitive' societies are too complex for 'civilized' people to understand with either ease or confidence.

Negritude expressed itself mainly, but not entirely, in poetry. Ironically it got its first chance in Cuba—as *negrismo*—when there was a European craze for all things African. (This craze did not represent a sudden awareness of the riches of African culture, but a reaction to the First World War.) In Haiti there was a similar revival. Caribbean Africans, thus encouraged, began to look at their true heritage. There were magazines—in Cuba *Revista de Avance* (1927–30) and in Haiti *La Revue Indigène*. Then, in Paris, a group of students, including Césaire and Senghor (qq.v.), published one issue of a magazine called *The Black Student*; later *Volontés* printed Césaire's *Return to My Native Land* (1939; tr. J. Berger and A. Bostock, 1969). This was ignored at the time; but André

Breton (q.v.) found a roneoed copy of it in 1940, visited Césaire in Martinique in 1942, and publicized the poem when he returned to France. When it was republished in 1956 it was already famous both as a surrealist poem and as the quintessential expression of negritude.

AIMÉ CÉSAIRE (1913) was born in the kind of appalling circumstances suffered by most poor African peasants in Martinique. His house was 'a shack splitting open with blisters like a peach-tree tormented by blight, and the roof worn thin, mended with bits of petrol cans, this roof pisses swamps of rust on to the grey sordid stinking mass of straw. . . .' Now Césaire is a deputy to the French Assembly, representing the independent revolutionary party of Martinique (which has association with France). *Return to My Native Land* is his main work, though he has written much else. Its style has been profoundly influenced by surrealism (q.v.)—the logical weapon with which to assail the polite and dreamless language of the oppressor—but it is misleading to call it a surrealist poem: its structure, and much of its content, are too immediately comprehensible to the rational conscious mind. But it is disorganized enough—in terms of what 'poetry-loving', paternalistic colonials would expect—for its purpose. Césaire's negritude is here a state of the soul: 'I want to rediscover the secret of great speech and of great burning. . . . The man who couldn't understand me couldn't understand the roaring of a tiger'; 'my negritude riddles with holes/ the dense affliction of its worthy patience'.

LÉOPOLD SÉDAR SENGHOR (1906), now President of Senegal, is often thought of as the leading apostle of negritude; but in fact his version of it now differs from his friend Césaire's. His father was wealthy (Senghor remembers his being visited by a king); he has retained his Catholicism; and where Césaire is well to the left of organized communism Senghor is a passionate pan-Africanist (his own experiments in federation have failed) whose sympathy with Marxism is tempered by his conviction that it is an unsuitable system for under-developed peoples. In Césaire's negritude there is at least an element of what is now known as 'black power': the militant movement that advocates seizure of power, by black people, from a white society that they see as rapidly falling into a capitalistically induced decay. Senghor, on the contrary, is an integrationist, who has in more recent years been influenced by the Jesuit Teilhard de Chardin's ideas of 'cosmic complexification': a number of organisms fitting symbiotically together to form a united whole. He would thus see the black African states united in a federation, and, in a wider context, this federation as a part in a still larger federation. His own political record is more humanly honourable than most; for example, his erstwhile associate Mamadou Dia, tried in 1962—after a crisis the details of which are not fully known—languishes in a prison and not a grave. . . . 'Negritude', Senghor has written, 'is the *sum total of the values of the African world . . . intuitive reason, reason which is embrace and not reason which is eye . . . the communal warmth, the image-symbol and the cosmic rhythm which instead of dividing and sterilizing, unified and made fertile.*' Other aspects of negritude include: rhythm (incantation); style—of sympathy; humour ('laughter to keep from crying'—as the American Negro poet Langston Hughes, q.v., put it); the

3

haunting presence of the dead. . . . It was poetry reflecting this complex attitude—embracing *non-whiteness* as well as blackness—that Senghor included in his important *Anthology of New Negro and Malagasy Poetry*, introduced by Sartre (q.v.), in 1948.

Senghor's poetry has appeared in several volumes, of which the first was *Songs in Shadow* (*Chants d'ombre*, 1945). There is a good English selection: *Prose and Poetry* (tr. J. Reed and C. Wake, 1964). Senghor's presentation is in the tradition of Claudel (q.v.): free verse in 'versets'. He also resembles Claudel in his use of elemental imagery and copious rhetoric. His most important poem —from a literary point of view—is the dramatic poem 'Chaka', in which he deals movingly with the problem of reconciling his poethood with his role as politician. (AWT; AP)

LÉON DAMAS (1912), an associate of Senghor's and Césaire's in Paris in the Thirties, comes from French Guiana. He made some successful innovations in French versification before Césaire or Senghor. *Pigments* (1937), the first volume of 'negritude poetry' to be published, was destroyed by the French police. His most recent volume is *Black Label* (1956). BIRAGO DIOP (1906), a Senegalese veterinary surgeon (now his country's ambassador to Tunis), is usually classed as a poet of negritude; he is most distinguished, however, as a short-story writer. Both his poetry and his prose incorporate Senegalese folklore in a subtle and sophisticated, and yet apparently artless, manner. He is one of Africa's most accomplished and elegant prose stylists. (MPA) DAVID DIOP (1927–60), of mixed Senegalese-Cameroonian blood, published one book (1956); all his manuscripts were lost when he died in an air crash. In Diop's poetry we see an aggressive affirmation of negritude, immature but of great power. (AWT; MPA)

In Diop's Congo contemporary TCHICAYA U TAM'SI (ps. FELIX TCHICAYA, 1931) the influence of Césaire is much more evident. A good selection is available: *Selected Poems* (tr. G. Moore, 1970). U Tam'si combines his surrealism with angry topical satire (he was in the Congo at the time of its crisis, and witnessed at first hand the ambiguous role of the United Nations in the murder of the Congolese Prime Minister, Patrice Lumumba); this aspect of his work is perhaps more original. He so far seems to have failed to integrate into his poetry the more personal theme of disturbed sexuality, which nevertheless haunts it. It is claimed, however, that his placing of disparate symbols—many of them violently sexual, or in sexual contexts—side by side, descends from Bantu poetry. This may be so; his work still conveys the impression of a powerful, gifted but not yet fulfilled poet.

The Malagasy JEAN-JOSEPH RABÉARIVELO (1901–37), included by Senghor in his 1948 anthology, was a victim of 'assimilation': the persistent refusal of French clerks to allow him to go to France, whose culture he loved, caused him first to take to drugs and then to kill himself. He is rightly regarded as the founder of modern Malagasy literature in French. He just had time to perfect his style. From self-consciously symbolist poetry in faulty French he graduated to masterly adaptations of Malagasy vernacular poetry:

What invisible rat
come from the walls of night
gnaws at the milky cake of the moon?
Tomorrow morning,
when it has gone,
there will be bleeding marks of teeth. . . .

And all will snigger
and, staggering, will fall.
The moon will no longer be there:
the rat will have carried her into his hole.

(MPA)

JEAN-JACQUES RABEMANANJARA (1913) was luckier than his countryman Rabéarivelo, whose disciple he early proclaimed himself: as a civil servant in Madagascar he managed to get to France on a tour of duty, and the Second World War prevented his return. He began by imitating French models; then he followed Rabéarivelo in his adaptations of popular indigenous ballads. His later style, however, imitates that of Senghor and, beyond him, Claudel; but rhetoric usually swamps invention. Rabemananjara was imprisoned in 1947 for his part in the uprising against the French; but became a minister in the first independent government (1960). His most original work is contained in his plays, which include *The Malagasy Gods* (1947).

FLAVIEN RANAIVO (1914), more poetically gifted, has carried on where his compatriot Rabéarivelo left off in the exploration of Malagasy popular poetry, particularly in the ballad form known as '*hain-teny*'. His collection *My Songs of Always* (*Mes chansons de toujours*, 1955) has been generously introduced by Senghor. (MPA)

II

CAMARA LAYE (1928), born in French Upper Guinea of a Malinke family, began his literary career while he was a student in Paris. Although attacked for his alleged lack of commitment (his first book was enviously described as a 'colonialist pot-boiler' by African nationalists), he is the most serious French-language writer in Africa; no other novelist approaches him in artistry or in psychological insight. Laye grew up in Kouroussa, in an environment largely untouched by French colonialism. His father was a smith; since he was respected as a master not only of metalwork but also magic, Laye came to acquire a full understanding of an ancient, and now vanishing, way of life. *The Dark Child* (*L'Enfant noir*, 1953; tr. J. Kirkup, 1954) is an autobiography in fictional form: written lucidly and straightforwardly, it is a candid lament for the past; there

5

is no resentment against colonialism. But, for all that, Laye's imagination is 'committed' to the all-important matter of the preservation of his own (black) identity. The book's chief importance is its unique evocation of Malinke traditions and customs. *The Radiance of the King* (*Le Regard du roi*, 1954; tr. J. Kirkup, 1956) is an ambitious allegory, written in colloquial style, on the theme of a white man's search for a King he wishes to serve (not, as some have suggested, God—except in an ironic, 'white' sense). Undoubtedly influenced by Kafka (q.v.), this subtle novel operates on both a serious and a comically ironic level. The white man Clarence goes to Africa, loses his money, and is enslaved. Only at the end is he redeemed. This moves out of the negritude phase and into the integrationist. It has all the mysterious life and infinite suggestiveness of a great work of art. Two of its main themes are the search, by the 'civilized' European, for the irrational that eludes him (but not the African), and the necessity for the European and the African to meet.

Camara Laye's most recent novel is *A Dream of Africa* (*Dramouss*, 1966; tr. J. Kirkup, 1968). This is again autobiographical: the narrator returns from a long sojourn in Paris to an Africa on the verge of independence. It is an anti-technological book, and in effect calls on Africans to renounce violence and to learn from their ancient ways. Camara Laye lives in exile in Senegal, where he teaches at Dakar University. (AWT; MAP)

The two chief writers from the French Cameroons are MONGO BETI (ps. ALEXANDRE BIYIDI, 1932), who began his literary career with two books written under the name of EZA BOTO, and FERDINAND OYONO (1929). Both are satirists of and mockers of colonial ways. Beti's style is as original and vigorous but not as elegant as Laye's. His first novel, *Cruel Town* (*Ville cruelle*, 1954), promising in its abundant energy, is not well accomplished and has been disclaimed by him. Beti has always been more obviously 'committed' than Laye and is in fact a cruder writer. His earlier novels, like Oyono's, were written at a time when European ways were being savagely rejected by Africans. *The Poor Christ of Bomba* (*Le Pauvre Christ de Bomba*, 1956; tr. G. Moore, 1962), is written in the form of a diary: that of an acolyte who accompanies his master on a Catholic missionary circuit through a remote region of the Cameroons. It is a cruel satire on the values of the Catholic Church: the missionary, a sincere priest, hopes for more suffering in order that his churches may be filled. . . . The same pattern is repeated in the more succinct *Mission to Kala* (*Mission terminée*, 1957; tr. P. Green, 1958), and in *King Lazarus* (*Le Roi miraculé*, 1958; tr. P. Green, 1961). Beti is a boisterous, disenchanted writer, who possesses—one would imagine—a considerable quota of personal cynicism. In recent years he seems to have become disillusioned with literature, and has increasingly turned to political journalism. (MAP; AP) Ferdinand Oyono takes a similar approach to similar material. His novels include *Houseboy* (*Une Vie de Boy*, 1956; tr. J. Reed, 1966) and *The Old Man and the Medal* (*Le Vieux Nègre et la medaille*, 1956; tr. J. Reed, 1967). (AWT; AP)

*

AMOS TUTUOLA (1920), a Nigerian who writes in English, became famous before his countrymen and contemporaries Chinua Achebe and Wole Soyinka (qq.v.). Since he is the most truly naïve (q.v.) major writer (for his book is indisputably major) in the whole of modern world literature, he has been badly misunderstood by his own countrymen, who dislike his total lack of commitment—and his lack of interest in commitment—his unsophisticatedly incorrect English, and what they insist are his debts to Yoruba legend, to the Nigerian novelist DANIEL O. FAGUNWA (c. 1910–63), who wrote popular novels in Yoruba, and to *The Pilgrim's Progress*. Tutuola is, indeed, indebted to Yoruba legend and to Fugunwa; but *The Palm-Wine Drinkard* (1952) is none the less a naïve masterpiece—and his own. This is really a loosely constructed epic, a mixture of native lore, poetry, children's tall tale, innocently observed modernity and *grotesquerie*. The palm-wine drinkard loses his tapster, and goes to seek him in the Dead's Town. Tutuola certainly has an imperfect grasp of grammatical English; but the English he talks is real—his own—and one of its chief virtues is its oral directness. When Tutuola tried again (*My Life in the Bush of Ghosts*, 1954, *The Brave African Huntress*, 1958, etc.) he found inspiration only in isolated passages. He is a natural to whom thought—in even the sense of a professional writer's thought—is fatal.

CHINUA ACHEBE (1930), born in Iboland, presents a complete contrast. He is an intellectual, whose chief debt is not to any African writer but to such English novelists as George Eliot and Joseph Conrad (q.v.)—who, although a Pole, chose English as his means of literary expression. Achebe is penetratingly intelligent, and his realistic treatment of Nigerian life is as valuable anthropologically and sociologically as it is creatively. He was actively involved on Biafra's side in the Nigerian civil war. His first novel, *Things Fall Apart* (1958), is the tragic and moving story of Okonkwo and his village of Umuofia. Achebe is detached, cool—but more penetrative of the nature of both his Nigerians and his Christian missionaries than any previous African writer. *No Longer at Ease* (1960) is about Okonkwo's grandson Obi, turned into a corrupt civil servant by pressure of superstition and prejudice. *Arrow of God* (1964) is set in the Twenties, in Eastern Nigeria, about a chief priest who comes to trust an ignorant and essentially cruel British District Officer (portrayed by Achebe with great restraint). *A Man of the People* (1966) is more satirical and comic, and is perhaps not quite so effective as its predecessors. Its central episode is frighteningly reminiscent of the military *coup* in 1966, when many people were murdered. *Girls at War* (1971) collects short stories. Achebe believes that the writer should be 'in the thick of . . . at the head of' 'the big social and political issues of contemporary Africa': 'I *am* a protest writer', he has said, but 'Restraint—well, that's my style, you see'. (AWT; MAP)

Another important Nigerian novelist is CYPRIAN EKWENSI (1921), also a supporter of Biafra. Ekwensi is a sometimes crude and flamboyant writer, but also an observant and amusing one. His best novel, *Beautiful Feathers* (1963), is about how Lagos people spoil their lives in trying to imitate Western models. Ekwensi can be superficial, and he has not solved the problem of rendering

Nigerian speech into the English language, as Achebe has; but he sees his country and its faults with clarity. GABRIEL OKARA (1921), also Nigerian, has had more linguistic success: his novel *The Voice* (1964) incorporates renderings of Ijaw idiom that have rightly been described as exciting. TIMOTHY ALUKO (1920), born at Ilesha in Nigeria, is another intelligent observer; but his three novels are possibly nearer to good journalism than to fiction.

*

African poetry in English runs into more serious linguistic difficulties. None of the African poets seems to have found his own voice in English. And yet the poetry is strikingly honest—especially compared to the pretentiousness of much pseudo-*avant garde* verse produced in Great Britain and America by writers who have nothing to say. The Africans seem to be most self-conscious just when they are trying to be most African—as if the English language cannot accommodate their Africanity. Even Gabriel Okara, so successful in *The Voice* seems self-conscious in this way:

> The mystic drum beat in my inside
> and fishes danced in the rivers
> and men and women danced on land
> to the rhythm of my drum
>
> But standing behind a tree
> with leaves around her waist
> she only smiled with a shake of her head. . . .

(MPA)

But interesting poetry has come from: LENRIE PETERS (1932), from Gambia, the Ghanaian G. AWOONOR-WILLIAMS (1935) and the Nigerians JOHN PEPPER CLARK (1935), and CHRISTOPHER OKIGBO (1932–67), killed while fighting for Biafra, whose *Labyrinths with Path of Thunder* has now been added to a series of *African Writers* published in London (1971). (All MPA)

The Nigerian WOLE SOYINKA (1934), who was in prison for a time in Lagos during the Biafran war, has written a novel and poetry; but it is in his plays that he is outstanding. His ambition is to develop a Nigerian theatre, and no matter how much this has been disrupted by political events, he has gone some way towards doing so in his own plays, which number more than a dozen. His short plays were gathered into a volume in 1963: *Three Plays*; in the same year appeared *The Dance of the Forests* and *The Lion and the Jewel*. *The Road* (1965) is a full-length play. Soyinka's technique is basically expressionist, but his strong rhythms and use of Nigerian folk themes give his dramatic verse a toughness and a resilience that no other African verse in English possesses. E. KOLAWOLE OGUNMOLA (1925) is the other Nigerian playwright of note. An

8

actor, he writes in Yoruba. He has dramatized *The Palm-Wine Drinkard* (q.v.), and is the same kind of 'innocent' writer as Tutuola: his folk-plays all possess vigour and considerable imaginative power—as well as a strong element of simple-minded Christian dogmatism that is wholly irrelevant to them.

III

George Lamming (q.v.) pointed out in 1960 that 'the West Indian novel, by which I mean the novel written by the West Indian about the West Indian reality, is hardly twenty years old'. The main reason for this has been the high rate of illiteracy in the West Indies (I refer here to the formerly British islands, and to Guyana), the direct responsibility of British administrators, whose nineteenth-century policy towards education of the Negroes has rightly been described as 'criminal'. The West Indian literary capital is still London. And it is as well to remember that the language of the West Indian novelist is an English which veers, not always easily, between what authorities call West Indian Standard (the correct language, surely, for West Indians), English Standard—and, of course, the dialects.

The first professional West Indian novelist was the Jamaican CLAUDE MCKAY (1890–1948), who was also a poet. McKay went to America to study just before the First World War; there he discovered the American Negro W. E. B. DuBois' *The Souls of Black Folk*. (DuBois and Marcus Garvey, a Jamaican described by McKay as a charlatan, were the two great founding—and feuding —fathers of Pan-Africanism; DuBois, mocked by Garvey for his light skin, believed in the maintenance of the black diaspora; Garvey did not.) Financed by a man named Gray ('there was a greyness in his personality like the sensation of dry sponge'), McKay in 1920 visited England, but was disappointed. His poetry is in a Victorian idiom and is of little value; but his fiction, which he began writing in the late Twenties, is of more interest: his novels are: *Home to Harlem* (1928), *Banjo* (1929) and *Banana Bottom* (1933), described by Kenneth Ramchand as the 'first classic of West Indian prose'. This is a vivid and affirmative evocation of Jamaican village and town life, and a skilful portrait of a woman's achievement of freedom from social and racial fear. It contains also a memorable portrait of an itinerant musician, Crazy Bow:

> You may wrap her up in silk,
> You may trim her up with gold,
> And the prince may come after
> To ask for your daughter,
> But Crazy Bow was first.

Many West Indian novelists are now better known than McKay, but few have bettered his work.

There was a general exodus of West Indian novelists to London in the early Fifties: to a place where they could feel the presence of readers. After the Second World War the British Broadcasting Association ran a programme called 'Caribbean Voices', and magazines started up (*Bim* in Barbados, *Focus* in Jamaica, *Kyk-over-Al* in what was to become Guyana); but the obstacles to local recognition remained formidable. Two novelists were in the forefront: EDGAR MITTELHOLZER (1909–65), who set fire to himself in a field after writing a novel with just such a suicide as its main incident, and ROGER MAIS (1905–55), who had distinguished himself already as a short-story writer and poet in Jamaica in the Thirties and Forties, but who did not become a novelist until the last three years of his life—two of which were spent in London, although he died in Jamaica.

Mittelholzer was an uneven, over-prolific novelist, whose work consists of ghost stories, Gothic horror tales, historical fiction and studies of decayed gentry. His novels of the past, despite fine passages, are spoilt by an indulgence in the exotic for its own sake; better is a more straightforward novel such as *A Morning at the Office* (1950), an acutely observed and painful account of racial division. In Mittelholzer the humanist observer and the neo-romantic experimentalist jostle against one another uncomfortably, and seldom work together. Possibly his best book is the autobiographical *A Swarthy Boy* (1963). It is a tragedy that his last terrible gesture should have been real and not fictional.

Mais wrote three novels, *The Hills Were Joyful Together* (1953), *Brother Man* (1954) and *Black Lightning* (1955). These have been collected as *The Three Novels of Roger Mais* (1966). The first two are grim sociological studies of poverty and prison life; they are of very high quality. The third is one of the few successful accounts in modern fiction of a Christ-like figure. Bra'Man's followers reject him; but he is saved by sexual love. This portrait of a holy man is neither Christian nor Reichian—but is convincing and original.

West Indians of a younger generation who have written good novels include: GEORGE LAMMING (1932), from Barbados, whose finely written *In the Castle of My Skin* (1953) and *The Emigrants* (1954) are autobiographical; ANDREW SALKEY (1928), born in Panama of Jamaican parents, who gives accurate and sometimes depressing pictures of Jamaican life in *A Quality of Violence* (1959) and *Escape to an Autumn Pavement* (1960); JOHN HEARNE (1926), another Jamaican (born in Canada), whose *The Faces of Love* (1957) brilliantly examines the insecurity of a mulatto woman; and H. ORLANDO PATTERSON (1926), a sociologist, whose *The Children of Sisyphus* (1965) gives a vivid and sympathetic account of the Rastafarian cult, who believe their religious destiny lies in Ethiopia, and who still await the call to go there.

Dominating all these is V. S. NAIPAUL (1932), born in Trinidad of a Hindu family. Naipaul is a gentle ironist whose work—which has fallen off in the Sixties—may have become slightly overrated; but he is undoubtedly an important novelist within traditional modes. He satirizes the aspirations of semi-educated West Indians, has a flair for the linguistically comic, and can make the bizarre convincing. His first books were *The Mystic Masseur* (1957) and *Miguel Street* (1959), comic and grotesque tales of a street in Port of Spain. His best novel is *A House for Mr. Biswas* (1964), a sad portrait of the dissolution of Indian family life in the West Indies over the period of Mr. Biswas' short lifespan of the first forty-six years of this century. Mr. Biswas, an Indian who marries into an Indian family, is doomed from the start: he is alienated from the dissolving present of his own race, but also from the cultural emptiness of colonial society. The physical sense, conveyed with the utmost sadness and nostalgia, of this decay is one of the chief features of the book. Its successors, though intelligent and sensitive, have been disappointing.

*

TOM REDCAM (ps. THOMAS MACDERMOT, 1870–1933), novelist as well as versifier, was the unpromising colonial father of West Indian poetry. A slightly better poet was W. ADOLPHE ROBERTS (1886–1962), born in Kingston (CV); but it was McKay (q.v.) who—even if not a good poet—brought the necessary theme of Africa into Caribbean poetry. The best Thirties poet was Roger Mais (q.v.). The form in which he was finally to find himself, shortly before his early death, was the novel; but his free verse and his manner show that he fully realized that Caribbean verse, to achieve anything beyond 'local colour', must break free of sunlight, sea—and the Victorian poetical poesy. Love, he knew, spoke 'With accents terrible, and slow'. Clearly he had read the imagists (q.v.), and his poetry has a sharpness otherwise entirely lacking in the West Indian poetry of the period. His now celebrated 'All Men Come to the Hills' was in part an exhortation to his countrymen to give up the touristic sun and sea and look at the nature of Jamaican society. (CV) But the future of Caribbean verse in English is undoubtedly in the hands of DEREK WALCOTT (1930), born in St. Lucia. Walcott has a superb ear, knows his limitations (important in a poet) and is intelligent without allowing this to undermine his initial poetic impulse. As well as effective plays, he has published three collections of poetry: *Twenty-five Poems* (1948), *In a Green Night* (1962) and *The Castaway* (1965). His poetry gives a record, often in exuberant language, of growth to maturity against a West Indian background more fully and truthfully and painfully realized than in any previous West Indian poetry. His play *Dream on Monkey Mountain* was published in London (1972).

Albanian Literature

I

Albania (the Illyria of ancient history), wild, mountainous and beautiful—and the last country in Europe to come entirely under the domination of a central government (this is claimed to have occurred under the communist regime over the past twenty-five years)—did not come into existence until 1913. The only periods of freedom it had previously known were intermittent, under rule by chieftains in the fourteenth century—and under the Turks until they finally established it as a province in 1748. But they had subdued it by 1468, after a long struggle in which the Albanians were led by the man who remains the most famous of his race, George Castrioti—Iskander Bey, known as Scanderbeg. He is supposed to have died before the Turks achieved full domination. It was the Turks who imposed the Moslem religion on the originally Roman Catholic Albanians. Today, for what the figures are worth under a communist authority that issues no information to the West or to its communist neighbours, the population is about two-thirds Moslem; the rest are Roman Catholic (perhaps a tenth) or Greek Orthodox. The population is by now probably two million.

The Albanians, a highly independent and warlike people, became increasingly conscious of their national character during the universally nationalistic nineteenth century; after the First World War had wrecked the officially proclaimed independence of 1912 there was chaos, with the continual threat of Italian colonization. There was a short-lived communist government under Fan Noli (q.v.) in 1924; a kind of stability was achieved with the establishment of a republic under the presidency of Ahmed Zogu, known most familiarly as King Zog—for he proclaimed himself King in 1928 and ruled, although as a pawn of Mussolini's, until 1939, when Italy once again invaded the country and chased its protegé out. Since the democratic elections of December 1945 Albania has had a communist regime under the dictatorship of Enver Hoxha. This was the first genuinely independent Albania. At first Hoxha followed a rigidly Stalinist line, and was rewarded with generous Russian aid; but by 1961 Albania had entirely gone over to the Chinese, and was expelled from the Warsaw Pact. She is now in the curious position of being the sole European communist state to support the Chinese line (Rumanian fellow-travelling probably indicating little more than determination to maintain a degree of independence of Russia). Aid from China is not on a level with what Hoxha would like, but he is probably acting traditionally in preferring an uncomfortable measure of independence of his near neighbours to a comfortable dependence on them. Diplomatic relations with Great Britain were broken off in 1951 when the Albanians refused to pay compensation for the mining of British destroyers in the Corfu Straits; there is hardly any contact with the West, even with Western communist parties in democratic countries. For this reason little can be said about literary developments in Albania since 1945.

The Albanian language is a somewhat mysterious one. It is unrecorded before the fifteenth century, although its history must be ancient. It is Indo-European, latinized, inflected, with an archaic grammar. It bears a strong resemblance to ancient Phrygian. The two main dialects (technically no more than dialectical variations), which are mutually understandable, are Tosk, spoken in the south, and Geg—the standard—spoken in the north. There are colonies of Albanian speakers in Italy, Greece, Yugoslavia and U.S.A.

Albania was impervious to Western culture until the late nineteenth century, and its literature was mainly a folk one. Konstantin Kristoforidhi (ps. K. Nelko, 1827–95), who studied for three years at London University, translated the New Testament, and some of the Old, and compiled an Albanian-Greek dictionary. His other work is mostly religious and didactic. Much of the literature of the twentieth century, until the beginning of communism, consists of lyrical poetry, patriotic history and reworked folk material. There has been little incursion of European movements such as symbolism, and the current 'socialist realists' and tractor novelists, the only permitted writers, are building on a foundation that is still primitive; they cannot be said to have produced any works that transcend their time and place. It is possible that the most nourishing element to the contemporary literature is not indigenous work, but translation: from the classic Russian novelists and from Dickens and other nineteenth-century writers. That the literature is primitive is not to be wondered at: the language was still proscribed at the beginning of this century (except for the Roman Catholic clergy in Scutari, who had special privileges, q.v.); and the ideologically rigid attempt since 1945 to create a viable society out of so intractable a people and land, now completely isolated from its neighbours, can give little encouragement to cultural activity.

II

Nineteenth-century romanticism manifested itself in Albania as nationalism and, in the literature, as a folk cult. The Congress of Berlin, by dealing high-handedly with Albanian territory, made certain of fostering the ferocious spirit of independence that already existed—not only among Albanians at home, where illiteracy was deliberately maintained by the Turks, but also in Italy and Greece, where Albanian colonies had been established by fifteenth-century refugees from the victorious Turks.

The pioneer of the preceding period had been JERONIM DE RADA (1813–1903), who was born in Calabria, son of a priest, in an Albanian-speaking village. He went to the only Albanian school then in existence, which was also in Calabria. He collected heroic ballads of Albanian and Calabrian revolt which he wove together into epics interspersed with folk-songs. The first of these, *The Tale of Milosao, Son of the Despot of Scutari* (1836), is also the best. In due course De Rada became a member of the Calabrian revolutionaries; his reputation grew, and he attracted the attention of such apostles of liberty as the French poet Lamartine. Eight years before the Congress of Berlin and the formation of the Prizrend League (q.v.) for the defence of Albania's rights De Rada was able to found his own press and publishing house at Corigliano. He published his own *Scanderbeg* in 1873, and reprinted such earlier works as *The Song of Seraphina Thopia, Princess of Zadrima* (1843). Most of these ill-organized but fluent productions are in the well-known rhythm of Longfellow's *Hiawatha*. In 1883 De Rada launched a journal, *Flag of Albania*, to promote the cause of the country he had never visited; but this, owing to lack of funds, did not last more than four years. When De Rada lost his family he despairingly destroyed his folk collection, which he spent his last years remorsefully trying to rebuild. But before he died, in extreme poverty, his work had begun to bear fruit: his suggestion that an Albanian Chair should be established at the Oriental Institute at Naples was taken up, and De Rada's successor as folklorist, Zef Schirò, was appointed to the post. De Rada's poetry is not distinguished, as he lacked the grasp necessary to pull his varied material together into a coherent form; but he did succeed in conveying some of its freshness and charm.

ZEF SCHIRÒ (1865–1927) was a member of the Albanian colony in Sicily. He was less haphazard than the impractical De Rada, and, a better scholar, paid more attention to his education. The knowledge of Greek poetry he gained as a young man—some of his earliest work consists of translation from Anacreon and other Greek poets into Albanian—gave his poetic style a sound basis. Parts of his epic *Mili and Hajdhia* (1891) have probably not been bettered in Albanian literature. Schirò should not have tried to inflate this odd and slightly decadent tale into an epic, and the stories of Scanderbeg he introduced into it would have been more effectively confined to a separate work; but it is a great improvement on De Rada's work, and some of its lyrical passages are excellent. In the year of his appointment to the Chair of Albanian at the Oriental Institute of Naples (of which he eventually became director) he published another epic, *In a Foreign Land* (1900), which tells the story of the Albanian settlement in Sicily in the fifteenth century. Schirò's shorter poems, mostly martial, gracefully summarize Albanian passions. 'The Old Men' is typical:

> The translucent veil of aureate light
> that spread from sky to earth
> was smashed
> by the guncrack of abrupt war.
> Fearfully the swallows failed to find

the sweetness of their nests
but our heroes ran along the streets
to join together in the fight;
their women sang them on
with battle songs
but their fathers sadly watched
the flashing rifles
and deeply cursed their age.

Although AGOSTIN RËBEKU (1867–1928), born in Calabria, was deeply involved in the cause of an independent Albania (like Schirò, he saw the cultivation of friendship with Italy as the best way to achieve it), his real gifts were as a minor but elegant anacreonitic poet. He made many more technical experiments than his contemporaries.

However, the Albanian 'nationalist poet par excellence' was NAIM FRASHËRI (1846–1900). He and his two brothers Abdyi Frashëri (1839–92) and Sami Frashëri (1850–1904) were famous as patriots, educationists and writers. It was Abdyl who set up, with another, the Prizrend League, whose ultimate aim was the achievement of self-government. This lasted only a year before the Turks suppressed it; but it helped to delay some territorial concessions arranged at Berlin—and to unite the Albanians of different religions. Sami Frashëri invented an alphabet (later dropped) that he hoped would be acceptable all over the country; and books began to circulate, clandestinely, in Albania itself.

Naim Frashëri was born at Frashëri in southern Albania. His literary grounding was in Persian and Arabic rather than classical literature, although he knew Homer and Virgil, and his first verse was written in Persian. He worked as a civil servant for the Turkish government in Istanbul, where his and his brothers' patriotic activity was tolerated as it could never have been in Albania. In religion Naim was a Bektashist, a liberal Mohammedanism that originated in the fourteenth century; Naim wanted to establish this as the Albanian religion because it also embraced Christianity, because it was against orthodox Islam and particularly against its original expansionism, and because it suited his own pantheistic inclinations. Naim, a prolific writer, was both lyric and epic poet. Some of his work was so popular that people risked their lives to smuggle it into Albania. It is ironic that Naim, in order to be an Albanian patriot, had to live not merely in exile but at Istanbul, the centre of the world of Albania's chief oppressor. His most popular work was the collection of lyrics *Herds and Pastures* (1886: most of Naim's works appeared in this year, from a press in Bucharest, which was another headquarters of nationalistic activity). They do not now seem any more distinguished as poetry than Naim's epic, on the inevitable *Scanderbeg* theme. More interesting is the misleadingly entitled *Bektashi Journal* (1896), which is really a collection of his own poetry on themes connected with Bektashism; 'Qerbela' contains his most aggressive statement of this. He translated the first book of the *Iliad*. Naim was less a poet than a skilful pioneer; but Albanian literature, whatever its future, will not cease to be grateful to him. His best poems recall, from exile, the beauty of his homeland.

Sami Frashëri wrote, in Turkish, the first play of the Albanian revival, *Loyalty*, which was translated into Albanian in 1901. Sami's proposals for an independent Albania were detailed and on the whole sensible, and his writings helped to spread the cause to all the Albanian colonies in exile, including that in Egypt. Here the poet SPIRO DINE (1846–1922) lived, the modest author of a number of poems and satires included in his own anthology, *Waves of the Sea* (1908), which he published at Sofia. ÇAJUPI (ps. ANTON ÇAKO, 1866–1930) was like Dine born in Albania, but left it for Egypt as a youth. He studied law and had a successful and lucrative career as a barrister in Cairo, where, although Albania had attained independence, he chose to die. Çajupi, a man of wide culture, was a more interesting because more complex man than any of the Albanian writers so far discussed. Genuinely gifted as a lyricist, and as fervently patriotic as any, Çajupi had another side to him: cynical, world-weary, sophisticated. In him the lawyer's view of honour—a mere word, a key weapon in rhetoric's armoury—lived uncomfortably side by side with a fiery native one. Thus his work consists not only of straightforward lyrics but also satires. His lyrical output is more varied and more sensitive to literary influences than that of any of his contemporaries, although he never produced the major poetry that the intelligence and tension in him were capable of creating. But his theatre is considerable; his plays, which include comedies and tragedies, are still successfully produced: *After Death* and *Fourteen Years a Son-in-law* are the best known. *Dad Musa the Naked* is verse satire on the Albanians themselves —and obliquely on its shrewd author. Çajupi, a somewhat aloof figure, is altogether the most lively of the earlier Albanian poets—more lively and interesting, perhaps, than the esteemed Gjergj Fishta (q.v.).

Another centre of Albanian resistance in this period was Sofia, where there was a printing press. *The National Calendar* (1897–1927), purposely made small in format so that it could be more easily smuggled into Albania, was an almanac that also contained original poetry and book reviews. This was founded, with Kristo Luarasi, by LUMO SKENDO (ps. MID'HAT FRASHËRI, 1880–1949), a son of Abdyl Frashëri (q.v.) who had been lovingly educated by his uncle Naim (q.v.). In accordance with the traditions of his family, he was an educationist, moralist (he published many 'self-help' manuals) and activist as well as a writer. During Zog's rule he became a bookseller in Tirana. In the war he led right-wing resistance to fascism, but was eventually pushed out by Hoxha's Tosk communists. He spent the rest of his life trying to rally Albanian opinion against them. In 1909 he wrote the first history of Albanian literature. His original work is limited to short stories, the best known collection of which is *Ashes and Embers* (1915). These have the purpose of civilizing the Albanians out of their pagan habits, and of correcting abuses. Often ironic, and clearly written by a man of intelligence and learning, they perform their self-appointed task well, and sometimes—in observation and description—even transcend it.

Bucharest was yet another centre of Albanian activity; the best known of the so-called Bucharest exiles is the lyrical poet ASDREN (ps. ALEKSANDËR S. DRENOVA, 1872–1947), who was a disciple of Naim Frashëri's (q.v.). His earlier poetry occasionally reaches Naim's competent level. GJERGJ BUBANI (c. 1898) was a highly cultured and witty poet of this group; he founded a short-lived but influential periodical called *Dodona*. In 1945, on his return to Tirana, he was sentenced to a term of imprisonment on a charge of collaboration.

LAZGUSH PORADECI (ps. LAZËR GUSHO PORADECI, 1899) is Albania's most cosmopolitan poet, and, with Mitrush Kuteli (q.v.), its only remotely 'modernist' one. He was born near what was then the border with Macedonia, at the town of Pogradec on the shores of Lake Ochrid in central western Albania. A teacher in various Albanian schools and colleges, he studied abroad, chiefly in Budapest. Poradeci is the only notable Albanian poet of his generation to be seriously aware of new developments, and his verse has been influenced by the proto-modernistic Rumanian poet Eminescu (q.v.), by symbolism and by surrealism. However, his most usual theme is the landscape around Lake Ochrid. He lives in Tirana. He is certainly one of the few Albanian poets whose work should be seen in translation into European languages. MITRUSH KUTELI (ps. DHIMITËR PASKO, 1907), also born in Pogradec, followed in Poradeci's footsteps, although his poetry is even more thoroughly Rumanian in character. MIGJENI (ps. M. G. NIKOLLA, 1911–38), reared in Yugoslavia, was Albania's first poet of social protest.

Another literary figure more important as a pioneer than as an original writer is FAIK KONISTA (1875–1943), who was born in a Greek Albanian colony but educated at Scutari. He was a scholar, politician and the most intelligent Albanian critic of his generation. He edited *Albania* (1897–1910) in Brussels and London. He was a witty and incisive writer, with a shrewd awareness of the exiguous nature of the young literature of his country.

FAN S. NOLI (c. 1880), Archbishop (1919) and founder of the Albanian Autocephalous Orthodox Church (he proclaimed it in Boston in 1908), was born in an Albanian colony near Adrianople in European Turkey. Once again, his importance—which is perhaps greater than Fishta's—is mainly historical. With his translations of Shakespeare, Ibsen, Blasco Ibañez, Cervantes, Gorki, Poe and others, Noli undoubtedly infused new and essential blood into Albanian literature. Active in politics before independence, and leader of the Democratic Party, in 1924 he was Prime Minister of a communist government for six months, until driven out by a group of southern landowners led by Zog. Albania would doubtless have done better under his rule than it did under that of Zog, who was little better than a gangster as well as the Duce's puppet. During the Second World War he failed to bring Zog, the liberals and the communists together in a common cause. He is a talented composer of music, and his book on Beethoven was praised by Bernard Shaw (q.v.).

III

The Roman Catholic clergy at Scutari, in the far north of Albania, had for long enjoyed special privileges from the Turks. The missionary matter written by gentle Franciscans and Jesuits seemed to the authorities to offer no political threat. The Geg literature of the later nineteenth century consists exclusively of pious tales and Christian lore. But most of the men who perpetrated it—some of them, like LEONARDO MARTINI (1830–1923), Italo-Albanians—were discreet supporters of Albanian independence. They prepared the way for the historically important figure of GJERGJ FISHTA (1871–1940), a Franciscan friar born in the Zadrima highlands of the north who inaugurated modern Albanian literature in Albania itself. He helped to introduce the Albanian language into the schools, worked on a modification of Sami Frashëri's alphabet, and was later (1921) elected to the parliament in Tirana. He spent his last years in the Franciscan monastery at Scutari. Fishta's work, although that of a gifted and highly educated man, possesses little distinction or originality. His real importance is as an initiator, leader and example, although the stream of Albanian literature of which he is the fount continues in exile rather than in his own country. He founded two periodicals. Fishta was best known both inside and outside his own country for his pastoral and epic trilogy *The Highland Lute* (1905; rev. 1931), since it appeared in a German translation—but German-speaking Albanians have called this version 'feeble'. Fishta also wrote lyrical poems, highly competent and pioneering plays and translations—of Molière, Euripides, the *Odyssey* and the fifth book of the *Iliad*—and a number of vehement, no-nonsense, satirical denunciations of what he saw as frivolity and decadence among his own people as well as of the Turkish tyranny. It is unfortunate that Fishta's work has every surface virtue, but little more. 'The Ballad of Euphrosyne' is characteristic: an Albanian girl is ordered to attend the Turkish ruler, but drowns herself instead: 'the land of Albania is full of girls who prefer death to dishonour'. Beyond the commonplace allegory and the grace of form, there is nothing.

No member of Fishta's 'Scutari Catholic' school could be regarded as more than locally important. HIL MOSI (1885–c. 1935), a politician as well as poet who became Minister of Education in 1930, had ambitions to write a cosmopolitan poetry and had a superficial grasp of German and Hungarian late nineteenth-century romanticism which his contemporaries lacked; but his work, some of which is unusually erotic in content, seldom rises above the level of pastiche. VINÇENC PRENUSHI (ps. VIÇ PRENDUSHI, 1885–1946), another Franciscan, who was made a Bishop by the occupying Italians during the Second World War, was little more than a shadow of his friend Fishta. He made an important collection of Geg folk-songs in 1911, and brought out his sole volume of original poetry and translations in 1925: *Leaves and Flowers*.

ERNEST KOLIQI (1903), born in Scutari, is superior to these in that he is more original. An Italian sympathizer, he became involved with the fascists to the extent of accepting the Presidency of the Grand Council in Tirana from 1943 until 1945, when he fled to Rome, where he now lives. He has written poetry, but is best known as Albania's finest short-story writer. His short-story collections, *Mountain Shades* (1929) and *The Flagseller* (1935), are slight, but break refreshingly away from the didactic tradition, and skilfully combine folklore and realistic themes. The stories are set in his native northern highlands. He has translated many Italian poets, including parts of Dante, into Albanian; and since his exile has translated some Albanian poets, such as Zef Schirò (q.v.), into Italian. He taught Albanian at Rome University. It is mistaken to think of Koliqi as a fascist: he misguidedly became involved with the Italian fascist powers because he believed that this would help to improve educational standards in his country—and the Italians naturally led him on.

IV

Most of Albania's few novelists and playwrights come from the south. The best known is the prolific KRISTO FLOQI (1873–?), who was born in Korça. He was prominent in the early struggle for Albanian independence, and an associate of Fan Noli and Faik Konitsa (q.v.). A lawyer, he was a Counsellor of State under Zog; his books and plays are proscribed under the present government. He translated Sophocles, Euripides and Molière, wrote some 'epic' tragedies (including one on Scanderbeg) and, chiefly, a number of polished comedies and satirical playlets. These, mostly intended for amateur readings—Albania's first theatre came under the communists—introduced French wit into Albanian theatre. More serious was the melodrama *Faith and Nationality* (1914), which used as its material the conflicting religious faiths in Albania. Floqi was also a poet, historian and essayist. Although a serious thinker, Floqi's best work was done in the realm of not too profound comedy.

The leading pre-communist novelists were both natives of Korça: MIHAL GRAMENO (1872–1931) and FOQION POSTOLI (1887–1927). Grameno wrote several novels and short stories, of which *The Kiss* is of particular interest for its successful exploitation of the mores of simple southern Albanian people. He also wrote one of the earliest plays, *The Death of Pyrrhus* (1906), a well-constructed tragedy. Like Grameno, Postoli was mainly a patriotic writer; but he was not perhaps as skilled at holding the reader's attention. His books, among them *In Defence of the Homeland* (1921) and *The Flower of Remembrance* (1924), begin well but the original impulse tends to diffuse itself into a mass of trivial incident.

Right out of any of the main streams of Albanian literature of this century is the wealthy southerner ANTON ZAKO (?–1930), a poet and playwright.

From 1910 until his death he lived a quiet life in Heliopolis, an opium-smoker with a girl companion. He wrote melancholy lyrics about his longing for Albania, but preferred to stay in Egypt.

The self-regalized brigand Zog spent most of the Second World War living it up in the countryside north of London, and was no threat to the Tosk communist partisans when they occupied Tirana, with the blessing of the Allies, in 1945. Little can be said of literary developments since then; there is no information. Until the late Fifties there was translation into and from Russian. Partisan experiences inspired some fiction of the late Forties and early Fifties. Since the rapprochement with the Chinese the permitted Albanian literature has presumably taken a new, and possibly drearier, turn. Of subversive literary activities in Albania itself there is not a whisper. Among the leading poets are SHEFQET MUSARAJ (1914), who in 1950 spoke up in Warsaw for the co-existence of Marxism with non-Marxism, and who may not now be in favour, and ALEKS ÇAÇI (1916), who is also a playwright. One of the leading novelists of the Russian period was DHIMETËR SHUTERIQI (1914), translator of Aragon. The first director of the new theatre was the playwright KOL JAKOVA (1917).

That some independent literary activity exists, at least in embryo, seems likely, since educational progress has certainly been speeded up under Hoxha. When it manifests itself it will doubtless embarrass whoever is running the country: that is its usual function, and is, alas for politicians, one of the hazards of education.

The most important Albanian writers are either in exile or in the autonomous Albanian part of Yugoslavia (where there are more than a million people): Kosmet. Here the language is Geg. Leading poets include ESAD MEKULI, ENVER GJERGJEKU and MARTIN CAMAJ, the most innovatory of all the younger Albanian poets with the exception of ARSHI PIPA, in whose hands the future of Albanian poetry may be said to lie. Pipa spent many years in prison under Hoxha, but he was eventually able to leave Albania and now lives in the United States. His most substantial collection is *Meridiana* (1969), which was published in Munich. This contains a selection of poems, in revised form, from *Prison Book* (1959), poetry conceived and sometimes written in prison. Pipa is a genuine visionary with an acute awareness of contemporary European poetry.

American
Literature

I

Henry James's statement, made in a letter of 1872, that 'it's a complex fate, being an American, and one of the responsibilities it entails is fighting against a superstitious valuation of Europe' is hackneyed; but it sums up, with splendid aptness, the heart of the American dilemma at the time he wrote it. (In 'Europe', of course, he included England: the parent country whose political, but not literary, shackles had been wholly thrown off.) The Americans as a whole were slow to recognize their native geniuses: no country likes to discover its true nature too quickly. Emerson was widely acknowledged and highly influential, but, although a major writer, he was not a major creative writer. The American public took Longfellow, an inferior poet, to its heart, but was not happy with Melville; and Whitman—the first wholly American poet—was to the end of his life read only by a minority, and at that a minority which misunderstood the nature of his achievement, leading to the establishment of a legend that took more than fifty years to dispel. Many Americans of the nineteenth century tended to regard their own literature patronizingly, as an inferior cousin of English literature: they reckoned that English earth, and not that of America itself, the new country, was the proper place for its roots.

This situation has now changed drastically. If there is a cultural capital of the English-speaking world, then it is New York—that it might be London is now no more than a joke. Since America is by far the bigger and more varied country, and since English literature has temporarily exhausted itself, it is not surprising that this state of affairs should have come about. What is more interesting is how American self-discovery developed into a major world literature. This may be seen most clearly in the way American writers discovered and achieved realism.

*

America had her indisputably great nineteenth-century writers: Melville, who failed to achieve real success and was forced to spend all but six of his last twenty-five years as a customs inspector; Whitman, who had even less popular

23

success; Hawthorne, who did achieve fame with *The Scarlet Letter*, but who was not fully understood. But these had done their best work by the end of the Civil War: Hawthorne died (1864), Melville 'retired' to his custom-house, Whitman began his long decline into mage-hood, and added nothing of consequence to *Leaves of Grass*. Few in the quarter-century after the Civil War would have thought of these writers as particularly important. The fashion was first for the so-called 'Brahmin' (the name was good-naturedly applied, by analogy with the highest caste of Hindus) poets and thinkers (Longfellow, J. R. Lowell, Holmes, Prescott and others), centred in Boston—once revered, then too severely misprized, now more temperately revalued as creatively limited but tolerably liberal gentlemen—and later for such popular pseudo-realist fiction as that written by 'the Beau Brummell of the Press', RICHARD HARDING DAVIS (1864–1916), a clever newspaper reporter, the more skilful romantic novelist F. MARION CRAWFORD (1854–1909), every one of whose forty-five novels has dated, the solid 'conscientious middle-class romantic' historical novelist WINSTON CHURCHILL (1871–1947), and the more gifted O. HENRY (ps. WILLIAM SIDNEY PORTER, 1862–1910), a writer of short stories of humour and technical adroitness (his speciality was the surprise ending) but no psychological depth. The more important writers were not at first much heeded. But there is a major exception: MARK TWAIN (ps. SAMUEL LANGHORNE CLEMENS, 1835–1910), a nineteenth-century figure the importance of whose legacy to the twentieth is beyond question. The 'Brahmin' James Russell Lowell as well as the so-called 'literary comedians' ('Artemus Ward', 'Josh Billings', 'Bill Arp' and so on) of the Fifties and Sixties had tried to create a truly indigenous prose style, and had failed. In *Huckleberry Finn* (1884), sequel to *Tom Sawyer* (1876), Twain portrayed a complex but free American boy, in genuinely American prose; he also wrote a great novel of innocence and experience. But, like Whitman, Twain was a naïve (q.v.) writer, the one great naïve American novelist of the latter half of the nineteenth century. He had also lived close to nature and to the experience of action. He could always write directly and uninhibitedly of experience; but only once, in *Huckleberry Finn*, did he produce a masterpiece. The realists were, however, for the most part sentimentive (q.v.) writers. They admired Twain—Howells (q.v.) was his friend and collaborator—but could not emulate him; nor, to do them justice, could he help them much in their aims: to portray truthfully, and to anatomize psychologically, American urban society.

Howells, James and the other realists had honourable precursors: writers whose realism was more than nominal, superficially regional—in the sense of patronizingly recording quirks and customs—and fashionable. Such was JOHN WILLIAM DE FOREST (1826–1906), who influenced Howells. De Forest, born in Connecticut, fought as a captain on the Union side; he wrote a number of readable novels, the most important of which is *Miss Ravenel's Conversion from Secession to Loyalty* (1867). This is didactic and its plot is sentimental, but its realism consists not of photographic set pieces but of a serious examination of the origins of the 'Southern' prejudices of Lillie, daughter of an abolitionist

24

New Orleans doctor who has voluntarily come north at the outbreak of the war. Particularly well done is the portrait of one of her suitors, John Carter, a Virginian officer in the Union army, dashing, dissipated, heroic, morally ambiguous. It was in his battle scenes, however, that De Forest was most in advance of his time. His more happily titled *Honest John Vane* (1875), about a corrupt congressman, is also realistic in its study of political background. De Forest had impulses towards realism, awakened by his war experiences, which might, as a critic has suggested, have borne even richer fruit if he had lived later.

The clergyman EDWARD EGGLESTON (1837–1902), founder of a 'Church of Christian Endeavour' in New York, was one of the best of the many regionalists then writing. Encouraged by J. R. Lowell, and an important influence on Hamlin Garland (q.v.), Eggleston described Indiana backwoods life in *The Hoosier School-Master* (1871), based perhaps on the experiences of his brother. Overall this is a sentimental and didactic novel, but it is important for the author's use of Indiana dialect and the realism of some isolated passages. Eggleston wrote a number of other novels, none as good as this, but nearly all distinguished by some realistic facet. EDGAR WATSON HOWE (1853–1937), who was also born in Indiana, was another forerunner—one who lived to see the aftermath. Howe was essentially a small-town sage, in the American tradition; a sort of provincial H. L. Mencken (q.v.). He edited newspapers and magazines, produced cynical and homely aphorisms and wrote memoirs. But when a young man he wrote one powerful, crude novel of the midwest: *The Story of a Country Town* (1883). Howe was not a good novelist, and the plot of this book is so melodramatically pessimistic as to be absurd. It is also monotonous. But Howe's savage misanthropy caused him to look for unpalatable facts, and since he was intelligent as well as completely sincere (as Mark Twain told him) Howe selected some facts that had not previously been presented in fiction. Howe's picture of midwestern life and human scullduddery and scullduggery (for example, the stern patrician farmer-preacher turns out to be a randy hypocrite) is not vivid—but is more truthful than anything that had preceded it in its category, and with its intended scope. It helped to set a tone for such later writers as Sherwood Anderson (q.v.).

WILLIAM DEAN HOWELLS (1837–1920), son of a newspaperman and printer, was born in Ohio. During the middle years of his long life Howells was considered by most critics to be the doyen of American writers. He was important not only as a pioneer realist, but also as a judicious and generous—but not indulgent—critic of the American writers of half a century, and as the introducer of much vital foreign literature. As a young man Howells, who knew how to get on, was taken up and blessed by Brahmin culture. He wrote a campaign life of Lincoln (1860) and was rewarded with the consulate at Venice, where he spent the years of the Civil War. Highly thought of by his elders, Howells joined the *Atlantic* in 1866 and soon became its editor (1871), and printed both their work and that of promising newcomers such as Henry James (q.v.). During the Seventies he began to form his ideas about fiction and to write novels. The best of these came between 1881 and 1892. Howells' reputation declined during his final years, and he was in due course equated with Victorianism, prudery (it was unfairly asserted that he had 'censored' Mark Twain) and facile optimism. Now Howells was a 'gentleman', and he did not think it right to be profane, obscene or gloomy; nor did he have the genius of Mark Twain. But he was not a pre-Freudian relic: his criticism is still valuable, and the best of his fiction has subtlety and depth. It comes from a mind that, even while it believed in a 'respectable' facade, was well aware of the violent impulses that rage beneath the surface of consciousness: he knew and admitted (to Twain) that the whole 'black heart's-truth' about himself could not be told. That was not something that more than one nineteenth-century liberal gentleman in ten thousand would admit; not many gentlemen will admit it now. Howells' achievement is a monument to what can be done in literature without genius. To understand him it is necessary, as one of his recent critics has well said, to have a taste for 'both James and Twain'. . . . Certainly it is grossly unjust to dismiss Howells and yet absolve James. For it was Howells above all who helped to make the decently written novel an acceptable form in America: who helped American readers to understand that fiction, too, could have a 'moral' message—that the absolutely serious writer need not confine himself, as had Howells' mentors, to the oracular essay or to verse. And his own best novels courageously, if never dynamically, examined American mores. *Dr Breen's Practice* (1881) traces the private and public fortunes of a woman doctor; it sympathizes with her ambitions, but in making her a puritan fit for satire Howells reveals, perhaps with deliberate slyness, lurking anti-feminist prejudice. His two best novels are *A Modern Instance* (1882) and *The Rise of Silas Lapham* (1885), both of which were more unusually subtle and penetrating for their time than is realized today. *A Modern Instance*, which handles divorce and got Howells blamed both for over-boldness and 'moral timidity', is a study in the spiritual squalidity of a relationship in which hatred has replaced attraction (not, I think, love). This, written under the direct influence of Zola (q.v.), is Howells' boldest book. In *The Rise of Silas Lapham* Howells satirized the hollow snobbishness of Brahmin families (reflecting his committedness to his own kind) and at the same time showed how a vulgar, self-made man could attain moral authority. Lapham is a brash paint-manufacturer with high social ambitions for his family. He is humbled and forced out of Boston society because, although his way to wealth has been ruthless, he refuses to commit a dishonest act; thus he grows in stature, but, as Howells remarks, 'It is certain that our manners and customs go for more in life than our qualities'. Some critics have hailed the panoramic *A Hazard of New Fortunes* (1890) as Howells' best work—and so it might be if it had the power of the psychological novels. After *An Imperative Duty* (1891) Howells' fiction became more self-consciously didactic and illustrative of the Tolstoyan socialism he had now adopted. But until the very last novel, *The Leatherwood God* (1916), published when he was seventy-nine, he maintained his high standards of craftsmanship and style. It is, strangely enough, this last book—a moving study of a historical character, an Ohio smallholder of the mid-nineteenth century, who persuaded a number of women to regard him as God—that is the least didactic of them all.

It is probably correct to regard Howells as one of the native sources of what we may call the naturalist strain in American fiction—if only because others followed where he led. But his own realism was never really naturalistic, even in *A Modern Instance*. Howe's rudimentary *The Story of a Country Town* was nearer. The fact is that there is always something 'ungentlemanly' about true naturalist fiction—even when, as it seldom is, it is written by gentlemen such as Frank Norris (q.v.). Howells was also, and more obviously, an exemplar for—and frequently an encourager of—the other American realists who eschewed naturalism. Many of these, both major and minor, were temporary or permanent expatriates. If you stayed in the new America, it seems, you thought you understood it in assured, scientific, Darwinian—evolutionary—terms: you were a sort of determinist. Otherwise your impulse was to escape from a reality that you could neither deny nor affirm.

Escapism at its most obvious is seen in the case of the eccentric LAFCADIO HEARN (1850–1904). Lafcadio Hearn was born on the Aegean island of Santa Maura (once called Leucadia, hence his name) of Irish-Greek parentage, with a goodly admixture of gipsy, English and Arabic—but no American—blood. However, he spent twenty-one years (1869–90) in America as a journalist before sailing for Japan, where he married into a Japanese Samurai family, raised a family, turned Buddhist, and became a lecturer in English literature at the Imperial University at Tokyo. (His successor was Natsume Soseki, q.v.). As a journalist Hearn presented himself as a believer in the evolution of human society into complex higher forms; but really he wanted to get away from the ruthless drive that this 'evolution' implied. When competitiveness became increasingly evident in the life of Meiji Japan, Hearn made plans to return to the States, but died before he could put them into effect. His real inclinations are revealed in the exotic character of his novels, *Chita* (1889), about a girl who survives a tidal wave on an island in the Gulf of Mexico, and even more in *Youma* (1890), on the theme of a slave-girl's devotion—till death—to the girl whose 'mammy' she is, and whom she has promised never to desert. Hearn never showed any inclination, despite the optimism of his journalism, to harness his creative imagination to the purpose of analyzing modern society. He knew that had he done so he would have taken a view too gloomy for the comfort of his social conscience.

His case is one of simple escapism. That of HENRY ADAMS (1838–1918), great-grandson of the second President of the U.S.A. and grandson of the sixth, is more complicated. The two novels he wrote, *Democracy* (1880) and *Esther* (1884) —the first anonymous, the second pseudonymous—are not important as literature; but Adams as a thinker is. He was the first great American pessimist. Where his illustrious family had been public servants, he took refuge in letters. Had he, however, sought to express himself creatively rather than philosophically he would perhaps have discovered an objective correlative for the personal problems of his marriage (1872) which ended in 1885 with the suicide of his wife. But this period of his life (with the seven years following it), is missed out of his remarkable autobiography, *The Education of Henry Adams* (privately issued 1907; published 1918). Adams was a distinguished historian, and in writing his huge *History of the United States during the Administrations of Jefferson and Madison* (1889–91) he had seen something like evolution at work; his argument here was that men cannot change the course of history. He wrote, it must be remembered, as a member of a family who had actually made history. . . . So he had a superior, or a stronger—less journalistic—sense of evolution than Hearn. But, like Hearn, he sought to escape: in restless travel to Mexico, Japan, Europe. In *Mont-Saint-Michel and Chartres* (privately issued 1904; published 1913) the religiously sceptic Adams postulated a unified medieval universe, the centre of which was the Virgin. This was perhaps more fictional, if unwittingly, than either of his novels: thirteenth-century stability is to a large extent a myth in the mind of nineteenth- and early twentieth-century Catholic apologists. He showed the world of 1150–1250 as in equilibrium, 'pre-evolutionary', centripetal. In the *Education*, he shows the modern 'multiverse' as accelerating towards disaster, centrifugal, spinning towards what in a letter he called 'an ultimate, colossal, cosmic collapse . . . science is to wreck us . . . our power over energy has now reached a point where it must sensibly affect the old adjustment. . . .' He used the Second Law of Thermodynamics to show the individual, the victim, as so to say being whirled (by the symbol of the Dynamo, opposed to the Virgin of the earlier book), run down and dissipated into a nothingness: into entropy, disorder. Here and in the posthumous *The Degradation of the Democratic Dogma* (1919)—which was edited by his brother, the historian Brooks Adams (1848–1927), who shared his gloomy view of history—Adams rationalized his theory into an exact prophecy, with dates. This prophecy was wrong—the date of final dissolution was doubtless made early in order to fall into Adams's own lifespan—but few intelligent men reading Adams fifty years after his death are likely to find his apprehensions entirely unjustified. He published his two most important books after the first heyday of American naturalism was over; he had no influence on it. But his thinking in these books—and even more so in his *Letters* (1930; 1947), where he is at his most fascinating and vigorous—is more representative than merely influential. Of course he has nothing in him of the material or cultural optimism that was then one of the characteristics of America, nothing of the pure joy in becoming and feeling pure American, un-English, that distinguishes, say, William Carlos Williams (q.v.). But his work is a response to the same sort of mental crisis that Hofmannsthal describes in his *Chandos* letter (q.v.). Not being a poet, Adams does not see the problem in terms of language. Basically he fears for the integrity of his human, and therefore the human, personality in the face of scientific advance. The proto-fascist and futurist Marinetti (q.v.) hailed the new technology. Adams shuddered before it, his sardonic mind casting fearfully back for a static and stable paradise, for 'some great generalization which would finish one's clamour to be educated'. 'Modern politics is, at bottom, a struggle not of men, but of forces', he wrote. In the new 'multiverse' 'order [is] an accidental relation obnoxious to nature'. Adams, however, was a historian, not a creative writer: all he wanted was to get out, have nothing to do with it: 'All the historian won was a vehement wish to escape'.

Each man sees his own death differently: he colours his apprehensions of it according to his personal and historical circumstances. Adams, a historian, a scion of mighty history-makers who had more excuse than most for treating the world as his particular oyster, faced by a crazily accelerating and already over-confident science (the 'score or two of individuals' who controlled 'mechanical power' he described as 'as dumb as their dynamos, absorbed in the economy of power'), coloured his idea of death with zestful meaninglessness. It is instructive to compare his non-creative reaction to the creative one of the first German expressionists (q.v.), with its distorting rapid wobble between ecstatic hope and horror. Adams's importance is that he shared such men's awareness of the time.

AMBROSE BIERCE (1842–?1914), born in Ohio, was as sardonic as Adams— and more creative. But although his best short stories are distinguished, he never wholly fulfilled his genius, preferring for the most part to substitute for the wisdom he could have attained a mordant but too folksy and self-indulgent cynicism. Bierce was a man of principle (he refused the back pay he had earned as a soldier in the Civil War), and a soul genuinely tortured by what Henry Adams called 'the persistently fiendish treatment of man by man'; but in his case journalism, and the pleasure of being literary dictator of the Pacific States (for a quarter of a century until he resigned in 1909), distracted him from literature; it was easier to indulge himself in his vitriolic epigrams—often cheap and gratuitous, and in any case never on the level of his best stories—than to write creatively. The epigrams are in *The Devil's Dictionary* (1911), originally called *The Cynic's Word Book* (1906); the stories are in *Can Such Things Be?* (1893) and, notably, in *In the Midst of Life* (1898), which was originally called *Tales of Soldiers and Civilians* (1891). The famous Civil War tales, including 'An Occurr- ence at Owl Creek Bridge' and 'The Horseman in the Sky', in which a young Union soldier has to shoot his father, make a valid use of Poe—and remain original, economic, appropriately macabre: they are secure minor classics. But Bierce did not want to use his imagination to grapple with the problem of contemporary America—his cynical journalism was in a sense as much of an 'escape' as Japan was for Hearn. He made his final escape when he disappeared into Mexico, in 1911, to join Pancho Villa. He was never heard of again.

*

The achievement of HENRY JAMES (1843–1916), born in New York and educated mostly abroad, is so great as hardly to abide all questions of American realism. Son of a formidable, eccentric Swedenborgian father, and younger brother of William James—an important and seminal thinker—Henry offers in one sense a contrast to Howells: his achievement is a monument to how literary genius can surmount crippling personal difficulties. For James was fated to be only an observer. His friend Henry Adams complained that he knew of women only from the outside—'he never had a wife'. But, as Alfred Kazin rejoins, 'because he knew so little, he could speculate endlessly'. His mind was a brilliant and sensitive instrument of speculation. He is certainly one of those whose work transcends its psychological and historical occasions; the only question is to what extent.

James expressed one important theme of his fiction when he passionately expostulated at the unfairness of fate's treatment of Howells's daughter, Winifred, who died young after a long, disabling, mysterious and unrelieved illness: 'To be young and gentle, and do no harm, and pay for it as if it were a crime'. James as an adolescent had felt himself crushed by his father and his clever older brother; he had not gone to the war as his younger brothers had, and never felt himself able to fulfil a masculine role. His biographer Leon Edel has now revealed, for those who had not detected it from the work, that James's sexual impulses (at least as a middle-aged man) were homosexual, and that he had a bad conscience about it. Whether or not he was ever an active homosexual is an as yet unanswered question. Probably not. Hugh Walpole (q.v.), whom he fell for ('Beloved Little Hugh') and overrated as a writer, is supposed to have offered himself to the master and to have been repudiated with 'Si la vieillesse pouvait!'. These facts throw new light on such works as 'The Turn of the Screw' (printed in *The Two Magics*, 1898), *The Other House* (1896) and *What Maisie Knew* (1897), all written at the height of James's crisis of homosexuality—which coincided with his humiliation in the theatre and with the trials of Oscar Wilde. It was in 'The Turn of the Screw' above all that James (unconsciously) analyzed his condition, defensively referring to it as a 'jeu d'esprit', hoping to throw himself and his readers off the scent. James's personal sexual predicament actually affects our interpretation of all his work, from his first novel *Roderick Hudson* right up until his last unfinished one, the posthumous *The Ivory Tower*. For the young novelist not only wanted to get away from America—although not from his Americanness, a different thing—but also from the 'masculine' obligations of love for a woman and the heavy commitments of marriage. The 'horrid even if . . . obscure hurt', probably a strained back, he claimed to have suffered while helping to put out a fire at about the time of the outbreak of the Civil War, served him in a number of ways: it linked him with his father, who when a child had lost a leg while fighting a fire; it excused him from joining the army; it enabled him to be passive, feminine; the nature of the 'injury' was supposed to be sexual, but no one could of course ask about it directly—thus giving 'sex' the *frisson* it nearly always has in James's fiction. The hurt was 'obscure'—but mere mention of it none the less drew a kind of attention to it. It reminds us of those 'things' little Miles, in 'The Turn of the Screw', said to those he 'liked', and which were 'Too bad' to write home about'. . . .

Europe attracted James from the beginning. He felt that America was too crude for his own artistic purposes. His first novel, *Roderick Hudson* (1876), explores his dilemma: Europe is beautiful, sinister, wicked—like Christina Light, who tortures the genius hero into 'horrible' dissipations which all, of course, as always in James, take place off-stage, and which eventually lead to his death. In *The American* (1877), not one of his most convincing novels, he rationalizes his doubts about his inadequacies. Wealthy American Christopher Newman (the name is significant) goes to Paris (where, said James elsewhere at this time, modern French books resembled 'little vases . . . into which unclean things had been dropped') and falls in love with an aristocratic girl whose family are most reluctant to approve the match. Christopher finds an ally, however, in her younger brother Count Valentin. He discovers that the mother of the girl he loves is a murderess, but eventually decides not to use the information to gain his objective: he will not use such knowledge for material ends. Thus James launched himself into fully fledged writerhood.

By 1881, at the age of thirty-eight, with *The Portrait of a Lady*, he had become an undisputed master, for all his shortcomings one of the most important of all English-language novelists. It was in the Eighties that James wrote the novels of his so-called 'middle period': the most notable are *The Bostonians* (1886), *The Princess Casamassima* (1886) and *The Tragic Muse* (1890). The novels of the last period—*The Ambassadors* (1903), *The Golden Bowl* (1904)—are more difficult: the sentences are long, the motivations that are examined are ambiguous: the whole approach seems anfractuous, not to say tortuous. And yet many regard *The Wings of the Dove* (1902), with good reason, as James's masterpiece. This is the story of an innocence betrayed and of the terrifying and irrevocable corruption of spirit that this betrayal brings in its wake. Kate Croy persuades her lover, a poor journalist, to attach himself falsely to a rich, dying girl, Milly. He does so, and gets her money. But he cannot take it, and asks Kate to have him without it. Now herself 'infected' by the innocence of Milly, she will not do so because she rightly suspects him of loving the dead girl's memory. In this hideously accurate portrayal of how a man acts in bad faith, of unmelodramatic evil, James the detached observer triumphed—as he did in so many of his short stories (ed. L. Edel, 12 vols., 1962–5).

Right through his fiction, from *Roderick Hudson* onwards, James had maintained a technique for suggesting, without ever detailing, evil. He had not, of course, experienced evil—only his 'evil' homosexual impulses. He was highly professional, as well as emotionally rather innocent, in the way he dealt with this problem. It is actually one of his strengths that the horrors he hints at are not really, by normal sophisticated standards, particularly horrible at all. The point is that this highly sentimentive (q.v.) writer was not, in calling 'debauchery' 'unclean', simply being reactionary or hypocritical. It was his lack of knowledge that lamed him; but he turned it into a crutch. We do not look, in James, for any kind of enlightenment about or illumination of actual sexual matters: his fiction deals with the innocent or inexperienced preliminaries to them. They lie horribly in wait at the ends of twisting and turning corridors.

In *The Portrait of a Lady* the good and generous Isabel Archer is not experienced enough to realize that the widower Gilbert Osmond—a shallow pseudo-aesthete whose worst failing, however, is his capacity to manipulate others' emotions for his material advantage—wants her fortune. She marries him, and discovers too late that she can do nothing for him—as she had hoped to do for whatever man she might love. Eventually she admits to her former American suitor that she loves him, but nevertheless chooses to return to her husband: to give up her freedom in return for that of his bastard daughter, Pansy, whose interests she will continue to protect. The reader can and does easily fill in the missing sexuality here: Osmond is as self-indulgently lustful for Isabel's virginity as for her money; her own disillusion is as much sexual as psychological. If any reader wonders how she could be taken in by so evidently insincere a man, then he need not wonder for long: the reason is sexual. James had the feminine sensitivity and intuition to understand these things: he earned it by the integrity of his self-analysis—for, in one aspect, all novels are either rationalizations or self-analyses. In *The Portrait of a Lady* James is Ralph Touchett, the tubercular (crippled) observer who loves Isabel, and renounces her from the start (because of his condition) but who stolidly looks after her interests. The real tragedy of the book lies in his death: James's touching account of his own death to sexual life. But he also presents himself as Isabel, who initially turns down both a straightforward New Englander and a decent English aristocrat, then falls into the snare of a cosmopolitan—finally choosing, now a natural and detached moralist, to endure him (as James chose to remain in Europe—but he was happier in England than Isabel was with Osmond, for he found there 'an arrangement of things hanging together with a romantic rightness that had the force of a revelation'). James wrote criticism of great subtlety, travel books and a number of interesting but bad plays and adaptations from his novels (*Complete Plays*, ed. L. Edel, 1949). When the First World War broke out James was agonized: 'that to have to take it all now for what the treacherous years were all the while really making for and *meaning* is too tragic for any words'. He became a British citizen, did what war-work his failing health would allow, received the Order of Merit, and died in 1916. James understood that 1914 meant the disintegration of the old order of things, but was too old to contemplate it. He was one of the greatest of the writers of that vanished world. But he has relevance to the literature of today because his fiction is ultimately a commentary, often exquisite, on what it is to be a creator. Most of the important considerations—the relationship between virtue and creativity among them—are there. James saw with some ruefulness what he could never be; but he never hid from his creative responsibilities. There will always be controversy about the stature of his last three major books—*The Wings of the Dove, The Ambassadors, The Golden Bowl.* Are they a 'trilogy' that embraces a new form, akin to the drama of Racine? Or was the profound self-adjustment (after his failure to capture a big audience or even to avoid ignominy as a dramatist) of which these books are undoubtedly the fruit, achieved at a high cost to the universality of his art? *The Wings of the Dove* is surely exempt; of the other two novels one is less sure. But all the work of James has much more to yield. Supposing he did, in his last period, create a new kind of fiction; he was still not an innovator in the sense of clearing ground for anyone else; but he cannot be ignored because his whole life was in one way an anticipation of the practice of the writers who came after him: he created his own world, understood that he was God in it—and took his responsibilities with the utmost seriousness. He has been denigrated both by Marxist critics and members of the indigenous, 'Black Mountain' school (q.v.); there also existed in the Forties and Fifties an over-fanciful image of James that had little relationship to the man or the writer. Close study, new understanding, increase our respect for him.

His friend EDITH WHARTON (1862–1937), although pessimistic in her view of life, was another who rejected the determinism of naturalism. She came of a distinguished family and, like James, was introduced to Europe in childhood. Her marriage was unhappy, since Edward Wharton became mentally ill; this helped to drive her into literature. She settled in France in 1907 and five years later divorced her husband. Mrs. Wharton insisted that the duty of a novelist was to discover what the characters, 'being what they are, would make of the situation'—but in reality her people are less free than James's. In her world, usually of high society, vulgarity overwhelms fineness; the choice to go against the conventional leads to disaster; opulence corrupts; where James's women are convincing angels, Mrs. Wharton's are defeated harpies. Edith Wharton wrote well of a society she knew, but as a whole her fiction lacks tension. The author knew too well from the beginning, one feels, that vulgarity would triumph: her characters do not assert themselves strongly enough to be tragic in their defeats. The short stories (*Best Short Stories of Edith Wharton*, 1958), ironic and satiric, are slight but in this respect more satisfactory. However, there are amongst the novels some notable exceptions; and Mrs. Wharton invariably maintains a high standard. Her observation is impeccable. One compares her to James and inevitably finds her wanting; and yet she is incomparably better than the Nobel-winning Galsworthy was, even at his best. In her best works she partially overcomes her shortcomings, and has something entirely of her own to offer. An account of *Ethan Frome* (1911), which is one of the only two novels (*Summer*, 1917, is the other) Edith Wharton set outside polite society, makes it sound naturalist; but it is no more than bleak. The story is told wonderingly, by a stranger. Ethan Frome barely wrings a living from the barren earth of his Massachusetts farm; his hated wife Zeena (Zenobia) is a whining hypochondriac. Her cousin Mattie comes to live with them, and Ethan and she fall in love. Zeena forces her out; when Ethan is taking her to the station he yields to the impulse to end it all by crashing the sledge in which they are travelling. But the couple are crippled. Zeena is transformed into their devoted nurse, leaving Mattie to become the whining invalid and Ethan to his despair and certain economic failure. This is not absolutely convincing, but the portrait of Zeena—the nagging, loathed wife—the growth of affection between Ethan and Mattie, and the ironic ending are all beautifully done. Her two other major books are both society novels: *The Custom of the Country* (1913) and *The Age of Innocence* (1920). The character of Undine Spragg, the ruthless social climber of the first, has been objected to on the grounds that Mrs. Wharton's disgust with her type is too great to permit of psychological accuracy. This is not altogether fair. Undine Spragg is a shallow monster driven by ignoble motives; but when critics object that the drama of her marriage to a Frenchman more decent than herself is 'weakened' by this, they are in effect trying to tell novelists what kind of characters to use in order to get their plots right. People like Undine Spragg do exist, and *The Custom of the Country* is better than is generally allowed. *The Age of Innocence* is an acid, ironic but touching study of a love whose happiness is destroyed by adherence to a code, and by the kind of people 'who dreaded scandal more than disease, who placed decency above courage'. *Hudson River Bracketed* (1929) is not wholly successful, but is peculiarly subtle and poignant in its portrait of the creative side of its hero, a novelist who discovers that the 'people' he understands best are the ones he has invented. . . . There is something very attractive about Edith Wharton even at her worst—when she is too gloomy or when she is copying Henry James in some of her supernatural tales—for she is always intelligent and humane. Probably her best work has been underestimated and her originality not fully recognized.

*

'New England transcendentalism' is even less susceptible of exact definition than most such phenomena. But, although it was never a school, it is important, for all subsequent American movements may be seen to stem from it. Essentially it is a first religious step after the repudiation of the Christian doctrine; it can fairly be called a form of rationalistic religion. Its chief figure was of course Emerson, and his lecture 'The Transcendentalist' came in 1841, when transcendentalism was at its peak. One can most profitably study transcendentalism as it manifested itself in individuals—in Henry David Thoreau, in Emerson himself, in the poet Jones Very—but, while there was never a doctrine, some ideas were held in common. Every transcendentalist is a Platonist, and the inclination towards Oriental religions (exemplified in the later Emerson), 'creedless creeds', is typical. The spirit of transcendentalism was eclectic, individualist, reformist. On the specifically American subject of slavery the transcendentalists were abolitionist, although initially they were more sympathetic than active—but for the honourable reason that they were sceptical of all group action.

In the fiction of Henry James the implications of transcendentalism were realized. Its consistent background was a non-dogmatic—indeed, a being-sought-for—moral system, something as ghostly but as effectual as that of any Platonic realm of perfections. Thus Mrs. Wharton, despite her gloom and her apparent belief that men's circumstances are stronger than themselves, is no naturalist: she follows James when she says: 'Every great novel must first of all be based on a profound sense of moral values . . .'. And one does feel her sense of values more strongly than her gloom, which in any case does not arise from an intellectual determinism. That same moral sense lurks behind Howells' fiction, too.

The source of naturalism—which only in America produced a crop of major or potentially major novelists—is, as Charles Child Walcutt has pointed out in an essay on Dreiser (q.v.), the 'Divided Stream of . . . transcendentalism'. The transcendentalists, not always unconfusedly, regarded spirit and matter as two aspects of the same thing. But, as Walcutt observes:

> The monist stream did not stay One . . . time and experience divided it into poles of optimism and pessimism, freedom and determinism, will and fate, social reformism and mechanistic despair . . . the Nature which was assumed to be a version of man's spirit and therefore of his will appeared under scientific analysis as a force which first controlled man's will and presently made it seem that his freedom was an illusion, that there was no such thing as will but only chemicals performing reactions which could (theoretically at least) be predicted.

First, Walcutt continues, Americans believed that the human spirit could be liberated by mastering nature; but their 'devotion to science and fact' led them to the point where the natural law seemed to deny both freedom and spirit. . . .

The atmosphere that produced the powerful movement of American naturalism was well summed up by Henry Adams in 1894 when he wrote '. . . if anything is radically wrong it must grow worse. . . . If we are diseased, so is all the world. . . . Europe is rather more in the dark than we are. . . .'

But there is more in a major novelist than a philosophy or, more usually, a pseudo-philosophy. As Nietzsche (q.v.) once said, talking about realists: 'What does one see, and paint, or write? In the last analysis, what one *wishes* to see, and what one *can* see'. And so, grateful as we are to determinism and gloom for sometimes inspiring such as Dreiser, we do not go to him for his thinking (God forbid). As always, the truly gifted went altogether beyond dogmatism, to produce something certain and knowable. But let us first look at the minor novelists who anticipated or participated in naturalism.

HAMLIN GARLAND (1860–1940) is more interesting as a pioneer than as a novelist. Harold Frederic (1856–98), a similar pioneer, produced, in *Seth's Brother's Wife* (1887) and *The Damnation of Theron Ware* (1896), novels psychologically far in advance of anything of Garland's; but the latter does have his importance. An autodidact, Garland was born in Wisconsin. As a young man he sweated on the land: he knew the farmers he wrote about, and the conditions under which they worked. He was influenced by Howells, and even more by the economist Henry George (1839–97). George, a lucid and fervent writer, was highly influential. Imbued with the Pelagianism that still characterizes most Americans, he devised an economic scheme by which he believed social justice might be ensured: a 'single tax' on land. By means of this, he believed, the community would recover what it had lost in rents. George's effect on economic thought probably amounted to little more than the stimulation of more lucid theories of rent (as an economist, it is said, he was 'a little more than a child'), but his passion for justice and the style of his thinking, were and to some extent still are influential (to the dismay of some economists). George's theories lie behind Garland's early short stories, collected in *Prairie Folks* (1893) and *Wayside Courtships* (1897): these villainize landlords and mortgage-holders. In the mid-Nineties Garland put forward a theory of literature that he called 'veritism'. This may be described as a meliorist extension of realism. It was naturalist only in that in proposing a literature that would change social conditions it assumed that those conditions determined men's lives. Garland's best work is a short novel called *A Little Norsk* (1892), about a Dakota farm-girl's hard lot; next best is the longer *Rose of Dutcher's Coolly* (1895), the story of another farm-girl—but this one studies at the University of Wisconsin and succeeds in becoming a writer in Chicago. Garland projected himself into his heroine, but then got interested in her for her own sake. The result is a convincing realist novel. Garland's most serious work was not popular, and before the turn of the century he began to write romances of the far West; after this he turned into a dull memoirist and, ultimately, weak-minded devotee of psychical phenomena.

ROBERT HERRICK (1868–1938) was not a naturalist, but like Garland he anticipated and influenced the mood by his critical and reformist attitude. A graduate of Harvard, he was a professor of English at the University of Chicago. An older professor, writing of him in 1909, could allude to him as 'something of a pessimist, but not unwholesome'. Herrick partly made up for his lack of power and psychological penetration by his honesty. He was perhaps temperamentally a determinist, but frustrated by guilt about the consequences of such an attitude. The scientist of his first novella, 'The Man Who Wins' (1897), believes in the freedom of the will—but his very circumstances seem to deny it. Herrick did not resolve his problem, but turned to the (sometimes acute) analysis of the corruptions and strains in industrial society. In his best novels he succeeded in his aim of dealing with social problems 'less in an argumentative . . . manner than as crises in human lives'. *The Web of Life* (1900), his most psychologically ambitious book, indicates the direction he might have liked to follow. Herrick was obsessed with the figure of the doctor, the healer (an inferior 1911 novel is called *The Healer*), and this early book is about one who saves the life of an alcoholic by an operation in which, however, he injures the brain. He falls in love with the man's wife; she collapses under the strain and kills herself. This was melodramatic and, except in parts, unconvincing; Herrick was wise to turn to the more social theme of *The Common Lot* (1904), his best novel, which traces the moral degradation of a young Chicago architect in his dealings with crooked builders, which finally lead to a fire and a number of deaths. His moral 'regeneration' by his wife is tacked on as a gesture. Herrick later became more ponderous, his characters less interesting. His greatest success, the sentimental novella *The Master of the Inn* (1908), is now dated and unreadable.

The prolific UPTON SINCLAIR (1878–1969) was from any kind of 'Jamesian' point of view never more than a simplistic romancer, but he cannot quite be ignored—he is, as one critic has said, 'an event in nature'. *The Jungle* (1906) displays real power and concern, and is possibly the most sheerly vivid exposée in American literature of humanly intolerable economic conditions. It tells of the exploitation of an immigrant Lithuanian family in the meat-packing industry. The message is socialist, but what was heeded was the revelation of the filthy conditions in which meat was packed in Chicago—Sinclair had himself investigated the situation. The Federal Pure Food and Drug Act was hastened through, with the assistance of Theodore Roosevelt; but the lot of the workers was not improved for many years. Sinclair was humourless, a crank and an idealist—but of a personal nobility enough to make most humorous and sensible realists feel at least a pang of shame. He wrote well over one hundred books. He remained a socialist all his life, but was one of the first to rumble the nature of the Russian regime. After *The Jungle* his best known novels are the 'Lanny Budd' series, beginning with *World's End* (1940): these feature Lanny Budd, the bastard son of a munitions king who is, in his grandiosely well-intentioned way, a kind of Yankee Jules Romains (q.v.) in that writer's unfortunate self-appointed capacity of world's chief trouble-shooter. Lanny knows everyone, including the top men, and they take note of him. Sinclair, who sunk his money into or took part in several Utopian projects, including Helicon Hall (burnt down), and a single-tax colony, was at heart a big, dear romantic booby. But he was not middlebrow: he did not tell his audience anything at all they wanted to hear. And although, like Henry George (q.v.), he believed in the innate goodness of man, he was a true naturalist at least in the sense that he was able to bring to the notice of a reluctant public the evils they lived amongst.

STEPHEN CRANE (1871–1900) was almost forgotten until some quarter of a century after his death from tuberculosis. Then the novelist, pleasantly ironic short-story writer and critic THOMAS BEER (1889–1940)—famous for his later study of the Nineties, which he christened *The Mauve Decade* (1926)—wrote his *Stephen Crane* (1923), which was one of the initial steps in the rehabilitation of a major writer. (Beer himself combined the economy of Lytton Strachey with the sardonic style of Henry Adams, q.v., and was a notable biographer; unfortunately he later came to over-sound the sardonic note, and some of *The Mauve Decade* reads like self-parody). Since Beer's book and the issue of his *Collected Works* in twelve volumes in 1926 Crane has, and without doubt properly, attained the status of a classic. The fourteenth son of a Methodist preacher and a religiously zealous, well-educated mother, Crane was a thorough rebel by the time he came of age. Part of the secret of his achievement lies in the absoluteness of his rejection of the values of his age—which went with an intelligent curiosity, a sense of humour, and a natural compassion in acute competition with a bitter and sardonic nihilism. Even when Crane seems to throw the whole of himself into what he is describing, a part of him is usually detached and amused.

Crane starved, worked as a freelance journalist, and then, in 1893, published his first book, under the name of 'Johnston Smith', at his own expense. *Maggie: A Girl of the Streets* was reprinted, in a slightly abridged form, in 1896. At the time of its first publication only Garland and Howells noticed it. *Maggie*, whatever its faults, is a pretty remarkable effort for a twenty-two-year-old: what it lacks in maturity it more than makes up for in attack, candour and confidence. Critics have suggested several sources of this stark tale of a pretty girl forced by the brutal squalor of her home, and then by seduction and desertion, into prostitution and suicide: '*Madame Bovary* recast in Bowery style', the novels of Zola, or a sermon of De Witt Talmage which visualizes the suicide of a prostitute called Maggie. . . . It is not certain how much Crane had then read. But the book's tone is Crane's and no one else's. It is, as a critic said, 'violent and absurd like a primitive film'—but not, as the same critic incautiously adds, 'dated'. The 'primitive film' effect is an impressionism that anticipates the innovatory pointillism of *The Red Badge of Courage*. The scenes in which Maggie's parents quarrel are perhaps absurd; they are also vivid and powerful—one feels how the hopelessly pretty, weak girl was deafened by them. (An old woman asks Maggie, amid shrieks, 'Is yer fader beatin' yer mudder, or yer mudder beatin' yer fader?') Regardless of whether naturalism is a 'true' philosophy or not, Crane gave an unforgettable account of one poor creature whose life was quickly snuffed out by her environment. And he strengthened his novel by bringing to it the moral indignation of his preacher father, but not the moral judgement. Its abundant irony is apparent only to the sensitive or humane reader. It remains as truthful a picture of Bowery life as could at that time have been achieved. It has the authority of imagination and a painterly exactitude that reminds one of the fine New York slum paintings of George Bellows and the 'Ashcan' group of painters whom he joined.

Encouraged by Howells and Garland although ignored by almost everyone else, Crane continued to write. In his laconic, debunking poetry, published in *The Black Riders* (1895), *War is Kind* (1899) and collected in 1930 and again in a variorum edition, by J. Katz (1966), Crane created a tough, rhythmical free verse: it was well fitted to accommodate what John Berryman (q.v.) has called his 'sincerity . . . bluntness . . . enigmatic character . . . barbarity'. It is subtler than the directness of its manner makes it seem, and in it Crane has absolutely no truck with respectability—or anything that seems to him to be respectable. This poetry, influenced as much by the verbal compression of Emily Dickinson as by the cynicism of Bierce (q.v.), has not perhaps had its full due in spite of the full recognition now accorded to Crane. However, his did not wholly succeed in finding his own poetic voice, which might well have combined his parabolic with his symbolist, 'Baudelairian' manner, when the had been purged of its immature neo-romantic tendencies. Crane's poetry is important, though, because in it he is investigating the meaning of his deepest and most mysterious impulses.

Crane subscribed to Garland's 'veritism', but had had no personal experience of war, the subject of *The Red Badge of Courage* (1895). This is an extraordinary demonstration of the complex nature of fiction: it may be 'realism', it may even be 'naturalism' in so far as it presents men helpless in the grip of events—but the 'reality' it embraces is evidently wider than that of mere reportage. As one of Crane's leading critics, R. W. Stallman, has pointed out, it 'is a symbolic construct'. And because it succeeds so triumphantly on the realistic level, it is also about many other things: the fearful plunge of men into maturity and responsibility, into sexuality, into the raw, chaotic unknown. Henry Fleming is not named until half-way through the book. A farm-boy, he swaggers to himself, is frightened, is reassured, is caught up in battle and runs, gains his 'red badge' by an accident, returns and becomes a demon of aggressive energy. But it is all for nothing: his regiment takes up its former position. If he has become a 'man' (as he tries to believe) then what, asks the ironic structure of the book, is a man? In a short sequel, 'The Veteran', Henry really does become a 'man' when he goes into a burning barn to rescue two horses; but after that conversion he is a dead man. Another interesting thing about Henry Fleming and some of Crane's other characters is that they have nothing dishonestly to offer outside his own pages. As Berryman points out, they are not 'types', but they are not 'round' characters either: they move significantly only in their context, of Crane's impressionistic imagination. This not only anticipates but also disposes of all the philosophical claptrap surrounding the *nouveau roman* (q.v.). He does not tell us meaninglessly that the *sun shone red*. He puts it honestly into the text that is his own picture, his invention of a battle: 'The red sun was pasted in the sky like a wafer'.

Crane's novel 'The Third Violet' (1897), on bohemian life, is more conventional than *George's Mother* (1896), a competent tale of a working-class mother whose son is the opposite of what she fondly and pathetically imagines he is. Besides novels, poetry, unfinished plays and fiction, and a mass of journalism, Crane left behind him a number of short stories as classic as *The Red Badge of Courage*. The most famous of these are 'The Open Boat', based on Crane's experiences when, sent as correspondent to cover an expedition, he was shipwrecked off Cuba, and 'The Blue Hotel', a wickedly knowing tale about a Swede who creates the death-trap, the hostility of tough Nebraskans, that he most fears.

Crane drove himself ever more frenetically towards an early death. He took jobs covering the Spanish-American and the Graeco-Turkish wars, got into debt, desperately and vainly tried to write himself out of it. His last years were shared in England in a dilapidated manor house at Brede, Kent, with Cora Taylor, divorcee, prostitute and madame. There he made close friends of H. G. Wells, Ford Madox Ford and Joseph Conrad (qq.v.), and enjoyed as much friendship and understanding as any young writer has had. But he wore himself out entertaining on a regal scale, projecting—and writing. It was characteristic that he should have taken no heed of a serious warning (a lung haemorrhage) six months before he died. His self-destructiveness remains enigmatic, but one senses an enormous secret despair behind the sardonic and even gay phthisic energy. We can suspect that as his Henry Fleming turned after the battle to 'tranquil skies' with 'a lover's thirst', so he turned to death. Certainly Hemingway was right in saying that modern American literature begins with *Huckleberry Finn*; but rivers do not come from one spring, and it is as true to say that it flows from Crane's fiction. This may become increasingly apparent. It is sometimes objected that Crane's fiction and 'perverse' poetry ultimately function only 'as a fresh symbol of the universe's indifference to human needs' (Alfred Kazin). Crane did feel that. But there is something else locked away in that blandly autonomous prose, a creative intelligence like a great bird of prey, anticipating American writing not yet seen.

Chicago, to become the centre of the new literature, was an appropriate birthplace for FRANK NORRIS (1870–1902), who shared the given names of 'Benjamin Franklin', but little else, with Wedekind (q.v.). Norris did not have Crane's genius or sense of style, but he left some powerful fiction, and usefully demonstrates the limitations of such terms as naturalism when they are allowed to apply to anything beyond conscious method: we cannot heed Nietzsche's warning too much: 'What does one see, and paint, or write? . . . what one *wishes* to see, and what one *can* see'. Norris was a romantic who studied art in Paris at seventeen, and while there became hooked on medieval chivalry (or what passed for it) rather than realist or naturalist literature. Later, however, at Harvard, he chose the naturalist method as he had observed it in the novels of Zola (q.v.) in order to have a literary principle, and thus to get his fiction written. He carried out journalistic assignments, including one in Cuba, married, and became well known as a novelist before his death. Norris wrote his best novel, *Vandover and the Brute* (1914) while at Harvard during 1894 and 1895; the manuscript was believed lost for a time, in the San Francisco earthquake; it was not published until twelve years after his early death of peritonitis. *McTeague*, written at about the same time, was published in 1899, after the issue of the later and inferior *Moran of the Lady Letty* (1898). Norris' reputation rests on *Vandover*, *McTeague*, and the first novel of a planned but uncompleted trilogy on the production and distribution of wheat: *The Octopus* (1901); *The Pit* (1903), the second, is inferior. His first published work, a long phoney-medieval poem in three cantos called *Yvernelle: A Tale of Feudal France* (1892), is of no literary value but is useful as an indication of the romanticism that he never wholly shed.

Norris' importance has been acknowledged, but his achievement has been underrated because he has been judged as a naturalist and therefore by the standards of realism. Norris was, however, like Crane, a symbolist, and his three best books are all symbolic novels; but unlike Crane, he had no inkling of the fact, and when he announced, 'By God! I told them the truth', he equated the telling of truth with the simple act of holding a mirror up to the unpleasanter facts of nature. He had been very worried by the consequences of his (apparently ordinary) sexual excesses, and suffered from some measure of the gentility then endemic in America. The simple fact of sex existing at all haunts his fiction as a terrifying background grossness. *McTeague* is about a huge and physically gross dentist who is driven to bestiality, and the murder of his whining, miserly wife Trina, because of the circumstances created when his jealous friend betrays him to the authorities for practising illegally. *McTeague* is indebted to Zola, and even to actual incidents in his novels, and it is plainly intended as a naturalist novel, with simple symbols (such as the huge, gilded tooth that Trina gives McTeague for his sign: 'tremendous, overpowering . . . shining dimly out . . . with some mysterious light . . .', or his canary). McTeague is usually described by critics as 'stupid and brutal', and as thoroughly deserving of his fate; and possibly Norris himself consciously thought this. Actually, however, he is initially a sympathetic character, not in the least brutal except when aroused—as when a friend bites his ear. His lapse in 'grossly' kissing Trina while she is anaesthetized is not too serious, since he goes no further—and in any case the episode too obviously arises from Norris' own anxiety about sexual desire originating in a menacing beasthood (which he was simultaneously trying to resolve in *Vandover*). In *McTeague* each incident and object, and not just that gilded tooth, has symbolic force. The whole does not quite hang together, but the clumsy and deliberate style (like that 'of a great wet dog', John Berryman suggests) is more appropriate than is at first apparent. McTeague's degeneration—after his friend has denounced him—is convincing; but is it 'realistic'? Not more than the detail of his carrying his little singing canary about with him under impossible circumstances, or more than the habit he gets into of biting his wife's fingers (which have to be amputated) to punish her.

The Octopus is a more truly realistic novel. The 'octopus' of the title is the railroad, which threatens California wheat-ranchers. The description of the battle between the farmers and the railway men is justly famous, and the whole novel—although like all of Norris' fiction it has grave faults, one of the chief of which is unconvincing and stilted dialogue—deserves its reputation. *Vandover*, however, remains his masterpiece. It deals with the descent into madness, despair and penury of a decent and well-bred man. It quite transcends its origins: Norris's fear of syphilis, which masked his even profounder terror that sexual indulgence might drive him into a mysterious insanity; and a programmatically naturalist desire to show a man at the mercy of his 'bad' heredity. This is not a moral tale, as is sometimes alleged, because Vandover's fate is ironically contrasted with the good fortune of his vulgar friend Geary, a dishonest man who sows as many wild oats as Vandover, but merely prospers. Vandover's illness is not venereal, as has been suggested, but mental: once a promising painter, he sinks into a fatal decline, ending up by prowling naked and barking like a dog, earning his living by cleaning up filth. His decent friend Haight, however, does get syphilis—apparently from a mere kiss and the accidental slippage of a court plaster. Out of a neurotic anxiety and a fairly crude programme Norris produced a satisfying comment on the nature of both sexuality and creativity. It has been objected that he was inconsistent, putting the blame for Vandover's madness variously on himself, an indifferent universe, and society. . . . But Norris' creative bewilderment is honest; the pert critical objection is sterile. The book has a power and cohesiveness that cause us to take it on trust. Norris did more than enough to ensure survival.

If THEODORE DREISER (1871–1945), the Indiana-born son of a crippled and intermittently employed mill superintendent, had sought fame as a thinker he would have been lucky to get as far as the middle pages of a local newspaper. His fiction, the best of which is not far below the best of the century, is related to his ideas (if we care so to dignify them); but it is fatal to an understanding of the fiction to try to interpret it in terms of the ideas. Most people with such sets of notions as Dreiser possessed remain comparatively inarticulate cranks, or, at best, write books whose appeal is strictly limited to the semi-educated. But Dreiser's fiction is what his ideas were really about. And although his determinism is philosophically shabby and his 'science' a vulgarized jargon and travesty, H. L. Mencken (q.v.) was entirely justified in his remark that 'Dreiser can feel, and, feeling, he can move. The others are very skilful with words'. And when a critic as highly intelligent as Lionel Trilling, an academic rationalist and intellectual incensed by such reactions as Mencken's, tried to demonstrate that Dreiser was not good and wrote poorly (clumsily and not like a professor) because he thought poorly (not like a rationalist professor), instead of damaging Dreiser's status (who, admiring him, does not know that his style and thinking are not models for emulation?) he most painfully and needlessly exposed his own shortcomings. Dreiser is an exception that tests almost every known rule.

Dreiser was an emotional, not an intellectual man. We have to treat his ideas as simplistic rationalizations of his feelings; in his fiction they become transformed. Since his parents were poor, Dreiser was all his life profoundly moved by poverty. Few if any serious modern writers actually believe in capitalism as a system, although many do believe that liberalized forms of it may be the least of a number of evils; Dreiser, however, loathed it, and at the end of his life he joined the communist party, convinced that a Marxist revolution would provide the only just solution. On the other hand Dreiser, himself a compulsive womanizer, was obsessed by capitalist tycoons and crooks, and by the compulsive sexuality they frequently display. The character of Frank Cowperwood, the central character in the trilogy comprising *The Financier* (1912), *The Titan* (1914) and the posthumous *The Stoic* (1947), is partially based on the swindler and transport magnate Charles Yerkes. (Dreiser himself, after a year at Indiana University and some years working on newspapers, attained huge success before he became a famous writer: although his first novel failed in 1900, he went on to become editor of the women's magazine *The Delineator* at the then unprecedented salary of $25,000.) Brought up as a strict Catholic, he came to hate religion and to profess to see the workings of the mind as 'chemisms', mere predetermined chemical reactions. But he remained as interested in religion as in socialism and communism; his last novel—most of *The Stoic* was written many years before his death—*The Bulwark* (1946), some of which was written at the end of his life, has for its hero Solon Barnes, who is sympathetically portrayed as a Quaker and a seeker after religious truth. As for 'chemisms': he could never fully make up his mind about free will (what novelist really can if he tries?), and one of the strengths of his fiction is its ambiguity on this point (for all the unnecessary pseudo-philosophical asides). As Dreiser drifted into communism, he also drifted into a sympathy with the transcendentalism of Thoreau, and with Hinduism.

In terms of thought all this is of small interest. But when Dreiser came to write his fiction he stopped thinking, his imagination started to work, and he dramatized the conflict within himself. Those asides that disfigure even the finest of his novels are irrelevant to them. Critics say that Dreiser in *An American Tragedy* 'makes society responsible' for the tragedy of Clyde Griffiths' execution. That is not so. Dreiser does not know. He shows us Clyde's pitiful moral weakness, the terrible unwitting callousness with which he plans Roberta's death. Beside this he shows us the hypocritical and equally callous indifference of society, concerned with procedures and not at all with understanding or even guilt. Dreiser's book is important in that it gives us the actual grain of, the sense of being of, a specific human being going towards extinction; it warns that 'life' is frightening because it is 'like that'; but it offers—whatever Dreiser himself may say when he abandons his proper business of rendering Clyde and his story—no easy junketing of responsibility onto society. Clyde is forced to leave Kansas and the Green-Davidson by chance (the running down of a child, for which he is not responsible); thus he meets his uncle, his good fortune—and his end. Here Dreiser offers no facile comment as to whether there is free will. There is nothing essential to the novel that demonstrates choice as an illusion—except in that universal and bitter sense which the retrospective view confers.

Sister Carrie (1900) was accepted for Doubleday by Frank Norris (q.v.), but Doubleday himself—influenced by his wife, who was horrified because in it 'sin' is not 'punished' (it is the duty of society to keep this dark, lest the under-privileged should try it)—'privished' it: he kept to his contract, printed and bound one thousand copies—but did not push it at all hard. So Dreiser had to wait until 1911 and the publication of *Jennie Gerhardt* for recognition. After the first two of the 'Trilogy of Desire' (on Cowperwood) came *The Genius* (1915). *An American Tragedy*, which was occasioned by the Chester Gillette-Grace Brown case, was published in 1925. Apart from these novels and the final posthumous two, Dreiser wrote many short stories, travel and political books, essays and (atrocious) verse.

The view (later modified) of the influential biographical critic Van Wyck Brooks (1886–1963) that American literature was impoverished by puritan dualism (isolated idealism starved by practical materialism) was over-simplified, especially since it wrote off Mark Twain and Henry James as failures; nor was it a new idea; but it had truth in it. Dreiser helped American literature out of the 'genteel tradition'; again, although critics do not enjoy admitting it, he offered something that Henry James could not offer. Where Dreiser is massive is in the illusions he gives of lives as they are lived, of people as they seem: Clyde weakly appealing in his good looks and ambitiousness (right from when the 'captain' at the Green-Davidson engages him as bellboy), Carrie Meeber and Jennie Gerhardt innocent—although in different ways—of the nature of the lusts they arouse in men. . . . Dreiser—notwithstanding the philosophies in which he was interested, ranging from Herbert Spencer to Elmer Gates'

Laboratory of Psychology and Psychurgy—can convey the texture of life itself as few other novelists can. It is the kind of 'realism' for which there will always be a place.

Dreiser's best novels are *Sister Carrie* and *An American Tragedy*, followed by *Jennie Gerhardt*—here the heroine, whom some critics still describe as 'sinful', is morally superior to the other characters, whereas Carrie was morally neutral —and *The Financier*. Then, a long way back, come the last two of the Cowperwood trilogy. Here there are too many authorial asides—we hear too often the voice of Elmer Gates of the Laboratory of Psychurgy—and Dreiser's confusion over Cowperwood loses dramatic power. *The Genius* (1915), whose chief character Eugene Witla is a self-portrait—with some added details drawn from a painter and an art-editor Dreiser knew—was banned and then drastically rewritten. It is the odd one out of Dreiser's books. Here Dreiser tried to resolve his sexual difficulties, but pseudo-intellectual scruples interfered; there are far too many irrelevant intrusions. However, some sections of the novel—such as that describing Witla's decision, after a breakdown, to give up painting and become a manual worker—are extremely good. *The Bulwark* is interesting, but lacks creative steam.

A word about the so famously bad style and the gauche dialogue. Too much is made of this. Dreiser was not a sophisticated writer; a sophisticated or elegant style would not have suited him. His style is admirable—for its purposes. That it is rebarbative, 'as lacerating to the sensibility as the continuous grinding of pneumatic drills' (Walter Allen) is neither here nor there: so is the life and death of Clyde Griffiths, so is the fact that only a little ruthlessness on his part would have brought him success, so is the transformation of the matter of his guilt or innocence into a political issue, so is the massive and never withdrawn pity. To lament that Dreiser's style was not 'better' is to miss the whole point of what Dreiser was. It is not of course sensible to praise Dreiser at the expense of a very different writer, Henry James. It is less sensible to condemn him, as Lionel Trilling tried to do, because he was not James (or, more precisely, James-as-seen-by-Trilling). Trilling sneers at the concept of Dreiser's 'great brooding pity' and attacks him for the 'failure of his mind and heart'. It is an interesting and curiously contorted bitterness—in a fine critic— that can miss Dreiser's achievement in *An American Tragedy*. What has gone wrong here? It is something more fundamental than Dreiser's doubtless hideously non-professorial notions of culture. . . . In a comment on *An American Tragedy* Irving Howe shrewdly quotes George Santayana (q.v.) on one kind of religious perception, that 'power of which we profess to know nothing further', and through which we feel 'the force, the friendliness, the hostility, the unfathomableness of the world'. As Howe says, this power 'flows, in . . . feverish vibration, through *An American Tragedy*'.

JACK LONDON (1876–1916), bastard son of a wandering Irish astrologer whom he never saw, is wrongly regarded in Russia as a great writer. He is, however, a remarkable one, with a gift for story-telling unsurpassed in his time. Before he found fame and a huge public in the early years of the century Jack London (he adopted his mother's husband's surname) had roughed it: had drunk heavily, whored, been to jail, poached oysters, slaved in a canning factory, prospected for gold, been a tramp, gone sealing. . . . He is another writer whose achievement need not be discussed in terms of his crude attempts to systematize his reading; but he has neither the compassion nor the weight of Dreiser. London achieved enormous success, wrote fifty books in sixteen years, married twice— and finally killed himself (unpremeditatedly) with an overdose of morphine when ill health (uraemia), financial worry and legal troubles exerted too great a pressure upon him.

The main influences on London, apart from the fact of his bastardy, which he suppressed and which drove him to seek fame, fortune and respectability, were the writings of Kipling (q.v.) and Stevenson, then in the ascendant in America, and the ideas of Marx, Darwin (through his popularizer Haeckel) and Nietzsche. There is usually something worth while in all London's fiction, if only narrative and descriptive vigour. But as he grew older he tended to dissipate his gifts in his increasingly frenetic quest for security. His best books are: *The Call of the Wild* (1903), which dealt with his own problem (compare Norris) of wildness by giving an account of a dog that returns to its ancestors, the wolves; *The Game* (1905), a boxing tale (perhaps only for those who like and have a knowledge of its subject); *The Iron Heel* (1907), which prophesied a 300-year period of fascism, followed by socialism; *Martin Eden* (1909), an autobiographical novel in which London made the more personal prophecy of his suicide seven years later; and *The Star Rover* (1915), interconnected short stories about a convict who learns to transfer himself to another body. London was acutely aware of the conflict between instinct and reason, retrogression to primitivism and progress to utopia; in his inferior fiction he too crudely advances either socialism or his misunderstanding of Nietzsche. It was in *The Call of the Wild* that he discovered his most satisfactory objective correlative (q.v.). He wrote beautifully about animals, with whom he had a sympathy that extended beyond his obsessions with brutality and strength. London is not only still readable, but still worth reading (a different matter).

SHERWOOD ANDERSON (1876–1941), born in Camden, Ohio, does not always get his due, even in America. To some extent this is understandable. At his death Lionel Trilling (once again) struck; he has reprinted his vicious and patronizing obituary piece, with added material, in his widely-circulated collection of essays *The Liberal Imagination* (1950). This helped to put Anderson out of fashion. Furthermore, the best writing of his last twenty years (written off too confidently by Trilling as a time of absolute and 'poignant' failure), the autobiographical material, was unavailable. Paul Rosenfeld's *Sherwood Anderson's Memoirs* (1942), however good its editor's intentions, was bibliographically a disgrace, consisting largely of rewritten material. Not until 1970 did *Sherwood Anderson's Memoirs: A Critical Edition*, impeccably edited by Ray Lewis White, appear. The best writing in this has the kind of impact of the stories of Anderson's undoubted and acknowledged masterpiece, *Winesburg, Ohio* (1919).

Anderson's moment of truth at the age of thirty-six is a legend. He was sitting in his paint factory in Elyria, Ohio, dictating to his secretary in the winter of 1912, when he suddenly walked out. He turned up in a Cleveland hospital four days later, with 'nervous collapse'. This myth that Anderson himself established about his escape from soulless commercialism to creative freedom contained an element of truth. For he did eventually reject the non-values of his existence as an advertising copywriter and salesman of paint and, previously, other merchandise. But he had been struggling for some years with writing before he made the famous break; and he did not give up writing advertising copy until 1923—as he tells us in the memoirs he wrote in the Thirties, when his fame had passed. Superficially the businessman Anderson was not very different from his neighbours: public churchgoer and private out-of-town brothel-patronizer, country club member, and so on. There are similar men in almost every small town in America, and some of them even walk out. But Anderson differed from them because, in the privacy of an attic, out of the way of his university-educated wife who was always informing him of his inability to become the kind of man she envisaged as a writer, he indulged himself in what at first seemed like fantasies but later turned out to be the imaginative realities of a born writer. Although the actual moment of walking out came to symbolize for him his dramatic escape from the crass materialism of America, the process really took a number of years. The incident of walking out was the result of a real breakdown, occasioned by domestic tension and financial anxiety; these elements were played down, and led first to Anderson's being lionized as a great anti-philistine and enemy of Babbittry (q.v.), but later to his being attacked and subsequently neglected as a crude apostle of instinct. And yet in 1956 William Faulkner (q.v.) affirmed that Anderson was 'the father of my generation of American writers and the tradition of American writing which our successors will carry on', and he asked for 'a proper evaluation'.

Six of Anderson's seven novels amount to little more than a distraction from his real achievement, which lies in his short stories and in the sections of auto-biography collected together by Ray Lewis White. Parts of the first, *Windy McPherson's Son* (1916), are good, and in all of them, even the disastrous *Dark Laughter* (1925), there are fine passages. The best, and worth revival, is *Poor White* (1920), a successful projection of the author into Hugh McVey, a 'poor white' telegraph operator who becomes successful when he invents a corn-cutter. He awakens from his mathematical dreams only when Bidwell, Ohio, has been turned into a strife-torn industrial hell. *Poor White* has the faults of too glaring symbolism, but the grotesque and then distorted character of Hugh, and much of the detail of Bidwell's transformation into a factory town, are described with the power and subtlety of *Winesburg, Ohio*.

But Anderson was superior in shorter forms; the pressure put upon him to write long fiction was not good for his work. He was a lyrical and truly naïve (q.v.) writer; his outbursts against criticism, some of it sensible criticism, did not help readers to understand him or critics to follow him. Hemingway (q.v.), an inferior writer, pillaged him and then tried to parody him in his *Torrents of Spring*. After a difficult period in the Twenties, Anderson met his fourth wife, with whom he was happy, and retired from the literary scene to edit two Virginia newspapers, one democratic and the other republican. It was in this period that he did much of the autobiographical writing that provides a full answer to Trilling's charge that 'what exasperates us is his stubborn, satisfied continuance in his earliest attitudes'. After his first great success Anderson was too eager to publish whatever he wrote, and in his efforts to fulfil his genius in a novel he momentarily lapsed into the midcult image of himself that had been created by the widest section of his public: that of prophet and mystic. But he was too fond of life itself to stand the strain of this falsity for long. He refused to become or to pose as a mage—the fate of so many naïve writers, from Hauptmann through Jammes to Giono (qq.v.)—and instead, never stubbornly or satisfiedly, strove for self-knowledge. In the best of his autobiographical writings his effortful honesty comes naked off the page: it *is* embarrassing in so sophisticated, so intellectual and so reticent an age. But literature would entirely dry up without its stream fed so copiously by Anderson. The *Memoirs* contain writing that is genuinely inspiring (again, an embarrassing concept today): it fills the reader with the desire to search for and try to attain a similar simplicity and similar honesty. There is very little like it in twentieth-century literature. It is beautiful in the important sense that it illuminates and adds meaning to that increasingly difficult word.

For so seminal and original a book *Winesburg, Ohio* has some strangely obvious sources. The structure is that of the poems of Edgar Lee Masters' *Spoon River Anthology* (q.v.); the self-revelatory characterization is reminiscent of Turgenev's *A Sportsman's Sketches*; the deliberately oral, indigenous style owes much to Mark Twain (q.v.), though it up-dates him; the tone sometimes approaches Howe's in *The Story of a Country Town* (q.v.). Finally, Gertrude Stein, whom Anderson early recognized as being essentially, 'a writer's writer', liberated him from conventional usage, teaching him what she could not herself achieve: the lyrical expression of intuitions. The episodes in *Winesburg, Ohio*, all centring around the writer-figure of George Willard—a man who brings out something in each of the characters, if only the desire to confess—reveal men as both cursed and blessed by their gift of language: even as they are trapped, they live, they exist, they believe. This arises from a profound scepticism, set out in the prologue to the book and too often ignored. Anderson saw the citizens of Winesburg, and the whole of the modern world, as trapped in what Keats so famously called 'an irritable reaching out after facts and certainties'. Rejecting that multiplicity of apparently contradictory truths that is the actual sum of human knowledge—refusing to be in those 'uncertainties, mysteries, doubts' (Keats) that are proper to the human condition—we (Anderson said) grasp at and appropriate single truths; this distorts us and turns us into grotesques. Anderson's notion throws more light on the nature of society than many searchers after or possessors of systems may care to admit. There are some other short stories by Anderson that reach the level of *Winesburg, Ohio* from *The Triumph of the Egg* (1921), *Horses and Men* (1923) and *Death in the Woods* (1933). These may be found in *Short Stories* (ed. M. Geismar, 1962). Hart Crane (q.v.)

said of this unique writer that his strong sense of nature 'colours his work with the most surprising grasp of what "innocence" and "holiness" ought to mean'. Despite what we know about the financial and domestic pressures, the quiet and beautiful work of Anderson's last decade does, after all, take us back to that winter afternoon in Elyria. . . . He at least did not spoil his myth.

The connection between Anderson and GEORGE SANTAYANA (ps. JORGE RUIZ DE SANTAYANA Y BORRÁS, 1863–1952), who was born in Spain and retained his Spanish nationality, may seem tenuous. Santayana was an intellectual, and was more important as a philosopher than as a creative writer. Yet he and Anderson are curiously bound together by the sceptical and eclectic philosophy that Santayana ambitiously formulated in *Scepticism and Animal Faith* (1923) and its successors. If Anderson typifies the naïve (q.v.) approach to a certain apprehension of reality, then Santayana typifies the sentimentive (q.v.). Santayana left Spain at the age of nine and was educated in Massachusetts. From 1889 until 1912 he was a professor at Harvard. Then, on receipt of a legacy, he resigned. After many productive years he settled (1939) in a Roman nursing home—the fascists left him alone in the war because of his Spanish nationality. Santayana has written the best prose of any philosopher of the century. His poetry, although technically graceful by the standards of its time, entirely fails to reconcile the disparate sides of his nature; had it succeeded he would have been a great poet. As it was he called himself, rightly, 'almost a poet'. His philosophy is essentially an attempted reconciliation of idealism and realism. It is rightly described by orthodox philosophers as not being thorough-going or 'of [philosophical] consequence': it is more important than any of their sets of rigorous games, in that it may be immediately related to how men actually feel and live. It is significant that Santayana's initial approach resembles that of a philosopher who stands behind much modern literature, Husserl (q.v.): the application of strict logic results in everything being doubt-able. But 'animal faith' compels us to believe in a matter from which what Santayana called 'intuitive essences' have arisen. It is a subtle philosophy, and a profoundly intelligent and ironic modification of scepticism (it is by suffering, Santayana says, that we gain the clue to matter, which we must affirm in a suitably sardonic manner); it contains anticipations and understandings of modernism in literature. Santayana wrote one distinguished and interesting novel, *The Last Puritan* (1935), in which he contrasts Oliver Alden, the last puritan of the title, with other, hedonistic characters. For a reason that no one could explain, this became a best seller.

In 1931 Santayana had written a book called *The Genteel Tradition at Bay*. This attacked, although with much more cogency, the same tradition that had been Van Wyck Brooks's (q.v.) target. But Santayana was specifically criticizing the movement of the 'new humanism', which was led by IRVING BABBITT (1865–1933), who taught French at Harvard for most of his life, and PAUL ELMER MORE (1864–1937), a more interesting figure who interrupted his teaching career to become a distinguished journalist (he edited *The Nation* 1904–14). T. S. Eliot (q.v.) was loosely associated with this movement, although critical of it. The new humanism was thin-blooded, anti-romantic, classical conservative, anti-modernist, intellectual, with some elements of authoritarianism. Essentially it was a foredoomed attempt, by men in general non-creative, to revive what they thought of as transcendentalism. It drew on Christianity, but substituted for its central tenets a universal ethical code. Babbitt advocated an 'inner principle of restraint'. This movement flourished in the Twenties but petered out, after being much attacked and defended, in the Thirties. It is one of the least distinguished of the theories that have come from the better minds of our century. Santayana revealed the new humanism, which claimed to be opposed to decadence, as itself decadent and attenuated. He was particularly withering on the question of the new humanists' supernaturalism, upon which they were vulnerable. *The Last Puritan* was conceived both as a criticism of and a satire on this continuation of the genteel tradition; it was also for Santayana a happy return to the Nineties, when he was still young enough (he said) to sympathize with youth but old enough to understand it. However, in the character of Oliver Alden, and the tragedies of his love and end, Santayana got beyond satire.

*

Four important woman fiction writers emerged in this period. KATE CHOPIN (1851–1904), born in St. Louis, did not begin to write seriously until after the death of her Creole husband in 1882. She won a notoriety (unwelcome to her) with her novel *The Awakening* (1899). Interest in her has grown so much that her *Collected Works* have recently been issued in a scholarly edition, in two volumes (1970), edited by Per Seyersted. Among the many 'local-colourists' then working she is immediately distinguished by her superior objectivity and psychological conscientiousness. Her best stories are in *Bayou Folk* (1894), often poignant and sometimes ironic studies of the Creoles of Louisiana. In 'Désirée's Baby', her most famous tale, a wealthy aristocrat turns his wife and son out of the house because he suspects them of having Negro blood; then he discovers that he has; meanwhile Désirée kills herself and her child. Kate Chopin's stories are slight, but are among the earliest of their kind to show real sensibility and freedom from prejudice.

Her major work, however, is her novel *The Awakening*. This tells the torrid story of Edna Pontellier, who fails in love but succeeds in lust—and kills herself. This could fairly be described as a kind of Creole *Madame Bovary* (Kate Chopin had read Flaubert), although its purpose is different. It is a tragedy that the hostile reviews of this fine book should have broken her spirit.

Another gift that deliberately confined itself to a single locality (Maine), but that displayed itself in tales rather than novels, is that of SARAH ORNE JEWETT (1849–1909). It would be impertinent to describe her as a local-colourist: her wide culture and worldly humour are always in evidence. Her novels are negligible, and the series of sketches with which she made her reputation, *Deephaven* (1877), are slight in comparison with those of her acknowledged masterpiece, *The Country of the Pointed Firs* (1896). By then she had assimilated the influence of James as well as of Flaubert, Tolstoy and other Europeans; but she wisely confined herself to the limits of her experience. *The Country of the Pointed Firs* consists of loosely connected tales about the people in the beautifully evoked seaport town of Dunnet. This deserves its status as a classic because in its unobtrusive way it says so much about old age (most of the characters are elderly) and the manner in which a place may embody both decay and hope, as well as about Maine. Willa Cather (q.v.) was deeply influenced by it.

ELLEN GLASGOW (1874–1945), born of an aristocratic family in Richmond, Virginia, came to revolt against the tradition into which she was born and in which she began—although not with absolute obedience—writing: the sentimental tradition of the old domain of the South as a lost cause, and of the Civil War as an affair between honour and commerce. Ellen Glasgow's fiction set out to investigate this legend. She had a highly developed sense of humour, and, like Sarah Orne Jewett, she chose to write about the locality, Virginia, that she knew best. The teacher and critic H. S. Canby claimed, with justice, that Ellen Glasgow in her nineteen novels 'was a major historian of our times, who, almost singlehandedly, rescued Southern fiction from the glamorous sentimentality of the Lost Cause'. The work in which she accomplished this was mostly done in the Twenties; in old age she became over-conservative, though not unintelligently so, in the sense that she found she could not accept such manifestations of the modern age as bad manners or William Faulkner (q.v.). Her main theme was the consequences of the Southern myth on Southerners themselves. She is also notable for her resistance to the notion that all Southerners are alike. She always, in her own words, 'preferred the spirit of fortitude to the sense of futility'. To some extent Ellen Glasgow anticipated the concerns of the 'Fugitives' group (q.v.), but her approach was more mordant and even, judged just as an approach and not as a breeding ground for poems, preferable. There was not so much to recommend about life in the South before 1860 as Margaret Mitchell's best-selling romance, *Gone With the Wind*, suggests. But later Southerners, and much more intelligent and sensitive ones than Margaret Mitchell, have cherished such an image.

Like most of the novelists of her generation, Ellen Glasgow was of a pessimistic turn of mind, although it was doubtless personal experience that led her to the limiting view that life consists of specifically sexual disappointment followed by stoical acceptance. In her treatment of her thus sexually defeated people there is sometimes an element that goes beyond irony and becomes gloating and almost cheap. From the quality of this irony and of her not always successful epigrammatic writing, one may discern, in fact, that she is not of the first rank. But she is consistently adult, and her best books rise above her intentions. In *Barren Ground* (1925) the 'poor white' Dorinda Oakley, crossed in love, turns her father's barren ground into a farm with as much determination as Ellen Glasgow had put into her fiction writing just before the turn of the century; ultimately, having contracted one marriage of convenience, she marries the man, now a drunk, who turned her down, caring for him until he dies. Dorinda is a memorable creation. *The Romantic Comedians* (1926) is a surprisingly sympathetic treatment of a hypocritical and lustful old judge, Gamaliel Bland Honeywell. The book begins as he buries his wife. A respectable man who disapproves of sexual looseness, he marries a young cousin of his dead wife; she immediately makes him a cuckold, and runs off with her lover. The old man becomes ill and depressed, but we leave him cheered up by spring and the charms of his young nurse. Neither we nor the author dislike him half as much as we should. The Judge, shallow and self-deceiving, is rightly described by Walter Allen as a 'considerable comic creation'; but, as Allen goes on to point out, his fantasies of romantic love are—surprisingly and unusually—given a genuinely lyrical quality, so that he becomes a character actually touching in his defeat. *Vein of Iron* (1935) is not as a whole quite as psychologically acute, but contains fine passages, and effectively sums up Ellen Glasgow's attitudes to the South and to life. Her title expresses her recommended philosophy. Ada Fincastle displays this 'vein of iron' throughout all her and her loved ones' vicissitudes; it enables her to endure her father's lack of reality, the pregnancy she cannot (out of love) disclose, ostracism by the community, her husband's bitterness, poverty during the Depression. Ellen Glasgow makes an excellent 'introduction to the South' and to the more complex novels of Faulkner: she makes explicit much of the knowledge of the South that, as Walter Allen has said, Faulkner assumes in us.

But the most considerable woman novelist of the period was undoubtedly WILLA CATHER (1873–1947). She was born in Virginia but moved to Nebraska, whose people are the subject of most of her novels and stories, at the age of nine. She never forgot the pioneering spirit of the immigrants, who in her childhood often lived in sod houses or caves. Nor, it must be added, could her later fiction adjust itself to what America became. She was a late developer. She was educated at the University of Nebraska and had a tough journalistic apprenticeship on *McClure's Magazine* (1906–12). She had been writing verse and short stories since before the turn of the century, but did not publish her first novel, *Alexander's Bridge* (1912) until she was nearly forty. This was a failure because of a too intrusive symbolism; but the subtly flawed, nostalgic character of its engineer hero already indicated that Willa Cather's scope was larger than that of any previous American woman novelist. In the more successful *O Pioneers!* (1913) she went back to her greatest love and inspiration: the late nineteenth-century settlers in the Nebraska prairie. Like Ellen Glasgow, Willa Cather excelled in the portraiture of strong-minded women; here Alexandra has to assume responsibility for the farm after her Swedish father dies. Her moral superiority to those around her is convincingly conveyed. The episode of 'The White Mulberry Tree'—the story of the doomed romance of Alexandra's younger brother Emil with Marie, whose husband murders them both—fits in and perfectly complements the main narrative.

In *The Song of the Lark* (1915) Willa Cather tried unsuccessfully to deal more or less directly with the subject of herself: her opera-singer Thea Kronberg is clearly based on herself although supposed to be modelled on an actual singer's career. The author told herself that she was most interested in the way in which her heroine 'escaped' through a fortuitous falling together of commonplace events; actually she was interested in, but ultimately afraid to deal with, the nature of her sexuality. On the one hand she shows Thea as regretful of the ascetism that she feels is a penalty of art; on the other, it is clear that her irritation with men does not originate in her creativity but in lesbianism.

My Ántonia (1918) is probably Willa Cather's finest novel. It is an unhappy New York lawyer's middle-aged recollections of his Nebraska childhood, and of his dear companion, the Czech Ántonia. This is one of the most moving and powerful of pastoral evocations; the lawyer Jim Burden's present unhappiness is the result of his urban existence, with its betrayal of the values of his childhood. *A Lost Lady* (1923) is as moving but not as convincing: here Willa Cather is beginning to manipulate her characters in order to prove her point about urban corruption. Ántonia remains a saved character; in *A Lost Lady* Mrs. Forrester yields to the corrupting embraces of Ivy Peters, a vulgar, slick lawyer: her worth is destroyed. This is a good novel, but one may see in it the germs of Willa Cather's sentimentalization of the pioneer age: the idealized portraits of the pioneers themselves, the too easy dismissal of those born to a commercial and urban way of life. In her great success *Death Comes for the Archbishop* (1927) she goes back to the middle of the nineteenth century and the organization of the diocese of New Mexico by two close friends, Bishop Jean Latour and his vicar Father Joseph Vaillant. This is more satisfactory because Willa Cather is writing about the era she loves: there is no temptation to load the dice against the present. In this book Willa Cather's style reached its apogee, achieving epic qualities. There is deep understanding of both the missionary Roman Catholics' and the Indians' point of view. Willa Cather was a major writer, but not one big enough to take creative account of the changes in her century. This is not to say that her hatred of urbanization was wrong; only that it was too intense. She failed to understand that *some* men are victims of their circumstances. She did in the end turn spinsterish and difficult. But she gallantly resisted the intrusion of journalistic vulgarity (it must be remembered that she had been a journalist) into the novel, and her best books offer a unique evocation of the midwest of her youth.

*

Finally, an unclassifiable odd man out: will anyone ever revive even the best-known novels of JAMES BRANCH CABELL (1879–1958)? Cabell, born in Virginia, was an expert in genealogy—and was what might be described as a latter-day escapist. Hatred of modern life caused him to invent his own country, Poictesme, his epic of which is much and tiresomely concerned with the imaginary genealogy of its leading family. His books are 'naughty', and now seem desperately dated; indeed, his reputation collapsed in the Twenties because it had been founded, unfortunately, upon an unsuccessful prosecution of his novel *Jurgen* (1919).

This, irritating though it is in its highly self-conscious artiness and sly phallicism, may be a book that will deserve to be looked at again. In this sceptical tale of a middle-aged Poictesme pawnbroker who has a series of fantastic adventures Cabell examined his romanticism and found it wanting. An age only a little later than our own may more easily be able to penetrate the tortuous style and discover the wisdom that it obscures. Cabell was the victim of a cult and shaped his style according to it; unfortunately his bitterness when he went out of fashion did not result in any recapture of the genius underlying *Jurgen*.

II

Although American poetry did not show its true strength until after the First World War, the poets from whose example its most modern manifestations spring were active before that war—and nearly all of them had to wait a long time for public recognition. The first fully and authentically American poet was Walt Whitman. But Whitman was not fully understood until as late as 1955, when Richard Chase's book *Walt Whitman Reconsidered* was published. Interest in him continued to grow after his death in 1892 and he was the rallying cry of many splinter movements; but he was treated as a mystic, a mage, a socialist, a homosexual, a 'transexualist', anything rather than as a discoverer of an American voice who was also a complicated hider behind various masks. Whitman had his faults, and his intellectual equipment was hardly superior to Dreiser's; but he and Emily Dickinson, unknown in her lifetime, were the only major American poets of the nineteenth century.

The poets most highly considered in the first decade of this century have vanished from sight; nor is there much of value or even of interest to salvage from their work. RICHARD HENRY STODDARD (1825–1903), called in the year of his death 'the most distinguished of living American poets', was no more than an imitator of English Victorian poets who celebrated Abraham Lincoln in the English Victorian manner. THOMAS BAILEY ALDRICH (1836–1907) was not quite undistinguished as a novelist, but as a poet was a scented and weak imitator of Tennyson. Of somewhat more account was the Ohio poet PAUL LAURENCE DUNBAR (1872–1906), who was at least the first Negro to use Negro dialect (he was preceded by a number of white men); but he did not know the South, and the most that can be said of his best work is that it has some grace and style.

The 'Harvard generation' of the Nineties promised much, but performed little. WILLIAM VAUGHN MOODY (1869–1910) was intelligent and even tried to achieve a modicum of sexual realism; but in spite of his skill no poem he wrote deserves to survive, and his verse drama—*The Fire-Bringer* (1904) was the best known—is stilted. It is sometimes claimed that Moody influenced Wallace Stevens (q.v.), and this may be true; but only of the Wallace Stevens of juvenilia, which he destroyed. That Moody was a formative influence is unlikely. Moody's best work was done in the prose drama, and is mentioned in the section devoted to theatre.

More poetically gifted was Moody's Harvard friend JOSEPH TRUMBULL STICKNEY (1874–1904), whom Santayana (q.v.) recollected as one of the two most brilliant men he had ever known. Stickney's life was cosmopolitan. He was born in Switzerland, and spent his childhood in Europe. After he graduated from Harvard in 1895 he again left immediately for Europe. He was the first American to receive the *Doctorat des Lettres* from the Sorbonne. Stickney finally returned to Harvard, to the post of Instructor in Greek. After only one unhappy year of teaching he died of a brain tumour. Stickney, like his friend Moody, wrote plays; his *Dramatic Verses* (1902) made no impact whatever, but when Moody and two others collected his *Poems* (1905), interest was briefly aroused. The English poet James Reeves (q.v.), with Seán Haldane, made a selection, *Homage to Trumbull Stickney* (1968), which contains a valuable biographical and critical introduction. Messrs. Reeves and Haldane quote lines such as 'Your face possesses my despair', 'He stubborned like the massive slaughter-beast', 'That power was once our torture and our Lord' and 'I have it all through my heart, I tell you, crying' to illustrate their contention that he is 'more a rejected than a neglected American poet of genius'. Another view puts him on a level with Moody and suggests that both 'occasionally capture the modern manner, only to lose it again in a plethora of words' (Marcus Cunliffe). It seems to me that, moving though some of Stickney's poems are, his language would need to be considerably less archaic for him to be as exceptional as Reeves and Haldane claim. Cunliffe's 'the modern manner' is perhaps misleading; what Stickney needed was a language capable of expressing—primarily, indeed, of discovering—a set of highly complex prepossessions. Now Stickney certainly had a 'modern' sensibility but in almost all his poems he tends to lapse into a diction and tone which are alien to this sensibility. Feeling in his poetry tends to be robbed of sharpness and impact by muddy, self-indulgent diction, and sometimes by an ear that is more metrical than rhythmical. He lacks a formed style. But the essay by Reeves and Haldane is persuasive and well argued: it should be read. Undoubtedly Stickney has been undervalued; and certainly he is, as Donald Hall has said, one of America's 'great unfulfilled talents'.

While most of these poets and others—such as the Canadian-born BLISS CARMAN (1861–1929), whose 'carefree' verse now seems so laboured, the verse playwright PERCY MACKAYE (1875–1956), or JOSEPHINE PRESTON PEABODY (1874–1922), who was influenced by Moody—were enjoying some esteem, EDWIN ARLINGTON ROBINSON (1869–1935) was ignored. He did not achieve real recognition until he was fifty. For the duration of the Twenties he was America's most popular poet (Frost's ascendancy came later), but before he died of cancer in 1935 his stock had begun to go down, and between the Second World War and the beginning of the Sixties he was almost forgotten by critics (although his massive *Collected Poems* has sold consistently at about twelve copies a week since it appeared in 1937). In the last decade there has been a revival of interest: his excellent letters are now being collected, and eleven books have been devoted to him since 1963. Even at the height of his fame, which did not go to his head, Robinson was never at the centre of any coterie or cult, and no one knew much of his private life—except that he was unmarried, rumoured (I believe incorrectly) to be homosexual and had an alcohol problem. Neither Eliot nor the usually percipient, just and generous Ezra Pound (qq.v.) seem to have troubled to read him. The fact is that he was the only fully-fledged American poet to come out of the 'gilded age' (the title of Mark Twain's and Charles Dudley Warren's melodramatic novel denouncing its instability and acquisitiveness) that followed the Civil War; in this age Robinson was formed. Nor is Robinson as far behind the vastly more ambitious Frost as the difference between their reputations suggests. Robinson did not write the handful of nearly perfect poems that Frost did as a young man; but he had a wider range and wrote more penetratingly about people. In many respects he remained a child of the nineteenth century, his roots in Crabbe, Hardy, Browning; but if one compares the diction of his early poems to that of Stickney's (q.v.), the best of the poets who failed to attain a twentieth-century manner, it will be obvious that Robinson did at least find a language appropriate to what he had to say. That does not of itself guarantee the value of the poems themselves; but in this case they are good poems precisely because their author has discovered a new language to say new things. In Stickney the sentimentality and easy assumptions of the age linger on—alas—in the diction and style; Robinson's manner cuts through all this like a knife. What he can do in his best poetry, besides expressing some personal emotions, is to give an authentic account of what it is like trying to be a nineteenth-century man in a twentieth-century society. That is something.

He was born at Head Tide, Maine, but moved to Gardiner, in the same state, six months after his birth; this environment marked him for the rest of his life, and the Tilbury Town of his poems is Gardiner. Robinson became aware of his lonely poetic vocation there (he was an exceptionally lonely man), and there too he learned to identify himself with failure. His mother and father kept him at such a distance as to imply to him their rejection of him; his two brothers were always expected to outshine him. Ultimately, however, he was the success of the family: his father failed financially and went to pieces under the strain and the eldest brother turned from a promising doctor into a drug addict. Robinson himself attended Harvard until the money ran out, then turned— still in his twenties—into a lonely and alcoholic drop-out. He published two books privately, and for the third, *Captain Craig* (1902), the publishers Houghton Miflin had to be guaranteed against loss. President Theodore Roosevelt was given this book to read in 1905, enthused, and obtained a sinecure for Robinson in the New York Customs House, which he retained until the change in the presidency in 1909. During that time of comparative independence Robinson drank heavily and wrote little. It was the poems of *The Man Against the Sky* (1916) which finally gained him public acceptance; but it was not until the eve of his fiftieth birthday that critics and poets alike joined together in tribute to him. From 1911 until the end of his life Robinson spent his summers at the MacDowell

Colony, founded by the widow of the gifted (and, outside America, still neglected) American composer Edward A. MacDowell, as a refuge for creative artists of all kinds. He published two plays, which are interesting but not viable theatrically, and wrote fiction, all of which he destroyed. Eventually he confined himself entirely to the long verse narrative: *Tristram* (1927), a national success, completed an Arthurian trilogy; he was at work on *King Jasper* to within a few weeks of his death. It is always said that Robinson fails in these very long poems. And so he does. What is not said often enough is that he comes nearer to success in this form than any other poet writing at the time.

One of Robinson's subtlest and most characteristic poems is 'Flammonde', in which he exploits commonplace and cliché in a strategy that is quite certainly 'modern' in its implications. Yvor Winters dismissed it as 'repulsively sentimental'; but William J. Free, in an important essay, has shown how Robinson in this instance did succeed in finding a suitable, if ambiguous, language to express his uneasy situation. As Free says, 'he was trying to restore life to a worn-out language without abandoning that language'. Flammonde is just such an enigmatic and alienated character as Robinson felt himself to be, but Robinson ironically presents him as seen through the eyes of the townspeople: he has wisdom, but this is remarkable because he is not respectable; he has 'something royal in his walk' and has been 'accredited' 'by kings', but has been banished from that kind of life. Robinson turns Flammonde's *noblesse oblige* into a caricature by making him befriend an ex-'scarlet woman'—one of the worst clichés of the period. In his brain the kink is 'satanic'. Flammonde is the poet seen from the angle of the crowd, vulgarly mysterious, cheaply sinister, and yet necessary:

> We cannot know how much we learn
> From those who never will return,
> Until a flash of unforeseen
> Remembrance falls on what has been.
> We've each a darkening hill to climb;
> And this is why, from time to time
> In Tilbury Town, we look beyond
> Horizons for the man Flammonde.

'Flammonde' demonstrates Robinson's inability to define his poetic function directly, and incidentally explains why he invariably expressed himself through a strategy of characterizations. Thus he found his Flammonde in an Englishman called Alfred H. Louis, a well-connected failure; when in the more famous and longer *Captain Craig* he tried to be more explicit, to dissolve some of the mystery, about the objective correlative he had discovered in this person he was not as successful—although this, too, is an interesting poem.

Robinson wrote a number of other excellent short poems. The celebrated 'Miniver Cheevy' sums up his own situation even more tersely. It has been pointed out that the fourth 'thought' of

> Miniver scorned the gold he sought
> But sore annoyed was he without it;
> Miniver thought and thought and thought
> And thought about it

'comes as an authentic kick in the womb of a stanza that proves the existence of a live poet'; it has the touch of a master. Equally good are 'Eros Turannos', 'Isaac and Archibald', 'Saint-Nitouche' and some others. The narrative poems, naturalistic in the sense that they show people at the mercy of their passions, are unrivalled in their field—Masefield's (q.v.) aim at so much less—in that they are all, even the lushest (*Tristram*), readable and interesting; one may come across a good passage at any time. A properly selected Robinson—still lacking—would have to include some of these, as well as the best of the shorter poems and such medium length narratives as 'Isaac and Archibald'. Robinson may have been a late romantic and even a transcendentalist, who allowed a false optimism to mar much of his poetry; but his was the only nineteenth-century sensibility to express itself effectively in twentieth-century terms. His influence has been considerable although, except in the case of Robert Lowell's *The Mills of the Kavanaughs* (q.v.), unobtrusive. His stock is certainly rising.

Now for three lesser, but undoubtedly important poets, all from the state of Illinois: EDGAR LEE MASTERS (1868–1950), CARL SANDBURG (1878–1967) and VACHEL LINDSAY (1879–1931). All of these were quintessentially American as distinct from English-style poets. In this sense, but only in this, each was superior to Robinson. Masters was the son of a lawyer who himself became a lawyer; born in Kansas, moved to Illinois at one, he wrote much both before and after *The Spoon River Anthology* (1915), but never produced anything remotely near to it in quality. A newspaper editor gave him Mackail's *Select Epigrams from the Greek Anthology* in 1911, and this acted as the catalyst required to manufacture the acid of his own genius, compounded of an innate bitterness, a passion for truth, and a rare sympathy for human beings. Spoon River was an amalgamation of Petersburg and Lewistown. In a flat, laconic free verse Masters makes the inhabitants of the Spoon River hill cemetery state their own epitaphs. He resembles Robinson, but is more direct and less officially optimistic:

> Did you ever hear of the Circuit Judge
> Helping anyone except the 'Q' railroad,
> Or the bankers . . .?

This was a poetry in the prose tradition initiated by Howe, Garland (q.v.) and others; but the compression he learned from the Greek Anthology enabled Masters to improve on it. However *The Spoon River Anthology* is better considered as prose than as poetry, as which it is undistinguished.

Vachel Lindsay, born in Springfield, Illinois, obtained a good education, and then studied art for five years; but he failed at it, and decided to become a tramp. His drawings look like meagre and talentless imitations of Blake.

Lindsay had always wanted to be a missionary, and in 1905 he alternated winter lecturing with summer tramping and declaiming; he would exchange leaflets of his poems for a bed and food. By 1913 he had become well known. Harriet Monroe began to publish his poetry, and *General William Booth Enters into Heaven and Other Poems* (1913) and *The Congo and Other Poems* (1914) were successful. For some fifteen years he enjoyed fame as declaimer of his own work all over America and in Great Britain as well. Public interest in him lessened soon after his marriage in 1925; in 1931, in despair and ill-health, he took poison.

Lindsay was a midwestern populist and revivalist whose views never altered or expanded with his experience of the greater world. His father was a Campbellite minister (member of the Church of the Disciples of Christ, which had broken away from Presbyterianism to a simplicity based solely on the Bible). Lindsay combined this evangelical creed with worship of Lincoln and other local heroes, religious ideas of Swedenborg, and the economics of Henry George (q.v.). He was vulgar and parochial, but at his best he knew it and exploited these very failings. His sources are revivalist hymns and sermons, Whitman's manner and tone, temperance tracts, Negro jazz, all the sayings and doings of Lincoln and other lesser known, local heroes, and Salvation Army brass band music. He learnt much about the performance of poetry from the readings of S. H. Clark, a professor at the University of Chicago. His best poems succeed because they are impassioned and wholly unsophisticated. To put it at its most simple: he meant every word of them, and for a few years he found exactly the right combination of sources. He introduced a genuinely new rhythm into American poetry; he was also America's first genuine folk poet—at his best he is superior to Sandburg. Later he went to pieces and produced too much weak and self-parodic verse. The novelist Richard Hughes (q.v.) heard him at Oxford, and has recorded for the British Broadcasting Corporation some remarkable and highly illuminating renderings of his poetry.

It was Harriet Monroe's *Poetry* that gave Sandburg fame. Born at Galesburg of Swedish immigrant parents, from thirteen he was an itinerant labourer all over the West; he served in the Spanish-American war, worked his way through college in his home town, and became a journalist and socialist. His master was Whitman, but although more genuinely 'of the people' than Whitman he is a minor poet by comparison because he is never more than a reporter. He used very free forms, and his poetry resembles Masters' in that it is by no means certainly properly judged as poetry, but rather as a rhythmical prose. At his worst he is whimsical, sentimental and falsely tough; at his rare best colloquial, tender and precise. He could be defined as an ideal 'unanimist' (q.v.): he responded to and thoroughly understood the corporate longings of the new industrial folk, and he fervently believed in their happy future. His weakness is that he has no creative means of confronting evil. The famous stanza about John Brown.

> They laid hands on him
> And the fool killers had a laugh

And the necktie party was a go, by God.
They laid hands on him and he was a goner.
   They hammered him to pieces and he stood up.
They buried him and he walked out of the grave, by God,
   Asking again: Where did that blood come from?

owes all its strength to the presentation of John Brown's vitality as a folk hero; Sandburg could not cope with, and was a child in trying to deal with, the forces of evil. But his best poems reflect midwestern speech and in rigorous selection they will continue to survive. He wrote a monumental biography of Lincoln (1926–39) and made two important collections of local American folk ballads, *The American Songbag* (1927) and *The New American Songbag* (1950).

At his death ROBERT FROST (1874–1963) was America's most famous poet and unofficial laureate. No other American has reached his eminence in letters. And yet he waited as long as—and even more bitterly than—Robinson for recognition. He was born in San Francisco of a New England father and a Scots mother; when he was eleven his father died, and the family moved to Salem, New Hampshire, where his mother taught in a school. Frost worked in mills and as a newspaper reporter, taught, married, spent two years at Harvard and tried to be a poultry farmer—all unsuccessfully. At the age of thirty-six he sold his farm in Derry and went to England, where he settled down to write. In England he met Wilfred Gibson, Ezra Pound, Lascelles Abercrombie and, most importantly, Edward Thomas (qq.v.), whom he encouraged to write poetry. While he was in England his first two books of poetry were accepted: *A Boy's Will* (1913) and *North of Boston* (1914). The second was published in America by Holt in the same year, and when he returned to the States early in 1915 he found he was the author of a best seller. For many years after this he spent periods as poet-in-residence in various academic institutions. The rest of the time he spent on farms he bought in Vermont and, finally, in Florida. He had much sorrow with his children: one died of puerperal fever, and his son Carol shot himself. At the end of his life, although an outspoken and fierce conservative, and a lifelong enemy of all things academic, he had twice been greeted by the Senate (on his seventy- and eighty-fifth birthdays), taken part as unofficial laureate in the inauguration of John F. Kennedy, and received nearly fifty honorary degrees (including ones from Oxford and Cambridge).

To say that Frost has been overrated is not to say that he is unimportant. He was a naïve (q.v.) poet, and when he took thought never more than a skilled folksy epigrammatist, who in order to cling on to his so hardly won fame had to write too much and not always in his natural vein. His pose as sage seldom led to wisdom, and hardly does the true poet in him credit. The poems of *A Boy's Will* are less certain than those of *North of Boston*, his best book, and the confidence of this extends into some of the poetry of its two successors, *Mountain Interval* (1916) and *New Hampshire* (1923). After this Frost was increasingly intent on subscribing to an image of himself largely formed by people who had little knowledge of or love for the arts in general. His poems can be optimistic

and cheerful when he does not really feel like that—he conceals his blackness—
and he can be arch and self-consciously Yankee.

But when this has been said Frost is still a unique and original poet both in
short lyrics and in certain comparatively short narrative poems. The famous
'Mending Wall' is a good enough example of his strength; it alone is enough
to give pause when we are told that the claim that Frost is a major poet is
'ridiculous'. This is a genuinely tragic poem: it spells out how things are between
people. Lawrance Thompson, Frost's biographer, suggests that 'the conclusion
resolves the conflict in favour of the poet's view. . . .' It seems to me that this
judgement does not do it justice: it is more than an expression of a mere point
of view, for while the wall is a real wall, it also stands for that barrier of reserve
which neighbours erect between each other—to avoid being friends, or to
protect themselves. We are told that 'Something there is that doesn't love a
wall': frosts break it up. Hunters have the same effect. At 'spring mending-time'
he gets in touch with his neighbours, and together they make the repairs, piling
the boulders up. It's only a game, the narrator tells us: a wall isn't necessary
at this point, since his neighbour is 'all pine' and he is apple orchard. He tackles
his neighbour with this—'Spring is the mischief in me', he explains, thus surely
negating Thompson's assertion that the notion of having no wall is his seriously
held point of view—but the neighbour only says 'Good fences make good
neighbours'. However, mischieviously he continues to taunt his neighbour, who
goes on rebuilding the wall 'like an old-stone savage armed'; and the narrator
concludes

> He moves in darkness as it seems to me,
> Not of woods only and the shades of trees.
> He will not go behind his father's saying,
> And he likes having thought of it so well
> He says again, 'Good fences make good neighbours'.

This is 'about' the barriers between people and the worth of love; maybe the
conservative neighbour is right. Frost could and did moralize in his lesser
poems; in this good one he is content to leave things as they are, tragically in
balance. Yes, spring has made him challenge (with 'mischief') the notion of a
wall; but there is no pat conclusion, no suggestion that it is his neighbour's state
of mind that is responsible for the state of affairs. . . . The poem works so well
because its full meaning arises so naturally out of the situation it describes;
there is no straining for a meaning in the account.

Again, it would surely be risky to dismiss the narrative 'The Death of the
Hired Man', also from *North of Boston*, as only a minor poem. It is true that
Frost's people are cardboard, and that they do not act upon each other or
change each other; it is also true that his technical arrangements are static—
the oft-made claim that he used American speech-rhythms cannot be carried
far. But this account of the return of a hired man, and the differing views of a
husband and wife about charity and their duty, attains such simplicity—

'Home is the place where, when you have to go there,
  They have to take you in.'
'I should have called it
  Something you somehow haven't to deserve.'

—that it cannot be ignored. It offers, for the time being, something other than the urban sophistication of Eliot (q.v.). So do a half dozen other similar narratives, most of them included in *North of Boston*. Frost is not usually a 'nature poet', for he does not observe natural objects minutely; he rather observes man in natural surroundings, and tries to find consolations for nature's indifference. He can be falsely sweet, as when he asks us to come with him while he cleans out the pasture spring (he does not mean it); but he achieves true sweetness when he reveals his desire for a valid and unsentimental universal love, as at the end of 'The Tuft of Flowers', from his first book:

'Men work together,' I told him from the heart,
'Whether they work together or apart.'

Frost's influence on American poets of account may, surprisingly, be somewhat less than even that of Robinson. Robinson remains enigmatic, unexplored; there does not at present seem to be very much to go to Frost for. The same can under no circumstances be said of the prince of American regionalist poets, WILLIAM CARLOS WILLIAMS (1883–1963), who was born in Rutherford, New Jersey, practised there as a doctor all his life, and died there. He studied dentistry at the University of Pennsylvania, where he met Pound, and later went to Europe to study medicine. By 1912 he was married and settled into his lifelong practice at Rutherford, the Paterson of his long poems of that name.

'Williams . . . is . . . the most innocently tedious, insufferably monotonous, and purely mental of modern poets . . . polythene verse. . . . [His] form conceals that he is saying very little, and has very little to say. . . .' (An English critic.)

'Williams' poems contain a generosity of spirit, a humane warmth, ability to translate daily life and ordinary objects into an unsentimental order of personal and universal significance, which are unique in modern poetry and rare at any time. . . . His ear for rhythm is practically perfect. . . .' (An American critic.)

The first judgement may be turned somewhat to Williams' advantage if we grant that, for all his multifarious pronouncements, Williams was a naïve (q.v.) poet—a good deal more naïve than Frost, himself disingenuous in his intellectual pose. His overriding passion (it was never a thought) from early on was that poetry should reflect experience exactly and that therefore rhyme and metre were falsifications: non-American, Anglophile devices. He attacked Eliot and Pound for not staying in America, and imagism (q.v.) for being mere free verse. His 'objectivism' (q.v.) postulated the poem itself as object, presenting its meaning by its form. 'No ideas but in things', he insisted, seeking until the end to describe the universal only in the stubborn particular. He went his own singular way, inconsistent, obstinate, publishing his poetry with obscure small presses— and ended up as a grand old man of American letters, inspirer not only of

Olsen, Ginsberg, Creeley (qq.v.), but, less logically, also of the formalists Roethke and Lowell (qq.v.). He wrote autobiography, impressionistic criticism (*In the American Grain*, 1925), plays, short stories and fiction.

All Williams' work flows out of his insistence upon the local and the particular. He saw the world 'contracted to a recognizable image'. His poems are his namings of the objects in his world as it unfolds itself to him. His own words, written when he was at his most energetic, and when he was hardly heeded, are incomparably the best expression of his intentions:

> There is a constant barrier between the reader and his consciousness of immediate contact with the world. . . . I love my fellow creature. Jesus, how I love him . . . but he doesn't exist! Neither does she. I do, in a bastardly sort of way. . . . In the composition, the artist does exactly what every eye must do with life, fix the particular with the universality of his own personality. . . . The only realism in art is of the imagination. It is only thus that the work escapes plagiarism after nature and becomes a creation. . . . [Shakespeare] holds no mirror up to nature but with his imagination rivals nature's composition with his own. . . .

That last remark gives us the clue both to Williams and the appeal he had for so many Americans. Here is a man who insists on the evidence of his own perceptions. As Marianne Moore (q.v.) shrewdly said of him: he has 'a kind of intellectual hauteur which one usually associates with the French'. Indeed, we have only to remember the philosophy behind the French *nouveau roman* (q.v.) to recognize this: but this is a doggone, non-intellectual, Yankee approach. Williams exists on the strength of his perceptions or he does not exist. After some early imitations of Keats, he began writing in the vein that he maintained until his death. It is seen at its best in 'This Is Just To Say'—surely an irresistible lyric?

This Is Just To Say

I have eaten
the plums
that were in
the icebox

and which
you were probably
saving
for breakfast

Forgive me
they were delicious
so sweet
and so cold

Williams' long poem *Paterson* (1946–58), his attempt at an epic, in five books, is distinctly American in its attempt to recover innocence and a sense of community. It is characteristically impressionistic: in large part it consists of seemingly casual collage of undoctored raw material: heard conversation, private letters, news clippings, official reports, bald anecdotes, and so on. It contains some vigorous and compelling passages, but suffers from two contradictory defects. Williams wants to appear non-literary, ordinary, and so to this end he includes far too much unedited material in the poem; this makes it tedious. However, at the same time the essentially naïve poet artfully and disingenuously tries to superimpose a symbolic pattern on the poem: for example, an analogy is worked out between the poet's and the physicist's function, even to the extent of comparing the splitting of the atom to the splitting of the (metrical) foot. . . . The first two books hold together better than the rest, but even these contain dull passages; the rest fails to convince or to cohere, although some enthusiastic critics have stated otherwise. Williams' technique here more closely parallels that of painters than poets: 'he strives', writes a critic, 'for a poem that will, in its own process, answer the question it continually poses'. This is no more than the old, anti-mimetic insistence on creation, the necessity he felt to 'rival nature's composition with his own. . . .' It does not work, but comes near enough to doing so for us to wish that Williams had not tried to be so artful: he was not good at it.

However, Williams' anti-mimetic preoccupation is enough to demonstrate that he is no spurious modern, as the English critic quoted above has suggested. It is true that in an intellectual or metaphysical sense Williams has nothing whatever to say. But is he that kind of writer? Is he not, rather, simply a recorder of his perceptions? That these are often simplistic is beside the point. They are almost inevitably unspoiled. However, can Williams, on the strength of his best things—such fragments as 'El Hombre',

> It's a strange courage
> you give me ancient star:
>
> Shine alone in the sunrise
> toward which you lend no part!

—be called a major poet? As a pioneer he is obviously of importance. But is his poetry intrinsically major? The poem of his old age, of some 350 lines, called 'Asphodel, That Greeny Flower' is probably his crowning achievement. It is hard not to respond to it. But are we not perhaps responding to the integrity and sweet cussedness of personality, to a devoted life, rather than to a poetic achievement? The answer to the question is not to be easily found. In my own judgement there is as much of the simple-minded as of the simple about Williams, so that he is finally a physician and minor poet rather than a major poet and a physician. He always wanted desperately to be 'average', and I think that his simplicities, too, were near the average. . . . (Evidently Wordsworth's, say, weren't.) One appreciates the way he lived and felt and talked; but even 'Asphodel, That Greeny Flower' offers no insight, only a chance to applaud that performance. In order to attain to it he eschewed all alien devices, so that his poems lack tension. And a whole poetry that lacks tension is inexorably minor.

And now, since it is relevant to most of the American poetry that follows, a word about Williams and poetic technique. Williams many times announced that he had discovered a new, American poetic technique, which he referred to as the 'variable foot'. Williams was no prosodist, and his attempted definitions of this variable foot are worthless. But it does mean something in terms of his own practice:

> Of asphodel, that greeny flower,
>   like a buttercup
>   upon its branching stem—
> save that it's green and wooden—
>   I come, my sweet,
>   to sing to you.
> We lived long together
>   a life filled
>   if you will. . . .

Each of those 'lines' is a 'variable foot'; at one time Williams would have called it a 'triadic foot', comprising a single 'line'. And the reader will quickly appreciate that while Williams himself achieved a personal rhythm by writing in this way, his imitators have not. This way of writing verse should be discussed, and there are new elements in it (even though one can treat Williams' verse in terms of the various traditional approaches to prosody); but it has not been usefully discussed yet—least of all by Williams, who waded thigh deep into the old bog of confusion between accent and quantity that has bedevilled English prosodic studies since Elizabethan times. Williams' confused theory comes nearest to the 'temporal' prosody advanced by the American poet Sidney Lanier, who died in 1881. What is original in his practice—'not that,' he wrote, 'I know anything about what I have myself written'—is the accommodation he gives to quantity without straining its function in the vernacular: without, as the Elizabethan Stanyhurst, and Bridges (q.v.), and even Tennyson, did, trying to destroy accent. If his pronouncements on Thomas Campion are embarrassing, his poems do achieve a kind of musicality, and a new musicality at that, which most others of this century lack.

It is appropriate at this point to deal with a movement in which Williams played a major part. Objectivism never hit any headlines, even though Pound (q.v.) was officially associated with it, and besides Williams only one other 'objectivist' has since become at all well known: LOUIS ZUKOFSKY (1904). But this small group is important both as a refinement of imagism (q.v.), and as a forerunner of a now flourishing branch of American poetry exemplified in the work of Robert Duncan, Robert Creeley, Gary Snyder (qq.v.) and many others. It began when a wealthy young man (the description is Williams'), GEORGE OPPEN (1908), decided to lose his money on publishing poetry. At first his press was called TO, and in 1932 it published *An "Objectivists" Anthology*, edited by Zukofsky. Then it became the Objectivist Press, with an advisory board consisting of Williams, Zukofsky and Pound; the other poets involved were CARL RAKOSI (ps. CALLMAN RAWLEY, 1903), born in Berlin, and CHARLES REZNIKOFF (1894), a lawyer born in New York. Acknowledging Williams as their master, these poets (this does not include Pound, whose relationship was avuncular and postal) published his *Collected Poems 1921–1931* (1934), with an introduction by Wallace Stevens (q.v.). But their own work has its importance in twentieth century American poets' search for simplicity. All possess an integrity and a lack of interest in personal fame—as distinct from poetic achievement—that could be a lesson to their modern successors. There is much in the claim that while the American poetic tradition appeared to be, during the Thirties, in the hands of such as Tate and Ransom (qq.v.), it was really in the hands of these relatively obscure poets. That this tradition, stemming directly from Whitman and running through Sandburg and Williams to Creeley and others, has not yet produced a truly major poet since its originator does not constitute a negation of the claim.

The objectivists were agreed that imagism, having helped to get rid of mere verbiage, had 'dribbled off into so much free verse. . . . There is no such thing as free verse! Verse is measure of some sort . . . we argued, the poem . . . is an object . . . that in itself formally presents its case and its meaning by the very form it assumes . . . it must be the purpose of the poet to make of his words a new form: to invent, that is, an object consonant with his day . . .' (Williams). These words bear heeding, because they sum up the credo of every kind of disciple of Williams.

Zukofsky is a quiet, unassertive man who has been possibly the most persistent and courageous experimentalist in the English-speaking world in this century. Once again, it is his procedures that are important—as indeed one might expect in a work that 'in itself formally presents its case and its meaning by the very form it assumes. . . .' To the reader nourished on conventional pap Zukofsky's poetry and criticism seem thin and insubstantial; nor indeed does he display anything of the emotional robustness of a Williams. But this should not distract attention from the significance of what he has been doing in the last forty years. It is characteristic of Zukofsky that his chief work, the long poem —unfinished—*A*, should be continuous, a day book. For Zukofsky it is absurd to be a good poet at one point of one's life, then a bad one, and so on. So *A* is his continuous poetic reaction, as often concerned with sounds as with music. He reminds us of Gertrude Stein (q.v.) at least inasmuch as meaning in his verse is very often no more than an overtone to sound. (All the objectivists shared Gertrude Stein's important notion of words as words, things-in-themselves.) Zukofsky is continually playful, and yet he is always thinking—if in a somewhat primitivistic (and why not?) sense of the word—very closely indeed about words as meaning and words as sound. The context of his work is almost always his domestic life; his wife and son Paul (now a well-known violinist) are both musicians. The theme of *A*, in fact, is marriage: marriage as a bastion against the ruins of 'civilization'. For poets at least it is always readable, always an evocation of a sweetly lived life. Some clues to the passages that look like nonsense, but which are in fact various sorts of experiments with sound, may be gathered from Zukofsky and his wife Celia's *Catallus* (1969), in which they have transliterated the entire works of Catullus from Latin into an American that 'tries . . . to breathe the "literal" meaning with him'. Thus the famous

> Odi et amo. quare id faciam, fortasse requiris.
> nescio, sed fieri sentio et excrucior

becomes

> O th' hate I move love. Quarry it fact I am, for that's so re queries.
> Nescience, say th' fiery scent I owe whets crookeder.

Now: can the texture of the sound of Latin be woven into that of American? Apart from one or two remarkable *tours de force*, it seems not. The vast majority, however well disposed, would consider the above transliteration, for example, a grotesque failure: not only in terms of the literal Latin meaning but also in those of the American language. But it is the failure of an intelligent man; and the experiment is not a useless or a foolish one. However, the question that wholehearted partisans of this version of Catullus (few of whom, curiously, seem to possess the Zukofsky's knowledge of Latin) need to answer is: what can be the function of such a language as is here invented? What is interesting is that an answer can be made. Just as sense can be made of Williams' 'theory' of prosody so even 'O th' hate I move love' for 'Odi et amo' can be defended. We must consider it—and Zukofsky. The poems have been collected in *All: The Collected Shorter Poems 1923–1958* (1966), *All: The Collected Shorter Poems 1956–1964* (1967), *"A" 1–12* (1967), *"A" 13–21* (1969). Criticism is in *Prepositions* (1967), and fiction (a useful method of approach to this important poet) in *Ferdinand* (1968). *Bottom: on Shakespeare* (1963) is criticism combining poetic and musical interests.

Carl Rakosi, a social worker and psychotherapist, is the least well known or committed of the objectivists, but his poetry is as clean as it is slight; *Selected Poems* appeared in 1941, *Amulet* in 1967. Oppen is more substantial. *Materials* (1962) collects thirty years of his work, and he has published three collections since then. He has been described, in terms characteristic of recent criticism, as being 'one of the best and one of the worst of poets'. He has been important to some of the Black Mountain poets (q.v.) because his project has been to express his existence and the use he has made of it:

> Yet I am one of those who from nothing but man's way of thought and
> one of his dialects and what has happened to me
> Have made poetry

Oppen, unlike Zukofsky and Olson (q.v.), has not received even belated critical recognition, despite his Pulitzer Prize of 1969. And yet his understanding of the problems of diction has been as acute as Williams', and since his first book appeared in 1934 he has provided an object-lesson: a poetry that 'presents its case . . . by the very form it assumes'. Like Zukofsky, he aims for a full articulation of his engagement with life; he is fascinated, too, with objects-as-themselves (cf., again, the *nouveau roman*), objects not anthropomorphized. But his method is complex; cutting across his purely objectivist preoccupations are intellectual and abstract concerns that might contort the face (often the Black Mountain equivalent of raising the eyebrow) of a true disciple of Williams. Sometimes he has been guilty of smuggling thought into his poetry, in such lines as those describing women in the streets 'weakened by too much need/Of too little'; and yet careful study of his poetry shows that he, more than any other poet in his tradition, has seen the possibilities of using content to create its own form. He is not trivial, and his methods are more original than some of his admirers think.

Charles Reznikoff, a considerably older man, has written distinguished prose in his novel *By the Waters of Manhattan* (1930), and in *Family Chronicle* (1963); as a poet he is more of an imagist:

This smoky morning—
do not despise the green jewel shining among the twigs
because it is a traffic light.

His poetry, much of which is collected in *By the Waters of Manhattan: Selected Verse* (1962), is as enjoyable (in the full sense of the word) as any imagist's could possibly be; though evidently sometimes impelled to widen his scope, he has chosen to limit himself to the minimal, with in this case excellent results. Reznikoff has not been, like Oppen, a pioneer; but because he has decided to narrow his scope, his picture-making impulses have not been frustrated, and many of his poems have the freshness of such paintings as 'Early Sunday Morning' by Edward Hopper, with whom he has indeed been compared.

EZRA POUND's (1885–1972) part in the new American poetry has been more cosmopolitan. No writer of the twentieth century has had more personal influence on modern literature or has known and encouraged more individual poets. His importance in connection with imagism (q.v.), vorticism (q.v.), W. B. Yeats (q.v.), T. S. Eliot (q.v.), William Carlos Williams (q.v.) and other men and movements has been or will be noted. His immense historical import-ance has never been in question; the matter of his individual achievement is more controversial.

Pound was born in Idaho. He began to attend the University of Pennsylvania, Philadelphia, at the age of fifteen, owing to his good Latin. Here he met William Carlos Williams, then a student in dentistry. After two years he transferred to Hamilton College in New York State. By 1906 when he received his M.A. he had for some time been experimenting with various forms of verse. He had also already begun to develop the eccentric behaviour—a mixture, it seems, of exhibitionism, excitability, devotedness to his ideals and something that looks like hypomania—that was to characterize his life, and eventually lead him to incarceration in a mental hospital for thirteen years. After a short time spent in an academic job, for which he was totally unsuitable, Pound left for Europe. He published his first book of poems, *A Lume Spento* (1908; reprinted as *A Lume Spento and Other Early Poems*, 1965—with a note by Pound addressed to William Carlos Williams referring to it as 'A collection of stale cream puffs . . . why a reprint? No lessons to be learned save the depth of ignorance . . .'). Soon afterwards he arrived in England and, with typical effrontery, 'took over' T. E. Hulme's (q.v.) and Henry Simpson's 'Poets' Club' of 1909 and turned it into the imagist group. In 1914 T. S. Eliot (q.v.) called on him in London; his poetry immediately aroused Pound's enthusiasm. Before this he had met Yeats (q.v.), and the Irish poet was to acknowledge his influence.

Pound was active on the English literary scene until after the end of the First World War. He helped, encouraged and publicized the work of James Joyce (q.v.), Wyndham Lewis (q.v.) and many others, a few of whom are still almost unknown today. Pound has never bothered much about reputation, and has frequently treated his own simply as a means of helping other writers' work to become recognized. In this sense he has been the most generous poet of the century. He began writing his (still unfinished) Cantos in 1915, but had been planning them for some time before that. The first collection, *A Draft of XXX Cantos*, was published in Paris in 1930 (Pound's *Cantos* are now available as follows: *The Cantos of Ezra Pound*, 1957; *Thrones: 96–109 de los Cantares*, 1959; *Drafts and Fragments of Cantos CX–CXVII*, 1970). He lived in France and then in Italy until his arrest at the end of the Second World War.

In 1918 Pound met Major C. H. Douglas, who had devised an economic scheme called Social Credit, which, he claimed, could avert economic depressions. Pound very soon became taken up with these ideas; he was convinced that in monetary reform lay the key to the creation of a society in which perfect beauty and perfect justice would co-exist. Previously his views on art and society had been less unusual: the writer was to be valued by the degree of his clarity and precision (compare the programme of imagism); of society and social systems Pound was contemptuous: only the individual deserved respect.

Douglas' ideas have never been taken seriously by economists—not necessarily an indictment of them, but perhaps of their originator's sense of tact—but they have had some influence on minority politics in Canada and elsewhere. Douglas himself was not a fascist, and he did not see his theories as being implemented either in Mussolini's Italy or in Hitler's Germany. Pound, unhappily, despite his later confused denial that he had ever been 'for Fascism', was deluded into thinking that Italy's fascist government was leading the country in the cultural direction he found desirable. His anti-semitism, never personal, now began to flare up dangerously; it became increasingly distasteful as the Nazi attitude towards the Jews became clearer. Pound gradually came to see all wars and social misery as a conspiracy of 'top' Jews, based in usury. Markedly greater than his anguish at the unhappiness caused to ordinary people by wars and poverty, however, was his own frustrated rage at not getting his ideas accepted. An element of grandiosity entered his calculations—or projects, as they had better be called—even as his anti-semitic language became more abrasively insulting (and puerile); he thought seriously of gaining the ear of American government officials, and at the same time developed a violent dislike of President Roosevelt. He did have some doubts about fascism, and on occasions he even tried to be fair, in his own terms, about the Jews; but more attracted him in fascism than did not, and he was clearly ideologically committed to it by the late Thirties. His thoughts and utterances were a fantastic ragbag of theories both wild and sane, and indignations just and unjust. He seems to have had not the faintest idea what the war of 1939 was really about: he told the popular novelist and Nobel prizewinner Pearl Buck that it was 'mainly for moneylending and three or four metal monopolies'. When America entered the war Pound seems to have made an effort to leave Italy, but finally to have been prevented from doing so. It is likely that he found it hard to make decisions.

It is clear that Pound's mind began to cloud, seriously, from the beginning of the Thirties—although a tendency to retreat into a position from which reality was inaccessible had been apparent since early youth. In 1933 he gained an audience with Mussolini, the only one he was ever to have, and came away with the delusion—amazing in anyone of his intelligence—that the dictator really cared for poetry and beauty, and was working passionately for a just society. Pound even thought, from a polite remark, that Mussolini had read and understood the *Cantos*.

It is evident that throughout the war years Pound was in a state of considerable distress. He had been taking small sums of money—which he needed—for broadcasts from Rome radio since before the American declaration of war. He continued to do so after it. The broadcasts were rambling, ill-delivered, dense and perhaps technically treasonable. They had no adverse effect on anyone on the Allied side: since they were almost always on the subject of economics or literature, very few could have understood them. His wife could not follow them for the same reason that some of his readers cannot follow his poems: because of the abrupt jumps from one subject to another. These radio talks were clearly the work of a man at the verge of, or perhaps at times immersed in, insanity.

At the end of the war Pound was eventually arrested and sent to the Disciplinary Training Camp at Pisa. Here he suffered exceedingly, at one point collapsing into a state of 'violent and hysterical terror'. But he recovered sufficiently to write the continuation of his *Cantos*, called *The Pisan Cantos*, and published as such (1948). Brought back to America to face treason charges in 1945, he was correctly judged to be unfit to plead, and was confined to St. Elizabeth's Hospital in Washington. His state at this time was worse than it had ever been: symptoms included scattered wits, inability to concentrate, and an insistence that his new versions of Confucius were the only rational foundation upon which to build a new world. He maintained throughout that he had not committed treason; it was plain that the matter had worried his conscience at all times.

Released (after too long) in 1958, Pound went back to Italy, where he died.

He suffered from periodic depressions, and was never wholly coherent. He said on several occasions that he had 'botched' his life work, and made 'errors'; but he continued to publish fragments of poetry. The *Cantos* remained unfinished.

Pound has of course aroused great controversy. This reached its height when he had not long been in St. Elizabeth's, and was awarded the Bollingen Prize for *The Pisan Cantos*. Since many of his disciples then appeared to share his political views, it was natural that his detractors, however unfairly, should identify his poetry with those views—with, in fact, a virulent brand of anti-semitic fascism. One of these erstwhile disciples, Pound's best biographer (*The Life of Ezra Pound*, 1970), Noel Stock, has put all this into a proper perspective. 'I will not dwell on the rubbish which we, his correspondents, fed to him [in St. Elizabeth's], or the rubbish which he in turn fed to us . . . a good number of us . . . helped to confirm him in the belief that he alone possessed a coherent view of the truth. . . .'

The fact is that Pound's political views, such as he has expressed them, would not do credit to a sixth-former. They were partly inherited from the American populism of the Nineties of Pound's childhood, a movement that originated in poverty and was quickly dissipated by a return to prosperity. Like all populism, Pound's is characterized by a practicality (he had been a good handyman all his life), a love of folk poetry, a genuine love of and feeling for the very poor and a cluster of negative attitudes: anti-capitalistic, anti-legal, anti-semitic and (tragically and confusedly in this case) anti-intellectual. Certainly the brilliance of some of Pound's insights has been vitiated by his evident insensitivity to human suffering (e.g. the suffering going on around him in Italy during the war) and his increasing tendency towards incoherence. Fortunately this is only half the story.

Pound's first book to attract wide attention, *Personae* (1909) was attacked both for being incomprehensibly 'modern' and for being absurdly archaic. Much of the modernism was actually Browning put into a distinctly new rhythm. Here Pound writes of a down-at-heel old scholar (these lines, from 'Famam Librosque Cano', come originally from *A Lume Spento*);

> Such an one picking a ragged
> Backless copy from the stall,
> Too cheap for cataloguing,
> Loquitur,
>
> 'Ah—eh! the strange rare name . . .
> Ah—eh. He must be rare if even *I* have not . . .'
> And lost mid-page
> Such age
> As his pardons the habit,
> He analyzes form and thought to see
> How I 'scaped immortality.

But where Pound was already most original was in his method. He adapted from the Provençal, mixed archaism with modern slang, resurrected (to adapt his own words from his *Credo*) forgotten modes because he found 'some leaven' in them, and because he saw in them an element that was lacking in the poetry of his own time 'which might unite' it 'again to its sustenance, life'.

In the succeeding years Pound produced more books of short poems, and a brilliant adaptation (complete with presumably deliberate howlers, such as a rendering of the Latin 'vates' as 'votes') of the poems of Sextus Propertius called *Homage to Sextus Propertius* (1934; written 1917–18). *Hugh Selwyn Mauberley* (1920), a group of poems originally prompted by the correct conviction that the free verse movement had 'gone too far', was written just afterwards. For those critics who see the *Cantos* as a failure not substantially relieved by excellent or beautiful passages, these two works represent the height of Pound's achievement. Free verse has probably never been handled more firmly or effectively in English than in *Homage to Sextus Propertius*, which, like *Hugh Selwyn Mauberley*, has a coherence that Pound never found again. 'Mr Nixon' is as acid and yet serenely good-mannered a satire against literary opportunism, commercialism and lack of integrity as the twentieth century has seen; and the famous 'Envoi (1919)' that Pound offers as his own poetic credo is as beautiful as anything he has ever written:

> *Go, dumb-born book,*
> *Tell her that sang me once that song of Lawes:*
> *Hadst thou but song*
> *As thou hast subjects known,*
> *Then were there cause in thee that should condone*
> *Even my faults that heavy upon me lie,*
> *And build her glories their longevity.*
>
> *Tell her that sheds*
> *Such treasure in the air,*
> *Recking naught else but that her graces give*
> *Life to the moment,*
> *I would bid them live*
> *As roses might, in magic amber laid,*
> *Red overwrought with orange and all made*
> *One substance and one colour*
> *Braving time.*
>
> *Tell her that goes*
> *With song upon her lips*
> *But sings not out the song, nor knows*
> *The maker of it, some other mouth,*
> *May be as fair as hers,*
> *Might, in new ages, gain her worshippers,*

When our two dusts with Waller's shall be laid,
Siftings on siftings in oblivion,
Till change hath broken down
All things save beauty alone.

And yet even in this poem, as good as anything ever written by Pound, we may see his limitations. 'Beauty' is still sensed as itself something of a generalization. There is nothing in Pound's poetry about human behaviour as such: no psychological hint as to what beauty itself might consist of, either behaviouristically or in understandable, human terms. The beauty in Pound's verse is nearly always elusive in its nature.

Pound had previously defined the image as 'an intellectual and emotional complex in an instant of time. . . . It is the presentation of such an image which gives that sudden sense of liberation; that sense of freedom from time and space limits; that sense of sudden growth, which we experience in . . . the greatest works of art'. His own participation in the imagist movement had really only been a dramatization of his own developing programme; and yet, like Reznikoff (q.v.), but on an infinitely grander scale, he was to remain an 'imagist' all his life.

Pound first learned about Japanese poetry from F. S. Flint (q.v.), but he soon took over as the pioneer in the study of it. In fact, although he did not understand the Japanese language, he understood some of the more important qualities of Japanese poetry long before they were fully explained to Western readers. It is in this understanding, and the use he made of it, that his greatest achievement lies. His famous poem 'In a Station of the Metro',

> The apparition of these faces in a crowd;
> Petals on a wet, black bough

perfectly illustrates his discovery: a straightforward non-metaphorical statement is followed by a striking image, in the manner of the Japanese *haiku* (q.v.). In this 'super-pository' method one idea 'is set on top of another'. The beauty and the meaning of the poem are to be discovered in the imaginative leap necessary from the statement to the metaphor for it. In a slightly longer poem, 'Coitus', Pound employs essentially the same method to describe a well-known experience:

> The gilded phaloi of the crocuses
>   are thrusting at the spring air.
> Here is there naught of dead gods
> But a procession of festival,
> A procession, O Giulio Romano,
> Fit for your spirit to dwell in.
> Dione, your nights are upon us.
>
> The dew is upon the leaf.
> The night about us is restless.

Pound's inspiration here was Japanese—specifically the Japanese *haiku*. Now this is essentially a miniature art—one that the modern Japanese poets have themselves found largely inadequate. Pound's genius perceived its possibilities for English verse, but nevertheless could not turn miniaturism into epic—which is, however, exactly what he tried to do in the *Cantos*. In the epic he hoped that his own unifying sensibility would successfully gather together all the fragmentarily presented poetries and cultures. Instead, the poem became a game for adepts, as Noel Stock has demonstrated (*Reading the Cantos*, 1967). As Stock says, they 'do not constitute a poem, but a disjointed series of short poems, passages, lines and fragments, often of exceptional beauty or interest, but uninformed, poetically or otherwise, by larger purpose'. They are, he insists, poetry—not poems. Although there are books, notably one by Donald Davie (*Ezra Pound: Poet as Sculptor*, 1964), which claim that the *Cantos* do possess a unifying purpose, these are not convincing, they have not on the whole convinced readers, and it seems unlikely that the view they put forward will prevail. It is very difficult indeed to credit the epic poet Pound with a 'unifying sensibility'—as difficult as it is to credit the man with one; and there is, after all, his own recent view of the poem, which cannot altogether be attributed to senile depression: 'I picked out this and that thing that interested me, and then jumbled them into a bag. But that's not the way to make a *work of art*.' As Santayana (q.v.) put it to Pound in a letter in 1940: '. . . Your tendency to jump is so irresistible that the bond between the particulars jumped to is not always apparent'; and he himself, in Canto CXVI, has confessed: 'I cannot make it cohere'. It is both ironic and significant that Pound's greatest triumphs and failures should consist of 'leaps'. In the *Cantos* the leaps too often become impenetrable ellipses.

In Pound mental instability has certainly vitiated poetic achievement. His imagery of beauty and its permanence, and of light, is often strangely beautiful; but even his achievement here may ultimately be seen to have been vitiated by a lack of emotional solidity, an absence of wisdom, reflecting an inability to learn through experience. Probably his reputation has been unduly inflated, and he has certainly attracted a large number of inferior cranks.

But Pound stood notably, if never very diplomatically or tactfully, for poetic values against commercial ones; he was generous and perceptive; and he searched, as well as his wrecked mind would allow him, for the truth. Posterity may dub him a minor poet: minor because even in his best poetry he lacks conviction; but he will be called a vital critic (sometimes in his poetry), and the failure of his mind will always be regarded as tragic.

The novelist and poet H. D. (ps. HILDA DOOLITTLE, 1886–1961), born in Bethlehem, Pennsylvania, went to Europe in 1911, was for a time married to the English writer Richard Aldington (q.v.) and was associated with the imagists in England; but she remained essentially an American poet in her attitudes and her use of the short line. Like Williams, she was much influenced by the hard precision of Greek poetry. Read by almost every poet of the century and recognized by them as an exquisite minor poet, H. D. has been extraordinarily neglected by critics. Her translation of Euripides' *Ion* (1937) is probably the best translation from Greek drama of the century—only MacNeice's *Agamemnon* can rival it—if faithfulness to the text be taken into consideration. H. D.'s gift, slight but tempered, survived: alone of those imagists who did not merely travel through the movement, she continued to write well. Her earlier poems subscribed exactly to the imagist programme; but she differed from the other imagists, such as her husband Richard Aldington, in that the manner was natural to her. She did not come to imagism; imagism came to her. Her style rigidly excludes sentimentalities, and concentrates on producing objects (poems) that do not pretend to evoke, but instead present themselves as themselves. Her poems have a dateless quality, which calls attention not only to their strength but also to her general weakness: commonplace emotion may be subsumed in 'classical' style, as such lines as

> your insight
> has driven deeper
> than the lordliest tome
> of Attic thought
> or Cyrenian logic

hint. Except at their very best, there is in her poems always an element of pastiche that raises suspicion. This suspicion is partly confirmed by the trilogy she wrote during the Second World War: *The Walls Do Not Fall* (1944), *Tribute to the Angels* (1945) and *Flowering of the Rod* (1946), which dealt with themes of war. In style and taste this is an impressive work; but the symbolism and thought behind it are almost tawdry. When H. D.'s poetry is not at its best the manner conceals this; when she is at her best the manner itself is, becomes, the poem. She wrote a number of novels, including an interesting *roman à clef*, *Bid Me To Live* (1960), about London in 1917. This contains a valuable portrait of D. H. Lawrence (q.v.).

MARIANNE MOORE (1887–1972), who was born at St. Louis, Missouri, has been praised and loved by poets of every persuasion. It was H. D. and the English novelist Bryher who, unknown to the author, published her first book, *Poems* (1921), which collected twenty-four poems that had appeared in periodicals. She was editor of the magazine *The Dial* from 1925 until its demise in 1929. Hers is a reputation that has never suffered vicissitudes.

Marianne Moore's *Complete Poems* were issued in 1968, but one also needs her *Collected Poems* (1961): her alterations are revealing. She is unique in that she alone has made a 'modern' (by means of procedures) poetry out of an experience that deliberately excludes that rawness which we associate with the modern. She cut, in her eighty-first year, the twenty-odd lines of her famous poem 'Poetry' to just these four:

> I, too, dislike it.
> Reading it, however, with a perfect
> contempt for it, one discovers in
> it, after all, a place for the genuine.

The end of the original version, which includes the celebrated lines about 'imaginary gardens with real toads in them' (it is the real toads she eschews), runs:

> ... if you demand on the one hand
>   the raw material of poetry in
>   all its rawness and
>   that which is on the other hand
>   genuine, you are interested in poetry.

Miss Moore really does dislike it; but she is interested in it, and in a thorough-going, respectable manner that is not shared by many other poets.

All this is not a mask. Miss Moore's external personality is what she presents it as: she is a Presbyterian (like her father) who approves of Bible classes. Hart Crane (q.v.) called her 'the Rt. Rev. Miss Mountjoy', and protested 'What strange people these ——[the omission is by the editor of Crane's letters] are. Always in a flutter for fear bowels will be mentioned. . . .' This aspect of Marianne Moore must, I think, be faced up to. And Crane's verdict is the right one: 'She is so prosaic that the extremity of her detachment touches, or seems to touch, a kind of inspiration'. This is the shrewdest remark ever made about her poetry, which is indeed about rejecting almost everything in modern experience—but rejecting it without loss of grace or authenticity. Out of a sensibility applied to a world she rejects she has created a genuinely poetic style, a body of work that confers vitality and meaning upon a propriety that we might otherwise reject as either incredible (in a poet) or absurdly provincial.

Her most sustained and exact and, in its way, confessional poem is 'The Pangolin'. This has been taken as a description of an animal so precise and loving that its object becomes a paradigm of a certain kind of human virtue. But it is both more and less than this. For here she describes her own life-style. And in the gentleness of the poem there is an implied rejection of an ungentle world:

> to explain grace requires
>   a curious hand. If that which is at all
>   were not forever,
>   why would those who graced the spires
>   with animals . . .
>   have slaved to confuse
>   grace with a kindly manner, time in
>   which to pay a debt
>   the cure for sins . . .?

In Marianne Moore's poetry the disliked 'poetry', the peerless, imaginative thing that she sees she must reject, is relentlessly eschewed by a technique that makes enjambement a rule and not an exception, and takes as often as not an almost cynical, mechanically syllabic pattern as its norm—and yet the poetry returns, as a gift, in the form of subtle rhythms and light rhymes, as delicately as a butterfly alighting.

WALLACE STEVENS (1879–1955), born in Pennsylvania, was admired by Williams, but is on the whole eschewed by the 'native American' school; academic critics and poets, however, have taken him up. Stevens is not only modern in appearance—recondite, wanton in his imagery, holding back explicitness—but in substance as well. Thus two of his best-known lines are: 'The poem is the cry of its occasion/Part of the res itself and not about it'. He wasted much of his gift in meandering, ineffectual poetry ('The Man with the Blue Guitar') that is little more than an appropriate screen for the projections of ingenious critics; he needs rigorous selection; but at his second-best he is delightful, and at his rare best, superb. His first book, *Harmonium*, appeared in 1923 when he was nearly forty-four, and, unusually, he wrote the bulk of his poetry after he was fifty. He was at Harvard, then read law, and then joined the Hartford Accident and Indemnity Company in 1916; in 1934 he became its vice-president, a position which he held until his death. He was, then, a full-time business man for the whole of his life. This is often remarked upon. Perhaps the only relevant comment is that he is the only poet of the century, of comparable stature, thus to combine business with poetry; and that this is a formidable undertaking simply because the values of insurance and those of poetry do not appear to mix too easily.

Stevens' manner is polished, aesthetic, literary, exotic—at its worst whimsical and contrived—alogical and rhetorical. In terms of feeling his poetry is thin and deliberately reticent: that kind of experience is not its subject. Stevens is above all a civilized poet; his project is usually taken to be philosophical, but it can also be described as a search for a style, an answer to the question, 'How can an insurance man also be a poet?' 'What! Wally a poet', one of his illiterate colleagues exclaimed when told of it. The usual critical approach is to grant that there is what Professor Frank Kermode calls a 'poetry of abstraction', and to judge Stevens as a master of it. However, Stevens is at his best when he is being non-abstract—even if about the pains and difficulties of trying to maintain abstractness. The whimsical, recondite surface of the inferior poems is not always as masterly as it appears. As Stevens told his future wife when he was a very young man: 'Perhaps I do like to be sentimental now and then in a roundabout way. . . . I certainly do dislike expressing it right and left'. Thus 'The Man with the Blue Guitar' conceals not feeling but sentimentality beneath its artful veneer of vaguely symbolist preciosity; the complex aesthetic philosophy it contains may provide grist for such interesting neo-scholiasts as Professor Frank Kermode (a fine if contentious expositor of Stevens), but poetically this is neither here nor there. Too often Stevens was practising: a business man who, instead of questioning the moral sources of his affluence, played scales on an old chocolate bassoon (as he might have put it). Kermode says 'There is a poetry of the abstract; if you do not like it, even when it is firmly rooted in the particulars of the world, you will not like Stevens'. It is not quite as simple as that. One may dislike or not accept as valid the existence of 'a poetry of the abstract', but one may still like a little of Stevens. The trouble with 'The Man with the Blue Guitar' is that it is wholly cerebral: there is nothing to anchor it to any sort of emotional particular. 'Owl Clover', a longish poem rightly omitted from the *Collected Poems* (1954) but restored in its original version in *Opus Posthumous* (1957), shows him to least advantage: not because it maintains a poet's right to pursue his function despite politics, but because its view of Marxism, for all the sonorities, is as vulgar and insensitive as one might expect from an insurance man (no more than an 'it', in E. E. Cummings', q.v., words, 'that stinks excuse me'). But William York Tindall has reminded us that Stevens was a 'Taft Republican who thought Eisenhower a dangerous radical', and in a poet of his sensibilities what is 'fine and private . . . heroic . . . the romance of lost causes finds its happiest concentration here'. However, Stevens skated on thin ice; we have good reason to suspect his aestheticism—if we are among those who do not believe the possession of genius is an excuse for lack of sensibility. 'Owl Clover' is crass reactionary propaganda from a man who never visited Europe in his life, and knew nothing of it at first hand—as bad as crass communist propaganda or tractor doggerel, and perhaps worse because wrapped up in an aestheticism that looks so advanced. (Stevens once wrote in a letter: 'The Italians have as much right to take Ethiopia from the coons as the coons had to take it from the boa-constrictors'; he then nervously qualified this by saying his own sympathy was with the coons and the boa-constrictors—but finally stated that Mussolini was 'right, practically').

Still, that is enough said. If he kept off politics, especially the kind that threatened his good living and his picture collecting (he believed, and wrongly, that people who could afford to buy pictures were better judges of them than those who could only talk about them), he was, after all, subversive: his early poetry, with its new words and gaiety, deliberately sought to annoy. 'The Emperor of Ice Cream' (equally, 'The Emperor of "I Scream" ') analyzes its material into its Freudian components in spite of himself.

Stevens' first inspiration may well have been Moody (q.v.); at all events, those poems (his juvenilia), he said, 'gave him the creeps'. The sources for his mature manner were mostly French, and perhaps his greatest debt was to Léon-Paul Fargue (q.v.), whom he sometimes resembles quite closely. His American forebears were inferior poets: DONALD EVANS (1884–1921), a now forgotten Greenwich Village decadent who killed himself, and ALFRED KREYMBORG (1883–1969), a lesser imagist and a friend of Stevens', from whom he may have gathered some more general hints. Lacking (or eschewing) a central core of experience that compelled poems from him, Stevens' chief theme is the supremacy of the creative imagination. Like Robbe-Grillet (q.v.), Stevens sees order, form, as coming only from the creators of imaginary worlds. For all his sophistication he is, as Marius Bewley has observed, a romantic, who believes in the transmuting powers of the imagination. This faith is most succinctly defined in the sequence called 'Notes Towards a Supreme Fiction', which some would put amongst his best poems. However, 'Sunday Morning' and the subtly autobiographical 'Le Monocle de Mon Oncle', both early poems, have the feeling this often verbally beautiful, but over-cerebral sequence lacks. In both Stevens' manner functions as vitality, but is subdued by personal concerns rather than philosophizings. Nothing touches the note of such lines as 'but until now I never knew/That fluttering things have so distinct a shade' or 'We live in an old chaos of the sun' until the serene final poems, when the threat of death edged safe business and prime living out of the foreground:

> Ariel was glad he had written his poems.
> They were of a remembered time
> Or of something seen that he liked.

It has been claimed that Stevens is the most important poet of the first half of the century with the 'possible' exceptions of Eliot, Pound and Frost: 'There are no other serious competitors'. This, it seems, is to put philosophy above poetry. Williams' poetry is surely much more 'important'; and Ransom's (q.v.) achievement in individual poems is as great or greater. But to exegetic critics, it is true, Stevens offers most of all; ironically, it is his best work, mostly in *Harmonium*, that most strongly resists such attentions.

E. E. CUMMINGS (1894–1962), born in Cambridge, Massachusetts, is still regarded by some as a 'modern' poet. But he was a quirky traditionalist in all respects save two: he showed that typography—visual variations—could be useful; and his ear for the vernacular was sometimes, though not always, good. There are two Cummings: a versifier who disguises his sentimentalities and sometimes irregular but always conventional metrics by typographical tricks; and a magnificently aggressive comic and satirical poet who—alas—never quite grew up. Cummings had wanted to be a painter, and he did in fact execute strangely atrocious paintings all his life (his sense of colour can only be described as nauseous). Instead of maturing he surrendered to—as his photographs and self-portrait show—self-love and arrogance: his language lost its edge, and he descended increasingly into the cliché from which his love poetry had never been wholly free. No amount of critical interpretation can disguise the tawdry third-rateness of the language in the following poem (drawn from Cummings' later work):

> now all the fingers of this tree(darling)have
> hands,and all the hands have people;and
> more each particular person is(my love)
> alive than every world can understand
>
> and now you are and i am now and we're
> a mystery which will never happen again,
> a miracle which has never happened before—
> and shining this our now must come to then
>
> our then shall be some darkness during which
> fingers are without hands;and i have no
> you:and all trees are(any more than each
> leafless)its silent in forevering snow
>
> —but never fear(my own,my beautiful
> my blossoming)for also then's until

This is the work of a man who has gone soft at the centre and likes himself too much to be able to see it. And yet he had once been very good indeed; more, I think, than the 'slight and charming' which has been allowed to him by his detractors. He had been able to criticize false patriotism and outworn literary language to admirable effect in such poems as 'come, gaze with me upon this dome'. Cummings has always been enormous fun, and if one sounds a dissenting note it is only because during his lifetime he had too much attention as a serious lyrical poet. He certainly deserves respect for his part in dismantling the genteel tradition. But diligent search fails to produce a single completely effective love poem: every one is marred by tentativeness or portentousness if not by that unquestioning sentimentality that is so odd in so fierce a satirist. The early poems are full of promise, but it was a promise that did not fully materialize. Cummings' originally childlike whimsicality and tweeness ('the little/lame balloon man'; 'hist whist/little ghostthings'—and so on) need not have been offensive; but he came to indulge it and, eventually, to confuse it with lyricism. The early love poems contain hints of a manner that Cummings might have developed, but most of them only conceal, by their eccentricity, which is of course often typographical, Cummings' failure to find a language. An exception is the fifth of the 'Songs' in *Tulips & Chimneys*: 'Doll's boy's asleep', in which a nursery rhyme insouciance is transformed into a note of genuine menace. But Cummings chose not to investigate his sexual emotions—he chose to avoid the crux of sexuality—and his best energies went into a satire that can be piercingly accurate, or merely hilarious—or funny but curiously diminishing, uncompassionate and perhaps insensitive. There are many poems like the one ending 'i try if you are a gentleman not to sense something un poco putrido/ when we contemplate her uneyes safely ensconced in thick glass', and they are certainly funny; but there is an absence, elsewhere in Cummings' work, of a compensating pity: perhaps he imagined that the lyrics filled this role. The fact is that for most of the time Cummings' fun is not quite good enough: not quite first class. The vernacular he reproduces has not always been listened to carefully enough—the poet has been too keen to impress. If he does not diminish he patronizes. It has, however, been salutary to have someone like Cummings to ridicule and generally slam our philistine society of politicians and business men—and the pseudo-culture that nurses and sustains it. And then there are the splendid tough-guy poems, and the descriptions of low life. Cummings is seldom as empathic as Williams in his descriptions ('It really must/be Nice, never to', XIII from *Is 5*, is one of the fine exceptions), since he is concentrating on a kind of audience that Williams has rejected, but his immense gaiety and humour ('what's become of maeterlinck/now that april's here?') give him a unique importance. The oft-repeated judgement that he is 'the Catullus of the modern movement' is quite wrong; he is cheerfully and most enjoyably obscene (as in his car poem: 'she being Brand/-new; and you/know consequently a/little stiff I was/careful of her . . . just as we turned the corner of Divinity/ avenue i touched the accelerator and give/her the juice, good . . .'), as Catullus is, but the Latin poet could never have indulged in Cummings' sentimentalities.

We are grateful to Cummings; but the reservations have to be made. It is astonishing how many readers and critics take Cummings' late nineteenth-century, neo-romantic love poetry to be modern because of its careful but logical surface pyrotechnics. What has not yet been fully grasped is that Cummings' experiments are extensions of traditionalism, not reachings-forward into the unknown.

Cummings went to France in the First World War as a volunteer ambulance driver; as a result of his violation of the French censorship laws in a letter home, he was arrested and spent some time in a French prison camp. *The Enormous Room* (1922) was the result, a classic of its kind—in which, incidentally, Cummings shows his capacity to master the vernacular. *Eimi* (1933), an account of a visit to Russia, is less good, but contains some memorable passages; in it, too, we see Cummings' romanticism at its strongest and least self-indulgent. *Complete Poems* (1968) supersedes previous collections.

A rather more important, but less striking and less heeded writer is CONRAD AIKEN (1889), born in Savannah, Georgia. Aiken is a distinguished novelist, critic and short-story writer as well as a poet. It is often said of him that he has not realized his enormous gifts. But this is to ignore too much: *Senlin* (1918), the *Preludes for Memnon* (1931)—his best poems, still undervalued—the novel *Great Circle* (1933), a number of short stories, the autobiographical *Ushant* (1953). The four main influences on Aiken have been: his physician father's killing of his mother and subsequent suicide (in 1900), music, Freud, and nineteenth-century romantic poetry (from Poe to Swinburne). He combines a luxuriant style with a psychological subtlety that has not been fully appreciated. Famous for such finely simple poetry as 'Discordants' (from *Turns and Movies*, 1916),

> Music I heard with you was more than music,
> And bread I broke with you was more than bread;
> Now that I am without you, all is desolate;
> All that was once so beautiful is dead

Aiken can sustain such feeling in more complex poetry, as in the tragic Rilkean twenty-ninth prelude which begins:

> What shall we do—what shall we think—what shall we say—?
> Why, as the crocus does, on a March morning,
> With just such shape and brightness; such fragility;
> Such white and gold, and out of just such earth.
> Or as the cloud does on the northeast wind—
> Fluent and formless; or as the tree that withers.

It takes much to maintain such pantheistic lyricism against the harsh sense of being human.

Aiken's weakness is his romantic imitativeness; but at his best he has—as in the lines above—been able to find his own voice. He has been neglected because he has chosen to express himself, for the most part, in long poems or sequences, and these have simply not been explored. They should be. More than any other poet, he has wanted to allow the subconscious mind to speak for itself; but—paradoxically—he has organized the surface of his poetry most elaborately to that effect. This is to say that he has modified his flow only by such devices as have suggested themselves at the moment of composition; but the devices themselves are often complicated.

His short stories often deal poignantly with psychotic situations; more than any others, they are the stories of a poet. *Ushant* treats of the men he has known: it was he who showed Eliot's poems to Pound; he who helped to orient Malcolm Lowry (q.v.) imaginatively, truthfully and yet with a tact that he may have learned during his long stay, between wars, in England. Of his novels, *Great Circle* (1933), a treatment of the catastrophe of his childhood, seems certain to be revived and admired. An 'essential Aiken', which would be a very fat volume, would contain some of this century's best writing. His *Collected Poems* appeared in 1953.

By contrast, ROBINSON JEFFERS (1887–1962) seems unlikely to survive, perhaps because his extreme pessimism is uncompensated for by any linguistic energy. He was born in Pittsburgh, Pennsylvania; from 1924 he lived in a stone house and tower—in Carmel, California—which he built himself. His philosophy is not new, but is not in itself uninteresting: man's intellectual capacities are a terrible delusion and they disgrace him and lead him into trouble. Stone, the sea: these endure. Animals: these have dignity and no aspiration. But nothing whatever happens in Jeffers' language, which is cliché-ridden and more often than not suggests that he was by no means convinced of his own beliefs, which were perhaps formulated as a response to his father's theological certainties. He had some narrative gift, of an old-fashioned kind; but his poems and plays hardly bear re-reading. His *Collected Poems* was published in 1948.

LOUISE BOGAN (1897–1970), whose *Collected Poems* (1954) shared the Bollingen Prize with Leonie Adams (q.v.), was best known for her poetry reviews in *The New Yorker*. She was skilful and precise and did enough to win gallant accolades such as 'the most distinguished woman poet of our time' (Allen Tate); but she lacked attack, and nothing she wrote is memorable.

LÉONIE ADAMS (1899), born in Brooklyn, is a different matter. Not too well known in her own country, she remains unpublished and unknown in Great Britain. Yet she is a most distinguished and original poet. She has been called romantic, but wrongly: rather, she has preserved the metaphysical tradition in a romantic diction. Of a gull alighting without a feather being stirred she says,

So in an air less rare than longing might
The dreams of flying lift a marble bird.

Both these poets are vastly superior to EDNA ST. VINCENT MILLAY (1892–1950), who survives in Edward Wilson's poignant memoir of her as a person but hardly at all as a poet. Once very widely read, her proper place (as has been pointed out) is beside Rupert Brooke. A few of her lines have descriptive precision, but she left no single satisfactory poem. Her capacities are well illustrated by her lines: 'God! we could keep this planet warm/By friction, if the sun should fail'.

III

The late nineteenth century in America was a time of highly effective, bewitching actors (Robert Mantell, William Gillette, Richard Mansfield, John Drew, Jr.), but of mediocre drama. Ibsen made a late impact, and the plays through which the Americans were introduced to realism now seem melodramatic as well as sentimental. The energetic actor-manager and dramatist Steele MacKaye (1842–94) developed stage machinery and lighting, and trained actors. He was, if mostly in what he aspired to, an important influence on the future American stage. But not as a playwright: his own plays were pioneer in subject (*Hazel Kirke*, 1880, is the most famous) but weak in structure and dialogue. Much of the work of the real pioneer in playwriting, BRONSON HOWARD (1842–1908) does not now seem an improvement; but, although his primary purpose was always to entertain, he was one of the first to treat his material thoughtfully—and he did develop. He was also the first American to make his living by writing for the stage. The loose ends of *Young Mrs. Winthrop* (1899), first produced in 1882, are sentimentally tied up in the last act; but its situation is realistic. One who did not hinder—though he hardly helped—the emergence of a realistic theatre was DAVID BELASCO (1859–1931), who also wrote plays—Puccini's opera is based on his *Girl of the Golden West* (1905). AUGUSTUS THOMAS (1857–1934) was in the main simply a successful playwright, but he did have the serious purpose of showing the United States as it was, and he did help—with, for example, *As a Man Thinks* (1911), on faith healing—to clear the way for the 'problem play'. Neither CLYDE FITCH (1865–1909) nor JAMES A. HERNE (1839–1901) wrote what we should call a good play. But both contributed in a small way to a specifically American theatre. The former's best plays were his study of a pathologically jealous woman, *The Girl with the Green Eyes*, and his last, *The City* (1909), which is one of the early stage attacks on political corruption. James A. Herne's *Margaret Fleming* (1890), about adultery, is superior. It seems maudlin and artificial to us now, but its theme deeply shocked the audiences—for the adultery is forgiven. It was praised by Howells and Garland (qq.v.). It is unfortunate that all these men worked to create the star system as well as an American theatre, since the star system is in many ways one of the banes of the modern American (and British) theatre; but they had little alternative if they wanted to eat. However, by 1896, with the formation of the first Theatrical Syndicate, the days of the actor-managers were effectually at an end. Philistinism and commerce moved into the theatre: it was hardly to be wondered at that business men, seeing a potential source of profit, should move in. In the first two decades of the century philistinism was countered by the formation of groups who, in one way or another, managed to make themselves independent. Winthrop Ames (1871–1937) inherited a fortune from his father, who was a railway magnate, and made three gallant efforts to found true repertory in New York; later he built two theatres. More important was the equally non-commercial Theatre Guild (1919), which began as the Washington Square Players in 1914. And most important of all was the Provincetown Players. This was founded in 1915 by the novelist and playwright SUSAN GLASPELL (1882–1948), whose plays were competent although not inspired, and her husband George Cram Cook. Their experimentalism was important for giving Eugene O'Neill (q.v.), America's only great dramatist, the chances he needed to develop without commercial restrictions. As vital an influence on American theatre was George Pierce Baker (1866–1935), a Harvard professor who in 1905 set up the '47 Workshop', a course in playwrighting that was taken by, among others, Winthrop Ames, O'Neill, Philip Barry, John Dos Passos, S. N. Behrman, Sidney Howard, Thomas Wolfe (qq.v.). Baker went to Yale in 1925, where he continued until his death. Wolfe's Professor Hatcher, in *Of Time and the River*, is a portrait of him.

The verse plays of William Vaughn Moody (q.v.) have already been mentioned; he was an intelligent man and an able craftsman, but he did not possess enough originality to achieve a real breakthrough. The best of all his works are *The Great Divide* (1909), a revision of an earlier play, about a girl who marries a man who has bought her against her will, and *The Faith Healer* (1909), about a genuine faith healer whose gift is destroyed by the scepticism of those around him. It was in this latter play that Moody came nearest to a truly modern style; but he was too inhibited to try for the rhythms of ordinary speech, and this failure seriously vitiates his achievement. EDWARD SHELDON (1886–1946) had similar difficulties with language, but had had the benefit of attending George Pierce Baker's classes. He was in fact its first distinguished graduate playwright, and his *Salvation Nell* (1908) was actually produced by the group. *The Nigger* (1909) and *The Boss* (1911) were both profoundly shocking in their day, the first because a white girl finally decided to marry the governor of a Southern state who discovers that he has Negro blood. Sheldon was blind and paralysed for the last fifteen years of his life, but continued until the end to act as consultant to actors, actresses and all connected with the theatre. His worst play, *Romance* (1913), a piece of skilfully executed midcult trash, was easily his most popular. It was Sheldon's skill as an entertainer— and, perhaps, the weakness induced by his progressive disease—that prevented his work achieving real seriousness.

Steele MacKaye's (q.v.) son Percy MacKaye (q.v.) wrote an effective verse drama called *The Scarecrow* (1908), from Hawthorne's tale 'Feathertop'; but although this was the best thing he ever did, it solved no problems for the theatre.

Towering above these, and over all his successors, is the figure of EUGENE O'NEILL (1888–1953), the New York born son of the well-known romantic actor James O'Neill, who was most celebrated in the part of the Count of Monte Cristo. O'Neill's mother was a drug addict and his brother an alcoholic. O'Neill himself suffered from ill-health for most of his life, and was, besides, a tortured soul—so much so that one of his biographers called his book *The Curse of the Misbegotten* (after O'Neill's title *A Moon for the Misbegotten*), and hardly descended into melodrama. O'Neill wrote successful plays in two styles, the realistic and the expressionist (q.v.); he also might be said to have pursued two careers in the theatre, since he was silent for the twelve years between 1934 and 1946. In 1936 he was awarded the Nobel Prize.

The theatre was in O'Neill's blood; but before he came to it he tried Princeton (a year), poetry, mining, marriage (secret and dissolved), the sea (he voyaged to South America, South Africa, several times to England), newspaper reporting, sickness, tuberculosis; and then, after writing some short plays, he joined Baker's course. In 1915 he went to Provincetown, and the Provincetown Players' performance of his one-act *Bound East for Cardiff*—on a makeshift stage in a fishermen's shack at the end of a pier, while fog seeped through the wooden walls—initiated the true birth of the American theatre. It was also the début of a playwright whom no other of his century would outdo. Baker, and the men and women of the Provincetown Players—Robert Edmond Jones, the stage designer, is important among them—had heard of what was going on in Europe: of Antoine (q.v.) in France, Reinhardt (q.v.) in Germany, Strindberg (q.v.) in Sweden, Stanislavski (q.v.) in Russia. . . . The American theatre had come of age, and its chief playwright had the required genius and nerve.

O'Neill had passion, gloom and an absolutely uncompromising realism; at the end, anguished, ill and personally unhappy though he was, he achieved a mood of something like reconciliation. The key to his achievement was stated by himself in a letter he wrote about his play *Mourning Becomes Electra*:

> It needed great language . . . I haven't got that. And, by way of self-consolation, I don't think, from the evidence of all that is being written today, that great language is possible for anyone living in the discordant, broken, faithless rhythm of our time. The best one can do is to be pathetically eloquent by one's moving, dramatic inarticulations.

O'Neill was right. No nineteenth- or twentieth-century dramatist has come near to what he called 'great language' (perhaps he was thinking of Shakespeare, as we all do), but he alone authentically yearned after it. Brecht achieved great language—but in his lyrical poetry. Only O'Neill achieved a dramatic framework whose interstices surround poetic silences, and whose 'inarticulations' are truly 'pathetic'. He has been attacked for not producing 'heroes of stature'; but that is one of the reasons why he is truly modern.

Beyond the Horizon (1920), his first full-length play, is a naturalistic study of two brothers, each of whom makes the wrong choice in life, and is defeated through mistakes induced by sexual drive. *The Emperor Jones* (1921) is a piece of expressionism conceived before O'Neill knew anything of the European expressionists: a Caribbean Negro dictator flees from his victims to the sound of a relentlessly beating drum. *The Hairy Ape* (1922), another expressionistic play, deals with a brutish stoker (a sort of McTeague, q.v.), Yank, who yearns for a more human fulfilment; he ends by trying to retreat into what he thinks he is, by embracing a gorilla—which kills him.

Desire Under the Elms (1925), largely prompted by O'Neill's interest in Freudian psychology, is a return to realism, and is one of his most powerful plays.

The Great God Brown (1926) is probably too experimental for the stage, although it reads well. In it O'Neill used masks to try to define the difference between the bourgeois and the creative temperaments—but his chief character Dion Anthony (Dionysus-St. Anthony) is too symbolic, even though his anguished vacillation between pagan creativeness and Christian morality is at times most intensely and movingly conveyed. In *Marco Millions* (1928) O'Neill turned unsuccessfully to satire: this lampoon of materialism is both too obvious and tedious. There is no tension. *Dynamo* (1929) is O'Neill's worst and most theory-ridden play. Aware that he was troubled by the loss of the Catholic faith of his childhood he tried an experiment in which he did not really believe, melodramatically showing a young man's failure to substitute faith in a dynamo for the Calvinistic faith of his childhood. *Days without End* (1934) has two actors playing the same (divided) man: a sceptic and a believer. Nothing demonstrates more clearly O'Neill's failure to rediscover Catholicism, although at the time it was widely believed that he had returned to it.

Between these two disastrous attempts, O'Neill had written the finest of all the plays of his earlier period: the trilogy, *Mourning Becomes Electra*, based on Aeschylus' Orestean trilogy. O'Neill took a New England family in the aftermath of the Civil War and fairly carefully paralleled the Greek story: the returning General Ezra Mannon is killed by his wife Christine, whose lover Adam Brant is then killed by their son Orin, egged on by their daughter, Lavinia. Christine kills herself, Orin goes mad and commits suicide, whereupon Lavinia shuts herself up for ever with an unrelievable guilty conscience in the family mansion. This was presented in relentlessly Freudian terms, which led many critics to describe it as a case-study rather than a tragedy. O'Neill has also been attacked for his prosaic language at moments of enormous stress. But may we not, in retrospect—having had the opportunity to study the 'great language' of the wretched Christopher Fry or even that of Tennessee Williams (qq.v.)—be grateful for this alleged 'flatness'? O'Neill knew he could not attain the great language he yearned for. And so, unlike so many lesser playwrights, he did not attempt it. One suspects that his critics would too easily forgive a heady, contrived rhetoric of the kind so often produced by Tennessee Williams— a pseudo-poetry; dramatic occasions demand 'high' language. I think O'Neill was right, and that the plays are better without such language.

By 1934 O'Neill had made two more marriages, the latter of which was not unsuccessful. He went into a state of semi-permanent depression from about the mid-Thirties until the end of the war. He destroyed much that he wrote in this period, but by 1946 he felt able to release *The Iceman Cometh* (1946), which he had written in 1939. O'Neill's experiments were necessary to him, but he always returned to the realistic mode. *The Iceman Cometh*, set in a disreputable dive for down-and-outs and outcasts, is entirely realistic; no gimmicks are required. The Iceman of the title is death, which is the only release from the illusions that torment mankind. The salesman Hickey tells all the drinkers in Harry Hope's bar that their only chance of happiness is to renounce hope. Previously happy in their absurd and drunken way, they now disbelieve Hickey and go out to prove him wrong. But each returns: broken. Then Hickey turns out to have killed his wife. When he gives himself up to the police, all but one of them return to their old contentment. Like Dreiser (q.v.), though in an utterly different and more poetic manner, O'Neill here richly conveys the actual grain of life. It does not much matter if you agree with his philosophy or not. Its torpor is counteracted by the lyricism of the outcasts' hope—and of their despair.

O'Neill wrote a number of other plays, none of which was performed in his lifetime. *A Moon for the Misbegotten* (1952) was withdrawn while on trial. *More Stately Mansions* (1964), a study of the breakdown of a poetic soul into madness, has only been tried out in a cut, Swedish version. *A Touch of the Poet* (1957), the sole survivor from a projected eleven-play cycle called *A Tale of Possessors Self-Dispossessed*, contains an unforgettable portrait of a man who seems to attain stature through self-deceit and selfishness. In the one-act *Hughie* (1959) and *Long Day's Journey into Night* (1956) O'Neill rose to the heights of his achievement. In *Hughie* he perfectly captures a vernacular more difficult than that of his early sea dramas: the speech of seedy, boastful New York drifters of the Twenties. *Long Day's Journey into Night*, a semi-autobiographical family-drama, is his simplest play. Here O'Neill demonstrates his genius beyond doubt: there is no plot and no drama, the play is very long—and yet it holds the attention. Alan S. Downer has written wisely of it: 'It cannot be overemphasized that this is a play of reconciliation; the audience that has experienced *Long Day's Journey* cannot go out of the theatre without a greater capacity for tolerance and understanding. . . .'

Not one of O'Neill's contemporaries and successors can be compared to him: his plays are torn from him; theirs are, at best, made. American theatre, like the British, lacked vitality in the Thirties, and this lack was made even more manifest by the example of O'Neill, who could be criticized for all sorts of faults, but never for lack of vitality or attack.

The verse drama does not seem to be a viable form in our century (the German habit of writing in verse is hardly relevant here), despite valiant attempts; it has been as successful in America as almost anywhere.

ARCHIBALD MACLEISH (1892) wrote *Nobo-daddy* (1926), the labour play *Panic* (1935), and *J. B.* (1958), his most successful play, in which a contemporary Job acts out his story in a circus tent. He also wrote several effective verse plays for radio, including *Air Raid* (1938). MacLeish began as a poet, and his *The Hamlet of A. MacLeish* (1928), one of those long poems inspired by the success of *The Waste Land* (q.v.), was taken with seriousness. He shifted from the extreme subjectivity of this poem to advocacy of full political 'engagement'. He was Librarian of Congress 1939–44 and was influential in the Roosevelt administration. He ranks, David Ray has written, 'with Robinson Jeffers and Carl Sandburg in the penetration of public taste'. But not, one has to add, with Brecht. MacLeish has written sincere and unpretentious verse, and has been an admirable public man—one of the most admirable of the time, a genuinely well-intentioned link between poets and an establishment that cannot take them into account. The poetry of his plays, however, contributes nothing whatever to them. *J.B.* was apparently personally inspiring to a number of those who watched it; this is admirable. But the nature of the inspiration is nearer to that of a good sermon or exhortation than to, say, Sherwood Anderson's (q.v.) various autobiographical writings. These are true literature because they never exhort: the author lives entirely in his imagination. MacLeish appears to have no such imaginative, internal centre.

The same applies to MAXWELL ANDERSON (1888–1959), who wrote plays in verse (and, in 1925, one book of poetry) and yet who was not a poet. He tried for the 'great language' that O'Neill knew could not be got: he felt that there could be no 'great drama' without 'great poetry', and he did not claim that his own verse was well written. He may have been right about 'great drama'; the trouble was that he thought anyone could write poetry—if 'badly'—not realizing that it takes a poet. The career of Anderson, a worthy, gifted and sincere writer, and a fine craftsman of the theatre, affords an illustration of the harsh fact that art and commerce do not and cannot really mix. Art may or may not be successful in terms of the market; once a writer orients himself towards the market, however, he destroys his credibility. Anderson was a serious man who nevertheless conceived it as his duty to entertain middlebrow audiences. His and LAURENCE STALLINGS' (1894) *What Price Glory* (1924), on the American soldiery of the First World War, was a great hit. It was outspoken for its time, but its realism is in fact tawdry and its comedy as second-hand as it is second-rate. Anderson improved on this, but always conceived of a play not only as a dramatically viable entity but also as suitable fare for commercial audiences, whom he believed he could convert to his own humane point of view. And so he did; but this, like a response to Billy Graham, was temporary, because Anderson did not write from his imagination. Verse operates in his drama as an effective rhetoric. *Elizabeth the Queen* (1930), on Elizabeth and Essex, was the first modern blank verse play to pay at the box-office. *Both Your Houses* (1933) attacked political corruption. Probably Anderson's most famous play was *Winterset* (1935), his second attempt to deal with the tragic material of the Sacco-Vanzetti case. It was a success at the time, but a total failure in literary terms: as Edmund Wilson wrote, 'in the text I could not discover anything that seemed to me in the least authentic as emotion, idea or characterization'. He rated Anderson more highly as a prose playwright. Anderson's best is in fact the relaxed musical comedy *Knickerbocker Holiday* (1938), which had a score by Kurt Weill (q.v.). Anderson came off in his lifetime, and deserved to; it seems unlikely that any of his plays will survive.

SIDNEY HOWARD (1891–1939), a Californian who died prematurely in an accident with a tractor on his farm, was as skilful as Anderson, but more orthodox. He was a member of Baker's '47 Workshop'. His first play, in verse, flopped; he took the hint and did not return to this medium. Howard went on to do fine, conscientious work of all kinds—translations (Vildrac's *S.S. Tenacity*, q.v.), adaptations (*The Late Christopher Bean*, 1932), documentaries (*Yellow Jack*, with Paul de Kruif, 1934) as well as original plays. *They Knew What They Wanted* (1924), which was granted a second lease of life in 1957 as the musical *The Most Happy Fella*, was a lively comedy about a Californian grapegrower and his mail-order bride, and immediately established Howard. In the same year Howard collaborated with Edward Sheldon (q.v.) on *Bewitched*. *The Silver Cord* (1926) was an unsentimental and psychologically accurate portrayal of a possessive mother. *Paths of Glory* (1935), adapted from a novel by Humphrey Cobb, was an excellent anti-war play. Howard listened carefully to common speech, and reported it accurately. He is an example of the man who does the best he can—rather than compromise himself—with a limited imagination.

ROBERT SHERWOOD (1896–1955), a forthright radical who was gassed in the First World War and put much of his energy into anti-totalitarian activities, was perhaps as skilful, but more trivial. *The Petrified Forest* (1935), although its theme is ostensibly the disintegration of the artist in modern society, suffers from technical slickness and sentimentality. The 'continental' comedy *Reunion in Vienna* (1931) is not as intellectually ambitious, and is Sherwood's best play. A psychiatrist thinks that a love-affair his wife is conducting with Prince Maximilian Rudolph, whose mistress she has been, will cure her of an obsession; his complacency is shattered. Apart from this and *Tovarich* (1936), which he adapted, Sherwood is probably better regarded as an admirable journalist than as an imaginative writer. He wrote some of Roosevelt's speeches.

ELMER RICE (ps. ELMER REIZENSTEIN, 1892–1967), a worthy man of the theatre, may be described as an experimentalist of abundant gifts but no genius. Rice, like Sherwood, is a radical, and has on several occasions taken a stand against censorship and witch-hunting by the authorities. His first play, *On Trial* (1914), a thriller, used the movie technique of flashback. *The Adding Machine* (1923), depicts Mr. Zero, executed for the murder of his boss, dissatisfied in the Elysian Fields and returning to the earth to become a perfect slave of the machine age. This is wholly expressionistic in technique, and a fine satire, which Rice has not bettered. Unfortunately Rice has no capacity for psychological penetration or characterization—even of the workmanlike sort practised by Howard (q.v.)—and this has tended to impoverish his drama. His best plays after *The Adding Machine* are the realistic *Street Scene* (1929), *Dream Girl* (1945) and *Cue for Passion* (1958).

PHILIP BARRY (1896–1949), another of Baker's pupils, collaborated with Rice in *Cock Robin* (1928). Barry was another prolific, intelligent and workmanlike playwright. Many of his plays are comedies with a serious note; the others tend to be his best. *You and I* (1923) is a poignant study of a father who discovers his own frustrations when he tries to turn his son into an artist. *Hotel Universe* (1930) was perhaps unfortunate: this drama of an old man who helps people to find themselves was rather too well made and contrived, but some of the individual portraits—including a man who has lost his faith and a girl whose love is unrequited—are excellent. He realized his potential most fully in *Here Come the Clowns* (1938), an odd and disturbing play about the effects of a magician's hypnotic powers on a vaudeville troupe. Barry was also responsible for the smooth and entertaining *The Philadelphia Story* (1939).

s. n. behrman (1893), yet another of Baker's pupils, tried to combine comedy with social drama, and dealt, in *No Time for Comedy* (1939) with his own predicament. Once again, too much skill at entertainment vitiates seriousness. He adapted, with Joshua Logan, Pagnol's *Fanny* (q.v.) as a musical comedy in 1945.

george s. kaufman (1889–1961) and marc connelly (1890) began in collaboration, with several plays, the most successful of which was *Beggar on Horseback* (1924), an expressionist satire on the oppression of the artist (here, a composer) by bourgeois society. Kaufman went on to write several smooth farces, some with moss hart (1904–61), including the famous, and deftly written, portrait of Alexander Woollcott, *The Man Who Came to Dinner* (1939). Connelly's Negro play, *The Green Pastures*, has a little more weight; but this well-meant picture of the Negro conception of the Old Testament is at heart both folksy and patronizing rather than dignified and poetic.

The Thirties saw the rise of a more aggressive social theatre, whose white hope was clifford odets (1906–63). Odets was a protégé of the important Group Theatre, founded by Harold Clurman, Lee Strasberg and Cheryl Crawford in 1931. The actor and director Elia Kazan was early associated with this venture, which devoted itself to Stanislavsky's (q.v.) principles of group acting. (Kazan later, 1947, founded the influential Actors' Studio, which taught the Method, a technique in which the actor is exhorted to 'become' the part he is playing. The Method is less different from other methods of training actors than some have thought, since every actor should in one way or another 'become' the stage-person he is representing—provided he does not forget the audience.) Odets began with *Waiting for Lefty* (1935), an effective and bitter piece, without characterization, about a taxicab strike. *Awake and Sing* (1935), ecstatic, well made, at times funny, established him as the leading playwright of his generation. *Golden Boy* (1937) is so well done that its central character, a musician who turns under economic pressure to professional boxing, is made almost credible. By the time of *The Big Knife* (1948) Odets, while he retained all his skill, had become affected by the pressures involved in producing big, successful plays: this indictment of Hollywood seems to come right out of Hollywood itself.

sidney kingsley (1906) was another competent social dramatist, responsible for the originals of the movies *Dead End* and *Detective Story*. His first play, *Men in White* (1933) about a young doctor's indecisions, is among his best. *They Shall Not Die* (1934) by john wesley (1902) and *Stevedore* (1934) by paul peters (1908) were more strident: written with the leftist fervour of Odets, they lacked his passionateness and concern for character.

john howard lawson (1895) preceded all these left-wing or Marxist playwrights. Lawson began with expressionist plays, such as *Roger Bloomer* (1923) and *Processional* (1925), all of which harped on class distinction. In 1936 he wrote a Marxist textbook of proletarian theatre. Once again, although he is a very skilful writer, he is best considered as a journalist and a propagandist for social change. Really only Odets, of the social and Marxist dramatists, achieved anything beyond the journalistic—and he did not altogether fulfil his promise.

LILLIAN HELLMAN (1905), who was born in New Orleans, is as radical as any of these, but is less ideological and more interested in characterization. Her one attempt at a proletarian piece, *Days to Come* (1936), about a strike, failed. She is one of the most able and effective of modern dramatists in the old 'well-made' technique. Her first play, *The Children's Hour* (1934), about a schoolgirl who maliciously accuses her two headmistresses of being lesbian, is skilful but ambiguous in that it leaves the audience in doubt as to whether the greater vileness in the play is the child's false accusation or lesbianism itself; Lillian Hellman might well now rewrite the play so that the two headmistresses actually are discreetly lesbian—and show them as still victimized. *The Little Foxes* (1939) is an excellent study of greed and unpleasantness: a Southern family seizes its opportunities as industrialism rises there. Her next two plays, *Watch on the Rhine* (1941), and *The Searching Wind* (1944) were finely made propaganda against fascism and opportunistic appeasement respectively. Then came her best play: *Another Part of the Forest* (1946), a comic study, rightly described as Jonsonian, of hateful people cheating each other. *Toys in the Attic* (1960) embodies Lillian Hellman's most memorable portrait of an evil person, and her most hopeful (if defeated) one. Charges of misanthropy against Miss Hellman are frivolous, and come from those whose optimism is flabby. But the 'well-madeness' of her plays does tend to vitiate them, even though one recognizes that she cannot proceed except in this way. *Another Part of the Forest* is a picaresque comedy, and is freer from the limitations of 'sardoodledom' (q.v.) than any other of her plays. (*The Little Foxes*, written earlier, is its sequel in time.)

WILLIAM SAROYAN (1908), born of Armenian parents in California, has exuberance, energy and tenderness; he might have been a major writer, and as it is he is now an undervalued one; unfortunately he has seldom been able to control his sentimentality, or force himself into moods in the least discriminatory. For this naïve (q.v.), all that matters is the glory of the dream. 'He puts everything in', one critic has said, 'in case he misses anything important'. He never went beyond his fictional début, *The Daring Young Man on the Flying Trapeze* (1934), short stories written with a strikingly innocent eye and a direct, appealing lyricism. Saroyan went on to produce much more fiction of the same sort, but the good bits become harder to find. He made his début as a playwright with *My Heart's in the Highlands* (1939) and *The Time of Your Life* (1939), the curious opposite of O'Neill's *The Iceman Cometh* (q.v.) since the somewhat similar central character dispenses happiness, not despair. For a time it looked to many people as though Saroyan might become an important figure in the theatre, but he lacked craftsmanship and discipline, and all his promise petered out into showy, patchy, sentimental drama such as *The Beautiful People*

(1941) or improvisations such as his more recent, *Sam the Highest Jumper of them All* (1960). One play stands out among all the others: *Hello Out There* (1942), a genuinely tragic one-act piece about the lynching of a tramp. Saroyan can be silly ('I am so innately great by comparison others who believe they are great . . . seem to me to be only pathetic, although occasionally charming'), and he has produced masses of rubbish; but his best is worth looking for.

THORNTON WILDER (1897), born at Madison, Wisconsin, novelist and play-wright, has certainly been an odd man out throughout his career; his work, unquestionably skilful, intelligent and technically resourceful, has been the subject of much controversy: is he at heart a middlebrow charlatan exploiting the discoveries and procedures of his betters, or is he an original writer with something of his own to say? The truth is that Wilder seems pretentious because (as he himself has come near to admitting) he can never answer the huge questions he asks. He is by no means a middlebrow in intention, and he has specifically stated that one of the problems of the modern dramatist is to create a theatre that will be genuinely disturbing to the bourgeoisie. But in actually dealing with this problem he has succeeded in pleasing rather than worrying them. He lacks an inner core of imaginative resilience, or passion, and con-sequently too quickly falls back on mere cleverness, laced with folksiness and sentimentality. In other words, his unconventionality resides in his daring technique rather than in his somewhat unoriginal content. The impact of his plays (and novels, with one exception) is perfectly middlebrow in that it provokes 'discussion' rather than meditation or wonder. *Our Town* (1938) gives the intimate history of a New Hampshire town by means of a bare stage (a shrewd reaction against the theatre's obsession at this time with décor) and a choric stage manager, who describes the characters and talks casually to the audience. It is a dazzling performance, but all it ultimately offers is the rather mundane thought that there is 'something way down deep that's eternal about a human being': a Yankee inarticulateness underlies the high articulateness of the bright presentation. In *The Skin of Our Teeth* the Antrobus family represent humanity and the escape, by the proverbial skin, from most of the terrors that are known to have beset the race. This is again brilliant; but an arch folksiness precludes real warmth.

Wilder's first popular success was the novel *The Bridge of San Luis Rey* (1927), which traces the fortunes of a number of people killed when a South American bridge collapses. But this was meretricious compared with his first novel, *The Cabala* (1926), or with the most solid of all his works, *Heaven's My Destination* (1935), about a book salesman called George Brush, a foolish saint, who reminds one of Duhamel's Salavin (q.v.). In this comic story Wilder found his own voice, and although his plays have their moving moments, they never measure up to this (he did not come back to fiction until 1967, with *The Eighth Day*; this has all the old brilliance of technique, but is otherwise sadly disappointing), which is a major work.

*

Since the Second World War the theatre almost everywhere has got increasingly into the hands of the directors; in certain cases the public are even more interested in the producers of plays than their authors. Americans have reacted to this by going 'off Broadway', and now this is where most of the dramatic energy lies. Great Britain is beginning to follow suit. The development is a healthy one, because it means that playwrights, writing for tiny audiences, are able to get away from commercial demands to fulfil artistic ones. This kind of theatre sees as much rubbish as the commercial theatre; but the good writers have more chance. However, the playwrights who dominated the immediate post-war scene—Tennessee Williams, Arthur Miller and, to a lesser extent, William Inge—had to fight for recognition in the commercial theatre.

TENNESSEE WILLIAMS (PS. THOMAS LANIER WILLIAMS, 1911) was born in Mississippi. His father was a salesman who was probably (according to a gossipy book Williams' mother wrote) a mean drunk; at all events, in his childhood he knew more anger and alienation than love. After much struggle to establish himself, Williams found an agent who believed in him, and in 1945, with *The Glass Menagerie*, he became accepted. His persistent theme is the agonized, even shrieking alienation of violent and crippled eccentrics: homosexuals, madmen, sex-driven women. The air his characters naturally breathe is that of romantic hysteria; without it they would wilt and die immediately. He combines lush vulgarity with lyrical despair to produce plays of undeniable power. But their language is not enduring, and they fade in the mind. He is adept at presenting nerve-shot situations, but has never written a successful play of reconciliation. His characters are happiest at not being happy, and when his plots contrive to satisfy them they protest by being totally unconvincing: a tribute to the power of his depiction of despair. Williams shows sensitive people as being ravished by the brutal and materialistic demands of society. But this is not genuine social comment: his sensitives are too often hopeless and irremediably crippled neurotics, and 'society' is represented by persons whose greed or lust or dishonesty is pathological. He loves the grotesque, and in effect he pays tribute to it by lyrically depicting hells on earth.

His first success, *The Glass Menagerie*, is his tenderest and best play: this account of a slightly crippled girl's coming briefly out of the world of dreams she lives in—symbolized by a menagerie of glass animals—is moving within a non-pathological realm. The rest of Williams' plays are set in a pathological world that does not often allow the spectator to visualize his own world—equally tragic—that is not entirely peopled by freaks. *A Streetcar Named Desire* (1947) almost succeeds, but Blanche, its heroine, destroyed and driven into madness by the hideous Stanley, is herself too impossible to gain full sympathy. *The Rose Tattoo* (1951), about Gulf coast Sicilians, declines into sentimentality and a false vitality. *Camino Real* (1953), a fantasy, is another failure: it has theatre-life, as a clever rhetoric, but a cool reading exposes its pretensions—and reveals the meagreness of linguistic resource which is Williams' basic weakness. The more realistic *Cat on a Hot Tin Roof* (1955), dealing with the frustrations and anguishes of a Southern family, contains some marvellously evocative individual portraits —Big Daddy, his alcoholic son Brick who cannot face up to the homosexual component in himself, his wife Maggie—but does not altogether succeed in setting them against each other. This is a play in which Williams, not dishonestly, tries to suggest the possibility of future happiness (for Maggie and the too detached Brick); but it remains unconvincing. In the Gothic *Suddenly Last Summer* (1958) the homosexual 'poet' Edward, the unseen hero, is eaten by the boys he has used (a typically vague allusion to Orpheus being devoured by furies). His mother, in order to inherit his fortune, is glad to submit her daughter-in-law to a lobotomy. The language here is particularly thin, and the intentions confused; but there are moments of power. More recently Williams has written *Sweet Bird of Youth* (1959), the factitious *The Night of the Iguana* (1961) and *The Eccentricities of a Nightingale* (1965). Williams, gifted as a realist, has chosen—and on balance the choice is probably a correct one—to work in more or less expressionist modes. This leads him into some difficulties with language; but he does gain poetic, and sometimes heartrending, effects from his juxtapositions of characters and settings. He is a writer as flawed as any of his heroes; but more of a genius, too, than any of them. In 1969 he joined the Roman Catholic Church, perhaps as a substitute for the writing of plays, which had served (he has said) as 'therapy' to reduce tension. He is the author of a not outstanding novel, *The Roman Spring of Mrs. Stone* (1950), many short stories (*One Arm*, 1948; *Hard Candy*, 1954) and some fuzzy, mystical verse that is collected in *In the Winter of Cities* (1956 rev. 1964). He has not really, as a writer, faced up to the problem that obsesses him: sexual anguish.

ARTHUR MILLER (1915), who was born in New York City, has by contrast more of the journalist and social reformer than of the poet in him, but is as important as Williams. Miller began to write plays while at the University of Michigan, won prizes, and after graduation (1938) worked for the Federal Theatre Project. (This, which lasted from the autumn of 1935 to the summer of 1939, was the first American state-sponsored theatre project, a typically New Deal enterprise which invented such devices as the Living Newspaper, and encouraged Negro theatre; it was suppressed by reactionary elements in Congress.) *Situation Normal* (1944) was a rather flat and starry-eyed piece of reportage about military life; *Focus* (1955) is an ironic novel about anti-semitism: the protagonist is an anti-semitic Gentile who gets demoted when a new pair of spectacles makes him appear Jewish; but he is slow to learn the lesson, and when he finally does his transformed character is unconvincing.

In 1947, with the strong drama of *All My Sons* (1947), Miller established himself as, with Tennessee Williams, America's leading young dramatist. This is a straightforward, traditional play, which shows the strong influence of Ibsen (whose *Enemy of the People* Miller adapted in 1951). Joe Keller has in the war allowed some faulty engine parts to be sent to the air force, which has meant the deaths of some pilots; his partner has been wrongly blamed and imprisoned, while he was exonerated. Now, after the war, his son discovers his guilt —and that his own elder brother, having realized their father's guilt, has allowed himself to be killed as a kind of expiation. Joe, after trying to wriggle out of his responsibility in every way, kills himself when he realizes that those dead pilots were all his sons. . . . This is a good, well constructed play, but nothing out of the ordinary. Far superior is *Death of a Salesman* (1949), which was directed by Elia Kazan (q.v.) and had the excellent Lee J. Cobb in the leading role. Willy Loman, who is presented with great compassion, is perhaps still the most vivid example on the modern stage of the 'other directed' man of modern industrial societies that David Riesman postulated in his (and collaborators') *The Lonely Crowd*: the social character who is controlled by the expectations of other people, the 'marketing character' of Erich Fromm (who has influenced Riesman), who becomes anxious when he lapses from the standards of selling himself to other people. Like all his kind, Willy preaches the bourgeois virtues to his family; but in reality he accepts dishonesty. But Miller shows him as possessing a humanity that, deep down, recognizes this. His suicide is genuinely tragic.

The Crucible (1953), about the notorious Salem witch trials, was performed at a time when witch-hunting for communists was prevalent in the United States. This is a play about commitment, and the French movie script was written by Sartre (q.v.): condemned to die for witchcraft, John Proctor confesses to it to save his life—but then refuses to live, and thus triumphs.

In 1956 Miller married the film-actress Marilyn Monroe, and became the object of a good deal of publicity which did not help his creative life. He wrote a film for her, *The Misfits* (1961), which is presented in its published form as a kind of novel; this is interesting, but its attempt to show how innocence (Miller had seen Marilyn Monroe as innocent) is destroyed was vitiated by the nature of the medium itself. The ending is sentimental—and Miller does not really suffer from sentimentality. He and Marilyn Monroe were divorced in 1960.

After the Fall (1964) is overtly autobiographical: Maggie is clearly a representation of Marilyn Monroe (who had recently died) and Quentin is the 'intellectual' Miller. It is as good as any of Miller's previous plays, and is most notable for its maturity—a maturity beyond that of any commercial audience —and its refusal to find easy or glib solutions. In *Incident at Vichy* (1964), a semi-documentary, about the Nazis' treatment of various Frenchmen, he seemed to be marking time.

It is in Miller that 'social realism', in the most intelligent, Ibsenian sense, has found its best and most compassionate playwright. The future of this kind of play, which requires audiences more educated than most at present are, could well be in his hands.

WILLIAM INGE (1913), who was born in Kansas, is more conventional in technique than either Williams or Miller; his plays are not as ambitious, but he has successfully portrayed midwest people, intelligently revealing them as they are beneath the public surface. *Come Back, Little Sheba* (1950) is one of the best of modern plays on the subject of alcoholism. *Picnic* (1953) and *Bus Stop* (1955) became famous in movie versions; in the latter the old technical device of bringing strangers fortuitously together is given new life by fine characterization and convincing dialogue. *The Dark at the Top of the Stairs* (1958) is that darkness into which both the child of a family and its parents dare not—

whatever they pretend—climb up to. *A Loss of Roses* (1960) was a disappointment: the relationship between a mother and her son clearly springs from a psychiatric textbook rather than from a human situation. Inge is perhaps not more than a useful playwright (in the sense that Telemann and Hindemith are useful composers)—but this is something considerable in its own right.

The off-Broadway movement has not yet brought many playwrights to prominence; but prominence may not be what the real theatre needs. However, three dramatists who have graduated from this milieu to some commercial success should be mentioned. The best known, EDWARD ALBEE (1928), is not necessarily superior, although his *Who's Afraid of Virginia Woolf?* (1963) is more substantial than anything so far written by JACK GELBER (1932) or JACK RICHARDSON (1934). Albee is unusual in that he seems to have nothing in him of American optimism, and actually began—with *The Zoo Story* (1959)—with an example of the Theatre of the Absurd (q.v.). Even so, this brilliant dialogue does end both violently and sentimentally: a gesture, it seems, to the American insistence on one or the other (in the absence of actual Utopian choruses). Its theme—a young homosexual inveigles an ordinary bourgeois into killing him —foreshadowed that of its successors, except for *The Death of Bessie Smith* (1959) and *The American Dream* (1960). The adventure into realism of the former has a shocking subject: the real reasons for the refusal of a hospital for whites to admit the injured blues singer, whom they could have saved. But it is no more than a dreary and uninteresting protest piece. *The American Dream* abandons realism, and is better. This is a send-up of America in terms of its clichés, beautifully heard and reproduced, that resembles Karl Kraus (q.v.) even more than Ionesco (q.v.), upon whose techniques it greatly depends.

Who's Afraid of Virginia Woolf? (1963) is superbly inventive theatre, but is ultimately sterile inasmuch as it amounts to an a-lyrical assault not merely on marriage but on all heterosexuality. Or that is how I read it. But its dialogue is masterly in its capture—or deadly parody—of a certain kind of upper middle-class Americanese; and throughout there is a yearning for understanding. *Tiny Alice* (1965) is a kind of disguised well-made play. A story of the richest woman in the world who seduces, marries and destroys a Catholic lay-brother, it works well on the stage, but reads badly except to critics set on interpreting its incredibly complicated symbolism. Once again, the real theme is the horror any man lays in store for himself by having truck with the evil trickster Woman. But for some the mood and language raise the play above this. In *A Delicate Balance* (1966) Albee returns to more realistic family horrors, but the message is similar. Albee does not of course load the dice against women, or make his men paragons—he is too intelligent; it is simply that one gets a strong sense, from his plays, that for him femininity is the ultimate destroyer and spoiler of happiness. But the greatly inferior William Burroughs (q.v.) is completely (and stupidly) explicit on this point, whereas it would certainly be doing Albee an injustice to suggest that this is his rational view. Albee has made excellent adaptations of Carson McCullers' *The Ballad of the Sad Café* (q.v., 1963) and *Malcolm* (1965), James Purdy's (q.v.) novel.

Jack Gelber's *The Connection* (1960) vacillates too uncertainly between realism and expressionism—Gelber is not sure whether he wants to protest against the drug laws or to depict a group of junkies waiting for their fix—but is nevertheless a vivid and accurate presentation of people who simply don't want anything to do with society. Its form is interesting: a jazz quartet improvises on the stage, two film cameramen become involved in the action; the aimless dialogue is authentic. *The Apple* (1961), an improvisation, departs more radically from the conventional theatre, but is less successful. *On Ice* (1965), a novel about a hipster called Manny, is surprisingly low in energy and humour.

Jack Richardson's *The Prodigal* (1960), an acerb and witty treatment of the Orestes theme, came from off Broadway; so did his *Gallows Humour* (1961). *The Prison Life of Harris Philmore* (1961) is a novel.

Another American dramatist who has attracted attention by serious work is PADDY CHAYEFSKY (1923). He began as a television playwright, and became famous when *Marty* (1953) was filmed, with Ernest Borgnine. *The Bachelor Party* (1954), a touching but not quite unsentimental play, was also filmed. Chayefsky was attacked for his 'tape recorder' realism, and has unwisely tried in his stage plays for symbolic effects which do not really suit him. For *The Tenth Man*, his best play, he combined an authentic Bronx setting with the Jewish legend of the Dybbuk.

IV

GERTRUDE STEIN (1874–1946), born of a wealthy family near Pittsburgh, was not altogether modern—she has even been put forward as one who belonged essentially to the 'sunset phase' of the nineteenth century—but she understood the importance of modernity. Her writings were not, as Sherwood Anderson (q.v.) saw, necessarily very important in themselves; but they provided incomparable signposts for others more imaginatively gifted. Gertrude Stein studied at Radcliffe under, among others, Santayana and Moody (qq.v.); the most important influence on her there, however, was William James. She planned to become a psychologist, and so began medicine, including brain anatomy, at Johns Hopkins. In 1903 she went abroad, learnt about art from her brother Leo, who—though he kept in the background—was always a better art critic than she, and set about establishing herself as an expatriate queen and patron of artists. She bought the work of Picasso, Braque, Matisse and others, and amassed a famous collection. She lived with her secretary and companion Alice B. Toklas in Paris for the rest of her life (except for a period during the war, when they lived in Vichy), only returning to America once—for a lecture tour in 1934. Her early books appeared so difficult that she had to publish or guarantee them herself. But when she had acquired fame as a personality, through both her *salon* and her assumption of the headship of the *avant garde* of the Twenties, she was able to write a popular book: *The Auto-biography of Alice B. Toklas* (1933), which purported to be her life as told by her friend. She repeated this with *Everybody's Autobiography* (1937). Gertrude Stein encouraged Anderson, Hemingway, Wilder, Fitzgerald (qq.v.) and others gifted, talented—and mediocre. No poet gained anything from her example. But she was certainly regarded as the most influential English-speaking writer in Paris in the early Twenties—Pound ('Gertrude Stein liked him', said Miss Stein in *Toklas*, 'but did not find him amusing. She said he was a village explainer, excellent if you were a village, but if you were not, not') and Ford Madox Ford (qq.v.) were also there. In her last years she and Miss Toklas entertained many American soldiers; she had known the Americans of two wars, and wrote of them in the popular *Wars I Have Seen* (1944) and in *Brewsie and Willie* (1946). This latter was her last; it reconstructs the language of the G.I. Joes of 1944–5 with brilliance and affection as well as sentimentality.

Apart from her popular works, which are not only witty and readable but also sometimes egocentric and surprisingly arch, *Three Lives* (1909), and some posthumously printed earlier writings, Gertrude Stein's books are hard to read: child-like but repetitious, monotonous and not always justifiably inscrutable. It was after *Three Lives* (her best work) that she began to evolve the style for which she is known. By that time she had come to understand what Pablo Picasso and his friends were trying to do in painting: to elevate the picture itself over its 'subject'. Thus, for her, words became objects-in-themselves. Meaning became an overtone. Picasso and the others concentrated on *the painting*; she concentrated on *the writing*. (This offered, perhaps, a convenient enough way of evading the issue of self-appraisal). Her teacher William James had 'discovered' the 'stream of consciousness'; as a psychologist he was interested in the flux itself—whereas she was more interested in the moment of 'the complete actual present': in the capturing of instants. One of the intentions of her repetitions is to convey an illusion like that of a motion picture: each sentence is a 'frame', and differs only slightly from its predecessor. Once the novelty has worn off, this tends, of course, to be as boring as exposing each frame of a movie not for a fraction of a second but for several minutes. But perhaps it had to be done. Gertrude Stein had the effrontery and self-confidence to do it.

She was also against the 'objective' or transcendent self: the self of which James claimed psychology could give no account. In that hopeful, Utopian manner common to many Americans she believed in the present—and thought the future was a rosy one. Perhaps such optimism requires to ignore sequence, structure and what I have called, in relation to Dreiser, the grain of life. The substantial, or transcendent, or objective self—what Wyndham Lewis (q.v.) thought of as 'the eye of the artist'—did not interest her any more than 'realism': she was peculiarly modern in this concentration on the qualities of objects, and in her opposition to 'stories'. She tried to get rid of narrative and put into its place a technique of extracting the essential quality of a thing or person. For example, this piece called 'A Cloth' from *Tender Buttons* (1914): 'Enough cloth is plenty and more, more is almost enough for that and besides if there is no more spreading is there plenty of room for it. Any occasion shows the best way'. Witty, intelligent—but trivial, and, when in bulk, tiresome. . . . This was the trap into which she fell. Not perhaps wishing her imagination to be free to investigate her personality, she allowed herself to create abstractions that were inexorably separated from life or anything like it. *Ida, a Novel* (1941), for example, is really 'about' all that is least important in its protagonist's life—or at any rate it tells us nothing that is significant. The mimetic or representational was for Gertrude Stein a vulgarity and a sentimentality. Her writing tried to be 'abstract' in the sense that painting is abstract. It is curious that of her modern non-representational or would-be non-representational successors (Olson, Creeley, qq.v. etc., etc.) only the American poet Robert Duncan has shown any real interest in her; but he is an 'intellectual', as she was; the others cannot really be described as such.

Gertrude Stein was in her own way, from her 'home town' of Paris, an American pioneer. She saw how American procedures—indecorous and adventurous—differed from English, which are neat and traditional because 'Nothing is perplexing if there is an island. The special sign of this is in dusting'. In other words, she saw the right direction for American literature. But she became increasingly megalomanic and remote, and it is not strange that she early turned from novelist to critic (demonstrator of how things ought to be done). *Things As They Are* (1950), a straightforward (though not 'obscene') treatment of a lesbian theme, written in 1903, gives us some clue as to why she chose the course she did. It is fortunate that she wrote *Three Lives* (1909) before she made this choice, for it is a masterpiece—as well as being the most accessible of all her writings. There are hints of the future manner, but it has not degenerated into a method and become tiresome. The book consists of three stories of women, all of whom are defeated by life. Outstanding is 'Melanctha', about the daughter of a Mulatto mother and a Negro father who hates her: this, as has many times been pointed out, is almost the first American fiction to treat a Negro as a human being. The vigour and scope of this book make it clear that Gertrude Stein abandoned imaginative for critical fiction for reasons other than experiential capacity.

*

No fiction could have been further from Gertrude Stein's than that of SINCLAIR LEWIS (1885–1951); if she was super-literary, he was never more than super-journalistic. He is one of the worst writers to win a Nobel Prize (he was the first American to do so, 1930), and the worst American writer to achieve fame on a more than merely popular level. Yet although he was in no way as serious or as good as Gertrude Stein, he was in a certain sense as historically important as her. The son of a doctor of Sauk City, Minnesota, he went to Yale, became a journalist, and fell under the influence of the journalist H. L. MENCKEN (1880–1956), an important debunker and satirist who despite his crudities was a magnificent destroyer of hypocrisy, cant and pretentiousness. Lewis wrote a number of realistic and partially satirical novels, but did not achieve recognition until *Main Street* (1920). This attacks Sauk City (here called Gopher Prairie) and every similar town in America on very much the same lines as Mencken and the critic George Jean Nathan (1882–1958) were currently doing in their magazine *The Smart Set*—but rather more ambiguously. For Lewis makes his symbol of freedom, Carol Kennicott, return to the dull doctor husband she has walked out on; not only that, but we can now see very easily that Carol Kennicott herself is an extremely sentimental and middlebrow creature—she is merely a bit smarter than the others. Lewis followed this with *Babbitt* (1922), a portrait of an average American business man which its readers took as satirical at the time but which may now be seen as loving as well as critical. Still, this added a new word to the language. *Arrowsmith* (1925) is about a scientist, and *Elmer Gantry* (1927), by far his best novel, is an almost Dickensian extravaganza about the attractions of phoney religion and a fake preacher who takes advantage of them. *Dodsworth* (1929) is a sentimental novel on the obligatory theme of the American being educated in Europe. The books of Lewis' last twenty years are more overtly in favour of what he began by satirizing; but the tendency was always there.

Lewis appealed to so vast a readership because he was 'safe'. As he confessed, he had written of Babbitt with love and not with hate. He could oppose nothing to the materialism of the small towns he portrayed. He was intellectually feeble. His powers of characterization were nil. What, then, were his virtues? First, he had a masterly journalistic grasp of his material: he really knew about the society of which he wrote. And if he did not really hate it, he none the less depicted it with vitality. He owed something to Wells, but most of all to Dickens. For essentially he was a caricaturist of great energy and zest. His readers were easily able to kid themselves that they were not like Babbitt; but the accuracy of his fine detail still fascinates—and in Elmer Gantry he has created a monster of Dickensian proportions and of some complexity.

*

WILLIAM FAULKNER (1897–1962), born in New Albany, Mississippi, and raised in Oxford in the same State, won the Nobel Prize nineteen years after Lewis, and was the fourth American to do so (if Eliot is regarded as British); he was incomparably the better writer; he is regarded by some, in fact, as the greatest of all American novelists. Faulkner joined the Royal Canadian Air Force in 1918, after the American Air Force had rejected him because of his smallness (5 feet 5 inches); he did not see any active service, but was able to enter the University of Mississippi, for which he could not qualify academically, as a veteran. He stayed there for just over a year, and then took a variety of jobs. He worked on a newspaper and in 1924 published a book of poor, imitative verse called *The Marble Faun*. His first novel, *Soldiers Pay* (1926), published with the help of his friend Sherwood Anderson (q.v.), *fin de siècle* in style, is about a dying soldier's return. *Mosquitoes* (1927) is a mannered satirical book; no one would notice it now if it had not been Faulkner's second novel. In 1929 he published his first important novel, *Sartoris*. For this he drew on his family history (his great grandfather's colourful life was ended by a bullet fired by a rival only eight years before Faulkner's birth), and created the domain for which he became famous: Yoknapatawpha County, county seat Jefferson. This place has a relation to Lafayette County, and Jefferson has a relation to Oxford (and other towns, such as Faulkner's birthplace, New Albany). It is also Faulkner's 'world': a world as untidy as the real one, and as vivid as any created by a novelist in this century. Within this world, with certain inconsistencies that make it more rather than less convincing, Faulkner traced the decline of certain families (the Compson, Sartoris, Benbow and McCaslin families) and the rise of the Snopes. The scheme is a vast map of Faulkner's imagination: it blurs somewhat at the edges, and there are undefined areas; but much is illuminated and illuminating. Faulkner is an example of a writer who managed, for a period—of about twelve or fourteen years—to keep his powerful imagination under control. His genealogies and complex accounts of the 'history' of his region were essential parts of this process. He had to bring his internal world into line with the external world. In the end, and understandably, he gave way under the strain of maintaining his gloomy but not life-denying vision: his speech of acceptance of the Nobel Prize is dutiful, a series of clichés almost worthy of a politician, unworthy of the creative writer. The view implied in Faulkner's works is not the view expressed by the winner of the Nobel Prize: '. . . man will not merely endure: he will prevail . . . because he has a soul, a spirit capable of compassion and sacrifice and endurance'. The view of the best work is more sombre. It has been well summed up as follows: '. . . the Faulkner novel is designedly a silo of compressed sin, from which life emerges as fermentation'. Faulkner believed in no system; he was at his best when he tried to discover the patterns of his internal world—this is of course, in part, a result of the impact the external world made on him. The values of Christianity will do for him; but there is no evidence that he believed that God had ever intervened in human affairs. His late novel *A Fable* (1954), an attempt to re-enact Christ's Passion against the background of the First World War, is imaginatively an atrocious failure: laboured, its bitterness misplaced, its use of the Christ-theme palpably erroneous because of Faulkner's clear lack of belief in it.

His first wholly characteristic novel was *The Sound and the Fury* (1929). Here the Compson family are shown degenerating, fallen from their former gentility, leading a doomed life. The story is told through the consciousnesses of three members of this family: Benjy the idiot, the sensitive Quentin and the twisted, mean Jason. Quentin kills himself through shame at his incestuous desire for his sister Candace; Jason's is a tale of pettiness and greed. A final section centres on the Negro servant, Dilsey, whose goodness and wholesomeness contrast with the horror of the Compsons' decline.

Faulkner made the interior monologue his chief technical device. He enters too bodily into his characters—white, black, successful, defeated—ever to speak confidently of men prevailing. . . . His world is infinitely more complicated than the platitudinous one in which such utterances can be made.

Faulkner's best work was written between *The Sound and the Fury* and *Intruder in the Dust* (1948), the story of how a Negro is saved from lynching by a white boy who has grown into understanding and humanity. After this—which is itself seriously vitiated by the introduction of a character who will insist on interpolating his unconvincing theories about race relations into the narrative —although none of his books is without some virtue, Faulkner tended to make optimistic intellectual inferences from his earlier works and elevate those into a kind of moral system. The three finest novels of all came early in Faulkner's career: *The Sound and the Fury*, *As I Lay Dying* (1930) and *Light in August* (1932). *As I Lay Dying* deals with the last journey of Addie Bundren: in her coffin as her family—her husband, her three legitimate sons, her bastard and a pregnant daughter—carry her to Jefferson. When there her husband finds himself new teeth and a new wife. This is a great novel because it reads perfectly as a realistic novel, and yet its symbolic possibilities are infinite. *Light in August* sets the bastard Joe Christmas, who may be half Negro but in any case feels and behaves as if he were, amongst a strict Calvinist community. This book touches, more closely than any of its predecessors, on one of Faulkner's main themes: that the doom and decline of the white man springs from his inability to treat the Negro as a fellow human being. This conviction—that all people should treat others as human beings—is one of the mainsprings of Faulkner's creative impulse. It is not 'political', but merely human. But there are characters as primitive and evil, in Faulkner's books, as some Southern demagogues with whom we are familiar: he penetrates their minds with his understanding, too. His job is not to satirize or to make judgements: he presents people as they are, and he can do so. Although *Light in August* is a grim book, it is a positive one because it is made clear, from the beginning to the end, that Joe Christmas' tragedy is his refusal to take or give love, and that he got into this condition because he was originally denied love.

Absalom, Absalom! (1936) brings back Quentin Compson, who is preparing for suicide in *The Sound and the Fury*, but only as narrator. The story is of Thomas Sutpen, the 'demon' poor white who has ambitions to achieve aristocracy and destroys everyone who gets in his way. Sutpen marries a planter's daughter and they have a son, but he abandons them when he discovers they have Negro blood. He goes to Yoknapatawpha County, obtains land by dishonest means, marries again, and has a son and a daughter. Later his son Henry goes to the University of Mississippi and meets and admires Charles, not knowing who he is. Charles falls in love with his own half-sister, Judith—and it is Henry who kills him when he learns about his Negro blood. Then Henry disappears. Sutpen is obsessed with begetting a male heir, and when he abandons a poor white girl on his land because she bears him a daughter her grandfather kills him with a scythe. Ultimately it is only Sutpen's Negro heirs who live on his land; in the end, finding the aged Henry come back and hidden in his own house, one of them burns it down. Thus Faulkner gives his most complete version of the doom of the South; once again he spells out the message: the fatal flaw is its refusal to accept the Negro on equal terms. This working out of the flaw is presented with passion, for Faulkner truthfully shows it to come of a horrible innocence. A Marxist explanation of the South simply will not do—and it is Faulkner who shows this most clearly. It would be more comforting if it would do. To have to report that this attitude to other human beings arises from an innocence is agonizing; but Faulkner, himself a Southerner, found the courage to tell the truth. There is a sense in which he had earned the clichés of his Nobel Prize acceptance. What else could he say but read *Absalom, Absalom!*? *The Unvanquished* (1938) linked episodes previously published as short stories into a novel about the fortunes of the Sartoris family in the Civil War. There are many more short stories, collected in *These Thirteen* (1931), *Doctor Martino* (1934), *Go Down Moses* (1942), *Knight's Gambit* (1949) and then in *Collected Stories* (1950). *The Wild Palms* (1939) relates the defeat, through love, of a New Orleans doctor who performs an abortion on his mistress.

The Hamlet (1940), *The Town* (1957) and *The Mansion* (1960) are a trilogy on the Snopes family; the first part is the best, but the second two contain the most humorous writing of Faulkner's latter years.

Faulkner is a very difficult, even forbidding writer. He is also, perhaps largely because of the strain and responsibility imposed upon him by his concern with the nature of evil, the most uneven of all the major writers of our time. His metaphors and similes can seem forced and even jejune. He can be pretentiously complex. He can be portentous and confused. But his best work is not more difficult than it has to be. Those long and intricate sentences are not too long and intricate when they are describing the processes of a mind. Few techniques more effective in doing so have been evolved. The subject of the beauty and innocence contained in evil is a difficult and paradoxical one, which can lead to misunderstandings. The sheer energy of Faulkner's stories of perversion, horror and despair gives the lie to those who would accuse him of doing the dirty on life itself, for his own creative ends.

*

F. SCOTT FITZGERALD (1896–1940), born at St. Paul, Minnesota, was the laureate of the Jazz age, of what Gertrude Stein called 'the lost generation'. These were people who were 'so deliberately and determinedly cynical that [they] became naïve'. Fitzgerald belonged to this age, but he knew that it was all wrong. In *The Great Gatsby* (1925), he achieved a balance between empathy and analysis, and produced the most memorable and accurate description of the American Twenties—a devastating criticism that is none the less rich and romantic, for Fitzgerald was an out-and-out romantic, and it was in large measure his offended romanticism that produced his disgust.

He began as very much one of his age. His family was prosperous, and when he went to Princetown in 1913 he was anxious to distinguish himself in every field including football; in 1920 he published his first successful novel, *This Side of Paradise*, which is about Princeton. Here Fitzgerald romantically sets his (immature) notion of true love against the corrupting power of money; the novel's strength, apart from its brilliant descriptive passages, lies in Fitzgerald's convincing grasp of what is unselfish in his initially snobbish and hedonistic hero. Fitzgerald had married a beautiful girl, Zelda, and he now began to live it up in one plush hotel after another, going from party to party, consuming himself rapidly but of course, in his twenties, imperceptibly. Zelda wanted to be a ballet dancer—she was very good, but she had started too late, and was not mentally stable—and she insisted on competing with Fitzgerald, which upset him, tearing him in two directions. Eventually she entered an institution; she was in one—in America—when she was burned to death in an accidental fire in 1947. Fitzgerald, earning a lot of money but increasingly in debt, wrote two volumes of short stories, a novel—*The Beautiful and Damned* (1922)—and a play before his first masterpiece, *The Great Gatsby*. The action takes place in the valley of ashes, beneath the huge eyes of Doctor T. J. Eckleburg (an advertisement). The story is told by Nick Carroway, a device that gives Fitzgerald the precise distance he needs between himself and his material. Poor Jay Gatz from Dakota quickly becomes one of the rich ('They are different from you and me. They possess and enjoy early, and it does something to them, makes them soft where we are hard, and cynical where we are trustful, in a way that, unless you were born rich, it is very difficult to understand') because he wants to win back Daisy Buchanan, Nick's cousin. After an affair with Jay when he was an army lieutenant, she had married the brutal, materialistic proto-fascist, Tom Buchanan—a prophetic portrait. Through Nick Gatsby meets Daisy again, and is able to make her his mistress. Tom takes a garage proprietor's wife for his mistress; her jealous husband locks her up, she runs out into the road—and is killed by Daisy, who does not stop. Gatsby takes the responsibility and Tom tells his own mistress's husband, Wilson, that it was Gatsby who killed her and drove on. Wilson shoots Gatsby in his swimming-pool, and then turns the gun on himself.

The Great Gatsby is another of those seminal books that manage to exist simultaneously and convincingly on both the realistic and the symbolic plane. Fitzgerald depicts the rich society into which Gatsby hoists himself as empty of all but putridity, the object of his simple romantic dreams, Daisy, as no more than a treacherous whore without the discrimination or inclination to diagnose the evil in her cruel and stupid husband. But Gatsby, as is often and rightly pointed out, comes, 'divided between power and dream', to represent America itself, and he (Nick says) 'turned out all right at the end; it is what preyed on Gatsby, what foul dust floated in the wake of his dreams that temporarily closed out my interest in the abortive sorrows and short-winded elations of men'. Fitzgerald is able to see Gatsby as both ex-criminal, vulgar member of the *nouveau riche*, and as a dreamer: as the man who had believed in Daisy's kiss so fervently that he had dedicated his whole being to what he thought it represented. In this way Gatsby embodies the American dream, which will

(Fitzgerald implies) founder on its preference of appearance to reality.

Tender is the Night (1934; rev. ed. 1951) is the love story of Dick Diver, psychiatrist, and his rich patient Nicole Warren. This is a more personal, more autobiographical book (for Nicole's schizophrenia he obviously drew on his experience of Zelda's); it does not have the universality of *The Great Gatsby*. It is none the less a masterpiece. The manner in which sick Nicole attracts Dick, and well Nicole corrupts him, is truly tragic. He loses his sense of vocation and becomes merely charming. Even though a schizophrenic and utterly dependent when she is sick, Nicole is somehow superior, the victor: she destroys her husband because in their marriage there is a tacit understanding that he is being paid for staying with her. In the end Dick returns to America, to—it is implied—rot away and waste his substance.

The Thirties were bad years for Fitzgerald. He worked in Hollywood, drank too much, behaved in such a manner as to give inferior men the opportunity to pity him, and almost stopped writing. At thirty-nine, in 1936, he experienced what he himself called a crack-up: Edmund Wilson (q.v.) edited the interesting notebooks, papers and essays describing this nervous breakdown in the volume *The Crack-up* (1945): why, Fitzgerald asked himself, had he gone so far as to have become identified with all he loathed and pitied. He had a daughter by Zelda, and it is clear that he desperately wanted to appear to her as a good and decent father—and that he felt he could not do so. Luckily for his personal happiness he met a journalist, Sheilah Graham, who sweetened his difficult final years, and helped him to get himself into a fit state to attempt his last novel, *The Last Tycoon* (1941). Fitzgerald died, after two heart attacks, before he could finish it. Essentially it is a self-portrait: Monroe Stahr, a film-producer at the end of his rope, tries to struggle on although he no longer believes in life. It is clear that Fitzgerald's alcoholism and involvement with commerce had not weakened his powers, and if this had been finished it might be safe to agree with those critics who find it his best novel. Fitzgerald wrote many short stories, of varying merit; there is a selection of eighteen of the best of them in *The Stories of F. Scott Fitzgerald* (1951).

ERNEST HEMINGWAY (1898–1961) also came from the midwest—he was the son of an Illinois doctor—and, as Fitzgerald had done, but to much greater point, he sat at the feet of Gertrude Stein in Paris. As a young man he made many hunting and fishing expeditions; his descriptions of these activities were one of the high points of his writing. Hemingway was a reporter in Kansas City, volunteered as an ambulance driver and was wounded in Italy in 1917. He served with the Italian infantry until the Armistice. In Paris he came to know Gertrude Stein, Ford Madox Ford and Ezra Pound (qq.v.), all of whom encouraged him. (His memoirs of his Paris years were published posthumously in *A Moveable Feast*, 1964. This is an example of Hemingway at his worst: self-parodic, arch, untruthful.) His early short stories were collected in *In Our Time* (1925). The tedious *The Torrents of Spring* (1926) parodied Sherwood Anderson's (q.v.) style—a style from which Hemingway had already appropriated what he wanted. *The Sun Also Rises* (1926), called *Fiesta* in Great Britain, his first novel, is his best. This was followed by the short stories *Men Without Women* (1927) and the novel *A Farewell to Arms* (1929); the short story collection *Winner Takes Nothing* (1933) was Hemingway's last book of account.

Hemingway was famous for his style, his four marriages (only the final one, lasting from 1944 until his death, took), and his various sporting exploits. The record is not very clear on his prowess as a sportsman. It seems that he was not always as good as he said or thought he was. When he went to the front in the Spanish Civil War he nearly killed someone with a grenade, and was regarded as a nuisance. But he could fish and he had enthusiasm for bullfighting. During most of the Thirties Hemingway lived in Key West in Florida. After the Second World War, during which he was a correspondent with the Fourth Division of the First Army, he lived on an estate near Havana, Cuba, until the Castro revolution. After this he settled in Idaho. But he was already mentally and physically ill, and in 1961 he shot himself. After 1933 his main publications were: *To Have and Have Not* (1937), *For Whom the Bell Tolls* (1940), on the Spanish Civil War, the badly received *Across the River and into the Trees* (1950), *The Old Man and the Sea* (1952), all novels, and *The Green Hills of Africa* (1935), on big game hunting. *The Fifth Column*, a hollow and cliché-ridden play about a newspaperman in Spain, was included in his collected short stories: *The Fifth Column and the First Forty-nine Stories* (1938). A posthumously issued, excruciating novel, *Islands in the Stream* (1970), is best ignored.

Hemingway, especially the late Hemingway, has been an overrated writer; but this does not mean that he was not a good one. The earliest influence on him, RING LARDNER (1885–1933), whose style he was imitating at school, deserves a paragraph to himself.

Lardner was better known as a sports columnist than as a short-story writer. He did not fully realize his genius, but he was the first to listen properly to and carefully reproduce the speech of the lower classes, the speech of people who went to prize fights and baseball matches. He refrained from judgement, and his idea of what was comic was also very often (as he knew) tragic; he missed greatness because there was just too much of the casual about his misanthropy. His lunatic short plays anticipate the Theatre of the Absurd, although they did not influence it.

The mature Hemingway of the Twenties owed the authenticity of his dialogue and his toughness to Lardner's example; in the latter the toughness was unassumed, in Hemingway it functioned laconically and truthfully as a guard against sentimentality.

Hemingway's style was self-conscious and carefully worked out, but it arose from a simplicity of feeling that he gradually lost. Apart from Lardner, its sources are in the economy of the newspaper report, the purity of Gertrude Stein, the honesty and lyricism of Anderson, the innocence of Huckleberry Finn, the simplicity of Stephen Crane (qq.v.). The Hemingway of the Twenties is complex; but he has not yet fallen prey to cliché or to noisy exhibitionism about 'action'. He is not as much of a 'man' as he would like to be: the hero of *The Sun Also Rises* has been emasculated by the war. But he lives to a code—the famous Hemingway code of 'grace under pressure'. For Jake Barnes there can be no meaning in life except to live gracefully. He cannot have the girl he loves, Brett; but she returns to him at the end because the novelist Robert Cohn, to whom she has briefly given herself, has nothing to offer—he is the victim of mere words and fine sentiments—and because she fears she will injure the bullfighter she loves if she stays with him. This is Hemingway's most moving novel, fine in characterization, pellucid in style, and contrasting without sentimentality the anguish of futility with the dignity of a few people's graciousness. *A Farewell to Arms* is poignant but the English nurse, Catherine Barkley, is quite unreal. Aside from Brett in *The Sun Also Rises*, whom he observes but upon whose qualities he does not comment, Hemingway could not create women. There was, it seems, a homosexual component in his nature which led him both to want to establish himself as masculine (i.e. not 'feminine'), and to make up soft, yielding, sweet women—too obviously the ideal complement for strong and hairy warriors. Catherine is the beginning of this line of girls, who get younger and more improbable as his heroes age along with him. But apart from this *A Farewell to Arms*—with its implied comments on the futility of war, its descriptions of battles, and its depiction of the state of mind of the hero—runs *The Sun Also Rises* very close.

The best short stories are in the first three collections. In them Hemingway was getting nineteenth-century culture out of his system, and saluting a primitivistic, non-industrial kind of life in which males (the females are out except for purposes of comfort, and as something a man 'needs') must learn to live and die with courage and grace: people must behave well. The best stories, particularly those about Nick Adams, are laconic and as pure as spring water. Hemingway's fascination with death (he chose it rather than life at the end) was genuine, and he is especially good in describing encounters with death.

But in many ways he never grew up. The kind of badness of his posthumous novel reveals him to have been capable of fantasies of action so puerile that it is hard to believe the author of *Fiesta* could have perpetrated them. His longest novel, *For Whom the Bell Tolls*, has good passages, but is flawed as a novel by its meaningless and sentimental love affair. The symbolism of *The Old Man and the Sea* is portentous, its simplicity false. It is, it is true, a skilful performance, and—the Christian symbolism apart—a sincere one. It conveys Hemingway's message: life is futile, but we must still live it nobly and with courage. However, it is not fresh, but lucubrated; the words have not been drawn up from a deep well, but pondered and put together by 'Papa Hemingway'.

The message itself is not and never was much, of course. Hemingway will be valued, surely, for the discovery of a style that enabled him to make vivid, lyrical and piercingly accurate descriptions of graciousness and male companionship (as in the fishing trip in *The Sun Also Rises*). He is a moving writer, but it is an error to go to him for 'philosophy'.

THOMAS WOLFE (1900–38) was less gifted than Hemingway, and his failure to grow up was more comprehensive. But he cannot be ignored. He was born in Asheville, North Carolina, where his father made grave masonry and his mother ran a small hotel. A giant in height—he was six feet six inches tall—he poured out a gigantic torrent of thinly fictionalized autobiography which his publishers, first Maxwell Perkins of Scribners and then Edward C. Aswell of Harpers, edited into four books (themselves massive novels). He had graduated from the University of North Carolina and then gone to Harvard to try George Pierce Baker's (q.v.) course in playwriting. He took his first novel to Perkins in 1923, and between them they put it into shape—meanwhile Wolfe was an instructor of English at New York University. *Look Homeward Angel*, in which he appears as Eugene Gant, was published in 1929, and was immediately successful; it was followed by *Of Time and the River* (1935). In his next two novels, both posthumously published, Gant becomes George Webber. Shortly after delivering the Webber manuscript Wolfe caught pneumonia; he died of a brain infection. Aswell edited and published the material Wolfe had left as *The Web and the Rock* (1939) and *You Can't Go Home Again* (1940). Since his death Wolfe's reputation has somewhat declined—no competent critic recommends him wholeheartedly—but he is still read. Clearly, for all his lack of self-discipline and failure to consider any phenomenon or person except in the light of his own interests, he is a writer of some importance.

He is most important to the young. Go back to him after thirty and you will find yourself selecting; before thirty you take it all in. In the first novel Gant tells the story of his father and mother. Even as edited by Perkins it is badly, inflatedly written; but this does not seem to matter, because Wolfe does create an unforgettably vivid picture of a savagely quarrelling, mutually recriminative family. Probably he could not have done it in any other way. The continuation, and the unsuccessful attempt to cover the same ground more objectively in the Webber novels, tell his own story: of the search for success (rather than meaning), for a father (found in his editor Maxwell Perkins) and for a mother (found and finally repudiated in the stage designer Aileen Bernstein, almost twenty years older than himself). And yet through all the inchoateness something does emerge: the ghost of man trying to find, fumbling with, sometimes finding and using, his own self-expression. Wolfe is a romantic rather than a novelist: the author of a vast body of work that seeks to define the myth of the American artist. But he failed—except as a writer of fragments—because he could not altogether discipline Wolfe into the artist, could not sensitively enough separate the ego from the creativity. But for all Wolfe's adolescence, for all the egoism that he drags into his fiction, much of what his prose recreates—his childhood, his tortured romance with Mrs. Bernstein, his relationship with the homosexual Francis Starwick—is as vividly evoked as anywhere in the fiction of our century. It is often as paranoiac, adolescent and unpleasantly egocentric as Wolfe himself was; but it is of legendary proportions, and we do not forget it.

*

Not much of the proletarian literature that flourished during the depression of the early Thirties, and only subsided with the Stalinist purges, the Nazi-Soviet pact, and then (ironically) the alliance with Russia, has survived or deserves to. But there were important writers who sympathized with the proletarians without subscribing rigidly to their Marxist point of view. No writing that subscribes rigidly to any dogma (Christian, Marxist or whatever), where there is a choice, survives for long: this kind of writing is, after all, criticism, or propaganda in which the work of the resolutely non-dogmatic imagination may take only second place.

Chicago-born JOHN DOS PASSOS (1896–1971), whose grandfather was a Portuguese immigrant, had gained fame and flourished before the Depression, but his important work fits most appropriately in with, and even influenced, proletarian literature. He had grave faults; his retreat into conservatism after the Second World War is unconvincing and adds nothing to his literary stature —and he is most important as a technician. But whatever may spoil his work, of whatever period, it is never dogmatism or rigidity.

After graduating from Harvard (1916) Dos Passos saw service in France. His first book was an autobiographical novel about an ambulance driver: *One Man's Initiation—1917* (1920; rev. as *First Encounter*, 1945). His next, *Three Soldiers* (1921), was more characteristic, and although it does not incorporate his later technical innovations it does conveniently illustrate his strengths, weaknesses, and chief preoccupations. During the Twenties Dos Passos wrote plays incorporating 'movie' techniques, and he translated Blaise Cendrars (q.v.), whose panoramic methods of composition were to influence him considerably.

Three Soldiers takes three different men and traces the impact of war upon them: the optical worker Fuselli, who wants promotion; the farm-labourer Chrisfield, who only wants to go home; and the educated musician, Andrews. All are destroyed. Fuselli gets not promotion but syphilis. Chrisfield kills a sergeant and deserts. Andrews is unjustly sent to a labour battalion, escapes, is let down by his girl, and is eventually recaptured. He faces a bleak future (death or years of imprisonment), and the sheets of music he has composed blow away.

This is the real, gloomy Dos Passos. *Three Soldiers* was one of the first novels to describe the war as it really did affect people; those who thought it a fine thing, and patriotism meaningful, upbraided Dos Passos; but he manfully defended himself. The novel is vivid, and it manifests the nihilism from which Dos Passos guiltily suffered all his life: he feared anarchy for the obvious reasons, and was not an anarchist; but even more he feared the society for whose portrayal he became so famous: he feared for the survival of the individual. In *Three Soldiers* he shows the destruction of three men by society; this he really, and reasonably, believed to be the fate of individual man in the twentieth century. But naturally enough he wanted to offer some hope, and so he turned to the portrayal of society itself in the hope of reforming it. Whether he had read Romains' *Death of a Nobody* (q.v.) is not clear; but from *Manhattan Transfer* (1925) onwards his thinking had—or tried to have—something in common with unanimism (q.v.). He knew French literature well. But he could never make up his mind whether his entities with a life of their own were good or bad. However, one suspects that society itself was for Dos Passos an evil entity; he never, for all his reformist zeal and his active leftism of the Thirties, caught a sense of that authentic corporate life that is explored by the sociologist Durkheim. And, as *Three Soldiers* already makes clear, he could not create character: even his leading figures are types, and they are portrayed without psychological richness.

However, the naturalism of *Manhattan Transfer* and the trilogy *U.S.A.* (1938) escapes drabness for three reasons: his technique is lively as well as skilful; he is responsive to poesy, and had been exposed to imagism and other colourful new developments while at Harvard, so that his writing, too, is often gay and fresh; and although his creative imagination was deficient he was driven by real passions: passion against the injustices caused by the social and economic conditions between wars, and passion against the bigger injustice of life itself. For Dos Passos the naturalist gloom was all-pervading because he had no real imaginative life to set against it. His counterweight was provided by travel; and his travel books, particularly *Orient Express* (1927) are superb—at a time when his novels are, understandably enough, more known about than read, these travel books ought to be reissued.

The technique Dos Passos invented is very fine indeed, and I think it is still useful and valid. It has been utilized, notably, by Döblin and Sartre (qq.v.), both much superior as novelists to Dos Passos—but both fertilized considerably by his method. Dos Passos himself derived it mainly from Joyce (q.v.), but he added much of his own, and his approach, although lyrical, was realistic rather than introspective. He was not interested in language but social reality; Joyce's books are increasingly an investigation into language itself.

Dos Passos first used this technique in *Manhattan Transfer*, which deals mainly with the teeming life of New York City over a period of some years, and in particular with certain defeated individual lives. Dos Passos takes a number of characters and deals with the rise and fall of their fortunes in parallel (sometimes converging) episodes. These episodes are combined with three other devices: brief 'biographies' of important people (giving obvious opportunities for irony when contrasted with those of poor people); the 'newsreel', a collage of headlines, phrases from popular songs and so on that define the general atmosphere; and 'the camera eye', in which the author himself enters the field, mixing prose poetry with impressionistic and stream-of-consciousness passages. These, with some exceptions, are the weakest passages in *Manhattan Transfer* and *U.S.A.*, which consists of *The 42nd Parallel* (1930), *1919* (1932) and *The Big Money* (1936), with a new prologue and epilogue. *U.S.A.* takes twelve characters and treats them with what Marcus Cunliffe well calls 'circumstantial unloving competence'. Each one is supposed to be subordinate to the life of the city; but Dos Passos does not succeed in concealing his despair—a rather sterile despair. His later books—among them the trilogy *District of Columbia* (1952), *Chosen Country* (1951) and the very poor *Most Likely to Succeed* (1954)— collapsed, doubtless from exhaustion, into facile phoney patriotism, flat reportage and a nearly whining self-indulgence. It would certainly be unfair to judge Dos Passos' earlier work by them. He began as a pessimistic individualist and in fact remained one all his life. But in his best works his commitment to collectivism is sincere, arising from that streak of Utopian idealism that runs through most American consciousnesses. Nor does he falsify his sense of doom: both *Manhattan Transfer* and *U.S.A.* are ultimately depressing books. What the novel owes Dos Passos is a still viable method; it was a considerable achievement.

Of Irish-Catholic background, JAMES T. FARRELL (1904), who was born in the South Side section of Chicago that provides the background for his works, set out his literary principles in *A Note on Literary Criticism* (1936), which is Marxist but never in a crude or oversimplified sense: it opposed the official communist literary line. In *The League of Frightened Philistines* (1945) he defends realism sensibly; some of his arguments are reminiscent of those of the French 'populists' (q.v.). Farrell owes debts to his Catholic upbringing, to Marx, to Sherwood Anderson, to Proust, and, especially, to Joyce (for his use of stream-of-consciousness) and Dreiser (qq.v.). He resembles Dreiser in being at bottom a true naturalist, with little hope for the poor or the ill-fashioned, but much pity; his prose style is not distinguished. Because Farrell's later prose and many short stories are the products of a comparatively exhausted talent, his *Studs Lonigan* trilogy has been undervalued since the Thirties. Studs is his doomed character; Danny O'Neill makes it, but the pentalogy through which he does so is not much more than competent; in the Bernard Carr trilogy, in which Farrell traces his own literary aspirations, the energy is even more dissipated. But *Studs Lonigan—Young Lonigan: A Boyhood in Chicago Streets* (1932), *The Young Manhood of Studs Lonigan* (1934) and *Judgement Day* (1935)—is different. This at least is worthy of Dreiser. Studs comes from a poisoned place—Chicago's South Side— and his fundamental decency is shown as stifled by it. He has the usual adventures; he wants to be a real human being; but the desire to appear like his gang companions—tough, unsentimental, ruthless—prevails. When he grows up he becomes a crook and torturer, and learns to drink unwisely; his girl rejects him. Finally he marries and tries to make it; but his weak heart, his lack of real or wholesome experience, the indifference of society—these conspire to defeat him. He dies at twenty-nine. This reveals, as it sets out to do, the 'concrete facts' of 'spiritual poverty'. It has force and passion. It is the most powerful work of naturalism in a post-naturalist era.

Although he won the Nobel Prize in 1962, JOHN STEINBECK (1902–68), who was born of German-Irish parentage in Salinas, centre of the Californian lettuce industry, never produced a single work quite as rawly effective and moving as *Studs Lonigan*; but he was a gifted novelist, who has written many more novels of interest, even if they are flawed, than Farrell. Steinbeck did not share the natural pessimism of Dos Passos or Farrell, but—although evidently a sturdy rationalist, and just as indignant an enemy of injustice—substituted for it something very like the unanimism of Romains (q.v.). But in some of his better books (they all belong to the Thirties), such as *Tortilla Flat* (1935), he seems to have grasped a sense of that 'Durkheimian' corporateness the lack of which has been noted in Dos Passos. *Tortilla Flat* consists of tales about the *paisanos* of Tortilla Flat, on the outskirts of Monterey: people who do not share the 'values' of society and have opted out from it, so that they are idle and thieving but untainted by commerce and generous to those in need. There is a strong vein of sentimentality running through *Tortilla Flat*, but it does not quite spoil the freshness and liveliness of his conception.

Steinbeck's unanimism was derived from his friend, the biologist Edward Ricketts, whose interest was in groups of marine creatures functioning as one organism. Writers and others began to get interested in unanimism in this century when the corporateness of behaviour of human groups became less evident (especially in the religious sphere). That this interest is fruitful we have seen from the sociology of Durkheim and the novels of Romains (qq.v.), to name only two writers; Steinbeck did add something of his own, in his insistence on bestowing a loving consideration upon all living things, even freaks—an attitude he opposed to morality. This produced the best of his novels, really a novella, *Of Mice and Men* (1937). This, too, is flawed—some of the characters are wooden; the symbolism is lucubrated; Lennie's hallucinations at the end are wildly unconvincing; but the theme of the animal-child, the giant who does not know his own strength, protected by the little, intelligent, physically weak man, is not sentimental even though it is fundamentally homosexual (Lennie is led from 'good' non-sexual friendship to murder by vile uncomprehending women).

Unfortunately Steinbeck did not realize the contradictions in which his unanimistic ideas involved him: why be sorry for the individual if the individual does not matter? Of course Steinbeck cared about the plight of individuals, and about injustice, and with *In Dubious Battle* (1936), the story of a strike of fruit-pickers, he aligned himself with the proletarian school. *The Grapes of Wrath* (1939), about the Joad family which with thousands of others came to California to find work, is epic in proportion and gripping as narrative; the coming of the sharecroppers from the Oklahoma dustbowl to California is seen as a vast instinctive migration. Again, brilliant impressionistic writing is mixed in with some intolerable folksy sentimentality. But the novel's chief fault is that it does not cohere: Steinbeck makes it clear that he believes the behaviour of the profiteers in California is humanly inadequate, but he cannot show why; there is a conflict in him between the philosophical unanimist and the humane socialist. The book's message, that everything that lives 'is holy', is vitiated by its philosophy—and in any case it conveys this message not in imaginative but only in sentimental terms. Steinbeck's later books do nothing to resolve this paradox, and the ambitious *East of Eden* (1952), although it contains some passages of good writing, is pretentiously symbolic.

ERSKINE CALDWELL (1903), from Georgia, is less gifted, but too easily dismissed by critics today. Like Steinbeck, Caldwell tends to deal in inarticulate or simple characters not only because he wants to depict people depressed by economic and social circumstances but also because he cannot create complex or articulate ones. However, his early work illuminates the lives of Southern poor whites in the Thirties—the backwoodsmen and sharecroppers, whose lives he knew well—in a way that they had never been illuminated before. In *Tobacco Road* (1932), a dramatization of which ran in New York for eight years, and *God's Little Acre* (1933), all these wretched and degraded creatures have is sex. They have been so reduced by circumstances that they are only parodies of human beings—and Caldwell writes of them forcefully. That what he writes is sometimes very funny is beyond his own intention (perhaps), but has its irony. Caldwell should not be judged by the self-parodic novels that keep him rich nowadays, but by the two novels already mentioned and by *Journeyman* (1935), *Georgia Boy* (1943), *Trouble in July* (1940), about a lynching, and, an exception, the recent *Miss Mamma Aimee* (1967). A few of his stories are excellent—they were collected in *Complete Stories* (1953)—especially 'Kneel to the Rising Sun' (1935), a tale of racism that has classic stature and ought to be better known than it is.

NELSON ALGREN (1909), once the lover of Simone de Beauvoir (q.v.), and written about by her, was born in Detroit and reared in poverty in Chicago, his home for most of his life and the scene of most of his novels. He is connected with the proletarian movement and its predecessor, naturalism, because his immature first novel, *Somebody in Boots* (1935), was deliberately Marxist—and because his fiction seems to resemble Dreiser's or Farrell's in its relentless build-up of detail. Actually his mature work is highly original in its effect. He is, one might say, a naturalist without a philosophy or even interest in a philosophy—he has stuck to his own vision of life. Caldwell's subjects are the dregs of a rural, Algren's those of an urban, society—usually from the slums of Chicago's West Side. He soon lost his political interests, and was honest in doing so—for he is properly the laureate of these doomed dregs: content to perform this minor function, his novels and stories are remarkably successful within their limitations. Algren really isn't trying to say anything at all: just, by implication, to claim human interest for his people, who are tramps, petty criminals with grandiose dreams, hustlers, prostitutes, bar-flies. *Never Come Morning* (1942) is about the Polish immigrants in Chicago, and in particular about Bruno Bicek, whose dream is to be heavyweight champion of the world. He ends by committing murder. In *The Man with the Golden Arm* (1949) Frankie Machine (Majcinek), another Pole, has genius at gambling—and heroin. He could escape; but the poetry of his environment as well as its hellishness, which he recognises, drags him back: he fails, and kills himself. *A Walk on the Wild Side* (1956) is set on the way to and in New Orleans, and records the self-destruction of an innocent strong man, Dave Linkhorn. *The Neon Wilderness* (1947) contains memorable short stories. Algren is too often ignored; but he is one of the most consistent of American novelists, and while the fact that he does not try to see further than his characters' world limits him, it also gives him purity and power. He has written less than Farrell, but his fiction has not fallen off.

EDWARD DAHLBERG (1900), born in Boston and a friend of Herbert Read, D. H. Lawrence (qq.v.), and many others, is a difficult writer to place. His literary criticism is mystical, his indictment of civilization both Jewish and vituperative, his philosophy learned; but he began as a novelist of the proletariat even if not as a proletarian novelist, as a realist if not as a naturalist. *Bottom Dogs* (1929) is to a certain extent his own story: Lorry Lewis is the bastard of an itinerant woman-barber of Kansas City; he goes to an orphanage and then drifts. This is interesting because although its material is similar to that of Farrell, Dahlberg's method is impressionistic. *From Flushing to Calvary* (1932) less convincingly treats of similar material. Dahlberg, whose *Bottom Dogs* was introduced by D. H. Lawrence, does not seem to have fulfilled its promise, although he has retained a certain small following.

Farrell and Algren were often bracketed together, as 'Chicago realists', with a third: the distinguished Negro writer RICHARD WRIGHT (1908–60). Wright was born in Mississippi and migrated to Chicago on the eve of the Depression. He was a communist from 1932 until 1944. He educated himself during the late Twenties and Thirties, studied sociology, whose compilations of facts, together with his experiences in dozens of jobs, gave him the background for *Native Son* (1940). This, which is often described as 'a Negro *American Tragedy*', tells the story of the Chicago Negro boy Bigger Thomas. Although Wright had already written the four novellas collected in *Uncle Tom's Children* (1938; rev. 1940), this is still the work of a prentice writer. But for all the crudities of its writing, and the structural collapse of Book III owing to confusions between Marxist and creative imperatives, is remains a powerful and seminal book. In essence this novel is as critical of communists as of everyone else; where it isn't, as in the long speech of Bigger's communist lawyer—a Marxist plea that society has made Bigger what he is—the material is extraneous. And it must be admitted that the heart of *Native Son* is a savage and demonic nihilism. Bigger, as under-privileged and conspired against as Studs Lonigan, but black into the bargain, becomes reluctantly involved with the communist friends of the daughter of his white employer. In a moment of panic he accidentally kills her. While in flight he kills his own girl. He is captured, tried and, after rejecting both Christianity and communism, is executed. What is interesting about *Native Son* is that its power comes not from its revelation of society's responsibility for Bigger Thomas but from its nihilism: clearly society is not altogether responsible for him, because he is shown as vicious even amongst his own equally under-privileged contemporaries. The power comes from his violent assertion of himself, his defiance of the whole city of Chicago, his final affirmation of his murderous self.

Wright followed this with *Black Boy* (1945), an autobiography and his best and least confused book. This gives a clue to his nihilistic attitude, for in it he confesses to the extent of his horror of the Negro's collaboration with the white man to keep himself down. Since Wright had been brought up by a strict mother, a Seventh Day Adventist, he had felt doubly alienated in his childhood; when he grew up he was able to sublimate his self-hatred—usual in all creative people—in a generally critical attitude towards his people as a whole. He underestimated Negro culture; tended, in fact, if only by implication, to see the Negro as actually inferior because of his lack of self-assertion. Yet *Black Boy* is a masterpiece, a series of episodes that demonstrate with a terrible dramatic exactitude the predicament not only of the Negro, but of the artist who sees the ills in his society, is punished for it, and yet is of it.

After the Second World War, partly at the behest of Gertrude Stein (q.v.), who had liked a review, Wright settled in Paris. He remained in France until his premature death, at only fifty-two, from a heart attack. Wright was by then a famous man; much of his time was taken up entertaining visitors, travelling and lecturing. The books he wrote in these years did not fulfil the promise of *Native Son* and *Black Boy*. Robert Bone has summed him up admirably: he cannot, he points out, 'convincingly exorcise his demon. His sense of self is too deeply rooted in revolt. To opt for love is to give up his identity as a picaresque saint, metaphysical rebel, lonely outsider'. This explains the failure of his long novel *The Outsider*, which betrays his imagination because it is contrived, stilted, pompous—ultimately, egocentric and insensitive. Because industrialization had freed him from the stultifying traditions of the South, he came to invest too much in it—to ignore the evils inherent in it. But in the posthumous *Eight Today* (1963) there is one novella, dating from the early Forties, in which Wright wholly succeeded. It is called 'The Man Who Lived Underground', and it bears some close resemblances to Ralph Ellison's almost classic *The Invisible Man* (q.v., 1952). Here Wright more or less abandons a painstakingly realistic surface, and concentrates on the sensations and consequences of being driven underground. His hero, Fred Daniels, resembles Bigger Thomas in that he breaks the laws of the white masters and defies them. Furthermore, unlike Bigger, he penetrates to the absurd centre of their inauthentic world, based as it is on exploitation and falsehoods. Here Wright's indignation goes well beyond the Marxist line: it reaches beyond the political. But Fred Daniels wants to integrate himself (as the expression goes): he tries to return, from the sewer where he has been living, to the world. But that white world does not know him, even when he confesses to the crimes he has committed. Eventually he is murdered by policemen, determined not to accept his reality, in his own sewer. On account of this story alone Wright must be given a place in the front ranks of modern American writers of fiction. But the first two books of *Native Son*, and parts of the third, and *Black Boy* also entitle him to this position.

RALPH ELLISON (1914) was born in Oklahoma City, the son of a construction worker and tradesman who died when he was three, leaving his mother to support him, which she did by working as a domestic cleaner. Ellison was and has always been as interested in jazz as in literature. He played the trumpet in his school band, knew Hot Lips Page, is a lifelong friend of Jimmy Rushing. He chose first to study music. Then in 1936 he went to New York, met Richard Wright and LANGSTON HUGHES (1902–67), another Negro writer, mainly a poet with a fine ear for colloquial speech, but also a novelist (*Not Without Laughter*, 1930), playwright and influential and intelligent leader of Negro culture—and began writing. After war service in the Merchant Marine he worked on *Invisible Man* (1952). Ellison's high reputation is unusual since it is based on this novel alone; in the nearly twenty years that have elapsed since its publication he has added to it only a volume of essays, *Shadow and Act* (1964), and fragments from his novel in progress, printed in periodicals.

The style and method of *Invisible Man*, a novel whose prophecies have been realized in its own time, have as many antecedents as those of other highly original novels. The one that is most often pointed to is Kafka (q.v.): the hero is not named, and is manipulated in ways mysterious to him. But this resemblance to Kafka, while it does exist, is somewhat misleading. So is the oft-made comparison with surrealism (q.v.). For the Negro's consciousness of his predicament—and *Invisible Man* is first and foremost about that—is prophesied, so to speak, by Kafka. And Ellison can hardly be said to be indebted to Kafka for that. As for surrealism: 'reality is surreal', as Ellison himself has said. Joyce is a more certain influence: Ellison has learned much from Joyce's use of modern methods, including stream of consciousness and the introduction of comedy. An even greater debt—or is it a resemblance?—is owed to Nathanael West (q.v.). It is often held to be essentially a 'backward-looking-novel'; but this is where the Kafka comparison is misleading. After all, *Invisible Man* is the first Negro novel to transcend its genre. This even led Philip Larkin to (inadvertently) insult Ellison by calling him 'a writer who *happens* to be an American Negro'. That this is wrong is clear from Ellison's proposition that 'we view the whole of American life as a drama acted out upon the body of a Negro giant, who, lying trussed up like Gulliver, forms the stage and the scene upon which and within which the action unfolds'.

Invisible Man uses symbolism, allegory, myth and any other modernist device to hand, but never to the detriment of the mad narrator's account of his alienated and 'invisible' state. He begins as an idealist, studying at a college for Negroes in the South run by an 'Uncle Tom' called Dr. Bledsoe. His rejection by the South is redolent with irony: through the 'accident' of being no more than he precisely is, the narrator brings the school into disrepute. He travels North and, like Fred Daniels in Wright's 'The Man Who Lived Underground', holes up in a Harlem basement: 'invisibility' is for the time being the only endurable condition. His ultimate wisdom—reached after working in a nightmare paint factory, and becoming a noted member of an underground liberal party whose policy, he comes to see, is betrayal and totalitarianism—is disillusionment. The end of the book, describing a Harlem race riot, might have been a piece of impressionistic reporting of events that took place more than ten years after it was written. The narrator ends by asking: 'Who knows but that, on the lower frequencies, I speak for you?'

The most impressive of the fragments from his work in progress that Ellison has published is called 'And Hickman Arrives'. It concerns a small boy acting out, in a coffin, 'the meaning of resurrection', and shows even more daring and power than *Invisible Man*.

*

The truly ideological representatives of the proletarian movement—ROBERT CANTWELL (1908), who wrote *Laugh and Lie Down*, MARY HEATON VORSE, author of *Strike—A Novel of Gastonia* (1930), and so on—did not leave any important fiction behind them. And even the more enduring work of Richard Wright (but not of Ellison, who was six years younger and in any case waited until he was thirty-eight before publishing his novel) is flawed by political conviction rather than otherwise. Steinbeck's view was confused; Farrell's was limited, enabling him to complete only the one satisfactory book, the Lonigan trilogy. However, there are three novelists of the Thirties, all Jews, whose fiction goes beyond politics to, as Walter Allen has rightly claimed, confront 'the human condition in its naked terror'. That is not to say that these men were not affronted by the hideous injustices of the Thirties. They certainly all were. But in their books they went straight to the reasons for them; they did not see the reasons as primarily political or economic. And their general superiority perhaps proves that it is not at any rate the writer's business to see things in economic terms—but rather to examine the human disease that produces the economic symptoms.

DANIEL FUCHS (1909), the least gifted of these writers, but nevertheless a substantial talent, was born in New York City; he long ago turned to the writing of movie scripts as a way of life; his three novels of the Thirties, *Summer in Williamsburg* (1934), *Homage to Blenholt* (1936) and *Low Company* (1937), attracted no attention until they were reissued in 1961 as *Three Novels*, when they were immediately acclaimed. Fuchs's apparently lightweight, Jewish humour, his good-natured irony, anticipated the manner of the 'Jewish novel' with which we have become perhaps too familiar in the last decade. He seems to stand squarely behind Bellow and Malamud (qq.v). And yet he was writing like this—about Jews in New York's Lower East Side during the Depression— long before either of these writers began. Fuchs is a comic novelist; his characters inevitably fail, usually humorously; they are incapable of inspiring any reader with a sense of tragedy. They are knowing, but their knowledge gets them nowhere: they are innocently without innocence, and some of them intuitively realize their futility. There is no tragic resonance in Fuchs's work, but his comedy is the genuine article. Above all he is truthful and never gratuitously unpleasant. He is detached from his characters, but he understands them.

HENRY ROTH (1906) is the author of one masterpiece, *Call it Sleep* (1934). He found himself unable to complete a second novel, and he has never been able to return to writing again—apart from the odd short story. This has been a real loss. Essentially *Call it Sleep* is the story of the anguish of a small boy, David Schearl, the son of European Jewish immigrants to America in 1907. His father is a withdrawn paranoiac who is useless to this sensitive son; so the boy goes to his mother, who is herself alienated from her surroundings by language and custom. The boy haunts the streets, learning about sex, crime and cruelty, all the time in an abject terror of something his irritable Rabbi teacher calls God. At last he finds a way to unify his disparate fears into something meaningful and divine. His teacher has spoken of the coal of fire with which God cleansed the mouth of his prophet, Isaiah. And two young toughs have forced him to drop a piece of metal into the crack between the two electrified streetcar rails. The resultant flash has struck him as something fearful but divine. One day he is forced to fly from his father's sick rage. This phantasmagoric flight through the streets, and its outcome, is one of the most intensely related episodes in American fiction. Had Roth gone on to write more fiction at this pitch he would have been of at least the stature of a Faulkner; Hemingway never wrote better. The boy thrusts a metal ladle into the electrified crack, and is shocked into an insensibility which purges him of the horrors he has endured. As he recovers he has a reconciling vision. He does not know how to describe this unconsciousness: 'call it sleep'.

NATHANAEL WEST (originally NATHANAEL WEINSTEIN, 1903–40), who lost his own and his wife's life when he failed to stop for an oncoming car in California, was a close friend of many writers, including Farrell, William Carlos Williams and Fitzgerald, but his four novels were not generally appreciated until the early Fifties. He drifted around in the late Twenties in such jobs as sub-managing or managing hotels; and for a time he edited the magazine *Contact* with Williams. He had spent some time in Paris in the mid-Twenties, and he thoroughly absorbed surrealism—but he hardly ever reproduced it. He spent the last six or seven years of his life in Hollywood, a sexually solitary and perhaps tormented man. Then he met Eileen McKenney, the heroine of the silly book *My Sister Eileen* by Ruth McKenney; he married her and they had a few months, it appears, of great happiness before they died in the car accident.

West was not a more powerful or poetic writer than Henry Roth, but he developed a wider range. His first book, *The Dream Life of Balso Snell* (1931), entirely ignored when it appeared, is nothing much in itself, although brilliant in promise. It is a fantasy inspired by surrealism, in which Balso Snell discovers 'while walking in the tall grass that has sprung up around the city of Troy', Homer's 'ancient song'; he decides to enter the wooden horse, and discovers the 'posterior opening of the alimentary canal', by which he enters it, 'O Anus Mirabilis!'

West was not only original in his own right, but he was the original black comedian (and with a surer touch than his successors)—after all, *Miss Lonelyhearts* (1933) preceded Fuchs's first novel by a year. This is not his best book—*The Day of the Locust* (1939) is that—but because in it he discovered the procedures most suitable to his genius, it does sometimes reasonably seem to be. It is certainly a very good, and a very grim book. The journalist hero is given the job of answering the 'lonely hearts' letters on a popular newspaper. He collapses under the pressure of the job and of the cynicism of his colleague Shrike ('Why don't you give them something new and hopeful? Tell them about art'). He needs to become nothing less than Jesus Christ; and he means it. But he perishes (crucified?), the accidental victim of a cripple whose wife he has seduced and whom he (too sentimentally?) wants to save.

The irony and terror of this was already beyond anything modern America had yet produced. West's next novel, *A Cool Million, or The Dismantling of Lemuel Pitkin* (1934), was a departure from the realistic surface of *Miss Lonelyhearts*. It has been criticized, and probably underrated, because it adopts a parody of a woman's magazine style. It is sometimes a little jejune, but also very funny—and in the end horrific. There are still few more effective exposures of naïve 'Americanism' and capitalist optimism than this story of the honourable, trusting and parodically innocent Lemuel Pitkin, who loses an eye, his teeth, his scalp and his leg, and after being jailed and used as a tool for both communist and fascist conspiracies, is killed and becomes a martyr in the fascist cause. It disappoints only because it fails to transcend its immediate object—the Horatio Alger legend of the rise to fame and fortune of the honest poor boy—and become a major work of the imagination. The same cannot be said of West's last novel, *The Day of the Locust* (1939). This was composed in a straightforwardly realistic style, and with the great economy West had achieved. Despite its refusal to compromise facts or situation or character with sentiment or, indeed, with emotion of any kind, and despite the despair which pervades it, *The Day of the Locust* is redolent with pity and understanding as well as the terror of the previous books. The events he depicts are outrageous—he knew and lived in Hollywood, which is enough—but he nurses their vitality, celebrating it sadly.

West's decade was that of Jean Harlow, who initiated a line of sex-symbols that culminated in Marilyn Monroe. Both girls died young. In the character of Faye Greener West displays a more perfect understanding of the type, and what it represents, than any writer since. What would his wry, intellectually cruel and yet compassionate genius have made of the Arthur Miller-Monroe marriage, in which the intellectual, however briefly, 'caught' the dream girl? His description of the relationship between his intelligent hero, the painter Tod Hackett, and Faye Greener, suggests an answer. Tod knows what Faye is, but she nevertheless captivates him. He feels that if he can possess her honourably, everything may change. . . . He has qualms about approaching her as a client while she is working in a brothel. He travels hundreds of miles in order to see her misperform brief scenes in movies she has made. 'Her invitation wasn't to pleasure', West writes. The truth of such books as this often has to wait years before it is heeded. 'It is hard to laugh at the need for beauty and romance', West wrote in it, 'no matter how tasteless, how horrible, the results of that need are. But it is easy to sigh. Few things are sadder than the truly monstrous.' West's work relentlessly depicts the truly monstrous, but also expresses the exact and human quality of its sadness.

JEROME WEIDMAN (1913), another New York Jewish novelist, is always a trifle unlucky, I feel, to be given no credit at all by critics. Certainly he is slick and sentimental in his later work (which is nevertheless readable and amusing light reading), but few novelists have been as good at portraying repulsively ruthless (Jewish) characters. His first three books are his best: *I Can Get It for You Wholesale* (1937), *What's in It for Me?* (1938) and the short stories collected in *The Horse That Could Whistle 'Dixie'* (1939). Here, as in none of his succeeding work, Weidman displays a cynicism so shocking that, whatever its motives, it is really fascinatingly effective, even if in a thoroughly minor way. Weidman cannot possibly be considered on a level with Daniel Fuchs, let alone West; but he has his tiny niche as caricaturist of Jewish go-getters.

JOHN O'HARA (1905–70), born in Pennsylvania, is another novelist famous for his portraits of heels and for his brutal realism. He had somewhat more merit than Weidman, especially as a craftsman in the short story. After the Thirties O'Hara's work grew increasingly pretentious, vulgar and lurid; little of it needs to be taken into account, although some of the short stories of his final decade are finely observed and compressed. His best novel is his first: *Appointment in Samarra* (1934). This tells of the events leading up to the suicide of Julian English, of Gibbsville, Pennsylvania. While drunk at the country club English throws a highball into the face of a man who could help him in business. It leads to his self-destruction. For although he promises his wife that he will try to make it up the next evening, events conspire to make him drunk again; he goes off to a roadhouse and dances with the mistress of a powerful local boot-legger; then later gets into a fight and finds himself ostracized on all sides. English's motives are not clear, but presumably the throwing of the drink into his potential business friend's face is seen as a decent (anti-materialistic) gesture that he has not the resilience, the decent substance, to sustain. The analysis of Gibbsville and its mores is masterly and utterly fascinating. But one feels even here that O'Hara is an excellent journalist and sociologist, but not a novelist. He has little insight into human character, and his accounts of it resemble good newspaper reporting rather than fiction. All his skill and readability cannot save him from his obtuseness about individuals. The best of his later novels was *Ourselves to Know* (1960), about the life of a successful murderer.

Very different from O'Hara, superior but less well known and prolific, is the Wisconsin novelist GLENWAY WESTCOTT (1901), who was encouraged but then disliked by Gertrude Stein ('. . . Glenway Wescott at no time interested Gertrude Stein. He has a certain syrup but it does not pour'). Wescott, though an expatriate for many years, has remained obsessed by Wisconsin, and might even be described as its reluctant laureate. Wescott found the repressive puritanism of his native region restricting and oppressive; but it fascinated him, as did the history of his tough pioneering forbears. He began as a poet, and his best fiction tries to recapture the bitter poetry of Wisconsin. *The Grand-mothers* (1927), his best work, is in its quiet way of classic status. Although very American it is a highly original novel; the only discernible influence, that of Proust (q.v.), has been thoroughly assimilated. Alwyn Tower, a young man living on the French Mediterranean coast, recreates the lives of his relatives: his three grandmothers (for one grandfather had two wives), his parents, and others. This sometimes painfully nostalgic book recreates the American past with the accuracy and love of a Willa Cather. The short stories in *Goodbye Wisconsin* (1928) have similar power. Later novels—*Pilgrim Hawk* (1940), set in Paris, and *Apartment in Athens* (1945)—have been distinguished but not of similar high quality.

High claims have occasionally been made for JOHN P. MARQUAND (1893–1960), but they can hardly be sustained. At its very best, his writing is that of a bland, shrewd and gentlemanly journalist. He began as a journalist, popular romancer and detective-story writer, but then graduated to a higher-middlebrow comedian of manners. He at once satirizes and indulges New England society, but never so as to offend. On the other hand, he is observant and he writes smoothly and amusingly. Some of his well known, rather smug (but pleasantly readable) books are *The Late George Apley* (1937), *Wickford Point* (1939), *H. M. Pulham, Esq.* (1941). His two best books are *So Little Time* (1943) and *Sincerely, Willis Wayde* (1955). The first expresses his own regrets at his creative mediocrity in the form of a story about a New York play editor who would like to have done something serious; the second is a knowledgeable study of a business man's rise to power.

Rather more extravagant claims have been made for the Chicago-born JAMES GOULD COZZENS (1903), even by serious critics—one of whom has compared him to C. P. Snow (q.v.), and perhaps not without unwitting point. For Cozzens is an arch-middlebrow, although by no means an inoffensive one. The book that rocketed him to fame, *By Love Possessed* (1957), is perhaps the most repulsive of all the pretentious midcult novels of the twentieth century. Its successor, *Morning Noon and Night* (1969), is almost deliriously bad in the pretentiousness of its language. However, no critic takes these books seriously; attempts to put Cozzens forward as a serious writer have mainly centred on *Men and Brethren* (1936), *The Just and the Unjust* (1942) and, in particular, *Guard of Honour* (1948). What can be said for him? The last book is a fairly meticulous account of three days at a United States Air Force training field in Florida in 1943; but it lacks characterization, and the attitude behind it is that of a business man who has made his pile and simply wants to leave everything to the experienced chaps who know best. In other words, Cozzens has nothing whatever to say. He is a man with a commonplace temperament who has, with happy results for himself, strayed into the field of literature. Cozzens, as *By Love Possessed* shows, has gathered no wisdom, and never had warmth—all one can discern is an extraordinarily virulent hatred of sex. Cozzens hides his coldness and civil servant's smugness behind what his admirers take to be a stoical irony. The combination in him, of sly authoritarianism, unwisdom and iciness, is unique. One must grant him, especially in *Guard of Honour*, a certain technical skill. But his 'objectivity', much vaunted by admirers, is simply insensitivity—a human stupidity of remarkable dimensions. A world that grants Cozzens a place in literature is on a long, steep slide into indifference.

*

HENRY MILLER (1891) is probably best regarded as an educationist. His reputation has been distorted because some of his books were for years banned in Great Britain and the United States. He has been thought of variously as a writer of dirty books (his notorious *Tropic of Cancer*, whined the semi-literary entertainer, Leon Uris—knocking, as Leslie Fiedler has implied, at the gates of gentile heaven—in a court case, 'goes beyond every bound of morality I've ever known in my life—everything I've been taught'), mage, mystic, daddy of the beats. . . . Miller was born in New York City and worked in a variety of jobs, eventually becoming employment manager for Western Union. He was nearly forty when he went to Paris and took up a literary and bohemian life. He has told the story of his early life in a series of autobiographical books, including *Black Spring* (1936) and *The Rosy Crucifixion* trilogy, consisting of *Sexus* (1949), *Plexus* (1953) and *Nexus* (1960). His writing about his family and his earlier life is his best, and is run a close second only by the account of his travels in Greece, *The Colossus of Marousi* (1941) and by his account of Conrad Moricand, an astrologer he had known in Paris and unwisely invited to Big Sur, in the section of *Big Sur and the Oranges of Hieronymus Bosch* (1957) called *A Devil in Paradise*, which appeared as a separate volume in 1956. For the past thirty years Miller has lived in Big Sur, California.

Miller resists classification inasmuch as he cannot be called critic, poet, novelist, essayist—or even all of these things together. Actually he does not have an imagination, and his attempts to write 'poetically' (in imitation of Rimbaud, q.v., whom he does not understand and about whom he has written very poorly) are disastrous. But this gives no cause for puzzlement once it is realized that Miller is a simple-minded and literal heir of American nineteenth-century romanticism. Since he lives in the twentieth century, his romanticism has developed a defensive, nihilist edge: he is famous for his denunciations of America (*The Air Conditioned Nightmare*, 1945). But it is wrong to call this side of him satirical: it is merely vituperative.

Miller is a true naïve (q.v.), as his embarrassing compilation called *The Books in My Life* (1952) demonstrates: here Rider Haggard rubs shoulders with Mary Baker Eddy and Shakespeare in one of the most haphazard lists ever made. The sage of Big Sur, the Whitmanesque celebrator of the body and the enemy of literature, became for the most part a highly 'literary' writer. It is a sad end to the career of the man who tried harder than any other twentieth-century American writer to realize the specifically American dream of absolute freedom. However, Miller has his intrinsic importance as an autobiographer, and his historical importance as a kind of educator of the beat generation. Leslie Fiedler is quite correct in saying that the years of Depression, unemployment and appeasement produced no 'brand of apocalyptic hysteria . . . so eccentric or so heartless as Miller's', and that, deliberately hilarious at his best and undeliberately so at his worst, he is the 'first important . . . anti-tragic writer in America'. But in freeing himself entirely from morality and responsibility— this involved 'being a swine' in the sense of sleeping with his benefactors' wives or stealing the car-fare home from the bag of a woman while laying her—he played a significant role. He has carried 'innocence' as far as it can be carried in this century; those who want to study the results need look no further. He thinks living is more important than writing, and we can judge him as liver as well as writer from his prose. In *Sexus* he tells us: 'I was approaching my thirty-third year, the age of Christ crucified. A wholly new life lay before me, had I the courage to risk all'. This, one might say, is bad life but good writing: good writing because it is true, as true as Miller's lifelong devotions to pseudo-religions and phoney prophets.

Miller is certainly not important for his contributions to the sexual life of the twentieth century. Sex unsettles him so much that a good deal of his writing about it is fairly describable as a way of filling in time (and not much time at that) between orgasms. In his writings about sex Miller proceeds frantically from one encounter to another, a gentle person desperately trying to brutalize his sexual role, not knowing what he is looking for beyond his need to degrade woman, make her comic, not to be tender towards her. He can be compassionate about anyone unless it is a woman in a sexual role; but he tries to push all his women into sexual roles. . . . He is the less likely to represent a woman as already degraded (simply by the fact of her being physically capable of fulfilling his mindless pleasure) the more she genuinely puzzles him or reminds him of his mother. Thus his second wife, Mona, lesbian, taxi-dancer, whore and pathological liar fascinates him more than any other woman in his writings: his sexual use of her does not exhaust her meaning. Somewhere behind all this, it seems, there is a Whitmanesque homosexual impulse that not even the so much vaunted innocence of total freedom can erase.

Miller is the authentic non-intelligent, natural, 'anti-tragic', free man. One can rightly call him 'eccentric and heartless'. But in him, one might also say, mankind has come some way—from employment manager to lucid autobiographer and clown. His despair, if he has any, has no quality; and his writings about sex are disappointingly pornographic. But can one say more of the silence of employment managers?

Another odd man out of American letters, although in almost every respect at the other end of the scale, is VLADIMIR NABOKOV (1899). Miller is odd because he is *so* representative, Nabokov is odd because he is, of course, not. One might treat him as Russian, since he was born of a noble Russian family in St. Petersburg (now Leningrad), and he wrote in Russian until 1940. But Nabokov was educated at Cambridge, has been an exile all his adult life, is an American citizen, and has written his more important books in an expert and confident English, and has written them about America. Nabokov taught Russian literature at Stanford and Cornell in the United States before his literary success enabled him to retire. He is a distinguished entomologist.

Nabokov's Russian books, most of which have now appeared in English, deal coldly with the anguishes of exile, which none the less come through strongly. They are brilliant, but only one or two of the short stories show feeling towards the characters. The best is *Laughter in the Dark* (*Camera Obscura*, 1933; tr. W. Roy, 1936), about a man's fatal infatuation for a cinema usherette, the worst—foreshadowing the ignominious depths plumbed by *Ada* (1969)—is *King Queen Knave* (1928; tr. D. and V. Nabokov, 1968). Nabokov's best books came in his second, American phase, when he decided to accept exile and to become—so far as he could—American. Then he began to analyze, with the genuinely innocent eye of the foreigner, his surroundings. *Pnin* (1957) tells of a Russian professor of entomology at a college in New York State. *Lolita* (1955), banned for a time, is Nabokov's best book. Humbert Humbert becomes obsessed with a twelve-year-old 'nymphet', and in order to gain possession of her marries her mother. After a flight across the United States, as vivid a description of it as has ever been made by a non-American, Lolita is seduced by a playwright, whom Humbert kills.

Nabokov might have been a major writer, but self-congratulatory cleverness has killed the intensity in him. His stylistic tricks—punning, anagrams—have energy but very soon become monotonous; they do not add anything funda- mental. His style is so hard that it is sometimes brittle, and that brittleness indicates that his aristocratic sensibility—early battered beyond repair by exile —is accompanied by an innate romanticism. Nabokov's course as a writer has been to challenge, combat, even at times to deny this romanticism, acknow- ledging it only as a sort of baroque nostalgia for St. Petersburg. However, in *Lolita* Nabokov was able, by means of a detachment he had cultivated with care and skill, convincingly to describe the enslaving effect of a certain kind of sexual passion—perhaps one of the things he 'means' by Humbert's passion is romantic love—and the opportunities for evil that it opens up. It is not the novel it might have been because it fails to examine the nature of Humbert's sexual pathology; Nabokov's lack of interest in this is a positive defect. The clue to Nabokov's deficiencies lies in *Ada*, where his delight in himself is anything but aristocratic. The only interest in this appalling book partakes of the nature of the solution to a crossword puzzle; but Nabokov has sufficient imagination and literary breeding to learn from the shame he must now feel at perpetrating it.

*

MARY McCARTHY (1912), born in Seattle, was orphaned when both her parents died in the influenza epidemic of 1918; she has recorded her experi- ences at the hands of various relatives in one of her best books, *Memories of a Catholic Girlhood* (1957). For a time she was the wife of EDMUND WILSON (1895– 1972), one of the best of American literary journalists and, with Geoffrey Grigson (q.v.) and one or two others, the last representative of a dying race of literate and informed periodical critics. Wilson, notable for his generosity and his shrewd judgements as a reviewer, also wrote some good fiction, including *I Thought of Daisy* (1929) and *Memoirs of Hecate County* (1946). Like her ex- husband, Mary McCarthy has always remained a journalist; in recent years she has written persuasive criticism, in magazines, of the American involvement in Viet Nam, which she has visited. She is a readable, successful and intelligent novelist, often described as 'scathing'. Her subject is usually the unwisdom of those who in our time regard themselves as wise: the cultured and the intel- lectual. She has little love for her own kind, and this may be the reason why she appeals to a middlebrow readership (she has stooped to its level only twice, in her two books about Venice and Florence); it is likely that she has been somewhat undervalued, although her characters tend to be manipulated for the benefit of her admirable wit, and she has little warmth. Her best novels are *The Oasis* (1949), about a modern would-be Utopia; *A Charmed Life* (1955), in which the artistic are castigated; *The Groves of Academe* (1952) and *The Group* (1963), a novel about the fates of eight girls who graduated from Vassar at the same time as Miss McCarthy. This is not psychologically profound, and like all Mary McCarthy's work it lacks a sense of poetry; but it is a brilliant and compassionate piece of social history, which deserves to survive.

The output of JEAN STAFFORD (1915), who was born in California and grew up in Colorado, has been slender but genuinely distinguished. From 1940 until 1948 she was married to the poet Robert Lowell (q.v.), and later, after a second marriage, she had a short (1959–63) marriage to the late A. J. Liebling, journalist and sports writer. Her perceptive and sharp first novel, *Boston Adventure* (1944), subjects Boston society to the scrutiny of Sonia Marburg, the daughter of an immigrant chambermaid; Sonia works as secretary to the wealthy spinster Miss Peabody. *The Mountain Lion* (1947) is one of those rare novels that can penetrate the world of children without shattering or sentimentalizing it. *Children Are Bored on Sundays* (1953) and *Bad Characters* (1965) are collections of short stories.

The South is a violent place, and a conservative one. It is not an easy place for its sensitive or liberal inhabitants, who, like Faulkner, form part of its tradition and yet oppose it—thus opposing a part of themselves. Perhaps the painfulness of living in the South is one of the reasons why the New Criticism— essentially an attempt to evolve an objective criticism—came from there. Following the period of reconstruction after the Civil War the South, given the best will in the world, had nearly insoluble problems. Where, above all, was it to deploy the mass of freed slaves? The problem is not, of course, solved; the South-eastern United States throws up Faulkners, and it also throws up Wallaces. Literature often flourishes under difficult conditions; the Southern renaissance has added greatly to the literature of modern America, even if its contribution has been markedly pessimistic. This has been a defeated area, not one of hope; but it is also a perfect microcosm of crazy modern man as he ruins his world. Faulkner towers above everyone else in this renaissance of letters, both in scope and depth; if in his life he had to hit the bottle, and if he ended in self-parody, in his best works he still sums up the South: its aspirations, its despairs, above all its doomed sense of itself. But there were others besides Faulkner. Some writers, although Southerners, contributed little to Southern literature as such: Thomas Wolfe (q.v.) is one; Erskine Caldwell is another. The first of these is an individualist (or an egocentric); the second is excellent on poor whites, but does not even try to see them in their context. They certainly do not build on the foundations laid by Kate Chopin and Ellen Glasgow (qq.v.).

In 1962 KATHERINE ANNE PORTER (1890), born at Indian Creek in Texas, published a long novel, which had become a legend, having been announced as imminent over a period of twenty years. This was *Ship of Fools*. An 'appallingly obvious and dull' (Leslie Fiedler) 'moral allegory' about a voyage, it is a surprising middlebrow negation of her previous and most distinguished work, which consists of short stories and novellas. In these earlier works—*Flowering Judas* (1930), stories, *Pale Horse, Pale Rider* (1939), three novellas and *The Leaning Tower* (1944), stories—she studies the effects of the changes in the South on the personalities of individuals; many of the stories deal with a girl called Miranda—into whose figure Katherine Anne Porter doubtless projects some of her own history—at various stages of her life.

Although Katherine Anne Porter has travelled all over Europe, and has lived in many parts of America (New Orleans, Chicago, Denver, Mexico City, New York, and elsewhere), the central concern of her writing is her Southern heritage. Her life has been dedicated to the subsidization of her creative writing, a vocation she once said she would not herself have chosen; in her earlier days she had to perform many unwelcome journalistic chores. She has destroyed 'trunkfuls' of material. She spoke of herself (1933) as 'a woman who goes with her mind permanently absent from the place where she is'. Her aim was 'to tell a straight story and to give true testimony'. One might describe her best writings as imaginatively in quest of the meaning of herself and of her peculiar heritage. She reveals her awareness by means of 'epiphanies' (q.v.), moments of sudden illumination: the child Miranda, curiously alienated from the tradition of which she is a part, even a kind of freak, understands her situation through seeing a circus performance. Almost always these moments of revelation indicate a tragic situation, meticulously and exquisitely set forth. The nearest to such illuminations is to be found in some of Emily Dickinson's poems. Few writers have been able to suggest such vast accumulations of fact, such complex histories, in so short a compass. *Noon Wine* (1937), included in *Pale Horse, Pale Rider*, is characteristic. It works perfectly on the realistic level, but sets up extraordinary resonances both parabolic and symbolic. Mr. Thompson, married to an invalid, unhappily and inefficiently runs a Texas dairy farm. Then the work of an enigmatic new hired man, Mr. Helton, puts things right. After nearly a decade Homer T. Hatch turns up: he claims that Mr. Helton is an escaped lunatic, and tries to capture him for profit. Thompson kills him, but is acquitted of murder; however, Hatch posthumously succeeds in ruining his life, for he cannot bear his guilt, and kills himself. What really happened? The question forms itself as naturally as it does when we seek explanations in the non-fictional world.

Since Miss Porter is so excitingly and uniquely gifted a writer, the failure of *Ship of Fools* was little short of a tragedy. There are of course fine touches in it; but these touches are those of a writer of short stories or novellas. Miss Porter is not a novelist, and it is a pity that she allowed her understandable ambition to write a long novel to develop into a pressure to produce a 'great' one; inevitably, *Ship of Fools* was turned into a big, *kitsch* movie. But this massive failure in no way detracts from the original achievement of the earlier fiction.

Since most of the members of the Southern Agrarian movement were poets, it is dealt with in the following section. One of the leading spirits was Allen Tate (q.v.), who for over a quarter of a century was married to the Southern novelist CAROLINE GORDON (1895). Caroline Gordon was born in Kentucky; her people on both sides had been tobacco-planters 'since the weed was first cultivated by white men'. Her novels are exceptionally skilful, but their austerity has prevented them from having a wide effect. *Penhally* (1931), her first novel, set the tone for its successors. An account of a Kentucky family over several generations, it demonstrated the author's grasp of the details of Southern history. *None Shall Look Back* (1937), a study of the Confederate general, Nathan Bedford Forrest, is her most severe novel. It gives her picture of the old South: gracious, heroic, feudal but benevolent to its slaves (who are represented as ungrateful!), and yet is, as Walter Allen has said, somehow 'abstract . . . static': has life ever actually been lived like this? But this is nevertheless an important novel, even if an obviously limited one: it gives, at an entirely serious level of intelligence (however its sensitivity is to be judged), the picture of the old South that so many people still hold—and have great nostalgia for. Unfortunately *None Shall Look Back* appeared in the shadow of Margaret Mitchell's *Gone With the Wind* (1936), a piece of midcult trash about the South that made history as a best seller and then as a movie. The best of Caroline Gordon's later novels is *The Malefactor* (1956), which puts to good use her extensive knowledge of literary people, including Tate himself.

Another close associate of the Agrarians, although somewhat younger than the rest of the group, was the Kentuckian ROBERT PENN WARREN (1905), who is a critic, poet and academic as well as a novelist. It was Warren, who cannot be described as other than a liberal, who first saw that Faulkner was being misjudged, in the Thirties, for 'having the wrong politics'; who saw that Faulkner's work went well beyond any kind of politics. A considerable writer in every genre that he has attempted, Warren has some affinities with Faulkner, in particular with his tendency to treat of violence and evil. But Warren's approach is more cerebral, and sometimes tends to lose in power. He has a colloquial liveliness that is rare in a 'new critic' of his generation; certainly, reading some of his criticism, one would not imagine him to be the kind of novelist he in fact is. As a poet Warren is consistently interesting and evidently of high quality; but he has not often succeeded in discovering a voice that is distinctively his own. His and Cleanth Brooks's *Understanding Poetry* (1938), a text book of the New Criticism, revolutionized the teaching of poetry in American universities, and its effects are still felt; it is possible that Warren's critical self-consciousness has weakened or dispersed his poetic impulse. His best poetry is to be found in *Promises* (1957).

He is a self-conscious novelist, too; and again, whatever weaknesses his fiction has may be traced to this (he and Brooks wrote an *Understanding Fiction*, 1943, as well . . .). For example, might not his surprising rhetoric be an attempt to escape from his over-intellectualism? His fiction has rightly been seen as developing straight out of Faulkner; one senses that he would sacrifice much of his critical intellect in order to attain to Faulkner's power. Certainly one sometimes gets the notion that Warren hates being a thinker, and wants to escape from it. And yet this is to judge by the highest standards. Warren is a serious writer, of undeniable quality; it is this that makes his failure to reconcile his strong creative impulses with his intellectual processes a serious and disappointing one. In his most famous novel, *All the King's Men* (1946), a study of a Southern politician suggested by the career of Huey Long (for some—

inexplicable—reason Warren denied this), there is an imbalance that results from Warren's attempt to escape his critical self-consciousness. This is a pity, because few more gifted novelists have tackled a more fascinating theme: that of the problem of how or when doing good by corrupt means is wrong or ultimately destructive. Willie Stark does good ruthlessly, and one of Warren's intended messages is perfectly clear: that nothing, even reform and justice and a square deal, is worse than totalitarianism. But Warren chooses as narrator a newspaperman called Jack Burden, a history graduate. Burden begins by accepting Stark at face value, and idealistically supports him. He even causes the suicide of a respected judge by digging something discreditable from his past—only to discover that this judge was his father. Eventually, when Stark is assassinated by an idealistic doctor—but not for political reasons—Burden is supposed 'to understand'. However, he is an unconvincing figure, and the novel as a whole leaves one with a strong impression that Willie Stark is, after all, a hero—that had he not become personally (sexually) corrupted by power, he might have survived to do even more good. Burden is supposed to understand by the end that Willie has been corrupted by power; but Burden is an intellectual, a representative of Warren, and he is not convincing. *All the King's Men* therefore fails, for one reason or the other, to demonstrate that power does corrupt.

Warren has written some notable short stories, collected in *The Circus in the Attic* (1948). His 'tale in verse and voices', *Brother to Dragons* (1953), is his most formidable effort to recapture the horror of the Jacobean era; much more successful than the lurid and theatrical novel *World Enough and Time* (1950). *Brother to Dragons* tells the story of the axe-killing of a Negro by the sons of Jefferson's sister; the author introduces himself as 'R. P. W.', an interlocutor of the twentieth century. This is, again, a powerful work, and yet it is a little too calculated, for all its concentration on evil and the deliberateness of its melodrama, to quite come off.

Claims have been made for Warren's later fiction, especially for *Flood* (1964). But it is likely that posterity will endorse Walter Allen's view that Warren's best novel is his first: *Night Rider* (1939). This is, in a way, on the same theme as the more ambitious *All the King's Men*: Percy Munn joins the Night Riders, an illicit organization formed to destroy a tobacco-buyers' ring that threatens the small growers of Kentucky, out of idealism; but the nature of its activity, which he helps to direct, corrupts him. The scenes of violence here are superbly described, and reinforce the suggestion that the full expression of a tragic vision of life has been prevented by too zealous an adherence to a critical theory.

A lesser novelist, but an interesting one, is T. S. STRIBLING (1881–1965), who was born in Tennessee. He is interesting because his obvious starting-point, his inspiration, was Sinclair Lewis (q.v.): his first significant novel, *Birthright* (1922), appeared just two years after *Main Street* (q.v.). This applies Lewis' methods to a different kind of problem: not one of mere smugness but one of savage injustice. An educated mulatto returns to a Tennessee town to try, as is his just and human due, to make his way. He fails horribly. The novel has more point than Lewis', although it is worse written by any standards, and much less clever; and Stribling, who had practised law in the South and knew his rogues as well as the others, displays as much knowledge as Lewis—which makes this and some of its successors rather neglected novels (two years after his death not a single book by him was listed as in print). *Teeftallow* (1926) is an even more Lewisian study, this time of a confidence-trickster, a small-time Southern politician, Railroad Jones, who climbs to wealth and influence by exploitation of the vileness of the people of his Tennessee mountain town. The couple who love each other and fail to conform are destroyed. Again, this is a novel whose corrosive bitterness is not forced. But better was to come from Stribling: a trilogy consisting of *The Forge* (1931), *The Store* (1932) and *Unfinished Cathedral* (1934). This traces the history of a family, the Vaidens, in Florence, Alabama. It is not a major work of the imagination, nor is it well-written, but it is none the less a truthful novel. Jimmy Vaiden rises from poor white to a position of dominance in the region; but he loses his slaves after the Civil War, and gets into debt to the local storekeeper. His son Miltiades, Klansman and ex-colonel, unscrupulously and dishonestly acquires the store. Finally we see him in his power, president of the local bank, feared and 'loved'. He is building a cathedral as his monument. Stribling is crude and his satire is laboured. But he was a pioneer. We meet the Vaidens again, after all, in the Snopes. Faulkner purchased the Vaiden trilogy as it appeared, and kept it until his death. He owed much to it.

EUDORA WELTY (1909) was born in Mississippi, yet in one important sense she chose to be Southern, for her father was from Ohio and her mother from West Virginia—which does not count, culturally, as a Southern state. Although she has written good novels, Eudora Welty is plainly at her best as a writer of short stories and novellas. She is an original, even an idiosyncratic writer, who was admired and encouraged by, among others, Ford Madox Ford, Katherine Anne Porter and Robert Penn Warren (qq.v.). A writer who has influenced her is Henry Green (q.v.), about whom she has written interestingly.

Eudora Welty is at her strongest in the short forms of fiction probably because she is best of all at compressed portraits of eccentrics. These are often called caricatures, but this is not the right word: Miss Welty seizes an individual at a self-revelatory moment, and the resultant portrait often appears as a caricature. In fact it is more often a truthful account of the person. She has the capacity to create characters that puzzle as much as those from everyday life. Is the postmistress of China Grove, Mississippi, in 'Why I Live at the P.O.'— in the collection *A Curtain of Green* (1941)—schizophrenic or merely alienated? That the story generates arguments on the point is tribute to Miss Welty's powers of characterization. It is true that the characters in the stories are frequently neurotics, eccentrics or in a few cases psychotics; but they are nevertheless seen as they are, and if they provide comedy, they provide quite as much pathos. Of course, dealing with such material invariably produces risks, and when Miss Welty tries consciously for symbolic effects she fails. But when she concentrates on the small-town Mississippi life that she has observed so carefully and understands so well, she frequently makes more universal statements. Besides *A Curtain of Green*, her story collections include *The Wide Net* (1943), *The Golden Apples* (1949) and *The Bride of the Innisfallen* (1955). *The Shoe Bird* (1964) is for children. *Delta Wedding* (1946) and *The Ponder Heart* (1954) are novels. It has been suggested that Eudora Welty is not essentially Southern. The answer is to imagine her fiction without the South. The strangeness of her characters is a Southern strangeness.

Two important Southern woman novelists are CARSON MCCULLERS (1917–67) and FLANNERY O'CONNOR (1925–64). Carson McCullers was born Lula Carson Smith in Georgia. She studied in New York, and married Reeves McCullers when she was just twenty. She published *The Heart is a Lonely Hunter* in 1940, at just about the time when she and her husband had agreed to divorce. For the next five years she lived mostly in New York, publishing *Reflections in a Golden Eye* (1941) and a number of short stories. She remarried Reeves McCullers, who had been wounded in the war, in 1945; this broke up in 1951, for Reeves had turned into a drug- and alcohol-addict—he killed himself in Paris soon after Carson McCullers left him. She herself suffered intermittently from heart disease, paralytic strokes, and pneumonia; when she died from a stroke she was also suffering from breast cancer. Her health had been deteriorating since her marriage in 1937. She managed, however, to produce several more books: *The Member of the Wedding* (1946), which she dramatized (1950), *The Ballad of the Sad Café* (1951), an omnibus volume containing her first three novels as well as collecting most of the stories, the play *The Square Root of Wonderful* (1958) and the final novel, *Clock Without Hands* (1961). Edward Albee (q.v.) successfully dramatized her short story *The Ballad of the Sad Café* in 1963. Although her last years were such a struggle against illness and incapacity, Carson McCullers published in 1964 a charming book of children's poetry: *Sweet as a Pickle and Clean as a Pig*.

Like the other Southern woman writers of fiction (Katherine Anne Porter, Eudora Welty, Flannery O'Connor, qq.v.) Carson McCullers deals in eccentrics and grotesques. This is an effect that the South has upon the minor writer. (It may well be that in trying to meet the challenge with major fiction such a writer as Warren has fallen short of the achievement of this quartet; certainly Wolfe failed so abjectly, so far as the South is concerned, that his fiction has scarcely any relevance to it.)

Carson McCullers is essentially a minor writer, and she has strengthened her best work by keeping strictly to her limitations. She has been misunderstood when critics have judged her analyses of crippled individuals as dissections of poisoned cultures. Miss McCullers was enough of a medical freak to be able to feel sympathy for more drastically maimed persons. But there is no sense, in her books, of horror at physical or mental deformity. She is in one important sense an affirmative writer, for she shows the world of her crippled characters to be beautiful and loving rather than horrible; true, her sense of the whole world is not an altogether beautiful one—but she does show, as few other modern writers have done, that what seems or is taken to be ugly is not necessarily so.

Her best work is in *The Heart is a Lonely Hunter*, the short story, almost a novella, 'The Ballad of the Sad Café', and *The Member of the Wedding*. *Reflections in a Golden Eye*, set in a pre-war army camp in the South, was a rather disastrous experiment in the macabre and is a thoroughly bad and, by its author's standards, pretentious piece of Gothic. *The Heart is a Lonely Hunter*, set in a small Georgian mill town, is concerned with an intelligent deaf-mute called John Singer and his effect on four people. He lives with the feeble-minded Spiros Antonapoulos, whom he loves. (There is no hint of homosexuality.) When Antonapoulos becomes ill and anti-social and has to be taken to a mental hospital, Singer enters into the lives of four other people, none of whom have an inkling of the grief he is feeling. Most beautifully drawn of these is the twelve-year-old girl Mick, who wants to be a composer. Finally Antonapoulos dies, and Singer kills himself; his disciples are puzzled—for they have never understood or cared about him personally. But each of them, too, is defeated. This book is flawed by over-writing, by a too conscious use of allegory that sometimes ruins the action on a realistic level, and by some too consciously taken—and contradictory—decisions about what Singer represents (Christ? Satan?). But it remains an important and beautiful book; the enigmatic, ambiguous nature of Singer, which is really the point of the novel, is maintained despite such details as his age at death (thirty-three) and his 'look of peace'.

'The Ballad of the Sad Café' is the most perfect of Carson McCullers' fiction. In this grotesque tale of Miss Amelia Evans, grasping merchant and generous healer, her imagination found its real shape; simultaneously she discovered her true voice. In all her other books, even *The Member of the Wedding*, her language is uncertain: she is given to ineffective comparisons and has a penchant for lofty pseudo-poeticisms. *The Member of the Wedding* is Carson McCullers' most realistic book, and her best full-length work. It tells the story of the entry of Frankie Addams into adolescence, and introduces the most straightforwardly sympathetic of all the author's characters, the four-times married, black cook, Berenice Sadie Brown. This is a lyrical, comic and hardly ever sentimental novel, moving and refreshing. *Clock Without Hands* never comes up to this level; its chief weaknesses are linguistic slackness and, again, unfulfilled symbolic pretentions. However, it is at least evident that had its author not been so seriously incapacitated (mainly by paralytic strokes) she could have gone on to write the major novel of which *The Heart is a Lonely Hunter* had shown her capable.

Flannery O'Connor, another Georgian, was also the victim of painful and crippling ill health: she inherited disseminated lupus from her father, and became progressively crippled by the complications the necessary treatment set up, and she must have known that she would die prematurely. Flannery O'Connor was born a Roman Catholic and remained one all her life. She began by trying to become a cartoonist, but soon changed over to fiction. Despite her illness and the discomfort it caused her Flannery O'Connor was a gay and wisecracking woman, who accepted as many invitations as she could to lecture and to appear in public. She found time to write two novels, *Wise*

Blood (1952) and *The Violent Bear it Away* (1960), and two collections of short stories, *A Good Man is Hard to Find* (1955) and the posthumous *Everything that Rises Must Converge* (1965).

Flannery O'Connor is a difficult writer, who mixes Southern Gothic (but in a more controlled form than Carson McCullers), grotesque humour and an extremely complex symbolism. Once again, her characters are grotesque. But her Catholicism (her religious 'position' seems to have approximated to, or at least to have been sympathetic towards, that of Teilhard de Chardin) gives her a completely different perspective from any other Southern writer. Her first remarkable novel is about nothing less than an anti-Christ, one Haze Motes who loses his (Protestant) faith while in the army and thereafter tries to establish a Church Without Christ, 'the church that the blood of Jesus don't foul with redemption', in the Tennessee mountains where he lives. Haze believes his blood is wise because it is natural; but his blood is actually wise, since he is, despite himself, the voice of the living God: even if he preaches an anti-Church, his preachings are more authentic than those of the secular contemporary Church: he is holy. Haze, in a book whose symbolism becomes more and more complex and theological, finally blinds himself with lime. Although herself of the Catholic faith, Flannery O'Connor sees Southern Protestant primitivism as an authentic Christianity—as hideously authentic as the truth (to her) of God's love and Christ's redemption. (It is only fair to add that her theme has also been interpreted as 'the spiritual distortions that are the consequence of Protestant primitivism'.) The symbolism of *Wise Blood*, which is very theological, tends to show Haze's life as comic—and distorted—but as a comic and distorted parallel to Christ's. Its fault is that, because of the bizarre and comic elements, no sense of anguish is allowed to come across. The things the author writes about (wearing barbed wire next to the skin, blinding oneself with quicklime) are so painful, so Grand Guignol, that they defeat their own ends: this gospel is ultimately eccentric rather than authentic. However, the manner in which Flannery O'Connor has set up an anti-Christianity is subtle and intelligent, even if, finally, a kind of sermon lies at the very back of it all.

The Violent Bear it Away (1960) has more imagination and less ingenuity, and is the better book. Francis Marion Tarwater's great-uncle, a mad prophet and illicit whisky-distiller, dies; but he has instructed his great-nephew to become a prophet, and to begin his ministry by baptizing his cousin Bishop Rayber. Tarwater, who does not wish to be a prophet, carries out this order—but also drowns him, as directed by Satan, previously only a voice in his head. He does all he can to avoid his calling. But ultimately, drugged and sodomized by Satan, he is driven into madness and authentic prophecy. Tarwater is certainly representative of the true Church, which must become itself—lose reason—to save the world. Clearly Flannery O'Connor, like so many other contemporary Catholics, was desperately unhappy about the present Church, which she saw as betraying itself.

It is possible that posterity will see the best of Flannery O'Connor's short stories—such stories as 'The Artificial Nigger', 'The Lame Shall Enter First' and

'Parker's Back'—as her most enduring work. On the whole these are easier to read in the sense that, while they possess as formidable a symbology, it is not as relentlessly calculated a one. But this view has been challenged, on the grounds that she put everything that was really important to her into the novels. The answer to that might be that she put in everything that she thought most important to her into the novels. . . . Certainly she is the most unusual of the Southern woman writers. As Stanley Edgar Hyman has pointed out, she goes back not to Faulkner but to Mark Twain, as her brilliant use of dialect shows; further, the writer by whom she was most influenced (this again was Hyman's discovery) was Nathanael West. She also resembles certain French Catholic writers such as Bernanos and, even more, Bloy (qq.v.): for example, racial integration is for her a sentimentality: what is important is beyond life. And yet, for all her important differences from her fellow Southern writers, it is impossible to consider her as anything but a Southern novelist: 'I have found that any fiction that comes out of the South,' she said, 'is going to be considered grotesque by the Northern critic, unless it is grotesque, in which case it is going to be considered realistic'.

JAMES AGEE (1909–55) was almost the only one of all the serious writers who went to Hollywood to script movies that were above average: *The African Queen* is a real improvement on its original. Agee was a good film critic, one of the best; but he destroyed himself in the interests of the cinema industry—even if he was trying to improve it. He wrote some poetry of quality, though not of genius, and only took to fiction towards the end of his life. *A Death in the Family* (1955), which is an unfinished, partly autobiographical, novel, is one of the few positive novels to come out of the South. It tells of the shattering effect on a happy Tennessee family of the father's death in a car accident. It is important for its picture of decency in Tennessee—not a thing much celebrated in fiction.

The Virginian WILLIAM STYRON (1925) is a most gifted writer who has become progressively the victim of an ambition to write the great Southern novel. *Lie Down in Darkness* (1951) was acclaimed. Since then, with the exception of the novella *The Long March* (1953), he has succumbed to the temptation to try to contain the whole Southern story between the two covers of one book. He has only completely failed, however, with *The Confessions of Nat Turner* (1969), the story of the slave insurrection of 1831 and its leader, in which he simply took on more than he could handle. This novel is of course interesting, but Styron, consciously a liberal and consciously a subtle and sophisticated novelist, left his invention and his imagination too little room. *Lie Down in Darkness*, for all its debts to Joyce and Faulkner and its lofty rhetoric, is, like its successor *Set This House on Fire*, an impressive book, with passages of first-class quality. The latter has the courage to try to take a leaf out of Dostoevski's book; at least it does not make itself look foolish. One can certainly say that Styron's novels do not cohere, and that the Nat Turner book was a mistake, an attempt to take on too much; but one must concede that his first two books are both readable and continuously intelligent. His potential is still great.

The admirers of Nebraska-born WRIGHT MORRIS (1910) invariably complain that he is neglected. To the extent that he does not enjoy huge sales and that not one of his novels has been a total critical success, this is true. But he is very much an intellectuals' writer: he makes no concessions. (And yet there are many snobs and fools among his admirers.) Wright Morris is an off-beat, original writer, whose sardonic approach to life—which he regards as absurd without making any fuss about it whatever—has not attracted the 'general reader'. His books have not been kept in print. Morris' outlook is neither comforting nor discomforting; he is, rather, acutely sophisticated. He is, apart from his fans (many of whom cannot read him), awaiting discovery. His first novel, *My Uncle Dudley* (1942), is about a long trip and a successful confidence man. Morris is a professional photographer, and two of his books are illustrated with his own photographs. *The Inhabitants* (1946) set out to show 'what it is to be an American', and failed; but the photographs are interesting. *The Home Place* (1948) is a novel about a writer who returns to Nebraska with his wife and children to live; *The World in the Attic* (1949), without the nostalgic photographs, is its sequel. These combine an aching love for the past, felt to be pointless, with a horror of the present that spends itself as nervous comedy. His first substantial, and his most moving, novel was *The Works of Love* (1952), about a midwest egg-farmer who is successful in business but comically unsuccessful with women. This is a subtle variation on the 'holy fool' theme, as exploited in Wilder's *Heaven's My Destination* (q.v.). Wright Morris is a most peculiar and unusual writer in that he expects nothing good whatever from life—but this is none the less a bitter book in effect, since no one to whom the egg-farmer offers his love even recognizes it for what it is. *The Huge Season* (1954) is about money and its corrupting effects. *Love Among the Cannibals* (1957), his most sheerly comic novel, deals with two bad song-writers and the girls they pick up on their way to Acapulco. *What a Way to Go* (1962) is a relentless study of the marriage of a middle-aged small-college professor to a very young girl. Morris is often an over-subtle and too self-conscious writer; he has not always succeeded in being simply the 'photographer' he wanted to be in the sense he meant when he said 'The windmill, the single plough, the grain elevator, the receding horizon, are both signs and symbols at the same time. They speak for themselves. They would rather talk than be talked about. The man who loves these things . . . is a photographer.' He also suffers from an archness and an involuteness, a lack of straightforwardness. But he is serious and sensitive, and his peculiar methods force his readers to see things from new angles.

SAUL BELLOW (1915) spent his first nine years in his birthplace, Canada. His parents were Russian Jews who had emigrated two years previously. The family moved to Chicago in 1924, and Bellow went to Chicago and then to Northwestern University, graduating (1937) in anthropology and sociology.

Bellow was America's first major writer to shift the central concern of his fiction from the social and political to the existential. Although one of the most intellectual of all American novelists, he has discouraged critical examination of his work; his admiration for Dreiser and Hardy, not intellectual writers, is significant. For all his wit and brilliance, Bellow's subject is ultimately what a critic has called 'the porous quotidian texture which is squeezed between the accidents of birth and the fatal sicknesses which end in death'. He is a realist (emphatically not a 'new novelist') armed with a formidable, vigorous poetry – his style. Bellow is above all an individualist, a man concerned to demonstrate that, although society has become so gigantic, individual human beings have not become smaller. He has tended to show Kafkaesque, put-upon man in his absurdity but also in his glory. It is mistaken to miss this essential simplicity in Bellow. One must remember that he has said, of Dreiser, 'I often think criticism of Dreiser as a stylist at times betrays a resistance to the feelings he causes readers to suffer. If they can say he can't write, they need not experience these feelings'. This unfashionable statement tells us much about the novelist who made it; fashionable interpretation of him does not always take it into account.

Although Bellow has developed, by widening his scope and his style accordingly, he sees all his protagonists as 'victims' of life in search of a cure in the Godless twentieth century. In his first novel, *Dangling Man* (1944) he introduces the first version of his hero, Joseph (not Joseph K.; but he has no surname), who is 'dangling' because he has given up his job and is waiting to be called up. The form is a journal. Joseph is passive, resigned, but hypersensitive about life; finally he begs for defeat by asking to be called up as soon as possible. *Dangling Man* shows modern man burdened, bored, by his very liberty—and yet alienated from those around him by his concern. *The Victim* (1947) goes more deeply into the question of Jewishness. Asa Leventhal, a journalist, worries about his position; he is picked up by a mad, drunken, anti-semite who accuses him of having once done him a wrong. Leventhal becomes aware, through being persecuted by this creature, that he needs something to hate, that he too carries within him an anti-human virus. There is a marvellous scene, characteristic of Bellow at his most powerful and moving, in which the two men come into physical contact—to blows; Leventhal is suddenly aware of his complicity, with his antagonist and torturer, in life itself. The two men are 'brothers'. This novel ends on a serene note, and one of the characters makes a remark that might serve for an epigraph to all Bellow's fiction: 'Choose dignity. Nobody knows enough to turn it down'. This is, of course, an anthropologist speaking.

In the picaresque, technically unambitious, loose *The Adventures of Augie March* (1953) Bellow presents what has been called his first 'above ground' hero, Augie, who refuses to accept defeat although he recognizes that 'everyone got bitterness in his chosen thing'. Augie is different from Joseph or Leventhal: although still a victim, he affirms rather than questions everything. He becomes a gangster, a kind of gigolo, a husband: he accepts it all.

But this (*Henderson the Rain King*, *Herzog* and *Mr. Sammler's Planet* are its successors) is the first of Bellow's 'big' books, of which only *Herzog* really comes off. There is a sense of strain here. The novel does not cohere: it is a series of episodes, some superb, where its predecessors clearly were not. The novella *Seize the Day* (1956), which as originally published appeared with a play and another shorter story, accomplishes more in a tenth of the length. This is about a failure—as a breadwinner, as a husband, as a son—the most clearly defined of all Bellow's victims. He knows he is unworthy and a fool, and yet he must hand his money over to a crooked psychiatrist, Tamkin, to be 'multiplied on the stock exchange'. He can fulfil himself only as the dupe of a confidence man; must sit and watch as his money is lost. In the end, defeated, stripped of money, turned away by his rich, valetudinarian old father whom he merely embarrasses, Tommy Wilhelm burst into tears in a chapel at the funeral of a complete stranger ('It must be somebody real close to carry on so', someone says). The music plays: 'He heard it and sank deeper than sorrow, through torn sobs and cries towards the consummation of his heart's ultimate need'. This is, curiously or otherwise (as one looks at it), one of the most moving endings in the whole of twentieth-century literature.

Henderson the Rain King (1959) is a comparative failure. This story of a (non-Jewish) millionaire who goes to Africa in quest of wisdom incorporates Bellow's anthropological interests, and despite its exuberance is ultimately bogged down in intellectuality. *Herzog* (1961) is, however, a successful long study of a middle-aged Jewish intellectual, a kind of Tommy Wilhelm but without the final masochistic need to submit to fate. Herzog is, of course, another victim; he is betrayed by his friends and wives and even his doctor, and he is forever writing letters of carefully reasoned complaint. These letters are really to God, the architect of his misery, in whom he continues to believe, 'Though never admitting it'. The greatest challenge to Herzog has been the one who makes him suffer most acutely, his second wife, who is unfaithful to him with the repulsive Valentine Gersbach. Without her choice treachery and her insane charges that he is insane, he feels nothing: she makes him remarkable. The vigour of this novel is the shrill vigour of nervous exhaustion; and yet Bellow succeeds in portraying an intellectual (a brilliant one) more convincingly than any other novelist of his time. *Mr. Sammler's Planet* (1970) is another exercise in the picaresque. Since Bellow's is a major talent, it has exquisite passages. But it hardly coheres around its central character as *Herzog* does. It is largely a vehicle for Bellow's (counter-revolutionary) philosophy. This philosophy, 'old-fashioned' in terms of today's youngest university rebels but in no way reactionary, seems wise and mellow to many of Bellow's readers; but this does not make his novel more than a series of episodes, a product of thought rather than imagination.

Bellow has written a play, *The Last Analysis* (1965), which was produced in 1964, and a volume of short stories, *Mosby's Memoirs* (1969).

BERNARD MALAMUD (1914), born in New York, is like Bellow the son of parents who had emigrated from Russia not long before his birth. It is Malamud who made the famous remark, 'All men are Jews', by which he meant that all men are at heart sensitive, alienated—'chosen'. His first novel, *The Natural* (1952), was a comic masterpiece, a treatment of baseball in terms of the American hero. This contained the germ of Malamud's method—a marriage of realism and fable that has been called 'magic realism' (q.v.)—as well as exploiting his pride in being a Brooklyn baseball afficionado. His next novel, *The Assistant*

(1957), a work of rare beauty and affirmation, is on his theme of 'All men are Jews'. It remains his best novel, and is on a level with anything of Bellow's. Bellow undoubtedly has the greater intellect and perhaps the greater potential; but he has not bettered this. *The Assistant* is about nothing less than goodness. Frankie Alpine is a Gentile hoodlum who robs a poor Jewish shopkeeper. Out of a pity he tries to resist—one is reminded of Flannery O'Connor's heroes resisting their vocation—he goes to work for him, and gradually becomes involved in his defeated and unsuccessful life. He falls in love with the grocer's daughter, Helen, and accepts her criticisms of him. In the end he actually becomes the grocer (who dies), running the store and grumblingly performing the same acts of charity. He has himself circumcised and becomes a Jew.

A New Life (1961) is a campus novel, tracing the progress of Seymour Levi from rock bottom to a realization that life is holy. This, although richly comic, is not altogether free from sentimentality. *The Fixer* (1967) is Malamud's most ambitious novel. It is not as good as *The Assistant* because its effects have been strained for too hard: it is an attempt to rival Bellow with a 'big' novel, and an attempt to write the great 'All men are Jews' novel. Considering this— the sense of strain is apparent—it is remarkably successful. It is loosely based on the case of Mendel Beiliss, an innocent Jewish workman who was tried in Tzarist Russia for the 'ritual' murder of a boy—and acquitted in spite of the conspiracy against him. *The Fixer* (handyman) describes the ordeal of Yakov Bok; the result of *his* trial, however, is left open. *Pictures of Fidelman* (1969) is a picaresque novel set in Italy. This is Malamud's weakest work, in which he experiments unsuccessfully with surrealism, and where his invention often seems less comic than farcical. Much better are his short stories, collected in *The Magic Barrel* (1958) and *Idiots First* (1963). The Jewish stories in the first collection remind one of the Yiddish-American author, Isaac Bashevis Singer (q.v.); the later stories try to get away from Brooklyn, as if in preparation for *The Fixer* and *Pictures of Fidelman*.

We get another and very different version of American Jewish fiction in the work of NORMAN MAILER (1923), who was also raised in Brooklyn. The accent here has been increasingly on performance; the fiction has deteriorated as the journalism has improved. The radical sociologist has turned into the white Negro hipster. Mailer is the most vivid figure on the American literary scene; he is decidedly not a playboy, although he is, of course, an exhibitionist—and he has come dangerously near to fragmenting himself. However, he is con- temptuous of any kind of official literary criticism, and with some justification; and he has to be saluted for his courage in trying by every means in his power to capture and bring up out of himself what is unconscious and mysterious. His seeing of himself as a *performer*, his unabashed self-appraisal in *Advertisements for Myself* (1959), where he tells of his vanities and aspirations, may irritate some. But they should look into their own minds. He is often silly; but it would not be possible for him to fulfil his existential project in any other way.

His first novel, *The Naked and the Dead* (1948), the best of the American

Second World War books, was in the realist tradition; but it foreshadowed the rest of his work. It concerns two different kinds of proto-fascist, a general and a sergeant, and an ineffective liberal lieutenant—in retrospect one can see that this figure is Mailer himself, unhappy in the role of a traditional radical writing a war book in conventional terms. This is a good book, containing in particular shrewd analyses of the motivations of the authoritarian types. But it has little characterization and, curiously enough, little compassion.

In *Barbary Shore* (1951) and *The Deer Park* (1955) we see Mailer making more effort to put himself meaningfully into his fictions. He goes into first-person singular narration and drops pretence of strict realism; the prose is messy, but some of the portraits, such as that of Eitel the radical film director, are unforgettable. However, these are based on real people. They are not invented: they are very good journalism. As one reads on in Mailer's fiction, coming to *An American Dream* (1965) and the disastrous *Why Are We in Vietnam?* (1967), one begins to suspect that he does not have an inventive imagination at all. Certainly he has evolved a 'position', one that is derived in large part from the psychoanalyst Wilhelm Reich and resembles D. H. Lawrence's. Reich preached the necessity of full, creative orgasm, and towards the end of his life could detect the 'orgone energy' in the universe (it gave off a blueish light). Mailer is not quite so set on the orgasm, or at least not on its blueish light; but the central theme of his later work is the necessity of living life according to instinct. The 'White Negro' or hipster is distinguished from the passive Beat by his active, energetic quest for pleasure. Rojack in *An American Dream* is simply an embodiment of this new kind of overman—and if his story is not biblical in its import, then one has to take it as being very silly and, worse, dangerous in its implications. We have to applaud Mailer for his courage (as he wants us to do); but we are also entitled to ask how much, in fact, he cares about anything but the quality of each of his particular performances. The generalization 'love', which comes easily to the lips of his disciples, is unconvincing in the absence of an answer. Commitment to Reich is one form that current American Utopianism takes. (Another, following Norman O. Brown, is against Reich's 'full genitality', and insists on a return to bisexual 'polymorphous perversity' and play without orgasm.) Bellow has been said to be committed to Reich; but at his best he is a writer rather than a philosopher, and even when he is a philosopher he builds himself a very respectable structure. Mailer is a public man, and he functions as such—like a boxer always forced to put on a performance. The question is whether in this way, without solitude, with public pressures upon him, he can properly function as a writer. The answer may well be that, unless he gets beyond his competitiveness, he is doomed to sink into confusion and fashionably hip reportage—as his report on the 1970 American moonshot, *A Fire on the Moon* (1970), suggests. The energy that drives him is phenomenal; but it can end by driving a husk.

HERBERT GOLD (1924), from Cleveland, is an inventive and often comic novelist who has ambitions to be a Bellow but remains trapped in the meandering picaresque. Even his best novels fragment into comedy or farce just as something interesting is happening in the mind of the central character. His novels include *Birth of a Hero* (1951), *The Prospect Before Us* (1954), *The Optimist* (1959), his best character study, on a man who wants to succeed *and* be loved by all, and *Therefore Be Bold* (1960), a sensitive first-person account of a Jewish adolescence in Ohio in the late Thirties. *Love and Like* (1960) collects short stories.

*

WILLIAM BURROUGHS (1914), born in St. Louis, for much of his life an expatriate, is part of an American sociological phenomenon. The Beat (exhaustion, but also beatification) movement began spontaneously in San Francisco in the Fifties, and was at first entirely sociological. People who were dissatisfied with bourgeois society reacted against it not by rebellion but simply by dropping out. The original Beats had no leaders; their aims were passive. They were influenced by, but did not understand, Zen Buddhism, and they sought private illumination by means of drugs and/or drink. Their spiritual fathers included Whitman and Henry Miller (q.v.); and the good-natured, unconscious business man who put them on the map, and invented several reputations—including that of Burroughs—was the poet Allen Ginsberg (q.v.). Burroughs' best book was his first, published in 1953 under the pseudonym of William Lee: *Junkie*. This is an account of his life as a drug addict. He had held a number of jobs in New York (private detective, factory-worker, barman); then in 1944 he became addicted to heroin and moved to New Orleans and Mexico, where he shot his wife in an accident. *Junkie* was a relatively straightforward book. In 1957 he flew from Tangier to London for the apomorphine treatment, and apart from two relapses immediately afterwards has not touched the drug since. Nowadays Burroughs, having delivered himself of his works— *The Naked Lunch* (1959), *The Soft Machine* (1961), *Nova Express* (1964), and others—is mainly a prophet-interviewer. What is perhaps most impressive about him is his monumental stupidity and naïvety. He discovered Reich late, and refreshes himself in one of those boxes—to gather orgone energy—that earned their inventor a prison sentence he did not survive. He is (or was) a 'scientologist'. He postulates, with apparent seriousness, an all-male community in which reproduction would be confined to test tubes. He admired China's Red Guards not because he could understand anything about them, but because (like Hitler?) 'they feel they have something important to do'.

His creative work is unoriginal but none the less looks different. His techniques consist of: the use of various aleatory devices to produce associations that arise from illogic, especially the illogic of dreams; these are superimposed on pulp type plots; bad SF or gangster books. His 'cut-out' and 'fold-in' techniques, consisting of certain semi-aleatory ways of manipulating existing material, are merely variations of old surrealist games. *The Naked Lunch* counterpoints a realist account of a junkie's life with the subjective horrors he experiences; it is supposed to have been given what little coherence it has by the shrewd Ginsberg, whose own incoherence is voluntary. The real subject, which is what a junkie experiences in withdrawal, is nausea. The organization of *The Naked Lunch* is naïve in the extreme. The themes are *addiction, control* (leading to more control), *power* and *means of cure*. His other works do not radically depart from this scheme. Burroughs submits his original material (which is probably bathetic and ill written) to his various techniques, spicing it up with clippings from his 'favourite' cut-in sources, such as the novels of William Golding (q.v.). But his chief obsessions emerge: the erections of hanged men, anal rape. . . .

What is pitiful is that Burroughs, an essentially simple-minded man, and one perhaps less unintelligent on than off narcotics, has been treated by some critics (including, amazingly, Mary McCarthy, q.v.) as an innovator. He is historically important; but his importance is as, in Leslie Fiedler's words, a 'pioneer mutant', pledged to become a child.

JACK KEROUAC (ps. JEAN-LOUIS KEROUAC, 1922–69), who 'died of drink and angry sicknesses' (Ted Berrigan), had a grotesquely inflated reputation; but as a latter-day Thomas Wolfe (q.v.), though a vastly inferior writer, he has historical importance. Kerouac was always a wanderer, and was twice married and twice divorced, both times in less than a year. Originally he was a drunken drifter who managed to commit to paper a bad Wolfeian novel called *The Town and the City* (1950). It contains in embryo his stale message: ignorance, incoherence and illiteracy are beatific, crime is lovely, do as you want, get stoned, learn to be naïve, attain sweetness and light. But it took the astute Ginsberg to launch him as a legend. *On the Road* (1957), type-written on a continuous roll of art paper in three weeks flat, has distinction as being the most non-structured book of its decade. In writing it Kerouac simply followed his own nose. It is in no sense fiction, but a record of the wanderings of three bums; Sal Paradise (Kerouac), Carlo Marx (Ginsberg), and Dean Moriarty (a friend of theirs called Neil Cassady). *The Dharma Bums* (1958) is similar, but puts emphasis on Kerouac's search for realization through some kind of Zen Buddhism. If anyone doubts Kerouac's pretentiousness, and the self-delusion in which he existed, he should read *Satori in Paris* (1966), in which he humourlessly describes a journey to Paris in search of his French ancestry, drinking bouts, and a final Buddhist illumination—as convincing as the 'satori' claimed by an English Buddhist, the judge Christmas Humphreys. Kerouac wrote many books, and in all of them he splashed, a critic rightly said, 'everything energetically with his own boisterous, messy ego'.

*

TRUMAN CAPOTE (1924), who was born in New Orleans, is clos o Tennessee Williams(q.v.) in atmosphere; all his books up to *In Cold Blood* (1966) sugar and prettify the same kind of Gothic-invert world. Leslie Fiedler calls Capote a representative of the 'Effete Dandies or . . . Decadents' school, which he sees as deriving from Faulkner. Certainly Capote is flip and his 'amusement' at evil is tiresome and even irresponsible—he can give a sense of a perverse boy liking to annoy his reader by being sick and crippled; but that is only one side of the picture. Capote is a consummate artist, a writer very serious about his craft, who, no matter whether his reader likes it or not, does create a world of his own. Things are seen by Capote not with an innocent but with the goblin eye of a self-retarded soul. In his first book, *Other Voices, Other Rooms* (1948), the boy Joel Knox sinks into a decadent homosexual relationship with the transvestite Randolph in just the same way as his paralyzed father's rotting house sinks gradually into the swamp on which it is built. As John A. Aldridge has said, Capote here achieves a purity, of 'the sort that can be attained only in the isolation of a mind which life has never violated, in which the image of art has developed to a flowerlike perfection because it has developed alone'. Capote is no surrealist; but his world is more dream than real. He does not like to call himself a Southern writer, but there is no doubt that his dream is a Southern one. Its inner coherence is admirable; but its relationship with any-body else's world is problematical. If Joel Knox's pilgrimage is for the father or the Holy Grail then these are fathers and grails few others would know any-thing about. *The Grass Harp* (1951) is about an eleven-year-old orphan who, with one of his elderly aunts and three others, is driven, by the nastiness of the world, to live in a tree-house. This little community is presented as innocent and even improved in its efficacy to deal with reality; there are allusions to Noah's ark and to Huck's raft. There is much sharply perceptive, fresh writing; but the pretty vision is corrupted by Capote's lack of interest in people as people. With *Breakfast at Tiffany's* (1958) Capote tipped his talent in the direction of the middlebrow: this traced the adventures of a playgirl, Holly Golightly, against the background of modern Manhattan. The book may well have achieved its popularity because Holly is utterly superficial, flip, all phoney; the book has a kind of false vitality, but is quite without warmth. And yet the writing is on an altogether higher level than the cult of the child which the book is advocating. *In Cold Blood* (1966) is a piece of gripping and highly intelligent journalism reconstructing a peculiarly brutal murder; Capote investigated the case in depth. This marked a complete break with the first three, narcissistic novels; but *In Cold Blood*, in spite of its author's claim to have invented a new form, 'the documentary novel', is no more than very good journalism. *Tree of Night* (1949) collects short stories.

Mark Twain was the first American to see the Noble Savage as a child (Huck), and writers have not stopped imitating him, or sharing in his vision, ever since. Truman Capote is a good example. Another is J. D. SALINGER (1919), whose *The Catcher in the Rye* (1951) achieved heights of popularity denied to any other 'quality' novel since the war. Salinger had studied at various establish-ments before the war without getting a degree; he ended up at Columbia in a short-story class taught by Whit Burnett, founder and editor of *Story*—not to be confused with the writer of superior gangster fiction W. R. BURNETT (1899), author of *Little Caesar* (1929)—a magazine which published his first story in 1940. He entered the army in 1942, and took part in five campaigns. It has been suggested that his military experiences brought his nausea with modern existence to the surface.

Salinger became so popular, a star *New Yorker* writer, because in *The Catcher in the Rye* he discovered the exact tone and flavour of post-war middle-class, adolescent alienation. The use of the vernacular owes much to Ring Lardner (q.v.); but it is Salinger's own (and greatest) achievement. The book is about Holden Caulfield, who flunks school and must go home to tell his parents about it. He spends a weekend in New York failing to connect, being nauseated by everybody, finding everything phoney. Only two nuns he meets at breakfast strike him as genuine. After an experience of feeling 'damn happy', which anticipates the *kitsch* Zen of the later stories, Holden goes home, falls psychiatrically ill, and is psychoanalyzed. The monologue which is *The Catcher in the Rye* is (presumably) part of a healthful therapy. But to what purpose? The book ends: 'Don't ever tell anybody anything. If you do, you start missing everybody'. *The Catcher in the Rye* is limited by its failure to go beyond Holden: it catches a style, and one must concede that it does so marvellously; but it has no wisdom, can imply no alternative either to the phoney world or the, ultimately, tiresome Holden. Here lies another reason for its popularity (although Salinger should not be blamed for this): the young do not want alternatives, or to acknowledge the necessity of compromise with the adult world they reject; so they seized on Holden Caulfield. As Walter Allen has said, Salinger's is the *New Yorker* version of the Beats and hipsters. For his older readers, whose notion of the ultimate in intelligence is to be found in the pages of the *New Yorker*, he had a comforting message: junior has been sick like you once were, but next week he will be coming home and he will go back to school. . . . I do not think this was the intention, but Salinger would have been a really important writer only if he could have written of the defeat (or victory?) of an adult Holden Caulfield; and if he could then have peopled his world not with cliché-shams (that is what the 'phonies' of *The Catcher in the Rye* are) but with real people—shams, yes; but shams with the varyingly concealed humanity that they do have. But the successors to *The Catcher in the Rye*, all short fictions, skilful though they are, do not suggest this possibility; and it is significant that except for a single story published by the *New Yorker* in 1965 Salinger has, in the Sixties, dried up. *Nine Stories* (1953), *Franny and Zooey* (1961) and *Raise High the Roof Beam, Carpenters;* and *Seymour: An Introduction* (1963) form a chronicle of the eccentric Glass family, including Buddy Glass, who is a representation of Salinger himself. Even by the side of *The Catcher in the Rye*, these tend to be cute and to fall back not on any kind of mellowness or comprehension of the real nature of the world, but on pseudo-religiosity.

JOHN UPDIKE (1932) worked for the *New Yorker* after leaving Harvard, and is now the brightest, funniest, most intelligent and entertaining from that stable. His first novel, *The Poorhouse Fair* (1959), is about a revolt of the old people in an institution against their liberal director. *Bech* (1970), his most recent, tells the story of a successful middle-aged Jewish writer who can do everything except write well. It is clearly Updike's effort to justify his own middlebrow success, which has led Leslie Fiedler to say of him that he provides 'the illusion of vision and fantasy without surrendering the kind of reassurance provided by slick writing at its most professionally *all right*'. It fails to explain Bech at all; but Updike does manage to convey a sympathy for this husk, who is presented not as a bad writer but a victim of the middlebrow public. . . .

JAMES BALDWIN (1924) was born in Harlem. He never knew his real father, to whom his mother was not married; but his stepfather, a preacher, rejected him and told him he was ugly—all against a background of bigotry and religious fanaticism. At fourteen Baldwin, in competition with his stepfather and wanting to draw bigger audiences than he did, became a preacher, a Holy Roller in the Fireside Pentecostal Church in Harlem. Except for the few years in which he wrote his two first (and best) novels, Baldwin has been a preacher ever since. His first novel, *Go Tell it on the Mountain* (1953), describes the conversion of a fourteen-year-old; this is a vision of ecstasy brought about by the guilts and stresses of initiation into puberty, by the hatred of his father, and by the desire to escape altogether to a new world. *Giovanni's Room* (1956) is set in Paris and deals with a conflict between homosexual and heterosexual love. *Another Country* (1962) mixes fine fiction with homosexual preaching. As Leslie Fiedler has been most articulate in pointing out, in America Jew, Negro and homosexual have become to some extent identified—because, of course, all are discriminated against. In Baldwin's third novel ('precisely because he is a homosexual as well as a Negro', claims Fiedler) one of the messages—the most important message, to Baldwin—is that hate between white and black is exacerbated by male-female relationships but healed by homosexual ones. Now the predicament of Negroes and homosexuals (how long before we write this word with an initial capital?) is similar (although the real enemies of homosexuality are themselves homosexuals, but repressed); the future of an over-populated world may well have to be homosexual; but, unless one takes negritude to be a disorder, the nature of the Negro and the homosexual *may* not be similar. At all events, Baldwin has to manipulate his people and his situations to elevate homosexuality into a panacea for the racial human illness. This approach does not really help to resolve the tension between the two ideas which Baldwin has recognized that any writer—but most particularly a Negro writer—'must hold . . . forever in his mind': '. . . the acceptance, totally without rancour, of life as it is . . . [and the idea] that one must never . . . accept . . . injustices as commonplace . . .'. Eric Jones, the bisexual actor who dominates the second part of *Another Country*, is an unreal figure. *Tell Me How Long the Train's Been Gone* (1968) deals with Baldwin in his role of publicist in the person of Leo Proudhammer; it seems to have been thrown hurriedly together, and shows a marked deterioration. However, as his creative work has declined, so his strength as an essay writer has increased. His function has changed: from imaginative writer to inspired Negro publicist.

There are at least a score of American novelists under fifty who have some fair claims to importance. Some, like Philip Roth, have gained commercial success; others, like John Hawkes, have not. The greatest *succés d'éstime* has been JOHN BARTH (1930), though so far critical enthusiasm tends to be expressed around publication time. The immensely ambitious *Giles Goat-Boy* (1967) is one of those novels that is either a masterpiece, albeit a flawed one—or something very much smaller. Barth is an academic and has been one ever since he graduated from Johns Hopkins. His novels, however, are as anti-academic as they are academic. He is amusing, inventive of situations, a trained philosopher, a polymath. His work is by a large number of people (including Nabokov, Kafka, Borges, Beckett, qq.v., Bunyan, Lewis Carroll) out of James Joyce (q.v.). He relies on puns, slang of all sorts and pastiche (and parody). His own ability to write prose has so far been concealed by these intellectual pyrotechnics (his use of slang is photographic). Barth is an author of 'in-books'; that so astute a critic as Leslie Fiedler can admire them is evidence that they contain in-jokes about academe that are good jokes; but a number of reviewers have knowingly saluted the achievement without, however, understanding it in the least.

Giles Goat-Boy is the ultimate in the *Bildungsroman* (q.v.); like Barth's preceding three novels—*The Floating Opera* (1956, rev. 1967), *The End of the Road* (1958, rev. 1968) and *The Sot-Weed Factor* (1960, rev. 1967), only more specifically and ironically, it deals in 'education'. Here the universe is a university, into which are launched a false Messiah—and a counter-claimant, Giles Goat-Boy, a 'horned human student'. This is dazzlingly clever, and I suppose some of those who combine crossword-puzzle mentalities with philosophical inclinations might have got through its 700-odd pages. The fact is that *Giles Goat-Boy* is a prototype for a certain kind of book: the new, scholastic, inturned Joycean epic. The justification comes out of Borges: the novelist is to re-invent the universe, but adding the coherence 'God' lacks. The self-caressing, 'fiendish' ingenuity comes from Nabokov, the Nabokov of such books as *Pale Fire* (1962) and, alas, *Ada*, with its whiff of exalted *kitsch*. Barth is serious, a comedian, a man with marvellous ideas—but his own language offers no clue to the presence of a creative imagination.

The enormous success of the 'masturbation novel', *Portnoy's Complaint* (1969), by PHILIP ROTH (1933), who was born in New Jersey, makes it difficult to assess him. It is an amusing comic book, an eminently worthwhile variation on the American Jewish novel; but it is not in the top flight. Roth belongs, as a critic puts it, in the tradition of American writers 'which examines the individual's posture of optimistic wilfulness and finds it wanting'. Thus, the compassionate sensibility of the hero of *Letting Go* (1962), Gabe Wallach, is crippled by his sentimentality and his weakness. But this book was ill organized, and its author's flipness drowned his delicacy of insight. *When She Was Good* (1967) is his best book. Lucy Nelson revenges herself for her inadequate childhood by turning herself into a castrator, a possessor of men-objects; and yet the vitality that throbs in her, tragic substitute for humanity, is vividly conveyed. *Portnoy's Complaint* is intelligent black Jewish comedy; but sheer professionalism, a facility for skating over the difficult explanations, spoils it. Alexander Portnoy cannot learn that his feelings of imprisonment arise from his failure to relate to others; but masturbation is not an adequate symbol for this.

American critics are mostly hostile to JAMES PURDY (1923), who was born in Ohio. One can see why: his homosexual Gothic is unmitigated and his control of it is doubtful, and, in any case, inelegant. But he has unquestionable power. He experienced fierce rejection until Edith Sitwell (q.v.), doubtless in a receptive mood, since she possessed small judgement in her last monomanic years, found him an English publisher. In America he was eventually, and predictably, taken up by CARL VAN VECHTEN (1880–1964), a dilettante old critic who was born out of his time and whose pussy predilections Purdy fulfilled with suitable modern garishness. In Van Vechten's decadent, well written novels—*Peter Whiffle* (1922), *The Tattooed Countess* (1924) and the excellent *Nigger Heaven* (1926)—we may find foreshadowed not only Purdy's anguished quest for love in violence but also a source (or anticipation) of much American fiction concerned with homosexuality. Purdy gets less attention than many inferior writers because, although he has humour, he does not pretend that his view of life is other than despairing. He is unacceptable to the *New Yorker* public because his misogyny is not comfortingly conveyed: not smuggled in, so to speak, between cocktails. *63: Dream Palace* (1956), the novella that made Purdy's name when it was published with other stories in *Colour of Darkness* (1957), portrays a man, lost and misused in a small town, who kills the brother he loves. He is seen as a victim of urban technology; but the author's Calvinist ancestry is more obvious than any desire to criticize modern society. . . . *Malcolm* (1959) projects homosexual anxiety onto a fifteen-year-old boy who wanders through a world of depravity in search of his lost father, only to be destroyed by ugly and evil forces. This, written in terms of bitter comedy, is a horrifying story, but it illuminates the urban indifference of evil with a real poetry. *The Nephew* (1960), a more integrated novel, and the high point in Purdy's writing, describes a spinster's search for the personality of the nephew, missing in Korea, whom she brought up; she does not find what she seeks— predictably, this nephew was among other things homosexual. The author cleverly and with surprising gentleness reveals the mainsprings of her own personality as she puzzles over her discoveries. If *Cabot Brown Begins* (1965), whose central character makes contact with others by means of rape ('at the rate of about $1\frac{1}{2}$ per diem') is Grand Guignol then *Eustace Chisholm and the Works* (1968), set in the Chicago of the Depression, is fashionable Gothic. The eponymous hero writes 'the Works' in charcoal on old pages of the *Chicago Tribune*. Another character is only able to express his true homosexual bent when sleepwalking; he is disembowelled by a mad Captain, also—it need hardly be added—homosexual. It is sad to see so eloquent a writer reduced to this; but criticism of Purdy, mostly hostile, is oddly silent about why he is granted attention at all—which is because of the quality of his style. This is very carefully based on the speech of Ohio, and is an achievement in itself. Purdy cannot (surely) indulge in more extensions of the Gothic; if he is to survive as a writer he must, it seems, allow this style to lead him into his subject.

JOHN HAWKES (1925), born in Connecticut, has a number of faults, the main one being a tendency to very heavy rhetoric; all his work, too, is uneven. But he is that very rare article: a genuine experimental writer. This is something for which a price usually has to be paid. Hawkes, like Barth, is concerned with the creation of fictional worlds, not with the transcription of events. But his approach is quite different; and less intellectual. Whatever the faults of his prose, it is always evident that an imagination of great power is struggling to express itself—with Barth one does not feel that the great energy arises from more than ingenuity. Hawkes' books are something like dreams, and so is their logic. He has been called a fabulist and a surrealist, but neither term really helps. The fact is that, for all the suddenly emerging rhetorical crudities and fallings-back on brutality when his own procedures break down, Hawkes is one of the most original writers of his time. It is true that his peculiar methods resemble those of DJUNA BARNES (1892); but he seems to me, although not to all critics, superior. Still, the comparison (originally Fiedler's, who called one of Hawkes's novels 'Brighton Rock rewritten by Djuna Barnes') is useful.

Djuna Barnes, born in New York, for long a member of the between-the-wars Paris expatriates, is a minor Gothic decadent—who was somewhat irresponsibly commended by T. S. Eliot (q.v.), with the predictable effect that she became a cult-object. Eliot wrote that her Nightwood (1936) had a quality 'very nearly related to that of Elizabethan tragedy'. This was, quite simply, wrong: the quality of this surrealist study in psychopathology (mostly sexual) is actually related to the French decadence of the Nineties. Djuna Barnes has also written The Book of Repulsive Women (1915), A Book (1923; rev. as A Night Among the Horses, 1929), the stream-of-consciousness novel Ryder (1928), and The Antiphon (1958), a tedious play in blank verse written perhaps under the influence of Eliot's linking of her with the Elizabethans. Her Selected Works were published in 1962. Djuna Barnes undoubtedly possesses originality; she adds to it an element of pretentiousness; and when all else fails her she retreats into irresponsible surrealism; attempts to demonstrate how her images cohere have not been convincing.

Hawkes's work resembles Djuna Barnes's in the integrity of its peculiar atmosphere. Nightwood is too long and too full of forced Gothic to be a major book; but it does have its own extraordinary atmosphere. Hawkes' The Cannibal (1949), his first novel, has a similar integrity but is less spoilt. It is no more about the horrors of devastated Germany than Robbe-Grillet's The House of Assignation (q.v.) is 'about' Hong Kong. Hawkes' post-war Germany is, however, as valid as any other: such fiction implies the question, Whose Germany can be viable? The Lime Twig (1961) is possibly based on Greene's Brighton Rock (q.v.) in the way Golding's Lord of the Flies (q.v.) is based on Ballantyne's Coral Island. It takes place in what Hawkes calls the London blitz. But this is only his surrender to a certain image he has (uncorrected by any historical investigation) of this event. The Beetle Leg (1951), perhaps his most successful novel, is about a worker buried alive while building a dam. It is certainly not realistic, but it is not symbolic either. One might better say that Hawkes' world here illuminates the reader's. . . . Of course he can be merely quaint; one of the stories collected in Lunar Landscapes (1970) begins: 'Early in the morning in a town famous for the growing of some grape, I arose from my bed in the inn and stepped outside alone to the automobile'. But that was perhaps to get a start. Hawkes, who has also written the novel *Second Skin* (1964) and some plays, is one of the leading writers of his generation, and one from whom we may perhaps expect the most.

EVAN S. CONNELL (1924) is one of the most accomplished of American novelists. He is always professional, but this never obtrudes into his work; he does not make concessions to gain entertainment value. He is not a loud novelist, but the way he distances himself from his material should not lead any reader to suppose that he lacks feeling. His less good novels (for example, *Diary of a Rapist*, 1966) do, it is true, strain after effect at the expense of feeling; but *Mr. Bridge* (1969) amply demonstrates that this is not lacking. At his worst Connell writes too tastefully well; but his mastery of technique stands him in good stead in *Mr. Bridge*, in which he portrays a modern Babbitt more skilfully and unambiguously than Sinclair Lewis (q.v.)—but not with the same raw power. Here he composes in vignettes, some not more than a page long; the cumulative effect is remarkable, and conveys the picture of a whole man. Connell is not a major writer; but within the limits he sets himself he is an excellent minor one. His other novels include *Mrs. Bridge* (1959); *The Anatomy Lesson* (1957) and *At the Crossroads* (1965) collect short stories. *Notes From a Bottle Found on the Beach at Carmel* (1963), a long poem in the manner of Pound's *Cantos*, is not poetry but is interesting, intelligent and readable.

HUBERT SELBY (1928) achieved notoriety through *Last Exit to Brooklyn* (1964), which the British government tried and failed to ban. It is a book of short stories, essentially in the realist tradition, about homosexuals and transvestites in Brooklyn. Few have written so vividly about the miseries of the extreme forms of homosexuality. It is ironic that Selby should have been selected for prosecution, because his attitude towards his material is somewhat puritanical. Doubtless it was his truthfulness and starkness that offended: he is one of the few writers of his generation to prove the continuing viability of realism.

V

The general tendency in American poetry in the last thirty years might be said to be towards Williams and away from Frost or Ransom (qq.v.), with the figure of Pound in the middle. Thus, such a poet as Marianne Moore is right of centre, whereas Roethke (q.v.) is to the left of it. But this is no more than a useful generalization. The recent poetry of John Berryman (q.v.), although it is disliked or ignored by the Beats and their associates, is not really classifiable.

Two 'schools' do exist side by side, however, and for the most part they sullenly ignore each other. On the one hand there are such poets as Creeley (q.v.), Edward Dorn, Gary Snyder (q.v.)—the sort collected by Donald Allen and Creeley in their *New Writing in the U.S.A.* (1967); on the other there is an academic group, more traditional: this includes Lowell, Wilbur, Snodgrass (qq.v.); James Wright, Robert Bly (qq.v.) and some others occupy a middle position—or, perhaps it is fairer to say, an independent one.

The last serious conservative, traditionalist movement in American poetry was promulgated by the Southern group of poets who called themselves the Fugitives. *The Fugitive*, a bi-monthly little magazine, appeared between 1922 and 1925. The contributors were mostly associated with Vanderbilt University, and their leader was JOHN CROWE RANSOM (1888), the son of a Tennessee Methodist minister. After studying at Vanderbilt and Oxford, England (as a Rhodes scholar), Ransom went back to Vanderbilt as an instructor in English. He stayed there for a quarter of a century and played a leading part in the Southern renaissance—that 'renaissance' which was preceded by nothing.

Southern Agrarianism was conservative, but the individuals who propounded it were not illiberal. The Agrarian programme is set forth in the 1930 symposium *I'll Take My Stand*, to which Ransom, Warren, Tate (qq.v.) and other Southerners contributed. One could make out a case for this programme being crypto-fascist, especially since its philosophy flowed from Plato; or a case for its being over-scholarly and, in politics, naïve—which in some aspects it is. Its importance, however, is not as a political programme—whatever its proponents may have thought at the time—but as the matrix for some important creative writing. The programme itself is essentially nostalgic, but being intellectual and scholarly it is carefully non-populist. The Agrarians advocated a non-industrialized, Agrarian South, and thus one not exploited by the North; they wanted culture to take the place of politics in an aristocracy. Their version of the Civil War is, of course, a complicated one; but we may be forgiven for interpreting it as a fight between culture (the South) and politics (the North). Agrarianism was not, however, obscurantist: regarded as something to be re-created. It would have to grow up as the men of the South learned to mould their lives to the natural geography of their region.

What all this actually represented was the last really intelligent, gifted traditionalist movement in American (or British) poetry. A poetry for the most part content to work within the limits of what has gone before it, needs to be attached to a set of real beliefs. (The trouble with the routine Georgians, q.v., in England, or, indeed, with any routine middlebrow versifiers, is that they have only a set of pseudo-beliefs, and slackly sentimental ones at that.) For a short time Agrarianism provided such a set of beliefs. Not all people will condemn a movement that referred to science and technology as new barbarisms 'controlled and directed by the modern power state'. And when it was clear that Agrarianism was no longer viable the same group, the Fugitives, turned to the development of the 'new criticism'. This term had been used as early as 1910 by the critic Joel E. Spingarn to describe his own methods; but what Ransom meant by it—in his book *The New Criticism* (1941)—was different. Taking into account all the critics who have been described as new critics one can fairly say no more than that the new criticism, as generally understood (Ransom's text of 1941 has had a considerable effect on that understanding), introduced higher and more responsible standards into criticism, and put it onto a more, but not of course a wholly, scientific basis. Eventually the movement petered out into the sometimes apparently half-hysterical pseudo-science of such critics as W. K. Wimsatt ('The Structure of Romantic Nature Imagery'). But in its heyday, for all its excesses, and in particular its tendency to artificially isolate works of literature from their contexts (this had begun as an admirable redirection of attentions that had wandered from texts), the new criticism represented a renaissance of sense and sensibility after a period marked mainly by sentimentality and soft thinking.

Ransom's own criticism is ingenious and important but somewhat frigid. Its frigidity, at any rate, confirms the truth of Dryden's remark that 'the corruption of a poet is the generation of a critic'; although 'corruption' is perhaps in this case too strong a word. If we do not (as he does not) count the crude, commonplace and often clumsy *Poems About God* (1919), then Ransom's fecund period—there are only four poems dating from the Thirties—lasted for only four years, from the beginning of 1922 until the end of 1925. In this time, in a series of remarkable poems, he held the balance between an archaic, mannered and ornate conservatism and his own personal, emotional concerns. Invariably these poems are cast in the form of elaborate fictions, sometimes learnedly historical and sometimes ironically idyllic. Everything is carefully removed from direct utterance; but a dark passion imbues every poem.

For Ransom, man was once whole, and able to perceive the world as it really is; now he is split into reason and sensibility, body and soul. Science, for Ransom, is materialism; it gratifies rational impulses. His kind of poetry, 'metaphysical', 'miraculist', is made up of *structure* (the logical sense, the syntax, the metre), and *texture* (tone, imagery, sound, subject). The texture needs to be supported to a certain extent by the structure, but the two may nevertheless be almost independent of each other: in any case the resultant poem is independent of either a rational or a 'platonic' (this is the kind of poetry Ransom dislikes) impulse. Essentially, it will be noted, the poem is a strategy; and as a critic Ransom has undoubtedly enjoyed isolating it—to that extent—from its author, for one of the oblique themes of his poetry is how a passionate man may viably live at a distance from himself.

Ransom's criticism is important and has deserved its wide influence. It is important, incidentally, because based on the experience of being a poet—and not because it is good theory. But it is essential to recognize that the criticism is a transformation of the poetic function into a series of the very abstractions the poet hates: for it is less criticism of specific poetry, illumination of texts, than a theory. In other words, we have to sit patiently on the banks of a pond of theory to trick the secret fish of poetic intuition into biting. The poet Ransom, the anti-abstractionist, is one of those who think of a theory as what someone has called 'a structure of interrelated empirical propositions'; the critic Ransom, who all but renounced poetry (many poets do in one way or another) because it began to bring him too uncomfortably close to himself, is a theorist, a prescriber of rules upon which poetry should be written and read. And by now, forty years after he could not continue with poetry, Ransom (in the definitive *Selected Poems*, 1969) ruins his earlier poems, 'pairing' the original texts of eight poems with 1968 versions, and adding commentaries in most cases longer than the poems themselves.

> Conrad, Conrad, aren't you old
> To sit so late in a mouldy garden

becomes the intolerable, arch

> Evening comes early, and soon discovers
> Exchange between two conjugate lovers.

> 'Conrad! dear man, surprise! aren't you bold
> To be sitting so late in your sodden garden?'

The critic has sat in judgement on the poetry.

In one sense the critic Ransom is a strategist leading us away from one of the main features of the poetry: that the poet got more into his poems than their rigorous composer had planned. In his smaller poems, such as 'Janet Waking', Ransom does get the effects he plans: here he shocks the reader out of sentimentality into a realization of what the death of Janet's hen, her first experience of death, really means to her. In the justly famous *Captain Carpenter* he goes beyond himself, achieving a major poetry. The personal price paid is great. As he said in his poem about what the poets ate and drank:

> God have mercy on the sinner
> Who must write with no dinner. . . .

Poetry comes out of experience, and there are points at which it becomes intolerable to question experience too deeply.

ALLEN TATE (1899), born in Kentucky, is a critic, historical biographer (of Stonewall Jackson and Jefferson Davis) and the author of a novel, *The Fathers* (1938, rev. 1960), as well as a poet. He was a pupil of Ransom, and was the first undergraduate to be invited to join the Fugitives. Tate's poems were from the beginning brilliantly phrased; he was always an adept at sustaining one manner or another: a brilliant student. All his work is elegant and accomplished, and yet there is a curious neutrality about it: not a lack of distinction, but the lack of a voice distinctive enough to suggest any personal unifying view. His poem 'Ode to the Confederate Dead' (1936) does sum up an ethos—roughly, the ethos of a typical Southern Agrarian—but even this, for so sheerly accomplished a poem, lacks personality. Almost always Tate's poetry seems to be trying to discover a literary language to define *a* position; but one has to persuade oneself that it is his position. Thus, although he has seldom been criticized (by the Williams-Olson-Black Mountain School he has been ignored, like Ransom, simply as an antique) or attacked, Tate has also seldom been warmly praised. There is not often either warmth or passion—or the notion of such feelings being suppressed—in his poetry. He attracts praise, but it is seldom enthusiastic. Conrad Aiken, who has much personal regard for Tate, was forced—in defending him against a severe appraisal—to resort to the word 'useful', hardly a compliment. Is he no more than a model of what a good twentieth-century metaphysical should be? Such a judgement would be unfair to the best of his relatively sparse poetic output. Usually Tate has simply taken too much thought ('So many fine things have a way of coming out all the better without the strain to sum up the whole universe in one impressive pellet' Hart Crane, q.v., once wrote to him); and for all his insistence on tension ('Tension in Poetry' is the title of his best known critical essay), the intellectual ingenuity of his poems tends to rob them of that very quality. But in such a poem as 'The Swimmers', where the poet remembers the lynching of a black man and a swim he shared with some other boys, he achieves a personal note of indignation and sadness—as in one of his sonnets, where he tells of how he got a Negro beaten unjustly. In the long meditative 'Seasons of the Soul' Tate is at his weakest: the poet is at all times clothing his thinking in suitable linguistic terms—the language is not arising of its own volition. This language has, somehow, a second-hand flavour: 'The living wound of love', 'the mother of silences', 'Irritable spring': very good modern metaphysical poetry, but it fails to convince.

Tate's single novel, *The Fathers* (1938), is a greater achievement than any-thing in his poetry—not because it is anything very different, but because if you are as clever as Tate is then you can get away with more in fiction than you can in poetry. *The Fathers* is about the old South, the time the months during which the Civil War broke out. It is narrated by an old man, but its central character is really Major Buchan, the narrator's father, a feudal gentle-man and an anti-secessionist who has no defences against the commercial, materialistic North. His son-in-law, George Posey, represents man uprooted from tradition. This is beautifully done, and the character of Major Buchan is most movingly conveyed. And even if one is left wondering if Tate's old South is not somewhat idealized, one accepts it as his legitimate view of the way in which the good life has disintegrated.

MERRILL MOORE (1903–57), born in Tennessee, was another member of the Fugitives. For most of his life he practised psychiatry in Boston (he was able to give valuable help to Edwin Arlington Robinson, q.v.); his immense poetic output consisted entirely of sonnets. He did not, eventually, take literature seriously; but if his comic verse were better known it would perhaps rival that of OGDEN NASH (1902–71), who though himself inexorably middlebrow and writing comfortingly for middlebrows, did smuggle a few truths into his deliberately banal and mostly irritating verse.

LAURA RIDING (ps. LAURA REICHENTHAL, 1901) was born in New York. Her father was an Austrian tailor, a naturalized American, and a lifelong socialist. She went to Cornell University, and there married a history instructor, Louis Gottschalk. Her first poems were signed Laura Riding Gottschalk. From her divorce in 1925 she was known as Laura Riding; since she married Schuyler B. Jackson (died 1968), in 1941 her few published works have been signed 'Laura (Riding) Jackson'. From 1926 until 1941, in England, Mallorca, Rennes (France) and finally America, she was associated with Robert Graves (q.v.), with whom she published a number of books and pamphlets. The Fugitives awarded her a poetry prize and made her an honorary member of their group; she was highly enthusiastic, and devised schemes to publicize their work. Soon after she published her *Collected Poems* (1938) she came to the conclusion 'that poetry had no provision in it for ultimate practical attainment of that rightness of word that *is* truth, but led on ever only to a temporizing less-than-truth (the lack eked out with illusions of truth produced by physical word effects)'. She worked with her husband on a project 'that would help to dissipate the confusion existing in the knowledge of word-meanings', and she is now trying to complete it alone. In the magazine *Chelsea* (12 and 14, 1962, 1964) she has detailed her reasons for rejecting poetry, and told 'the story of human beings in the universe' (*The Telling*, in *Chelsea*, 1967). In 1970 her *Selected Poems* appeared in Great Britain, with a Preface explaining why she considers even her own poetry an inadequate approach to her function of truth-telling. She knows, she says, of 'no one besides myself and my husband . . . who has put feet beyond the margin on the further ground—the margin being the knowledge that truth begins where poetry ends. . . .' *The Telling* appeared in England in 1972.

The notion of poetry—and, indeed, all writing—as humanly inadequate is not new. Rilke, Broch and Thomas Mann (qq.v.) all had similar forebodings, and so have many others. In a century in which everything is questioned it is unlikely that art would not have been, too. But Laura Riding has been more specific about it than anyone else. She calls the vanity of 'artistically perfect word-use' 'a parasitic partner in the poetic enterprise'. How American this is! And how interesting that where she, in her own word, '*stopped*', such writers as Charles Olson (q.v.) simply tried to make a new sort of poetry. But, her personal peculiarities apart (they involve her in continual complaints that everyone has ill-treated her and stolen their styles and ideas from her, and have been said to constitute a 'Jehovah complex'), she has drawn attention to a crisis of poetry in our time—and she has done so whether, with her, we abandon poetry, or whether we go on trying to make it.

Laura Riding's own poetry, which has interested only a minority, but a distinguished one—the Fugitives, Graves, Auden, Cameron, Larkin (qq.v.)—is difficult but at its best, as in her first collection, *The Close Chaplet* (1926), astonishing: almost a definition of a sense of the poetic. Here is the kind of absolute dedication to poetry of a Rilke: all experience is continuously subjected to the heroically objective scrutiny of a truthful heart. Her quality is as well illustrated in 'The Mask' as in any other short poem:

> Cover up,
> Oh, quickly cover up
> All the new spotted places,
> All the unbeautifuls,
> The insufficiently beloved.
>
> With what? with what?
> With the uncovering of the lovelies,
> With the patches that transformed
> The more previous corruptions.
>
> Is there no pure then?
> The eternal taint wears beauty like a mask.
> But a mask eternal.

In a way the rejection of the poetry that came in 1940 is already there, in the poems: 'if poetry', she often seems to imply, 'won't get me further in my quest for the perfect and the pure, then poetry will have to go'. Her assertions of her knowledge of the direction of truth do not make for her best poetry; the best lies in her descriptions of the sufferings of a woman of genius, with aspirations towards goodness: 'Nor is it written that you may not grieve./There is no rule of joy . . .' is a notable example. This is a poetry that either makes no appeal or deeply fascinates; the full, important and fascinating story of it, and of its aftermath, has yet to be told.

*

HART CRANE (1899–1932), born in Ohio, failed to escape the demons that drove him to drink and homosexual encounters; he died when he jumped from a ship after a bad night gambling with some sailors, who had beaten him up. He was travelling with a woman with whom he had had a satisfactory hetero-sexual relationship in the previous months; but she came too late into his life to help him to achieve stability. He published *White Buildings* (1926), short poems, and the American epic, *The Bridge* (1930), in his lifetime. *Collected Poems* (1933) incorporates a last group of shorter poems. His *Letters* (1952) are full of acute and generous critical insights into his own and his contemporaries' poetry. Crane, who was patchily self-educated and who was, in an academic sense, unfamiliar with the history of his own country, was quintessentially American and poetically enormously gifted; he is the subject of an increasing number of contradictory monographs, certain of which reach the fantastic in their projections of their authors' involved symbolisms onto Crane's often historically confused conceptions.

Crane was not, it should be emphasized, naïve (q.v.) in the modified Schillerian sense in which I have used it in this book. He was just badly educated, and too frenetic to do anything about it. His parents were unhappily married, and both seem to have been thoroughly unpleasant people. He was a classic victim; and when he emerged from adolescence he was dangerously mother-attached, bisexual with an almost ritual emphasis on the homosexual side, and a problem drinker (whether he suffered from the specific disease of alcoholism, which was even less well understood then than now, is not clear). But Crane's letters make it perfectly clear that his intelligence, when allowed to function unimpeded, was powerful. He has been compared, inevitably, with Dylan Thomas (q.v.); but—as a comparison of the letters demonstrates—Crane was by far the more intelligent of the two (and infinitely the better and more important poet).

The more academic the approach to Crane—that is to say, the more his poetry is approached as an entity separate from his drunken and hell-driven self—the more emphasis is put on *The Bridge* as a more or less successful American epic. But Crane, unlike some other poets, is not well served by an exclusively academic approach. His poetry embodies the drives of his own frenetic personality.

No really aware critic considers *The Bridge* a success. He conceived this epic in a state of desperation in order to get money from a business man patron, Otto Kahn (whose $2,000 he soon spent in drink and debauchery, as well he might—perhaps Wallace Stevens, by then fairly well-heeled, should have advanced the cash). Crane told Kahn that the poem was supposed to represent the American past by showing the present in its 'vital substance'; but it is only good when Crane is doing something else; it can only be judged as a ragbag of fragments, some sentimental and forced, others beautiful. Nothing in *The Bridge* coheres. The concept of it belongs to the semi-literate side of Crane: his *conscious* Americanism is exceedingly laboured. He was not, at twenty-five, equipped to write any kind of an epic.

Crane had a number of mediocre and, worse, pretentious friends and acquaintances; he had very little more than his superb intuition to distinguish between the fake and the real. Yet he was not himself pretentious: rather, he overwrote, putting out hot gusts of rhetoric to the sound of jazz and the glug-glug of his throat as he poured alcohol down it. He would interrupt his bouts of drink-writing to indulge in equally heroic bouts of homosex.

Yet after all this has been said, Crane is one of this century's major poets. In some dozen or so poems—they include the 'Voyages' sequence and several other poems from *White Buildings*, and the late 'The Broken Tower'—he found a language as suitable to his time as to himself. It cost him immense pain; the real reason for his death, apart from the local remorse that occasioned it, was that he believed his powers were failing. Crane has much to tell us: of the nature of romantic love; of gentleness, for he was gentle; of sexuality; of the anguish of homosexuality; of poetry and of being a poet. No twentieth-century poet has written more moving poetry. 'The Broken Tower', the poem he believed had failed, is perhaps more moving than any other. This combines the themes of his bisexuality and his capacity as a poet in a complex image of bell-ringing at dawn (which he had helped to do in a Mexican town). Its strength and poetic confidence make a tragic contrast with his state of mind a few weeks after he had written it. These are its last six stanzas:

And so it was I entered the broken world
To trace the visionary company of love, its voice
An instant in the wind (I know not whither hurled)
But not for long to hold each desperate choice.

My word I poured. But was it cognate, scored
Of that tribunal monarch of the air
Whose thigh embronzes earth, strikes crystal Word
In wounds pledged once to hope—cleft to despair?

The steep encroachments of my blood left me
No answer (could blood hold such a lofty tower
As flings the question true?)—or is it she
Whose sweet mortality stirs latent power?—

And through whose pulse I hear, counting the strokes
My veins recall and add, revived and sure
The angelus of wars my chest evokes:
What I hold healed, original now, and pure . . .

And builds, within, a tower that is not stone
(Not stone can jacket heaven)—but slip
Of pebbles—visible wings of silence sown
In azure circles, widening as they dip

The matrix of the heart, lift down the eye
That shrines the quiet lake and swells a tower . . .
The commodious, tall decorum of that sky
Unseals her earth, and lifts love in its shower.

Like Rilke's, Crane's poetry in its very different way nakedly poses the dangerous question of just what poetry itself is.

*

YVOR WINTERS (1900–68), born in Chicago, was much better known as critic than poet. He taught at Stanford University from 1928 onwards. He began as an experimental imagist poet, recording life as a series of ecstatic perceptions in an ineffective free verse. Then he became, or tried to become, the moral and classical spokesman of his generation. Since Winters could really think, it is probably fair to call him an exponent of the new criticism (which was never a school); but his criticism does not otherwise resemble that of other well-known critics such as Warren or Ransom (qq.v.). He was ill-tempered, racked with envy and frustration, and pompous; at its frequent worst his criticism is grotesque (as when he claims that Bridges', q.v., verse drama is the best in English since Shakespeare). But at his best, as when he attacks Hopkins and Yeats and Crane (qq.v.), he demands an answer, and is thus provocative. His own poetry, however, tells us why he became the enemy of romantic self-discovery and expressionism. First, there are the early 'modernist' poems. These are commonplace and affected. Then come the 'restrained' models for his contemporaries (almost the only one he wholly applauded was Elizabeth Daryush, Bridges' daughter). These are restrained because there has been no feeling to restrain. This enemy of romanticism does not understand what he hates. Many of the poems, such as 'On the Death of Senator Thomas J. Walsh', are disguised tributes to himself:

An old man more is gathered to the great,
Singly, for conscience' sake he bent his brow. . . .

Why did he become so famous as well as unpopular? Because, I think, the deliquescent hatred, product of envy and poetic inner emptiness, that inform his criticism does give it an energy, and when that energy is harnessed to logical argument the results are interesting and stimulating. Here egocentricity shrieks contortedly in the name of 'reason' and 'classicism'. And his passionate exhortations to young poets towards restraint did occasionally have useful results, particularly in the cases of J. V. CUNNINGHAM (1911) and the English poet Thom Gunn (q.v.).

Cunningham was born in Maryland and studied at Stanford. He has interestingly transformed Winters' aim; and his motive is not an impoverished emotional life or an inability to create an energetic language. Therefore his project, at least, is of great interest—particularly to those who are concerned with what I have termed *Künstlerschuld* (q.v.). Poetry, and his own poetic impulse, Cunningham wants humbly to reduce to the level of other 'ordinary' activities: Poetry 'is a concern of the ordinary human self. . . . Its virtues are the civic virtues. If it lacks much, what it does have is ascertainable and can be judged'. This is very much the view of W. H. Auden (q.v.) (dealt with as an English poet), who believes that poetry changes nothing and regards it as an entertainment (and yet continually acts as a public man who believes in the civilizing virtues of art). Thus Cunningham writes a good deal of 'light' verse—much of it highly accomplished and amusing. His more serious poetry, in such volumes as *The Judge is Fury* (1947), *To What Strangers, What Welcome* (1964), is difficult but of great integrity. He is a neglected poet—but probably not one who would appeal to upholders of the civic virtues of the average American town, which is perhaps ironic. *Selected Poems* appeared in 1971.

DELMORE SCHWARTZ (1913–67), born in Brooklyn, was an extremely brilliant man who perished under the burden of his gifts. In him were uneasily combined two traditions: the Brooklyn Jewish (he planned a baseball novel before he was thirty, but it was Malamud, q.v., who wrote *The Natural*) and the intelligent academic. When he died he was a mental and physical wreck, whose gift had long ago choked on itself. Schwartz's Marxist inclinations (he was at various times concerned with editing *Partisan Review* and *The New Republic*) often clashed with those of his imagination; this may have been one of the reasons why he failed, in poetry, to discover his own voice for more than a few lines at a time. A trained philosopher with an intellect too clear for his own good, he wanted simply to observe, pessimistically; but his acute Jewish conscience would not allow him to do this. Hence the title of his first book, *In Dreams Begin Responsibilities* (1938). He is forever philosophizing against the horrors his imagination involuntarily reveals. Towards the end he became too consciously 'symbolic': the bright heart of his work had entered into a tunnel of gloom. In his poetry the language that his self-consciousness, his guilt, struggles to produce is expected—but never comes. But the Jewish stories of *The World is a Wedding* (1948), the acute criticism—and the so nearly successful poetry, much of which is collected in *Summer Knowledge* (1959)—gave him an important place in modern American literature, as a writer of high quality destroyed, to an alarming and poignant degree, by his predicament and his honesty.

The poetry of MURIEL RUKEYSER (1913), born in New York, is more specifically directed towards socialism than Schwartz's; what isn't tends to the too exuberantly feminine. It is not that the sense of it is embarrassing; but the poet writes too much in the 'open' tradition of Sandburg and does not bother to discover her own voice. She was influenced by HORACE GREGORY (1898), from Wisconsin, a distinguished translator who has not found his own voice, either— because of too easy philosophical and Marxist predilections. Both these poets have floundered intelligently about, but have been too much at the service of simplistic ideas. Better, because resolutely minor, was KENNETH FEARING (1902– 61), born in Chicago, who in his fiction—notably *The Big Clock* (1946)—achieved a level of intelligence seldom seen in the thriller: he influenced the Englishman Julian Symons, who achieved a similar distinction. His poetry (*New and Selected Poems*, 1956), in free verse, is funny and sometimes compassionate: a readable and sarcastic rebuke to the pretentious excesses of others more ambitious.

Minnesota-born RICHARD EBERHART (1904) has experimented with too many forms; he has diffused his considerable gift into a too rambling poetry, which ranges from the metaphysical through the allegorical to the descriptive-romantic. He protests against the anonymity of the 'system' that pseudo-orders life, but cannot seem to set against it anything personal enough to convince us of more than his own, rather than his poems', excellence. He has published his *Collected Poems* (1960), *Selected Poems* (1965), and two volumes since then. No clearly serious poet is, perhaps, so uneven. His 'philosophy' shifts between a pessimism that he will not sufficiently explore and a mild religiousness that is unconvincing. One of his best known poems begins

> You would think the fury of aerial bombardment
> Would arouse God to relent. . . .

It is slack, careless, undistinguished writing: too generalized even to call forth a personal rhythm. And yet when the poet becomes personal, his poetry leaps into life: that same poem ends with these four lines:

> Of Van Wettering I speak, and Averill,
> Names on a list, whose names I do not recall
> But they are gone to early death, who late in school
> Distinguished the belt feed lever from the belt holding pawl.

The long quarry into the vague mud of his poetry yields similar jewels, and is worth while.

STANLEY KUNITZ (1905), born in Massachusetts, whose *Selected Poems 1928–58* appeared in 1958, is one of the most skilled poets of his generation. His achievement stands, like Eberhart's, but more solidly, behind the poetry of Lowell and others; but this is not yet fully acknowledged. His first book, *Intellectual Things* (1930), appeared when Lowell was twelve years old. His is one of the earliest poetries to concern itself exclusively with the naked, solipsist self, unconsoled, in a hostile world. There is in the earlier poems too much dependence on Yeats, and a corresponding rhetoric; but personal suffering and a refining of style has modified this to a spareness of diction in the later work. He has recently made excellent translations from Russian poets.

*

American poetry since the war has divided itself into two diverging streams. Some of the more or less traditionalist poets—such as Lowell, Jarrell, Roethke, Elizabeth Bishop, Snodgrass, Hecht (qq.v.)—have been influenced by, or at least enjoy, the poetry of William Carlos Williams (q.v.), who is the real twentieth-century father of the anti-traditionalists—Olson, Creeley, Duncan, Snyder. But these latter will have no truck with the Fugitives ('antiques'), Frost, or Lowell himself. The one figure to which nearly all acknowledge allegiance is Pound (q.v.). It is the Black Mountain poets and their disciples, however, who have most decisively broken away; and their immediate prophet is Charles Olson (q.v.). To be fully aware of what they have broken away from it is necessary to look, first, at the continuers of the tradition: those who, whether in fact *avant garde* (as Lowell is) or not, have not been self-consciously, pro-grammatically so. Mostly they are poets of self-revelation, who have written 'confessionally' in the belief that by exploiting their verbal gifts in the interests of self-analysis they may create a world comprehending enough to allow the realization of all individual values. The danger, as one soon sees, is that under the strain of confession they become self-publicists, cultural film-stars: that their imagination may be robbed of authority, so that they themselves subscribe to sentimental photographs of themselves as midcult poet-heroes. Thus society pulls them into the very life-impoverishing system they set out to destroy: gives them a glossy place, reports on their pain, panders to their ideals.

Thus, ROBERT LOWELL (1917), scion of a great family, is now a public figure whose poetry has lately (whether temporarily or not remains to be seen) degenerated into a sterile, exhibitionist journalism: the confessionalist puts himself on show, inserting into an account of his selected private and public activities the odd striking line. This is *Notebook 1967–8* (1969, rev. 1969, rev. 1970). No mistake should be made about this: it is rank bad, a coffee-table book, and if its author does not go back on it he ends his serious career as poet.

Lowell's early poems, the best of which are to be found in *Poems 1938–49* (1950) and *The Mills of the Kavanaughs* (1951), were metrically tight and invariably rhymed. Lowell had learned about prosody from Bridges (q.v.)—that master technician who had nothing of poetic importance to say—as Auden did, and these early poems show him as the leading technician of his time. These youthful, livid, melodramatic poems look rather like a magnified, violent revision of Allen Tate (Tate and Ransom were Lowell's first masters):

> Wallowing in this bloody sty
> I cast for fish that pleased my eye
> (Truly Jehovah's bow suspends
> No pots of gold to weight its ends);
> Only the blood-mouthed rainbow trout
> Rose to my bait. . . .

The tone has been well described as one of 'baroque exaltation'. During the war Lowell ('a fire-breathing Catholic C.O.') was a conscientious objector and went to prison; the themes of the early poems are generally speaking Jansenist (he left the Catholic Church in the Fifties), and harp on the punishment that man must resign himself to for his failure to fulfil his obligation to God. Their mood, if nothing else, is not unlike that of the earlier novels of Mauriac (q.v.). From the beginning Lowell carried within him a consciousness of a certain regality; he studied, so to speak, to assume the regal duties of appraising Boston and, in due course, his family. He had evaded his background at first; but during the Fifties, experiencing divorce (from the novelist Jean Stafford), remarriage and madness, he went back to it: the result was *Life Studies* (1959). The fuller American edition of this contains a prose autobiography and auto-biographical poems—the method of which, Lowell has acknowledged, he borrowed from his pupil W. D. Snodgrass. This collection included the famous 'Skunk Hour', with the lines:

> One dark night
> My Tudor Ford climbed the hill's skull;
> I watched for love cars. Lights turned down,
> they lay together, hull to hull,
> where the graveyard shelves on the town. . . .
> My mind's not right.

These are the poems, beautifully accomplished in their relaxed rhetoric, for which Lowell is most celebrated. His *Imitations* (1961), often deliberate distortions or alterations of European poets, are also admired—and arouse interest as part of the education of an allegedly major poet. But some have preferred the crabbed, tightly restrained energy of the earlier Lowell, seeing in *Life Studies* the beginnings of the process that leads through *For the Union Dead* (1964) and *Near the Ocean* (1967)—some original poems and more translations—to the self-vulgarizing disaster of the *Notebooks*, which read, says Donald Hall cruelly but justly, 'like prayers to Stockholm'. The poems of *Life Studies*, and some of those that come after them, are masterly in technique; but the autobiographical ones often seem less good than the prose. Comparison establishes that the poem is often a fiercely worked up version of the prose: often nothing has come up from the well of the unconscious—rather, the poet has manufactured a poem out of his raw material, tricking it up and making it rhetorical. The best poems, the ones to Ford, Schwartz and Santayana (qq.v.), 'Skunk Hour' and others, are minor rather than major: the distinction is nearly all in the way style manipulates tone and feeling. The poetry is impressive, fashionable, superbly appropriate for treatment in approved critical modes. One can see why Lowell got into a state of mind in which he felt obliged to imitate his friend John Berryman (q.v.)—to the extent of even copying the form of the *Dream Songs*. *Notebooks* often looks like what it is: a rival to *Dream Songs*. The career of Lowell, and the embarrassing impasse into which it has led him, exemplifies the difficulties of poetry in our time. The poet is transformed into politician; he has to justify himself, get glass eyes; his imagination is threatened. That Lowell in 1970 came quietly to England for a period gives hope that he means to retreat into himself and keep away from publicity; only thus can his poetry survive.

Another poet who suffered from bouts of madness throughout his difficult life was THEODORE ROETHKE (1908–63), the Michigan-born son of the Prussian owner of a huge and well-known nursery business, the details of which figure greatly in his poetry. Roethke's subject is the state of his being as it comes into contact with reality. He is not 'confessional', is not, like Lowell, interested in making his subject his own awareness of his behaviour. He presents his biography in lyrical, semi-mystical terms that were notably influenced, at various times, by Blake, Yeats, Eliot, Auden, Dylan Thomas and Léonie Adams (qq.v.). His first poems, published in *Open House* (1941), were in strict forms; but those of *The Lost Son* (1948) are in a freer verse. They consist of interior monologues, in which Roethke incorporates microscopic descriptions of plants that are not in fact scientific or even very carefully observed—rather they remind one of Graham Sutherland's close-up paintings, which try to define the nature of their subjects by pictorial metaphor. *Praise to the End* (1951), which contains much pastiche of Yeats (q.v.) and mimicry of Dylan Thomas (q.v.), is at once less original and more visionary.

Roethke's poems were collected in *The Waking* (1953), again in *Words for the Wind* (1958), and finally and posthumously in *Collected Poems* (1968). He was an insecure poet, and his most serious fault is his parodies—or mimicries—of other poets. It makes most of what he has to say unconvincing. Such tender poetry as 'The Meadow Mouse' is spoiled because, in it, all that is not imitated from John Clare is petty moralizing. Eliot is drawn upon not only for manner but for a whole symbolic method that Roethke himself was not close to.

What is left and may survive is a small body of minor love poetry, such poems as 'The Apparition', 'Her Reticence' and 'The Happy Three'—all of these from his posthumous collection *The Far Field* (1964).

Roethke often looks very good indeed. His poetry nearly always has a most attractive surface. His technique seldom let him down. But close investigation usually shows the poetry to be second-rate and second-hand, the ecstatic voice something the poet jollied himself into. The long para-surrealist poems about greenhouses and plants have a certain value, but ultimately they fail to take us beyond the experiences of mental disintegration and regression to childhood which they record. Again, the purely physical love poetry, which is not as plagiaristic as most of the rest of his work, is of little value because when one comes down to it, it does no more than find various ingenious ways of describing physical desire. Roethke's 'mystical vision' consists of nothing at all. But his breathless, lyrical manner (often, in him, trite—as in 'The Geranium', with its banal ending) had a wide and probably beneficial because releasing influence.

A poet admired by Lowell and others of his group is ELIZABETH BISHOP (1911), who published her complete poems in 1970. If this quiet and fastidious poet, who was born in Massachusetts and has spent much of her life in South America, has a model then it is Marianne Moore (q.v.). She is not immune from awfulness ('Invitation to Miss Marianne Moore' begins 'From Booklyn, over the Brooklyn Bridge, on this fine morning,/please come flying' and continues in that vein), but in general she is more discriminating in what she publishes than most. Although she has written competent ballads and done some translations from the Portuguese of some Brazilian poets, she is mainly a poet of description so accurate and skilful that she suggests something beyond her subject. She owes part of the curiosity of her style to Marianne Moore, and her method is rooted in imagism—but a Bishop poem has its own unmistakable stamp. When she tries anything other than this she is liable to sentimentality and tweeness, as in 'Cootchie'. But, with a group of some twenty-five poems, such as 'The Fish' and 'The Weed' she has made a special place for herself in modern American poetry.

There can be no more technically skilful poet living than RICHARD WILBUR (1921), who was born in New York. Wilbur is graceful, learned, civilized—but he cannot allow himself to mean as much to his readers as they would like. He cannot be wild. His discretion, his control, insists on decorum. He observes well, writes beautifully, translates exquisitely; but of course it is all just a little too good to be true. No one really important, alas, *could* be that fastidiously perfect. And yet. . . . One finds oneself lamenting that Wilbur, so intelligent and decent, lacks 'attack'. Even 'Beasts', one of his finest poems, lacks a really cutting edge. Yet *Poems 1943–56* (1957), published in England and collecting the best of three American volumes, contains many pleasurable poems, as do his next three books, the most recent of which is *Walking to Sleep* (1970). Perhaps a British critic, writing of this latest volume, has put his finger on the trouble when he suggests that Wilbur's poetry may not cost him enough. Much bad verse doubtless costs dear; but all good poetry must do so.

SYLVIA PLATH (1932–63), who was born in Boston and died in London, was the exact opposite of Wilbur: at the end of her life, her marriage to the English poet Ted Hughes (q.v.) broken up, the surface of her life was, quite literally, poetry. She had had a nervous breakdown in America in 1951, when she had tried to commit suicide. She wrote about this time of her life in her novel *The Bell Jar*, which was first published in 1963 under the pseudonym Victoria Lucas. When she became seriously ill in London in 1963 she had no one to look after her, and she finally gassed herself. She had published *The Colossus* in 1960; but it is generally agreed that it is the poems of the posthumous *Ariel* (1965) that are her most important. More has been and will be issued; but none of this appears to have much intrinsic value.

Most people are dedicated to the surfaces of their lives, and this protects them from the stresses of poetic thinking: from caring intensely about what does not, in material terms, matter. Because for a few months Sylvia Plath made all her existence into poetry (her children were her only distraction), critics have too confidently assumed that her ostensible subject matter, of concentration camps and of the plight of Jewishness, is their real subject matter. One, calling her a 'minor poet of great intensity', yet states that 'the last, greatest poems culminate in an act of identification, of total communion with those tortured and massacred'. This is mystical. Another critic (no doctor) assumes that her illness was schizophrenic and pronounces that her poetry 'defines the age as schizophrenic'. But the chances are that her illness was a form of manic-depression—a form in which euphoria and depression may mysteriously co-exist (cf. Campana, Bacovia, qq.v.). That, certainly, is the mood of the last poems.

These are minor poems—although they may in an age of increasing urban stress and consequent madness be historically prophetic—because their subject is never really more than her own illness. So 'minor poet of great intensity' is right. But that is enough. For they tell us much of the nature of her mental and therefore of human illness. But fashionable criticism has been wrong in emphasizing 'the contemporary predicament' in her poems. They should read the French diarist and essayist Simone Weil to find this: she really writes about the contemporary predicament. Sylvia Plath was writing about herself. The comparison is a revealing one.

When A. Alvarez (q.v.), an able critic and, to a point, good on Sylvia Plath, says that she 'gambled . . . and lost', implying she 'did it' for poetry, he is projecting his own poker-playing preoccupations onto her. For it evades the issue. Her predicament was not to gamble but to remain truthful while she suffered madness; and the best of her poems do remain truthful, if only to her condition of a suicidal depression shot through with euphoria. They tell us about this condition—not about 'the schizophrenic world', a critic's ambitious and rhetorical abstraction.

However, Sylvia Plath did find apt words to describe her condition as she waited to die. In 'Death & Co.' she imagines death as two business men calling, one of whom 'exhibits

> The birthmarks that are his trademark—
> The scald scar of water,
> The nude
> Verdigris of the condor.
> I am red meat. His beak
>
> Claps sidewise: I am not his yet
> He tells me how badly I photograph. . . .
>
> The other . . .
> His hair long and plausive.
> Bastard
> Masturbating a glitter,
> He wants to be loved. . . .'

The tone comes straight out of Roethke's greenhouse poems, but it is sharpened by knowledge of self-inflicted death. These are suicide poems. They are not at all, and cannot be, about any kind of love. They are about horror. But however much this diminishes their stature, they will remain important for the chilling accuracy of their descriptions of terror.

ANNE SEXTON (1928) is usually described as of the 'confessional' school, although she would prefer to be classed as 'an imagist who deals with reality and its hard facts'. She writes, inevitably, in the shadow of Sylvia Plath, since some of her poems are about mental breakdown. The title of her first book was

To Bedlam and Part Way Back (1960), and this dealt with, among other things, a suicide attempt. She published her *Selected Poems* in 1964. Two more collections followed: *Live or Die* (1967) and *Love Poems* (1969). Anne Sexton is an excellent writer of lyrical autobiography. She writes of her own experiences—illness, motherhood, love—descriptively, not moralistically or squeamishly. Her poems set up few resonances, are autobiographically 'regional'. Her love poems, for example, are splendidly physical, and extremely feminine inasmuch as they make no attempts to extrapolate 'meanings' from the pleasures they record. As that kind of love poet, writing as a woman, she is probably unsurpassed.

JOHN BERRYMAN (1914–72), who was born of strict Roman Catholic parents in Oklahoma, and whose father shot himself in front of the twelve-year-old son's window, could well be described as the confessional poet *par excellence*. His style is frequently cryptic, mannered, convoluted; but the subject (beginning with his *Sonnets*, which he wrote in the Forties but did not publish until 1967) of his poetry has increasingly been himself: his mental instability, his adultery, his friends, his general agony. Obviously Berryman is in the *Dream Songs*—*77 Dream Songs* (1964), *His Toy, His Dream, His Rest* (1968)—frequently a very bad poet indeed: impenetrably obscure, ruthlessly making use of private references, crabbed, archaic, over-dramatic. . . . This is hardly denied unless by the kind of uncritical reader whom no one wants. The question, in the *Dream Songs* as much as in the *Sonnets*, is whether by taking these risks Berryman has achieved a new, more lucid, better poetry. Well, he has achieved a very fascinating and different kind of poetry, which demands to be studied. Berryman does not pretend that he does not lust for fame:

> He can advance no claim,
> save that he studied thy Word and grew afraid,
> work & fear be the basis for his terrible cry
> not to forget his name.

And yet he said (in an interview on British TV) that he had only six readers who really understood what he was doing. . . . Did he mean this? The number of private references in his poems suggests that in one sense he did—but it is unfortunately not a question he chose to answer, perhaps because he remained Roman Catholic enough to leave such matters to God. Berryman, an alcoholic, killed himself during a spell of depression partly caused by his going off drink.

Berryman began as an almost academic poet, writing in tight stanzas; Dudley Fitts found in them 'an aura of academic contrivance'. He collected together such of his early poems as he wished to preserve in *Short Poems* (1967); but these are quite different from the three later sequences. *Homage to Mistress Bradstreet* (1956) is a poem-sequence based on the twin conceits that the Puritan Anne Bradstreet, America's first poet, is his mistress—and that she is his alter ego. By participating in her life—into which Berryman made research —the poet illuminates his discovery of his own country.

The organization of *Dream Songs* is calculated to allow the writer to explore himself and his world in as free a manner as possible. Each poem consists of eighteen lines divided into three stanzas of six lines each; but lengths and stress of line, and rhyme pattern, vary. Berryman projects himself into several voices: Henry, a white man in black face, who speaks like a nigger minstrel (Berryman says the poem is 'essentially about' him), an unnamed friend who calls him Mr. Bones, and some other not definitely identified voices. This Henry and his friend are not more than acknowledgements on his part that no poet can himself be the 'I' of any poem; he can only pretend it. This pretence is not necessarily reprehensible; but it will not do for so long and ambitious an epic—a rival to the *Cantos*?—as Berryman planned. The poem has rightly been called artificial, uneven and pretentious. The question is: How much more artificial, uneven and pretentious than its author (or its readers)? Could one get such comic effects as Berryman gets in the following stanza by not being 'quirky'?:

> Henry sits in de plane & was gay.
> Careful Henry nothing said aloud
> but where a Virgin out of cloud
> to her Mountain dropt in light,
> his thought made pockets & the plane buckt.
> 'Parm me, lady.' 'Orright.'

This of course shows a poet being himself (in just the way Wilbur will not be himself) with a vengeance. It has attendant risks, and it can lead to an egocentric and even offensive verse. But someone who cared about the past of poetry, and for the notion of effort in making it, had to take this plunge. It could prove of more historical than intrinsic interest: it is very uneven, and we must wait to see what cumulative effect it has after at least a decade. But its importance is unquestioned.

RANDALL JARRELL (1914–65), who was born in Tennessee, threw himself under a truck at the age of fifty-one. He was a leading member of the gifted generation of Schwartz, Lowell and Berryman (qq.v.), and like them, he taught in universities. In the Second World War he served in the United States Air Force. He was a critic of genius (*Poetry and the Age*, 1953), being particularly funny at the expense of the wholly academic critics; and he wrote a good novel satirizing small college life, *Pictures from an Institution* (1954). Jarrell was a poet of, above all, sensibility: sensibility about man's doomed quest for decency and goodness. He wrote much about childhood because innocence was what interested him. He was a very friendly poet—the friendliest of all of his generation. But he fell into sentimentality, his obvious temptation, less often than Schwartz into windy abstraction, Lowell into regal exhibitionism. Roethke into pastiche, Berryman into private and idiosyncratic muttering. . . . He will no doubt be called a minor poet; he is not as ambitious as Lowell (although history will see him, I think, as effective), and does not try for so much as Berryman; Robert Fitzgerald was possibly justified in his stricture that we 'admire' Jarrell's poetry, but are 'unrelieved; we miss the great exhilarations of art'. Or was he? When one remembers Lowell and his recent struggles to achieve something that *looks* like those great exhilarations, one is thankful for the more modest Jarrell. But then Jarrell was more sceptical and less personally ambitious; he might even, at his best, have avoided the phrase 'the great exhilarations of art'. One is above all grateful for him when thinking of the gush that has gathered around such apocalyptics as Dylan Thomas (q.v.): like Thomas, Jarrell stood for poetry, and was against its impoverishment by the sort of criticism he called 'nearly autonymous'; but unlike Thomas he resisted the fake-Bardic in himself.

His war poetry, *qua* war poetry, is probably the best to come out of the Second World War. It has some of the bitter irony of Owen, and great compassion. Reading it one really does wonder about those 'great exhilarations': doesn't he have here what Fitzgerald meant?

> In bombers named for girls, we burned
> The cities we had learned about in school. . . .

> The soldier simply wishes for his name. . . .

> Strapped at the centre of the blazing wheel,
> His flesh ice-white against the shattered mask
> He tears at the easy clasp, his sobbing breaths
> Misting the fresh blood lightening to flame,
> Darkening to smoke. . . .

The best of these, with others, were included in *Selected Poems* (1955). The postwar Jarrell, with his love of Grimm and the *Märchen*, could not always keep away from the whimsical. And such poems as 'Nollekens', based on the famous book, are a little too wide-eyed ('All that my poem says he did, he did . . .'). Then, in his last years, Jarrell found a more suitable style. Although it was not Browning's, Browning, with his dramatic monologues, pointed the way. The poems, most of them dramatic monologues spoken by women, are in the posthumous *The Lost World* (1966). At their best these have the exact quality of the nostalgia of his admired Proust. 'Thinking of the Lost World' begins

> This spoonful of chocolate tapioca
> Tastes like—like peanut butter, like the vanilla
> Extract Mama told me not to drink.
> Swallowing the spoonful, I have already travelled
> Through time to my childhood. It puzzles me
> That age is like it. . . .

and later occur the lines:

> All of them are gone
> Except for me; and for me nothing is gone—
> The chicken's body is still going round
> And round in widening circles. . . .
> Mama and Pop and Dandeen are still there
> In the Gay Twenties.

It ends:

> I hold in my own hands, in happiness,
> Nothing: the nothing for which there's no reward.

It has been given to few American poets to write so beautifully and so simply—and to avoid the psychopathic, the abnormal, the terrible, at the same time.

*

HOWARD NEMEROV (1920), born in New York, has not embraced the Beats or the school of Olson; but he is a very knowing, humorous traditionalist—by no means a citizen of Squaresville. His first poems were sophisticated and metaphysical, and often spoiled by their cleverness. But he has evolved to a greater simplicity. And even if there is no special virtue in having simplicity for an aim, there is every virtue in a poet's working to attain the greatest simplicity commensurate with what he has to say. This is what Nemerov, it seems, is trying to do. He is one of the most gifted American poets born in the Twenties—and in many ways the most representative of his time. He has slowly but surely forged his own style, as the carefully edited *New and Selected Poems* (1960), taking only forty-three poems from four volumes and adding fifteen new ones, shows. Nemerov has come to the all-important point of asking why he writes:

> The time came
> He had to ask himself, what did he want?
> What did he want when he began
> That idiot fiddling with sound of things.

Although he appears at present to believe that the answer to this lies in philosophy, it is to be hoped that he will continue to search for his answer in his imagination. The kind of poem he now writes is well illustrated by the fine 'The Iron Characters':

> The iron characters, keepers of the public confidence,
> The sponsors, fund raisers, and members of the board,
> Who naturally assume their seats among the governors,
> Who place their names behind the issue of bonds
> And are consulted in the formation of cabinets,
> The catastrophes of war, depression, and natural disaster:
> They represent us in responsibilities many and great.
> It is no wonder, then, if in a moment of crisis,
> Before the microphones, under the lights, on a great occasion,
> One of them will break down in hysterical weeping
> Or fall in an epileptic seizure, or if one day
> We read in the papers of one's having been found
> Naked and drunk in a basement with three high school boys,
> Of one who jumped from the window of his hospital room.
> For are they not as ourselves in these things also?
> Let the orphan, the pauper, the thief, the derelict drunk
> And all those of no fixed address, shed tears of rejoicing
> For the broken minds of the strong, the torn flesh of the just.

Nemerov has written some highly intellectual, comic fiction: four novels and a number of (uncollected) short stories; and two volumes of non-fiction, the second, *Journal of the Fictive Life* (1965), an interesting account of his inability to finish a novel. It seems likely that this pessimistic but humorous writer has his best work in front of him.

W. D. SNODGRASS (1926), who was born in Pennsylvania, first wrote on very personal subjects; since he tried to widen his range, and deliberately made his language, once straightforward, more complex, he has been notably less good. But this might happen to any poet who has run low on inspiration. His poetry is collected in two books: *Heart's Needle* (1958) and *After Experience*. . . .(1969). Essentially, when one has ruthlessly cut out the over-mawkish, the complacent and sentimental, Snodgrass is another good autobiographical poet like Anne Sexton.

New York-born ANTHONY HECHT (1923) has sometimes been associated—misleadingly—with the 'confessional' school. Actually he is a factitious poet, wholly traditional, who would not dream of letting slip a confession that had been undoctored with wit or irony. Behind all this care, though, lurks an Old Testament Jewish voice, sometimes very angry; Hecht mutes it but its prophetic bray is still there. *The Hard Hours* (1967) selects from the earlier *A Summoning of Stones* (1954).

W. S. MERWIN (1927), also born in New York, is a most skilful constructor of poetic surface. He began by writing poems, of excellent technique, that looked as though they were meant to satisfy all the requirements of the new critics. They analyzed beautifully, one might say; but they lacked a distinctive voice, and they were not moving or convincing. The experience they reflected was that of thinking about being an acceptable poet. Since then Merwin has gone through a Williams (q.v.) phase, and is now writing in the style of the French poetry that stems from Reverdy (q.v.). He is a good craftsman, and is evidently sincere—he least of all needs to switch from traditional to unrhymed and free modes—but his new poetry looks too much like translation. And he is of course a notable translator from Spanish and from French: he translated Jean Follain (q.v.) in 1969, in a volume called *Transparence of the World*, and the French poet's influence is evident. Merwin's first verse was collected in *A Mask for Janus* (1952); recent books include *The Moving Target* (1967) and *The Lice* (1967).

*

There are probably more than a thousand published Beat poets. We need consider only one: ALLEN GINSBERG (1926). Ginsberg is a socio-anthropological phenomenon, a shrewd business man, and now, ironically, a part of the way of American life. He was educated at Columbia University, after which he went on the hoof. Then in 1955 he published the long poem *Howl*, and he was made: the Beat Generation was accepted. And Ginsberg cannot rebel again; so he boasts 'I . . . achieved the introduction of the word *fuck* into texts inevitably studied by schoolboys'. This is again ironic (if, of course, we accept that he alone did it): for this amiable pseudo-Zen droll is by no means a propagandist for heterosexuality. His poetry, he says, is 'Angelical Ravings'; but he is too comfortable to do more now than worry about his influence. His poetry is actually simply the manifestation of the eclectic, syncretic, 'redskin' American tradition. The first poems, although incoherent, had a pressure of indignation behind them. Their literary badness was deliberate. The poet 'simply followed his Angel in the course of compositions'. There *was* just a tiny bit of Blake in all this: the poet meant it. It expressed the drop-out's attitude to organized society. Ginsberg did have something that Lowell did not. But all this became corrupt, a way of life; and life has not changed. Ginsberg's latest verse is publicly performed, chopped-up prose, incoherent and self-indulgent. It is preferable to the antics of politicians; preferable even to what passes for literature in the 'literary world'; but if it is indeed the new poetry, then a poetry in which thought, care and effort play a part is dead. And that is false to Gods Ginsberg himself appeals to: Blake, Smart, Shelley. Ginsberg's is a way of life. And so far we have not had a poetry that went along with any accepted way of life—certainly not ones that are sponsored by national institutions like Ginsberg. Whatever Ginsberg does, he is trapped: society has tamed him.

The Black Mountain school of poets, of whom I shall here discuss Olson and Creeley, did not arise from the Beat movement, although Creeley welcomed Ginsberg, who had previously been endorsed by Williams (who endorsed, in fact, pretty well anyone, including Lowell). Black Mountain College began in the Thirties and finally collapsed in the late Fifties. The emphasis was at first on the visual arts, on the art-object as thing-in-itself, and the tradition was that of American pragmatism. So far as literature is concerned, with the exception of Olson's doctrines (to be outlined below) the preoccupations were those of the objectivists (q.v.).

CHARLES OLSON (1910–70), who was born in Worcester, Massachusetts, was fifty before he became well known; and when he did it was in an atmosphere partly created by the Beat generation. At the end of Williams' life all American poets admired and respected him—as they did and do Pound. But Olson, who drew on Williams and Pound, only knew the admiration of disciples. He represents an apostle of Americanness: another step in the voyage of American self-discovery. He published many small volumes; but his main work is to be found in *Selected Writings* (1967), *The Maximus Poems* (1953; 1956; 1968); collected poetry is in the posthumous *Archeologist of Morning* (1970).

Olson's doctrines are to be found in the now famous essay 'Projective Verse'. They too spring directly from the American pragmatic tradition: verse is to be of *'essential* use', must reflect the breathing of the poet. Energy must be immediately transferred from writer (speaker) to reader (listener). This is 'kinetic': 'COMPOSITION BY FIELD'. The old method ('closed verse . . . which print bred') interposes the ego of the writer between himself and his audience; Olson claimed, contentiously, that this was what Keats meant by 'the Egotistical Sublime' (rather as if Keats had been born in Massachusetts in 1910: neither Olson nor his disciples are very strong on the past, except in their own terms of '*essential* use'). The new poetry Olson demanded in his essay, which was published in 1950, was to put rhyme and metre in the background, and let 'the syllable . . . lead the harmony on'.

All this, written in sometimes old-fashioned professorial slang ('And the joker? that it is in the 1st half of the proposition that, in composing, one lets-it-rip. . . . Consider the best minds you know in this here business . . .' and so on), was interesting as a theory: it was just one more, rather dogmatic and slapdash, way of looking at the problem of prosody, about which no one has ever been able to agree beyond the most elementary points. It was also a plea, of course, for more poetry readings—but would, in the course of these, the ego of the poet still not obtrude? Olson's own poetry does not seem less egocentric, or 'egotistically sublime', than anyone else's; in fact it is a very noisy poetry. And his theory wholly ignores the fact of a form (selected or invented by the poet: not necessarily failing to 'extend the content', one of Olson's prerequisites, which, given his instructions to poets to let their own breathing determine their lines, are excessively rigid) and a content acting as two poles to generate a poetic tension. It also ignores the ritual element in poem-making, which leads to the creation of arbitrary forms. All men live within a recognisable bodily pattern: two ears, two eyes, a nose, and so on. And yet all bodies are different. . . . One way of approaching the problem is, of course, Olson's. What is distressing is his insistence that only his own way is valid. . . His own poetry noisily insists, too: is as philosophical and bullying as his criticism. It is so American that it can have no more than historical interest to British readers; it looks unlikely to survive long.

ROBERT CREELEY (1926), also born in Massachusetts, began as an avowed disciple of Olson's although his lines have always been short where Olson's were long. It is ironic that when he writes at his best, as in 'Kore',

> As I was walking
>   I came upon
> chance walking
>   the same road upon.
> As I sat down
>   by chance to move
> later
>   if and as I might,
>
> light the wood was,
>   light and green,
> and what I saw
>   before I had not seen.
>
> It was a lady
>   accompanied
> by goat men
>   leading her.

> Her hair held earth.
>> Her eyes were dark.
> A double flute
>> made her move.
>
> 'Oh love,
>> where are you
> leading
>> me now?'

there is nothing peculiar about his rhythms. This is a fair lyric in a distinctive manner: its occasion is emotional rather than theoretical. Much more recently Creeley has written:

> Could write of fucking—
> rather its instant or the slow
> longing at times of its approach—
>
> how the young man desires,
> how, older, it is never known,
> but, familiar, comes to be so.
>
> How your breasts, love,
> fall in a rhythm also familiar,
> neither tired nor so young they
>
> push forward. I hate the metaphors.
> I want you. I am still alone,
> but want you with me.

Now this, unless Creeley adds something special to it in his performance of it, seems to me (as poetry) commonplace. Where the ballad-like clumsiness and archaism of the early poem added something essential to it, the form of this indicates the writer's tiredness. It is very like bad conversation. It—like Olson's theory and indeed any other theory if a poet has nothing to say—leads to the production of work that lacks tension.

Creeley's tightly held dogmas are, of course, a way of life. His novel *The Island* (1963), although autobiographical, and dealing with a hard time in his life, resolutely concentrates upon its author's perceptions (except when it slips); he thus misses much he might achieve. He cannot, or refuses to, say *of what use making poetry is*. Now that is a difficult, a primitive, even a philistine, position to be in if you are a poet. 'Things continue, but my sense is that I have, at best, simply taken place with that fact. . . . Words will not say more than they do. . . .' It is not enough to arouse interest outside the hall where the poem is being performed. Creeley's poetry is collected in *Poems 1950–65* (1965), in *The Finger* (1970) and in many small volumes.

GARY SNYDER (1930), who has studied Zen Buddhism in Japan and has been regarded as a Beat, is a good deal less intransigent about learning from the tradition. His poetry actually works by means of images (in Olson's or Creeley's theory interpositions of the ego), and it has developed in a manner reminiscent of poets working in the tradition. Yet Snyder has learned something from Ginsberg and from Olson and Creeley, for he eschews any kind of literary style. His sense of the world as he records it in his poetry is relaxed, pleasurable and without exhibitionism. Much of his best work is contained in *A Range of Poems* (1966), *The Back Country* (1967) and *Regarding Wave* (1970).

*

ROBERT BLY (1926), who was born in Minnesota, founded the magazine *The Sixties* in 1958, and pioneered—with JAMES WRIGHT (1927)—many important translations (of Vallejo, Trakl, Jimenez, qq.v., and others). Bly is not a disciple of Olson in any sense, but he has bitterly attacked the whole concept of the new criticism—and the poetry of Robert Lowell. His ideal poet is probably Trakl (q.v.); which means that he eschews rhetoric, and is a poet who dislikes 'talk' in poems: as he has said of Trakl, the images speak for themselves. His own procedures resemble those of Trakl. But in his first book, *Silence in the Snowy Fields* (1962) he has introduced a bareness, an austerity. He wants to allow the things of Minnesota to speak for themselves. Later, in *The Light Around the Body* (1967), he finds he cannot: they are too spoiled by the world. And by now he is hopelessly (one feels in some sense reluctantly) involved in work against the Viet Nam War, which has led him dutifully to a kind of poetry of which, in a peaceful world, he might disapprove. Who is to question him? But his best work has been done peacefully and alone.

James Wright has been much influenced by Bly. He began as a disciple of Frost and Robinson (qq.v.), and had been a pupil of Ransom and Roethke (qq.v.). But he was affected by Bly's war against rhetoric, and the poems of his third book, *The Branch Will Not Break* (1963)—the first two were *The Green Wall* (1957) and *Saint Judas* (1959)—are in free verse, and are almost Japanese in their spontaneity and freshness. His most recent poems, in similar style, are collected in *Shall We Gather at the River?* (1968). *Collected Poems* appeared in 1972.

Although LOUIS SIMPSON (1923), who was born in Jamaica, was associated with friends of Bly as an anthologist, he cannot be regarded as one of the 'Sixties' school. His best poetry is in his *Selected Poems* (1965). Simpson, who believes that poetry 'arises from the inner life of the poet and is expressed in original images and rhythms', is a lyrical poet of great power who, perhaps unusually, is also an accomplished ironist. He has absorbed enough of the native American schools, without sacrificing his notion of the uses of knowledge, to suggest that he may be a pioneer of style.

Arabic Literature

The literature of the Arabs has its own magnificent tradition. But its contact with modernism, as this is understood in the West, has been comparatively slight and small-scale. Understandably, the demands of Arab nationalism have continually conflicted with those of literary modernism, which is European. The great debate in Middle Eastern literature at the turn of the century revolved about the question of what a writer's subject ought to be. It was a Syro-Lebanese faction living in the United States who, at about the beginning of the First World War, took over the leadership of a school, modern at least in that it advocated the assimilation of the European literatures. These Syro-Lebanese originally left their countries owing to Turkish oppression (the Albanians, q.v., suffered similarly); first they went to Egypt—where they helped to create an Arab press—and then to Brazil and North America. These writers were nationalist, but urged their compatriots not to reject European discoveries and methods but, on the contrary, to employ them. The forces of conservatism are so strong in the Middle Eastern countries, however, that this group did not at first make a strong or general impact. Later Egyptian literary activity became dominant; but this, too, had its roots in the Syro-Lebanese movement of the Eighties and after. The debate between the conservative and cosmopolitan factions goes on to this day in Arab letters, confused only by such essentially modernist concepts as 'arabism' (cf. negritude, q.v.).

*

The difficulties facing the Arab novelist in the later nineteenth century were almost unsurmountable. The potential readership—the educated classes—were more or less anti-European and regarded story-telling as a disgusting and vulgar activity. Literary Arabic was unsuitable for modern narrative and sounded ridiculous when used as dialogue. The earliest important novelist, JIRJI ZAYDAN (1861–1914), the self-educated son of a poor Christian family, tried to solve the problem by writing historical novels. He became a noted scholar, writing a standard history of Islamic literature. His twenty-two novels are imitations of Scott (cf. the development of the Japanese novel, q.v.), and have no literary value; but they did in their modest way begin something. YAQUB SARRUF (1852–1927), a Lebanese who eventually established himself in Egypt (which had just then come under British rule), devoted much of his life to the popularization of science. His novels, which include *Egypt's Daughter* (1905) and *The Prince of Lebanon* (1907) are poor—and, of course, deal with the past. But they do attempt some description of society. In *The Story of Isa Ibn Hisham* (1907) the

Egyptian MUHAMMAD MUWAYLIHI (1858–1930) cleverly and sensitively preserved the old form of the *maquama* (a usually picaresque tale told in an ornate way in rhymed and rhythmic prose) but introduced a cautious note of social criticism. An early nineteenth-century Pasha dreams of Cairene everyday life in 1900— thus giving Muwaylihi the chance to compare the old with the new. In Lebanon the art of the short story was cultivated with some success. But in general, fiction lagged far behind the essay: it was clumsy, sentimental and lacking in interest. The chief writers of the Syro-Lebanese diaspora (*mahjar*) added little or nothing to the development of fiction. MIKHAIL NUAYMA (1894) wrote some competent but not innovatory short stories; his friend GABRAN KHALIL GABRAN (1883–1931) was a master of the modern prose poem, but his novels are rhetorical and sentimental; AMIN RAYHANI (1876–1940) initiated the Arabic prose poem, but, like Nuayma, has not written novels. All three of these authors wrote in English as well as Arabic.

The first true modern novelist in Arabic is the Egyptian MUHAMMAD HUSAYN HAYKAL (1888–1956) who, significantly, studied in Paris. His *Zaynab* (1917), published anonymously, was a study of a village girl of the Delta, and introduced colloquial dialogue for the first time. It is not a good novel by Western standards, but is a pioneer Arab work. Haykal, who was in the Egyptian cabinet in the late Thirties, exercised a powerful influence by his advocacy of modern usage. His last novel, *She Was Created Thus, She is Like That* (1955) is cast in the form of an Egyptian woman's biography. MUHAMMAD TAYMUR (1892–1921) introduced, under the influence of Maupassant, realistic vignettes of everyday life, in which his brother, MAHMUD TAYMUR (1894), followed him with even greater success. His *The Call of the Unknown* has been translated by H. Haren (1964). These two between them helped considerably to rid serious fiction of the moralizing element.

By 1945 the way was prepared for better and longer regional and social fiction. NAGIB MAHFUZ (1912) covered the years in Cairo between the European wars in a comprehensive and lucidly written trilogy: *Bayn al-Qasrayn* (1956), *Qasr ash-Shawq* (1957), *as-Sukkariyya* (1957). (Each is the name of a suburb of Cairo.) This trilogy marks the beginning of the urban Egyptian novel, and has not been equalled in its genre. But ABD AL-RAHMAN ASH-SHARQAWI wrote, soon after the socialist revolution that toppled King Farouk's corrupt regime, *The Earth* (1957), a well-written novel about the landowners.

EHSAN ABDEL KUDDOUS moved from journalism to the novel, of which he is an extremely popular expositor. He has long been associated with all the progressive movements in Egypt. His best novel is *Something Inside Me*, which deals with the life of a millionaire. *Don't Shut Off the Sun* is an intelligent treatment of the 1956 Suez scandal.

KAMIL HUSAYN, an eminent Cairo doctor, wrote about the trial of Jesus in *City of Wrong* (1954; tr. 1959; 1966). YUSUF IDRIS, another doctor, is the leading socialist realist (but only by his own wish). Technically he is the best of the short story writers, as he shows in *Nights of the Unloved* (1954). With SONALLAH IBRAHIM (1935) the Egyptian novel comes of age: *The Smell Of It* (1968; tr.

D. Johnson-Davies, 1971), a novella of a young man's sexual and social frustrations in Cairo, was banned in 1968, and was only allowed to appear when substantial cuts had been made. The leading woman author is ANDRÉE CHEDID, who writes in French. She has written plays, poems and novels. However politically progressive Egypt may be, writers are up against it.

Good writers have now begun to appear in other Middle Eastern countries. LAYLA BALABAKKI (1936), from the Lebanon, has published two novels of sexual and social revolt in *I Live* (1958), of which there is a French translation (1958), and *The Monstrous Gods* (1960). The Iraqui ABD AL-MALIK NURI (1914), in *The Song of the Earth* (1954) is gloomy and nihilistic. DHU N-NUN AYYUB (1908), his countryman, a professor of physics and chemistry, is a 'committed' writer. His best work is about his years of exile (1954–8) in Vienna: *Stories of Vienna* (1957).

*

Apart from Mahmud Taymur (q.v.), who has written some excellent comedies rather in the style of his short stories, there are only two outstanding Arabic dramatists of this century: AHMAD SHAWQI (1868–1932), who was of noble birth, was close to the court and, although an ardent nationalist, never made any serious attempt to face the grave social problems of his time. But he was a man of wide learning and humanity. His lyrical poems are in the strict classical tradition. His plays—the fruit of his last four years—are important because in them Shawqi, who had had a European education, imported the spirit of the European and English classical theatre, in particular that of Corneille. *The Death of Cleopatra* (1929) is, in fact, Corneille done over into Arabic; pastiche perhaps, but the pastiche of an educated man and not of a charlatan.

TEWFIQ-AL-HAKIM (1902), who was born in Alexandria and lived in Paris for many years, is a sharp, realistic novelist as well as a poetic dramatist. He is still Egypt's most cosmopolitan and sophisticated writer—as at home in France as in Cairo. His novels include *The Return of the Spirit* (1933), of which there is a French translation (1937), about ancient Egypt, and a Simenon (q.v.) -like mystery story—in the form of a journal by the investigating officer—about murder in a Delta village: *The Maze of Justice* (1937; tr. A. Eban, 1937). (This English translation is by Israel's present foreign minister.) Tewfiq-al-Hakim is a versatile playwright, ranging from the fantastic and symbolic—*The Cavern of Dreams* (1939), *Scheherazade* (1934), a masterpiece—to the modern.

*

Arabic poetry has changed in form over the past hundred years; its content has remained almost consistently dull. The leading poet, the Egyptian HAFIZ IBRAHIM (1871–1932), is a case in point. Skilled in technique, he had nothing to say, and concentrated on conservative social pronouncements and obituary poetry for notables (for example, Queen Victoria and himself). The poets of Egypt remained neo-classical in style and spirit for some years; but the Syro-Lebanese broke with the past (mainly represented by the *quasida*, the sanctified traditional form), and initiated freer forms. This had its effect in the Arab

world itself only after the Second World War. Meanwhile, in Baghdad the poet
MARUF RUSAFI (1875–1945) remained faithful to the classical forms, but was able
to produce a less indifferent content because of his awareness of modern life
and the changes that had come over it.

The great exception in this era was the Lebanese Gabran (q.v.), who lived
outside his native country from the age of twenty. Gabran was a traditionalist,
but one with an acute awareness of the West and of the changes that were
taking place there. His work became something of a cult.

After 1945 Arab poetry came under the direct influence of contemporary
European writing. It is not hard to explain why the modern poet found most
congenial was Lorca (q.v.). There is much experimentation with form, usually
resulting in modifications of blank verse; the most substantial poet to emerge
so far has been Syria's ADONIS (ps. ALI AHMED SAID, 1930), a selection of whose
poetry has appeared in an English translation by S. Hazo: *The Blood of Adonis*
(1971). In 1960 Adonis became a citizen of the Lebanon, where he has been
active in literary affairs. Here he has run two magazines and edited an important anthology of Arabic poetry. His poetry reflects French influences, but
remains Arabic in character. Notable contemporary poets of his include the
Iraquians JALIL HAIDAR, MOAYAD EL-RAWDI, the Egyptian FRANÇOIS BASSILY and
the Syrian MAHMUD ADWAN.

Australian Literature

Twenty-five years ago it was widely held, even by academic critics of repute, that there was no Australian literature worth mentioning outside Australia itself. Today that is an untenable view. Patrick White (q.v.) is a Nobel candidate —a deserving one—and the work of at least three Australian poets (Slessor, Judith Wright, Hope, qq.v.) is well known throughout the world. Australian woman prose writers have been especially notable. And in the period since the Second World War a specifically Australian consciousness has emerged.

Australian literature developed along familiar colonial patterns. There was poetry before (creative) prose, and this was carefully and inhibitedly based on that of England. Thus an anonymous poet of the late eighteenth century wrote: 'And none will doubt but that our emigration/Has proved most useful to the British nation'. The work of the three leading poets of the colonial period— Harpur, Kendall and Gordon, none of them really good except in flashes— must be judged mainly in terms of the late romantic or decadent literature into which their Australian experience happened to fit. More truly native writing, whether superior or otherwise, is to be found in such fugitive writing as J. F. Mortlock's important *Experiences of a Convict*, which was not published (ed. A. G. Mitchell and G. A. Wilkes) until 1965.

The foundation of the *Bulletin* in Sydney in 1880 established the nationalist movement, which lasted until well after the Second World War, and which still exercises a certain influence—though not at a high level. That this movement has been shown to embody a tradition which is largely mythical is hardly surprising; most movements are susceptible to similar retrospective reassessments. Not all the important Australian writers of the early part of the modern period can be fitted into it. But it is nevertheless useful to define the 'myth', if only to see much of it fall apart in considering some individual writers—and, indeed, in considering some aspects of Australia itself. For, as has been pointed out by more thoughtful critics, the glowing, American kind of optimism could never have existed in Australia: the earliest settlers were convicts, the interior was vast and hostile and apparently unconquerable; there were criminal heroes in plenty, but no 'great men' who struggled for and gained independence— which did not have to be fought for. Sin and the melancholy loneliness of the individual in vast and mysterious places lie at the heart of the true Australian consciousness. This new world was never wholly brave. And, last but not least, the early development of the economy depended upon corporate rather than individual effort—which has had its oblique effect.

The nationalist movement tried, naturally enough, to ignore this darker side. It was chauvinistic, democratic (in the early, broad, populist American sense of setting the ordinary man up against the privileged), and in that sense 'left-wing', Utopian, and anti-literary (in that it opposed aristocratic 'polish' as genteel). The main literary figures were HENRY LAWSON (1867–1922), TOM COLLINS (ps. JOSEPH FURPHY, 1843–1912) and ANDREW BARTON, 'BANJO' PATERSON (1864–1941). After the heyday of these men, themselves in some ways exceptions, most of the really interesting or major Australian writers are to be found outside nationalist tradition.

Lawson, the laureate of 'mateship' (the sense of corporateness that keeps Australians going in the face of hardship) and the outback, had a hard time on his father's farm in his youth—but spent most of his life in Sydney. His bush ballads were popular in his lifetime, but it is his short stories that will survive. Lawson is a sardonic realist, writing of the bush and its inhabitants with naturalistic resignation but also with humour and energy. Early reading of Dickens encouraged his capacity for taking pleasure in eccentric or roguish characters, whom he describes with brilliant zest. His best prose is admirably simple and sharp. It is seldom vague and its observation is keen and exact. Despite lapses into sentimentality, repetitiveness and unevenness, Lawson has recorded the Australian bush of the Nineties. After the turn of the century the quality of his work fell off, and he sought refuge in drink, unhappily divided in mind between outback and city.

Tom Collins, now usually referred to by his real name because he only became well known some thirty years after his death, is an altogether more substantial writer. Furphy was born in Victoria, and had a harder life than Lawson. After he was married, a farm he had taken failed, and he became a bullock-driver for some seven years before going to work in a factory. By 1897 he had finished 'a full-sized novel'; this is lost. But it was published in an abridged, revised form as *Such is Life* (1903); some of the material rejected for it appeared in shorter works. *Such is Life* was the first Australian novel to break with the English tradition. It made no attempt at a plot, and satirized effete British gentlemen (understandably but possibly unfairly). Furphy famously described the book as in 'temper, democratic; bias, offensively Australian'. Furphy was a semi-naturalist, fascinated by the notion of ineluctable destiny stemming from choices made in a moment (thus, because at one point he does not fill his pipe, the narrator, Tom Collins, gets involved in a series of mishaps). *Such is Life* is crude, but crude in an authentically Australian manner; it is also comic and impolite in a manner that (in book form) would have shattered a true Britisher of the time. The title is in itself a criticism of the carefully plotted Victorian novel; and I have called Furphy a *semi*-naturalist because, while he acknowledges destiny as a force, his experience had taught him a measure of scepticism about all aspects of life.

Of Banjo Paterson, author of the unofficial national anthem *Waltzing Matilda*, there is less to say. He is a literary balladeer who frequently reflected native Australian rather than colonial experience; his poems should be read aloud. His verse tends, under careful analysis, to collapse into components of patronization (he was, unlike the people he wrote about, an educated man), chauvinism and populism. But there is an authentic note: 'Clancy's gone to Queensland droving, and we don't know where he are'. This vein of popular poetry was continued in the work of CLARENCE JAMES DENNIS (1876–1938), in *Songs of a Sentimental Bloke*.

The Victorian BERNARD O'DOWD (1866–1953) will probably survive only as a figure of historical interest. He corresponded with, and to a certain extent imitated, Walt Whitman, whose subtleties and complexities he lacked. His manifesto is *Poetry Militant* (1909), which is contained in his *Collected Poems* of 1941: this postulates a poet who understands history and can therefore contribute to the building of the future. O'Dowd was a clever versifier of a conventional kind, but his work is too overloaded with rhetoric—and suspiciously free of personal concerns—to be of any but historical interest today. (BAV) The cosmic abstractionist and crypto-fascist WILLIAM BAYLEBRIDGE (1883–1942), a crude misinterpreter of Nietzsche, is infinitely less attractive and equally unlikely to survive as a poet. (BAV)

SHAW NEILSON (1872–1942), who was born at Penola in South Australia, was a poorly educated manual worker who suffered for most of his life from bad eyesight. He used to compose his poetry in his head and then wait for a suitable amanuensis; many poems, he himself said, were lost in this process. Neilson is a minor poet, at his very best resembling Blake (whom he never read); he was the first unselfconsciously Australian poet, in whose simplicities lie a few jewels of insight and genuine ecstasy. He modelled himself on Thomas Hood, and often his insufferably 'poetical' language ('Plague me no more') spoils his effects. But occasionally his poetry comes through breathtakingly:

> Shall we assault the pain?
> It is the time to part:
> Let us of Love again
> Eat the impatient heart.

His *Collected Poems* appeared in 1934; *Unpublished Poems* in 1947. (BAV)

Neilson's was a delightful and touching achievement, and greater than that of the more sophisticated and learned CHRISTOPHER JOHN BRENNAN (1870–1932), who went to Sydney University (where he was later a professor), travelled in Europe, and was deeply conscious of the European poetic tradition. To put it briefly, the gifted Brennan went adrift on that notorious sandbank for the poets of his generation: sex. He felt he had to deal with his own failure to find sexual fulfilment in marriage, but he did so—as James McAuley (q.v.) has pointed out —pretentiously. An evader of the true nature of his experience—a central feature of which was that the hopefulness contained in his innocent, over-forcefully applied wedding-night lustiness was shattered by his virginal wife's shuddering revulsion—he posed as a 'confessional' poet. (He had waited, Victorian-like, for some years for the ecstasy of sexual fulfilment—and when it came he found it, of course, not only a let-down but also a focal point for every kind of guilt.) Actually he drew on French symbolism (q.v.). German romanticism and Pre-Raphaelite womanology in order to construct an edifice that would look like sexual wisdom. But he was the first Australian poet to be intelligently aware of a poetry outside the Anglo-Australian tradition, and is important for this reason. His ultimate ambition, in conscious terms, was to create a complete symbolist myth; in unconscious terms to erect a Platonic paradise that would compensate him for his sexual disappointment. And his poetry is always interesting and skilful. He came under the influence of most of the important poets of his time—Verhaeren and George (notably) as well as the early French symbolists (qq.v.)—and he never indulged in pastiche. As a minor poet Neilson does sometimes come off; but Brennan had to come off as a major poet or not at all. And he fails because his rather impressive structure of intellect, scholarship and literary awareness cannot subsume his personal experience. The definitive edition of his poetry is *Verse* (1960). (BAV)

HUGH McCRAE (1876–1958) has been important to almost every Australian poet. This seems curious to the outsider, because his poetry does appear, in any context except its own, to be not only limited but tiresome. The commonplaceness of McCrae's vitality is only to some extent compensated for by its abundance; his 'paganism' (satyrs, fauns and so on) is irritatingly simplistic and inadequate as a poetic response to his times. But everyone feels like him sometimes, and he has purity—even when crying, as at the end of his long life, '*Bibamus!*' He was the hero of the *Vision* group that gathered round Norman Lindsay (q.v.) in the Twenties—Australia's first clearly defined literary group. They, like other Australians, chose McCrae as a hero because he seemed so energetically anti-bourgeois. He was the obvious alternative to the new middle-class smugness. The poet R. D. Fitzgerald (q.v.) edited and selected his lively *Letters* (1970). Of his poetry one can now say little; like Lindsay's own work and personality, it became one of the weekend treasures of the very class whose values it set out to challenge. (BAV)

The communist poet MARY GILMORE (1865–1962) declined into what James McAuley calls 'a repulsive example of a formidable will, cannily sucking homage indiscriminately out of the environment' some years before this attitude was properly rewarded by the D.B.E. (1937). But earlier in the century she had successfully avoided (as McAuley again observes), in her unpretentious short lyrics, most of the vices of inflated diction and the poeticism that disfigured the poetry even of a Neilson. She was a pioneer feminist, and a devotee of Aboriginal culture. (BAV)

The next stage in Australian poetry came after the First World War, with the publication of the magazine *Vision* (1923). Its inspirer, NORMAN LINDSAY (1879–1969), has to be considered both as an influence (in Australian terms, immense) and as a novelist (minor). He was, of course, primarily an illustrator. Like his close friend McCrae, Lindsay had boundless energy as mannered draughtsman and crude philosopher of 'vitalism' or 'biologism'.

His 'philosophy' is expressed in *Creative Effort* (1920), an extraordinarily inconsistent mish-mash of pseudo-Nietzschean vitalism, Godless immortality and heavy-handed amorous innuendo. The obvious message of this book, as of *Vision*, is 'vitality, vigour', of any sort—and not necessarily Australian. And this was what the writers in a more settled Australia wanted; they could thus evade their melancholy destiny (a thing we all wish to do) and yet oppose bourgeois complacency. All the members of this group did their best work after leaving it. For it was essentially a backwards-looking movement, which avowedly preferred 'being alive' to 'being modern'—and this was inadequate to the inner needs of the best Australian poets. *Vision* vanished from Australia and reappeared in London (briefly) as *The London Aphrodite* (1928), edited by Norman's son JACK LINDSAY (1900), who remained in England and poured out an immense amount of lively Marxist historical fiction, useful translation and interesting reminiscence.

The best of all Norman Lindsay's books is his children's novel *The Magic Pudding* (1918), because here the sheer thoughtlessness of his exuberance cannot offend. As he himself said, its basic themes are 'eating and fighting'. It is a children's classic. But his adult fiction, although stylistically offensive, is not negligible. It is probably a testimony to the accuracy of *Redheap* (1930), about life in the Australian Nineties, that it was for over twenty years banned by the Australian government. Perhaps his best novel is *Saturdee* (1933), which helps to explode the myth of boys as angels.

The most gifted member of the *Vision* group was KENNETH SLESSOR (1901–71). But his early poetry consists of little more than energetic and linguistically promising literary inventiveness—sophistications of the subject-matter of McCrae. He is descriptively brilliant, playful (often archly so) and has no content beyond a generally bristling sexuality and materialism. Later Slessor became a more interesting poet; but it is only in a few individual poems, mostly noted by critics, that he has wholly succeeded. 'Gulliver' shows very appropriately what sort of experience his uneasy later poems can explore with success (although even here the exasperated tone of the monologue is a little forced and lucubrated):

> I'll kick your walls to bits, I'll die scratching a tunnel,
> If you'll give me a wall, if you'll give me simple stone,
> If you'll do me the honour of a dungeon—
> Anything but this tyranny of sinews.
> Lashed with a hundred ropes of nerve and bone
> I lie, poor helpless Gulliver,
> In a twopenny dock for the want of a penny,
> Tied up with stuff too cheap, and strings too many.
> One chain is usually sufficient for a cur.
>
> Hair over hair, I pick my cables loose,
> But still the ridiculous manacles confine me.
> I snap them, swollen with sobbing. What's the use?
> One hair I break, ten thousand hairs entwine me.

Love, hunger, drunkenness, neuralgia, debt,
Cold weather, hot weather, sleep and age—
If I could only unloose their spongy fingers,
I'd have a chance yet, slip through the cage.
But who ever heard of a cage of hairs?
You can't scrape tunnels in a net.

If you'd give me a chain, if you'd give me honest iron,
If you'd graciously give me a turnkey,
I could break my teeth on a chain, I could bite through metal,
But what can you do with hairs?
For God's sake, call the hangman.

Clearly McCrae's vitalism is too simplistic for him, and yet he resents a universe in which this should be so: the giant trapped by 'hairs' therefore wants to die. To McCrae himself he said (most Australian poets have written poems to McCrae): 'We live by . . . your masks and images/ . . . But you take passage on the ruffian seas/And you are vanished in the dark already'. One continually feels, reading the poetry of Slessor, that one is just about to encounter a linguistic revelation; but it seldom really comes. 'Five Visions of Captain Cook' is an interesting and important Australian poem, with some good passages; but as a whole it is not quite *réussi*: the thought and the language only fall together sporadically. However, 'Five Bells', a meditation on the death of a friend by drowning, is a perhaps major poem of despair: here at last Slessor is wholly able to see his vitalism for the nihilism it is, and respond with words that haunt the mind. Slessor frequently revised his poems in the course of his life; the definitive edition is *Poems* (1957). (BAV)

The poet REX INGAMELLS' (1913–55) Jindyworobak school of the late Thirties, with its emphasis on the importance of the Aboriginal culture, produced no important poetry even though it hit the (literary) headlines. The *Jindyworobak Review* ran from 1938 until 1948.

R. D. FITZGERALD (1902) contributed to *Vision* but was not associated with Lindsay's group as closely as Slessor. Some see Fitzgerald as Australia's major poet of the century: the writer who succeeded where Brennan (q.v.) failed. Certainly he has been as aware as Brennan of European poetry, and his goal has been ambitiously philosophical. An intellectual poet, he also suffers from a brash optimism ('I regret I shall not be around/to stand on Mars') that either attracts or repels; but is in any case honest and unaffected. He is to be seen at his best in such poems as 'The Wind at your Door' (AWT), a sensitive and skilful meditation on an ancestor, a doctor, 'caught in the system', which broadens out into a lyrical and humane exploration of the original sin that lies at the back of the Australian experience (a nation of convicts and, as bad, their no less criminal oppressors). 'I find I lack/the hateful paint to daub him wholly black' Fitzgerald says of this ancestor: 'Perhaps my life replies to his too much/through veiling generations dropped between'. The language of this poem is simple almost to clumsiness; but retrospectively one sees that it suits the awkward and agonized honesty—and makes the poet's vain wish to be a descendant of the flogged man who (under the medical supervision of Fitzgerald's forbear) guiltily haunts the poem. Fitzgerald has probably received most praise for his collection of 1938, *Moonlight Acre*; but these philosophical poems are on the whole less spontaneous than *Between Two Tides* (1952), an epic of eighteenth-century Tonga, and the lyrics of *This Night's Orbit* (1953). (BAV; AW)

A. D. HOPE (1907) did not publish his first collection, *The Wandering Islands* (1955), until he was nearly fifty. Since then he has exercised an increasing influence on Australian poetry. He is an original rather than a conservative: his apparent conservatism and rejection of modernism (including that of Eliot) are seen on closer examination to be an expression of Swiftian disgust at all developments in human history since about 1750; this disgust also incorporates, one may add, a profound self-dissatisfaction: Hope *feels* modern in that he has no faith (except in the familiar Australian sex-fun: McCraean healthy pagan rompings), but he yearns for at least Augustan deism. He is a sexual romantic, highly energetic (again in a familiar Australian way), operating in severely classical modes of his own choosing. A similarly gifted poet, JAMES MCAULEY (1917), a witty and astringent critic, has displayed a similarly intelligent but unhappy conservatism. Like the New Zealand poet James K. Baxter (q.v.), he has become a Catholic; but his poetry tends hotly to limit his own faith rather than to affirm it. Australians bitterly attack their own 'way of life', but, watching the developments in the outside world (of which they are acutely aware: they are not 'cut off') are unwilling to let in pop-culture.

A. D. Hope has been a 'literary nuisance' on the Australian scene, sometimes silly but usually excellent; he is at his best when caught between the nervous tension of his deliberately Augustan formalism and his sexual wildness. And yet even here one wonders if the Australian predicament itself is not responsible for a refusal to allow rhythms to develop in their own idiosyncratic way: the traditional forms seem to trap Hope, at his most personal, in poeticisms that the term 'irony' cannot quite accommodate:

> She does not tire of the pattern of a rose,
> Her oldest tricks still catch us by surprise.
> She cannot recall how long ago she chose
> The streamlined hulls of fish, the snail's long eyes.

McAuley, who has criticized Brennan's personal inadequacies in no mean terms, has brought the influence of Rilke (q.v.) into Australian poetry—something Brennan could not have done. It was after his first book, *Under Aldebaran* (1946), and after the Ern Malley hoax—in which he and another poet, Harold Stewart, faked a Dylan Thomas-like poet and successfully put him across on Australian letters—that McAuley became a Roman Catholic and defined his anti-sceptical position: the danger, as he saw it, was that everyone was being encouraged to be *uncommitted*, 'without fixed principles or certainties'. Considering the self-limiting nature of his own faith, one is bound to have the reservation about McAuley that he was merely urging himself to take arms against the sea of his own troubled scepticism. His own poetry, as in 'A Letter to John Dryden', is less celebratory of the joys of understanding the true God than shot through with hatred of scepticism. It seems a highly provincial kind of position for so gifted a critic and poet. So far the lyrics of McAuley's first book have been his best work: he has made the mistake of taking up a critical position in his poetry—afraid, perhaps, of what he might find if he did otherwise. (BAV)

Not a great deal has happened in Australian poetry since the emergence of Hope and McAuley. Its third force (as she might be called) is JUDITH WRIGHT (1915), who published her first book, *The Moving Image*, in 1946. She has written intelligently on her contemporaries, and in poetry has been less ambitious and perhaps more healthily stark in her use of language. But she is better on her non-sexual experience than on her position as wife and mother: here, while she is translucently sincere, a puritanically bourgeois attitude becomes too apparent; that so typically Australian, frozenly ineffectual resistance to what is happening in the world causes her to cast a rosily sentimental glow over 'family life'. One's own experience is one thing; lack of understanding through a dogged refusal to understand is another—and there is a residue of the latter in her over-fragrant attitude. She has rightly emphasized that poetry must finally depend upon emotion; but she has tended to diminish the role of that hard thought which must so often precede the statement of emotion. Her early despair at loneliness relieved only by sexual contact, which produced her best poems, has given way to a less self-explorative assertion of 'old-fashioned' values. (AW; BAV)

DOUGLAS STEWART (1913) was born in New Zealand, where he learned to write nature poetry. He belongs to the still flourishing Antipodean tradition of conservative formalism; by not forcing himself into an intellectual stocktaking he has managed to continue writing poetry and vigorous, if conventional, verse drama. 'The Sunflowers' demonstrates his strength and his limitations:

> 'Bring me a long sharp knife for we are in danger;
> I see a tall man standing in the foggy corn
> And his high, shadowy companions'—'But that is no stranger,
> That is your company of sunflowers; and at night they turn
> Their dark heads crowned with gold to the earth and the dew
> So that indeed at daybreak, shrouded and silent,
> Filled with a quietness such as we never knew,
> They look like invaders down from another planet.
> And now at the touch of light from the sun they love—'
> 'Give me the knife. They move.'

This is in certain respects poor: no one can say that the clichés of observation and language are exploited, either ironically or otherwise—and yet it was worth doing. (BAV; AW)

The most interesting poets now active are ROSEMARY DOBSON (1920), who has been influenced by Robert Lowell (q.v.) (BAV) and EVAN JONES (1932), the best of the younger critics, who has achieved a colloquial directness not often seen in Australian poetry. VINCENT BUCKLEY (1925), another helpful critic, has written some poetry of recollected experience that is moving in the honesty of its attempt to capture exactly the mood and feeling of the past moment.

*

Australian dramatists have been few and far between. Douglas Stewart's (q.v.) verse plays have vigour, but their language—read over—is prosy. The one authentic Australian play that has so far been written is by the actor RAY LAWLER (1913): *The Summer of the Seventeenth Doll* (1955). This thoroughly deserved its world-wide success. It is an examination of the legend of the tough Australian outdoor man and his innate superiority; the notion it gave non-Australians of Australia was both truthful and moving. It was not flaw-less—sentimental box-office concessions were made—but its final departures from psychological accuracy do challenge the basic conceptions of the play. *The Piccadilly Bushman* (1959) was not as successful, and later plays by Lawler have settings other than Australia. There have been good plays by Patrick White and Hal Porter (qq.v.), but so far no Australian of Lawler's calibre has emerged.

*

The first Australian novelist of importance was HENRY HANDEL RICHARDSON (ps. ETHEL FLORENCE LINDESAY RICHARDSON, 1870–1946). She was in Europe studying music until 1903, and her first essays into literature were translations from the Scandinavian; Jacobsen's *Niels Lyhne* (q.v.), so important to Rilke (q.v.) and others, she acknowledged as a formative influence—her translation of it appeared in 1896. *Maurice Guest* (1908), autobiographical in many diverse ways, none of them quite direct, is naturalistic, Freudian and 'amoral'. Although Henry Handel Richardson visited Australia only briefly—she lived in England, where her husband was a professor of German literature, and she died at Hastings in Sussex—she is still to be considered an Australian novelist, for the subject of her most important novel, *The Fortunes of Richard Mahony* trilogy (1930), is Australian. It is a brilliant work, a late flowering of naturalism; its theme, of an English Victorian doctor's emigration to Australia and the crushing of himself and his decent qualities by fate, in the form of his own characteristics and circumstance, is never forced. The societies of Australia and England (to which Mahony at one point returns) are acutely described, and Mahony's defeat and moral collapse are observed with feline attention to detail. Pity is withheld; but not understanding.

Naturalism has flourished longer in Australian writing than elsewhere: the fatalistic habit of mind has not yet been dispelled. The best poets insist on retreating into conservatism (or, like Slessor, give up after a final nihilistic fling); the novelists can cling on to naturalism, which after all—with its insistence on exact mimesis and cruel destiny—is a kind of faith. A novelist who has had his due neither in his native Australia nor outside it is LEONARD MANN (1895), a bleak and clumsy writer whose best fiction approaches the power of Dreiser's (q.v.). Mann tries to irradiate the darkness he sees over the world with socialistic hope, but gloom dims his effort; the resultant glow in his novels is one of courage in adversity. *Flesh in Armour* (1932) is one of the best of the First World War books, and has been unduly neglected. The ex-schoolmaster Frank Jeffreys is the typical Mann victim: he tries to make himself into a soldier with the A.E.F., but cannot manage it; he shoots himself in the hour of the Allied victory. Mann presents this early anti-hero, the man who *could* not kill, as in one sense superior to his companions—but doomed. After *Human Drift* (1935) came *A Murder in Sydney* (1937), a subtle and once again gloomy metropolitan study of crime and redemption (through the agency of a Dostoevskian maimed lover), which is set in the years of the Depression. *The Go-Getter* (1942) is Mann's tensest and finest book: Chris Gibbons is redeemed from cheapness by his tough challenge to fate. His heartless project to seduce a girl turns into love. *Andrea Caslin* (1959) and *Venus Half-Caste* (1963) maintain the high standards of this powerful and unheeded novelist beneath the crust of whose pessimism, the late H. M. Green said, one 'can feel the glow'. The key to Mann's fiction may be found in his minor but not undistinguished poetry. (BAV)

FREDERIC MANNING (1882–1935) produced one classic; it appeared anonymously in Paris in 1929 under the title *The Middle Parts of Fortune*; but it is better known under its English title of *Her Privates We* (1930)—the author called himself 'Private 19022'. This is a contrast to Mann's pacifistic *Flesh in Armour*, than which it is a more artistically successful—but not more powerful —work: Manning treats the war as a test of character. Where Mann is deliberately anti-heroic Manning is heroic—but not by choice. It is simply that his Bourne *can* what Mann's Jeffreys *cannot*. But there is as much irony in *Her Privates We*: Bourne is, in effect, murdered (by being forced to go on a suicidal sortie) by an officer who fears and envies his qualities. Manning, who had written other graceful minor prose, suffered from asthma even while serving in Flanders; he died in Italy.

VANCE PALMER (1885–1959), a competent and serious author, was a better writer of short stories than novels: he could deal with the apparently trivial, but whatever struck him as important seemed to inhibit him. But his novels contain much excellent work. His best books are *Separate Lives* (1931), *Sea and Spinifex* (1934) and *Let the Birds Fly* (1955), all collections of stories, and the novel *The Passage* (1930), in which he fails with the love relationships but succeeds with the description of the stresses and strains experienced within a family. His big trilogy about a socialist politician, *Golconda* (1948), *Seedtime* (1957) and *The Big Fellow* (1959), is honest but more mediocre.

KATHERINE SUSANNAH PRICHARD (1884–1969), although she played some part in the formation of a specifically Australian novel, never produced a masterpiece. Her first efforts were feeble, and almost all her books are flawed by too great a reliance upon a crude Marxism. Like Mary Gilmore (q.v.), Katherine Prichard was a communist, but a rather simple-minded one; it did not do her writing that much good. She is at her best in *Haxby's Circus* (1930), a humorous and continuously vivid account of circus life which contains no manipulation of character in the interests of theory, and no preaching. *Coonardoo* (1929), reckoned by most to be her best book, is a moving story (based on what used to be called 'real life') of a black Australian's romance with a white man. It is flawed by the poor handling of its melodramatic plot and its inept attempt to emulate D. H. Lawrence's (q.v.) manner of dealing with 'elemental' sex ('deep inexplicable currents of his being flowed towards her'); but the author makes Coonardoo herself understandable. Later books, particularly the gold-field trilogy—*The Roaring Nineties* (1946), *Golden Miles* (1948) and *Winged Seeds* (1950) —are worthy: always worth reading for their author's mastery of the facts of her material and her sincere treatment of it.

For Katherine Prichard the naturalistic gloom of imagination was replaced by Marxist socialism; KYLIE TENNANT (ps. MRS. L. C. RODD, 1912) is a more thoroughgoing naturalist, whose contribution was several vivid novels of city life. *Tiburon* (1935) is about unemployed relief-workers in the country during the Depression; but *Foveaux* (1939) is a vivid picture of Sydney slum-life in the years 1912–35.

Of the expatriates since Henry Handel Richardson, CHRISTINA STEAD (1902) has been easily the most distinguished. She went to London in 1928, and settled in America permanently in 1937. She was mainly a 'critic's author' until the reprint in America, in 1965, of *The Man Who Loved Children* (1940). Her first book was a collection of stories, *The Salzburg Tales* (1934); this was followed by *Seven Poor Men of Sydney* (1934), a novel about young revolutionaries in Sydney in the Twenties, and remarkable for its realistic picture of the Sydney docks. *The Man Who Loved Children* is undoubtedly her masterpiece: a study of the savage warfare between a wild but intelligent woman and her neurotic, even proto-fascistic husband, and of the seven children's varying means of evading permanent damage. This is set in America, and it is hard to see anything Australian about it: Christina Stead is a cosmopolitan novelist, nominally left-wing (but without party) and she has studied French fiction—particularly that of Louis Guilloux (q.v.), whose influence she has acknowledged. But *The Man Who Loved Children* is entirely original; sovereign among its many qualities, perhaps, is the detachment of its portrayal of Sam Politt, the husband who drives his wife to suicide and 'never thought she meant it'. Other books by Christina Stead include *For Love Alone* (1944), the earlier part of which is set in Australia, *Letty Fox, Her Luck* (1946), *A Little Tea, A Little Chat* (1948), *Cotter's England* (1966) and the four superb novellas in *A Puzzleheaded Girl* (1967). One can at least see the fascination that Guilloux had for Christina Stead: like him, she horrifiedly and fascinatedly dwells on the tiny details of obsessions. *For Love Alone* dwells thus on the behaviour of an Australian girl who falls in love with a student and follows him to London. *Cotter's England*, set in England, looks at the lives of a couple somewhat reminiscent of Sam and Henrietta in *The Man Who Loved Children*. Nell, an unsuccessful left-wing journalist, 'collects' women and fills her house with them; her husband George is more important in the world, less neurotic and cares less about other people. Christina Stead is one of the most gifted novelists of her generation. Her realism is only apparent: she is a master of significant detail.

MARTIN A'BECKETT BOYD (ps. MARTIN MILLS, 1893–1972) improved on his expatriate fiction after he returned to Australia in 1948. Boyd is not a sensational novelist, and although generally readable his books do have their *longueurs*; but he is an intelligent and gifted analyst of the Australian past, who deserves rather more attention than he has had. *The Montforts* (1928) traces the history of his mother's family over five generations; *Lucinda Brayford* (1946), however, which deals with the same subject-matter, is superior. It traces the fortunes of the Vanes from William Vane's emigration to Australia after being sent down from Cambridge for cheating at cards until the death of his great-grandson in England in the Second World War. This is an intelligent and sensitive 'family saga' novel, and avoids the sentimentalities and dishonesties into which Galsworthy (q.v.) fell. The 'Langton' tetralogy—*The Cardboard Crown* (1952), *A Difficult Young Man* (1955), *Outbreak of Love* (1957) and *When Blackbirds Sing* (1962)—suffers more from sentimentality than *Lucinda Brayford*, but is more substantial and contains as much of value.

SEAFORTH MACKENZIE (ps. KENNETH MACKENZIE, 1913–55), whose novels but not poetry collections were published under the name of Seaforth because his publisher had a Kenneth Mackenzie on their list, could well have been treated as poet, for he was equally—perhaps more—distinguished in this field. He has been compared, and not unfruitfully, with Dylan Thomas (q.v.): he was Australia's latter-day *poète maudit*: alcoholic (meths drinker sometimes), an isolate, always poor, usually desperate, died young (by drowning). But in his shrugging, complex, sardonic despair he resembles Malcolm Lowry (q.v.) rather than the simpler Thomas. At all events, Mackenzie is certainly an odd man out of Australian letters—and an important one. Not one of his four novels is an absolute success, but each achieves something. *The Young Desire It* (1937) and *Chosen People* (1938) are sometimes marred by pastiche of Lawrence's (q.v.) vitalism, or by youthful awkwardnesses. But both introduce something new into Australian fiction. The most successful feature of the first is its sympathetic portrait of an unhappy homosexual schoolmaster. (Clearly Mackenzie had had some adolescent trouble with homosexuality, though he seems to have emerged as a fully fledged heterosexual at adulthood.) There is also some excellent observation of the narcissism natural to certain types of adolescent. One critic, Evan Jones (q.v.), has most unfairly confused his dislike of the manifestation with Mackenzie's portrayal of it. *Chosen People* is a vile story told with hideous conviction and power: a beautiful woman gives up her young paramour—already sucked dry by her—and grooms her equally beautiful daughter for marriage to him. *Dead Men Rising* (1951) is disappointing; but Mackenzie's last novel, *The Refuge* (1954), shows a return to the form of *Chosen People*, and is his best-written book. This is the story of a love affair ending in murder; it reads straightforwardly on a realist level, but has unmistakable symbolic overtones that have not yet been investigated. Lloyd Fitzherbert falls in love with a young woman, a double agent who has renounced both her employers; Lloyd Fitzherbert renounces her offer of herself to him. Later, however, they marry secretly; the girl takes his beloved son (whose mother died in giving birth to him) as lover; Fitzherbert kills her, with, it seems, her consent. This has mythological and incestuous overtones; it is also about isolation and the tragedies this can lead to: in a diary Mackenzie wrote: 'Perfect moonlight—absolute, utter silence of windless night, cold'. This is the spiritual atmosphere of *The Refuge*.

Mackenzie's poetry, a properly definitive collection of which is only just now in preparation (by Evan Jones and Geoffrey Little), is at its best as good as any Australian's of the century, and perhaps suggestive of greater gifts. From his personal hell Mackenzie seems to have been unique in breaking free of that stultifying kind of traditionalism which even the most brilliant of Australian poets seem to oblige themselves, in one way or another, with varying reluctance, to cling to. Mackenzie at his best has a voice more unmistakably his own than any of his contemporaries; you can never confuse it, as you can even McAuley's and Hope's, with that of a dead age.

> Blackness rises. Am I now to die
> and feel the steps no more and not see day
> break out its answering smile of hail all's well
> from east full round to east and hear the bird
> whistle all creatures that on earth do dwell?

Mackenzie did not always write well, and his poetic achievement will not be truly measurable until we have his complete work; but we have enough to be sure that he almost (although not quite) alone of contemporary Australians was prepared to risk himself in the quest for an adequate response to his time.

HAL PORTER (1917) has, after Patrick White (q.v.), the most versatile and vigorous talent of all Australian contemporary writers. His best prose is in his magnificent autobiography, *The Watcher on the Cast-Iron Balcony* (1963 pt. AW), which has extraordinary control and detachment as well as a Proustian sense of the past. This is one of the most quintessentially Australian books to be published since 1945—because Porter's experience has been Australian and because his book remains true to it. Its exuberant manner owes something to Dylan Thomas' Welsh idylls. A sequel volume, *The Paper Chase*, followed in 1966. Much influenced by Katherine Mansfield (q.v.), Porter writes well, in short stories, of innocence betrayed by maturity: *A Bachelor's Children* (1962) and *The Cats of Venice* (1965). In his novel *The Tilted Cross* (1961), set in mid-nineteenth-century Tasmania, Porter seemed to be going out of his depth in trying to follow Patrick White. So far his best fiction has been in short stories.

PATRICK WHITE (1912), born of Australian parents in London, educated at Cambridge, only returned to Australia permanently after serving in the Second

World War. He began with a book of poems, *The Ploughman* (1935), which has considerable value as an index to his later works. His first really important book was *The Aunt's Story* (1948). This dealt with what is really his central theme, the Nietzschean (q.v.) one of the lonely atheist's agonized capacity for insight into the nature of existence. Comparisons with Dostoevski and other such writers are not, in White's case, foolish, although he continually experiences difficulty in sorting out rhetoric from what is a kind of truly mantic utterance. *The Aunt's Story* is concerned with Theodora, who in her desire to lose personal identity—she rejects love as a threat to this process—becomes mad, but possibly feels at peace. In *The Tree of Man* (1955) White tried to resolve this problem of solitude by anchoring his characters—husband and wife who build up a large farm from a smallholding—in everyday life; but one can see his obstinate and guilt-ridden obsession with the necessity of loneliness even in this most realistically conceived of his novels. *Voss* (1957) goes entirely the other way: its hero's project is, by making an expedition into the Australian interior, to become God: to turn himself into what is not. Although this profound and beautiful book has sources in the journeys of actual explorers, the most instructive general background to it is undoubtedly the thought of Nietzsche. Voss has to transcend his sense of beauty (one is reminded of Hopkins, q.v., punishing himself for having taken too much pleasure from the landscape) in order to achieve his project: he must not yield to the sensuous. Perhaps he loves his dog: he kills it. In *Riders in the Chariot* (1961), perhaps his greatest book, White achieves on a major level, with alienated freaks, what Carson McCullers (q.v.) could only hint at. This takes place in Sarsaparilla, the Sydney suburb that White has made as real as Faulkner (q.v.) made Yoknapatawpha County. All the freaks are in quest of a loss of identity that is not a suicide or an escape. *The Solid Mandala* (1966) is about twins, one apparently simple, the other clever, who are brought to Sarsaparilla by their English parents when young. First we see life from Waldo's point of view: he is 'superior', but he fails and ends his life hating his twin Arthur because he knows that Arthur is his only contact with life. Then we see the same events from Arthur's point of view: Arthur is a 'holy fool', a wise man who from childhood has wanted to climb to 'the red gold disc of the sun'—but he is judged by all but a neighbour, Mrs. Poulter, as a madman. The apparently sordid *dénouement* is seen through her eyes. This is a difficult but immensely powerful novel, another milestone in a strange and poetic journey. White has written short stories (*The Burnt Ones*, 1964) and four plays of varying dramatic effectiveness but extreme significance in the context of his fiction.

The novelist and poet RANDOLPH STOW (1935) is the most gifted follower of White, and is at least in Australian terms a major talent. He leans heavily on White; but it is hard to see how a still young man who genuinely shares White's predisposition to the symbolic could fail to do so. His first two novels were powerful but melodramatic; only in the third, *To the Islands* (1958), about a sixty-eight-year-old Antipodean Lear, did he really begin to find himself. Heriot, a missionary, loses his faith and goes off on a voyage of exploration, accompanied by an old aborigine, to the islands of the dead. *Tourmaline* (1963) is about a ghost-town stricken by drought; a water-diviner who comes there persuades the inhabitants of his magic qualities, but proves to be a fake. This intended fable of man's capacity for self-deceit does not come off: Stow is dealing in fact with his own religious feelings, but tries to rationalize this into generalized comment. In *The Merry-go-Round in the Sea* (1965) Stow abandons conscious symbolism for a vein of tender realism, and does much better. He only falters at the end, when he tries to contrast the old world of childhood with the new one of adult reality. In his poetry Stow expresses a vision much akin to that of Sydney Nolan (who has illustrated one of his collections); he speaks of his 'sad-coloured country/bitterly admired'. What James McAuley, in a lecture on Australian poetry, has called 'the personal element' has so far been missing or ineptly expressed; but of linguistic resources there is no doubt.

British Literature

I

Although no country had more good novelists than Great Britain at the beginning of this century, the European naturalist movement had little direct effect on British fiction. It did, however, influence the work of GEORGE GISSING (1857–1903), who in his turn has exercised a strong, although largely subterranean, influence on later writers (particularly on Orwell, q.v.). Gissing, an unhappy and unhealthy man, led a life of almost unrelieved misery. At college he stole to help a prostitute he had befriended; after serving a prison sentence he went to America for a year; he failed to support himself there, returned—and married the same woman. She was a nagging psychopath, and Gissing's life was made hell for ten years. Then she died, and he went out and picked up and married a similarly impossible woman. When she became insane Gissing found a Frenchwoman with whom he was happier. He never achieved financial stability, and only kept his head above water by constant overwork—which subsequently weakened his constitution and led to his early death. His close friend H. G. Wells (q.v.), who was with him at his death, wrote of him with great acumen: he called him 'an extraordinary blend of a damaged joy-living human being hampered by inherited gentility and a classical education'.

There is something a little repulsive about Gissing: a genteel defensiveness and a not always wholly repressed whining self-pity. Yet at his best, as in *Born in Exile* (1892), Gissing is not merely a good but a major novelist—greater in achievement than, for example, his older, more sophisticated and more gifted contemporary George Meredith (q.v.). Some of Gissing's twenty-two novels are poor and thin, and the writing is cliché-ridden and weary. But at least in *Born in Exile*, the bitter tale of a free-thinker who destroys himself by pretending (against his principles) to be a Christian in order to gain love and position, Gissing wrote a major novel—and one of Dostoevskian overtones.

His original model had been the Dickens who recorded the seamy side of life; he wrote of this with sourness and no humour—but managed to add something. Personally doomed by his own foolish propensity to 'redeem' and 'genteelize' lower-class women, he was a naturalist in spite of himself: his characters are often driven—sometimes one must read between the lines—by their anguished sexual preoccupations, as he was. There is much worth reading in him beside *Born in Exile*, his masterpiece: *Demos* (1886), in which he expresses his distrust of the people *en masse*, *A Life's Morning* (1888), *New Grub Street* (1891), *The Private Papers of Henry Ryecroft* (1903), and more. He still requires his due.

GEORGE MEREDITH (1828–1909), although nearly thirty years older than Gissing, is a modernist *manqué*. He deserves credit for his intentions; and if he must ultimately be said to have failed then his was a very notable failure. The spirit of naturalism also influenced Meredith, although in a different and even less direct way: he retained a somewhat obstinate conviction that everything may be explained mechanically—this is at the heart of both his (uninteresting and unconvincing) optimism and his (interesting) sense of the comic, which in some respects anticipates that of Wyndham Lewis (q.v.). He had a hard time establishing a reputation—even at the height of his Victorian fame there were influential cliques who had no use for him—and he had not long been dead before he became widely unread. And yet he was a tireless experimenter; he will never quite lie down. No one's novels sound more interesting in detailed summary. He would have liked to have been an ironic comedian in the manner of the Brazilian Machado de Assis (q.v.), whose work he did not know; but his subtle and intelligent novels usually become victim to his meretriciousness, his false philosophical optimism and the puzzling manner in which he trans-forms his huge imaginative energy into something merely whimsical or even plain crazy. And yet, as Henry James carefully said, he did 'the best things best'. He has his magnificent moments, and these are prophetic of what is to come in the novel.

Meredith was badly hamstrung by the Victorian necessity for sexual reticence: his realistic view of women and of sexual matters in general cut sharply across the Victorian fantasy, which enshrined women only to patronize them and neutralize their (in anthropological terms) magical qualities. His imaginative sympathy really was with women—as victims of this male distortion—and it involved him in the kind of extreme difficulties with which we, in turn, must sympathize. Meredith's sympathy with women and his understanding of sexual problems led to some inspired passages (such as the scene, in *The Egoist*, where Clare watches Vernon Whitford asleep under the cherry tree; or, earlier, the masturbation scenes in *The Ordeal of Richard Feverel*) but never, alas, to a completely successful novel. The only book in which the notorious Meredithian difficulties are wholly absent is the comparatively early and simple *Rhoda Fleming* (1865). However, despite the existence during his lifetime of a band of loyal (but not all comprehending) 'Meredithians', he has not had his due even for what he attempted. He is, after all, as V. S. Pritchett has said in an excellent study of him, 'a storehouse of ways and means' and 'rather hard and intelligently merciless—which is refreshing in the nineteenth century'. And the best of his poetry, despite his unfortunate penchant for trying to sound—and sometimes sounding—Shakespearean, is at the least interesting.

GEORGE MOORE (1852–1933) deserves to be considered both as a nineteenth-and a twentieth-century writer. He is the most seriously neglected major novelist of the past century: too many critics have confused his best work with his frequently sloppy and foolish persona (even if he was ultimately, in Sherard Vines' oddly apt words, 'a dear good soul'). He was a pioneer, as the 'English naturalist'—a category he may be said to have invented for himself, in order to get a real start as a novelist—as autobiographer and as post-realist novelist; he is one of the best writers of short stories in the English language (yet, in a recent survey of this form by a reputable critic, he gets exactly one sentence). Moore is a remarkable illustration of the fact that great writing frequently springs from personal humiliation: the sources of his energy certainly include his boastful foolishness and his sexual voyeurism. He turned both these humiliating characteristics to creative account.

The key to Moore's imaginative attitude is summed up in a remark from his *Reminiscences of the Impressionist Painters* (1906): 'Life is a rose that withers in the iron fist of dogma. . . .' Creatively he was a consistent sceptic; his diagnosis of the disease that threatens twentieth-century humanity is subtler and profounder than his non-creative (critical) pronouncements, frequently inane, would lead one to believe. Ford Madox Ford (q.v.) called him 'infinitely the most skilful man of letters of his day—the most skilful in the world'. One of Moore's skills consisted in filtering his considerable Irish silliness out of his writings, and yet preserving the energy from which it sprang.

His first important book was the autobiographical *Confessions of a Young Man* (1886 rev. 1926): he needed to satirize what he had been as a very young man in Paris. This book conveys an accurate sense of the genuine (as distinct from the theatrical) element in his immature paganism of those early days—by isolating it and thus keeping it at a proper comic distance. As early, then, as 1886 Moore had abandoned any serious attempt to present himself in conventionally realist terms. This is so incongruous as coming from the later self-styled champion of Zolaesque naturalism that it has been overlooked. By the time he came to write the autobiographical trilogy *Hail and Farewell* (1911–14) he had perfected the process. By then he knew, as he put it in a letter (1913) to Robert Ross, that a 'man only seems natural when he is speaking aside or to himself; he seems quite mechanical when he is uttering little phrases to people standing. . . . .'

But his first undoubted masterpiece was a work avowedly naturalist, and certainly realist: *Esther Waters* (1894). This is a tender study of a servant betrayed and left pregnant, and of her fight for her son. Grudgingly acknowledged as a classic, it has nevertheless been consistently underrated. Virginia Woolf (q.v.) claimed that Moore 'had not the strength to project Esther from himself'; but she merely put a finger on a weakness of her own. All Zola's naturalism did for Moore was to give him a method to get started. *Esther Waters* is naturalist in intention, but its effect is, eventually, anti-naturalist: the 'message' is that compassion is all, not that character or environment is destiny. However, naturalism taught Moore not to be reticent about sexual matters, and it purged him of the gentility that even today bedevils English literature and most of the criticism of it.

Moore went on to produce at least three more major novels. The first was *The Lake* (1905); later came *The Brook Kerith* (1916), the story of Paul's betrayal of a Christ who, rescued from the cross, has come to reject his earlier fanaticism; *Héloise and Abelard* (1921) is hardly read now, and is not in print—but it is another masterpiece. These later novels (the new manner began with *The Lake*, but was not developed until *The Brook Kerith*) demand to be read aloud if the reader is fully to appreciate how so lyrical and uninterrupted (but varied) a 'seamless' flow can contain so much complex material. There is, after all, a part of ourselves that perceives our experience as an unstitched and seamless whole; Moore seized on this aspect of perception and made himself its master.

And yet his greatest achievement of all is in the realm of the short story: from the relatively early *Celibates* (1895), through *The Untilled Field* (1903) and *A Story Teller's Holiday* (1918) to the perfection of *Celibate Lives* (1927), which is the final revision of *In Single Strictness* (1922). 'Albert Nobbs', originally from *A Story Teller's Holiday* but included in *Celibate Lives*, is the greatest comic short story of the century in any language. *The Untilled Field* (as Graham Hough has observed) precedes Joyce's *Dubliners* (q.v.) just as *Confessions of a Young Man* precedes his *Portrait of the Artist as a Young Man*.

There were once excuses for not looking at Moore: in his famous quarrel with Yeats (q.v.) he made himself look foolish; his disciples (they included Charles Morgan, q.v.) were the most mediocre any great writer has ever gathered around him. These excuses are no longer viable: Moore is a very important—and modern—writer indeed, both extrinsically and intrinsically: far from ever having left him behind, there is a whole readership that has yet to catch up with him.

w. h. hudson (1841–1922) was of American parents who emigrated to Argentina; he returned to England in 1870 and became an English citizen in 1900. Although he gained wide recognition with *Green Mansions* (1915), he is now a rather neglected writer. Conrad said of him to Ford: 'He writes as the grass grows. The Good God makes it be there. . . .' He was a brilliant and unusual observer of countless small natural things; his observations fly, like richly coloured birds, across the bleakness of his recollections of Spanish-American savagery and of his own poverty and neglect. *Green Mansions*, the story of a bird woman, is still insufficiently acknowledged as a classic; that it was derived from an earlier and inferior novel (Lady Morgan's *The Missionary*) makes little difference, since it transforms and improves it.

r. b. cunninghame graham (1852–1936), once the toast of many distinguished authors (including Ford), is now buried in oblivion. This is not quite deserved. Three-quarters Scottish and the rest Spanish, he was a fierce and flamboyant personality, who lived an adventurous life: as a young man he pioneered in South America and America; later, in England, he got himself jailed for championing the then unpopular cause of justice for working men. He should be revived in selection. Edward Garnett's selection, *Thirty Tales and Sketches* (1929) and *Rodeo* (1936), edited by A. F. Tschiffely, reveals an original minor writer, one of the few British masters of *costumbrismo* (q.v.), a portraitist of wild places, whose lawlessness bohemianism has—despite its over-dependence on rhetoric—a fine and genuine quality. Cunninghame Graham is a Kipling-in-reverse: he suffers from the same violent anarchic

passions, but channels them into socialism instead of imperialism. He shamelessly indulged himself in both his Scottish-dour and Spanish *hidalgo* aspects,
but had a clear sense of the places he wrote about, and his uncompromisingly
shame- (as distinct from guilt-) directed approach is sincere—more sincere,
less puerile, than that of, say, Roy Campbell (q.v.).

JOSEPH CONRAD (originally TEODOR JOZEF KONRAD KORNZENIOWSKI, 1851–
1924), a Pole, was the son of a literary man who was sent into political exile;
he went to sea, and soon began serving in English ships—he passed for master in
1880, and took up British citizenship in 1886. He began writing while still at
sea. His first novel, *Almayer's Folly*, was published in 1895, and gained critical
success; but he did not get public recognition and the relative financial independence that flows from it until *Chance* (1913). He wrote English much better
than he spoke it; and each of his novels cost him an inordinate amount of
nervous energy. The influence and help of Ford Madox Ford (q.v.) has been
deliberately underestimated by critics; it was, however, vital in his development. Conrad and Ford wrote three novels in collaboration: *The Inheritors*
(1901), *Romance* (1903)—and *The Nature of a Crime* (1924), which was written
in 1906–7 and first published by Ford in his *English Review*.

The best of Conrad's fiction has been the subject of an exorbitant amount of
critical exegesis, both in Great Britain and the United States. Recognition of
his supremacy as a novelist was a cornerstone of the ultra-dogmatic school of
the critic F. R. Leavis (q.v.) at Downing College, Cambridge, which was
influential between 1930 and 1960 (Leavis has written well on him). There
have been remarkably few dissentients from the basic assumption of his greatness; his position as a great novelist remains secure and undisturbed. The case
for the prosecution (if there is one) has never really been presented. And at the
very least this does pay tribute to Conrad's massive seriousness, his great
struggle with himself, his wide range—and his extraordinary mastery of written
English. Henry James (q.v.), it seems, could turn his sexual deficiency into a
triumph of art; Conrad, likewise, turned both a clumsy incapacity for full
human relationships (perhaps this culminates in the partial portrait of his wife
Jessie as Winnie Verloc in *The Secret Agent*), and a difficulty with the English
language, into a triumph. Here is another sceptic, anxiously probing at heroic
and moral truisms, masterfully avoiding what he hardly understood, though
personally yearned for: friendship, love, communion. It so happened that
Conrad's genius coincided in certain respects with that of the English language,
which (as is natural in a Pole) he approached for its Latin rather than its
Anglo-Saxon qualities. But he worked desperately hard to achieve the
coincidence.

Conrad's masterpieces are *Typhoon* (1902), *Heart of Darkness* (1902), *Nostromo*
(1904), *The Secret Agent* (1907) and *Under Western Eyes* (1911). *Heart of Darkness*,
which contains the quintessence of his art, is set in the Congo—where Conrad
himself, in difficult circumstances, discovered his true vocation. This is Conrad's
exploration of his narrator, Marlow's, recollections (on the Thames in London)
of a nightmare journey into the interior. It demonstrates the firmness of his

control, through style and tone, of his material; agonizedly, it shows a human sympathy existing where an 'official' view would allow of none.

Conrad's chief subjects include revolution—its causes, its excesses and its betrayal; and the evils of acquisitiveness. His concern is always imaginative rather than political. There lies at the heart of Conrad's best fiction a horrified awareness of evil, a scepticism about the validity of human attitudes, and a terrified recognition of human solitude. In *The Nigger of the 'Narcissus'* (1897) he shows how sympathy itself can threaten survival; in *Lord Jim* (1900), again narrated by Marlow, he demonstrates how imagination and idealism can corrupt and lead to cowardice—and also how impossible non-intuitive moral judgement (the prerogative of establishments and the systems they perpetuate) is to achieve (in *Heart of Darkness* we find two moral opposites in profound kinship. . . .). In *The Secret Agent* Conrad found a sardonic objective correlative (q.v.)—Ford provided the material—for his uneasiness over his marriage (which was, at bottom, an unhappy one) and over the role of the writer (his treatment of the *Künstlerschuld*, q.v., theme), whom he projects into the morally insensitive dealer in pornography, Verloc, who gets more involved in the game of spying and terrorism than he had intended (he thought he could play with evil); but the characters transcend their origins in the author's mind. It is probably true to say, as a critic has, that Conrad does not 'explore human relationships'; but he does use this incapacity to show how they can fail to exist; at other times he can imply them very cleverly. The lack of one between the comically sinister Verloc and his wife is one of the most chilling things in the whole of his work. There is often a ponderousness about Conrad's style that not everyone finds to their taste (he is sometimes a bit too much the Polish 'master of English prose'); but of his stature, his subtlety, his seriousness, there can be no serious doubt.

RUDYARD KIPLING (1865–1936) is a strange case indeed. He is certainly not less than a major writer of fiction (though only a minor poet) and yet, more than any writer of his stature, he seems to suffer, not simply from ignorance or lack of education, but from an advanced philistinism and, at times, an insensitive proto-fascism. His attitudes, taken simply as attitudes, form an offensive constellation: racist, blindly imperialist, British 'public school' in the worst sense, feudal. . . . But actually, of course, his thought is confused. The real man does not hold these views at all: unlike his actually philistine counterpart, the stupid British Tory (not the intelligent one, of whom Ford's Tietjens, q.v., was the last), Kipling has an imagination. A good deal of Victorian imperialistic sentiment (which was not of course as 'offensive' then as it is now) undoubtedly released repressed sexual energies: Elgar's symphonies, for example, are as much 'about' a series of sexual climaxes and sexual guilts as they are 'about' anything else. It is hardly necessary to point out, at this date, that one of the functions of the British Empire was phallic. But Elgar was a robust and relatively uncomplicated Roman Catholic. The evidence suggests that Kipling—and here lies the secret of his creative strength—was a sadomasochistic bisexual. His rationalizations of his (in his own Victorian terms) hideous impulses took two forms: one was his political doctrines; but the other was often a true objective correlative, a creative resolution of his severe emotional and sexual problems. And in many of Kipling's stories and one or two of his novels we find instinctive wisdom, love, kindness—and, sometimes, terror. As a writer he was, after all, at his best, very good—his Nobel Prize of 1907 is not incongruous, as is, say, Galsworthy's—and that is perhaps what is important in a writer. He is one of the best of the immensely popular writers of the twentieth century.

Kipling was born in Bombay; after some unhappy years in England with a relative and then four years at school in Westward Ho in Devon, he returned to India. W. E. Henley, who among other better things was a chauvinist, enthused about his early *Barrack-Room Ballads,* and printed them in the *National Observer.* Kipling collected his first stories in *Plain Tales from the Hills* (1888) and *Soldiers Three* (1888). *Barrack-Room Ballads* were collected in book form in 1890 and 1892. In the latter year Kipling married the sister of an American journalist, Wolcot Balestier; he seems to have been in love with both brother and sister, and he lived in Vermont until 1896, when a quarrel with Wolcot caused him to leave. After this he settled in Sussex, eventually building himself a large house, Batemans, from which august headquarters he continued to issue prose and verse until the end of his life.

Kipling's tales are at their best when their sheer realism becomes independent of the code of 'honour' that he consciously built up—and which was largely responsible for his immense popularity. Kipling, when he was not trying to think, possessed an uncanny insight into the mind of the common soldiers and officers about whom he wrote so vividly. Kipling's code consists of 'fair play' (approximating rather to the 'fairness ethic' that Erich Fromm has wryly distinguished as a capitalist contribution to society), British public school solidarity and loyalty (this was partly fantasy on Kipling's part, as he showed in *Stalky and Co.,* 1899, where he transformed his own timid role at a rather enlightened non-public school into that of a rebellious hero playing the game against the game), self-reliance and paternalism. He applies this, in the course of his fiction, to many situations, in particular to animals (*The Jungle Books,* 1894, 1895) and to simple masculine situations—military, engineering and so on. As C. S. Lewis pointed out, Kipling longed to be in on all masculine mysteries, to be 'one of the boys'. Max Beerbohm (q.v.) put his finger on Kipling's motivations when he wrote: 'Mr. Kipling is so far masculine that he has never displayed a knowledge of women as they are; but the unreality of his male creatures, with his worship of them, makes his name ring quaintly like a pseudonym. . . . Strange that these heroes . . . were not . . . created out of the inner consciousness of a lady novelist. . . .' This is malicious but just. Eliot (q.v.) tried to defend Kipling from the charge of fascism by calling him a Tory. But Kipling was not a Tory: he was a Tory-anarchist—a passionate, confused man—whose confusions, however, passionately appealed to the thousands of Englishmen like him. Ford's Edward Ashburnham, from *The Good Soldier* (q.v.), would have read and admired Kipling; but he would not have seen that Kipling projected his own 'cheep cynicism about the female sex', his own propensity and 'relish' for 'The ugly word, the ugly action, the ugly atmosphere' (Beerbohm) into his characters. He has, too, a pathic slyness and cunning that give his tales, with their pristine and lyrical feelings, not only technical mastery but also great power. His best novel is *Kim* (1901): here the writer took over entirely, and the British and Indian characters are seen with equal imaginative sympathy.

In verse Kipling is what Orwell (q.v.) called 'a good bad' poet. 'Danny Deever' has an authentic *frisson*, but the conflict in Kipling's mind between his false code ('a sneakin' shootin' hound': ''e shot a comrade sleeping') and his sexual and sadistic fascination with hanging is too nastily apparent, and the poem doesn't have the strength to resolve it. His poems, whether ballads or nostalgic lyrics, seldom get beyond the bounds of self-indulgence.

Kipling's best work arose out of confusion and even viciousness; it also has a strange beauty, something not altogether definable—a gentleness and child-likeness—that functions as a soother and a neutralizer of the violence of the 'Freudian' elements. He was ungenerous in his views; but it would be un-generous of us to take these at face value, and to refuse to judge him from his best books. His collected works were published in thirty-one volumes (1913–38), and are still available.

If ARTHUR CONAN DOYLE (1859–1930) will eventually be forgotten as a historical novelist, he will be immortal for his creation of Sherlock Holmes. His historical romances are excellent, and some remain in print; but they are romances. His photograph of his fantasy-self as Sherlock Holmes, however, is an offbeat literary achievement: a Victorian portrait of an eccentric, with innumerable implications, and embellished with a splendid and absorbing ingenuity. Conan Doyle's Holmes is the dream-paradigm of the brilliant decadent, cunningly written from a non-decadent point of view; it transcends most of the decadent literature of its time.

H. G. WELLS (1866–1946), despite his huge and continuing popularity with all sections of the public, is with critics a persistently underrated and mis-understood writer. He himself disclaimed interest in his literary reputation and stated, in a mock-obituary of 1936, that he was 'much more the scientific man than the artist, though he dealt in literary forms'. But he was a major novelist, praised fulsomely by Henry James (q.v.), and told (1920), by Ford, one of the most perceptive men of this time, that he was a 'genius' who wasted too much of his time on 'social speculation'. The reasons why Wells the propa-gandist, the inconsistent and irascible generalizer, was led to betray the creative writer in himself, and the ways in which he unconsciously rapped himself over the knuckles for this betrayal, are exceptionally interesting.

The most destructive criticism of Wells the 'thinker', the Utopian, is Max Beerbohm's (q.v.) deadly parody 'Perkins and Mankind', in which he has Wells writing an account of an old man happily going to the 'Municipal Lethal Chamber' on 'General Cessation Day', 'walking with a firm step in the midst of his progeny. . . . He will not be thinking of himself. . . . He will be filled with joy at the thought that he is about to die for the good of the race . . . for the beautiful young breed of men and women who, in simple, antiseptic garments, are disporting themselves so gladly on this day of days. . . .'

But Wells the Utopian, the public figure with 'brains but no tact' (his uncle said this of Wells when he was fourteen), is only the least important part of a story that is more complicated than is generally acknowledged. The popular idea of Wells—publicist, novelist, pioneer of science fiction—seems to be that he betrayed the glowing optimism of a lifetime only in his gloomy last work, *Mind at the End of its Tether* (1945). Nothing could be further from the truth. The root of the false view lies in the notion that Wells was an optimist. He was nothing of the sort. He was, it is true, a cheeky satyr, full of good humour and tactlessness, who thoroughly enjoyed gatecrashing a high society that he despised; but his continuous sexual curiosity (he was exceptionally good to his many cast-off mistresses) and his ebullience hid a gloomy dreamer: a man of profound imaginative capabilities, who read Blake as well as science text-books. Allying itself to this pessimistic streak was Well's feeling of social inferiority, which never really left him, and which he exploited to superb comic effect in his early straight novels. It was the submerged poetic, subversive elements in Wells, working through the scientifically trained exterior, that led him to make his most startling prophecies and anticipations. For besides the better known scientific prophecies, some of which we cannot yet assess, Wells made many astute sociological guesses; all of these are negative, satirical, gloomy.

The cannibals of Rampole Island (in the neglected dystopia *Mr. Blettsworthy on Rampole Island*, 1928) who call their enemies 'cannibals' are as good an example of doublethink as anything in Orwell's *1984* (q.v.); their failure to refer to unpleasant manifestations of state authority by their proper names (criminals are 'reproached', not punished) is worthy of Swift. Compare this morbid side of Wells—the far future envisaged in *The Time Machine* (1895), the death of Griffin in *The Invisible Man* (1897)—with the antiseptic, imagination-free, laboured naïvety of a *Modern Utopia* (1905) or the lecture on the World Encyclopaedia project (1936). . . . . In all the fiction in which Wells tried to create a Utopia he never quite knew what to do with it: he did not believe in Utopias.

Wells's range is very wide. As a writer of science fiction he has not been equalled for versatility, ingenuity or credibility; the atmosphere of those early tales is unforgettable, unrepeatable, poetic. He is a great comic novelist: *Kipps* (1905), *Tono Bungay* (1909), *The History of Mr. Polly* (1909). His later and more complex fiction has been unjustly neglected: *Mr. Blettsworthy on Rampole Island*, although flawed, is one of the most memorable of modern dystopias; *The Bulpington of Blup* (1933), in part a portrait of Ford (q.v.), is a notable psychological study. Wells's work as would-be shaper of human destiny and popularizer of science did partly undermine his creativity: he never, after *Mr. Polly*, reached the point at which his imagination could function positively. But his earlier work deserves the praise James conferred on it ('You are a very swagger performer indeed' who 'makes even dear old Dickens turn . . . in his grave'); the best of his later work demands responsible reconsideration.

By contrast the talent of JOHN GALSWORTHY (1867–1933) is drab. He cannot hope to achieve more than his recent enshrinement as author of the original script (so to speak) of the (for ever?) current soap opera of *The Forsyte Saga*. His best work, which is very modest in achievement, is in the drama and the earlier part of the *Saga*. He won the Nobel Prize in 1932. Easy as it is to sneer at him, D. H. Lawrence's (q.v.) attack on him as 'a sneaking old cynic' cannot really be countered: we find ourselves apologizing rather than pointing to positive virtues.

Galsworthy wrote nothing of account before *The Island Pharisees* (1904) and the first of the *Forsyte Saga*: *The Man of Property* (1906). The latter remains the best of his novels, and even Lawrence conceded that its satire on the upper crust of society 'really had a certain noble touch'. But even this and its successors *The Country House* (1908) and *Fraternity* (1909) can hardly be described as important books. One has only to think of Ford's *The Good Soldier* (q.v.) to realize just how ordinary they are. The characters are flat and lifeless; the redeeming factor is the author's genuine social indignation, which expresses itself in the form of satire. By 1922, introducing the first Forsyte trilogy (*The Man of Property; In Chancery*, 1920; *To Let*, 1921), he was able to say: 'Human Nature, under its changing pretensions . . . is and ever will be very much of a Forsyte, and might, after all, be a much worse animal'. He remained a courteous, considerate, conscientious man; but as a serious writer he was finished. The Forsytes who had been the villains of the early novel now became the heroes; nor, in the later volumes (the trilogy is called *A Modern Comedy*, 1929) did Galsworthy display the least understanding of the post-war generation. And in all these later novels Galsworthy indulges himself in the middlebrow habit of manipulating his characters according to his emotions, which became progressively more sentimental and conservatively 'worthy'. He was not at any time a major writer. His dramas, notably *The Silver Box* (1903), *Strife* (1909) and *Justice* (1910), are well made, restrained, and display a genuine passion for social justice. They represent Galsworthy at his most skilful and agreeable. But his undeservedly high reputation justifies the harshness of D. H. Lawrence's verdict: 'Vulgarity pays, and cheap cynicism smothered in sentimentality pays better than anything else'.

ARNOLD BENNETT (1867–1931) is both more gifted and more puzzling. To many readers of modern poetry he is no more than a footnote to Ezra Pound's unkind poem 'Mr. Nixon':

> . . . 'Consider
> Carefully the reviewer.
>
> I was as poor as you are;
> When I began I got, of course,
> Advance on royalties, fifty at first,' said Mr. Nixon,
> 'Follow me, and take a column,
> Even if you have to work free. . . .

I never mentioned a man but with the view
of selling my own works. . . .

And give up verse, my boy,
There's nothing in it.' . . .

This goes well enough with 'I write for as much money as I can get' and the admonition by Bennett to those 'parasites' (poets) to try to understand that nothing matters so much as cash and the preservation of 'decency'. Galsworthy, possibly to his credit, would never even have considered such philistine sentiments; the irony is that Bennett was, incomparably, the better novelist. Even in the late Twenties, when rising critics such as Edwin Muir (q.v.) found it necessary to dismiss Bennett, they would admit that in *The Old Wives' Tale* (1908) he had 'beautifully and profoundly expressed the passing away of human delight in possessions'.

The truth is that Bennett's 'philistinism', while tactless and reprehensible in itself, was part of an ironic self-defence. He could not quite understand how his ambition had driven him into being a *writer*: there must have been something wrong there: he had been a cocky, self-confident law-clerk and prentice-journalist down from Hanley (one of the Five Towns) to escape from a puritan-ical atmosphere and his father's domination: a man with an eye on the brass should have been able to do better than *that*. The puritan in him felt guilty, too, about the self-indulgence (he was a famed sybarite) that success in letters had allowed him. As a popular recommender of books to a middlebrow audience (in his capacity as critic of *The New Age* and *The Evening Standard*) he did much to push his fellow authors, displayed as consistently high standards as any such columnist ever has, and was remarkably unspiteful and unpre-tentious. 'Mr. Nixon' is a fair comment on the value of certain of Bennett's pronouncements, many of which were as absurd as George Moore's (q.v.); it is not a fair comment on the man himself—who was generous, sensitive and vulnerable—or on his best work.

Bennett is a strange case. Throughout his life he issued a stream of pot-boiling novels, instructive handbooks on *Self-Help* lines and popular 'philos-ophies of life'; yet this did not corrupt his creativity. As late as 1923, when he was fifty-six, he produced a novel whose flaws of style and presentation cannot prevent its being a masterpiece—in creation of atmosphere, in psycho-logical acuteness and, above all, in warmth of feeling: *Riceyman Steps*. His really important books are: *The Old Wives' Tale*; the *Clayhanger* trilogy (*Clay-hanger*, 1910; *Hilda Lessways*, 1911; *These Twain*. 1915); *The Card* (1911): *Riceyman Steps*; *Lord Raingo* (1924). His last novel, *Imperial Palace* (1930), is as sceptical about great hotels as it is awe-inspired; and is a lively and amusing performance. He knew nothing whatever about poetry, and was silly when he talked about it (hence Pound's justified satire); but although he regarded literature as a business, his imagination never became corrupt; the quality of *Riceyman Steps* is as high as that of anything he ever wrote.

Bennett's first models were the 'French' George Moore (q.v.) and the later French nineteenth-century novel. He was always more at home in French than in English literature. Although influenced by naturalism, Bennett was a realist without (in his novels) any philosophy; however, the grim puritanism and drab ugliness of the Five Towns affected him deeply, and are reflected in his best books. *The Old Wives' Tale* is his greatest achievement: its people, as Frank Swinnerton (q.v.) has said, 'are within his heart as well as his head'; he is at his best here because he is 'both humorous and humane'. This is a great unsophisticated classic. *The Card* (called *Denry the Audacious* in America), a kind of delightedly objective self-study, did something that had not previously been done in English fiction, even by Wells—the thread was taken up again by William Cooper (q.v.) forty years later; but *The Card* has not been bettered. For all his lapses, his spasmodic puritanism, his unevenness, Bennett succeeded in achieving the 'all-embracing compassion' that he believed to be the 'essential characteristic of the really good novelist'.

STEPHEN HUDSON (ps. SIDNEY SCHIFF, 1868–1944) presents a complete contrast: a member of the so-called Bloomsbury Group (centred in Cambridge and the Bloomsbury district of London, and including Leonard and Virginia Woolf, q.v., the art-critics Clive Bell and Roger Fry, the painter Duncan Grant, the writers Lytton Strachey, E. M. Forster, the economist John Maynard Keynes, and many others; chief common or overlapping interests were Fabianism, beautiful young men—such as Rupert Brooke, q.v.—and humanism), he was self-consciously literary. He completed Scott Moncrieff's famous translation of Proust—notoriously badly. But his fiction deserves to be remembered. His best book is *A True Story* (1930, rev. 1949), which is a revision and condensation of three earlier novels and part of a fourth: *Richard Kurt* (1919), *Elinor Colhouse* (1921), *Prince Hempseed* (1922) and *Myrtle* (1925). This, the story of Richard Kurt, is an original and economically written study of motivation—and of, as Walter Allen has pointed out, 'the Oedipus Complex working its doom throughout a man's life'. Hudson was aware of the discoveries of psychoanalysis, and his unobtrusive use of them was both intelligent and pioneering. The beginning of *A True Story* is the best part: the account of Kurt's adolescence and of his life in America. I agree with Walter Allen (who has been largely responsible for drawing attention to Hudson's distinction) that the succeeding parts, in which Kurt's relationships with two women are explored, are less satisfactory: Hudson was weak when dealing with women, and he cannot disguise this. But when he deals with Kurt's own motivations he remains impressive. His technique consists of selecting certain incidents in his hero's life, and concentrating upon them with great psychological intensity. *Tony* (1924), a portrait of Kurt through his brother's eyes, is more interesting than the modest and over-sophisticated Hudson himself would allow.

The Powys brothers—JOHN COWPER POWYS (1872–1963), T. F. POWYS (1875– 1953) and LLEWELLYN POWYS (1884–1939)—sons of a Church of England parson, were a remarkable trio of eccentric writers; the first two have become the subjects of cults. John Cowper's virtues, and in particular his sexual philosophy, have been urged by the critic G. Wilson Knight; and T. F. Powys is or was compulsory diet for budding Leavisites (q.v.). The least unconventional of the three was Llewellyn, who spent most of his life struggling with tuberculosis, to which he finally succumbed. He wrote well of this struggle (*Skin for Skin*, 1925) and of his travels (*Ebony and Ivory*, 1924); he was also a competent biographer. But he was hardly a creative writer, and his two novels are negligible.

John Cowper is a writer on a huge—even cosmic—scale; Theodore Francis is a miniaturist. But both brothers see the universe—as do Bernanos and Jouhandeau (qq.v.)—as a battleground for the forces of good and evil. Both writers have been overrated by their admirers; both had genius; both too rapidly become bores by harping on their particular obsessions. Of the two, T. F. Powys is more likely to survive: he used shorter forms.

John Cowper Powys' best book, by far and away, is his *Autobiography* (1934); this should be read in conjunction with the American edition, *The Art of Happiness* (1935), which differs considerably. Powys' self-insight and honesty are here displayed at their best. His massive novels tend to be both boring and pretentious; there is an element of charlatanism in them. The imagination of the author is less in evidence than the grandiose schemes suggest: there is usually more of his philosophical world-view than of invention: he tells us about his characters' conflicts, but cannot convince us of their existence. The 'imaginative power' with which he is so often credited consists in large measure of a vulgarly 'cosmic', pseudo-mystical approach to life, which ignores individuality and concentrates on mere largeness of conception. *A Glastonbury Romance* (1933), a modern treatment of the Grail legend, is unreadable except by those who want to escape from themselves into a vague pantheism. *Wolf Solent* (1929) is better, but suffers from the same grandiosity. And yet there was a grand obstinacy here, and an occasional achievement of colloquial style (when Powys tried to be archaic he was excruciating; but his vernacular is often excellent). At the heart of all this high intention and self-inflation is a minor writer of distinction, best savoured in short passages. Like his brother Theodore Francis, John Cowper Powys was a miniaturist; but he would not accept this limitation.

T. F. Powys is superior. Certainly his sadistic morbidity becomes absurd when taken in quantity. The perverseness and cruelty of his rustic characters are too easily caricatured. It is not that he had an exaggerated picture of the beastliness inherent in human beings; it is rather that he usually (he wrote eight novels and more than twenty collections of short stories) fails to place this beastliness (often sexual) in a convincing context. It becomes *grand guignol*, too much of a joke. In *Mr. Tasker's Gods* (1925), a notorious example, a rapist feeds his father to his pigs, who are his Gods. Despite the power and the conviction, it does not come off. Powys is not, in H. Coombes's words, a 'great and extraordinary writer' who has 'the terrifying honesty of genius'. But he is an extraordinary writer and he sometimes has genius; but even he is neither great nor quite terrifying. One can see (this has often been pointed out), in Dylan

Thomas's (q.v.) early short stories in *The Map of Love* (1939), how this kind of semi-surrealist perversity can spill over into a sick and ill-accomplished nastiness. From the difference between Thomas and Powys one may discern that whereas Thomas (in this aspect at least) was a dirty little boy playing with evil, Powys was genuinely and more maturely obsessed; he might, indeed, have been a great writer if he could have got things into better balance. But he fails (unlike another similarly obsessed writer, Céline, q.v.) to reveal his charity. One needs at least one 'normal' rustic as a foil for the others. His best novel, *Mr. Weston's Good Wine* (1927), an allegory in which God appears in Dorset, has a lightness of touch and a gentleness that neutralize his usual concentration on the bestial side of man; but one must resist, as grotesque, the comparisons with Shakespeare that have been made. However, for this, the novel *Black Bryony* (1923), and for a handful of the short stories, Powys has his place as an original minor writer.

c. e. montague (1867–1928), one of the last of the great journalists, wrote four competent but now dated novels, of which the best is *Rough Justice* (1926), and one masterpiece of non-fiction: *Disenchantment* (1922), a description of the Western Front, and one of the earliest and finest denunciations of the cruelty and stupidity of militarism. *Fiery Particles* (1923) contains some good short stories.

norman douglas (1868–1952) is possibly more memorable as a personality than as a writer. But at least *South Wind* (1917), *Old Calabria* (1915) and his two books of autobiography—*Looking Back* (1933) and *Late Harvest* (1946)—will survive. *South Wind* is a unique light satirical novel, a study of a group of expatriated English on Capri (an island which he made, so to speak, his own). Nothing is as harmless and tolerant as Douglas' 'hedonism'.

max beerbohm (1872–1956) is just about as substantial as a minor writer can become—and a warning to those who regard minor writers as mere *repetiteurs* of their elders and betters. Beerbohm was, in fact, minor entirely by choice: he preferred to wound with arrows shot from the periphery. He is distinguished as an essayist, as a parodist and a short-story writer ('Enoch Soames' is a masterpiece). He was also a notable caricaturist. He understood more than his deliberately lightweight style suggests—as the parodies in *A Christmas Garland* clearly demonstrate.

g. k. chesterton (1874–1936) could never be uninteresting, as man or writer. It has been said that he is a 'master who left no masterpiece'; and this seems just—or does some masterpiece-like quality inform at least the conception of Father Brown? . . . The vitality of Chesterton's best writing is not a consequence of his Roman Catholicism, the intellectual content of which may now be seen as an accidental. Chesterton spent his creative life indulging his nihilism, but rendering it powerless with brilliant final twists. Terror is the father of his ingenuity. His ostensible message—bluff, matter-of-fact, 'jolly', beery, genial—is 'Everything's all right *really*: see how harmless I render these fascinating horrors'. But a little examination reveals a profound unease: a spirit wrestling with the notion of absurdity as far as it dared without madness. The wonderfully ingenious *The Man Who Was Thursday* (1908), the best of his novels, reveals all evil as non-existent: six of the anarchists are really detectives, and the seventh is God. But the figure of Sunday (God behind the mask of Nature) is ambiguous and ill-defined: a confession of 'faith' but a failure of the imagination.

HILAIRE BELLOC (1870–1953) never achieved the creative level of his friend Chesterton, but he did certain small things well. He is most distinguished of all as a writer of comic verse: here he was relaxed; his essential decency and gaiety found their best and purest form in parodying smug, false Victorian didacticism.

SAKI (PS. HECTOR HUGH MUNRO, 1870–1916), who was killed in the First World War, was born in Burma; but at the age of two he was sent home to Devon in the care of two sadistic maiden aunts. This experience formed him as a writer. He first became known as a journalist, but before his death he had established a reputation for his grotesque short stories about Reginald and Clovis, those clever young assailants of the pretentious, the fake-adult and the orthodox. His short stories were collected in 1930; he wrote one novel, *The Unbearable Bassington* (1912). Saki could be as cruel and sick as those maiden aunts: they prompted in him (and in his sister) a desire for revenge that lasted all his life. His standard procedure is original: the gruesome or sinister is wrapped up in a farcical package. The novel is an exception: here Saki seriously tries to account for his hero's sadism; there is evidence that he took this book more seriously than his short stories. It was on an unusual theme for its time, and psychologically it is penetratingly accurate; it suggests that, had he not been killed (by a sniper), he might have developed into a major novelist. He has been compared with Beerbohm, Wilde and Firbank (q.v.); a more telling comparison, allowing for nationality, might be with Wedekind (q.v.): Saki has the same gay grimness, the same hatred of gentility and of its life-denying emptiness.

OLIVER ONIONS (1873–1912) is a now somewhat neglected writer who wrote one minor masterpiece: *In Accordance with the Evidence* (1912), the first of a trilogy, about a clerk who murders a rival and gets away with it by tricking him into writing a suicide note. This is a powerfully unpleasant novel, with an uncanny and oppressive air of reality about it. Its two successors (*The Debit Account*, 1913; *The Story of Louie*, 1913) are not quite as good. The whole trilogy was issued as a single volume in 1925. There are a few effective stories in the *Collected Ghost Stories* (1935). The best of his later fiction is *The Story of Ragged Robyn* (1945).

FORD MADOX FORD (originally FORD MADOX HUEFFER, 1873–1939), if only for five novels (he wrote, counting collaborations, thirty-two, plus countless other books of criticism, travel, history and belles lettres), is one of the dozen greatest novelists of the century. The most generous of men—only Pound (q.v.), himself conspicuously loyal to Ford, has been as generous and helpful to other writers—Ford was a boastful and often grotesquely silly liar and, like Coleridge, made a mess of his life; yet, like Coleridge, he was a better human being than most of those who denigrated him. Stella Bowen, who lived with him for many years and bore him a daughter, said: 'Ford's weakness of character, unfairness, disregard of truth, and vanity *must* be accepted. . . . On the other hand, his tenderness, understanding, wisdom (about anything that didn't apply to himself!) and the tremendous attraction of his gorgeous mind, must make him always regretted. . . .' England, to its eternal discredit, more or less rejected him; in recent years Graham Greene (q.v.) has crusaded for him almost alone; all the substantial studies of him, as well as the standard biography by Arthur Mizener (1971), are American. When he is praised by English critics it is almost always grudgingly, or in the shadow of his friend Conrad (of whom his study remains one of the best), than whom, however, he was not in his own way less good. No man was more persecuted by women—Ford suffered unreasonably from his wife, but more from the woman he left her for, Violet Hunt—and he was lucky to find some happiness with Stella Bowen and then even more, in the last nine years of his life, with Janice Biala. Robert Lowell, who met him, sums it all up in the last line of one of the most moving of his poems: 'You were a good man, Ford, and you died in want'.

Ford's five great novels are: *The Good Soldier* (1915) and the Tietjens tetralogy, consisting of *Some Do Not . . .* (1924), *No More Parades* (1925), *A Man Could Stand Up* (1926) and *Last Post* (1928). His good, if flawed novels include the *Fifth Queen* trilogy (1906–8), on Henry VIII's Katherine Howard, and *When the Wicked Man* (1931). Throughout his life he wrote charming poetry; the series of poems he wrote in the Thirties to Janice Biala, *Buckshee*, are rather more than charming, and deserve revival: they convey a sense of the absolute—and holy—sweetness at the heart of Ford the bumbling, romantic, self-deceiving, vain man. That wise sweetness glows at the heart of all his best work.

Pound, Joyce, Wyndham Lewis, Eliot (qq.v.) and Ford are sometimes, because of their pioneering spirit and innovations, known as the 'men of 1914'. Pound, Joyce and Eliot have had their due (and more); Lewis and Ford have not. And yet in terms of intrinsic importance Lewis' and Ford's achievements are greater: their best prose is of higher quality than Pound's or Eliot's poetry.

Ford, thrust by his parents into the Roman Catholic Church when a youth, remained a nominal Catholic all his life; when it suited him, as his biographer Arthur Mizener has said, he could be very Catholic indeed. But he was never a believing Catholic. Considering the impartiality of his treatment of Roman Catholics in his novels, particularly in *The Good Soldier*, Ford cannot other than disingenuously be claimed as a real member of the fold. (Nor, to be fair, has the claim been made: few groups, to their shame, have wanted Ford among them.) By 1914 he had painted a picture of himself—it was not truer to life than anyone else's picture of himself—as an honourable, radical, romantic Tory. This Toryism was of the old-fashioned sort (as George Orwell said in 1946, and it still applies, there are now no Tories: only 'liberals, fascists and the accomplices of fascists'). He was always thoroughly humanitarian in his political opinions, which seldom showed any of the silliness of which he was so capable. His sense of history and of current political situations was excellent.

There is an important sense in which Christopher Tietjens, although a character in a book and not a real man, really is the 'last Tory'. Much has been written about Ford's personal involvement in the characters of *The Good Soldier*; but while it is of course true that there are elements of both his wife and Violet Hunt in the two chief woman characters, and of himself in Dowell, the narrator, and in Edward Ashburnham, he here entirely transcended his own difficulties. No better novel in the realist mode has appeared in this century in any language. The story is simple enough: of the American narrator's unconsummated marriage to a shallow but lustful and deceitful woman, and of their apparently placid but actually fatal relationship with an English couple: a 'good soldier', an honourable and brave man who is corrupted into a liar and a betrayer by his compulsive womanizing, and his Irish Catholic wife. There is disagreement about the narrator: is he a sexual and moral idiot, or a sensitive man? The first view, which depends on a Lawrentian (or Reichian) view of men as undeveloped unless fulfilled sexually, of course reads more irony into the novel as a whole. It is, I believe, untenable: nothing in the text suggests that Dowell would be 'better' as a sexual he-man. There is enough irony in the fact that these four people are 'well behaved': Edward Ashburnham is stupid, but he is a conscientious magistrate and a benevolent and humane landlord. And there is irony in Dowell's well-bred failure to get sexual possession of his wife (and evidence that he wants her); but he is by no means an idiot. *The Good Soldier* is the complex and ironic presentation of an Edwardian tragedy. The novelist is always in perfect control. There is no more formally perfect novel in the language.

Ford became dissatisfied with *Last Post*, the final novel of the tetralogy *Parade's End*; but as Arthur Mizener says, 'it cannot be made to disappear': it was undoubtedly a mistake to reprint the series, as was done in recent years, without it. Fundamentally *Parade's End* is the story of how the Edwardian Tory Christopher Tietjens transforms himself into a modern man: the story of endurance (of war, of a fearsome bitch, of misunderstandings) and finally of survival and love. Christopher's brother Mark, by contrast, chooses to die rather than live in a new age. No books, fiction or non-fiction, reflect more exactly or more profoundly the radical changes that British society underwent between 1910 and 1925. Walter Allen has suggested that the 'Tory Christian' character of Christopher Tietjens is laid on a little too thickly: that it is difficult not to see him as a sentimental creation. This is not a frivolous charge —nothing Allen says is less than sensible and carefully considered—but I think it misses one of the central ironies of the book as a whole: whatever Ford's conscious intentions, Tietjens does not come across simply as the wholly 'good man', who will not break his code. There is an element of caricature in him—of self-criticism. Ford's picture of him hovers, throughout the book, between these two views—as a piece of music may hover between a major and a minor key. He is too good to be true. . . . But is he? This adds to, rather than detracts from, the excellence of *Parade's End*.

Much else might be said of Ford: as a critic, as a writer of travel books, as an editor (the most impractical, but the best of the century), as a man. Arthur Mizener's fat biography is sound, sensible and sensitive, and should do much to gain Ford his rightful place—even if it tends slightly to underestimate him. There has been no English novelist like Ford; it is time he had some of the praise that has been so willingly lavished on his contemporaries.

w. SOMERSET MAUGHAM (1874–1965) wrote many skilful but now mostly dated (though still playable) plays and farces; his fiction cannot be so easily dismissed. With the exception of Franz Werfel (q.v.), he is the most serious popular writer of this century; if he wrote nothing as good as Werfel's earliest poetry, he wrote nothing as nauseous as *The Song of Bernadette* (q.v.). His fiction, even at its slightest, was always intelligent and craftsmanlike, and although he appealed to a middlebrow public he was neither pretentious nor did he manipulate his characters in accordance to set formulas. Maugham is neither brilliant nor profound; he is a sardonic, or sometimes merely wondering, observer of human nature. Even at his tritest he serves up an interesting assemblage of odd facts about human nature. In his best work he is not as limited as some critics have made him out to be. His first novel, *Liza of Lambeth* (1897), written out of his experiences as a medical student, is a warmly indignant book, influenced by Zola but not much resembling him. He wrote a number of other goodish but not spectacular realistic novels, conquered the London stage (*Lady Frederick*, 1912, ran for over a year) and then, in the second year of the First World War, produced his finest although not his best written novel: *Of Human Bondage* (1915). This is a fine realistic novel, and it is not a minor one. It is largely autobiographical, although in it, because of the time at which it was written, Maugham was unable to face his problem of bisexuality. The waitress to whom Philip Carey becomes enslaved may well have been (in Maugham's own life) a vicious and beautiful young man; but the transformation is in any case entirely successful. The 'bondage' in which Philip feels himself to be is not only that of the waitress with whom he is infatuated, but also the whole constellation of beliefs that he has inherited; finally he succeeds in casting them off. But the world of the book is nevertheless an exceedingly bleak and hostile one. This is a novel to which one returns gratefully: for the account of Philip's schooldays, of his years as an art student in Paris (this is particularly vivid and well-realized), above all of his fatal infatuation. What prevents Maugham from being a major writer, the mundane (although beautifully styled) quality of his point of view, is, paradoxically, one of his strengths: he is never pretentious. At his worst, as in *Theatre* (1937), he is simply trivial— but even here he manages to be entertaining. The rest of Maugham's best work is to be found in various short stories and in one more novel, *Cakes and Ale* (1930), a malicious and subtly observed tale about writers; it contains an unfair but uproariously funny caricature of Hugh Walpole (q.v.) as Alroy Kear.

E. M. FORSTER (1879–1970) is Great Britain's chief representative of humanism. He published five novels in his lifetime—*Where Angels Fear to Tread* (1905), *The Longest Journey* (1907), *A Room with a View* (1908), *Howards End* (1910) and *A Passage to India* (1924)—a number of short stories (collected in 1948), criticism, essays and biographies; *Maurice* (1971), a weak novel dealing with his own problem of homosexuality, is posthumous. His finest achievement is, without doubt, *A Passage to India*; after it he wrote no more creative work of significance. Forster's stature as a major novelist undoubtedly depends on this novel: his earlier books are seriously flawed and over-contrived, and in them his blandly old-fashioned technique is usually a hindrance. In *A Passage to India* Forster's creative impulse was strong enough to generate an organic plot, hinging on an ambiguity (what happened in the Marabar Caves between Adela Quest and Aziz? Aziz is tried for attempted rape; but we never know). He conveys a unique sense of the tragedy of the gap that lies between Indians and English-men, even if they do not desire it. Further, while this novel works perfectly on a realistic and psychological level, it also functions on a symbolic level—with the Marabar Caves themselves, and the strange figure of Mrs. Moore, as the two central symbols.

In an excellent (because intelligent and provocative) book of criticism, *Aspects of the Novel* (1927), Forster very interestingly examined and then rejected Henry James's (q.v.) notion that the writer of fiction must above all avoid giving his own point of view; and in his own fiction he is very much the omniscient narrator. And yet, apart from Jane Austen and Samuel Butler, his master is Proust (q.v.). . . . His technique was deliberately old-fashioned, then; but his practice in the last and best of his novels was twentieth-century. The wisdom of Mrs. Moore, although it consists of no more than human good will, is thoroughly 'modern' in its function, and it is still as valid as it was in 1924.

The formative influences on Forster were his life at Cambridge at the turn of the century, his extensive travels—and Cavafy (q.v.), whom he knew. He might well have achieved more had he been able—which he was not—to come to terms publicly (as a novelist) with his homosexuality. The posthumous *Maurice* is sensitive, but it shows how far off he was from facing up to the aspect of himself which so disturbed him.

COMPTON MACKENZIE (1883–1972) wrote two excellent novels, *Sinister Street* (1913–14) and the less well known *Guy and Pauline* (1915), many distinguished others—and a number of light novels that are among the funniest of their time (*Buttercups and Daisies*, in America *For Sale*, 1931, is perhaps the funniest of all). As late as 1956 he turned out a first-class story of a homosexual politician who becomes the victim of blackmail: *Thin Ice*. He has written many books of essays, travel and autobiography. Like Maugham, Mackenzie expresses no higher aim than to 'entertain'; in his comic novels that is just what he does, and without offence; the earlier novels—and to some extent *The Four Winds of Love* (1937–45)—possess a lyricism, a keenness of observation and a psycho-logical insight that go beyond entertainment. Most of his other fiction is spoiled by over-indulgence in sentimental romanticism or deliberate Gaelic eccentricity; but *Sinister Street* at least is genuinely realist throughout.

R. H. MOTTRAM (1883–1971) wrote competent and worthy traditional fiction throughout his long life; but his *The Spanish Farm Trilogy* (1924–6) is important. It is a valuable document of the First World War—the first part, *The Spanish Farm*, was one of the first books in any language to take a detached view—and a notable work of fiction. Mottram was a friend and an admirer of Galsworthy, who encouraged him; but *The Spanish Farm Trilogy* is superior to anything of Galsworthy's: as a critic has pointed out, it escapes Galsworthy's 'social evangelism' (which is not genuine—as D. H. Lawrence saw) and his 'worse sentimentality'. *The Spanish Farm Trilogy* is a quiet book, full of compassionate and restrained observations of the horrors and the courage that characterized the First World War.

FRANK SWINNERTON (1884), who has written invaluable (though not always critically discriminating) friendly-malicious memoirs of his friendships with Bennett, Wells (qq.v.) and many others in *The Georgian Literary Scene* (1935 rev. 1950) and its successors, has been another practitioner of competent fiction throughout a long life. He began with some good (and now neglected) novels in the mode of Gissing (q.v.): he had come up the hard way, and he had known bad health. His study of Gissing (1912) is still one of the best. He has written only one really distinguished novel, *Nocturne* (1917), a charming and memorable love story; as Wells said, 'he can count on this much of his work living'. The best of his later novels is *A Woman in Sunshine* (1944).

HUGH WALPOLE (1884–1941), gifted, promising, immensely successful, never achieved more than competence. The best of his many readable novels is his third, *Mr. Perrin and Mr. Traill* (1911), a psychologically acute study of two schoolmasters. Walpole was intelligent—so much so that Henry James admired him, and not for wholly extra-literary reasons—and he had feeling; when he did not try to do too much he could be highly effective. But he preferred keeping his name in front of the public to cultivating his craft; consequently he produced some atrocious work, such as the pseudo-historical *Rogue Herries* (1930) and its sequels. One of the reasons for this may well have been that he was a (notorious) homosexual with sadistic inclinations (the flogging scene in *Jeremy at Crale*, 1927, clearly shows this)—but he could hardly work out this theme in public. When he tried to do so, as in *Portrait of a Man With Red Hair* (1925) he was near his best. There is a sympathetic biography of him by Rupert Hart-Davis (1952).

II

Victorianism and its last burst of (partial) vigour, Pre-Raphaelitism, survived into this century as Georgianism. This was an actual movement, named after Edward Marsh's anthology *Georgian Poetry 1911–12* (1912), which was the first of five similar collections. The movement itself is unimportant, because Marsh was (by literary standards) a conservative dilettante. It was his love for Rupert Brooke (q.v.), and for Brooke's youthful enthusiasm for some of his contemporaries, that first set him off. (Brooke is Georgian, but, for reasons of contrast, is dealt with as a war poet.) Not all those represented in *Georgian*

Poetry were in fact Georgians: D. H. Lawrence and James Stephens, for example, certainly were not. The word 'Georgian' has come to have a pejorative meaning, and understandably so. One's sympathy must be historical or sociological. As a literary movement it has no redeeming features. It was really a commercial venture (only Marsh's pleasant sentimentality conceals this); and it cannot really be said to have succeeded in its aim of creating a large reading public for poetry (the volumes were to sell very well, as of course verse does in wartime) because what it actually created was a large reading public for verse (with a bit of poetry accidentally thrown in). Georgianism, even as war-clouds gathered, insensitively aimed to perpetuate Victorian values at a time when Victorian standards, procedures and practice were no longer adequate. What may fairly be described as Georgian poetry continues to be written today, both in Great Britain and America: it is escapist in the worst sense (rural fantasies set in a countryside both unthreatened by technology and commerce, and inhabited by servile dream-peasants), flatly traditionalist and uninventive in form, sentimental in attitude, crudely mechanistic in its assumptions about human nature. Much verse that looks modern, either because it is in free verse or because it is spiced up with fashionably up-to-date mannerisms, is also fundamentally Georgian. Here I shall discuss only those Georgian poets who transcended the insulting category. But what of the background out of which both Georgianism and imagism developed?

Of the Victorians ROBERT BRIDGES (1844–1930), the Poet Laureate (1913), THOMAS HARDY (1840–1928) and ALGERNON CHARLES SWINBURNE (1837–1909) survived into this century. Little need be said of Swinburne, who was a spent force long before the turn of the century. It is impossible to say what kind of poet—with his enormous metrical facility, his vigour and his learning—Swinburne might have been had he possessed emotional maturity. Unfortunately he never grew up sexually, and this seriously affected his intellect. It was natural enough for the poets of this century to react against the rhetoric of even his earlier, better poetry; the imitation of Swinburne's lush and imprecise manner (at its most reprehensible in Gilbert Murray's translations of Greek drama, as Eliot, q.v., observed) would have been fatal to a viable new poetry.

Bridges was a conservative innovator (in matters of technique), but wrote not one single good poem. He lacks the energy necessary to a poet. Attempts have been made to rehabilitate him as a poet (notably by Yvor Winters, q.v.), but they are unconvincing. He is at his least conventional in the conversational 'Poor Poll' (in its least attractive aspect an envious and ineffective parody of Eliot's polylingual *montage* in *The Waste Land*, q.v.), but this is not incisive enough, and is too labouredly and exasperatedly eccentric (in place of the modernism Bridges knew he could not achieve) in manner to be of much appeal today. All his poetry, especially the long philosophical *The Testament of Beauty* (1929), is marred by artificiality, lack of feeling (once called restraint but now recognized as frigidity) and unintelligent conservatism. He shrank too much from life—nor could he examine his reasons for doing so. The age still allowed such lack of robustness to be 'good form'. The last long poem, which purports to prove that the natural order is 'good', does not do so in spite of its length. His friend Gerard Manley Hopkins (q.v.) praised Bridges' poetry in general but criticized it in particular. The critic Sir Walter Raleigh, his contemporary, summed up Bridges best: 'Just a shade too little of a blackguard. . . .' Bridges' experiments with classical, quantitative metres have some importance, and doubtless he deserves credit for dimly recognizing the genius of Hopkins—and for eventually giving his poems to the world.

Hardy's novels were all written in the nineteenth century; I shall not discuss them here, since they are essentially of their century. He continued to write poetry, however, until his death. Although he was a traditionalist in both conscious attitude and technique, his poetry has been influential in this century. He is a major poet, and the sheer bulk of his best work continues to surprise. Nor is the good easily separable from the bad. Hardy's poetry springs from a tension between overpowering feelings (for people, for landscape, for justice and for women—whom he saw as instruments of men, whose function in this respect he equated with careless or malign fate) and a courageous and toughly held conviction that life is purposeless or even subject to the dictates of a wanton or malevolent God:

> Let me enjoy the earth no less
> Because the all-enacting Might
> That fashioned forth its loveliness
> Had other aims than my delight.

Hardy represents the tragic and imaginatively articulate side of Victorian unbelief; but he was not an intellectual. He had simplicity. But what continually buoys him up above his faults (they would have been faults, at least, in other writers)—clumsiness of diction, reliance on the poetical rather than the poetic expression ('all-enacting Might'), the simplistic polemicism of his naturalism (for this can be seen as a version of naturalism, even though Hardy believed in fate rather than character or environment as destiny) when it is functioning unimaginatively—is, quite simply, beauty of spirit. To state that a man means what he says is to make no claim at all for him creatively; but to say that he means it when he says such things as Hardy said is to make a very large claim. And Hardy is, indeed, the last indisputable great naïve writer in the English language. He is also the most accomplished portrayer of women in English literature since Shakespeare. Like all naïve writers, he was content to be a part of his times—but he imaginatively transformed the drab rationalism of the late nineteenth century, with its various humanistic consolations: at the heart of his work, as at the heart of Shakespeare's, is a vision of absurdity quite as complete as Camus' (q.v.)—but more robustly tragic. That is why Hardy is 'modern'. He is intrinsically of more importance than any British or Irish poet of the twentieth century, if only because his poetry is validly accessible to a greater audience without playing down to that audience; and his range is wider. And, as Ford (q.v.) wrote in 1925, it was 'first Browning and then . . . Hardy' who 'showed the way for' the imagists (q.v.); '. . . his power to excite—is that . . . he simply takes his lines by the throat and squeezes them until they become as it were mutinously obedient. . . .' Hardy has not attracted the same volume of academic criticism as Eliot and Yeats, but he has been as much read and assimilated. He is an infinitely greater writer.

A. E. HOUSMAN (1859–1936) published his first collection of poems, *A Shropshire Lad*, in 1896; within a few years he was one of the best selling of all twentieth-century poets. He issued *Last Poems* in 1922, and *More Poems* appeared in the year of his death. The best collected edition is *Complete Poems* (1960). While at Oxford Housman fell in love with a fellow-student, Moses Jackson. The exact nature and extent of their relationship is not known, but it affected Housman so much that, a gifted classical scholar, he failed his finals. To make up for this he turned himself into one of the most formidable classical scholars of his day, ending up at Cambridge, 'the other place'. As a poet he worked within the limits of a narrow epigrammatic tradition. Much of his poetry is trite and speciously pessimistic; and it is hardly 'classical', as its admirers used to claim. One of Housman's models is Heine, another is the Greek Anthology; a third, less happily, is Kipling (and his imperialistic ideas). However, despite his frequently poetical triteness, he is at his best an exquisite and moving poet. His poetry arose from the conflict between strong homosexual feeling and a genuinely acute horror of this, reinforced by convention. He remained emotionally immature, as possibly many homosexuals do; but within his limits he did something no one else has done. His 1933 address *The Name and Nature of Poetry*, published separately and then in *Selected Prose* (1961), is wrong-headed in places (as when it equates 'nonsense' with 'ravishing poetry') but contains an understanding of poetry greater than that of the critics (themselves incapable of any poetry) who deplore it. His best poetry is not pessimistic—as he glacially intended—but heartrendingly gloomy and yet tender. His brother LAURENCE HOUSMAN (1865–1959) was an efficient minor essayist, novelist and illustrator; he is most famous for his dramatic biography of Queen Victoria, collected in *Victoria Regina* (1934); this is skilful but sentimental.

No account of modern British poetry is complete without mention of Gerard Manley Hopkins (1844–89). Hopkins, although he was an innovator, was a Victorian poet and a Jesuit priest and he needs to be considered in those contexts if he is to be properly understood. But (with the exception of a few poems that appeared in an anthology published after his death) his poetry did not become available until 1918. Within a decade he had become a major influence.

Hopkins was caught between his duties as a priest (one of the factors in his decision to enter the Society of Jesus two years after his conversion must have been his discovery of his homosexual leanings) and his intense and sensuous joy in the details of nature. His observation of these details was so sharp that he was impelled to invent an ecstatic language to match it. He also expressed his negative moods in violent and vivid language. Hopkins succeeded in his aim of rejuvenating poetic language; he showed the way for the poets of the twentieth century who were trying to break away from the stale Victorian conventions. His 'sprung rhythm' is, essentially, a more flexible, musical way of looking at poetic technique than the metrical one. It is an accentual system, taking into account rising and falling movement; the poet is in effect freer and has more equipment at his command. Attempts to imitate Hopkins' own extreme use of his technique are invariably grotesque: it is too much his own. But the example he set had enormous influence on both the development of 'free' (or irregular) verse and the amount of licence poets allowed themselves. It was Hopkins, too, who first turned to the seventeeth century and the 'metaphysical' tradition of deliberate exploitation of the ambiguities inherent in language.

A rather better and more interesting poet than Bridges was THOMAS STURGE MOORE (1870–1944), a classicist of some skill who 'made' poems rather than dealt with any strong pressure to do so, but whose work is executed with taste and precision—and in an awareness of the exhausted state of fashionable Victorian diction. His poems were collected in four volumes (1931–3); the 1934 *Selected Poems* is still a useful introduction. His correspondence with Yeats (q.v.) is interesting (1953).

Thirteen years older, and considerably less well adjusted to the world, JOHN DAVIDSON (1857–1909), a Scot, was a more gifted and incisive poet who became a victim of what Hugh MacDiarmid (q.v.) admiringly calls 'giantism': the disease of attempting to create a grandiose system, a 'philosophy of life'. When he killed himself a journalist said of him that he had been murdered by Nietzsche (q.v.), of whom he was one of the earliest English explicators. He was a prolific writer: the author of fiction, criticism, translations, epic poems and plays. . . . His philosophy was that 'Man is but the Universe grown conscious'. It is a pity he did not leave it at that. Davidson was right in seeing the need to destroy the pseudo-values of his environment and (this he learned from Nietzsche) the 'Christianity' that it had erected as a defence against the terrors of authenticity. But he expressed this more effectively as a lyrical poet than as an epic poet and dramatist—although there are good things buried in the five *Testaments* (*The Testament of a Vivisector*, 1901; *The Testament of a Man Forbid*, 1901; *The Testament of an Empire-Builder*, 1902; *The Testament of a Prime Minister*, 1904; *The Testament of John Davidson*, 1908). His best poetry, which was popular for a time but then went out of fashion, was published in the Nineties. *John Davidson: A Selection of his Poems* (1961) is an excellent introduction. Among the best of his ballads are 'Thirty Bob a Week', 'A Ballad of a Nun', 'A Ballad of Hell'. Davidson began as a Pre-Raphaelite and decadent, but soon developed out of this manner, discovering his true voice in the ballad-form, in which he has a strength most of the Pre-Raphaelites lack. At his best he was a fine urban poet. And few of his contemporaries could equal 'The Runnable Stag' as a lyric.

W. E. HENLEY (1849–1903) was an invalid (a tuberculous disease brought about the eventual amputation of a foot), and he consequently worshipped not only health, and the feelings of strength that stem from its possession, but also imperialism. His politics were, in fact, offensively jingoist; and one has to say that the spirit of the too famous 'Invictus', rousing at first, is specious. But Henley had another and preferable manner: light, impressionistic, sensitive, delicate. He is at his best in the 'Hospital Sketches', graceful and vivid impressions, in a nearly free verse, of his ordeal in hospital.

The unhappy career of FRANCIS THOMPSON (1859–1907) is a monument to the failure of more or less traditional methods to express the complex and baroque. One has only to compare Thompson's poetry, particularly the famous 'The Hound of Heaven', with that of Hopkins (q.v.) to see its shortcomings. Thompson was a passionate Roman Catholic (his parents were converts) who tried, first, to become a priest, but was refused as unsuitable, and, secondly, to enter his father's profession of physician—he failed here, too. He took to opium and the streets, and for a while lived off the earnings of prostitutes. By the time he was discovered and rescued by a magazine editor, Wilfred Meynell, his health was ruined. Thompson, though gifted, was weak, lazy and without inner resource. 'The Hound of Heaven', influenced by the seventeenth-century poet Richard Crashaw, has some academic virtues (speed, shape, high style), but does not achieve real poetic success: Thompson tries for tough, metaphysical paradox but lapses into semi-hysterical self-indulgence. Hopkins, who dealt with his tendencies towards hysteria and self-indulgence by embracing a strict monkhood, never found the way to God so easily. However, there is something touching about Thompson's work, which is not quite at its best in 'The Hound of Heaven': he manages, at times, to convey both his observation of nature and his profound suffering. His weakness is that he lacks originality of style, and falls back on earlier manners: he is not strong enough to transmute Crashaw's baroque ecstasy, and depends too much on a vague, 'Shelleyan' style.

ERNEST DOWSON (1867–1900) was similarly weak, but a few of his poems are more effective than anything of Thompson's, because he had less grandiose aspirations. He, too, embraced that brand of Roman Catholicism peculiar to the decadents of the late nineteenth century. As a member of the Rhymers' Club he knew Lionel Johnson, Oscar Wilde and W. B. Yeats (qq.v.), its co-founders. The famous 'Non Sum Qualis Eram Bonae Sub Regno Cynarae' ('I have been faithful to thee, Cynara! in my fashion') is only limited, so to speak, by its innate decadence: it perfectly sums up the attenuatedly romantic attitudes of the Nineties poets; it is well done, and, as Eliot observed, it escapes the traditional metres of the time 'by a slight shift'. Better and even more original, however, is 'Spleen'.

OSCAR WILDE (1856–1900) is of course primarily a playwright; but all his plays belong to the nineteenth century, and form no part of modern literature. As a poet he was simply another decadent—although parts of *The Ballad of Reading Gaol* have a certain crude power.

The most gifted of this group of poets was LIONEL JOHNSON (1867–1902), a brilliant classical scholar who, although English, identified himself with his Irish contemporaries: Yeats was his close friend. Johnson had much more to offer, in the way of learning, intelligence, skill and inner poetic resource, than

Thompson or Dowson. His critical book on Thomas Hardy (1894) remains one of the best. He became a Roman Catholic in 1891; when he fell off a bar-stool (he drank heavily) eleven years later he cracked his skull and killed himself. Johnson looked intelligently to the Caroline poets of the seventeenth century for inspiration; through this he was able to achieve a more austere poetry than that of others in his group. He had assimilated Greek and Latin poetry, and unlike most of his contemporaries he designed his poems; even his over-ornamentation (which we can now see as a fault) has elegance. Johnson was not a major poet: his mystical outlook is too vague: his hard-headedness comes out in style but not enough in irony (this was needed to slash sarcastically across the too inebriating God-yearnings). But he was a distinguished minor poet.

Nothing need be said of the turgid poetaster STEPHEN PHILLIPS (1868–1915), whose vastly inflated verse plays, which lack any vestige of merit, captured, for a few years, an audience that could not stomach Kipling or Masefield (qq.v.). His cousin LAURENCE BINYON (1869–1943) is in a different class altogether. Binyon was a scholar and art historian; his translation of Dante's *Inferno* (1933) is still the best: it solves more problems than any other version, including even that of new ones. His poetry was traditional and restrained; his poetic drama (*Brief Candles*, 1938, is the best) is well executed. He did many graceful translations from the Japanese. Then, in old age, he produced his best sequence of poems: *The Burning of the Leaves* (1944), first published in Cyril Connolly's (q.v.) magazine *Horizon* in 1942 under the title of 'Ruins'. All Binyon's poetry had up till then been marred by excessive restraint: here is an example of a fastidious, discerning and deep-feeling poet whose energy was certainly the victim of gentility as well as native diffidence. This was partly overcome in the collection *The North Star* (1941), and then more so—but not wholly—in the final sequence. Binyon's achievement in these poems should not be exaggerated: ultimately he evades the issue (of the Second World War and what it stood for); and the influence of Eliot—on one who had hitherto been a traditionalist—is sometimes unfortunate. But they do show an unusual sensitivity—and flashes of linguistic power. Binyon's earlier poetry, which is also worth investigation, was collected in two volumes in 1931.

ALFRED NOYES (1880–1958), encouraged by the ageing Swinburne and by Meredith, entirely failed to fulfil his early promise—which lay, in fact, in his Swinburnian metrical facility. But the promise, slight though it was, was there—it has been forgotten because of the spurious nature of his popular verse, from which Harold Monro fairly inferred that 'prudent management of rhyme, economy of epithet, love of the true substantive, pleasure in the right verb; imaginative curiosity . . . these apparently, one and all, are unknown to him'. His few decent, very minor poems are in his first collection, *The Loom of Years* (1902).

JOHN MASEFIELD (1878–1967), who became Poet Laureate on the death of Bridges, is now undervalued. It is true that he never quite realized his poetic gifts; but he achieved something vivid and vigorous in the difficult realm of narrative verse (*The Everlasting Mercy*, 1911, and *Reynard the Fox*, 1919, are his best) and he was a competent novelist in the vein of Robert Louis Stevenson (*Lost Endeavour*, 1910; *Sard Harker*, 1924). None of his later verse, or his verse plays, is of account. The forthrightness of the earlier narrative poetry, which shocked some people at the time, is not absolute, and seems tame enough now; but it did introduce a new anti-genteel element (Masefield went to sea and knocked about a good deal before settling down to a literary career); the story of the poacher Saul Kane's conversion in *The Everlasting Mercy* is by no means wholly specious, though when it came to it Masefield could never face up to the full implications of the non-respectability that he implied. One of the most intelligent general comments on Masefield's poetry was made by the critic John Middleton Murry: 'He is seeking always to be that which he is not, to lash himself into the illusion of a certainty which he knows he can never possess. . . .' The illusion was that he could ever be wholly free of that stifling gentility which he seemed, to his first admirers, to be so effectively challenging. But all his prose remained vigorous; and *William Shakespeare* (1911 rev. 1955), although unscholarly, is stimulating where many more sophisticated or learned performances are not.

CHARLOTTE MEW (1869–1928), an eccentric figure, wrote a few memorable poems in an idiom that she forged for herself out of an extremely unhappy life that ended in insanity and suicide. Her talent was recognized by Monro, Hardy, Masefield and de la Mare (qq.v.). Charlotte Mew had something of the gnarled wisdom of W. H. Davies (q.v.); she wrote not of a fanciful world, as she might be expected to have done, but of the unhappy real world that she observed, bird-like, from her sad, shabby-genteel experience: of prostitutes and sailors, in a dramatic verse that is from time to time remarkably effective and moving. Her poetry was collected in 1953.

A younger woman poet of similarly eccentric and lonely demeanour ANNA WICKHAM (1884–1947), may conveniently be classed with Charlotte Mew. She hanged herself when the Chancellor of the Exchequer increased the tax on cigarettes, of which (like Charlotte Mew) she was an inveterate consumer: she lived the latter part of her life in poverty and neglect. She had begun with marriage and hope. Anna Wickham's poetry, which has never been collected, lacks Emily Dickinson's linguistic power, but has something of her epigrammatic quality, and is distinctly individual and, at its best, wisely sardonic. She published three books: *The Contemplative Quarry* (1915), *The Man with a Hammer* (1916) and *The Little Old House* (1921). The contents of the first two books were gathered together in America under the title of the first (1921).

By comparison with these two, ALICE MEYNELL (1847–1922), although a sensitive mind, is ungifted: the language of her poetry never comes near to doing justice to the delicacy of its impulses.

*

J. C. SQUIRE (1884–1958) was a typically Georgian figure: he was critically

GUIDE TO MODERN WORLD LITERATURE

obtuse, being all for 'straightforwardness' (but at times robustly sensible in spite of this beery pseudo-simplicity), over-prejudiced against poetry he could not understand; and he usually stifled his genuine poetic impulses with a blanket of bluff Englishness. In his parodies (*Collected Parodies*, 1921), however, he was often brilliantly funny, for he had the parodist's knack of intuitively catching his victim's manner and then caricaturing it. He was a highly influential editor, and champion of Georgianism, and was knighted in 1933. He ended his days as a forgotten, agreeable drunk, occasionally giving lectures to schools for small fees (he would frequently turn up on the wrong day, or on the right day of the wrong week). He was a kind and generous man, and a better poet than many who now enjoy temporary reputations and have not heard of him. His *Collected Poems* appeared in the year following his death.

EDWARD THOMAS (1878–1917), who was killed in France, is sometimes classified as a Georgian, but he did not appear in Marsh's anthology; nor is he really one of the 'war poets' (Rosenberg, Sorley, Graves, Sassoon, Owen, qq.v.). Though claimed by the Georgians, he does not deserve the epithet except in a few isolated instances. He spent most of his life as a hack critic and editor, under conditions of great poverty (asked for his address, he retorted: 'Ask any publisher in London'); he wrote one novel, *The Happy-Go-Lucky Morgans* (1913). His work in prose is discerning but not distinguished, although his nature essays contain descriptions that anticipate his poetry. He did not begin to write in verse, in his adult life, until persuaded to do so by Robert Frost (q.v.), who was visiting England (1912–14). His first collection, *Poems* (1917), appeared under the pseudonym 'Edward Eastaway'; he was dead before he acquired fame. His *Collected Poems* (1920 rev. 1949) represents, there is no doubt of it, a major achievement. Norman Douglas (q.v.) said of his years as a hack writer (three books a year) that 'the lyrical love of his mind was submerged, imprisoned, encysted in an impenetrable capsule'. But in the last four years of his life this capsule exploded. His range is wider than the frequent label, 'nature poet', implies. He is not a merely descriptive poet: although his observation of the English countryside is exact, he is almost all the time probing the core of sexual melancholy, of solitude, of nostalgia. He used only the technical equipment available to him, but was plainer, less rhetorical, freer, than any true Georgian—and as a whole Georgian editors did not much respond to him. They could not find enough metre or full rhyme; the poems are too conversational; there is an originality that would have disturbed a Georgian.

Thomas often falls into what looks like cliché ('The glory of the beauty of the morning') but then successfully invests the tired phrases with life (he can do it because he means it) as he illustrates them with the beautifully observed particular ('The cuckoo crying over the untouched dew;/The blackbird that has found it, and the dove/That tempts me on to something sweeter than love. . . .'). He knew that he could not penetrate to the heart of what he felt as beauty ('I cannot bite the day to the core'), but in his poetry he strove for a language that would do so. Miraculously he avoided, but without ever evading, the ugly and the urban; his is the last body of work that seeks to define a rural concept of beauty that was finally invalidated by the First World War, by the growth of technology—and by that complex process whereby the anti-human has crystallized, or is still crystallizing, into the political. Given the hideous context of today, the kind of solitude Thomas' poetry explores—as a man he had wandered through it for his nearly twenty years as a hack writer—no longer exists. But it still functions as a metaphor for solitude and for solitudes relieved and/or threatened by love. One of his most remarkable poems is 'The Other', in which he follows a phantom of himself, and tries to come to terms with it; this beautifully illustrates his quality of toughness, by which he refuses to depend on any body or thing to arrive at his answers.

HAROLD MONRO (1879–1932) hardly realized his considerable poetic gifts. Ezra Pound (q.v.) summed it up in a letter to him (of about 1922): 'only HELL—you never had a programme—you've always dragged in Aberbubble and Siphon. . . . One always suspects you of having (and knows you have had) sympathy with a lot of lopp . . .' Monro did weakly succumb to Georgianism, and as generous proprietor of the Poetry Bookshop he did sympathize with far too much 'second-rate lopp'. None of his own verse is as bad, as flaccid and uninventive, as really bad Georgian; but some of it is undeniably Georgian. Monro compromised with his own standards, as the unevenness of his book *Some Contemporary Poets* (1920) clearly shows. And yet Eliot's tribute to him is justified: 'His poetry . . . is more nearly the real right thing than any of the poetry of a somewhat older generation than mine except . . . Yeats's . . . like every other good poet, he has . . . done something that no one else has done at all'. Monro's achievement rests on about a dozen poems, nearly all of them written towards the end of his life. In at least two of these poems ('Friendship', 'The One, Faithful . . .') Monro went further towards a resolution of his bisexual problems than most English-language poets of the twentieth century in similar predicaments have been able to do:

> But, probing, I discovered, with what pain,
> Wine more essential in the end than you,
> And boon-companionship left me again
> Less than I had been, with no more to do
> Than drop pale hands towards their hips and keep
> Friendship for speculation or for sleep.

Even if Monro did dissipate his poetic energy by giving aid to inferior talents, this arose from a generosity that is apparent in the best poems, the most famous of which is 'Bitter Sanctuary', a poem surprisingly far, in manner, from the sonnet-sequence 'Weekend', or the much anthologized 'Milk for the Cat'. What he did in this poem is indeed 'something that no one else has done at all'. There is a valuable (and painful) portrait of the man Monro, as Arnault, in Conrad Aiken's (q.v.) *Ushant*.

W. H. DAVIES (1871–1940) was self-educated; he had been a tramp and pimp in America and England, and wrote lucidly and well of this in *Autobiography of a Super-Tramp* (1908), a minor classic that has remained in print. Before that he had hawked an ill-printed collection of his poems—*The Soul's Destroyer* (1905)—from house to house. It was through the encouragement of Shaw (q.v.) that he became established as a writer. His *Complete Poems* (in texts not impeccable) appeared in 1963. Most of Davies' later poetry and prose is bad: artfully simple, deliberately appealing, slyly mock-innocent (Davies was nothing like as 'simple' as he liked to make out), banal, insipid. But, when he was not trying, he wrote some highly original lyrics—charmingly whimsical, blackly melancholic, mysteriously impudent (as in the famous 'The Inquest'), or, very occasionally, of a genuinely Blakeian simplicity. Davies has been neglected because the bulk of his output is poor and because there is nothing in him for academics; but the reader who does not take the trouble to pick out the jewels from the rubble of imitation stones is missing an exquisite and highly individual minor poet.

WALTER DE LA MARE (1873–1956), undoubtedly in certain respects a Georgian, is a very difficult case; he has not had the serious critical attention he deserves, although there is a general awareness of his worth. The best study of him (1929) is by Forrest Reid; later criticism has been poor. He is distinguished not only as a poet but also as a children's poet (indisputably the greatest of his time), novelist, anthologist and short-story writer. At his weakest De la Mare is lush, excessively romantic and imprecise (as in 'Arabia'); at his best he is unique: quite certainly a poet of major proportions. He has often been described as an 'evader of reality', even by his admirers; this seems obtuse. What is usually called unreality was, for De la Mare, a reality. It is of no use to try to judge the achievement of his finest work by the values propounded in his more self-consciously poetical verse, where he is often thoughlessly romantic. But although he did so often make what H. Coombes has well called 'a routine use of the properties [of] verbal magic and romantic symbol', De la Mare was a master of the world of childhood. Such lines as

> Grill me some bones,' said the cobbler,
>   'Some bones, my pretty Sue;
> I'm tired of my lonesome with heels and soles,
> Springsides and uppers too;
> A mouse in the wainscot is nibbling;
> A wind in the keyhole drones;
> And a sheet webbed over my candle, Susie.
>   Grill me some bones!'

from the (ostensibly) child's poem 'At the Keyhole' make his mastery perfectly clear. He is rhythmically inventive; and he can enter into the world of children —sinister and cruel as well as innocent—with uncanny ease. 'The Song of the Mad Prince' is unthinkable outside the context of childhood, but it is not simply a children's poem: it is unusual in that it is for both child and adult. This poem, in which de la Mare takes on the mask of the 'mad' Hamlet, is one of the subtlest, dramatic and most beautiful that he ever wrote; it shows him at strength: rooted in literature, but not in the literature of escape:

Who said, 'Peacock Pie'?
  The old King to the sparrow:
Who said, 'Crops are ripe'?
  Rust to the harrow:
Who said, 'Where sleeps she now?
  Where rests she now her head,
Bathed in eve's loveliness'?
  That's what I said.

Who said, 'Ay, mum's the word'?
  Sexton to willow:
Who said, 'Green dusk for dreams,
  Moss for a pillow'?
Who said, 'All Time's delight
  Hath she for narrow bed,
Life's troubled bubble broken'?
  That's what I said.

There is rather more of this calibre in De la Mare than has usually been allowed, as his *Complete Poems* (1969) made apparent. A reading of the whole of this strengthens the impression that De la Mare is a major poet. What he alone does, he does so well. It has been something to have, in this century, so exquisite a ponderer on the various mysteries that life offers (even such simple ones as described in the haunting 'The Railway Junction'); after all, the crasser scientists and the least creative critics have between them attempted to remove all element of mystery from life.

De la Mare's fiction is uneven, but at its best it, like the poetry, does what no one else has done. The novel *Memoirs of a Midget* (1921) is a sinister *tour de force* that would long ago have been seen as genuinely expressionistic if it were not for its unashamedly archaic manner. It is a strange and degenerate book; attempts to neutralize its undoubted power and originality by attributing 'unsound' opinions to De la Mare have failed. As to the short stories: as Graham Greene has written, here 'we have a prose unequalled in its richness since . . . Robert Louis Stevenson'. It is, of course, a certain kind of richness ('Stevenson', says Greene, 'comes particularly to mind because he played with so wide a vocabulary—the colloquial and the literary phrase'), and it has its obvious limitations; but as the investigator of what is odd or spectral or puzzingly 'lost' in experience De la Mare has no peer. His total achievement is undoubtedly an important one.

WILFRED WILSON GIBSON (1878–1962), a Yorkshireman, began as a Victorian, but later developed into a determinedly realist poet. During the Thirties he sank into oblivion, although most people are aware of his name through certain narrative poems by which he was well represented in school anthologies. He was one of those (De la Mare was another) who inherited Rupert Brooke's estate. Most of Gibson's best poetry—there is not much of it—is to be found in

Collected Poems 1905–1925 (1926): shrewd, Hardyesque character studies, dramatizing ordinary lives. Unfortunately, although Gibson deserves credit for helping to purge poetry of pseudo-romantic trappings, he is on the whole a somewhat dull and linguistically uninspired poet. He fought in the First World War as a private; his war poems are lucid and realistic, but they lack power— as does most of his work. Yet, mainly in the character studies (not in the school-book narratives, which lack sufficient edge), he did achieve a tiny distinction: a reward for fifty years of 'worthy' writing. His last collection, *Cold Knuckles* (1947), shows no falling off. He wrote a number of moderately efficient verse dramas.

LASCELLES ABERCROMBIE (1881–1938) stands out from amongst the Georgians for his intelligence and excellent criticism. He showed a greater awareness of the seventeenth century than any of his Georgian contemporaries; his *Colloquial Language in Literature* (1931) shows that he wanted to transcend the Georgian limitations. But he was, as one might fairly put it, 'no poet'. His imagery is sometimes interesting and original, but its source seems to be Abercrombie's interest in the metaphysical poets rather than in his poetic impulse. His language as a whole, notwithstanding his images, continually lapses, just as his theme is becoming interesting, into Victorian bathos. He is at his best in his plays (the best are included in *Collected Poems*, 1930), where his psychology is powerful and his plots subtle; but once again it is his language that lets him down. Had he employed prose in them he might have been a major dramatist. His *A Plea for the Liberty of Interpreting* (1930) has some marginal importance in the history of Shakespearean bibliography.

RALPH HODGSON (?1871–1962), who may have been even older than he gave out, was a tough eccentric who from 1940 lived in Ohio (U.S.A.), where he owned a farm. Before that he had worked on newspapers in America and as a graphic artist—and had bred and judged bull-terriers; he was a dedicated spectator of boxing. He is most famous for his poems condemning cruelty to animals. Such a poem as 'The Birdcatcher' not only categorizes the malevolent hunter himself but also, by extension, a certain kind of frigid intellectual. Hodgson, a man of steadfast integrity and strong personality, possessed true distinction; the following famous short poem, 'Reason', displays his epigram-matic and lyrical power:

> Reason has moons, but moons not hers
> Lie mirrored on her sea,
> Confusing her astronomers,
> But O! delighting me.

Hodgson (like Andrew Young, q.v.) is an excellent example of the man who can write really good and relevant poetry strictly within the tradition (De la Mare, who has seemed so much part of it, has unwittingly strained and distorted it to a point where, paradoxically, he is considerably more 'modern' than, say, Cummings, q.v.). His *Collected Poems* appeared in 1961, and is an essential book for real connoisseurs. In both 'Song of Honour', an ecstatic meditative poem

reminiscent of Smart, and 'The Bull', which comes as near to Clare's unsentimental sympathy with animals as any poet has, Hodgson achieved convincing poetry.

JAMES ELROY FLECKER (1884–1915), whom tuberculosis early killed off, was
regarded as one of the central figures of the Georgian movement. And he was,
it is true, low in vitality, firmly anti-realistic and a somewhat pallid pursuer of
'beauty'. However, his poetry is stylistically more distinguished than that of a
mere Georgian: he was intelligently aware of foreign literature—particularly
that of France—and he learned from the Parnassian (q.v.) poets, whom he
tried to emulate in English. His poetry does have a fastidiousness, a deliberate
and studied lack of diffuseness, that is alien to the vague Georgian ideal—
and for this he should be remembered. Flecker spent most of his adult life
in the East, in diplomatic posts. He wrote a good deal, including some readable
fiction and the verse dramas *Don Juan* (1925) and the more famous, lush, dated
but not ineffective *Hassan* (1922).

W. J. TURNER (1889–1946) was born in Australia; but he came to England
as a very young man and remained there until his death. He was a well known
music critic, a novelist—and a notable playwright in *The Man Who Ate the
Popomack* (1922). Turner seldom succeeded in reconciling his wild romanticism
(so wild that it sometimes ran over into irresponsibility and irascibility) with
his satirical impulses; but he was an interesting although uneven poet, who
sought for subtler and profounder themes than he was able to cope with. His
passion for music led him to treat his poetry as a sort of music; this spoiled
much of it. But at his best he is memorable and deceptively simple:

> The sun has come, I know,
>> For yesterday I stood
>> Beside it in the wood—
> But O how pale, how softly did it glow.
> I stooped to warm my hands
>> Before its rain-washed gold;
>> But it was pebble-cold,
> Startled to find itself in these dark lands.

There is a *Selected Poems* (1939); his last collection, *Fossils of a Future Time?*
(1946), is as interesting as anything he did. Yeats (q.v.) was an admirer of his
poetry.

*

Some poets of the Georgian generation remain entirely immune. For all that
the poetry of the Scottish parson (he changed from nonconformist to Church
of England, and was vicar of a parish in Sussex for many years until his retirement) ANDREW YOUNG (1885) is firmly traditional in form, it is never tainted
with the poetical, and it always has acuteness of observation and fine sharpness
of style. Furthermore, Young remained a minority taste until after the Second
World War—his first collections were pamphlets issued somewhat late in life;

his first collection from a regular publisher, *The White Blackbird* (1935) was issued when he was fifty. His poetry has no Georgian affinities, and he, a fastidious user of words, could never have tolerated the slack and styleless meandering that generally characterizes Georgian verse. Young is a tough, precise, even dour poet who says almost all that he has to say through a rapt contemplation of nature. Watching birds through binoculars, he feels his shoulders prick as though he himself were sprouting wings. He has much—if only incidentally—to say about the phenomenon of anthropomorphization. Above all, because of his remarkable sensibility, he is a describer of the natural world of Great Britain that no discerning reader could do without. His *Collected Poems* appeared in 1950. This includes all his lyrics; a later, narrative poem, *Into Hades* (1952), which begins with the poet's funeral, is lively and interesting but less successful. *Nicodemus* (1937), included in the *Collected Poems*, is a straight-forward and effective verse play, quite as good as most essays in this, in the twentieth century, impossible genre.

HUMBERT WOLFE (1885–1940), a Jewish civil servant born in Milan and brought up in Bradford (Yorkshire) was an extremely popular poet: so much so that he stands in danger of being forgotten. This would be a pity, for when not trying to be lushly lyrical (a vein he was very clever at emulating, but in which in fact he never got beyond sentimentality) Wolfe was an accomplished minor satirist and ironist, with a devastating sense of humour. No one has quite this touch ('The Grey Squirrel'):

> Like a small grey
> coffee-pot,
> sits the squirrel.
> He is not
>
> all he should be,
> kills by dozens
> trees, and eats
> his red-brown cousins.
>
> The keeper, on the
> other hand
> , who shot him, is
> a Christian, and
>
> loves his enemies,
> which shows
> the squirrel was not
> one of those.

This is an admittedly fragile and slight exposure of Christian pretensions; and Wolfe usually spoiled such an effect as he gains here by his own pretentiousness. But in the early *Kensington Gardens* (1924) and in *Requiem* (1927) there are several poems as good. He cannot be dismissed as easily as most coffee-table poets.

CHARLES WILLIAMS (1886–1945), poet, dramatist and novelist, had his admirers—including such critics as C. S. Lewis. But his work normally raises grave doubts. His 'cosmic thrillers' are frankly middlebrow, written to raise money. In them the 'belief in the supernatural' is insincere and vulgar: he so patently *disbelieves* in their action. They are nearer to the crudely written occult romances of Dennis Wheatley than to literature. He was a confused, unsatisfactory critic: an obscurantist without even the resources of a C. S. Lewis. His early poetry is a semi-Chestertonian attempt to revive a Victorian style. His most highly praised poetry is in *Taliesin through Logres* (1938) and *The Region of the Summer Stars* (1944), a sequence on the Arthurian legend. No critic, however, has made out a satisfactory case for it: C. S. Lewis could only call it 'gorgeous', with 'profound wisdom'. In fact it is muddy work; what looks like originality is simply disguised archaism; the 'grand style' proceeds to nothing. Behind all Williams' work—particularly the novels—there seems to be something thoroughly unpleasant: the orthodox Christian apologetics conceal a human rather than a merely Christian heresy: one senses Williams hanging masturbatorily over his nasty, midcult images of evil.

FRANCES CORNFORD (1886–1960), wife of the classical scholar Francis Cornford, is most famous for the clever triolet 'To a Fat Lady Seen from the Train' ('O why do you walk through the fields in gloves,/Missing so much and so much?/O fat white woman whom nobody loves. . . .'); but she wrote other tiny but charming and distinctive poetry. She seldom, unless in her diction, fell victim to Georgian sloppiness. Her *Collected Poems* appeared in 1954.

ARTHUR WALEY (1889–1966) has exercised a considerable influence on the development of English poetry through his brilliant and poetic translations from the Chinese. These, admired by Pound (and superior to Pound's essays in the genre) and Yeats, represent a remarkable achievement, and are perhaps as substantial a contribution to modern poetry. The translations—*170 Chinese Poems* (1919), *The Book of Songs* (1937), *Chinese Poems* (1946)—are done into a sensitive, rhythmically impeccable free verse; the sense is not really Chinese (how could it be?), but it introduced into English poetry as many new attitudes as new procedures. Waley's translations helped English poets to regain something of the spontaneity and lyricism that are so difficult to attain in twentieth-century poetry without resort to cliché. Again, in his less direct way, Waley has influenced the use of imagery in English poetry almost as much as Pound: the Chinese poems he translated employed concentrated images in place of mere description. His influence has been subterranean but (almost) all-pervasive.

*

The burst of creative activity that took place in Ireland at the turn of the century is sometimes called the Irish literary renaissance. It was not, however, a movement, but rather the result of the sudden diversion of national energy from politics to literature after the Parnell scandal (1892). The main activity was in the drama (this is discussed in the appropriate section), but there was also a Gaelic revival (and some translations out of the language of Ireland's only wholly native culture) and a resurgence of poetry. PADRAIC COLUM (1881–1972), dramatist (he helped to found the Irish National Theatre), auto-biographer and folklorist, wrote attractive poetry for almost the whole of his long life. (He came to America at the beginning of the First World War and remained there until his death.) Colum's poetry has a quality with which, as L. A. G. Strong said, 'literary criticism has little to do': 'simplicity', which 'cannot be analyzed'. Colum's plays, discussed elsewhere, are important; but so is his poetry, which ought to be better known. Some of it has passed back into the folk tradition from which it came. . . . It is remarkable that Colum never spoiled the purity of his gift in his near sixty years of exile in America (and Hawaii); his fairly frequent visits to Ireland seem to have protected him from sentimentality and feyness. His *Collected Poems* (1953) is an essential part of any comprehensive library of twentieth-century poetry in English. Although his poetry always has a lilt, it is not a monotonous one—he has an exquisite and original ear, as the deservedly famous 'She Moved Through the Fair' demonstrates. His subtlety, elegance and fine craftsmanship are all evident in 'Wild Ass':

> The wild ass lounges, legs stuck out
> In vagrom unconcern:
> The tombs of Archaemenian kings
> Are for those hooves to spurn.
>
> And all of rugged Tartary
> Lies with him on the ground.
> The Tartary that knows no awe
> That has nor ban nor bound.
>
> The wild horse from the herd is plucked
> To bear a saddle's weight;
> The boar is one keeps covert, and
> The wolf runs with a mate.
>
> But he's the solitary of space,
> Curbless and unbeguiled;
> The only being that bears a heart
> Not recreant to the wild.

Colum, 'whose goodness and poetic innocence speak at once to all that is good and innocent in his audience' (L. A. G. Strong), is one of the very few English-language poets to draw his strength from tradition throughout his career.

Poet's Circuits (1960), a collection of poems published in his eightieth year, is as pure and strong as ever.

Æ (ps. GEORGE WILLIAM RUSSELL, 1867–1935)—he wrote an early article under the pseudonym 'Aeon'; the printer dropped the last two letters, and he stuck to the result—was a prolific and active member of the Irish revival: in fact, he and his close friend Yeats dominated it. He was an interesting man, helplessly divided between active social idealism (half his time was given up to founding co-operatives and trying to persuade the farmers to abandon their wasteful and inefficient methods) and a mysticism that he acquired from the reading of oriental literature. His activities are often described as political. This is unfair: Russell was no purveyor of clichés or seeker after power, but was honest, meant what he said, and was a competent economist and, far from being an 'expert' (in the meaningless manner of politicians), was actually an authority on agricultural matters such as soil conditioning; he retained his sympathy for the poor. Furthermore, Russell so disliked Irish politics after the First World War that he spent his last years in England, where he died of cancer. One may learn much about the personality of Russell from his *Letters* (1961), which have been well edited and annotated by Alan Denson. So far as his poetry is concerned (there is a *Collected Poems* of 1926; *Selected Poems*, 1935, contains much of his best poetry) Æ (he kept this name for his 'mystical' and poetic identity) is essentially an Irish Platonist: this world is unreal, and our only clues to that real world, of which it is the shadow, are dreams and visions of beauty. Yeats said, brilliantly, that his poems had 'a mind of scented flame consuming them from within'. At their best they faithfully describe their author's trance-like mood—for Æ was not a vague dreamer: he had experienced what he tried to convey. But whereas Yeats, who shared his combination of interests, was able to evolve his own style, Æ had to fall back on a diction and manner not quite his own: he could only talk of 'the breath of Beauty', where Yeats could eventually supply actual particulars of beauty. . . . But as a minor Celtic twilight poet Æ is distinguished: delicate, sincere, with a subdued glow. 'Exiles' is characteristic:

> The gods have taken alien shapes upon them,
> Wild peasants driving swine
> In a strange country. Through the swarthy faces
> The starry faces shine.
>
> Under grey tattered skies they reel and strain there:
> Yet cannot all disguise
> The majesty of fallen Gods, the beauty,
> The fire beneath their eyes.
>
> They huddle at night within low, clay-built cabins;
> And, to themselves unknown,
> They carry with them diadem and sceptre
> And move from throne to throne.

One of Æ's most valuable books, which deserves revival, is about his own poetry and how it came to be written: *Song and its Fountains* (1932). His religious thought, which contains some cogent criticisms of Christianity, is interesting and original; as thought—although not as a vehicle for poetry—it is superior to Yeats' elaborate system. There have been few kinder literary men in this century.

It was Russell who rescued JAMES STEPHENS (1882–1950) from life in an office, and introduced him to the literary world. A few years afterwards, with the generosity and shrewdness characteristic of him, he spoke of him as 'a poet without a formula', 'perplexed' but moving 'down to earth'. Russell was referring to the division in Stephens between comic, faun-like, impudent elf— and poet-as-angel; this conflict was resolved in his best poetry. In his prose Stephens succeeded admirably both as realist and as fantasist. Joyce (q.v.) regarded him very highly. His first success was the novel *The Crock of Gold* (1912), one of the best of modern fairy stories. The stories in *Etched in Moonlight* (1928) show him in more realist vein: he is in debt to Moore (q.v.) for his material, but introduces a lyrical quality that is his own. As a poet he is most attractive: more sophisticated than Colum, he is nevertheless simple and innocent without guile. His Irish charm (of the best variety) is revealed in the celebrated 'The Centaurs'; occasionally he strikes a deeper, almost Blakean note, as in 'The Shell' and 'What Thomas An Buile Said in a Pub': here God is going to strike the unsatisfactory earth, but Thomas (he claims) tells him

'Stay,
You must not strike it, God; I'm in the way:
And I will never move from where I stand.'
He said, 'Dear child, I feared that you were dead,'
And stayed his hand.

'Little Things', too, strikes exactly the right sweet and simple note. Some of the poems in *Strict Joy* (1931) and *Kings and the Moon* (1938) are as good as anything in the *Collected Poems* (1926); Lloyd Frankenberg's *A James Stephens Reader* (1962) is an excellent job—but a more substantial selection from the poetry is still urgently needed.

The poetry of WILLIAM BUTLER YEATS (1865–1939) has attracted much criticism and exegesis, a high proportion of which consists of wilful projection (of the critics' own predilections) or frigid abstractions. Considering his intrinsic and extrinsic importance he has, in fact, attracted surprisingly little really good, lucid criticism—although a few of the straightforwardly explanatory guides and handbooks collect facts that are indispensable to an understanding of his poetry. Yeats is clearly a major poet; but the high reverence in which he is held frequently conceals an inability to come to terms with him. The 'philosophical' system which he developed is, in fact, one about which it is impossible not to have reservations.

He was the son of J. B. Yeats, a lawyer turned painter, whose family originally came from England—but had been in Ireland since the seventeenth century;

his mother's family, also English, had been in Ireland for a considerably shorter period. Yeats began as a vaguely Pre-Raphaelite poet; but from the beginning his manner was different from that of his friends Dowson and Johnson (qq.v.) because he had Sligo folk-lore to fall back on: this acted as an effective antidote to his Pre-Raphaelite vagueness and dreaminess. Of the poems of this first period, much of it spent in London, the Irish ones are the strongest: they are the most down to earth, precise, natural, unforced. That Yeats was likely to develop into a poet of genius was already apparent in 1889, when he wrote 'Down by the Salley Gardens', 'an attempt to reconstruct an old song from three lines imperfectly remembered by an old peasant woman' in Sligo. Clearly the author of this beautiful song understood how real poetry sounded. During the Nineties Yeats wrote plays, and was active with Lady Gregory (q.v.) and Douglas Hyde in founding the Abbey Theatre (1900).

As he matured Yeats sought to purge his language of excessive romanticism (the extent to which he succeeded may be seen in the *Variorum Edition* of his poems, 1957; the fullest, definitive *Collected Poems* appeared in 1956). He clung on to the poetically formal (he never really abandoned it) as his expression of the high, aristocratic calling of the poet, and as an appropriate response to the mysteriousness and magic of the natural—as distinct from the 'ordinary', sordid, commercialized—world. But he laced his formal language with colloquialese, to achieve an effect unique in English poetry. The style he wanted to create eschewed abstraction and cliché, and yet it was based in Irish tradition. Yeats, although he fell early under the influence of Blake, Shelley and neo-Platonic ideas in general, could not remain immune to Irish aspirations. The conflict between the ethereal, the immaterial, and the concreteness of Irish nationalism produced, in fact, some of his best poetry. During the Nineties he was associated with the Socialist League; but in the first ten years of this century, under the influence of visits to Lady Gregory's country house, Coole Park, and of his convictions of the poet's high calling, he began to evolve his feudal idea. This, which involved a total rejection of middle-class materialism, an enlightened aristocracy and a partly idealized peasantry (which knew how to keep its place), was both unrealistic and politic-ally naïve; but it did not prevent Yeats writing meaningful poems in the important collections *The Green Helmet* (1910) and *Responsibilities* (1914). It was in this period that Yeats was in love with the actress and patriot Maud Gonne, who refused to marry him and caused him much sexual frustration and despair. In 1917 he married.

By this time his poetry had entered into a third phase: in response to Pound (whom he knew well) and imagism (qq.v.) he began to evolve a laconic, even epigrammatic manner; at the same time, more independently, he had become increasingly concerned with mysticism (oriental and neo-Platonic) and with the 'occult'. His wife claimed mediumistic powers, and she faked (with the best of intentions: to help him) 'automatic writing', which he used as raw material for his poetry. Yeats believed that this writing was dictated by spirits, and it helped him to evolve the symbolic system he outlined in *A Vision* (1925 rev. 1937). The poetry of *The Wild Swans at Coole* (1919), for all its conversational quality, is technically finer than anything preceding it. It is rhythmically more subtle, and it plays an important part in freeing English verse from metrical (i.e. iambic) monotony.

From here on Yeats proceeded into his penultimate phase. This is the period of his richest poetry, in which he combines a number of themes: the conflicts between the spirit and the flesh, 'madness' and cool reason, permanence and change. In 1934 he underwent the Steinach 'monkey gland' operations—for sexual 'rejuvenation'—and this ushered in the poetry of his final phase: wild, lustfully romantic once again—and yet conscious of 'sin' and 'the foul rag-and-bone shop of the heart'. Yeats won the Nobel Prize in 1923. Since his death he has been almost universally regarded as the greatest English-language poet of this century. However, the viewing of him from a position of over-reverence has not helped towards an understanding of him—any more than it has helped in the case of Shakespeare. . . . A good deal of nonsense has been written about Yeats by academic critics who know nothing of poetry's roots in real life. It has become exceedingly difficult to tell the truth about him—to criticize him at all —without heaping abuse upon one's head. Thus, when Conor Cruse O'Brien (the most gifted Irish critic of his generation), who admires him, asked the question, 'How can those of us who loathe [Yeats's] politics continue . . . to love the poetry . . .?', he brought coals of fire upon his head. However, he convincingly proved that Yeats's politics, *qua* politics, were naïve, disagreeable and opportunistic (his record as a Senator in the Twenties, when he supported Protestant landed interests, is not good by any standards); and critics do have the right to ask the question. The relationship between poetry and virtue is hardly an irrelevant one; and Yeats's politics, naïve or not, are humanly reprehensible. Auden (q.v.) has asked a similar question of the 'occult' beliefs: 'How on earth . . . could a man of Yeats's gifts take such nonsense seriously?' And he goes on to point out, further, that since Yeats was a 'snob' (it is a fair word, and it fits in with his politics), it is all the more remarkable that he believed in 'mediums, spells, the Mysterious Orient'.

The problem is this: Yeats's politics are stupid or humanly disgraceful, or both; his 'philosophical' system, as outlined in *A Vision*, is a synthesis of vulgar rubbish, intellectually ill-digested lore from neo-Platonism and what Auden calls the 'Mysterious East', and Ancient Greece and elsewhere—and of the insensitive, authoritarian politics, too; and yet the poetry is admired—and is almost always interpreted in the terms of *A Vision*. . . .

The short answer is that it does not matter in the least what Yeats's ideas actually mean—*but what, in his poetry, he meant by them*. By no means all the elements in his system are specious in themselves; one may argue, without granting intellectual or philosophical respectability to the system itself (it simply doesn't have it), that Yeats responded intuitively to what was important in it, and that his responses are contained in his poems rather than in his obscure and difficult expository prose. Or one might agree with L. C. Knights: 'Measured by potentiality, by aspiration, and by the achievement of a few poems, it is as a heroic failure that one is forced to consider Yeats's poetic career as a whole'. For, as Knights goes on to say, Yeats thought that 'Unity of Being' is impossible without 'Unity of Culture'; and yet he realized that 'Unity of Culture', in the face of a mechanized society drifting towards culture-less technocracy, is itself increasingly impossible.

The fundamental symbolism of the poems in the two books regarded by the majority of critics as Yeats's greatest—*The Tower* (1928) and *The Winding Stair* (1929)—and of the later poems, is fairly simple: our life is a walk up a spiral staircase in a tower; we keep covering the same ground, but at a different height; because we travel in a 'gyre' (Yeats's word for a spiral), we both go round in a circle and yet make progress; the point, of final understanding, the tip of the spiral, where we are 'above' every place we have been before, is also the point of death; thus the summit of the tower is ruined. History, too, is for Yeats composed of gyres (cycles), as he makes most clear in 'The Second Coming', which he wrote in 1920 and published in 1921:

Turning and turning in the widening gyre
The falcon cannot hear the falconer;
Things fall apart; the centre cannot hold;
Mere anarchy is loosed upon the world,
The blood-dimmed tide is loosed, and everywhere
The ceremony of innocence is drowned;
The best lack all conviction, while the worst
Are full of passionate intensity.

Surely some revelation is at hand;
Surely the Second Coming is at hand.
The Second Coming! Hardly are those words out
When a vast image out of *Spiritus Mundi*
Troubles my sight: somewhere on sands of the desert
A shape with lion body and the head of a man,
A gaze blank and pitiless as the sun,
Is moving its slow thighs, while all about it
Reel shadows of the indignant desert birds.
The darkness drops again; but now I know
That twenty centuries of stony sleep
Were vexed to nightmare by a rocking cradle,
And what rough beast, its hour come round at last,
Slouches towards Bethlehem to be born?

This is an example of Yeats at his most powerful; it embodies both his rejection of Christianity as a system, and his religious sense; furthermore, it does not really depend for its full poetic effect on a knowledge of the system of thought behind it: the opening image of the first two lines is self-evident: the falcon breaks free, goes out of control.

It is often asserted that the two famous Byzantium poems, 'Sailing to Byzantium' and 'Byzantium' (they appear, respectively, in the 1928 and 1929 volumes), written some years later, exercise their power before any knowledge of their symbolic patterns has been gained by the reader; this is true, but perhaps to a more limited extent than has been realized or admitted. These and other poems of the late Twenties and early Thirties contain magnificent lines, but they also contain elements as pretentious as the 'system' upon which they are too carefully and calculatedly based; either the spontaneity of the original impulse has been eliminated (Yeats first wrote them out in prose), or there never was a true impulse; after they have been fully examined they shrink into something less profound than their grand surface suggests. Perhaps the poems in *The Wild Swans at Coole*, however, have had less consideration than they deserve: are not these more central to humanity, less concerned with the poet himself, than the more spectacular ones of the late Twenties and early Thirties?

In any case, Yeats is not on the level of Rilke, Vallejo, Valéry, Blok. . . . He failed because his sophistication failed. Being sensitive to and monumentally aware of the demands of this century, he tried to transform himself from a naïve to a sentimentive poet (qq.v.); his effort appeared to be much more successful than that of (say) Gerhardt Hauptmann (q.v.); but ultimately it was not successful. He possessed consummate technical skill and epigrammatic mastery —but his intellect was not strong, and he sought refuge in the over-factitious. The metaphysical complexity of the Byzantium poems, for example, is ultimately a factitious rather than a poetic element in them. The much vaunted 'intellectual power' of these poems has been exaggerated; whatever qualities they may have, real intellectual power is hardly one of them. Passion is. But, despite the public air, it is an egotistic passion. The incredible richness of most of these poems has been bought at a price; the comparative simplicity of the poems in *The Wild Swans at Coole* suggests this. And yet they, too, can attain simplicity:

> When such as I cast out remorse
> So great a sweetness flows into the breast
> We must laugh and we must sing,
> We are blest by everything,
> Everything we look upon is blest.

*

T. S. Eliot (q.v.), although not officially one of the imagist poets, stated (1953) that the London imagist group of 1910 is 'usually and conveniently taken, as the starting-point of modern poetry' in the English language. Ezra Pound (q.v.) was the moving spirit behind this group; but others in it were important. Imagism was never clearly enough delineated to allow of precise definitions; however, one can fairly say of it that it represented 'British-American expressionism'. It was, however, less violent and aggressive, generally less self-confident and extensive in its aims, and more limited in its results, than German expressionism (q.v.). Its poets were on the whole less gifted. The intrinsic importance of every self-consciously 'imagist' poem is minor—or even trivial. But to claim that 'apart from Pound, and also Lawrence, . . .' the imagists 'have no importance' (John Holloway) is plainly wrong: Eliot's statement that modern Anglo-American poetry has its starting-point in imagism is authoritative. The actual poetry of the imagist anthologies was trivial, theoretical. But it was not unimportant.

Apart from the effervescent and ever-active Pound, the chief figure in the imagist group was the philosopher T. E. HULME (1883–1917), a victim of the First World War. Hulme did not have time to mature, but he is none the less an important and prophetic thinker. The work he left was collected by his friend Herbert Read (q.v.) in *Speculations* (1924; 1960) and *Notes on Language and Style* (1929); *Further Speculations* was edited in 1955 by Sam Hynes. Five of his poems were printed by Pound at the end of his own *Ripostes* (1912) as 'The Complete Poetical Works'; further poems were added by Alun Jones in his useful *The Life and Opinions of T. E. Hulme* (1960). Hulme's poems, delicate, elegant, beautifully phrased, are the best produced by the imagist movement; we have tended to take them for granted. His thinking was confused: he preferred, as Read wrote, 'to see things in the emotional light of a metaphor rather than to reach reality through scientific analysis', and this led him to some foolishly extreme conclusions, such as that *all* romantic poetry was sloppy, or that 'fancy' is to be preferred to 'imagination' (his argument on this point is peculiarly confused and inane). However, it is unfair to call him a 'premature fascist'. He was perceptive about the faults of democracy and made noises about authoritarian or monarchist regimes—but he was never exposed to the reality of fascism, and actually put to the test; there is much in the fragments he left behind that could be taken as 'proto-anti-fascist'. . . . He studied for a time under Bergson (q.v.), and from him he gained his pre-dilection for the concrete and for the notion of qualitative, 'real time'. Bergsonism hardly chimes in with authoritarianism. . . .

However, this is not the place to examine the inconsistencies of Hulme's thought; the main point is that he was prophetically aware of the fact that the twentieth century would see a drastic break away from types of thinking that had been traditional since the late fifteenth century. He misdiagnosed the nature of this revolution, confusing it with his own brash neoclassicism, and he was guilty of over-simplifications (as when he claimed that blank verse, being new, had alone been responsible for the Elizabethan efflorescence); he wrongly thought of all romantics as Pelasgian optimists. But his programme for poetry—and for intellectual life and art in general—was, although confused, sympto-matic: neoclassical, abstract (non-representational), 'royalist', 'hard' (as against 'romantic', 'softness' or sloppiness), intellectual (not emotional), precise (not vague), 'religious' (in the broad, public sense), pessimistic (man is seen as a limited and sinful creature; only his art raises him above the status of an animal). We can see many of these lines of thought converging in the positions

233

taken up by Eliot and Wyndham Lewis—and by the anarchist Herbert Read. Yet Hulme's own poetry, instructive in intention, is by no means, of course, non-romantic:

> Three birds flew over the red wall into the pit of the setting sun.
> O daring, doomed birds that pass from my sight.

The actual starting-point of imagism may be traced back to Hulme's formation of a 'Poets' Club' at Cambridge in 1908; he wrote and published one of his most famous poems, 'Autumn', in that year. Soon afterwards he got into a fight in a pub and was expelled from the university, whereupon he appeared in London. Here he met F. S. FLINT (1885–1966) and Pound. In 1909 a group of poets, including Hulme, Pound and Flint, began meeting in a Soho restaurant. Out of these meetings, the subject of which centred on poetic technique and French and Japanese poetry, was eventually evolved the following credo (published by Flint in 1913): '1. Direct treatment of the "thing" whether subjective or objective. 2. To use absolutely no word that does not contribute to the presentation. 3. As regarding rhythm: to compose in the sequence of the musical phrase, not in sequence of a metronome'. And Pound added a note in the course of which he referred to an image as 'that which presents an intellectual and emotional complex in an instant of time'.

By 1913 Pound, as was his wont, had taken over: the group he now called 'Les Imagistes' (active in 1912–14 and rightly regarded as the true imagists), which did not include Hulme but acknowledged his influence, was organized and publicized by him. The chief members, besides Pound and Flint, were the American H.D. (q.v.) and the Englishman who became her husband for a time: RICHARD ALDINGTON (1892–1962). The first anthology of imagism, *Des Imagistes*, appeared in 1914. The British poets included, besides Aldington and Flint, were Ford and Joyce (qq.v.). Soon after this the American poetastress Amy Lowell gained control of the imagist group—and imagism quickly turned into what Pound called 'Amygism'. (This is a part of literary history— several good poets, including Lawrence, q.v., and some of the original imagists, were represented in Amy Lowell's anthologies—but it is not important.)

Many of the attitudes subsumed under the term imagism are peculiar to Pound, or were initiated by him, and have been discussed in the section devoted to him. The imagist poems themselves were, as has been mentioned, small or trivial affairs; but the state of mind which produced them was modernist. The actual imagist poem concentrates so hard on being visually exact and vivid that it hardly has time, in its brief life, to demonstrate the anti-logical direction of its origins. But both Hulme (through Bergson) and Pound rejected ordinary logic as an acceptable surface for poetry: Hulme spoke (1908) of a new impressionism, and of an introspective (rather than heroic) poetry that would deal 'with expression and communication of momentary phases in the poet's mind'; Pound resorted to the Chinese ideogram (q.v.), or to his understanding of it—which was entirely alogical. It was the imagists—again, chiefly Hulme and Pound—who put forward 'free verse' as the most appropriate vehicle for poetry. This, then, was what was most modernist, most expressionist, about imagism: its assumption that poetry communicated metaphorically rather than logically.

Milton and, in the nineteenth century, Arnold had written 'free verse': verse in irregular lines. Whitman had not obeyed metrical laws—although his verse is by no means 'free'—and neither had a number of other nineteenth-century poets after him. But imagist free verse is not really 'free' at all; rather, as Pound wrote, it is 'a rhythm . . . which corresponds exactly to the motion or shade of emotion to be expressed'. This left the poets themselves free of rules; it did not mean that poetry was now to become a kind of chopped up prose.

Whenever English poetry has radically changed its direction (in, for example, the sixteenth and twentieth centuries) it has turned to foreign poetries. Surrey and Wyatt and their minor contemporaries turned to Italy for the sonnet and blank verse; Pound and his contemporaries turned to the poetry of China and Japan, and of the French symbolists. Directly and indirectly, then, English-language poetry of this century has taken sustenance from elsewhere.

Flint, an important figure in the history of imagism, but possessed of an 'almost imbecile modesty' (Aldington), was a civil servant (Chief of the Overseas Section, Statistics Division); he translated Verhaeren (*Love Poems*, 1916; *Plays*, 1920) and others, and published three volumes of original poetry—the last of these appeared as long ago as 1920. Flint, whom Ford called 'one of the most beautiful spirits of the country' (did he suggest some aspects of Tietjens, also in the Statistics Division?), had an exquisite gift; unfortunately it was too slight—or perhaps fragile is the apter word—to fully convey the acuteness of his sensitivity. He rather too frequently fell back on visual preciosity: 'Under the lily shadow/and the gold/and the blue and mauve/that the whin and the lilac/pour down on the water,/the fishes quiver. . . .' (Flint) is not of the quality of the briefer 'Green arsenic smeared on an egg-white cloth. . . .' (Pound). Nor do Flint's longer poems ('Hats', 'Otherworld') quite come off. 'Hats', an attack on the complacent bourgeoisie very much in the manner of Richard Aldington, lacks originality and linguistic edge. However, a few of his shorter poems have the vivid sharpness of good etchings: this one is actually called 'Eau Forte':

> On black bare trees a stale cream moon
> Hangs dead, and sours the unborn buds.
>
> Two gaunt old hacks, knees bent, heads low,
> Tug, tired and spent, an old horse tram.
>
> Damp smoke, rank mist fill the dark square;
> And round the bend six bullocks come.
>
> A hobbling, dirt-grimed drover guides
> Their clattering feet—
>   their clattering feet!
>   to the slaughterhouse.

Richard Aldington, poet, novelist, translator, critic and biographer, never realized his potentialities. A man of learning, sensibility and even some genius, he turned into an exhausted hack. His last works, critical and biographical, are worth reading; but they are enervated and frequently exasperated in tone (especially the biography of T. E. Lawrence). Aldington, who fought in the First World War, suffered from a tendency to incoherence and bitter, convulsive rage; it is most apparent in his novel *Death of a Hero* (1929)—about war and its prelude and aftermath—which has passages of power but which is written in too headlong a style. When Aldington had his emotions under control he was interesting; too often he is either debilitated or hysterical; he seldom does justice to his intelligence. His *Complete Poems* appeared in 1948. One of his best and most self-revealing books is the autobiographical *Life for Life's Sake* (1941).

As a poet, Aldington was seldom self-confident enough even to search for his own voice. From elegant imagist he moved (perhaps under Pound's influence) to pastiche of the styles of previous centuries (in his 1923 collection, *Exile*). The phantasmagoric *A Fool i' the Forest* (1925), one of the long poems of disillusion written as a response to Eliot's *The Waste Land* (Aiken's *Senlin* is another), is his most original work, and the one that most nearly pinpoints the nature of his disabling pain—an alarming combination of cynicism, sense of failure, blurred emotionalism, hysteria, frustration and satirical indignation. As a whole Aldington's poetry fails to throw off sufficiently the mere posture of romanticism; surprisingly, a good deal is taken for granted, and this operates as a sort of background of cliché. Aldington knew ancient Greek poetry well, but did not learn enough from it. His violently anti-bourgeois attitude is unsubtle and over-romanticized.

The poetry of Eliot, which to a large extent developed out of imagism and the poetic mood in which that movement originated, was one of the factors that led to the clear emergence of a 'modern' style in the Thirties. Another, less immediately obvious, factor was the poetry of some of the men who fought in the trenches in the First World War; their work originated in an ambience more or less Georgian—the exigencies of the war jerked them out of this complacency.

The Sitwells offered a third, minor but lively challenge to Georgianism. The comment that this trio belong 'more to the history of publicity than to the history of poetry' (Leavis) is manifestly unfair in the case of SACHEVERELL SITWELL (1897), and both EDITH SITWELL (1887–1964) and OSBERT SITWELL (1892–1969) did many things that transcend mere publicity. Undoubtedly the Sitwells, especially Edith, were frequently tiresome and exhibitionistic; the 'progressive' anthology *Wheels* (1916), edited by Edith, contained mostly mediocre work; there was a strident egocentric note about most of Edith's public statements and critical pronouncements; her fiction (*I Live Under a Black Sun*, 1937, on Swift), criticism and biography are spoiled by a jarring, sometimes hysterical note that is in fact, not confidence or certainty, but spinsterish self-love. None the less, although she became a bore, Edith's earlier poetry has seldom, since her death, had its due.

Osbert Sitwell was an amusing, accomplished and clever satirist (*England Reclaimed*, 1927, 1949; *Wrack at Tidesend*, 1952; *On the Continent*, 1958); but, as Conrad Aiken (q.v.) said in 1928, he 'never disturbs us, he never reveals'. As an essayist and critic he is pompous but often shrewd and informative. His best book, and this really is 'revealing', is his five-part autobiography: *Left Hand, Right Hand* (1944), *The Scarlet Tree* (1946), *Great Morning* (1947), *Laughter in the Next Room* (1948) and *Noble Essences* (1950). The autobiography is good because it does not take up a defensive position ('I belonged by birth, education, nature, outlook, and period to the pre-war era'), but simply records. Not the least excellent passages deal with the eccentric Sitwell father, Sir George, who, among other things, invented a toothbrush that played 'Annie Laurie' as it brushed the teeth and a 'small revolver for shooting wasps'. Osbert Sitwell also wrote one perceptive novel about the provincial England of 1914, before the holocaust of the First World War: *Before the Bombardment* (1926).

Sacheverell Sitwell is a more limited writer. His many travel books are self-consciously aesthetic, and evade seriousness; his writings on baroque art and architecture are learned but curiously neutral in their effect. His poetry, notably *Canons of Giant Art* (1933), is eccentric, accomplished, artificial; it has unmistakable quality, but the most diligent investigation fails to yield an answer to the question, 'What quality?' What Sacheverell Sitwell has is a manner; but this, elegant and assured, conceals a total lack of poetic conviction —the sad emptiness of a man born into the wrong time.

Edith was at once the most eccentric and most poetically gifted of her family. She was never more than a minor poet; but her verbal virtuosity and dexterity have hardly been equalled, within traditional limits, in this century. She chose not to draw upon her personal experience, but instead to construct an aristocratic-surrealist world that owed much to her interest in painting. The value of this lies in its style and its arch pseudo-innocence; resolutely avoiding the serious, the grotesqueness of Edith Sitwell's play-world reflects the grimness of the sexual experience (itself a narcissistic indulgence, or even celebration, of lack of sexual contact) she eschewed. 'Colonel Fantock', one of the more revealing of her poems, is haunted by the shadow of incest and degeneration. The most successful of her poems is undoubtedly *Gold Coast Customs* (1930), a rhythmical *tour de force*.

With the advent of the Second World War Edith Sitwell adopted a new, earnest, apocalyptic manner, which culminated in her (surely too triumphal) entry into the Roman Catholic Church in 1954. This new style, cruelly refer-red to by James Reeves (q.v.) as 'death-bed repentance', was disastrous. Edith Sitwell attempted to fuse the richness of Yeats, a grand high style, and the seventeenth-century complexity of such poets as Crashaw and Vaughan. The result is pretentious, vacuous, rhetorical, as at the beginning of 'Dirge for the New Sunrise', which has the solemn epigraph 'Fifteen minutes past eight o'clock, on the morning of Monday, the 6th of August, 1945':

Bound to my heart as Ixion to the wheel,
Nailed to my heart as the thief upon the cross,
I hang between our Christ and the gap where the
world was lost. . . .

Rhapsodies of praise flowed from certain knighted cultural *entrepreneurs*, but not from critics. These later effusions of Edith Sitwell—Dr. Leavis, having been read one of them in a suitably lugubrious manner by an enthusiastic pupil, is supposed to have asked 'What do I do now? Ejaculate?'—are now for the most part unread. Edith Sitwell's *Collected Poems* appeared in 1957; this is supplemented by *The Outcasts* (1962).

*

RUPERT BROOKE (1887–1915), a dazzlingly good-looking young man who held Henry James (he 'took for *his* own the whole of the poetic consciousness he was born to, and moved about in it as a stripped young swimmer. . . . Rupert expressed us *all*. . . .') as well as Edward Marsh spellbound, was in many ways the epitome of Georgianism. But he is best treated as a war-, or rather a 'pre-war-', poet, because here he provides the clearest example of the limitations of Georgianism. He wrote some pleasant (and graceful) light verse, but was not a good poet and could never have been one. His rebelliousness is schoolboy—his father was a master at Rugby School, which he attended and apparently enjoyed; nothing he wrote is ever in bad taste, nothing is profound. The excitement he caused in his male contemporaries was largely sentimental and homosexual in origin, although he himself was heterosexual. Because of his energy, his skill and his accomplishment, he seemed more original to his contemporaries than he actually was. Had he not died of blood-poisoning (at Skyros) while on his way to Gallipoli he would not have continued to write verse—his proficiency at it was but one of his accomplishments: there is no pressure behind his work—but would have become a publisher, or, most likely, a moderately reformist politician and then a peer. His famous sonnet 'The Soldier' sums up a mood that was almost universal among young people in the autumn of 1914; one can hardly blame Brooke himself for it. But it is bad poetry: under the guise of specious patriotism the poet celebrates a racial and therefore personal superiority ('a richer dust') that he has in no sense earned: God ('the eternal mind') is coolly equated with all things English. Now Brooke could hardly have known what the First World War was going to be like; but this sonnet is none the less non-poetry, a piece of inadequate traditionalism that sets out to supply what its public desires. It is still better known and more widely read than any single poem by any of the genuine poets of the First World War. Brooke's fundamental unoriginality is shown in one of his better poems, 'Dust': this, we realize, is all he can do with the new and exciting influence of Donne: all that comes through is a self-consciously bluff, 'young' tone.

The first poet—and an incomparably more important one than Brooke—to realize the true nature of war in this century was CHARLES HAMILTON SORLEY

(1895–1915), killed before he had time to develop his remarkable poetic gifts. His *Letters* (1919) are, for their time, extraordinary: they anticipate attitudes not taken up until after his death. In one of them he condemns Brooke for his 'fine words' and sentimentality. 'There is no such thing as a just war', he wrote: 'England—I am sick of the sound of the word. In training to fight for England, I am training to fight for that deliberate hypocrisy, that terrible middle-class sloth of outlook . . . after the war all brave men will renounce their country and confess that they are strangers and pilgrims on the earth'. Before writing this he had diagnosed the hypocrisy underlying the British public school system (he experienced it at Marlborough); there is enough here to make it clear that the loss to English literature and life occasioned by his death is incalculable. His poetry is, for the most part, no more than immensely promising. But its eloquence, studiedly unrhetorical, already points to an astonishing integrity of purpose.

ISAAC ROSENBERG (1890–1918), a Bristol Jew who began as an art-student, is not often given his due. The usual verdict is 'greater in promise than achievement'. His *Collected Works* (1949) suggests that this is an unfair verdict. He is patronized for his 'imperfect education', but this did not in fact 'obscure his genius' any more than the more 'perfect' education of other aspiring poets illumined theirs. . . . On the whole critics have failed to understand that his poems, far from being 'unfinished', are rhythmically original—and they have failed to recognize the intense Jewishness that underlies everything he wrote. Sorley (who was not twenty-one when he died) apart, Rosenberg was the most naturally gifted of all those who fell in the First World War: although of course war drew poetry from him (he suffered greatly at the front, as his health was poor: he was not in fact medically fit for service), it was not a decisive factor— as it was in the case of Owen. There is a complexity (sometimes wrongly referred to as 'verbal awkwardness') in Rosenberg's poetry that is absent from that of any of his contemporaries. Siegfried Sassoon saw it as a fusion of British and Hebrew culture, 'a strenuous effort for impassioned expression . . . he saw things in terms of sculpture . . . a poet of movement. . . . Words which express movement . . . are essential to his natural utterance'. The most substantial and sensitive critical account of him so far is in C. H. Sisson's (q.v.) *English Poetry 1900–1950* (1971).

'Expression' illustrates the intensity of Rosenberg's poetic awareness—and his courage in not limiting the complex sense of what he is trying to say:

> Call—call—and bruise the air:
> Shatter dumb space!
> Yea! We will fling this passion
>   everywhere;
> Leaving no place
>
> For the superb and grave
> Magnificent throng,

The pregnant queens of quietness
    that brave
And edge our song

Of wonder at the light
(Our life-leased home),
Of greeting to our housemates.
    And in might
Our song shall roam

Life's heart, a blossoming fire
Blown bright by thought,
While gleams and fades the infinite
    desire,
Phantasmed naught.

Can this be caught and caged?
Wings can be clipt
Of eagles, the sun's gaudy measure
    gauged,
But no sense dipt

In the mystery of sense.
The troubled throng
Of words break out like smothered
    fire through dense
And smouldering wrong.

The 'wit' (in the metaphysical sense) of this poem works: here—in a poem written in 1914 or 1915, before Rosenberg enlisted—is 'modern' writing apparently arising from nowhere. Actually Rosenberg sensed the 'seventeenth-century' aspirations in the poetry of the intelligent Lascelles Abercrombie (q.v.) —one is tempted to say that he admired it because of what it tried to do rather than for what it did—and put these to work. . . . Rosenberg's view of the war that destroyed him was extraordinarily objective and comprehensive (more so than Owen's): he realized that the hideous destructiveness of 'shrieking iron and flame/Hurled through still heavens' nevertheless called forth, from men, what D. W. Harding (one of Rosenberg's editors) calls 'a simplified greatness which they could never have reached before'. Rosenberg is quite as 'modern' as Eliot; but he has more experience—and much more to say. The neglect in which he has been held is puzzling; probably the main reason for it lies in the difficulties his poems present. He is unique in English-language poetry inasmuch as, like Vallejo (q.v.), he passionately seeks to turn his poems into actual *things*, spells; too often this differentness has been dismissed as 'immaturity'. For the ex-painter Rosenberg, however—he did not finally decide to devote himself solely to poetry until 1915, when he was staying with a married sister in Capetown, South Africa—words had a magical value: they existed for him, as they do for some contemporary writers in Spanish, as the actual mysterious doubles of the things or qualities they denote (cf. Asturias, q.v.). He sees, in 'On Receiving News of the War' (1914), the ill tidings as 'Snow', 'a strange white word'. In 'Dead Man's Dump' a 'choked soul stretched weak hands/To reach the living word'; the dead lie in 'great sunk silences'. Rosenberg's poetry only requires close attention to be more widely recognized as the greatest to come from any soldier poet in this century. No contemporary English-language poet has had greater potentiality.

WILFRED OWEN (1893–1918), who was killed only a week before the Armistice, was unknown to the public in his lifetime; he saw only four of his poems in print. Owen was the son of a Shropshire railway clerk. The account of him by his brother HAROLD OWEN (1897) in his memoirs, *Journey From Obscurity* (1963–5)— itself a masterpiece of reluctant, doggedly honest self-revelation—suggests that he was in many ways a prissy and self-absorbed youth. His earliest poems are Keatsian exercises—without anything very special about them. His parents could not afford to keep him at London University, where he matriculated in 1910; instead he was forced to take up a post as assistant to a vicar; he was supposed to decide whether to take orders. This exposure to the Church itself led him to a mental crisis: naturally enough, he lost the simple Christian faith of his childhood. Between 1913 and 1915, when he enlisted, he was a private tutor near Bordeaux. In September 1914 he wrote from France to his brother Harold (Owen's *Collected Letters* appeared in 1967) about a visit he had made, in the company of a doctor, to a hospital where some of the earliest casualties of the war were being cared for. Considering that Owen was the man who, less than four years later, was prepared to sacrifice the poetry ('Above all I am not concerned with Poetry' he wrote in the famous preface he drafted to a future volume) for the pity ('The Poetry is in the pity'), this is an odd letter: ostensibly written to 'educate' Harold 'to the actualities of war', it gives a clinical account, with illustrations, of the wounded. 'I was not much upset', Owen told his brother. But nearly all the poems of pity by which he is now remembered were written in the last eighteen months of his life.

Now that we have Owen's letters and his brother's remarkable reminiscences we are able to see more clearly that his rather frozen and forbidding manner as a young man arose largely from sexual confusions. Joseph Cohen has shown in his *Owen Agonistes* (1967) that Owen was in fact a passive homosexual and what he aptly calls an 'injustice collector'. It seems that he fully discovered this fact about himself when he was in hospital at Craiglockhart after his first spell of active service (1916–7). While there he met Siegfried Sassoon—who was also a homosexual; one letter to Sassoon settles the matter beyond dispute. (There is, furthermore, a fairly well-founded suggestion that he was seduced by C. K. Scott-Moncrieff, the translator of Proust.) All that we know about Owen tends to support this view: there is sometimes a certain morbidity in him which, despite the indignation and the anger which undoubtedly seared him, is not even, perhaps, primarily compassionate. This is particularly apparent in 'The Show', whose subject is not only the 'pity of war' but also an undiagnosed sickness in Owen's mind:

> My soul looked down from a vague height with Death,
> As unremembering how I rose or why,
> And saw a sad land, weak with sweats of dearth,
> Gray, cratered like the moon with hollow woe,
> And fitted with great pocks and scabs of plagues.
>
> Across its beard, that horror of harsh wire,
> There moved thin caterpillars, slowly uncoiled.
> It seemed they pushed themselves to be as plugs
> Of ditches, where they writhed and shrivelled, killed.
>
> By them had slimy paths been trailed and scraped
> Round myriad warts that might be little hills.
> From gloom's last dregs these long-strung creatures crept,
> And vanished out of dawn down hidden holes.
>
> (And smell came up from those foul openings
> As out of mouths, or deep wounds deepening.)
>
> On dithering feet upgathered, more and more,
> Brown strings towards strings of gray, with bristling spines,
> All migrants from green fields, intent on mire.
> Those that were gray, of more abundant spawns,
> Ramped on the rest and ate them and were eaten.
> I saw their bitten backs curve, loop, and straighten,
> I watched those agonies curl, lift, and flatten.
>
> Whereat, in terror what that sight might mean,
> I reeled and shivered earthward like a feather.
> And Death fell with me, like a deepening moan.
> And He, picking a manner of worm, which half had hid
> Its bruises in the earth, but crawled no further,
> Showed me its feet, the feet of many men,
> And the fresh-severed head of it, my head.

This is one of Owen's most powerful and self-revealing poems: often he remains himself curiously uninvolved in the 'pity' he describes—it is a legitimate criticism of the body of his later anti-war poems—but here he is a part of the horrible murder-process he is describing. Almost all of the anti-war poems are of course effective and deeply moving. However, we have, I think, to look again at Vallejo's (q.v.) poetry to see clearly that in Owen there is something morbid —something that actually *enjoys* the suffering that is being described, something nearly self-indulgent. (This is to judge by the high standards that the poems demand.) Further, the poems do not altogether avoid a note of personal resentment: 'Miners' ('. . . they will not dream of us poor lads/Lost in the ground') does read like the poem of an injustice collector: it has that note. Sassoon was wrong when he said 'he did not pity himself'; had he said it of Rosenberg he would have been nearer the mark. There is a sullen, homosexually oriented resentment of women that, every so often, surfaces in the poems ('all women, without exception, *annoy* me', he wrote in 1914).

But this is only to redress a balance: Owen has long been slightly over-rated, Rosenberg miserably underrated. Owen at his best is a poet of great power, who discovered, in his complex response to the war, new poetic procedures that were to influence the next generation of poets. His experiments with half-rhyme and what Edmund Blunden called 'para-rhyme'—most effective in the famous 'Strange Meeting', where he meets the man he has killed—were extensive and intelligent. His blend of irony and pity, too, was new in English poetry.

SIEGFRIED SASSOON (1886–1967) was the most satirical of the war poets. He had started (in his anonymous *Poems*, 1906, *Hyacinth*, 1912, and other collections of pre-war poetry) as a fairly conventional post-Pre-Raphaelite; his originality first made itself evident, not in his war poems of *The Old Huntsman* (1917) and *Counter-Attack* (1918), but in *The Daffodil Murderer* (1913), published under the pseudonym of Saul Kain: this was intended as a parody of Masefield's *The Everlasting Mercy* (q.v.), but it ended as a serious poem. Sassoon's attitude to the war was at first orthodox ('war has made us wise/And, fighting for our freedom, we are free'); experience of it soon changed this, and he became the most savage satirist of war that has, perhaps, ever been known. A captain in the Royal Welch Fusiliers, he was a close friend of Robert Graves (who held the same rank in the same regiment) and, later, in hospital at Craiglockhart, of Wilfred Owen—upon whom he exercised a decisive influence both sexually and poetically. *The Daffodil Murderer* (which Sassoon never made re-available) revealed what can only be described as a strange inner twistedness: a kind of half-crazy, delirious, pathic decadence, mixed in with strong feelings of guilt, lyrical compassion (expressed in the famous 'Everyone Sang') and whatever love for the 'wholesome', aristocratic, distracting 'sport' of fox-hunting represents. . . . Sassoon never succeeded in resolving his problems; but the horrors of war—which turned him into a lifelong pacifist—brought out in him a (valid) satirical ferocity and power: paradoxically, he found a kind of spiritual peace in the hellish sufferings of war. The war poems are crude and even uncontrolled, but in that lies their power: as D. J. Enright has written, they are 'so clearly written out of honest rage and decent indignation'. It took war, however, to push him into this kind of honesty and decency. His only effective poetry between the end of the First World War and his death is satirical; most of it is in the short sequence called *The Road to Ruin* (1933). During and after the Second World War he reverted to facile patriotism—a kind of 'dash . . . of Winston Churchill in an ocean of water' (D. J. Enright). He ended in the Roman Catholic Church (he entered it at 70). His many volumes of fictionalized autobiography, such as *The Complete Memoirs of George Sherston* (1937) and *Siegfried's Journey* (1945) have been much admired; *The Old Century and Seven More Years* (1938) is the least contrived, the most lucid and touching and informative, of these. But for the essence of Sassoon, a good minor satirical poet, one must go back to those angry poems of the war which he so hated and in which he fought with such courage.

Although he saw longer service and was badly wounded, the war did not prompt such powerful work from ROBERT GRAVES (1895), who matured considerably later. His poetry may, allowing for anticipations and regressions, be divided into four main phases: from his schoolboy beginnings in 1906 until his discovery of the poetry of the American poet Laura Riding (q.v.) in 1926; the duration of his literary and personal association with her (1926–39); the period of his war-time sojourn in a South Devon farmhouse and of the first years of his return to Mallorca (1939–56); and what may be called the years in which he has emerged into world fame. The two main events in his poetic life have been the impact upon him of four years' trench warfare in the First World War, and his response to the poetry and personality of Laura Riding. While the effect of Graves' war experiences has been adequately appreciated by his critics, the influence of Laura Riding has been very seriously under-estimated—owing, one feels, to failure to understand her poetry.

Graves's faith in the poem he has to write—although not attended by careless arrogance about his capacities to write it—has been as great as that of any English poet, perhaps greater. In this sense the poem, for Graves, is a thing outside himself, a task of truth-telling—and not a thing to be invented or 'composed'. Poem-writing is a matter of absolute truthfulness to the mood of self-revelation. Graves is not the kind of craftsman who invents shapes in stone, to his own desires; but one who seeks, by means of intuition, to discover the exact shape in the middle of the stone, in which he has absolute faith.

If one of the signs of a major as distinct from a minor poet is development, then Graves is certainly a major poet. Yet his technical experiments have always been within the limits of tradition. As a schoolboy he worked on hosts of complicated rhyme-schemes and verse-forms, including the Welsh *englyn*, as well as with assonance and dissonance. For his subject-matter he drew on the worlds of chivalry, romance and nursery rhyme. Much of his technical facility and his capacity to use folk-themes without parodying them he owed to his father, ALFRED PERCEVAL GRAVES (1846–1931), himself a graceful minor Irish poet.

Graves has rejected not only nearly all his war poetry but also much of his immediately post-war poetry, written under the twin (and opposing) influences of war-trauma and pastoral marriage. This is technically accomplished, charming, and with an underlying complexity that is by no means as typically Georgian as its surface. Graves was at this time working—under the influence of W. H. R. Rivers, the anthropologist—on the Freudian theory that poetry was therapeutic, a view he largely abandoned in the later Twenties.

Little of the poetry of Graves's first period has been preserved in his *Collected Poems*; but its main positive features—delight in nonsense, preoccupation with terror, the nature of his love for women—have survived into his later poetry. What was purged was softness and cloying over-sweetness. Yet it was not Laura Riding's procedures that influenced him, but the content of her poems— and the personality that went with this. The poems of his maturity are in no sense at all imitations of hers; but her remarkably complicated view of life (and therefore the work in which she expressed this) are relevant to them: he shared, or rather, attempted devotedly to learn, this view, and the material of the poems is his struggle to accommodate himself lovingly to it and to her. The process proved impossible in the end, as he foresaw in 'Sick Love', written in the late Twenties: 'O Love, be fed with apples while you may', this begins; and it ends,

> Take your delight in momentariness,
> Walk between dark and dark—a shining space
> With the grave's narrowness, though not its peace.

The poems Graves wrote in his second period record, with great directness and in a diction of deliberate hardness and strength, the nerve-strains of impossible love ('To the galleys, thief, and sweat your soul out', one begins) and his attempt to achieve an existence that accorded with the goodness that Graves and (at that time) Laura Riding saw as residing in poetry above every other human activity. These are therefore 'existential' poems, and to be understood they must be read in this way: they are at once an account of the condition of romanticized devotedness, of a search for perfection (always tempered with ironic realism and earthy masculine robustness) and of human failures. Poems such as 'The Legs' describe the distractions that Graves saw as tempting him from the concentration his single-minded quest for poetic wisdom required. His 'historical grammar of poetic myth', *The White Goddess* (1947 rev. 1952), is essentially a generalization from his experiences of these years of devoted struggle to serve a savagely demanding muse, whom in 'On Portents' he had seen as a vast propeller, a 'bladed mind' strongly pulling through the 'ever-reluctant element' of Time. These poems, by which—together with those of the succeeding phase—Graves will probably be chiefly remembered, provide what will almost certainly become the classic latter-day record of romantic love; this is so not least because of their unsentimentality, their tough and un-idealistic acceptance of the author's strong masculine recalcitrance. Thus, his mood changes from confidence—

> We tell no lies now, at last cannot be
> The rogues we were—so evilly linked in sense
> With what we scrutinized that lion or tiger
> Could leap from every copse, strike and devour us.

to zestful gloom—

> Yet why does she
> Come never as longed-for beauty
> Slender and cool, with limbs lovely to see . . .?

As he wrote in 1965, 'My theme was always the practical impossibility, transcended only by miracle, of absolute love continuing between man and woman.' It is the tension between 'practical impossibility' and 'miracle' that gives Grave's poetry its power.

The poems of Graves's third phase, written when he had abandoned his prodigious enterprise of creating—with Laura Riding—an existence in which poetry and what it represents would be a natural way of life—reflect upon the meaning of his experience:

> her image
> Warped in the weather, turned beldamish.
> Then back came winter on me at a bound,
> The pallid sky heaved with a moon-quake.
>
> Dangerous had it been with love-notes
> To serenade Queen Famine. . . .

They also discover new love, in some of the most beautiful love lyrics in English:

> Have you not read
> The words in my head,
> And I made part
> Of your own heart?

Finally, they humorously state his position and accept that fame has caught up with him, as in 'From the Embassy', where he refers to himself as 'ambassador of Otherwhere/To the unfederated States of Here and There'.

The poetry of Graves's most recent phase lacks the tension of the earlier work. It owes a good deal to the Sufist ideas by which Graves has been influenced in recent years; it discovers, but not wholly convincingly, the peaceful figure of the Black Goddess who lies behind the crueller one of the White Goddess. Love, to Graves in these new poems, walks 'on a knife-edge between two different fates': one fate is to consort with the White Goddess, and is physical; the other, more difficult yet more rewarding, is to find peace in the domains of the Black Goddess. Frequently the poems are so lapidary as to remind the reader of Landor; but they reach a greater power than Landor usually achieved when they envisage the hell of a world made dead by a too great reliance upon physical passion. Of one who is trapped in this hell, who in departing too casually has said, 'I will write', he says in a poem of the same title:

> Long letters written and mailed in her own head—
> There are no mails in a city of the dead.

These late poems provide, in their explorations of the possibilities of a world purged of what he calls 'the blood sports of desire', and of the agonies of alienation from such a world, a fitting sequel to those of his earlier years. He will be, perhaps, the last romantic poet to operate within traditional limits. His mastery of these is not in question.

Graves has also written some important prose. The best of his many historical novels are the two Claudius books: *I, Claudius* (1934) and *Claudius the God* (1934), *Wife to Mr. Milton* (1943)—an account of the first marriage that has been called 'distorted', but never on evidence—and *The Golden Fleece* (1944). His autobiography, *Good-bye to all That* (1929) is rightly regarded as a classic. *The Nazarene Gospel Restored* (1953), which he wrote in collaboration with Joshua Podro, is a remarkable reconstruction of the Gospel story; it was damned out of hand by orthodox theologians, but has gained wide currency—and was highly praised by Reinhold Niebuhr.

For EDMUND BLUNDEN (1896), too, the war (in which he was gassed) was a devastating experience; but for the most part he reacted to it in a very different way: in a pastoral, although gnarled and highly original poetry. Blunden, a self-effacing and modest man, has been a useful although not a trenchant critic—he has been absurdly although touchingly over-generous to his contemporaries; carrying on where Norman Gale and Arthur Symons left off, he became the pioneer of the major eighteenth-century poet John Clare; *Undertones of War* (1928), though somewhat archly written, is one of the better prose books to come out of the First World War.

Nearly all Blunden's best poetry was written between about 1914 and 1929; it may be found in *The Poems of Edmund Blunden 1914–1930* (1930); the most substantial later collection is *Poems of Many Years* (1957), which is supplemented by *A Hong Kong House* (1961). The best of the poems, with a very few notable exceptions such as 'Report on Experience', come into the category perhaps unfortunately called 'nature poetry'. Blunden's poems about nature combine accuracy of observation with an odd (and by no means always 'pleasant', in the sense that this word is understood by devotees of the pastoral and the bucolic) imaginative malice. This is when he is at his best and most disturbing. At other times he is artificial and literary. 'The Midnight Skaters' shows him at his best:

> The hop-poles stand in cones,
> The icy pond lurks under,
> The pole-tops touch the star-gods' thrones
> And sound the gulfs of wonder,
> But not the tallest there, 'tis said,
> Could fathom to this pond's black bed.
>
> Then is not Death at watch
> Within those secret waters?
> What wants he but to catch
> Earth's heedless sons and daughters,

With but a crystal parapet
Between, he has his engines set.

Then on, blood shouts, on, on,
   Twirl, wheel and whip above him,
Dance on this ball-floor thin and wan,
   Use him as though you love him;
Court him, elude him, reel and pass,
And let him hate you through the glass.

Blunden edited a selection of the *Poems* (1954) of his friend, the Gloucester-shire man IVOR GURNEY (1890–1937). Gurney, who was a gifted composer of songs as well as a poet, is unaccountably neglected: as a poet he was far superior to, for example, Brooke. Though he survived it, Gurney was really a victim of the war: soon after it was over he became afflicted with mental illness, which resulted in his spending most of the last years of his life in institutions. He published two volumes in his lifetime: *Severn and Somme* (1917) and *War's Embers* (1919); much of his poetry has never been published. It is often painfully inchoate and rambling, reflecting his disturbed mentality; but every so often it flashes into its own unique and passionate life. Gurney's manner, in his best poems, is very far from Georgian.

HERBERT READ (1893–1968), who also fought in the First World War, was unquestionably a great eclectic critic. He was also an influential art critic. Probably his finest creative work is the novel, *The Green Child* (1935). His poetry (*Collected Poems*, 1966) is very seldom as successful as one feels it should have been. He was a man of great sincerity and exquisite sensibility—over-tolerant towards bad art because of his generous assumption that others shared his qualities—but, like Bridges (q.v.), 'just a shade too little of a blackguard'. He was, of course, a stronger poet than Bridges; but he very seldom achieved a manner of his own ('To a Conscript of 1940' is an exception). Ultimately he acknowledged this, quoting Yeats' remark to the effect that 'perfection' is to be found in the 'life' or in the 'work', but not (presumably) in both. However, his acknowledgement of the fundamental problem of *Künstlerschuld* (q.v.) made him into an important creative critic.

*

HUGH MACDIARMID (ps. CHRISTOPHER MURRAY GRIEVE, 1892) is—as he would wish it—unclassifiable. He has been somewhat overrated by Scottish critics, who tend, as David Daiches does—to confuse his extrinsic importance to Scots literature with his intrinsic value as a poet; but he is undoubtedly a figure of stature. Until the Sixties he was unjustly neglected outside his own country; since then there has been a good deal of irrelevant hullabaloo; there is no proper collected poems (the book of that title, 1962, is not nearly what it purports to be; it is only partially supplemented by its successors: a decently edited retrospective collection is badly needed). MacDiarmid's achievement is uneven. His egotism (he can seldom write about anyone else without concentrating upon himself—although he is not ungenerous) and much of his militant communism often seem frustratingly irrelevant to his poetry. His endorsement of the Russian invasion of Czechoslovakia (1968)—'fraternal entry'—as of Hungary twelve years earlier has raised doubts about his decency and, indeed, his historical judgement. But for half a century he has waged war against philistinism and against the tendency of the vast majority of his fellow Scots to affect an unnatural Englishness—thus emasculating themselves and undermining their native genius, of which they are as timidly afraid as a law-clerk of a cut lily (to adapt a phrase of Pablo Neruda's, q.v.). The strain, accompanied by neglect and hostility, has told: MacDiarmid's external *persona* is not wholly attractive: he thinks too much of himself too solemnly, and his grandiosity is frequently a bore. But it is a natural enough response to the treatment he has had, and it may easily be disregarded.

MacDiarmid is the pioneer of, and the most gifted figure in, the Scottish literary renaissance (which came twenty-five years later than the Irish); he provided its 'programme . . . focus, and . . . models' (David Daiches).

MacDiarmid has done more than any other Scottish writer to develop Lallans, a synthetic language that draws upon Middle Scots, English and modern local dialects. Lallans has unique vitality in the right hands; in the hands of inferior poets it is laboured and tedious. As Daiches has pointed out, Lallans is in fact no more 'synthetic' than the language of Dunbar or Burns; it has closer links with Anglo-Saxon than modern English; it preserves English words that English has lost. . . . Here, in a well-known poem, 'Lourd on my Hert', is MacDiarmid using it as it should be used:

> Lourd on my hert as winter lies
> The state that Scotland's in the day.
> Spring to the north has aye come slow
> But noo dour winter's like to stay
> > For guid
> > And no for guid.
>
> O wae's me on the weary days
> When it is scarce grey licht at noon;
> It maun be a' the stupid folk
> Diffusin' their dullness roon and roon
> > Like soot
> > That keeps the sunlicht oot.
>
> Nae wonder if I think I see
> A lichter shadow than the reist
> I'm fain to cry 'the dawn, the dawn!
> I see it brackin' in the East.'
> > But ah
> > —It's just mair snaw!

MacDiarmid's concern for Scotland is better shown here than in his many cantankerous utterances on the subject. Practically all his best work was done by the mid-Thirties, including the long poem-sequence *A Drunk Man Looks at the Thistle* (1926), a linguistic *tour de force* of immense vitality in which satirical verve exists side by side with self-contemplation. Here Lallans is triumphantly appropriate: it functions as the poet's pure voice. MacDiarmid never reached this level again, although some of his short Scots lyrics are arresting in their freshness and depth of emotion. Much of MacDiarmid's later verse is in English: long poems (such as *In Memoriam James Joyce*, 1955, and 'A Raised Beach') setting forth arguments. Most of this resembles dull prose: MacDiarmid is not impressive as a thinker (there is something distinctly ingenuous about his polymathic enterprises), and he lacks an ear for English rhythms. Intelligent critics speak of 'the cumulative pattern of meaning' (much of this English verse consists of mere catalogues of facts), but this is over-charitable. The claim that MacDiarmid is the best Scottish poet since Burns is a just one; but this is on the strength of his earlier Scots poetry.

Of poets born in the nineteenth century, the most distinguished successor to MacDiarmid was WILLIAM SOUTAR (1898–1943), who was a bedridden invalid for almost a quarter of a century. Soutar's Scots poems (his English are negligible) are narrow in range of subject and feeling, but none the less exquisite in tone, style and execution. His *Collected Poems* appeared posthumously, in 1948; *Poems in Scots and English* (1961) adds more good poems. Soutar's moving and perceptive journal, *Diaries of a Dying Man* (1954), deserves to be better known.

The most eminent Scots poet to use English was EDWIN MUIR (1887–1959), one of the most modest and self-effacing of contemporary writers. Muir, who came from the Orkneys, had a bitter struggle to establish himself: for nearly twenty years he lived a grim and miserable life in Glasgow. His first book, of literary criticism, appeared under the pseudonym of 'E. Moore' in 1918, when he was already past thirty. Muir and his wife Willa Muir made many translations from contemporary German writers; the most important were from Kafka (q.v.). Muir was one of the best critics of his time (the book-reviewing he did towards the end of his life is his least important criticism: the best is in *The Structure of the Novel*, 1928, comparable in importance to Lubbock's *The Craft of Fiction* and Forster's *Aspects of the Novel*). His three novels —*The Marionette* (1927), *The Three Brothers* (1931) and *Poor Tom* (1932)—are of a high standard as well as being important guides to the nature of his complex sensibility. Muir's unambitious and diffident nature gives his poetry a unique quality; unfortunately these qualities were also responsible for his too frequent lack of linguistic distinctiveness and energy. He could rarely develop a rhythm of his own: his poetry, traditional in form, relies too much on metrical norms; he often evades, one might say, the sound of his own voice. And yet he is a remarkably original poet, who avoided both the Scottish and the English traditions. There is nothing of the Georgians and little of Eliot in his work. He took his inspiration from fable and myth, and from his observation of the natural world of animals. He was not a major poet only because he lacked procedures adequate to fully express the combination of the visionary and the metaphysical that characterizes his attitude. And yet he is a rewarding and often beautiful poet, in whom there is no fatal failure in humour (see 'Suburban Idyll'); one is prepared to accept his faintly stilted, strained diction and his awkwardness—arising from the fact that his poetic impulses usually fail, very oddly, to find their complete verbal counterparts: there is little verbal excitement in Muir—because one has such faith in his integrity, sweetness of disposition and wisdom. He is not a sensuous poet—this means that he lacks the force and conviction of a Yeats or a Graves—and he is sometimes given to a kind of too obviously symbolic, abstract writing that lacks experiential reference ('The Actor on the Tree'; 'like the happy doe/That keeps its perfect laws/ Between the tiger's paws/And vindicates its cause'), but his best poems, such as 'The Horses', have their own substance. Muir's first book of poetry appeared in 1925; the definitive *Collected Poems* was published in 1965. His *An Autobiography* (1954; originally *The Story and the Fable*, 1940) is deservedly a classic.

*

Two woman poets born in the Nineties stand out above others: RUTH PITTER (1897) and SYLVIA TOWNSEND WARNER (1893). The latter is a distinguished novelist, and her fiction is mentioned elsewhere; but her poetry has been unduly and strangely neglected. Ruth Pitter is less resourceful and usually less interesting linguistically, but she is a graceful craftsman, and her quiet manner can be attractive. She is one of those rare woman poets who, like Marianne Moore (q.v.), can make a poetic virtue out of an apparently genteel and orthodox respectability. Often her themes are Christian; her gentle optimism functions pleasantly, as a kind of innocence. She has just a handful of truly distinguished and original poems which, beneath an unruffled surface, combine pastoral charm with emotional vitality. 'Time's Fool' ends with lucidity and serenity:

> I knew that the roots were creeping under the floor,
> That the toad was safe in his hole, the poor cat by the fire,
> The starling snug in the roof, each slept in his place:
> The lily in splendour, the vine in her grace,
> The fox in the forest, all had their desire,
> As then I had mine, in the place that was happy and poor.

Sylvia Townsend Warner is a musician learned in the church music of the fourteenth, fifteenth and sixteenth centuries. Her prose achieves what T. F. Powys (q.v.)—an admirer—tried but so seldom succeeded in achieving. Her poetry only needs to be better known to be more widely acclaimed. She has never had her due; perhaps this is because she knows her limitations too well. 'Nellie Trim' is one of the most effective of modern literary ballads, and conveys an authentic poetic *frisson* in a way that many more ambitious poems do not. She has an epigrammatic style, a fine technique, and the capacity to employ traditional diction without distorting her meaning. Her best poetry is to be found in longer works, such as *Opus 7* (1931). But 'Song from the Bride of Smithfield' illustrates her skill and wit:

> A thousand guileless sheep have bled,
> A thousand bullocks knelt in fear,
> To daub my Henry's cheek with red
> And round the curl above his ear.
>
> And wounded calves hung up to drip
> Have in slow sweats distilled for him
> To dew that polishes his lip,
> The inward balm that oils each limb.
>
> In vain I spread my maiden arts,
> In vain for Henry's love I pine.
> He is too skilled in bleeding hearts
> To turn this way and pity mine.

Sylvia Townsend Warner's poetry has not been collected; it may be found in *The Espalier* (1925), *Time Importuned* (1928) and *Whether a Dove or a Seagull* (1933), half of the poems in which are by her lifelong friend Valentine Ackland.

*

T. S. ELIOT (1888–1965)—who, although loosely associated with the imagists, requires separate treatment—was born in St. Louis, Missouri, and educated at Harvard. After study in Paris and Germany, and a short period as an assistant in the department of philosophy at Harvard, he settled permanently in England. He gained his living as an editorial director of the distinguished publishing firm of Faber and Faber (originally Faber and Gwyer). He married an Englishwoman (who subsequently became insane) in 1915. In 1927 he became an English citizen; it was in the following year that he issued his famous statement (influenced by *Action Française*, q.v.) that he was 'Anglo-Catholic in religion . . . classicist in literature, and royalist in politics'. He won the Nobel Prize in 1948. He made a second marriage in the Fifties.

Eliot's enormous extrinsic importance is undoubted. It is so great that Geoffrey Grigson's (q.v.) comparison of him with Cowley, the minor late seventeenth-century poet who in his lifetime was regarded as a major figure, is hardly appropriate: Grigson is certainly correct to draw attention to Eliot's extremely limited intrinsic achievement—but he was very much more influential, and accomplished, than even Cowley.

Eliot poses a formidable problem: the distance between his remarkable critical sensibility and perceptiveness, and his poetic achievement, is so great as at first to seem impossible; furthermore, he possessed the technical accomplish-ment—if not the rhythmical energy—of a major poet. Eliot was one of the first to see that, as he put it in his tribute to John Davidson (q.v.), it was necessary for a poet to 'free himself completely from the poetic diction of English verse of his time. . . .' Eliot saw this more clearly than anyone else of his generation (he owed much to Pound, who established him; but his mind was always clearer than Pound's); he had the capacity to demonstrate it in a practical form—in 'The Love Song of J. Alfred Prufrock' (written while Eliot was at Harvard and published, with other poems, in *Prufrock and Other Observations*, in 1917). This poem, like most of its successors, is full of technical excellencies: the control of tone and the juxtaposition of the literary and the colloquial are perhaps the main ones. At all times Eliot demonstrates a superior intelligence —in fact, when one thinks of the English-language poets who dominated the scene at the time Eliot was actually writing the poem this intelligence is not short of astonishing.

But it is primarily a critical intelligence. 'Prufrock', like the best of its successors, is a minor poem. Eliot is a minor poet: he cannot write about love; he lacks real sympathy, or empathy; he is frigid. . . . Skill, accomplishment, sensibility—even these are not enough to make a major poet. Emotional substance is needed. 'Prufrock' is the best as well as the earliest of Eliot's important poems: it is the only one that tries to deal, fully, with his own problem: with his lack of feeling. That is to say, it states his predicament and it laments it; ultimately it is thin stuff, for all the delicacy of manipulation and the cleverness and the sensitivity. Eliot's use of Laforgue and other French poets is masterly; his importation of French symbolist techniques into English poetry has been valuable; but even as early as 'Prufrock' his procedures tend to function as a substitute for an original poetic impulse. This he never really has. That is why, in later poems, his technique of *montage* becomes poetically reprehensible: the reason for it is that he cannot make his own poetry, and so— with that exquisite sensibility that can so beautifully discern poetry, he uses other people's. It amounts to a splendid and judicious patchwork; but it is critical, anthological—not, in the final analysis, poetic.

The fact is that Eliot, although extremely sophisticated in literary matters, was sexually and politically naïve to a quite extraordinary degree. His in-ability to write about love is illustrated by the disastrous 'A Dedication to my Wife', written to his second wife: however touching this may seem in everyday terms, it amounts to a confession of total poetic failure in an area that is surely important. Again, Eliot's political position—although not 'fascist' as has often been urged—is simply naïve, insensitive and humanly ignorant. The celebrated disdainful contempt for humanity that emerges in Eliot's plays, particularly in the final comedies (*The Cocktail Party*, 1950; *The Confidential Clerk*, 1954; *The Elder Statesman*, 1959), is not the product of suffering or bitterness, but of a near-giggling frigidity and an ultra-conservative insensitivity. The crucifixion, on an ant hill, of his character Celia—in *The Cocktail Party*—is the supreme, atrocious example of this element in his attitude: of his failure to see ideas in terms of their human results. His attitude was not 'fascist', but it was insensitive; thus he could subscribe, at the end of his life, to a lunatic-fringe right-wing newspaper (now happily out of business, its owner bankrupted). Eliot's notion of the England he adopted as his own country was as simplistic as that of one of its military servants in the last century, and it had less justification. The contrast between that fantasy and his literary judgement—when this operated freely and autonomously—is extraordinary.

The Waste Land (1922) coincided with a universal mood of disillusion and despair. Its near-nihilism is more dignified than that of the icy and sneering little commercial verse-comedies of the Fifties—for in the early Twenties Eliot had no sustaining orthodoxy to cling to. The notion that *The Waste Land* is a unity, however, is incorrect: it is a ragbag of satirical and pseudo-lyrical and sensitively dramatic pieces, all on the general theme of present decay and past beauty. The satirical feeling is poetic, but the carpentry is obtrusive— and already the positive element, the beauty of the past, is factitiously presented, and is unconvincing. The sense of present degradation is well conveyed; there are scenes of genuine comedy; but the non-satirical sections (especially at the end) are pretentious. As a satirical poem—or, rather, a series of satirical poems —*The Waste Land* is successful. As a poem it fails: all traces of the experience that prompted it have been carefully removed. The critic John Peter implied, in an essay that was withdrawn (out of courtesy) when Eliot's solicitors threatened to take action, that it is (in part) an elegy for a young man who was killed at Gallipoli. . . . Whether this is so or not, there is little doubt that, at a personal level, it examined the problems of 'the waist land': the fact of sexual as well as spiritual loss and frustration.

Eliot's poetry after his conversion to the Anglican religion becomes empty. E. M. Forster, writing in 1929, put his finger on the reasons for this conversion: 'if it [religious emotion] exists [in Eliot's books], it cannot be relegated. He has not got it; what he seeks is not revelation, but stability. . . . Most writers . . . ask the reader in, to co-operate or to look. . . . Mr. Eliot does not want us in. He feels we shall increase the barrenness. . . . He is difficult because he has seen something terrible, and (underestimating . . . the general decency of his audience) has declined to say so plainly'. Eliot saw not one but two 'terrible' things: he saw not only the repellently commercial and mechanized nature of modern life—but also the arid nature of his own heart. The *Four Quartets* (1936–42) consist of theological and philosophical abstractions piled up on one another in a skilful and sometimes entrancing manner; but they represent an evasion of experience, a failure to examine an incapacity for experience. For all the many ambitious exegeses that have been made of them, it is safe to predict that they will not survive as major poetry.

Eliot, then, is a vitally important influence; but the enormous edifice of his authority stands on a pin-point of actual poetic achievement. It remains to say that in his public life he was courteous, scrupulous, modest and generous.

III

The drama in Great Britain in the Nineties was in just such an attenuated and totally exhausted state as it was in Europe. Although Ibsen (q.v.) had been known to a devoted few since about 1880, London audiences refused to accept him. He did not pay. Oscar Wilde's comedies, particularly *The Importance of Being Ernest* (1895), represented the very best that could be commercially viable. ARTHUR WING PINERO (1855–1934), of Portuguese-Jewish ancestry, represents the best of the popular theatre outside Wilde and Shaw. Like many playwrights Pinero began as an actor (with Irving's company); his many plays show a mastery of the technical side of the theatre. He made his reputation with *The Second Mrs Tanqueray* (1894), a social tragedy which still plays entertainingly. Pinero manipulated his characters; they do not develop; they are two-dimensional. But he lacked the innate vulgarity of his German contemporary Sudermann (q.v.), and within his limitations he is an effective, extraordinarily skilful and sometimes witty dramatist.

GEORGE BERNARD SHAW (1856–1950) is a part of history; he made the world of his intellectual or enlightened contemporaries a more lively place; he was a skilful technician; he was an on the whole humane and generous man; he had a most engaging personality. But he was a superficial thinker and a third-rate creative writer. His career as a whole is a monument to the failure of reason alone to solve human problems. His importance in the history of the theatre, as an Ibsenite revolutionary, has been exaggerated. Shaw is an excellent dramatist of ideas; few can go to the theatre and fail—in the theatre itself—to respond to the lively entertainment he usually offers. He is a man of almost infinite theatrical skill. But his drama is not literature, and his characters are not alive—actually they don't even pretend to be so. His portraits of real creative writers (the 'poet' Marchbanks in *Candida*, 1894, is the chief one) show no understanding whatever of the creative process or the creative character: they are, in fact, hopelessly conventional. Shaw was brilliant and he was lucid; but he entirely misunderstood the nature of the imagination. He thought himself to be in the tradition of Molière, and was seriously disturbed because no one would agree with his own estimate of himself as superior to Shakespeare. His attempt to write an imaginative, a 'great', play, which deals with emotion, is *St. Joan* (1924): when it tries to be moving it is execrable— as embarrassingly false as the 'passion' expressed in his letters to the actress Mrs. Patrick Campbell (published in their *Correspondence*, edited A. Dent, 1952). Shaw's lack of emotion, which was not accompanied by any sort of unkindness, enabled him to be acute on occasions, as well as obtuse (as in his failure to see anything wrong with Mussolini's 'castor oil treatment' of his political opponents, or his sentimental worship of 'great' men). Shaw undoubtedly belongs to the history of the theatre; his place in literature, however, is a very minor one. One may say, indeed, that the place of the 'drama of ideas' itself—when it is no more than that—in literature is a very minor one. Given the audiences of today, it has been little more than midcult journalism. Shaw won the Nobel Prize in 1925.

In attacking the complacency of the Nineties theatrical audience—*The Quintessence of Ibsenism* (1891)—Shaw concentrated on the reforming, didactic element in Ibsen, entirely ignoring the imaginative; his own plays, while full of outrageous (rather than genuinely vital) dialogue were structurally conventional. With his long and elaborate stage directions he helped to create the anti-linguistic, 'director's' theatre that still dominates the English and American stages, and stifles real drama. He did help to initiate a theatre with more life in it; but, as is now generally recognized, it was in no sense really new.

The most important and enduring work of HARLEY GRANVILLE-BARKER (1877–1946) is contained in his *Prefaces to Shakespeare* (5 volumes, 1958); but, a man of quite exceptional intelligence, he was also a more than competent playwright. Long a protegé of Shaw's, he was one of the earliest pioneers for the British National Theatre—which has still not actually been built. In 1911 he published his 'paraphrase' of Schnitzler's *Anatol* (q.v.). He also translated plays by Romains and the Quintero Brothers (qq.v.). His best plays, *The Voysey Inheritance* and *Waste* (published, with *The Madras House*, as *Three Plays*, 1909), are reminiscent of Galsworthy; but Granville-Barker is better at the creation of character.

The failure of JAMES BARRIE (1860–1937) to fulfil his high potential has most usually been attributed to his over-attachment to his mother. Certainly this played a part in his life and work: his best play and his greatest success, *Peter Pan* (1904), about the boy who wouldn't grow up, is clearly related to his maternal problems. But Barrie's unresolved Oedipus complex was by no means as crippling to him as has been supposed; he failed to fulfil his gifts because he wilfully and slyly chose to indulge his sentimentality (and the sadism that went with it)—and he refused to remain in Scotland and become a Scottish instead of a popular British writer. . . . It was Edwin Muir who first pointed out that he was really tough, not soft at all; but Beerbohm (q.v.) had hinted at it when he said, a propos of the newly produced *Peter Pan*: '[Barrie's preoccupation with children] forces me to suppose that Mr. Barrie has, after all, to some extent, grown up. For children are the last thing with which a child concerns itself'.

Barrie began as a journalist, then succeeded as a novelist in the 'kailyard' tradition, which exploited Scottish humour and peculiarities in a manner that combined whimsicality, sentimentality and acute observation. His best book was *My Lady Nicotine* (1890), about his journalistic experiences; this is delightful. After this he sank into a cunning utilization of his audiences' most immature and crude instincts: a hard, subtle little Scot almost cynically purveying the cult of the child. *Peter Pan*, like the later *Mary Rose* (1924), is a masterpiece of polymorphous perversity, a Freudian joy-ride whose whole existence furiously denies the efficacy of beastly Freud. . . . It is as irresistible and as horrible as a nasty day-dream.

*

More important than Shaw or anyone operating in England or Scotland was the group of playwrights associated with the Abbey Theatre in Dublin. This came into being in 1903. It gathered its inspiration from a desire to treat Ireland and her problems in an honest manner (the recalcitrance of the censor was thus a negative stimulus) and from the austere style of acting just then initiated in Paris by Antoine (q.v.). Because of the cosmopolitan policy of Edward Martyn (1859–1924), Moore's cousin, the Abbey Theatre became more than a mere platform for Irish peasant plays: it looked beyond England, to the continent. Yeats (dealt with here in his capacity as a verse dramatist), George Moore, Colum, Joyce and Æ (qq.v.) were among those who were concerned with the venture; the most gifted playwright of the first period was J. M. SYNGE (1871–1909). Synge trained as a musician, but became interested in literature while in Germany. In Paris he met Yeats, who encouraged him and sent him off to the Aran Islands to express 'a life that has never found expression'. Synge was a naïve (q.v.) writer who never had time to ruin his work with 'thought'. Yeats said to Moore of him: 'Synge has always the better of you, for you have brief but ghastly moments during which you admit the existence of other writers; Synge never has'. And he added that he did not think that Synge 'disliked other writers': 'they did not exist'. And Moore himself spoke (1914) of Synge's strangeness and solitariness; he 'was interested in things rather than ideas'. (Moore also suggested that Yeats 'could not keep himself from putting rouge on Synge's face and touching up his eyebrows'.) What Synge, second only to O'Neill (q.v.) in the English-speaking theatre of this century, gave to an enervated drama was the vitality of non-literary, country people and their speech. But he rejected realism: his greatest play, *The Playboy of the Western World* (1907), is poetic in all but its actual prose form. Synge, even though his greatest achievement lies in the theatre, was primarily a poet. An excellent linguist, he made some fine translations (many of them in prose) from the Gaelic, Hebrew, French, Italian and German (his *Translations* were collected in 1961). In the Aran Islands he spoke Irish and listened to the English that the Irish spoke—the English of which Yeats said: it 'takes its vocabulary from the time of Malory and of the translators of the Bible, but its idiom and vivid metaphor from Irish'. His own poem 'In Kerry' reflects this linguistic experience—and Synge's own fear of death:

> We heard the thrushes by the shore and sea,
> And saw the golden stars' nativity,
> Then round we went the lane by Thomas Flynn,
> Across the church where bones lie out and in;
> And there I asked beneath a lonely cloud
> Of strange delight, with one bird singing loud,
> What change you'd wrought in graveyard, rock and sea,
> To wake this new wild paradise for me. . . .
> Yet knew no more than knew those merry sins
> Had built this stack of thigh-bones, jaws and shins.

Synge died of cancer in 1909 just as he was beginning to achieve fame. His plays deal with and draw their energy from the untamed wildness of Ireland; the greatest, *The Playboy of the Western World*, functions at a number of levels. The language is as fresh as Jacobean English (it is interesting and significant that, like O'Neill, Synge knew better than to employ verse): exuberant, extravagant, tender, beautiful. It is splendidly primitive—its first audiences were profoundly shocked because it cut sharply and neatly across their pseudo-sophisticated gentility and false patriotism—with its roots deep in the true Irish tradition. Its theme, that a man can become what people think of him, anticipates the contemporary drama of Europe rather than that of Ireland or Great Britain. A properly edited *Collected Works*, edited by Robin Skelton, began to appear in 1962. Synge, a truly poetic dramatist, has never really been understood or accepted by the Irish urban audience, to whom he is superior. As a critic has said, 'his plays demand that kind of attention from ear and brain and heart, which appears to have been lost to the English-speaking theatre three centuries ago'. He stands almost alone in a century in which most theatre has belonged to managers and directors.

None of the other Irish playwrights of the first decade of this century (with the exception of Yeats) was of Synge's stature; but many vigorous plays were written. Padraic Colum's *The Saxon Shillin'* (1903) was effective both as nationalist propaganda (it protested the enlistment of Irishmen in the British army) and as drama; his *Thomas Muskerry* (1910), set in a small rural community, recalls both Ibsen (in its social awareness) and Synge (in its language). ISABELLA GREGORY (1852–1932), Lady Gregory, manager of the Abbey, was a graceful minor dramatist whose *The Rising of the Moon* (1907) and *The Gaol Gate* (1908) deserve to survive. LENNOX ROBINSON (1886–1958), who also ran the Abbey Theatre for many years, produced a number of workmanlike realist plays; he lacked Synge's or even Colum's power over language, but he was absolutely faithful to Irish experience. *The Lost Leader* (1918) is about Parnell; his best play, *The White-Headed Boy* (1920), is a shrewd comedy of peasant life. Later, in *Church Street* (1934), he successfully attempted a Pirandellian experiment.

LORD DUNSANY (EDWARD DRAY PLUNKETT, 1878–1957), a somewhat isolated figure, should also be mentioned. Dunsany developed a highly individual style as a writer of fiction as well as of one-act plays. He was educated at Eton and Sandhurst, and saw service with the British army in the Boer War and the First World War—he had, in fact, a sardonic *persona* as a 'correct', cricketing, Englishman; but, as Ernest Boyd shrewdly pointed out, he failed 'in some slight . . . details to conform exactly to type'. It is easy to see why Dunsany is one of Borges' (q.v.) favourite authors: he is a thoroughgoing fantasist, one of the few who succeeds in this form. As the marvellously perceptive Ford (q.v.) put it, 'Says he: "I am sick of this world. . . . I will build up a world that shall be the unreal world of before the fall of Babylon. . . ." And all [his] effects . . . are got by the methods of sheerest realism'. One need add little more. He was a master of the one-act play and the short story (his verse has dated); one who builds his own worlds, and adventures in them—rather than indulging himself in them. Yeats introduced a *Selection* from his earliest work in 1912; there are a number of collections of the plays and stories.

The next major Irish dramatist to emerge after Synge was SEAN O'CASEY (originally JOHN CASEY, 1880–1964), whose best plays are his first three: *Shadow of a Gunman* (1925), *Juno and the Paycock* (1925) and *The Plough and the Stars* (1926). O'Casey came from the slums of Dublin and educated himself. His three great plays are set against the background of the Irish revolution and civil war. O'Casey, too, rejected that kind of realism of which Yeats had said that it 'cannot become impassioned, that is to say vital, without making somebody gushing and sentimental'. He chose highly melodramatic plots, but these were no more obtrusive than Shakespeare's. O'Casey, in these early plays, was able—as Synge had done before him—to create something that was so intensely Irish as to transcend it. These will continue to be played as long as the theatre lasts; they bring out the best in their audiences. By the time O'Casey arrived, the true genius of the Irish theatre had been almost stifled; but at first the Dublin audience accepted him, if only because his tragedy is screened by an inspired, savage farce. His vision is pessimistic, but tempered by comic irony; in *Juno and the Paycock* the violence and the horror are continuously redeemed by ebullience and vitality. O'Casey's indignation and hatred of priestly bigotry later got the better of him: where once his sense of the comic had operated lovingly and affirmatively, as an organizing and controlling factor, his later work tends to be either frozen into too consciously expressionist modes or merely chaotic (as in the case of his six volumes of autobiography, 1939–54). But in *The Plough and the Stars*, which caused so much anger that he left Ireland for England, O'Casey was still at the height of his powers. No play, even *Juno*, so successfully describes and defines the peculiar tragedy of Ireland—a tragedy that continues into our own times. Of course O'Casey's later plays contain much excellent work. Some critics have even seen *The Silver Tassie* (1929), which is certainly one of the fiercest and most moving anti-war plays ever written, as his finest. And his expressionist experiments, influenced by film techniques, are valuable. But it is a pity that O'Casey's hatred of the capitalist system led him to embrace the *dogma* of communism: the imagination—so far as any dogma is concerned—is a sceptical instrument. Too much of the language of the later plays is factitious; too many of the targets are objects set up by the author simply to indulge his rage. O'Casey began as an eloquent, compassionate and comic diagnostician of the Irish tragedy— of both the beauty and the terror in the Irish soul. He ended as a victim of violence and hatred, sustained only by the lyricism of his sense of justice and love of humanity. He failed (as, after all, even Marx did not) to see that individual members of an oppressive class may be as, or even more, 'human' than individual members of an oppressed class. . . . His plays were collected in four volumes (1949–51); *The Bishop's Bonfire* (1955), *The Drums of Father Ned* (1960) and three shorter plays, collected under the title of *Behind the Green Curtains* (1961), followed.

The only Irish dramatist of real stature since O'Casey is DENIS JOHNSTON

(1901), who has been living in America since 1960. Johnston was a co-director of the Gate Theatre (which became a rival of the Abbey when the latter became state subsidized and respectable) for a number of years before joining the British Broadcasting Corporation. He lacks the sheer power and wildness of O'Casey, but has more control and perhaps more intelligence. He is one of the few English-language dramatists who has thoroughly absorbed and understood expressionist (q.v.) techniques. His first two plays are his best: *The Old Lady Says 'No'* and *The Moon in the Yellow River* (published together in 1932 under the latter title, and now included in *Collected Plays*, 1960). The first explores both sides of the myth of Ireland. The second, Johnston's simplest play in terms of technique, contrasts the reality of an independent Ireland with the dream: a German engineer comes to Ireland to supervise an electrical power project. The time is the Twenties, when the Irish had newly won their independence. Johnston, while characteristically refraining from actually making judgements (this is one of his strengths), shows that the impact of technology on a rural society is not a happy one—it must be remembered that when the play was first performed the notion of 'progress' was more respectable among intellectuals than it is now. In 1936 Johnston adapted a play of Ernst Toller's (q.v.) as *Blind Man's Buff*. Johnston has continued to produce highly intelligent plays, including *The Dreaming Dust* (1940), about Swift, and *The Scythe and the Sunset*, which is set in Dublin in 1916.

One more Irish playwright deserves mention. BRENDAN BEHAN (1922–64) was a diabetic alcoholic; the dangerous combination killed him early. He had little skill of any kind, but his enormous energy partly compensated for this. Wilful egocentricity and self-adoration drowned his gift, and before he died he had become a pitiful and tiresome self-publicist; but he produced three memorable works: the plays *The Quare Fella* (1954) and *The Hostage* (1958), and his memoirs, *Borstal Boy* (1958). *The Quare Fella* is a fine, moving, indignant exposure of the villainy of capital punishment and of the cruel hypocrites who believe in and operate it. *The Hostage* is a lively, if formless, depiction of the Dublin underworld. *Borstal Boy*, an account of authoritarian and official infamy and stupidity, is sharp, amoral, objective.

*

Unlike James Barrie (q.v.), JAMES BRIDIE (ps. O. H. MAVOR, 1888–1951) remained in Scotland: for most of his adult life he practised as a doctor in his native Glasgow. But his star, once thought to be rising, fell into the sea with a hissing plop: he simply could not be serious enough. He could write superb scenes, but he never managed to produce a single satisfactory play. His weakness springs not only from lack of imaginative self-confidence but also from a feyness that archly replaced creative recklessness. Like Shaw, whom he resembles, Bridie lacks emotional substance and tries to make up for it by ingenuity. And yet he has enormous energy and inventiveness, and his best work (*The Anatomist*, 1931; *Jonah and the Whale*, 1932; *The Black Eye*, 1933; *Dr. Angelus*,

1950) reveals what is best and worst in the middlebrow Scottish audience—and that is one way of being superior to it. But he disappointed many serious Scots by his failure to initiate a revival in the theatre that would match the one begun by MacDiarmid (q.v.) in poetry.

NOËL COWARD (1899) is middlebrow in all but one respect: he has never been pretentious. His sophisticated comedies of modern life (the best are *Hay Fever*, 1925, *Private Lives*, 1930, and *Blithe Spirit*, 1941) are, within their admittedly—but unashamedly—extremely narrow limits, accurate, truthful, cynical and funny. He also has a sentimental, semi-jingoist, 'patriotic' vein (*Cavalcade*, 1932; *This Happy Breed*, 1942), which is surprisingly inoffensive: one has never been asked to take him seriously, and one accepts this as part of him. His movie *Brief Encounter* (scripted and directed by him) is rightly considered a cinema classic: this tale of a provincial love-affair is marred only by a sentimental fifty-second sequence at the end, and even this is defensible within its context. His books of autobiography—*Present Indicative* (1937), *Future Indefinite* (1954)—are well written and shrewd. Coward's fault is brittleness; but when one considers his work as a whole one is impressed by the tolerance and decency that—I use the word advisedly—shine through. This is particularly apparent in the short stories, collected in 1962. Coward is the most successful of all the non-'profound' writers in the theatre because he has a generous heart as well as being a professional to his finger-tips.

FREDERIC LONSDALE (1881–1954), though less gifted, was similarly professional. His greatest success was *The Last of Mrs. Cheney* (1925), a clever post-Wildean comedy with a melodramatic plot. He wrote for the moment. 'He delighted the millions', wrote W. Bridges-Adams, and 'the party over, his mirror reflects an empty mask'.

Some other successful playwrights who emerged in the pre-1956 (that is, pre-*Look Back in Anger*, q.v.) period are TERENCE RATTIGAN (1911), an excellent technician, PETER USTINOV (1921) and RODNEY ACKLAND (1908). All of these, and some others, have provided intelligent and skilful fare for London's theatregoers. But their techniques, and with it the whole notion of the 'well-made play', have been repudiated by the post-Osborne dramatists.

*

As Eugene O'Neill (q.v.) realized, great drama needs 'great language'—which is usually in verse rather than prose. Has any English-language dramatist of the twentieth century been capable of great language? Only Synge, perhaps. . . . Certainly the contemporary attempt to revive verse drama has been an almost unrelieved failure. The most poetic verse play of this century, Hardy's *The Dynasts* (1903–8), was not designed or written for the theatre. There has been no audience for real, contemporary poetry in the English theatre (and there is no sign of one's developing). Hardy saw this, and in *The Dynasts* he anticipated the technique of both radio and cinema. It is not free from faults, but it is considerably more profound that its sometimes portentous surface suggests.

When one compares it to Bridges' attempts at verse drama ('I spake too roughly, Margaret; I was angry:/I knew not what I said. Margaret, I am sorry. . . . My God, oh, if I have killed her! Margaret, Margaret!') one realizes its strengths. *The Dynasts* has not yet been subjected to really intelligent, extensive, critical examination. Its stage directions alone represent a high point of English prose— and once it is realized that no verse at that time could have come much nearer than Hardy's to success in dealing with so comprehensive and vast a theme, the magnitude of his achievement may be grasped. Kenneth Muir's verdict that he writes in a 'strange jargon', an understandable enough response, is not, however, a fair one. This 'jargon' expresses a remarkable complexity of thought.

The century's best verse dramatist in the theatre itself is certainly Yeats. But (and surely this is as significant as O'Neill's conscious eschewal of 'great language' and Hardy's refusal to write for the actual theatre) his finest play, *The Words Upon the Window Pane* (1934), written in the last years of his life, is in prose. . . . In the verse play Yeats very nearly, in the words of his compatriot Frank O'Connor, 'made good': he, almost alone, came to understand that no verse play in which the verse is merely ornamental to the action (the fault of, e.g., Fry, q.v.) can be poetic. His very early *The Countess Kathleen* (1891) has some good (minor) poetry in it—but this has no relevance to the action. Later Yeats came to realize that his drama could only appeal to a minority; this minority did not constitute the kind of audience that could have prompted a real revival of poetic drama—but it enabled Yeats to do almost as well as anyone could have done. The best of his verse plays are in one act. He had a good sense of theatre (he learned this while trying to run an actual theatre), but was poor in characterization. However, since most of his plays are on mythological themes, this hardly matters. His plays were collected in 1952.

The history of the verse drama since Yeats is uninspiring. Masefield (his best play is *The Tragedy of Nan*, 1909, which is in dialect) and Binyon made serious efforts, but they have dated. Abercrombie, as already noted, failed as a playwright actually because he chose to write in verse instead of prose. . . . Eliot's verse drama, which lay very near to his heart, was a disastrous affair that would not have attracted attention but for his fame in other fields. When *Murder in the Cathedral* (1935) is stripped of its Christian pretensions it is revealed as an empty, pseudo-liturgical affair, devoid of psychological interest; skilfully executed though it is, it can only be of real interest to churchgoers. *The Family Reunion* (1939) has dated. The comedies of the Fifties have already been mentioned. In his plays Eliot betrayed poetry by trying to make it unobtrusive: his fashionable audiences believed they had been watching drawing-room comedies—and so, as it happens, they had.

GORDON BOTTOMLEY (1874–1948) wrote accomplished verse; but not one of his plays, which include glosses on *Macbeth* and *King Lear*, really hits the mark. He was always devoid of dramatic sense, and as he grew older he tried to turn his plays into rhetorical performances. His verse is better than that of most Georgians, and for this reason one searches in it for something more than mere verbal beauty—but, alas, in vain. His gift consisted of little more than a capacity for concealing clichés.

Auden, Spender and MacNeice (qq.v.) all wrote verse plays during the Thirties. Three of Auden's were written in collaboration with Isherwood (q.v.), who supplied the plots. *The Ascent of F6* (1936) and *On the Frontier* (1938) are no more than lively reflections of fashionable preoccupations; *The Dog Beneath the Skin* (1935) anticipates the later interest in Brecht and in the 'musical'. Verse is not an essential element in any of these. MacNeice made a splendid verse translation of *Agamemnon*, but his original verse play, *Out of the Picture* (1937), is weak. His plays for radio are excellent, but ephemeral. The best of the Thirties verse plays, although it is gravely flawed, is Spender's *Trial of a Judge* (1938): this is more mature than anything comparable of its time, and has at least the virtue of trying to make use of poetry to express an agonizing situation—that of a liberal judge trapped between extremes. The language fails; but the attempt is testimony to Spender's political and critical awareness.

After the Second World War there was a revival of Eliotian 'Christian' drama; some of this was moderately successful in the theatre, but none has survived. Andrew Young's *Nicodemus* (q.v.), written earlier, is superior to all these productions. Then CHRISTOPHER FRY (1907) burst on the scene. Fry began as an imitator of Eliot, but soon switched to comedy with *A Phoenix too Frequent* (1946) and *The Lady's Not for Burning* (1949). Later he did *Venus Observed* (1950). Soon after this he began to go out of fashion, although he has tried to make several comebacks. Fortunately for himself he was able to earn money writing scripts for Hollywood. Fry's verse is perhaps most clearly defined by the adjective 'non-poetic': his language is inorganic, over-confident, slick, pseudo-effervescent, grovelling for the superficial response of an inattentive audience. His sense of 'wonder' and 'delight' is as meretricious as his sense of character. One feels sorry for him as a victim of fashion (the fickleness of the middlebrow audience is one of its chief characteristics)—but on the other hand he has perpetrated an offensive pretentiousness (thus a newspaper critic once spoke of his 'great hymns to living'): a smug prosiness snuggles cosily at the heart-cavity of the false vivacity: '. . . in the heart/Of all right causes is a cause that cannot lose. . . .' His skill works most effectively in translation, where he is controlled by meanings outside the area of his own self-indulgent fancy.

*

The English theatrical revolution is usually dated from 8 May 1956, when JOHN OSBORNE's (1929) play *Look Back in Anger* (1956) was staged. This was certainly an important date in the history of the theatre: theatrical impresarios —who are seldom intelligent in a literary sense—became interested in the work of young authors, and the theatre became more lively: the age of the drawing-room comedy was past. A shrewd journalist and theatrical historian, John Russell Taylor, has claimed that, now, 'there is a hard core of exciting new writing in the theatre'. This is partly justified, although the influence of

Osborne's play (which has already begun to date badly) is limited to its effect on the mentality of the people who run the theatre—as Taylor himself remarks, there was no 'School of Osborne'. There were more active good playwrights in 1970 than there were in 1950. . . . However, Taylor's term 'exciting' should not be taken to imply that there has been a genuine theatrical revival: there has not. This would have required an audience, and it could not take place in the commercial theatre—or under the present star system. The general improvement of the British theatre in the third quarter of this century is largely due to the belated influence of Brecht (q.v.)—and of other continental playwrights. The theatre of an essentially conventional playwright such as ROBERT BOLT (1924), for example, is probably rather more lively for its cautious assimilation of Brechtian and other innovations; but Bolt writes for stars, and never strays over the boundary of the generally acceptable. The other beneficial influence on the new British theatre has been that of the music hall. N. F. SIMPSON (1919), for example, is too confidently treated as an absurdist by Martin Esslin in his book *The Theatre of the Absurd*: he is (as Taylor, again, has pointed out) much nearer to the wartime radio show *Itma* (*It's That Man Again*) and the Goons than to Ionesco (q.v.). *One Way Pendulum* (1960) is theatrically excellent—'it plays itself', as one experienced member of the original cast put it—but its nonsense is that of the old variety comic rather than that of a Lear or a Carroll or a Morgenstern (q.v.). . . . When Simpson has tried to be allegorical or 'significant' the result has been disastrous.

Osborne's own progress since *Look Back in Anger* has been disappointing. *Look Back in Anger* was a muddled but passionate play which caught the muddled and passionate mood of young people in the Fifties, and provided a younger generation with a portrait of itself in Jimmy Porter. *Epitaph for George Dillon* (1958), written, before *Look Back in Anger*, in collaboration with ANTHONY CREIGHTON, is an even better, more psychologically dense play, about a playwright who decides to sell out. (The situation is the same, Allardyce Nicoll has discovered, as that of a 1910 farce; he might have added that it is also an English variation of Renard's *The Sponger*, q.v.) In *The Entertainer* (1957) Osborne's confusions vitiate the play; nor does he successfully convey the spirit of the old Edwardian music hall which he so admires. *Luther* (1961) is simply pseudo-Brechtian documentary; the words (mostly Luther's) are effective, but the dramatist's selection of his material is oddly uncreative. *Inadmissible Evidence* (1965), although admired by some, and certainly the best of Osborne's plays since 1956, is basically a rehash of *Look Back in Anger*. At his best Osborne is, in Raymond Williams' words, 'uncontrolled, unresolved but directly powerful'. A major playwright needs more than that. When Osborne takes control he becomes a writer of (perfectly good) commercial documentary; and he loses power. The worst of his faults is his inability to rid himself of trivial obsessions.

JOHN ARDEN (1930) is more original than Osborne, but has not achieved comparable commercial success. Arden uses verse in parts of some of his plays, but this is not poetic—or, I think, intended to be so. Arden, though himself what would be described in newspapers as a 'radical', does not write 'committed' plays. In fact it is this that upsets his audiences, who expect him to take sides. Actually he is an individualist, a man more in love with vigour of personality and vitality than with morality. He has more control over language than Osborne, and more complexity. His first substantial play, *Serjeant Musgrave's Dance* (1959), met with a fairly hostile reception because, although 'about' pacifism, it had no comforting message. It showed instead a man of semi-pathological personality spearheading a confused pacifist movement in a provincial town in the North of England. This is 'about' Arden's own confusions, and it resolves them in human terms: Serjeant Musgrave, the central figure, is as splendidly puzzling as Brecht's Mother Courage (q.v.), with whom he has often been compared. The language is the richest in the modern British theatre. It ran for twenty-eight performances, but was later presented as a television play. *The Workhouse Donkey* (1963) is a comedy: a caricature of local politics in a northern town. *Armstrong's Last Goodnight* (1964), set in sixteenth-century Scotland, fails because Arden has invented an unsuccessful and pointless equivalent for the Scottish speech of the time; but in other respects it is an impressive and subtle play.

Few approach the level of seriousness achieved by John Arden, although there are many skilful dramatists who can put together effective theatre pieces. Arden's one genuine rival is HAROLD PINTER (1930), a Jewish actor from the East End who continues to write brilliantly original plays. Pinter is an ironic super-realist whose first three plays hold up a mirror to nature—to life as she is really lived—with a quite remarkably artful artlessness. When asked what his work was about he replied: 'The weasel under the cocktail cabinet': in 'real life' there are weasels under cocktail cabinets; but not in fiction. . . . Again, the oddness of Pinter's dialogue is simply that it reproduces everyday speech—which, in dramatic contexts, seems very odd indeed. The 'Kafkaesque' elements in Pinter's plays, the hired killers, the strange instructions given down the shaft of a dumb-waiter, the menacing atmosphere (of the first three plays: *The Room, The Birthday Party, The Dumb Waiter*)—all these are super-realistic: the author merely witholds the 'explanation': why is Stanley to be killed in *The Birthday Party*? Who gives the instructions in *The Dumb Waiter*? You only need to be supplied with a limited number of answers, and you have solved the riddle. Pinter, then, is a very different kind of 'absurdist'. There are elements of caricature (of reality), and an atmosphere of horror as well as comedy—but the dramatist's position is still basically realist. These plays were published in 1960 under the title of *The Birthday Party*.

The Caretaker (1960) is even more overtly realist: although the play is strange in atmosphere, and one of the characters is (medically) depressed, there is a perfectly acceptable 'explanation': Mick wants to get rid of an old tramp his depressed brother has picked up—but without offending the latter. *Tea Party*, written like a number of Pinter's other plays for television, is a masterful study of a man descending into catatonic schizophrenia—it ends with his complete paralysis. Again, this is absolutely realist once we have the explanation (which in this case we do have). *The Homecoming* (1965), written for the stage, is also realist; it moves yet nearer to the conventional realist formula. The notion that Teddy—who comes home, having achieved success in America, to confront his awful family—is a liar has no more evidence to support it than any other unverifiable statement by anyone else. . . . That is one of Pinter's points. And in the case of this play we can even begin to discuss it in 'Bradleyan' terms: in terms of the characters' psychological motivations. With Arden, Pinter stands head and shoulders above his contemporaries in the theatre.

The third substantial post-war English dramatist, JOHN WHITING (1915–63), died prematurely. He did not, in fact, fulfil his potential—nor did he ever have a real commercial success. *Saint's Day* (*Three Plays*, 1957), winner of the Festival of Britain Play Competition, anticipated a good many future techniques: 'absurdity', deliberate lopsidedness of structure, abandonment of realist intentions. *Marching Song* (*Three Plays*, 1957) is one of the few really outstanding post-war plays: so much so that John Russell Taylor calls it 'formidably intelligent' but 'a little cold and lifeless': it 'could never take an unprepared audience by storm'. For *The Devils* (1961), commissioned by the Royal Shakespeare Company, Whiting drew on Aldous Huxley's study of mass hysteria, *The Devils of Loudon*, but treated the material in the light of his own unusual preoccupation with man's tendency to undermine his material position —in which process Whiting discovers much poetry. *The Devils* should not be judged by realist standards: it needs (like Shakespeare's histories) to be judged in its own, not in historical, terms.

ARNOLD WESKER (1932) is less gifted, but his *Wesker Trilogy* (1960) at least— *Chicken Soup with Barley* (1958), *Roots*, (1959) *I'm Talking About Jerusalem* (1960) —deserves to survive. The first of these is set in Wesker's native East End, the last two in Norfolk. These are sprawling, muddled—but passionately alive. They do not succeed in portraying the post-war working-classes, but they do present some convincing characters—notably Beatie in *Roots*. However, the plays, for all their vitality, do not stand up well to close examination: the Norfolk speech is badly done, there are some pointless faults of construction and inconsistencies, and at times Wesker's simplistic idealism is revealed in all its stupidity—not as innocently lovely or Blakean, but as something a little awkward. . . . *Chips with Everything* (1962), a portrait of life in the R.A.F., has its moments—but in general Wesker's attitudes (which are not the result of processes one would normally describe as intellectual) are obtrusive. During the Sixties Wesker worked hard on his impossible and noble Centre 42 project, and his plays of that period (*The Four Seasons*, 1966; *Their Very Own and Golden City*, 1966) have increasingly reflected his over-optimistic view of society—a view that unfortunately has less and less, of a lyrical nature, to sustain it.

JOHN SPURLING (1938) is the most promising of the new playwrights. He combines hard neutrality of outlook with interest in Latin-American possibilities, and is already technically adept. *Macrune's Guevara* (1969) is a relentless and yet moving examination of a legendary character, and is one of the most outstanding and serious plays of its decade.

IV

D. H. LAWRENCE (1885–1930), despite his international reputation, was one of the most English of all English writers. He wrote novels, stories, drama (at the end of the Sixties this was revived, in London, with some deserved success), travel books, criticism and poetry. Much of his best poetry (the fullest edition is *Complete Poems*, 1964) is about birds, beasts or flowers; but in this form he tends to be over-diffuse: very few of his poems are wholly successful. They aim at truth to feeling, but too often language fails. However, judicious selections from his poetry show clearly that it cannot be lightly dismissed: apart from any other consideration, it contains invaluable indications of his attitudes. His criticism (conveniently assembled in Anthony Beal's *Selected Literary Criticism*, 1955) is frequently whining, self-indulgent and unfair; it is, quite as frequently, piercingly brilliant in its insights.

Whether one ultimately likes Lawrence or not, he is undoubtedly a writer of immense importance, undisputable genius, and power. He lived and died poor; although a sick man—he suffered from tuberculosis for much of his life, and it killed him—the concept of compromise with commerce was totally unknown to him. He was the most honest of all writers. Moreover, there are some things he could do perfectly (like the sketch 'Adolf', about his father; and some of the short stories): things that no one else has done. 'There was', his friend Richard Aldington said, 'no taming him'. And so even if he could be vicious (as in his letter to Kathleen Mansfield, q.v., as she was dying), unkind, prejudiced, a would-be sex-mage whose practical grasp of his subject was notably imperfect —still, this century has needed and still needs more like him: untameable, dedicated to their project, undeflectable from it by any pieties—political, academic, polite or dogmatic. . . . The price of all this is likely to be a personality difficult to deal with; but it is a price worth paying.

Lawrence's father was a Nottingham miner married to a woman who was— and felt herself to be—a little above him socially and intellectually. For the whole of his life he sought (unsuccessfully) to resolve his fierce Oedipal feelings, which were complicated by his extreme (and equally unresolved) difficulties in relating to women. Almost always a petulant, small-minded egoism undermined his marvellous tenderness. He refused to recognize his limitations—which in terms of technique (as his poetry demonstrates) were considerable—and too frequently tried (angrily and aggressively) to express his attitude in its entirety in single works. His marriage to Frieda Lawrence, originally the German wife of an etymologist at Nottingham University, was probably about as stable as any marriage he might have made; but neither Frieda, nor any other woman, could have supplied his demands, which were unquestionably neurotic. In so far as Lawrence is a creative writer, he is liberating; but in so far as Lawrence was a sexual prophet, he was a dangerous man, insensitive to the effects of the tyranny of himself and others. His philosophy, that what is right is what feels right—in the 'solar-plexus', the 'blood'—is certainly much more dangerous and ambiguous than Nietzsche's (q.v.) philosophy, which was the result of intellectual processes far more complex, and of a much deeper self-insight. Lawrence acted on his instincts and intuitions, but, at some relatively early stage, his sexual self-exploration became arrested: he became identified with the position in which he found himself. He furiously and truculantly generalized from this position, refusing to try to create better balanced books. Even though he preached instinctive life, his own instinctive life was evidently more crippled than that of many men; the power of his message surely derives from the fierceness of his compensation for this—in the Adlerian sense. He seems to have suffered from some kind of impotence (his friend John Middleton Murry, the critic, Utopian and 'professional sufferer', stated that he did), and the descriptions of love-making in his novels are embarrassing and unconvincing, and are decked out with vulgar and pretentious language. However, his descriptions of male contacts are often authoritative (the wrestling in *Women in Love*, the massage in *Aaron's Rod*): there was a quality in women that sent him into a retreat whose ignominy, like his concomitant homosexual inclinations, he entirely refused to face. Thus, in the middle of *The Rainbow* (1915), in which the characters have been allowed a life of their own, Lawrence hysterically intrudes with something entirely personal to himself. . . . 'What is the meaning', asks David Daiches, 'of the incident' in which 'Ursula and Skebrensky have some sort of tremendous crisis . . . symbolized by Ursula's compulsive desire to lie on her back . . . and by the particular way she accepts Skebrensky's love-making'? The meaning is that Lawrence is substituting himself for his imagination at the point where this fails. . . . He, the prophet of sexual liberation, was not sexually liberated. . . . He was, in fact, sexually ignorant: his defensive sexual dogmatism destroyed his sexual freedom. It is strange that so few critics have thought it worth while to examine this discrepancy. But it is interesting, in this connection, that Lawrence's wholehearted admirers are never only critics, but also themselves committed to sexual or moral prophecy. Since it is Lawrence whom Dr. F. R. Leavis has set above all other writers of this century it is appropriate at this point briefly to discuss this influential and gifted critic—whose own excellence is so similarly flawed. Leavis is a self-assertive moralist, and he has chosen to select what he likes from Lawrence's work and then to erect this as a kind of monument of twentieth-century genius—while 'wilfully' (Daiches) ignoring Lawrence's limitations. Now Lawrence's faults, which are bad ones, go along with great virtues—the chief of them is the intuitive capacity to present hidden truths about human beings and their relationships in terms of their apprehensions of nature—but the faults need to be mentioned.

Leavis as a critic suffers from similar limitations: he is a critic of great gifts, insight and integrity; but those who are not entirely for him are wholly against him; he seeks not pupils but 'disciples'; those disciples he has attracted who have not broken away have been, like the master, rancid and fanatic in manner: the chip on the shoulder of every 'Leavisite' (as his followers are called) is a splinter of the cross upon which the master himself has been crucified by society's less than absolute acceptance of his creed.

It is no wonder that Lawrence has been raised up, in this atmosphere, as a God. And it is a pity: while Leavis in his book on Lawrence's novels, *D. H. Lawrence: Novelist* (1955), gives a valuable account, he has also been responsible for an uncritical acceptance of Lawrence's dangerous, because so confusingly presented, ideology: that life is a mystery, not to be solved by dogmas, and only to be known by itself: by acceptance of itself, by vitality.

There are of course inspired passages in every one of Lawrence's twelve novels; but each one is flawed in the same way as Daiches points out that *The Rainbow* is flawed: by a sudden, raw, personal, ideological intrusion into the imaginative texture. The best of the novels are *Sons and Lovers* (1913), for which he drew on the experiences of his own childhood—and in which he managed to be fair to his father (who appears as Morel), *The Rainbow*, and *Women in Love* (1920) in part—but this is ruined by his attempt to *judge* Gerald Crich instead of explaining him, and by the untruthful presentation of Birkin (himself) as a sexually self-fulfilled man.

But Lawrence's supreme achievement is in the best of his short stories, which were collected in three volumes in 1955 (the short novels appeared in two volumes in 1957). Here, in this relatively short compass, he did not always feel impelled to intrude. Here his sense of humour (in Lawrence's writing this seldom manifests itself more specifically than as a sense of general relaxation) emerges. In 'The Prussian Officer', one of his greatest stories, he is able to draw upon his homosexual proclivities without strain: writing it, he did not have time to become upset and confused about this problem. It is in the stories that Lawrence reached perfection uninterrupted by the sort of neurotic turbulence that led him, in his final novels, to authoritarianism and (in *Lady Chatterley's Lover*, unexpurgated version 1961) hysterical manipulation of a female character —the noble lady in the arms of the gamekeeper, a wishful portrait of Lawrence —under the disguise of writing a hymn to the life of the instincts. It has been said that although we must condemn 'the murk and unassimilated excitement' when 'it comes into the novels', we nevertheless pay the price 'for the Lawrentian genius . . . gladly'. We do pay it; but not 'gladly': we are only 'glad' when we discover the genius unpoisoned, as in the best stories.

VIRGINIA WOOLF (1882–1941) was a very different sort of writer. The daughter of the Victorian man of letters Leslie Stephen, and the wife of Leonard Woolf— a liberal and humane journalist, publisher and (latterly) autobiographer—she suffered for most of her life from a type of manic-depression. Eventually she drowned herself. That Virginia Woolf was a genuinely innovatory novelist, critically aware of the changes in sensibility that were taking place around her, goes without question. The extent of her actual achievement, however, has been challenged. Just how much more conventional was she than she thought? Are her innovations chiefly technical?

Her theories will sound familiar to anyone who knows something of modernism. The novel was not to be a photograph, not even a critical photograph, of life: it was to be a recreation of experience. 'Clock'-time was to cease to dominate it. But Virginia Woolf's work frequently suffers from her own lack of experience. She understood that trivialities were only apparent, but—herself always rich and protected—she tended to underrate the obviously non-trivial: 'it's not catastrophes, murders, deaths, diseases, that age and kill us; it's the way people look and laugh, and run up the steps of omnibuses'. One knows what, in reaction to the realism practised by Bennett and Wells and by a host of poor novelists, she meant; but these things *do* age and kill (too)—and all the more amongst the poor, about whom Virginia Woolf failed to be as sensitive as she would (to her credit) have desired. She would have done better if she had worried less. One might say, without being wholly unfair, that her aware-ness of the inadequacy of conventional realism was an advantage to Virginia Woolf: she employed it as a strategy to avoid the 'cruder' aspects of life (murder, death, diseases—poverty) with which she guiltily could not deal. She remains, despite her immense potentialities, very 'literary'; she could not quite escape from that into literature, as other greater modernists (Joyce, Céline) have done. Joyce chose the stuff of 'normal' life (to reveal that it was there, rather than anywhere else, that abnormalities were to be found). Virginia Woolf was less at ease about her subject matter. In her two most important novels (*Mrs. Dalloway*, 1925; *To the Lighthouse*, 1927) her technique suggests new and rich possibilities; but clearly the imaginative stuff on which she is concentrating, even in these books, is somewhat lacking in substance: her imagination cannot quite visualize a world, a society: her characters swim in water that has been sterilized and distilled—its salt, its fish, its teeming life destroyed—by purely literary considerations. Thus, those significant moments that it was her so intelligent intention to capture are not always particularly revelatory; her world seems impoverished because it is composed of people like herself. The ghost of her father's Victorian rationalism is nearly always lurking in the shadows: as a 'philosophy' to console us for our loss of belief; thus the imagina-tion's freedom is curtailed. But *Mrs. Dalloway* succeeds at least in its vivid, impressionistic evocation of London and in its consciously Proustian revelation of life-as-flux. Her finest novel, *To the Lighthouse*, is much influenced by Romains' *Death of a Nobody* (q.v.), which her friend Desmond MacCarthy had translated: although it is in no sense a product of 'unanimistic' thinking, its theme is the influence of a person after her death, and its concept of time is the Bergsonian one of Romains. And although it is limited by Virginia Woolf's usual lack of substance, by an emphasis on sensibility that is made at the expense of robust-ness, it is none the less a beautiful book. *The Waves* (1931), which consists of a series of interior monologues keyed in with the progress of the sun over the sea, has its admirers; but it is too self-conscious, the life-substance ebbs away like the waves: Virginia Woolf was not a poet, and when she tried to be she was inclined to be embarrassing. Throughout the Thirties, except for occasional flares, the flame of Virginia Woolf's genius guttered; her last novel, *Between the Acts* (1941), shows all the old intelligence, but lacks power and conviction (although it is worth noting that Walter Allen, q.v., seldom a critic to dismiss lightly when he has had time to consider, regards it as her best novel).

Less need be said of DOROTHY M. RICHARDSON (1872–1957)—for a time one of H. G. Wells' many mistresses—whose sequence of twelve novels *Pilgrimage* (1915–38) is rather lucky to have attracted the amount of attention that it has. She was certainly a pioneer of the stream-of-consciousness (q.v.) method; but in an ultra-realist rather than a phenomenological direction. Dorothy Richardson's protagonist Miriam is not an interesting woman, and the progress of her life is (alas) made more dull and more monotonous by the author's dogged and humourless refusal to leave much of it out. The method is of course interesting; but it is not as interesting as some have made it out to be. After all, it cuts out the physical; it ignores (as Walter Allen has pointed out) the entire implications of what Freud and others of his generation brought out into the open. Dorothy Richardson held feminist views; but her feminism is impoverished by her refusal to acknowledge woman's sexuality (she herself was not short of sexual experience: she was married, and in any case H. G. Wells would have educated her in any shortcomings—if that term may be used advisedly).

The most important of experimental writers of his generation in English literature is JAMES JOYCE (1882–1941), a Dubliner who lived in exile from 1904 until the end of his life—in Zurich, whither he had fled from France, after an operation. Joyce has often been attacked for his insensitivity to contemporary history, but in his case this is hardly just: his subject-matter was not the life of literary people (far from it), but of 'ordinary' people (he wanted above all— he, too, saw the awful, tragic irony of it—to reconcile the function of good-bourgeois-husband-and-father with that of writer): he saw that he could not do this in a priest- and politician-ridden Ireland, and he left it. *Ulysses* (1922) is a celebration of, a monument to, the life of ordinary, 'vulgar' people; had Joyce directed his energies to polemical indignation over Irish—and, later, European—politics he could not have created this monument, which in itself is an antidote to the dehumanized and dehumanizing efforts of politicians. (Joyce's admirer Eliot cannot be acquitted of the same charge: in his work there is neither indignation nor pity.)

Joyce received a good although painful education in Jesuit schools. He soon rejected the ideals of the Irish literary revival as being too nationalistic; he even went to Paris with the intention of studying medicine. The poems of *Chamber Music* (1907)—the pun is, of course, intentional—which went unnoticed, reveal the lyrical springs of his genius. He had already written the stories in *Dubliners* (1914), but could not find a publisher for them. These describe the Ireland from which he had deliberately chosen to exile himself, from which he had painfully torn up his roots. They render it with perfection: the prose loves compassionately the dreary awfulness even while it comments ironically upon it. Joyce had already taken the guts and bone out of Catholicism: he left behind only the bloated skin of its tired dogmatic insistencies. He had learned from Ibsen to be realistic; his awareness that life consisted of moments of continuous 'sin' (the official Roman Catholic word for a constellation of emotions including guilt, shame, anxiety, lovelessness) redeemed by equally continouus moments of joy and blessedness was his own. Until after *Ulysses* he was an optimistic writer.

The protagonist of *A Portrait of the Artist as a Young Man* (1916) is Stephen Dedalus, who reappears in *Ulysses*, which, in tracing the progress of an artist to maturity, represents him as necessarily uncommitted and free—and lonely.

In *Ulysses*, a masterful combination of realism (of an undeniably naturalist flavour) and symbolism, we find Stephen confronted with Leopold Bloom, an 'ordinary' man. Gradually, throughout the twenty-four hours of time covered by the novel, these two come together. Bloom is the father whom Stephen seeks; but he must finally refuse his offer of hospitality (a bed for the night). Significantly it is Bloom, Ulysses, the 'ordinary', 'dirty', 'little' man whose experiences are the richest: the artist is represented as the calculating son of the universal, decent, threatened man. This is Joyce's resolution of the universal problem of what I have called *Künstlerschuld* (q.v.). Even Joyce, one of the most dedicated writers of the century, once thought of being a physician. . . . *Ulysses* is a colossal celebration of life—including its miseries—biologically (in Marion Bloom's final thoughts as she goes off to sleep) emotionally (in Bloom's mind) and intellectually (in Stephen's mind). To describe his technique as an exploitation of 'stream-of-consciousness' is inadequate; his own theory of 'epiphanies' is more revealing. In scriptural terms an epiphany is a 'showing-forth'; for Joyce it was 'a sudden spiritual manifestation, whether in the vulgarity of speech or of gesture or in a memorable phase of the mind itself'. *Ulysses* is a subtle and rich book, but it is not a difficult one. It is, at once, a despairing, amoral, drunken Irish joke, a retelling of an ancient myth in symbolic terms, an immense, rueful parody of Catholic 'order', a quasi-naturalist tragicomedy. . . .

Joyce's wife (they lived together from 1904, but did not get legally married until 1931), Nora Barnacle, was a non-literary woman ('Why don't you write sensible books that people can understand?')—as 'ordinary' (but how extraordinary she was!) as one would expect from the author of *Ulysses*. She bore him two children, a son and a daughter. The latter, Lucia, became schizophrenic and eventually had to be permanently hospitalized. This broke Joyce: it touched off his enormous guilt. The guilt was not connected with his leaving the Roman Catholic Church, but with the price (paid by others) for his devoting himself to creative writing. Like most of the great writers of this century, he blamed himself for being creative. In *Ulysses*, as I have suggested above, he had been able to some extent to resolve this problem. The progressive dissociation of Lucia's personality revived his guilt. *Finnegans Wake* (1939) is his anguished response to his daughter's gradual retreat from reality. He took her to Jung, who told Joyce that she had schizophrenic tendencies. Desperately he objected: why were her verbal games not just like his own? 'You are both going to the bottom of the river', Jung replied, 'but she is falling and you are diving'. Joyce had his own troubles, too: fame had by no means made him rich; he was almost blind; *Ulysses* ran into trouble in almost every country in which it appeared: he may well have felt that he was being driven deeply into himself. *Finnegans Wake* is the dream of H. C. Earwicker (*Here Comes Everybody*) and of Joyce himself, written in multiple puns. Although it has become a book to which a number of scholars have written keys, *Finnegans Wake* is an inaccessible failure, the work of a man whose masterpiece had already been written. It is fascinating, comic, ingenious; but as a whole it fails. Joyce's associative technique becomes a desperate, empathic parody of Lucia's disastrous compulsion: the guilty father searches the bottom of the river for the daughter he feels he has abandoned and allowed to drown. *Finnegans Wake* is wonderful food; but we cannot really eat it. 'I could not', he wrote of this book, which was seventeen years in the making (scrawled out painfully, between eye operations) 'I felt I could not, use words in their ordinary connections. . . . When morning comes of course everything will be clear again. . . . I'll give them back their English language. . . .' But morning (Lucia's miraculous recovery; his own clear sight) never did come. The project of *Finnegans Wake* arose as an intuitive response to the oddness apparent in the fifteen-year-old Lucia: to the effect that Joyce saw himself having, as a dedicated writer, upon his family's life. But the answer to his doggedly private and bitter attempt to turn words into nothing but counters is to be found in the humanity of *Ulysses*. Joyce's letters have been collected (1957), and his *Critical Writings* (1959). Richard Ellmann's excellent biography appeared in 1959. *Giacomo Joyce*, a short but exceedingly interesting story from about 1914, was published in 1969.

As important (and exciting) a writer as Joyce, though few have recognized it, was PERCY WYNDHAM LEWIS (1882–1956). Although Joyce learned much from Lewis, no two writers could be more different. Lewis was a painter of genius, as well as a writer; he, too—although much later in life—went blind. Wyndham Lewis (who is not to be confused with an often witty humorist, Catholic apologist and biographer called D. B. Wyndham-Lewis, also blind in his old age and now also dead) was literary critic, art critic, polemicist, satirical poet—and, above all, novelist. In general Wyndham Lewis has been, and is, ignored; when granted a place in surveys of literature it is usually as a right-wing obscurantist. But discerning critics (T. S. Eliot was one of them; Pound, Grigson, Walter Allen, qq.v., are others) have recognized his strange genius.

Lewis embarrassed everyone, including—in the end—himself. His faults are soon dealt with—sooner, indeed, than some, because of the lack of attention he has suffered. But these must be enumerated.

He frequently tried to do too much at the same time: some of his polemical writing is inexcusably slapdash—as well as being irrelevant to his real concerns. He became too involved in his function as polemicist, and neglected to develop his imaginative and intuitive gifts—until it was almost too late. For much of his life (until he found himself exiled in Canada, during the Second World War) he used the intellectual side of himself as a protective shield against compulsions that can only be described as romantic. These he nervously rationalized as 'privacy': it is as well to remind his detractors that, while he wilfully over-indulged his paranoid tendencies, he also enjoyed a tenderly happy marriage. But in his capacity as the hard-headed, self-styled 'Enemy', this (personally) timid, kind and gentle man wilfully refused (1931) to see Hitler as anything but a comic 'gutbag', and even appeared to praise him. This was a worse case, as Lewis finally saw, than merely doing it to annoy because he knew it teased the left. He failed to discern the humanity and sense of alarm that were genuine elements in the liberal protest against Hitler. *The Hitler Cult* (1939) was his official apology; but he later examined the causes of this failure (and what it implied) in one of the most self-castigating novels of the century: *Self-Condemned* (1954), published only three years before he died. He lived to suffer for his excesses, and to expose his failures to himself— and in the process to write a work, *The Human Age* (1955–6) that, although it is unfinished, will in due time be seen to be a classic (as T. S. Eliot said, alluding to the treatment of people as puppets—'hallucinated automata': here 'the puppets begin to get the better of the puppet-master'). So Lewis' grave faults did not destroy or even diminish him as a creative writer. He is ultimately a giant of letters not in spite of them but—like all such giants—because of them. Most of Lewis' novels are in print, and there are two excellent selections from his work: E. W. F. Tomlin's *Wyndham Lewis: An Anthology of his Prose* (1969) and Raymond Rosenthal's paperback *A Soldier of Humour and other Writings* (1966), which contains much otherwise inaccessible early work.

What Lewis the critic, satirist and sociologist was interested in was what he called, in *The Art of Being Ruled* (1926), 'the life of the intelligence'; the pride of 'its servants', he wrote, 'if they have it, is because of something inside themselves which has been won at no one else's expense, and that no one can give them or remove from them'. Lewis the satirist was at his best an apostle of the life of the intelligence unique in his time. Savagely humorous (usually over the heads of his targets), he used *thought* where most *literati* slackly used fashion or facile emotion. He cast himself into isolation partly by exercising his human right to objectivity. His thinking about time, flux, and the role of the intellect may most conveniently be found in *Time and Western Man* (1927), a book which anticipates and transcends many of the more important ideas of the four decades that followed its publication; here he is at his least rigid in his application. The basis of his notions about art arose from his practice as a painter: '. . . I am for the Great Without', he wrote, 'for the method of *external* approach'. And he tended to describe his people in wholly external terms. So far as satire was concerned, this was effective: in the massive *The Apes of God* (1930), a fearful account of the silliness of *literati*, the dehumanizing process is justified. But that was Lewis functioning as the Enemy—and in him there lurked an enemy of the Enemy. . . . Even in his most ferocious satire (probably this is contained in *The Roaring Queen*, which he himself withdrew at proof stage in 1936) Lewis was always straining after something else, something imaginative and creative; but this was not really compatible with his dehumanizing descriptive technique. His satire became phantasmagoric horror: the romantic element cannot express itself, but is held rigidly down by the cold technique (in such paintings as 'The Surrender of Barcelona' the romantic richness is more apparent, because Lewis was able to use actual colour). Lewis' powerful imaginative yearnings hid beneath the cool or comic surface, a metaphor for the graphic, a result of the ruthless and behaviouristic exploitation of the 'eye' —like red-hot lava waiting to erupt. It has been asked why the strangely original early writings—'Bestre', 'The Cornac and his Wife'—'had no later fulfilment'. But they did: partially in *Self-Condemned*, fully and linguistically in the last great unfinished tetralogy. Lewis was in 1914 a pioneer of the short-lived vorticist movement: in other words an English cubist. Vorticism (of which Pound, q.v., was the chief champion) in painting and literature was essentially an anti-mimetic movement: the artist was urged to *invent* in his own right (cf. cubism, q.v.). As Walter Allen has remarked, 'Lewis's prose at its best is as exciting as any written in English this century'. And in Lewis' earlier prose we may see the germs of an astonishing experimentalism. Consider the beginning of 'Cantleman's Spring Mate' (1917):

> 'Cantleman walked in the strenuous fields, steam
> rising from them as though from an exertion,
> dissecting the daisies specking the small wood,
> the primroses on the banks, the marshy lakes,
> and all God's creatures. The heat of a heavy
> premature Summer was cooking the little narrow
> belt of earth-air, causing everything innocently
> to burst its skin, bask abjectly and profoundly. . . .'

Or this from the 'advertisement' to 'The Enemy of the Stars' (it is not possible here to reproduce the startling typography):

DRESS. ENORMOUS YOUNGSTERS, BURSTING
EVERYWHERE THROUGH HEAVY TIGHT
CLOTHES, LABOURED BY DULL
EXPLOSIVE MUSCLES, full of
fiery dust and sinewy energetic
air, not sap. BLACK CLOTH
CUT SOMEWHERE, NOWADAYS, ON
THE UPPER BALTIC.

VERY WELL ACTED BY YOU AND ME.

Lewis tinkered with this amazingly original style, in which disparate elements seem to clash, diverge and come together, until *The Childermass* (1928), in which he tried to discover to where it might lead in a full-scale work. Then, in illness and possibly in despair, he abandoned it and fought his battles in a different way. (This negative phase of his creative life is perhaps best described as one of heroic behaviourism.) But towards the end of his life he resumed the task, with renewed lucidity and courage: *Monstre Gai* and *Malign Fiesta*, which, with the revised *Childermass*, form *The Human Age*, explore the meaning of existence. The mass of humanity, in a limbo outside heaven, awaits examination by the Bailiff. This visionary work, 'magnificent and dreadful' (Walter Allen), which will undoubtedly be seen as one of the major achievements of the present century, was written by Lewis when he had become (by a savage stroke of irony) blind (the pressure of an inoperable tumour on his optic nerve) and was dying.

Other notable works by Lewis, one of the major art critics of his time, include *The Demon of Progress in the Arts* (1954) and the novels *Tarr* (1918) and *The Revenge for Love* (1937).

L. H. MYERS (1881–1944), like T. F. Powys, has long been championed by F. R. Leavis and his school (q.v.); without the critical attention thus accorded to him he would perhaps have been forgotten—which would certainly be critically unjust. Myers, especially in the trilogy *The Root and the Flower* (1927–35)—*The Pool of Vishnu* (1940), a sequel, is not on the same level—is a distinguished philosophical novelist; in fact, he is so distinguished that he clearly shows the limitations of this genre. Myers, son of F. W. H. Myers the psychical researcher, was rich, fastidious and mystical. As a young man he had a mystical experience: a sense of the goodness of man as seen from the eye of God. This—together with his guilty hatred of his own class—remained his guiding light until his suicide. He began as a verse dramatist, and did not publish his first novel, *The Orisers* (1922), until he was forty-one. Myers failed to resolve the problem of his sense of alienation from his environment until he set his fiction in the past (in sixteenth-century India). Even here he does not entirely succeed in a creative capacity, for, subtle and intelligent as he is, his real purpose is didactic: briefly, it is to demonstrate that personality and all that man does to form it and exercise it is an obstacle to his self-realization. In *The Root and the Flower* a young prince, Jali, is shown as being presented with various temptations, the main one being that of becoming a personality instead of a fulfilled person. Myers' thinking is interesting and important—but it precedes his invention and conception of character. Finally he rejected art and fiction altogether, became a somewhat desperate communist, and tried to pinpoint the evils of society in an autobiographical study; he destroyed this before destroying himself, thus incidentally answering the question that had plagued him for the whole of his life: why do men choose to live? Like Martin Buber, the author of *I and Thou*, to whom he owes much, Myers fiercely resisted the tendency of the modern, commercial world to treat people as objects—and, as G. H. Bantock has remarked, 'he has . . . a sense of evil'. Judged by the highest standards, he failed; but no novelist of greater imaginative power has yet tackled his subject-matter. He is an important figure.

A. E. COPPARD (1878–1957), a short-story writer who never essayed a novel, is nowadays almost as neglected as Myers. His *Collected Tales* appeared in 1948; it was followed by *Lucy In Her Pink Jacket* (1954). Coppard came up the hard way: apprentice to an East End tailor, office boy, professional athlete, clerk. He was well over thirty before he began writing poetry and stories seriously. His poetry is not successful; but his best short stories are among the most poetic of his time. Although self-educated, he was an exceedingly cunning and studied writer, who worked very hard (sometimes too hard) to gain his apparently spontaneous effects. A grand anarchy lay at the heart of his work; his most deeply felt stories (such as 'Dusky Ruth') involve characters whose real concerns are entirely anti- or non-social. He also has charm, comedy and beauty. Coppard, who came from Kent, is one of the most English of writers.

CARADOC EVANS (1879–1945), although one of the most ferocious satirists of Wales (he was a Welsh-speaking Welshman writing in English), was as Welsh as Coppard was English. His first collection of short stories, *My People* (1915), was remarkably original, even though the author went back to the style of the Bible for his sharp, gleefully realistic and honest accounts of the dark idiosyncrasies of his people. After two more volumes of stories he brought out a satirical play, *Taffy* (1923), which caused a stir when it was produced in London: a critic said it 'hit, hurt and heartened'. His first novel, *Nothing to Pay* (1930), embodied an even more deliberate and angry caricature of the Welsh than he had yet attempted—and it did not increase his popularity in his own country. Evans was above all the denouncer—often in its own brand of powerful rhetoric—of the Welsh nonconformist institution known as Chapel. It is in Evans' novels and collections of stories that we may find a more morally engaged, less self-indulgent version of the more popular *Under Milk Wood* (q.v.).

RONALD FIRBANK (1886–1926), a cultivated taste if ever there was one, presents a complete contrast. He was a pathetic and yet genuinely agonized trivialist, a chic fugitive from life who hid, in aestheticism, what his giggling response to terror could not neutralize; his substanceless fiction attracts fellow-homosexuals—and writers whose roots are in, or half in, the Nineties. His technique and mood have influenced writers as diverse as Osbert Sitwell, Anthony Powell, Carl Van Vechten, Aldous Huxley, William Gerhardie, Evelyn Waugh, Ivy Compton–Burnett (qq.v.). He wrote twelve novels and a play; the best known novels are *Valmouth* (1919) and *Concerning the Eccentricities of Cardinal Pirelli* (1926); *The Works* appeared in 1928, later to be supplemented by *Santal* (1931), stories, and *The Artificial Princess* (1934). Firbank cannot be called serious, and he was also silly—but it must be conceded, even by those who are repelled by the pointlessness of his concinnity, that, in Evelyn Waugh's words, he 'negligently stumbled' upon 'technical discoveries': the efficacy of dialogue, conversational nuance, the withdrawal of the kind of cause and effect associated with conventional *mimesis*. . . . *Sorrow in Sunlight* (1924), called *Prancing Nigger* in America, played an important part in the cult of things negro which swept France in the Twenties—and which indirectly influenced the progress of negritude (q.v.). Firbank's work, always valetudinarian, hovers between the ingenuous and the cunning; its tittering nihility has no more than a touching, childish quality—but in Waugh it becomes a blackness, in Powell an observational position, in Van Vechten a self-caressing pussiness, in the early Huxley a cleverness. . . . Firbank belonged inexorably to the Nineties, but he managed to anticipate—largely by influencing—that twentieth-century vein which exploited, more or less successfully, decadence.

Another source for these writers, as for Firbank himself, was FREDERICK ROLFE (1860–1913), self-styled baronet and priest, who was both more comic and more poisonous than Firbank. He was a confidence-man, pauper, tutor, blackmailer, paedophile, translator—and author of seven novels and a number of short stories. Rolfe was a trickster whose failed life stank to himself as to the few friends whom he had and betrayed. But he was a fascinating figure: a bore, but also a pseudo-Borgian freak whose vindictiveness and paranoia have deservedly become legendary—largely through A. J. A. Symons' famous biography, *The Quest for Corvo* (1930). Rolfe's one decent novel, *Hadrian the Seventh* (1904; 1950), is by no means the 'masterpiece' Symons called it; but it is a psychopathological *tour de force*, an autobiographical fantasy about a man who, rejected as a priest (as Rolfe was), is elected Pope and proceeds to revenge himself upon—or to reform?—the Church. . . . Even this novel, told in an over-mannered and hysterical prose, depends upon our knowledge of Rolfe himself to gain its full effect: it is the self-recorded case-history of a remarkable patient.

IVY COMPTON-BURNETT (1892–1969), whose novels are constructed entirely out of dialogue, is a unique phenomenon in English fiction: a very respectable and aristocratic lady (one thinks of Marianne Moore, q.v.) whose one 'moral failing' (in purely Victorian terms), her lesbianism, gave her uncannily sharp intelligence a window onto the world of real human evil: this bitter and severe intelligence, in the privacy of the author's consciousness, made its ironic decision some time between the publication of a first, wholly conventional tale, *Dolores* (1911) and that of *Pastors and Masters* (1924), the first genuinely 'Compton-Burnett' novel. Ivy Compton-Burnett was an artful prestidigitator: her bland procedure—the recording of dialogue—conceals: the very highly melodramatic nature of her plots; her lack of interest in realism—all her 'characters', after all, share in their creator's delight in style and epigram; her limitations (the late Victorian upper middle-class world), which are as severe—she recognized it—as her opinion of existence; her lack of psychological expertise—of knowledge of actual mental process; the strong, uncreative, mushy element of sentimentality in her. . . . Here is a case of the triumph of a self-prescribed, drastic therapy. Her theme, most broadly defined, is exploitation: she sees her specimens as exploiters or exploited—but the former may prove to be the latter in disguise, or the position may become transformed. One can be sure of only one thing: that the surface of the story will remain conversational, an imperturbable parody of the ravaged and ravaging minds of the protagonists. Her plots almost invariably involve such vicious, violent or sensational crimes as incest, murder, forgery and so on. Ultimately these are not, perhaps, novels at all—but marvellously entertaining Indic fantasies, in which nothing really happens in peoples' minds. As she has said, with a characteristically misleading, sardonic directness: 'real life' is 'of no help at all'.

This hardly matters, though: ultimately the quality we gain from these observations is as tragic as their classically educated progenitor intended. There are more than twenty novels, from which one might select *Brothers and Sisters* (1929), *Parents and Children* (1941), *Manservant and Maidservant* (1947), called *Bullivant and the Lambs* in America, and *A Heritage and its History* (1959) as being particularly excellent.

ALDOUS HUXLEY (1894–1963) was more versatile and, during his lifetime, very much more widely read than Ivy Compton-Burnett. In the years following his death his reputation has slumped drastically, doubtless because he had throughout his career—right from clever young man through fashionable mystic to psychedelic vulgarian—a journalistic flair. This may seem odd in so esoteric and highly educated a man; but Huxley bristled with contradictions— his failure to resolve them prevented him from progressing from brilliance to the seriousness of a major writer. The adroit, studiedly cruel young imitator of Firbank jostled in Huxley with the aesthete of guiltily ascetic tendencies; the theoretical hedonist with the deficient monk. Because Huxley began as an entertainer and ended as a mystic it is often supposed that he changed drastically; such is not the case. As D. S. Savage, one of the most astute of modern critics, has pointed out, both the early attitude of 'Pyrrhonic hedonism' and the later mystical one—essentially this amounts to rejection of the ego and its works, including time, for the sake of union with the absolute—'originate in a common dislocation of being'. The early Huxley of those bright comedies of manners, *Chrome Yellow* (1921), *Antic Hay* (1923) and *Those Barren Leaves* (1925), felt himself to be as detached from the crude, raw stuff of life as did the later mystic. The early writer has no mercy on his characters; he caricatures the disgustingness of human physicality in them; the later writer has dropped caricature and learned compassion (although he was never able, in his fiction, to achieve warmth); he still rejects physicality.

The three early novels are coruscating, farcical, worthy successors to the Ben Jonson of the 'humour' plays. *Those Barren Leaves*, more serious, is more questionable because its characters, which ought to be endowed with their own vitality, are rather too obviously vehicles for Huxley's own reflections on futility. *Point Counter Point* (1928), a *roman à clef* that owed a good deal to Gide's *The Coiners* (q.v.), is Huxley's best, most felt, novel—although it is significant that even here the most moving episode revolves around a Beethoven quartet. Huxley lacked warmth as a novelist; but he had decency and gentleness, and *Point Counter Point* does succeed to a limited degree in exhibiting sympathy towards that humanity which does not aspire but simply suffers and lives. Huxley examines himself in the person of the novelist Philip Quarles and finds himself wanting: 'All his life he had walked in . . . a private void, into which nobody . . . had ever been permitted to enter'. He throws himself (humbly) up against the vitalistic Mark Rampion (D. H. Lawrence, a friend of Huxley's), and in the book gives Rampion the edge ('the intellect', Quarles ends by believing, 'ought to humble itself. . . and admit the claims of the heart, aye and the bowels, the loins. . . .'). But that was to falsify the true state of affairs. Savage calls the novel an inept failure, shoddily written, 'puerile in conception and presentation'. . . . There is something to this judgement, and even to the charge that here more than anywhere Huxley betrays 'the fatal juvenility which . . . vitiates his understanding of life'. But it is none the less too severe. Huxley is only juvenile as a novelist when compared to, say, Lawrence at his very best; at times *Point Counter Point* is far from inept; the sincerity and, perhaps more to the point, the seriousness of Huxley's project is evident on every page, and Rampion is realized with power and some understanding. After this Huxley's powers as a novelist collapsed: *Eyeless in Gaza* (1936), *After Many a Summer* (1939) and all its successors are intelligent; but they are thesis-fiction, written in an entire absence of imaginative pressure. *Brave New World* (1932) is a clever but somewhat cold dystopia. Of Huxley's retreat into mysticism the less said, perhaps, the better: it never seems, even to a reader of good faith who is interested in mysticism and not prejudiced against it, to be more than journalistic; one assumes, or at least hopes, that his personal experience was of a more substantial calibre. His two best later books are historical studies: *Grey Eminence* (1941) and *The Devils of Loudon* (1952). *Texts and Pretexts* (1932) is one of the most lively and provocative anthologies—linked by commentary—of its time. His *Letters* (1971) are interesting.

WILLIAM GERHARDIE (1895)—the final 'e' is his own recent reversion to an older family spelling—is a better novelist, who has never had his due; even a uniform edition initiated in the late Sixties has not really established him. He did in truth 'go off' (like the ladies in Mrs. Oliphant's Victorian novel *Miss Marjoribanks*) very badly during the Thirties, and his latter-day manner (in letters to the press and so on) has been irritating and off-putting; but this is not an excuse for the neglect of his accomplished and unusual early novels. His originality owes much, no doubt, to the fact that Gerhardie—an Englishman—was brought up in Petrograd: he looks at things from a very unusual point of view. That is his strength. *Futility* (1922) and *The Polyglots* (1925) are both true English-Chekhov—and both deal with Englishmen abroad. Here Gerhardie is both sad and comic, with a certain modest deftness of touch that he later mistakenly sacrificed in the interests of a wider scope. *Resurrection* (1934), about a young man who has the mystical experience of becoming divorced from his body, is his attempt at a major novel, and it almost comes off. But Gerhardie is too ambitious and self-consciously experimental, as if he wishes to produce a rival to *Ulysses* or *Point Counter Point*; and it is here, too, that a self-defeating tone of superiority begins to creep in (just the same kind of preening but mistaken self-delight that wrecks Nabokov's *Ada*, q.v.). *Of Mortal Love* (1936), a sentimental love story of the Twenties, shows his talent stretched to its utmost—and fragmenting under the strain.

EVELYN WAUGH (1903–66), another predictable admirer of Firbank, has the same horror of life as Huxley; he has more energy, Dickensian inventiveness, but is much sicker—he early (1930) rationalized his inability to respond to people into an all-embracing orthodoxy: Roman Catholicism. Essentially, however, his world is the nihilistic one of Firbank; but it was enriched by the manure of an intelligent and religious gloom. It is obvious enough that Waugh dwelled darkly and at length upon the mysteries of Christ; but it is equally obvious that, whatever he achieved in his own life, self-centredness deflects his work from true seriousness. Religion in his work seldom functions as more than something to console his sense of hatred (not dislike or distaste) for the world—and everyone in it. His aggressive Catholicism has assured him of many more readers than Huxley—but he is not really a better novelist, even if he looks like one (and it must be conceded that he usually does): his religion is seen, by his readers at least, as his excuse for condemning not merely the modern world but also the people in it. Waugh's early novels differ from Huxley's in that they are fantasies where Huxley's are farces; they are less brilliant, but more crazy. In *Decline and Fall* (1928) and *Vile Bodies* (1930) there is a sense of autonomous life missing in even the earliest Huxley; the atmosphere is entirely antinomian. Only the kind of seriousness that expresses itself in the form of solidity is absent—present, instead, is an indifference of which the author is obviously unaware. It might have been youth; later books showed that it was not. *A Handful of Dust* (1937), the story of a man's falling apart under the strain of his broken marriage, has been admired as Waugh's best novel and a masterpiece; but it is neither. It is rather, as Graham Martin has suggested, a piece of elaborate and skilful fakery: Waugh uses his famous detached manner—much vaunted as 'objectivity'—to cover up his own incapacity for that psychological understanding which amounts to compassion. Whereas in the comic novels (*Scoop*, 1938, and *Put Out More Flags*, 1942, are to be included in this category) Waugh could to some extent rationalize his terror into shuddering, quick laughter, here he inhibits himself by attempting to deal with ostensibly realist material. All Waugh's later fiction—with the exception of the scarifying satire, *The Loved One*, 1948, on the Hollywood cult of death—is spoiled in this way. The trilogy formed by *Men at Arms* (1952), *Officers and Gentlemen* (1954) and *Unconditional Surrender* (1961) is an imitation of Ford's *Parade's End* (q.v.), and collapses by the side of it: Guy Crouchback is a wistful technicoloured photograph of Waugh, whereas Tietjens has an existence independent of Ford. It is true that in this trilogy, especially in the concluding book, Waugh tried to assert an interest in humanity; but it came too late to make any difference to his creative achievement: the relevant passages read like (admirable) sermons preached by worthy but linguistically ungifted parsons. The best of the later novels is *The Ordeal of Gilbert Pinfold* (1957), a realistic treatment of his own alarming experience of a series of hallucinations. A gifted and interesting writer—but either neutral or nasty in just the places where niceness counts.

*

JOYCE CARY (1888–1957) did not publish his first novel, *Aissa Saved*, until 1932, when he was forty-four years old—so that as a writer he belongs to a generation later than his own. He is an exuberant novelist, whose poor sense of form is

281

usually more than counterbalanced by his remarkable gift for identifying with his characters. What matters to Cary is vitality and integrity: these are more important than morality—and in the life of an individual they are more important qualities than success. Cary's earliest novels, written out of his experiences in the Nigerian Political Service, are as good as anything he ever did. *Aissa Saved* is an objective account of the effect of missionaries upon those they convert, *Mister Johnson* the memorable story of an African who tries, with first pathetic and then tragic results, to live like an Englishman. The sequence *Herself Surprised* (1941), *To Be a Pilgrim* (1942) and *The Horse's Mouth* (1944) is a study in different sorts of innocence and integrity; the novels are narrated, respectively, by Sara Monday, Mr. Wilcher and Gulley Jimson. The first and the last of these are criminal; Wilcher is a senile exhibitionist. But all three represent life to Cary, and, whether they irritate the reader or not, there is no mistaking the gusto and the energy which have gone into their making. *A House of Children* (1941) recreates an Irish childhood with great charm and verve. It is true that the actual world of Cary's novels is unvaried and limited, and even that he is unimaginative ('there is . . . much less . . . than meets the eye' in his writing, wrote Anthony West); but he is inventive, and he does convey the sense of life in which he so desperately believed. Cary is a representative of the same religious tradition as Bunyan, but in his hands it becomes secularized into a kind of humanism, a combination of pragmatism and ecstasy that for many readers is unsatisfactory—but is nevertheless a fact of British life and is not artificial.

ROSE MACAULAY (1889–1958) was a humane, shrewd and witty novelist whose best work will assuredly survive. Her best novels are *Potterism* (1920), an excellent, rather Forsterian satire on the society of its time, and her last, *The Towers of Trezibond* (1956), the self-told story of a man who goes to Turkey to escape from an adulterous love-affair—an extremely unusual and sad comedy.

STELLA BENSON (1892–1933), who died young of tuberculosis, should not be forgotten. Probably her diary, which is allowed to be published in 1973, is her most important work; but *The Poor Man* (1922) and *Tobit Transplanted* (1931) are both original, painfully self-probing, witty novels; the latter tells the story of Tobias and the Angel in a modern, Manchurian setting.

REBECCA WEST (ps. C. I. FAIRFIELD, 1892) is very much a novelist of her period: intelligent, solid, sensibly feminine, determinedly enlightened. She is a brilliant journalist—though in this field her work, of which *The Meaning of Treason* (1949) is the most notable, remains journalism. Her second novel, *The Judge* (1922), was hailed as the 'best psychoanalytical novel'; and so it was, but now it reads just a little too pat. In fact Rebecca West's best novel is the comparatively late *The Fountain Overflows* (1956), which is the first of a sequence in progress. This is a retrospective account of an Edwardian family broken up by the defection of the brilliant but self-destructive father. *Letters to A Grandfather* (1933) is an unusual work about the religious impulse, in which God appears as a tired Negro in faded scarlet evening dress.

More gifted as a novelist than any of these, and now unduly neglected (not a single book of hers is in print) is Rebecca West's older contemporary MAY SINCLAIR (1865–1946). Like Rebecca West, she is very much of the Edwardian period (she was a suffragette, or at least took part in some marches), but her grasp of character is greater; clever, again like Rebecca West, in her best fiction she transcends this entirely. *Mary Olivier: A Life* (1919) and *The Life and Death of Harriett Frean* (1922), both acute psychological studies of women, are probably her finest novels; but *A Cure of Souls* (1924), the portrait of a sybaritic vicar, runs these very close. May Sinclair was also a very good writer of short stories; one of these, 'Where Their Fire is Not Quenched', is a small masterpiece of the supernatural.

ELIZABETH BOWEN (1899), as obviously a disciple of Henry James as L. P. Hartley, has written about a dozen worthy novels, full of delicate and sensitive descriptions of moods and places, but has never equalled *The Death of the Heart* (1938), the story of the destruction of a young girl's sensibility and capacity to love by a group of cold-hearted, affected people. In her other novels, one of the best of which is *The Little Girls* (1964), Elizabeth Bowen is better, so to speak, at description than psychology. And she has made her incapacity to deal with any but a specific type of upper-class person into a more severe limitation than it needs to be by trying, from time to time, to overcome it.

DAVID GARNETT (1892) wrote some unusual novels of fantasy—'a perfect literary nick-nack', Desmond MacCarthy said of the first, *Lady Into Fox* (1922) —but gradually dried up until in the middle Fifties he produced a very ordinary comedy of manners. *Lady Into Fox* is, indeed, a slight work; but it is beautifully done, with exactly the right touch, as are its successors *A Man in the Zoo* (1924) and *The Sailor's Return* (1925). Sylvia Townsend Warner (q.v.) began in something like the same vein with her story of a witch, *Lolly Willowes* (1926); but she went on to produce a much more substantial novel, a remarkable account of fourteenth-century convent life, *The Corner That Held Them* (1948). Garnett wrote *No Love* (1929), a realistic picture of life in the first quarter of the twentieth century, which is marred by preciosity of style, but contains some vivid portraits. He wrote no fiction between 1935 and 1955; when he began again he had lost his touch.

J. B. PRIESTLEY (1894) has been a best-selling novelist since the panoramic *The Good Companions* (1929); he has also had successes as a playwright—sometimes an interestingly experimental one. It has long been fashionable to dismiss him from serious consideration—but this is not fair. Priestley does have certain middlebrow vices: long-windedness, over-heartiness—an insecure, bluff, Yorkshire manner—sentimentality; and he is in the realm of fiction an entirely conventional realist. But he has virtues: and he is a better novelist than his master and close friend Hugh Walpole (q.v.), with whom he collaborated in a letter-novel. Even *The Good Companions*, the tale of a concert party, has virtues: strong characterization, a good sense of place, a sense of the comic. But he has written better than this: good, intelligent thrillers (*Black-Out in Gretley*, 1942, is the best) and *Lost Empires* (1965), a really moving story of the old-time music-hall. His plays are well made, and the 'time' plays—*Time and the Conways* (1937) and *I Have Been Here Before* (1937)—and *Dangerous Corner* (1932) are as good as anything seen in the commercial theatre in their decade.

L. P. HARTLEY (1895–1972) is an uneven writer—some of his tales of the supernatural are really shoddy—but at his best he earns the comparison with Henry James (q.v.) that is often made. *Simonetta Perkins* (1925) is as much an exercise in the manner of James as Lubbock's *The Region Cloud*. Hartley's strength lies, rather surprisingly, in his stern morality. His attitudes are what would be called 'old-fashioned', and one assumes that he would reject such things as psychoanalysis as tending to excuse 'evil' conduct. And yet his own work is very 'Freudian': it gains its power from the fact that the evil in it is never really defined. *The Go-Between* (1950) is a Jamesean tale of the adult world interpreted by a boy. The *Eustace and Hilda* trilogy—*The Shrimp and the Anemone* (1944), *The Sixth Heaven* (1946), *Eustace and Hilda* (1947)—is the subtle and beautifully told account of a brother and sister doomed, by their characters, to destroy each other; terror and comedy are perfectly blended here. Although Hartley is himself a moralist (his non-fiction work leaves this in no doubt) he is not in fact a moralist as a writer, but rather what Paul Bloomfield has described as 'the transmitter of a civilized ethos'. He has not only an awareness of evil but also an awareness of inevitability; moreover, he makes no judgements in his novels. *Facial Justice* (1960) is a powerfully imagined dystopia.

L. A. G. STRONG (1896–1958) never fulfilled his early promise. A prolific and successful writer of competent and intelligent novels, the really substantial novel just eluded him. He was highly professional—perhaps too much so—but could only create types, rather than developing characters. His best work is to be found in the early novels *Dewar Rides* (1929), *The Garden* (1931) and *Sea Wall* (1933), and in his short stories of Irish rural life. He was a graceful minor poet: *The Body's Imperfection* (1957) collects his poems.

CHARLES MORGAN (1896–1958), regarded by the French as a leading British novelist, has gained the unenviable reputation of the middlebrow novelist *par excellence*: he is pretentious, 'deep' without depth, politely mystical—and pompous (one of his favourite phrases was 'the eternal verities'). 'X marks the spot where I read *Sparkenbroke*' (1936) V. S. Pritchett said of his most pretentious book. But Morgan did write one good novel: his first, *The Gunroom* (1919), based on his naval experiences. This was relatively simple, and came out of real suffering. Within six years, with *My Name is Legion*, Morgan had learned how to get himself compared with Dostoevski in *The London Mercury*. . . . His elaborate prose style is as bad as his 'philosophy': he became a Golf-Club novelist, and entirely deserves his bad reputation.

The Irish writer LIAM O'FLAHERTY (1896) wrote some excellent short stories and one good novel, *The Informer* (1925), but seems to have dried up in mid-career. The stories in *Spring Sowing* (1924) were lyrical, elemental, highly readable without, however, making any concessions to popularity. They marked him out as one of the leading writers in this form of his generation; but the two collections since *The Short Stories* (1937; 1948) have not been on the early level.

Another writer who lost his fine early form, perhaps because he decided to tackle novels—for which he has a commercial but not really an artistic capacity —is H. E. BATES (1905). Bates' early stories, in such volumes as *Day's End* (1928), *The Woman Who Had Imagination* (1934) and *The Beauty of the Dead* (1940), are unsurpassed in English in their time. 'The Kimono' for example, a magnificent story, could have been written by no one else. But since serving in the R.A.F. during the Second World War Bates' work has coarsened considerably, although it has remained highly professional. The earlier Bates is a sensuous, powerful writer, expert in portraying women and their moods and the atmosphere of the countryside or the small town. Latterly he has become mannered, and has sometimes declined into self-parody.

V. S. PRITCHETT (1900) was never, perhaps, as good as Bates at his best. But he is more versatile and his work has not fallen off. His stories—collected in 1956—are often about eccentric characters or absurd situations. His novels, which contain passages of exquisite comedy, are studies of tormented puritans: *Nothing Like Leather* (1935), *Dead Man Leading* (1937) and *Mr. Beluncle* (1951), the best, a sympathetic and penetrating study of an enthusiast for odd and out-of-the-way nonconformist religions. Pritchett is one of the very few good contemporary literary journalists.

*

We now come to the three novelists, all born in the first decade of the century, who are generally regarded as the most important of their generation: Graham Greene, C. P. Snow and Anthony Powell.

GRAHAM GREENE (1904) is, like Waugh, with whom he is sometimes bracketed because of it, a convert to Roman Catholicism. But he is a very different sort of Catholic. For one thing, while Waugh was obviously of a Tory mentality, Greene is aggressively left-wing; again, where Waugh revered orthodoxy and decorum, Greene is openly against the conservative elements in his Church— and in his obsessive concern with seediness and evil he has even appeared to many of his fellow Roman Catholics to be heretical. However, Greene's Catholicism is an even more essential element in his fiction than Waugh's. Essentially Greene is concerned with what in Catholic terms is the idea of the mercy of God; but we do not need to be Catholics ourselves to respond to his work—for this idea functions in it as human compassion. Thus, in *Brighton Rock* (1938), the first major novel, the young gangster and murderer Pinkie is presented as in some sense 'holy': he is at least dedicated to evil, whereas his pursuers are merely decent—they lack Pinkie's faith in God, which continues to exist in spite of his desperate project to deny it. This is not in fact a realist novel (how would a semi-literate young gangster remark 'Credo in unum Satanum'?), although the seedy realist background is superbly filled in. Greene has never seriously sought to imitate life (as, say, Snow does so industriously). *Brighton Rock* is a thriller-as-metaphor (Paul West calls it a 'structural oxymoron'), a superb novel that misses real distinction only because of a certain patness on the part of the author, a professionalism that most unfortunately functions as an over-simplifying, even a coarsening, agent. This criticism applies in more or less degree to all Greene's novels, and is perhaps the reason why they do not wear as well as one expects them to. And yet I think it is truer to put it in this way than in the way the Leavis-inspired (q.v.) F. N. Lees (1952) put it. He spoke of 'popular fiction . . . crude analysis, the obtrusive and deformed emotionalism . . . defective presentational technique. . . .' That is to say, I believe Greene's view of life has more power and creative validity than this approach allows: one does see it as modified by sensationalism, but at least its power is always there. His view of life, repellent to so many people, is not really 'popular' (i.e. middlebrow): it involves no manipulations of reality, and it cannot be called sentimentality.

His first novel, *The Man Within* (1929), was influenced by both Robert Louis Stevenson and—thematically—Conrad, a novelist whom he closely resembles. Even here Greene's hero is educated by guilt into grace. And for those who are not Catholics, and doubtless for some of those who are, grace in Greene often means simply *being human* rather than being *moral-before-the-event*: defensively rigid, reaching forward aggressively into the texture of life to make judgements. Greene's whisky-priest in *The Power and the Glory* (1940) is a coward, dirty, the father of a bastard—but he is none the less a priest. He represents man, doomed to sin (always depicted in Greene as various kinds of squalor or shabbiness), redeemed by grace. He is the only priest in a Mexico that has prohibited both Catholicism and alcohol, and his enemy is a policeman who is as dedicated as himself. Before the priest is shot the two come together, in a passage whose irony is sometimes missed, to recognize each other's type of goodness.

Greene has tended to parody himself in some of his later novels, in particular in *The Heart of the Matter* (1948), which is technically one of his finest achievements. This dramatization of theological abstractions (how can a sinner in the eyes of God's Church be a saint in the eyes of God?) is almost convincing; but Orwell (q.v.) was right to charge that it led to 'psychological absurdities'. However, although the context into which Greene has put his hero, Scobie, is unsatisfactory, the man himself is nevertheless invested with a kind of life. The best of the later novels are *The Quiet American* (1955), which contains a masterful portrait of a hysterically bad man, and *The Comedians* (1966), about Haiti under the malevolent regime of the late Duvalier, 'Papa Doc'.

Although C. P. SNOW (1905) has by now attracted almost as much attention as Greene, he is not in the same class. He provides, in fact, an excellent example of an approach that is not merely traditional—Greene is not an innovator in the technical sense, but no one can accuse him of refusing to confront the problems of the twentieth century—but also positively inadequate and obscurantist. As Rubin Rabinovitz has demonstrated in his *The Reaction Against Experiment in the English Novel 1950–1960* (1967), Snow as a critic has been resolutely against every kind of modernism. His favourite novelists include —as well as Proust, whom he wishes to emulate—Daphne du Maurier, James

Gould Cozzens (q.v.) ('one of the few novelists now practising whom a grown-up person can read with respect'; 'intellectually and morally hard'; 'the soundest of his generation . . . which includes . . . Faulkner. . . .'), Nevil Shute and Nancy Mitford. Of satire he has said that it is 'cheek'; and he has quoted with approval his wife Pamela Hansford Johnson's remark that it is 'the revenge of those who cannot really comprehend the world. . . .' Snow, who has been a scientist, civil servant and government minister, is the author of a *roman fleuve* called *Strangers and Brothers* (1940–70). The narrator is Lewis Eliot—a figure resembling Snow himself in education, background, profession and temperament. The books' reading order is *Strangers and Brothers* (1940), *The Conscience of the Rich* (1958), *Time of Hope* (1949), *The Light and the Dark* (1947), *The Masters* (1951), *Homecoming* (1956), *The New Men* (1954), *The Affair* (1960), *Corridors of Power* (1964), *The Sleep of Reason* (1968) and *Last Things* (1970). They trace the progress of Eliot from a Midland working-class childhood through legal training and practice as a barrister, wartime service at a Ministry, to eminence in the political world; Eliot's two marriages and his friendships are reviewed. Now this novel-sequence is an achievement. But it is not a literary achievement. The reason is, simply, that Snow lacks imagination. His Lewis Eliot is a mostly flattering photograph of himself: the stiff-lipped man of affairs, compassionate and understanding, but controlled in the interests of the commonweal. It has as much relationship to life—life in the sense the novelist must feel it: life out there, not-as-I-want-it, the lived, mysterious thing—as a well-run office of the civil service. Admirable, perhaps; but certainly limited. That definition of satire—'cheek'—is surely relevant. Not all literature, of course, is satire; but all except the rare literature of pure joy (and no one is going to accuse *Strangers and Brothers* of being that: it is as drab as Monday morning at the Ministry of Social Security) springs out of what may be described as the difference between man as he is and man as he might be. . . . Snow's attitudes, although humane, function throughout his sequence as a kind of self-satisfaction. The man writing this book is an excellent public man (if public men can be excellent), but he is not what we usually think of as a novelist. Walter Allen speaks of Snow's 'massive fairness' (he is thinking particularly of *The Masters*, 1951, about the struggle for power in a Cambridge college), but is this not the fairness of an enlightened civil servant? Is not the 'moral agnosticism' from which it springs a result, not of a mature scepticism, but of an impoverished imagination? Is not his 'wonderfully subtle' (Paul West) sense of character merely the shrewdness of an interviewer quick to smell out a candidate with problems or habits that might lead him to put himself before The Firm? Shrewd, yes. But understanding?

One might say that it was, at least, all very worthy—if it were not so clearly inadequate, so sociologically unsophisticated (has he read Romains or Durkheim? Does he think he comprehends them? One would give much to know the answers)—and if the self-satisfaction of Lewis Eliot, the man (after all) of affairs, were less apparent. What is shocking in the sequence is that Eliot, the great inside-man to whom supreme reality is bureaucratic procedure, is so uncritical of the world in which he lives. Nothing is *really* wrong—but if only officials wouldn't indulge in so much humanity: the great reality isn't being yourself at home but compromising in committee. Snow has little style, no humour, no recognition of the religious side of man (even in the sense that the sociologist Durkheim wrote of it) or of its function. Eliot's world is colourless: no tenderness, no lyricism—no enthusiasm or passion. However, Snow treats politicians and the lives they lead with absolute solemnity—indeed, with reverence. No 'cheek' or 'revenge' here. And Eliot himself ('in depth . . . myself' admits Snow): is he admirable—or, as Geoffrey Wagner has put it, 'obnoxious'? The answer is not relevant to Snow's achievement. The more important question is, Is he real? The answer must, I think, be that he is not real in terms of his century: he is as blind as his creator to the real nature of twentieth-century man. Snow, the most reactionary of novel reviewers (he is not and presumably has not set out to be a literary critic), has consistently attacked all forms of modernism; he and his wife's violent objections to 'absurdity' and 'cruelty' are as well known as they are one-sided; the nature of his attitude is revealing. As Frederick R. Karl has pointed out, the characters in Snow's novels are not real; the code they live by is illusory: 'Snow is not really concerned with people . . . he gives a sense of the *things* that exist. . . . This way of treating *things* is carried over to people. . . . What pompous fools these administrators and scientists are as Snow describes them, and yet he takes them seriously. . . .' Let us grant Snow's good intentions; let us grant that he is nice enough to attract kind criticism from people who ought to (and no doubt, privately, do) know better. We still cannot escape from judging him with the utmost severity. His enormous yarn, or head-boy's prospectus-in-form-of-tale, is extremely ambitious: it demands an answer of the same magnitude. That answer is that it is reprehensible—I use the mildest term available—to treat human beings as objects in any kind of games—even in office games. Our response must be: 'No, people are *not* like this; and we must not allow them to become so'.

ANTHONY POWELL (1905) provides a complete contrast: his attitude is sardonic 'High Tory' (Snow is nominally a socialist); he has the aristocratic background that Snow makes it obvious that he lacks; he is sophisticated and has a sophisticated style; above all, he has a highly developed sense of humour. Members of Parliament can read Snow with pleasure; one cannot imagine their having much time for Powell.

Powell wrote five novels before the Second World War, of which the last, *What's Become of Waring?* (1939), is perhaps best. They established him as the best comic novelist of his generation; but recognition of this fact has been slow to come, despite the fame of his novel-sequence (still in progress), *A Dance to the Music of Time*, begun in 1951 with *A Question of Upbringing*. Powell's method in the early novels is decidedly aristocratic and omniscient; but he knows not to try to do more than expose the follies and stupidity of his characters. There is more than a touch of Wyndham Lewis, although the tone is softer, and the laughter elicited considerably less strident.

A Dance to the Music of Time continues the comic work with confidence, brilliance and an admirable coolness; it is also a technical *tour de force*. Powell is one of those novelists who make a virtue of their limitations. While it is true that his attitude is unmistakably upper-class—as a novelist he cannot take the lower classes seriously—it is to his credit that he has not tried to change this: *A Dance to the Music of Time* never purports to be more than an upper-class comedy. However, it must be conceded that the sequence lacks variety, that the reasons for 'strangely formalized dialogue' are not yet fully apparent, and that the area it covers is small. All these are valid objections to its evaluation as a major work.

Powell's narrator, Nicholas Jenkins, is evocatively unobtrusive, a worried ironist whose own personality is for most of the time in the background. His narrative consists of carefully selected recollections; objectivity is attained by a balletic scheme in which 'human beings, facing outwards like the Seasons, move hand in hand in intricate measure'. Whether or not this is a viable or even relevant concept, the spell of the storyteller is present. Powell's type of comedy has been compared to Evelyn Waugh's; but the hypomanic and cruel element in Waugh is absent; where he is frenetically gleeful, shrieking the truth of (his own) religion, Powell is thoughtful, as if in his attitude he were trying to define what social sanity might consist of.

The sequence opens with *A Question of Upbringing* (1951). After a Proustian introductory paragraph, Nicholas Jenkins is back at school, at Eton. Its successors are: *A Buyer's Market* (1952), *The Acceptance World* (1955), *At Lady Molly's* (1957), *Casanova's Chinese Restaurant* (1960), *The Kindly Ones* (1962), *The Valley of Bones* (1964), *The Soldier's Art* (1966), *The Military Philosophers* (1968) and *Books Do Furnish a Room* (1971).

Some objections to the consideration of Powell as a major novelist have been mentioned. Against these is the fact that—despite the restricted area of life treated—few fictional techniques employed in the English language today convey as well as Powell's the sense of life as it actually passes before us: hence the plotlessness, the wild improbabilities and coincidences, the flatness of narrative manner. The passing of time is for once seen—without metaphysics or passion—as it is: without even such feelings about it as Powell himself possesses. But this does not create a sense of boredom. Widmerpool, one of the true monsters of modern fiction, is anything but a bore. There is residual wisdom enough in the sequence for us to want to know, not what Powell will do with Widmerpool, but what life will do with him. . . . We shall not be sure of the status of *The Music of Time* until it is finished: certainly, however, Widmerpool is a major comic-evil creation. Behind Powell's comedy and irony, and perhaps behind the Proustian ambitions, lies a serious concern with what human obligations are, or might become. The American critic Charles Shapiro's judgement, 'England's best comic writer since Charles Dickens', may well prove to be right.

*

RICHARD HUGHES (1900), a good poet and pioneer of radio drama as well as a novelist, has written so little that he probably has not had his full due. Each of his three novels is excellent and highly original. The first, *A High Wind in Jamaica* (1929), is the story of some children in the Sixties of the last century; on their way home from a Jamaican plantation they are captured by pirates; eventually they are rescued, and learn to accept an adult version of their experience. But the subject of the novel is the truer nature of this experience: its nature as seen from the viewpoint of a child. This lucid tale of children, brutal and yet strangely gentle, is poetic in the best sense. Hughes' now unjustly forgotten poems (they are collected in *Confessio Juvenis*, 1926) were successful— they are influenced by Skelton and by Hughes' friend Robert Graves, yet are original and eloquent—but lightweight. *In Hazard* (1938), equally unusual and beautifully accomplished, is about a steamer caught in an unexpected hurricane. The narration seems to be artless, but is in fact highly sophisticated and carefully planned—one presumes that Hughes has written so little because he revises at length. The revelation of the true characters of some of the ship's officers and crew is done with consummate skill and subtlety; the descriptive writing is masterly. Hughes' third novel, *The Fox in the Attic* (1962), the beginning of a three- or four-volume work with the rather unhappy title of *The Human Predicament*, is 'a historical novel of my own times'. A young Welshman, just too young to have fought in the First World War, comes down from Oxford and goes to the Germany of the Weimar Republic. Here we meet Hitler, Goering, Röhm and other historical personages; the hero, a curiously innocent and bewildered creature, understands little of what is going on around him. It will be impossible to judge this novel until we have the whole.

EDWARD UPWARD (ps. ALLEN CHALMERS, 1903), close friend at Cambridge of Isherwood (with whom he devised the private, satirical world of 'Mortmere'— as Isherwood recounts in his autobiography *Lions and Shadows*, 1938), was the only British writer of fiction—as Gascoyne (q.v.) was of poetry—successfully to absorb both Kafka and surrealism (qq.v.). This was in the novel *Journey to the Border* (1938), and in a few short stories (now collected, together with the novel, in *Railway Accident*, 1969). This early work is brilliant and exciting, but it has been a little overrated; the stories are better than the novel because the latter peters out into crude communist propaganda. Communist dogma is what frustrates Upward's very different novels *In the Thirties* (1962) and *Rotten Elements* (1969), which are the first two of a projected trilogy. They trace the progress of Alan Sebrill, who, like Upward himself, joins the communists in the Thirties but leaves them in the Forties. Sebrill is an unsympathetic character: a humourless puritan rigidly devoted to his creed. The writing is deliberately muted: it is as if Upward had determined to sacrifice all his imaginative gifts. However, the account of Sebrill's dedication to communism is of historical interest. In effect Upward recounts the process of a man's destruction by his lack of humour and flexibility; but he does it unwittingly.

Upward's early prose was more effective than that of the overrated REX WARNER (1905). Warner is a gifted stylist and a classical scholar of distinction, but in his fiction he has consistently failed to find a satisfactory objective correlative (q.v.). It is obvious that he has feelings and ideals, but his fiction is always spoiled by coldness and over-intellectuality. In the earlier, Marxist books—*The Wild Goose Chase* (1937) and *The Professor* (1938)—Warner created, with undoubted skill although little conviction, a Kafkaesque atmosphere; but this tended, in fact, to obscure his intentions—which were simply allegorical. In *The Aerodrome* (1941), his least unsuccessful novel, the allegory becomes more explicit, although an over-complicated plot interferes with its impact. Since the end of the war Warner has written efficient but less ambitious historical novels.

ARTHUR KOESTLER (1905) has treated the problems of fascism and communism with more success. He is a Hungarian whose better fiction was written in Hungarian and German rather than English. Before becoming an Englishman and settling in England Koestler spent some time in gaols in Spain (under sentence of death) and France; he has written books about this. After temporarily giving up fiction Koestler wrote a series of useful, influential books on sociological and religious subjects. His first two and best novels were written in Hungarian and German respectively: *The Gladiators* (tr. E. Simon, 1939) and *Darkness at Noon* (tr. D. Hardy, 1940). The first is an intelligent and moving account of the slaves' revolt of Spartacus in ancient Rome; that it examines it in twentieth-century terms does not subtract from its power and force of characterization. *Darkness at Noon* is Koestler's finest novel: it is the story of an old-guard communist who falls victim to Stalin's purges. He is a 'just' victim to the extent that in his heart he regards Stalin as a betrayer of communism. This was one of the earliest really lucid revelations—in the West—of the true nature of Stalin's rule. But its political implications are incidental—they gain their strength from Koestler's very matter-of-factness. Rubashov, the protagonist, is presented not only as a victim of a tyrannical system and a mad logic: we see him attaining an ultimate freedom as he contemplates his destruction. That the book is so convincing psychologically is a strong argument against those who hold that it is not really a novel at all. Koestler's later novels are in English. None is dull, and all are acutely intelligent; but they lack the power of the two already discussed. *Thieves in the Night* (1946) is an impassioned but propagandist tale of the struggle of the Zionists in the Palestine of 1937-9; *Arrival and Departure* (1943) tries to demonstrate that ethical imperatives transcend neurosis—a secret agent is shown by psychoanalysis that his motivations are private, but he continues the fight—but the bones of the argument show through the thin psychological skin and flesh much too obtrusively.

GEORGE ORWELL (1903-50), who died young, of tuberculosis, has been much discussed since he published *Animal Farm* (1945), his satire on the Soviet Union; but his fiction apart from this has been consistently underrated. He has been called many things: leftist, conservative, sick satirist. . . . His last great novel, *Nineteen Eighty-Four* (1949), has been systematically denigrated, despite its great power: it is too near the truth. Even David Daiches, usually a reliable critic, calls it 'masochistic' and tiptoes backwards into the safety of the drawing-room (home of 'serious political reflections') as he gasps, 'as a criticism of English socialism it is fantastically irrelevant and even as a picture of the ultimate evil of the totalitarian state it is too obsessed and self-lacerating to arouse serious political reflection'. *Nineteen Eighty-Four* is not a criticism of English socialism, but a warning of the consequences of contemporary 'politics' in general. What Daiches may have failed to realize is that it is just conceivably possible that Orwell's warning has actually postponed or even prevented the horrors that he foretold. This novel represents an entirely valid resolution of Orwell's conflicts. Big Brother and the rest are convincing: the critics have shrunk back in horror. Irving Howe is right when he observes that the book 'trembles with an eschatological fury that is certain to create . . . the most powerful kinds of resistance'. Once that fury is recognized, the timid little Aristotelian and other objections of the awed critics can be seen for what they are—and ignored. For, as Howe points out, of course we should all 'feel more comfortable if the book could be cast out'. It is certainly, to employ C. P. Snow's unforgettable term, 'cheek'; but it will take more than Snow or even Daiches to transform the nature of twentieth-century affairs into something genteel and acceptable at office- or cosy seminar-level. *Nineteen Eighty-Four* is a vision of Swiftian proportions which belongs, horribly, to our time.

Orwell was a fine (if often confused) journalist—all his occasional writing is in *The Collected Essays, Journalism and Letters of George Orwell* (1968). He can be obtuse (what columnist is not from time to time?) but he makes up for this with his many unique insights. He is, in fact, for decency and readability and intelligence combined, the best journalist of the century—and it is by studying his journalism all together that we can best see that his potentialities, in the realm of psychological fiction, were enormous. But his best work is in *Down and Out in Paris and London* (1933) and in his novels (a fact not sufficiently recognized), chiefly of course in *Animal Farm* (a classic), and the final book. It has been said that Orwell was not interested in character; but to condemn him as a novelist because of this is to misunderstand both his purposes and the type of fiction he wrote—as well as to ignore his actual achievement. After all, *Animal Farm* is an animal fable. And a characterization of Winston Smith, the protagonist of *Nineteen Eighty-Four*, would be wholly out of place: the man is fighting for the right to have a personality. Thus he makes effective his ultimate verdict on those who are *not* interested in character. His autobiographical sketch of pre-school life, *Such, Such Were the Joys* (it is in the *Collected Essays*), shows considerable aptitude for presenting character, and suggests that, had he lived, he could have carried out his intention of breaking away entirely from polemics to write about 'human relationships'—this is what he told his wife in the last days of his life. But his earlier novels are better than is often admitted: *Burmese Days* (1934), *A Clergyman's Daughter* (1935), *Keep the Aspidistra Flying* (1936), *Coming up for Air* (1939): all these have lasted for over a quarter of a century or more—and they will survive as invaluable and sensitive portraits of the Thirties where more ambitious books will fall into oblivion. They are the nearest we have in fiction to the novels of Gissing (q.v.):

they evince a similar kind of disgust at all the manifestations of modern life, and a similarly obstinate belief in integrity. But I cannot agree with Walter Allen that Orwell resembles Gissing in deficiency of 'human sympathy'. True, some of Gissing's novels are thus deficient; but I do not think one feels this in Orwell. He is not concerned with the compassionate portrayal of character; but he is concerned with the portrayal of the conditions that cause men to lack compassion. Did Swift lack compassion? Allen admires *Burmese Days*, but feels that an impression of misanthropy 'finally chills'. But how was the young Orwell, fresh from Eton and service with the police in Burma, to deal with such conditions? Was there anything at all likeable about the British administration there? I think that what Allen feels as misanthropy is in fact despair of Swiftian proportions: compassionate concern. Orwell achieved more in his fiction than almost any critic is prepared to allow.

CHRISTOPHER ISHERWOOD (1904), once a great hope of English fiction, petered out into a skilful and intelligent entertainer—a novelist of high quality, but not of the first or perhaps even the second rank. His genius all but vanished, possibly under the pressure of personal problems, in a cloud of mysticism: like Huxley, he took up the study of Eastern religion—which he at first combined with writing film scripts in Hollywood. Isherwood, as all his novels and his autobiography (*Lions and Shadows*, 1938) show, writes very well indeed—too well, perhaps, for his own good, since he is able to make trivialities pass for more substantial stuff. Between 1928 and the outbreak of war (and his departure to America, where he has eventually settled—as an American citizen) Isherwood wrote four good minor novels. He was as gifted in prose as his friend Auden was in verse. But, again like Auden—many of whose characteristics he shares—he has never really grown up. Hence his retreat into an unconvincing mysticism. The early novels were comic and brilliant, but depthlessly so; the later ones well describe the miserable lives of immature men, but fail to explain the misery or the immaturity. For all the recommended mysticism (or Quaker austerity), one's strongest impression is of a clever, seedy, hopped-up kid. . . . The first two novels, *All the Conspirators* (1928) and *The Memorial* (1932), are clever and well observed Audenesque indictments of the bourgeois for their sickness of mind and acceptance of falsity; they do not go deep psychologically, but are technically adept. *Goodbye to Berlin* (1939) is Isherwood's best novel (the third, *Mr. Norris Changes Trains*, 1933, is an amusing, in-joke novel partly based on the exploits of a real-life homosexual): a series of sketches that superbly evoke the atmosphere of pre-Hitler Berlin; Isherwood is the neutral observer—and is at his best in this relaxed and undemanding position. *Prater Violet* (1945) was a disastrous attempt at a Hollywood novel; its successors are more readable and amusing, but entirely fail to account for their protagonists' inability to come to terms with themselves or the world.

A less clever, stylistically inferior, vastly more substantial (and, alas, more neglected) novelist is JAMES HANLEY (1901). Hanley is an irritating writer: he has obstinately refused to learn much about technique through over forty years of writing; he is diffuse and humourless; but he has a power and intensity of vision that all but a very few of his contemporaries lack. In certain respects he may be compared with Thomas Wolfe (q.v.); he does not run to length, and is generous and outward-looking where Wolfe was egocentric—but he has the same kind of crude energy, and is moved by the spectacle of life in somewhat the same way. *Boy* (1931), the stark tale of the ordeal and death of a twelve-year-old boy on a sea voyage, was foolishly banned, which discouraged the sensitive Hanley—who, however, continued with the first of his *Furys* tetralogy, about a Liverpool-Irish family (Hanley was born in Dublin): *The Furys* (1934), *The Secret Journey* (1936), *Our Time is Gone* (1940) and *Winter Song* (1950). This suffers from Hanley's usual faults of diffuseness and clumsiness—but it does have the inestimable advantage of reading like an account of a 'real' family. His most sombre work, however, is *Say Nothing* (1962), which deals with the despairing inhabitants of a boarding-house; this has a truly Dostoev-skian power. Hanley's adaptation of this novel provided British television's finest play of the Sixties. Hanley's technique has not advanced, but he has developed into one of the subtlest exponents of inarticulate emotion; it is time that he gained the recognition that he deserves.

*

CYRIL CONNOLLY (1903) is not primarily a novelist; but *The Unquiet Grave* (1945), the book for which he will be remembered, is certainly an imaginative work. For many years Connolly—editor of the widely read magazine *Horizon* (1940–9)—was, with Pritchett and Grigson (qq.v.), one of the few literary journalists whose critical opinions were worth noting. His best criticism is collected in *Enemies of Promise* (1938 rev. 1949), *The Condemned Playground* (1945), *Ideas and Places* (1953) and *Previous Convictions* (1964). He is often provocative, and is unreliable on poetry—but always civilized (in the best sense) and worth reading. Like Jocelyn Brooke, Isherwood and Rayner Heppenstall (qq.v.) he writes with a rare lucidity. He is an ironic pessimist of the civilized Irish variety ('It is closing time in the gardens of the West' . . .), puckish, an expert parodist, an authoritative historian of the educated sensibility of his age. Most of what may be said against him has been said by him in *The Unquiet Grave*, which he published under the pseudonym of 'Palinurus'. Since for the past few years Connolly (no longer at his most interested) has been chief literary columnist of the London *Sunday Times*, this book is in danger of being forgotten—or at any rate of being ignored by a generation too young to remember it. It is a work of courageous self-revelation, whose chief achievement is to cut self-love out of the self-portrait it renders. It is said that many intel-lectuals of Connolly's generation immediately recognized themselves in *The Unquiet Grave*; what is more surprising is that almost any cultivated person born not later than 1932 (or thereabouts) can still recognize something of himself in this wry, rueful and self-mockingly sensitive account of an intellectual's attempt to lead a tolerable existence. Connolly has found it hard to be at his best—the novel *The Rock Pool* (1935), about a young man's disintegration when he falls into the hands of an arty group in France, is amusing but resolutely minor—but *The Unquiet Grave* is a classic, and it has not dated. *The Missing Diplomats* (1953), on Burgess and MacLean, both of whom he knew well, is a superb piece of journalism. Connolly, who produced little because he has not wanted to produce mediocre work, is the last of a dying breed: the genuine man of letters.

FLANN O'BRIEN (ps. BRIAN O'NOLAN, 1911–66), a civil servant, journalist and Gaelic scholar, who was born and lived all his life in Dublin, is a very different kind of Irishman, but is similarly unclassifiable in the context of the more or less conventional novel. O'Brien's prose combines Joyce (q.v.), who praised his first book, with the great nonsense writers—Lear, Carroll and Morgenstern (q.v.); only his tendency to whimsicality prevents his being a major comic writer. His lightness of touch, however, does not detract from his achievement: it is, indeed, a relief to have one of the most familiar of modern themes (a novel about a man writing a novel about men writing a novel, which is the subject of O'Brien's best book, *At Swim Two Birds*, 1939) treated lightly rather than heavily. *At Swim Two Birds* is funny in a unique manner. It is the quintessence of Irish responsibility, which means that it lacks serious emotional substance but not wisdom. A characteristic notion introduced by O'Brien is that the water we drink is too strong. . . . The other novels, *The Hard Life* (1961), *The Dalkey Archive* (1964), *The Third Policeman* (1967), are excellent comic tales on a smaller scale.

*

HENRY GREEN (ps. HENRY YORKE, 1905), a Midlands industrialist, is a major novelist who pursued the trivial, of which he has an exquisite sense, to the point where his subject-matter disappeared and he stopped writing. But his achievement is a major one. *Living* (1929) is about life in a Midlands foundry just such as Green worked in after he came down from Oxford; it is a joyfully optimistic novel, simply celebrating the fact of life against a background of drabness, personal disappointment and hard work. Although it was for years taken as a proletarian novel, *Living* is concerned essentially with what Green considers the proper subject of modern fiction: 'the everyday mishaps of ordinary life'. Green is often called a symbolist; but the fog (*Party Going*, 1939) and birds (*Living*, *Party Going*, *Loving*, 1945) and other entities that haunt his novels are both more or less than symbols: they 'stand for' qualities just as such entities do so—if they do so—in 'real life'. Green, for all his carefully selective technique and lyricism, is a realist more than a symbolist. In *Party Going* a group of idle parasites are waiting to set off for France, but are delayed by fog in a hotel that becomes surrounded by workers waiting to go home. The scales are not weighted: this is a realist treatment. The metaphor for the 1939 situation is all the more effective for not being contrived—as in the novels of Rex Warner (q.v.) or some of the poetry of Auden (q.v.). *Caught* (1943) is about life in the London fire-service just before the German Blitz began in earnest. *Loving*, set in an Irish country house in the early years of the Second World War, is Green's most beautiful and subtle novel. It is the love story of the English butler, Raunce, and the housemaid Edith. Raunce is one of the most complex and solid portraits in modern British fiction. Raunce emerges so clearly because morality (judgement) never intervenes: the result is a product of pure imagination, a character as rich in contradictions as a real man. Green was not able to maintain this standard; in *Loving*, one of the most original novels of its time, he exactly caught the elusive poetry of 'everyday life'; his work was done. Its successors—*Back* (1946), *Concluding* (1948), *Nothing* (1950), *Doting* (1952)—concentrate, Pinter (q.v.)-like, on capturing exact nuances of speech, and become slighter and slighter.

JOCELYN BROOKE (1908–1966), another writer of unusually lucid prose, never achieved anything near the recognition he deserved, although his highly original autobiographical works—*The Goose Cathedral* (1950) and *The Dog at Clambercrown* (1955) are the best—received good notices. His finest book is *Private View: Four Portraits* (1954), four beautifully delineated, shrewd portraits of people whom he had known well. Brooke was at his best in this shadowy area between fiction and reminiscence, but one of his straight novels comes nearer to creating a genuinely Kafkaesque atmosphere than anything except Edward Upward's (q.v.) fiction of the Thirties: this is *The Image of a Drawn Sword* (1950), a beautifully written account of a nightmare that begins when the protagonist is awakened in the middle of the night and drafted into an unknown, mysterious army. . . . This at least of his fiction should survive; as a Proustian autobiographer he seems certain to be remembered.

ROSAMOND LEHMANN (1903) derives, like Elizabeth Bowen (q.v.), from Henry James as much as she derives from anyone. She is a sensitive writer, gifted with compassion and psychological understanding; but it sometimes seems that she seeks, vainly, to escape from her own feminine intensity. She has never found a really distinguished style, and her main subject—the sufferings of women in love—often becomes cloying and over-obtrusive. She has maintained a high standard, but probably has never done better than her first novel, *Dusty Answer* (1927), and *The Weather in the Streets* (1936). Both of these are excellent period pieces. In the much later *The Echoing Grove* (1953) her real intentions (to dissect and perhaps destroy, or reveal in its full unworthiness, the male object of female suffering) seem to be at odds with the story she tells, in which her gentleness and reconciliatory nature operate against her impulses. Her brother JOHN LEHMANN (1907) has written fiction, autobiography, criticism and graceful minor poetry; but he is most famous for his discriminatory help to young writers through his magazines (*Penguin New Writing*, *The London Magazine*) and his publishing firm.

WILLIAM COOPER (ps. HARRY S. HOFF, 1910) is a disciple of C. P. Snow (q.v.), but is a more gifted novelist. The Joe Lunn of his *Scenes from Provincial Life* (1950) is the first of the unlikeable nonconformist heroes of whom Kingsley Amis' Jim Dixon is the most famous. In *Scenes From Married Life* (1961) Joe has settled down into a useful member of the community as a civil servant (he is also, of course, a well known writer) and accepted that what he once disliked and rebelled against is really the best of all possible worlds. . . . In this and his other novels Cooper is only as funny as an establishmentarian can be. There is, however, one exception: *Disquiet and Peace* (1956), a most perceptive and moving study of a woman afflicted with depression, set in Edwardian times. This is a distinguished and delicate novel, and stands in strange contrast to the mixture of crude, cocky brashness and conformity that characterize the other, markedly inferior, books.

PATRICK HAMILTON (1904–62), famous as the author of the excellent stage thriller *Rope* (1929), and of a really remarkable and underestimated play called *The Duke in Darkness* (1943), was a novelist who never received the critical attention he deserved. He was an expert (and envenomed) castigator of the speech habits and stupidity of the pseudo-gentry—the sort that congregate in the saloon-bars of large pubs (exactly the kind of people who refer to the lower classes as 'the great unwashed' and to Harold Wilson as 'Flash Harold'). This infinitely foolish and pathetic section of society is triumphantly well represented in *Mr. Simpson and Mr. Gorse* (1953), but too facetiously in the trilogy *Twenty Thousand Streets Under the Sky* (1935), the important parts of which, however, are entirely successful—and compassionate. Hamilton realized the poetic side of his genius most fully in *The Duke in Darkness*; he never went on to do, in the novel, what *Twenty Thousand Streets Under the Sky*—a touching and psychologically acute story of ordinary, underprivileged people—had promised. He became over-obsessed with evil (rather as L. P. Hartley, q.v., is, in his terror-driven 'punish bad children' mood, when his imagination is not functioning fully), with stupidity and with vulgarity. Still, the three novels about Ernest Ralph Gorse (a cross between the post-war British psychopathic multiple-killers Heath and Haigh) are effective and intelligent: *The West Pier* (1951), *Mr. Simpson and Mr. Gorse*, which anatomizes the pseudo-genteel of Reading, and *Unknown Assailant* (1955). It is a pity, however, that Hamilton did not present Gorse in the round instead of simply as a psychopathic villain. It is probably true that some human beings cannot avoid being evil; but even these have motivations—and Hamilton does not try to explain these. His best novel is *Hangover Square* (1941).

*

MALCOLM LOWRY (1909–57), born in England and educated at Cambridge— but resident abroad (America, Mexico, Canada) for most of his life, although it was at the little village of Ripe in Sussex that he finally put an end to his life— was a heroic alcoholic who succeeded, more than any other who resembled him, in resolving his terrible problems in creative form. His *Selected Poems* (1962) show him to have been a gifted poet; his posthumous fiction—which includes *Hear Us O Lord from Heaven Thy Dwelling Place* (1961) and *Lunar Caustic* (French tr. 1956; 1968)—reveals massive gifts; his early hallucinated sea-story *Ultramarine* (1933), which was influenced by and written with the help of Conrad Aiken (q.v.), is full of promise. But his masterpiece, one of the most powerful novels of its time, is *Under the Volcano* (1947). Lowry dedicated himself to work on this as desperately as he dedicated himself to self-exploration and self-destruction through drinking. Its setting is Mexico—a Mexico that symbolizes Hell—on the Day of the Dead, and its hero is an alcoholic, Geoffrey Firmin, the last day of whose life this is. Firmin is dedicated to his own death, and *Under the Volcano* is the terrific vision that his voluntary sacrifice of his life vouchsafes him. Finally he is murdered and thrown into a ravine; but it is of course drink, or rather what drink stands for, that kills him. Lowry knew his subject well, and only ten years after finishing this novel he killed himself. Firmin, British Consul in a Mexican town between two volcanoes, represents Lowry himself—and, on the level that matters to the reader, the artist. If Vallejo (q.v.) and some other writers have given us a positive answer to the problem of what I have called *Künstlerschuld* (q.v.), then Lowry certainly gives us a terribly negative one. Perhaps it is a limitation. And yet Firmin—himself in deliberate flight, to hell, from all those who love him and seek his salvation (his ex-wife, his anti-fascist brother)—knows of heaven as well as hell. His self-destructive drinking (a Faust figure, he has taken drink to gain the power of insight—and now he must pay) enables him to see heaven—as well as to anaesthetize him from a rotten world that (1939) is destroying itself just as he is. *Under the Volcano* operates successfully on both the realist and the symbolic planes; Firmin is a true modern Faust, a tragic figure of our times. Lowry, after all, endured the agonies of alcoholism (some details appear in Aiken's *Ushant*, where he figures as Hambo) to some purpose: perhaps in his own terror-haunted mind Lowry did equate the Faustian drunk Firmin with an ineluctably guilty artist; but in relentlessly recording his anguish he showed a courage and sense of compassion (this, of course, is apparent in the characters of those who desire to save Firmin) that merit our gratitude.

A writer who has something of Lowry's power, and who is regarded by some as Britain's leading living novelist, is WILLIAM GOLDING (1911). Although he had published a volume of poetry as early as 1934, Golding did not attract attention until he was forty-three, with *Lord of The Flies* (1954), still his most famous novel. This is a savage gloss on the Victorian writer R. M. Ballantyne's *Coral Island*, in which some British boys are wrecked on a desert island, and create a decent Christian society. Golding's boys create as memorably horrible a dystopia as anyone has thought up since Wells' Rampole Island. There is something modish about Golding's vision of these prep-school boys' vileness, and I am not even sure that all 'the disagreeables', in Keats' famous phrase, fully 'evaporate'; but there is no denying his conviction and force. He is, however, a writer who requires to be separated rather firmly from the many fashionable critics that his work has attracted. These critics have represented him as every kind of writer: allegorist, fabulist, realist, mythographer, Christian —and so on. This is, as Walter Allen has pointed out, 'a considerable confidence trick'. Here there really is a negative vision—and one in which, when we think about it, Golding has cheated somewhat: this is fantasy. Yet, because of the modishness I have mentioned, because of a certain element of pretentiousness, *Lord of the Flies* escapes the censure that *Nineteen Eighty-Four* (q.v.) attracted. . . .

Of Golding's later novels *The Inheritors* (1955), *The Spire* (1964) and *The Pyramid* (1967) seem to me to be the best. *The Inheritors*, about Neanderthal man, is flawed by the same wilfully negative attitude (I mean that the negativity seems to be contrived, to deliberately omit something from the author's response, in the interests of fashion or rhetoric), but it is a *tour de force* by virtue of its brilliant presentation of the Neanderthal people. Golding gives no reason why *Homo Sapiens* (supplanter of Neanderthal Man) should be vile, murderous and predatory; but his picture of his predecessor does have a kind of gentleness. *Pincher Martin* (1956) and *Free Fall* (1959) fail to cohere, although they contain superb passages; *The Spire*, a medieval novel about the erection of a phallic spire, without proper foundations, to the glory of God, is another study of the evil grounds upon which the apparently good establishes itself. It is too confused to be satisfactory, but the portrait of the Dean, Jocelin, is superbly clear. In *The Pyramid*, his best, least pretentious, novel so far, Golding appears to take up a realist approach; but closer examination reveals that it is as symbolic, if less obtrusively so, as its predecessors. However, the treatment of the background, a provincial town (Stilbourne) in 1930, and its Operatic Society's production of *The King of Hearts*, is well done in a realist mode. Golding has been overrated; his symbolism is strained; but he remains one of the most interesting of contemporary novelists.

Golding's contemporary RAYNER HEPPENSTALL (1911) is yet another neglected British novelist. Heppenstall, like Connolly and Jocelyn Brooke, is an excellently lucid writer; but he has always been uneven—and latterly he has become off-puttingly eccentric in reviews, putting forward such views as that Thomas Hardy is a bad writer because his prose cannot be translated into French, or that the pornographer Ian Fleming (perpetrator of James Bond) is the finest stylist of our time. . . . This must be ignored, for Heppenstall is almost the only English novelist to have properly absorbed the influence of the modern French novel. He has written well on Léon Bloy and Raymond Roussel (qq.v.). Heppenstall's best novel is *The Connecting Door* (1962), which renders the surface of things with great acuteness and feeling. *The Lesser Infortune* (1953) and *The Greater Infortune* (1960) are also interesting novels. *The Fourfold Tradition* (1961) is one of the most illuminating books on the differences between French and English fiction—and on the French 'new novel' (q.v.).

WALTER ALLEN (1911), author of deservedly standard books on the novel in English, is in danger of being ignored as a good novelist in his own right. This would be unjust, for he is a master of colloquial understatement and an unusually careful observer of society. His modest, almost casual manner is deceptive. His first mature novel was *Rogue Elephant* (1946), a comic and ironic study of an ugly and unpleasant writer. *Dead Man Over All* (1950), which gained scant appreciation, is one of the best of modern novels about technocracy. Allen does not have Snow's (q.v.) reverence for the public, official over the private, individual, life, and he traces the real lives of his characters with a compassionate psychological adeptness. But his best novel is *All in a Lifetime* (1959), which traces, through a bedridden narrator, the changes in British working-class life since the latter years of the reign of Queen Victoria. This is a subtle sociological study, in which Allen's knowledge of fictional techniques has stood him in good stead. It is moving, as well as shrewd and skilful: the most successful working-class novel since Green's *Living* (q.v.).

The fiction of PAMELA HANSFORD JOHNSON (1912), wife of Lord Snow, has been progressively impaired by a simplistic, authoritarian, anti-imaginative moralism. She began with real gifts—of comedy and of character realization. By *The Honours Board* (1970) these had been entirely squandered in the interests of her prurient, neo-Victorian obsession with the 'permissive society': thus, in this disastrously poor novel, the villain reads 'dirty books': all is manipulated to the simple-minded, self-indulgent pseudo-sociological fantasies of the author. There was always in Pamela Hansford Johnson's fiction a basic, unsophisticated, perhaps semi-hysterical, appeal to middlebrow (i.e. a manipulative, self-indulgent) morality; but this did at least reflect a concern with the results of the loss of official morality. That she was ever a seriously excellent novelist is a frag-rant British myth. American critics have always been puzzled by it: as Carlos Baker wrote of the characters in *Night and Silence! Who is Here?*: 'These, one and all, are people whose predicaments can be enjoyed without our feeling the slightest compulsion to believe in their actuality'. But it is a pity that her pre-occupations should have eventually led to something as non-creative as *Cork Street, Next to the Hatters* (1965)—a weak, because uncomprehending, satire on aspects of modernism misunderstood by the author—and *The Honours Board*. For it might have resolved itself into something more creatively viable: the humour, psychological accuracy, skill and elegance of the earlier fiction certainly gave some compensation for the basic orthodoxy of attitude underlying it. Her most amusing novel is *The Unspeakable Skipton* (1958), in which she takes a Rolfe (q.v.)-like character, a bad and selfish novelist, and traces his career of exploitation.

LAWRENCE DURRELL (1912) was for many years best known as a poet and youthful friend of Henry Miller (q.v.). His *Collected Poems* (1960) contain, in fact, his most enduring work. An Irishman born in India, and for much of his life a British government official in the Middle East, Durrell's most consistent characteristic is his anti-puritanism, and his best poetry presents an Anglicized, thoroughly heterosexualized, wafer-thin but absolutely genuine slice of Cafavy (q.v.): it is an achievement. What brought Durrell real fame, however, was the tetralogy known as the Alexandria quartet: *Justine* (1957), *Balthazar* (1958), *Mount Olive* (1958) and *Clea* (1960). This has been an enormous popular success, hailed by modish critics; it amounts, however, to little more than what Leslie Fiedler has called 'warmed-through Proust'. The French see the same kind of profundities in it as they saw in Charles Morgan (q.v.). The clue to its lack of real quality is contained in Durrell's pretentious prefatory note to the second novel in the series: 'Three sides of space and one of time constitute the soup-mix recipe of a continuum. . . .' The vulgarity of 'soup-mix' is characteristic. How could the coffee-table public fail to fall for something that was not only as 'deep' as this pompous statement implies but also sexy and overwritten ('beautiful' or 'poetic' writing)? Durrell based the series on a vulgarization of the relativity principle. As Pursewarden, one of the characters, pronounces: 'We live our lives based on selected fictions. Our view of reality is conditioned by our position in time and space—not by our personalities, as we like to think. . . . Two paces west and the whole picture is changed'. The quartet is full of such gobbets of 'wisdom'. The four books deal with the same material—a series of (mostly sexual) incidents in Alexandria—from different viewpoints. The whole is supposed to be an investigation of modern love (of physical sex as the true reality), or perhaps a representation of life as significant only when it becomes art. But it is muddled, and the self-consciously lush writing is an indication of its essential meretriciousness. The characters have no solidity; the entire conception is robbed of whatever atmospheric power it might have had by its author's ambitious, polymathic vulgarity: his adolescent obsession with decadence, his preoccupation with occultism, his fatal penchant for potted wisdom. This is the kind of thing that naturists read aloud to one another after sunset and before exchanging sensual essences (or whatever). If Colin Wilson —who perpetrates a rather similar though vastly less well educated mixture of Nietzsche-and-water, sexiness, personal immortality, 'superman crime' and the occult—is the mage of the lounge, then Durrell is the savant of the drawing-room. By 2000 his quartet will be as dead as *Sparkenbroke* is today—and orgasms will still be non-philosophical.

ANGUS WILSON (1913) is an altogether more serious and substantial writer. He has been much misunderstood ('scrupulously prolongs the tradition running from Trollope to Hugh Walpole') for two reasons: he is a brilliant realist, and he has made attempts to revive the solid, Victorian novel. In fact he is not a traditionalist—and even if his attempts to create a twentieth-century equivalent of the nineteenth-century novel are over-ambitious failures, they are nevertheless experimental failures, for Wilson is a sophisticated critic, well aware of the difficulties confronting him in his project. Wilson is a very gifted novelist and one eminently justified in harbouring major ambitions: he is a deadly satirist of the stupid and the pretentious, he has the sort of compassion that goes with a capacity for self-criticism (this is all too clearly what the latter-day Durrell has lost), he can construct his big novels properly. . . . But his very ambitiousness is in a sense his worst enemy: it has led him to attempt the impossible, the construction of massive realist novels, when his real gift is for the fantastic, the grotesque—the richly imaginative. His best novel, *The Old Men at the Zoo* (1961), is in fact satirical fantasy: set in (what was then) the future, 1970. We see England invaded by Europe and the Zoo taken over so that the new rulers can throw their opponents to the beasts. All this is presented as if it were 'ordinary' subject-matter; but the result is merely an increase of ironic tension. Wilson's first novel, *Hemlock and After* (1952), is his most successful purely realist work (outside the short story); it suffers from its failure to build up a complete enough portrait of the hero, Bernard Sands, a novelist who falls victim, in middle life, to the homosexual impulses that he has so far successfully repressed. Wilson has a Dickensian gift for caricature, and this has never been seen to better advantage than in his devastating picture of London's homosexual underworld. This is hardly, alas, an advertisement for what in the United States of America is called the Gay Liberation Front. *Anglo-Saxon Attitudes* (1956), full of excellent things, and an acute character study, is nevertheless too long; it tries to achieve what is today an inappropriate kind of solidity. *The Middle Age of Mrs. Eliot* (1958) is, as has often been pointed out, too near to clinical case-history. *Late Call* (1964) is less novel than satire—on the deadness of modern life as lived (or not lived) in a British New Town.

P. H. NEWBY (1918) is an excellent minor comic novelist, but when he has tried to be more ambitious he has not succeeded in writing more than a few superb but isolated scenes. The context is always highly intelligent, but it is not really imagined: one feels that Newby has taken too much thought, that he lacks a single vision of his own because of his awareness of others'. And yet the potentiality is there to such an extent that one wishes that Newby would abandon his nervous, play-safe pastiche of other writers' life-views (Conrad's, Lawrence's, in particular), and abandon himself to himself. As it is, a certain meanness of spirit (a deliberate avoidance of robustness), an over-prudence, seems to vitiate what could clearly be—and in part is—a major achievement. If only, one feels, Newby could sustain the power and sensitivity of *A Step to Silence* (1952), the first of two books about Oliver Knight (the sequel is *The Retreat*, 1953): the descriptions of Midland landscape, of the teachers' training college which Oliver attends before joining up, of (in particular) Oliver's older friend Hesketh's model geography lesson, given to satisfy the examiners of his efficiency as a teacher. But even this novel fails to hold together: Newby is too reticent with Knight; and he is too eager in the sequel to turn him into a freak, to disown him as a character and transform him into a stock symbol of alienated man. Basically what has happened is that Newby's empathy has failed. In later novels the symbolic intentions are excellent, and there are always sensitively rendered scenes; but there is a lack of psychological conviction. In *The Picnic at Sakkara* (1955) and *A Guest and his Going* (1959) Newby has set his sights lower: the result is superbly executed light comedy.

DENTON WELCH (1917–48) died at thirty-one as a result of a road accident sustained when he was a boy; he lived in extreme discomfort and, in the last stages of his illness, acute pain. His books, *Maiden Voyage* (1943), *In Youth is Pleasure* (1944) and *A Voice Through a Cloud* (1950)—there was also a volume of stories and sketches, *Brave and Cruel* (1948)—are candid, subjective explorations of his self-pity and homosexuality. His was only a minor talent, but a sufficiently exquisite one to have kept his work alive for a quarter of a century. Like Jocelyn Brooke, who edited some of his literary remains, Welch wrote autobiography in the form of fiction; his unbaring of his personality is quite remarkable—and even unnerving. His technique consists of a series of extremely detailed impressions; there is no generalization. Welch's narcissism and hypersensitivity sometimes obtrude into his work (especially in *In Youth is Pleasure*), but when these are under control his writing provides a unique insight into the homosexual mentality.

ANTHONY BURGESS (1917) is unquestionably the most gifted English novelist of his generation; but he has not yet produced the major novel of which he is so clearly capable. He is a talented musician, learned in linguistics, and with a real grasp of all sorts of knowledge. He is also an active journalist and critic. No writer of our time is more obviously highly intelligent—and aware of the essentially subversive function of the writer. No contemporary novelist more clearly displays genius. And yet no single book has yet contained all this genius and sensibility. This is partly because he is too clever, too aware, too self-conscious, too versatile: swarms of objective correlatives present themselves to him, and become too articulate too soon; he can't help knowing too well what he is doing. But in too many cases this extremely sentimentive (q.v.) type of writer allows himself to be inhibited into complete silence; we are grateful for Burgess' prodigious output, for the fecundity for which he has unfairly been blamed. Notable among his novels is the *Malayan Trilogy* (1956–9), which is essentially a tragedy on the subject of Britain's withdrawal (of interest as well as power) from its empire. Burgess is a Tory (in the old, Johnsonian, sense) unable to recover from the shock of realizing that Toryism died with Ford's Tietjens (a statement with which he would certainly agree). This horror has led him into over-frenzied journalistic activity, into a no-nonsense, professional approach to his craft that tends to obscure his seriousness, dedication and stature—and into excursions into the area where horror merges with comedy. *Nothing Like the Sun* (1964) is a *tour de force* on Shakespeare's life—the only tolerable novel on the subject—which seems to be based on Fripp's rather than Chambers' better known biography. Perhaps his most powerful novel, in which we see more of the author himself than elsewhere, is the devastating *Honey for The Bears* (1963).

It is the habit of literary journalists to compare all woman novelists with Jane Austen—which is both an injudicious and a foolish procedure. Two writers who have had too much pseudo-critical attention paid to them are MURIEL SPARK (1918) and IRIS MURDOCH (1919). Neither of these has come near to the writing of a major novel, but both are fluent, skilful and creatively ambitious. Muriel Spark is clever and sometimes amusing (her jokes go less far than her admirers claim, however), but her Roman Catholicism seems to function as something more distinctly personal than universally divine (if one may so put it). She writes well and concisely, and this has tended to obscure the psychological superficiality and sheer petty malice of her content. Like Evelyn Waugh she indulges herself in callousness; but she doesn't have Waugh's intelligence or weight. Her stature is exactly summed up (if unwittingly) by a phrase thrown off by the ladies' columnist Katherine Whitehorn: 'top-notch Spark'. This mock-critical ejaculation exactly echoes her real voice—even if it filters out the uncanny literary adroitness. *Memento Mori* (1959) is the most successful of her novels. She lacks wisdom, emotional substance and all compassion, but the surface of her novels is exceedingly attractive. Her limitations were not fully revealed until she attempted a large-scale novel, *The Mandelbaum Gate* (1964), in which most of the writing is simply dull.

Although considerably less adroit, Iris Murdoch is more serious. She (unlike Muriel Spark) has the potentialities of a good novelist; but she has in effect refused to write a novel, and has instead resorted to desperate tricks: pretentious symbolism and crass sentimentality. At times both her characterization and her dialogue are at a woman's magazine level (as in *The Nice and the Good*, 1968); she leaves us with the impression that she dares not contemplate her true attitude towards life, but instead must hurry on to the next novel. She is a teacher of philosophy by profession, and her own philosophy (it is outlined in the astonishingly entitled pamphlet *The Sovereignty of Good Over Other Concepts*, 1967) gives a useful indication of her fictional intentions. These are not (apparently they dare not be) imaginative—but philosophical. Alas, philosophy has never been a satisfactory *raison d'être* for the creative writer. And Iris Murdoch's philosophy is not distinguished: a pallid and sentimental Kantian substitute for Christianity. In the later novels some of the characters search for Murdochian virtue; the results are as mediocre as the philosophy, and they are not improved by the author's insertion of clothes- and pet-notes of interest only to an audience for whom the public library is now a (doubtless unsavoury) substitute for the defunct circulating library. The earlier novels are superior— the least organized, *Under the Net* (1954), is in some ways the best of all because it has no pretentious control superimposed on it, and the hero is simply allowed to wander. For in Iris Murdoch control is nearly always pretentious in terms of the creativity—the ability to create autonomous character and situation— that has been revealed. She can descend to such depths as this piece of dialogue, supposed to be exchanged between a very young man and woman after their first sexual encounter:

> 'Was that really it?'
> 'Yes.'
> 'Are you sure you did it right?'
> 'My God, I'm sure!'
> 'Well, I don't like it.'
> 'Girls never do the first time.'
> 'Perhaps I'm a Lesbian' . . .
> 'Oh Barb, you were so wonderful, I worship you.'

The novel that demonstrates that Iris Murdoch is above the kind of thing she is now content to perpetrate is *The Bell* (1958), which most critics have agreed is her best. Here the action, which concerns a homosexual founder of a religious community, is convincing in itself—with the result that the author's symbolic intentions do not seem to be contrived. Otherwise, despite excellent passages, the 'mysteriousness' of Iris Murdoch's fiction, even if it is regarded as 'deep' in some quarters, is no more than meretricious trickery. What has happened to this talented writer by now is that she cannot see her people as people, and so in her despair she has become increasingly reckless, using every modish cliché—spying, sex, incest, mythological allusion, the Gothic, whips—to distort her and her reader's attention from her inability to imagine situation.

KINGSLEY AMIS (1922) caught a universal post-war mood in his very funny first novel *Lucky Jim* (1954). In this book the Pooterish Jim Dixon represents honesty; a university lecturer, he rejects culture not so much because of what it is as because of its snobbish and hypocritical associations. He is not likeable: he is not only exasperated, anti-phoney and furious, but also a sly and ambitious go-getter. He resembles Denry of Arnold Bennett's *The Card*, but lacks his mobility and warmth: there is something feral about his snarl: this is a deprived young man who is going to be revenged. The high comedy does not obscure the inner determination. But Jim Dixon is real, and his preoccupations are powerfully conveyed. Nor are we entitled to assume that the author has put Dixon forward simply as a hero; on the contrary, I doubt if Amis objects in the least if we object to his boorishness and pity his accident-proneness. We laugh at him as much as we laugh with him. This was an unusual novel, a necessary variation on the theme initiated in *The Card*. It is all the more unfortunate, then, that Amis' fiction has, over the past twenty years, consistently deteriorated. This seems to be because Amis has identified with the simplistic, materialist side of himself—at the expense of the sensitive side, as is sometimes presented in his earlier poetry. In a word, he is coarse; rather than be driven by his comic imagination and his dislike of sham, he has allowed himself to be taken over by the aggressive, conservative moralizer who features so unpleasantly in the press: the taunter of 'lefties' and advocate of British participation in Viet Nam. He is now no more than a popular novelist who turns his private conflicts to good commercial account. One might put it in another way: that Amis was not intellectually capable of developing the *Lucky Jim* theme any further than he did; that the succeeding novels simply exploit various kinds of smartness and cynicism until the author became tired and settled into a straight novel-a-year man. . . . But one cannot help wondering if Amis did not once possess the capacity to illuminate the reactionary slyness which he portrays so uncannily well.

JOHN WAIN (1925) is less accomplished but more straightforward. *Hurry on Down* (1953) was—as Anthony Burgess seems to have been the only critic to note—an inept performance, ill-written and almost insultingly badly constructed; but its subject-matter, the rejection of bourgeois values by an educated anti-hero, was fashionable; and, as far as it went, it was well-meant. Better was Wain's Empsonian (q.v.) early verse, with which he apparently took some trouble. The successors of *Hurry on Down* have been, if anything, less distinguished; the poetry has degenerated through want of direction; but in his short stories Wain exhibits some of the control he so badly lacks in his other work. He seems in this form to be able to master his excitement about himself, and his sensitivity and feeling are given fuller expression.

THOMAS HINDE (ps. THOMAS CHITTY, 1926), who has been somewhat neglected by the critics, is a master-delineator of the British at their nastiest and most small-minded, and is one of the best realist novelists of his generation. *Mr. Nicholas* (1952), his first novel, is also his best—and one of the best to appear in England since the Second World War. He set himself a very high standard with it. It is about the tyranny of nastiness, age and insanity—a memorable and deeply-felt portrait of an impossible-to-love, and yet pathetic human being, together with an account of how the young struggle in the cruel nets laid by their elders and betters. Hinde conveys the sense of decency (this is not, alas, definable in public-school, Christian, or any other moralistic terms), of the decent man's helplessness in the face of bourgeois malice or ill-will, better than any novelist of his time. He shows this in many of his later novels, including *Happy as Larry* (1957), *For the Good of the Company* (1961) and the African novel *The Cage* (1962). It is possibly a matter of regret that he has latterly turned to a self-conscious symbolism, for his social observation is so acute that one misses it —and the symbols do not arise from the action, but are arbitrary. But clearly he is a novelist, still young, of major potential.

The novels of ALAN SILLITOE (1928) are all more or less wrecked by their author's extreme simplicity of mind. Few writers who have managed to acquire his reputation can have been so much at the mercy of crude emotion. The nature of his mental difficulties is probably best illustrated by an equation made in one of his poems—between 'cancer' and 'racism'. His first novel, *Saturday Night and Sunday Morning* (1958), is as atrociously written as Wain's *Hurry on Down*, and is not particularly pyschologically plausible, but has the power and freshness of youth. *Key to the Door* (1961) is distorted by wishful thinking and poor construction; the succeeding novels consist mostly of puerile anti-authoritarian fantasy, although there are flashes of good description. Sillitoe is better in his short stories, and has never been more powerful than in *The Loneliness of the Long Distance Runner* (1959): in this narrative of a Borstal boy Sillitoe's hatred of injustice, hypocrisy and exploitation found an effective objective correlative (q.v.). He has written other simple, precise and moving stories; one of the best is *The Ragman's Daughter* (1963), also the title of a collection.

V

The Thirties in Britain were dominated by the four poets whom Roy Campbell (q.v.), in an otherwise poor satire, conflated as 'MacSpaunday'. Actually CECIL DAY LEWIS (1904–72), LOUIS MACNEICE (1907–63), W. H. AUDEN (1907) and STEPHEN SPENDER (1909) were never all together in one room until after the Second World War, and the notion of them as a genuine foursome is a wrong one. But all four, like many intellectuals in the Thirties, were Marxist (or at least left-wing), and all four were associated in the public mind. What they had in common was age, an admiration for Hopkins and Eliot's *The Waste Land*, and a feeling that revolutionary changes were needed. They were, however, very different. The Irishman Day Lewis, despite his gestures towards modernism, was not a modern poet at all, and was never able to deal with modern issues. Presumably his odd penchant for writing verses on public occasions got him the laureateship. Day Lewis had energy and strong feeling, and was a brilliant pasticheur (Hardy, Emily Bronte and others); but diligent search through his *Collected Poems* (1954) and its successors yields all too little poetry in Day Lewis' own voice. His best poetry appears in the wartime collection *Word Over All* (1943) and in his translations—from Valéry (q.v.) and Virgil. As early as 1939 Philip Henderson noted that Lewis is 'only a poet . . . when he forgets the Marxist mountain [today one would substitute Her Majesty, the bully-boys in the back rooms working for good old Britain, and so on] . . . and allows his natural, and after all quite Georgian, lyrical talent free play'. Day Lewis is the sort of poet one would like to praise more than one is able to; even in his modest neo-Georgian vein he is too frequently tepid or over-parodic, his rhythms metrical rather than personal (they have been called slick).

Louis MacNeice, also an Irishman, was the most extroverted of the poets of the Thirties: as well as being a student of the classics, he was a keen player of games and (like Norman Cameron, q.v.) a popular boon-companion. He was a minor poet who never really took poetry quite seriously enough. A good deal of his output, particularly *Autumn Journal* (1939) and *Autumn Sequel* (1954), consists of prosy pseudo-philosophical rambling. But he was intelligent and honest: if his poetry gives most pleasure to members of the middle classes who feel doomed, bewildered and sorry, but still continue as they are, he cannot fairly be called a middlebrow—in the sense that Day Lewis is middlebrow, a substitute for 'difficult' poets: poetry was for MacNeice a limited instrument, and he was never pretentious. But his poetry does little more than reflect the fears, hopes and anxieties of his class; it describes much, sometimes felicitously, but illuminates nothing. His work abounds in the tired, sophisticated clichés of the audience at which it is aimed; whenever he becomes serious the atmosphere becomes highbrow-taproom. His best poetry is satirical-funny, as in the famous 'Bagpipe Music'—he exploited the same vein very successfully in one or two of his radio plays. It is often said that in his last poems, published in *The Burning Perch* (1963), he reached a new intensity; and certainly he succeeded here, at last, in purging his language of its unfortunate Chelsea-like glibness ('May come up with a bouncing cheque,/An acid-drop and a bandage') and professionally blasé tone. These poems do, too, expertly describe what it is like to be middle-aged, in love, intelligent, tired, possessed by forebodings of death; but the slick, journalistic manner had been with MacNeice too long: none is more than neat and appealing. The elements of surprise, a truly individual voice and technique, the capacity to express the intensity of feeling that was, I think, genuinely there, are missing. MacNeice, whose *Collected Poems* appeared in 1967, could entertain poetically, and he could touch the heart; he could be appealing; but his poetry is not durable.

W. H. Auden's early *Poems* (1930) was the most energetic and promising collection of its time; its excitement still casts a spell—and there are many of Auden's own generation who have never escaped from this spell, and who consequently have never been able to judge his achievement dispassionately. The poems in his first collection are frequently incoherent, and their author is clearly hopelessly confused between a Kiplingesque imperialism and a Marxist-

Freudian revolutionary attitude; there are echoes of other poets—Blunden, de la Mare, Graves, Laura Riding (qq.v.), and so on; but excitement and feeling are both present: this is a poet of technical brilliance who has a genuine lyrical gift. *The Orators* (1932), which again mixed Freud, Groddeck and Kipling, was just as confused; but in *Look Stranger* (1936) Auden had reached his lyrical apogee, and had purged himself of his more irritating public-school mannerisms. From then on the story of his poetic career is one of steady decline and disappointment: like his friend Isherwood, he has never grown up. One is presented with the extraordinary spectacle of a man of great facility, with fine intuitions about poetry (Auden is one of the best anthologists of our time), who has nothing of intellectual and little of emotional substance to say. For all his energy and versatility and intellectual curiosity, Auden has no more to offer than the following messages: that poetry changes nothing (he agrees, in fact, with Laura Riding, q.v.—but continues to write), that poetry should be entertaining above all else (this is consistent: entertainment is all it is good for); and that life should be led as graciously as possible. Thus, Auden's 'philosophical' poems, the poems in which he tries to make 'major' statements—*New Year Letter* (1941), 'The Sea and the Mirror' (1945: included in *For the Time Being*, 1945), *The Age of Anxiety* (1948)—are essentially superficial. *New Year Letter* contains Auden's ideas (of that time) about all subjects; it is rather like a glossy 'dictionary of thoughts', and when it surprises it does so because Auden is so adept at the expression of truisms. *The Age of Anxiety* is just what it seems: the prelude to a conversion to Christianity that can make sense only to Auden himself. But not many critics claim that the later Auden, the Auden of the later Fifties and Sixties, carries real weight. If he is really the major poet he has for so long been supposed to be then this is for the poetry collected in the earlier *Collected Shorter Poems* (1950) and perhaps for the poems in *The Shield of Achilles* (1955). Now if vigour and the ability to move the reader (Auden lost both these qualities during the Fifties) were enough to make a major poet, then Auden would be major. But they are not. Again, if what Alfred Alvarez has called 'catching the tone of the age' ('catching the tone' is just right: it does not imply explaining, exploring or illuminating) were the attribute of a major poet, then certainly Auden would be one. But it is not; and he is not. He is an important phenomenon; he had excellent qualities; but he failed to develop—and became the greatest disappointment of his age. Even in the most celebrated of his poems—the elegies on Yeats and Freud, 'Musée des Beaux Arts'—there is a spurious quality. In the best poems the superbly memorable phrases are isolated, have no context: they are the notes and impressions of a clever and sensitive adolescent, not of a mature man. The immaturity of which the clowning was a symptom in the earlier poetry has persisted: this poet has failed to examine his personal situation: his casual stance towards poetry may be more the result of this than conviction. And yet until about the mid-Fifties—when his poems began to deteriorate into facetious trivia—Auden concealed his emotional rawness and intellectual superficiality with remarkable skill. Sometimes he did this by apeing another poet—he is a superb mimic. A good example of this is 'Their Lonely Betters' (1951), which is, as one would say, 'pure Graves'—but without being pastiche-homage in the manner of Day Lewis. Auden injects his own casual manner. (Graves himself once called Auden 'a synthetic poet who probably never wrote an original line in his life'.) Auden has real feeling for the poets whose procedures he appropriates. Indeed, those of his best poems that are not imitative owe what viability they have to their quality of sincerity. *Spain* (1937 rev. 1940), on the Spanish Civil War, remains moving in spite of its rhetoric; 'In Praise of Limestone' (1951), when one looks carefully at it, has little meaning—but does embody a fascination with England. A great deal of the responsible admiration that Auden attracts is actually admiration of his *performance* rather than of his achievement; future critics who cannot be dazzled by his performance will assuredly wonder why we saw so much in him.

Stephen Spender had markedly fewer technical resources than Day Lewis, MacNeice or Auden; his ear is considerably less sure; but his poetic impulses were deeper and more serious—and have survived longer. He has written much lush, tentative, over-sensuous poetry, but his best has qualities more enduring than that of most of his contemporaries. In recent years he has been able to integrate his sense of humour—often in evidence in his criticism—into his poetry. Spender has written an outstanding novel about life in an unpleasant preparatory school, *The Backward Son* (1940), and a book of stories, *The Burning Cactus* (1936); two later stories, published under the title *Engaged in Writing* (1958), are less successful. He is also an uneven but always stimulating critic.

The poems in Spender's first collection, *Poems* (1933; there were two earlier, privately printed pamphlets), were altogether more emotionally *réussis* than the earlier poems of Auden, MacNeice or Day Lewis. There are obvious faults—lack of humour, obscurity resorted to in order to avoid sentimentality, confusion—but one is drawn into the unmistakable presence of a poet. And although Spender has remained a poet (in a way that Auden and Day Lewis quite certainly have not), has not become corrupt or tired or mechanical, has retained his sensibility, has learned to do certain things better—I doubt if he has ever written a more exciting and appealing book. There is a sweetness and a breathlessness about Spender's early poetry that he has never quite been able to recapture. This quality is seen at its most vulnerable but nevertheless most potent in the very early 'Epilogue':

> Time is a thing
> That does not pass through boredom and the wishing,
> But must be fought with, rushed at, over-awed,
> And threatened with a sword:
>
> For that prodigious voyager, the Mind,
> Another self doth find
> At each hour's stage, and riven, hewn and wrought
> Cannot foretell its port.

Let heart be done, shut close the whining eyes,
And work, or drink, or sleep, till life defies
Minute, month, hour and day
Which are harrowed, and beaten, and scared away.

Spender charmingly foresaw the weaknesses of his later poetry: he 'expected always', in a manner genuinely Shelleyan, 'Some brightness to hold in trust,/ Some final innocence/To save from dust'. But this was not always apparent: Spender's lyricism and sensitivity were not usually strong enough to shore him up against the shocks of war and of the kind of personal sexual difficulties common to us all. He lacks the less often acknowledged, sceptical, toughly intellectual side of Shelley. *The Still Centre* (1939) and *Ruins and Visions* (1942) showed a falling off after *Poems*, and there was not even quite enough in *Collected Poems* (1955) to state positively that Spender had either fulfilled his promise or developed satisfactorily. But adjudgement of his performance now means less to him, and in more recent poems, now collected in *The Generous Days* (1971), he has notably succeeded in integrating his subtle sensibility and his intellectual intricacy, although everything has been transposed into a minor key. Whereas Spender had previously always been open to the charges of clumsiness, emotional over-indulgence and unnecessary ambiguity, the author of these less grandiose poems is firmly in control. Is this new modesty a gain? One can only repeat what George Barker said of the *Collected Poems* ('. . . if you come across a cripple walking you can be . . . sure that he wants to get somewhere'): 'the true presence itself . . . moves and operates'. With Spender this has always been the case, and one has learned to be grateful for it.

However, just as the homogeneity of 'MacSpaunday' was false, so was the concept of their dominance of the Thirties. There were other poets as good— or better. Chief among these was NORMAN CAMERON (1905–53), whose genius is only just now in the process of being recognized—though he has had imitators since the Fifties. Cameron, a Scot with a Calvinistic conscience and a penchant for occasional reckless behaviour, wrote a witty and metaphysical poetry—frequently laced with deep feeling—that foreshadowed the style of the so-called Movement (q.v.) of the Fifties. He resembled Graves and was a close friend of his and of Laura Riding's—but he was not substantially influenced by either. He formed his style while still at Oxford, as the sequence of poems included by Auden in *Oxford Poetry 1927* shows. Perhaps nothing demonstrates the general insensitivity to real quality in poetry of official, academic or fashionable critics, anthologists and literary historians so much as their neglect of Cameron, whose excellence and originality are evident to anyone who truly cares for poetry. Cameron made the best English translations from Villon and Rimbaud; his *Collected Poems*, a slim volume, appeared posthumously in 1957. He did not really develop (he was doubtful and suspicious about the importance of poetry)—in this respect he resembles his compatriot Andrew Young—but his sardonic, tender sensibility was always capable of dealing with problems as they arose. Cameron's was the perfect twentieth-century traditional manner:

he had no innovatory ambitions and was (over-) modest about his achievement —but cliché and poeticism are so entirely absent from his poetry as to render it exemplary in style alone. Its emotionally dense texture is the result of stubborn honesty and of intellectual and emotional self-appraisal. Cameron's is a poetry that will appear increasingly strong and original as work more ambitious in scope, but ephemeral, falls away.

RONALD BOTTRALL (1906) is not in Cameron's rare class; but when one compares his achievement (*Collected Poems*, 1961) to, say, that of MacNeice, one is again struck by the obtuseness of the regular critics. For Bottrall, while a poet of limited means and ends, nevertheless far exceeds MacNeice both in dedication and performance. Possibly his reputation was harmed when both F. R. Leavis (q.v.) and Edith Sitwell—a notoriously hysterical and unreliable critic—praised him. Bottrall's faults are obvious: when his response is not individual he tends to be metrical (rather than rhythmical), he is derivative (Pound, Empson, Graves), humourless and over-cerebral. But at his best he has real style and feeling; above all, he truly feels the pressure of the modern world (Auden tends to enjoy his own success in it, however he may protest), and it evokes a complex and lively response from him. Moreover, he has an original lyric gift, as he shows in 'Four Orders':

> I am a trembling leaf
> I am a withered arm
> I am a sunken reef
> I am a trampled worm.

> Leaf, be the caterpillar's joy
> Arm, enfold the new-born boy
> Reef, flower into a coral isle
> Worm, fertilize the soil.

JOHN BETJEMAN (1906) could have been a poet, but—in Spender's words— he has never been able to escape being 'the schoolboy who pretends that he is only pretending to be a poet'. Betjeman is bound to irritate serious readers of poetry for this reason: so much wilful silliness, thumping metre, and deliberate pastiche of earlier and now inadequate modes from a writer so clearly capable of sensitivity and rhythmical tact. By silliness one means the sort of impulse that can lead him to say—on one of his too frequent appearances on television —that he prefers 'Tom Moore' to Donne. . . . This refusal to be serious haunts and ultimately vitiates his verse, which is enjoyable but none the less coffee-table. One has to be crass to be a best-selling poet in these days, and Betjeman is crass; but he has qualities that other best-selling poets have not usually possessed. He is capable of real feeling; his nostalgia has style. One is not inclined to praise him for this, however: he has squandered his gift—and, even worse, has used it to slyly persuade those who buy his books that they are reading serious poetry. Most reprehensible is the cunning manner in which he indulges his own sentimentality: some of his lines move his non-literary readers, while his sophisticated audience may take them as satire. The most complete edition of his *Collected Poems* appeared in 1970. He is now Poet Laureate.

GEOFFREY GRIGSON (1905) published his *Collected Poems* in 1963; most unusually, he has written nearly all his best poetry since then. Grigson, a tough, scholarly and always provocative critic, is another of that dying breed, the genuine man of letters. Grigson edited the influential poetry magazine *New Verse*, which he had founded, throughout the Thirties. Since then he has supported himself by a series of critical and other works of a high standard; outstanding among these is the autobiographical *The Crest on the Silver*. His early poems were impressionistic, even imagist (q.v.)—and correspondingly slight. During the Sixties he broadened his scope without sacrificing the precision and luminosity that, at his best, he had always had.

It is through Grigson that the memory of CLERE PARSONS (1908–31) has been kept alive. Parsons did not have time to fulfil his promise, but what he did accomplish shows that he was potentially a major poet. He was mainly influenced by his contemporaries at Oxford (Auden, Spender) and by Laura Riding.

Curiously, since he is famed for his cerebral qualities, the keynote of the poetry of WILLIAM EMPSON (1906) is repressed passion. His output is small. He has published two collections; his *Collected Poems* appeared in 1955. He is best known as a critic—for *Seven Types of Ambiguity* (1930 rev. 1953), *Some Versions of Pastoral* (1935) and *The Structure of Complex Words* (1951). And he is, too, one of the most suggestive and subtle, although recondite, critics of his time. But he is also a good poet, and one who has been consistently misunderstood. The reason for his extreme intellectuality is his extreme intensity and depth of feeling, both political and personal; this feeling is apparent, but has not been searched for diligently enough by his critics and even his disciples. Thus, Alfred Alvarez, who began as a disciple of Empson and then swung (predictably enough) to D. H. Lawrence—and then to confessionalism and suicido-confessionalism—called his subjects 'impersonal'. Now it is true that from time to time Empson indulges in 'crossword puzzle' poetry—his enthusiasm for this, as a critic, has sometimes led him into an indiscriminating attitude— as in such poems as 'Rolling the Lawn' ('You can't beat English lawns. Our final hope/Is flat despair. Each morning therefore ere/I greet the office, through the weekday air,/Holding the Holy Roller at the slope. . . .'). But the essential Empson has 'learned', as the last line of 'This Last Pain' announces, 'a style from a despair'. This is, however, as Alvarez insists, a limited achievement. Empson was concealing deep feelings—but not a rich lyrical gift. The achievement has been important because it kept 'wit' alive over a period when it counted for little in poetry: Empson's best lines—'Not to have fire is to be a skin that shrills'; ''Twixt devil and deep sea man hacks his caves'—have an Augustan toughness as well as a metaphysical concentration of feeling. Empson had his reasons for turning poetry into a minor project—it is one of the features of his minor poetry—and it is not his fault that the poets of the Fifties imitated his manner and produced no more than a series of drab anti-romantic statements. He himself has disliked his influence, and has pleaded, by implication, for 'honey' and for 'a singing line'—although his own lines never 'sing'.

W. R. RODGERS (1909–69), an Ulsterman who had been a protestant priest and who wrote highly praised radio features, was at one time held up as a possible rival to Dylan Thomas and George Barker (qq.v.); but his poetry has now, it seems, been almost forgotten. In his first poems, collected in *Awake* (1941), he was over-intoxicated by words and too heavily influenced by Hopkins ('Now all our hurries that hung up on hooks'); verbal pyrotechnics, assonance and dissonance and rhetoric too often obscured the fact that he had something to say. He was always plainer than Thomas and Barker, though: a strong-thewed Augustanism lay behind even the comparative exuberance of the earlier poems. The American poet and critic Kenneth Rexroth compared him to Marvell; this is not too far-fetched, as the poems in *Europa and the Bull* (1952) demonstrate. But Rodgers failed to develop: his poetry was too uneven, too unexcitingly 'physical' (it remained difficult to justify most of his verbal effects), too little worked out. The strength and unfashionable openness were there; but so was an unaccountable carelessness. His best poetry is simple, like his description of the airman who must be pitied because 'he'll/Halt, hang hump-backed, and look into his crater'.

BERNARD SPENCER (1909–63) was associated with Lawrence Durrell (q.v.) in Cairo during the Second World War; a few of his poems had appeared in such magazines as Grigson's *New Verse* (q.v.) in the Thirties, but he did not publish a book—*Aegean Islands*—until 1946. He killed himself. His *Collected Poems*, which drew on two later collections and added ten more poems written in Vienna at the end of Spencer's life, appeared in 1965. His poems resemble him: well-bred, restrained, fastidious, acutely sensitive (to the point of breakdown) behind a tight-lipped reserve. His early poetry is elegant, unpretentious, over-civilized, passive; but a note of menace begins to creep in about 1950 (he ends a poem of that year by asking 'what towns born on what darker coast of sleep,/how many histories deep?'). It is a profounder note; but Spencer never gave it a quite full expression. But he did find single images into which he concentrated his feelings of sexual guilt and shame, and his premonitions of death: for example, in 'By a Breakwater' he sees what he takes to be lovers— but the man, 'middle-aged', is emptying a syringe into the woman's arm. . . . Spencer's work was never trite, and it deepened in intensity as he grew older. He is most likely to be remembered for his later poems; but *Collected Poems* is a distinguished volume, a testament to integrity and seriousness and purpose.

KATHLEEN RAINE (1908), who published her *Collected Poems* in 1956—*The Hollow Hill* followed in 1965—has since the Forties been an uncompromising Platonist and symbolist. Her poetry is limpid, musical, deeply serious; frequently it is so removed from life that it hardly touches the ground (after all, even the Platonist is rooted in life); but when Kathleen Raine writes of the real mystery she helps to restore meaning to it:

We look up and the sky is empty as always; only
Assembling the scattered for-ever broadcast light
Here, or there, in his creatures, is seen that Face.

JAMES REEVES (1909) is widely read but has not had the attention of critics. For long it was commonplace to hear him referred to as of the 'school of Graves', on the strength of his friendship with the older poet and because Laura Riding prefaced his first collection, *The Natural Need* (1936). In fact the early poems included in this owe at least as much to Eliot, Pound, Richard Aldington and the imagists (qq.v.) as they do to Graves or Laura Riding. On the other hand, Reeves' later poems, most particularly those collected in the two volumes published since his *Collected Poems* (1959), owe more to Edmund Blunden, Andrew Young and John Crowe Ransom than to Graves—whose consistency of energy and 'attack' his poetry has never pretended to have.

Reeves' poetry requires selection. There are some metrical wastes, where energy and linguistic inventiveness have been low, and where consequently the effect is commonplace and even Georgian in the worst sense. *Selected Poems* (1967) is a valuable pointer towards what he can achieve at his best.

Reeves writes in three distinct manners; but, as Edwin Muir (q.v.) wrote in reviewing one of his volumes, 'Perfection does not call attention to itself': the surface of the poems is not striking. Most approachable of Reeves' manners is his quiet pastoralism, which in its way is as authentic as Blunden's, although it is less observant of natural detail and frequently takes a wryly satiric look at human obtrusions. In 'Ghosts and Persons' he writes of 'slow heads drowsing over sums' and the 'mower's distant sound' whining through high windows, but also of 'The forward smile and stupid eyes/Of a youthful village charmer'. Human 'progress' in its urbanizing forms amuses Reeves, but finally, especially in pastoral settings, arouses his resentment.

Reeves' angry, Kafkaesque manner, as beautifully exemplified in 'Greenhallows'—ostensibly an account of a journey to an interview for an important position—is less familiar, more original and harder to interpret. In this vein, Reeves appears violently to reject his normally calm acceptance of—even refuge in—his bourgeois backgrounds and to express attitudes quite alien to his usual self as expressed in poetry. The same kind of uncharacteristic energy is to be found in the sequence 'Letter Before a Journey' and in some of the satirical poems included in *The Questioning Tiger* (1964).

Finally, Reeves is the author of a handful of deeply felt, and powerfully expressed lyrics, such as 'All Days But One', which begins:

> All days but one shall see us wake to make
> Our last confession:
> Bird notes at dawn revive the night's obsession.

Guilt, regret, anger, desire for stability—these are among the staple elements in Reeves' best poetry. Few have more memorably portrayed the pains, pleasures and sinister or unhappy nature of the conventional life than Reeves; few are more startling beneath a tranquil surface. *Subsong* appeared in 1969, *Poems and Paraphrases* in 1972.

*

'MacSpaunday' and those whom they influenced (Kathleen Raine, who had not discovered her true manner, and Bernard Spencer were among them) were sometimes called the 'New Country' school: this was the name of an anthology, edited by MICHAEL ROBERTS (1902–49), a distinguished intellectual —he wrote a good book on T. E. Hulme (1938)—and a minor poet of some distinction (*Collected Poems*, 1959). Roberts had also edited *New Signatures* (1932); he went on to produce what is arguably the most influential anthology of this century, the original (the revised versions of it are worthless) *Faber Book of Modern Verse* (1935). Roberts included in this excellent collection three poets whose work was recognized at the time as reacting away from the socio-political concerns of the so-called 'New Country' poets. It was not that GEORGE BARKER (1913), DYLAN THOMAS (1914–53) and DAVID GASCOYNE (1916) were anti left-wing—all three were sympathetic, for example, to the legal government of Spain—but that their main concerns in poetry were non-political.

Of the three Barker is at once the most uneven and the most gifted. It is unfortunate that he has had to write under the shadow of his more immediately striking but also more meretricious contemporary Dylan Thomas. The general verdict is that Thomas is the better poet; but this is not the case. Barker is a prolific, hit-or-miss poet who can write quite indescribably badly—and with great power and authority. Barker was not much influenced by surrealism; his confusions came naturally to him, and harked back to Smart and the Blake of the prophetic books rather than to France. His early poetry was tragic and guilt-laden, consisting of great clusters of words that are flung at the reader with a deliberate lack of tact. In many ways Barker anticipated Berryman (q.v.), who looks somewhat less original when put by his side. Barker, a capable prosodist, distrusts neatness and can inflict hideous cacophonies upon his readers—'Satan is on your tongue, sweet singer, with/Your eye on the income and the encomium'—he has not really developed his procedures since his early days—but he scores a rather higher proportion of successes. However, it is perhaps fair to say, as David Daiches does, that he has never integrated 'his talents into a wholly satisfying poetic complexity'. But he is not that kind of poet: we have to look for his best and most integrated work in single poems. Barker, a most original poet (he is in fact more original than Thomas), is in love with the paradox—sometimes too facilely, but at others with surprising authority. Not afraid to be absurd, he can be more successfully elemental than almost any of his contemporaries:

> Step, Primavera, from your bed,
> Dazzling with existence;

315

Put the Sun and the Moon and the Systems right;
Hang heaven on circumstance:
Lean from all windows like waterfalls,
Look, love on us below:—
And so from their somnolence in sense
All things shall rise to you.

Barker needs rigorous selection (his *Collected Poems* appeared in 1957). There is no doubt that he is one of the most rewarding and interesting of contemporary poets—and one who deserves a great deal more critical attention than he has had. Although the generally accepted notion of Barker as an uneven poet is correct as far as it goes, there is more to him than this: he has plenty of wit and skill, and quite often his failures are considerably less disastrous than they appear. Finally, Barker has done things no other English poet has even dared to try.

Dylan Thomas has been overrated and overpraised, largely, no doubt, because of his somewhat spectacular life and death. He was a simpler and less prudent man than Barker; despite the many books—particularly in America— that have been written about his poetry, this is usually not well accomplished, and leans heavily on violent rhetoric. Thomas' early inspiration came from James Joyce (q.v.), translations of Rimbaud (perhaps by Norman Cameron, who became his close friend) and the Bible; the wild and whirling, irrational manner of his early volumes (*Eighteen Poems*, 1934; *Twenty-five Poems*, 1936) was certainly highly original. But, as his leading critics themselves admit, he is never lucid (Barker very often is). If, then, he is the major poet that we are so often invited to celebrate, we should need to discern a method in this lack of lucidity. But there is none. When we have conceded the powerful effect of the rhetoric and the unfamiliarity of his surrealist-like verbal juxtapositions (but he is always closer to a Welsh revivalist spell-binder than to a genuine sur-realist), we have to admit that Thomas is frequently irresponsible in his use of words. There is a strong emotional pressure behind his poetry, and a feeling for the sound of words (though his ear was faulty, as in 'There is a s*a*viour/ R*a*rer than r*a*dium. . . .'); but Thomas suffered from an insensitivity to the *meanings* of words, a result of his inability to come to terms with reality. Like many alcoholics, he was at bottom an appealing man; but he never grew up, or even tried to. He was no Baudelaire or Rimbaud; his counterparts are to be sought in the nineteenth century, among similarly immature men: Swin-burne, Dowson, Francis Thompson. Where Thomas is comparatively lucid, as in the elegy for Ann Jones, he is usually weakly adjectival: strip the poem of its not, on second inspection, so striking adjectives and nothing is left. Thomas is in some respects a dirty little boy, and the imagery of the earlier poems (many of them about masturbation) is simply 'dirty'. The much vaunted complexities and profundities of his work invariably prove to be the projections of critics.

But Thomas does have vitality—and, where he is not too ambitious, some small successes, such as 'The Hand That Signed the Paper'. But it is a pity that this vitality, and his sensuousness, have led even such sensible critics as David Daiches to over-praise him, and to regard him as a profound thinker. Daiches' account of his 'thought', in fact, unwittingly reduces it to the series of commonplaces that it is. Thomas' later poems—'Over Sir John's Hill', 'In Country Sleep'—do attain a greater simplicity than his earlier in that they are less clotted and wilfully sexual in their imagery; but the kind of simplicity they seek is rhetorical, and their individuality is restricted to tone. The most complete edition of Thomas' *Collected Poems* appeared in 1971. He wrote some exquisitely funny prose, printed in *Quite Early One Morning* (1954) and *Adventures in the Skin Trade* (1955); but the success of the radio drama *Under Milk Wood*, skilfully done though it is, is not artistically deserved: Joyce is plundered, T. F. Powys is imitated—the script is ingenious rather than felt, and a lack of real clarity is everywhere apparent.

David Gascoyne was more directly influenced by surrealism than either Barker or Thomas—or, indeed, any other English poet. Gascoyne's first book of poetry, *Roman Balcony*, appeared when he was sixteen; his novel *Opening Day* followed in 1933, when he was seventeen; *A Short Survey of Surrealism* (1936) was published when he was twenty. When he published *Poems 1937–42* (1943) he had reached his maturity, although he was not yet thirty. Influenced by Jouve (q.v.) and by the philosophy of existentialism, Gascoyne is a most unusual phenomenon in English poetry; yet his 'Europeanness' does not give his poetry an un-English flavour. On the contrary, he remains the most English of poets, a genuine visionary writing in the tradition of Blake and Dante Gabriel Rossetti's 'The Woodspurge'. His early surrealism, where successful, achieves innocence. Unfortunately, however, the latter stage in Gascoyne's development is wanting: his later poetry has the strength of sincerity, but is grey, defeated and lachrymose.

> Not from a monstrance silver-wrought
> But from the tree of human pain
> Redeem our sterile misery,
> Christ of Revolution and of Poetry,
> That man's long journey through the night
> May not have been in vain.

This is too deeply felt and dignified to be platitudinous; but it is disappointing in the light of the earliest poetry. Gascoyne's *Collected Poems* appeared in 1965.

VERNON WATKINS (1907–69) was considerably older than Thomas and Barker, but did not become known until the Forties. His first book, *The Ballad of the Mari Lwyd*, appeared in 1941. Watkins was the best of the British poets to be associated with the so-called romanticism of the Forties, and until the end of his life he continued to write in his own unfashionably lyrical or Platonic styles. He began as a self-consciously Celtic imitator of Yeats; but at his best his manner is seventeenth- rather than nineteenth- or twentieth-century. He is humourless and often takes himself too bardically seriously; much of his poetry is monotonous and dull; but every so often he is pellucid, illuminating and original. It is ironic that so heavyweight an effort as Watkins' should in the end produce only a few lyrics; but it is also an object-lesson. A *Selected Poems* appeared in 1948.

The poetry of JOHN HEATH-STUBBS (1918) suffered for many years from its author's theoretical neoclassical preoccupations; but his *Selected Poems* (1965) reveal a poet of more strength and individuality than is perhaps generally realized. Heath-Stubbs is a genuine literary conservative. As a craftsman in traditional forms he has few peers; and his light verse is perhaps the most readable of his time. Mainly he is a graceful occasional poet, for whom style represents passion; but he has written a handful of personal poems (for example, the beautiful and subtle elegy 'Address Not Known') of great distinction.

HENRY REED (1914) has published only one collection of poems, *A Map of Verona* (1947), but this is widely read—it has remained in print for a quarter of a century. He has earned his living as a translator and writer of radio scripts —including the famous 'Hilda Tablet' series. Reed has written several distinctly different kinds of poem: the metaphysical, influenced above all by Marvell; a narrative, contemplative poetry influenced by Eliot; parody—as in 'Chard Whitlow', which was Eliot's own favourite parody of himself; a narrative poetry influenced not by Eliot but by Hardy—such as 'The Auction Sale'. Reed's justly famous 'Lessons of the War' sequence is in his metaphysical vein, exploiting *double entendre* to its limit, varying the tone from the wistful to the broadly comic (as in the third poem of the sequence). The less well known 'The Auction Sale' handles narrative as well as it can be handled in this age. Reed is a poet of greater range than is usually recognized; only his Eliotian contemplative poetry really fails to come off, and even this is eloquent and rhythmically interesting.

*

Two Irish successors of Yeats are outstanding: PATRICK KAVANAGH (1905–69) and AUSTIN CLARKE (1896). Yeats had preferred F. R. HIGGINS (1896–41), but Higgins never really progressed beyond a pleasantly expressive occasional poetry. Kavanagh (*Collected Poems*, 1964) wrote a narrative poem about the poverty of the land and the people in his home county, Monaghan: 'The Great Hunger'. He also wrote a good autobiographical novel, *Tarry Flynn* (1949); he was for some years a newspaper columnist. His best poetry is subtler than his ostensibly careless, conventionally romantic attitude ('. . . this soul needs to be honoured with a new dress woven/From green and blue things and arguments that cannot be proven'), combining self-satire with lyricism in an unusual and moving way. Clarke (*Later Collected Poems*, 1961) is a fastidious minor poet who has over the years performed a number of technical experiments, within the tradition, of interest and importance. He is above all a classical poet, and is an honourable example of one; but although his integrity is beyond question, the usual fault of his work is that there seldom seems to be sufficient emotional impulse to draw it together. However, Ireland has not yet produced—leaving aside the more robust Kavanagh—a worthier successor to Yeats.

*

During the Second World War itself, it was the loss of SIDNEY KEYES (1922–43) that attracted the most attention. Keyes (*Collected Poems*, 1946) was certainly promising, but it is hardly possible to prophesy what he might have done: his poetry is (understandably) a hotch-potch of influences (Rilke, Yeats, Eliot —and others), and there are hardly as yet the glimmerings of an original manner. Two other poets, lucky enough to have a little more time to develop than Keyes was allowed, were more important: the Welshman ALUN LEWIS (1915–44), whose *Collected Poems* finally appeared in 1966, and KEITH DOUGLAS (1900–44): *Collected Poems* (1951 rev. 1966).

Alun Lewis, who seems to have died by his own hand, while serving in Burma, had time to develop, to purge his poetry of triteness and over-romantic diction (often apparent in his first collection, *Raider's Dawn*, 1941). His greatest difficulty lay, it seems, in knowing when to stop. But he was a poet of great power, who described the loneliness of military life in the early Forties with unique eloquence and accuracy; he wrote, too, exciting and original love poetry.

Douglas did not actually achieve more (he had less time), but his extrinsic importance would probably have been greater. In him we see romanticism not rejected, but tempered by intellectuality—and a poetic intelligence not equalled by any poet since. His poems often lack finish, but this does not obscure his tough fusion of feeling and 'wit', his generous awareness of the world around him.

ROY FULLER (1912) also made his reputation during the war, in which he served but which he fortunately survived—he had in fact been publishing poetry, criticism and fiction since the mid-Thirties. His *Collected Poems*, which appeared in 1962, established him as a major poet among the younger generation: it was generally felt that here was the best living poet of his generation, one just a few years younger than that of MacSpaunday. But his poetry does not make as clear an impression as it should. He is intelligent and sensitive, but lacks power and drive. His early poetry is too evidently influenced by Auden, his later by Yeats (this is particularly important, because here he apes a manner that rather clearly does not suit him). He began well, but chose a disappointing direction in which to develop. For all his later poetry's interesting and intelligent unravelling of small Freudian knots, its chief function seems to be to keep any real kind of poetic vision at bay. Thus Fuller—in his weakest type of poem—mourns his political impotence and bourgeoisdom (he is a Marxist), but does absolutely nothing about it. His parodies of Yeatsian richness do not complement this apathy, because they entirely fail to convince. And yet there is enough that is good in Fuller to compel us to judge him from high standards: he has always tried to deal honestly with his experience, and even his latter-day posturing is rhetorical in intention, rather than self-deceit. He

319

has written enough to make us regret that his ultimate stance should be to defend so limited a position.

It is difficult to understand why Fuller's near contemporary, C. H. SISSON (1915), who did not become known until the publication of his first collection of poems, *The London Zoo*, in 1961, is not better appreciated. The author of an extraordinary novel, *Christopher Homm* (1965), Sisson's voice is unquestionably contemporary. His diction is chaste, sometimes almost puritanical in its clarity and savage directness; but beneath this temperamental severity fires burn—fires which throw up passionate and memorable lines, such as 'If we have reasons, they lie deep'. The 'if' here is characteristic: Sisson appears to be an extreme pessimist—intelligence and gloom have never, of course, been fashionable attributes—part of whose theme is corruption, or, in theological terms, original sin. But the careful reader of his poems (*Numbers*, 1965; *Metamorphoses*, 1968) will discover that they are coloured by an extreme, though subtly ironic, good humour. For another part of his theme is grace: both the grace inherent in the human creature to endure its terrible corruption, and the grace that is therefore inherent in the situation itself. The 'if' in the line quoted above is characteristic, then, because Sisson refuses, with unobtrusive courage and a poetic sharpness of intelligence, to exploit his own certainties, to step beyond the known grounds. Sisson's poetry displays a tough, curious, informed mind under continuous pressure from experience; it ranges from exuberant and deliberately villainous scatology ('The Theology of Fitness' is the prime example of this) to sustained passion.

*

Scotland has not yet produced another poet of the calibre of MacDiarmid; but at least three poets writing in Lallans, and four in English, are worthy of note. ROBERT GARIOCH (ps. R. G. SUTHERLAND, 1909) is a good, witty, acerb poet in Scots; many of his best poems are satires. He is well represented in *Selected Poems* (1967). He uses Lallans as though it were his own language, not a literary device, and expresses comic and outrageous emotions in it that could not possibly be expressed in any other language. SYDNEY GOODSIR SMITH (1915), who also writes in Scots, is more ambitious and more uneven. Many regard him as the natural successor to MacDiarmid; but MacDiarmid's own lyrical successes very often show up his lyrics as forced and artificial. Nor does his Rabelaisian, comic verse always succeed. But when it does it is revelatory; 'Sydney Slugabed Godless Smith', upon whom 'Auld Oblomov has nocht on' can be genuinely exhilarating. What one finally misses in his work, however, is the ability to modify his romanticism (in which he over-indulges himself under the disguise of linguistic gusto) or his sense of fun, which spills over into facetiousness. TOM SCOTT (1917) is altogether more austere; but his use of Lallans, while not as exuberant as Goodsir Smith's, is ultimately more responsible. He began by writing in English, but in 1953 produced his remarkable *Seeven Poems o Master Francis Villon made owre into Scots*.

NORMAN MACCAIG (1910), originally a member of the extreme romantic group who called themselves the 'New Apocalyptics', writes in English—but has, as has been pointed out, an unmistakably Scottish sensibility. He has, perhaps, written too much; but he has never written badly, and has developed consistently towards a truer self-expression. He has the acute observation of his countryman Andrew Young, and he has combined this (latterly in free verse forms) with metaphysical speculation. His best books include *The Sinai Sort* (1957) and *Measures* (1965). W. S. GRAHAM (1917) had verbal energy, best displayed in *The Nightfishing* (1955), an obscure but exciting sequence; *Malcolm Mooney's Land* (1970), in which he indulges his intellectual confusions rather than purges them, shows that he has failed to develop. G. S. FRASER (1915) wrote, in *Home Town Elegy* (1944) and *The Traveller Has Regrets* (1947), some of the most honest and carefully wrought poetry of the Forties; readers will turn back to it when the time comes to reappraise the period. *Leaves Without a Tree* (1952), published in Japan, is his most substantial collection of poetry, and contains most of his best poems. At his best, when he is not susceptible to the influence of Yeats, he is a gritty, subdued poet—certainly one of the best of his generation. IAN CRICHTON SMITH (1928) is an uneven poet; but no one writes more densely or compassionately than he does at his best. His main collections are: *The Law and the Grace* (1965), *In Bourgeois Land* (1970) and *Selected Poems* (1971). He combines a subtle humanitarianism with a brooding, self-deprecatory Calvinism that gives his poetry great strength and originality.

*

The Fifties saw a reaction to the romanticism of the Forties, although the name of the 'Movement' given by a journalist to such poets as Davie, Gunn, Larkin and Amis (qq.v.) was unhelpful. The Sixties and early Seventies saw a great proliferation of versifiers of all kinds (mostly bad because lazy, careless, ignorant or derivative). It remains here to pick out the more outstanding. ELIZABETH JENNINGS (1926) has been cruelly used by fashion. Her first collection, *Poems* (1953), was rightly praised for its modest and sober strength, and its unusual way of looking at landscape and experience. The chief influence on these early poems was Edwin Muir (q.v.), whom Elizabeth Jennings also resembled in lacking a personal, 'attacking' rhythm. Throughout many volumes (*Collected Poems*, 1967), she has sustained her sobriety and honesty of tone—but she has run out of experience. It is as if she gave up all to be a poet, and now has nothing to write about except her approach to the writing of poetry and her acute disappointment. But her potential as well as her earlier achievement remain.

DONALD DAVIE (1922), one of the most intelligent and aware critics of his generation, has never quite been able to escape from his didactic inclinations. His poetry is brilliant, but nearly all of it is factitious—verse not as poetry (which is produced under the kind of pressure that cannot be faked) but as various kinds of didactic criticism. He has wit, ingenuity and technique—but his work is controlled by what he prescribes as necessary ('for poetry') at the time of its composition: everything is for 'the good of poetry'. The best poetry does not come into being in this way: experience is primary in it, and its author is first a poet—and then (if he likes) a critic. Davie is first a critic. But there is a wry and bitter feeling which takes over in some earlier poems; and no critic illustrates his prescriptions more cleverly or more interestingly. His wit and the remarkable movement of his intellect are his own; it is a pity that the emotion in his poetry should so often be non-existent or aped. Much of his best work is in *New and Selected Poems* (1962), *Events and Wisdoms* (1964). *Essex Poems* (1969) is less good.

Davie's exact contemporary PHILIP LARKIN (1922) aptly reveals his severe limitations (it is a matter of the difference between actually being moved and simply being in a state of admiration or intellectual fascination); it is ironic that he, in his turn, should exhibit severe critical limitations, the chief of which is his refusal to consider European poetry as being of interest. But the student of true poetry becomes used to such ironies. For Larkin, although a minor poet, is the best since 1945. His first collection, *The North Ship* (1945), is not more than promising (it was Charles Madge, q.v., alone who prophesied his future from this volume); *The Less Deceived* (1955) and *The Whitsun Weddings* (1964) contain his important poetry; it has traces of Hardy and Graves, but there is no doubt of its originality. That this is apodictically as good as it is demonstrates the sceptical quality of the imagination. Larkin faces what seems to be a merely squalid predicament ('truth', for him, is a 'trite truss advertisement'), and yet he moves us. His best poems remain on the right side of sentimentality. One may sympathize with Charles Tomlinson (q.v.) when he complains that 'a movement in which he is the star performer can scarcely be thought of as having the energy to affect the ultimate destinies of English poetry'. But Tomlinson, like Davie, is a critic-poet and not a poet-critic: the 'ultimate destinies' of any poetry exist only retrospectively; meanwhile, poets do what they can. As Tomlinson points out, Larkin's subject is 'largely his own inadequacy'; he goes on to deplore 'Larkin's refusal to note what had been done by the French before 1890 in the ironic self-deprecating mode'. But if Larkin could 'note' Laforgue and Corbière's poetry then he would certainly not be capable of the fine ironic self-deprecating poetry he wrote in English in the Fifties and Sixties. . . . So much for criticism.

CHARLES TOMLINSON (1927) is, like Davie, an excellent and sensitive critic. He has a fine sense of landscape, a fascination with decay (which he seems not to acknowledge), and he is a good craftsman. An American admirer of his perception and his intelligence, however, has characterized him as 'no poet'. One sees what he means. Tomlinson has all the equipment of a poet except the capacity to deal with emotion. This has led him to try to realize himself in other men's styles: he has thus imported the procedures of Williams, Vallejo (qq.v.) and other poets into English poetry—but he has not absorbed them, and he has been unable to compensate for his own deficiencies. He is a frustrated painter, and his best effects have been gained from poem-pictures, where landscape acts as a metaphor for mood; but self-satisfaction or complacency (reflected in the prissy and exasperated tone of his criticism) seem to preclude the self-criticism, the self-exploration, the irony and the humour to which he would need to subject himself if he were to succeed in recording more than a series of moods. This is a loss to poetry. But as it is his poetry is far too cool and delighted with itself: one can hear the taps of the ferule as he sets about instructing his calm little world in how to organize itself—all ignorant of another, rougher world outside. His books include *The Necklace* (1955), *Seeing is Believing* (1958), *A Peopled Landscape* (1963) and *The Way of a World* (1969).

BRIAN HIGGINS (1930–65), by contrast, was a hit-or-miss poet (somewhat in the manner of his friend George Barker, q.v.), who had too little time to exercise control over his considerable intelligence. His poems were published in *The Only Need* (1960), *Notes While Travelling* (1964) and *The Northern Fiddler* (1966). His best poems were full of urgency (an urgency that now seems poignant), primitive energy and directness of purpose. They combine passion, humour and subtlety. 'Genesis' demonstrates something of his quality:

> Language is the first perversion of the senses.
> The alphabet was written on the gates of Eden.
> Reason is an angel in mathematics, a castration
>   in literature, and a devil in life.
> The first and last speech was a curse.
> When the moon was numbered the stars grew pale.
> It was God who conspired with Satan in that garden
> When, lowering the snake, he sent words to prove
>   the Fall.

Of poets of Higgins' generation the two most discussed are TED HUGHES (1930) and THOM GUNN (1929). Hughes began (*The Hawk in the Rain*, 1957; *Lupercal*, 1960) as an elemental poet of power; he was inchoate, but fruitfully aware both of the brute force of creation and of the natural world. Then—a naïve (q.v.) poet—he began to assume a mantic role; he has now turned into (*Crow*, 1970) a pretentious, coffee-table poet, a mindless celebrant of instinct. Gunn's best poems were in his first book, *Fighting Terms* (1954 rev. 1962), of which the original version is preferable. His later poetry (*My Sad Captains*, 1961; *Moly*, 1971) has remained interesting, but the tug between the classicist influence of Yvor Winters (q.v.) on the one hand and the 'tough', male, leather-jacketed world of American pop on the other has proved destructive: it is not, perhaps, a fundamental conflict.

Of poets younger than this IAN HAMILTON (1938) and DOUGLAS DUNN (1942) are the best. Hamilton (*The Visit*, 1970), a good critic, needs nerve and humour (which he does not lack) to stiffen his not yet explicit enough, though sensitive and fastidious, poems. Dunn (*Terry Street*, 1969) has feeling and a sense of occasion; he is the most substantial poet of his age-group.

Bulgarian Literature

The modern state of Bulgaria came into being in 1878. Before this the literary activity, directed towards national liberation and the foundation of a literary language, was mainly in the hands of the patriotic poet Hristo Botev (1848–76), the poet and educationist Petko Slaveykov (1827–95) and the story-writer and populist Lyuben Karavelov (1835–79). Of these men only Karavelov showed much concern for art and psychological truth. IVAN VAZOV (1850–1922), who was a minister of education for a short while in the closing years of the nine-teenth century, became the leader of the traditionalist and nationalist group which dominated Bulgarian literature until the end of the Second World War. Vazov, a just and never narrow-minded critic, believed literature should be devoted to the interests of the whole people. His novel *Under the Yoke* (1894; tr. E. Gosse, 1894; M. Alexieva and T. Atanasova, 1955), written in exile, deals with the savagely crushed April Rising of 1876. It made the world aware of Bulgarian literature. Certain of Vazov's other work—poetry and drama—is somewhat primitive and hastily composed. But his satires on bureaucrats, army snobbery and pseudo-intellectualism make it clear that he was a man of high mental stature. Although his work now inevitably seems dated, he remains the dominant figure in modern Bulgarian literature. (MBL)

KONSTANTIN VELICHKOV (1855–1907), who was minister of education before Vazov, was the most notable poet in the traditionalist group. His chief con-tribution to Bulgarian poetry was his expansion of its techniques—for example, he wrote the first good sonnets in the language. This facility he gained from his French education. His best work, however, is in his travel books.

STOYAN MIHAYLOVSKI (1856–1927), also educated in France, was the satirist of the Vazov circle. He appointed himself the castigator of all the evils of the new Bulgaria. He was in fact a savage pessimist, with a fine technique and a vituperative style, who might (with more creative imagination) have been as happy with Pencho Slaveykov's *Thought* group (q.v.) as with Vazov's. His theatre comedies of family life—*When the Gods Laugh* (1922), *The Tragedy of Conjugal Love* (1927)—show the less bitter side of his nature.

VENELIN (ps. TODOR VLAYKOV, 1865–1943), although also a follower of Vazov, was caught for the whole of his long life between his social and his individual aspirations. He wrote some of the first realistic stories of Bulgarian village people, using colloquial language and dialect. He was dedicated to the interests of the peasants all his life.

ANTON STRASHIMIROV (1872–1937) also wrote stories of peasant life, though in a less colloquial language, and with sometimes more conventionally literary 'colour' and plot. He was more prolific than Vlaykov; many of his novels and plays (the outstanding one is *The Vampire*, 1902) are vivid evocations of the history of Bulgaria at the end of the nineteenth century. (MBL)

Naturally, there arose a school of writers who were sharply opposed to Vazov's nationalist conception of the function of literature. Its leader was the poet PENCHO SLAVEYKOV (1866–1912), the son of Petko Slaveykov; its organ of expression was the magazine *Thought*. His aim, he said, was to 'extricate the man from the Bulgarian'. He travelled abroad, mainly in Germany, and imported into the literature of his country ideas from German idealism, English romanticism and Russian humanism. Naturalism (q.v.) he rejected altogether. Slaveykov was crippled from youth, and tended to see his country's predicament as his own. The myth of Prometheus is central in his work. From Nietzsche (q.v.) he extrapolated the notion of 'exalted personality', which he equated with 'aesthetic man'; he saw Bulgarian destiny as involving a transcendence of national dogma. One of the most gifted poets associated with this group was PEYO YAVOROV (ps. P. KRACHOLOV, 1878–1914). Yavorov was the first truly tormented soul of Bulgarian literature. He became disillusioned with populism and socialism in 1903, after having fought (though not a Macedonian) on behalf of Macedonia, withdrew more and more into himself, and finally committed suicide (after one unsuccessful attempt). The poetry of the years 1904–11, which was written much under the influence of Russian and then French symbolism, is his best. The characteristic title of his 1907 collection is *Insomnia and Intuitions*. In order (it is said) to please his wife he turned to poetic drama, and wrote *At the Foot of Mount Vitosha* (1911), *When the Thunder Rolls* (1912) and *As the Echo Replies* (1912), misty Chekhovian (q.v.) plays with an undertone of menace and despair.

The works of PETKO TODOROV (1879–1916) consist of 'idylls' (a form he took from Schlaf, q.v.) and plays. The idylls are symbolist recreations of ancient folk tales in which heroes tragically fail to achieve reconciliation of their own aspirations with the needs of society. His plays combine Ibsen's techniques with folk themes. *The First* (1912) is a more straightforward play, about the wealthy Bulgarians who collaborated with the Turks.

The poet KIRIL HRISTOV (1875–1944) was certainly of an individualistic persuasion, although in fact he took Vazov's side in the controversy between him and Slaveykov, who was his friend. He spent most of his life in exile—the lot of many Bulgarians. Hristov was the first uninhibited poet of Bulgaria: personal, fresh, erotically descriptive, he shocked the readers of the Nineties. The poems are now dated; but they served their purpose. He also wrote plays and novels.

ELIN PELIN (ps. D. IVANOV, 1877–1949), Bulgaria's greatest writer of short stories, became the best known Bulgarian writer after Vazov's death. In his writings he conducted a love-hate relationship with the Bulgarian peasants of the countryside around Sofia; but, although he travelled and lived in foreign cities (France, Russia), he could never come to terms with urban life. Whereas

Todorov and Vlaykov (qq.v.) had in their different ways portrayed the old peasantry as they had always been, Pelin portrayed them under the impact of modern life: he saw them under the threat of change. He understood them better than Todorov and Vlaykov, and portrayed them not in any romantic spirit but in that of psychological realism. He is Bulgaria's first realist—and a good one. He cheerfully accepted the Revolution—and did not live to see it betrayed. (MBL)

YORDAN YOVKOV (1880–1937) is another writer still in communist favour. His subject is usually the same as Pelin's, but his approach—while never urbanly slanted—is more cosmopolitan. He wrote a fine satirical comedy about the greed and nastiness of the provincial bourgeois which would have been quite beyond Pelin's range: *The Millionaire* (1930). He wrote many stories and story-cycles (which amount to novels) about Bulgarian peasants and the impact upon them of war and other circumstances outside their control. Pelin analyzes the effects of change; Yovkov does the same, but his range is wider. His style is still held up as a model. (MBL)

As time went on the tendency to literary individualism grew stronger in Bulgaria. But it would be misleading to suppose that nationalism, even in the most modernist writers of Bulgaria, was not a considerable element. Slaveykov (q.v.) himself had opposed the Vazov circle only on the grounds that Bulgarians needed more than Bulgaria. What he was saying, by implication, was that the writer has a duty to his own function, too. The Bulgarian symbolists got their doctrine from France. But their interests were Bulgarian: in the medieval Bogomil heresy—the Bogomils were, to put it briefly, Bulgarian Cathars or Albigensians—and in the ancient history of the region.

DIMCHO DEBELYANOV (1887–1916), who was killed in Greece during the First World War, into which Bulgaria's rulers had led it on the side of Germany, was the leading symbolist poet. He saw French symbolist doctrine as a key to the mysteries of Bulgarian history. He left just a handful of rhythmically haunting poems, in some of which he has premonitions of his early death; but has been highly influential because of their quality, their evocation of the Bulgarian past, and their peculiarly Bulgarian unhappiness—that sense of having been cheated by history of the primitive right to one's own roots.

NICOLAY LILIEV (ps. N. MIHAYLOV, 1885–1960) was Debelyanov's friend and fellow symbolist. He had a powerful influence in post-war Bulgaria, and in 1934 became the director of the National Theatre in Sofia. His knowledge of foreign literatures, particularly English and French, was unsurpassed. He wrote comparatively few poems; most of them are collected in *Poems* of 1932. A sad man, hating the modern world and loving only the memory of his childhood, his search for an inner world manifested itself mainly in his emphasis upon form, melody and delicate elegance of utterance.

HRISTO JASENOV (ps. X. TUDŽAROV, 1889–1925), murdered by police for his leftist sympathies, was another symbolist with considerable mastery of style.

ELISAVETA BAGRYANA (ps. E. BELCHEVA, 1893) is Bulgaria's leading woman poet. She travelled much abroad, saying that she 'had a husband in every country', and generally titillated the Bulgarian bourgeoisie between the wars by enjoying many love affairs and writing about them with candour. One of her best cycles of love-poems is about Britain, where she had what polite critics once used to call 'a passionate liaison'. She has written beautifully of the Bulgarian landscape, and passionately against modern technology and the insensitivity of the men who implement its humanly menacing programmes. She is a prolific poet, sometimes too content to express conventionally romantic sentiments; but at her best she is vital and impressive. Her books include *The Eternal and the Saint* (1927), *The Sailor's Star* (1932), *Five Stars* (1953) and *From One Bank to the Other* (1963). The two latter volumes contain a good deal of 'socialist' poetry, in which genre Elisaveta Bagryana is clearly uneasy. Many of her first poems appeared in the magazine *Golden Horn* (*Zlatorog*, 1922–44), which was, in general, devoted to perfection of form and simplicity of expression. It was an eclectic and anti-dogmatic magazine, intelligently edited by the critic Vladimir Vasilev, and was the most important in Bulgaria in its time. *Hyperion* (1922–32) was devoted to symbolist poetry, and advocated a language and a content aloof from the common understanding. Also active at this time, but not yet very influential, was a Marxist group of critics.

The leading novelist of this period, and after the First World War, was the Macedonian DIMITAR TALEV (1898–1966). His main works are *The Years of Proof* (1928–30), the trilogy *The Iron Candlesticks* (1952) and *The Bells of Prespa* (1954). These are historical works, tracing the difficult and exciting history of the Macedonian peoples. Talev has narrative power and what has been called an epic serenity; his style, already formed, was not much affected by the advent of socialist realism.

Bulgaria's most successful writers of urban fiction are GEORGI STAMATOV (1869–1942), GEORGI RAYCHEV (1882–1948), whose psychological novel *Sin* (1923) was much praised, and DIMITAR SHISHMANOV (1889–1945), whose *Shadows on the Acropolis* (1938), on the relations between the ancient and the modern, reached a new level of sophistication. Stamatov introduced psychological analysis into Bulgarian fiction. His tales of city life are pitiless, revealing the corruption of officials and the misery of the poor. First an army officer and then a judge, Stamatov was one of the most sharply gloomy of all Bulgarian writers; but his sense of psychology is acute, and his cynicism often, alas, justified. He is probably the best Bulgarian writer of fiction of this century. Raychev has carried on in the same tradition. Shishmanov, executed by the communists for his conservatism at the end of the Second World War, treated eccentrics in a markedly unconservative manner.

NIKOLAI VAPTSAROV (1909–42), murdered by a firing-squad as a communist and resister of fascism, has aptly been called 'Bulgaria's Mayakovsky' (q.v.). He was indisputably the most gifted poet of his generation, and would no doubt have been shot by the communists if the Germans had not done it for them. He was no more subject to slogans or clichés than Mayakovsky. And, again like Mayakovsky, his feeling for everything modern and mechanical is suffused with genuine optimism and energy. In the hours before his death he wrote some remarkably moving poems to his wife. His only collection was *Motor Songs* (1940); but his *Collected Works* appeared in 1959.

Vaptsarov's most distinguished successors among a generation who were only children during the Second World War is LYVBOMIR LEVCHEV, who is the leader of a number of revolutionary young poets. He writes in free verse and, while he keeps in with the authorities (as he must), he has managed to achieve an authentic voice of his own. He is a predominantly urban poet, simple-minded and perfervid but not insincere.

Névéna Stefanova's *La poésie bulgare* (1968), published in Paris, is the only comprehensive guide to an obscure subject.

*

The theatre has flourished in Bulgaria since the communists took over. Playwrights have not. Almost the only play criticizing the system appeared in the very brief Bulgarian Thaw (1956): *Fear* (1956), by T. GENOV. This showed an opportunist climbing through the ranks of the communist party. In 1957 controls were brutally applied again. Bulgarian writers have been as repressed as any in the world. Socialist realism (q.v.) is absolute dogma, and literature is directed by a set of semi-literate culture-clerks. There are innumerable and interminable discussions, conducted on a low cultural level. Approved writing is monotonous, repetitive, lacking in psychological depth: the writer's situation is an abject one. Bulgaria's literature in exile is, unfortunately, an undistinguished one: 'hampered', says an exile, 'by its old-fashioned ideas and polemics—continually turning back to the past instead of looking towards the future'.

Canadian Literature

Canadian literature follows the usual colonial pattern, except that the pressures on her writers have been more diverse: there have been two 'home cultures', French and British—and the presence of the strongly-developing American culture to the immediate south. The fact that the French and the British (one should perhaps say English and Scottish) cultures exist side by side brings up the question of whether there is actually such a thing as a single, indigenous *Canadian* culture even now. Certainly it is only very recently that young Canadian writers have felt anything like confidence that there is—and this is largely owing to the emergence of an international feeling (among young people) that racial and political differences belong to an older generation. . . . And yet from this supposedly 'boring', archaic and 'square' society has emerged the first 'unsquare', new-style prime minister in the history of the modern world: Pierre Elliott Trudeau (Olof Palme of Sweden was the next). It is true that when a Canadian politician was kidnapped and subsequently killed by Canadian separatists Trudeau in mid-crisis looked (and spoke and acted), suddenly, very much like any other conventional politician; but it is still their world—not his.

There is not much in the poetry and fiction of the nineteenth-century Canadians that can honestly be offered as interesting except in a historical or purely local sense. The one exception, Isabella Valancy Crawford, whose poetry contains some magnificent lines and passages, died in 1887, aged thirty-seven. It was not until during and after the war that Canadian literature really developed. It is true that STEPHEN LEACOCK (1869–1944) began writing his humorous sketches in 1910 (he had previously written serious works on politics), but he was merely an Englishman commenting on Canadian provincial society. The crude balladeer ROBERT SERVICE (1874–1958), whose frontier verses are still popular, has no poetic merit. The fiction of WILLIAM KIRBY (1817–1906) served a function in its day, but is now of no interest.

As is usual in colonial literatures, it was poets who first made themselves heard—in the Twenties. But two early French-Canadian poets should be mentioned. The invalid ALBERT LOZEAU (1878—1924) was not a modernist, but his short lyrics—written from his bed—were, when not sentimental, elegant and moving records of a life necessarily devoted to reverie. The precocious ÉMILE NELLIGAN (1879–1941), born in Montreal, had an Irish father and a French-Canadian mother; before he was twenty he had become hopelessly insane, and spent his last forty years in an asylum. He can justifiably be thought of as Canada's Rimbaud. He is really a part of the French rather than the

French-Canadian tradition, but this makes him all the more important: he introduced symbolism to Canada, whose English poets, however, made nothing of it. He read his poems aloud, but they were not published until 1903; the *Complete Poems* (*Poésies complètes*) appeared in 1952. The chief influences on his work were Rimbaud and Verlaine, and the theme of his lush but suggestive poetry is the inaccessibility of beauty in the ordinary world. (OBCV)

The English-Canadian poets became active in the mid-Twenties, but their group anthology, *New Provinces*, did not appear until 1936. Canadian publishers were not much interested in issuing poetry until the years of the Second World War. The father-figure of modern Canadian poetry is undoubtedly E. J. PRATT (1883–1964), born in Newfoundland. Pratt is a good, forceful narrative poet who has affinities with Masefield and Roy Campbell (qq.v.); he had little lyrical gift but his language is admirably lucid and his versification masterly within its limitations. He broke with the old, mechanically picturesque procedures to form a poetry that actually observed both natural and urban processes. Pratt is a truly dynamic poet, who will introduce any kind of relevant scientific information into his work. In this (alone) he resembles MacDiarmid (q.v.); but he is never prosy. He takes public themes (*Towards the Last Spike*, 1952, is on the building of the Canadian Pacific Railway) but spices them with irony. If he failed to gain an international reputation then this is because, finally, he never resolved his ambiguous attitudes: his vitalism, sometimes jaunty like Campbell's, but never schoolboyish, veers between grimly ironic naturalism—with much emphasis on 'nature red in tooth and claw'—and a compassionate calm. He never found a language of resolution, and therefore lacks that ultimate wisdom which characterizes the work of a major poet. The fullest retrospective edition of his work was published in Canada in 1944.

The poets of the so-called 'Montreal School' of the Twenties learned from Pratt to widen their scope to include all aspects of life; but they employed shorter forms. A. J. M. SMITH (1902) has been important as an influence and anthologist as well as a poet. He appeared in *New Provinces* with Pratt, Klein and Scott (qq.v.). He is essentially a cautious modernist, and his work remains more or less in the formal tradition, often reminding one of the Sitwells (qq.v.), and drawing on the English metaphysical tradition. His deliberate pastiche of such poets as Yeats (q.v.) and Vaughan is brilliantly educated and displays extraordinary sensitivity and skill; but since his best effects are in this kind of poetry one wonders if his function is not predominantly critical. He has an admirably hard style in his 'own' poems, but seems too often to lapse into rhythmical obviousness and a tone slightly false to his own educated sophistication. F. R. SCOTT (1899) is a satirist, a love poet and a nature poet—in that order. As a young man at McGill University he played a large part in making his contemporaries aware of Pound and Eliot. He has led a public life, as Professor of Law at McGill and as an active socialist (he was chairman of the C.C.F., the Canadian socialist party, 1942–50), and has been a lively figure. He is more successful as a satirist than in other modes, as the opening lines of 'The Canadian Authors Meet' suggest:

Expansive puppets percolate self-unction
Beneath a portrait of the Prince of Wales.
Miss Crotchet's muse has somehow failed to function,
Yet she's poetess. . . .

(OBCV)

The most interesting and gifted of this Montreal group was the Jewish poet
A. M. KLEIN (1909), who has remained poetically silent since 1948, when he
published *The Rocking Chair*, his fourth collection. His first volume was called
Hath Not a Jew . . . (1940). This was followed by *The Hitleriad* (1944) and *Poems*
(1944). *The Second Scroll*, an experimental novel, appeared in 1951. Klein, 'a
Jewish poet in the sense that Claudel [q.v.] was a Catholic poet' (A. J. M.
Smith), is the poet of Quebec, whose French-Canadian conservatism he views
from his own Hebraically conservative position. He is very much an odd man
out, although his work is held in high regard. He writes from the point of view
of a sophisticated but committed Jew; even when dealing with such themes as
an Indian Reservation he considers them—if only obliquely—in the terms of
an alienated, tortured Jew who yearns for Jerusalem. But he is unique because
of his involuntary (and still very Jewish) irony, and his remarkable use of
language. One feels that he has not gone to secular Israel (he works in public
relations in Montreal) because, under such circumstances, he would rather work
in a less frustratedly secular Canada. Nevertheless, he was zealously concerned
with the establishment of Israel as well as with protest against the Nazi
atrocities. His latest poetry achieved an idiosyncrasy of diction which was
necessary for the complex feelings it expressed. Has Klein been an influence on
John Berryman? He ends his poem 'Montreal', in *The Rocking Horse*:

City, O city, you are vision'd as
A parchemin roll of saecular exploit
Inked with the script of eterne souvenir!
You are in sound, chanson and instrument!
Mental, you rest forever edified
With tower and dome; and in these beating valves,
Here in these beating valves, you will
For all my mortal time reside!

Here is the same kind of mixture of heroic poesy, old high manner, archaism
and quaintness that characterizes much of Berryman's later work. Certainly
Berryman's own manner differs from Klein's; but this approach among others
could well have provided him with the confidence to go forward. Despite his
long silence, Klein is Canada's most original poet, and perhaps the only one
of his generation who, although so rooted in the past of his race, was entirely
unsatisfied with the poetic procedures of the nineteenth century. (OBCV)

The younger poets whose work began to appear in the Forties had less
creative confidence than Klein, and consequently a more eclectic and 'international' approach. They were galvanized into activity by an energetic

Englishman, PATRICK ANDERSON (1915), who became a Canadian citizen, but eventually returned to Great Britain. He was only in Canada for ten years. What Anderson really did was to export to Canada the styles and preoccupations of the English poets of the late Thirties; his own poetry was a sensitive instrument for the recording of these (particularly of Auden, MacNeice, Barker, Gascoyne, qq.v.) rather than an *œuvre* in its own right. But his application of this Thirties-style sensibility was intelligent and fluent, and his presence in Canada entirely beneficial. His best published work is contained in autobiographies (*Snake Wine*, 1955) and travel books. Although called with some justice 'a kind of tea-drinking Dylan Thomas', on account of some of his over-fluent Canadian poems, Anderson is an exceptionally intelligent man who has an engaging line in criticism of his earlier selves. (OBCV) Anderson established the magazine *Preview*, and it was there that the work of P. K. PAGE (1917) first appeared. P. K. Page was born in Swanage, Dorset, England, but was educated and grew up in Canada. A characteristically rigorous selection of her best work, with new poems, was included in *Cry Ararat!* (1967), her most recent volume. Her start as a poet of social protest under the influence of Scott and Anderson (qq.v.) was in fact a false one; her real concerns emerged in the poems of *The Metal and the Flower* (1954): satire of lonely bourgeois personalities merges into psychological and biographical concern. These were perhaps her most successful poems: her more recent work, for all its purity of line (reminiscent of Kathleen Raine, q.v., and of some other good woman poets), is not entirely convincing. Such thoughts as 'A single leaf can block a mountainside; / all Ararat be conjured in a leaf' are better left where they belong: with William Blake. But if its mysticism fails, this is still an attractive and limpid poetry. (OBCV)

EARLE BIRNEY (1904), a noted scholar and critic, born in Alberta, was in his early years a farm labourer, logger, bank clerk and sailor. He has been the most independent of Canadian writers, and is now a universally respected veteran. The influences on his verse have been manifold. Much of its strength comes from his scholarly concern with early English poetry and Chaucer. Then there is his non-dogmatic, tough radicalism and feeling of kinship with the working-classes. More recently—for Birney will cheerfully expose himself to any influence that he feels may be of use to him—there have been the Beats and the American Black Mountain poets (qq.v.); such as is silly or brutal about these has been resolutely rejected. Chiefly, however, Birney has written out of himself: out of an innate scepticism and humanitarianism, and a vision rooted in the Canadian Rockies where he spent his childhood. He is in fact at his best when writing in terms of nature, as in 'Slug in Woods',

> For eyes he waves greentipped
> taut horns of slime. They dipped,
> hours back, across a reef,
> a salmonberry leaf.

where his attention is directed onto the minute detail of what he has observed. But he is never unreadable or pretentious. His *Selected Poems* appeared in 1966.

He has written two excellent novels: the picaresque *Turvey* (1949) and *Down the Long Table* (1955). (OBCV)

Another Canadian original is IRVING LAYTON (1912), who was born in Rumania. His parents emigrated to Canada when he was only one year old. Layton is a highly gifted poet, a 'natural', who simply has to mix in his sillinesses and rushes of blood to the head with his more straightforward lyrical poems. He can seldom express his opinions about affairs without a childish rage or petulance; his experience is deliberately withdrawn. But when he writes of that experience which ought to temper his opinions he is a bright minor poet, and justifies the comparisons—often made—between himself and Blake and Whitman. He has been overrated (he is nowhere near so accomplished a poet as Klein, even though he has been referred to as 'great') because his immense energy tends to obscure his incapacity, even at his best, to organize his emotions. The concluding stanza of 'The Birth of Tragedy' gives a good sense of his achievements and his limitations:

> A quiet madman, never far from tears,
>   I lie like a slain thing
>   under the green air the trees
> inhabit, or rest upon a chair
>   towards which the inflammable air
> tumbles on many robins' wings;
>   noting how seasonably
>   leaf and blossom uncurl
> and living things arrange their death,
> while someone from afar off
> blows birthday candles for the world.

There is more cliché here than the sincere vitality of the surface suggests there might be, and there are confusions; the last two lines insufferably indulge a penchant for whimsy; but the emotion which the poet is not altogether success-fully trying to capture is pure, powerful and moving, and the line 'and living things arrange their death' has been its reward. Layton's *Collected Poems* were published in 1965. (OBCV)

The Montreal poet LOUIS DUDEK (1918) has been a vital and helpful influence on Canadian poetry without, perhaps, contributing much to its permanent qualities. He originally appeared in the *Preview* anthology, *Unit of Five* (1944), which introduced P. K. Page. Dudek's friend RAYMOND SOUSTER (1921) is a useful, generous and lively influence; his poetry is direct, pleasant and prosy. For many years he was also at the centre of Montreal literary activity. A *Selected Poems* appeared in 1956, and he has published many other collections.

Later English-Canadian poets seem to have divided themselves into academic and U.S.A. schools. JAY MACPHERSON (1931), a university teacher who has stated that she stopped being a poet in 1957, makes poetry out of previous poetries, of which she has extensive knowledge. She was first taken up by

Robert Graves, who printed her *Nineteen Poems* (1952) on his long-defunct Seizin Press (he revived it again for Terence Hards in 1964); but her best-known, and much-acclaimed, book is *The Boatman* (1957). These poems represented one of the cleverest and most attractive literary retreats from sexuality of their decade. Reluctantly influenced by Graves' pagan beastliness (as one might, from the general tone of the poems, put it), they combined elements of fable and learned Biblical reference with great skill and charm. The subtly organized scholastic surface does not conceal a wistfulness for robust experience. (OBCV) The work of JAMES REANEY (1926), centred in life where Jay Macpherson's is centred in learning, forms a contrast. Reaney founded, and edits, a magazine called *Alphabet*, which follows the theories of the important Canadian critic Northrop Frye (1912), an episcopalian priest and university teacher who has been described by Mordecai Richler (q.v.) as 'our keeper of true standards'. Frye's most ambitious and influential book is *Anatomy of Criticism* (1957), in which he contentiously attacks value judgements and makes a prophetic bid to reduce literature to its socio-anthropological and mythopoeic components. Reaney's poetry seeks to order his experience into recognizably Fryean categories, and to subsume them under a general Christianity. The most interesting and original of his four books are *Twelve Letters to a Small Town* (1962), written in a mock-infantile style, and *A Suit of Nettles* (1958), satirical mock allegory. Despite some surrealism, Reaney has yet to burst out of his over-scholastic theorizings and to face himself in his poetry; but it already displays the lineaments of experience. (OBCV; CWT)

BERTRAM WARR (1917–43), killed in the Second World War, should also be mentioned. He did not have time to realize his gifts, but the poems in *Yet a Little Onwards* (1941) display remarkable sophistication and potential—as the final lines of 'The Deviator' illustrate:

And as I sat here this morning, thinking my thoughts amid the sounds,
Suddenly, all these, the definables, began telling their meanings to me,
Saying there is no aloneness, there can be no dark cocoon,
With room for one, and an empty place, if love should come.

*

In French-Canadian poetry only ROBERT CHOQUETTE (1905) rivalled E. J. Pratt's (q.v.) gift for creating on an epic scale. His first volume *Through the Winds* (*A Travers les vents*, 1925), contained passionately lyrical poems about the northern part of Canada. He is a rhetorical and romantic poet, in some ways a French counterpart of Birney (q.v.)—but with smoother rhythms and much less toughness of mind. (OBCV) The first really important poet after Nelligan (q.v.) was HECTOR DE SAINT-DENYS-GARNEAU (1912–43), whose volume *Gazes and Games in Space* (*Regards et jeux dans l'espace*, 1937) initiated the modern movement in Canadian poetry. Saint-Denys-Garneau did almost all his work between 1935 and 1938—he suffered from a heart condition—and, like Nelligan, was

more a part of the French than the French-Canadian tradition. He was aware
of Rilke (q.v.), and his poetry is more individual and more pioneering in its
use of free verse than any of his Canadian-English counterparts. 'Birdcage'
demonstrates his quality.

> I am a bird-cage
> Bone-cage
> With a bird
>
> The bird in his bone-cage
> It is death who makes his nest
>
> When nothing happens
> You hear his wing-ruffle
>
> And after a burst of laughter
> If you suddenly stop
> You hear his coo
> Deep down
> Like a tiny bell
>
> It's a captive bird
> Death in my bone-cage
>
> Wouldn't he love to fly away
> Is it you who holds him back
> Or me
> Or what
>
> He can only escape
> When he's eaten me all
> My heart
> My source of blood
> My life
>
> In his beak will be my soul

Saint-Denys-Garneau's cousin ANNE HÉBERT (1916) has written with similar
purity and insight: 'Manor Life', in F. R. Scott's (q.v.) version, is one of her
most characteristically sombre and exact poems. It concludes:

> See, these mirrors are deep
> Like cupboards
> There is always someone dead behind the quicksilver
> Who soon covers your reflection
> And clings to you like seaweed
>
> Shapes himself to you, naked and thin,
> And imitates love in a long bitter shiver.
>
> (CWT)

Anne Hébert has also written a surrealistic novel, *The Wooden Rooms* (*Les Chambres de bois*, 1958). (OBCV)

The best known French-Canadian poet of the younger generation is JEAN-GUY PILON (1930), whose poetry is however more deliberately cosmopolitan than personal. (OBCV; CWT)

*

Fiction that is not merely provincial has been even slower to establish itself than poetry in Canada. The chief places of honour must go, in English, to MORLEY CALLAGHAN (1903), and in French to GABRIELLE ROY (1909). Callaghan, a tough Canadian newspaperman, was first encouraged to write fiction by Hemingway (q.v.), who later introduced him to the American expatriates in Paris, about whom he has written brilliantly and understandingly in *That Summer in Paris* (1963), one of his best books. Callaghan is a realistic novelist of very high quality, whose achievement has not been fully recognized except in his native Canada, and then belatedly. Callaghan's harshness is somewhat modified by his devout Catholicism, but this is never really to the fore (unless compassion be a solely Christian quality). *Strange Fugitive* (1928), his first novel, was about a bootlegger. Much better was *It's Never Over* (1930), a haunting account of the sufferings of the friends and family of a man hanged for murdering a policeman. His major work is *Such Is My Beloved* (1934), dealing with a Roman Catholic priest's attempt, which leads to his destruction, to redeem two prostitutes. Here Morley dwells upon the dangerous resemblances between Christian love and opportunistic lust. His attitude towards his prostitutes is, for the Thirties, refreshingly unsentimental and unhysterical. *The Loved and the Lost* (1951) examines, with the same poignancy, Negro-white relations in Montreal; this shocked Callaghan's fellow Catholics. *A Passion in Rome* (1961) is a story of a love affair between two Canadians living in Rome, and raises the same issue as Callaghan's earlier work: to what extent is love sexual opportunism? Callaghan's short stories, mostly written in the Twenties, owe much to Hemingway, but are excellently observed. They are collected in *Morley Callaghan's Stories* (1959).

Gabrielle Roy was born in Manitoba; she was a teacher and an actress before becoming a writer. Allowing for differences of culture and sex, Gabrielle Roy shares Callaghan's approach: she is first and foremost a realist. Her first novel, *The Tin Flute* (*Bonheur d'occasion*, 1945; tr. 1947) is a humourless but moving study of slum life in Montreal, with a bitter undertone of social accusation. *The Cashier* (*Alexandre Chenevert, caissier*, 1954; tr. 1955), her subtlest book, presents a bank-clerk, a character reminiscent of Duhamel's Salavin (q.v.). The well-written *Street of Riches* (*Rue Deschambault*, 1955; tr. 1957) consists of autobiographical sketches. *The Hidden Mountain* (*La Montagne secrète*, 1961; tr. 1962) tries to trace the mainsprings of artistic inspiration through the career of a painter who seeks beauty in Canada and then in Paris; this excursion into symbolism is unconvincing. Gabrielle Roy's strength as a novelist lies in her uncluttered view of ordinary lives, and her refusal to regard commercial 'progress' as a true human benefit.

HUGH MACLENNAN (1907), born in Nova Scotia, is another writer who from the beginning showed an awareness of the real problems facing Canadians, and he has continually urged his countrymen to abandon their collective inferiority complex and to face their problem of a divided culture with realism and maturity. After Princeton MacLennan went on to Oxford as a Rhodes Scholar, and while there travelled widely in Europe. He wrote, but did not publish, two novels in the early Thirties, while teaching in Canada; but then became aware that there was 'no known contemporary fiction being written in Canada' (either he had not read, or had misunderstood, Callaghan), and so set himself the task of rectifying the omission. The result was *Barometer Rising* (1941), about the great munitions ship explosion in Halifax Harbour in 1917 (which he witnessed). *Two Solitudes* (1945) was the first Canadian novel to explore in depth and with real understanding the conflict between the descendants of the British and the French. *The Watch that Ends the Night* (1959) is a rather over-solemn novel about communism and Canadian intellectuals; but it is intelligent and humane. Like Gabrielle Roy, MacLennan has little humour; in this respect both writers are overshadowed by the cosmopolitan and witty Callaghan.

Although of an older generation, ETHEL WILSON (1890) did not publish her first novel, *Hetty Dorval* (1947), until she had reached almost sixty. The wife of a Vancouver doctor, Ethel Wilson is justly honoured by the younger generation as a shrewd, ironic and intelligent experimental novelist. *Hetty Dorval* is a subtle study in promiscuity. All its successors are about love or emotions and attitudes that pose as love. *Equations of Love* (1952) describes a love affair through the eyes of a number of people, and then examines it in terms of the person who experienced it. *Love and Salt Water* (1956) is more overtly satirical. Ethel Wilson shares at least an acerbity of mind with Ivy Compton-Burnett (q.v.).

The French-Canadian novelist, ROGER LEMELIN (1919), 'the bad boy of present-day Canadian literature', began brilliantly with two realistic novels about the Lower Town of Quebec, where he had worked. Again like Gabrielle Roy, Lemelin compels attention by his refusal to settle for a complacent view of French-Canadian society. *The Town Below* (*Au Pied de la pente douce*, 1944; tr. S. Putnam, 1948), a disrespectful and satirical tale, won a prize in France. *The Plouffe Family* (*Les Plouffe*, 1948; tr. M. Finch, 1950)—taken up as a weekly serial on television—is about an opera-singer who becomes a monk but then leaves his monastery to fight Nazism.

Two minor novelists, exact contemporaries, who share a concern with the Canadian creative predicament, are ERNEST BUCKLER (1908) and SINCLAIR ROSS (1908). Buckler's most outstanding novel is his depressing and partly symbolist study of a mute artist in *The Mountain and the Valley* (1952). Ross is less pessimistic; *As for Me and My House* (1941) is about a clergyman's and his wife's struggle to exist physically and spiritually in a prairie town. More interesting and vivid is the analytical *The Well* (1958), which deals shrewdly and sympathetically with a young man of criminal mentality.

Younger prose writers include MORDECAI RICHLER (1931), who has long made his home in London, BRIAN MOORE (1921), who lives in California, JACK LUDWIG (1922), who works as a university teacher in the state of New York and MARGARET LAURENCE (1926), who lived in Africa before settling in England. The fact that these and other highly self-consciously Canadian writers live abroad must mean something; it is probably, however, an indictment of the social rather than the strictly cultural environment. The French-Canadians tend to stay at home, although most of them publish in France—a few in France only.

Richler, a lively and intelligent writer much concerned with Jewish problems, has not yet—despite massive and somewhat irrelevant publicity campaigns—written the novel of which he is capable. His novels deal with the same kind of material as the poems of Klein (q.v.): he was brought up in a Jewish family in Montreal. He has not bettered his second novel, *Son of a Smaller Hero* (1955), about Jewish life in Montreal. *The Apprenticeship of Duddy Kravitz* (1959) is less sure in touch, but is written with great verve and humour. The satirical *The Incomparable Atuk* (1963), about an Eskimo writer's success with Toronto intellectuals, is slighter but extremely funny. *Cocksure* (1968) is very much more ambitious and less effective.

Brian Moore is a Belfast Irishman who emigrated to Canada after the Second World War. *The Lonely Passion of Judith Hearne* (1955) is a tender-tough study of an alcoholic spinster. His best known book, *The Luck of Ginger Coffey* (1960) is also his most specifically Canadian. Ginger Coffey is a middle-aged Irish immigrant in Canada: he finds himself bereft of wife, job and a sense of virility, and he can only respond by fantasizing and self-deceit. The processes through which he discovers the truth about himself and his situation are described with acute psychological penetration and feeling. He has not yet bettered this novel, one of the finest to come from Canada since the Second World War; but its successors, which include *The Emperor of Ice-Cream* (1965), have been of a uniformly high standard.

Jack Ludwig is more experimental, and has learnt from Saul Bellow (q.v.), with whom he has collaborated on a review. Of his two novels, the earlier *Confusions* (1963) is by far the better. Especially notable in this study of an American Jew who goes to teach in California is Ludwig's grasp of the speech-habits of North American Jews (one of Bellow's special provinces). Margaret Laurence sets the best of her three novels, *Jest of God* (1966), in a small Canadian town. The story of an unhappy and unfulfilled teacher's love affair is told by herself with dignity and insight. The best parts of the novel describe small-town pressures on the individual.

The leading younger French-Canadian novelists are ANDRÉ LANGEVIN and CLAIRE MARTIN (PS. CLAIRE FAUCHER). The more vigorous talent is that of Langevin, whose best novel remains, however, the early *Dust Over the Town* (*Poussière sur la ville*, 1953). Claire Martin is at her best as a short story writer

(*With and Without Love, Avec et sans amour,* 1958) and autobiographer (*In an Iron Glove, Dans un gant de fer,* 1965); but her later novels, including *Doux-Amer* (1960) are shrewd, and lucidly written.

*

A good deal of theatrical activity goes on in Canada, but there have so far been few really successful dramatists worthy of consideration. The French branch has had more vitality than the English. The dominant theatrical personality in Canada for the past thirty years has been the versatile actor, producer and playwright GRATIEN GÉLINAS (1909), known as Fridolin because of the series of revue sketches he wrote and played in between 1938 and 1946: these featured himself as the Chaplinesque Fridolin. *Lil' Rooster* (*Tit-Coq,* 1948; tr. 1950), a shrewd comedy about French-Canadians in the overseas Canadian armies during the Second World War, was more substantial, and enjoyed an immense and widespread success (except in New York). *Bousille and the Righteous* (*Bousille et les justes,* 1959) was another success in both English and French. Other French-Canadian playwrights include GUY DUFRESNE, FÉLIX LECLERC— both authors of fairly successful plays—and the more serious PAUL TOUPIN, whose *Brutus* and *The Lie* are interesting, but have not attracted the public. However, JACQUES LANGUIRAND, a close disciple of Beckett and Ionesco, has aroused some interest. The leading playwright of the younger generation is the prolific MARCEL DUBÉ, whose *Zone* and *Florence* are black farces of some originality.

English-Canadian drama is sparse on the ground, although there are numerous performances in many cities. James Reaney (q.v.) has written interesting verse plays. Canada's most distinguished English-language playwright is ROBERTSON DAVIES (1913), also a novelist (whose work has been praised by Bellow, q.v.). Davies, an ex-actor and now an academic, gained success with the one-act *Eros at Breakfast* (1948), which he followed with the full-length *Fortune My Foe* (1949). His novels portray small-town Canadian life satirically but lovingly. He adapted *Leaven of Malice* (1954), a satire on intellectuals, for the stage in 1960. He is an intelligent writer whose work is unfortunately not free from a sentimentality that too often masquerades as wisdom.

Chinese Literature

Modern Chinese literature begins late: in 1919, with the movement called the Literary Revolution. This was a logical development from the political revolution of 1911, which, although not really successful, created a climate of change. Of all the literary languages of the world not yet supplanted by the colloquial, the Chinese was probably the most helplessly and hopelessly out of touch with the actual life of the first two decades of this century. It was a language foreign to the common people. And however well or badly, intelligently or unintelligently, the common people react to literature, it is an unwritten law that any literature written in a language remote from them is an attenuated and diffuse copy of reality, of little value. It cannot be said that since 1919 Chinese literature, whose past poetry, at least, is one of the glories of the world, has attained much distinction. Between then and 1937 China was torn apart by civil war and then by the war with Japan (1937–45); there followed four more years of civil war. In 1949 the communists came to power. Little is known in the West, and less understood, about their impact upon Chinese society. But literature has for the time being been a casualty, if we are to rely on the trans-lated material that is sent out of Pekin, which consists of abject socialist realist (q.v.) fiction that is quite certainly more simple-minded than the government of Mao Tse Tung, himself once a minor poet, and now advertised in his own country as a major one.

It is necessary, before discussing the very few Chinese twentieth-century writers of any distinction, to make some remarks on the political background. Too frequently it is assumed that the peasants—still the vast majority of the huge population of China—have been plunged, by communism, into a hell that contrasts with an idyllic past. Whatever one may feel or think about com-munism, this is not so. Until 1937, when it became necessary for the Chinese to unite against the common enemy, the country was alive with war: not only the civil war, but also feudal wars between warlords—for power and plunder. Communism may or may not be bad for the peasants—we are in no position to judge the communes—but the past, it may safely be said, was worse.

On 4 May 1919 Chinese students, supported by intellectuals, rose in violent protest against the Versailles Treaty decision to cede former German territory in Shantung to the Japanese. Intellectuals were putting forward their claims to judge and to control foreign policy. Magazines in the colloquial began to appear. The young suddenly felt emancipated. Their spirit was Chinese—this is often misunderstood—but the ideas came from the West. Eventually this led to con-fusions: the Chinese civilization is not Western, and the greatness of its literature is based in Chinese and not Western concepts. This, perhaps, underlies some of the difficulties experienced by the Chinese in adapting themselves to the complex and self-contradictory theories of a complex and self-contradictory nineteenth-century German Jew; it also explains the complex nature of Chinese political attitudes towards the West, which are not simply 'Marxist', and are certainly not as simply hostile and aggressive as many of us may be led to believe.

The leading spirit in the literary revolution was the critic, versifier and scholar HU SHIH (1891–1962), who studied at Cornell University in the U.S.A., and then at Columbia. Hu Shih pronounced the literary language (*ku-wen*) to have been dead for two thousand years, and proposed to substitute for it a form of the vernacular (*pai-hua*) that had been employed in the popular literature, which was regarded as vulgar by the classical writers. He was a professor at Pekin University from 1917 until 1926, and was thus in a position to get his ideas put into practice. But he was not revolutionary by temperament, and was glad to leave the polemics to his friend and supporter, the essayist Ch'en Tu-hsui (1879–1942), who wrote (1917): 'Down with ornate toadying aristocratic literature to build a simple and lyrical literature . . . a fresh and sincere realistic literature . . . a clear, popular social literature'. New translations of important European writers, including Ibsen, Tchekov and Strindberg (qq.v.), into the vernacular followed. All this was part of the great process, begun under the impact of the West, of the breaking down of the supremacy of the intellectual élite: both Confucianism and the old examination system had gone; now young Chinese, as young Japanese almost fifty years before them, were anxious to acquire knowledge of foreign languages and Western technology.

One opponent of the literary revolution deserves brief mention: LIN SHU (1852–1924), who had himself paraphrased 156 works of Western fiction—although not into the vernacular—and thus helped to prepare the way for it. Novelist, poet and painter, he was the last significant member of the old school, known as *T'ung-ch'eng*. (His paraphrases of Dickens, Scott, Dumas and others were done from oral translations made by friends who knew English and French, which he did not.)

By the beginning of the Twenties the language battle had been won, and the vernacular (now renamed *kuo yu*, or national language) was established. There was a spate of social realism in the drama and in fiction (nearly always in the form of the short story). Poetry did not fare so well, as Hu Shi's *Experimental Verse* (1916) had already made clear. In this less than thirty years of freedom (until 1949, when socialist realism was imposed) modern Chinese literature did not of course have time to develop. The literature of its classical period had lasted for nearly three millennia; it is not yet time to judge that of its modern period.

The political background in those thirty years was not conducive to the growth of a new literature. Civil war existed between Chiang Kai-shek's ruling Kuomintang, the warlords and the Chinese Communist Party (formed 1921). By 1927 writers had become disillusioned. In 1922 the Creation Society had been formed, chiefly inspired by the poet and critic KUO MO-JO (1893). The

344

writers of this group were influenced by European romanticism and, like their earlier Japanese counterparts, by *fin de siècle* decadence; but all were social revolutionaries, if of varying hues. The group was proscribed in 1929 by Chiang Kai-shek, who thus dealt a blow to the development of his country's literature—just as his fascism disguised as democracy prepared the way for the communism which he (at any rate) maintained would ruin China. A number of the Creation writers and critics returned to Japan (until 1937), the country where they had originally learned about Western literature.

Kuo Mo-jo is a well known and favoured writer in communist China. He represents writers in the People's Congress. He has always been a passionate radical. His early poetry is influenced by Tagore (q.v.) and Whitman; later he became a crude, declamatory poet, a Chinese equivalent of Becher (q.v.) rather than of Mayakovski (q.v.) or even Vaptsarov (q.v.).

The outstanding figure in modern Chinese literature, and the fullest artist so far to manifest himself, is LU HSIN (ps. CHOU SHU-JEN, 1881–1936). (His name is variously written, as Chinese is variously transcribed; he often appears as Lu Xun.) Lu Hsin was dissatisfied with Chinese society from his earliest student days, and he set out to be a writer in order to provide a cure. Until his disillusioned last days, when he cooperated with the communists, he was remarkably consistent in his objectives. As a young man he studied medicine in Japan, taught at various universities, and translated some Russian stories. He wrote his first short story, 'Diary of a Madman', in 1918 especially for the inaugurators of the literary revolution; twenty-five more followed. Besides this first one, 'The True Story of Ah Q' (tr. 1926; 1956) is his most famous. He was an important critic, whose *Brief History of Chinese Fiction* remains the best Chinese criticism of this century. Three of his stories are translated in *Modern Chinese Stories* (1970; tr. W. J. F. Jenner and G. Yang). Lu Hsin's style is laconic, and although he sets out to satirize national defects, his sense of comedy is also artistic.

Lu Hsin spent his last years issuing polemics from Shanghai, under various pseudonyms, against the nationalist government. He was continually in danger of assassination by Chiang Kai-shek's hired killers. But he never joined the communist party—although he is still revered by it—and a year before he died he wrote: 'Once a person goes inside the Party he would be bogged down in meaningless complications and quarrels. . . .' Lu Hsin was an individualist, whose social indignation was essentially non-dogmatic. No writer of modern Chinese prose can match either his economy or the degree of human feeling that he gets into stories.

MAO TUN (ps. SHEN YEN-PING, 1896), in favour until recently—and for a time Minister of Culture—wrote some realistic novels in the Thirties, including *Midnight* (1933; tr. 1957). He was severely censured for allegedly supporting the ownership of private property in *The Lin Family Shop* (written before the revolution but translated in Pekin in 1957).

TING LING (1907), who vanished from the literary scene in 1957 when she was accused of rightist tendencies (this was not long after she had unsuccessfully denounced her ex-husband SHEN TS'UNG-WEN, 1903, a popular story-teller, as bourgeois), wrote some of the best Chinese fiction in the period before the Japanese invasion of 1937. It is sensationalist by Western standards; but the subject-matter of *Water* (1933)—group-life—and of certain short stories—sexual incompatibility between communists and non-communists—represented a sincere attempt to deal realistically with the personal problems of people living in politically disturbed times.

PA CHIN (ps. LI FEI-KAN, 1904), at one time an anarchist, is best known for his trilogy *Torrent* (1933–40), of which the first volume, *Family* (1933), was translated in 1958. This effectively describes his own struggles against, and escape from, his traditional upbringing in a wealthy family; but it is excessively sentimental. Since 1949 he has written little fiction.

*

The new Chinese poetry at first seemed crude. The poets threw their traditional forms entirely overboard and concentrated on imitation of Western models. WEN I-TUO (1899–1946) was one of the first to realize that the Chinese tradition itself, although worn out, had something essential to offer. Having studied the English romantic poets, he tried to fashion—in his few rather dilettante poems —successful new forms in the vernacular. He joined the Democratic League in 1944, and was killed by one of Chiang Kai-shek's murder-squads.

Associated with Wen was HSU CHIH-MO (1896–1931), whose life was cut short by an air crash. A friend of H. G. Wells and Katherine Mansfield (qq.v.), and a pupil of Harold Laski, he learned much from his study of English poetry, some of whose rhythms he successfully adapted to Chinese. The content of his poetry is perfervidly romantic.

*

The most important playwrights of modern China are TSAO YU (ps. WAN CHIA-PAO, 1910) and T'IEN HAN (1898). T'ien Han, such as he is, is the first pioneer. A member of the Creation Society (q.v.), he has been an active communist since the mid-Twenties, and is still in favour. His plays of the Twenties were ludicrously sentimental—they would be jeered off the stage as parodic farces by Western audiences—but they did introduce an element of social criticism. Themes of his later plays are predictably socialist realist. Tsao Yu is somewhat superior, and has more successfully assimilated the influence of Ibsen; but his plays since 1949 have shown no dramatic merit. His first play, *Thunderstorm* (1934; tr. 1958), was influenced by Greek tragedy, but its real aim was to show the terrible fate (death, insanity) of those who were brought up under the old Confucian family system.

*

It cannot be pretended that any literature of merit has manifested itself in

China since 1949. The position of the serious writer is so impossible that there appear to be no true 'revisionists', although every so often some slavishly unoriginal writer is purged for this offence. What will come in the future is anyone's guess; but nothing good, it is safe to say, will see the light of day for some considerable time to come. If Chinese communism wants a literature worth the name, it must give its writers freedom.

There are one or two worthlessly sentimental Chinese writers in exile; the only novelist worthy of note writing outside China is EILEEN CHANG (ps. CHANG AI-LING), whose *The Rice-Sprout Song* (1954; tr. author, 1955) is perhaps the outstanding Chinese novel of its period. Her *Collected Stories* appeared in Hong Kong in 1954.

Czechoslovakian Literature

I

Czechoslovakia came into being in autumn 1918. However, a vigorous literature was already extant in Czech and, to a lesser extent, in Slovak. Literary Czech was fully developed in 1348, when Prague University was founded; the nineteenth-century patriots had the rich tradition of the earliest Slavonic literature to draw upon. Czech and Slovak are similar (the Czecho-Moravian dialect is actually a transition between the two languages, with a largely similar vocabulary). The Czechs have dominated the modern period (with the exception of the immediate post-1945 period), but there have been a few important Slovak writers. The only two writers to have achieved an international reputation are Hašek and Čapek (qq.v.), although Holub (q.v.) seems to be in the process of doing so, if on a more modest scale.

ALOIS JIRÁSEK (1851–1930), historical novelist, was most important for his role in reminding Czechs of their past greatness. His novels, while vivid, are poor in characterization; but they draw attention to the other than individual forces which form history, and are still widely read. SVATOPLUK ČECH (1846–1908) was a more complex character. He used to be regarded mainly as a poet; but his epics have not stood the test of time, and nowadays it is his satirical *Hanuman* (1884; tr. W. W. Strickland, 1894) that we should read: this, with its portrayal of a progressive ape leader and nationalist (his slogan: 'Back to the ape!') would have pleased Orwell (q.v.). The satire *Mr. Brouček's Excursion to the Moon* (1886) and its sequel were made familiar in Janáček's fine operatic version.

Czechoslovakian literary development parallels that of Europe: liberalism and nationalism were followed in the Nineties by scepticism (the future first President of the Czechoslovak Republic, T. G. MASARYK, 1850–1937, then Professor of Philosophy at Prague University, was the leading anti-romantic), which existed side by side with the decadent *fin-de-siècle* mood common to every country. JAROSLAV VRCHLICKÝ (ps. EMIL FRIDA, 1853–1912), often contrasted with Čech—because where the latter represented 'nationalism' he represented 'cosmopolitanism'—was receptive to all these phases, and then to symbolism (q.v.). His epic poetry is marked by skill and superb craftsmanship, but is bogged down in solemnity. However, his technical influence, and the example he set of going to French and English rather than to German literature, have been of importance in the development of Czech poetry. Undoubtedly his influence is more important than his work. For the last four years of his life he was mad.

The beginning of Czech poetry is always dated from Karel Hynek Mácha's (1810–36) epic poem *May* (tr. H. H. McGoverne, 1949): this not only embodies the romantic revolt of the individual against society, but also foreshadows the Nietzschean revolt against God—and even the universe itself. This attitude conflicted with the upsurge of Czech nationalism that followed Mácha's death; but it is always as well to remember that this (philosophically) thoroughgoingly negative epic lies at the back of all the Czech poetry that followed it. This applies in approaching the work of OTOKAR BŘEZINA (ps. VÁCLAV IGNÁC JEBAVÝ, 1868–1929), a great thinker and the first major Czech poet after Mácha. Březina, born in southern Bohemia, became a schoolmaster. In him we see the impact of Schopenhauer and Nietzsche, and then of French symbolism, on a mind wholly Czech. It was Březina who imported symbolism into Czech poetry. The usual account of him claims that he convincingly transformed his bleak pessimism into an optimistic vitalism; this is somewhat misleading. His first book of poetry, *Mysterious Distances* (1895) is immature in content—decadent, Nietzschean, sorrowful—but assured in style. By the time of *Polar Winds* (1897), his third book, he had found his own voice: in a highly disciplined free verse, which has had a great influence, he expressed a Spinozan acceptance of all things, including evil and suffering, as part of an incomprehensible pattern. *Builders of the Temple* (1899; tr. O. Pick, 1920) concentrates, however, on the suffering rather than the pattern. *Hands* (1901), his last collection of verse, has possibly been misunderstood; it is not his best work, and he withdrew into a disgruntled twenty-eight-year silence after it. It returns to the earlier mood of Spinozan acceptance, but its return to more traditional forms and hymning of life are not altogether convincing. The essays in *The Music of the Springs* (1903) are much more so, and their subtlety has hardly been noticed. Březina was a true symbolist in that he preferred his inner world to the outer one; his real message is not more optimistic than Mácha's—but he felt obliged to mute it.

The opposite tendency is to be found in KAREL TOMAN (ps. ANTONÍN BERNÁŠEK, 1877–1946) and VIKTOR DYK (1877–1931). Both began as ironic decadents, but then turned into nationalist poets—melodious but superficial. The latter became a politician and polemicist during the last decade of his life. Toman lived to see himself, in the last year of his life, promulgated as 'national poet'.

The Czech version of expressionism (q.v.), the most important phase of which was 'poetism' (q.v.), at first took the form of an earthy naturalism, the chief exponent of which was the communist STANISLAV KOSTKA NEUMANN (1875–1947), who wrote novels and influential criticism as well as poetry. His best poems—personal and relaxed—are contained in *Love* (1933); his most influential book, however, was *New Songs* (1918). He had begun as a crude vitalist, then developed, under pressure of war, into a poet of everyday things; *Love* represents his early sexual vitalism modified by experience. JOSEF HORA (1891–1945) was a more interesting and complicated poet. His expressionism at first took a political form—his first volumes reveal him to be a proletarian and even unanimistic (q.v.) poet. *A Tree in Blossom* (1920) and *Working Day* (1920) are devoted to wartime Prague: its collective will to freedom and independence during the First World War, and its individual workers. Hora became a communist, but both the ruthless programme of the party and the pull of his native countryside induced him to leave it in 1929. Then, consciously following the romantic pessimism of Mácha, he wrote his most convincing poems, especially those in *Variations on Mácha* (1936), one of the most overwhelmingly Czech of all modern collections, in which nineteenth-century Gothic (tombs, witch-lovers, death) is subjected to a thoroughly modernistic sensibility. Eventually, under the pressure of the betrayal of Czechoslovakia and the pending Nazi occupation, Hora paradoxically regained some of his faith in life. *Jan the Fiddler* (1939) subsumes under its story of a musician who leaves his homeland for many years of exile, only finally to return, Hora's own development. He meets the lover he parted with years before, long married, as a stranger:

> A black piano. Katie dressed in black,
> black hair above her forehead braided high.
> So was it that she met her friend come back
> after some twenty years had passed them by.
> His lamp-lit room seemed darkened to her eye.
> 'Autumn? Let us not think of that tonight.'
>
> (PP)

JIŘÍ WOLKER (1900–24), who died of tuberculosis, was eventually a more thoroughgoingly proletarian poet. Convinced that he was of English descent (from a family named Walker), he was a typically expressionist figure, and reminds one slightly of Georg Heym (q.v.), in that he was a keen open-air type and loathed, or said he loathed, all forms of bohemianism. And, just as Heym kept a skull on his desk, so he read and studied Oscar Wilde. He came to Prague to study law, but the misery of the working classes contrasted with the ancient magnificence of the city called forth from him the extraordinary poetry of *A Guest into the Home* (1921), which is not only unanimist and Tolstoian in its call for universal love and brotherhood but also shot through and through with Czech country lore and magic. One is reminded of Esenin (q.v.) in his optimistic phase, and of Else Lasker-Schüler (q.v.). But the main inspiration is Wolker's own. Čapek's (q.v.) important anthology of French poetry in translation (1920) also played an important part in Wolker's development—as it did in that of many other Czech poets. Then Wolker came under the influence of Hora's *Working Day* (q.v.), and produced the classic collection of the proletarian movement: *The Difficult Hour* (1922). The viewpoint behind this combines a Dostoevski- or Bloy-like reverence for the poor—God's chosen ones—with a new radicalism, religious in its fervour. The poems are beautiful in their intensity, and their radicalism resembles Soviet poetry in its great early phase —not in its 'socialist realist' phase. Wolker was not an innovator in matters of form; but, more important, he created his own poetics. He was attacked, even by his friends, for his ideological views—and not wrongly—but in the best of his own poetry he entirely transcends these. The notion of human brotherhood transcends any possible notion of 'politics'; and even if Wolker embraced these as an entity on the literary scene, his poems go beyond them.

Czech 'poetism', whose chief spokesman was the critic and art-critic Karel Teige (1900–51), arose out of two previous rival groups: the *Devětsil* group—dedicated to revolution in all spheres of life—and a more conservative one, which produced the magazine *Host* (*The Guest*), and of which Wolker was the leading spirit. Teige had been the leading theoretician of the proletarian *Devětsil* group; but in 1924, following the poetic example of his friend VÍTĚZSLAV NEZVAL (1900–58), he returned to the anti-dogmatic, non-political attitude from which he (rightly) deduced that the best of Czech poetry had emerged. Teige could not advocate pessimism, and so he defined 'poetism' as 'airy and playful, full of fantasy, unfettered and unheroic, with a bias towards love'. This provided the right kind of basis—a better one than social or socialist realism could have offered—upon which individual poets could build: nearly all the important Czech poets of the Twenties were associated with poetism, which later (1928) transformed itself into surrealism—a surrealism that had only tenuous links with Breton's (q.v.) movement, since the Czechs had their own rich past of love-horror, miracles and magic to draw upon. It is important to realize that the Czech modernist poets of the period between the wars did not personally reject political socialism and communism, even if they reserved the right to go their own way poetically. This can be seen most clearly in the work of Nezval: its contradictions are instructive.

Nezval began with *The Bridge* (1922), a collection reflecting 'proletarian' intentions but shot through with the poet's own characteristically Czech vision, and much influenced by his reading of decadent poetry. The effect is already proto-surrealistic. His justification for making and living in his own world came from his conviction—crystallized when he heard JAROSLAV SEIFERT (1901), a minor poet whose style has intelligently changed with the times, read a paper in 1922—that truly revolutionary poets could only reach the uneducated common man through 'lowbrow' art: what was wanted was not Marx, incomprehensible to the worker in his bourgeois environment, but fantasy—fantasy that he would take as entertainment but which was really training him for the socialist millennium. In other words, Nezval, like Seifert, was one of those who anticipated pop-art. (Pop-art has now, in the Sixties and Seventies, become a commercial parasite on true folk art, as Nezval would now have seen.) But in fact Nezval, a truly gifted poet, was suffering from an acute case of *Künstlerschuld* (q.v.)—a disease which also troubled his fellow-Czechs Rilke and Kafka (qq.v.). The silent cinema, the Czech folk-heritage of fantasy and fairy-tale: all this had not yet been devitalized by commerce; besides, it offered him the excuse he needed to create his own world. His massive output between this time and 1938, when he broke with surrealism, is characterized by a violent and guilty confusion between two moods: an individualism undoubtedly felt as morbid (death, night, horror), and a lyrical affirmation of the brotherhood of

man. In these ten years of frenzied activity Nezval reflected one of the confusions that haunt the heart of modern man. Thus his ideal poet of the
remarkable epic *The Amazing Magician* (1922) is conceived in optimism; but
he is in fact a tortured figure, who gains his power at the expense of his reason.
Eventually the strain of fulfilling this role proved too much for Nezval, and he
turned to communism and to the writing of patriotic poems. During the
immediate post-war years he wrote routine hymns to Stalin and 'peace' (*Song of
Peace*, 1950; tr. J. Lindsay and S. Jolly, 1951), which display verbal dexterity
but no poetic conviction. But he quickly became disillusioned (the suicide of
his fellow-poet and close friend Konstantin Biebl in 1951 deeply disturbed him),
was associated with elements hostile to socialist realism, and tried to intervene
in cases of writers imprisoned under the Stalinist regime. His situation was not
an easy one. His *Collected Works* appeared in twenty-four volumes (1950ff.)
(TMCP)

FRANTIŠEK HALAS (1901–49) also began in the proletarian movement and
passed through a poetist phase; but he abandoned himself more fully than any
other poet of his generation to subjectivism. That subjectivism in poetry is not
necessarily equivalent to indifference to events is suggested by his collections
Wide Open (1936) and *Torso of Hope* (1938). His collections between *The Squid*
(1927), his first, and these, had indeed been 'morbid' (one of the official Stalinist
adjectives to be applied to his work after his death, when 'Halasism' became a
word of opprobrium among the mediocre lackeys then in charge of 'culture'),
most particularly *The Cock Alarms Death* (1930), in which he wrote:

> The world grown so familiar
> lies on your dream
> The grub within the rose.
> (PP)

But in *Wide Open* (1936) he had so withdrawn from the external world as to
picture himself being borne away, helplessly, by his dream. So that his return
to a care for his country in *Torso of Hope* is not unconvincing: the only alternative would have been silence, and silence (as the poems indicate) was not
his response to the disaster that threatened Czechoslovakia and the world. His
wartime and post-war poetry certainly reflects a deepening pessimism, but it is
never irresponsible. Probably his most characteristic volume of poetry is *Old
Women* (1935; tr. K. Offer, 1947), where he mixes brutality with charm to
illustrate the meaningless tragedy of ageing. His death in 1949 may be taken, in
George Theiner's words, as a 'symbolic event': his kind of poetry could not
exist under Stalinism.

The tradition of Catholic mysticism, strong in Czechoslovakia, was represented by the Moravian JAKUB DEML (1878–1961), a renegade priest who spent
much of his time 'feuding', in Alfred French's words, 'with its living officers'.
Deml reminds one in certain respects of Bloy (q.v.) whose work he knew well:
his onslaughts on his enemies (including at one time or another everybody)
were characterized by a similar convoluted bitterness, if not scatology. Like

Bloy, Bernanos and Jouhandeau (qq.v.), Deml sees life on earth as a conflict between God and Satan; but his vision is of course Czech; his poetry recreates the world of the nineteenth-century romantics and of Březina (q.v.) in his own peculiar but none the less modern setting. One is often led to feel that his Catholicism was only another name for the inner world which he regarded as paramount. However, his work would be impossible to understand without the idea of a single God at its centre: a God who beckons him into this inner world. Deml, who translated Rilke (q.v.) into Czech, was regarded by Nezval as his master. The neglect into which he has fallen is due not only to his own scorn for readers and critics but also to the fact that he refused, after 1948, to have anything to do with the communists, and published no more in the remaining years of his life.

The main argument amongst the modernist Czech poets between the wars revolved around the question of social commitment; Catholicism was frequently seen as politically reactionary and conducive to artistic self-withdrawal or 'ivory-towerism'. The polemics were as transitory as most such polemics are; and the advent of socialist realism (q.v.) put paid to them for more than a decade. The more seriously a poet was identified with a position the less serious his work: the best poets were, like Nezval, confused and inconsistent: for it is in poetry, not polemical prose, that poets resolve their confusions.

VLADIMÍR HOLAN (1905), whose first book appeared in 1926, emerged in the Thirties as a representative of 'pure poetry'; he has styled himself a 'sombre poet, an apocalyptic poet'. It was not until the Thaw in Czechoslovakia that his poetry could be collected and appraised. He is now a dominant figure in Czech literature. He owes more than any other contemporary Czech poet to Valéry (q.v.). His earlier poetry was more abstract and intellectual than anyone else's of the time, and this cut him off from potential readers. He has since developed, as 'The Old Priest' makes clear:

> We met on Charles Bridge, it was snowing.
> I had not seen him for almost twenty years.
> Did I complain? I suppose so, since he comforted me,
> and when I spoke of sin, said gently:
> 'Yes, how else should we know you
> at the Last Judgement!'
> And when that did not help, he said all of a sudden:
> 'My son, it seems to me that in your verses
> you now reject abstraction . . . Your desire for simplicity
> would be praiseworthy if only it were subtle . . .
> But it is as if you, with a part of your spirit,
> the most adventurous part,
> did not wish to partake of the divine power.
> Do you mean to say that you don't like to drink wine?'
> (NWC)

Several new poets emerged in the Sixties—it would have been impossible for them to do so before. The position for the Czech writer now, since the 1968 Russian invasion and the establishment of a government subservient to Moscow, is not yet quite clear.

The leading poet of the younger generation is MIROSLAV HOLUB (1923), who is as distinguished a scientist (he is an immunologist) as he is a poet. He has been translated into English extensively (*Selected Poems*, tr. I. Milner and G. Theiner, 1967; *Although*, tr. I. and J. Milner, 1971; NWC), which might give the impression that he is a more important poet than, say, Halas (q.v.)— who has not. This is not the case—or has not yet become wholly apparent. But Holub is an interesting and gifted poet: an anti-dogmatic ironist, an experimentalist concerned with the achievement of the maximum freedom to create as he wishes. Like Seifert and Nezval long before him, he wants to create a poetry that 'ordinary people' can read 'as naturally as they read the papers, or go to a football game'. He is against the lyrical-romantic Czech tradition, and uses a stark free verse. A. Alvarez (q.v.) has put him forward as a matter-of-fact poet of the electronic and industrial present, refusing to commit himself but rather accepting reality as it is. Whether this is wholly true or not, Holub has not rejected compassion or the nostalgia for the past that Alvarez condemns. As he writes, in 'Water Sprite',

> no one has the time today
> just to sit and do a little haunting.

Clearly a man of immense intelligence and sophistication, Holub's poetry lacks emotional robustness and linguistic excitement. It is as cerebral in its way as Holan's earlier work. Whether he will move forward to denser forms of self-expression remains to be seen.

*

In this century the Czechs have achieved more in poetry than in fiction, with the exception of Hašek and Čapek. JAROSLAV HAŠEK (1883–1923), joker, anarchist and great novelist, was in himself a paradigm of the subversive artist. No wonder Brecht (q.v.) loved him. He would not have been happy for long under any authority. Hašek drank a good deal and frequently engaged the attention of policemen, whom he regarded with disfavour; he edited a fortnightly magazine called *The Animal World* in which he would from time to time invent animals or to which he would contribute articles with such titles as 'The Rational Breeding of Werewolves'; he twice seems to have falsely notified the authorities of his death, and to have composed an obituary of himself headed 'A Traitor'; he ran a dog-stealing business and even wrote a guide on how to steal dogs; he stood as parliamentary candidate for his own Party of Moderate Progress Within the Limits of the Law; worst of all, his most famous book had to be banned to the armies of three countries (Czechoslovakia, Poland, Hungary) as 'detrimental to discipline'. . . . Hašek's famous masterpiece *The Good Soldier Schweik* (1920–23) was left unfinished; the conclusion by Karel Vaněk is trivial. But the English translation, made by the late Paul Selver in 1930 with the best intentions, and hamstrung by the fashions of the time, is a monument to gentility and ignorance rather than an adequate version of *Schweik*: first, it is bowdlerized; secondly, it is incomplete, such passages as the translator wrongly felt would be incomprehensible to English-speaking readers being cut. (A new, full English version is in preparation.)

Hašek wrote a great deal other than *Schweik*, of which only *The Tourist Guide* (tr. 1962) is available in English translation; his other work—short stories, sketches, humorous and subversive essays—has been hidden for years, but is slowly becoming available and will presumably be translated in due course.

Schweik is based on Hašek's experiences in the Austro-Czech army in 1915, before he deserted to the free Czech armies in Russia. The correct interpretation of the hero is undoubtedly that he is an anarchistic and anti-social figure. He is also, of course, a Czech making fun of his Austrian masters. But this fat dog-fancier who entered the hearts of the people long before he entered the minds of the critics is essentially a man who despises authority and who knows how to get round it. Hašek and all his works should certainly be banned from any respectable society. For years *Schweik* could be written off as irresponsible fun; events have caused it to be revealed for what it is: a comic exhortation to individuals to defy the tyranny of officials and oppressors. It is magnificently there—as are the multiplying officials: a bible for the decent.

KAREL ČAPEK-CHOD (ps. K. ČAPEK, 1860–1927) lacked Hašek's comic genius, but shared, though from a socially more viable stance, his point of view. Čapek-Chod was a naturalist, but only because he enjoyed demonstrating man's pointless struggles. The happy chronicler of the decay of the Prague bourgeoisie, he is Hardyesque in that he projects his own nihilism into Fate, making it into a teaser. But this is because he has aspirations to challenge his sense of absurdity; eventually he stopped short, merely telling bizarre tales of trapped men. Sometimes called 'the Zola of Prague', his gusto in describing decline is far greater than Zola's, and he incorporates into it much Czech grotesquerie. *Antonín Vondrejc* (1917–18) is a satirical portrait of Prague intellectuals and bohemians; his best novel, *The Turbine* (1916), which was translated into French in the year of its publication (*La Turbine*; tr. J. Chopin) is a prophetic account of the impact of technology, with comic pictures of the kind of men who believe in it. *The Jindras* (1921) is a less satirical novel about a father-son relationship. Čapek-Chod published many excellent collections of novellas and short stories, such as *Five Novels* (1904) and *Four Audacious Stories* (1926). He was a tough, mocking and excellent writer who awaits an English translator.

IVAN OLBRACHT (ps. KAMIL ZEMAN, 1882–1952), originally a lawyer and a lifelong communist, became a fairly important politician after 1945. Although politics tempted him from his literary function, he was regarded by many critics as Czechoslovakia's leading novelist. *Of Evil Solitary Men* (1913) consists of sketches about tramps and circus people, and rather uneasily combines the attitude of the early Gorki (q.v.) with an almost *kitsch* romanticism. It was his novel *The Strange Friendship of the Actor Jesenius* (1919) that established him. This is the story of a comedian, Jesenius, and his double, the actor Veselý; it is divided between the battlefront and the world of the Prague theatre. *Anne the Proletarian* (1928) is a tendentious failure. His best novel is *Nikola Šuhaj—Robber* (1933; tr. R. Finlayson-Sansour, 1954): here Olbracht projected his less respectable and more anarchistic feelings into the hero, a bandit of sub-Carpathian Ruthenia who lived by his own laws, but who was a popular hero among the poor people of the area because he divided much of his booty among them. This has an epic sweep, and incorporates much Czech and Jewish lore. He also wrote *The Darkest Prison* (1916), a powerful psychological novel of a blind man's jealousy, *Valley of Exile* (1937; tr. 1965), again set in Ruthenia, and *The Conquerors* (1947), ostensibly about the conquest of Mexico but really about the Nazis. During the occupation he wrote children's books.

KAREL ČAPEK (1890–1938), who died, it was said, of a heart pierced by Chamberlain's umbrella, was one of the most intelligent of Czechoslovakian writers. The creative life of Čapek, who was novelist, playwright, essayist and journalist, exactly paralleled the life of Masaryk's Czech republic, which was also killed by 'Chamberlain's umbrella'. Čapek was the chief dramatist of the republic, but his novels are superior to his plays. He was a close friend of Masaryk's. Čapek at first studied science, and his early novels owe much to H. G. Wells (q.v.). His important and influential volume of translations from French poets has already been mentioned; in spite of this, he chiefly turned to English and American literature. He threw himself heart and soul into the affairs of his country, but his real attitude to life is expressed in his dictum that 'A short life is better for mankind, for a long life would deprive man of his optimism'. His brother Josef Čapek, primarily a cubist and primitivist painter but the co-author of some of the earlier works, perished in Belsen.

Čapek's plays include *R.U.R.* (1920; tr. P. Selver, 1923), *The Macropoulos Secret* (1922; tr. 1925)—made into an opera by Janáček—and, with his brother, *The Insect Play* (1921; tr. 1923). *R.U.R.*, written in the spirit of, and anticipating, Huxley's *Brave New World* (q.v.), gave the name 'robot' to the world. The robots revolt against their masters.

Čapek's novels, written in a clear language, try to educate his countrymen into democracy and vigilance against fascist aggression by means of Wellsean fantasy; but they involuntarily express a profound pessimism. *The Absolute at Large* (1922; tr. M. and R. Weatherall, 1944) tries to deny the absolute—which is released among mankind as a gas. *Krakatit* (1924; tr. L. Hyde, 1925) prophesies the atomic bomb. But Čapek's finest novel is *War with the Newts* (1936; tr. M. and R. Weatherall, 1937), in which he satirizes and foresees both the coming Nazi holocaust and post-war West European capitulation to commerce. A Czech sailor discovers some newts which resemble human beings; humanity exploits them; they revolt (led by a mad corporal) and triumph.

Čapek cannot be called a great writer; but he is a good and important one. Banned by Nazis and Czech Stalinists alike, he was only 'rehabilitated' in Czechoslovakia in the late Fifties when his work had been made available in Moscow.

JAROSLAV DURYCH (1886–1962), a doctor, was a historical Catholic novelist whose sympathies with the working classes never wavered. This led him into inconsistencies—his enthusiasm for the Counter-Reformation, for example, is hard to reconcile with his hatred of oppression—but his most outstanding work, *The Descent of the Idol* (1929; tr. L. Hudson, 1935), is strengthened by the tensions thus generated. This is a story of the Thirty Years' War, and is the best of the many novels (and biographies) that have been written about Wallenstein, with whose career it deals. Durych's poems and dramas were unsuccessful, but in his best novel he succeeded in creating the kind of symbolist art advocated by his master Březina (q.v.).

VLADISLAV VANČURA (1891–1942), also originally a doctor, was a steadfast communist throughout the Twenties and Thirties; he was shot by the Nazis as one of the reprisals for Heydrich, who had been executed by Czech patriots. Although his last novel, *The Family Horvat* (1938), shows some signs of the crudities which often characterize the socialist realist (q.v.) approach, Vančura was in fact a highly experimental writer, who introduced both colloquial and archaic words into the literary language. His books differ markedly from one another except in the densely baroque nature of their style. The best of his many novels are *The Baker Jan Marhoul* (1924), which although not always convincing in its portrayal of a man dedicated to communism, is none the less often powerful, *Markéta Lazarovà* (1931), an adventure story set in medieval days, *The End of Old Times* (1934; tr. in French *La Fin des temps anciens*, 1936), another adventure story—this time more satirical and with debts to the eighteenth-century French novel—and *Three Rivers* (1936), an analysis of a Czech intellectual's response to communism during and after the First World War. Vančura was proscribed by the Stalinists, but his works have had a strong influence on such writers as Kundera.

MILAN KUNDERA (1929), born in Brno, was the first of the younger Czech novelists to react sharply against the dreary socialist realism of the Stalinist years. His chief novel is *The Joke* (1966), a proper English translation of which —replacing an innacurate one—appeared in 1971; this is at once a satire on the fake communism of the Stalinists, on the opportunists who thrived under it, and on the Czech character itself. (NCW) JOSEF ŠKVORECKÝ (1924), now in Canada, wrote the first novel to look dispassionately at the Red Army's 'liberation' of Czechoslovakia in 1945: *The Cowards* (1958; tr. J. Němcová, 1970). This differed considerably from the official version of these events, and was soon banned. One of the chief official objections was that the liberating army were described by Škvorecký as 'Mongolians'; from Canada he has retorted that he sees no objection to this, since he is not a racist. He has written a number of other books, including *Reflections of a Detective Story Reader* (1965) and *The Lion Cub* (1969), which is now being translated. (NCW)

BOHUMIL HRABAL (1914), now one of Czechoslovakia's most distinguished writers, did not begin to publish until he was fifty. He studied law, but the Nazi occupation made practice an impossibility. He was obliged to take a variety of manual jobs. But in 1962 he decided to devote himself to literature. *A Pearl in the Depths* appeared in 1963. His best-known work is *A Close Watch on the Trains* (1965; tr. E. Pargeter, 1968), which became famous as a movie under the title *Closely Observed Trains*. This is narrated by its anti-hero, Miloš Hrma, who works on the railways (on which Hrabal worked) when the Nazis are rushing troops through Czechoslovakia to their collapsing eastern front. It is hilarious, moving and heroic by turns, and leaves the reader in no uncertainty as to why its author shot suddenly to fame. He writes in a colloquial, apparently uncontrolled language which is highly effective for his debunking purposes.

The most distinguished Czech writer in exile is EGON HOSTOVSKÝ (1908), who resigned from the diplomatic service in 1948 after the communist *coup*, and went to the U.S.A. He was also in exile during the Second World War. His exciting novels, whose plots are sometimes as melodramatic as those of thrillers, deal with the experiences of alienated and displaced personalities. His earlier fiction—*The Closed Door* (1926), *The Case of Professor Körner* (1937)—dealt with the plight of alienated Czech Jews. His finest work—*Missing* (tr. E. Osers, 1952), *The Charity Ball* (tr. P. H. Smith, 1957), *Three Nights* (1964)—probes the inner world of refugees from tyranny with intensity and understanding but without self-pity. He is one of the few contemporary novelists who have learned from Dostoevski without parodying him.

II

The Slovaks had been separated from the Czechs since 906; the creation of Czechoslovakia in 1918 was a bringing together of two natural cultural partners; but while the Czechs had had their own state under Austria, the Slovaks had simply been part of Hungary. Until the middle of the eighteenth century the Slovaks had used Latin, Hungarian or Czech to write their literature; a standard Slovak was devised in the mid-nineteenth century.

The father of Slovak realism, the prolific novelist MARTIN KUKUČÍN (ps. MATEJ BENCÚR, 1860–1928), a doctor, spent most of his life abroad: in Dalmatia, then in Chile, and finally back in Yugoslavia. He was in Czechoslovakia for a few years after 1918. He had a confident style and his fiction is solid, well observed and humorous. His early work deals with Czech life, but his best novels—*The House on the Slope* (1903–4) and the five-volume *Mother Calls* (1926–7)—deal with Dalmatia and the lives of Croatian emigrants in South America. The posthumous *Bohumil Valilost Zábor* (1930) is once again set in Czechoslovakia.

JANKO JESENSKY (1874–1945), like Hašek (q.v.) and other future Czechs loyal to their aspirations, deserted from the Austro-Hungarian army during the First World War and joined the free Czech army in Russia. A lawyer, he held a political post in the republic; during the Nazi occupation he circulated anti-fascist verses, collected in *Against the Night* (1945). Though Jesensky thought of himself primarily as a poet, and had been associated with Krasko (q.v.) as one of the leading poets of the pre-1914 Slovak 'modern' school, his chief work is the novel *Democrats* (1934–7; tr. J. Edwards, 1961), a scathing satire on upper-class Slovak life under the republic. Like Čapek, Jesensky was dedicated to the republic without much hope of its survival. Always an enemy of Slovak separatism, he made cruel fun of the Nazi puppet-state, the 'independent' Slovak Republic of 1939–45.

PETER JILEMNICKÝ (1901–49), a Czech by birth, began to write in Slovak when he went to Slovakia as a schoolmaster in 1922. Jilemnický was a good socialist realist (voluntary) who wrote well of the Slovak peasantry in *The Step that Rings* (1930), *The Fallow Field* (1932)—his best novel—and *Our Compass* (1937). He was taken by the Gestapo in the Second World War and spent three years in concentration camps. He spent the rest of his life—shortened by his sufferings—as Czechoslovakia's cultural attaché in Moscow, and as a model for younger writers to emulate.

MILO URBAN (1904) was a brilliantly realistic observer of the process of transition from Hungarian to Czechoslovak rule. He has never bettered *The Living Scourge* (1927), a novel about Slovak peasants during the First World War. A Slovak separatist, he collaborated with the Nazis as a journalist during the Second World War, and was imprisoned at the liberation; but by 1958 he was allowed to publish a socialist realist view of the Chamberlain-Hitler dismemberment of Czechoslovakia: *The Extinguished Lights* (1958).

A long novel by FRANTIŠEK HEČKO (1905–60), written before he became hamstrung by socialist realism, is even more successful in the same *genre* as *The Living Scourge*, though it deals with a later period: *Red Wine* (1948).

LADISLAV MŇAČKO (1919), who defected to Israel in 1967, supported the Stalinist line in the early years of communism, but later (1964) publicly recanted, confessing his own guilt. *Death is Called Engelchen* (1959; tr. G. Theiner, 1961) is about the resistance to Nazism; *The Taste of Power* (1968; tr. P. Stevenson, 1967) describes the life of a top communist.

*

SVETOZÁR HURBAN VAJANSKÝ (ps. SVETOZÁR HURBAN, 1847–1916) was equally important as poet and novelist, but it is probably his poetry that will survive the longer. He was an ardent and mystic Slavophile who believed that the West was morally corrupt; he was nevertheless influenced, especially in his poetry, by German models. His lyrics introduced a new lucidity into Slovak poetry. Although he was himself a staunch fighter for Slovak liberty, several times imprisoned by the Magyars, his novels are remarkably objective in their account of the difficulties of wealthy Slovaks, torn between a convenient loyalty to the authorities and loyalty to their own people.

The reputation of HVIEZDOSLAV (ps. PAVEL ORSZÁGH, 1849–1921) has perceptibly declined; but during and for a quarter of a century after his lifetime he was regarded as the doyen of Slovak poets. As a precocious boy poet he was a Hungarian patriot, but from his nineteenth year all he wrote was in Slovak. He was a lawyer, but gave up the profession early in order to devote himself to literature. He undoubtedly enriched the language and range of Slovak poetry, and he broadened his themes; but his work has dated. His best poetry is probably contained in the *Blood-red Sonnets* of 1918, a protest against all war and the First World War in particular. He was influenced by Vrchlický and Čech (qq.v.), and did perhaps more than any other Slovak writer to internationalize his literature. He translated *Hamlet* and many other classics.

IVAN KRASKO (ps. JÁN BOTTO, 1876–1958), although all his work is contained in two volumes—*Nox et Solitudo* (1909) and *Poems* (1912)—was really a superior poet. He was an important political functionary in the Masaryk republic. But his poetry, usually described as 'decadent', is in fact based on a recognizable system of symbols; he can certainly be called a symbolist. The influence of his pessimism has been as great as that of Hviezdoslav, but more subterranean. Where Hviezdoslav extended Slavonic poetry, Krasko broke more decisively with its traditional forms, substituting for them ones taken over from French and Italian poetry.

EMIL LUKÁČ (1900) and JÁN SMREK (ps. JÁN ČIETEK, 1899) were the two leading poets of the Twenties and Thirties. Lukáč was widely influenced: by Hviezdoslav, French symbolism, Valéry, Jammes (qq.v.)—he spent two years at the Sorbonne—Rilke and Ady (qq.v.). His translations from French poetry —*Trophies* (1933)—were influential. Lukáč, a religious but profoundly pessimistic man, condemned as a 'cosmopolitan decadent' in 1948, remains an 'old-fashioned' symbolist. Smrek underwent the same kind of influences, but was more responsive to the wave of surrealism which manifested itself in both Czech and Slovak literature between the wars—and which was to be condemned in 1948. Where Lukáč—like Urban (q.v.)—supported the short-lived 'independent' Slovak state Smrek opposed it.

LACO NOVOMESKÝ (1904), who took an active part in the great Slovak uprising against the Nazis in 1944, is now considered to be the chief older poet. Like most of the better poets of the between-wars period, Novomeský was strongly influenced by the Czech proletarian and poetist phases; he was a leading light in the communist and *avant garde* Masses (*Dav*) Group, whose magazine of that name ran from 1924 until 1926. Novomeský came to reject 'committed' in favour of 'pure' poetry, but his work of the period reflects confusions and tensions similar to that of Nezval's. His books include *Sunday* (1927), *Rhomboid* (1932) and *Open Windows* (1935). At the liberation he gained high office in the Ministry of Slovak Education, but was one of the victims of the Stalinist purges of the early Fifties. He was released and 'rehabilitated' in 1963: the state went so far as to promulgate him (1964) a 'national artist', a high Czech honour accorded posthumously to Toman, the murdered Vančura (qq.v.) and others. He has since written informatively on the Slovak *avant garde* between the wars.

The chief figure in the conservative Catholic movement in poetry was the Franciscan priest RUDOLF DILONG (1905), another Slovak separatist and supporter of Tiso's German-protected Slovakia. He fled at the end of the war and remains in exile.

Since the early Sixties the Czech and Slovak cultures have tended to move nearer together; the number of translations to and from the two languages has increased. At present, however (1971), the puppet rulers of Czechoslovakia can get no change from their writers. 'Offer them more money', advises Moscow. 'But we do,' a harassed culture-lackey is reported to have answered: 'We offer them Hollywood salaries, but they just won't write'. . . .

III

Čapek (q.v.) is undoubtedly the best known Czechoslovak playwright of this century; whether he is an important one is another matter. His plays are ingenious and enjoyable, but his fiction is of considerably more interest— and the plays add nothing to theatrical development. The Czechs are enthusiastic theatregoers; but much intelligent and imaginative theatrical activity has failed to produce a dramatist of major stature. The best theatre of the Masaryk republic was probably the 'Unfettered' Theatre of the two actors Jiři Voskovec (1905) and Jan Werich (1905), and the experimental theatre of E. F. Burian (1904–59). On the advent of communism, Voskovec chose exile, but Werich and Burian remained. Both played some part in the theatrical revival after Stalin's death. There was also a short-lived 'Dada Theatre' in the Twenties. The only tolerable socialist realist in the Stalinist period was the lively JAN DRDA (1915), who skilfully used the folk-tale tradition to gild the bitter pill. The most promising *avant garde* dramatist JIŘÍ FREJKA (1904–52) killed himself.

In the Sixties a new *avant garde* theatre grew up. The best known young playwright is VÁCLAV HAVEL (1936), who has worked in the theatre for most of his life, and was until 1966 literary manager of the important Balustrade Theatre in Prague. *The Garden Party* (1964), his first play, was an international success. *The Memorandum* (1966; tr. V. Blackwell, 1967) is a memorable satire on bureaucracy, in which a deputy outwits his boss by introducing into the business a synthetic language, Ptydepe, which revolutionizes communication. This is one of the funniest, most penetrating and disturbing satires to come out of the communist world since the war.

IVAN STODOLA (1888) was the dominant figure in the Slovak theatre in the between-wars period, with such plays as *The Shepherd's Wife* (1928), a tragedy, the historical *King Svatopluk*, on the Slovak anti-Hungarian uprising of 1848–9, and *Tea with his Excellency the Senator* (1929), social satire. The leading post-war playwright is PETER KARVAŠ (1920), who has applied himself as intelligently as the times have allowed to the individual psychological problems of 'socialist man'. *The People of Our Street* (1951) and *The Scar* (1963) are among his plays.

Dutch Literature

I

The literature of the Netherlands differs from that of the Flemish Belgians, which is treated in a separate section—though under the general heading of 'Dutch'. For the two languages are very similar. Flemish was a Frankish dialect which after the sixteenth century fell into disuse and was revived by Belgian writers in the nineteenth century; these drew, however, on literary Dutch as well. The spelling of Flemish is more archaic than that of Dutch. Dutch is gaining ground amongst Flemish speakers, but the University of Ghent continues to be a centre of Flemish learning and literature. The two literatures are gradually coalescing; but important differences are still manifest.

In the Netherlands many people speak English, German and French; the Dutchman's literary education is considerably higher than that of his British counterpart. But he tends to have a somewhat low regard for his own literature. This may account for Dutch literature's relative lack of self-confidence. The feeling is unjustified: the Netherlands in this century have produced two, perhaps even four, major novelists, and two major poets; and a host of important minor talents.

II

The Dutch literary revival of 1880, in the hands of the Eightiers (*Tachtigers*) as they called themselves, paralleled similar movements in other European countries; but it was—and had to be—more drastic. The way had been prepared by the novelist Multatuli (the pseudonym, meaning 'I have suffered much', of Eduard Douwes Dekker, 1820–87). The Eightiers, whose magazine was called *The New Guide*, attacked the effete romanticism, then too solidly established, for its sentimentality, conventional religiosity and unctuousness. They changed the Dutch literary language by their insistence upon precision and eschewal of cliché.

The chief poet of this group was WILLEM KLOOS (1859–1938), whose cult of beauty and art for art's sake now seems dated, but whose influence on Dutch poetry was great because of his originality of diction, his evocative rhythms, and the consistency of his critical thinking, which is basically Shelleyan. For him the function of art is the creation of beauty, and his position in Dutch poetry may fairly be described as similar to Shelley's in England. (The Keats of the Netherlands is certainly Jacques Perk, Kloos's close friend, who died in

1881 at the age of twenty-one. Perk was a better poet than Kloos: his sonnet-sequence to a Belgian girl he met briefly is one of the best things in the Dutch literature of the nineteenth century, and is far less lucubrated than anything by Kloos.) Kloos's first book, *Poems* (1894), is famous for its sonnets, which are, in their literary way, extremely beautiful. Kloos gradually declined into an emotionally lifeless perpetrator of philosophically pretentious verse; but his cult of worship of the elevated self was a necessary reaction to the complacency that had characterized Dutch literature before the Eighties. He is a vital figure in Dutch literature.

ALBERT VERWEY (1865–1937), like Kloos, was one of the early editors of *The New Guide*, but he severed his connection with Kloos in 1889, becoming critical of his worship of the irrational and his views about the non-political nature of literature. He was a friend (not a disciple) of George's (q.v.), and his manner is often reminiscent of the German poet's. He ended by seeing the function of poetry as a social binding of all peoples and times. Verwey was a skilful but largely artificial poet, at his best when he felt that his 'eternal self' was 'doomed to solitude'—a view against which he later reacted. Verwey underwent many changes of mind, and gives the impression of continually forming groups only to break away from them. But his progress was intelligent, and he, too, was an essential figure.

Dutch late nineteenth-century prose was directly influenced by Zola's naturalism (q.v.); but it also drew upon its own great pictorial tradition. There was a tendency to try to turn writing into a kind of painting, in which everything was to be described with minute and photographic accuracy. One is inevitably reminded of Holz (q.v.) and his search for an art that would exactly reproduce life. This is realism at its utmost limits; it sometimes even appears modernist because its syntax is stripped down until it resembles a diagram. LODEWIJK VAN DEYSSEL (ps. K. J. L. A. THIJM, 1864–1952), a friend of Kloos's and a fellow 'Eightier', began with an admiration for Zola, although his aestheticism led him to condemn Zola's moralism. His two early novels, *The Little Republic* (1888) and *A Love Story* (1887), are not really so much naturalist as defiantly realistic; they included some descriptions of sexual scenes which caused a twitter then, but which nowadays seem innocuous. His impressionistic prose poetry, attempts at making pictures with words (they are collected in *Apocalypse*, 1893), are failures. Until about this date he could profitably be compared to Holz (q.v.) in his tendencies; but soon afterwards he drifted into a whimsical mysticism on the pattern of Maeterlinck (q.v.). He was influential in Dutch literature, but left no really successful book except for his biographies.

The Dutch novel of this period seldom transcends national boundaries: the photographic accuracy of its portrayal of bourgeois society lacks psychological penetration, and the prose is clumsy. These novels are to literature precisely what sober, competent and unexperimental photography is to painting. 'Naturalist' should only really be used of this kind of fiction in its (in literature) misleading sense of 'like nature'.

There are exceptions amongst this generation of realists: the main one, LOUIS

COUPERUS (1863–1923), is the only Dutch writer of this century to achieve a truly international reputation. He was a cosmopolitan character, of Javanese blood, who lived in Italy until the beginning of the First World War; he said of himself that although he loved the Netherlands he felt more Italian than Dutch. He began as a realist-naturalist under the influence of Flaubert, Zola and, to some extent, Tolstoi; but Zola did little more than provide him with a method. In *Footsteps of Fate* (1890; tr. C. Bell, 1890) the characters are the victims of inexorable fate in a manner typical of naturalism, but even here there is a hint that character is not destiny. For Couperus had an oriental bent in his make-up that led him to view man as unnecessarily concerned with his fate: he who resigns himself may find peace. The tetralogy *Small Souls* (1901–4; tr. A. T. de Mattos, 1914–18) gives a picture of Dutch family life on the scale of Galsworthy's *Forsyte Saga* (q.v.), but is infinitely more subtle and sensitive than that overrated work. Here Couperus compassionately traces the progress of a mentality from pettiness to desire, through suffering, for wisdom—and incidentally gives an incomparable picture of Dutch middle-class life. *Old People and the Things that Pass* (1908; tr. A. T. de Mattos, 1918; 1963), the story of the effect on two very old people and their ageing children of a murder committed sixty years back, in the colonies, shows him at his best. Although its impressionistic prose is sometimes unnecessarily hard to read it is masterly in its presentation of a present haunted by memories of the past. Couperus is a fascinating writer who only needs comprehensive republication in the English-speaking world to draw attention to his genius. Nearly all his work was translated into English. J. VAN OUDSHOORN (ps. J. K. FELYBRIEF, 1876–1951) is much more neglected. He is a mysterious, rewarding writer, whose *Alienation* (1914; tr. N. C. Clegg, 1965), about a man who feels himself to have been ruined through masturbation, is a pioneer masterpiece. FRANS COENEN (1866–1936) was naturalistically inclined; his posthumous *The House on the Canal* (1937; tr. J. Brockway, 1965) is, however, a tense psychological study.

P. C. BOUTENS (1870–1943), the best translator of his generation, was a poet similarly aloof from the Eighties. He gradually withdrew into himself, but unlike Kloos he understood the nature of his introspection: rather than indulging in an egocentric programme he tempered his romanticism with thought. He was a natural symbolist, in that his poetry, essentially, seeks out a world beyond that of the senses. He was a classical scholar who achieved a mastery of form; but his poetry suffers from his lack of understanding of the sensual world, which seems to exert little pull on him. He was as good as an academic poet, trapped in thoughts of beauty but never ensnared in desire, can be—but no better.

The poet and novelist FREDERIK VAN EEDEN (1860–1932), a psychiatrist, was a co-founder of *The New Guide*, but soon reacted to Kloos's dedication to art for its own sake. More interestingly than Kloos or, indeed, Boutens, he oscillated between social conscience and individual realization, discovering—in so doing —a language of his own. But this tension between opposites, evident in his novel *The Deeps of Deliverance* (1900; tr. M. Robinson, 1902) and in his poems of the late Nineties, did not last. To combat the anti-social villain in him, which produced his best work, he founded a semi-communist community, which (because of his admiration for Thoreau) he called Walden; this collapsed, as all such communities do, and eventually (1922) he fell into Roman Catholicism. *The Deeps of Deliverance*, a study of a young girl's development, is in bourgeois terms 'morbid', although it struggles out of such morasses into a false pleasantness before it finishes. Its best passages emphasize the difficulties of reconciling female sexuality with a male world, and are full of the kind of insight one might expect from a psychiatrist; when it rationalizes these into 'joy' it becomes programmatic and is as unconvincing as it is dated and boring. He wrote with humour and understanding of the failure of his Tolstoian community in *The Promised Land* (1909). He also wrote some of the best plays of his time, of which the most outstanding is *The Brothers' Feud* (1894).

The most important playwright of this generation, however, was HERMAN HEIJERMANS (1864–1924). Influenced in his technique mainly by Ibsen, he was a socialist who depicted, in a naturalist manner, the miseries of the poor. His most famous play, about oppressed North Sea fishermen, was *The Good Hope* (1900; tr. L. Saunders and C. Heijermans-Houwinck, 1928), which was played all over the world. At the very end of his life he wrote a poignant novel, *The Little Dreaming King* (1924), about a boy's growing up in a slum. He was a Jew, and his comic sketches about Jewish life in Dutch cities, published under the name of Samuel Falkland, are unique in the language for their raciness and insight.

The writer who eventually most decisively broke with photographic realism was ARTHUR VAN SCHENDEL (1874–1946), who was born in Java. Van Schendel wrote of events in the external world, but described them through the eyes of a dreamer. He spent some years teaching in England and then in Holland before devoting himself entirely to writing. Curiously enough, although he was the first major novelist to break completely with the naturalist manner, one of the chief themes of all his fiction is man's impotence against his destiny. His first stories and novels, set in medieval times, were Pre-Raphaelite in mood. And yet the germ of his future work is contained in his first story, *Drogon* (1896): a dreamy, eccentric young man is 'fated' to seduce his brother's wife. *A Wanderer in Love* (1904) and *A Wanderer Lost* (1907) tell of a monk and his struggles against sexual desire. These have an irresistibly lush quality, somewhat reminiscent of Rossetti; but they are self-indulgent, and the pseudo-medieval background palls. Van Schendel continued in this vein, more or less unprofitably, until 1921, when he went to live in Italy. His Italian stories show signs of a change. The period of his maturity begins in 1930, with *The 'Johanna Maria'* (tr. B. W. Downs, 1935), the biography (set in the nineteenth century) of a sailing vessel. This is written in the impassive style for which Van Schendel became famous: there is no dialogue, and the events described have an oneiric quality. There followed novels of high quality, in which Van Schendel more seriously explores his fatalistic theme: *The Waterman* (1933; tr. N. C. Clegg, 1963), *The House in Haarlem* (1935; tr. M. S. Stephens, 1940), *Grey Birds* (1937;

tr. M. S. Stephens, 1939). *Oberon and Madame* (1940) and other books of this period are actually gay in their romanticism. The posthumous *The Old House* (1946) is perhaps Van Schendel's finest work of all. Van Schendel was at his best when imposing a fierce restraint on his innate romanticism: when, as in *The Waterman*, he is showing how destiny—in the form of unobtrusive but stifling social pressure—overrides such romanticism. It was in *The Old House* that he brought this to near perfection. He is a difficult writer—as difficult to come to terms with as such Japanese as Toson and Soseki (qq.v.)—but an original and compelling one.

Poetry immediately before the First World War was represented mainly by Gorter, Holst and Leopold, as well as by Verwey. HERMAN GORTER (1864–1927) was a member of the Eighties movement, and up until *The School of Poetry* (1897) he indulged himself in an entirely subjective verse. This accorded with Kloos's prescription, but Gorter was in earnest in a way that Kloos could never have known: he flung himself into his own feelings and conducted an exploration of them so frenzied that he nearly lost his reason. The resultant poems were in freer verse than anything the Netherlands had seen. At this point Gorter really left the best of himself behind. After a study of philosophy he became a Marxist —but a curiously rigid one. His epic *Pan* (1916) is a grandiose work, highly doctrinaire—and hopelessly remote from ordinary experience, let alone that of the proletariat. Gorter's communism was characterized by so intense a degree of intellectual absolutism (his Marxist studies of Aeschylus, Dante and Shakespeare are unimpressive) that one must suspect that he clung to it as a man clings to a raft: for reasons of preserving his sanity.

The early work of HENRIETTE ROLAND HOLST (1869–1952) appeared in *The New Guide* (q.v.), but, in company with Gorter (of whom she wrote a biography, 1933) she became an adherent of William Morris socialism and then of communism. In the mid-Twenties she turned to a religious socialism. Her poetry suffers from lack of control. Probably her best work was in the realm of biography. She was married to the painter Richard Roland Holst.

The symbolist poetry of JAN HENDRIK LEOPOLD (1865–1925), whose output was small, resembles an island half-enveloped in haze: nothing is quite in focus or quite discernible. No doubt this remoteness (not at all like that of Gorter's epic) arose largely from the deafness from which he suffered. Like that of another deaf poet, David Wright (q.v.), his poetry has a sensuous musical quality. He made the best Dutch translation of Omar Khayyam. He was deeply influenced by the philosophy of his countryman, Spinoza, as well as by ancient Sufic poetry. During most of his lifetime he was not well known; now there is a revival of interest in his poetry. Verwey (q.v.) described his lyrics as 'like the swelling and fading of a wave that never breaks'. His world, particularly as expressed in the long poem *Cheops* (1915), is eminently worthy of investigation.

A. ROLAND HOLST (1888), one of the most lively literary members of the underground war against the occupying Nazis in the Second World War, is another important symbolist, who combines the Celtic esotericism of Yeats (q.v.) with the kind of pre-temporal paradises of which we catch so many glimpses in the French poetry of the first thirty or forty years of this century. Writing from the viewpoint of innocence (though not assuming it) he either celebrates the eternal lost world or, with perhaps more effect—and in a more hallucinated poetry—records visions of himself in the corrupted temporal world. His imagery is elemental, and in this and in his paganism he is reminiscent of Saint-John Perse. Some earlier collections are *The Confessions of Silence* (1913), *Beyond the Distances* (1920), *A Winter By the Sea* (1937); more recent is *In Danger* (1958). Dutch literature needs only to be better known for Roland Holst to have an international reputation. His language, like that of Saint-John Perse, matches his grand theme.

Dutch expressionism was imported from Germany and re-named 'vitalism' by its leader HENDRIK MARSMAN (1899–1940), who was supported by the humanist critic Dirk Coster (1887–1956). Marsman's vitalism differed very little from the second phase of German expressionism, which he had imbibed while in Germany as a very young man; but he was one of the first outside Germany to perceive the genius of Trakl. His *Poems* (1923) and *Paradise Regained* (1927) contain explosive and implosive poetry, too experimental and programmatic to be effective, but suffused with undoubted energy. In 1930 he began to revise his ideas; the resultant collection of essays, *The Death of Vitalism* (1933), marks the beginning of his maturity. Where the young Germans who had influenced Marsman in 1921 became Nazis, he looked into himself, rejecting the nihilistic and violent side of expressionism. His consistent self-consciousness saved him from his grandiose tendencies, but robbed most of his later poetry of spontaneity. In the Thirties he led a wandering life, searching for but not really finding a faith; always pursuing his idea of 'Gothic ardour'. His last poem, *Temple and Cross* (1939), on the theme of the conflict between Christ and Dionysus, comes down in favour of the pagan God. Perhaps the best of all his creative works is his novel *The Death of Angèle Degroux* (1933), the strange tale of a love affair between two 'superior' beings. The boat in which Marsman was escaping to England from France in 1940 was torpedoed, and all but his wife and one other passenger were lost.

EDDY DU PERRON (ps. CHARLES EDGAR DU PERRON, 1899–1940), Marsman's exact contemporary, was one of the liveliest and most valuable members of this generation. The son of rich parents, he came to Paris to work as a journalist when they lost their money. He was a close friend of Malraux (q.v.), who dedicated *The Human Condition* (q.v.) to him. He had an especial admiration for Stendhal, whom he physically resembled, for Multatuli (q.v.), whose work he helped to popularize, Larbaud (q.v.) and for Simenon (q.v.). Of the very best type of tough, intelligent, individualist left-wing intellectual, Du Perron exercised a strong influence on the generation that came after him; his death from heart disease at only forty-one was a tragedy. His poems are amusing, deliberately lightweight and in the intentionally matter-of-fact, colloquial 'parlando' style that he and his *Forum* (q.v.) associates cultivated. But Du Perron wrote one classic, a book that demands to be better known outside Holland: *The Country of Origin* (1935). This autobiographical novel consists of descriptions of his life in Paris alternated with extraordinarily vivid memories of his Javanese childhood. There are few books as good on the East Indies; and few books recapture the mind of a child so exactly. Du Perron also wrote two other novels, some excellent short stories, and much fine informal critical prose.

Du Perron was the co-founder, with Menno ter Braak (1902–40), of the *Forum* group, which was originally formed as a counter to Marsman's 'vitalism'. This group, which advocated lucidity, objectivity and quietude in place of expressionist rhetoric and noise, almost exactly parallels the German 'new objectivity' (q.v.), although it manifested itself rather later: it was in fact a modified expressionism, but wanted to shed the frenetic aspects while retaining the ground that had been won. The leading figure of the group was SIMON VESTDIJK (1898–1971), who became the Netherlands' most important writer after the death of Van Schendel (q.v.).

Vestdijk studied medicine, psychology and philosophy before he became a writer. He was among the most prolific: translator of Emily Dickinson, R. L. Stevenson and others, he found time to write thirty-eight novels, ten collections of short stories and twenty-two books of poetry—as well as twenty-eight non-fiction books. He wrote, it was said, 'faster than God can read'. He combines in his novels (his best work) a lust for life with a psychiatrist's objectivity. After the Second World War he was put forward as an exemplary writer by the Dutch existentialists (q.v.), whose leader was the poet and critic PAUL RODENKO (1920), a left-wing polemicist (who compiled the standard anthology of the work produced by the 'experimental' poets of the Fifties q.v.). Vestdijk's outstanding work is the eight-novel autobiographical sequence *Anton Wachter* (1934–50). This has Proustian elements, but is generally characterized by Vestdijk's special, and at first off-putting, combination of vitalism and cerebral analysis. He has been unlucky in his translations: the only good novel of his that has appeared in English is *The Garden Where the Brass Band Played* (1950; tr. 1965). This is an account of how beauty and trust are destroyed in a small Dutch town at the beginning of the century. Nol, a judge's son, loves his piano-teacher's daughter, Trix; but trivial prejudices triumph. Vestdijk is more consistent in the shorter forms, however, when his ideas are most subordinated to his imagination, which gets free range. At one time put forward as the Netherlands' candidate for the Nobel Prize, Vestdijk undoubtedly diffused his gift by too great a prolificity; but his best fiction will survive.

FERDINAND BORDEWIJK (1884–1965), a genial joker who took in earnest critics more than once, was an independent writer who successfully developed certain aspects of nineteenth-century Gothic. His *Fantastic Tales* (1919–24) combined the elements of Poe and the modern detective story. After this, becoming aware of surrealism, he turned to a more fantastic manner. *Groaning Beasts* (1928) is about a motor-race. *Bint* (1934) exposes the fascism latent in vitalism, and was itself accused of fascism. His finest novel, *Character* (1938), is written in a more conventional style. Grandly evocative of Rotterdam, the port of its setting, it tells of a father whose method of bringing up his (illegitimate) son is to oppose his every whim. Bordewijk was a versatile and eccentric writer the main function of whose work is to reveal the inadequacy of social structure and morality to human needs. He is notable as a recreator of the atmosphere of old places.

The figure of MARTINUS NIJHOFF (1894–1953) stands behind much of the Dutch poetry written since 1945, even though Achterberg (q.v.) is regarded as a more important poet. Nijhoff passed through a semi-expressionist phase, but by 1924, with *Forms*, had discovered the resigned and melancholy manner natural to him. He is a religious poet, searching for a means of redemption from adult corruption, which he sees in sexual terms: he postulates a Christ who is the equivalent of the child-in-the-man, through whom the man may gain salvation. Wise innocence may illuminate the adult's mundane and degenerate life. His language is deliberately sober and non-poetical. It is his awareness of the existence of an inner world rather than any specific poetic procedure that has made him important to the poets of a later generation.

GERRIT ACHTERBERG (1905–62) was the most gifted of the Dutch modernist poets. Words for him are in themselves magical, and his poetry is to be approached firstly for its necromantic qualities. He suffered from incapacitating mental illness, and wrote his poetry for therapeutic reasons; but he regarded it as therapeutic only because he thought of it as spiritually efficacious. He believed in the transmuting power of poetry, which he regarded as prayer. This belief gives his work a surrealist (q.v.) air. He eschews the ordinary materialistic meanings of words and tries to return to their true, primitive meanings—which centuries of corrupt usage have obscured and distorted. His central theme, expressed in various ways, is a version of the Orpheus myth: Orpheus does not want to bring Eurydice back to life, but to join her in death. This is Achterberg's response to the actual loss of his beloved. Inasmuch as a poet 'is', in a Sartrian (q.v.) sense, 'what he prefers', Achterberg is a poet of earth. He wryly contrasts the trivial nature of 'ordinary' life, with its little projects, with the depth of being itself. His verse became increasingly traditional in its forms. At his most eloquent he is a poet of purity and magic; but some of his work is spoiled by an eccentricity—arising from mental instability—that is irrelevant to his central vision. His poems were collected in 1963.

LUCEBERT (ps. L. J. SWAANSWIJK, 1924) tries, like Achterberg, to create an objective reality of language; but the process is less natural to him, the pressure to write less intense. He is an abstract painter and photographer as well as a poet, and since the Fifties has turned to drawing in preference to writing. He was then the most important representative of the 'experimental' school of poetry, with *The Triangle in the Jungle* (1951) and *Of the Abyss and Aerial Man* (1953). He is a cheerful rebel against all kinds of conformity, who writes a lightweight, playful neo-surrealist verse that mixes humour in equal proportion with social indignation. 'Atonal' (the author's term), it is full of neologisms, nonsense-propositions and startling juxtapositions—sometimes clothed in parodically solemn, hymn-like forms.

WILLEM FREDERIK HERMANS (1921) is the leading contemporary Dutch experimental writer of fiction. His initially sceptical approach may be compared to that of Robbe-Grillet (q.v.), from whom, however, he differs in other respects. Hermans began as a poet, but changed to fiction in 1949 with *The Tears of the Acacias*, a savagely cynical, scatological story set in occupied Amsterdam and in Brussels at the time of the liberation. Hermans, whose exasperated tone—in fiction and polemics—often recalls that of Céline (q.v.), has written in various experimental forms, but his main theme is the unavoidability of human chaos and individual anomie. With *The Dark Room of Damocles* (1958; tr. R. Edwards, 1962) Hermans begins a new and less desperate approach: man's situation is the same, but the existence of values is obliquely conceded. *Memoirs of a Guardian Angel* (1971) reflects the same concerns.

After the war the individualist tradition of Du Perron was continued in the magazine *Libertinage*, edited by the poet H. A. GOMPERTS (1915). This has steered a middle course between the socialism of *Podium* and the aesthetic *The Word*. The chief 'experimentalist' was Lucebert (q.v.); the most interesting poet of a more traditional bent is A. MARJA (ps. A. T. MOUJI, 1917), a 'committed' writer who calls his poetry 'anecdotic'.

JAN HENDRIK WOLKERS (1925), who is also well known as a sculptor, is a best-selling author—and a serious one. There is an element of sick meretriciousness in his work; but this is no more than incidental and irritating. He has a sense of wry and ironic humour that is genuine—and more understandable than his fiction as a whole, which is perhaps the reason for his wide appeal. Wolkers' novels that have been translated into English are characteristic work. *A Rose of Flesh* (1963; tr. J. Scott, 1967) is a study of a self-pitying, guilty man whose daughter has died in a scalding accident by his neglect (and that of his wife). He continually re-enacts this trauma, his own spirit scalded. *The Horrible Tango* (1964; tr. R. R. Symonds, 1970) is about a similarly sick but younger man. Wolkers' is one of the most brilliant gifts of his generation; as yet he has not wholly realized it.

GERARD KORNELIS VAN HET REVE (1923) wrote *Evenings* (1947), a description of a week in the life of an adolescent 'drop-out'. This compassionately traces the anguish that lies at the heart of his unease, and is one of the best studies of the younger generation written in the post-1945 period. HARRY MULISCH (1927) is self consciously European. *The Stone Bridal Bed* (1959; tr. 1962) is a semi-surrealistic study of the post-war mentality of sometimes horrifying power.

III

The magazine *From Now On* was the vehicle for the Flemish revival, which closely paralleled those of the French-speaking Belgians and the Netherlands. The Flemish literature being insecure, the magazine was all the more fiercely assertive of its uniqueness. The father-figure for all Flemish writers at this time was the poet-priest Guido Gezelle (1830–99), who had almost alone re-created Flemish as a literary language. The poetry of Gezelle, a lovable man, persecuted for his love of Flemish by government and Church alike, is unlikely to survive except as a demonstration of linguistic skill and virtuosity. But as a whole it breathes warmth and simple faith in nature.

CYRIEL BUYSSE (1859–1932), a close friend of Maeterlinck (q.v.), was equally French in outlook. But unlike his associate he decided to write in Flemish in order to enrich and invigorate a literature he felt had become impoverished. He was a prolific author of short stories, travel books and essays; but did his best work in fiction and the drama. He published his first novel in the Dutch *New Guide* (q.v.) in 1890. Resembling Maupassant in lucidity, but influenced by Zola (q.v.) as a kindred spirit, he depicted farming and middle-class life without sentimentality. His most famous novel is the early *The Right of the Strongest* (1893), a portrait of a coarse farmer who gets his way with his girl and everyone else; this is naturalist, but with the emphasis on the Darwinian doctrine of the survival of the fittest. As a dramatist Buysse, who was made a Baron in the last year of his life, was influenced by Hauptmann and, closer to home, the Dutch Heijermans (qq.v.). He wrote neat comedies and, most notably, *The Paemel Family* (1903), about a farmer exploited by landowners and his struggle against them. Buysse had much contact with Dutch writers, including Louis Couperus (q.v.).

Gezelle's nephew STIJN STREUVELS (ps. FRANK LATEUR, 1871–1969), who rivalled Chiesa (q.v.) in longevity was for fifteen years a village baker. He read widely, and his natural countryman's fatalism was reinforced by Dostoevski, Hamsun, Zola, Hardy (qq.v.) and the other novelists he devoured. Ultimately, however, he eschewed literary influence and found that he could most effectively simply record the life he saw around him in Western Flanders. His early book of stories described life in the depressed flax-growing areas: *The Path of Life* (1899; tr. A. T. de Mattos, 1915). All the ingredients of his later work are apparent: fatalism, delicacy of observation of human aspirations, a poetic sense of inexorable, beautiful, cruel nature. He has in his succeeding fiction—short stories and short novels—no lesson to teach, only a fact to demonstrate; but, like Hardy (q.v.), whom he somewhat resembles, he sees man as at the mercy of a blind destiny—in this case the natural cycle of the seasons; those who rebel suffer; it is better to be like Jan Vandeveughel in *Old Jan* (1902; tr. E. Crankshaw, 1936), and endure. Although he does not have Hardy's massive sense of tragedy, and often takes refuge in an assumption that God's in his heaven and all's really right with the world (in which his shocked imagination does not believe), Streuvels deserves to be better known and more widely translated. There is an element of Flemish mysticism or fatalism running through his work that raises it above regionalism. *The Flax Field* (1907), for example, a drama of the conflict between father and son, is so intense and psychologically accurate that it transcends mere regionalism. Fortunately some of Streuvels' earlier work is available in a French collection, *August* (*L'Août*, 1928). *Life and Death in Den Ast* is available in an English translation.

HERMAN TEIRLINCK (1879–1967), son of ISIDOOR TEIRLINCK (1851–1934)—who with RAIMOND STIJNS (1850–1904) wrote *Poor Flanders*, a truthful picture of poverty and social injustice—expanded the horizons of the Flemish novel. He was first led to experimentalism by his failure to write with real effect about the peasants, whom he approached with urban preconceptions (he was born in Brussels). He became famous for *Mijnheer Serjanszoon* (1908), a tale of an eighteenth-century hedonist; this is witty and amusing, but is now as hopelessly dated as most of Anatole France's (q.v.) books; it is certainly not his best work, which it is too often claimed to be.

As a dramatist Teirlinck set himself the task of revitalizing, on broadly expressionistic lines, the Flemish theatre. His *Slow Motion Picture* (1922) is one of the most successful of all the later expressionist plays. Two lovers jump into a canal. As they drown they re-live their experiences together, including the birth of a now dead child; when the police rescue them they part as strangers— cured of love. This was one of the earliest plays to make effective use of cinema techniques, and Salacrou was clearly influenced by it in his *The Unknown Woman of Arras* (q.v.). *The Bodiless Man* (1935) employs the familiar expressionist technique of splitting one man into his component parts. *The Magpie on the Gallows* (1937), perhaps Teirlinck's best play, reveals the evils of puritanism.

The novel *Maria Speermalie* (1940) gives the history of a passionate and polyandrous woman who rises to the aristocracy. *The Man in the Mirror* (1955; tr. J. Brockway), which addresses its old business-man hero in the second person throughout, is a tragi-comic masterpiece. The protagonist sees his past self, with its transgressions of bourgeois values, as someone else. *The Struggle with the Angel* (1952), which ranges over six centuries, is less successful as a whole.

The leading Flemish poet, and perhaps the only other major twentieth-century poet in Dutch besides Achterberg (q.v.), was KAREL VAN DE WOESTIJNE (1878–1929). Van de Woestijne was initially influenced by the narcissistic decadence of Kloos, by George and Rilke, and, above all, by the ideas of Baudelaire (qq.v.). In his best poetry he achieves a manner entirely his own, compounded of nostalgia for childhood, sexual guilt and unrelieved bitterness. He died of tuberculosis. A robust, not to say lush, sensuality is challenged and penetrated by a cruel and almost metaphysical shrewdness. He was very much of his age, a typical tormented soul of the first quarter of the century; but he is particularly interesting because he felt his symbolist procedures, at which he grasped like a drowning man, to be continually threatened by his lack of faith in the Platonic assumptions underlying them; this explains much of the intensity of his bitterness and his supposed obscurity. He saw his own lust as a luxurious and hellish dissolver of the beauties of nature. He saw himself as a hazel-nut and, simultaneously, as the greedy worm within it; as it devours his robust centre he becomes 'an emptiness that does not speak or heed'; but, touched by a child's hand, he sings. His epic, systematizing poems of the Twenties are less successful than the early ones, but contain many fine passages. He wrote several volumes of literary criticism and prose, all of which are suffused with his own unhappy and melodious style.

No later Flemish poet of Van de Woestijne's stature has emerged. Elsschot (q.v.) wrote some good poems, but was primarily a novelist. PAUL VAN OSTAIJEN

(1896–1928) was an expressionist and experimentalist who did not live long enough to entirely fulfil his gift. *Music Hall* (1916), however, was a really remarkable and original first collection of poems from a man of only twenty. The chief influence was the unanimism (q.v.) of Romains and the *Abbaye* group (q.v.); but the poems in it, all evoking a great city, incorporate (and frequently anticipate) elements of the grotesque; van Ostaijen is never starry eyed as were some of the *Abbaye* group—on the contrary, he is deeply and naturally cynical in an extremely modern, specifically urban manner. After the surrealism of *The Signal* (1918) and *The Occupied City* (1921) van Ostaijen did in fact reach a more sombre and idealistic mood in *The First Book of Schmol* (1928), in which he essays a self-styled poetry of 'organic expressionism', which amounts to an attempt to combine words irrationally, in order to attain new meanings. He wrote a number of Kafkaesque prose works, such as *The Brothel of Ika Loch* (1925). Van Ostaijen exercised a strong influence on the post-1945 Flemish poets.

RICHARD MINNE (1891) is the most intelligent representative of the traditionalist group, which strongly opposed the modernism of van Ostaijen. KAREL JONCK-HEERE (1896) began under the influence of Van de Woestijne, and although he reacted against him has retained his essentially expressionist attitude.

HERWIG HENSEN (ps. FLORENT MIELANTS, 1917) has also followed in this direction rather than in a modernist one. He began as an imitator of Van de Woestijne (q.v.), but later developed into an atheist-humanist poet of moderate though not great interest. He is a better playwright, especially in *Lady Godiva* (1946); in Hensen's version her sacrifice is wasted. Hensen's intelligent if not inspired plays are immensely popular with Flemish playgoers.

BERT DE DECORTE (1915) is the leading contemporary modernist poet, much influenced by Rimbaud as well as van Ostaijen. He is more interesting as a poet than Hensen, but does not seem to have decided what course to take. His best collection is *The Passage of Orpheus* (1940), in which Greek mythological themes are set off against a Flemish background. He is a learned poet, who writes in Latin and translates well from the Greek.

*

Until well after the First World War the regional fiction of Buysse and Streuvels —and that of their inferior imitators—was regarded as the only kind of effective fiction that Flanders could produce. Even Teirlinck did not come into his own until between the two wars, and Elsschot was shamefully neglected by all but a few.

WILLEM ELSSCHOT (ps. ALFONS DE RIDDER, 1882–1960) was for long better known in the Netherlands (he was 'discovered' by the *Forum* group) than in his native Belgium. At one point he remained silent for fifteen years. He is an unsensational, sophisticated, parodic, tender realist of genius; a delightful writer, and a major one. Elsschot is full of subtle feeling; and 'near sentimentality' (a term used by one critic) is less apt than saying that he always avoids it. His style is highly economical and lucid. Three of his novels have been translated by A. Brotherton (*Three Novels*, 1963): *Soft Soap* (1924), *The Leg* (1938) and *Will-o'-the-Wisp* (1946). *Soft Soap* is about the advertising world (Elsschot himself was the director of an advertising agency), and introduces his Chaplinesque character Laarmans—and the bourgeois crook Boorman, who can live with his conscience but sometimes comically tries to appease it. He appears again in *The Leg*, as does Laarmans, and in *The Tanker* (1942). *Cheese* (1933) is probably Elsschot's funniest book: an account of a man's dream of becoming a big cheese importer, which is very rudely shattered when he attempts to realize it. His best book, however, is his last: *Will-o'-the-Wisp*. A girl has given three Indian sailors a false address. Laarmans meets them and tries to help them find her, listening to their awed praises of her beauty until he wants her himself. Here Elsschot, in a novel of wide application, achieves a tenuous, sad sense of human brotherhood, of broken dreams, of sweetness. His poetry, all written about 1920, published in 1934 (*Yester Year*), has similar qualities: lucid, cynical, compassionate.

FELIX TIMMERMANS (1886–1947) is a minor figure by comparison, although he achieved an international success. He had skill, but his invention of the painter Breughel's environment is as swashbucklingly artificial in *Droll Peter* (1928; tr. M. C. Darnton and W. J. Paul, 1930) as his Rabelaisian peasant in *Pallieter* (1918; tr. 1924). *Peasant Hymn* is available in English.

GERARD WALSCHAP (1898), an inspector of public libraries for much of his life, has written acerb novels of protest against the Flemish Catholic establishment. His heroes are amoral and instinctive men or women who obey nature and therefore find themselves ranged against society. His faith in a purely vitalistic approach to life, manifested in his best known novel, *Houtekiet* (1940), about a Utopian village community, seems naïve and inadequate; but the portrait of his hero has power and some depth. *Cure through Aspirin* (1943; tr. 1960) is more sophisticated and psychological in its approach. *Congo Insurrection* (1953) is a prophetic analysis of the shortcomings of Belgian colonialism. *Marriage* and *Ordeal* have been translated in one volume.

MAURICE ROELANTS (1895) is a novelist and critic who has tried to take Flemish letters in the direction of Dutch internationalism and away from provincialism and local elements. He writes psychological novels in the French classical tradition: there are few characters, and nothing much happens except in their minds. The short story collection *The Jazz Player* (1928) contains his best work; but his few tense, intelligent novels are excellent studies of middle-class *angst*. They include *Come and Go* (1927), *Life as We Dreamed It* (1931) and *Prayer for a Good End* (1944).

LOUIS-PAUL BOON (1912) began as a vitalistic follower of Walschap, and he has remained a severe critic of society. But he is more modernistic in method, and his long novels are more reminiscent of Céline's (q.v.) than of Walschap's. He is concerned, without in the least disguising his own angry and exasperated feelings, to reveal the moral and physical corruption that underlies modern life.

His novels are peopled with scores of characters, and in this at least seem to have been influenced by Dos Passos (q.v.); although his technique is modernistic, there is more than a trace of the old, pessimistic naturalist about him. His people are not usually intelligent or nice—and they are, of course, his choice. His finest books are the ironically entitled *My Little War* (1946), the vast *Chapel Road* (1953; tr. A. Dixon, 1972) and *Summer in Ter-Muren* (1956), the moving story of a little working-class girl. Boon introduces himself into his own novels as a participant in the action and by holding conversations with his characters. Prolific and bursting with energy, Boon is Belgium's most gifted novelist writing in Flemish.

Boon's contemporary JOHAN DAISNE (ps. HERMAN THIERY, 1912) is a more cerebral writer. He describes himself as a 'magic realist' (q.v.), and this is useful inasmuch as he has the power to compel belief in his fantastic narrations. *The Stairway of Stone and Clouds* (1942) rather too sentimentally relates aspirations to reality; but the cinematic *The Man Who Had His Hair Cut Short* (1947), narrated by a man on the verge of madness, is more convincing. The long Joycean narration describes, at one point, the post-mortem of a girl whose body is rapidly rotting.

MARNIX GIJSEN (ps. JAN-ALBERT GORIS, 1899), a Belgian diplomat, has written a remarkable modern reinterpretation of the Susanna and the Elders story, *The Book of Joachim of Babylon* (1946; tr. 1951); like his near-contemporary Vestdijk (q.v.) Gijsen is Freudian in his approach and uses much autobiographical material. He is also bitterly anti-clerical, intellectual, sceptical and anti-nationalist. *Telemachus in the Village* (1948) is a vivid, shrewd, sad picture of life in a Belgian provincial town, *Lament for Agnes* (1951) a nostalgic story about an unhappy love-affair.

*

Teirlinck's contribution to the Flemish theatre has already been discussed; but certain other notable playwrights should be mentioned. GASTON MARTENS (1883) is a delightful minor playwright, whose *Birds of Paradise* (1944) enjoyed a huge success (in a French translation) in post-war France as play and movie. PAUL DE MONT (1895–1950), whose health was permanently impaired by his service in the First World War, was a notable satirist whose finest play, *The Trial of Our Lord* (1925), inspired Ghelderode's *Barabbas* (q.v.); it is an excellent play in its own right, and presents (better than in any of those well-made but *kitsch* 'courtroom dramas' of the period between the wars) all human justice as no better than a conspiracy. Johan Daisne (q.v.) has written effective, rather Teutonic plays illustrative of his Platonic and idealistic theses; none come up to the artistic level of *The Man Who Had His Hair Cut Short* (q.v.).

The leading figure of the younger generation of Flemish writers is the versatile poet, novelist and dramatist HUGO CLAUS (1929). A poet highly experimental and modern in style, he seeks to reinstate man in a context of pre-'civilized' innocence. His theatre is powerful and highly coloured: in particular

The Dawn Fiancée, which enjoyed a success in a French version, is a robust treatment of a brother-sister incest theme, in which society's attitude to incest, rather than incest itself, is regarded as corrupt. His novel *Dog-Days* (1952) resolutely describes a young man's doomed quest for existential purity. *Shame* (1972) cleverly explores the emptiness of a Belgian TV team who are filming a passion play on a Pacific island.

Eastern Minor Literatures

Colonization by various European countries—the Netherlands, Great Britain and France among them—has meant that most Eastern countries have produced little more than embryos of indigenous literatures. The native languages themselves—let alone their scripts—have had little opportunity to develop. Those that have been insubstantially productive, and have shown no true development, have not been discussed, although (as in the case of Malta) individual writers have been mentioned. (Eastern literatures of countries within the USSR have been assigned to Western Minor Literatures.)

Burmese modern literature—written in the now official language of the Union of Burma, Burmese—has not been particularly substantial, nor has any writer of real stature arisen. Its development, however, started relatively early: with the introduction of printing, which began about 1870, and the fall of the monarchy in 1886. British rule provided fewer impediments than are usual to the development of a popular colonial literature. From 1875 onwards popular works began to appear, particularly the dramatic form known as the *pya-zat*—a kind of musical play—and sentimental romances.

The traditional Burmese drama has had a long and distinguished history; but by the beginning of this century it had entirely vanished. The modern novel in Burma begins in 1904 with an adaptation by JAMES HLA GYAW of *The Count of Monte Cristo*. Only two or three other novels appeared, however, in the first two decades of the century: U KYI's *The Rosette Seller* (1904) and two novels—*Sa-be-bin* (1913) and *Shwe-pyi-zo* (1913)—by U LAT.

By 1920 literature was fast deteriorating; the foundation of the University of Rangoon in that year partially halted the process. Between then and the Japanese invasion (1942) there arose a new generation of writers who began to write in a Burmese not too far removed from the colloquial. A number of adequate translations from European literatures were made; prose fiction was developed; poems that were at least serious in intention were written. The major influence in these years was the Experiment for a New Age (*Khit-san*) movement. This, based on Rangoon University, attempted to hold the balance between Western and Burmese. The most substantial literary achievement was the novel *The Modern Monk* (1936) by THEIN PE.

Since 1948, with the creation of the republic and the replacement of English by Burmese as the official language, interest in the national literature has increased. U NU (1907), one-time prime minister, then political prisoner (now released), is one of modern Burma's better known writers. Apart from political essays and translations of Western novels, he has published a memoir, *Five Years in Burma* (1945), and a Western-style play, *The Victorious Voice of the People* (1953; tr. 1953). Two leading novelists have been MIN AUNG, who wrote *The Earth under the Sky* (1948) and the woman novelist JA-NE-GYAW MA MA LAY, author of *Not that I Hate* (1955). It is disappointing, however, that since independence the foundations laid in the rather more exciting 1920–40 period do not seem to have been built upon.

*

The modern literatures of Cambodia, Laos and Viet Nam (both South and North) are in general exceedingly impoverished, although there is no lack of trash in the form of detective stories, romances and semi-pornography (usually cast in a highly moral framework). In certain of these countries the ancient literatures are being made available once again; this is probably the most significant aspect of their literary activity. This is certainly the case in Bali (now, however, increasingly under the influence of the Indonesians), in Cambodia, and in that part of Lower Burma inhabited by the Buddhist Mons (where worship of the ancient literature actually inhibits the creation of a new). In the earlier modern period many paraphrases of Western—mostly French—realistic novels were published; these have no independent literary merit.

*

It is owing to Truong Vinh Ky, known as Petrus Ky (1837–98) that nearly all Vietnamese literature today is written in Quoc Ngu, a romanized script. In this century most of the better writing emanated from the literary group calling itself Tu-Luc Van-Doan. This, influenced by French realism, flourished in the Thirties. No outstanding single work was produced, but the whole direction of Vietnamese fiction was changed.

*

The main exceptions to the general picture of Oriental literary impoverishment (the oriental Russian states being dealt with in the Western section) are Indonesia, Persia and the Philippines; but Thailand (formerly Siam) has a fairly flourishing literature. The main influence has been Buddhist; but the Hindu influence has not been negligible. It was the circle of the King of Siam, Rama VI, VAJIRAVUDH (1881–1925) and of the Prince BIDYALANKARANA (1876–1945) that first introduced modernism into Thai literature. Vajiravudh translated from the French and the English (he went to Oxford), wrote stylish short comedies that were original at least in Thai literature, and an intelligent epistolary novel called *The Heart of a Young Man*. Bidyalankarana was more creatively gifted: his short stories—clever and humane—count among the best of Thai prose.

One of the most gifted of modern Thai novelists has been SI BURAPHA (ps.

KULAP SAIPRADIT, 1904). Si Burapha, influenced by Marxist theory though not a thoroughgoing Marxist, has persistently opposed the tendencies to sentimentality that disfigure most of Thai fiction—even that by relatively talented writers. *A Man Indeed* (1928), a bitter story of a man's struggle to overcome his inferior social position, introduced a new note of realism into Thai literature. *Behind the Picture* (1938) and *The Struggle of Life* (1944) treat of sexual themes with great restraint and subtle psychological understanding.

DOK MAI SOT (ps. MOM LUANG BUBPA SUKICH NIMMANHEMINDA, 1906–63) was the leading woman novelist. Her theme—the social and other harms resulting from crude and mechanical Westernization—is best illustrated in *Thus the World Is* (1935); she wrote nine other novels, all of them containing intelligent and often amusing writing.

SOT KURAMAROHIT (1908) is a gifted anti-fascist and socialist; his novels are graphic and skilful without having high literary pretensions.

The versatile MOM RATCHAWONG KHU'KRIT PRAMOJ (1912), a leading liberal journalist and satirist, is still the most lively figure in contemporary Thai literature. He is a critic, radio and short-story writer, and playwright as well as a novelist. *Four Reigns* (1953), a long saga, intelligently reconciles the past with the future, the ancient and oriental with the new and Western. *Many Lives* shows acute awareness of social differences in modern Thailand.

*

Maltese is a language with affinities with Tunisian Arabic, ancient Phoenician and Sicilian. It replaced Italian as Malta's official language in 1934. So far only one man has written in it with true distinction: this is DUN KARM (ps. CARMELO PSAILA, 1871–1961), a Roman Catholic priest. In Psaila's poetry, which can be read in the original by fewer than half a million people, many of the unique characteristics of the Maltese literature of the past are preserved: among these are conciseness, dignity and lack of sentimentality. Psaila turned from Italian to Maltese poetry in 1912. His predecessor G. MUSCAT AZZOPARDI (1853–1927) was less gifted, but deserves mention as a pioneer and as Psaila's teacher and the one who persuaded him to write in Maltese. Others who contributed to the development of Maltese poetry are A. CUSCHIERI (1876) and NINU CREMONA (1880). But Psaila, or Dun Karm as he is usually called, is the outstanding Maltese poet. He is not a great author, but his poetry is original and interesting. Fortunately, a selection of it has been translated by A. J. Arberry in *Dun Karm: Poet of Malta* (1961). The diction of the following translation of a poem called 'Ashes' is somewhat unnecessarily archaic, but still conveys a sense of Psaila's integrity and emotional range:

> She was beautiful, and I saw her bowing her head
> before the priest. Black, black as the night
> was the veil over her brow, and her sweet gaze
> never lifted from the ground, neither her hands
> loosed one from the other.

Locked in his thoughts
the Man of God made the sign of the cross in ashes
over the girl's head. 'Remember,' he spoke, 'woman,
that thou art dust and to dust shalt return.'

Concentrated
upon that counsel, the girl went forth slowly,
slowly out of the church, and scattered not her gaze
along the road as she passed. Many eyes were cast
upon her and followed her as she went, many
hearts beat fast, beat fast, fast as the tread
of her hurrying steps; and when behind her
the door was shut that hid her from every gaze
the eyes still yearned, and the hearts still sighed.

(tr. A. J. Arberry)

G. AQUILINA, although not as gifted as Psaila, has done more than any other towards the development of Maltese prose, particularly in his historical novel *Under Three Regimes*, and in his plays.

*

The literature of modern Korea has been serious in its aspirations as well as energetic; but few writers of real originality have emerged. The so-called Era of Enlightenment, involving imitations of European and American realism, began in 1876, when Korea began to make contact with other countries. It represents a clean break with the literature of the past, which had stretched back over two thousand years. Until 1910 Korean literature was dominated by the 'New Novel', which, while crude, melodramatic and nationalistic, did introduce the use of the colloquial. The most notable examples are novels by YI IN-JIK (1862–1916)—*Tears of Blood* (1906), *The Voice of the Devil* (1908)— who inaugurated this type of fiction.

In 1910 Korea was forced to accept the 'annexation' to Japan; from this time dates the second modernist phase known (for reasons obvious enough) as the Independence era. YI-KWANG-SU (1892–?), whose fiction has still not been surpassed in this century, became active at this time. (The date of his death, or even whether he is dead, is not known: he was captured by the communists during the Korean War and taken off to North Korea.) *The Heartless* (1917) is the first truly modern Korean novel: apart from attacking the Japanese annexation, it attacks the injustices inherent in Korean society itself, and yet maintains a high standard of psychological accuracy. *Love* (1936) is even more outstanding. Yet Yi-Kwang-su, for all his personal success in restoring a partially non-propagandist role to fiction, none the less believed in the dogmatic, nationalistic function of literature.

After the Japanese suppression of the Korean revolt of 1919 a group of writers arose who felt that literature, by working for independence, was betraying its true purpose. The members of this 'Creation Circle' (called thus after their magazine, *Creation*) admired the achievement of Yi-Kwang-su, but opposed themselves to his theory of literature's social function. These writers, on the whole pessimistic and anti-political in mood, fell under the influence of Zola (q.v.) and other late nineteenth-century naturalists.

At roughly the same time as the Creation Circle was formed, however, a proletarian group arose; this became stronger within a few years, and by 1923 there was an active New Trend group, practising social realism. Less good writing came from this than from the Creation Circle; in any case the whole left-wing of Korean literature was rigidly repressed, by the Japanese, by 1935. After the Second World War and, again, after the Korean War in South Korea (the writers of North Korea practise a crude form of socialist realism, q.v., or nothing; there is no discussion), the debate between those who believe in literature as a social and political instrument and those who believe in it as a means of revealing truth has continued. South Korea is an unhappy country, ruled by a virtual dictator; there are indications that a novel and a drama heavily influenced by European radical modernism will emerge; but as yet there is no substantial writer.

Modern Korean poetry has been superior in quality. Ko Won has compiled and translated an excellent selection from it in *Contemporary Korean Poetry* (1970). Modern poetry begins with CH'OE NAMSON's (1890–1957) free verse poem 'From the Sea to Children', a vernacular poem that seemed—with its ironic levity of tone and its idiomatic language—as modern to Koreans as 'Prufrock' (q.v.) did to Americans and Englishmen. As a poem it is not more intrinsically important than, say, Jakob Van Hoddis' 'World's End' (q.v.); but it happened to inaugurate a new poetry and a new poetics. Later, after 1919, symbolism (q.v.) began to play its role. KONGCH'O (ps. O SANG-SUN, 1894–1963), a 'nihilistic wanderer, never married', educated in Japan, introduced a resigned, Buddhistic note in his free verse poetry. YI CHANG-HUI (1902–28), who killed himself, was Korea's leading symbolist and hermetic poet of the early period; he wrote poems of elegant despair and solipsist ecstasy. CHONG CHI-YONG (1903–c. 1951), probably killed in the Korean War, cultivated a similar note, and is influential today. The best of the younger poets is KIM CH'UN-SU (1922), who combines Japanese with Western influences in a poetry that evokes the modern sensibility with great sensitivity and feeling, as in 'Prelude for a Flower', included in the comprehensive anthology mentioned above:

> I am now a dangerous animal.
> The touch of my hands makes you
> an unknown, remote darkness.
>
> On the end of a branch
> of an existence, you bloom
> and fall without a name.
>
> I cry all night having lit a wick
> of memory in this nameless darkness
> sunken in my eyelids.

My cry will gradually become
a night whirlwind shaking a tower,
and then gold, having pierced stone.

. . . Veiled bride of mine. . . .

*

Modern Persian literature has for the most part reflected the political situation. This has not yet been resolved, since the regime now in power is essentially reactionary: there is no freedom of speech or opinion. The literature of the early period (1905–21) is one of liberal revolt against tyranny and religious obscurantism. There seemed to be some hope for a liberal constitution until the *coup d'état* of 1921, when the reign of Riza Shah was inaugurated. The dominating figure of this period is the poet MALIK AL-SHU'ARA (ps. MUHAMMAD TAQI BAHAR, 1886–1951), who was forced (some less cautious contemporary poets were murdered) to take refuge in scholarly activities. He had been a leading member of the liberal revolution (1905–12), and was an M.P. Always a classicist, he was nevertheless a tireless experimenter within the limits of the traditional forms, and he believed in both free discussion and the abolition of privilege. In retrospect his character and the example he set are more intrinsically important than his own poetry, skilful and often eloquent though this is.

Contemporary Persian poetry resembles Turkish, but there are fewer and less gifted practitioners; and the situation for writers is rather worse. Probably the best known of the modern poets is PAJMAN BAKHTIYARI.

The two most important prose writers have been MUHAMMAD HIJAZI (1899) and SADIQ HIDAYAT (1902–51), Persia's most important modern novelist, and a major figure by international standards. Hijazi managed to attain to, and retain, popularity during the reign of Riza Shah; his subject was the nature and the lot of Persian women. His first mature novel, and the one that brought him fame, was *Ziba* (1931). This, the most penetrating and detailed portrait of twentieth-century Persian life yet to appear, deals with Ziba, a charming *femme fatale*, and a young theological student who is driven to delinquency by his involvement with her. *Ziba* is a devastatingly ironic exposure of Persian bureaucracy. Unfortunately Hijazi himself became increasingly involved in the world he depicted in this early novel; nothing he has written since—skilled and clever though it is—comes near to equalling it.

Sadiq Hidayat, orginally a student of dentistry, visited France and absorbed much of its culture. The chief influence on the younger generation of Persian writers, he was profoundly aware of the Persian past (he was learned in its folklore) and yet as receptive to Western influences. At bottom a nihilist, thrown into despair by the fierce and cruel obscurantism still (twenty years after his death) the dominant factor in Persian life, he gassed himself in his Paris apartment in 1951. He is a fascinating writer, who combines in his fiction (one novel and several collections of short stories) brutal naturalism (q.v.)

with the magical and fantastic elements of Persian folklore. He also wrote plays. One of his earliest books had a theme unusual, even unique, in modern Oriental fiction: *Man and Animal* (1924) deals with mankind's cruelty to animals. His best stories were written between 1930 and 1937. His short novel *Haji Aqa* appeared in 1945; this is a study of a charlatan. Hidayat translated works by Schnitzler, Kafka and Sartre (qq.v.) into Persian. One of his most distinguished successors is ALI-MUHAMMAD AFGHANI, about whom little is known save that he was an army officer and that he spent much of the Fifties in prison because of his interest in freedom ('leftist tendencies'). Afghani has written (it is said in prison) one enormous novel: *Mrs Ahu's Husband* (1961). This may well be the masterpiece that some Persians (but not the conservative majority) claim it to be. It describes the decay of the last thoroughgoingly reactionary generation (born around the turn of the century) of Iranians. It deals unerringly and movingly with the position of Persian women. The main plot concerns the eventually successful efforts of a woman to win her husband, a worthy baker, from the clutches of an adventuress. The book is over long, but it represents the best in Persian literature since the death of Hidayat.

SADEGH CHUBAK, who began publishing in the Thirties, combines decadent influences from the Nineties with an ill-absorbed modernism, although he can achieve power in isolated passages. *Sang-e Sabur* (1967) is characteristic: as a novel it does not hold together, and each element is nihilistic or decadent: a corpse eaten by worms; an impotent junkie; brutal murder; sexual orgies. The younger ESMAIL FASIH shows more promise, and his first novel, *Sharab-e Kham* (1969), although uneven, is more psychologically convincing. FERYDOUN HOVEYDA writes in French. His best novel is *The Quarantines* (*Les quarantaines*, 1967). A notable work by a Persian written in English is F. M. ESFANDIARY's *Identity Card* (1966): this, which gives perhaps the grimmest picture of the Shah's Persia yet available, had to be smuggled to America.

*

The literature of modern Indonesia is a comparatively flourishing one; among the literatures dealt with in this section only that of the Philippines can rival it. A few natives of the modern Indonesia write in Balinese (q.v.), Javanese and Malay; but the vast majority write in the modernized form of Malay now described as Indonesian. One of the more talented of the earlier pioneers, the first modern poet in Indonesian, was MUHAMMAD YAMIN (1903–62), a Sumatran who played some part in the creation of modern Indonesia. His first collection of poetry, *Fatherland*, appeared in 1922. But Yamin is in no way modern in his use of language, and his forms are traditional and conservative; his poetry was new only because of its nationalistic content. ROESTAM EFFENDI (1903) is more versatile and sophisticated; as a communist M.P. between the two World Wars he spent much time in the Netherlands. His poetry draws much on European models, but is none the less rooted in his experience of his native West Sumatra.

Even more influential, however, were the brothers SANUSI PANÉ (1905) and ARMIJN PANÉ (1908), and SUTAN TAKDIR ALISJAHBANA (1908). Sanusi Pané wrote some attractive lyrical verse as a young man, then turned to drama and finally to literary journalism. His brother, whose language assimilates European constructions to Malay in a remarkable manner, is a gifted novelist: *Shackles* (1940) is the first true psychological novel in Indonesian. Takdir Alisjahbana is a more polemical writer: he has always fervently believed in the assimilation of Western techniques as the chief means of raising Indonesia to her rightful position in the world, and his advocation of an Indonesian culture based on European rather than Hindu concepts has given rise to much controversy. His own creative work (poetry, fiction) is less important than his influence as a critic and essayist (he posits a version of social realism, as well as nationalism, against the artistic self-sufficiency of a writer such as Sanusi Pané); he has held high cultural posts since independence. He, Armijn Pané and the poet AMIR HAMZAH (1911–46)—killed in pre-independence fighting—founded a magazine in 1933 that was to prove the rallying-point of Indonesian literature over the next nine years: *New Man of Letters*.

The 'Generation of 1945', upon whom Du Perron (q.v., born in Indonesia) was an important influence, has so far produced a handful of outstanding writers. The poet CHAIRIL ANWAR (1922–49)—who died of a combination of syphilis, alcoholism, typhus and tuberculosis—is undoubtedly the most gifted writer Indonesia has yet produced. Anwar, another 'nihilistic wanderer', an 'agony writer', was a natural expressionist who used Rimbaud and the Dutch Marsman (q.v.) as his models. His poetry, disturbed, vital and powerful—it has something in it of the haunted quality of Campana's (q.v.)—was published in collected form after his death. *The Complete Poetry and Prose of Chairil Anwar* (tr. B. Raffel) appeared in 1970. Although haunted by despair and restlessness, Anwar found some hope in the aspirations of his people, in whose destiny he was able (at times) to believe, since he could project into it his own dynamic, if chaotic, spirit. This anonymous translation of one of his best known poems is quoted in Wignesan's *Bunga Emas* (q.v.):

> When my time arrives
> I wish nobody will cry
> Not even you
> You needn't weep for me
> I'm only a wild animal
> Expelled from its herd
> Let the bullets strike me deep
> I'll still growl and rush ahead
> Poison and wound run with me
> I'll flee
>
> Till pains and sorrows have gone
> Nothing bothers me any more
> And I shall live a thousand years longer.

Anwar was able to create an Indonesia in which he projected the entire gamut of his confusions—and his insight.

Three outstanding contemporary Indonesian poets are w. s. RENDRA (1935), SITOR SITUMORANG (1924) and AJIP ROSSIDHY (1938).

PRAMOEDYA ANANTA TOER (1925) is the leading contemporary novelist. He is an objective realist who deals—in such novels as *A Guerilla Family* and *No Fun Fair*—with the themes of the Japanese occupation and the post-war struggle against the Netherlands. As Toer became more communist, his fiction coarsened. He may now be dead or in prison. MOCHTAR LUBIS has written, in his loosely constructed, episodic *Twilight in Djakarta* (1963) the most savage indictment of Indonesian life under the now deceased Sukarno. Indonesian literature continues to develop.

*

Literature in Malay has received some stimulus from that of Indonesia; but rather more of intrinsic value has been produced in the non-Malay literatures of Malaya and Singapore: those written in English, Chinese and Tamil. The leading poet in English—and he is a talented and aware one, if somewhat given to facile imitation of fashionable European and American models—is WONG PHUI NAM (1935); some of his poetry may be found in *Bunga Emas: An Anthology of Contemporary Malaysian Literature* (ed. T. Wignesan, 1964). Good short stories have been written, notably by LEE KOK LIANG (1927), who received his university education in Australia and has been influenced both by Australian realists such as Leonard Mann (q.v.) and by Faulkner (q.v.); none the less, the background of his stories is strictly regional. Chinese prose writing in Malaya is represented by WEI YUN, originally from China, and MIAO HSIU, who writes mainly of the period of Japanese occupation. The best poet writing in Chinese is TU HUNG (ps. TAY AH POON, 1936). All the Tamil writing consists of short stories, radio plays and poetry. The most gifted of these writers in the Indian language is B. SUBBA NARAYANAN (1929), who came to Malaya from India in 1940. He is chiefly a playwright, but has also written short stories and poems.

*

The modern literature of the Philippines, the third-largest English-speaking country in the world, has been and continues to be flourishing and individual, although many younger writers find it hard to establish themselves. Doubtless this vitality has much to do with the American occupation, which followed that of the Spanish and was benign and encouraging to the development of the native culture ('Filipinization'). Although the literature of the latter half of the nineteenth century was in Spanish—even the important novels of the nationalist José Rizal (1861–96), murdered by the Spaniards, were in Spanish; and they could not have been in any other language—the Spaniards' influence ceased abruptly as soon as they were driven out by the Spanish-American war (1898). The nationalist phase had produced a flowering of native talent (in

Spanish); and there were, of course, works in Spanish published in the first twenty-five years, and later, of American rule. But most of the important Filipino writing has been in English. However, there are two writers in Filipino, the national language derived from Tagalog (the language of Manila and its environs) and nine other regional vernaculars. These are A. G. ABADILLA and the social realist AMADO V. HERNANDEZ. Abadilla is a novelist; Hernandez a playwright and poet as well as the author of one novel. These are the only writers so far to have given life to a language that is still under attack for its artificiality.

Modern Filipino literature of the earlier phase, beginning in the late Twenties and maturing in the mid-Thirties with the granting of commonwealth status (1936), was best represented in the short story; contemporary Filipino literature is mainly distinguished by its interesting and original poetry. Good novels remain an exception. One of the first and most gifted of the writers of short stories was MANUEL ARGUILLA (1911–44), executed by the Japanese when they discovered he was working against them. Most of his best stories are collected in *How My Brother Leon Brought Home a Wife* (1940). Influenced—but not to his detriment—by Hemingway (q.v.), Arguilla was at his best in telling stories through the eyes of a child. At the same time as he was active José Garcia Villa (q.v.) was also writing short stories; but Villa is primarily a poet, and is something of an odd man out. His stories were published in America, but not in his own country. Other important pioneers in fiction include N. V. M. GONZALEZ (1915), author of some of the best Filipino novels, including *The Bamboo Dancers* (1959), the physician ARTURO B. ROTOR (1907), who writes vivid stories based on his own experiences in his first and best collection, *The Wound and the Scar* (1937) and KERIMA POLOTAN, whose novel *The Hand of the Enemy* (1962) is one of the best novels to appear since 1945.

NICK JOAQUÍN (1917) is a subtle, if stylistically lush, writer of fiction and drama that mostly searches for the Filipino essence in the Americanized present. He was once going to be a priest, and he has been concerned all his writing life to reconcile the pagan past of his country with the spirit, not of any modern Church, but of the Gospels. Filipino drama has been slow to develop; Joaquín's *Portrait of the Artist as Filipino* (1953) is the best of the plays so far written. He has written one novel: *The Woman who had Two Navels* (1961). This was developed from a novella Joaquín completed shortly after the end of the Second World War, and published in *Prose and Poems* (1952). It juxtaposes two stories, one set in the Spanish past and one in the present, in a skilful and meaningful manner.

JOSÉ GARCIA VILLA (1914) is the first Philippine writer since Rizal to gain a truly international reputation. His early and promising short stories, mostly about his boyhood and strict upbringing, were collected in *Footnote to Youth* (1933) and published in New York. Villa had enrolled at the University of New Mexico at the age of sixteen. He has made his home in America since this time, although he has held teaching posts (including one at the University of Quezon, which had expelled him at the age of fifteen for publishing a poem it considered obscene) in the Philippines. Not many Filipino critics rate him highly: they accuse him of solipsism and prophesy that the novelty of his poetry will quickly wear off. And yet Marianne Moore (q.v.), among others less distinguished, has given serious critical attention to his poetry, which is unquestionably serious. His famous 'comma poems', in which the words are separated from one another by commas, are by no means ineffective or merely 'novel'. (An experiment that came after the 'comma poems' is 'reversed consonance': Villa claims that, for example, the word 'sings' 'mirrors' the word 'begins'.) What at first may look like a specious rhetoric in his best poetry (the most substantial selection is in *Poems* 55, 1962) is in fact the product of an original and often astute mind. At the back of much of the poetry is his early rejection of his wealthy father and all he stood for (Villa rejects not the Philippines but his family). Villa is a genuine eccentric, a poet of interest and some fascination; he may not possess major status, and he may have disfigured some of his poetry by over-ingenious tricks; but his integrity has never really been in doubt. The genuine puzzle his work offers is well exemplified in 'Inviting a Tiger for a Weekend':

> Inviting a tiger for a weekend.
> The gesture is not heroics but discipline.
> The memoirs will be splendid.
>
> Proceed to dazzlement, Augustine.
> Banish little birds, graduate to tiger.
> Proceed to dazzlement, Augustine.
>
> Any tiger of whatever colour
> The same as jewels any stone
> Flames always essential morn.
>
> The guest is luminous, peer of Blake.
> The host is gallant, eye of Death.
> If you do this you will break
>
> The little religions for my sake.
> Invite a tiger for a weekend,
> Proceed to dazzlement, Augustine.

The outstanding poet of the younger generation—and he deserves a higher reputation than he has so far gained outside his own country—is ALEJANDRINO G. HUFANA (1926). Hufana studied in America, and has assimilated all that he needs from twentieth-century American poetry (for example, the epigrammatic gravity of Masters, q.v., the narrative mastery of Robinson, q.v.). His basic theme, like that of Joaquín, is the quest for whatever is authentic in the Filipino past. He writes brilliantly and poetically, in a clean verse that most would-be narrative poets contemporary with him should envy, of both the past and the present of 'primitive' peoples. He is possibly the finest 'anthropological poet' writing in English today, as 'Pygmy Reservation', whose language so precisely reflects its complex and alien subject-matter, suggests:

> Unclothing so the Zambal Bali Dag
> May for her dead infanta deep be soft
> The black she-parent grieving on the crag
> A lullaby invokes: 'Arrow aloft
> Time for your sleep, piece-of-my-thigh,
> The fletcher is not false, time for your dream,
> Meat will be yours.' But deer is famine-shy
> And in the tough grass armour-wearers gleam,
> Who cut off headmen of the tribe, then in
> The place of thorns their barbed wire strains as far
> As christenings and unctions, light of skin,
> Succeeding through supplying men-of-war
> Whose monuments outbear orangoutan
> And birds of paradise, breast-sucked man.

FEDERICO LILSI ESPINO Jr. is the leading writer in Tagalog; he also writes in English. So far his work, collected in *Pasternak's Balalaika* (1967) and *A Rapture of Distress* (1968), and other small volumes, is self-consciously experimental: cosmopolitan influences have not yet been fully absorbed. But Espino clearly has something to give to Filipino literature. His best work so far has been in English prose, in the tense and well-written tales of *The Country of Sleep* (1969). EDELBERTO K. TIEMPO, who writes in English, shows a similar promise in the stories in *A Stream at Dalton Pass* (1970). The outstanding writer in Spanish is the woman poet ADELINA GURREA, whose most substantial collection is *Other Paths* (1967).

Finnish Literature

Finnish, a Uralian language with nothing in common with Swedish, is now the vernacular of nine-tenths of the population of Finland. Modern Finnish literature proper dates from 1880, with the so-called Young Finland movement. The new native literature was of course influenced by both Swedish and Russian literatures, but also looked to the rest of Europe. Its main aim, however, was to create a genuinely Finnish culture. Probably the most important single influence, particularly on the novel, was Alexis Kivi (1834–72).

The leading writers of the Young Finland movement were: the brilliant woman writer Minna Canth (1844–97), playwright and author of short stories influenced by Ibsen, and still recognized for her ear for authentic dialogue; JUHANI AHO (ps. JUHANI BROFELDT, 1861–1921) and ARVID JÄRNEFELT (1861–1932). Aho, a parson's son, got to know Maupassant, Daudet and Zola (q.v.) in Paris in 1889. He was and remained a basically romantic writer; but his discovery of French realistic procedures did his work nothing but good. Prior to his visit to Paris he had written *The Railway* (1884) and *The Parson's Daughter* (1885). The former is a study of a primitive couple living in the backwoods; the latter deals with provincial middle-class life and touches on the question of the emancipation of women—a theme as common in Finnish as in Scandinavian literature. His first mature work, however, was the series of sketches he began to write while in Paris, *Shavings* (1891–1921), and which he continued to publish throughout his life. In these realism and romanticism are most attractively and effectively mixed; stylistically they influenced later writers. *The Parson's Wife* (1893) describes, in a fine detail not previously seen in Finnish, the misery of a woman tied to a partner she despises. *Panu* (1897) is a historical novel about Christianity's conquest of paganism. *Juha* (1911), a love story, studies the Finnish character; by this time Aho's romantic inclinations had fully emerged. But he always kept his realistic head, and, apart from the *Shavings*, *Juha* is his best novel. In his last phase he was influenced by Selma Lagerlöf (q.v.). Some of the *Shavings* have been translated into French; all that is available in English is a volume of selected short stories: *Squire Hellman* (tr. R. Nisbet Bain, 1893).

Arvid Järnefelt was a lawyer who early came under the influence of Tolstoi. He gave up his legal career in favour of a writing life on a small farm. His novel *Fatherland* (1893) sensitively examines the difficulties experienced by a student, a peasant's son, in acclimatizing himself to bourgeois society. He finely described his Tolstoian change of heart in *My Conversion* (1894). Over the next thirty years he was regarded as an eccentric recluse, and was out of the main stream: even though some of his concerns (feminism, sexuality, the future of peasants) were Finnish, his Utopianism was out of place. Then, in 1925, he scored a major success with the religious novel *Greeta and his Lord*, which he followed with the three-part *Novel of my Parents* (1928–30). Järnefelt had a tendency to moralize, but his work is important for its psychological penetration and clear style.

The leading lyrical poet of this generation was EINO LEINO (ps. ARMAS EINO LEOPOLD LÖNNBOHM, 1878–1926), who became involved in the Young Finland movement while at university in the mid-Nineties. He was the first poet of real skill and flair since Runeberg, 'Finland's national poet' who died in 1877. But Runeberg wrote in Swedish, as of course did his important Swedo-Finnish contemporary Edith Södergran (q.v.). Leino did not clearly understand what could be done with the Finnish language in poetry, but his instinct told him that a change had to be made from a prosody ingeniously but unhappily based on German models. Leino began as a brilliant journalist and youthful national romantic; but his personal life became clouded when his marriage broke up towards the end of the first decade of the century, and he moved from a nationalist to a confused Nietzschean (q.v.) position. The brilliant lyrics of the young Leino, collected in *Songs of Man* (1896), represent the spearhead of the neo-romantic reaction to-naturalism. His chief work, *Helka Songs* (1903–16), contains elements from folk-lore—particularly the great Finnish epic, the *Kalevala*—and combines patriotism with menacing undertones of a personal nature; here, drawing on the old oral tradition, he came near to creating truly Finnish rhythms. He wrote some twenty verse plays, fiction and criticism. The quality of Leino's purely patriotic verse is demonstrated in 'A Legend of Finland':

> In days of yore (or so the legends say)
> God and St. Peter passing on their way
> O'er land and sea, when night was near at hand
> Touched on the shore of this, our blessed land.

> They sat them down upon the sloping ground
> Where birch trees grow down to a quiet sound.
> No sooner there, than Peter, who was wont
> To argue, opened with this taunt:

> 'O Lord, what land is this we've come upon!
> What people rudely poor and bent with brawn!
> Soil rocky, rugged with but scanty yields
> Of mushrooms and poor berries from the fields.'

> But in His quiet strength the Good Lord smiled,
> 'The land may neither fruitful be, nor mild;
> Cold and uninviting lies each farm,
> But every heart is beautiful and warm.'

Thus saying, the Good Lord smiled silently
And lo! a splendor spread o'er all the sea.
The marshes dried, the wilderness was cowed,
And frozen fields soon yielded to the plow.

God and St. Peter then did take their leave,
But it is said, 'If on a summer eve
You sit beneath the birch, you still can see
God's smile move on the water—quietly.'

(TCSP)

The works of Leino's final years were tired, but it is still amusing to read that the 'second half of his short life was marred by bohemian debauchery'—and from the pen of a relatively modern critic.

The other poets of the turn of the century were not as naturally gifted. OTTO MANNINEN (1872–1950), a lecturer at Helsinki University and Finland's leading translator (Homer, Heine, Ibsen, Petőfi, Runeberg, etc.), wrote comparatively little. He began in patriotic and romantic vein; but later achieved a lyrical compression and elegance of form unique in at any rate conventional (i.e. based on Germanic metres) verse. His manner is often bitingly satirical. Although he did not achieve a personal rhythm, he did make interesting experiments within the stultifying tradition. His *Complete Poems* appeared in the year of his death.

VEIKKO ANTERO KOSKENNIEMI (1885–1962), another academic and scholar—he was an authority on Goethe—was even more traditional, as critic and poet, than Manninen, whose reputation was for a time rather unfairly obscured by his. Most of his poetry—such as *Spring Evening in the Latin Quarter* (1912)—has already begun to date. The early work is influenced by French Parnassian (q.v.) poetry and Levertin and Fröding (qq.v.); later he turned to the poetry of classical antiquity. The most famous Finnish poet during his lifetime, his reputation is fading rapidly: it is not just that he refused modernism, but that he failed to understand it—and even resented it.

LARIN-KYÖSTI (ps. KYÖSTI LARSSON, 1873–1948), the son of a Swede living in Finland, was in the troubadour tradition; his first collection was called *The Spring Hummings of This Fellow* (1897). He wrote plays; and at one time turned unsuccessfully to symbolism (*Ad Astra*, 1907).

MARIA JOTUNI (1880–1943) was important as a novelist and a playwright. Her earliest short stories, influenced by Aho (q.v.), dealt with simple people, and were written in a clipped, laconic style which combines humour, an acute feminine psychological insight and a sense of tragic destiny. She later turned from naturalism, but never lost her underlying sense of the tragic. Eventually she refined her techniques to a distinctly modernistic degree of concentratedness. Her use of dialogue is celebrated for its skill. Perhaps the finest of her work is to be found in *The Young Girl in the Rose Garden* (1927), a collection of short stories. However, *Everyday Life* (1909), a comedy describing one summer's day in the life of a rural community, is also a minor masterpiece.

Another distinguished prose writer of the earlier period is VOLTER KILPI (1874–1939), who began as a Pre-Raphaelite aesthete but graduated from this in a manner uncannily reminiscent of his exact contemporary, the Dutch novelist Arthur van Schendel (q.v.), whose work he could hardly have known. It must be added that Kilpi was more cosmopolitan from the start. His most substantial work is his epic trilogy, *In Alastalo's Room* (1933–7), about a patriarchal island community in the days of the decline of the sailing-ship. (Van Schendel, too, was interested in the sailing ship.) Kilpi used modernist techniques, including stream-of-consciousness, in this vigorous and often moving work.

KERSTI SOLVEIG BERGROTH (1886) wrote in Swedish until 1920, when she turned to Finnish. A highly prolific writer of stage comedies, journalism, girls' tales and novels, she lives in Rome. She is one of the relatively few writers (cf. Bely, q.v.) to have been influenced by Rudolf Steiner's anthroposophy.

The most eminent of modern Finnish novelists, however, has been FRANS EEMIL SILLANPÄÄ (1888–1964), Finland's only recipient of the Nobel Prize (1939). Sillanpää was at first influenced by Hamsun's (q.v.) vitalism. He had studied natural science at Helsinki, and his belief in the universe as a single living object dominates all his fiction. *Life and the Sun* (1916), his first novel, is a now somewhat dated piece of Finnish vitalism: it describes a summer in the life of two urban lovers, and represents them as but two aspects of nature coming together. It recalls Hamsun, Lawrence and Romains (qq.v.). Far superior is *Meek Heritage* (1919; tr. A. Matson, 1938), the best constructed of all Sillanpää's works; this deals with the events of the Finnish civil war of 1918 between Bolsheviks and 'Whites'. (Finland had taken advantage of the situation in Russia in 1917 to declare its independence; it gained this in 1918, and adopted a democratic and republican constitution in 1919.) The central figure of *Meek Heritage* is a tenant-farmer, a character who is resigned to his fate. Sillanpää's treatment is not profound; but it is humane. After this Sillanpää came under the influence of Maeterlinck (q.v.), and entered a more mystical period. He became famous with *Maid Silja or Fallen Asleep While Young* (1931; tr. A. Matson, 1933), his least satisfactory book. Sillanpää's short stories are possibly superior to his novels: better constructed and with a deeper psychological penetration. Here Sillanpää displays his genius for noting tiny inner movements of the mind and heart, and for suggesting unconscious motivation.

TOIVO PEKKANEN (1902–57) is in some ways a more interesting and enigmatic writer than Sillanpää. His work has been subjected to various interpretations. Is he a naturalist, a realist or a symbolist? The answer is that he has been all three. *My Childhood* (1953; tr. A. Blair, 1966) is a starkly objective account of the struggle of a working-class family. This came late in Pekkanen's surprisingly versatile writing career. Earlier had come the undoubtedly naturalistic *On the Shores of My Finland* (1937), describing a strike, and *Black Ecstasy* (1939), a psychological novel about love between peasants. His novel-cycle about his native port of Kotka (1957–8) employs the techniques of Dos Passos (q.v.), presenting its inhabitants in the dreary world in which they live, but also showing them in moments of true humanity, when their resignation changes to desire for a better life.

PENTTI HAANPÄÄ (1905–55), a self-taught writer, paid for his accurate savaging of the life of Finnish conscripts in the short-story collection *Field and Barracks* (1928) by being ostracized as every kind of insect: red, godless, enemy of security. These were the days of the rise of the fascist *Lapua* organization, which attempted *coups d'état*, and was a strong influence in the land. Haanpää's work later became accepted; but he compromised only to the (reasonable) extent of supporting his country against the Russians when they treacherously attacked it. *War in the White Desert* (1940) is the most vivid of all descriptions of the Russo-Finnish 'winter' war over whose fierce fifteen weeks the Red Army was humiliated—before using sheer extra might to force Finland to cede nearly 16,000 square miles of land. *War in the White Desert* was translated into French by A. Sauvageot (*Guerre dans le désert blanc*, 1942). Thereafter Haanpää became a brutally powerful writer: ironic, uncompromising in his pessimistic view of life. After his accidental death by drowning there appeared *Magic Circle* (1957), perhaps his greatest achievement. Haanpää's view of life resembles that of Camus (q.v.); but he is not interested in solutions or protests. He relishes the comedy of human aspirations, played out against the wholly indifferent, and yet mockingly beautiful, background of nature. In this he recalls Bunin (q.v.).

Although not as gifted a writer, MIKA WALTARI (1908) has attracted much more attention outside Finland, with his skilful, well-written, intelligent but *kitsch* historical novels, most of which have been translated (*Sinuhe the Egyptian*, 1945, tr. and abridged N. Walford, 1949; *The Secret of the Kingdom*, 1959, tr. 1960; etc., etc.); but he has done his more serious work in the short story. Waltari was associated with the *Tulenkantajat* (*Torchbearer*) group when a very young man. The Torchbearers, 1924–9, were a left-wing, outwards-looking group: their motto was 'The large windows open onto Europe'. This group contained most of the Finnish writers influenced by expressionism, q.v., but it also belatedly incorporated some elements of futurism, q.v. It quickly dissolved, although an important left-wing magazine bearing the same name continued until 1939.

Though Waltari caused something of a stir with his precocious first book, *The Great Illusion* (1928), about rebellious youth, he soon calmed down. His most interesting work is to be found in *Moonscape* (1953; tr. 1954), short stories. Here the cinemascope effect and relentlessly mindless piling up of historical detail are lacking, and there is some understanding of psychology. But essentially Waltari remains a good-natured purveyor of midcult fodder: his seriousness is continually swallowed by his reprehensible desire to fill the lounges of the West with pseudo-mystical consolation.

VÄINÖ LINNA (1920) caused one of the biggest recent sensations in Finnish letters with the publication of *The Unknown Soldier* (1954; tr. 1957), the story of a grousing soldier in the winter war. This sold half a million copies, which was unprecedented in a country of under five million. It is a vivid and vigorous book, making brilliant use of dialogue; polite society was shattered by its candour, but also fascinated. The trilogy *Under the Polar Star* (1959–62) deals with the Civil War of 1918, and again provoked controversy. Linna's views of the extremely complex issues behind the war are controversial, but they are undoubtedly more penetrating than those of the historians. He has been particularly anxious to dispel what he believes is the myth of a disinterested White army.

VEIJO MERI (1928) shares the post-war generation's disillusionment with war and bourgeois war-values (such as 'heroism', which he considers a mythical quality). *The Isolated* (1959) and *Events of 1918* (1960)—on the Civil War—portray individuals lost and isolated in the hell of war. *A Story of Rope* (1957; tr. in French P. Sylvain and F. Bolgár, 1962) is set in the First World War. Meri has also written about modern Helsinki. ANTTI HYRY (1931) is an experimentalist, who cultivates a naïvely objective style that is interesting but apt to become monotonous. His best novel is *The Edge of the World* (1967).

*

Despite the genius of Leino, Finnish poetry has adapted slowly to this century. What the Finnish poet ANSELM HOLLO (1934)—he now writes in English and lives in Great Britain and America—has called 'Finnitude' grew up, and 'was liable to bog poetry down in either of two kinds of neo-romanticism: the "cosmic" . . . or the folkloristic. . . .' This was understandable in a new nation. But almost all poets until the Fifties tried to write Finnish poetry in predominantly German forms; since, as Hollo points out, Finnish is a Uralian and not an Indo-European tongue, the results were often 'somewhat repulsive'. The modernist poets of the Fifties therefore have less use for the Torchbearers (q.v.) as pioneers than they otherwise might. One cannot say that any of the Twenties poets discussed below really understood their reading of Nietzsche and French poetry. Like Ady (q.v.) in Hungary, they brought back something; but Finnish soil was less fertile than Hungarian.

Most of Finland's leading poets of the between-wars period were associated with the Torchbearers group (q.v.). UUNO KAILAS (ps. FRANS UUNO SALONEN, 1901–33), who died—like so many of his countrymen—from tuberculosis, was its leading spirit: he introduced the German expressionist poets into Finland in a volume of translations published in 1924. For a whole year (1928–9) he was seriously ill with schizophrenia. His early poetry is violent and tormented in a typically expressionist style; after his illness he reacted against this, to produce a more controlled—although not less disturbed—poetry. His first mature collection was *Sleep and Death* (1931): here for the first time his turbulent guilts, anguished self-scrutiny and hallucinations are subsumed under an iron discipline—representative, of course, of Kailas' need for restraint and fear of mental collapse. His thinking about poetry was influenced by that of JUHANI SILJO (1888–1918), who was killed in the Civil War. Siljo believed in poetry as a means of self-revelation and of achieving a perfect life; Kailas clung to this without believing in it. (TCSP) P. MUSTAPÄÄ (ps. M. HAAVIO, 1899), a distinguished scholar, has drawn on Finland's early literature. The surface of his

delightful poetry is deliberately light and easy; but this conceals a masterful
adaptation of early manners to modern needs, and a profound humour:

> I am still far away.

> I will arrive tomorrow.
> Hey, my pack, my laughing pack!
> Hey, my friendly walking stick!
> Tomorrow we shall arrive.

> At a beautiful time.
> Just when the old sexton opens the loft of the belfry.
> Steam bath, Saturday steam bath.
> The music of the round
> Sounds in the village.

> I am still far away.
> A mist, a wild wizard's mist
> Seeks the hollows, mounds, shadows,
> Groups of aspen trees.

> Slippery rocks under foot,
> Stumps with staring eyes along the roadside.
> Welcome to you,
> Welcome, I am a bridegroom,
> The bridegroom of happiness.

> And so wildly in love.
> (TCSP)

LAURI VILJANEN (1900), another leading light in the Torchbearers group, is
more important as an influence than as a poet. He is an intelligent conservative
humanist, sometimes intolerant in his more recent criticism. He has kept Finns
in touch with European developments for nearly fifty years. His own poetry is
well-made but rather conventionally humanistic in content.

The leading woman poet of the Torchbearers was KATRI VALA (ps. ALICE
WADENSTRÖM, 1901–44), who is often compared, for her intensity, to Edith
Södergran (q.v.). Like the latter, Katri Vala died of tuberculosis. She introduced free verse to Finland. Her poetry of the late Twenties is her best—'I
cycle my hunger's orbit/Bare and dreary as a prison yard./My senses and
thoughts are rough from work'—because of its freshness, spontaneity and firmness of line. The later, more politically radical poetry is less important. Katri
Vala died in Sweden; her *Collected Poems* appeared in 1945.

AALA TYNNI (1913), Mustapää's (q.v.) wife, is an interesting poet, who has
assembled an important anthology of European poetry—translated by herself—
from A.D. 1000 to the present: *A Millennium of Song* (1957). Her most interesting

original poetry explores the nature of human evil. LAURI VIITA (1916–65), who died prematurely in a car crash, was a predominantly urban poet (his first collection was called *Concreter*, 1947) who alternated between a grandiose 'cosmic' poetry—ineffective—and a simple, ballad-like style of great charm. He graduated into an impressive novelist: *Moraine* (1950), set in the Civil War, a study of urban life, is successful on sociological and psychological levels. HELVI JUVONEN (1919–59) was influenced by Emily Dickinson and, above all, Marianne Moore (q.v.): she projects herself into various animals in the same way, although her manner is considerably more personal. With Haavikko she was the leading Finnish modernist of the Fifties.

The most gifted Finnish post-war modernist is PAAVO HAAVIKKO (1931). A selection of his poems has been translated into English: *Selected Poems* (tr . A. Hollo, 1968). Haavikko is an extreme modernist: his poetry combines hermeticism with a strong sense of, as he puts it (in the form of a question), 'How can we endure without falling silent when poems are shown to mean nothing?' He has indignantly repudiated the reactionary 'Finnitude' of his elders, and he shares his contemporary Meri's (q.v.) view of war. His poetry rejects any kind of easy way out, any neatness, and consequently often runs the risk of being found impenetrable. His poem-sequence 'The Winter Palace' is his most impressive work, and has attracted praise from Enzensberger (q.v.) and other poets.

JUHA MANNERKORPI (1915), who was born in Ohio, is a more run-of-the-mill modernist, whose poetry, drama and short stories seldom transcend their influences (mainly Beckett); but he has made important translations from Beckett and other French writers into Finnish. TUOMAS ANHAVA (1927), a more original poet, has absorbed the influence of classical Chinese and Japanese poetry, which he has finely translated. A substantial retrospective selection appeared in 1967. MARJA-LIISA VARTIO (1924–66) began as a poet but then went on to write a series of highly poetic novels: essentially she was a poet. Her early death was a serious loss to Finnish letters. The posthumous *The Birds Were Hers* (1967) is her finest novel, the subtle and original story of a widow who, obsessed with birds, can only relate to others through her maid. With Haavikko at the forefront of the modernist movement is EEVA-LIISA MANNER (1921), who has graduated from the traditional to surrealist free verse; she has written fiction and drama.

*

Maria Jotuni (q.v.) was as distinguished in the theatre as in fiction. She began as an Ibsenian (q.v.) but soon branched out into comedy—her forte—with such plays as *Man's Rib* (1914). Her most powerful tragedy is her drama dealing with Saul, *I Am to Blame* (1929). Kersti Bergroth's (q.v.) comedies in the Karelian dialect have enjoyed a deserved success. LAURI HAARLA (1890–1944) wrote a number of successful dramas (and novels) on medieval subjects. A number of Finnish writers best known for their work in other fields—Waltari and Haavikko (qq.v.) among them—have written plays, but no major dramatist has emerged.

French and Belgian
Literature

I

ÉMILE ZOLA (1840–1902),son of an Italian engineer (a naturalized Frenchman), is a logical point of departure in a survey of the modern French novel. The fiction that followed his may be described both as developing from and reacting to it. Just as modernism was a redefinition of romanticism rather than a return to classicism, so Zola's naturalism, with its pseudo-scientific programme and its over-simplified determinism, was essentially a necessary curbing of his own romantic extravagance. No true classicist would, for example, call a work of art 'a corner of creation seen through a temperament', as Zola did. His project as defined in *The Experimental Novel* (*Le Roman expérimental*, 1880; tr. 1894), though not privately believed in by him, is romantic in its grand excessiveness, and amounts to a romantic assertion of the authority of the artist. He claimed, for example, that mechanistic interpretations of the interplay of characters could guide government. As Jean-Albert Bédé has remarked, 'the *petite fleur bleue* will never fail to blossom in the corner of even his darkest novels'. Nor, he might have added, do the essentially romantic elements of horror and sexual decadence often fail to materialize: as in *Thérèse Raquin* (1867; tr. L. W. Tancock, 1962), or in the lust and death scenes in *Nana* (1880; tr. B. Rascoe, 1922). For Zola 'science', really a constellation of pseudo-sciences in which he did not seriously believe, was among other things a means to romantic ends. But truth was always his aim, and his scientific aspirations are more important than his pseudo-science. One of his strengths lies in his depiction of various kinds of corruption. In the first instance corruption fascinated him as it fascinates almost all writers; but his scientific aims increased the power and sharpness of his writing on the subject.

Zola, like Dreiser (the only other great naturalist), is paramount in his account of individuality oppressed by social vastness. This illustrates the principle of determinism—man at the mercy of destiny; but just as surely it gathers the theme of alienation into its scope. Romanticism had concentrated on the uniqueness of individualities. Now positivism and scientific advance inevitably concentrated on the resemblances between individuals. Literature, in spite of itself, continued to concentrate on their uniqueness. . . . And hence it became pessimistic (although Zola, in other respects a nervously inhibited man, relished escaping to his desk to dramatize his gloom).

However, the nature of Zola's creative imagination should not distract attention from his own conscious dedication to, or the widespread belief in, the salvation of mankind through the use of scientific method. The novels of Zola's middle period, the extensive Rougon-Macquart series, were considered by him to be a naturalist project; in this series he was the first to exploit the idea of hereditary determinism. Zola admitted that he did not believe in the bogus theory he used; but that he chose this instead of another framework is significant. He always employed a simple kind of symbolism to achieve his effects—in, for example, his study of the Parisian meat industry, *The Fat and the Thin* (*Le Ventre de Paris*, 1873; tr. E. A. Vizetelly, 1895), the actual descriptions of piles of food are undoubtedly symbolic, as, more effectively, is the mine (= the birth of social revolt) in *Germinal* (1885; tr. H. Ellis, 1894). In his last novels this element of symbolism became stronger.

Zola's novels, like Dreiser's, are a monument to the fact that literature can never become 'science'—any more than science alone can embrace truth. His way of writing, vigorous and crude, is impressionistic, not based on actual observation (although he uses a carefully gathered series of reported details). He reflects the true nature of nineteenth-century faith (or hope) in science; he anticipates modern sociology. It was Zola who forced the reading public to accept harrowing descriptions of poverty, disease and other largely industrial or urban phenomena in the place of insipid romantic fiction—or, at best, fiction containing characters with whom it could comfortably identify.

Naturalism originated in France with the documentary *Germinie Lacerteux* of the Brothers Goncourt, but did not gain acceptance until Zola's heyday and the record-breaking sales of *Nana*. Then the group around Zola, who now lived at Médan, published in 1880 a collection of supposedly 'naturalistic' short stories. It is interesting that the only stories here that accurately demonstrate the naturalist theory are by the least gifted members of the group. PAUL ALEXIS (1847–1901) remained a naturalist, many of whose works agreeably reflect his real distinction as champion whore-hunter of Paris; but there is not much in his novels (the best is *Madame Meuriot*, 1891) to remember. HENRI CÉARD (1851–1924) was another minor talent; the well-intentioned first of his two novels, *A Lovely Day* (*Une Belle Journée*, 1881), about a planned adultery that does not come off, has rightly been called 'a triumph of . . . dullness'. The novels of the Guadeloupean-born LÉON HENNIQUE (1851–1935) were not less dull. Of the other two contributors to the 1880 volume—their stories, like Zola's, quickly transcend naturalist doctrine—Maupassant (1850–93) early developed out of naturalism, and Huysmans (q.v.) travelled along one of the main channels of reaction to it: the reawakened interest in religion.

Naturalism lasted for thirty years (1865–95), but its heyday amounted to little more than a decade. The influential critic Ferdinand Brunetière (1849–1906) attacked it and inflicted serious damage as early as 1883. The claims of science and positivism rapidly lost their appeal. People became interested in psychology, philosophy (such as Bergson's) and religion. The run-of-the-mill naturalist novel, such as Céard's *A Lovely Day* (q.v.), was regarded by the public as being as monotonous as it actually was. But while naturalism proved inadequate, no really important new novelist emerged until the end of the decade.

JORIS-KARL HUYSMANS (ps. GEORGES CHARLES HUYSMANS, 1848–1907), born in Paris, began as a naturalist, at least in the sense that his fiction was documented, but later extended his technique to treat of more evidently subjective material. Huysmans, who was of Dutch descent, was much admired by Oscar Wilde and other English writers of the Nineties for his 'decadence'; but he soon rejected the 'Satanism' of his most famous novel *Against Nature* (*A rebours*, 1884; tr. R. Baldick, 1959) and returned to Catholicism (1892), reflecting the general revival of interest in religion.

There is not much to choose between his early short fictions. *Marthe* (1876; tr. R. Baldick, 1948), on prostitution, is meticulous and humanitarian; perhaps *The Vatard Sisters* (*Les Sœurs Vatard*, 1879), on Parisian woman book-stitchers, contains the most clearly delineated characters. But in *Against Nature* he expressed for the first time his own sense of frailty and preciosity; his elaborately constructed rococo defence of aestheticism against coarseness, ugliness and boredom was what appealed to Wilde. The behaviour of Des Esseintes, the hero, doubtless provided a programme for Huysmans himself to follow. The tendencies were certainly already there in the Eighties: in what the poet Jules Laforgue christened the decadent spirit (*l'esprit décadent*) of that time: an anti-dogmatic and intensely anti-bourgeois hatred of restraints, with a consequent seeking out of perversities that would shatter *ennui*—but not too noisily because this was essentially a pseudo-aristocratic, affected and enervated spirit. It goes without saying that Des Esseintes is a worshipper of Baudelaire (q.v.). He is also a reader of an unknown poet called Mallarmé (q.v.): this novel awakened interest in him.

The rest of Huysmans' work describes the progress of his Catholicism. Now the hero, a later version of Des Esseintes, is called Durtal, and his experiences are largely Huysmans' own. In *Down There* (*Là-bas*, 1891; tr. 1924) he experiments with Satanism and occultism; but in the trilogy of novels *En Route* (1895: tr. 1896), *The Cathedral* (*La Cathédrale*, 1898; tr. 1898) and *Oblate* (*L'Oblat*, 1903; tr. 1924) Durtal finds the true, non-radical, Christian light. Huysmans was a gifted writer, in any of whose works characters are apt to leap to life; but his spiritual progress from exquisite dandy to monk-like devotee of God, while as sincere as his refusal at the end of his life to accept drugs for the painful cancer of which he died was courageous, is not altogether convincing. George Moore (q.v.) treated the same material with considerably more penetration. The interest of Huysmans' novels lies more in the light they cast upon the nature of the aesthetic reaction to positivism than in their account of religious experience. It is his style that betrays him: involute, mannered, as artificial at the end as at the beginning.

The Provençal ÉLÉMIR BOURGES (1852–1925), less talented, was another of those to react against naturalism and the climate from which it sprang. His attempt to elevate man above the gutter of naturalism was Teutonically inspired; but his abilities in the realm of the long novel, which he unfortunately favoured, did not match his erudition or give much scope to his miniaturist's capacity to evoke country scenes and customs. Consequently most of his novels fall grotesquely short of their intended effect. Bourges was less clear-minded than Huysmans, and his project was correspondingly vaguer. He disliked everyday reality, but blamed the naturalists for depicting it without beauty—which he offered as the only avenue of escape. Bourges, as a transcendentalist, was influenced by symbolism, though not very fruitfully. His philosophy is pretentious; but he does have a tiny niche in the French tradition of heroic exultation in the face of malign or indifferent fate (he admired the Greek tragic dramatists). His best novel, a first-class adventure story, is *Under the Axe* (*Sous la hache*, 1885), a story of the Chouannerie—the Royalist insurrections in Brittany and Normandy during the Revolution. This is more straightforward and less ambitious than the long, Wagnerian *The Twilight of the Gods* (*Le Crépuscule des Dieux*, 1884) and *The Birds Fly Away and the Leaves Fade* (*Les Oiseaux s'envolent et les feuilles tombent*, 1893), or the prose-poem on the Prometheus theme, *The Nave* (*La Nef*, 1904–22).

PAUL BOURGET (1852–1935), born at Amiens, was most gifted as a critic, but his novels are not quite negligible even today—and were once very widely read. Bourget, a friend of Henry James's (q.v.), ended as a Catholic fascist and supporter of *Action Française* (q.v.). The ultra-conservative moralist in him was in evidence from the outset; but until his conversion to Catholicism in 1901, and for some years after that, his intelligence remained in control. After some Parnassian (q.v.) verse of no account, Bourget published a series of essays in which he searched various leading literary figures (among them Baudelaire and Stendhal) for the flaw in them that had led to the pessimism he saw all around him. He derived his methods from his study of the critic H. Taine, but this led him to different conclusions from Zola. His first novel of consequence, *The Disciple* (*Le Disciple*, 1889; tr. 1898), condemns naturalism and decadence, and contains self-criticism (Bourget had been a member of the decadent café society called *Les Hydropathes* in the earlier part of the decade). This readable anti-positivist tract describes the malign influence, on a youth's morals, of a dear old determinist philosopher. Bourget is usually called a psychological novelist, and such indeed his approach seems to be; but he was really a conservative dogmatist, a smooth stylist with enough skill to dress his thesis, that France's sickness lay in the betrayal of her traditions, into respectable fictional clothes.

More attractive and more serious as an imaginative writer was RENÉ BAZIN (1853–1932), born at Angers. Bazin's staunch Catholic conservatism may have limited his range as a writer, but it was not tainted with the frenetic and viciously insensitive dogmatism (for all his long concealment of it) of Bourget. Shocked by naturalism, Bazin's sympathy with the humble and oppressed gives him more in common with Zola, for all their difference of approach, than he would have cared to acknowledge. His outstanding novel was not happily titled in its English translation: *Autumn Glory* (*La Terre qui meurt*, 1899; tr. E. Waugh, 1899). This is a melancholy description of the exodus from the Vendée countryside of men tempted by the town; this might have been obscurantist, but, even if the peasants are unreal, it has instead the effect of a series of pictures by Millet, whom Bazin deeply admired. This and *The Children of Alsace* (*Les Oberlé*, 1901; tr. A. S. Rappaport, 1912), on the tragedy of an Alsatian family divided among itself between German and French claims, are certainly conventional; but in these examples of his fiction at least Bazin's eye is on the object and not on polemic.

More substantially gifted and complex was RENÉ BOYLESVE (ps. RENÉ TARDIVEAU, 1867–1926), born in Touraine. His youthful association with symbolists and experimentalists left little mark on his work. His best novel is *Daily Bread* (*La Becquée*, 1901; tr. H. V. Marrot, 1929): a large Touraine household is seen through the eyes of a small boy. This contains a remarkably unsentimental portrait of a tough, dominating old woman. The sequel, *The Child at the Balustrade* (*L'Enfant à la balustrade*, 1903; tr. H. V. Marrot, 1929), deals with the remarriage of the boy's father, and is more comic. Boylesve was one of the best of the provincial novelists, in whose best work there exists a tension between the restrained style and the lyrical content.

ÉDOUARD ESTAUNIÉ (1862–1943), born at Dijon and brought up by Jesuits, was a distinguished engineer as well as a novelist. He chose to put his vitality into his engineering and his melancholy into his fiction. Basically Estaunié resented the impression the Jesuits had left upon him; and in his most famous novel, *The Imprint* (*L'Empreinte*, 1896), he demonstrated with great psychological skill how the effects of such an education were indelible. But this was as far as he ever went in protest; later he even felt obliged to publish a novel—*Le Ferment* (1899)—exposing the dangers of a rationalist education. He was a timid but subtle soul, whose chief unhappiness—to a large extent hidden away in his subconscious—was that he could not be a free thinker. But the Jesuits, a good-looking, possessive and intelligent mother (widowed) and her rigid disciplinarian father standing in for his own, combined to instil into him, early on, a sense of inevitability. He stoically bore the burden of his inability to be free; but developed into an interesting analyst of unhappy men. His later books were not discussed as *The Imprint* was, and have been correspondingly undervalued. Estaunié was too sensitive and too honest to become a preacher of conservatism—and no doubt his engineering success (he became a Commander of the Legion of Honour and received the Belgian Order of Léopold) did his fiction good by relieving him of the burden of literary ambition. Estaunié's subject became secret unhappiness, and his later fiction—almost unknown abroad—will be read again, and reappraised; that of contemporaries more famous in the first decade of the century may not merit further attention. To read such novels as *The Secret Life* (*La Vie secrète*, 1909) or *The Ascension of Mr. Baslèvre* (*L'Ascension de Monsieur Baslèvre*, 1919) as biased towards Roman Catholicism is to miss their real subject: the tragedy of the paralyzed will.

His last novel was *Madame Clapain* (1932). The meticulously observed fiction of this modest but distinguished writer is long overdue for rediscovery.

PAUL ADAM (1862–1920), who once had a wide reputation, possessed literary skill but little mind of his own. He began as a naturalist, soon became a symbolist (and 'decadent': he compiled a glossary to guide readers in the mysteries of 'auteurs décadents et symbolistes') and ended up as a middlebrow nationalist. To call him a forerunner of the unanimists (q.v.) is to exaggerate the powers of his mind: his accounts of collective emotions are more reactionary and sentimental than analytical. But his *The Mystery of Crowds* (*Le Mystère des foules*, 1895), which is about the Boulangist movement (q.v.), may have influenced Romains. Adam was a prolific author given to the production of cycles: the most famous series was called *Le Temps et la vie* (1899–1903), and consists of sixteen novels.

But better known as novelists at the beginning of the century were France, Barrès, Bourget (qq.v.) and Loti. The work of PIERRE LOTI (ps. LOUIS MARIE JULIEN VIAUD, 1850–1923), who was brought up in a Protestant household by a widowed mother and her sisters at Rochefort, will perhaps survive longer than that of Barrès, and as long as that of Anatole France. His fiction represents a reaction to naturalism in the form of regionalism and exoticism. Loti, for all his sentimentality and intellectually feeble vanity, has a residual charm that the socially genial and personally generous Barrès does not possess.

Viaud was a naval officer nicknamed Loti by the Tahitian heroine of his second novel; his first book, *Constantinople* (*Aziyadé*, 1879; tr. M. Laurie, with sequel tr. J. E. Gordon, 1928), set in Turkey, was published anonymously. He then published the autobiographical *Rarahu: The Marriage of Loti* (*Le Mariage de Loti*, 1880; tr. C. Bell, 1890), an account of how he 'married' and then abandoned a Tahitian girl. This combined the exoticism of the far-away with a vague sensuality, all in a musical prose that was then new, but quickly cloyed. Readers liked the wrapped-up sexiness, made legitimate because the girl was a 'savage'. But the book, like nearly all Loti's work, is not quite awful: the melancholy nostalgia and expectation of death that pervade it are genuine emotions. *The Romance of a Spahi* (*Le Roman d'un Spahi*, 1881; tr. M. L. Watkins, 1890) depicts a French soldier's sexual life amongst Senegalese women. Loti's best novels, however, were on Breton fishermen: *My Brother Yves* (*Mon Frère Yves*, 1883; tr. W. P. Baines, 1924), *An Iceland Fisherman* (*Pêcheur d'Islande*, 1886; tr. W. P. Baines, 1924). The second of these, brilliant in its impressionistic descriptions of the countryside of Brittany and of the sea, is a monument to 'pity and death' (as one of Loti's own travel books was called). Loti's best work was done by the time of his admission to the French Academy in 1891, but his subsequent travel books, notable for their ridicule of tourists, are readable. Loti's was an attenuated and egocentric talent at best; and as he became famous, which he did early, his style became too self-consciously *douce* and regretful of the passing of time. But his Debussy-like impressionism and his vision of nature as an agonizingly beautiful commentary on the ephemerality of existence cannot be ignored. At its very best his descriptive prose endows landscapes or the sea with the ecstatic transitoriness of orgasm, which is doubtless what he really—if unconsciously—meant.

The nationalist and anti-semitic MAURICE BARRÈS (1862–1923), who came from Lorraine and was responsible for the cult of it later so skilfully exploited by General de Gaulle, was always a gentleman, and one who charmed his opponents. For him literature was a substitute for action; his self-imposed role was that of educator of his generation. But behind this lay what Gide (q.v.) shrewdly discerned as a 'great anxiety about the figure he cuts'. He wrote, if one includes his posthumously published diaries, over a hundred books. An artificial writer, he had intelligence and even a kind of passion—but behind the charm was no heart, only vanity. His political position is even now some-what ambiguous: one could make out a reasonable case for excluding him from the ranks of the French right. Essentially, perhaps, he was an aloof populist.

Barrès began, like Anatole France, as a detached ironist under the influence of Renan; he maintained this intellectual manner in his style for ever after. But his content is by no means always intellectual, and he quickly abandoned a non-partisan position for a political one: that of *Boulangisme*.

Général Georges Boulanger was regarded as the 'general of the revenge'—against Germany—and for a time he was the figurehead of a semi-populist, militarist and nationalist movement directed against the Third Republic; eventually his nerve failed him, and his movement collapsed.

The Jewish Army Captain Alfred Dreyfus had been sent to Devil's Island for treason in 1894; by 1898 his cause had become that of the radicals, because it was discovered that he was innocent—and that forgery had been used in the case against him; and that, furthermore, since then facts had been suppressed. Dreyfus was not properly rehabilitated until 1906. Meanwhile the affair split France. Barrès had become Boulangist deputy for Nancy at the age of twenty-seven; in 1898, like most other Boulangists, he rallied to the anti-Dreyfusard cause: it did not matter whether Dreyfus was guilty or not: his supporters were international socialists, un-French, trying to cut themselves off from the living past.

Barrès the writer does not deserve the space he gets here; but his ideas, though less extreme than those of Maurras (q.v.), are important to an under-standing of modern French literature. He had begun as a kind of rationalist, and personally remained an unbeliever; but he came to elevate instinct above reason, and to regard nationalism as the fate, so to speak, of all men: men's attempts to uproot themselves can lead only to disaster. Barrès' well-written novels are no more than an illustration of this thesis (which was itself disastrous for France), and because of it they do not achieve, imaginatively, even as much as those of the humbler if equally conservative Bazin (q.v.).

The first trilogy of novels, entitled *The Cult of the Self* (*Le Culte du moi*, 1888–91), portrays Barrès as Philippe, a young man who cannot recognize any reality but that of self. The next trilogy, *The Romance of National Energy* (*Le Roman de l'énergie nationale*, 1897–1902), of which the most important is *The Uprooted* (*Les Déracinés*, 1897), is devoted to a demonstration of the necessity for the solipsistic individual to recognize his oneness with his race and region. Actually this, like all Barrès' subsequent novels, presents a rationalized version of the solipsism of the first trilogy. Barrès had seen his home occupied by the Germans in 1870, when he was eight, and the experience had been traumatic. In his books he either devises means of defence against such occupation (projecting them on to a national canvas), or escapes from the whole problem by going abroad (he was a restless traveller). In *The Sacred Hill* (*La Colline inspirée*, 1913; tr. M. Cowley, 1929) he advocates, although not without confusions, the Catholicism he did not believe in as the only solution for a unified and strong France, incorporating its past and assimilating its 'scientific' future. This, richly written, pulsating with the sort of 'sincerity' practised by statesmen, was almost convincing. At the very end, in the last novel, *A Garden on the Orontes* (*Un Jardin sur l'Oronte*, 1922), he advocated, in a style persuasively serene but faked, a sensuous 'inner' mysticism. Barrès was a bad influence and a bad writer, a polemicist concealing his cruel message under a sometimes bewitchingly 'magical' style. But it is hard not to sympathize with him: a spiritual guttersnipe, his actual books, like his famous courtesy, have a disarming effect. And at the heart of his racist malevolence there lurked the simple fear of the eight-year-old boy who had seen strange conquerors take over his own territory. As Gide said of him, a propos of his theories: 'This is the most touching, most moving thing about Barrès: his obstinate perseverance in the absurd'.

ANATOLE FRANCE (ps. ANATOLE-FRANÇOIS THIBAULT, 1844–1924), winner of the Nobel Prize (1921), son of a Paris bookseller, had until a few years after his death an international reputation far surpassing that of Barrès, and one out of proportion to his achievement; he is now, however, too summarily dismissed unread. There is nothing like as much to be said for him as for another neglected Nobel Prize winner, Hauptmann (q.v.); but there is something. What rightly militates against him, as against Bernard Shaw (q.v.), is his self-indulgent lack of critical rigour and his general air of dilettantism, in which seriousness gives way to elegance. But he was less superficial than Shaw, and more erudite and sensitive.

France began, like Barrès, as a disciple of Renan; he changed less in the course of his life. He retained his scepticism, combining it with a love of French pagan antiquity and a cynically irresponsible surface manner. His early Parnassian (q.v.) verse is important only for the clues it affords to the sensuality underlying this unconcerned persona. Under the influence of a literary mistress and of the socialist politician Jaurès, France developed into a socialist: he was a leading Dreyfusard, a pacifist (he tried to join up, at seventy, in 1914, but this was a temporary aberration in keeping with the spirit of that year) and, at the end of his life, a supporter of the Russian Revolution and the French communist party.

As well as personal reminiscences and *belles lettres* France wrote many novels. They are all marred by bookishness and contrived plots; he was always too much the literary man (his father had a passion for the eighteenth century) to survive in any important sense; but the reasonable enough reaction to him—

Valéry, his successor in the Academy, failed to mention him in his traditional speech of praise—was surely really more to the inflated middlebrow reputation than to the inoffensive works themselves, which are amusing. *The Crime of Sylvestre Bonnard* (*Le Crime de Sylvestre Bonnard*, 1881; tr. L. Hearn, 1891), the story of an old hedonist's capture for himself of the daughter of a former mistress, is pitched at exactly the right level, and can still give pleasure. *The Red Lily* (*Le Lys rouge*, 1894; tr. W. Stephens, 1908) is a notable study of an enlightened woman, and contains a shrewd and valuable partial portrait, in the poet Choulette, of Verlaine. *The Amethyst Ring* (*L'Anneau d'améthyste*, 1899; tr. B. Drillien, 1919) over-indulges France himself but contains memorable and telling caricatures of bishops and of anti-Dreyfusards more stupid than Barrès. *Penguin Island* (*L'Île des pingouins*, 1908; tr. A. W. Evans, 1909) contains some *longueurs*, but is representative of an intellectual's satirical view of emotion- or religion-driven man. France was frivolous, perhaps; but his genuine gift for conciseness should survive his overblown reputation.

Three other novelists, Philippe, Renard and Bloy, are exceptional. CHARLES-LOUIS PHILIPPE (1874–1909), a poor cobbler's son from Bourbonnais, has been curiously undervalued, in spite of the admiration and friendship of Barrès (who personally assisted him by getting him a civil service post), Renard and Gide. Philippe was neither a naturalist nor one who reacted against naturalism; he was instead influenced by Nietzsche (q.v.), Dostoevski, and, in his own country, Renard. He was an original, a painstaking realist who wrote without much conscious artistry—but who achieved that marvellous art which results from the reportage of the innocent eye and the humble heart. It is a pity that he should have been preserved only through a minority cult. *Bubu of Montparnasse* (*Bubu de Montparnasse*, 1901; tr. L. Vail, 1932), his second novel, is one of the most exquisite of all the stories of young man and prostitute with whom he falls in love; it came from his own experience with a girl called Maria, whom he had tried—like his bank-clerk Pierre Hardy—to reclaim from her enslavement to a brutal pimp. It has been called sentimental; but this is a grotesquely unjust charge. One might just as well call the paintings of the Douanier Rousseau primitive. . . . Philippe made no attempt to emulate the Tolstoy of *Resurrection* (q.v.) in Pierre's bid to redeem the girl, as has been suggested. He simply wants her for himself, away from the pimp Bubu; there is no high moral intention—after all, he first meets her when he hires her, and he never has moral thoughts about this. Philippe's fiction has the same rain-washed brightness as the painting of the Douanier Rousseau, and he sees life from a similar kind of perspective. Before this he had written *Mother and Child* (*La Mère et l'enfant*, 1899), the story of his mother and childhood. *Bubu* was followed by *Le Père Perdrix* (1903), *Marie Donadieu* (1904) and *Croquignole* (1906); *Charles Blanchard* (1913), perhaps his masterpiece, about his father's struggles in early life, was left unfinished when he died of meningitis.

Philippe was a 'natural', who complained of the tendency to make the novel 'the pretext for social and psychological studies': 'What is important', he said, 'is the creation of living characters'. Perhaps his greatest achievement, apart from his ability to evoke the pathos of poverty (leading to the aforesaid unfair and snobbish accusations of sentimentality), is the dateless quality of his prose. Despite 'science', life has not changed much since Philippe died in 1909, and *Bubu* could as well happen now as then—it reads like it.

JULES RENARD (1864–1910), born in Châlons-sur-Mayenne but brought up from the age of two in a remote part of Burgundy, was another original: a sharp, clever, sensitive countryman (and yet at home enough in the Paris literary world to be a co-founder of the magazine *Mercure de France*) quite out of key with his time. To try to relate his precise prose, which now has classic status, to any movement of the time is fruitless and misleading. His extreme bitterness reflected his rurally suspicious temperament and concern for creative as opposed to mundane values; but he did not lead or condone the bohemian life. He married in 1888 and from then divided his time between Paris and his old home town of Chitry, of which he was conscientious socialist mayor from 1904 until his death. He is most famous for *Carrots* (*Poil de Carotte*, 1894; tr. G. W. Stonier, 1946), the story of how a country boy bullied by his mother and ignored by his father learns to put a shell around himself. His sourest and finest novel preceded this: *The Sponger* (*L'Écornifleur*, 1892; tr. E. Hyams, 1957) is about a man who takes advantage of a couple's foolish admiration for his literary qualities. This, which is classic in its precision, is the book of an honest man driven to despair by the nastiness and falsity of the bourgeois attitude towards art. He wrote a number of successful plays of the naturalist sort, of which *The Bigot* (*La Bigote*, 1909) is a bitter portrait of his own mother, whose treatment of him may have formed his unhappy temperament. His most original writing is contained in *Hunting with the Fox* (*Histoires naturelles*, 1896; tr. G. W. Stonier and T. W. Earp, 1948), brilliantly concentrated and poetic sketches of country phenomena, mostly animals. Renard was for some time after his death seen as a too affectedly pessimistic writer ('not a river but a distillery', commented Gide); but the publication of his important *Journal* (1925–7) demonstrated that he was a more complex personality than this imperceptive judgement allows for.

The frenetically destructive, impetuous LÉON BLOY (1846–1917) was born in Périgueux in Dordogne of a republican anti-clerical father and a mother of Spanish extraction. He became a Catholic at eighteen, on his first visit to Paris, under the influence of the novelist Barbey d'Aurevilly. From a free-thinker Bloy turned overnight into a fervent and fierce mystic, a man from whom each one of his works—essays, studies, novels and stories—was a confession extracted (he said) by torture. Those who confuse the profession of Christianity with the practice of charity will be more confused by Bloy: although he believed that history was pre-ordained, 'a vast liturgical text', expressing the will of God, he was none the less savagely unkind to those instruments of it that God had pre-destined him to dislike. The vituperative and scatological nature of his attacks was proverbial. But Bloy's writing has a visionary quality; his are not simply the ravings of a dissatisfied and vicious nature. He has unique (and carefully calculated) powers of invective. He was excessive, but possessed absolute integrity. For most of his life he lived in dire poverty. When the racist and proto-fascist Édouard Drumont wrote his attack on French Jewry in 1886 Bloy replied, 'to the glory of Israel', six years later, with a book claiming that the Jews above all provided a testimony of the divine will. However, this may be construed as being anti-semitic in effect, since for Bloy all degradation was glorious. Much of the anger that Bloy directed at the complacency of his times—as well as at naturalists, rationalists and Victor Hugo—made people feel uncomfortable, and he was ignored and ostracized. He castigated his co-religionists—particularly the putative father of Apollinaire (q.v.), Pope Leo XIII, while he lay dying—as he did everyone else.

Bloy's first novel, *The Desperate One* (1886), glorifies Barbey d'Aurevilly, attacks the Establishment and presents Bloy the crusader as Caïn Marchenoir. The saga is continued in *The Woman who was Poor* (*La Femme pauvre*, 1897; tr. W. Collins, 1939). Bloy believed that the world was going to be ended and transformed, and that he had a special role in the transformation. *Pilgrim of the Absolute* (ed. R. Maritain; tr. J. Coleman and H. L. Binsse, 1947) contains much of his best writing.

One other odd man out, very different from Bloy, deserves to be mentioned: JULES VERNE (1828–1905), who was born at Nantes. Verne is frequently omitted from literary histories, but wrongly: although hardly a stylist, and certainly not a 'literary man', his impact on poets and writers has been considerable.

Indeed, the misanthropic and sinister Captain Nemo, and some other of his characters do possess a poetic appeal, even if this is of an adolescent nature. Verne began by writing opera libretti and plays in collaboration with Dumas *fils*, but discovered his métier in his early thirties with *Five Weeks in a Balloon* (*Cinq Semaines en ballon*; tr. 1870). The interest in Verne's stories, many of them set in the future, coincided with the rise of science; but even now, when science is in disrepute with the thoughtful, they are still read. Verne was—like Conan Doyle (q.v.), the creator of Sherlock Holmes—a boy at heart; but an ingenious and inspired boy.

ROMAIN ROLLAND (1866–1944), born at Clamecy in Burgundy, winner of the Nobel Prize (1915), was more important as a socialist and idealist than as a novelist. But he remains a significant figure in the late nineteenth-century reaction against determinism and gloom. He supported Dreyfus, was a pacifist in the First World War—he withdrew to Switzerland—and was a moderate partisan of the Bolshevik uprising. Later he protested against the Munich agreement. His inspiration came mostly from Beethoven—he was a musicologist—and Tolstoy (q.v.), whose condemnation of art (q.v.) he could not, however, entirely accept. Rolland was a fine biographer (Beethoven, Gandhi and others) and a competent playwright. *The Wolves* (1898; tr. 1937) is on the Dreyfus affair. The cycle of ten revolutionary dramas, *The Triumph of Reason*, incorporates the best of all his plays: *Danton* (1900) and *The Fourteenth of July* (1902; tr. B. H. Clark, 1918). Rolland's long novel *Jean-Christophe* (1904–12; tr. G. Cannan, 1910–13), for which he was awarded the Nobel Prize, is now unreadable. It is the worthy study of a musician of genius (a kind of modern

Beethoven), but it remains imaginatively sterile. Rolland failed to understand the problem of evil, and events have not justified his optimism; but he possessed the kind of nobility of which the world is always in need.

II

Few of the so-called 'Parnassian' poets survived into the twentieth century; but it is necessary to begin this survey with the publication, in 1866, of Lemerre's anthology *Le Parnasse contemporain*. This was followed by two more volumes (1871, 1876), and contained poems by Verlaine and Mallarmé as well as by poets actually considered Parnassians. This school, of whom Leconte de Lisle was the acknowledged leader, in certain respects reflected the positivist spirit of the age; it reacted against romanticism and technical freedom, tended towards the art for art's sake (*l'art pour l'art*) that Gautier had advocated in 1836 in the introduction to his novel *Mademoiselle de Maupin*, and evoked exotic foreign cultures. The Parnassians were influenced by the development of archeological studies, by Buddhism (interpreted as a pessimistic religion of acceptance) and by Schopenhauer's philosophy, which is akin to Buddhism, that the phenomenal world is no more than a representation in man's mind. Above all, the ideal Parnassian poem was emotionally restrained, descriptive, often pictorial: in a word, it set out to achieve '*impassibilité*': impassiveness. It was therefore highly artificial. However, more important than any of this was the fact that behind this school of modified romanticism was the all-important figure of Charles-Pierre Baudelaire (1821–67). It is not possible to understand twentieth-century French poetry without knowing something of him and of two others who came after: Arthur Rimbaud (1854–91) and Stéphane Mallarmé (1842–98).

Baudelaire was the first poet of modern sensibility in these respects: he explored, rather than merely sympathized with, or 'excused', what in bourgeois terminology are the 'evil' elements in humanity; he pursued detailed investigations into sexual 'degradation' (his poems were called *Flowers of Evil*, *Les Fleurs du mal*, 1857); he was self-critical; he wrote of the city; he cast the poet in the role of 'dandy', a *persona* at once out of the common run and bizarrely artificial. In other respects Baudelaire was not so modern: his thought, judged simply as thought and not in the context of his poetry, is puerile; sometimes his language and assumptions retain many of the worst elements of romanticism. His essential modernity, however, is revealed in his famous sonnet 'Correspondances'. Here for the first time the poetic possibilities inherent in neo-Platonism were fully realized.

The Enlightenment of the previous century had been brought about in the first place by the apostles of reason, the *philosophes*. But the irrational elements in humanity obstinately remained. Once people had looked to the Church to contain, control and interpret these elements. Now, more doubtfully, they were obliged to look to, among other things, art. The artist suddenly found himself a putatively responsible figure: he was either a priest who could interpret the will of the universe (God), or a prophet who could change the world—or both. Imaginative literature was no longer a commentary within an accepted system.

There was a definite *symboliste* movement in French poetry, dating from 1886. There were also reactions to it, such as the *École romane* and *naturisme* (qq.v.). But to look to the poets and practice of this particularly named school for the essence of symbolism is misleading: the school is long dead, whereas symbolism was with us before it and is still with us. Its essence is contained in Baudelaire's sonnet:

> Nature is a temple whose living pillars
> Sometimes give forth indistinct words;
> In it man passes through forests of symbols
> Which watch him with familiar glances.
>
> Like long echoes which from a distance fuse
> In a dark and profound unity,
> Vast as the night and as the radiance of day,
> Perfumes, colours, and sounds respond to one another.
>
> There are perfumes fresh as a child's skin,
> Sweet as oboes, green as meadows,
> And others, corrupt, rich, triumphant,
>
> Having the expansion of infinite things,
> Like amber, musk, balsam and frankincense,
> Which sing the raptures of the spirit and the senses.
>
> (FBS)

Here the poet is postulated, by implication, as a *seer*, as one who by use of his intuition may unravel the mysteries of the universe: penetrate to the hidden reality behind phenomena. There are 'correspondences' between different sense-impressions (synesthesia), and between *emotion* and *imagery*. This latter is very important, for it gets rid, at a stroke, of the necessity for a logically coherent surface in poetry: it introduces a new range for the responsible poet, even if it lets in charlatans and poeticules. Finally, there are correspondences between appearances (phenomena) and the reality which they conceal.

The view that modern French poetry stems from two aspects of Baudelaire —from the artist, via the Parnassians and Mallarmé to Valéry (qq.v.); and from the seer, via Rimbaud to the surrealists (q.v.)—is of course an over-simplification, but a useful one if not taken too seriously or literally. One line of development emphasizes intellect (Mallarmé, Valéry), the other emotion (Verlaine, Rimbaud, the surrealists).

Arthur Rimbaud (1854–91), the apotheosis of revolt, began as an imitator of the late (and still insufficiently appreciated) Hugo and of Baudelaire. The 'problem' of Rimbaud, who had renounced poetry by the age of nineteen, has not been solved, and will not be. It is enough to say here that it was Rimbaud who called Baudelaire 'the first seer, king of poets, a true God!' and that it was Rimbaud who considered the 'disorder of his senses' 'sacred' (this leads straight into surrealism).

Stéphane Mallarmé (1842–98) was very different. He, too, found Baudelaire as seer a springboard; but where Rimbaud concentrated on a disorder of the senses, he concentrated on the discovery—by means of a highly cerebral and hermetic poetry—of the world of appearances that lay behind phenomena. Baudelaire had defined the painter Delacroix as 'passionately in love with passion and coldly determined to find the means of expressing it'; as Marcel Raymond says in his classic account of modern French poetry, *From Baudelaire to Surrealism*, he 'defined himself at the same time'. And if Rimbaud followed his passion, Mallarmé followed his cold determination: his faith in artistry. Mallarmé's life, as an ineffective teacher of English, was uneventful, although he became increasingly well known after Huysmans' homage to him in *A rebours* (q.v.) in 1884. For Mallarmé poetry was sacred, and therefore an esoteric mystery ('Every holy thing wishing to remain holy surrounds itself with mystery'). He deliberately made his poems obscure, as a defence against vulgarity. It is a common criticism of him that he went too far in this. And yet he wrote 'Le sens trop précis rature / Ta vague littérature' ('Too much precision of sense destroys your vague literature'); the question of his obscurity is not easily settled. He believed that poetry was a sort of magic; his own poetry indisputably casts a spell. Like his successor Valéry, he resisted 'ordinary life'; in his case it filled him with a panic so intense that it may have been pathological. There is nothing as withering as the scorn of children, and Mallarmé's lack of success as a teacher must have influenced him considerably. Certainly he moved away from direct towards suggestive statement; from a 'Parnassian' poetry to one that has itself constituted, for many critics, a definition of symbolism.

Not many of the so-called Parnassian poets are read now. CATULLE MENDÈS (1842–1909), son of a Bordeaux Jewish banker, once a name to conjure with, is now only a part of literary history. Gide, who did not know him personally and was able to observe him closely at a theatre because of this, called him a 'Moloch'. Novelist, playwright and poet, he was too metrically facile and too versatile to write anything worthy of survival. Larger claims are occasionally made for the Parisian SULLY-PRUDHOMME (ps. RENÉ-FRANÇOIS-ARMAND PRUDHOMME, 1839–1907), and not only for the anthology-piece 'The Shattered Vase' ('*Le Vase brisé*') or because of the Nobel Prize he won in 1901. He made a sustained effort to transform his extensive knowledge of science and philosophy into poetry, in a series of optimistic epics, but ended by devoting himself to prose. His initial lyrical gift was in any case so slight that it would have vanished at any provocation. His cult of brotherhood through self-sacrifice, while well-intentioned and backed up by book-learning, was unrealistic.

The best of the Parnassians—better than their leader Leconte de Lisle—is the half-Spanish JOSÉ-MARIA DE HEREDIA (1842–1905), who was born in Cuba. It is true that his only original work, *The Trophies* (*Les Trophées*, 1893), a series of 118 Petrarchan sonnets, does not nearly constitute the history of civilization that he intended; but the sonnets are triumphs of sonorous artificial poetry, of pure artistry, and represent French frigidity and emotional superficiality at its rhetorically most gracious and magnificent. One might with some reason say that he was no poet; but he was a superb craftsman and his rhetoric influenced poets (arguably, Mallarmé).

One likes to, and is probably right to, think of FRANÇOIS COPPÉE (1842–1908), Parisian poet, dramatist and novelist, as a simple soul. In his day 'the poet of the poor' enjoyed enormous prestige; he is now only slightly less unreadable than the Victorian poetaster Martin Tupper. Beginning with sentimental pastiche of Parnassian poetry, he proceeded to a fluent 'plain style' in which he expressed specious pity for the poor. He ended as an anti-Dreyfusard and innocent anti-semite.

LOUIS MÉNARD (1822–1901), another Parisian, is a more interesting figure, since he influenced Leconte de Lisle and through him the whole Parnassian group and beyond, with his ideas of a 'mystical paganism'. His epic poetry is not important in itself; but his search for a humanistic and viable substitute for organized religion that would recognize the importance of the symbolic and the irrational, is intelligent as well as symptomatic of its time.

One of the main features of the symbolist school was a demand for a 'new prosody', that of free verse (*vers libre*), a term that embraces anything from prose to a verse that is only faintly irregular in a strictly metrical sense. The chief theorist of *vers libre* was GUSTAVE KAHN (1859–1936), poet and art critic born in Metz. In France *vers libre* developed from *vers libérés*, which had sought to do no more than free French verse from the strict classical conventions that the Parnassians had reimposed upon it. *Vers libre* sought to free poets from every restriction except a personal rhythm. Kahn made out a responsible and intelligently argued case for this at a time when it was needed. His own verse, in *Wandering Palaces* (*Palais nomades*, 1887), is striking but inchoate; nor, ironically, was he able to free himself as successfully as some other poets from formalistic inhibitions.

Here may be mentioned two Americans who (like the more notable Julien Green, q.v., a novelist, after them) came to regard themselves as French, and wrote French poetry of some technical mastery if not of genius. FRANCIS VIÉLÉ-GRIFFIN (1864–1937) was born in Norfolk, Virginia, but his parents were of French descent and he was educated in France. He was one of the pioneers of free verse, and was a more successful practitioner of it than Kahn. His earlier poems (after a youthful period of 'decadence'), which are permeated with the spirit of the Touraine he loved so much, are his pleasantest; he is always at his best when writing of nature. He saw little evil in the world, but the optimism of his verbose later poems—for all their fluency—is simplistic rather than innocent in the manner of Thomas Traherne.

STUART MERRILL (1863–1915), born on Long Island, was of French descent on his mother's side. He was educated in France, but returned to America to study law and pursue socialism before finally settling in Versailles at the age of twenty-seven. Merrill was a gifted linguist, critic and translator, and he played a considerable part in the French symbolist movement; he was not a poetic genius, and his verse is not much read today except in the large anthologies representing his period. In these he has a rightful place. Like most of the symbolists, he was influenced by the music of Wagner; his poetry experiments not so much with *vers libre* as with 'orchestration' of sounds: assonance, alliteration, vowel-sounds in combination. This elegantly handled but too finely wrought style gave way to an emotionally more substantial one in the collections *The Four Seasons* (*Les Quatre Saisons*, 1900) and *A Voice in the Crowd* (*Une Voix dans la foule*, 1909) which were inspired by socialism and influenced by naturism (q.v.).

The lush, mannered verses of ALBERT SAMAIN (1858–1900), born at Lille, were once the subject of a cult. They were little more than neatly turned Nineties notions of what poems ought to be: sweet, 'classical' (in the worst, artificial sense), and expressing vaguely melancholy longings for a 'romantic' life. Samain was a Dowson (q.v.) *manqué*. The 'sponger' who is taken up by the Vernets in Jules Renard's novel of that name (q.v.) would have been thought of by them as a kind of Samain: a defused poetaster.

The eccentric but unquestionably important SAINT-POL-ROUX (ps. PIERRE-PAUL ROUX, 1861–1940)—called the 'magnificent' because after inaugurating a new kind of poetry called 'l'idéoréalisme' he settled upon another, 'le magnificisme'—in his first poetry sometimes tended to obscure his considerable gifts in too great a welter of matter. He did not share the manner of the symbolists, but had their aim of animating and making apparent the world behind phenomena. Mallarmé referred to him as 'my son'. But before the turn of the century and the advent of Apollinaire, Reverdy, and Saint-Pol-Roux's close friend Max Jacob (qq.v.) he had anticipated the new developments, most particularly the notion—the faith—of the artist as God: as omnipotent creator of his own world. Saint-Pol-Roux is the so-to-speak missing link between the new and what preceded it. He never wrote with ponderousness or conceit, and the resultant, most eloquent mixture of Breton medieval myth and Baudelairian investigation is sweetly readable.

There is more than this to the matter of Saint-Pol-Roux, however, involving a most poignant history. Before he was fifty Saint-Pol-Roux retired to Brittany in disgust with the literary world and disappointed at his failure to achieve recognition. The surrealists organized a noble tribute in 1924, but this made little impression, and he remained in semi-oblivion. He was one of the first to protest, in *Supplication of Christ* (*Supplique du Christ*, 1933), at the Nazis' treatment of the Jews. In 1940 a drunken German soldier entered his house and tried to rape his daughter. Saint-Pol-Roux and his housekeeper went to her aid, whereupon the German began shooting: he badly wounded the daughter and killed the housekeeper. This was embarrassing for the German authorities, and while the old poet was recuperating with friends they ransacked his house and destroyed the work of thirty years: this included the second and third parts of a dramatic trilogy, the first part of which he had published in 1899. He was a legendary figure amongst the surrealists if not amongst the general readers; it is just possible that among what the Nazis destroyed were masterpieces. He was a gentle man, of absolute integrity, who ceased to try to please the literary world at about the turn of the century—hence the oblivion into which he fell. His competence as a commercial or merely fashionable writer is proved by the fact that (clandestinely) he wrote the 'book' for Gustave Carpentier's vastly successful *Louise*. What we have of Saint-Pol-Roux is never less than interesting; what the Nazis destroyed is likely to have been a mass of work at once more humane, humorous and enduring than that of Claudel. This was a true triumph of barbarism. (PBFV4)

JEAN MORÉAS (ps. IANNIS PAPADIAMANTOPOULOS, 1856–1910), a Greek who became an adopted Frenchman, was successively a decadent and a symbolist before founding his own school. (It is his—extremely confused—'manifesto' in the newspaper *Le Figaro* of 18 September, 1886 that marks the launching of the actual symbolist movement.) However, he was never a symbolist in the Baudelairian sense, but rather a highly artificial poet whose search for a pro-gramme was more important to him than any programme itself: the process enabled him to conceal, from himself and others, the inclinations—chiefly the sexual inclinations, whatever these were—of his volatile nature. Moréas was a café-performer, a holder-forth, one who sought emotional stability in a 'posi-tion'; he was more publicist than poet. His earlier poetry is pastiche, but the cultivated work of his last years, *Stanzas* (*Les Stances*, 1899–1920), more austere, is more his own: it concentrates on the processes of avoidance of particular emotions, and is interesting though not appealing. It attempts to freeze an unbearable reality (but Moréas seems to have kept his secret) by imposing upon it a reason, a perfection, that does not exist; but its 'significance and humanity' suggest 'the disorder that preceded it' (Marcel Raymond).

Six months after being acclaimed as a symbolist, Moréas characteristically founded the neo-classical Romance School (*École romane*, 1891), with such fellow poets as CHARLES MAURRAS (1868–1952) and RAYMOND DE LA TAILHÈDE (1867–1938). This was not important in itself, but it represented a certain over-idealistic, classical-Mediterranean element in French verse that has persisted. Romanticism was seen as the corrupting influence on French letters, whose fundamental principle was Graeco-Roman. (The classical principles advocated by these poets had little relation to antiquity.) Moréas hunted for archaic words and imitated Ronsard, but did not produce good poetry; in his own case the project was an attempt to model French literature on the history of Iannis Papadiamantopoulos' evasions of self-knowledge. . . . Maurras became the rabid spokesman of this group, which he characteristically deluded himself into believing had great topical importance. Little need be said here of the Provençal Maurras as a writer; but his failure as a poet may well explain the fanatic rigour with which he pursued his nationalist and monarchist ideals. For most of his life he was stone deaf. In 1899 he founded, with others, *Action Française*; he saw much of its programme put into effect with the setting up of Vichy—which he appeared to imagine had true freedom of action, though he resented the German 'influence'. To Maurras all enemies of French glory and perfection (the Germans, the Jews, emotion) were anathema. Both claimants to the French throne, and the Pope himself, condemned him. He displayed little charity in the course of an unhappy and lonely life, only an aesthetic taste that might, in the absence of anti-romantic bias, have amounted to something. The French President released him from life imprisonment, to which he had been condemned in 1945, a few months before he died. Maurras was a mentally sick man, more obstinate than courageous, a monument to self-delusion whose self-confidence led even his 1945 prosecutor to a mistaken belief in his 'genius'. When he was condemned his comment was that Dreyfus had had his revenge. Maurras is unimportant, but the dream in which he lived—of classical restraint, of a glorious authoritarian France under a king, of the dross of life purified in the fire of the mind and turned to a finite beauty, of the blossom from 'the universal mud'—is an important theme in French literature. This was at once a reaction against romanticism and against the sense of loss it had brought with it, and a means of avoiding the anguish of personal experience—hence Maurras' lifelong admiration for Moréas. Not infrequently this limiting classicism was the result of an envy felt by the creatively feeble or sterile. Maurras, for example, could not express his love of and nostalgia for the ancient with real imaginative power; his skilfully achieved neatness of form is not enough to record this really passionate emotion. And so he erected it into a theoretical principle.

The most gifted poet, albeit a minor one, associated with the Romance School was probably Raymond de la Tailhède; he ceased to adhere strictly to its rules, and his poems became less mannered. He remained an artificial poet, but his later verse has the same kind of interest as Moréas'. (PBFV3) Some critics, however, regard MAURICE DU PLESSYS (1864–1924) as the most gifted of the group. Du Plessys, utterly dedicated to the idea of poetry, was a master of pastiche—in which he wasted much of his gift—whose pathetic life of poverty and sacrifice is almost too good to be true. But occasionally poignant lines shine forth from amongst his voluminous work.

The so-called 'naturist' protest was more immediately significant than that of the *École romane*, and was attended by poets less psychologically crippled. We may locate it most precisely in Charles-Louis Philippe's (q.v.) exclamation, from a letter of 1897: 'What we need now is barbarians. One . . . must have a vision of natural life. . . . Today begins the era of passion'. This was much later quoted with approval by Philippe's friend André Gide (q.v.), who had himself reacted against the inevitable preciosity into which symbolism had declined. Naturism's most important and representative figure, FRANCIS JAMMES (1868–1938), who came from the Hautes-Pyrénées, actually began by publishing a manifesto (one gets used to these in French literature) attacking it and sub- stituting 'le Jammisme': a return to naturalness, truth—and God. The confused manifesto of the poetaster and playwright SAINT-GEORGES DE BOUHÉLIER (ps. STÉPHANE-GEORGES DE BOUHÉLIER-LEPELLETIER, 1876–1947), the initiator of naturism, was less well worked out and more artificial; but what Jammes and those he began by attacking had in common was a fervent desire to return to life itself, life as it is lived; they were ardent for 'real' and not mental experience. In other words, 'naturism' (never under any circumstances to be confused with naturalism) was nothing more than one of those returns of realism, those reassertions of common sense elements, that punctuate *avant garde* movements when they become diffused, or end them when they peter out. Jammes was a naïve (q.v.) writer *par excellence*. He began as a new, clean, instinctive poet, of charming clumsiness and simplicity; the poems of *From the Dawn Angelus to the Evening Angelus* (*De l'angélus de l'aube à l'angélus du soir*, 1898) are indubitably poems of adolescence, but they have a remarkable freshness and earthiness after the life-starved preciosities of the minor symbolists. The following is an exampae, from that collection, of the poetry whose quality Jamme's friend Gide called 'aromatic'.

> I love the memory of Clara d'Ellébeuse,
> pupil in old boarding-schools,
> who on warm evenings used to sit beneath the may
> and read old magazines.
>
> I love no one but her; upon my heart I feel shining
> blue light from her snowy breast.
> Where is she now? Where was my joy then?
> Into her bright room the branches grow.
>
> Maybe she's living still; maybe
> we both were ghosts.
> The cold wind of summers' ends
> swept dry leaves through the manor yard.
>
> Remember those peacock's feathers, in the big vase
> By the ornaments made of shells? . . .
> We heard there'd been a wreck
> And we called Newfoundland: *the Bank*.
>
> Come, come my darling Clara d'Ellébeuse,
> let's love—if you are real.
> In the old garden the old tulips sprout.
> Oh come quite naked, Clara d'Ellébeuse.

This is certainly an original and evocative poetry of nostalgia; but Jammes, who went on to write many novels, and more poems, gently declined into a pious and self-indulgent bore. The values of his sorrowful, early novel, *Clara d'Ellébeuse* (1901: she was one of his several passionate, excitingly chaste heroines) were as pagan as those of the poem quoted above; but Jammes, losing some of his initial energy, his fine innocence shattered by failures in love, drifted from the sphere of Gide's influence to that of the Catholic and morally rigid Claudel (q.v.). This surrender, even if in one sense a logical development and no sudden decision, slowly but surely sapped his creative energy, until little more was left than his delightful habits of observation, his lack of insipidity and his rhythmic prose. He contracted a respectable marriage (1906) and affected a dogmatic rigour that did not really suit him (his best work arose from a state of sexual tension, when he was priapically in pursuit but kept from consummation by being, so to speak, trapped in a frieze); worst of all, he himself subscribed to the legend of the simple, pious man living the village life close to God. People made pilgrimages to see him. And yet the poet in him, repressed, lingered on—just as the hare in his charming and prophetic book *The Story of the Hare* (*Le Roman du lièvre*, 1903) had sighed, in dull heaven, for the adventurousness of his existence on earth. But Jammes left enough behind him to ensure his survival as a poet of greater stature than nearly all his Catholic contemporaries, and as a lively prose writer. Jammes kept clearer too, of authoritarian right-wing politics, the 'Catholic Revival', than any other of his co-religionists.

Also usually classified with the so-called naturists was the over-prolific PAUL FORT (1872–1960), the son of a Rheims miller. He numbered Gide, Moréas, Valéry (with whom he edited the review *Vers et Prose*) and Verlaine among his friends. In 1912 he was elected 'Prince of Poets' by some 400 of his contemporaries; he succeeded the inferior Parnassian Léon Dierx, who had succeeded Mallarmé. He founded the *Théatre d'Art*, later the *Théatre de l'Œuvre* (q.v.), in 1890, in opposition to the naturalist theatre. Fort regarded himself as a *trouvère* (the *trouvères* were the medieval poets of Northern France, influenced by the *troubadours* of the South, authors of the *Chansons de Geste*), a balladeer and modern folklorist. What links him with naturism is his treatment of 'ordinary' subjects. He wrote plays, and was much influenced in his poetry by the spoken word. His verse is free but strongly rhythmic; often he printed it as prose. Fort, as agreeable a poet as he was a man, was essentially another naïve writer; he wrote far too much, but his lyric gifts and sensitivity, combined with his transparent sincerity, saved him from triviality or pretentiousness.

ANNA ELIZABETH DE BRANCOVAN, COMTESSE MATHIEU DE NOAILLES (1876–1933), born in Paris of a Greek mother and the Rumanian Prince Bibesco, gained her title by marriage. 'Quite a great lady,' said the novelist and diarist PAUL LÉAUTAUD (1872–1956), 'but not quite simple enough.' As she grew older she cultivated an affected and fashionable hedonistic paganism, influenced by Nietzsche (q.v.); but her poetry is better than her 'philosophy', and is among the most technically outstanding written by French women. She is at her best in her earlier poems, which express sexual happiness and contain sensitive descriptions of landscape; the pessimism of her later poetry, despite sincerity and her fine rejection of Christian solace, tends to seem forced. She wrote three bad novels, but her autobiography (1932) is of great interest. The earlier work at least is due for reappraisal.

III

In Belgium two languages (Flemish, which is almost identical to Dutch, and French), two literatures, and two races, exist side by side. Here there is a separate section devoted to Flemish literature; the Walloons and those of Flemish and mixed blood who write in French are discussed here.

Modern Belgian literature begins with the launching of *La Jeune Belgique* (1881), edited by Max Waller, and *L'Art Moderne* (1880), edited by Edmond Picard. The groups, which had many members in common, around these magazines were dissatisfied, socialist-oriented young men: their main complaint was that Belgian literature had not received sufficient recognition in the general context of French letters, or established itself as an autonomous entity. Their chief mentor was the novelist and art critic Camille Lemonnier (q.v.), and the senior writer they most admired besides him was Albert de Coster, author of *Thyl Ulenspiegel*. As might be expected, the main French influences upon them were naturalism and Baudelaire and his Parnassian followers (q.v.).

ALBERT GIRAUD (ps. ALBERT KAYENBERG, 1860–1929), not quite accurately described by one authority as a 'man of highly unpleasant nature', was born in Louvain, and was a member of the *Jeune Belgique* group. Like so many Belgian writers of his time, he began by studying law. Giraud, a shy rather than an unpleasant man, affected a haughty aloofness of manner and a coldly precise, colourful style in the manner of Heredia (q.v.). Like Moréas (q.v.), he emphasized style to the detriment of content: his poems are careful to avoid any personal intimacy, and in adhering to the Parnassian ideal of art for art's sake, he was trying to create an art that embraced only form.

The genius of ALBERT MOCKEL (1866–1945), from Liège, one of the most intelligent minds produced by modern Belgium and the most astute and witty critic of his generation, did not come out fully in his poetry. But he as much as any other one man was responsible for turning Belgian verse away from the Parnassian frigidity of Giraud to an intelligent practice of symbolism and relaxed form. He lived in Paris after 1890, returning to Brussels only when war began to threaten in 1937. Mockel was never over-doctrinaire, and his remain the most intelligent claims made for the symbolist movement in itself, even though he tends to overrate individual poets. He wrote the best critical accounts of Verhaeren (q.v.), a sensible book on Mallarmé, and a charming book of *Tales for Yesterday's Children* (*Contes pour les enfants d'hier*, 1908). His poetry is mainly musical, but never pretentious. It was this admirable man who, by the publication of his magazine *La Wallonie* (1886–92), ensured the acceptance of modern poetry in his country.

Vernon Mallinson, the excellent historian of modern Belgian literature, has pointed out that whereas in France the symbolist movement acted as, among other things, a channel of protest against Third Republic drabness and Parnassian perfection of trivia and bourgeois complacency, in Belgium it was both more vital and more native: the Belgian temperament is in itself, one might say, 'symbolist': 'artistic', mystical, aesthetic. One sees this quality to excess in Maeterlinck (q.v.).

CHARLES VAN LERBERGHE (1861–1907), born near Ghent, was at his best when his natural gaiety broke through his delicate, pre-Raphaelite timidity, as in his anti-clerical and anti-bourgeois *Pan* (1906). Otherwise he somewhat resembles his friend Maeterlinck in his vagueness. His most characteristic poetry, *Song of Ève* (*La Chanson d'Ève*, 1904), is a dreamy evocation, in a limpid verse, of woman from primal innocence to the renunciation of paradise. But it has poetic overtones. His play *The Scenters-Out* (*Les Flaireurs*, 1889), a morbid and tense drama of a girl doomed to death, is more powerful; it reveals latent sadism and anti-feminine tendencies. When chased by an Italian girl the fascinated but horrified Van Lerberghe could not bring himself to marry her; unfortunately he never seriously explored the nature of his ambiguous view of women. Nevertheless, his poetry does not mean what it sets out to mean, and is interesting because of this. The tension between the conscious aim and the repressed emotion produces some memorable lines, such as 'All still neglects that we must die' ('Et tout ignore encor qu'il faut mourir'). (PBFV4)

GRÉGOIRE LE ROY (1862–1941) was a lesser poet, but is rightly remembered for his power to evoke landscape—a tradition strong in a country so distinguished for its painters. His unconquerable despair and nostalgia came out pictorially; it is hardly surprising to learn that he tried to become a painter. For a time, exasperated by his 'artistic inactivity', he became a successful business man.

The Catholic MAX ELSKAMP (1862–1931), the wealthy son of a banker who remained for nearly all of his life (except for university studies at Brussels and youthful travels, and the years of the First World War, which he spent in Holland) in his native Antwerp, is a more fascinating poet than any of the preceding. An eccentric, and uninterested in fame, he published his earlier poetry in small privately printed editions illustrated by himself; only in 1898 did he collect them all into the volume *Praise of Life* (*La Louange de la Vie*). In youth he was a gifted athlete. His engravings have quality. Elskamp, a notable student of popular culture who founded an important Antwerp folklore society, is too often dismissed as a 'pious dilettante', an over-delicate Verlaine. It is an understandable judgement; but there is more in his poetry than that. His welding of sophisticated and often complex thought to simple, popular rhythms is not of merely academic interest. This kind of poetry is characteristic of him:

> I'm sad about my wooden heart
> And sadder still about my stones
> And those cold houses where
> On wooden-hearted Sundays
> The lamps eat light.

Elskamp combined the primitive with the metaphysically ingenious in a highly original and new way, and his successors outside Belgium (where he is regarded as a master) have not given him his due. Although he would not travel, Elskamp was no recluse; nor was he a Parnassian perfectionist eager to escape from experience. On the contrary, he was a man of agonized sensibility; a little experience went a great way with him. Nostalgia made the end of his life almost intolerable; but the poems he then wrote, after a long silence, are his most powerful, combining Blakean simplicity with existential anguish in a poetry that yet remains to be fully recognized.

But the most important Belgian poet, the greatest Belgium has ever produced, is ÉMILE VERHAEREN (1855–1916), who was born near Antwerp. Whereas the Nobel Prize winner Maeterlinck is unlikely to be rehabilitated, the best of Verhaeren's poetry will certainly come back into favour. His vehement optimism is often condemned as facile and tiresome; but his detractors have not read him, and attack him for the least important although most strident aspect of his art. He possessed a force, a boldness and a robustness that his Belgian contemporaries lacked. His optimism, fostered in the years before the First World War, may seem over-idealistic to us; but it is a reflection of his enormous creative drive as well as of his guilt and regret at loss of belief in God. Verhaeren, too, was a lawyer. After extensive travel he produced his first collection, *The Flemish* (*Les Flamandes*, 1883). The exuberance of this celebration of modern pagan man produced guilt, a nervous breakdown and a subsequent celebration of monkish life 'as voluptuous as the joyousness of living illustrated in *Les Flamandes*' (Vernon Mallinson): *The Monks* (*Les Moines*, 1886). He now began to produce a more mature poetry, a savage attempt to reconcile his socialist faith in the future with his despair at the erosion of rural life by the growing cities. Verhaeren was in a sense the prophet of industrial doom; but with immense courage, which never modified the squalor revealed by his vision, he went forward to meet it. 'You command your heart's unease by indulging it', he said. This struggle reached its climax in his most ruggedly powerful book of poetry, the immensely influential *The Tentacular Cities* (*Les Villes tentaculaires*, 1895). Although this ends with a statement of faith in science, it is a deeply pessimistic collection, a thrilled and hallucinated account of the desecration of nature by machinery. Unlike his pessimism, Verhaeren's optimism is always, in fact, modified or ambiguous; at times it attains a true nobility. Fatally run over by a railway train at Rouen in 1916, Verhaeren's last words were 'Ma patrie. . . . Ma femme!'; but he meant it, and in the light of his life the words are moving. In this poet lack of irony is a positive strength; and he is one of the very few upon whom Whitman's influence was not fatal. His real voice may be heard in his terrifyingly lucid description of 'The Peasants', whom he loved, in his first book: 'dark, coarse, bestial—they are like that . . . they remain slaves in the human struggle for fear of being crushed one day if they rebelled'. Verhaeren was Flemish, and in him we have perhaps the most powerful literary expression of the Flemish genius, which consists of an almost mystical capacity for redeeming a reality not quite believed in by an unparalleled fierceness of sensuality. (PBFV3).

By comparison, the poetry of FERNAND SÉVERIN (1867–1931), the lifelong friend of Van Lerberghe, is minor; but it is distinctly original in the context of the *Jeune Belgique* group. He shared the common Belgian inspiration of painting, but concentrated upon it exclusively, producing a classical poetry of landscape that is as serenely charming as it is limited.

The novelist CAMILLE LEMONNIER (1844–1913), who was born in Brussels, may reasonably be described as the father of the *Jeune Belgique*. In common with theirs, his inspiration was pictorial; throughout his life he wrote art criticism. Lemonnier, now a too neglected novelist, began as a naturalist (Zola admired his work), but like all the other really gifted naturalists he soon found the theory constricting. He was a thoroughgoing romantic, in spite of his capacity for portraying the brutal and animal passions. He resembles Verhaeren in the loving truth with which he portrays peasants. He wrote nearly thirty novels, most of them eminently readable and intelligent, and many short stories. *A Stud (Un Mâle*, 1881), a non-moralistic account of country life in all its freedom, coarseness and pictorial beauty—the hero is a sexually well-endowed poacher—is more typical than the spate of, technically, more naturalist novels that followed it. The best of his other works of fiction are *Madame Lupar* (1888), a study of miserliness, *The End of the Bourgeois (La Fin des bourgeois*, 1893) and the mystery tales of *The Secret Life (La Vie secrète*, 1898). Few of his successors have been on a level with him.

Also from Brussels was the, at least by comparison, pallid EUGÈNE DEMOLDER (1862–1919), mainly an art critic but also author of three novels. One of these, *The Emerald Road (La Route d'émeraude*, 1899), a recreation of the seventeenth century and the life of Rembrandt, deserves mention because it so aptly if tritely illustrates one of the chief characteristics of Belgian writing: competently executed, it tells its story in vignettes reminiscent of actual pictures.

GEORGES EEKHOUD (1854–1927), from Antwerp, is Lemonnier's only serious rival. At first associated with the *Jeune Belgique*, he broke away when it seemed that the group was tending to make a cult of objectivity. Eekhoud, although his attitudes are not without a nineteenth-century affectedness and tiresomely exaggerated pseudo-romanticism, was essentially genuine in his view of criminals and outcasts as saints. Anarchistic by temperament (his love for the lumpenproletariat ruled Marxism out for him), his lusty vitalism is too inchoate to have really sinister undertones; he has something in common with Gorki (q.v.), but had he lived to read Genêt (q.v.) one may guess that he might have done so with sympathy. His best novel, an uncompromisingly pessimistic tale of the destruction of Antwerp by well-meaning 'modernizers', *The New Carthage (La Nouvelle Carthage*, 1888; tr. 1917), could be called sociologically irresponsible or prophetic—according to how the reader feels about urban progress towards the end of our own century.

LOUIS DELATTRE (1870–1938), a doctor from the province of Hainaut, wrote unpretentious, vivid short stories, dealing with incidents in the lives of patients and friends. These avoid sentimentality by the careful exercise of the Belgian virtue of pictorial exactitude.

ANDRÉ BAILLON (1875–1932), born in Antwerp, is urgently due for re-discovery outside France: for all that he owes to Jules Renard and Charles-Louis Philippe (qq.v.), he was an original who projected his violent quest for himself, which ended in suicide in Paris, into a stream of autobiographical fiction that anticipated its time by some quarter of a century. Baillon had a full and eventful life. His parents died when he was six, and he was put in the care of a pious and cruel aunt. Then he was cheated of all his money by a confidence-man, and so tried to kill himself. After this he was, successively, café-proprietor, writer and chicken-breeder. He wrote his first novel, *Somewhere Myself* (*Moi, quelque part*, 1920), when he was over forty, during the war. It tells of the simple life he had led in a Flemish village earlier in the century, and of how he renounced the literary life. Soon afterwards he went to Paris, where he published the story of his long liaison with a pianist and prostitute called Marie, *History of a Mary* (*Histoire d'une Marie*, 1921). Other of his books describe life in the mental hospital at which he was twice a patient, and give more of his autobiography. He killed himself when his mind seemed to be giving way completely. It is strange that Baillon, a profoundly original writer with a shrewd understanding of human nature, should still be unknown—and untranslated—in the English-speaking world.

The novelist, art critic and short story writer FRANZ HELLENS (ps. FRÉDÉRIC VAN ERMENGEM, 1881), born in Ghent, is another writer neglected outside France. Whereas Baillon remained in a strictly realist tradition, Hellens is at least a fellow-traveller with the surrealists; but he cannot be classified as a surrealist because his prose, as distinct from the situations in his fiction, clings to a common-sense coherence—as an editor of poetry he resisted surrealism in the Twenties. Hellens conveys in his writing his sense of unreality as he passes through life; for him dreams are truer than life. This feeling of un-reality stems partly from Hellens' feeling of uprootedness: he is a man of pure Flemish extraction who was educated entirely in the French tradition. His fiction describes the impingement of the medieval past of architecture and paintings, and the world of dreams, upon mundane modern reality. *Nocturnal* (1919), in which his mature technique first appears, is an account of a series of dreams. Hellens does not begin with a mystery and then proceed to explain it; he does just the opposite, taking delight in demonstrating the inexplicability of the apparently obvious. His most famous work, *Mélusine* (1920), which features Merlin and Charlie Chaplin (under the name of Locharlochi), was written in a trance that lasted several months. *Eye of God* (*Œil-de-Dieu*, 1925) is also about a Chaplin-like figure. This may remind us of another Belgian, Henri Michaux's (q.v.), obsession with Chaplin—and of his character Plume. Hellens' most characteristic title is the collection of short stories called *Fantastic Realities* (*Réalités fantastiques*, 1923). His strangest and most powerful, however, is *Moreldieu* (1946), in which he creates a repulsively fascinating and squalid criminal called Marcel Morel, and describes his project, which is to be equal to God. This is a highly original book, which in many respects anticiqates and outdoes the *nouveau roman* that came just after it. Hellens was the moving-spirit of a group that in 1937 declared against the regionalism of Belgian writing on the grounds that this was keeping it out of the mainstream of European literature. His own work has certainly not been regional; and like Baillon's, it is hard to see why it is not better known outside Belgium. Mervyn Peake's fantastic novels have had great success in England since his death, but such a work as *Moreldieu* immediately exposes their dependence upon a rather undistinguished whimsicality. Hellens' work is important because it has seized upon that unmistakably Belgian quality of poetic awareness of the unknown that we find in Maeterlinck, and has tried to purge it of its vagueness. His influence on the development of Belgian poetry is discussed below.

CHARLES PLISNIER (1896–1952), from Hainaut, was another writer who began as a lawyer. He was at first a Trotskyite, but abandoned politics for literature in the early Thirties. The main theme of his fiction, however, remained destructive criticism of bourgeois institutions, particularly the family. His first novel, *Nothing to Chance* (*Mariages*, 1936; tr. P. Morris, 1938) is tendentious— but perhaps ironic; one of the faults is that this is not clear—in plot, but deadly accurate in its exposure of the hypocrisy of the religious and social sides of marriage. Plisnier's next novel, *Memoirs of a Secret Revolutionary* (*Faux-Passeports*, 1937; tr. G. Dunlop, 1938) won him the Prix Goncourt and led him to settle in Paris. Just as *Nothing to Chance* had anticipated the psychological novel of family life, so this anticipated the fiction of disillusioned communism. It consists of five separate narratives by five communists expelled from the Party for Trotskyist deviationism. The fervour with which they embrace their creed is religious in its intensity; and some of their sacrifices of outward appearance to attain inner grace remind one of those made in Graham Greene's (q.v.) novels. Plisnier next brought out a *roman-fleuve* in five volumes under the title of *Murders* (*Meurtres*, 1939–42); this is an intensive study of the effect of a capitalist economy on personal and family life. It contains much detailed description of bourgeois corruption, but is essentially a *roman à thèse* in that the hero and heroine are seen passing through various phases before achieving the state of Christian (Catholic) communism to which Plisnier now aspired. It was filmed with Fernandel and the young Jeanne Moreau in 1950. Plisnier failed to reconcile the aggressive anarchist and the pious lover of God in himself. His figure of the mediating, ever-loving mother, which appears in his fiction and his poetry, is mostly sentimental wishful thinking. But he will be remembered as an at times powerful chronicler of modern family life, and as an acute investigator of the effect of capitalist *mores* on the hearts of men. His style unfortunately became progressively more tedious.

Belgium has made a distinctive contribution to the French theatre through its special—and once again, pictorial—perspective of distortion and hallucination. The elements of the theatre of the absurd (q.v.) have always lain dormant in Belgian (and Flemish) drama; even its realism is so Gothic as to be distorted, its farce mirthless and grimly cruel. One of those seeking new forms in which to express the Belgian genius was Lemonnier (q.v.), with his 'tragic farce' and pantomime, *Death* (*Le Mort*, 1894). This tendency was finally established in Van Lerberghe's full-length *Pan* (q.v.) in 1906.

We must now consider the Belgian writer who achieved the widest international fame (and the Nobel Prize in 1911): MAURICE MAETERLINCK (1862–1949), born in Ghent. He was yet another who gave up the law for literature. He began as a poet, with *Hothouses* (*Serres chaudes*, 1889), but it was his never-performed play *La Princesse Maleine* (1889; tr. G. Harry, 1892), hailed by the playwright, novelist (he wrote the sharp, humane *Diary of a Chambermaid*, *Le Journal d'une femme de chambre*, 1900; tr. D. Garman, 1966) and critic OCTAVE MIRBEAU (1850–1917) that made his name. This was heralded as the breakaway from naturalism that everyone had been awaiting; Maeterlinck was indeed fortunate to have written it at the right time. He did not look back for twenty years.

Maeterlinck's early poetry, much of it in free verse and much influenced by Whitman, came to be very influential—Yeats, Rilke, Hofmannsthal, Edward Thomas and Eugene O'Neill (qq.v.) were amongst his keen readers. Certainly these poems, ultimately derivative like all Maeterlinck's work, now seem to us sickly and affected: listless, falsely morbid, repetitive. But the free verse is effective, and the emotions—derivative though they may be—are genuine enough.

Maeterlinck's later successes include *Pelléas et Mélisande* (1892; tr. L. A. Tadema, 1895), one of the most oppressive plays ever written, made by Debussy into an opera that unlike its original has survived, and *The Blue Bird* (*L'Oiseau bleu*, 1908; tr. A. T. de Mattos, 1909), an optimistic and charming crib of Barrie's *Peter Pan* (q.v.) that won him the Nobel Prize and was popular until the outbreak of the Second World War.

Maeterlinck began in fashionable (but true) fear and ended in false (but sincere) peace. Like Macpherson with *Ossian*, Maeterlinck with his plays struck a European mood. He was a modest and retiring man, who would have been quite content to remain the minor writer he in fact was. His death-haunted early work attracted and pleasantly scared those who were exhausted by scientific materialism; the optimistic fake mysticism of his later phases, which embraced spiritualism and pseudo-scientific meditations on ants, bees and aspects of nature, delighted middlebrows as 'deep', and conclusively demonstrated that Maeterlinck's responses to his age were inadequate.

The early Maeterlinck did not have to affect a symbolist way of looking at things, for this was the way he actually saw them. People, he believed, were at the mercy of a mysterious destiny, and this destiny was their unknown life. Parallel to it was the 'ordinary' world, which in his early theatre he depicts as interpenetrated by this pagan mystery. *The Sightless* (*Les Aveugles*, 1890; tr. L. A. Tadema, 1895) is typical: the guide of a group of blind people suddenly drops dead, and they (humanity?) are left to grope in terror until they meet a stranger—death. It is certainly jejune; and yet its mood has not yet passed. The 'message' is the same as that of Beckett's *Waiting for Godot* (q.v.). Maeterlinck's best play, curiously enough, did not come until 1918, and was written out of his sense of rage at German atrocities in the First World War: the

German brutality in *Le Bourgmestre de Stilemonde* (1919; tr. A. T. de Mattos, 1918) is fairly and truthfully portrayed, and the characters have psychological depth.

Maeterlinck was at his best when communicating an atmosphere of human terror at the true nature of destiny; when he essayed to explain this destiny in any detail he became a second-rate exploiter of silence, mystery and cheap *frisson*; when he tried to invent consolations he became third-rate. His voice will not speak to any succeeding generation, but it spoke strongly to his own.

Although some of the important modern Belgian playwrights—notably Crommelynck, Ghelderode and Soumagne (qq.v.) were born before 1900 and had work performed in the early years of the century, their mature work does not date from before 1920, and they will accordingly be discussed in the later section devoted to more recent Belgian literature. There were several commercially successful dramatists as well as Maeterlinck; but probably no better play was written than Verhaeren's powerful though over-romantic and stylized *The Cloister* (*Le Cloître*, 1900; tr. O. Edwards, 1915), the best of his five dramas; this strongly characterized and well-structured play is still effective to read, although it would probably not stand stage revival.

IV

The history of modern French drama begins with the actor André Antoine (1858–1943), originally a Paris gas clerk, the founder and director of the *Théâtre Libre*. It was Antoine who gave the predominantly naturalistic playwright Henri Becque (1837–99) his first chance, and later EUGÈNE BRIEUX (1858–1932), who was born in Paris. Brieux was a typical dramatist of the turn of the century, and enjoyed a vogue in Great Britain, where he was over-praised by Shaw (q.v.). He was a 'problem playwright', and his plays—of which *Damaged Goods* (*Les Avariés*, 1901; tr. J. Pollock in *Three Plays*, 1911), a competent crib of *Ghosts* (q.v.), on the ravages of hereditary venereal disease, is the most famous—became increasingly didactic. Less ambitious and more important was GEORGES COURTELINE (ps. GEORGES MOINEAUX, c. 1858–1929), born at Tours, many of whose later plays were put on by Antoine at the *Théâtre Libre* and its successor the *Théâtre Antoine*. Courteline's many farces have their origin in the popular music-hall sketch, many of whose later techniques, however, he actually anticipated and perhaps influenced; but there is an undercurrent of savagery and malice—always informed by intelligence—running through his work that gives it stature as literature. He is superior to another author of farces, much performed today, GEORGES FEYDEAU (1862–1921), whose manipulative technique is beyond question brilliantly elegant, but who has nothing whatever to say, and the resemblance of whose work—in its sheer craziness—to some modern drama is accidental. Nor is Courteline so far behind Alfred Jarry (q.v.) as the present vogue for the latter would suggest.

Courteline's comic characters, although conceived as types, do achieve a life of their own; he is an accurate observer of manners, not content merely to raise a laugh, but intent on doing so by isolating and ridiculing a habit. He sees, within the strict and modest limits he set himself, as clearly as any writer, how conventions—from the loose ones of marriage to the rigidly enforced ones of military life—distort the human in people. Hence his brutality—which is not a whit too intense. *The Bureaucrats* (*Messieurs les ronds-de-cuir*, 1893; tr. E. Sutton, 1928) are prose sketches worth reviving. His most famous plays are *Boubouroche* (1893), an archetypal cuckold figure comparable to Ben Jonson's Kitely in *Every Man in His Humour*, or Crommelynck's Bruno in *The Magnificent Cuckold* (q.v.), *Peace at Home* (*La Paix chez soi*, 1903; tr. V. and F. Vernon, 1933) and *Lidoire* (1892).

ALFRED JARRY (1873–1907), born at Laval in Mayenne, was one of those iconoclasts whose ideas, a generation or two after they fail with one public, are taken up by a new public—and even become commercially successful. He inherited his genius for the absurd from an unstable, brilliant mother. The germ of *Ubu Roi* (1896; tr. B. Wright, 1951) was a play written, mostly by Jarry at the age of fifteen, to ridicule a pompous schoolmaster. This master, Hébert, had been nicknamed Hébé by successive generations of boys—and this got transformed into Ubu. So Père Ubu, hero of *Ubu Roi* and other of Jarry's works, originated—like a good deal of anti-bourgeois humour—in the subversive fun of intelligent schoolboys. Although *Ubu Roi* ran for only two performances at the *Théâtre de l'Œuvre* (q.v.), it brought him notoriety—and the admiration of Yeats (reluctant: 'After us the Savage God'), Mallarmé, and Renard (qq.v.), who were present. When Jarry was not posturing in cafés he wrote more, and founded the College of Pataphysics (see below); but he ruined his health with absinthe-drinking, and died aged thirty-four.

Jarry's undoubted importance as a forerunner of dada (q.v.) and surrealism (q.v.)—and incidentally of such commercial phenomena as the profitable pseudo-surrealism of the Sixties—has led many critics to exaggerate his individual importance. Creatively he never grew up; his role is rather one of a culture-hero than an important author in his own right. He was rightly important to the surrealists; but need not be as important to us. He is not a hero of literature, but of the politics of literature—and of nonconformity. For most of Jarry's 'absurd' utterances are merely private, oblique expressions of his unhappy sadism, emotional inadequacy and misogyny. The fact that he made these utterances is more important than their intrinsic content, for ultimately we judge a writer's value by the quality, the integrity, of his attempt to come to terms with the existence of himself and others. Jarry's *Ubu Roi*, and its successors featuring the same gross hero, clever though they are, fail miserably by such standards. And Jarry himself took on the personality of his creation, adopting the pompous manner—until the mask became the face of the wearer. As far as *Ubu Roi* itself is concerned, one must accept David I. Grossvogel's judgement: 'the truth apparently lay in the revelation of a rather pathetic figure, a wizard of Oz amplifying his own fractious voice through the sound-box of what were to have been masks larger than life'.

Jarry spent the remaining eleven years of his life acting out his Ubu fantasy in private and in public (some of the successors to the first play are translated in *Selected Works*, 1965). But he did find time to write what is by far his best book, a brilliant short novel called *The Supermale* (*Le Surmâle*, 1902; tr. B. Wright, 1968). Enthusiasts taken up with Jarry's capacity for anticipating the future have failed to see that this cruel tale of a machine that falls in love with its creator is an indictment of his own loveless life and solipsism.

Another game of the absurd that Jarry lived out in his own life was his College of Pataphysics—whose members today include Queneau, Prévert and Ionesco (qq.v.). Pataphysics was originally what Ubu professed himself to be a doctor of; but Jarry took this over from him, too. He defined pataphysics as 'the science of imaginary solutions, which symbolically attributes the properties of objects, described by their virtuality, to their lineaments' (cf. expressionism). It is only by a knowledge of pataphysics that Jarry's own transformation into Ubu, the personification of all the bourgeois vices which he loathed, may be explained—a tribute to its sense but not its warmth as he practised it. But Jarry is an important link between the old and the new.

The reaction to conventional or naturalist drama, and the skilful but lifeless 'well made' plays of VICTORIEN SARDOU (1831–1908), came, as we have seen, with Maeterlinck (q.v.). Another and rather different playwright was EDMOND ROSTAND (1868–1918), who was born in Marseille. Rostand intensified the reaction, but is a somewhat curious case: his *Cyrano de Bergerac* (1897; tr. H. Wolfe, 1937) is still a favourite, and is performed by reputable companies. But, like all his drama, it is anachronistic, a throw-back to late romanticism. Rostand, who was genuinely witty, was also unfortunately superficial, sentimental and often vulgar. His glitter is really his only true quality: fun for an evening, but embarrassing if not soon forgotten. It was apt that his Cyrano, the story of the huge-nosed, self-sacrificing, romantic swordsman, should have been translated by his English counterpart, the sickly-sentimental but skilful and witty poetaster (once immensely popular) Humbert Wolfe (q.v.). The play, his best, survives mainly because it provides a marvellous role for an actor. Rostand's other two notable plays are *The Young Eagle* (*L'Aiglon*, 1900; tr. B. Davenport, 1927), on Napoleon's son, the so-called Duc de Reichstadt, who was played by Sarah Bernhardt, and *Chantecler* (1910; tr. H. D. Norman, 1921), which is his most ambitious attempt to break away from stultifying theatrical convention. Rostand's *kitsch* fluency and vulgar artifice are fatal to his better intentions.

However, the giant of the French theatre of this time, whose works have only become really well known in the last quarter of a century, is the diplomat, Catholic and poet PAUL CLAUDEL (1868–1955), who was born in a small village in the Tardenois, between Ile-de-France and Champagne. His recognition was delayed not only because his diplomatic career (he eventually became a French ambassador to Japan, America, and Belgium) isolated him from his country but also because he was unfashionable—and his dramas were desperately hard to produce. One problem of assessing Claudel lies in the fact that he has become identified with his religion: critics tend to like or dislike him according to whether they like or dislike Catholicism. Another is that he was in certain respects a repellently intolerant man, who remorselessly quarrelled with those who would not agree with him. His political opinions were unpleasant (though he was not an anti-semite or a supporter of Hitler); nor can he be cleared, for all his apparently intransigeant rectitude, of charges of opportunism. In 1940 he wrote an atrocious ode welcoming Pétain ('Lift up your eyes and see something great and tricoloured in the heavens!') which reflected not only his warm approval of Vichy but also his desire to get Pétain's old job of Ambassador to Spain. In 1944 he wrote another equally effusive ode welcoming the arrival of Pétain's enemy de Gaulle. But there is more in his work than in the attitudes he revealed in his life. And even if his lack of humour and his pomposity ultimately keep him from the ranks of the most outstanding writers of the century, he can hardly be called a minor. As a playwright and poet sure of his Catholic mission his integrity was absolute. Inevitably, of course, it is to Catholics that he must appeal; that is as he would have wished. A Freudian interpretation would put the other side of the case—but this could not diminish the power of the work.

Claudel had a run-of-the-mill Catholic education, lost his faith, then regained it as the result of a mystical experience in Notre-Dame when he was eighteen. This was owed in large part to his reading Rimbaud's (q.v.) *Les Illuminations*, through which he claimed to have discovered the meaning of the supernatural. He learned from Mallarmé (q.v.); but for Claudel the mystery that poetry tried to decipher was always God's; to Rimbaud's and Mallarmé's teaching he added that of St. Thomas Aquinas. From this point, reached in his early thirties, he did not (unusually for a major writer) develop; he merely added. A large proportion of his creative work, especially poetry, was written before he was forty; he spent his last twenty-five years on biblical exegesis (whose value and validity only a minority, and this Catholic, will wish to establish).

Most of Claudel's plays were considerably revised; not so that they should succeed in the theatre, but so that they should express his meaning more clearly—this makes him, as a playwright, almost unique. In the end it was the stage that had to come to him. . . . The success of his old age began with the production by Jean-Louis Barrault (q.v.) of his last epic play, written between 1919 and 1924, *The Satin Slipper* (*Le Soulier de satin*, 1929; tr. 1931) at the Comédie-Française in late 1943. Previously he had scored theatrical hits abroad with *The Hostage* (*L'Otage*, 1911) and *The Tidings Brought to Mary* (*L'Annonce faite à Marie*, 1912; tr. 1927); the former had been produced at the Comédie-Française in 1934, and might be said to signal the beginning of his acceptance, though not his success, in his own country. His most personal and powerful play, *Noontide* (*Partage de midi*, 1906), 'written with my blood', was performed privately in 1916 but not publicly until 1948. This concerns a woman, Ysé, and her husband and two lovers—one of whom is Mesa, undoubtedly a repre-

The Coiners (*Les Faux-Monnayeurs*, 1926; tr. D. Bussy, 1950), Gide's only novel according to his own criteria (the others he called *récits*), is among other things a clever book—so clever that the majority dismiss Gide's own claim that it matches the untidiness of life, and accuse him of artificiality. Gide (a highly accomplished amateur pianist) was much influenced by musical structure in its composition. *The Coiners* consists of a number of themes but is mainly concerned with a group of young men around the novelist, Édouard, who is writing a novel called *The Coiners*. The plot is carefully and ironically melodramatic: one may interpret it, as one may interpret life, as having a complex pattern or having none at all. *The Coiners* is still a source book for novelists, and it antici- pates many of the later developments in the novel. *The Coiners* lightly and good- manneredly demonstrates the consequences of living a forged life: not a popular message in an age when to be rated at all, in almost any field, is to be distorted into a puppet manipulated by publicists. . . . *The Coiners*, for all its fame, has not had its critical due; but one suspects that in this case the balance is restored by a continuing, wide and understanding readership.

The prolific Gide can be guilty of inflating the trivial by apeing the classically profound (in some of his drama, to some extent in *Corydon*, and in the *récit Thésée*, 1946). Other of his work is undernourished as the result of an excess of narcissism. But his best writing (and the *Journals* as well as *The Coiners* must be included among this) has a vitality and subtlety that still joyfully and teasingly eludes the solemn or censorious.

MARCEL PROUST (1871–1922), born at Auteuil, the son of a Jewish mother (the centre of his existence—though she died in 1905—from birth to death) and a distinguished doctor (who invented the phrase '*cordon sanitaire*'), is regarded by some as the greatest writer of the century, and by all as one of major importance. Proust suffered from chronic asthma from the age of nine, but he did a year's military service (1889–90) and was a well known society figure and entertainer until the early years of the century, when he withdrew from the world into the famous cork-lined room on Boulevard Haussmann (1907) to devote himself to his seven-volumed, unfinished novel, for which we now know —his contemporaries did not—he had been preparing since youth: in his translations from Ruskin, his elegant *Pleasures and Regrets* (*Les Plaisirs et les jours*, 1896; tr. L. Varese, 1950), with its preface by Anatole France (q.v.), in his unfinished novel *Jean Santeuil* (1952, tr. G. Hopkins, 1955) and in the critical and introspective studies of *By Way of Sainte-Beuve* (*Contre Sainte-Beuve*, 1954; tr. S. T. Warner, 1958). *Remembrance of Things Past* (*A la recherche du temps perdu*, 1913–27; tr. G. K. Scott-Moncrieff, 1922–5; last vol. tr. A. Mayor, 1970) is the collective title of his life's work. He published the first volume, *Swann's Way*, at his own expense in 1913, but it did not do well, largely owing to the war. But in 1919 *La Nouvelle Revue Française* brought out the second volume— Proust's reputation having gradually grown—and Léon Daudet, son of Alphonse Daudet and an anti-semite and, later, collaborator with the Nazis, saw to it that this ex-Dreyfusard half-Jew received the Prix Goncourt. For the last three years of his life Proust was famous. He would spend much of his time in bed, in a fur coat, writing, going out only at night, to gain material for his work. He was a genuinely sick man who used his sickness to protect himself and (as Gide observed) his writing. He was also a helpless victim of neurosis, caused largely by the homosexuality that dominated his nature but which he could never, although he indulged in it, accept. He was inordinately sensitive, often radiantly kind; but he could indulge in sadistic viciousness, as when he had rats beaten and stuck with hatpins, a procedure the viewing of which brought him to orgasm. However, there is comedy and robustness in his writing, which was the result of a determination not at all delicate, sickly or precious— but, on the contrary, remarkably tough. It was in art that Proust realized himself. Like Flaubert, and like many of his successors, he believed that art was the only real universe.

The narrator of *Remembrance of Things Past* is called Marcel; he resembles Proust in being neurotic, sensitive and asthmatic, but he is neither half-Jewish nor homosexual (a feature that leads to certain confusions and distortions, though some argue that these can be satisfactorily untangled). Almost everyone of importance or interest in the Paris society of Proust's time is involved in *Remembrance*; but no character 'is' a real person. Even the homosexual Baron de Charlus, besides being modelled on the poetaster Comte Robert de Montesquiou (who also served Huysmans for Des Esseintes, the hero of *Against Nature*, q.v.), combines traits exhibited by several other notables. Proust was well aware that he was creating an illusory world on paper, rather than providing a description of a real one. But he believed the fictional was superior to the real, since (as Aristotle said of poetry) 'its statements are of the nature of universals'.

The discovery that *Remembrance* made for its author, and makes for its readers, is that all our pasts remain within us, capable of rediscovery. Proust's famous example is how the taste of a cake dipped into a cup of tea awakens an involuntary memory that expands like the ripples from a stone thrown into a pond. Like the important romantic philosopher Henri Bergson (q.v.), Proust returned to 'the immediate data of consciousness'—not for philosophical purposes but because he sought to perfect, through art, a life he found agonizing. Thus, as he lay dying he tried to perfect a passage in his novel describing the death of the novelist, Bergotte.

Had Proust not been a brilliant stylist he could hardly have prevented such a mass of analytical material from being boring; but although he is frequently abstruse, he is never abstract: all the processes he describes are the stuff of life. He can be criticized for some boring passages, especially those in which he dwells for too long on social rank. Again, it is likely that homosexual love is emphasized at the expense of (to avoid the tendentious term 'normal') heterosexual. Nevertheless, *Remembrance* is indisputably one of the world's paramount novels. It will be read long after Proust-worship, which is often tiresome, snobbish and uncritical, has passed.

The French produced surprisingly few distinguished war novels. An exception was provided by HENRI BARBUSSE (1873–1935), who was born near Paris, with *Under Fire* (*Le Feu*, 1916; tr. F. Wray, 1917). Barbusse had originally been an unsuccessful writer. He began as a fashionable and bad poet—a protégé of Catulle Mendès (q.v.), one of whose daughters he married. His fiction made so little impression that he had to earn his living as a journalist. At the outbreak of war, though ill, he joined up in an access of the patriotic feeling from which almost everyone else in France (and Great Britain and Germany) was suffering at the time. Like Sorley, Sassoon, Owen and other English writers, he quickly became disillusioned. *Under Fire* is the story of a doomed squad of men and their corporal in the perpetual winter of the trenches. The book convincingly shows men as exploited creatures fighting a war that can in no way benefit them. No French literature of the time so closely matched, in mood, the German left-wing and pacifist expressionism (q.v.). *Under Fire* was enthusiastically received in Geneva. After the success of this, Barbusse's earlier *Inferno* (*L'Enfer*, 1908; tr. J. Rodker, 1932) was revived: this was a naturalist work, a series of Zolaesque *tranches de vie* that often display the lucid power with which Barbusse was to depict the filthy and squalid side of war in *Under Fire*. *Light* (*Clarté*, 1918; tr. F. Wray, 1919), another war book, was militantly socialist; from this point Barbusse became a propagandist rather than a creative writer. *Under Fire* remains the best direct account, in French, of the life of ordinary men in the trenches; by comparison the war tetralogy of MAURICE GENEVOIX (1890), collected in one volume under the title of *Those of Verdun* (*Ceux de Verdun*, 1915)—good straight reportage though it is—is pale. Genevoix, however, went on to write some good regional novels (about the Nivernais), of which the best known is *Raboliot* (1925), which won the Prix Goncourt. ROLAND DORGELÈS (ps. RENÉ LECAVELÉ, 1886), originally a humorous writer, wrote a highly successful imitation of *Under Fire* in 1919, *The Wooden Crosses* (*Les Croix de bois*; tr. 1921), but avoided Barbusse's impassioned grimness.

The Burgundian COLETTE (ps. SIDONIE GABRIELLE COLETTE, 1873–1954) remains an essentially *fin de siècle* writer, but a versatile and subtle original of undoubted stature. All her values and interests stem from the Bohemian Paris of her youth: nostalgia, the cult of youth and regret, a relaxed attitude towards morality. Colette was a writer of more range than is usually acknowledged: she could subtly trace the progress of moods in young people, evoke the urban life of the *demi-monde* (she was herself a dancer and mime for some years after her first divorce in 1906) and describe the countryside—landscape, animals, birds and flowers—with meticulous ease. Her first books, the Claudine stories, were written under the direction of her husband Willy, who signed them himself. *The Vagabond* (*La Vagabonde*, 1911; tr. E. McLeod, 1954) is basically her own story. *Chéri* (1920) and its sequel (*La Fin de Chéri*, 1926; both tr. R. Senhouse) form the exquisitely told story of a young man's love for a woman of fifty, and of his gradual decline. *Duo* (1934) is a study of a marriage destroyed and a man self-destroyed by jealousy. *Gigi* (1944), impeccably observed and unsentimental, gained fame as a sentimental film.

The two chief criticisms of Colette have been that her identification with nature is falsely sensuous, or even gushing, and that she is really no more than a woman's magazine writer with a superior style. It is true that when writing of her country childhood she occasionally slipped into sentimentality, and equally true that the material of her novels (which draw greatly on her own experience) is concerned with sentimental and weakly 'romantic' people. But she herself is not sentimental. Although no moral lens distorts her vision of them, her tracery of her characters' moods and caprices and deeper longings has the effect of sharp analysis. Although as a character in her novels she may be sentimental, she is not so as writer. She brings instinctive (not intellectual) female wisdom to the novel; with this she enchants it (as in her autobiographical writings, dealing with nature and animals) or brings to it a glowing tolerance of the unchecked life of instinct. Her exquisite libretto for Ravel's opera, *The Child and the Spells* (*L'Enfant et les sortilèges*) is characteristic, and is one of the most beautiful and tender children's stories ever written.

RAYMOND ROUSSEL (1877–1933), born in Paris, was a rich and leisured eccentric who, because he anticipated them in so many ways, was taken up by the surrealists (q.v.) in the late Twenties, and then again by the exponents of the *nouveau roman* in the Fifties. After having had initial ambitions, Roussel had no interest in fame or fashion, and wrote for himself alone. He suffered from mental illness—his case was described in print by his doctor, Pierre Janet, in 1926—and spent his time travelling the world but not looking at it. Rather, he laboured to construct his own world on paper. This world seems—on the psychological level—to amount to an attempt to construct a denial of reality. The mechanics of Roussel's paranoia are of extreme interest; but he is not always successful in holding the attention of the reader. However, this is the kind of self-defeating process that attracted—and not foolishly—the surrealists and others; it makes him important as an influence. Furthermore, an understanding of his state of mind and intentions in his best works makes them more accessible. However, his procedures, some of them phonic, render him well nigh untranslatable into English, although what has been done has been done well. He was influenced by a host of diverse writers (for example, Verne, Loti, qq.v., Dumas *père*) but exploited these rather than viewed them critically.

Roussel wrote two novels in verse: *The Understudy* (*La Doublure*, 1896), a projection of himself as a failed actor making his masked way through the Carnival of Nice (life), and *The View* (*La Vue*, 1901), and several wildly antitheatrical plays (which, though they were derided, he could afford to put on with good casts): these would perhaps lend themselves to modern productions, but are probably best regarded as significant personal gestures.

Roussel's major works are *Impressions of Africa* (*Impressions d'Afrique*, 1910; tr. L. Foord and R. Heppenstall, 1966) and *Locus Solus* (1914), which was adapted by the prolific and skilful novelist PIERRE FRONDAIE (ps. RENÉ FRAUDET, 1884–1948) into a more viable play than he himself ever achieved. Roussel had already, at nineteen, anticipated the method of his later works, of combining precise description (of the Nice Carnival, for example) with situational fantasy. Now he was concerned with words themselves: he proceeded by pun and homophone, trying to superimpose a purely verbal logic upon a (recondite) representational one. *Impressions of Africa* is divided into two halves. The first presents a series of isolated scenes involving a number of people shipwrecked in Africa who are celebrating their captor King's coronation. The second begins at an earlier point of time and re-presents the whole action in the form of a parody (sometimes tedious) of conventional storytelling. Roussel's intention was not unlike Proust's: to recreate lost perceptions—but his method was linguistic. He anticipated not only the *nouveau roman* but also, as a critic has pointed out, that modern psychoanalysis (one of the chief British practitioners is Charles Rycroft) which defines its formulas as 'semantic ones . . . able to free the tongues of those for whom to be speechless is to suffer'. He left a key to his intentions, without which his most enthusiastic critics would be lost, in *How I Wrote Certain Books* (*Comment j'ai écrit certaines de mes livres*, 1935). He is a very important writer rather than a freak, as some have called him; but it should perhaps be pointed out that he failed to achieve a wholly satisfactory work. Attributing his mental illness to the 'violent shock' he experienced at the failure of *The Understudy*, he said that he vainly sought to recapture 'the sensation of mental sunlight' that he had experienced while he was writing it. He killed himself in Palermo.

VICTOR SÉGALEN (1878–1919), born in Brest, is a neglected writer. Novelist and poet, he was the friend and the influencer of Claudel, Perse and Jouve (qq.v.), who edited his poetry. He wrote *The Immemorial* (*Les Immémoriaux*, 1907) after visiting Tahiti—on the ship whose doctor he was—three months after Gauguin's death. This, one of the earliest books—half novel and half autobiography—to describe 'uncivilized' people accurately, sympathetically and unpatronizingly, and to lament the destruction of primitive wisdom, anticipates the work of the French anthropologist Claude Lévi-Strauss. Ségalen worked with Debussy on a lyrical drama, *King Orpheus* (*Orphée Roi*, 1921), travelled on an archaeological expedition to China, and visited Tibet. He absorbed much from the Orient, which he distilled into the highly original poetry of *Steles* (*Stèles*, 1912), *Paintings* (*Peintures*, 1916) and *Escapade* (*Équipée*, 1929). *René Lys* is a posthumous novel about China. He vanished when on an expedition in the forest of Hoelgoat.

CHARLES-FERDINAND RAMUZ (1878–1947), friend of the composer Stravinsky (for whom he wrote *The Soldier's Tale*), was born at Cully, a town on Lake Geneva, in Switzerland. He spent a number of years in Paris as a young man, but returned to Switzerland after 1914. Ramuz is a regional writer, who frequently employs the local Vaud dialect in his roughly told stories. Considering the fame of Giono (q.v.), to whom he is in some respects close, Ramuz is undeservedly neglected. True, several of his books have been translated into English, but he is seldom discussed; in his own country he was almost sixty before he gained popular recognition. His first novel, *Aline* (1905), on the well-worn theme of the village girl who is deserted by her seducer and kills her baby, is direct and deeply felt, but went unheeded. Critics told him to apply his gifts to a wider field than that of the Vaudois; the result was the semi-autobiographical *Aimé Pache, Vaudois Painter* (*Aimé Pache, peintre vaudois*, 1910), in which the artist-hero goes to Paris but discovers his roots in his native Vaud. Similar was *The Life of Samuel Belet* (*Vie de Samuel Belet*, 1913; tr. M. Savill, 1951). After 1919 followed—with the exception of the brilliant collaborative effort *The Soldier's Tale*—Ramuz's creatively least successful phase, in which he experimented with satire—*The Reign of the Evil One* (*Le Règne de l'esprit malin*, 1917; tr. J. Whitall, 1922), in which the thinker destroys the novelist—and with modernist techniques unsuited to his genius. *Terror on the Mountain* (*La Grande Peur dans la montagne*, 1926; tr. 1966) marked the beginning of his maturity, in which he evolved an inimitable 'anti-literary', no-nonsense style (described by one critic as consisting of 'syntactical eccentricities . . . provincialisms, archaisms, neologisms, ellipses, missing verbs and Biblical echoes') perfect for his purposes, impossible for almost anyone else's. The most fully satisfying of his twenty-two novels is *When the Mountain Fell* (*Derborence*, 1935; tr. S. F. Scott, 1949). In this story of a young man who emerges from beneath the rocks of an avalanche some weeks after it has occurred Ramuz combines his brilliance of regional understanding with the more universal theme of self-discovery. To some critics Ramuz's style is monotonous; here at least, where the author creates the oral illusion of his own voice almost as remarkably as Céline (q.v.) does, this claim is difficult to sustain. Ramuz's *Journal* (1943; 1949) is of the utmost interest. This gruff writer, whose journey to self-fulfilment was as arduous and courageous as anyone's of his time, has not had his due.

LOUIS HÉMON (1880–1913) was born in Brest and emigrated to Canada in 1911. He was run over by a train while walking along a track in Ontario. Hémon, who worked as a journalist in England for eight years, published only one novel in his lifetime: *Lizzie Blakeston* (1908), about English life. *Maria Chapdelaine* (1916; tr. W. H. Blake, 1921), serialized in 1914 in Paris without attracting notice, brought him posthumous fame, and was immensely influential in French Canadian literature (q.v.), since it represented an enraptured treatment of the 'new Frenchness' in terms of the old France from which this sprang. An excellent novel by any standards, *Maria Chapdelaine* is one of those books that define the spirit and the aspirations of a whole community, in this case the *défricheurs* (clearers of and settlers in new land in forested Quebec) and their families. Maria's father Samuel wrests a comfortable home from the forests, but must always move further north to repeat his victory. A memorable section of the book is devoted to the isolated family's joyous recognition of the signs of spring. The man Maria loves is killed by the harshness of nature (he is lost in the snow), and her mother dies; but, although offered a city life in America, she decides to remain and to marry a neighbour—a decision that is as moving as it is convincingly conveyed. Hémon was always a devotee of sport and physical fitness, and one of the most amusing of the short works that were issued after his death is *Battling Malone* (1925). *Maria Chapdelaine* was filmed twice, memorably by Duvivier with Madeleine Renaud and Jean Gabin (1934); René Clément in 1953 filmed *Monsieur Ripois et la Némésis* (1926; tr. W. A. Bradley, 1924).

The novelist and dramatist ROGER MARTIN DU GARD (1881–1958), born in the Paris suburb of Neuilly, won the Nobel Prize in 1937. A close personal friend of Gide's (q.v.), he spent his life in strict seclusion and did not involve himself in literary affairs. Trained as an archivist—this is significant in view of the massive build-ups of detail in his fiction—he fought in the First World War and for a while worked with Copeau (q.v.) at the Vieux-Colombier (q.v.). He left behind him an immense novel called *The Journal of Colonel Maumort*, on which he worked between 1940 and his death; this is so far unpublished. It is possible, even likely, that it will prove a masterpiece. Several other works have not yet been issued. It is often suggested that the reticent Martin du Gard was not quite able to compensate for his lack of genius, that his fiction is superbly intelligent documentary, but more finely industrious than imaginative. This is certainly true of his second novel, *Jean Barois* (1913; tr. S. Gilbert, 1950) although it is an incomparable picture of France (in particular the Dreyfus affair) in the thirty years before the First World War; it is arguably so in the case of the *roman-fleuve* for which he was awarded the Nobel Prize, *The World of the Thibaults* (*Les Thibault*, 1922–40; tr. S. Haden-Guest and S. Gilbert, 1939–40); but it is not true of his comic novel *The Postman* (*Vieille France*, 1933; tr. J. Russell, 1955) —which is surprisingly robust—and emphatically not true of the more seriously intended short novel about incest, *African Confidence* (*Confidence africaine*, 1931). *The Journal of Colonel Maumort* may surprise some critics. Martin du Gard has written two subtle farces and a technically more conventional but none the less excellent realist drama, *A Silent One* (*Un Taciturne*, 1931), on the subject of homosexuality (Gide wrote interestingly about it in his *Journal*). Roger Martin du Gard was a versatile writer whose worth has not yet been assessed.

The Thibaults concentrates on the relationships of the two Catholic Thibault sons, Jacques and Antoine, with their father and with the Protestant family of Fontenin. Jacques is an open rebel; Antoine, a doctor, is a moderate prepared to accept conventional ways if he can throw off Catholicism. Roger Martin du Gard saw clearly into the nature of French Catholicism. Both sons die as a result of the war, which the author pessimistically regarded as the end of the last tolerable chapter in human civilization. There is much remarkable detail: the slow death of Thibault senior from uremia (Antoine eventually puts him out of his misery); the actions of Antoine's love-rival Hirst, who kills his daughter, with whom he has been to bed, and her husband—and then takes Antoine's mistress back from him although she knows this. The detail in *The Thibaults* has been described as tending to dullness, and this cannot always be denied; but to take risks is necessary in this kind of novel—the slick, meretricious, unreal surface of C. P. Snow's sequence (q.v.), incidentally exposed by such a serious work as *Les Thibault* for the middlebrow journalism that it is, demonstrates the fact—and Martin du Gard is not often actually dull. Here the realist tradition, because it is sensibly used, lives effectively on. Roger Martin du Gard has been called a naturalist, but this is misleading; he is pessimistic about the nature of man, but has no special deterministic philosophy.

The Catholic FRANÇOIS MAURIAC (1885–1970), from Bordeaux, also received a Nobel Prize (1952). Mauriac's Catholicism is more attractive than Claudel's: less self-centred, more self-questioning, more merciful, more liberal-minded.

Perhaps the human indignity reached by Claudel in his ode to Pétain is the automatic price of the pomposity of a too high self-regard; Mauriac could never, in any case, have erred in this respect. He attacked Franco, supported the Resistance (but denounced the savage witch-hunting of the years following the war) and was a critical and independent supporter of de Gaulle. In the latter half of his life Mauriac practised journalism, and became France's leading commentator on current affairs.

Mauriac writes on the same theme as Claudel—the meaningless misery of existence without God—but he finds less radiance in himself or the world. He was brought up strictly, in an atmosphere of Catholic puritanism, and has often been called a Jansenist. (The followers of the heretical Jansen 1585–1638, one of whom was Pascal, introduced a strongly pessimistic and puritanical streak into Catholicism; above all, they emphasized natural man's helpless inability to turn to God.) The gloomy novels of Mauriac's first and 'Jansenist' period, lasting until the early Thirties, are his most powerful. The change of heart he then experienced, which led to a softening of his general attitude— and, in particular, to a higher estimate of the spiritually regenerative powers of love—was totally sincere; but tension in him slackened, and his characters no longer make the same tragic impact. The attempted poisoner of her husband, *Thérèse Desqueyroux* (1927: all the Thérèse books tr. G. Hopkins, *Thérèse: A Portrait in Four Parts*, 1947), is an absolutely typical Mauriac character, tempted by boredom with her deadly marriage into sin. In the later stories one can see the mellower and more orthodox Mauriac struggling with himself and her; it is less convincing, but he will do no more than bring her closer to official salvation. A priest did tell Mauriac (he said) how Thérèse might be saved. But the creative writer can hardly believe in such solutions.

Mauriac, who was encouraged by Barrès (q.v.), began with verse. His first mature novel was *A Kiss for the Leper* (*Le Baiser au lépreux*, 1922; tr. G. Hopkins, *Collected Novels*, 1946 ff.), about an ugly man and his wife, who devotes herself piously to his memory after he dies. *Génitrix* (1923; tr. G. Hopkins, ibid), Mauriac's first undoubted masterpiece, is a bleakly pessimistic study of a murderously intense maternal possessiveness defeating itself in the moment of its apparent victory—and of the loneliness of a weak man to whom love has been nothing but a stultifying disaster. These novels, like most of Mauriac's others, are redolent of Bordeaux and the sandy, pine- and vine-filled country-side that surrounds it.

In *The Desert of Love* (*Le Désert de l'amour*, 1925; tr. G. Hopkins, ibid) Mauriac reached the height of his achievement. Masterly in technique, this book does end with a moment of love, as a hitherto estranged father and son—both doomed by their characters never to find fulfilment in love—briefly recognize each other and the desert of love in which each dwells. It is a bitter moment, but its lyricism is enough to clear Mauriac's earlier work of the charge of over-pessimism. *The Vipers' Tangle* (*Le Nœud de vipères*, 1932; tr. G. Hopkins, ibid) marks the stage when Mauriac was becoming dissatisfied with (and perhaps orthodoxly ashamed of) his own bleak pessimism. Most of the book is on a level with his best: Louis, a millionaire, keeps his family, whom he hates, in the vipers' tangle of the title. Spite is so strong in him that he even writes a diary in which he expresses his hatred of his wife. She is to read this on his death. Then she dies before him, and he turns—but not at all convincingly, psychologically—to Christ. However, the conversion is moving—its energy being gained from Mauriac's desire for change.

The fact is that Mauriac need never have chosen to portray this kind of character. There are people less depressing in life than the inhabitants of his fiction. . . . While the tension in him, between dutiful love of God's human creation and despair at its vile helplessness, remained strong, Mauriac was a novelist of great power; but he cannot convincingly resolve such a tension (except temporarily, in the kind of momentarily non-solipsistic illumination provided at the end of *The Desert of Love*), because his imagination (unlike Claudel's) cannot fully believe in, record, the psychological detail of the amazing dynamics of such conversions as Louis', in *The Vipers' Tangle*, to Christ. The situation is further complicated by the fact that Mauriac has to equate a change of heart with a turning to Christ: he is not only religious but also Christian.

But Mauriac's fiction, though it deteriorated, never became less than interesting and intelligent. And in *A Woman of the Pharisees* (*La Pharisienne*, 1941; tr. G. Hopkins, ibid) at least, he returns to his old form. This deals with the sort of character with whom Mauriac has always been obsessed: the tyrannical *bien-pensant*. It is only at the end of the novel that Mauriac allows the sour and cruel monster he has created to glimpse the grace of inner sweetness; this cannot but be psychologically unconvincing. Sartre (q.v.) in fact accused this author of creating characters who were incapable of change (the strongest Calvinist element in Jansenism is its belief in predestination). This was damaging criticism, and angered the Catholic in Mauriac. It is true that doctrine finally caused him to manipulate his characters; but then his belief in doctrine, his faith, was the positive pole of the generator of his whole creative effort. . . . However, it must be conceded that the comparative serenity of the later fiction is, by the highest standards, false and morally imposed.

In his second phase Mauriac wrote some well-constructed plays, and continued until the very end to produce fiction of a high standard. His restrained style, of a classical purity, is universally praised.

VI

Although that extraordinarily fascinating and versatile writer JULES ROMAINS (ps. LOUIS FARIGOULE, 1885–1972), who was born in a village of the Cévennes, could claim to have invented 'unanimism', it was actually something—like all the contemporary philosophies worthy of note—that was very much in the air in the years before 1914, a French equivalent to the German 'O Mensch!'

side of expressionism (q.v.). These were years of idealism more intense (and perhaps more complacent) than anything we have since witnessed. The men who started the First World War did not know what had happened; those who tried to make a settlement in 1919 were sentimental and pompous mediocrities without an elementary grasp of reality. The serious men of before 1914 may be forgiven for regarding politicians as human beings as responsible as themselves —and more gifted in action. No such mistake is made today except in the literature of *kitsch*: in the fantasies of Snow (q.v.) or Allen Drury. Hope for mankind was still not quite a drastic or startling emotion to hold—or an official's trick-cliché. Politicians had not yet fully emerged as the foci of the human sickness, as men behind whose comfortingly featureless masks the essence of criminality has been refined. This kind of idealism has tended to persist, if only as one element, in the work of Romains and of some of those others who began with him as unanimists and then went their different ways. We have seen it, too, in the influential poetry of Verhaeren (q.v.): it operates as an extreme cosmic excitement about mankind's new prospects. But here it is seriously challenged and undermined by knowledge of human nature: by guilt-inducing but irrepressible pessimism.

Unanimism—under any of its names, for its spirit was apparent in the work of men who had never heard of it—was also a response to the tendency of the world to contract (McLuhan's 'global village') owing to more and faster ships, railways, telegraph, etc. This group theory, by which collective emotions—of two people, of small rural communities, of cities, of countries, and finally of the whole world—transcend and are superior to individual ones, was also an attempt to rediscover the God who had given mankind a kind of unity, but who had vanished with the enlightenment of the eighteenth century. At a more scientific level, anthropologists and sociologists were examining the exact ways in which individuals are related to their groups. Émile Durkheim (1858–1917), one of the greatest of sociologists, a thinker of true profundity, had been led to postulate social facts as entities (not abstractions) in themselves. The supreme collective fact, he postulated, is religion. This was the field that Romains and others were to explore creatively: writers-as-scientists, but new scientists, uncertain of science's capacities. They extended rationalism.

It was in this spirit—the spirit not only of Verhaeren but of Whitman and the idealistic side of Zola—that Georges Duhamel, his brother-in-law Charles Vildrac (q.v.) and others founded a Utopian community, *L'Abbaye*, at an old house at Créteil near Paris in the late summer of 1906. These men were making an experiment in living partly based on the idealistic prescriptions of the eighteenth-century sociologist François Marie Charles Fourier (to whom André Breton, q.v., wrote an ode). They were in effect repeating the nineteenth-century American Brook Farm venture, about which Nathaniel Hawthorne wrote his novel *The Blithedale Romance* (1852). One of Duhamel's *Pasquier Chronicles* (q.v.) similarly describes life at Créteil. Marinetti (q.v.) was a frequent visitor, as was Romains himself, and LUC DURTAIN (ps. ANDRÉ NEPVEU, 1881–1959), a doctor by profession, who wrote a novel, *The Necessary Step*

441

(*L'Étape nécessaire*, 1907), which may be regarded as the group's manifesto. Durtain, who was a conscientious and humane man but not a gifted or profound writer, probably remained most faithful to the immediate ideals of *L'Abbaye*. The community remained in existence only until the autumn of 1907.

Romains began, as *L'Abbaye* group had, with mainly poetic aspirations. He published a book of poems at nineteen; in 1906, 'a muscular, blue-eyed cyclist', he turned up at Créteil with the manuscript of a collection called *The Unanimous Life* (*La Vie unanime*). As a student, while walking the streets, he had experienced a 'concept of a vast and elemental being, of whom the streets, the cars, the passers-by formed the body', and of whom he (the writer-scientist in embryo) felt himself to be the consciousness. Romains' programme was (and to some extent always has been) concerned to employ the poet's intuition of the *Unanime* in aiding individuals to integrate themselves into it. The social and Utopian elements in this are obvious; it also lends itself to religious and mystical interpretations.

Romains' poetry, which is better than that of most novelists, and which he has continued to write, is spoiled by his didacticism; but it is still anthologized, read and studied, and has perhaps sufficient qualities to deserve this, The non-philosophical, lyrical poems in *Love Colour of Paris* (*Amour couleur de Paris*, 1921) are his best. His fine early novel *Death of a Nobody* (*Mort de quelqu'un*, 1911; tr. D. MacCarthy and S. Waterlow, 1914), often rather misleadingly described as his masterpiece, quite transcends its author's didactic intentions. A retired employee, who has felt no collective radiance in his commonplace life, dies. His aged father comes to bury him. Gradually, in his death, he takes on 'collective' significance. This significance is his survival. Thus death gives meaning to his senseless life. Philosophically this book proves nothing. But it is highly original, establishes a not unimportant aspect of existence, and is above all authentic in its portrayal of people. In *The Boys in the Back Room* (*Les Copains*, 1913; tr. J. LeClerq, 1937) Romains allowed his gift of humour, often a saving one, to emerge. Seven young men, by a series of crazy jokes, awaken the bourgeois of two towns. This may instructively be compared to Frank's *The Robber Band* (q.v.), written seven years later. The subject matter of the trilogy *The Body's Rapture* (*Psyché*, 1922–9; tr. J. Rodker, 1937) is erotic: Lucienne is awakened into love and lust by Pierre, whom she marries. The frankly sensual writing here is a great improvement on D. H. Lawrence's in *Lady Chatterley's Lover* (q.v.); the bisexual and puritanical Lawrence was ill at ease with his material, while Romains was more relaxedly trying to communicate his mystical sense of the pleasures of sexual love.

The twenty-seven volume *roman-fleuve*, *Men of Good Will* (*Les Hommes de bonne volonté*, 1932–47; tr. W. B. Wells and G. Hopkins, 1933–46), which has the longest list of characters of any novel, and covers the period 1908–33 in historical detail, as well as in terms of its characters' personal lives, is almost always described as a failure. Of course. The question is: how much does it actually achieve? And the answer is that it achieves more than is usually allowed. Romains put some of himself into one of the main characters, Jean Jerphanion;

the writer he portrays in Pierre Jallez. If one reads *Men of Good Will* not as a bible of unanimism but simply as a survey (surely a heroic one) of elements of French society over twenty-five years, it is a rewarding experience. There are some thin and boring passages. But there are also some excellent volumes, mixing valuable records (of, for example, the fighting at Verdun, and of Soviet Russia), comedy (the pretentious writer Georges Allory), and psychological drama (the crime of the bookbinder Quinette, the gratuitous nature of which recalls that of Lafcadio in Gide's *The Vatican Cellars*, q.v.).

Romains' work raises some odd parodoxes. Why does *Men of Good Will*, by the apostle of unanimism, fail precisely in a 'unanimistic' way? How can one of the century's funniest writers produce work on current affairs so pompously absurd? Why in his drama does Romains seem to satirize the collective more than he advances it?

The answer is that he is a naïve (q.v.) writer, a lyricist who should follow his own imaginative bent and never try to philosophize or play a part in politics (this most unfascist of men even got himself called fascist by refusing to pursue his proper function of writer, and vainly meddling in public affairs). Had Romains confined himself to the creative exploration of his intuitions of the collective, instead of becoming a busybody in public matters—one book written in America at the beginning of the Second World War appears to discuss that catastrophe in terms of the author's own activities—he might have achieved the greatness he so narrowly misses.

Romains is an outstanding dramatist. His most famous play, *Knock* (1923; tr. H. Granville-Barker, 1935), which was directed and acted by Louis Jouvet, is a classic: a doctor sends a whole community to bed with an imaginary sickness. Other plays showed similar gullings of the populace by practical jokers or dictators, and Romains has been accused, by some, of admiring the jokers and showing contempt for the crowds. Actually the plays reveal Romains' creative misgivings about the over-simplifications inherent in his theories. But his public statements repudiating Hitler's kind of 'unanimism', while clearing him of fascist sympathies, lack imaginative conviction. Characteristically, Romains, who was gifted with a good grasp of the sciences, wrote an early and not foolish book on 'vision without sight'. He has always been interested in parapsychology.

GEORGES DUHAMEL (1884–1966), son of a muddling, lovable Paris chemist who qualified as a doctor at the age of fifty-one, began himself as a doctor. While at Créteil he wrote poetry and plays, but after war-service as a doctor he returned to fiction, and produced two *romans-fleuve*, *Salavin* (*Vie et aventures de Salavin*, 1920–32; tr. G. Billings, 1936) and the more famous but not superior *Pasquier Chronicle* (*Chronique des Pasquier*, 1933–45; tr. B. de Holthoir, 1937–46). He began his literary career in earnest with two compassionate, ironic books about the sufferings he saw in the First World War: *The New Book of Martyrs* (*Vie des martyrs*, 1917; tr. F. Simmonds, 1918) and *Civilization* (1918; tr. E. S. Brooks, 1919). These stories, as good as anything he wrote, are excellent examples of the writer fulfilling his proper function: they are committed to no more than humanity and compassion. *Salavin* is not an innovatory novel, nor a startling feat of imagination; it is nevertheless a lovely, often humorous, but ultimately sombre book. The hero is a failure and an idealist. He tries to be a saint, but fails comically—and terribly sadly for himself. His (gratuitous?) impulse to touch his boss's ear costs him his job; his vow of chastity costs his wife's happiness. Only as he dies, through an over-generous act, does he see that he has always lacked spontaneous love. Duhamel here performs the extra-ordinary feat of irradiating mediocrity, and demonstrating, with absolute honesty, how it may attain nobility. Of course it has been objected that Duhamel has spread out his material too thinly. But in this case the criticism has less force: the nature of the material is deliberately unmelodramatic, and yet it has an undoubted intensity. There is a trace of Futabatei's (q.v.) Bunzo in Salavin. To suggest, as one critic has done, that *Salavin* is modelled upon Dostoevski (simply because it has a 'negative' hero), and that by this standard it is 'thin', is misleading and unfair. It is more original than this. Its subtle and humane criticism of both kinds of Christianity makes it an interesting contrast to the work of Christian novelists.

The Pasquier Chronicle is delightfully written, but here Duhamel's humanity has become too diffused for completely successful fiction: the book really is too long, and lacks energy. The portrait of his own father, however, is loving and accurate; and there are other continuously interesting volumes. The whole is certainly superior to the middlebrow sham of, say, all but early fragments of Galsworthy's *Forsyte Saga* (q.v.). However debilitated he is, Duhamel always has a radiant mind, and is ever anxious to avoid self-deceit. A post-war novel, *The Voyage of Patrice Périot* (*Le Voyage de Patrice Périot*, 1951) is doubtless correct in representing scientists as naïve and politicians as vicious; but the human stuff of the story is missing. Duhamel's critical works, essays and autobiographical volumes—*Light on my Days* (*Inventaire de l'abîme*, 1945, *Biographie de mes fantômes*; tr. in one vol., B. Collier, 1948)—are all of interest. During the Second World War he and his family stayed in France and suffered from the Nazis, though fortunately not drastically. Duhamel, in his war sketches and in *Salavin*, has left a literary testament to his radiant nature.

The idealism felt by Duhamel, Romains and so many others before the catastrophe of 1914 was modified or altered by events—but it was in most cases sharpened rather than destroyed. For most of those who came to manhood before 1914, and who then experienced the war, the future of the world was, and for reasons obvious enough, a major issue. Some writers, however, displayed their concern in a more oblique manner than the naïve Romains or the gently liberal Duhamel. For such as Claudel or Mauriac (qq.v.), of course, the answer lay with God. For those of the only temporarily weakened, mystical *Action Française* (q.v.) it lay in nationalism, new disciplines, and an acknowledge-ment of a Crown and Church (in which one did not necessarily have to believe as a private citizen). For unanimists and others it lay in new understandings, new hopes, new *rapprochements* (Romains wanted a Franco-German *rapproche-ment* in spite of Hitler). Some of those who had fought towards the end of the war, younger men, turned, as we shall see, to surrealism and to other allied movements of protest. One important aspect of all these movements was their antagonism, so profound as to amount to rejection rather than criticism, to the systems of living that had collapsed in war.

However, there is another group of writers, many of genius, who have at least these features in common: they do not share in nihilism or communism— or in the liberal humanism of such writers as Romains, Gide or Duhamel. They are (or have been called) 'right-wing' or 'fascist'. The category, like all categories, is a loose one. What characterizes all those included in it is not their 'right-wingedness', but rather the intensity of their repudiation of left-wing solutions. In Great Britain the category embraces a wide spectrum: from Belloc and Chesterton (qq.v.) to (an aspect of) Wyndham Lewis (q.v.); for its survivors—mostly deintellectualized, hysterical pseudo-writers or guttersnipe journalists—the Heath 1970 government was a Vichy, now (late 1972) betrayed.

GEORGES BERNANOS (1888–1948), who was born and died in Paris, was a true spiritual son of Léon Bloy (q.v.). He undoubtedly belongs to the vituperative, enraged, frenetic wing of French Catholicism. But he is a subtler and more gifted novelist than Huysmans or Bloy, and even his fiercest detractors do not deny that he left behind him at least one masterpiece. The English writer one immediately thinks of in connection with him is Graham Greene (q.v.); but there are important differences, not the least among them being Greene's left-wing position. But if we speak of Dostoevski as Bernanos' conscious model, we shall not—as in the case of Duhamel—mislead.

Hate distorts and disfigures—in an almost 'expressionist' manner—the by no means ignoble passion of Bernanos' polemic (but he was considerably saner than Bloy, who must be described as to some extent unbalanced); yet his fiction is powerful and transcends its Christian terms of reference.

The young Bernanos was a supporter of *Action Française* and an admirer of the anti-semite Drumont. But he differed from most *Action Française* supporters in being obsessed (as Mauriac was) with the materialism of the bourgeois. This Bloy-like strain of spirituality runs through all his work, and is stronger than the other emotions which possessed him: royalism, hatred of atheists, patriotism. Basically Bernanos is a visionary, as he showed in no uncertain terms in his febrile and tormented first novel, *Star of Satan* (*Sous le soleil de Satan*, 1926; tr. P. Morris, 1940), in which a priest struggles with Satan (a horse trader) for his own soul and for that of a precocious village girl. There is melodrama here, but also power and a genuine apprehension of the mysterious and the supernatural. Bernanos' vision of life on earth, a theatre of struggle between God and Satan for the soul of man, is perhaps simplistic; but his view of human nature, although lurid, is neither unsubtle nor ignorant of the dynamics of lust and despair. His next two novels, *The Deception* (*L'Imposture*, 1927) and *Joy* (*La Joie*, 1929; tr. L. Varèse, 1946), deal with a hypocrite priest. The second of these, whose main character is a saintly girl, introduces Bernanos' most Dostoevskian figure: a Russian chauffeur who murders the joyous girl, but then kills himself and thus brings the priest back to faith.

445

In 1931 Bernanos wrote the most savage of his diatribes, *The Great Fear of the Well-Disposed* (*La Grande Peur des bien-pensants*): this is an attack on those un-believers who are merely Catholic out of tradition—and it amply demonstrates Bernanos' fundamental lack of sympathy with *Action Française*. He was a believer in God's kingdom; they were 'patriots'. Unfortunately the book is tainted with anti-semitism.

Diary of a Country Priest (*Journal d'un curé de campagne*, 1936; tr. P. Morris, 1937) is Bernanos' most famous book. It is another story of a saint: sick and unworldly, the priest of Ambricourt (in Northern France) tries to serve the poor. But the poor are vicious and abuse him. Finally, defeated in everything but his own sense of grace, absolved by an unfrocked priest, he dies. This, Bernanos' quietest and most carefully composed novel, is his most intensely moving.

Two books of Bernanos' that have been undervalued are *A Crime* (*Un Crime*, 1935; tr. A. Green, 1936) and its extraordinary counterpart, written in 1935 but not published until 1950: *Night is Darkest* (*Un Mauvais Rêve*; tr. W. J. Strachan, 1953).

In 1936 Bernanos was in Mallorca and saw the fascist atrocities committed there, blessed and encouraged by his own Church. In *Diary of My Times* (*Les Grands Cimetières sous la lune*, 1938; tr. P. Morris, 1938), one of the greatest of books of impassioned protest, he condemned what he saw. His *Action Française* friends, who had been taught by Barrès (q.v.) and others to regard the truth as the enemy of tradition, and therefore as something not to be uttered, condemned him in their turn. During the war he lived in Brazil, from which he periodically denounced the compromise of Vichy. However, Bernanos did not cease to oppose parliamentary democracy; but his resistance to it is based on his belief that it affords no protection from bourgeois greed for money and power. This makes him as anti-capitalist as any communist; but (unlike Greene) he will have no truck at all with godless communism. His hatred of fascism was inspired by human decency, not by any intellectual conversion to liberalism. He was an early supporter of de Gaulle—and while Gaullism was against the fact of Vichy, it remains in certain ways close to its conservative ideals.

One more novel of Bernanos' must be mentioned; it is regarded by many as the height of his achievement: *The Open Mind* (*Monsieur Ouine*, 1943, rev. 1946, correct text 1955; tr. G. Dunlop, 1945), which he had been working on since 1934, and first published in Buenos Aires. This concerns an utterly depraved populace, who are observed by the cynical Monsieur Ouine, who was in part a satirical caricature of the liberal, godless André Gide (q.v.) that is Bloy-like in its savagery, hysterically unjust in a personal sense, and yet full of meaning. The evil is depicted with gusto; but the note of grace is clearly sounded. Bernanos' technique here is almost *pointilliste*: the town is presented in a series of discrete episodes. However, this is a fragmented realism rather than an anticipation (as is sometimes claimed) of the *nouveau roman* (q.v.). *The Open Mind* is an important and powerful book, but not a better one than *The Diary of a Country Priest*. When he died, of cancer, Bernanos was working on a biography of Christ. His reputation was well served by the French composer Francis Poulenc, who turned his film-script *The Carmelites* (*Dialogues des Carmélites*, 1948; tr. G. Hopkins, 1961), based on Gertrud von Le Fort's novel *The Song at the Scaffold* (*Die Letzte am Schafott*, q.v.), into a successful opera.

In this writer we find French conservative Catholicism at its most honest and least unattractive—as well as a creative power that continually transcends the crudities and over-simplifications in which his convictions involved him. His best work represents a kind of justification of Bloy; and it is perhaps the most profound of all modern expositions of one of Bloy's chief themes, an extremely important one in French Catholicism: vicarious suffering. It is safe to say that the reader who remains emotionally immune to Bernanos at his most powerful is a remarkably insensitive one.

MARCEL JOUHANDEAU (ps. MARCEL PROVENCE, 1888) was born in Guéret, Creuse, which is some forty miles north-east of Limoges, and is the 'Chaminadour' of his books. Less widely known than Bernanos, he has a number of distinguished admirers (Gide, Claude Mauriac, Jean-Louis Curtis, Thornton Wilder, qq.v., Havelock Ellis—and many more), and is clearly a writer of importance, a genuine eccentric (he has affinities, as a critic has shrewdly pointed out, with T. F. Powys, q.v.), a heretical Catholic who can only be ignored at the peril of missing strange and valuable insights. A schoolmaster in Paris from 1912 until 1949, he has written over seventy books, some of which are mere hack work, lives of saints and so on. He has been called a 'demented and ranting exhibitionist'; but this does not characterize him. His mysticism and pessimism are, perhaps, less offensive to his critics than the unique frankness of his *Marital Chronicles* (*Chroniques maritales*, 1938, 1943), which tell of the difficulties (and pleasures) of his marriage, made in 1929, to a dancer and choreographer called Caryathis. His creative writing is tormented by an inchoate but powerful vision: of the world as the scene of Satan's winning battle with God for the soul of humanity; but when Jouhandeau tries to articulate this in his non-fiction it varies bewilderingly, and loses force. An anti-semite, public egoist, and bisexual, Jouhandeau fell victim to Nazi propaganda and visited Berlin during the occupation, a self-indulgence for which he was eventually forgiven.

Jouhandeau is a versatile and prolific writer. There are the novels of Chaminadour—including *Chaminadour* (1934–41) and *Mémorial* (1948–58)—comic and cruelly bitter accounts of the seamy side of life, but always bathed in the light of the supernatural. These works have something of the sensuous, thick-lined brutality of Rembrandt's drawings; occasionally Jouhandeau manipulates his situations to the benefit of this texture. His 'marriage' books, which include *Monsieur Godeau Married* (1933) and *Élise* (1933) and many others, as well as *Marital Chronicles* (he is Godeau; and Caryathis, who was recommended to him by Marie Laurencin, the painter and erstwhile mistress of Apollinaire, is the remarkable Élise), are lighter in tone, but still confessional in a unique manner; they contain much agonized self-appraisal. (*Marcel and Élise*, tr. Martin Turnell, 1953, is a selection from them.) Jouhandeau also published novels under his own name, including *The Germans in Provence* (*Les Allemands en Provence*, 1919), much more grimly naturalist in style than his later work; but here he had not found his true *métier*. Jouhandeau is above all a lucid chronicler of human secrecies, and in this sense a writer of great courage. He combines an extraordinary number of conflicting qualities: piety, impudence, sweetness, nastiness, affection, malice. . . . He will continue to be valued, but in rigorous selection.

PIERRE-EUGÈNE DRIEU LA ROCHELLE (1893–1945), born in Paris, is a less complex, less gifted conservative than the preceding writers. His is a tragic case. He invested his entire life with the heroic recklessness that Jouhandeau hoarded—for the most part—for use in his books; and Drieu La Rochelle's life was anguished and disgraced, his books mostly inferior. . . . Confusing creative exploration of his nearly demonic aggressiveness and driving need for women with politics in a peculiarly French manner, Drieu, who fought in the First World War and was spiritually lost after it, threw himself into almost every literary and political movement (communism, Catholic mysticism, surrealism, *Action Française* . . .) that came into existence during the inter-war years: this was both to escape from and yet, vainly, to discover some system that would accommodate him. His mystiques of sport and sex, however, remained consistent. Hysterically lacking in control though he was, it was an inner despair that impelled him—not an innate cruelty or even an urge to power. Like all Frenchmen, he had bad precedents to draw upon. (His Whitman-like war verse was hailed by Barrès, whom he reverenced, as the best to come out of the war.) As well as polemics, Drieu wrote novels and short stories in which he portrayed both his own and France's emptiness. Of these *The Fire Within* (*Le Feu follet*, 1931; tr. R. Howard, 1961) is representative. The writing is powerful; but the author fails to penetrate analytically the internal hell that he is describing. That was to come later. In the Thirties Drieu's aching pessimism found a haven in Doriot's shabby French Nazi party (*Parti Populaire Français*), and he wrote a book called *With Doriot* (*Avec Doriot*, 1937). His novel of 1939, *Gilles*, reaches his fictional nadir: the style is still powerful, reflecting its author's inner discontent, but the hero's involvement with Franco's fascists only pretends to solve his problem (it would be disturbing if it succeeded). With the occupation Drieu took over the *Nouvelle Revue Française* and turned it into a pro-Nazi paper. When he heard about this Aldous Huxley (q.v.) wrote to his brother: 'My old friend . . . has, alas, carried his pre-war infatuation with Doriot to its logical conclusion. . . . He is an outstanding example of the strange things that happen when a naturally weak man, whose talents are entirely literary, conceives a romantic desire for action and a romantic ambition for political power . . . there was something very nice about Drieu. . . .' When the game was up in 1944 Drieu tried to kill himself, failed, and went into hiding, where he wrote his best (unfinished) novel: *Mémoires de Dirk Raspe* (1966), in which he projected himself into a fictional figure inspired by Van Gogh. Here, in full anticipation of his successful suicide of April 1945, he does not succeed in reconciling his concept of 'heroic energy' with his temperamental blackly cynical nihilism; but he does not try. He desperately relaxes, and invents the character he might better have been, scraping the bottom of the barrel of his memory for his old personal decencies. He is an important representative French writer, a genius crippled and destroyed by fervour.

HENRI DE MONTHERLANT (1896–1972), one of the most distinguished and versatile European writers of his generation, was born in Paris. He is very frequently described as a 'fascist', a 'collaborationist' and even as a 'soul kindred to Drieu La Rochelle'. All this is untrue. There may be things about Montherlant that are not palatable to everyone: he is aristocratic in attitude, he can perhaps be accused of *snobisme*, he does not believe in the Utopian capacities of mankind, he does not wear his heart on his sleeve, he has criticized romantic love, he has spoken uncomfortable truths at tactless times. . . . However, as one of his shrewdest critics has said, his worst political crime as a writer is to have a tendency 'to see moral problems in terms of aesthetics'. Some of the essays in *The June Solstice* (*Le Solstice de juin*, 1941), originally banned by the Nazis and only allowed to appear because a German official had translated some of Montherlant's work, suffer from this fault. However, they are also courageous essays: in them Montherlant was trying to maintain his independence as a writer. The suggestion that he was a collaborator has no foundation. Although more aloof from politics than most French writers, he has been unable to resist some involvement (partly to tease: it is not widely realized that he is a humorist who enjoys this aspect of the literary life); his 'record' is rather more 'left', or independent, than 'right'. For example, at the time of the Spanish Civil War he was unequivocally opposed to the fascists, and was known to be so. He refused an invitation to Barcelona in 1936 not only because he was ill but also because he felt he would be tempted to join in the fight against Franco. His apparently ambiguous political attitude recalls that of Wyndham Lewis (q.v.), who was more careless and less cautious, but is also widely misunderstood as politically reactionary. He shot himself when threatened with blindness.

Montherlant has made remarkable achievements as an essayist, a novelist, and, more recently, as a dramatist. Unlike Hemingway (q.v.), a writer almost infantile in comparison to him, he had some experience in fighting bulls, and in other sports, and he wrote much that is self-revealing on this subject (his best writing on bullfighting, which incidentally exposes Hemingway's *Death in the Afternoon* as naïve swagger, is in the novel *The Bullfighters, Les Bestiaires*, 1926, tr. 1927). He also wrote about his experiences as a soldier in the First World War in his first novel, *The Dream* (*Le Songe*, 1922; tr. T. Kilmartin 1962). This could be called 'hard', for it extols the Spartan virtues; but one has only to read Ernst Jünger (q.v.) to understand that it is not. Rather it reflects a romantic young man's determination to engage a bitterly hard world with honour and virtue. Although Montherlant has often chosen a generally Catholic as opposed to Protestant line, his 'Catholicism' is an essentially non-programmatic version of the specifically French brand of atheistic, external Catholicism: he is basically hostile to Christianity, not least because he believes it leads men to have false hopes and thus to be 'soft'. Not all critics have seen that *The Dream* is a shocked book, in which romanticism is brutally and deliberately deflated—but only to re-emerge in the rather self-conscious rhetoric of the style (and in the clumsiness with which the ideal of brotherhood is substituted for that of love).

His tetralogy *The Girls* (*Les Jeunes Filles*, 1936–9; tr. T. McGreevey and J. Rodker, 1937–40; T. Kilmartin, 1968) is one of his most celebrated and controversial works, but, although a superb *tour de force*, not (by his own high standards) his best. It has been widely misunderstood, taken for an anti-feminine tract where it is in fact a comic and ironic study of one aspect of its author. Its hero, Pierre Costals, is a brilliantly successful novelist who experiments with women. It is an error to try to extract a 'philosophy' from this novel, although one might well extract Montherlant's self-criticism. The worst mistake is to equate Montherlant with Costals. Montherlant, a public ironist, was always intelligently struggling to create non-subjective works; hence his post-war concentration on drama, in which he increasingly demonstrates unpalatable facts but remains stoically withdrawn from them. In this book, which is funny for those who are able to see Costals as simply a creation and not a vehicle for a philosophy, Montherlant did indulge an inclination; but he punished it. It is true that the girls who cling to Costals are seen by him as morally leprous, possessively draining the writer of his creative sap. But the Arab girl who does not cling is physically leprous. Embodied in *The Girls* is a close and rueful criticism of romantic love that, as a careful reading shows, involves Costals as closely as his women. The book is an exploration, not a statement. It is, after all, by a man who has said that most of the people around us who are capable of noble deeds are women.

The Bachelors (*Les Célibataires*, 1934; tr. T. Kilmartin, 1960) is one of Montherlant's most perfect and most moving novels. Here he was able to combine his regard for truth with his humour, tenderness for old age and fascination with the aristocracy. This is the story of two old penniless aristocrats, a baron and his sixty-four-year-old nephew: a senile madman and an obstinate, foolish old man who none the less achieves tragic grandeur in his unvictorious bid for both independence of his uncle and his aristocratic place in a society no longer constructed to accommodate him.

Montherlant finished a long novel about Africa called *The Black Rose* (*La Rose de sable*) in 1932; so far only a part has been published, *Desert Love* (*L'Histoire d'amour de 'La Rose de sable'*, 1954; tr. A. Brown, 1957). On the strength of this (self-contained) section, the novel, a sympathetic study of a weak officer, serving in Africa, would seem to be one of his best. Certainly in *Chaos and Night* (*Le Chaos et la nuit*, 1963; tr. T. Kilmartin, 1964) he achieves the depth and feeling of *The Bachelors*, and seems to confirm his position as France's leading living novelist. Here again the heroic spirit of a man triumphs over his own absurdity and failure: an old Spanish anarchist, grown near to madness after years of exile in Paris, returns to Madrid and an obscure and yet tragic and noble death. The theme is matched by the lucid beauty of the writing.

Montherlant had written for the stage before 1939; but it was not until the occupation that he turned seriously to it. *The Dead Queen* (*La Reine morte*, 1942; tr. J. Griffin, 1951), played in occupied Paris, was a subtle gesture of the author's independence; but there can be no doubt of his anti-German sympathies. One of his most famous plays is *The Master of Santiago* (*Le Maître de Santiago*, 1947; tr. J. Griffin, 1951), which portrays renunciation and adherence to principle at the expense of personal happiness. In *Those One Holds in One's Arms* (*Celles qu'on prend dans ses bras*, 1950), which was not a theatrical success, he contrasts a refined but involuntarily depraved old man with the noble girl who obsesses him. He has continued to produce excellent plays, including the vigorous *Malatesta* (1946), *Port Royal* (1954) and *The Cardinal of Spain* (1960). In early 1971 his moving play about a priest who loves one of his pupils (based on an experience of his own), *The Town Where the Prince is a Child* (*La Ville dont le Prince est un enfant*, 1951), was at last performed publicly and in its entirety. A long novel about the Roman Empire is scheduled for future publication.

Montherlant has been called a 'man of the Renaissance'. It would be even truer to describe him as a writer profoundly concerned with the problem of how to re-introduce, into the universal guilt-culture of the 'civilized' world, the most life-enhancing elements of the shame-cultures of the past. Much of what his readers find unattractive in him may be thus explained. His essays and notebooks are essential to a proper understanding of him. *Selected Essays* (tr. J. Weightman, 1960) is excellent in this respect, and contains a substantial selection from the notebooks.

JEAN GIONO (1895–1970), who was born at Manosque near Aix, offers a complete contrast. His father was a protestant shoemaker born in France of Piedmontese parents, his mother a Parisian. He is a rich writer, combining the bleakness of Faulkner (q.v.), the ecstasy of Whitman, the relentlessness of the Greek tragedians, a Hardean love for his peasants and a crudely Melvillean *penchant* for 'big' symbols. He is a true naïve (q.v.) and he has not, on the whole, tried to be a thinker. His experiences during the First World War were decisive, and led him to a lifelong pacifism. He was highly thought of during the Thirties, but his behaviour during the occupation lost him his popularity, which he only partly regained by his remarkable assumption of an entirely new style. Treatment as a sage advocating a return to the soil and an end of urbanism (pilgrimages were made to him, as they were to Jammes and Hauptmann, qq.v.) perhaps coarsened his sensitivity to people's individual sufferings and magnified his self-importance: he preached pacifism and then, in the defeat, gave every appearance of finding the Nazis no more repulsive than the French. He wrote for a collaborationist periodical, went to prison briefly (in 1939 and again in 1945), and eventually re-emerged in the new guise of historical novelist. His indifferent attitude to the Nazis was a compound of ignorance of the sophisticated nature of modern life and a sullen obstinacy rather akin to that of the British Mosleyite, also a lover of nature (though a trivial one when compared to Giono), Henry Williamson. The damage inflicted by war must ultimately be held responsible.

The novels of Giono's first and best period are nearly all set against Provençal rural backgrounds. He became famous with the trilogy *Pan: Hill of Destiny* (*Colline*, 1929; tr. J. LeClerq, 1929), *Lovers are Never Losers* (*Un de Baumugnes*, 1929; tr. J. LeClerq, 1931) and *Harvest* (*Regain*, 1930; tr. H. Fluchère and G. Myers, 1939). The last two were made into successful and effective movies, as was the comic short story *La Femme du Boulanger*, in which Raimu appeared. All six of the films from Giono's books were made by Marcel Pagnol (q.v.). One of the finest of all Giono's many novels is *The Song of the World* (*Le Chant du monde*, 1934; tr. H. Fluchère and G. Myers, 1937). This, a tale of violence and lust, and of a search (in Giono's native region) for a pair of lovers, has an epic grandeur which clearly shows Homer as one of the formative influences on the author. At his best Giono is unsurpassed in his communication of the rhythms of lives lived in accordance with nature's laws; unsurpassed, too, is his expression of the simple happiness of simple people. However, when he is not trying to be polemic, or to implement his programme for the abolition of industry (our possible sympathy for his point of view cannot, alas, modify its naïvety), he can deal with more complex material. His most powerful novel, *Joy of Man's Desiring* (*Que ma joie demeure*, 1935; tr. K. A. Clarke, 1940), certainly expresses Giono's disillusion with and disbelief in the viability of the urban world; but this work of the imagination is very different from any of his works of prophecy. And indeed, in the central figure of the book, a charlatan but a true prophet, there are those elements of self-criticism that so often mark the greatest literature.

After the war Giono wrote a series of historical 'Chronicles', including *The Hussar on the Roof* (*Le Hussard sur le toit*, 1951; tr. J. Griffin, 1953) and *The Straw Man* (*Le Bonheur fou*, 1957; tr. P. Johnson, 1959), in which Angelo Pardi, a Piedmontese officer, figures. These were a skilful new departure. In them he broke away from the dense, lurid, organic style of the earlier books to a new simplicity. They are refreshing and full of vitality. But, brilliant though they are, they have the status of potboilers in comparison to the earlier work. The Second World War had done something irreparable to Giono: for, whatever his errors, the early books had been generated by hope as well as despair; their sweeping lyricism had come from hope. In *Joy of Man's Desiring* Bobi had given the community joy and brotherhood until sexual jealousy intervened —was his death, stabbed by a flash of lightning as he ascended a mountain in a storm, prophetic of the fate of Giono's complex hope?

Giono's post-war rural comedies are pale parodies of what had come thirty and forty years earlier. His best book of this period was non-fiction: *The Dominici Affair* (*Notes sur l'affaire Dominici*, 1956; tr. 1956), in which he brought his understanding of his region to bear upon the curious murder, by peasants, of an English touring family. But in spite of the falling-off, Giono's achievement is a substantial one. The earthy, impassioned style of the novels of his first period is not the least part of it.

There is as much confusion about the work of LOUIS-FERDINAND CÉLINE (ps. LOUIS-FERDINAND DESTOUCHES, 1894–1961), who was born and died in Paris, as about the facts of his life. What is certain is that, whether wittingly or willingly or not, he devised new procedures. Céline (he took his maternal grandmother's maiden name) was the son of the minor employee of an insurance company and a maker of antique lace. He enlisted in the Cavalry in 1912, was severely wounded in 1914, and awarded a seventy-five per cent disability pension. After a series of voyages and a sojourn in wartime London, Céline began to study medicine in 1918; in the following year he married the daughter of the director of his medical school. His writing career begins with his doctoral thesis on Semmelweiss (1924), the embittered discoverer of the cause of puerperal fever, who proved his point to his incredulous colleagues by slashing his fingers and plunging them into the putrescent corpse of a fever victim: he died soon after. This appealed to the then ambitious and bourgeois-oriented young doctor, and prophesied his own career: the misanthropist's suicidal gesture carried within it the seeds of a desperate humanitarianism. But Céline, whose self-infection began in earnest with *Journey to the End of the Night* (*Voyage au bout de la nuit*, 1932; tr. J. Marks, 1934), lived with his anguish and fever for nearly thirty more years. This hallucinated account of his spiritual adventures, in the guises of one Ferdinand Bardamu and his double Robinson, made him famous; but he continued to practise as a doctor among the poor. *Death on the Instalment Plan* (*Mort à crédit*, 1936; tr. J. Marks, 1938) tells of a nightmare childhood. It is not influenced by surrealism (q.v.), but partakes with huge greed of the blackness and despair, but not the hope, out of which the larger and inclusive movement of expressionism (q.v.) had come. Céline's own childhood had not been nightmarish; but his conscience, stimulated by the poor patients he treated, and by the misery and stupidity he saw around him—as well as the spite and envy that were a part of his character—compelled him to invent one. In those two books, the critic Roland Barthes has said, 'writing is not at the service of thought . . . it really represents the writer's descent into the sticky opacity of the condition which he is describing'. One thinks of Sartre's (q.v.) 'viscosity': that foul quality he ascribes to non-authentic experience, to all objects and persons who betray the individual's movement towards his freedom, to the self recalcitrantly clinging to its fear of existence. For Céline the world is in headlong decay. The physical voice of the self- and world-sickened physician, a kindly and humanitarian specialist in children's diseases, devotee of the music halls, dear and gay friend of such as the actress Arletty and the novelist Aymé (q.v.), gives the illusion of coming straight off the page: exasperated, always vigorous and spontaneous, enchanted, ribald, furious, eager, abandonedly vile, agonized. Céline called himself a classicist because he had worked hard to achieve this unique tone of voice. The bourgeois readership recoiled in horror, not wanting to listen to this ghost of their own internal monologue (but they bought his books); the patients came to the doctor.

Then Céline fell victim to the endemic French disease of anti-semitism. He may have been jealous of the number of successful Jewish refugees in the medical profession in Paris. At all events, his tone clearly reveals that he knew, all the time, that these emotions were vile. *Trifles for a Massacre* (*Bagatelles pour un*

453

massacre, 1937) impressed Gide (q.v.) as a comic satire of a bestial Nazi blue-print for the destruction of European Jewry. Essentially, Gide was right. As a critic has pointed out, Céline's 'Jew' 'is a projection . . . of his own class's worst tendencies'. But his balance of judgement, always precarious, began to desert him. Like Jouhandeau (q.v.) he was a difficult and irascible man, an enemy to his literary friends, to all but his boon-companions. He became identified with the parodic *persona* of his anti-semitic pamphlets. Such madness, in a man of his sensibility, is not excusable at such a time. The first, character-istically, incorporates three of his magical 'Ballets', celebrations of all he loved in life. Then the war came. He volunteered but was rejected. During the occupa-tion he called Hitler a Jew, predicted his defeat, repelled advances from the Germans on some occasions, incoherently approached them on others: put himself in an unnecessarily dangerous and foolish position. He associated with collaborators and practised medicine. He never denounced any individual. He later admitted to having been mixed up in doings, 'stuff connected with Jews', that were not 'his business'. In 1944, hearing himself condemned to death on the radio from London, he fled to Germany with the Vichy govern-ment, whom he served, with gleeful hatred, in a medical capacity. Then he escaped to Denmark, where he was imprisoned but not handed over to the French. Finally, sick with paralysis and pellagra, but cleared of all charges by a military tribunal, he returned to Paris (1951). Here he practised spasmodically, often for no fees, until his death. He had published *Guignol's Band* (*La Bande de Guignol;* tr. B. Frechtman and J. T. Niles), about his time in the London of the First World War, in 1944. His remaining books deal with his seventeen years of exile: they include the posthumous *Rigadon* and his hilarious account of Vichy in exile, *Castle to Castle* (*D'un Château l'autre*, 1957; tr. R. Manheim, 1969). It is usually stated that the later Céline is a shadow of the one of the first two books. This is an exaggeration. The first two novels are undoubtedly epoch-making. But the later ones are remarkable, and have not had their due. There are no autobiographies like them. When the history books have been reduced to lists of whatever indisputable facts they contain, it is to Céline's accounts of twentieth-century life that the truly curious will turn.

Every novelist who survives is, of course, ultimately unclassifiable; but most may be usefully seen against the background of one tradition or another. An exception is BLAISE CENDRARS (ps. FRÉDÉRIC SAUSER, 1887–1961), who was entirely his own man even when temporarily involved with movements.

Although he claimed at various times to have been been born in Paris, Egypt and Italy, Cendrars was in fact born in Switzerland, near Neuchâtel. He has been described, with justice, as 'one of the greatest liars of all time'. However, this likable eccentric and continual traveller, who lost an arm fighting voluntarily for France in the First World War, certainly knew most of the French writers worth knowing during his lifetime; his lies were self-protective, strategic and humorous—not boastful, which they never needed to be. His father was Swiss, his mother a Scot. After several adventurous failures—as businessman, student and horticulturalist—he began to write seriously in about

1908. His poetry is impressionistic, formless, evocative; an Englishman would call it poetic prose; like all his work, it tends towards the journalistic, not troubling itself about aesthetic levels. His breathless, lyrical manner, anticipating itself, running on beyond itself and never catching up with itself—often highly effective—was influential, as was his philosophy: 'There is no truth other than absurd life shaking its ass's ears. Wait for it, lie in ambush for it, kill it'. *Easter in New York* (*Pâques à New York*, 1912) and *Panama* (1918; tr. J. Dos Passos, 1931) contain some of his best poetic writing.

Cendrars' most conventional novel is *Sutter's Gold* (*L'Or*, 1925; tr. H. L. Stuart, 1926). This tells the story of the Swiss General who discovered and created California, was ruined by the discovery of gold beneath his lands, but then made a new discovery of inner fortitude almost as resilient as that of any of Montherlant's (q.v.) characters. *Antarctic Fugue* (*Dan Yack*, 1927, 1929; tr. 1929) and *Moravagine* (1926; tr. A. Brown, 1969) complement one another: the first, constructive and optimistic, delineates the survival of a pragmatist, and is against creativity; the second is destructive (the name of the intensely anti-feminine hero means, of course, 'Death-to-the-vagina') but for creativity. Cendrars' work thus certainly touches on the matter of *Künstlerschuld* (q.v.); but he is casual, and regards his creativity as a matter of survival as well as of morals. Cendrars, whose prose veers without unease or embarrassment between journalese and exquisite and inspired expression, was not primarily a writer; he was an adventurer highly suspicious of literature, but drawn to it as a con-man is drawn to a promising mark. He was gifted as a storyteller, and was much influenced and aided in this and other respects by an early visit to Russia. It is not easy to see his seriousness through the clouds of what many English-speaking readers would call his irresponsibility, and he does share with his admirer Henry Miller (q.v.) a certain naïvety that leads him (like Miller) into foolishness as well as innocence. None the less, he is an important anti-literary writer, and one of whom a more detailed study should be made.

Two novelists who died young play an important part in French literature. ALAIN-FOURNIER (ps. HENRI-ALBAN FOURNIER, 1886–1914) was possibly the most severe loss French literature sustained during the First World War: he was killed in action during its first weeks. He left one novel, *The Lost Domain* (*Les Grandes Meaulnes*, 1913; tr. F. Davison, 1959), some short stories (*Miracles*, 1924), and a correspondence (1948) with the critic and editor Jacques Rivière (1886–1925) that is both fascinating in itself and wonderfully revealing of the feelings and aspirations of the literary young of that period. He came from the marshy and flat countryside around Bourges in Cher, and his fiction is redolent of its fenny, brooding atmosphere. His one finished work has irritated many critics because of what they take to be its immaturity and even 'nastiness'. The cult of childhood seems to these critics to be over-extended: the tragic ending, they maintain, is contrived in its interests. Others see the book as the one successful novel to come out of symbolism. There is some truth in both views, although the severity of the first should be modified by the fact of the author's inability to demonstrate whether and how he would have developed.

The story is one of a dream world, a manor, discovered and dreamingly enjoyed, abruptly lost, then rediscovered and destroyed. It is a classic of immaturity and adolescence, and possibly irritating for that. But it is told with lucidity, grace and even magic. Besides, what adolescent fantasy—and this is one—is not 'nasty' as well as lovely? Alain-Fournier showed, even within the limitations of this one book, that he was aware of the precarious nature of the lost paradise of childhood. What he could not quite cope with, except in the vaguest possible way, were the intimations of lust that bring it down upon its foundations. The 'love' in this book is unconvincing: the question is evaded. But Alain-Fournier might well, had he not disappeared (his body was never recovered), have developed the capacity to deal with this problem.

RAYMOND RADIGUET (1903–23), born in Paris, achieved success as an adolescent with some ambitious, precious, wicked, clever little *fantaisiste* poems (collected in *Cheeks on Fire, Les Joues en feu*, 1920), wrote two novels, and died of typhoid at twenty. He was introduced to Paris literary society by ANDRÉ SALMON (1881), a minor poet and close associate of the surrealists. Radiguet was greatly promising, but has been overvalued and turned into a cult; perhaps this has something to do with the fact that two of the men who first took him up, Cocteau and Jacob (qq.v.), were homosexuals with a tendency to sentimentality. His two novels do not fulfil their promise because they are emotionally immature. One does not expect every precocious adolescent to be a Rimbaud. But they are more than brilliant classical pastiche. *The Devil in the Flesh* (*Le Diable au corps*, 1923; tr. K. Boyle, 1932), which is partly autobiographical, tells of a youth's love for an older married woman whose husband is at the war. The thoughtful austerity with which the tale is told is distinctly more concentrated than the feeling Radiguet put into it; but nothing is false or forced. *Count d'Orgel Opens the Ball* (*Le Bal du Comte d'Orgel*, 1924; tr. M. Cowley, *The Count's Ball*, 1929; tr. V. Schiff, 1952) is closely modelled on Madame de La Fayette's *La Princesse de Clèves* (regarded as the first French psychological novel). The role of the epigrammatic sage was too much for Radiguet to manage: this novel does not escape affectation, although it is keenly intelligent. Radiguet was very much under the spell of Cocteau, and, in portraying women, possessed a similar sexually oblivious (pathic?) sensitivity, sympathy and gentleness. Radiguet did not have time to grow a heart, and the people of his novels are pale and a little too consciously classicized reflections of real people; but he had remarkable control over them, and might well have outgrown his dependence on the eighteenth century, to which he turned not because he understood it particularly well but because it offered him the artificiality and the stability he needed to fortify the legend of precocity that he was creating.

Mention should be made here of the so-called 'populism', an intelligent neo-realism that has persisted from the late Twenties until the present day. The prize for the best novel embodying 'populist' aims was instituted by Mme Antonine Coulet-Tessier in 1931, and is still awarded. No great novel has come out of this tradition, but many good ones have been written in it—and it could have its importance yet. There is no school; and from the outset the manifestos were sensible: in essence, no more was asserted than that a realist tradition (as well as middlebrow fiction) should exist by the side of the *avant garde*. The novelists LÉON LEMONNIER (1890–1953) and ANDRÉ THÉRIVE (ps. ROGER PUTHOSTE, 1891–1967) began by reacting to the literature of *snobisme*, of 'those trivial sinners who have nothing to do but put on rouge' of high society. They postulated an eclectic realism, which would incorporate 'mysticism' (as an authentic aspect of human experience) and which would guard itself against 'petty pessimism'. The movement was shortlived, but while it lasted it was supported by such as Simenon, Duhamel, Romains, Barbusse, Sinclair Lewis, Heinrich Mann and Aragon (qq.v.). The original populist group is often called 'neo-naturalist', but this is misleading and arises from a semantic confusion. What Thérive and Lemonnier were trying to establish was simply a fluid, adaptable realism—but Lemonnier called it a 'true and indispensable naturalism': a vehicle, he meant, for the honest and loving depiction of the ever-changing reality of the world: 'we are sure to prolong the great tradition of the French novel, which always disdains pretentious acrobatics in favour of writing simply and truthfully.' But perhaps the term naturalist was partially justified: in the sense that the original populists did intend 'to depict the people'. There was, in their pronouncements, a hopeful and even a socialist note. In many of their actual novels, however, there existed more than a trace of gloom. We find pessimism in Thérive's own early *Without Soul* (*Sans âme*, 1928), as in his later *Voices of Blood* (*Les Voix du sang*, 1955). But it is materialism that arouses his gloom. His portraits of weak, life-battered eccentrics are effective, but his style is in general too elegant for his material. Lemonnier's *Woman without Sin* (*Femme sans péché*, 1931), not a pessimistic book, is a psychological study of a proletarian woman.

The most considerable 'populist' novelist, however, was EUGÈNE DABIT (1898–1936), son of a Paris labourer. Dabit worked at menial jobs, joined up and served at the front, and then began to educate himself. He discovered the angry nineteenth-century writer Jules Vallès (one of the generous, hate-impelled ancestors of Céline), the gentle Charles-Louis Philippe (q.v.), and others, and he conceived the ambition to illuminate the lives of the humble of Paris as they had not been illuminated before. He did not succeed in this; but his novels, and especially the first, are today unduly neglected. *Hôtel du Nord* (1929; tr. H. P. Earle, 1931), based on some of what he had seen in the hotel his parents now managed, was awarded the first populist prize. He wrote several more novels, including *Villa Oasis* (1932) and *A Brand New Death* (*Un Mort tout neuf*, 1934). Dabit was a depressed personality whose experience had taught him that the world was a place without consolations. He died of scarlet fever while in Russia, where he had gone (with Gide, q.v.) to attend Gorki's (q.v.) funeral. *Hôtel du Nord* was made into a good movie by Marcel Carné.

Dabit had a deep suspicion of the 'populist' label. This was reasonable. No one likes to be labelled—and thus put away. But his work is in fact firmly in the realist tradition Lemonnier and Thérive so undogmatically tried to consolidate.

The populist movement was certainly ephemeral; it is quite often dismissed. I have chosen to give it space because so many realists, in no way attempting to fulfil its programme, in fact do so.

Thus the Breton LOUIS GUILLOUX (1899), who was with Dabit on his final trip to Russia, wrote in this tradition until he was past fifty, though, as Malraux (q.v.) said of him, he has 'an eternal grudge against reality' so powerful that it compels him to express himself, not lyrically, but 'through this same reality': his characters, observed in a minute detail reminiscent of the heyday of naturalism, 'give the impression of being seen in a kind of phosphorescent light. . . .' His early novel *The House of the People* (*La Maison du peuple*, 1927), a close study of poverty, received praise from Camus (q.v.). His masterpiece, a remarkable novel that finds a perfect objective correlative for the conflict in the author between his poetic and his political inclinations, is *Bitter Victory* (*Sang noir*, 1935; tr. S. Putnam, 1938). This is set in 1917, in Brittany, and concerns the last day of Merlin, a schoolmaster who indulges his nihilism and hatred of the bourgeois, and yet meanly clings on to his bank securities. And since he cannot attain inner freedom, and believes in nothing, he kills himself. Since the war, during most of which he was in hiding in Toulouse, Guilloux has become more disillusioned, but has retained his passion for delineating all aspects of urban life in meticulous detail: *The Game of Patience* (*Le Jeu de patience*, 1949), immensely long, analyses the life of a Breton town over fifty years. Much more interesting and more like *Bitter Victory* is *Parpagnacco* (1954), in which the author entirely (as if heeding Malraux's remarks, made in the Thirties) abandons his usual method. This strange book tells of a search for a girl in Italy undertaken by two Swedes, who remain possessed by an icy Northern evil. *The Confrontation* (*La Confrontation*, 1968) is also a successful novel, combining the old realism with procedures well assimilated from more recent novelists: an old man recreates the life of a stranger, in a town between Paris and Brest, in a quest to discover his 'worthiness' (if he is 'worthy', he will be given money by a mysterious rich man). Guilloux, if he has never quite repeated the achievement of *Bitter Victory*, with its stiflingly accurate account of an acute intelligence trapped in 'viscosity' (q.v.), is none the less a considerable and, in England, too easily ignored novelist.

JULIEN GREEN (1900), who was born in Paris of American parents, has in common with Guilloux a concern with the inner world of his characters. Apart from the years 1939–45 he has lived in France. He is bilingual, and writes his novels in French. *Memories of Happy Days* (1942), a moving autobiography, is in English. His *Journals*, which have been appearing since 1928, give a full account of his Jansenist anguish (pt. tr. J. Godofroi, *Personal Record, 1928–39*, 1940; tr. A. Green, *Diary 1928–57*, 1962). No Roman Catholic writer has a more tortured soul than Green, but it is misleading to call him a 'Catholic novelist': until *Moïra* his novels do not deal with problems of faith, but with problems of anguish and illusion—particularly with the false promises held out by sexual release and physical love. Green's technique is Victorian-Gothic—his novels are highly melodramatic—but he is a modernist because his subject is the Nietzschean one of 'man without God'; for Green godlessness is epitomized in man's condition of lustfulness and panic. He has perhaps learned more from Balzac than anyone else, although when he was young he read Dickens, Hawthorne and others with rapt attention.

Green, says a critic, is 'incapable of the exhibitionism which delights other Catholics also dwelling in Sodom'. He has always been a restrained writer, but has never concealed the fact that he was 'crucified in sex'. *Avarice House* (*Mont-Cinère*, 1926; tr. M. Best, 1927) was a Gothic tale of a miserly woman trapped in a hate relationship with her daughter. *The Dark Journey* (*Léviathan*, 1929; tr. V. Holland, 1929), equally Gothic, comes nearer to the bone of Green's concerns: a man, in raping a servant girl, scars her face by lashing her with a branch; she falls in love with him and flees with him. *The Dreamer* (*Le Visionnaire*, 1934; tr. V. Holland, 1934) shows the other side of the penny: the ecstatic hero realizes that life is anguish but that there really does exist another and perfect world.

However, Green's best work lay in front of him, and belongs to the post-war period. One of his three plays, *South* (*Sud*, 1953; tr. 1955), set in the American South, has power; but the two novels *Moïra* (1950; tr. D. Folliot, 1951) and *Each in His Darkness* (*Chaque Homme dans sa nuit*, 1960; tr. 1961) represent the peak of his achievement. In the first a puritanical young student at an American university murders a girl with whom he has been to bed. Here faith does have some say, if only obliquely, for without it Green could not have achieved the serenity of his characterization of the people whose sexuality so violently disturbs them. *Each in His Darkness* approaches the problem of Catholicism more openly. Wilfred Ingram, target of many homosexual approaches, is a draper's assistant who wants to live a good Catholic life but whose sensuality torments him. Ingram's 'Catholicism' as contrasted with his sexually disturbed life makes sense whether the reader is Roman Catholic or not. It might be objected that Green's idea of erotic pleasure is an unrealistic one; the answer is the question, Who's is not? He is a frenetic writer—but no novelist has exploited modern Gothic to such effect.

*

Before considering Saint-Exupéry and Malraux, two novelists of action, it would be wrong to leave unmentioned the eccentric, versatile armchair adventurer PIERRE MAC ORLAN (ps. PAUL DUMARCHAIS, 1883–1970), born at Péronne, in Picardy. Before the First World War, in which he fought, he was a cartoonist, and assumed his Scottish pseudonym. His early novels were fantasies, the best known of which is *Yellow Laughter* (*La Rire jaune*, 1914), a parody of H. G. Wells (q.v.) in which the earth is invaded and overcome by the yellow laughter of the title. Mac Orlan, who was an outer member of Picasso's circle, flirted with a poetry that never, as a critic has said, became more than prose: *Complete Poems* (*Poésies documentaires complètes*, 1954). However, it is a pleasantly readable prose. But his adventure stories at their best are at least reminiscent of Conrad or Stephenson; and in his tough studies of port life he reaches the peak of his achievement, Marcel Carné captured the exact taste of it all in his 1938 movie (with Jean Gabin, Michèle Morgan and Pierre Brasseur all playing magnificently) of *Quay of Shadows* (*Le Quai des brumes*, 1927). Mac Orlan, also an art critic and essayist, was a thoroughly competent professional writer. He has written novels about magic and the supernatural, of which he has an extensive knowledge. The excitement and action in his tales spring from a philosophy that prefers the stable adventures of the mind to the cruel and dangerous ones of actuality.

ANTOINE DE SAINT-EXUPÉRY (1900–44), however, could not live happily without facing the actual challenge of death. He belongs to the long line of literary men of action, which includes figures as diverse as d'Annunzio (q.v.), T. E. Lawrence, Ernst Jünger and Malraux (qq.v.). It is likely that the legend (he had, like T. E. Lawrence, a genius for 'backing into the limelight') and the man himself—much loved, mysterious and heroic—have become confused with the worth of his actual books. Born at Lyon, he had a radiantly happy childhood: this was the paradise that he fell back upon when his search in dangerous action—flying—for release from inner tensions and for human brotherhood exercised intolerable strains. His first book, *Southern Mail* (*Courrier-Sud*, 1928; tr. S. Gilbert, 1933) is a relatively crude adventure story, based on Saint-Exupéry's experiences as a pioneer of commercial flying; but it does contain some of the descriptions of flying for which Saint-Exupéry is famous. *Night Flight* (*Vol de nuit*, 1931; tr. S. Gilbert, 1932) is a great improvement. It contains two well drawn characters: the externally ruthless but inwardly tender head of a newly established South American airline, and his mystical chief pilot. This essentially simple and well constructed book may well be Saint-Exupéry's best, although it does not contain all his best writing, which is distributed between the two non-fiction books, *Wind, Sand and Stars* (*Terre des hommes*, 1939; tr. L. Galantière, 1939), on being a flier in the Thirties, and *Flight to Arras* (*Pilote de guerre*, 1942; tr. L. Galantière, 1942), on his experiences as a reconnaissance pilot at the time of the defeat of France. He left a charming children's book, *The Little Prince* (*Le Petit Prince*, 1945; tr. K. Woods, 1945) and an on the whole inferior posthumous collection of aphorisms and meditation slung together under the title of *The Wisdom of the Sands* (*Citadelle*, 1948; tr. S. Gilbert, 1950). One must not look for more in Saint-Exupéry than he can truly give; when he tries to be metaphysical he can be portentous and even pretentious—but when he sticks to the task in hand, as he did in *Night Flight*, and simply projects his feelings and sensations and his accurate memories (he had been in South America operating an airline), then, as Gide observed, he is truly metaphysical. Furthermore, he still has no rival in the literature of flight.

The spectacular ANDRÉ MALRAUX (1901), born in Paris, is another who writes from experience of various kinds of action. But he is more effective as an intellectual than Saint-Exupéry; and when, after his pro-communism (he was never a Marxist) of the Thirties, he became Minister of Propaganda and then Culture in de Gaulle's governments (he departed when the General did), he dried up as a novelist, and has concentrated on the history of art. In his youth he was an archaeologist and an adventurer, and became involved, in the Twenties in Indo-China, with the smuggling of statues. He was also involved in revolutionary activities in China. In the Second World War he was in the tank corps and was taken prisoner. He escaped and became a guerilla leader, was recaptured; and then set free when his comrades raided Toulouse Prison where he was held. During the Spanish Civil War Malraux fought against the fascists as an airman.

Malraux is important among modern writers as one who, despite his (self-styled) Dostoevskian imagination, has always wanted to do something, to be 'engaged'. Not for him the notion of the writer committed to no more than his function as writer. A consistent theme throughout his fiction has been a Spenglerian notion of the decline of the West, in which he has perhaps continued depressedly to believe: thus the post-novelist elevates only graphic art above fatal history; the Minister, instead of pursuing fiction, has the historic buildings of Paris cleaned and restored—and, alas, vulgarized. Malraux's 'swing to the right' after the war should be regarded not as political but as springing from a conviction that the Russian form of communism is more of a threat to Western freedom than the corruptions of capitalism; doubtless there was an element of personal ambition. There was enough 'leftism' in de Gaulle to satisfy him; his complacency about the system that the General would leave behind him on his departure (the uneasy France of Pompidou) is more criticizable. In any case, the choice of so shrewd and sensitive a man cannot be ignored. The key to his behaviour is to be found in *The Voices of Silence* (*Les Voix du silence*, 1951; tr. S. Gilbert, 1953), the book on art in which he reveals himself as pessimistic determinist arguing for the deliberate assertion of art over history: because art is the only permanent expression of man's will over fate. The inevitable corollary is that forms of society (even the General's) are not in this way permanent. However, Malraux does, at times thrillingly, put forward art as the only common denominator of mankind. It would be *logical* for a man holding such views to be Minister of Culture in any government.

Malraux established himself as an important writer with his third novel, *Man's Estate* (*La Condition humaine*, 1933; tr. A. Macdonald, 1948), the background of which is Chiang Kai-Shek's coup against the communists of 1927. This is a novel without a 'plot' in the conventional sense: it consists of a series of scenes, cinematic in technique, throughout which a lurid drama of deceit and murder is played out. This was one of the earliest serious novels to have many of the features of a thriller, and in this way led on from Conrad (q.v.), by whom Malraux must have been influenced. It was perhaps the first book to reveal the true nature of twentieth-century politics in action; those who read it and then accused Malraux, twelve years later, of betraying the left were far off the mark: he had never, as a writer, pledged himself to them (nor, of course, has he ever repudiated some measure of communism, at some appropriate time, as a necessary form of change). After a more straightforward novel, *Days of Contempt* (*Le Temps du mépris*, 1935; tr. H. M. Chevalier, 1938), the unequivocally anti-fascist story of a communist imprisoned by the Nazis and freed by a comrade's strategem so that he may continue the fight, Malraux produced what is probably the best of all his books: *Days of Hope* (*L'Espoir*, 1937; tr. S. Gilbert and A. Macdonald), on the tragic prelude to the Second World War, the Civil War in Spain. This employs the same highly effective cinematic technique as *Man's Estate*, and contains a classic account of the heroic defence of Madrid. It reflects the Spanish Civil War more fairly than any other book (Barea's, q.v., reporting was from the inside), in its desperate untidiness, its marvellous hopes, and in its irony—men of intellect riddling one another with bullets. It is frequently, and rightly, compared with Hemingway's sentimental but best-selling *For Whom the Bell Tolls* (q.v.) to the detriment of the latter. There was only one more novel to come. While in prison Malraux began a long novel, much of which the Germans destroyed. The surviving part of *The Struggle with the Angel* (*La Lutte avec l'ange*) is *The Walnuts of Altenburg* (*Les Noyers de l'Altenburg*, 1943, 1945; tr. A. W. Fielding, 1952), a 'dialogue novel' of great interest, but a failure as fiction. The story offers a framework for discussions of Malraux's ideas; freed from the pressures of his imagination, he becomes (as all human beings do) more philosophical, rhetorical, consciously noble; it represents a diffusion of imagination. But there are memorable passages, in particular an extraordinary recreation of the madness of Nietzsche (q.v.).

It seems that Malraux, when he was driven by his imagination, sought in action some kind of reification of his ideals; driven by his (considerable) intellect, he has postulated art as man's eternal escape in books that may well be bad art-history, but which are none the less important. He and Saint-Exupéry served as models for many writers. Of his involvement with politics we may at least say that his shame is his own business. How must he have felt as he 'briefed' Nixon for his Chinese adventure (1972)?

The novelist, geographer, historian and art-historian ANDRÉ CHAMSON (1900), who was born at Nîmes, resembles his wartime comrade and friend André Malraux in a number of ways: he is concerned with personal courage as a way of life; he, too, was associated with left-wing activities in the Thirties, and was actually in politics; again, a qualified archivist, he became director of the art gallery of the Petit Palais, in Paris, after the war; he wrote on the Spanish Civil War. Chamson, who has written poems in Provençal and is an admirer of Mistral (q.v.), is essentially a regionalist, although not a militant one like Giono. On the whole his social concerns have emerged most fruitfully in his regional rather than in his metropolitan novels; an exception is *The Year of the Vanquished* (*L'Année des vaincus*, 1935), on Nazi Germany and its blighting of Franco-German proletarian friendship. This was in the same international spirit as Pabst's movie, *Comradeship* (*Kameradschaft*, 1931), which showed German miners coming to the aid of French in a disaster. Unfortunately the imagination of Chamson, who is an admirably humane and intelligent man, is not sufficiently powerful to give his fiction as a whole much colour or conviction. In that respect he has written little better than his first novel, *Roux the Bandit* (*Roux le bandit*, 1925; tr. V. W. Brooks, 1929), about a tough peasant who refuses to join up, and is sought by *gendarmerie* while the locals fête him and turn him into a hero—and its successor, *The Road* (*Les Hommes de la route*, 1927; tr. V. W. Brooks, 1929), a vivid and sympathetic depiction of nineteenth-century Provençal peasants leaving the country to live in the town. *The Sum of Our days* (*Le Chiffre de nos jours*, 1954) is a lucid re-creation, in fictional form, of Chamson's Cévanole childhood. Chamson has always been obsessed by Catholic cruelty to his Protestant ancestors, and in *The Superb* (*La Superbe*, 1967) he traces the history of the persecuted *camisards*, the Huguenots who eventually rose up in the early eighteenth century. This is often an effectively dispassionate picture of persecution, though the struggle for objectivity is a painful and over-lengthy one. Chamson is important for his understanding of his region and as a representative of the minority Protestant tradition.

VII

PAUL VALÉRY (1871–1945), born at Sète on France's Mediterranean coast near Montpellier, represents an end-development of nineteenth-century symbolism as much as a beginning to twentieth-century modernism. Universally considered to be France's greatest poet of the century, he has had little direct influence. He was austere but also smilingly humorous; indeed, his sense of fun was probably the chief factor in the stability he maintained in despite of a mind stretched in many directions. Valéry's coldness, for all his natural reticence, was only apparent; otherwise the surface of his poetry would merely look like a picture of the sea—and not resemble the sea itself: glitteringly delicate, richly suggesting its hidden depths.

Valéry's external life was uneventful. He studied law, did military service, worked as a civil servant and then for a news agency for over twenty years until 1922, when he retired. He married in 1900. To begin to approach his highly abstruse but beautiful poetry—perhaps the most sheerly 'beautiful' of the century—it is necessary to consider his hermetic beginnings under the influence of Mallarmé, whom he knew well; and to understand that he desperately desired not to be a poet—or a writer at all—but just a thinker.

Thus, after some prolific early poetry in the manner of the symbolists and Mallarmé, Valéry gave up writing poetry—in an access, one may guess, of sceptical despair, as well as because of an unhappy love affair—and invented the cruelly impossible Monsieur Teste, master of thought, who only lacks the 'weakness of character' that is necessary to become a universally acclaimed genius. But of course Monsieur Teste—*Monsieur Teste* (*La Soirée avec Monsieur Teste*, 1896, 1919, 1946; tr. J. Matthews, 1947)—was only one side of Valéry. In 1912 he took up work on some of his early poems, including 'The Young Fate' ('La Jeune Parque', 1917), which he expanded into one of his major works, and in 1922 brought out a further volume, *Enchantments* (*Charmes*, 1922).

All his life he worked on his *Notebooks* (*Cahiers*, 1957–61; pt. VCW), which since their publication in twenty-nine volumes have been seen to form an essential part of his prose work. He combined within himself, perhaps more successfully than any other modern writer, the roles of scientist and poet. No philosopher will ever regard him as a philosopher; but the work he did in the 257 *Notebooks*, lucid dawn research (he favoured the early rather than the late hours) on the mental origins of his poems and other writings—should eventually be considered as far more important than any twentieth-century philosophy; they suggest, indeed, that philosophy (in at least the British sense) is now an exhausted vein. The conscious basis of his poetic art had been anti-romanticism; but in 1912 he became involved in a struggle to push back to the utmost the limits of irrationality. The result, especially in 'The Pythoness' (' La Pythie'), 'The Cemetery by the Sea' ('Le Cimetière Marin') and 'The Young Fate' is a poetry of weight, sonorous beauty and, above all, extraordinary Mediterranean wildness and robust sensibility. During the twenty years of his poetic silence Valéry had pondered on the problem of creativity, and had discovered that, in the words of his most famous single line, 'Le vent se lève! . . . il faut tenter de vivre!' ('The wind rises! . . . We must try to live!'). He set out to investigate the unconscious origins of his early poetry; to examine the method by which the irrational is made significant. The project grew; the campaign against romanticism became a reluctant definition of it, its iron surface redolent of its secret beauties and mysteries. Valéry's finest poetry has an emotional substance that his original master Mallarmé's usually lacks: at its core is an educated Latin sensuality, even at times a smiling hedonist ('the astonishing spring laughs, violates. . . .'). The theory-bound French critics who accused him of turning poetry into an intellectual exercise (this was a mid-century phase of reaction, and has now been dropped) ignored all but the strict classicism of form that his temperament required. That first great rediscovery of his poetic power, 'La Jeune Parque', makes this clear: 'without doubt the most perfect and the most difficult poem in the French language', an enraptured account of a young girl's apprehension of spring and desire, of the poet's own abandonment of the shadowless death of thought for the disturbing uncertainties of life:

> Were purpose clear, all would seem vain to you.
> Your ennui would haunt a shadowless world
> Of neutral life and untransforming souls.
> Something of disquiet is a holy gift:
> Hope, which in your eyes lights up dark alleyways,
> Does not arise from a more settled earth;
> All your splendours spring from mysteries.
> The most profound, not self-understood,
> From certain night derive their riches
> And the pure objects of their noble loves.
> The treasure that irradiates your life
> Is dark; from misty silence poems arise.

T. S. Eliot (q.v.) was right when he asserted that it is Valéry who will be, for posterity, 'the representative poet' of the first half of our century. This is not to say that he was 'better' than, for example, Rilke; but he does represent the absolutely sentimentive (q.v.) artist. He is the major poet who is also the major critic, in the most acutely self-conscious, the most 'sentimentive' century. What he wrote about the composition of his poetry is among the most searching of all criticism; doubtless it is significant that it is by a poet, and that it is self-criticism.

As one may gather from reading Gide's *Journals*, Valéry (whom Gide loved none the less) seemed in certain respects to be a cold, irritating and even an ungenerous man. He was, Léautaud says, 'violently anti-Dreyfus'—but not too seriously. Unable to reach in conversation the precision he achieved in writing, he tended to substitute for it a sweepingly superior condemnation of everything. However, he was also gay and vivacious, 'the depths of his soul broken open by laughter', said Cocteau. But the oft-repeated charge of 'cerebral narcissism' must stand—indeed, a cerebral narcissism was essential to this poetry. Valéry carries one aspect of the French poetic genius to a point of richness that no one without passion could have done; no one will deny him his place as one of the four or five of France's supreme poets.

*

While Valéry was going his own independent way, much was happening in French poetry. The First World War did not produce the quality of poetry from France that it produced from Great Britain and Germany: against Sorley, Owen, Sassoon, Rosenberg (qq.v.) in Britain, and Stadler, Stramm and Trakl (qq.v.) and others in Germany, France can really only offer Apollinaire.

Some would class CHARLES PÉGUY (1873–1914), who was born at Orléans and died at the head of his troops on the Marne in the first weeks of the war, as a war poet. He had anticipated and ardently desired the war since 1905. But the lines 'Happy are the dead, for they have gone back to / The first clay fed by their bodies . . .' ('Heureux sont ces morts, car ils sont retournés / Dans ce terre au nourris de leur dépouille . . .'), too famous outside their context in the long poem *Ève*, while they reflect the universally keen war-spirit of 1914, are not about the realities of war itself (which Apollinaire's poems, for all their ironic playfulness, are), and were in any case written before it. Judged by the poetic standards of the war poetry of Owen and others, these lines are as specious, although less egocentric, than Rupert Brooke's (q.v.) popular 'war' sonnets. Péguy was a playwright and poet, but owes his high, possibly too high, position in French literary history to his essays and to his foundation and editorship of the influential *Cahiers de la Quinzaine* (1900–14), the files of which provide an indispensable guide to the France of its period. Péguy began as a socialist and an agnostic, but ended as a right-wing Catholic crusader. A supporter of Dreyfus, he quarrelled with the manner of the Dreyfusards' exploitation of their victory. Péguy was always high-minded, a man of passionate integrity and sincerity; it may well be that the legend (hagiography is not too strong a word) of the man has seemed to invest his visionary verse with qualities that it does not possess. It is interesting to speculate upon what the always just Péguy, who loved his country and its army, would have felt about the glory of the war by 1917. One can be sure that he would not have pretended.

The historical importance of the indisputably noble Péguy and of his changing convictions, from intellectual agnostic international socialist to unorthodox Catholic patriot and Bergsonian anti-intellectual, is evident. But how will he be judged as a poet? He stands outside the mainstream of twentieth-century European poetry because he speaks absolutely directly and offers no linguistic difficulties whatever. His poems, long and repetitive, can only (and then remotely) be compared to those of Claudel—to no one else's. Péguy is even more anachronistic, and writes, with a countryman's simplicity, of the 'supernatural' itself as 'carnal'. The main poems are a recast of his earlier play, *The Mystery of the Charity of Joan of Arc* (*Le Mystère de la charité de Jeanne d'Arc*, 1909; tr. J. Green, 1950), the poem of his 1908 reconversion, *Ève* (1913)— 10,000 lines—and *The Mystery of the Holy Innocents* (*Le Mystère des Saints Innocents*, 1912; tr. with other poems P. Pakenham, 1956). Passionate, incantatory, diffuse, this poetry compels attention by its sheer force of conviction; it rings true; but it cannot come to the point ('like a cunning peasant', said a critic, remembering Péguy's peasant origins of which he was so proud), and nothing in it compensates for the monotony of the repetitions. It should perhaps be judged not as poetry but as a rhythmical prose of the same kind as that of Ramuz (q.v.), to whose fictional style it has been compared: 'full of knots and slag . . . harsh and strong . . . primitive . . . concrete and spoken. . . .' (PBFV4; FBS)

Most of the other twentieth-century French poets (few of whom approach Valéry in seriousness or importance) may be considered in relation to, or at least seen against, the background of that exceedingly Gallic phenomenon, surrealism—which critics take too seriously at grave risk. Dada (q.v.), which manifested itself in Switzerland during and as a protest against the First World War, was the movement out of which it sprang; and dada, of course, was one of the outcomes of expressionism (q.v.). The co-founder of dada, TRISTAN TZARA (1896–1963), originally a Rumanian, collaborated with the surrealists from 1929–34. Previously Breton had supplanted him as leader of the Paris dada group (1919). Dada was necessary to literature, although in its extremity of romanticism it could ultimately only laugh at itself ('true dadas are against dada'): by being at all, it contradicted itself, was pacifist and yet nihilist, totally destructive and yet hoped (Tzara's words) for 'a purified humanity'. Dada, picked out at a very apt random by Tzara from a *Larousse* with a paper-knife, means 'hobby horse', 'obsession'; it also, of course, mocked at the bourgeois God, the authoritative father (cf. expressionism)—rather as Blake more than a century before had with his 'Nobodaddy'.

Predictably, Tzara abandoned nihilism and became more politically committed. His long poem *Approximate Man* (*L'Homme approximatif*, 1931) tries to express his revolutionary hopes, but most of it is bogged down in an obsessional verbalism. After the Second World War, during which Tzara had engaged in anti-Nazi activities in the South of France, he moved to a more conventional and lyrical poetry. Important as a literary symptom, his own work is moving in the context of his struggles—but scarcely effective in its own right.

Surrealism was, in basic literary terms, a revolution against *all* kinds of formal literary expression (but with literary antecedents: including de Sade, Nerval, Isidore Ducasse, self-styled Comte de Lautréamont, 1846–70—the overrated sick adolescent who wrote *The Songs of Maldoror, Les Chants de Maldoror*, 1868; tr. G. Wernham, 1944—the more gifted and important Charles Cros, 1842–88, Jarry, q.v., and, with reservations, Baudelaire, q.v.). The surrealists proper, those who lived for the movement—officially promulgated in 1922—and never broke away, were not over-gifted writers, but confused romantic theoreticians. One cannot take André Breton, the chief surrealist, at times a veritable Stalin with his purges, wholly seriously as a creative writer: his confusions require to be studied; he is a symptom of twentieth-century unease. The history of surrealism proper is no doubt the history of Breton (its custodian). Nihilistically humorous though it often is, surrealism, in broadest terms, is an attempted answer to 'the absurd', a desperate appeal to the unconscious, to dreams, to the irrational, to establish 'a new declaration of the rights of man'. The movement eventually split up into political activists (such as Aragon) and 'explorers of the marvellous' (such as Breton).

For the truly gifted writers, on the other hand, surrealism provided a new beginning, a break with conventions; they went on to new pastures. The surrealists proper either busied themselves, like Breton, with coercion and polemic (*Manifeste du Surréalisme*, 1924; *Qu'est-ce que le Surréalisme?*, tr. D. Gascoyne, 1936, etc., etc.) or, unable to discover any commitment, killed themselves. JACQUES VACHÉ (1896–1919), the chief influence on Breton, killed himself in 1919. JACQUES RIGAUT (1899–1929), after breaking with literature (logically enough) and trying marriage with an American girl, killed himself in 1929: he had condemned himself to die, at the precise date and time he did die, in 1919. Surrealism naturally attracted such war-victims. In it, nihilism was engaged in a continuous struggle with hope; Breton, Éluard and other lesser poets tried to reconcile these in the figure of a mysterious woman; later some, but not Breton, substituted for her the communist party. God (meaning) was pitted desperately against death (meaninglessness, the 'absurd'). But now the conflict resolved itself as a battle between *signs* and *chance*. You pursued the meaningful mystery, the strange woman, and waited for the revelation; or you killed yourself; or you joined the proletariat.

ANDRÉ BRETON (1896–1966), born in Tinchebray in Normandy, wrote poems, but these are mostly of documentary interest: nine-tenths of his energy went into his concern for the movement he had been foremost in creating. In seeking to save dada from its self-destructiveness, he turned it into surrealism (the actual word was coined by Apollinaire), the concept of which, for the rest of his life, he strove to promote as a key to self-knowledge and human freedom.

Breton began as a disciple of Valéry; then, as an army psychiatrist in the

First World War, he became interested in the ideas of Freud, to which he remained loyal. His strongly anti-literary bent came from Vaché, who was not a surrealist on paper but in life; this loyalty was reinforced by his 'comic' suicide. *The Magnetic Fields* (*Les Champs magnétiques*, 1921), Breton's experiments in automatic writing in collaboration with PHILIPPE SOUPAULT (1897), was the only technical innovation introduced by surrealism. It was an important one, because it opened the way not only to unconscious writing (if in fact that can be achieved) but also to the operations of chance—and to the establishment of those significant coincidences that Jung called synchronicity. All subsequent surrealist experiments can be traced back to this, as can every one of the antics of the pseudo-*avant garde* of the Sixties—and, indeed, every one of the experiments of writers such as William Burroughs (q.v.).

Breton, 'the glass of water in the storm' (the surrealists gave themselves and each other such names), continued to defend surrealism against subordination to any ideology, even to specifically anti-bourgeois ones such as Marxism. This amounted to a defence of literature, if only a certain kind of literature, against commitment; as such it is important.

Breton's actual poetry (PBFV4; FBS; BSP) suffers from a certain rigidity; one feels that he needs a visual medium, so that rather than strain for highly emotional or dramatic effects he cannot achieve, he could attain the sort of casual charm of a Dali composition—second-rate art at its best, but unpretentious. However, in what is his most important creative work, the prose *Nadja* (1928; tr. R. Howard, 1963), he comes close to the definition of the mad, psychic, liberating woman whom he sought, and who haunted his imagination. The long surrealist prologue is irrelevant; but the part dealing with the strange Nadja, written in more coherent form, is one of the more memorable of modern attempts to penetrate the mechanical face of the everyday and inhabit the mysterious reality behind it. Nadja's unpredictable nature is presented as emanating from this super-reality.

Many writers and poets who never joined the movement as such were 'fellow travellers'—or genuine ancestors. Saint-Pol-Roux (q.v.), though a survivor from symbolism, is clearly one of them, and was recognized as such. But no predecessor was closer to surrealism than the half-Polish, half-Italian GUILLAUME APOLLINAIRE (ps. GUILLAUME-ALBERT-VLADIMIR-ALEXANDRE-APOLLINAIRE DE KOSTROWITSKY, 1880–1918). Apollinaire was a bastard: his mother Angelica, a 'demoniacal coquette' and gambler who brought him and his younger brother up in Monte Carlo, had worked in the Vatican. Apollinaire may never have known who his father, most often assumed to have been an Italian army officer, was, but he never denied that it had been Pope Leo XIII, and would have liked nothing more than for posterity to thus settle the matter. Another story, which he did not discourage, has it that he was descended from Napoleon.

Apollinaire, a quintessentially inquisitive spirit, loved by his friends, a legend in his own lifetime, was a characteristic early twentieth-century man: he was everything at once: scholar and vagabond, traditionalist and innovator, aesthete and pornographer, atheist, agnostic and religious man. When the Mona Lisa was stolen the police put him in prison. He was that kind of person. Close friend of Picasso and Braque, he was fascinated by painting, and wrote about it; he was, one might say, in on the discovery of cubism, although he did not fully understand it until the very eve of the publication of his *The Cubist Painters* (*Méditations esthétiques: Les Peintres Cubistes*, 1913; tr. L. Abel, 1949), whose sub-title he added at the last moment. In art cubism, which originated in the practice of Cézanne, was an attempt to give more than merely a representation of objects: to give a full account of their structure, and their positions in space. Several views of an object, including geometrical ones, would be superimposed on one another. Literary cubism is necessarily a somewhat vaguer term; its tendency, however, may be summed up in Apollinaire's own invention of the term 'Orphic Cubism', which he used to describe the painting of Robert Delaunay: 'the art of painting new structures out of elements that have not been borrowed from the visual sphere but have been created entirely by the artist himself, and have been endowed by him with the fullness of reality'. Substitute 'writing' for painting and add a substantial quantity of salt and we know as much about the programme of literary cubism as is good for us. What it actually *is* may most clearly be seen in the poetry of Reverdy (q.v.). Apollinaire went from -ism to -ism, continually being reproached for betrayal; after two years on the front and a serious head-wound he became more sympathetic to traditional procedures, but continued until the end (weakened, he died of influenza on 10 November, the day before the Armistice), to preach the spirit of the new. He coined the word surrealism in one of his programme notes for the Cocteau-Picasso-Massine-Satie ballet *Parade*, and used it to describe his play *The Breasts of Tirésias* (*Les Mamelles de Tirésias*, 1918; tr. L. Simpson in *Odyssey*, December, 1961). This is chaotic and impudent, but not really at all like the *Ubu Roi* of that egocentric precursor of surrealism, Jarry (q.v.): it can be variously interpreted, but its high spirits undoubtedly conceal a self-disquiet and a dissatisfaction with the role of *avant garde* clown and travelling king of all the -isms. After all, Apollinaire was no poetaster searching in theories for the substance of a genius he lacked: he was a lyric poet of genius, but one who in 1898 had found the scented perfectionism of the symbolists totally inadequate.

Most of Apollinaire's poetry is in *Spirits* (*Alcools*, 1913; tr. W. Meredith, 1964; A. Greet, 1965) and *Calligrammes* (1918); it is collected, with the theatre, in *The Poetic Works* (*Œuvres Poétiques*, 1956). The so-called calligrammes follow on from earlier poets who wrote their verses in the shapes of hour-glasses, diamonds, and so on: Apollinaire shapes a poem on rain like rain, on a car like a car, and so on. He had been doing it since the early years of the century. In these charming poems, inevitably slighter than some of his others, he took 'concrete poetry' (q.v.) as far, poetically (but not graphically), as it could go. Other poems read rather uneasily: like a mixture of the crude Italian, Marinetti (q.v.), Whitman and Verhaeren (q.v.). But the best, 'Zone', 'Song of the Badly Loved' ('Chanson du mal aimé') and many others, combine a melancholy lyricism, eroticism, sweetness, out-of-the-way knowledge, cosmopolitanism and passionate feeling. Apollinaire removed the punctuation of *Alcools* at the proof stage: 'I cut it out . . . for the rhythm itself and the division of the lines are the real punctuation'. But in technique he was less anti-traditional than he appeared and felt. When he is most moved his rhythms are usually regular.

Apollinaire's war poetry, much of which was published posthumously, eroticizes, and, at its most effective—when nervousness becomes power—transcends violence. There will always be readers ready to accuse such poems as 'The Horseman's Farewell' of 'bad taste' or 'lack of feeling'; but it is not less serious in quality than anything by Sassoon or Owen:

> Oh God how pretty war is
> With its songs and long rests
> I have polished this ring
> I hear your sighs in the wind
>
> Goodbye! Here is his gear
> He vanished from sight
> And died over there while she
> Laughed at fate's surprises

War for Apollinaire represented the emptiness within himself, which in the later poems becomes a secret grief. This secret grief is, as has been pointed out, fear of poetic inadequacy; it is also fear of the restless 'incertitude' (his own word) that had kept him on the move, from -ism to -ism, for the whole of his life. A poet of genius, the proto-surrealist who died before surrealism, he already lived at the heart of two of surrealism's profoundest paradoxes, in one of which hope wrestles with despair; the other is summed up in Valéry's laconic statement that 'the ideal of the new is contrary to the requirements of form'.

Apart from his amusing and efficient pornography, done for money, Apollinaire wrote two novels: *The Assassinated Poet* (*Le Poète assassiné*, 1916; tr. M. Josephson, 1923) and *The Seated Woman* (*La Femme assise*, 1920). These are indispensable to a study of him, but neither succeeds as a whole. Much more successful are the delightful short stories of *The Wandering Jew* (*L'Hérésiarque et Cie*, 1910; tr. R. M. Hall, 1965), in which Apollinaire shows his scholarly and Slavic side, and revels in mystery, colour and magic with the natural facility of an Isaac Bashevis Singer (q.v.) and the confidence of a poet. (ASW; ASP; PBFV4; FBS; MEP; PI; Selected Writings, tr. R. Shattuck, 1950).

The Parisian LÉON-PAUL FARGUE (1876–1947) might be described as a prince of minor poets. In certain respects, especially in his sense of humour, he resembles his friend Erik Satie, the composer whose loveliness and importance (suppressed by music journalists, fearfully oblivious to him, for fifty years) is just becoming apparent—Satie set some of his poems. Fargue was never a surrealist, but Breton pronounced him 'surrealist in atmosphere': and, like Saint-Pol-Roux, he is a link between symbolism and surrealism. He was as famous, in literary Paris, for his bohemian personality, conversation and inveterate telephoning of friends from far-flung bars as for his poetry. He has been solemnly criticized for 'wasting himself' on trivial literary activity, but the roots of his poetry, which has more substance than is immediately apparent —and little more whimsicality than Satie's massively strict music—needed the nourishment of this kind of life. The solitary Fargue is the poet of Paris and of its streets, and to evoke it accurately and vividly he frequently and increasingly used prose forms. His earlier poetry, written while he was a disciple of Mallarmé (also his schoolmaster at the Collège Rollin), groped to define small nostalgias:

> Charitable hand that chastely
> Warms the other, frozen hand.
> Straw that a bit of sun kisses
> Before the door of a dying man.
> A woman held out but not embraced
> Like a bird or a sword.
> A mouth smiling far off
> To make certain that you die well.
>
> (FBS)

Later he relied on Paris itself to make these definitions, training his apprehension of it to become ever sharper: 'poetry is the only dream in which one must not dream'. Much of Paris and Parisian bohemian and literary life died with him. He is wrongly described as an escapist: one does not 'escape' into one's own loneliness and nostalgia. Like Satie, Fargue mistrusted 'greatness', and his unpretentiousness too easily encourages his neglect. His occasional reminiscences, such as the contrast between Mallarmé as schoolmaster and teacher of 'Twinkle, twinkle, little star', and Mallarmé as poetic sage (included in *Refuges*, 1942), are charming and wise. His most famous book, whose title describes him so well, is *The Paris Pedestrian* (*Le Piéton de Paris*, 1939); much of his work appears in *Poésies* (1963), which was introduced by Saint-John Perse. *Lanterne Magique* (1944) was translated in 1946. (FBS; PBFV4)

MAX JACOB (1876–1944) was born of Jewish parents at Quimper in Brittany. He too was a legendary personality: friend of Picasso and Apollinaire, painter, homosexual, Catholic, recluse, one-time astrologer, humorist. He was taken by the Gestapo to the concentration camp at Drancy, where he died, not long before the liberation of Paris. He even made a pun about that (in a message to a friend he wrote: 'Pris par la Gestapo. Prononcez "J'ai ta peau" '). Jacob was above all a gentle and good man, whose existence was one long striving to keep at bay and yet to understand the keen misery of his childhood, when he had three times tried to kill himself. No one could penetrate the various masks —clown, martyr, saint—beneath which he lived. His refusal or inability to be himself weakens his work, which none the less has enormous charm and wholesomeness. His life, which in one of his relatively few serious moments he called 'a hell', was most unfortunately complicated by a homosexuality which he could not accept. He made no attempt to deal with this anguish in his work, which consisted of poems, prose poems, short stories and surrealist texts. He had visions of Christ in 1909 and in 1914—this one in a cinema, 'in the one-and-threes'—and in 1915 he was finally received into the Roman Catholic Church. Like most surrealists, Jacob believed in signs, and waited for them. From 1921, just as he had become famous, he retired to an Abbey at Saint-Benoît-sur-Loire. It seems that his homosexual tendencies played a great part in his decision. He did not finally settle there until 1936, after which he is said to have succeeded in leading the life of humility and prayer he so desired. He did not, however, cut himself off from poetry, painting or his friends (who visited him regularly until the war).

Jacob's most enduring writing is probably to be found in his letters; although that judgement might be shown to be unfair by a really rigorous selection from all his humorous poems, including those written in Breton. *The Dice Box* (*Le Cornet à dés*, 1917), prose poems, his most influential collection, contains the sharpest expressions of his mental crisis: he reluctantly discovers his anguish in a series of casual apprehensions, anecdotes, 'cubist' visions of 'ordinary' objects. But Jacob did not in his work achieve the serenity he may have found towards the end of his life. He was himself a work of art, a mystifier whose holiness some of his closest friends regarded as just one more joke. (JDP; FBS; PBFV4)

VALÉRY-NICOLAS LARBAUD (1881–1957) was born of rich parents in Vichy, and never entirely shrugged off the burden of the fortune he inherited. A friend of Gide's and of most of the other writers of his generation, he was never affiliated to any movement. A traveller and scholar, he did much for English literature in France, translating Coleridge and, later, some of James Joyce's *Ulysses* (q.v.). In his *Poems of A. O. Barnabooth* (*Poèmes d'A. O. Barnabooth*, 1923; first issued 1908 as *Poems of a Rich Amateur*, *Poèmes d'un riche amateur*; tr. W. J. Smith, *Poems of a Multimillionaire*, 1955) and in the prose *Intimate Journal of A. O. Barnabooth* (*Journal intime d'A. O. Barnabooth*, 1913) he projects himself into a cynical young South American who searches for his true identity while fervently responding to twentieth-century mechanization. His best work is probably the faintly sinister short novel *Fermina Marquez* (1911), describing the havoc played in an exclusive boys' school by the advent of two beautiful girls. Larbaud was intelligent, civilized and super-cultivated, but his vein of creativity was a thin one. (PBFV4)

JULES SUPERVIELLE (1884–1960), born of French-Basque parents in Montevideo, is an influential poet, a pantheist whose gentle meditations offer an interesting contrast to the more explosive surrealists. Supervielle has introduced into French poetry the South American traditions of acceptance of the harshness of existence, and of playfulness. He is a tragic poet, but not a pessimistic one:

> When the horses of time stop at my door
> I always hesitate a little to watch them drink
> Since it is with my own blood that they quench their thirst.

They turn toward me with grateful eyes
While their long draughts fill me with weakness
And leave me so weary, so alone and uncertain
That a passing night invades my eyelids
And suddenly I feel the need to rebuild my strength
So that one day when the team comes to drink
I may live again and slake my thirst.

(FBS)

Supervielle's most frequent theme is death: as the inevitable end of life (although he lived to a good age, he had a serious heart condition), as the thief of life, and as the goal of life. In his quiet and technically highly accomplished poems we do not see him (and ourselves) protesting, but rather hiding from a threat we ought to but cannot accept. A good part of his mature poetry, which begins with the collection *Gravitations* (1925) may be seen as a series of rueful, graceful strategies for spiritual or physical survival:

Presences, speak low,
Someone might hear us
And sell me to death
Hide my face
Behind the branches
And let me be indistinguishable
From the shadow of the world.

(FBS)

In Supervielle, as Laura Riding (q.v.) once said of another poet, 'fear is golden'. An unusually accessible poet who is yet truly 'modern' in spirit, he offers an excellent introduction to contemporary French poetry and its concerns. He has also written drama, novels, fine short stories—*Souls of the Soulless* (*L'Enfant de la haute mer*, 1931; tr. D. Japp and N. Nicholls, 1933)—and children's stories, of which *The Colonel's Children* (*Le Voleur d'enfants*, tr. A. Pryce-Jones, 1950) is the most enchanting. (SSW; PBFV4; FBS; MEP)

Recently rediscovered and reassessed, the work of the scholar and diplomat OSCAR VENCESLAS DE LUBICZ MILOSZ (1877–1939) contains, buried within a mass of gorgeous reconditeness, some poems of quite astonishing beauty. Milosz was a Lithuanian who learned French as a child and early chose it as his language of literary expression. A linguist and expert in philosophy and physics (it has been claimed that he evolved the theory of relativity at the same time as Einstein), he travelled in the East and wrote fairly conventional symbolist poetry. After the war he represented his country in Paris; in 1926 he retired to Fontainebleau, to a home he filled with birds. He became a French citizen (1930). His metaphysics have been described as 'an exotic blend of Catholicism, Swedenborg, Böhme, Eastern traditions and modern physics'—a mixture heady enough to enrapture any symbolist. His best poems sense the Platonic world of perfect objects as a pre-human paradise through the window of his mundane existence:

> Go down on your knees, orphan life,
> Feign prayer, while I count and count again
> Those patterns of flowers that have no sad and grimed
> Suburban garden counterparts
>
> Such as are seen hanging on doomed walls through rain.
> Later you will lift your gaze from the blank book:
> I shall see moored barges, barrels, sleeping coal
> And the wind blowing through the sailors' stiff linen. . . .

Milosz's collected works, in eleven volumes, were published 1960–3. He wrote plays—*Miguel Mañara* (1912; tr. 1919)—and philosophical explications. (MSP; PBFV4; FBS)

Recognition abroad came late for PIERRE-JEAN JOUVE (1887), who was born at Arras; he has been influential among poets in France, but until recently not much read by the general public. As well as a poet, he is a novelist, music- and art-critic, essayist and translator of Shakespeare. Never a poet easy of access, it is best to approach him in terms of his influences: unanimism (soon repudiated by him, however, as '*néfaste*': ill-omened, unfortunate; but it is symptomatic of his high serious honesty); Romain Rolland (q.v.); Freud (decisively); Roman Catholicism; Blake; Mozart (he has written well on *Don Giovanni*: *Le Don Juan de Mozart*, tr. E. B. Smith, 1957); the English meta-physical poets; the composer Alban Berg (on whom he has also written illuminatingly).

Jouve began as a 'unanimist' poet; but he has proscribed all his work before the 1929 collection, *The Lost Paradise (Le Paradis perdu)*. After emerging from the influence of Romain Rolland he underwent what he describes as a 'moral, aesthetic, spiritual crisis'; he became a Catholic and a Freudian; and at about this time he married a psychoanalyst. As he puts it, 'I have two fixed objectives: . . . to work out a poetic language that would hold its own entirely as song; to find in the poetic act a *religious* perspective—the only answer to the void of time'. Jouve, like Claudel, but from the standpoint of an entirely different temperament, saw God's kingdom of the world threatened by an engulfing Eros, the twin of death. He found no pleasure in a world from which God appeared to have withdrawn himself, and his poetry until the war (and his Swiss exile) seems, as one critic has expressed it, 'repellent and grandiose'. But acquaintance with his later work makes the earlier, which appeared in such books as *Nuptials (Les Noces*, 1928) and *Blood Sweat (Sueur de sang*, 1933), more accessible because more understandable. The poetry of the first and disturbed period is highly original, an example of a poet obstinately going his own way and finding ultimate acceptance. It is not always successful in holding its own as 'song' ('*chant*'), and its theological themes are often obscure; but Jouve does convey, urgently, his sense of the ambiguities of an eroticism whose irresistibly holy-seeming exaltations divorce him from God. These poems describe the impossibility of a physical renunciation that is nevertheless seen as necessary to salvation. They are not (like Milosz's) symbolist poems: Jouve's God is 'dead' (in the sense of the modern theological controversy). The predicament is summed up in 'The Death Tree': if man is 'saved from the sun' (of desire) by the death tree, it is in the absence of the 'Angel'—but this saving tree's roots are 'convulsed in desire', and the tree 'shuts', trying to kill the man. Then the Angel returns, and 'The dark uncertain fight took place in confusion'.

War jerked Jouve from what threatened to become an obsession, and he began to write

> for god and fire
> For a love of place
> Let the void be rid of man
> Frozen by a flame.
> (IN)

His resistance poems, collected in *The Virgin of Paris* (*La Vierge de Paris*, 1946), discovered new concerns; the collection contained his most famous poem, 'Tapestry of Apple-trees', welcoming the 'iron beasts of love', the invading armies of the allies, into Normandy in 1944.

Jouve's novels, the best known of which is *Paulina 1880* (1925), all belong to the Twenties and Thirties, and describe people who are, like himself, simultaneously obsessed by the erotic and the mystical. (IN; PBFV4; FBS)

The premier 'poet's poet' of our time, SAINT-JOHN PERSE (ps. MARIE-RENÉ ALEXIS SAINT-LÉGER LÉGER, 1887), who was born on a small coral island his family owned near Guadeloupe, chose to earn his living in the diplomatic service. He was General Secretary of the Ministry of Foreign Affairs from 1933 until the fall of France, when he went into exile in America. He lived in Washington for some years, but finally returned to France. Only Saint-John Perse's first collection, *Eulogies* (*Éloges*, 1910; tr. A. MacLeish, 1944; tr. L. Varèse, 1956), was published under his own name. In 1960 he was awarded the Nobel Prize. He is a modest and self-effacing man, who has stated that his name 'does not belong to literature'. His admirers and translators include many of the illustrious names of the twentieth century: Rilke, Eliot, Hofmannsthal, Ungaretti (qq.v.) and others.

Saint-John Perse was influenced by Claudel in his use of form: he writes in long, incantatory lines. His poetry is rooted in the early twentieth-century rediscovery of the past, most famously represented in Stravinsky's *Rite of Spring* and Eliot's *Waste Land*. He is encyclopaedic, technical, concrete, cryptic—but only as cryptic as the history of the earth as recreated in the mind of the poet. His descriptions of the world follow, it has been suggested, not recognized roads or currents, but 'isobars or isotherms, hitherto unsuspected but real paths'. He wishes to recapture the lost language, not of God—for Saint-John Perse, too, that particular God is dead—but of the Gods: the manifold voices of nature. He explores the universe historically, geologically, above all anthropologically, in his irresistibly epic terms—and in doing so discovers himself; he is a kind of Lévi-Strauss who is also a *chanteur*. His language is stately, ceremonious; he is an atheistic priest, conducting rites of nature. He has all the ecstasy of a Claudel, but sees no horror or tragedy or senselessness in a creation without Christianity. *Eulogies* contains his most personal poems, inspired by his marvellous childhood on the coral island, with a nurse who was, secretly, a pagan priestess, and by his blissful discovery of the world in those surroundings.

Anabasis (*Anabase*, 1924; tr. T. S. Eliot, 1930) is perhaps the most optimistic major work of the century. The sweeps of conquering armies of which it is full, the establishment of a town by nomads that it celebrates—these show the poet conquering the word, discovering language: 'Saint language', which contains all the Gods and is man's profoundest experience. With this poem Saint-John Perse confidently took up the mantle of Orphic poet. *Exile* (*Exil*, 1942; tr. D. Devlin, 1954), his unhappiest volume, but not a pessimistic one, describes the hero-poet cut off from his quest. *Winds* (*Vents*, 1946; tr. H. Chisholm) both enhance and disturb life; *Rains* (*Pluies*, 1943) wash it clean; in these poems and in *Snows* (*Neiges*, 1944) Saint-John Perse literally describes the elements, at the same time as integrating them into his huge single metaphor. *Seamarks* (*Amers*, 1957; tr. W. Fowlie, 1958) similarly describes the sea, but in treating it as loving the earth he also (for the first time) deals with the erotic. *Chronique* (1960) welcomes old age; *Birds* (*Oiseaux*, 1963; tr. R. Fitzgerald, 1966) traces the same mystery in the ways of the birds.

Saint-John Perse is a consistent Platonist: he seeks the true order of things in the entire universe; he also seeks to return to his enchanted childhood. His work shows no development. Except for its affinities with Claudel—himself an anachronism—it is detached from modern literature; it employs figures of medieval and Renaissance rhetoric hardly remembered today; yet it has, for those who have read it, a nearly Biblical value. Saint-John Perse's vision of paradise has not reached many readers directly—but in a diffused manner: through the many poets whose work it has nourished. (PBFV4; PI)

PIERRE REVERDY (1889–1960) was the son of a Narbonne winegrower ruined in the disaster of 1907; always something of a recluse, he was associated with the group around Apollinaire, and then with the surrealists, but never entered wholeheartedly into any *avant garde* activities. He was only in his mid-thirties when he retired to the Abbaye de Solesmes, where he lived for most of the time until his death. Although he did not have so acute a personal problem as the homosexuality of his friend Max Jacob, he was afflicted with religious doubt, which arose from his anguish at his inability to penetrate the mystery of the universe—a failure he attributed to his own inability to apprehend God. He did not find the peace he hoped for in the ascetic life he chose. He is rightly described as 'the' 'cubist' poet: he continually tries to understand, and in doing so superimposes one view (one image) of his subject-matter onto another. But what Reverdy most distrusted was the ordinary perception of his senses.

His strangely fragmented and difficult poetry, arranged geometrically on the page, is like that of a man who insists to another: 'I know that our words agree on what we see, but I do not believe that we see in the same way'. His effort, which remained consistent and unchanging all his life, was to express his own sense of the real behind the perceived. His desolate poems might be those of a frustrated painter (he wrote commentaries on paintings); certainly, to be approached at all, they must first be approached as cubist paintings:

> Someone has just gone by
> And in the room
> > has left a sigh
> Life deserted
> > The street
> > An open window pane
> A ray of sunshine
> On the green plain
> > (MEP)

Reverdy is trapped (as he often said) between reality and dream: between (in fact) the agonizedly perceived, and the intangible and elusive emotions that it conjures up—those, for Reverdy, are intimations of the existence of a true world. Poems are 'crystals precipitated after the effervescent contact of the mind with reality'. His is possibly a too remote, difficult poetry ever to have much general appeal; but he is important to other poets. For a time, in Paris during the First World War, he came under the influence of—or perhaps initiated—Huidobro's 'creationism' (q.v.): 'whatever the eye looks at, let it be created'. But the eventual difference was that while creationist poets subscribed to the notion of the poet as 'a little God' 'bringing the rose to flower in the poem' itself, Reverdy remained in a position of humility, regarding his poetry as a means of apprehension of the world—not as a way of becoming independent of it, and of compensating for godlessness by becoming god. *The Sackcloth Glove* (*Le Gant de crin*, 1927) is his intensely fascinating poetics. (RSP; PBFV4; MEP; CFP)

PAUL ÉLUARD (ps. EUGÈNE GRINDEL, 1895–1952), one of the surrealists ('the nurse of the stars') who became a communist, has achieved the widest popular fame of any of his generation as a love poet. Éluard was born and died in Paris, and was always an essentially urban poet. He was a surrealist, generously searching for the elusive purity of the erotic and for a human brotherhood that his high sophistication—rather than his intelligence—kept warning him was inaccessible. Intimately associated with Breton in the surrealist movement, Éluard possessed the poetic genius Breton lacked; like Breton, he was obsessed with the feminine figure in which all conflicts would come to rest and be reconciled. It was his broad human sympathies rather than any intellectual Marxist conviction that caused him to break with Breton and surrealism, and to join the communist party (to which, characteristically, he remained faithful until his death). His political poetry is forced and embarrassing—especially in the light of the (now more evident) betrayal of communism by those who have acted in its name; but his innocence preserved him from falsity. The fact is that while Éluard needed the liberation from convention that surrealism offered him, and the anti-bourgeois and humanitarian ideals that communism seemed to offer him, he was not convincing either as a surrealist or a communist: he was a naïve (q.v.) writer moved by the notion of human freedom, and made indignant by poverty. His poetry has a touch of folk-song about it, which makes it accessible to a non-literary public; indeed, he is an anti-literary poet, but not a proletarian one—he is too sophisticated, and has too many moments of loneliness. Until 1936 Éluard's subject was, almost invariably, the relationship between men and women. With the Spanish Civil War he came to believe that a poet's duty was to be 'profoundly involved in the lives of other men'. During the war he became, with Aragon, the leading poet of the resistance, in which he was active. At one point he had to hide in a lunatic asylum, about which he wrote one of his most moving prose works, *Memories of the Asylum* (*Souvenirs de la maison des fous*, 1946); this experience may have reminded him of his 1930 experiment in collaboration with Breton, when they tried to simulate various kinds of mental disorder: *The Immaculate Conception* (*L'Immaculée Conception*). After the war he became increasingly active as a cultural ambassador, and his poetry lost its intensity. No better tribute to him could be devised than the fact that his best poetry is loved and intuitively grasped by the intelligent young. (ESW; VTT; PBFV4; FBS; MEP)

LOUIS ARAGON (1897), born in Paris, was successively dadaist, surrealist and communist. An *enfant terrible* when young, surrealism for him, too, was a liberating phase rather than a matter of conviction. His own lyricism is usually more important than the various surrealist experiments in which he is supposed to be participating. He visited Russia in 1930 and was so impressed with what he saw that he broke with surrealism and became a realist. Breton could never have written: 'If by following a surrealist method you write wretched stupidities, they are wretched stupidities. And inexcusable'. 'We have no talent', said Breton at the time of their inevitable quarrel. 'Under pretext that this is all surrealism', replied Aragon, 'the next cur who happens along thinks himself authorized to equate his slobberings with true poetry, a marvellous comfort for vanity and stupidity.' Aragon had written a hallucinatory, surrealist novel about Paris, *The Peasant of Paris* (*Le Paysan de Paris*, 1926). Now he turned to solid novels of socialist realism, beginning with *The Bells of Basel* (*Les Cloches de Bâle*, 1933; tr. H. M. Chevalier, 1937); this was followed by many others, under the general title of 'The Real World'. These are readable and competent rather than inspired; *Aurélien* (1945; tr. E. Wilkins, 1946) is perhaps the best of them.

Aragon's best moment came with the war. Not only was he one of the leaders of the literary resistance, but also, through his poetry, he became the spokesman of France. The poems of *Heartbreak* (*Le Crève-cœur*, 1941) and *The*

Eyes of Elsa (*Les Yeux d'Elsa*, 1942) celebrated both France and his love for his wife, the writer Elsa Triolet. *The French Diana* (*La Diane française*, 1944) contained dramatic ballads, some of them among Aragon's best poetry, to keep up morale against the Nazis and their French collaborators. In the Elsa poems Aragon used traditional techniques with great skill; they were as appropriate for the times as poetry can be. But they were written only for those times, and have not worn well. Much that was moving in the heat of the moment now appears as sentimental cliché, however effectively exploited. Literature is no more, to Aragon, than a weapon in the service of social revolution; he remains an exceptional author of this kind of writing. In the post-war years his fiction has been less crudely propagandist than his verse. (PBFV4; MEP; PI)

The Parisian ROBERT DESNOS (1900–45) did not, alas, live to take up the important place in French post-war poetry he would undoubtedly have had: he died of typhus soon after the war as a result of ill treatment in a Nazi concentration camp. An early surrealist, who used to deliver long 'automatic' monologues, he broke with the surrealists in 1929—one of the victims of Breton's overzealousness. Surrealism helped him, but, like Éluard, he was a natural lyric poet and his best work is not composed only with the subconscious, however it may have seemed at the time. Desnos wrote in the belief that a poet in his lifetime produces one poem, but is only capable of bringing parts of it to the surface. His surrealist poems, some of them produced in a trance-like state, were collected in 1930, and they remain his best. Much of the poetry of his latter years was rather too self-conscious. However, the famous 'Last Poem', written to his wife not long before he died (he had been taken for resistance activity), is a good example of his gift, poetically slight but pure and sincere:

> I have so fiercely dreamed of you
> And walked so far and spoken of you so,
> Loved a shade of you so hard
> That now I've no more left of you.
> I'm left to be a shade among the shades
> A hundred times more shade than shade
> To be shade cast time and time again into your sun-transfigured life.
>
> (MEP; see also PBFV4; FBS)

VIII

JEAN-PAUL SARTRE (1905), born in Paris, dominated French literature for a quarter of a century. He is a philosopher (but in the French, not the British sense: professional British philosophers shudder at his name and think of bedrooms, spit and semen; they only read him on holiday), political activist, refuser of the Nobel Prize (1964), critic and playwright as well as novelist. His existentialist philosophy derives from Heidegger, Kierkegaard, the phenomen-

ologist Husserl and (indirectly) from Nietzsche (qq.v.). Very briefly, Sartre
sees man in an absurd and godless universe, but capable of achieving meaning
if he will only make the choice to exist as himself. However, his activity
(bourgeois, and in 'bad faith') consists in a perpetual attempt to alienate both
himself and his neighbours from the freedom involved in choice. Sartre was
attracted by phenomenology because (again briefly) this is a philosophy that
seizes upon phenomena as they present themselves to consciousness—rather
than debating upon their nature. Sartre sees man as trapped in 'viscosity':
his first semi-autobiographical novel *Nausea* (*La Nausée*, 1938; tr. R. Baldick,
1965) describes the nauseousness of this state with brilliant conviction, and is on
a level with his greatest achievements. It contains most of the essential matter
of his metaphysical *Being and Nothingness* (*L'Être et le Néant*, 1943; tr. H. E.
Barnes, 1957): this, written partly while Sartre was a German prisoner of war,
is often shrugged off as bad philosophy. So much the worse, perhaps, for the
philosophy that can thus shrug it off. Sartre is and always has been quasi-
Marxist, a 'fellow traveller'; it is certainly possible to re-interpret his philosophy,
to adapt it to Christianity or to an attitude not involving support for any
political party; but his restatement of the situation of human authenticity in
an atheist century is too important to be ignored. It is only when he turns
Marxist, advocating violent revolution in place of individualism, that he
becomes seriously contentious; but this Marxist role is not one with which he
himself has been wholly happy. From the time he thus committed himself he
ceased to write fiction, undoubtedly the form in which he has most distinguished
himself.

His short stories, collected in *Intimacy* (*Le Mur*, 1939; tr. L. Alexander, 1956),
are essentially sympathetic but gloomy accounts of the various mechanisms by
which people remain trapped in boredom, abstraction, essence (as opposed to
existence; being as opposed to becoming). *Nausea* analyses the psychology of
the condition at greater length and with detailed imaginative penetration.
The trilogy *The Roads to Freedom* (*Les Chemins de la liberté*: *The Age of Reason*,
L'Âge de raison, 1945; tr. E. Sutton, 1947; *The Reprieve*, *Le Sursis*, 1945; tr. E.
Sutton, 1947; *Iron in the Soul*, *La Mort dans l'âme*, 1949, tr. G. Hopkins, 1950),
which is unfinished, is an ambitious and full-scale treatment—and one of the
most outstanding works of fiction of the century. The writing of it caught Sartre
in full indecision between individualism and collectivism. His hero, Mathieu,
goes in the direction of commitment, following the direction of his creator's
intellect; but his impulsions towards individualism are as energetically and
sympathetically described as are those towards political cohesion. As a true
representation of intellectuals of Sartre's generation (Mathieu, like Sartre, has
studied philosophy and is a teacher), the novel transcends its thesis. It is also
a demonstration of the fact that a masterpiece need not be innovatory in form.
Sartre drew on what suited his imaginative convenience: the 'simultaneism' of
Romains and Dos Passos, the epic structure of Zola, the demotic language of
Céline (qq.v.). Mathieu's personal drama of freedom, culminating in what is
usually taken to be his death in action (although Sartre has stated that Mathieu

was not in fact killed), is played against that of many other characters, which is in turn related to France's descent into the self-disgrace of Vichy and defeat—in its turn seen against international events: the abject selling of Czechoslovakia to the Nazis, symbol of man's desperate need to imprison himself.

Sartre is also an expert dramatist. Nearly all his plays have been written from the intellectual standpoint of a man who is prepared to dirty his hands in the interests of the future of society (compare Brecht's carefully ironic and ambiguous verdict on Stalin: 'a useful man'). But they frequently betray individualist sympathies; and it is to the credit of their author that this should be allowed to be so. Doubtless he, too, has observed the case of Brecht. The human drama is often more absorbing than the thesis. (It is surely significant that Sartre has never joined the communist party, and is a critic of such Russian actions as the invasions of Hungary and Czechoslovakia.) No play he has written actually succeeds in showing how it is possible to remain 'authentic' and at the same time 'dirty one's hands' in the cause of the future, and this is Sartre's chief problem—one which he preferred, however, not to solve in his friend Camus' manner. His best play is the one in which it is not touched upon: *In Camera* (*Huis-Clos*, 1945; tr. S. Gilbert, 1946). Here three people, each of whom has been guilty of 'bad faith' (refusing the choice of an authentic existence) find themselves shut up, after death, in a drawing-room in hell. They discuss their lives, and become trapped in an eternal vicious circle: the coward man loves the lesbian who loves the infanticide girl who loves the coward. . . . 'Hell is other people' ('L'enfer, c'est les autres'), says one of the characters, thus crystallizing Sartre's view of bad faith: the failure to define oneself by reference to other people. This brilliant and grim comedy is as likely to survive in the theatre as any post-war play; there are few modern plays on its level.

Other plays by Sartre include *Crime Passionnel* (*Les Mains sales*, 1948; tr. K. Black, 1949), his most moving play, and in effect an attack on the inhumanity of communist tactics—but it can, of course, be looked at in another way. *Nekrassov* (1955; tr. S. and G. Leeson, 1956), a satire on anti-communism, is his funniest play; but it irritated most theatre critics by scoring unforgivable points against the press and therefore against their way of life. *Loser Wins* (*Les Séquestrés d'Altona*, 1959; tr. S. and G. Leeson, 1960) deals with the theme of personal responsibility by way of German war-guilt; it is a highly effective drama, which seems (to me) to contain some self-criticism in the figure of the Nazi recluse, Frantz, who justifies himself to a jury of crabs in a secret upstairs room (Sartre has experienced hallucinations of marine crabs).

Sartre's drama has consistently tended to humanize his Marxist ideology, which is made vulnerable by the actual behaviour of Russia, the 'Marxist state'. His debate with Camus is absolutely central to the concerns of our time, and therefore to its literature.

ALBERT CAMUS (1913–60) was born in Algeria of an Alsatian father (killed in the First World War) and a Spanish mother; he grew up poor, but his childhood was not an unhappy one. He had a brief period (1934) in the communist party, but left at that time because he disliked its attitude towards the Arabs. He studied philosophy at the University of Algiers, became a journalist there and was involved—as actor, writer and director—in left-wing theatrical activities. His early essays, collected in *The Wrong Side and the Right Side* (*L'Envers et l'endroit*, 1937) and *Nuptials* (*Noces*, 1938) lay the foundations of his later work: they oppose the sensual pagan values of the sun-drenched Mediterranean to those of the gloomy, intellectual North. He went to Paris, worked for a while on the newspaper *Paris Soir*, and then returned to Algeria to teach. His first two important books, *The Outsider* (*L'Étranger*, 1942; tr. S. Gilbert 1946), and the long essay, *The Myth of Sisyphus* (*Le Mythe de Sisyphe*, 1942; tr. J. O'Brien, 1955), were published when he returned to Paris. He joined the resistance and edited and contributed to the resistance journal *Combat*. Until he was over thirty Camus suffered from recurrent bouts of tuberculosis. After the war he was an editor at the leading publishing house of Gallimard. He received the Nobel Prize in 1957; less than three years later he was killed (he was not driving) in a car smash resulting from an, apparently, 'absurd' bout of speed not unusual on French roads.

Camus' first novel, *The Outsider*, is about Patrice Meursault ('the only Christ we deserve', Camus said later), who kills an Arab on a beach in apparent self-defence, 'because of the sun'; through his indifference and his incompetent lawyer he is condemned to death. Superbly effective in its psychological presentation of the protagonist and in evoking the atmosphere of Algiers, it deals on another, more symbolic, level with the problem of 'sun-drenched' pagan values versus those of a more northern and 'serious' society; with hedonism and the search for happiness within a framework of meaninglessness. The novel is relentless, too, in its demonstration of how remote the relationship of Meursault's trial is to his act: it exposes, often satirically, the hideous inadequacy of public versions of private events. Meursault reaches a state of happiness because he has refused to subscribe to meaningless social rituals, to mourn at his mother's funeral, to plead 'innocent' or 'guilty', to act as a 'concerned' person when accused of a crime. He rejects society's values, but cannot discover his own until the point at which he is suspended between life and death; then he understands his existence as itself a happiness.

The essays in *The Myth of Sisyphus* represent man as like Sisyphus in his absurd task, but happy in his losing battle. It is necessary, he argues, to go through two stages: to accept that you live in an absurd universe, and then to fight against this acceptance. 'This *malaise* in front of man's own inhumanity', he wrote there, 'this incalculable let-down when faced with the image of what we are, this "nausea" as a contemporary writer [Sartre] calls it, also is the Absurd'. The key word is *malaise*: Camus insists, as Sartre insists, on man's duty to attain a 'good faith'. But their solutions differed.

His play *Caligula* (CTP) had been drafted in 1938 and was performed in 1945. It is interesting to compare this treatment of the notion of the 'absurd' with that of the dramatists of the absurd: Camus demonstrates the absurdity of such a life as Caligula's (or Hitler's); the dramatists of the absurd present it *as such*.

Camus soon developed his sense of the mad logic of nihilism (which in his work is always equated with the madness of a Caligula, or a Hitler) into a humanist defiance of it, which he spent his life in trying to formulate. 'Every negation contains a flowering of *yes*'. In the novel *The Plague* (*La Peste*, 1947; tr, J. O'Brien, 1960), whose occasion is a plague that afflicted Oran in the Forties, the rat-carried virus is despair, total acceptance of absurdity. It is easy to see why Camus should have been associated with Sartre as an existentialist. Both, in their different ways, were saying the same thing about man's condition. The German expressionists had sensed it, but in general they overreacted and became lost in abstractions; these were statements as lucid as the century's literature had seen.

The disagreement between Camus and Sartre arose from a review, in Sartre's paper *Les Temps Modernes*, of Camus' book *The Rebel* (*L'Homme révolté*, 1951; tr. A. Bower, 1953). This book was a refutation of communism, an attack on some aspects of Marx—particularly his historical determinism—and a condemnation of the Russian concentration camps, on the grounds that no ends could justify unjust means. He drew unwelcome attention to the 'fascism' that came in the wake of the French and Russian revolutions, to the 'Caesarism' that 'Promethean' revolutionary endeavour invariably seemed to flounder into. In effect Camus was postulating a non-violent, liberal, democratic, multi-party alternative to communism. He was in no way, of course, condoning capitalism; and no serious person suggests that he was. But he was putting forward the notion of a state of 'ethically pure' revolt, which could continuously humanize all tendencies to revolutionary absolutism. The book was reviewed in Sartre's paper by Francis Jeanson, who objected to it on the grounds that while Russia was imperfect it was none the less the only Marxist state and therefore in a privileged position. Camus replied arrogantly and injudiciously, ignoring Jeanson and addressing himself to Sartre. Sartre's own reply was excellent to the extent that he attacked Camus' tactics. And he was right in pointing out that anti-communists rejoiced in the sufferings inflicted on anyone by the enemies of their convenience—rather than deplored them because they were actually cruel. But on the question of the existence of concentration camps in Soviet Russia—and the lack of human freedom in that country—he was plainly embarrassed. Defending Marx, whom Camus had attacked, he was careful to describe himself as 'not a Marxist'; he pointed out that his own paper had not ignored the question of the camps; he was effective in drawing attention to a certain arrogance and egocentricity in Camus' character. . . . But he was uneasy on the central question. And he paid Camus a magnificent (subconscious?) compliment, born of profound respect, when he told him that his attitude left him nowhere to go but the Galapagos Islands: these are remote and hardly populated, true; but another who had gone there and been stimulated to extraordinary activity was Charles Darwin. . . . The debate, of course, continues—and is central to modern literature, which is, predominantly, a literature of the thus divided left.

Camus had shortcomings as an arguer. The criticism that his proposals lacked a sociology is not without point; but nor is his reply: that authoritarian Marxism puts sociology above humanity. Again, there is some substance in the description of Camus as one with the mentality of a 'poor white', no more than —on the Algerian question—a 'conscience-stricken paternalist liberal'. His sense of absurdity is then explained as arising from the dilemma of one who feels moral responsibility for Arab society, but can never belong to it. Useful criticism; but it assumes enormous moral superiority in its maker—who, freer in the first place, can truly 'belong' to alien, oppressed societies?; and it ignores the possibility of psychic ('Freudian') imperatives turning into ethical ones.

Camus wrote several more plays and a series of stage adaptations of prose works; his version of Dostoevski's *The Possessed* (*Les Possédés*, 1959; tr. J. O'Brien, 1960) is perhaps the most dramatically effective of his theatre. *The State of Siege* (*L'État de siège*, 1948; CTP) was a fiasco when Barrault (q.v.) put it on in 1948; *The Just* (*Les Justes*, 1950; CTP), about the assassination of a Grand duke in Russia at the beginning of the century, was more skilful but still over-didactic. In his adaptation of Dostoevski Camus concentrated more on character and achieved greater dramatic success.

In *The Rebel* and in other works such as *The Just* Camus had come out in favour of individual integrity against 'party solidarity'; in his novel *The Fall* (*La Chute*, 1956; tr. J. O'Brien, 1957) he made a defiant gesture in favour of the unpredictable, mysterious, autonomous creative imagination; it is also a savage, but not altogether unsympathetic, gloss on Sartrian existentialism. Camus here pitted creative subversiveness against intellectual social conscience. His anti-hero, Jean-Baptiste Clamance, is a caricature of the artist as God: a Gallic Felix Krull (q.v.), a con-man, a disembodied voice 'confessing' a 'judge-penitent' in a Dutch bar, a Paris lawyer abdicated from 'business' to the Amsterdam waterfront because he 'fell' when he failed to rescue a girl from drowning. But Camus makes Clamance enjoy his 'fall'. And in *The Fall* the guilty and famous artist Camus expatiates upon, but enjoys, his guilt and fame; he comes to rest in a diabolical scepticism, gleefully and slyly—as Germaine Brée has remarked—presenting a 'penitent' who will not make the existentialist 'choice' to 'leap' into authenticity. Certain sentimental or puzzled journalists attributed a 'conversion' to Christianity to Camus on the strength of *The Fall*; but he quickly disposed of any such notion.

Exile and the Kingdom (*L'Exil et le royaume*, 1957; tr. J. O'Brien, 1958) contained six short stories, each employing a different technical approach. It seems as though Camus was trying to escape from 'morality' into the not so certainly responsible area of the imagination; from philosophy, or his approximation to it, into the more alarming and (possibly) more reprehensible reality of creativity; from the idea of freedom into the dangerously unknown element of freedom itself. His posthumously published *Notebooks* (*Carnets, 1935–1942*,

1962; tr. P. Thody, 1963; *1942–1951*, 1964; tr. P. Thody, 1966) tend to confirm this.

It is unfortunate that Camus was taken up by the American and French right-wing as a hero. He is, most emphatically, a writer of the left—but not of the 'committed' left. Thus he was able to condemn Stalin's Russia along with Franco's Spain, and to urge the Algerians to work out a union with France. This last proposition was a politically naïve one. But if politics is never to be more than 'the art of the possible' then it may well become a humanly worse activity than it already is. . . . One can pay no greater tribute to Camus than Sartre did in his obituary notice: 'Camus could never cease to be one of the principal forces in our cultural domain, nor to represent, in his own way, the history of France and of this century'.

*

The approach of the novelist, poet and pataphysicist (q.v.) RAYMOND QUENEAU (1903), born at Le Havre, offers a striking contrast; but if his emotional intensity is less, his awareness is not. Queneau is an erudite encyclopaedia editor, grammarian, philosopher and historian of mathematics as well as creative writer. Since 1936 he has been an associate of the publishing firm of Gallimard. He was a surrealist until 1930, when he broke with Breton.

Queneau's poetry and song is ingenious, and some of it has been successful in cafés and cabaret. But, the pleasant—and never offensive—pop element apart, it is more experimental than substantial. The do-it-yourself sonnet kit, *Hundred Thousand Billion Poems* (*Cent mille milliards de poèmes*, 1961) is an amusing way of expressing distrust of the efficacy of 'sonnets', but cannot stand the strain of being solemnly hailed as a major *avant garde* piece—as, alas, it is in some quarters. The best poems are in *Les Ziaux* (1943), Queneau's first collection.

Queneau's deep knowledge of mathematics, linguistics, science and philosophy must be accounted one major influence upon him. The others are: Céline (q.v.), who caused him to continue (in his very different way) to try to reintroduce the colloquial into the literary language; surrealism, which taught him disrespect for established values but respect for the irrational; the sheer clownishness of Charlie Chaplin (cf. Henri Michaux, Franz Hellens, qq.v.); and the linguistic games of James Joyce in *Finnegans Wake* (q.v.). He has a sappy good humour that makes the best of his work delightful, clever and influential where influence matters; but his distrust of passion or passionate commitment, intellectually decent though it is, robs it of the ripe wisdom that one feels its author possesses. Despite the amount of subtle material crammed in, much of it over the reader's head, there is always also a sense of something emotional being held back.

Queneau's first novel, *The Bark Tree* (*Le Chiendent*, 1933; tr. B. Wright, 1968) 'the *nouveau roman* [q.v.] twenty years before its time' (Robbe-Grillet, q.v.), is one of his best: written in his inimitable brand of demotic French, it gives meaning to an abstract philosophical meditation on 'I think therefore I am' by transforming it into a 'story' about a bank clerk. In *The Sunday of Life* (*Le Dimanche de la vie*, 1952) Queneau achieves his most perfect balance between humour (which does not here degenerate into whimsy) and humanity: an amiable young man opens a shop and passes on the confidences of customers to his wife, who has enormous success as a fortune-teller; when she is ill he disguises himself and replaces her. *Zazie* (*Zazie dans le métro*, 1959; tr. B. Wright, 1960) sympathetically and feelingly recounts the adventures of a little girl who, by her innocence and because of their corruption, creates havoc among adults. The ultra-sceptical *Exercises in Style* (*Exercices de style*, 1947; tr. B. Wright, 1958), a *tour de force*, describes the same trivial—but is it?—incident on a bus in ninety-nine different styles.

Few writers have succeeded better than Queneau, who found what he wanted in Céline and made it into a thoroughgoing technique, in reproducing the spoken language; he uses phonetic spelling, incorrect grammar and any other aid in order to capture it. If anything in Queneau's work comes near to being sacred, then it is certainly the language as it is spoken. In his humour Queneau recalls his fellow-pataphysicist Boris Vian (q.v.) and the Irish humorist Flann O'Brien (q.v.).

The anthropologist, novelist, poet and autobiographer MICHEL LEIRIS (1901), who was born in Paris, was until recently one of the most neglected of living writers. He too began as a surrealist, and has written surrealist poetry, the most recent of which is collected in *Nights without Night* (*Nuits sans nuit*, 1946). His anthropological works, including *Race and Culture* (*Race et civilisation*, 1951; tr. 1951), are of importance; he specializes in Africa. But his greatest achievement is in his autobiography, consisting of *Manhood* (*L'Âge d'homme*, 1939; tr. R. Howard, 1963) and the books, *Erasures* (*Biffures*, 1948), *Gear* (*Fourbis*, 1955) and *Fibrils* (*Fibrilles*, 1966) that make up *The Rule of the Game* (*La Régle du jeu*). These are not 'novels'; but in the ambience of Leiris' subtle considerations such distinctions become pointless: he does not doubt that all writing is in a sense 'fiction'. And he immediately acknowledges that the writer's subject is himself: his project is to write a book that is an act: 'the danger to which I expose myself by publishing my confession differs radically, on the level of *quality*, from that which the matador constantly assumes in performing his role' —but none the less, because by confession he exposes and maltreats his extreme timidity he does endanger himself, and because in language he commits himself to the rule of his game with as much courage as the *torero*, so he sees the project as parallel to his. Leiris' honesty is not merely conventional candour: in his autobiography he faces (as the *torero* faces the bull) that horror of death, of annihilation, that has always prevented him from pursuing physical life whole-heartedly. Such a project could be wholly pretentious, the work of a concealed journalist or, more tiresome, of one anxious to please journalists; the quality and sincerity of Leiris' self-examination ensure that the opposite is true. Furthermore Leiris rejects—and no doubt this is one of the reasons for which his fellow anthropologist Lévi-Strauss admires him—chronology as dull and rational: he chooses to examine his life as a synchronous phenomenon, analysing it as one block, in terms of the formation of his own language.

Leiris broke with surrealism, perhaps mainly because it changed the field of the unknown in so assiduously searching for the unknown; but he remained steeped in it (as he admits): his thoroughgoing Freudianism assured his receptivity to everything given, most particularly dreams—and his hostility to selective procedures. *The Rule of the Game* is a tragic work in the sense that its author could not tell himself, or us, that he had been able to find meaning, pattern, in his lived—as opposed to his written—life. However, he tried to kill himself because of it. His life was saved by a tracheotomy. The scar from this he calls his *fibule*. At this point the man becomes the writer, the writer becomes the man. Although still not known well in English-speaking countries, Leiris has had increasing influence in France.

MARCEL AYMÉ (1902–67), born at Joigny in central France, an uncommitted and ostensibly metaphysical satirist of all human manifestations, comedian, friend of Céline's, offers a complete contrast. A prolific and popular writer, he has been described as an unacknowledged genius by some and as a facile waster of comic gifts by others. The truth, as so often, lies between the two extremes. He does have comic power, but in his novels he does squander it—in monotonous repetitiousness, wild fantasy or gratuitous and insensitive cruelty. His first great success, *The Green Mare* (*La Jument verte*, 1933; tr. N. Denny, 1955), contains the same mixture as its numerous successors: a robustly Rabelaisian approach to a provincial community, every aspect of whose affairs is satirically surveyed within the limits of a cleverly tailored plot. Aymé is always highly professional—sometimes too much so. His plays, with which he was also successful, are on the same pattern; but here the professionalism is too obtrusive, and they do not rise above the level of entertainment. Aymé's best work is in the short story: two volumes in English draw on several collections: *Across Paris* (1958; tr. N. Denny) and *The Proverb* (1961; tr. N. Denny). Here the fantastic element is not drawn thinly out, or over-elaborated, but is concentrated into something that is usually pointed. In 'The Walker through Walls' a clerk discovers that he has the power to acquire wealth dishonestly (by walking through walls), but is destroyed by sex. This has real point, which is satisfyingly presented in terms of an entirely logical tale.

Aymé is merely Rabelaisian, something that even the most repressive male communities have been able to excuse (they set up a delicately etherealized image of women and then, presumably, relieve the strain of its unreality by unkindly upsetting the obliging ladies themselves). Other twentieth-century writers, usually following on de Sade, have evolved a literary pornography. The three most important of these are GEORGES BATAILLE (1897–1962), PIERRE KLOSSOWSKI (1905) and 'PAULINE RÉAGE', whose identity is unknown. Bataille (to whom Leiris' *Manhood* is dedicated) was always cheerfully surrealist in spirit, in that he never took his literary project as anything but a game. His erotic novels, the best of which are *Story of the Eye* (*Historie de l'œil*, n.d.) and *L'Abbé C* (1950), parody eighteenth- and nineteenth-century pornography, including its deliberate intention to arouse sexually; but, discovering in this way a means of circumventing the conventional reticence about sex, they reveal hidden ('shocking') facts about its sado-masochistic component. *L'Abbé C* deals with a prostitute and a priest whom she tempts, seduces and destroys—the psychological relationship between these two is delineated with an ironic subtlety of originality and brilliance. Bataille is a writer of importance. Klossowski is a scholar, translator of Virgil, Catholic, essayist and exegetist of de Sade, whose approach is quite different: he treats his highly erotic material in a frigidly aloof, philosophical style. The most important of his novels is the trilogy *The Laws of Hospitality* (*Les Lois de l'hospitalité*, 1953–60) whose hero— a theologian, 'K'—prostitutes his wife, Roberte, to other men, in order to know her better; she also prostitutes herself. Roberte, however, is a politician— and bans a book by her husband. All this is presented in a theological framework, stemming from the 'discovery' of the point of view that Roberte may prostitute herself to her nephew because the body is only a vessel for the spirit. . . . There are three novels: *Roberte, This Evening* (*Roberte, ce soir*, 1953; tr. 1969), *The Revocation of the Edict of Nantes* (*La Révocation de l'Édit de Nantes*, 1959), *The Prompter, or Theatre of Society* (*Le Souffleur, ou le théâtre de société*, 1960). This was followed by *So Fatal a Desire* (*Un si funeste désir*, 1963) and *Baphomet* (1965). Klossowski's chief awareness is that, like de Sade, he is creating erotic fantasy in the form of words; his abtruse fiction probes the relationship between actual fulfilled lusts and verbal fantasy. He is a most interesting, although difficult writer. 'Pauline Réage's' *The Story of O* (*Histoire d'O*, 1954; tr. S. D'Estrée, 1956; 1970) is the virtuoso classic of female masochism, and demonstrates the limits of pornography as an art. It is an intelligent, humorous, distressing book; no one has 'revealed' its author. This is a novel to ignore or to come to terms with; but not to condemn. It is cleverly truthful to a sexual mood. When a trade edition appeared in Great Britain during 1970 it quickly flushed out those whose highest sexual satisfaction comes from moralizing.

It is not perhaps so great a jump from 'Pauline Réage' to PAULE RÉGNIER (1890–1950), who has become famous, since her suicide, for her journal and her letters. Badly deformed by a childhood illness, she was a devout Catholic and a recluse, who loved unhappily in youth and lived on, miserable and poor, for over thirty years. Her novel *L'Abbaye d'Évolayne* (1933) is a classic of its kind, for in its simple plot she was able to project her own situation, in which she felt emotionally rejected (the poet she loved, killed in the war, had liked but not loved her, as she discovered after his death), sexually frustrated, devoutly Catholic. A passionate girl's husband decides, owing to his war experiences, to become a monk; she agrees to become a nun, but suffers from jealousy and finally kills herself in front of him. Beneath the surface of this moving book there is a good deal of raging sexuality. Paule Régnier wrote several other novels, but none approaching this one.

A good number of French men and women did not deserve their fates at the hands of the over-jubilant and revengeful anti-Vichyssois who gained power in 1945, but LUCIEN REBATET (1903) is hardly one of them. His book *The*

Rubbish (*Les Décombres*, 1943) was one of the more repulsive to be written under the German occupation. His guttersnipe fascism and racism would not now be remembered had the sentence of death passed on him after the war been carried out. Fortunately and rightly he was reprieved, and in prison wrote a very long novel, *The Two Flags* (*Les Deux Étendards*, 1951), which, although unduly long, is nevertheless a remarkable and powerful work. There are no politics in it. It resembles *L'Abbaye d'Évolayne* inasmuch as it portrays a young couple who agree to indulge their religious and not their sexual vocation: as a Jesuit and a nun respectively. In *The Ripe Corn* (*Les Epis mûrs*, 1954) he traces the defeat and ultimate death in battle of a composer. He convinces the reader of his hero's genius and the obstacles to it. Here Rebatet actually succeeds in transforming into a valid criticism of society the nihilism that had previously led him into fascism. Rebatet is a little overpowering, but there can be no doubt of his gifts.

SIMONE DE BEAUVOIR (1908), born in Paris, the lifelong companion of Sartre, has made vital contributions to existentialism, but is also an important novelist. *She Came to Stay* (*L'Invitée*, 1943; tr. R. Senhouse and Y. Moyse, 1949) is an acute analysis, in existentialist terms, of a *ménage à trois* that ends in murder. *The Blood of Others* (*Le Sang des autres*, 1944; tr. R. Senhouse and Y. Moyse, 1948) is set in the Thirties and early Forties, and is a study of a girl who discovers through love her ability to die for freedom: at first accepting Nazi doctrine, she ends by fighting in the maquis. These two novels are distinguished by their characterization and convincing action. The next, *All Men are Mortal* (*Tous les hommes sont mortels*, 1946; tr. L. Friedman, 1955), is an experiment that fails. By tracing, from the fourteenth century to the present day, the existence of an Italian who drinks an immortality potion it tries to prove that immortality is meaningless, because any individual would see his own projects ruined; it is ingenious and often amusing, but remains a thesis novel. The partly auto-biographical *The Mandarins* (*Les Mandarins*, 1954; tr. L. Friedman, 1957) is a shrewd *roman à clef*, with portraits of Sartre, Camus, the sociologist Raymond Aron, and Nelson Algren (q.v.)—with whom Simone de Beauvoir herself was involved somewhat as she describes her psychiatrist protagonist as being involved here.

Nothing Simone de Beauvoir writes, from fiction to sociology (*The Second Sex*, *Le Deuxième Sexe*, 1949; tr. H. M. Paishley, 1960) is less than absorbing and of the highest intelligence, but none of her later fiction has equalled her first two novels—better have been her volumes of autobiography: *Memoirs of a Dutiful Daughter* (*Mémoires d'une fille rangée*, 1958; tr. J. Kirkup, 1959), *The Prime of Life* (*Lâ Force de l'âge*, 1960; tr. P. Green, 1962) and *The Force of Circumstance* (*La Force des choses*, 1963; tr. J. Kirkup, 1965). These are vivid, exact and in certain respects—as in the passages about adolescence—unsurpassed in modern French literature.

VERCORS (ps. JEAN BRULLER, 1902), born in Paris, was before the Second World War a well-known illustrator and etcher. After the war he invented a highly effective technique for reproducing paintings. He founded, with friends, the clandestine publishers Les Éditions de Minuit, whose first book was his own *The Silence of the Sea* (*Le Silence de la mer*, 1942; tr. C. Connolly, 1944), the story of a 'good' German, who loves music—and of silent resistance to the enemy. When the book appeared in England and America many famous French writers—Mauriac, Gide, Aragon (qq.v.)—were suggested as its author. It is a simple, moving tale, which had a profound effect on the oppressed Frenchmen of the time. Vercors did not equal it until 1961, with *Sylva* (tr. R. Barisse, 1962), the charming story of a vixen turned woman and 'tamed'—but not completely—by an English squire.

ROBERT MERLE (1908), a Frenchman born in Algeria and a professor at the University of Toulouse, spent some time before the Second World War in America. Later he was at Dunkirk. *Weekend at Dunkirk* (*Week-end à Zuydcoote*, 1949; tr. K. Rebillon-Lambley, 1950) reflects both experiences. It is too self-consciously 'tough' (where it need not have been) and too obviously destined to become a 'screen epic' (1965); but the descriptions of action are excellent. The historical and anti-racist *The Island* (*L'Île*, 1962; tr. H. Hare, 1964) is probably his best: Merle has the unusual gift of being able to write 'adventure' without distorting or over-simplifying character. His radicalism is doubtless a crude element, but it is only reactionaries who find it—in the unpretentious context of such a book as *The Island*—offensive. *Behind the Glass* (*Derrière le vitre*, 1970) resorts, honourable and usefully, to the 'simultaneism' of Romains and Dos Passos, to make a sincere and objective examination of the day of 22 March, 1968, when the students rose in revolt at Nanterre. Merle is a competent and honest writer whose work always repays reading.

The Parisian ROGER VAILLAND (1907–65) was one of the surrealists who turned Marxist—and in 1952 joined the communist party, only to break away from it within a few years. Vailland was a fine writer and an elegant stylist who succeeded only once in producing a work that reconciled the disparate elements in himself. The conflict in him is not so much between erotic hedonism and humanitarian concern as between erotic hedonism and a guilty conscience posing as humanitarian concern. His best novel was his first: *Playing with Fire* (*Drôle de jeu*, 1945; tr. G. Hopkins, 1948), a study of life in the underground (in which Vailland played a part). Marat is a hero, but for him the risks and the adventure are an exciting game that symbolizes life as a whole. Vailland here both resolves his own problems and gives a memorably acute and amusing portrait in depth of the kind of man for whom war and its concomitants are a heaven-sent opportunity for self-realization. But Vailland was a naïve (q.v.) writer; the attempt to be a 'social realist' distorts, in varying degrees, the true intentions of all his other books—none of which, however, lacks vivid or comic passages. The cynical, stylish egoist was very much uppermost in Vailland's fiction; the communism is unconvincing. Unhappily he never, after *Playing with Fire*, found a suitable objective correlative. The predominant influence on him was the eighteenth-century writer Choderlos de Laclos, author of *Dangerous Acquaintances* (*Les Liaisons dangereuses*, 1782; tr. R. Aldington, 1924), a detached and aristocratic analysis of sexual relationships in the years before the Revolution.

SAMUEL BECKETT (1906), born of a Protestant family in Dublin, usually writes in French and often translates his work into English himself. He went to Paris as an exchange lecturer in English at the École Normale in 1928, and had soon become a member of the literary circle around James Joyce (q.v.)—and had written on him. In 1937, after a period of travel, he settled permanently in Paris. He was quite close to Joyce, and occasionally took down passages of *Finnegans Wake*—but he never, as is often stated, acted as his 'secretary'. As a writer Beckett is not as comic as Joyce; but it seems that he is less gloomy as a man, although when young he suffered from a legendary apathy. Where he resembles Joyce is in his close knowledge of philosophical meditation, of the metaphysical and theological speculations of such thinkers as Aquinas, Vico and Descartes—and in his preoccupation with languages. He was a keen athlete at school; soon afterwards all the energy he spent on this went into lie-abed 'metaphysical games'. During the war he was a member of the resistance; finally he had to flee to unoccupied France. His great creative period occurred in the five or six years after the war. He gained universal recognition with the play *Waiting for Godot* (*En attendant Godot*, 1952; tr. S. Beckett, 1956). In 1969 he was awarded the Nobel Prize. He is a cricket enthusiast.

Beckett writes in French as a discipline: to protect himself from lapsing into rhetoric, from which his concentration on composing in a language not his own deflects him. His manner and material are almost exclusively Irish, and the chief influence upon him is certainly Swift, the Englishman who returned to the Ireland of his birth to experience the quintessence of its despair. The rigour of Beckett's investigations into existence, often functioning as a bleak parody of the precise trivializings of linguistic philosophers, probably derives from his Protestant ('almost Quaker') upbringing. His work embodies all the anguish and anxiety of theological speculation, but icily transfers this from its 'safe' context of the Christian system to one of utter meaninglessness. This is familiar—the world of the modern writer. But Beckett's account of it is made peculiarly desolate by his concentration on the solipsist isolation of his characters, who meditate ceaselessly upon their coming extinction, continuing the while to contemplate language, their only weapon—a useless one.

Beckett's first excursions, in English (*Poems in English*, 1961), were poor verse but may now be seen to contain—in the way the early poetry of prose writers so often does—the germs of his later concerns. His first novel, *Murphy* (1938), written in English, also contains all upon which the later work would elaborate. Murphy's world is South London. He is for a time kept by a prostitute (the only tender portrait in the whole of Beckett), but eventually becomes an assistant male nurse in a lunatic asylum. He is happy here, but dies in a fire caused (accidentally) by himself. His ashes are scattered, also accidentally, on the floor of a Dublin pub. The influence of Joyce is more apparent in this early book than anywhere else in Beckett.

Beckett's 'trilogy', consisting of *Molloy* (1951; tr. S. Beckett and P. Bowles, 1955), *Malone Dies* (*Malone meurt*, 1951; tr. S. Beckett, 1956) and *The Unnameable* (*L'Innommable*, 1953; tr. S. Beckett, 1958), has been published as a single volume (*Three Novels*, 1959). These reverse the Cartesian *cogito ergo sum* by reducing existence to pure thought. They are not philosophy, however, but a violently negative parody of philosophy. They define 'Irishness'—hopelessness, helplessness, perennial passionate despair at pointless passion—perhaps as precisely as it has ever been defined, but hardly transcend it. (There is no hint to be found, in Beckett's writings, of why he should have loathed and fought against Nazism; whereas such concern is actually one of the characteristics of the work of that other proponent of man's absurd condition, Camus.) Molloy, crippled, sets off on a bicycle to find his mother, in which archetypal project he fails. Malone characterizes the artist: he writes confused and absurd tales in a room of whose location he is ignorant. There is no *Künstlerschuld* (q.v.) here, it seems—but is there? Beckett's books are certainly on the theme of the absurdity of existence; they gain their strength from being about, more particularly, the absurdity of his (writer's?) existence. The Irish are always desperately repentant of their nihilistic violence; one feels that Beckett entertains similar feelings about the results of his own examination of existence: in enjoyably reducing it to a squalid, mad game he omits to give an account of the fine, hopeful, unsqualid detail. . . .

The Unnameable is a monologue in a void, as potent of philosophical misery as an Irish hangover. In *How It Is* (*Comment c'est*, 1961; tr. S. Beckett, 1964) Bom and Pim crawl belly down in the primeval slime with their sacks containing tinned fish—and their tin openers. It is this syntaxless book, above all, that shows Beckett to be, not a pointer forward to new literary ways, but the last parodic naturalist: his fiction has stripped life of such 'illusory' details as provided the realist and naturalist novelist with all his matter, and concentrated upon the naturalist thesis. In quest of reason, and finding none, he has elevated purposelessness itself into a reason.

His plays are theatrically effective presentations of the same themes, and because their mood coincided with that of Europe they achieved enormous commercial success. He has since revenged himself for being thus taken up by 'writing' plays in which nothing happens at all—much praised by reviewers of plays, for many of whom 'the void' may be a comforting thought. *Waiting for Godot* was widely misinterpreted as a 'statement' with a 'meaning'; critics searched in it for meanings. But it is no more than a brilliant (quintessentially Irish) portrait of human uncertainty. It 'says' nothing whatever about God(ot), only that when he is expected he does not come. It says more about (God)ot— i.e., as has been pointed out, Charlot, the French name for Charlie Chaplin— God's little victim enmeshed in life and, amazingly, laughing. Hence the vaudeville energy of Beckett's play, and its gaiety. The enjoyment of the play itself, and the enjoyment Beckett got from writing it, provide some answer to the inevitable charge of pessimism. *Endgame* (*Fin de partie*, 1957; tr. S. Beckett, 1958) is a dramatic parallel to *How It Is*. In *Krapp's Last Tape* (1959), written in English, which undoubtedly deserves the status of a stage masterpiece, an old man plays back, on his tape recorder, some of the tapes upon which he has kept records of his experiences. Here we see most clearly the Beckett who was influenced by Proust (q.v.), and who wrote a book on him (1931). His last substantial work, *Play* (1963), pushes nearer to stillness, silence and death, and points to a further withdrawal of Beckett's art from life. The short *Lessness* (1970), neither play nor novel, neither poetry nor prose, tries to record, using language itself, the final failure of language to provide a secure refuge. Beckett, always a writer of great integrity, has finally pared away everything sensual and sensuous; it seems that there can be nothing left now but silence.

'The absurd' is an important but minor literary genre; Beckett, however, is not a minor writer: he has never been content simply to accept, and thus present, the apparent absurdity of the human condition. His work is ultimately ambiguous, for while it is obviously pessimistic about the human chances of achieving metaphysical happiness, it does not promote (as Sartre and Camus do) atheism: Beckett is too sceptical to do this, whatever his mood or expectations. His importance is undoubted; but he is pre-eminently a historian of mental anguish: his art has increasingly rejected quotidian detail, and inevitably it lacks richness.

Thief, pimp, professional masturbator, betrayer, queer, JEAN GENÊT (1910) was born in Paris but abandoned by his mother to the Public Assistance—a gesture that has taken him his life to answer. Branded by his foster-parents as a thief, Genêt between the ages of ten and thirty-eight conscientiously sought out trouble. In 1948 he was let off a sentence of life-imprisonment because of his literary achievements. For Jean-Paul Sartre, who with others made this sensible and humane act of clemency possible, Genêt is a modern existentialist hero, as he explains at length in his fascinating *Saint-Genêt* (*Saint-Genêt, comédien et martyr*, 1952; tr. B. Frechtman, 1964). For Sartre Genêt is exemplary because of his choice to become the image (thief, criminal) that his foster-parents— and then society—thrust upon him. This view of him has validity, but only the validity of an abstraction. Until Genêt gained a literary reputation, just after the end of the Second World War, his project was an essentially bourgeois one. It is a testament to his genius that, especially as a playwright, he then proceeded to develop. For the author of the novel *Our Lady of the Flowers* (*Notre-Dame des fleurs*, 1944; tr. B. Frechtman, 1964), written clandestinely in pencil on brown paper in prison in 1943, and of the autobiography *Thief's Journal* (*Journal du voleur*, 1948; tr. B. Frechtman, 1964), the nadir of existence lies in an elaborate—and itself ritual—denial of bourgeois rituals, an antithesis of the French version of the British public school 'code': to be filthy, to steal, to be a coward, to masturbate, to fart sensuously and enjoy the smell, to betray, to be a studiedly conventional 'enemy of society'. The 'nastiness' of Genêt's content, which deals with the degraded underbelly of society, is directly contradicted by the stylistic beauty of his prose: the kind of prose taught mindlessly in the 'best' schools, a kind of prose at which Genêt happens to excel. There is, then, an irony in *Our Lady of the Flowers*: the 'rotten', 'perverse' criminal uses a highly academic, 'proper' style to relentlessly record petty vilenesses, which range from how to produce an especially satisfying type of fart ('a pearl') to tossing off into a murdered man's mouth—all to offend and affront the beloved, repudiating mother into a gesture of attention that will cancel the original abandonment—Genêt's notion of this unknown real mother quite clearly being derived from the petit-bourgeois figure of his foster-mother. More inventive is *Querelle of Brest* (*Querelle de Brest*, 1947; tr. G. Streatham, 1966), Genêt's best novel: here, in a terser prose, the author seems to have taken thought (but not too much) and set himself to examine the nature of 'immorality' from a more general standpoint. The sailor Querelle is an autonomous creation, into which a hero-worshipping, sexually thrilled author has breathed real power.

Genêt's theatre explores the sociological implications of the project he pursued before President Auriol (who invited him to dinner) pardoned him and thus rehabilitated him, in his own eyes, by acting as his mother (who was a whore) ought to have acted. His main theme, although approached in a totally different way, is the same as that of Max Frisch (q.v.): that society (and other people) impose an image upon the individual by which he is deprived of his freedom. In his life as thief, beggar, homosexual prostitute and convict, Genêt's writing was all fantasy (and masturbation fantasy at that); his theatre represents the act of breaking free. *The Maids* (*Les Bonnes*, 1947; tr. B. Frechtman, 1954), a powerful play (fuelled, perhaps, by misogyny) shows how fatal decisions may be made in illusory situations. His best play, *The Balcony* (*Le Balcon*, 1956; tr. B. Frechtman), shows false dignitaries acting out their erotic fantasies in a brothel while a revolution goes on outside; finally the make-believe events within the brothel become interwoven with the 'real' facts outside—but political power is brilliantly postulated as having its origins in erotic fantasy. This is obviously a limited view, and the play is too subjective to have universal validity; but it demonstrates Genêt's progress from rhapsodic narcissist to skilful satirist.

MARGUERITE DURAS (1914) was born in Indochina and did not come to Paris until she was eighteen. She has dispensed with some of the trappings of the conventional novel, but her greatest debt is to those who have tried to extend the resources of realism rather than to those who have made radical alterations in technique. She became famous through her script for Alain Resnais' lushly middlebrow film *Hiroshima mon amour* (1959), which uses new techniques without real urgency. She is a skilful, ingenious and intelligent writer, but she is prone to create characters who seem unusual but are in fact no more interesting than any shallow follower of fashion. Anna, the heroine of *The Sailor from Gibraltar* (*Le Marin de Gibraltar*, 1952), hunts for a love once casually tasted, but eventually accepts what is to hand. This remains curiously unconvincing, almost as if the boring Anna were being invested by the author with the virtues of a spurious 'modernity'. *The Square* (*Le Square*, 1955; tr. S. Pitt-Rivers and I. Murdoch, 1959) is an ordinary and even sentimental story of a young housemaid who falls into conversation with a salesman; it is tricked out with such devices as repetition, and 'explanation' is withdrawn pretentiously: the content is highly suitable for ladies' hairdressing saloons. Marguerite Duras' novels are, indeed, most voraciously devoured by women who do not read the romantic magazine serials only because they are ashamed to, and because they would like to feel capable of reading 'something deep': their discussions of their reading are keyed to remarks made by newspaper reviewers of novels. Iris Murdoch (q.v.) is an appropriate translator here, since her own interminable series of novels fulfil a similar function in Great Britain. But *Moderato Cantabile* (1958) and *Ten-Thirty on a Summer Night* (*10.30 du soir en été*, 1960; tr. A. Borchardt, 1962) are superior, and the latter in particular contains some writing finely evocative of a small Spanish town on a rainy summer evening. And yet both (unnecessarily) promise more than they deliver: they would be better literature if they did not pose as 'literature', every other page or so asking to be 'the latest Duras'. It is not that Marguerite Duras is stylistically insincere or an 'opportunist', as has been alleged; but it seems that she could not accept that her gifts were largely those of a realist: this feeling led her, honourably enough, to experiment. . . . Her attitude towards and use of time in her fiction is seriously discussed by some critics; but it amounts to no more than an often ponderous emphasis on the fact that it passes.

HERVÉ BAZIN (1917), a grand-nephew of René Bazin (q.v.), made a stir with his first novel, *Viper in the Fist* (*Vipère au poing*, 1947; tr. W. J. Strachan, 1951). He came from a Catholic and conservative family, and violently rebelled against it by writing this account of a boy's psychological conflict with his detestable mother. *Viper in the Fist* is powerful, although the character of the woman is too unrelievedly evil; excellent, too, is the indignant documentary realism of *Head Against the Walls* (*La Tête contre les murs*, 1949; tr. W. J. Strachan, 1952), an exposure of the conditions in French mental hospitals. But Bazin thereafter failed to develop his gifts, and instead fell back upon a sensationalism that soon began to seem artificial.

JULIEN GRACQ (ps. LOUIS POIRIER, 1910), the friend of Breton (q.v.) and author of the best book on him, translator of Kleist and satirist of the literary establishment (he declined the Prix Goncourt) is a history teacher, as well as a novelist and essayist. He was profoundly influenced by surrealism—and by Breton more particularly—but has never been a surrealist or practised aleatory or 'automatic' techniques. When his first novel, *The Castle of Argol* (*Au Château d'Argol*, 1939; tr. L. Varèse, 1951) appeared Breton saw in it the 'flowering' of surrealism, which 'doubtless for the first time . . . freely turns around to confront the great experiments in sensibility of the past and to evaluate . . . the extent of its achievement'. Gracq is a highly studied, 'exquisite' writer, whose prose often reads like a surrealized parody of eighteenth-century Gothic; he has also been much (perhaps over-) influenced by Lautréamont (q.v.). He is steeped in the world of the German *Märchen* and of all the later versions of the Grail legend. He made his reputation with *A Dark Stranger* (*Un Beau ténébreux*, 1945; tr. W. J. Strachan, 1951), a novel of the same kind. That a real and infernal place of the spirit exists in Gracq's books is undeniable, as is his integrity (the charge of 'fake', which has been levelled, is absolutely wrong); but he does not often do much more than evoke the atmosphere of this place.

Only in *A Balcony in the Forest* (*Un Balcon en forêt*, 1958; tr. R. Howard, 1960) has Gracq chosen a modern setting: his literary Lieutenant Grange commands a small post on the Belgian frontier during the autumn of 1939. He and his three men are lulled into an enchantment by the thickly forested Ardennes countryside and by the women they find. Then the Germans come. This has magnificent passages, but is none the less over-written; even here, the magical revelation promised by the rich prose does not come. Gracq's work is too like a wonderful sauce—for meat but served without it.

JEAN-LOUIS CURTIS (1917), who was born in Orthez near the Basque country, is one of the best of the 'conventional' novelists now writing in France: he is not worried about originality of technique and prefers to concentrate upon what he can do well, which is to anatomize bourgeois societies and 'artistic' communities. His second and so far most successful novel was *The Forests of the Night* (*Les Forêts de la nuit*, 1947; tr. N. Wydenbruck, 1950): this, set in Curtis' native region, was the first book to portray France as much of it really was under fascism. Satirically, but always sympathetically where it matters, Curtis shows how, in a little town on the borderline between Vichy and the occupied zone, present attitudes to the Nazis and the collaborators have their origins in the past. Sociologically this is a more adult book than Vailland's *The Rule of the Game* (q.v.). Curtis has not equalled it, but has continued to write intelligent fiction: *Lucifer's Dream* (*Gibier de Potence*, 1949; tr. R. Chancellor, 1952) is an acid picture of post-war Paris, but always a sensible one. *The Side of the Angels* (*Les Justes Causes*, 1954; tr. H. Hare, 1956) is a distinguished *roman à clef*.

FÉLICIEN MARCEAU (originally ALBERT CARETTE, 1913) was born in Belgium and worked for the Nazi-controlled radio during the occupation; he was imprisoned, exiled from Belgium, changed his name and became a French citizen. He achieved fame with a finely made comedy, *The Egg* (*L'Œuf*, 1956; tr. C. Frank, 1958), on the theme of the hypocrisy of society, which execrates crime but admires criminals. Marceau is not an innovator, but is a highly original stylist. When his elegant, fanciful idiom does not dissolve into preciosity he achieves subtle and sometimes moving effects. *The China Shepherdess* (*Bergère légère*, 1953; tr. D. Hughes and M. J. Mason, 1957) is a fantasy that is actually not tiresome. But Marceau's best novel is *The Flutterings of the Heart* (*Les Élans du cœur*, 1955; tr. D. Hughes and M. J. Mason, 1957), a study of a provincial family on the decline which combines wit, compassion and freshness of observation. He has written well on Casanova and what is perhaps the best of all the many books on his favourite, Balzac: *Balzac and His World* (*Balzac et son monde*, 1955; tr. D. Coltman, 1967).

ROGER NIMIER (1925–64), who was killed in a car crash, was a kind of Gallic equivalent of the middle-aged Kingsley Amis (q.v.): slick, heartless, sly, anti-progressive but brilliant, talented and puzzled—and ambitiously curious about human feeling. *The Blue Hussar* (*Le Hussard bleu*, 1950; tr. J. LeClerq, 1953; tr. J. Russell and A. Rhodes, 1953) gives a sharp picture of a French regiment in the Germany of 1945; it is an unpleasant and even a shallow book, but it accurately reflects the attitude of a generation which was in 1945 terrified of its cruel emptiness but which forms, a quarter of a century later, the 'backbone' of Pompidou's France. Nimier wrote nothing else of interest, and faded out some ten years before his premature death. His essays are on a level with those of the reactionary British Catholic journalist and popular romancer John Braine; but he possesses a better education, a better intellect and a better style.

ANDRÉ GORZ (1926) was born in Austria of a Jewish family that emigrated to Switzerland. He became a naturalized Frenchman, and deserved the enthusiastic preface Sartre wrote for his autobiographical *The Traitor* (*Le Traître*, 1958; tr. R. Howard, 1959): the important thing about this book was that Gorz literally 'redefined' himself—and created an authenticity—by writing it. Sartre's claims for it as 'an invitation to life' after the great slaughter of the twentieth century are justified.

MICHEL DEL CASTILLO (1933), who is wholly Spanish, was born in Madrid; at six, as a refugee from Franco, he was taken to France, where he was interned in a concentration camp; he was then sent to another camp, in Germany— then to a Jesuit school in Spain, from which he ran away, at the age of sixteen, in order to return to France and his mother. He tells this story in his first and best novel, *A Child of Our Time* (*Tanguy*, 1957; tr. P. Green, 1958). In *The Guitar* (*La Guitare*, 1957; tr. H. Hare, 1959) he tried a more inventive kind of fiction. A dwarf seeks to melt the hearts of his fellow men by the magic of his guitar, but they regard this as witchcraft, and stone him. Del Castillo called this 'a book of utter despair'. The successors to this powerful tale, which is set in Galicia, have proved disappointing.

FRANÇOISE SAGAN (ps. FRANÇOISE QUOIREZ, 1935) has one distinction: her lucid style. She writes of bored, shallow, boring, spoiled people seeking relief in brief sexual contacts. Her great successes have been *Bonjour Tristesse* (1954; tr. I. Ash, 1957) and *Aimez-vous Brahms?* (1959; tr. P. Wiles, 1960), both of which have been enshrined in *kitsch* celluloid. Francoise Sagan's 'sophisticated' manner is as effective a cover for mental vacuousness as money is an effective substitute for intelligence—we may judge of this from her devoted readers as well as her characters.

IX

The Fifties in France was the decade of the emergence of 'anti-literature', '*choisisme*', the 'anti-novel', the 'new wave', the 'new novel'; the phenomenon as a whole is important, but its many components should not be taken too seriously. With two or three exceptions no exponent of the 'new novel' has shown signs of possessing more than a minor talent. Like all blanket terms, *nouveau roman*, which was invented by journalists—mainly hostile—to describe the work of Ollier, Pinget, Robbe-Grillet and others, can be misleading; but it is none the less more useful than most such terms.

In 1948 NATHALIE SARRAUTE (1902), who was born in Russia of Russian-Jewish parents who separated soon after her birth, published her first novel, *Portrait of a Man Unknown* (*Portrait d'un inconnu*, 1947; tr. M. Jolas, 1959). Her *Tropisms* (*Tropismes*, 1939, rev., add., 1957; tr. M. Jolas, with essays, 1964), short sketches contrasting the exiguousness of bourgeois habits with their rich subconscious origins, had passed unnoticed. Sartre wrote a famous preface to her novel, in which he hailed the arrival of the *anti-roman* (a term used by the seventeenth-century writer Charles Sorel to describe the reprint of a novel in which he had mocked the pastoral artificialities of his day). What Sartre—whose own *Nausea* (q.v.) is, although in a different way, itself clearly an anti-novel—meant was that Nathalie Sarraute's fiction questioned its own validity: its writer questioned the moral propriety of writing fiction, and the effectiveness of fiction itself. 'Where is the invented story that could compete with that of the . . . Battle of Stalingrad?' she asked. '. . . The character as conceived of in the old-style novel (along with the entire old-style mechanism that was used to make him stand out) does not succeed in containing the psychological reality of today . . . the whole problem is here: to dispossess the reader and entice him, at all costs, into the author's territory'.

The nineteenth-century novel, with its characters and plots, had the confidence of a society that was successfully expanding. Nineteenth-century criticism liked to insist upon 'consistency of character', 'soundness of plot'. The programme of the new novel rejects this: it is morally reprehensible to lead the reader to expect to see consistent characters and 'plots' around him. Again, it is false to present characters whose lives are determined by 'clock time': we do not recollect experience in terms of clock time. The new novel deliberately returns to what Henri Bergson (who, perhaps because his ideas became vulgarized by Shaw, q.v., himself and others, seldom gets his due in discussions of the new novel) called 'the immediate data of consciousness'. The new novelist is a phenomenologist: a subjective realist.

The average British reader remains cut off from the developments of continental philosophy, whereas the French are aware of the phenomenology of Edmund Husserl (1859–1938) through the work not only of Sartre but also of his friend Maurice Merleau-Ponty. Phenomenology played an essential part in the formulation of the existential position; it is not too much to say that its world is the world of the new novelists (and, although less deliberately, of many more writers in many countries). Husserl began by relating states of mind to objects: all states of mind, he pointed out, are directed to real or imaginary objects. The new novel reinstates the object-for-its-own-sake, elevates it (Robbe-Grillet) to the status of an independent world. Like Butor (q.v.), Husserl was interested in the difference between states of mind towards the same object: the man who led the Free French is different from the man whose daughter died young, and *he* is different from the man who resigned power in 1969. Husserl was not, as a philosopher, interested in the actual: his investigations were 'eidetic' (conceptual); he is concerned not with what is perceived but with the mechanics of perception. Anything can be discussed in Husserl's philosophy because anything can be 'constituted' in the mind; hell-fire, then (one could argue), may be 'reinstated'. Husserl is not troubled by the 'ridiculousness' of the notion of a flat earth: it may be studied as a phenomenon in consciousness. The later Husserl increasingly tended to interpret common-sense reality (it gets reasserted in philosophy every so often) as mere 'data for consciousness'—once again, his relevance to literature is obvious. This development in his philosophy may be linked to one of the gravest objections that has been made to the new novelists: that the horrors of Viet Nam or Czecho-slovakia are no more than data for their consciousness. . . .

And so the new novelist takes you inside his laboratory, shows you what he is doing and how he is doing it, and frankly admits that what he is giving you is not susceptible of verification. Like a 'new cook' he dispenses with the opaque wall and substitutes one of glass (it makes his cooking cleaner, but it also turns him into a more narcissistic exhibitionist—one who has to turn his back with an elegant gesture and a pretence of pinching in a subtle flavouring as he pisses into your soup). The new novelist is not likely to be a Christian, since he does not believe in order: his fiction does not demonstrate the existence of a concealed order (as does, say, Saint-John Perse's poetry), but draws attention to the fact that his own selective procedures and patternings are false impositions of order on the chaos of life; he admits that it is only his consciousness which imposes duration on a discontinuous series—but, unlike the essentially romantic Bergson, prefers to leave the matter at that. However, the new novelist is likely to be 'left-wing'—at least to the extent that he rejects the essentially right-wing (and authoritarian) myths of social stability and order in the best of all possible worlds.

This thinking is of great importance, and its impact upon other literatures (such as that of Great Britain) will (or would) undoubtedly prove fruitful. But it is critical and philosophical thinking. The imagination is relegated to a secondary position; in the case of the sly behaviourist Robbe-Grillet it is actually discredited as wholly mythical, in favour of the 'geometry'—the hard measurable facts of the external world—that he naïvely sees as 'factual' (though science, considered in the terms employed by Robbe-Grillet, is actually as mythical as anything else). The phenomenon of the new novel is ambivalent: it seeks to recharge the batteries of creativity, but it also jealously seeks to destroy the intuitive richness of creation by cerebralizing it.

All *avant garde* notions eventually fragment, and 'common sense' reasserts itself—but it can be an enriched common sense, because it has absorbed the essential revolutionary elements. This will be the fate of the new novel, at least as it is exemplified in the work of most of those now called new novelists, which uniformly lacks robustness. To achieve robustness, to avoid the boring effect created by detailed—and inevitably narcissistic—mental self-exploration, at the same time avoiding the error of false objectivity: this is what novelists should now be trying to do, and they should be doing it through the writing of fiction rather than of criticism, or criticism disguised as fiction. But they will certainly in one way or another have taken account of the new novel, will have absorbed it. Familiar disparagement of it is, alas, based on ignorance—or a preference for the erection of dream-yarns.

*

'Tropism' is a biological term for the automatic, i.e. the instinctive, turning of an organism in a certain direction in reaction to a stimulus; this is, for Nathalie Sarraute, who must certainly be regarded as one of the chief pioneers and anticipators of the new novel (although she is less programmatic than her successors), a description of instinctive human authenticity that is concealed by the clichés of speech and the (bourgeois) rituals of society. Tropisms are 'inner movements . . . hidden under the commonplace . . . they . . . seem to me to constitute the secret source of our existence . . . veritable dramatic actions . . . constantly emerging up to the surface of the appearances that both conceal and reveal them'. Her technique must not be confused with that stream-of-consciousness (q.v.) which is a pushing-out of the frontiers of realism; Sarraute tries to describe, by means of metaphor, or what she calls 'images', the 'tropisms' that 'glide quickly round the border of our consciousness'.

The anonymous narrator of *Portrait of a Man Unknown* describes selected details of the suspicion between a miser (or one 'the others' call a miser) and his daughter. *Martereau* (1954; tr. M. Jolas, 1964) is narrated by a sick, indeterminate young man playing at art, living in the spacious home of relatives, fascinated by the character of Martereau, whom he suspects to be a crook. The narrator (who is as much a representative and critique of the novelist as any of Kafka's central characters) is seen as himself creating the other characters; but he cannot create—'fix', deal with in his mind—Martereau, whom he has idealized. There is much suspicion, here, on the part of the creator, of what she is creating. In *The Planetarium* (*Le Planétarium*, 1959; tr. M. Jolas, 1961), her best novel, the egocentric savagery hidden by the social behaviour of shallow, 'polite' people is depressingly revealed. The hero of *The Golden Fruits* (*Les Fruits d'or*, 1963; tr. M. Jolas, 1965), her most comic novel, is itself, a 'worthless' book called *The Golden Fruits* (or is this not, perhaps *The Golden Fruits* we are reading?): its rise and fall. A savage work doubtless drawing on experience of the long period in which the author was entirely neglected (her first book got only one review), *The Golden Fruits* formidably exposes the mindlessness of a certain section of the 'reading public'. Since this novel Nathalie Sarraute has published two radio plays, *Silence* and *The Lie* (*Le Silence* suivi de *Le Mensonge*, 1967), commissioned and broadcast by West German radio (Stuttgart), where she has been received with great interest.

ALAIN ROBBE-GRILLET (1922), born in Brest, was trained as an agronomist and then worked as a statistician and in research on tropical fruits. He is as clever as any French writer of his time; but frigidity and a childishly brash over-confidence rob his fiction of imaginative significance. He is ingenious to a degree; a brilliant publicist; but never wise or mellow: a scientist come into literature in order to show its inferiority, indeed, its meaninglessness; not

merely a philosopher disguising himself as a novelist, but a bad philosopher—
adhering to the discredited and simplistic theory of behaviourism—disguising
himself as an advanced novelist. What he writes is of undoubted interest;
but it has the quality of the production of a computor that has somehow been
endowed with the orientations of a statistician on heat in a shop full of dirty
pics and girlie magazines. In Robbe-Grillet we have the purest possible case of
the artist-as-solipsist, although he rationalizes his solipsism into a complaint
(irrelevant to literature) that only Robbe-Grillet of all mankind is capable of
taking the geometrical world as-it-is. Robbe-Grillet sees the world of objects
and wants to accept it without anthropomorphizing it; of human beings who
have the habit of anthropomorphization—the whole human race, including
his unwitting self—or of human beings who discern purpose in the universe,
or who are sceptical, he can tell us nothing. The mean little grid he clamps on to
phenomena is simply his own: phenomenology here is transformed into a
sullen, bored (*In the Labyrinth*) or smutty (*The House of Assignation*) assertion of
self. It is a fascinating and repellent enterprise. But it is an odd and ambiguous
one, so that Robbe-Grillet—who is the centre of a cult—has been credited with
a number of high-minded intentions. For example, he has been presented as
the pioneer revealer of the world as-it-is: indifferent, unconnected with man,
incapable of being 'humanized' into a sentimental system on a theological
model. This was Robbe-Grillet as *choisiste*: presenter of things as simply there.
Since Roland Barthes put forward this Robbe-Grillet, others have postulated
other Robbe-Grillets—the most ambitious one following the author's own
evaluation of himself as in 'the Stendhal-Balzac-Flaubert-Proust-Gide tradition': 'as a result [of his work], man is enabled to enter uncharted domains of
fiction in search of a new reality which he can only attain through works of
art . . . [he] appears to stand at the most advanced point of evolution of the
twentieth-century novel and film' (Bruce Morrissette). This is from an intelligent and illuminating study, and I quote it as contrast to the view I have put
forward. The fact is that only those who 'like' Robbe-Grillet's cerebral
behaviourism will 'like' his fiction. His importance as an influence and as a
stimulus is undeniable. But if the literary value of his work depends on the
truth of his philosophy, as it surely does, then his admirers are in the position
of dogmatists.

The Erasers (*Les Gommes*, 1953; tr. R. Howard, 1964) is a diabolically ingenious, perhaps parodic, adaptation of the Oedipus theme. It is full of tricks:
duplicated events, symbols, contradictions, 'clues', scenes that are 'imagined'
and therefore do not really take place in the novel, and so on. The 'plot' is
simple: a detective, Wallas, kills the supposed victim (his father) of a murder
that he is sent to investigate. The novelist desperately tries to 'erase' the notion
that the Oedipus myth has any relevance to modern man: this is his way of
saying that it ought not to. There is a good deal of *choisiste* description—of a
tomato, the rubber (eraser) that Wallas seeks throughout the book, the paper-
weight that the supposedly murdered man keeps on his desk. Each of these
objects does in fact have a significance outside itself: the rubber is an erotic

object, the segment of tomato is 'perfect' but for an 'accident': 'a corner of the skin, detached from the flesh over the space of one or two millimetres, sticks up imperceptibly'. This accident, for Robbe-Grillet a horrifying wrecker of symmetry, with the force of an emotion spoiling a thought, is the novel itself. This book has everything, one might say, except feeling; its successors are elaborations of it: *The Voyeur* (*Le Voyeur*, 1955; tr. R. Howard, 1958), *Jealousy* (*La Jalousie*, 1957; tr. R. Howard, 1959), *In the Labyrinth* (*Dans le labyrinthe*, 1959; tr. R. Howard, 1960), *The House of Assignation* (*La Maison de rendez-vous*, 1965; tr. A. M. Sheridan-Smith, 1970) and the 'film-novels', including *Last Year at Marienbad* (*L'Année dernière à Marienbad*, 1961; tr. R. Howard, 1962), partly a successful middlebrow hoax (it had its audiences busily discussing its 'meaning') and partly a sincere visual exploration. *The House of Assignation* is a largely sadistic pornography played against the 'Hong Kong' of the popular cinema; once again, it is ingenious and even humorous, but the only accessible feeling is the 'eroticism' offered by dirty booksellers. Robbe-Grillet's frenzy is directed at his inability to be a machine; if the world of *The House of Assignation* is the one in which he feels himself trapped then one can understand his aspiration and his error in treating the scientific view as an absolute. He is a fascinating and undoubtedly important critic, using the form of fiction to discredit fiction itself. A real novelist will benefit from his speculations—which is hardly what this icy playboy himself, desperately trying to disembarrass himself of the furtive eroticism that is the surface of his romanticism, can have intended.

The theories of the new novelists do not agree, and they lead to very different results. The 'new' novels have only one thing in common: they are conscious and critical of themselves. Thus MICHEL BUTOR (1926), who was born in Lille, does not share Robbe-Grillet's overriding desire to divest himself of humanity and merge himself into the geometrical, neutral world; on the contrary, although as intellectually subtle as Robbe-Grillet, he is clearly in full possession of his emotional faculties. Whereas Robbe-Grillet has exploited surrealism, Butor has been influenced by it. His early poetry he himself characterizes as irrational and demonstrative of his confusion at the time. Butor studied philosophy at the Sorbonne; one of the only two of his teachers for whom he felt respect was Gaston Bachelard, by whose thought he has been profoundly influenced. His novel, *Passage of Kites* (*Passage de milan*, 1954) tries to study the corporate as well as the individual life of the inhabitants of a block of flats throughout one evening and night; in certain respects it represents a highly sophisticated excursion in, and extension of, unanimism (q.v.). The intricate *Passing Time* (*L'Emploi du temps*, 1957; tr. J. Stewart, 1961) gives an account of a young Frenchman, Jacques Revel, as he tries to find his bearings in the British industrial city of Bleston. Butor had spent two years as a lecturer in Manchester, and Bleston—the 'hero' or anti-hero of the book—is not unlike it. Like so many novels of its kind, *Passing Time* incorporates elements of the detective story: the Bleston murder mystery Revel reads becomes 'real' to him, and its author becomes himself involved in a murder mystery similar to the one he has invented. . . . The whole thing is mysterious, but the mystery is something like that of real life—and the search for 'meaning' and 'solution' has a resemblance to any person's bewildered desire for 'a place' when he suddenly becomes conscious—when he breaks or is awoken out of habitude.

In *Second Thoughts* (*La Modification*, 1957; tr. J. Stewart, 1958) the narrator addresses himself throughout in the second person. It traces the decision, made on a rail journey, of a typewriter salesman (i.e. writer) to leave his wife for his mistress. Really, it is a study of a man who pretends to himself that external actions can achieve inner freedom; *Second Thoughts* is a novel in which one can aptly trace the shift from a moral to an existential viewpoint: Léon is not judged, but presented as incapable of escaping from his own 'bad faith', his failure to respect the freedom of himself or others. *Degrees* (*Degrés*, 1960; tr. R. Howard, 1962) projects Butor the moralist as Pierre Vernier, teacher in a lycée, agonizedly attempting to preserve the detailed truth of life at the lycée for the sake of his nephew—so that he should have understanding of it. It is Butor's most ambitious, fearsomely complex and painstakingly honest novel—the teacher has to hand over his job of recorder to others, but it becomes apparent that until nearly the end he is only pretending to allow them to speak—and it illustrates his dilemma. Butor believes that the function of the writer is to improve the world; but he is not prepared to compromise by oversimplification. In an oblique way, he rejects Sartre's (not happily held) theory that it is necessary to have 'dirty hands'. He is highly intellectual: he has been accused of using 'tricks' when in fact he has been intellectually scrupulous. His difficulty is to hold the attention of the reader without sacrificing the subtleties and sophistications that he feels necessary to describe the truth. One might put it in this way: a wholly 'sentimentive' (q.v.) writer, he is in danger of cutting himself off altogether from nature—and what matters most of all to him. He has tried to resolve his difficulties by writing books that cannot be classified as novels, such as *Mobile* (1963), a 'structural' presentation of American society, and by his 'serial opera', with music by Henri Pousseur, *Votre Faust*. *Mobile* builds up a picture of its subject from advertisements, quotations, the author's own descriptions and other elements, all presented in a complex typographical scheme. Unfortunately some degree of self-satisfaction has obtruded here: this is a book that requires another book to explicate it, and that has attracted an undesirable cult. Butor, a sensitive instrument and originally a writer of imaginative power, is declining into a fragmenting intellectual, an explicator of explications; thus, much of his recent work consists of increasingly complex essays explaining the development of his fictions. Ironically, as he vanishes into what amounts to hermeticism, he preaches the necessity of hermeneutics; but this becomes a passion directed only at himself.

CLAUDE MAURIAC (1914), the son of François Mauriac, is a polemicist for 'the new literature', on which he wrote an influential book, as well as a novelist himself. All his novels, including *The Dinner Party* (*Le Dîner en ville*, 1959; tr. M. Lawrence, 1960) and *The Marquise Went out at Five* (*La Marquise sortit à cinq heures*, 1963; tr. R. Howard, 1965), deal with Bertrand Carnéjoux, a successful novelist and womanizer. Mauriac has faithfully and intelligently followed those precepts of the new novel that militate against traditional realism, but (unlike Butor) he does not really believe in his characters, and the reader becomes aware that this fiction is a conscientious critical exercise.

CLAUDE SIMON (1913), born of French parents in Tananarive in Madagascar, looked at first towards Camus and Faulkner (qq.v.); his novels themselves have perhaps looked towards rather than been influenced by the new novel, although his imagination has been fertilized by its eruption. Butor's is a formidable intellect, but Simon may emerge as the finer and more natural novelist. One can extract a philosophy from Simon: the notion of everything as in flux and unstable—which is once again a feature of Bachelard's thinking. But what are more important are his portraits of human beings: these, not the abstractions, came first. Simon does not set out to abolish the 'story' of the traditional novel, but rather seeks to trace it in the unconscious and painful making: he is the fascinated chronicler of what must happen in life before fictions can be made, and is much less conscious of himself as writer than Robbe-Grillet or Butor. His first novel, *The Trickster* (*Le Tricheur*, 1945) was conventional; its themes, and those of his next two novels, were not to find adequate expression until *Wind* (*Le Vent*, 1957; tr. R. Howard, 1959). This is the story, in dense prose, of a man who cannot but bring disaster to all he touches. Antoine Montès, a sailor, comes to south-eastern France to recover some vineyards he has inherited: everything, his human relationships and his vines, collapses before the wind. Of Simon's other novels, all impressive, *The Flanders Road* (*La Route des Flandres*, 1960; tr. R. Howard, 1962) is the best. Like Karl in Frank's much inferior *Karl and Anna* (q.v.), Georges has heard throughout his war (the Second World War) of a woman; after it is over he has an affair with her. She is Corinne, for whom Georges' Captain probably committed suicide: she had been unfaithful to him with his batman. The character of the dead Captain is reconstituted, too, in Georges' and his companions' minds as they spend their aimless war. He 'comes to life' in their memory as meaningfully to them as when he was in fact alive. And so the Corinne of Georges' invention is as real to him as the true Corinne he seduces after the war. Simon shows everything as changing, and individuals therefore falling back into themselves and superimposing their images of reality upon reality itself. Robbe-Grillet preaches the perniciousness of this; Simon sees the acceptance of it as salvation. He shows order as perpetually destroyed by chance, life as having significance only in the mind, death as having significance only in the memories of the undead. For him, it seems, the tragedy is not that life is 'tragic', but that people do not accept it. He therefore presents his characters as tragic because their consciousness is directed upon their experience in such a way that their hopes of order actually create disorder. Like Faulkner, to whom he owes so much, he seems to gloat over man's helplessness in confused flux. *The Palace* (*Le Palace*, 1962; tr. R. Howard, 1964) contrasts his realization of this situation with his revolutionary aspirations, in a powerfully evocative story of the Spanish Civil War, of the assassination of a revolutionary leader by other revolutionaries. In Simon we see the determinist gloom of naturalism replaced by a conviction that chaos must supervene: he is the novelist of entropy, of running down. When C. P. Snow (q.v.) launched his 'Two Cultures' he postulated the literary man as one who did not understand the Second Law of Thermodynamics; he forgot (or was ignorant of?) Simon, who is its laureate.

CLAUDE OLLIER (1922) met Robbe-Grillet in Germany during the war when they were both working in Nuremburg as deported labourers; it is said that much of the latter's system originated in Ollier's mind. There may even be some injustice in describing him as the disciple of Robbe-Grillet. His first novel, *The Setting* (*La Mise en scène*, 1958) is about an engineer mapping a road across the African desert; he is puzzled by traces of someone who has been there before him. *The Maintenance of Order* (*Le Maintien de l'ordre*, 1961) describes, again in an African setting, two assassins stalking their intended victim. The second of these novels builds up a considerable tension of curiosity; the first, which is open to the unique interpretation of each of its readers, is less penetrable than anything of Robbe-Grillet's. (Nothing, incidentally, could be more 'anthropomorphized' than the desert in this book.) Ollier has said that he is interested in creating other worlds, not in order to 'counterweigh' 'this' one, but to compare with it. He is that rare phenomenon: a genuinely experimental writer, a pioneer, who works intelligently in strange territory in order to discover the results.

An important if difficult writer is MAURICE BLANCHOT (1907), a distinguished critic as well as novelist, who unites in himself almost every modernist tendency. Although his fiction is read by few, Blanchot is highly respected in France as a thinker and writer of unimpeachable integrity. In Great Britain he would be a laughing-stock, although perhaps recognized by journalists in his declining years; in America he would perhaps live in a community that had contracted out. France, by respecting him, allows such a man to attain to his full serious-ness; Great Britain would torment him into personal eccentricity—and then pity him.

Paul West aptly quotes Blanchot's question:

> what can this thing be, with its eternal immutability which is nothing but a semblance, a thing which speaks truth and yet with nothing but a void behind it, so that in it the truth has nothing with which to confirm itself, appears without support, is only a scandalous semblance of truth, an image, and by its imagery and seeming withdraws from truth into depths where there is neither truth nor meaning, not even error?

This should be compared to what Broch (q.v.) said on the same subject (q.v.); it is one of the questions at the heart of *Künstlerschuld* (q.v.). Blanchot, however, has an affirmative attitude towards creation: man may recreate himself as he writes; the creation of the great definitive 'fiction' for all time may change the world because in the writing of it man may change himself. Literature is the expression of man's progress from silence to silence, and 'above all the domain of the "as if" ' (Maurice Nadeau).

In *Thomas the Obscure* (*Thomas l'obscur*, 1940, rev. 1950) Thomas seeks himself in various settings, some or even all of which may be hallucinatory. This is much less easily readable than Gracq (q.v.), but less playful: the writer is seeking to purge himself of the 'ordinary', which poisons his perception. The effect is somewhat akin to that created by Kafka's work, but, as has been pointed out, Blanchot's real ancestor is Mallarmé. However, Blanchot's novels considerably outdo Mallarmé's poems in obscurity; they may even qualify for the title of the most recondite in the world. And yet time, one feels, will make them more accessible.

The Swiss ROBERT PINGET (1919) was born in Geneva; he is a collaborator of Beckett's, and has an undoubted kinship with him in metaphysical direction although less in style. His novels are less individual and interesting than his plays, although the writing of novels has been important to him in releasing his full creative potential; and some of his best plays have been dramatized from novels. *Monsieur Levert* (*Le Fiston*, 1959; tr. R. Howard, 1961; tr. A. N. Coe, *No Answer*, 1961) is an unsent letter written by a father to his prodigal son, of whose whereabouts he has no idea. His reports on events in his town, which are repeated in different forms, get mixed in with his observations on his feelings; it all seems the work of a fumbling and drunken old fool, until one realizes that the writer is trying to abolish the reality of his grief—just as a new novelist softens the anguish of living by writing novels that try to abolish reality. When he put this on the stage in *Dead Letter* (*Lettre morte*, 1960; PP) Pinget made the old man speak his helpless piece to a post-office clerk (whom he asks vainly for a letter from his son) and a bartender, both of whom are played by the same actor. Then some strolling players come into the bar and idly repeat passages from their current farce, about the return of a prodigal son. . . . Becket has brilliantly transferred a radio play of Pinget's, *The Old Tune* (*Le Manivelle*, 1960), in which two old men chatter crazily together, from a French into an Irish idiom. Pinget's themes are exceedingly close to Beckett's, and he will inevitably suffer by comparison. But this is so because of a real affinity; and Pinget's genuine Frenchness contrasts strangely and interestingly with Beckett's Irishness. *Baga* (1958; tr. J. Stevenson, 1967), a fantasy, is more original but less confident and substantial.

J. M. G. LE CLÉZIO (1940) was born in Nice of a Mauritian family (his father's forbears emigrated from England in the eighteenth century), and is English by nationality. He studied at the Universities of Bristol and London, and, like Van Gogh and other unfortunates, has taught in an English school. Le Clézio is brilliantly accomplished—perhaps almost too much so. His first novel, *The Interrogation* (*Le Procès-verbal*, 1963; tr. D. Woodward, 1964), is his most powerful and convincing. Adam Pollo, a student who has lost his memory, goes mad in the solitude of a seaside villa into which he has broken. He goes into the town and addresses a crowd, whereupon he is put into a mental hospital. This may be read as a study in madness and as 'philosophy' in the manner of the new novelists; but there is at present more imagination and interest in psychology than philosophy in Le Clézio. His second novel, *The*

Flood (*Le Déluge*, 1966; tr. P. Green) appeared in English in 1967.

PHILIPPE SOLLERS (1936), editor of the influential magazine *Tel Quel* and a highly intelligent critic (he has written on Francis Ponge, q.v.), is less successful as a novelist. *The Park* (*Le Parc*, 1961; tr. A. Sheridan-Smith, 1967), in which a man invents or recalls (which?) three other characters, in an orange exercise book, never achieves a more than philosophic interest. Character has an extraordinary and mysterious way of 'taking over'. Philosophically this is reprehensible—perhaps too reprehensible for it to happen here.

X

With new producers active, the French theatre after the end of the First World War became as lively as and considerably more interesting than the German. AURÉLIEN MARIE LUGNÉ POË (1869–1940), who had put on Jarry's *Ubu Roi* (q.v.) in 1896, was still active at the Théâtre de l'Œuvre. JACQUES COPEAU (1879–1949) carried on with the experimental Théâtre du Vieux-Colombier, which he had started in 1913, until 1924—when he went to Burgundy to train a new generation of actors. This band eventually became his nephew Michel Saint-Denis' Compagnie des Quinze. One of Copeau's actors was the director and actor LOUIS JOUVET (1887–1951), who established his own theatres soon after the war. Jouvet was closely associated with Giraudoux (q.v.), and he lived to stage a play by Genêt. Jouvet also found time to star in a number of memorable movies. The Russians Georges and Ludmilla Pitoëff produced many Russian and Scandinavian plays. Not long before the outbreak of the Second World War Jouvet was invited to produce at the Comédie-Française, and Copeau's work was recognized when he was appointed a director. Another of Copeau's pupils had been CHARLES DULLIN (1885–1949), who had founded his own *avant garde* Théâtre de l'Atelier in 1921; his pupil JEAN-LOUIS BARRAULT (1910) has been one of the chief forces in the French theatre since the occupation, during which he put on Claudel (q.v.).

JEAN COCTEAU (1889–1963), poet, novelist, illustrator, film-maker, was one of the most versatile of all modern writers; but his greatest achievement is undoubtedly in the theatre; he was a successful playwright in both *avant garde* and traditional forms. And yet it is unlikely that anything by Cocteau will survive the century; nor was he influential except as a personality. Homosexual, drug-addict, socialite, Cocteau's desire was to astonish and surprise; he did astonish and surprise people, but never for long. His genius was for talent. The friend of Proust, Radiguet, Picasso, Cendrars, Apollinaire, Max Jacob, Poulenc —of everyone who mattered—he understood them and surprised even them; yet it is hard now to see even his best plays as possessing real substance. He was ultimately more interested in the topical, in the cleverest possible exploitation of the very best fashion, of the very best people, of the immediate moment.

He did it all in the name of the poetic, the eternal, the anti-fashionable. He understood this; and we believe him. Yet there was at his heart some kind of tragic emptiness—perhaps to do with his disturbed sexuality—that seems to have prevented him from achieving emotional solidity in his life or in his work.

So runs one judgement. But as soon as we agree with it we want to question it. For the worth of this man is as elusive as was his emotional centre of gravity. We have to look again. Perhaps he will survive. . . .

His verse is fantastic, precious, virtuosic, charming, modish; never more than poesy at best, but it can be touching even while it is stylish. What characterizes it most is Cocteau's fancifulness. His fiction is less rarefied. *The Potomak* (*Le Potomak*, 1919) was a mixture of texts and drawings, not a novel; but *The Grand Ecart* (*Le Grand Écart*, 1923; tr. L. Galantière, 1925) is a conventional, and charming, 'education novel'. *The Impostor* (*Thomas l'Imposteur*, 1923; tr. D. Williams, 1957) is a hymn to the cult of youth of which Cocteau was the supreme embodiment; if it does not survive as reading matter it will, like its author, be an essential part of literary and sociological history. Cocteau's best novel followed in 1929: *Children of the Game* (*Les Enfants terribles*, 1929; tr. R. Lehmann, 1955), a sinister study of four young bourgeois who create their own world, with disastrous results. In 1950 Cocteau made a memorable film of this novel.

Some of Cocteau's earliest ventures were in ballet; he wrote the sketch for *Parade* (1917), Satie's masterly score for which evokes its time, complete with Cocteau and all the others, with haunting perfection; and he went on creating ballets until the Fifties. His first major play, and still the one by which he will live in the theatre if he lives at all, was *Orpheus* (*Orphée*, 1926; tr. C. Wildman, 1962); this was on a theme that obsessed him for the whole of his life. It was produced by Georges and Ludmilla Pitoëff. In Cocteau's version of the myth, which is comic and ironic but never flippant, the lovers are not happy until their departure to the next world. *Orphée* depends on an ingenious director and many props; but its reconciliation of the mythical with the modern is no more certainly a confidence trick than it is a *tour de force*. . . . The dying Rilke (q.v.) began to translate it, and sent a telegram: 'Tell Jean Cocteau I love him, for he alone has access to the world of myth. . . .' *The Human Voice* (*La Voix humaine*, 1930; tr. C. Wildman, 1951), in which a woman tries to get her lover back, on the telephone, shows two Cocteaus: the homosexual Cocteau revenging himself on women by showing one in a humiliating position, and the showman Cocteau manufacturing a piece of impeccable middlebrow theatre in order to do it. Even *The Eagle with Two Heads* (*L'Aigle à deux têtes*, 1946; ad. R. Duncan, 1948; tr. C. Wildman, 1962), his most pretentious play, a romantic Ruritanian melodrama, has a residue of poetry.

Opinion is nowhere more sharply divided than on the subject of Cocteau. Certainly much of his work lacks spontaneity; certainly the rebel was also a socialite. But he was a magician: real magic or sleight of hand? It is hard to say, because Cocteau's case may resemble that of a genuine medium who, in terror of failure, arranges to cheat. . . . There is a unique quality in his work, an elusive quality like the true personality of its creator: alarmed, secret: the pale face of the showman caught in an accidental beam of light is seen, for a fleeting moment, at some private task. . . . If the secret comes out anywhere, it comes out in *Orphée*, and in the film (1949) of the same title. Cocteau will continue to fascinate.

JEAN GIRAUDOUX (1882–1944), born at the Limousin town of Bellac, was a professional diplomat and Germanophile whose first literary successes were with a series of clever, bright novels about adolescence. The best of these, and Giraudoux's best single work, was *Simon the Pathetic* (*Simon le pathétique*, 1918, rev. 1926), the most famous *My Friend from Limousin* (*Siegfried et le Limousin*, 1922; tr. L. C. Willcox, 1923), which became *Siegfried* (1928; tr. P. Carr, 1930) in the theatre. This was an attempted resolution of Giraudoux's own problem: the pellucidity of his fanciful world was threatened by the fogginess of German 'thought'. In *Siegfried* Jacques, the hero, is a Frenchman who loses his memory in the war, and consequently becomes a leading figure in German politics; he is rescued and returned to his proper Frenchness by one of Giraudoux's many delightful, undefined women—but he is still 'German-minded'. In fact Giraudoux never did resolve the conflict; but Jouvet (q.v.) saw what he could make from Giraudoux's scripts, and the fundamental crack was skilfully papered over to yield a quarter of a century of solidly successful theatre. The first international hit was *Amphitryon 38* (1929; ad. S. N. Behrman, 1938); revivals suggest that this rhetorical, meretricious, beautifully made farce about the Gods depended largely upon the right actors (Jouvet, Michel Simon in Paris; Lunt and Fontanne in New York) at the right time. *Tiger at the Gates* (*La Guerre de Troie n'aura pas lieu*, 1935; tr. 1963) found the perfect translator in Christopher Fry (q.v.), another sentimental fantasticator, though on a smaller scale. This anti-war play is one of his best.

Giraudoux tried to fuse seriousness with comedy and delight; but his seriousness consisted too much of a soft-centredly Teutonic romanticism and woman-worship, and he was too tempted by the opportunity of middlebrow dramatic success, to which his great skill and elegance gave him relatively easy access. At the very end of his life he wrote *The Madwoman of Chaillot* (*La Folle de Chaillot*, 1945; ad. M. Valency, 1949), an uncomplicated satire on greed: this has no intellectual distinction but is inspired by a passion for decency. In it Giraudoux may have found his true, modest level.

JEAN ANOUILH (1910), from Bordeaux, is yet a third playwright who has been accused of a basic superficiality; he is perhaps fortunate to have had so much critical attention lavished upon him; but he has been a major figure in the French theatre since the Second World War because he has maintained consistently high standards despite a remarkable prolificity—and, above all, because his mastery of his craft is assured. If in the last decades he has degenerated from bitter critic of society into entertainer, he must nevertheless be the finest entertainer in the modern theatre. Although Anouilh's early plays (the first was *The Ermine*, *L'Hermine*, 1932; tr. M. John, 1955) were produced by such as Jouvet and Lugné-Poë (q.v.), it took him some ten years to attain to a stable position in the theatre. The earlier plays reflect the poverty in which Anouilh lived: individuals obsessed by purity reject the corruptness of society and lead private existences. But even in the best of this period Anouilh reveals a certain fundamental paucity of thought. One of the first of his plays to achieve a success, *Traveller without Luggage* (*Voyageur sans bagage*, 1936; tr. J. Whiting, 1959), deals with an amnesic ex-soldier who returns home to discover from his family, who are not sure of his identity, that he has been a vicious and cruel character. He chooses, as circumstances allow him to, not to re-become himself, but to assume the identity of one who was a pleasanter person. The play is gripping and, in terms of technique, formidable; but as has been well said: 'the hero has made no effort to understand his past, he has simply dismissed it'. This is the fatal flaw that Anouilh's consummate theatricality and sure sense of atmosphere conceal: his bleak pessimism is the bleaker for being, beneath the flashing froth of skill and gaiety, shallow and incapable of self-examination. None the less, his stage people, unlike Giraudoux's, have a reality in their 'all-too-humanness', so that his plays remain interesting spectacles. *Ring Round the Moon* (*L'Invitation au château*, 1947; tr. 1950), among other plays by Anouilh, attracted that master of the scented epigram—the 'sheer verbal magic' of suburban dramatic clubs—Christopher Fry, who incidentally removed its 'French' beastliness by excising the impurity of the heroine; in this form it provided a feast for London theatregoers. Anouilh has produced two impressive updated versions of myth: *Point of Departure* (*Eurydice*, 1942; tr. K. Black, 1951) and *Antigone* (1942; tr. L. Galantière, 1946), which played during the occupation to audiences who slowly realized that the plausibly presented Creon represented Vichy compromise, whereas the pure and idealistic Antigone represented unsullied France. Anouilh has divided his production into 'Pièces roses', 'Pièces noires' and, more recently, 'Pièces grinçantes' (grinding). Both these are 'black' pieces. Characteristically, Anouilh's version of the Orpheus myth revolves around the question of Eurydice's purity; she is killed in a car-crash, but returns to tell Orpheus of her corrupt past—he chooses to join her in death. In *Waltz of the Toreadors* (*La Valse des toréadors*, 1952; tr. L. Hill, 1956) Anouilh concentrates, with success, on the sexual atmosphere generated by his unhappy pseudo-philosophy: General Saint-Pé (who appeared in the earlier *Ardèle*, 1948, tr. L. Hill, 1951), tormented by his crazy, nagging wife, tries vainly to escape from his lonely eroticism by re-idealizing the object of each new sexual episode, and ends as he began. *Becket, or the Honour of God* (*Becket ou l'honneur de Dieu*, 1959; tr. L. Hill, 1961), successfully filmed, is dramatically effective, but the brilliant *coups de théâtre* hardly conceal that no more is stated, in psychological terms, about the reasons for Becket's change of heart than was explained about the amnesic Gaston's choice of a 'good image' in *Traveller without Luggage*. The best one gets from this consummate master of the theatre is sharp characterization and a despair at the glib falsity of life—and at the inefficacy of the theatre-as-life.

ARMAND SALACROU (1899), born at Rouen, also took some ten years to establish himself; during this time he was supported and encouraged by Jouvet. His very early plays were produced by Lugné-Poë. A man of great intellectual mobility, Salacrou has been influenced by, and has sometimes anticipated, all the *avant garde* movements of the century, from socialism to the theatre of the absurd. But his most substantial plays are essentially realistic in form; the stronger his feelings in them, the more realistic they are likely to be; even where the situation is not realistic the treatment tends to be. Unfortunately his dramatic skill, in all but a few of his many plays, is such that he seems to resolve his genuinely complex themes too glibly. But in a handful of plays he rises above this. One of them, *Time Confounded (Sens interdit*, 1953), is a remarkably successful experiment, as theatrically clever as almost anything by Anouilh, and with more genuine intellectual content. It postulates a world in which time is reversed and life is lived backwards: people eagerly await their youth, their innocence—and their illusions. *No Laughing Matter (Histoire de rire,* 1939; tr. L. Hill, 1957), by contrast, shows Salacrou in his role as author of Boulevard plays; it was filmed in 1941, with Fernand Gravey. Even here there is a caustic sting in the tail for alert members of the audience. His best play is often taken to be *Men of Darkness (Les Nuits de la colère,* 1946; ad. R. Morley, 1948), a resistance drama, set in Chartres; after the action, which involves betrayal and murder, the characters defend their own positions. *The Earth is Round (La Terre est ronde,* 1938) anatomizes fascism, in the religious fanaticism of Savonarola, with fairness and intelligent sensitivity. In *The Unknown Woman of Arras (L'Inconnue d'Arras,* 1935) a man sees his whole life in flashback in the minute before he dies, a suicide because of his wife's unfaithfulness. Here this is no mere device: the events are presented as though observed in a final moment. Salacrou's drama, which frequently illuminates those depths of human anguish upon which Anouilh's more sparkling theatrical edifice only floats, deserves to be introduced more generally into the English-speaking world.

CHARLES VILDRAC (ps. CHARLES MESSAGER, 1882) began as a poet, and was one of the Abbaye group (q.v.). His early poetry expressed Whitmanesque ideals of camaraderie and human goodness; but his optimism found its most effective outlet in the drama. *S.S. Tenacity (Le Paquebot Tenacity,* 1920; tr. S. Howard, 1922), a good popular play which was put on by Copeau at the Vieux-Colombier, showed two comrades after the same girl while the boat that is to take them to a new life in Canada is held up in dry-dock. The go-ahead one gives it all up, marries and settles for a bourgeois existence in France; the shy dreamer goes ahead to adventure. This provides an excellent example of the conventional play that does not owe its success to pretentiousness or to the advancement of offensive philosophies. Vildrac's usual procedure is to take 'humble', 'insignificant' people (such as workmen or factory workers), put them in situations of stress, and then depict the true structure of both their characters and their humanity. In *The Misunderstanding (La Brouille,* 1930), about a realist and an idealist who quarrel over business methods, he shows a fine awareness of his own idealism. *Three Months of Prison (Trois mois de prison,* 1943) was written while Vildrac was playing an active part in resisting the

Nazis. He has written notable children's books.

JEAN-JACQUES BERNARD (1888–1972), a Frenchman born at Enghien in Belgium, was the son of TRISTAN BERNARD (1866–1947), who wrote ingenious moralistic comedies. Bernard's theatre is essentially a development out of Maeterlinck's (q.v.), but with more emphasis on psychology and unconscious motivations. His earlier plays formed a series called 'the theatre of silence' (tr. J. L. Frith, *The Sulky Fire: Five Plays*, 1939): characters are put into miserable love-situations, and their speech either feebly tries to contradict or brokenly hints at the mysterious morass of feeling into which missed opportunity has plunged them. *The Sulky Fire* (*Le Feu qui reprend mal*, 1921), the first of the 'theatre of silence' series, broods for its three acts over a returned soldier's suspicions of his wife's fidelity. Effective within his extreme limits, Bernard failed in his later attempts to broaden the horizons of his theatre.

MARCEL PAGNOL (1895), born near Marseilles, is an even better example than Vildrac of the naïve (q.v.) writer who is aware of, or simply keeps within, his limitations, and entirely avoids distortion or offence. All who have seen his earthy films, on his own and other writer's scenarios, have been grateful. His occasional vulgarities and sentimentalities are unimportant, and may even be enjoyed. *Topaze* (1928; tr. A. Rossi, 1963) is about a schoolmaster who is dismissed for conscientiousness. He is taken up by a racketeer for use as an innocent front-man; but he learns about life and outdoes his exploiter. Pagnol's other important work is his trilogy about the Marseilles waterfront: *Marius* (1929), *Fanny* (1931), *César* (1937). This, some of which has been filmed in Italian and German as well as French (with the incomparable Raimu), is simple fare—but its comedies and tragedies are faithful to the simple lives it depicts. If not taken more seriously than intended, it is delightful.

JEAN SARMENT (ps. JEAN BELLEMÈRE, 1897), born at Nantes, was an actor with Copeau and Lugné-Poë; he evolved into a writer of minor, but delicately melancholy plays involving characters who prefer to escape from life by way of dreams or impostures. His first and best play, *The Cardboard Crown* (*La Couronne de carton*, 1920), shows the self-defeat of a young romantic who can only win his girl when he is acting a part; this knowledge causes him to cease to love her. *Fishing for Shadows* (*Le Pêcheur d'ombres*, 1921; tr. P. Ustinov, 1940) deals with illusion and identity: a poet kills himself because he cannot prevent himself from conjecture about the identity of a girl who drove him mad and who returns to him. Marcel Pagnol directed the excellent movie version (1934) of *Leopold the Well-Beloved* (*Léopold le bien-aimé*, 1927), which starred Sarment himself, and Michel Simon. This is a sad comedy about an ageing failure with women who is persuaded that he is, after all, a roaring success with them. His youthful autobiographical novel, *Jean-Jacques of Nantes* (*Jean-Jacques de Nantes*, 1922) has interest and charm.

*

The notion of man as in an absurd situation in the universe is not new in literature; as one aspect of his feeling towards his existence it is implied in Greek tragedy. But for the twentieth century perhaps the aptest expression of it was made by Albert Camus in *The Myth of Sisyphus* (q.v.): man is seen as Sisyphus trying to push a stone to the top of a hill in the full knowledge he will never, can never, succeed. The so-called theatre—or literature—of the absurd was never a school; it was a term applied to certain writers, nearly all of them playwrights, who shared this attitude. Argument about whether one or two of them—such as Beckett and Genêt (qq.v.)—really or completely 'belong' to the theatre of the absurd is fruitless. What distinguishes the playwrights of the absurd from predecessors and successors who share their philosophical attitude is that in their case the attitude shapes the actual form of the play. This is why the movement had spent itself by the early Sixties: no matter how philosophically desirable, it is difficult to write a full-length play on these principles that will hold the attention of an audience. Paris, the headquarters of the *avant garde*, was also the headquarters of this kind of theatre; but the movement had influence in America (Albee, Kopit, qq.v.), England (Pinter, Simpson, qq.v.), Italy (Buzzati, q.v.), Germany (Grass, Hildesheimer, qq.v.), Czechoslovakia (Havel, Mrozek, qq.v.), Switzerland (Frisch), Poland and Spain. It is a movement of sociological importance; but no dramatist who has not clearly transcended its boundaries can be called more than a minor talent.

Although one of the roots of the theatre of the absurd is in the ridiculous, 'absurd' here means more than this: it has its original meaning of 'out of harmony with reason or purpose'. This drama tries to express the notion through its structure. Other important roots of the theatre of the absurd are: the literature of nonsense (Morgenstern, Ringelnatz, even Busch, qq.v., and Edward Lear and Lewis Carroll); the world of vaudeville and the circus; the early silent comedy movies, notably those made by Mack Sennett; Valle-Inclán (q.v.).

Martin Esslin, the excellent historian of the theatre of the absurd, has distinguished from it a theatre of the 'poetic *avant garde*', which 'relies on fantasy and dream reality' to the same degree as the theatre of the absurd; but 'basically . . . represents a different mood . . . more lyrical, and far less violent and grotesque . . . [it] relies to a far greater extent on consciously "poetic" speech . . .'. Esslin is probably right to class the plays of Audiberti, Ghelderode (qq.v.) and of the delicate but exceedingly slight HENRI PICHETTE (1924), who is half-American, among this 'poetic *avant garde*'.

EUGÈNE IONESCO (1912) was born in Slatina in Rumania, of a Rumanian father and French mother. He was educated in France, and has lived there except for a dozen or so years spent in Rumania between 1925 and 1938. He did not start writing plays—although he published Rumanian poetry and criticism—until 1948, when he was suddenly stimulated into it by the 'absurd' world conjured up to him by the phrases contained in an English manual. The result was *The Bald Prima-Donna* (*La Cantatrice chauve*, 1950; IPI), in which the text-book clichés of two bourgeois families are exploited for far too long. It was a highly amusing event, but not a very exciting beginning. Ionesco is not in fact a writer of great importance, although one feels impelled to say this only because he has had too much solemn attention; within his essentially pataphysical (q.v.) limitations, Ionesco is a good playwright. But he has little emotional substance, and his work rests on the philosophical tenets of absurdity and linguistic futility. He has written many plays, and is an amusing though not always unconfused controversialist. One of the best of the plays is *Rhinoceros* (*Le Rinocéros*, 1960; IP4): there is feeling and real bitterness in this ferocious fable about the progressive transformation of humanity into rhinoceroses (fascist conformists; worshippers of nature); Béranger, Ionesco's 'average citizen', whom he first introduced in another of his better plays, *The Killer* (*Tueur sans gages*; IP3), does not resist the 'mastification' because he wants to, but because he must: at the end it is 'too late' to become one of them. He does not care enough. . . . In this bitter twist we catch a glimpse of a profounder Ionesco. *The Killer* cleverly depicts death as a pointless and cheap giggler. Ionesco is an expert and intelligent critic of bourgeois conformity; but so far he has had little of significance to add to what other writers have said about the particular area he inhabits. It is in one sense excellent that Ionesco should enrage conformists of the political left and right; but he himself does appear to suffer from Béranger's clownish indifference: its nature could provide him with the theme of a more satisfying drama.

ARTHUR ADAMOV (1908–70) was born in the Caucasus. His father, a rich oil man of Armenian extraction, educated him in French, and French is his main language. At the age of sixteen Adamov was associating with surrealists. Later he edited a magazine and became a friend of Éluard's (q.v.). He then underwent a crisis, which he described in his autobiographical *The Confession* (*L'Aveu*, 1946; pt. tr. R. Howard, *Evergreen Review*, 8, 1959). Martin Esslin isolates from it the following quotation, which he rightly calls 'the basis' of both existentialist literature and of the theatre of the absurd:

'What is there? I know first of all that I am. But who am I? All I know of myself is that I suffer. And if I suffer it is because at the origin of myself there is mutilation, separation.

I am separated. What I am separated from—I cannot name it. But I am separated.'

Adamov's first plays were influenced by expressionism (q.v.) inasmuch as they reacted against the presentation of named characters, and reverted to types. This work is a clear demonstration of the fact that all *avant garde* movements are but facets or developments of the original expressionism; it was even partly inspired by one of the founding fathers of expressionism, August Strindberg (q.v.).

It is interesting that Adamov, although always sympathetic to communism, should gradually have shifted from a primarily 'metaphysical' centre of gravity to an unquestionably Marxist one, closely allied to Brecht's idea of an 'epic theatre' (q.v.): it seems that too rigid adherence to the theory of the absurd leads to sterility. But Adamov's plays have always had more substance, mystery and passion about them than Ionesco's. Although he intends to present Alien$_s$ ated Man rather than alienated men, a realistic sense of the latter pervade. most of his plays. He is interested in individuals as well as in abstractions- Adamov sees man's alienation from the unnameable ('Formerly it was called God. Today it no longer has any name') as mutilating him, and in one of his plays he shows this literally: in *The Large and the Small Manœuvre* (*La Grande et la petite manœuvre*, 1950) the victim of opposing political factions is cut down to a useless trunk in a wheelchair—but the activists are depicted as just as helpless. *The Invasion* (*L'Invasion*, 1950) is about Pierre's quest for what his brother-in- law's eminent literary work meant. Jean has bequeathed all his immense mass of papers to him; but they are in an appalling physical state and cannot be reduced to order. Pierre finally destroys the papers, which have by this time destroyed him.

Professor Taranne (*Le Professeur Taranne*, 1953; MFC; AD) is based on a dream of the author's. Professor Taranne is accused of obscenity and plagiarism, and finds himself in a situation that can only be described as Kafkaesque; he ends by exposing himself, the act of which he had originally been (falsely) accused. Once again we have the theme of the artist exposed as a fraud. Soon after this Adamov came to his best play, and the best produced by the theatre of the absurd: *Le Ping-Pong* (1955; tr. R. Howard, 1959; D. Prouse, 1962), in which, far more horribly, subtly and effectively than in Elmer Rice's *Adding Machine*, a machine (a machine, it should be noted, that is a game of chance) is shown as gaining control over human affairs. Two young men who play on a pinball machine in a café come to regard it as both a work of art and a good business investment. They become slaves to the pinball machine, and are at the last seen as two foolish old men playing ping-pong—one of them drops dead, the other is left alone. This, as may easily be seen, is open to a Marxist as well as to an 'absurd' interpretation; and with his next play *Paolo Paoli* (1957; tr. G. Brereton, 1959) he turned his back on the absurd and embraced the activist theatre of Brecht—but not in any simplistic manner. *Paolo Paoli* deals with the years 1900–14, during which the First World War was brewed. Paoli lives by killing rare butterflies, his friend deals in ostrich feathers; beauty is destroyed by the profit-motive. In this intricate play Adamov's skill is almost the equal of Brecht's; but a writer ought not, perhaps, to be so certain of where he is going. *Sainte Europe* (1966), a satire on General de Gaulle (who seemed to obsess him), is an almost disastrous failure.

JEAN TARDIEU (1903) was before the Second World War a poet somewhat in the vein of Ponge (q.v.); he translated Hölderlin with conspicuous success. After 1945 he seemed to find a new and stronger confidence, and in 1947 began to produce short experimental plays and sketches for radio and cabaret. These are slight, but have often anticipated the larger-scale works of better known dramatists. Tardieu is unambitious and playful, and his work carries little weight; but it is delightful and makes no large claims.

BORIS VIAN (1920–59) trained as an engineer but abandoned this career to play jazz and to write. If anyone could be described as the French Flann

O'Brien then it would certainly be Vian, who was full of the same kind of lore; but his activities were wider, and included pornography, singing, acting, drinking, translating, inventing gadgets—and, alas, dying young. He wrote an opera to music by one of France's foremost composers, Darius Milhaud (once Claudel's secretary in South America), four tough thrillers, one of which was banned (Vian was an adept at enraging 'public moralists'), five novels rather disappointing as wholes but containing passages of great power, two of which have been translated, short stories—and plays. Vian's remarkable gift, which ought however not to be exaggerated as it occasionally has been (for example in Great Britain), may have been weakened by its wide application; in the drama it found its proper outlet. Cocteau was excited by his first play, *The Knackers' ABC* (*Équarrissage pour tous*, 1950; tr. S. W. Taylor, 1968), a 'paramilitary vaudeville' which finely mocks patriotic and other pompous pretensions; it caused great offence. *The Empire Builders* (*Les Bâtisseurs d'empire ou le Schmürz*, 1959; tr. S. W. Taylor, 1963, rev. 1967), a theatrical success, was put on after Vian's death from the painful heart disease from which he had been suffering for some time. This is a superior production, and is almost certainly the best thing Vian ever did. A family runs away from a terrible noise, going to higher and higher floors and smaller and smaller flats in the same building. Ultimately the father is cut off from his family and dies in terror. The *Schmürz* is a bleeding, bandaged figure, silent, struck continually by the characters and yet never noticed by them. In this personal statement about his doomed flight upwards from death Vian succeeded in making a universal one: we grandiosely build higher and higher, and our world gets smaller and smaller —we ignore and ill-treat our authentic selves (our *Schmürz*es), which represent both our freedom and the possibility of accepting death without fear. Just before the father succumbs to terror and dies his *Schmürz* (*Schmerz*: pain) dies: his chances of freedom have vanished. But after his death other *Schmürz*es enter: a reminder of the possibilities for man. If one must classify, this impressive play is surely more 'existentialist' than 'absurd'.

FERNANDO ARRABAL (1932) was born in Melilla in what was then Spanish Morocco; he studied law in Madrid, but left Spain for France in 1954. He writes in French. Arrabal, a minor playwright with a resourceful technique who owes most of all to Beckett, cruelly contrasts innocence with reality, as in his first play *Picnic on the Battlefield* (*Pique-nique en campagne*, 1958; tr. J. Hewitt, *Evergreen Review*, 15, 1960), in which a mother and father come to join their son in the front line for a picnic; they are all wiped out. His most savage play is *The Two Executioners* (*Les Deux Bourreaux*, 1958; AD), an exposure of conventional morality—most particularly, perhaps, of the type of brutal obscurantism practised in fascist Spain. Here 'justice' is revealed as hatred and torture, and 'duty' is to condone it (there is an analogy here with Franco's establishment of tyranny in Spain). Arrabal has more recently, and disappointingly, been experimenting with abstract spectacles—less with texts than with the theatre itself.

*

The influence of ANTONIN ARTAUD (1896–1948), who was born at Marseille, is by no means exhausted. In fact, except in France, where he has profoundly influenced Barrault and the leading director associated with the Theatre of the Absurd, Roger Blin, his views have so far been mostly misapplied—by such as the British director Peter Brook, who has modified his demands for a revolutionary theatre into something eminently acceptable to pseudo-radical audiences, and therefore commercially viable. Artaud, 'the magic cudgel', began as a symbolist poet and leading light of the surrealists; 'expelled' by Breton, he, Robert Aron and Roger Vitrac (q.v.) founded in 1927 the *Théâtre Alfred Jarry* and put on Strindberg's *Dream Play* (a performance that Breton was prevented by the police from disrupting), the last act of Claudel's *Partage de Midi* (q.v.) produced as farce, and plays by Vitrac himself. Artaud had already acted in films (including the role of the young monk in Carl Dreyer's silent *La Passion de Jeanne d'Arc*) with Lugné-Poë, Dullin and Pitoëff: he knew the practical and theoretical theatre intimately. Artaud's impassioned theory of the theatre, which may yet prove to be the main force in taking it out of the middlebrow domain, is set forth in the collection of essays called *The Theatre and its Double* (*Le Théâtre et son double*, 1938; tr. M. C. Richards, 1958); in this are republished his manifestoes of 1932 and 1933, both called *The Theatre of Cruelty* (*Le Théâtre de la cruauté*). In 1935 he was able to find funds to form his own theatre of cruelty, and with the help of Barrault and Blin he put on a performance of his own play, *Les Cenci* (in *Complete Works*, *Œuvres Complètes*, 1957–67). This failed, and Artaud's capacity to conduct everyday life began to collapse. He had suffered from mental instability since childhood. After a visit to Mexico and a session on drugs (with which he had been experimenting for many years), he had to be given electric-shock treatment and hospitalized at Rodez (1937), where he stayed for nine years. He had many devoted friends, including Barrault and Adamov; but his condition would not allow of his release until two years before his death, of cancer.

Artaud's thinking was most profoundly influenced by his own experiments with himself, which went farther than those of any surrealist (with the exception of RENÉ DAUMAL, 1908–44, a consumptive surrealist novelist and disciple of Gurdjieff's who allowed himself to die in the interests of self-exploration); drugs were merely incidental, for Artaud's entire life was dedicated to the realization of his ideal. Outside influences on Artaud included (predictably) vaudeville and comic films—and, particularly, a performance by a troupe of Balinese dancers that he witnessed in 1931.

Artaud's ideas are important and revolutionary: they faithfully represent the spirit of modernism, demonstrating its essential romanticism—and, incidentally, once again, the extent to which the expressionist movement contains this. Hofmannsthal's 'Chandos letter' (q.v.) and Artaud's *Theatre and its Double* are not as far apart as might be imagined. A *Sprachkrise* (q.v.) is at the heart of both. Artaud was tormented personally (not just intellectually) by the collapse of the illusions about words in their relation to the things they denote. His is an anti-language as well as an anti-psychological theatre. He

517

wanted a return of myth, a ritualized theatre of movement and gesture, shapes and lights; a theatre that would confront the audience's problems so extremely, so 'cruelly', that it would liberate from the chains of rationality. Actors and audiences should be 'victims burnt at the stake, signalling through the flames'. The terror of the plagues of history, Artaud said, released men from the restraints of rationality and morality, and purified them, giving them a primitive power (cf. Camus' *The Plague*, q.v.). Thus the stage must surround the audience, and terrify it. But no account of Artaud's theatre can convey the brilliance of his detail and the subtle passion of his language.

Artaud's own *The Cenci* does not fulfil its author's programme; his most powerful work is contained in his correspondence (1923) with Jacques Rivière (q.v.), his letters to Jean-Louis Barrault (1952), and some of his poems and short plays. Such a theatre as his must doubtless be modified—but not by the values of the drawing-room, the beauty saloon or the theatre critic's local. In this sense much of the lip-service paid to his ideas, especially in Great Britain, is not always of much more value than the genteel opposition that vague notions of it arouse. Artaud will be even more important to the theatre than he has already been.

His friend ROGER VITRAC (1899–1952), born at Pinsac, was one of the best playwrights to come out of surrealism. His plays lightly mock the bourgeois and their idols; had he emerged at the same time as Ionesco he would have been regarded as his equal. *The Mysteries of Love* (*Les Mystères de l'amour*, 1927) is quite as 'absurd' as anything of Ionesco's, and has passages of greater linguistic suggestion. *The Werewolf* (*Le Loup-garou*, 1939), set in an expensive madhouse, is masterly in its capture of the speech of the mentally ill.

XI

GEORGES SIMENON (PS. GEORGES SIM, 1903), born at Liège of a French father and Dutch mother, has on occasion been over-praised—as when a critic adjudged him superior to Balzac. But Simenon is one of the very few writers (others are Kenneth Fearing, Julian Symons) who have consistently raised the thriller to a literary level. Simenon can evoke the exact atmosphere of a place, of a kind of day, as acutely as any of his contemporaries. A true 'naïve' (q.v.), he is admired by almost every 'intellectual' in the world. His technique is to take a character and then—he works very quickly—go along with him in a situation that takes him to the end of his tether. His great strengths are his natural sense of poetry and his freedom from distorting moral preconceptions about conduct, which he is able to present with a remarkable empathy. The objectivity of his treatment of ruthlessness, greed and murderousness provides an example of a sort of compassion that contrasts oddly with the psychologically limited charity of orthodox morality. As a faithful entertainer of the best minds, Simenon is indeed a strange case: how should such as Ford, Eliot, Montale, Graves (qq.v.), all admirers, avidly read one who gives them such honest fare, fare they could not themselves provide? In 1931 Simenon invented his famous detective, Maigret, the only credible fictional detective of the century. But much of his best work has not featured Maigret. *The Stain on the Snow* (*La Neige était sale*, 1948; tr. J. Petrie, 1953) is about life under Nazi domination, and traces the motives and fate of a man who kills a German. *Pedigree* (1948; tr. R. Baldick, 1965) is autobiographical, telling of his Liège childhood. In *The Little Saint* (*Le Petit Saint*, 1965) Simenon successfully tells the story of a dwarf who becomes a painter. Simenon's detractors, often puzzled academics for whom his *tranches de vie* are too frighteningly raw, accuse him of lacking intellect; this is to miss the point—we should send such critics back to Schiller. Here is an author the legitimate enjoyment of whom may be seriously interfered with by the frequently egregious urge to evaluate.

One other modern Belgian novelist of some distinction is FRANÇOISE MALLET-JORIS (1930), who was born in Antwerp and is the daughter of the writer Suzanne Lilar (q.v.). Her father is a lawyer and politician, who has served in the Belgian government. She studied in America and Paris and made an immediate impression with what remains her best novel: *Into the Labyrinth* (*Le Rempart des Béguines*, 1950; tr. H. Briffault, 1953), a story of the narrator's lesbian affair with her father's mistress. This was a well deserved success. The novels that succeeded it have all been competent and intelligent; she has not yet written again as coolly and as effectively.

*

The Belgian contribution to the French theatre has been considerable; most of it has been on the part of Flemings, such as Maeterlinck, who wrote in French. This Belgian vein, of other-worldliness paradoxically combined with immediate sensual grasp of phenomena—and most characteristically emerging as a type of comedy or farce—is in fact a vital component of French-speaking theatre. Drama, it seems, is a form in which Belgian genius naturally manifests itself.

FERNAND CROMMELYNCK (1885), another Fleming, was born in Brussels, but early established himself in Paris as a precocious young actor and playwright. His mother was French, his father an actor from whom he learnt much. Between the wars Crommelynck had a high reputation; he has published nothing since a play on Shakespeare's Falstaff in 1954, and outside France at least the reputation has rather unfairly faded. He wrote some fairly successful plays as a very young man, but he was thirty-five when he had his first international hit, *The Magnificent Cuckold* (*Le Cocu magnifique*, 1920; TGBP), produced in Paris by Lugné-Poë. He then moved back to Paris, and he and his family shared a house with Verhaeren's widow. In their distortedness and grotesqueness Crommelynck's plays are undoubtedly expressionist (in the sense of expressionism that includes Grünewald and other artists of the past, and is as much a part of the Flemish as of the German genius); Sternheim (q.v.), who lived in Belgium, must at least have read Crommelynck with pleasure. *The Magnificent Cuckold*, at first mounted by producers as a farce, but more recently presented as tragedy, is undoubtedly a black (though not a 'sick') play. It shows the destruction of a happy marriage by the demon jealousy. Bruno, the village scribe and poet, is in effect played by two actors, one of whom—his secretary Estrugo (an Iago)—represents the jealous and curious element in him that must know what it is that possesses him. Bruno has affinities with the jealous Kitely of Ben Jonson's *Every Man in his Humour*—as Crommelynck himself shares something of Jonson's truculent, subtle approach. Bruno looses his wife Stella to every male in the village, in order to discover the nature of the sexual hold she has on him. (As in the case of Kitely, there are hints of voyeurism.) Even when he finally loses her, to a foolish suitor, he cannot believe it, and jokes about it: this is a trick. In other words, Bruno becomes more interested in the mechanism of his sexuality than in its object; the sentimentive, one might say, undermines and destroys the naïve component of his personality. There is an underlying theme, here, of criticism of the artist, for whom love is less important than its analysis; the result is that Stella is doomed to a commonplace existence at the hands of an utterly commonplace man—but the moral is obvious. This play, whose language is unusually beautiful and poetic—in this respect it outruns anything by Giraudoux or Anouilh—is one of the century's highest dramatic achievements. De Meyst's 1946 Belgian movie, of the same title, with Jean-Louis Barrault and Maria Mauban, is a classic.

Golden Guts (*Tripes d'or*, 1925) has been compared to Molière's *The Miser* (*L'Avare*), but is closer to Jonson's *The Alchemist*; Crommelynck makes it clear by the name of one of the characters, Muscar (reminiscent of Mosca, Volpone's 'parasite'), that he is aware of Jonson—whose mantle, indeed, he is more entitled to wear than any other contemporary playwright. In this, produced by Jouvet in 1930, a miser is persuaded by his doctor to cure himself of his avarice—for this interferes with the course of his love—by swallowing his gold. After a month of constipation he dies in voiding himself of it. Although painstakingly realistic on the surface, this is essentially symbolist, brilliantly exploiting the age-old equation between excrement and gold (tormentedly apprehended by Luther and made explicit by Freud). Outside the action, haunting it and at one moment desperately seeking entrance to the stage, is Azelle, the beloved of the miser.

Another notable play by Crommelynck, whose output is small, is *Hot and Cold* (*Chaud et froid*, 1934), in which an unfaithful wife becomes a faithful widow. He is one of the century's half a dozen most distinguished dramatists. He has also written two amusing novels, both of which deserve translation: *That is the Question* (*Là est la question*, 1947) and *Is Mr. Larose the Killer?* (*Monsieur Larose, est-il l'assassin?* 1950).

MICHEL DE GHELDERODE (1898–1962), another Fleming, and a devout Catholic, was born in Ixelles in Brabant. An eccentric recluse who lived in a room full of puppets, armour and seashells, Ghelderode was another natural expressionist; one cannot understand his work without recognizing its roots in the art of Brueghel and Bosch—and its affinities with the pre-expressionist Belgian painter (whose father was English), his friend James Ensor. He is the most Flemish of all Belgians using the French language, but the closest in spirit to the Elizabethan farce of Marlowe (*The Jew of Malta*) and Middleton or Tourneur (*The Revenger's Tragedy*). Much of what seems unfamiliar in his drama—deformed puppets, cruelty accepted as inevitable, tormented medieval characters—is a part of Flemish folk-lore, and, especially, of the tradition of the Belgian puppet-theatre. For Ghelderode, as for Bernanos (q.v.), life is a perpetual struggle between good and evil, and the devil is real. But Ghelderode's Catholic faith keeps him happier than Bernanos': he does not feel himself to be the centre of the drama, and instead concentrates on recreating a world where this drama may be seen more clearly: medieval Flanders. Ghelderode seems as strange in this century as his French language must have seemed to him in his authentic Flemish world. Yet he is steeped in the theatre —in the kind of theatre that hardly exists any longer in Great Britain: the folk theatre that has no eyes whatever on, not even an awareness of, the 'rewards' of stardom, or notoriety in a cultural capital; a theatre that concentrates on what it is. From 1927 until 1930 he was closely associated with the Flemish Popular Theatre, and many of his plays (some of which are for puppets) were first given in Flemish translation. The world of Ghelderode's plays might remind one of that of Gracq (q.v.); but it is in sharper focus, it is natural to Ghelderode, and its novelty does not fatally engage his intellect. No mists obscure its darkness. It is a world that has fairly been called 'putrid'; but, unlike the equally putrid world of bourgeois reality, it has the beauty of the Flemish masters. Almost every one of his many plays has at its centre a surrogate for a lonely, psychically mutilated—impotent or crazily sadistic—creator. In *The School for Jesters* (*L'École des bouffons*, 1942) it is Folial who, ennobled (the playwright 'taken up' by the public?), has to tell his disciples the secret of his art ('cruelty'). In *Hop Signor!* (1935) a married virgin lusts in 'an old, forgotten cemetery' for a virgin executioner, who finally beheads her. This was put on by Barrault in Paris in 1947, and gave Ghelderode fame—his *Chronicles of Hell* (*Fastes d'enfer*, 1929; GSP) caused a scandal in 1949, to which he was quite indifferent. He attended no performances.

Barabbas (1928; GSP), still performed in Holy Week in Flanders, is the most vivid and moving of all modern versions of the drama of the crucifixion, the agony of which is set against a Brueghelian funfair. In *Pantagleize* (1929; GSP) a revolution is started when the saintly innocent, Pantagleize, says 'It's a lovely day'. No 'civilized' theatre can afford to ignore Ghelderode, any more than in the long run it can neglect Artaud—and it is a hopeful sign that both have made a considerable impact on the American theatre. Ghelderode wrote several short novels, of which *The Comic History of Klizer Karel* (*L'Histoire comique de Klizer Karel*, 1923) is typical.

HENRI SOUMAGNE (ps. HENRI WAGENER, 1891–1951), who was born in Brussels, has been shamefully neglected outside France—especially when one considers that not even the best British dramatist of the past half-century has produced anything remotely on a level with the masterpiece that made him famous in the Twenties: *The Other Messiah* (*L'Autre Messie*, 1923). Soumagne, like many other Belgian writers, was a lawyer. (Whereas in Great Britain the majority of solicitors and barristers are, from the first, arch-conservatives and careerists, in Belgium as elsewhere many more young men enter the law from a sense of idealism.)

The Other Messiah deals with Kellerstein, a rich Jew who returns one Christmas Eve to one of the scenes of his early struggles, a Warsaw bar with 'that characteristic smell of fried onions, sweat and intelligence that so often permeates places where Jews hang out'. Kellerstein does not believe in God because he has failed to find a firm-breasted woman. Another character bets him that God exists, and the matter is settled by a 'boxing match': a series of arguments that register as 'punches', under which the characters reel. This is one of the most brilliantly and subtly handled scenes in the whole of modern theatre. Kellerstein loses (unfairly), and has to admit that God does, after all, exist: hasn't the landlord's daughter got firm breasts? Who is he, then? By now the characters are all drunk, and it becomes clear that Kellerstein himself is God: his father was a carpenter. . . . When will he proclaim the new laws? 'Soon. . . . But right at this moment God's as pissed as a newt. . . . And he can't preach a Sermon on the Mount from under a table.' This, which provoked riots in Prague, is neither a religious nor an anti-religious, but a sceptical play, an oblique attack on argumentativeness. Soumagne's later plays were, with one partial exception, ingenious and provocative, but did not have the feeling or the really audacious brilliance that distinguished *The Other Messiah*. The exception, *Madame Marie* (1928), gives a version of the Christ story in which Jesus is ironically postulated as being so divine—sympathetic, understanding, comforting, strengthening—that he is embarrassed by being turned into a legend: he does not wish to be burdened with religion. Matthew, the villain, is seen as 'arranging' for the divinity of Christ, in which he does not believe; but finally he is forced to believe in what he has devised. Soumagne wrote little more for the theatre after this, but turned instead to the reconstruction of actual crimes, including *The Strange Mr. Courtois* (*L'Étrange Monsieur Courtois*, 1943), about a policeman who was also a thief and killer.

HERMAN CLOSSON (1901) resembles Soumagne in that he sees the historical image of heroes or saviours as false; but where Soumagne sceptically seeks a true basis for feeling Closson is more narrowly cynical and aggressive. His first play, which is unpublished, consists of the monologue of an old woman sitting on a lavatory. He is a technically accomplished dramatist, but in none of his plays has he been able to surpass his cynicism or even to point, with total effect, the contrast between history and the reality it purports to depict. His best play is *False Light* (*Faux-jour*, 1941), about three men, long resident in the tropics, who invite a cover-girl to spend a holiday with them. She does so— and nothing happens. This is on the familiar Belgian theme of men searching for the identity of the emotion or desire that impels them (cf. the motive for

Bruno's self-destructive jealousy in *The Magnificent Cuckold*). Can it be that Belgian writers seek for a visual representation of their emotions? The native genius is for making such representations. . . .

SUZANNE LILAR (1901), the mother of Françoise Mallet-Joris, wrote a clever variation on the Don Juan theme in *Burlador* (*Le Burlador*, 1947; TGBP): her Don Juan is pure and a self-deceiver, who really loves all his women. The philosophy behind this approach is outlined in an interesting book (we do not often find the wife of a Minister of Justice vaunting a theory of *l'amour fou*): *Aspects of Love* (*Le Couple*, 1963; tr. J. Griffin, 1965).

*

The leading spirit in the foundation of the magazine *The Green Disk* (*Le Disque Vert*, 1922) was Franz Hellens (q.v.), the most advanced of the Belgian *avant garde*. But the programme sensibly proposed by Hellens was so eclectic as to amount to no programme: he wanted the poet to do no more than to discover and to adhere to his own vision of life. Closely associated with *The Green Disk* was ODILON-JEAN PÉRIER (1901–28), who died of heart disease. Périer found a clear and lucid style, and much of his poetry is touching in its brave intimations of early death; but he never found a language in which to describe the difference between his own anti-romantic austerity and the puritanism he loathed; when he offers justifications of his position they are too obviously second-hand. And one feels that by so resolutely denying himself any romantic self-indulgence he failed to discover his own mind. Perhaps his best work, in which he came nearer to this than in his poetry, was the novel *Passage of Angels* (*Le Passage des anges*, 1926).

ERIC DE HAULLEVILLE (1900–41), born in Brussels, who married the sister of Aldous Huxley's first wife, was yet another victim of the Nazis: he died after fleeing from them, when ill, to the South of France. His earliest poetry, uncertain of direction and heavily influenced by surrealism, is his most vital.

The leading Belgian poet of modern times is HENRI MICHAUX (1899), who was born at Namur and who describes himself in an autobiographical note as 'Belgian, of Paris'. Michaux, who is also an artist, is a writer of international stature. He had already established himself as such when Gide (q.v.) devoted a pleasant and chatty little book to him in 1941; since then his reputation has been assured. Michaux, although a very different kind of writer, resembles the Argentinian Borges (q.v.) in that he gladly forgoes the world of the flesh for that of the mind. For Michaux, therefore, to write a poem is in a sense to 'kill' it: once the word is made flesh it goes the way of all flesh. But a certain robustness, evident in his sense of humour and satirical bent, rescues Michaux from any tendency to preciosity or solipsistic over-obscurity. There is, especially in *A Certain Plume* (*Un Certain Plume*, 1930; pt. MSW) a distinctly engaging quality to his work. Everything he writes bears the stamp of authentic experience. He has frequently experimented with drugs, since hallucinations and similar experiences are as interesting to him as external affairs are to others. Like Borges, he is important because his concern with inwardness is not a pose or a game. He has been put forward as a surrealist; but this is misleading, because his poetry and prose arise from a deliberate intensity of self-exploration rather than from a wilder rummaging of the unconscious or a total yielding to impulse. It was Supervielle (q.v.) rather than any surrealist who first encouraged him. His early work appeared in *The Green Disk*.

Michaux, a poet who has never sought to hide his anguish, writes to 'exorcize': to keep at bay, really, the irrational demons of desire or impulse that lead men into action—and to neutralize 'the surrounding powers of the hostile world'. He is too tempted, too human, to be able to live inside himself except in the act of writing, by which he forces himself to do so. What he clings on to is the magic of words, which are like spells against the madness that he continually invites by his almost fanatic refusal to become 'engaged' or committed. When Michaux ran away from home as a young man, to become a widely faring sailor, he was literally trying to disengage himself from the whole accumulation of individual 'facts' that comprised Henri Michaux. The impulse behind his quest was ambivalent: to withdraw in horror, to refuse; but also to wash clean and recreate a rational—in the Swiftian sense—being. He meticulously described South America and Asia in his travel books *Ecuador* (1929) and *A Barbarian in Asia* (*Un Barbare en Asie*, 1932; tr. S. Beach, 1949), but excluded accounts of history or culture.

A remote and impossibly difficult writer? On the contrary, a remarkably accessible one. Michaux wears his fine seriousness with an agreeable and unconceited humour; the poet of inner space remains—the point can hardly be over-emphasized—human. His Monsieur Plume is his own apotheosis of Charlie Chaplin: defenceless, a creature whose lack of offence releases the vilest impulses of perversion and tyranny in others—but a poet, different. If he goes into a restaurant it will be to order something not on the menu; his request will strike the management as sinister, his excuses will fail to convince, the place will become a turmoil, the police will be involved. . . . On another occasion he wakes up to find that his house has been stolen. Tried and condemned for allowing his wife to be run over by a train (which rushed at where their house had been, and damaged him) he tells the judge that he has not been following the case. The early Chaplin could have made movie versions of each of the fifteen episodes in this book without taking thought. In the satirical fantasies of *Elsewhere* (*Ailleurs*, 1948), which collects earlier works, the influences of Swift and Voltaire are apparent. His poetry has about it an elegiac quality that X. J. Kennedy catches well in this first stanza from 'Nausea or This is Death Coming On?':

> Give yourself up, heart.
> We've struggled long enough.
> Let my life draw halt.
> Cowards we were not.
> Whatever we could we did. (MP)

In a prose poem Michaux introduces camels into Honfleur (which changes the place), and flees on the fourth day. . . . Since the accidental death of his wife in a fire in 1948 (he wrote *We Two*, *Nous deux encore*, 1948, about their life together) Michaux has concentrated more exclusively on his painting —a retrospective exhibition was held in 1965—and on writing careful accounts of his experiments with drugs. He has actually spoken of renouncing literature, and certainly he finds his paintings more self-expressive. Posterity, however, will value him most as a writer. Gide has been sneered at for not understanding Michaux; but he could recognize a delightful and important writer—and this is, perhaps, understanding enough. (MEP; PBFV4; CFP; FWT)

In Belgium itself one of the most highly regarded of the poets and critics born within this century is ROGER BODART (1910). He, too, trained as a lawyer. He is an authoritative, generous and sympathetic critic of his Belgian contemporaries. As a poet he is strictly traditional—as traditional as his unquestioning religious belief. But the poems are finely made and their classicism serves a purpose, because its very rigidity produces an effect of great suggestiveness. Bodart seeks to manipulate his tendency to sentimentality into a valid warmth, and he sometimes succeeds. His optimism rests on assumptions too easily made for him to be an important poet, but when he writes of his love for nature, specifically the landscape of his native land, he achieves a touching authenticity.

EDMOND VANDERCAMMEN (1901) is more distinctly Belgian, and has been more influenced by Flemish literature. He has been related to unanimism (q.v.), already introduced into Belgian literature by the Flemish poet Paul van Ostayen; but he is really more concerned with the primitive mystery of being. His poems express a pantheism that is commonplace but deeply felt; their strength lies in the details he gives of his attitude rather than in the attitude itself. He has been much influenced by Spanish poetry. Some of his best poetry is collected in *September Bees* (*Les Abeilles de septembre*, 1959).

Leaving aside the unique Michaux—a genuinely 'denationalized' author? —the chief contribution of French-speaking Belgian literature has been to the theatre; this has been considerable. The younger Belgian poets, aware of this, seem to be turning theatrewards. CHARLES BERTIN (1919), author of *Black Song* (*Chant noir*, 1949), has written a number of interesting plays. The poet JEAN MOGIN (ps. JEAN NORGE, 1921) wrote a play of remarkable power and psychological penetration in *To Each According to His Hunger* (*A chacun selon sa faim*, 1950), which is a portrait of a religious fanatic.

XII

France has always been the home of -isms as well as of good writers. One or two, such as unanimism, naturism and, particularly, surrealism (qq.v.), were important, although of course less so than the individual writer. Among other trivial -isms of this century, we may note intimism, synthesism, integralism, musicism, floralism, aristocratism, druidism, totalism and lettrism. This last movement was inaugurated by ISIDORE ISOU (ps. JEAN-ISIDORE GOLDMANN, 1925) in the years immediately following the end of the Second World War. Isou was a Rumanian who came to Paris in 1945. It did not change the course of French poetry, and it was not important; but it does usefully illustrate the manner in which Paris remains the headquarters of the *avant garde*—'the *avant garde* of the *avant garde*' as the faintly megalomaniac Isou puts it. No doubt there is in France, as has more than once been suggested, a somewhat dull 'conformity to non-conformity'; but because such creatively ungifted writers as Isou, the novelist MARC SAPORTA (1923), or the 'concrete' poet PIERRE GARNIER (1928), editor of *Les Lettres*, are not insincere or even pretentious, but simply an orthodox and agreeable part of the French scene and honourable and dedicated men, they do act as a stimulus to literature everywhere. Lettrism was a fearsome theory involving typography and phonetics, and is really connected with concrete poetry, though it is more intellectual than most concrete poets (as apart from their specially appointed critics) are prepared to be. Since the radical breaking down of language that lettrism involved was supposed to lead to the annihilation of the difference between the letter and the spirit, it is not surprising that reports of its success have not yet filtered through, nor that it has passed out of fashion; nevertheless, it was not quite contemptible, and in certain intellectual respects it reflects the preoccupations of the age.

However, the mainstream of French poetry since the war may be seen to parallel—if only very approximately—the developments in philosophy (not of course as non- or anti-literary as in the Anglo-Saxon countries) and fiction. Thus it is no accident that Philippe Sollers (q.v.) has devoted a book to FRANCIS PONGE (1899), who was born at Montpellier. Ponge, along with Michaux, is now one of the 'old masters' of French poetry. He has been a teacher, a journalist and a publisher; from the late Thirties until the end of the Second World War he was a committed communist. He did not begin to attract attention until 1942 with *The Set Purpose of Things* (*Le Parti pris des choses*). Paul Bowles was translating him by 1945. He had had some association with the surrealists, but had apparently no serious literary ambitions. He did not achieve real fame, however, until he was nearly sixty. Ponge himself repudiates the label poet; and if from the very broad Gallic interpretation of that term he is a poet, few British critics would think of applying it to him. But he is a writer of interest to poets—of this there can be no doubt. Ponge might most appropriately be described as a practising phenomenologist: instead of philosophizing, however, like Husserl (q.v.) and his successors, he describes his approach to and mental involvement with objects. These descriptions are frequently lyrical and humorous. (*Dix cours sur la méthode*, 1946, is a characteristic title: it irreverently recalls one of Descartes' masterworks, *Discours de la méthode*.) Ponge is no more concerned with the inner life than Robbe-Grillet (q.v.); but his art does not attempt to erect a philosophy;

ineffably modest, it simply describes a certain way of looking at the world, which in the prose poems presents itself as a number of isolated fragments. There is no behaviourism here—unless the reader wishes to infer it. Furthermore, his world of objects is humanized by what only some Frenchmen might not recognize as the most preposterous romanticisms, ironies and suggestive metaphors: a cigarette has passion as it is smoked, it's 'rough work' opening an oyster, as 'the prying fingers get sliced, the fingernails are snapped off', of a match 'Only the head can burst into flames, in contact with a harsh reality'. Probably *Soap* (*Le Savon*, 1967; tr. L. Dunlop, 1969) is his most famous poem: it is a long meditation, begun in 1942 when soap was a valuable commodity, on every aspect of this 'stone-like object with its marvellous powers of dissolution and rebirth'. He collected much of his work—essays on his procedures and poems —together with new material in the three volumes of his *Great Miscellany* (*Le Grand Recueil*, 1961). He is certainly an important ancestor of the *nouveau roman*, but this is because of his method which has classical but, as I have pointed out, not behaviourist implications. Ponge can be and has been overrated; but he is a genial and thoughtful writer. (PBFV4; CFP; FWT)

The Parisian JACQUES PRÉVERT (1900), once a surrealist and then a Marxist, is a casual and cheerful anarchist. He did notable work in films, writing the scripts of a number of Carné's best films, including *Le Jour se lève* and *Les Enfants du paradis*. Prévert is a true cabaret poet, a gleeman, a professional, whose technical skill is very considerable. His themes are often sentimental, but never offensively so—although the best setting for such work is usually the authentic (not the slick or pretentious) night-club for which it was created. Prévert's work, however thin—and much of it is this—always possesses vigour and the authority of tough experience. He has achieved the genuinely popular poetry that has eluded nearly every poet who has tried it; and yet at the same time he demonstrates, so to speak, that popular poetry has its limitations. For although he is an effective poet, he is inevitably a superficial one. His simplicities ring true, but their reverberations are strictly limited. The finest feature of his work is its lucid onslaught on the 'official', the pompous and the dehumanized. Although the magazine *Commerce* had published the long comic satire, *A Try at a Description of a Dinner of Disguised Guests in Paris, France* (*Tentative de description d'un dîner de têtes à Paris-France*, 1931) which is one of his best and most characteristic works, and other poems and stories, Prévert did not become really well known until in 1946 a friend—René Bertelé, author of a study of Michaux—collected together, from newspapers and even from the tablecloths on which they had been written down, all the poems he could find and brought them together in *Words* (*Paroles*, 1946; pt. tr. L. Ferlinghetti, 1958; 1966), which was a phenomenal and deserved success. Several collections have followed, and it is hardly to be wondered at if some of the poems in them are exceedingly slight. But they are slight rather than self-parodic or factitious. Prévert's poetry justifies the claim made for it by one critic: it is 'both public and innocent'. (MEP; PBFV4)

One of the most fascinating and original poets of Prévert's generation is

527

JACQUES AUDIBERTI (1899–1965), who was born in Antibes, the son of a master mason. He was a journalist who did not start serious writing until he was almost thirty. After that he wrote plays, novels and criticism as well as his extraordinarily dense, rich poetry. In all his work Audiberti combines wide erudition and verbal exaltation with an unobtrusive psychological sensitivity. His many novels, such as *Abraxas* (1938), *Urujac* (1941), *Gardens and Rivers* (*Les Jardins et les fleuves*, 1954) are virtuoso performances, treating fantasy, pagan story and myth in a remarkable variety of styles. They reflect his view of life more chaotically than his other work, although they contain superb passages. The drama form concentrated his mind, and his parodic procedures gained in significance. *Quoat-Quoat* (1946) combined his favourite theme of paganism asserting itself through a veneer of pretence, with a parody of nineteenth-century melodrama. The effect is that of a kind of modern hilarody. The passengers on a ship bound for Mexico become prey to the savage and primitive forces of the stone of the ancient Mexican God Quoat-Quoat. *The Transient Evil* (*Le Mal court*, 1947), which was a commercial success, is set in the eighteenth century; it shows an innocent princess shrouded in the inevitable evil of experience. In the superb *Natives of the Bordeaux Country* (*Les Naturels du Bordelais*, 1953) Audiberti presents one of the most vital charlatans of modern drama: La Becquilleuse, poet, aphrodisiac-seller and top-fuzz. The entire cast is transformed—into critics and into beasts. *Pucelle* (1950) is his subtle adaptation of the Joan of Arc story. Audiberti was affected by surrealism, and found it liberating; but he early saw that its eventual outcome could be to destroy literature by denying it the pole of tension offered by form. Even his first collection (1929), the poems in which were about Napoleon, was by no means surrealist. He drew upon the entire tradition of French poetry, particularly upon Hugo, to produce a highly intricate, rhetorical poetry. This is as versatile as the prose fiction, but every so often is precipitated a poem of quite astonishing metaphysical brilliance compounded with passion:

> People suffer. As for suffering, suffering does not consider it.
> She demands everything, except herself on the gallows.
> Absent from the star where you named her. . . .
> (CFP)

Rampart (*Rempart*, 1953) is devoted to his native Antibes. The whole body of Audiberti's poetry, with its self-styled 'abhumanism', involving a re-thinking of life, a literal re-making of it on paper, is already overdue for review; it seems to have important implications for the difficult future of poetry everywhere.

RENÉ CHAR (1907), born in the province of Vaucluse in the South of France, where he now lives, was a fully-fledged member of the surrealist movement and a close friend of Éluard's (q.v.); but his heart was never fully in it and his style cannot be called surrealist. Surrealism was for him no more than a liberating force: although his collected poems in the manner of surrealism, *The*

Masterless Hammer (*Le Marteau sans maître*, 1934), are classics of the genre, he was still looking for his own style. He was a brave resistance leader in the Second World War, and was described by his friend Camus (q.v.), whose assumption that modern man needs to recreate his moral world he shared, as the greatest of modern French poets. Char is a hermetic (q.v.) poet in that he seeks to substitute poetry, for him a celebration of eternal truths in a language that entirely transcends that of the everyday, for the 'religion' that he has rejected for reasons identical to those of Camus; furthermore, he uses, or tries to use, words divorced from their traditional associations. His pre-war work consisted of a search for the meaning and function of poetry; since he was involved, as a freedom fighter, in a reassertion of a straightforward humanism, it has become a communication of his inner apprehensions about truth. One might compare him to Saint-John Perse, but the older poet began with and has retained a sense of the friendliness of the natural world that René Char does not possess. He loves his native Midi, and his poetry is soaked in its atmosphere; but the simple celebration of its mysteries is not enough. His poetry, which has tended increasingly to freer forms and thence to prose, seeks to recreate its often fleeting occasions. His style is as oracular as that of the fragments of Heraclitus, the pre-Socratic philosopher whom he profoundly admires; but he is not a mystic: his poems are offered as revelations, and the external world is very much present to him. What he calls 'fascinators', common events that may suddenly illuminate or reveal, are really poetic 'epiphanies': thus 'The Lark':

> Last cinder of sky and first ardour of day,
> She remains mounted in dawn and sings perturbed earth,
> Carillon master of her breath and free of her route.
>
> A fascinator, she's killed by being dazzled.
>
> (CFP)

It is easy to misconstrue this as surrealist, for surrealism has so clearly been a part of its author's apprenticeship. But it is aphoristic, gnomic, in a way no truly surrealist poem can be: it seeks, like all Char's poems, to capture an aspect of the eternal in the instant. There is an effort here to create a poetic language that recalls the intentions of Stefan George (q.v.); but Char does not reject life as the German poet did. On the contrary, he affirms it, with, as one of his critics (Alexander Aspel) has well said, 'an exasperated serenity'. In the lark Char sees not only the lark itself but also creatively free man, capable of exercising his possibilities. The last line is illuminated by his famous statement, made apropos of his *Leaves of Hypnos* (*Feuillets d'Hypnos*, 1946; pt. tr. J. Matthews, *Botteghe Oscure*, XIV, 1954), that he practised a 'humanism aware of its duties, discreet about its virtues, wishing to keep in reserve the inaccessible as a free field for the fantasy of its suns, and resolved to pay the price for this'. The main difficulty encountered in reading Char's work is that words do in fact have traditional associations; even if a poet can intimate processes of actually becoming—as Char does—the ghost of old poetic techniques lingers and to some extent interferes with communication. The creation of this kind of hermetic poetry does not perhaps lie within the English language; but it is worth attending to Char, whose integrity is beyond question: all foreign example, properly understood, acts invigoratingly. (HW; PBFV4; PI; FWT; CFP; MEP)

Such a poet was bound to attract gifted followers, and three leading poets who have thoroughly assimilated his influence are YVES BONNEFOY (1923), born in Tours, the Parisian ANDRÉ DU BOUCHET (1924) and JACQUES DUPIN (1927), born at Privas in Ardèche. Bonnefoy, who is distinguished as a translator of Shakespeare and as a critic, is the most highly regarded French poet of his generation. Like Char, Bonnefoy is a hermetic poet; but he has read Valéry (q.v.) and learned much from his grave and sonorous manner, and Jouve (q.v.), and is both more urban (or less rural) and more literary than Char. His philosophical ambitions are not, like Char's, unobtrusive. The basis of his outlook is that death illuminates and makes sense of life, and he prefaced his first sequence of poems, *Of the Movement and Immobility of Douve* (*Du mouvement et de l'immobolité de Douve*, 1953; pt. tr. A. Rudolf in *Selected Poems*, 1968) with Hegel's dictum that 'the life of the spirit . . . is the life which endures death and in death maintains itself'. What symbolized the truly sacred has now become meaningless to men, who have therefore lost the sense of the sacred altogether; now death must be the sacred. He sees his poems as a series of intuitive approximations to this sacred reality—which is, so to speak by definition, indefinable. Douve is the beloved ('at each moment I see you born, Douve, / At each moment die') who is glimpsed as herself and as various aspects of nature or landscape. Although Bonnefoy's poetry has a certain magnificence, and brilliantly succeeds in creating a new style that sedulously avoids perfection of form (as an artificiality), there is a certain monotony and lack of warmth about it; with the warm and gentle Char we feel that the poet has to speak as he does, and we seek to penetrate his utterance; with Bonnefoy there is often a feeling that the poet's intellect has played a much greater part in the poem's creation than its pretentions acknowledge. None the less, as the impressive—and in this case moving—poem 'Threats of the Witness' (CFP) demonstrates, this is a poetry of authority. (PBFV4; MEP; CFP; FWT)

Du Bouchet is less ambitious, or less philosophical, than Bonnefoy. Like Ponge's, his poetry is one of things; but in this work only an austere world is presented. Aside from Char, the chief influence on du Bouchet has been Pierre Reverdy (q.v.). Like Reverdy, he agonizedly searches for moments of communion with a nature stripped of all lushness or sensual pleasure: a nature bleak, galvanic, elemental. This is a convincingly honest poetry, but one whose terms of reference are so far limited. (PBFV4; CFP; FWT)

In the post-surrealism of Jacques Dupin, who is a publisher and art-critic, there is greater positiveness of feeling, and more humanly satisfying imagery. Such poems as 'The Mineral Kingdom' (CFP) recreate an experience of hope

('The fire will never be cured of us, / The fire that speaks our language'), rely more upon words themselves than upon the lay-out of the poem on the page (as in du Bouchet). His seeing of all experience in elemental terms— stone, minerals, mountains—is rendered in harsh and demanding imagery; and his world is more limited than Char's full-blooded, sun drenched one—but his apprehensions have been wrung out of him, as in 'Air':

> The body and the dreams of the lady
> For whom the hammers whirled
> Are lost together, and return
> Retrieving from the storm clouds
> Only the tattered rags of the lightning
> With the dew to come.

(CFP)

This is a highly elliptical account of a love-encounter, from which the 'essence' has been extracted, in the manner of Char. The second line transforms 'lust', 'feelings of love', into an image that is redolent both of pagan mystery (Jupiter or Thor making thunder) and of quarrymen's techniques. The decrease of interest in this love-figure, a romanticized and archetypal one, since she is 'la dame', 'comes back' to the poet as a storm's end, with dew of the succeeding morning to come. The anthropomorphism is so intense that the experience itself is eliminated from the account of it. . . . (PBFV4; FWT)

GUILLEVIC (ps. EUGÈNE GUILLEVIC, 1907) who was born at Carnac in Brittany, the son of a policeman, is in a sense a less ambitious poet. A civil servant for most of his life, he joined the (clandestine) communists in 1943. He was a friend of the ill-fated Drieu La Rochelle's, and of Éluard's (qq.v.). Guillevic, too, is concerned with matter, and in the uniquely French manner of this century wishes to abolish his personal identity (hence his abandonment of his Christian name). But no philosophical programme can be inferred from this. Once he committed himself to the Marxist task of analysing society in terms of exploiters and exploited he lost much of his original power—particularly since, a naïve (q.v.) poet *par excellence*, he tried to use his earlier procedures to achieve this. He is essentially a 'poet of elementary matter' (Alexander Aspel): a namer of the nameless origins of humanity: the mud, the slime, the water, the foul depths of caves. But after his first two collections he became more self-conscious, and most of the startling effects of his later poetry may be traced to genuine insights in the earlier ones. (CFP; FWT)

JEAN FOLLAIN (1903), born at Canisy in Normandy, is more casual—partaking of the manner of Fargue (q.v.)—but not necessarily less significant. He describes his moments of illumination without fuss, cheerfully, charmingly; he is frank in his nostalgia, recalls his childhood openly. He is one of those delightful minor writers the effect of whose modest vignettes is that of a fresh, beautifully observed impressionist painting: an improvement upon life, thus adding to our and his life—without metaphysics. (CFP; MEP)

ANDRÉ FRÉNAUD (1907), born in a small town in Saône-et-Loire, Burgundy, wrote quieter but ultimately more deeply felt and illuminating poetry about the German occupation than Aragon's (q.v.), in *The Magi* (*Les Rois mages*, 1943). Frénaud has rightly been referred to as an existentialist poet. He is concerned with a quest for self, and his best poems express, beautifully and simply, moments of authenticity and freedom won from misery, or recognitions of loveliness in things that had become sordid. He is a lyrical, affirming poet, who combines something of the tenderness of Éluard with a good-tempered ruefulness that is all his own. (CFP; FWT; PBFV4)

The poet and novelist ANDRÉ PIEYRE DE MANDIARGUES (1909), born in Paris, is undoubtedly an important writer. He was associated with the post-war surrealists, and is often called a surrealist, but once again, the function of surrealism for him has been no more than a liberating one. His novels, of which *The Motorcycle* (*La Motocyclette*, 1963; tr. R. Howard, 1965) is famous as a film (a poor one), are certainly as realist as they are surrealist. Pieyre de Mandiargues brilliantly and accurately shows people behaving in what psychiatrists call 'fugues'. In *The Motorcycle* a girl bored with her husband speeds off, fatally, to meet her lover. She is doomed by her attachment to speed and lust; the erotic detail is described with a redoubtable psychological accuracy. This same precision applies to his poetry and prose poems, which often begin on surreal premises but soon concentrate into careful, uninhibited description. Pieyre de Mandiargues' greatest achievements are probably his novels; but in these he is a poet in the power of his description of the actions of people in despair. (CFP; FWT)

PATRICE DE LA TOUR DU PIN (1911), born in Paris, educated in Sologne (which is the background of his poetry), offers a contrast to all the foregoing: he is one of the few poets of merit to have been honoured as 'an answer to surrealism'. He has given force to this interpretation by declaring, misguidedly, that his work is 'absolutely independent of the modern spirit'. And, in mistaken emulation of Claudel (q.v.) and with high Christian zeal, he has embarked on an enormous project (patently beyond his powers) of assembling a *A Summa of Poetry* (*Une Somme de poésie*, 1946, 1959, 1963), which he is still continuing. In fact, and against his orthodox wishes, his poetry is rightly described as 'hermetic and personal': he is the Gallic equivalent of a Wilson Knight crossed with J. C. Powys and T. H. White: violently eccentric, obstinate, conceited, medieval, foolish to ignore. *The Quest for Joy* (*La Quête de joie*, 1933), which was acclaimed, was extraordinary: a kind of grail poem, in traditional form, incorporating ghosts of the medieval past as reinterpreted by the Victorians. But the question was whether the young poet would or could eventually achieve the precision lacking in the poem. He did not. A prisoner of the Germans for much of the Second World War, he returned and inflated himself into a poet-philosopher: his lyrical gift departed. His ideas about poetry are summed up in *The Dedicated Life in Poetry* (*La Vie recluse en poésie*, 1938; tr. G. S. Fraser, 1948). (PBFV4)

PIERRE EMMANUEL (ps. NOËL MATHIEU, 1916), born at Gan in the Pyrenees and educated partly in America, is another Christian traditionalist, but of a very different kind; he is a disciple and a friend of Jouve (q.v.), but his amiable and superficial fluency, which functions as a kind of inoffensively optimistic journalism, has prevented him from ever attaining Jouve's eminence. He has a slick, pleasant and sincere style, but has failed to develop it into anything serious.

PHILIPPE JACCOTTET (1925) was born at Moudon in Vaud, in Switzerland, but settled in France in 1946. He shares the same concerns as his contemporaries, but is less austere and more conversational, less hermetic, seeming to address the reader more directly and in a more friendly way. He writes gently and subtly of death—

> Don't worry, it will come! You're drawing near, you're getting warm! For the word which is to end the poem more than the first word will be near your death. . . .

—addressing lovers, equating their 'coming' with the intimation of death and with the end of his poem. He has translated Musil (q.v.) into French. Jaccottet has written what are perhaps the most satisfying and substantial poems of any poet of his generation who has absorbed and understood modernism. Others of this age group, such as MICHEL DEGUY (1930) have demonstrated both intellectual agility and feeling, but have not yet—as Jaccottet has—found the means to combine them. (PBFV4; FWT; CFP)

German Literature

I

There was a German literary renaissance between 1880 and 1900. In 1880 literature was debilitated; by 1900 there was a host of new talent. Poetry was in 1880 represented at its worse by a multitude of mediocre narrative romances, but at its better only by the monotonous and self-consciously 'beautiful' verses of PAUL HEYSE (1830–1914), the first German to win a Nobel Prize (1910). Heyse did good work as a collector of German short stories, and some of his own, particularly *L'Arrabbiata* (1855; tr. 1855) and the English collection *The Dead Lake* (1867; tr. M. Wilson, 1870) deserve to survive; his poetry, plays and novels are now unreadable. The better poets, among them von Eichendorff, Mörike and above all Heine, were dead. The Swiss C. F. Meyer (1825–98) wrote lyrics that sometimes anticipate later poetry in their tentative symbolism; significantly, this poetry originated in a pathological melancholia. But such an excellent example of his best work as 'Lethe' (PGV) has its roots firmly in romanticism. These writers influenced such twentieth-century poets and novelists as Ricarda Huch (q.v.), but did not impel them towards modernism.

It is unnecessary to speak of the theatregoers' average diet in the early Eighties: this consisted of farces or ponderous imitations of Schiller's historical plays.

In fiction there were a few exceptions to the general rule of sentimental family tales and massively erudite but poor historical novels in imitation of Scott. Some memorable novellas were written. The Swiss Gottfried Keller published the final revision of his major novel, *Green Henry* (*Der grüne Heinrich*, 1880; tr. A. M. Holt, 1960), in 1880. The most shining exception was Theodore Fontane, who did not begin to write novels until he was in his middle fifties. Fontane was claimed by, and encouraged, the naturalists. But he was a non-romantic realist, not a naturalist; his work in any case transcends that of the programmatists whose admiration he gained. Two other forerunners of the naturalist movement that was so soon to erupt do, in terms of lifespan, belong to this century. The novels of FRIEDRICH SPIELHAGEN (1829–1911) were once admired. He was a socialist who advocated social realism in his criticism, but who could not achieve it in fiction because he had neither grasp of character nor conception of a prose style appropriate to his material. His best book is *Faustulus* (1898), a satire on the Nietzschean idea of the superman.

WILHELM RAABE (1831–1910) is, by contrast, a major figure. A genuine humorist, influenced by Dickens and Sterne, he combined a temperamental pessimism with decency, detachment and a sharp intelligence. His best work, *Stopfkuchen* (1891), belongs to his final period. *Abu Telfan: Return from the Mountains of the Moon* (*Abu Telfan, oder Die Heimkehr vom Mondgebirge*, 1868; tr. S. Delffs, 1881) is a shrewd criticism of his Germany.

Six more nineteenth-century figures are relevant. Four are poets and two are thinkers, the influence of whose ideas cannot be ignored. WILHELM BUSCH (1832–1908), caricaturist as well as poet, is as famous in Germany for his *Max and Maurice* (*Max und Moritz*, 1865; tr. A. Esdaile, 1913) as Edward Lear is in the English-speaking world for his nonsense verses; but he was not as poetically gifted as Lear, and his 'nonsense' is not true nonsense, as Morgenstern's (q.v.) is. But Busch was a genuinely comic poet. There is rather more, in fact, of Hilaire Belloc (as comic poet) in him than of Lear or Carroll; he has Belloc's stolidity and cheerful, sincere dismay. Of a pious girl burned to death he says:

> Here we see her smoking ruins.
> The rest is of no further use.

Busch had to satisfy a large and indiscriminate audience (from 1884 onwards he produced an annual); his aggressiveness and contempt for bourgeois religion do not always save his work from mediocrity. But he never entirely lost his gift.

PAUL SCHEERBART (ps. BRUNO KÜFER, 1863–1915), novelist and poet born in Danzig and a friend of Dehmel's and Przybyszewski's (qq.v.), was possibly more important than Busch. Certainly he was carefully read by Ringelnatz and Hans Arp (qq.v.), to mention only two. He wrote fantastic 'cosmic' novels (adventures in space in a bottle, dancing planets, and so on) that may be considered, although they are so whimsical, as early prototypes of Science Fiction. His nonsense poetry (*Katerpoesie*, 1909), which was republished in Germany in 1963, should be more widely known. Like Fritz von Hermanovsky-Orlando (q.v.) Scheerbart was a friend of the Prague painter and writer Alfred Kubin.

DETLEV VON LILIENCRON (1844–1909), impoverished Baron, soldier, perpetual debtor, adventurer, wag, good fellow, wrote plays and fiction, but is now remembered for his poetry. Like Roy Campbell (q.v.), another not altogether convincing laureate of the soldier's life, Liliencron was a stylist rather than a thinker; his modest innovations—the abolition of some archaisms, the introduction of a few everyday (but not colloquial) words—were accidental, a result of his military forthrightness. Wounded in the two wars of 1866 and 1870, Liliencron was forced to resign his commission in 1875 because of debts; he spent two 'lost' years in America (house-painting, horse-breaking: the usual), and then took a job in Germany as a bailiff and, finally, parish-overseer. He was a scamp (this is, surprisingly, the right word): he had suffered too much, said his friend Richard Dehmel, not to be beyond dignity and honour. Liliencron was best when most subdued, although in his sporting-voluptuous vein ('With a plume in my helmet in sport or in daring, Halli!/Life gave me no lessons in fasting or sparing, Hallo!/No wench so unwilling but yields her to me. . . .' and so on) he has undoubted verve even when he prompts a smile. But while he was the best of the so-called 'impressionist' poets, it is going much too far to claim, as one critic does, that his technique is a precursor of expressionism (q.v.) because, it is claimed, 'he gives a series of realistic impressions (rather in the Japanese style) from which everything unnecessary has been eliminated'. 'Day in March' is characteristic. Beginning with pure description of cloud-masses, cranes, larks, it concludes: 'brief fortune dreams its way across wide lands./Brief fortune swam away with the cloud-masses;/I wished to hold on to it, had to let it swim away' (TCG; see also PGV, CGP). The description here is for the sake of the observation about 'brief fortune'; and even in his poems where the essentially late romantic observations are absent, they are implied. Liliencron is a late nineteenth-century poet, not a proto-expressionist.

The poet RICHARD DEHMEL (1863–1920) was until his death rated far too highly; he is hardly read now. His historical importance, as one influenced both by Nietzsche (q.v.) and socialism, is undoubted; his inconsistency—militarism, worship of ruthlessness, socialistic sympathy—is symptomatic. Dehmel's development as a poet is illusory; his ideas are as uninteresting as his over-sexed brand of vitalism, leading to a transparently spurious programme for 'spiritualizing' sex.

But when he was not intellectualizing, Dehmel was better as a poet. He translated Verlaine well, and learnt from him. The handful of satisfactory poems he left are evocations of landscape. To him this was doubtless an exercise in creating 'atmosphere' rather than in the more important matter of expressing his thoughts. But it was then that he came closest to expressing himself: 'The pond is resting and/The meadow glistening./Its shadows glimmer/In the pond's tide, and/The mind weeps in the trees./We dream—dream–. . .' (TCG; see also PGV, CGP).

FRIEDRICH NIETZSCHE (1844–1900) was insane (he had had syphilis at the age of twenty-two) for the last eleven years of his life, so that his work was all done well within the limits of the nineteenth century. But no discussion of modern Western literature can avoid referring to him: his influence upon our century has been decisive. His creative work consisted only of poetry: the long prose poem *Thus Spake Zarathustra* (*Also sprach Zarathustra*, 1883–5; tr. T. Common, 1909; R. J. Hollingdale, 1961) and the shorter lyrical poems *Dionysus-Dithyrambs* (*Dionysos-Dithyramben*, 1884–8).

Nietzsche, until 1889 one of the most lucid of nineteenth-century German prose writers, has been interpreted in a variety of conflicting ways: as proto-Nazi, as proto-communist, and as existentialist prophet of human freedom. He was not himself consistent, but his complete (syphilitic?) breakdown at the age of forty-five prevented him from reconciling some of the most glaring contradictions in his work.

First and foremost, Nietzsche consistently attacked the *status quo*. His work was unheeded until the Dane Georges Brandes (q.v.) began to lecture on it in 1888; there had been no such forceful denunciation of bourgeois complacency in the century. Nietzsche rediscovered the Dionysian and anti-intellectual principle that life is tragic: he hailed the Greek tragedy of Aeschylus and Sophocles as the supreme achievement of art ('We have art in order not to perish of truth') because it emphasized that man must suffer to know joy ('All joy wants the eternity of all things, wants honey, wants dregs, wants intoxicated midnight, wants graves, wants the consolation of graveside tears, wants gilded sunsets'), and celebrated the irrationality of the instincts that he believed had been weakened by Socrates, by Euripides and, then, finally and fatally, by Christianity.

Nietzsche's advocacy of a 'superman' ('Übermensch'), now perhaps better rendered as 'overman' if only because of its unfortunate associations, was used by fascist ideologists; but they certainly misunderstood it. His appeal to the youth of his day to reject knowledge for its own sake, and to live by instinct, was not as crude as the Prussian militarists, and then the Nazis, liked to pretend. (When he attacked the acquisition of knowledge for its own sake he was, if only in part, reacting against the German educational system, which undoubtedly crammed its victims with accumulations of meaningless facts to a dangerous degree.) Nietzsche's overman gives his life meaning by learning to create, to love his enemies, to be virtuous; he would have seen the Nazi, as Nietzsche himself saw Bismarck, as a failed overman—a mere crude pursuer of power.

Unfortunately Nietzsche's descriptions of his 'new man' are themselves partly responsible for later misinterpretations (some would put it more strongly than that); and he certainly had a sinister side to him, as may be seen in his hysterical glorifications of force, war and the military. Nietzsche was a formative influence on expressionism (q.v.). His message 'God is dead', and consequent exhortation to man to turn against his narcissistic, death-resisting intellect, profoundly affected the succeeding generation of expressionist (and then surrealist) poets, who put all the emphasis upon intuition rather than upon rational perception.

Nietzsche's idea of 'the eternal recurrence of the same', another of his re-discoveries, was part and parcel of his demand that literature should revitalize itself by means of myth (myth naturally being preferred to debilitating 'morality' and rationalism); it had a profound effect, as may be seen in the fact that well over half the major works of this century have employed or drawn upon myth.

Freud said of Nietzsche that he probably had more knowledge of himself than any other human being. Certainly no pre-Freudian writer, with the possible exception of Coleridge, formulated so many 'Freudian' concepts. Thus, he said: 'One's own self is well hidden from oneself: of all mines of treasure one's own is the last to be dug up'. His use of a new psychology was all-pervasive in its influence, not only upon writers who did not hear of Freud until during or after the First World War, but on Freud himself. Nietzsche could be strident, even horrisonous; but he is a key figure. The difficulties raised by his overman exactly parallel the difficulties that lie at the heart of expressionism: both raise the urgent question, When does a nihilism become a barbarism?

The philosopher WILHELM DILTHEY (1833–1911) is important for the emphasis he put on psychic as distinct from materialistic manifestation, and for his confidence in the capacity of poets to make meaningful statements about the mysteriousness of life, which can thereafter be intellectually analyzed. For Dilthey, too, intuition is primary. His poetics, the most important to be published in Germany in his lifetime, concentrated upon the creative process and the experience of the creator—and thus played a part in the genesis of expressionism. His frequent insistence that 'the origin of all genuine poetry is in experience' has been of importance both to poets and to some critics, as has his subtle treatment of the nature of the experience that can lead to poetry: something actively and intensely felt, and subsequently transformed; something that is processed by the poet in his totality—by 'the whole man'. Later Dilthey saw certain shortcomings in his formulation of the problem; his criticism of individual poets is sometimes theory-bound; but the value of his always sober insistence upon the primacy of experience and intuition, and his account of the imaginative process, is undoubted, and helped greatly to prepare the atmosphere for the eruption of genuine poetry that began at the time of his death. (One might say the same of the English 'pre-romantic' poet and critic Edward Young, who influenced Dilthey and was hailed by the surrealists.) His work is ably summarized by H. A. Hodges in *The Philosophy of Wilhelm Dilthey* (1952).

II

The most indefatigably polemical of the German naturalists (q.v.) was ARNO HOLZ (1863–1929). He was no more than a competent writer at best, but he has importance as one of the leading figures, with his friend and collaborator JOHANNES SCHLAF (1862–1941), of German naturalism; above all he was generous in his encouragement of writers better than himself. In his treatise *Art: Its Nature and Its Laws* (*Die Kunst: ihr Wesen und ihre Gesetze*, 1890–2) he gave an almost fanatic definition of naturalism, in which he went so far as to assert that art is different from nature only in its means. He formulated the law that 'art has the tendency to return to nature'. The problem was a scientific one: art was photographic, and its only limitations were its means. Earlier (1885) he had written a book of lyrics conventional in form but decidedly 'modern' in that it dealt with social and sexual themes: this was *The Book of the Age* (*Das Buch der Zeit*, 1885). At the turn of the century, he began, under the influence of Whitman, to advocate free verse rhythms: metrical form is 'smashed', and its place is taken by rhythmical form. There are to be no rhymes or stanzas, and the poem turns on an invisible central pivot: that is to say, each line is centred on the page—making Holz's own examples look rather like some concrete poetry (q.v.). The basic notion behind this, that of an 'inner rhythm', is by no means silly: it characterizes all literature. But Holz, although his ideas are of interest as an extreme development of French naturalist theory, was over-confident and over-theoretical; and his creative powers were limited. The truth is, he and nearly all the other early German naturalists were critics at heart: they recognized that the romanticism of their day was outdated, that Goethe had exhausted its soil; and that the political progress of their country had been retarded. But they had no inner creative urge, such as characterized almost all of the writers associated with the first phase of expressionism. Holz's creative sterility is well shown in 'Its roof almost brushed the stars. . . .', ostensibly a 'naturalist lyric' about a starving young man in a garret who could only stammer 'O Muse! and knew nothing of his destitution' (TCG; see also PGV). This succeeds only in achieving the banal and outworn romanticism against which the naturalists were reacting.

Other naturalists of historical interest who should be mentioned are the critic and novelist MICHAEL GEORG CONRAD (1846–1927), who made personal contact with Zola, the brothers HEINRICH (1855–1906) and JULIUS HART (1859–1930), critics, dramatists and poets, and the Scottish-born poet, novelist and anarchist JOHN HENRY MACKAY (1864–1933): these championed Zola intelligently and not uncritically, but could not convincingly emulate him in their own creative work. All were members, with Holz and others such as the critic and novelist WILHELM BÖLSCHE (1861–1939) and Gerhart Hauptmann (q.v.), of an *avant garde* literary club called *Durch*. The heroes of *Durch* were Ibsen and Tolstoi (qq.v.). The Free Stage (Die freie Bühne), modelled on Antoine's Théâtre Libre (q.v.) in Paris, lasted from 1889 until 1891 (but later if special performances are counted), and put on plays by Ibsen and Zola as well as Holz and Hauptmann. The heyday of German naturalism may be measured by its duration.

Holz and Schlaf scored a success with a volume of three stories called *Papa Hamlet* (1889), which they published under the name of Bjarne P. Holmsen (chosen because of the esteem in which Scandinavian writers were then held). These tales are an attempt to be totally objective and photographic; but the subject-matter is sensational (thus betraying subjectivity) and the disjointed style—called 'Sekundenstil' (i.e. style that tries to reproduce the passing of seconds), an early forerunner of 'stream of consciousness' (q.v.) technique—produces an effect of dullness. This, with its short scenes, came close to drama, and Holz's and Schlaf's next effort was a play, *The Family Selicke* (*Die Familie Selicke*, 1890), which followed the same technique and had the same sensational, sordid subject-matter.

MAX KRETZER (1854–1941) is the most typical of all the German naturalist novelists, and although he sold well until 1939, he is today forgotten. Here is an example of a writer with the same kind of impulses as Theodore Dreiser (q.v.), but without the genius or sensibility. Much of his work stems from painstaking imitations of individual novels by Zola or Dickens, but he is at his unimpressive best when writing of his own experiences, as in his most famous novel, *Meister Timpe* (1888), where he traces a family's decline from the middle to the lower classes, or in *The Signwriter* (*Der Fassadenraphael*, 1911). He pretended not to have read Zola.

HERMANN SUDERMANN (1857–1928), like Kretzer an East Prussian, achieved enormous success as playwright and novelist. A clever if not wholly honest craftsman, he gave the middle classes just the kind of pseudo-controversial material they wanted: he was readable, and seemed to have a social conscience. Sudermann's play *Honour* (*Die Ehre*, 1889; tr. H. R. Bankrage, 1915) set him up for a quarter of a century as Germany's leading popular playwright. In it he combined a bow towards the 'new' ideas with a masterly grasp of old-fashioned stage technique. Like Sardou's (q.v.), his plays are mechanically 'well made', and thoroughly deserved Shaw's (q.v.) epithet of 'Sardoodledom'. An arch-middlebrow, Sudermann exploited naturalism for commercial ends—not, doubtless, because he so planned it, but because, along with his undoubted skill, he had a commonplace mind. His literary reputation was eventually destroyed by the implacable opposition of the critic and poet ALFRED KERR (ps. ALFRED KEMPNER, 1868–1948), who understood true naturalism as it was exemplified in Ibsen and Hauptmann (qq.v.). Sudermann also wrote novels: regional (his best), historical and sensationalist. *The Song of Songs* (*Das hohe Lied*, 1908; tr. Beatrice Marshall, 1909), about a loathsome aristocratic General and the girl he 'corrupts', was a *cause célèbre* in Germany and England. Its moral, that a high society which does not work must be 'rotten', was peculiarly edifying to its bourgeois audience. All Sudermann's work was directed at the public, who devoured him avidly; he is today unreadable, for he wrote from no inner compulsion.

MAX HALBE (1865–1944), another of those whose intense naturalism is now outdated, came from near Danzig. Influenced first by both Ibsen and Gerhart Hauptmann (qq.v.), he later became friendly with Wedekind (q.v.). *The Breaking of the Ice* (*Der Eisgang*, 1892), in which rivalry between two brothers is depicted against the background of the gradually unfreezing Vistula, draws from Ibsen for its symbolism (socialism flooding forth) and Hauptmann for its psychology. Halbe's great success was the play *When Love is Young* (*Jugend*, 1893; tr. S. T. Barrows, 1916). This is his best work because it stems from the conflicts of his own youth; however, its language, once admired, now seems more poetical than poetic, and its machinery creaks. As a tragedy of adolescent love it is a genuine predecessor of Wedekind's *Spring's Awakening* (q.v.); but the latter unkindly exposes its shortcomings. Halbe did try to participate in some proto-expressionist theatrical activities, but these were short-lived experiments. His autobiography *Turn of the Century* (*Jahrhundertwende*, 1935), telling of his years of association with Wedekind and others between 1893 and 1914, is valuable for the background of German naturalism and of the group around Wedekind.

PAUL ERNST (1866–1933), novelist, poet, critic, playwright, developed through theological, naturalistic and Marxist phases to his own abstract position, which involved a crude, neo-classical cult of a super-hero, the lifeless star of 'meta-tragedies', of which Ernst left a number. By means of his theories he was able to condemn *King Lear*. He ended up as a kind of transcendental Christian, praised by the Nazis. His output is as enormous (one verse epic extends to 100,000 stanzas) as it is undistinguished.

The poet, novelist, critic and historian RICARDA HUCH (1864–1947), more interesting, and for long acclaimed as modern Germany's outstanding writer

('Germany's first lady', said Thomas Mann), allowed herself to be by-passed by naturalism and the movements that succeeded it. Her high-bred loftiness would not have allowed her to dabble in anything that dealt in detail with such crude material as the lives of the poor. She did not lack concern, but it was aristocratic. Instead she drew her inspiration from C. F. Meyer, Heyse, Keller (qq.v.), and earlier writers. She lacked a sense of humour, and was unable to see the shortcomings of nineteenth-century German bourgeois respectability—she signally failed to take a critical view of it in her smooth, lush first novel, *Unconquered Love* (*Erinnerungen von Ludolf Ursleu dem Jüngeren*, 1893; tr. W. A. Drake, 1931). Her verse is sentimental and wooden. In retrospect a rather stupidly grand old lady, perhaps—but one who was a scholar, who proudly refused Nazi honours and secretly opposed their regime, and who, in her small way, developed. Her only work of interest now is the detective story, *The Deruga Trial* (*Der Fall Deruga*, 1917; tr. L. Dietz, 1929): superior and intelligent detective fiction, this stands up today: it displays most of Ricarda Huch's virtues and powers in a, for once, congenial and creatively modest framework.

Finally we come to the man within whose work the imaginatively sterile German naturalist movement became transformed. GERHART HAUPTMANN (1862–1946), dramatist, novelist and poet, was once a literary giant, and his 1912 Nobel Prize surprised no one. Now he is little read outside his own country, except by academics; yet critics accord him more than mouth-honour, and it seems certain that a substantial amount will remain to be rescued and rehabilitated from the vast mass of his drama and fiction, though not from his verse. New and improved English versions of his works continue to be made, and his plays are still being performed. His importance is more than historical.

His elder brother CARL HAUPTMANN (1858–1921), gifted, but not as a writer of fiction, was a rather embarrassing imitator of Gerhart—even to the reading of his plays to devoted disciples and the acceptance of the title 'Master'. However, his play *War* (*Krieg*, 1914; tr. in *Vision and Aftermath, Four Expressionist War Plays*, 1969), the last and best of a trilogy, is exceptional. It prophesied with remarkable accuracy the real nature of what, at the end of 1914 (the play was written in 1913), was still felt by the vast majority to be a noble and holy war, and in doing so partook of the spirit of expressionism. Hauptmann's gloom here was generated not by the cast of events suiting a dark temperament —as often happened with expressionist writers—but by a keen and early understanding of what the cataclysm would really mean. *War* still reads remarkably well. Unfortunately nothing else Hauptmann wrote matches it.

Gerhart Hauptmann was born in Silesia, and at first intended to be a sculptor. After a Byronic poem (later withdrawn) and some fiction, he took the German-speaking world by storm with his drama *Before Dawn* (*Vor Sonnenaufgang*, 1889; tr. L. Bloomfield, 1909. All Hauptmann's dramas before 1925 were collected and tr. L. Lewisohn and others in *Dramatic Works*, 1913–29). Here he was influenced by Holz: there can be no doubt of the 'consistency' of his determinism here. A family of Silesian farmers become drunks when coal is discovered on their land. An idealist who believes in 'scientific determinism' comes amongst them and falls in love with the one alcoholically uncorrupted member of the family, the daughter Helene. The reformer, Alfred Loth, rejects her on the grounds of her heredity, and she kills herself. Very much a young man's play, and delightfully close to naturalist theory for Holz. . . . But it had real dramatic impact: one could already have discerned, from the depiction of the main characters, both Alfred Kerr's much later tribute, 'this is not accuracy; this is intuition', and Thomas Mann's even more remarkable one, 'He did not speak in his own guise, but let life itself talk'.

However, these tributes were to, and are really only applicable to, the plays of Hauptmann's earlier period: it is for these that he will be remembered. *The Weavers (Die Weber,* 1892; tr. T. H. Lustig in *Five Plays by Gerhart Hauptmann,* 1961), about the 1844 revolt of Silesian weavers (his grandfather had been one of them), was one of the first plays in which the hero was the crowd. This transcends both politics and naturalist theory by, to adapt Mann's remark, 'letting the weavers themselves talk'. This, along with *The Assumption of Hannele (Hanneles Himmelfahrt,* 1893; tr. T. M. Lustig, ibid.), in which a poor, dying girl has visions of her ascent to paradise, was banned. In revenge Hauptmann wrote one of the best and liveliest of all German comedies, *The Beaver Coat (Der Biberpelz,* 1893; tr. T. M. Lustig, ibid.). Authority has seldom been more accurately caricatured. The thieving, cunning washerwoman Wolffen is done with a vitality that acts as a perfect contrast to the absurd official Wehrhahn. This will play almost anywhere and in almost any language with success. Two other plays of Hauptmann's early period that will also continue to survive are the tragedies *Drayman Henschel* and *Rose Bernd (Fuhrmann Henschel,* 1898; *Rose Bernd,* 1903; tr. T. H. Lustig, ibid.).

Gerhart Hauptmann was—in the terms of Schiller's distinction between 'naïve' and 'sentimentive' (q.v.)—a 'naïve' writer. The playwright who was translated by James Joyce (q.v.) and admired by pretty well every important writer in the world, became, as Michael Hamburger has well said, 'defeated by the tension of the age'. In deep sympathy with humanity, he failed to understand the changes that were taking place around him. Hauptmann the old mage, who modelled himself on Goethe and imagined that he had improved Shakespeare's *Hamlet,* is a figure of little interest. His enormous dull epics, in monotonous verse, are of no value; his final tetralogy, again in verse, on the subject of the House of Atreus is inadequate because its turgid language fails to function except as an outmoded notion of grandeur. The bright, empathic young playwright becomes 'a great man', and so his work declines: instead of positive achievements, he produces nothing that is more than 'interesting'— such as his treatment of *The Tempest* theme in *Indipondi* (1920), in which he celebrates incest. He accepted the Nazis, but never actively collaborated; later he published attacks on them.

Hauptmann's intentions oscillated between naturalism and what may be called a kind of neo-romantic symbolism, seldom free from sentimentality. At his best, naturalism functioned as a matrix for his intuitions. In fiction, too, Hauptmann vacillated between two extremes: an erotic paganism and a pious Christianity. In *The Fool in Christ, Emanuel Quint* (*Der Narr in Christo*, 1910; tr. T. Selzer, 1912) he shows a modern misunderstood Christ coming to grief; but in *The Heretic of Soana* (*Der Ketzer von Soana*, 1918; tr. B. Q. Morgan, 1960) his subject is a priest converted to sensuality and neo-paganism.

Hauptmann was a true naïve, who would have done better work throughout his life if he had observed reality more calmly and been content simply to celebrate nature—as he always did in his heart.

His attempt to synthesize his inner and outer worlds was a conspicuous failure: an object lesson in how not to approach the twentieth century.

III

It is customary to associate three poets of the turn of the century: the Hessian Stefan George, the Austrian Hugo von Hofmannsthal, and the German-Czech Rainer Maria Rilke. At this time a number of '-isms' were in currency: impressionism, symbolism, even a 'beyond naturalism'. But, as a critic has written, 'the dark horse with the staying power will be found wearing the dun colours of *Sprachkrise* [crisis in language]'. The question being asked by the important poets was, Can language communicate?

The work of STEFAN GEORGE (1868–1933) is the least enduring and important. However, despite his limitations and ridiculosities, he was one of the men who helped to bring into Germany a viable poetry; and he did write a handful of fine poems. Authorities appear to differ on the subject of his influence. One critic calls it 'profound and extensive'; another says he 'has had comparatively little influence in Germany, and none outside'. This last is an incautious remark: George's influence on Rilke and Hofmannsthal was certainly extensive; he had followers outside Germany, especially in Holland. His undoubted genius was too often vitiated, first by the self-consciousness of his decadent-symbolist pose, and later by his assumption of a mantic role.

He went to France as a young man, became friendly with both Mallarmé and Verlaine (qq.v.), and returned to Germany full of certainties: 'A poem is not the reproduction of a thought but of a mood', he wrote. 'We do not desire the invention of stories but the reproduction of moods.' As he grew older he became increasingly dogmatic. He had a vein of real poetry in him, as such individual poems as 'The Master of the Island' (PI) clearly show; but he wrapped this around and eventually concealed it with rhetorical and critical paraphernalia: a bizarre pomposity, that can, retrospectively, easily be seen as psychologically defensive. He was a master of conventional form—his typographical eccentricities are acutely fastidious but not innovatory—and over his life he succeeded in imposing a rigid discipline. He is not a likable poet, but to call him a proto-Nazi is misleading. The Nazis were far too vulgar for him: when they came to power he went into voluntary exile in Switzerland, and refused all the honours they offered him. The imperious George did, however, attract proto-Nazis, and he himself did envisage a 'new Reich' (*The New Reich, Das neue Reich*, 1928, is the title of his last book); but his was a cerebral vision of the future.

George began and ended as a symbolist and preacher of 'art for art's sake'; but he was less original than his first master Mallarmé (q.v.). Some of his best poems are in *The Year of the Soul* (*Das Jahr der Seele*, 1897), and owe much to Verlaine. From its most famous poem, and George's, we can see that for all his 'hardness' George was essentially a neo-romantic: for all his dogmatic pronouncements his real gift lay in an unspectacular but exquisite capacity to reflect his inner states in landscapes:

> Come into the park they say is dead and look: the gleam of distant smiling shores, the unhoped-for blue of the pure clouds shed a light on the ponds and the variegated paths.
>
> Gather the deep yellow, the soft grey of birches and of box—the breeze is mild—the late roses have not yet quite withered; choose them, kiss them, and wind the garland,
>
> And do not forget these last asters either; twine in with gentle hands the purple round the tendrils of the wild vine and, with the autumn scene before you, whatever there is left of the green life. (PGV)

This is a self-portrait: the heart of this homosexual only seems dead: a little 'green life' remains. The behest to gather and kiss the roses is excessive but pathetic because so sentimental and unrealistic.

George's 'philosophy', which is hardly worth taking seriously, but which did not seem so ridiculous at the time it was propounded, derived immediately from Nietzsche, but was severely limited by its furtive homosexual orientation. It was a philosophy of the spirit. The poet (George himself) is priestly reconciler of nature and the intelligence: an unmistakable, if idiosyncratic, version of Nietzsche's 'overman' (q.v.). The poem, static, sculpted, perfect, is literally holy: transcendent of all the experiences that occasioned it; and the poet (*qua* poet) is no single personality but a cosmic ego: in short, a priest-God owing allegiance to nothing and no one beyond himself (except, if he is not George, to George). Hence the mathematical nature of the forms imposed upon his poetry, and the involved structure of his sequences. No concession is to be made to the reader, who either possesses the magic key to the system or—more likely—does not. The attitude to language is resolutely anti-demotic: a poem is profaned if it employs words 'conversationally' or even simply prosaically. The ideal is Greek antiquity (or George's idea of it), by the example of which the new Germany —in reality a renewal of the old hero cult—is to be created and Europe saved.

Of more consequence is George's actual poetic method. He achieved a certain austerity of diction by dropping unnecessary words (yet another rejection of ordinary idiom), and by reducing punctuation to a minimum. He employed a 'centred' full-stop or period, in which he has been imitated by, among others, the roughneck American poet James Dickey. Since he considered his poetry to be the apotheosis of beauty and truth, it required special typography; from 1897 this was provided by Melchior Lechter, 'the William Morris of Germany'.

George's 'system' finally lost what claim to respect it had possessed when, at the beginning of the century, he met and fell in love with a very young, good-looking poet called Maximilian Kronberger ('Maximin'), who died at sixteen. George's worship of this young man was excessively, perhaps wholly, narcissistic—'I, the creature of my own son, am attaining the power of the throne', he wrote—but none the less became a cult. *The Seventh Ring* (*Der siebente Ring*, 1907–11) sublimates his lust for the boy into a massive, mathematically systematized cycle of poems.

George's ideas about poetic language reappear in much more viable and convincing form in Rilke, who wrote: '*No* word in a poem . . . is *identical* with the pure-sounding word in ordinary usage and conversation; the purer legitimacy, the large relationship, the constellation which receives it in verse or in artistic prose alters it to the very kernel of its nature, makes it useless, unfit for mere intercourse, inviolable and lasting'. George lacked the sensibility to write like this; but he must be given credit for his insight.

His best will emerge more clearly when more critics are willing to examine his work in the light of his homosexual state of mind, and consequently to locate those moments when his landscapes most faithfully reflect his despair. His image was that of a poet-priest, a master who read his poems by candlelight in darkened rooms; but the real George is a man in love with men-in-his-own-image—and afraid of the consequences. He introduced new poetic methods into Germany; but his own answer to the 'crisis of speech' was negative. (The fullest translated selections from George are in *Poems*, tr. C. N. Valhope and E. Morwitz, 1944; *More Poems*, tr. C. F. McIntyre, 1945; and *The Works of Stefan George*, tr. E. Morwitz and O. Marx, 1949. See also PI, TCG, TCGV, PGV, CGP, CGPD.)

Most of George's disciples were talented cranks; others were brilliant but not creative. The chief exceptions were Borchardt, Wolfskehl and Schaeffer. Not one of them was wholly committed to George.

The most interesting of the three was KARL WOLFSKEHL (1869–1948), born at Darmstadt, who was Jewish. He died in New Zealand, where he found refuge from the Nazis. His was a less doctrinaire, more attractive and friendly personality than that of George. Author of dramas and epics as well as poems (in freer forms than those of George), Wolfskehl is most likely to survive in his posthumous collection of letters from New Zealand, *Ten Year Exile: Letters from New Zealand 1938–1948* (*Zehn Jahre Exil: Briefe aus Neu Seeland*, 1959). These are warm, intelligent and generous; above all, they demonstrate the predicament of a German Jew who had lost a Germany in which he was once at home (MGP).

RUDOLF BORCHARDT (1877–1945), another Jew (he fled to Italy before 1933) was independent-minded, erudite and almost self-destructively eccentric. He was predominantly a critic, but some of his poetry—if not his translated epics in his own brand of Middle High German—is due for re-examination. He also wrote a number of short stories, novels, and a play. Borchardt is almost impossibly ponderous; but his intentions may be compared to those of Doughty (attempts to revivify the present language by use of the archaic), Pound ('creative' translation) and, less happily, Swinburne. His brilliance finds it difficult to struggle free of his laboured style, but it is interesting trying to rescue it.

ALBRECHT SCHAEFFER (1885–1950) came from West Prussia. He, too, left Germany on account of the Nazis: he lived in the U.S.A., and died in the year of his return to Germany. He was poet, critic, dramatist and essayist; but his best work is in his fiction. His first mentor was George, and it was under George's influence that he formulated his lifelong view of the world as 'Spirit', whose medium is the poet. None of this is of account, nor are Schaeffer's 'lyrical epics'; but his short fiction, in which his intellectual preoccupations are sometimes swallowed up by other and more pressing concerns, is more substantial. He dealt with prostitution in *Elli, or the Seven Steps* (*Elli oder Sieben Treppen*, 1920) and incest in *The Lattice* (*Das Gitter*, 1923). In the first of these he satirized both Wolfskehl and the cult of George.

A writer who had contact, but no more, with Stefan George, as well as with Dehmel (q.v.), was MAX[IMILIAN] DAUTHENDEY (1867–1918), born in Bavaria of a Russian mother and a German father of French ancestry. He was painter, novelist, short-story writer, dramatist, and, above all, poet. As a painter he was, like the contemporary Englishman Charles Tomlinson (q.v.), frustrated; his poems, often captivatingly, try to paint impossible pictures. Doubtless he formed his passion for colour when serving a seven years' apprenticeship in his father's black-and-white photography business. He gained some success as a novelist (for which he was denounced by George, who regarded the novel as mere reportage), but his poetry remained little read until after his death. For Dauthendey nature is suffused with living atoms: stones and mountains have feelings. Life is tragic, but must be lived as a sensitive orgy. His position resembles that of Edith Sitwell (q.v.), another gifted but dead-end experimenter with synaesthesia (the concurrent use of several senses or types of sensation; or the description of one sensory experience in terms of another: air sings, taste sounds, sounds or colours taste, and so on). Dauthendey spent his last years in the Far East, where he wrote two volumes of markedly German 'oriental' short stories, full of transcendent sexuality. He also wrote travel books and humour in the vein of Wilhelm Busch (q.v.).

The Viennese HUGO VON HOFMANNSTHAL (1874–1929), who had Jewish and Italian blood, is one of the most astonishing poets of the turn of the century. If the humourless George is representative of a certain morbid and proselytizing streak in the German temperament, then Hofmannsthal, altogether more attractive, represents the best of Vienna in its palmy days—before the collapse of the Austro-Hungarian empire in 1918. All his writing could be said to be about this heady disintegration and collapse. Taken up by George when a precocious and attractive young poet, he was rejected when he gained success through drama. Yet the young poet Hofmannsthal had something in common with George: poetry is the language of inner life; the words it employs must *belong* to the inner life; each prose word has a poetic 'brother-word': itself, used in a different, purer, truer sense. But the theorizing was an afterthought: the young poet was in the throes of creation. Hofmannsthal was a creative and critical genius: what happened to him, and his account of it, is of immense importance for a fuller understanding of what the term 'modern' in literature means.

The boy Hofmannsthal, almost as precocious as Rimbaud, began by writing lyrical poetry of an exquisite quality; in those few years, his confidence was unbounded. He was 'anti-naturalistic', because naturalism, as he saw it, tried to expunge or at best distort the mystery of life; but his poetry transcends theory. Two examples will demonstrate his lyrical mastery. The first, 'The Two' (*Die Beiden*), is a love poem, a perfect expression of the violence that lurks behind tenderness and passion:

> Like the full wine-cup in her hand
> Her smiling mouth was round;
> Her steadfast tread was light and sure,
> No drop spilled on the ground.
>
> The horse that carried him was young;
> As firm as hers the hand
> That with a careless movement made
> His horse beside her stand.
>
> But when he reached to take the cup,
> Their fingers trembled so,
> They saw between them on the ground
> The red wine darkly flow.
>
> (*tr. James Reeves*)

This is effective on a purely realistic level. It also expresses the inevitably brutal side of love: the spilt wine represents (i) the spilt blood of virginity, (ii) the 'wounds' of that discord which romantic love precedes, and (iii) lust's waste of 'holiness'; the communion wine, Christ's blood, flowing on the ground (Hofmannsthal began and ended as a Roman Catholic).

The other poem, 'Ballad of External Life' ('Ballade des äusseren Lebens') may be (and has been) too easily misunderstood as wholly pessimistic:

And children grown up with deep eyes that know of nothing, grow up and die, and all men go their ways.

And sweet fruits grow from the bitter ones and drop down at night like dead birds and lie there a few days and rot.

548

And always the wind blows, and again and again we hear and speak many words and feel the joy and weariness of our limbs.

And streets run through the grass, and places are here and there, full of torches, trees, ponds, and threatening and deadly withered . . .

Why were these constructed? and never resemble one another? and are innumerable? Why do life, weeping, and death alternate?

What does all this profit us and these games, we who are grown up and eternally alone and wandering never seek any goal?

What does it profit to have seen many such things? And yet he says much who says 'evening', a word from which profound meaning and sadness run

like thick honey from hollow honeycombs.

(TCG)

The critic who has stated that here Hofmannsthal 'reflects the emptiness of human existence' and 'has . . . no answer to all his questionings' has not considered the Platonic world that almost gaily haunts this vision of despair. This functions as what we call 'beauty'—a 'beautiful' melancholy—and as the poet's own sheer energy: his joy in extracting the non-materialistic truth from the gloomy life-situation. As a critic has pointed out, while the poem does say that 'Outer life is futile', 'this outer life as reflected in poetry is "much" ' ['he says much who says "evening" ']: 'the reader should remind himself that, according to Hofmannsthal, words used referentially [i.e. in an 'everyday' way: to 'get' things: for materialistic, and finally futile purposes] must be distinguished fundamentally from the same words used poetically'. His poem 'can be called dreary and decadent only if the words that compose it are understood as being carriers of a life content'.

Hofmannsthal's score or so of youthful lyrical poems, cast in traditional forms, adumbrate his later, tragic predicament. Hofmannsthal is a poet of 'the romantic agony', who sees the lover, the lunatic and the poet as intuitive, helpless, passive possessors of the secret of a lost and yet, paradoxically, attainable world: the Platonic realm of perfection, of which this world is but an imperfect and distorted copy.

However, Hofmannsthal—increasingly erudite, a student of cultures foreign to him—had a tough streak of intellectual scepticism: very early he condemned the aesthete (an aspect of himself) as a dreamer who must die without ever having lived. And in the poems, incomparably the best things he ever did, he continually hints at the necessity for 'engagement' (but not political), for life —for the very thing that the autocratic George guarded himself against. He was, as he put it in the prologue to one of his short plays: 'Full of precocious wisdom, early doubt, / And yet with a deep, questioning longing'.

Hofmannsthal's poetry depicted a precious unity (implied partly in the wholeness of the poem itself), precarious because—like the faith of ages, like the Austro-Hungarian Empire, like European culture, like the poet's own inspiration—threatened with final disintegration. This explains the baroque element in Hofmannsthal: he was fascinated by the sugary putrescence of the expiring body, as his librettos for the lush Richard Strauss show; this led him to an admiration for the 'decadent', and for such comparatively inferior writers as Swinburne (q.v.), a delirious and metrically gifted but ultimately superficial poet. Little of this rococo extravagance leaked into his lyric poetry.

Why did Hofmannsthal abandon lyrical poetry? He answers himself in one of the most prophetic of modern literary documents: *The Letter of Lord Chandos to Francis Bacon* (*Ein Brief des Lord Chandos an Francis Bacon*, 1902; tr. M. Hottinger and T. and J. Stern in *Selected Prose*, 1952).

The 'Chandos letter', as it is usually called, is an expression of a personal psychological crisis; it was also prophetic of an international cultural cataclysm. In it Hofmannsthal takes on the *persona* of a fictitious Elizabethan, a 'younger son of the Earl of Bath', who writes to Bacon to apologize for (and in a sense justify) his 'complete abandonment of literary activity'. In a sense Hofmannsthal solves his problem. But the solution is temporary. The crisis here related was repeated every time Hofmannsthal attempted a creative work (i.e. perpetually); it was seldom resolved. The subject of the letter is really that *Sprachkrise* of which George was aware but with which he failed to deal.

Suddenly, for Hofmannsthal, the world appeared as without meaning or coherence; he lost his faith in the customary modes of thought. As a consequence language itself, and his faith in it, failed: 'Words fell to pieces in my mouth like mouldy mushrooms'. Chandos-Hofmannsthal is 'forced to see everything . . . in uncanny close-up'; he can no longer approach men or their actions 'with the simplifying eye of custom and habit'. In other words, *scepticism* and *curiosity*—those qualities so dangerous to Catholicism, and for so long resisted by it—have entered into his soul. Words 'turn and twist unceasingly', and at the end they reveal 'only emptiness'. There can be no more lyrical poetry because the author has lost confidence in the magic of words; the successful young poet had maintained the tension between love of death and resistance of it, between a cynical, sceptical solipsism and an outward-looking love. Such maintenances are little short of miraculous.

In such early playlets as *Death and the Fool* (*Der Tor und der Tod*, 1893; tr. J. Heard, 1913–15; E. Walter, 1914; *The Fool and Death*, H. E. Mierow, 1930; and in M. Hamburger, *Poems and Verse Plays*, 1961), as well as in the poems, the urge to create takes precedence over intellectual anxieties. The protagonist of *Death and the Fool* is Claudio, an aesthete—cynical, impressionist (everything, for him, 'passes'), sexually selfish—who is confronted by death in the guise of an elegant violinist. Certainly, the play may be said to have a 'moral': the young nobleman, named after the condemned man in *Measure for Measure* who is not ready for death, finally discovers, to his horror, that he has not lived. But *Death and the Fool* is not an 'explicit . . . warning against aestheticism', although it has been described as such: there is too much vitality in Claudio's monologue, too much ambiguity of approach. What still fascinates Hofmannsthal—although he clearly sees the sterility of his hero's life—is decadence, the mystery of death, the denial of conventional morality.

Michael Hamburger has implied that Hofmannsthal's work did not lose power: that he 'reversed' the well-established German process of turning from prose to (over-dignified) verse, and moved from the lyrical dramas of his youth to 'the poetic prose' of his 'last and greatest tragedy, *Der Turm*; a prose both highly colloquial and condensed'. (Another critic describes it as 'creeping'.) Hofmannsthal did remain intelligent and aware; but the large-scaled *Der Turm* does not equal, let alone develop from, his early lyrics. . . . Even if the 'greatness' of his latter years was more intellectually viable and less empty than that of, say, Hauptmann—still, he had, in his way, been forced to abdicate as poet. This is not discreditable: many poets have refused to abdicate. . . .

We may trace through Hofmannsthal's dramas the fate of his desperate attempt to preserve and reinvigorate the traditions of the nineteenth century. After 1902 he was essentially a progressive conservative (never a reactionary). He shunned expressionist techniques, and cultivated a symbolist realism which he regarded as 'conservatively revolutionary'. He tried in a public capacity to preserve European culture (he founded, with Max Reinhardt, the Salzburg Festival). His comments on individual writers were penetrating, but his programmatic criticism is rightly described as 'cloudily ineffectual'. Hofmannsthal remained true to himself: a 'modern', an expressionist or surrealist Hofmannsthal would have been wholly factitious. But most of his later work, udged in the light of the earliest, lacks, for all its admirable qualities, inner strength, originality and conviction of language. Hofmannsthal was a traditionalist, but one who saw into the abyss, that 'emptiness' or 'void' of which he had written in 1902. It is ironic, to say the least, that he had to pay such a price for his sensitivity, intelligence and social conscientiousness. His youthful phase he called a 'pre-existence'.

After 1902, creatively 'blocked', he began to adapt and recast plays of the past (he had done this before, but in a different spirit, with Euripides' *Alcestis*, 1893): *Electra* (*Elektra*, 1903; tr. in T. H. Dickinson, *Chief Contemporary Dramatists*, 1930; M. Hamburger, *Selected Plays and Libretti*, 1964), *Oedipus and the Sphinx* (*Oedipus und die Sphinx*, 1905), three of Molière's plays, *The Play of Everyman* (*Jedermann*, 1911; tr. G. Sterling and R. Ordynski, 1917). This last was highly successful. For his final play, *The Tower* (*Der Turm*, 1925, rev. 1927; tr. M. Hamburger, *Selected Plays and Libretti*, 1964), he drew on Calderon's *Life is a Dream* (*La Vida es Sueño*): a prince is imprisoned in a tower by his father, who fears that he will supersede him before the time falls due. Sigismund, the prince, represents the spiritual authority by which a country needs (Hofmannsthal implies) to be ruled; he becomes the leader of a non-Marxist proletarian revolution, but is poisoned by the proto-Fascist Olivier. In the 1925 version his deathbed is visited by an orphan who pledges to carry on his peaceful and purifying work. But in 1927 there is only Sigismund's last despairing remark: 'Witness that I was here, though none has recognized me'. Soon afterwards Hofmannsthal, shattered by his son's suicide, died.

In *The Tale of 672. Night* (*Das Märchen der 672. Nacht*, 1904), a novella, Hofmannsthal tried to do justice to the theme of *Death and the Fool*. A late, and posthumously published, fragment—begun, however, before 1914—was yet another attempt to solve the problem of 'aesthetic sterility': *Andreas, or the United Ones* (*Andreas, oder Die Vereinigten*, 1930; tr. M. Hottinger, 1936) deals with temptation in Venice (like Mann's *Death in Venice*, q.v.); the hero has, significantly, almost the same name as that of the seventeen-year-old Hofmannsthal's first play, *Yesterday* (*Gestern*, 1891). But none of his late fiction equals his few 'pre-Chandos' short stories, notably 'Cavalry Patrol' ('Reitergeschichte', 1899). There was cruel justice in Hermann Bahr's (q.v.) remarks that 'I cannot forgive him for not having died at twenty [twenty-eight would have been nearer the mark]; if he had, he would have been the most beautiful figure in world literature', and that he had mistaken, in Hofmannsthal, 'the smiling death of Austria for a holy spring tide'.

RAINER MARIA RILKE (1875–1926), christened René, was born in Prague, of German descent, and Austrian nationality; in 1918 he found himself a Czech. His story of an aristocratic ancestry may have been invented: actually Rilke was descended from Sudeten tradesmen and peasants, and received a middle-class upbringing ordinary in everything save his peculiar mother, who pretended until he was five that he was a girl called Sophie, with long hair and dolls. Rilke was one of this century's great originals, and for this reason it would be misleading to call him an 'expressionist': he incorporated what expressionism stood for in his work, but much more as well. He was not associated with the expressionist or with any other movement. The crisis he suffered before the First World War, out of which the *Duino Elegies* came, coincided with the expressionist movement. (All Rilke's important poetry has been tr., some many times, into English, most devotedly but not always successfully by J. B. Leishman, who sentimentally lamented Rilke's fundamental hatred of Christianity. The best complete tr. of his masterpiece, *The Duinese Elegies*, *Duineser Elegien*, 1912–22, is by Ruth Spiers: this has not yet been published in book form owing to copyright difficulties. *Duino Elegies*, tr. J. B. Leishman and S. Spender, 1939; *Poems 1906–1926*, tr. J. B. Leishman, 1959; *New Poems*, *Neue Gedichte*, 1907, 1908, tr. J. B. Leishman, 1964; *Sonnets to Orpheus*, *Sonette an Orpheus*, 1923, tr. J. B. Leishman, 1936; *The Book of Hours*, *Das Stundenbuch*, 1905, tr. A. L. Peck, 1961; *Poems from The Book of Hours*, tr. sel. Babette Deutsch; *Selected Letters*, tr. R. F. C. Hull, 1946. See also MEP, PGV, CGP, CGPD, MGP, TCG, TCGV, PI.)

Rilke wrote poetry in Italian, French and Russian, as well as German; he also wrote fiction and drama (between 1895 and 1901). (His early autobiographical novel, *Ewald Tragy*, c. 1898, published in German, 1944, has not been tr.; but *The Notebook of Malte Laurids Brigge*, *Die Aufzeichnungen des Malte Laurids Brigge*, 1910, tr. J. Linton, 1930, and the earlier *The Tale of the Love and Death of Cornet Christopher Rilke*, *Die Weise von Liebe und Tod des Cornets Christoph Rilke*, 1906, tr. M. D. Herter Norton, 1932, are available.)

Rilke, who rightly called himself 'a bungler of life', tried to behave responsibly, but remained in certain respects innocent, childlike—and selfish. He was, if it were an adequate term (which it is not), a 'womanizer'. His being was dedicated to his poetry; essentially the facts of his life interested him only inasmuch as they affected this. The Russian-born German novelist and critic LOU ANDREAS-SALOMÉ (1861–1937), to whom Nietzsche had proposed and who was later to become a valued associate of Freud, became his mistress when he was twenty-two, and throughout his life he turned to her as a confessor and (almost) a muse. 'She moves fearlessly midst the most burning mysteries', he wrote, 'which do nothing to her. . . .' But he could not live even with her, and their physical relationship ended when he married the sculptress Clara Westhoff in 1901. However, he could not live with Clara either, and before long he was alone in Paris. Until his death he pursued a number of relationships with women younger than himself; these always stopped short, not of sexual contact, but of permanent domestic cohabitation, which he would not endure.

Once in Paris, Rilke became secretary to the sculptor Rodin. He had had important enthusiasms before: Italy (where he met Stefan George, whom he continued to admire); the Danish novelist Jens Per Jacobsen (1847–85), a sensuous realist who made an ideal of flawless work (as distinct from life) and who celebrated an autonomous nature; Russia; monkhood; and then the painters' community near Bremen to which his wife belonged. But this new admiration was the most intense of all: Rodin, like Rilke himself, insulated his work from 'ordinary life'; it was (Rilke said) 'isolated from the spectator as though by a non-conducting vacuum'. Rilke told his wife in 1902, possibly tactlessly, that Rodin had told him that he had married 'parce qu'il faut avoir une femme': another bond between them. He had chosen not bourgeois—or even bohemian—happiness, but art. 'Rodin has lived nothing that is not in his work.' However, Rodin overworked him, and he left his household abruptly; but later there was a reconciliation.

Rilke's first notable poetic work was *The Book of Hours*, divided into 'The Book of Monkish Life', 'The Book of Pilgrimage' and 'The Book of Poverty and Death'. He called these poems 'prayers'; but the God he invokes in them is not God the Creator—or any Christian God. Rilke consistently maintained his animosity to all forms of Christianity, and to Jesus Christ in particular, all his life; on his death-bed he refused to see a priest. His God has 'no use for the Christians': he is a figure existing only in the future, utterly meaningless, in fact non-existent, without humanity, and above all *living truly*: he is a partly Nietzschean God who will be perfected by artists, and of course in particular by Rilke himself.

The later Rilke may be discerned in some of the poems in *The Book of Hours*, but in general fluency, in the form of technique, takes over and submerges the sense. The author is still a thoroughgoing romantic.

It was in some of the *New Poems* published in 1907 and 1908 that Rilke first succeeded in translating external phenomena into 'inwardness'. Since at least 1899 it had been his ambition to express the 'thingness of things' by understanding their spirit and then expressing this in new forms of words: to destroy the killing material necessity of making *definitions*. It is significant that at about this time Hofmannsthal, in 'Chandos', was worrying about exactly the same problem: how can we be sure, he asked, what the word 'apple' really 'means'? It means one thing to one person in one context, and so on. . . . Rilke distrusted language, too; but eventually, unlike Hofmannsthal, he found confidence in himself as a worthy sounding-board for nature. Hofmannsthal declined material irresponsibility: he felt impelled to care for the future, to be a guardian of what was best in the tradition; to found a Salzburg Festival. Rilke, seeing with cruel shrewdness that 'ordinary life', political or merely humanitarian activism, required *definitions*, over-simplifications, rejected that kind of life: he deliberately cultivated what he called 'the child's wise incapacity to understand'.

The very first of the so-called *New Poems* to be written, in the winter of 1902–3, was the famous 'Panther', which he saw in the Jardin des Plantes in Paris. This poem, whose method Rilke was not to adopt fully until about 1906, is self-descriptive, but only by dint of extreme concentration upon the object itself.

> His gaze those bars keep passing is so misted
> with tiredness, it can take in nothing more.
> He feels as though a thousand bars existed,
> and no more world beyond them than before.
>
> Those supply-powerful paddings, turning there
> in tiniest of circles, well might be
> the dance of forces round a centre where
> some mighty will stands paralyticly.
>
> Just now and then the pupil's noiseless shutter
> is lifted.—Then an image will indart,
> down through the limbs' intensive stillness flutter,
> and end its being in the heart.
>
> (tr. J. B. Leishman)

This deals, despairingly, with the poet's own problem of 'images': the panther, imprisoned by bars, lives in a world of bars. His will, and his enormous energy, are stupefied. He does sometimes experience a picture, an image, of the real world beyond the bars; but this is then 'killed' by his trapped, disappointed and frustrated heart. Rilke had written in an earlier poem: 'You are murdering what you define, what *I* love to hear singing'. The bars stand for both the habit of constricting reality by defining it, and the materialism that leads to this habit; thus truth 'ends its being in the heart'. Almost a quarter of a century after writing this, Rilke said in a letter: 'A house, in the American sense, an American apple or one of the vines of that country has *nothing* in common with the house, the fruit, the grape into which have entered the hope and meditation of our forefathers. The lived and living things, the things that share our thought, these are on the decline and can no more be replaced. *We are perhaps the last to have known such things'*. Rilke always had a true love for things—the objects, persons, situations of his poems; and 'The Panther' was his first poem to success-fully express the anguished discrepancy that he felt between his inner vision and the destructive external world.

But the *New Poems* were also influenced by the formal, anti-romantic elegance and concentration achieved by such French poets as Verlaine and Mallarmé as well as by Stefan George and Hofmannsthal: his interest in Parnassian poetry helped Rilke to struggle against the fluency that, because it becomes so facile, spoils *The Book of Hours*. These new poems may be seen as a reconciliation of the aims of different schools: of the 'romantic', with its insistence on the importance of the poet, with the more 'classical' views of poets such as Mallarmé, who wished to achieve an autonomous poetry that was divorced from the life of the poet; a reconciliation, indeed, of feeling and thought.

It was by submitting himself to the strict discipline necessary for the com-position of the *New Poems* that Rilke was later able to complete *The Duinese Elegies* and their successors, *Sonnets to Orpheus*. But before he could write this last work he endured a mental and physical crisis, during which he questioned the value of poetry itself. It is because Rilke fought to dedicate himself to poetry, because he so fiercely questioned the validity of what he had chosen to do with his life—to absorb it into art—that we cannot call him a facile or superficial devotee of 'art for art's sake'. 'Art', he said in the years immediately before the writing of the first elegies, 'is superfluous. . . . Can art heal wounds, can it take away the bitterness of death?' And he would have liked, he said, to be a country doctor. Yet he miserably and increasingly succumbed to erotic temptation—temptation because in every case he reached a point at which he felt that he had to dissociate himself, thus causing unhappinesses which deeply distressed him. He could not resist sex, although he desired to; but he could not accept its human consequences. He went some way towards resolving this dilemma in his poetry, which is more than most of his kind can do, and he thus gave a valuable account of the manner in which the creative imagination threatens personal virtue. Whether that account is worth his transgression of virtue (by causing unhappiness) is an unanswered question—but one he never hesitated fearlessly to ask himself. The main theme of *The Duinese Elegies* is 'the virtually anti-human or extra-human lot of the poet' (Eudo C. Mason).

Rilke's crisis was partly precipitated by the writing, in Paris, of *The Notebook of Malte Laurids Brigge* (begun in 1904). This consists of a series of notebook-jottings by a Danish poet who has come to Paris. It has been said that Malte 'was' Rilke, but Rilke denied it. Of course he was not Rilke: no fictional character can 'be' a real one, whether this is intended or not. Malte was, however, a picture of the 'human' Rilke: a mixture of the man as he was in his 'non-poetic' existence, the man he wished to be, and the man of whose life and death (Malte perishes in a terrible unspecified way) he was mortally afraid. The story is of one who has, like the prodigal son, fled from love—

as Rilke always did when it seemed that he might be caught and trapped by it. Malte was made Danish both because Rilke could thus distance himself from him, and because the writings of J. P. Jacobsen (q.v.), particularly the reminiscences of childhood in *Niels Lyhne* (1880; tr. H. Astrup-Larsen, 1919), and other Scandinavian writers such as Herman Bang (q.v.), had always excited and moved him. The re-creation of Malte's childhood is based on an idealization of Rilke's own childhood (Malte is, of course, of aristocratic descent) and on his thrilled response to Jacobsen, from whom he also took over and developed the notion of 'authentic death' (*der eigene Tod*): a dignified, profoundly sceptical and anti-Christian desire to accept death as a part of life. (Sartre, q.v., spoke, in his moving obituary of Camus, q.v., of the 'pure . . . endeavour of a man to recover each instant of his existence from his future death'.) Malte's city is a nightmare; his contact with urban life is continuously horrifying.

It is often suggested, especially by those who wish to claim Rilke as a potential Christian, that this novel is representative of a cult of decadence and 'disease' found in the work of Maeterlinck and Verhaeren (qq.v.). Rilke read both these poets, but the judgement is altogether misleading. For *Malte* may fairly be looked upon as both a negation and a culmination of the *Künstlerroman* (q.v.): the artist's true education is death: 'everyone carries within him', he wrote, 'his own death'.

Rilke, then, underwent the most serious crisis of his life in these years of the composition of *Malte*: his faith in language, in his own capacity to achieve a dedicated poetic life, in art itself, was threatened. He solved—or partially solved—the problem, which had affected his delicate health, by the sporadic achievement of a trance-like state in which he was able to write poetry. In May 1911 he wrote to his rich, intelligent friend and patron Princess Marie von Thurn und Taxis-Hohenlohe: '. . . this long drought is gradually reducing my soul to starvation . . . . as if I had completely lost the ability to bring about the conditions that might help me . . .'. The Princess invited him to her castle at Duino, on the Adriatic coast, and after Christmas left him there alone. In a letter to Lou Andreas-Salomé, to whom he nearly always addressed himself in moments of crisis, he pointed out that psychoanalysis 'was too fundamental a help' for him: he did not want to be 'cleared up'. And he spoke of his life as 'a long convalescence'. A few days later, in another letter to Lou, he astonishingly diagnosed the 'inward' aspect of the disease (leukaemia) that was to kill him in fourteen years' time: 'It may be that the continual distraughtness in which I live has bodily causes in part, is a thinness of the blood'. This indeed is an apt characterization of Rilke the human being. He has been called 'cold'; but that epithet does not accurately describe him. His poetry is anything but cold. However, his relationships can legitimately be called 'thin-blooded', and with just the sinister overtone that our retrospective knowledge of his death adds to the passage in the letter: Rilke was well aware of how sinister poetry itself was. But now in the castle at Duino he waited for his anguish to awaken his creative powers in the dangerous process he called 'reversal', in which he received his poetry almost, as it were, by dictation. One day he did 'hear' a voice calling the words with which the first elegy begins: 'Who, if I shrieked out in pain, would hear me from amongst / The orders of angels?' He wrote the whole of the first two elegies; then, in three short spells—oases in a decade of silence—he wrote three more. The rest were written in early 1922.

Rilke has frequently and wrongly been approached as a thinker or philosopher rather than as the poet he was. His poems must be read as accounts of the destiny of a dedicated poet tormented by the need for religious certainties in a godless universe. Rilke's angels represent many things, but chiefly the terrible and beautiful heart of a universe that can offer no hope of immortality. They are neither Christian nor 'real'. To call them symbols, however, is to over-simplify. They are poetic destiny, hard truth, apostles of 'inwardness': whereas ordinary perception simply sees, the poet, in Rilke's term, 'in-sees': discerns the *thingness* of things. Again, these angels call upon the amorous poet to put aside his sexual curiosity. In his life Rilke was morally humiliated, selfish and disingenuous in his tiresome search for a woman who, having been enjoyed by him, would 'withdraw': become an 'Eloisa' (i.e. Heloise). In his poetry he ceases to be disingenuous. Rilke's elegies trace the course of his engagement with his angels, from despair to rejoicing, back to despair, and finally to a kind of acceptance of himself.

The first lines of the first elegy ask the question, 'How can we endure beauty in a godless universe?':

> Who, if I shrieked out in pain, would hear me from amongst
> The orders of angels? Even if one would take me
> To his breast, I should be overwhelmed and die in his
> Stronger existence: for the beautiful is nothing
> But the first apprehension of the terrible,
> Which we can still just endure: we respect the cool scorn
> Of its refusal to destroy us. Each angel is terrible.
>
> And so I swallow down the signal-note of black sobs.
> Alas, with whom can we share our solitude?
> Not with angels and not with men; but even
> The percipient animals well understand
> That we are lost in the interpreted world.
> Perhaps there is just one tree on a hillside
> Daily to reassure, or yesterday's street,
> Or a trivial habit enduring for its own sake. . . .

For a gloss, in English poetry, on the difficulties of the phrase 'the interpreted world', one cannot do better than turn to Robert Graves's (q.v.) poem 'The Cool Web' with its evocative line, 'There's a cool web of language winds us in'.

After Rilke had finally completed all the elegies—they were at least partly delayed by erotic complications of his own making—he wrote, very rapidly, the sequence of fifty-five free sonnets called *Sonnets to Orpheus*, who is addressed as the God of poetry (and as an idealized Rilke). This is a more modest sequence than the elegies, but it in some ways equals it. It is important to recognize that Orpheus here is not the 'angel' of the elegies, but 'the exact opposite. . . . Whereas the Angel had been the apotheosis of self-sufficient Narcissism . . . Orpheus is conceived of as freely giving himself . . . to all things . . .' (Eudo C. Mason). In this sequence Rilke went a long way towards redeeming the human side of himself from the charge of coldness and remoteness; and he himself became, in his last years, more approachable.

Rilke, a pagan poet, possessed as much scope and linguistic capacity as any poet of the century. To regard him as primarily a thinker or mystic is a serious mistake; but his attitude towards death may have something to teach his readers, inasmuch as it can help them (Christian or not) to overcome the disastrous complacency of official Christianity, with its promise of an earth-like heaven. In his repudiation of bourgeois pseudo-certitude he showed much courage; as much as other more politically orientated writers who exposed other failings of the bourgeois life. Although Rilke transcends all the theoretical aspects of the modern movement, he is essential to an understanding of it.

IV

Most of the clear-cut forerunners of expressionism were dramatists. The most important was the Swedish August Strindberg (q.v.), but the others were mostly Austrians and Germans, social satirists and critics among them. Expressionism as a phenomenon in poetry and fiction is best approached via the drama, where it takes its simplest form—as the externalization of internal events. This was preceded by the deliberate depiction of unreality, or the baffling mixture of it with reality.

The most famous play of the Austrian HERMANN BAHR (1863–1934), *The Concert* (*Das Konzert*, 1909; CCD), a farce about a wife's clever plot to recover her pianist husband's errant affections by making him jealous, foreshadows expressionism in no way at all; but its author, primarily a critic and publicist but a novelist as well as dramatist (about eighty plays) and theatrical producer, eventually became a spokesman of expressionism; his book *Expressionism* (*Expressionismus*, 1914; tr. F. Henderson, 1925) was not a merely opportunistically late one.

Bahr was an intelligent although never profound man, genuinely sensitive to literary movements and to the impulses behind them. First an Ibsenian naturalist and an associate of Holz (q.v.) and his circle, he soon fell under the influence of French symbolism, and became the leading spirit (as he claimed, the founder) of the *Jungwien* (Young Viennese) group, which included Hofmannsthal and Schnitzler (qq.v.). He understood naturalism better than any of its leading proponents, and brilliantly prophesied that it would be succeeded by 'a mysticism of the nerves'. His novel *The Good School* (*Die gute Schule*, 1890), a polemic in favour of sexual experience (the 'good school' of the title), tried to put decadent 'nervousness' into effect, but is not more than a patchwork of French influences. Eventually Bahr returned to the Roman Catholic Church and to repentant championship of the baroque that he now considered to be the cradle of all Austrian genius.

PETER ALTENBERG (ps. RICHARD ENGLÄNDER, 1859–1919), who was born and died in Vienna, has been amusingly described as 'a bizarre character frequenting literary cafés' who fervently 'loved ladies noble and very ignoble'. A friend of Bahr's, Altenberg was a poseur most of whose energy went into his café life—'a presidential poet with his halo of harlots'—but his impressionistic prose sketches, when not too studied, have sharpness and charm. Hedonistic but hypochondriacal advocate of a healthy open-air life and frequent baths, Altenberg was more a man of his time than he or most of his friends realized, but his fragmented method of writing had some influence, especially in Russia —he was certainly read, for example, by Elena Guro (q.v.). There was something pathetic and insubstantial about the semi-invalid Altenberg with his insistence on physiological perfection as the basis of all other perfection and his hymns to his own health; but Hofmannsthal (q.v.) paid him just tribute when he said that his books 'were as full of dear little stories as a basket of fruit'.

The Viennese Jew ARTHUR SCHNITZLER (1862–1931), novelist and dramatist, trained as a doctor, was much influenced by Freud, with whom he conducted a correspondence from 1906. He did not begin writing creatively until his late twenties, when he began contributing to Viennese periodicals under the name of 'Anatol', the name he selected for the hero of his first series of playlets.

Schnitzler accomplished much in spite of limited technical resources. He combined an understanding love-terror of his disintegrating milieu, a Don Juanism rather resembling Rilke's (q.v.), and, most importantly, an intuition of subconscious sexual motivation. When Freud read his play *Paracelsus* (1897; tr. H. B. Samuel, 1913) he remarked that he had not thought an author could know so much. . . . He is most famous for the sexually cynical, meticulous but essentially lightweight *Merry-go-round* (*Reigen*, 1900; tr. F. and J. Marcus, 1953; filmed as *La Ronde*, 1950); but Schnitzler's best full-length play is probably *Professor Bernhardi* (1912; tr. H. Landstone, 1927; L. Borell and R. Adam, 1936). This is a subtle and objective study of the position of the Jew in pre-war Vienna. A Jewish doctor refuses a priest access to a girl who is dying of an abortion: she is in a state of euphoria, and will spend a happier last hour in ignorance of her fate. (Actually, she is informed of it by the ward-sister, so the Professor's gesture is useless.) After much unpleasant intrigue, Bernhardi goes to prison—from whence, however, he is triumphantly released when a Prince requires his services. The priest calls on Bernhardi to tell him that he has agreed with him in this case—but could not say so in public.

In *Anatol* (tr. H. Granville Barker, 1911 and 1933–4), and other plays on the autobiographical theme of philandering, Schnitzler has many keen insights into the sadistic, masochistic and other nerve-strains of romantic love, but does not always succeed in rising above his own personal difficulties. Further, his account of the love-process (his own), its rapture always declining into pathological jealousy, boredom or disgust, is too specifically decadent-Viennese: Schnitzler, whose psychiatric knowledge caused him to question the scientific efficacy of naturalism, is always the analyst of the decadent culture; but he was humanly very much of it, for all his capacity for detachment. When, as in *Playing with Love* (*Liebelei*, 1895; tr. P. M. Shand, 1914), he succeeds in presenting a woman whose substantial and wholesome emotions genuinely expose the shallowness of a philanderer, he ultimately collapses into rhetoric, facile moralization and sentimentality.

He is at his best when he avoids too much heady, decadent elegance on the one hand, and guilty morality on the other. Then he does adumbrate a non-naturalistic method of describing internal reality adequate to his needs. The interior dialogue (an early example) of the short story 'None but the Brave' ('Leutnant Gustl', 1901; tr. R. L. Simon, 1926) is less an ambitious extension of naturalism than a genuine foreshadowing of modern techniques: the human deficiencies of the horrible Leutnant as he contemplates suicide are unerringly revealed. Even subtler is the later novella, 'Fräulein Else' (1924; tr. F. H. Lyon and E. Sutton, 1930): a financier names as price for the redemption of a girl's father that she strip for him in her hotel room at midnight; she does strip, but in the lobby of the hotel—and then kills herself.

The first and best of Schnitzler's two novels, *The Road to the Open* (*Der Weg ins Freie*, 1908; tr. H. B. Samuel, 1923) portrays a vast social canvas with a success surprising to those who think of the author only as a miniaturist: once again, the author is at his best in his remarkably objective treatment of his fellow Jews.

Schnitzler is a pioneer in interior monologue and invented, out of his technical inability to create dramatic action, a new kind of 'cyclic' play. Most likely of all to survive are some dozen or more of his novellas. Ten representative ones are collected, in an excellent translation by Eric Sutton, in *Little Novels* (1929); also notable for its foreshadowings of methods to come is 'Bertha Garlan' ('Frau Bertha Garlan', 1901; tr. J. H. Wisdom and M. Murray, 1913), a meticulous tracing of different kinds of sexual processes.

The poet, novelist and playwright RICHARD BEER-HOFMANN (1866–1945), another Viennese Jew, and a close friend of Hofmannsthal (q.v.), was not as gifted as Schnitzler, though in the earlier *Jungwien* period he was more prominent. Beer-Hofmann, who was a talented theatrical producer, began as a typical neo-romantic and ended as an unequivocal upholder of the Jewish tradition. He was a more lush and flamboyant writer than Schnitzler, and had none of his consulting-room dryness—for which he substituted a lyrical, quasi-religious element. His first play was *The Count of Charolais* (*Der Graf von Charolais*, 1904; pt. tr. *This Quarter* [Paris], II, 3, 1931), an adaptation of the English Elizabethan play *The Fatal Dowry* by John Ford and Philip Massinger. This is decidedly decadent—a very proper little lady is turned into a lustful tart by a professional seducer—but naturalistic at least inasmuch as all its characters are represented as driven by an uncontrollable destiny. The most successful character is a senile judge who gives his daughter away to a 'noble' man who will presumably spare her the horrors of sex. He never completed his intended trilogy on the life of King David, but the frankly Zionist *Jacob's Dream* (*Jaakobs Traum*, 1918; tr. I. B. Wynn, 1946), the prelude, proved popular on the stage; the first and only one of the cycle itself to be completed was *Young David* (*Der junge David*, 1933). One of his poems, 'Lullaby for Miriam', written in 1898, was once famous, but has not survived the test of time. The death-ridden novel *The Death of George* (*Der Tod Georgs*, 1900), about the premature death of a gifted man and the terminal illness of an imaginary woman is as a whole oppressive and even affected; but it is not without psychological merit. The narrator, Paul, may fairly be described as a 'nerve mystic': the presentation of his state of mind is more interesting than a bald account of the plot suggests. Like his creator, Paul eventually escapes from his mystical longings into a not ignoble but unfortunately creatively sterile Jewishness.

OTTO JULIUS BIERBAUM (1865–1910) has been referred to as a 'gifted university scholar' who took 'to light literature much as a prostitute takes to her trade'; but this is to misunderstand him. He was a sort of German Alfred Jarry (q.v.) without the dedication to self-destruction. He was a co-founder of two important periodicals, *Pan* and *Die Insel*, which later became the famous publishing house Insel-Verlag. Neither his poems nor his novels have depth, because they were conceived in self-satisfaction; but his consciously Wildean flippancy, irreverence and hatred of sexual hypocrisy were genuine qualities. His cabaret verse and his initiation of the 'Literary Cabaret' movement ('Überbrettl'), conventional in form but truly gay, indirectly influenced Brecht (q.v.). His various novels are deliberately decadent fantasies after the manner of Wilde and Huysmans (qq.v.).

The poet and translator RUDOLF ALEXANDER SCHRÖDER (1878–1962), who was born in Bremen, helped Bierbaum to found *Die Insel*. Versatile and talented, he was a modest man, with, as the saying goes (creatively speaking), much to be modest about. His conservative protestantism was too rigid to allow of much originality, as may be seen in his too formal poetry, which is full of orthodoxly Christian platitudes.

He wrote a number of hymns. Much of what little creative energy he had was vitiated by his pious dogmatism; but then it might well be said that the latter was but a reflection of the former. A fine classicist, his best work is undoubtedly his translation from Greek and Latin poetry—Homer, Virgil, Horace. During the years of the Third Reich he maintained a dignified neutrality; some of his poems circulated secretly. Despite his undoubtedly blinkered vision, Schröder possessed personal nobility and courage.

The playwright FRANK WEDEKIND (1864–1918), born in Hanover but brought up in Switzerland, was a less fortuitous anticipator of expressionism and surrealism. Wedekind was successively secretary to a Danish confidence-man (whom he portrayed in *The Marquis von Keith*), circus-worker and cabaret-entertainer (he sang Überbrettl songs to his own guitar) before he took to writing plays. Cripple (he was lame) and showman (he liked to present and act in his own plays), Wedekind fought all his life against the censors; it is important to realize that he achieved his present reputation only at the end of his life. He sang many of his famous ballads at 'The Eleven Hangmen' ('Die elf Scharfrichter'), the literary cabaret in Munich. He was for most of his life regarded as a clown. It is said that even as he died (of acute appendicitis) he sang his own song 'Search fearlessly for every sin/For out of sin comes joy. . . .' And he himself was surely, in some way, author of the final hilarious scene: the speaker of the graveside eulogy read from his paper: 'Frank Wedekind, we loved you. Your spirit is with us. Here falter, tears. . . .'

It is sometimes said that Wedekind is a 'naturalist-expressionist'. But although his plays incorporate some realism, his main impulse, besides gaiety (that should not be forgotten, and only will be in petit-bourgeois disgust), is indignation rather than a sense of an inexorable fate. Wedekind was a solitary figure, best regarded—as has been suggested—as a bridge between the *Sturm und Drang* period (the 'Storm and Stress' movement of the German 1770s, characterized by a reaction against reason, and by reliance upon inspiration), particularly its doomed prodigy, the brilliantly gifted dramatist Georg Büchner (1813–37), and expressionism.

Wedekind's first important play *Spring's Awakening* (*Frühlings Erwachen*, 1891; FTS) is his most lyrical and human. Hideous adults—caricature schoolmasters and 'respectable' parents, all representative of the tyrannical and repressive father—penalize and attempt to destroy adolescents who have discovered the powers of sex. A boy impregnates a girl, who dies of the abortion her parents force upon her. He, expelled from school, is tempted to commit suicide by the ghost of a fellow-pupil (carrying his head under his arm) who has shot himself for failing an examination; but he is saved from this by a moralist in evening dress (Wedekind). The mechanisms of the adults' anti-human behaviour are brilliantly revealed; and there is more feeling in the depiction of the young people than Wedekind ever again displayed.

Earth Spirit and its sequel *Pandora's Box* (*Der Erdgeist*, 1895; *Die Büchse der Pandora*, 1904; FTS) combine social satire with a morbid but always energetic dissection of femininity. Alban Berg made his unfinished opera, *Lulu*, out of them. Wedekind wrote the play as one whole, but was forced by censorship troubles to divide it. *Lulu* certainly had some effect on Brecht. The stage is peopled by crooks, whores and perverts; their centre is the destructive Lulu, whom Wedekind regarded as the archetypal woman. But he had two sides to him: the moralist-prophet of the joys of sex; and a more personal fear of women, perhaps originally connected with his deformity. In the final scene Lulu is murdered by Jack the Ripper. We see an aspect of Wedekind himself in the role of Lulu's discoverer, Dr. Schön (Dr. Beautiful), an absolute hedonist. He is destroyed by Lulu, since he understands her and is therefore a hindrance to her own total triumph. Clearly Wedekind feared the consequences of his own view of life. He was not a profound thinker, but his work reflects admirably the beginnings of our nerve-shot age. He picked up much of his attitude towards women from Strindberg (q.v.), whose second wife was for a time his mistress.

The Marquis von Keith (1901; FMR 2) celebrates a confidence-trickster: cynical, it is also gay. *Such is Life* (*König Nicolo oder So ist das Leben*, 1902; tr. F. J. Ziegler, 1916) is one of Wedekind's most interesting plays, and his most lucid spiritual autobiography. A king (Wedekind, the artist) is dethroned by a butcher (the common herd). He takes on various humiliating jobs, and finally becomes an actor. The butcher-king is entertained (like the herd) by his acting, and offers to make him court jester (Wedekind as clown entertaining the bourgeois). He dies, and is buried in the royal tomb. This perfectly embodies Wedekind's view of himself as tragic and trapped clown.

Wedekind also wrote some notable short stories in the Nineties, of which 'The Fire of Egliswyl' (in *Fireworks, Feuerwerk*, 1905) is the most outstanding. A promiscuous village boy falls in love with a frigid servant-girl; when at last he climbs into her bedroom he finds that her coldness and that of the weather, combined, have made him impotent. He then sets fire to all the houses in which his previous victims live, and returns triumphantly to his servant-girl. But she, cheated of her own satisfaction, denounces him. In another delightful tale a husband calls on a friend. This friend has his wife in bed with him. He covers her face, thus exposing her body: the husband, not recognizing her, congratulates him on his good taste.

Another important pre-expressionist was CARL STERNHEIM (1878–1942). The son of a Jewish banker, Sternheim was born in Leipzig, but spent the latter part of his life in Brussels. His third wife was Wedekind's daughter, Pamela.

Sternheim, who was prey to increasing depression and restlessness, is one of the few successful twentieth-century German comic playwrights; his humour is savage, stemming from his Jewishness and consequent sense of belonging to an isolated minority, and it lacks Wedekind's sexual morbidity. He was the creator, in his dialogue, of what is often called a 'telegraphic style': a parodically staccato series of epigrammatic exchanges which at least hint at the 'alienation effect' (q.v.) later to be created by Brecht. His best plays move very fast, and their characters are clearly conceived of as 'stage people'. Sternheim punished the bourgeois, in fact, by exploiting an exaggeration of their own clipped speech—a speech-style in which, as Walter Sokel has said, 'they aped the Prussian ruling caste'.

Sternheim's most famous work is the eleven-play collection *From the Heroic Life of the Bourgeoisie* (published 1922); the best are the first two of a trilogy consisting of *The Knickers, A Place in the World* and *1913* (*Die Hose*, 1911; MT6; *Der Snob*, 1913; tr. B. Clark and W. Katzin in *Eight European Plays*, 1927; *1913*, 1914), and *Bürger Schippel* (1913), which the Hungarian composer Ernst von Dohnanyi turned into an opera.

The trilogy tells the story of the Maske family. *The Knickers* begins with

Theobald Maske, a Prussian petty official, beating his wife for threatening his position: watching the passing of the Kaiser in the Zoological Gardens, her knickers have fallen to her ankles and halted the royal progress. . . . In fact, the mishap has attracted two male witnesses of it to apply for lodgings in Maske's house: a pseudo-romantic poet and an awkwardly sentimental, Wagnerite barber. The young wife, a sentimental dreamer, imagines herself in love with the poet—but he, like her, is a day-dreamer, and at the crucial point he chooses to lock himself up and write bad verse rather than seduce her. The barber, when given his chance, prefers a night in his own bed. Meanwhile Theobald has been overcharging these two lovers for their rooms, and generally exploiting them. Here, with suitable irony, we see the ignorant bourgeois as the invincible superman—the poet, Scarron, is no match for him—and trickster. The next two plays trace the vicious history of the Maskes' son, Christian. Sternheim's attitude is ambiguous, for while he reveals the Maskes and his other bourgeois characters as absurd, he nevertheless presents them as heroes: because they ruthlessly exploit society, they are more admirable than the people they crush and trick. Sternheim hates and intellectually despises them; but there is an element of admiration in his attitude. This stems from his essentially cynical view of society: everyone wants only to achieve respectability, as the comedy *Bürger Schippel* demonstrates.

Sternheim's plays (with some unimportant exceptions) are mainly satirical: he does not examine or scrutinize his ambiguously vitalist attitudes towards basic drives. They resemble Wedekind's in that the characters are dehumanized, stripped of such characteristics as might soften the harsh outlines of their biologically predetermined ambitiousness; this was the foot, so to speak, that Sternheim had in naturalism, and it prevented him from ever becoming a fully-fledged expressionist. In his unduly neglected fiction Sternheim made more effort to express and examine the consequences of his pessimistic view of human nature. There was, after all, a frustrated man of warmth—if not a lyricist—in Sternheim: he had wanted to be the German Molière, but failed because of his flat, cold characters. Some of his best stories are collected in *Annals of the Origin of the Twentieth Century* (*Chronik von des zwanzigsten Jahrhunderts Beginn*, 1918). Several are ironic parables, like Wedekind's *Such is Life*, of the artist's plight. In 'Schuhlin the Musician' ('Schuhlin', 1913; tr. in R. Eaton, *Best Continental Stories of 1927*, 1928) the eponymous hero lives off a rich pupil and his wife, whose whole lives are devoted only to serving him. The chef of 'Napoleon' (1915), clearly a representation of the artist, achieves understanding of (and conceives scorn for) society by learning how to provide them with superior food. The comparison of the writer with the chef was prophetic. Sternheim's highly concentrated and fragmentary methods of prose technique (he wrote it out 'ordinarily' and then 'treated' it) were carried to their logical fulfilment in Robert Musil's *The Man without Qualities* (q.v.). An important and competent writer, Sternheim never quite achieved his great potential. But his prose does not today get the attention it deserves, even if its experimentation is ultimately more suggestive than creatively successful. He would be amused to hear that in the Sixties he was still being accused by journalists of 'wilful' experimentalism and (in *The Knickers*) of bad taste. . . .

Pessimism, tempered by a strong religious sense, replaces the urge to satire in the work of ERNST BARLACH (1870–1938). Born in Holstein, Barlach began as sculptor and only took to the serious writing of plays when he was over forty, by which time he had withdrawn into the virtual seclusion, in Mecklenburg, of his last twenty-eight years. Barlach's sculpture, which is nearly all in wood, is 'modern [i.e. purposefully distorted] Late Gothic', and has great power; the Nazis destroyed some of his work as 'decadent', but a good many of his single figures survive. He was probably lucky not to have been sent to a concentration camp. He illustrated his plays with his own engravings. He was a genuinely isolated figure who has some affinities with Blake, and who may be compared to similar eccentric, non-urbanized semi-recluses such as David Jones, in at least the fact that he combines a strong folk-element with a sort of 'rough', untrained but formidable intellectualism, an obstinately persevering drive towards precise self-expression that looks, as one approaches it, first wilfully recondite or 'mad' (cf. Blake), then odd, then unexpectedly sophisticated and, finally, self-fulfilling. Barlach came from a region of dark clouds and murk near the North Sea; a certain Scandinavian gloom pervades all his work, and a genuine sense of the comic can do little to dispel it; but of his power and sensibility there is no doubt. He visited Russia for two months in 1906, and the suffering human beings he saw there, sharply etched against grey infinities of space, strongly affected him, and taught him humility.

What links Barlach to expressionism is his concern with 'inwardness': the exterior of his carved figures is patently expressive of their inner natures. In fact, he is more truly expressionist in his sculpture than in his writing, for he always tended towards establishing a realistic basis in the latter, and criticized his closest friend, the poet Theodor Däubler (q.v.), for trying to express himself in incomprehensible ciphers.

Barlach was a happy pessimist, in that his enjoyment of his transcendentally loving struggle with inevitable human imperfection came to be greater than his *angst*; thus his best work is saved by a refreshingly unmystical earthiness.

Barlach's first completed play, *The Dead Day* (*Der tote Tag*, 1912) ought to have remained on the realistic plane of its beginning. Barlach should have concentrated on expressing his theme at this level. Despite its power, the play is overridden by a windy abstractness. Mother and son live together in a vast hall, in perpetual twilight; the 'spiritual' son tries to break away from the 'physical' mother, who plots continually to keep him in immaturity. His father is pure spirit—he turns up with only a stone, which symbolizes sorrow. He has sent a magic steed to take the boy into bliss, but the mother murders it, and all ends in the 'dead day' of stifling physicality, not very happily symbolized here by Barlach as mother-love. It is interesting that while he wrote this play he was bringing up his four-year-old bastard son, Klaus: he had spent the years 1906–9 in legal battles to get him away from his (stifling?) mother. (The less precise and more divine the afflatus, the more strictly earthy, perhaps, its occasion.)

The best scenes in *Blue Boll* (*Der blaue Boll*, 1926) depict Boll's lusty self-confidence, and amount to a convincing realistic portrait of a certain kind of guilty, lively upstart; but Boll's transfiguration is more doubtful.

Barlach's best work is in parts of his posthumous autobiographical novel *Seespeck* (1948), where the style is precise and the self-examination continually revealing. Here the grotesque sometimes becomes prophetic, and Barlach achieves the quality of his best figures: man, his mind in the configurations of his body, reaches desperately out to 'God', to powers outside himself—and we are spared the transcendental definitions. There was much that was superfluously mystical in Barlach, but there is a validity in his view of life as a struggle between non-materialistic aspiration and physicality—though none in his 'philosophical' solution, described by one critic as a 'profounder cosmic emotion'. When, as in his carvings and in parts of his plays and novels, he is content to describe the plight of modern man as a believer who has lost his belief he is a moving writer.

V

Most of the expressionists proper, as well as Brecht and Rilke, admired [LUIZ] HEINRICH MANN (1871–1950) more than his younger brother THOMAS MANN (1875–1955); now this is rightly regarded as having been because Heinrich was cruder, less complex and more sensational. But, ultimately superior though Thomas is, it is problematical whether full justice is now done to Heinrich Mann's best work.

Born in Lübeck, son of a wealthy Senator and a partly Brazilian mother, Heinrich was at least as prolific as his brother, and published more than fifty books in his lifetime, mostly fiction, but also plays, essays, memoirs, and an anthology. The obvious difference between him and his brother is that he early decided that literature should be politically committed, which the more conservative Thomas always denied.

The Mann brothers have a theme in common: the creative artist's relationship to society. But the early Heinrich can be classified with Wedekind and Sternheim as an unequivocal castigator of the Wilhelmine bourgeoisie; his brother cannot. He soon made up his mind that the artist represented, or ought to represent, revolutionary progress. Practically all Heinrich Mann's literary inspiration came from outside Germany: from Stendhal, Maupassant, Zola and D'Annunzio (qq.v.) in particular. Even before he was forced out of Germany by the Nazis he had spent much of his time in Italy. In his work the conflict between southern and northern blood is more unevenly fought out than in that of his brother: the south is the victor.

His first book of consequence was *Berlin, the Land of Cockaigne* (*Im Schlaraffenland*, 1901; tr. A. D. B. Clark, 1929), in which the unbridled but vital sexuality of the hero, Andreas Zumsee (a German version of Maupassant's womanizer, Bel Ami), is contrasted with the debilitated and worthless society of Berlin, whose rottenness is portrayed with memorable savagery. The trilogy *The Goddesses, Diana, Minerva, Venus* (*Die Göttinnen*, 1902–3; *Diana*, tr. E. Posselt and E. Glore, 1929) has affinities with Wedekind's *Lulu* (qq.v.), but is more calculatingly frenzied. Like Mann, Violante d'Assy, the *femme fatale* heroine, has mixed northern and southern blood; a Nietzschean superwoman (rich, emancipated), she nevertheless feels herself to be artificial. This is a historically interesting novel, but quite unreadable today: Mann's own concerns are too inexorably submerged in a neo-romantic programme.

It was in the novella 'Pippo Spano' (TT), included in his collection *Flutes and Daggers* (*Flöten und Dolche*, 1904–5) that Mann came closest to his brother and anticipated expressionism. Here and in the famous *The Blue Angel* (*Professor Unrat*, 1905; tr. 1932 and, as *Small Town Tyrant*, 1944) of the following year Mann first expressed his deeper as opposed to his more superficial and programmatic self: for there was a distraughtness and nervousness in him which undermined his over-confident polemics, but which gave his best fiction its cutting edge.

In 'Pippo Spano' Heinrich Mann is frightened about himself. Mario Malvolto, a poet, uses his art as a means of preserving his narcissism intact. He feels himself, like Violante, to be *artificial*—this is Heinrich Mann's great theme— but he cannot accept reality because he fears and despises it. (Thus the Mann of *Berlin, the Land of Cockaigne* had tried to pretend that reality consisted solely of swinish and contemptible bourgeoisie.) But he keeps a portrait of one Pippo Spano, a strong and passionate *condottiere*, in his study: here, he feels, is an authentic, not an artificial, man. Such characters fill his books. A girl, Gemma, falls in love with him on the strength of his work. He determines to respond— at last—as Pippo Spano would. Then scandal supervenes, and the 'authentic' thing to do is for the lovers to enter into a suicide pact. They do; but having stabbed Gemma, Mario cannot kill himself: he will create a masterpiece from his experience. Dying, she calls him 'murderer!' but his agreement is 'comic': his masterpiece is a comedy, and 'one does not kill oneself really at the end of a comedy'.

The original Josef von Sternberg movie of *The Blue Angel*, with Jannings and Dietrich, and with an admirable script by Carl Zuckmayer (q.v.), was a work of genius, but in some ways, perhaps inevitably, misrepresented the novel. In the film the schoolmaster is finally seen as an object of pity; in the novel there is no such compassion. Ostracized by the community because he has fallen for the singer Rosa Fröhlich, at the Blue Angel, Professor Unrat ('Filth') revenges himself by using her as bait to lead his judges into the same humiliating situation; previously he had been the most rigid of all of them, a stifler of youthful love and life like the adults in Wedekind's *Spring's Awakening* (q.v.). The downfall of the tyrant Filth is in a sense the downfall of the whole community, which beneath its respectable and placid exterior is seething with lust and anarchy.

The conflicts of 'Pippo Spano' are partially resolved, but painfully and artificially, in *Without a Country* (*Zwischen den Rassen*, 1907): the protagonist, Arnold Acton, a spokesman for Mann, preaches thoughtful action: the intellectual must learn to defascinate himself of the strong man, the Pippo Spano, and to act for himself; thus Arnold is at first fascinated by his politically reactionary rival in love—but is regenerated when he realizes that he must fight. As he triumphs, and his mistress returns to him, there is a victory of Social Democracy: it is the dawn of a new age. . . . This is a very bad book; indeed, Heinrich's lapses were always more drastic than his brother's.

In *The Little Town* (*Die kleine Stadt*, 1909; tr. W. Ray, 1930), however, this optimism receives more convincing treatment. The inhabitants of an Italian town are affected by the arrival of an operatic troupe in just the way that those of the German town of *The Blue Angel* were by Rosa Fröhlich; but this time, in a novel of charm and comedy, they are led to discover their own natures and to attain a degree of harmony. However, a pair of lovers from the troupe die tragically. Is this a sacrifice of art to the common good?

The trilogy *The Kaiserreich*, *The Patrioteer* (*Der Untertan*, 1918; tr. E. Boyd, 1921; and as *Man of Straw*, 1947), *The Poor* (*Die Armen*, 1917; tr. E. Boyd, 1917) and *The Chief* (*Der Kopf*, 1925; tr. E. Boyd, 1925), deteriorates as it proceeds; but the first part, with *Henri IV* (q.v.), is undoubtedly his best work. Diederich Hessling is the first large-scale proto-Nazi in German literature, and he was created before 1914 (the novel waited until 1918 for publication). No one saw what could happen in Germany more clearly than Heinrich Mann. His brother supported the 'decent war', and there was public controversy between them; but Thomas later came to criticize his own attitude. Thomas was the subtler writer, but at this stage his innate conservatism prevented him from attaining the insight of *The Patrioteer*, in which Heinrich Mann provides the first psychological dissection of the fear, stupidity and ruthlessness that went to make up a mentality which, within a year or two of the end of the war, was to be the property of an average Nazi. *The Poor* is more polemical—in *The Patrioteer* satire provides most of the creative energy—and *The Chief* (which does not continue the story) is a failed experiment in documentary fiction.

Heinrich Mann's creative powers subsequently became submerged in his political programme. But they were to erupt once more in his two historical novels about Henry IV of France, the enlightened and tolerant ruler whom he set up as his ideal: *King Wren: the Youth of Henry of Navarre* and *Henry, King of France* (*Die Jugend des Königs Henri Quatre*, 1935; *Die Vollendung des Königs Henri Quatre*, 1937; tr. E. Sutton, 1937, 1939). Unlike Thomas, Heinrich always wanted to repudiate his German origins. Here he pays unequivocal tribute to Mediterranean blood: Henry, in Mann's idealized version of him, combines the reason of Mario Malvolto with the ability to act of Pippo Spano, but on a suitably grand scale. This Henry retains emotional innocence (from which his sexuality benefits, in manifold love-affairs), but his intellect is subtle. And in this characterization Mann was able, perhaps disingenuously, to resolve his doubts about the intellectual artist being an *actor*: Henry acts the part of regal splendour because it is good for his people. This, Mann's last important book, can be shown to avoid the complex moral problems that his brother faced. For Thomas, shrewd and often opportunistic irony; for Heinrich, political commitment. But *Henry IV* is none the less a major work of the second rank—and is easier to read than any of the more massively complicated works of Thomas. As an imaginative writer, Heinrich Mann's best is usually to be found in satire; when reasoning takes over, he is less convincing. But in *Henry IV* he managed a non-satirical monument to his beliefs.

In Thomas Mann we find the *Zeitgeist*, in all its violence, concentrated within the stolid limits of a phenomenally intelligent, though not intellectually original, conservative. No wonder that Mann, whose external life was uneventful, struggled for years with guilt at abandoning his family role of 'Bürger'; being a writer made his inner life a continuously hard one. He was always reticent and careful—even cunning—about where his sympathies lay, and he retained to the end the mercantile acumen of his forebears. Heinrich was the opposite: 'right' about the kind of war the 1914–18 one was going to be, where his brother was patently wrong (and later admitted it), he has less to offer. The Hungarian Marxist critic Georg Lukács has posited Mann as a realistic bourgeois writer who clearly saw that time for his class had run out; and his sympathy for Mann is so great that, since as a Marxist he could not honestly claim him as a 'revolutionary' he calls him a 'naïve' (q.v.) writer, in Schiller's sense. But Mann is a 'sentimentive' writer *par excellence*, whose strictly 'non-confessional' methods conceal more subjective expression. There is more of Thomas in his work than of Heinrich in his. Thomas was an artfully, almost deceitfully, sophisticated manipulator of his audience: he conserved the cultivated merchant in himself, survived as an old-fashioned bourgeois, secretly tried to achieve within himself a compromise between a solid decent commercialism and spirituality, between optimism and pessimism, throughout his writing career of almost sixty years. He was not a dishonest or an inhumane man; but he became, perhaps inevitably, pompous—although no doubt parodically and comically so. One of the most revealing stories he ever wrote, 'Tonio Kröger' (1903; tr. H. T. Lowe-Porter in *Stories of a Lifetime*, 1961), contains this paragraph, in which he sees himself with absolute clarity (the fourteen-year-old Tonio is, like Mann, the son of a rich grain merchant and a Latin mother):

> The fact that he had a note-book full of such things [poems], written by himself, leaked out through his own carelessness and injured him no little with the masters as well as among his fellows. On the one hand, Consul Kröger's son found their attitude cheap and silly, and despised his schoolmates and his masters as well, and in his turn (with extraordinary penetration) saw through and disliked their personal weaknesses and bad breeding. But then, on the other hand, he himself felt his verse-making extravagant and out of place and to a certain extent agreed with those who considered it an unpleasing occupation. But that did not enable him to leave off.

Later, when a young man, Tonio realizes that 'knowledge of the soul would unfailingly make us melancholy if the pleasures of expression did not keep us alert and of good cheer'. This was something that Rilke understood; and it is evident from this story and his other early work that Mann's problem, too, was the nature of the relationship between art and human virtue: is it necessary to 'die to life in order to be utterly a creator'? This is what Tonio soon tells himself, as, successful in his work, he cuts himself off from 'the small fry' who do not understand the nature of the difficulty. He knows that 'Nobody but a beginner imagines that he who creates must feel. . . . If you care too much about what you have to say, if your heart is too much in it, you can be pretty sure of making a mess'. We can see from this that Mann was no more a straight-forward romantic than he was a 'naïve' writer. But he is not simply attacking imaginative writing here; he is criticizing it from the inside (as an imaginative writer); drawing attention to an aspect of its nature. And yet, like Tonio, the twenty-eight-year-old Mann was 'sick to death of depicting humanity without having any part or lot in it. . . .' It was the observing *coldness* (his own, as a writer), too, that shocked him: 'To see things clear, if even through your tears, to recognize, notice, observe—and have to put it all down with a smile, at the very moment when hands are clinging, and lips meeting, and the human gaze is blinded with feeling—it is infamous . . . indecent, outrageous. . . .' Tonio makes this declaration to a sensible girl, and when he ends by saying that he loves life none the less, she tells him that he is 'a bourgeois *manqué*'. When, after thirteen years in the south, he visits his home town, he finds that his parents' house has become a public library; he is also mistaken for a 'swindler' —the artist as swindler was to be one of Mann's chief themes. Finally Tonio resigns himself to the fate of being a writer, but affirms his faith in 'the human, the living and usual. It is the source of all warmth, goodness, and humour. . . .'

This was an advance, in Mann's terms, from the novel that brought him phenomenal success at the age of twenty-six: *Buddenbrooks* (1901; tr. H. T. Lowe-Porter, 1930). This superficially resembled Galsworthy's *Forsyte Saga* (q.v.); but in fact it embodied a profound pessimism, and was, as has been well said, 'a novel of death, resignation and extinction'. In it the heir of the great nineteenth-century mercantile family dies simply because he has not the will to survive. Mann himself did survive, respectable and 'happy' with his good marriage; but there was always a reluctance to do so. He is one of the most anti-creative creators of his century: trapped in nostalgia for nineteenth-century stolidity, whose faults he sees clearly, he opts for a bourgeois democracy and a bourgeois solution. Humane culture, the public man continuously pronounces after his post 1914–18 War conversion to democracy, can provide the answer. He posits an artist who will combine self-discipline with the necessary 'licence' to perform his function; but this is artificial. Mann the creative writer horrifies himself with visions of the sick creative writer; Mann the publicist seeks refuge in what, compared with his novels, are sonorous pomposities. He fails to solve his problem, because he can never be committed; but he provides priceless insights. It is interesting that as early as *Buddenbrooks* Mann sees the decline of the great bourgeois family as the result of the lack of a will to live; and this weakening of the will he sees as being in its turn the result of 'artistic' blood and sexual licence. Mann made a fiction both effectively popular and genuinely 'highbrow' (an unusual achievement) out of the change of heart indicated in 'Tonio Kröger'; but of his 'message' he never really convinces either himself or the astute reader. Throughout his life he refused to adopt a philosophy; but it is necessary to regard him not as a sceptic but as an ironic comedian: a comic exploitation of his own indecision characterizes his work.

It is probably heresy to suggest that Mann's 'great' works, the full-scale novels, are less good than one short work he wrote in 1912; but here the story entirely transcends the moral. In *Death in Venice* (*Der Tod in Venedig*; tr. H. T. Lowe-Porter in *Stories of a Lifetime*, 1961) the forces of perversely apprehended beauty function with as much power as the novelist's implied judgement. One of Mann's chief poses was as poet of the process of regeneration and redemption; but this pose is the least convincing aspect of his fiction—and the 'bigger' it is the less convincing. In this novella he describes with uncanny accuracy how being a writer affected him. When the great writer Aschenbach, hitherto a self-disciplined character, falls in love with the beautiful Polish boy Tadzio (to whom he does not even speak), and gives way to fantasies of passion, he realizes that the moral order has collapsed: 'the moral law' has fallen in ruins and only the monstrous and perverse hold out a hope. Thus, and most memorably, the alarmed (not didactic) Mann exorcized the spectre of moral licentiousness in himself. He said that Aschenbach was suggested by the composer Mahler as well as by a passage in the diary of the homosexual poet Platen—but he was at least as much suggested by himself. His passion has the authenticity of Rilke's lines, quoted above: 'For the beautiful is nothing / But the first apprehension of the terrible. . . .'

The Magic Mountain (*Der Zauberberg*, 1924; tr. H. T. Lowe-Porter, 1927) most ambitiously expands on this; but its heart, for all the brilliant comedy—and, indeed, the subtle majesty of its structure—is sterile. An engineer, Hans Castorp, goes to a Swiss sanatorium for a visit of three weeks; he stays seven years, during which he is 'educated' (*The Magic Mountain* is, as Mann himself often said, 'a queer, ironical, almost parodic' version of the *Bildungsroman*) out of his obsession with death. But his regeneration is comic rather than tragic in spirit, for he is ridiculous. In a sense, Mann is on the side of the devil. The sickness of the world in which Castorp compulsively moves is what he enjoys; the thesis of sickness as a sign of distinction, to be overcome and replaced by a 'life'-enhanced health, is, for all the apparent profundity with which it was advanced, academic in Mann: this does not act upon him as a creative but as a pseudo-philosophical yeast. Mann was a realist in most of *Buddenbrooks*, but elsewhere only by fits and starts; as a conscientious humanitarian made intelligently aware of the *national* consequences of Schopenhauer, Nietzsche and Wagner, his problem was to evolve a fiction that at least appeared to be positive. So Castorp is a comic caricature, a 'representative' rather than (in a realist sense) a man at all; the time (1907–14) is the past; the structure is fashionably based on myth (that of the hero in quest of adventure): the whole huge apparatus looks impressively positive. And once this is seen, *The Magic Mountain* is even funnier in its sly cunning. It is significant that Mann never, here or elsewhere, can define or communicate the nature of the 'love' by which 'death' may be outwitted. The only love he can communicate with true power is that of Gustav von Aschenbach for Tadzio; and this is a love of death. All Mann can do at the end of the novel, when Castorp finally leaves the death-enchanted mountain in order to enlist as a soldier, is to hope that 'Out of this universal feast of death, out of this extremity of fever, kindling the rain-washed evening sky to a fiery glow, may it be that love one day shall mount?' This is the rhetoric of a liberal activist, not the insight of a creative writer.

In the novella 'Mario and the Magician' ('Mario und der Zauberer', 1930; tr. H. T. Lowe-Porter in *Stories of a Lifetime*, 1961) Mann presents a Hitler or Mussolini type figure as, significantly, an evil artist: a hypnotist who fascinates his audiences. The 'wholesome' Mario's defeat of this charlatan is unconvincing. Mann was wrong, too, in his wishful public belief that the Germans would repudiate Hitler.

The Biblical tetralogy *Joseph and his Brothers* (*Joseph und seine Brüder*, 1933–43; tr. H. T. Lowe-Porter, 1948) builds up, with an immense panoply of learning, the figure of a 'chosen one', a suffering, regenerated, redeemed con-man who reconciles simplicity with sophistication, superstition with scepticism, *Geist* with *Leben* ('spirit' with 'life': an opposition fundamental in the German temperament), to achieve an enlightened society: a democratic Germany. In exile in America, Mann could relax enough to fantasize this Joseph, an artist turned successful business-man, and a society that could exorcize its demons. The cheerfulness of the ending has been as brilliantly stage-managed by Mann as, in the novel, Joseph has stage-managed the scene of his 'recognition'; it is only in the light of reflection that it strikes the reader as incongruous.

In *Doctor Faustus* (1947; tr. H. T. Lowe-Porter, 1949) Mann attacked what he so reluctantly and secretly was: an 'expressionist' artist; but his composer Adrian Leverkühn (born 1885) went the whole hog, which Mann himself did not. Mann here regards music as specifically 'devilish': Germanic (Hitlerian). Leverkühn comes to realize, with the help of the devil, that creativity has been bought at the price of syphilis: his manic-depressive personality is, literally, devilish. Mann saw that 'expressionism' run riot had led to fascism; but he did not see the other side of the picture, and—in portraying a *non-*charlatan as positively evil—he emphasized that the humanly successful artist must be a confidence man: himself.

In *The Holy Sinner* (*Der Erwählte*, 1951; tr. H. T. Lowe-Porter, 1951) the protagonist is born in incest, marries his 'sister' who is his mother, and becomes Pope (so that his mother can call him 'father'): its nihilism is decked out in a mannerist prose that makes the vicious message look noble and even positive— at least to the middlebrow audience whom Mann delighted in hoodwinking.

The Black Swan (*Die Betrogene*, 1953; tr. W. R. Trask, in *Stories of a Lifetime*, 1961) is undeniably 'sick'; and Mann, who was getting old and tired, is for once slick and facile in his execution. *The Holy Sinner* looks like a 'regeneration' story, but in fact the author is splitting his sides; *The Black Swan* is a solemn (and pitiless) rehash of the old theme that it is bad for society when people go against nature. The 'characters' are garishly unreal. A widow of fifty falls for a young American. She becomes unduly sensitive to scents, only to trace one to a compost-heap. She experiences a return of menstruation: but this is cancer of the womb (described in repulsive detail), and she dies.

Then Mann had a last renewal of energy, and—appropriately—decided to tell the truth. *The Confessions of Felix Krull, Confidence Man* (*Bekenntnisse des Hochstaplers Felix Krull*, 1954; tr. Denver Lindley, 1955) is supposed to be unfinished —but it was finished by Mann's death. His zest in this picaresque novel is greater than it had been for forty years. Certainly the relaxed story of yet another 'chosen being', a gay criminal amorist, is his best novel since the first, *Buddenbrooks*.

Mann was a black pessimist trapped in the Germanism he so vigorously resisted. The author who wrote an early story in which a man dances himself to death in women's clothes, to music composed and played by his wife and her lover, may well have felt he had something to live down (and he, unlike many decadents, had meant it). He distrusted 'inwardness', but ignored or failed to discern the fact that such poetry of 'inwardness' as *The Duino Elegies* (q.v.), wrung out of a tortured selfishness (not hedonism), does have a glow of love towards others—because it is not meretricious, does not cheat the easily cheated audience, does insist on communicating its uncompromising message. Mann does not achieve this degree of poetry: in terror of his inwardness, he tried to turn it into a kind of outwardness. But he remained humorously aware of this, and at the end, in *Felix Krull*, he openly and amusingly confessed his inadequacy.

VI

Expressionism—the literary movement of approximately 1910–1925—was the first, and the most violent and explicit, manifestation of modernism. The term— an early application of it was made by German art critics to an exhibition of French paintings by Picasso and others held in Berlin in 1911—was not liked in literary circles until after the outbreak of the First World War, when the movement became increasingly political, and was taken up by more or less polemic critics such as Hermann Bahr (q.v.). Marinetti (q.v.) and his futurist manifesto were welcomed in Berlin in 1912, and there was a widespread movement by then, exemplified in the founding of two (rival) magazines, *Die Aktion* and *Der Sturm*, and of literary clubs and cabarets. A good many untalented poeticules and criticasters could and did jump on the bandwagon. The impact had first come from the visual arts, and the German visual expressionist movement (e.g. *die Brücke*, the Bridge group founded in Dresden in 1905, and incorporated into *Der blaue Reiter*, the Blue Rider group, in 1911) predates the literary. It was Bahr who said that the chief characteristic of the movement was the shriek, an expression of inner agony—aptly depicted, in a famous and hysterical painting, by the Norwegian Edvard Munch, a friend of Strindberg's (q.v.).

The German reaction to the disintegration of the old culture and to the impending catastrophe of the war, to the growing notion that man was alone in a hostile universe, was the most anguished of all; frequently it took violent or gruesome forms. Equivalents of expressionism arose elsewhere, but there is an expressionism that is a peculiarly German phenomenon: apart from its intensity, its most notable feature is the hostility of the younger towards the elder generation, often manifesting itself as hatred of the father or father-figure. Expressionism 'is part of the great international movement of modernism in art and literature; on the other hand, it is a turbulent and vital chapter in the catastrophic history of modern Germany': 'the antithesis (and chief victim of) Nazism as well as its forerunner and kin' (Walter H. Sokel). The imagists (q.v.) in England—whose actual work is less drastically 'modern' than that of the German expressionists—concentrated upon the formal, stylistic aspects of poetry; the Germans were from the beginning as concerned, however vaguely, with wider implications: being Germans, they were more philosophical in their approach. But their initial failure to make satisfactory aesthetic formulations testifies to their initial creative strength: theoretical programmes inevitably sap creativity. And, of course, the more considerable the gifts of those poets or writers now usually called expressionist, the more isolated or remote from the movement they tended to be. Neither Trakl nor Kafka (qq.v.) had anything seriously to do with any programme, and the work of both transcends programmatic concerns.

The first nominally expressionist poem appeared in the periodical *Die Aktion* in 1911. It was called 'World's End':

> The bourgeois' hat flies off his pointed head,
> the air re-echoes with a screaming sound.
> Tilers plunge from roofs and hit the ground,
> and seas are rising round the coasts (you read).

> The storm is here, crushed dams no longer hold,
> the savage seas come inland with a hop.
> The greater part of people have a cold.
> Off bridges everywhere the railroads drop.

> (MGP; see also TCG)

This was by JAKOB VAN HODDIS (ps. HANS DAVIDSOHN, 1887–1942), who went mad in 1914 and was, after nearly thirty years in an asylum, murdered ('deported') by the Nazis. His poem was 'expressionist' because, as well as satirizing bourgeois complacency and ironically predicting disaster, it presented what Michael Hamburger has called 'an arbitrary concatenation of images derived from contemporary life . . . a picture, but not a realistic one'. Van Hoddis was a comparatively crude poet; more gifted was ALFRED LICHTENSTEIN

(1889–1914), who was killed in action in Belgium at the beginning of the war. His poem 'Twilight' (whether dawn or dusk is not specified) was admittedly modelled on van Hoddis' 'World's End', but, as Hamburger has pointed out, he allows 'the images to speak for themselves'. 'Twilight' is less contrived than 'World's End', for while Lichtenstein was a genuine poet, van Hoddis was probably not more than a gifted and zestful perpetrator of sardonic *montage*. In Lichtenstein's poetry there is a wholeness of vision: integrity of surface is preserved even while the familiar world is cruelly, gaily or sadly dislocated:

A fat boy is playing with a pond. The wind has got caught in a tree. The sky looks wasted and pale, as though it had run out of make-up.

Bent crookedly on long crutches and chattering two lame men creep across the field. Maybe a blond poet is going mad. A pony stumbles over a lady.

A fat man is sticking to a window. A youth is on his way to visit a soft-hearted woman. A grey clown is pulling on his boots. A pram screams and dogs curse. (TCG; see also MGP)

Lichtenstein, as is now often pointed out (following Hamburger), paralleled Eliot and Pound in a number of ways: in his use of *collage*, his introduction of an ironic *persona* (called Kuno Kohn) and his mocking and deprecatory tone. He also wrote a children's book.

AUGUST STRAMM (1874–1915), a poet and dramatist who was killed on the Russian front, combined a respectable life in the Central Postal Ministry with study at university and some of the most violent experiments yet seen. He is a crude writer, but one of exceptional integrity. For many years he could not get his work published at all; but Herwarth Walden's *Der Sturm* took his play *Sancta Susanna* (1914; tr. in *Poet Lore*, XXV, 1914), and he soon became its co-editor. Stramm's work, like that of E. E. Cummings (q.v.), is less radical than it immediately suggests; he owes much to Arno Holz (q.v.) and to the shrill Marinetti (q.v.). But he sought for self-expression, not sensationalism, in his war-poems. It is misleading to describe him as an expressionist or a pre-expressionist, although he was hailed as such when his work became widely known after the war: in the typical expressionist poem the external scene expresses the poet's inner state. In Stramm there is no external scene: there are no images; and conventional logic, syntax and all description are eschewed. The weakness of his poetry is lack of feeling; but this arises not from coldness but from undue concentration upon technique. Under the pressure of war, however, Stramm wrote to greater effect.

Stramm's plays are less successful. Intended for intimate theatres, they exploit gesture, pause and (even the intimate theatre not then being quite what it is now, only verbal) ejaculation. Doubtless *Powers* (*Kräfte*, 1915) seemed effective in Max Reinhardt's production; but the text left it all to him.

Before passing to others who died in the war, it is necessary to consider a poet who had nothing to do with the expressionist movement, and yet can only be classified as an expressionist (if he can be classified as anything)—and one whose most earnest work falls lamentably short of his ostensibly least serious. CHRISTIAN MORGENSTERN (1871–1914), a consumptive, was lucky to live as long as forty-three years, and it is unlikely that he would have had he not been so devotedly cared for by his mistress Margarete Gosebruch; certainly he lived, from his early teens onwards, in the shadow of a premature death.

Morgenstern knew Ibsen and translated both his and Strindberg's plays into German. He was influenced first by Nietzsche, then by mysticism both Eastern and Western, and finally by the 'anthroposophy' of Rudolf Steiner, a partly mystical and partly practical system that embraced the whole of life; it still survives. Morgenstern believed that his philosophical poetry was his most important contribution to literature. It is in fact, as Leonard Forster has written, *innig*: 'sincere-fervent', linguistically uninspired and over-intense. His 'nonsense-verse', however, which he began writing (relaxedly: this is the clue to its achievement) in his twenties, puts him on a level with, and possibly even above, Lear and Carroll. His earnestness as a serious poet is pathetic; but it allowed him to relax in officially non-intense off-moments, and thus, in his ostensibly 'light' verse, to comment more pungently on his problems than he ever could when he was trying.

One of his chief problems was the way in which words are related to the things they denote. Morgenstern's approach is one of laughter; but he created his own autonomous poetry. The world of Baron von Korf and Professor Palmström is even more self-contained than that of Lewis Carroll. Morgenstern the mystic struggled hard and with humourless solemnity with the universe: everything was at stake. As soon as he played with it, with nothing at stake, he became a major poet: probably the most successful 'nonsense' poet in the history of literature. Man is a linguistically endowed animal. Morgenstern played with his language as few had played with it before; he demonstrated both its inadequacies and its capacity to create a world of its own. Although he himself saw no essential difference between his 'serious' and his 'nonsense' poetry, in the latter he unobtrusively mocks his mystical pretensions,

> Palmström's grown nervous; henceforth
> He will sleep only to the North. . . .

without really undermining them. In 'The Dreamer' he sees himself even more lucidly:

> Palmström sets a bunch of candles
> on the table by his bedside
> and observes them slowly melting.
>
> Wondrously they fashion mountains
> out of downward-dripping lava,
> fashion tongues, and toads, and tassels.

Swaying o'er the guttering candles
stand the wicks with flames aspiring,
each one like a golden cypress.

On the pearly fairy boulders
soon the dreamer's eyes see hosts of
dauntless pilgrims of the sun.

(MGP)

At rock bottom Morgenstern was a sceptic, who dissolved his kindly immortal longings in metaphysical laughter:

There was a fence with spaces you
Could look through if you wanted to.

An architect who saw this thing
Stood there one summer evening,

Took out the spaces with great care.
And built a castle in the air.

The fence was utterly dumbfounded:
Each post stood there with nothing round it. . . .

(tr. R. F. C. Hull)

His inimitable and still by no means widely enough known poetry has been much translated. (Notably by Max Knight, *The Gallows Songs*, 1963, and by W. D. Snodgrass and Lore Segal, *Gallows Songs*, 1968. See also MGP, TCG, TCGV, PGV.)

GEORG HEYM (1887–1912), poet and short-story writer, escaped the war only because he was drowned while trying (vainly) to rescue a friend with whom he was skating on the River Havel. Heym was influenced by Baudelaire and, above all, Rimbaud; he was also another of those Germans who were fascinated by the early poetry of Maeterlinck; he must have owed much, too, to the poems of Émile Verhaeren (q.v.), with their visions of the encroaching cities, for one of the main themes of his talented, death-intoxicated poetry is 'the God of the City', with his 'slaughterer's fist' shaking as devouring fire rages along a street. Yet Heym, who was physically a giant, had a side to him as conventional as his verse-forms: he wanted to be a soldier or a consul, and was quite as full of zest for life as he was fascinated by death. His joy in horror, which parallels that of Benn's (q.v.) poems of almost exactly the same time, may have stemmed, like Wilfred Owen's (q.v.), from a repressed homosexual streak; but the athletic Heym would have recoiled from this in more terror than Owen did. He had extraordinary difficulties with women. As has often been repeated—it was first stated by Ernst Stadler (q.v.)—his poems achieve such tension because he contained the turbulence of their emotions in strict verse forms. There is some truth in the judgement that 'the general impression of Heym's poetry is that of a boyish elaboration of the macabre', but it fails to do justice either to the authenticity that lay at the heart of expressionism or to Heym's poetic confidence. It is true that he made a fetish of a schoolmate's suicide—as a courageous act— and had a skull decorated with vine leaves on his desk; but he was an equally intense sports lover. Shame (as he recorded in a diary) at his 'delicacy' was the reason for this. The truly lived-out dichotomy produced the tension from which the poems arose.

> They tramp around the prison yard.
> Their glances sweep its emptiness
> Searching for some meadow or some tree,
> Sickened by the blankness of the walls.
>
> Like a mill-wheel turning, their black tracks
> Go round and round and round.
> And like a monk's shaved head
> The middle of the yard is bright.

There is social indignation here; but more than that. The prisoners are trapped bourgeois who march pointlessly—de-sexed like monks—on the periphery of the 'brightness' that is their birthright. Heym could achieve a deeper and more mysterious, personal note, as this opening stanza from 'Why Do You Visit Me, White Moths, So Often?' shows:

> Why do you visit me, white moths, so often?
> You dead souls, why should you often flutter
> Down to my hand, so that a little
> Ash from your wings is often left there?
>
> (MGP; see also TCG, PGV)

The Alsatian ERNST STADLER (1883–1914), who was killed early in the war, was a notable scholar (he studied at Oxford 1906–8) as well as an influential poet. He had founded a periodical, *Der Stürmer* (*The Assailant*) as early as 1902, together with his friend René Schickele (q.v.); its object was to accomplish a cultural *rapprochement* between France and Germany. Stadler was influenced by French poets, notably Jammes and Péguy (qq.v.), both of whom he translated, Verhaeren, Hofmannsthal and George (qq.v.) as well as by Whitman. He was one of the most considered, quiet and intellectual of the early modernists. Of the gifted young poets—French, British, and German—who were slaughtered in the First World War, he is the most likely one, had he lived, to have developed procedures that would have enabled him to fulfil his undoubtedly major potentialities. He was one of the most intelligent critics of his generation.

Stadler has been described as a 'semi-modernist', and with some justification. His optimism and idealism led him to have hopes for the real world, so that his repudiation of conventional reality—his 'expressionism'—was less absolute than that of Trakl or even Heym (q.v.). He belongs mainly to the functionalist, sober, 'responsible' side of expressionism, and he anticipated by some years the so-called New Objectivity (*Neue Sachlichkeit*).

His first book was derivative, even 'decadent'—and some poems in his second (and only important) collection, *Decampment* (*Der Aufbruch*, 1914), are marred by an immature voluptuousness. Stadler was wholeheartedly against the disintegrating, rotten-ripe society of his time; but unlike Trakl, Benn (qq.v.) and others, he believed in the future and maintained that 'true art' existed to serve it. He often used a long, rhyming line to evoke what Michael Hamburger calls 'an elemental vision that is religious and erotic'. Probably just as years of war would have shattered his idealism, so they would have shattered this only occasionally convincing technique. He summed up his dilemma most acutely in 'Form is Joy'; and this can be taken, too, as a prophecy of the direction in which he might have gone:

> First mould and bolt had to burst, and world press through opened conduits: form is joy, peace, heavenly content, but my urge is to plough up the clods of the field. Form seeks to strangle and to cramp me, but I desire to force my being into all distances—form is clear hardness without pity, but I am driven to the dull, the poor, and as I give myself limitlessly away life will quench my thirst with fulfilment. (PGV; see also TCG, MGP.)

GEORG TRAKL (1887–1914) was an Austrian poet who managed, despite an almost completely deranged life, to achieve a body of poetry of absolute integrity—which incidentally fulfilled the expressionist programme of 'visionary poet' and anticipated certain aspects of surrealism. Trakl was born in Salzburg, the son of an ironmonger. He did badly at school, and before he had left was sniffing chloroform and drinking heavily. He decided to become a pharmacist—probably because of the opportunities it would and did give him to indulge in the drugs of his choice—trained in Vienna, did a year of military service, and then returned to Salzburg. His sister, Margarete, who was a concert pianist, committed suicide. A sister figures in Trakl's poetry, as does the theme of incest; no reliable biographical conclusion can, however, be drawn. Only one book of poems appeared in his lifetime, in 1913; this was a selection made by Franz Werfel (q.v.).

Trakl's letters show that he had as deep a seriousness about his poetic vocation as Rilke, whom he influenced and who was one of his first understanding readers; but unlike Rilke, who never touched any drug or stimulant, Trakl could not endure his existence without their help. Fortunately he was physically very strong, although his way of life would inevitably have destroyed him had he not destroyed himself. The philosopher Ludwig Wittgenstein, recognizing Trakl's genius although admitting that he could not understand his poetry, made a considerable sum of money available to him through his patron—Ludwig von Ficker, who published most of his later poetry in his magazine *Der Brenner*—but even this upset his delicate sensibility.

When the war came Trakl was called up as a lieutenant in the Austrian Medical Corps. After the battle of Grodek, the title of one of his last poems, he was given the task of caring for ninety seriously wounded men: he had neither the skill nor supplies, and broke down. He was put under observation as a possible case of what used to be called *dementia praecox* (schizophrenia), an unlikely diagnosis. He developed a delusion that he would be executed as a deserter (he had seen the hanged bodies of deserters at Grodek), there was no intelligent person within reach, and he died of an overdose of cocaine, probably unintentionally.

Trakl, while he is one of the most individual poets of the century, typifies not only the 'visionary poet', as has been mentioned, but also the 'alienated artist'. He is an early case of a man driven deep into himself by a world he finds intolerable. The process was at least helped along by his family's ridicule of him for writing poetry, their equation of 'poetry' and 'failure'. Poetry was his only real therapy—for his 'anti-therapy' was the alcohol and drugs which he used simultaneously to protect and destroy himself. His life paralleled that of a fictional expressionist hero, well defined by W. H. Sokel as one whose 'superiority is the bane of his life . . . [and] . . . casts him into outer darkness. His nature is unique; his words find no echo.' Not for nothing did Trakl poetically identify himself with the 'righteous' Caspar Hauser (q.v.), who 'truly adored the sun, as, crimson, it sank from the hilltop . . . and the joy of green', and into whose heart God had spoken 'a gentle flame': 'O man!'—but who was pursued by 'bush and beast' and sought by his murderer, and who at the end

> Saw snow falling through bare branches
> And in the dusking hall his murderer's shadow.
>
> Silver it fell, the head of the not-yet born.

(tr. D. Luke in *Selected Poems*, 1968, the best and most representative English collection; see also MGP, TCG, PGV, MEP and R. Bly and J. Wright, *Twenty Poems*, 1961. *Decline*, tr. M. Hamburger, 1952, contains one version not subsequently republished.)

The expressionist 'message' is well concealed in Trakl's poetry—it is never advanced polemically; but those who think of him as predominantly morbid should be reminded that his gloom arose from a consciousness of joy rather than from decadent self-indulgence. He is an absolutely ambiguous poet, and it is as wrong to speak of pure ugliness in his work as it is of pure beauty: they go together. He used colour more than any poet before or since. The philosopher Martin Heidegger tried to show, in a controversial essay, how his use of colour implies two opposed qualities. Thus 'green' (which appears as frequently in his poetry as it does in that of Lorca or Hagiwara, qq.v.) is both spring-like, pristine—and decay. But Michael Hamburger has challenged this view as an over-simplification. The world of Trakl's poetry, his inner world, is built up, like a dream-picture, from disparate images of the external world. Much has been written attempting to explicate this world, for all sensitive readers intuit that it is meaningful, if in no familiar manner.

Trakl was first influenced by Rimbaud, the French symbolists and Nietzsche; the chief influence on his later and more doom-ridden poetry was the Swabian poet Friedrich Hölderlin (1770–1843), a prophetic and visionary figure who—mad for the last thirty-seven years of his life, anti-orthodox but profoundly religious, above all the expressor of a sense of hopeless isolation—was gratefully rediscovered in this century. As Trakl grew older and progressively failed to make satisfactory contact with his environment, or to fulfil his conviction that (as he said in a letter to von Ficker) 'all human beings are worthy of love', or to find anything to contradict his sense of impending doom, his guilt assumed gigantic proportions. His poetry is impenetrable because, as Walter Sokel has pointed out, 'withdrawal and disguise' were the keynotes of his existence: he could not face himself any more than he could face the world. And yet his poetic integrity, even in a disintegrating culture (the Austrian decay was the most immediately evident and poignant of all), was such that it forced him to face himself; and so, in Sokel's words, 'Upon the visionary screen a carefully masked biography of the poet's essential existence is projected in fragments'. Trakl haunts his own poetry, a ghost possessed by already tainted joy, and then by guilt and death. His theme is of decline into death; a recurrent, and often final, image is of the falling head: 'Fading, the head bows in the dark of the olive tree', '. . . the wine-drunk head sinks down to the gutter', '. . . O how softly/ Into black fever his face sank down', 'From the stony wall/A yellow head bowed down', 'Silver it fell, the head of the not-yet born', '. . . he bows his head in purple sleep'. This, doubtless prompted by his own drug- or alcohol-induced sinkings-into-trance, suggests the resignation of the intellect to extinction. In Trakl's poetry everything sinks unhappily but intoxicatedly downwards, through a Nature seen as through the eyes of a painter (Rilke shrewdly pointed out in a letter that 'a Trakl [one thinks] . . . could have exercised his painting and music instead of poetry'—Rilke could not), into oblivion. He is the mythical youth Elis, whose own 'decline' is when the blackbird calls in the black wood, and who is dead, or at any rate not yet born. Death implies innocence, perhaps even ignorance, of human corruption. Trakl's poetry does not so much refer, however, to the state of innocence itself as to the anguish or corruption that modern life (particularly the city) thrusts upon the individual. One of the functions of poetry, for Trakl as for certain other expressionists, was the creation of a separate world—this one being too painful. But the poet's own 'autonomous', subjective world is shot through with intimations of the 'real' world: there is a tension between the 'real' and the 'unreal', between the world of pure imagination and the world upon which it depends. Thus Trakl the man is involuntarily haunted by guilt about his sexual desire for, or possibly relationship with, his sister; but Trakl the poet, even while expressing this guilt, questions its validity—if only by implication. Trakl's last poem is called 'Grodek', and one may see in it—dramatically—how the poet was related to, dependent upon, the man. For it was at Grodek that Trakl endured the experiences that led him to attempt suicide, to be removed to a military hospital, and there to die of an overdose of cocaine:

> At nightfall the autumn woods cry out
> With deadly weapons and the golden plains,
> The deep blue lakes, above which more darkly
> Rolls the sun; the night embraces
> Dying warriors, the wild lament
> Of their broken mouths.
> But quietly there in the pastureland
> Red clouds in which an angry god resides,
> The shed blood gathers, lunar coolness.
> All the roads lead to blackest carrion.
> Under golden twigs of the night and stars
> The sister's shade now sways through the silent copse
> To greet the ghosts of the heroes, the bleeding heads;
> And softly the dark flutes of autumn sound in the reeds.
> O prouder grief! You brazen altars,
> Today a great pain feeds the hot flame of the spirit,
> The grandsons yet unborn.

(MGP)

The 'world' of this poem is not more incoherent than a dream is incoherent; but it needs as much effort of understanding as a dream—and the means of its interpretation are as various and as uncertain. . . . However, the figure of the sister is here, a ghost ambiguously 'greeting' ghosts. And this last of Trakl's poems most poignantly illustrates the dilemma common to all would-be denizens of autonomous worlds. . . .

It is his most sensitive translator, Michael Hamburger, who has pointed out that the many mythical figures in Trakl's poetry frequently stand, not merely for childlike innocence, but for actual exemption from original sin: feeling trapped by his own narcissism (with, it should be added, a sensitivity more intense and articulated than the normal), the poet postulates the impossible, or at least the unknown—the unknown of which he yet has a vague premonition, which he catches, ghost-like, haunting that terrified consciousness of decline.

It is tempting to try to interpret Trakl's poetry in symbolist terms; but while this may sometimes indicate his own conscious intentions, it does not, I think, lead to the richest response. For example, Hamburger has interpreted him as 'a Christian poet', and by this he presumably means a poet who believed—in the core of his being—in Christ as redeemer. I can find no evidence of this; his use of Christian material seems to me a pagan use. The way to read him is intuitively; his poems must be seen as paintings, but also as desperate attempts to visualize his inner landscape. This is an enigmatic poetry that has no trace of pretentiousness in it. Unlike Dylan Thomas (q.v.), Trakl did not become increasingly submerged in beery rhetoric—for all the alcohol and drugs he took.

His poetry is about himself, and if we want to discover the universal in it we must, I think, approach it—first—in that way. He 'perished', Rilke said, 'under the too great weight of his creation and the darkness which it brought upon him'.

VII

There were other expressionist poets, or poets intimately associated with the expressionist movement. When expressionism went into its second and inferior phase in about 1914, and became strident, sociological, political and programmatic, these multiplied to such an extent that only a directory—and that in small type—could deal with them all. Time has in any case extinguished most of the reputations. However, a number of more important poets were either on the fringes of the movement, or claimed by it.

ELSE LASKER-SCHÜLER (1869–1945), as well known for bohemianism as for poetry, was friendly with Dehmel, Kraus, Kokoschka, Däubler, Werfel and Benn (qq.v.). Her first liaison was with the not conspicuously talented vagabond poet and novelist PETER HILLE (1854–1904), whom she commemorated in *The Peter Hille Book* (*Das Peter Hille Buch*, 1906–7). Trakl (q.v.) met her briefly and dedicated a poem to her. She was for a time married to Herwarth Walden (ps. Georg Levin), the editor of the expressionist magazine *Der Sturm*. But even though she was an enthusiastic propagandist for expressionism, she was a true eccentric original, and could never have belonged to any movement. Her remark 'I die of life and breathe again in the image' is marvellously evocative of expressionism; but her inner world was largely a product of fancy (rather than imagination), and had been formed from her Westphalian childhood and (mainly) from her Jewish background.

She lived for the last eight years of her life in Jerusalem, where she was regarded as a national Jewish poet: a fitting apotheosis, for Judaism—both religious and secular—had been her chief inspiration. She wrote novels and a play, but her important work is in poetry. At their best, her poems have the colourful, grotesque, humorous quality of the paintings of Chagall; apparently surrealistic, they are actually rooted in a warm primitivism. The expressionists welcomed her because of this primitivism, but her alliance with the movement harmed her art by making her take thought—which was not her strong point. Her 'mysticism' is deliberate, an attempt at thinking, not felt at all; her impersonations of oriental princesses are merely tiresome. When she is at her weakest, which she often is, she is not evoking an inner world but merely seeking an escape from reality. Too many of her fabulous inventions are of this character. Her romanticism is often profoundly bourgeois in type, for all her detestation of the species: it is, after all, a bourgeois habit to 'hate love among the common plebs' as she did, adding 'love is for Tristan and Isolde, Romeo and Juliet. . . .' She is at her best in those short poems where she is least obsessed with the intellectual nature of her symbols—colour, the East in general, the search for God—and more impelled by powerful emotion into the creation of an uncalculated language. (The grotesque and sometimes nightmarish humour of her autobiographical *My Heart, Mein Herz*, 1912, is appealing but relatively trivial.)

OVER SHINING SHINGLE

O to go home at last—
The lights fade fast—
Their final greeting gone.

Where lay my head?
Mother, say soon.
Our garden, too, is dead.

A bunch of grey carnations lies
In some lost corner of the house.
Every ounce it took of all our care,

It wreathed the welcome at the door,
And gave itself, in color generous,
O mother dear.

It spread the sunset gold,
And in the morning soft desires,
Before this downfall of the world.

None of my sisters live now and no brothers live.
Winter has played with death in every nest
And frozen cold our every song of love.

(MGP)

This poem, beautiful in its simplicity, was written in the Forties, under the strain of knowledge of the fate of so many of her race, and included in the collection *My Blue Piano* (*Mein blaues Klavier*, 1943), in which for the first time she recaptured the purity of her poems of thirty years before that (these were collected in the book she most prized: *Hebrew Ballads, Hebräische Balladen*, 1913). She illustrated most of her own books. (MGP, TCG, CGP, CGPD.)

A less influential but equally enthusiastic proponent of expressionism was the 'bearded Oceanus' THEODOR DÄUBLER (1876–1934), who was born, of German parents (he had an Irish grandmother) in Trieste. He evolved a tiresome mystical system—sun is father, earth mother, and the earth is perpetually struggling to join the sun—and wrote an epic, *The North Light* (*Das Nordlicht*, 1910, rev. 1921) of over 30,000 lines to illustrate it. He had connections with the semi-expressionist group *Charon*, founded by the poet OTTO ZUR LINDE (1873–1938), which aimed to penetrate to the ultimate meaning in sound. Out of this came his famous synaesthetic poem 'I hear a million nightingales singing', which is something of a *tour de force*. He knew Yeats (q.v.), who was doubtless sympathetic to his astral claptrap; he was also a close friend of the proto-Nazi critic Moeller van den Bruck. But Däubler, novelist and critic as well as poet, was no Nazi. His fate, it seems, is to be represented in anthologies by short poems that are described as 'uncharacteristic'. Much of his best work is in *The Way of the Stars* (*Der sternhelle Weg*, 1915). In such a poem as 'Cats' (MGP) he writes a characteristically 'expressionist poem' of high quality. (TCG, CGPD.)

ALFRED MOMBERT (1872–1942), a Jew from Karlsruhe, was not as involved in expressionism as Lasker-Schüler and Däubler, but was nevertheless included in some anthologies. Mombert's inoffensively grandiose work is now largely forgotten, but in his time he was regarded by a few as the outstanding genius of his generation. Benn (q.v.) names him and Däubler as pioneers of expressionism. Mombert began by writing shorter poems, but about 1905 began a lifelong attempt to base a 'modern myth' on his spiritual life. Mombert's virtues of nobility and courage were personal rather than literary; his best writing is contained in the posthumous collections of his letters made in 1956 and 1961. The later works, of which the most notable are *Aeon* (1907–11) and *Sfaira der Alte* (1936–42), are cast in the form of 'symphonic dramas'. They were not intended for the contemporary stage, but for the 'new humanity' of ages hence. The lovely and wise old poet who figures in the latter of these 'symphonic dramas', who holds converse with trees, parks and other inanimate things, is a curiously appealing figure—but the work is none the less a penance to read. At the end of his life Mombert was sent to a concentration camp, but a friend ransomed him and he was able to go to die in Switzerland. The man, in this case, is better than the work.

Neither WILHELM LEHMANN (1882–1968) nor his friend OSKAR LOERKE (1884–1941) was involved in any programme; but both have enough in common with early expressionism to be considered here. Both are more important poets than Däubler or Mombert, and both continue to exercise a powerful influence on post-war German writing. Lehmann, who was born in Venezuela, began with a volume of stories in 1912 and a novel four years later. His first book of poetry did not appear until 1935, when he was well over fifty. His life, with the exception of a spell of captivity as a prisoner-of-war in England in the First World War, was uneventful. He was a teacher until 1947, when he retired. He was perhaps the most serene of all modern poets, and one of the very few who did not lose the faculty of lyricism.

Lehmann is an esoteric, not a hermetic (q.v.) poet: the reader needs information, but this is available from books on natural history; and the best poems stand on their own. Lehmann has a passion for 'nature'—flowers and animals—and is a 'nature poet' of comparable stature with, but very different from, Robert Frost and Andrew Young (qq.v.). 'The true poet can be singled out by his close connection with natural phenomena', he has written, 'and his belief in the power of language'. Lehmann's poems are ' "deeds" ', he says, 'of my eyes'. 'God and the world only appear to the summons of mysteriously definite planned syllables'. For Lehmann, exact description of the world in minute particulars is a magical act; the English might respond more readily and fully to the poetry of Andrew Young (q.v.) in the light of this. This is really the limit of Lehmann's 'mysticism', which is refreshingly less ponderous and complex than that of, say, Däubler (q.v.). He is passive, rather than prosily inventive of vast schemes, in the face of what the natural world does to him. Thus two of the chief features of his poetry are exactitude of detail and a dislike of abstraction. . . . When the wind seemed to be 'moved to pity' by the horror of post-war starvation and desolation, in 1947, he watched spring return: 'It is nothing. Abortive magic? It worked. I am nourished. I hear song'. Lehmann's fiction is autobiographical, and essential to an understanding of his poetry, although not on the same high creative level. His criticism illuminates his own practice more than that of his subjects. The integrity of his faith in Nature and its power to survive even the 'second flood' of the Second World War, are most apparent in his poetry, much of the best of which was written in old age. (MGP, TCGV, PGV.)

His close friend Oskar Loerke worked for most of his life in Berlin as a reader for the important publishing firm of S. Fischer Verlag. Like Lehmann's, his work has come to the forefront only since the war; neither writer was taken much account of before, and both were frowned upon—though not proscribed— by the Nazis. Loerke wrote book reviews, two novels, and some musical studies as well as poems. His attitude (the last of his seven volumes of poetry appeared in 1934, a year before Lehmann's first) has much in common with Lehmann's, but he is more incantatory, and more melancholy. Lehmann would never have written that 'The mountain of care stands . . . glassily in front of every goal, and everyone who seeks happier regions finds it barring his way to the world' ('Summer Night over the Country', PGV). He much resembles Heym and Lichtenstein (qq.v.) in that he writes 'modernist' poems in strict forms. His poems often dramatize his spiritual adventures in a series of vivid and violent metaphors; they are both more personal and more mythographically ambitious than those of Lehmann. (MGP, PGV, TCG.)

ELISABETH LANGGÄSSER (ps. ELISABETH HOFFMANN, 1899–1950), born in the Rhineland, was partly Jewish; she became a Roman Catholic. She established a modest reputation as a poet and novelist before 1933, but it was the novel *The Indelible Seal* (*Das unauslöschliche Siegel*, 1946) that brought her fame. The persecution she suffered at the hands of the Nazis, including forced labour, brought about her early death. Her daughter was imprisoned in Auschwitz Concentration Camp, but survived.

As a novelist Langgässer was perfervid and humourless, but undoubtedly gifted and original. Her Catholicism is remorseless and would be tiresome even to fellow converts; but in her poetry and shorter fiction her imagination takes precedence over her religious obsessions, with happier results. And yet so discerning a critic as Broch (q.v.) suggested that *The Indelible Seal* might be the first genuinely distinguished surrealistic novel. Certainly the crudity of Lang-gässer's lifelong view of existence as a battleground for Satan and God is in direct contrast to the complexity of other aspects of her work. Perhaps, like Graham Greene (q.v.), she should be treated as one of those who are Roman Catholics in order, so to speak, to be novelists. . . .

As a poet Langgässer made no secret of her debt to Wilhelm Lehmann (q.v.), whose view of nature she consciously Christianized. She is not as distinguished a poet because her dogmatic ardour, not necessarily in tune with her imag-ination, imparts a sense of strain to her language; her devotion never strikes one (as does, say, George Herbert's) as being 'natural'. But she has insight as well as dignity and beauty of feeling, and can at her best find an appropriate language. Her terms of reference, even in moments of extreme emotional stress —as exemplified in 'Spring 1946' (TCG) when she was reunited with her eldest daughter after the latter's imprisonment—are mythical or Christian, or both. One of her obsessive themes was the reconciliation of the pagan with the Christian world—in other words with the effective Christianization of herself. The poem 'Rose in October' (TCG) perfectly illustrates both this and her usually recondite general methods. If Langgässer lacks simplicity, she does at her best convey an ecstatic sense of nature. (See also PGV.)

Her first novel, *Proserpina* (1932), reflects her concerns: the techniques are varied and sophisticated, but the content—the struggle between good and evil for the soul of a small child—is crude in the extreme. *The Indelible Seal*, which reminds one as much of J. C. Powys (q.v.) as of Greene, Bernanos and Faulkner (qq.v.) with whom she is so often compared, is concerned with the soul of Lazarus Belfontaine, a Jew converted to Roman Catholicism for extra-religious reasons. 'Enlightenment' is here unequivocally pictured as hideously evil: the result of Belfontaine's lapse is spiritual emptiness and moral foulness. But his baptism, fraudulent or not, is literally an 'indelible seal', and after the murder of his second wife he is redeemed, and finally appears during the war as a saintly beggar. Langgässer's rather puritanical but none the less fanatically anti-Lutheran Catholicism was as dogmatic as her vision was wild; here Belfontaine is saved from hell by a miraculous 'grace'. But it is the hell, not the grace, in which Langgässer is really interested. The grandly pious structure of the novel is not really of literary interest. In this author the complexities of narrative and style reflect extra-Catholic fascinations, which are consequently consigned to hell. Thus Belfontaine's unbelieving hell is surreal.

The Quest (*Märkische Argonautenfahrt*, 1950; tr. J. B. Greene, 1953) is the story of a pilgrimage, made in 1945 by seven people, in search of just such a vague, radiant grail as the author depicts in the poem, 'Rose in October', already referred to: 'Deep in the azure—Condwiramurs [wife of the Grail-questing hero Parzival] and Grail at once—the rose, red in blue, not spirit, not flesh, carries its structure high over field and lea into the ether'.

Langgässer's earlier books, such as *The Way Through the Marshland* (*Der Gang durch das Ried*, 1936), about a butcher's son who runs away and joins the Foreign Legion, are less complex but not less mannered. Her best work is to be found in *The Torso* (*Der Torso*, 1947), a collection of short stories mostly about war-time Germany. Here she is less ornate and spiritually ambitious. However, even at her most convoluted, she remains an engrossing novelist. The dogma she professed only appeared to resolve her violent confusions; but of the quality of her feeling, when not exacerbated by theological rationalizations, there can be no doubt.

The Silesian MAX HERRMANN-NEISSE (1886–1941) was a distinguished poet who associated with and was influenced by individual expressionist poets (for example, Loerke and Schickele, qq.v.) and the expressionist movement, but was never of the movement. His sense of his own doomed hideousness—he was huge-headed, his face that of an aged man, his body tiny and hunchbacked—was modified by his inherent sweetness and his grateful love for his wife Leni. He began as a more or less strident ironist, in the spirit of the times; but his irony became muted and more effective as he grew older. Herrmann-Neisse is still underrated today: he is a more individual poet than he has been given credit for. Expressionism gave him the courage to follow his own instincts, but while his usually traditional form does not function, like that of Heym or Loerke, as a pole of tension, his practice has nothing in common with 'neo-romanticism'. His mood of ironically tinged melancholy, perfectly poised in his best poems, is unique. After 1933 Herrmann-Neisse left Germany as a voluntary exile; he died in 1941 in London, where his last collection of poems had just appeared. He wrote several entertaining farces and novels, notably *The Dying Man* (*Der Todeskandidat*, 1927). (MGP, TCG, CGPD.)

GOTTFRIED BENN (1886–1956) was both an expressionist and (later) a historian of expressionism. He was also the only German poet of indisputable genius who (for a short time) embraced Nazism. He is certainly, in his way, a seminal twentieth-century figure, whether the praise of his poetry since 1945 has (as has been claimed) been 'largely uncritical' or not.

Benn, son of a Prussian Lutheran pastor and a French-Swiss mother, was a doctor. He served in the Medical Corps during 1914–18 and 1935–45; otherwise he practised in Berlin as a specialist in skin and venereal diseases until his retirement in 1954. He had been 'non-political' until 1933, and therefore profoundly shocked his friends when he gave support to Hitler—though he never joined the Nazi Party. When his work came under attack from the Nazis, he withdrew into 'inner exile' (his own term, widely adopted), saw his works banned, and sweated it unhappily out until 1945—when the Allies once again banned him (for his former Nazi sympathies). His subsequent response to fame and adulation was privately exultant, but publicly cynical, sardonic and dignified. He had never been lovable, and was not going to be now. But the old man, while continuously resisting emotion as he always had, was moved: he would even have liked to make a full, positive public gesture. Death, however, saved him from such an indignity, although he did give some lectures and interviews; probably death was right.

Two things may be said about Benn; each has an element of truth. On the one hand, he was hailed as 'one of the grand old men of literary Europe'; on the other, he was 'a highbrow charlatan ["It is not a bad word", he wrote. "There are worse".] and a lavish stylist' who 'in spite of his nihilism and his voluptuary's fingering of futility . . . makes a sharp verbal impact' (Paul West). His readers are repelled at the insensitivity that led him to support Hitler, that led the exquisite master of cerebration to fail to discern the nature of Nazism, and yet they are compelled to admit that he spoke 'from the innermost core of our time' (Wilhelm Grenzmann). Unlike another and more committed Nazi supporter, the Austrian poet Weinheber, Benn always had taste; yet this collapsed, if temporarily, when Hitler came to power. Reluctant to do more than impertinently and shockingly examine the body of life, Benn at his best is impelled to probe deeply into its unanaesthetized body; the explanation of the disturbing effect he has must be, at least in part, that he, too, is this body.

The first book was a collection of poems, *Morgue* (1912). The surgeon plays at enjoying the horrors (the aster someone had stuck between the truck-driver's teeth, which he 'packed into the chest' during the post-mortem; the dead girl's body harbouring a nest of rats; the mortician's mate who stole a dead whore's gold filling because 'Earth alone should return to earth'), but his pity, too, is evident. In *Sons* (*Söhne*, 1913) and *Flesh* (*Fleisch*, 1917) the poems are less sensational, on the whole subtler. But not many of the poems in these first collections are memorable. However, Benn never wrote more effectively than in the two early 'Songs' of 1913, the first of which states an attitude he strove to hold all his life:

> Oh that we were our primal ancestors,
> A little lump of slime in tepid swamps,
> Our life and death, mating and giving birth
> a gliding forth out of our silent sap.
>
> An alga leaf or hillock on the dunes,
> Shaped by the wind and weighted towards earth
> A dragonfly's small head, a seagull's wing
> Would be too far advanced in suffering.
>
> (tr. Michael Hamburger)

After a short period in the early Twenties when he did not write at all, Benn's work began to reflect his reaction against the optimism and the hope inherent in the expressionist movement (if not always in certain of the best poets associated with it). Always influenced by the nihilist side of Nietzsche, he now read Oswald Spengler's *The Decline of the West*, which he agreed with, and which caused him more pleasure than despair. There was a strange moral and emotional obtuseness about this undoubtedly gifted man—or was it an obstinate bloody-mindedness? In any case, it amounts to the same thing: a crass, monstrously egoistic insensitivity, a moral stupidity not unakin to that sometimes displayed by the Scottish poet Hugh MacDiarmid (q.v.). Benn, who had never previously subscribed to a view more optimistic than that the sole way of transcending the absurdity of life was by means of an autonomous art, now spoke of a 'bestial transcendence'. His transition to a support of Nazism is thus easily explicable on merely intellectual grounds. And yet his 'Answer to the Political Emigrants', written in reply to a thoughtful, shocked letter from Thomas Mann's son, the playwright Klaus Mann (q.v.), makes sickening reading; Goebbels had it featured prominently in the press. Suddenly the non-political, fastidious Benn was moved to speak of Hitler as 'magical'—and to state that 'all thinking persons' must recognize his true function. Alas, one cannot doubt Benn's sincerity. It is likely that he was surprised when in the following year he found he had to 'defend himself' against the charge of Jewish ancestry; one would give a great deal to know exactly how he felt as he sat down to perform this task. He had never been an anti-semite. His early prose writings now also brought him trouble: they were 'degenerate'. Indeed, if Benn had really shared in the Nazi brand of vitalism, then he should have been the first to condemn them. For the Dr. Rönne—justifiably referred to by critics as Rönne-Benn—of the short stories collected in *Brains* (*Gehirne*, 1916) is un-doubtedly 'degenerate', not only by the Nazis' but by any 'civilized' standards.

Rönne can only affirm consciousness of himself: this is all he makes of 'reality'. He cannot 'bear' or 'grasp' reality, knows only 'the opening and closing of the ego'; 'confronted with the experience of the deep, unbounded, mythically ancient strangeness between man and the world, [he] believed com-pletely in the myth and its images'. Rönne's is an apathetic personality because, disbelieving in the possibility of communication, he does not try to achieve any. Rönne, who also figures in some dramatic sketches, is a frigidly theoretical creation—but a very remarkable one.

Benn was forbidden by the Nazis in 1937 and by the Allies in 1945 to publish; but in 1948 the ban was lifted (it was an anti-Nazi who arranged this). He now emerged as one who championed aestheticism rather than any other form of transcendentalism. Thus his new poems were called *Static Poems* (*Statische Gedichte*, 1948): they manufactured a sense of order, a purposefulness, which was to be set against the absurdity of life, especially the absurdity of change—or so Benn intended, and so most of his critics have followed him. Benn's only novel, *The Ptolemean* (*Der Ptolemäer*, 1949; pt. tr. E. Kaiser and E. Wilkins in E. B. Ashton, ed., *Primal Vision*, Selected Writings, 1961: this contains much prose and poetry), about a beauty-specialist, makes the same point: his Ptolemean is a transparent if ironic symbol for the poet, Benn, who creates beauty in a pointless world: 'From foreign papers I see a single *maison* offers sixty-seven different brands of hair lotions and cosmetic waters, so *that* is not dying out—but when it is all up, they'll find something else, oils for robots or salves for corpses'. Meanwhile, the only sense you can make out of life—Benn says—is what you do, literally, *make*: in that way you can decide.

Benn was convinced, from early on, that the only possible intellectual attitude to adopt in the face of the twentieth century was a nihilistic one. And he was always ready to evolve theories with this notion as a basis. But he did not tell the whole story in his theoretical writings, which have none the less caused almost all his critics to call him a 'wholly cerebral', or an 'Apollonian' poet. Actually, Benn was here perpetrating a fraud: he was an intelligent man, blessed with a lucid style, posing as an original thinker; and he was a poet of romantic impulses posing as a voluptuous, clinical hedonist. What people have taken as theorizing in good faith is in fact a series of brilliant self-protective devices. Michael Hamburger has well exposed the tawdriness and moral dubiousness of Benn as a public thinker; and we know that the consequences of his public attitudes resulted in his disgraceful public endorsement of the Third Reich. But of the private man we seem to know nothing.

We need not here indulge ourselves in the so-called 'biographical fallacy'. It is sufficient to say that critics, hypnotized by Benn's brilliant, disgusting or shocking public performance, choose mainly to relate this to his poetry. Other facts, however, are equally public, if not—so to say—equally performed: Benn had a private life, he practised as a doctor (attended to the sick, whether in civilian or military life), had women and wives, deplored Hitler but continued ('objectively', as someone has said) to help him. Benn never said why he chose to heal the sick—surely mercy to venerealees is a pointless activity in a pointless world? Neither, although appearances may suggest the contrary, did he ever adequately explain his poetic impulse. His 'theory of poetry', most carefully set out in *Problems of the Lyric* (*Probleme der Lyrik*, 1951), is a coruscating artifact, designed to portray his own poems as coruscating artifacts—and as nothing else. Benn's criticism and self-explication is a cunning affair, because it sets out to conceal as much as to reveal.

It is probably a mistake to call any poet 'purely cerebral' or 'purely Apollonian'; certainly it is so in the case of Benn. What his best poetry is about, what it describes the act of, is the strangling at birth of romantic or sentimental or (sometimes) aesthetic impulses. Thus, he juxtaposes a warm, ecstatic not always devulgarized 'South' with a harsh, no-nonsense Nordic nihilism. This he systematizes into a sort of negative 'philosophy of life'; but it is not really a philosophy at all, and it will not stand up to serious examination. One of Benn's 'philosophical' tenets was that 'change' was 'absurd'; this was merely a screen for his acute nostalgia. Loving the stable past, represented by among other things a God-loving father, and yet wanting—often slickly—to be up with the times, Benn marred even his finest set of poems, those of the mid-twenties, with extraordinary neologisms: clevered-up technical and scientific jargon. As Hamburger has rightly objected, these 'have no business to be there'. Benn's poetry is seminal because in it he is recording the disturbances of an intelligent modern sensibility; but it is as though he doubts his own modernity, and feels obliged to assert it in this strident manner.

Benn was embarrassed by beauty and tenderness and delight and tried to turn his affirmations of these qualities into hedonistic negatives. Consequently, his poetry is crippled: faces that wear masks for too long must themselves come to resemble them. But his poetry, despite its faults, does have its element of integrity, and it does contain a secret history of what this clever century does, in its agony, to simplicity—to delight, love, affirmation. Even the distortions in

Benn's work, stylistic and mental, are ultimately an affirmation, an attempt to create the communication and love he denies, to make beauty. He preaches a selfhood as unavoidable, but loathes it and wants to return to the ancient unity of the original slime. The dense blocks of language of which some of his poems of the Twenties consist, in which the verb and sometimes even syntax itself are eliminated, are primeval in just this way: they seem to point to a regression to a more archaic utterance, and they provided Benn himself with a means of escape from his terror of death by dissolution into absolute cerebration. Analyse how Benn's poetry actually works, ignore what he says, and sometimes even what the poetry seems to try to say, and you come closer to the heart of the poet.

We can seldom ignore in Benn's work the cruel obtuseness of the self-styled hedonist; but nor can we always ignore the tenderness of the doctor who preserved life while officially not believing in it. It is significant that in a late poem (1948), characteristically a mixture of self-love and tender idealism (here for once not distorted out of recognition), Benn should have postulated himself as Chopin ('he for his part was unable/to explicate his nocturnes'): a 'minor' composer, exquisite, 'romantic', loved by the vulgar as by the discriminating— and full of 'emotion': not a 'mathematical' or 'scientific' type; and that one of the very last poems should end:

> Often I have asked myself, but found no answer,
> Where gentleness and goodness can possibly come from;
> Even today I can't tell, and it's time to be gone.
>
> (MGP)

Perhaps Hofmannsthal should have the last word: like many readers of Benn's poems, he saw him (in an essay) as the 'man lurking beneath the bridge over which every man passes, the unknown beggar at his own hearth'.

(As well as in the comprehensive *Primal Vision*, see TCG, PGV, CGVD, MGP, MEP.)

VIII

Expressionism proper, the self-conscious movement permeating all spheres of thought and activity, flourished in the theatre as nowhere else (except, perhaps, in the cafés). There was, significantly, no single outstanding dramatist. The typical expressionist play might combine features of the drama of Strindberg (the supernatural) and of Wedekind and Sternheim (satire on the bourgeois); it would probably be more strident, more obviously experimental. As well as in the dramatic fragments or sketches that nearly all the expressionists wrote (e.g. Benn, Stramm, qq.v.), it is in the drama proper that we hear most loudly the ecstatic or agonized cry that is so characteristic of the movement.

The Austro-Czech OSCAR KOKOSCHKA (1886) is an important figure and a great painter, but not a major writer. However, his first play, *Murder, Hope of the Women* (1907; GED) has been called the first expressionist drama—and certainly it is an early and pure example. In Vienna, in the summer of 1908, it created an outrage, as did *Sphinx and Strawman* (*Sphinx und Strohmann*, 1907), which was performed with it—neither is more than a few hundred lines long. The characters have no names, and much of the dialogue consists of exclamation and disjointed sentences. The very violence of the conception, and the lack of an element of reality, anticipate dada and surrealism (qq.v.) as much as expressionism. Later came *The Burning Bush* (*Der brennende Dornbusch*, 1911); once again, the subject is man and woman, their love and hate for each other, and their eventual regeneration. These first plays reflect Kokoschka's sexual turbulence at the time; but in typical expressionist fashion he exploits this to present—or attempt to present—a frenetic picture of the situation between the sexes. Later *Sphinx and Strawman* was expanded into the three-act *Job* (*Hiob*, 1917; GED), the nearest Kokoschka came to writing a 'normal' play: it has some relaxed sparkle and wit, in the Viennese manner. *Orpheus and Eurydice* (1919) reflects the author's sufferings in the war, when he was very seriously wounded, and his consequent pacifism, as well as his continuing obsession with the conflict between man and woman.

Kokoschka's plays have intrinsic worth as well as historical importance (Thornton Wilder, q.v., is an unexpected acknowledger of their influence on him); but because his gift is not for language their excesses seem melodramatic; they are mainly to be regarded as an essential part of his development. Kokoschka drew most of the illustrations for Walden's *Der Sturm* (q.v.). (A volume of Kokoschka's short stories has been translated: *A Sea Ringed With Visions, Spur im Treibsand*, 1962.)

REINHARD SORGE (1892–1916) was first influenced by Nietzsche; then, just after his only work of importance had been performed, he discovered Christ and tried to give publicity to his repudiation of Nietzsche's overman. He can hardly be said to have repudiated his expressionism, however, because his mood was continuously fervent in the expressionist manner: his conversion to Catholicism merely anticipated by a few years the conversion of scores of minuscule expressionists either to some form of Christianity or to communism. Yet his verse-play *The Beggar* (*Der Bettler*, 1912; tr. Acts 1–3 only, GED), while of little literary value, anticipates many innovations and notions, including that of the 'theatre as hospital' (if, indeed, this can really be said to be new at all, in view of Aristotle's *Poetics*). A beggar-poet is presented as in conflict with his insanely materialistic engineer-father. The play now seems intensely puerile, but it does give a clear notion of what expressionism as a movement was about: the spiritual poet feels compelled to regenerate the people, rather than to entertain them; and in doing so he has to destroy his father, whose 'insanity' takes the form of wanting to aid the world from without (by utilizing the canals on Mars). The beggar-poet-son wants to regenerate it from within. After writing some grandiose mystical dramas and verse, Sorge was killed on the Somme. His impassioned attitude had been carried over into his life: he and his wife spent the first nine months of their marriage in mutual prayer so intense that they forgot to consummate their union.

PAUL KORNFELD (1889–1942), who later successfully turned to bizarre comedy before he was murdered by the Nazis in a Polish concentration camp, wrote two scarcely more dramatically effective expressionist plays, one bleakly pessimistic, the other ecstatically optimistic: *The Seduction* (*Die Verführung*, 1913) and *Heaven and Hell* (*Himmel und Hölle*, 1919). Kornfeld eschewed all characterization, and sought to portray his heroes as lonely souls embattled with bourgeois authority and heartlessness. His hero performs a 'gratuitous act', the murder of a bourgeois he dislikes on first sight, and is sent to prison, where he is surrounded by grotesque functionaries. Persuaded to escape for love, he is himself destroyed. The second play is even more nakedly programmatic, and contains less satire and more sentimentality: the redeemer is a repulsive Lesbian tart who, after sacrificial execution, rises—with others—to heaven on a cloud to divine choruses. Kornfeld, whose later less ambitious comedies show more of his gift, exhorted actors to ignore the objective (which did not exist), and represent only abstract ideas.

Of more account than these was WALTER HASENCLEVER (1890–1940), who was another victim of the Nazis: he committed suicide in an internment camp in France, having emigrated there in 1933. Hasenclever, a friend of Werfel's and Kokoschka's, began as a 'shocking' poet (confessing his sexual adventures), and became a highly successful writer of film-scripts and musical comedies after the heyday of expressionism; but he was best known for *The Son* (*Der Sohn*, 1914, produced 1916), the best of all the many parricidal plays produced in Germany during this period. The plot is crude—the son, ecstasy-possessed, is eventually forestalled from shooting his father only by the latter's fatal stroke—but the language is more convincing; and by casting his play in a traditional form Hasenclever maintains dramatic tension. The expressionist theatre owed much to its producers—mainly Erwin Piscator and Leopold Jessner; but Hasenclever's particular friend was the more conservative Max Reinhardt (q.v.), which may possibly account for the comparatively more conventional form of *The Son*.

This doubtless helped the Viennese ARNOLT BRONNEN (ps. ARNOLD BRONNER, 1895–1959) to write the most publicly shocking of all the plays on this popular subject: *Parricide* (*Vatermord*, 1915, produced 1922), in which the son, about to be seduced by his naked mother, despatches his father (Herr Fessel = fetter) with a coal shovel as he breaks into the bedroom. Bronnen went to East Germany after the defeat of 1945. But for a time he had been in charge of Nazi radio drama. His latter-day confessions are of interest, though produced for communist consumption.

Three other expressionist playwrights contributed drama of more permanent value. ERNST TOLLER (1893–1939), a political activist who took part in the workers' November revolution of 1918 and went to prison for five years (1919–24) as a consequence of his Chairmanship of the Bavarian Soviet Republican party, killed himself in New York after six years of exile. Toller's abundant dramatic genius was to some extent vitiated by his political passions—although he would not have accepted the charge. His first play was *Transfiguration* (*Die Wandlung*, 1919; tr. *Seven Plays*, 1935), in which for perhaps the first time the established expressionistic technique of alternating reality with dream is presented with real dramatic effectiveness. But although it is expressionist in technique, this play could also be regarded as symbolist. The pacifist hero is portrayed in realistic scenes, which alternate with dream ones that contrast with his idealism: there is no 'inwardness', only a beckoning towards Utopian socialism. Toller was an agonized Utopian (some of his most moving work consists of lyrics written in prison) but, despite his skill and passion, his language does not really measure up to his convictions. He feels impelled to write of man the frustrated socialist animal, rather than to record the details of his own suffering: the lack of selfishness spoils, or at least vitiates, his art. His most famous play is *Masses and Man* (*Masse Mensch*, 1921; tr. *Seven Plays*), in which the characters are anonymous. Dramatically this is one of the most effective of all expressionist plays, but from its realistic scenes one infers how much more powerful it might have been if Toller, instead of concentrating on a 'message', had concentrated on finding an 'objective correlative' for his emotions in a human situation. Almost always in his plays the human situation in which the imaginative writer is interested gives way to a programme that has to be 'expressionistically' realized. The exception is *The Machine-Wreckers* (*Die Maschinenstürmer*, 1922; tr. *Seven Plays*; Ashley Dukes, 1923), his finest achievement. Doubtless this is because it is his most realistic play, and realism happened in fact to be where he excelled. This is based on the 1815 Luddite revolt in England, and is largely historical. Although this has a 'message'—man's enslavement by machinery, and all the capitalistic consequences—it grips the spectator and the reader because of its dramatic situation: its irony (the hero is murdered by the men he works to free) goes beyond any programme: Toller had become temporarily fascinated by reality rather than theory. None of his many other plays reaches this standard except *Hinkemann* (1923; tr. *Seven Plays*), on the not uncommon theme of the soldier who has been emasculated through war injury (compare Ernest Hemingway's *The Sun also Rises*, later *Fiesta*, q.v.). Here Toller does become interested again in his character as a character, rather than as a symbol: Hinkemann could not be happy even in a socialist Utopia, and this tragic fact is what fascinates Toller.

Such is life (*Hoppla, wir leben!*, 1927; tr. *Seven Plays*), produced by Piscator (who with characteristic ruthlessness added some fifty minutes of his own business, mostly consisting of filmed material), deals with the emergence from isolation in a mental hospital of a revolutionary, Karl Thomas. His betrayer, also a former revolutionary, is now a minister in the capitalist government. Thomas plots to kill him, but is forestalled by a fanatic; however, he is arrested for the crime, and in prison (prophetically) commits suicide: here Toller projected his own sense of ineffectuality. His later plays could only demonstrate his sense of hopelessness and frustration. If he could have examined his disillusion in non-political terms, he might have found creative satisfaction; as it was, the events of 1933 in Germany broke him both as man and playwright. He could never

examine in enough depth his disappointment that 'mankind' rejected 'the poet':
'Men make them suffer', he wrote in prison. 'Men they love/With inextin-
guishable ardour,/They, who are brothers to the stars and stones and storms/
More than to this humanity'.

FRITZ VON UNRUH (1885–1970), who was born at Coblenz, is a forgotten man
of German letters. Unruh was the son of a general who insisted—against
advice—on his son's taking up a military career. The whole of his writing
may be seen as a protest against this. Unruh left the Imperial Guard in 1912 in
order to devote his life to literature, but was recalled in 1914. After the war
Unruh became a political activist, and was a member of the Reichstag. He left
Germany in 1932. He was not successful in re-establishing his reputation there
on his return, although he continued to write.

Unruh's first, pre-1914 plays are on the theme of duty and aristocratic revolt,
and led to his being compared with the Prussian dramatist Heinrich von Kleist
(1777–1811), who had also resigned from the army to devote himself to
literature. On the surface the early plays are aristocratic in sympathy; actually
they foreshadow Unruh's expressionist future: the heroes are vitalists in love with
death, although they call their nihilism relief from tedium and the achievement
of glory. Unruh's change of heart, which led him to recognize nationalism as a
symptom of the death-wish, came within a month or two of the beginning of the
war: it was a logical step. The now somewhat embarrassingly hysterical
dramatic poem *Before the Decision* (*Vor der Entscheidung*, 1919) was written in
October 1914, but not published until five years later. This is a record of
Unruh's 'transfiguration'; it ends as the soldier hero, Ulan, calls his troops to
battle—against their own masters. But it was his one-act *A Family* (*Ein Geschlecht*,
1917) that turned him into a leading expressionist dramatist overnight; this
remains his best play. The verse in which it is written is not poetry, but is
effective in the theatre. This, too, ends in an army's revolutionary march on its
masters. The Eldest Son, who denounces the Mother for carrying both life and
therefore death in her 'moisted womb', has committed rape, as a soldier, and is
condemned to die. (His brother has just been killed in battle.) His behaviour
incidentally exposes the hypocrisy of this judgement, but it goes further: his
aggression towards everything (except his sister, for whom he lusts) is prompted
by his sense of the absurd—and thus, as W. H. Sokel has pointed out, foreshadows an 'existential' attitude. He kills himself. The Mother, who is executed
as the leader of the rebellious soldiery, represents the life-force—she figures in
other expressionist works, particularly those of Werfel (q.v.), and is ultimately
derived from the anthropologically incorrect postulation of an ancient matri-
archy in *Das Mutterrecht* (1841) of the Swiss J. J. Bachofen (1815–87), which has
been no less uncritically accepted in our own time by the English poet Robert
Graves (q.v.). However, the Youngest Son, who was also condemned to death
for cowardice and desertion, takes her place as leader, and the soldiers march
off: he lacks the father's hardness, and has heeded his mother's last call for the
creation of a new race. *Square* (*Platz*, 1920), the sequel, lacks the fierce passion
that lifted its predecessor out of the commonplace. The Youngest Son (now

called Dietrich) resigns his leadership, chooses a spiritual lover rather than a sensual one, and looks forward, from amongst the ruins of his political dreams, to the creation of 'a new man', the stock-figure of 'Phase II' expressionism. *Bonaparte* (1927; tr. E. Björkman, 1928), the only one of Unruh's plays to be translated, prophesied the rise of the Nazis.

Unruh continued to write plays, the most recent being the comedy *Bismarck* (1955), and he achieved fame in this form; but his best work has been in prose. His best book, written while at the front at Verdun in 1916, has been translated: *Way of Sacrifice* (*Opfergang*, 1918; tr. C. A. Macartney, 1928). If this is not a classic of description of war itself, it is a classic of description of man's mind when he is at war. *The End is Not Yet* (1947, in English; German version: *Der nie verlor*, 1949) is about Nazism. Unruh had a grotesque, unusual sense of humour, which has more often been seen since the war in his comedies and novels. *The Saint* (1950, in English; *Die Heilige*, 1951) is about Catherine of Siena. Unruh has believed throughout his life in the primacy of 'ideas' over 'facts'; his work, however, has been at its best when the facts rather than the ideas pressed themselves upon him.

GEORG KAISER (1878–1945) is certainly the paramount dramatist of expressionism; whether he was more than that is doubtful. His enormous output has now dated, and it remains to be seen whether his greatest successes, such as the *Gas* trilogy, could stand revival. Besides some seventy dramatic works, he wrote two novels and over one hundred poems. His vision was the one common to most expressionists: the regeneration of man. Kaiser was a brilliant theatrical craftsman, but like every one of the expressionist dramatists his language is scarcely adequate to sustain the explosive content of his plays. He has been revived on the post-war German stage and occasionally elsewhere, but usually in his capacity as a satirist rather than as a pioneer of expressionism.

Kaiser's theories of dramatic presentation, like his personality as a whole, were violently forthright—and crude. His plays are shorn of 'facts' so that the 'ideas' may emerge the more forcefully. His chief models were Plato's dialogues (in his consideration 'the greatest plays'). When his landlord prosecuted him for selling some of the furnishings of the villa he rented him, Kaiser's defence was that he was an artist who had needed the money; he was sent to prison (only in France might he have got away with this line of defence). There is no distinction between thinking and feeling; 'the intellect is a wound'. His earliest plays owed much to Wedekind (q.v.), although Kaiser went further with caricature. In *Headmaster Kleist* (*Rektor Kleist*, 1905) a boy commits suicide because of his teachers' tyranny. This is farcical satire, full of hate for the school system. He first attracted attention with *From Morn to Midnight* (*Von Morgens bis Mitternachts*, 1912; tr. A. Dukes, 1920), about a bank clerk's embezzlement of a large sum and his discovery that it is of no use to him. He is finally betrayed by a Salvation Army girl (for the reward) after attending a gigantic bicycle race—an impressive scene, for Kaiser was a master of the theatre—and kills himself. Kaiser achieved real fame, however, with a play written in 1914 but not performed until 1917: *The Burghers of Calais* (*Die Bürger von Calais*), based on the famous story, but with an additional hero: a successfully activist intellectual who sacrifices himself in order to achieve a universal rebirth.

Kaiser's most famous play was the trilogy *Gas*: *The Coral, Gas I, Gas II* (*Die Koralle*, 1917, *Gas I*, 1918, *Gas II*, 1920; tr. in 25MP). In the first the Billionaire gains self-identity and (expressionist) freedom by murdering his secretary and double, and is executed. In *Gas I* his son continues the management of his gas producing factory, giving the workers a share of the profits. It explodes, and the son tries to deliver his workmen from their enslavement to the machine, but they oppose him (cf. Toller, q.v.) and stone him to death; he expires as he affirms a vision of regenerated man. In *Gas II* the workers have already become slaves, and an entirely impersonal war is in progress. However, the war is lost and the workers gain control of the factory from the state. The end is cataclysmic. Not only did Kaiser thus prophesy the atom bomb, but also his faceless and nameless villains truly resemble the horrifyingly dehumanized politicians of today.

The true dramatic situation did not interest Kaiser, and his plays, for all their passion, have no more warmth or humanity than Shaw's (q.v.); but Shaw was witty, and Kaiser was not. Although his later plays are more realistic in style, they continue to explore the world of ideas rather than that of situation, of psychology: Kaiser never even succeeded in depicting the kind of personality (like his own) that is driven by a vision from an objective viewpoint. He himself gradually withdrew from reality, since—as for so many of the expressionists—it proved so unaccommodating to his ideas. (One of his two novels, *Villa Aurea*, 1940, appeared first in English tr.: *Vera, or a Villa in Sicily*, 1939.)

One other of the many expressionists deserves notice. HANNS JOHST (1890) may be treated as symptomatic of the 'evil wing' of expressionism, and of its totalitarian tendencies: his plays, novels and verse are derivative, and whatever small promise they had is easily discountable in his later commitment of 'unchanging loyalty' to Hitler. *The Lonely One* (*Der Einsame*, 1917) is about the nineteenth-century poet Christian Grabbe, one of those hailed by the expressionists as a precursor. Johst, an opportunistic anti-semite who was showered with honours by the Nazis, reached his nadir with *Schlageter* (1933), in which a saboteur executed by the French in the Ruhr in 1923 is made into a hero. One can see the future Nazi and honorary SS man foreshadowed even in the earliest of Johst's plays and novels.

IX

The major novelists, apart from Mann, are Kafka, Musil, Hesse, Broch—and, I would add, the unfairly forgotten Döblin (qq.v.). These are discussed in the following section. Here I deal with a selection from the vast number of other novelists, beginning with those usually classed as expressionists.

The Prague-born FRANZ WERFEL (1890–1945) was an ecstatic sensitive who almost inevitably lapsed into best-selling middlebrowdom. He began as an expressionist poet, continued as an expressionist dramatist, and ended as a progressively inferior 'epic' novelist. As has been well observed, the 'rhetorical plush and pathos of his verse have not worn well', and it is necessary to select rigorously. The single poem Hamburger and Middleton choose to represent him by in their *Modern German Poetry* is an excellent example of his touchingly ecstatic—and typically expressionistic—manner, and his stylistic brilliance:

> Tell me, what brought you safely
> Through all the nightseas of sand?

> In my hair shone unfailing
> A nest a nest of blue light.

> (MGP)

This is more attractive than the injunction to us all, in *Veni Creator Spiritus*, to 'rise from our stricken lowlands' and 'storm into one another like flames'. Werfel's early poetry, which contains his best work, possesses the skill and charm that never left him. In the Twenties, when his verse had lost its early fervour, he wrote a revealing little poem about himself as conductor, reproving 'applause as he acknowledges it' and showing the 'harassed features of a saviour'. This has been called ironic; but is perhaps more appropriately regarded as revealing a charming and decent awareness of his essential vulgarity. W. H. Sokel is correct when he says that in his final works Werfel achieved 'a happy and profitable blend of commercialism and Judaeo-Christian sentiments', and his accusation that Werfel achieved 'communion with the masses' by oversimplifying and sentimentalizing his fiction is a fair one—but he was not exactly a charlatan. It was simply that his original creative gift, a lyrical one, was very small and delicately balanced; but his skill was disproportionately high, and he fell an easy victim to self-inflation. His sweetness turned syrupy, and he fell in love with his own religiose image. His 'spiritual quest', inspired by Gustav Mahler's widow, whom he married, might easily have been filmed in technicolour: its culmination is all too easily understandable. His nauseous *The Song of Bernadette* (*Das Lied von Bernadette*, 1941; tr. L. Lewisohn, 1958), turned into an even more nauseous film, made (as Sokel rightly says) 'millions of shopgirls weep and rejoice'. The vulgarizing tendency appears at least as early as the novel *Verdi: a Novel of the Opera* (*Verdi: Roman der Oper*, 1924; tr. H. Jessiman, 1924). Werfel genuinely loved Verdi's music, and edited an important edition of his letters as well as adapting two of his operas into German; but the Verdi of the novel, a kind of Werfel, bears no resemblance to the historical Verdi. Here is a *Wandlung* indeed.

Werfel was an important figure in the expressionist theatre from the time of his adaptation of Euripides' *The Trojan Women* (*Die Troerinnen*, 1915), with its religio-pacifist message. In *Goat Song* (*Bocksgesang*, 1921; tr. R. Langer, 1936), peasants in rebellion worship a monster only half-human; destroyed, this beast leaves his legacy in the form of a child. This is typically ambivalent: it can be taken as a condemnation of the bestial in man, or as a vitalistic affirmation—or, confusedly, both. Perhaps Werfel, having lost the poetic faculty of his youth, found himself most truly and least offensively in the comedy *Jacobowsky and the Colonel* (*Jakobowsky und der Oberst*, 1944; tr. N. S. Behrman, 1944), in which a clever Jewish refugee gets an anti-semitic Polish colonel through the enemy lines. Here a more than usually relaxed Werfel disguises mockery of his own pretensions as a tribute to Jewish ingenuity. (There are translations of Werfel's poems in MGP, PGV, TCG; and in *Poems*, tr. E. A. Snow, 1945; most of his novels appeared in English.)

Werfel, as a Jew, could not but have chosen exile—nor, doubtless, would he have wished to do so. JOHANNES R. BECHER (1891–1958), who would have been a minor figure without the existence of the expressionist movement, unlike his almost exact contemporary Johst (q.v.), chose the way of the left. A communist in 1918–19, he spent 1935–45 in Russia, and then became Minister of Culture in East Germany. His prolific verse is in the frenzied 'poster' style of Mayakovsky (q.v.), but, like the English pseudo-satirist Christopher Logue's, without any underlying genius. He began by expressing the sense of loneliness felt by the individual in large cities, but soon found a facile way of merging himself with these masses, only miserable when divided. His best work is the novel *Parting* (*Abschied*, 1948): in so far as it is polemic it fails (the boy-hero solves his problems too easily, by becoming a revolutionary and refusing to join up in 1914); but the effects of stultifying bourgeois existence on the young before the First World War are often sharply recollected.

LEONHARD FRANK (1882–1961), novelist and dramatist, was accused of being a vulgarizer of expressionism, and this would be true if the movement could have been vulgarized. But he was a genial, humorous, unpretentious writer who increasingly tended towards crudity and the (inoffensively) middlebrow; his best work, based in experience, had real substance; the disjointed techniques of expressionism added nothing essential to it: at heart, Frank was an optimistic naturalist. His sympathy with the proletariat was by no means theoretical: the son of a carpenter, he had known poverty and had been a worker. His best novel was certainly his first, *The Robber Band* (*Die Räuberbande*, 1914; tr. C. Brooks, 1928), which must have influenced Erich Kästner (q.v.). Frank offers what Sokel calls the 'best example of the Expressionist's *Wandlung* from self-abasement to human dignity through revolt, and thereby shows us the genesis of the activist attitude'—but the novel's energy comes, too, from the element of sheer fun of the plot, which involves a gang of boys who form themselves into a secret society and have various anti-social adventures. It should be compared with Jules Romains' nearly contemporaneous *Les Copains* (q.v.). However, *The Robber Band* is also a sour variation of the *Künstlerroman* (q.v.), since its hero (ironically named Old Shatterhand, after the fantasy-German—noble, tough, and so on—created by the Wild West Adventure author KARL MAY, 1842–1912, Hitler's favourite writer), a painter, utterly lacks self-conviction or the will to live, and eventually kills himself. In *The Singers* (*Das Ochsenfurter Männerquartett*, 1927; tr. C. Brooks, 1932) Frank shows his 'robber band' turned into timid bourgeois. In his next novel, *The Cause of the Crime* (*Die Ursache*, 1915; tr. C. Brooks, 1928) Frank turned rather ostentatiously to Freud. The hero, a masochist like Old Shatterhand, discovers through self-analysis (of, among other material, his dreams) that his inferiority is the result of humiliation which Mager, a sadistic teacher who figures in *The Robber Band*, forced upon him. He decides to visit him to discuss the matter, but when they meet finds that Mager is still a sadist—and so strangles him. Again, expressionist though it was in style and message, this novel had such a wide appeal because of its realism and the suspense that Frank built up. The murderer, Anton Seiler, uses his trial as an opportunity to broadcast his message—just as Kaiser (q.v.) had in real life.

Man is Good (*Der Mensch ist gut*, 1917), the most explicitly expressionist of all his works, written in Zurich—where he had joined Schickele (q.v.) and other German pacifists—was notorious for the picture it gave of the suffering caused by war and for its possibly deleterious effect on the German home front. Frank was a writer of international stature by the time the Nazis came to power in 1933—when he found it necessary to flee. His *Carl and Anna* (*Carl und Anna*, 1926; tr. C. Brooks, 1929) shows him at his most sentimental; it was taken as seriously all over the world as Muriel Spark (q.v.) is now. *Heart on the Left* (*Links wo das Herz ist*, 1952; tr. C. Brooks, 1954), an autobiographical novel, is the best of his later books, doubtless because, in the words of one literary historian, it displays 'scant regard for elementary decency'.

JAKOB WASSERMANN (1873–1934), a German Jew who spent most of his life in Austria, had sincerely grandiose pretensions not unlike those of Charles Morgan or Lawrence Durrell (qq.v.), and these led middlebrow critics to regard him— in the Twenties—as an equal of Dostoevski and Thomas Mann (q.v.); none the less, unlike at least Morgan, he deserves rescue from the total oblivion into which he has now fallen. His best book is his autobiography, *My Life as German and Jew* (*Mein Weg als Deutscher und Jude*, 1921; tr. S. N. Brainin, 1933), but his novels are not entirely negligible. Wassermann was a public figure in much demand as a Jewish liberal—a kind of 'exposed nerve of humanity', like the more substantial Arthur Koestler (q.v.). His friends, who included the composer Busoni and the writers Döblin, Schnitzler, Mann and Hofmannsthal (qq.v.), were mostly of superior creative calibre to himself. His later novels are well-meaningly pretentious; they ape profundity but are not rooted in his own German experience. Hence his popularity amongst a wide middlebrow readership in the English-speaking world. But even if he could not adequately reveal the reasons for human cruelty, he was a true humanitarian. His best novels are *The Dark Pilgrimage* (*Die Juden von Zirndorf*, 1897; tr. C. Brooks, 1933), in substance an attack on Jewish religiosity, and *The Maurizius Case* (*Der Fall Maurizius*, 1928; tr. C. Newton, 1929), about an old case reopened. This latter novel often falls into pastiche of Dostoevski, but remains an effective crime story. *Caspar Hauser* (*Caspar Hauser oder Die Trägheit des Herzens* 1908; tr. C. Newton, 1928) is mannered and laboured, but the passion of its message does come through: on the familiar motif of the imprisoned prince, used by Hofmannsthal in *The Tower* (qq.v.), the real theme is the destruction of innocence by the 'system'. (Caspar Hauser, 'the wild boy', had appeared on the streets of Nuremberg in May 1828. He was like an animal, yet able to give an account of himself: he said he had been kept in a hole by 'the man'. After becoming transformed into a handsome youth, in 1833 he was found shot in the breast. Probably he was a hysterical impostor; but the story naturally attracted many German novelists and poets, especially those of the expressionist generation. Georg Trakl, q.v., was obsessed with it.) *The Goose Man* (*Das Gänsemännchen*, 1915; tr. A. W. Porterfield, 1922) is an over-ambitious attempt to improve upon Heinrich Mann's *The Little Town* (q.v.) in that it tries to portray the artist reconciled with society; its shortcomings may be seen by comparing it to Heinrich Mann's earlier book.

Sometimes described as the initiator of expressionism (because of an occasion in 1910 on which he publicly read a poem of his Austro-Czech compatriot Werfel in Berlin), MAX BROD (1884–1968) is certainly best known as the friend of Franz Kafka (q.v.), preserver (against his instructions) of his works, and editor and interpreter of them. Inevitably his views on Kafka have been violently challenged, although all are grateful that he disobeyed the instructions. However, he has been a prolific author on his own account. A good deal of his work has been translated into English, but not the most outstanding: *The Great Risk* (*Das grosse Wagnis*, 1919). This subtle dystopian novel anticipated many aspects of *Brave New World* and *1984* (qq.v.), and is in some respects superior to Zamyatin's *We* (q.v.), a much more widely acknowledged prototype. Here a society that was started on idealistic but intelligently realistic principles turns into a nightmare totalitarian state. *The Great Risk* dissects and condemns expressionist activism; but Brod continued to believe in Israel as a possible Utopia, and lived there from 1939 and was the director of the Habima Theatre in Tel Aviv. Brod was a passionate Zionist from when he came under the influence of the philosopher Martin Buber, soon after 1908.

Brod's novels have not been very successful in English, largely because his style is cumbersome and turgid; he lacks his friend Kafka's narrative facility, and this even applies to *The Great Risk*. *The Redemption of Tycho Brahe* (*Tycho Brahes Weg zu Gott*, 1916; tr. F. W. Crosse, 1928) sets the mystical Danish astronomer against the 'scientific' Kepler in a Bohemian castle; an account of it, alas, is more inspiring than its text. This is more straightforwardly expressionist than *The Great Risk*, since it unashamedly uses an unhistorical version of the past (cf. Werfel's *Verdi*, q.v.) in order to explore the problems of the present. Brod wrote many plays, including dramatizations of Kafka's *The Castle* and *America* (qq.v.), some volumes of verse, and critical books, including *The Kingdom of Love* (*Zauberreich der Liebe*, 1928; tr. E. Sutton, 1930), which, as well as being autobiographical, is about Kafka, who is seen as an expressionist saint. *Mira* (1958) is about Hofmannsthal (q.v.).

Although KARL KRAUS (1874–1936) was one of Robert Musil's (q.v.) pet hates—'There are two things against which one can't fight because they are too long, too fat, and have neither head nor foot: Karl Kraus and psychoanalysis'—

perhaps partly owing to the latter's jealousy, he was none the less one of the most notable of all modern satirists. Success never made him complacent or less critical of his audience. For well over half his life he ran and wrote most of his own satirical paper, *The Torch* (*Die Fackel*, 1889–1936). A Jew, he was born in what is now Czechoslovakia and was then a part of the Austro-Hungarian Empire: at Jičin in north-eastern Bohemia. However, he became to all intents and purposes a Viennese. Kraus was a writer who understood and accepted the fact of the disintegration of the Empire—and its implications—and (the fun apart) his life may be seen as dedicated to an intelligent and just reappraisal. If his themes—the corrupting effects of commerce, the enslavement of men by machinery, sexual hypocrisy—seem familiar, then he was one of those who helped to make our century aware of them. He fought the press and what it represented—lack of values, hypocrisy, vulgarity—all his life; in turn journalists suppressed mention of him whenever possible. His support of the Catholic-fascist Dollfuss, towards the end of his life, was an unfortunate miscalculation, not a change of heart: he believed that Dollfuss could save Austria from annexation by the Nazis. The other side of the picture, which the socialist friends he lost never saw—it did not appear until sixteen years after his death—is to be seen in his attacks on the Third Reich, *The Third Walpurgis Night* (*Die dritte Walpurgisnacht*, 1952).

Kraus's finest work, however, is an enormous play that has never, in fact, been performed in full: *The Last Days of Mankind* (*Die letzten Tage der Menschheit*, 1922). This is partly documentary, with a cast of hundreds—it anticipates the methods of Brecht and Weiss (qq.v.) and makes some use of expressionist technique. When performed, it was necessarily condensed. With adjustments, it would make—were the terms not almost a contradiction—intelligent television. *The Last Days of Mankind* is an attack on war and on the press, which Kraus saw as representing and maintaining the forces that cause war. He was fifty years ahead of the irresponsible arch-popster McLuhan (q.v.) in pointing out that 'printed words have enabled depraved humanity to commit atrocities they can no longer imagine. . . . Everything that happens happens only for those who describe it and for those who do not experience it'. In *The Last Days of Mankind* the continuation of selfish life, with the people still on their diet of cliché, is contrasted with the horrors of war. At the end the Voice of God speaks the ghastly words attributed to the aged Franz Josef in 1914: 'I didn't want this to happen'. Kraus also wrote some pungent criticism and poetry (*Poems*, tr. A. Broch, 1930, including sel. from *The Last Days of Mankind*). He still has not had his full due because modern literary journalists who do investigate him prefer hastily to redraw the curtains they have unwittingly opened: his work is a mirror of smallness and irresponsibility. Only at times of crisis or international despair is he reprinted and praised. He is important, too, for his colloquial style and his shrewd concern for the German language. He was a man who foresaw almost all the excesses of our post-1945 age, and to that unhappy extent would have been at home in it; it desperately needs, moreover, a man of his integrity, imagination and ability.

The early death from consumption of KLABUND (ps. ALFRED HENSCHKE, 1890–1928) moved his friend Gottfried Benn (q.v.) to the least restrained peroration of his life. Klabund was a poet, free adapter from other languages (notably oriental), short-story writer, dramatist and novelist. His historical novels such as *Rasputin* (1929), *The Incredible Borgias* (*Borgia*, 1928; tr. L. Brink, 1929) and *Peter the Czar* (*Pjotr*, 1923; tr. H. G. Scheffauer, 1925) are tedious, though they enjoyed some middlebrow success (as the title of the Borgias one amply shows). His oriental adaptations, though often too deliberately and voluptuously concinnous, brilliantly construct exquisite alien worlds. Klabund was undoubtedly gifted; he was as undoubtedly capable of crass vulgarity. Although he was never nominally one of the group, he may be regarded as a typical expressionist; his undoubted talents never quite lifted him out of the rut of a mere category, unless in a few of his adaptations and short stories, and in the play *Circle of Chalk* (*Der Kreidekreis*, 1924; tr. J. Laver, 1928), on a theme also used by Brecht (q.v.). Sokel mentions a story of Klabund's as exemplifying the 'crassest example of the vampire-personality in Expressionism': in 'The Man with the Mark' the protagonist becomes a writer only when his face is disfigured by a disease. Now he wears a mask and waits in the café for people from whom to gain material for his writings; he has none of his own (cf. Musil's infinitely subtler study of a 'man without qualities', q.v.). A girl falls in love with him, asks to see what is behind his mask, and when she is shown kills herself. He writes a story about this. As Sokel points out, this is a crudely naïve attack on the concept of 'art' and on the artist as a user of a mask, a 'romantic fraud', to hide the horror of his empty self. . . . (Cf. Thomas Mann, q.v.)

More substantial, but formidable and bewildering, was the eccentric organ-builder, music-publisher and horse-breeder HANS HENNY JAHNN (1894–1959). Jahnn made his reputation as a playwright, with such plays as *Pastor Ephraim Magnus*, which caused an uproar when staged by Brecht and Bronnen (qq.v.) in 1919. In his play *Die Krönung Richards III* (1921) the deformed King, decidedly a sick 'expressionist artist', kills because of his ugliness. But posterity will be more interested in his strange, genuinely original but not uniformly readable novels *Perrudja* (1929) and the trilogy *Shoreless River* (*Fluss ohne Ufer*, 1949–50: I. *The Ship*, tr. C. Hutten, 1961). This latter work occupied him for the sixteen years before its publication. Jahnn is the kind of writer who is excessively praised by a very small minority; universal recognition never came to him, although his reputation is now slowly growing.

Jahnn is generally spoken of as having been influenced by Joyce and Freud, which he was; but Kafka was a more potent and first-hand influence than either. His obsessive emphasis on sexual violence springs naturally from an expressionist background, but is in its context entirely his own. It was the Pole Witold Gombrowicz (q.v.) who suggested that when approaching 'difficult books' we should in the first instance 'dance with' them; it is obvious what is meant by this excellent advice. Unfortunately it is not easy to 'dance' with Jahnn's prose for very long at a time, so that his monumental trilogy presents almost insuperable obstacles to the reader. *Shoreless River* is based on theoretical musical principles; but sometimes these vitiate literary effectiveness. Jahnn's dark mysticism endows his work with power—especially when retrospectively contemplated—but it detracts from its actual viability. However, there can be no doubt that he is an important writer.

The central figure of *Shoreless River* is Gustav Anais Horn, who sets out on a voyage on a ship, 'Lais', with a mysterious cargo. His fiancée is murdered, but it is not until the second volume that we discover by whom. Horn enters into a friendship with her murderer, and lives first among South Americans and then (as the pacifist Jahnn did during the 1914–18 war) in isolation in Norway. He remains haunted by the fate of the *Lais*, and by the injustice meted out by the 'civilized' minority to their more or less primitive fellow-humans. But while living by his own laws, he discovers his musical potentialities. Jahnn, whatever his shortcomings, remains an intensely fascinating writer, although one never perhaps in complete control of his material. Is the 'river' of the trilogy an 'inward' or an 'outward' stream? There is controversy on the point; we should not ignore the possibility that Jahnn failed fully to resolve his confusions.

LION FEUCHTWANGER (1884–1958) was born in Munich. Another immensely popular middlebrow novelist, he was not as gifted as Werfel (q.v.), although he had talent; but he never wrote as offensively. A good and honest man, Feuchtwanger is one of those prolific creative writers whose most distinctive work is to be found in autobiography: *Moscow 1937* (*Moskau, 1937*; tr. I. Josephy, 1937) and *The Devil in France* (*Der Teufel in Frankreich*, 1941; tr. P. Blewitt, 1941). He collaborated with Brecht (q.v.) on three plays. The most famous of his many novels is *Jew Süss* (*Jud Süss*, 1925; tr. W. and E. Muir, 1926), which plagiarises a novel by the early nineteenth-century German imitator of Walter Scott, Wilhelm Hauff. Others treat historical subjects such as Elizabeth I, Nero and the French Revolution. Feuchtwanger's knack was to make 'modern' treatments; associated with left-wing expressionism, his method of exploiting history proved exceedingly popular. The results are profoundly vulgar and strictly unhistorical, but never unintelligent.

The attempt of the noble-minded Bavarian doctor HANS CAROSSA (1878–1956), poet and autobiographical novelist, to reconcile science with poetry is intellectually unconvincing, and, like his poetry, has dated badly; but his effort had style, character and dignity. Carossa has a niche as a minor writer. His chief inspiration was Goethe. One of Carossa's most beautiful books, which will survive as a classic of childhood, is *A Childhood* (*Eine Kindheit*, 1922; tr. A. N. Scott, 1930), the first and best of an autobiographical sequence which includes *A Rumanian Diary* (*Rumänisches Tagebuch*, 1924; tr. A. N. Scott, 1929), *Boyhood and Youth* (*Verwandlung einer Jugend*, 1928; tr. A. N. Scott, 1931) and, finally, *The Young Doctor's Day* (*Der Tag des jungen Arztes*, 1955). Carossa's solution to the problems of evil is mystical, over-dependent on Goethe and therefore inappropriate to his century; but in his refusal to deny evil, and in his own life-style (which his literary style well reflects) he achieves true quality.

GERTRUD VON LE FORT (1876), daughter of a Prussian officer, is a more notable and original, and less pompous, traditionalist and conservative than

Ricarda Huch (q.v.). While some German writers claimed after the event to have practised an 'inner emigration'—so that the term became discredited—Gertrud von Le Fort's withdrawal was absolute in its dignity and integrity. She fled to Switzerland after her books had been banned and her family estate confiscated. She had become converted to Roman Catholicism in Rome in her late forties, but being of Protestant stock—and studiously tolerant—she maintained an ecumenical bent. All her more important work follows her conversion. Like so many German writers, she chose to use history as a means of illuminating the present. She is not as readable as Bergengruen (q.v.)—not, that is to say, as energetic and in love with life and its colour—but her intellect is more potent: she has even prompted Carl Zuckmayer (q.v.) to remark that she is 'the greatest metaphysical writer of the twentieth century', which would not be an exaggeration if modified to 'woman writer'. Although in no sense 'modern', Gertrud von Le Fort has been consistently intelligent; her work is still much studied and read, and since the war many of her books have been translated into Eastern languages, especially into Japanese.

For all her over-heavy emphasis on the spiritual, Gertrud von Le Fort's fiction is cast in a realistic form. It hardly does justice to her to declare (as is often done) that her three great subjects are the (German) Empire; woman as virgin, bride and mother; and the Church. Her fiction is, so to speak, better than this, although it is unlikely that further interest will be taken in her ponderous poetry. *The Song of the Scaffold* (*Die Letzte am Schafott*, 1931; tr. O. Marx, 1953), a novella, the basis for Bernanos' (q.v.) libretto for Poulenc's opera *Dialogue des Carmélites* (1956), is probably her most intense and effective work. Although religious faith is shown as the only answer to the nihilism and despair felt by the expressionist generation, this story of a nun faced with execution during the French Revolution gives as accurate a portrayal of *non-*Catholic anguish as most fiction of its time.

Another converted Roman Catholic novelist is WERNER BERGENGRUEN (1892–1962); he fell foul of the Nazis, and was forced to retreat to the Tyrol, where he spent the war years until he was smuggled into Switzerland by friends a few months before the unconditional surrender. Like Le Fort, he did not become a Catholic until he was nearly fifty. Born in what was then Russia, of a noble family, Bergengruen is representative of the right-wing, aristocratic opposition to Hitler, who banned his works. He is at his best as a short-story writer; but his novels have the virtue (not as common in Germany as in some other countries) of being eminently readable without ever being ponderous, vulgar or slick. *The Last Captain of Horse* (*Der letzte Rittmeister*, 1952; tr. E. Peters, 1953) is a series of connected tales told by an old Czarist Captain-of-horse, who reappears in other volumes in his capacity as story-teller.

Bergengruen is better in the shorter forms, in which he was influenced by E. T. A. Hoffmann (of whom he wrote a study), because his natural vitality and his delight in story-telling are nearer to the essence of his creative imagination than his conservative 'philosophy'; but this is not negligible, and *A Matter of Conscience* (*Der Grosstyrann und das Gericht*, 1935; tr. N. Cameron, 1952), in which

Nazidom is transferred to a small Italian Renaissance state, is one of the most successful of modern German historical allegories. Here moralizing and psychological analysis are excluded in favour of dialogue, a technique that works well. *On Earth as it is in Heaven (Am Himmel wie auf Erden*, 1940), personally banned by Goebbels (himself once the author of a pitiful 'Dostoevskian' 'novel', *Michael*) is set in sixteenth-century Berlin, and once again treats history with more success and less vulgarity than most German novelists. Bergengruen is also an attractive minor poet in traditional modes, being best known for his lyrical 'resistance poems', *Dies Irae* (1945).

RENÉ SCHICKELE (1883–1940), like the Manns, Arp, and Benn (qq.v.), was divided from birth: he was an Alsatian, his mother being French and his father German. All his life he worked to heal the split between the two countries, and he deserves to be regarded as one of the fathers of whatever cultural residue there may remain in the notion of the E.E.C. . . . He wrote poetry, fiction, criticism and drama. His poetry gained him the reputation of an expressionist, but he was never committed to the movement, and his fiction is mainly conventional in form: he believed too firmly in the concrete ever to be seriously influenced by the movement. Of his many novels the trilogy *The Rhineland Heritage (Das Erbe am Rhein*, 1925–7; tr. H. Waller, *Maria Capponi*, 1925; *Heart of Alsace*, 1929; the third part, *The Wolf in the Fold*, *Der Wolf in der Hürde*, has not been translated) is probably the most outstanding, although his earlier and more obviously 'expressionist' novel *Benkal the Consoler of Women (Benkal der Frauentröster*, 1914) is interesting because of its unusual emphasis on character delineation. The sculptor Benkal is a typical expressionist 'artist as his own victim' figure. Feeling incapable of love, this narcissist destroys his masterpieces and drinks a toast to life.

Not one of the Nazi exponents of 'Blood and Soil' belongs in this book, which deals with literature. The East Prussian poet and novelist ERNST WIECHERT (1887–1950), who wrote novels protesting against technology and intellectualism, and preached the virtues of a life close to the soil, does; that he was in no way akin to the Nazis is surely proved by the fact that they imprisoned him for a time in 1938. His account of this, *The Forest of the Dead (Der Totenwald*, 1945; tr. U. Stechow, 1947), is his best book. His fiction is evocative of the East Prussian landscape, but traces less convincingly (and with a too obvious indebtedness to Knut Hamsun, q.v.) his attempts to escape from misery and his slow acceptance of a Christian feeling. The best novel is probably *The Baroness (Die Marjorin*, 1934; tr. P. and T. Blewitt, 1936), about a woman's fight to reconcile an embittered soldier to life.

ARNOLD ZWEIG (1887–1968), a Silesian Jew, became a pacifist and socialist after the First World War. *Claudia (Novellen um Claudia*, 1912; tr. E. Sutton, 1930), a psychologically accurate but saccharine series of accounts of 'artistic' people, in particular of a fragile girl and her timid academic lover, showed the influence of Thomas Mann rather than any politically left-wing or expressionist influences. His *The Case of Sergeant Grischa (Der Streit um den Sergeanten Grischa*, 1927; tr. E. Sutton, 1927) was not, as J. B. Priestley (q.v.) pronounced, 'the greatest' of the war novels; but it was among the first half-dozen. Certainly it was Zweig's own best book. Few modern authors have traced the pitiless nature of bureaucracy more truthfully than Zweig in this tale of a Russian prisoner murdered ('executed') because, although he is not guilty, the system demands a victim. Also remarkable was the thoroughness and fairness of Zweig's picture of the German army. Here was a novel that *demonstrated* the human monstrousness, the inevitable injustice, of war.

In 1933 Zweig, who had become a Zionist in the Twenties, went to Palestine; but he returned to East Germany in 1948, and became identified with the regime to the extent of becoming President of the Academy of Arts. The novels that Zweig intended to stand with *Grischa* in a series, as exposures of bourgeois hypocrisy, are competent but more doctrinaire: the best is *Young Woman of 1914* (*Junge Frau von 1914*, 1931; tr. E. Sutton, 1932), in which the criticism of the pre-war society, although justified, is too angry to be altogether good for the fiction. His later work is of little interest. He was blind for the last forty years of his life.

It is extraordinary, on the face of it, that HANS FALLADA (ps. RUDOLF DITZEN, 1893–1947) wrote any novels at all; yet his output, considering his relatively short life, was large—and he has yet, perhaps, to receive his proper due. His subject was most often and certainly most famously 'the little man', the innocent victim; but he was not much like a 'little man', and was anything but an innocent victim. A novel that told the story of his life would be criticized as straining the reader's credulity. Son of an eminent Prussian judge, he ran away from home, tried to kill himself, was accused of writing obscene letters to the daughter of one of his father's colleagues, and shot and killed a young friend in a suicide pact whose terms he did not honour. He escaped trial for this, and war service, on the grounds of insanity. During the war he became addicted both to drink and morphine; at the same time he displayed his lifelong flair for survival against high odds by becoming a successful farmer. Finally he went to prison for stealing in order to maintain his drug supply.

At this point writing came to his rescue. Ernest Rowohlt, publisher of so many of the best writers of the time (Kafka, q.v., among them), gave him a part-time job in his Hamburg firm so that he could write.

He obliged with what, although it is early work, is most probably his best novel: *Peasants, Bosses and Bombs* (*Bauern, Bonzen und Bomben*, 1930). He had been working at it intermittently throughout the Twenties. It remains one of the most vivid and sympathetic accounts of a local revolt (of farmers, in Holstein, a town where he had worked selling advertisement space for a paper) ever written: 'marvellously accurate', the verdict of a critic writing as late as 1968, is no exaggeration. His enormous success of 1932, *Little Man What Now?* (*Kleiner Mann—was nun*; tr. E. Sutton, 1933) is not quite as good only because its range is smaller. It remains one of those few world best-sellers that merit attention to this day. Fallada—the name came from Falada, the cut-off horse's head, in the Grimm tale, that told the truth despite the uncomprehending world—could tell a story; in this respect he was perhaps no more remarkable than Feuchtwanger (q.v.) or half-a-dozen others; but his very psychopathic disabilities enabled him to achieve a naked sympathy with all the oppressed. This gives his work a special quality. He did not seriously deteriorate as a writer: his own personal troubles saw to that. When Hitler came, he stayed in Germany—perhaps too drunk and indecisive to get out—and wrote whimsical tripe that nevertheless has in it a yearning for better things. In *Wolf Among Wolves* (*Wolf unter Wölfen*, 1937; tr. P. Owens, 1938) he could get away with it as far as the Nazis were concerned because he was dealing with the inflation and allied problems they 'solved'. *Iron Gustav* (*Der eiserne Gustav*, 1938; tr. P. Owens, 1940) is a less easy compromise: the protagonist becomes a Nazi; but there is muted criticism, and the sensation of being up against it is vividly conveyed. Fallada suffered anguish under the Nazis, but his wildness did not allow him to make more than a token protest. He got rid of his first (helpful, teetotal) wife, and married a fellow-alcoholic. Then he shot and wounded his first wife, and was once again imprisoned. The Red Army happened to appear at this somewhat crucial time, and he found himself 'elected' Mayor of Feldburg in Mecklenburg. It is probably a pity that he was not an ironist. But his case is remarkable enough, and why the Nazis did not do away with him is a mystery. After he died there appeared *The Drinker* (*Der Trinker*, 1950; tr. C. and A. L. Lloyd, 1952), which explains something of his own predicament—but not enough. As one who felt the anguish of his times quite as strongly as any more 'committed' writer, and whose own private hell strangely failed to vitiate his achievement, Fallada demands critical attention. His real theme was his own weakness of will—and its concomitant eruptions of violence; for this he found an occasionally perfect objective correlative in victims of fate, in men who were as 'ordinary' as he was extraordinary. He was one of those writers who will be looked at again in depth.

LUDWIG RENN (ps. A. F. VIETH VON GOLSSENAU, 1889) who now lives in East Germany, is famous for one book, his first: *War* (*Krieg*, 1928; tr. E. and W. Muir, 1929). This utterly matter-of-fact, non-judging, terse account of war is probably the best book on the subject to be written in the century. It has, above all, what one critic has called 'the severity of objective eloquence'. It moves at great speed, and perfectly conveys men's necessarily dehumanized habits of mind in the trenches. *War* might seem 'hard', insensitive, easy to write; but the perspective is continuously human: recording this is one who is patently not dehumanized. Renn came from an old and noble family, and had begun life as a soldier (1911). The war changed everything for him, and eventually turned him into a lifelong communist. He himself dates the change in his outlook to when, on the front, he 'ceased to drink'; indeed, *War* does read exactly like the narrative of a man who has suddenly ceased to drink, and who awakens, starkly, to what is going on around him. It has that profoundly moral awareness that never goes with what Renn here so studiously avoids: moral judgement. It is above politics; it is scrupulously fair and attaches 'blame' to no one. Instead it portrays human weakness and human misery. The difference between its compassion and that of *All Quiet on the Western Front* (q.v.) is just the difference between matter-of-fact, practical aid, and effusive sympathy. Renn's account of the final collapse of the Germans is perhaps the most remarkable part of a remarkable book—undoubtedly one of the greatest on war of our time.

It is ironic that the chief formative influence on the future communist Renn's deservedly much admired style was the Swedish geographer, explorer and travel writer Sven Hedin (1865–1952): Hedin, gifted but personally repellent, was an unrepentant Nazi sympathizer, who was decorated by a grateful Hitler in 1940. Renn was never able to write another book like *War*. In its sequel *After War* (*Nachkrieg*, 1930; tr. W. and E. Muir, 1931) he tried to portray the confusion of the Weimar Republic, but failed to grasp the material. After twice being made a prisoner by the Nazis, he escaped to Switzerland, and then took an active part in the Spanish Civil War. From then his history is one of increasing intellectual commitment to communism. He went to East Germany in 1947, and there has written run-of-the-mill novels, autobiographies, travel books and children's books.

ANNA SEGHERS (ps. NETTY RADVANYI, 1900), who also now lives in East Germany, won the Kleist prize with her first novel, *The Revolt of the Fishermen* (*Der Aufstand der Fischer von St. Barbara*, 1928; tr. M. Goldsmith, 1929); it is a concise and psychologically accurate account of the revolt of Breton fishermen against their grasping employers. She wrote nothing less tendentious except her famous *The Seventh Cross* (*Das siebte Kreuz*, 1941; tr. J. A. Galston, 1945), which was filmed; this meticulously documented description of Nazi Germany remains the best book she has written. It tells of the escape of seven victims from a concentration camp, only one of whom avoids the cross set up for him by the camp commandant. Some of her later books contain vivid passages, but have become increasingly propagandist.

ERICH MARIA REMARQUE (ps. ERICH PAUL REMARK, 1898–1970), who was born at Osnabrück, in Hanover near the Dutch border, was a soldier in the First World War and then, before the phenomenal success of *All Quiet on the Western Front* (*Im Westen nichts Neues*, 1929; tr. A. W. Wheen, 1929), a teacher, business-man and sports reporter. This novel of the war seen through the eyes of an ordinary soldier is not in the same class as Renn's *War* (q.v.), which it neverthe-less eclipsed: characterization is lacking, and the claim that it 'speaks for its generation' is false—in certain respects it said, as Renn's book reveals by contrast, just what this generation wanted to hear. However, it is only a vastly overrated, and not a bad book: within the author's fairly narrow limits, it is truthful, it does show war as being unheroic, and the point of view of the 'cannon fodder' is faithfully adhered to. But the horrors are crudely piled on. *All Quiet on the Western Front* is not in fact better than a book that helped to prepare the way for its success, the fictionalized war-diary *Private Suhren* (*Soldat Suhren*, 1927; tr. 1928) by the poet, painter, translator and dramatist GEORG VON DER VRING (1889–1968). Remarque afterwards became the popular recorder of human heroism in the face of horrors economic and personal—as in what is his best novel, *Three Comrades* (*Drei Kameraden*, 1937; tr. A. W. Wheen, 1937)—or racial. His heart was as big as his truly literary skill was small. He left Germany in 1933, became an American citizen in 1947, and a film star in 1956, when he played in the movie of his own *A Time to Live and a Time to Die* (*Zeit zu leben und Zeit zu sterben*, 1954; tr. D. Lindley, 1954).

ERNST JÜNGER (1895), brother of the poet F. G. Jünger (q.v.), is another writer—an interesting, but rather repugnant one—whose primary inspiration was derived from war. In Jünger an impulse towards violent and dangerous action—he ran away at seventeen to join the Foreign Legion, saw four years' almost continuous warfare between 1914 and 1918, and was then again a soldier in the Second World War, at the beginning of which he performed an act of conspicuous and suicidal heroism—is contradicted, rather than balanced by, its exact opposite: a need for static contemplation, reflected in his botanical and naturalistic studies. Jünger has been mistakenly revered since 1945, by injudicious critics and by himself, as a 'great' writer; his combination of aristocratic nihilism and soldierly virtue conceals the frigidity of an intrinsic behaviourism and even, perhaps, a streak of plain middlebrow vulgarity: a tawdry ideology posing as a profound one. The effectiveness of his prose depends to a surprisingly high degree upon frigid abstractions that are either meaningless or, worse still, heartlessly insensitive. But he is a fascinating writer.

Jünger's first book, *The Storm of Steel* (*In Stahlgewittern*, 1920; tr. B. Creighton, 1929), which he has continually revised, might be said to be the earliest of all the 'anti-war books', except that, realistic though its descriptions of the horrors are, it does not reflect a hatred of war. These are ecstatic, depersonalized etchings, achieved through participation in violence. A bombardment of shells is 'the spectacle of a greatness that no human feeling can match', and it thus quells fear. This is the key to Jünger's earlier work: he sought God in war. He found danger an anaesthetic. After the First World War he busied himself with botany and allied sciences: ever in pursuit of the static, the rigid, the ordered, the hard. There is no sweetness in his botany, and little feeling for beauty.

Jünger's most interesting, original and probably best book is the collection *The Adventurous Heart* (*Das abenteuerliche Herz*, 1929, withdrawn, curtailed, revised and reissued 1936), which anticipates Robbe-Grillet's (q.v.) behaviourism by a quarter of a century. Like Robbe-Grillet, although more gifted, Jünger's only passion is for the world-as-it-is: he has hardly an inkling that his 'detached', 'reasonable', 'scientific' objections to anthropomorphism provide an excuse to participate in a process of dehumanization, of denying love.

Jünger was politically involved, at least until 1933, with a totalitarian 'National Bolshevist' group; but all that was 'Bolshevist' about it was that it favoured a *rapprochement* with Russia against the West. In the psychologically inept *The Worker* (*Der Arbeiter*, 1932) Jünger advocated a semi-mystical workers' revolution—but by 'workers' he only meant 'technocrats'. The Nazis themselves did not suit him, and he withdrew from their scene; but they made liberal use of his ideas—and he could not complain. His system had little more concern with people than the Nazis'; in his desire for a political situation in which everyone would 'unite' with everyone else to win a 'war', Jünger was—and is—indulging himself. In Paris as a German officer in the Second World War he enjoyed being a 'cultivated' member of the master-race, and the 'sympathy' he shows for French and other suffering in his war-diaries is intellectual rather than emotional. He possesses conscience as a pedigree dog possesses breeding, and this is petrified like a flower plucked and under botanical observation—not like a growing flower. His breeding, this cerebral notion of decency, prevented him from being bad-mannered enough to join the Nazis, and even led him, in his first novel, *On the Marble Cliffs* (*Auf den Marmorklippen*, 1939; tr. S. Hood, 1947) to perpetrate a work that they eventually, after it had sold well over a quarter of a million copies, banned—but without reprisals against himself. The term 'magic realism', often associated with the works of Hermann Hesse (q.v.), has been applied to this work: a fantastic situation is realistically treated. The narrator and another man settle, in isolation, just as Jünger did, to botany and meditation after fighting in a long war. But a pillaging, plundering Despot lives in the forest surrounding them, and they are forced to join battle with him (though they were once in his band). It has not been doubted that this was a thinly disguised attack on Nazidom; actually, in creative terms, it was a rationalization of Jünger's own predicament: the meditative life is portrayed with spurious mysticism, and Jünger's fascination with the Despot's lust and cruelty is hardly concealed. *The Peace* (*Der Friede*, 1943, 1945; tr. S. Hood, 1948), written in 1943 and circulated in typescript, reflected the views held by the participants in the June 1944 *putsch* against Hitler; but Jünger managed to remain 'uninvolved'. His friend and protector in Paris and after the war was General Speidel, who was arrested by Himmler in 1944—and thus managed to rise to a high position in the Nato hierarchy. It should be emphasized that Jünger was never an anti-semite or a member of the Nazi party, and that he has never lacked courage; but he contributed through his human coldness and insensitivity to the nihilism that made Nazidom possible. It is significant that *The Peace*, the nearest he came to protest, was written just after his eighteen-year-old son Ernestel was killed in action in Italy; but its philosophy is exactly the same as that of *The Worker*.

In the long futuristic novel *Heliopolis* (1949) Lucius de Geer (Jünger) sees human conflict as inevitable. Now this may be so. But it is all too obvious that Jünger, for his part, sees it only because he draws his nourishment from it. He has no despair. This implies that, however fascinating his work may be, it is inevitably second-rate. *Visit to Godenholm* (*Besuch auf Godenholm*, 1952) once again explores the military frustrations of ex-soldiers: here two of them go to a magician to regain the power they have lost. *The Glass Bees* (*Gläserne Bienen*, 1957; tr. L. Bogan and E. Mayer, 1961) is shorter, lighter and more overtly satirical: a more attractive note has crept in. But still there is coldness rather than wisdom, or even warmth, at its heart. Jünger is at fault not because his view of life is nihilistic, but because this view does not go further than an ingenious self-indulgence. He has not neutralized the demonic element in his militarism, and we must shudderingly agree with H. M. Waidson that 'one need have no regrets that he has never been let loose to operate on the patient' of modern man. It is all very well to say that 'when he deals with objects, forces, intellectual perceptions, he is unapproached by any German writer of this century'; but when the same critic adds, 'it is precisely with human beings that he breaks down', he is adding a very great deal.

The lifelong left-wing commitment of THEODOR PLIEVIER (1892–1955) led him to settle in East Germany in 1945, where he had an official position in the cultural hierarchy; but, soon disillusioned, he fled in 1947 to Bavaria, and died in Switzerland. Plievier, whose name is sometimes spelt 'Plivier', was a journalistic novelist, more concerned with politics than with literature. The son of a poor Berlin tile-cutter, Plievier was a sailor from an early age, and was one of the leaders of the sailors' revolt at Wilhelmshaven. *The Kaiser's Coolies* (*Des Kaisers Kulis*, 1929; tr. 1931) made him famous; it is written in a deliberately flat, non-literary style, and while not as effective as Renn's *War* (q.v.), is nevertheless a powerful book, containing the most vivid of all descriptions of the Battle of Jutland. Before Plievier fled to Russia in 1933 he wrote *The Kaiser Went, the Generals Remained* (*Der Kaiser ging, die Generäle blieben*, 1932; tr. 1933), which is more tendentious. Plievier became disillusioned with the Russians in 1936, but could not get away until nine years later. The book that put his name before a world-wide public, *Stalingrad* (1945; tr. H. L. Robinson, 1948), is a massively effective piece of journalism: crude, clumsy and lacking in characterization, it yet conveys a convincing picture of the collapse of the German military machine in Russia. This is documentary, but Plievier rightly gives himself the freedom of fiction. *Moscow* (*Moskau*, 1952; tr. S. Hood, 1953) and *Berlin* (1954; tr. L. Hagen and V. Milroy, 1956; reissued as *The Rape of a City*, 1962) are the sequels. Throughout this vast work the viewpoint changes from avidly pro-Russian to anti-Russian (but not anti-communist). The finest of Plievier's writing is to be found in *Berlin*, in the section that describes the final destruction of the city.

HERMANN KESTEN (1900), born in Nuremberg, fled to Amsterdam in 1933, and then in 1940 to New York. He now lives in Rome. He was always radical, but not communist. His earlier novels, such as *Joseph Breaks Free* (*Joseph sucht die Freiheit*, 1927; tr. E. Sutton, 1930) were rebellious in theme in a rather conventional manner, but psychologically they were solid enough. In *The Charlatan* (*Der Scharlatan*, 1932) he characterized Hitler. His Spanish trilogy, the middle part of which, *I, the King* (*König Philipp II*, 1938; tr. G. Dunlop, 1939), has been translated, studied the present in terms of the past, in the German fashion. *The Children of Guernica* (*Die Kinder von Guernica*, 1939; tr. G. Dunlop, 1939) is set in Northern Spain at the time of the Civil War. His best novel, in which his sense of irony at least equals his indignation, is *The Twins of Nuremberg* (*Die Zwillinge von Nürnberg*, 1947; tr. A. St. James and B. B. Ashton, 1946). One twin, Primula, marries a Nazi; the other Uli, marries a writer who, like Kesten, has to emigrate. The time span is 1918–45, and the account of a Germany that the author had not known is in its way as remarkable as that of Carl Zuckmayer in *The Devil's General* (q.v.). It is in this remarkably un-Teutonic and lucid book that Kesten's usually somewhat too crude, or at any rate unsubtle, notion of the tyrannical dogmatic enemy is most effectively modified, and it deserves to be better known.

The melancholic STEFAN ZWEIG (1881–1942), an almost over-gifted Viennese Jew, was the archetypal casualty of the collapse of the Austro-Hungarian Empire; that he killed himself in 1942 (he and his wife committed suicide in Brazil) rather than a quarter of a century before sometimes seems like an accident. Zweig had an acute sense of historical crisis, but could not respond adequately to it in creative terms; so it was his vulgarity that came to the fore, in a series of worked up biographies, brilliant and intelligent, but lurid, over-simplified and ultimately little more than autobiographical in significance. He wrote on, among others, Verhaeren, Romain Rolland (qq.v.), Masaryk, Hölderlin, Kleist, Nietzsche (q.v.), Casanova, Freud (who considerably in-fluenced him in his approach to biography), Stendhal, Tolstoy (q.v.), Marie Antoinette, Queen Elizabeth and Mary Queen of Scots. . . . Nine of the shorter of these 'analyses', as he called them, may be found collected in *Adepts in Self-Portraiture* (*Drei Dichter ihres Lebens*, 1928; tr. E. and C. Paul, 1929), *Three Masters* (*Drei Meister*, 1920; tr. E. and C. Paul, 1930) and *Master Builders* (*Baumeister der Welt*, 1925; tr. E. and C. Paul, 1939). These amount to little more than superb journalism. Zweig had a wide circle of artistic friends (Verhaeren, Rolland, the composer Richard Strauss and hosts of others), and it may be that most of his genius came out in sympathetic friendship. Certainly the promising *Jungwien* (q.v.) poet and dramatist was destroyed by the dis-integration of his world. He was at his best in the short story, and if he is to be remembered it will be for such examples as *Amok* (1922; tr. in *The Royal Game*, 1944). His posthumous autobiography, characteristically entitled *The World of Yesterday* (*Die Welt von Gestern*, 1943; tr. E. and C. Paul, 1943), is a moving work.

Life struck from the very beginning at the Austrian novelist JOSEPH ROTH (1894–1939), a half-Jew: before he was born his father left his mother; he died in a lunatic asylum in Holland without Roth's ever seeing him. Roth was only forty-four when, an alcoholic, he died in a Paris hospital, down on his own luck and agonized by events in Vienna. He was basically conservative—he wrote in 1939 that he 'desired the return of the Empire'—but his sufferings prevented his becoming a reactionary. His theme is invariably, directly or indirectly, the results of the dissolution of the Austro-Hungarian Empire. He cannot, as Hofmannsthal (q.v.) did, see the broader implications of this event, but records its effects on himself realistically and self-critically. An officer in the First World War, he was accidentally involved in the Russian Revolution; his wife went mad soon afterwards, and he was forced to take jobs such as cinema-usher to survive. His greatest success was *Radetzkymarsch* (1932; tr. G. Dunlop, 1933), which nostalgically but unsentimentally depicts the Austria of Franz Josef. It is a memorable book, as are *Job* (*Hiob*, 1930; tr. D. Thompson, 1931) and his last novella, *The Legend of the Holy Drinker* (*Die Legende vom heiligen Trinker*, 1939; HE). *Hiob*, the story of a wandering Jew, is as autobiographical as *The Holy Drinker*, a bitter-sweet picture of Roth's final demoralized years in Paris, drinking and living on despair and chance.

About the Viennese novelist HEIMITO VON DODERER (1896–1966) there is some controversy. Like Stefan Zweig's his point of departure was the collapse of the Austrian monarchy (and of the Russian Czardom, which he saw as a prisoner-of-war in Siberia during the Revolution); but, although a monumentalist, Doderer's Austrian sense of the comic saved him from Zweig's anguish and sense of permanent exile. Is his reputation, however, grossly inflated, or is he really one of the outstanding writers of the century as is sometimes claimed? The question can best be answered by comparing his work to that of the novelists who most influenced him: Dickens, Proust and Musil (qq.v.). By the side of this, his novels are quickly seen to lack an inner core of vision, to reflect no very profound response to the disintegration of European life. His major novel is *The Demons* (*Die Dämonen*, 1956; tr. R. and C. Winston, 1961), a continuation of *The Strudlhof Steps* (*Die Strudlhofstiege*, 1951) and *The Illuminating Window* (*Die erleuchteten Fenster*, 1951). The message of this large-scale portrait of Vienna is that concrete actuality is the only reliable touchstone; that all our 'demons' arise from imagination. Doderer utilizes the techniques of Proust and Musil, only to deny the validity of their vision. And this seems to stem not from conviction but from creative inferiority. There is some fine and humorous writing, and when Doderer forgets his message in his enthusiasm for his characters he is lively and amusing. But the problem of length defeated him. His monumentalism is pretentious, because attended by no inner compulsion: the pattern he tries to create is artificial. Broch, Musil (qq.v.), and others, did not overcome the especially Teutonic problem of length; but for them it was a genuine problem; Doderer could better have written realistic short novels. Doderer is a writer well aware of the impulses inherent in literary modernism, but he is, in his own words, a 'naturalist'; it is a pity that his fiction does not behave as though this were more straightforwardly so. A contrary critical view represents Doderer as a neglected master. The chief objection—apart from the fact that so many of Doderer's tricks, particularly his punning, have an element of charlatanism—is the crudity of his 'naturalism', in which even character itself is subordinated to luck or chance. Furthermore, the dependence on *The Man Without Qualities* (q.v.) and the desire to outstrip it are too much in evidence. But Doderer, it must be admitted, often *looks* very like the major novelist he aspired to be. Such a perceptive critic as Paul West would clearly like to prefer him to Broch or Musil; but when he says that Doderer is 'in favour of such an ostentatious sensibleness as that recommended by C. P. Snow' (q.v.) then some of us will not be tempted to go further.

In contrast to Doderer, the Swiss ROBERT WALSER (1878–1956) was a miniaturist with a fastidious conscience. A humble and diffident man, he was the younger brother of a fairly well known decorative painter, Karl. Before going to Berlin in 1905 he was a banker and clerk. There he wrote his three published novels (at least one other, most probably more, were destroyed). He became mentally ill in 1913 and returned to Switzerland, where he struggled vainly to live as a writer. In 1929 he gave up and entered hospital. Four years later he transferred to another hospital at Herisau, where he remained for the last twenty-three years of his life.

Walser's gift was delicate and fragilely held, but quite as considerable as that of most 'monumentalists'. Christopher Middleton has pointed out—in the introduction to his translations of Walser's short stories: *The Walk* (*Der Spaziergang*, 1917; tr. 1957)—that behind Walser's charm and clarity lies a sense of nightmare, and that his stark simplicity influenced Kafka (q.v.). In Walser's shorter sketches men move through a dreamlike world. For example, in the sketch 'The Walk' a young writer goes to a town to lunch with a patroness, visit a tailor—and convince a tax-man that he deserves special consideration. But the subtlety of style gives this work several levels, of which one is humour and another nightmare. What is unusual in Walser is his ability to transform the commonplace into the remarkable. His freshness and his lyrical quality are evident even in his first immature collection of sketches, *Fritz Kocher's Compositions* (*Fritz Kochers Aufsätze*, 1904), which are represented as posthumous schoolboy essays. The device was characteristic and apt: there was always a strong element of the child-like in Walser, but there was also an ironic playfulness about him, which he could perfectly express through a schoolboy *persona*. This, with its deceptively simple descriptions of his home town and so on, is a lovely book, and enables us to see at once that Middleton is right when he describes Walser's 'archetype' as 'the Holy Fool'.

Walser's three novels are extraordinary, and all the more so for being, not consciously experimental or 'modern', but rather intensely his own. 'Not caring about artistic propriety, I simply fired away', he told Seelig regretfully in 1937; but we can be grateful that he did not care, even if later, when his mental state was too precarious for him to leave hospital, he wished he had. *The Tanner Family* (*Die Geschwister Tanner*, 1907) was hardly a novel by the standards of its time, since it consists of a series of relatively brief sections: letters, monologues and narrative passages. *The Assistant* (*Der Gehülfe*, 1908) is a (mainly) comic treatment of what we may call 'the man without qualities' (cf. Musil) theme: the restless Joseph Marti would like, so to say, to realize himself without ever committing himself. He is a gentle and quiet man in conflict with a loud, coarse and yet not wholly unlovable one—his employer, the engineer Tobler, a portrait that only needs wider currency to be acknowledged as a comic classic.

Jakob von Gunten (1909; tr. C. Middleton, 1970), which influenced Kafka perhaps as much as any single book, is another novel that demands to be better known. Jakob attends the Institut Benjamenta, where there is only one, indefinitely repeated, lesson, given by the principal's sister. Instruction consists of learning the school rules by heart, and tasks are limited to sweeping and scrubbing. Like the pupils in ostensibly more conventional establishments, most are cheerful—but since their destiny is to be valets they entertain no hope. Ironically, Jakob's presence here is an act of rebellion against his family. . . . But although he begins by hating the principal Benjamenta and his sister, later, by reaching an understanding that even these two are human in their need for love and sympathy, he comes to love and eventually to identify himself with them. When the school breaks up with the death of Benjamenta's sister, Jakob sets off with Benjamenta—satisfying the latter's craving—on an aimless journey.

In certain respects this beautiful and subtle book is preferable to Kafka's unfinished novels: though haunted by mystery, it is none the less not so starkly non-realistic: humanity does not even have to keep breaking in, for it is there all the time. Walser was a major writer who has yet to be fully discovered in the English-speaking world.

FRIEDO LAMPE (1899–1945), born in Bremen, accidentally shot by Russian troops, remained almost unknown until ten years after his death, when his work was republished. Like Walser's, his stories employ ostensibly realistic methods to achieve far from naturalistic effects. *On the Edge of Night* (*Am Rande der Nacht*, 1933) gives an account of various peoples' activities at twilight in autumn in Bremen; the matter-of-fact, almost lyrical realism has a sinister quality, which also characterized the novella *September Storm* (*Septembergewitter*, 1937).

Carl Zuckmayer (q.v.) described the Viennese ALEXANDER LERNET-HOLENIA (1897) as the most distinguished Austrian writer after Hofmannsthal; he is his close friend, but this does approximate to Lernet-Holenia's reputation just before the war. He is not a good poet or a lasting dramatist, but his novels are superior to the better known ones of Werfel (q.v.). Outstanding is *The Standard* (*Die Standarte*, 1934), a roguish but intelligent story of the decadence of the Austro-Hungarian monarchy. *Mars in Aries* (*Mars im Widder*, 1941) counterpoints an ironic account of the mobilization of 1939 with the personal experiences of an Austrian officer, and was in its necessarily ultra-subtle way an anti-war and anti-Hitler novel.

We all know ERICH KÄSTNER (1899) from his *Emil and the Detectives* (*Emil und die Detektive*, 1929; tr. 1930; E. Hull, 1960). This is a charming children's book, in which the author avoids sentimentality, and is able to portray the innocence that forms the basis of his more important work, his satirical poetry. He began as a conscious exponent of the 'new objectivity' (q.v.), but his irreverent sense of humour puts him out of reach of any theory. He has remained very much his own man, and has failed only when he has tried to bear too earnest witness to the horrors of his time (as in the drama *The School of the Dictators*, *Die Schule der Diktatoren*, 1956). He is one of the outstanding children's writers of the century, because—whatever he may intend—his poker-faced moralism appeals to the child (and to the child in the adult mind) as a mask just teetering on the edge of collapse into total and uncontrollable laughter.

Kästner's ideal style is laconic. When he lapses into other styles, as in his novel *Fabian, the Story of a Moralist* (*Fabian, die Geschichte eines Moralisten*, 1932; tr. C. Brooks, 1932) the results are embarrassing. His children's fiction is charming; his poetry (the largest selection is in *Let's Face It*, ed. P. Bridgwater, 1963; also TCG, MGP), for all its surface humour and even whimsy, is more serious and substantial. As a poet Kästner was from the beginning a self-styled 'workaday poet' (*Gebrauchslyriker*), one who deliberately set out to be functional, to be useful. His achievement is to have written such simple and yet penetrating poems. Not many modern poets have succeeded in preserving lucidity at so little cost to integrity of content. 'Evolution of Mankind' (TCGV) is typical: once 'these characters used to squat in trees . . . then they were lured out of the primeval forest and the world was asphalted . . .'. Then follows an account of what men do: 'tele-phone . . . tele-view . . . breathe in the modern way. . . . split atoms . . . cure incest. . . . Thus with head and mouth they have brought about the progress of mankind. But apart from this and taking a wide view they are still basically the same old apes'.

HERMANN KASACK (1896–1966), who was born in Potsdam, regarded himself primarily as a poet, but is more celebrated as a novelist and usually classed as one. He was a doctor's son, and for most of his life worked in publishing. He was a friend of Oskar Loerke (q.v.), edited his diaries, and was much influenced by him in his poetry, for which he was well known in the Thirties. During the years of the Third Reich he lay low, but he did publish a retrospective selection of his poems in 1943: *Life Everlasting* (*Das ewige Dasein*). As a young man Kasack wrote plays—one of them about Van Gogh—without much success. His present reputation is almost entirely based on his novel *The City Beyond the River* (*Die Stadt hinter dem Strom*, 1947; tr. P. de Mendelssohn, 1953), which was written during and immediately after the war years.

Kasack's ultimate literary origins may fairly be described as expressionist. In an article on him W. F. Mainland has quoted a piece of his early poetry that makes this abundantly clear: 'The horror, Night, destroys the evening walk. Emptiness of talk ungulfs gesture with a sob. Mouth's dark chasm holds the cry —so take me. Street tears apart, men silhouette. I fall, rubble weighs on my head. Hands flutter apart with the hat raised in greeting, and still in dream this hovering lingers; its moan dies away at the sight of mask; hair makes strand of face. Horrified, hunted, body lashes drifting space'. As Mainland says: '. . . this was the fibre from which grew the admired economy of Kasack's style; he found the significance of gesture, discovered the motif of the mask which was to recur with the deeper significance in his post-war novels'.

The first part of *City Beyond the River* is a genuinely imaginative and complex response to the nightmare conditions of the defeated Germany of the immediate post-war years. Robert Lindhoff, an orientalist, crosses a bridge into a strange city. The book remains on a high creative level until about half-way, when Lindhoff discovers that he is in a city of the dead, of ghosts awaiting final dissolution. Then, although still interesting, the narrative becomes abstract; creative pressure yields to cerebration. Kasack's pantheistic-Buddhist solutions are not convincing; but his diagnosis of human illness, including the hideous misuse of technological advance, is brilliant and edged; his subtlety and integrity are not in question. *The Big Net* (*Das grosse Netz*, 1952) has good passages, but is a failure as a whole. The satirical intelligence with which it exposes human stupidity in dependence upon press, statistics and 'images' put across is worthy of Kraus or Wyndham Lewis (qq.v.), and those of its episodes that are imaginatively charged are powerful (and often comic); but too much of the novel is contrived. Nevertheless, *The Big Net* has been underrated: lack of integration should not blind us to the quality of the intelligence that underlies it.

Forgeries (*Fälschungen*, 1953), although it lacks the scope of the two earlier books, is rightly regarded as Kasack's best-integrated work. A collector comes to prefer his antiques to his wife or his mistress; when he sees his mistake he has to destroy all he loves—both the fakes and the genuine articles. This is a psychologically convincing story which raises questions of truth and falsity and of the righteous kind of self-deception that may be practised by those who are dedicated to beauty and to the past.

X

The Czech FRANZ KAFKA (1883–1924), born, like Rilke, in Prague, has been both more widely influential and more widely interpreted than any other single modern writer. Known during his life by only a select few, he wanted his three unfinished novels to be burned after his death, but his friend Max Brod (q.v.) published them. Research into his life has shown him to have been a painful neurotic, especially in his relationships with women; but he could be gay and happy, and the popular portrait of him as 'the sick artist' is too one-sided. Kafka's father, a self-made Jewish haberdashery merchant, was a dominating personality, and profoundly affected his son's attitude to life. On the one hand, Kafka wanted to win his approval; on the other, he despised his materialism and the respect for bureaucratic procedures that naturally went with it. If he is not ultimately, for all his enormous influence and his unerring finger on the pulse of his century, a supreme writer, then this is because he lacks human warmth—and that, in turn, is because he could never reconcile his emotional desire for patriarchal approval (and all that this implies) with his sophisticated rejection of it. Kafka worked as an insurance clerk until tuberculosis forced him to retire. He published six collections of stories, fragments and aphorisms in his lifetime, and was not as obscure as is sometimes supposed; but it was not until Brod issued *The Trial* (*Der Prozess*, 1925; tr. W. and E. Muir, 1955), *The Castle* (*Das Schloss*, 1926; tr. W. and E. Muir, 1953) and *America* (*Amerika*, 1927; tr. W. and E. Muir, 1938) that he achieved world-wide fame. These three unfinished novels are his most famous but not his best—or at least not his most fulfilled—work, which is to be found amongst the short stories. Also published and in translation are his diaries and some of his letters.

Kafka is not interested in character: he is a writer of fables, but of fables in the intrinsically ironical style of the tales of the Hasidim and other traditional Jewish writings. A man seldom serene in himself, his narrative calm—especially in such a tale as *Metamorphosis* (*Die Verwandlung*, 1912; tr. W. and E. Muir, 1961)—can be appallingly serene. This is partly because his work is oneiric in quality—and dreams speak in the 'pictorial language speech once was'.

Kafka, I repeat, is not interested in character: he is a writer of fables, but of fables that evoke the bewildered, humiliated or defensive states of mind of a single protagonist. He read widely, and was influenced by such diverse writers as Dickens and the Freud of *The Interpretation of Dreams*. Indeed, his fiction is most usefully approached as dream. He is still one of the most consistently 'modern' of twentieth-century writers: attempts to interpret him in terms of any modes that preceded him—even of those practised by writers who influenced him—are doomed to failure.

One of Kafka's most characteristic short stories is *Metamorphosis*. Gregor Samsa's life is dedicated to supporting his parents; his father has had a business failure. He wants to send his sister to music school, where she may develop her talent for violin playing. He works as traveller for a warehouse. It becomes clear in the course of the narrative that Gregor is the kind of man most other men would call 'an insect': he has no 'backbone'. It is into an insect, in fact, that he finds himself turned: 'As Gregor Samsa awoke one morning from uneasy dreams he found himself transformed in his bed into a gigantic insect', the tale begins. His first thought is that he will not be able to go to work. And throughout he feels no self-pity, no surprise that he has been thus transformed (is it not natural?)—only a rather mild instinct for survival, which quite soon subsides into an acceptance of death; as soon, in fact, as he sees himself unable to resume his job. He ends up 'quite flat and dry', expiring without complaint. Gregor is Kafka's most passive hero: he has no defence against his family's loathing of him. He could bite, but does not. Literally, he turns into what he is: a repulsive and filthy insect. All his hatred and resentment of his father are submerged in guilty approval-seeking; he feels himself obliged to compensate for the business failure to the extent that he does not even think about it: his whole wretched existence, humiliated and criticized by his employers, has been dedicated to serving his family. And so, of course, his involuntary metamorphosis is a final and definitive coming-to-the-surface of his hatred, a distortedly and exaggeratedly cruel revenge; this insect that cannot even assert itself enough to acquire a personality revenges itself by *turning into itself*. There is no escape from guilt and sin and wretchedness. This is what the insurance clerk Kafka thought of himself for giving in to what he interpreted as 'his father's wishes', instead of devoting himself to writing. Gregor is certainly a self-portrait. But he is more than this. He is, too, like almost every other of Kafka's protagonists, the imaginative artist, the creator. For this 'insect' has had at least this power: the strength, as secret from himself as from others, to become what he is: to make metaphor reality. In that situation he is entirely alienated, since although he at first imagines he is speaking he soon discovers that what comes out is a series of insect squeaks (the public's 'understanding' of writers?). When he wants to express good intentions, he hisses horribly, and his father throws fruit at him.

Metamorphosis belongs to Kafka's early maturity, and originates in self-punitive fantasy. Gregor's punishment for not being his true self is to become the untrue self he was. His function as 'artist' is only to confer power and horror; Kafka was as yet unconscious of this aspect of his work, and his guilt at being a creator is at this stage swamped by a more subjective and neurotic guilt. But that the repulsive insect-form did already represent the creator is evident from the very early sketch 'Wedding Preparations in the Country'. The hero Raban's fantasy is of splitting himself into two: an image would perform 'duties', while the true self would stay in bed—a giant beetle.

Walter Sokel's division of Kafka's maturity into three phases is useful and not too arbitrary: 'In the first phase of his maturity (1912–1914) the protagonist represses his inner truth, but his truth erupts in a catastrophe—accuses, judges, and annihilates him. This is the phase of . . . the powerful tales of punishment and death which are Kafka's most . . . popular. . . . The second phase (1914–1917) begins with *The Penal Colony* and continues with the short parabolic pieces of the *Country Doctor* volume. . . . In this phase a detached perspective views and contemplates a paradoxical discrepancy between self and truth. The final phase (1920–1924) is Kafka's . . . most profound. It comprises the four stories of the *Hunger Artist* volume . . . "Investigations of a Dog" and "The Burrow" and . . . *The Castle*. In . . . that phase . . . Kafka presents the protagonist's deception of the world, perpetrated by his desperate need to create and fulfil his existence'. (*America* was written 1911–14, *The Trial* 1914–15 and *The Castle* 1921–2.)

America, although apparently more realistic than anything else Kafka preserved (he destroyed some novels in manuscript), is essentially of the same pattern with the rest: the protagonist is accused, judged and condemned. Sent to America by his family for, he thinks, *being seduced*, he enters a similar situation and is similarly exiled—and so on. In *The Trial* the hero is arrested for an unknown crime of which he nevertheless feels guilty—and is eventually 'executed'. The basis of the states of mind of nearly all Kafka's heroes is their sense of alienation and, further, their agonies of guilt because of this.

Max Brod, and his translator Edwin Muir (qq.v.), thought of Kafka as a religious novelist. His victims, they assert, represent Mankind in a state of original sin or truth-seeking. A fabulist, Kafka can perhaps be so interpreted. But the trouble with this view is that it posits a Kafka who at heart believed in a purposeful universe; and one of the essential features of his work, taken as a whole, seems to lie in its agonized doubts on this very point. His anguished protagonists have, precisely, no certainty of anything. The Divine, which Brod and Muir postulate as being symbolically or allegorically omnipresent in his work, actually remains undefined in it: the nature and quality of the sinister threat, functioning externally as bureaucratic menace to life and freedom, and internally as *angst*, remain unknown. Kafka is, as Günther Anders has said in the most provocative of all the studies of him (*Kafka: Pro et Contra*, 1951; tr. A. Steer and A. K. Thorlby, *Kafka*, 1960), a sceptic who doubts his own scepticism —and, one may add, doubts that doubt to the point where he asks that his work be destroyed.

This request of Kafka's that such of his works as were not published should be destroyed was not simply neurotic. In his writings he had got beyond neurosis, and he knew it: he could not have perpetrated the bad taste, the personal ambitiousness, the ignorance, or the stylistic confusion of Hitler's *Mein Kampf* —but he could have invented its spirit. And he had come to see that those who invent, in words, may be responsible for more than words. His decision may have been right or wrong; but it must be respected as essentially beyond private neurosis.

One of Kafka's last fragments was the novel *The Castle*. Whereas the hero of *The Trial* was Josef K., the hero of this is simply K. The connections with Kafka himself are obvious and, of course, have not been overlooked. 'A Hunger Artist' (published in 1922), which was written in the same period, is a more successful treatment of the same theme. As Sokel has noted, 'The perspective of the punitive fantasies, seeing the protagonists as victims of external injustice and outrageous fortune, tends to prevent us from noting the submerged inner force that drives them to their catastrophes'. This applies equally to the works of Kafka's last phase: the hunger artist, like K, is so put upon as a victim that we do not notice what Sokel rightly calls 'the crucial fact': that he is a fraud. The difference between the punitive fantasies and these later works is that now Kafka's protagonists (all unequivocally himself) 'oppose a unified self to truth'.

I agree with Sokel and other commentators in seeing K's claim to an appointment of Land Surveyor as a colossal confidence-trick—a confidence-trick from which the reader's attention is distracted by K's blandly righteous and urgent attitude. In fact K has no more right to the position than any other person. Were the claim legitimate, this would be made clear. Of course, we may see K as confidence-man or the unhappy victim of a delusion that involves an un- witting confidence-trick—as we wish. But indisputably he is guilty of deception. His degree of guilt is ambiguous—sickeningly so. Kafka lived in a world, as we all do, in which blame is no longer precisely measurable (and therefore no longer precisely expiable) and in which no authority can go unquestioned.

While Kafka may legitimately be regarded both as a spokesman for the Jews (as a German-speaking Jew in Prague he was doubly alienated; but he also felt alienated from his own race because of his lack of instinctive sympathy with Zionism) and as an ambiguous but revealing commentator upon the loss of religious certainty in his century, he is most directly to be considered as the most potent of all modern doubters of the human sufficiency of art. As Günther Anders writes, he considered his work suspect and ordered it to be destroyed because 'his writing possessed *only* artistic perfection'. (Here he may be linked with at least two others, also Jewish, who arrived at similar although more overtly stated conclusions by different paths: Hermann Broch and the American poet Laura Riding, qq.v.) The reasons for Kafka's wish to destroy his work are most evident in *The Castle*. Kafka's intended ending to this book (he told Brod) was to be that as K lay dying, exhausted by his struggles, word was to come from the Castle that although his legal claim is not recognized, 'taking certain auxiliary circumstances into account' he will be allowed to 'live and work in the village'. Such a fate doubtless seemed appropriate and even merciful for so persuasive a charlatan. But when Kafka postulated the artist as a charlatan he drew attention to an issue wider than that of the artist in society: for the predicament of the writer, with his egotistic concern to achieve 'artistic perfection', may not be so different from that of any other human being, also non-altruistically concerned with the establishment of mere perfection of an external *persona*. However, the creative predicament, not a whit mitigated by its universality, is in the godless twentieth century paradigmatic of this state.

Kafka, with his acute sensitivity, exemplified it both as man and writer.

GUSTAV MEYRINK (ps. GUSTAV MEYER, 1868–1932) was born in Vienna but spent much of his life in Prague. His early short stories combine Jewish grotesqueness with more conventional satire against the bourgeois. Sometimes mentioned as having an affinity with Kafka (but this is far-fetched) even his best work—e.g. *The Golem* (*Der Golem*, 1915; tr. M. Pemberton, 1928)—suffers from superficiality, as though he could never quite develop confidence in himself. His conversion to Buddhism had a charlatan element in it. The Golem is a robot-figure—from Jewish lore—who accidentally gets out of his rabbi-owner's control, and starts to smash up the city. This has great energy and colour, but little depth.

Another, less well-known, author occasionally mentioned as akin to Kafka is FRITZ VON HERZMANOVSKY-ORLANDO (1877–1954), who was born in Vienna. His collected works did not appear until after his death (1957–63), and he published only one novel in his lifetime. Herzmanovsky-Orlando's fiction is in the mainly Czech-Jewish tradition of grotesquerie, and he was friendly with Kubin and Scheerbart (qq.v.). But it is not really 'kafkaesque' to any greater degree than Kafka's own work partakes of this particular half-whimsical, half-Jewish tradition. Herzmanovsky-Orlando's fiction is less whimsical and rather more serious than either Meyrink's or Kubin's, and at the same time more wildly grotesque.

HERMANN BROCH (1886–1951) has aptly been called 'the reluctant poet' ('poet' being used more in the sense of 'artist'). English-speaking writers have found his fiction difficult of approach. Not even his German readers have found him easy. A novelist of unquestionable importance, altiloquent but not pretentious, Broch could be obscure, prolix, humourless and plain boring. But he was a pioneer, and is as important in literature as he was heroically virtuous in his life—especially in his American years.

Broch was born in Vienna, the son of a Jewish textile manufacturer. Until the age of forty-two he ran the family's mills, and became a well-known conciliatory figure in Austrian industrial relations. As well as gaining a theoretical and practical mastery of the techniques of milling, Broch studied philosophy, mathematics, logic and physics at the University of Vienna, and knew many of the leading writers, who did not consider him one of them. Broch became a convert to Roman Catholicism well before he was thirty, but this was never much more than a gesture to the solidarity of the Catholic middle ages. Although he made efforts to disembarrass himself of the connection in the last years of his life, his thinking had always been 'post-Christian'.

In 1928 Broch sold the mills and returned to the University of Vienna in order to obtain a doctorate in philosophy and mathematics. His sense of the approaching economic depression probably made this a less difficult decision. After a year he left the University. He discovered that neither philosophy nor mathematics was adequate to express his ideas: he was forced to turn to literature. He then produced *The Sleepwalkers* (*Die Schlafwandler*, 1931–2; tr. W. and E. Muir, 1932), *The Unknown Quantity* (*Die unbekannte Grösse*, 1933;

tr. W. and E. Muir, 1935), and began the novel now known as *The Tempter* (*Der Versucher*, 1953), upon a drastic revision of which he had not finished working at the time of his sudden death of a heart-attack. It was also in the Thirties that Broch wrote his famous essay on James Joyce (q.v.). After the *Anschluss*, he was put into prison by the Gestapo; when released, he managed to escape from Austria, and eventually went to America. While in prison and literally facing death, he began to elaborate on an eighteen-page story he had read—by invitation—on Viennese radio in 1936, 'Virgil's Homecoming'. This had been an expression of his scepticism about literature. By 1940 what is by some regarded as his masterpiece, *The Death of Virgil* (*Der Tod des Vergil*, 1945; tr. J. S. Untermeyer, 1946) was completed—but he worked at details for five more years. After this publication he once again renounced literature, teaching and devoting himself (effectively but at high personal cost) to helping individual refugees; but when a publisher desired to reprint five of his earlier stories he found himself unable to resist the temptation to change these into a 'novel in eleven stories': *The Innocents* (*Die Schuldlosen*, 1950). Much loved by many friends, Broch none the less died poor and alone.

Broch saw history dialectically, as a process of cycles of two millennia (cf. Yeats, q.v.). The Christian era arose from the ruins of the pagan, but is now —having achieved its fullness in the Catholic middle ages—itself in ruins. Our era, like Virgil's, is one of 'no longer, not yet'. There are now 'partial systems': war, business, literature—all these are examples. Literature is as inadequate as, but more noble than, the other systems. The result of combining several of these partial, inevitably secular systems is by no means a valid syncretism, but increasing chaos. Broch's solution, in so far as he successfully formulated one, is for the individual to eschew all frenzies of eroticism and religiosity—as well as all partial systems—and to behave 'realistically'. Those who feel tempted to look to the nominally Catholic Broch for support for a 'new Christianity' should note that his system cuts God out altogether.

His first novel, which is the first of the trilogy *The Sleepwalkers*, is taken to be his most successful by perhaps the majority of critics. It is decidedly easier to read than *The Death of Virgil*. The trilogy as a whole reveals Broch's dialectic theory: *Pasenow the Romantic* is contrasted with *Esch the Anarchist*; both are found wanting. The 'new' man is to be seen in *Huguenau the Realist*. The triad is: Romanticism—Anarchy—Actuality. However, Broch was by no means simple enough, or lacking in subtlety, to try to portray Huguenau as a 'nice' or a 'good' man: he is, however, for a time, a truly 'objective' man (we may compare him, perhaps, to what Brecht called Stalin: 'a useful man'), and Broch admitted that in him he saw his own 'super-ego'. This notwithstanding that he is an army deserter, rapist, swindler and murderer. In technique *The Sleepwalkers* is influenced by Dos Passos, Joyce, Gide (of *The Counterfeiters*) and Huxley (qq.v.), but the overriding design is unquestionably Broch's own. He had no hesitation in making use of any technique that might help him to achieve his complex purpose.

Broch found philosophy inadequate: it could not consider the irrational.

But when he turned to fiction he incorporated all of the philosophy he knew (he had studied under distinguished philosophers) into it. Scrupulous to the last degree, Broch saw that everything in fiction must be conditioned by the personality of the writer, and he therefore took care to present the personality of the 'author' of his first novel: this Dr. Bertrand Müller is the author of both an essay and a lyrical ballad that are incorporated into the work. He is not Broch; but he probably 'is' Broch self-observed.

The Tempter (*Der Versucher*), which Broch finally proposed to call *The Wanderer*, is a study of the rise of Nazism. Marius Ratti comes to the mountain village of Kuppron and corrupts it. The novel as it was posthumously published is the result of extensive revision at the end of Broch's life; in respect of readability, which is not unimportant (when a basic intelligence in the reader is granted), it is his best novel. Marius, a false prophet, exploits the people of Kuppron. But the central character is the doctor who narrates the story.

The Death of Virgil, which deals with the last eighteen hours of Virgil's life, has been too confidently disposed of. Broch will be remembered, it is asserted, for *The Sleepwalkers* alone. The later novel certainly contains some of the longest sentences in literature, which have been characterized as 'page-long sentences with their cottonwoolly thump of pointless repetition'; but explained thus: 'Undoubtedly this prolixity is meant to indicate the endlessly trivial nature of human experience. . . . These sentences roll on because in nature there is no full stop'. And so, even if repetitions are boring or 'cottonwoolly', they are not 'pointless': the over-confident dismissal of *The Death of Virgil* is insensitive, if only to Broch's intentions. He himself described the book as 'a poem . . . that extends in a single breath over more than five hundred pages'. This novel is a monumental literary account of the insufficiency of literature. The dying Virgil comes ashore at Brindisi in the train of the Emperor Augustus, and is borne to the palace. He spends the final night of his life in regret. Then he speaks to his friends, and finally to Augustus, who persuades him to hand over his manuscript rather than destroy it (Virgil in return is given the right to free his slaves). The last part is a description of Virgil's transition from life into death.

Must we condemn *The Death of Virgil* because, as Aldous Huxley complained to the author, it is unreadable? (Huxley put it politely, saying that 'quantity destroys quality', and that Broch had imposed too great a 'strain' on the reader to guarantee obtaining 'an adequate response'.) No: for however strongly we may feel about Broch's portentousness, his failure to incorporate into his work the sense of humour he undoubtedly possessed, his ponderousness—in two words, his Teutonic heaviness—to dismiss *The Death of Virgil* is in itself an inadequate response. It may fail, but its treatment of the two themes of the reconciliation of life and death, and the insufficiency of art, is heroic; it is also radiant with intelligence. So few have persevered with the formidably difficult prose of *The Death of Virgil*, especially that of the long second section in which Virgil goes over his past life and its wastefulness in denying the truth of ugliness for the sake of artistic beauty, that we require further reports of the experience of concentrating upon it. Like his Virgil, Broch sought for 'a potency of expression . . . beyond all earthly linguistics . . . a speech which would help the eyes to perceive, heartbreakingly and quick as a heartbeat, the unity of all existence . . .' and he believed that 'the effort to approach such a language with paltry verses was rash, a fruitless effort and a blasphemous presumption'. Even a sceptic, who cannot believe that such a 'potency of expression' is humanly accessible, cannot but be impressed.

Although HERMANN HESSE (1877–1962), critic, poet, short-story writer, water colourist and—above all—novelist, lived in Switzerland from 1911, and became a Swiss citizen in 1923, he was born in Swabia. He won the Nobel Prize in 1946. Although Hesse was not as ambitious in his aims as Broch, he had much in common with him, chiefly an over-riding desire to reconcile such opposites as death and life; but he was more drawn towards the East, and to such thinkers as Jung, than Broch. He has been more heeded in the East than in the West; there have been two editions of his complete works in Japan alone.

The novel with which Hesse made his reputation, *Peter Camenzind* (tr. W. J. Strachan, 1961) is nearer to Keller (q.v.) than to anyone else: it is a charming, idealistic, derivative novel, soaked in neo-romanticism but partially redeemed from this by its integrity. A Swiss peasant becomes a famous writer, but renounces the decadent city and goes back to his native countryside. It was self-prophetic. In *The Prodigy* (*Unterm Rad*, 1905; tr. W. J. Strachan, 1957) he relived his early years, when he ran away from theological school, but showed the hero, Klein, collapsing under the strain and drowning himself. Married to a woman nine years older than himself, and with three sons, Hesse was a prolific success. But he was unhappy. Yearnings very like those that stirred Broch prompted him to travel, first to Italy and around the Continent, and then, in 1911, to India. This made a deep impression upon him, but one which he could not assimilate. He felt it ought to be his spiritual home, but could not make it so. In fact he was not ready for India; he was tired of his 'happy' marriage, and wanted to find good 'artistic' reasons to cast it off. He tried to rationalize these impulses in *Rosshalde* (1914), the story of a dedicated painter with a similar problem; it is the least honest of his books.

With the war Hesse turned pacifist, and although he worked to relieve the sufferings of German prisoners-of-war he became unpopular and lost many friends. He went through the familiar crisis in which art can offer no solace: it seems insufficient. He left his wife (whose mental health had broken down) and underwent Jungian analysis. The result was his first major novel, *Demian* (1919; tr. N. H. Priday, 1923; M. Roloff and M. Lebeck, 1965), which made him an entirely new (and wider) reputation.

This is the first-person narrative of Emil Sinclair (the pseudonym under which Hesse published it). Sometimes described as an expressionist novel, it is certainly so in that Emil's exploration of a 'dark' world is undertaken in defiance of his bourgeois parents, for whom such things do not even exist: it is an 'anti-father' novel. Otherwise it is an original synthesis of lyricism and symbolism both Christian and Jungian, whose theme is a quest for individual values. But Emil's young friend Demian is a kind of expressionist 'new man': he performs miracles, has followers, and is sacrificed in the war. His mother Eva is a 'wife-mother figure', a fount of the life-instinct, who makes herself available to Sinclair whenever required. Everything that takes place is 'real' enough, and yet the overall effect is 'magical'; hence the term 'magic realism'. The quest for personal values is seen as essentially a magical one. As Hesse picks up each influence—Nietzsche, Christianity, Jung—he transcends it in favour of his own semi-mystical synthesis; for him the solution must always be in individual terms, and must therefore be unique. *Demian* is a fascinating and readable novel—much more easily readable than anything by Broch—and has the glow of genius. But its glow is suspect, as though poisonous feverishness were concealed by flushed sweetness: Hesse was anticipating an achievement he had not yet reached. But from this time he was increasingly regarded as a mage, and he prided himself on acting as what he described as a 'counsellor' to many young people. T. S. Eliot was so impressed by the non-fiction *In Sight of Chaos* (*Blick ins Chaos*, 1920; tr. S. Hudson, 1923)—no doubt his close friend Sydney Schiff, who wrote under the name Stephen Hudson (q.v.) and who translated it, drew his attention to it—that he paid the author a personal visit (and quoted from him in the notes to *The Waste Land*).

In *Siddharta* (1922; tr. H. Rosner, 1957) the increasingly antinomian Hesse drew on his Indian experiences. The hero, son of a Brahman, is first an ascetic then a sensual materialist, but does not learn anything until he becomes the assistant of a ferryman-mage who plies between the two worlds of spirit and flesh. . . .

Der Steppenwolf (1927; tr. B. Creighton, 1929; rev. W. Sorrell, 1965) shows Hesse both at his strongest and weakest. Of all the considerable pioneers in fiction of his time, Hesse was perhaps the most conservative: unlike Broch, he liked to rely as far as possible on traditional forms, and often he would take a specific nineteenth-century model. Here he drew on the realistic fairy stories of E. T. A. Hoffmann, the pioneer of 'magic realism'. Harry Haller, who is Hesse projected, is forty-eight and has decided upon suicide at fifty; but he finds a more meaningful solution in the 'MAGIC THEATRE. ENTRANCE NOT FOR EVERYBODY: FOR MADMEN ONLY'. The German conflict between Nature and Spirit is age-old, and to outsiders it can become wearisomely oversimplified and tiresome. It does so in the inferior works of late expressionism. But it has seldom been so charmingly presented (if not resolved) as in Hesse's *Steppenwolf*. The agonized Haller has devoted himself to pure spirit; now he finds himself entranced by the world of the flesh—and yet feels himself to be a half-wolf, and only half-man. At the end, when his prostitute Hermine has been shrunk 'to the dimensions of a toy figure' and put into the pocket of the musician Pablo, the proprietor of the 'magic theatre', he determines to 'begin the game afresh', although he knows he will 'shudder again at its senselessness': 'One day I would be a better hand at the game'. Unlike Broch, Hesse was learning to go in a more relaxed direction: to modify his Germanic philosophical certainties with humour and forbearance. In the fifteenth-century *Narziss and Goldmund* (1930;

tr. G. Dunlop, 1932) he presents the same conflict, but in a less imaginative and more self-indulgently symbolic manner.

Hesse's most successful novel, *The Glass Bead Game* (*Das Glasperlenspiel*, 1943; tr., as *Magister Ludi*, M. Savill, 1949; tr. R. and C. Winston, 1970), took him eleven years to write. The glass bead game is Hesse's own 'game' (the irony is characteristic): the quest for perfection, for the possibility of stating what Klein had only been able to feel as he drowned. The protagonist is Joseph Knecht, the imagined country Castalia, an idealized society that is nevertheless dis-integrating because of its commitment to the spirit. We read of Knecht's education in Castalia, his two years in a monastery outside Castalia, and his eight years as Magister Ludi. Finally, like Ibsen (q.v.), who gave up esotericism in order 'to build houses for ordinary people', he decides to try to introduce life into the impoverished and abstract world of his country. The book ends ambiguously with his death by drowning. This could suggest despair of ever achieving a reconciliation; but since Knecht leaps into the water in order to leave an example of sacrifice for the young man to whom he has been tutor, some kind of hope remains. Knecht's suicide is one of those acts that go entirely beyond their author's intentions, and pose a meaningful question. The narration is made after Knecht's death, and subtly implies a Castalia that is no longer impoverished (or de-culturized).

The Glass Bead Game creates its own convincing world, and works its problems out entirely within that context. Hesse retained the gift of pure lyricism: the ability to find simplicity and sweetness at the heart of complexity.

With the Austrian ROBERT MUSIL (1880–1942) we come to an absolute scepticism. Born in Klagenfurt, Musil gave up military school in order to qualify as an engineer. Later he studied philosophy and psychology. He had a distinguished record as an officer in the First World War. After this he worked for a while as a civil servant and a magazine critic; then he tried to settle down as a playwright and freelance writer, but his small private fortune was lost in the inflation. A society was formed to help him financially, but with the *Anschluss* Musil left for Switzerland. The last four years of his life were poverty-stricken, and doubtless contributed to his early death.

Musil wrote two novels, *The Confusions of Young Törless* (*Die Verwirrungen des Jünglings Törless*, 1906; tr. E. Wilkins and E. Kaiser, 1955) and the unfinished *The Man without Qualities* (*Der Mann ohne Eigenschaften*, 1930–43; rev. ed. 1952–7; tr. E. Wilkins and E. Kaiser, 1953–60), some short stories, collected in English in *Tonka* (tr. E. Wilkins and E. Kaiser, 1965), a drama, *The Visionaries* (*Die Schwärmer*, 1921), a farce, *Vinzenz and the Girl Friend of Important Men* (*Vinzenz und die Freundin bedeutender Männer*, 1924)—characterized by Brecht and Zuckmayer, when submitted to them as playreaders for the Deutsches Theater in Berlin, as being, in Brecht's word, 'shit'—and many essays and reviews.

It should first be stated that the German edition of Musil's major novel, edited by Dr. Adolf Frisé, has come under very heavy fire from his English translators, Mr. and Mrs. Ernst Kaiser: they argue that after the fourteenth chapter of Part III—Musil had revised only as far as this when he died—Frisé has presented no more than an unwarranted and arbitrary construction, based on early and sometimes rejected drafts. Their case seems to be proven.

Young Törless is certainly a masterpiece. Its ostensible subject is homosexuality and sadism at just such a military academy as Musil himself had attended; indeed, a meticulously realistic account of this is given, one quite good enough to satisfy the most demanding realist. However, the true subject is the 'growing up' of Törless, his shift from pure (innocent) subjectivity to an awareness of objectivity, and his consequent sense of the gap between 'experience' and 'reason'. True, there seems to be something almost monstrously cold about him, in his capacity for analysis; but we feel repelled as though by a real young man. Musil had been tough enough to survive life at a military academy, and no doubt it hardened him; but, as Mr. and Mrs. Kaiser have pointed out, 'no adult Törless ever came into existence'—either as Ulrich in *The Man without Qualities* or as Musil himself.

Musil's few short stories are exquisitely written and realized. If anyone has doubts about either his psychological or his imaginative grasp, then these will be quickly dispelled by the first of his stories 'The Perfecting of a Love' ('Die Vollendung der Liebe', 1911), Musil's own favourite, in which a woman achieves a sense of love for her husband by allowing herself to be seduced by a ridiculous stranger. 'The Temptation of Silent Veronika' ('Die Versuchung der stillen Veronika', 1911), a study of a psychotic woman who has been buggered by a dog, is even more unusual for its time, although not perhaps as successful. It has been compared to both the Rilke of *Malte Laurids Brigge* and Trakl (qq.v.), with the proviso that whereas these writers' methods were 'an organic part of their subjects and of themselves . . . the garment Musil wears in his story was put on for the occasion'.

Musil's other stories, really better considered as novellas, collected in a volume entitled *Three Women* (*Drei Frauen*, 1924), are as subtle and original, but possess somewhat more of the surface realism that characterizes *The Man without Qualities*. They are better than his two plays, neither of which is good theatre, although both are interesting to read in the light of the novel that followed them. *Vinzenz* had a short-lived success.

The Man without Qualities is one of the longest novels ever written, but its action is confined to a single year, that of 1913–14. It has been called a 'great novel' but 'an unsuccessful work of art' because it is unfinished. However, if one were required to define its form in one word, then this would be 'unfinishable'. Its hero Ulrich, 'not godless but God-free', has withdrawn from life, paralysed by uncertainty. In view of Broch's (q.v.) explanation of our age as one of 'no longer, not yet', it is interesting to compare Ulrich's reaction: 'His view was that in this century we and all humanity are on an expedition, that pride requires that all useless questionings should be met with a "not yet", and that life should be conducted on interim principles. . . .' Again, one is reminded of Broch's 'partial systems' by Musil's view that any individual quality becomes useless when it is independently propagated for its own sake. But Musil is temperamentally more Swiftian than Utopian, although he does not deny the possibility of a solution. One of his basic concerns is what might be called 'the solipsist problem': the problem of the dichotomy between each man, enclosed in his own private world, and all men, somehow (how?) concerned in 'society'. Musil's approach is comic and ironic. One of the main themes of *The Man without Qualities*, which is a plotless although realistic novel, is the so-called 'Collateral Campaign'. This is a project by 'important' people to celebrate 1918, the seventieth anniversary of the ancient Emperor's accession to the throne. It is 'collateral' because the Germans have similar plans for their Emperor. Ulrich becomes honorary secretary of this campaign: a campaign that the reader knows, retrospectively, could not come off. That year, 1918, in fact saw the end of the Austro-Hungarian Empire. Musil's novel exists deliberately on the edge of the precipice of 1914, but does not really ever dive headlong over it: the novel teeters; but Austro-Hungary (the Kakania of the novel) did fall.

Another major theme is the affair of the sex-murderer Moosbrugger, with whose fate Ulrich feels strangely linked. 'If mankind could dream collectively', Ulrich thinks, 'it would dream Moosbrugger'. Austria and Germany did, of course, dream the psychopath Hitler collectively. . . . This theme is indeed, as the Kaisers have remarked, 'the sombre reflection' of the Collateral Campaign.

Musil shared with Rilke a realization of how the impersonality of modern technology strangles the inner life of man. But unlike Rilke he remained an uncommitted sceptic: for him and for his hero Ulrich, any choice, any action, is only one out of a number of possibilities, and has no more validity than its alternatives. Thus life, like Hardy's (q.v.) 'fate', is for Musil indifferent, open-ended; it is inferior, unrealistic to be attached to single causes (again, we recall Broch's 'partial systems'). Man, reckoned Musil, is tempted by life as a fly is to a fly-paper; the fate of the committed is to perish in its stickiness. And yet, paradoxically, in *The Man without Qualities* he is searching for a total reality, even though it eludes him. Scepticism is stretched to its utmost limit, and ironically tested as the only intelligent basis upon which to conduct life. Musil's Ulrich is, in one important aspect, the artist; but he is paralysed rather than sick—and, because of Musil's view of the nature of 'engagement', he is not seen as evil. *The Man without Qualities* was the latest of the great novels of the first half of this century to gain recognition; it will throw up more and richer interpretations.

The prolific ALFRED DÖBLIN (1878–1957) did not achieve as much as any of the preceding writers dealt with in this section. He is nevertheless unduly neglected, and his best fiction will come back into its own. Döblin is often classified as an expressionist, and with some justification; but his position was an unusual and original one. He came from the seaport Stettin in Pomerania (now Polish), and qualified as a doctor in 1905; after an interlude as a newspaper correspondent he settled down as a psychiatrist in the working-class Alexanderplatz of Berlin in 1911. He had written the novel *The Black Curtain* (*Der schwarze Vorhang*, 1912) by 1903, although he did not publish it until he had made contact with literary, particularly expressionist, circles. He became a contributor to Walden's *Der Sturm* (q.v.), and his novel *The Three Leaps of Wang-Lun* (*Die drei Sprünge des Wang-Lun*, 1915) made him famous. As a Jew Döblin could not have lived in Germany after 1933, but as a socialist he would not have done so anyway. He went to Russia, Palestine, France and, finally, America, where in 1941-2 he became a Roman Catholic. After the war he returned to West Germany, where he edited a magazine and continued to write.

Döblin's work always contained a strongly religious element. The stories and sketches in his collection *Murder of a Buttercup* (*Die Ermordung einer Butterblume*, 1913), which are linguistically as interesting as anything he ever wrote, are mainly expressionistic and socialistic—in the title-story, as a business man decapitates a butterfly, the nature of the profit-motive is revealed. But *The Three Leaps of Wang-Lun* (these 'leaps' are vital decisions in his life) is religio-political rather than merely political. Wang-Lun is a fisherman's son who founds the sect of 'truly weak ones', intelligent hippies, who are destroyed by the Chinese establishment. This novel incidentally reminds one of how meticulously some sections of modern youth are now fulfilling an expressionist programme.

Wadzek's Struggle with the Steam-Machine (*Wadzeks Kampf mit der Dampfturbine*, 1918) is more satirical and grotesque, and foreshadows *Mountains, Seas, and Giants* (q.v.) in its posing of the problem of man and machinery. *Wallenstein* (1920) is a long, intelligent and subtle historical novel in which Wallenstein, the man of action, is set against the passive man, the Emperor Ferdinand; it is also, in the fashion of the time, a comment on the current situation.

The distinctly Wellsean dystopia *Mountains, Seas and Giants* (*Berge, Meere und Giganten*, 1924; rev. as *Giganten*, 1931) is the culmination of four years of frenzied satirical and attempted dramatic activity. Under the pseudonym of 'Linke-Poot' Döblin wrote a series of political satires, which he collected into a volume in 1921; his plays of the same period were not successful. *Mountains, Seas and Giants*, which has, surprisingly, been misinterpreted as a Utopia, is set in the period A.D. 2700-3000. Man has mastered machinery to the extent of making Greenland free from ice (by use of Iceland's volcanoes); but nature takes its revenge.

Berlin Alexanderplatz (1929; tr. E. Jolas, 1931) is often, but most misleadingly, compared with Joyce's *Ulysses*. Its genius—it is very nearly a great novel—is not comic. Technically Döblin borrowed from Dos Passos' *Manhattan Transfer* (q.v.), and also used every device of *montage, collage* and interior monologue: advertisements, popular songs, radio announcements, mythological parallels. There are two heroes: Franz Biberkopf, a simple-minded proletarian, a victim of 'the system'; and the teeming life of Berlin.

When the novel opens Franz Biberkopf has just been released from a four-year sentence for the manslaughter, in a rage, of the girl with whom he has been living. He cannot understand his freedom, which has a traumatic effect on him but he manages to find a job as a street-vendor. He can only solve his problems by drink; but even this very simple man is able, through suffering, to learn in the end. He gets in with criminals, and in particular with a vicious but shrewd gangster called Reinhold, by whom he is thrown from a car. He loses an arm. He flirts with the Nazi movement. Old friends help him, and he begins a happy association with a prostitute. However, she is murdered by Reinhold when she will not yield to his demands. This drives Biberkopf mad, and he spends a long time in a mental hospital in a semi-catatonic state. We leave him working as a hospital porter; he is not prosperous, and never will be; but he has learned, despite his simple and over-trusting nature, to try to steer a decent course: he had earned an identity.

The most remarkable element in *Berlin Alexanderplatz* is the success with which it depicts the mental processes that motivate the behaviour of a man so simple and unsophisticated as to be almost (but not quite) 'wanting'. Döblin portrays this distinctly non-literary figure with no patronage at all, and is able to invest him with the humanity that is his due. Döblin deserves a higher status than he has been accorded: he achieved something here that no other German achieved. I doubt if there is any more convincing, accurate and sympathetic portrait of a proletarian in twentieth-century literature. Faulkner (q.v.) was of course a masterly presenter of idiots and primitives; but Franz is neither idiotic nor primitive.

Berlin Alexanderplatz lacks greatness only because it lacks cohesion: in the very last analysis, teutonic nobility of purpose, a didacticism, is seen to stand in place of compassion; and the poor effects can be traced to an attempt to conceal elements of a detached clinicism that is disingenuously not self-acknowledged. And yet it is the experience of a number of readers that when the novel is considered in retrospect, these shortcomings seem less vitiating.

Men Without Mercy (*Pardon wird nicht gegeben*, 1935; tr. T. and P. Blewitt, 1937) is the only novel besides *Berlin Alexanderplatz* by Döblin to have been translated into English (pt. *November 1918*, q.v., is in HE); one would not have chosen it, although it usefully illustrates his concerns. Set in an anonymous, totalitarian country, it traces a lifelong process of self-destruction originating in an adolescent moment of self-betrayal—this, however, being almost forced upon the hero by his bitter, ambitious mother. In this book Döblin hovers uneasily between realism and fable, between a Marxist-Freudian and a religious attitude. The hero's mother prevents his joining a revolutionary comrade, and he becomes a highly successful capitalist and, indeed, an enemy of the revolution to which his young heart had been pledged. Eventually he is killed during a riot. In his younger brother we see, although in a somewhat ambiguous and unsatisfactory portrayal, a passive semi-religious revolutionary. *Men Without Mercy* is an interesting but not fully resolved novel, in which shrewd socio-political analysis is unfortunately not supported by a convincing or consistent psychology.

This was followed by a long work about South America, *Land Without Death* (*Das Land ohne Tod*, *Der blaue Tiger*, 1936-8), and by the trilogy *November 1918*, begun in 1939 and finished in 1950: *The Betrayed People* (*Verratenes Volk*, 1948), *Return from the Front* (*Heimkehr der Fronttruppen*, 1949) and *Karl and Rosa* (*Karl und Rosa*, 1950); this dealt with the Spartacus League and the events in Berlin between November 1918 and January 1919 leading up to the murder of Rosa Luxemburg and Karl Liebknecht. This work is shrewd, mature and politically balanced; the reasons for the failure of the revolution—misplaced idealism—are made manifest.

Döblin was a versatile writer of short stories and novellas, and the absence of a comprehensive selection in English translation is a matter for regret. As in *Berlin Alexanderplatz*, he adopted every kind of technique or form—from the expressionistic and the fantastic through the realistic to the detective story—that would suit his purpose.

His last novel, *Hamlet* (*Hamlet oder Die lange Nacht nimmt ein Ende*, 1957) shows no falling off of power, and is one of his most interesting. It is about an Englishman, shattered by the war, returning home to find his marriage in as great a state of ruin as his mind. Again, Döblin combines a remarkable number of different techniques—flashback, interior monologue, reference to myths—in a lucid narrative.

Döblin is a difficult writer, but this cannot account for the comparative neglect into which he has fallen. Germany has not produced more than half a dozen better ones in the course of the century.

XI

The movement known as dada was founded in 1916 in Zürich, which was, significantly, the headquarters of German pacifism; it was there that René Schickele (q.v.) edited his pacifist *Die weissen Blätter*, in whose pages Hans Arp's poetry appeared. It was not a specifically German, but rather a European pacifist movement. It may be regarded as an offshoot of, or as originating in, German expressionism because its form was a protest against the war—this had existed in Germany from before 1914, whereas its first expression in, for example, English is probably seen in the poetry of Charles Sorley (q.v.)—and because it was clearly an evolution of cabaret-literature. By 1924 the initiative had passed to Paris; the surrealism into which dada developed is a French movement.

'The eel of the dunes', HANS ARP (1887–1966), sometimes referred to as Jean Arp, was born in Strasbourg, of parents who favoured a French Alsace-Lorraine, only a few years after its annexation by the Germans. He was tri-lingual, having a fluent command of French, German and Alsatian (in which his first poem was written). Arp was a sculptor and graphic artist of international stature; and although he made no creative distinction between the visual and verbal aspects of his work, regarding them as complementary, he has always been very much better known as an artist than as a writer. However, his were the only literary contributions to dada that are likely to survive. In this respect he differs from his fellow German MAX ERNST (1891), 'Loplop, the Superior of the Birds' (the surrealists, q.v., gave themselves or each other such names), who engaged in literary activity—such as the production of collage novels, and some poetry—but never of a more than peripheral sort. For Arp poetry was a necessary means of expressing his essentially surrealistic response to existence: childlike, spontaneous, cheerfully and mockingly aleatory in the face of a supremely confident assumption of the total absurdity of everything.

Arp's poetry provides a clear illustration of the close relationship of surrealism to expressionism (of which it was one development). Arp was himself associated with *Der blaue Reiter* and the magazine *Der Sturm*. One of his most characteristic poems, of which he made several versions because of the importance to him of its theme, mourns the death of that expressionist saint, Caspar Hauser (q.v.) (TCG, MGP). His poetry at its best, being cast in the form most natural to his temperament, incidentally reveals the sterility of almost all 'concrete' poetry (q.v.)—at its worst in the cleverly neat, frigid, devitalized experiments of the Scot Edwin 'bloodless magpie' Morgan—for verbal dexterity and re-arrangement are two of Arp's chief means. When he searches for himself amidst the light he finds himself thus: 'L-ich-t'. This characteristic makes his poetry all but untranslatable. Arp is not a casual poet: his regret at the loss of the innocence of childhood, as in the 'Caspar' poem, is deeply felt and expressed with a simple, sweet lyricism rare in its time:

> woe our good Caspar is dead
> who's going to hide the burning flag in the cloud-tail now and play a black trick every day.
> who's going to grind the coffee-mill now in the age-old barrel.
> who's going to charm the idyllic roe now from out of the petrified paper-bag. . . .
> woe woe woe our good Caspar is dead. holy ding dong Caspar is dead. . . .
> his bust will grace the fireplaces of all truly noble men but that is small consolation and snuff for a death's head.

> (tr. R. W. Last, *Hans Arp*, 1969)

The charm and lightness of tone only mute the poet's sense of loss. Arp plays, but not for relaxation. He made many versions of his poems, and there is as yet no satisfactory edition; the nearest approach is in the two-volume *Collected Poems* (1963–4). Arp fully deserves the title given to him by R. W. Last, his leading British interpreter: 'the poet of dadaism'. His poetry is a genuine and never calculated response to experience.

Arp's friend HUGO BALL (1886–1927) was born not far from him, at Pirmasens near the French border. He was always a fierce critic of all things German, and for the latter half of his short life lived in Switzerland. A student of philosophy and a very influential figure, he left little of creative value: his poetry (MGP) compared with Arp's is merely programmatic. His best-known poems invent new words—'Ensúdio tres a sudio mischumi' and so on; but Morgenstern (q.v.) had anticipated him: 'Kroklowafzi? Semememil!/Seiokronto-prafriplo. . . .' He worked with Max Reinhardt (q.v.) before the war, then went to Zürich as a pacifist, and in 1916 was the leading spirit in the founding of dada; he played the piano at the Café Voltaire, the home of dada cabaret. Within little more than a year he had repudiated all this activity on the grounds that dadaism was not, in reality, a revolt against war and its allied demons (as it was supposed to be) but a dangerous and egotistic endorsement of it. In other words, he saw in this extreme manifestation of expressionism negative, totalitarian and demonic symptoms. His small creative capacity did not survive this shock, and he fell into a pious Roman Catholicism; his last book was about saints. He also wrote an acute study of Hermann Hesse (q.v.), whom he knew well. Ball's letters (*Briefe 1911–1927*, 1958) are an invaluable source. His wife Emmy Hennings (1885–1948) was among the performers on the first evening of dadaist entertainment on 2 February 1916.

Another German who helped to found dada in 1916 was the poet RICHARD HUELSENBECK (ps. CHARLES R. HULBECK, 1892). Huelsenbeck, a psychiatrist, went to the U.S.A. in 1936. His poetry, which was collected in *The Answer of the Deep* (*Die Antwort der Tiefe*, 1954), is slight; his contribution to dada was mainly personal. His autobiographical *With Wit, Light and Guts* (*Mit Witz, Licht und Grütze*, 1957) is another valuable source.

KURT SCHWITTERS (1887–1948), born in Hanover, was another sculptor and painter who was also a poet and member of the dadaist circle. He called his own form of dada, 'abstract collages' that made up poems and paintings, *Merz* because of a fortuitous piece of advertisement, *Commerz und Privatbank*, on an early one. In art he was chiefly influenced by the abstract painter Wassily Kandinsky, in poetry by Arp. His poetry is more merely eccentric, slight and less poised than Arp's; but it is not aleatory junk. The best known poem is 'To Anna Blume', 'beloved of my twenty-seven senses. . . . Anna, a-n-n-a I trickle your name. Your name drips like soft beef-dripping. . . . Beef dripping trickles over my back. Anna, you dripping creature, I love you' (TCG). Schwitters emigrated to Norway in 1937, and escaped from there to Britain, where he was treated shamefully, in 1943. He died at Ambleside, after having worked as a portrait-painter. Only one of his three immense (as big as a house) *collages*, *Merzbau* as he called them, survives, and this is unfinished; it was moved from Ambleside to Newcastle University in 1965.

The Saxon JOACHIM RINGELNATZ (ps. HANS BÖTTICHER, 1883–1934) is one of the few 'functionalists' whose verse is still printed in anthologies. 'Ringelnatz' means 'watersnake', 'ringed adder' or 'little seahorse'. He was a clown and vagabond by choice; during the First World War he efficiently commanded a minesweeper. Previously he had been, among other things, a seaman, newspaper-boy, librarian and bar-poet. He devoted most of his life to successfully performing his grotesque and comic cabaret poetry, especially in Berlin and Munich. His two novels about his war experiences show his other side. He was also a talented painter.

Ringelnatz's clowning was a conscious and intelligent form of relaxation, with an undertone of savagery. His most famous pose in his cabaret acts was that of an experienced ordinary seaman. He wrote, charmingly, that his '*Ideal*' was to have, after his death

A little street . . . given my name,
A narrow twisty street with low down doors,
Steep stairways and cheap little whores,
Shadows and sloping windows I want.
It would be my haunt.

(MGP)

Even his trivial songs have charm and quality (two tr. in TCG). . . . *liner Roma* . . . (1924), prose poetry, is often mentioned as having some affinities with dada, as has Ringelnatz's choice of the cabaret as his main medium.

Surrealism (q.v.) was predominantly a French movement; dada, its earliest group manifestation, cannot be described as German, although it was certainly expressionist. The one really gifted dada writer, Arp, was as French as he was German. German writers have had a greater awareness of surrealism than, for example, British and American writers; but not one besides Arp and the relatively minor figure of Schwitters can usefully or accurately be described as a surrealist. There are no English or even American novelists as surrealist as Kasack or Langgässer (qq.v.); but even these owe as much to Kafka, who was not surrealist, as they do to surrealism.

XII

The so-called *neue Sachlichkeit*, the new 'reality'/'objectivity'/'sobriety'/'matter-of-factness', was not a reactionary or anti-modernist movement: though pessimistic and down to earth, it was neither a return to the naturalism of thirty years before, nor to the Ibsenian realism from which that sprang. It was a move away from the violent extremes and abstractions of what Michael Hamburger calls 'Phase II' expressionism. Again, more stable forms, more concrete situations, reflected the comparative stability of the Weimar Republic between 1923 and the 1929 economic slump that brought about its downfall. But the new objectivity, as we view it retrospectively, did not repudiate the basic methods of expressionism; it repudiated only the empty (and almost wholly unimaginative) idealism into which it had turned. Thus, such a clear-cut practitioner of the new objectivity as Erich Kästner had no desire to return to the literary situation of 1900—only to correct the false optimism (largely dispelled by the failure of the 1918 revolution to usher in a new Utopia) of the later expressionists. The degree of pessimism in the new objectivity varied considerably; it is delicately balanced by optimism in the most notable of all the novels, *Berlin Alexanderplatz* (q.v.). Rather than pessimistic, the approach was *matter-of-fact*; but perhaps such an attitude is bound to tend towards pessimism—in the absence of just that fervency which the new objectivity above all eschewed.

The movement manifested itself most explicitly in drama. Language re-

636

mained concentrated and terse, new ideas continued to flow, but the visionary element vanished. For the time being there was no background of disquietude and agitation. Most of the expressionist dramatists felt that they had 'grown out' of their former ecstatic beliefs, although their best work lay behind them. Only a few, such as Johst (q.v.), flung themselves into the new barbarism of Hitler. Some, such as Hasenclever and Kornfeld (qq.v.), wrote cynical comedies.

There developed, alongside this, a brand of 'idealistic' realism, usually nationalistic; but it was crude and consistently unsophisticated, and attracted no writer of real merit. None of the many *Heimatkunst* (literally, 'native-land-art') novels, the most successful of which was *Winter* (1927; tr. D. L. A. Hobman, 1929), by FRIEDRICH GRIESE (1890), came up to the level of Wiechert's or Carossa's (qq.v.) fiction. But while Wiechert went to Buchenwald for a time, many of those classed as 'idealistic' realists became Nazis or fellow-travellers.

HANS GRIMM (1875–1959) was not a Nazi, but he was a racist, and was a favourite in the Third Reich. As recently as 1947 he was described as 'indisputably the greatest living master' of the longer short story, which ought perhaps to go on record as one of the dozen silliest judgements ever attempted. The not ill-intentioned Grimm, a Kipling without genius, wrote an enormously long and now unreadable novel called *People Without Room* (*Volk ohne Raum*, 1926). It sold in millions. The style is modelled on that of the Icelandic sagas; the content, whether the result of an inner viciousness or mere foolishness, is nauseous. It relates, at insufferable length, the ordeals of Germans both in their own overcrowded country and in South Africa. Thus literature at its best under Hitler.

The Berliner HANS JOSÉ REHFISCH (1891–1960), who sometimes used the names GEORG TURNER and RENÉ KESTNER, was a prolific and facile but not unintelligent writer. His best and most successful play was *Who Weeps for Juckenack?* (*Wer weint um Juckenack?*, 1924). Rehfisch had, as H. F. Garten says, 'a remarkable talent for presenting vital topics of the day in a somewhat conventional form'. *Chauffeur Martin* (1920) was expressionist—the hero accidentally knocks a man over, rebels against God and is spiritually reborn. *Who Weeps for Juckenack?* is firmly in the spirit of the 'new objectivity': the hero's project for rebirth, in putting him outside the pale of the law, results in his madness and death.

More substantial if not more representative of the new mood were Ernst Toller's *Hinkemann* (q.v.), Frank's dramatization of his novel *Karl and Anna* (q.v.) and the strongly anti-war *Miracle at Verdun* (*Wunder um Verdun*, 1930; tr. J. Leigh, 1931; E. Crankshaw, 1932) by the Viennese HANS CHUMBLERG (1897–1930), in which the dead of the First World War arise to prevent another war. Chumblerg, who died in an accident at the dress-rehearsal, enclosed this action in the framework of a dream. Ironically, the play is set in the late summer of 1939.

It was natural that in this period the war should be viewed more dispassionately and calmly. The spate of 'war books' began in Germany, as elsewhere, at the end of the Twenties. People found that they were now able to write soberly about their war experiences. The retrospective sobriety and precision of Remarque's journalistically effective *All Quiet on the Western Front* or Renn's profounder *War* (qq.v.) would have found little or no response at the beginning of the Twenties.

Other popular topical themes were no newer, but were given new treatment. As controls became less hysterical and rigid so works dealing with the theme of adolescence versus parental or educational authority tended to become less critical of the establishment. Thomas Mann's son KLAUS MANN (1906–49) wrote, at the age of nineteen, a play called *Anja and Esther* (1925) in which the younger generation are portrayed as fostering a sickly cult of eurhythmics, decadent romanticism and homosexuality; Sternheim's last important play, *The School of Uznach*, subtitled 'the new objectivity', satirized this. Other works dealt with law-cases and incidents from history. Two playwrights, Brecht and Zuckmayer, were markedly superior; but several others were distinguished craftsmen who wrote intelligent plays.

FERDINAND BRUCKNER (ps. THEODOR TAGGER, 1891–1958), a Viennese, began as a violently expressionist poet in the 'telegram style' initiated in the theatre by Sternheim and in poetry by Stramm (qq.v.); his poetry in this vein was wholly derivative. Then he emerged as a differently named, cynical and shocking realist, creating a sensation with his first, skilfully constructed play *The Malady of Youth* (*Krankheit der Jugend*, 1926), in which youth sees itself as a disease. If you grow up, you die spiritually; the only solution is suicide. The atmosphere here is expressionist—but drained of all ecstasy or even hope. The play ends with death, and no other solution is offered. *The Criminals* (*Die Verbrecher*, 1928) exposes, again with great technical skill, the processes of law as neither just nor humane. Both these plays are realistic in form but thoroughly expressionist in temper: the one depicts a cult of death, the other takes pleasure in revealing the law, beloved of the bourgeois mentality, as an institution set up to insulate behaviour from conscience. But this, of course, is the sober (*sachlich*), deromanticized expressionism of the new objectivity. The techniques employed in Bruckner's next, historical play, *Elizabeth of England* (*Elizabeth von England*, 1930; tr. A. Dukes, 1931), which made him world famous, were again expressionist: as in *The Criminals*, Bruckner used the device of 'simultaneous action', in which the stage is divided into two sections (to depict the Spanish and English side by side). Lytton Strachey's *Elizabeth and Essex*, the least convincing and psychologically most lurid of his books, had appeared in 1928, and Bruckner drew on this to provide a 'love interest'. It was his worst, most successful play. *Timon* (1931), based on Shakespeare's play, was expressionist self-criticism, its ostensible moral being that the individual must fulfil the needs of the community; but most of *Timon*'s energy derives from Bruckner's non-programmatic fascination with his hero's misanthropy. The theme continued to interest Bruckner: he made two more versions, the last one *Timon and the Gold* (*Timon und das Gold*) in 1956, two years before his death. *Races* (*Die Rassen*, 1933; tr. R. Langner, 1934), about an Aryan who loves a Jewish girl, was written after Bruckner had left Germany. Apart from Brecht, Zuckmayer and Wolf (qq.v.), Bruckner was the only playwright able to re-establish himself in the post-war German theatre. He had written two historical anti-Hitler plays in exile, and made a successful comeback in 1946 with the second of these: *Heroic Comedy* (*Heroische Komödie*, 1942–6). *Fruit of Nothing* (*Früchte des Nichts*, 1952) returns to the theme of *The Malady of Youth*, this time treating of the young at the end of Hitler's war. *Death of a Doll* (*Der Tod einer Puppe*, 1956) is in verse and is influenced by Greek classical models. Bruckner was a good working dramatist: he never achieved a major work, but seldom fell below a certain level of competence and integrity.

Bruckner's only serious rival for the position of leading dramatist after Brecht and Zuckmayer is FRIEDRICH WOLF (1888–1953), who was born at Neuwied in the Rhineland. Wolf was a member of the communist party who returned to East Germany after the war, and was there held in an esteem second only to Brecht's. Like Bruckner, Wolf began as an expressionist. Although his 'message' was unequivocally Marxist, he had a gift for vivid if not deep characterization, and his plays still grip. *Kolonne Hund* (1927), about a land reclamation scheme in which he had taken part, was his first effective play. His great success was *Cyanide* (*Cyankali*, 1929), an exposure of the inhumanity of the law forbidding abortion. *The Sailors of Cattaro* (*Die Matrosen von Cattaro*, 1930; tr. K. Wallis, 1935) is a documentary play about a mutiny in the Austro-Hungarian navy in 1918. *Professor Mamlock* (1933), on the subject of the Nazi persecution of the Jews, is his most famous play because of the widely shown Russian film. His best, and certainly most interesting, play, however, is *Beaumarchais* (1940), in which he portrays his own dilemma: an emotional revolutionary who cannot accept the revolution himself. He was unhappy in East Germany, where he wrote only light comedies and reproached himself for not more openly criticising the regime.

The modern theatrical giant of Germany is BERTOLT BRECHT (1898–1956), who was born in Augsburg, Bavaria. Essentially Brecht was a poet (and a legendary performer of songs to his own guitar accompaniment); and although his previously underrated poetry has begun in recent years to receive its due, his chief fame is as a playwright. Yet while his plays will certainly survive, his poetry will survive longer.

Brecht served as a medical orderly in the last year of the First World War; the experience was decisive, inasmuch as it left him with no illusions about what man could so easily be ordered to do to man. It seems that he had already reacted against the chauvinism, militarism and economic greed that characterized the German society of his adolescence. The most studiously anti-literary of all twentieth-century writers, Brecht certainly first conceived his scorn for bourgeois '*Kultur*' when he observed the hypocritical nature of pre-war Augsburg society's devotion to it. By the age of twenty he had started to write poetry and drama. In 1922 his *Drums in the Night* (*Trommeln in der Nacht*, 1923) was produced in Munich, and soon afterwards awarded the Kleist Prize. Although wholly individual, this also managed to be a typical (and early) product of the new and more sober mood. But Brecht added a poetic tang to the sobriety. Andreas Kragler comes back from prisoner-of-war camp to discover that his girl has been sleeping with a blackmarketeer. He becomes involved with the revolution of 1919, but eventually decisively rejects it in favour of taking up again with his faithless girl. Here perhaps we see the cynical Brecht, the one who will on no account 'rot in the gutter' so that a mere (communist) 'idea may triumph'; but we also see a Brecht who was already fascinated by communism. At the end of this play, Kragler abuses the audience and hurls his drum at the Chinese lantern that serves as a stage moon, which falls into the waterless river: Brecht's concern to do away with stage illusion, later to be developed into the theory of 'alienation effect' and 'epic theatre' (qq.v.), was thus apparent in his second play.

The eponymous hero of his first play, *Baal* (1922; GED), written in 1918 and produced in Leipsig in 1923, is illustrative of the same side of himself; but here his nihilism and antinomian zest for life emerge rather more strongly. Brecht's Baal is a coarse, kindly criminal—tramp, drunkard, poet, homosexual, murderer, joker, honest and disillusioned man. He enjoys his life. *Baal* was an anti-sentimental comedy. Its amorality, whether or not the result of youthful excess, was dramatically justified: it presented the late expressionists with the reality of their dream, and ironically created a character morally no worse— but decidedly less pompous, idealistic or acceptably fragrant—than the heroes of the still militaristic bourgeois.

The greatest individual success Brecht ever had was with *The Threepenny Opera* (*Die Dreigroschenoper*, 1929; MT; BP); this is based on John Gay's *Beggar's Opera*, and has music by Busoni's brilliant pupil Kurt Weill. The criminal gang whose exploits everyone so much enjoyed, were supposed, by Brecht, to be bourgeois capitalists. But however ingeniously he directed the piece to be produced, this is not quite how it can be taken. Once more, it is essentially nihilistic, and may be taken as a satire on communist revolutionaries as well as on capitalists. Its real mood is one of gay cynicism: nobody in authority is respected, and who is going to stand up (at any rate to be counted) to deny that such authorial aggressiveness as is contained in Macheath's incitement to the audience to 'smash the faces of the police with heavy iron hammers' is directed at *all* police, and not merely at capitalist police?

At this time, when National Socialism was making headway in Germany, Brecht had been studying Marxist communism, including *Das Kapital*, very carefully. How well he grasped it, in an intellectual sense, is not clear; but he has been accused of treating the twentieth century as though it were the nineteenth, and of a general lack of sophistication. 'In his theoretical efforts', writes Peter Demetz, 'Brecht is like an eagle whose eyes triumphantly and sharply view the future of the arts—but the eagle's feet drag the rusty chains of Marxist iron and lead'. His next short plays—after one more satirical opera, again done with Weill, *The Rise and Fall of the Town of Mahagonny* (*Aufstieg und Fall der Stadt Mahagonny*, 1929)—were 'theoretical efforts', *Lehrstücke*, 'teaching pieces', in the sense that they were consciously didactic pieces, designed to bring their audience to an awareness of the inevitability of the historical process as envisaged in Marxist theory. These are by no means bad playlets; but because they are theory-bound, they are Brecht's weakest. They include *Baden-Baden Cantata of Acquiescence* (*Das Badener Lehrstück vom Einverständnis*, 1930; tr. G. Nellhaus, *Harvard Advocate*, CXXXIV, 4, 1951; L. Baxandall, *Tulane Drama Review*, IV, 4, 1960) and *He Who Said Yes / He Who Said No* (*Der Jasager / Der Neinsager*, 1930; *Der Jasager*, tr. G. Nellhaus, *Accent* VII, 2, 1946). They were followed by longer plays of the same kind: *St. Joan of the Stockyards* (*Die heilige Johanna der Schlachthöfe*, 1932; FMR) and *The Measures Taken* (*Die Massnahme*, 1931; MT). The thesis of each play is that it is necessary to renounce individual, incidental compassion—and even to be cruel—in order to create a better world, in order, that is to say, to follow the party line. For by now Brecht was, or believed himself to be, a convert to communism. *St. Joan of the Stockyards*, loosely adapted from, or suggested by, Shaw's (q.v.) Salvation Army play *Major Barbara*, is set in Chicago. Johanna begins by preaching the Gospel to and helping the oppressed workers; having caused a general strike to fail, she ends by attacking all religion (he who asserts the claims of spirituality, she says, must 'have his head beaten on the pavement till he croaks') and by affirming that 'nothing should be called honourable but what / Finally changes the world'. In *The Measures Taken*, based on a Japanese No play (q.v.), four communist infiltrators are sent into China. One of them gives way to his immediate humanitarian impulses, with the result that no long-term progress is achieved, and the mission itself is threatened. The 'emotional socialist' then emerges as an individual—he tears off his anonymous mask—and agrees to be liquidated. The lesson, of course, is that the aims of the party come before any manifestation of individuality—even pity.

Compared to the plays of Brecht's later period, these polemics of the Thirties are crude works; and they are crude because they are dogmatic. *Fear and Misery in the Third Reich* (*Furcht und Elend des dritten Reiches*, 1941; tr. 1942; as *The Private Life of the Master Race*, E. Bentley, 1944) is superb on the realistic level, but sickeningly disingenuous when it toes the communist line. *Round Heads and Pointed Heads* (*Die Rundköpfe und die Spitzköpfe*, 1938; tr. N. G. Verschoyle, *International Literature*, May, 1937), a satire on Nazi anti-semitism, is a total failure, and even appears to be itself anti-semitic. The earlier *The Mother* (*Die Mutter*, 1933), an adaptation from Maxim Gorki's (q.v.) novel, is perhaps the best of all the Thirties plays: it is frankly party propaganda, but in the cunning and vitality of the leading character we already get a hint of Mother Courage (q.v.). Something goes on despite, or as well as, the call to come to the aid of the party. *Señora Carrar's Rifles* (*Die Gewehre der Frau Carrar*, 1937; tr. K. Wallis, *Theatre Workshop*, II, 1938), based on a play by Synge (q.v.) and set in Spain, is in Brecht's most realistic vein.

Brecht went to Denmark when Hitler gained power; when this was overrun he escaped through Sweden, Finland and Russia (he had been there before, in 1935, and apparently did not wish to stay—perhaps because Russia was then in alliance with the Third Reich, perhaps because he did not savour the prospect of living there) to America, where he lived in California until 1947. He was then brought before the notorious Committee on Un-American Activities, whose chairman praised him for his 'co-operation'; yet he left America and waited for nearly two years, in Zürich, to get into Western Germany; but the occupying powers refused him permission. The East Germans, by contrast, offered him a theatre. He settled in Berlin in 1949, and ran the Berliner Ensemble from then until his death of a coronary thrombosis in 1956. It is now run by the actress Hilda Weigel (whom he had married in 1928 after divorcing his first wife). He retained Austrian citizenship and a Swiss bank account. The workers' riots of 1953 upset him, and he is supposed (famously) to have suggested that the government dissolve the people and elect another one; but he made no open protest. However, the charge that he wrote a regulation 'ode' or 'odes' to Stalin, made by Hannah Arendt as though she had read them (she calls them 'thin'), has not been substantiated: no 'odes to Stalin' have been produced or quoted, and Miss Arendt's silence when courteously challenged on this point has been puzzling to her admirers. Nothing Brecht said about Stalin is less than highly ambiguous. When he came back from Moscow in the Thirties and was asked why he had not stayed there, he said that he had not been able to get enough sugar for his tea and coffee (did not find enough sweetness?).

Mother Courage (*Mutter Courage und ihre Kinder*, 1949; tr. H. R. Hays in *New Directions*, 1941; MT; SP), a chronicle of the Thirty Years' War based on a story by Grimmelshausen, the seventeenth-century German author of *Simplicissimus*, portrays the indomitable lust for life of a greedy, mean, malicious, amoral, uncharitable, cunning and yet vital canteen-woman. Brecht's intentions here were as Marxist as ever: war is commercially motivated and destructive, and those who live off it like the sutler woman, who loses all her family, cannot see what they do to themselves. But his imagination and his own love of life created a work that transcends any thesis. After the first performance in Zürich in 1941, when the audience responded sympathetically to Mother Courage, Brecht tried to emphasize her inhumanity by rewriting parts of the text, and as director (of his wife, who presumably played the part as he required it). But it was as though he were trying to rewrite and re-direct the part of his own anti-virtuous, opportunist, cynical Baal—with the aim of demonstrating his essentially bourgeois character and motivations. He could not take away Mother Courage's humanity; even rigidly Marxist critics still saw her as human. Brecht was not a man who would not conform: he could not.

Brecht's other major plays are: *The Life of Galileo* (*Leben des Galilei*, 1955; FMR; SP; BP), which was translated into English by Brecht himself with the help of Charles Laughton, who played the main role in America; *The Good Woman of Setzuan* (*Der gute Mensch von Sezuan*, 1953; SP); *The Caucasian Chalk Circle*; and some would add the more straightforwardly comic *Herr Puntila and his Man Matti* (*Herr Puntila und sein Knecht Matti*, 1948). *The Life of Galileo* portrays the scientist as a man avid and voracious for life (Laughton's 1947 performance, in which he returned to the stage after eleven years in films, is legendary) and for truth; but not one prepared to sacrifice his life for a principle. Like the real Galileo, who is supposed to have muttered '*Eppur si muove!*' (And yet it moves) after recanting, he gives way out of fear; but a copy of his work is smuggled abroad. Brecht's Galileo is, significantly, a mixture of Baal and Schweik (q.v.). But Brecht lets us know that had he behaved boldly, he would not have been tortured. . . .

The detail of *The Good Woman of Setzuan* and of *The Caucasian Chalk Circle*, Brecht's tenderest play, again seems to challenge the comparative crudity of their 'message'.

Brecht's dramatic theories, although criticized by himself as abstract, if not actually disowned ('I developed—oh calamity!—a theory of the epic theatre', he once said), and inconsistent, are very important for the enormous influence they have wielded since the end of the Second World War.

Brecht's theorizing was not consistent, but the notion basic to it was that the audience at a play should be made to *think* rather than to become emotionally identified with the characters. Aristotle had said in his *Poetics* that 'tragedy . . . is a representation of an action that is worth serious attention . . . presented in the form of action, not narration; by means of pity and fear bringing about the catharsis [untranslated] of such emotions'. Now until recently *catharsis* had been understood by nearly everyone, including Brecht, to mean 'purgation' (the best guess is probably more like 'a healthy emotional balance'). Brecht thought of the theatre that had preceded him as an 'Aristotelian' theatre in which the spectator was 'purged' of his fear and pity—fear and pity aroused, for example, by portrayal of tragic injustice—and therefore rendered a harmless member of society. Brecht, in the words of his Russian friend Sergei Tretiakov, wanted an 'intelligent theatre . . . not [one that left] the spectator purged by a cathartic but [that left] him a changed man . . . to sow within him the seeds of the changes which must be completed outside the theatre'. These changes, needless to say, were revolutionary in nature. 'The performance must not be a closed circle where the heroes and villains balance, where all accounts are settled . . . . it must be spiral in form . . . the spectator must be brought out of equilibrium'. Brecht called the 'Aristotelian' theatre 'dramatic', his own 'epic'. His type of theatre is calculated to make the spectator observe (not become involved); to awaken him to action (not to accept tragedy but to join the communist revolution in order ultimately to remove tragedy from the face of the earth); to argue (not state); to present man not as already known and unalterable but as an evolving object of investigation; to cause the spectator not to feel but to reason; to present theatre in tableaux (montage), not as 'organic' ('well made').

H. F. Garten has said that Brecht's 'conversion to communism was not actuated by any genuine sympathy for the poor. . . . It was born from a deep-rooted hatred of the bourgeois class from which he himself had sprung; and it was a desperate effort to escape from the total nihilism of his earlier years . . . .'.

This is partly true; but the matter is more complicated, and the first statement is as unjust as it is incorrect. Brecht's poetry—in which is embodied his most substantial achievement—leaves no doubt whatever of his sympathy for and intuitive understanding of other human beings. These lines of verse occur in the play, *The Good Woman of Setzuan*; the poet who wrote them sympathized with his fellow creatures—and possessed that faculty so rare in male writers, understanding of women:

> I saw him at night, puffing out his cheeks in his sleep: they were evil.
> And in the morning I held his coat up to the light: I could see the wall
>   through it.
> When I saw his cunning laughter I was afraid, but
> When I saw the holes in his shoes, I loved him very much.

(SP)

That Villon was always a strong influence on Brecht is no accident. Villon presents himself in his poetry as a damned soul. Brecht is progressively less explicit, but is always something more than a mere *polisson*. He likes delinquents. Like Villon, he feels at home with criminals. However didactic *The Threepenny Opera* is supposed to be, there can be no doubt that its vitality is derived from Brecht's sheer pleasure in the refreshingly sincere vitality of the criminal classes. He preferred, as many do, their kind of criminality to the version of it practised by 'respectable' society in its pursuit of business, war and the maintenance of 'law and order'. But he knew that it was not socially preferable; and Garten is right in saying that Brecht wanted to escape from his nihilism. This nihilism he saw as identified with the values of the individual, and he was deliberately hard on the claims of the individual in his early communist plays. But he was fundamentally 'Schweikian' in the face of all authority; and not even his strong sense of guilt at his instinctive nihilism (it almost amounted, in communistic terms, to a sense of identification with the *Lumpenproletariat*) could scotch his sly and yet lusty sense of humour—or his undoctrinaire sympathy with all human creatures. Brecht was in fact so fascinated by Schweik (q.v.) that he devoted a whole dramatic sequence to him, *Schweik in the Second World War* (*Schweik im zweiten Weltkrieg*, 1957).

Brecht felt guilty because in pursuing this vein of poetry he thought he might be renouncing the happiness not only of himself but also of the whole species. We have encountered the problem of what may be called *Künstlerschuld* (artist-guilt) before: in Rilke, in Mann, and, most particularly, in Broch; Brecht was not immune to it. His solution is not to his discredit, nor does it reflect a lack of sympathy with the poor—as Garten suggests. Communism advocated what seemed like an anti-bourgeois solution, and entailed a discipline of the intellect over the emotions; this was what Brecht required, and he felt himself 'converted' to it. After persecution by the Western authorities, who first impertinently hauled him in front of a committee to question him on his beliefs and then prevented him from entering his own country, he went to East Germany, who had offered him the theatre he wanted. After the workers' riots of 1953 he wrote 'A Bad Morning':

644

The silver poplar, a beauty of local fame
An old hag today. The lake
A puddle of dirty suds—do not touch:
The fuschia among the snapdragons cheap and vain.
But why?
Last night in a dream I saw fingers pointing at me
As at a leper. They were callous, stained with work and
They were broken.

You don't know! I cried,
Conscious of guilt.

(MGP)

Brecht's first commercially issued book of poetry, *Manual of Piety* (*Die Hauspostille*, 1927) has been translated by Eric Bentley; a selection is in *Selected Poems* (tr. H. R. Hays, 1947). (See also MGP, TCG, PGV, MEP, PI.) He is one of the foremost lyrical poets of his time, and is unsurpassed in the modern ballad form. In German his collected poems comprise seven volumes; and now that his achievement is becoming better known the claim that he is 'a great and major lyricist' no longer strains credulity. A subtle and sensitive manipulator of tone, he has a remarkable variety of modes, ranging from the ironic, lugubrious ballad through the autobiographical disguised as folk-poetry to the pellucid nature lyric—very often nature is as seen by cynical urban man. His gravelly, world-weary tone does not conceal his power and depths of feeling. More perhaps than any other writer of his times he 'touches the ordinary human heart' without recourse to sentimentality. Adherence to communist dogma led Brecht to compromise his creative freedom—but not more seriously, perhaps, than (say) T. S. Eliot's adoption of Christian dogma led him to compromise his.

CARL ZUCKMAYER (1896), who was born in Nackenheim in Rheinhessen, is Germany's leading living playwright of the elder generation. He has found less favour with reviewers in the past decade because he has not tried to keep up with fashion. But critics have become increasingly aware of him and of his achievement, not only as a dramatist, but as poet and writer of fiction and outstanding autobiography. Zuckmayer, who has always worked within the traditions of the realistic theatre, is not an innovator; nor does he see as much as Brecht saw. But within his limitations he is a considerable writer. His genius is best characterized, perhaps, in terms of an instinctive moral decency. When we read his remarkable autobiography, *A Part of Myself* (*Als wärs ein Stück von mir*, 1966; tr. R. and C. Winston, 1970—it must be added that this translation, without declaring it, abridges Zuckmayer's text in an unsatisfactory manner), we feel grateful to the life out of which his work has sprung.

Zuckmayer fought throughout the First World War, and then went to study law at Heidelberg. His first two plays were in the expressionist vein, entirely foreign to him, and they flopped. He was obliged to take many menial jobs before he found success with his comedy *The Merry Vineyard* (*Der fröhliche Weinberg*, 1925). This, set in the Hessian Rhineland, yoked splendid mockery of a pompous young pseudo-patriot and proto-Nazi with broad rustic humour. It was the result of real *joie de vivre*, not of a calculated attempt to give the public what it wanted. And its cheerfulness caught the German public at just the time when it was least distressed and most relaxed.

The best of the early comedies is *The Captain of Köpenick* (*Der Hauptmann von Köpenick*, 1931; tr. D. Portman, 1932), which was a success but earned Zuckmayer the permanent hostility of the Nazi party. It is set in Berlin in the early part of the century; its target is militarism. The hero, a cobbler called Voigt, is forced into the position of rebel by the heartlessness and injustice of bureaucracy. The system will not allow him to get a pass without a job, or a job without a pass. Had he been in the army he could have obtained either. . . . Eventually he masquerades as a captain in order to get his way. In the end he fails; but the point of his human superiority has been established. Zuckmayer rightly felt himself to be the successor to the Gerhart Hauptmann who wrote such comedies as *The Beaver Coat* (q.v.), and Hauptmann himself praised him.

Soon after this success Hitler came to power, and Zuckmayer went to Austria. Here he wrote two historical plays, *The Rogue of Bergen* (*Der Schelm von Bergen*, 1934) and *Bellman* (1938; rev. 1953 as *Ulla Winblad*). The first is little more than a potboiler; the second, on the life of Carl Michael Bellman, the eighteenth-century Swedish poet, is a gay and delicate *tour de force*.

After the *Anschluss* Zuckmayer moved to America, went briefly to Hollywood, and then became a farmer in Vermont. Here he wrote his most famous play, *The Devil's General* (*Des Teufels General*, 1946), which is known throughout the English-speaking world as play and film. Suggested by the suicide by air-crash of the First World War fighter-ace Ernst Udet when, as a quartermaster-general in the German air-ministry, he fell foul of the Gestapo, *The Devil's General* captured the atmosphere of Germany under the Nazis with uncanny accuracy. Alexander Lernet-Holenia (q.v.) exclaimed to the author, 'You never left!' Like Udet, Zuckmayer's Luftwaffe General Harras hates Nazidom, but does no more about it than make risky, sarcastic jokes. Harras discovers that his chief engineer, Oderbruch, has done more about his own anti-Nazi convictions: he has been sabotaging aircraft production. Harras finally takes to the air in one of the sabotaged machines.

Zuckmayer, as he has become older, has tended towards conservatism and a sympathy for Catholicism; in his two most recent plays the desire to make a moral point to some extent spoils their psychological credibility. *The Cold Light* (*Das kalte Licht*, 1956) is based on the case of Klaus Fuchs, the atom spy, although there seems to have been no attempt to represent Fuchs' character. Kristof Wolters, a German refugee, is shipped off to Canada but released as a useful scientist. Wolters is not presented as a dedicated communist but as one embittered by his experiences. Northon, a British security agent, causes him to confess by 'converting' him—but from exactly what? This is a confused play,

646

for Zuckmayer has tried to solve his problem—of how validly to temper a wild and anti-social disposition—in too crude terms. Northon is presented as a 'saved character'; but he is unconvincing.

The Clock Struck One (*Die Uhr schlägt eins*, 1961), in nine scenes, tries to deal with too many problems at once, but possesses a more authentically human hero than Wolters. It has been well said that the theme of all Zuckmayer's later plays has been, in one way or another, 'the guilty hero'. But he has been successful only when he has created an autonomous character such as Harras; there is a dignity about the way such a character achieves redemption—but compare the cardboard Wolters' decision to confess.

Zuckmayer's best novels are *The Moon in the South* (*Salwàre*, 1937; tr. M. Firth, 1938), a long story about the love affair of an 'intellectual' with a peasant, and *Carnival Confession* (*Die Fastnachtsbeichte*, 1959; tr. J. and N. Mander, 1961), in which immense vitality is once again partially undermined by a moral intensity that the author seems to be forcing upon himself against his creative will.

Zuckmayer's poetry (TCG, PGV) is traditional in form, as one would expect; it is relaxed, colloquial and unambitious—but whatever mood, small scene or event Zuckmayer describes is newly illuminated. In his poetry his voice is seldom analytical—and this suits him, since his natural way of seeing is more valuable than his thinking.

XIII

Nothing illustrates the nature of the German genius more clearly than the German novel. As Paul West has remarked, 'German writers mythologize easily and naturally'; there have tended to be in even the best of German novels 'too many possibilities'. An ordinary enough realistic tale can suddenly turn into a symbolic history of the human (or at least German) soul, or an ambitiously guilty account of the fatal split between Nature (*Natur*) and Spirit (*Geist*). This is why the rare miniaturists, such as Lampe or Walser (qq.v.), are so welcome and so remarkable when they appear. Again, almost every German novel is vitiated by ponderousness, length and guilt. And yet who will now accuse such Germans or Austrians as the Manns, Hesse, Musil, Broch (qq.v.) of having, in their pre-1939 novels, something too big on their minds? The guilty sense of being German was shared by writers, from the communist Brecht to the conservative Thomas Mann; this demonstrated more than an irresistible tendency towards grandiosity. We grumble, justifiably, of there being a too grand, too suffering element in most of those great German novels. Perhaps they do share one specifically German characteristic possessed by the Third Reich: that was intended to endure for a millenium; they plan with similar ambitiousness to solve the whole mystery of human evil. . . . Yet the Third Reich in a dozen years performed evil on a scale unprecedented in history, and not a single writer of undisputed genius gave them serious, continuous, unequivocal support.

Expressionism contained within itself elements that the Nazis transformed into reality; the Nazi episode itself may itself be seen as a 'formless scream'. The 'new objectivity' that succeeded expressionism and tried to modify its extremism even while remaining loyal to its real achievements was a reflection of a more than literary mood in Germany; but it was not strong enough to avoid the cataclysm of 1939–45. When literary activity started up again in 1945, when the older writers emerged from exterior or interior exile, and newer ones came into being, the situation was a fluid one. One German critic spoke of the literature of 'the Year Nought' (*Nullpunkt Literatur*). It was an understandable and popular concept; but a quarter of a century of writing has shown it to have been an invalid one. The post-war German writing is as recognizably teutonic as that produced by those who began before 1939. It would be surprising if it did not display some distinctively new features; but these features were not nearly as innovatory or drastic as those that began to appear in German literature in about the year 1910—and this in spite of the fact that post-1945 writers (especially poets) have been, for obvious reasons, much more open to foreign influences. As Rodney Livingstone has pointed out, the possibly unexpected 'continuity was provided by both the Inner and the Outer Emigration'. If I have chosen to deal with some older writers—such as Hans Erich Nossack—on this rather than on the other side of the historical watershed of 1945 then this is only because their work seems to me to belong to the later rather than to the earlier period: the work of their maturity comes after rather than before the final catastrophic realization of 1945. This is certainly true of Nossack (born 1901), Günter Eich (born 1907) and probably of Stefan Andres (born 1906); but it is not true of Anna Seghers (born 1900). That this decision as to who belongs to the later period and who does not has often had to be arbitrary makes its own point: the distinction is artificial and therefore not of great importance. A 'new' German literature came into being at the end of the first decade of this century; but it did not come into being in 1945. As a whole German literature is as it always was: 'philosophical', intensely and ambitiously over-anxious to probe colossal fundamentals (even when it begins with modest and solely realistic intentions), and simultaneously gloomy about the loneliness of the solipsist, the socially unengaged self and the threatening nature of society.

All this becomes evident in the retrospective consideration of the first post-war literary star in the (West) German firmament, WOLFGANG BORCHERT (1921–47). Borchert was regarded as the spokesman of the *Nullpunkt*, and has been called 'a monument of unique artistry to the . . . disillusion of Germany in the immediate post-war years'. And in those years he did seem to Germans, and even to others, to be 'unique'.

Born in Hamburg, Borchert was whisked into the army almost before he had had time to grow up. He spent just over a year as a bookseller's assistant, during which time he lived unconventionally and marked himself out as a

648

critic of the Nazi government. (The Gestapo arrested him for having had a homosexual affair with 'one Rieke': they meant Rilke.) He was happier when, between December 1940 and June 1941, he acted with a touring company. This came to an end when he was called up. He was severely wounded on the Russian front, and in addition suffered from jaundice and diphtheria in military hospitals. Acquitted of wounding himself in the hand, his letters home were intercepted and he was sentenced to death, pardoned (a Nazi strategy) and returned to the front—only to be arrested again, after discharge from the army, for displaying a defeatist and anti-Nazi attitude. He died only two years after the end of the war, on the day before his only extant play *The Man Outside* (*Draussen vor der Tür*, 1947; tr. D. Porter in *The Prose Works of Wolfgang Borchert*, 1952), which had previously been broadcast, received its first highly successful performance. He wrote some poetry while he was in the army, but is remembered for his prose sketches and the single play.

Borchert was highly gifted and in the case of at least one story, 'Billbrook', he showed genius; but, his brilliance notwithstanding, he was not original and he was, and by some still is, overrated.

The Man Outside, for all the angry satirical energy and the promise in manipulation of language that it shows, is a neo-expressionist *Heimkehrerdrama* (homecoming-drama). Negatively, that is to say satirically, this depiction of the return of a prisoner-of-war to his ruined homeland and ruined life is effective; positively it is a failure, drawing upon outworn expressionist techniques and a torrent of what Rodney Livingstone rightly calls 'pompous' cliché. The fact is that, although the quality of Borchert's language is superior (and that of course is important), judged solely in terms of content his play is not intrinsically different from any typical late expressionist drama. The mood of *The Man Outside* oscillates between satirical nihilism and pseudo-ecstasy (with an understandable emphasis on the former); this successfully reflected the mood of 1947. No critical self-examination emanated from Borchert, whose fragile, three-quarters stifled genius operated only in established channels. One may even go so far as to say of *The Man Outside* that it is not only the old, but the old posing as the new, the different—and morally superior. There is nothing in it that is not in Toller's *Hinkemann* (q.v.), except that the latter pays some attention to reality whereas the former is not really more—not even in that smoking rubble!—than the familiar 'formless scream'.

Borchert's essentially miniaturist fiction—short, plotless, colloquial, evocative —is more modest, and achieves a good deal more. In 'Billbrook' a young Canadian pilot sets out joyfully to explore a district of Hamburg that bears his own name (Bill Brook), but he meets nothing but despair, rejection and emptiness. In this short story Borchert comes nearer than he did in his play to an understanding of the spiritual poverty of his own nihilism: here the genius of his ability, remarkable in his circumstances, to descry the truly human amongst the dehumanized, is intimated. Borchert's fiction is sensitive and poetic, but the large amount of attention it naturally received when it was published is misleading: judged by what he achieved, Borchert was a minor writer.

KARL WITTLINGER (1922) carried on the more or less expressionistic tradition of Borchert with *Do You Know the Milky Way?* (*Kennen Sie die Milchstrasse?*, 1956). As in a number of German novels and plays, the returning soldier finds himself superfluous. He ends up in a mental home, and his psychiatrist (in a twist that showed the influence of the theatre of the absurd), after acting out his patient's life-story, becomes a milkman. A later play, *Transmigration of the Soul* (*Seelenwanderung*, 1963) is a slick, but inoffensive and entertaining version of the Faust legend.

However, not all post-1945 German literature is as clearly traditional as that of Borchert, who reacted to the situation immediately and instinctively. For one thing the German language itself has been turned into a more straightforward instrument; to a large extent it has, literally, been cleaned up. The younger writers do not try to be inventive with language, only to employ it directly. (This is why such a writer as the linguistically reprehensible Ernst Jünger so clearly does not belong to the post-war period.) The hysteria, the sentimentality, the rhetoric—these at least have been purged away, even if their cause has not.

This cooling down and cleaning up of the language was in accord with the spirit of the movement—or, as appropriately, anti-movement—called *Gruppe 47*.

Many members of *Gruppe 47*, most notably the poet Günter Eich, have expressed themselves through the medium of the *Hörspiel*, the radio-play, which has been more fully developed in Germany than anywhere else in the world. Radio is an appropriate medium for the practitioners of expressionist and post-expressionist methods: there is no 'Aristotelian' formality, scenes ('sound-tableaux') follow one another in a succession rather than a progression, and different actions may be almost simultaneously presented. The first *Hörspiele* were written and broadcast in the mid-Twenties—there were similar efforts in Great Britain by Richard Hughes (q.v.) and Tyrone Guthrie—but the form did not come into its own until after the war.

The founder of *Gruppe 47*, HANS WERNER RICHTER (1908), the son of a North Prussian fisherman, is a writer of documentary fiction not unlike that of Plievier (q.v.), but more polished and less powerful. Richter, well known for his opposition to Hitler, fled to Paris in 1933 but was forced by poverty to return to Berlin in the following year; he unwillingly joined the army in 1940, and fell into American hands three years later. On release he edited a left-wing magazine, *Der Ruf*, until it was banned by the occupying forces; it was good enough to upset everyone. Richter himself is a comparatively crude realist, and his fiction is of little literary interest; but *Gruppe 47*, founded as a successor to *Der Ruf*, has accommodated many more versatile and gifted writers—a fact that does much credit to Richter.

Gruppe 47 has continued to meet every year for discussion and reading of new work. Its prize is the most coveted in West Germany. It is anti-programmatic, profoundly sceptical and tends to straightforward language. The right wing is excluded, and has not tried to enter. Nothing, it seems, has been lost by this. Because *Gruppe 47* has been so eclectic—a Roman Catholic liberal, Heinrich Böll, is one of its most characteristic writers—allowing itself to represent what responsible German literature actually is rather than (beyond the insistence on 'clean', non-visionary language) trying to shape it, it has lasted. Its strength lies in the fact that one cannot be dogmatic about it. Few of those German writers who established themselves after 1945 who have not been associated with it could be described as fundamentally alien to its modest aims.

XIV

Borchert's was the only important new name in the German theatre in the immediate post-war years. Switzerland, where Brecht's plays were seen during and after the war, provided what continuity there was; two of the leading German dramatists of the post-war years, Max Frisch and Friedrich Dürrenmatt (qq.v.), are Swiss. The Austrian theatre survives in the works of Lernet-Holenia (q.v.) and FRANZ THEODOR CSOKOR (1885–1969); but the work of the Viennese Fritz Hochwälder (q.v.), who emigrated to Switzerland in 1938, is not in this tradition. It is only with Rolf Hochhuth (q.v.) and his few successors that new beginnings have been made.

MAX FRISCH (1911) was born in Zürich. During the Thirties he was a university student and reporter before he decided to become, like his father, an architect. He was a soldier (guarding the frontiers of his neutral country) for a short time at the beginning of the war. After he gained literary success Frisch gave up his architect's practice (he had been awarded a prize for the design of a municipal swimming bath); he now spends most of his time in Rome.

The Swiss have been unkindly described as 'typical Germans who escaped two world wars'; this is an unfair generalization, but is an aspect of Switzerland that deeply concerns both Frisch and Dürrenmatt. Bourgeois Switzerland is proud of its 'sensible' approach, its decision to remain 'minor', its financial solidarity, the perfect, tiny gloriousness of its watches, its neutrality. Its intellectuals, however, see its 'sense' and 'minority' as cruel and petty; its neutrality as a matter of luck and lack of commitment. Neutral Switzerland is a particularly apt vantage-point for the consideration of the possibility that the Second World War and its aftermath were caused, not by Germany alone, but by the whole world's failure to achieve a properly human sense of responsibility. This 'Swiss guilt', this refusal to smugly accept neutrality, pervades the work of both Frisch and Dürrenmatt, more particularly that of the former.

Frisch's first performed play, *Now They Sing Again* (*Nun singen sie wieder*, 1945), in which the dead mix with the living, was an unremarkable latter-day essay in expressionism, and showed no more promise than the autobiographical novel *Jürg Reinhart* (1934).

Frisch's chief theme, his serious handling of which gives him higher status than the cleverer Dürrenmatt, is the search for identity—for an authentic existence. It is not clear whether Frisch believes in the existence of a single, true identity for the individual; but he believes in the search for it. His attempts to define the nature of the love that makes it a possibility are sober and unsentimental.

Frisch made friends with Brecht while the latter was in Switzerland, and although he shares only Brecht's critical attitude towards the bourgeois, and not his communism, he was deeply influenced by him. This immediately showed itself in *When the War Came to an End* (*Als der Krieg zu Ende war*, 1949), in which the heroine steps out of her role to comment upon it. In 1951 came his best play to that date, *Count Öderland* (*Graf Öderland*, 1951, rev. 1956, 1961; FTP), a brilliant *tour de force* in which a public prosecutor suddenly becomes a terrorist—only to find himself, as dictator, obliged to rule. To escape—whether from fantasy or fact—he kills himself. This reveals the identity of prosecutor and gangster as well as hinting at the true nature of 'revolution'; but the central character is unfortunately not made convincing as either human being or 'stage person'.

The more comic *Don Juan or Love of Geometry* (*Don Juan oder Die Liebe zur Geometrie*, 1953) presents Don Juan as a misogynist devoted to mathematics and therefore irresistible to women. He arranges his own legendary 'death' in front of his assembled girl-friends, but is found out and trapped into a respectable marriage. As critics have pointed out, the basic form of Frisch's mature works is that of the parable, for the incidents he depicts make little sense detached from some kind of 'moral'. The moral here is that the image the world has of a man is actually more real than the man himself. At the end of the play a book about Don Juan the seducer is introduced: this legend will outlive the mathematician and even the trapped and domesticated married man. Thus, when we think of others as having a certain character, we withdraw love from them—and threaten the possibility of their free development—by clamping a mask upon them.

Frisch's most famous play, originally written for radio, *The Fire Raisers* (*Biedermann und die Brandstifter*, 1958; FTP), is certainly a parable, although its form owes something to the theatre of the absurd (q.v.). The bourgeois Biedermann is a cruel and relentless businessman, but, as his name ('honest man') implies, he regards himself as being a respectable and decent fellow. When sinister characters infiltrate his house and begin to pile up petrol he welcomes them and relies upon his good nature to prevent them from carrying out their intention. Finally he hands them the matches with which they fire his own property and the whole town. (An epilogue in hell, added later to the stage version, did not improve this short play.) Apparently the theme was originally suggested to Frisch by the Czech President Beneš's acceptance of the communist coup of 1948, whereby Gottwald was able to establish a dictatorship. But it applies equally to the German acceptance of Hitler and to mankind's possession of the atomic bomb. Furthermore, given the personality of Biedermann, the question arises as to who really is the 'fire raiser', and whether he deserves a better fate. . . . Frisch here represents the plight of modern man, trapped between the bourgeois viciousness of Biedermann and the true nature of 'revolution'.

Frisch's most substantial play is *Andorra* (1961; FTP), in which the country depicted is 'any country'—but most aptly neutral Switzerland, smugly aware of its virtue, and confident of its ability to dissuade the neighbouring 'Blacks' from invading it. The young hero Andri has been presented by his school-master father as a Jew he adopted; actually he is his bastard son, the result of an affair with a 'Black' woman. He proposes to teach his countrymen the fallacy of racism by eventually revealing Andri as no Jew, but his son. But Andri's identity is shown as having been destroyed by the opinion of others, who impose upon him the 'image' of a Jew. Finally he dies as a Jewish scape-goat for the murder of his own mother by Andorrans. This is one of the most moving of all post-war dramas, and incidentally reveals what the modern theatre owes to Brecht in a technical sense: between the scenes each character (named only by his trade or profession) enters a dock and tries to excuse himself of the crime of Andri's murder.

Frisch has also written three novels. *I'm not Stiller* (*Stiller*, 1954; tr. M. Bullock, 1961) deals with a sculptor's forced rediscovery of an identity he had successfully shed. In some respects this goes more deeply into the question of identity than Frisch's plays. Stiller refuses the image forced upon him by society; but fails to discover himself. Frisch seems to hint here, as he has elsewhere, that the only way of achieving 'authenticity' is to 'accept God'—but what he means by this he has not made clear. *I'm not Stiller* eventually resolves itself as yet another elaborate artist's expiation piece: Stiller, who can't be himself, therefore makes images. Is this, Frisch asks, 'responsible'?

Homo Faber (1957; tr. M. Bullock, 1959) again explores the consequences of human creativity. The technologist hero (called Faber: 'maker') is trapped by various failures of intricate machinery (razors, engines) into marriage with his own daughter; he is thus inexorably an Oedipus, for all the brilliance with which he and his 'civilization' have distanced themselves from 'nature'.

Wilderness of Mirrors (*Mein Name sei Gantenbein*, 1964; tr. M. Bullock, 1965) is Frisch's most difficult and ambitious work, an attempt to deal truthfully with human lack of identity that, according to one bemused critic, is 'so uncompromising as to shatter the very foundations of the medium of the novel'. As in Musil's *The Man without Qualities* (q.v.), only more deliberately and systematically, and as a matter of structural policy, every conjecture and possibility is envisaged; characters are 'tried out' under different images. Gantenbein's marriage is 'happy' because he can be 'blind' while his wife deceives him with other men. . . . This is a contrived novel, which probably fails because of an absence of human richness. But, of course, in the state of affairs it reveals—the absence of fixed identity—human richness is not even possible. . . . Somehow Frisch's attempt to convey the poignancy of this—as a result of a residual, reluctant scepticism about 'God'?—fails. Yet he is a sensitive, acutely intelligent and never frivolous writer, and one of those who carry the future of literature in their hands. His *Diary* (*Tagebuch 1946–1949*, 1950) is another important book.

So far FRIEDRICH DÜRRENMATT (1921), son of a Berne pastor, has not revealed himself as of quite the calibre of Frisch. The difference between the two is apparent in their fiction: Frisch is the author of major novels, Dürrenmatt of highly competent, original and intelligent detective stories: *The Judge and His Hangman* (*Der Richter und sein Henker*, 1950; tr. C. Brooks, 1954), *Suspicion* (*Der Verdacht*, 1954) and *The Pledge* (*Das Versprechen*, 1958; tr. R. and C. Winston, 1959). But he is ten years younger than Frisch, and his flippancy is perhaps less natural to him than defensive.

Dürrenmatt, whose first aspiration was to be a painter, has withdrawn his first two plays, *It is Written* (*Es steht geschrieben*, 1947) and *The Blind* (*Der Blinde*, 1948), although they have been published. In *Romulus the Great* (*Romulus der Grosse*, 1949, rev. 1957; DFP) and *The Marriage of Mr. Mississippi* (*Die Ehe des Herrn Mississippi*, 1951; DFP) he at last found his style. Both are comedies, and both overturn bourgeois values. Romulus, the (unhistorical) last Roman emperor before the invasion of the barbarians, is a clown who finally achieves human dignity by refusing to regard himself seriously as a martyr. Romulus is a convincing figure, who develops throughout the play, whose unobtrusive message is for mankind to give up self-esteem. The surrealistic *The Marriage of Mr. Mississippi* is brilliant but less successful, since its characters remain abstractions and it ultimately depends upon stage effects.

An Angel Comes to Babylon (*Ein Engel kommt nach Babylon*, 1953, rev. 1957; DFP) is again brilliant, but too much reflects its author's philosophical bewilderment—Dürrenmatt's profusion of tricks is not wholly successful in concealing his yearning (even if ironically qualified) for a 'system'. This play is supposed to have a sequel whose theme will be the construction of the Tower of Babel.

After this Dürrenmatt produced what is still probably the best of his plays, although it has not attained the international success of *The Physicists* (q.v.). The central character, a shopkeeper called Ill, attains much the same kind of dignity as Romulus does in the earlier play. In *The Visit* (*Der Besuch der alten Dame*, 1956; tr. P. Bowles, 1962) an old millionairess, whom in youth Ill has seduced and impregnated, returns to her home town when it is running through a hard time. She offers a large sum of money—if the burghers will enable her to have her revenge on Ill by killing him. In the end they do it: they lose their integrity, but the ordinary little Ill achieves a stature he never previously had as he comes to accept his fate.

But it was *The Physicists* (*Die Physiker*, 1962; DFP) that provided Dürrenmatt with his greatest commercial success. It is, undoubtedly, one of the most sheerly skilful plays of its time, and is perhaps the most effective, literate and unpretentious of all the 'black comedies'. It is set in a mental home, where we encounter three apparent lunatics, who claim to be Newton, Einstein and the spokesman of King Solomon. Actually, however, this third man is a brilliant physicist who has sought refuge, in the sanatorium, from the terrible power of his own discoveries. In the first act all three men murder their nurses: each has fallen in love with her patient and has discovered his sanity. The other two madmen are agents of the two main world powers, sent to abduct the genius,

Mobius. While a police inspector investigates the murders, Mobius persuades the others to help him save the world by staying put. They agree, but unfortunately the female psychiatrist in charge of their 'cases' has taken copies of Mobius' manuscripts before he burned them; herself mad, she proposes to exploit them. Whether 'a certain flippancy about the treatment' actually 'introduces a note of insincerity' (H. F. Garten) or not, it is certain that Dürrenmatt fails to do full justice to his ingenious plot. An excellent play, *The Physicists* should also be a moving one—and for some reason it is not.

Dürrenmatt has written short stories and radio plays, one of which, *A Dangerous Game*, was translated (R. and C. Winston, 1960). An immensely gifted writer, it remains for him to do justice to the emotional seriousness he displays in his thoughtful criticism.

FRITZ HOCHWÄLDER (1911) was born in Vienna, but left for Switzerland in 1938. He has continued to write plays (for radio and TV as well as the stage) of a consistently high standard for over a quarter of a century, but has never repeated the commercial success of *The Strong are Lonely* (*Das heilige Experiment*, 1947; ad. E. le Gallienne, 1954), which was first performed in 1943. This deals with the destruction of the theocratic Jesuit state in eighteenth-century Paraguay and with the conflict in the mind of the Father Provincial—between his own spiritual interests and the needs of his Church as a whole. Hochwälder was a friend of Georg Kaiser (q.v.), and based his second play *The Fugitive* (*Der Flüchtling*, 1945) on a scenario written by him just before his death in Switzerland. This story of the conversion of a frontier guard to a belief in freedom—a fugitive takes his wife from him—is his least convincing play; it was made into a successful film. *The Public Prosecutor* (*Der öffentliche Ankläger*, 1949; tr. K. Black, 1958) is as good as anything he has written. Fouquier Tinville, the public prosecutor of the period after Robespierre's death, conducts a case against an anonymous enemy of the people: himself. *Donadieu* (1953), based on a ballad by C. F. Meyer (q.v.), is a convincing and dramatically effective account of a man's renunciation of the right to revenge himself upon his wife's murderer. In *The Inn* (*Die Herberge*, 1956), once again a finely constructed and highly effective play, the theft of a bag of gold brings to light a more serious crime. *The Innocent* (*Die Unschuldige*, 1958) is a comedy in which a man's life is changed when he is accused of a murder of which he is not, but—as he realizes—might have been, guilty. *Thursday* (*Donnerstag*, 1959), written for the Salzburg festival, is a miracle play, and one of the few in which Hochwälder has used a modern setting and drawn on the traditions of his native theatre. Pomfrit, an Austrian Faust, wins his struggle against the devil's temptation. *1003* (1963) is Hochwälder's most experimental play. It shows the author creating a character, and at the same time is concerned with his usual theme of the humanization of man: his awakening of conscience, and acquirement of qualities that entitle him to the definition of human: the transformation of '*Nichtmensch*' into *Mensch*. *The Raspberry-picker* (*Der Himbeerpflücker*, 1965), a farce, is based on Gogol's *Government Inspector*. *The Command* (*Der Befehl*, 1967) is for television.

Hochwälder is a prolific playwright, well known to the public for his

Paraguayan success, but perhaps not enough heeded by critics. His technical skill extends, as *1003* demonstrates, to the non-conventional play; and it never conceals a superficial or sentimental approach.

WOLFGANG HILDESHEIMER (1916), from Hamburg, was originally a painter (he trained in England), but is probably best known as one of the comparatively few German so-called dramatists of the absurd. He emigrated to Palestine in 1933 and, an Israeli citizen, now lives in Switzerland. He is certainly the leader of such dramatists in German. He is also the author of short stories, and radio plays and a radio opera (with music by Hans Werner Henze). His first stage success, *The Dragon Throne* (*Der Drachenthron*, 1955), was based on his *Hörspiel* on the Turandot story, *Prinzessin Turandot*, of the previous year. His first venture into the theatre of the absurd was the trilogy of one-act plays *Plays in Which Darkness Falls* (*Spiele in denen es dunkel wird*, 1958). His earlier radio plays were bizarre and witty variations on 'Ruritanian' themes. Now he consciously drew upon the techniques of the theatre of the absurd to depict the grotesque manner in which non-material values lay buried in the commercial details of the new prosperity. *Pastoral or Time for Cocoa* (*Pastorale oder die Zeit für Kakao*), the first of the three 'darkness' plays, is very close to reality in its depiction of a number of men mixing business talk with sham culture—but condenses the action to expose its absurdity. Hildesheimer's use of the absurd has been characteristically German in that he has made it as didactic as possible—since (he says) 'life makes no statement' so the absurd play becomes a parable of life by itself making no statement. His first full-length play of the absurd is *The Delay* (*Die Verspätung*, 1961), which is set in a village inn. An old professor is waiting for the arrival of a fabulous bird, while all public services have ceased to function. This is a moving play, but owes much to Beckett and Ionesco. Hildesheimer is gentle rather than gloomy or savage. The use of this technique by RICHARD HEY (1926) is less convincing. As H. F. Garten implies, his plays *The Fish with the Golden Dagger* (*Der Fisch mit dem goldenen Dolch*, 1959) and *Woe to Him Who Doesn't Lie* (*Weh dem der nicht lügt*, 1962) are essentially romantic dramas conveniently cast into the fashionable form of the absurd.

PETER WEISS (1916), who was born near Berlin, and who is often referred to as Brecht's natural successor, was an early member of *Gruppe 47*, but did not attain his present high reputation until he was well over forty. Best known in the English-speaking world as the author of *Marat/Sade*, which was eventually filmed, Weiss is the author of several other plays and novels. His father was a Czech Jew (converted to Christianity), his mother Swiss. When Weiss was eighteen, the family left for London, and he studied photography at the London Polytechnic. In 1936 he went to Prague to study at the Academy of Art. In 1938 he fled to Switzerland. He went to Sweden in 1939, to rejoin his parents, and eventually became a Swedish citizen. For the next twenty years he devoted himself mostly to visual arts: first as a painter and then as a film-maker. He published two small collections of poetry in Swedish in the Forties, but did not take up writing seriously until the late Fifties. Weiss met and was encouraged by Hesse (q.v.). Other influences are his experience in the documentary cinema, the gruesome, alogical world of Grimms' tales and the Märchen, surrealism, Kafka, and Breughel and Bosch and their re-appearance in the work of Kafka's friend the painter, novelist and illustrator Alfred Kubin.

Weiss's first book in German, his 'micro-novel' *The Shadow of the Coachman's Body* (*Der Schatten des Körpers des Kutschers*, 1960), was written eight years before its publication. This is a child-narrator's account of the events in an isolated house in some undefined fairy-tale past; the cinema has influenced the descriptive terms, chiefly compounded of light and shadow; the atmosphere is menacing, the attitude of the narrator unmistakably paranoid. This is an experiment, not entirely successful because it becomes repetitious and boring; but it is a remarkable and original piece of writing.

The two autobiographical pieces, *Leavetaking* and *Vanishing Point* (*Abschied von den Eltern*, 1961; *Fluchtpunkt*, 1962; tr. C. Levenson, 1967), usefully appear in English in a single volume. This narrative, covering the years 1916–47, makes evident the purely personal difficulties that account for Weiss's slow start: what his best English critic Ian Hilton describes as 'extreme alienation'. The partial attempt in his first prose work to describe the world in terms of 'scientific' perception failed because it did not correspond closely enough to Weiss's own alienated point of view. It was simply another, frozen, point of view. The autobiographical narrative, in which there is some excellently lucid and minutely observed detail (technically of a conventional sort), is more successful.

But Weiss was to find his true *métier*, and his first release from the severe feelings of alienation that afflicted him, in the drama. He has said that when he writes a book he feels alone; but when his work reaches the stage he feels 'alive'. His play, *The Persecution and Assassination of Marat as Performed by the Inmates of the Asylum of Charenton under the Direction of the Marquis de Sade* (*Die Verfolgung und Edmordung Jean Paul Marats, dargestellt durch die Schauspielgruppe des Hospizes zu Charenton unter Anleitung des Herrn de Sade*, 1964; tr. G. Skelton and A. Mitchell, 1965), known simply as *Marat/Sade*, is an original amalgam of the theatres of the absurd and cruelty (qq.v.), and of Beckett, Wedekind, Genet, Ionesco and Strindberg (qq.v.); but the strongest influence of all came from Brecht (q.v.), whose political ideas Weiss took with absolute seriousness. He was to offend many of his left-wing admirers in the West when, in the year following his greatest success, he announced his allegiance to East Germany. (Since he chooses to remain in capitalist Sweden, this is doubtless to be interpreted as a gesture within the Western camp—or perhaps as a kind of autobiographical alienation effect.)

Clearly, however, Weiss's requirements for feeling alive included widespread success as well as the dramatic form. His earlier plays had been failures. In *The Tower* (*Der Turm*, 1963; tr. PWGT, 1967) and *The Insurance* (*Die Versicherung*, 1967), written in the late Forties and early Fifties respectively, there is insufficient dramatic element; and in *Night with Guests* (*Nacht mit Gästen*, 1963) the rhyming doggerel in which the play is written merely helps to emphasize its slightness. *Marat/Sade*, certainly superior to anything Weiss has done before or since, finely and inventively dramatizes the tension within him—and in history

—between imagination and action, individualism and socialism. It lacks German ponderousness, and, like the plays of Brecht that were its main inspiration, it offers enormous possibilities to its director—and it has attracted distinguished directors, including the greatest of them all, Ingmar Bergman. Like its predecessors, *Marat/Sade* lacks true dramatic action; but it is a *tour de force* because it creates the illusion of it, smuggling in a good deal of almost Shavian discussion of ideas. Against a background of insane babbling Sade directs his play of the murder of Marat. The date is 13 July 1808, fifteen years after the actual event. Acting out Weiss's own conflict between what he felt to be creative solipsism and desirable but unattainable revolutionary socialism, *Marat/Sade* mirrored a universal conflict. Every production, from Peter Brook's simplistic one to the infinitely subtle, individualistic Ingmar Bergman's, added a new dimension. Significantly, Weiss preferred the most 'committed' production, in which Marat is made the revolutionary hero. He revised the script five times, each time in this direction. From his own act of political commitment may be marked—after all too brief an ascent—his creative decline, a decline that is, however, gradual and, doubtless, not irreversible. This has nothing to do with the merits of Marxism or the deficiencies of capitalism; it is simply that nothing Weiss has written since *Marat/Sade* is on the same imaginative level because it lacks its high tension.

In *The Investigation* (*Die Ermittlung*, 1965; tr. A. Gross, 1966), staged in Germany by Erwin Piscator (q.v.) not long before his death, Weiss allows a selection of facts to substitute for imagination. This oratorio is a series of extracts, pretentiously broken up into free verse, from reports of the proceedings at the Auschwitz trial at Frankfurt-on-Main in 1964. It is, of course, unbearably moving; but attempts to demonstrate that this is so because of Weiss's selective brilliance are misguided. Almost any such juxtaposition would be equally effective. Offered to us as a work of imagination, *The Investigation* is merely impertinent. As one critic remarked, 'it wrote itself'. *My Place* (*Meine Ortschaft*, 1965; GWT), a prose account of Weiss's visit to Auschwitz, is superior. Of the three successors to *The Investigation*, only the 'everyman' piece *How Herr Mockinpott Was Relieved of his Sufferings* (*Wie dem Herrn Mockinpott das Leiden ausgetrieben wurde*, 1968), although its situation is over-indebted to Kafka, is better: non-documentary, it is more inventive and more vital in its detail. *The Song of the Lusitanian Bogey* (*Gesang vom lusitanischen Popanz*, 1967), about the brutal Portuguese suppression of the Angolan uprising of 1961, and *Vietnam Discourse* (*Viet Nam Diskurs*, 1968)—the one in the form of a song-and-dance revue for (ideally) an all-Negro cast, and the other 'tub-thumping documentary' (Ian Hilton)—are slavishly Brechtian in technique and have no claim at all as imaginative works. Rather, they are political acts. Weiss has turned into a higher middlebrow entertainer in the most fashionable modern manner of left-wing conscience-stirrer. It does not much help his work that the attack is really less on the capitalist West, admittedly as corrupt as Weiss likes, than on the solipsistic tendencies of the author. Beneath their superficially bang-up-to-date, fashionable appearance, Weiss's propaganda pieces are curiously old-fashioned, and hark back to the days of expressionist activism; furthermore, they tend increasingly to over-simplify matters, a risk often run by those who abandon the objective function of the writer for the necessarily subjective one of changing the world (which is Weiss's avowed aim). His latest work, *Trotsky in Exile* (*Trotzki im Exil*, 1970), once again documentary, diminishes the humanity of Trotsky in the interests of its message. Weiss, a sincere man, remains desperately naïve about the nature of revolutions. He can hardly have carefully considered the state of his master Brecht's mind at the end of his life. He sees, he has written, 'no reason why artists in a Socialist state should be restricted in their own natural development'. One can only sadly append one's own mark of exclamation. He and literature would be better served if he concentrated more upon his natural—and not his intellectual—development. One may see in him another example, and in this case a victim, of *Künstlerschuld*: instead of, like Rilke, yearning to be a 'country doctor', he has decided to be a doctor to the world from which he cannot help feeling so distant. And yet the feeling for other people displayed in some of his prose of the early Sixties—for, say, the Swedish forestry workers in *Vanishing Point*—is stronger and purer and certainly more beautiful and natural than that displayed in the more or less cleverly manipulated puppets of his propaganda plays. The masters of Auschwitz itself regarded their charges as puppets; had they regarded them as people they could not have abused them as they did.

It is easy to understand why the post-war Germans evolved a documentary-drama form as a means of solving their problems: theoretically, in place of ecstasy, or mere interpretation, the facts would speak truthfully, would clarify the situation, and would deter the tendency to excess. The more 'documentary' such works are, of course, the less imaginative they are likely to be. But creativity itself has come under strong suspicion in Germany: better, therefore, to have facts than figments of the imagination.

This form is also, however, a logical development of epic theatre (q.v.), and the documentary drama has tended to become less an objective theatre—fulfilling the role of the good newspaper, which of course no commercially viable newspaper can for long fulfil—than either a theatre of protest or, as in the case of Peter Weiss, an agent for social change. Ours, furthermore, is an age of the 'directors' theatre': as one critic has written, 'The play is no longer the thing; it is what producer and director make of it that counts'. The documentary drama, one might say, is one manner—and an important one—in which the authors connive at this arrangement. It mostly suits playwrights in whom the springs of invention or imagination are weak; but it might be a prelude to a genuinely co-operative phase in the theatre, in which individuals need not be distinguished.

The best known, or some would say most notorious, of the documentary-dramatists is ROLF HOCHHUTH (1931), who was born near Kassel in Northern Hesse. Hochhuth has written both short stories and a novel (neither are published in book form), but it was his play about the Roman Catholics and the Nazis, *The Representative* (*Der Stellvertreter*, 1963; tr. R. D. MacDonald, 1963) that made him famous. Appropriately in the age of director's theatre, the German text consists of much more than anyone has ever seen in any production: what goes in depends on the director. This play, first produced by Piscator in Berlin, is undoubtedly an indictment of Pope Pius XII for his indifference to the plight of the Jews and his failure to denounce Nazi persecution of them. It aroused much controversy, all of which tended to obscure the question of its dramatic merit. Pope John XXIII is supposed to have exclaimed, when asked what could be done to neutralize the effects of the play, 'Do against it? What can you do against the truth?' Hochhuth has been compared with Schiller, and this is apt so far as *The Representative* is concerned, for the structure is old-fashioned and 'plotted' as distinct from, say, Weiss's documentaries; but *Soldiers* (*Soldaten*, 1967; tr. R. D. MacDonald, 1969) his second play—again a textually massive work from which the producer must select—is more chaotic, and its dialogue is flatter and less effective. This is clearly intended as a condemnation of the inhumanity of war in general, based on Hochhuth's belief that history (tragically) expresses itself in a few strong personalities who make decisions; its effect is to suggest that the British were as morally culpable as the Germans. Now this point of view—if Hochhuth intended it—might no doubt convincingly be set forth in an imaginative work; here it functions simply as journalism. The question of whether or not Churchill connived at, or ordered, the death of the Polish General Sikorski has nothing to do with the literary value of *Soldiers*.

Hochhuth has written some powerful scenes; and his technique, in his first play, of interspersing heartless official cliché with concentrated verse does convey his indignation and his humanity. But *Soldiers* is more decisively a directors' play; furthermore, its imaginative worth seems to have been wilfully vitiated by polemical considerations. *The Representative* was a mixture of pamphlet and drama, displaying creative gifts of a high order; *Soldiers* is skilful journalism, and should be judged on that level.

XV

One of the most characteristic of post-war West German writers is the novelist, critic and playwright MARTIN WALSER (1927) born in Wasserburg. He is not a profound writer—but he is a useful one, a responsible and scrupulous social critic and satirist who knows his limitations. It is typical of him that, as a critic, he should approach drama as essentially historical. It is wrong, he asserts, to re-interpret any drama of the past. He does not, in other words, fully grasp the critical problem of the drama that is ephemeral and the drama that transcends its time: his own work, although not frenetic or over-programmatic like some of Weiss's, is written specifically for its time. A dialectical writer, and excessively intellectual, he lacks the confidence of inspiration—an understandable attitude in an intelligent German of his generation. But he rationalizes this into a critically unconvincing distrust of words' capacities. For Walser, the artist is not guilty but incapable: pressure to write in him is low. He first attracted wide attention with his novel *The Gadarene Club* (*Ehen in Philippsburg*, 1957; tr. 1959), a satire on business and the German 'economic miracle'. *Half-Time* (*Halbzeit*, 1960) is a more comprehensive satire on the same subject-matter. *The Unicorn* (*Das Einhorn*, 1966), his most amusing and psychologically pointed novel, deals with the experiences of a man commissioned by a woman publisher to write a novel about love. He gets his copy from an affair with her.

Walser, almost always an accomplished and argute writer, is at his most adroit in the *Hörspiel* and in stage drama. *The Rabbit Race* (*Eiche und Angora*, 1962; ad. R. Duncan, 1963, with *The Detour, Der Abstecher*, 1961) is unoriginal inasmuch as it patchily draws on almost every dramatic source available in the half-century preceding its composition; but it is both intelligent and entertaining. The central character is Alois Grübel, representative of the exploited German, 'nice' but naïve, who submits to all manner of evil. *The Detour* is a sinister comedy which Walser subsequently turned into a radio play, heard in Great Britain in 1962. *The Black Swan* (*Der schwarze Schwan*, 1964) continues Walser's study of the German character and of German guilt in particular. A son tries to discover if he contains within himself the seeds of his father's guilt. Like nearly all Walser's work, the penetrating intelligence of this play is undermined by a failure to create—perhaps arising from a lack of interest in—individual character. In so far as Germany has produced a 'new writer' since 1945, the cool, non-incandescent Walser is typical. His workaday creative talent, operating in more or less 'intelligible' forms, stands in contrast to the paucity of that of many self-conscious, non-representational *avant gardists*.

HANS ERICH NOSSACK (1901), from Hamburg, is older and, by contrast, wholly introspective; but, with his constant theme of self-renewal, he is indisputably a post-war writer. Forbidden to publish by the Nazis in 1933 on account of his left-wing views, he gave up the hand-to-mouth existence (factory-worker, salesman, clerk, reporter, unemployed) that he had deliberately chosen rather than continue to study law and philosophy at Jena, and joined his father's coffee-importing firm. His manuscripts were destroyed in the Hamburg air-raids of summer 1943, although it seems that an unfinished drama about Lenin written in the Thirties, *Elnin*, survives. Virtually all of the work—novels, plays, poems, essays—by which he is known arises not from early left-wing interests but from experiences of the war; and what started this off was his witnessing, from the country outside Hamburg, its destruction by Allied bombers. He felt that he was literally watching the destruction of his own past, and his subsequent writings are an account of his difficult rebirth: of his struggle to find himself as a real person and to survive as one. He has developed into one of the strangest of contemporary writers; and his writing, always difficult, has consistently gained in power.

His first works—they can be classified as short stories although English-speaking readers might call them autobiographical essays; and he himself calls them 'reports'— described the Hamburg raids, and were praised by Jean Paul Sartre. All these pieces were revised and collected together as *Dorothea* (1950). In his fiction Nossack uses surrealistic devices to express bewilderment, disgust and a Bergsonian (q.v.) disbelief in time. Like most German writers, he has directed his satirical attention at the *Wirtschaftswunder* society, the prosperous and smug perpetrators and maintainers of the 'economic miracle'. But he remains obsessed by what he saw from outside his native Hamburg; paradoxically, its chaos preserves him from the anti-human horrors of the *Wirtschaftswunder*. The first novel he published, *At Latest in November* (*Spätestens im November*, 1955) tells—from her point of view—of a woman torn between her husband, an industrialist, and a writer. The husband, a 'good fellow', uses her beauty as an advertisement for the firm; she meets the writer because he is the recipient of the firm's prize (more advertisement). Thus the writer depends on the crass businessman for cash, prestige and sex. Nossack shows relentlessly that the love between these two people sets up no authentic values in opposition to the industrialist's rosy materialism. Marianne, the wife, returns to her husband, but leaves him again—to meet death with her lover in a car crash. This, Nossack's most technically conventional work, is wholly pessimistic. *The Younger Brother* (*Der jüngere Bruder*, 1958) is an even sharper indictment of the capitalist present.

We Know That Already (*Das kennt man*, 1964) is the paranoid—or is it?—narrative of a dying prostitute of Hamburg's Reeperbahn district. She has been run over—by a genuine accident or by the machinations of the people who live 'over there', on the other side of the river? The surface of this multi-layered book is (for Nossack) a fairly straightforward account of the breakdown of a simple mind, which takes to paranoically interpreting kindness as hostility. But, ironically, this colloquial monologue, hardly surrealist in terms of the dying girl's delirium, has its sinisterly realistic side. The book has great distinction of style; the demotic nature of the girl's narrative does not so much question as cut through the parodistically teutonic sections of the plot (for example, 'over there', in a quiet glade, where time is non-existent, at the secret centre of the slave-run industrial complex, dwells the great mistress whose servant the narrator was in a previous incarnation).

Nossack's best novel, *The Case d'Arthez* (*Der Fall d'Arthez*, 1968), again deals, in a complex plot, with the problem of discovering an 'authentic' existence in a political state that regards such authenticity as treason. For Nossack there is no modern state that would be able to tolerate a truly free individual. The anonymous narrator, d'Arthez, and his friend Lambert, are all shown as in search of self: the narrator gives up his post with the security service, d'Arthez renounces name and fortune, Lambert (whose name is a pseudonym) refuses success. Nossack, in a novel that is surprisingly easy to read, makes the quest for self and truth mean something in psychological as well as mythical, or parabolic, terms. To a large extent it may be seen as what his earlier and sometimes recondite work was leading up to. He has also written poetry, criticism and plays.

EDZARD SCHAPER (1908) was born near Posen, now in Poland; he lived in Esthonia and Finland from 1930 until after the war, and finally settled in Switzerland. A Baltic background predominates in his work, which is un-equivocally Christian. The solution he offers to the problems of terror and tyranny, to which he is acutely and honestly sensitive (as his background might suggest)—a solution involving the cultivation of a Christian stoicism in order to attain inner freedom—is not sufficiently worked out to be convincing to readers. But his accounts of the struggle to survive of an Orthodox Christian community in Esthonia in *The Dying Church* (*Die sterbende Kirche*, 1935) and its sequel *The Last Advent* (*Der letzte Advent*, 1949) are touching and always truthful. Nor are they without some humour. He is at his best, however, and least hortatory, in the novella. 'The Shipwrecked Ark' (1935), in which a cargo of circus animals perish in a storm as a young couple try to resolve their difficulties, is the most delicate example

ALBRECHT GOES (1908), who was born in Würtemberg, is another Christian traditionalist, but one of greater power and range. He is a Lutheran pastor who served as an army chaplain on the Russian Front. His poetry (TCG) is traditional and occasionally achieves an impressive serenity in the manner of Mörike, of whom he has written a study (1938). He is well known as an essayist. His best work is contained in the two novellas (*Arrow to the Heart* (*Unruhige Nacht*, 1949; tr. C. Fitzgibbon, 1951) and *The Burnt Offering* (*Das Brandopfer*, 1954; tr. M. Hamburger, 1956). In the first a chaplain on the Russian Front has to comfort a young soldier who is going to be shot in the morning for desertion. *The Burnt Offering* describes how a butcher's wife becomes aware, through her work, of the true nature of the Nazi attitude towards the Jews. This admirably straightforward, brief tale is Goes's masterpiece.

STEFAN ANDRES (1906–70), a Roman Catholic from the Moselle valley, began as a trainee-priest, but abandoned this in favour of study at the university and extensive travel. He lived in Italy from 1937 until 1949. His simplistic first novel, *Brother Lucifer* (*Bruder Luzifer*, 1932), is autobiographical: a not extraordinary account of conflict between spiritual aspirations and physical instincts. He was a prolific author of plays, novels, novellas, poetry, short stories and *Hörspiele*: a competent writer whose lusty sense of humour and vitality continually redeem his books from dullness. The novella that made him famous after the war, *We are Utopia* (*Wir sind Utopia*, 1942; tr. C. Brooks, 1954), is his best book, an example of ingenuity fully exploited. A monk, Paco, leaves his monastery in Spain to devote himself to the establishment of that heaven upon earth that his superiors have told him not even God has been able to create. Fighting against the fascists in the Civil War he is captured—and confined in his old cell in the very monastery from which he had fled. The officer in charge of the prisoners, a bullying rapist and killer, is terrified of dying unconfessed, and comes for help. Paco, with his knowledge of the place, could kill him and help his friends to escape. However, although knowing that the officer's intention is to machine-gun them all, he both confesses him and allows him to carry out his murderous plan. Andres turned this powerful and unostentatious story into a moving and effective *Hörspiel*, *God's Utopia* (*Gottes Utopia*, 1950). The dystopian trilogy *The Deluge* (*Die Sintflut*, 1949–59) is about an ex-priest, Moosethaler, who becomes a Hitler in an imaginary country. *The Journey to Portiuncula* (*Die Reise nach Portiuncula*, 1954) is a clever and amusing novel, full of Andres' love for the south, about a rich German brewer who revisits the place in Italy where thirty years before he betrayed a girl and his youthful ideals.

GERD GAISER (1908), the son of a Würtemberg priest, has been one of the leading writers of fiction since 1950. Like Andres, he began by training for the priesthood but abandoned this for art studies and travel. Then he was an art teacher until the war, when he joined the Luftwaffe. After being released from a British P.O.W. camp in Italy he became a painter; then an art teacher again. His creativity, too, was stirred by experience of war. His use of symbolism is effective in short stories, but sometimes obtrusive in his novels. *A Voice is Raised* (*Eine Stimme hebt an*, 1950), his first novel, on the ubiquitous theme of the returning soldier, has an unusually optimistic conclusion, and gives an honest portrayal of a man who regains his hold on life after devastating experiences. The dense style, however, vitiates much of the novel's effect: it appears pretentious. *The Falling Leaf* (*Die sterbende Jagd*, 1953; tr. P. Findlay, 1956) relates the disillusion of a fighter squadron based in Norway with both their task and the war they are fighting. This is in a realistic style throughout. Gaiser, in what is possibly the most outstanding of all the German novels about the Second World War, has been accused of treating the question of moral guilt 'superficially'. But what he actually does is to give an unforgettable picture of what his bored and disgusted pilots actually do: go on fighting, although they know that they will lose, that there is no honour or chivalry left, and that their cause is worse than unjust. *The Ship in the Mountain* (*Das Schiff im Berg*, 1955) more ambitiously sets out to explore the relationship between man and nature, but succeeds only in some of its details: a poor community discover caves in the mountain side upon which they live and plan to make them a tourist attraction. *The Last Dance of the Season* (*Schlussball*, 1958; tr. M. Waldman, 1960) satirizes the 'economic miracle' yet again; but one has only to compare this with, say, Martin Walser's competent *Half-time* (q.v.) to see that Gaiser is a truly imaginative writer, whose language is richly suggestive. That he is not a moralist, and will not facilely condemn the behaviour of either his disillusioned pilots or even his bourgeois participants in the *Wirtschaftswunder* seems admirable: his committal is creative. Gaiser has achieved most, however, as a writer of short stories, in which he is better able—perhaps more intuitively and less consciously—to handle his extra-realistic impulses without becoming laboured. His best work arises from a self-exploration conducted by the means of writing; excellent novelist although he is at his best, the length of the form causes him to take too much thought in what, for him, is the wrong way. 'Antigone and the Garden Dwarf' (GSS) is an excellent example of his subtle humour and poetic sense of language. On the face of it a light-heartedly grotesque tale about a struggle between two men to buy a garden-dwarf from an unconfident florist, it is at the same time an account of the horrors and violent impulses that lie only just beneath the surface of 'civilized' life. It is witty and readable. Gaiser has attracted some hostile criticism from younger writers; but it is he, with his cautious modernism, who seems to have more to say than they, with their too often reckless and externally rather than internally dictated search for new forms.

GERTRUD FUSSENEGGER (1912) was born in Pilsen in Czechoslovakia, the daughter of an Austrian army officer. A distinguished writer, she has not had the critical attention she deserves. Many of her novels deal with the Czecho-slovakian past: *The Brothers from Lasawa* (*Die Brüder von Lasawa*, 1948) is about two brothers in the Thirty Years War; and her two most substantial novels, *The House* (*Das Haus der dunklen Krüge*, 1951) and *The Masked Face* (*Das verschüttete Antlitz*, 1957) are dense sociological studies of the immediate Bohemian past. The short story 'Woman Driver' (GSS), about a bored and unhappily married woman who drives to her death, gives a good example of how, by means of a lyrical style, she can gain new insight into a commonplace theme.

ALFRED ANDERSCH (1914) was born in Munich; as a communist he spent six months in Dachau when Hitler gained power. He was an unwilling factory worker and then soldier, and deserted in 1944, preferring to be a prisoner-of-war in the U.S.A. Later he edited the eventually banned *Der Ruf*, helped with the founding of *Gruppe 47*, and worked for Stuttgart Radio. Andersch, who is now more of an anarchist than a communist, is the same sort of writer as Martin Walser—but on the whole he is less efficient as well as less satirical and sharp. After an autobiography describing his desertion from the army, he published *Flight to Afar* (*Sansibar oder Der letzte Grund*, 1957; tr. M. Bullock, 1958). This describes how people could behave decently even under the hideous pressure of Nazidom, but is more journalistic than imaginative, and because of this makes unconscious concessions to its readers. Rodney Livingstone's charge that Andersch, for all his personal courage and fine record of resistance to the Nazis, provides fashionably vague solutions for fashionably vague guilts is difficult to answer. But Andersch, an intelligent and capable writer, took to fiction in the first place because the Allies stopped him running *Der Ruf*. The people in his novels are products of his thinking rather than of his imagination, which does not function autonomously. Lacking Martin Walser's satirical edge, his writing is transparently sincere (as the often im-passioned style indicates) but remains vague in the very diagnoses it desperately wants to make. In *The Redhead* (*Die Rote*, 1960; tr. M. Bullock, 1961) he portrays a woman, herself successful in business, who becomes suddenly nauseated, while on holiday in Italy, with her husband and the commercially comfortable Germany he stands for. So far so good. But Andersch can do nothing psychologically convincing with her: her love affairs, and final decision to work in a factory, are hopelessly contrived. Andersch is committed to the *avant garde*, but is himself an essentially conservative writer. His stories, some of which are collected in *The Night of the Giraffe* (tr. C. Armstrong, 1965), are at their best when autobiographical, or when describing events the author has witnessed. If Andersch cannot but simplify his material, however, he undoubtedly possesses genuine dramatic power; probably his best work has been done in radio-drama. His best known *Hörspiel, Driver's Escape (Fahrerflucht,* 1965), has been published, with three other volumes devoted to his work for radio.

The poet and short-story writer WOLFDIETRICH SCHNURRE (1920), a founder of *Gruppe 47* (q.v.) (which he later left), was born in Frankfurt-on-Main, but grew up in north-east Berlin, the setting of much of his work, from 1928. He spent over six years in the army. He is the author of some highly distinguished *Hörspiele*—indeed, certain critics see these, some of which have been collected in the volume *Furnished Room (Spreezimmer möbliert,* 1967), as his best work. Schnurre, who sometimes provides lively illustrations to his books, crosses bitter satire with humour both charming and 'absurd'. He thus combines, without pretentiousness, the traditions of Heine, Tucholsky and Brecht (corrosive satire), Busch (stolid nonsense) and Morgenstern (poetic humour). He became well known with his first novel *Stardust and Sedan Chair (Sternstaub und Sänfte,* 1953), the diary of a confidence-poodle who writes sonnets. The title story in the collection *People Ought to Object (Man sollte dagegen sein,* 1953) is one of his best known. A man reads an advertisement in the paper announcing that God has died, and goes to his funeral. Only the parson and the gravediggers are there, and they are bored. Only the sordid and drab world remains. Perhaps the moral is Voltaire's 'Si dieu n'existait pas, ils faudrait l'inventer'. Schnurre's poetry (MGP, TCG, GWT) is compressed, satirical and frequently sinister, as in 'Denunciation', about the moon whose 'employer is known to us; / he lives on the far side of love'. However, he has also written straightforwardly lyrical poetry. The short story 'In the Trocadero' (GSS) offers an excellent example of this sensitive and original writer at his best. Comparison of Schnurre with Swift—whom he has studied and written well about—to the disadvantage of the latter has been attempted and is very silly; but he is a powerful writer, whose anger is in no sense misanthropic, like Arno Schmidt's, but based rather in his intelligent humanitarianism.

ARNO SCHMIDT (1914) is the most thoroughgoing *avant gardist* in Germany; he has no trace of teutonic ponderousness—on the contrary, there is something positively Gallic about his procedures, whose excessively cerebral nature is, however, consistently modified by his sense of humour and unfrivolous integrity of purpose. Because it is difficult, his work has not attracted the attention it deserves outside Germany. Born in Hamburg, he was a mathematical child-prodigy whose studies were forbidden by the Nazis. He was in the army that occupied Norway as a cartographer (maps and map-reading play a large part in his fiction). He has written many critical essays, a book on the popular adventure-author Karl May, and translations of such authors as Wilkie Collins and William Faulkner. There is no doubt of his subtlety and brilliance; and whatever view be taken of the success of his large-scale experiments, it is certain that they have no pretentiousness. Schmidt is acutely self-critical, and frequently parodies German writing of the 'magic realist' type—and his own style. Only one passage—it is from his novel *Die Gelehrtenrepublik*—seems to be available in English translation (GWT). The novella *Leviathan* (1949) describes a train journey out of the ruins of Berlin towards death. *Nobodaddy's Children* (*Nobodaddys Kinder*, 1951–63) consists of three novels, series of diary entries by three progressively younger characters. The last book, *Black Mirrors* (*Schwarze Spiegel*) consists of the writings of the last man in the world. Sardonic, atheistic ('The "Lord", without Whose willing it no sparrow falls from the roof, nor are 10 Million people gassed in concentration camps: He must be a strange sort —if He exists now at all'), sceptical, exceedingly clever, Schmidt attracts some critics but few book reviewers, who find him 'perverse' and are horrified, as journalists always seem to be, by his biting pessimism. Paul West (who admires him) has said that for Schmidt life is a 'cheerless conundrum'—but he might as well have written 'cheerful'. *From the Life of a Faun* (*Aus dem Leben eines Fauns*, 1953), the first of the trilogy, evokes the atmosphere of (civilian) wartime Germany as well as any book. The middle novel, *Brand's Heath* (*Brands Haide*), describes an ex-POW's researches into the life of an obscure author and his relations with a mistress who eventually deserts him—but sends him food parcels from America.

Schmidt's most massive book is *Zettel's Dream* (*Zettels Traum*, 1970). This breaks up and rearranges several languages (including English), and was originally printed in facsimile, with handwritten corrections and additions— and parallel columns of typescript.

Schmidt is not a behaviourist; but he writes in constant awareness of modern scientific discoveries. Narratives that give the illusion of life being a continuously efficient process are, to him, inadequate. He seeks to build up a truthful picture out of the fragments of conscious perception. Essentially Schmidt is (like Joyce) a comic writer; he is an important one.

The Roman Catholic HEINRICH BÖLL (1917), born in Cologne, is, with Günter Grass, the most celebrated—and translated—of all post-war German novelists. He is a prolific, versatile and gifted writer, always sensible. Before being conscripted he was a bookseller. He served in the ranks of Hitler's army, and was wounded four times on the Russian front. Eventually he was taken prisoner. Soon after the war he began to write. His big public success came with *Acquainted with the Night* (*Und sagte kein einziges Wort*, 1953; tr. R. Graves, 1955). A satirical and humorous writer, Böll, although a moralist, is as un-dogmatic and undidactic as it is possible for a Roman Catholic to be. He is reticent, and his Catholic point of view is only implied. He was never a Nazi; but neither has he been leftist (for example, he can express admiration for individual freedom and the dignity of poverty—compare another Catholic, Léon Bloy, q.v.—in Eire, where he has a home); his energy was and remains directed against war. Böll's starting point is, once again, desolation; but he is in a slightly different position from such a writer as, say, Gaiser (q.v.), who undoubtedly felt some kind of patriotism (if not sympathy for the Nazis themselves) at the very beginning of the war (as his early poetry shows).

A basic theme in all Böll's fiction is man's inability to change the course of his destiny. This is something Böll deals with without philosophical or (apparently) religious preconceptions. He is no determinist; but he does not provide the unconvincing solution, of Christian stoicism, of a Schaper (q.v.): that his powerless heroes must suffer is not accepted stoically by them, since he refuses to teach by manipulating them. Böll tries to proceed from human situations, and to record first of all what people actually feel and actually do. His use of relatively modern techniques—flashback, interior monologue and so on—is invariably functional. He won the 1972 Nobel Prize.

His first two books were about the war. In *The Train was on Time* (*Der Zug war pünktlich*, 1949; tr. R. Graves, 1956) the hero is being taken by train to the Russian front; in *Adam, Where art Thou?* (*Wo warst du, Adam?*, 1951; tr. M. Savill, 1955) he is retreating from Rumania back into Germany. These do not have the meticulousness of Gaiser's study of disillusion, *The Falling Leaf* (q.v.), but are more impressionistic accounts of men as so much rubble being carted back and forth to inevitable destruction. The horror of war struck deep at Böll, and few modern writers have conveyed it to their readers with such force.

Next, as well as writing short stories and radio-plays, Böll turned to writing novels about the effects of war on family life. *Acquainted with the Night* is devoted to a single weekend in the life of Fred Bogner, a poor and numbed survivor of the war. *The Unguarded House* (*Haus ohne Hüter*; tr. M. Savill, 1957) is more complex, contrasting the fate of two families, one rich and one poor, made fatherless by war. In *Billiards at Half-past Nine* (*Billard um halbzehn*, 1959; tr. P. Bowles, 1961) his technique becomes yet more elaborate; and the time-span is now reduced to only one day. This tender and compassionate study of the concerns that keep generations apart and together was Böll's richest achievement to date, although with it he may have sacrificed some of his more facile readers. But his best novel is the simplest of all: *The Clown* (*Ansichten eines Clowns*, 1963; tr. L. Vennewitz, 1965), a book in which his Catholicism is, if anything, even more radical than that of Graham Greene (q.v.). Hans Schnier, a clown, finds his work tolerable while he lives with Marie; but Catholic intellectual friends influence her to leave him, and she marries elsewhere. Now the time interval is reduced to a few hours, although (as always) there are many flashbacks. The anti-Catholic Hans is defeated, reduced from clown to beggar, in a process that reveals him as possessed of a grace that the Catholics of the book lack.

Böll admits to having been influenced by Dickens and Joseph Roth (q.v.). His short stories bear the influence of Hemingway (q.v.), whose terse style seemed like a tonic to the post-war Germans. An author to whom he is very close, although his techniques are more modern, is Graham Greene (q.v.). The reasons are obvious enough. Like Greene he is drawn to the sordid; he is also highly professional—although not to that point where, occasionally, the sense of art vitiates Greene's work, making the reader feel that everything is so well-tailored that, after all, it must only be a story.

Böll has been translated into at least seventeen languages, and is probably the most commercially successful of all the serious post-war German writers. But this success has been thoroughly earned, and none has been gained by making concessions—either consciously or unconsciously. He has written many memorable short stories, which some critics regard as his greatest achievement. Some of these are collected in *Traveller, if you Come to Spa* (tr. M. Savill, 1956) and in *Absent without Leave* (tr. L. Vennewitz, 1967). Typical of his ironic but lusty humour is the story, contained in the latter collection, called 'Bonn Diary', in which a bunch of officers heartily prove that their former commander was responsible for more deaths than the official estimate. 'Pale Anna' (GSS) encapsulates in a few pages his attitude to war: the war veteran seeks for the physical equivalent of his own mental scars in a girl's face, ruined by bomb blast. One can discern Hemingway's influence here; but it has been wholly assimilated; and Böll in any case understands the possibilities of love (particularly heterosexual love) more profoundly and less histrionically than Hemingway. Another well-known story is 'Dr Murke's Collected Silences', from the volume of that title (*Doktor Murkes gesammeltes Schweigen*, 1958), in which an assistant radio producer collects snippets of silent tape in order to preserve his sanity. Böll has also written many *Hörspiele*, a stage play, and several volumes of essays, including an *Irish Notebook* (*Irisches Tagebuch*, 1957).

The Viennese ILSE AICHINGER (1921), wife since 1953 of Günter Eich (q.v.), studied medicine for a time before taking up writing. Her first fiction was a novel, *The Greater Hope* (*Die grössere Hoffnung*, 1948); since then she has preferred the short story and *Hörspiel*, and has become one of the most outstanding practitioners of her generation. Some of her earlier short stories are collected in *The Bound Man* (*Der Gefesselte*, 1953; tr. E. Mosbacher, 1957). Her novel, based on her own experiences of persecution during the war, deals with the short life of a young, partly Jewish girl from the *Anschluss* until her death in street-fighting seven years later. Ilse Aichinger's prose is lucid in the manner of Kafka, whom she also resembles in that she is less a surrealist than a fabulist. She will not accept the surface of life—what is ordinarily called 'reality'—and all she writes is permeated with wonder. Her style is lyrical, or at least semi-lyrical; and often her prose comes close to verse in its regular rhythms. 'Story in Reverse' (GSS) is characteristic, being on exactly the same theme as Günter Kunert's (q.v.) 'Film put in Backwards' (GWT)—the executed soldier wakes in the 'black / of the box. . . . The lid flew up and I / Stood, feeling: / Three bullets travel / Out of my chest / Into the rifles of soldiers . . .'—except that the subject is a young girl suffering from a fatal disease. This is treated with great pathos.

WALTER JENS (1923) is a classics teacher who was born at Hamburg. He has had wide influence as a critic, in which capacity he is preferable as commentator on individual works to propagandist for post-war German literature. His fiction is less tendentious. *No—The World of the Accused* (*Nein—Die Welt der Angeklagten*, 1950) is a variation on Zamyatin's *We* and, more directly, Orwell's *1984* (qq.v.). It is one of the more effective of the many post-war dystopias. A future world-state has divided mankind into judges, witnesses and accused. The ruling terror is the Palace of Justice. The hero betrays his girl and becomes a witness; but when he refuses to become a judge he is killed. Owing much to Orwell, this nevertheless refined his vision and further defined the anti-human nature of the totalitarian state. *The Blind Man* (*Der Blinde*, 1951; tr. M. Bullock, 1954), a novella, works well on both levels: as an account of a teacher suddenly overwhelmed by blindness, and an allegory of man lost in darkness. *Forgotten Faces* (*Vergessene Gesichter*, 1952) is a more realistic story about a home for retired actors. Jens's best novel, however, is *The Man Who did not Want to Grow Old* (*Der Mann, der nicht alt werden wollte*, 1954), which mixes satire and psychological analysis to produce a sad comment on the limitations of academicism and the differences between generations. A German student commits suicide in Paris, and his old professor investigates the reasons. He considers the young man's literary remains, part of a novel, to be outstanding, and analyses them accordingly. This gives Jens a chance to reveal the character of the professor; he never takes advantage of it to gain cheap effects, and the final impression is a tragic one, of an intelligence life-starved and wasted.

GÜNTER GRASS (1927), who was born of German-Polish parents in the Free City of Danzig (now Gdansk), has achieved the greatest success of all post-war German writers. Unlike Böll, who is a writer of similar status, he has not alienated the pseudo-progressive element, as powerful and vociferous in Germany as it is ignorant. Grass's integrity is hardly in doubt, but he has a more flamboyant and colourful personality than Böll; this keeps him in the newspapers and therefore in the forefront of the minds of reviewers. Grass, who fought in the army towards the end of the war and was captured by the Americans, began, like so many German writers (one needs to think only of Hauptmann, Arp, Weiss, Hildesheimer. . . .) as an artist: a sculptor. He had become known both for his art and his radio plays by the mid-Fifties. He wrote *The Tin Drum* (*Die Blechtrommel*, 1959; tr. R. Manheim, 1961) in Paris in the latter part of the decade. *Gruppe 47* awarded him a prize for it before publication. Since then Grass has written three more novels, a full-scale stage play, poetry and several essays and speeches. Committed to the establishment of socialism in West Germany, he campaigned for the Social Democrats in 1965 and 1969 (when they were just successful); and in 1972 when they did well.

Grass is a linguistically exuberant, ingenious and highly inventive writer, whose work is a unique combination of vitality and grotesquerie. He is old enough to have taken part in Nazi activities and the war (he was a member of the Hitler Youth when Germany seized Danzig) without being responsible. This, as has been pointed out, makes him eager to probe the immediate past, an activity that puzzles those too young to have experienced Nazidom, but annoys those who once accepted it. Grass insists that the artist, however committed he may be in life, should be a clown in art. There is, however, much pained irony in this pronouncement—which not all his critics have realized. But Grass, an intelligent and sensible as well as a clever and amusing man, has made good sense of the division between his art (which is sceptical about human happiness) and his life (unequivocal political activity for a party of which he is critical). Such an arbitrary division must not, of course, be taken too literally; but Grass remains extraordinarily relaxed, a remarkable feat for a really gifted German writer.

The Tin Drum is a historically meticulous examination of the period 1925–55, narrated by the dwarf Oskar Matzerath. Fantasy of the specifically German sort is brilliantly counterpointed with historical detail. We can understand that Oskar's childhood need for tin drums, his glass-shattering screams if denied them, is not merely fanciful. *Dog Years* (*Hundejahre*, 1963; tr. R. Manheim, 1965) begins in 1917, and, with three narrators instead of one, therefore takes in even more history. *Cat and Mouse* (*Katz und Maus*, 1961; tr. R. Manheim, 1961) is a novella: the oversized Joachim Mahlke's schoolfriend tells the story of his successful military career. *Local Anaesthetic* (*örtlich betaubt*, 1969; tr. R. Manheim, 1970) comes up to date to examine the nature of the student revolt. Characteristically, Grass spreads himself, or at least his inclinations, among the characters: Scherbaum, the boy who is going to burn his beloved dog in front of a Berlin cakeshop in protest against the Viet Nam war; Starusch, his liberal form-teacher who persuades him not to do so, and whose dental problems are (it is said) the same as Grass's; and the unnamed dentist, maker of 'corrective bridges', who lives on Senecan principles. This novel, part of which appeared as a play, *Davor*, early in 1969, solves nothing for Grass or anyone else; but it reveals the German conflict between activism and quietism as soberly—although ebulliently in terms of style—as it has ever been revealed. Grass has angrily parodied Rilke for his 'inwardness', but has never failed to acknowledge it in himself.

Grass is a charming, most often playful or satirical, minor poet (*Poems of Günter Grass*, tr. M. Hamburger and C. Middleton, 1967). In the Fifties he wrote several violent comedies, certainly to be classified as of the absurd type; *The Plebeians Rehearse the Uprising* (*Die Plebejer proben den Aufstand*, 1966), which did not work well on the stage, is a Brechtian drama ironically depicting Brecht's refusal, as he rehearsed his adaptation of *Coriolanus*, to side openly with the East German workers in their uprising of 1953.

UWE JOHNSON (1934) was born in Pomerania. He left East Germany in 1959 to settle in the West. Once again, he is concerned with the problem of expressing truths in literature—and not with playing omniscient Balzacian games. This problem becomes—or seems to become—more acute when, as in Berlin, a community is artificially divided and the hapless individual is trapped by conflicting—and in the case of the East, politically directed—mores. Demotic in style, Johnson aims at a meticulous and detailed realism. He put his point of view in 'Berlin, Border of the Divided World' (GWT) before the Wall was built in August 1961. *Speculations about Jakob* (*Mutmassungen über Jakob*, 1959; tr. U. Molinaro, 1963) is a delicate exploration of the psychological facts about the death of a worker. This, written before he came to the West, remains his best novel. Its successors, *The Third Book about Achim* (*Das dritte Buch über Achim*, 1961; tr. U. Molinaro, 1966) and *Two Views* (*Zwei Ansichten*, 1965; tr. U. Molinaro, 1967), put more emphasis on technique and do not provide, except fleetingly, imaginative illumination.

OSKAR MARIA GRAF (1894–1967) was a left-wing, pacifist Bavarian who left Germany for Czechoslovakia in 1933, and then settled in the U.S.A. from 1938.

There he wrote intellectually over-ambitious novels of the future, such as *The Conquest of a World* (*Die Eroberung einer Welt*, 1948). Much better, because in a more deliberately 'minor' tradition, were his coarse, comic novels about the Bavarian peasantry. As has been well said, these 'produce the effect of having been related by word of mouth over the beer and radishes to an eager circle of listeners, who bang the table with their fists in token of assent'. These include, *The Stationmaster* (*Bolwieser*, 1931; tr. M. Goldsmith, 1933), *The Wolf* (*Einer gegen alle*, 1932; tr. 1934) and *The Life of my Mother* (*Das Leben meiner Mutter*, 1947; tr. 1940). The best of his last work is to be found in his short story collections, where he reverts to his earlier subject-matter.

XVI

All post-war German literature is, naturally enough, one form or another of reaction to Nazism and its disastrous end: this necessarily entered into the very fibre of the thought or feeling of all Germans. Of a somewhat older generation, such poets as HANS EGON HOLTHUSEN (1913) and RUDOLF HAGELSTANGE (1912) continued to write in traditional styles, but devoted themselves entirely and consciously to the immediate situation. Even GÜNTER EICH (1907), author of the most distinguished and highly thought of *Hörspiele* of the age (all of them distinctly modernist in technique) has not abandoned regular syntax or employed surrealist effects.

Eich, born in Lebus near Frankfurt-on-Oder, is one of the most influential writers of his time. What makes his poetry (TCG, MGP, GWT) 'modern' is its laconic directness and conspicuous lack of rhetoric. He published a volume in 1930, but this may be regarded as juvenilia. Technically, his poetry is more conservative than his radio work, which is as *avant garde*, particularly in its use of dream situations, as anyone could require. But its content, like its tone of voice, is radical—a fact that its form brings out with an at times shocking force. In the famous 'Latrine', one of the best poems to come out of Germany in the last quarter of a century, he squats 'over a stinking ditch' over bloody, fly-blown paper, watching gardens, a lake, a boat. 'The hardened filth plops' and 'some lines of Hölderlin ring madly' in his ears: ' "But go now and greet the lovely Garonne".' The clouds are reflected in the urine, and swim away beneath his 'unsteady feet'. This is taking 'nature poetry' to its extreme limits, by juxtaposing the fleetingly beautiful—the poetry and the clouds—with the disgusting—the uncomfortable evacuation of hard 'filth' plopping into a pulp of bloody, fly-blown decay. It reflects ruined Germany, but only from a basis of keenly observed and honestly felt experience. Eich, than whom there is no better poet in modern Germany, is the true heir of Lehmann and Loerke (qq.v.).

Holthusen, from Schleswig-Holstein, was influential in the years immediately after the war, but has written little poetry since. He is well known as an intelligent critic, oriented to the earlier period of modernism. His chief concern, never obscurantist, is with the valid survival of the old values into the present. His 'Tabula Rasa' (TCG), written in a style reminiscent of early Rilke and influenced by T. S. Eliot, spoke for all sensitive Germans in 1948: 'What demon is this which, pitiless, grips us and wrings us and impels us to and fro! We pile our dead, bewildered, we grow poorer from year to year. O frenzied inferno!' (TCG, MGP, TCGV.)

The Prussian Rudolf Hagelstange wrote a series of anti-Nazi sonnets, which were widely circulated, while he was a serving soldier. He is, unusually, a poet who combines a deep religious faith of a traditional sort with a full awareness of modern atheistic tendencies. His *Ballad of the Buried Life* (*Ballade vom verschütteten Leben*, 1952; tr. H. Salinger, 1962) is the outstanding modern narrative poem on a contemporary theme in Germany; it is about six German soldiers trapped underground for six years by an explosion. It is tendentiously Christian and somewhat predictable; but the material is impressively handled. (TCG, MGP.)

The poet FRIEDRICH GEORG JÜNGER (1898), like his brother Ernst Jünger (q.v.), has been fascinated by aristocratic, non-Nazi forms of totalitarianism. He was involved in Ernst Nickisch's 'National Bolshevism' with his brother, and had to fly to Switzerland in 1937 when he offended the Nazis with his clandestine but well-known poem 'The Poppy'. His opposition to the regime was considerably less equivocal than that of his brother, who gladly helped to fight Hitler's wars (if only because he believed in the war itself, and not its cause).

Jünger has written criticism and (latterly) fiction; but it is as a poet that he is chiefly known and respected. He has not eschewed modern concerns or sought refuge in inadequate or outmoded attitudes, but he has consistently made use of traditional forms (he has also revived some), of which he is a skilful practitioner.

In terms of content, Jünger's poetry is a fairly uninteresting—and un-attractive—combination of aristocratic stoicism and emotionally unconvincing but accurate observation of nature. Like his brother's, his position seems an artificial one. But his hardness of style, elegant control of expression and intelligence give his poetry a certain distinction. Its intellectual spuriousness is somewhat compensated for by the fact that it reflects a genuine attempt to combat both disorder and sexual confusion. What is interesting is the nature of his failure to achieve this.

His best poem remains the anti-Nazi 'The Poppy' (TCG), in which he expresses his indignation at the Nazi betrayal of good-mannered totalitarian ideals. This is impressive and courageous.

KARL KROLOW (1915), born in Hanover, was originally closer in feeling and style to Lehmann and the tradition of nature poetry than Eich; but he has found it necessary to experiment with surrealism, and to attempt a more hermetic and impenetrable type of poetry than either Lehmann or Eich would write; Krolow has even been criticized, not altogether unjustly, in the sense that he is over-prolific and his experiments frequently fail, for following merely fashionable trends. He has translated much from Spanish and French (Apollinaire, the surrealists, Lorca) and one of the most powerful influences upon him has certainly been Lorca (q.v.), particularly in the way he uses colour. Krolow is a poet of great lyrical gifts and a charming surrealist; possibly his involvement with experimentation has caused him to be somewhat over-valued, and has led readers of his poetry to look for or to assume the existence of depths that are not in it. (TCG, GWT, MEP, MGP and *Invisible Hands*, tr. M. Bullock, 1969.)

PAUL CELAN (ps. PAUL ANTSCHEL, 1920–70), who was born in Rumania and whose parents were murdered by the Nazis while he was sent to forced labour, is a conspicuously modern poet; but he is more certainly a substantial one than Krolow. He became a naturalized Frenchman, and made his living as a language-teacher in Paris. He is generally considered, despite the undeniable difficulties offered by his hermetic poetry, to be the leading German poet of his generation—and the most outstanding to appear since well before the Second World War. Without doubt he is Germany's foremost surrealist poet. He made some distinguished translations from modern poets. Like Krolow he was deeply influenced by the French surrealists; also by Trakl and Goll. Another influence not so often mentioned was really a part of his Jewish background: that fabulous Jewish lore which figures so strongly in the paintings of Chagall and has been mentioned in connection with Kafka. His chief fault is his lack of humour—understandable though this is. Celan is profoundly serious, and seldom exhibitionistically frivolous in the manner one sometimes suspects in Krolow and recognizes in many others. His integrity is never in doubt: he desperately wants to communicate, but must confront the problems both of a cliché-ridden poetic language, and of the inefficacy of any language against the hideousness of such facts as the Nazi oppression of the Jews, which is one of Celan's main themes. This theme functions in his poetry as an acute sense of loss: that whole Rumanian community, with its irreplaceable lore, from which Celan came was wiped out. Only one thing, he said, was not lost: language. But even this 'had to pass through its own inability to answer'. Celan's most famous poem, 'Fugue of Death' (TCG, MEP, MGP), is a fitting representative of his genius. Unlike many of his poems, particularly the later, it is not in the least obscure— yet it is a poem that one can produce as evidence of the quality of the poetry of 'uprooted metaphor': autonomous poetry that uses language as an explorative instrument. Here we all drink the 'Coal-black milk of dawn', and 'Death is a master from Germany' who 'whistles his Jews'.

Towards the end Celan had serious difficulty in expressing himself in poetry, and doubtless would have done better to remain silent. He became derivative, and occasionally he even copied frivolous 'modernists', producing post-surrealist nonsense that had an air of desperation about it. He began to play with words; but his lack of humour made this an unsuitable activity for him. Yet his best poems express responses to life that are unique in the century:

> Gorselight, yellow, the slopes
> fester to heaven, the thorn

woos the wound, bells ring
in there, it is evening, the void
rolls its oceans to worship,
the sail of blood is aiming for you.

(GWT)

Responsible criticism has hardly yet come to terms with such poetry; but it must and will do so.

ERICH FRIED (1921), a Viennese, has lived in London since 1938; for some years he worked for the British Broadcasting Corporation, and is well known for his efficient and sensitive translations into German of Shakespeare, E. E. Cummings, Hopkins and Eliot (qq.v.). Fried is not a poet of the incantatory power of Celan, but he has often, and fairly, been compared to him: he experiences the same kind of difficulties with language as Celan did. The point has been made that he writes his poems in a language which he does not use in daily speech; they treat words with special reverence. He writes densely and punningly, and exhibits a considerable sense of humour (in contrast to Celan), and is strongly and openly committed to the left (one of his books is called *and Vietnam and, und Vietnam und,* 1966). Fried, like Krolow, has had a book of English translations devoted to him: *On Pain of Seeing* (tr. author and G. Rapp, 1969; also TCG, GWT, MGP).

Fried believes 'with Ernesto Che Guevara . . . that the main task for art is the fight against alienation [in the Marxist sense of men being alienated by capitalist forces from a meaningful and creative existence]'. This is what he means when he says that his poetry is 'committed' (he has been at the centre of a controversy on this subject in Germany, where he is highly thought of). His use of language in poetry is a fight against alienation, a fight he also (he says) wages with himself. Latterly he has been experimenting with sounds and word associations in the manner of the 'concrete' poets. This work, while it may well be necessary to Fried, is no more convincing than the later poetry of Celan. In English Fried's poetry tends to appear trite, aphoristic or, sometimes, even gnomic; in the original German it is clearer that he is exploring the nature of language itself. Most effective in his more recent work have been his poems of protest.

The Prussian HELMUT HEISSENBÜTTEL (1921) is the most extreme modernist, if we except 'concrete' poets such as Jandl, Mon or Gomringer, whose work has perhaps less relationship to literature than to the graphic arts, showmanship and entertainment. Heissenbüttel is an associate of these artists, but is altogether more literary. Whatever his readers may think about his abandonment of syntax, they must concede him intelligence and the fact that his is a genuine rejection of traditional modes. Christopher Middleton, a shrewd and well-informed enthusiast, dedicated to the *avant garde*, says of him: 'his so-called "texts" are a kind of linguistic spectral analysis of modern forms of consciousness, atomized, disoriented, admassed'.

Heissenbüttel, much influenced by Wittgenstein (q.v.), has rejected the term 'experiment' in art and therefore calls his first novel, *D'Alembert's End* (*D'Alemberts Ende*, 1970), an *Ausprobieren* (test: trial and error). This extremely complicated fiction—it makes almost any French exponent of the *nouveau roman* seem elementary by comparison—requires both concentration and a high degree of previous admiration in order to read right through. It is a testament to Heissenbüttel's philosophical and critical acuteness, but more doubtfully to his imagination. This attacks the notion of story-telling, and simultaneously explores problems of identity and satirizes foolish or misguided intellectuals. Like Arno Schmidt (q.v.), Heissenbüttel takes note of the new physics, and distrusts conventional grammar because it establishes false relationships and hierarchies; like Schmidt again, but more thoroughgoingly and less comically, he presents reality in disparate fragmented parts (a 'master of discontinuous consciousness'). In himself Heissenbüttel may well be only a minor writer, of limited imaginative capacity; but he is a theorist and critic of whom it is necessary to take account. (MGP, GWT, TCG.)

Of the several woman poets now writing in German the Austrian INGEBORG BACHMANN (1926) is the most highly regarded. A book of her short stories, *The Thirtieth Year* (*Das dreissigste Jahr*, 1961; tr. M. Bullock, 1964) has appeared in English; she has also written opera librettos and radio plays. She wrote her doctoral dissertation on Heidegger, and all her poetry is essentially a means of discovering 'authenticity' in his special sense. She has travelled a great deal. Her poetry, which has been described both as a skilful amalgam of many other poets' styles (Rilke, Trakl, Hölderlin, Goll, Benn, and very many others), and as highly original, is lyrical, tender in its allusions to nature, sporadically surrealist ('the fishes' entrails/have grown cold in the wind' is typical) and above all confessional. Bachmann is a fluent and always impressive poet, but often she seems to be lost in her own rich flux, and to have discovered not authenticity but a self-induced trance.

HANS MAGNUS ENZENSBERGER (1929) was born in Bavaria. Often referred to, in a foolish phrase, as 'Germany's angry young man', he is nevertheless a vociferous opponent of what he dislikes: the economic prosperity, uncommitted literature, the pseudo-*avant garde*. He lives in Norway. Enzensberger is a shrewd and sensitive critic torn between 'personal' poetic impulses, which he distrusts because he believes that the indulgence of them leads to political indifference of the kind exercised by Benn (q.v.), and 'public' impulses—the desire to share his poetry, not make it a dangerous esoteric mystery. Enzensberger's master is Brecht—but he responds to Benn. Unlike Brecht, Enzensberger cannot write poetry of the ballad type: poetry that can communicate with 'the people' and yet contain subtleties of which only more 'literary' folk would be likely to be aware. Brecht's slyness was built in. Enzensberger is honest, and a fine critic—his attack on the *avant garde* for trying to be new when for the time being 'newness' has exhausted itself is important. But his position is so ingenuous that his lyrical impulse has been at least half-strangled; indeed, he will resort to rhetoric, laboured satire and journalistic tricks in order not to indulge it. Michael Hamburger, who has introduced a selection of his poems in English translation (*Poems*, 1968; tr. the author, J. Rothenberg, M. Hamburger), draws attention to this deadlock between 'public purpose and private impulse' and suggests it will have to be broken; but he considers the poetry to date to have been successful. Certainly it has a refreshing directness, and certainly it testifies to Enzensberger's poetic gifts. But his refusal to indulge his private impulses and concomitant lack of a Brechtian vein of balladry or the equivalent sometimes force him into writing a sort of poetry that he might not otherwise perpetrate. 'Foam', for example, reads like a parody of Ginsberg's *Howl*; of course it is more intelligent, but the rhetoric and anger give the impression of having been manufactured as a substitute for other, politically more ambiguous, emotions. The later 'summer poem', another longish piece, is more successful in expressing the quality of Enzensberger's own emotion; but in it he does not yet dare to face, within himself, the threat (as one might put it) of his poetic impulse. An important critic, probably a gifted lyrical poet, his position is really only another version of that *Künstlerschuld* that in one way or another has assailed nearly every modern German writer. His attitude has been a significant one; his surrender to himself might have even more interesting consequences. So we still see him at his best only in such excellent satires as 'Middle Class Blues' or such exceedingly interesting poems as 'Lachesis Lapponica', where he nevertheless nervously distances himself from his motivations.

XVII

We have already seen that a number of writers committed to communism, eventually including Brecht, returned to East Germany (Deutsche Demokratische Republik) rather than to the West (Bundesrepublik Deutschland). In this country, one of the most repressive in the Russian bloc, literature and the press are under the direct control of the party. Therefore literature is defined as a weapon of the revolution, and is subject to the same kind of restrictions as have developed in Russia. East Germany is one of the communist countries where *avant garde* or 'formalist' art has small chance (like Bulgaria, but in contrast to Czechoslovakia, Poland and Hungary). The influential writers are not necessarily the officially recognized ones (Becher, q.v., has had no influence at all; and few have heard of the novelist HANS MARCHWITZA (1890–1965), hailed as an important social realist). The authorities have to stomach Brecht's reputation; but they do not like him. The writers worthy of note are those who, in one way or another, manage to express themselves as well as toe the party line. As we see elsewhere, this is always difficult and sometimes impossible. For this reason the published fiction in the German Democratic Republic tends to be of a low quality; where it has strength this lies in depiction of facts or situations: in what may be called naïve realism.

The Leipzig-born BRUNO APITZ's (1900) *Naked Among Wolves* (*Nackt unter*

Wölfen, 1958), set in Buchenwald concentration camp—Apitz, as a communist, spent nine years in various of these—has been highly praised. An account of the preservation of a smuggled baby, it is a moving book; but the plainness of its style amounts to crudity, and the psychology is unsubtle. This is not nearly as 'real' as even the comparatively crude Plievier (q.v.). It is not a book one would wish to dispraise; but a better one would have revealed the psychology of men under intolerable conditions in considerably more depth.

STEFAN HEYM (ps. HELLMUTH FLIEGEL, 1913) came from Chemmitz, and left Germany in 1933. He went to Prague and then to America, where he did military service. He returned to East Germany in 1953. He has written in English and German. Like many uncomplicated, straightforward communists, Heym's work is readable but crude in psychological detail. *Hostages* (1942; *Der Fall Glasenapp*, 1958), on resistance to the Nazis in Prague, is at least as exciting as a John le Carré thriller, and more intelligent; but it flourishes best in the mind of the indignant reader. Later novels become increasingly bombastic, and *The Eyes of Reason* (1951) dishonestly exploits Heym's considerable skill to give a false account of the communist takeover in Czechoslovakia.

More interesting—and more cunning—are the Prussian ERWIN STRITT-MATTER (1912), president of the East German Writers' Association, and MANFRED BIELER (1934), both of whom work in the picaresque tradition, which in an atmosphere of social realism can cover a multitude of sinfully unpalatable truths. Strittmatter—who deserted from the Nazi army, became a communist civil servant and worked on newspapers before taking to writing—was first taken up by Brecht, who himself produced his first play, a comedy, *Katzgraben* (1954). The best of his novels, *Ole Bienkopp*, is subversive of East German political procedures if not of communist theory; but not in any too obvious manner. It tells of a man who tried to get new methods adopted in his locality. He is destroyed by the party, and does not live to see his ideas accepted. This was accepted by Strittmatter's party as high comedy. . . . It would be preferable to have a translation of this rather than of Bieler's *The Sailor in the Bottle* (*Bonifaz, oder der Matrose in der Flasche*, 1963; tr. J. Clark, 1965), for while this satire (mostly on the capitalist West) has its moments, it is not Bieler's best work. More effective are his short stories (GWT).

The East German theatre is almost destitute of significant new plays. Only PETER HACKS (1928), who was born in Breslau and went to East Germany (to join Brecht's Berliner Ensemble) until 1955, has dealt with the social problems of his adopted country with anything like a critical vigour. His *Moritz Tassow* (1965) satirizes collective farming.

But in poetry East Germany has produced at least two major talents and several minor ones. STEPHAN HERMLIN (ps. RUDOLF LEDER, 1915), who returned to Germany from Palestine in 1947, was criticized for writing 'personal' poems; his later work, more conformist, is less interesting. However, a poet such as PETER HUCHEL (1903) has seldom (hardly at all, in fact, except in 'Das Gesetz', on the East German agrarian reforms), in his poetry at least, appeared to be politically committed in any sense. Removed from the editorship of the important magazine *Sinn und Form* in 1962, he has at last been able to get to the West. Huchel has always written in the German nature tradition; but he is different from Lehmann or Eich (qq.v.) in that he is essentially, for all his realism and careful imagery, a meditative poet. For all his courage in developing *Sinn und Form* into an organ independent of mediocre sub-literary meddlers, Huchel is nearer to an independent nature-poet than a rebel. His poetry has in it something of the melancholy of Edward Thomas (q.v.), although freer in form. (TCG, MGP, GWT.)

JOHANNES BOBROWSKI (1917–65), who did not become well known until two or three years before his death, is no more a typical figure in the East German situation than Huchel. Bobrowski was a prisoner-of-war in Russia for eight years, until 1949, when he went to Berlin. Apart from a children's book, he did not publish a volume of poetry until 1961. He received a *Gruppe 47* prize in 1962. *Shadow Land*, his selected poems in English translation, appeared in 1966 (tr. R. and M. Mead). He wrote some fiction.

Bobrowski is a brooding poet who writes of the landscapes and obscure or extinct folkways of Eastern Europe. His style is haunting and beautiful, and yet impersonal. He reminds one a little of a dark, non-Jewish, and un-gay Chagall. (GWT, TCGV.)

WOLF BIERMANN (1936) was born in Hamburg and did not go to East Germany until 1953, the year of the workers' uprising. In 1965 his work was suppressed. The genius of this explosive balladeer is more doubtful than that of Bobrowski; but he belongs to a newer generation. GÜNTER KUNERT (1929) deserves to be called a successor to Brecht. He was helped by Becher (q.v.). He is the most gifted and subtle of a number of practitioners of what Michael Hamburger has called 'minimal poetry': they resemble Brecht in that they remain committed to the general direction their society is taking, but insist on retaining their freedom to criticize—and to be the best judges of what is good and what is bad for the progress of mankind. Kunert leaves the gaps to be filled in by intelligent readers. (GWT, MGP.)

Greek Literature

The literature of modern Greece consists almost entirely of poetry. To an educated Greek, poetry is a natural response to experience. The struggle for expression in vernacular, demotic (*demotike*) as opposed to artificial, literary Greek (*katharevousa*: 'purist' Greek introduced in an attempt to recreate the language of classical Athens) absorbed most of the energies of the liberal writers of the Eighties(who arose in the literatures of all the European countries). This struggle was eventually won for poetry; but it must be emphasized that the problem has not yet been solved. Greek poetry still hovers between the demotic and the purist. (Officialdom insists on the *katharevousa*, which is used in all public communications.) The demotic, while it is the living language, lacks abstract words, which frequently makes it difficult for the poet.

YANNIS PSYCHARIS (1854–1929) was the pioneer of the demotic. His philological polemics are as unimportant as his novels; the controversy he started off with the satirical *My Journey* (1888; it ostensibly described a journey to Greece) led eventually to the prevalence of the demotic. He lived most of his life in Paris, and was a friend of Moréas (q.v.). His theories were put into practice by Dragoumes and Palamas, two writers who possessed the gift he lacked. ION DRAGOUMES (1878–1920), who was influenced by Nietzsche and then by Barrès (qq.v.), is also important for the style he achieved in the demotic.

KOSTIS PALAMAS (1859–1943) began by writing in the *katharevousa*, but soon became converted to the demotic. Palamas was an academic (he was at the University of Athens until he was seventy), and a literary and self-conscious poet; but he was at all times a sincere and vigorous one, and if nearly all his own work seems dated and lucubrated, he opened the way for others more poetically gifted. His sense of Greece has been important for later poets. A good deal of his work is spoiled by his belief in Orphic doctrine, in which he was learned; by means of this he prophesied the resurgence of Greece. By now such nationalistic systematizations have inevitably dated. But there is a lyrical residue of deep feeling and understanding of Greek antiquity. *The Grave* (1898; tr. D. A. Michalaros, 1930), a collection of poems on the death of his small daughter, is exceptional. *The Twelve Words of the Gipsy* (1907; tr. F. Will, 1964), is an ambitious epic: it fails because of a too great weight of learning and intellectual organization; spontaneity is lacking or smothered. Palamas educated Greek poetry; if his own work lacks greatness, his influence and example do not. (PBGV; see also *The King's Flute*, 1910, tr. F. Will, 1967) By contrast, the poet CONSTANTINE VARNALIS (1884) has made an intelligent Marxist interpretation of the ancient Greek world. The poems of GEORGE DROSINIS (1859–1951) were popular for a long time, but his reputation has faded since his death. (PBGV)

*

At this point it is necessary to consider a poet—probably one of the dozen greatest of this century, and certainly a major one—who has no place in the history or development of modern Greek poetry proper. CONSTANTINE CAVAFY (1863–1933), a 'Greek gentleman in a straw hat, standing absolutely motionless at a slight angle to the universe' (E. M. Forster, q.v.), the scourge of Christianity, nationalism and heterosexuality (all sacred to Western society), was an Alexandrian of Greek parentage who spent nearly all his life in Alexandria as a civil servant. Cavafy was a consummate modernist: ironic, utterly contemptuous of cliché and the small talk of politicians about large matters, cynical and sceptical. But he was quiet; and he mixed *katharevousa* with the demotic as and when he felt like it. (English was his first language, and he spent some of his childhood in England.) Beneath his urban and sophisticated manner, Cavafy concealed a hatred of modern life—more, perhaps, a nostalgia for the picture of the classical past that he carried within him than anything else—and anguish at the nature of his sexuality, which was exclusively homosexual. Bored in the day, he was in his seedy Alexandrian evenings a typical homosexual of his generation: a thorough, furtive pederast. His mixture of 'purist' archaic Greek and the colloquial is subtle and consummately artistic: he lived partly in the past and used its language (but always so that it could be understood in the present) to evoke a sense of it. His is the poetry of the resigned, alienated and learned intellectual in modern times: he condemns the barbarians, but accepts them—and wryly admits this. His poetry has been much translated into English, but the translations can hardly convey the subtlety of his language: to mix English archaic language with the colloquial would provide no kind of accurate parallel, and the translators have not tried it. His poetry was translated by the falconer John Mavrogordato (*Poems*, 1951), by Rae Dalven (*Complete Poems*, 1961) and, perhaps most satisfactorily, in *Four Greek Poets*. (PBGV; MGL)

Cavafy began as a fairly unoriginal romantic poet; he suppressed all his early work. His genius did not manifest itself until he was forty. Then he pruned and revised the many poems he wrote, to leave only 154 of the best twentieth-century poems in any language. As a critic has said, in these he discovered 'the obverse of the Boy Scout Creed': 'Cowardice, disillusion, sordidness, contradiction, paradox'. There is a sense in which he is the most subversive of all modern poets. And he is great because, unlike so many who in their hearts share his attitude, he put his roots down into his own misery, thereby discovering to what extent his self-disgust was determined by his unauthentic, bourgeois environment. As the cliché has it, he faced himself. And in his poetry, at least, he acquired wisdom. No single poem, perhaps, can so appropriately illustrate this as 'Waiting for the Barbarians', which I quote in the excellent translation by Edmund Keeley and Philip Sherrard:

What are we waiting for, gathered in the market-place?

The barbarians are to arrive today.

Why so little activity in the senate?
Why do the senators sit there without legislating?

Because the barbarians will arrive today.
What laws should the senators make now?
The barbarians, when they come, will do the legislating.

Why has our emperor risen so early,
and why does he sit at the largest gate of the city
on the throne, in state, wearing the crown?

Because the barbarians will arrive today.
And the emperor is waiting to receive
their leader. He has even prepared
a parchment for him. There
he has given him many titles and names.

Why did our two consuls and our praetors go out
today in the scarlet, the embroidered, togas?
Why did they wear bracelets with so many amethysts,
and rings with brilliant sparkling emeralds?
Why today do they carry precious staves
splendidly inlaid with silver and gold?

Because the barbarians will arrive today;
and such things dazzle barbarians.

And why don't the worthy orators come as always
to make their speeches, say what they have to say?

Because the barbarians will arrive today;
and they are bored by eloquence and public speaking.

What does this sudden uneasiness mean,
and this confusion? (How grave the faces have become!)
Why are the streets and squares rapidly emptying,
and why is everyone going back home so lost in thought?

Because it is night and the barbarians have not come.
And some men have arrived from the frontiers
and they say that barbarians don't exist any longer.

And now, what will become of us without barbarians?
They were a kind of solution.

(FGP)

*

ANGELOS SIKELIANOS (1884–1951), despite his immense learning and skill, is not in the class of Cavafy as a poet because his poetry—like some of Palamas', but more so—is clotted up with grandiose palaver: where he should be stripping his utterance of rhetoric and ornament, preparing it for the task of defining his guilty secrets, he is inventing such irrelevancies as the 'Delphic idea', which would lead to a rebirth of civilization. But he was a colourful personality, and much of himself, particularly his sensuality, lingers in his poetry. His attempt to fuse Christianity with paganism into a non-dogmatic general religion is noble and sincere, but it often distracts his poetry from its proper themes. But Sikelianos possessed great resources of language and he enriched modern Greek poetry. Drawing on the great epic traditions of the past, his narrative poetry can be enthralling. His strengths and limitations are well seen in 'Sparta' (the speaker is Lycurgus, who in Plutarch is said to have introduced his young wife to a young man and to have recognized 'the offspring of their generous blood as his own':

> 'As if from ambush now for a long time
> I've held you in my eye, and from all others
> have chosen you as if you were a star;
> your countenance has gratified my heart.
> Hearken: now let me tightly grasp your hand,
> for youth is like a stallion thus subdued:
> for one night only shall you lie upon
> my bed, and be my own wife's counterpart.
>
> Go; she is small in waist and as compact
> in beauty as majestic Helen was,
> and fill her generously with your seed.
> For one night take her in your strong embrace,
> and then uplift my desolate old age
> before all Sparta with a worthy son.'

(MEP; see also PBGV; MGL)

The Athenian TAKIS PAPATSONIS (1895), an economist and lawyer who worked as a higher civil servant, has not perhaps had his due outside Greece—even now when its poetry is much discussed and translated in the English-speaking countries. Papatsonis' verse published in the Twenties anticipated later styles. Like Sikelianos, he advocates a universal religion; but he puts more emphasis on the figure of Christ. His poetry is much nearer to surrealism, and is frequently recondite to the point of impenetrability. He sometimes employs liturgical forms. (MGL)

The greatest modern Greek poet, a writer whose work has most of the qualities—clarity, precision, hardness, true dignity—associated with ancient Greek poetry, is GEORGE SEFERIS (ps. GEORGE SEFERIADES, 1900–71), who was born in Smyrna and spent his working life in the diplomatic service: he was his country's ambassador to Great Britain (1957–62). He won the Nobel Prize, the first Greek to do so, in 1963. Seferis' poetry may be seen as a definition of what it is to be fully human and fully Greek. His disillusion with Greek political life up to 1967 was absolute: the politicians he saw as 'petty' and 'often . . . of a confused and unformed sentimentality': 'we have not made one inch of progress . . .' (1966). But on the ridiculous and yet tragic military coup of 1967 he made himself clear: 'I see before me the abyss towards which we are being led by the oppression which has spread over the land. This situation must be brought to an end. It is imperative for the good of the Nation. I return now to my silence and I pray to God that he will not again oblige me to speak' (1969). The colonels replied to this by accusing Seferis of association with communists and of 'selling' Cyprus to foreign interests while ambassador in London in return for the Nobel Prize. . . . Meanwhile, Pattakos—second to Papadopoulos in the new authoritarian hierarchy—has given his opinion of all intellectuals: 'They should summarily be sent to the gallows'. These facts are worth recording, as is the fact that no writer worthy of the name will collaborate in any way with the regime—many are in prison or restricted.

Seferis, who studied in France, was at first influenced by French poetry; but while on duty in England he became acquainted with the work of T. S. Eliot (q.v.), which he later translated. Seferis' mind is harder and intellectually more distinguished than Eliot's; but he recognized the authoritatively dry and poetic manner of the older poet, and learned from it. *The Waste Land* (q.v.) deals with the disintegration of civilization, and this, too, was Seferis' concern—even though his basically sceptical temperament is such that any kind of retreat into religious orthodoxy is impossible. Seferis' poetry dwells wonderingly and horrifiedly on the modern void: the old closed systems and beauty's permanence could so nearly fill it. . . . He improves on Palamas and Sikelianos (qq.v.), whose skill and evocative power he shares, because he is forced to deny the present viability of the past: they tried to revive it or adapt it. Thus, his use of Greek myths (these are not merely a part of a Greek's cultural background: they are alive to him, a part of him) is never archaic: the time in Seferis' poetry is always very much the present, an achingly empty framework in which the past hangs suspended.

Seferis has been much translated, most satisfactorily (again) by Philip Sherrard and Edmund Keeley; *Collected Poems—1924–1955* (1967), in parallel text. There are also versions by Rex Warner (q.v.)—*Poems* (1960)—and a joint effort by Bernard Spencer (q.v.), N. Valaoritis and Lawrence Durrell—*The King of Asine* ((1948). Seferis' mature manner, the result of his long stay in England, became apparent in the collection *Novel* (1935), whose title is best rendered as *Myth-History*. In this book he moved from formal to freer techniques, and his subject-matter became more explicitly Greek. His view of poetry is aptly expressed in a section from one of *Three Secret Poems*, which he published in Athens in 1967; I quote it in a version by Peter Thompson (*Agenda*, 7, 1, 1969: *Greek Poetry Special Issue*):

> The white paper, a hard mirror
> that reflects only what you were.

The white paper speaks with your voice,
your very own voice
not the one that you like;
it's your own composition, this life
that you have wasted.
Perhaps you can redeem it if you want to
if you fasten upon this indifferent thing
that throws you back
to where you started from.

You travelled, you saw many moons and many suns
you touched the dead and the living
you felt the pain of the young man
and the moaning of the woman
the bitterness of the ungrown child—
but all you felt will crumble to nothing
unless you trust this emptiness.
Perhaps to find there what you thought was lost:
the budding of youth, the just foundering of age.

Your life is what you have given
this emptiness is what you have given
the white paper.
          (See also PBGV; MEP; MGL)

Other distinguished poets of Seferis' generation include GEORGE THEMELIS (1900), who was born on Samos, and DEMETRIOS ANTONIOU (1906), born in Mozambique. Both poets have achieved a hard and highly personal style. Themelis is melancholy, an explorer of mood and nostalgia (MEP; MGL); Antoniou, a sea-captain, writes a dense and compressed poetry. It is interesting to compare his 'Poem' with the passage quoted from Seferis immediately above.

To conquer this blank paper! now
securing in words that fill it this bruised
necessity, in half-feelings and in the mirror
of resolution that becomes an immovable mountain in our way . . .
What do you long for?
The star will no longer rise nor turn to sleep
as your road is ending, there where you
shall say: and a little more and day will break . . .
The simple daisy in the green meadow does not stay you,
nor shall you weep ever again
over the nameless small flowers of the field.
Thus drunk with melancholy
we murmured until yesterday, strolling in the countryside:
we recall all of this today and pass it by

as we might consent to the course of the wind in a blossomed almond tree,
your ring turning to rust on the finger of another.
Your pleading voice brings our years to their knees,
those years I spent in an open sea blossomed by sails of return.

(MEP)

A number of important Greek poets became involved in surrealism (q.v.),
a movement of which Seferis showed awareness, but did not join. The leader
of the Greek surrealists was the psychoanalyst and amateur photographer
ANDREAS EMBIRIKOS (1901), born in Rumania; he lived abroad before settling
in Athens. He has acknowledged the influence of André Breton (q.v.). His
Blast Furnace (1935) was the first surrealist publication in Greece. What may
seem odd is that Embirikos, who used the techniques of dada and automatic
writing, writes mainly in 'purist' Greek; this results in some odd—but not
archaic—effects. He has written three long erotic novels, which he has not yet
published. Embirikos' poetry is important for its influence, and is brilliantly
attractive; but as poetry it is, like all purely surrealist poetry, minor. (MGL)

YANNIS RITSOS (1909), born in the South Peloponnese, is Greece's most
prolific modern poet (over forty volumes). He has been imprisoned by the
present regime. He was also in prison between 1948 and 1952. Like his friend
and fellow-communist the composer Theodorakis, with whom he has collaborated, he suffers from tuberculosis. The fatal fault of his Whitmanesque
earlier poetry is that it runs to an enormous length, and nothing quite compensates for this. However, this does not arise from a prosy MacDiarmid-like
(q.v.) egoism, but from a Mediterranean expansiveness. There are lyrical
passages—characterized both by love of Greek landscape and by his radical
socialism—which are irresistible in their appeal. But his more recent and more
compressed poetry is superior, and sacrifices nothing of lyrical effect whenever
he wishes to achieve it. 'Estimation', on the subject of Cavafy (q.v.), is an
example:

> This man who died was, indeed, remarkable,
> unique: he left us a unique standard
> to measure ourselves and above all to measure
> our surroundings;—one man this size,
> very short, another thin, the third
> long as a pair of stilts: no one
> with any value; never, no never.
> Only we who make proper use
> of that standard—but which standard do you mean?—
> that is Nemesis, the Archangel's Sword,
> have it already sharpened, and we
> can set everyone in order now and decapitate them.

(tr. P. Merchant, *Modern Poetry in
Translation*, 4, 1968; see also MEP; MGL)

A new volume of *Selected Poems*, 1968–1970, translated by Nikos Stangos (1971) contains sixty-seven hitherto unpublished poems which he wrote during his recent imprisonment.

The Cretan ODYSSEUS ELYTIS (ps. ODYSSEUS ALEPOUDELIS, 1912) was influenced by between-wars surrealism, but his poetry has never been wholeheartedly surrealist like that of Embirikos. There is, allowing for inevitable differences of race, something of Char (q.v.) in Elytis' response to landscape and to the exigencies of modern life. In his poetry of the Thirties he is trying to find his own voice, mixing evocations of Greek landscape with surrealist experimentation; his war experiences on the Albanian front led to 'A Heroic and Mournful Song on the Lieutenant Killed in Albania' (1945), an extraordinary elegy that combines straightforward emotion with more complex and purely verbal explorations of ideas. After this he published nothing until 1959, when he issued *Worthy It Is*; *Six and One Regrets for the Sky* appeared the following year. It is here that his development matches Char's. The poetry is difficult, but rescued from impenetrability by its incantatory qualities, and by the integrity of its purpose: to record his discovery of Greece in resolutely non-rhetorical language, although sometimes using a framework reminiscent of the Byzantine liturgy. (MEP; FGP; PBGV; MGL)

There are a number of other contemporary Greek poets of some importance. NIKOS GATSOS (1912), born in Arcadia, deeply influenced by the Heraclitan notion of flux, has combined surrealism and folk-song into a poetry of unmistakably Greek quality. His main collection is *Amorgos* (1943). (FGP; MEP; MGL) TAKIS SINOPOULOS (1917), a pathologist born in Olympia, was for a time a painter as well as a poet, but gave this up to concentrate on his literary work. He has an epigrammatic quality lacking in nearly all his contemporaries— 'Tell me what light your hands have, darkening as they do/whatever I protected from you and preserved and was?'—and he writes less of the Greek landscape and more of inner mental states. He has been influenced by post-surrealist French modernist poetry, but his voice is very much his own, as he demonstrates in 'Death feast', a haunting poem (unpublished in Greece but tr. P. Merchant, *Modern Poetry in Translation*, 4, 1968) which combines personal elements with memories of the Greek Civil War.

ELENI VAKALO (1921) is in some respects Greece's most ambitiously modern poet. She believes that poetry is a part of living or else nothing; also in the poem as an object in itself. Her approach to the writing of poetry is explorative: her poems are solutions to her existential problems. The results are attractive but lack weight.

Two Greek poets who have written well in English should be mentioned. DEMETRIOS CAPETANAKIS (1912–44), a Smyrnan like Seferis, died of leukaemia in London. After studying in Germany he had come to England, and became so attracted to the country and its language that he began to write poetry in English. Against all the odds, this worked. His work has been preserved by John Lehmann (q.v.), who championed his literary cause, in *A Greek Poet in England* (1947). Capetanakis, who anticipated the post-war concern with the absurdity of human existence, wrote English poetry with true Greek directness; he was also a superb—and now neglected—critic.

CONSTANTINE TRYPANIS (1909), born in Chios, came from Athens University to Exeter College, Oxford, in 1947. He is now Professor of Classics at the University of Chicago. Like Capetanakis, he has incorporated into English poetry a Greek directness; he also has an almost uncanny flair for the British colloquial. His themes come from the Greek world, but he has adapted them to his understanding of the English present. His collections include *Grooves in the Wind* (1964) and *Pompeian Dog* (1965).

*

There has been little Greek prose at an international level. ALEXANDROS PAPADIAMANTIS (1851–1911) wrote too much too fast, but his intuitive socio-logical grasp and his profound sympathy give his short stories a unique sweet-ness. He was a devout member of the Orthodox Church, and his language, while 'pure' (although containing elements of the colloquial) is different from the official language. He was not a naturalist, since he portrayed life as interfused by the promise of the life to come; but his observation was as keen as that of a naturalist. He wrote accurately in his many nostalgic short stories of poor people, and could on occasion excel himself, and overcome his Christian optimism, in harsher psychological studies.

The Cretan NIKOS KAZANTZAKIS (1885–1957) has claims to be treated primarily as a poet; but it is in his prose that he will live. Kazantzakis' work is undoubtedly magnificent, but he meant it to be: his grandiosity somewhat vitiates it. It is not his confusion between Bergsonian vitalism (he studied under Bergson, q.v., in Paris) and Nietzschean despair that causes suspicion—this is a familiar enough conflict in our century—but his restless pretensions to a great-ness that his writings never quite earn. His enormous 33,333 line epic, *The Odyssey* (tr. K. Friar, 1959), which takes up the story where Homer left off, is unfortunately designed as, among other things, a challenge to Homer himself. Despite some magnificent passages, it fails to come off as a whole: Kazantzakis misjudged his age, and tried to achieve a sort of greatness that it cannot accommodate. But he was a noble-minded man, and his effort can be noted—and need not be condemned. He moved excitedly from influence to influence, absorbing the nature of virtually every major teaching the world has known. His translation of Dante's *Divine Comedy* into Greek is monumental. He is of course famous for the crude, near-*kitsch*, but vital and evocative novels of his later life: *Zorba the Greek* (1946; tr. C. Wildman, 1952), which was turned into a popular film, *Christ Recrucified* (1954; tr. J. Griffin, 1954) and a number of others. He died in Germany from leukaemia. (MEP; MGP)

STRATIS MYRIVILIS (ps. STRATIS STAMATOPOULOS, 1892), who was born in Mytilene, first studied law and literature, and was then a fighting soldier between 1910 and 1922—serving in the Balkan wars, the First World War and the war against Turkey. Myrivilis was for long considered to be the most gifted Greek novelist. Certainly he wrote the best Greek novel about war: (*Life in a Tomb*, 1930; tr. 1931), in the form of a soldier's letters home, has the same kind of realism to be found in Manning or Renn (qq.v.). One can compare it, although it is in prose and lacks modernist elements, with Elytis' *A Heroic and Mournful Song* (q.v.): it, too, combines horror and terror with humour, idyllic evocation of landscape and love of life. After this important book, which belongs in the select company of First World War classics, Myrivilis turned to his native Lesbos: *The Schoolteacher with the Pretty Eyes* (1932) is a love story set there. *The Mermaid Madonna* (1949; tr. A. Rick, 1955), a broader study of island ways, is the classic book on modern Lesbos. Myrivilis has shown, in style and content, what can be done with modern Greek. He has written many excellent short stories, in which he combines shrewd psychology, comedy and love of life.

ILIAS VENEZIS (ps. ILIAS MELLOS-VENEZIS, 1904) fought in the Graeco-Turkish war of 1921–2, and was taken prisoner. His experiences in a concentration camp led him to write *Number 31328* (1931; tr. French, *La Grande Pitié*, 1946). Although realist, this was a more modernist kind of war book than Myrivilis' *Life in a Tomb*: not only was it written in more colloquial language, but also it put more emphasis upon inner than on outer events—although these were not neglected. Thus, where Myrivilis' book describes events, Venezis' is more of a psychological study of man in adversity. *Serenity* (1939) is a novel about people from Asia Minor (Venezis was born in Anatolia) settling in a remote part of Greece; it is a brilliant study of their feelings in this situation. *Aeolia* (1943; tr. E. D. Scott-Kilvert, 1949) is an autobiographical novel of Anatolian life before the First World War. Most critics agree, however, that Venezis excels himself in the short story, in which he gains his profoundest—and sometimes mysterious —effects by combining a realistic treatment with a poetic evocation of atmosphere. *Block C* (1944) is a powerful play. (MGL)

GEORGE THEOTOKAS (1906–66), who was born at Constantinople, was an excellent realist who was twice Director of the National Theatre. *Argo* (1936; tr. A. Brook and A. Tsatsopoulos, 1951) gives an outstanding portrait of Greek life in the Twenties. His friend Seferis (q.v.) quotes him as having written, in 1932: 'I am attempting to construct (if the gods will) a style which shall be pure and simple, mature and expressive, flexible and disciplined, a living language without barbarities, classical without academicism'. Theotokas did succeed in constructing such a style in his novels—*Leonis* (1940), about his childhood in Constantinople, is one of the most notable; and, as Seferis has said, 'such a style was absolutely necessary in our country'. He has also written notable plays, of which *The Game of Folly vs. Wisdom* has been translated into English. (MGL)

ANGELOS TERZAKIS (1907) only needs to be translated into English to be internationally appreciated as the major novelist he is. *Captives* (1932) is a comprehensive, almost naturalist portrait of the life of a lower-middle-class Athens family. *The Decline of Skleroi* (1933) is a subtle psychological study of two boys subjugated by their mother, who eventually drives one of them to kill the other. *Voyage with Hesperus* (1946) is a brilliant portrait of the lives of young people. *Mystic Life* (1957), more modernist in technique, is an apparently haphazard autobiographical manuscript, whose author is as futile as Svevo's Zeno (q.v.). Here Terzakis has gained complete mastery over his material.

The older KOSMAS POLITIS (1893) is now regarded as an important influence in modern Greek prose. *Lemon Grove* (1928) was conventional but exquisitely done. *Eroica* (1938), in a more modern and realist tradition is regarded as 'a landmark in . . . Greek prose'. He writes penetratingly of the crucial experiences of adolescents.

PANDELIS PREVELAKIS (1909), born in the beautiful little Cretan town of Rethymnon, made his first reputation as a poet; but he is most famous for his historical novels, which have not been equalled in modern Greek literature. The trilogy *The Cretans* (1948–52) is a magnificent and entirely unsentimental embodiment of his people. *Story of a Town* (1938) was a charming book about Rethymnon. *The Sun of Death* (1959; tr. P. Sherrard, 1965) is set in Crete during the First World War; it is slightly spoiled by the author's unnecessary asides, but is nevertheless an unforgettable portrait of an island community wrecked by war and yet persisting in senseless vendettas. His plays include *The Lost Tournament* (MGL). He has written on Kazantzakis, whom he regards as his master.

The Cypriot LOUKIS ACRITAS (1909–65) wrote good psychological studies of the victims of social evils, including *Young Man with Good References* (1935) and *Under Arms* (1947), about the struggle with Albania. He also wrote plays. (MGL)

In *The Third Wedding* (1965; tr. L. Finer, 1967) COSTAS TAKBIS gave a memorable portrait of the Greece of the first half of the century. The narrative, in the hands of Nina, the chief character, is a breathless *tour de force*, in which one reacts to her moods as one might to those of an actual speaker.

*

The leading Greek dramatist of the Greek dramatic revival was IANNIS KAMBISIS (1872–1902), who was influenced by Ibsen (q.v.). SPYRO MELAS (1883), influenced by Gorki (q.v.), wrote plays about the struggle for Greek independence in which heroism mixes, sometimes incongruously, with naturalism. He formed *The Theatre of Man* (1925). The outstanding man of the theatre, however, was the radical GREGORIOS XENOPOULOS (1867–1951), best known for his 'problem play', *Stella Violanti* (1909), which also shows the influence of Ibsen. His main concern was with the emancipation of women. He also wrote novels and criticism. Kazantzakis, Theotokas and Prevelakis (qq.v.) have all written plays; Prevelakis has translated Euripides into modern Greek.

Hungarian Literature

The same applies, in more or less degree, to Hungarian literature as applies to the literatures of other similarly placed, politically precarious countries such as Poland or Czechoslovakia: there is a definite relationship to Western European (mainly French) literature, but this tends to be disguised by the fact that the native literature is a natural instrument of nationalism. Even hermetically inclined poets become patriotic in times of trouble (as was the case in Czechoslovakia, q.v., where poets of every possible type published elegiac, patriotic books in the year of the Chamberlain-Daladier-Hitler dismemberment, 1938). Movements tend to arrive late in such countries. There is an additional reason why, in the case of Hungary, the general Western European pattern appears distorted: whereas such a country as Poland proudly acknowledges a strong Latin influence, Hungary—whose language is Finno-Ugric—has its own special standards. At first these were extremely conservative; then—after a brief interval —with the advent of the communist state, they have been the official, false, mediocre and anti-literary ones of socialist realism (q.v.). Of course, socialist realism can give rise to excellent writings when it follows a long period of corrupt, conservative repression; but the viable movement is invariably short-lived.

The liberal spirit developed late in Hungary, and it does not appear in so clear-cut a form as it does in some other countries. There is no 'Young Hungary' or 'Awakening' as such. The reason for this is not only to be sought in the continuation of the stultified Dual Monarchy, which controlled official literary life, but also in Magyar pride and self-sufficiency. One cannot describe PÁL GYULAI (1826–1909), a minor poet but an enormously influential critic, as in any sense liberal. He was, on the contrary, a conservative nationalist; and even if he could—and did—recognize the genius of someone like Ady (q.v.), he could never have approved of or aided and abetted Ady's intentions. Gyulai persistently criticized the fiction of MÓR JÓKAI (1825–1904), who was ultimately no more truly liberal than he was—but was more creatively gifted. Jókai was introduced to the literary world by Hungary's great nineteenth-century poet (and the outstanding figure in Hungarian literature) Sándor Petőfi (1823–49), the spirit of whose romanticism he maintained in his own work. Jókai, whose early radicalism, inspired by the French Revolution, was later modified to a cautiously liberal conservatism, is a characteristically romantic figure. He was an exuberant and inventive writer of historical fiction, who deliberately wrote for the masses—and made a large amount of money. Considering this, it is remarkable that he managed to attain to the status of a major writer. He has rightly been described as a 'guileless soul'; but the fictional world of his best books, although it bears more relation to fancy than to reality, will stand intelligent investigation. He wrote over 100 novels, all set in various periods of the past. If his characterization is weak and crude, it impresses by its diversification and energy; and in his descriptive powers he far excels Dumas, a writer with whom he has been unfairly compared. Many of his books have been translated into English, and they remain readable today. But Jókai was in no sense a modernist, and his work has to be considered in the light of nineteenth-century Hungarian romanticism.

JÓZSEF KISS (1843–1921) was not, perhaps, a more modern poet than Jókai was a modern novelist; but as editor of the periodical *Week* (*Hét*) he helped considerably in preparing the way for the important and influential *West* (*Nyugat*, q.v.). Kiss, influenced by folk ballads, was the first Hungarian poet to take Jewish life as his material. Later in his career he wrote popular poetry about the city of Budapest, where he lived.

The early fiction of KÁLMÁN MIKSZÁTH (1847–1910) was greatly influenced by Jókai; later he developed an original brand of satirical and humorous realism that represented, sociologically, some advance on Jókai. But he is still essentially a nineteenth-century writer, although a very important and gifted one. The same applies to two lesser writers: GÉZA GÁRDONYI (1863–1922) and the short-story writer ISTVÁN TÖMÖRKÉNY (1866–1917). Gárdonyi's descriptions of peasant life are humorous but remain idealistic in a sense that Móricz's (q.v.) are not. Tömörkény's descriptions of the peasant life on the great Hungarian plain are equally classic, but show little awareness of the origins of social injustice.

At the end of the nineteenth century such Hungarian literary programmes as existed possessed, in terms of the actual situation, no viability. The impetus towards new directions came—as it usually had in the Hungarian past—from lyrical poets. The first landmark in the history of Hungarian modernism is the launching of the radical periodical *West*. This was founded by the man of letters, publicist and minor poet, IGNOTUS (ps. HUGÓ VEIGELSBERG, 1869–1949), and the critic Ernő Osvát in 1908. *West*, which did not cease publication until 1941, and even then carried on for a few years under a different name, introduced the poet ENDRE ADY (1877–1919), the real father of Hungarian literary modernism.

Ady is the leading figure in Hungarian letters of the first quarter of this century, and, although there have been superior poets and more intelligent men, he can never lose his importance. The degree of his intellectual grasp of French symbolist techniques was probably slight; but he was as intuitively aware of symbolism as of the spirit of radicalism. His politics, at a time when Hungary was ruled by reactionaries in their last violent throes, caused him to be reviled by conservative critics.

Ady, born of an impoverished Protestant family in Érmindszent, studied law and then became a journalist in Nagyvárad, in Transylvania; this town was then rivalled as a centre of literary activity only by Budapest. It was here that he met his mistress and first muse, 'Leda', a wealthy married woman who paid for him to visit Paris in 1904 and again in 1906–7. Later he settled in Budapest and married a woman, the 'Csinszka' of his poems, much younger than himself. Ady, a fundamentally naïve (q.v.)—as most if not all major Hungarian poets seem to have been—poet, combines within himself several pairs of opposites: he is an imitator of the French symbolists, and yet he is equally an authentic, indigenous Magyar poet; he is a prophet of Hungary's destiny, a passionate advocate of freedom—and yet he is also a *poète maudit* in the tradition of Verlaine; he is politically responsible, and yet an egoistic narcissist. Ady, whose suffering was great and whose 'irregular' life led to his early death, has been described both as a great lyrical poet and as a great metaphysical poet. . . . The truth is that for much of the time Ady, as a poet, is confused, or divided between his national aspirations—his radicalism and his awareness of the sickness and injustice of Hungarian society, and the evil of the First World War (which he, in common with many of his countrymen, opposed)—and his personal concerns. Ady wanted to believe in artistic (and amorous) hermeticism, in art for art's sake; but as a Hungarian he could not. In Hungary, as in other similarly situated countries, the sense of individual self-preservation is closely linked to that of national self-preservation. The poet, as he seeks his own identity, tends to seek the identity of his country. (One contemporary Hungarian woman poet has even gone so far as to assert that she cannot be primarily a poet because she is a Hungarian. . .) In Ady's best poetry, however, he reconciles these two often violently opposing themes, and incidentally discovers the most precious aspects of his own disturbed and unhappy personality. The mainspring of expression in Ady's less personal poems—such as those about money—is, as Joseph Reményi remarked, 'the cleavage between his sense of values and the sense of values of those in power'. And Reményi goes on to describe Ady as Hungary's 'apocalyptic poet' because his 'symbolism . . . unfolded the image of Hungary, victimized by outer and inner forces'. Ady never rationalized Hungary's position in the world; he felt it and, sometimes, personalized it. His pessimism on the subject of his country's future ('. . . Hungary's Messiahs./ A thousandfold they perish/. . . . For vain is their affliction. . . !), and his consequent tendency to berate her, are exactly matched by his personal pessimism and guilt, and his tendency towards self-castigation. Ady's poetry has been translated by A. Nyerges in *Three Score Poems of Endre Ady* (1946), in *Poems* (tr. Vajna and Bokor, 1941) and by Watson Kirkconnel in his anthology *The Magyar Muse* (1933). In all these cases the translations are into a more or less nineteenth-century English idiom that hardly does justice to Ady's own language. But some of his distress—trapped between subjectivism and nationalism—and intensity do come across. In 'Walk Around my Birthplace' he speaks evocatively of the place where he was born, and then exclaims 'Here life is curs'd; men choke and burn'. Characteristically, he continues:

> Yet this, perhaps, am I myself,
> The blacken'd embers of old fires
> And overhead the wind of fate
> That howls out: Shun me! Curse and hate!
> Be fiercely proud in your desires! (HWL)

Ady is undoubtedly an important European poet who still awaits a translator.

MIHÁLY BABITS (1883–1941), who edited *West* (q.v.) from 1929, was a very different and more austere kind of writer, one of Hungary's rather few genuinely 'sentimentive' (q.v.) writers; he has been misrepresented as both 'emotionally sterile' and impelled by too narrowly academic motives. It is true that he distrusted violent emotion, and that he remained a too cautiously conservative liberal for most of his life (until he saw the results of fascism, both Hungarian and Nazi). But his poetry is by no means devoid of feeling; and his pacifism during the First World War was passionately advocated. His opponents tended to confuse his immense learning, caution and reverence for classical order, with lack of emotion. Babits fought—until nearly the end—to keep politics out of his literature; he failed, one might fairly say, because he was Hungarian.

Babits was an important critic (*History of European Literature*, 1935, is a classic) and novelist. It was in his poetry that he tried to express himself most fully; but it may nevertheless be that his most enduring work is in fiction. *The Son of Virgil Timár* (1922), the best of his novels, is a subtle study of repressed homosexuality, written after its author had thoroughly assimilated Freud. In it he realized himself more fully than elsewhere. His poetry has nobility and every kind of skill; but its language is seldom inspired.

Like Babits, the poet, novelist and critic DEZSŐ KOSZTOLÁNYI (1885–1936) tried to keep his art clear of politics. Although he never rejected politics as unimportant, he remained a more or less consistent advocate of 'art for art's sake' —but in the Rilkean (q.v.) rather than the 'decadent' sense. (The poetry and personality of Rilke deeply fascinated and influenced him.) After the First World War he became involved for a time in political journalism, supporting the fascistic forces that took over after the flight of the communist Béla Kun; but this episode merely displays his political innocence. He gained a large measure of unpopularity for himself by his criticism of Ady (q.v.), the adulation of whom he considered—with some justice—to be largely uncritical and indiscriminate in nature. As a poet Kosztolányi was generally more concerned with metaphysical states of mind—most particularly with the fear of death— than with the analysis of experience. But his material is never thin. Probably his best volume is *Naked* (1928), in which he found a new freedom as a result of reading the *vers libre* of the German expressionist (q.v.) poets. The subject-matter of these poems may be summed up as a quest for personal meaning, or for personal identity, in an absurd or cruel environment:

> Just a stick and some linen,
> Yet not a stick and linen,
> But a flag.
>
> Ever it speaks,
> Ever it waves,
> Ever it is restless. . . .
>
> Above the street

It soars aloft,
Untorn in the sky,
And proclaims something
Eagerly.
If men grow used to it and heed it not,
If they slumber also
By day and night,
So that it is wholly wasted away
And stands, like a gaunt apostolic orator,
On the peak of the roof,
Still alone,
Wrestling with the calm and the storm,
Fruitlessly, ceaselessly, ever majestically
It waves
And speaks.

My soul, be thou too, thou too—
Not stick and linen,
But a flag.
(HWL)

More justice would have been done to Kosztolányi if the archaic details were expunged from this version; but it nevertheless adequately conveys a sense of his complexity if not of his linguistic capacities and his technical mastery.

Kosztolányi was a close friend of Sándor Ferenczi, one of Freud's earliest associates (there are widely differing versions of Freud's rejection of him, and of the degree of mental disturbance from which he was suffering at the time of his death). Kosztolányi's fiction—intelligent, lucid and stylistically distinguished —clearly shows this influence. *The Bloody Poet* (1924; tr. C. Fadiman, 1927), the best and most psychologically acute of all the many novels about Nero, concentrates not upon the cruel ruler but on the jealous poet; this is a brilliant and dramatic study in psychopathology. *Wonder Maid* (1927; tr. A. Hegedűs, 1947) deals with a servant girl who suddenly slaughters her master and mistress with an axe; much of it is taken up with the doctor's defence of her in court, which saves her from execution. This is an unusual and most original novel; it fully answers those who accuse Kosztolányi of lack of feeling or excessive aestheticism. Both here and in his short stories he is an adept at describing the sensations of 'ordinary' people. He was also a distinguished translator.

Another important contributor to *West*—like many of these, her first works appeared in Kiss's *The Week* (q.v.)—was MARGIT KAFFKA (1880–1918), Hungary's first important woman writer. Her life was cut short by the influenza epidemic that swept over Europe (killing Apollinaire, q.v.) at the end of the First World War. She began as a poet, but reached maturity as a novelist. Her main subject-matter is the position of women in society, and in this respect she may be compared to other similar European women writers of her generation, such

697

as Selma Lagerlöf or Cora Sandel (qq.v.). Margit Kaffka, despite the fineness of much of the detail in her poetry and prose, did not have time to develop into a major writer; but she liberated Hungarian feminine writing from sentimentality and male dictation, and she is therefore more important than her actual literary achievement. A friend of Ady's (q.v.), she was an ardent advocate of reason and social equality, and a pacifist. She was twice married.

Her poetry is intense but lacks—as, with the exception of a few short stories, all her work tends to do—a sense of form. The best of her four novels is *Colours and Years* (1912), an acute study of feminine alienation in the turn-of-the-century Hungarian provinces; the heroine's lack of sexual and psychological fulfilment is traced to her inability to express herself socially as a woman. Probably the very best of her work is to be found in her short story collections, which include *Quiet Crisis* (1909) and *Summer* (1910).

Of a slightly older generation, both SÁNDOR BRÓDY (1863–1924) and JENŐ HELTAI (1871–1957) stood well to the right of the eclectic liberalism of *West*; but both deserve mention. Bródy, an over-prolific author of fiction who too usually indulged himself in sentimentality and facile plots, was nevertheless the first to use the Budapest colloquial; he mixed this into a fluent and often meretricious narrative—but he did introduce it. He seemed to some of his readers to have introduced the spirit of French naturalism (q.v.) into Hungarian; but in fact he was a sentimental romantic whose treatment of poverty appealed because it was essentially sentimental. His best work in fiction is his earliest, represented by the short-story collection *Poverty* (1884). The poet, playwright and novelist Jenő Heltai began as a clever and popular light versifier, but achieved greater stature with his fiction. He was the first Hungarian writer to learn from French literature; his view of it was even less deep than Ady's, but he deserves credit for his small contribution.

A more important figure was the novelist and critic ZOLTÁN AMBRUS (1861–1932). Ambrus also anticipated Ady in drawing his inspiration from French literature—chiefly from Flaubert and Maupassant; but he differed from him in being sensitive not to symbolism, or to any other poetic movement, but only to prose realism. He is a lone wolf in Hungarian letters, for—again unlike Ady —he never succeeded in reconciling the precepts of French realism, to which he was devoted, with the Hungarian spirit. So although he was one of Hungary's first truly modern writers, he failed—where Ady, despite his limitations, succeeded—in becoming more than a French author writing in the Hungarian language. His critical insistence upon the role of reason—much influenced by Anatole France (q.v.)—hardly fitted into the Hungarian situation, as readers of the impassioned lyrics of Ady will readily understand. But he was a good 'French' writer: an acute psychologist, whose novels—*King Midas* (1906) is the best of them—and short stories provide sharply critical analyses of emotional behaviour. Because of his links with France, Ambrus was not popular; but he was regarded with respect by his contemporaries.

GYULA SZINI (1876–1932) produced mostly hack work; but there is a portion of his writing, consisting of short stories, that will endure. He published regularly in *West*. He translated plays by Oscar Wilde and Wedekind (q.v.) into Hungarian.

GYULA KRÚDY (1878–1933), born in central Hungary of a well-to-do family, was an uneven writer; but in his best work he not only reveals a turn-of-the-century decadent sadness, but also anticipates the unreal, dream-like atmospheres created by more recent writers of fiction. He was as isolated a figure as Ambrus, and a more odd one; but there is no disputing his Hungarianness. His characters, faintly bizarre and almost always unhappy, move through their world as through a dream; they share their creator's sense of unreality, and often his sense of humour. Essentially a short-story writer—his novels are expanded short stories—some of his finest work is to be found in *The Youth and Sorrow of Sindbad* (1912). Krúdy is still something of an enigma; it is likely that his work will become still more widely read and admired.

FERENC MÓRA (1879–1934), a museum-director, one of the chief regionalists of this century, gained more appreciation in his own lifetime than Krúdy. He was born in Kiskunfélegyháza, but spent nearly all his life in Hungary's second largest city, Szeged, to whose region he devoted his fiction. He evolved a pleasant musical style which has been much admired. Although he had no connections with the writers gathered around *West* (q.v.), Mora shared their radical viewpoint—if more by instinct and temperament than by intellectual conviction. His most famous novel is *Song of the Wheatfields* (1927; tr. G. Halász, 1930), a powerful anti-war novel containing starkly authentic portraits of peasants. The main plot concerns the disastrous effect upon a married couple when they learn that the former husband of the wife, believed killed in battle, is in fact alive ('prisoner' of a Russian woman, who demands a ransom for his safe return).

ZSIGMOND MÓRICZ (1879–1942), Hungary's great naturalist (q.v.), is also his country's most important twentieth-century novelist; some rate him above Ady in importance. The bluntness and brutality of his realism, which stems from an innate and angry honesty and a profound sensitivity, are both less self-conscious and less fundamentally squeamish than that of Zola (q.v.). In general, Móricz may fairly be compared to the French novelist. He became famous with the publication—in *West*—of his short story 'Seven Pennies' (1909), about extreme poverty. He took his early inspiration from the poetry of Ady—although he himself spoke no language other than his own, and read Zola in translations—of whom he later became a friend. His great strength lay in the power of his portrayals of peasants and their immediate social superiors; he delighted in their coarseness—he was more than once accused of 'bad taste'—and he had no capacity to portray intellectuals. His own grasp and authority were wholly instinctive; the son of a peasant and a parson's daughter, his intelligence, his eye for important detail, resembled that of a peasant rather than that of an intellectual. Undoubtedly he relished the plebeian gusto of his characters; he was also driven by a strong sense of justice. In his own way Móricz was as aware of the way in which social stagnation had led Hungary to the brink of disaster as was Ady; he was in any case the first writer of fiction to smash through the old and convenient tradition by which the relationship between the peasant and his landlord was viewed in a rosy and sentimental light. He shared Zola's determinism, but put a greater emphasis upon the erotic; it is safe to say that no realist of his generation wrote more graphically (and zestfully) of what seems, to 'civilized' readers, 'beastly' in the lives of peasants. He always professed contempt for any kind of idealism. Thus marriage is never, in his books, more than a battleground. His first novel, *Golden Mud*, is a portrait of the same kind of super-sexed male peasant as the Belgian Lemonnier had written about in *A Stud* (q.v.). *The Torch* (1917; tr. A. Lengyel, 1931) studies an idealistic young priest destroyed by the brutal realities of his rural parish. *Be Faithful Unto Death* (tr. L. Körösi, 1962), his finest novel, sets the innocent world of a growing boy against the corruptness and cruelty of his adult environment, especially that of his Calvinist school. *Transylvania* (1922–35) is a historical trilogy set in the seventeenth century. Móricz wrote dramas as well as fiction; his short stories, including *Shawl of Many Colours* (tr. L. Wolfe, 1936), are notable. The vitality and conviction of his work have not been excelled in later Hungarian fiction.

The fiction of DEZSŐ SZABÓ (1879–1945) was vitiated by his violent temperament. Something of a chauvinist, and never capable of moderation of tone, Szabó for a time supported the fascism of Horthy's government between the wars, including its anti-semitism; then, seeing the growing menace of the Nazis, he turned anti-German—and courageously attacked them in the writings of his last years. He ended as a pro-Russian, and it is said that the Nazis tortured him to death. Szabó made his reputation with *The Lost Village* (1919), about a near-peasant who returns to a village in order to awaken the inhabitants to a realization of Magyar greatness. This is a reactionary novel, but none the less a powerful one. Its successors, though all distinguished by some excellence of detail, are less impressive.

ZSOLT HARSÁNYI (1887–1944) is the Hungarian writer who has the most in common with Stefan Zweig (q.v.). His fictionalized biographies—Liszt, Rubens, and so on—have much in common with those of Zweig, including the Freudian approach; he also shares Zweig's vulgarity. It cannot be said that he does not entirely deserve the English titles of some of his books: *Immortal Franz* (tr. 1937), *The Star-Gazer* (tr. 1939)—this is Galileo—*Through a Woman's Eyes* (tr. 1942) and *The Lover of Life* (tr. 1942). However, he possessed true flair and insight, and he has some place in Hungarian letters. His style is fluent and his observations keen; his intelligence does not leave him even in the moments of his most intense vulgarity.

The humorist FRIGYES KARINTHY (1888–1938), a member of the *West* group, is more important. Translator of Swift, Heine and Mark Twain—as well as, incongruously, the sentimental twentieth-century English pseudo-humorist A. A. Milne—he was Hungary's most brilliant modern satirist: her leading writer in the thoroughgoingly sceptical post-1914 tradition. He was Hungary's representative of expressionism, and he wrote as adeptly for cabaret audiences as for literary men. He did not, Reményi says, 'lead a well-regulated life': he never took a moral view. Much of his work was done in the form of short newspaper articles. Like nearly all humorists, he was a profoundly melancholy man, who regarded the quietness of death as the true aim of life. In *The Way You Write* (1912) he satirized the literary conventions of his time with a bitter good humour and intelligence. He took a sardonic view of love; but this concealed an idealistic view of women—a critical one of men. It is fortunate that his finest work, *A Journey Round my Skull* (1937; tr. V. D. Barker, 1939), is available in English. Karinthy suffered from a brain tumour; despite an operation by a famous Swedish surgeon, it killed him within a year of writing this book, which is a classic. In it Karinthy tries to describe his experience in an 'undisturbed' state of mind; furthermore, and most symptomatically of his age, he states that he was 'the victim of a sense of guilt . . . some forgotten sin that had never been condoned because the memory of it remained outside my conscious mind'. This sense of guilt explained to him why he was 'incapable of complaining or rebelling' against his fate. Doubtless this guilt originated in his lack of sense of values; yet his objectivity here suggests that, whether wittingly or not, he finally attained one.

Of a later generation, SÁNDOR MÁRAI (1900), who has lived outside Hungary since 1947, is another who has resolutely tried to keep his writing apart from politics. He began as a journalist, and also wrote poetry and plays; but it is as a novelist that he is outstanding. In his fiction he has resisted, not altogether without success, his tendency to satisfy a middle-class audience. There is, however, some substance in the charge of Marxist critics that he remains tied to a decadent civilization: there is no evidence in his pages, psychologically excellent though some of them are, that he finds fault with the mores of the society he depicts. He has been compared to Thomas Wolfe (q.v.) both for his fluency—and his inability to control his flow of words. *A Diver* (tr. L. Wolfe, 1936) is his only novel to be translated into English; since he has lived in the USA he has published a novel, *Peace in Ithaca*, and his *Journal 1945–1947*.

LAJOS ZILAHY (1891) is one of the few Hungarian writers (Molnár, q.v., is outstanding in this respect) whose works are relatively well known in the West. He is a playwright as well as a novelist. Like Márai, he left Hungary with the advent of communism; since 1947 he has lived in New York. Again like Márai, he eschewed politics (although a pungent critic of society, who had to hide from the Nazis and was investigated by the Russians) and was a popular author; but he has had more luck in the West, and at least six of his books have been translated into English. He became widely known with the publication of *Two Prisoners* (1931; tr. G. Collins and I. Zeitlin, 1931). There is a certain superficiality about his work, but it is consistently intelligent and well made. His early fiction was written under the influence of Krúdy (q.v.). *Two Prisoners* has all the ingredients of a highly popular novel, including that tediousness which untrained readers tend to take for 'depth'; but it does have some actual depth as well. . . . It is a story of a marriage shattered by the First World War (during which Zilahy was a prisoner of the Russians). *The Deserter*

(1930; tr. G. Halász) is another war novel. *The Dukays* (tr. J. Panker, 1949) chronicles the collapse of a wealthy aristocratic family; *The Angry Angel* (tr. T. L. Harsner, 1953) is a continuation.

TIBOR DÉRY (1894), a communist between the wars, was imprisoned for three years after the Hungarian uprising of 1956; he has always been an opponent of socialist realism (q.v.). His fiction—novels and short stories— portrays the life of workers with compassionate exactitude. His most famous book, an international best-seller, is *Niki, the Story of a Dog* (tr. E. Hyams, 1958), which manages to be both sentimental and delightful.

ÁRON TAMÁSI (1897–1966) was a latter-day regionalist; he wrote exclusively of the Sekler peasant environment into which he was born. The Seklers, who number some half-million, are a people of uncertain origin who live in south-eastern Transylvania. There was a strong Transylvanian movement between the wars; the whole of this region, rich in folklore, was annexed to Rumania in 1920, which merely exacerbated the Hungarians. The two chief figures in this Transylvanian movement were Tamási and the poet Sándor Reményik (q.v.). Tamási was one of the few surviving masters of the modern folk-tale; he successfully absorbed the influence of traditional poetry. His first book consisted of short stories: *Soul's Trek* (1925). His most famous books are the *Abel* trilogy: *Abel in the Wilderness*, *Abel in the Land* and *Abel in America* (1934). Abel is a shrewd Sekler shepherd boy who outwits more sophisticated people in great cities, and, finally, in America. Only *In Praise of a Donkey* (tr. L. Wolfe, 1936) and *Orderly Resurrection* (tr. I. Duczynska, 1963) have been translated.

ANTAL SZERB (1901–45), a Jew born in Budapest, was persecuted by the Horthy regime and finally murdered by the Nazis. He was best known as a critic and essayist; but his novels—*The Pendragon Legend* (1934; tr. L. Halápy, 1963) and *Love in a Battle* (tr. L. Wolfe, 1936)—are unusual in their subtle irony.

The erudite novelist, translator, critic and playwright LASZLÓ NÉMETH (1901) was a leading member of the younger *West* generation. His fiction, in which he explores the predicament of the intelligent Hungarian middle classes of his time, is better than his journalism, which is often confused. Thus, his belief that the small Hungary created after the First World War provided an opportunity to build an ideal country ignored too many realities. He allowed himself to be involved in too much controversy: his imagination, working in fiction, provided sounder if more complex analyses of his environment. One of his novels, *Revulsion* (1947), has been translated (1965). This is the story of an unhappy woman whose husband is kind but insensitive to her profounder feelings. He has written successful plays of some literary merit.

*

It has already been noted that the chief impetus in the Hungarian modern movement came from lyrical poetry, with Ady as its spearhead. GYULA JUHÁSZ (1883–1937), born at Szeged, at first bade fair to become as famous as his friend Ady, whose revolutionary ideas profoundly influenced him. He was a leading member of the first *West* group, and his poetry owed much to French models—though more to the Parnassians (q.v.) than to the symbolist (q.v.) school. But he gradually withdrew from the world, falling into an acute melancholy that disabled him even as a teacher. Though not really a political poet, he supported Béla Kun's regime in 1919, and for this was persecuted by the inter-war fascists. He took to drinking, and finally withdrew almost entirely into himself; he frequently attempted suicide, and eventually succeeded. Juhász's poetry is simple and refined; but modern in spirit. More than any other Hungarian poet he expressed the differences between Hungary and the West; this fitted in well with his own alienated mood:

> Today this town is dull, my world confin'd,
> And distant Indies beckon to my mind. . . .
>
> Is there not some spot beneath the sun
> Where thou, my soul, mayst rest, the longing done?
>
> (HWL)

Some of his best poetry is written to 'Anna', an actress he loved hopelessly— no doubt he chose her because she was incapable of loving anyone. . . .

ÁRPÁD TÓTH (1886–1928), the leading translator of his day (Baudelaire, Flaubert, Keats, Milton, and others), was a more active member of the *West* movement; but his poetry, too, is beset with gloom: he suffered from tuberculosis, knew that he was destined to an early death—and succumbed at the age of forty-two. He was born in Arad, which was assigned to Rumania after the First World War. Tóth was a scholarly man, who failed as a journalist but did better as a professor; his closest friend was Babits (q.v.), who edited his works after his death. He, too, was a pacifist during the First World War; but he was a supporter of Béla Kun, which has ensured his position in communist literary history. His poetry is learned and literary, influenced by the late French symbolists and by Keats, but Magyar in its tone and rhythms. It is deliberately removed from experience; but his metaphysical anguish is everywhere apparent. He wants to warn men of the dangerousness of time:

> But Silences within the darkness break
> And choke my words. Through leagues of midnight there
>
> Only a myriad pendulums are awake,
> Blind, swaying splendours and mysterious miens,
> Relentless sickles, golden guillotines.
>
> (HWL)

There is a paradox at the heart of the work of LAJOS KASSÁK (1887–1970): he is Hungary's leading proletarian writer of this century—Reményi compares him to Nexø (q.v.)—and yet it is not unfair to describe him, as J. F. Ray has, as 'the chief representative of Hungarian abstract literature'. He was a pacifist in the First World War, and then an enthusiastic communist; but he has stated his belief that literature is not bound up with politics. In other words, he is no advocate of socialist realism (q.v.). The town where he was born is now in Czechoslovakia. His early life was typical of that of a proletarian writer of his generation: he became a travelling blacksmith, both inside and outside Hungary, and all the while preached socialism. He has told his story in his autobiographies *Addressed to my Mother* (1947) and *The Life of a Man*. For a time he lived in Vienna, exiled on account of his socialism. His early poetry, reminiscent of Whitman in form, is heroic in its mood about the future of the working classes:

> We sat at the base of dark tenement-houses; in speechless fulfilment like the individual substance itself.
> Yesterday we wept, and tomorrow perhaps the century will marvel at our deeds.
> Yes! for from our blunt, ugly fingers fresh power already strikes forth, and tomorrow we drink a toast on the new walls.
> Tomorrow out of asbestos, iron and massive life in the ruins, and do away with State democracies, moonlight and orpheums! . . .

He looked upon literary life, as he had the right to do, with the disdain of a workman. And yet much of his poetry is painfully abstract, and reminds one of an inferior expressionist such as Becher (q.v.); but there is another, more solitary side of him that is more authentic. He has also written novels and short stories. Despite his unevenness, he is historically important: his poetry opened up a highly accessible way to modernism.

The poet, critic and novelist MILÁN FÜST (1888), born in Budapest and an important member of the *West* group, is another somewhat abstract poet. Like Tóth's (q.v.), his poetry is deliberately removed from experience; but in his case the energy is supplied by philosophy rather than by anguish. He yearns for a better world without wholly convincing us that he knows very much of this one. However, his command of free verse is impressive.

SÁNDOR REMÉNYIK (1890–1942) is, with Tamási (q.v.), the great Transylvanian regionalist. But where Tamási was a Sekler from the south-east, Reményik was born in Kolozsvár, the chief city of Transylvania. One of the chief concerns of his life was the plight of the Hungarians in Transylvania, which was handed over to Rumania in 1920. Much of his poetry has this as its theme, and does not always transcend its occasion. It does so most successfully when Reményik—always a sick man—expresses his personal melancholy. Such poems as 'Star Beneath the Water' are not profound in content, but have an incantatory quality that testifies to Reményik's remarkable integrity.

LÁSZLÓ MÉCS (1895), a Roman Catholic priest, taught in Košice in Slovakia, and was for many years the leading literary figure in the Hungarian minority in Czechoslovakia. His poetry has little emotional substance, but is distinguished in the field of modern devotional Catholic poetry by its sincerity and gracefulness of expression; he was, between the wars, a highly successful declaimer of his own verse. After 1947 he vanished into seclusion; he is not now listed in any official 'critical' publications. *I Graft Roses on Eglantines* (1968) contains selected translations by Kirkconnel and R. J. Conrad, with an introduction written by Valéry in 1944 for a volume of French translations.

LŐRINC SZABÓ (1900–57), born in Miskolc, was one of the leading poets of the younger *West* group—of the late Twenties and early Thirties. He began as an expressionist rebel, denouncing both urban values and the social system; then he came under the influence of Stefan George (q.v.); eventually he retreated into a kind of nihilism occasionally relieved by bursts of positive and constructive energy. As in Ady, narcissism in Szabó struggled with social concern. He is one of the most eloquent as well as one of the most interesting poets of his generation. 'The Hay-wagon' affords an excellent example of his earlier manner, even though the 'Georgian' (q.v.) idiom used by Watson Kirkconnel in his translation does not do justice to Szabó's use of language:

> During the night a wagon-load of hay
> Pass'd through the town along the moonlit street.
> Oh, how the stuffy rows of houses stirr'd
> And hearken'd! How the boulevard's poor trees
> Stretched out their creaking, mutilated arms!
> A wagon-load of hay passed through the town.
> It came, it went, it rustled, sang, and sway'd,
> Swam in the moonlight, swam and sang to me,
> Chanted to me! And in the song it brought
> The village-moon again, the cricket's voice,
> The shaggy collie, reapers' pleasant songs,
> Ploughs, harrows, pails, the gypsy fiddle-bow,
> And grumbling bag-pipes' murmurous refrain.—
> It brought to me the sooty-waisted bulls,
> Their lustrous eyes, the ardour of the sun,
> Barnyard manure, skies a-flood with rain,
> Hillsides a-stream, and humble human strength,
> Human endurance, selfishness and love
> Deep though austere.—All, all it brought to me,
> All this to me. And while that wagon pass'd
> Through the perverted and discouraged town,
> I listen'd on the boulevard of night,
> With throbbing pulses, how around me grew
> The trees and grasses, and on far-off peaks
> How with vast slumbering body sprawled supine
> The mountains' God, shock-hair'd and oaken-brow'd,
> Breathed, in his age-old dream of death and life.
>
> (HWL)

GYULA ILLYÉS (1902) has for long been regarded as the finest living Hungarian poet; only Sandor Weőres and Ferenc Juhász (q.v.) seem in recent years to have supplanted him in popularity. Illyés is admired by such younger poets as

Ferenc Juhász for the same reasons as many critics of his own generation distrusted him: he ignored traditional rules, and seemed 'to delight in stylized primitiveness' (Reményi). Like other major Hungarian poets, Illyés has been heavily influenced by European, particularly French, models. When in Paris as a student he was a friend of Malraux (q.v.) and others. He wrote of this period of his life in the novel *Huns in Paris; People of the Pusztas* (1936; tr. V. Biro) is a classic autobiography. His best poetry, heroic in mood and subject, is suffused with a melancholy that he cannot suppress in spite of his communism:

> The sharp dust rattles on the window-pane.
> Bury your face, with shut eyes, on my breast!
> Fill the glass, father! If our future flies
> With dust and rubbish down the wind of time,
> Let it, 'mid leaves, go eddying with song!
>
> (HWL)

The doomed hero of modern Hungarian poetry, regarded by some as a greater poet than Ady, is ATTILA JÓZSEF (1905–37). He was born in Budapest and grew up in atrocious poverty. He is justly called a proletarian poet; but, influenced by Ady, he surpassed the older man both in his understanding of foreign influences and in his assimilation of them to an astonishingly original, and yet absolutely Hungarian, style. The strain of life, and chronic poverty, eventually became too much for him, and he became mentally ill (it is said that he was schizophrenic) and committed suicide by jumping in front of a train. His assimilation of folk poetry, and transformation of it into something new and his own, has rightly been compared to what the composer Bartók did with folk music. He became a member of the communist party—illegal under Horthy's regime—but, unable to live with any set of dogmas, was soon expelled. The authorities persecuted him. He was an urban poet; but the rural world, which he intuitively understood and responded to, exists in his poetry like a dream.

József's father, a soap-factory worker, left his family and went to America; his mother was a washerwoman. By enormous effort he was able to enter the University of Szeged, but he did not complete his education. His youthful poems, full of promise, appeared in *West*. The rest of the story is one of increasing withdrawal, punctuated by bursts of poetic activity and attempts to rescue himself from his wilful narcissism and nihilism. But the poetry he created was entirely his own. Influenced by surrealism, it was no more surrealist than that of Lorca (q.v.), a poet with whom he has sometimes been compared—not for his musical qualities, but for the idiosyncratic nature of his poetic world. His strength is that he succeeded in creating an absolutely self-sufficient poetic world: a perfect expression of his inner state, which itself reflects his country's helplessness between 1920 and 1925. His poetry resembles Magyar folk poetry in form and rhythm, but its content frequently reflects his reading of Marx and Freud. It is surprising that no recent English translator has yet tackled József; existing translations are inadequate, for they give little idea of his achievement in the realm of language. The best translations of József's poetry have been into Italian: *Poesie* (tr. U. Albini, 1957) contains a substantial selection. This translation by A. Nyerges of 'I Did Not Know' conveys a sense of his nightmare mood but does less than justice to his language.

> I always lent my ear as to a tale
> When schooling was of sin. And without heed
> I ever laughed—how stupid are these words!
> He prates of sin who cowers before the deed!
>
> I did not know so many monsters housed
> Within the cavern of my heart. I thought
> That as a mother rocks her sleeping babe,
> So are the pulsing beats with dreaming fraught.
>
> But now I understand. Within the light
> Of this appalling truth the primal blight
> Grows black like a catafalque in my heart.
>
> Should I not speak, my lips would still make moan:
> Were you but all so sinful, not I alone,
> That I might not be utterly apart.
>
> (HWL)

It is József who is the founder of modern Hungarian poetry; he will, at least retrospectively, be seen as a figure as important as Ady.

MIKLÓS RADNÓTI (1907–44), born in Budapest, is remembered as Hungary's finest poet of protest. Horthy's regime persecuted him; the Germans arrested and murdered him. He made his reputation as a translator (Shelley, Cocteau, q.v.), but in the very early Thirties began to write a defiant anti-fascist poetry; this gradually gave way to a more sombre and more personal type of work, in which the themes of freedom and justice combine with those of Radnóti's love for his family and his all-too-justified fears that his attitudes would lead to his early death. His poetry—which he continued to write until the day of his murder—aptly reflects the nobility and courage of his aspirations and is technically highly accomplished.

Two poets of minor distinction, both born in Budapest, deserve to be mentioned here: ISTVÁN VAS (1910) and GYÖRGY FALUDY (1913). Vas began as a conventional although technically distinguished poet; later he came under the influence of the *West* poets, and took up a classical position. Faludy, of Jewish descent, was persecuted by the Nazis and the communists; he has lived in Great Britain since the uprising of 1956. He has translated Villon into free Hungarian. His poetry is lyrical and graceful without being unusual or disturbing. Probably his finest achievement is the prose autobiography *My Happy Days in Hell* (1962; tr. K. Szász, 1962).

The reputation of SANDOR WEŐRES (1913), born in Pécs, increased enormously during the Sixties: he is now regarded as Hungary's leading living poet. A near contemporary of Dylan Thomas (q.v.), whose poetry is currently much admired in Hungary, he somewhat resembles him in manner; but his poetry is less optimistic and his philosophy both more complex and more nihilistically extreme. His style is eclectic, and reflects the influence of German expressionism and surrealism as well as the Celtic verbal exuberance of Dylan Thomas, to whose work his is immensely superior. He is a noted translator. Weöres is perhaps even more important as an influence than as a poet in his own right. A selection from his and Ferenc Juhász's (q.v.) work was published in English translation in 1970, in the Penguin European Poets series.

The poetry of FERENC JUHÁSZ (1928), who was born in a village near Budapest, has had more attention bestowed upon it outside Hungary than that of any other Hungarian writer—including Petőfi. This is unfair on Ady, József, Illyés and others; but Juhász is clearly a gifted poet. The authoritative translation of his poetry in English is by Kenneth McRobbie and Ilona Duczynska: *The Boy Changed into a Stag* (1970). Juhász has been accused of opportunism— he was in some disfavour after the 1956 uprising for publishing his poetry during the Stalinist period—but this has now largely been forgotten. The first thing to be said of him is that he is, apodictically, a lyrical poet of great gifts, who can produce such lines as '. . . the heart of the Universe shall break when the song ceases'. He feels a special kinship with, and has written a moving poem to, József. Juhász is a convinced Marxist (though not in any sense a Stalinist, whatever pressures he may—or may not—have yielded to when a young man) who sees life as a slow and essentially painful evolution towards a better state. There is nothing dogmatic in this Marxism. He is a highly personal and sombre poet. The subject of his famous 'The Boy Changed into a Stag' is the death of his father (this may recall József's anguished intimate cries of 'mama!' in his poems to his mother); 'Seasons' and 'Four Voices' are about his wife and her mental breakdown. Juhász is so fluent that many of his poems tend to run on for too long at a level just below that of the excellent; he has many of the faults of Dylan Thomas (q.v.), whom he admires: he becomes too intoxicated with his own rhetoric; he lacks control. But his voice has an unmistakable authority, as we may discern in 'At the Grave of Attila József' or in this uncharacteristically short poem (quoted here in the McRobbie-Duczynska translation), 'On the Margin of My Years in Suspended Animation':

> Talk too much, then did I?
> Will dumbness be my fate?
> For my seer's heart, worry?
> Has drought dried up my throat?

> What skeleton armies have
> by my star-fate been summoned?
> Have they devoured my faith?
> Is my face a gravemound?

*

With the exception of Molnár (q.v.), the modern Hungarian theatre has not produced a major dramatist. The first dramatist to introduce the colloquial Budapest idiom into the theatre was Bródy (q.v.). His plays have this virtue in common with his novels—and they suffer from the same commercially orientated vices. Bródy's best play is *The Schoolmistress* (1908).

For the first quarter of a century the Hungarian stage was dominated by FERENC HERCZEG (1863–1954), an extremely conservative writer whose skill is practically cancelled out by the superficiality of his psychology. In his novels and, chiefly, plays, he cynically glorified the corrupt feudal life of the Hungarian gentry at the turn of the century. His lack of social concern is repellent; but one is able to gather from his work something of the mood and tone of the last mad fling of the wealthy Hungarian classes. He was of German descent. His best play is the historical *Byzantium* (1904); in this drama of the dissolution of the Byzantine Empire he comes nearest to a feeling of the impending collapse of the Austro-Hungarian Empire.

MENYHÉRT LENGYEL (1880–1957) is more important, though not more skilful. He settled in the U.S.A. after the First World War. He had many world-wide successes, the most famous of which is perhaps *Typhoon* (1909; tr. L. Irving, 1913), which deals with the lack of moral courage of a brilliant Japanese scientist. He had a wide range of subjects; his plays on folk-topics— such as *The Miraculous Mandarin,* upon which Bartók based his ballet (from which the famous suite is derived)—are particularly good.

FERENC MOLNÁR (1878–1952), born in Budapest, died in New York, to which he had emigrated twelve years earlier. He had great success outside Hungary: his plays were filmed, and *Liliom* (1909; tr. B. F. Glazer, 1921) is more famous under the title of *Carousel,* the musical still successful on stage and screen. Molnár has been described as superficial outside and, more often, inside his native country; this is not altogether fair. Comparisons with Schnitzler and Pirandello (qq.v.) are somewhat more apt, although he lacks the stature of either. He is sentimental; but his sentimentality does not dominate his concept of the play: it is merely one element. He is also intellectually astute, deeply humorous and often wise. *The Guardsman* (1910), technically impeccable, has seemed to some mere comic froth; but, in fact, it has dimensions worthy of Pirandello. An actor disguises himself as a Russian officer in order to 'test' his wife. This fits her world of fantasy, and she agrees to go to bed with him. But just before the seduction he declares himself; she pretends that she has known all along. . . . Molnár was also an important novelist: *The Paul Street Boys* (1907; tr. L. Rittenberg, 1927), as important to Hungarians as De Amicis' *Heart* (q.v.) was to Italians, is a juvenile classic. His plays, when collected in English translation in 1929, were introduced by David Belasco (q.v.).

Most of the plays of GYULA HÁY (1900) are in German: he lived in Germany for many years as a young man. As a good Marxist (he left Germany in 1933 and spent the next twenty-three years in Moscow) he was arrested after the 1956 uprising and not released until 1960. His *God, Peasant, Emperor* (1932) was produced by Reinhardt (q.v.). Outstanding among his plays are *Tisza*

Nook (1946), on the Horthy regime, and *The Horse* (1964), about Caligula; the latter was seen in the West.

Illyés' (q.v.) theatrical début, in the Thirties, was unsuccessful; but in the Fifties he wrote some remarkable historical plays, including *The Example of Ozora* (1952) and *Dozsa* (1956), an outstanding drama on the subject of the abortive peasants' revolt of 1514: this had strong overtones, and might well have got Illyés into trouble.

Of a younger generation, the most gifted are LAJOS MESTERHÁZI (1916), whose conformity to the official line cannot quite stifle his skill, and IMRE SARKADI (1921–61), who committed suicide. Sarkadi's *Simeon Stylites* (1967) is a powerful portrait of a man who neither can nor will conform. FERENC KARINTHY (1921), son of the great humorist, has written *Four-Handed Piece* (1966), which has many of the qualities of the drama of the absurd (q.v.); so also has the grotesque *The Tót Family* (1966) of ISTVÁN ORKÉNY (1912), which played in Paris in 1968.

Indian and Pakistani Literature

India (the division of India and Pakistan—Bangladesh is too young to consider in literary terms—makes no political sense, of course, until 1947) is a country of many languages. The now official language of Hindustani (Urdu) is only one of literally hundreds of distinctive languages and dialects. Bengali, Malayalam, Marathi, Tamil, Assamese, Kannada, Kashmiri, Oria, Punjabi, Sanskrit, Sindhi, Telugu and Gujarati are some of the more important ones. However, modern Indian writers have on the whole failed to make an international impression. This is not unjust. Most of the Indian fiction of the last eighty years is poor, whatever its sociological value. It neither properly embodies the purely Indian culture, nor (when it tries, as it so often does) succeeds in exploiting Western techniques. Forster's *A Passage to India* (q.v.) remains the best 'Western' Indian novel. The exceptions, more or less gifted, I discuss here.

RABINDRANATH TAGORE (1861–1941), who was knighted in 1914 (presumably because he won the Nobel Prize in 1913), has been one of the few Indians to gain an international reputation. Born in Calcutta, he wrote in Bengali. He was a lyrical poet, novelist and dramatist. He was a noble (in the Elgarian sense) man, who did much good; but his work has dated badly. His own English translations of his best work—his lyrical poetry—are, although competent, banal. His main object, to synthesize Eastern and Western cultures, was value-less because based on an idealization of the chief elements in each. He is most important in the development of Bengali literature for his use of the colloquial (*chalit blasha*); his once enormous British reputation was based on work that will not be revived. He put personal before national freedom, and should be honoured for his stand—whether he confused the issues or not. Much of the best of him, which resides in his direct style and in his humanistic and cautiously anti-conservative attitude (he was by no means a major imaginative writer), may be found in *A Tagore Reader* (ed. A. Chakravarty, 1961).

The leading contemporary Bengali novelist is MANI SHANKAR MUKHERJI (1933), whose first novel *Kata Ajanare* deals perceptively with his experiences as the assistant of an English barrister. He has since developed into a skilful, intelligent and readable recorder of Indian life.

There are not many important twentieth-century novelists. Bankimchandra Chatterji (1838–94) was the first true Indian novelist, but died at fifty-five. PREM CAND (ps. D. R. SRIVASTAV, 1880–1936), born near Banaras, wrote in

Urdu until about 1914, but thereafter wrote in both Urdu and Hindi. Prem Cand, much of whose work is available in English translation, acquired his literary background in Urdu, but is generally regarded as having developed the Hindi novel. The first novel of his maturity, *Sevasadan* (1919), was published in Hindi but had been first drafted in Urdu. Prem Cand wrote other novels, but is at his best in short stories (he wrote more than 250), in which he often transcends his dogmatic idealism and presents humorous and touching character studies. There is a *Prem Cand Reader* (1962).

Perhaps the best of all modern Indian novelists, however, was until recently neglected: BIBHUTIBHUSHAN BANERJI (1894–1950) was well known only to experts in the Bengali language (few and far between) until Satyajit Ray's famous film of *Pather Panchali* (1928–9), which was then translated in 1968 by the late T. W. Clark and T. Mukherji. This is the only modern Indian novel (written in an Indian language) of true artistry. It is full of changing moods and changing styles, all expressed with mastery. Banerji was born in a village north of Calcutta; his father—this is reflected in *Pather Panchali*—was gifted but impractical: he could not earn enough as family priest and singer of traditional songs to keep his family from poverty. But Banerji won an education for himself. For a time he was a teacher; he then left this profession to become in turn an Inspector to the Society for the Protection of Cattle, and clerk in an estate office. Eventually he returned to teaching. He wrote some fifty works, including a translation of *Ivanhoe* and books on astrology and the occult. He was immensely popular, but none of his books reaches the level of this one fictional masterpiece of twentieth-century Indian literature. It is a haunting study of four characters, the chief two being children: Opu, a boy, and his sister Durga; the other two main characters are their parents. The book is essentially about a difficult and yet beautiful childhood—in many ways, but not all, Banerji's own. The village of Nishchindipur is certainly Banerji's own childhood village, the parents his own; and yet the imagination has played its part. This is a world classic as well as a Bengali masterpiece.

The most distinguished contemporary Tamil poet is N. PICHAMURTHI, whose work sensitively reflects the agonizing complexities of modern Indian life: the painful contrast between atrocious poverty and a developing technology that seems to achieve nothing.

Probably nothing in twentieth-century Indian literature, in prose or poetry, comes to the level of *Pather Panchali*; but other writers have reached high standards. The poet MOHAMMED IQBAL (1873–1938), father of Pakistani literature and one of the earliest advocates of a separate Moslem state, was born at Sialkot in Punjab. He was the Moslem counterpart to the Indian Tagore: a contemporary giant. He began by writing in Urdu, then, finding that he could express his philosophical ideas better in Persian, switched to that language—in which he published his most famous work, *Secrets of the Self* (1915; tr. R. A. Nicholson, 1920). This attracted a midcult readership in the English-speaking world, but hardly deserved it: he was a learned philosopher, and at least as sensible as any of his Western counterparts. Ironically, its subject-matter is anti-Western: an exhortation to Islam to abandon passivity and to seek instead to change the world, it arose from his strong feelings about the West's attitude towards Islam. None the less, he accepted a knighthood in 1922 (Tagore, q.v., had done the same—but later resigned it). Another long philosophical poem, again in Persian, followed: *Mysteries of Selflessness* (tr. A. J. Arberry, 1953). These long poems have no poetic value; and Iqbal's main importance is indeed as a historical figure; his best poems are in Urdu, and are short and lyrical. They may be found in V. G. Kiernan's *Poems from Iqbal* (1947; rev. 1955).

V. G. Kiernan is also the authorized translator of the poetry of Iqbal's acknowledged successor as national poet of Pakistan: FAIZ AHMED FAIZ (1905), a communist whose best and most approachable poems are about being in prison, an experience he knows well. Faiz is popular in Russia, where all his poetry has been translated. His political poetry is less impressive; but his more personal lyrics—many are in the bilingual *Poems by Faiz* (tr. V. G. Kiernan, 1971)—have something of the wistful quality of those of another communist prisoner, the Turkish Nazim Hikmet (q.v.).

The poet VALLATTOL NARAYANA MENON (1897–1958), who wrote in Malayalam (the language of Kerala), was famous in India but less known abroad for lack of translators. He introduced into Malayalam a new type of poetry, based on ballad and popular song, and very carefully wrought. His early poems are centred in the struggle for independence. Then he came under the influence of Sanskrit poetry, and wrote a long epic, *Komappan*, in Sanskrit style. The work of his last phase is mellow and tolerant, but less poetically interesting.

India's innovator and experimentalist, influenced by Eliot and Pound, was the Marathi poet BAL SITARAM MARDHEKAR (1907–56) who wrote in an impersonal, condensed style. P. S. REGE (1910), a professor of economics, is a prolific writer of novels, stories and poems. He is a serene, aphoristic writer of unusual sophistication; his poems have been translated into several languages. But better known, especially abroad, is the Bengali poet, novelist, critic and short-story writer BUDDHADEVA BOSE (1908). Bose is also an innovator and an advocate of Western modernism, which has made his position in Pakistani letters a controversial one. His name is familiar in English-speaking countries, but rather as a witty, intelligent, learned and trenchant critic than poet or novelist. He is extremely prolific, having over forty novels to his credit, as well as many volumes of poetry and criticism.

AHMAD ALI (1906) began by writing short stories of strongly socialist content in Urdu, but later switched to English for his more substantial *Twilight in Delhi* (1940), a touching portrait of a Delhi Moslem family in decline at the turn of the century. The Pakistani SA'ADAT HASAN MANTU (1912–55), journalist and worker in the Indian cinema, was notorious for the sexual and bizarre nature of his short stories, which led to his legal persecution on several occasions. In fact the stories—a selection is in *Black Milk* (tr. H. Jalal, 1955)—are merely candid. Early in his writing career Mantu had been influenced by Gorki (q.v.) and other Russian realists, whom he translated, and this formed his style. His best stories are subtle and penetrating. He drank himself to death in Lahore.

MOHANDAS KARAMCHAND GANDHI (1869–1948) is important in the Gujarati language (in which all his voluminous political, historical and other works were at first written) for his remarkable simplicity and terseness of style. An important modern Gujarati poet was the late RAVJI PATEL, whose death-haunted poetry, while it reflected influences as diverse as Eliot and Lorca (qq.v.), had its own distinctive voice.

The Telugu novel developed late; its most distinguished although as yet unrecognized exponent is the gifted woman novelist MUPPALA RANGANAYAKAMMA (1939); she writes as yet only of social problems, but her talents are such as to suggest that she will develop into a novelist of considerable literary merits.

The most outstanding novel by a Pakistani writer is regarded as *The Shore and the Wave*, by AZIZ AHMAD. This has now been introduced to English readers in a translation added to the *Unesco Collection of Contemporary Works* (1971).

A word should be said about that pathetic blind alley: Indian poetry in English. Its chief representative is P. LAL (1929), who runs the Writers' Workshop in Calcutta. He maintains that he 'spearheaded the "Indo-Anglian" revolt against traditional Indian poetry in English'. Even this can lead nowhere; but Lal is a better and more interesting poet than DOM MORAES (1939), who has apparently settled in England permanently. Moraes made a strong impression when he came to Oxford as a very young man; but his poetry and reputation have faded rapidly. In retrospect even his earliest verse may be seen as basically Georgian (q.v.), with a good admixture of George Barker (q.v.), spurious high emotion, and zany intellectual incoherence.

Italian Literature

I

Giuseppe Prezzolini, one of the most distinguished Italian critics of his generation, believed that the Italians, in unifying their country (1861), 'deprived cultured Europeans of their second fatherland; Italy became a little competitor among other nations, and no longer the dream nation of those who already had their own country'. It must be added that Italy has had barely a century to build up a truly native literature. Carducci (q.v.), superior to D'Annunzio, did not acquire a European reputation. D'Annunzio did—but because of his Europeanness, not his Italianness. One of the more important thinkers of this century, BENEDETTO CROCE (1866–1952), never succeeded in reaching a really European audience: only his aesthetics are widely known outside Italy—but he treated almost every other subject under the sun. Furthermore, what D'Annunzio stands for is opposed to what Carducci stands for; it is more immediately impressive, but of less value.

The modern Italian novel begins, of course, with Alessandro Manzoni's (1785–1873) *The Betrothed* (*I promessi sposi*, 1825–7; rev. 1840–2; tr. D. T. Connor, 1924; A. Colquhoun, 1951). This contains the seeds of subsequent Italian social realism, which concentrates almost exclusively upon the poor. The poverty and squalor of Italy were and, alas, are famous; and although the Italian communist party is the largest in the West, the country has never experienced the rule of a left-wing party (the socialists in coalition have forced some measure of reform on their centrist partners, but there has not been a serious approach to radicalism). It is not surprising that one of the persistent themes of Italian literature should be the lives of the poor and humble. Manzoni's masterpiece is not only about love, but also about exploitation. But realism, the European movement, reached Italy rather late, because the times were not ripe for it in the first half of the nineteenth century—as they were in sophisticated France. The native brand of realism was called *verismo*, and was developed mainly by Verga and Capuana (qq.v.).

The tendency begins, but is hardly developed, in the fiction of EDMONDO DE AMICIS (1846–1908), who was born at Oneglia in Liguria. He was criticized by Carducci (q.v.) for his langour and sentimentality; but his sincerity gives his best work a quality that will ensure its survival. He was for many years an army officer, and wrote his early books about his military experiences. He wrote many travel books; and then a long novel about illiterate emigrants, *On Blue Water* (*Sull'oceano*; tr. 1897). But his best book, a sentimental classic, is *Heart of a Boy* (*Cuore*, 1886; tr. C. S. Godkin, 1895; S. Jewett, 1960), sketches about a boy at school and his relationships with his teacher and other pupils. De Amicis openly declared his socialist sympathies in the Nineties, but his fiction about the poor is too idealistic to be effective.

It was the Sicilian LUIGI CAPUANA (1839–1915) who imported the ideas of French naturalism into Italian literature. Capuana tried to put into practice the critical precepts of Zola (q.v.). He envisaged the novel as a purely scientific study, a case history; fiction was to be at the service of social progress. But he was a lively and versatile man—'bird-fancier', practical joker and gallant, 'he never had an idle moment'—and his best fiction is a little better than his critical theory suggests. He did change his views late in life, coming to an elevation of form over all other considerations; but he had by then exercised his influence. He failed with his first novel, *Giacinta*, which is pseudo-clinical and wildly romantic, dabbling in the occult. Better is *The Marquis of Roccaverdina* (*Il Marchese di Roccaverdina*, 1901), a kind of early detective story about a Sicilian landowner and his murdered agent. (The Italians are often at their best studying the effects of crime.) Capuana's most effective fiction is to be found in his short stories about Sicily, such as 'The Reverend Walnut' (BISS), in which he shows the ability to evoke character vividly and powerfully. But Capuana, who wrote plays, children's stories, parodies and dialect works, is important, too, for his influence on his fellow-Sicilian GIOVANNI VERGA (1840–1922), who is always awarded the place of honour after Manzoni in Italian fiction.

Verga's creative life is always, and with good reason, divided into two phases: that of the so-called first manner (*prima maniera*), which attained popularity but is of little account; and the mature works of his final, naturalistic period, in which he practised *verismo*—truth to nature. His short story, later adapted as a play and as a libretto for Mascagni, *Cavalleria rusticana* (1880; tr. D. H. Lawrence, 1928; libretto, 1890), has achieved an independent fame. Verga's earlier work, sentimental, melodramatic and skilful, requires little discussion: he became famous with *Story of a Linnet* (*Storia di una capinera*, 1871), about a young nun in love. The fiction of this period appealed to a foolish audience, eager for fantasy dressed up as realism; but he was not satisfied with it or with himself for writing it. Although there are some isolated passages of merit in this work, Verga did not find himself until he began to write of his native Sicily, which interested him and engaged his attention in a way that the crude invention of bourgeois love-plots did not.

His first Sicilian fiction consisted of novellas and shorter stories (some are collected in the *Cavalleria rusticana* volume translated—badly—by D. H. Lawrence; see also *Little Novels of Sicily*, tr. D. H. Lawrence, 1925; BISS), of which the first was 'Nedda' (1874). This was the story of a young Sicilian peasant girl who goes off to make some money, becomes pregnant and loses in turn her lover and her baby: a grim, uncompromising study of the hardness of poor Sicilian life and of the primitive attitudes of those who suffer it. The first major novel, generally considered to be Verga's masterpiece, was *The*

House by the Medlar Tree (*I Malavoglia*, 1881; tr. M. A. Craig, 1890; E. Mosbacher, 1950). This deals with the impact of malign fate upon Sicilian fisherfolk. Ironically, part of this fate lies in the 'honour' persisted in by 'Ntoni. This was the first of a projected cycle, *The Conquered, I vinti*, which was to explore the 'flood of human progress' at all social levels: a 'phantasmagoria', he wrote in a letter, 'of life's struggle, extending from the ragpicker to the minister of state and the artist, assuming all forms from ambition to avidity of profit, and lending itself to a thousand representations of the great, grotesque play of mankind, the providential struggle guiding humanity through all appetites, high and low, to its conquest of truth'. Only two of a projected five novels got finished: *Mastro–don Gesualdo* (1888; rev. 1889; tr. D. H. Lawrence, 1928), a study of a peasant who acquires wealth but is none the less defeated: sponged on by relatives, relegated to the attic of his ducal son-in-law to die disappointed. Some of the detail is brilliant; but as a whole this novel does not come up to the level of its predecessor. Verga could not finish his announced (in the introduction to *The House by the Medlar Tree*) series of novels; he only managed to begin the aristocratic one, which was to examine the life of Gesualdo's Duchess daughter. But he continued to write plays, including the dramatization of the short story 'The She Wolf' (BISS), which is as good as any fiction he ever wrote, and distinctive in the Italian drama of its time. He was silent for the last twenty years of his life.

Verga was always a pessimist: his first works are not good, but his basic attitude—man is inevitably defeated by fate, whose agents are both character and villainy—may be traced even in them. Capuana influenced him to write in the manner of Flaubert and Zola, and praised his regionalistic brand of naturalism; but Verga was not imitative and did not need to be inculcated with any theory of gloom: his view of life was gloomy. Although he is the supreme exponent of *verismo*, he is not in any meaningful sense a programmatic writer. He writes to express his view of life; and here lie both his strength and his weakness. His method—to withdraw himself entirely from the narrative—was new in Italian literature, even though he inevitably projects his own concerns into plot and character. In Verga's fiction people cannot find peace even when they kill. The 'she wolf' in the story of that name cannot stand life without her son-in-law, Nanni, even if he kills her; and he has in the end to kill her with an axe in order to resist her sexual attraction for him. In *The House by the Medlar Tree* the moneylender who bleeds the family white is seen —one feels—more as an instrument of destructive fate than as a villain. And yet his fiction expresses both the terror of fate—particularly as this takes the form of vagaries of the weather—and passion of primitive people with an incomparable vividness and tenderness. He may (or may not) be wrong in his 'philosophy'; but he understands the life of his Sicilians. And his notion of the nature of life is itself not unjustified in the light of the nature of life in Sicily: 'The donkey must be beaten, because he can't beat us; if he could, he'd smash us under his hooves and rip our flesh apart'. In any case, he contrasts fate's malevolence with the will to survive—and with, in

The House by the Medlar Tree, the fact of survival against all odds.

But Verga's greatest achievement was to invent a language which, while it would not shut him off from the general reader who could not understand the Sicilian dialect, would validly express the thoughts, feelings and speech of Sicilians. Thus, he withdraws his own voice from the narrative and tells his story through his characters' thoughts, feelings and actions. He successfully translates from the Sicilian into a literary vernacular. He is modern, then, whether consciously or not: unlike some naturalists of other countries he no longer aims at 'photography', mimesis: he is as concerned to make an imaginative reconstruction as he is to create an imaginary language. He is at his best when he is at his least dialectical, at his most intuitive. Then he is the most distinguished regional novelist—with the exception of Hardy—of the nineteenth century.

If Verga had a rival in the latter half of the nineteenth century then it was the very different ANTONIO FOGAZZARO (1842–1911), who was born in Vincenza, near Venice. Fogazzaro was the pupil of the priest-poet Giacomo Zanella (1820–88), whose programme of reconciliation between Catholic faith and scientific advance he inherited. Fogazzaro's romantic first novel, *The Woman* (*Malombra,* 1881; tr. F. T. Dickson, 1907), incorporates a dash of realism into its torrid romantic and sentimental Gothic, but is not important. *Daniele Cortis* (1885; tr. I. R. Tilton, 1887; S. L. Simeon, 1890) is an improvement. Cortis is a politician who loves his cousin; duty to the Church wins, but not before the author has made his own liberal views clear. Fogazzaro's four subsequent novels form a loosely connected series: *The Patriot, The Man of the World, The Saint* and *Leila* (*Piccolo mondo antico,* 1895; *Piccolo mondo moderno,* 1900; *Il santo,* 1905; *Leila,* 1910; all tr. M. Prichard-Agnetti, 1906–11; the first has been tr. W. J. Strachan, *The Little World of the Past,* 1962). The best of these is the first, because in it Fogazzaro maintains a convincing balance between the rational and irrational. Its 'little old world' is that of the Fifties, before the Austrians were driven from Lombardy. It is a study of a husband and wife, Franco and Luisa. Eventually their little girl is drowned; Franco accepts this as God's will; Luisa will not do so, and tries to contact her through spiritualism —previously she has been a practical, no-nonsense woman. Eventually she is able to come to terms with her loss by having a new child—a son who will figure in the later books. This is rightly considered one of the leading novels of the latter half of the nineteenth century: it is strong in characterization, brilliant in its use of dialogue, and, above all, delightful in its humour. Its successors are more obvious pleas for the Church to humanize and modernize itself (the Church's response was to place them on the Index), and they do not achieve such complex portraits as those of Franco and Luisa.

D'Annunzio's chief work was done in verse, and he is considered as a poet here. One associated with him, and like him hailed by the fascists, was ALFREDO ORIANI (1852–1909), who exploited all the worst aspects of both decadent romanticism and squalid naturalism. His first novels are theatrical self-indulgences; his later books, with one exception, are concerned with enterprises

as well as terrible. He increasingly indulged, in the last twenty years of his life, in a sort of exasperated causticity and false bitterness. It seems that only an inferior novel, *Wanted—a Wife* (*Io cerco moglie*, 1920; tr. F. T. Cooper, 1923; N. L. Brown, 1929) has been translated into English. Much better is *Lesbia's Kiss* (*Il bacio di Lesbia*, 1937), where his neurotic view of women turns into something of interest.

*

ITALO SVEVO (ps. ETTORE SCHMITZ, 1861–1928), like Saba (q.v.) a native of Trieste, had to wait until he was sixty-five before he gained recognition. His subject could be described as literature as an antidote to failure. Svevo was born of German-Italian and Jewish parentage. His early education took place in Bavaria. He then had a business training, but around the age of thirty turned to literature. He wrote *A Life* (*Una vita*, 1892; tr. A. Colquhoun, 1963), and published it at his own expense. Then came *As a Man Grows Older* (*Senilità* 1898; tr. B. de Zoete, 1962). Neither did well, and Svevo decided to abandon literature. His business—paint, out of which he made a large profit in the First World War—took him from time to time to England, and he went to an Irishman living in Trieste for his English lessons (1906–14). This teacher, James Joyce (q.v.), encouraged him to continue writing. At the end of the First World War Svevo was able to take the advice, and produced *Confessions of Zeno* (*La coscienza di Zeno*, 1923; tr. B. de Zoete, 1962). Joyce arranged for it to be translated into French, and in 1926 Valéry Larbaud (q.v.) presented the author, in his review, as a neglected master. Svevo became famous overnight; the Italians felt resentful, and tried to prove either that Svevo was a bad writer or that their own Montale (q.v.) had 'discovered' him before Larbaud. Svevo enjoyed all this for only a short while before he died in a car crash. A collection of his short stories was published posthumously (1930): *Short Sentimental Journey* (tr. B. de Zoete et al., 1967).

Svevo was a number of different people: the business man, citizen of his city, which he loved; the married man; the alienated Jew; the writer; the invented hero of his own books and stories. He is a peculiar writer. His Triestine people and language—his style is sophisticated but not distinguished—are not typically Italian; he was, indeed, an Austrian citizen until 1918. Svevo can only be called an Italian writer; but he can best be considered in a non-Italian context. It is quite inadequate to call him an Italian regional naturalist: his art is more modern—more nerve-bound, inward-looking—than this will allow for. His characters are helpless: adept at psychoanalyzing themselves, they are not good at succeeding at what they most desire: writing. Zeno is successful at business, as Svevo was, only because he does not want to be a business man and is not interested in business. Svevo's characters even, taking into account the environmental differences, anticipate Bellow's (q.v.) inasmuch as they are trapped self-analysts; however, they are nastier and more fundamentally neurotic than Bellow's. Above all, Svevo is the chronicler of the modern non-man-of-action, the fantasist, the man whose unconscious answer to life is the same as K. Edschmid's (q.v.): 'The world is *there*; it would be foolish to reproduce it'. Svevo's heroes reject life in a series of increasingly refined ways. Alfonso Nitti in *A Life* kills himself; Emilio in *As a Man Grows Older* retreats into fantasy; Zeno actually achieves a triumph, even if it is a comic one.

The first novel, *A Life*, is about insincere love. Alfonso Nitti, working in a bank as Svevo had, becomes the lover of his employer's daughter, whose insincerity corrupts him to the point that, when they inevitably part, he is driven into a boredom that leads him to take his own life. The next novel, *As a Man Grows Older*, is an improvement in subtlety and psychological penetration, and led Joyce and many others to applaud it as his best novel. Emilio falls in love with a vulgar tart; he is not cured until his spinster sister, in dying, reveals her qualities. Then he retreats into a fantasy life in which he can happily live with the 'memory' of a blend of the two women. This is the supreme example of Flaubert's influence intelligently exploited to the full. *Zeno* is one of the comic masterpieces of the century; as Svevo had previously used Flaubert more intelligently than any Italian before him, here he uses Freud in a way that no Italian has done since. Zeno is well aware that his memories are false, that his life-in-the-mind is a lie; his narration of the events of his life, for the purposes of his psychoanalysis, is a 'new novel' (q.v.) both more human and entertaining —and perfect—than the work of any of the modern French exponents of this genre. And Svevo transcends his own sense of mediocrity and misdirected purpose because he succeeds in showing, through the weak-willed Zeno, how even the strong-willed are at the mercy of their own inventions. Basically his work is about art, and about art in its relationship to commerce. In 'The Hoax' an unsuccessful author is tricked by a colleague into believing that an Austrian firm wants the translation rights of his ignored novel; the trick leads him to make a fortune inadvertently. Svevo the detached writer is the satirist of his own bourgeois nature; Zeno seeks, through psychoanalysis, his salvation: authenticity (in the existentialist sense). But Svevo ended *Zeno* by prophesying the invention of the atomic bomb. . . . The problem has not been solved, and he remains a great—and thoroughly untypical—writer. The flatness of his style, which is sometimes grammatically incorrect, suits the commonplaceness of his characters; but it is not altogether a virtue, since it means that certain ex-plorations of experience are unavailable to him.

Italian fiction, having ignored Svevo, did not take advantage of him when he was 'discovered'. He was a true cosmopolitan, speaking both Italian and German (imperfectly), and belonging to a city that did not even become Italian until he was nearly sixty years old. Only Moravia (q.v.) has learnt much from him.

Another odd man out of Italian fiction, although of a very different com-plexion from Svevo—and only a minor writer—is the centenarian FRANCESCO CHIESA (1871), who belongs to Italian Switzerland: the Ticino and the southern valleys of Grisons. Chiesa, an aloof schoolmaster who made his first public pronouncement on cultural matters at the age of eighty-five, is a typical regional writer, who created in his fiction an original, lyrical style. *March* (*Tempo di marzo*, 1925), which is autobiographical, is his best book: an inward history that is remarkable for its restraint and careful craftsmanship. Chiesa, who has written poetry in the style of Carducci, and who single-handedly defended the culture of the Ticino—and thus founded a whole minor school—is the last surviving nineteenth-century figure of the twentieth century; in the Ticino he has been able to maintain this role validly.

*

Futurism, although it originated in Italy, was more important in Russia; in any case it was associated mostly with poets and is dealt with in that category. One critic and novelist who was briefly a futurist—but he, too, began as a poet —was MASSIMO BONTEMPELLI (1878–1960)—an interesting writer, not much heeded outside Italy—who was born at Como. Bontempelli invented his own version of 'magic realism' (q.v.): 'to clothe in a smile the most sorrowful things, and with wonderment the most common things: to make art a miracle instead of a weariness: instead of the clearing away, the dispatching of some routine, an act of magic'. This seems removed from the kind of magic realism that is associated with Hesse and Jünger (qq.v.); and yet Bontempelli wanted to discover 'surreality in reality'. He was a restless but intelligent writer who after his flirtation with futurism founded a magazine that opposed both *avant garde* extravagance and nineteenth-century orthodoxy. His own fiction, written in a severe but readable style, seeks to expose the non-existence of 'ordinariness' by demonstrating that it is composed of atoms of 'magic'. His best novel is *Life and Death of Adria and her Sons* (*Vita e morte di Adria e dei suoi figli*, 1930). He also wrote plays, and was Italy's wittiest aphorist.

BRUNO CICOGNANI (1879), playwright as well as novelist, was born in Florence. He is a more conventional novelist than Bontempelli. He began under the influence of both *verismo* and Fucini's (q.v.) Tuscan realism; the best of his earlier novels is *The Shrike* (*La velia*, 1923). Later Cicognani's approach became more psychological: *Villa Beatrice* (1932), his best book, is a memorable study of a frigid woman. Most of his work since 1940 has been non-fictional: *The Fabulous Age* (1940) is a fascinating account of Cicognani's gifted family and of the Florence he knows so well.

The Sicilian GIUSEPPE ANTONIO BORGESE (1882–1952) is better known and more important as an influential critic, politician, and, at the end of his life, spinner of idealistic schemes for world unity, than as a writer of fiction. But this fiction—notably *Rubè* (1921; tr. 1923), the short stories in *The Passionate Pilgrim* (*Il pellegrino appassionato*, 1933), and those collected in *Novelle* (1950)— had considerable merit. As a critic Borgese was essentially a romantic, although he deplored the fascistic style of his former friend D'Annunzio (whom he described as an 'alluring *mauvais maître*'), and was a partisan—and subsequently a modifier—of Croce's intuitionist philosophy (Croce published his first book, a history of Italian romantic criticism, in 1905). The heroes of his novels are impoverished intellectuals who do too much thinking and not enough acting, and thus destroy themselves. Borgese left Italy soon after the fascists took power, and for the rest of his life was a professor in American universities. His second wife was a daughter of Thomas Mann's (q.v.). Borgese was a better novelist than philosopher—his philosophical equipment was not impressive— and *Rubè* is not only a justified prophecy of disaster but also a moving portrait of a powerless and doomed intellectual. This was what Borgese really felt himself to be; but he tried to compensate for it by his sentimental although well-meant work for peace and world federation.

ENRICO PEA (1881–1958), an autodidact, was born in Seravezza. He worked as a marble cutter and, he says, as a 'workman, manufacturer and merchant' in Egypt before deciding to become a writer. Pea was never wholly accepted by critics or public. His work is unusual but not wholly original, being based on old and sometimes deliberately obscure literary patterns. His best work, the novel *Moscardino* (1922), the first part of which Ezra Pound (q.v.) translated but did not publish, combines conventional realism with a rich style and some fine descriptions of nature. *Zutina* (1949) is his most outstanding later work.

FEDERIGO TOZZI (1883–1920), who came from Siena, resisted his early education and worked, for a time, for the railways. His earlier books are auto-biographical and somewhat D'Annunzian; but the three novels upon which, with his short stories, his now considerable reputation rests—*With Closed Eyes* (*Con gli occhi chiusi*, 1919), *Three Crosses* (*Tre croci*, 1920; tr. 1921) and *The Farm* (*Il podere*, 1921), are outstanding in Italian fiction. Pirandello (q.v.) admired Tozzi; but it was Borgese (q.v.) who waged the campaign that established his reputation. Tozzi's work looks naturalistic; but in fact it served him as a ritual magic by which he could neutralize or even gain power over what frightened and alienated him: people. 'Naturalism narrates by virtue of ex-plaining', Giacomo Debenedetti said, 'whereas Tozzi narrates inasmuch as he cannot explain'. And as Debenedetti has shown, Tozzi's central myth, of blindness to life, a particularly drastic sensation of alienation, arose from an almost frantic castration anxiety: this is most forcefully expressed in the scene in *With Closed Eyes* when Pietro, with stunned horror, witnesses all the male animals of the farm being castrated indiscriminately—at his father's order. *Bestie* (1917) is autobiographical, and contains some magnificent, subtle and sensitive writing about childhood. *With Closed Eyes* is also autobiographical in inspiration; Pietro deliberately fails in love. In *Three Crosses* Tozzi objectifies his concerns: this is the powerful story of three Sienese brothers who have forged a promissory note and dread exposure—which, with death, rapidly overtakes them. *The Farm* is more autobiographical: Remigio Selmi leaves his job on the railways to take over the farm his father has left him (as Tozzi did). He proceeds to destroy this property with a savage determination, falling into the hands of every crook he can find. But in the end Remigio, defeated at law, branded as a criminal, has triumphed: he has overcome his father. Mention should be made of Tozzi's comparatively early work (written in 1910), the revealing *Diary of a*

Clerk (*Ricordi d'un impiegato*, 1927) whose text was curtailed and remodelled by Borgese; it did not appear in its proper form until 1960, when Tozzi's son published it. Tozzi used to be unfavourably compared to his early idol, D'Annunzio; now it is beginning to be realized just how superior he was.

MARINO MORETTI (1885), who was born in Romagna, began as one of the *crepuscolari* (q.v.). Moretti himself fiercely resists this classification, but there is no doubt that the manner of his early poems and prose-poems is crepuscular: everything is soaked in the uniform grey of helpless melancholy.

Although Corazzini and Gozzano (qq.v.) are superior poets, and the chief *crepuscolari*, it was to a collection of poems by Moretti, in fact, that Borgese first applied the term crepuscular. Moretti's poetry, and the provincial short stories he turned to when he found the poetic mode unsuitable, are characterized by a 'humble' and colloquial style—a deliberate reaction to D'Annunzio's bombast. Indeed, all Moretti's fiction—he first turned to the novel in 1916— may be seen as a reaction to D'Annunzio: his characters are 'ordinary', battered by meaningless life. The heroine of *Saturday's Sun* (*Il sole del sabato*, 1916) has nothing—not even wisdom—except courage. This is one of the earliest and best of those many Italian novels of this century which portray the nobility with which women face their ordeal from the selfishness of men and the un- friendliness of fate. The successors to this novel present similar characters, mostly women. Only *L'Andreana* (1935), often regarded as his best book, presents a character who is not entirely passive. Moretti has very definite limitations, but within them he is a delicate and penetrating psychologist.

RICCARDO BACCHELLI (1891), born at Bologna, is a more substantial novelist, and one of infinitely wider range: he has tried poetry, drama and pretty well every kind of novel. Bacchelli began his literary career as an associate of the writers around the magazines *La Voce* (Florence) and *La Ronda* (Rome), both of which he edited for a time. These periodicals represented a more or less intelligent and traditionalist neo-classical approach, and Bacchelli has remained a traditional writer. Bacchelli, as his best known novel, the massive *The Mill on the Po* (*Il mulino del Po*, 1938–40; tr. F. Frenaye and S. Hood, 1952–5), demonstrates, is a master of straight narrative in an age that has on the whole rejected it. He is gifted enough to have profited from Manzoni and Fogazzaro (q.v.), from whom he has learned, writes one critic, 'to cover his robust sensuality under a veil of Catholic unction'. *The Mill on the Po* deals with several generations of a family of millers, the Scacerni, from 1812 to 1918. This is an efficient and well written nineteenth-century novel, which deserves its reputation. Earlier novels by Bacchelli include *The Devil at Long Bridge* (*Il diavolo al Pontelungo*, 1927; tr. O. Williams, 1929), about Bakunin's attempt to organize a revolutionary movement in Emilia, and *Love Town* (*La città degli amanti*, 1929; tr. O. Williams, 1930). The first is a vivid and effective historical novel; the second—about a love-Utopia built by an American tycoon in which, of course, true love cannot flourish—is too self-conscious. *The Fire of Milan* (*L'incendio di Milano*, 1952; tr. K. Nott, 1958), which sensitively traces the fate of various people at the time of Mussolini's downfall, and *Son of Stalin* (*Il figlio di Stalin*, 1953; tr. K. Nott, 1956), about Stalin's son Jacob, are excellent in their straightforward way, as is *The Three Slaves of Julius Caesar* (*I tre schiavi di Giulio Cesare*, 1958). *Hamlet* (*Amleto*, 1919) is a modernization of interest and merit. *The Aphrodite* (*L''Afrodite'*, 1969) is an acute and sensitive psychological study of a woman set on a ship off the Salentrio Peninsula, which is evoked with mastery.

Bacchelli's contemporary, the Milanese CARLO EMILIO GADDA (1893) has received more critical attention, and rightly so: he is a pioneer who was content to remain unapplauded for many years in order to accomplish exactly what he wanted. He has the best-developed sense of humour of all the Italian writers of the century. He belongs to the non-establishment side of Italian literature—a considerable achievement in itself. His wildly exuberant, macaronic style—an interfusion of colloquialisms, obsolete, foreign and technical words and dialect—is inimitable. Gadda does owe something, however, to CARLO DOSSI (ps. ALBERTO PISANI, 1849–1910), a Pavian who failed to achieve himself ('the lamp was soon clogged by too much oil and afterwards only smoked') but whose neologisms and insistence on the introduction of idiomatic Italian into his style were prophetic and influential. Dossi's fury at human crassness overcame his love, but he remains a badly neglected writer.

Gadda, who was an engineer (he built the Vatican power-stations, and wrote the official descriptions of them) before he took to full-time writing, is a difficult writer; he is both anti-literary and anti-middlebrow: he certainly protects the 'average reader' from contamination: by erecting a learned barrier of language. Although satirical in effect (but who, writing truthfully of modern society, can avoid this?), Gadda is not a moralist. For him words are things—magic and mysterious things. Thus his approach is poetic. Writers to whom, in certain respects only, he might be compared are Céline (q.v.)—creation of a 'voice' on a page—and the younger German writer Arno Schmidt (q.v.)—'preposterous', deliberately narcissistic experimentation. One thing is certain: Gadda is untranslatable. William Weaver's literal rendering (1966) of the best known of the novels, *That Awful Mess on Via Merulana* (*Quer pasticciaccio brutto de Via Merulana*, 1957), which is expert and hardly improvable, functions as little more than a kind of guide to the original. Further, Gadda is as unfriendly to the literati as he is to the middlebrow audience. He is solitary, pessimistic, sophisticated. Gadda works on words and then sees what his workings become. His writing does not describe, but expresses.

Much of Gadda's earlier work has been collected in *Dreams and Illumination* (*I sogni e la folgore*, 1955). His two major novels came late. *That Awful Mess* is a detective story in which the bourgeois reader is teased and mocked by having a 'solution' withdrawn from him. Two crimes, a jewel theft and a brutal murder, are investigated by Ingravallo, a police officer who is really no more than the sensitive, ironizing instrument of Gadda's own sensibility. The time is 1927, the place Rome, the air heavy with fascism. The two crimes reveal the existence of untold viciousness and corruption. The autobiographical *Acquainted with Grief* (*La cognizione del dolore*, 1963; tr. W. Weaver, 1969) is a more fragmentary work set in an imaginary South American country that is in fact based on the author's recreation, in his mind, of Lombardy. . . . The hero suffers from a mysterious illness which makes his life impossible. Gadda's most recent work is *Eros and Priapus: From Frenzy to Ashes* (*Eros e Priapo: da furore a cenere*, 1967); this is as complex as anything he has written: an analysis of what happened to the Italian people under fascism—and of why it happened. This writer, who describes himself as 'a solitary glutton, unmarried and melancholy, and subject to fits of cyclothymia', is one of Europe's more important. (ISS; BISS)

CORRADO ALVARO (1895–1956), born in Calabria, made his living by journalism. He began as a poet. In Alvaro there is a characteristically modern conflict, never fully resolved, between liberal realism and a solipsist escapism born of disgust and despair. His masterpiece is undoubtedly *The People in Aspromonte* (*Gente in Aspromonte*, 1930), in which he in effect contrasts the innocence of his childhood recollections of Calabria (how Calabria could, should be) with the harsh reality (how Calabria is). The tension between poetic dream and reality is not as successfully maintained in the cycle of novels about Rinaldo Diacono: *The Brief Age* (*L'età breve*, 1946), *Mastrangelina* (1960) and *Everything is Happening* (*Tutto è accaduto*, 1961). (BISS)

GIUSEPPE TOMASI, PRINCIPE DI LAMPEDUSA (1896–1957), was a wealthy Sicilian Prince who wrote his single novel *The Leopard* (*Il gattopardo*, 1958; tr. A. Colquhoun, 1960) in the last three years of his life. It was posthumously published, and he never knew the enormous fame that it brought him. The typescript was discovered by Bassani (q.v.). This story of the Sicilian Prince Fabrizio in the Sixties of the last century is frankly archaic; but its archaism is at every point tempered by the most sophisticated considerations. It is a masterful, confidently delineated portrait of one complex man: cruel, lustful, brave, always sure in action, uncertain in mind. No nineteenth-century writer could have written this nineteenth-century tale; but few twentieth-century writers could have handled its simplicities in the way this one does. The Prince watches the Garibaldian destruction of the Bourbon monarchy, to which he is tied, with what the author called 'historic nausea', and yet with a strange calm. *Two Stories and a Memory* is a partial translation (A. Colquhoun, 1962) of *Racconti* (1961), more posthumous fiction and some finely written auto-biography.

IGNAZIO SILONE (PS. SECONDO TRANQUILLI, 1900), born in Aquila, has developed from communism to Christianity. His brother was murdered in jail in Mussolini's early years; Silone himself escaped and finally settled in Switzerland. He returned to Italy in 1944. His standing as an anti-fascist and socialist activist is high in his country; but his fiction is more admired outside Italy. When we compare the quality of his response to fascism to Gadda's we see his shortcomings as a writer, for it is the latter who is so much more penetrating—if also, of course, more difficult. *Fontamara* (1933; tr. G. D. and E. Mosbacher, 1934) is not, as has often been pointed out, a realistic novel: its Abruzzi peasants are too idealized, and some of its fascists are too caricatured. The nobility arising from this book (Silone's best) and from its author's life has a quality perhaps more philosophico-political than literary. By this is meant that his imaginative exploration of reality is vitiated by his devotion to causes that, however dignified in human terms, are abstract. There is in Silone's work little creative autonomy. The techniques of *Fontamara* were almost exclusively those of Verga (q.v.); but it is only at the distance of forty years, perhaps, that we begin to see that this version of reality is rather a theorized humanitarian photograph than something that welled up from its creator's imagination. Its successors have tried to rationalize Silone's predicament; but too often a crude and obtrusive symbolism has replaced subtlety of observation. *Bread and Wine* (*Pane e vino*, 1937; rev. as *Vino e pane*, 1955; tr. H. Fergusson II, 1964) and *The Seed Beneath the Snow* (*Il seme sotto la neve*, 1941; tr. F. Frenaye, 1943) deal with Pietro Spina, who eventually dies for another man's crime; in this character Silone describes his own evolution from communist to primitive Christian socialist. *A Handful of Blackberries* (*Una manciata di more*, 1952; tr. D. Silone, 1954), which is technically almost disastrous—careless, tiredly written, badly put together, with a crude central symbol—treats of the disillusion of a communist when he is forced to choose between party discipline and the peasants who love and trust him. The discussion of this problem remains on an emotionally naïve level, and not all Silone's skill in anecdote, his strongest quality, can rescue it. The instinct of Silone's countrymen about his fiction seems right.

CARLO LEVI (1902), born in Turin, trained as a doctor; like Silone, he has been active in anti-fascist politics. He is also a painter. Essentially Levi is a journalist rather than a novelist; but at his best he is a journalist of genius. Levi's most famous book is *Christ Stopped at Eboli* (*Cristo si è fermato a Eboli*, 1945; tr. F. Frenaye, 1948); he wrote it out of his experiences when he was exiled, by the fascists, to the remote region of Lucania. He treats of a village so secluded that Christianity has never come to it—Christ having stopped at Eboli. This remains one of the most vivid and poignant descriptions of the Southern way of life to have been written in the past half-century. More convincing as fiction, however, is *The Watch* (*L'orologio*, 1950; tr. J. Farrar, 1952), about the liberation and its chaotic aftermath.

FRANCESCO JOVINE (1902–50), a teacher, came from Abruzzi. He wrote a number of novels and short stories, but completed his single masterpiece (which incidentally contains far more authentic portraits of peasants than *Fontamara*) at the very end of his life: *The Estate in Abruzzi* (*Le terre del Sacramento*, tr. A. Colquhoun, 1952). Jovine is Italy's worthiest successor to Verga as a regionalist; and his attitude (certainly anticlerical and left-wing) does not obtrude in *The Estate in Abruzzi*, which is a most impressively truthful picture of life in the region. Jovine's selection of detail is masterly; most striking of all is his vision of the peasants, who seem half legendary in their grand isolation from history and civilization.

DINO BUZZATI (ps. DINO BUZZATI TRAVERSO, 1906–72), born at Belluno in the extreme north of Venetia, was one of Italy's veteran *avant gardists*. Kafka is the chief influence upon him—indeed, to such an extent as to become a positive hindrance to his own development. But he is a more considerable novelist than

Kafka's English imitator, Rex Warner (q.v.): the manner comes naturally to him, whereas Warner took it over without well understanding it. Buzzati has in any case written one undoubted classic: *The Bears' Famous Invasion of Sicily* (*La famosa invasione degli orsi in Sicilia*, 1945; tr. 1946). This is for children, but let no one be deceived. . . . Perhaps Buzzati is at his best when writing in this relaxed style. But the indisputably adult *The Tartar Steppe* (*Il deserto dei Tartari*, 1940; tr. S. Hood 1952), about a garrison waiting to prove its valour, is an impressively profound anti-fascist novel published at a time when it was an achievement to criticize the regime at all. The young officer Giovanni Drogo waits for an enemy attack in vain; only when he is an old man does there seem a chance that the garrison will be forced to defend itself. *Larger Than Life* (*Il grande ritratto*, 1960; tr. H. Reed, 1962) is an unsuccessful novel about a computer. Better is *A Love Affair* (*Un amore*, 1963; tr. J. Green, 1965): this is Buzzati's most realistic book, and in spite of passages of boredom, the central theme—of the unwittingly commercial nature of the architect Antonio Dongo's obsession with a call-girl—is well brought out. Nothing Buzzati wrote is without intelligence and interest; a children's writer of genius, he always seems on the verge of an adult masterpiece. *Poem in Cartoons* (*Poema a fumetti*, 1969) is a *tour de force* in which he combines his talents as a painter with his experimental literary genius: it retells, in modern terms, the Orpheus legend. Buzzati's plays are discussed further on.

MARIO SOLDATI (1906), from Turin, was educated by Jesuits. He is known as a film-director as well as a novelist. He has reacted against his upbringing, but only in his short stories (the form in which he has done his best work) does he succeed in escaping from it. He writes too much, but is skilful, professional and readable; his feeling of freedom from his upbringing tends to make him deliberately flippant, and one often feels that his intelligence and sensibility are somewhat wasted. His best fiction is in the form of sketches evoking a single mood; 'Footsteps in the Snow' (ISS), a good example, sums up a man's entire sexuality in a few short sentences. *The Commander Comes to Dine* (*A cena col Commendatore*, 1950; tr. 1952) contains three more of his best stories. His later writing has tended to be increasingly tedious, predictable and flippant.

ALBERTO [PINCHERLE] MORAVIA (1907), a Roman, has gained a wide international reputation since the Second World War. But opinion on his merits is sharply divided, especially in his own country. Moravia was an ardent anti-fascist, and after having seen his books personally vetoed by the Duce had the honour of seeing them put (1952) on the now discontinued Index. Moravia is an exceptionally intelligent man, of great integrity and creative gifts, who has somehow not been able to go far enough beyond his main original theme, which is that men indulge in sex because they cannot love—and that they enjoy prostitutes because in that way they can find contact with other bored, frustrated, guilty men. But Moravia's approach to this is so unusual, so full of feeling and incidental observations of human behaviour, that almost all his work is none the less remarkable and rewarding. Only very recently has it shown signs of falling off. Like Svevo, whose influence Moravia is the only Italian writer to have thoroughly absorbed, he is a Jew. His response to his anguish at the destruction of individuality and individual freedom in our time has been to try to identify himself with those who cause this destruction and with those who suffer it. He has succeeded to a remarkable degree. He has much utterly genuine tenderness for the downtrodden. He has been regarded by good critics as a great writer; and if great writing were simply a matter of empathy with those whom it describes, then the judgement would be correct. But Moravia has not yet quite succeeded in analyzing his own sense of sexual *ennui*. He has only succeeded—and this is of course a distinction in itself—in portraying a memorable gallery of characters. He has not succeeded, as some would say Svevo did, in penetrating to the terrible heart of human solitariness; perhaps it might be argued that it is his very lack of coldness which prevents him from doing so. The question of his stature remains a difficult one. Most of his novels and stories have been excellently translated into English by Angus Davidson.

If Moravia is a great writer then it is for three books: his first, *The Time of Indifference* (*Gli indifferenti*, 1929; tr. 1953), the novella 'The Epidemic' ('L'epidemia', 1944) and *The Woman of Rome* (*La romana*, 1947; tr. 1949). *The Time of Indifference* gives an unforgettable picture of middle-class Rome under the corrupting influence of fascism, of people using one another as sexual machines and yet desiring to change this. 'The Epidemic' is a fable about a society that adapts itself to a loathsome epidemic, a foul stench of death (fascism), by regarding it as a sweet scent. In *The Woman of Rome* Moravia examines the life of a Roman prostitute with love and in fascinated and often brilliantly sensual detail.

It is one of the few modern novels in which woman is seen as the victim of men's anguished attempt at communication with one another; but it is a novel without homosexual slyness or hatred. Modern urban life frustrates man's need to communicate socially, and therefore sexually, in a meaningful way. Woman suffers. That is what *The Woman of Rome* is about, but Moravia does not fully realize this, even intuitively; but he does describe Adriana, his heroine, with a compensatorily full love and bewilderment—the bewilderment emerging as an obsession with physical description of her. Other fine novels by Moravia include his third, containing a grotesque picture of Mussolini, *The Fancy Dress Party* (*La mascherata*, 1941; tr. 1947) and *The Empty Canvas* (*La noia*, 1960; tr. 1961), almost exclusively about frantic sexual activity failing to alleviate the monotony of an existence in which the hero does not believe. But Moravia's limitation remains, really, his insistence on realism. When persecuted by fascists he was forced to turn to fable and even to a sort of semi-surrealism. He now needs to make similar explorations in order to fulfil his enormous potential. Some of his criticism has been collected in *Man as an End* (*L'uomo come fine*, 1963; tr. B. Wall, 1965): it is as consistently humane and intelligent as his style is impeccable.

One might say that VITALIANO BRANCATI (1907–54), who was Sicilian, represents the sexual conscience the Southern male does not want to possess. His first novel, the uncharacteristic *The Lost Years* (*Gli anni perduti*, 1941), is a graceful caricature of provincial Italian society. In later novels—*Don Giovanni in Sicilia* (1942), *Antonio, the Great Lover* (*Il bell'Antonio*, 1949; tr. V. Kean, 1952), *Paul the Hot* (*Paolo il caldo*, 1955)—he explores the motives of Southern promiscuity. In the first this is satirized as wholly empty: a product of fear of impotence, swagger and fantasy. In the second the hero is actually impotent. The third is more complex, and tries, without complete success, to deal with the problem of the conflict between convention and sexual need. Brancati was a lively and comic minor writer: readable, liberal in outlook, and intelligent. The short story collection *Old Man in Boots* (*Il vecchio con gli stivali*, 1945) contains some effective portrayals of fascist types.

The journalist, literary critic and novelist GUIDO PIOVENE (1907), from Vicenza, was trained as a philosopher. He is a shrewd exposer of the (in existentialist terms) 'bad faith' (q.v.) of respectable people; he is often criticized, not altogether without justice, as abstract and lacking in vigour; but nevertheless he has not by any means had his due. It may be true that Piovene writes of his wealthy, pious, aristocratic Catholics as though their 'world . . . were the only possible one'; but this is just what such people, whose depravity and criminal impulses Piovene so brilliantly lays bare, themselves assume. Furthermore, Piovene understands this sick world more thoroughly than any living Italian writer. And he may be defended from the charge of negativism on two grounds: the society he portrays is an effete one, and in any case in showing his characters playing little pleasure-games with their consciences he also shows them at their nearest to a human authenticity: they yearn to be themselves rather than a bundle of depraved impulses. Piovene's first novel was *The Merry Widow* (*La vedova allegra*, 1931); this was directly in the tradition of the eighteenth-century French psychological novel. Its successor, the scathing *Confessions of a Novice* (*Lettere di una novizia*, 1941; tr. E. Wilkins, 1950), revived the epistolary form. *The Furies* (*Le furie*, 1963), in which he returned to the novel form after fifteen years, is in fact hardly a novel at all, but rather an account of why the author cannot write one. The furies of the title are what prevented Piovene from putting imaginary characters in the real setting of the district of Venetia where he spent his childhood. In *The Furies* he meets the real people of that district—and he meets his own invented people. This was as badly received as it was misunderstood; but it is a haunting and deeply interesting book by Italy's leading heir to and developer of the tradition of Fogazzaro.

CESARE PAVESE (1908–50), novelist, poet, translator, born near Cuneo in Piedmont, killed himself in Turin in August 1950. His suicide shocked all literate Italy, and set sensitive people to examining themselves in much the same way as Hart Crane's (q.v.) death seventeen years previously had affected Americans. Pavese had his own neuroses and hopeless yearnings—he would attach himself romantically and unhappily to sexual objects that he knew (if only unconsciously) could never relate to him—but he was close enough to the sensibility of his generation in Italy to reveal, when he decided to end his life, a crisis of conscience and determination. He is an important and a good writer;

but he may none the less have been slightly overrated. But by this I mean no more than that such remarks as 'Incontrovertibly the greatest "European" writer produced by Italy' are insufficiently cautious—and in any case not perhaps very useful. After all, why compare Pavese with Svevo? Let us have both. As to categories: like Moravia, Pavese is unquestionably a neo-realist— but in the case of an author as sensitive as this, the term becomes inadequate: a whole poetic and symbolic system arises from the narrative.

Pavese remained convinced throughout his life, as his diary of fifteen years, *This Business of Living* (*Il mestiere di vivere*, 1952; tr. A. E. Murch, 1961) continually reveals, that life is not worth living unless for others. An acutely sensitive man, who took himself with a desperate seriousness that his playful and intelligent irony could not hide, he found relating to other people very difficult. His suicide is thus important because it was only partly neurotic; the element of neurosis in it was possibly his sexual self-loathing: with women he was undoubtedly as difficult as Kafka (q.v.). But Pavese's disillusion with politics was certainly not neurotic. His gesture was ultimately a return to himself— even a sparing of others. In the solitude of mysterious death he may have felt he could find not only peace but self-sufficiency.

Pavese's style was profoundly influenced by the English and American authors he (excellently) translated: Defoe, Dickens, Melville (his *Moby Dick* is a masterpiece of the art of translation), Gertrude Stein and Faulkner (qq.v.). Throughout his life he worked as an editor in the Turin publishing firm he co-founded: Einaudi. He was imprisoned for being involved with anti-fascists in 1935, and spent a year at Brancaleone Calabro.

Pavese wrote poetry all his life, and his first book was of poetry (*A Mania for Solitude: Selected Poems*, tr. M. Crosland, 1969). Here, although he was not at his best in this form, is to be discovered the key to his complex personality: the stark and tragic contrasts between town and country, experience and innocence, adulthood and childhood—and that questing for the meaning of the state of maturity which led him to quote the 'ripeness is all' passage from *King Lear* as the epigraph to his last and best novel, *The Moon and the Bonfire* (*La luna e i falò*, 1950; tr. L. Sinclair, 1952).

Among Pavese's novels the most outstanding are *Before the Cock Crows* (*Prima che il gallo canti*, 1949); the three novellas contained in *The Beautiful Summer* (*La bella estate*, 1949), consisting of the title-story, *The Devil in the Hills* (*Il diavolo sulle colline*, tr. D. D. Paige, 1954) and *Among Women Only* (*Tra donne sole*, tr. D. D. Paige, 1953); and, above all, *The Moon and the Bonfire*. This, written in Pavese's uniquely evocative style (a mixture of Piedmontese and literary Italian), establishes its own extraordinary rhythm, and at the same time reveals that the past was as fundamentally the basis of Pavese's art as it was of Proust's. Anguilla ('eel' in Italian: the eel returns to its birthplace) returns to his Italian mountain village after twenty years in America. The novel is about Anguilla's re-creation, with his friend Nuto's help, of his idyllic past; and about the anguish of seeing these painfully constructed memories disintegrate in the present. It is a tragic novel, which indicts the present and future in such a way as to give an unmistakable pointer to Pavese's ragingly bitter, although still gentle, mood when he finished it. He saw no sexual hope for himself. He might have surmounted that; but, as he said in a letter a few days before he took the dose of sleeping pills that ended his life: 'I've finished with politics'. Much of his subtle and sensitive thinking is to be found in *Dialogues with Leuco* (*Dialoghi con Leuco*, 1945: tr. W. Arrowsmith and D. S. Carne-Ross, 1953).

ELIO VITTORINI (1908–66), born at Syracuse in Sicily, is more important than his putative position as Italy's leading post-war advocate of social realism, although of a modified sort, might lead us to suppose. Like Pavese (than whom, however, he was a much more vociferous partisan of 'neo-realism') Vittorini had in the fascist Thirties to confine himself largely to the making of translations: he chose Defoe, D. H. Lawrence, Faulkner, Hemingway and Saroyan (qq.v.). This apprenticeship, and Vittorini's own vigorous anti-fascism, grafted a 'tough guy' element onto his natural lyricism. (His method of learning English was to translate *Robinson Crusoe* by looking up each word in a dictionary.) Vittorini's political commitments involved him not only in the usual difficulties connected with social realism, but also in personal ones: he is hardly to be described as a natural realist, and his literary criticism by no means resembles that of a simple-minded advocate of socialism twinned with cheering mimesis. No man who said, 'Poetry is poetry for this reason: because it does not remain tied to the things from which it originated and can be related, if it is born out of pain, to any pain', as Vittorini did, could be described as a simplistic critic. And it was that kind of 'poetry' to which Vittorini aspired, although he was also concerned to show how all men are brothers because their physical experiences are the same: that the kind of loneliness from which Pavese suffered is a tragic illusion, a sinister and distorting filter. Vittorini's first novel—*The Red Carnation* (*Il garofano rosso*, pt. 1933–5; 1948; tr. A. Bower, 1953)—was suppressed by the fascists. It deals sensitively with the growth of an adolescent at the time of the emergence of fascism; this is one of the books to which one would go—in preference to most of the histories—for information about the Italian young of the Twenties. Then came Vittorini's finest achievement: *Conversation in Sicily* (*Conversazione in Sicilia*, 1939; tr. W. David, 1949). It was the censorship that helped to give this novel its great power: Vittorini was obliged to modify his political emotions, which (as Donald Heiney has pointed out) emerged as poetry. The narrator, Silvestro, lives in Milan but has returned to his native Sicily to visit his mother. His journey represents a dark night of the soul. *Conversation in Sicily* is so successful a study of the human rottenness that led Italy into fascism just because it avoids (has to avoid to achieve publication) overt politics. The three novels Vittorini wrote after this—*Men and Non-Men* (*Uomini e no*, 1945), *Tune for an Elephant* (*Il Sempione strizza l'occhio a Frejus*, 1947; tr. E. Mosbacher, 1955), *The Women of Messina* (*Le donne di Messina*, 1949) contain useful and sometimes successful experimental writing, but fail as wholes: the author has become theory-ridden. *Woman on the Road* (*Erica*, 1961; tr. F. Keene and B. Wall, 1961) contains three tales, of which 'Erica', about prostitution, is entirely successful. Vittorini remained an aware

733

and valuable critic to the end, as the posthumous collection *The Two Tensions* (*Le due tensioni*, 1967) clearly demonstrates.

The Florentine vasco pratolini (1913) although he began as a left-wing supporter of the regime, a national *socialist*, is another anti-fascist realist. During the war he was a partisan. Pratolini is a kind of vitalist in the sense that his love for humanity, not always justified intellectually but none the less deeply felt, shows itself even when he intends to convey disgust. In *A Tale of Santa Croce* (*Il quartiere*, 1945; tr. P. and P. Duncan, 1952) he explores Florence's poorest quarter and discovers, in a highly rhythmical prose, an ancient pattern even in the squalor. He tries to find deeper meaning by taking a bird's-eye view; but he never loses sight of individual misery or joy. This exploration is continued in *A Tale of Poor Lovers* (*Cronache di poveri amanti*, 1947; tr. 1949). Later novels, in which he has attempted to trace the history of the poor from the end of the last century to the present—notably *Metello* (1955) and *Waste* (*Lo scialo*, 1959) —have sometimes presented a sentimental picture; but they also contain passages about collective life that recall and sometimes even surpass Romains (q.v.).

giorgio bassani (1916), born in Bologna, is the novelist who has most sensitively portrayed the fate of the Jews under fascism. *The Garden of the Finzi-Continis* (*Il giardino dei Finzi-Contini*, 1962; tr. I. Quigly, 1963), tracing the pathetic history of a wealthy Jewish family as it pursues its life within its garden walls while inhumanity and menace grow outside, is remarkable; but the earlier *The Gold-Rimmed Spectacles* (*Gli occhiali d'oro*, 1958; tr. I. Quigly, 1960), the study of a homosexual doctor driven into shame and suicide by a vicious young man, while the society around becomes progressively madder, is an even more masterly piece of neo-realism, and one of the most moving of all post-war studies of alienation and cruelty. Bassani's exposure of the origins of fascism in 'respectability' deserves wide currency even in the democracies that have not known fascism. *Behind the Door* (*Dietro la porta*, 1964) is about schoolchildren, in whose transitory life Bassani pessimistically traces the seeds of adult anguish. *The Heron* (*L'airone*, 1968) is about a man who, in the author's own words, wants 'to be like [a stuffed heron] . . . beautiful, motionless, eternal. . . .' The novel is about his last day and his suicide. (BISS)

carlo cassola (1917), a Roman, has remained independent of all schools; he is one of Italy's most popular authors. The chief influence on him, according to himself, is the early Joyce (q.v.). He is an *avant garde* writer, who has rightly been described as in some ways akin to the French 'new novelists' (q.v.); but his main quest is for absolute objectivity. Thus nothing really 'happens' in the stories with which he began his career. He is here an interesting writer, but is sometimes in some danger of becoming a bore inasmuch as one feels that he is putting forward a philosophy rather than creating anything. His novels, often expansions of the earlier stories, represent a great advance. *Fausto and Anna* (*Fausto e Anna*, 1952; tr. I. Quigly, 1960) is about a young man who gives up his love to join the communists, becomes disillusioned by them, and then tries unsuccessfully to reclaim his former love. This is a lyrical and delicate study;

but his outstanding novel is *An Arid Heart* (*Un cuore arido*, 1961; tr. W. Weaver, 1964), about the retreat of a simple girl into lonely isolation after the experience of two unhappy love affairs. (ISS; IWT)

ELSA MORANTE (1918), a Roman like her husband Moravia (q.v.), whom she married in 1941, is Italy's leading woman novelist, although she has published little. Her language is as fine a blend of dialect and standard Italian as that achieved by Pavese. Elsa Morante may with justice be described as a 'magic realist'. The finest of her fiction, *Arturo's Island* (*L'isola di Arturo*, 1957; tr. I. Quigly, 1959), about a boy's loves first for his father and then for his step-mother, does magically mix the fantasy world of childhood with the disillusion of adolescence: one sees childhood crack and break under the strain, and is led to understand how and why it happens.

PIER PAOLO PASOLINI (1922), from Bologna, is an internationally known film-director as well as a poet and novelist. With his obvious gifts and vitality, his 'revisionist' Marxism, his fierce rejection of bourgeois values, his experimentalism, his restlessness, he may in some ways be described as Italy's equivalent to Günter Grass (q.v.); his increasing interest in Christian values and a Catholic way of life (he made a film about Christ) adds a specifically Italian ingredient. He is in his own way as isolated a figure as Cassola; but, unlike Cassola, he is 'news'. Pasolini rejects 'literary' language because he feels that it is that of the ruling classes; he is intent—and here Gadda (q.v.) has exercised a strong influence on him—upon reproducing the speech of ordinary people, but with scholarly accuracy. He has edited a volume of popular poetry. His own poetry, lucid and full of attack, provides an index to his literary personality: constructive, intelligent, indignant—even shocked at the human condition. His two best known novels, *The Ragazzi* (*Ragazzi di vita*, 1955; tr. 1968) and *A Violent Life* (*Una vita violente*, 1959; tr. W. Weaver, 1968), form a a desperate account of the Roman slums, in which the protagonists do not so much speak to one another as to themselves—in strings of savage imperatives, blasphemies, obscenities. . . . The first of these is one of the most brutal and pessimistic books of its age; it appears to offer no hope. *A Violent Life* is less effective because more explicitly Marxist: here a slum boy is politically 'educated', and this education is quite simply unconvincing. What is good here, as in the earlier novel, is Pasolini's descriptive power, his lyrical evocations of filth (somewhat resembling, in their lyricism, Wilfred Owen's, q.v., of conditions and suffering in the First World War trenches). If this is 'nihilist' then polite readers who do not like it must keep away, as indeed they have every right to do. Pasolini's literary work has somewhat declined in power since he self-consciously abandoned his nihilism; his films have improved.

A Sicilian of Jewish parents, NATALIA GINZBURG (1916), was a close friend of Pavese's; her husband Leone, another co-founder of Einaudi, was murdered by Nazis in 1944 after he had been arrested for editing an anti-fascist newspaper. Natalia Ginzburg is, after Elsa Morante, Italy's best known woman writer. She has an extremely personal style—marvellously exemplified in the portrait of her second marriage, 'He and I' (IWT)—sometimes over-influenced

GUIDE TO MODERN WORLD LITERATURE

by Hemingway in its flatness, but at others remarkably effective in its restraint and muted lyricism. Like Pavese, Natalia Ginzburg resolutely avoids sentimentality. Her two first books were published together in one volume in English as *The Road to the City* (1952). All her novellas have been collected together in an Italian edition: *Five Short Novels* (*Cinque romanzi brevi*, 1965). Perhaps her best books are the short stories *Voices in the Evening* (*Le voci della sera*, 1961; tr. 1963) and the autobiography *Family Sayings* (*Lessico famigliare*, 1963; tr. D. Low, 1967). Her excursions into playwriting have met with some commercial but little literary success. (IWT; ISS)

ITALO CALVINO (1923), born in Cuba but brought up at San Remo, has been on the editorial board of Einaudi since 1947. Without shedding his left-wing views, he has moved from a strongly 'committed' position to one of science fiction fantasist and metaphysician in the tradition of Borges (q.v.). His first books dealt with the Resistance: *The Path to the Nest of Spiders* (*Il sentiero dei nidi di ragno*, 1947; tr. A. Colquhoun, 1956) and the story collection *Adam One Afternoon* (*Ultimo viene il corvo*, 1949; sel. tr. A. Colquhoun and P. Wright, 1957). The novel's hero is no political animal, but a tough fourteen-year-old called Pin, who despises everyone until he discovers true warmth and comradeship among a group of partisans. This warmth has arisen spontaneously not from political ideology but from common hatred of fascist inhumanity.

Calvino's later novels are absolutely different in mood and type. His trilogy has been translated into English in two books as *The Non-Existent Knight* and *Baron of the Trees* (*I nostri antenati*, 1952–9; tr. A. Colquhoun, 1959, 62). These are fantastic—in one the viscount-hero is 'cloven' by a cannon-ball into two halves, one good and one bad; in another the protagonist does not in fact exist —but they also look back to the eighteenth-century tradition. The collection *Cosmicomics* (*Le cosmicomiche*, 1965; tr. W. Weaver, 1969) consists of stories the protagonist and teller of each of which is Qfwfq, who is the age of the universe. Each story begins with a different premise. *You with Zero* (*Ti con zero*, 1967) projects even further into the past: Qfwfq now recounts how it felt to be a one-celled creature on the point of dividing into two; then, in a third section, Calvino exploits his theme (of the immortality of protoplasm) to illuminate a modern love-affair. Calvino is a sparkling and humorous writer whose more recent work has not yet quite succeeded in conveying the seriousness of his despair about society and the possibilities of meaningful communication between human beings. (IWT; ISS; BISS)

The prevailing form in Italian fiction after the end of fascism was for many years neo-realism. By 1963 the wheel had come full circle: an *avant garde* movement was formed; it called itself *Gruppo 63*, *Group 63*, in imitation of the German *Group 47* (q.v.). The time-lag is significant. Both Calvino and Pasolini have been associated with the experimental spirit of this group, but little other prose of real significance has yet emerged from it. Gadda still reigns supreme as Italy's experimental writer. There are more *avant garde* poets than writers of *avant garde* fiction; but more critics than either. The more successful of the creative *avant garde* writers have avoided extremism and over-emphasis on technique. This applies to GIOVANNI ARPINO (1927), a Piedmontese, whose *A Crime of Honour* (*Un delitto d'onore*, 1962; tr. R. Rosenthal, 1963) is an outstanding novel on the theme of the Southern male notion that crimes committed to revenge sexual betrayal are 'honourable'. Arpino's treatment of this kind of material is very different from Brancati's (q.v.). A doctor tries to remake a peasant girl into the image he desires, marries her, discovers she is not a virgin— and kills her and another woman, whom he believes to be responsible. The story is told with black irony, but also with understanding of the traditions involved. *The Darkness and the Honey* (*Il buio e il miele*, 1969) is not wholly successful, but contains a memorable portrait of a blinded, embittered but tender army officer (IWT)

BEPPE FENOGLIO (1922–63), who was born and died near Pavese's birthplace, has been saluted as a progressive spirit. In his posthumous and unfinished novel *A Private Question* (*Una questione privata*, 1963; pt. IWT), he discovered a language which illuminated previously unexpressed aspects of the partisan experience (in which he shared). (IWT)

PIER ANTONIO QUARANTOTTI GAMBINI (1910–65), rather an isolated figure, was born at Pola (now Yugoslav). He wrote some fresh, penetrative studies of childhood and adolescence, and of his own native country: *Our Fellow Men* (*I nostri simili*, 1932), *The Hot Life* (*La calda vita*, 1958), and many others. The lucid and evocative quality of his prose is well illustrated in the extract from the novel *Norma's Games* (*I giochi di Norma*, 1964), translated by Gwyn Morris (IWT): all of his that is available in English.

LEONARDO SCIASCIA (1921), a Sicilian, is notable for his powerful evocation of the mentality of the people of his native island. *Death of the Inquisitor* (*Morte dell' Inquisitore*, 1964) is a collection of historical stories about the Inquisition in seventeenth-century Sicily (pt. BISS). Other of his novels both explain and expose the Mafia: *Mafia Vendetta* (*Il giorno della civetta*, 1961; tr. 1963) and *A Man's Blessing* (*A ciascuno il suo*, 1966; tr. A. Foulke, 1969), a truly horrifying tale of a Mafia lawyer who has a chemist and a doctor killed, then a school-master who finds him out—and who then marries the doctor's widow. *The Council of Egypt* (*Il consiglio d'Egitto*, 1963; tr. A. Foulke, 1966) is on a larger scale: the story of a colossally impudent forgery set in late eighteenth-century Palermo, it begins as comedy and ends as real-life *grand guignol*. It is one of the most informative books on Sicily of our time, and has established its author as a fine novelist in the realistic tradition. (IWT)

The Roman ANNA MARIA ORTESE (1915) began as a short-story writer, and then came into some prominence with *The Bay is not Naples* (*Il mare non bagna Napoli*, 1953; tr. 1955), which rather curiously blends realism with a dreaminess and stylistic inconsequence. *The Iguana* (*L'iguana*, 1965) is a fantasy. (IWT)

RENZO ROSSO (1927), from Trieste, has so far written one major novel: *The Hard Thorn* (*La dura spina*, 1963; tr. W. Weaver, 1966), a study of a womanizing pianist whose sexuality and playing are becoming eroded by age. This is an exceedingly subtle study of the decline of an artist who is not quite of the first rank—his performances are syntheses of other artists'; he loves not the music but its form. The ageing process is vividly and subtly conveyed. *The Bait* (*L'adescamento*, 1959; tr. W. Weaver, 1962) consists of short stories. (IWT)

Both PAOLO VOLPONI (1924), from Urbino, and the Roman OTTIERO OTTIERI (1924) are *avant garde* writers who work for Olivetti (no connection is suggested). Both have written experimental sociological novels about industry. Volponi's *My Troubles Began* (*Memoriale*, 1962; tr. B. Sevareid, 1964) created a stir when it came out; but his *The Worldwide Machine* (*La macchina mondiale*, 1965; tr. B. Sevareid, 1967), a study in madness, is a more interesting and original book, with wider implications. An ignorant peasant becomes interested in science and thought; when he gets hold of books he creates a religion for himself out of them, in which man is the botched creation of superior beings. He has it all wrong—or has he?

Ottieri's *The Men at the Gate* (*Donnarumma all'assalto*, 1959; tr. 1962), which is sometimes tedious but always intelligent, sees the opening up of new industry in southern Italy through the eyes of a personnel manager—his own job at Olivetti's.

II

The story of the drama of united Italy is almost, although not quite, exclusively that of Luigi Pirandello. Italian theatre at the beginning of this century was still entirely tied to the past. Dialect theatre had declined and lost its vitality. The best of this period outside Verga (q.v.) is to be found in the Piedmontese GIUSEPPE GIACOSA (1847–1906). But although Giacosa was best known as a dramatist in his own time, and although his plays were skilful, he did his most enduring work in the short story (BISS). He could write every kind of drama— Ibsenite, *verista*, verse melodrama, and so on—but none memorably. He will doubtless survive only as the librettist of three of Puccini's best known operas: *La Bohème*, *Tosca* and *Madame Butterfly*. Although much earlier in time than Galsworthy (q.v.), his was essentially the same sort of theatrical achievement: solid, unadventurous, decent until it came to the threat of criticizing the roots of bourgeois morality or of really offending his audience—fundamentally mediocre.

Various writers better known for their work in other fields wrote dramas that held the stage for a while: D'Annunzio, Capuana, Marinetti (qq.v.; Marinetti wrote most of his plays in French: *Le Roi Bombance* had a première at Lugné-Poë's theatre that resembled that of *Ubu Roi* in all but the quality of the text) and, of course, Verga. But more dramatically percipient were ENRICO BUTTI (1868–1912) and ROBERTO BRACCO (1862–1943), the last part of whose life was ruined—he died in poverty—because he could not get his plays staged under the Mussolini regime. Both of these dramatists went through naturalistic periods, but both reacted away from naturalism. Butti, a Milanese, was a chronically sick man whose natural vitality and humour were modified by a crepuscular (q.v.) melancholy. He was a poor novelist, but his plays were done with skill and a certain disregard for their audience's worst predilections. After his naturalist apprenticeship he tackled a number of 'problem' themes in the manner of Ibsen: mercy killing, agnosticism and so on. He ended as a weary conservative; *The Storm* (*La tempesta*, 1901) attempts to demonstrate the uselessness of revolution.

Bracco, a Neapolitan, is more interesting and much more gifted. Because he opposed the fascists—he was an anti-fascist member of parliament—he was persecuted, and died in poverty. Like Butti, he wrote plays in the naturalistic and Ibsenite traditions; but he went further, to develop a number of his own ideas, and is rightly described as the progenitor of the 'theatre of silence' that was later made famous by Jean-Jacques Bernard (q.v.). He was a versatile playwright who graduated from pastiche of Shaw to drama of genuine psychological depth, which succeeds, often brilliantly, in tracing human motives to their subconscious origins. Bracco is less well known than Bernard—but is a better and more versatile dramatist. *The Holy Child* (*Il piccolo santo*, 1909) and *The Madmen* (*I pazzi*, 1922)—a neglected masterpiece of prophecy which demands revival—are his best dramas. *Bitter Fruit* (*Il frutto acerbo*, 1904) is recognized as one of his funniest comedies. Although an excellent journalist and lively dialect poet, Bracco was before anything else a man of the theatre, whose work foreshadows not just Bernard's theatre of silence but also many other more important developments. One of the earlier, naturalist plays, *Lost in Shadows* (*Sperduti nel buio*, 1901) was filmed in 1914 and then again in 1947, this time with da Sica. The eclipse and persecution of this outstandingly intelligent and gifted dramatist by the forces of evil is one of the major tragedies sustained by Italian literature. Bracco has yet to regain his due on the stages of the world.

Italy's contribution to modern European theatre (leaving the individual genius of Pirandello aside) is the movement known as *teatro grottesco*, the theatre of the grotesque. But even this is really a reflection of expressionism. LUIGI CHIARELLI (1884–1947) called his play *The Mask and the Face* (*La maschera e il volto*, 1916; very freely ad. C. B. Fernald, 1924) a 'grotesque in three acts', and he is often given the credit for the break with realism. *The Mask and the Face*, nearly a first-class play, certainly marks a new departure in Italian theatre: a sick, bored and hypocritical society was ultimately bound to find a satirist who would depict it as grotesque rather than real. Here a cuckolded husband pretends to have killed his wife—in fact he can't bring himself to do it —in order to conform to custom; he stands trial, is acquitted, is congratulated by his wife, and with her flees the country to escape the 'obligations of society'. None of Chiarelli's other plays comes up to the level of *The Mask and the Face*, and even this is somewhat spoiled by an out-of-place sentimentality. However, he wrote some memorably comic scenes, such as the one where a foolish young dancer becomes a cabinet minister and, while haranguing a huge crowd with clichés, bursts instinctively into dance—and is applauded. However, Chiarelli was on the whole an artificer of trite dialogue and situation, and hardly did justice to his 'grotesque' intention of showing characters as anguished ghosts, half-way between torture and glazed laughter.

The futurist poet ENRICO CAVACCHIOLI (1885–1954) learned, as Pirandello did, from Andreyev (q.v.), and wrote at least two plays that amount to a little more than technical *tours de force*: *The Bird of Paradise* (*L'uccello del paradiso*, 1919) and *Pierrot the Lottery Clerk* (*Pierrot impiegato al lotto*, 1925). More important are LUIGI ANTONELLI (1882–1942) and PIER MARIA ROSSO DI SAN SECONDO (ps. PIETRO MARIA ROSSO, 1887–1956), the most important playwright of this group. Antonelli, a thoroughly craftsmanlike dramatist, wrote many plays, of which *The Man Who Met Himself* (*L'uomo che incontrò se stesso*, 1918) and *The Lady in the Shop Window* (*La donna in vetrina*, 1930) are two of the best known. His themes were usually Pirandellian—the sad uselessness of wisdom, man's exploitation of his dream world—and he may have been unlucky to have been Pirandello's contemporary. His characters are more substantial than Chiarelli's, and he is less sentimental.

But Rosso is the most interesting of the exponents of the *grottesco*. Novelist as well as playwright, he is a lyrical and optimistic (in contrast to his friend and fellow Sicilian, Pirandello, who guided him in his career) demonstrator, directly in the tradition of Vico, of man's ultimately poetic nature: Rosso sees all men as exiled from a Platonic world of ideals, and consequently in a bewildered state of mind. Quotidian activity is vile—and Rosso expends his spleen upon it—because the objects of this world reflect the colours of their ideals so palely. Rosso sees life as futile; but his is not—as is sometimes stated— a negative view of life. He is not a sceptic because he is a Platonist. *Marionettes, What Passion!* (*Marionette, che passione!*, 1918) is his most famous play: three actors reveal themselves as the mere puppets of passion as they confess to, and berate one another in public. Their lives have no meaning. They are mad; but only their failure to realize the truth—that life has no meaning—makes them mad. But by 'life' Rosso means 'this life', not 'all life always'. *The Sleeping Beauty* (*La bella addormentata*, 1919) ironically offers hope in the form of the 'Black Man from the Sulphur Pit', a primitive and romantic figure who helps the pregnant village prostitute to get for husband the lawyer who jilted her. Rosso's grimness and cynicism were for long widely misunderstood, partly, perhaps, because of the energy of his attack on life as it is lived. But—leaving the ignored Bracco aside—he was rightly regarded as being second only to Pirandello. His greatest commercial success was *La scala* (1926). Perhaps his most important play, written in 1933 but not produced until the Fifties, will ultimately be seen to be *The Rape of Persephone* (*Il ratto di Proserpina*), the culmination of his lifelong concern with the Persephone myth, in which he found the meaning of life. This makes his Platonic intentions more clear.

LUIGI PIRANDELLO (1867–1936), winner of the Nobel Prize (1934), was a figure as important in world drama as Strindberg or Ibsen (qq.v.). It is quite often suggested, especially by theatre-critics who dislike his pessimism and seek for more comfort from their theatre evenings than he can provide, that his impact on the theatre was not justified by his achievement. This is a suspect judgement: Pirandello is one of the giants of the twentieth century, a wholly sentimentive (q.v.) writer who lived a cruelly unhappy life and who has been badly misunderstood and misinterpreted from the beginning. Although he has been presented in Great Britain, the contemporary British theatre's treatment of him has been somewhat shabby. A Sicilian, he began as poet and philologist, became a teacher and novelist, and was forty before he completed his first play. He went on to write forty-three more; many of these are re-workings of earlier short stories. Pirandello was the son of wealthy parents who lost all their money in 1903 when their sulphur mines were flooded. This drove his beautiful wife, already suffering from nervous illness after the birth of her third child, into an incurable paranoia. Pirandello would not put her into a nursing home until sixteen years later, and then only because her delusions that he was conducting a sexual relationship with his daughter were a threat to the girl's physical safety. He compromised with fascism, and was for a time a member of the fascist party. Privately he considered Mussolini to be a vulgarian; but he so loved the theatre, into which Mussolini poured state money, that he misled himself into eulogizing the fascist system in highly abstract terms. His involvement with fascism is a discredit to him, and his dislike of capitalist democracy on the grounds that it is a concealed tyranny—a perfectly valid dislike, as the 'free world' is now beginning to discover—provides him with little excuse for supporting a system that some other Italians well understood. But his only alternative would have been silence. And he said enough, perhaps, to indicate what he really thought about fascism. But it is undoubtedly disappointing—though some would say it is irrelevant to a consideration of his art—that this great sceptic and mocker of human falsity did not leave a more public and unequivocal condemnation of the fascist system, and of its strutting and disastrous progenitor. Pirandello's behaviour (giving his Nobel medal to the state to be melted down; declaring to an anti-fascist group in Brazil that outside Italy Italians were not fascists or anti-fascists but Italians; typing out the word 'buffoonery' as he talked to journalists after his Nobel award) was well above the head of any power-politician, let alone Mussolini—when he died (having opened the list of those who would come to pay their final respects with 'Pirandello') Mussolini cried: 'There he went, slamming the door'—but it was also above the heads of people who were, after 1926, victims of the regime. . . . His sincerity, however, is no more in question than that of Benn (q.v.): he joined the party after the Matteotti murder, by personal request to Mussolini, and while the press was still free.

Croce, the philosopher, criticized Pirandello for treating of philosophical problems as though they were ones of everyday life. But this was Pirandello's intention. He understood philosophy well; but when faced with a choice between abstractions of philosophy that were soluble in unreal terms, and realities that were insoluble he chose, as Vico had before him, to concentrate on reality. If he thus betrayed God, or Croce's spiritual flux (to which the fascist period offered an apparent interruption) then so do all imaginative writers. Pirandello left great fiction (a number of short stories and a batch of novels that add up to a great achievement) and great plays. He first worked out his approach in his fiction; but this did not find complete expression until he put it into dramatic form.

Pirandello began as Verga's verist successor. He shared Verga's view of the proper artistic programme: the creation of a valid compassion to counter the malignity of fate—a compassion to be built up from truthful observation. Later Pirandello was to extend this to *in*-seeing: to a *verismo* of the soul. But he has anticipated most of the concerns of his successors; the individual man as a myriad men and therefore no one (his understanding of relativity), or as his dreams and illusions, or as several people, or as others see him; the 'reality' of fictions in the minds of their progenitors; the sanity of madness; the comedy of evil; the buffoonery of moral earnestness; the sadness of maturity. Pirandello's art is a perfect example of the interdependence of the regional and the universal, for he is always himself: a Sicilian. And yet he learned from a number of sources: from Andreyev (q.v.) certainly, and from the early German ex- pressionist theatre. He anticipated, too, and made cunning authorial provision for, the director's theatre (q.v.) that developed out of the Russian and German theatricalism of the first two decades of the century and is now almost universal: his texts deliberately lend themselves to the gimmicks of directors (who are not often intelligent in a literary sense, even when they are effective), but they have a tough inner resilience that resists all the 'ideas' of directors. The texts act as challenges to just what is rightly creative in theatrical production, a quality not intellectual. Most of Pirandello's short stories—BISS; *Short Stories*, tr. L. Duplaix, 1959; *Short Stories*, sel. tr. F. May, 1965—have been translated. He also wrote seven novels. The first two are regional and concentrate on plot. The third, *The Late Mattia Pascal* (*Il fu Mattia Pascal*, 1904; tr. A. Livingstone, 1923; W. Weaver, 1964), really marks the beginning of the *teatro grottesco* and of Pirandello's turning inwards. Now the story no longer dominates. Pascal is out of place in his life: he is henpecked by his wife and her mother, he has been cheated of his money, his job as librarian is pointless and the library is useless. He escapes, wins money by gambling, discovers that he has been written off as a suicide, and so goes to Rome under an assumed name. Now he has to invent an identity; but he cannot. And so he has to return home—but his wife has remarried, and he finds that, although alive, he is 'dead'. This contains the germ of all Pirandello's succeeding works. We live and do not watch ourselves, he said; the corollary is that we do not know who we are. Are we anybody? But Pirandello found that the dramatic form was necessary: in order to confront man with himself, so that he should feel a pain that would lead him to an authentic existence. Besides, the multi-facetedness of the human condition (one of Pirandello's basic themes) can most effectively be shown in dramatic terms.

Of his other novels, the most controversial last one, *One, None, and a Hundred Thousand* (*Uno, nessuno e centomila*, 1926; tr. S. Putnam, 1933), is the most fascinating. This is a study in the fragmentation of a personality, a sinking into madness. Moscarda begins to realize that he is unknown to himself and to those around him: does he exist? He decides to play the game of his life as though in fact he did not. He ends in a poor-house, having 'succeeded' in his project.

Pirandello's first play of real consequence is *Right You Are—If You Think So* (*Così è—se vi pare*, 1917; PTP), about the relative truth of three differing points of view. But his masterpieces are *Six Characters in Search of an Author* (*Sei personaggi in cerca d'autore*, 1921; PTP; tr. F. May, 1954), *Henry IV* (*Enrico IV*, 1922; tr. F. May, 1960), *Each in his Own Way* (*Ciascuno a suo modo*, 1924; tr. A. Livingstone, 1924) and *Tonight We Improvise* (*Questa sera si recita a soggetto*, 1930; tr. S. Putnam, 1932). The first and last two of these may be described as a trilogy, since each one uses a theatre-within-theatre technique: *Six Characters*, the play within the play, *Each in his Own Way* the play outside the play, and *Tonight We Improvise* the scripted improvisation. In each case here Pirandello dissolves the external form, the hallowed structure, of the drama; he undoubtedly anticipated the spirit of Brecht's epic theatre (q.v.). He had already, so to speak, smashed the form of the traditional solid novel, built up from character, by writing a novel which 'proved' that such character did not exist —or by showing it in a logically correct process of dissolution. In the playwithin-play drama he attempts to establish, with the kind of irony—*umorismo*— he had already defined in a book of critical essays of 1908, the true autonomy of the world of the imagination. *Henry IV* is more personal, since Pirandello was in his life much concerned with the problems presented by his wife's incurable insanity (it was his grief over this that provided most of the feeling inherent in the work of the latter half of his life); *Henry IV* deals with insanity and its relation to sanity and reality. Pirandello continually holds reality up to question. He also holds identity up to question: as in *Right You Are—If You Think So*, where the wife comes forward and tells the audience that she is just what they want her to be; and in *As You Desire Me* (*Come tu mi vuoi*, 1930; tr. S. Putnam, 1931). Pirandello was particularly vulnerable because his jealous wife continually believed him to be something that he was not—for example, the incestuous possessor of his daughter's virtue. Was he? he of course asked himself. To say that Pirandello is not interested in character itself invites the retort that he did not believe in it; still, he himself, despite his *umorismo*, did have a character—and his *umorismo* failed him when Mussolini came on the scene. This is in fact a weakness in his work: a bit of wisdom about what common sense calls 'character' would have helped him with Il Duce; so his dramatic work does sometimes seem to lack richness.

Pirandello has exercised an enormous and frequently unacknowledged influence on the modern theatre and, through it, on modern fiction as well. It is impossible to imagine so excellent a writer as Max Frisch (q.v.) without Pirandello as his predecessor. Nearly all his work, with the exception of a single early novel (*The Succession*, *Il turno*, 1902), some stories, and a few plays, has been translated, much of it twice or more. The one-act plays, some of them very fine, have been collected in *The One-Act Plays of Luigi Pirandello* (1928) in translations by various hands.

*

The only outstanding Italian dramatist since Pirandello has been UGO BETTI (1892–1953), who began as a disciple. Like Rosso, however, Betti is an optimist; but unlike Rosso, a Christian. All this hell, he suggests, is God's will: his message is that it must be accepted. He was a judge, which much influenced his production. He began as a rather bad, nebulous poet; and his nebulosity and good-hearted Christian vagueness have continued to vitiate all but two or three of his twenty-six plays. However, he was a judge who faced reality; one wonders how he squared his conscience to sentencing men and women to the unspeakable hell of Italian prisons. Perhaps a belief in a higher world is the only answer to such promptings of an essentially decent, as well as lyrical, conscience. Certainly Betti has a tendency to set his plays outside earthly limits—significant in a conscientious judge. He took some time to find himself. His first plays were proletarian melodramas in which good redeems evil and squalor, and society is indicted in an almost unanimist (q.v.) spirit for its responsibility for the anguish within it. The later, non-realistic plays are the more interesting. In *Crime on Goat Island* (*Delitto all' isola delle capre*, 1948; tr. H. Reed, 1960) he altogether transcends his concerns in depicting a grotesque revenge by women on the men they have used. Betti was something of a weakling as an artist—weakened, perhaps, by his necessary omniscience as a decider of punishment? —and came under too many influences as he tried to subdue his crepuscular (q.v.) gloom; but he did in one important sense, in his final plays, ask the question that Pirandello's drama poses but never answers: If we have no identity, what is human responsibility? These plays include *Corruption in the Palace of Justice* (*Corruzione al palazzo di giustizia*, 1944) and *The Burnt Flower Bed* (*L'aiuola bruciata*, 1952; tr. H. Reed, 1957). *Our Dreams* (*I nostri sogni*, 1937) is a charming and wise comedy, not as ambitious as Betti's other plays, but one of his best.

No playwright of calibre has since emerged, which leaves the Italian stage still dominated by the relatively senior figures of EDUARDO DE FILIPPO (1900) and DIEGO FABBRI (1911). De Filippo comes of a celebrated Neapolitan family of actors. In 1931 he and his brother and sister opened a theatre in Naples, and he wrote mostly for this—taking time off to write some film scripts—until after the Second World War. Although De Filippo writes in Neapolitan he is not a true dialect writer, since his language is literary rather than colloquial. He has imported the attitude of Pirandello into a lighter Neapolitan structure; but even his farce has an undertone of seriousness: he is always the champion of the oppressed against their hypocritical and greedy masters.

De Filippo did not emerge as a playwright of international importance until after the war. His most famous plays are *Filomena Marturana* (1946), which travelled the world as a Loren-Mastroianni movie, and *These Phantoms* (*Questi fantasmi*, 1946).

Fabbri is a skilful playwright, but everything he writes is more or less compromised by sentimentality and his eye for midcult audiences and their desire not to be fundamentally upset. But he has an excellent sense of humour, and is intelligent. He has done his best work in adaptations from Dostoevski, especially

The Demons (a novel often known as *The Possessed*). His position as Italy's leading playwright since Betti's death is not a secure one. He is explicitly Christian in his approach, and has been much influenced by Betti in his 'unanimist' concept of responsibility. *Inquisition* (*Inquisizione*, 1950) is one of his best plays: a clever study of two priests who find themselves advising the husband and the wife respectively in a disintegrating marriage.

Italy has made little contribution (since Pirandello) to the theatre of the *avant garde*. Dino Buzzati (q.v.) wrote *A Clinical Case* (*Un caso clinico*, 1953), which was adapted by Camus (q.v.) and presented in Paris in 1955. This has been classed as an 'absurd' play, and so in one sense it is; but it transcends any mere genre, and is probably the best single play to come from Italy since the death of Pirandello. It is a frightening allegory of man's pointless progress through society to death, and is one of the most powerful and intelligent of Italian indictments of bureaucracy. *A Worm at the Ministry* (*Un verme al ministero*, 1960) is a satire on the totalitarian future now in process of being unwittingly created by the Western bourgeois 'democracies'.

Finally, an interesting and neglected figure in Italian letters whose most distinguished work has been done in the theatre: EZIO D'ERRICO (1892). D'Errico, now an old man, is a painter, a writer of good thrillers, a journalist and an art- and film-critic. He started to write plays when he was nearing sixty; most of them have been performed outside his own country, whose audience for *avant garde* art is small. His most important play is *The Forest* (*La foresta*, 1959), a parable of man's self-imprisonment in a technological nightmare. Here Ezio D'Errico is a romantic furiously condemning society's eager desire to destroy the individuality of its members; it is an impressive and compassionate play.

III

There are five major modern Italian poets: Campana, Saba, Ungaretti, Quasimodo and Montale. Some might dispute the status of the first two; that of the last three is assured. But in addition to these are a number of other writers of excellent or at least historically important poetry. And the main achievement of Italian poetry, its contribution to the modern European consciousness, has been the establishment of the perhaps misleadingly named *poesia ermetica*, hermetic poetry.

But we must begin with three lesser figures, all of whom are, however, of immense historical importance in nineteenth-century Italian literature. These three—Carducci, Pascoli, D'Annunzio—dominated Italian poetry in 1900. They had no doubt laid, in their different ways, the foundations for the emergence of a poetry that would be at once Italian (in the national sense) and European. Now their romanticism had to be overcome, superseded—in a word, destroyed. GIOSUÈ CARDUCCI (1835–1907), born in Tuscany, was Professor of Italian Literature at the University of Bologna until he retired in 1904. He was awarded the Nobel Prize two years later. Carducci, an extremely combative man, combined romanticism with a reaction against it which was not truly classical but which was certainly influenced by his classical education. Carducci, who did much for scholarship, was Italy's great public poet, proudly anti-Christian as well as anti-clerical. He opposed effusive romanticism by manufacturing a poetry—of fine technique—that had a civic, national function. *The Barbarian Odes* (*Odi Barbare*, 1877–9; tr. W. F. Smith, 1939) are important experiments with classical metres, but few are of much value as poetry. For all his fervour, Carducci was a humdrum thinker, and all but a little of his poetry smells much too heavily of the lamp. His best is melancholy, impressionistic description—anticipating the *crepuscolari* (q.v.) in its mood. (PI; PIV)

GIOVANNI PASCOLI (1855–1912), born at San Mauro, was a modest minor poet, whose work as a whole is of greater value and interest than Carducci's. He, too, anticipated the *crepuscolari*. His childhood was tragic (his father was murdered, his mother and three brothers and sisters died soon after), and this and a general note of gloom in the air just at the time he reached his maturity fixed his attitudes for life. He is a gifted poet, but his gifts seem to lead him nowhere. He can express sadness with sweet perfection, but the tragic is beyond his reach. He tries to achieve a profound symbolism, he uses a simplified diction, but too often he ends up being merely trite. However, he is a prince, if a petty one, of minor poets, and he sounded a new, precise note in the Italian poetry of nature. Whatever his poems lack, it is not melody. He excels among poets for readability: he is never, like Carducci, a learned, pompous bore. He was once thought of as an 'advanced' poet; it is now easy to see him for what he was: a sometimes exquisite nineteenth-century minor. (PIV; PI)

GABRIELE D'ANNUNZIO (1863–1938) came from Pescara (Abruzzi). He soon came to represent all that is most detestable in Italian life and literature, and his real importance lies in the example he set other writers: what he did they avoided doing. And yet he had small, genuinely romantic beginnings, and when he was content to be himself could be a fair poet. He also had enormous vitality. D'Annunzio was one of the progenitors of Italian and therefore European fascism, one of the monsters of his time; it is significant that he should have become megalomanic to the point of insanity. He wrote novels, plays and poetry and lived a 'scandalous' life until the First World War, when he indulged himself in a number of heroic exploits, and lost an eye. In 1919 he led 12000 'Arditi', proto-fascist bullies, into the Port of Fiume, of which he made himself commander ('Even if the citizens of Fiume do not desire annexation, I desire it against their wishes'). After declaring war on Italy he returned to it ('Citizens, Gabriele D'Annunzio is here. Not a word. Continue to weep for joy.'), supported Mussolini from the beginning, and lived on in increasingly eccentric state as a crazy and superstitious spiritual gigolo attended and worshipped by his cast-offs as well as his current fancies.

D'Annunzio's first poems and short stories were much influenced by Carducci and Verga respectively, and they were fresh and lyrical; he was possessed of undoubted skill, and his yearnings to become a part of nature, when they are subdued, have considerable charm. His only novel of any real literary interest is *The Triumph of Death* (*Il trionfo della morte*, 1894; tr. G. Harding, 1898): it is a repulsive and immature tale, by one who had turned himself into an arch-decadent by means of misunderstanding Nietzsche; but it is written in an irresistibly vivid style, and has considerable descriptive power—as in a scene of cripples seeking a miraculous cure. The main theme is hedonistic eroticism; this could have become good art only if D'Annunzio had approached the subject pornographically rather than, as he thought, passionately and philosophically. But one must grant D'Annunzio enormous, although decadent, linguistic power. He was morbid, but always adventurously so. His intrinsic merit is all stylistic. But he lacked conscience—artistic or otherwise—and usually his linguistic gift is distorted in the interests of his own vanity and glory: his swaggering lushness led to the reaction, first, of crepuscular humility of language, and finally to the decent hermetic precision. (PIV; PI)

The *crespuscolari* represent the beginning of Italian modern poetry: the first real modification of romanticism, partially forced upon Italian literature by the excessive D'Annunzio. Borgese first used the term 'crepuscular' of Moretti, whom we have met as a novelist. The two chief *crepuscolari*, however, were Gozzano and Corazzini. In the sense that both these poets regard their poetic life as *unhealthy*, they are decadent and derive from D'Annunzio. But their approach is importantly different: unlike D'Annunzio, who loudly rejoices in his morbidity and hedonism by application of pseudo-Nietzschean principles, they murmur in a subdued voice, in twilit melancholy, about the approach of death (both Gozzano and Corazzini did die young) and the vain desire to escape from oneself. Partially these poets are complaining about how their native simplicity is tainted with a decadence that is exaggerated in the work of D'Annunzio. And because that kind of decadence really was a taint, their work gained merit. The complaint was not frivolous. Gozzano complains of being old at twenty-five, but since he died of tuberculosis at thirty-three, and probably feared that he would, he had some justice in so feeling ('Twenty-five years! I am old, indeed/I am old! My prime of youth fled fast/and left me only emptiness and need'). Borgese's 'Crepuscular' was a brilliant summary term: night (death) is approaching, there are very long shadows, things appear preternaturally soft. . . .

GUIDO GOZZANO (1883–1916), an entomologist, was born in the province of Turin. He is one of the most enjoyable of all European minor poets. He has a charming and ironic humour, as when he addresses a goose:

> . . . you don't think. Yours is a happy fate!
> For to be roasted is not sad at all,
> What's sad is the thought that we must roast.

He is at his best when least serious: in that mood, common in all Italian literature, between comic pleasure and anguish, between objectivity and suffering. His manner reminds one of the mocking one, more familiar to us, of the early Eliot; and his poetry is as good. A characteristic example is 'Toto Merùmeni' (PI): Toto is very like one of E. A. Robinson's (q.v.) failures; this suggests the link, not often acknowledged, between Robinson's sad people and Eliot's Prufrock. But Gozzano's poetry has more urgency of feeling than Eliot's, more passion in the background. (CIP; PI)

The Roman SERGIO CORAZZINI (1887–1907) also died of tuberculosis, and almost before he had had time to develop. His precocious poetry was much influenced by Laforgue and Verlaine, whose work he hardly had time fully to absorb. He catches the crepuscular mood perfectly when—in contradistinction to the hedonistic grandiosity of D'Annunzio—he declares

> I love the life of common things.
> How many passions have I seen deflower themselves, little by little,
> for every single thing that slipped away!
> But you don't understand me and you smile,
> and think that I'm ill.

(CIP)

On another occasion he asks people not to refer to him as a poet: 'I am only an infant squealing'.

The components in crepuscular poetry that were truly modern were the new simplicity of language and the ironic self-appraisal: the late romantic decadence turns in upon itself.

Some of the poets who passed through futurism, a necessary but intrinsically unimportant movement, had begun as associates of the *crepuscolari*. Futurism itself was no more than an extreme manifestation of the movement to integrate Italian with European culture (not to destroy Italian culture—only its isolation). The review *Leonardo* was founded with just this in mind, by GIOVANNI PAPINI (1881–1956) and the critic Giuseppe Prezzolini. Papini, a Florentine, was anything but a consistent man. After his cosmopolitan beginnings as the philosophically orientated co-editor of *Leonardo*, he became a futurist; he then became a nationalist. He was in his time an agnostic and a Christian, for and against the Church. On paper he was often like D'Annunzio: arrogant, exhibitionist, sunk in self, not at all emotionally in control of his more than adequate intellect. As a man, however, he was unlike D'Annunzio: lovable, devoted to culture, helpful to others. His father had been an atheist, his mother a devout Catholic, which may partly explain his continual oscillations. His best book is *A Man— Finished (Un uomo—finito*, 1912; tr. 1924), a classic in which he describes his difficult childhood with candour and insight. But in general Papini is a writer to whom one goes for incidental insights. One will not find them in the conversion-document *The Story of Christ (Storia di Cristo*, 1921; tr. 1923), a kind of half-disguised autobiography of no historical value. Papini was a powerful force in Italian letters, however, because of his sincerity and enthusiasm: literatures need men like him. And some of his poetry describes, as nothing else in his vast opus does, the confusions of his existence: it puts a quiet index-finger on the excitements, angers, enthusiasms and personal despairs. For just as he despised the 'literary life', so he desired fame:

> I march at instinct's urge; I look
> around me, master of the desert;
> in the hollow silence I listen
> to my convinced and open words. . . .
>
> I become everything I see:
> I am the shadow of the wall, the light of lights. . . .
>
> I am the beloved lover of myself,
> I kiss lip with lip, I squeeze
> one hand with a burning hand,
> fully I possess myself, I don't pretend. . . .
>
> But when at day's end,
> tired and cold, I find again the road's ditch,
> in the lilac dusk of my return
> I am the sad creature nobody heeds.
>
> (CIP)

Not all his poetry is on this level; but it is in general a poetry in which he examines himself in depth. He was guilty of compromise: he took on a Christian mask in which he did not believe. He lacked inner consistency. But in his poetry he looked at his confusions, and found a dignity the man so given to facilities lacked.

Little space needs to be given to the founder of futurism, FILIPPO TOMMASO MARINETTI (1876–1944), who was born in Egypt. He launched his futurist programme, demanding the entire destruction of the past (museums, rules of grammar and composition) and the tapping of the technologically new for inspiration, from Paris. Such a moment, more or less, has had to come in all non-primitive cultures in this century: many gifted Italians passed through futurism: it represented a quite proper—if of course unbalanced—dissatisfaction with the status quo. But so far as Marinetti himself was concerned (none of his own works—poems, novels and plays in French as well as Italian—are of the least interest) this was no more than D'Annunzio writ new. This is one of the ironies of literary history of which we should take note: the violent and deliberately illiterate nature of the very latest British and American manifestation of pop posing as *avant garde* is equally totalitarian in its implications: its intellectually impoverished, egotistic and egoistic idiocy is based upon a similar spiritual emptiness and intellectual laziness. The Jesuit-educated Marinetti's programme, like D'Annunzio's, called for fascism before Mussolini had even begun his bid for the leadership of Italy. (D'Annunzio himself, in 1909, pronounced himself an admirer of Marinetti's; Capuana, q.v., could only regret his inability, owing to age, to become a futurist; the authoritarian Claudel, q.v., also fell under the spell.) He himself became an enthusiastic fascist. The actual futurist programme—though not its use as a temporary outlet for feelings of frustration—is a useful index of those components of modernism that contribute to tyranny. Marinetti himself, a shabby enough writer, was personally charismatic. But his kind of nihilism gloried in war, the subjugation of women to men's casual lust, the abolition of quietude, the rape of nature by machinery. He was a manifestation of a great evil. (*Selected Writings*, tr. 1972.)

The year of the futurist manifesto was 1909. In 1908 Prezzolini, co-founder of *Leonardo*—which had collapsed in 1907—founded *The Voice* (*La Voce*). The group associated with this magazine—one of them was of course Papini—who were known as the *vociani*, had no more in common than an urgent desire to discover a new and intelligent awareness of the changes that were taking place at the time. This was futurism discarded and re-thought.

CORRADO GOVONI (1884–1965), from Ferrara, passed through the gamut of all the movements: a close friend of Corazzini (q.v.), he began as crepuscular poet, but, not feeling doomed (he lived, after all, to eighty-one), he joined the futurists; he discovered himself when he became one of the *vociani*. He remained a basically impressionistic poet, lucid and sometimes powerful. (CIP)

ALDO PALAZZESCHI (ps. ALDO GIURLANI, 1885), is, by contrast, an important figure. He, too, wrote crepuscular verse, and then briefly joined the futurists. He is an anti-rhetorical humorist who comes nearer than any other Italian to the mood of Morgenstern (q.v.). Even when, as a young man, Palazzeschi was strongly influenced by D'Annunzio, he parodied him. He began as a poet but turned into a novelist. He is a relaxed and deliberately minor artist, who has been content to mock society (and himself) without attempting to create any set of values in opposition to it. A satirist, he is also a self-satirist; a very gentle nihilist. His playful poetry, with its undertones of regret, provides the key to his later work in fiction. *Allegory of November* (*Allegoria di novembre*, 1908) is his most personal novel. It is a sensitive study of a Roman prince who falls in love with an Englishman and then tries to cure himself of it by isolating himself from him. Palazzeschi fought shy of returning to this delicate problem—it leaves this immature first novel as his most interesting but not most accomplished —and instead elected to become a sceptic in the best Italian tradition. The decision lay between becoming a major writer and a minor one; Palazzeschi became a good minor one, and his choice may well have been correct. He turned himself, in *Perelà, the Man of Smoke* (*Perelà uomo di fumo*, 1911, rev. 1954; ad. 1936), into a Pirandellian non-existent man. A man of smoke who has lived for thirty-two years in a chimney emerges into the world to get to know it; he is successful in life, but is suddenly condemned to life-imprisonment—and is of course able to vanish. This has rightly been regarded as a novel prophetic of fascism. It also presents, in a veiled way, Palazzeschi's own predicament: the world would not allow him to be himself (or, alternately, he feels he has no self), and so he becomes 'a man of smoke'. This novel must be read in close conjunction with the author's first, in which Prince Valentino destroys himself rather than compromise his love for the Englishman John Mare. Palazzeschi has continued to write novels. Of these *The Duke* (*Il Doge*, 1967) is as brilliant and ingenious as anything he has written. *The Materassi Sisters* (*Sorelle Materassi*, 1934; tr. A. Davidson, 1953) is a deadly study of two old maids fascinated, horrified and finally destroyed by the machinations of their nephew. *Stefanino* (1969) satirically describes society's reception of a foundling who is deformed but prodigiously intelligent. Recently he has returned to poetry.

The Milanese CLEMENTE REBORA (1885–1957) is Italy's most important modern Christian poet. He was a teacher, then joined the army in the First World War. His wounds and experiences nearly destroyed his reason; he entered a monastery in 1931 and five years later became a priest. Rebora represents the wholly spiritual answer to modern man's discovery of human absurdity or 'the void'; doubtless his war experiences helped to determine the nature of his reaction to his futurist beginnings. It is interesting to contrast him with Max Jacob (q.v.), whose reaction was essentially similar but more complex. Rebora's poetry is written in a kind of breathless expectation of apocalypse: 'With tense imagination/I count the seconds/In imminent expectation. . . .' The moment when the void will be filled by a new message from God does not come, and the poet transforms his hopes into a faith in death. This is a poetry that interestingly describes a life of nervous anguish, muffled by piety and by seeing a purposeful God everywhere—especially in nature, which sadly reassures. (CIP)

The Genoese PIERO JAHIER (1884), who spent most of his working life as a state railway employee in Bologna, was closely watched by Mussolini's policemen throughout the fascist period. His last book appeared in 1919, but he has retained the high regard of critics as one of the most faithful of the *vociani*. The nihilism of futurism and then the horrors of war personally experienced led Jahier to a poetry that asserted a humanistic faith with a paradoxically mystical fervour. Jahier's masters were Gide and, in particular, Claudel (qq.v.), to whom he owes the form of his work. He is revered by the discriminating because of his unaffected sincerity—indeed, his is one of those small *œuvres* that one might instance as evidence, even in our sophisticated century, that sincerity is still a meaningful concept. He wrote three books: *Boy* (*Ragazzo*, 1919; rev. with early poems added 1939), about his Protestant family and boyhood, *Gino Bianchi* (1915), which satirizes life in the railroad office in prose and in certain respects anticipates Gadda (q.v.), and *With Me and the Alpini* (1919), on the war and the heroic characteristics of the soldiers he commanded. Jahier is an original and lucid poet. His fragmentary utterances are bound together by a Claudelian formal ecstasy; but his accounts of inner conditions of simplicity and peace certainly anticipate the poetry of Ungaretti. *Some Poems* (*Qualche Poesia*) appeared in 1962. (CIP)

CAMILLO SBARBARO (1888), born on the Italian Riviera, was another of the *vociani*. He taught Greek in Genoa. Essentially he is a crepuscular intellectual, his poetry an acrid record of his disenchantment: nothing at all can defeat his sense of life's indifference. His mood is one of resignation: 'Alternating joys and sorrows/do not touch us. The siren of the world/has lost its voice, and the world is a vast desert./In the desert/with dry eyes I behold myself'. (CIP)

But the first major twentieth-century Italian poet—he was associated with those around the review *La Voce*, but can hardly be classified as one of them—was the mentally disordered vagabond DINO CAMPANA (1885-1932). Campana was born in the small town of Marradi, north of Florence. Even as a young boy he felt alienated, and the bourgeois of his town—where his father was a headmaster—labelled him 'odd'. The University of Bologna threw him out as dangerous—for his ideas and for his chemical experiments. He published his only book, *Orphic Songs* (*Canti orfici*; collected ed.: *Canti orfici e altri scritti*, 1952) in 1914. He roamed Europe (including Russia) and South America, sojourning as a worker (knife-sharpener, fireman, labourer, bandsman, cop, sailor, porter, circus hack, etc.), as a prisoner and as a mental patient. He joined the army, was made a sergeant, went mad—and was once again thrown out. He died in a mental hospital before he was fifty. At his worst Campana is a mentally confused, rhetorical decadent, whose wild rococo flourishes conceal his anguished sensibility. But at his best he belongs to the best in his tradition, which is that of the *poète maudit*: a child of grace, whose personal anguish still makes itself poignantly felt. His intellectual confusion is exemplified in his statement that he was an 'imperialistic anarchist'; this is silly, of course, and ninety-nine times out of a hundred the person who said it would be silly, too. But Campana's best poetry is in fact a reconciliation of just such opposites: of love and hate for the gipsy girl who figures in them; of pagan and moral feelings; of depression and exaltation. Mentally he seems to have suffered from an affective disorder that put him into states in which depression and euphoria blended into a kind of intolerable paranoia—a paranoia false in medical terms, but agonizing enough to the sufferer. (His case was diagnosed by doctors as 'dementia praecox', the old name for schizophrenia—not of course an affective disorder—but it is often hard to distinguish between certain affective states and schizophrenia; most poets are in fact manic-depressive by disposition. I doubt if the doctors' diagnoses were much better than their treatment.) Campana is a visionary poet, who records his fruitless quest to lose his hated (sick) personal identity in new experiences and new themes; the lyrical note is one of hope, which he never gives up. But after 1916 he seems to have written no more. Campana erected beautiful places in his imagination, and for a time walked in them, as in 'Autumn Garden':

> To the ghost-garden, to the clipped laurel
> Of poets' whispering green crowns
> To the lands of autumn
> A last goodbye!
> To the parched rough slopes
> Reddening in sunset
> Distant life cries out
> In a rattle of shrieks:
> Cries to the sinking sun
> That bloodies beds of flowers.

A fanfare's heard,
Raised knife of noise: the river sinks
Into its gilded sand; quiet
At the ends of bridges, their heads turned away,
The white statues stand.
The past is gone.
And silence rising deeply from itself
Like a tender and majestic choir
Yearns to my tall balcony
And in the laurel's scent,
In the laurel's sour and torpid scent,
Among the ageless statues in the final sun
She comes to me, is there.

Here inner and outer experience are fused; and yet the beautiful vision is heavily charged with menace. 'She' is Campana's gipsy girl; and the place is a Florence (the Boboli Gardens, where Rilke met George, qq.v.) transformed in the poet's imagination. He gives us a portrait of his gipsy girl in the terrifying and marvellous 'A Strange Gipsy' (PIV), in which he contrasts his threatening dream with the reality it seems to wrong. In such poems Campana achieves a hallucinated purity rare in the twentieth century. (CIP; PI; MEP)

*

VINCENZO CARDARELLI (1887–1959), born near Rome, co-founded the post-war traditionalist magazine *La Ronda* in 1919, and was a literary journalist all his life. *La Ronda* was always an intelligently conservative magazine, and it exercised a wide influence; but it failed in its bid to establish a new Italian poetics based on the example of Leopardi: because this was unrealistic. Cardarelli's own poetry, however, although classical in form—consciously modelled on Leopardi and Baudelaire—is both modern in spirit and extremely sensual. This quality is illustrated in 'Adolescent' (CIP), which however contains more than an evocation of physical desire. Cardarelli was no re-actionary conservative—indeed, his *La Ronda* could be and has been spoken of as '*avant garde*'. He was, however, decidedly in the realistic tradition, an anti-hermetic: he was for 'order, not images', and so his own poems come off the page with a great and often surprising directness. (MEP)

LUIGI BARTOLINI (1892–1963), a victim of fascist persecution, was born in Cupramontana, near Ancona on the Adriatic coast. He was a painter and etcher as well as a writer. He wrote the novel upon which the script of da Sica's justly famous movie *The Bicycle Thief* was based. His poetry, more optimistic and cheerfully warm in tone than most Italian work, has a touch of the whimsicality of Palazzeschi.

CARLO BETOCCHI (1899) was born in Turin and is, like Rebora, a Catholic poet. But he is more placid: his work glows with an inner certainty: he imbues the landscapes of the world with the fervour of heaven ('. . . gardens full of roses/that flourish beyond this world, and far away . . .'), and with a verbally fastidious elegance and a faithfulness to his own vision that give his poetry a unique flavour.

The Perugian SANDRO PENNA (1906) is an impressionistic minor poet of great charm. One of his best known poems is also one of his most characteristic:

> The little Venetian square
> mournful and ancient, gathers
> the fragrance of the sea. And flights
> of pigeons. But memory
> retains—bewitching
> the very light—the flying
> young cyclist
> turning to his friend: a melodious
> whisper: 'Going alone?'
>
> (CIP; CIV)

However, the most important Italian poet outside the hermetic tradition— an odd man out, certainly, but a major one—is UMBERTO SABA (1883–1957), a Trieste bookseller who (partly because he came from Trieste) played little part in what became, in 1918 when he was already thirty-five, his country. He spent the whole of his life in Trieste, except that during the Second World War he hid in Florence, as he was half-Jewish. Saba is only superficially a simple and quiet poet: his intimate and spontaneous manner—a remarkable achievement —conceals much distress, high psychological intelligence and some melancholy. His work has not really had its due outside Italy. In *The Story and Chronicle of my Work* (*Storia e cronistoria del canzoniere*, 1921, 1948, final version, 1961) Saba gives a uniquely valuable blow-by-blow account of his poetry. One of his best known poems, 'The Goat' (PI), contains most of the characteristics of his poetry:

> I talked to a goat,
> Alone in the field, tied to a post,
> Full up with grass, soaked
> Through with rain, bleating.
>
> That monotone was brother
> To my grief. I answered back: first
> For fun, but then because sorrow's
> Forever, and is monotonous.
> I heard its voice
> Sounding in a solitary goat.
>
> From a goat with a semitic face
> I heard all ills, all lives,
> Lamenting.

Here there is sardonic humour, love of animals, a refusal to be distinguished from 'ordinary' humanity (very characteristic of Saba). Also typical is the final equation of 'ills' with 'lives': Saba is a cheerful or at any rate humorous poet in his tone, but his content makes it clear that he regards existence as largely a matter of suffering. His achievement is considerable, because he can do almost anything that a hermetic poet can do; and yet his work reads like an intimate diary. He may yet emerge as the most considerable Italian poet of his time, because the most consistently approachable.

GIUSEPPE UNGARETTI (1888–1970) was, like Marinetti, an Italian born in Egypt. He too spent his formative years in Paris, where he was a friend of Apollinaire's (q.v.). The term 'hermetic poetry' was first used pejoratively (by Francisco Flore) in 1936; but Ungaretti had started writing it during the First World War, in which he took part. His aim was not anti-romantic: his quest within himself precluded the search for such abstractions, since he could not know what he would find. What he insisted upon was the purging of poetry of all rhetoric: a return to inner truth, to confidence in the purity of the word itself. If the right word could be found, then this word would be at once utterly subjective and yet utterly universal. His poetry reduces the voice of the poet himself to an inner whisper; it is bare, full of clusters of words and white meaningful silences. His poetics, entirely without pretension, searches for the original function of words, and thus concentrates upon old meanings (the project Laura Riding, q.v., the repudiator of poetry, reports herself to be engaged on with her dictionary)—meanings divorced from those attached to them by the materialism of centuries. It is I think misleading to call Ungaretti a Platonist, for his poetry shows no actual faith in an ideal world: rather, it sceptically but with stubborn hope explores his experience for the true, original status of language. (His later, Christian, acceptance is not always as convincing as his toughly won early work.) Looking at an Ungaretti poem, we can understand a great deal about how 'modern poetry'—that to some readers justifiably terrifying phenomenon—works. The war poem about San Martino del Carso, a ruined town on the Austrian front that literally becomes the ruined heart of the poet, is utterly simple—and yet 'hermetic' just because of this simplicity:

> Of these houses
> nothing's left
> but certain
> strands of wall
>
> Of so many
> whom I loved
> nothing's left
> not even those
>
> But in my heart
> no cross is missing
> My heart is
> the most tormented town

Ungaretti saw his work as a unity, which he called *Life of a Man*. After the war poems of *Joy of Shipwrecks* (*Allegria di naufragi*, 1919) he developed considerably; *Sense of Time* (*Sentimento del tempo*, 1933) shows him searching for, but never certain of, the lost innocence of pristine speech: for the original word. One of his most celebrated poems is the minuscule 'Morning':

> I flood myself with the light
> of the immense

One can hardly claim greatness for Ungaretti on the strength of this—he was violently attacked for it—but in the context of his work it does have a significant function: it shows him, as a critic has noted, stating that however huge the universe is, the soul's recognition of it is exhilarating—and not dismaying as Pascal (with his infinite spaces) found it. (MEP; CIP; IQ; PI; AU)

The Genoese EUGENIO MONTALE (1896) is correctly grouped with Ungaretti as 'hermetic': the quality of his language is similarly inwards-looking, shy of rhetoric and sentimentality: 'closed'. But he is a very different kind of poet. If Ungaretti learnt from Apollinaire, Montale learnt from Ungaretti and Mallarmé. His pessimism, related to that of T. S. Eliot, whom he translated, is his own, and goes deeper than that of Ungaretti, in whom one may finally perhaps sense a discovery of meaning in the universe (he never departed from Christianity). Montale is no Christian, and he has never given his allegiance to any other party. He actively although quietly rejected fascism. But otherwise he has not pretended that he has any comfort to offer; indeed, the 'message' of his poetry is certainly that the light of cold reason reduces existence to a dismaying fact. Fortunately, however, there is more to it than that: he records his experience of life faithfully, and in a sober language as purged of extraneous accretions as Ungaretti's. His output has been small: *Bones of the Cuttlefish* (*Ossi di seppia*, 1925), *Occasions* (*Le occasioni*, 1939), *Finisterre* (1943) and *The Storm* (*La bufera*, 1956). There are two volumes of good or useful English translations: *Selected Poems* (tr. G. Kay, 1964) and *Selected Poems* (ed. G. Cambon, 1965).

Montale's stoical view of life is less important than the poetry which describes it. 'The Eel', for example, is a lyrical and affirmative poem about the natural animal urge in man to search, even as he journeys to death, for life:

> The eel, the siren
> of icy seas, who leaves the Baltic
> in quest of our waters,
> our estuaries, our rivers,
> which it deeply travels against the flow
> from rivulet to rivulet and then
> from trickle to trickle, and as these vanish
> into the heart of rock filters
> through packs of mud
> until one day
> a through-chestnuts-flash of sun

captures its glide through stagnancies
of ditches that run
from the Apennine cliffs to Romagna—
eel, torch, whip,
earth's arrow of Love,
which our gullies or parched,
Pyrenean creeks alone lead back
to fertile paradises;
the green soul seeking
life where only
dryness and desolation gnash
the spark that says
all starts from ashes,
a buried stump,
brief eye-rainbow twin
of what your gaze attacks,
keeps shining, safe, amid humanity
trapped in your slime—
O can you call her sister?

This is more difficult than anything of Ungaretti's; partly because it shifts from metaphor to metaphor without any help to the reader. But it is only in this way that we can see the eel becoming transformed—in the mind of the poet—into the spirit of renewal and regeneration. For although the eel, like any other object, is an eel, it also functions as a metaphor for something else. Montale's poem is concerned with this process of mental transformation from perception to metaphor. Thus, in other poems he invests his native Ligurian landscape with the quality of myth: he re-creates it for his reader. He differs from Ungaretti chiefly, perhaps, in his greater concern with the impact of sentences and whole poems rather than with single words. Ungaretti continually pared down; Montale's impulse is to build up.

The Sicilian SALVATORE QUASIMODO (1901–68), although originally also classed as hermetic, is a very different poet from either Ungaretti or Montale. He won the Nobel Prize in 1959. Of the three hermetic poets, Quasimodo was the most native in his inspiration. His severe early work was much criticized for being a 'metaphysic of aridity: a retreat into Sicilian gloom and secretiveness'. But Quasimodo later showed that this emotionlessness was the result of a deliberate withdrawal; when the war came he began to write a poetry of anger and sorrow. He rather incautiously defined the poet's task as being to 'remake man'—and he was promptly told, by the earlier critics of his harshness, that he was not competent as an exponent of what he has called 'social poetry' (*poesia sociale*). The culmination of the early, rarefied, semi-surrealistic, often truly 'hermetic' poetry was his book of exquisite translations called *Greek Lyrics* (*Lirici greci*, 1940). This confirmed his integrity, and helped to make clear that the early poetry aimed at a precise definition of the nature of harsh, sunlit

Southern experience. The refusal to entertain illusions—so easy to nurse and so disastrous in Sicily—was a necessary phase for him. It was from his study of Greek that Quasimodo gained his elegance and grace; as a stylist he is the most distinguished of modern European heirs of the Greeks. Besides, one can hardly call the famous short poem from his first collection—

> We stand alone on the world's heart
> stabbed by a ray of sun:
> and suddenly it's night

—'harsh': it has as much emotion in it as any fragment of such shortness can possibly have. *And Suddenly it's Night* (*Ed è subito sera*, 1945) was in fact the title of Quasimodo's collection that won him more readers than any other hermetic poet. On the whole Quasimodo's defence of his shift from 'private' to 'public' poet is convincing: we expect it to be so, for—again on the whole—the public poetry is convincing. His argument is that to the exact degree he creates beauty so is a poet morally responsible. And when he writes about Auschwitz it is immediately clear that he does so without pretentiousness: his indignation arises directly into language. And so while it is true that some of Quasimodo's early poetry is over-abstract, and that some of his later is unconvincing and weak, the best of both stands up well. 'Poetry', he said, 'is the liberty and truth of [the poet's] time, and not abstract modulations of sentiment'. It is not irrelevant that he was imprisoned by Mussolini. The following poem, 'From the Fortress of Upper Bergamo', dating from some time after the Second World War, is a good example of his later manner. The 'you' addressed here is chiefly himself; but it is also, perhaps, an old lover; a dead soldier now a ghost; and, of course, the reader. (It should be mentioned that the antelope and heron are, for Quasimodo, symbols of his innocent childhood in Sicily.)

> You heard cockcrow in the air
> outside the towers and walls
> chill with a light you lost,
> a lightning-cry of life
> and dungeon-mutterings
> and the bird-call of the dawn-patrol.
> And you said nothing for yourself,
> were trapped in winter's sun:
> antelope and heron had no message,
> lost in gusts of filthy smoke,
> emblems of a pristine world.
> And February's moon sailed over clear,
> but to you was memory
> alight with silence.
> You too are moving now, and silent,

between the cypress trees
and here all rage
is silenced by young death's green:
muffled pity's almost joy.

Quasimodo's verse has been selected and paraphrased by Jack Bevan (1965), but more reliable translations are to be found in *Selected Writings* (tr. A. Mandelbaum, 1960) and *To Give and to Have* (tr. E. Farnsworth, 1969). (MEP; CIP; IQ; PI; PIV)

*

The rest of modern Italian poetry arises out of hermeticism or anti-hermeticism. No independent figure of the calibre of Saba has made an appearance. The Florentine MARIO LUZI (1914) is a gifted descriptive poet who began in the hermetic tradition but has broken out of it into a new explicitness. He has emerged, during the Sixties, as Italy's leading poet of his generation. Luzi is at his best in such poems as 'Ménage' (CIV), in which he contemplates a situation (a woman listening to a record, 'Not in This Life') and then so to speak allows its subtle truths to emerge without making biographical manipulations:

'Not in this life, in another' exults more than ever
her proud look, shedding an unbearable light
and meaning other thoughts than those
of the man whose yoke are caresses she bears and perhaps desires.

Luzi is above all a poet of sad but serene tone and manner; there is much rhetoric, but even this is not manufactured, but rather issues from the poet in a sweet flow. The 'I' of his poems is a perpetual balancer of reason and emotion. Luzi has been said to have reached towards 'a new Christian realization', and perhaps in Italian terms this is understandable; in international terms, however, he may be seen as the author of an authentic and instructive poetry. (MEP; CIP; CIV; IWT)

VITTORIO SERENI (1913), who was born in Lombardy, has also passed from hermeticism to a new simplicity; of all Italy's considerable poets now writing, he is in fact the easiest to understand. It was his experiences in the Second World War—when after seeing some action he was taken prisoner—that turned him into something more than a magazine-poetaster. He sometimes writes ('Hallucination': MEP; CIV) rather over-obviously allegorical poems, but never without grace. He has been profoundly influenced by, and has a special reverence for, the poetry of Guido Gozzano (q.v.), which has given his poetry its partly deceptive air of matter-of-factness. He has also translated and been influenced by William Carlos Williams (q.v.). One might call Sereni a neo-crepuscular except that his minor-keyed poetry is shot through with social conscience and even anger:

I am all this, the commonplace and its reverse
beneath the vault that darkens more and more.
But can do nothing against a single look
from others, confident in itself, that lights itself
from my own look
against the guilty eyes,
against the furtive steps
that bear you away.

(IWT)

ALFONSO GATTO (1909) was born in Salerno. In 1938 he founded a magazine
with Pratolini (q.v.), was active against fascism, and at the end of the war was
fighting with the resistance. His earliest poems, collected in *Island* (*Isola*,
1932), were little more than evocations of southern landscapes and moods.
Later, under the influence of Quasimodo, he became almost surrealistic. With
the war he again followed Quasimodo into a new social awareness. Much of
his more recent poetry has concentrated on death and the reasons for death.
(CIV; CIP; IWT; MEP)

The leading poet of a younger generation, although evidently this is by no
means accepted in all circles, is BARTOLO CATTAFI (1922), born in Barcellona
(Messina, Sicily), who now lives in Milan. Trained as a lawyer, he has
wandered restlessly, trying out various occupations. He shows no sign of
becoming a major poet; but, like Luzi, he writes quite attractive verse. One
meets the manner often—a few English and American poets, such as W. S.
Merwin (q.v.), have affected it without making it seem spontaneous—but
seldom does it sound natural; it was recently described as 'the continental
manner' with some justice. Yet Cattafi has his own poetic impulse:

What about wingspan?
It varies; it can be
microns, inches, yards wide.
Depends on the model, on materials, on
motor power; the aim, to attain altitude.

Here the establishment of a set of facts releases a genuine lyricism; such catalogue
poems are not often as successful as the one which begins with the lines quoted
above. (CIV; MEP; PIV)

The Milanese LUCIANO ERBA (1922), of the same generation, is more aloof
from fashionable literary currents and *avant garde* styles than Cattafi. His style
is reticent, but conceals a sly irony: he is a subtle, deliberately minor poet, who
deals in juxtapositions such as:

Schooner, most gentle craft, O swift
prodigy! if the heart only
knew how to sail as you do
among the azure island chains!

But I go back to my house above the harbour
around six, when my Lenormant
pushes an armchair forward on the terrace
and settles down to her embroidery—
new napery for the altars. . . .

(MEP; see also IWT)

FRANCO FORTINI (ps. FRANCO LATTES, 1917), a Florentine, is Italy's leading Marxist critic, and has been more influenced by Éluard and Brecht (q.v.) than any other Italian. He is also probably the most influential of critics of modern Italian poetry, which he has analyzed exhaustively from a Marxist point of view. His own poetry shows an intelligent awareness of the problems confronting modern poets. (CIV)

CAMILLO PENNATI (1931), born in Milan, now works in London at the Italian Institute of Culture. He has translated some well known English poets. He is concerned with the ambiguous relationship between man and nature, and many of his poems record explorations of natural scenes or phenomena in which he is finally defeated: cannot understand, cannot merge, cannot be (therefore) what he is. An example of such a poem is 'Wood'. (IWT)

Japanese Literature

I

The conditions for modern Japanese literature were created when the country was opened up to the outside world—after 218 years of isolation—at the end of 1857. Until 1853, when the American Commodore Perry arrived in Edo (later Tokyo) Bay and 'requested' the opening of relations between Japan and the U.S.A., Japan had been almost entirely cut off from the rest of the world for over two centuries. Under the feudal Tokugawa system, inaugurated by Tokugawa Ieyasu at the beginning of the seventeenth century, Japan was ruled from Edo by the *shogun* ('barbarian-subduing great general': in modern parlance, 'generalissimo'); the imperial court was relegated to Kyoto, and the emperors wielded no power. In 1639 the country cut itself off from all outside influence except for the Dutch—who were confined to the island of Nagasaki—and some Chinese. Christianity, which had previously been encouraged, was virtually extirpated. Subjects were forbidden to go abroad. Thus the Japanese were effectively cut off from the Renaissance and from the technological discoveries that came in its wake, their natural expansionist energies were frustrated, and they were forced to turn in upon themselves—with eventually, but not immediately, bad results for their literature. The Tokugawa instituted a highly efficient secret police system, and, in order to retain power, did all they could to keep their warrior-dominated, rigidly hierarchical society as static and as uncontaminated by the outside world as possible.

But change was bound to come, if only because such a static society could not survive indefinitely amongst the dynamic, expansionist societies of the nineteenth century. Internally, the population had grown. By 1800 the warrior aristocracy (*samurai*), although they traditionally despised the acquirement of money (and therefore arithmetic), had got into debt to the despised but economically powerful merchant class. Rice economy was giving way to money economy. In the last years of the Tokugawa period the country was only formally feudal, and the thirteenth *shogun*, Iesada, was in 1857 forced to answer Townsend Harris, the diplomatic representative of the U.S.A. and (more important) symbol of his country's naval force, in the following terms: 'Pleased with the letter sent with the Ambassador from a far distant country, and likewise pleased with his discourse. Intercourse shall be continued for ever'.

During the following decade Japan suddenly became filled with foreign diplomats and traders. The Japanese were puzzled, and the *shogunate* lost its power and initiative to such an extent that it collapsed when challenged by an alliance of noble families from western Japan who united themselves under the long subordinated royal house. The eighteen-year-old Emperor Meiji gained full powers in 1868, and until his death in 1912 presided over the modernization and the expansion of Japan. The Taisho period, 1912–26, was followed by the yet unfinished Showa.

The Japanese are an avidly curious people, and in general they took to the ways of the West with great imitative enthusiasm. Extraordinary progress was made both industrially and militarily. At this point the story becomes more familiar: the gaining of Formosa, South Manchuria and Korea in the Nineties, the victory over Russia of 1904–5, the rise to power—against the wishes of the Emperor—of a *führer*-less but nevertheless fascistic (and fanatic) nationalism in the Thirties, the consequent victories and final cataclysmic defeat, leading to the occupation (1945–52)—and to what may fairly be described as the bizarre *shogunate* of the vain, touchy, grandiose, remote and fundamentally mediocre General MacArthur. Since the granting of independence Japan has been ruled by a succession of moderate conservative governments; extreme left-wing opposition amongst the intelligentsia is strong, and most active writers are left-wing (although the most spectacular, Mishima Yukio, q.v., was a fanatic right-wing nationalist); but the socialist party (which held control for a short time under the occupying powers) has so far made a disappointing showing with the electorate, although its share of the vote has increased.

II

Prior to 1868, Japanese literature falls into four main periods. The first, the Yamoto and Nara periods (A.D. 400–794), saw the transition from Chinese to Japanese. (The latter language is polysyllabic and has nothing syntactically or otherwise in common with the monosyllabic former; but written Japanese evolved from the adoption and adaptation, probably in the fifth century, of the Chinese ideographs.)

The next period, the Heian, is the classical period, sometimes known as the 'golden age'. Murasaki Shikibu's *The Tale of Genji*, sometimes regarded as the world's first great novel, and certainly one of the most delightful of all time, was written about 1000. This was the age of refinement, delicacy and technical achievement. Many of the writers were women, and nearly all were aristocrats.

After this comes a dark and unstable period (1185–1603), subdivided into Kamakura, Nambokucho and Muromachi eras, which was characterized by uprisings and civil wars. Naturally enough against this background, Buddhist meditations—as well as war tales became popular. The *Noh* play evolved in this period.

The long Tokugawa, or Edo, period (1603–1868) at first witnessed a literary renaissance. The writers were now mostly neither aristocrats nor monks, but warriors and merchants. The growth of *ukiyo*, 'the floating world', the new kind of society that developed around places of entertainment and relaxation—theatres, geisha houses—led to a new kind of literature, a semi-picaresque literature of everyday life. The puppet theatre, *joruri*, arose; and along with it the *kabuki*, domestic or historical drama played by males only. Both types of theatre continue to be popular today. In poetry the *haiku* was developed.

But by the beginning of the nineteenth century the whole of this energy was spent. The central government was undergoing serious difficulties—but would not allow any writer to mention them. Poetry became trivial, the novel absurd. Most fiction consisted of series of unintegrated episodes, bad jokes, monotonous pornography or moralizations on the lowest level. Gaiety and vitality left the fiction of the *ukiyo*, which became no more than 'spicy'. It was believed—and the government encouraged it—that the function of literature was to impart moral instruction. The most popular and, indeed, gifted of the novelists of this decadence, Kyokutei Bakin (ps. Takizawa Okikuni, 1767–1848), stated that the purpose of his books was to 'encourage virtue and reprimand vice'. He wrote more than 300 works; but, the best of his age, he reveals its inadequacies: his plots are wildly improbable, his tone unconvincingly idealistic. Had he been younger and survived into the Meiji period, he could in no way have responded to its challenge.

*

Japanese differ amongst themselves as much as any other people. They are not, of course, a primitive tribe, although Westerners have tended to treat them as such. However, it is true to say that the Japanese character, so far as one may generalize, is a volatile and unstable one. Therefore it is natural that the kind of stability and serenity advocated by the official religion of Buddhism should be their ideal. However, while Buddhism—originally introduced from China—remained the official religion, the very different and earlier polytheism known as Shinto has had a strong influence. This, while it has its quota of vigour, is comparatively ethnocentric and crude, and was exploited by the nationalists when they took control in the Thirties; but it represents and satisfies the aggressive side of the Japanese character. One of the distinctive features of Japan has been that this—to use the language of anthropologists—'shame culture' (where honour, proper external behaviour, counts for more than private conscience—the most famous works of literature in which this state of affairs obtains are the Homeric epics) has never been wholly supplanted by a 'guilt culture', as has happened in the West. Instead, alongside it have developed the mystical and fatalistic tenets of Buddhism. Those leaders condemned to death by the Allies in the post-war trials, who had embodied the heroic, nationalistic, ruthless spirit of Shintoism were easily—but remarkably to Western observers—able to die in Buddhist serenity.

It was the writers of Japan who most of all responded to the element of abstract morality in Western thinking. Because Japan did not entirely abandon feudalism until 1868, the notion of *individuality*, and with it the notion of individual morality that Europe had been aware of at least since the Renaissance, did not make itself apparent there until very late indeed. And yet when the modern novelists and poets tried to imitate Western models the best of them produced something unmistakably Japanese. Like their compatriots, they restlessly and excitedly—and with great humility—turned to the West; but, sometimes painfully, they discovered themselves.

Japanese literature, especially the poetry, had until 1868 been above all delicate, anxious to capture the transitory beauty of the world. By the side of the lusty *gunki monogatari*, the war stories of the 'dark' period of Japanese literature, had existed such typically meditative and observant verse as Priest Saigyo's

> Trailing on the wind,
> The smoke from Mount Fuji
> Melts into the sky.
> So too my thoughts—
> Unknown their resting-place. (PJV)

What was not simply moralistic (in a Confucian, indeed, often pseudo-Confucian, sense) concentrated, in the long Tokugawa period, upon the exquisite, the subtle, the miniature, the revealing, the evanescent and the beautiful. Japanese poetry is technically easy to write because there is virtually no stress or quantity: all depends upon syllable-count (the number of syllables in the line). Basho (ps. Matsuo Munefusu, 1644–94) developed the famous *haiku* (sometimes transcribed as *hokku*), a three-line form consisting of seventeen syllables: five, seven, five. An understanding of the spirit of this is essential to an understanding of Japanese literature. Most educated Japanese citizens today write *haiku*, and the poets themselves have not abandoned the form.

The most important thing about the *haiku* is that it leaves the reader himself to complete the 'meaning' of the poem: it is not self-contained, but suggestive and impressionistic, like so much of Japanese literature. This alone explains why it has influenced twentieth-century Western poetry. Basho wrote:

> Still baking down—
> The sun, not regarding
> The wind of autumn.

It is up to each reader to interpret this for himself, to form his own peculiar response to it. The success of the poem depends entirely on two qualities: the sharpness, the exactness, of its observation; and its ambiguity, that is, its lack of a personal conclusion such as 'I am sad', or 'this makes me pleased'. . . . Thus, Japanese poetry might be said to be, in one strictly limited sense, prophetic of modern Western poetry: it accepts transitoriness—which most nineteenth-century Western poets did not (or dared not) accept, and it effortlessly perceives the reality that the poem is as much the property of the reader as of the writer. But the *haiku* is, essentially, a miniature form: it can do no more than suggest; the perfection it seeks lies precisely in its power to suggest as widely as possible. The sensitive writer of the Meiji period, possessed of and understanding this capacity, found himself bewildered and fascinated by the concrete and in certain respects threatening prospects of the new world that had suddenly been opened up to him. A businessman (and therefore a politician) could simply enthusiastically imitate and learn from Western models, and profit thereby. Prosperity soon compensated him for his native bewilderment.

But the writers were left to ponder upon the meaning of this 'miracle': this transformation, over only half a century, of a broken-down feudal monarchy into a first-class military and economic power. It is true that the breakdown, owing to industrialization, of the traditional Confucian family system— zealously maintained by the Tokugawa *shogunate* as conducive to general acquiescence in its power—did in the long run have a traumatic effect on the Japanese character. The writers were the first to sense this in themselves. Thus, by the first decade of the century, Japan had developed its own psychological novel; it was much less like its prototype, or inspiration, than was, say, a Japanese locomotive.

III

The changes in fiction after 1868 took longer than in other fields, such as the technological; indeed, the new fiction of Futabatei Shimei and subsequently of Natsume Soseki and others is quite as much a reaction to the changes in Japan itself as to the impact of Western ways. The first Western novels to appear in Japan were Bulwer-Lytton's *Ernest Maltravers*, and its sequel, *Alice, or the Mysteries*, in 1878–9. This 'Byronic' romance about a rich young man's love and loss of a beautiful working-class girl, sentimental and melodramatic but innocuous, was entitled in Japanese *A Spring Tale of Flowers and Willows*. Even the justly described father of the modern novel, TSUBOUCHI SHOYO (1859–1935), called the first part of his inaccurate translation of Scott's *The Bride of Lammermoor* (1880), *A Spring Breeze Love Story*: this followed the pre-Meiji custom of giving everything a vaguely erotic title, partly in the hope of gaining readers by a tacit suggestion of pornographic appeal. Readership consisted of people who still wanted the old kind of fiction; but these same people had bought Samuel Smiles' *Self-Help* in hundreds of thousands.

The most important and influential literary group was the Kenyusha, whose chief representative was the novelist Ozaki Koyo (q.v.). This group, whose ideals can best be summed up as anti-political (in so far as literature is concerned), realist and urban, controlled the literary world for some time from about 1885 onwards. It originated in a determination on the part of certain writers to treat literature as literature.

Tsubouchi Shoyo was the critic, translator and essayist whose *The Essence of the Novel* (*Shosetsu shinzui*, 1885–6) was by far the most important and influential critical work to be published in nineteenth-century Japan. Tsubouchi's underlying thesis, revolutionary in a Japanese context, was that the novel was self-sufficient, a law unto itself, something not only to be distinguished from the popular tale or the romance but also requiring no justification beyond its mere existence. 'There is a simply staggering production of books, all of them extremely bad,' he began. All contemporary fiction, he went on, is either faked or in imitation of Bakin and other classics; he even, though an admirer, refuted Bakin's didactic view of the novel. He blamed not only the writers but also the indiscriminate readers: 'It has long been the custom . . . to consider the novel as an instrument of education. . . . In actual practice . . . only stories of blood-thirsty cruelty or else of pornography are welcomed. . . .' And he hoped that his book would help authors to improve upon Japanese fiction until it surpassed that of Europe in quality.

Tsubouchi attacked the traditional poetic forms, including the *haiku*, as unsuitable for modern life, and suggested that a viable poetry, of a Western kind, was closer to the Japanese novel than to its poetry. He attacked the distortions of plot and the careless psychology of the didactic novelists. The primary objective of the 'artistic' novel that he desired to promote was to portray human emotions, to probe and penetrate the human psyche. Most important is his prescription for the language in which the new novel should be composed.

Previous Japanese fiction had come in three different styles, which we may here call rhetorical, colloquial and rhetorical-colloquial (i.e. a standardized combination of the first two). *The Tale of Genji* (*c.* 1022) is the most famous example of the first; remote from common speech, its style is unsuitable to convey a sense of modern life. The same (Tsubouchi believed) applies to the colloquial style, because of the frequent discrepancy between literary and demotic words: for this, and other reasons peculiar to the Japanese language, he could not himself conceive of a satisfactory style that employed only the spoken language—although he hoped that it would be developed to a point where it was suitable. (Chinese, in which much of Japanese literature—particularly poetry—had been and was still written, was of course regarded as even less suitable.) His solution was a combination of both styles: the rhetorical was to be used for narrative, the colloquial for dialogue.

Thus Tsubouchi most intelligently applied the methods of Western criticism to the problems of Japanese literature. Unfortunately he was less successful in applying his principles to his own practice. A pleader for accurate translations, his own translations were inaccurate; a pleader for realistic fiction, he was himself unable to write it. His novel *The Character of Present-day Students* (*Tosei shosei katagi*, 1885–6), hopefully written to demonstrate his critical theories, does not do so. It is, in fact, didactic—although not in the worst sense. Written to illustrate worthy and sensible theories, it fails to come to life. Tsubouchi made too much of the habits of his students, and not enough of their characters.

However, a younger man than Tsubouchi, FUTABATEI SHIMEI (ps. HASEGAWA TATSUNOSUKE, 1864–1909) was able to produce a novel along the lines he had prescribed: *Drifting Clouds* (1887) is well described as 'Japan's first modern novel'; it added elements of its own, in fact, to Tsubouchi's prescription.

Futabatei, son of an ex-*samurai*, had at first had military ambitions, and it was only when these were thwarted by short-sightedness that he concentrated his energies on literature. One of the influences that he brought to Japanese literature was Russian criticism and fiction, of which Tsubouchi had been unaware. Yet originally Futabatei's interest in Russian grew out of his patriotic conviction that Russia posed the most serious threat to Japan's future: the best weapon to guard against this would be a knowledge of the Russian language. However, in his own words, 'At first neither [my 'excessive chauvinism'] was stronger than the other [interest in Russian literature] but soon my nationalistic fervour was quieted and my passion for literature burned on'. After a period of interest in socialism, Futabatei decided on a literary career. During his Russian studies he became a student of Japanese musical narrative, which, as his American biographer and translator Marleigh Grayer Ryan points out, helped him to cultivate *goro*, 'that indefinable quality in . . . language of what sounds right to a cultivated ear'.

Futabatei read *The Essence of the Novel* when it was published and subsequently became friendly with Tsubouchi. Under his guidance he began to translate Russian fiction—and to write *Drifting Clouds*. But the older man soon realized that Futabatei was more sensitive to literature than he was. The Russian novel, particularly as exemplified by Turgenev, fertilized his imagination in a way that Tsubouchi could only admire.

Drifting Clouds (*Ukigumo*, 1887; tr. M. G. Ryan, 1967) is important for two reasons. One is the language that Futabatei wrote it in—this was not quite what Tsubouchi had had in mind, although his theories had a marked influence. The other is that in its protagonist, Bunzo, Futabatei summed up all that is most melancholic, sensitive and ineffectual in the Japanese character—as it had never been summed up before. It is somewhat ironic, perhaps, that he was able so well to portray the bewildered Meiji Japanese through his understanding of the Russian 'negative hero'.

As we read the novels written after *Drifting Clouds* we meet men like Bunzo again and again. And while the cast of mind is specifically Japanese, the depiction of it is meaningful to Western readers because it represents a certain response to that sense of absurdity, of contingency, to which all modern literature is itself in some way a response.

In his style Futabatei was a pioneer. He realized, as Tsubouchi had, that in narrative the colloquial mode was not satisfactory; but he wanted to move as close to it as he could. By the end of his first novel he had modified the rhetorical style more considerably and more effectively than any of his contemporaries; his knowledge of Russian techniques, such as interior monologue and the relation of events through his hero's eyes, undoubtedly helped him to achieve this. He was engaged in translating Turgenev while writing *Drifting*

Clouds; his version of *Diary of a Hunter* became the accepted model for future translations.

Futabatei wrote more novels: *Chasengami* (the name of the hair style adopted by widows), a fragment of 1906; *An Adopted Son* (*Sono Omokage*, 1906: tr. B. Mitsui and G. M. Sinclair, 1919) and *Mediocrity* (*Heibon*, 1907: tr. G. W. Shaw, 1927). *Chasengami* seems to have been intended as in part a study of the human cruelty of traditional social customs. *An Adopted Son*, like *Drifting Clouds*, portrays moral inertia; *Mediocrity*, which is autobiographical, attacks intellectuals, and gives point to the fact that Futabatei never mixed happily (or, indeed, much at all) with the writers of his day. *Mediocrity* contains many moments of acute self-insight, and is in some ways a more interesting and substantial book than *Drifting Clouds*. But Futabatei was a difficult and obstinate man who frequently protested—one suspects undue bitterness—that he was not a writer at all. Distress over his difficulties with *Drifting Clouds* led him, in 1889, to take up a post in the office of the gazette of the Japanese Government. In 1908, dissatisfied with literary expression, he visited Russia, Germany and England, but died (1909) on the voyage home.

What is most important about *Drifting Clouds* is that Futabatei was concerned to portray the society of his day truthfully and realistically. His largely successful efforts to do this nearly cost him his sanity: he contemplated suicide while engaged on it, and could not attempt any further fiction for almost twenty years. His standards were those of the Russian novelists, not those of his contemporaries—not even, in the last analysis, those of Tsubouchi, though it was Tsubouchi who gave him the impetus to write.

Drifting Clouds concerns a hapless young government clerk, Utsumi Bunzo, who will not ambitiously seek to please his civil service employers, and so loses his job. He lives with his aunt and her daughter Osei, with whom he is in love. Contrasted to Bunzo is the energetic 'new man', the toady and decision-maker Honda Noburo, a colleague of Bunzo's who is clearly cut out for a successful career. Osei, superficially westernized and enlightened, is skilfully and subtly presented as being untrue to her own Japanese nature. She turns from Bunzo to Noburo, who (it is implied) will have an affair with her and then reject her to make a more useful marriage. Bunzo is represented as possessing standards and sensitivity, but as being totally mediocre in the realm of action. He drifts from one situation to another. He loves Osei and wants her, but despises her—and cannot make up his mind to win her and then try to change her: he lacks the crude, calculating, coarse energy of Noburo, who gains her affection by cunning.

Drifting Clouds is partly satirical, or at least critical to the point of caricature, of the Meiji 'enlightenment'. Thus, Futabatei shows the nastiness and the spiritual superficiality of Noburo, and the shallowness of Osei's acceptance of current fashions. Bunzo himself, although able to make private qualitative judgements in the materialistic context of his office (run by a foolish hypocrite who pays lip-service to democracy while acting as a tyrant), betrays his own principles of Confucian honesty and decency by remaining incapable of action.

Indeed, Edward Seidensticker has described the novel as 'a drably realistic study in fecklessness'—and it is true enough that there is an element of fecklessness in Bunzo.

But Futabatei went beyond satire. Apart from the fact that his characters 'come to life', in Bunzo he created the first genuinely 'alienated character'—in the modern sense—in Japanese fiction. Thus he may be said to have possessed a truly 'modern' sensibility. Like Futabatei himself, Bunzo was a *shizoku*, a gentleman, an ex-*samurai* forced to abandon his traditional, easy role and make his own way in the world. Bunzo will not make his own way, however: he will not compromise—though, ironically, his passivity results in compromise.

As I have already pointed out, Futabatai learned of this type of character from the Russians, who were divided amongst themselves as to the propriety of depicting it in fiction. But in taking it over he added a specifically Japanese quality. 'It is almost an accident,' writes Marleigh Grayer Ryan, 'that Futabatei was the first to portray him; another author would surely have created such a hero in any case. The amazing thing is that, being the first, Futabatei succeeded so well'. It might be added that, in succeeding so well, Futabatei virtually incapacitated himself as a creative writer: for in creating Bunzo he had partially to portray his own sense of alienation and isolation—never an easy thing for a man to do. His pseudonym—it is customary for Japanese writers to employ them—is, Marleigh Grayer Ryan tells us, an 'approximation of the profanity, *kutabatte shimae* . . . "go to hell" '. There is something 'modern', too, in that.

The intelligent and sensitive Japanese suffered an excruciatingly sudden transition from feudalism to industrialism. Hence the proverbial—and to many Western readers highly irritating and frustrating—impotence and hopelessness of the heroes of so many Japanese novels. And yet to other Western readers these heroes, with their self-defeating type of involuntary scepticism, seem peculiarly prophetic. As such comforting bourgeois conceptions as God, the inherent goodness of man and the wisdom of leaders have been progressively exposed as illusions or at best uncertainties, Western man—his landscape illuminated by the two atom bombs he dropped on, of all places, Japan, in 1945—begins himself to feel traumatized: lost, unable to act on the old values or to believe in the efficacy of new ones: in the situation of, as Broch (q.v.) put it, 'no longer, not yet'.

Bunzo's isolation is peculiarly Japanese in that it does not arise from a sense of aggression; his bosses distrust him because he seems dull and unambitious, not because he attacks them or criticizes them. When a redundancy arises they pick on him to sack. But Bunzo sees himself as superior: 'The fellows still . . . there aren't especially competent,' he thinks, '. . . they're so damned obsequious. It's downright obsequious to be so submissive and grovel for the sake of a little pay'. However, Bunzo flatters himself when he sees himself as capable of such tough independent-mindedness.

Drifting Clouds, had it been translated into English in the Eighties, would have met with incomprehension; today, making allowances for some stylistic

771

archaisms, it reads quite naturally. It hints at sexual anxieties that were later to be developed in Western and Japanese fiction, for example in this passage, where the growth of Bunzo's love for Osei is compared to the growth, not of flowers but of worms:

> Since Osei had come home to live, worms had been breeding inside poor, unsuspecting Bunzo's heart. At first they were very small and did not occupy enough space to give him trouble. But once they started actively crawling around, he felt as though he were peacefully departing from this world and entering a blissful paradise. It was like lying among exquisite flowers and glittering leaves on a spring day, wafting on scent-filled air, dozing, half awake and half asleep, hearing the drone of a fly growing ever more distant. It was an indescribably glorious sensation.
>
> But all too soon the worms grew fat and powerful. By the time Bunzo had begun to suspect that he was infatuated with Osei, they were enormous and were crawling about, anxious to be mated. They depended on her encouragement for their survival, and if she had been cold they would surely have died. But as it was, they were being half killed. The worms seem to have found this state of affairs horribly painful—they wriggled around and chewed away at his insides, making him utterly miserable.
>
> (tr. M. G. Ryan)

Futabatei—although he does not go as far as to question the reliability of human perception itself—abandons the omniscience of the narrator that characterized Western novels of this time; like Bunzo himself, he does not pretend certainty. Describing strained relations that occur between Osei and Noburo, he tells us that 'She was cold and distant, treating him like an estranged relative.' But then, instead of telling us more, he asks, 'Had they quarrelled or had she just grown tired of him? Perhaps the novelty of her infatuation had worn off. It is impossible to tell'.

Drifting Clouds ends on an inconclusive note. There have been well grounded suggestions that it is unfinished; but it seems that the ending as we have it, although 'unpolished', does represent Futabatei's final intentions—or rather lack of them. The existence of several varying outlines for different endings indicates that, like Bunzo, Futabatei could not make up his mind, and that therefore the ending as it stands represented, even if it did not satisfy him (what could?), his real intentions.

In this ending Bunzo is momentarily cheered by a smile from Osei, who seems to have lost some of her snobbishness and to have given up Noburo. Are the 'knitting-lessons' to which she goes out in heavy make-up real; or has she, rejected by Noburo, decided to 'have a good time'? Bunzo, pleased by the smile, nevertheless discerns that 'something is wrong', and determines to talk to Osei on her return from the bath. 'If she would not listen, he would leave that house once and for all.' And the book ends: 'He went upstairs to wait.' We know, of course, from what has become of Bunzo's decisions before, that he will allow himself to be fobbed off: will continue to drift in obscurity and lack of self-fulfilment.

I have devoted considerable space to this novel because of its relevance to the fiction that comes after it. Bunzo, for all that he owes to Goncharov's *Oblomov*, may almost be seen as a prototype for the hero of the modern Japanese novel. That quality which in Western terms makes *Drifting Clouds* and other slightly later Japanese novels prophetic is also partly fortuitous—it is largely due, as I have pointed out, to the speed of transition from nominally feudal to industrial Japan; but it is none the less there, and none the less relevant to modernism.

However, not too much emphasis must be put on Futabatei's originality. It so happens that his first novel has lasted as literature, whereas fiction by others who were working, if less resolutely and intelligently, in the same direction as Futabatei has not. The literary group known as the Kenyusha, founded to oppose superficial westernization and to bring about a return to earlier fictional modes, had as one of its members YAMADA BIMYO (1868–1910), whose stories certainly contained colloquial elements. Futabatei, though less conservative, had some things in common with the Kenyusha group. Again, it is not possible to state to what extent Futabatei influenced Toson and Soseki, both writers superior to him. Still, *Drifting Clouds* certainly deserves its reputation as 'Japan's first modern novel', and it equally certainly does foreshadow many of both its more and less distinguished successors.

OZAKI KOYO (1867–1903) wrote many more novels than Futabatei, and possessed perhaps as much skill; but he is less important, despite the influence he wielded during his short life. Nor did he ever write as subtle or as penetrating a novel as *Drifting Clouds*. Koyo's realism is in fact superficial, although his presentation is vivid. He was able to analyze emotions—especially sexual and amorous emotions—but was less successful with character. The best passages in his fiction are peculiarly erotic in that wholly Japanese manner which is most effectively exploited by Tanizaki Junichiro and after him by Kawabata Yasunari (qq.v.). For example, in *Purple* (*Murasaki*, 1894), which deals with a thrice-unsuccessful medical student's anxieties (typically, Koyo deals brilliantly with the anxiety, but mechanically with the student), his teacher's daughter presents him with a purple cushion for use as an elbow rest. Koyo's last work, which is unfinished, was *The Gold Demon* (*Konjiki yasha*, 1897): about a woman who gives up love for wealth, and thereby turns her rejected lover, Kanichi, into a miserly demon of a usurer. It is interesting to compare this treatment of greed for money with that of Frank Norris (q.v.) in his almost contemporary *McTeague* (1899).

IV

Some lines of poetry that might quite appropriately have been written by Bunzo of *Drifting Clouds*—provided we can postulate a Bunzo with the resolution to sit down and write a serious poem—are:

I am like the morning cloud
That brought rain the night before;
Or I am like the evening rain
That tomorrow will be a floating cloud.

Like leaves that have fallen
I was carried by the wind;
And with the clouds of the morning
Came over the river at night.

Perhaps here, in Miyagi Plain,
In this ancient wilderness without a path
I shall cease to wander,
And find some rest.

The grass has withered under the northern sun;
And in this barrenness of Miyagi Plain
My troubled heart
Shall find a home.

In loneliness I listen to the northern wind;
To my ears it is like the sound of the harp;
And to my eyes the stones
Are like flowers in bloom.

(tr. E. McClellan)

This passage is taken from a longer poem, 'Pillow of Grass', by SHIMAZAKI TOSON (ps. SHIMAZAKI HARUKI, 1872–1943). As a pioneer of the 'modern-style' poem, Toson will be discussed in the context of poetry; but he was also a novelist, one of Japan's most distinguished.

However, before discussing Toson and his most outstanding contemporaries, it is necessary to insert a word of warning. The Japanese themselves have a mania for classification, and since 1868 they have divided writers of the past and present into innumerable schools, sub-schools, and even sub-sub-schools. . . . This is not useful to the Western reader; probably it is also confusing and distracting to the Japanese. All that it is necessary to know is that modern Japanese literature is fundamentally romantic: the writers are mostly egoistic, and their fiction is almost invariably autobiographical. The early craze for European naturalism (q.v.), the emphasis on realism, should not mislead us as to this. Some Japanese might have liked to write in the style of Zola (q.v.), giving a solidly factual, scientific picture of the life of their industrial society— and, of course, in the spirit of naturalism, with its insistence upon man's helplessness. The general gloom inherent in naturalism was something that the Japanese could respond to; but their society was changing far too quickly for them to exploit it as Zola had French society, or Frank Norris (q.v.) American.

774

Furthermore, Japanese gloom tended more towards nihilism; despair there frequently has a suicidal edge, and unhappiness is often violent. The Japanese writer, more sharply and personally disturbed than his Western counterpart, turned to himself for material: it was his own personality that he subjected to meticulous examination. So he was really quite unlike Zola; and resembled more, as has been pointed out, Rousseau. As for Zola's 'frankness': this was matter-of-fact to Japanese writers, who are not prudes.

Toson's first novel did deal with a social theme; but it was an exception, and he never wrote another on an invented subject. Nor would it be useful to call Toson a true naturalist at any stage of his career. Whatever was written in a naturalist spirit before about 1910 tended to be imitative and unconvincing, and therefore forgettable. Later we shall encounter exceptions. But not more than incidental notice need be taken of the 'schools' of literature that have proliferated in Japan since the Restoration: they merely distract attention from individual achievement (and non-achievement).

Toson was born in what was then a remote part of Japan, Nagano, a district that often figures in his novels. He was educated in Tokyo, and later attended a Christian school where English, in which he had developed an interest, was well taught. He was baptized, but the influence of Christianity on his fiction is negligible. He began as a journalist, then, in 1892, became a schoolmaster. He was associated with the group surrounding the poet and essayist Kitamura Tokuku (1868–94), who committed suicide and who figured as Aoki in *Spring* (q.v.). Toson married in 1899. He first made his reputation as a poet, but in 1899 began to write prose seriously. When his first novel, *Broken Commandment*, was published he abandoned teaching and settled down as a writer. His wife died soon afterwards, but he did not marry again until 1929. Toson represented Japan at the International P.E.N. Conference in Buenos Aires in 1936. He died in 1943 while at work on his seventh novel.

Toson's first fiction, consisting of short stories, was pseudo-realistic, immature and untypical. But *Broken Commandment* (*Hakai*, 1906; pt. tr. MJL), which was successful with the public, remains one of the best of all Japanese novels. Its most unusual features in its time were that it was wholly based on an imaginary situation, and that it explored a social problem; Donald Keene has called it 'a pioneer Japanese problem novel'.

Segawa Ushimatsu, the hero, is an *eta*. During the Tokugawa period the *eta* and *hissin* were two outcast groups, inferior by law to ordinary commoners. The *eta* were placed higher than the *hissin*, but could not—as could the latter —become commoners. The *eta* class, whose position was somewhat like that of the 'untouchable' in India, was hereditary: it was segregated, and limited to the practice of occupations generally regarded as unpleasant, such as executioner's assistant, butcher, sandal-maker. All discrimination against the *eta* was forbidden by law in 1871, but even now feeling against them, amongst some, is strong. In 1906 it was more general and more intense, as Toson's novel clearly shows.

Ushimatsu's father has commanded him never to reveal to anyone that he is an *eta*. When he dies, he goes so far as to arrange for himself to be buried quietly and obscurely in the hills, so that the formalities necessary for a temple burial in the city should not accidentally reveal his origin. Such a promise carries with it a very strong sense of obligation—more so in Japan than in the West—but Ushimatsu finally breaks it.

Although influenced by the interest of Western novelists in social problems, *Broken Commandment* is completely Japanese until nearly the end; it is an example of successful assimilation of literary influence. Ushimatsu is less passive than Bunzo; but he might well irritate some Western readers by his gormlessness. His state of mind, unhappily ambivalent until events force him to action, is portrayed with consummate subtlety and skill. He has gone through school and then become, by concealing his origins, a schoolmaster in the normal fashion. It is a natural enough deception in the face of so manifest a social injustice. Yet Ushimatsu is uneasy. On the one hand he is terrified of discovery. He uses his father's instruction to rationalize his fear. On a yet deeper level, exposure represents for Ushimatsu a terrifying immersement into his alienated state. When an *eta* guest at the inn in which he lodges is asked to leave, Ushimatsu himself moves to a more uncomfortable room in a local temple.

On the other hand, Ushimatsu has a deep sense of shame: he is a secret admirer of an *eta* called Inoko Rentaro who, forced to resign from a school because of his origin, has devoted his life to championing the *eta* cause. He partners an *eta* boy at tennis. But he cannot bring himself to confess, either to Inoko Rentaro himself (whom he gets to know) or to anyone else. In fact he is continually haunted by the fear that his rash actions will cause people to guess his secret.

The strain upon him becomes worse when his father dies and his uncle suggests that he should steer clear of Inoko Rentaro: the reason is that Inoko Rentaro is an *eta*! It is clear that both Ushimatsu's father and uncle (by lying) accept their alienated position as being just; but the young man cannot. Eventually it is somewhat melodramatic circumstances that force Ushimatsu, after Inoko has been murdered, to tell the truth about himself. It was at this point that Toson over-succumbed to Western influence. He should h ve left things as they were. As it was, he contrived a job in Texas for his hero; a girl-friend accompanies him. Thus the whole moral dilemma is evaded: the quetsion of how the self-confessed *eta* would survive is avoided. Perhaps it was this forced and incongruous ending that caused Toson to abandon the 'invented' for the autobiographical novel: all his other fiction is based in his personal experience, although the last completed novel is about his father rather than himself. It was left for other writers, such as Soseki, to pursue the 'invented' novel in modern Japan. Why did Toson not try another novel, based on purely imaginary material, when he had come so close to success? Edwin McClellan, who has written a book about him, suggests that he was one of those novelists who find it 'extremely difficult to avoid banality in imaginary situations'. This is probably true; and the reason may well be that he was, essentially, a lyrical and 'confessional' poet—one for whom no objective correlative could be wholly satisfactory. He felt, as McClellan says, 'more comfortable, less strained' when dealing with familiar facts. But *Broken Commandment* is a remarkable novel. It is impossible to consider it now without thinking of the position of the Jews, the Negroes—or any other of the persecuted minorities of the world, from the Northern Irish Catholics to the British Gipsies. Again, Ushimatsu's father and uncle accept their unjust predicament in the same way as the human race accepts *its* unjust predicament; Ushimatsu himself, however, stands for the 'alienated artist'. His predicament represented Toson's own; but the poet/ novelist could not, of course, escape happily married to Texas and prosperity.

With *Spring* (*Haru*, 1908) Toson found a mode more congenial to him. It is a deliberately rambling, impressionistic and lyrical account of Toson's connection with the group, called the Bungakkai, centring around the poet Kitamura Tokuku. Toson appears as Kishimoto, a young man who feels purposelessness, like Futabatei's Bunzo, but struggles against it. It is objected that *Spring* has no 'design'; that it is too 'impressionistic': 'the reader has no idea . . . what emotional response is expected of him'. But should the reader have such an idea? It is objected that Katsuko, the girl Kishimoto loves (but cannot have because she is engaged to another), is a key figure, but is not glimpsed for more than an 'unilluminating moment'. But surely Toson was right in not trying to superimpose a design—a solid, nineteenth-century novelistic design—on his essentially fleeting material. This was an advance—at least for a Japanese novelist—on Western realism. We need to read Toson more in the spirit of today than in that of, say, George Eliot. If the reasons for Aoki's (Kitamura Tokuku's) suicide are unexplained then this is not necessarily a failure on the part of the novelist; it is simply another way of depicting Japanese reality. The Japanese are on the whole an anti-intellectual people, and analytical explanations appear to them as abstractions. Toson was representative in this respect.

The Destiny of Two Households (*Ie*, 1911) is a long and detailed account of the married life of Toson, and of his elder sister. Once again, the voice of the novelist himself seldom intervenes to offer explanations or interpretations. At times, as in the scene where two brothers decide to send their feckless and irresponsible elder brother, Minoru, off to Manchuria where he cannot plague them, the writing is masterly in its restraint and in the sense of sadness it conveys. Like all Toson's fiction, this is pervaded with a sense of helplessness and hopelessness. The writing—restrained, lyrical, touching, infinitely sad—is often very beautiful indeed. Like Zola, Toson tried to work with a meticulous accuracy. 'I eliminated any description of the things which happened outside the houses [the two houses of the novel], and confined the scenes and events to the household. I went into the kitchen to write about it. I wrote on the porch where certain incidents took place. . . .' The differences from Zola and from naturalism were that the material so treated was not sociological, and that Toson brought his Japanese and poetic vision to bear on it.

In *When the Cherries Ripen* (*Sakura no mi no juku suru toki*, 1917) Toson went back to the difficult adolescent days when he lived, in Tokyo, with friends of his family. But his next novel, *A New Life* (*Shinsei*, 1919) is the most fascinating of all his books, in which he anticipated more modern writers of the West in creating a frankly 'confessional' novel, whose theme is incest. Once again he appears as Kishimoto, and the experiences he describes are clearly his own. After his first wife died Toson took in a grown-up niece as housekeeper (called Setsuko in the book): he slept with her, she became pregnant—and he fled to Paris for three years (1913–16). When he returned—the child having been given away, a practice easier and commoner in Japan than in the West—he resumed his relationship with his niece. Finally he decided to write a novel, called *A New Life*, in order to examine his conduct. Again, Kishimoto's uncertainty as described in the novel will irritate readers used to the techniques of Victorian fiction. But for readers less confident in human beings' ability to explain their motives clearly, it is eminently satisfactory. The reader himself is left, on the evidence provided—which consists of exactly what the writer can in fact remember of his feelings and motives (it does not consist of invention, for that would have been afterthought)—to make up his own mind if he wishes to. The effect is uncannily like that of 'real life'. This—as Tanizaki's *The Makioka Sisters* (q.v.) also shows—is a kind of realism the Japanese can handle better than Western writers. The novel is no longer used to 'clarify' life or to endow it with certain moral purposes; it is used to describe it. This is offensive to the moral or the dogmatic, and may partly account for the patronizing attitude towards Japanese literature often encountered in the Occident. When Kishimoto's brother Yoshio, father of Setsuko, hears of the publication of the first part of *A New Life*, he writes: 'What a sorry business writing must be, when in order to eat you have to wash your dirty linen in public'. That, too, with its awareness of the existential difficulties of being a writer, has a very modern ring about it.

Toson's last completed novel, *Before the Dawn* (*Yoakemae*, 1935), describes the doomed life of a character much resembling his own father. Hanzo is an idealist and a scholar, the head-man of a village, who greets the Meiji Restoration with hope and loyalty. But its crassness, and his own failure to come to terms with himself, destroys him: he becomes a drunkard, and then a madman. The historical background is filled in with meticulous detail, and there is throughout a sense of high tragedy and sad waste of a noble life. But for all the Dreiseresque grandeur he achieves, Toson is not philosophically committed enough to be called a true naturalist. Here as elsewhere, he is a lyrical realist, employing a most careful technique, the chief feature of which is avoidance of explanation or of abstraction. It is certain that if Toson's novels were translated and published in the West, they would be acclaimed as the work of a master.

V

NATSUME SOSEKI (PS. NATSUME KINNOSUKE, 1867–1916), Japan's most popular modern novelist, has been luckier than Toson: many of his novels have been translated. He, too, is one of the undoubted masters of the twentieth century. His books have a unique flavour which, once tasted, can never be forgotten. He was the most distinguished Japanese poet to write in Chinese. The following lines, called 'Self-derision', suggest many of the qualities of his fiction: originality ('audacity', it has been called), bitterness, psychological subtlety, unhappy remoteness, intelligence:

> With hateful eyes I wait withdrawal from the world,
> Lazy, with this doltish ignorance, to try its fame.
> Turning my back upon the days, I slander my contemporaries;
> I read old books to curse the ancients.
> With the talent of a donkey, a lagging roan,
> Head vacuous as the autumn locust's shell,
> Abounding only in passion for the mists,
> I shall rate rivers, from my rude hut classify the hills.

> (MJL)

This poem sums up Soseki's attitude as a novelist. It is, self-evidently, characteristically Japanese. The feeling is not so much one of lack of self-confidence as semi-nihilism and despair. His life was an unhappy one: his parents did not want him and he was adopted by a childless couple, who returned him to his real parents when they divorced. He became a noted scholar of Chinese and English, and after graduation accepted a teaching post regarded as a surprisingly humble one for a man of his capacities. Probably it was taken up in a spirit of Buddhist renunciation. Unlike Toson, who regarded Buddhism as alien to the Japanese character and ultimately harmful, Soseki remained obsessed with the spirit of it all his life. A Buddhistic resignation haunts all his work—in contrast to that of Toson, which embodies no definable attitude (unless it be that of a dedicated, conscientious realist). Soseki, a humorous but exceedingly neurotic man, married a girl whom he liked because, although she had bad teeth, 'she made no attempt to hide them'. The marriage was happy for a time, but, as two or three of his novels reveal, became desperately unhappy in the last years of his life.

In 1900 he went to England for two years on a government scholarship. He did not like the English, and was lonely; but he read and assimilated much English fiction. On his return he became a lecturer at the First National College in Tokyo. In 1907 he went to work, at last on a satisfactory financial basis, for a newspaper. He began late—at the age of thirty-seven—as a novelist. He died, probably as a result of stomach ulcers, in 1916. It has been considered, on the evidence of his terrifying rages, that he was 'insane', or 'very near it'. Perhaps the misery his uncontrollable manifestations caused him explains his orientation towards Buddhist self-denial. He was a man of much more dramatic psychological make-up than Toson. But he had more humour. His theory was that there were 'leisure novels' (i.e. entertainments) and non-leisure novels. He wrote both.

After a historical novel, a false start, he had an immediate popular success with *I am a Cat* (*Wagahai wa neko de aru*, 1905; tr. K. Ando, 1906–9; K. Shibatu and M. Kai, 1961), which is really a series of satirical episodes, and is the lightest and slightest thing he did. Through the eyes of a cat, he satirizes certain aspects of himself in the character of Kushami, an ineffectual man whose imagination of himself is as just the opposite. He also put various 'Meiji types' under the microscope for the first time: in particular the vicious, gross business man and the charlatan right-wing 'philosopher'. He derived some of his satirical procedures from Meredith (q.v.).

Soseki discovered a richer vein in his next novel, *Young Master* (*Botchan*, 1906; tr. M. Yasutaro, 1918; U. Sasaki, 1922; pt. MJL), the Japanese title of which means something like 'sonny boy'. This is among the first of the so-called 'I' novels—i.e. novels written in the first person—in modern Japanese literature. Its hero is a young man who has inherited the outlook and the virtues of his *samurai* parents; unfortunately these qualities will not be of the least use to him in the new, crass Meiji world; and, like Bunzo's, his life is doomed. This is not autobiographical in the way Toson's *A New Life* is; but there are many more autobiographical elements in it than in the (technically) meticulously objective *Broken Commandment*. Botchan is not represented as being intelligent; but shares with Soseki a romantic, non-commercial emotional outlook. Whereas Toson in his moving last novel showed the defeat of a man already mature in 1868, Soseki shows the similar predicament of one no more than born into the old order. The most depressingly ironic incident in the novel is when Botchan and a friend catch two of their schoolmaster colleagues—coarse, cunning, machinating, 'modern' men—coming out of a brothel. Botchan's only argument against them—against their hypocrisy and lack of human quality—resides, alas, in his fists. . . . This in itself constitutes a biting social comment.

The opening paragraph of *Young Master* gives a good example of Soseki's economy and skill in quickly establishing the characteristics of his protagonists. Here Botchan's fatally 'old-fashioned' attitudes are made clear in a few lines; and his comparative lack of intelligence is also more than hinted at:

From childhood I have suffered because of the reckless nature I inherited from my parents. When I was in elementary school I jumped out of the second story of the school building and lost the use of my legs for a week. Some people might ask why I did such a thing. I had no very profound reason. I was looking out of the second-floor window of the new schoolhouse when one of my class-mates said as a joke that, for all my boasting, he bet I could not jump to the ground. He called me a coward. When the janitor carried me home on his back, my father looked at me sternly and said he did not think much of anyone who dislocated his back just by jumping from the second floor. I said next time I would show him I could do it without getting hurt.

(MJL)

It is strange that a man subject to violent rages, whose own children went in terror of him, should have contributed to the Meiji novel qualities of relaxedness, humour and wit, and freedom from melodramatic—if not always from emotional—tension. But Soseki seems to have sought for the opposite to himself in the atmosphere, if not in the characters, of his fiction. Of his ten further novels, three are outstanding.

Pillow of Grass (*Kusamakura*, 1906; tr. Alan Turney, *The Three-Cornered World*, 1965; U. Sasaki, 1927; K. Takahashi, *Unhuman Tour*, 1927), is Soseki's gentlest book, which he called 'a novel in the manner of a *haiku*'. But for all its delicacy and gentleness, *Pillow of Grass* foreshadows the anguish of his later works. It is about a painter and a woman who try to live in friendship, in a beautiful mountain village, without passion. The artist tries to subject himself to an aesthetic discipline: to seek the real world of the senses, in which the impersonal eternal lies enveloped, and to reject the false one of the heart, which can only distract human attention—by passion and pain—from the meaning of existence. Nature is presented in the exquisite Japanese manner, as fleetingly and uncapturably beautiful; thus, in spite of their desire for it, is peace uncapturable for the painter and his woman friend, Nani. *Pillow of Grass* operates on many levels of meaning, but one of its chief functions is as comment on the nature of creativity (contrast Toson's concern with the same subject in *A New Life*). Its conclusion—that human beings cannot live without pain, can know only the possibility of resignation, not resignation itself—is made more explicit at the end of the trilogy of novels that came soon after it, *Sanshiro* (1908), *And Then* (*Sore kara*, 1909) and *The Gate* (*Mon*, 1910; tr. F. Mathy, 1971), when Sosuke, the hero, tries but fails to find peace through Buddhist meditation. In this phase Soseki is depicting a kind of man who desires Buddhistic peace but cannot find it—almost as if he feels that this peace is an illusion, but a necessary illusion.

The Heart (*Kokoro*, 1914; tr. K. B. Shinkokai, 1939; E. McClellan, *Kokoro*, 1957) is not only the most popular of all Soseki's phenomenally popular books, but also probably the finest of them. Exquisitely simple in structure and sure in its touch, it is unusual in that it explores, though delicately, a homosexuality that Soseki had previously only hinted at.

The Heart, a story within a story, is a study in loneliness. Although not wholly autobiographical, there is much of Soseki himself in both the young student-narrator and in Sensei (this means, roughly, '*maître*', and is not a personal name), the older man to whom he becomes so attracted.

The plot is simple. The novel is told in three parts. The first, narrated by the young student, describes how, holidaying at the resort of Kamakura, he sees and is attracted by an elder stranger on the beach. Though it is never explicitly stated, it is perfectly clear that the narrator's motives, whether conscious or unconscious, are vaguely homosexual—homosexual in the sense that this type of relationship is looked for as an escape from 'life'—pain, passion and the 'ties' as uncomfortably symbolized by women. This is to say that the feeling is homosexual—not that the student physically desires the older man. The narrator succeeds in making friends with the faintly forbidding Sensei, who is married, and who clearly reciprocates the young man's affection, but never the less rather mysteriously keeps him at his distance.

In the second part the younger man describes his summer visit to his family in the country, where his father is dying. The father is a complete contrast to Sensei: though dying he is emphatically not a lonely man, but a respectable and happy one. However, when a letter from Sensei arrives containing the sentence, 'By the time this letter reaches you, I shall in all likelihood be dead', his son rushes off to the city in the hope of finding Sensei alive. Such neglect, guilt-inducing enough anywhere, is catastrophic in conventional Japanese terms.

The third part of the novel consists of Sensei's letter. This, too, is a story of cruelty and betrayal. He tells the story of his youth and of how, lodging in a private household while a student at the university, he fell in love with the daughter of the house. He has a friend, called simply K, who is the son of a priest. K has made up his mind to renounce all worldly pleasures—in the Buddhist fashion—and is actually starving when Sensei persuades him to move into his lodgings. Now K falls in love with Ojosan, their landlady's daughter, and Sensei suddenly becomes jealous and destructive. He sneers at K for his abandonment of those very aspirations from which, a short time before, he had tried to dissuade him. In short, he does all he can to ruthlessly destroy his friend. Then he becomes engaged to Ojosan. K, hearing about it, kills himself. Sensei's guilt pushes him into the inescapable loneliness of his life, ended by suicide. He tells his young friend in his final letter that loneliness is the inevitable price of having been born into the modern age, even though it seems so full of freedom and independence.

This novel may correctly be read as an expression of modern loneliness; it also has the undoubted homosexual overtones to which I have referred. Sensei's jealousy of K is partly homosexual in origin; it is also based on envy of his courageous asceticism. When the young narrator of the first two sections comes into his life his emotions become exacerbated, and in despair he destroys himself.

It has been suggested that, because of the bareness of its style and the dearth of proper names, *The Heart* was intended as a kind of allegory. But it stands so well on its own as a piece of psychological realism that this interpretation may be discounted. An allegory would have been strained, and *The Heart* is not. Besides, only if we do not attempt to extract any one single meaning from it can we appreciate its full richness.

Soseki's last completed novel, *Grass on the Wayside* (*Michikusa*, 1916; tr. E. McClellan, 1969), is his only straightforwardly autobiographical work. It deals with the period of his life between his return from England and his decision to become a full-time writer, and therefore with the period when the happiness of his marriage began to break down.

Here Soseki expresses his sense of personal isolation most poignantly and bitterly. One is acutely reminded of the lines of verse quoted above: the novelist rates rivers and classifies hills—but the man has withdrawn from the world with 'hateful [i.e. 'full of hate'] eyes'. *Grass on the Wayside* is a bitter 'classification' and 'rating' of the man, alone in his wretchedness, unable to activate even the residual affection that exists between himself and his wife.

Kenzo (Soseki) meets by chance his old foster-father, Shimada, who tries to extract money from him and to re-enter his life. Kenzo's relations, including his wife, take the conventional view: all they are frightened of are the legal consequences. Kenzo is not, for he knows Shimada has no claim upon him; but in spite of himself he feels guilt. Eventually he buys the old man off. The end of the novel is bitterly ironic:

> 'What a relief,' Kenzo's wife said with feeling. 'At least this affair is settled.'
>
> 'Settled? What do you mean?'
>
> 'Well, we have his signed statement now, so there's nothing to worry about any more. . . .
>
> 'Hardly anything in this life is settled. Things that happen once will go on happening. But they come back in different guises, and that's what fools us.' He spoke bitterly, almost with venom.
>
> His wife gave no answer. She picked up the baby and kissed its red cheeks many times. 'Nice baby, nice baby, we don't know what daddy is talking about, do we?' (tr. E. McClellan.)

He was only part of the way through *Light and Darkness* (*Meian*, 1916; tr. V. H. Vigliemo, 1971), a psychologically meticulous study of an unhappy marriage and regarded by many as his greatest achievement, when he died.

Two themes haunted Soseki: the desirability and impossibility of resignation, peace, calm, submergence of self; and betrayal. No doubt the latter arose from his feeling of unwantedness as a child, when his real parents put him out to adoption (though this in itself is as acceptable a practice in Japan as marriage is in the West) and were then forced to have him back when the foster-parents divorced. Soseki is undoubtedly a major novelist in terms of world literature. Like Toson, he succeeded in postulating a figure resembling the now familiar 'anti-hero' against a modern background.

These two novelists dominated their period. Probably only Tanizaki Junichiro has equalled them in all-round stature as a writer of prose—although the poet Hagiwara Saguturo, whose gifts have yet to be recognized in the West, is as eminent. But the earlier period produced several writers and individual works of importance.

VI

As a stylist HIGUCHI ICHIYO (1872–96) was the last of Japan's notable traditionalists; but the subject-matter of her masterpiece, the novella *Growing Up* (*Takekurabe*, 1895; MJL) is pure Meiji: it is an account of precocious children, of tough young boys and a prostitute, growing up in the Tokyo licensed quarter. Higuchi's observation was sharp and inexorable, her fatalism poignant, and there seems little doubt that she would have accomplished even more substantial works if she had lived.

MORI OGAI (ps. MORI RINTARO, 1862–1922), novelist, poet, essayist and translator, was an army doctor who studied in Germany for four years (1884–8). His translations of foreign poetry were influential, and he became famous for his rather ponderous but effective style; he is now remembered mainly for individual works of fiction. Not being a full-time writer, like Toson and Soseki, he saw the novel less as an art to be developed and more as an intelligent entertainment, although his standards were not less rigorous. His first novel, *The Dancing Girl* (*Maihime*, 1890; tr. F. W. Eastlake, 1907), was autobiographical (the first notable 'I' novel), and was thought of as initiating the romantic movement in Japanese literature. Heavily influenced by Goethe and German romanticism, it tells of Mori's love-affair with a German dancer. The 'japanization' here is not as complete as it is in Soseki—or even in Futabatei. Later Mori became more polemically inclined, opposing himself to the facile naturalists of the time, who were too self-consciously and philosophically concerned to depict life as subject to the sexual drive. His finest novel, *The Wild Geese* (*Gan*, 1911–13; tr. Goldstein and Ochiai, 1959; pt. MJL), dates from this period. It tells of how Otama is taken up and betrayed into a bigamous marriage by a policeman, who then abandons her; she becomes the mistress of a moneylender, and consequently suffers from social ostracism. Finally she falls in love with a medical student (Mori himself, writing in retrospect), but before the affair can develop he leaves for Germany. *The Wild Geese* is notable for its delicate and sympathetic portrayal of a woman. Mori's last books—he wrote more than sixty—are mostly modern versions of ancient legends; they lack the genius and uniqueness of Akutagawa Ryunosuke's (q.v.) adaptations of similar material, but are more readable than has been allowed. Against Edwin McClellan's judgement that 'as novelist, he seems to have lacked originality and imagination . . . Ogai, one feels, was basically a professor of genius who happened to write fiction . . .' we must balance the touching and gentle qualities of *The Wild Geese*.

TOKUTOMI ROKA (ps. TOKUTOMI KENJIRO, 1868–1927, usually referred to as Kenjiro) was the younger brother of the critic, essayist and historian Tokutomi Iichero (1863–1957). The feud between the brothers, never more than partially resolved, became famous. Kenjiro was not a novelist of the stature of any of those so far discussed; but at least one of his novels, his second popular success, *Footprints in the Snow* (*Omoide noki*, 1901; tr. Kenneth Strong, 1970), deserves mention. It is still widely read in Japan. His first success, *Namiko* (*Hototogisu*, 1898; tr. S. Shioya and E. F. Edgett, 1905) is of less interest. Kenjiro was a Christian and a socialist, and was often—in his later years—called mad. He was not mad, however, only exceedingly eccentric—a kind of Japanese combination of Tolstoi and D. H. Lawrence. He had to struggle to achieve marital stability, and used to lay into his wife with a stick (then a little less unusual in

Japan than in the West) in the process. He went to Russia to meet Tolstoi, whom he much admired. The visit was not a complete success—but at least the Japanese was able to show his admiration by imitating Tolstoi when, on a walk, the great man stopped to piss without ceremony. Kenjiro's life represented, for many Japanese, the attempt—characteristic of the Meiji era—to escape from the stultifying effect of traditional family ties. Yet *Footprints in the Snow*, which was over-influenced by *David Copperfield*, is based more on the career of his brother Iichiro than on his own. It tells of the struggles of a poor boy, Shintaro, for education and emancipation. Kenjiro was highly independent both as a stylist and a technician; but he lacked the psychological depth of Japan's best Meiji novelists, and was essentially much more in tune with conventional Meiji ideals than they. He was more of a reforming idealist than a novelist; but *Footprints in the Snow*, for all its faults, compels affection.

KINOSHITA NAOE (1869–1937), less personally eccentric than Kenjiro, was another dedicated socialist. *The Confessions of a Husband* (*Ryojinnojihaku*, 1904–5; tr. A. Lloyd, 1905–6) was more propaganda than literature. *Column of Fire* (*Hinohashira*, 1904), although another piece of propaganda, was more vivid, particularly in its description of the coal mines. Horrified by the rise of fascist nationalism in the Thirties, Kinoshita became a recluse.

KUNIKADA DOPPO (ps. KUNIKADA TETSUO, 1871–1908), was an influential and much read novelist around the turn of the century. At least *The Fatalist* (*Unmeironja*, 1902), a striking and early treatment of an 'Oedipus situation' —the drinking hero is forced into an incestuous situation—may be worthy of revival. (A more lyrical, simple, short story has been tr.: *Old Gen, Gen oji*, 1897.)

TAYAMA KATAI (ps. TAYAMA ROKUYA, 1872–1930) began as a pupil of one of the leading novelists and poets of the Kenyusha group (q.v.), OZAKI KOYO (1867–1903). His most famous novel, *The Quilt* (*Futon*, 1907), is well-written, sensational autobiography: the story of his jealous love for a young woman student, a lodger in his house and a pupil of his in fiction-writing. This was the first of a remarkable trilogy, completed by *The Wife* (*Tsuma*, 1908) and *Karma En* (1908), in which Katai describes with great frankness the nastinesses between him and his wife as well as the fate of his former pupil, whom he had unkindly sent away. If any Japanese novelist of this period can be said to have come near to the European conception of naturalism, then it was Katai in this trilogy and, even more particularly, in *One Soldier* (*Ippeisotsu*, 1908; MJL). Based on what he had seen of the Russo-Japanese war as a newspaper correspondent, this is a movingly stark description of a soldier's thoughts and fears as he dies of beri-beri. It has something of the quality of Stephen Crane. Katai, who is unusual among Japanese novelists in not having had an academic training, is still regarded as one of the pioneers of realistic fiction. He did not have the complexity of character that—expressed and brought to the surface —confers greatness upon Toson, Soseki and others of the finest modern Japanese writers, but his realism and straightforward style are admirable. He demonstrates that there is a place for directness and unequivocal pity in Japanese literature.

IZUMI KYOKA (ps. IZUMI KYOTARO, 1873–1939) was another pupil of Ozaki Koyo. He was not any kind of a realist, but went back to the Edo period for his inspiration. In his symbolical and even mystical novels reality only has meaning when it serves to exalt the romantic spirit. One of his best novels, *The Night-Duty Policeman* (*Yako junsa*, 1895), is about a conscientious policeman who tries to help a criminal and causes his own death. Typical of his work is *A Tale of Three Who Were Blind* (*Sanniu no mekura no hanashi*, 1912; MJL), a fine and intelligent story of the macabre.

MASAMUNE HAKUCHO (ps. MASAMUNE TADAO, 1879) was a popular and prolific member of the 'naturalist' school, whose consistently bleak mood is characteristic of Japanese fiction. He was an admirer of Chekhov. His earlier novels are somewhat over-ebulliently nihilistic (in *Dust*, *Jinai*, 1907, city people breathe 'day after day the dust . . . until at last the germs in the dust eat their lives away'); but his sense of loneliness—the real subject, it has rightly been said, of the modern Japanese novel—was always authentic. His work was notably free from sentimentality, and his realism deepened. His most substantial novel is *Clay Doll* (*Doro ningyo*, 1911; tr. G. M. Sinclair and K. Suita in *Tokyo People*, 1925), which traces the process of his own marriage of the same year. Moriya Jukichi (Hakucho) despises women, having had too many of them; when he comes to marry, he cannot regard his bride as anything but a clay doll, although he loathes himself for it. The picture of an empty marriage reflects the emptiness and meaninglessness of life itself—Hakucho's real theme. *Near the Inlet* (*Irie no hotori*, 1915) contains a notably objective portrait of a paranoiac. Later Hakucho's prose became more mannered, and he turned increasingly to drama, where he scored some commercial success. He wrote little after 1930.

With NAGAI KAFU (ps. NAGAI SOKICHI, 1879–1959), whom his biographer Edward Seidensticker has called 'perhaps the best reason one can think of for learning Japanese', we come to an unquestionably major writer, although in his best work he is perhaps the least 'modern' of the few of his stature. Kafu, pimp, voyeur, perpetual hetero- and occasional homosexual adventurer in Tokyo's *demi-monde*, his spiritual home, is a delightful writer. His contempt for 'affairs' and all respectability was magnificently absolute; it extended to his attitude towards the fascists during the war. He was perhaps not a less good man, in his personal relationships, than many who are in the habit of expressing higher aspirations.

He began, like Katai, as an avowed naturalist, and *Flowers of Hell* (*Jigoku no hana*, 1902), his first novel, is a competent piece of Japanese realism conceived in the spirit of Zola. But during the first decade of the century he travelled in France and America—and when he returned in 1908 he found himself horrified by the new-style 'Western' Tokyo, and consequently beset by nostalgia. After this, though realistic in detail, his fiction became a series of remembrances of things past: of survivals of customs from the Tokugawa period, which he has made very much his own, and the old Meiji Tokyo of his boyhood and youth. Kafu's return to the past is less a result of intellectual dislike of modernization than of a thoroughly nostalgic temperament. He is the only important modern Japanese writer to employ on occasion old-fashioned, and sometimes unlikely, plots. He too learned his craft from a 'master', a writer of realist fiction.

Some critics have objected to Kafu's 'lack of feeling for his characters'. This is frivolous as well as unjust. In his masterpiece *The River Sumida* (*Sumidagawa*, 1909; MJL), an evocation of the Tokyo of about 1890, there is every indication of sympathy with the characters.

The River Sumida, like so much other Japanese fiction, depicts people destroyed by the Meiji era. Ragetsu is a middle-aged '*haiku* master'; his younger sister Otoyo teaches *tokiwazu* (a kind of recitation to music); her son Chokichi, around whom the story centres, is passionately interested in only two things: to be an actor and to marry Oito. But his mother wants him to go to university and have a 'western' style career; and Oito is taken from him to train to become a geisha. Ragetsu, who as a young man has been disinherited because of his dissipated behaviour, takes the side of his sister when she remonstrates with Chokichi. The boy, unable to cope with examinations and the harsh realities of modern life, wanders around in the waters of a flood and catches typhoid fever; it seems that he will not recover. Significantly, not long before his tragic final gesture, Chokichi experiences a moment of 'strange fascination and sorrow':

> He wanted to be possessed by that sweet, gentle, suddenly cold and in-different fate. As the wings of his fancy spread, the spring sky seemed bluer and wider than before. He caught from the distance the sound of the Korean flute of a sweet-seller. To hear the flute in this unexpected place, playing its curious low-pitched tune, produced in him a melancholy which words could not describe.
>
> For a while Chokichi forgot the dissatisfaction with his uncle that had taken root in his breast. For a while he forgot the anguish of actuality.
>
> (MJL)

This exquisite passage perfectly captures the essence of Kafu, a writer for whom perhaps any present—because of the manner in which the past permeates it—would have been agony. *The River Sumida* ends with Ragetsu sitting in Otoyo's house, despairing of the boy's recovery, and bitterly regretting his betrayal. He thinks of 'the two young beautiful people—Chokichi with his fair skin, delicate face, and clear eyes; and Oito with her charming mouth and tilted eyes set in a round face. And he cried in his heart, "No matter how bad your fever is, don't die! Chokichi, there's nothing to worry about. I am with you."'

In the Thirties Kafu began to publish stories about prostitutes—women in whom he saw the ruined image of the old geisha. In *A Strange Tale from East of the River* (*Bokuto kidan*, 1937; tr. E. Seidensticker, *Kafu the Scribbler*) a middle-aged author searches for a story: he finds a prostitute who reminds him of the

Meiji women of his youth. All Kafu's feeling here flows into his nostalgia and regret. He is, above all, the prose-poet of Tokyo and its Edo past, the sniffer-out of whatever of the past endures in the present. He never represents the past as having been 'better' than the present: his theme, apart from the evocation of place, is the sadness nostalgia confers on the sensitive life. There is a touch in him of Jorge Luis Borges (q.v.), which becomes evident when we read the latter's descriptions of old Buenos Aires. Kafu, however, is unhappy rather than pessimistic or intellectual.

SHIGA NAOYA (1883) is another novelist almost as important. The doyen of living Japanese writers, today he writes nothing—although he has endorsed some left-wing activities. He began as a member of an 'anti-naturalist' faction, but soon broke away. He is a highly original, stylistically distinguished writer, but took many years to find himself. He was early associated with MUSHAKOJI SANEATSU (1885), a crusading anti-naturalist novelist and playwright whose idealism—strongly influenced by Christianity—had some influence. Mushakoji is peculiar in Japanese literature in that he is forthrightly optimistic about the nature of man. He has even tried to establish model communities. When Shiga became discouraged about his own abilities as a writer, in the second decade of the century, Mushakoji encouraged him and was instrumental in persuading him to continue. But Shiga is creatively more gifted, and shares little or none of Mushakoji's idealism.

Shiga's qualities of lucidity, deceptively plain style and psychological perceptiveness are nowhere better illustrated than in the short story *Han's Crime* (*Han no hanzai*, 1913; MJL). A young Chinese knife-thrower kills his wife in the course of their act. He is arrested, and the course of his trial is described in detail. He and his wife have been in conflict for a long time, and this is known to the witnesses. Han decides to be honest: he says to the examining magistrate, 'I decided that my best way of being acquitted would be to make a clean breast of everything . . . why not be completely honest and say I did not know what happened?' *Han's Crime* is a *tour de force*, a slab of utterly uncompromising psychological realism. When Han tells the judge that he not only feels no compunction at all at his wife's death, but 'Even when I hated my wife most bitterly in the past I could never have imagined I would feel such happiness in her death', the judge feels 'strangely moved', and immediately writes down the words 'not guilty'. That, clearly, is the writer's own partly ironic judgement.

A Western judge would not have been as compassionate as this one; nor, in fact, would most Japanese. Yet it is the only sensible verdict—and any good lawyer in the West could, technically, argue Han's case and quite properly plead 'not guilty'. This treatment should be contrasted with Theodore Dreiser's (q.v.) of the almost exactly similar situation in *An American Tragedy*. The story also anticipates the Italian Michele Prisco's much longer but not more pointed *A Spiral of Mist*, which dealt with the theme, very fashionable by the late Sixties, of whether a man really meant to shoot his wife. . . . And the sharp reader will of course think immediately of Meursault's 'crime' in Camus' *The*

Outsider (q.v.)—and of his indifference to his mother's death. *Han's Crime*, however, is twenty-five years earlier.

It is ironic, of course, because we have to reflect that in 'real life' no one would or perhaps could be so honest and self-analytical; and how many courts would appreciate this kind of thing? What *Han's Crime* demonstrates, then, as does Camus' *The Outsider*, is the inability of organized society to deal with such truthfulness as Han exhibits. Shiga is a markedly humanitarian writer—much more specifically so than, say, Toson—but *Han's Crime* displays no idealism: as I have pointed out, the merciful judgement is, ironically, all too clearly that of the author; mercy and understanding are not the kind of treatment men can expect to get.

It has been suggested that Shiga's concentration, in his stories and novels, on themes of conflict—Han's with his wife is characteristic—is to be explained by his own protracted quarrel with his father. He movingly described this quarrel, and the reconciliation that ended it, in the novel *Reconciliation* (*Wakai*, 1917).

Shiga, though he wrote autobiographical and semi-autobiographical fiction, is no sensationalist; it has been suggested that his long silence has been due to his unwillingness to live a sensational life (in the sense that the life described by Toson in *A New Life* is sensational). He spent fifteen years on a semi-autobiographical novel, *Journey into the Dark* (*Anya Koro*, 1922–37), which was very widely read. This is perhaps a self-portrait, but its incidents are invented. Stylistically it goes straight back to the realism of Futabatei's *Drifting Clouds*. Shiga shares with Soseki the distinction, not as usual in Japanese fiction as elsewhere, of a sense of humour.

VII

TANIZAKI JUNICHIRO (1886–1965), one of the paramount writers of the century in any language, possessed a true complexity, all of which he succeeded in distilling into his fiction. The method of his maturity was not strictly impressionistic, but he has—with evident critical deliberation—eschewed omniscience of narration. Tanizaki's later books represent a triumph of artistic effort over a lurid, 'decadent' imagination. Each of the three periods into which his career may be divided yielded undoubted masterpieces.

Tanizaki began as an eroticist working under the influence of such 'decadent' Western writers as Poe, Wilde and Baudelaire. The themes of degeneration and decadence, linked with sex, have always fascinated him; in his early books he explores this quite overtly. It was *The Victim* (*Shisei*, 1909; MJS) that first brought him to the attention of the public. A tattooer persuades a beautiful girl to allow him to imprint a design on her back; she agrees, and the artist destroys himself—dies exhausted—as, in shaping a weird spider, *Nephila clavata*, he brings out her hidden cruelty, leaving her savagely exultant and transformed. This brilliant tale is thoroughly Japanese, but the author's overriding concern with sexuality is plainly a Western import. At this time Tanizaki was 'progressive' in the sense that he actually took the side of those who held that Japan was being too slow in the process of Westernization. He lived among foreigners, and was known for his interest in Western ways. Later there was a reaction; it is too simple to say that the devastating earthquake of September 1923, which destroyed the whole of Yokohama (where Tanizaki lived) and more than half of Tokyo, changed his mind for him—but this national catastrophe certainly profoundly influenced him. He moved to Kyoto, and became increasingly interested in the Japanese traditions and past. But his interest in eroticism has never been extinguished for long. Another more substantial work from this early period is *A Springtime Case* (*Otsuyagoroshi*, 1914; tr. Z. Iwado, 1927): this is a highly melodramatic tale of lust and murder, but is written with great control. Tanizaki showed his interest in historical themes from the very beginning. His first publication was a historical drama; and a story from 1910, *Prodigy* (*Kirin*), is about Confucius as well as about a prince who (typically of an early Tanizaki character) tells his wife: 'I hate you. You are a horrible woman. You are a demon who will finally ruin me, but still I cannot leave you'. Stories of the next two years deal almost exclusively and quite explicitly with masochistic themes. *The Demon* (*Akuma*, 1912), for example, tells of a young man who licks the handkerchief into which his girl-friend has sneezed.

In *A Fool's Love* (*Chijin no ai*, 1924–5) Tanizaki made his change of mood evident by subtly adapting Somerset Maugham's (q.v.) *Of Human Bondage* (1915) to a Japanese setting. The pathetic anti-hero, ashamed of his Japanese attributes—shortness, protruding teeth—picks up a barmaid who reminds him of the then very famous American film-star, Mary Pickford. This girl's name, Naomi, might even be foreign—which fascinates her lover all the more. He takes her to live with him, and encourages her to be 'Western', with the inevitable result that she becomes a torment to him. At the end he is content to tolerate her foreign lovers provided that she will not leave him. Certainly *A Fool's Love* was meant to be a kind of warning to those who wanted to 'go Western'; but in it Tanizaki also pursued his perennial theme of the damaging nature of sexual fascination. He is as interested in his hero's masochism, of which there is much description, as he is in his fatal orientation towards all things Western. This novel seems in part to represent Tanizaki's self-criticism of his interest in Westernization, transferred—characteristically—to a sexual plane.

Some Prefer Nettles (*Tade kuu muhi*, 1928; tr. E. Seidensticker, 1955) is Tanizaki's most overtly autobiographical novel. It is based on his relationship with his first wife, whom he divorced in 1930 (he remarried the next year). This is a study in lassitude and, again, in the nature of sexual interest. Tanizaki seems to have polarized women into Western and Japanese types; in him the conflict in Japanese life between the Western and the Japanese is seen in almost exclusively sexual terms. Kanname, the hero of *Some Prefer Nettles*, has grown bored with his 'modern' wife (she has a lover—in real life the poet Sato

Haruo, q.v.), and is attracted by her father's mistress, an old-style Japanese beauty. He also, however, carries on an affair with Louise, a Eurasian prostitute. Here dislike of Japan's modernity is more evident than in any other of Tanizaki's fiction. The *ennui* and lack of energy of both partners in the hero's unhappy marriage are brilliantly conveyed. The novel was an immediate success when it appeared in the West almost thirty years after its original publication.

After this Tanizaki entered his third and final period as a writer, although with his last two novels he might (by some) be said to have regressed. For a 'decadent' writer, such as Tanizaki was held to be, the Thirties and early Forties, with the fascists in power, were a dangerous period. During the Thirties he wrote a number of novellas whose central theme was the Japanese past as embodied in the traditional Japanese woman. Of these, *Ashikari* (1932) and *Shunkinsho* (1933) were translated together in one volume by R. Humpherson and H. Okita: *Ashikari and the Story of Shunkin* (1936). When the authorities became even tougher on writers, Tanizaki concentrated on his adaptation of the most famous of all Japanese novels, the eleventh-century *Tale of Genji*, by Murasaki Shikibu. During the Forties he wrote a long novel, *The Makioka Sisters* (*Sasameyuki*, 1943–8; tr. E. Seidensticker, 1957); the Japanese title means 'Light Snow'. The government would not allow him to continue publication of this, as they regarded it as incompatible with the war-effort—a judgement with which one must agree.

This was an entirely new departure. It tells, with delicacy and in perhaps uniquely fine detail, the story of four sisters in the Japan of 1936–40. There is no plot; and the approach is 'photographic' in that Tanizaki tries to recreate life as exactly as it can be recreated in fiction. There is no description of emotion. As Donald Keene has written, it 'is a true *roman fleuve*, a slow and turbid river of a book, which moves inevitably and meaninglessly [but one may question this adjective] to its close'. It contains some beautifully realized descriptions, such as one of a firefly-hunt. There is and probably always will be some controversy about this novel's ultimate worth; but as an experiment in photographic realism it has not been surpassed in any language. It seems likely that Tanizaki was trying to recapture what he felt to be the essence of the Japanese cultural genius. By the Thirties he had come to feel that its delicacy was threatened by the comparatively crude methods of the West. *The Makioka Sisters* combines total realism with traditional Japanese delicacy. Its chief theme is the finding of a husband for one of the sisters. There are, as often in Tanizaki, a number of medical details—vitamin shortages, visits to the lavatory, etc. The positive cumulative effect of these is a tribute to his art.

In 1950 he wrote a historical novel, *The Mother of Captain Shigemoto* (*Shosho Shigemoto no hana*, 1950; pt. MJL). Based on Heian accounts of actual events in ninth-century Japan, it deals with an old man's vain attempts to forget the beautiful young wife out of whom he has been tricked. It is interesting in that it deals, more directly than the novels of the middle period, with what is in fact the basic theme of the early period: the male sexually deprived of his woman, be she wife, lover or mother. The masochism of his characters springs from a fear of such deprivation. In *The Mother of Captain Shigemoto* both the man and his son, who is the Captain Shigemoto of the title, are thus deprived.

The Key (*Kagi*, 1960; tr. H. Hibbet, 1961) portrays an elderly couple, and concentrates in particular on the sexual anxieties of the male partner, who examines his drunken wife under a strong electric light. *Diary of a Mad Old Man* (tr. H. Hibbet, 1966) is a portrait of the artist as an old man: the hero is seventy-seven, impotent, and obsessed by his daughter-in-law. She lets him suck her toes while she is showering (which nearly gives him a stroke) and he gives her a valuable jewel. The book is written in a tone of clinical understatement—it concludes with the old man's medical case-notes—and yet with great empathy. It has been suggested that the old man's 'perversions' (though this is an old-fashioned way of putting it) 'stand for the West's debasement of Japanese life'; but this seems unlikely: *Diary of a Mad Old Man* is best read as an ironic but sympathetic description of the sexual difficulties of old age. Those who reject it reveal themselves as the neurotic victims of their upbringing.

Tanizaki was the major figure of Japanese literature in the period from 1868, though not always regarded as such; he is also, without any doubt, one of the century's most important writers by any standards. Fortunately most of his books are available in good translations.

The prolific KIKUCHI KAN (ps. KIKUCHI HIROSHI, 1888–1948) wrote novels, such as *Victory or Defeat* (*Shohai*, 1932; tr. K. Nishi, 1934), and short stories, but his plays were best. His fiction provides a good example of straightforward realism communicated in a manner in no way patronizing from an intellectual to the 'ordinary' intelligent reader. However, Kikuchi is most important as the indefatigable and generous encourager of younger men (for example, the Nobel Prize winner Kawabata Yasunari, q.v.), whose work he printed in the still extant monthly *Bungei shunju*, which he founded in 1923. Kikuchi might be regarded as a kind of John Lehmann (q.v.) of Japan. He was particularly loathed and execrated by the much more gifted Nagai Kafu (q.v.), who regarded him (not unjustifiably, but very unsportingly) as a 'typical literary figure'. (Five plays are tr. G. W. Shaw in *Tojura's Love*, 1925.)

AKUTAGAWA RYUNOSUKE (1892–1927) is a short-story writer who has a particular appeal for Western readers. He is most famous for his *Rashomon* (1915; tr., with other stories, Kojima Takashi, 1952), but more recently claims have been made for his satirical late novel, *Kappa* (tr. S. Shiojiri, 1949; more authoritatively G. Bownas, 1970). Ryunosuke began as a member of a literary group that centred itself around Natsume Soseki (q.v.), but as he developed he became something of an odd man out in Japanese literature—one in whom intelligence and subtlety of outlook were exceptionally well developed. Unfortunately Ryunosuke was mentally unstable, perhaps schizophrenic, and in 1927 he killed himself by an overdose of sleeping tablets after experiencing what appears to have been a bout of severe paranoia. He is said to have felt guilty at basing his fiction on traditional tales (many of them of the thirteenth century, others from the tenth); he certainly supported the ideal of auto-biographical fiction as a critic and public debater. It is, however, discovery of the past as an objective correlative that makes him unusual in Japanese literature. He was superbly gifted, with a marked *penchant* for the macabre and the dramatic, as may be seen in his *Kesa and Morito* (*Kesa to Morito*, 1918; MJL).

Another powerful and extraordinary story is *Hell Screen* (MJL), an out-standing example of the kind of fiction that hovers on the border of the supernatural. Stylistically Ryunosuke is often called the most elegant and lucid of all twentieth-century Japanese. Certainly few modern writers anywhere have exploited the past as brilliantly and effectively; in this respect (only) Ryunosuke may be compared with Isaac Bashevis Singer and Ivo Andrić (qq.v.). He was an essentially brilliant, highly-strung writer, who could not face the ordeal of dealing with himself at length: instead he projected his psyche, always more or less critically balanced, onto the materials offered by fantastic episodes in history. He did, however, write some autobiographical fiction at the end of his life. He was cynical, but also fundamentally good-tempered and warm-hearted. Personally, he was probably partly the victim of the penetrative brilliance of his own insight (*Tales Grotesque and Curious*, tr. G. W. Shaw, 1938).

EDOGAWA RAMPO (ps. HIRAI TARO, 1894) deserves mention as the intelligent pioneer of the mystery and thriller story in Japanese. His name is a pseudonym based on the Japanese pronunciation of Edgar Allen Poe, his acknowledged master. His writing is brutally realistic. A good selection is *Japanese Tales of Mystery and Imagination* (tr. J. B. Harris, 1957).

OSARAGI JIRO (1897) is a popular but not inferior novelist, who writes in a Western style. His best known work is the story of a Japanese expatriate who returned to Japan from Malaya after the war, *Homecoming* (*Kikyo*, 1948; tr. B. Horowitz, 1955).

YOKOMITSU RIICHI (1898–1947) was associated with, and sundered himself from, a number of literary schools in his time: he edited a magazine with Kawabata Yasunari (q.v.), and became involved with a group of writers who preached what they called 'New Sensationalism'. But Riichi was a less effective polemicist than novelist and short story writer. He was a genuine independent, against both political and autobiographical literature. Whatever his position with regard to Japanese naturalism, he may fruitfully be compared to certain genuine naturalists such as Dreiser (q.v.), for his main theme is man's struggle against his fatal destiny. However, Donald Keene regards his concern with 'the hell that man creates for himself on earth' as 'essentially Buddhist'. Of Japanese writers, he was most influenced by Shiga Naoya (q.v.).

Yokomitsu is 'morbid' inasmuch as most of his fiction is about illness, death and disaster; but he has a sense of humour, a warmth and an interest in human nature that save him from mawkishness or affectation. Donald Keene has translated a characteristically moving, realistic and vivid story, *Time* (MJL). (See also MJS: and M. M. Suzuki's collection, *The Heart is Alone*, 1957).

IBUSE MASUJI (1898) is, like Osaragi Jiro, a popular novelist of genuine creative gifts. He writes both whimsical contemporary, and historical novels. *No Consultation Today (Honjitsu kyushin,* 1949; tr. E. Seidensticker, *Japan Quarterly,* VIII, 1, 1961) gives a formidably professional and psychologically accurate portrait of a whole town through a series of accounts of treatments of patients by a police doctor. *A Far-Worshipping Commander (Yohai taisho,* 1950; tr. J. Bester, *Japan Quarterly,* I, 1, 1954) is about an officer who believes the war is still on. Ibuse Masuji's masterpiece, however, is *Black Rain (Kuroi Ame;* tr. J. Bester, 1969), an authoritative account of the atomic disaster that manages to combine the documentary, the realistic and the poetic. *Black Rain* is good enough to transcend even its terrible subject. (See also MJS.)

KAWABATA YASUNARI (1899–1972) is Japan's only Nobel Prize winner (1969). Critically he was the most sophisticated of modern Japanese writers, always excepting Tanizaki; his techniques would undoubtedly appear as immediately understandable to a young *avant garde* writer of any country in the Seventies. The Japanese writer with whom he had most in common is Tanizaki, although Kawabata took 'decadence' yet one step farther. He dealt in even more detail with what happens beneath the surface of eroticism, and in most aspects had a decidedly more 'modern' approach to fiction. He began by publishing stories in Kikuchi Kan's *Bungei shunju* (q.v.), and followed Kikuchi's example by generously encouraging younger writers. His chief gifts lay in the creation of atmosphere and, more recently, in the exploration of sexual feelings, which were usually broken down into their disturbingly bizarre components.

His first important novel, *The Izu Dancer (Izu no odoriko,* 1926; pt. tr. E. Seidensticker, *Atlantic Monthly,* 195, 1955), an autobiographical account of Kawabata's youthful infatuation with a dancer, was influenced by European surrealism and was one of the first responsibly 'modern' works to appear in Japan. Kawabata understood the resemblances between the traditionally abrupt transition from subject to subject in Japanese poetry, and modern European methods, and he successfully, because thoughtfully, assimilated the latter. *The Snow Country (Yukiguni,* 1935–47; tr. E. Seidensticker, 1957) combines a nostalgia for old Japan (perhaps brought on by the rise of the militarists) with a treatment of a sexual relationship between a Tokyo roué and a geisha in a winter resort.

Thousand Cranes (Sembazuru, 1949–51; tr. E. Seidensticker, 1959) may not find sexual degeneracy at the heart of normal behaviour; but it chooses to study it, in the form of a group of people whose relationships are all determined by guilt or incestuous wishes. *The Mole (Hokuro no nikki,* 1940; tr. E. Seidensticker, MJL) is characteristic: a woman has a habit of fingering a mole, a habit that enrages her husband. She tries to determine, in a letter to him, what causes her to do it, and to answer the question why she won't go to the doctor to have it removed as her husband wishes. She goes into the matter in detail: 'That was the frightening thought. I trembled when it came to me of a sudden that there might be men who would find the habit charming'. 'I do think . . . I cannot get over thinking, that it would have been better if you could have brought yourself to overlook my habit of playing with the mole'. Eventually she loses the habit, but continues to dwell upon its meaning, and to dream of it. This is a sinister study of feminine psychology, with distinctly sado-masochistic overtones. It shows Kawabata at his best, quietly dredging the depths of individual sexual feeling for grotesque, bizarre and disturbing truths. *House of the Sleeping Beauties* (tr. E. Seidensticker, 1969) collects three stories: two new and one, 'Birds and Beasts' (1939), from an earlier period. The title story concerns the sixty-seven-year-old Eguchi who, although not impotent, is advised by a friend to visit a brothel where old men sleep the night with passive and silent young women (drugged? in a trance? The essence is that we are not told). Eguchi is fascinated, and returns again and again—until he is taught the true nature of his eroticism. In 'One Arm' a young man has a dialogue with his girl-friend's arm, which she has lent him for the night. 'Birds and Beasts' is a sort of elegy: a man keeps birds, and watches them die at the same time as he considers his affair with a dancer who is also dying. Kawabata was enigmatic, cruel, a master of female erotic psychology. He was also intensely Japanese, for all the effect that Western writing had upon him. His limits confined him more or less exclusively to the erotic, but here he was a master. He committed suicide in 1972.

KOBAYASHI TAKIJI (1903–33) was the chief member of the so-called 'proletarian literature' movement, which lost its ground when the militarists gained effective power in 1932. Kobayashi was the only really gifted novelist produced by the group. He became a communist, and was murdered in a Tokyo prison by policemen. He wrote a number of political novels, but the most famous and the best is *The Cannery Boat* (*Kani kosen*, 1929; tr. 1933: pt. MJL). This described, in a manner reminiscent of Upton Sinclair (q.v.), the conditions in a crab-canning boat that is dominated by a fiendish and sadistic superintendent, Asakawa. The philosophy behind it is inexorably Marxist. Some of the crew discover that conditions in Russia are different; there is a mutiny, suppressed by the navy. *The Cannery Boat* is powerful and vivid, but gives a convincing picture of a group of men as distinct from a set of individuals.

An associate of and sympathizer with the 'proletarian movement', though not herself to be classified as part of it, was the moving chronicler of the poor of Tokyo, HAYASHI FUMIKO (1904–51), probably Japan's most distinguished modern woman writer. Born to hardship, she profoundly understood the lot of Tokyo's lower classes, and depicted them with an unobtrusively skilful realism and without a trace of sentimentality. She wrote a series of novels in diary-form, under the general title of *Journal of a Vagabond* (*Horoki*, 1922–7); Western critics would probably classify these as autobiographical. Her moving account of a struggling woman in post-war Tokyo, and of her optimism even in the face of atrocious luck and emotional deprivation, has been finely translated by Ivan Morris (*Shitamachi*, 1948; MJL). Her most famous novel has the same title as Futabatei's pioneering work, *Drifting Clouds* (*Ukigumo*, 1948; tr. Y. Koitabashi, *Floating Cloud*, 1957). This tells of a young woman who goes to Indo-China to act as a typist for the Japanese occupying armies. She had been a timid young woman, dully acquiescent in the austerities forced upon her by the war. Influenced by the comparatively luxurious conditions of her new life, she turns into a sophisticated and sexy good-time girl. She has a love affair; but when she and her lover get back to Japan everything changes. He leaves her, and she has an affair with an American soldier. Nothing means anything. Donald Keene praises the authenticity of this sombre book, but feels that it 'is too close to the facts which inspired it to permit any real literary quality'. This could be a harsh judgement; but in fact there is a 'documentary' quality about *Floating Cloud* that somewhat vitiates its imaginative power: *Tokyo* is more accomplished.

HINO ASHIHEI (1907–61) became famous on account of *Sanitary Tales* (*Funnyotan*, 1937), a humorous account of local government affairs. He then consolidated his reputation with four books of brilliant reportage from the Chinese front: *Barley and Soldiers* (*Mugi to heitai*, 1938; tr. K. and L. W. Bush, 1939), *Earth and Soldiers* (*Tsuchi to heitai*, 1938; pt. MJL), *Flowers and Soldiers* (*Hana to heitai*, 1939), and *War and Soldiers* (*Umi to heitai*, 1938). (L. W. Bush published a complete translation, as *War and Soldiers*, in Tokyo in 1940.) These are more journalistic than literary; but they are journalism at its best, whatever we may think of Hino's apparent lack of sensitivity to the type of war his countrymen were being made to fight. Later, after a period in which he was forbidden by the Americans to publish, Hino told the story of his parents' life in the much praised novel *Flower and Dragon* (*Hana to rnu*, 1952).

DAZAI OSAMU (ps. SHUJI TSUSHIMA, 1909–48), variously drug addict, communist opponent of the militarists, drunkard, man of courage, and suicide (unless he was pushed into the water by the woman who drowned with him; but he had frequently tried to kill himself before), was notorious during his lifetime as the dissipated son of a rich landowning family from northern Japan. He is one of Japan's most important writers; probably the most important of all those born in this century. If he can be compared to any Western writer, then it would be to Malcolm Lowry (q.v.): the frequently sceptical, mocking tone of Lowry's letters, concealing an innocent seriousness in helpless struggle with an alcoholic despair, is similar; and Lowry, too, anticipated alcohol and destroyed himself. Both were amazingly cool artists at the centre of roaring, disastrous personal vortices. Both were indisputably writers of genius. But Dazai's fiction was different from Lowry's. He was a most unhappy young man, who continually tried to kill himself. But at the same time he was learning to write fiction, seeking (as is an excellent tradition in Japan) the guidance of such senior writers as Ibuse Masuji. He had gained a reputation by the mid-Thirties for such black novels as *A Clown's Flowers* (*Doke no hana*, 1935). *No Longer Human* (*Ningen shikkaku*, 1937; tr. D. Keene, 1958) is a diary, a form frequently adopted by Japanese writers. These are brilliant books: ironic, self-mocking, clever, unbearably miserable and conscience-stricken.

In 1939 Dazai married, and—oddly, since he was an uncompromising opponent of the fascists—spent during the war the happiest, or at least the most stable, years of his life. After the war, possibly partly owing to the fame into which he suddenly emerged—C. J. Dunn has observed that he symbolized 'the return to a cultural existence that many Japanese were yearning for'— his urge to self-destruction returned, as did his need for drink. A number of fine short stories date from these years (see *Encounter*, September, 1953; MJL; MJS; *Japan Quarterly*, October–December, 1958): acutely self-critical in a manner that is very rare even in modern literature, and most discomfiting. However, Dazai's masterpiece is undoubtedly *The Setting Sun* (*Shayo*, 1947; tr. D. Keene, 1950), in which he aimed at, and notably achieved, objectivity. This story of the aristocracy dispossessed by the war became so popular that the people with whom it dealt, a new class, became known as 'setting sun people': *Shayozoku*. This book, at the very least, put Dazai into the international class; his death was a loss to world literature—although at such a pompous cliché he would only have laughed.

OOKA SHOHEI (1909) began as translator and critic of Stendhal. Then, in 1944, he had to join the army; his experiences, in the Philippines, were atrocious; eventually he was taken prisoner. Out of his sufferings came his finest novel, *Fire on the Plain* (*Nobi*, 1951; tr. I. Morris, 1957), a study of a soldier trying to survive as an individual even while his army disintegrates around him. He had made his reputation with *Records of Imprisonment* (*Furyoki*, 1948), and a series of successors. These, like *Fire on the Plain*, look back to Tayama Katai's *One Soldier* (q.v.) as well as lean heavily on Stendhal. Ooka also wrote a study of a woman's out-of-character adultery, *The Lady From Musashino* (*Musashino fujin*, 1950).

Fire on the Plain, whose 'fabling character' has been compared to stories by William Golding (q.v.), is narrated by a mental patient who is trying to remember what happened to him after his unit threw him out as a sick liability. It is a nightmarish work, and an apt answer—one might say—of the Japanese writers to the Japanese militarists. Ooka has been attacked as being unable to place his characters in their social contexts; but this is a strength, too—as in his masterpiece, where the narrator's social context has been totally and brutally eroded.

NOMA HIROSHI (1915), who made a special study of French literature, is a Marxist who was imprisoned after his conscription into the army in 1941, and later dismissed the service. Somehow he survived. His *Zone of Emptiness* (*Shinkuchitai*, 1952; tr. B. Frechtman, 1956) is an account of army life that transcends polemic and is one of the best of its kind in the literature.

The leading writer of the younger generation in Japan, and one of the most successful in the world, was undoubtedly MISHIMA YUKIO (1925–70), whose work was singled out for praise by Kawabata Yasunari (q.v.). Mishima graduated in law in 1947, but had published a book of short stories at the age of nineteen. He became a full-time author before 1950. Mishima was a talented writer; nearly all of his books have appeared in English translations. They seem less Japanese than the work of the other writers discussed here, not only to English-speaking readers but also to the Japanese themselves: they were a product of the sophisticated, American-dominated post-war generation.

He was deeply influenced by Western psychoanalysis, but this did not improve his work. He has written some successful modern versions of *Noh* plays, original plays, and a travel book.

Although he married in 1958, and had a child, Mishima was a homosexual addicted to body-building and weight-lifting. In 1968 he published a book of repulsive photographs of semi-nude men, including some of himself. This obsession, which also embraced the ancient Japanese art of sword-play, slotted in easily—in Mishima's sick mind—with his nostalgia for Japan's military might. He founded an extreme right-wing association dedicated to 'protecting the Emperor' and to the reversal of the pacifist policy undertaken by Japan as one of the conditions of her independence. On 24 November 1970, Mishima led a fanatic sword-waving attack on an army HQ in Tokyo, tied up the commander, harangued troops from a balcony for a few minutes on the military decline of Japan, and then committed hara-kiri. Neither Mishima's books nor his political commitments can be wholly explained in any except psychiatric terms. As the Japanese prime minister commented: 'He must have gone mad'.

Mishima's ultimate value as a writer has been questioned on the grounds of psychological superficiality and sensationalism, although his talent has not been denied. Certainly his fiction tends to the sensational (though an early novel, *Thirst For Love*, *Ai no kawaki*, 1950; tr. Alfred H. Marks, 1970, is less offensive in this respect), and he is open to the charge of superficiality; at one time he showed some sign of outliving his sheer cleverness, but this promise was not maintained. His *The Sailor Who Fell From Grace with the Sea* (*Gogo no eigo*, 1963; tr. John Nathan, 1966) is characteristic. Noboru, a thirteen-year-old, spies on his widowed mother as she makes love to a sailor. When she decides to marry him, Noboru 'reports' him to 'No 1' of the sinister schoolboy élite of which he is 'No 3'. They deal horribly with the sailor, being certain of themselves in the light of 'Penal Code, Article Fourteen: *Acts of juveniles less than fourteen years of age are not punishable by law*'. This is brilliantly done, but has a certain fashionably 'sick' gloss on it, and hardly conceals a psychopathic hatred of women. Partially successful, its 'disagreeables', in Keats' famous phrase, fail to 'evaporate' sufficiently: we get an impression of unpleasantness being indulged in for its own sake. However, in *The Temple of the Golden Pavilion* (*Kinkakuji*, 1956; tr. I. Morris, 1957) the 'unpleasant' nature of the material—a trainee-priest burns down his temple—vanishes to a greater extent in the psychological accuracy of the portrait. Both *Confessions of a Mask* (*Kamen no kokuhaku*, 1949; tr. M. Weatherby, 1960) and *Forbidden Pleasure* (*Kinjiki*, 1952) are immensely skilful and interesting studies in homosexuality, the former a partially autobiographical account of a boy's discovery of his inclinations, and the latter a (nastier) one of an old man's passion for a young man. But Mishima failed to write a substantial novel, or one of any more than technical authority, and it is likely that his reputation will vanish, if not like a puff, then at least like a large cloud, of smoke. He combined an insatiable Japanese curiosity about all things Western with an increasingly disturbed homosexuality: eventually this erupted in a 'Japanese' gesture—but one perhaps as empty as his books are of real feeling.

VIII

Neither the drama nor the poetry of Japan has been as distinguished as its prose. There has been no dramatist of international stature, and only a handful of poets.

In drama the Japanese audience has on the whole preferred the period pieces: the *Kabuki* theatre and the *Noh* plays. There is an especially sensitive account of *Kabuki* performances in the late Twenties by Tanizaki in *Some Prefer Nettles* (q.v.).

Plays of Ibsen, Strindberg and Pinero as well as Shakespeare were performed in the first decade of the century; since then the majority of non-traditional Japanese plays have been imitations of Ibsen or Strindberg—competent entertainment but not of high literary value. Kikuchi Kan's (q.v.) plays (see *The Madman on the Roof*, MJL) were popular, but do not possess exceptional merit. Mishima Yukio's modern *Noh* plays have been praised, as have the folk plays of the left-wing academic KINOSHITA JUNJI (1914). Kinoshita runs a theatre group and is the most lively, powerful and influential force in the Japanese theatre of today. His plays have been performed in London, New York and Moscow. He has had more success than any other Japanese dramatist in the creation of a vigorous drama based on folklore—a drama that can communicate with its audience through their own myths. The most famous of his plays is *Twilight Crane* (*Yuzuru*, 1949; tr. A. C. Scott in *Playbook*, 1956), which is highly effective in performance and well above the level usually achieved by modern Japanese drama. It is sensitively based on the legend of a crane-wife who was driven to renounce human form by the greed of her husband and others.

Shimpa (new school) drama, started in 1888, was intelligent but basically political; really it belongs to the history of commercial entertainment rather than to that of literature. *Shimpa* aimed at realism and contemporaneity; some Western plays were performed, but most were adapted from novels and failed to avoid melodrama. *Shimpa* eventually evolved into a modernized version of *Kabuki*: the actors had been classically trained, and were never at home in the new form.

The real founders of the modern theatre movement in Japan, the *Shingeki*, were the indefatigable Tsubouchi Shoyo (q.v.) and OSANAI KAORU. Their initial efforts, at the beginning of the century, had little more success than *Shimpa* had had; but in 1924 Osanai founded the Tsukiji Little Theatre (destroyed in the Second World War), through which Western theatre was established in Japan. The fascists disbanded all *Shingeki* troupes; but since the end of the war it has made considerable progress, while the traditional theatre is gradually—and sadly—losing its hold. But *Shingeki* still has only one substantial theatre, the Haiyuza Gekijo in Tokyo, and so the many companies wishing to do non-traditional plays are forced to present them on inadequate stages. As in Great Britain, a long-standing plan for a National Theatre has met with no serious interest from philistine politicians. The modern Japanese stage has not yet evolved into a stable form: no major dramatist has yet emerged, and it is uncertain just how much the new theatre is going to owe to the old— to *Kabuki*, to *Noh*, and to the *Kyogen*, the comic interlude of the *Noh* plays. It seems likely that the director will further increase his power over the actor, to establish a 'director's theatre' (q.v.). But what the Japanese stage awaits is a great dramatist.

Poetic activity is wider and more varied than the dramatic, although there have been few poets of international stature. The particular difficulty encountered by twentieth-century Japanese poets has been to build on the severely restricted traditional forms. Unfortunately too much energy has gone into polemics and theory—and into the formation of schools and misleading categories. But there have been some real developments.

At the beginning of the Meiji era the Japanese wrote their poetry either in Chinese or in one of the traditional forms, of which the most popular was still the *haiku*. Japanese verse consisted of variations on a basic pattern of alternating five- and seven-syllable lines (*tanka*), which is known as *shichi go cho*. Since there is no appreciable accent, or quantity, in the spoken language, rhythm is established syllabically. Rhyme is very seldom used, as every Japanese syllable ends in a vowel. Two important traditional devices of Japanese poetry are the 'pillow-word', a kind of stock epithet, but with special characteristics; and the 'pivot-word', a single word which is employed so that, by functioning in two senses (as a pun, in fact) it acts as a hinge.

For some years after 1868 no kind of poetry was written in everyday, colloquial language; but this essential breakthrough was eventually achieved. In 1882 three professors of Tokyo University, not one of whom held a literary post, issued *An Anthology of New Style Poetry (Shintaishiso)*. This consisted of innocuous stuff—translations of Gray, Campbell and others—but the editors did state in their introduction that 'The poetry of Meiji should not be the poetry of the past but that of Meiji itself', and they avoided archaic terms, trying to work out a poetry 'on the European pattern'. This was followed by *Vestiges (Omokage,* 1889), in which the leading spirit was Mori Ogai (q.v.); and, most importantly, by VEDA BIN's (ps. VEDA RYUSON, 1874–1916) *The Sound of the Tide (Kaichoon,* 1905), which introduced further and more drastic colloquialization as well as translations from Hugo and the 'symbolist' (q.v.) poets (in whom he was most interested) such as the overrated Albert Samain (q.v.). Many foolish notions were put forward, such as Yamada Bimyo's proposal, rightly derided by Mori Ogai, to apply Western prosody to Japanese poetry. But amid the welter of 'schools', the titles of which are often misleading, a little real poetry was achieved.

At first the main stream of Japanese poetry was only marginally affected by the importation of foreign influences. For example, Toson, whose novels have already been discussed at length, was in most respects a traditional poet. He used the resources and the material already available to him. But before he took to fiction he wrote some of the best poetry in the language: as Ninomiya Takamichi and D. J. Enright note, 'here was a receptive soul, confronted suddenly with a fresh and vast view of poetry's potentialities'. His 'Crafty Fox' has a laconic toughness and complexity about it that remind one of Robert Graves (q.v.):

> There in the garden, a little fox
> Steals out at night, when no one is about,
> And under the shadow of the autumn vines
> He eats in secret the dewy bunch.
>
> Love is no fox,
> Nor you a bunch of grapes.
> But unbeknown my heart stole out
> And plucked you in secret, when no one was about.
>
> (PLJ)

'Otsutu' (PLJ) has a similarly foreboding subtle irony at the end. When the works of Toson have been fully translated, the West will realize what a magnificent writer it has been deprived of for so long. His poetry is modern in spirit, in the sense that it should be read in the light of a modern, and not a nineteenth-century sensibility.

The most influential poet during the Meiji period was MASAOKA SHIKI (ps. MASAOKA TSUNENORI, 1867–1902), a close friend of Soseki's (q.v.). Masaoka, who was not as gifted as Toson, died young as a result of tuberculosis contracted while a war correspondent in the Sino-Russian war. His main critical efforts, which became phthisically intense as his disease progressed, were directed towards the purging of artificiality from *haiku*: 'prefer real pictures', he advised his followers. He sought inspiration in the simplicity of the earliest, eighth-century, period of Japanese poetry. But his poetry, never more than miniaturist, is usually banal or polemic. He is seldom better than in this *haiku*:

> A snake gourd [used as cough-medicine] is blooming—
> Clogged with phlegm
> A dying man. (JLME)

Other early or essentially traditional poets include YOSANO AKIKO (1878–1942), YAMAKAWA SHIRAHAGI (ps. YAMAKAWA TOMIKO, c. 1880–1910) and, above all, the short-lived ISHIKAWA TAKUBOKU (ps. ISHIKAWA HAJIMI, 1885–1912), the author of a remarkable posthumously published private diary—he wanted it burned (pt. tr. MJL).

Yosano Akiko married Yosano Hiroshi (later called Yosano Tekkan), an influential editor who also wrote verse. Akiko might, in English terms, be compared to a somewhat superior English Georgian (q.v.) poet—someone of the order of Frank Prewett. The first notable Japanese woman poet since the eleventh century, she wrote vast quantities of whimsical, narcissistic and sentimental verse; but at her rare best she expresses her feelings with an attractively uncluttered straightforwardness. Her first collection, *Tangled Hair* (*Midaregami*, 1901; tr. S. Sakanishi, 1935), contains most of her best work. But such poems as

> Spring is short:
> Why ever should it
> Be thought immortal?
> I grope for
> My full breasts with my hands.
>
> (PJV)

demonstrate her virtues and limitations. After the eclipse of her husband's magazine and of its 'romanticist' programme she changed too self-consciously to a 'symbolist' style, and her work became mannered.

Ishikawa Takuboku was well known as a writer in both traditional and 'new style' forms. Technically, however, he was no modernist—and at the end of his consumption-racked and poverty-stricken life he turned to socialist politics rather than to literature. Nevertheless, his sensibility was an essentially 'modern' one. Japan lost a more accomplished and gifted poet by his early death than Great Britain did by that of Rupert Brooke (q.v.). He has a bitter, sometimes meaningfully convoluted humour, a 'blackness', that anticipates both Hagiwara Sakutaro (q.v.) in poetry and such modern prose writers as Yukio Mishimo (q.v.). His poetry never, perhaps, achieves the amazingly lucid self-searching of his seventh, *Romaji* diary (so called because it was written in Roman letters); but Keene's words about this diary may none the less be applied to his best poetry: 'it reveals a man of a depth, complexity, and modernity of thought and emotion that could not have been predicted from earlier literature'. The achievement, of course, lies in Ishikawa's capacity to make the revelation. The following fragment demonstrates his complexity and irony,

> Carrying mother on my back
> Just for a joke.
> Three steps, then weeping—
> She's so light.
>
> (PJV)

if not his other qualities. His 'new style' poems look forward to the density of Hagiwara, but are seldom unified. Where Hagiwara is able to set down his poetic experience, Ishikawa still uses devices such as dreams (as in the impressive *Rather Than Cry*, MJP): writing for no one's eyes, in prose, he dared the utmost; when composing for the public eye, he was slightly constrained.

However, Japan's most important poet of modern times is HAGIWARA SAKUTARO (1886–1942). Recognition of this has for some reason been grudging, even amongst the Japanese, but it cannot be put off for long. Graeme Wilson's brilliant selection of poems translated into English, *Face at the Bottom of the*

World (1969), should help the inevitable process. Hagiwara was the first gifted Japanese poet to use *spoken* colloquial Japanese in his poetry. There had been experiments before him, by SUSUKIDA KYUKIN and in a more thorough-going way by KAWAJI RYUKO in *Dustbin* (*Hakidame*, 1907); and in the same year SAKURAI TENDAN published a translation of the German poet Detlev von Liliencron (q.v.) into colloquial Japanese; later, in 1911, Ishikawa himself published a few semi-colloquial poems in a magazine—but they were blatantly political rather than poetic in content. Hagiwara's claim that 'all new styles issued' from his first book, *Baying at the Moon* (*Tsuki ni haeru*, 1917), is, as his translator says, on the whole a fair one. No one actually denies it; but the editors of *The Penguin Book of Japanese Verse* include only one poem by Hagiwara, and even Ninomiya Takamichi and D. J. Enright complain in *The Poetry of Living Japan* of his 'exposed nerves' and 'morbidity'. Donald Keene, however, in observing that most of modern Japanese poetry 'seems curiously lacking in substance', says: 'The poems of Hagiwara Sakutaro are perhaps the best of recent years. They seem the deepest felt, and although clearly influenced by European examples, retain a feeling for the music and potentialities of the Japanese language'.

In introducing Hagiwara's first book to the public the brilliant and eccentric poet Kitahara Hakushu (q.v.) compared its quality to that of 'a razor soaked in gloomy scent', to 'the flash of a razor in a bowl of cool mercury'. He has been compared to Baudelaire, and was obviously deeply influenced by him; but much more revealing is Graeme Wilson's comparison with Lorca, whom we may be sure Hagiwara had not read. Wilson cites his

> Here is a little flute
> Whose music is pure green

and mentions the poets' common affinity for rivers, moonlight, the barking of dogs and, above all, for music (Hagiwara was a gifted musician, although too lazy to make anything of it).

Certainly nothing had ever been written in Japan resembling Hagiwara's bitter, resonant, almost 'metaphysical' and beautifully organized poetry; no Japanese poetry has so successfully and unstrainedly assimilated Western influences. 'Murder Case' perfectly illustrates these qualities:

> There sounds a shot of pistol
> In the faraway sky; and then
> A pistol-shot again.
>
> Two pistol-shots; and my
> Detective dressed in glass
> Warps in from that clear sky,
> Vitrescent but to find
> Behind the window pane
> He takes such pains to pass
> The floorboards cut from crystal.

Between the fingers wind
Ribbons of blood more blue
Than words for blue contain,
And from the glazen dew
That glints like cellophane
On that sad woman's corpse
A chill, chill cricket chirps.

One morning of an early
November, dressed in glass,
The sad detective, surly
From sadnesses, came down

And, where the two roads cross
To quatrify the town,
Turned. At his point of turning
An autumn fountain waited.

Already isolated
In knowingness, he only
Can feel the real bereavement,
The long slow wrench concerning
Identity's decay.

Look, on the distant lonely
Acres of marble pavement
The villain, quick as silver,
Glides silverly away.

(tr. G. Wilson)

Hagiwara was friendly with Yosano Akiko (q.v.)—his gift for friendship somewhat sweetened his last, sour days, spent in drinking himself, though with reasonable self-regard, into incoherence—and with Kitahara Hakushu, Yamamura Bocho, Muro Sasei and Miyoshi Tatsuji (qq.v.).

KITAHARA HAKUSHU (ps. KITAHARA RYUKICHI, 1885–1942), well known for folk-songs and nursery rhymes as well as 'modern' poetry, had a gift for the grotesque, the whimsically telling phrase, the poetically appropriate epigram. There is a touch in him of Erik Satie and Ramón Gómez de la Serna (q.v.). When young his work had an attractively naughty 'unhealthiness'. He was highly intelligent, and had, with the possible exception of Nagai Kafu (q.v.), the best developed sense of humour of his literary generation. His poetry, almost invariably but never the less misleadingly referred to as 'symbolist', gives a vivid account of irrational terrors: finding itself unable to explore these, it falls back on the poetically well-bred humour and intelligence that have already been described. Hakushu's poetry is minor because of his inability—

in contrast to Hagiwara—to inhabit his own world and speak from its centre; but he had a world, and his descriptions of it are authentic, and he remains a delightful and skilful poet.

YAMAMURA BOCHO (1884–1924), a Christian priest who lived in poverty and eventually died of tuberculosis at forty, anticipated the self-conscious and poetically dull surrealist school. At their best his short poems have the freshness of pictures by Paul Klee:

> At the bottom of the river
> In the afternoon
> A moving motor-car—
> Giving a fish a ride
> And running it over—
> Causes a brilliant disturbance.
>
> (PLJ)

MURO SAISEI (1889–1962) edited a magazine with Hagiwara, and wrote some competent realistic fiction as well as poetry. His simple, lyrical poems, which were written in the colloquial idiom but in a rather self-consciously literary style, do not translate well, but were at one time very popular. Muro's was a minor, but pure talent.

MIYOSHI TATSUJI (1900–64) began as a disciple of Muro and Hagiwara, and has been called Japan's best poet between the death of the latter and his own. A 'lyricist' poet, he was one of the founders of *Four Seasons* (*Shiki*, 1934–44), the most influential of all the many hundreds of Japanese poetry magazines. He is less intense than Hagiwara, although such poems as 'Lake' (PJV) show what he could achieve in his modulated version of the same manner. A prose poem, 'Nostalgia', demonstrates his maintenance of a balance between thought and feeling:

> Like a butterfly, my nostalgia . . . The butterfly flies over hedges, sees the sea around the afternoon street-corner . . . I hear the sea inside the wall . . . I shut my book; I lean against the wall. It strikes two in the next room. 'Sea! Far-off sea! . . .' I write down on the paper: SEA. In our language you contain a 'mother' in you. And MOTHER—in the language of the French, you have the 'sea' in you!
>
> (PLJ)

TAKAMURA KOTARO (1883–1956), who with his use of free verse was something of an innovator, spent four years abroad after graduating from Tokyo University; but in his interesting poem 'My Poetry' (PLJ) he makes it clear that he does not propose to abandon his poetic nationality: 'My poetry is not part of Western poetry;/The two touch, circumference against circumference,/But never quite coincide. . . .' Takamura's poetry has an intellectual content, but is at the same time straightforward. As the son of a famous sculptor, and sculptor himself, he studied under Rodin for a time. Like Rilke's (q.v.), his poetry was for some time affected by this: the expression of inner *angst* accompanies lyricism in his work, which makes a quasi-religious effort to mould the raw material of life into significant forms, and which often (like Rodin) presents fragments as finished work. His favourite poet was Émile Verhaeren (q.v.), and the influence of Walt Whitman is almost as apparent.

> Stop, stop,
> What's this city of insect life? What's this city of insect life?
> With noises like that of a piano when you sit on the key board,
> And turbidity like that of a hardened palette. . . .
>
> (JLME)

There is also a vein of playfulness running through his verse, as exemplified in 'Chieko Mounting on the Wind' (PJV). As a person he has been described as 'sober . . . almost a puritan', a self-conscious artist who never lost himself in drink or even in poetry. This makes him unusual among Japanese writers, most of whom tended, especially at that time, to lose themselves in what the bourgeois would have called vice—or in the pleasures of alcohol.

FUKAO SUMAKO (1893), the only modern woman poet to gain a substantial reputation, is a more fastidious poet than Yosano Akiko (q.v.). For some reason she is excluded from *The Penguin Book of Japanese Verse*, but *The Poetry of Living Japan* includes good translations of two of her poems, which, elegant and thoughtful, never take refuge in 'femininity', that trap for the unwary or not quite sufficiently talented woman poet. She shares this unusual characteristic with an English poet of similar stature, E. J. Scovell.

MIKI ROFU (1889–1964), influenced by and a friend of Nagai Kafu (q.v.), was an indefatigable experimenter. He passed through a number of phases before seeking temporary refuge in a Trappist monastery. At its best, Miki's poetry, although always somewhat artificial and 'literary', elegantly expresses nostalgic moods; his melancholy and tendency towards nihilism are less convincing. Memory is a recurrent theme: 'At dusk, upon my heart/The snows of memory fall . . .'; '[The tree's] face is of a melancholic sphinx/With a stigma of sorrow impressed by "the Past" . . .'; and, in 'Home' (PJV), he asks a girl, listening to the flute, how her 'same heart' differs from itself after ten years and the loss of her mother, 'After the Kiss', (PLJ),

> 'Are you asleep?'
> 'No,' you say.
>
> Flowers in May
> Flowering at noon.
>
> In the lakeside grass
> Under the sun,
> 'I could close my eyes
> And die here,' you say.

uncannily resembles the manner of the young English poet Ian Hamilton (q.v.) in his first book, *The Visit*.

KAMBARA ARIAKE (1876–1952), often known as Kambara Yumei, was a disciple of Toson (q.v.), and later became known as an important 'symbolist'. This is less misleading than usual, since his poems are more self-consciously and genuinely symbolic than those of nearly all his notable contemporaries. His best known poem, 'Oyster Shell' (PJV, PLJ) presents man's plight as 'unbearable', since his 'shelter' is 'destined to decay'. Ariake's content now seems rather unsensational to Western readers, but he did much to strengthen the impact of French symbolism upon Japanese poetry—and was, however tamely, a true symbolist. He also imitated D. G. Rossetti in a series of longer, ballad-style poems. The chief weakness of his poetry is its reliance on invented emotion and amorous experience: it consequently lacks immediacy. Possibly he recognized this, since he published nothing new after 1908, and spent the rest of his life revising his earlier work.

The prolific SATO HARUO (1892–1964) began as a novelist, then turned to poetry. Like his friends Tanizaki and Nagai Kafu (qq.v.), he was fascinated by the lives of prostitutes in the old 'pleasure' quarters of the cities, and was at various times called 'decadent' and 'epicurean'. He is 'the other man' in Tanizaki's *Some Prefer Nettles* (q.v.), and did in fact marry Tanizaki's second wife. It is interesting to compare Tanizaki's version of the affair with his own no less candid one, in the poem 'To a Person':

Last night was the second time you have appeared in my dream:
Your husband, however, has done so no less than six times . . .

With you I find little to talk about, even in a dream:
With him, however, I walk and talk and am merry.

Even the dream world, I find, is against me;
Hence my doubts as to the Other World . . .

After both dreams I wake and cannot sleep for long;
Your dream, though, is ephemeral—

Whereas your husband's always lasts too long,
And leaves me with a headache on the morrow.

I confess how much I wish to see
Your husband killed by me in my dream—

And wish to see
How much I shall regret the killing . . .

(PLJ)

By the mid-Twenties an aggressively 'proletariat' school had split itself off from all other developments. This in turn fragmented into a formidable number of groups, variously short-lived. Although these poets naturally enjoyed a new vogue after the defeat in 1945, very few have emerged as poetically gifted. The most outstanding is NAKANO SHIGEHARU (1902), whose main poetic activity coincided with the period immediately preceding the militarist take-over; since then he has been active as a novelist and, notably, a communist politician. He can most profitably be compared with Mayakovsky (q.v.), by whom he was certainly influenced. But the vitality and satirical edge of his short-lined poems is his own; his is a much less complicated character.

The 'dadaist' and 'surrealist' (qq.v.) schools have also been more or less closely associated with the 'proletariat' school; the only 'dadaist' poet of substantial gifts and integrity is TAKAHASHI SHINKICHI (1901), who reached his dadaist position in 1921 via journalism and six months of Buddhist monasticism. He has also written fiction. His talent is slight, but genuinely surrealistic. In certain ways he reminds one of the surrealistic side of Pablo Neruda's (q.v.) poetry: his good-humouredly irrational world has its own effortless logic and integrity.

The eccentric KATSUE KITASANO's (c. 1914) magazine *Vou* (1935–   ) is courageously maintained and maintains contact with Ezra Pound, Charles Olson, Robert Creeley (qq.v.) and many others of the past or present *avant garde*.

The other modern Japanese poets are supposed to be representatives of the 'realist', 'lyricist' or 'intellectual' schools. As I cannot sufficiently emphasize, these categories are of little value in determining the nature of the work of those who are placed in them. Although they do mean a little more to the Japanese themselves, there can be little doubt that critical abstractions tend to impoverish their literature and drain it of energy. However, it has been pertinently pointed out that in Japan the argument about 'life' and 'Art' still rages; hence the proliferation of groups taking one side or the other. For example, KUSANO SHIMPEI (1903), who is regarded as the leader of the 'realists', is also described as a 'fauve'. . . . Actually Kusano is something of a comedian; and perhaps the term 'realist' as applied to him will mean a little more to Western readers when they know that this implies a rejection of over-theorization (which supposedly characterizes the 'intellectuals'). Kusano was in China from 1921 until 1939, and his first book arrived in the middle of this period of exile, in 1928. It was about frogs, whom Kusano described as 'heaven', 'anarchists', 'proletariats' and many other things. The effect of the poems in this volume was not unlike that of the Scottish poet Ian Hamilton Finlay's earlier poems collected in *The Dancers Inherit the Party*: cheerful, deliberately bathetic, innocent, quasi-surrealist, minor, whimsical. Another leading realist is the rather older KANEKO MITSUHARU (1895), who was once a symbolist. Kaneko has the deserved reputation, unusual in a poet, of having done his best work after reaching the age of fifty. He is a different and more serious kind of poet, sharply and bitterly satirical where Kusano is comic. His general attitude is well summed up in this stanza from 'Opposition':

Of course I'm opposed to 'the Japanese spirit'
And duty and human feeling make me vomit.
I'm against any government anywhere
And show my bum to authors' and artists' circles.

(PJV)

The chief 'intellectual' poet is NISHIWAKI JUNZABURO (1894), a professor
who has translated T. S. Eliot's *The Waste Land* (qq.v.) into Japanese. Another
of this group is HISHIYAMA SHUZO (1909), translator of Valéry and other French
authors. In general the poetry of this group is—as the realists claim—vitiated
by its members' excessive interest in poetic theory. Nishiwaki, however, is a
highly intelligent man, and his poetry—even if it be judged as essentially that
of a critic—is intellectually attractive. Occasionally, as in 'Rain' (PLJ, PJV),
his poems hint at something more erotic and personal.

The leading group in recent years has been that of the 'lyricists', an essentially moderate, eclectic, liberal-conservative movement that rejected over-
theorization and crude political propaganda, and tried to preserve whatever
was viable in the native tradition. Miyoshi Tatsuji (q.v.) was the most gifted
of them; others include TANAKA KATSUMI (1911), whose 'Chance Encounter'
(PLJ) well illustrates the competent traditionalism achieved by the more
distinguished members of the group:

Halley's Comet appeared in 1910
(And I was born in the following year):
Its period being seventy-six years and seven days,
It is due to reappear in 1986—
So I read, and my heart sinks.
It is unlikely that I shall ever see the star—
And probably the case is the same with human encounters.

An understanding mind one meets as seldom,
And an undistracted love one wins as rarely—
I know that my true friend will appear after my death,
And my sweetheart died before I was born.

(PLJ)

The smaller and more recent 'Waste Land' group has been highly influential
in the Sixties; its magazine was started in 1939 and resuscitated after the war.
Its foremost member is Japan's leading poet of the generation born in the
Twenties, TAMURA RYUICHI (1923). Tamura has been accused, by implication,
of writing in an 'international' style (q.v.), 'a cold collation of tentative,
repetitive, sometimes stammering incoherence'. There is such a style; but it
does not occur in Tamura, although his poems do translate remarkably well
out of Japanese. 'October Poem' seems altogether appropriate as the work of
one who was twenty-two when the atom bombs were dropped on his country:

Crisis is part of me.
Beneath my glass skin
Is a typhoon of savage passion. On October's
Desolate shore a fresh carcass is cast up;

October is my empire.
My gentle hands control what is lost.
My tiny eyes survey what is melting.
My tender ears listen to the silence of the dying.

Terror is part of me.
In my rich bloodstream
Courses all-killing time. In October's
Chilling sky a fresh famine erupts.

October is my empire.
My dead troops hold every rain-sodden city.
My dead warning-plane circles the sky above aimless minds.
My dead sign their names for the dying.

(PJV)

Jewish Literature

Jewish literature consists of two branches: writings in the Hebrew language, which are merely the most recent developments in a great and ancient literature (familiar to everyone in the Authorized Translation of the Bible); and writings in Yiddish, which began to develop as a literature only about a century ago, and today, regrettably, shows some signs of dying out. The Hebrew language has a history of at least three thousand years, and is one of the most ancient in the world. It fell into decline; but its revival, begun at the end of the last century, has proved successful. Its closest relative is Arabic. Yiddish, named after *Jüdische-Deutsch*, derives from the Frankish dialect of High German spoken by Jews in medieval Germany; it contains elements of English, Russian, French and Polish as well as of Hebrew. Its surviving form is written in a modified form of the Hebrew alphabet. The Yiddish literature first arose from the lower sectors of the Jewish population; it was rejected by the wealthy as vulgar. But, even upon those writers who chose Hebrew, it had an important effect. Thus Mendele (q.v.) is as important for his role in creating a new and viable Hebrew language as he is for his work in Yiddish. Yiddish was spoken by some eight million people before the Second World War. This number must now be much less.

I

Yiddish literature reached its peak at the beginning of this century. It flourished in Palestine (but has declined since the establishment of Israel, whose official language is Hebrew)—and in the U.S.A., Poland and Russia. Many of the Jews who remained in Russia after the Revolution were murdered in Stalin's purges; the regime under Lenin gave them hope, and their culture was encouraged—but things soon changed, and their situation is still rather precarious.

The three great founders of Yiddish literature are Mendele Moicher Seforim, Y. L. Peretz and Sholem Aleichem. MENDELE MOICHER SEFORIM (PS. SHOLEM JACOB ABRAMOVITCH, 1835–1917), who wrote in Yiddish and Hebrew, is called a 'grandfather' of both literatures. He lived in Russia. His first works were in Hebrew. But then he turned to Yiddish; hitherto merely the lingua franca of Jews, in his hands this became a means of artistic expression. His pseudonym means 'the bookseller', and by this he meant 'carrier of knowledge'. Sadly, he believed in the viability of Jewish life in Russia, and (as director of the Jewish school in Odessa) worked for it all his life. He was a great describer both of the Russian natural scene and of the realities of Jewish life. He wrote short stories and novels, of which *Fishke the Lame* (1869; tr. A. Rappoport, 1929; G. Stillman, 1960) is one of the most famous. His fiction is colourful, sometimes satirical, and always in touch with reality.

Y. L. PERETZ (1852–1915), who spent his life in Poland, also began by writing in Hebrew. After he published his first Yiddish story in 1888 he quickly became a centre of Yiddish literature. He combined Jewish nationalism with social realism, and while most of his own work is not of more than historical interest, it prepared the way for the best Yiddish literature. There are three volumes of selections in English: *Stories and Pictures* (tr. H. Frank, 1906), *Prince of the Ghetto* (tr. M. Samuel, 1948) and *Selections* (tr. S. Liptzin, 1947).

SHOLEM ALEICHEM (ps. SHOLEM RABINOVITCH, 1859–1916), born in the Ukraine, is superior to either Mendele or Peretz as a writer. As a young man Sholem Aleichem was a Government Rabbi in Luben; but in his mid-twenties he went to Kiev to devote himself to writing and to the dissemination of Jewish culture. He lost a fortune in his publishing ventures, and went bankrupt. His work from the early Eighties onwards was mostly in Yiddish. His pen-name means 'Peace be unto you'. He helped to launch Yiddish as a living literature by editing the first literary annual ever to pay its contributors. Although he was himself attended by financial ill-luck—towards which his attitude was characteristically good-humoured—Aleichem became famous all over the world. He travelled extensively, and finally settled in New York, where he died.

His short stories are vivid and, above all, humorous; it is rightly claimed that he played an important part in helping the modern, oppressed Jew to laugh at both his misfortunes and his Jewishness. His own financial reverses are reflected in those of his hero Menahem Mendel. His flexible idiom is unique, although rooted in the folkways of Jews down the ages. Yitzhak Berkowitz's (q.v.) translations of his works into Hebrew have always exercised an influence on that language, helping to give it flexibility. Nearly all his work has been translated into English (and into the other main European languages), although with some inevitable loss of vigour and tang. Among the best versions are: *Stories and Satires* (tr. C. Leviant, 1959), *Old Country Tales* (tr. C. Leviant, 1966), *Jewish Children* (tr. H. Berman, 1920). His autobiography (1920) is overdue for translation.

Although he is a critic and essayist and not a creative writer, Shmuel Niger (ps. Shmuel Charmi, 1884), born at Minsk, is an important figure in Yiddish literature. He considers it as necessary to Jewish survival; his accounts of Yiddish writers, such as Sholem Aleichem and Peretz, are indispensable; and his arguments for a vigorous Yiddish literature are convincing in the light of the continuing diaspora.

DAVID BERGELSON (1884–1952) was born at Uman in the Ukraine; although a supporter of the Soviet regime, he eventually became one of Stalin's victims. His early work is regional, dealing with Jewish small-town life; later he turned to the subject of the Revolution and its aftermath. The novel *After All* (1919) is considered to be his finest work, and is outstanding in Yiddish literature.

SHOLEM ASCH (1880–1957), born at Kutno in Poland, was the most famous Yiddish novelist of his generation, and most of his books have appeared in English translation. He travelled extensively, became a naturalized American citizen in 1920 and lived in Florida, Israel, and London—where he died. Asch's first fiction, short stories, was written in Hebrew; but he took early to Yiddish, although continuing to write in Hebrew. His method differed from that of Peretz and Seforim (qq.v.), and his vision in no way resembled Sholem Aleichem's comic one: he introduced an element of romanticism into what had been a primarily realistic field. But the sordid realism of his play *The Vengeance of God* (1907; tr. 1918) shocked Germans when it was produced in Berlin in 1910 by Reinhardt (q.v.). He was a skilful writer, and a good popular one; but he is not important. His best fiction is his earliest: here he portrays small Jewish communities with compassion and shrewdness. His *Collected Short Stories* (tr. M. Samuel and M. Levin) appeared in English in 1958. His later fiction is more pretentious, seeking, without conviction, to combine the Jewish and Christian religions. He wrote of Christ—*The Nazarene* (1939; tr. M. Samuel, 1939)—and of Moses and of Mary, in a series of semi-midcult pseudo-historical novels which are unimpressive.

LAMED SHAPIRO (1875–1948), who was born in the Ukraine but settled in America and died there, was a less famous but not less good writer. He is important for his stylistic modernism, which was influential on later writers, and for the uncompromisingly stark realism of his stories of the Tsarist pogroms. He translated Hugo, Dickens, Kipling (q.v.) and other writers into Yiddish— and also wrote the first Yiddish sea-stories.

JOSEF OPATOSHU (originally JOSEF OPATOFSKI, 1887–1957) came from Mlava in Poland; he settled in America as early as 1907. His importance lies in the introduction of a new form into Yiddish literature: the historical novel. His trilogy on Jewish life in nineteenth-century Poland, published in the early Twenties—it has not been translated—thus helped to make the historical novels of Isaac Bashevis Singer (q.v.) possible. (Sholem Asch's historical fiction made no such contribution.) Actually Opatoshu's 'novels' consist of a series of loosely associated, sometimes vivid sketches; but his feeling for the past and his way of handling it has influenced Yiddish literature.

Y. J. SINGER (1893–1944), in style a follower of Shapiro (q.v.), became famous before his younger brother ISAAC BASHEVIS SINGER (1904), with *The Brothers Ashkenazi* (1936; tr. M. Samuel, 1936), the best of his novels. Although Isaac Bashevis Singer is more important—probably the most important of all Yiddish writers—he undoubtedly learned much from Yisroel, who was a leader of the modern school. He has further explored themes of Yisroel's. Both were born in Lublin, Poland, where their father was a Rabbi. Isaac Singer's *The Family Moskat* (1945; tr. 1950) is dedicated to his brother: 'not only the older brother but a spiritual father and master'.

All Isaac Bashevis Singer's books were originally written in Yiddish, although not all are available in that language. He has lived in America since 1935, and has translated much of his own fiction either alone or in collaboration. The essence of Singer's greatness as a writer is that, as the American critic Irving Howe has put it, he can write of a vanished past as if it still existed. The power of his writing in this respect is uncanny. He has written novels, short stories and memoirs. He has an unmatched knowledge and understanding of Jewish-Polish folk-lore—he had, he says, picked this up long before he read the only source for it: Trachenberg's *Jewish Magic*. His work has a special appeal to writers of the Sixties (Saul Bellow, q.v., has translated him) perhaps mainly because of the religious needs of a secular age. Singer believes in 'Higher Powers', as his books make clear; but he is not a dogmatist. Apart from *The Family Moskat*—'a Jewish *Buddenbrooks*' (q.v.) set in Poland in the first half of this century, and chronicling the decay of a Jewish family—he has written: *The Magician of Lublin* (tr. 1960), concerned with a womanizing circus-magician and acrobat in late nineteenth-century Poland, *The Slave* (tr. 1967), about a young seventeenth-century Jewish scholar sold into slavery, *The Manor* (1953–5; tr. 1967), again set in late nineteenth-century Poland, and *Satan in Goray* (1935; tr. 1955), about religious fervour and the birth of Chassidism, again in seventeenth-century Poland. Short story collections in English are: *Gimpel the Fool* (1957), *The Spinoza of Market Street* (1961), *Short Friday* (1967), and *The Séance* (1968). Also notable is *In My Father's Court* (1956; tr. 1967)—the English translation differs somewhat from the Yiddish original—a collection of memories of a rabbinical court in Lublin, and an invaluable description of a way of life now vanished. Singer writes without sentimentality, and his themes are often terrible; but no modern writer's work has so rich and so affirmative a glow to it. Many of the short stories are classics: 'Gimpel the Fool', translated by Saul Bellow (q.v.) for *The Partisan Review* in 1949, takes its place amongst the best of all stories about the simple man exploited by his neighbours; 'The Séance', about a sick old man living in New York who deliberately allows himself to be exploited by a crooked and sadistic medium so that he can somehow keep contact with his European Jewish past; 'Alone', one of the greatest—and shortest—stories of the supernatural ever written. Singer's stature will continue to grow.

BENJAMIN SHLEVIN (1913) was born in Brest-Litovsk, but went to France in the early Thirties and has since become a Frenchman. A soldier in the French army in the Second World War, he was taken prisoner (1940–5) but managed to survive. All his work, with the exception of his first novel—which appeared in Warsaw in 1933—has been published in Paris, where he is highly regarded.

*

One of the first to start writing poetry in Yiddish was SIMON SAMUEL FRUG (1860–1916). Frug was born in an agricultural community at Herson in Southern Russia, and his education and environment were less intensely Jewish than those of most of his contemporaries. He gained a reputation as a poet in Russian, but began writing in Yiddish in 1888. He helped to bring modern standards to Yiddish poetry; but his work in Russian remains his best.

A more substantial precursor of modern Yiddish poetry was MORRIS ROSEN-FELD (ps. MOSHE JACOB ALTER, 1862–1923). It was translations of his poetry that brought Yiddish literature to the attention of the English-speaking world. He left Russia—he was born at Boksa in Russian Poland—for Warsaw as a child; at twenty he was in London in an East End tailor's sweatshop; then he learned diamond-cutting in Amsterdam. He arrived in the United States in 1886, where he lived in the New York ghetto and worked as a presser in even worse sweatshops than those of London's East End. *Songs from the Ghetto* (1898) finally extricated him from poverty: Leo Wiener, a Harvard professor, made a Latin transcription of the original, and supplied an introduction, a glossary—and a prose translation. The poems—wrathful, lush, heavily rhythmical—earned him the title of the 'mouthpiece of victims of a dehumanized society'. As befitted a Yiddish poet, he wrote of the conditions of poverty and of the proletariat. His poetry has not lasted, but its fervour was sincere and still conveys itself.

ABRAHAM REIZEN (1875–1953), born at Minsk, a pioneer of the Yiddish language—he edited a weekly devoted to translation from European into Yiddish—was perhaps the first poet to achieve a truly poetic stature. His intensely personal sketches about his miserable childhood were new in the literature. His verse is compassionate and musical without sentimentality.

MENAHEM BORAISCHA (originally MENAHEM GOLDBERG, 1888–1949) began as a religious poet, but then became the scourge of the anti-semitism of his native Poland. On going to New York (where he died) he became the poet of exile, his theme being the Jew in a Gentile environment. His most important work is *The Wayfarer* (1943), his longest and most personal poem, in which he sums up his life.

HALPER LEIVICK (1888–1962), born in Minsk, was sentenced to life imprisonment by the Tsarist government in 1912; but he escaped to New York. After Rosenfeld he has been the most popular of all Yiddish poets. His harsh experiences directed him towards mysticism rather than realism: he is a visionary—sometimes inchoately so—poet, of some power.

ITZIK FEFFER (1900–?1948) was a socialist realist poet whose work has some merit because of its sincerity and vigour. He fought for the Red Army at the Revolution and against the Nazis. Soon afterwards he vanished in one of Stalin's purges.

ITZIG MANGER (1900) was born and grew up in Rumania. He moved to Warsaw, then London (1941–51), then to New York, where he now lives. He has written prose and drama—but his song-like poems, spontaneous in manner and drawing upon folk and biblical themes, are his best works, and are unique in Yiddish poetry. A Jubilee edition of his works appeared in Geneva and Paris in 1951.

ABRAHAM SUTZKEVER (1913), born in Lithuania, is one of the few poets living in Israel to write in Yiddish; he is unquestionably the leading Yiddish modernist. He played an important part in Russian Jewish culture before 1941. He then escaped from the Nazis to Siberia. Sutzkever lived in Russia, then in Poland, before emigrating to Israel at the beginning of the Fifties. *Siberia* (1950) was translated by J. Sonntag in 1961. He edits a leading literary quarterly in Tel Aviv.

*

Since Yiddish was the spoken language of the Jews, the Yiddish theatre came into being some time before the Hebrew. Its modern father was the actor, song-writer, producer, manager and playwright AVRAHAM GOLDFADEN (1840–1908), who was born in the Ukraine and died in New York. He founded the first professional Yiddish theatre at Jassy, in Rumania, in October 1876. Some of his plays—for example *The Witch* (1879), *Shulamit* (1880)—are still in the repertory. After the Russians had banned his theatre he came to New York, where he lived for the last five years of his life. His plays have immense verve, but much of his genius was involved in the establishment and running of his theatre, rather than in the study of contemporary European drama, from which he could have learned much that would have improved his work. This, however, is still popular enough to be given in Hebrew in Israel.

JACOB GORDIN (1853–1909), another Ukrainian who settled in America, was a pupil of Tolstoi, and—like Asch (q.v.)—advocated a reconciliation of Judaism and Christianity. He knew the European theatre better than Goldfaden, and many of his seventy plays are clever adaptations of Shakespeare (*Jewish King Lear*, 1892), Ibsen and others into terms of the Jewish theatre. He was not as creatively gifted as Goldfaden, but he is important in the history of Yiddish theatre. AN-SKI (originally SOLOMON SAMUEL RAPPAPORT, 1863–1920), born at Vitebsk, is remembered for his play on a classical Jewish theme, *The Dybbuk* (1916; tr. H. G. Alsberg and W. Katzin, 1917). DAVID PINSKI (1872–1960), born in the Ukraine, lived in Switzerland, Germany and America before emigrating to Israel in 1950. He wrote novels (at first socialist in theme, but later on folk themes), essays (including important ones on Yiddish drama) and, above all, plays, the best of which is *The Treasure* (1905; tr. L. Lewisohn, 1905). Sholem Aleichem's (q.v.) plays helped to further enliven the Yiddish theatre in Europe. Halper Leivick's (q.v.) plays have power, particularly *The Golem*, a traditional theme to which he accords an unusual treatment. Leivick wrote a number of social dramas: *Rags* (1921), *Chains* (1930). *The Miracle of the Warsaw Ghetto* (1945) is inspired documentary. David Bergelson (q.v.) had plays produced in Russia. PERETZ MARKISCH (1895–?1948), when arrested by Stalin's secret policemen after the Second World War, bravely denounced their methods at his 'trial'. A poet as well as a playwright, he played an important part in the Russian Yiddish theatre in Kiev. His theme was often Jewish heroism against Nazi oppression.

II

Most of the older generation of Hebrew writers had their roots in the diaspora; the new type of Jewish writer is of course inspired by (or, latterly, bitterly

816

despondent about or highly critical of) the new state of Israel. The modern revival of Hebrew literature may be traced back to the German philosopher Moses Mendelssohn (1729–86), who insisted that the language used by the Jews in their struggle for deliverance—and the release from medievalism that was necessary before this could come about—should be Hebrew, which alone had the dignity and the character to move the whole of the people. In the course of time Hebrew literature became one of the chief instruments of the great Jewish revival—a revival much encouraged by the Balfour Declaration of 1917, and of course horrifyingly discouraged (and yet finally made more determined) by the holocaust. The linguistic pioneer, and planner of the great *Dictionary of Ancient and Modern Hebrew* (1908–59), was Eliezer Ben Yehudah (1858–1922).

The modern Hebrew literature is not a gay one; this element is more to be found in the Yiddish, the spoken language of the Jews—not the newly recreated one of men earnestly determined to revive their heritage. . . . One of the historians of modern Hebrew literature, Reuben Wallenrod, has usefully divided it (up to the foundation of the state of Israel) into four phases, which may be summarized thus: the romantic literature of the first wave of immigration to Israel, 1882–1905; the more complex work of 1905–18, where the idea and ideal of pioneering clashed with disillusion and reality; an expressionist phase, in which modernism was assimilated; and the 'mystical' phase (preceding the establishment of the state of Israel), in which tragic realism (the millions murdered) yielded to an ecstatic purpose.

MOSHE SMILANSKI (1874–1950) came to Israel (as I shall, throughout, call the Jewish Palestine of before 1947) from the Ukraine in 1890. He wrote not only of the early pioneers, but also of the Arabs, whom he loved. He described the difficulties experienced by the early Jewish settlers with a depressed, dutiful accuracy. But his most imaginative achievements are his romantic tales of heroism: his disillusioned writing is nearer to excellent journalism.

JOSEPH CHAIM BRENNER (1881–1921) is representative of the second phase of modern Hebrew writing. He was born in Bulgaria, but settled in Israel in 1908. He was assassinated in the 1921 Arab riots. He wrote fine realistic short stories of the horrors of the European ghettoes; but his later fiction is more complex, reflecting the impact of his own experience upon his Zionist idealism. *Between the Waters* (1920), a novel, demonstrates how the difficult situation in the Israel of the time too easily transformed young and wholesome emotion into falsehood and emptiness. *Bereavement and Failure* (1922) is Brenner's most important book. Like all his novels, it is episodic and loosely knit; but it is the first fiction to undermine the simple-minded romanticism of the early settlers: in it Brenner portrays hypocrites and self-deceivers, and expresses his fear that Israel will become just another 'ordinary' country, losing its special character. He is not a major novelist: his characters do not develop, but remain types; he is, however, an important realist. The argument between him and his friend, the influential philosopher A. D. Gordon (1856–1922), is instructive. Whereas Brenner—as he made clear in his novels—could not find solace in his despair at man's universal selfishness (he was bitterly disappointed to discover that the new Utopian possibilities offered by settlement in Israel did not appear to alter human nature for the better), Gordon made a virtue of his own more Nietzschean (q.v.) despair: it led him to call for action. Gordon nobly typifies the philosophical approach—he exhorts the Israeli to work in order to solve the problem of human evil; Brenner is the typical imaginative writer, always discovering evil and selfishness at the source of personality, unable to take much comfort in abstraction.

The work of ABRAHAM KABAK (1881–1945), born in Russia, may be divided into two phases: his studies of Jews under alien conditions, written while he was in Russia, and his novels about Jews living together, written in Israel. *Alone* (1905) deals penetratingly with the conflict between Zionistic and communistic aspirations amongst Russian Jews. In the historical *Solomon Molko* (1928–30) Kabak found his true voice: he recreates the colour and horror of the medieval period with vigour and skill, and convincingly shows how aspirations on behalf of all Jews may be reconciled—though at tragic personal cost—with the individual need for self-realization.

YITZHAK DOV BERKOWITZ (1885), who came to Israel from Russia via residence in the U.S.A., married Sholem Aleichem's (q.v.) daughter, and is best known for his excellent and important renderings of his father-in-law's work (complete) into Hebrew. But he also wrote his own fiction: a novel and some short stories. His stories deal sensitively with the crumbling of the old customs, particularly with conflict between conservative fathers and rebellious children.

SHMUEL YOSEF AGNON (originally S. Y. TSCATSKY or CZACZES, 1888–1970), was born in a part of Galicia, then Austrian, now Russian; he settled in Israel in 1908. He was among the best known of Hebrew writers for many years, but gained a truly international reputation only when awarded the Nobel Prize (1966). His main subject is the European Jewish diaspora; not until towards the end of his long life did he begin to write about the country in which he had lived for so long. His first important story was called 'Agunot' ('Deserted Wives'), and he signed it 'Agnon' in assonance to its title. When it was successful he adopted this name as his own. It was unusual, since it combined extreme modernity—a psychoanalytical treatment at a time when psychoanalysis was not of age—with equally extreme conservatism: the language is a Hebrew more medieval than modern, and the subject-matter is Jewish-traditional. His first stories were collected in 1916: *And the Crooked Shall Be Made Straight. The Bridal Canopy* (1922; tr. I. M. Lask, 1937) is his most famous and probably his best book. This is set in early nineteenth-century Galicia, and very cleverly and memorably employs the ancient technique of 'inset story' (*Rahmenerzählung*: a cycle or mosaic of stories all contained within a single story). Reb Yudl, a kind of Don Quixote, travels all over Galicia to collect dowries for his three daughters; he is accompanied by a Sancho Panza figure, Notté, his driver. The unifying elements in the series of episodes of which *The Bridal Canopy* consists are Reb Yudl's deeply religious passivity, and the strength of Jewish life at this period of history. In this book Agnon is at his happiest: where his contemporaries tended to portray the old-fashioned pious Jew as a figure of fun, he rejoices in his qualities. In *A Guest for the Night* (1945), written in 1939 after a visit to the land of his birth, he gave a sombre and spiritually terrified picture of Galician life between the wars: for Agnon, all cohesion has gone, and life is lived chaotically in a waste land: the coming holocaust is foreseen.

Just Yesterday (1947) is about Galicians living in Israel before the First World War; it combines Kafka-like allegory with implied social criticism. Other books by Agnon include *In the Heart of Seas* (1935; tr. 1948), some stories in *Tehilla* (tr. 1956), both translated by I. M. Lask, and *Two Tales* (1966; tr. W. Lever). Agnon is an extremely sophisticated writer, well aware of both Freud and Kafka (q.v.), and an expert employer of almost every kind of literary device. In the widest context his theme may be described as man's alienation from his own nature: his failure of individual and social function owing to the collapse of traditions. He is less conservative, perhaps—he conveys no obscurantist sense of wishing, willy-nilly, to re-impose the ancient ways—than simply tragic. He merely records, with much insight, the fatal split in the mind of the modern Jew; and if, as Malamud (q.v.) suggests, all men are now Jews, then this is all the more reason for paying attention to Agnon's work. Despite a basic difference of approach, the writer with whom Agnon has most in common is Kafka (q.v.); but in Kafka the nihilistic element is absolute. Agnon clings to Jewishness and its rich past.

ASHER BARASH (1889–1954) was also born in Galicia and came to Israel as a young man. Like Kabak's, his earlier work is about the European diaspora, his later about life in Israel. Barash, who has an admirably lucid and direct style, is the only Hebrew novelist who may with some justice be described as a naturalist (q.v.). He is charitable towards people and their motives, but fate may always be heard knocking on the door. His main earlier novels are *Pictures From the Brewery* (1928) and *Strange Love* (1938), both describing Jewish life in Galicia. The splendidly characteristic title of a later story, about Israel, is 'He and His Life Were Ruined'.

ELIEZER STEINMAN (1892), born in Russia, has written of the effect of the strains of modern Jewish life on sexuality; he was influenced by Gorky and, later, by Freud. SHRAGA KADARI (1907), born at Lvov, has been misunderstood and taken too literally. His Freudian interpretations of modern Jewish observance of ancient traditions are intelligent and unusual.

One of the most widely read of the younger novelists is MOSHE SHAMIR (1921), whose best book is the historical *King of Flesh and Blood* (tr. D. Patterson, 1965). S. YIZHAR (1918) is somewhat less traditionalist in his approach, although by no means an innovator. He has written the best fiction about the men who fought to establish Israel, or to defend her from Arab attack.

Only in the fiction of the Sixties has the spirit of modernism really begun to manifest itself. A generation of writers who grew up in the state of Israel have begun to question the bases of the Jewish religious faith—one of the chief unifying factors in the diaspora—and even to challenge what they consider to be the dangerous chauvinism of the present government. This attitude is well illustrated in the best novel to come from Israel in the Sixties: AHARON MEGGED'S (1920) fine *The Living on the Dead* (tr. M. Louvish, 1970). Jonas Rabinowitz, a Jewish writer of more promise than achievement (but his promise is genuine), is on trial for breach of contract. On the strength of a fragment from an uncompleted novel, published in a magazine, he has been commissioned to write the life of one of Israel's legendary heroes, Davidov; but when he learns the truth about him—that he was both good and bad—he finds he cannot sanctify him. There is a brilliant and valuable picture of the contemporary Israeli literary world in the coterie Jonas joins. The book ends with the situation unresolved: the trial will go on for years, Jonas will go on stalling. . . . This book is an allegory of the situation of 'Young Israel': the situation of those who inherited the benefits of the struggle. Davidov, with all his faults—compulsive womanizing, cruelty to his wife and family—made Israel possible. When Jonas discovers, however, that the *legend* of Davidov is not true, a 'block' is formed, which threatens his entire creativity. No character in the book is able to see that Jonas is really 'on trial' for being unable to subscribe to an acceptable view of the Israeli past. . . . This is a depressing book; but the boldness with which it raises issues, and the directness with which it faces them, is a sign of a cultural health that no culture-committee could recognize.

*

Ancient Hebrew poetry is known to every educated person all over the world: the most familiar examples are, perhaps, the psalms—and *Job* and *Ecclesiastes*. The poetry of the Old Testament was superseded by the poetry of the *Aggadah* (this means 'folk-tale', but in the Jewish consciousness it has come 'to mean almost everything that is not canonical law, known as *Halakhah*', to which it is complementary rather than opposed). In the early Middle Ages Hebrew religious poetry co-existed with secular poetry. Between 1300 and the second half of the nineteenth century there was virtually no Hebrew poetry: it could, writes Abraham Birman, 'be written off as an almost total loss'. The first signs of a revival came with Yehudah Leib Gordon (1830–92), known because of his initials as *Yalag*. His poetry at least had energy—if little else. Then there emerged the 'triumvirate' of Bialik, Tchernikhovsky and Schneour (qq.v.), which made Hebrew poetry into a once more viable entity.

The most important of these three poets, and still the most important poet in modern Hebrew literature, was CHAIM NACHMAN BIALIK (1873–1934). Born in Russia, as a young man Bialik reacted against the strict Talmudic upbringing that his grandfather had given him, and came under the influence of the 'enlightenment' (*Haskalah*). A disciple of Mendele's (q.v.), Bialik's poetic gifts manifested themselves early, although at first he tried (disastrously) to make a living as a lumber merchant. He is a lyrical poet of depth and power, whose best known poems, such as 'The City of Slaughter', denounce both Israel's Russian oppressors and the Jews themselves for allowing it. A. M. Klein (q.v.)

has made an excellent translation of this furious poem (AMHP), unique in its heat and indignation. Bialik wrote it after he had visited Kishinev in the aftermath of a cruel pogrom:

> No lustre in the eye, no hoping in the mind,
> They grope to seek support they shall not find:
> Thus when the oil is gone the wick still sends its smoke,
> Thus does an old beast of burden still bear its yoke.
> Would that misfortune had left them some small solace . . .
> And thou, too, pity them not, nor touch their wound;
> Within their cup no further measure pour.
> Wherever thou wilt touch, a bruise is found.
> Their flesh is wholly sore.
> For since they have met pain with resignation
> And have made peace with shame,
> What shall avail thy consolation?

This is one of the *Songs of Wrath*, in which he accused his fellow-Jews of 'stuffing their souls' down the throats of the oppressor. But this is only a facet of Bialik's poetic genius: he can be comic, racy and passionate as well as railing. The structure of his poetry is Biblical; but, as Abraham Birman has observed, 'the minutiae of his craft . . . all borrow largely from the *Aggadah*' (q.v.)—of which he made a famous and influential anthology. In 1924 he left Russia for Israel, where he was welcomed as the natural leader of Hebrew culture. He transferred the publishing firm he had founded in Odessa to Tel Aviv, and was active in every field—but he wrote no more poetry until shortly before his death, when he produced *Yatmut*, reckoned by some critics to be his best poem. *Aftergrowth* (tr. I. M. Task, 1940) is a selection of stories.

SHAUL TCHERNIKHOVSKY (1875–1943), also born in Russia, did not come into contact with the Hebrew language until he was seven, and although he always loved it, and wrote in nothing else, the emphasis in his work is more on the Jewish desire to be as other peoples than on their desire to fulfil a special destiny. Tchernikhovsky practised medicine all his life, even in his last years, when he settled in Tel Aviv. He made many translations into Hebrew, including Homer, *Gilgamesh* and Shakespeare. He is a frankly 'pagan' poet, although profoundly Jewish in spirit. His earlier poetry is sensuous, and frankly that of a philanderer—a unique tone in the Hebrew poetry of the time; then came pantheistic poems, addressed to heathen gods in deliberate defiance of Jewish monotheism. He is a warm poet, sometimes too lush—but always passionately sincere. His poetic gift was not as great as that of Bialik, but he was as original. (AMHP)

ZALMAN SHNEOUR (1887–1959) was not very original in style; but he is the best Jewish egotistic poet ('a true follower of "the style of the big I" ') of his time—a kind of Frank Harris of decency. He possessed an extraordinary intuition, prophesying the holocaust, the discovery of the Dead Sea Scrolls and the atom bomb. . . . His early poetry is his best. (AMHP)

AVIGDOR HAMEIRI (ps. EMIL FEUERSTEIN, 1886), deeply influenced by Ady (q.v.)—he was born in Hungary—was perhaps the best Hebrew poet to express the themes of hope and despair of the years before the establishment of the state of Israel. He also wrote fiction.

AVRAHAM SHLONSKY (1900) came to Israel—where he had been educated—from Russia in 1921; he was deeply influenced by Mayakovsky (q.v.) and other Soviet modernists, and he introduced modernism—in a somewhat over-flamboyant manner—into Hebrew poetry. It has been pointed out that his own best poetry is more traditional in form; Birman quotes an excellent passage, which he has himself translated:

> The room here is right-angled, as in all hotels,
> But very long
> And not too high
> And narrow.
> Here in the gloom you manage all too well
> To whisper 'God' in adolescent terror.
>
> To press a torrid brow against a window-pane
> (The eye, you know, can hear at such an hour),
> And like a dog whose master has been slain
> Frustrated silence in the darkness howls.
>   (AMHP)

Shlonsky is the easiest of all modern Hebrew poets to recognize, even through the veil of translation, as a true poet.

NATHAN ALTERMAN (1910), who came to Israel from Poland as a boy, is generally thought of as the first *Sabra* poet (*Sabra* is the fruit of the prickly pear, and is the name given to Israelis born in Palestine—brash, prickly, sweet at the heart), even though he was not actually born in Palestine. Alterman, laureate of Tel Aviv, is a strident, urban poet, who has been most notably influenced by Shlonsky (rather, perhaps, than by the Russian revolutionary poets who were his models). A critic has well characterized his best work as having an 'innocuous alcoholic element'. (AMHP)

DAVID AVIDAN (1934) is Israel's angry young man: neo-surrealist in manner, wildly hit or miss, inchoate, he has probably done Israeli poetry some good; he is at his best when less angry and more feeling.

There is no major playwright in Israel, but the theatre flourishes, and competent plays have been written, notably, by Alterman, Megged and Shamir (qq.v.). The most interesting activities go on in the 'little' theatres.

Latin-American
Literature

I

Modern Spanish-American literature begins, appropriately enough, with *modernismo* (modernism), which I have here called by its Spanish name in order to avoid confusion with the generic term 'modernism'. (The Brazilian *modernismo* of 1922 is referred to, where confusion could arise, as 'Brazilian modernism'.) Before the publication in Argentina of José Hernández' poem of gaucho life, *Martín Fierro* (1872–9), which is among other things a protest against a Europeanized, urbanized government's treatment of rural dwellers, Spanish-American literature had exhibited most of the usual characteristics of a colonial literature. The often bizarre and always colourful reality of the Spanish-American nineteenth century is practically ignored; there are no movements to speak of—just a number of individual versions of romanticism. Spain and things Spanish were of course nominally rejected; but, so far as the literature is concerned, this rejection is in favour of non-Spanish Europe rather than the native South America. The conditions were not yet conducive to the creation of a truly indigenous literature: ceaseless and often violent political activity effectively hindered the development of an intelligent and educated reading public. The only indigenous culture, although magnificently vigorous, was rural, illiterate and entirely cut off from the other, Europeanized one. Hernández' *Martín Fierro*—which is, most successfully, written not in a gaucho dialect but instead in a Spanish that conveys the whole gaucho spirit—is important because it is the first serious attempt to bridge this gap. It is a romanticizing and even, fundamentally, a conservative work; but it also has revolutionary elements. Whether Hernández' original purpose was didactic or not, his work shows—for the first time in South American literature—a sophisticated mind achieving imaginative identification with the non-literate population.

The countries of South America and the Antilles have known little social or political justice; there has recently been drastic social reform in Cuba, but it is not yet clear at what price. Allende's socialist Chile is not yet of age; meanwhile the difficulties it finds, even as the legally elected government, in instituting reforms are symptomatic of South American political life. Under these circumstances it is hardly surprising that South American literature as a whole is profoundly concerned, directly or indirectly, with social and political issues. There are of course important exceptions, such as Borges (q.v.); but they are very much exceptions, and even Borges has upset some of the Argentine younger generation by his refusal, over the past few years, to take a public stand against the reactionary governments of his country. As Jean Franco has pointed out, whereas in Europe the names of movements refer to technique (cubism, expressionism, symbolism, and so on) the names of South American movements 'define social attitudes' (modernism, new worldism, Indianism, and so on). She continues: 'This difference . . . has meant that . . . movements in the arts have not grown out of a previous movement but have arisen in response to factors external to art'.

Yet it is likely that Latin America as a whole will be an important cradle of a new and reinvigorated literature. Its mysterious, unknown, unconquered interiors are representative of the unknown depths of men's minds, and of the wise past; in Latin America the political drama of mankind is being dramatically worked out. . . .

*

'Modernismo' was, of course, like all literary movements, an abstraction; but it is one of the most easily definable—even if critics have called it everything from a wholesale crisis in Western civilization to the procedures of a single poet, Rubén Darío (q.v.). The latter view is foolishly narrow; the former is nearer to the truth, and was held by Juan Ramón Jiménez (q.v.), the leading representative of *modernismo* in Spain. The Spanish-American *modernista* poets share at least a subjectivism and a desire to rise, like phoenixes, from the ashes of an age from which all spiritual sustenance had been sucked by nearly a century of narrowly intellectual utilitarianism and positivism. Clearly the old kind of universal Christianity would not and could not fill this vacuum; *modernismo* reflects at least an attempt to do so, mostly with a self-awareness— which varies from narcissism to acute self-observation (more often than not it is a mixture of both). Its deficiency, in retrospective terms, is that although its intentions were nationalistic, its manners were European. But it was an essential phase in Spanish-American self-awareness.

In general, the *modernista* poets were aware of one another—and of the attitudes they shared. Thus, they were generally 'Spanish-American' rather than rigidly nationalist (in terms of their particular countries—as the Argentinian gaucho movement, for example, had been). The man who—not always scrupulously—made himself into their leader, the Nicaraguan Rubén Darío (q.v.), was in every sense the opposite of regionalistic; indeed, one of the reasons why he succeeded in dominating the movement was his cosmopolitanism.

It may seem paradoxical that *modernismo*, the first truly Spanish-American literary manifestation, should have been at least in part an 'art for art's sake' movement—in the history of a literature that has rightly been characterized as predominantly social. But there is ample reason for this. Hispanic romanticism as a whole had been half-hearted in comparison to French or English or

German; the old neo-classical critical assumptions had not even been substantially challenged. That is why both the Generation of '98 (q.v.) in Spain and the specifically Spanish-American *modernismo* that influenced it may be seen as in certain respects late manifestations of romanticism itself (as well as a reaction to some of the more superficial aspects of it). Both the men of '98 and the *modernistas* turned to Bécquer (q.v.), the only really good nineteenth-century Spanish poet—and certainly a romantic. This being so, the writers needed to do what their counterparts in most other countries had done seventy and eighty years earlier: establish literature on a higher plane than neo-classical conceptions of it had ever allowed. It is not surprising that during this process some degree of artistic hermeticism should be expressed. In any case, it may be argued that even the more aloof, bohemian and aesthetic of the *modernista* poets (Julio Herrera y Reissig, q.v., comes immediately to mind) were—whatever their attitude—engaged in a social act: the creation, for the first time, of a national literature.

Finding nineteenth-century Spanish literature impoverished, the Spanish-Americans turned to France: to the Parnassian poets (q.v.), with their emphasis on style, elegance, and art, to Hugo, Baudelaire and to Verlaine (whom Darío met in Paris) and to the symbolists (q.v.). However, *modernismo* tried to be essentially Spanish-American: the poets sought to make the Spanish language adequate to deal with reality by bringing it up to date. To accomplish this they turned to French sources; they were also influenced by German and English writers, but these languages were less well known. It cannot be emphasized too strongly that the *modernista* poets did not intend to 'become' French: they were, on the contrary, seeking in French examples means of attaining an identity of their own.

Though Darío, a prodigy who was also something of an opportunist, gave *modernismo* its name and carried its influence to Spain ('the return of the galleons'), he was not its initiator. Its point of beginning is to be found in the poetry of the Cubans José Martí (1853–95)—a great poet—and Julián del Casal (1863–93), the Mexican Manuel Gutiérrez Nájera (1859–95) and the Colombian José Asunción Silva (1865–96). There are also some hints of the *modernista* manner in the earlier poetry of the Peruvian MANUEL GONZÁLEZ PRADA (1848–1918)—his collection of thoroughgoingly *modernista* poetry, *Minúsculas*, was not published until 1901; the earlier poetry was not collected until after his death. González Prada represents the revolutionary, sociological side of *modernismo*. In the earlier poems, particularly in his German-influenced ballads, he attained a new simplicity and directness. He was a political agitator: variously a Marxist, a Tolstoian anarchist and an enemy of the reactionary Church. He was one of the first partisans of the Indian majority in Peru, and he effectively punctured the arguments of the racist 'sociologists' who argued that the Indians were inferior beings. González Prada's *modernista* poems in *Minúsculas* are among his least effective; but in his earlier search for simplicity, adaptation of divers foreign poetic forms to the Spanish, experiments with semi-free verse ('polyrhythm without rhyme'), use of Baudelarian synesthesia—in all these things he shows himself a typical *modernista* poet. His best poetry is in the posthumous *Peruvian Ballads*, in which the Indian appears for the first time not as exotic ornament but as an Indian. His prose, chiefly criticism and political and satirical essays castigating the cruel complacency of his countrymen, is as important as his poetry. Vallejo (q.v.) loved and was influenced by him. (SCO)

In RUBÉN DARÍO (ps. FÉLIX RUBÉN GARCÍA SARMIENTO, 1867–1916), the organizer and namer of *modernismo* if not its real pioneer, the confusions of the time worked themselves out—sweetly, sentimentally, sadly, angrily or softly.

He steered a perpetually tortured course between compulsive sensuality and a yearning for the innocent Catholicism of his childhood. He maintained his Christian faith, but did not believe in it. He grew up in a small town in a small country, Nicaragua; he had Negro and Indian as well as Spanish blood. Darío was publishing poetry in periodicals at the age of twelve; in 1881 he went to El Salvador, where he learned about Hugo and the Parnassians from the poet FRANCISCO GAVIDIA (1863–1955), only four years his senior. Gavidia's first collection of original poems, of 1884, deserves to be regarded as genuinely pre-*modernista* for its careful imitations from French models. Rubén Darío, an inveterate traveller, soon became well known all over South America. The Parnassian *Azure* (*Azul*), prose-poems and stories, appeared in Chile in 1888; for some critics it initiates *modernismo*. His duties as a diplomat and cultural ambassador carried him to Europe in the early Nineties and thereafter; there he came to know almost everyone of importance in Paris and Madrid. During the first decade of this century he visited Europe even more extensively. He succumbed to an attack of pneumonia in 1916 almost certainly because of lack of resistance caused by years of alcoholism. Married twice, Rubén was in his private life a compulsive womanizer; after each romantic episode he would be attacked by, successively, guilt, remorse and disillusion.

Whether one views Rubén Darío as a great poet or not, he is certainly one of the more fascinating of his time. Of his historical importance there can be no doubt. The subtlest and most suggestive critical account of him is by the Spanish poet Pedro Salinas (q.v.). As a poet Darío possessed enormous skill and courage; it has rightly been pointed out that he has some resemblances to Swinburne (q.v.), not only in his skill but also in his deliberate and brassy cultivation of the erotic and the hedonistic. However, his personal experience was psychologically deeper and richer than the unfortunate Swinburne's, and he is a more substantial poet. Although Darío rationalized art into a personal and aristocratic device for the reconciliation of God and mammon, his sympathies—if somewhat vague—were socialistic. It was chiefly his sexual problems that kept him from thinking deeply about society; and even as late as 1905, in the preface to what is probably his best collection of poetry, *Songs of Life and Hope* (*Cantos de vida y esperanza*), he cannot take up an entirely aristocratic position. Thus while he denies that he is 'a poet for the masses', he also declares that 'I must inevitably go to them'.

One of Rubén's most famous poems, 'The Swan', established the chief symbol of the *modernista* spirit:

It was a wondrous hour for all humanity.
Before, the swan would sing when death was drawing near.
The hour that Wagner's Swan sent forth its melody
Was just at dawn; it meant that new life would appear.

Prevailing over tempests on the human sea,
The singing of the Swan is heard, we can still hear
It rule the mace of Thor, the Nordic deity,
And trumpets singing of the Sword of Argantir.

O Swan! O sacred bird! If Helen, fair of face,
Came forth from Leda's azure egg, replete with grace,
Immortal princess of the Beautiful and Real,

New Poesy conceives beneath your wings of white
Amidst a brilliancy of harmony and light,
Eternal Helen, pure incarnated ideal.

(SCO)

All of the familiar ingredients of *modernismo*, including Nordic mythology, have been incorporated into this now rather dated poem. The Swan is chosen as symbol because it was in the form of a swan that Zeus raped Leda (for Rubén Darío this was a particularly convenient rationalization: the artist as God fulfils his sexuality—he wrote a poem on the subject of this rape, which he sees as a gorgeous affair), because it is white, beautiful, aloof, virginal (until raped by a poet-God) and because its neck is enigmatic in shape—somewhat like a question-mark.

Darío's poetry has, with justice, been compared, in its shimmering effects, to impressionist painting; it has also been called superficial and insensitive. Now while it is always mannered, it is not always superficial. He is not quite always adopting a pose or stating an artistic programme. On certain occasions the extreme anxiety underlying his attitudes, particularly his attitude to death —shudderingly manifested in the short-lived fulfilment of sexual desire—as the fearful solver of life's enigma, makes itself powerfully felt. 'Nocturne' contains a suggestion of this:

You who diagnose the heart of night,
who in massive sleeplessness have heard
a door shutting, a carriage's far sound,
a vague echo, a tiny noise. . . .

At the moments of mysterious silence
when the unremembered arise,
at the hour of the dead, the hour of rest—
you will know how to read these acrid lines.

I pour into them, as into a glass, my griefs
for memories of long ago and sad misfortunes—

and for the nostalgias of my dismal soul, drunk with flowers,
and the pain of a heart that is weary of play.

And repentance for not becoming what I should,
the loss of a kingdom I was meant to have,
and the thought that, once, I might have avoided birth,
and the dream that my whole life's been.

All this comes amid the deep silence
in which night wraps up this dream of life.
And I seem to hear an echo from the world's heart
Which pierces, and then fills, my own.

His important books, in addition to those already mentioned, are *Profane Prose* (*Prosas profanas*, 1896), *The Strange Ones* (*Los raros*, 1896) and *Sunny Lands* (*Tierras solares*, 1904)—all prose. His collected works were published in Madrid (1950–55). (PSV; SCO; PLAV)

It is an unintelligent, or at least a pedantic, use of the concept of *modernismo* that refuses to accept the Mexicans SALVADOR DÍAZ MIRÓN (1853–1928) and MANUEL JOSÉ ORTHÓN (1858–1906) as *modernista* poets. Díaz Mirón's poetry prior to *Splinters* (*Lascas*, 1901) was bombastic, patriotic and Byronic, 'like a herd of wild American buffalo', said Rubén Darío, an admirer. Then in 1892 he shot a man in self-defence in a brawl in Veracruz, during an election campaign, and was sent to prison for four years. As a result of this experience (he was arrested again in 1912, this time for attempted murder) he changed his style, aiming for a new elegance and polish that are certainly *modernista*; at the same time he wholly rejected the aristocratic conception of literature that Rubén Darío affected. His later and much better poetry played no part in the *modernismo* movement; but it was a result of it. Díaz Mirón is one of the best South American poets of his time. The sonnet 'The Example' shows him at the height of his powers: laconic, terse, technically (in the original) assured, rich in meaning:

On the branch the naked body putrefied.
Like a foul fruit hanging near the trunk,
witness to an unlikely sentence,
swinging, like a pendulum, above the road.

Its obscene nudity, the protruding tongue,
the hair tufted like a cock's comb, made it clownish;
and by my horse's feet a group of urchins
joked and laughed.

And the sad corpse, with head hung low,
scandalizing and yet shy on its green gallows,
spread its stink on the fresh breeze,

still like a censer swinging. And the sun
climbed up in the flawless blue; the countryside
was as in an old poet's lovely song.

(The word 'fallo' in the third line, meaning 'sentence', puns on the other meaning of 'one declared past hope'; and on 'falo', phallus: the hanged man's 'unlikely', ironically useless erection.) (PLAV)

There is perhaps more excuse in not counting Othón as a *modernista*, for he persistently attacked *modernismo*, and his formula, 'we must not express what we have not seen', strikes at the symbolic roots of the movement. But he was a close friend of the man whose ideas he fiercely attacked, Manuel Gutiérrez Nájera (q.v.), wrote a warm and generous tribute to him when he died of alcoholism in 1895, and contributed to his *modernista* magazine, the *Azure Review* (*Revista Azul*). Furthermore, his supreme achievement—one of the greatest in Spanish-American poetry of the century—the *Savage Idyll* (*Idilio salvaje*, 1928), written in 1905, is unquestionably *modernista* in its tone and technique. Certainly this sequence of sonnets inspired by a young girl with whom Orthón, a married man (he tried to attribute his emotions to a friend, a respectable unmarried historian, in a hopelessly unconvincingly preliminary poem), had fallen in love, is not the poetry of a man looking directly or carefully at nature. The spectacular landscape of Northern Mexico, with which Othón compares his love- and death-haunted mind, fulfils an undeniably symbolic function:

Look at the landscape: immensity below,
immensity, immensity above;
in the distance the huge mountain
sapped by an appalling ravine.

Gigantic blocks that quakes
have ripped from living rocks
and on that menacing and sullen plain
no path nor track.

The incandescent lonely air's
encrusted with serene and massive birds,
like nails hammered slowly home.

Huge obscurity, silence, fear,
which only the triumphal thud of deer
momentarily half-breaks.
(See also PLAV)

The Bolivian poet and scholar RICARDO JAIMES FREYRE (1868–1933), a close friend of Rubén Darío's and of Lugones' (q.v.), was a professor of literature and history—until in 1923 he was sent to the United States as Bolivia's ambassador. Later he joined the government. His first book, *Pagan Fountain* (*Castalia bárbara*), which appeared in 1899 (and not two years earlier, as is usually stated), consisted of a number of drastic and effective experiments with rhythm; the themes were generally Nordic and Wagnerian. Jaimes Freyre's *modernista* exoticism had its roots in knowledge as well as imagination. His account of his theories of Spanish versification (1912) seems as eccentric as W. C. Williams' (q.v.) scattered remarks on technique; his practice, which seldom approximates to genuine free verse, is masterly. Jaimes Freyre was in a number of respects more modernist (not *modernista*) than Rubén Darío. His poems of the lonely and frozen north look forward to the condition of man in the second half of this century. 'The Sad Voices' comes from his first book:

Across the whitened steppe
The sleigh glides on its way;
The howling of the wolves far in this distance
Joins with the laboured breathing of the dogs that pull the sleigh.

It snows.
It seems that space has been enveloped in a veil,
That has been trimmed with lilies
By a sweeping northern gale.

Infinitude of whiteness.
Over desert's vast extent,
There floats a vague sensation of deep anguish,
Supreme abandonment, and sombre and profound discouragement.

Afar is silhouetted
A solitary pine,
Against a background formed of mist and snow,
A skeleton's long line.

Between the two white shrouds
That earth and sky unfold,
Advances in the east
The early winter morning, freezing cold.

(SCO)

This sense of bleakness and loss becomes stronger in Jaimes Freyre's later poetry, collected in *Dreams Are Life* (*Los sueños son vida*, 1917). (PLAV)

The Argentinian LEOPOLDO LUGONES (1874–1938) was another close friend and associate of Rubén Darío; they worked together, when young, as clerks in the Department of Posts in Buenos Aires. Lugones began as a rebellious young anarchist, but ended—sadly—as a fascist nationalist; he killed himself. He was the most versatile of the *modernista* poets; he was also—to the detriment of some of his poetry—an exhibitionist: an inveterate performer. Much of his work is marred by ill-considered rhetoric; right from the first collection, *Gilded Mountains* (*Las montañas del oro*, 1897), one can see—if only incipiently—the frenetic state of mind that was ultimately going to drive him to fascist nationalism and self-destruction. (The Argentinian writers have tended to be less socially oriented than their neighbours; but they have not usually been fascist.) His second collection, *Garden Twilight* (*Los crepúsculos del jardín*, 1905) modified the frequently violent tone of *Gilded Mountains*; *Sentimental Lunarium* (*Lunario sentimental*, 1909) is even quieter in tone, and imports the procedures of the French symbolists, together with some Japanese quaintness, in an imaginative and extremely self-assured manner. This volume, written it seems mainly under the influence of Laforgue, contains his best work: ironic, intelligent minor poems in which Lugones humorously and attractively distorts his sentimentality into something self-mocking and occasionally psychologically revealing. But for all his accomplishment and mental brilliance Lugones is essentially a frigid poet; he possessed little true feeling; and his selfishness led him, in the end, to an attitude that lacked good will towards other men. His later nationalist poetry, and his posthumous ballads, though much admired by certain sections of the public, and of historical importance, are of small account poetically. Lugones has been exceedingly influential in South American poetry, both for his early importations from the European *avant garde* and his later treatment of the Argentinian countryside as a kind of Utopia. The best of his fiction is the novel *The Gaucho War* (*La guerra gaucha*, 1905). (SCO; PLAV)

The poetry of the Mexican AMADO NERVO (1870–1919) began and ended poorly; he was at his most original in his *modernista* phase, which covered roughly the first decade of this century. He wrote in a variety of styles, ranging from the romantic preciosity of his immature verse to the tiresome, superficial and moralizing religiosity of his final collection, the poems of which unconvincingly spiritualize his eroticism. Largely because of these Nervo was at one time one of the most widely read of poets writing in the Spanish language. Since then critics more discerning than this sentimental public have whittled down his large output (fiction, essays, criticism—as well as verse) to a few poems and stories. Nervo was intelligent but also self-indulgent; indignantly aware of the isolation of the writer and the lack of an educated audience, he was himself too seldom concerned with standards. At his best he has a tinselly grace and a kind of saccharine sincerity; but, judged in poetic terms, his mystical pose conceals an emotional vacuity. (SCO)

The most aesthetic of the *modernista* poets was the Uruguayan JULIO HERRERA Y REISSIG (1875–1910). He was highly accomplished in a Parnassian way, and he well understood the procedures of the French symbolists; but he was no more than a minor poet; what is unaffected in his work, which consists entirely of sonnets, is negligible. He was utterly dedicated to poetry, but for him poetry represented all that is most artificial in the works of his masters, who included certain of the poorer symbolists (for example, Samain, q.v.) as well as Baudelaire and Verlaine. He was foolishly aristocratic in his attitude, and was consequently neglected in his lifetime except by his immediate literary circle. He cultivated 'ivory towerism' and did, in fact, inhabit a garret, from which he would from time to time issue silly decrees. He died from heart disease.

Herrera y Reissig exercised a considerable influence; but his poetry, exquisite though it is, is too literary to be convincing. The Spanish landscape—from which, although he never saw it, he felt himself to be unnaturally separated—that figures in his poetry is less a landscape of his imagination than of, in the Coleridgian distinction, his fancy. The inner life he records is less a life than an act put on to regale himself. Actually, Herrera y Reissig has nothing relevant to say; but for those who enjoy the artificial poetry of evasion he is an important example. His hermeticism may have influenced Huidobro (q.v.). (PLAV)

More important, because at his best more authentic, is the Peruvian megalomaniac, fascist and killer JOSÉ SANTOS CHOCANO (1875–1934). Chocano was both a Peruvian and a South American nationalist; as a child he witnessed the defeat of his country by Chile. He was sent to prison at the age of nineteen for taking part in an unsuccessful revolution; from prison he issued a book of vigorously liberal revolutionary poetry appropriately printed in red type. His best poetry came while he was comparatively young: in 1906, with *Soul of America, Indo-Spanish Poems* (*Alma América. Poemas indo-españoles*). His connection with *modernismo* is a technical matter: his study of the work of Rubén Darío, and of the Parnassians in translation, taught him to control and make evocative his wild vision of South America. Rubén Darío himself recognized Chocano as 'the poet of America'; because of his sense of identity with the Indians and their past, and his fear of United States imperialism, he has been called the poet of 'New Worldism' (*mundonovismo*). Unfortunately Chocano's empathy (strengthened by his own Indian blood) soon spilled over into a hysterical fascism. He became a close friend and adviser to one of the most repulsive of all the South American dictators, Estrada Cabrera of Guatemala. When Cabrera was overthrown in 1921 the revolutionaries sentenced Chocano to death. Petitions to save 'the poet of America' succeeded; he was released. He returned to Peru, where he loudly and unrepentantly continued to support the causes of tyranny and militarism. After the celebrations of the centenary of the Battle of Ayacucho in Peru he shot and killed a young Peruvian critic. He was himself gunned down while travelling in a tramcar in Chile in 1934.

Most of Chocano's earlier poetry is declamatory and has no chance whatever of survival; he himself disowned it when he came to publish *Soul of America*. His championship of the Indian has sociological and political significance; his empathy with the Indians has genuine poetic value. But Chocano's best poetry is concerned with South America the place: its landscape, flora and fauna. He is not a major poet—his eye is always too vulgarly on the main chance of swaying his audience with fulsome rhetoric rather than poetry—but his best work is truly evocative of the teeming beauty and variety of the tropics, and Neruda (q.v.) may have learned something from it. (PLAV)

Less sensational, but as important, is Chocano's fellow-countryman JOSÉ MARÍA EGUREN (1874–1942), who did not gain the recognition he deserved until the last decade of his life. He began (*Simbólicas*, 1911) as a somewhat whimsical *modernista*; the early poetry reminds one more than a little of Apollinaire (q.v.) in his more playful mood and of the great neglected Icelander Þórbergur

Þórðarson (q.v.) as well as of Lugones (q.v.). Later Eguren withdrew more into himself; but not to the extent that he could not effectively communicate his own hallucinated world. He has been called (LAP) the 'first Peruvian symbolist', but this seems highly misleading; it is more to the point to recall Neruda's (q.v.) words about Vallejo (q.v.), the great Peruvian poet who followed Eguren: 'In Vallejo [the Indian element] shows itself as a subtle way of thought, a way of expression that is not direct, but oblique. . . .' This applies equally to the less substantial, less convulsively agonized Eguren, who walks in his own landscapes (where Vallejo, with stunning and unique courage, walks in the real world) and who conveys his sense of remoteness by description of them. (LAP; PLAV)

The Mexican ENRIQUE GONZÁLEZ MARTÍNEZ (1871–1952), who was originally a doctor of medicine, and then became a diplomat (like so many South American writers), has often been called the last of the *modernista* poets. There is a certain justification for this view; but one could with equal conviction apply it to the Chocano of *Soul of America*. . . . Almost all the Spanish-American poetry of the past hundred years has been *modernista*; thus, the so-called *post-modernismo* is as much a part of *modernismo* as the new objectivity (*neue Sachlichkeit*, q.v.) is of expressionism. González Martínez' first, immature books were as *modernista* in technique as his later ones; the content of these in fact deviates less from the original Parnassian-symbolist spirit of *modernismo* than does the poetry of Lugones or Chocano. González Martínez wrote the following famous (and controversial) poem in 1911. Originally he called it 'Wring the Neck of the Swan'; in 1915 he reprinted it, in a new collection, under the title of 'The Symbol':

> Then twist the neck of this delusive swan,
> white stress upon the fountain's overflow,
> that merely drifts in grace and cannot know
> the reeds' green soul and the mute cry of stone.
>
> Avoid all form, all speech, that does not go
> shifting its beat in secret unison
> with life . . . Love life to adoration!
> Let life accept the homage you bestow.
>
> See how the sapient owl, winging the gap
> from high Olympus, even from Pallas' lap,
> closes upon this tree its noiseless flight . . .
>
> Here is no swan's grace. But an unquiet stare
> interprets through the penetrable air
> the inscrutable volume of the silent night.
>
> (LAP)

It used to be thought that the 'neck' was that of Rubén Darío; but this was a misinterpretation—as González Martínez was much later at great pains to point out. Clearly the opening exhortation refers to Verlaine's recommendation to 'wring the neck' of rhetoric. But González Martínez was not proclaiming a programme; he was making a rule for himself. His swan is not so much Darío's as the tawdry one of his minor followers. This does not represent a termination of *modernismo*, or even a full reaction to its artistic hermeticism; rather it is a development of it: an attack on rhetoric and the over-ornamentation of a debilitated and life-denying Parnassianism. The air in the *modernista* closet had become over-stuffy.

González Martínez is a pantheistic poet who sets himself the task of expressing the inner nature (rather than the glittering surface) of the world. Like the Othón of *Savage Idyll* (q.v.), although in a very different way, he spiritualizes landscape. His is a *modernismo* purged of mannerism and rhetoric. (PSV; SCO; PLAV)

*

González Martínez had a considerable influence upon the poets of the so-called *postmodernismo* movement (really this is a tendency, not a movement), all of whom searched, in their different ways, for a new simplicity of expression. Four women poets emerged, all of whom wrote romantically, passionately and directly. The common themes in poetry, in these years before the advent of the *avant garde* movements, are specifically American ones: cosmopolitanism gives way to a new sort of *costumbrismo* (q.v.); but these poets had throughly absorbed the cosmopolitanism of *modernismo*—even as they rejected it.

The Mexican RAMÓN LÓPEZ VELARDE (1888–1921), once a judge but then a minor bureaucrat in Mexico City, suffered from Rubén Darío's eroticoreligious problem; but, unlike Rubén, he yearned for the 'ordinary', the simple, and he was more articulately and devoutly nationalist (although he was in no way chauvinist in a *criollista*, q.v., manner). The poems of his first collection, *Devout Blood* (*La sangre devota*, 1916), were regionalist in the best sense. It is a poetry of extreme subtlety and complexity, but always vivid and of a lucid surface, as in his memories of 'My Cousin Agueda':

> My grandmother invited my cousin Agueda
> to spend a day with us
> and my cousin arrived
> in a paradoxical
> prestige of starch and of frightened
> ritual mourning.
>
> Agueda arrived shining
> with starch, and her green eyes
> and ruddy cheeks
> protected me from that sinister
> mourning . . .
>   I was a child

and knew *o* by its roundness
and Agueda who knitted
doggedly and patiently in the echoing
corridor made me
secretly afraid . . .
(I think I got from her the heroically insane
habit of talking to myself)

when we ate, in the placid shadows
of the dining-room
I was under the spell of the delicate
and intermittent sound of plates
and of the caressing smoothness
of my cousin's voice.
                    Agueda was
(mourning, green eyes, ruddy cheeks)
a many-coloured basket
of apples and grapes
in an old cupboard's ebony depths.

Here the lovely and dangerous mind of a child is evoked as wonderfully as it is in Gabriela Mistral (q.v.). The theme of another of López Velarde's best poems, 'The Maleficent Return', is of the malignancy of the modern town; with great linguistic brilliance and concentration López Velarde describes a battle-ruined, now nature-corrupting town as a metaphor for twentieth-century sexual and intellectual sophistication. This, more successful than the poetry in which he attempts to reconcile his morbid eroticism and fear of death with his more optimistic religious impulses, remains one of the most powerful of all modern Spanish-American poems. It is better, he advises, not to go back to the 'shattered paradise that lies silent/after its mutilation by artillery'; and he draws an unforgettable picture, throughout over fifty lines, of its sinister ill-health. A definitive collection of López Velarde's poetry was published in Mexico in 1957. (SCO; PSV; PLAV)

ENRIQUE BANCHS (1888–1968), of Buenos Aires, seems to have stopped his poetic activity before the age of twenty-five; although a few of the poems of a small collection of fugitive pieces of 1950 were written after 1910, when he published the last of his four books, *The Urn* (*La urna*). Banchs is an exquisite minor. His poems, many of which are carefully wrought sonnets, are masterpieces of understatement and ironic modesty in varying styles. In keeping with the reaction against artifice of which he formed a part, he prefers charm to rhetoric. He distrusts deep emotion—and yet many of his poems convey it. (PLAV)

Banchs' compatriot BALDOMERO FERNÁNDEZ MORENO (1886–1950), who was a doctor, is not so much *post-* as simply non-*modernista*. His language is unsensational, technically traditional and deliberately simple; he is perhaps the most distinguished traditionalist of his generation. (PLAV)

835

Another Argentinian poet often described as a *postmodernista* is RAFAEL ALBERTO ARRIETA (1889), who has spent his life in his native Buenos Aires as an academic and editor of literary and scholarly reviews. Like his younger compatriot Borges (q.v.), Arrieta is a student of the English language, and has made a number of translations of, among others, Shakespeare. Arrieta, like Banchs, sought a new simplicity of style—but he lack Banchs' technical mastery. One of the persistent themes of his poetry is nostalgia; he wants poetry to do what nothing else can do: fix and capture exquisite moments. The same concern is present in Azorín (q.v.), and, in its most developed and significant form, Jorge Guillén (q.v.). (LAP)

The Mexican ALFONSO REYES (1889–1959), another diplomat, may be remembered less for his poetry than for his influential critical prose. This would be a tragedy, for his poetry has been neglected: to some extent his role as humanist essayist and publicist tended to distract attention from it. He was a distinguished scholar and editor, and an authority on many Spanish writers, Cervantes, Góngora, Quevedo and Lope de Vega among them. He also wrote fiction and travel books. His collected works (1955–   ) are in process of being published in Mexico. So far eighteen volumes have been issued, of which the tenth is devoted to his poetry.

Reyes was a product of what in Spanish America is called the Arielist tradition —after an essay of 1900, by the important Uruguayan essayist José Enrique Rodó (1871–1917), called *Ariel*. This employed the symbolism (Ariel as aristocratic spirit, Caliban as gross, plebeian matter) used by Ernest Renan in his rationalistic, anti-democratic *Caliban*—but not for similar purposes. Rodó did not, like Renan, fear that the advent of democracy would destroy the spirit: his essay (written, and with a good deal of sympathy for Spain, just as the Spanish-American War was ending) tries to prescribe how a democracy might function without destroying spiritual values. The United States is seen as on the whole a materialistic threat, a common theme in South American literature; but Rodó's intentions here were soon exaggerated—which gave rise to the dangerous and incorrect conception of a spiritualized South America in morally triumphal opposition to a coarse, commercialized and materialistic North America. Essentially *Ariel* is a plea—not hopelessly idealistic—for social justice without a rejection of spiritual values. It exercised an enormous and beneficial influence, helping to counter the personal malevolence and human ill-will represented by the many military dictators of twentieth-century South America.

Reyes' prose—intelligent, flexible and humorous—is conceived in this spirit; so, more obliquely, is his poetry, which reflects an early and apparently direct awareness of expressionism (q.v.). Reyes is a highly original writer and critic, and considering his achievement, a neglected poet. (PSV; LAP; PLAV)

We now come to two unclassifiable writers, both of importance and considerable originality, who are usually associated (if only for convenience, and because of their ages) with the *postmodernista* group. The Chilean PEDRO PRADO (1886–1952), poet, prose-poet and novelist, deserves to be better known outside

South America. Trained as a lawyer, he was gifted in many fields—painting, sculpture, science, architecture—but, until illness forced him in the late Thirties to retire, he devoted himself to diplomacy and journalism. He founded and organized a Chilean literary group called 'The Ten' (*Los Diez*); this was loosely knit, and the real common factor was friendship. Like the Serapion Brothers (q.v.), although possibly under better auspices, 'The Ten' tried 'to do nothing more than cultivate art with complete freedom'. The young Prado of his first book, *Thistle Flowers* (*Flores de cardo*, 1908), was one of the chief South-American pioneers of free—or semi-free—verse; in its successor, *The Abandoned House* (*La casa abandonada*, 1912), he turned to the prose poem. He was attacked by conservative critics both for his views and for what they considered to be his poor technical accomplishment. Prado gave them the lie when, in a final phase, he turned to the sonnet, a form which he handled with some mastery. The theme of these last poems is the love affair, and its aftermath, that he had in spite of his happy marriage, at the age of forty-eight. These are over-esoteric (and perhaps over-discreet), but always of the greatest intelligence and interest. Between 1914 and 1924 Prado wrote a number of novels, the best of them being the last, *A Rural Judge* (*Un juez rural*, 1924), one of the finest Latin-American regionalist novels of the century. His allegory *Alsino* (1920), about a little hunchbacked boy who learns to fly, is the most famous of his books.

The Guatemalan RAFAEL ARÉVALO MARTÍNEZ (1884), poet and novelist and inventor of 'psychozoological' fiction, is another unclassifiable writer. For many years he was Director of the National Library of Guatemala. Arévalo Martínez is among the most fascinating and unusual writers of his generation; it is surprising that so well known a tale as *The Man Who Looked Like a Horse* (*El hombre que parecía un caballo*, 1914) should not have been translated. The essence of the psychozoological tale, which is not supposed to be too solemn or rigid a literary category, is that it is a technique for describing human beings more fully and exactly—by reference to their animal counterparts. Arévalo Martínez wrote stories about a man-dog, a man-elephant and a man-tiger as well as the more famous man-horse who finally gallops away. The collection of which *The Man Who Looked Like a Horse* is the title story contains elements of social criticism (an account of the exploited Central Americans who work in the Alaskan salmon fisheries) and caricature (the man-horse was in part based on the legendarily homosexual Colombian poet PORFIRIO BARBA JACOBS, ps. MIGUEL ANGEL OSORIO, 1883–1942, who was a failed but interesting and talented mixture of decadent, *poète maudit* and clown, a kind of South American Max Jacob, q.v.—PLAV); but is a highly original tragi-comic collection—an early example of genuine expressionism (in the wider sense). Arévalo Martínez is doubtless as important for this type of fiction as for his poetry; but this poetry is as distinguished and unusual, in that it reflects his complex and subtle sense of humour, his restraint and his 'psychozoological' interests. Some of the poems are charming, sweet and simple in that Spanish-American manner which manages to steer a course that just avoids sentimentality; others are deceptive in their simplicity. His main theme, and the original motive of his psychozoological investigations, is the conflict between spirit and instinct. He expresses this in 'The Men-Wolves':

> At first I called them 'brothers,' with my hands extended;
> But soon their thieving in my sheepfold was begun;
> The call of brotherhood then in my soul was ended;
> Approaching them, I saw that they were wolves, each one!
>
> What happened in my soul that it was so unseeing,
> In my poor soul that is so prone to love and dream?
> I should have seen in their long strides the roving being,
> And in their eyes the cruel predatory gleam.
>
> Since then I also left the straight road for another;
> A wolf myself, in what deep mud holes I would fall!
> Then I could recognize in each of them a brother;
> Approaching them, I saw that they were men; yes, all!
>
> (SCO)

Other important works by Arévalo Martínez include his Utopian *The World of the Maharachías* (*El mundo de los maharachías*, 1938) and *The Torlanian Ambassador* (*El embajador de Torlania*, 1960). (SCO; LAP)

*

It was in this period that four Latin-American women poets attracted the attention of the public: the Uruguayans DELMIRA AGUSTINI (1886–1914)—murdered by her estranged, horse-dealing husband—and JUANA DE IBARBOUROU (1895), the immensely popular 'Juana of America', the Argentinian ALFONSINA STORNI (1892–1938) and the Chilean GABRIELA MISTRAL (ps. LUCILA GODOY ALCAYAGA, 1889–1957). Delmira Agustini's highly charged super-erotic poetry ('O love, it was upon a tragic sobbing night,/That I heard singing in my lock your golden key') caused ladies to protest; it retains its intensity, but its scope (pleasure-pain, frustration) is so limited that it has none the less dated: Delmira Agustini's intuitions did not match her magnificently romantic-decadent lusts, which she did not have time to outgrow. (SCO; PLAV)

Juana de Ibarbourou eventually became the most conventional of these four poets, and has throughout her life maintained a radiant image as 'wife and mother'. But while this might well be suspect in an advanced and sophisticated democracy (say in America or Great Britain), in South America—where poverty still abounds and where gangster-politicians may wreak their will on entire populations—there is a greater depth of genuinely popular, 'conventional' feeling. It was the sophisticated Reyes—no fragrant sentimentalist—who (in 1928) gave Juana de Ibarbourou her title 'Juana of America'. In any case, in her early love poetry, she ignored stuffy convention as much as Delmira

Agustini—even if one would not now go to her for any profound revelations about the nature of woman. (LAP; SCO)

Alfonsina Storni, who drowned herself at the age of forty-six, was a woman whose greatest happiness was to work creatively with young children. Her love-poetry is subtler and more bitter, although not less sensual, that that of Juana de Ibarbourou. She longs, as has been pointed out, to be indifferent to men, but she cannot bring herself to be; she is also critical of men: while Juana Ibarbourou at one point goes so far as to 'deeply regret' her femininity, Alfonsina Storni writes:

> You told me: My father did not weep;
> You told me: My grandfather did not weep;
> They have never wept, the men of my race;
> They were of steel.
>
> Speaking thus, a tear welled from you
> And fell upon my mouth . . . More venom
> Have I never drunk from any other glass
> As small as that.
>
> Weak woman, poor woman who understands,
> Sorrows of centuries in the drinking of it:
> Ah, this soul of mine cannot support
> All of its weight!   (LAP)

Alfonsina Storni is the most gifted, except Gabriela Mistral, of this group of poets; further, she deals with themes not touched upon by the latter. Her haunted last poetry, often composed in trance-like moods brought on probably by the strain (under which she finally collapsed) of the knowledge that she was suffering from cancer, was collected in *Death-Mask and Clover* (*Mascarilla y trébol*, 1938). Alfonsina Storni is an interesting poet whose conflicts anticipated many of the themes of women poets (of all nationalities) of the generation after hers. (LAP; SCO)

Gabriela Mistral was the first woman poet, as well as the first Latin-American, to win the Nobel Prize (1945). She wrote only four collections of poetry; but many unauthorized editions have been issued. She continued, unsystematically, to revise her poems all her life; thus they exist in many versions. The *Collected Poems* of 1958 (Madrid) does its best, but is bibliographically unsatisfactory. Gabriela Mistral began as a schoolteacher; she first made her mark with 'Sonnets of Death' (1914), for which she gained a prize. Shortly before this (1909) the man with whom she was in love (and whose mistress she presumably was) committed suicide under circumstances that have never been satisfactorily explained; one authority says he did it 'for honour'. Gabriela Mistral experienced at least one other great and unhappy love; but she never married, and she never became what she so passionately desired—as her poetry tells us so expressively—a mother. She did, however, adopt her nephew as a son; in the third great (known) tragedy of her life, he killed himself (1944)—again under mysterious or undisclosed circumstances. Her country afforded her the unique honour of appointing her Consul—in the country of her own choosing. She travelled extensively in Europe and the U.S.A., where she died (of cancer). She suffered from mental disturbance from time to time in these last years. In the late Forties she met an American woman with whom she lived until her death. Her four collections are: *Desolation* (*Desolación*, 1922; rev. 1923; rev. 1926; rev. 1954), *Tenderness* (*Ternura*, 1924 rev. 1945), which mostly consists of revisions of the poems from the first book, *Felling of Trees* (*Tala*, 1938) and *Winepress* (*Lagar*, 1954). There is a selection of English translations made by Langston Hughes (q.v.), *Selected Poems* (1957), and one by D. Dana with the same title (1971). She wrote much delightful prose.

Gabriela Mistral was both a devout Roman Catholic (although her Christianity is more of a Tolstoian—compassionate—than an orthodox sort) and a devout lover of men. Her candid—but not really erotic—poetry of love makes even that of Anne Sexton (q.v.) look a little over-affected and tawdry; that of Judith Wright (q.v.) looks suburban by the side of it. Gabriela Mistral is not, perhaps, an innovator—although both her demotically 'coarse' or 'rough' language and her indifference to academic pedantry were extremely influential—but she hardly needs to be; like almost all major poets, and all Spanish-American major poets, her roots are obviously and deeply in the naïve (q.v.). One can see that Gabriela Mistral and Pablo Neruda (q.v.) are both Chilean: there are passages in *Winepress* that resemble Neruda quite closely. She wrote with as deep an insight into children as any poet of her generation.

She is in many ways a primitive poet, as in 'God Wills It':

> The very earth will disown you
> If your soul barter my soul;
> In angry tribulation
> The waters will tremble and rise.
> My world became more beautiful
> Since the day you took me to you,
> When, under the flowering thorn tree
> Together we stood without words,
> And love, like the heavy fragrance
> Of the flowering thorn tree, pierced us.
>
> The earth will vomit forth snakes
> If ever you barter my soul!
> Barren of your child, and empty
> I rock my desolate knees.
> Christ in my breast will be crushed,
> And the charitable door of my house
> Will break the wrist of the beggar,
> And repulse the woman in sorrow.

The kiss your mouth gives another
Will echo within my ear,
As the deep surrounding caverns
Bring back your words to me.
Even the dust of the highway
Keeps the scent of your footprints.
I track them, and like a deer
Follow you into the mountains.

Clouds will paint over my dwelling
The image of your new love.
Go to her like a thief, crawling
In the boweled earth to kiss her.
When you lift her face you will find
My face disfigured with weeping.
God will not give you the light
Unless you walk by my side.
God will not let you drink
If I do not tremble in the water.
He will not let you sleep
Except in the hollow of my hair.

If you go, you destroy my soul
As you trample the weeds by the roadside.
Hunger and thirst will gnaw you,
Crossing the heights or the plains;
And wherever you are, you will watch
The evenings bleed with my wounds.
When you call another woman
I will issue forth on your tongue,
Even as a taste of salt
Deep in the roots of your throat.
In hating, or singing, in yearning
It is me alone you summon.

If you go, and die far from me
Ten years your hand will be waiting
Hollowed under the earth
To gather the drip of my tears.
And you will feel the trembling
Of your corrupted flesh,
Until my bones are powdered
Into the dust on your face.

(LAP)

Yet this, by virtue of its intensity, its lack of pretentiousness or sentimentality, does brilliantly and movingly summarize a certain mood; further, it has pantheistic overtones that take it out of the realm of the merely simple-minded or pathologically possessive. The poem can fairly be read as a romantic metaphor for the kind of conditions love imposes. Gabriela Mistral's poetry, disturbed and yet trusting, is in accord with the teeming nature which she so loves; it is one of the most distinguished non-intellectual poetries of this over-sophisticated and intellectual century. (LAP; LWT; PLAV)

*

Chile, with its two Nobel Prizes for poetry within twenty-six years of one another (Gabriela Mistral, Neruda), has maintained a distinguished or at least a lively poetry from the beginning of the century until the Seventies. The earlier period is well represented by MANUEL MAGALLANES MOURE (1878–1924), an elegant lyricist. It was in Chile, of course, that Darío (q.v.) chose to publish *Azure*. CARLOS PEZOA VÉLIZ (1879–1908), almost unknown in his short lifetime, was a gifted and original 'sociological' poet, whose poetry in *Chilean Soul* (*Alma Chileana*, 1912) reflects his sensitivity to the poverty he saw around him; he was also a fine descriptive poet.

One of the liveliest and most controversial if not necessarily greatest Chilean poets was the vain, flamboyant, gifted, untruthful, quarrelsome VICENTE HUIDOBRO (1893–1948), the inventor of creationism (*creacionismo*), which is really an extreme form of cubist poetry (q.v.). Huidobro, a literary publicist as well as a writer, made false claims—and faked editions of his early work—about his early activities; but it appears that he was responsible for at least the formulation of creationism, although his friend Reverdy (q.v.) played some part in this, too; and it is certainly true that Huidobro exercised a strong influence on Spanish literature. He was active in Paris during the First World War and in Spain after it.

For some years Huidobro's bases were in Madrid and Paris; he wrote many of his poems in French. He has therefore been subjected to much criticism in South America. But he was a genuine representative of the *avant garde*, and his own poetry is often ingenious and charming; it is not bogus. And creationism, although hardly original, is a useful concept inasmuch as it brings together most of the basic tenets of modernism in its second ('*avant garde*') phase.

Huidobro pretended that he had begun as a creationist poet; but his first four collections are facilely romantic, conservative and unpromising. It seems that it was the impact of the poetry of Apollinaire (which he read in South America) that started Huidobro off as a modernist poet. He was associated with Reverdy in the review *North-South* (*Nord-Sud*), but quarrelled with him at the end of 1917. It seems that, after the eclipse of creationism, he took to fighting in wars: against Franco in Spain and against Hitler in the Second World War. He is said to have been shot in the head and to have died prematurely as a result. He took part in Chilean politics at various times.

The essence of creationism is that a poem should be autonomous: 'Why do you sing of the rose, O poets?/Make it blossom in the poem'. The poet must ignore 'nature' and live in and create his own world; 'nature' has no beauty of its own, and so the poet must himself invent beauty—and give it to the reader; the poet is, of course, 'a little God', as Huidobro called him in 'The Art of Poetry' (LAP).

Huidobro's own poetry is fun and sometimes rather more than that; but it does not quite achieve his aesthetic aims. However, poems like 'Drowned Enchanter', which he wrote in both French (LAP) and Spanish, have a bewitching fluency:

Drowned enchanter what time is it?
Tell me how dreams that can change
Into revolutions could agree

Peace is dense with sheep's wool
And I know nothing

In the griefs that walk over life
White clothes dry night and day
On the horizon's rope
(We can't go very far away)

Drowned enchanter
The lovely music of equinoxes drags lovers together
Only the law of gravity
Can pull down drawing-room walls

Drowned enchanter
If you could see now
The tamed waves
Bowing to our feet

Drowned enchanter
What did Our Lady tell you
Does she still hold the rise of the winds
In her transparent fingers
What are the other saints talking about
In aeroplane language?

His novel *Satyr or The Power of Words* (*Satyr o El poder de las palabras*, 1939) anticipates Nabokov's *Lolita* (q.v.)—and one of the chief concerns of Frisch and Sartre (qq.v.): think of a man as being something, and you help to take away his freedom to be himself. Here Huidobro ironically questions his own creationism—which pronounces that the word should become flesh—and produces a masterpiece. (LAP; PLAV)

*

In this rich field (possibly, with the exception of the Russian, the richest of the century) there are perhaps only two more unquestionably major poets that have not been dealt with: Vallejo and Neruda. The Peruvian CÉSAR VALLEJO (1892–1938) is one of the greatest poets of the century—and the most puzzling and 'advanced' of all. In considering him we must bear in mind Neruda's remarks, already quoted during the discussion of Eguren (q.v.), about Vallejo's 'Indianness': his possession of a magical intuitiveness that is somehow oblique—and yet does not lose, but rather gains, from this. In the poetry of Vallejo the social and political anguish of this century is seen more authentically than elsewhere. Rilke (q.v.) illustrates the crises of sex, death and the end of a corporate God—but in order to perform his function he had (at times painfully) to withdraw his attention from social and political problems. So, after all, did Valéry (who was even insensitive enough to be, admittedly in his youth, anti-Dreyfusard). I have from time to time spoken, in this survey, of the concept I have called *Künstlerschuld*, artist-guilt (q.v.): the problem in a writer's mind of whether his writings help humanity, 'other people'—and of whether the capacity to produce these writings is not bought at the price of his own humanity. Thus: Rilke feels he wants to be a country doctor; Laura Riding (q.v.) wants to abolish poetry and substitute her own (and her late husband's) dictionary as a basis for existence; Broch (q.v.) does not want to be a writer and tries not to be one; Mann (q.v.) fails entirely to resolve the conflict—remains a bourgeois anti-writer opposed, in the same body, by a 'devilish', 'syphilitic' artist; and ends by regarding himself as a confidence-man.

In the work of Vallejo we find a resolution of this problem. His last agonized poems, written in Paris as Franco and his Nazi and Italian allies raped Spain, actually *are* 'political agony'. But they rise far above the clichés of any politician this century has known, for they represent an entirely new and intense use of language. Here we see political passion—with its malignant, abstract components—transformed into purely human and compassionate feeling. The poems of *Spain, Take Thou this Cup from me* (*España, aparta de mí este cáliz*, 1940), printed by defenders of the Republic on paper of their own making—the edition was entirely destroyed, appropriately enough, in the collapse of Catalonia—are not overtly political: they are about the agony of war, and the loss of humanity it entails. Here, as in the *Human Poems* (*Poemas humanos*, 1939; tr. C. Eshleman, 1968), written during the Thirties, Vallejo rejects a use of words that is soiled by materialism or even, one sometimes feels, by any kind of selfhood. Many of us, as we study Vallejo more deeply, come to feel that he may be, after all, the supreme poet of this century: here is one who truly lived poetry, who sought to instil into language its authentic, its human, its original meaning. For Vallejo words were things: the mysterious doubles of what they denote (cf. Asturias, q.v.). As he dies moaning 'Spain! Spain! I want to go to Spain!' he himself turns into words.

Vallejo's first book, published soon after he had taken his university degree, was *The Dark Messengers* (*Los heraldos negros*, 1918). It is one of the most astonishing first books of poetry in the whole of world literature. The forms used are mostly traditional, but they nearly burst under the strain of what they have to accommodate; it is Vallejo who above all at this time suggests the inadequacy of these forms for major poetry. The book was fairly well received in Peru; but it was not understood.

All the themes of Vallejo's later poetry are present in embryonic form in this first book. He was a member of a closely-knit, piously Catholic family, part of a poor community trapped helplessly between acute poverty and the intransigent inhumanity of the operators of the tungsten mines which employed it. All this is reflected in *The Dark Messengers*, with its Christian imagery and its moving evocations of family love. Vallejo, though not a practising Roman Catholic, always retained a love for the Catholicism of his childhood. In this first book he literally feels himself into an empathy with the poor and oppressed. An attitude is not enough: right from the beginning, for Vallejo, the poem has somehow or other itself to *become* an act of compassion. The title poem provides an example:

> Life deals such fearful blows . . . I don't know!
> They seem to come from God's own hate, as though
> the flood of everything that's suffered in the world
> were dammed up in the soul . . . I don't know!
>
> They're few; but they exist . . . They rip black holes
> in the most savage face and in the broadest back.
> Perhaps they're barbarous Attila's steeds—
> or Death's dark messengers.
>
> They are the stunning falls of soul-Christs
> from some sweet faith profaned by Destiny.
> Those bloody blows are the cracklings
> of flaming bread at the oven-door.
>
> And man . . . poor . . . poor! He turns his gaze
> as one does when one's startled by a clap behind;
> he turns his mad gaze, and the whole of life
> is dammed up, like a lake of blame, in sudden eyes.
>
> Life deals such fearful blows . . . I don't know!

Soon after the publication of *The Dark Messengers* Vallejo was imprisoned for over three months on false charges of arson and political agitation. This experience marked him for life. The poems of his next book, *Trilce* (1922)—the title was adopted as a result of a stammering slip of the tongue on the part of the poet, but clearly it combines *dulce* (sweet) with *triste* (sad)—were written in prison. They break with convention altogether, burst the dams of form: anything that needs to be wrenched by the emotions of love or indignation is wrenched—syntax, typographical convention, logic. Undoubtedly Vallejo, who was widely read and passionately interested at this time in French literature, knew about dada (q.v.) and about developments in French poetry; but the poems of *Trilce*, although they owe much to the proto-surrealistic activities of French poets between 1916 and the time of their composition, are not surrealistic. They have at their heart a 'primitive' Indian wisdom (Vallejo's mother was Indian, and so was his father's mother): that 'oblique' quality of which Neruda spoke. They also fear loss, not of selfhood, but of personal uniqueness: they have the faith that what a human being *really is* is beautiful— and would function beautifully. But why, Vallejo asks, is life so bitter? 'And they make us pay, when we/who were young at that time, as you see/couldn't have taken anything/from anyone; when you gave it to us,/isn't that right, mummy?' He ironically rejects the significance of clock-time by, so to speak, showing its separateness from existence—by isolating it from phenomeno- logically observed experience: 'The second of November sadly tolls', 'June you are ours' and so on. He points—sometimes ironically, sometimes helplessly— to the fact that words are not the same as the things or qualities they denote, and to underline this he even puts initial capitals at the ends of words. And thus words often become something they have not been in the life of civilization. In one poem (*Trilce* consists of seventy-seven numbered, untitled poems) he 'objectifies the dialectic of the human personality' (Jean Franco):

> It frightens me this stream,
> lovely memory, puissant Lord, implacable,
> murderous sweetness. It frightens me.
> This house comforts me, it's a good place
> for that not-knowing-where-to-be.
>
> Don't let's go in. It frightens me this gift
> of going back in moments, over blown bridges.
> I'm not going on, O darling lord,
> valiant memory, sad
> skeleton singing.
>
> But what strange contents, those of this enchanted house:
> They give me deaths of mercury and I solder
> with lead my graspings at parched reality
>
> The stream that does not understand us
> makes me fear and dread.
> Valiant memory, I'm not going on
> Whistle, whistle: skeleton of sad gold.

This is an example of a 'phenomenological' poem that—unlike many of its French counterparts—fully expresses human anguish; it is one of the most remarkable poems about memory ever written. The difficult third stanza surely means that the present, too, is compounded of successive moments. It gives him 'deaths of mercury' (which is glistening and elusive) because each moment represents a hopeless attempt to seize actuality; these are bound together 'with lead' (which is heavy and dull).

Vallejo was at first anti-Marxist, opposing the introduction of rigid or abstract systems to cure the social ills of South America. But after he had been deprived (for political reasons) of his teaching position and had left for Paris (never to return), he became convinced, in his anguish, of the necessity of communism. He went to Russia twice, and in 1931 joined the Party. He wrote some more or less socialist realist fiction—the novel *Tungsten* was published in 1931—and some drama of the same sort. He became more and more certain that it was necessary for the writer to support the workers in their struggle, and he increasingly resisted what he thought of as the falsifying role of reason— as distinct from intuition and instinct. But his poetry of the Thirties, his expression of his true self, is by no means Marxist: it transcends the linguistic falsity (or actual murderous villainy) of politicians, as well as the tawdry abstractness of mere systems: Vallejo's poems about the anguish of the Thirties and of Spain in particular represent, in themselves, acts of compassion. Vallejo can use cliché words and phrases that in anyone else's work would be disastrous: we know from their context that he means them, that they are utterances torn out of him. When he spoke of identifying with 'ordinary' people, with the proletariat, he was not like most other communist intellectuals: he meant exactly that. His poetry, although difficult, ultimately reaches lyrical intensity. One of his very last poems, 'Masses', from his last book, is as simple as anything he ever wrote:

> At the end of the battle,
> the soldier dead, one came to him
> and begged 'O do not die; I love you so!'
> But alas, the corpse went on being dead.
>
> Two came to him and once more begged:
> 'Don't leave us! Courage! Return to life!'
> But alas, the corpse went on being dead.
>
> Then there came to him twenty, a hundred, a thousand, five
>   hundred thousand,
> all crying: 'O so much love, and to have no power over death!'
> But alas, the corpse went on being dead.
>
> Then millions came round him
> all crying together: 'O please stay brother!'
> But alas, the corpse went on being dead.

Then every man on earth
came to him; and tears sprang to his opened eyes:
slowly he rose,
kissed the first man; and walked. . . .

It is frustrating—whether there are good reasons for it or not—that not all the prose, criticism, journalism and drama of this supremely important writer has yet been collected. But—even, so far as the later work is concerned, if in his widow's possibly imperfect copies—we have the best of him. Vallejo lived nearly all his own life in poverty; he above all is the poet of poverty, of misery, of the oppressed. Not every poem he wrote is successful; but all is part and parcel of the same prodigious effort. He is, one feels, the poet of the future: the poet for the intelligent, compassionate and enlightened young. In his poetry— as in his death, surely caused by the anguish of Spain—he at least answers the question (of *Künstlerschuld*, q.v.) that convoluted Mann, Broch and even Rilke (qq.v.): he showed that the words of poetry can, after all, have a social and 'political' function. (LAP; PSV; MEP; PI; LWT; NVSP; PLAV)

The Chilean PABLO NERUDA (ps. NEFTALÍ RICARDO REYES, 1904), who won the 1971 Nobel Prize, got his pseudonym from the nineteenth-century Czech poet Jan Neruda, whom he admired. He is the son of a railway worker, who died, in a fall from a train, while Neruda was still a boy. His huge output is uneven —some of it, while poetic in atmosphere, is irresponsibly wandering and without concentration—but at his best he has written a marvellous poetry, evocative of both the teeming natural mysteries of South America and of his own tough amorousness. As a young man he said, 'In my day to day life, I am a tranquil man, the enemy of laws, leaders, and established institutions. I find the middle class odious [this, of course, has been a major theme, implicit or explicit, in poetry since at least Baudelaire], and I like the lives of people who are restless and unsatisfied, whether they are artists or criminals'. He has been much translated into English, and his works are easy to find in libraries; incomparably the best translations, however, have been made by Robert Bly and James Wright. (NVSP)

Neruda has been through a number of distinct phases. His first book, *Song of the Fiesta* (*La canción de la fiesta*, 1921), was fairly conventional. In the second, *Crepuscular* (*Crepusculario*, 1923), an original voice emerges—but the tone is still often *modernista*. Neruda cannot be categorized in terms of influences; but the early influence upon him of the Uruguayan poet CARLOS SABAT ERCASTY (1887) is important. Sabat Ercasty began as a *modernista* and a decadent; but in 1912 he burned all his earlier poetry and began to write, under the influence of Whitman (also a decisive influence on Neruda), a new and entirely different kind of poetry: diffuse but exuberant and evocative of the South America of the past and future. (PLAV) Another important influence on Neruda was French surrealism.

His first really original collection was *Twenty Poems of Love and One Desperate Song* (*Veinte poemas de amor y una canción desesperada*, 1924). This, which is still his most popular book, is an account of a love affair: the beloved becomes identified with the world, and is sometimes beautiful and desirable and at others threatening and strange. It was in these poems Neruda decisively broke away from tradition. *Twenty Poems* has its roots in experience; the next book, *Attempt of Infinite Man (Tentativa del hombre infinito,* 1925), is merely experimental; although it was for Neruda an important and liberating excursion into surrealism.

Neruda, who had been given a position as a diplomat, began to travel extensively in the late Twenties; in 1933 he published the first volume of his collection called *Residence on Earth (Residencia en la tierra)*—a second volume followed in 1935, and a third in 1947. Neruda later rejected the contents of the first two books as negative, and understandably so; but this is perhaps his most powerful poetry. In *Residence* I and II Neruda plumbs his own terrified, mysterious and alarming depths. 'Walking Around' aptly illustrates his state of mind at the time he wrote these poems:

> It so happens I am sick of being a man.
> And it happens that I walk into tailorshops and movie houses
> dried up, waterproof, like a swan made of felt
> steering my way in a water of wombs and ashes.
>
> The smell of barbershops makes me break into hoarse sobs.
> The only thing I want is to lie still like stones or wool.
> The only thing I want is to see no more stores, no gardens,
> no more goods, no spectacles, no elevators.
>
> It so happens I am sick of my feet and my nails
> and my hair and my shadow.
> It so happens I am sick of being a man.
>
> Still it would be marvellous
> to terrify a law clerk with a cut lily,
> or kill a nun with a blow on the ear.
> It would be great
> to go through the streets with a green knife
> letting out yells until I died of the cold.
>
> I don't want to go on being a root in the dark,
> insecure, stretched out, shivering with sleep,
> going on down, into the moist guts of the earth,
> taking in and thinking, eating every day.
>
> I don't want so much misery.
> I don't want to go on as a root and a tomb,
> alone under the ground, a warehouse with corpses,
> half frozen, dying of grief.

That's why Monday, when it sees me coming
with my convict face, blazes up like gasoline,
and it howls on its way like a wounded wheel,
and leaves tracks full of warm blood leading toward the night.

And it pushes me into certain corners, into some moist houses,
into hospitals where the bones fly out the window,
into shoeshops that smell like vinegar,
and certain streets hideous as cracks in the skin.

There are sulphur-colored birds, and hideous intestines
hanging over the doors of houses that I hate,
and there are false teeth forgotten in a coffeepot,
there are mirrors
that ought to have wept from shame and terror,
there are umbrellas everywhere, and venoms, and umbilical cords.

I stroll along serenely, with my eyes, my shoes,
my rage, forgetting everything,
I walk by, going through office buildings and orthopedic shops,
and courtyards with washing hanging from the line:
underwear, towels and shirts from which slow
dirty tears are falling.

(NVSP)

This poetry could not have been written without surrealism; but it is more than surrealist, and although it is a poetry of disintegration and fragmentation, the images are certainly connected.

In the Thirties Neruda, like Vallejo, put all his energies into the fight for Spain; he became a close associate of Rafael Alberti (q.v.), published a surrealist magazine, and got to know such poets as Lorca and Hernández (qq.v.) well. Like Vallejo, he became a communist. Has he 'sacrificed his lyricism to politics', as many critics have claimed? In this case the answer is negative— perhaps because Neruda's communism is so undogmatic and compassionate. He has continued to write a great deal of poetry, and the best of this has shown no falling off. *Spain in the Heart* (*España en el corazón*, 1937) contains his first 'public' poems. In 1947 he published the third volume of the *Residence* poems: *Third Residence* (*Tercera residencia*). In 1950 there came the long descriptive poem about South America called *Canto general* (pt. tr. N. Tarn, *The Heights of Macchu Picchu*, 1966). This is divided into fifteen sections. The best parts are descriptions of the fauna and flora of South America ('there are in our countries', he has said, 'rivers which have no names, trees which nobody knows, and birds which nobody has described. It is easier for us to be surrealistic because everything we know is new'). In his odes of the Fifties—*Elemental Odes* (*Odas elementales*, 1954) and its successors—Neruda has reached through to a new simplicity. Although one of the most advanced poets of his generation, he now seems to wish to take an anti-expressionistic direction: away from distortion and complexity, and towards simplicity and accessibility. There are odes to 'ordinary', useful things: a pair of socks, wood, the salt in a salt-cellar, the watermelon; most of these avoid the whimsical—but few achieve more than a minor status. It is unmistakably poetry of quality—such as may be found in Neruda's collections of the Sixties, which include *Full Powers* (*Plenos poderes*, 1962). Neruda's humanity and large generosity are conveyed with considerable power by his poetry; he is unusual in being a major poet with a truly valid message that is optimistic and positive rather than pessimistic and negative. He is Chilean ambassador in Paris. (LAP; MEP; PSV; LWT; PLAV)

*

No one else in contemporary Latin-American poetry is of Neruda's stature; but there are a number of important poets. One of the most distinguished is the Cuban mulatto NICOLÁS GUILLÉN (1902), the leader of the school of negro poetry (*poesia negra*). As has already been mentioned (in the section dealing with African and Caribbean literature) negrophilism received its first impetus from Europe. Picasso and other cubists were painting objects in a 'primitive' African manner—as they 'thought' them rather than as they saw them—early in the century; later there was a snobbish (and often disgusting) Parisian vogue for all things negro. However, and for obvious reasons, the real roots of negro poetry are in South America and most particularly in Cuba, Domenica and Puerto Rico. One of the earliest negrophile poets was the white Puerto Rican LUIS PALÉS MATOS (1898–1959), whose work, circulated widely in typescript, was extremely influential; it is politically more restrained than N. Guillén's, but equally lively. (LAP; PLAV) Hispanic negro (or, where appropriate, Afro-Cuban) poetry incorporates a number of elements: 'primitive' sexuality and frenzy, pagan religious attitudes, incantation, mystery, a degree of 'negritude' (q.v.). Guillén himself began, under the influence of Lorca (q.v.) as well as of Palés Matos, with a popular and humorous verse, steeped in folklore and in the ways of Cuban negroes. His first collection, *Motives of Sound* (*Motivos de son*, 1930), contained brilliant pastiche of Afro-Cuban popular songs. Later, after he had fought in Spain against Franco and become a communist, the subject-matter of his poetry became wider—to include the oppressed of all races. Guillén is also a powerful satirist, as in *West Indies Ltd* (1934). His later poetry has the vitality of the earlier, but has tended to the over-didactic. (LAP; PSV; PLAV)

The other Spanish-American *avant garde* movements have failed to produce poets of such marked gifts as N. Guillén; but they have some historical importance. The loud-mouthed Peruvian egocentric ALBERTO HIDALGO (1897), a devotee of war, German militarism and Stalin, invented simplism (*simplismo*), a Latin-American equivalent of futurism (q.v.). This had some effect on later production, though the less said of Hidalgo's own the better. It is by the study of Hidalgo's work—only tolerable when absolutely trivial—that we can perceive the comparative quality of Huidobro's (q.v.). The confused stridentism (*estridentismo*) of the Mexican MANUEL MAPLES ARCE (1898), whose *Metropolis* was translated by John Dos Passos (1929), is another Latin-American version of futurism—but this time more politically radical. It was less interesting than his own, often amusing, light poetry. Maples Arce has been an important diplomat.

Surrealism (often called *superrealismo* in Latin America) had its most fruitful influence on Neruda; but it also made some impact on the work of an attractive and individual minor poet, the Ecuadorian JORGE CARRERA ANDRADE (1903), whose work appealed to William Carlos Williams (q.v.). Carrera Andrade's poetry, much of which is on the theme of his extensive travels, is charmingly and (as Williams remarked) primitively descriptive. It can be over-whimsical, but at its best it has a unique freshness. He learnt much from Jammes (q.v.), but surrealism gave him an enlarged sense of freedom. (LAP; PSV; PLAV)

RICARDO MOLINARI (1898), an Argentinian, began in the ultraism (q.v.) brought back to Argentine by Borges (q.v.), but soon proceeded to an individual method that drew heavily on tradition and Catholicism, even though free verse was an important part of it. He is respected by the younger generation, even though, when writing on spiritual themes, he is inclined to pompousness and monotony. Molinari is at his best when writing of the landscape, especially of the wide open plains, of Argentina. He is always a highly accomplished stylist. (PSV; PLAV)

The literature of Mexico has, since the second decade of the century, had distinctive characteristics. This is the only South-American country in which there has been a definitive Revolution. Although the present rulers are now accused of having largely forgotten this fact, it cannot be cancelled out: the 1917 constitution assured the distribution of land to the peasants—and other things still unheard of (except in 'communist plots') in Mexico's northern neighbour. The spirit of this Revolution has had influence on Mexican fiction; but its effect on poetry was less direct—the leading poets of the Twenties reacted against all forms of social realism in favour of the exploration of private areas of experience. XAVIER VILLAURRUTIA (1903–50) was much influenced by the modern poetry of the U.S.A., where he lived for some time. He is a leading representative of the non-political stream in Latin-American literature. The haunted mood of some of his poetry somewhat recalls the Neruda of *Residences* I and II:

> If anyone should utter, at a given moment,
> in one word only, that which he is thinking,
> the six letters of DESIRE would form a huge shining scar. . . .

Villaurrutia's most important work, however, was done in the realm of drama. (PSV; LAP; PLAV) SALVADOR NOVO (1904) is also a dramatist; his poetry is more playful, though its lightness conceals a serious terror of the unknown. (PSV; LAP) Both Villaurrutia and Novo were associated with the Ulysses group—after the review *Ulysses* (*Ulises*)—which maintained close ties with France; so also was JAIME TORRES BODET (1902), a somewhat more substantial poet. Torres Bodet is the most 'European' of the Latin-American poets of his generation, in that his anguished speculations about his identity have a less regionalistic flavour about them; a theme that haunts him is a search for himself in corridors of mirrors. His poetry, even at its most painful, has lyrical appeal. Like Villaurrutia and Novo, but with more success, he wrote novels: the best are *The First of January* (*Primero de Enero*, 1934) and *Shadows* (*Sombras*, 1937). (LAP; SCO)

OCTAVIO PAZ (1914), now regarded as the doyen of Spanish-American poets of his generation, followed in the footsteps of these poets, but has developed procedures that are unclassifiable. A committed leftist, his poems are none the less non-political; the consequences of his theory of poetry appear to be anarchist: poetry and society, he maintains, seek 'a mutual dialogue', but are fundamentally opposed to each other; he seeks 'the transformation of society into a creative community, into a living poem; and the poem into social life, into an incarnate image'. His own poetry is less idealistic, and suggests that he experiences difficulties similar to those of Torres Bodet—as in 'Mirror':

> Before the mirror's fatuous games
> my being is pyre and ash,
> breathes, is, ash,
> and I burn myself, I blaze, I glow, I pretend
> I've built a self that, though consumed, grips
> the smoke-knife imitating
> the proof of the wound's blood,
> and one self, the last-but-one,
> which begs oblivion, shadow, nothingness—
> the final lie that burns it whole.
>
> From one pretence to one more
> there's always that last-but-one: asking.
> I drown in myself. I will not touch myself.

In the cunningly contrived *Sun Stone* (*Piedra de sol*, 1957; tr. M. Rukeyser, 1963) Paz searches for an intuitive grasp of the meaning of the so-called primitive, for he believes (and surely correctly) that man's only chance, now, of avoiding disaster is to try to regain the wisdom that has been lost. (LAP; PSV; LWT; MEP; PLAV)

The Chilean NICANOR PARRA (1914) is most famous for his *Poems and Anti-poems* (*Poemas y antipoemas*, 1954), powerfully satirical anti-literary and anti-establishment poems that often incorporate blandly naturalistic (q.v.) descriptions of misery or enforced conformity. He began, like N. Guillén, with skilful pastiche of popular song. (LWT; PLAV)

One of the most distinguished of the Spanish-American poets under fifty is the Peruvian CARLOS GERMÁN BELLI (1927), whose sour and ironic parodies of *modernista* exquisiteness, incorporating tortured contemporary emotions, are effective.

II

Spanish-American poetry was outstanding in the first half of the century; the fiction has until comparatively recently been considerably less so; there are few exceptions. Now, however, as Gabriel García Márquez (q.v.) has said, the liveliness of the Latin-American novel is the only answer to the sterility of the French *nouveau roman* (q.v.). In the earlier period the strong religious feeling of the people—for it takes a readership as well as a writer to establish a literary genre—made the establishment of naturalism, a useful phase in the development of modern fiction, difficult, as happened in Spain. Nor were there really any prose writers of the nineteenth century capable of conveying the nature of the South-American landscape: unexplored, wild, teeming, mysterious, menacing. There was in the earlier part of the period no true novelist, but rather several writers of fiction. All too often the imaginative powers of even the intelligently aware novelists were vitiated by their paternalistic and patronizing assumptions, or by didacticism. Even the best of the nineteenth-century Spanish-American novelists, such as Jorge Isaacs, produced adaptations of European models.

The historical novels of the Uruguayan EDUARDO ACEVEDO DÍAZ (1851–1921) —the best is the trilogy about Uruguayan independence: *Ismael* (1888), *Nativa* (1890) and *Cry of Glory* (*Grito de gloria*, 1893)—incorporate intelligent realistic description, but are marred by their pompous didactic passages and failures of psychological insight. Acevedo Díaz is a good writer, but hardly a novelist. Other writers concentrated—and for even longer than did their Spanish counterparts—on local colour: they desired above all to create a Latin-American literature—one which would be common to all the countries of the continent and which would rival any European literature; but their intentions were largely defeated because there was no one of sufficient stature to take on the whole Latin-American experience. The *modernista* prose writers were conspicuously less successful than the poets in matching style to content.

There are one or two exceptions. The Colombian TOMÁS CARRASQUILLA (1858–1940) was more than merely a good regionalist—his novels are set in the provincial town of Antioquia—for he insisted on psychological realism, and he was (unusually at that time) opposed to the concept of literature as an instrument of social change; he also had a keen sense of the comic and considerable psychological insight; his dialogue is vigorous and faithful to common speech; but he often wrote carelessly and never succeeded—or, indeed, tried—to deal with the unique experience of his whole continent. Nevertheless, he is a remarkable writer, who wrote in a noble solitude (he cared nothing for popularity), and whose work anticipates at least two important characteristics of modernism: its concentration on the demotic and its tendency to distort 'normal' reality. Much of his best work is to be found in his short stories. His best novel, though carelessly slung together, is *The Marquise of Yolombó* (*La Marquesa de Yolombó*, 1926); his collected works were published in Madrid in 1952.

By contrast the Peruvian RICARDO PALMA (1833–1919) was in one—technical —sense a miniaturist. He invented his own genre, the 'tradition': his *Peruvian Traditions* (*Tradiciones peruanas*) began to appear in 1872 (all but one excellently bawdy example were collected in a definitive edition in Madrid in 1957). But Palma resembled Carrasquilla in his use of the colloquial. He also went further than Carrasquilla in building up, for his readers, a sense of Latin-American tradition. But in his mixture of every aspect of history and folklore and local record he did not get far outside the boundaries of Peru. *The Knights of the Cape* (tr. H. de Onís, 1945) is a selection.

The Chilean anti-romantic novelist ALBERTO BLEST GANA (1830–1920), although he spent four years in France as a very young man, made up his mind to bring Chilean reality to Chilean readers. His earlier novels deal with events in Chile; even *The Uprooted* (*Los trasplantados*, 1904), which is set in Paris, is really about the lack of moral values displayed by a Chilean family. Blest Gana's younger Chilean contemporary BALDOMERO LILLO (1867–1923) was a less heavy and more forceful writer who learnt from Zola (q.v.) rather than from Balzac, Blest Gana's master. Lillo's best tales (in *Sub Terra*, 1904) are harshly realistic, sensitive, sympathetic accounts of the hardships endured by miners in Southern Chile; he is the first uncompromising social realist, and his feelings towards his characters are not condescending. Lillo's successor, MARIANO LATORRE (1886–1955), a less powerful writer, was not less but more Chilean in his preoccupations. He was the initiator in Chile of the creolist (*criollista*) school, which was essentially a development of *costumbrismo* (q.v.): a Creole in Latin America is a Latin-American of Spanish descent; the blanket term *criollismo* refers to literature dealing with peasants but infused with local colour. Latorre was a poor stylist, but in some of his stories he made early attempts to portray the mysterious savagery of nature in Chile (and, by implication, the whole of South America).

Perhaps the best Argentine novelist of his generation to fall within the scope of this survey was MANUEL GÁLVEZ (1882–1962), if only for *Metaphysical Anguish* (*El mal metafísico*, 1916). Gálvez was a strange mixture of commercial writer, harsh realist, sloppy Catholic and crypto-modernist. His best novel takes a characteristically *modernista* type, Carlos Riga, and manages to give a sharply objective and ironic account of his attempts 'to live for art': Gálvez was taking a critical glance at his own aloof and decadent aspirations. And yet though Riga is in certain ways ridiculous, he fails not because of this but because he is too sensitive (and sensible) to adapt himself to the modern world. Gálvez continued to write competent novels until almost the end of his life, but none came near to *Metaphysical Anguish*. This is superior to anything by another popular Argentine realist, BENITO LYNCH (1880–1951), the quality of whose work is, however, higher overall. Lynch's best novel is *The Englishman of the Bones* (*El inglés de los huesos*, 1924), about a cold-hearted English archeologist who comes to Argentina. ROBERTO PAYRÓ (1867–1928), an Argentinian journalist of a slightly older generation than Gálvez and Lynch, was a prolific writer of fiction; but only three of his novels, all belonging to a single short phase of his life, stand out: *Laucha's Marriage* (*El casamiento de Laucha*, 1906), *Pago Chico* (1908)—both are translated in *Tales from the Argentine*, 1930—and *The Diverting Adventures of Juan Moreira's Grandson* (*Divertidas aventuras del nieto de Juan Moreira*, 1910). These mix regionalism and humorous picaresque with serious social intent. Payró always keeps his temper, and he takes pleasure in his rogues—but his portrait of the corrupt social and political conditions in his country is a disturbing one.

The best of Uruguayan fiction in this period came from the provincial realist CARLOS REYLES (1868–1938), a wealthy landowner; Reyles was a feudalist and a conservative, but he was intelligent, was not a reactionary— and he had a sense of responsibility towards the peasants (so long as they remained in their proper place). Furthermore, Reyles' grasp of character and the scope of his imagination transcend his ideas. *Beba* (1894) is about a farmer who tries to improve his cattle-breeding by using new methods, but is defeated by apathy and fear of the new. *The Race of Cain* (*La raza de Caín*, 1900) deals with city and business life. *The Homeland* (*El terruño*, 1916) gives a memorable portrait of an intuitive, instinctive woman who runs a farm and its workers far more successfully than her morally more aware and intellectually gifted son-in-law. Reyles' fellow-countryman JAVIER DE VIANA (1868–1926) presents a contrast. His realism is deliberately more brutal: so much so that he may almost be called a naturalist. It is universally conceded that Viana's early work is superior to his later, which is monotonous. His best fiction—which is unusual in that it gives an uncompromisingly anti-romantic portrait of the Uruguayan half-caste peasants as lazy, sordid, dirty and insensitive victims of malign fate— is to be found in his many collections of short stories, such as *Countryside* (*Campo*, 1896) and *Gurí* (1901). Viana's view of the peasants recalls Verhaeren's poem 'The Peasants', part of which is quoted in this book; but the former had little of the Belgian poet's optimism.

The Bolivian ALCIDES ARGUEDAS (1879–1946) is a novelist with more regard for people. His *Race of Bronze* (*Raza de Bronce*, 1919), the final revised version of a book he worked on for twenty years, is in many ways a crude novel; but as a celebration of the Indian way of life and an exposure of the brutality practised against them by Creoles and mestizos it is an important and salutary document. Arguedas failed to penetrate the minds of his Indian characters; but his attempt do do so was a serious and notable one.

*

The Latin-American fiction of the Twenties tended to remain regionalist, but this was a new kind of regionalism. There was at this point still no Latin-American novel proper (such as has now come into being), because no writer confronted his environment purely imaginatively; but there was a development towards it. The Venezuelan RÓMULO GALLEGOS (1884–1969), a liberal politician who was president for a short period before being overthrown by a military coup (1948), is probably more a gifted pamphleteer than a real novelist; but his aspirations, and much of the detail in his books, are important. His most famous novel is *Doña Bárbara* (1929), about the conflict between the instinctive, primitive life and educated 'civilization'; the outcome is sentimental, and although the book has elements of a novel it never becomes one; but the atmosphere of the Venezuelan plains is often well conveyed, and some of the scenes of brutality are powerful. Gallegos' best novel is *The Climber* (*La trepadora*, 1925): here the central character, a ruthless but not unlovable businessman, comes alive—and the author occasionally neglects his (admirable) intellectual intentions: to advocate miscegenation and social reform.

The Colombian JOSÉ EUSTASIO RIVERA (1888–1928) was a more gifted writer, although as a whole his single novel, *The Vortex* (*La vorágine*, 1924; tr. E. K. James, 1935), is a considered approach to history and politics rather than an act of the imagination. *The Vortex* deals with a sensitive urban poet and his confrontation with the savage life of cowboys on the plains of Colombia and rubber-tappers in its jungles. Rivera succeeded to some extent in conveying the violence and mystery of the untamed wilds, but he is too simply scared of it: like his poet Arturo Cova (brutalized and finally destroyed by nature), his sense of art is too sculptured and deliberate. And yet Rivera had at least an intuition of what had to be done to create an authentic Latin-American novel.

The most famous Spanish-American novel of the Twenties, regarded as a classic, is *Don Segundo Sombra* (1926; tr. H. de Onís, 1935), by the Argentinian RICARDO GÜIRALDES (1886–1927). Güiraldes was at first, in both his poetry and his fiction, influenced by European symbolist models; but later, unimpressed by either the social or the literary models provided by Europe, he turned to what may fairly be called the 'intrahistory' (q.v.) of his own country. *Don Segundo Sombra* is his fullest expression of it. There are two views of this novel: one regards it as a masterpiece, the first work to present the gaucho not according to European values but as an Argentinian fully equipped to grow to maturity within his own environment; the other regards it as a historically important and accomplished work, but one in which, essentially, the 'gaucho myth' is 'poeticized'. The truth is that because it deliberately falsifies, for aesthetic reasons—as we may more easily see retrospectively—on the realistic level it is perhaps not quite a great novel: this is to say, it sacrifices to aesthetic interests a truth that then badly needed revealing. However, it has value as an allegory, and this has often been overlooked. Borges (q.v.), an admirer of Güiraldes, has in his different way much the same point of view; but his best work has been written at a later stage, and he is more fully (and regretfully) aware of his absolute incapacity to achieve realist fiction; he is, as Neruda (q.v.) called Mallarmé (whom he admires), a great writer 'of closed rooms'; he has made a triumph of his defect. Güiraldes was not of this calibre. But *Don Segundo Sombra* can well strike some readers as so beautiful and mysterious as to be great; possibly that is enough.

Whether this is so or not, there is certainly a case for putting forward the death- and disaster-haunted suicide (he had cancer) HORACIO QUIROGA (1878–

1937), a Uruguayan, as a more important and gifted writer. Quiroga, most of whose life was spent in lonely struggle with severe psychoneurosis and worse (his father, first wife, son and daughter all killed themselves, and he himself accidentally shot and killed a friend while inspecting a gun), began as a fairly simple decadent and *modernista*—and even wrote an early volume of bad poetry as evidence of it. By the time he reached forty he had also reached maturity as a writer; his macabre short stories, collected in *Tales of Love, Madness and Death* (*Cuentos de amor, de locura y de muerte*, 1917), *Anaconda* (1921), *The Beheaded Chicken* (*La gallina degollada*, 1925) and many other books, have not been more than equalled in their genre in this century. It is a limited genre; but Quiroga, by looking inwards, found a more appropriate metaphor for South American nature (he lived in the Argentinian jungle, and it is often the setting for his stories) than any writer before him; after all, their attempted realism was no more, whatever he may have thought, than another less deliberate metaphor. He has been called 'in the last analysis' 'maladjusted'. But what is adjustment? Latin-American fiction needed such 'maladjustment'. Quiroga's short stories (his two novels are poor) are more successfully realistic than *Don Segundo Sombra* because, while they do not pretend to portray communities, they intimately communicate the harshness of man's struggle with nature or the struggle of animals (with which he displayed uncanny sympathy) to survive. Quiroga was an expressionist at a time when expressionism was needed if Latin-American fiction was to reflect the Latin-American experience adequately. In him the nerve-crisis of two generations came to the surface. *Stories of the Jungle* (*Cuentos de la selva*, 1918) was translated in 1923 by A. Livingstone.

Ultraism (q.v.), which originated in Spain, was brought to Argentina by Borges in the early Twenties. It did not produce any major work; even Borges himself can hardly be said to have discovered his own genius in his passage through it, although in its aim, to reduce 'the lyric to its essential element—the metaphor', one may see a trace of his (for once) magnificently life-effacing formula. But one writer who grew up with the ultraists, and who first became known as a poet (LAP), is of interest, if only for one novel: LEOPOLDO MARECHAL (1900–70). His *Adam Buenos Aires* (*Adán Buenosayres*) was published in 1948, but he had been writing it since 1930. This is certainly over-dependent on the Joyce of *Ulysses*; but it is a brilliant performance, 'the first tentative approach to a complete novel in our literature' (Luis Harss and Barbara Dohmann). It characterizes Buenos Aires more fully than any 'socially aware' writer had been able to characterize it (when the hero descends into hell it is of course merchants and officials he finds there). *Adam Buenos Aires* is not completely realized, but it does represent, despite the author's Catholicism and reprehensible support of the Perón regime, a complete rejection of stereotyped versions of reality. In 1965 Marechal came up with a structurally even more complex and fantastic work: *The Banquet of Severo Archangel* (*El banquete de Severo Arcángelo*). This develops logically enough out of the earlier book, and underlines the debt owed to Marechal by Cortázar (q.v.). Marechal derived his basic approach from medieval theology (one is reminded of Joyce's use of Vico). He wrote a number of interesting plays, the best of which is *The Battle of José Luna* (*La batalla de José Luna*, 1970).

ROBERTO ARLT (1900–42), the Argentinian son of German immigrants, was in his life a doomed neurotic; in his fiction and drama he was a poetic naturalist reminiscent of Céline. He is a landmark in the history of South American fiction: a great writer.

His first book, *The Angry Toy* (*El juguete rabioso*, 1927) is tough social realism in the manner of Gorki (q.v.), but his two best novels deal with Erdosain, a portrait of himself as a criminal: *The Seven Madmen* (*Los siete locos*, 1929) and *The Flame Throwers* (*Los lanzallamas*, 1931). These are episodic, and sometimes very clumsily written; they lack the exquisite art (or is it anti-art?) of Céline; but they are more important than many better executed literary works contemporary with them; and often the clumsiness is effective. There is indeed a sense in which Arlt's nightmare galleries of city-dwellers are more 'serious' than *Don Segundo Sombra* (he used to ask Güiraldes when he would begin to write 'seriously'). The difference is that Güiraldes was a wealthy man, lapped in literary comforts and pleasures; Arlt was unlearned, negative and irrational— but he knew despair, and his picture of Buenos Aires is as authentic as Céline's is of Paris. *Anthology* (*Antología*, 1967) is a useful selection. He is important in the theatre. His novels and short stories were collected, in three volumes, in 1963. Arlt is the most important of the novelists to anticipate the *tremendista* (q.v.) novel of the Spanish Forties.

*

Mexican poets seemed almost to ignore the Revolution; the novelists did not. The subject-matter of most of the novels of MARIANO AZUELA (1873–1952), generally considered a pioneer of social realism, is the Revolution or the issues it raised. Azuela, as profoundly influenced by naturalism as Lillo (q.v.), was one of the most successful of Latin-American realists of his generation. His three most important novels are *The Underdogs* (*Los de abajo*, 1915–16; tr. E. Munguía, 1963), *The Bosses* (*Los caciques*, 1917; TNM) and *The Flies* (*Las moscas*, 1918; TNM); of these the first is as accurate a portrayal of the Revolution as realist techniques (or perhaps any techniques in 1915) could give. There are unanimist (q.v.) elements in Azuela, one of whose greatest achievements is his ability to portray the behaviour of men *en masse*; he can show them as individuals, and then the change in them when they become part of a movement with potentialities greater than they could realize alone. Azuela went on writing novels until the end of his life; he even underwent a modernist stage in the Twenties, but the results clearly show his dependence on straightforward realist techniques. Azuela is a true realist because while he depicts social change as desirable he depicts its instruments as incapable of carrying it out; at this point his imagination fails—but his achievement, within its limitations, is secure. His *Marcela*, a love story, was translated in 1932 by A. Brenner.

As intelligent an approach to the Revolution is made by MARTÍN LUIS GUZMÁN (1887) in the episodic, semi-fictional *The Eagle and the Serpent* (*El águila y la serpiente*, 1928; tr. H. de Onís, 1930), the outstanding aspect of which is a vivid portrait of Pancho Villa. Guzmán wrote an even more powerful novel, *The Shadow of the Leader* (*La sombra del caudillo*, 1928), an indictment of the ruthlessness and lack of human responsibility of the political manipulator and virtual dictator Calles, and of the men surrounding him. If anyone wants to understand why South America is a politically unstable continent, with few examples to show of genuine democracy (even of the shabby and dishonourable, but at least very much more bearable and infinitely less cruel, sort that we are used to in the democratic West), then he should probably read this book. It is one which Orwell (q.v.), who invented Big Brother, would have well understood. Guzmán's *Memoirs of Pancho Villa* (*Memorias de Pancho Villa*, 1940; tr. V. T. Taylor, 1965), whom he knew, is among the most fascinating books about revolution of our time.

JOSÉ RUBÉN ROMERO (1890–1952), although he rose to be a distinguished diplomatic employee of post-revolutionary governments, took it out on what they stood for in some of his books. He is acerb, pessimistic, scatological and comic, with a nicely restrained vein of nihilism. It probably afforded him amusement to do his political work well, and gain promotion. His best books are *My Horse, My Dog and My Rifle* (*Mi caballo, mi perro y mi rifle*, 1936), *The Futile Life of Pito Pérez* (*La vida inútil de Pito Pérez*, 1938; tr. J. Coyne, 1966) and *Rosenda* (1946). The first is a savage tale of a young revolutionary's disillusionment; the second, a picaresque classic, is about a ne'er-do-well and drunkard whose self-debasement and scurrilous hatred of both rich and poor are contrasted with the narrow and hypocritical complacency of the people of his town; *Rosenda* is a more conventional portrait of a courageous country girl.

*

Straightforward realism did produce masterpieces (nearly all of them nineteenth-century), but few of these came from Spanish America, whose novel really only began to come alive when her writers developed expressionist techniques. However, certain of the more notable attempts to create a viable realistic novel should be mentioned: eventually these led into the necessary innovations. ENRIQUE AMORIM (1900–60) was born in Uruguay but lived for most of his life in Buenos Aires—and is counted as an Argentinian writer. In *Countryman Aguilar* (*El paisano Aguilar*, 1934) the hero returns from the city to the countryside, which absorbs him until he becomes a part of it. *The Horse and Its Shadow* (*El caballo y su sombra*, 1941; tr. R. O'Connell and J. G. Lugan, 1943) studies the effect of the Argentine on an Italian immigrant. *Outlet* (*La desembocadura*, 1958) traces the history of a pioneer and his family. Amorim's novels, which become increasingly symbolic, illustrate the difficulties confronting an intelligent Spanish-American realist.

The only other outstanding Uruguayan novelist of this generation is FRANCISCO ESPÍNOLA (1901), who writes with harsh realism and understanding of the lives of very poor people. His best book is *Blind Race* (*Raza ciega*, 1927).

He also wrote a good surrealist play: *Flight in the Mirror* (*La fuga en el espejo*, 1937). His short stories (*Cuentas*) were collected in 1961.

In Chile there were three outstanding realists. The eldest was EDUARDO BARRIOS (1884–1963), mainly a psychological novelist, but also the author of one important regionalist (as well as psychological) work, *Gentleman and Hell-Raiser* (*Gran señor y rajadiablos*, 1948). Barrios' first novel, *The Boy Who Went Mad for Love* (*El niño que enloqueció de amor*, 1915), was a powerful study, in the form of a diary, of a boy's pathological obsession with a woman. *A Failure* (*Un perdido*, 1917), which may be considered in parallel with Gálvez's *Metaphysical Anguish* (q.v.) as the study of an intellectually superior man's struggle to realize himself in an alien society, is a brilliantly observed account of Chilean social life as well as a gallery of psychological types. *Brother Ass* (*El hermano asno*, 1902) is the story (again in diary form) of monastery life and of the hypocrisy of those in power. Barrios' concerns were always intelligent; though not expressionist in technique, his last novel, *The Men in the Man* (*Los hombres del hombre*, 1950), about the various personalities (one of them pathologically jealous) in one man, is genuinely modernist. Barrios is a good enough novelist to demonstrate, even in the difficult and fictionally impoverished conditions of South America, that certain forms of modified realism are still viable.

Barrios may have been influenced by his contemporary AUGUSTO D'HALMAR (ps. AUGUSTO GEOMINNE THOMSON, 1882–1950), whose early *Juana Lucero* (1922) is one of the best of the many naturalist novels about prostitution that appeared in Spanish America in the first quarter of the century. D'Halmar's best novel was *Passion and Death of the Priest Deusto* (*Pasión y muerte del cura Deusto*, 1924) about the homosexual passion of a priest and a young Basque.

MANUEL ROJAS (1896), an admirer of Quiroga (q.v., disgracefully neglected at the end of his career as a writer), had unusual aspirations for a novelist of his generation: he wanted to achieve cosmopolitanism, and, like Barrios, he was more interested in people than in social realism—he thus achieved a greater measure of the latter than most of his contemporaries. His finest work, one of the major realist works of Latin America of this century, is *Born Guilty* (*Hijo de ladrón*, 1951; tr. F. Gaynor, 1955), which was followed by two more novels to make up a trilogy; this relates the life of the young son of a burglar (as the Spanish title indicates), from his release from prison to his decision to go to work. Rojas remains politically detached from his material, but humanly he is extremely involved in it, as he shows by his brilliantly selective descriptions of riots, poverty, prison and the effects of friendship. Other books by Rojas, all of them distinguished, include *Boats in the Bay* (*Lanchas en la bahía*, 1931), *Better than Wine* (*Mejor que el vino*, 1958)—the third of the trilogy beginning with *Born Guilty*—and *The Biretta from Maule* (*El bonete maulino*, 1943).

Ecuador produced the most distinguished realist school of this century. The same country had already produced one notable naturalist, LUIS A. MARTÍNEZ (1868–1909), whose powerful *Towards the Coast* (*A la costa*, 1904; tr. M. J. Calle, 1906) initiated social realism there. This, which is only occasionally crude in style, traces the history of a law student, Salvador, from the time when he decides to leave his native town for Quito, the capital. He gives up his studies, becomes involved in the revolution of 1895, then finds employment as manager of a plantation on the coast. He is ultimately destroyed; but before he dies he realizes that all his aspirations and loves were mere illusions. This attacks (by implication) middle-class complacency (Salvador's fanatically Catholic mother is an excellent character study) in trying to force sons to take up 'respectable' professions in the cities instead of allowing them to find salvation by working on the land; it is also a meticulous social study. But it was not taken up until twenty-five years later, when its example fired a number of young writers (most of them militant socialists and communists) to treat the social problems of Ecuador in a similarly forceful and radical manner. The best of these, because the least psychologically crude, was josé de la cuadra (1904–41), whose *The Sangurimas* (*Los Sangurimas*, 1934) is a memorable and admirably objective study of the destruction of the power of a violent old man—and of the murders and vendettas that beset his descendants. enrique gil gilbert (1912) wrote an almost equally objective account of the owners of and workers in the rice-fields in *Our Daily Bread* (*Nuestra pan*, 1941; tr. D. Poore, 1943); it is only spoiled at the end by the intrusion of propagandist material. jorge icaza (1906) is less gifted as a stylist, but his *Huasipungo* (1934; tr. M. Savill, 1962) gathers power because of the author's own strange but in some way effective detachment from his violent material, which concerns the exploitation of the Indians. Icaza does not idealize the Indians; on the contrary, he presents them as beasts; but the unmistakable implication is that they are made so by their masters.

Indianism (a self-explanatory term), of which *Huasipungo* is one of the best examples, was never a wholly successful genre: it was, until it re-emerged imaginatively transformed in the innovatory novels of Asturias (q.v.) and others, too theoretical. The many Indianist novels are admirable in their social and political intentions, but they seldom reach the level of literary excellence. As Jean Franco has pointed out, the superior, later Indianist novelists broke 'with realism precisely because of the limitations of the genre when it came to representing the Indian'. Thus Asturias (q.v.) in his Indianist novel *Men of Maize* (*Hombres de maíz*, 1949) breaks with conventional chronology and presents the systematic degradation and dehumanization of the Indian in the form of a series of myths. In the language, Asturias has said, he was searching for 'an American idiom', 'a biological dimension': he goes back to, or at least attempts to go back to, the wholly forgotten time when words were the 'doubles' of entities and attributes, and were therefore actively magical (cf. Vallejo, q.v.). That, of course, is being truly Indian. And Asturias is not only fully aware of the social history of the Indians; he is also deeply versed in their myths. His Spanish, in *Men of Maize*, is an intuitive version of the Indian languages.

Another leading Indianist writer is the Peruvian josé maría arguedas (1911–69), partially brought up by Indians. Like Asturias, though to a lesser degree, his scope is wider than the term 'Indianist' implies. His two chief novels are *Deep Rivers* (*Los ríos profundos*, 1958) and *All the Bloods* (*Todas las sangres*, 1964). Arguedas' achievement is to have demonstrated the terrible loss to Peruvian culture of its Indian component—a loss for which the rigid ferocity of the Catholic Church and the greed of the landlords are chiefly responsible. But Arguedas has been less successful, less intuitive, than Asturias in handling the linguistic problems of metamorphosing Indian (the language he first learnt is Quechua) into Spanish.

*

The Argentinian JORGE LUIS BORGES (1899) hardly fits into any category except the generally anti-realist one. He is unique in world literature. And yet he found himself as a writer only by a minute investigation into his own 'Argentineness'. This process of self-discovery took a long time. He was educated in Switzerland, and then lived in Spain; he returned to Buenos Aires in 1921, to a period he later called the 'ultraist mistake'; however, he did say in a poem that the 'years spent in Europe are an illusion. I have always been, and always will be, in Buenos Aires'. Some of the chief influences on Borges, who has known English since his childhood (he had an English governess, Miss Tink, as well as an English grandmother) have been Schopenhauer (q.v.), Robert Louis Stevenson, Ramón Gomez de la Serna (q.v.), his Argentine compatriot and friend MACEDONIO FERNÁNDEZ (1874–1952)—one of those metaphysical jokers which the religious intensity of Spain and Spanish America throws up from time to time—with whom he edited a magazine *Proa*, in the Twenties, H. G. Wells, G. K. Chesterton, Léon Bloy (qq.v.), the seventeenth-century Spanish novelist, satirist and poet Quevedo. . . . For Borges the only relief from Schopenhauer's 'restless will-driven flux' is in literary creation . . . 'to kill and to beget are divine or magical acts which manifestly transcend humanity'. Time extinguishes man's glory; attempts to escape from time are evasions ('Time is a substance of which I am made'). For this sceptical metaphysician the compensation for the loss of God is to become God. Borges is a great teaser and self-parodist: it is characteristic of him to have postulated, for example, a Céline (q.v.) who wrote the *Imitation of Christ*, or a critic who rewrites two fragments of *Don Quijote*, which he has only read once in the distant past, word for word—to create a much 'richer' work. . . . Borges' position is unequivocally phenomenological; he quotes Schopenhauer: 'The present is the form of all life'; he points out that it is not the order in which books were written that is important, but the *order in which we read* them. . . . 'It is venturesome to think that a co-ordination of words (philosophies are nothing more than that), can resemble the universe very much.' Everything, he says, that man tries to do against the incomprehensible fact of the universe is—by definition—a fiction. That is the kind of fiction, then, that Borges writes.

Borges began as an attractive but undoubtedly minor ultraist poet (SCO; LAP; PLAV; *Selected Poems 1923–1967*, ed. N. di Giovanni, 1972). His origins in ultraism are logical enough: this was an anti-humanistic, anti-rhetorical and anti-anthropomorphic movement, which regarded man as part of the flow of all things, not as the centre of the universe. But poetry is a dead end for Borges because he does not think poetically: the mystery of linguistic creation is not a source of energy in him (as it so obviously is in Vallejo). His poetry is merely a charming second string; in it he indulges his simple nostalgia for nineteenth-century Buenos Aires, and his fancies. In his stories, which he began to write in the Thirties, he takes up the position of extreme sceptic; specific nostalgias are incidental.

In all these stories he eschews psychological detail or the implication of it; he plays games which have their starting-points in philosophical systems that intrigue him. But these games, though beyond the 'chaotic idols of blood, earth and passion', have their deadly seriousness. Eliot said that for John Donne a thought was an experience; the same applies to Borges, with the difference that for him thought is the primary source of experience.

In the Thirties Borges, a librarian, edited anthologies of Argentinian literature, wrote ingenious detective stories (some in collaboration or under pseudonyms). During the Second World War he was resolutely anti-Nazi. In 1946 he signed a petition against the dictator Perón, who promptly removed him from his library and appointed him poultry inspector. He resigned and became a teacher and script-writer. On the fall of Perón he became director of the Argentine National Library. For over a quarter of a century his sight has deteriorated; he is now almost totally blind, and has to dictate. Although translations of his most important work already exist, Borges is now collaborating with the American writer Norman T. di Giovanni on authorized English translations of all his books. So far *The Aleph* (*El Aleph*, 1949 rev. 1957; tr. 1970) and *The Book of Imaginary Beings* (1969) have appeared. Other translations include *Labyrinths* (tr. D. A. Yates and J. E. Irby, 1962), an excellent comprehensive selection—and, less reliable, *Fictions* (*Ficciones*, 1944 rev. 1961; tr. A. Kerrigan et al, 1962) and *Dream tigers* (pt. *El hacedor*, *The Maker* 1960; tr. M. Boyer and H. Morland, 1964).

Borges has been described as a mystic; but he is only in fact an explorer of mysticism. After all, it is as characteristic of a Spanish-American (or Spanish) writer to postulate writers as Gods as it is for Frenchmen to postulate them as cooks. . . . With Gide (q.v., so very different a writer), Borges is the nearest in the twentieth century to the spirit of Montaigne. For those who are not blinded by one or other of the many contradictory versions of 'the truth' about the universe, the sixteenth-century essayist seems astonishingly 'modern'; so, in four centuries' time might seem the work of an Argentinian writer who recognized in the twentieth century that things had gone beyond the point when mere verbal assertions of humane values (by politicians) were of much use. . . .

In his fiction, which consists entirely of short stories (most are very short), Borges actively seeks to overthrow the reader's confidence in external reality. To a certain extent this is an act of revenge, since, as he has himself implied, he has had small experience of 'life in the raw'. The earlier stories, in *Fictions*, do this more playfully; the stories in *The Maker* are briefer, more mordant. What Borges has done, above all, is to triumph over his deficiencies without being dogmatic about it; to erect a number of possible worlds on parodically 'scholarly' bases. He, a sceptic, has made the century's most thorough investigation of the philosophical element in human experience. (LWT)

Three more Argentinian writers deserve serious consideration. EDUARDO MALLEA (1903) is the Latin-American existentialist novelist *par excellence*. His struggle, and that of his agonized characters, is to achieve an authentic existence; but this involves (and here we are at least reminded of Borges) dissolving, destroying, the hostile, non-authentic environment. For Mallea, despite his sympathy with those (the poor, oppressed or exploited) whose human authenticity has not been wholly destroyed, the inner life is the only real life (and there we are reminded of Rilke, q.v.). Of his many novels the best are: *The Bay of Silence* (*La bahía del silencio*, 1940; tr. S. E. Grummon, 1944), a bitter story of a man's discovery of peace in a solipsism that wholly rejects life; *All Green Shall Perish* (*Todo verdor perecerá*, 1941; tr. J. B. Hughes, with other novels, 1967), a bleak study of a woman's complete loneliness, in which the past is cunningly counterpointed with the present; and *Sinbad* (*Simbad*, 1957), which is—and is 'about'—a drama being composed by a playwright. Mallea is a powerful, intelligent and honest novelist; he is also a tragic one, for he finds no solution to his problem except in solipsism.

ERNESTO SÁBATO (1911), a mathematician, is also concerned with the nature of solipsist experience. *The Outsider* (*El túnel*, 1948; tr. H. de Onís, 1950) is about a painter who murders his mistress because he cannot communicate with her. *On Heroes and Tombs* (*Sobre héroes y tumbas*, 1961; rev. 1964) is a longer novel, with more characters; here Sábato enters into the vision of an incestuous paranoiac who is murdered by his daughter. This is a novel of great power, in which the author demonstrates the insanity of Argentinian society as it reflects itself in the shattered mind of the protagonist.

The fiction of JULIO CORTÁZAR (1914), who lives in France, contains most of the ingredients of the *nouveau roman*, but also possesses imaginative zest and a contempt for philosophical abstraction, which he links with the habit of intellectual calculation—this in spite of the fact that he himself confesses that he is 'over-intellectual'. He resembles Borges, who has influenced him, in being a joker; but his fictional games are less desperate. Apart from short stories, Cortázar has written three novels: *The Winners* (*Los premios*, 1960; tr. E. Kerrigan, 1965), *Hopscotch* (*Rayuela*, 1963; tr. G. Rabassa, 1966) and *62. A Novel to Put Together* (*62. Novela para armar*, 1968). These require progressively more 'audience-participation', and the weakness of the most recent is that it hardly achieves an identity of its own into which even the most willing reader can project. *The Winners*, relatively straightforward, deals with a mysterious voyage taken by the winners of a lottery. These divide into two groups: one accepts the rules (of not asking where they are going, and not going on the bridge), the other does not. *Hopscotch* is more radical and anti-literary; it contains elements of self-criticism, but is essentially a Borgesian postulation of a personality who *accepts* absurdity.

*

One novel, *Men of Maize*, by Borges' only equal in Latin-American fiction, the Guatemalan MIGUEL ÁNGEL ASTURIAS (1899), has already been discussed. Asturias won the Nobel Prize in 1967. He began writing poetry (LAP) and prose well before the Second World War, while he was in Paris studying anthropology and the Maya civilization; but his first important book, although begun in 1922, did not appear until 1946. This was *Mr President* (*El señor presidente*; tr. F. Partridge, 1963). Asturias grew up under the shadow of the reign of Chocano's (q.v.) vicious friend, Estrada Cabrera, and he drew on his experiences for his phantasmagoric novel of dictatorship. This supplements Guzmán's *The Shadow of the Leader* (q.v.) as an impression of what it is like to live under tyranny, and of what tyranny does to a society. The country of the dictatorship in *Mr President* is not mentioned: it is any Latin-American country. This has been called Asturias' 'greatest novel', but it is not that: it is too full of crudities. Yet its genuinely Gothic vision, and the poetic accuracy of its diagnosis of the evil that tyranny is and does, foreshadows his later work. One may see here the influence of that so strangely neglected Spanish novelist Valle-Inclán, in his *The Tyrant Banderas* (q.v.), with its *esperpento* (q.v.).

Of *Men of Maize* Asturias says 'there is no story line. Whether things are clear or not doesn't matter. They are simply given'. He followed it with a trilogy: *The Cyclone* (*Viento fuerte*, 1950; tr. D. Flakoll and C. Alegria, 1967), *The Green Pope* (*El Papa verde*, 1954; tr. G. Rabassa, 1971) and *The Eyes of the Buried* (*Los ojos de los enterrados*, 1960). This deals with United States exploitation of Guatemalan banana plantations, but chooses as 'saved characters' two North Americans who want to change things. This is not as successful as *Men of Maize* because, at certain points, Asturias' indignation has pre-empted his imagination; the too obvious device of making North Americans into the heroes hardly helps. But this trilogy is nevertheless clearly the work of a genius —and never more so than when Asturias forgets his social intentions.

Weekend in Guatemala (*Weekend en Guatemala*, 1956), which describes the army coup that overthrew the Árbenz government in the early Fifties (and sent Asturias into eight years of exile), are not on a level with his other work.

With *The Mulatta and Mr Fly* (*Mulata de tal*, 1963; tr. G. Rabassa, 1967) Asturias returned, for the first time, to something like the form of *Men of Maize*. But this is in popular rather than mythical or religious language, and the time is the present: Yumí barters his wife for money and marries the Mulata, who turns out to be malevolent. He thereupon joins up again with his wife to wall up the Mulata. The two of them undergo many terrifying metamorphoses. Asturias has said that basically this is a retelling of the Indian myth of the sun and the moon. The Mulata will only give Yumí her arse when he makes love to her: 'the sun as a male and the moon as a female would breed monstrous children'. This novel often wanders; but it remains unique, and we should be grateful to have the insights it offers in any form.

A Cuban novelist sometimes, and not very usefully, grouped with Asturias as a 'magic realist' (q.v.) is ALEJO CARPENTIER (1904), who has won considerable success in English translation. Carpentier, who has been a musicologist and radio script writer, is an eclectic and highly intelligent novelist who manages to produce work with a considerable middlebrow appeal (at least in Great Britain). There is an element of syncretic and allegorical pretentiousness in some of his novels (such as *The Lost Steps, Los pasos perdidos,* 1953; tr. H. de Onís, 1956). This seems to be involuntary; and it is only one element; Carpentier's work cannot be dismissed, for it is acutely serious and skilful. He began as an Afro-Cuban poet; he then became increasingly concerned with the necessity of social and political change, and today he is one of the most distinguished supporters of Fidel Castro's revolution. He was born in Havana; but his father was French, his mother Russian. Carpentier is both a pioneer of the Latin-American new novel and a proponent of it. After a period of imprisonment under the dictator Machado Carpentier went into exile to France; it was the French poet Desnos (q.v.) who helped him to leave Cuba.

His first novel was *Praised Be the Lord* (*Ecué-Yamba-O,* 1934), an unsuccessful and over-intellectual attempt to depict Afro-Cuban culture from the inside. In *The Kingdom of This World* (*El reino de este mundo,* 1949; tr. 1957) he dealt with the reign of the nineteenth-century Haitian Negro king Henri Christophe (subject of a play by Aimé Césaire, q.v.); the chief character is a slave who changes hands continuously as circumstances change. This book consists too much of 'set pieces' (such as Henri Christophe's death), which, although magnificently done, do not hang at all well together. Carpentier seems unable to resist the temptation to indulge himself—either as a high stylistic performer or at least as a 'deep' (midcult version) philosopher.

This was a pessimistic version of the revolutionary theme. *The Lost Steps* goes the other way: a musician, sometimes an irritating, pretentious and humourless character, goes on an expedition to seek primitive musical instruments. He is in the company of a group of people who want to recapture the ancient 'primitive' wisdom; but when it comes to the time to make a decision the musician returns to 'civilization'—nor, when he tries to return, can he find the way. *Explosion in a Cathedral* (*El siglo de las luces,* 1962; tr. 1963) is more explicitly political; the truly impressive erudition and heavy rhetoric seem, however, unnecessary in this study of the merchant Victor Hugues and his vacillations in the age immediately following the French Revolution. Carpentier has a deep-rooted ambivalence towards revolution, and his novels do not really begin to resolve this. Here he seems to want to prove that eventually Marxism will be humanly realized; but he never convinces us. In his shorter fiction, where he tries less hard to cover up this failure of resolution with over-literary richnesses, he is a better writer. *Manhunt* (*El acoso,* 1956; tr. 1959) studies a revolutionary who informs (after torture) on his companions and is hunted down and killed in a concert-hall where he has been listening to Beethoven; here, where Carpentier has confined himself to a relatively short space—and to the requirements of his imagination rather than of his political beliefs—he has been most successful. This appears in *The War of Time* (*Guerra del tiempo,* 1958), with three shorter stories, two of which, 'The Road to Santiago' and 'Journey to the Seed' (LWT) are as good as anything Carpentier has written.

*

The chief pioneer of Mexico's 'new novel' has been AUGUSTÍN YAÑEZ (1904), whose *On the Edge of the Storm* (*Al filo del agua*, 1947; tr. E. Brinton, 1963)—the sense of the title is 'on the brink'—seeks, with success, to study the social state of mind of a country on the verge of revolution. This is a valuable and objective account of the collapse of the authority of 'God': of the Church in a Mexican town that can no longer make do with pretences, of ecclesiastical authorities whose religious self-confidence has collapsed into terror. It is one of the best of modern novels to deal with the sociological nature of revolution. The sequel to *On the Edge of the Storm*, *The Creation* (*La creación*, 1959) is less subtle and wide in scope, but is nevertheless a fine novel. *Prodigal Earth* (*La tierra pródiga*, 1960) deals with the land and the way those who exploit it feel about it. Yañez is one of South America's most accomplished and penetrating novelists.

The novels of JOSÉ REVUELTAS (1914) are less convincing, possibly because he cannot entirely separate his (communist) political convictions from his creative insights, which are considerable. In 1940 he was sent to prison for what the Mexican government termed 'subversive activity'; his first novel, *The Walls of Water* (*Los muros de agua*), dealing with political prisoners, followed in 1941. In 1943 he published his best book, *The Stone Knife* (*El luto humano*; tr. H. R. Hays, 1947); here he gives a compelling account, by the skilful use of Faulknerian interior monologue, of a group of rural people trying to save themselves from destruction by a flood. This novel contained elements of nihilism as well as of tragedy. Revueltas' later novels are all more or less vitiated by his enslavement to communist theory; he has even obediently 'renounced' a novel that gave offence to the party.

JUAN JOSÉ ARREOLA (1918), who trained as an actor in France and has been active in many cultural fields, is Mexico's leading contemporary practitioner of the short story. His two collections, *Varied Invention* (*Varia invención*, 1949) and *Confabulario* (1952; tr. G. D. Schade, 1964) were gathered together into a single volume, *Confabulario total*, in 1962. He has also written an effective play, an exposure of the emptiness of a potentate's life: *Everyone's Day* (*La hora de todos*, 1954). Arreola's stories are deceptively modest: ironic, light in touch, they probe good humouredly into the modern society's various sicknesses. In 'Verily I Say Unto You' the rich become poor in their efforts to get a camel through the eye of a needle. Arreola, who has been influential in Mexico, published a novel, *The Fair* (*La feria*) in 1963. Here Arreola seems to have come almost as far as Butor (q.v.): *The Fair* is an assemblage of material—including press-cuttings, accounts of certain people's lives, history, legend—dealing with a single town in Jalisco.

JUAN RULFO (1918) also made his now considerable reputation with a book of short stories: *The Burning Plain* (*El llano en llamas*, 1953; tr. G. D. Schade,

1967). These stories of Mexican rural life differed greatly from the fiction of most of Rulfo's contemporaries: they were laconic, apparently without feeling— almost neo-naturalist in mood. Rulfo wrote in simple, lucid prose. But he was not simply reviving traditional realism and regionalism. Rulfo is candid, strictly human (rather than political); he looks for the strange and the destroyed. This is a new, stark, unconfident naturalism. Rulfo has written only one novel, *Pedro Páramo* (1955; tr. L. Kemp, 1959). This is one of the most important and original books in modern literature in the Spanish language. It is about the dead as well as the living. Like Asturias and Paz (qq.v.), Rulfo seeks wisdom in the 'primitive': in this story of a tyrannical, brutal, love-obsessed landowner, Pedro Páramo, we read of the Mexican 'life of the dead' as well as of the protagonists' lives. For when Juan Preciado goes to seek his father at Comala, to get his due, his father is already dead; so is Comala; so is his mother, who sent him; so is the woman who first receives him. Later he, too, dies; but the story continues. In this extraordinary and difficult novel Rulfo goes more deeply into Mexican 'intrahistory' (q.v.), and into the living meaning of its myths, than any politically motivated writer could possibly have done. Páramo is revealed not only as a man—typical of the period covered by the novel, the first quarter of our century—but also as a legend; the legend that made him possible is also revealed. He is shown as the victim of his own brutality, hate and virility (his horse, symbol of this, kills him); yet also as a nobly hopeless lover. Rulfo has been influenced by Faulkner (q.v., a generally strong influence on Spanish-American fiction); but more so by various European writers, such as Korolenko, Andreyev, Hamsun, Laxness and, in particular, Giono and Ramuz (qq.v.), two regionalists with, like Rulfo himself, a differ-ence. He is now working on a novel, *The Mountain Ridge* (*La cordillera*), which begins in the sixteenth century in Jalisco, the harsh region of his birth. (LWT)

ROSARIO CASTELLANOS (1925) has written notable novels about Indian life: *The Nine Guardians* (*Balún Canán*, 1957; tr. I. Nicholson, 1959) and *Office of Shadows* (*Oficio de tinieblas*, 1962). Both—the latter more successfully—deal with confrontations between Indians and other races. Rosario Castellanos is also an accomplished poet. (LWT)

CARLOS FUENTES (1928) is the leading Mexican novelist of his generation, with a growing international reputation. Fuentes, son of a diplomat, has worked in the cinema (with Buñuel, among others, on an adaptation of Carpentier's *The Pursuit*). After a preliminary collection of stories Fuentes published his first novel, *Where the Air is Clear* (*La región más transparente*; tr. S. Hileman, 1960), in 1958. This is about Mexico City, 'where', in a famous phrase, 'the air is clear'. It was a runaway success. It is the story both of the city itself and of the ruin of one of its inhabitants, an ex-revolutionary whose complex financial affairs have reached the point of no return. This is a brilliant and disenchanted study of modern Mexico, which is portrayed as a country corrupted by money and power. (The translation of this novel is said by the leading American authority on the Mexican novel to be in 'second-rate . . . prose' which 'belongs to the translator, not to Fuentes'.)

Fuentes has continued in his prolific fiction to work out the theme of Mexican self-dissatisfaction. Possibly this theme dominates the Mexican literature of the past fifty years because of the failure of the Revolution: Mexico's moderate, reformist governments (since the reign of the virtual dictator Calles came to an end) have shown no inclination to stamp out capitalism or its attendant evils. His next novel, *The Good Conscience* (*Las buenas conciencias*, 1959; tr. S. Hileman, 1961), is technically superior because less ambitious. It is set in a town that epitomizes Mexican self-regard, conservatism and obscurantism; it deals with the gradual corruption and moral self-destruction of a young man, son of wealthy parents, who begins as a radical in revolt against the values of his society.

Aura (1962) is a minor, 'decadent' ghost story; but in *The Death of Artemio Cruz* (*La muerte de Artemio Cruz*; tr. S. Hileman, 1964), published in the same year, Fuentes achieved his greatest success. As in Rulfo's *Pedro Páramo*, the hero is finished as we begin the book: he is dying in hospital. Artemio Cruz is a man who rose through the Revolution, but then betrayed it. As he dies we hear not only the voice of his murderous and self-assertive ego, but also that of his conscience, or perhaps of what might be called his 'under-self'. Technically assured, complex, panoramic in its view of Mexico, *The Death of Artemio Cruz* is also a triumph of characterization; it is undoubtedly Fuentes' finest book. *Change of Skin* (*Cambio de piel*, 1967), which contrasts real consciousness of self with a man's ('an ageing beatnik's') idea of what it ought to be, has its moments, but fails to fall into one piece. Despite the occasional presence of an element of slickness in his work, Fuentes is one of the more important Mexican writers of his generation. (LWT)

LOUIS SPOTA (1925) is a journalist, and one can tell this from his many and popular novels. But despite their over-facility and sensationalism, his best books cannot be ignored. Spota is a neo-naturalist who exposes (often, but not always, too obviously) social evils. His best novel, and one of the best to have been written on the subject of bull-fighting is *The Wounds of Hunger* (*Mas cornadas da un hombre*, 1950; tr. B. Conrad, 1957). *Almost Paradise* (*Casi el paraíso*, 1956) is an at times intolerably crude, but at times highly effective revelation of the worthlessness of Mexico City's 'high society'. Spota provides an excellent example of a popular novelist who also possesses some literary merits.

*

There having been, until comparatively recently, no Uruguayan market, most novelists tended to go to Buenos Aires. The most gifted of his generation, Amorim (q.v.) is even thought of as an Argentinian writer. Quiroga lived for much of his life in the Argentine. Uruguay's leading contemporary novelist, JUAN CARLOS ONETTI (1909)—the name is not Italian, but was originally Irish: O'Nety (if this is not a characteristic joke)—also lived and worked in Buenos Aires for many years. His *The Well* (*El pozo*, 1939) is a Latin-American *Nausea* (q.v.); but the chief influence on him, particularly on his style, as on so many other writers, has been Céline (q.v.). Technically he has learnt from Dos Passos and Faulkner (qq.v.)—the two North Americans who have exercised the most influence outside their own country. Much of Onetti's short fiction has been usefully collected in *Short Novels* (*Novelas cortas*, 1968). Onetti is one of the most pessimistic of modern writers; but he has a humour and a verve to modify his bitterness, Sartrian sense of disgust and conviction of the solipsist state of man. He is, he says, 'a lonely man smoking somewhere in the night . . . turning toward the shadow on the wall at night to dwell on nonsensical fantasies'.

In his early novel *No Man's Land* (*Tierra de nadie*, 1941) Onetti was clearly under the influence of Arlt; its 'hero' is Buenos Aires, and this is seen as the finally disrupting force in the lives of people: as the malevolent power that prevents communication. Onetti is, one might say, an existentialist who hardly believes in the possibility of authenticity: there are too many small obstacles to its achievement.

Of Onetti's many books, all of them excellent, two stand out: *Short Life* (*La vida breve*, 1950) and *The Shipyard* (*El astillero*, 1961; tr. 1968). In the first he introduces the world of his later fiction: the town of Santa María. The narrator, who suffers from *ennui*, dreams up a fictional character, Díaz Gray (Dorian Gray, someone has suggested), who is actually the narrator of several later works. . . . The narrator Bransen dreams up some other characters, too; but Díaz Gray comes to dominate them all. *The Shipyard* is about the attempt of an ageing and shady man, Larsen, to make a dilapidated shipyard into a working concern. He pretends to devote himself to this task, while he courts the mad daughter of the owner in the pretence of hoping that in this way he may eventually gain control. *Juntacádaveres* (1965) takes us back to the time when Larsen ran a brothel in Santa María (he was expelled for it). Onetti is an original, with an especial gift for the comic; although his concerns are by no means philosophical, the intellectual implications of his work are profound. (LWT)

MARIO BENEDETTI (1920) is a poet as well as a novelist. He is also a useful and informative critic. His best work is in the collection of short stories entitled *Montevideanos* (1959), in which he explores with sensitivity and compassion the lives of 'ordinary' people in Montevideo. His novel *The Truce* (*La tregua*, 1960) deals with similarly humdrum material: an ageing clerk falls in love with a young girl who works in his office. *Thanks for the Light* (*Gracias por el fuego*, 1964) diagnoses the moral paralysis and corruption of modern Uruguayan society (LWT)

Paraguay's most important novelist is AUGUSTO ROA BASTOS (1917); he, too, protests against his country's situation and its social causes. *Thunder in the Leaves* (*El trueno entre las hojas*, 1953) consists of short stories written in a mixture of Spanish and the Indian language, Guiraní; these contrast individual freedom with the checks it meets from an over-industrialized and cruel society. Roa Bastos' finest work, however, is his novel *Son of Man* (*Hijo de hombre*, 1959; tr. R. Caffyn, 1965). This, loosely constructed in a series of episodes, reveals a whole society sacrificing its chances of human self-realization to greed and power; in portraying the tragic history of the Paraguayan people Roa Bastos succeeds in creating a violent allegory of the human social situation.

There have been relatively few Colombian literary figures of note: Silva, Carrasquilla, Rivera (qq.v.) are exceptions in a desert of mediocrity. Today only GABRIEL GARCÍA MÁRQUEZ (1928) is outstanding. Significantly, he lives in exile in Mexico (where he works writing movie scripts): Colombia is perhaps the most obscurantist of the republics in South America. Like Onetti, García Márquez has created his own imaginary place: the small tropical town of Macondo. Like any enlightened Colombian, García Márquez is of course on the side of social reform; but as a writer he is essentially explorative and anti-dogmatic: he is aware of the necessity of inoculating his imagination against idealogical infection. In his first novel, *Withered Leaves* (*La hojarasca*, 1955), he portrays the rottenness and ruin of a whole town (Macondo) over the first quarter of this century in a bundle of interior reminiscences that are experienced in a period of less than one hour. The central character is a mysterious doctor, the kind of 'stranger' portrayed with such subtle strategy by Edwin Arlington Robinson in his poem 'Flammonde' (q.v.): is he Macondo's evil genius or its hidden conscience? Soon after this came García Márquez' most accomplished novel to date: *No-one Writes to the Colonel* (*El coronel no tiene quien le escriba*, 1961). This portrait of an eccentric old soldier who awaits a pension that never arrives is optimistic because of the sheer power of its characterization: the colonel remains lovable and vigorous even in his moments of worst defeat. *One Hundred Years of Solitude* (*Cien años de soledad*, 1967; tr. G. Rabassa, 1970) is again set in Macondo: this is the history of its founding and of its 'progress', a quintessenti-ally Latin-American novel that finally demonstrates, as Jean Franco points out, that realism is an inadequate technique in dealing with this mysterious and frequently fantastic environment. (LWT)

Of the younger generation of novelists, the most distinguished is the Peruvian MARIO VARGAS LLOSA (1936). One of Vargas Llosa's main themes is the *macho* complex: the Spanish-American version of the famous Southern Italian obsession with virility that Brancati (q.v.) deals with in his novels; *machismo* implies not only virility but also a bullying attitude, and its existence is unquestionably one of the chief reasons for the political backwardness of South America as a whole. (It is interesting that Sicily, where a similar attitude prevails, is similarly corrupt and backward.) His first novel, *The City and the Dogs* (*La ciudad y los perros*, 1962; tr. 1967) tells of 'education' at a military school; there has been nothing as scarifying since *Törless*. Vargas Llosa obtained his material from his school-days in Lima, and even retained the name of his school, which retaliated by officially burning one thousand copies of the book (this honour must be envied by almost every writer who went to more or less that kind of school). The 'dogs' of the title are first-year students, confined to quarters: they are being taught 'virility' by undergoing a series of tests. But all the characters, even the one decent member of the staff, fail real tests of character.

The Green House (*La casa verde*, 1965; tr. G. Rabassa, 1968) is the story of a brothel in Piura—and of Peruvian corruption, exploitation and cruelty. On the one hand there is an expedition into the jungle—back into what Vargas Llosa has himself called the Stone Age—by Church, army and whores, eager to exploit its possibilities, ignoring its wisdom and its beauty. On the other hand there is the brothel. This book is full of irony, of fine characterization, of insights—and of poor, too experimental passages and even writing that looks suspiciously phoney. But Vargas Llosa approaches his South-American theme with understanding and a high measure of intuition; clearly he is a force to be reckoned with.

There is much talent in the younger generation of Spanish-American novelists. The Chilean JOSÉ DONOSO (1924) has already achieved a high reputation. *Coronation* (*Coronación*, 1957; tr. 1965) traces the collapse of an upper-class family as its stately home becomes invaded by proletarian members of the younger generation (LWT) The Cuban GUILLERMO CABRERA INFANTE (1929), who lives in exile from the Castro regime, wrote *In Peace as in War* (*Así en la paz como en la guerra*, 1964; pt. LWT) and *View of a Tropical Dawn* (*Vista del amanecer el trópico*, 1964), a large-scale portrait of Cuba under Batista. (WNC; LWT) The *avant garde* poet JOSÉ LEZAMA LIMA (1912), also a Cuban, has written much interesting verse (LAP; PLAV)—and one remarkable novel, *Paradise* (*Paradiso*, 1966), a work that may be classed with that of such writers as Roussel and Blanchot (qq.v.). It is one of the most erudite and complex of all modern novels, comparable with the best of its type of this century; certainly it is the most important novel ever to come out of Cuba.

Two writers from Ecuador should be mentioned. From an older generation, PABLO PALACIO (1906–46), who went mad, was a notable and humorous eccentric whose short stories in *A Man Kicked to Death* (*Un hombre muerto a puntapiés*, 1929) are worth preserving. The Mulatto poet ADALBERTO ORTIZ (1914) wrote a good novel, *Juyungo* (1943) about a Negro who runs away into mysterious regions in Ecuador during the Peruvian invasion of 1941.

III

The Spanish-American theatre, which has yet to reach maturity, has not produced a single major playwright (if there is an exception it is probably Arlt, q.v.). This is in spite of the facts that the theatre has flourished in Buenos Aires, Mexico City and, at times, in Lima and Santiago, and that the roots of Spanish-American theatre reach down into soil not only European but also Indian and (in certain cases) African. Has this soil so far proved too rich? Or have the Spanish-American theatre and its audience not yet outgrown colonial inhibitions? These questions are not easy to answer. However, the main reason for dramatic impoverishment seems to lie in the absence, until very recently, of the kind of audience that produces theatre of significance. That audience must be stiffened by a non-intellectual element that is not, however, in search of pseudo-profound, 'advanced' midcult pap (such as the crass and uncomprehending but commercially viable pastiche of 'mod theatre' perpetrated by the English entertainer Tom Stoppard in *Rosencrantz and Guildenstern are Dead*). One thinks of the complex nature of Shakespeare's audience—or of the audience for the Belgian and Flemish theatre of today. Such an element seems to be lacking, so far, in South America—where elementary social progress is hindered (for the most part) by obscurantist and reactionary modes of thought. Again, it is possible that the cinema, as popular in South America as anywhere in the world, has attracted much of the potential theatrical audience.

Every country has a playwright who imported what may, broadly, be called the Ibsenite theatre. In South America it was the Uruguayan FLORENCIO SÁNCHEZ (1875–1910), who wrote minor dramas, for the Argentine stage, of social realism, often dealing with gaucho or slum life. Sánchez believed in the philosophy of optimistic naturalism (which even Zola privately rejected), and he had little imaginative power. But he had pity, and one or two of his plays are moving. *My Son the Doctor* (*M'hijo el dotor*, 1903) deals with a father's failure to understand his son's urban ways. *The Immigrant's Daughter* (*La gringa*, 1904), which is interesting to compare with Amorim's *The Horse and Its Shadow* (q.v.), is about the clash between Argentinians and Italian immigrants. Sánchez' best play is *Downhill* (*Barranca abajo*, 1905), on the collapse of an old Creole family under the pressures of modern life. These and other plays appear in English in *Representative Plays of Florencio Sánchez* (tr. W. K. Jones, 1961).

As effective as Sánchez, but not acknowledged as such, was his disciple, also Uruguayan, ERNESTO HERRERA (1886–1917), who was a fully-fledged anarchist-naturalist. His study of a South American bully in *The Blind Lion* (*El león ciego*, 1911) is powerful. *Our Daily Bread* (*El pan nuestro*, 1913), which is about a Madrid family in process of deterioration, is one of the best social dramas of its period.

Most of the Argentine dramatists have been managers. Such is the most famous of them, and the most famous South American playwright of his generation: SAMUEL EICHELBAUM (1894). Eichelbaum has followed in the tradition of Sanchez and Herrera, but is psychologically more subtle. Furthermore, although basically a realist, he has tried to eschew sensationalism by concentrating not so much upon action as upon its effects on people's minds. His drama has some affinities with the theatre of silence (q.v.) initiated by the Italian Bracco and continued by Bernard (qq.v.). Among his most successful plays are *A Tough of the Nineties* (*Un guapo del novecientos*, 1940), about a professional assassin—Eichelbaum solves his 'moral problem' with neat irony—and *Clay Pigeon* (*Pájaro de barro*, 1940). Alone of the Spanish-American realist playwrights Eichelbaum achieves international stature. His work was suppressed by Perón's censors, but he re-emerged.

Roberto Arlt (q.v.) wrote eight plays, one of which, *Saverio the Cruel* (*Saverio el cruel*, 1936), is the best single drama to emerge from twentieth-century South America. Of all the playwrights influenced by Pirandello (q.v.), Arlt was the most intelligent and original. Other plays include *Africa*, 300 *Million* and *The Desert Island* (*La isla desierta*). Arlt's theatre was at once more intelligent and 'advanced' than anyone else's of its time; he had a full grasp of psychological reality, but was never under the illusion that his characters were other than stage-people: i.e., were his own creations. His drama, as energetic as his fiction, probes this mystery with sensitivity and, at times, relentless cruelty. Theatre in the Argentine collapsed under Perón; it has hardly revived since his departure. Arlt's complete plays appeared in 1968.

In Chile three leading elder generation dramatists were ARMANDO MOOCK (1894–1942), ANTONIO ACEVEDO HERNÁNDEZ (1886–1962) and GERMÁN LUCO CRUCHAGA (1894–1936). The first contributed only the virtues of sound technique: he was an inveterate sentimentalist and never concealed this for long. Acevedo Hernández was a sometimes powerful naturalist in the tradition of Herrera; Luco Cruchaga is famous for his *Apablaza's Widow* (*La viuda de Apablaza*, 1928), a still effective drama of rural passion.

In the Thirties in Chile there arose an interesting experimental theatre, encouraged by the universities. This has continued to develop. The best playwright to emerge out of the movement was LUIS ALBERTO HEIREMANS (1928–64), whose premature death was a severe loss to the South American theatre.

The leading Cuban dramatist of the earlier part of the century was JOSÉ ANTONIO RAMOS (1885–1946). Much of Ramos' drama is vitiated by his radical preoccupations; but there are exceptions: *The Quaking Land* (*Tembladera*, 1917) is the chief of these. Its theme is social enough: the sale, by the political gangsters in charge of Cuba, of the sugar plantations to foreigners and the misery this caused. But all Ramos' indignation went into the human situations that arose from this corruption; the social message is thus all the more powerful. *The Legend of the Stars* (*La leyenda de las estrellas*, 1935) was written in a different style, and reflected the influence of Pirandello. The best known of the post-revolutionary Cuban dramatists, who have produced disappointing work, is JOSÉ TRIANA (1933), whose *Night of the Assassins* (*Noche de los asesinos*) is one of the most intelligent and effective of plays to deal with the complex and difficult existentialist theme of the meanings of 'love' and 'love-relationship'; Triana here postulates a situation where parental 'love' means 'death', since it involves the destruction of the beloveds' freedom. It was seen in London (1967).

The Mexican theatre produced, first and foremost, RODOLFO USIGLI (1905), who was originally much influenced by Shaw's coldly rational and yet 'preposterous' approach to the drama. His best known play is *The Gesticulator* (*El gesticulador*, 1937) which was not performed until ten years after its publication because of its supposed reactionary elements. Usigli, who is a skilful and intelligent but not really penetrating playwright, shares the view of Mexican society and character taken by most Mexican writers: he regards Mexicans as incapable of authentic behaviour because of their need to play out roles, to accept lies instead of truth. Thus, in *The Gesticulator* a professor called César Rubio impersonates—at first for financial reasons—an assassinated revolutionary leader of the same name; this game acquires a dangerous reality of its own that not even Rubio's confession can break. Usigli has written a number of other plays, chief among which is *Crown of Shadow* (*Corona de sombra*, 1943; tr. W. Stirling, 1946), which questions the conventional version of the Mexican past (the time of the Emperor Maximilian).

Usigli was intimately associated with the foundation of a theatrical group in the Thirties, *Orientation* (*Orientación*), originally Ulysses Theatre; the founder was the poet Xavier Villaurrutia (q.v.), who wrote a number of outstandingly lucid psychological dissections of middle-class life. His finest play, however, is *Invitation to Death* (*Invitación a la muerte*, 1944), which dramatizes the Mexican instability more poetically and understandingly than anything by Usigli, whose work looks pallid and superficial beside it. Salvador Novo (q.v.) has written his best dramatic work since 1950, but he, too, was associated with *Orientation*. *Cuathtémoc* (1962) questions the Mexican past even more profoundly than Usigli's *Crown of Shadow*.

The presence in Buenos Aires from 1939 until a year or so before his death of the Spanish playwright Alejandro Casona (q.v.) had important consequences for the Latin-American theatre: it is one of the reasons why most younger playwrights are exponents of European *avant garde* techniques. Much of what is produced is trivial or ephemeral; but this has always applied more to the theatre than to the other serious arts; the situation has never been more lively in Spanish-America than it is now. There is only one outstanding realist: the Argentine CARLOS GOROSTIZA (1920)—but the content of his plays, as distinct from their presentation, is anything but conventionally realist. *The Bridge* (*El puente*, 1949) presents the same action from differing points of view. The ironically entitled *The Neighbours* (*Los prójimos*, 1966) shows the murder of a girl taking place beneath the eyes of her indifferent and selfish neighbours. OSVALDO DRAGÚN (1929), another Argentinian, has been influenced by Brecht (q.v.), whose effects he employs to create savage indictments of his own generation. Also influenced by Brecht is the Mexican LUISA JOSEFINA HERNÁNDEZ (1928), whose *Popol Vuh* (1966) is a successful play on Mayan themes. The Chilean ALEJANDRO SIEVEKING (1934) has some affinities with Salacrou (q.v.), especially in *Souls of a Clear Day* (*Animas de día claro*, 1962), which has its starting-point in a folk superstition. Lastly, the Puerto Rican RENÉ MARQUÉS (1919) should be mentioned. Puerto Rico was for half a century torn between its own Spanish culture and that of the United States. Only Marqués rose above the level of polemic, both in short stories, in *Another of Our Days*, (*Otro día nuestro*, 1955) and drama. His play *The Little Cart* (*La carreta*, 1952) deals, in psychological rather than political terms, with peasants forced into an urban existence and, ultimately, tragic emigration. Later plays, such as *A Blue Child for That Shadow* (*Un niño azul para esa sombra*, 1958), show an increasing control of theatrical potential and a deepening sensitivity. Of all those South American writers who deal with the theme of various types of North American cultural and economic aggression Marqués is the subtlest and the least polemical.

IV

Brazil differs from the rest of the South American states not only for the obvious linguistic reason, but also because it has an independent monarchical past, which lasted from Pedro I's declaration of Brazilian independence in 1822 until the abolition of slavery in 1888. Furthermore, Brazil is one of the five largest countries in the world—virtually as big as the United States. It has all the South American problems—but they loom larger. Although there have of course been nationalistic trends in the rest of South America, these have been at their strongest in Brazil. There are more variations in the climate and landscape of Brazil, with its dry *sertão* in the north-east, than elsewhere.

The roots of romanticism went more deeply into the soil of Brazil than elsewhere. One critic stated it thus: 'Romanticism appears here less as a doctrine than as a vital impulse . . . in Brazil, romanticism was a national religious and social force . . . it . . . reestablish[ed] letters in the high dignity they deserved . . . it took the side of freedom, at one with the very existence of the young nation'. *Modernismo* did not touch Brazil, whose own modernism (q.v.) did not erupt until 1922. However, the spirit of naturalism (q.v.) was more prevalent than elsewhere: Brazil can boast of at least one thoroughgoing naturalist novelist.

Brazilian fiction had begun late (with Teixeira e Sousa's *The Fisherman's Son* in 1845), securely under romantic auspices. It was the skilful José de Alencar (1829–77) who first saw that the novel could be turned into an adequate vehicle for the expression of Brazilian experience. But Brazil was even readier than the rest of the South American continent to absorb the message of positivism. Of course, its naturalist novel is produced by men as romantic (about the 'scientific' truth as well as other things) as Zola himself; but this is a naturalism altogether tougher and more uncompromising than anything seen in Spanish America. It was, of course, bitterly attacked by bourgeois elements. Its chief exponent was ALUÍZIO AZEVEDO (1857–1913), who had carefully studied the fiction of both Eça de Queiroz and Zola (qq.v.). Azevedo, who wrote six novels for the popular market as well as six serious ones (his collected works were published in fourteen volumes in 1941), could write well, but did not often bother to try to do so. He was above all romantically excited by the notion of delineating the sordid truth. He is a good example of a naturalist. His chief merit is that although he made use of Zola, his material was genuinely Brazilian. He became increasingly more candid in his treatment of sexual themes, until in *The Man* (1887), a study of a sexually hysterical woman, he created a scandal. His most important works are *The Mulatto* (1881), *The Boardinghouse* (1884) and *A Brazilian Tenement* (1890; tr. H. W. Brown, 1928). The first describes a young man's struggle against racial prejudice; the second and third, better as novels, are epoch-making not only for the directness of their treatment of the lives of the lower classes but also for their use of demotic speech. Azevedo can be classified as a genuine naturalist because all his characters are seen by him as at the mercy of irresistible forces. Other naturalists included Julío César Ribeiro (1845–90), the hero of whose *Flesh* is driven by a sexual instinct over which he has no control, HERCULANO MARCOS INGLÊS DE SOUSA (1853–1918), Adolfo Caminha (1867–97), DOMINGOS OLYMPIO (1850–1906) and Raul Pompéia (1863–95), whose *The Athenum*, about boarding-school life, has been called 'one of the ten best Brazilian books of all time'. The sources of the fiction of HENRIQUE COELHO NETO (1864–1934), who was at the end of his life put up by the Brazilian Academy as a Nobel candidate, are naturalist, although he himself rejected the theories. He was initially more influenced by Flaubert than by Zola; but his master was undoubtedly Eça de Queiroz. His most thoroughgoingly naturalist novel is *Mirages* (1895), in which there are effective descriptions of the *sertão*. There was never an organized naturalist movement in Brazil—in this sense it may be called frustrated—but the genre left its mark indelibly on the literature. The influence of the environmentalist, materialist and proto-behaviourist Taine is decisive in Brazilian literature, even if it charges only one pole of the dynamo generating it.

Naturalism thus affected Brazil's greatest novelist—one of the giants of world literature—the 'myopic, epileptic quadroon', 'rickety' and stammering JOAQUIM MARIA MACHADO DE ASSIS (1839–1908), the quintessential Brazilian whose genius shook Brazilianism to its foundation by questioning its every aspect. He began as a moderately sentimental romantic; but the mature work of this rather frigidly mannered, publicly restrained but privately warm pessimist entirely transcends categories and movements, whose exaggerations he as a critic always resisted. Machado de Assis, who spent most of his life working as a bureaucrat, is not a wholly nineteenth-century figure: in many respects he anticipates the modern novel; his attitude, although influenced, inevitably, by romanticism, realism, naturalism and symbolism, is not nineteenth- but twentieth-century. For Machado de Assis the imagination is autonomous; he claims that he exists validly not in his life but in his writing; he does not believe in human progress or in the changeability of man for the better; he creates his own world, but deliberately leaves ellipses; he knows that fiction is fiction, that characters in books are characters in books; he is an ironic comedian in the modern manner —the modern manner that Meredith (q.v.), whom he must have read, tried to but could not quite achieve. Machado de Assis was, above all, an absolute sceptic: 'the most completely disenchanted writer', says one of his translators, William Grossman, 'in occidental literature'. Machado de Assis has something of the nobility of a Hardy (q.v.) in face of terrifying convictions: though less obviously emotional and more of a comedian, he feels deeply; even as he condemns Brazil, the subject—at one level or another—of all his novels, Machado de Assis loves and cares for it. His greatest work is in the last five of his nine novels, and in his 200 short stories—three are in *Brazilian Tales* (tr. I. Goldberg, 1921), and twelve more in *The Psychiatrist* (tr. W. Grossman and H. Caldwell, 1963). One of the earlier novels has appeared in an English translation: *The Hand and the Glove* (tr. A. I. Bagby, 1971). Machado de Assis also wrote journalism, opera libretti, drama and a considerable quantity of possibly overrated, but often touching poetry.

Epitaph for a Small Winner (1880; tr. W. Grossman as *Posthumous Memoirs of Braz Cubas*, 1951; 1952) is Machado de Assis' first mature work. In the manner of Stern in *Tristram Shandy*, Machado de Assis begins with the death of his narrator. This Braz Cubas is good-humoured; but there is no mistaking (even if some too cheerful critics have tried) his residual bitterness: when he comes, in the last of 160 (mostly short) chapters, to sum it all up, he can only console himself with one 'small surplus': 'I had no progeny, I transmitted to no one the legacy of our misery'. Machado de Assis, refusing to concede the absolute greatness of Eça de Queiros, whose *Cousin Bazílio* had just taken Brazil by storm, had written (1878) that Luiza 'slips in the mire without . . . repugnance, without compunction . . . she simply wallows'. But a part of him, like his Braz Cubas, is a naturalist. . . . *Epitaph for a Small Winner* parodies the picaresque novel and all 'philosophies', particularly positivism. But what is even more interesting is that Machado de Assis begins with this novel to conduct the same kind of dialogue with his selves as Pessoa (q.v.) was to do in his poetry. In the last five novels Machado de Assis introduces various characters who recur: in *Epitaph* the mad philosopher Quincas Borba appears; the sixth novel, *Philosopher or Dog?* (1891; tr. C. Wilson, 1954), is devoted to him. This is a tragic novel, which features the schoolmaster Rubião and Borba's dog, Quincas Borba, as well as the mad philosopher himself. *Don Casmurro* (1900; tr. H. Caldwell, 1953 rev. 1966)—'casmurro' meant, in Machado de Assis' day, 'stubborn, pig-headed'—is an exception: this is Bento Santiago's own account of how he found himself cuckolded by his own best friend, Escobar. In reality it is an account of a person dehumanized, made horribly aware of his deliberate denial of his own humanness, by deliberately choosing to adhere to his self-pity, his illusory 'rights'. The last two novels, *Esau and Jacob* (1904; tr. H. Caldwell, 1965) and *Ayres Memorial* (1908) are both 'written' by a retired diplomat, Ayres: another old man and another writer. All these 'writers' (Braz Cubas, Bento Santiago, Ayres) are aspects of Machado de Assis himself; so are Quincas Borba, Rubião and others.

Machado de Assis is almost certainly the greatest of all Portuguese-language novelists. He is also a novelist far ahead of his time. There is little in the twentieth-century novel that his subtle, ingenious and sardonic technical procedures do not anticipate. His style—elegant, cool, always restrained—is unsurpassed in the Portuguese language. It is curious that critics invariably ask: where did Machado de Assis acquire his pessimism (those who do not ask the question pretend that he is not really pessimistic). The answer lies in the steadiness of a vision that remained as undistracted by dogma as it was by genteel illusions. But in any case, is 'pessimism' quite the correct word? It is often employed as an opposite to bourgeois cheerfulness; but that is a false cheerfulness, equivalent to self-satisfaction about nothing real. Machado de Assis had his own satisfactions at arriving nearer to the truth.

Brazilian poetry at the end of the nineteenth century came under the influence of the French Parnassian poets (q.v.). The chief representatives of this anti-romantic school were ALBERTO DE OLIVEIRA (1857–1937), a fine technician who had nothing to say, RAIMUNDO CORREIA (1860–1911), whose pessimistic philosophy, although it resembles Machado de Assis', now seems dated—and, above all, OLAVO BILAC (1865–1918). Bilac, who belongs firmly to the nineteenth century although he outlived it, attained great popularity. He, too, was a good technician, and in his erotic and fervid poems he captures about as much poetry as Brazilian Parnassianism was capable of releasing: but even Bilac's work seems dated now. (PLAV)

Those who came under the influence of the French symbolist poets were in a minority, and they were little read; but they now seem superior to their Parnassian contemporaries. Especially superior is the Negro João da Cruz e Sousa, who died in 1898 at the age of thirty-seven. Although a 'Satanist', as decadent in his attitudes as any poet of the Nineties anywhere in the world, Cruz e Sousa's morbidity was genuine—and his poetry is strangely suggestive. He was hailed as a master by the Brazilian modernists (q.v.). The other leading symbolist, though not on a level with Cruz e Sousa, was JOÃO ALPHONSUS DE GUIMARAENS (1870–1921). (PLAV) Apart from these two, Brazilian poetry of the pre- (Brazilian) modernist period was moribund; only Cruz e Sousa responded adequately—in his strange way—to his age.

*

The most important event in Brazilian literature before 1922 was the pub-lication of *Rebellion in the Backlands* (1902; tr. S. Putnam, 1944; 1967; abridged as *Revolt in the Backlands*, 1947), by a journalist called EUCLYDES DA CUNHA (1866–1909). During the years 1896–7 the Brazilian government had sent no less than four military expeditions into the *sertão*, the backlands, of Northern Brazil, in order to crush one 'Antonio the Counsellor', whom the ignorant and poor gathered around and regarded as a holy man. These people, half-Portu-guese and half-Indian, founded a village called Canudos and made it a head-quarters for various kinds of criminal and revolutionary activity. The Messiah himself forecast the end of the world (as Christ had before him) and built his own church. His outlaws inflicted serious defeats on federal troops before being slaughtered by a force that vastly outnumbered them. Cunha, a victim of nineteenth-century ideas about racial superiority, could not understand why these half-breeds (whom he really admired) could have put up such fierce and intelligent resistance. His book (originally written as a newspaper account) contains some fictional elements, but it is not a novel; nevertheless, it is a work of art, and one in which creative imagination takes precedence over racist theories (held in good faith at that time by most, though by no means all, 'educated' people). This book, which described the *sertão* in all its aspects, awakened many consciences: Cunha asked why its inhabitants had been left to dwell in ignorance. He assumed the superiority of 'civilized' and European ways; but he did not lie. And he wrote well. *Rebellion in the Backlands* is the first literary work in Brazil—Machado de Assis cannot be described as a social novelist—to face Brazilian social problems adequately and with imagination. The part of the picture that he was unable to see, or failed to convey accurately, was filled in by an important sociological work published in 1933: Gilberto Freyre's *The Masters and the Slaves* (tr. S. Putnam, 1946 rev. 1956). This followed another valuable work, not heeded at the time of its publication in 1917: Alberto Torres' *The Problem of Brazilian Nationality*.

Another influential book that appeared at the beginning of the century was the novel *Canaan* (1902; tr. M. J. Lorente, 1920) by JOSÉ PEREIRA DE GRAÇA ARANHA (1868–1931). This is about two Germans who join a community that has settled in the interior. One of them believes in the future of a European-directed society; the other believes that the Western world is in decline. There is some disagreement as to whether this gives a truthful picture of the Brazilians, or whether Graça Aranha was basically conventional in his attitude. Certainly he is successful in recording the impact of the fantastic Brazilian world on European sensibilities. Later Graça Aranha, who has been described as a 'literary opportunist', supported (without properly understanding) the Brazilian modernist movement.

The satirist MONTEIRO LOBATO (1882–1948) wrote, in *Urupês* (1918), a humorous classic: the account of a real—rather than an official—Brazilian, Jeca Tatú, who is lovable but hardly a man likely to solve any of the problems of society. He is a hard-headed peasant, and is presented with devastating realism. Lobato at first attacked Brazilian modernism; later he became converted to it. *Urupês* is certainly a part of its history.

The movement known as Brazilian modernism began officially with the Modern Art Week Exhibition in São Paulo in February 1922. But it had been gathering force for a decade. The only satisfactory definition of modernism is, quite simply, the whole modern movement in Brazilian letters. As so often happens, it was a painter who was among the first to employ modernist procedures: this was Anita Malfatti, who had been to Europe and the U.S.A. and had developed a colourful and expressionist style. She showed her pictures in 1914 and 1917, and was in each case (as the modernists put it) 'martyred' by the reviewers. The fiercest attack came from Lobato, who even after his conversion to modernism would not change his mind about her work. Later the modernists found a new idol: the Rodin-influenced sculptor Victor Brecheret, who worked in France and kept his Brazilian friends informed of developments there.

Brazilian modernism was unquestionably expressionist (q.v.). Its sources, like those of German expressionism, included futurism and cubism (qq.v.). The modernists were united more by what they were against (the kind of society that had produced Parnassianism; academic values; respectability; 'backwardness of spirit') than what they were for. But their protest exploded into life during the Modern Art Week, during which a number of them read their poems and called for a new approach. This event became unmentionable in 'decent' circles in São Paulo: modernism had come to stay. The movement was a response to the same sense of self-awareness that produced (1922) a political revolution; this revolution failed, but it produced a party of conscience ('the Lieutenants' Party').

The modernists were determined to break with stuffy, pedantic Portuguese dominance of their literature, and with the 'syphilitic lyricism' (Bandeira, q.v.) of Brazilian poetry. They wanted a poetry written in the Brazilian vernacular, which in turn they sought to discover. They wanted a fused nation—of Blacks,

Indians and Europeans—and they loudly cried out for it. The influences on them were mostly French: Romain Rolland (q.v.), the 'fostering in modern art of an intuition of the tragic spirit of the octopus-like big city'—clearly this was inspired by Verhaeren (q.v.). And, just like German expressionism, Brazilian modernism eventually split up into factions: the Green and Yellow group, which became fascistic; the Brazilwood group, which was socialist but insisted on artistic autonomy; and others.

It was OSWALD DE ANDRADE (1890–1954) who, on returning from Europe in 1912, had been largely instrumental in introducing the ideas of the European *avant garde* into Brazil. But his own poetry is mostly trivial. His historical part in the establishment of modernism in Brazil is important, but he merits the title awarded him by Samuel Putnam: 'enduring playboy of Brazilian letters'. His best work is in the short story and in the novel *The Sentimental Memories of João Miramar* (1924). Oswald de Andrade in his later career resorted to an extreme primitivism (anthropophagy: he used the pleasing and apt idea of a Bishop being eaten by Indians as a symbol), both anti-European and anti-Christian.

More gifted was 'the Pope of modernism', MÁRIO DE ANDRADE (1893–1945), of mixed Indian, Negro and Portuguese blood, who bore much of the brunt of the initial scandal caused by modernist activity. He wrote poetry, fiction and criticism, and was one of the most versatile and forceful personalities in the history of Brazilian literature. If his namesake Oswald ensured the initial impact of modernism, then it was Mário's energy and devotion that ensured its survival. His poetry on the whole fails: it is too courageously and consistently experimental, and most of it functions more usefully as an intelligent (and daring) critical response to his environment than as something fully realized in itself. His fiction is a different matter. When the novel *Macunaíma: the Hero Without Any Character* was published in 1928 it was regarded as a failure. But its language, a 'Brazilian' synthesized from 'all the idioms and all the particular dialects of all the localities of Brazil' and 'combined arbitrarily', was unique in Brazilian writing; one is reminded of Reymont's similarly successful synthesis of Polish peasant dialects in The Peasants (q.v.). The novel is about a kind of Brazilian Robin Hood, a legendary rascal who epitomizes the Brazilian character. Mário de Andrade was the acknowledged leader of the modernist movement in Brazil from the time of the publication of his poems, *Hallucinated City* (1917; tr. J. E. Tomlins, 1968)—the title recalls Verhaeren—until at least 1930. Despite his iconoclastic temperament, Mário de Andrade was a consistently devout Catholic. Unusually for a modernist writer he was a happy and optimistic man who knew (he said) 'how to love giddy youth, defenseless childhood, the Januaries and the dawns'. (PLAV)

Another prominent member of the modernists was the journalist and diplomat RONALD DE CARVALHO (1893–1935), who helped to organize the Modern Art Week in 1922 and who lectured during it on Heitor Villa-Lobos, whose fine music the modernists championed. He had travelled to Portugal in 1912 and established connections with the Portuguese *avant garde* magazine *Orpheus* (q.v.).

His poetry is attractive but indubitably slight, reading (as Bandeira pointed out) like a 'less naïve, less "innocent" ' version of Walt Whitman. (LAP) Of similar stature was PAULO MENOTTI DEL PICCHIA (1892), whose best work was his early long poem *Joe Mulatto* (1917), in some ways a kind of poetic counterpart to Lobato's *Urupês* (q.v.). He was one of those who remained consistently *avant garde* in his outlook, although he rejected Marinetti (q.v.) and the futuristic label. His poetry became progressively more trivial. *Joe Mulatto*, however, remains an achievement: Menotti del Picchia successfully gave the over-tired poetical language of 1917 a much needed transfusion of fresh blood—that of popular and vernacular poetry. (LAP) Other minor modernists include GUILHERME DE ALMEIDA (1890), a master of technique and a fine translator (especially of Villon), CASSIANO RICARDO LEITE (1895), a vivid describer of Brazilian landscape, and RAUL BOPP (1898), whose greatest achievement, the long 'cannibalist' poem *Cobra Norato* (1921), 'the equivalent of the tragedy of fever', is an exciting and inspired exploration of the Amazon jungle.

Of greater stature than any of these is the more independent modernist MANUEL BANDEIRA (1886–1968), whose international reputation rapidly increased during the Sixties. Bandeira, born in Recife, was the great old man of Brazilian letters. For the whole of his long life his health was delicate, the result of tuberculosis contracted when he was a young man. Sensitive, humorous, intelligent, generous, Bandeira is undoubtedly a representative figure; but his achievement may have been somewhat exaggerated: his poetry, good as it is, is not on a level with that of the greatest of the century. Haunted until his middle age (when his tuberculosis was cured) by the prospect of an early death, Bandeira was a poet of enormous simplicity: anti-rhetorical, anti-moralistic, he loved life and, like Mário de Andrade, remained tenderly optimistic. The difference between his and Andrade's poetry, however, is that he touched the edge of despair—it is for this reason that Bandeira wanted 'the delight of being able to feel the simplest things'. He is a master of the colloquial, and his sympathy with the lives of 'ordinary', non-literary people is absolute. Like the theologian Karl Barth, he has had a vision of Mozart in heaven: the angels are astonished and ask 'Who can that be?', and he becomes the youngest of them. His first book, *The Ashes of the Hours*, appeared in 1917—this had its roots in the nineteenth century; his collected works, including prose, were published in two volumes in 1958. Bandeira's attitude and tone are aptly illustrated by the short poem 'Dead of Night':

> In the dead of night
> Beside the lamp post
> The toads are gulping mosquitoes.

> No one passes in the street,
> Not even a drunkard.

> Nevertheless there is certainly a procession of shadows:
> Shadows of all those who have passed,
> Of those who are still alive and those already dead.

The stream weeps in its bed.
The voice of the night . . .

(Not of this night, but of one yet vaster.)
(LAP; see also PI; PLAV)

Another important modernist, whose work takes in all aspects of the movement, is the north-eastern Mulatto JORGE DE LIMA (1893–1953), who practised
medicine for the whole of his life. Jorge de Lima's work could understandably
be classified as 'Negro'; but really it transcends categories. He wrote (initially)
neo-Parnassian, modernist, 'Indianist' and religious poetry; he wrote both
naturalist and surrealist fiction. Although he was sensitive to the exploitation
of the Negro, Jorge de Lima's best early poetry is content to celebrate his nature.
It will ironically state the injustices to which the Negro is subjected ('The white
man stole Daddy John's wife/to be wet-nurse to his children') but does not
usually protest in a strident manner. The narrative 'That Negress Fulô' (1928)
is ultimately more poignant than ironic. *Time and Eternity* (1935), written in
collaboration with another neo-Catholic modernist, MURILO MENDES (1902),
contains more conventional poetry on mystical Catholic themes, written in a
fluent free verse. *Seamless Tunic* (1938), more powerful, describes a world
haunted by strange creatures who disturb the poet's consciousness; his solution
is to reject the world and 'reconstitute poetry in Christ'. He is one of the most
convincing of twentieth-century Catholic poets. He often wrote in a state of
trance-like intensity, which had been preceded by a period of spiritual anguish.
His last, long poem, *Invention to Orpheus* (1952) is flawed by the sections in which
no control is apparent; but there are other sections of great power. Both he and
Mendes became Catholic in 1935. (LAP; PLAV)

Brazilian poetry has gone through two more phases, which are often called
the Generations of 1930 and 1945. The leading figure in the earliest phase, the
second stage of modernism, is the brilliant and versatile CARLOS DRUMMOND DE
ANDRADE (1902). Drummond's early poetry is often fragmentary, ironic, joking,
cryptic. One of the most controversial of the early poems is 'In the Middle of
the Road':

In the middle of the road there was a stone
there was a stone in the middle of the road
there was a stone
in the middle of the road there was a stone

I will never forget that event
in the life of my exhausted retina
I will never forget that in the middle of the road
there was a stone
there was a stone in the middle of the road
in the middle of the road there was a stone.

884

This is a perfect—and a characteristically perfectly casual—statement of one aspect of the modern situation. The proper path is blocked: we must go one way or another, but we remain obsessed with the obstacle. For Drummond de Andrade life itself is an 'impossible' idea. But he seeks brotherhood. He is deeply concerned with the process of writing poetry, and with its 'impossibility'; his own manner is lyrical (as if in direct contrast to his minute metaphysical and phenomenological investigations), humorous, relaxed; he distrusts and ironically uses language to question its own capacities. He is a fascinating poet because the surface of his work is a deliberate refutation of his intellectuality. He is too clever to propound social solutions; but in such famous poems as 'José' he achieves as positive a statement of the position as is possible: 'Key in hand/ you'd like to open the door—/there's no door;/ you'd like to drown in the sea./ but the sea's dried up. . . .' This is positive, since if enough people had understood it they would have acted. . . . In his later poetry Drummond has become more, rather than less, optimistic, seeing love as the ultimate destiny of all human beings—as the substance into which they will turn. He continues, remarkably, to develop. (LAP; LWT; PLAV)

CECÍLIA MEIRELES (1901–65), a Catholic poet, was never exactly a modernist; but she exercised a strong influence on Brazilian modernism, and was regarded as a major poet during the last twenty years of her life—'the greatest woman poet in the Portuguese language'. She is an aesthetic poet, achieving a purity of tone reminiscent of the English poet Kathleen Raine (q.v.) at her best. Her universe is an ordered one, in which all depends on God. But she is not pious; rather she is precise, restrained, unsentimental, exact. (PLAV)

The most important figure in the most recent phase of Brazilian modernism (it is a reaction against it) is JOÃO CABRAL DE MELO NETO (1920), who, like Bandeira, is from Recife. João Cabral is a hermetic (q.v.) poet, who seeks to create an autonomous poetry that will cohere despite the incoherent nature of the universe (his apprehension of which is opposite to that of Cecília Meireles). He has been much admired by the so-called 'concretists'—the pioneers of concrete poetry, which has flourished in Brazil more than elsewhere. João Cabral is a more important poet than any of the concretists; but this movement is significant in the Brazilian context—if trivial in many others—and it casts light on João Cabral's achievement. He has written notable plays.

Concretism has its sources in many things: the experiments of the Swiss Eugene Gomringer; the calligrams of Apollinaire (q.v.); in Brazil, the games of Oswald de Andrade (q.v.); abstract graphic art; the need to abolish mimetic logic and present an *immediate* and precise perception of things-as-they-are; the desire (not realized) to restore to words their original significance. Concrete poetry is essentially based in an aesthetic attitude to the world, and it lacks emotional substance (it tries to lack it, but this is beside the point: its theoreticians are afraid of emotion); it is also an attempt to turn poetry into a graphic art (which it can never be more than partially); it represents an effort to eschew the real, existential issues of poetry. But in the Brazilian context it is also motivated by a desire to create a new artistic hermeticism: to capture the new sociological reality, in a politically vicious context, by aesthetic means. Its Brazilian pioneer is FERREIRA GULLAR (ps. JOSÉ RIBAMAR FERREIRA, 1930), whose poems are trivial experiments but whose project has socio-anthropological significance. The chief defects of concretism, even in a country where it does not attract charlatans, are its solemnity and its basis in pompous aesthetic abstractions.

João Cabral has absorbed all this, but has sensibly decided not to remain limited by it; his poetry is consequently wider in range than that of any concretist, and more healthily open-ended. (LWT; PLAV)

*

The Brazilian theatre, like that of Spanish America, is only just coming into its own. In the nineteenth century only Luíz Carlos Martins Penna (1814–48) was truly distinguished; Machado de Assis's plays are intelligent but not dramatic. ROBERTO GOMES (1892–1922) was a disciple of Maeterlinck (q.v.) who failed to discover an authentically Brazilian objective correlative (q.v.), and killed himself. A dramatist who has achieved international recognition, for his 'mad' monologue *The Hands of Eurydice* (1945), is PEDRO BLOCH (1910). GUILHERME FIGUEIREDO is the best neo-realist. Perhaps the best play to come out of Brazil in the past twenty-five years is *The Rogues' Trial* (1955; tr. 1963) by ARIANO SUASSUNA (1927), which develops north-eastern folk-theatre in a strikingly imaginative manner. João Cabral de Melo Neto (q.v.) has turned his poem 'The Death and Life of Severino' (pt. LWT) into an effective play. The best of the Brazilian Marxist or quasi-Marxist playwrights is ALFREDO DIAS GOMES (1924), whose *The Holy Inquest* (1965) movingly exposes the savagery and hypocrisy of the Brazilian inquisitors. His best play, *To Pay Vows*, was made into a prize-winning film.

*

Most of the important Brazilian novelists of the past fifty years have been concerned with the north-east and its problems, and they have consequently been influenced by both Cunha and Freyre (qq.v.), and by the political events of the Thirties, during which the once (1930) democratic President Getúlio Vargas set up a fascist-type constitution (1937) to protect his personal power from the left (whose spirit, despite a murderous purge, he failed to crush) and (ironically) the right, represented in the person of the futurist and now fascist writer PLÍNIO SALGADO (1901). Another influence on this north-eastern school of writers has undoubtedly been the obstinate and frequently over-extreme anti-traditionalism of the modernist poets. The most distinguished non-north-eastern writer of fiction is MARQUES REBELO (ps. EDDY DIAS DA CRUZ, 1907), whose *The Star Rises* (1938) is an effective evocation of Rio de Janeiro.

The pioneer of Brazil's north-eastern novel is JOSÉ AMÉRICO DE ALMEIDA (1887), who was at one point a liberal presidential candidate against Vargas, having come to this from being a member of Vargas' first cabinet. He is a popular figure in Brazil, and a man of integrity; but his literary achievement has certainly been vitiated by his political involvements. Before his single major novel, *Cane Trash* (1928), he had written an important sociological work, deeply influenced by the work of both Cunha and Freyre. *Cane Trash* deals with a group of north-easterners driven from their homes by drought and their exploitation by the owners of the sugar plantation on which they find work. This is crude as a novel—its stilted language is its chief fault—but the characterization is powerful and the 'message'—that even a man of good will must be defeated when he tries to reconcile the *sertanejos*, the refugees, and the Negro workers—is transmitted without compromise. But it remained for Américo's more imaginatively gifted successors to make even profounder statements about this subject-matter. Five writers are outstanding; each of them is a major novelist by international standards (perhaps this is less surprising when the size of Brazil is taken into consideration).

GRACILIANO RAMOS (1892–1953), whose death was hastened by persecution in the Thirties, is often regarded as the natural successor to Machado de Assis. Too genuinely revolutionary to be a convinced member of the communist party, Graciliano Ramos lived a difficult and unhappy life, in which he remained consistently modest about his own work. But this is as triumphant in the psychological as in the social realm. His first novel, *Caetés* (1933)—this is the name of an old cannibalistic tribe—is naturalistic and gloomy, but Graciliano's Dostoevskian power is already in evidence. After *St Bernard* (1934; tr. 1940), about a man who feels that he cannot change himself (but none the less decides to write a novel) came *Anguish* (1936; tr. L. L. Kaplan, 1946), a masterpiece. The technique employed here has been called that of the interior monologue, but in fact it should be referred to as 'phenomenological monologue': here Graciliano broke with realism. This novel of passion, jealousy and murder is narrated by a madman: a metaphor for the author's own shattered hopes (he wrote it in prison). *Barren Lives* (1938; tr. R. E. Dimmick, 1965) is Graciliano's most positive novel: it deals with a cowherd from the backlands who remains uncontaminated by urban 'civilization'. As a stylist Graciliano Ramos (who published only short stories between 1938 and his death fifteen years later) is unparalleled in twentieth-century Brazilian fiction.

Graciliano wrote much about the towns. JOSÉ LINS DO RÊGO (1901–57) wrote of the sugar plantations. He is celebrated for his five novels that constitute *The Sugar Cane Cycle* (1932–6). This is a partly autobiographical chronicle in which Lins do Rêgo traces the fortunes of a plantation from its heyday to its decline. This is regional literature of universal significance; particularly memorable is the first novel, *Plantation Boy*, about the childhood of Carlos de Mello, grandson of a sugar-planter. The final novel, *The Sugar Refinery*, deals, with candour, with homosexuality in prison. The first three of the series have been translated as one volume: *Plantation Boy* (1966). What he loses by carelessness of style, Lins do Rêgo regains in keenness of observation and psychological accuracy. He added, however, only two more novels of real distinction to his initial achievement: *Wondrous Rock* (1939), which deals with an incident related by Cunha (q.v.), and *Dead Fires* (1943; tr. 1944), which is again set in the late nineteenth century.

JORGE AMADO (1912) has been translated more extensively than Graciliano and Lins do Rêgo, and is better known; but, though a good writer, he is not of their stature. Several of his books are available in English translations: *The Violent Land* (1942; tr. S. Putnam, 1945), *Gabriela, Clove and Cinnamon* (1952; tr. W. L. Grossman, 1962), *Home is the Sailor* (1962; tr. H. de Onís, 1964). The first of these novels is by far Amado's best. Although he is a skilful writer, the bulk of his work is marred by his tendency to distort his material in the interests of a leftism that often seems over-rigid. *The Violent Land* concerns the struggles between various planters for the cocoa groves at the beginning of the century. This is an excellent and objective realist novel.

RACHEL DE QUEIRÓS (1910), who is concerned with the role of women in Brazilian society as well as with her region of the north-east, began her short career as a writer of fiction with an extraordinary achievement for a girl of nineteen: *The Year Fifteen* (1930), an account of the drought of 1915 through which she had lived as a small child. She published only three more novels in the Thirties, and then settled down as a distinguished translator and essayist. (In 1942, however, she collaborated on a novel with Amado, Lins do Rêgo and Graciliano Ramos: *Brandão Between his Love and the Sea.*) *The Year Fifteen* is a sombre and lucidly written piece of realism. *The Three Marias* (1939; tr. F. Ellison, 1963) is a study of the development of a woman's personality against the unsympathetic background of her environment. Its most memorable section deals with the hell of life at a convent boarding-school for girls, whose natural feelings dulled nuns vainly seek to torment into piety.

Of these four novelists, only Graciliano Ramos' technique approached the modernism of JOÃO GUIMARÃES ROSA (1908–69) in *The Devil to Pay in the Backlands* (1956; tr. J. Taylor and H. de Onís, 1963). Guimarães Rosa is Brazil's greatest novelist since Machado. The language of his long, subtly written monologue of a north-eastern bandit who believes that he has sold his soul to the devil is at first reminiscent of Joyce; but where Joyce's interior monologue is part naturalist, part phenomenological, Guimarães Rosa's is (like that of Graciliano in *Anguish*) wholly phenomenological. This is a book about the inside of a man's mind, and for the first time in Brazilian fiction the savage, wonderful and surreal interior is unequivocally equated with the unconscious and instinctive regions of the human mind.

It has been said, and rightly, that Guimarães Rosa both takes up where da Cunha (q.v.) left off and 'on another level' goes far beyond anything '. . . [he] dreamed of'. It is in this writer—rather than in the too ideological Amado, or even Graciliano Ramos and Lins do Rêgo—that the modern Brazilian novel reaches fullest maturity. Like so many Brazilian modernists, Guimarães Rosa has retained his Catholicism, although he has enriched it by his study of Eastern religions. Learned in many fields, he began as a physician, but abandoned this (1934) for diplomacy. Guimarães Rosa is most famous for *The Devil to Pay in the Backlands*—'the English-translation title . . . exactly combines the two elements of myth . . . and the American setting. . . .' (Jean Franco); an 'inane title' (Luis Harss and Barbara Dohmann)—but he made his reputa tion with *Sagarana* (1946), nine stories written in 1938. *Corps de Ballet* (1956) consists of seven short stories and novellas, all dealing with one or other aspect of the *sertão*. It was in this collection (published in the same year as *The Devil to Pay*) that Guimarães Rosa first demonstrated his full confidence and genius. But *The Devil to Pay* is certainly his masterpiece; it is a novel that, although not without (perhaps inevitable) pretentious elements, deserves to be considered along with works by Musil, Broch, Hesse, Joyce, Ford, Lewis, Proust, Céline, Toson, Soseki, Anderson (qq.v.): with the greatest of the century.

The bandit Riobaldo is an ex-jagunço—one of those of whom da Cunha wrote—who tells his story to a modern listener. He became a maverick of the plains because (it seems homosexually) he loved Diadorim—who turns out, however, to be a woman in disguise, after all. Riobaldo's adventures ultimately teach him that the 'devil' has really been his own unconscious impulses: the unknown parts of himself. At times the elaborate and ambitiously allegorical structure of this novel tends to collapse under the weight of its massively observed detail; but of its importance there can be no doubt. In his *New Stories* (1962; tr. *The Other Side of the River*, 1969), very short stories, Guimarães Rosa seemed to be feeling towards what, in a very different way, Broch was trying to do in *The Death of Virgil* (q.v.): to pinpoint reality at what has aptly been described as a 'subliminal' level. He was a writer of similar stature. His last book of stories was published in 1967.

New Zealand Literature

New Zealand has not only to look at the mother-country, but also, jealously and out of the corner of her eye, at Australia; this has affected her literature, which feels itself to be, and is, smaller than that of its neighbour. New Zealand has as yet produced only one major writer, Frank Sargeson (q.v.), but the quality of much of its run-of-the-mill, competent writing—especially the poetry —is somewhat higher than that of Australia. Geographically New Zealand presents a contrast to Australia: where the interior of the latter is harsh, hostile and mysterious, New Zealand is greener and more—in geography-book terms— 'scenic'. Beautiful and mysterious it may be, but it is undoubtedly rather more welcoming.

The beginnings of literature in New Zealand were English. Writers have never had prestige with the New Zealand middle-class, which does not regard creativity as 'honest work'. This has led to some of the sharpest of contemporary English-language satire. Writers have none the less instinctively felt that one of their functions is to record specifically New Zealand experience, which is neither British nor Australian—nor, as C. K. Stead has well said, 'the product of some strange mutation of spirit induced by Pacific sun'. No one can today be interested in the Victorian verses of WILLIAM PEMBER REEVES (1857–1932), who in any case relinquished his interest in literature for politics. The socialist JESSIE MACKAY (1864–1938) aspired to create a genuinely New Zealand literature, and was more intelligent than Reeves; but she did not understand enough about imagination as distinct from worthy social causes, and most of her verse is crude. Superior to Jessie Mackay was BLANCHE BAUGHAN (1870–1958), who was born in Putney, London, and went to New Zealand in 1900. She had less skill, but she looked more closely at what was going on around her, and she also created a popular form all on her own—unlike Australia, New Zealand had no ballad tradition to fall back upon. She was an active socialist and a fighter against injustice and the cruelty of the prison system. She wrote some notable sketches, collected in *Brown Bread from a Colonial Oven* (1912). One might claim her as New Zealand's first innovator, even if a few poeticisms are mixed up in her generally colloquial and unpretentious offering. Her counterpart in prose is FRANK S. ANTHONY (1891–1925), whose works were published after his death. *Follow the Call* (1936) and *Me and Gus* (1938) portray the life of pioneer farmers in a prose that draws fully and freely on genuine New Zealand idiom.

The novelist WILLIAM SATCHELL (1859–1942) made what can only be called the first attempt to describe the New Zealand scene. *The Toll of the Bush* (1905) is about the New Zealand outback; his most famous novel, *The Greenstone Door* (1914), is about the troubles with the Maoris in the Sixties that resulted in their being granted part of the North Island (1870). This is weak in characterization as well as being sentimental, but Satchell's intended objectivity is evident.

KATHERINE MANSFIELD (ps. KATHERINE MANSFIELD BEAUCHAMP, 1888–1923), who married the English critic John Middleton Murry in 1918 (a marriage to George Bowden in 1909 had resulted in an immediate separation), certainly escaped provincialism—she was educated in London, and finally came to Europe at the age of twenty. She was a gifted and delicate author, but has been somewhat overrated as a short story writer. Her stories are often auto-biographical ones; the best, about her childhood in New Zealand, were written soon after the death of her brother Leslie Beauchamp in action in France in 1915, an event which upset her profoundly, since she had just previously spent some months in his company recreating their common childhood back home. It can now more easily be seen that even in these tales—published in the collection *Bliss* (1920)—Katherine Mansfield sacrificed a certain amount of spontaneity to 'art'. Later stories are more tragic; reflecting her fear of loneliness and the consequences of arrogance; they distil the essence of lonely or embittered lives. She died in 1923 of tuberculosis, in Gurdjieff's community at Fontainebleau, after publishing *The Garden Party* (1922); two posthumous collections followed: *The Doves' Nest* (1923) and *Something Childish* (1924). At her very best (in the stories of innocence, about New Zealand, and in later work such as 'Life of Ma Parker') Katherine Mansfield does reach a lyrical perfection, even if her scope is limited in the interests of stylistic effect. But her more substantial writing is to be found in her *Letters* (1928; 1951) and her *Journals* (most complete ed. 1954): here she records her coming to maturity in the face of imminent death, and describes her relationship with the Lawrences—D. H. Lawrence (q.v.) ended their friendship when, in one of the most terrible letters ever written, he attacked her for suffering from the very disease that was to kill him. *Collected Stories* was published in 1945. She is a minor writer of great interest; and she is particularly relevant to New Zealand literature because she wrote her best stories about life there. Probably the supreme example is 'At the Bay', which opens *Something Childish*.

A truly indigenous New Zealand literature began to appear at home in the Twenties. JANE MANDER (1878–1949), in contrast to Katherine Mansfield, was artless and sentimental, but she showed a shrewd understanding of the problems of women living in rural conditions. Her best novel is *The Story of a New Zealand River* (1920); *Allen Adair* (1925) was her most popular.

It was R. A. K. MASON (1905), who studied classics at Auckland University, who wrote the first truly native poems. He made an early reputation, but then more or less dried up in his mid-thirties. Mason is an angry pessimistic radical, a finely lucid poet, a non-Christian concerned wonderingly with Christ. Clearly he has been influenced by Housman and Hardy, and yet his voice has its own rawness and harshness:

> Oh I have grown so shrivelled and sere
> *But the body of John enlarges*
> and I can scarcely summon a tear
> *but the body of John discharges. . . .* (ANZP)

His example has been important to the poets who followed him. Allen Curnow (q.v.) has called him New Zealand's first 'wholly original, unmistakably gifted poet'. Harold Monro (q.v.) took up the cause of his poetry in the Twenties. His achievement may be small, but his place is secure.

MARY BETHELL (1874–1945), whose best poems are perhaps superior to any written by a native New Zealander, was born in England thirty-one years before Mason, but did not publish her first book, *From a Garden in the Antipodes* (1929), until six years after his. This appeared under the pseudonym of 'Evelyn Hayes'. Mary Bethell spent her middle years in England, and did not try to be a 'New Zealand poet', but to adapt the English tradition to the New Zealand scene—in which she was remarkably successful. She is at her best when writing about her garden, at her worst when trying to draw philosophical conclusions. Clearly she had read Lawrence (q.v.), who influenced her first poems, which are, however, more plainly descriptive of nature. Her later work, upon which the influence of Hopkins has been suggested, is more ambitious but not less successful or original. Her *Collected Poems* appeared in 1950. (AZNP)

ROBIN HYDE (ps. IRIS WILKINSON, 1906–39) produced much before her early death. She was born in South Africa, came to New Zealand when young, went to China in 1938 and then on to England, where she died. She was a novelist and poet of high distinction, and her death was a major loss to letters. Her poetry is lucid and tender, and often of considerable subtlety. *The Houses by the Sea* (1952) consists of autobiographical poems, some almost transparent in their intense nostalgia and purity of feeling. Her distinction is well shown in these lines from her sequence 'The Beaches'. She has been watching two lovers—a man seducing a girl—and has afterwards gone to lie in their 'bed':

> I never meant
> To tell the rest, or you, what I had seen;
> Though that night, when I came in late for tea,
> I hoped you'd see the sandgrains on my coat.

Most of her best poetry is in this autobiographical vein. Her fiction was the best written in New Zealand in the Thirties. *Passport to Hell* (1935) and its sequel *Nor the Years Condemn* (1938), in the form of reminiscences told to her by a friend, portray New Zealand before and after the First World War. *Check to Your King* (1936), about the adventurer Baron de Thierry, has been described as New Zealand's best historical novel. (ANZP)

The four writers who dominated the literary scene of the Thirties, associated either with the magazine *Phoenix* (1932) or with the Caxton Press (founded 1935), were all poets. A. R. D. FAIRBURN (1904–57), a lecturer at Auckland University, was the most limited. A kind of more genial and soft A. D. Hope (q.v.), he had a tendency towards rather obvious satire. This was balanced by a not unsentimental lyricism, as in

> He was such a curious lover of shells
> and the hallucinations of water

that he could never return out of the sea
without first having to settle a mermaid's bill. . . .

He is better when sardonic, as in 'I'm Older than You, please Listen', and conversational, but even in this vein he lacks edge. He was most useful as a personality on the literary scene. (ANZP)

CHARLES BRASCH (1909), founder of the important post-war periodical *Landfall* (1947), lived and studied abroad and did not return to New Zealand until after the war. His earlier poetry was less regional in tone than that of his contemporaries, although obviously written by a New Zealander. Like the baby Sebastian in his poem 'Photograph of a Baby' he

> has the air of one looking back, by death set
> free,
> Who sees the strangeness of life, and what things are
> trying to be.

The real subject of his later poetry is just how much it is possible and proper to establish as true, out of a general scepticism. His answers are often in terms of South Island landscape:

> Ask in one life no more
> Than that first revelation of earth and sky,
> Renewed as now in the place of birth
> Where the sea turns and the first roots go round. . . .
>
> (ANZP)

DENIS GLOVER (1912), typographer and founder of the important Caxton Press, is an acerb poet of narrow range but more achievement than he is sometimes given credit for. He has been a significant influence in his capacity as publisher and as printer. He began as a satirist (*Six Easy Ways of Dodging Debt Collectors*, 1936), but in the Fifties broadened out into a sardonic observer of the human scene in New Zealand—with work that is satirical in tone but also often lyrical. His best work in this vein is in *Sings Harry* (1951). Harry is a tough and lonely character through whom Glover seems to be able to express himself most effectively and fully.

> Once the days were clear
> Like mountains in water,
> The mountains were always there
> And the mountain water;
>
> And I was a fool leaving
> Good land to moulder
> Leaving the fences sagging
> And the old man older
> To follow my wild thoughts
> Away over the hill,

Where there is only the world
And the world's ill,
                                    sings Harry.
(ANZP)

ALLEN CURNOW (1911) is the most considerable poet New Zealand has yet produced. He has a versatile technique at his command, and his statements about New Zealand poetry are authoritative. He contends—sensibly—that the New Zealand poet must be regional in order to be international; his own poetry fuses his sophisticated knowledge of New Zealand history with the New Zealand present. He, too, began as a satirist—*Enemies* (1937) was published by Denis Glover—but his scope widened soon, and amply. His potentiality had been shown early on in such lines as 'Fear made the superior sea/The colour of his new car'. Poems such as 'Landfall in Unknown Seas', on the 300th anniversary of the discovery of New Zealand by Tasman (1642), are highly intelligent and display a graceful rhetoric, but are not as successful as his more personal poems. Then he has a wholly original manner of investigating the metaphysical aspects of his experience, both plain in language and yet not over-simplified:

> What it would look like if really there were only
> One point of the compass not known illusory,
> All other quarters proving nothing but quaint
> Obsolete expressions of true north (would it be?),
> And seeds, birds, children, loves, and thoughts bore down
> The unwinding abiding beam from birth
> To death! What a plan!

Curnow's language seems to have been slightly influenced by Dylan Thomas (q.v.), but more considerably by the English Elizabethan and Jacobean poets. His poems, of which there is as yet no collected edition, are rather more impressive in bulk than read singly or in groups in anthologies. (ANZP)

The best-known poet of the younger generation was JAMES K. BAXTER (1926–1972), who established an international reputation. He has been called the 'focus of highest hopes for the future'. He believed in poetry as 'a cell of good living in a corrupt society' and mixed socialism with what has been called a 'histrionic' Catholicism (he was a convert). Rather a self-consciously wild man, although well endowed intellectually, Baxter has written in a number of styles, none of which coheres absolutely. His ballads are fairly successful, but superficial; his most convincing mode is that employed in *Pig Island Letters* (1966): the conversational. His 'wild youth' has remained a consistent theme in Baxter's poetry, which is largely of the hit-or-miss kind: he rejected his own intellectualism as a distraction. Baxter's energy and intelligence are probably sufficient to justify his high position in New Zealand poetry; but except in a few landscape and seascape poems he failed to prove himself a satisfying poet. He remained, disappointingly, over-intoxicated with his own energy, and never manifested convincingly qualities of restraint to balance it. (ANZP)

KENDRICK SMITHYMAN (1922) is possibly the more gifted poet, although the obscurity of much of his work has robbed him of an international audience. But this obscurity represents a struggle for self-expression that is at least sometimes less self-indulgent than Baxter's bursts of vitality. Smithyman can certainly indulge himself in windy rhetoric ('. . . the days of the weeping woman/between the terror of love and the tremor/history shakes in a bride bed. . . .'), and one suspects that he has been over-influenced by George Barker and Dylan Thomas (qq.v.); but when he builds a poem around an objective situation rather than a set of only nominally personal and romantic clichés he discovers a language of his own, as in the syllabic 'Waikato Railstop'. (ANZP)

There are other New Zealand poets of promise and achievement: HONE TUWHARE (1922), LOUIS JOHNSON (1924), C. K. STEAD (1932), an excellent critic, FLEUR ADCOCK (1934), who has published two volumes in England, VINCENT O'SULLIVAN (1937). All these from time to time display linguistic resources of their own to meet their situations.

*

Three writers of fiction are outstanding in contemporary New Zealand literature: Roderick Finlayson, Frank Sargeson and Dan Davin. The work of RODERICK FINLAYSON (1904) is not as well known as it should be. His contribution has been towards the understanding of the Maoris of the country around Auckland, where he was born. He has written a standard work on the Maoris and their culture: *The Maoris of New Zealand* (with J. Smith, 1959). Finlayson portrays the Maoris with humorous sympathy but no patronage, and has reproduced their speech to great effect. *Tidal Creek* (1948) and *The Schooner Came to Atia* (1952) are novels; short stories are collected in *Sweet Beulah Land* (1942). Where Satchell (q.v.), although a pioneer, was forced to oversimplify his Maoris, Finlayson has taught his contemporaries that this is not necessary.

The novelist FRANK SARGESON (1903), born at Hamilton, south of Auckland, is the most important—and influential—writer so far produced by New Zealand. He is an undisputed master of the vernacular, and while never prepared to sacrifice coherence he has not been afraid to experiment—as in the autobiographical *Up Onto the Roof and Down Again* (serialized in *Landfall*, 1950–1). Sargeson belongs to the same hurt, puzzled, liberal-humanist tradition as E. M. Forster (q.v.), who praised him, and James Hanley (q.v.); and the same kind of bruised sensitivity exists below the tougher and more amused surface-skin of his writing. Like so many New Zealand writers, Sargeson began as a satirist, stung to expression by a bourgeoisie that is apparently, judging by what it has invited in the way of protest, peculiarly complacent. His first pamphlet of stories, *Conversation with My Uncle* (1936), satirized suburban life from an orthodox left-wing point of view. But since then he has gone on to make emancipation and spiritual redemption his main theme. His earlier stories suffer from a somewhat crude distinction that he makes between capitalism and the values of the working classes; eventually Sargeson became more concerned with general human values, although he has remained a radical. Sargeson has dealt with homosexual themes more fully and frankly (for example, in *That Summer*, q.v.) than Forster was able to do, but his women—although beautifully observed—are never as subtly presented as Forster's in *A Passage to India*.

It was in *That Summer* (1943-4) that Sargeson's genius first fully emerged: for the first time he revealed both his unfailing ear for local dialogue and his unsentimental compassion. A more leisurely narration replaces the cryptic and laconic style of the earlier stories. *I Saw in My Dream* (1949), a novel set in the early years of the century, traces the revolt of a son from respectable parents to his eventual spiritual victory. Sociologically rich, this is also a skilful presentation of a rather negative figure; critics who said that the hero was 'too negative . . . to excite interest' missed the subtlety that Sargeson had by now developed. *I, For One* (1954), in the form of letters, is a more overt study-in-depth of suburban mentality. *Memoirs of a Peon* (1965) represents a new departure. Its narrator, John Newhouse (i.e. Giovanni Casanova), is intelligent and fully articulate; his account of his rakish progress in the New Zealand Depression is the first picaresque novel in Antipodean fiction. *The Hangover* (1967) deals with the pressures that build up in adolescence; no more convincing picture of the motives behind the behaviour of what is usually known as a 'juvenile delinquent' exists in modern English-language fiction. Sargeson is a major writer, legendarily modest, who continues to go from strength to strength. *Collected Stories* (1969) includes *I, For One*. *Wrestling with the Angel* (1964) contains two plays: *A Time for Sowing*, about the missionary who wrote the first primer of the Maori language, and *The Cradle and the Egg*.

DAN DAVIN (1913), who has for many years worked as a publisher in England, has never actually bettered the short stories in his early collection *The Gorse Blooms Pale* (1947). These are set in the area of South Canterbury, and in the Middle East during the Second World War. His novels cover much the same ground. In a Scandinavian country they would probably be described as a 'novel-cycle', since thematically they are intimately linked. They make use of autobiographical material: Davin differs markedly from Sargeson in having little—some would say too little—faith in his imagination: he deliberately eschews invention. His first novel, *Cliffs of Fall* (1945) is highly melodramatic; it seems to consist in part of bitter self-appraisal, and it probes expatriate guilt. His next, *For the Rest of Our Lives* (1947), based on his war experiences and set in the Middle East, is his best. There is no better account of the New Zealander at war. *Roads From Home* (1949) is set in New Zealand, *The Sullen Bell* (1956) in London. Davin is a sensitive novelist, meticulous in his social observation, but so far without the imaginative depth of Sargeson. His earliest work in the short story suggests, however, that inventiveness is a quality he restrains rather than lacks. Recent novels have been disappointing.

JAMES COURAGE (1903-63) lived for the latter half of his life in England. He wrote well (*The Young Have Secrets*, 1954; *Desire Without Content*, 1950) of the wealthy landowners in Canterbury, showing how their attempts to be 'English' amounted to self-destruction. In 1959 he published what must have been up to that date the most physically candid (though in no sense 'pornographic') English novel in English about homosexuality: *A Kind of Love*. He also left a handful of exquisite short stories. RUTH PARK, who lives in Australia, wrote an excellent comedy of New Zealand working-class life in *The Harp and the South* (1948), but her later books declined into a more forced robustness. MAURICE SHADBOLT (1932) is the most promising of the younger writers. His novel, *Among the Cinders* (1965), is a kind of New Zealand *Catcher in the Rye* (q.v.). *This Summer's Dolphin* (1969) is a more carefully written symbolic work, but too obviously influenced by Patrick White (q.v.); however, it reveals its author as a novelist of potential.

Polish Literature

I

The Polish nation was dismembered in 1795; it did not come into existence again until after the end of the First World War. One of the results of this was that society remained stratified throughout the nineteenth century, and that relatively little industry was developed. But Polish literature is still the most important Slavonic literature (after Russian), and there has been no dearth of good writers since the beginning of the nineteenth century. The great romantic triumvirate consisted of Adam Mickiewicz, Juliusz Słowacki and Zygmunt Krasiński, all of whom flourished in the first half of the nineteenth century. These three poets, in particular the 'national bard' Mickiewicz, helped to inspire the national mood which led to the unsuccessful revolutions of 1863–4. After this defeat 'positivism' came into play: a natural enough reaction to romanticism, and one which fitted in well enough with what was going on all over Europe. Romanticism, it was all too easy for a Pole to feel, led to disappointment and frustration. Positivism ushered in a period of prose.

The four most representative writers of this phase are Prus, Eliza Orzeszkowa, Żeromski and Reymont. All of them, however, transcend the philosophical implications of the positivist movement. BOLESŁAW PRUS (ps. A. GŁOWACKI, 1845–1912), often called the Balzac of Polish literature, took part in the uprising of 1863 and was badly wounded. Although considered the chief representative of Polish positivism, Prus's mature fiction rises above such criteria: the subject-matter of his greatest novel, *The Doll* (1890), is basically romantic, and one must look upon his positivism as innate good sense, a counter to his own romanticism, to the excesses of romanticism (including the excitements of revolution, which almost inevitably spill over into horror)—but not to the romantic spirit as a whole. His early work consists of humorous, observant sketches of Polish life; then he became interested in character, and began to explore it in a series of major novels. *The Doll*, partly autobiographical, contrasts a wealthy merchant's social and commercial aggressiveness with his amorous masochism and wantonness in loving a poor, frigid, aristocratic girl, who spurns him. *The Pharaoh and the Priest* (1896; tr. J. Curtin, 1902) is a brilliant historical novel about a young Pharaoh (invented) who quarrels with his priests. Like *The Doll*, it is a study of integrity and failure. Prus's fiction explores what the American poet Laura Riding (q.v.) referred to in the line 'To each man is given what defeat he will'. Prus himself was a small and timid man, who suffered so badly from agoraphobia that he could not manage to travel away from the suburb of Warsaw in which he lived. (IMPL)

ELIZA ORZESZKOWA (1841–1910), born near Grodno, the wife of an aristocrat who was exiled to Siberia, was another whose 'positivism' was tempered by reservations. She was not against the uprising—indeed, she was associated with it; and she was always a moralist. She wrote over fifty volumes of fiction; the best of it is invariably the least didactic. Her views were confused —her noble ideals of tolerance jostled uneasily with her personal religious bigotry—but when she simply gave accounts of provoked or oppressed people (for example, the Jews) she was perceptive and sympathetic at the same time.

She influenced STEFAN ŻEROMSKI (1864–1925), who was similarly divided, but more tormentedly so. Żeromski, born near Kielce, had a disturbed and unhappy youth, which plunged him into a despair from which he never really recovered. His career perfectly exemplifies the predicament of the post-positivist Polish intellectual brought up in the shadow of the events of 1863–4. All the works of Żeromski's first period, lasting from 1889 (when he made his début) until the turn of the century, are studies in frustrated idealism. The chief novel from this phase is *The Homeless* (1900), about a young doctor whose Promethean dreams of bringing justice to his people destroy him. *Ashes* (1904; tr. H. Stankiewicz-Zand, 1928) is a confused but rapturous Napoleonic epic, unsuccessfully mixing lyrical descriptions of Polish landscape, realistic treatment of battle scenes and philosophical asides. Better as a whole than these, for all their power, is *The Faithful River* (1913; tr. S. Garry, 1943), where the lyrical note predominates. Żeromski's last novel, *Early Spring* (1925), is ambiguous in its attitude to communism (and was accused, in the course of a controversy, of favouring it). It begins with his greatest single piece of writing: a fascinated, terrified description of the Bolshevik Revolution; but it ends with a picture of a free Poland that seemed communist to the officials of the unstable Polish government of the time (in the following year Piłsudski staged a military coup, and Poland remained under a dictatorship until it was invaded in 1939). What is most interesting about Żeromski is not the conflict in him between romantic aristocrat and social realist (shading into naturalist)—which is perfectly understandable, and not unusual—but that between his irritable diabolic impulses and his bland, ecstatic lyricism. His demons, it has been pointed out, 'were perhaps too clearly of Polish origin'; and so he is not perhaps as well known outside Poland as one might expect. (IMPL)

WŁADYSŁAW REYMONT (1867–1925), portrayer of the Polish peasantry, was born in Kobiele Wielkie near Radom. Son of a village organist, he failed both at school and in his first jobs—tailor, vagabond actor, railway clerk, novice monk. He found himself only when he began to use his own experiences in short stories and novels; he learned to become a good writer from life and from actually writing—not from books. In *The Comedienne* (1896; tr. E. Obecny, 1921) and *Ferments* (1897) he described the life of wandering actors; in *The Promised Land* (1899; tr. M. Dziewicki, 1928) he revealed the dehumanizing horrors of urbanization in a story of workers in a Lodz factory. Then, wishing to outdo Zola (q.v.), whose peasant novel *Earth* he found unauthentic, Reymont came to his masterpiece, for which he got the 1924 Nobel Prize: *The Peasants*

(1902–9; tr. M. Dziewicki, 1924–5). This is markedly superior to any of the other peasant epics of the period: Reymont was at the height of his creative powers, he knew and loved what he was writing about—and he was at just the right distance from this material. *The Peasants* is a veritable guide to the Polish village of its period. It is divided into four parts, each corresponding to a season. There is an immense cast of characters, brilliantly handled. The main theme is a father-son conflict, in which Reymont's psychological mastery is seen to much better advantage than it is in his later more self-consciously 'psychological' novels. Undoubtedly *The Peasants* is one of the greatest prose epics of this century; the language Reymont invented to represent peasant speech, without regionalizing it, is entirely successful. His later fiction is less good, although there are hints of a new, Swiftian manner in *Bunt* (1924), in which men are seen from the point of view of animals. Reymont was a naïve (q.v.) writer, whose one masterpiece is the result of intuition rather than thought; his attempts at psychological, religious (*The Vampire*, 1911) and historical (*The Year 1794*, 1914–19) fiction are comparative failures, though not dishonourable ones.

When he was poor and unknown, Reymont's master and model had been HENRYK SIENKIEWICZ (1846–1916), born of a family of rural gentry in the village of Wola Okrzejska in Russian Poland. Sienkiewicz is best known outside Poland for *Quo Vadis?* (1896; tr. J. Curtin, 1898; C. J. Hogarth, 1941), which is not quite fair on him, in view of the renowned and progressively more vulgar film versions that have been made of it. This is a skilled recreation of Nero's Rome: the author indulges his relish for Nero's bestial paganism under cover of some rather repellently over-fragrant Christian nobility. The book, a world best seller, does have merit in its vitality, however. Its formative influence has been acknowledged by, for example, Montherlant (q.v.).

Sienkiewicz began as a positivist, but abandoned this programme when he discovered his flair for the colourful historical novel. He became successful with a war-trilogy set in the seventeenth century: *With Fire and Sword* (1884; tr. J. Curtin, 1895), *The Deluge* (1886; tr. J. Curtin, 1895), *Pan Michael* (1887–8; tr. J. Curtin, 1895). Sienkiewicz's handling of a vast historical canvas is masterly, his power of description magnificent. But in his well-known works—for which he got the Nobel Prize (1905)—he displays no real interest in character. This lack of psychological penetration does weaken some of his more popular work. And yet it is important enough to have inspired Reymont's greater *The Peasants* (q.v.)—and, as has been fairly claimed, the free Poland of Piłsudski that appeared in 1918. A selection of his *Tales* has for many decades had a place in a standard English series of classics. *The Teutonic Knights*, written in the nationalistic style of Sir Walter Scott, and the greatest of Sienkiewicz's historical novels, was available in England from 1944 and helped inspire exiled Polish intellectuals and resistance fighters.

One of Sienkiewicz's most interesting books is the youthful *In Vain* (1872; tr. J. Curtin, 1889), a description of his own disturbed sexuality, set at a university. He was a fine stylist, very badly served by his translators. Another more psychologically oriented novel, possibly his best, is *Without Dogma* (1891;

tr. I. Young, 1893), in which Sienkiewicz examines the division, within himself, between Christian and pagan with more honesty than in *Quo Vadis?*. On the one hand is his sceptical, dilettante hero, in whom decadence is less satirized or caricatured than skilfully analysed; on the other is an over-earnest Christian girl whose sexuality is destroyed by her quest for purity. (IMPL)

Poland's romantic counter-revolution of the Nineties, 'Young Poland', represented the return of European influences (including symbolism, q.v.) and a nostalgia for the values of lyrical poetry as contrasted with those of positivism, which had run itself out as a movement. 'Young Poland'—centred on Cracow in Austrian Poland—was, however, a highly amorphous group, embracing naturalists as well as symbolists, verse dramatists and lesser decadents. What was called 'Tatraism'—after the southern mountains, the Tatras, where the new poets found inspiration—soon gave way to 'satanism' and the artistic hermeticism of STANISŁAW PRZYBYSZEWSKI (1868–1927). Przybyszewski lived in Berlin and wrote in German until he was thirty, when he returned to Cracow. He was a typical *fin de siècle* figure: bohemian, sexually 'shocking', exhibitionist. His novels and plays, though ingenious, are no longer of much interest; but he did, without having a very deep understanding of them, import new and important ideas into Poland: notably those of Nietzsche, and of his friend Strindberg (qq.v.).

The chief novelist of this period was WACŁAW BERENT (1873–1940), who began—*The Expert* (1895)—by satirizing the positivists' optimism and idealism. His own lifelong project was itself partly scientific, however: to reveal 'the genealogy of the Polish soul' through fiction. (He was a marine biologist who both admired and distrusted the objective spirit of scientific enquiry.) *Winter Wheat* (1911) is a remarkable experimental novel in which he gives an account of a night at a fashionable Warsaw house. *Living Stones* (1918) is a recreation of the Poland of the Middle Ages. *The Twilight of the Leaders* (1939) is about the men who ruled in Piłsudski's stead after his death in 1935. Berent is one of those whose intelligent experiments in ultra-realism look somewhat like modernism; but he was no more innovatory in technique—although influenced in his thinking by Nietzsche—than is, say, conventional stream-of-consciousness.

The novelist, painter, playwright and theatrical reformer STANISŁAW IGNACY WITKIEWICZ (1885–1939), born in Cracow, in certain respects never outgrew the *fin de siècle* affectations of his youth; but his eccentric restlessness produced some unusual although strangely carelessly written work. One of his novels predicted communism in Poland; its successor a Chinese invasion of Europe. . . . All his fiction, like his most important drama (q.v.), anticipates post-war concern with sexual fantasy. Witkiewicz committed suicide on the day after the Russians entered Poland in 1939. He is a figure of some importance in the *avant garde*, although his own works are all vitiated by their pointlessly slack artlessness.

MARIA DĄBROWSKA (1892–1965), born near Kalisz in German Poland, continued the tradition of Prus (q.v.): she wrote good, solid, sensible, realist novels. *Nights and Days* (1932–4), a tetralogy dealing with Polish rural life between the uprising of 1863 and the outbreak of the First World War, is her finest achievement: it records—compassionately—the collapse of a social system, and contains several memorable portraits of women. *People from There* (1925), her first book, consisted of short stories evoking the wretched and yet dignified lives of landless peasants. In the Stalinist period she was obliged to translate Pepys into Polish (it being unsafe to write anything but slavishly socialist realist fiction), a task she performed excellently. At the end of her life she was regarded as Poland's greatest living novelist. (IMPL)

The gift of JULIUSZ KADEN-BANDROWSKI (1885–1944), chief spokesman of the Piłsudski group after it returned to power in 1926, was partly destroyed by his eventually fanatic political opinions; to support the official literary policy of any government is a mistake, and this is what Kaden-Bandrowski increasingly did. But his *Black Wings* cycle (1928–33) has sociological value; and there is a wistfully visionary quality about his writing which suggests that his imagination would like to have broken free. *Call to the Cuckoo* (1926), a volume of short stories, was translated into English by H. Linn in 1948. (IMPL)

JÓZEF WITTLIN (1896), who has lived in New York since 1941, is a poet as well as novelist. As a poet he was influenced by Kasprowicz (q.v.) and by the German expressionists (q.v.) and pre-expressionists. Originally he was a member of a group of young expressionist and pacifist writers gathered round the Poznan magazine *Spring*. He is best known for his novel *Salt of the Earth* (1935; tr. P. de Chary, 1939). This was the first of a trilogy; the manuscript of the last two parts was lost when Wittlin was caught in France in 1940; he has been working on a reconstruction. This is a modern epic of 'a patient foot soldier', a bewildered Galician drafted into the Austro-Hungarian army in 1914. This is a lyrical and humorous novel, unobtrusively contrasting the hideous events of history—set in train by the power-crazed—with the sweetness of a simple and innocent man. (IMPL)

FERDYNAND GOETEL (1890–1960), one of the earliest genuine modernists in Polish fiction, had a hard life. Born in Sucha in the Tatras, his father was a poor railway employee. A socialist in his youth, he was interned by the Russians during the First World War and deported to Turkestan. He underwent much hardship there—as he did when he escaped back to Poland through Persia and India. His best writing was done in the Twenties; in the Thirties he was, like Kaden-Bandrowski, a propagandist for the militarist government in power. He was obliged to escape from Poland when the communists gained power, and he died, in poverty, blind and unknown, in London. His important books are the exotic *The Messenger of the Snow* (1923; tr. M. Słomczanka and G. K. Murray, 1931) and *From Day to Day* (1926; tr. W. Cooper, 1931). The second of these, his best, is cast in the form of a diary of a resident of Cracow who is writing a novel about Turkestan, which he incorporates into the text. This is a major novel, and the creative strength that produced it is maintained in two books about Iceland: *An Island of the Cloudy North* (1928) and *Glacier's Heart* (1931). Then—although he was no fascist—despair at his country's predicament drove him into an ideological position, and his work petered out until in 1938 he was turning out such stuff as *Under the Fascist Banner*, preaching 'heroism'. . . .

JAROSŁAW IWASZKIEWICZ (1894), now rightly described as the 'Nestor of Polish writers', was a close friend of the Polish composer Szymanowski. He was one of the founders of the magazine *Skamander* (q.v.); and is as well known as a poet as he is as a novelist. His novels, plays and poetry, however, are not as good as his short stories, in which he reaches the height of his highly self-conscious artistry. He still edits a monthly review. His best work has been done since the Second World War—in, for example, the stories of *The Fragrant Reed* (1960). Decadence and disillusion have been the keynotes of all Iwaszkiewicz's work.

MICHAŁ CHOROMAŃSKI (1904), brought up in Russia, came to Poland in 1924. He began by translating Russian poetry into Polish and vice versa. *Jealousy and Medicine* (1932; tr. E. Arthurton, 1946) anticipates some of the habits of the practitioners of the French *nouveau roman* (q.v.), such as their obsession with objects, but Choromański is more interested in human psychology and less in philosophy. It deals with an obsessed surgeon, Tamten, and a phantasmogoric operation during which he re-lives his jealousies. *The White Brothers* (1931) is a collection of short stories.

WITOLD GOMBROWICZ (1904-69), who lived in Argentina after 1939, began with *Memorials* (1933), a series of fantastic short stories. Gombrowicz, although he blends elements of nonsense, the absurd, irony, social satire and the grotesque into a highly unconventional and unique product, is an unmistakably Polish writer, whose gay humour continually threatens to turn into a convoluted bitterness before the reader's shocked eyes. *Ferdydurke* (1937; tr. E. Mosbacher, 1961), his best book, is one of the oddest concoctions of its time, into which Gombrowicz poured all his concerns with human drives. It is a crazy and yet wise novel (if it should be called a novel), with which the author advises the reader to 'dance'—and not to ask for meanings. He has also written *Pornografia* (1960; tr. A. Hamilton, 1966), *Transatlantic* (1955) and a quirky, intimate diary, much of which appeared in the Paris magazine *Kultura*. This last may prove to be his most enduring work. (IMPL)

ADOLF RUDNICKI (1912), born into a Jewish family at Zabno, has been called the 'Jeremiah of the Warsaw Ghetto'; he is the outstanding Polish chronicler of Jewish life. In *The Soldier* (1933) he gave an account of his military service which aroused some controversy in the Poland of the time (rather as Pennti Haanpää had three years previously in Finland, with *Field and Barracks*, q.v.). Some of Rudnicki's short stories were collected in *Ascent to Heaven* (tr. H. C. Stevens, 1951). Rudnicki is even more than the recorder of Jewish and Polish suffering under the Nazis: he is also an investigator of the psychology of suffering. Even more anguished and sad are the stories of TADEUSZ BOROWSKI (1924-51) who, brave as he was in his stoic endurance of the horrors of Auschwitz, apparently found he could no longer face a pitiless totalitarian aftermath. He committed suicide, but left behind him grim, bare stories of 'man's inhumanity to man' in the hell of the concentration camp.

JERZY ANDRZEJEWSKI (1909), born in Warsaw, is Poland's leading living contemporary novelist. His first novel, *Harmony of the Heart* (1938), was a Roman Catholic exercise of considerable merit, somewhat in the manner of Mauriac (q.v.). *Ashes and Diamonds* (1947; abridged tr. D. J. Welsh, 1962) is an account of the difficulties suffered by Poles during the Second World War; called politically ambivalent—and made into a famous Polish film—it is in fact an essay in realism, which takes the side of communism but refuses to condemn its opponents. He played an important part in the thaw in Polish letters that followed the accession of Gomulka in 1956—in that year he published three allegories, collected as *The Golden Fox*, and in the next resigned his membership of the party in protest against censorship. *The Inquisitors* (1957; tr. 1960) is set in the time of the Spanish Inquisition but is, again, an allegory of modern Poland. *The Gates of Paradise* (1960; tr. J. Kirkup, 1963) is a novel consisting of a single sentence—an achievement for an avowed disciple of nineteenth-century literature. Andrzejewski's earlier work was characterized by a moral passion that not all found attractive; but his most recent book, *The Appeal* (1968; tr. C. Wieniewska, 1970), completes his shift from this position: it is ostensibly a study of the paranoia of a meat-packer, Koniegy, who believes the Polish Counter-Intelligence employ 30,000 agents to watch him . . . It is also a classic satirical account of the experience of ordinary men in Poland today. (IMPL)

The fiction of KAZIMIERZ BRANDYS (1916), who studied law at Warsaw University in the Thirties and stayed in Warsaw throughout the Second World War, arises from the horrors of the Nazi occupation—and then, less obviously, of the Stalinist aftermath. *The Wooden Horse* (1946) and *The Unvanquished City* (1948) are both about the Nazi occupation. The tetralogy *Between the Wars* (1948–51) was less obedient to the rules of socialist realism (q.v.) than any fiction published in its time; *The Citizens* (1955) was actually attacked by official Polish critics. (IMPL; PWT)

MALEK HŁASKO (1931) is a leading representative of the protest literature that emerged after 1956. He is self-taught. He is in the peculiar position of having been attacked both by orthodox socialist realists and by bourgeois Catholics. He left Poland in 1958, and now lives in Munich. His novella *The Eighth Day of the Week* (1957; tr. N. Guterman, 1959) contrasts young love with the dreariness of modern Warsaw. *Next Stop—Paradise and the Graveyard* (1958; tr. N. Guterman, 1961) is an attack on Stalinism. Hłasko is an authentic social (not socialist) realist, with a passionate hatred of injustice and corruption. At heart he is a romantic, appalled at the affront, presented by the shabbiness of power-mad politicians, to the decencies of individuality—and to human nature itself.

II

Adam Mickiewicz, one of those poets so great that his influence has eventually to be challenged for the good of poetry, asked to be called not a critic but a '*wieszcz*'—a prophet, an inspired poet who knows the future in his bones.

'I and my country are me./My name is Millions—because I love/And suffer millions' he wrote. For him Poland—whose unenviable geographical position has resulted in her tragic history—was Christ: it had to be crucified, die and be resurrected—as free and independent.

A reaction to this Polish Messianism, as it is called, had to come. And when it did it was ignored—as Hopkins (q.v.) was ignored in England, his poetry remaining unpublished until nearly fifty years after his death. Cyprian Norwid (1821–83), ridiculed in his lifetime, was only rediscovered by MIRIAM (ps. ZENON PRZESMYCKI, 1861–1944)—himself a minor poet, but important in Polish poetry for his devotion, which included invaluable bibliographical services, to this vital cause. For Norwid fought thoughtfully, and almost alone, against Polish Messianism. He moved from traditional verse into which colloquial rhythms are introduced, to a subtly rhythmical free verse. Norwid's Christianity was more international than that of Polish Messianism; he even interpreted technique in Christian terms. He stands behind modern Polish poetry—and is undoubtedly one of the greatest European poets of his generation. (FCP)

The impact of STANISŁAW WYSPIAŃSKI (1869–1907), mainly a playwright (in verse), was also important. He was a violently uneven writer, but when being himself—as in his play *The Wedding* (1901), based on a real wedding of a poet-friend and a peasant-girl, and on the structure of the traditional puppet theatre —was a great naïve (q.v.) poet. This play, like Wyspiański's best poems (he wrote few, and some are of despair at the syphilis that killed him), combines ecstasy and despair in a genuine folk-drama—a swan-song to the century that had just vanished.

The romantic tendencies implicit in 'Young Poland' first manifested themselves in the decadent, cynical and pessimistic poetry of KAZIMIERZ TETMAJER (1865–1940). But more important is the first major Polish poet of peasant origin (he was born in Szymborze), who enriched a Polish poetry not yet aware of Norwid (q.v.) with thoroughly assimilated elements of folk-lore: JAN KASPROWICZ (1860–1926). He did not reach maturity as a poet until the volume *To a Dying World* (1902), which consisted of 'hymns' whose free verse was based on the metres of medieval penitential hymns. He remained a romantic; but one who reinvigorated Polish poetry because he rethought his romanticism. 'My Evening Song' is characteristic:

> Blessed be the moment
> When the soul's evening hymn breaks forth!
> When from the quiet fields,
> From the stubble and the river bank,
> The lanes and the fallow land,
> The low-lying huts
> And the weather-beaten barns. . . .
> I fashioned you from a willow branch,
> Where flows the silver-blue river,

Where rises the murmuring grove.
Dew collects on the sleepy flowers,
On the meadows and dark wheat fields.
It rests on the lake's curving shore,
Does the soul of this far-spreading land,
And prayerfully stares in its depths.
Then it rises with mist-clouds on high,
O'er the silent, the praying waters.
It listens, and looks, and whispers
Perpetual prayers.
From the hamlets flow sounds of talking,
In the marshes the wild birds answer,
And far in a lonely corner, at a crossroad,
A single candle glimmers within some cottage.

(IMPL; see also FCP)

LEOPOLD STAFF (1878–1957), born in Lvov, began as a member of the Young Poland movement (q.v.), but soon broke with its decadent, *fin de siècle* tendencies. He reminds one, because of his transitions through each of the successive phases of Polish poetry, of the Czech Seifert (q.v.); but he is more poetically gifted, and a more authoritative figure. He did not find his own voice until he was an old man; but, a master technician, he had encouraged and taught younger poets for the whole of his life. (IMPL; FCP; PPP)

The first group signs of a Polish poetic revival came with the re-emergence of a free and independent Poland in 1918: with the foundation of the Warsaw magazine *Skamander* (the river upon which Troy stood). They worked within traditional forms, but were determined to adapt them to modern needs; one may describe the *Skamander* group as moderate modernists. One of their leaders was ANTONI SŁONIMSKI (1895), born in Warsaw. Although he was a pacifist-rationalist, his sardonic manner retains a trace of resigned and self-mocking decadence—an attitude he rejects, but not without irony. He was in London during the Second World War, and returned to Poland in 1950; in 1956 he was in the forefront of those who demanded free conditions for writers. He remains a sarcastic liberal in spirit, profoundly ironic, contrasting the rational with the romantic: 'The moral is in me and the starry sky/Is above me. So what, if Law is disgraced by Oppression?/Let the moons turn unchanged in their courses,/Let at least the sky remain pure'. (IMPL; PPP)

Another co-founder of *Skamander* is Słonimski's near contemporary KASIMIERZ WIERZYŃSKI (1894), who comes from the region of the Carpathian mountains. In his violent youthful poetry he reminds one both of Roy Campbell (q.v.) and (more) of Montherlant (q.v.) in his praise of physical prowess: one of his early poems was called *The Olympic Laurel* (1928), and won a prize for a work honouring sport. His poetry of the Thirties—*Tragic Freedom* (1936)—takes up the theme of the life-force denied by Nazi and communist brutality. He has lived in the United States, in a painful exile, since 1940. His more recent poetry much resembles that published in Poland since the thaw of 1956. His poem 'Europe' demonstrates the force and the linguistic resources of his essential lyricism:

> O bitter, disconsolate love,
> Europe, our Mother,
> Among ancient stones I roam,
> A wood of memories I comb,
> One footprint after another.
>
> I repeat your names,
> I must wonder and admire
> That despite the paltry human span
> You did create some men
> Like Bach, and Shakespeare's lyre.
>
> A golden-pink façade
> In Salamanca smiles with grace,
> And your seductive spell,
> Smiles at the Venetian shell,
> The secret of your hand and face.
>
> O lovely Mother, this rescues me,
> To save you, too, my thought aspires,
> Europe, the requiem for my closest deaths, you
> Motherland of evening melody,
> Of Parisian revelry,
> Of Gothic rose-windows,
> And holy spires.
>
> (IMPL; see also PPP)

The two other main *Skamander* poets are JULIAN TUWIM (1894–1954), born at Lodz, and JAN LECHOŃ (1899–1956), most of whose poetry was written when he was a young man. Tuwim, one of the popular Polish poets between wars, was essentially a light poet—metrically skilful, exuberant, urban, colloquial—but not always a superficial one. Lechoń, who killed himself as an exile in New York, was once a diplomat; his poetry was the least unusual of the four leading *Skamander* poets, but it has its own academic distinction. (both FCP)

The *Skamander* poets had no set programme: when expressionism (q.v.) and dada (q.v.) were rampant, something more violent was bound to challenge what may have appeared to be their complacency. The chief challenge came from ALEKSANDER WAT (1900–67), although it was not much heeded at the time. The impact of surrealism in the Poland of the Twenties was negligible. Wat edited a left-wing review and became an unorthodox and sometimes provocatively intelligent critic. He spent the Second World War in various Russian prisons, as he was arrested in Lvov by the Soviet secret police for 'obstruction'. Then, after a difficult period under Stalinism, during which he contracted a

serious heart condition, he suddenly published, in 1956, a volume of poetry—
Poems—which attracted the enthusiastic attention of the younger generation.
It was, in fact, a literary sensation. As Czesław Miłosz has observed, 'For a
literary critic it is a curious example of belated fulfilment, and at the same time
of a once-defeated movement taking its revenge. . . .' Wat's poems, written
during the Stalinist period with no hope of publication, are profoundly
pessimistic ('Nothing is final/and evil is fathomless. . . .') but not heavy in tone.
They cram in an enormous amount of learning—Jewish, religious, philosophical,
architectural and other—and are extremely modest both on this account and
on account of the great physical and mental anguish which was their genesis
and is their theme. One of his poems prophesies an age of terror even more
horrific than that of Stalinism, ruled by the 'splendid Cybernetic Hangman
with a disinfected string'. From 1959 until his death Wat lived in the South of
France, where he wrote a small amount of less unhappy poetry. (IMPL;
FCP; PPP)

The Polish poetic *avant garde* is divided into two phases, usually known as
the First and Second Vanguard. As I have noted above, surrealism and allied
movements made no serious impact in this period. But the *Skamander* poets did
attract substantial opposition. The chief leader of this opposition—the First
Vanguard, based in Cracow—was JULIAN PRZYBOŚ (1901–70), who was born
into a poor peasant family in southern Poland. Przyboś wrote few substantial
poems; but he is acknowledged as an important influence on Polish poetry.
His rather dogmatic view of the nature of poetry may, with proper reservations,
be compared to that of the blander and more hermetic, but similarly theoretical,
Rumanian poet, Ion Barbu (q.v.): he saw the poem as an almost mathematical
construct, and objected to the form of poetry being used for the expression of
emotion. Przyboś also objected to the *Skamander* poets for their use of regular
rhythms and their statements of personal themes. A somewhat sour and rigidly
theoretical technologist, Przyboś was not an altogether attractive figure. Indeed,
most of the poetry of the First Vanguard is nearer to prose than to free verse.
But Przyboś in his own best poetry can be oddly pleasant—especially, of course,
where he loses the complete control that he foolishly prescribed the poet to have
over his poem, as he did in his patriotic poetry. Przyboś, one of the few Poles
to give positive warnings against the Nazi menace in the Thirties, served as
Minister to Switzerland for some years during the Stalinist period; he wrote
a good deal of criticism. (PPP)

A more attractive and gifted poet is MIECZYSŁAW JASTRUN (ps. MIECZYSŁAW
AGATSTEIN, 1903), who has functioned independently of movements. He is a
distinguished translator from French, German and Russian—and has a close
affinity with Rilke (q.v.) in particular, as his translations from him demonstrate.
He is a poet torn between an urge to contemplate loneliness and an obligation
to witness external events. He was in Warsaw, teaching in underground schools
and publishing resistance poems, during the Second World War—he was in
particular danger, since he is partly Jewish. He therefore well understands
the nature of the conflict between the personal and the political that is

one of the characteristics of Polish poetry from at least 1795. One feels 'the poetry in the pity'—the Nazi oppression, the Stalinist Terror—in Jastrun as keenly as in any modern Eastern European poet. Jastrun's anti-Nietzschean (q.v.) faith—reminding one of Norwid (q.v.), one of his acknowledged masters —in history is beautifully and wistfully expressed in 'Beyond Time':

> I am not concerned at all with the golden age of these pines
> Or the white time of a carnation
> Or the time of dust on the highway
> Or the time of passing clouds.
> Whether I lived an age or an instant loses its importance.
> It is enough to glance into the eyes of a sunflower,
> To grind up thyme in your hand,
> Any scent in the infinitive suffices,
> Any of the usually unnoticed things of the earth,
> Suddenly perceived in such a way
> That their shape with eyelids not quite closed
> Denies transience (of water, of clouds, of man).
>
> (PPP; see also IMPL)

ADAM WAŻYK (1905), who was opposed to the *Skamander* and to the First Vanguard poets, anticipated—and was admired by—the Second Vanguard (q.v.). His early poems were influenced by French poetry and by Apollinaire's in particular. An extremely gifted, not to say 'over-sophisticated' (*mitosz*) man, he has had a most curious career. In his early period he opposed any kind of social commitment. Then, in Russia during the Second World War, he became a convinced socialist realist. During Stalinism he was a 'feared and hated' figure, living in 'an ecstasy of constant self purification, utterly subservient'. Then, after the death of Stalin, he helped to inaugurate the Polish thaw with his 'Poem for Adults' (pt. tr. IMPL), a passionate attack on the very features of the party authority that he had so loyally served. This clearly reflects a severe emotional crisis: 'The nation was working and/philosophical scoundrels attacked us,/they have stolen our brains bit by bit/and left us merely belief'; 'They drink sea-water/and cry—/Lemonade!/They return quietly home/to vomit,/to vomit'. And Ważyk quitted the party altogether. Ważyk is an important poet technically; but much of his work lacks real substance or content, being too satisfied with its own ingenuity or verbal sensitivity. (PPP)

JÓZEF CZECHOWICZ (1903–39), born in Lublin, and killed there by a Nazi bomb, was a more gifted poet, and was just as representative of the *avant garde* as Ważyk. He is important because, like Kasprowicz and Wyspiański (qq.v.), he understood intuitively that Polish poetry ultimately gains its strength from peasant sources. In a few of his poems Czechowicz has something in common with Esenin (q.v.); but his own intellectual urban sophistication is more controlled and integrated into his work: he is not as inspired by pastoral emotion, and is consequently more self-consciously *avant garde*. (FCPP)

The Second Vanguard, inaugurated in the early Thirties, was a reaction to quarrels about form in a time of political upheaval and threat. Because their poems reflected the uneasiness of the times—and prophesied disaster—the poets of this group were described as catastrophists. Its founder was CZESŁAW MIŁOSZ (1911), a cousin of Oscar Miłosz (q.v.). Miłosz left Poland in 1951 and is now a professor in America. Even in his pre-war poetry he tended towards classical forms: 'The term classicism applied to [my] poetry', he has written in a note, 'probably means that [my] experimentation is mitigated by an attachment to old Polish verse'. He is a victim of the same dilemma as Jastrun (q.v.): a modern metaphysical by inclination, concerned—in a manner somewhat reminding one of the Swede, Ekelöf (q.v.)—with the nature of the material universe and its relationship to mind, he is dragged away from contemplativeness by what he calls his 'civic passions'. Unlike Jastrun, however, he has a pronounced strand of sardonic, very Polish, humour. He has written two novels, the better of which is *The Valley of Issa* (1955–7), about his childhood in Lithuania. He is one of the very few poets to fully succeed in fusing elements of the traditional with elements of the truly modern. (FCP)

TADEUSZ RÓŻEWICZ (1921) is one of the most interesting of the post-war poets. He fought with the partisans against the Nazis, and spent the war as a guerrilla, hunted and killing. His experiences led him to dispense (or to try to dispense?) altogether with the problem of *Künstlerschuld* (q.v.) by inventing an anti-poetry that would deny 'art'—an offence to the kind of human suffering that he had witnessed. As Miłosz has said: 'Famine and death are more powerfully expressive than the most inspired poetic stanza or the most beautifully painted picture'. His poetry is stripped of what he calls 'devices'—but not for the brutally egocentric reasons of an Olsen or a Creeley (qq.v.). He is concerned to destroy sentimental or dream values (the solemn marvellousness, for example, of art—which in Poland is held in more profound awe than perhaps in any other European country). When he has sunk into nihilism he has realized it and has tried to pull himself out—but too often the result has been merely to achieve precisely the kind of sentimentality that he wishes to avoid. But Różewicz's 'naked' poetry can be highly effective, as in 'Proofs':

> Death will not correct
> a single line of verse
> she is no proof-reader
> she is no sympathetic
> lady-editor
>
> a bad metaphor is immortal
>
> a shoddy poet who has died
> is a shoddy dead poet
>
> set a cat among the pigeons
>
> a bore bores after death
> a fool keeps up his foolish chatter
> from beyond the grave   (tr. A. Czerniawski)

For a time Różewicz held to a belief in the Soviet Union; his disillusion led to further despair. His plays (q.v.) are also important. A selection of his poetry has been translated by Adam Czerniawski: *Faces of Anxiety* (1969). (PPP; PWT; IMPL)

However, the most celebrated living Polish poet is the less stark, more humanistic ZBIGNIEW HERBERT (1924). It is instructive to compare Różewicz's solution with Herbert's. Herbert had the same kind of war experiences as Różewicz. Herbert, possibly the most distinguished European poet of his generation, represents the independent poet; and yet, as A. Alvarez has pointed out, his poetry is 'unremittingly political'. How could it not be so? Yet his politics are, as Alvarez again well says, a 'minority politics of sanity'. In contrast to Różewicz his poetry is determinedly anti-nihilistic. He has not fallen for any dogma. He would not publish a volume of his poems until he could do so without compromising what he had to say. In style he is cool and laconic, restrained, writing, in short lines, a controlled free verse:

> The real duel of Apollo
> with Marsyas
> (absolute ear
> versus immense range)
> takes place in the evening
> when as we already know
> the judges
> have awarded victory to the god
>
> bound tight to a tree
> meticulously stripped of his skin
> Marsyas
> howls
> before the howl reaches his tall ears
> he reposes in the shadow of that howl
>
> shaken by a shudder of disgust
> Apollo is cleaning his instrument
>
> only seemingly
> is the voice of Marsyas
> monotonous
> and composed of a single vowel
> Aaa
>
> in reality
> Marsyas relates
> the inexhaustible wealth
> of his body
>
> bald mountains of liver
> white ravines of aliment
> rustling forests of lung

sweet hillocks of muscle
joints bile blood and shudders
the wintry wind of bone
over the salt of memory
shaken by a shudder of disgust
Apollo is cleaning his instrument

now to the chorus
is joined the backbone of Marsyas
in principle the same A
only deeper with the addition of rust

this is already beyond the endurance
of the god with nerves of artificial fibre

along a gravel path
hedged with box
the victor departs
wondering
whether out of Marsyas' howling
there will not some day arise
a new kind
of art—let us say—concrete

suddenly
at his feet
falls a petrified nightingale

he looks back
and sees
that the hair of the tree to which Marsyas was fastened
is white
completely

This gives an adequate idea of Herbert's wide range and sure technique. The
translation is from Miłosz's and P. D. Scott's edition of his *Selected Poems* (1968).
(IMPL; PPP; PWT)

III

GABRIELA ZAPOLSKA (ps. GABRIELA KORWIN-PIOTROWSKA, 1857–1921), daughter
of an aristocrat, began as an actress. It was after a scandal—she left her cavalry-
officer husband when she became pregnant by a well-known literary and
theatrical figure in Warsaw—that she took to the stage. In the early Nineties
she was a member of the *Théâtre Antoine* (q.v.), which served her in good stead
when she became a dramatist herself. Her first really important play, still a
Polish classic, was the mordant attack on middle-class hypocrisy, *The Moral
Code of Madame Dulska* (1907), which she called a 'tragi-farce of bourgeoisdom'.
Zapolska, who wrote a number of novels, was basically a sensational and over-

strident writer, but she served her purpose in shattering the conservatism and complacency of the Polish theatre.

The best things to happen in the theatre were in fact Wyspiański's *The Wedding* (q.v.) and his *November Night*, an account of the first night of the Polish insurrection of 1830. In both plays Wyspiański skilfully mixes the real and the unreal: in *The Wedding* men mingle with ghosts; in *November Night* Polish revolutionary heroes mix in with figures from mythology. But these were verse plays, and had little effect on the development of the ordinary theatre. However, they did influence KAROL HUBERT ROSTWOROWSKI (1877–1938), who used some-times to be called 'the Polish Mauriac'. He became a Roman Catholic soon after his theatrical début (1910), and all his plays thereafter are concerned—and, certainly, in a manner remarkably reminiscent of Mauriac—with human depravity and reconciliation with God. His symbolic method, however, is based on Wyspiański's. His best plays are *Judas Iscariot* (1912), *Caligula* (1916) and the trilogy *The Surprise*, *The Way Up* and *At the Goal* (1929–32), which traces the effect of a mother's unwitting killing of her son on two successive generations.

The plays of WŁODZIMIERZ PERZYŃSKI (1877–1930) are still often revived. He was also a poet and novelist; but it is his plays that will last. They are not deep, but few European playwrights of his generation had his mastery of dramatic structure—which he learned from a careful study of French models. He may be compared with Shaw (q.v.) both for his emotional superficiality, his skill and his unsentimentality; but his language is superior to Shaw's (he would never have been able to perpetrate the fake-passion of some of the speeches in *St. Joan*). His first play was *The Prodigal Sister* (1904), and it marked the beginning of a long run of deserved successes.

Stanisław Ignacy Witkiewicz (q.v.) anticipated the theatre of the absurd with his twenty plays parodying Polish classics and politicians of the time. His collected plays were published in Warsaw in 1962, and have attracted increasing interest ever since. Witold Gombrowicz (q.v.) anticipated the same genre. His best, *The Wedding* (1950), is a dream play. Tadeusz Różewicz (q.v.) began his dramatic career with *The Card Index* (1960), a grotesque exercise in overlapping self-memories. In *The Ridiculous Old Man* (1964) he mocks bourgeois child-molestors—and their judges.

The outstanding contemporary Polish dramatist is a satirist: SŁAWOMIR MROŻEK (1930). In *The Police* (1958) the secret police have been so efficient that there is no longer any opposition to the dictatorship—except one suspect, who finally declares himself for the regime. The police have to order some of their own men to become subversives. His most important play, *Tango* (1965; tr. N. Bethell, 1968), is a comic and grotesque attack on stupidity and power—not just the stupidity and desire for power of communist politicians, but of all politicians. Mrożek is an inventive dramatist of real satirical gifts.

Portuguese Literature

The Portuguese are markedly different from their Iberian neighbours (except, for obvious reasons, from the Galicians, q.v.). Although their language resembles Spanish (those with a knowledge of the latter need spend little time in acquiring a rough working knowledge of Portuguese), it yielded much less to the influence of Arabic, whereas it was more pervious to French—as is the culture of those who speak it.

Every one of the few major poets produced by Portugal has had to struggle against or rationalize his own proneness to the elegiac and highly subjective spirit that pervades the literature: *saudade*, which is the spirit of longing, yearning, of sad personal recollection in the sun: a particular, Lusitanian, version of the Mediterranean inclination towards more or less elegant torpor, resignation, acceptance, nostalgia, *laissez faire*.

In the nineteenth century liberalism was active in Portugal, and this eventually led to the flight of the King to England in 1910 and the declaration of a republic. However, no real progress was made in the next sixteen years (there were twenty-four revolutions in this time); in 1926 the army gained power. In 1928 Salazar gained virtual control, and he ruled the country as dictator until incapacitated by a stroke in 1968. In 1933 a constitution on the fascist Italian model was adopted. The government of Caetano, Salazar's successor, has granted no fundamental liberties to the Portuguese people, a majority of whom (for various reasons) probably do not want them. Portugal's exploitation of her African colonies means that an otherwise badly threatened economy is saved—which explains her brutal attitude towards them. However, even the most subtle Marxist analysis of the situation is inadequate—inadequate, at least, to fully illuminate modern Portuguese literature.

The beginnings of the modern literature go back to the formation of the Coimbra group, a heterogeneous movement bound together by a generally liberal and realistic attitude and a desire to relate Portuguese culture to that of Europe; this, arising from a feeling of malaise and decay amongst the Iberian peoples—long stripped of their mighty empires but highly self-conscious of national identity, in the great nationalistic century—was an earlier manifestation of the Spanish 'Generation of 98', and influenced it. In 1871 a number of leading members of the Coimbra group—including the poet Antero de Quental (1842–92) and Eça de Queirós (q.v.)—gave a series of lectures. It is symptomatic that the government suspended these as a threat to state religion. It is also symptomatic that Quental, associated with the foundation of the First International in Lisbon, became disillusioned—he could not reconcile Portuguese workers with his notion of an ideal proletariat—and finally committed suicide; and that another member of the group, the journalist José Duarte Ramalho Ortigão, should have turned into an exotic reactionary and enemy—in his last years—of the republic he had once desired.

The Coimbra generation opposed the milk-and-water, bourgeois romanticism of their time, and advocated a social and realistic literature. The most characteristic member of this positivist group was TEÓFILO BRAGA (ps. JOAQUIM BRAGA, 1843–1924), who was the head of the 1910 Republic (Portugal's only political chink of light). Called 'the most distinguished victim of the systematic method', Braga's creative powers were consistently undermined by his too rigid political and philosophical convictions: he never explores, only states; nobility (that vicious Iberian virtue) takes the place of private curiosity. He is important in Portuguese literature not for his own work but because he helped to draw attention to what he called 'lusismo' (the Portuguese national spirit) even if he got it wrong by over-systematization—and because of his work on popular literature.

The liberal spirit of the Coimbra generation has been maintained, but since the military *coup* of 1926 it has tended, for obvious reasons, to surface in non-political forms. The official authoritarian culture is as valueless as any other official culture. One of those who helped Catholic nationalism to triumph was ANTÓNIO SARDINHA (1887–1925), a proto-fascist and racist who helped to inaugurate the Portuguese version of *Action Française* (q.v.), called *Integralismo Lusitano*. Sardinha possessed considerable skill—as Maurras (q.v.) did—but his works, poetical and critical, provide a demonstration of how such skill may be misused in the interests of a morbid narcissism disguising itself as patriotism.

But the Coimbra generation produced only one creative writer of genius. JOSÉ MARIA DE EÇA DE QUEIRÓS (1845–1900) only just comes into the province of this book. He was an essentially nineteenth-century figure, the writer who established Portuguese realism; but he has dominated the Portuguese novel ever since. A member of the Portuguese consular service, he lived mostly abroad (in England 1874–80). Zola's naturalism was his starting-point, but he soon developed his own art. His fiction profited from being written at a distance from what it described. He wrote to expose the vices of nineteenth-century Portugal—the priest-ridden government, the defects of education, bourgeois hypocrisy—but mostly to jerk his fellow-countrymen out of their apathy. He ended in despair. His best novels are masterpieces of social analysis, and his characters are clearly delineated even when they only serve to illustrate a thesis. For his irony he has been compared to Shaw and France (qq.v.), but he was more creatively gifted than either of these. Besides stylistic elegance, he has the capacity to endow even his minor characters with life—and he is a subtly inventive comedian.

The best of the pre-symbolist poets were ANTÓNIO DUARTE GOMES LEAL (1848–1924) and ABÍLIO GUERRA JUNQUEIRO (1850–1923). Leal was a violently anti-clerical and anti-royalist writer, whose poetry was more distinguished by its technique and procedures than by its content. Junqueiro's fame was established by *The Death of Don Juan* (1874), in which he satirized bourgeois romanticism. His best collection was *The Simple* (1892), in which some have discerned symbolist elements. He was an energetic, audacious poet; but in retrospect is seen to be facile. He ended as an eccentric mystic.

EUGÉNIO DE CASTRO (1869–1944), who was born in Coimbra, was the first to introduce symbolism and *modernismo* (q.v.) into the Iberian countries. This is his chief claim to fame, for his poetry has dated badly: he was more influenced by Moréas, Catulle Mendès and the decadents in general, than by Baudelaire (qq.v.), and here his weakness shows. But he did help to renovate the language of poetry by challenging the empty rhetoric of his predecessors. After a sojourn in France he published *Intimate Dialogues* (1890), introduced by a manifesto; he condemned the poetry of the present as commonplace and asked for (and provided) a lush, archaic poetry in which art is celebrated for art's sake. The movement he inaugurated was given the name of *nefelibata*, cloud-treader. But Castro was a symbolist only in his reliance on word-music as distinct from meaning. He did not explore experience: his is a poetry of skilfully enriched cliché, for cliché lies at its heart. In his later years he gradually moved towards a more classical attitude.

ANTÓNIO NOBRE (1867–1903), from Oporto, was more gifted as a poet. A consumptive, he, too, had lived in Paris. His symbolist experiments, as decadent as—and more egocentric than—Castro's, are also more interesting. *Alone* (1892), published in Paris, collects poems that contrast lyrical regret for Portugal with his sense of alienation from it—on account of his critical attitude and of his romantic solitude, which he contemplated with loving anguish. If Castro contributed the externals of symbolism to Portuguese literature, Nobre's poetry was more fully in the symbolic spirit. (Cesário Verde, 1855–86, was more important than either of these; he anticipated the style and attitude of Verhaeren, q.v., and exhibited an urgency absent from the poetry of his contemporaries.)

TEIXEIRA DE PASCOAIS (ps. J. PEREIRA TEIXEIRA DE VASCONCELOS, 1877–1952) was born in Northern Portugal. Pascoais was a pantheist who believed in the possibilities of a man-created God, forged by effort against the pressure exerted by a supernatural evil. His evolution of his system, which combines the characteristics of unanimism (q.v.) with Bergsonian vitalism, represents yet another Portuguese attempt to overcome basic pessimism. In 1910 Pascoais launched his magazine, *The Eagle*, which inaugurated his cult of *saudosismo*. He claimed that his blend of Christianity and paganism represented the authentic spirit of Portugal, and could cure its ills. But, as is generally conceded, he was really defining the nature of his own genius; his dislike of French poetry and his objections to symbolism were, for example, personal and not Portuguese traits. In effect Pascoais used the framework of the *saudade* (q.v.) to accommodate his own pantheistic ideas: its element of pleasure-pain fitted in very well with his theories about God. *Saudosismo*, to the definition of which Pascoais devoted his poetry, postulates the movements of individual conscience as impulses towards God, who represents the unity of all things; but this unity is attainable only by understanding and effort; evil, the tendency to see things discretely, must be overcome. Pascoais is an interesting eccentric, whose poetry is exceedingly odd; but it is odd not, as one may at first think, because of any linguistic originality, but because of the sheer eccentricity of the ideas lying behind it. Pascoais' most interesting book is his exposition of his philosophy, *Shadow* (1907). His poetry is contained in *Maranos* (1911) and *Return to Paradise* (1912). He exercised a great influence on Portuguese literature. His original movement eventually split up into liberal and right-wing groups: the latter, Sardinha's *Integralismo Lusitano* (q.v.), laid the ideological foundations for the present fascist regime.

At about the same time as *The Eagle* was being launched a group of poets issued the Portuguese-Brazilian review *Orpheus* (1915), which, although only two numbers appeared, marks the beginning of modern Portuguese poetry. The futurism of this group soon petered out; but it led to the more sober modernism of those associated with the magazine *Presence* (1927). JOSÉ RÉGIO (ps. JOSÉ-MARIA DOS REIS PEREIRA, 1901–69) was the moving spirit behind this most important of Portuguese periodicals. A scrupulous and generous historian of Portuguese poetry, Régio's verse is technically conventional but truly modern in spirit in its recommendation of solitary creation as a solution to the problems of the division of spirit and flesh, individualism and communal feeling.

MARIO DE SÁ-CARNEIRO (1890–1916) was born in Lisbon and committed suicide in Paris in the middle of the First World War. He was a close friend of the only major Portuguese poet of the century, Pessoa (q.v.)—at whose instigation, in 1913, he first began to write poetry. Previously he had written only a play and some short stories. It may well be that Sá-Carneiro, in his turn, exercised an influence on his friend. For his time he was quite extraordinarily original. He was one of the leading figures of the *Orpheus* group (q.v.). The title of his first collection indicates his theme: *Dispersion* (1914). The dispersion is of his own personality, which he watched until he could bear it no longer. In one of the poems he predicts his death in Paris; the later poetry is written in a death-haunted awareness of his disintegrating condition. He and Pessoa evolved an essentially modernist procedure which they called intersectionism (*interseccionismo*): it amounts to a sort of primitive hermeticism (q.v.), in which subjective images are interlocked to produce a poetry that has an inner but not an outer coherence. His collection *Signs of Gold* (1937) is composed in this style. He wrote a novella, *The Confessions of Lúcio*, also describing his own mental decomposition; his *Letters to Pessoa* (1958–9) are of great interest. Sá-Carneiro is an important minor poet, with genuine affinities with Rimbaud.

The Portuguese *modernista* movement was influenced mainly by French poetry and by contemporary developments in the plastic arts. FERNANDO PESSOA (1888–1935), who was born, and died, in Lisbon, played his part in all this; but his best work was done later, in literary isolation: unquestionably Portugal's greatest poet since Camões, he was uninterested in the publication of his own poetry, much of which appeared after his death. He was brought up in Durban, and as a result understood English as well as Portuguese. He wrote his first poems in English: *Marais* (1914), *35 Sonnets* (1918), *Antinous* (1918), *English Poems* (1922). These poems are often homosexual in the furtively erotic, English manner of the time; they also imitate English poetry to bad effect. But the sonnets are fascinatingly mannered.

Pessoa spent most of his life in Lisbon, apparently eschewing all forms of sex, living precariously as a commercial translator, drinking, publishing the occasional poem in magazines, admired by a small coterie. He published one book, *Message* (1934), containing possibly ironic patriotic poems that are nearer to the spirit of *saudosismo* than to his own major poetry: this won a consolation prize in a competition.

The major poetry is composed by Pessoa himself and three 'heteronyms', three aspects of himself who, however, also exist in their own right—autonomous, biographically documented—as the poet's fictions. This tells us two things about Pessoa: that he is half-way to a sceptical, Pirandellian (q.v.) view of the non-identity or non-validity of individual personality; and that he wished, for some reason, to escape from his own personality—or to relieve himself of it.

Alvaro de Campos—a naval engineer educated in Glasgow—is a futurist modernist, who writes in a Whitmanesque form: long, rhapsodic lines. Ricardo Reis is a classical pagan, whose poetry is severe and traditional in form. Alberto Caeiro is an intellectual rustic, anti-urban. Pessoa's own poems discuss the difficulties of writing poetry at all. 'Autopsicografia' is characteristic:

> Poets pretend
> They pretend so well
> They even pretend
> They suffer what they suffer.
>
> But their readers feel
> Not the pain that pretends
> Nor the pain that is
> But only their own: that's real.
>
> And so upon toy rails
> Circling reason like an art
> Runs round the model train
> That's known by the name of heart.

This assumes that poetry does have a valid function, but it is ironically puzzled about how 'feigning' can produce such results.

Pessoa said that the poetry of Campos, into whom he poured the wilder side of his nature, was written as a result of impulse; that of Reis he wrote through intensive intellectual deliberation; that of Caeiro, to whom he gave the shortest lifespan, came from inspiration.

All this makes for one of the most remarkable bodies of work of the century: Pessoa's solution is not cubist (q.v.)—simultaneous expression of differing aspects of his vision—but 'heteronymous'. Pessoa, in his lonely isolation, is one of the few to have approached a solution of the problem of the sophisticated, sentimentive (q.v.) poet cut off from the poetically essential 'naïve' (q.v.) sources: he solves it by the grand imaginative act of granting autonomy to the sides of himself that most self-evidently crystallize. The result is really a dramatic dialogue (Pessoa had his poets engage in polemics with one another). Pessoa's own metaphysics are contrasted with Campos' modernism, this with Reis's traditionalism; and all is subsumed under Caeiro's awareness of the sensual world. Caeiro, significantly, is the poet of inspiration. Pessoa shows as great an awareness of the problems facing the twentieth-century poet as anyone of his time. *Selected Poems* (tr. E. Honig, 1971) is a useful comprehensive introduction.

By the time the magazine *Presence* had established itself, Pessoa had virtually withdrawn from literary life. One of the chief influences on the writers who founded it was the poet CAMILO PESSANHA (1867–1926), born in Coimbra. Pessanha could be described as Portugal's Arthur Waley (q.v.), since he translated Chinese poetry into a Portuguese verse very much of his own invention; but he was probably more original than Waley (whose own poems are negligible, as he tacitly acknowledged), and he was in any case not introducing an orientalist tradition, but merely sustaining it—the Portuguese had been in Macao long before he went there as a teacher, and had long been susceptible to its influence. Pessanha translated Chinese poems into an exquisite Portuguese, but his style owed as much to French as to oriental influences—and managed to make the result look entirely native. One might describe his poetry, therefore, as a cross between Chinese humorous disillusion and French symbolist yearning for a Platonic world to be located within the individual—but expressed in a wholly Portuguese, nostalgic manner. He was a careful poet, whose fragmentary phrases—attempts to capture the fleeting nature of experience—have a symbolic coherence only sometimes too deliberate. His poems are collected in *The Blue Bird* (1899) and *The Centaur* (1916); and then in the retrospective but incomplete *Clepsidra* (1920).

*

Portugal has had only one great playwright: Gil Vicente (c. 1465–1537). Since the sixteenth century, doubtless for political reasons, the Portuguese theatre has been largely dominated by authors interested mostly in captivating their audiences. JOÃO DA CÂMARA (1852–1908), a pretentious but skilful opportunist, held sway over the Portuguese theatre at the turn of the century: he wrote regional, 'scandalous', Ibsenite and pseudo-symbolic plays, as well as pompous historical dramas, but in none did he risk offending his audience. Since 1926 prospects for a creative writer who wishes to devote himself to drama have been so bad that no one of real stature has emerged. The censorship is vicious and foolish. The Experimental Theatre of Oporto (1953) provides the best possibilities, but the censor is ever present to mutilate the vigorous, the decent or the true—one cannot put it less strongly. The audience for an *avant garde* drama over the censor's head is severely limited. Conditions in this respect are worse than in Spain, where more people are interested in the modern theatre, and have asserted themselves to a greater extent. It is perhaps only a matter of time in Portugal, since the pressure for freedom of expression is continually building up. After the inevitable explosion of minor talent, it seems likely that a more substantial figure will emerge.

Of the older-generation Portuguese dramatists one of the more notable has been JÚLIO DANTAS (1876), who is a poet and writer of short stories as well as a dramatist. A psychiatrist, he could be called Portugal's Schnitzler (q.v.)—but the development-stage is more or less wanting: he has almost always fallen back on trivial subject-matter. His doctoral thesis dealt with the painters and poets in the Rilhafoles Mental Hospital. He made his reputation with the historical melodrama *Severa* (1901), a clever but unimportant decadent variation on an ancient Portuguese theme. The stories collected in *Sick People* (1897) had been better than this: they display considerable insight, and compassion partly replaces the desire to shock by titillation. Dantas' most famous play outside Portugal is *The Cardinal's Collation* (1902; freely ad. H. A. Saintsbury, 1927), a one-act play set in the Vatican. *Roses All the Year Round* (1907; tr. 1912), a sly glorification of sexual irresponsibility *au portugais*, was also popular. Dantas could not attain complete seriousness in his own drama, but he made some good adaptations from foreign dramatists.

Many leading writers better known in other genres have contributed plays: these include Eugénio de Castro, Sá-Carneiro, Brandão and Torga (qq.v.). AMILCAR RAMADA CURTO (1886–1961) was a clever expositor of popular themes such as unrequited love; mostly he wrote 'strong' historical dramas which he disguised as modern plays by the expedient of putting them in rural settings.

The leading younger playwrights are ROMEU CORREIA (1917), LUÍS MONTEIRO (1926), BERNARDO SANTARENO (1926) and LUÍS FRANCISCO REBELLO (1924). Correia scored a success with *The Vagabond with Golden Hands* (1961). Monteiro has been influenced by Brecht. Both Santareno and Rebello are dramatists of social protest (to such extent as they can be). Rebello, one of Portugal's leading dramatic critics, was influenced by the German expressionist theatre.

*

No novelist of the calibre or energy of Eça de Queirós has yet arisen in twentieth-century Portugal. One of the most independent of the novelists was RÁUL BRANDÃO (1867–1930). Brandão, who after a spell in the army made his living by journalism, began in the naturalist tradition, with tales of the poor; but even in his early fiction his philosophical preoccupations emerge. The fundamental conflict in Brandão's work foreshadows a problem of which his successors have chosen to make themselves particularly conscious: it comes down to the simple opposition between individual and social needs. Writers of Portuguese fiction tend to call themselves either 'social' or 'psychological' novelists. This came to a head in 1940, when there was a protracted controversy between the self-styled neo-realists and the *Presence* group, who favoured the psychological novel.

Brandão's work, as a critic has said, never reaches conclusions, but oscillates between 'the inner *ego* and the social *persona* . . . mystical idealism and anarchist nihilism'. The contradiction is partially resolved in his concept of life as a tragic farce, which he expressed as early as 1896 in his *Memoirs of a Clown* (rev. *Death of a Clown*, 1926). He then read Dostoevski; previously he had seen the poor as exploited, now he thought of them as the elect of God because of their wretchedness. But he continued to shift his emphasis from one view to the other: he remained aware of the dangers of the Dostoevskian viewpoint. In his four most important novels—*The Poor* (1906), *The Farce* (1909), *Soil* (1917) and the posthumous *The Poor Man of Pedir* (1931)—he presents the world as a savage arena in which men are driven by an inexorable life-force to seek power that will be useless to them even if they obtain it.

The prolific AQUILINO RIBEIRO (1885–1963), of peasant stock from Beira, was for most of his life regarded as Eça's most accomplished successor. He was a most distinguished writer, and one who never hid his detestation of Salazar's fascism. A supporter of both opposition candidates in the Portuguese 'elections' of 1949 and 1958, he was arrested in 1958, at the age of seventy-three, on the publication of *When the Wolves Howl* (q.v.); but Salazar's illiterate thugs, puzzled by the weight and extent of the resultant protest, especially from French intellectuals, hastily released him and recommended him for the Nobel Prize. He had been arrested before: by the monarchist police. He spent the first years of the dictatorship in France.

Ribeiro's first book was a collection of eleven short stories, *Garden of Torments* (1913), written in Paris. Some of these dealt with the Beira peasants. This book incorporates most of Ribeiro's later concerns: use of the vernacular, exposure of the corruptions of Portuguese society (hypocrisy, cruel and greedy exploitation, brutal Catholic tyranny), an almost Brechtian admiration of lower-class slyness in the face of adversity, anti-clericalism, love of sexual pleasure and hatred of the conventions that tend to inhibit it. The fiction of his earlier period is mostly regional, but later he passed to analyses of city life in many different styles. In *Mad Compass* (1938) he comes (not happily) under Proust's (q.v.) influence, whereas in other of his many novels he looked to contemporary developments in Brazilian literature. *When the Wolves Howl* (1958; tr. P. M. Pinheiro, 1963), Ribeiro's only book translated into English, and always said to be 'out of print' in his own country, led to his arrest for 'dishonouring Portugal in the eyes of the world' (i.e. for giving a true picture of her under fascism). It is not a masterpiece—the author's narrative powers showed some signs of flagging after forty-five years of continual writing, with over seventy books to show for it—but its intricate structure was (perhaps not undeliberately) misunderstood by certain British critics who see Portugal as a moral haven and 'bastion against communism'. Its main theme is the conflict between peasants and urban 'experts' who wish to foist an afforestation scheme upon them; secondary themes are a Brazilian hunt for treasure and an old man's pursuit of a peasant vendetta. The whole amounts to an intelligent and subtle exploration of Portugal's role in the modern and in the ancient world. Ribeiro had great feeling for animals, which he expressed in several charming children's books. He also wrote criticism and biography.

The north Portuguese JOSÉ MARIA FERREIRA DE CASTRO (1898) went to Brazil when he was thirteen and spent seven years there, the first four of them as a worker on a rubber plantation. He returned to Portugal in 1919, having begun writing in Brazil. Ferreira de Castro is Portugal's social realist; but he has been clever enough to avoid trouble. After a series of minor works, including *Black Blood* (1923) and *Theft in the Shadows* (1927), he achieved his first success, which is rightly regarded as Portugal's first modern social novel: *Emigrants* (1928). Loosely structured, impassioned, written in a photographic style, this is about the sufferings of Portuguese emigrants to Brazil. His next book, *The Jungle* (1930), an indictment of conditions on the Brazilian rubber plantations, achieved enormous success. Of his later novels *The Wool and the Snow* (1947), a powerful analysis of the producing and manufacturing sides of the Covilhã wool industry, is the most notable. Later fiction abandons the theme of the underprivileged and concerns itself with moral decisions in the face of difficult political circumstances. Ferreira de Castro is perhaps primarily to be considered as an excellent and humanitarian journalist—in the highest tradition. His non-fictional books, which include *Little Worlds and Old Civilizations* (1937–8), are as good as the novels, in which the necessity of invention frequently vitiates the purely descriptive effect.

MIGUEL TORGA (ps. ADOLFO CORREIA DA ROCHA, 1907), who is a Coimbra doctor, is now Portugal's most distinguished living man of letters; he is thought of as his country's automatic candidate for the Nobel Prize (for which Ferreira de Castro refuses to allow himself to be put forward). Torga began as one of the *Presence* group, but soon broke away; poet, diarist, dramatist, novelist and, above all, short-story writer, he is one of the most independent-minded of Portuguese writers. His *Diary*—really a sort of scrapbook—has been coming out at irregular intervals since 1941; each new instalment is regarded as a literary event. Torga is an atheist who uses transcendental language more, it seems, as a kind of rhetoric than to express anything important. He is a gifted writer, but only his short stories (and a single one of his novels) really lift him from a Portuguese to an international stature—perhaps because he aims less high in them. His poetry is his least effective writing: it is accomplished, but its good-tempered protest against life's pointlessness is emotionally and intellectually second-hand. By far the best of his novels, and a fine work by any standards, is *Vindima* (1945), about the ruination of a grape-crop on a Doura estate. Here Torga makes his pessimism convincing. This genuine piece of late naturalism, in which the characterization is outstanding, is reminiscent of Verga in its bright harshness and fatalism; it may interestingly be contrasted with Claude Simon's *Wind* (q.v.), a very different treatment of a similar theme. But Torga's finest work is to be found in his short stories: in *Worms* (1940) and the two *Stories of*

Montanha collections (1941, 1944). The stories of the first book are in that peculiar Latin and Latin-American genre, almost but not quite fabulous, of animal-human fiction. The Montanha tales are more straightforward, and depict—again with the rigour of a Verga—the life of the people in Torga's own province of Trás-os-Montes, where life is backward even in backward Portugal. Torga has also written four plays.

ANTÓNIO JOSÉ BRANQUINHO DA FONSECA (ps. ANTÓNIO MADEIRA, 1905) broke away, with Torga, from the *Presence* group to found a short-lived magazine called *Signal*. Later he took to a fairly conventional fiction, of which the best is *Minerva's Gate* (1947), a vivid and at the same time subtly observed depiction of life at Coimbra University.

JOAQUIM PAÇO D'ARCOS (ps. JOAQUIM CORRÊA DA SILVA, 1908) has a facile, popular side to him, as exemplified in the repulsively whimsical *Memoirs of a Banknote* (1962). His verse—*Nostalgia* (1952; tr. R. Campbell, 1960)—on conventional religious themes, is mediocre. But his *Chronicles of Lisbon Life* (1938–56), six novels, offer something better: altogether harder, in no way middlebrow, and quite different from his other work. They embody a number of sharp and authentic vignettes of Lisbon life. The best of them is *Anxiety* (1940).

ALVES REDOL (1911), who has lived in Angola, is now regarded as one of Portugal's leading novelists. His best novel, *The Man with Seven Names* (1959) was translated into English by L. L. Barrett in 1964.

An outstanding psychological novelist is FERNANDO NAMORA (1919), who is a country doctor, and who (like so many Portuguese writers) was a member of the *Presence* group. He writes, out of his own experience, of the ordinary people to whom he ministers. *Experiences of a Country Doctor* (1949) is a moving account of his struggle against ignorance. *The Disguised Man* (1958), a shrewd psychological analysis of urban life, is a new departure—although Namora's youthful books had tended in this direction.

*

The leading Portuguese poetry magazine was for many years *Cadernos de Poesia* (*Folios of Poetry*). The poets tend to oscillate even more violently between the extremes of order and disorder, structure and anarchy, religious and atheist emotion. No one of real calibre has emerged. A neo-realist movement, which issued a series of volumes called *The New Songbook* (1941), arose in reaction to the often facile modernism of the Thirties; but it was short-lived. Most of the poets involved either faded out or, like Fonseca and Namora (qq.v.), became novelists. However, the vaguely hermetic tendencies of the poets who came after it are only a little more satisfying. ALBERTO DE LACERDA (1928) is sometimes referred to as the leading Portuguese poet of his generation, and he was extremely fortunate to find so excellent a translator as Arthur Waley (q.v.) for his first collection, which is in parallel text: *77 Poems* (1955). Lacerda was born in

Mozambique, and when he came to Portugal his talent was quickly recognized and a whole number of *Cadernos de Poesia* devoted to him. He has subsequently published two more collections. His poems are short and, alas, typical of the best of the current Portuguese style: a somewhat slack mood-poesy, semi-surrealistic. At its best it has a kind of oriental charm, and doubtless this is what attracted Waley:

> Do not touch the lake.
> Do not throw pebbles in it,
> Nor boats of paper, nor dead leaves.
>
> The waters would suffer at being waves.

This has a tiny distinction; but it is a poetry of fancy and not of imagination.

More convincing poets are the politically committed and powerful lyricist EGITO GONÇALVES (1922), notable for his fine poem 'News of the Blockade', and the witty and sardonic ALEXANDRE O'NEILL (1924), a graceful minor poet who has exploited surrealism but is in no way subservient to its programme. The only true surrealist was ANTÓNIO MARIA LISBOA (1928–53), whose poetry wanly but authentically reflects his commitment to death by starvation. The work of the Portuguese 'concretists' (q.v.), the best known of whom is E. M. DE MELO E CASTRO (1932) is considerably less interesting than that of such experimental but non-graphic poets as PEDRO TAMEN (1934) or the effectively sexually explicit MARIA TERESA HORTA (1937). (*Modern Poetry in Translation* 13/14, 1972, contains a useful anthology of twentieth-century Portuguese poetry in translations of varying merit.)

Rumanian Literature

Rumania gained its independence in 1878, and became a kingdom in 1881. Between the wars there was continuous political unrest. In this period the Rumanian upper classes helped to ensure post-war communism by their sympathy with the Nazis. The communists gained complete control after 1947. Rumanian is a romance language, strongly influenced by the neighbouring Slavonic languages. However, the assertion of the Latin element in the Rumanian heritage plays an important part in the literature, the earliest oral manifestations of which are typified by the dramatic ballad *The Lambkin*, which the poet Vasile Alecsandri transposed into a 'correct' form in 1852.

The golden age of Rumanian literature was that of the storyteller Ion Creangă (1837–89), the dramatist Caragiale (q.v.) and the poet Mihai Eminescu (1850–89), 'Rumania's Hölderlin', who before he sank into pathological melancholy (he died in a mental hospital) constructed a body of Rumanian poetry that has never been equalled. The enchanted quality that his marvellous and original handling of the language produces—his themes are simple—is inevitably lost in translation. Eminescu established Rumanian as a literary language.

The literary movement called *Junimea* (Youth) with which Creanga and Eminescu were associated, was divided by a familiar controversy: Titu Maiorescu (1840–1917), a philosopher and critic who became prime minister, was the advocate of artistic hermeticism, while the revolutionary Constantin Dobrogeanu-Gherea (1855–1920), proclaimed the Marxist view. The latter led to the *Poporanist* (People's) movement, which eschewed 'Rumaniadom' and traditionalism in favour of the sponsorship of a socialistically inspired peasant literature. Nicolae Iorga (1871–1940), the historian and politician murdered by Rumanian Nazis, steered a middle course: a nationalist (but not a chauvinist), he sought a literature inspired by the Rumanian village, the institution within which he considered all Rumanian wisdom had been deposited: a kind of '*raison qui s'ignore*'. However, his aesthetics tended to lean towards those of Maiorescu (q.v.); and in fact he was an inconsistent thinker who typified Rumanian confusions rather than helped to resolve them. He, too, was prime minister for a time; one often feels that most Balkan writers of this period—however hermetic—were.

Between the wars the more traditional or independent writers grouped themselves round the magazine *Thought*, which achieved great prestige under the editorship of NICHIFOR CRAINIC (ps. ION DOBRE, 1889). This began in 1926 and ceased publication in 1944. Crainic is a devout and orthodox Christian whose poetic language is unfortunately not more unusual than the ideas he tries to express. Nor did his favoured magazine accommodate many of the better writers. The review *Rumanian Life* represented the opposite tendency. This had been founded in 1906 at Jassy by the revolutionary CONSTANTIN STERE (1865–1936), friend of Lenin—and author of an autbiographical classic, partly cast as fiction: *On the Verge of Revolution* (1932–6). After the First World War *Rumanian Life* moved to Bucharest. The communist magazine of the same title, founded in 1947 and rigidly dedicated to socialist realism (q.v.), cannot be regarded as a true continuation. In the period between wars, and in the two years before 1947, Rumanian writers were able to express whatever ideas they wished; in the past twenty-five years this has been less easy, since literature is state-directed on the usual communist ideological lines. Only poets have had some freedom to develop, and this is perhaps because the party bosses and their 'literary' henchmen do not know what to make of the proliferating styles. Since the deaths of Bacovia, Arghezi, Barbu and Blaga (qq.v.) no substantial figure has yet emerged. One can hardly yet speak of a thaw, despite Rumania's drawing away from Russia. But the Rumanians are a highly cultured people, whose programme of translation from foreign literatures is one of the finest and most ambitious in the world. Certainly a Rumanian Cultural Mission deserves better treatment from the British Council than what it got: entertainment at the Black and White Minstrel Show. One might call this adding British insular injury to the insult of Russian socialist realism: the Rumanians are not philistines. Contemporary Rumanian literature is not as sycophantic to communist theories of art as are those of, for example, Russia or Bulgaria. What is missing, however, is the ability freely to express or overtly make use of ideas alien to socialist realism without being accused of disloyalty to the communist state. A new pronouncement on literature by the Rumanian leader Nicolae Ceausescu in the summer of 1971 holds out little hope.

*

The father of the twentieth-century Rumanian theatre, regarded as the chief forerunner of socialist realism—Rumania's National Theatre (rebuilt since its destruction by a Nazi bomb in 1944) is named after him—is ION LUCA CARAGIALE (1852–1912), a writer of satirical comedies and short stories whose family, of Greek descent, were wandering actors. A humorous but sarcastic and contentious man who finally exiled himself to Berlin (1904), to enjoy a quieter life, Caragiale may be said to have invented the living Rumanian theatre by peopling it with believable characters. In his comedies, such as *A Stormy Night* (1879; tr. F. Knight, 1956), *Mr. Leonida Faces the Reaction* (1879), and *The Lost Letter* (1884; tr. F. Knight, 1956), he satirizes bourgeois life and bureaucracy. He understood far better than anyone of his generation the fundamental human conflicts involved in the modernization of his country; this is what he puts his finger on to such effect. His tragedy of peasant life, *False Accusation* (1889), although a powerful drama, involved him in so much controversy (including an accusation of plagiarism and an action for libel—which he won—against his accusers) that he abandoned the stage. His provincial and seedy suburban prose sketches, dealing brilliantly with humdrum lives, are classics of comic observation.

No other Rumanian writer has made this kind of mark on the theatre. There are, however, certain modern dramatists of merit. RONETTI ROMAN (1853–1908), a Jew who was educated outside Rumania, was a close friend of Caragiale and Eminescu, and, like them, a member of the Youth group. His single contribution to the Rumanian theatre is *Manasse* (1900), a vivid and technically adept picture of Jewish and Rumanian communities living side by side and misunderstanding each other in a Moldavian town. The Albanian-born VICTOR EFTIMIU (1889), whose wife Agepsina was one of Rumania's greatest tragic actresses, has been the director of the state theatres at Cluj and Bucharest. He has written scores of popular novels, but his verse drama is more important. He was the first effective Rumanian playwright to employ symbolic methods: in *Story Without End* (1911) and *The Black Cock* (1913). These deal with characters from Rumanian folk-lore.

The theatre under communism is active and highly developed but as yet too propagandist and rigidly controlled to accommodate truly radical talent. There are over ten times as many theatres as there were before, including special Jewish, Army and Youth theatres. This at least provides a foundation. The director of the National Theatre is Zaharia Stancu (q.v.). Only one man in modern times has looked as though he might have equalled Caragiale's achievement, but he died in a traffic accident: MIHAIL SEBASTIAN (1907–45). Sebastian wrote the two best Rumanian comedies of the century in his last two years: *Nameless Star* (1944) and *The Last Hour* (1945). He was also a substantial, if ostensibly light, novelist, and the author of a remarkably intelligent critical work, *The Past Two Thousand Years* (1934). His was the sort of mind that can change things around it; his premature death was a tragedy for Rumania.

*

DUILIU ZAMFIRESCU (1858–1922), a lawyer by training, began as a poet of promise but ended by becoming perhaps the first substantial Rumanian novelist (as distinct from short story or novella writer). He decisively rejected French influences in favour of Russian. The five-novel saga *The Comanesteanu Family* (1894–1911; pt. tr. as *Sasha*, L. Byng, 1926) is ponderous but of high psychological and sociological quality.

MIHAIL SADOVEANU (1880–1961) is a better writer but not so effective in the novel or in the treatment of urban subjects. He is at his best in novellas of peasant life such as *The Hatchet* (1930), which describes a peasant-woman's hunt for and revenge upon the killers of her husband. This has entered the

Rumanian consciousness perhaps less because of its sensational, though deftly and realistically handled, subject than because of the author's genius for evoking the Rumanian rural scene. A masterpiece, *The Hatchet* has not been translated into English, but is available in a French version: *La Hache d'armes* (tr. B. Vortines, *Le Temps*, 1936). Sadoveanu has written historical and modern novels, and innumerable short stories. He was sixty-seven when the communists came to power, and he decided to go along with them. *Mitrea Cocor* (1949; tr. 1953) is an uneasy essay in socialist realism. Sadoveanu's genius consists of his power to evoke the permanency of nature as contrasted with man's transitoriness. He is Rumania's greatest modern prose writer.

It was LIVIU REBREANU (1885–1944) who developed the Rumanian novel proper. He cannot rival Zamfirescu as a portrayer of urban life, or even as a creator of character; but he introduced objectivity into Rumanian fiction. His novels include *Ion* (1920), an objective and panoramic view of the life of peasants in his native Transylvania; *The Forest of the Hanged* (1922; tr. A. V. Wise, 1930), a war novel based on the story of his brother Emil, who was pressed into Austro-Hungarian service and murdered as a 'deserter'; and the posthumous *The Uprising* (1933; tr. P. Crandjean and S. Hartauer, 1964) on the Transylvanian peasant revolt of 1907.

CEZAR PETRESCU (1892–1961), who was one of Rumania's most popular authors, and who is often compared to Rebreanu, founded the magazine *Thought* (q.v.) in 1921; but it did not acquire its later characteristics until he handed it over to Crainic (q.v.) in 1926. His best novel, *Gloom* (1927), deals masterfully with Rumania's part in the First World War and its aftermath. After this Petrescu devoted himself to a huge and uneven cycle of novels of Rumanian life, of which *The Eyes of the Ghost* (1942) is the most impressive: this reintroduces a character from *Gloom*: a young officer who has been in a coma for twenty years and who escapes from hospital into the changed Rumania of 1937. Petrescu was a skilled novelist—and writer of charming children's books —who eventually diluted his genius by his journalistic facility; but he never lost it altogether.

PETRU DUMITRIU (1924) was originally a literary star of the communist regime, but defected to the West while on a cultural mission to Berlin in 1960. Since then he has started to write in French. His *Chronicle of a Family* (1956–7), the first two parts of which have been translated in an abridged form as *Family Jewels* (1961) and *The Prodigals* (1962), deals, rather in the panoramic manner of Rebreanu, with Rumanian high society from the beginning of the century. It gives a vivid and disturbing picture. Dumitriu, who is not a conservative, gloomily sees totalitarianism as a symptom of general Western decay. The picture of the opportunism of Rumanians in the period 1914–44 given in *The Prodigals* is especially critical. *Incognito* (tr. 1964), unpublished in Rumanian, is a memorable examination of the impact of the communist revolution on Rumanian society. *Westward Lies Heaven* (1964; tr. P. Wiles, 1966), written in French, is an indictment of the rottenness of the capitalist West. But Dumitriu, a worthy successor to Rebreanu and Petrescu, had to leave Rumania to gain the freedom to write as he wished. His later work gloomily suggests that he believes that what he saw in Rumania we shall eventually see here.

*

Eminescu has had few worthy successors: only Cosbuc, Arghezi, Bacovia, Barbu and Blaga (qq.v.) achieve an idiom that is of more than national interest. Eminescu's jealous rival, the quarrelsome ALEXANDRU MACEDONSKI (1854–1920), failed to realize his own poetic ambitions but did introduce symbolism (from France) into Rumanian poetry—and he encouraged Arghezi by publishing him in one of the many magazines he edited during the course of his life. The symbolist theories he himself could not effectively use proved fruitful influences on poets of the next generation.

GHEORGHE COSBUC (1866–1918) is the only important non-modernist successor to Eminescu, against whose pessimism he strongly reacted. He was a gifted translator (Homer, Dante, Byron) and the one conservative writer of real sensibility of his generation. Like Iorga (q.v.), but with fewer doubts and confusions, he regarded the Rumanian village as the proper foundation-stone for literature and political life. He writes eloquently and simply of the peasants and their ways, tapping genuinely primitive sources of wisdom.

TUDOR ARGHEZI (ps. ION N. THEODORESCU, 1880–1967) is Rumania's outstanding poet of this century. From a few years as a monk at the beginning of the century, he graduated to a reluctant acceptance of communism. An avid polemicist all his life, he was interned by the fascists—with many other Rumanian writers—during the Second World War. He had been imprisoned after the First for political offences. He was translated by Quasimodo and Alberti (qq.v.). He is a highly theatrical, frenzied poet, conducting first a vivid dialogue with God, in which blasphemy alternates with praise, and then moving to a poetry of ecstatic contemplation of a malodorous environment in which he still searches for beauty and peace. Later still he arrives at a quieter celebration of nature. His post-war (socialist realist) poetry, written when he was a very old man, is more forced and less convincing. His earliest and best poems are in *Matched Words* (1927) and *Mildewed Flowers* (1930). Arghezi is not perhaps a poet of quite the first rank: he never succeeds in resolving his conflicts, and is sometimes in love with violence and depravity for their own sake—the result of the not altogether assimilated influences of the French decadence and perhaps of Dostoevski. But his rhetoric is extremely eloquent, and he was certainly the first Rumanian poet to see the depraved and evil in the lyrical light of his favourite Baudelaire, whom he translated. He wrote remarkable novels about his monastery and prison experiences. (CRP)

The melancholy GEORGE BACOVIA (ps. G. VASILIU, 1881–1957) kept out of politics, and led an unhappy life of poverty and periodic bouts of pathological depression. He learned much from the French, particularly Laforgue, and was essentially a poet of gloomy cities. He might well have been a crepuscular (q.v.) poet had he lived in Italy; but in his later poems there is a note of Fargue (q.v.). His theme is sadness. But it is a sadness of self: he can welcome a socialist future (quite sincerely) for others. He is always a stylish poet, but an outstanding one when he describes the semi-surrealist, urban visions he experienced in states when his depression temporarily gave way to creative excitement. Bacovia still exercises an influence on young poets. They can learn from him, for he was not the romantic narcissist he seems: his poetry at its best, although keyed to a depressive mood, is one of keen and ironic self-observation: he portrays himself rather than speaks directly. (CRP)

ION BARBU (ps. DAN BARBILIAN, 1895–1961) was a distinguished and important mathematician who became Professor of Mathematics at the University of Bucharest. Understandably, the chief influences on his poetry were Valéry— and his master, Mallarmé (qq.v.). He published only three books of poetry. He spent much of his time towards the end of his life working at a translation of *Richard III*. Something of a poet's poet, he is Rumania's most distinguished representative of the school of what he called 'passion on ice': the expression of vitalist or exuberant emotions in intellectual terms and in intricate and strict forms. The poetry of his first book, *Looking for Snails* (1921) is Parnassian (q.v.) in style, but Nietzschean in content. *The Long View* (1930) contains poems celebrating Rumanian customs and landscape; the third, *Minor Games* (1930), his most important, is Mallarméan in the degree of its withdrawal from reality and reconditeness. The first stanza of the title poem of this volume indicates its subtlety and poetic quality:

> From the hour, deducted, depth of this calm crest,
> come in through the mirror, blue and pacified,
> split out of the drowning of flocks
> in clustered water—a minor game, pure.

(CRP)

LUCIAN BLAGA (1895–1961), a professor of philosophy, is the one important Rumanian poet to have associated himself with Crainic's *Thought* (q.v.). The roots of his poetry are to be found in George, Rilke (qq.v.) and the German expressionist poets; but his thinking was more akin to Iorga's. The communist take-over silenced him, but after his death his poetry began to attract attention again. At his best he recalls the young Werfel: humorous, tremblingly sensitive, sweetly ironic. (CRP)

Much of the poetry currently being written in Rumania is pleasantly surrealist or 'continental' in style, but little is outstanding. Despite his official positions (Director of the National Theatre, President of the Writers' Union, Member of Parliament), of which one may excusably be suspicious in a totalitarian state, ZAHARIA STANCU (1902) writes as well, if as typically, as any. Stancu is, however, an original novelist, and one of the best still working in Rumania. *Barefoot* (1949; tr. 1950) is his best known novel; *A Gamble with Death* (1962; tr. R. A. Hilliard, 1969) is set in 1917, when the Balkan Peninsular was in German hands. Two Rumanian conscripts are captured by police and made to dig trenches. They escape and make their hazardous way back home. One is a club-footed youth, the other a smoother ex-diplomat who has made the transition—if indeed any transition is involved—to con-man. This by no means fulfils the idea of a 'party' novel. (CRP)

Another Rumanian poet of some distinction, a friend of Tzara's (q.v.), and like him almost a Frenchman by adoption, was the surrealist and dadaist ILARIE VORONCA (1903–45), whose verse has more charm than that of many poets who try—as he did not—to be of consequence.

One of the leaders of the younger generation of poets is NICHITA STANESCU (1939), whose chief work is a sequence of *Eleven Elegies* (tr. R. MacGregor-Hastie, *Modern Poetry in Translation* 9, 1971). There is a metaphysical and intellectual quality about some of this difficult poetry that gives it a substance that most of the currently fashionable 'surrealist' or 'hermetic' poetry of Rumania and most other European countries does not possess:

> I fell again into the state of being Man,
> but so quickly that I bumped
> into my own body, astonished to find
> > that
> I had one, and hurt myself. . . .

Surrealism and other *avant garde* modes came very early indeed to Rumania, and some of its proponents have been praised. But most of them in fact tended to rely on modes rather than inner impulse. The poets already mentioned have been the most distinguished—and Arghezi the most distinguished of all; he was unlucky to miss the Nobel Prize in 1964, when he was a candidate.

Russian Literature

I

No Russian writer, whether Tsarist or Soviet, has been free, or has felt free, to express himself as he wished while he lived and published in his own country. The principle of Tsarist censorship was to suppress anything that might tend to subvert the authority of the central government. LEO TOLSTOI (1828–1910) was left alone, after his 1880 conversion to his own brand of Christian anarchism, only because the government judged that by arresting him they would give added potency to his alarming subversive doctrines. The principle of Soviet censorship was at first rather different, and may be summed up in the words of Lenin (whose literary taste was as conservative as his political principles were progressive) in 1905: 'Literature must become imbued with the party spirit. . . . Away with non-partisan writers!' The belief was that the Revolution would change human nature for the better, and that therefore literature must aid in this process. Lenin's own interpretation of this, when he came to power fourteen years later, was thoughtful and broadminded. He saw that literature written by non-communist 'fellow travellers' (Trotsky's term) could be valuable, even though he personally disliked modernism and, of course, as a communist could not allow art any kind of autonomy. Stalin's interpretation was quite different: it insisted on a crudely Marxist line, but in the interests of maintaining a Stalinist dictatorship. The position has remained essentially the same over the past two decades, although conditions have eased from time to time.

But although so tenuously achieved, Russian literature has had to absorb, in the absence of a free press, many of the functions of journalism. Russian literary criticism has thus always involved the consideration of social, economic and (if possible) political problems. Its authority in the creative field is a Russian, not a Soviet, phenomenon.

Tolstoi, although he survived well into the twentieth century, was a nineteenth-century writer who left an enormous legacy to the future—rather than a modernist. Of his three novels, only *Resurrection* (1899; tr. L. Maude, 1911) was written in his latter period. Tolstoi believed (*What is Art?*, 1897–8; tr. A. Maude, 1899) that literature which was not intelligible to the masses, and which did not in effect improve their lives, was valueless. This stands squarely behind 'socialist realism' (q.v.); but Tolstoi, who disliked all governments, would not have approved of those of Stalin and his successors. In the Nineties Russian novelists were in fact less influenced by Tolstoi the moralist than by the works he now eschewed, especially, of course, *War and Peace*

(1865-9; tr. R. Edmonds, 1957) and *Anna Karenina* (1878; tr. R. Edmonds, 1954).

Tolstoi's realism, sensitivity and compassion obviously influenced the works of V. M. Garshin, who died in 1888, and of VLADIMIR KOROLENKO (1853—1921), who was born in Western Russia. His father was a county judge, his mother Polish. At ten he saw his parents divided on the matter of the Polish rebellion against Russian rule; this would not have inclined him towards dogmatism. He was expelled from the University of St. Petersburg and eventually (1879) sent into Siberian exile. He supported the deposition of the Tsar, but not the Bolsheviks, even though they courted him. This was partly because his gentle nature could not accept their violent methods; but also because he had all his life supported the populist movement, which preached a form of agrarian socialism based on the Slavophile mystique of the Russian peasant. Much of his life was spent in exile; in 1881 he was sent to the sub-Arctic province of Yakutsk for refusing to take the oath to Alexander III. Although his prose was directly influenced by Turgenev's, Korolenko was near to Tolstoi in his attitude: he was sensitive to the needs of the poor and downtrodden, but his fiction, which consists of short stories, often goes beyond this to express a sense of the unity of nature. Neither his life, so much of it spent in icy exile, nor the horrors of what he saw, stifled his geniality and conviction that human happiness ultimately depends on an inner peace. *Makar's Dream* (1885; tr. 1892; tr. M. Fell, in *The Murmuring Forest*, 1916), which made his reputation, is a story about a drunken old Siberian peasant who dreams that he has died and is to be judged for his sins; its theme, that the most commonplace reprehensible life has significance, has been called sentimental—but the character of the old man is so vividly and lovingly presented that what might seem sentimental in the abstract is transformed into sentiment. Its quiet humour brought something new into Russian literature. His best work of fiction, and the most characteristic of his genius, is *The Blind Musician* (1885; tr. S. Stepnyak and W. Westall, 1890): this shows a Ukrainian composer, born blind, learning to live in harmony with nature and to accept his deprivation. The most fascinating of all his writings, *The Story of My Times* (1909-22), which he was still working on when he died, has not been translated into English; but Rosa Luxemburg made a version of the first part in German: *Die Geschichte meines Zeitgenossen* (1919). Korolenko is dwarfed by Chekhov, but posterity, especially outside Russia, should have accorded him more attention.

The dramatist and story-writer ANTON CHEKHOV (1860-1904), born at the small port of Taganrog on the Sea of Azov, is no more classifiable than any other great writer. He went to Moscow at the age of nineteen to study medicine, and qualified as a doctor five years later. However, he gained success as a writer, and in 1892 was able to buy a farm near Moscow. But his life was made difficult by his restless temperament and his health: the tuberculosis that killed him first appeared in the year he qualified, 1884. He numbered Tolstoi—in whose ideas he was perpetually interested—and Gorky (q.v.) among his friends in his later life, when he achieved further successes with the four most famous of his plays: *The Seagull* (1896; CP), *Uncle Vanya* (1897; CP), *Three Sisters* (1901; CP) and *The Cherry Orchard* (1904; CP). He died when he was writing at his best.

Chekhov gained his first successes by making his readers laugh. But as tuberculosis gained hold of him so his pessimism grew—but always tempered by natural good humour, care for and interest in the plight of others, and sometimes by political idealism (as in *My Life*, 1895, which was inspired by Tolstoi). Chekhov may be interpreted in many ways, so long as none of them fails to take account of his compassion and pity. He portrays hopeless people, dreaming of action; he does not pretend that they are profound or unselfish, but he is unusual in not satirizing or patronizing them. He recognizes the futility and comedy, but seems to regard the circumstances of life as being most conducive to futility. Soviet criticism has posited a Chekhov as portraying a rotten, passive society ripe for revolutionary change; but while there is every evidence of his deep compassion and understanding, there is none whatever of his faith in revolution. He would, however, have sympathized with this as with everyone else. He is one of the most undoctrinaire, charitable and tolerant of all the writers of really great psychological penetration. If he portrays the decaying gentry then he feels sorry for them. Even if he portrays a selfish *roué* he will somehow contrive to put the best face upon him—but without senti-mentality. Chekhov is very important for this kindliness. It is present in Korolenko; but Korolenko has not the range, the skill or, above all, the high intelligence. Chekhov's realism is not a whit mitigated by his kindness towards people.

During his short life Chekhov wrote six full-length plays, about a dozen one-act plays, some thousand stories and sketches, and miscellaneous non-fiction. As a story-writer he depends not on plot or surprise (as so often in Maupassant), but on atmosphere and the captivation of the sense of a whole life in just a single of its moments. He knew, too, that women were capable of greater nobility than men, and he observed them with the same love and shrewdness as Hardy (q.v.). It is right to see Chekhov as a comedian, a pessimist, a satirist. He is all these. He did not join the symbolist or decadent or realist movements because his art has its own mysterious quality: no one has defined it; but they argue about it as they argue about Shakespeare's. (TC)

The Russian realist fiction of the latter half of the nineteenth century has been muted by the same kind of politeness as the fiction of other countries, such as England and America. In the instances of Turgenev, Dostoevski and Chekhov this did not matter; but it did act as a brake on lesser but none the less gifted writers. The man who freed realism from its conservatism was MAXIM GORKY (ps. ALEXEI PESHKOV, 1868–1936), 'Maxim the Bitter', whose historical and personal importance in Russian literature can hardly be over-estimated. Gorky is indissolubly associated with the rise of the proletariat in Russia, and then with socialist realism. But he changed his attitude; his instinctive inclinations were never quite in accord with his critical pronouncements. However, he did form a bridge between the old and the new Russias. He was born at a town on the Volga that is now called Gorky after him; he was put to work, by the grandparents who brought him up, when only eight years old. The fiction of his earlier period, born of his tough experiences, is concerned with the *lumpenproletariat* rather than the proletariat: its hero is the tramp, and its attitude nearer to anarchistic nihilism than to any constructive political outlook. But there is an element of romanticism in these stories; later it became sentimentalized because the brutal realism contains nothing to justify the romantic dream. Gorky resolves these contradictory elements only in the early work. He oscillated between love and hate of the seamy side of life. On the one hand he saw brutality as simply a solution, which attracted him; but he recoiled from this, which led him to a weak idealism.

Nearly all Gorky's best writing is from his first period, when he was concerned not with a message but just with depicting life. Although he had neither imagination nor style, his reportage is inspired. His unique contribution is his portrayal of late nineteenth-century Russia in its totality, in such fiction as the title story in *The Orlov Couple* (1897; tr. E. Jakovlev and D. B. Montefiore, 1901), the doss-house portraits in *Creatures that Once Were Men* (1897; tr. J. K. M. Shirazi, 1905) and the novel, his first and best, *Foma Gordeyev* (1899; tr. I. F. Hapgood, 1901; H. Bernstein, 1928) and the short stories in *Twenty-six Men and a Girl* (1899; tr. E. Jakovlev and D. B. Montefiore, 1902) .The novel is episodic and its effectiveness somewhat reduced by Gorky's unreasonableness towards the bourgeoisie (his hatred of whose hypocrisy was really a stronger and more defined emotion than his hopes for a socialist future, in which—in his heart of hearts—he hardly believed); but all this fiction is first-hand story-telling of genius: journalism raised—by the author's intuition of what to select, and his masterful reproduction of colloquial speech—to the level of creative writing. In 'Twenty-six Men and a Girl' the only joy for a group of bakers is a girl who comes to buy rolls every morning. Then a soldier who comes to work with them boasts that he can seduce her as he can any other woman. He succeeds, they gather around her angrily—but she treats them with contempt, and their last illusion has been destroyed.

Gorky got himself into increasing trouble with the regime after the turn of the century; after the abortive revolution of 1905, which caused great gloom among all Russian intellectuals, he was arrested and released only through the intervention of Western writers. Until 1913 he lived abroad, keeping up his contacts with the Bolsheviks. *Mother* (1907; tr. I. Schneider, 1947), regarded by Lenin as a model of socialist literature, is sentimental and didactic. *The Confession* (1909; tr. F. Harvey, 1910; R. Strunsky, 1916), ignored in Soviet criticism of Gorky, is the work most uncharacteristic of his true genius; it unconvincingly portrays its hero, a seeker after truth, as rejecting system after system until he comes to embrace a kind of Marxist-Christian unanimism (q.v.).

Gorky returned to Russia in 1913 and supported the Bolsheviks right through until their victory. During and after the Revolution the great nobility and generosity of his personal character emerged: by means of commissions and loans he helped writer after writer to survive in those difficult days. But Gorky's own acceptance of Bolshevism was hesitant; he criticized its dictatorial methods; in 1921 he went to Italy, but kept in touch with the regime. He found himself, significantly, unable to write of Soviet Russia: he brought the novel *The Artamonov Business* (1925; tr. A. Brown, 1935), a fascinated study of the decay of a mercantile family ('a less sophisticated *Buddenbrooks*', q.v., a critic has written), to an end as the Reds commandeer the veteran business man's villa. His last epic tetralogy, *The Bystander* (tr. B. Guerney, 1930), *The Magnet. Other Fires* and *The Spectre* (tr. A. Bakshy, 1931–8), written over the last eleven years of his life, traces the rise of the revolutionary spirit; it is the work of a tired man, and of one who has committed himself to theory rather than imagination. For Gorky finally returned to Soviet Russia, in 1931, and committed himself to the regime. He was welcomed as a returning hero, and became Chairman of the Union of Soviet Writers and the advocate of socialist realism. Although he was Russia's unofficial laureate in the last years of his life, he died under mysterious circumstances—perhaps poisoned on Stalin's orders.

In 1934, at the First Congress of Soviet Writers, Gorky spoke of the main theme of pre-revolutionary literature as having been 'the tragedy of a person to whom life seemed cramped, who felt superfluous in society, sought therein a comfortable place, failed to find it and suffered, died, or reconciled himself to a society that was hostile to him, or sank to drunkenness or suicide'. Gorky the writer was essentially the laureate not of Soviet optimism but of these various kinds of defeat. After his first period the best of his work, aside from the occasional short story, is to be found in his autobiographical trilogy, *Autobiography* (1913–23; tr. I. Schneider, 1953). His *Reminiscences of Tolstoi* (1919; tr. S. S. Koteliansky and L. Woolf, 1948) is also remarkable. Gorky could only try to see the proletariat as the bearer of a rosy future. But he invented the term socialist realism, and although he would have been horrified at the narrowness with which it was later interpreted, the basis of the theory is to be found in his utterances. We cannot understand the climate of Soviet Russian letters unless we understand socialist realism—or its roots in an earlier Russia—and its political background.

After the terrible days of the Revolution itself, when to many people Russia seemed to have died, literary activity slowly renewed itself. For a time, as will become apparent, moderation prevailed. In 1917 the Proletkult was organized; but the good writing, encouraged by such as Trotsky, came from the Serapion brothers (q.v.) and others who supported the Revolution but were not necessarily communists. In 1920 the Proletkult had 300 literary workshops with 80,000 members; by 1924 they had seven, with a membership of 500. . . . The period of moderation more or less coincided with that of Lenin's compromise New Economic Policy (NEP) from 1922 to 1928. In 1928 another attempt to control literature was made; this coincided with Stalin's Five Year Plan. The Russian Association of Proletarian Pencraftsmen (RAPP) had been formed in 1925; in 1928 its spokesmen insisted that art be made into an integral part of the Five Year Plan. The non-political All-Russian Union of Writers, which contained all the best practitioners, and the 'fellow-travellers' (the original term was Trotsky's, and was not pejorative), had long attracted the hatred of the militants who came together to form RAPP. The period of comparative freedom of 1921–8 was ended when RAPP, inspired by a genuinely mystical and religious fervour, was allowed to proceed with a campaign of terror. Their methods, involving the victimization of one or two individuals in an attempt to cow a whole group into submission, were to become familiar in the succeeding decades. They picked on Boris Pilnyak (q.v.), who was Chairman of the All-Russian Union, and Evgeni Zamyatin (q.v.), head of its branch in Leningrad. First these were accused of publishing works abroad. When they answered this charge satis-factorily, their work was called anti-Soviet. Pilnyak gave in and made a recantation; Zamyatin asked Stalin for permission to emigrate, and was allowed to go to Paris.

Then, in 1932, when Russian writing in the hands of RAPP had become quite abject, Stalin dissolved RAPP, and the Union of Soviet Writers was founded. In 1934 socialist realism was promulgated. It was put forward by Zhdanov, who remained associated with 'culture' until his timely death. But the actual theory was devised by Gorky, in consultation with Stalin. Stalin's part in it was that of a man who loathed and feared true communists, and required only toadies with the ignorant gangster mentality of Zhdanov, or ex-bourgeois who would condone any of his own non-Marxist enormities. But Gorky was doing his best to keep Russian literature in the tradition in which he himself had played a considerable part: the realist tradition. Unfortunately his influence (he defended Pilnyak and helped Zamyatin to make his exit) did not prevail. Literary standards declined after his death, and many writers perished in Stalin's purges. The war provided a temporary let-up; but then Zhdanov in 1946 began the 1934 process all over again, this time attacking Akhmatova and Zoshchenko (qq.v.). Zhdanov died in 1948; but his and Stalin's policies continued until the latter's death in 1953.

The positive aspects of socialist realism, the aspects put in by Gorky, have their origin in the nineteenth-century criticism of Belinsky and others. The Russians have always written in order to change men's hearts or minds, doubt-less partly because they feel guilty about the effect of their gloom; Belinsky invented the term 'superfluous man' to describe the hero who could not fit into his times because they had not yet developed to the stage at which he could integrate himself with them. Socialist realism is therefore a characteristically Russian reaction to the twentieth-century artist's scepticism and inability to know his purpose. Gorky's pronouncements in the Thirties were not always very confident; but official criticism has held them up as authoritative. Realism, Gorky said, 'would best cope with its task if . . . it would describe man not as he is today, but also as he must be—and will be—tomorrow'. This is something he himself failed to do. Zhdanov demanded the combination of 'the truthfulness and historical concreteness of artistic description' with 'the task of the ideological transformation and education of the working people in the spirit of socialism'. This method he defined as socialist realism.

Literature means more to the average educated Russian than it does to his Western counterpart. Tolstoi's *War and Peace* really did play a part in Russian resistance to the Nazi attack; books played no comparable part in the morale of Great Britain in the period when she stood alone against the same aggressor. Russians expect good books to be a part of their lives. On the other hand, the Zhdanov line demands nothing less than the subordination of literature to politics —and not even to the politics of socialism, but to those of tyrants determined to retain power. The nineteenth-century realists set up values to attack the society of their time. The twentieth-century realists were supposed to employ the same techniques to defend their society. . . . While that society was experimental and hopeful it was easier; but soon after Stalin put himself in charge the situation for literature deteriorated.

*

In 1902 Gorky was appointed head of the *Znanie* (knowledge) publishing house; he thus gathered round him the best and most outspoken writers of the time. Most of these writers believed, like Gorky, in what can fairly be described as a programme of socialist realism—though not necessarily in an exclusively Marxist approach. Three, Andreyev, Bunin and Kuprin, abandoned the group when they attained success.

LEONID ANDREYEV (1871–1919), born in Orel, was (for a time) Gorky's only serious rival. Andreyev has rightly been blamed for sensationalism; but this was not opportunistic, for he was of a suicidal disposition from early in his life, when he studied law and unsuccessfully tried to support himself as a painter. Andreyev has been called a symbolist (q.v.), but he is better described as an expressionist (q.v.) hopelessly out of context. He was a (suspiciously) violent sceptic who owed his success to his appeal to the mood of Russian intellectuals at the turn of the century, a mood that intensified with the failure of the 1905 revolution. Andreyev was influenced by, or perhaps it is more accurate to say dependent upon, Tolstoi, Chekhov and Dostoevski; but his real subject was his own despair and bewilderment. He is stridently interested in the existence of problems; but not in their solution. Into his early stories—many of them translated in *The Little Angel* (1915; tr. W. H. Lowe)—Andreyev projects his own fear of death and sexuality into a number of helpless individuals. 'Silence' portrays a dour village priest who does not discover the reasons for his daughter's silence until she has killed herself. 'Snapper' characteristically sees the world through the eyes of a badly treated dog who has known just one moment of kindness. In *The Abyss* (1902; tr. J. Cournos, 1929), one of his best books, Andreyev convincingly shows an ordinary man suddenly possessed by an overwhelming and extraordinary sexual desire.

Andreyev's later style is crude and rhetorical; but there are exceptions, such as *The Governor* (1906; tr. 1947), a tense and entirely unsensational story about the last hours of a governor awaiting execution, and *The Seven That Were Hanged* (1908; tr. H. Bernstein, 1909). Most of Andreyev's plays are pretentious, but there are two exceptions: *The Life of Man* (1906; tr. C. J. Hogarth, 1915) and *He Who Gets Slapped* (1914; tr. G. Zilboorg, 1922). The latter is expressionistic, with anticipations of the theatre of the absurd (q.v.): 'He' is an arrogant intellectual who arrives at a circus to offer his services. The circus people can communicate, but He cannot; He smiles while He is slapped. There has been renewed interest in this play, whose form is undoubtedly original, in recent years. Andreyev reacted violently against the Bolshevik Revolution, fled to Finland, and died there an embittered man.

ALEXANDER KUPRIN (1870–1938), born in Narovchat, Penza, was another who ultimately left the Znanie group. He served in the army between 1890 and 1894, and this provided him with material for the book that made him famous: *The Duel* (1905; tr. 1916). In the meantime he had held a variety of jobs— dock worker, journalist, actor and fisherman among them. His work began to appear about a decade before *The Duel*, but this is his masterpiece. It is about an intellectual young officer who cannot stomach his sadistic and stupid colleagues, or the horrors of army life. Kuprin himself was essentially uninterested in politics; he was committed only to realism. But *The Duel* appeared just after the loss of the Russo-Japanese war, and was thus given a political relevance. Kuprin was a born story-teller; he was influenced by Kipling and Jack London (qq.v.), with whom he had real affinities. However, he later tended to choose sensationalist subjects that did not suit his genius: *The Pit* (1910; tr. B. G. Guerney, 1930), about prostitution in Odessa, is lurid rather than vivid; the author is not happy following Gorky, for this prevents his use of narrative—his great strength—and leads him to strain for realism rather than to achieve it. His best stories, where the influence of Chekhov is as apparent as that of Kipling, are to be found in *The Bracelet of Garnets* (tr. L. Pasvolsky, 1917) and *The River of Life* (tr. S. S. Koteliansky and J. M. Murry, 1916), especially 'Listrigony' (1911) in the latter volume. Kuprin left Russia at the Revolution, but returned in the last year of his life.

IVAN BUNIN (1870–1953) was born in Voronezh of an aristocratic family. He was the first Russian to win a Nobel Prize for literature (1933); he parted from Russia for ever at the time of the Revolution, but left many enthusiastic readers behind him. It is said that he got his Nobel Prize by a prolonged campaign of letter writing. Bunin was counted as one of Gorky's group, but never wholeheartedly shared its views. He began with poetry, in a Parnassian (q.v.)— he was never a symbolist—style, and although he is most famous for prose his poetry is distinguished (PRV; MRP). He is the only twentieth-century Russian writer to wholeheartedly carry on pre-Revolutionary traditions. He is one of the more important Russian writers of prose fiction in this century. Until he won his Nobel Prize he was little known abroad. He is also the only true cosmopolitan Russian writer of his time.

Bunin is a most impressive writer who may, since his death, have become somewhat neglected. He manages to mix romantic regret, mordant psychological objectivity and non-political social realism; the poet is always present. His earlier books were about the disintegration of the Russian gentry: *The*

Village (1910; tr. I. F. Hapgood, 1923), bitter, lucid, beautifully written; and 'Dry Valley' (in *The Elaghin Affair*, tr. B. G. Guerney, 1935), the depiction of the fall of a great landowning family. Bunin then turned to other parts of the world for his subject matter, revealing himself to be a writer of international stature. Many of the stories of this period (1912–16) are collected in *The Dreams of Chang* (tr. B. Guerney, 1923) and *The Gentleman from San Francisco* (tr. D. H. Lawrence, S. S. Koteliansky and L. Woolf, 1922). The title story of the latter volume, besides being his most famous, is his most characteristic, and is one of the more notable modern writings about death. It is about a millionaire who, after a lifetime spent acquiring his wealth, proposes to enjoy it; but he suddenly dies on reaching Capri. Bunin contrasts the fact of his death against the beautiful nature for which it has no meaning. In exile Bunin continued to write well: *Mitya's Love* (1925; tr. M. Boyd, 1926), about an idealistic boy who falls in love unwisely; and his last stories, *Dark Alleys* (1943), which are in very highly concentrated prose, are almost as good as anything he did before. Bunin refused to accept the Revolution, but during the war he was an adamant opponent of the Nazis, and is said to have sheltered a Jew in his house at Grasse throughout the occupation. His last years were spent in obscurity. He has been described as a father of 'magic realism' (q.v.).

M. P. ARTSYBASHEV (1878–1927), born in the Ukraine, is usually dismissed as a clumsy thesis novelist whose books are little more than 'amateurish' attempts to prove that all instinct can be reduced to sexual desire. Certainly his most famous novel, *Sanin* (1907; tr. P. Pinkerton, 1915), had a sensational vogue (particularly in Poland). But to regard it as merely a vehicle for proving that all life is a matter of carnal gratification is unfair. It was in fact written in 1903, and then rejected by publishers, only to be accepted after the war and 1905 revolution, when it fitted in better with the gloomy current thinking. Its message is more hopelessness (in the familiar Russian style) than joy-through-sex, and I suspect that many of the critics who have dismissed it have not read it. For it is certainly more of a realistic depiction of a group of people than a programme. Later Artsybashev, affected by the reception of *Sanin*, became boringly tendentious: *Breaking Point* (1912; tr. 1915) is a thoroughly unconvincing suicide-novel. Artsybashev left Russia in 1921 and spent the rest of his life attacking the communists.

Three other members of Gorky's group deserve mention. The dramatist and short story writer EVGENI CHIRIKOV (1864–1932), who became an anti-Bolshevik *émigré* after 1917, wrote about provincial Russia. *Marka of the Pits* (1911; tr. L. Zarine, 1930), a Gorky-like exposé of poverty and degradation of life in a Volga town, is a typical example of his fiction. His plays are competent. V. V. VERESAYEV (ps. V. V. SMIDOVICH, 1867–1946), born at Tula in Central Russia, was a doctor, as his philanthropic father had been before him. *Confessions of a Physician* (1900; tr. S. Linden, 1904) caused a sensation when it appeared because of some of its revelations, and its socialistic conclusions. He served as an army surgeon in the war of 1904–5 and indicted the Tsar's ineffective military machine in *In the War* (1908). He could not at first accept the Revolution, and in *Deadlock* (1923; tr. N. Wissotzky and C. Coventry, 1928) portrays a girl in his own predicament: she cannot accept either way out. However, in the tendentious *The Sisters* (1933; tr. J. Soskice, 1934) he has accepted Marxism. ALEXANDER SERAFIMOVICH (ps. A. S. POPOV, 1863–1949), one of the heroes of Soviet culture, was a Cossack born in the Don Region. He was an established writer before the Revolution; his first novel, *The City in the Steppe* (1905–12), was about the exploitation of factory workers in the Don region. He helped Sholokhov (q.v.) to publish his first book. Serafimovich's most famous book, supposed to be a model of socialist realism (but Gorky privately complained of its crudities) is *The Iron Flood* (1924; tr. 1935). This deals with the retreat of the Red Cossacks through the Northern Caucasus in 1918; its hero is the masses, moulded by party doctrine and discipline into good communists. This is rightly described as 'pseudo-impressionistic'; it is also rhetorical, badly written, boring and cliché-ridden. Zamyatin (q.v.) attacked it in the year it appeared as 'tinselly', its 'occasional apt images' being 'as scarce as the righteous in Gomorrah'.

*

However, there are some wholehearted supporters of the regime, and some socialist realists, who have more talent than Serafimovich. Chiefly there is COUNT ALEXEY TOLSTOI (1882–1945), a distant relative of Leo Tolstoi, who symbolized for the Soviets the reconciliation between culture and communism. He began as a symbolist poet in the early years of the century. His first fiction, with which he made a reputation before the Revolution, consisted of light, energetic tales of his native Volga region. His main gift for non-doctrinaire storytelling is already apparent. Blok (q.v.) even accused him of hooliganism and immaturity. The characters are grotesque and fantastic decaying gentry; what interests Tolstoi is their colour, wild absurdity and sexual vigour. Whatever Soviet critics may later have claimed, Tolstoi had no social intentions whatever, and his genius was somewhat distorted when he decided to become a Soviet writer. Given to obeying his immediate impulses, he turned against the Bolsheviks, fought against them, and went into exile in Paris. But in 1923, after sounding out various party officials, he returned to Russia: he found he could not live happily outside it. The trilogy *The Road to Calvary* (1919–41; tr. E. Bone, 1946) was begun as an anti-Russian work, but ended as a pro-communist account of the intelligentsia before, during and after the Revolution. This is a flawed but not dishonest work. Its hero, Teleghin, is not an ideological communist, but he does come to accept the Revolution, as Tolstoi himself did, for patriotic reasons. The flaws include some passages toadying to Stalin—Tolstoi was among other things an expert opportunist—a gradual diminution of power throughout, and a fragmentariness imposed on it by the episodic technique. But it is good storytelling, and the characters are well done; it gives a truthful picture of the kind of intellectual who was prepared to accept Bolshevism but not to join the party. *Bread* (1937; tr. S. Garry, 1938) is a piece of phoney socialist realism, written at a fairly bad time in Russian letters; it is

Tolstoi's worst book. Some of Tolstoi's adventure yarns written in the Twenties, when he was experimenting with science fiction modes, are excellent; they include *The Death Box* (1925; tr. B. G. Guerney, 1936), in which the inventor of a death-ray imposes his fascist rule on Europe. If Tolstoi's early tales are his best fiction, his unfinished historical novel *Peter the Great* (1929–45; tr. T. Shebunina, 1956) comes only a very little way behind. When he came to attempt it he had come to terms with the regime, was making money and living in high style, and had regained all his old confidence. It is one of the outstanding historical reconstructions of its time, full of verve and gusto: Tolstoi admired Peter's brute strength and virility, and he communicates the sense of it admirably.

FYODOR GLADKOV (1883–1958), a follower of Gorky, had known the hardship of pre-revolutionary Russia at first hand: his parents worked in Caspian fisheries and Caucasian mills on starvation wages. *Cement* (1925; tr. A. S. Arthur and C. Ashleigh, 1929), one of the first Soviet best-sellers, is a lurid and affected piece of pseudo-realism, in which hope is crudely portrayed as rising from the ruins of horror. A returning Red has both to come to terms with his wife's emancipated views, and to lead his fellow townspeople in the reconstruction of the abandoned cement works, in which he succeeds. Later Gladkov purged the novel of its decadent style, according to the tenets of socialist realism, but he could not improve it. However, it has some importance as the first Soviet fiction to be written to a non-literary formula—prescribed by the proletariat group—and it is still read. His Five Year Plan book, *Power* (1933; pt. SL), is an incredibly dull and crude novel.

ALEXANDER FADEYEV (1901–56) is a truly tragic case. Most of the Soviet literary dictators have been mediocre or semi-literate; Fadeyev, in the Twenties a RAPP theoretician and then an important member of the Union of Soviet Writers, seems to have been responsible for the exile or execution of a number of writers in Stalin's last years. But he had been a gifted writer; unusually among the proletarian writers, he had a sense of and interest in psychology. In *The Nineteen* (1927; tr. R. Charques, 1929; 1957) he successfully exploited the methods of (Leo) Tolstoi in regard to style and lucid psychology. This is the story of the civil war in Siberia, where the communist guerrillas fought both Whites and Japanese. Fadeyev does not try to see his guerrillas as one mass (as Serafimovich did), but treats them individually. The only true communist is their leader, the Jew Levinson; his transformation of his dissident band into a single fighting body is more effectively described than in Serafimovich's *The Iron Flood* or Gladkov's *Cement. The Last of the Udegs* (1929–36), which is unfinished, is longer and, because it too consciously strains after epic stature, less successful. This deals with more or less the same material—Fadeyev was in Siberia during the civil war—but its virtues are outweighed by its earnest attempt to realize the tenets of socialist realism. Fadeyev saw this; but unfortunately his desire to be a good party member was stronger than his creative self-confidence. Thus his *Young Guard* (1945), based on the true story of Russian teenagers' resistance to the Nazis occupying Krasnodon, was attacked because it showed older

Bolsheviks being inefficient. Fadeyev undertook to revise it— '. . . Bolsheviks are not bad organizers, and that is why they win. Therefore, in a work that was going to be read so widely, I should have shown this strong Bolshevik feature. . . .'—and he severely compromised his conscience by doing so. At the Twentieth Congress of the Communist Party in 1956 Fadeyev was bitterly attacked by Sholokhov ('. . . no writer wants to stand at attention in front of Fadeyev. . . .'); rumours went round Moscow that he had been directly responsible for the denunciation of Babel (q.v.) and others; he began to drink heavily and in May, presumably out of remorse for what—probably in all sincerity—he had done, he shot himself.

MIKHAIL SHOLOKHOV (1905), one of the outstanding Russian writers of this century, is a Cossack. Like Fadeyev, Sholokhov went back to Leo Tolstoi for his basic method of 'psychological realism', which amounts to no more, really, than the presentation of characters 'in the round', which in turn involves analysis and a distinction between appearance and inner motivation. In the last few years Sholokhov, who won the Nobel Prize in 1964, has published little; to the irritation of some younger Russians he lives in high style, drinking and hunting, on his large estate at Rostov-on-Don, where he has a private aeroplane and a private theatre. Sholokhov's first book, the short stories of *Tales from the Don* (1925; tr. H. C. Stevens, 1961) anticipated his later themes and displayed his regional limitations: he cannot deal convincingly with any non-Cossack material. Sholokhov's main work is his *Don* trilogy, translated in two parts by S. Garry as *And Quiet Flows the Don* (1934) and *The Don Flows Home to the Sea* (1940). He interrupted this to write the story of collectivization in the Cossack region, *Virgin Soil Upturned* (1932; tr. S. Garry, 1935) and *Harvest on the Don* (tr. H. C. Stevens, 1960).

Sholokhov's work is remarkable because of its objective treatment of anti-communists. In the *Don* trilogy the account of Grigory Melekhov is convincing. Demobilized from the Russo-German front, he is delighted with the abolition of Tsardom, but hates the Bolsheviks. He fights them; but the Whites distrust him, and eventually he joins Budenny's Red Cavalry. He recognizes that the old Russia is dead, but cannot accept the new; when he is demobilized and harassed by his new allies, he therefore again becomes an anti-Red. . . . Sholokhov failed to analyse Grigory; but he depicted his instincts rightly, and his feelings for the rhythms of his native countryside are superbly conveyed. Really this book is a lament for the vanishing rural scene; were Sholokhov to be asked to write such a novel as *Cement* (q.v.) he would be totally unable to respond. What is good in the *Don* trilogy is the lyrical affirmation of an agricultural life that has continued for centuries.

Sholokhov's other major work was written about Stalin's collectivization of the farmlands, which caused untold misery and upheaval. It gives a true picture of this misery, as it traces the fortunes of Davydov, who is sent to a Cossack village to enforce collectivization. Sholokhov is a naïve (q.v.) writer, and he is genuinely attached to Soviet communism; it seems likely that he really believed in collectivization. But its results clearly caused him much anguish, and the novel is distorted by verbosity and a plethora of comedy, not all of it successful. It is vigorous, and Cossack speech is brilliantly recorded; but it is fragmentary. Sholokhov's anti-intellectual pronouncements, made over the past thirty years, are distasteful, and have given younger Russian writers good reason to hate him.

*

The Serapion Brothers was a literary group formed in 1921 under the patronage of Gorky and Zamyatin (qq.v.). All admirers of E. T. A. Hoffmann, they followed one of his heroes who believed in the power of the imagination to conquer space and time. . . . These were the 'fellow-travellers' of Trotsky's phrase, all of whom accepted the Revolution, but: 'We are no school', they said, 'no direction. . . . In February 1921, at a time of widespread regimentation, registration, and barrack-room regulations . . . we decided to foregather without statutes or chairman. . . . We think that present-day Russian literature is amazingly decorous, conceited, and monotonous. . . . We demand but one thing: that a work of art . . . live its own peculiar life'. Under Stalin the influence of the Serapion Brothers was pronounced 'bourgeois'; but almost every good writer, even if not a member, felt close to them. Their aim was no more than to feel free to interpret the Revolution in an individual way. Some believed in following specifically Russian procedures; others, particularly Zamyatin, believed in learning from the West. But all were concerned to utilize every new technical device: they were rejecting the spirit of philistinism implicit in the Proletkult school, which held the ascendancy in the Thirties, Forties and early Fifties.

The moving spirit behind the formation of the Serapion Brothers was EVGENY ZAMYATIN (1884–1937). Zamyatin was a revolutionary in literature in a sense that Gorky was not. As we know, official Russian literature chose to go Gorky's way, not Zamyatin's; but some of Russia's writers have taken more heed of Zamyatin's views; and have looked elsewhere than their own nineteenth-century classics for inspiration.

To understand the spirit of Zamyatin's modernism it is necessary to look behind him: to two slightly older figures who profoundly influenced him and —largely through him and Pilnyak—modern Russian literature. These two writers are ANDREY BELY (ps. BORIS N. BUGAYEV, 1880–1934), 'Andrew the White', and ALEXEI REMIZOV (1877–1957).

Bely, chiefly a novelist and critic, wrote symbolist poetry (PRV; RP; SBRV) of distinction but little originality except of technique. However, he was the one symbolist who survived to carry forward the message symbolism had for Russian literature—the party wing of which was reluctant to receive it, and uncomprehending of it. Zamyatin wrote of him at his death: 'Mathematics, poetry, anthroposophy, fox-trot—these are some of the sharpest angles that make up the fantastic image of Andrey Bely'. And he added that Bely had been above all 'a writer's writer'. Bely, the son of a mathematician, was interested from an early age in art, music and the poetry of Goethe; he was encouraged by the philosopher and poet Solovyov (q.v.). It is no surprise that in 1914, by which time he had become the chief theoretician of the symbolists, he became attracted by Rudolf Steiner's syncretic anthroposophy, and joined an anthroposophical community in Switzerland. He welcomed the Revolution, not in its own materialistic spirit but as a preparation for a Second Coming. Disillusioned by 1921 he went abroad again, to Berlin, where his wife left him to be near Rudolf Steiner, beyond whose ideas Bely himself had passed. He drank heavily, nearly went mad; but in 1923 summoned up the strength to return to Russia, where his books were issued in small editions and he was left in peace until his death.

Bely's two most important works are novels written in a deliberately rhythmical prose that is itself half poetry: *The Silver Dove* (1909) and, chiefly, *Petersburg* (1913–16; tr. J. Cournos, 1960). Bely had already prepared the way for his new prose style in his *Symphonies* (1902–8), which were constructed on musical analogues. *The Silver Dove*, of which there is a German translation, is about the Flagellant sect (from which Rasputin had emerged) and a sensitive poet who is destroyed by his involvement with it; *Petersburg* paints the decline of Tsarist Petersburg and deals with the conflict in a young man whose father has been condemned by the revolutionaries, of whom he is one. *Kotik Letayev* (1917; pt. SL), begun in 1915, which has often been called Joycean, is one of the most extraordinary of Russian experiments. Bely, almost a Platonist, lived and suffered in a world in which he did not believe. This autobiographical novel, in which he tries to recreate the emergence of consciousness in his own infant mind, is an attempt to make a bridge between the two worlds. It is, as Zamyatin said, the only anthroposophical work of fiction in existence. Like *The Silver Dove*, it urgently requires translation into English in its entirety, for if it is not as important as *Ulysses* (q.v.) it is certainly more so than the deliberately obscurantist *Finnegans Wake*. In it Bely tries to do no less than show how the real (Platonic—or Solovyovan) world is contained in the false, empirical world: how the fourth dimension is absorbed into, secreted in, the familiar three-dimensional one. It is a failure; but a very notable one. Bely's later prose became more straightforward; but he continued to make verbal experiments. His memoirs have been rightly described as the best ever written inside Russia. The later novels—which include *The Moscow Crank* (1927) and *Masks* (1933)—are subtly satirical and ostensibly realistic, with conventional (and skilfully handled)) plots; unfortunately Bely's devices (his rhythmical prose, his neologisms) here become monotonous. Bely is regarded as important in Russian literature, though official Soviet criticism does not know what to do with him; were his works more readily available in English and French he would doubtless have the world stature he deserves: as a key symbolist. He has been an important influence, particularly stylistically, on Nabokov (q.v.).

Remizov, born in Moscow, is another writer's writer; he, too, has not been translated as extensively as he should have been. He was exiled in 1897, and never took part in politics again, even as an *émigré* in Paris for the last thirty-five years of his long life. Remizov was much influenced by Nikolai Leskov (1831–95), a writer who made use of Russian—and his own invented—vernacular by putting his incongruous or fantastic narrations into the mouths of provincial, usually only half-literate, characters. (This method of narration is called *skaz*, and influenced Zoshchenko, q.v., as well as Remizov.) Remizov could write straightforwardly, as in *On a Field Azure* (1922; tr. B. Scott, 1946), about a girl who becomes a revolutionary; but in the main he is a symbolist who anticipates Borges (q.v.) and other similar writers in positing the writer's world as being an improvement on God's. But Remizov believes in God notwithstanding—as Dostoevski, one of his masters, did—and for his own imaginary world he draws greatly on folklore, magic and dream. He is very Russian in combining a profound pessimism with a faith whose constant black heat irradiates all his works. *The Pond* (1907), his first novel, is a phantasmagoric picture of urban life, which Remizov clearly sees as devilish. Indeed, Remizov sees all life as devilish, and man's fate in it as unpredictable; but his belief in death (as the beginning of a new life) lightens the burden somewhat. And in this consolation, at least, he is not modern, but archaic. Some of his early short stories have been translated in *The Fifth Pestilence* (1912; tr. A. Brown, 1927) and *The Clock* (1908; tr. J. Cournos, 1924).

Zamyatin, the keenest critical mind of his generation in Russia, began as a student of and then lecturer in naval engineering. He was a communist when a very young man, and was twice arrested and exiled. He therefore suffered persecution under the Tsar and the Soviets: the latter arrested him in 1922—putting him in the same cell-block in which the Tsarist police had put him after the 1905 uprising—for a while, and he was lucky in 1931, after denunciation in 1929, to be allowed to go to Paris. He wrote many short stories and novellas, including two satires on English life—he spent some time there observing the making of Russian ice-breakers—which he saw as peculiarly stultifying and hypocritical: *The Islanders* (1922). *We* (1920; first Russian edition 1952; tr. G. Zilboorg, 1925; ARL; B. G. Guerney, 1960) found its way out of Russia to Prague, where it was translated into Czech without the author's knowledge. In 1929 this was used to discredit him, and after suffering ostracism for two years he was allowed, owing to the good offices of Gorky, to go to Paris. For the last six years of his life, poor and unhappy, he led the life of a recluse, remaining aloof from Russian *émigré* circles. He had written a play about Attila, whose era he found paralleled his own; at his death he was still working on a novel, *Scourge of God* (1938), on the same subject.

Zamyatin was an eclectic and a sceptic who believed in heresy and nonconformity and who resisted all kinds of dogmas; not at all a man to appeal to any kind of politician, let alone a Stalin; indeed, there are few cultural officials the world over who could stomach his statement that 'Real literature can be created only by madmen, hermits, heretics, dreamers, rebels, and sceptics, not by diligent and trustworthy functionaries'. Zamyatin saw human beings as trapped between entropy and energy: symbolism, the literary equivalent of solar energy, disrupted the tendency to come to (philistine) rest.

Thus, the creative urge is a tormenting one—the philistine passivity of exhaustion is blissful. Zamyatin's 'neo-realism' was really a kind of literary cubism (q.v.): a new, visionary putting together of mundane reality. As in Bely, fantasy is juxtaposed with reality. And the realism is neo-realism because, as he said, 'If you examine your hand through a microscope you will see a grotesque picture: trees, ravines, stones—instead of hairs, pores, grains and dust. . . . To my mind this is more genuine realism than the primitive one'. Zamyatin wrote a number of remarkable short stories (the best are collected in *Dragons*, tr. M. Ginsburg, 1967), including 'The Cave', which springs from a single metaphor, 'The Story About What Matters Most', his view of the Revolution, and the earlier 'At the World's End'. *We* anticipated both Huxley and Orwell (qq.v.) (Huxley, possibly disingenuously, claimed not to have read it), and is intellectually superior to both, but lacks the power of *1984*. The basis of the dystopia of 2600 is the destruction of individualism; at the end the hero submits to an operation for the removal of his imagination.

KONSTANTIN FEDIN (1892) was perhaps Zamyatin's most notable pupil. His gift has been slowly eroded by party demands, but he began independently, by writing objectively about the Revolution rather than mindlessly affirming it. The subject of his earlier books was the impact of the Revolution. 'The Orchard' (1920), his first notable story, tells of an old gardener who burns down the old manor house and orchard, now a children's colony, whose owners he served before the Revolution. 'The Tale of One Morning' (1921) is an ironic account of a hangman, containing a horrifying description of an execution. *Cities and Years* (1924; tr. M. Scammell, 1962), his first novel, tells of a vacillating intellectual who is eventually murdered for helping an anti-revolutionary German to escape. It irritated Soviet and other critics by its arbitrary treatment of chronology; but this device works perfectly in revealing the confusion of the time and of the hero's mind. *The Brothers* (1928), his best novel, written at the very end of the only decade of freedom that Soviet Russian literature has known, is less compromising: a plea, in effect, for an autonomous art. The composer Nikita Katev is portrayed as a victim of the revolution; the communist Rodian Chorbov, whom Nikita's girl marries but then leaves to return to him, may be seen as wooden—or satirically portrayed as wooden. Fedin's later work contains passages of depth and sensitivity, but is ruined overall by his obligations to socialist realism.

VSEVOLOD IVANOV (1895–1963) is known mainly as a playwright, but his short stories may survive his drama. Like Gorky, who helped him, his early experiences gave him an instinctive sympathy with tramps, hobos and confidence men: with, in fact, the *lumpenproletariat*. In his early days he was, among other things, a circus performer, sword swallower, fakir and wrestler. Gorky saved him from death when he was starving in St. Petersburg in 1920, and introduced him to the Serapion Brothers the next year. He had written some crude stories based on his experiences before that; but now he settled down to learn. His first stories recorded the course of the civil war in Asia with a thrilling amoral zest; he treats the hideous cruelty of both sides not with pleasure or horror, but as natural human phenomena. *Armoured Train 14–69* (1922; tr. G. Cowan and A. K. T. Grant, 1933), about a train led by a crazy White officer and besieged by Red guerrillas, gives an unforgettable picture of the mindless fury of the revolutionary drive. Later Ivanov became 'educated' to the Stalinist way of thinking, and rewrote some of his work, robbing it of much of its vigour. His attempt to portray the Five Year Plan sympathetically was sincere but as imaginatively impoverished as the rest. The last work that shows traces of Ivanov's old power is *Adventures of a Fakir* (1934; tr. 1936).

To VALENTIN KATAYEV (1897), born in Odessa, and another of the Serapion Brothers, belongs the credit of writing the least theory-ridden novel about the first Five Year Plan: *Forward, Oh Time* (1932; tr. C. Malamuth, 1933). This, influenced in technique by Dos Passos (q.v.), is funny as well as being orthodox, and manages to portray life as it is without traversing the party line. By sensibly sacrificing any desire to write major fiction, Katayev made his account of a concrete-mixing race against time both enthralling and meaningful. Previously he had written *The Embezzlers* (1927; tr. L. Zarine, 1929), into which he cleverly projected his own nihilistic feelings: two employees of a Moscow Trust have a good time with the money they have appropriated before giving themselves up to the law.

v. KAVERIN (ps. v. A. ZILBERG, 1902) has retained his integrity by writing excellent adventure books for children—*Two Captains* (1940; tr. E. L. Swan, 1942) is one of the best—and carefully edited reminiscences. Of all the Serapion Brothers, he was most interested in plot (unusual in a Russian writer), and his stories of the underworld were clearly influenced by Western models. *Artist Unknown* (1931; tr. N. P. Ross, 1947) is one of the most extraordinary defences of the autonomy of the romantic artist to emerge from Soviet Russia. Nor is it only a defence of the artist: it is also an attack on exactly the attitude which in fact prevailed in Stalinist Russia: the *mindless* acceptance of faith in the new order. Arkhinedov, the artist, is indeed a pitiful creature; Shpektorov the communist prevails. But Arkhinedov's 'useless' apprehensions, it is suggested, triumph. Before this Kaverin had more comically held the balance between Soviet good and artistic evil in *The Scandalizer* (1928), about effete scholars cut off from communist reality.

ILF AND PETROV (pss. ILYA A. FAINZILBERG, 1897–1937, and EVGENY KATAYEV, 1903–42) was a remarkable case of collaboration: these two really wrote as one man. The latter was the younger brother of Valentin Katayev (q.v.), and was killed while reporting the siege of Sevastopol. In *Twelve Chairs* (1928; tr. J. Richardson, 1961) and *The Golden Calf* (1931; tr. J. Richardson, 1962) they satirized those Russian vices that persisted in spite of the Revolution: red tape, bureaucracy and inefficiency. The influence of Zamyatin is seen in the ingenious and inventive style; but the tradition Ilf and Petrov wrote in is that of Gogol. Ostap Bender is certainly a swindler and a rogue determined to get what he can out of Russia before it becomes impossible for him and his kind. But he is also a human being: 'undesirable' but none the less full of warmth. In *Twelve Chairs* the authors give a picture of Russia as it was at the end of the

NEP; *The Golden Calf* is in a sense a 'Five Year Plan' novel, and is more serious: the opportunities for such criminal bourgeois as Ostap Bender (who, murdered at the end of *Twelve Chairs*, is resurrected for this novel) are over, and Ilf and Petrov gaily, but with an underlying sadness, note this. Their message is unmistakable: there's no fun in a 'perfect' society.

But the century's major Russian humorist, whose great gift was literally crushed and broken by Stalinism, was MIKHAIL ZOSHCHENKO (1895–1958), who still managed for a time to be an effective satirist of Soviet society. He was one of the most popular of all Soviet writers, both on account of his masterly *skaz* (q.v.) style—he used as a narrator in his often very short stories an ostensibly foolish, semi-literate observer, through whom Zoshchenko was able to make sly observations about Soviet society—and because his readers, who had their own difficulties in adjusting to the Revolution, were able to identify with his characters. He could fairly be described as a kind of Russian equivalent of Ring Lardner (q.v.), but he was less journalistic and more substantially gifted. Zoshchenko was, however, a misanthropist, not an anti-communist; the genius of his writings arises from a tension generated by his ambivalent attitude towards the little man whom he satirized: he loathed his philistinism, meanness and pettiness—but he pitied him as a victim of bureaucracy, of the revolution of simple-minded bullies, of life itself. One is inevitably reminded of Swift's attitude to the Irish, whom he said he loathed but whom he nevertheless fought to preserve from economic exploitation. The fact is that Zoshchenko loved life in spite of his opinion of it. He sees the humanity of his victims, and therefore he does not diminish them. Zoshchenko's methods are hilarious, but were displeasing to party officials less clever than he. In his play *Esteemed Comrade* (1929), for example, he shows a communist tyrannizing over the tenants of an apartment. He is a thoroughly despicable and stupid man, and Zoshchenko could well have been attacked for showing communism in a bad light. But he shows it in a good light, instead—by having the bully expelled from the party as a 'negative' character.

After 1929 Zoshchenko was forced to compromise with the party or remain silent. His novel *Youth Restored* (1933), a story of a professor of astronomy who tries to recover the youth he has too easily let pass by, is one of the most effective snooks ever cocked at the philistine establishment in Russia. Some European critics have purported to take it as a serious attempt on Zoshchenko's part at a reconciliation with the party; and official criticism, indeed, praised him at the time for 'introducing science into literature'. Actually Zoshchenko's professor is a comic demonstration of the impossibility of changing the laws of human nature by imposing theories on them. After almost killing himself with physical exercises, he studies himself and actually succeeds in feeling more vigorous; he leaves his wife to marry a tough whore, but has a stroke when he finds her in a young man's arms. He returns to his family, recovers from his stroke—and even manages to cure himself of 'political deviation' by joining a shock brigade. *Youth Restored* is one of the most delightful legpulls in Soviet literature; it even had the People's Commissar of Health gravely censuring Zoshchenko for 'overemphasizing biological factors' but praising him for showing how life may be organized. . . .

Zoshchenko wrote some propaganda books in the Thirties, such as the rewriting of the autobiography of a convict-turned-good-communist; but it is nearly always possible to see his tongue in his cheek—especially when he parodies worthless official literature. But it is clear that Zoshchenko was unhappy, particularly about having to produce weak children's tales about Lenin; his cryptic autobiography, *Before Sunrise* (1943; pt. tr. J. Richardson, *Partisan Review*, 3 and 4, 1961), in which he analyses himself on Freudian principles but repudiates Freud and praises Pavlov, was an attempt to do something more self-satisfying and serious. This is a confessional work, by a neurotic hypochondriac, and it was immediately condemned; further publication was prohibited. So Zoshchenko's desire to develop in a direction that in certain respects reminds one of Jouhandeau's, or even Leiris' (qq.v.) was thwarted—with incalculable results for Russian literature. In June 1946 Zoshchenko published a story called 'Adventures of a Monkey', which is not a 'vulgar lampoon on Soviet life' but a somewhat Swiftian portrayal of humanity in general. By the end of that year he had been expelled from the Writers' Union—the usual toadies made condemnatory speeches—and his work was outlawed. At the same time the poetry of Akhmatova was attacked and she was expelled. Both writers were personally attacked, in terms of gutter abuse, by the secretary of the Central Committee, Zhdanov (his ferocity reminds one of nothing more than the rage of a semi-literate failed writer). What upset the party about Zoshchenko was that in his most recent short story he had treated mankind as imperfect. But the Soviet society that had defeated Germany could not accept such things: they were not unhealthy. It was not until 1946 that the party began to change Russian history; Zoshchenko did not have a chance of surviving. And every other Russian writer now knew that there was only one target for satire: the West. The attack reduced Zoshchenko to a wreck, and he never recovered. But his stories, in censored form, have proved as popular as ever when reissued. There are translations of his fiction in *Russia Laughs* (tr. H. Clayton, 1935), *The Woman Who Could Not Read* (tr. E. Fen, 1940) and *The Wonderful Dog* (tr. E. Fen, 1942).

*

A number of writers were fellow travellers but not actually members of the Serapion Brothers. Ehrenburg, who became one of the best known apologists for Stalinism (as well as for writing *The Thaw*, q.v.), was actually an anti-Bolshevik *émigré*.

BORIS PILNYAK (ps. BORIS VOGAU, 1894–?1938) was so truthful to his own vision, for all his attempts to damp it down and conform, that Stalin had to destroy him: in 1937 he was accused of being a Japanese spy and murdered either immediately or soon afterwards in a camp. Pilnyak, who was of mixed Volga German and Jewish descent, was distrusted by the communists and disliked by conservative *émigrés*. He was influenced by Remizov and Bely (qq.v.), particularly by the former; but his views of the Revolution were all his own. He was not a Marxist, but the Revolution satisfied his Slavophile aspirations; he saw it as a triumph of the peasantry. He seems to have employed Dos Passos' 'newsreel' (q.v.) technique independently. But his prose style, a welter of words, is closest to Remizov's. Sometimes it is too close. The book that made him famous was *The Naked Year* (1922; tr. A. Brown, 1928), the first Russian novel wholly about the Revolution. This is a youthful novel, on the theme of the triumph of moral strength over artificiality. Its style is remarkable: long sentences, authorial asides about techniques, puns, and all manner of devices. For *Mahogany* (1929; tr. M. Hayward, *Partisan Review*, 3 and 4, 1961) he was denounced: it depicted a provincial town peopled by eccentrics, and it made clear that Pilnyak did not believe that any revolution could or should change the old Asiatic Russian way of life, and also that he believed all rulers were similar—whether Tsarists or Marxists. The truth is that he was an anarchist, a writer—not a political thinker. He had already upset the party with *The Tale of the Unextinguished Moon* (1926), in which he portrayed the party as soulless in its treatment of a General who had been ordered (against his will) to undergo an operation. Worse still, Pilnyak hinted here that Stalin had murdered Mikhail Frunze, Commander-in-Chief of the Red Army, by ordering him to have an operation. If this was not true then it was certainly 'philosophically true'; perhaps this was what lost Pilnyak his life later on. He did recant when attacked, however, and rewrote *Mahogany* as *The Volga Falls into the Caspian Sea* (1930; tr. C. Malamuth, 1932); but he could not conceal his anti-industrialism or his belief that environment could not alter human nature, nor did he modify his style sufficiently (so that it could be followed easily by philistine officials and cultural bureaucrats). This was not for want of trying: Pilnyak was neither courageous like Zamyatin, nor cunning like Zoshchenko. He wanted to succeed with the people in power. It is ironic that he should have so signally failed to change his own nature—just as he insisted that communism could not change humanity's. For a quarter of a century after his death his name was not mentioned in text-books of literature; even now the Soviet student dependent on books published in Russian cannot know how celebrated he was in the Twenties.

Another writer deeply indebted to Remizov is MIKHAIL PRISHVIN (1873–1954). Prishvin, an inveterate wanderer throughout Russia, was an agronomist, naturalist and ethnographer. He made a reputation as an ethnographic journalist before the revolution, but did not become famous until the Twenties, when he began to write about people as well as nature. The Revolution became increasingly an industrial one; the people therefore needed someone to satisfy their nature-worshipping tendencies. Prishvin did this; and was allowed to continue doing so. Prishvin is a symbolist, a pantheist and a precise, even scientific, describer of the natural scene. He feels most strongly those elements in man that do harmonize with nature, and he is an optimist who loves man and nature. There is something in him, as a critic has pointed out, of the seventeenth-century mystic Traherne; but equally there is something in him of the microphotographer Ernst Jünger (q.v.), though he has none of the

German's cruel and loveless remoteness. His first novel was *The Chain of Kashchey* (1923–30); the hero sets out to break the evil chain of Kashchey, which consists of all those things that divorce man from his own nature. *Nature's Diary* (1925; tr. 1958) consists of rural and archeological sketches throughout the seasons; it was from this writing, among the very best ever made about the Russian countryside, that Prishvin's most important follower, Konstantin Paustovsky (q.v.), learned. *Jen Sheng: the Root of Life* (1932; tr. G. Walton and P. Gibbons, 1936), in which the hero Louven searches for the Jen Sheng, the dream in his own heart, is really about the quest for serenity and an antidote for the human sicknesses of ambition. Other writings of Prishvin that have been translated include *The Lake and the Woods* (1951), and *The Larder of the Sun* (tr. W. Goodman, 1952).

LEONID LEONOV (1899), born in Moscow, fought for the communists in the Revolution. His first stories were written in the shadow of Remizov and Zamyatin, but, although a fellow traveller, he never joined the Serapion Brothers. And even his earliest works display the interest in psychology that distinguishes him from most of his contemporaries. Like so many other of the Russian writers of the Twenties, Leonov began by examining an aspect—in his case, the psychological—of the collapse of the pre-revolutionary intelligentsia. *The Badgers* (1925; tr. H. Kazanina, 1947) is a study in contrasts: the old capitalists and their children. The heroine rebels against her wealthy father, but remains a bourgeois at heart; and two of her father's employees, brothers, are also ready to destroy the old order. One becomes a Red, but the other becomes leader of peasants resisting communism. His brother is sent at the head of troops to destroy him. This is a lively novel, and the male characters are well done; but, as always in Leonov, the woman is a failure. Leonov's feeling about Bolshevism, as implied in *The Badgers* and in its successor, his best novel, *The Thief* (1927; tr. H. Butler, 1931), is that it cannot succeed unless it comes to terms with the peasant by trying to understand him.

It is in *The Thief* that Leonov shows his affinity to Dostoevski. He did not share his religion, but he did share his psychological approach to character—and something of his half-mystic Slavophile belief in the destiny of the Russian people, after having passed through the crucible of suffering, to lead the world. Leonov's view of communism was not too different from Bely's; but was less overtly religious. Communism was not for him the rational tool it was for those who strove to put it into effect. *The Thief* is set in the Moscow underworld in the middle years of the NEP. The hero is an ex-communist, Mitka, who has become disillusioned with the 'retreat' to a modified bourgeois economy forced upon Lenin by peasant disturbances. An author appears in the novel, who 'discovers' this hero, now a criminal, as excellent material for his novel (the technique is of course that of Gide's *The Coiners*, q.v.). Mitka is a bold thief, but he is tormented both by remorse for his past killing of a White officer and by his anarchic present. The luridness of Dostoevski is everywhere evident; but this author is up to his task. One of the most notable characters is the hideous Chikelyov—'degenerate epigone with a wound instead of a face', says the author—whose cringing subservience to the establishment and bullying of others personifies the Soviet bureaucrat: 'Thought, that is the cause of suffering. The man who can eradicate thought will be held in everlasting remembrance by a grateful mankind'.

Ultimately, we are told, Mitka finds self-respect and rehabilitation by work as a lumberman. Unfortunately Leonov published (1959) a 'party' version of this fine novel which is but a pale version of the original. (The Soviet establishment often likes to offer a man the chance to cut off his own balls before it does it for him.) In his more orthodox novels, *Sot* (1930; tr. I. Montagu and S. Nolbandov, 1931), named after the river, and *Skutarevsky* (1932; tr. A. Brown, 1936), both Five Year Plan novels, dealing with industrialization and the re-education of bourgeoisie, he does his best to introduce characterization and conflict, but gets little chance. *Road to the Ocean* (1935; tr. N. Guterman, 1944) is better, for in Kurilov the author has created one of the very few almost convincing dedicated communist heroes in Soviet fiction. Leonov was genuinely moved by the human effort put into the Five Year Plan, and he conveys this. But his interest in character nearly ran away with him, so that it is his socialist realism rather than his novel that is flawed. Certainly *Road to the Ocean* has its solemn moments: for anyone trying to write 'good communism', in the party sense, is not able to simultaneously hold on to his sense of humour. Thus, defending a girl, he can speak of her as 'nice. . . . She has never been sentenced . . . never engaged in trade, she has no record of harmful deviations'. But the difficulties of Kurilov's love life are well done, and his fears of death are sensitively conveyed, and Leonov's least unconvincing women figure in this novel. However, no one received it with enthusiasm. *Russian Forest* (1953; pt. tr. N. Lukoshkova, *Soviet Literature*, 6, 1954) is over-ambitious and disappointing; most of the steam seems to have gone out of the author's powers of characterization. Between these last two novels Leonov turned to the theatre. He is an excellent example of a writer who has successfully steered his way down the twisting path of party policy—he lacks humorous resources—but has done so without renouncing much personal integrity.

ISAAC BABEL (1894–?1941), another victim of Stalin's purges, was the son of a Jewish tradesman of Odessa. He has been irresponsibly hailed (by, among others, Lionel Trilling) as the only genius to come out of Soviet Russia, and his reputation is still—despite his rehabilitation in 1957—greater in the West. He was, nevertheless, a remarkable writer of short stories. His fiction exists in several translations; the best is *Collected Stories* (tr. W. Morison *et al.*, 1957). None of his plays has been translated. Babel was a more intense, literate, literary, thoughtful and gifted Vsevolod Ivanov (q.v.). His genius arose from his strict Jewish upbringing, which included the reading of Hebrew and the Talmud, French language and literature—he was so keen on it as an adolescent that he wrote his first stories in it—and, finally, the Russian Revolution itself in all its colour and cruelty. In Babel's stories the ghosts of Flaubert and Maupassant jostle with that of Gogol.

Babel fought in the First World War, then joined the Bolsheviks in 1917.

Although short-sighted and frail, he fought with Budenny's Red Cavalry in Poland. His experiences led to the most colourful version of that persistent theme of the Twenties, the intellectual and his relationship with the revolutionaries: the stories in *Red Cavalry* (1926).

Had Chagall been forced to paint scenes of bloody action he would perhaps have produced canvases possessing the same kind of impact as Babel's violent, sensual, stark tales. His eye for detail as he describes these killing Cossacks (Budenny himself protested that he exaggerated) is marvellous. A Jew about to die for spying shrieks; but when his executioner puts a headlock on him he quietens and 'spreads his legs'; then 'Kudrya took out a dagger . . . and carefully butchered the old man without bespattering himself'. The bespectacled intellectual is simultaneously fascinated and horrified by this kind of primitivism; but he is also a part of it. Babel is a painter; a non-moralist. *Red Cavalry* is as raw as his wounded, shocked, abject-proud sensibility. His later stories, good too but not as good as those in *Red Cavalry*, deal with the Jewish underworld of Odessa. Babel wrote little in the Thirties, before he was imprisoned; at the 1934 Writers' Congress he spoke of cultivating a 'new genre': silence. No such society as Stalin's could possibly have accommodated his brilliance, his intelligence, his irony.

ILYA EHRENBURG (1891–1967), born in Kiev, was creatively a minor talent; but he was a good journalist. Nothing Ehrenburg did is very convincing, because his response to all experience was superficial, journalistic. But he was humane, and he has been a useful and entertaining writer; until he returned to Russia in 1924 he was blown about by the prevailing wind of almost every possible fashion: he had written an anti-Bolshevik 'Prayer for Russia', and before that some gloomy pseudo-symbolist poetry. Even after his return he conceded both to the fashion for Stalin and then the fashion for liberalization. His nihilistic *Julio Jurenito* (1919; tr. A. Bostock and Y. Kapp, 1958) is imitation satire. Probably *A Street in Moscow* (1927; tr. S. Volochova, 1932) displays him at his best: this has the appeal and use of good journalism. It was characteristic of his luck that he should be thought of, in the West, as a leading liberal because of the apt title of his novel *The Thaw* (1954; tr. M. Harari, 1955).

Some of the work of MIKHAIL BULGAKOV (1891–1940), a much more gifted writer, was suppressed because he treated the anti-communists truthfully and sympathetically. *The White Guard* (1924), the novel on which the *The Days of the Turbins* (q.v.) is based, has Whites as its heroes. The five stories in *Diablerie* (1925) are fantastic: the title story is a satire on bureaucracy, almost Kafkaesque in detail, about a clerk who mistakes his new boss's name for the word 'pants' and consequently loses position and identity. *The Heart of a Dog* (1925; tr. 1968) is another satire, in which a famous Moscow surgeon makes a dog into a humanoid. His fantasy on the devil in modern Moscow was not published until 1967: *The Master and Margarita*. Bulgakov was fortunate to escape the attentions of Stalin's secret police.

KONSTANTIN PAUSTOVSKY (1892–1968) always just avoided trouble; but when the thaw came he stood out as one of the writers who had somehow lost no integrity. He played some part in the liberalization of the late Fifties. He was born in Kiev, and led a varied life until he settled down as a writer in the Twenties, when he knew many of the leading writers of the time. At his death he was the most venerated of all Russian writers. Paustovsky was the friend and biographer of a most curious case in Soviet literature, the ever-popular ALEXANDER GRIN (ps. ALEXANDER GRINEVSKY, 1880–1932). Grin's books take place in the imaginary country of Grinland, and are escapist fantasies of quality and charm. They contain no references to the Soviet present and were ignored by the censors until 1950, eighteen years after Grin's death of cancer: they were then discovered to be decadent and 'cosmopolitan', and between 1950 and 1956 were suspended from circulation.

Paustovsky was also a dreamer; but his scope was wider, and he was influenced by Prishvin, Zamyatin and Bunin (qq.v.). His earlier books were over-romantic and literary—the first of his novels was called *Romantics* (1923) —and often inspired by Western romances. His novels of the Thirties, *Kara Bugaz* (1932) and *Kolchida* (1934), fulfilled party requirements by recording achievements, such as the history of attempts to utilize sodium sulphate on the bottom of a bay in the Caspian Sea; but they are exotic, and contain evocations of the Russian landscape in its various aspects of bareness and lushness. But Paustovsky's main work is his vast autobiography (1946–64), translated by M. Harari and J. Duncan as *Story of a Life* (1964), *Slow Approach of Thunder* (1965), *In That Dawn* (1967). This is a work of enormous scope, preserving an essentially romantic and optimistic vision; historians will need to refer to it when they investigate the history of Russia in the twentieth century. However, it has been overrated in the West.

A close friend of Paustovsky's was YURY OLESHA (1899–1960), who is most famous for his novel *Envy* (1928; tr. L. and V. Woolf, 1936; P. Ross, 1947). Olesha, who disappeared into the camps in the late Thirties, suddenly reappeared, 'rehabilitated', in 1956. He wrote other books, and a play; but *Envy* is his masterpiece. As a critic has said: Olesha 'always succeeded in seeing the world through the eyes of lovers and children'. *Envy* is a completely fresh way of seeing the conflict between the old and the new Russias. It does not attempt a 'solution'. It could best be described as expressionist. Babichev, a director of the Soviet Food Industry Trust, one night sentimentally picks up Kavalerov, a drunken bum and anarchist, from the street and takes him into his house. Kavalerov is envious (hence the title) of Babichev, who is his inferior in every way—except in that of worldly success and 'social seriousness'. Babichev's brother Ivan is another misfit; he has invented a machine called Ophelia, with which he plans to dishonour the entire modern mechanized world—and in particular to destroy Babichev's model community kitchen. Some of the criticism of this complicated book, which should be better known in the West than it is, spoke of how valuably it exposed the enemies of the regime. . . . No wonder Olesha more or less stopped writing. This short novel embraces, with high responsibility, the whole tragi-comedy of technology and its destruction of life's pleasures, of Soviet communism and its creation of Babichevs—men not unlike, in their Soviet way, Sinclair Lewis' Babbitt. Olesha saw through to the heart of the paradox involved in Utopianism; his puzzlement at it led him into ironies which he may not have intended. (Short stories by Olesha are in SL, ARL.)

A literary organization close to the ideals of the Serapion Brothers, but much smaller, was called the Pau; it was founded in 1924. The most immediately successful of this group—many of whom vanished in the late Thirties, as Trotskyites—was P. PAVLENKO (1899–1951), who turned into an orthodox party servant. Better known now, however, is ANDREY PLATONOV (1896–1951), a selection of whose short stories Evtushenko (q.v.) has introduced to the West— *The Fierce and Beautiful World* (tr. J. Barnes, 1971)—by saying 'There is not an educated reader in the USSR who does not know Platonov'. This fame came to him after death and rehabilitation. His stories are simple, psychologically penetrating and yet have an epic sweep.

*

When Stalin dissolved all literary groups in 1932 it was up to Soviet writers to be 'educational'—or to cultivate Babel's new genre of silence. This means that there is very little to discuss in the decades between 1932 and 1954. As we have seen, even those who had been free to write more or less as they wished in the Twenties were forced to compromise in the Thirties, and wrote less well. So far they have few successors: the path of a writer worth the name in post-Stalinist Russia is not easy, as may be judged from the fates of Pasternak, Daniel and Sinyavsky, and Solzhenitsyn (qq.v.). The last named is the only major prose writer (known to the West) to emerge in Russia since Stalin's death. VLADIMIR DUDINTSEV (1918), author of one of the books that initiated the thaw, *Not By Bread Alone* (1956; tr. E. Bone, 1957), about an engineer's struggles against Stalinist corruption, is a somewhat verbose writer—his importance is mainly historical, since his book goes so far as to imply criticism of the entire communist system. One or two other writers have actually come to the West, but they are not distinguished—any more than is most of the material illegally circulated abroad.

It is possible, however, that the work of another Solzhenitsyn is circulating in *samizdat*, the system by which Russian readers get round the censorship: this involves the clandestine transmission of work in typewritten or mimeographed copies, and the practice probably began around 1955–6. Some of this finds its way abroad, where it is eagerly seized upon by anti-communist journalists who are no more interested in literature than are the Soviet censors.

YURI DANIEL (1925), who used the pseudonym Nikolay Arzak for his publications in the West, was in 1966 sentenced to five years for, in effect, supplying the 'reactionary' West with material for propaganda against the Soviet system. Tried with him was his friend, a more important writer, ANDREY SINYAVSKY (1925), whose Western pseudonym was Abram Tertz; he got seven years. Daniel, an accomplished stylist, is the son of a writer of Yiddish stories. His four best known stories, and the ones for which he was put on trial, are collected

GUIDE TO MODERN WORLD LITERATURE

in *This is Moscow Speaking* (tr. S. Hood *et al.*, 1968). Daniel is a realist, but he sometimes uses fantasy to point his satire—as in the title story of *This is Moscow Speaking*, in which the Russian government declares 10 August 1960 to be 'a Public Murder Day'. This is good satire; but it is rather anti-state than anti-Soviet.

Sinyavsky was a friend of Pasternak, and is an important critic; as a novelist and short story writer he is in the Twenties tradition: his fantastic techniques simply cannot be reconciled with the simple-minded party idea of a novel, which is what led him to circumvent both the official censor and his own sense of self-preservation and take the risk of expressing himself freely. The novel *The Trial Begins* (tr. 1960) and the stories in *The Icicle* (1961; tr. 1963) are evocations of the horrors of the Stalin period. *The Makepeace Experiment* (1964; tr. 1965) has a hero who can influence people by remote control, and tries to create a toy Utopia. His vision of his time is not political, but metaphysical; he is a true modernist, whose self-styled 'phantasmagoric art' has (like Borges' and so many others') 'hypotheses instead of a purpose'.

ALEXANDER SOLZHENITSYN (1918), born in Rostov, won the Nobel Prize in 1970—but was not allowed to go to Stockholm to receive it. He appears to have resisted all attempts to persuade him to live outside Russia. But of his four full-length novels only the first, *One Day in the Life of Ivan Denisovich* (1962; tr. R. Parker, 1963; G. Aitken, 1970), has appeared in Russia. He is still, in 1973, attempting to publish his fourth novel in Russia. Kruschev personally gave the go-ahead for the publication of *One Day*, which exposes the conditions in one of Stalin's camps through the eyes of the kind of simple man beloved by generations of Russian readers; but this was not because Kruschev loved freedom but because he wanted to scare off political enemies, and chose to create conditions resembling a fresh thaw in order to do so. Solzhenitsyn was soon in trouble: denounced in 1968 for having had, since 1957, the consistent aim of opposing the basic principles of Soviet literature, he was expelled from the Writers' Union in 1970.

Solzhenitsyn knew about Stalin's camps because, while serving as an officer in East Prussia in 1945 he had written to a fellow-officer of the military short-comings of 'the whiskered one'; for this he got eight years, which was followed by three years in exile—followed, in 1957, by complete rehabilitation. Since *One Day* he has written *Cancer Ward* (1968; tr. 1968), which is once again based on autobiographical material and *First Circle* (1968; tr. M. Guybon, 1968), which is about one of Stalin's 'special prisons'—for highly qualified political prisoners—and which has several chapters devoted to Stalin himself. *Stories and Prose Poems* (tr. M. Glenny, 1971) collects some famous stories, including 'Matryona's House' and 'An Incident at Krechetovka Station', in improved translations. His latest novel, *1914* (tr. 1972), part of a longer work, deals with events in Russia before the Revolution. He is constantly harassed by the government.

Solzhenitsyn has not been overrated because of his unfortunate position. *Cancer Ward* most aptly indicates the scope and stature of his fiction. It is one of those novels whose symbolism is profound and almost limitlessly resonant because everything works perfectly on the realistic level. *Cancer Ward* can and should be read at the realistic level. But the cancer suffered by the patients (Solzhenitsyn himself has suffered from cancer for eighteen years) stands for— one is tempted to say 'is'—other things: death, the suffering that regenerates (a persistent theme in Russian fiction) and the human sickness that is Stalin himself. This notion that all men—even the police informer Rusanov—are threatened by death contradicts the childish fantasy of immortality that Soviet governments try to put across on the people. We can say 'governments' because although this novel is set in the Stalinist era, Stalin's successors will not allow it to appear. . . . Stylistically *Cancer Ward* is less good than Solzhenitsyn's first novel, with its brilliant use of dialect; it is considerably longer, and some of its description is aimlessly weak. But this hardly matters, for it succeeds in demonstrating that in spite of terror and bureaucracy, humanity, in the Tolstoian sense, has survived. We need, in this age, such demonstrations. There is much goodness and unselfishness and self-sacrifice in the book; and there could hardly ever have been a more sympathetic portrait of an *apparatchik* than that of Rusanov, considering what he is. And Solzhenitsyn brings out the irony perfectly: this man, who thinks he led men and women to their deaths or imprisonments out of service to the state—and for his family's happiness—is a paradigm of bourgeoishood. What has communism been for?

Another side of Solzhenitsyn, the lyrical and simple, comes out in his prose poems, which can make such simple statements as 'As long as there is fresh air to breathe under an apple-tree in a shower, we may survive a little longer'. This occurs in a minor piece of writing. But its author's major works have the same simplicity on a grander scale—and the same heroism—that characterize his life.

II

The Soviet theatre is certainly the finest state theatre in the world. Actors are looked after like 'amateur' athletes. But, since the first rule of this theatre is that it should be 'a laboratory for the creation of Soviet plays' it has, as is well known, failed to produce any major playwrights. True, the average Soviet play is not inferior to its American or British counterpart; but where those countries have produced at least some gifted dramatists, Russia has produced dramatists of competence and no more. Had the theatre been allowed to reap the benefits of the experimental period in the Twenties then things might have been different. Soviet drama proves that when you try to reduce literature to a formula, you get no literature.

The new Russian theatre was built up before the Revolution. The process began in 1898 with the establishment of the Moscow Arts Theatre under V. I. Nemirovich-Danchenko and Stanislavsky. It was these men who did away with rhetoric and theatricality in favour of simplicity and atmosphere. Stanislavsky's influence on the 'method' style of acting (q.v.) was only a part of his contribution to the theatre; the over-emphasis on the psychological as opposed to the technical side of acting was hardly his. He was one of the first to realize that the staging of a play is a matter of creating an illusion; he concentrated on the style of the illusion rather than on crude mimesis or re-creation of reality. On the other hand, he believed devoutly in the illusion, and so has been characterized—and not wrongly—as being 'lovingly realistic'. But it is important to understand that his procedures were not mimetic. His own greatest triumphs were his productions of Chekhov's plays. After producing Gorky's *The Lower Depths* (1902), a flawed but powerful play, he turned between 1905 and 1916 to symbolic drama, including plays by Maeterlinck and Andreyev (qq.v.). Alexander Tairov founded the Kamerny Theatre (1914) to oppose Stanislavsky. He was not as far, in his deliberate theatricalism, from Stanislavsky as he and some others supposed; it was simply that he put less emphasis on the actor's role. Here he agreed with Vsevolod Meyerhold (a victim of the purges), who embraced Bolshevism, but whose theories increasingly displeased the authorities. Meyerhold was really a reluctant pioneer of 'director's theatre' (q.v.): the actor was reduced to a puppet in the director's hands.

The two most exciting plays presented in Russia after the Revolution were prose plays by Mayakovsky (q.v.). His second (the first had been the tragedy *Vladimir Mayakovsky*, produced and acted by himself) play, *Mystery-Bouffe* (1918; rev. 1921; MRP), had been a provocative pro-communist farce, parodying the Noah story. But ten years later, having thrown himself wholeheartedly into the revolutionary struggle, he began to feel gloom. *The Bedbug* (1928; tr. P. Blake, 1960) is a satire on the type of man who was soon to rise to the top under Stalin: the pseudo-communist Prisypkin, imprisoned in a zoo by future generations as a curious specimen, is the perfect Stalinist bureaucrat. *The Bathhouse* (1930) is an even more bitter attack, in the same vein. Both plays were produced by Meyerhold with great panache; but they were withdrawn as subversive, and did not reappear until 1954. Stalin later praised Mayakovsky as the best poet of the epoch, and he was thereafter made obligatory ('his second death', Pasternak, q.v., called it); but the textbooks ignored these plays.

Bulgakov (q.v.) adapted his novel *The White Guard* as a play, *The Days of the Turbins* (1926; SSP), and this was produced at the Moscow Arts Theatre with enormous success: Soviet audiences were genuinely interested in the psychology of enemies of the revolution—until this was discouraged. Bulgakov made himself more unpopular with the regime with *Zoe's Apartment* (1926) and *The Purple Island* (1928), which made fun of the censorship. In the Thirties he turned to adaptation rather than the writing of socialist realist plays.

Some writers besides Katayev who were primarily novelists made plays in the earlier, less restrictive period. Babel's (q.v.) best play is *Sunset* (1928), a colourful treatment of Jewish life. Leonov (q.v.) turned to drama between 1936 and the end of the war. His interest in individual psychology distinguishes his plays from the usual diet of the period; but his potentiality in this direction was modified by party demands. The rather Chekhovian *Untilovsk* (1926) earned him reproaches for making the cynical leading character more interesting than the good communists. *The Apple Orchards* (1938) was performed in England after the war. This exists in two versions, the second of which is a travesty of the first. His war drama *Lyonushka* (1943), ostensibly about guerrilla fighters, a burnt flier they hide, and the peasant girl who loves him, is really a symbolic drama.

An equivocal play of the Thirties was Olesha's adaptation of his novel *Envy* (q.v.), called *A Conspiracy of Feelings*; his *A List of Benefits* (1931) is more orthodox in that it comes down in favour of the Revolution—but it takes a critical look at it. It was this kind of critical scrutiny—by no means necessarily hostile—that Stalin set out not merely to discourage but to eliminate. He and his henchmen realized the powerful propaganda weapon they had in the theatre; but in their fear of criticism they robbed it of all vigour: the theatre was the most immediately vulnerable to a system that reduced literature to a matter of an imitation not of real life but of one man's (Stalin's) official image of it. Meyerhold and Tairov were condemned as 'decadent and bourgeois', and guilty of 'art for art's sake'. The situation was made considerably worse by the fact of Stalin's personal philistinism. The last flicker of life was extinguished at about the beginning of the Thirties, when Mayakovsky's farcical satires and most other 'undesirable' comedies were suppressed. Katayev adapted his *The Embezzlers* (q.v.); his satire on the NEP period, *Squaring the Circle* (1928; SSP), cast in vaudeville form, would not have been playable in the mid-Thirties.

NIKOLAY POGODIN (ps. N. F. STUKALOV, 1900–62), in the Thirties the most successful dramatist, produced the best official drama; he did so by concentrating on men actually at work. The theme of *The Aristocrats* (1934; tr. 1937) is the optimistic stock communist one of how criminals are morally regenerated by forced labour. Pogodin did what he could to redeem this unpromising material by the introduction of wit, humour and a cinematic technique. For personal problems he substituted ones involving the achievement of industrial feats. Thus, *Tempo* (1930; tr. 1936) hangs on the speed with which workers can construct a tractor factory—they are helped by a young American communist, a detail that might well have proved unacceptable by the late Thirties. *The Man with the Gun* (1937; tr. 1938) puts Lenin on the stage in a not too embarrassingly idealized manner. *Kremlin Chimes* (1940), a drama of electrification with a sub-plot about a workman who repairs the Kremlin Chimes so that they play the Internationale, reintroduces Lenin. *The Third, Pathetic* (1958), dealing with his death, completes the Lenin trilogy. *Missouri Waltz* (1950) is a sometimes amusing satire on President Truman.

VSEVOLOD VISHNEVSKY (1900–51), a talented man, is still regarded as a Russian classic. Vishnevsky began as an intelligent admirer of such Western writers as Dos Passos and Joyce (qq.v.). He was as gifted as Pogodin, but a fanatic communist—and, it seems, a most treacherous man—who was not above altering history so as to give Stalin a heroic role in it in his sycophantic *The Unforgettable 1919* (1949). But he is better than this makes him out to be. *The First Cavalry Army* (1929) sincerely glorifies the Revolution, and shows a mastery of crowd scenes. *The Optimistic Tragedy* (1934), which was produced by Tairov, is perhaps the most successful of all the propaganda drama of its period. It deals with the Red fleet and a woman commissar who works and dies with it in the years of the Revolution. What is remarkable about this heroic pageant is that it does not lack convincing characterization. But Vishnevsky never equalled this almost expressionistic play, in which he made use of a narrator, who comments on the action.

VLADIMIR KIRSHON (1902–?1938) was a leading 'proletarian' playwright, who insisted that plays should be politically correct. His plays are inevitably superficial, but some of them created sensations when they appeared. *Red Rust* (1927; ad. V. and F. Vernon, 1930) dealt with a controversy over whether a condemned murderer should be pardoned on account of his communism. Vishnevsky, his theatrical rival, publicly accused him of Trotskyism and he was arrested and murdered (some say that Fadeyev, q.v., had a hand in this, too). He was rehabilitated in 1956.

Such writers as Grin and Prishvin kept out of trouble with the authorities by limiting themselves to the realms of fantasy or pure nature. So, in the theatre, EVGENY SHVARTS (1896—1958) avoided dullness by confining himself to fantasy or children's theatre. His genre is perhaps a minor one, but within it he is enchanting. He has written for the puppet theatre and the cinema, as well as the theatre, on such characters as *Red Riding Hood* (1937), *The Snow Queen* (1938) and Don Quixote. He is one of those writers whose high and apparently conventional morality is the reverse of offensive: he inhabits the magic world he creates.

The Soviet theatre has not made much advance in the years since Stalin's death. Audiences have on the whole chosen to value plays of poor quality that make them laugh, such as those of ANATOLY SOFRONOV (1911), an author of musical comedies—one of which, *A Million for a Smile*, was seen in London in 1967. A. VOLODIN (ps. A. LIFSHITS, 1919) is better than this: his *The Factory Girl* (1956) was attacked by party officials, but was put on and enjoyed great success. This portrays a straight-speaking factory girl and ridicules a party organizer. Since then he has written several more independent-minded plays. VICTOR ROZOV (1913), who wrote the drama on which the well-known film *The Cranes are Flying* was based, has written some pleasant comedies.

Russia has had no major dramatist since Chekhov. But with the wrongly interpreted views of Stanislavsky, which dominated Russian theatre for nearly a quarter of a century, being challenged, and with the authority of the rehabilitated Meyerhold and Tairov persistently being quoted, it is now at least possible that one might, if his plays could get through to performance, emerge.

III

In the late nineteenth century Russian writers reacted against realism. The chief feature of this so-called Silver Age was symbolist poetry. Poetry had been almost eclipsed by the realist fiction. The only major poets were Afanasy Fet, Fyodor Tyutchev and the much loved Nikolay Nekrasov; Leo Tolstoi's distant relative Count Alexey Tolstoi, and the romantic Yakov Polonsky were pleasant minor poets. The critics of the mid-nineteenth century were so utilitarian (they foreshadowed, as I have noted, the Soviet critics) that one of them went so far as to say that Shakespeare's poetry (i.e. all poetry) was worth less than a good pair of boots. Obviously there was going to be a reaction to this; it came in the Nineties, and it took the form of symbolism.

The poetry and criticism that came into being at this time were later known as 'symbolist', 'decadent' and 'modernist'. The poet, novelist and critic DMITRI MEREZHKOVSKY (1865—1941) was the chief active pioneer. In a famous lecture of 1892 he emphasized that the greatest Russian writers all believed in a mysterious, ideal world: a higher reality. He attacked the crass realism that would not or could not acknowledge this reality. His own poetry is not as important as that of his wife, Z. Gippius (q.v.); but his early historical novel, the trilogy *Christ and the Antichrist* (1896-1905; tr. B. G. Guerney, 1928-31), in which he tries to reconcile the spirituality of Christianity with the physicality of paganism, is of interest. His later work is largely spoilt because he became obsessed with this reconciliation and projected it onto everything. He went to Paris at the Revolution and in time became a pretentious neo-fascist, frustrated at the West's refusal to stem the tide of Bolshevism.

The early symbolists preserved the French word *décadence* as *dekadens* in order to signify that they understood it not literally but as a genre. They had their own word for the literal term. Their enemies, who included Gorky (q.v.), translated *dekadens* into the Russian. . . . Thus arose a confusion between symbolism and decadence that the Soviet critics have naturally exploited: all individualists or romantics are 'decadent'.

Russian symbolism had its roots not only in the poetry of Baudelaire and his successors, but also in that of Fet and Tyutchev. A more immediate precursor was VLADIMIR SOLOVYEV (1853-1900), who was a particularly potent influence on Blok and Bely (qq.v.). Some of the symbolists held that the movement was literary; others, including Blok and Bely, believed that it was a religion, a whole way of looking at existence; their idea of the priestly function of the poet is somewhat akin to that of George (q.v.). In general, Russian symbolism had the hallmarks of a religious movement.

Solovyev is important as theologian, philosopher and poet. He was a syncretist who sought to reconcile humanism with Christianity; he wanted to effect a reunification of the Russian Orthodox Church with Rome; he evolved a system that he called theosophy, an 'organic synthesis of theology, philosophy and the science of experience'. What affected the symbolists in his thought was his exploration of the relation of 'that which truly is' to 'empirical reality'. This remarkable man also anticipated some of the work of Husserl (q.v.), and may therefore be regarded as a precursor of the phenomenonologists. This opening stanza of one of his poems, expressing a thought central in Solovyev's philosophy, makes it easy to see what in him appealed to the symbolists:

> Do you not see, Beloved?
> All that about us lies
> Is but the shade, the mirrored image
> Of things not seen with eyes.   (BRV)

His mystical celebration of his muse, the Eternal Feminine Sophia, the Divine Wisdom—she appeared to him in a vision in London, ordering him to Arabia, where he went—was extremely important to Blok. Solovyev's single book of poems, through which he wielded his influence, was published in 1891. It is surprising to find in them, in view of his philosophy, a strong element of playfulness—this was certainly inherited by Bely.

Before Merezhkovsky's lecture mentioned above some obscure poets had been publishing symbolist poems in magazines. But the publication of three issues of *Russian Symbolists* (1894) made more stir. This was partly a hoax, since many of the poems are signed with false names: they are actually by the editor, VALERY BRYUSOV (1873–1924). Bryusov succeeded in shocking the reading public by these rather intellectual imitations of French symbolist poems; but he himself was ostracized for some years, until in fact symbolism had become an accomplished school in the hands of other poets. He was later accepted as a brilliantly classical poet and a leader of the symbolist movement. After 1917 he became an enthusiastic communist. He wrote two intelligent historical novels, *The Fiery Angel* (1908) and *The Altar of Victory* (1913), short stories and criticism.

Bryusov is a somewhat curious case. Undoubtedly an initiator of symbolism in his country, he was too rational and impressionable to be a true symbolist: he gives no evidence that he believes in any other world; he is more interested, it seems, in form and procedures. His conviction is no more than that 'everything in life is but a means for the creation of vivid and melodious verses' and that 'from time immemorial the poet's cherished crown has been one of thorns'. And yet he was regarded by such very different poets as Blok and Andrey Bely as an indispensable teacher of technique. Essentially he was a persistent and always highly intelligent experimentalist. The strongest single influence on Bryusov's poetry was Verhaeren (q.v.), whom he translated; with Verhaeren he shares a certain excitement simply in what is happening, for its own sake. Of the Revolution he could write, without mysticism:

> O you fantastics, you aesthetic throng,
> must all your dreams have faint and faraway wings?
> Was it in books alone, made safe in song,
> you loved remarkable and shattering things?   (RP)

At the end of his life Bryusov, who had himself anticipated and influenced the futurists (q.v.), was attempting a 'scientific poetry' in something like their style. (BRV; PRV)

While Bryusov languished in unpopularity, KONSTANTIN BALMONT (1867–1943) enjoyed a great vogue. His verse was musical and, in its technically conservative manner, skilful; but he had nothing serious to say. He is a symbolist only because his true world is that of mellifluous music. He became an *émigré* in Paris after having at first greeted the Revolution with enthusiasm. His later work is of interest. (PRV; BRV; BRV2)

A more important and interesting poet is INNOKENTY ANNENSKY (1856–1909), who was born at Omsk. Annensky was hardly known as a poet until the posthumous publication of his second collection, *The Cypress Chest* (1910). He learned much from the French symbolists, but was never, although often referred to as a symbolist, a member of the Russian symbolist school, whose diffusiveness and mystical tendencies he criticized. His poetry was an immediate source of inspiration to the Acmeists and to Pasternak (qq.v.). He was a noted Greek scholar who translated the whole of Euripides into Russian. His poetry is about futility, hopeless longing and anguish, which is counterbalanced by little more than the sense of beauty residing in his lucidity, and brilliant use of form and description. Life is redeemed for Annensky only by the richness of its decay, of which his poetry is a celebration. (PRV; MRP)

With FYODOR SOLOGUB (ps. FYODOR K. TETERNIKOV, 1863–1927) we have a symbolist who really deserves to be called a decadent; but he was a fascinating writer, a major novelist and poet who, although his name is well known, has not had the Western critical attention that he merits. He remained in Russia after the Revolution, but Soviet criticism has largely ignored him because of his pessimism. For twenty-five years Sologub endured the life of a school inspector; then in 1907 he was able to retire to devote himself to writing. The key to Sologub is self-hate; from this he wanted to take refuge in the world of the imagination. He was so romantic that he could not stand, within himself, any kind of crassness: lust, greed, and so on—the things we must all bear within ourselves. His description of the world is therefore romantically corrupt, loathsome. In his deservedly famous novel *The Little Demon* (1905–7; tr. R. Wilks, 1962; A. Field, 1969) the schoolmaster Peredonov is the apotheosis of pettiness and baseness. The novel has been attacked on the grounds of its hero's vileness; but Sologub was experimenting with his nastiest side. His trilogy *The Created Legend* (1908–12), the background of which is the 1905 revolution, is an uninvestigated masterpiece; the first part was translated by J. Cournos (*The Created Legend*, 1916). Sologub's poetry resembles Annensky's in this: that the counterweight to despair resides in the sensuousness of the poems (they are incredibly numerous) themselves. Only Zamyatin (q.v.) seems to have understood him: his sickness, he said, was 'the Russian sickness': the love that demands all or nothing; in other words, absolute romanticism, hatred of less than the lush perfection that Peredonov seeks in his sadism and rejection of 'ordinary' decencies. Thus, while the content of many of his poems is perverse, its expression is beautiful. He casts his mad spell of desire for beauty in them; and the reader succumbs. His poet forgets the pleasures of wine and goes to his voluntary prison alone, without a lamp—the door has not been opened for a long time, and the place is dark, damp and unpleasant. But when he grows accustomed to the dark he notes strange marks on the walls and floor: he cannot understand them, but is confident that death will explain them. (PRV; BRV)

VYACHESLAV IVANOV (1866–1949), philosopher as well as poet, subordinated poetry to the religious life; he eventually became a monk. Ivanov's ideas are boring and obvious—Nietzsche is adapted so that Dionysus is the forerunner of Christ—but his poetry has a certain magnificence of style. (PRV; BRV; BRV2)

ZINAIDA GIPPIUS (1869–1945), the wife of Merezhkovsky (q.v.), was a skilful technician who might have written in any style, but actually wrote in a symbolist-decadent one because of her immediate circumstances. She sees her flaccid, dull and stingless soul, 'black and fearsome', as her limitation. Her content is often in this rather lurid vein; but her actual writing is elegant and metaphysical, and the sometimes sensational themes are always handled with intelligence and tact. It is not generally realized that she is as important a woman poet—and a more difficult one—as Akhmatova (q.v.). (PRV; MRP)

MAXIMILIAN VOLOSHIN (1877–1932), a painter as well as a poet, was born of a noble family in Kiev. He was a symbolist by belief, but the surface of his poetry is almost Parnassian (q.v.): in fact he lived in Paris for some years, translated from the French, and modelled his own first poetry on such poets as Heredia (q.v.). He was later involved with the beginnings of acmeism (q.v.). But with the Revolution his poetry changed: he hymned the cataclysm as a purging terror which would bring about a spiritual rebirth. This was, generally speaking, a Slavophile and symbolist reaction; certainly Voloshin believed that the Revolution would liberate Russia from foreign influences. Like Blok (q.v.), he became disillusioned; after 1924 he ceased to publish. His earlier poems, some of them sonnets, are impressionistic studies of landscape very much in the manner of Heredia; but Voloshin adds a sense of fear that anticipates his attitude to the events of 1917. This is shown most clearly in 'Holy Russia' (PRV).

The greatest of the symbolists, and one of the greatest of modern poets in any language, is ALEXANDER BLOK (1880–1921), who was born at St. Petersburg. He came from a highly literate family, and differed from most of the other symbolists in that his earliest models were nineteenth-century Russian poets, and not Frenchmen. He found himself as a poet when he discovered the poetry of Solovyev (q.v.) in 1902; but he rejected the Christian elements in Solovyev's syncretism: 'Nothing—and this is final—will ever make me turn to Christ for a cure'. This reminds us of Rilke, a poet of similar stature. Previously Blok had had a series of mystical experiences, all of which concerned the 'Lady Beautiful': a figure of perfection and (musical) harmony—Solovyev's intuition of Sophia Blok saw, of course, as equivalent to his own apprehension of the Lady Beautiful; in fact, as he himself said in his autobiography, it was Solovyev who gave him understanding of his experiences. His first book was called *Verses About the Lady Beautiful* (1904). In 1903 he had married, and he regarded his wife as a manifestation of the Lady Beautiful. As a young man (himself beautiful and with an extraordinary presence) Blok vainly sought to combine the ecstasies of romantic love with wisdom, but was full of forebodings even as he sensed the coming of the Lady Beautiful: 'How clear the whole horizon is! Radiance approaches. But terror pricks me: You will change your shape'. It is important to recognize that, however savagely the always troubled Blok satirized himself—as in *The Little Booth* (1906–7), part of a trilogy of dramas— he believed in the objective reality of those other realms from which the Lady Beautiful came. However, one side of Blok himself suffered from the ironic scepticism that characterizes the intelligentsia of the twentieth century; but he loathed this, because he saw it as challenging the spiritual reality in which he believed. But he had to go through with what his vision of life vouchsafed. The Lady Beautiful became a hideous sex-doll; he felt himself 'full of demons' which 'the caprices of his evil creative will form[ed] into ever-changing groups of conspirators', with whose help he hid 'some part of his soul from himself'. Art and poetic success were no substitute, for Blok, for the loss of his unifying Goddess in her most beneficient and healing aspect. He continued to 'believe' in her; it was in himself—doomed to be no more than an actor—that he ceased to believe. The revolution of 1905 gave him some hope; but he suffered more than any writer from the disillusion of its aftermath. A practising homosexual (inventors of 'Goddess' systems usually are, although not all practise), he took to drink, despair and extra-marital love. His poem 'The Stranger' reflects this period with great vividness and power. Here the mystery seems to be carried by a prostitute. He tried to establish contact with others, and to escape from his own anguish, by writing his first plays. These were directed by Meyerhold. Later he sought other means of uniting himself with his own people, and the peculiar destiny of that people: by working hard, by opposing himself to the disintegrating school of symbolism, by undertaking public activities. In 'On the Field of Kulikove' he prophesies cataclysm and disaster in giving an account of a famous victory:

> The heart cannot live peaceably.
> Now not for nothing does the air
> darken, armour hang heavily.
> Your hour has struck—To prayer!
> > (*The Twelve and other poems*: tr. J. Stallworthy
> > and P. France, 1970)

He believed in Russia as a 'lyrical force', but confessed that he did not believe in its past or future existence—an essentially symbolist utterance. All this time he displayed ferocious energy, wavering between eschatological ecstasy and helpless despair, but sustained by a social conscience of true nobility. He served in the war; then, when the Revolution came, welcomed it for reasons rather similar to those of Voloshin (q.v.)—but, perhaps owing to his unhappiness at losing the purity of his original vision and his dissatisfaction with his poetic role, Blok threw himself into the Revolution with high enthusiasm. He was uninterested in Marx and Lenin except as instruments of truth. His poem sequence 'The Twelve' shows twelve Red Guardsmen, scum, killers, turned into the twelve apostles led by the figure of Christ; the rhythms vary from those of folk-tunes to marches to revolutionary slogans. This of course pleased neither the Church nor the party. This Christ is certainly in no sense an orthodox one; he is the Tolstoian Christ of the Gospels, the good man in whom the churches take no interest (as Tolstoi saw); he is also the spirit of music. Blok went on working for the Revolution, as Zamyatin (q.v.) has recorded in a remarkable essay; but he was a broken man, and he died of heart-trouble after a difficult illness.

Blok was probably the greatest Russian poet since Pushkin; although internationally less well known than Rilke and Valéry (qq.v.), he is of their stature and importance. He revolutionized Russian versification by making use of a purely accentual technique. He knew, as so few now know, that only the poetry of suffering—whether it is a poetry of joy or not—can be great. His own poetry, for which he burnt himself out, demonstrates this. (PRV; BRV; BVR2; MRP; MEP; RP)

If Blok was the greatest of the modern Russian poets, he was by no means the only major poet. It is even arguable that from Russia more major poets have emerged than from anywhere else. . . .

The 'acmeist' revolution began with the launching of the magazine *Apollon* late in the first decade of the century, and with the homosexual MIKHAIL KUZMIN's (1875–1936) manifesto *Concerning Beautiful Clarity* (1910). Kuzmin began as a precious pasticheur of earlier styles; his later poetry is of great interest and originality. (MRP). His rebellion against the diffuseness and vague mysticism of minor symbolists expressed something in the air. He summed up the matter when he demanded clarity as well as beauty in poetry. NIKOLAY GUMILYEV (1886–1921) replaced this term by 'acmeism'. Acmeism is yet another example of a classical movement absorbing the main achievements of its romantic predecessor. Acmeism was concerned with exactitude, sharp and well-defined imagery and economy. Acmeism is not very important as a movement; its classical stylistic aims hid much romantic subject-matter; but it produced three major poets: Gumilyev, his wife (until their divorce in 1918) ANNA AKHMATOVA (ps. ANNA GORENKO, 1889–1967) and OSIP MANDELSHTAM (1891–1938). One of Gumilyev's school-teachers was Annensky (q.v.); with SERGEI GORADETSKY (1884) (BVR2) in 1911 he founded the Poets' Guild, as the acmeists called themselves. Gumilev fought in the First World War, returned to Russia and took part in various literary activities; and was then executed by firing squad for his part in a conspiracy against the Bolsheviks. That acmeism was mainly a stylistic movement is demonstrated above all by Gumilyev's poetry, whose subject-matter is exotic and romantic, and reflects his extensive travels, especially those in Africa. He is an elegant poet, who achieved the stylistic effects for which he aimed. He was particularly famous for his evocations of African landscapes. His poetry glorifies travel, adventure and heroism in a Parnassian manner; but adds a Kiplingesque vigour that no French Parnassian poet possessed. Gumilyev's last poems are his best; the life of action in the war and the Revolution (he was a monarchist) stirred him to profounder responses. Gumilyev's name embarrasses the Soviets, and of course his poetry has not often appeared in Russia; but he is read avidly, and has been extremely influential. 'The Tram that Lost its Way' is a famous and excellent illustration of his apocalyptic and intense final manner: the poet finds himself on a phantom tram that leaves a trail of fire in the air; he is executed, and his ghost searches for his lost betrothed; he understands that 'our freedom is but a light that breaks through from another world'. (PRV; BRV; BRV2; MRP)

Akhmatova was married three times. She suffered from Stalinism as much as any Russian not actually imprisoned or murdered; her son spent most of the years between 1934 and 1956 in concentration camps; her third husband was also arrested in the Thirties. She became known, at first, as a love poet who was not afraid to write in blunt terms of woman's passions. She, too, was a laconic and lucid poet. Her frank lyricism looked back to Pushkin; and Mandelshtam said that she 'brought to the Russian lyric the wealth of the nineteenth-century Russian novel'. She published nothing in the two decades before the Second World War; her later work combines the personal themes with the public one of suffering Russia. She was able to publish in the war; but Zhdanov selected her (with Zoshchenko, q.v.) for attack in 1946— calling her 'half nun, half harlot'—and she was forced into silence as well as out of the Writers' Union. Her longest and most complex work is 'Poem Without a Hero', the composition of which took her over twenty years. It is a poem that depends too much upon private knowledge to be completely successful as a whole, but it contains many fine passages. Akhmatova's earliest manner is typified in the beautiful 'Of the Cuckoo I Inquired':

> Of the cuckoo I inquired
> How many years I had left for living . . .
> The tops of the pine-trees trembled,
> A yellow sunbeam fell on the sward.
> But no sound disturbed the clearing . . .
> I walked homeward,
> And the cool breeze fondled
> My brow which was burning.   (MEP)

Later a note of menace came into her work, which sacrificed nothing in simplicity:

> If the moon's horror splashes,
> the whole town dissolves in poison.
> Without the slightest hope of sleep
> I see through the green murk
> not my childhood, not the sea,
> nor the butterflies' wedding flight
> over the bed of snow-white narcissi
> in that sixteenth year . . .
> but the eternally petrified round dance
> of the cypresses over your grave.
>
> (*Selected Poems*, tr. R. McKane, 1969)

'Requiem 1935–1940' is a moving sequence describing the author's own agonies in the worst years of Stalin; it is the best poetry to come out of that terrible period. (PVR; RP; BRV; BRV2; MRP)

Mandelshtam was the most complex of the three major acmeists. In 1934 he wrote a poem denouncing Stalin, for which he was persecuted, exiled and driven to his death. His widow has written a book, one of the most vivid accounts of the terrible years, telling all she knows of the affair: *Hope Against Hope* (1970; tr. M. Hayward, 1971). Mandelshtam's poetry shows a steady development from classicism to a near-surrealistic, even 'cubist' style— reflecting the disintegration of his health and hopes. This later work is more 'futurist' (q.v.) than acmeist. His first book, *Stone*, was published in 1913. In 1922 *Tristia* followed. His *Poems* of 1928 contained some seventy previously published poems and about forty new or previously unpublished ones. Some of his work was lost, but fifty-seven of his poems appear in his *Collected Works* (1964–6), published in New York. Mandelshtam was always influenced by classical literature, of which he had a wide and deep knowledge. Mandelshtam was of a highly nervous disposition, incapable of deviousness, and subject to attacks of *angina pectoris* (his first attack came while Samuel Marshak, a children's poet, translator and noted opportunist of the Stalin era, was defining poetry to him in a 'saccharine' voice). He was hopelessly out of tune with the Stalinist era because he insisted upon the right of a poet to dedicate himself to his own, truth-telling function, which he saw variously as priest-like and prophetic. This is a tradition in Russian criticism that the Soviets, of course, wholly crushed, wrongly labelling it as an 'art for art's sake' theory. His criticism is in *About Poetry* (1928). So far as happiness is concerned, Mandelshtam was a defeatist. Of his own age he wrote: 'your spine has been smashed, my beautiful, pitiful age. And you look back, cruel and weak, with an inane smile, like a beast that has once been supple, at the tracks left by your own paws' (PRV). One of his most persistent themes is St. Petersburg and the contrast between its past and its—to him—sad present:

> Petersburg! I still possess a list of addresses,
> Which will help me to hear the voices of the dead.
> I live on a black staircase, and the doorbell
> Ripped out with the flesh hits me on the temple.
>
> (MEP)

Against the instability of post-revolutionary Russia he posited a past in which rationality is perfectly balanced against irrationality; he did not really believe in its reality. In his later poetry he turned more and more to an elliptical search for the definition of a love that would act as reconciliation of beauty and upheaval, lust and death. He builds these poems up without much regard to logic. But the reader shares his own faith in inner integrity and coherence. Mandelshtam also wrote a collection called *The Egyptian Room* (1928): semi-autobiographical prose essays of unique distinction, invaluable aids to his difficult poetry. (MRP)

Futurism (q.v.) was the third of the movements in Russian poetry of this century. It did not have the same premises as Italian futurism. Russian futurism was urban, anti-aesthetic and anti-sentimental. Their famous manifesto of 1912 was called 'A Slap in the Face of Public Taste'; Pushkin, Tolstoi, Dostoevski: these were to be 'thrown overboard from the ship of modernity'. Futurism originated about 1910, a little after acmeism, and concentrated on dissonance, industrial reality (with a concomitant distaste for abstractions), and a trans-rational language they called *zaum*. As Mandelshtam wrote what may be called Russian expressionist (q.v.) poems, so *zaum* was a special form of surrealism (q.v.), varying from gibberish to carefully worked out neological and philological experimentation.

Minor futurists, or associates of the movement, include ELENA GURO (1877–1913), who wrote some impressionistic prose that ought to be remembered, DAVID BURLYUK (1882–1967), who was primarily a painter, and who went to America, and ALEXEI KRUCHONYKH (1886), an indefatigable *avant gardist* of small gifts but great energy, whose career of issuing small publications, often in various forms of *zaum*, ended when the period of Russian experimentation was ended by the authorities. There is now some interest in him again, and a critic has even remarked 'One ought to know who Kruchonykh was'. And so one ought, for unlike his imitators of today, he was in his minor way genuine. There was a brief vogue for the leader of the 'ego-futurist' school, IGOR SEVERYANIN (ps. IGOR LOTAREV, 1887–1942) (MRP); but there is little that is not pyrotechnic about his earlier poetry; after he went into exile he wrote in a more straightforward style. Burlyuk was the chief organizer of the movement, and it is usually claimed that without him there would have been no futurism.

More important is VELIMIR (really VIKTOR) KHLEBNIKOV (1885–1922), who died of typhus and malnutrition. Khlebnikov was a wanderer but also a genuine scholar of the Slavonic language, and his experiments have such value that their effect has not yet worked itself out—and will not until the atmosphere in Russia becomes less restrictive. He created new words from existing roots with the intention of doing away with cliché; this showed a real awareness of the worn-out nature of conventional poetic language. His experimentalism was combined, however, with a strong idealism: he welcomed the Revolution, but as the foundation of a new heaven on earth. But he is never unrealistic. The lyrical poetry of his last years is simpler, and deals directly with experience: travelling, people, the Russian landscape, the effects of the Revolution. These poems revealed another side of him: primitivist, visionary. His importance to Russian poetry is like that of Ezra Pound (q.v.) to Western poetry; but his poetry is better than Pound's. Unlike Kruchonykh, a mere experimentalist, Khlebnikov left few possibilities—traditionalist or otherwise—unexplored: he was less interested in form than in discovering means of expressing what he had to say. He is an important poet: less sensational than Mayakovsky (q.v.), but with as much substance. (MRP; SBRV; RP; PRV)

The Revolution split the Russian poets, acmeist and futurist, into exiles and Soviets. The finest poet amongst the former, although he has been shamefully neglected in the West, is VLADISLAV KHODASEVICH (1886–1939), who was able to leave Russia for Paris in 1922 through the help of Gorky. Khodasevich modelled his style on Pushkin, and equated the 'cancer' of futurism with that of the Revolution, which (unlike Blok and others) he refused to see as in any way apocalyptic, but only as one more and terrible example of the world's refusal to dissolve into spirits of pure beauty. For he remained an unrepentant symbolist. He 'choked' (as a critic has well said) into silence as the world defied his eschatological expectations. He became famous in Russia with the collection *The Way of Grain* (1920); his best poetry is in *The Heavy Lyre* (1922) and *European Night* (1927). No modern poet has been more inspired than Khodasevich was during the Twenties. The famous 'Ballad' is, in its way, as perfect an illustration of the symbolist attitude as Baudelaire's 'Correspondances' (q.v.); it should be quoted for that reason alone. There are a number of translations, but Vladimir Nabokov's (q.v.) best captures the sense (the *Penguin Book of Russian Verse* gives a literal prose rendering):

> Brightly lit from above, I am sitting
> In my circular room; this is I—
> Looking up at a sky made of stucco,
> At a sixty-watt sun in that sky.
>
> All around me, and also lit brightly,
> All around me my furniture stands,
> Chair and table and bed—and I wonder
> Sitting there what to do with my hands.
>
> Frost-engendered white feathery palm-trees
> On the window-panes silently bloom;
> Loud and quick ticks the watch in my pocket
> As I sit in my circular room.
>
> Oh, the leaden, the beggarly bareness
> Of a life where no issue I see!
> Whom on earth could I tell how I pity
> My own self and the things around me?
>
> And then clasping my knees I start slowly
> To sway backwards and forwards, and soon
> I am speaking in verse, I am crooning
> To myself as I sway in a swoon.
>
> What a vague, what a passionate murmur
> Lacking any intelligent plan;
> But a sound may be truer than reason
> And a word may be stronger than man.

And then melody, melody, melody
Blends my accents and joins in their quest,
And a delicate, delicate, delicate
Pointed blade seems to enter my breast.

High above my own spirit I tower,
High above mortal matter I grow;
Subterranean flames lick my ankles,
Past my brow the cool galaxies glow.

With big eyes, as my singing grows wilder,
With the eyes of a serpent maybe,
I keep watching the helpless expression
Of the poor things that listen to me.

And the room and the furniture slowly,
Slowly start in a circle to sail,
And a great heavy lyre is from nowhere
Handed by a ghost through the gale.

And the sixty-watt sun has now vanished,
And away the false heavens are blown;
On the smoothness of glossy white boulders
This is Orpheus standing alone.

(BRV2)

Khodasevich is a thrilling poet, yet to be discovered in the West. (BRV; MRP)

GEORGE IVANOV (1894–1959) is another quite unduly neglected poet (especially when one thinks of the fame of the trivial Evtushenko, q.v.). Ivanov, whose memoirs *Petersburg Winters* (1928) are fascinating, valuable and unreliable, began as a brief ego-futurist (his first book, under this aegis, was *The Embarkation for Cythera*, 1912), then became an acmeist—he was a close friend of Mandelshtam; as an exile his attitude was one of almost comic despair. He retained, in fact, some of the extremism of his ego-futuristic beginnings, when he pronounced that not only was Russian culture ended (a plausible hypothesis) but also that Russia itself was dead.

It is good there is no Czar.
It is good there is no Russia.
It is good there is no God.

Only icy light from stars.
Only yellow sunsets blushing.
Only years in endless flood.

Good—there's nothing to be found.
Good—that no one is around.
And blackness and death abound.

Life could not be more dead—ever.
There could be no blacker day.
And no one will help us. Never.
But who needs help anyway?

(MRP)

One might well think that Ivanov's nihilism would be tiresome and artificial; in fact, because he was as amused by it as we are, and because he is witty, it is not. He is not and does not try to be more than a minor poet, but he is a most cultivated one. His prose work *The Splitting of the Atom* (1938), which contains a recurring scene of necrophilia, upset its readers. (MRP; BRV2; PRV)

MARINA TSVETAYEVA (1892–1941), it has been said, was 'a nervous woman and a nervous poet'. The daughter of an artistic family, she went into exile in 1922; between 1917 and 1922 she had been in Moscow, where her youngest child died of malnutrition. She followed her husband back into Russia in 1939, as she had followed him out of it; he was shot on attempting to enter the country. When war came she was evacuated from Moscow to Elabuga, where she hanged herself. Perhaps her life gave her reason for nervousness. Tsvetayeva, at first popular in *émigré* circles and then ostracized, is a confused and uneven poet, and certainly not one of the calibre of Khodasevich. Her aristocratic tendencies were no less non-political than her rebellious ones. Sometimes one feels that it is only her violently modernistic technique that separates her from the pseudo-feminine 'intensity' characteristic of women poets who want to satisfy men's image of them. But she is better than this: a naïve (q.v.) whose commonplace emotions are transfigured by her technique, which is the index of her originality. Her poetry is now rightly being rediscovered in Russia; in the West it is overrated.

*

The distinction between Soviet and *émigré* is of course in poetic terms nonsense; I have used it here merely to distinguish the poets who left Russia at the Revolution from those who stayed. Once one begins to argue about the extent to which Soviet poets were and remained committed to the Revolution one strays into a highly specialized area. Thus, that VLADIMIR MAYAKOVSKY (1893–1930) threw himself into communism heart and soul should not cause us to interpret his poetry in wholly Marxist terms—even if Stalin did brand those who ignored this poet as criminals. . . . Mayakovsky, who was born in Georgia but came to Moscow in his boyhood, was an immensely talented, vital, energetic poet, and one who has remained in favour. But he is not quite of the calibre that the sheer confidence and vigour of the surface of his work suggests. He burnt himself out without quite achieving the major poetry that he might have come to if he had dealt with his own problems (for to deal with one's own problems is not necessarily to ignore mankind's, as Shakespeare's sonnets testify.) This may well be a tragedy. While most of his verse, even the stridently propagandist stuff ('Who marches there with the right? Left!/Left!/Left!'), is attractive, his best work results from the opposition between his own gaudy, and frequently immature, individualism, and the demands of the Revolution. He was like a boy: sometimes this comes out in an innocent vitality, at others in a stupidity or a petulance. He is a most overrated, most lovable poet; his suicide in 1930 remains one of the most potent protests against Stalinism, incipient as that (as we now understand it) then was: it was 'for purely personal reasons', said the party hacks. Mayakovsky began as a futurist, recited his poetry in a yellow blazer and with blue roses painted on his cheeks, made such pronouncements as that he'd rather 'serve pineapple sodas/to whores in a bar' than satisfy comfortable bourgeois expectations. He was arrested several times, was introduced to futurism by Burlyuk (q.v.), and became famous as a shocker of the bourgeoisie—all before 1917. He wrote in 'stepped' lines, in an un-doubtedly revolutionary style which put the emphasis on single words or phrases, giving an aggressive staccato effect. It is his spirit, however, rather than his achievement, that has persisted and exercised such an influence. He is a machine-gunner firing words: he has not the rifleman's time to aim. His suicide was partly caused by sexual frustration—he was not allowed to go to Paris to see Lili Brik, the married White émigrée girl he loved—but he had written:

> I am also sick
> with propaganda
> I too could write
> folk-songs about you—
> it's nicer and the pay is better—
> but I persuaded myself
> by planting my boot on the throat of my own song.

Often Mayakovsky's bulldozing and undoubtedly brilliant style conceals an absence of real matter; yet there is always an awareness of what it is to be a poet, so that the nervous, declaratory poems about Soviet society and the poet are authentic even where they frustrate by stopping short of revelation. Clearly the phantasmagoric nature of his very early poetry was inspired, and might have developed into something of gigantic proportions:

> I like to watch children dying.
> Do you not, behind the proboscis sighing,
> the vast, vague waves of the laughter's foam?
> But I—
> in the reading room of the streets—
> have so often leafed through the coffin tome.
> Midnight

with drenched fingers was groping
me
and the battered fence,
and the crazy cathedral was galloping
in drops of downpour on the cupola's bald head.
I have seen Christ flee from an icon
and the mud in tears kiss
the wind-blown fringe of his chiton. . . .

(MRP)

But this lonely man escaped the anguish of meditation by identifying his aims with those of the Revolution, by travelling and castigating the capitalist corruptions of foreign countries just as he had castigated those of Russia before 1917. Thousands of his verses appeared in newspapers: he was perhaps the only tolerable propaganda poet of all time: he meant it, and the energy he put into it was, as is frequently said, demonic. Later he became more satirical of the regime, especially in his plays, *The Bedbug* and *The Bathhouse* (qq.v.). His last (unfinished) poem was written for 'personal reasons'. The penultimate section runs:

Past one o'clock. You'll be in bed.
The Milky Way streams silver in the sky.
No need to smash your sleep with urgent wires.
It's as they say: the thing is finished.
Love's ship has foundered on the rocks of life.
We're quits: stupid to draw up a list
of mutual sorrows, hurts and pains.
See how the world's so still and silent now!
The sky pays out the night in stars.
At times like this one rises to address
time, history, the universe.

The last part is less often quoted and less well known:

I understand the power and the alarm of words—
Not those that they applaud from theatre-boxes,
but those which make coffins break from bearers
and on their four oak legs walk right away.
Sometimes, unseen, unprinted, they throw you aside,
but the word gallops on, tightens its girth,
sounds through centuries until the railway trains
creep up to lick the rein-scarred hands of poetry.
It looks nothing, like a flower beneath a dancer's heel.
But man in his soul, lips, bones. . . .

In one important and comprehensive—although infinitely subtle—sense Mayakovsky's failure is an index to that of the Revolution itself. (PRV; SL; MRP; MBSP; MHP; ARL; BRV; BRV2; RP; MEP)

The chief follower of Mayakovsky was his friend NIKOLAY ASEYEV (1889–1963), who wrote a novel of his life, *Mayakovsky Starts Off* (1940). He was born in Vladivostock, and began writing poetry there before he came to Moscow. Aseyev was never able to throw off Mayakovsky's influence; undoubtedly his mastery of the exciting style Mayakovsky evolved hindered his own poetic development, which might otherwise have taken a new direction.

A more original disciple of Mayakovsky is SEMYON KIRSANOV (1906). He is a lightweight poet who does not try to be more; but he has made intelligent use of Mayakovsky's techniques in his satirical, sardonic poetry, which since Stalin's death has often been highly critical of Soviet bureaucracy.

Even more popular than Mayakovsky, and probably of greater achievement, was the sophisticated but none the less genuine peasant poet SERGEI ESENIN (1895–1925), the son of a peasant of the Ryazan. It is a Welsh Esenin that Dylan Thomas (q.v.) might possibly have become if he could have stayed clear of booze and cities—these ruined his weaker gift, whereas Esenin's survived them until almost the day he died. He welcomed the Revolution, but as a renaissance of the old, peasant Russia; this displeased the masters, as did the violent hooliganism into which he eventually fell. He came from the country to recite his poetry, dressed in peasant smock, in the pre-revolutionary drawing-rooms of Moscow and St. Petersburg—audiences as nauseous and treacherous as those of the great nineteenth-century English country poet John Clare. Eventually he joined a group, basically anti-communist but accepters of the Revolution as an apocalyptic event, the 'peasant poets'. The most important of these was NIKOLAY KLYUYEV (1887–?1937) who died or was murdered in Siberia: Stalin had him put away on the excuse that he was a *kulak*, a wealthy peasant. Gorky was able to arrange for his release once; but he was re-arrested. Klyuyev, Esenin's friend and mentor, called by him an elder brother, was never a fake peasant poet—as Esenin himself, more richly gifted, certainly was at his worst (for example, in some of his poems welcoming the Revolution). Klyuyev is in fact more convincing than his pupil as a peasant poet; he did not have the poetic power, but he possessed a superior intellect, and his construction of a sophisticated and yet genuine poetry based on folklore and the mystical symbolism of the 'Old Believers' sect (in which he was brought up) was a considerable achievement. In fact, although his poetry is a folk poetry, it is also mystical:

> This young girl will die in childbirth soon . . .
> And the sickly midwife does not know
> That he pressed his shoulders hard to her
> With fuzz on his boyish groin below. . . .
>
> In the whites of eyes sperm whales will splash.
> In a walrus boat is death, eskimo iced . . .
> And this girl, fragrant as honeycomb,
> Will be cared for by the rainbow-Christ.   (MRP)

Esenin made three marriages, the middle one to the dancer Isadora Duncan; but as alcohol and drugs increased their grip on him and ate into his lyric gift he fell into depression; finally, in a Leningrad hotel, he slashed his wrists, wrote a short farewell poem in his blood, and then hanged himself.

For a time he was associated with and the leading poet of the group calling itself the 'imaginists' (imagists), which had no connection with Pound's earlier school of the same name (q.v.), but which did proclaim the supremacy of the image. However, Russian imagism—not an important movement; and it would be less so without Esenin—was not just a cleaning-up operation: it aimed at arousing subconscious response in the reader by a series of images. For Esenin it was a way of avoiding the Revolution—to which he had tried, unhappily, to commit himself—and of maintaining his own non-political view of life.

Esenin's main subject is country life—writing on this he can be very like Clare indeed: heartrendingly simple—viewed from a position of urban debauchery. This is reinforced by his disappointment with the industrial nature of the Revolution. One may say of him, because he was a pure enough poet, that Stalin's collectivization would have killed him if he had not done it himself. Towards the end of his life he ended a famous poem:

> The low house will crouch without me;
> My old dog has been long gone by now.
> It seems God has me destined to perish
> On the cold, crooked streets of Moscow.
> (MRP)

Esenin did go back to his old village. But he found it changed. His farewell poem ended: 'There's nothing new in dying—but not in living, either.' (MRP; PRV; BRV; BRV2; SL; RP; ARL)

BORIS PASTERNAK (1890–1960) was born in Moscow, of partly Jewish parents; his father was a noted painter, his mother an accomplished pianist. It is difficult to discuss Pasternak because he, too, has been made a pawn in the propaganda efforts of Western journalists who care almost less than they know about literature. The fact is that the novel *Doctor Zhivago* (1957; tr. M. Hayward and M. Harari, 1958), for which he is so famous in the West, has been overpraised (though it by no means deserved its truly hideous Western 'epic' film version): Pasternak's genius was not suited to long works, for his sense of structure was defective. But this novel and his two long poems—*1905* (1927) and *Lieutenant Schmidt* (1927)—are none the less extremely powerful works.

Throughout his life Pasternak remained as aloof as possible from politics and movements. Early influences on him included Tolstoi (whom he knew), a nanny who introduced him to the Greek Orthodox Church (and perhaps, like Saint John Perse's, q.v., nurse, had him secretly baptized), Rilke, and music—that of the mystical Scriabin, whom he knew, in particular. For six years Pasternak, always an intellectual—he had already studied philosophy—studied musical theory and composition; but he turned to literature. At first he was associated with the futurists: his first collection of poems, *A Twin in Clouds* (1914) had a preface by Aseyev (q.v.) and the second, *Above the Barriers* (1917), appeared under a futurist imprint. He published his best poetry in the Twenties, with *My Sister Life* (1922) and *Themes and Variations* (1924): he never wrote better than here. Most of his shorter prose works also date from the Twenties and early Thirties: short stories and the autobiographical *Safe Conduct* (tr. A. Brown and L. Pasternak-Slater, 1959); *The Childhood of Luvers* (1925), the best prose he ever published, is a fragment of a longer novel which was written very early on—it was destroyed in anti-German riots at the beginning of the First World War. His work was displeasing to the authorities, and probably he survived the purges only because Stalin liked his versions of Soviet Georgian poetry. During this time he translated many of Shakespeare's plays, and Goethe's *Faust*, into Russian. The poetry he published during the Second World War was simpler than his early work; he seemed to progress towards simplicity, and this is apparent in the poems appended to *Doctor Zhivago*, on which he worked for some fifteen years. This is a series of brilliant fragments, the study of the disintegration of an intellectual who died in 1923 after having welcomed the Revolution and been disillusioned by its aftermath. It is rightly described as a book of 'major interest', rather than a major work in itself. There are Christian overtones which, contrasted with Pasternak's pagan interpretation of nature in his best poetry, remain ambiguous and extremely baffling. It is not an attack on communism; but it does by implication criticize the Soviet betrayal of the spirit of communism. It is not at all what opponents of Russia would want as a blanket condemnation of non-capitalism. But it is not what the Soviet authorities want, either: it contains no endorsement of Marxism as such, and it does condemn revolutionary cruelty. Its optimism—it is an optimistic book—is of the spirit.

Pasternak's best work is contained in his richly suggestive poetry of the Twenties, when he had completely absorbed the influence of Blok and Mayakovsky. To understand these poems it is necessary to realize that Pasternak is essentially a symbolist, who continually implies his own vision by means of sound, half-meaning and metaphor:

> There are in the lines of great poets
> Traits of complete naturalness.
> And having sensed it there, one cannot
> But end in all silence, speechless.
>
> And feeling near to all things, greeting
> In daily life what-is-to-be,
> At last one cannot help but falling
> Into a rare simplicity.
>
> But if we do not keep it hidden,
> No mercy will be shown us here . . .
> It's what is needed most—but people
> Do find complexities more clear.   (MRP)

But the last, simpler poems are alive, too. The view that Pasternak tried towards the end of his life 'to take a seat at the table of the greats', possibly inspired by the envious Nabokov (q.v.), is hardly tenable. Pasternak was forced to refuse the Nobel Prize in 1958, and was persecuted for the rest of his life. There are a number of selections from Pasternak in English, of varying merit. (MRP; PRV; BRV; BRV2; SL; RP; ARL)

NIKOLAY TIKHONOV (1896–1971), born in St. Petersburg, did most of his best work early—as is the case with many poets. He began as an acmeist, came under the influence of Pasternak and Khlebnikov, and then became more Soviet-simple. But his poems of the civil war remain amongst the best; and he has always been at his best as an action poet—whether as soldier or mountaineer. The hardness of action tempers his rather commonplace romanticism. He has been notably successful with ballads. (RP; BRV2; SL; MRP; PRV)

PAVEL ANTOKOLSKY (1896), also born in St. Petersburg, spent his youth as an actor and theatrical producer. He is a minor poet of distinction, with a deep sense of culture and an acmeist precision. He has written a number of poems about Shakespeare and his plays.

ILYA SELVINSKY (1899–1968) founded the movement known as constructivism, basically an attempt to reconcile the *avant garde* spirit of futurism with the philistinism of the Russian communist administration. The object was simply to create a technological literature. Selvinsky's poems building on children's language—

> Dear Mummy my darling
> I. Love. You.
>
> . . . .
>
> I know the alfa bet already
>
> . . . .

—are charming. Some of his 'tough guy' ballads are also good. His later work is orthodox and uninteresting. (MRP)

EDUARD BAGRITSKY (ps. EDUARD DZYUBIN, 1895–1934), also nominally a constructivist, is a more interesting and gifted poet. He came from Odessa. *The Lay of Opanas* (1926) is the best orthodox poem about the civil war; it uses folk procedures with conspicuous success. He was a bright and lusty romantic, stupid but full of zest—rather like Roy Campbell (q.v.) at his best. (MRP; PBV)

More important than any of these is NIKOLAY ZABOLOTSKY (1903–58). He made his debut in 1929 with a series of bitter satires on Leningrad in the last years of the New Economic Policy. Later he published *The Triumph of Agriculture* (1933), which celebrated collectivization but nevertheless managed to run into trouble. He spent 1938–46 in a concentration camp on a false charge.

Zabolotsky is the last certainly important Russian poet—with the exception of Pasternak—and the only major poet whose work belongs entirely to the Soviet period. He began as a member of a circle who tried to combine the excitement and vision of futurism with the hardness and precision of acmeism. The poems in his first book, *Scrolls*, are influenced by Khlebnikov (q.v.); they brilliantly contrast realism with fantasy, and contain incomparable descriptions of every-day sights: herrings 'flash like sabres', a mongrel's eyes 'are like a dish'. The poem on collectivization is Utopian; the socialist transformation of agriculture is seen as the beginning of man's successful mastery of nature. But the poem was too difficult and was seen as a parody. His later poetry is much simpler, and has—like other Russians'—the colourfulness and strangeness of Chagall's painting. (MRP; ZS)

Zabolotsky's friend and colleague DANIL KHARMS (ps. D. I. YUVACHYOV, 1904–42) was a fairly well-known writer of children's stories, but published little of his poetry in Russia. It is the nearest, in Russian, to the 'absurd', and is certainly neglected. He died in prison. (MRP)

*

The four most distinguished poets of the younger generation in Russia are EVGENY EVTUSHENKO (1933), JOSEF BRODSKY (1940), ANDREY VOZNESENSKY (1933) and BELLA AKHMADULINA (1937). Brodsky, tried for 'parasitism' and exiled but soon afterwards released, has not published anything in Russia. Akhmadulina, once Evtushenko's wife, has published only one book.

Little needs to be said of Evtushenko. He has a clear style and has had much courage—as in his poem 'Babi Yar', a memorial to the Jews murdered by the Nazis. But he is no more than a talented poetaster—which is quite obvious to all but Western journalists—and it would be foolish to consider him as more than a likable self-publicist. (MRP; PRV)

It remains to see which way Voznesensky will go; but he is clearly a poet of larger potentiality. He is brilliant technically, witty, playful and sensitive. The entertaining side of Voznesensky has attracted W. H. Auden, who has trans-lated him superbly; but he has not yet written poetry of serious commitment. (MRP; PRV; VA)

Akhmadulina may well prove to have the most original and enduring talent of these four. Her poetry is traditional in form; but this is deceptive. She can write as beautifully of the commonplace as any living poet; and her sly humour is unique. (MRP; PRV; AF)

Brodsky is a non-political poet of much promise. His poetry has no pyro-technics, and one would not guess from it that he had read Mayakovsky. His work has so far been quiet and unambitious; but it may well herald a new development in Russian poetry. He now lives abroad. (BEJD)

Scandinavian Literature

I

There is controversy, into which I shall not enter, as to the exact meaning of the term Scandinavian. For the purposes of this book the following literatures are dealt with under the heading: Danish, Norwegian, Swedish, Finno-Swedish and Icelandic.

Scandinavia's literature offers as sharp a contrast to Latin as its climate. It is generally characterized by stoicism, seriousness, gloom, tragedy. This is to be expected in a region of long, severe winters—with their obvious consequences. But the compensatory aspect, mainly aesthetic, also exercises its influence: the landscape is majestic, and the bright sunlight that illuminates it for some of the year is of especial significance. The Scandinavians tend to be practical, and their contribution to philosophy has been small; they are disinclined to make abstractions. In terms of liberalism, modern Scandinavia is advanced and enlightened (the early abolition of capital punishment in Denmark is only one of many examples); the three chief nations have kept their monarchies, but these have for some scores of years been less anachronistic in form and function than their British counterpart. Illiteracy is negligible. To an educated Scandinavian the main languages are mutually intelligible in print if not in speech. There is a sharp division between 'town' and 'country' writing.

II

Just as no study of modern German literature is possible without taking Nietzsche into account, so must consideration of modern Danish, indeed, Scandinavian, literature begin with Georg Brandes (1842–1927), born of an unorthodox Jewish family in Copenhagen. Until Brandes lectured on him in 1888, the works of Nietzsche (q.v.) had been ignored. This gives an idea of his intelligence and his influence. But he was probably more of a cultural agitator than a critic; and he was not original. Nevertheless, he introduced European literature to Denmark—and to the whole of Scandinavia—in his Copenhagen lectures of 1871. Brandes influenced and was influenced by all the important Scandinavian writers of his time, including Strindberg and Ibsen (qq.v.).

Before 1871 Danish literature had been complacently romantic and unrealistic; Brandes demanded a radical realism and a discussion of social

problems. With his flamboyant positivism and his brilliant lecturing he introduced the spirit of naturalism into Denmark. There were inevitable reactions
against his ideas, but he dominated the Danish scene until his death. Brandes,
the inspirer of the Modern Awakening (*moderne Gennembrud*) movement in
Denmark—nearly every European country, of course, has an equivalent—had
an intuitive understanding of the needs of his time. He was called an atheist
and a socialist; actually he was—or turned into—an anti-democrat, a right-
wing disciple of Nietzsche, who preached an 'aristocratic radicalism': a sort of
proto-fascism. But Brandes would never have supported a fascist government.

The most important creative writer of the Modern Awakening was J. P.
Jacobsen, whose fiction fascinated Rilke (q.v.) so much. Jacobsen, who also left a
few poems of high quality, should have lived into this century, but died of
tuberculosis before he had reached the age of forty. Although his two novels
can justly be called classics of Danish naturalism, they transcend genre: they
are records of the struggle in the author's mind between a dreamy romanticism
and a harsh, cynical realism. Three other important novelists did, however,
live into this century.

HERMAN BANG (1857–1912), born on the island of Als, was influenced by the
French naturalists and Jonas Lie (q.v.); but his naturalism, pervaded with
fin de siècle gloom, is idiosyncratic. His impressionistic style, which employed
much dialogue, was formed from the example of his compatriot Hans Andersen,
but also from a desire to achieve a kind of modified version of the realism aimed
at in Germany by Holz and Schlaf (qq.v.). This attempt at objectivity, the
result of hatred of his own homosexual nature and desire to escape from it, was
attended by a highly subjective approach to his material: Bang continually
projected his own sense of gloom and alienation into his fiction, which is peopled
by characters whose dreams have been smashed; his achievement was seriously
weakened because he could not, in the circumstances of the time, deal with his
own problem. His first novel, *Hopeless Generations* (1880), was banned (but only
after it had achieved some success). He wrote many novels, of which the two
best are *Tine* (1889), about the Danish war with Austria and Prussia, and the
earlier *By the Wayside* (1886), a plotless saga of Danish provincial life and a
woman's helpless suffering. The novel in which he recorded his own miseries
most potently is *Denied a Country* (1906; tr. M. Busch and A. G. Chater, 1927),
the story of a wandering violinist, clearly a projection of himself. This is a
collection of glum vignettes, in which the meaningless conversations of the
characters have a vaguely menacing effect. Bang eventually approached an
almost expressionistic (q.v.) technique (*The Grey House*, 1901), consisting of
dialogue interspersed with description; explanation is eschewed.

HENRIK PONTOPPIDAN (1857–1943), who was born in Fredericia in East
Jutland, is regarded by some as Denmark's greatest novelist. He began as an
idealist: he married a peasant girl and attempted to live a Tolstoian (q.v.)
life. This experience is reflected in his first cycle of novels, *The Promised Land*
(1891–5; pt. tr. E. Lucas, 1896), about a clergyman (the profession of
Pontoppidan's father) who fails in his Tolstoian aspirations. He had previously

written a number of naturalistic short stories, a few of which appear in *The Apothecary's Daughters* (1886; tr. G. Nielsen, 1890). His later novel-cycles are the eight-volume *Lucky Peter* (1898–1904) and *Kingdom of the Dead* (5 vols., 1910–16). These are superior to the earlier cycle, but they remain untranslated into English despite his Nobel Prize (shared with Gjellerup, q.v.) of 1917. Pontoppidan's fiction massively and majestically portrays and analyzes Denmark between 1875 and the end of the First World War. For the first nineteen of these years progress and justice in Denmark were hindered by the governments of the malign J. B. S. Estrup, a fact that prompted Pontoppidan to increasingly eloquent denunciation. The early series deals with the neglect of the peasants and the disillusioned aftermath of the defeat of Denmark (when Jutland was annexed to Schleswig-Holstein, an event Pontoppidan witnessed). It presents a figure, satirically realized, who sacrifices everything and gets nothing in return except anguish and, finally, incarceration in a lunatic asylum. *Lucky Peter* is a subtler, more wide-ranging and more poetic book: its protagonist recalls Peer Gynt: Per Sidenius (a projection of the author) is one of those who finally discover themselves, but not without enduring a sceptical restlessness that for long alienates him from everything, including himself. It is a powerfully individualistic and socially pessimistic novel, in which Per at the end leaves his family in order to lead a hermit's life and to write down (rather than achieve in existential terms) his final, and fruitful, conclusions. *Kingdom of the Dead* is less autobiographical and even more socially pessimistic. It presents a number of characters all of whom fail in the realization of their fine ideas; it feels towards an indictment not merely of society but of man-in-society: 'you have', he remarks elsewhere, 'the tyrants you deserve'. Pontoppidan's last novel, *Man's Heaven* (1927), is his most morose and acrid indictment of the use made by his fellow-countrymen of the great opportunities offered to them; it is not convincing, however, as fiction. Better are his memoirs, the fruits of old age, called *On the Road to Myself* (1933–43): these are surprisingly good-tempered and optimistic: the gloom came out in Pontoppidan when he put his imagination to work. He wrote from a naturalist point of view, but his imagination's subject is self-discovery and self-realization in a hostile environment.

KARL GJELLERUP (1857–1919) shared the Nobel Prize with Pontoppidan, but retrospectively his work is of little interest. His Nobel Prize, in fact, came as a shock to everyone, including the Danes. At first he was a theological student; then he turned to Brandes and atheism. Not long after that he became attracted by German idealism. He settled in Germany and ultimately collapsed into a facile Christianity, having, characteristically, passed through Buddhism in the meantime. He was a superficial writer, although formally skilful, and underwent hosts of influences without assimilating, or really understanding, any of them. His first novel, *An Idealist* (1878), is atheistic. *Minna* (1889; tr. C. L. Nielsen, 1913) is a sickly paean to all things teutonic in the person of his wife. His only readable novel is *The Mill* (1896), which is set in Denmark and imitates Dostoevski—but not too slavishly.

*

The history of Brandes' influence befits that of a theorist: the best writers who came under it either broke away or transcended it. HOLGER DRACHMANN (1846–1908), for example, who was born in Copenhagen, was a true radical who mistakenly thought that Brandes was. Drachmann was chiefly a poet; with Holstein and Aakjær, he was the chief traditional poet of his generation. Too happy and healthy to be a *poète maudit*, he was none the less a genuine Bohemian and sincere denier of genteel values. He was conscious of the socialist movement, and, unlike Brandes, shared its aspirations; but as a poet he celebrated what he saw as the possibilities for individual anarchy inherent in it. His merit is all in his lyrical tone. His lines 'I wear the hat I want to./I sing the songs I want to/ And can' sum up his early attitude. He dropped this pose, however, in his mid-thirties, and wrote some introspective poetry of higher quality. He was a master craftsman of a rather obvious type; almost all his poetry is spoilt by Swinburnian pseudo-vitality (although his sexuality was more robust than that of the English poet). As well as plays and libretti for operettas, Drachmann wrote a long novel, *Signed Away* (1890), which is perhaps the best thing he ever did—his poetry having dated badly. Here he successfully represents the poles of his own personality as two characters: a vagabond poet and an industrious, aesthetic artist.

LUDWIG HOLSTEIN (1864–1943) is the lyrical celebrator of Denmark's natural scene. His pantheism is irrelevant, something he doubtless felt obliged—in his always sincere way—to affect; he is at his best when writing simply and directly of nature. Born on Zealand, the son of a count, he was an admirer of Jensen's (q.v.) materialism. Holstein was a simple materialist who desired above all to make the best of life, and this best he saw in the nature from which man comes and to which he returns. (TCSP)

JEPPE AAKJÆR (1866–1930) was born in Jutland, the son of a poor farmer, and wrote his best poetry in the Jutish dialect; he is often referred to as a Danish Burns. An autodidact and rabid socialist (he was gaoled), with a gift for epigram, he is still one of his country's most widely read poets. He began with crude socialist novels; but after spending some time in Copenhagen he developed intellectually and was able to devise a dialect poetry that is at once simple and subtle: it is held together by its original and haunting rhythms. He intelligently paraphrases Burns, and learnt much from him. As P. M. Mitchell has observed, he graduated from being a naïve (q.v.) to a sentimentive (q.v.) writer—but without, it must be added, losing his inspiration. (TCSP)

Aakjær's first wife MARIE BREGENDAHL (1867–1940) was one of the leading regional novelists; she attained fame with her descriptions of Jutland and its inhabitants. Her best book is a collection of short stories, *A Night of Death* (1912; tr. M. Blanchard, 1931). A later massive novel cycle of Jutland life is worthy but not of the same quality.

A group of regionalist writers, mostly from Jutland, gathered round Jensen (q.v.) and Aakjær; this was in part a reaction against Brandes (of whom Aakjær wrote: 'Sole giant in a field where critics perch/How much we revel in your deep research!/You write so finely of the mighty dead;/Why is so little of the living said?/Can Intellect not count you an apostle/Until its work is found to be a fossil?') and his positivist intellectualism. There was a similar reaction from the more cosmopolitan poets. In this group the so-called 'neo-romanticism' of the Nineties amounted to little more than a release of 'private' emotions that naturalism had seemed to proscribe. No one yet thought of eschewing realism —even if they did so. The three poets who represent this *fin de siècle* movement in Danish literature began as close friends: VIGGO STUCKENBERG (1863–1905), JOHANNES JØRGENSEN (1866–1956) and SOPHUS CLAUSSEN (1865–1931). They were originally followers of Brandes, but became interested in French symbolism as a result of some lectures on the subject given in Copenhagen in 1892 by Léon Bloy (q.v.), whose wife was Danish.

Jørgensen may be dealt with briefly. He drew apart from the others when, in 1896, he became a Roman Catholic; soon afterwards he went to Italy, where he lived. He became famous as a writer of religious prose—lives of saints, memoirs, and so on—which has been of interest to Catholics, and has given him a reputation in Denmark as chief (lay) representative of Catholicism. He abandoned his early symbolist leanings for a well written, but dull, devout verse. Stuckenberg, less prone to dogma, was a more gifted poet. He wrote one percipient novel of adolescence, *Breaking Through* (1888). His wife Ingeborg acted as 'muse' to himself, the young Jørgensen and Claussen, but left him ten years later. Stuckenberg's poetry is symbolic only in the most simplistic way; his real merit lies in his directness, his tenderness and the nobility of his resignation.

Claussen, a friend of Verlaine's, was not a better poet than Stuckenberg; but he deserves credit for being the first truly cosmopolitan Danish poet. He spent many years in France and Italy, and is the only out-and-out symbolic theorist his country, which remained largely impervious to the symbolist movement, knew. And yet, for all its attempts at a dutiful symbolism, most of his poetry remains explicit on a conventional level—as though it merely wanted to remind its readers that another kind of poetry existed. Because of his preoccupations with symbolism, which in retrospect seem academic, Claussen never resolved his own real problem, which was to reconcile his happily sensual love of life with his erotic guilt, which he recklessly and dishonestly rationalized as a hatred of technology. (TCSP) Another influential neo-romantic and symbolist, and friend of the Stuckenberg circle, was HELGE RODE (1870–1937), a religious mystic whose smoothly written, gentle poetry is usually spoiled by literary preciosity.

*

The conservative, neo-romantic, symbolic or regionalist reaction to Brandes attracted some undoubtedly reactionary figures. The poets HARALD BERGSTEDT (1877) and the prolific VALDEMAR RØRDAM (1872–1946), whose early work has some small merit, ended up by collaborating with the Nazis. These would not be of interest to readers outside Denmark. (Both TCSP) The North Jutlander

JOHANNES V. JENSEN (1873–1950), however, who was the leader of the counter-reaction to the Nineties neo-romanticism, was a writer of international stature, whose Nobel Prize (1944) was well deserved. Jensen is Denmark's last un-questionably major author; he is also the first real modernist. He went to America when he was twenty-two, and fell under the influence of Whitman and the pushing and aggressive vigour of the new world. His first novel, *The Fall of the King* (1900–1; tr. P. Kirwan and P. Federspiel, 1933), about Christian II's defeat by the Germans, is in fact an indictment of Danish indecision and lack of vitality, which Jensen saw as a national disease. Apart from this aspect of it, it is a penetrating study of sixteenth-century people. Jensen's tales of his native Himmerland (North Jutland), *People of the Himmerland* (1898) and its two successors *New Tales* (1904) and *More Tales* (1910), are among the best of all modern regional literature. Jensen also invented a new form, which he called the myth: this was a short piece, without plot, con-centrating upon essences. Here Jensen's best work may be found. Often Jensen begins with a description of a familiar object, but casts new light on it by applying to it a personal memory—or to his evolutionary philosophy. The results are poetic rather than merely odd. *The Myths* are in nine volumes (1907–44). Jensen, an inveterate traveller, was a convinced Darwinist: the huge novel for which he obtained the Nobel Prize, *The Long Journey* (1908–22; tr. A. G. Chater, 1922), treats of man's evolutionary journey from pre-glacial baboon to Columbus, whom Jensen makes into a teuton. His aim was to write a new Bible. This has isolated passages of great brilliance, revealing all the various influences on Jensen—Darwin, Kipling (q.v.), Heine, Wells (q.v.) and others—but it is imbued with the pseudo-Darwinist theory which he called 'Gothic expansion', according to which civilization began in the Scandinavian North. This dreary and charlatanic theory spoils the book as a whole—and many of its parts. 'Gothic expansion' has unpleasantly racist elements—but Jensen repudiated the Nazis. Jensen also wrote some poetry of high quality; most clearly influenced by Whitman, it is nevertheless prophetic of a more modern American, urban tone. 'At Memphis Station' (TCSP) is the most famous example. It begins characteristically:

> Half-awake and half-dozing,
> In an inward seawind of dadaid dreams
> I stand and gnash my teeth
> At Memphis Station, Tennessee.
> It is raining.

Jensen was a naïve (q.v.) writer posing as a thinker; his philosophy is worthless. This adversely affects his later fiction, but is irrelevant to his finest work: the tales of Himmerland and the myths.

There was one other Danish novelist of European stature: MARTIN ANDERSEN NEXØ (1869–1954), born in a Copenhagen slum and Denmark's foremost Marxist writer. Nexø was first a social democrat, but after the First World War he became a convinced follower of the communist party line; he escaped to Moscow in the Second World War and travelled extensively in Eastern European countries after it. He died in Dresden. His two most important novel cycles, *Pelle the Conqueror* (1906–10; tr. J. Muir and B. Miall, 1913–16) and *Ditte* (1917–21; tr. A. G. Chater, R. Thirsk, A. and R. Kenney, 1920–22) depend on his sympathy for and knowledge of the poor and downtrodden—but not on his socialism. *Pelle* is largely autobiographical, featuring Nexø himself in the person of Morten. *Ditte* is a poignant study, from cradle to early grave, of an illegitimate woman, and is chiefly impressive for its convincing portraiture of goodness in the face of adversity. None of this has to do with socialist realism.

Nexø had the same kind of beginnings as Gorki (q.v.), and his first novel, *Life Drips Away* (1902) is Gorkian. His first outstanding book, however, was the remarkably sensitive account of his sojourn among the poor in the Mediterranean, where he had gone to recover from tuberculosis: *Days in the Sun* (1903; tr. J. W. Hartmann, 1929). His *Memoirs* (1932–9; pt. tr. J. B. C. Watkins, *Under the Open Sky*, 1938) give a fascinating account of his early life and conversion to socialism. Nexø is a massive naturalist, and at his best—particularly in *Ditte*—he approaches Dreiser (q.v.). (His own poetic asides are only a little less beside the point than Dreiser's.) Two other well known shorter novels, *In God's Land* (1929; tr. T. Seltzer, 1933), an attack on the complacency of wealthy farmers, and *Morten the Red* (1945), a continuation of *Pelle*, are unsuccessful as fiction.

GUSTAV WIED (1858–1914) was the most humorous of Denmark's novelists. Moreover, he was the outstanding prose writer of the Nineties. Wied's ironic mask hid a bitter nihilism and sense of loneliness which finally led him, on the outbreak of the First World War, to suicide. He was in many ways a typical Dane: humorous, introspective, self-mocking but with a strong moralistic element. Wied was in some ways close to his compatriot Søren Kierkegaard (1813–55), that quintessential Dane who had no Danish followers: like Kierkegaard, he felt trapped between an 'either' and an 'or' (*Either/Or*, 1843, is the title of one of Kierkegaard's most famous books), between an aesthetic and an ethical life. In his unfinished autobiography he speaks of himself as a divided man: '. . . any time I run into trouble "the other" takes care of the matter and says "of what importance is it to you?" and I feel relieved'. But Wied, unlike Kierkegaard, was not a religious man: he saw life as a meaningless farce. He began by writing Strindbergian (q.v.) dramas, but these failed. His best mature work may be divided into four genres: the bitter, humorous sketches of *Silhouettes* (1891) and other volumes; his so-called 'satyr' plays—designed for reading; his comedies, including *Skirmishes* (1901), which was a commercial success; and satire. Some of his novels, such as *The Family* (1898)—his most seriously purposed book—and *The Fathers Eat Grapes* (1908), are good but not distinguished. He invented, however, a legendary character, Knagsted, in two satirical classics: *Life's Malice* (1899) and *Knagsted* (1902). One of Knagsted's recreations is the collection of famous Danish writers' commas. For nearly half a century, dating from a few years before his death, Wied's work was half-forgotten; during and since the Second World War it has enjoyed a deserved revival.

The two best known woman novelists of this period are AGNES HENNINGSEN (1868–1962) and, particularly, KARIN MICHAËLIS (1872–1950). Agnes Henningsen wrote a number of novels on the erotic problems of women that shocked the readers of their period; but her best work is her eight-volume *Memoirs* (1941–55). Karin Michaëlis, who was born at Randers in North-East Jutland, but spent much time outside Denmark, enjoyed an international reputation which she may not altogether have deserved: she was, it is true, a pioneer—but not a very distinguished one. She became famous through *The Dangerous Age* (1910; tr. B. Marshall, 1911), which is in the form of a diary written by a woman during her menopause. Very much of her time, Karin Michaëlis was a good woman: intelligent, and psychologically accurate, and she opened up new territory for novelists; but her work is not distinguished as fiction. She is, however, an interesting writer, especially of volumes of memoirs. Other woman writers included HÜLDA LÜTKEN (1896–1947) and THIT JENSEN (1876–1957), best known as a historical novelist. Possibly more distinguished than any of these was the wife of the poet Helge Rode (q.v.): EDITH RODE (1879–1956). Her poetry is skilful but has dated; her best fiction, mostly short stories, will last in a way that Michaëlis' cannot. Unfortunately nothing has been translated except one story, 'The Eternal Adorer' (tr. in *The Norseman*, 1950).

The Jutlander JAKOB KNUDSEN (1858–1917) was a minor novelist of the reaction against Brandes. He was an honest authoritarian: Christian, courageous, cruel, pigheaded, hero-worshipping, believing in inequality: the kind of proto-fascist who would never have supported a fascist government. He is often aptly called 'the Carlyle of Denmark'. (He would have loathed Christ, he said, as a gutless, repulsive, sexless and flabby type—but he happens to be the son of God.) Many of his novels are unpleasant in the manner of Carlyle: *Lærer Urup* (1909), for example, is an attack on the humane treatment of criminals. *Fear* (1912) is about Martin Luther. His best novel is *The Old Pastor* (1899), which boringly advocates society's right to kill bad men not legally guilty of any crime, but which portrays its degenerate beast-type with a certain romantic fascination. But Knudsen's only real virtue is the fine, homespun plainness of his prose. He was a priest, but when he divorced his wife and married again he was forced to become a lecturer.

The fiction of HARALD KIDDE (1878–1918), who came from Vejle in East Jutland, has its roots in the attitudes of J. P. Jacobsen and Herman Bang (qq.v.). Kidde was also clearly influenced by Kierkegaard. He is an introspective dreamer, but one who sounds a more hopeful note than either of his masters. *Aage and Else* (1902–3) and *The Hero* (1912) are his chief novels. The purpose of both seems to be to raise up forces stronger and more virile than Kidde felt himself to be. The first novel is too long; but it still has elements of a classic— not least because of the way in which it captures the *angst* and indecision of the central character, a self-portrait. As genuine if not as notable a precursor of the existentialist mood as Kierkegaard, Kidde's work is now attracting increasing attention. He died in the influenza epidemic that swept Europe in 1918 (claiming, too, Apollinaire, q.v.).

ALBERT DAM (1880), although of Kidde's generation, was not discovered until the early Fifties. He wrote two novels in the first decade of the century, another in 1934, and then, at the age of seventy, began to produce fiction that made the Danes realize they had amongst them a major modernist writer, of great wisdom. His short stories, none of which has been translated, begin where Jensen in his 'myths' (q.v.) left off. His is a genius somewhat akin to that of his contemporary, Karen Blixen (q.v.).

*

The Danish social drama begins with the not very effective plays of the brother of Georg, EDVARD BRANDES (1847–1931) and of the more interesting OTTO BENZON (1856–1927). A Danish playwright of the genius of Strindberg or Ibsen (qq.v.) is lacking. The theatre of Wied (q.v.) comes nearest to Strindberg in versatility and general attitude. His *Dancing Mice* (1905), a clearly pre-expressionist piece, portrays human beings as mice in a treadmill. His series of small 'satyr' plays, collected together as *Nobility, Clergy, Burgher and Peasant* (1897) are witty. His most successful play is $2 \times 2 = 5$ (1906; tr. E. Boyd and K. Koppel, 1923). Among the more conventional talents that of the Jewish HENRI NATHANSEN (1868–1944) stands out. He fled from the Nazis to Sweden, where he jumped out of a hotel window. He was for many years director of the Royal Theatre of Copenhagen. Many of his plays are about Danish Jews and their problems. The best of these was *Within the Walls* (1912). CARL ERIK SOYA (1896) is the natural successor to Wied, although he has been strongly influenced by Pirandello. Much of his work, particularly the more recent, is spoiled by a naïve desire to shock (he was almost fifty before he gained recognition). His most important dramatic work is the exuberant tetralogy called *Bits of a Pattern* (1940–8). Here his laconic dialogue and presentation are outstanding. His novel *Grandmother's House* (1943; tr. A. C. Hansen, 1966) is an evocation of Copenhagen at the beginning of the century, distinguished for its psychological acumen and its creation of an eerie atmosphere.

The two most important modern Danish dramatists, however, are KAJ MUNK (1898–1944), a parson murdered by the Nazis, and KJELD ABELL (1901–1961). Munk was a publicist and journalist who set out to break up the polite theatre by a return to high, poetic drama. He was less unsuccessful in this difficult project than any other playwright of the century. His theme was power. He passed from an early admiration of fascism to a practical hatred of it that cost him his life. He, too, was deeply influenced by Kierkegaard. His most powerful play is *The Word* (1932; PKM), in which a madman performs the miracle of raising the dead. This, which exploited the basic Romeo-Juliet theme, was freer than any other of his plays from his besetting sin of melodrama. Two other plays are *Herod the King* (1928; PKM) and *Cant* (1931; PKM) on Henry VIII of England. Munk, despite his heroism and martyrdom, has been somewhat overrated. But his plays made the Danes feel that they possessed a major dramatist—and the earlier ones do, for all their faults, have real power.

Abell is superior, both as craftsman and a thinker. His *The Melody that Got Lost* (1935; ad. F. Sinclair and R. Adam, 1939), which established his reputation, is a satire on the 'little man'; its technique is cinematic and impressionistic. His best play, *Anna Sophie Hedvig* (1939; tr. H. A. Larsen in *Scandinavian Plays of the Twentieth Century*, 1945), is about a seedy schoolteacher's murder of an unjust colleague. Abell presents this insignificant little woman as a symbol of resistance to Nazi tyranny; only the ending, where she is shot, along with an anti-Franco volunteer, jars. During the occupation Abell openly opposed the Nazis and was finally forced underground. Of his later plays *Days on a Cloud* (1947; tr. A. I. Roughton and E. Bredsdorff in *The Genius of the Scandinavian Theatre*, 1964) is the most outstanding. This, against a mythological background, portrays a scientist's apathy and retreat into cliché. Abell never wholly realized his gifts, but he is Denmark's best modern dramatist.

ERNST BRUUN OLSEN (1923) is Denmark's radical critic of society. His successful *Teenager Love* (1962) is an effective and scathing satire on the pop industry.

*

Of the poets who came into prominence between the wars one of the most important is PAUL LA COUR (1902–56), whose position in Denmark was something like Auden's (q.v.) in Great Britain—though he is a very different kind of poet. His real effect was on the poets of the post-1945 generation. He lived in Paris for many years, and wrote an influential critical book, *Fragments of a Diary* (1948), which is more important than his poetry. He began, a follower of Jensen (q.v.), with poems that showed his interest in painting. He had, in fact, started by trying to be a painter. His later manner was first manifested in the collection *I Demand All* (1938). It is not that he is a 'political' poet, but that he wants to find a valid reason why, in a disintegrating Europe, he and others should pursue the path of poetry. This is the theme of *Fragments of a Diary*, which acutely reflects the modern phenomenon I have called *Künstlerschuld* (q.v.). This is la Cour's main contribution, because in his actual poetry and fiction he seldom found the coherence, the method, he searched for. (TCSP)

More representative as a creative writer is NIS PETERSEN (1897–1943), better known as a novelist in the English-speaking world, but in fact more important as a poet. Petersen is Denmark's (rather late on the scene) *poète maudit*: a vagabond who has something (but not temperance) in common with Vachel Lindsay and, for metrical virtuosity, Roy Campbell (qq.v.). He is emphatically a naïve (q.v.) writer, very much hit or miss. *The Street of the Sandalmakers* (1931; tr. E. Sprigge and C. Napier, 1933) is a novel set in the Rome of Marcus Aurelius, but, in the German tradition, is really a comment on modern Denmark. *Spilt Milk* (1934; tr. C. Napier, 1935) is, curiously, about the Irish 'troubles'. Petersen also wrote readable, exaggerated accounts of his wanderings, in the form of prose sketches. But his poetry, in rigorous selection, shows him at his best; at times he can achieve the sultry eroticism of a D. H. Lawrence (q.v.).

TOM KRISTENSEN (1893), critic, poet and novelist, is the leading Danish expressionist, although his first master was Jensen (q.v.). Expressionism (q.v.) reached Denmark after the First World War; Kristensen used its violent techniques to express his own disillusion and programmatic modernism:

> In chaos I lift my rifle
> to take aim at the star of beauty

could serve as his motto. He has had little of his own to say, but has faithfully reflected the concerns of his generation; expressionism has come as naturally to him as it has, so to say, to his age. Between the wars he was the leading interpreter of writers such as Joyce and Hemingway (qq.v.). His poetry is exhilarated, basically traditional and simple despite the noise it makes and its sprawling presentation. His best novel is *Havoc* (1930; tr. C. Malmberg, 1968), a Hemingwayesque depiction of the Danish 'lost generation', in which 'drunkenness of the senses mingles with the dream of a revolution to come'. (TCSP)

Kristensen is a useful writer, an enthusiastic interpreter of foreign writers whom he does not always fully understand, but JACOB PALUDAN (1896) is a deeper one. He is an intelligent conservative, who resembles Aldous Huxley (q.v.), who has influenced him, in his loathing of the materialistic and the crass and the physical in modern life. In contrast to Kristensen, he deplores the modern—but in a consistently shrewd way. As a young man he went to America, which made him feel as disgusted and gloomy as it had made Kristensen ecstatic. After his major novel, *Jørgen Stein* (1932–3; tr. C. Malmberg, 1966), Paludan turned to criticism. *Jørgen Stein* is a pessimistic study of Denmark between wars. Jørgen Stein is in certain respects the kind of man Kristensen portrays (self-portrays?) in *Havoc*: he has lost direction; he has given up. In him Paludan symbolizes modern degeneration: he moves sceptically from one idea to another, and takes refuge in dreams. Here Paludan's conservatism vitiates his understanding of the conditions that produce scepticism, and he cannot see that in scepticism lies a hope for universal tolerance and understanding. But Jørgen himself is convincingly lost; Paludan has the warmth Huxley lacked.

KAREN BLIXEN (ps. Baroness BLIXEN-FINECKE, also known as ISAK DINESEN, 1885–1962) can hardly be related to the development of Danish literature; but to some tastes outside Denmark she has been the best modern Danish author —partly, no doubt, because her work has been consistently available. She ran a coffee-plantation in Kenya until 1931, and was remote from literary influences. *Out of Africa* (1937) is her account of this experience: a classic of tenderness and understanding. Her stories, in *Seven Gothic Tales* (1934), in English, *Winter's Tales* (1942) and *Last Tales* (1957) are eccentric masterpieces; ostensibly Gothic pastiche, their outward form conceals epic wisdom, profound feminine sorrow, and a clean magic almost lost today. She is undoubtedly the princess of modern aristocratic storytellers, a delight and a revelation. Her style is in fact not pastiche but precise, sober, studied and often ironically epigrammatic, the product of a full experience. In these sad and lovely tales, as men and women go through the rituals of love, adventure and dying, we sense a poet's wisdom.

*

The work of minor rather than major poets reflects the influx into Denmark of surrealism, dada and nonsense. SIGFRED PEDERSEN (1903) mixes the clichés of bourgeois politicians and newspaper commentators with Copenhagen slang in a delightful verse. JENS AUGUST SCHADE (1903) is a disrespectful poet, amusing when he is thumbing his nose at everybody but dull when he essays Whitman-esque poems. His erotic poetry somewhat resembles Cummings' (q.v.), as does his whole œuvre: he has the same satirical impulses, the same tendency to destroy by false diminution of his satirical target, the same saving humour. *Sjov in Denmark* (1928) a series of poems in which the archetypal Dane fails ludicrously in all his aspirations (revolution, suicide, and so on) is his best and most characteristic book. PIET HEIN (1905) calls his poems 'grooks': brief, epigrammatic, resigned verses in which Hein displays a sharp humour. HALFDAN RASMUSSEN (1915), ten years younger, Denmark's leading proletarian poet, is also a writer of the best nonsense poetry in the language (published in a series of volumes under the title *Tomfoolery*).

A newer generation, immediately influenced by la Cour (q.v.), has been less interested in humour and the surrealist approach than in Eliot, Rilke (particularly) and the symbolists. The most impressive is THORKILD BJØRNVIG (1918), the joint editor of the most influential post-war magazine, *Heretica*. His first master was Rilke, of whom he has perhaps purged himself by making some excellent translations. He seems, like other contemporary Danish poets, to be more obsessed with discovering viable procedures than with the expression of his own sensibility; but he is helping to prepare the way for a more urgent writer. (TCSP) ERIK KNUDSEN (1922) is, by contrast, certainly more urgent; but his attitudes—of savage disillusion with pop culture and of general scepticism—are so far more attractive than his over-diffuse poetry. (TCSP) MORTEN NIELSEN (1922–44), a member of the resistance, was killed in an accident before he had time to fulfil his promise. But his lucid poetry is still read in Denmark, in just the same way as Keith Douglas' (q.v.) is here. His participation in active resistance gave his doubtfulness an edge of lyricism. (TCSP)

TOVE DITLEVSEN (1918) is the best known contemporary woman writer, for both poetry and fiction. From a Copenhagen working-class family, she writes of the proletariat and of women's difficulties: a modern equivalent of Karin Michaëlis, but with a lyrical poetic gift and a better developed imagination. She has written acutely and candidly of her own problems, which included drug addiction.

*

Denmark's more recent novelists have achieved better results than her poets. This is not an unusual state of affairs: poetry requires not merely pressure to write, but a language to write in, and this is becoming increasingly difficult to create in the ultra-sophisticated atmosphere of the century.

HANS KIRK (1898–1962), a communist and a brilliant novelist, provides an example of socialist realism (q.v.) operating freely: not under a tyranny of mediocrities. Kirk chose to adhere to the method; but no one 'directed' or 'corrected' him. He left the Danish Civil Service to join a group of Jutland fishermen, and wrote an excellent and vivid novel about the experience: *Fishermen* (1928; tr. M. Gilliam, 1950), which transcends its conscious aims, and which incorporates elements of unanimism (q.v.) as much as of socialist realism. Kirk does not in the least share the fanatic religious faith (the 'Inner Mission' of the Danish State Church) of his fishermen, although he may admire it; but in any case he gives a remarkably objective presentation. Kirk never equalled this achievement. His two Thirties novels, *Labourers* (1936) and *New Times* (1939) are comparatively crude: here he presents a collective phenomenon of which he approves, rather than sympathetically studies one that he does not. *Son of Wrath* (1950), showing Jesus Christ as a Jewish proto-Marxist, contains some vivid passages.

An interesting contrast to Kirk's *Fishermen* is to be found in ERIK BERTELSEN's (1898) *Daybreak* (1937), which treats the 'Inner Mission' as a positive force; this is ultimately sentimental, but it is a useful complement to Kirk's book, and skilfully incorporates much dialect.

JØRGEN NIELSEN (1902–45), an outstanding psychological novelist, received no recognition in his lifetime, but is now regarded as an important writer. He wrote about the sullen, tough, solitary farming people of the Jutland heath. His first book was of short stories: *Low Land* (1929). He wrote several novels, of which the best is *A Woman at the Bonfire* (1933); it is an outwardly uneventful work, but possessed keen insight into the mental states of people who desire happiness but whose beliefs prevent them from attaining it. One novel, *The Haughty* (1930), is set in a town: a study of provincial post-war disillusion that parallels and even excels Kristensen's *Havoc* (q.v.).

However, the two most important novelists of modern Denmark have been H. C. Branner and M. A. Hansen. HANS CHRISTIAN BRANNER (1903–66) was born at Ordrup. After failing as an actor he went into publishing; he first made his name with radio plays. Then he published *Toys* (1936), a novel about the power-struggle among the employees of a Copenhagen firm. This already displays his individualism; but his main preoccupations did not come to the fore until later. Like Jørgen Nielsen, he is essentially a psychological novelist; but he dwells particularly in the area of fear and solitude. He discovered his true métier in the story collection *In a Little While We Are Gone* (1939); *Two Minutes of Silence* (1944; tr. V. L. Vance, 1966) contains his best stories. No contemporary except perhaps Conrad Aiken (q.v.) can match Branner as the revealer of the child's psyche, with its irrational terrors and its incomprehension of its parents' world. In *The Child Playing on the Shore* (1937) fear of this world

997

drives a boy to his death. Branner matured as a novelist with *The Riding Master* (1949; tr. A. I. Roughton, 1951), which shows him to have fully absorbed Freud: now he reveals his characters' hidden motives. *No Man Knows the Night* (1955; tr. A. I. Roughton, 1958) is the peak of his achievement.

MARTIN A. HANSEN (1909–55), who came from Zealand, enjoyed even greater prestige, at the time of his early death, than Branner. His first two novels, *Surrender* (1935) and *The Colony* (1937), are sober sociological examinations of farming life; the first tells of an experiment in collective farming. Then, forced by wartime conditions to write of apparently innocuous subjects, he wrote *Jonathan's Journey* (1941 rev. 1950), ostensibly a fairy tale about a smith who captured the devil in a flask and set out to visit the king. The whole is an allegory of the Nazi tyranny. *Lucky Christopher* (1945) is a historical novel, this time set in the sixteenth century. Then came his finest novel, *The Liar* (1950; tr. J. J. Egglishaw, 1954), a subtle study of a contemporary Christian. Hansen was a romantic Christian (like Kierkegaard, he was interested not in dogma but in faith) who finally evolved a kind of subtle Christian nationalism, a synthesis of Christianity and Jensen's (q.v.) Norse fantasies.

The leading figure in Danish letters today is the over-prolific KLAUS RIFBJERG, author of plays, poetry and novels. Rifbjerg can be superficial, sentimental and slapdash, but he is highly gifted; lately (*Narrene*, 1971) he has been writing excellent plays.

Several other novelists should be mentioned. AAGE DONS (1903), whose choice to write about alienated neurotics and bunglers of life links him with Bang (q.v.), first became well known with *The Soldiers Well* (1936; tr. T. Shiel, 1940). This is a convincing account of the series of frustrations that lead a woman to a murder—which is not discovered. An important later novel is *The Past Is Not Gone* (1950). LECK FISCHER (1904–56) was a reliable realist, writing with insight about ordinary lives. His best book is the trilogy *Leif the Lucky* (1928–9 rev. 1935), about two friends—one lucky and bold, the other timid—both afflicted by an inner insecurity. Fischer was modest but never middlebrow: a fine professional writer. KNUD SØNDERBY (1909–66) began with a competent Hemingway novel—a Danish equivalent of *The Sun Also Rises* (q.v.)—*In the Middle of a Jazz Age* (1931). His best novel, which was later made into a highly successful drama, is *A Woman is Superfluous* (1935), a fine portrait of an interfering mother. MOGENS KLITGAARD (1906–45) wrote proletarian novels in the Thirties; but the historical novels, *The Red Feathers* (1940) and *Trouble at Newmarket* (1940) are better. MARCUS LAUESEN (1907) is famous for *Waiting for a Ship* (1931; tr. A. G. Chater, 1933), a story of prosperous merchants in the region of the German-Danish border. Its successors, more philosophically ambitious, have not been as good. HANS SCHERFIG (1905) is another unpretentious professional: *The Idealists* (1945; tr. N. Walford, 1949) is his most outstanding book.

*

The Faeroe Islands, of only 25,000 inhabitants, have preserved a literature in their own dialect. Two Faeroese have written fiction in Danish: WILLIAM

HEINESEN (1900) and JØRGEN-FRANTZ JACOBSEN (1900–38). Heinesen's *Niels Peter* (1938; tr. J. Noble, 1939) is a psychological novel; *The Black Kettle* (1949) deals with the British occupation of the Faeroes in the Second World War; *The Lost Musicians* (1950) is an allegory. Jacobsen's *Barbara* (1938; tr. E. Bannister, 1948), published posthumously, is a warm novel about a woman who likes men in and out of bed. The chief writer of fiction in the Faeroese language is HEDIN BRU (ps. H. J. JACOBSEN, 1901): *Mirage* (1930); *Firm Grip* (1936).

III

From the sixteenth century until 1814 Norway was a province of Denmark. The movement that led to breakage of the link with Denmark also gave the impetus to the creation of a national literature. It was during the nineteenth century that the synthetic literary language, *landsmål* (national, or country, language), was formed. The original *riksmål* (state language) still exists, and most Norwegian literature is written in it; but New Norwegian (as *landsmål* is now called) is employed by a number of important writers.

In the Seventies Norwegian literature was still dominated by Ibsen, Bjørnson, Kielland and Lie (qq.v.). All survived into the twentieth century; but all are essentially nineteenth-century figures: forerunners but not part of modern literature.

HENRIK IBSEN (1828–1906) admired Brandes (q.v.), who made himself as felt in Norway as in his native Denmark. His 'social' period begins with *Pillars of Society* (1877), towards the end of the decade of Brandes' greatest influence. He had already written his poetic dramas, *Brand* (1866) and *Peer Gynt* (1867). Ibsen's theatre transcends movements, but his development through *The Wild Duck* (1884) and *Hedda Gabler* (1890) to *The Master Builder* (1892) can be seen to reflect the concerns of the time. In Norway the period of 'social' writing did not persist as long as in Denmark, and the impulses behind the neo-romanticism and decadence of the Nineties (reflected in *Hedda Gabler*) were stronger. Ibsen's influence is to be seen in every important European dramatist who came after him. Pirandello (q.v.) was particularly affected. Acquaintance with his work makes it clear that no aspiring playwright could fail to react to it and to learn from it. Ibsen gave European drama the depth it lacked, both by his technique —the masterly recreation of the past in terms of the present; the invention of a truly realistic dialogue—and by the diversity of his approach. He is an entirely international figure, who has been accepted in the English-speaking world as though he were a part of it; his major plays have been translated into the idiom of succeeding generations.

BJØRNSTJERNE BJØRNSON (1832–1910) was a greatly gifted writer of plays, novels and poetry; but in all but a few works he was overshadowed by the more cosmopolitan Ibsen, who lived abroad for many years. Where Ibsen was internationally minded, Bjørnson was nationally minded. It is appropriate that he should have written Norway's national anthem. But the element of chauvinism and conservative morality that runs through his work did not affect *A Gauntlet* (1883), a play in which he attacked the blindness and hypocrisy of authority. His novels are ponderous and didactic, but he left much charming shorter fiction. Most likely to survive are his tales of peasant life.

ALEXANDER KIELLAND (1849–1906), born at Stavanger, was the great Norwegian radical novelist of the nineteenth century. His masterpiece, *Garman and Worse* (1880; tr. W. Kettlewell, 1885), set in Stavanger, ironic, elegant and bitter, is an attack on the social system of his day. His other work, apart from early stories, hardly comes up to this.

More important was JONAS LIE (1833–1908), the antithesis of Kielland. He was not interested in social problems as such, but in people. His really important work is contained in his perceptive treatment of Norwegian middle-class life. *One of Life's Slaves* (1883; tr. J. Muir, 1895) gives an account of a disintegrating marriage. He was affected by naturalism; but saw trolls, those Scandinavian mischief-makers, as responsible for most of life's mishaps. His genius came out most fully in *Weird Tales from the Northern Seas* (1891–2; tr. R. Nisbet Bain, 1893), where he avoids, on the one hand, the crude spiritualism that mars his first novel, *The Visionary* (1870; tr. J. Muir, 1894), and on the other the sentimental and simplistic insistence on family harmony (never something to have a philosophy about) that renders *Life Together* (1887) commonplace.

*

ARNE GARBORG (1851–1924) was a quasi-naturalist who turned Tolstoian. He was profoundly affected by the suicide of his father, which had been brought about by an extreme piety. No Norwegian except Amalie Skram (q.v.) can be described as a true naturalist, but the implications of Garborg's first fiction are undoubtedly naturalistic. He was the first major Norwegian novelist to write in *landsmål* (whose opponents, it should be noted, were not and are not vicious pro-Danish anti-patriots, but objectors to what they see as its linguistically contaminating effects and its artificiality). His first two books, *Peasant Students* (1882) and *Menfolk* (1886) are on one level indictments of the circumstances under which young men had to acquire their education. But in reality they are desperately gloomy indictments of human circumstances. . . . Garborg, at this stage of his development, was Norway's Gissing (q.v.); he is consistently dour, and his would-be parsons are young men of infinitely unpleasant disposition. Laurits Kruse of *Menfolk* is one of the most outstanding young swine of the fiction of the latter part of the nineteenth century—and his callousness comes entirely naturally to him. By the time of *Peace* (1892; tr. P. Carleton, 1930) Garborg had reached his Tolstoian phase. The hero kills himself, but not before he makes a gesture of practical Christianity in the best Tolstoian tradition. The hero is partly based on Garborg's father, and the novel holds a balance between approval and disapproval that makes it Garborg's tensest and best. The later work, including poems and plays, is nobler but less imaginatively convincing.

AMALIE SKRAM (1846–1905) was born Bertha Amalie Alver, married a sea-captain, left him, and married the Danish critic Erik Skram (1884). Subject to mental disturbance, she wrote an excellent exposé of the shortcomings of psychiatric medicine, based on her experiences in a Copenhagen hospital in 1894, in *Professor Hieronimus* (1895), a novel that has a secure place in at least the history of the ill-treatment of the mentally ill. The subject-matter of Amalie Skram's earlier novels (*Constance Ring*, 1885; *Madame Inès*, 1891; *Betrayed*, 1892) is women who 'cannot love', from which it has been concluded that her problem was 'frigidity', a province in which many male critics of the early part of this century liked to pronounce themselves expert. Such is not the case. Her subject is actually the difficulty sensitive and inwardly emancipated women found, in her day, in dealing with husbands who sexually repelled them by their demands. Amalie Skram was the kind of woman who sought, temperamentally, for extra-marital sexual satisfaction. (She had it and enjoyed it.) Her greatest achievement is her naturalistic cycle called *The Hellemyr Family* (1887–98), which traces the decline (but from no heights) of a poor fishing family through three generations. These are the grimmest of all naturalist fiction; they are also among the most vivid.

KNUT HAMSUN (originally KNUT PEDERSEN, 1859–1952), who came from the north of Norway, was a powerful and important naïve (q.v.) writer who lived too long into this century to understand it. Recipient of the Nobel Prize (1920), he took up a strongly pro-Nazi attitude in the Second World War, and is only just now emerging from the shadow this cast upon him. His good work, which arose from instinct and not intellect, was done in the first half of his long life. But he is nevertheless one of the most important figures in Norwegian literature after Ibsen.

Hamsun began by attacking Ibsen's 'social' approach, and demanding a subjective literature. His first novel, *Hunger* (1890; tr. G. Egerton, 1899), is a brutally egocentric account of the mental perceptions of its hero, a friendless wanderer. It foreshadows the unwitting egocentricity of the American poet Charles Olson (q.v.), himself of Scandinavian extraction, in its curious insistence —implicit rather than stated—that what Olson called 'the ego' must not come between the writer and the reader. Olson meant by ego, 'thought; invention; calculation; art'. Hamsun was not as polemic; but his insistence upon emphasizing his hero's perceptions—at the expense of all else—reveals a similar state of mind. *Hunger* is a repulsive book; but a powerful one.

Hamsun's best novel, which gets way beyond his always unpleasant intentions, is *Mysteries* (1892; tr. A. G. Chater, 1927); a new translation (1971) is becoming an American bestseller. This is a great novel, carrying within it the seeds of most of the experiments in fiction that have been made since. A young man spends a summer in a small resort. He ends by destroying himself. The 'mysteries' of the title are the mysteries of his contact with others, through whom he searches for himself and his own motives. *Pan* (1894; tr. J. W. McFarlane, 1956) explores similar territory, but more sporadically. Most of the rest of Hamsun's output, including his plays and verse, is of little intrinsic interest: it celebrates, with some incidentally beautiful impressions of nature, his self-love. But *Mysteries* reveals the young man's lyrical bewilderment at the human failure of his solipsism, and is a classic. Hamsun evolved his remarkable style by remaining insensitive to whatever appeared to threaten his perceptive faculties. Hamsun was an unpleasant man, but his primitivism, when it remains intuitive, is instructive; the result of his attempting to rationalize it into 'thought' was his fascism (he even visited Hitler in 1943).

HANS ERNST KINCK (1865–1926), born in Finnmark, is more attractive and intelligent than Hamsun, but lacks his power and instinctive depth. Nor did he realize his genius except in fragments—because, ironically, he took so much painful thought. But he remains Norway's finest writer of short fiction. His novels are marred by the didacticism of his purpose, which is to reveal the differences between, and hence find means of reconciling, the cultures of peasants and townfolk. But his short stories exhibit understanding and insight; their imaginative and artistic excellence undermine his noble hopes for his country.

OLAV DUUN (1876–1939), who wrote in a *landsmål* tempered by his native Trøndelag dialect, was a leading modern Norwegian writer. He recalls Lie (q.v.) in his emphasis on the *strangeness* of the fate that controls human existence —the unique quality in Norwegian writing, familiar to us in the trolls of Ibsen's *Peer Gynt*. His novel-cycle *The People of Juvik* (1918–23; tr. A. G. Chater, 1930–5) traces the history of a family from the Middle Ages to the twentieth century. Duun is interested in the difficulties of adaptation of relatively primitive peoples to modern conditions, a problem he treats with sensitivity and insight. In *The Present Time* (1936) he too cleverly symbolized the world situation in terms of peasant life, thus somewhat distorting the latter. *Floodtide of Fate* (1938; tr. R. G. Popperwell, 1960), his last novel, is a more successful allegory; it describes how the people of a small island overcome the natural disaster of flood. 'If we lift the earth from beneath our feet and the sky above us, we are still men all the same, we go on in spite of cold, we don't even know ourselves how much we can bear'. Duun's style, which owed much to the Norwegian tradition of oral story-telling, may in its 'seamlessness' be compared to that of George Moore (q.v.) for narrative effectiveness.

The prolific JOHAN BOJER (1872–1959), also from Trøndelag, was a conventional realist of some merit. His novels achieved a popularity abroad, especially in France, that is possibly out of proportion to their merits. He is most famous for *The Last of the Vikings* (1921; tr. J. Muir, 1936), about the codfishers of the Lofoten islands. His best books provide excellent examples of barely written, effective psychological regionalism—they usually deal with Trøndelag people; much of his work, however, is trite. Translations of good novels include: *The Power of a Lie* (1903; tr. J. Muir, 1908), a powerful novel about the consequences of a forgery, and *Treacherous Ground* (1908; tr. J. Muir, 1912), which is on the favourite Norwegian theme of idealism: Erik tries to make up for the ruthlessness with which his father has exploited the workers in building up his fortune—but events prove the falsity of his intentions. Bojer wrote some plays and poetry.

PETER EGGE (1869–1959), another Trøndelagander, is also firmly in the realist tradition. *Hansine Solstad: The History of an Honest Woman* (1925; tr. J. H. Jackson, 1929), the story of a humble girl whose life is ruined by an unjust accusation of theft, is his most famous book. But incomparably his best is *Jægtvig and his God* (1923), a moving and exciting novel about a visionary young cobbler's fight to establish a new religion.

KRISTOFER UPPDAL (1878–1961), again from Trøndelag, was a more isolated and eccentric writer. He began his life as an itinerant navvy. Although the subject of Uppdal's massive novel-cycle *Dance Through a Shadowy Land* (1911–24) is the Norwegian technological revolution—occasioned by the development of hydro-electric projects—he is interested in the process of psychological transformation rather than in the social aspect. This is an example of a writer, as distinct from a politician, getting his priorities right. Uppdal worked out a grandiose philosophical system, involving Nietzschean recurrence, which is pretentious as a whole but incidentally interesting. This is presented in a large philosophical poem, *Cults* (1947), narrated by just such a navvy as he once was. It was written—and this is evident—under the cloud of madness, which afflicted Uppdal for the last twenty-five years of his life. Uppdal was certainly a proletarian writer; but he approached the problems of the proletariat less than ecstatically: he regarded the technological revolution as tragic. His verse is mostly trite; but the collection *Gallows Hill* (1930) is an exception.

JOHAN FALKBERGET (1879–1967) was born in the copper mining district of Røros (in South Trøndelag), and followed his father into the mines at the age of eight; he did not finally leave them until he was twenty-seven. An over-optimistic but good-hearted Christian whose first literary efforts were inspired by evangelistic tracts, his finest work is to be found in his unrelentingly truthful pictures of mining life at the end of the last century and the beginning of this: *When Life's Twilight Comes* (1902), *Black Mountains* (1907). His later historical novels have received higher praise, and this has been deserved—but the quality of the writing never quite comes up to that inspired by his early feelings of indignation. Of these *Lisbeth of Jarnfjeld* (1915; tr. R. Gjelsness, 1930) has been translated. *Christianus Sextus* (1927–35), in six volumes, is an epic of the Røros mining industry from about 1800. *Bør Børson* (1920) is a novel about the tragic results of industrialization.

SIGRID UNDSET (1882–1949) was born in Denmark, the daughter of a famous Norwegian archeologist. When she got the Nobel Prize (1928) she told reporters: 'I have not the time to receive you. I am studying scholastic philosophy'. She had joined the Roman Catholic Church in 1924. When at home she wore national costume. Her third novel, *Jenny* (1911; tr. W. Emme, 1921), which gained her her first success, is a semi-naturalistic account of a sensitive girl's failure to achieve happiness; it is of no promise. She became internationally famous with *Kristin Lavransdatter* (1920–2; tr. C. Archer and J. S. Scott, 1930), set in medieval Norway. This was a pioneer work in the historical novel, in that it applied modern pseudo-psychology to circumstances in which modern psychology did not exist. This method proved to have enormous middlebrow possibilities.

Kristin Lavransdatter is a skilful work, into which Sigrid Undset put much hard work; but it is not important as literature. It was followed by a less effective historical cycle. The tendentious Catholic fiction of her later years, all dealing with contemporary society, provided entertainment for bored middle-class ladies all over the world, but is worthless.

An incomparably superior and more serious writer is CORA SANDEL (ps. SARA FABRICIUS, 1880), born in Kristiansand. Since 1921 she has lived mostly in Sweden. Her studies of intelligent women trying to realize themselves are masterly in their subtlety and poetic qualities, as they are in the creation of atmosphere. She began late, with *Alberta and Jacob* (1926; tr. E. Rokkan, 1962), followed by *Alberta and Freedom* (1931; tr. E. Rokkan, 1965) and *Odd Alberta* (1939). Her masterpiece is *Krane's Café* (1945; tr. E. Rokkan, 1968), one of the century's most pitiless and accurate revelations of small-town nastiness and male selfishness. Katinka Stordal, deserted by her husband, supports her children by dressmaking. The women of the small Norwegian coastal town where she lives overlook her slovenliness and occasional tipsiness because she is superb at her job—and thus an ally of their vanity. But one day, in Krane's Café, the meeting place of the leading residents, a coarse but honest Swede shows an interest in Katinka for her own sake. She spends the day talking to him and then goes to bed with him. The town is scandalized—and put out by the fact that the dresses for a forthcoming ball may be delayed. Even Katinka's errant husband pleads with her. . . . This great novel was successfully dramatized by Helge Krog (q.v.). *Leech* (1958; tr. E. Rokkan, 1960) is also excellent.

RONALD FANGEN (1895–1946), whose mother was English, is most important for *Duel* (1932; tr. P. Wiking, 1934), an examination of the hostile friendship between two different types of men. His early dramas, *Descent into Sin* (1920) and *The Enemy* (1922), while over-influenced by expressionism (q.v.), had some merit. In 1934 he joined the Oxford Movement (now called 'Moral Rearmament'), and his work lapsed into the kind of simplistic vulgarity (if not concealed authoritarianism) that one associates with that unpleasant manifestation.

More gifted and important was SIGURD HOEL (1890–1960). Hoel was an intelligent and self-critical left-winger. He realized that 'social criticism and psychological analysis are aspects of the same phenomenon. . . . The fight for social, economic and moral liberation is the same fight on the same front'. He directed the 'Yellow Series', which presented such writers as Hemingway, Sherwood Anderson, Faulkner and Caldwell (qq.v.) to the Norwegian reading public. *Sinners in Summertime* (1927; tr. E. Sprigge and C. Napier, 1930) is a satire on members of the younger generation who imagine themselves emancipated but are in fact as bourgeois as the adults against whom they are in revolt. In *One Day in October* (1931; tr. S. and R. Bateson, 1933) he made a penetrating analysis of bourgeois puritanism in a series of portraits of middle-class marriages. *The Road to the End of the World* (1933) returns to the world of childhood. *Two Weeks before the Glacial Nights* (1934) and *Meeting at the Milestone* (1947; tr. E. Ramsden, 1951) are probably his best novels.

AXEL SANDEMOSE (1899–1965) was a Dane with a Norwegian mother. Having made his literary début in Denmark, he settled in Norway when he was about thirty, and made his entry into Norwegian literature in 1931 with *A Sailor Comes Ashore. A Fugitive Crosses his Tracks* (1933 rev. 1955; tr. E. Gay-Tifft, 1936), which appeared in America with an introduction by Sigrid Undset (q.v.), marks the beginning of his mature manner. It is a series of deep investigations into the mind of a murderer, a skilful assemblage of fragments. *Horns for Our Adornment* (1936; tr. E. Gay-Tifft, 1939) and *September* (1939) return to the subjects of the sea and sailors. *The Coal-Tar Seller* (1945) is about a swindler. Sandemose, one of Norway's most interesting writers, concentrated in most of his mature fiction on Strindbergian (q.v.) themes of love and murder: *The Werewolf* (1958; tr. G. Lannestock, 1966) is characteristic.

JOHAN BORGEN (1902), born in Oslo, began by writing in the manner of Hamsun (q.v.). Since the war he has established himself as a leading novelist with *Days of White Bread* (1948), the ironic *News on the Subject of Love* (1952) and with the trilogy *Lillelord* (1955–7), whose main theme is the problem of preserving individual identity under the Nazi occupation. This is an extreme example of his central concern: people's means of achieving themselves in the web of deceit in the midst of which they live.

*

Ibsen was a world figure; his immediate Norwegian successor, GUNNAR HEIBERG (1857–1929), did not reach this eminence. He was unfortunate in having a repulsive physical appearance, which frustrated his ambitions to become an actor. He was, like Ibsen, a follower of Brandes (q.v.), and he broke with the conservative traditions of his family in order to know what friends—including bohemians—he wished to know. His radicalism and cosmopolitanism naturally led him to attack Bjørnson. Because he had necessarily to live in the shadow of Ibsen, Heiberg has not had his due outside Norway. His first play, *Aunt Ulrikke* (1883), is an Ibsenian exposure of social hypocrisy. *King Midas* (1890) attacked 'the uncrowned King of Norway', Bjørnson, the darling of polite society, and caused a fierce uproar: Heiberg was determined to make the best of physical ugliness. It is in fact an effective attack on Bjørnson's brand of moral purity, which could be unpleasant. His best plays, however, are *The Balcony* (1894; tr. 1922) and *The Tragedy of Love* (1904; CCD). The first act of the former is hilarious. A woman just manages to conceal her lover, with whom she has spent the night, from her unexpectedly early husband by getting him onto the balcony. He has then to explain his early presence by evincing a desire to buy the house. The husband agrees, says that the property is sound, and to prove it leaps onto the balcony—which collapses, precipitating him to his death. All this and the comic sequel is presented deadpan: in a lyrical prose. It was attacked by the moralists for its 'unsoundness'. More amusing still, the 'modernists' praised it. Played in the right way today it would bring the house down; nor would Heiberg turn in his grave. The balcony (through which a lover no. 2 gains entry, and through which husband no. 2—the original lover—

then makes his departure) is not a 'crass' symbol (as it has been called) but a comic one—the whole thing, surely, anticipates Sternheim. To suggest that Heiberg is nearer to the truly crass Sudermann (q.v.) is to miss the point. *The Tragedy of Love* is on the theme of the artist as solitary as well as on that of woman-as-insatiable-lover (Heiberg had two bad marriages with only one satisfactory mistress between).

Lie, Kielland, Hamsun and Kinck (qq.v.) all made contributions to the theatre, as did other novelists, such as Bojer (q.v.), after them. But the modern Norwegian theatre belongs mainly to HELGE KROG (1889–1962) and NORDAHL GRIEG (1902–43). Krog, always a lively figure on the Norwegian scene, is in some ways the natural successor to Heiberg—but not in any narrow sense. He also achieved a more effective dialogue. Krog's social drama, all on the side of enlightenment and against bourgeois pseudo-morality, includes *On the Way* (1931; tr. H. Yourelle, 1939) and *Break Up* (1936; tr. M. Linge, 1939). He wrote *Don Juan* (1930) in collaboration with Sigurd Hoel. All these are very much in the Ibsenite tradition, and are well and unpretentiously done. His ostensibly light comedy, however, is also extremely good, and perhaps in this form he is more original. Typical of this genre is *Triad* (1933; tr. R. Campbell, 1934). Krog was a useful man to have around: intelligent, tolerant, highly talented, skilful and, above all, an excellent polemicist who thoroughly enjoyed being the bad boy of Norwegian literature between the wars.

Nordahl Grieg was the most influential member of the younger generation in Norway between the wars. He had been to sea and to Oxford, and was active as a journalist. He travelled widely: China, Spain, Russia. He was one of the enthusiasms of Malcolm Lowry (q.v.), who also went young to sea. Grieg was a poet, novelist and dramatist—but his chief achievement was certainly in the theatre. He was receptive to a host of influences, including those of Kipling (q.v.) and Marx. He did not have time to reconcile the man-of-action in himself with the intellectual. For a time he was a Marxist, as he demonstrated in the anti-war play *Our Honour and Our Might* (1935) and in *Defeat* (1937; tr. E. Arkwright, 1945), about the Paris Commune. The latter influenced Brecht (q.v.) in his own play on the Commune. He joined the free Norwegian forces in London, worked as a propagandist, and in 1943 was shot down on an American bombing mission over Berlin. Grieg wrote some lucid but unimportant poetry, a good novel about his experiences at sea, *The Ship Sails On* (1925; tr. A. G. Chater, 1927), and other excellent journalistic prose; but it is as a dramatist, especially in the two plays mentioned above, that he was really important. His role as Norwegian hero is really less significant. A volume of his war poems, *War Poems* (tr. G. M. Gathorne-Hardy) appeared in 1944; but this gives no idea of his real creative capacities.

Two other Norwegian dramatists should be mentioned. ASLAUG VAA (1889) is perhaps primarily a poet, but her lyrical plays, especially *The Stone God* (1938) are interesting and effective. The *landsmål* writer TORE ØRJASÆTER (1886), also primarily a poet, composed two notable expressionist plays: *Anne* (1933), and *Christophoros* (1948). The expressionism is of Strindberg's variety (both are dream-plays), but Ørjasæter uses that form only to put in a content very much his own. The younger TORMOD SKAGESTAD (1920) has tried to revive the verse drama, influenced by Eliot and, alas, Fry (qq.v.).

*

The first modernist in Norwegian poetry was a minor poet, the consumptive and mentally disturbed SIGBJØRN OBSTFELDER (1866–1900). Obstfelder was the first to recognize the importance of Edvard Munch (q.v.), the painter who has already been mentioned in connection with expressionism (q.v.). He was a kindred spirit. He wrote, in a lyrical free verse, of his feelings of alienation from the world. Unlike such a poet as Campana (q.v.), however, his anguish is not resolved in even a handful of poems, and the final impression is of a sickly rather than a dynamic decadence. One seldom finds anything better than:

> The day it is passing in laughter and song.
> Death he is sowing the whole night long.
> Death he is sowing. (TCSP)

VILHELM KRAG (1871–1933) is less decadent, and some of his poetry about his native Sørlandet has an old-fashioned charm; but he is similarly weak. (TCSP)

More important are Olav Aukrust and Olav Bull. OLAV AUKRUST (1883–1929) wrote in *landsmål*. He combines love of the Norwegian peasantry and landscape with a mysticism that he acquired by reading Indian and Persian literature. He is a lyrical poet of much greater power than Krag, but his work has inevitably dated. (TCSP)

OLAV BULL (1883–1933), however, is the first really important modern Norwegian poet: he is ironic, sophisticated, capable of assimilating cosmopolitan influence, and an excellent technician. Bull was, one feels, the first Norwegian poet to really understand what modernism was about. In fact some of his work has been condemned for 'introspection' by critics who understand it less well than he did. He learned particularly from the philosophy of Bergson and the poetry of Valéry. But because he was an intellectual it must not be thought that he was not a lyrical poet: he was, but a fastidious one. Comparison with Valéry is a little far-fetched; but at his best—not in such poems as the popular 'Metope'—when he is self-critical and ironic but still moved, he is very good indeed. (TCSP)

The leading living Norwegian poet in some people's minds is ARNULF ØVERLAND (1889), who swung from a strongly pro-German attitude in the First World War to a socialism that led the Nazis, provoked by the clandestine circulation of his patriotic poems, to put him in a concentration camp in 1942. When he was released in 1945 he was Norway's most honoured poet. But it must be admitted that his earlier, individualistic poetry is on the whole his best. This is tragic, romantic, lonely—but tersely expressed, as though the form criticized the content. This is the poet of such collections as *The Hundred Violins* (1912). By the time of *Bread and Wine* (1924) he had become almost a socialist realist, and he continued in this vein. But in his post-war poetry—having witnessed Russian leaders' betrayal of communism—he has developed a new and stridently anti-modernist manner that is not wholly satisfactory: it seems to reflect the critical intentions of his intellect rather than those of his imagination. However, all his work is characterized by vitality, formal excellence and a poetic know-how that prevents it from declining into prosy diatribes. (TCSP)

Tore Ørjasæter's (q.v.) concerns are broadly those of Uppdal and Duun (qq.v.)—the impact of the industrial revolution on the peasantry—but he has increasingly incorporated his own metaphysics into his poetry, which frankly anthropomorphizes nature, as in 'The Kiss'. (TCSP)

HERMAN WILDENVEY (ps. HERMAN PORTAAS, 1886–1959) introduced a new and welcome note of insouciant humour into Norwegian poetry, which on the whole is ponderous, like their winter, rather than sparkling, like the dance of sunlight on their fiords. Like Bull, Wildenvey enjoyed living as he wished to live. This led the aged Bjørnson (q.v.) to say of his first volume, *Bonfires* (1907): 'I suppose he is not such a swine as he makes himself out to be'. Wildenvey genuinely developed, for while he retained his easy, colloquial tone (of which he was a master), his poetry deepened in thought and feeling. He seems to have developed his happy manner from having studied for a year within the grim confines of an American theological seminary. But in his later poems a concern with religion returns. A selection of his poetry (*Owls to Athens*, 1934) was translated by Joseph Auslander.

It is difficult to classify TARJEI VESAAS (1897–1970), who was a *landsmål* writer, born in Vinje, Telemark: he has done equally good things in poetry, drama and fiction. He was a minor writer, but an exceedingly live and versatile one: the kind of intelligent, vital and curious author that no literature can afford to be without. Since 1946 he received a 'State Artist's Salary'—something which in Great Britain, if it existed, would betoken a mediocrity or an aristocrat, but which, in Norway, exercises few pressures, hidden or otherwise. He was an instrument sensitive to the developments of modern literature—and therefore to the developments of the world. His experimentalism amounted to no more than his desire to be this: to record his own complex reactions to life. His great gift was the consummately Norwegian one of relating people to landscape —and of symbolizing their unconscious feelings for one another through descriptions of landscape. He begins a poem:

> Talk of home—
> Snow and fir forests
> Are home.
>
> From the very first
> It is ours.
> Before anyone ever said it.
> That it *is* snow and fir forests,
> It is here within us,
> And then it remains
> Always, always.   (TCSP)

His plays for the theatre have not been as successful as his other work, but he cultivated the radio play more effectively. He realized himself most fully in his prolific fiction, to the complexities of which his poetry is a useful index. Only two novels have been translated: *The Ice Palace* (1963; tr. E. Rokkan, 1965) and *The Seed* (1940; tr. K. G. Chapman, 1966). *The Seed* describes a small island in the grip of a collective madness, brought on by a madman, that affects animals and human beings alike. *The Ice Palace*, more ambitious, is about identical twins, one of whom attempts to explore a frozen waterfall (the ice palace of the title) alone. She is destroyed when it melts, and her sister tries to recreate her perfectly in her memory. Both these books—clearly, like much of Vesaas' fiction, influenced by Kafka—are full of possibilities. Unfortunately characterization would have strengthened both—and here the author fails. He succeeds magnificently in evoking the landscapes against which the dramas are played, but almost perversely neglects psychology. Since his fiction is almost exclusively devoted to trying to pinpoint the kind of bestiality that produces fascists and tyrants, and therefore war, this is a serious lack. It is this that relegates Vesaas to the status of a minor writer. As the history of German expressionism shows, neither a wholly instinctive nor a wholly intellectual reaction to the obscene processes by which men desire to acquire power over one another is adequate. Mankind needs a sense of psychology to deal with its Hitlers and Stalins—as we see in the unhappy cases of Pirandello (q.v.) and Mussolini, and Wyndham Lewis and Hitler. But Vesaas was none the less dedicated and, in his sphere, of remarkable authority. His use of the *landsmål* was the most refined and effective that has yet been seen.

Norwegian poets since after the First World War have searched for new means of expression, means that would somehow reconcile and resolve their inner conflicts: between tradition and the new, order and anarchy, the collective and the individual. PAAL BREKKE (1922) translated *The Waste Land* (q.v.), which has had its effect—not a very impressive one, because it came more than twenty-five years after its appearance in English. TOR JONSSON (1916–51) is the chief representative of the neo-lyrical reaction to modernism. (TCSP) JAN-MAGNUS BRUHEIM (1914), a farmer, woodcutter and violinist from the Gubrundsdal Valley, in whose dialect he writes, is another lucid and deliberately unsophisticated poet (TCSP), as is GUNVOR HOFMO (1921), whose poems make an almost Platonic appeal to the secret world that resides in nature. (TCSP)

The leading modernist poets between the wars were CLAES GILL (1910), EMIL BOYSON (1900) and ROLF JACOBSEN (1907). In the Thirties Boyson wrote a love-poetry that reminds one more of the Victorian poet Coventry Patmore than of anyone else, although it is more genuinely philosophical than Patmore's. With *Hidden in Shadows* (1939) he became more self-consciously modernistic in style. (TCSP) Gill was much influenced by Boyson; his reading of Yeats has caused him to try to achieve a resonant, emotionally fully satisfying style that yet preserves the essentials of modernism. He has more recently been active in the theatre. (TCSP)

Jacobsen was Norway's violent and mindless modernist. An imitator of Whitman's technique, influenced by Jensen's (q.v.) more authentically Whitmanesque American verse, Jacobsen introduced this century's technological clatter into Norwegian poetry. He might have been a Cendrars or a Mayakovsky (qq.v.), but instead joined the Nazis when they invaded Norway, and thus more resembled the empty Marinetti (q.v.).

Much of GUNNAR REISS-ANDERSEN's (1896–1964) work was spoiled by over-fluency and preciosity, but he occasionally succeeded in recording his confusions in a memorable poem. His best work was written in the war in the spirit of Øverland's anti-Nazi poetry; he was able to escape to Sweden. (TCSP)

The outstanding post-war novelist is perhaps AGNAR MYKLE (1915). He is known in English-speaking countries for his trilogy: *The Hotel Room* (1951; tr. M. Michael, 1963), *Lasso Round the Moon* (1954; tr. M. Michael, 1960) and *The Song of the Red Ruby* (1955; tr. M. Michael, 1961); and for *Rubicon* (1966; tr. M. Michael, 1966). In all these novels the same character (although in two of them under different names) appears. Mykle combines elements of Thomas Wolfe and D. H. Lawrence (qq.v.) with Norwegian earthiness and a troll-like humour. Mykle is a powerful writer, an idealistic, amorous, socialist vitalist; but he is not a satisfactory one. He does not do as much with his energy as he should—it does not hide his rather simplistic bewilderment.

TERJE STIGEN (1922) has written good short stories–*Dead Calm on the Way* (1956)—and some intelligent novels of adventure, such as *The Saga of Åsmund Armodsson* (1958). His latest novel, *Infatuation* (1970), displays deep psychological understanding of the love between a girl student and her schoolmaster. ODD BANG-HANSEN (1908) wrote two impressive anti-war novels, *The Midge and the Lamp* (1949) and *Fly, White Dove!* (1953), and followed these up with some finely constructed novellas.

IV

Swedish letters would have taken a quieter course between the forces of conservatism and naturalism had it not been for the restless and frequently highly irritating genius of AUGUST STRINDBERG (1849–1912), the son of a shipping-agent. His mother was an ex-waitress, a fact that he chose to emphasize. Ibsen (q.v.) was a father of the modern theatre—he is indispensable—but Strindberg, who made his torment so much more evident to the world, is of equal historical importance. The founding-father of expressionism in the theatre, he is more obtrusive than Ibsen. One can confidently assign Ibsen to the century in which he lived most of his life; the same cannot apply to Strindberg. But this does not imply a judgement in favour of him; actually, the habit of postulating him as an alternative to Ibsen and then damning him is a wasteful exercise. He achieved less than Ibsen in the dramatic form—because he was too frenetic ever to relax into warmth of feeling—but the quality of his anguish none the less penetrates even into our own times. Ibsen is a classic, and carries the authority of a classic; Strindberg, not a classic, still worries us: we understand his difficulties too well.

Strindberg has rightly been described as 'incorrigibly subjective'; his self-absorption frequently appears and is perverse; but he had to clarify his motives and to explore himself. He became increasingly unstable in his personal life; for example, after his first marriage failed he imagined that European feminists had won his wife Siri over to their side and that they were persecuting him: he had a doctor come with him to a brothel to measure his erect penis in order to counter the rumour that he was 'not a man'. He had his gentle side, out of which came some fiction of charm and sweetness; but his major work is written not from a still centre of wisdom but from a whirling periphery of subjective torment. It does not cast a sober light on life, but illuminates it in lightning flashes. What is 'modern' about Strindberg is that he made no distinction whatever between art and life: he ignored the assumptions of the previous centuries. If expressionism (q.v.) is rightly characterized by a shriek, then Strindberg was the first to open his mouth.

Strindberg's brilliant first novel, *The Red Room* (1879; tr. E. Sprigge, 1967) was an exposure of social hypocrisy and city rackets—and an account of a young man's painful recovery from idealism. His *The Son of a Servant* (1886–1909; tr. E. Sprinchorn, 1967), with its characteristic title, retraces his spiritual development. Much of his prose (one cannot safely call it either autobiography or fiction) records the vicissitudes and major spiritual events of his troubled life: his first marriage (*The Confession of a Fool*, 1895; tr. E. Schleussner, 1912), the 'inferno' period in Paris, when he was experimenting with alchemy and the occult (*Inferno*, 1897; tr. M. Sandbach, 1962), the quieter time of his third marriage (1901–4), which ended less violently (*Ensam*, 1903). Other prose by Strindberg is strictly fiction and is, by his standards, objective. In *The People of Hemsö* (1887;. tr. E. H. Schubert, 1959) his sense of humour is most apparent, as is his gift for description. This is a story of the people of Stockholm skerries. Its successor, *In the Outer Skerries* (1890), disposes of a Nietzschean (q.v.) super-man, Borg, by the strict application of naturalist laws. It is typical of Strindberg that he should have been in the course of his life everything that it was then possible to be: socialist, aristocrat, feminist, anti-feminist, Nietzschean, anti-Nietzschean, Christian, democrat, occultist. . . . *In the Outer Skerries* is ambiguous, and illustrates the conflict between his Nietzschean ideas and his Darwinist convictions (inspired in the first place by reading Zola).

But drama was the genre in which Strindberg excelled. His earlier naturalistic plays—*The Father* (1887;. tr. M. Meyer, 1964), *Miss Julie* (1888; tr. M. Meyer, 1964)—mix morbid psychology, of which Strindberg had made himself a master, paranoid fear of women, and hereditary determinism. These do contain an element of Grand Guignol: we should protest at a classification of them as drama of the highest class if only because they exclude too much. But in technique they are nearly perfect, particularly so in their use of silence—and of the silences by which people torment one another.

Later, after his 'inferno' period, Strindberg became a Swedenborgian—and consequently a symbolist. (Emanuel Swedenborg, 1688–1772, was a Swedish scientist and theologian whose later ideas—which were not mystical—had an important influence on symbolism. Very briefly, he taught that creation is dead, except through God's intervention, through whom man lives. His law of correspondences is popularized by Baudelaire's famous sonnet, q.v.) The first part of his symbolist-expressionist play *To Damascus* (1898–1901; tr. G. Rawson, 1959), is considered by some to be the finest of all his work. Others prefer *A Dream Play* (1901; tr. E. Sprigge, 1963), a highly poetic evocation of human evanescence.

Strindberg exercised an enormous influence in the international theatre; he is also a crucial figure in the development of Swedish literature. He was the dominating figure of the Eighties, and the other writers of this period, who formed the rather amorphous group known as Young Sweden, are overshadowed. In Sweden even the ideas of Brandes filtered through largely by way of Strindberg.

In the Nineties there was the familiar neo-romantic reaction, which may of course be traced in Strindberg himself—as, in Norway, it can in Ibsen.

Sweden's great distinction in literature before Strindberg—whose own poetry is somewhat neglected outside his native country—had been in lyrical poetry. On the whole this has declined—diffusing itself into a number of minor writers rather than remaining in the hands of a few masters; the exceptions can hardly be described as lyric poets. The reaction to naturalism of the leaders of the Nineties, which took the form of a demand for wholesomeness and joy in life, rather than of decadence, were, however, mostly poets. (Count CARL SNOILSKY, 1841–1903, survived into this century but belongs to an earlier era; his attempts to reach the working classes in the early Eighties were not successful.) VERNER VON HEIDENSTAM (1859–1940), together with his friend, the Jewish OSCAR LEVERTIN (1862–1906), wrote *Pepita's Marriage* (1890), a manifesto satirizing naturalist gloom and exalting the role of the imagination. With Strindberg temporarily absent from the scene, this exercised a strong influence on a generation of poets. Heidenstam has been aptly called 'a great national poet *manqué*': he was an exquisite minor who inflated himself into a pretentious magus rather resembling the later Hauptmann (q.v.), who was, however, a far better writer. His poetry, the best of which is to be found in *Poems* (1895), is visual, pagan and exuberant; he was skilled enough not to misuse the influence of Goethe. But as he developed he tended to cover up his Nietzschean feelings of loneliness and poetic arrogance with, first, a rhetorical patriotism, and later (*New Poems*, 1915) a concentrated classical style. Some of his poetry was translated into English in *Sweden's Laureate* (tr. C. W. Stork, 1919) after he had won the Nobel Prize (1916). His historical fiction contains fine isolated passages, but lacks any real direction: he was a minor writer suffering from a condition of self-appointed greatness. The Nobel award quietened his aspirations, and he lived the last quarter-century of his life in a majestic isolation broken only by the pilgrimages of young men.

Levertin was infinitely more intelligent, more sensitive, more interesting, rather less gifted: the perfect sentimentive (q.v.) foil to Heidenstam's naïvety. Until his early death he was Sweden's leading critic. He began as a social writer, but soon turned to a more personal and romantic style. He is less canny than Heidenstam in hiding his preoccupations. His Pre-Raphaelite interest in antiques, expressed in his poetry, seldom conceals his death-haunted sexuality. The song-cycle *King Solomon and Morolf* (1905) contains some of his best work. Anyone who understands Dante Gabriel Rossetti will understand Levertin.

GUSTAF FRÖDING (1860–1911), who was born in the province of Värmland, produced his poetry against the heavy odds of progressive mental illness and chronic poverty. He spent the last thirteen years of his life in confinement. Before that he had failed socially and academically; but *Guitar and Concertina* (1891; tr. C. D. Locock, 1930), his first collection of poems, made him Sweden's most popular poet. In it, in clear and charming verse, he writes of the people of his native province. *Splashes and Rags* (1896) contained 'Morning Dream', for whose honest eroticism he was prosecuted. Although acquitted, this experience helped to drive him towards total withdrawal. His finest poetry is collected in *Grail Splashes* (1898); these poems, written on the verge of mental collapse, cluster about the sinister symbol of the grail—a pagan grail. They usually retain the simple surface of the earlier regional ones, but reach more deeply into their author's disturbed mind, in which sexual guilt threatened a Spinozan serenity and faith in the ultimately divine unity of all things. Fröding, especially in his last phase, is a European as well as a Swedish poet; a late romantic who can evoke delight as easily as terror, and whose lyrics have at their most powerful an almost unbearable intensity of feeling. C. W. Stork translated a useful *Selected Poems* (1916).

ERIK AXEL KARLFELDT (1864–1931) is a modern paradigm of Sweden's genius for lyrical poetry. He came from the province of Dalecarlia, and did for it what his friend Fröding had done for Värmland. He declined the Nobel Prize (he was on the committee for many years) in 1918, but was awarded it posthumously (1931). His early poetry was influenced by Fröding, but later he developed his own manner. His most popular collections, featuring his bachelor-poet Fridolin, are *Fridolin's Songs* (1898) and *Fridolin's Garden* (1901). These embody old peasant customs that he had noted as still practised in contemporary Dalecarlia. He is more than a country poet, however, for he uses flora and country customs as symbols for his restrained but ecstatic eroticism. His later poetry deepened in mood and texture: less overtly gay and carefree, it expresses moods of sadness and fear of death. Particularly notable are his versions of Biblical stories—set in Dalecarlia—which date from the turn of the century. These have the swing and verve of a Vachel Lindsay (q.v.), as in 'The Sea Voyage of Jonah':

And they grab him without heeding
His insistent, frantic pleading:
'Can't you see I am a prophet and a holy man at that!'
But they answer: 'Where you're heading
You can practise water treading
Though undoubtedly you'll float, O prophet, on your priestly fat!'
Upside down is Jonah in the midst of his descent
With his frock coat round his head and flapping like a tent.
In the horrid depths below
We behold a double row
Of the gaping monster's gleaming teeth on bloody murder bent.

(TCSP)

BO BERGMAN (1869–1967) had a long and distinguished career as a good minor poet and dramatic critic in his native Stockholm. His predominantly melancholy mood is caught in his lines 'Not happiness but yearning/Desire for it makes us sing'. He developed from a decadent pessimist into a humanist wryly concealing his scepticism in an elegant, urban poetry. He is the poet, above all, of the Stockholm winter. He was in fact one of the earliest of the European urban poets—what his close friend Söderberg did in prose he did in verse—and his prime historical importance lies in his initiation of a poetry entirely stripped of rhetoric and the habit of poeticizing. He is among the first of the anti-romantics: in his early poetry he distrustfully chops down emotion to an ironic slightness. Later he modified his powerful sexuality in a series of restrained urban descriptions and nostalgias. His mood is often that of Fargue, or, even more, of a Bacovia (qq.v.)—but in place of Bacovia's instability of mood he substitutes a robust humour. Bergman is a very good minor writer; he wrote excellent novels and short stories, including *The Ship* (1915), short stories.

Two other poets may be associated with Bergman in initiating this new and more restrained mood, although the approach of each was entirely different. VILHELM EKELUND (1880–1949), who came from Skåne, was an eccentric and semi-mystical sage whose influence is yet to be felt—or not felt. From 1908 until 1921 he was out of Sweden; when he returned he lived poorly, supported only by a small group of admirers. His importance lies in his introduction into Swedish poetry, in his early collections, of a skilfully modulated free (perhaps irregular is the better word) verse. From the year of his voluntary exile he turned to an aphoristic prose that reflects his intelligent successive assimilations of various thinkers and writers (including Nietzsche, George, qq.v., and others more ancient) rather than any personal development. For all but devotees, his best work is contained in his seven collections of poetry, in which he seems to be more himself. They are not perhaps much more than Shelleyan hymns to ineffable beauty, and anyone who is familiar with the best of romantic poetry will recognize their unoriginality; but their free form and phraseology are, respectively, masterful and beautiful; they helped by their example to free Swedish poets from restrictions. (TCSP)

ANDERS ÖSTERLING (1884), at first a symbolist, later brought his understanding of Wordsworth to bear on his poetry, and thus contributed importantly to the new simplicity of diction of which Swedish poets were in search. He was more distinguished as translator than poet, but his own simple poems about the places and people of Skåne, in southernmost Sweden, have their modest place. He adapted Wordsworth's direct treatment of rural characters to his own environment with conspicuous success. (TCSP)

DAN ANDERSSON (1888–1920), born in Dalecarlia, was concerned with the proletariat in his poems and novels, and is one of the initiators of modern Swedish 'proletarian' literature; but he was no Marxist. He was concerned less with class-struggle than with what he could make of the actual lives of poor people, which he knew because he was one. He was himself a charcoal-burner in a region of Dalecarlia where impoverished communities of Finnish origin lived their own idiosyncratic and deprived lives: he was concerned with the mystery of this kind of existence rather than with social improvement. His autobiographical novels, *Three Homeless Ones* (1918) and *David Ramm's Heritage* (1919), are clumsy but broodingly intense. *Charcoal-Burner's Ballad and Other Poems* (1915; tr. C. Schleef) was translated in 1943. *Black Ballads* (1917), however, contains his most achieved poetry. (TCSP)

BIRGER SJÖBERG (1885–1929) was an embryonic Brecht (q.v.), who in the years after the First World War sang his songs to his own guitar accompaniment. He began as an entertainer, but disgust with bourgeois society gradually drove him into a subversive attitude which he could not successfully integrate into his popular performances. He ended by being driven literally to madness and death. *Frida's Book* (1922) contains his ballads of small town life; *Crises and Wreaths* (1926) some of his later, more important and more angry poetry. Three posthumous volumes appeared: work reflecting his rancour and rage against bureaucracy and complacency. His conventional verse is charming but somewhat *kitsch*; his more serious poetry incorporates elements of terror and rage expressed in a racy language that has had an influence on later poets. (TCSP)

Perhaps less important, but nevertheless immensely gifted and vital, is EVERT TAUBE (1890), also a singer of his own songs. These are often about his early life as a sailor and his life in Argentine between 1910 and 1915. Taube is in a great Swedish tradition, running from Sweden's greatest poet Carl Michael Bellman to himself (with whom it seems it will die—falling into the hands of popsters and commercialites), of the singer-poet. He is a light poet, but an authentic one.

Little need be said of BERTIL MALMBERG (1889–1958) except that he was a skilful technician who varied from an inflated pseudo-philosophical poetry to jolly aphorisms. His late transformation to a modernistic style (which he attributed to the effects of a brain haemorrhage) is unconvincing and need not be taken seriously. He was for a time an adherent of the Oxford Movement: an indication of the quality of his mind, which did not match his capacities as a craftsman. Thus he could write: 'The one thing on earth/You may trust in still/Is not what you feel,/But what you will.' (TCSP)

HJALMAR GULLBERG (1898–1961), born in Malmö and for a long time a theatrical director of Swedish radio, had a more interesting development, rooted in his linguistic rather than in his emotional or intellectual reactions. His early poetry was traditional in form, concerning itself with themes both Christian and classical. He then used poetry to express a series of moods: he can be Hardyesque ('Someone from eternity/Arranges for his exalted pleasure/With comets and suns/A great display'), ironically sentimental, straightforwardly erotic, or, perhaps most characteristically, find a basis for his mysticism in the everyday. This early poetry is written in a deliberately conversational, anti-poetical style. It was extremely popular in the Thirties; but after the Second World War (in which of course Sweden remained neutral and unoccupied by the Nazis), the new generation not altogether fairly condemned it as tending to the middle-brow. He responded with three collections of poems in a new style: more highly charged, sceptical, closely packed. Gullberg was a fine translator from Sophocles, Lorca and other important European poets. (TCSP; sel. tr. F. Fleisher, *Seven Swedish Poets*, 1963)

*

By the beginning of the Thirties a 'culture debate' was in progress. Heidenstam's (q.v.) sentimental patriotism had been succeeded by a more socialistic and viable kind of nationalism. But this manifested itself in prose; it was insufficient for poets. Bourgeois culture was attacked by the proletarian Marxists, by the Freudians and by 'primitivism' (Martinson, Lundkvist, qq.v.). The most intelligent faction gathered around the magazine *Spektrum*.

KARIN BOYE (1900–41), a psychologist, Sweden's most outstanding modern woman poet, represented a synthesis of all three attitudes. Some of her earlier poetry—technically very influenced by Ekelund (q.v.)—is over-idealistic and over-intense: a compost of unassimilated influences. Translating Eliot's *Waste Land* (q.v.) in the early Thirties helped her to find a manner of her own. Karin Boye's was a tragic personality. She abandoned Christianity for Freud and socialism, and ended as a desperate and reluctant Marxist; but the rise of totalitarianism disturbed her essentially religious nature so much that she killed herself. Her best poetry describes the mysteries of transformation and ageing; her poetry of political anguish is less good, although moving. This was more effectively expressed in the totalitarian novel *Kallocain* (1940; tr. G. Lannestock, 1966), which belongs, in intensity and horror, with Orwell's *1984* (q.v.). *The Seven Deadly Sins* (1941) is her final, posthumous collection. Her early fiction was unsuccessful, but *Too Little* (1936), a novel about a writer of genius destroyed by his domestic environment, deserves mention. But Karin Boye was above all a poet, whose best poems are among the most beautiful and original to have been written in Sweden in the present century. She inevitably reminds the English-speaking reader of Sylvia Plath (q.v.); but her work, while it matches Sylvia Plath's in intensity of manner, is more substantial and controlled. 'My Skin is Full of Butterflies' is characteristic:

My skin is full of butterflies, of flutterwings—
They flutter out over the field, enjoying their honey
And flutter home and die in sad little spasms,
No flowerdust is stirred by gentle feet.
For them the sun—hot, boundless, older than the ages . . .

But under skin and blood and within the marrow
Heavily heavily move captive sea-eagles
Spread-winged, never releasing their prey.
How would you frolic in the sea's spring storm
And cry when the sun brought yellow eyes to glow?

Closed the cavern! Closed the cavern!
Between the claws, writhing, white as cellar-sprouts, sinewy strands

Of my innermost self.

(TCSP)

*

ARTUR LUNDKVIST (1906) was a Marxist and a 'primitivist'; but in the late Twenties Lundkvist, with Martinson (q.v.), treated here primarily as a prose writer—together with GUSTAV SANDGREN (1904), JOSEF KJELLGREN (1907–48), both now better known for their proletarian novels than for their verse, and one other—made his début in the collection *Five Young Ones* (1929). This marked an important stage in Swedish poetry, for it introduced to it such diverse influences as D. H. Lawrence (q.v.), Whitman, Sandburg (q.v.) and others, and drew attention to the neighbouring voice of Finnish-Swedish poetry (Björling, Södergran, qq.v.). There were elements of expressionistic vitalism and futurism in Lundkvist's earlier work; but he has gradually gained control over his hyper-idealism without sacrificing his spontaneity and free-flowing style. He has published a number of novels as well as many volumes of poetry.

The poet regarded by most critics as Sweden's most original and greatest of this century is GUNNAR EKELÖF (1907–68). Karin Boye may have been neglected in this respect; but Ekelöf deserves his reputation. He is a genuinely philosophical and mystical (rather than existential) poet, of great persistence and integrity. He lived much of the latter part of his life in seclusion. For Ekelöf thought and inner feeling *are* experience, and his poetry is a continual attempt to define his position. Ekelöf's poetry is primarily rooted in Swedish literature— in Fröding and, technically, in Ekelund (qq.v.); but he became aware of Rimbaud (whom he translated in the early Thirties) and surrealism (q.v.) before most other Swedish poets. His work also has affinities with the 'cubist' poetry of Reverdy (q.v.). There is also a strongly oriental—particularly Sufic— element in his poetry. His writing has always been exceedingly esoteric and personal, and none of it yields its meaning without long acquaintance. His first book, *Late Hour on Earth* (published by the Spektrum Press), surrealistic in manner, reflected his solipsist despair at being unable, as a person, to break through to the objects of his own perceptions, which consequently appear as hallucinated and menacing. The poet he is nearest to here is certainly Reverdy. The poet's isolation affects the whole field of his contemplation. (Experience in an existential sense apparently counts for nothing at all.)

> The nerves screech silently in the dying light
> which flows through the window grey and delicate
> the red flowers silently feel their wounds in the dying light
> and the lamp sings on lonely in a corner
> (tr. R. Bly and C. Paulson, *Late Arrival on Earth: Selected Poems*, 1967)

On a less personal level, these first poems assail—with a highly sophisticated irony—what is petrified in the bourgeois culture. Ekelöf does not of course exempt or spare himself. He has called the collection 'a suicide book' because in it he set out to do no less than strip himself of all bourgeois illusion—and his approach is not political but highly personal—in at least a mental sense. He risked self-destruction. Like Ungaretti (q.v.) he seeks to return to the primitive, the real, the human situation; but he does not take Ungaretti's specifically verbal approach, and he also desires a more denatured—philosophical—version of the primitive. It makes him into a formidable poet; but a good deal of the early work is over-programmatic and repeats the content of surrealist manifestos ('To the overwhelming and general stupidity, to the state and the laws, the family and the Church, lies and fears, with hatred,/In order to violate false innocence, to ravage the lovely false-fronts . . .').

In his books of the next twenty years Ekelöf, with some lapses, tried to 'become like himself': in other words, to locate himself among the objects (including people) of his perception. Erik Lindegren (q.v.), in an informative essay, has described Ekelöf's division of people into three categories: the naïve, innocent, timid, wild people who have not been tempted by dualism; the committed moralists, who identify with what they believe in, 'partly enlightened, partly prisoners'; and those who reject rationalism, who see morality as 'totalitarian opium'. This third ('authentic'?) type is familiar enough, although Ekelöf's division is highly original—and valuable. Ekelöf's search for a valid identity reveals itself in the later collections: *Trash* (1955), *Opus Incertum* (1959), *A Night in Otočac* (1961), *Diwan* (1965) and *The Tale of Fatumeh* (1966).

Ekelöf is undoubtedly a major poet, and one who repays close study. If he is not a great one then this would be because nearly all his poetry deliberately deals in abstractions: seems to lack flesh and blood. But then, it may be argued, his is a poetry of abstraction: of how man is assailed by abstractions. . . . 'Come and help me', he asks in 'Monologue with his wife': 'I am vanishing./He has a grip on me, he transforms me, the god over there in the corner whispering'. He is a true modern metaphysical, and he will almost certainly prove to be a prophetic poet. (TCSP; *Selected Poems*, tr. M. Rukeyser and L. Sjöberg, 1967).

Ekelöf's only slightly younger contemporary ERIK LINDEGREN (1910) was profoundly influenced by both him and surrealism; he is contemporary Sweden's foremost experimental poet. He first became known in the Forties, as one of those defenders of liberty (in a neutral country) who also assured the victory of modernism. Although Swedish compromise during the years 1939–45 was prudent in the circumstances, these writers (grouped around the magazine *40-tal*) nevertheless felt morally contaminated. The two most important members of this pessimistic group were Lindegren and Vennberg (q.v.). Others included RAGNAR THOURSIE (1919) and WERNER ASPENSTRÖM (1918), who founded and co-edited *40-tal*. Thoursie is a poet of menace, clearly influenced by Ekelöf but more on the attack: he arranges the familiar paraphernalia of everyday life in threatening patterns. (TCSP) Aspenström approaches the same material in a more lyrical manner. (TCSP) Lindegren, who feels that he is being 'fitted into the wall of hatred like the grey stone' even while he senses 'the community of stones', reacts to his predicament with a disjointed poetry, whose lyricism is only evident in fragments. His *The Man Without a Way* (tr. R. Bates and L. Sjöberg, *New Directions*, 20, 1968; pt. TCSP) consists of forty 'broken sonnets', and is self-evidently a preparation for action: a concrete statement of commitment, made in this form because no other (say, a conventionally coherent one) would be adequate. This work eventually became a classic statement for the succeeding generations. It consists of an 'inner' poetry of surrealistic surface but carefully worked out internal structure. Lindegren does not have Ekelöf's intensity, and there is something lucubrated about his most indignant poetry; but the sincerity of the mystical experience is unquestionable. By contrast KARL VENNBERG (1910) is both more accessible and tougher; his brand of socialism is also more straightforward. He is a polemicist (particularly for a 'Third World' attitude to the East-West conflict), and in his poetry a refreshing sceptic with an eye for the detail of the world of nature and sex that he loves and feels is being torn asunder by rigidly held ideas.

LARS FORSSELL (1928) is an experimentalist who blends together a specifically Swedish lyrical note, internationalism (sometimes glib and suspect), and a revival of old popular forms, and of the fable and idyll. In his earlier poetry he functioned behind the masks of a pathetic clown or a petrified bourgeois—for example, *F. C. Tietjens* (1954), a kind of Swedish Chaplin or M. Plume (q.v.). His later poetry is more mannered. Sheer virtuosity, versatility and a capacity for writing too irresponsibly in the vaguely surrealistic 'continental manner' are his worst enemies. (TCSP) Infinitely more serious is TOMAS TRANSTRÖMER (1931), a psychologist who has the rare ability to express his inner world in coherent external terms. Robert Bly has brilliantly translated *20 Poems* (1970).

*

The novelist SELMA LAGERLÖF (1858–1940) won the Nobel Prize (1909). An essentially naïve (q.v.) writer, she became in her later years stupid and out of touch; but the Swedish public loved her, and not foolishly. Few of her books (most of which were translated into English) are without merit and insight into the ways of her native Värmland; but it is for her first novel, *The Story of Gösta Berling* (1891; tr. P. B. Flach, 1898) that she will be remembered. This is a book that will survive, as those by her Norwegian fellow Nobel Prize winner,

Sigrid Undset (q.v.), will not. It is really a series of stories—rather than a novel —the hero of which is the womanizing Gösta, a defrocked priest, drunkard and poet. The time is an indeterminate past, the place, of course, Värmland. Selma Lagerlöf's style here is a mixture of rhetoric, inherited from Carlyle, and lucidity. *The Story of Gösta Berling* is epic in its range, shot through with real romance and vitality, and certainly a great book. Succeeding novels are often good, but lack the classic sweep of this. In *The Wonderful Adventures of Nils* (1906–7; tr. V. S. Howard, 1907) she wrote possibly the best educational book of all time: a geographical portrait of Sweden seen from the back of a goose. *Thy Soul Shall Bear Witness!* (1912; tr. W. F. Harvey, 1921) should be mentioned as a fine novel of the supernatural. Selma Lagerlöf is one of the last great naïve epic writers. Her intuitive genius enabled her to invent tales of great complexity from raw folk material.

PER HALLSTRÖM (1866–1960) remained in a conservative and moralistic tradition, but is perhaps neglected today. His self-conscious quest for beauty, in poems, novels and plays, is dull and dated; but his sincere pessimism (learned from Schopenhauer) and sense of the macabre emerge in certain short stories.

His contemporary HJALMAR SÖDERBERG (1869–1941), however, who went in the opposite direction, is a more important writer. He is a fascinating figure, whose sustained and systematic campaign against Christianity (mostly in his last, and creatively inactive, twenty-five years) has led to his work being undervalued. He was the friend of Bo Bergman (q.v.), and did in prose for turn-of-the-century Stockholm—where he was born—what Bergman did in verse: the city's atmosphere is conveyed more precisely and evocatively in *Martin Birck's Youth* (1901; tr. C. W. Stork, 1930) than in any other Swedish prose. Söderberg was a naturalist, but a Swedish naturalist: he believed in Darwinism and fate, but always at the back of his mind there lurked the more-than-suspicion that trolls, fairies and even more mysterious entities might be directing fate. He was ready, then, for Freud—whom he read and understood early. His fiction has a special glow, which comes out in his poetic and ironic short stories (*Selected Short Stories*; tr. C. W. Stork, 1935). *Doctor Glas* (1905; tr. P. B. Austin, 1963) is a neglected masterpiece: one of this century's great novels —and one of the earliest to utilize Freud's discoveries in an intelligent and unsensational manner. It was of course entirely passed by in its time. It tells of the murder, by the lonely Dr. Glas, of his attractive patient's husband, a repulsive and demanding Lutheran—a murder that brings him nothing. Cast in the form of Dr. Glas's own journal, it catches, inimitably, the moods of Stockholm in the early years of this century. Söderberg wrote one more novel, *The Evening Star* (1912), a love story, like his successful play, *Gertrud* (1906). His short stories have not been bettered by any Scandinavian writer. It is said that he lacks 'robustness'; but this judgement may well reflect a sly distaste for his unsensational and persuasive pessimism. His anti-Christian essays are as superbly argued as his stand against Nazism in the Thirties was prophetically accurate. He learned from Jacobsen, Bang and Anatole France (qq.v.), but discovered his own manner early. He is certainly a more important writer than France, who merely served him, in his youth, as a model of scepticism. His second wife was Danish, and he spent the last twenty-four years of his life in Denmark. He is a major writer, and urgently due for reappraisal.

*

Swedish 'proletarian' literature is unique in Europe: a number of largely self-taught writers have investigated working-class life without any discipline imposed from above. GUSTAV HEDENVIND-ERIKSSON (1880–1967) was one of the pioneers of this literature. He wrote with consistent intelligence about the lives of railway-constructors and, in the Fifties, of those employed in the modern Swedish timber industry. The self-taught MARTIN KOCH (1882–1940) was a more imaginative writer, whose silence in the last twenty years of his life is to be explained by his guilt at being more interested in the psychology of his pro-letarian characters than in their struggle to achieve social parity. Influenced by Upton Sinclair and Jack London (qq.v.), Koch was essentially an inspired chronicler of the dregs of Stockholm: *God's Beautiful World* (1916) is a memor-able depiction of oppressed scum: it is a novel of despair, paradoxically contrasting an evil urban vitality with a benign, moribund pastoralism.

VILHELM MOBERG (1898), another autodidact, belongs to the 'proletarian' school; he is a puzzling writer, since he has persisted in combining a facility for producing successful midcult fiction with literary qualities that cannot be ignored. *The Earth is Ours* (1935–9; tr. E. Björkman, 1940), a trilogy, about Knut Toring who leaves his south Swedish home for the big city but then feels impelled to return to and come to terms with it, is probably his best novel. It is markedly successful in its depiction of Swedish social and economic problems of the time. Moberg's famous novels about Swedish nineteenth-century im-migrants to the U.S.A.—*The Emigrants* (1949; tr. G. Lannestock, 1956), *Unto a Good Land* (1952; tr. G. Lannestock, 1957), *Last Letter Home* (1956–9; tr. G. Lannestock, 1961)—are less good. They have a pseudo-epic air; but at the same time they incorporate much valuable reportage.

More important than Moberg is EYVIND JOHNSON (1900), born at Boden: a subtler writer, more aware of contemporary mental stress. *The Novel of Olof* (1934–7) is a masterful autobiographical series, describing his adolescence and hard apprenticeship as a timberman. *Return to Ithaca* (1946; tr. M. Michael, 1952) is a modern version of the *Odyssey; The Days of his Grace* (1960; tr. N. Walford, 1965), Johnson's best novel, is a subtle dissection of the totalitarian spirit set in the time of Charlemagne. The massive *Krilon* (1941–3) trilogy should also be mentioned: an allegory of Nazism and neutrality, always subtle, some-times laboured, but never dull. Johnson is a brilliantly intelligent writer, prolific but sophisticated, restlessly experimental but coherent.

HARRY MARTINSON (1904) is internationally the best known of the Swedish 'proletarians'. Orphaned at six, he had a tough and nasty early life; eventually he became a sailor and continental wanderer. He has recorded some of his adventures in *Cape Farewell* (1933; tr. N. Walford, 1936). He began as an adherent of 'primitivism', and pretended to believe in the goodness of mankind and the imminent victory of the proletarian struggle; but actually he is and always has been a lyrical nihilist and loner. *The Road* (1948; tr. M. Michael, 1955), his best book, a novel about tramps, makes his position clear: the answer to industrialization and the technological plans of politicians is to preserve your individuality and freedom by taking to the road. Martinson's poetry in shorter forms is his best; the rest is spoiled by being inflated into grandiose statements of his 'philosophy', a tedious and pretentious mystical primitivism. *Aniara* (1956; tr. H. McDiarmid and E. H. Schubert), for example, a long poem in 103 cantos about a space-ship drifting irremediably into the void, is unfortunately as puerile in general conception as it is interesting in detail (its translator, Hugh McDiarmid, is himself a naïve polymath of the Martinson type). It should be added that this view of Martinson, although by no means new, is a minority one. The general consensus is that, in the words of Dr. Tord Hall, 'Martinson is a pioneer of the poetry of the Atomic Age. No poet before him has tackled the formidable task of studying Man with the aid of modern science . . . observing him in the astronomical perspective of the two-hundred-inch reflector at Mount Palomar . . . work whose symphonic breadth derives from one shuddering theme—Man's journey through his own emptiness, humanity's fall away from earth, into the trackless void'.

But Martinson has been overrated only as a 'thinker'. For once it is realized that his ideas are merely tiresome, he may be read for his immediate insights; and he is one of the greatest of all Swedish nature writers. Far more important, in fact, than his 'mysticism' is his feeling for the wilderness and for fauna and flora. His intuitive linguistic innovations are also of importance. His best poetry is to be found in *Trade Wind* (1945); this is vigorous and of high quality.

IVAR LO-JOHANSSON (1901) is another writer who had a rough early life, and had to find his own education. He is associated in the mind of the Swedish reading public with Johnson, Martinson and Moberg as a proletarian writer; but most especially with Jan Fridegård (q.v.), as the leading portrayer of the grim lives of the Swedish farm labourers before the First World War. Lo-Johansson's father was an illiterate who eventually acquired his own small farm; he pays him high and moving tribute in *The Illiterate* (1951). His massive 'collective' novels of the Thirties—including *Good Night, Earth* (1933) are aesthetically clumsy but impress by their sincerity and the accuracy of their portrayal of the labouring characters. He has also written of the city and of every kind of social problem: prostitution, old age, even sport. *Mana is Dead* (1932), a love story, sounds an entirely different note. *The Illiterate* was the first of a series of autobiographical novels—this is a well established Swedish genre—which is of considerable value. Lo-Johansson is a shrewd observer of both the mores and the psychology of his contemporaries; his later work has been improved by its unexpectedly relaxed quality and its humour.

JAN FRIDEGÅRD (1897) takes the same kind of subject-matter, but his approach is more indignant and cynical, and he concentrates on individual rather than collective fate. His best work is the tough *Lars Hård* (1935–42) tetralogy, showing how an ex-soldier is smashed down by the impersonal forces of society, and yet retains his own identity. It is a de-idealized self-portrait—Fridegård had been a navvy, a soldier and on the dole—which illuminates the lower end of Swedish society in the years before the Social Democrats came to power (1932) more fully than any historical or sociological work. *Lars Hård* is a latter-day naturalist novel of great power and depth, which Fridegård has not surpassed. Fridegård's later fiction, some of it historical, is however consistently skilful and intelligent.

*

GUSTAF HELLSTRÖM (1882–1953), who worked for some time in England and U.S.A., published many interesting autobiographical novels; but his finest work is to be found in *Lacemaker Lekholm has an Idea* (1927; tr. F. H. Lyon, 1930), a survey of a family over two generations. A grandson returns from the States to his grandfather's centenary, which gives the author his occasion. This has a naturalist programme—Hellström believed that character was determined by heredity—but its virtues lie in its psychological shrewdness, warmth and humour. *Carl Heribert Malmros* (1931) gets inside the skin of a chief of police.

LUDWIG NORDSTRÖM (1882–1942) had an English mother and knew English literature (as did Hellström) well. He was an uneven writer, whose advocation of a world-Utopia, which he called 'totalism' (based on a one-sided view of H. G. Wells, q.v.), vitiates most of his later work. But he was the first to write effective fiction about the Baltic region of Sweden (where he was born). Then he is racy, lushly comic and splendidly evocative of the quality of the people's lives. His finest work is undoubtedly to be found in his early tales: for example, *Fisherfolk* (1907) and *The Twelve Sundays* (1910).

The huge fictional output, much of it topical, of the popular author SIGFRID SIWERTZ (1882) is distinguished by intelligence and consistency of attitude; but two or three books stand out above the rest. He began as a decadent with atmospheric stories of Stockholm in the manner of Bo Bergman and Söderberg (qq.v.); but in 1907 he attended a series of lectures by Bergson (q.v.), and, as a critic has said, 'his *flâneurs* became activists'. *The Pirates of Lake Mälar* (1911) is a boys' adventure classic, and represented to its author a return to spiritual health. His masterpiece is *Downstream* (1920; tr. E. Classen, 1923), a savage and relentless attack on commercial values embodied in a selfish and profiteering family. *Jonas and the Dragon* (1928) dissects the world of journalism with almost equal skill. *Goldman's* (1926; tr. E. G. Nash, 1929) is about the world of big stores. His autobiographical books are excellent.

ELIN WÄGNER (1882–1949), Sweden's leading feminist, and the biographer of Selma Lagerlöf (1942–3), was a journalist and publicist as well as a novelist. Her feminism was quasi-mystical, and she was a strongly religious woman who found it exceedingly difficult to reconcile her convictions with her emancipated views on modern life. Her best book, *Åsa-Hanna* (1918), an evocation of Småland country life, is one of the finest of recent Swedish provincial novels.

This evokes a whole culture at the same time as it re-creates the mind of child-hood, and imaginatively explores the character of Hanna, who finds her way back to honesty from the life of crime into which she has innocently been lured. Elin Wägner's other novels are worthy but not on this high level.

HJALMAR BERGMAN (1883–1931), born at Örebro, the 'Wadköping' of his fiction, in central Sweden, offers a strong contrast to the other writers of his generation. 'Not always agreeable to conventional readers', Bergman is closer to Strindberg than any of his contemporaries, and he must certainly be treated as a fundamentally expressionist writer. A melancholic, much of his fiction presents a comic or tragi-comic surface. He attained great popularity in the last years of his life. A pessimist, hindered by his near blindness, ill health and depressive constitution, Bergman ironically took refuge in his own world; yet his gift for penetrating realistic writing is as great as anyone's. He found success with *God's Orchid* (1919; tr. E. Classen, 1923), the first of a series of recreations (he lived mostly outside Sweden) of his home town. Markurell has advanced ruthlessly from innkeeper to rich financier; he is obsessed with love for his son —who turns out not to be his. *Thy Rod and Thy Staff* (1921; tr. C. Napier, 1937) explores the same territory. *The Head of the Firm* (1924; tr. E. Sprigge and C. Napier, 1936) is a Freudian study in sexual fascination: a young man becomes obsessed with, and is destroyed by, his future mother-in-law. Finally Bergman showed himself, in *Clown Jac* (1930), as a clown haunted by fear and driven to his performance by it. Its object? To drive fear away by laughter.

PÄR LAGERKVIST (1891), who received (for his novels *The Dwarf* and *Barabbas*) the Nobel Prize (1951), is well known in Sweden for his lyrical poetry. His reputation is international; there are, one feels, other Swedish writers more deserving—for example, Söderberg, Hjalmar Bergman (qq.v.). Lagerkvist's very high philosophical intentions are rather more impressive than his creative solutions of them. Still, he is a gifted writer, with a brilliant capacity for integrating folk material into his fiction. His creative life has been a project to heal the wound made in him by the First World War—his first book of poetry was called *Anguish* (1916), of which the title poem begins:

> Anguish, anguish is my heritage
> My throat's wound
> My heart's cry in the world.

His later fiction has been distinguished for its beauty; but its hints at Christian reconciliation are not very impressive—are, in fact, detachable. It is important to read his autobiographical sketch, included in *Guest of Reality* (1925; tr. E. Mesterton and D. W. Harding, 1936) in order to gain the key to his later work. *The Dwarf* (1944; tr. A. Dick, 1953) presents a hideous creature against a colourfully drawn Renaissance background. *Barabbas* (1950; tr. A. Blair, 1952) is Lagerkvist's most tragic work, setting up Barabbas as a foil to the impossible Christ-figure, and presenting man as wounded by the loss of goodness but powerless to act in the interests of his own virtue. As good as this is the novella

The Hangman (in *Guest of Reality*), a medieval allegory of contemporary (Nazi) evil. Lagerkvist is a fine stylist, but as a whole his work is given too great a symbolic burden. He is lucky to enjoy the reputation he does.

OLLE HEDBERG (1899) is by contrast a realist whose work has no sense of ambitiously straining towards philosophic 'greatness'. He is a satirist and, latterly, a disenchanted moralist. He has been one of Sweden's most consistently probing and astute analysts of middle-class mores. *Animals in Cages* (1959; tr. E. H. Schubert, 1962) consists of two stories, in both of which dialogue plays so large a part (cf. Ivy Compton-Burnett, Henry Green, qq.v.) as to give them an almost dramatic quality. The first, 'A Smiling Procession of Triumph', gives an ironic and subtle version of the conflict between rebellious youth and experienced conservatism; the second, 'Awake in a Dormitory Town', is a mellower study of youth and age.

LARS AHLIN (1915) is a younger and different type of proletarian writer, who emerged later (in *40-tal*, q.v.) than the group already dealt with—and underwent the hardship of unemployment during the Thirties, when they had already become writers. Ahlin is an anti-naturalist and anti-theorist inasmuch as he believes in the autonomy of his characters. One of Sweden's most important active contemporary novelists, he is also one of the few modern authors to make something of the ubiquitous influence of Dostoevski. The long *My Death is My Own* (1945) is sprawling and unsatisfactory in structure but undeniably powerful. Ahlin is intelligently concerned with the religious impulse in modern men and women, and has become a master of discovering this when it takes other forms, such as neuroses or moral intentions. *Night in the Market Tent* (1957) deals with a man's evasion of love on the grounds that he has not deserved it. It is a remarkable work, sometimes confused, but always powerful and acute.

LARS GYLLENSTEN (1921) is predominantly an intellectual; but this does not prevent him from using an at times highly evocative language. Gyllensten has tended to dissipate his energy in a series of restless experiments; but there is no denying his gifts. The early *Children's Book* (1952) remains one of his best novels: a description of a man's desire to cling to childhood's innocence, and therefore to childhood, which results in madness and—ironically—a stunted personality. *The Testament of Cain* (1963; tr. K. Bradfield, 1967) is an original and clever re-creation of the Genesis myth: there are only a few documents of the Cainites' literature available, and the reader is invited to piece them together. This is, however, more intellectually than imaginatively attractive.

The death of STIG DAGERMAN (1923–54), a leading and most original writer of the Forties—he was closely linked with *40-tal* (q.v.)—was a serious loss to Swedish literature. A latter-day expressionist who owed a large but not crippling debt to Kafka (q.v.), his energy was prodigious. His suicide meant as much to the intellectuals of his generation as that of Pavese had to Italians four years before. Other obvious influences on Dagerman included the tough or primitive American novel (Hemingway, Faulkner, q.v.), and, nearer home, the symbolic procedures of the Norwegian Vesaas (q.v.). His later novels, *Burnt Child* (1948; tr. A. Blair, 1950) and *Wedding Pains* (1949), are brilliant but so shot through with anguish that the final effect is of a half-muted shriek. Better is his first novel, *The Snake* (1945), an evocation of the menace of the outside world to the individual. Dagerman's finest work is contained in the short stories collected in *The Games of Night* (1947; tr. N. Walford, 1960), in which his tendency towards symbolism is more controlled. He distinguished himself in the theatre, and, especially, as a radio dramatist.

SARA LIDMAN (1923), who has spent a considerable time in Africa, has most recently written sensitive and subtle novels about the oppressed minority in South Africa (by whose government she has been persecuted). Her earlier fiction was regionalistic, and looked back to the Thirties. Sara Lidman is able to portray both the tenderly innocent and the brutally egocentric—nowhere better than in her only translated novel, *Rain Bird* (1958; tr. E. H. Schubert, 1962), the record of a girl's bruised childhood and her evolution into a tough and selfish, but self-aware, woman.

*

No Swede since Strindberg has been a major dramatist, and no entirely serious writer has concentrated exclusively on the genre. But some Swedish writers have written notable plays. Per Hallström's (q.v.) *The Count of Antwerp* (1899) marked the beginning of a series of competent classical historical dramas. He translated most of Shakespeare into what may be described as a kind of Edwardian Swedish. Hjalmar Bergman (q.v.) was Strindberg's natural theatrical successor; in his first plays, tragedies, he chose Maeterlinck's (q.v.) cloudy manner but used it to demonstrate, often to sinister effect, how the unconscious mind rules behaviour. His last comedies are outstanding, especially *Patrasket* (1928), about a Jewish business man: here Bergman daringly and always entertainingly contrasts the commercial non-values of the business man with the conscientious ones of the Jew. Pär Lagerkvist (q.v.) is more expressionist in technique—and even more obviously indebted to Strindberg and Maeterlinck than Bergman. His best plays, however, belong to a period when he had tried to cast off these influences, and was trying for a 'magic realism', in which the fantastic is to be endowed with an everyday quality: *Victory in the Dark* (1939) and the dramatized version of his novel *Barabbas* (1953), which he also scripted for a movie directed by Alf Sjöberg (1953)—to be preferred to the more vulgar, better known, but not worthless Italian version directed by Richard Fleischer and starring Anthony Quinn, Silvana Mangano and Jack Palance. Lagerkvist's earlier technique has something in common, too, with the 'theatre of silence' (q.v.), although he hardly anticipated it as Bracco (q.v.) did. Stig Dagerman (q.v.) also wrote a remarkable adaptation of his story *The Condemned* (1948; tr. in *Scandinavian Plays of the Twentieth Century*, 1951).

V

Some 400,000 Finns, of Nyland and Åland islands, speak Swedish as well as Finnish—a language that has nothing in common with Scandinavian, and whose literature is of course treated separately. The Swedo-Finnish literature is more international than the Finno-Finnish, simply because while the latter had only native traditions to fall back upon, the former had Swedish—and all that this had absorbed. Because of its peculiar situation, it has developed an interesting and unique kind of independence. Like other modern European literatures, it is divided, in the opening period, into the traditional and the modern, and like those other literatures which develop in predominantly rural environments the two strands have in common the love of the native landscape and its customs. It was undoubtedly EDITH SÖDERGRAN (1892–1923), who was born in Russia, who introduced modernism into Swedo-Finnish literature; she was also influential in Sweden and in Finno-Finnish literature. Strongly influenced by Nietzsche, her 'cosmic' philosophy is not today of much interest. But her free-associative technique and consumptive ecstasy (she died of tuberculosis, to which she succumbed after fifteen years of poverty and illness) about nature are a different matter. Particularly moving is the humble, humorous and unhysterical acceptance of early death that she manifests in her less philo-sophically pretentious poems, such as 'The Portrait':

> For my little songs,
> The funny plaintive ones, the evening purple ones,
> Spring gave me the egg of a water-bird.
> I asked my beloved to paint my portrait on the thick shell.
> He painted a young leek in brown soil—
> And on the other side a round soft mound of sand.
>
> (TCSP)

Too high claims have been made for Edith Södergran; but in the context of Scandinavian and Finnish poetry her importance can hardly be underestimated.

The aggressive ELMER DIKTONIUS (1896–1961), who studied music and originally wanted to be a composer, once nearly starved; it was from this experience that (he said) his lifelong socialism mostly stemmed. There is something almost of Mayakovsky (q.v.) in his explosiveness; but he is more personal and, when being himself, more melodious. He translated many poets into and from Finnish. Diktonius, founder of two modernist magazines, was perhaps more vitally important as a lively influence than as a poet in his own right—his own poetry is almost always over-excited; but it is also bold and has a Whitmanesque tang. Like Södergran, he had a strong influence, during the Thirties, on Swedish literature.

Later manifestations of modernism such as surrealism and dada (qq.v.) were introduced into Swedo-Finnish poetry by GUNNAR BJÖRLING (1887–1960), who was again extremely influential in Sweden as well as in his own country. Björling remained resolutely faithful to dadaist, grammar-smashing procedures; but, paradoxically, this was for him a method of expression rather than a means of mental exploration. For he had a philosophy, an attempt to reconcile naturalist with vitalist impulses, and he stuck to it. But this philosophy is less important in his poetry, which is at bottom one of reification: objects of sense-experience are reconstituted and as such raised to significant status:

> Hear me, bird of the night
> Take me day
> Arising!
> Speak, shadow,
> Fill with morning devotion
> China's land and Peking's alleys
> And that oasis
> And all the boats are rolling
> Like a morning over the peasant's cart.
>
> (TCSP)

Björling was a minor poet, but a consistent one.

Most of the early poetry of RABBE ENCKELL (1903) is impressionistic and concerned with nature; although highly subjective and compressed, it is not notably modernistic; but he defended Björling and the modernist cause, and published in *Quosquo* (1928-9), the vehicle for the new poetry. He had studied art in Italy and France, and his early inspiration was painting. Like a number of other failed painters he tried to make poetry into a sort of painting. A little later he turned to the verse drama with classical themes—*Orpheus and Eurydice* (1938), *Jocasta* (1939). His later classical preoccupations, which recall and were perhaps influenced by Ekelund's (q.v.), are reflected in his collection *Copper Breath* (1946); a selection of his poems was included with the two dramas in *Nike Fleeing in the Garb of the Wind* (1947), which was introduced by Lindegren. Since then he has written more classical verse plays, including *Agamemnon* (1949), poetry, and intimate essays. His understanding of the classical spirit is profound, and he is its chief exponent in the Scandinavian languages. His later poetry is not pastiche; even more than H.D.'s (q.v.), it re-creates Greek elegance and elegiac calm for its own age. Enckell's voice is his own, but he has assimilated the lesson of Sappho:

> O, sun
> Thou who in the cobweb of thy rays
> Weavest, weavest
> Catching, tying hearts together,
> Bind,
> One morning before awakening
> A heart
> Closely to mine.   (TCSP)

But translation can give no impression of his stylistic achievement.

One of the most distinguished Swedo-Finnish novelists is TITO COLLIANDER (1904), who taught both art and (Greek Orthodox) religion in schools. His approach may well have been a decisive influence on Ahlin (q.v.), but his postulation of mystical Christian acceptance of suffering is more definite than Ahlin's. His characters are weak and passionate, and the spiritual peace they sometimes attain is convincing—but possibly more specious than Colliander intends.

WALENTIN CHORELL (1912), more modernist in outlook, although in his fiction stylistically conventional, is a leading playwright as well as a novelist. His plays, including *Madame* (1951), have been widely performed in Scandinavia and Germany. His most important fiction is the trilogy *Miriam* (1954–8). He chooses to deal, in an austere manner, with the world of people who have been stripped, by mental disorder, to their instinctive and primitive selves.

VI

In Iceland realism was inaugurated—under the influence of Brandes (q.v.), as elsewhere in Scandinavia—through the medium of *The Present* (1882–3), edited by students who had attended his lectures. But its impact was not quite as great —doubtless because the urban socialism that Brandes appeared to represent could have little appeal in a country of poor rural crofters and fishermen. It was not until the first two decades of this century that the drift to the towns took place. Its chief achievement was to decisively separate intellectual life from the gloomily narrow piety represented by the Lutheran State Church. Christianity reconstituted itself as the 'new theology', which threw out hell—doubtless sensing its unpopularity. (It is in this period, too, that the Icelandic vogue for spiritualism and theosophy has its origin. This trend is still so strong that it can co-exist with militant Marxism.) The movement produced no important writer; one of its leaders, the poet HANNES HAFSTEIN (1861–1922), went on to react against at least the pessimism inherent in Brandes' philosophy—and, indeed, to become prime minister (1904). STEPHAN G. STEPHANSSON (ps. STEFÁN GUÐMUNDARSON, 1853–1927), who had left Iceland for the New World in 1872, properly belongs to American-Icelandic literature, which belongs to Canada, North Dakota, and neighbouring states. He was the most important of the realists, among whom he belongs by virtue of his social satires. But he was primarily a poet, and was undoubtedly the dominant personality in the settlers' literature. He was a crude but worthy poet, who told vigorous stories, made nostalgic descriptions of his homeland, and expressed generally humanitarian beliefs. The pronouncement of one F. S. Cawley that he was 'the finest poet of the Western world' belongs more to the history of comedy than criticism; but he was a worthy figure.

Symbolism came to Iceland from Denmark, from whence it was brought by

EINAR BENEDIKTSSON (1864–1940). His five books of verse are, however, less important than his influence in turning Icelandic literature away from naturalism. His poetry is lofty, not to say pompous; his notion of symbolism is extremely limited—as is his notion of poetry itself, which he regards as the most suitable means of expression of noble and idealistic emotions. But he helped to prepare the way for better poets who were not, as he was, really interested in the wave of nationalism that swept over the country in the first years of the century.

HULDA (ps. UNNAR BJARKLIND, 1881–1946) went back to simple and folk forms. (TCSP) JÓHANN GUNNAR SIGURÐSSON (1882–1906) was probably the best of the neo-romantics. (TCSP) But much more important than these is ÞÓRBERGUR ÞÓRÐARSON (1889), who filled the traditional measures with nonsense and satirized the sentimentality of more conventional poets, as in 'Futuristic Evening Moods':

> Rant thy treble rhyme from stable,
> Rarest child mid life's defiledness!
> Spy! what gibberish were you saying?
> Sprung white lilies on scarlet tongue then?
> Glycerine is a godly oozing.
> Gling-glang-glo! who's got the low wretch?
> Nybbari good and Noah the scrubber!
> *Nonsense! Chaos! Bhratar! Monsieur!*
> (TCSP)

Þórðarson is the best modern Icelandic poet. Like so many Icelanders, he has been involved with theosophy and Yoga as well as Marxism; he was also an Esperanto enthusiast. He was a prominent anti-Nazi. *The Eccentric* (1940–1) is a lively and interesting autobiographical novel, in which he displays remarkable self-awareness and a superb humour. His massive, Boswellian fiction, *The Life of Pastor Arni Þorarinson* (1945–50) is a comic masterpiece. *The Hymn About the Flower* (1954–5) is written from the point of view of a child. Þórðarson is also important for *Letter to Laura* (1924), socialist and modernist essays that introduced much that was intelligent and new to Iceland. Considering the world reputation of Laxness (q.v.), who could never have got started without him, Þórðarson has been cruelly neglected outside Iceland; he is a superior writer.

The prolific GUNNAR GUNNARSSON (1889) made his reputation in Denmark as a writer in Danish, but returned to Iceland in 1939. He has been compared to Olav Duun (q.v.) as an interpreter of ordinary people. *Guest the One-Eyed* (1912–14; tr. 1920) is an over-romanticized historical novel about his own part of Iceland; nevertheless, it has enormous verve and descriptive skill. *Seven Days' Darkness* (1920; tr. R. Tapley, 1930), set in Reykjavík, is really much better. It records the collapse into madness of a doctor during the influenza epidemic of 1918. This is Gunnarsson's best book; what has followed it—including plays and poetry—has been no more than worthy.

HALLDÓR LAXNESS (1902), born in Reykjavík, is Iceland's leading writer; in

1955 he was awarded the Nobel Prize. No Icelandic writer in the last century can be compared to him except Þórðarson (who is a superior poet and who began the process of freeing Icelandic prose from archaism, which Laxness completed). As a young man Laxness travelled and absorbed many cultures and influences: German expressionism (q.v.), Catholicism (he was in a Luxemburg monastery for a time), French surrealism (q.v.), and America. Finally he arrived at a communism (about 1927) from which he has not retreated. (It should perhaps be mentioned that communism is not eccentric in Iceland: the party have for some time held nine seats in a parliament of sixty—nearly ten times as strong as the Liberal party's representation here.) Laxness is a lyricist and a satirist who has shown the kind of development characteristic of major writers. The novel *The Great Weaver from Casmïr* (1927) marks his emergence from Catholicism, whose intransigeance he savaged in his essays of 1929: *The Book of the People*. His fiction of the Thirties—*Salka Valka* (1931–2; tr. F. H. Lyon, 1936 rev. 1963), *Independent People* (1934–5; tr. J. A. Thompson, 1945), *The Light of the World* (1937—40)—all dealt with the contemporary Icelandic scene. They are conceived on too grand a scale to entirely suit all tastes—one can understand this tendency, however, in the literature that produced the Eddas—but they must undoubtedly be accepted as landmarks in Scandinavian literature. The first deals with the fishing community, the second with farming, and the third with a folk poet. These are fiercely critical of society, but ultimately must be treated as expressionist rather than social novels. *The Atom Station* (1948; tr. M. Magnússon, 1961) satirized the American presence in Iceland; likewise the play *The Silver Moon* (1954). *Paradise Reclaimed* (1960; tr. M. Magnússon, 1962) is at the expense of the Iceland Mormons. Laxness' style has become more formal with time; but it always reflects his own turmoil: cynicism clashes with lyrical acceptance, anger with gentleness. Of his historical novels, in which he owes most to the traditional literature of his country, only the satirical *Happy Warriors* (1952; tr. K. John) is available in English. *Iceland's Bell* (1943) is set in the early eighteenth century.

South African Literature

South African literature comprises literatures written in English, Afrikaans (a form of Dutch that eventually replaced Dutch as the official language of South Africa) and African languages.

I

A true Afrikaans literature began only in this century. On the familiar colonial pattern, the first truly native poetry preceded the prose. It was in EUGÈNE MARAIS (1871–1936), TOTIUS (ps. J. D. DU TOIT, 1877–1953), JAN CELLIERS (1865–1940) and C. LOUIS LEIPOLDT (1880–1947) that Afrikaans poetry first found its authentic voice. Marais, a lawyer, wrote only one volume of verse; it contained 'Winter Night', which is considered to open the Afrikaans epoch. His wife died young, his own health was broken, and he finally killed himself. He wrote well in prose of animals and insects, especially in *The Soul of the White Ant* (1934; tr. W. De Kok, 1937). (PSAV) Totius was a minister in the Dutch Reformed Church and a professor of theology. His verse is stark, simple and surprisingly effective; he was influenced by late nineteenth-century Flemish poetry and by protestant hymnology. (PSAV) Celliers was the least interesting of this group, but deserves his place for his technical ability. Leipoldt was one of the most gifted South Africans of his generation: he was a politician, journalist and doctor as well as poet. He was also a novelist, dramatist, botanist and notable personality. 'The Banded Cobra' is a fine poem showing at the same time his deep hatred of war and the love of nature in which his bitterness about humanity took refuge:

> The copper cobra comes out of his slit
>   On the ridge and slides around
> 'The rain has fallen; the veld is wet,
>   And wet the red-gold ground.'
> The meercat comes, his eyes two gleams,
>   And watches bolt-upright.
> The ancient porcupine says: 'It seems
>   It will rain again tonight.'
> But the lizard squeaks: 'Why, that's not rain,
>   It's red and sticky and dark:

Such rain will you ever see again—
    So smooth, so fine, so stark?'
And the wise rock-owl weighs in his words:
    'It's blood, it's human blood!
    It's living blood at the bushes' roots
That feeds them in its flood.'

(PSAV)

The only Twenties writer to make a lasting mark was C. M. VAN DEN HEEVER (1902–57), born in one of the world's first concentration camps (the British one at Norvalspont), whose fiction is probably more important than his poetry. His best novels are *Late Fruit* (1939) and *The Harvest Home* (1935; tr. T. J. Haarhoff, 1945); like much Afrikaans fiction, van den Heever's is weak in psychology; but he gives a poignant picture of farmers forced by failure to the city and exploitation. (PSAV)

The dominating personality in Afrikaans letters today, however, is still N. P. VAN WYK LOUW (1906), a university lecturer. He is a genuine intellectual, and has written criticism and a verse drama—*Germanicus* (1956)—of some importance. Some of his dramatic and yet metaphysical lyrics are distinctly unusual and original, as 'Oh the Inconstant':

Oh the inconstant child: young girl
fantasy-making, fantastic, neurotic—
bound forever to the hardest:
wood never could be hard enough for her knife;

lime was too crumbling
(granite again beyond her forbearance),
'form' she had in her, to her—oh the light
play-haunches that filled a universe—

but the role of free hetaira was
concentration-camp wire parting
her from the double-bed and babies
and the too wide sheet plus the pillow;

the cool sheet, and the separated pillows
were two mountains and a finlandic mere
between her and her 'sanctity',
between her bestowal and her desire.

(PSAV)

This plainly shows the influences of German and possibly Dutch expressionism.

Another important Afrikaans writer, a little younger than Louw, is UYS KRIGE (1910), who is an anthologist and translator into Afrikaans (from French, Spanish, Italian, Portuguese) of note as well as a poet. He has been influenced by the Latin-language poets from whom he translates, but has acclimatized them to his own Afrikaans voice. His subject-matter is usually war or the suffering inflicted by man upon man; but this he often sees against the natural background of South Africa, which he renders with a hard precision. The last two stanzas of 'Farm Gate' illustrate his lyrical powers:

> Now after all the years I'll open
> a gate again.
> Where have my paths
> till now not led
> to bring me to this farm-road gate
> with all illusions shed
> but hope, hope in my heart
> and clear dreams in my head?
>
> The gate stands in
> a maroola's shade.
> A wholeness in me, harmony
> and no bitterness, no hate.
> I lift the catch . . . and in my heart
> opens a gate.
>
> (PSAV; see also SAWT)

Uys Krige is the author of many stories, and of a book about his escape from an Italian prisoner-of-war camp during the Second World War.

D. J. OPPERMAN (1914), like Louw, continued to experiment within traditional forms, and is generally regarded as the leading Afrikaans poet of his generation. He is a clever and attractive poet:

> Under a dung-cake
> with the rain in spate
> two earthworms held
> a terse debate
>
> on 'you' and 'me'
> and 'my native land',
> on 'my mud-hut
> was first to stand'.
>
> A casual spade
> by chance sank through,
> the earthworms both
> were chopped in two:
>
> Four earthworms now
> jerk slimily along
> the 'I's' and the 'you's'
> doubt where they belong.

In the next thick mush
of a meeting place
politely each
greets his own face.

(PSAV)

ELISABETH EYBERS (1915), deeply influenced by Emily Dickinson, was the only outstanding Afrikaans woman poet until the advent of Ingrid Jonker (q.v.). She now lives in Holland. Her subject-matter is the same as that of the Australian poet Judith Wright (q.v.): motherhood, womanhood, loneliness. . . . But she is terser and less inclined to sentimentality, and there is a note of subdued bitterness running through her work. *The Quiet Adventure* (tr. O. Kirsch and E. Eybers, 1948) is a selection of her poems in English translation. (PSAV)

The suicide of INGRID JONKER (1933–65) has had an unquestionable symbolic significance for all South African writers. Her poetry is disturbed and disturbing. The comparison with Sylvia Plath (q.v.) is inevitable; but she yielded to the British influence of Dylan Thomas more than to that of Roethke (qq.v.), the figure most obviously behind Plath. But the poetry of both anguishedly explores the link between birth and violence: 'but sewer O sewer/my blood child lies in the water' writes Ingrid Jonker. And just before her suicide she expressed her feelings about the situation in South Africa:

My black Africa
follow my lonely fingers
follow my absent image
lonely as an owl
and the forsaken fingers of the world
alone like my sister
My people have rotted away from me
what will become of the rotten nation
a hand cannot pray alone.

(PSAV)

Selected Poems (tr. J. Cope) appeared in 1968.

II

With only a few exceptions, those South Africans who write in English and are known internationally are exiles; few of them are even thought of as being South African. ROY CAMPBELL (1901–57) did not stay in South Africa long, although long enough to make his mark as a satirist and to write his best poetry. He and William Plomer (q.v.) founded the magazine *Whiplash* (1926), to 'sting with satire the mental hindquarters . . . of the bovine citizenry.' Then

Campbell left, stormed London (challenging his literary enemies to duels), fought for Franco in the Spanish Civil War and then for the Allies in the Second World War, worked for the B.B.C., and finally went to live and farm in Portugal, where he died in a car crash.

Campbell never grew up, and as he grew older became increasingly brash and egocentric, while his satire became thin. He became a Roman Catholic, but an unpleasantly militant one, sharing the hysterically nihilist mood of some of the fascist rebels in Spain, who rationalized their brutality by the slogan, 'Live Christ the King'. He himself was no fascist, simply a naïve (q.v.) who lamented—but without ever bothering to take serious thought—modern technology's erosion of individuality. Much of his work, like his personality, was vitiated by his inability to examine the nature of his ultra-romantic compulsions. But he had real warmth, and his egocentricity—which occasionally involved hitting people he disliked in public—may be looked upon as an accidental sickness. Without it he could have remained a fairly good vitalist poet. His early satire, in which he attacked the pseudo-romantic self-indulgence of bad colonial poetry, was excellent: the famous epigram 'On Some South African Novelists'—

> You praise the firm restraint with which they write—
> I'm with you there, of course:
> They use the snaffle and the curb all right,
> But where's the bloody horse?

—gives a hint of his power and wit. Later satire is vigorous and ingenious in its compression; but its points of view are too often sick: Jews are funny, force equals Christ equals glory, and so on. There was, however, a lyrical purity in him; and before he came to London and became too involved with his own megalomania this came out in a handful of beautiful poems. The best is the comparatively long 'Tristan da Cunha', the real subject of which is that very poetic loneliness which drove him into egocentricity. It is a magnificent poem, of major proportions, more complex than its lucid surface immediately suggests; one prophetic stanza is:

> My pride has sunk, like your grey fissured crags,
> By its own strength o'ertoppled and betrayed:
> I, too, have burned the wind with fiery flags
> Who now am but a roost for empty words,
> An island of the sea whose only trade
> Is in the voyages of its wandering birds.

Campbell's poems and translations were collected in three volumes: *Collected Poems* (1949–60). David Wright (q.v.) has written of Campbell with wisdom and understanding.

The turning-point from colonial to South African came with Campbell and WILLIAM PLOMER (1903). The colonial had been mainly represented by such poets as F. C. SLATER (1876–1954), KINGSLEY FAIRBRIDGE (1885–1924) and the

Rhodesian ARTHUR SHEARLY CRIPPS (1896–1952), none of whom is more than historically interesting. Both Campbell and Plomer saw and accepted what the earlier poets had escaped from by rooting themselves in the Victorian British tradition: the nature of their new country. Both looked not to the worn-out home tradition, but to the vigour of the Africans themselves, and to European modernism. Plomer, a still undervalued writer, is a distinguished novelist and poet. He combines the humanism of his close friend E. M. Forster (q.v.) with a colourful sense of the bizarre. His *Collected Poems* appeared in 1960. His poetry may be divided into comic extravaganza on the one hand, and more personal work on the other. There is no one like him in the world in the former genre; as a 'light poet' he is preferable to John Betjeman—as fluent in traditional forms, his work is never vitiated by refuge in the poetical or high sentimental, and his choice of words is subtler, funnier and altogether sharper. In his other vein Plomer is fastidious, reticent, elegant and the author of some memorable and moving lines, such as (in his elegy, 'The Taste of the Fruit', for Ingrid Jonker and Nathaniel Nasaka, who killed himself in the same month): 'Where sour beer and thick smoke/Lewdness and loud/Laughter half disguise/Hope dying of wounds;/He is not there'. There is no doubt that Plomer has been underrated as a serious poet. He has had more of his due as a novelist, and it is on the whole well acknowledged that he was the first South African writer of English fiction to try to see the black man as he actually is. His first novel, *Turbott Wolfe* (1925), bears obvious signs of its author's youth; but it remains a passionate demonstration that a human way for South Africa would be through miscegenation. After three relatively minor books, Plomer produced his best novel: *Museum Pieces* (1952), a study of a man who cannot find a place for himself in the modern world. *Museum Pieces* is a sad novel, about a failure; but it affirms and even comes near to defining certain elusive personal values of the past that might be forgotten. Its equivalent at a lower social level is the English novelist Geoffrey Cotterell's *Go Said the Bird*.

Other English-speaking exiles from South Africa may be dealt with here. CHARLES MADGE (1912) left very early, and has never returned. He became associated with the leading English poets of the Thirties, and was for a time married to Kathleen Raine (q.v.). His only two books of poetry are *The Disappearing Castle* (1937) and *The Father Found* (1941). He was co-founder, with Tom Harrisson, of Mass Observation, and later became a publisher, planner in a new town, and, finally, a professor of sociology. He is now retired and lives in the south of France. Madge has since the Second World War been a much neglected poet, most of whose best work has not yet been collected. He began as a reasonably straightforward Marxist; but even his two early volumes contain indications of the direction he would take in his post-war work, of which the most important are the sequence, *Poem by Stages*, and the long poem *The Storming of the Brain*. That no honest publisher has yet taken these up (a publisher did, but left them unpublished) is not short of scandalous, for Madge is the one and only genuinely 'sociological' poet writing in English, and is also extremely original. His Marxism has become tempered by observations of practical communism (and its betrayal), by an increasing understanding of the anthropological bases of religious feeling, and by a personal—and sweetly old-fashioned—romanticism. The resultant poetry is of major interest, and a revelation. It should be made available without delay.

R. N. CURREY (1907), who has been a schoolmaster in Essex since 1946, did his most distinguished work as a war poet; his more recent development as a specifically South African poet (something Charles Madge never attempted) has been of a more academic nature. His war poems are in *This Other Planet* (1945). ANTHONY DELIUS (1916) did not leave South Africa until more recently. He now works for the B.B.C. in London. He has written a celebrated long poem, 'Black South Easter', satires, and a number of shorter poems on exclusively South African themes. F. T. PRINCE (1912), Professor of English at the University of Southampton, is a distinguished scholar whose elegant, fastidious, reticent poetry is collected in *The Doors of Stone* (1963). One of his poems, 'Soldiers Bathing', has become an anthology piece.

DAVID WRIGHT (1920), who is deaf, has not returned to South Africa except on visits. As well as a poet, he is a superb although unobtrusive critic (*Seven Victorian Poets*, 1965), a fine translator (Chaucer, *Beowulf*) and writer of travel books (about Portugal) in collaboration with the painter Patrick Swift. *Deafness* (1969) is the best general book on the subject; one is tempted to say the only good one. As a poet Wright has two styles: one romantic, more or less rhetorical, and the other sardonic, hard. In the first he seldom wholly locates his own voice; but there are exceptions which make the misses worth while. For example, on Wordsworth:

> There is a cragbound solitary quarter
> Hawk's kingdom once, a pass with a tarn
> High on its shoulder. Inscribed on a stone
> With graveyard letters, a verse to his brother
> Says it was here they parted from each other
> Where the long difficult track winding down
> A bald blank bowl of the hills may be seen
> Leading the eye to a distant gleam of water.
> After that last goodbye and shake of the hand
> A bright imagination flashed and ended;
> The one would live on, for forty years becalmed
> Among the presences he had commanded—
> Those energies in which the other foundered
> Devoured by wind and sea in sight of land.

Another aspect of Wright's more lyrical poetry is its fineness of technique: a deaf man's sense of music. In his sardonic manner, which comes to him as and when it can, Wright is both more detached—

> With paper and pen, with a room, and with time to think,
> Everything, in fact, unnecessary to the Muse. . . .

—and, as Anthony Delius has put it, 'dry-eyed'. He is an original poet, much read but little noticed by reviewers, who dislike the manner in which his anthologies studiously and obstinately ignore their own verses and their current preferences.

The Rhodesian novelist DORIS LESSING (1919) has lived in England since 1949. She made her reputation with her first book, *The Grass is Singing* (1950), which remains her best. This is about a white farmer and his wife, and their African servant. Here the author's social and political concerns are implicit in the story; they are not superimposed from without. Succeeding work has not fulfilled the promise of this book: although it has proved popular, and is worthy, it has not, on the whole, succeeded on a purely imaginative level. The most successful was *Five* (1953), short stories. *The Golden Notebook* (1962) impressively and despairingly records Doris Lessing's own creative problems. Essentially she is a writer searching for a new language to describe old truths; she finds it most nearly in her short stories.

LAURENS VAN DER POST (1906), of the generation of Plomer (q.v.), has also left South Africa. He is partially a humanist like Plomer; but he also has a mystical streak which he has not succeeded in integrating into the scheme of his fiction. His best work is non-fiction about Africa: *The Lost World of the Kalahari* (1958) and *Venture to the Interior* (1951). His novels are unquestionably the products of a distinguished and humane mind, but they fail to reconcile the scientist in him with the seer: rather than resolve his conflicts, they tend to make for more confusion. The best is *The Heart of the Hunter* (1961). Earlier novels include *Flamingo Feather* (1955) and *The Face beside the Fire* (1953). All his fiction contains magnificent descriptive writing; but he cannot decide how to handle or even to see his characters. He is, significantly, a 'Jungian'.

*

South African fiction begins with OLIVE SCHREINER (1855–1920), famous for her *The Story of a South African Farm* (1883), which founded the South African novel proper. This, set on an ostrich farm on the veld, is at the beginning a powerful novel, even if too obviously influenced by *Wuthering Heights;* it later becomes a piece of fine social preaching (reminiscent of Shaw, q.v.), rather than a novel. The description of the veld itself, and of a childhood on it, is magnificent. Jesus Christ comes to Mashonaland in *Trooper Peter Halket of Mashonaland* (1897) and preaches racial justice. But Olive Schreiner's most interesting book is her very early—but posthumously published—*Undine: A Queer Little Child* (1928), which describes both her morbid death-wish as a child, and the manner in which her family's Calvinism drove her to atheism. South Africans are proud of Olive Schreiner, a passionate and complex personality, of whom Roy Campbell (q.v.) wrote in 'Buffel's Kop (Olive Schreiner's Grave)':

> In after times when strength or courage fail,
> May I recall this lonely hour: the gloom
> Moving one way: all heaven in the pale

Roaring: and high above the insulated tomb
An eagle anchored on full spread of sail
That from its wings let fall a silver plume.

SARAH GERTRUDE MILLIN (1889), the wife of a judge, has been a prolific and worthy chronicler who writes lucidly and with great competence—if not more. She has covered most aspects of South Africa's recent history with sympathy, skill and accuracy, though not with any outstanding psychological penetration. She is particularly concerned with the plight of the 'coloureds' (those of mixed descent), who since the Second World War have been denied the right to vote, as in *The Dark River* (1919) and *King of the Bastards* (1950).

Racial conflicts between black and white were the theme of the single novel, *Bayete! Hail to the King* (1923) of the South African politician—previously police commandant—GEORGE HEATON NICHOLLS (1876–1942), who was born in England. This was certain, of course, to become the increasing concern of serious writers of South African fiction—which is why the contemporary novelists look back to Olive Schreiner, Sarah Gertrude Millin, and then to Plomer, rather than to the comfortable colonial writers who simply ignored the problem, or treated the Africans as picturesque furniture. FRANK BROWNLEE (1875–1952), although a minor writer, deserves honour in this respect. He lived among the people of the Transkeian territories and wrote stories about them which show understanding without a trace of patronage: *Ntsukumbini, Cattle Thief* (1929), *Corporal Wanzi* (1937), *Lion and Jackal* (1938).

It is quite possible that posterity will regard H. C. BOSMAN (1905–51) as the most outstanding South African writer of fiction in the first half of the century. An Afrikaner who wrote in English, and poet as well as prose writer, he served four and a half years in prison for shooting his stepbrother ('culpable homicide') in a family brawl. He was originally sentenced to death, but was reprieved. His first stories (some of them written in prison) were collected in *Mafeking Road* (1947); these are told by an old Boer farmer and trekker; the result is a remarkably objective picture of an isolated Afrikaner community. The laconic prose is outstanding. Bosman is the best of all South African story writers because he is the least compromising; yet no malice distorts the picture. If these men of the backveld are sly and mean, they are also courageous and— on occasion—generous. *Cold Stone Jug* (1948) is one of the best of the many books that have been written about life in prison. His novel, *Jacaranda in the Night* (1946), was not a success. He never bettered the sketches in *Mafeking Road*.

One might regard Bosman as an exile: he lived away from South Africa for a long time. But he went back there, and he regarded himself only as a South African writer. He has rightly been compared to Maupassant and (for his cruelty) to Saki (q.v.); but he has his own characteristic flavour.

Contemporary fiction in English from South Africa is somewhat disappointing. Not much written by supporters of the governmental policy of *apartheid* has any relationship with literature (this is a statement of fact, not of opinion);

nearly all the fiction by opponents of *apartheid* tends, naturally enough, to be on that subject. Unfortunately few of these writers have major imaginative talent—or energy. Most of the vigour comes from black writers with feelings of oppression. This is not to suggest that the humane, human, high journalistic value of such books as ALAN PATON's (1903) *Cry the Beloved Country* (1948) is not great; but such a book as Plomer's *Turbott Wolfe* quickly shows up their literary pretensions. Perhaps the outstanding contemporary writer of fiction living in South Africa is NADINE GORDIMER (1923), who is less overtly political and more concerned with the human results of *apartheid*. Thus, she emphasizes feelings rather than makes political arguments. She is at her best in the short story: *Six Feet in the Country* (1956), *Not for Publication* (1965) and two other collections. She has written five novels, all of which, like her stories, sensitively explore the psychological and emotional consequences of *apartheid*.

*

One poet who remains in South Africa deserves mention: GUY BUTLER (1918), Professor of English at Rhodes University. Butler is a versatile experimenter within traditional forms; his main concern is to bring together the strains of South African and European within himself; he is sensitive to European and English poetry, and tends to write poems that either record his South African experience in a European manner or to describe Europe (he is fond of and knows Italy well) from the point of view of a South African. His two main collections are *Stranger to Europe* (1952) and *South of the Zambesi* (1966). His poetry is elegant, subtle, lyrical and yet meditative, as these lines from 'Common Dawn' indicate:

> Submitting to a sentry's fate
> I concentrate
>   On the day's way of dawning—
>
> Grey clouds brighten, birds awake,
> Wings and singing shake
>   The curtained silence of the morning.
>
> As gentle as a bird, the breeze
> Brushes the grass about my knees
>   So softly that the dew remains
>
> On every blade from here to where
> Alien sentries, watching, share
>   The view of fatal plains. . . .
>
>   (PSAV; SAWT)

*

PETER ABRAHAMS (1919), son of an Abyssinian father and a coloured mother, was the first South African of mixed blood to make an international name for himself as a novelist. He escaped early from the native township where he was born to come and live in London. His novel *Mine Boy* (1946) was the first novel by a black South African to appear in sixteen years. He had previously published a book of short stories: *Dark Testament* (1942). Abrahams became well known on the publication of his autobiography *Tell Freedom* (1954). He is by no means a major novelist: characterization is not above average and plots, especially in recent novels, tend to creak. But he is an intelligent and valuable one. *Mine Boy* was one of the first novels to reveal the true effects of white exploitation upon black South Africans. The best of his other novels are *Wild Conquest* (1966), about the Great Trek of the Boers to the Matabele, *A Wreath for Udomo* (1956), set in West Africa and prophetic of the rise and fall of Nkrumah of Ghana, and *This Island Now*, which deals with the rough and tumble of politics in a Caribbean island (Abrahams now lives in the West Indies).

ALEX LA GUMA (1925), whose work may not be published or quoted in South Africa, was accused in the notorious Treason Trial of 1956, but the charge was dropped. In 1967 he escaped to Britain; the British version of *apartheid* introduced by the Maudling Act of 1971 (on the precedent of Callaghan's action against the Kenyan Asians, which actually introduced the principle of *apartheid* into the British constitution) has hardly yet been developed to a point where it will trouble him. But doubtless he watches with apprehension. *A Walk in the Night*, a long short-story, was published alone in 1962 and then in a story collection of the same title in 1967; it is one of the most vivid of all modern African stories. It is set in Cape Town's District Six, one of the toughest places in the world. Here lives Michael Adonis, sacked for answering his white foreman back. It has been compared to Paton's *Cry the Beloved Country* (q.v.) and to Doris Lessing's *Five* (q.v.); one is bound to say that it is superior to both: it really has, as one critic has claimed, 'Dostoevskian overtones'. *The Stone Country* (1967) is a novel about South Africa's prisons. (SAWT; AWT)

In *Road to Ghana* (1960) ALFRED HUTCHINSON (1924) memorably describes his flight from South Africa, where he was prosecuted by the government for his opposition to their policies. It has pace, lucidity and humour; and its record of stupidity and the brutality that this leads to amounts to one of the most powerful denunciations of some supporters of South Africa's Nationalist Party. (SAWT)

EZEKIEL MPHAHLELE (1919), banned from his profession of teacher because of his opposition to the Bantu Education Act, now lives in Nigeria. He has summed up a feeling common to many South African writers, in a remarkable statement: 'I feel very gloomy about the whole situation as far as creative writing is concerned. I think right now we are being sucked into this battle between the ruling whites and the Africans . . . our energies go into this conflict to such an extent that we don't have much left for creative work . . . why could this not be a spur towards creative writing? . . . I think it's a paralysing spur. . . . You won't get a great, white novel, I don't think, and you won't get a great black novel until we get to a point where we . . . [are] integrated'. *Down Second Avenue* (1959) is a vivid evocation of a ghetto area in Pretoria; the long, four-part *The Wanderers* (1970), is in part a semi-autobiographical account of a black journalist forced out of South Africa, in part a shrewd study of a liberal white journalist. It is an intelligent and moving work, as complex and subtle as anything to come out of Africa in the last few difficult and embittering years. (SAWT; AWT)

LEWIS NKOSI (1936), trenchant critic of much mediocre black literature, displays a similarly fine intelligence. He was barred from South Africa in the early Sixties. He is mainly a critic; but *The Rhythm of Violence* (1964) is a powerful play, set in Johannesburg, about racial tensions against a background of stupidity and violence. (AWT)

Spanish Literature

I

Modern Spanish literature is frequently divided into four distinct periods: the Generation of '98, consisting of writers born between about 1864 and 1880; the Generation of '25 (or, sometimes, '27, because that year marked the third centenary of the seventeenth-century Baroque poet Góngora), consisting of writers born between 1880 and 1900; the Generation of 1936, or of the Republic; post-Civil War writers. Overall, this arbitrary division is more misleading than helpful: too many writers overlap the divisions or transcend them.

But the first, the Generation of '98 (so named by Azorín, q.v., in 1913), is an exception: it has a real meaning in the development of modern Spanish literature, a literature whose scope and depth rival the literatures of France, Germany, the two Americas, Russia and (in the richer, earlier phase) Great Britain. The fascist victory of 1939, partly made possible by Russian and pro-Russian intervention on the side of the Republic, has dealt this literature a severe blow; but it now shows every sign of vigorous revival. The death of Franco may—at least in the long run—ease conditions still more.

The causes of the Civil War of 1936 are infinitely complex; but the main single one is the refusal—one might describe it more aptly as the inability—of the ruling classes to institute social and agrarian reforms. Less social progress has been made in Spain in this century than in any other European country. But Spain is, as Gerald Brenan has observed, 'psychologically and climactically at variance with its neighbours'. A large proportion of her people remains obstinately immune to change even now. She is more isolated than any other European country; her literature varies from other European literatures to the extent of this extra isolation.

Spain's tragedy may be seen most clearly, perhaps, in the failure of the ideals of the Generation of '98 to find fruition during the first seven decades of this century. Neither of the chief representatives of that generation—Unamuno and Ortega (qq.v.)—was happy with the Republic that Franco illegally overthrew; but the fascist victory of 1939 finally extinguished their hopes of establishing a Spain that would be truly European and yet preserve, at the same time, its own identity; a Spain that could influence Europe in a positive way. (It is true that one of the most prominent and gifted members of the Generation of '98, the essayist and political writer Ramiro de Maeztu,

1875–1936, eventually became a virulent fascist—and was in fact murdered by Republican troops for his opinions—but he had long ago decisively repudiated his early ideas, which were socialist.)

Spain's defeat by America in 1898, and the consequent loss of Cuba, Puerto Rico, the Philippines, Guam and Marianas, caused a severe blow to her pride; and, more importantly, it induced a mood of national self-appraisal. This mood is most brilliantly and fully reflected in the work of the Basque MIGUEL DE UNAMUNO (1864–1936), novelist, poet, essayist and inconsistent, asystematic, seminal thinker (to call him a philosopher would not only annoy philosophers but also imply that his scope is narrower than it is), born in Bilbao. His strain of thought is continued, as well as altered, in JOSÉ ORTEGA Y GASSET (1883–1955), philosopher and essayist, born in Madrid. Ortega was not, strictly speaking, a creative writer; but his thought is creative. An understanding of it is necessary to an understanding of the modern Spanish literary mentality. (Ortega is usually placed in the Generation of '25, but he belongs spiritually to '98 as well.) Both of these writers cultivated the essay, which is a more significant form in Spanish than in any other European literature.

If any one brief passage from the voluminous works of Unamuno contains the basic premises of his thinking then it is this, from the little posthumous collection of essays translated into English, *Perplexities and Paradoxes* (1945):

> . . . I do not nor can I affirm the existence of another life; I am not myself convinced of it; but my head just does not have room for the idea that . . . a real man, can not only resign himself to not participating in a life beyond, but also renounce and even reject it. The whole idea that we live on in our accomplishments, in our children, and in memory, and that everything is renewed and transformed and that we shall keep on doing our part toward forming a more perfect society [the great 'consoling idea', of course, of the rationalists of the latter half of the nineteenth century]—all these things seem to me like very poor subterfuges to escape the depths of despair.

This profoundly paradoxical view, in which it is doubt itself that confers meaning on life, is worked out in the course of Unamuno's criticism, novels, plays and poetry. We can see clearly in the work of Unamuno—who himself frequently fails to escape 'the depths of despair'—what we owe to the Spanish experience and the Spanish insight. His most lucid and mature expression of his position is to be found in *The Tragic Sense of Life* (*Del sentimiento trágico de la vida*, 1913; tr. J. E. C. Flitch, 1921; P. Smith, 1958). The 'tragic sense' here is the longing for personal immortality—which Unamuno saw as the basic force in individuals—which can never, in terms of life itself, be fulfilled. Unamuno, one of the leaders and chief representatives of the Generation of '98—and yet never a man with real disciples—consistently placed the subjective above what he considered to be the falsely or abstractly objective: the 'interior life' above the historical or sociological. The formative influences upon him were Bergson, Kierkegaard, and the pragmatism of William James. It was probably from Kierkegaard that Unamuno first derived the notion that the most convincing proof of the existence of God lies in the need for God: as he later put it, only one letter separates *creer* (to believe) from *crear* (to create). He is, of course, a forerunner of such French existentialists as Sartre (q.v.); but he is an entirely Spanish existentialist, and therefore very different from his successors of other nationalities: his whole purpose is to counter 'disgust' and 'absurdity'; he is as angry at such states of mind as he is at Shaw's (q.v.) socialism, which tries to limit the significance of human life to social experience and achievement.

Another important non-fiction work by Unamuno is *The Life of Don Quixote and Sancho* (*Vida de Don Quijote y Sancho*, 1905; tr. H. P. Earle, 1927), in which Cervantes' humour is shrewdly interpreted as an inversion of the tragic sense Unamuno diagnosed as fundamental to human existence. For Unamuno, the essence of Spain lay in what he called her *intrahistoria*, not in that 'glorious' external history of conquest which in 1898 came to an end, but in the real tradition—independent of events—that is passed from era to era by the *pueblo*, the humble common people. This conception could be compared to that of the French Catholics' 'La raison qui s'ignore' (q.v.); but it is different because it is not autocratic, and it concerns not the accumulated wisdom of institutions but the deep sense of identity (it may in some aspects be abject, as Unamuno fully realized, as well as noble) held by an entire populace; it is anthropological.

By profession Unamuno was a professor of Greek and Latin; he became Rector of Salamanca University in 1901. He lost this position in 1914 when he opposed German militarism; the dictator Primo de Rivera (who ruled from 1924 to 1930) exiled him to the island of Fuerteventura in 1924; he supported the Republic of 1931; then he opposed it, and even announced his qualified approval of Franco as an anti-communist; but he ended by publicly confronting and castigating the nihilismand anti-intellectualism of one of Franco's craziest followers, who at a public gathering at Salamanca shouted out 'Long live death!' Unamuno replied: 'You will conquer but not convince.' He probably escaped assassination at Franco's orders by dying on the last day of 1936. He had been put under house arrest. Although no anarchist, Unamuno could never have supported any government or system for very long: he was of too obstinate a nature, and little performed by politicians could satisfy him.

Unamuno was an active and prolific novelist, dramatist and poet. The official Spanish view of the Silver Age of her literature (between 1898 and the outbreak of the Civil War) is that it is in the essay (*ensayo*)—as represented in the work of Ortega, Azorín and others—that it reaches its highest point. There is much to be said for this view; one cannot as lightly dismiss Ortega as a creative writer as one can, say, Croce (q.v.). But then, against this view, one thinks of the poetry of Machado, Jiménez, Guillén, Lorca . . . And, too, one thinks of the power of Unamuno's novels, the evocative qualities of his best poetry; besides being an incomparably deeper thinker than the much more renowned Shaw (q.v.), Unamuno is also an incomparably superior creative writer. His first novel, *Peace in War* (*Paz en la guerra*, 1897), on the subject of the Carlist war and the siege of Bilbao (through which he had lived), is conventionally realistic in style. All his other fiction is modernist; attacked for this,

Unamuno scornfully replied that he would henceforth refer to his 'panting narratives of intimate realities' as *nivolas* rather than *novelas*(novels). These are by no means 'essays dressed up as fiction', as has been charged. The most successful are *Mist* (*Niebla*, 1914; tr. W. Fite, 1928), one of the subtlest and most original novels of its era, and *Abel Sánchez* (1917). The chief character in *Mist*, Augusto Pérez, has a character remarkably similar to that of his creator; in the scene where he confronts him, however, he demonstrates his disturbing autonomy. This, of course, anticipates, by six years, the concerns of Pirandello in *Six Characters in Search of an Author* (q.v.). It also contains elements peculiar to Unamuno himself: the attempt to ensure his survival by putting himself in a novel (but Pérez dies); the exploration of the relationship between a putative God (Unamuno) and his created one (Pérez-Unamuno).

Abel Sánchez is Unamuno's fullest expression of a theme that always obsessed him: that of Cain and Abel. (It is perhaps not surprising that this theme of fratricide should have haunted the mind of one of Spain's most representative writers.) This studies the envy of Joaquín Monegro, a character who immediately gives the lie to the accusation that Unamuno's people are really only abstractions. He is the moral superior of Abel Sánchez, and his lifelong struggle with his hate of him gives him a kind of tragic grandeur. Another remarkable novel is *Saint Manuel Bueno, Martyr* (*San Manuel Bueno, mártir*, 1933; pt. IMSL), about a priest who cannot believe in his own immortality—but continues to preach it to his parishioners. In all his fiction the characters are, in Unamuno's own word, agonists rather than protagonists.

Unamuno is at his least effective as a dramatist. His most interesting plays are *The Other* (*El otro*, 1932), a further exploration of the Cain-Abel theme, and *Brother John* (*El hermano Juan*, 1934), on the Don Juan legend.

It was Rubén Darío (q.v.) who first hailed Unamuno as a poet. But Unamuno rejected Darío's *modernismo* (q.v.) to develop his own crabbed and often rough style. The poet Unamuno cannot be fitted into any particular school; but neither can he be denied his unique place in modern Spanish poetry. He is versatile: he can write directly and lyrically of his own problems, especially of his anguish at the idea of death, evocatively of the Castilian landscape, philosophically of the meaning of religion. He always has warmth, and at his best his language is inspired. Many critics believe his long, blank-verse poem *The Christ of Velázquez* (*El Cristo de Velázquez*, 1920; pt. IMSL) to be his best; but, while interesting and full of good intentions, this relies too much on a highly complex and over-intellectualized symbolic conception to be successful. Unamuno is at his most moving in the shorter and more lyrical forms; an excellent and famous example is 'In a Castilian Village Cemetery' (PSV; PI). Here, as elsewhere, the language springs directly from contemplative emotion: the Basque identifies himself with the Castilian landscape and with the paradox of Spain itself that it seems to embody: the dead of 'In a Castilian Village Cemetery' lie in their corner of uncut grass, and when the sky falls upon them in rain 'they feel in their bones the summons of the gushing waters of life' (IMSL).

Unamuno played an important part in the life and thought of Ortega, who represents both the Generation of '98 (his first publication was in 1902), which he joined, and the reaction to it of the mid-twenties—a reaction that partly embodies, in the realm of thought, Ortega's exasperation with Unamuno's attitudes. Ortega, very much of a *torero* with words, whose deliberate aim is to make people become aware of their situation, in some ways represents a Unamuno who has decided to take the plunge, and who is less concerned with the foundation of a valid nationalism than with the creation of a climate in which the arts may flourish and man may develop without illusions. Although Ortega was Professor of Metaphysics at Madrid University for a quarter of a century, his most influential books, written between 1914 and 1930, consist of essays that originally appeared in newspapers: he always sought popular outlets.

Like Unamuno, only more decisively, Ortega is an existentialist; the core of his philosophy is contained in his famous variation on Descartes' 'I think therefore I am': 'I am myself plus my circumstances'. Ortega rejected the pure reason with which the academic philosophers play behind the walls of universities and substituted for it a 'vital reason' (*razón vital*), a reason 'rooted in life', a balance between something like the life force (*élan vital*) of Bergson and the dehumanized, logical reason that is the toy of philosophers: a mixture of instinct and reason that could, perhaps, be defined as intuition-in-action, choosing from moment to moment the direction in which life must go. As a young man Ortega studied in Germany, and became influenced both by post-Kantian philosophy and by the ideas of Dilthey and Husserl (qq.v.). In his first important book, *Meditation on Quixote* (*Meditaciones del Quijote*, 1914; tr. E. Rugg and D. Marin, 1964)—from which Heidegger (q.v.) drew much—Ortega concentrated on the genius of Cervantes rather than upon the character of Quixote. In Ortega existentialist *angst* is expressed in the brilliant metaphor of shipwreck (*naufragio*): man is floundering in a sea of insecurity, and he leans on conventional beliefs (*creencias*), habits, customs in order to sustain himself (hence the human inadequacy of the philosopher who relies on the concept of pure reason); but when he is alone, when orthodoxy fails, then he is himself, then he discovers himself—and leads an authentic existence.

Ortega's quarrel with Unamuno's attitude was rooted in his belief that, in order to survive, shipwrecked man needed to evolve a rigorous and scientific system: he found Unamuno guilty of failing to be systematic. One might say that Ortega rejected Unamuno's scepticism—as well as his belief in the necessity of a Catholic Church (Ortega deeply disapproved of the Church, particularly as a political force). Most of Ortega's main books are concerned with discovering the bases of a system. *The Modern Theme* (*El tema de nuestro tiempo*, 1923; tr. J. Cleugh, 1931) posits a modified vitalism, 'the succession of a new type of culture, the biological'. It is full of fruitful suggestions and insights but its thesis is unconvincing.

The Dehumanization of Art and *Ideas on the Novel* (*La deshumanización del arte e ideas sobre la novela*, 1925) is his most important book from a literary point of view. It is one of the century's most original and puzzling books on the nature and function of art. This relentless and perhaps largely ironic—certainly ambiguous—examination of modernist tendencies has often been misinterpreted as a downright prescription; but it is in part a lament for the old days when art could confidently be described as an imitation of reality, in part a deliberately cruel delineation of its limitations. Ortega takes up the position that a true work of literature is only artistic (*artístico*) to the extent that it is removed from reality; that it is aristocratic, and should be not merely un- but anti-popular (*antipopular*); that the more exquisite it is, the less socially useful it is; that it should distort reality by style (cf. *esperpento*); that it should 'dehumanize': progressively eliminate all those human elements that have corrupted realist modes; that it is for élites and never for the vulgar; that the novel is dead: devoid of themes or meaningful content. What Ortega asserts, or implies, then, is entirely modernist, particularly his insistence on the hermetic nature of literary works: these express, they do not describe. This was a deliberate carrying of the tendencies of one aspect of expressionism (q.v.) to an extreme; the analysis enabled Ortega to confront one aspect of himself. From this and from the élitist thesis of *The Revolt of the Masses* (*La rebelión de las masas*, 1929–30; tr. 1932), in which the modern world is represented as ruled by intellectually inferior 'mass-man', who loathes all distinction and individuality, it might be concluded that Ortega was of fascist mentality. Actually he was an anti-fascist who left Spain in 1936 and only returned (to divide residence between Madrid and Lisbon) nine years later when he saw that Franco (mass-man in the role of pious gangster) was there to stay.

Ortega is more a brilliant and seminal writer, perhaps, than an attractive one. His élitist sociology may be diagnostically nearer to the truth than some of his critics care to admit; but he is more deficient in love than some of them—and more so than Unamuno, who although he did fail to lead opinion in the years of the Republic, and thus added to the confusions of his country, never lacked love.

And yet in *The Dehumanization of Art* even Ortega comes nearer to a humane statement of the function of poetry than he himself may have thought. For when, in his theory of metaphor, he lays emphasis on metaphor as a means of evasion ('poetry is an evasion of the everyday names for things'), he cannot really escape from the implication that metaphor (the 'implement which God forgot and left inside one of His creatures when he created it, as the absent-minded surgeon leaves an instrument inside his patient's abdomen after an operation . . . Only the metaphor makes evasion possible, creates imaginary reefs among the real things . . .') *may*, rather than 'invent what does not exist', arrive at new truths. The use of God in Ortega's own metaphor is in this connection highly suggestive.

Ortega's style is a brilliant and creative one, which abounds in metaphors. He helped to maintain high literary standards in Spain (which was what he wanted to do); furthermore, in the agonized shifts of his thinking—not obscured by his frequently over-dogmatic manner and high rhetoric—may be discerned the background of much of the Spanish poetry and fiction written in his lifetime.

Both he and Unamuno represent a Spain that failed to find itself in the Republic —and lost itself utterly in Franco's cruel, fanatic and regressive dictatorship.

II

The true ancestor of Spanish fictional realism is not so much the socio-psychological aspect of the romantic novel as *costumbrismo*, the name for the novel, or—at first—sketch, of local colour and customs, which incorporated a considerable amount of social comment and satire. Most important of the *costumbrista* writers—who include Serafín Estébanez Calderón, Ramón Mesonero Romanos, José Somoza—was the critic Mariano José de Larra, whose romantic suicide after a drinking-bout (he shot himself, while looking into a mirror, in 1837) dramatized the violent and irreconcilable battle, in the Spanish mentality, between romantic liberalism and classical conservatism (which itself can spill over either into fascist fanaticism or Quixotic heroism). Larra was an inspired journalist (the newspaper article is—or was—a creative form in the literature of Spain, as it is nowhere else) whose life and writings were later held up by the men of '98 as embodying their own ideals. (His fiction, drama and poetry are less successful.) His most important work consists of 'essays on customs' (*artículos de costumbres*). These combine severe and intelligent criticism of Spanish backwardness with brilliant and loving description. Larra's accuracy of observation was developed by Fernán Caballero (ps. Cecilia Böhl de Faber, 1796–1877), who wrote about Andalusian life. The most famous of her many novels is *The Seagull* (*La gaviota*, 1849). This is an essentially romantic but none the less well observed and shrewd account of how a young German surgeon, Stein, falls in love with, socially transforms and marries a beautiful peasant girl, Marisalada; eventually she returns to her native village, where, Stein having died, she marries the barber. It is significant that in this early example of what may fairly be called Spanish pre-realism (the orthodox view, a justifiable one, is that the modern Spanish novel begins with Fernán Caballero) the main intellectual conception—that education perverts the naturally humble and simple—is a conservative one.

The great decade of Spanish realism was that in which Pedro Antonio de Alarcón (1833–91) was most active. Alarcón, who also wrote of Andalusia, was nearer in spirit and style to Fernán Caballero than to the realists (Galdós, Pereda, Emilia Pardo Bazán, Palacio Valdés, qq.v.), who come within the scope of this book; but the best fiction of this essentially naïve (q.v.) writer, whose output was immense, transcends categories, as does that of BENITO PÉREZ GALDÓS (1843–1920). Galdós is the leading Spanish realist of the nineteenth century; but his realism is tempered by a good deal more romantic sentiment than is that of, say, Flaubert. Nevertheless, it is not foolish to speak of him as on a level with Dickens, Balzac or Eça de Queiróz (q.v.); and Galdós is undoubtedly an excellent representative of the liberal, tolerant side of the

Spanish mentality. It is today sometimes stated that to speak of a particular writer's 'world' is to speak nonsense; Galdós gives the lie to this over-sophisticated view, for it is because of the 'world' he presents in, for example, *Fortunata and Jacinta (Fortunata y Jacinta*, 1886–7), that he may be compared to the greatest of the nineteenth-century novelists. Nearly all his important work, most of which has been translated into English, was done in the nineteenth century; it belongs to that century. The forty-six novels making up the series *National Episodes (Episodios nacionales)* describe the chief events of nineteenth-century Spanish history. These were his most popular books, but his best are on contemporary themes. *Fortunata and Jacinta* is a long and grim study of Madrid life in the Seventies, centring on the rivalry between a wife and a vicious mistress for the love and control of the young hero, Juanito Santa Cruz. Galdós' interest in severely neurotic or bizarre characters had always been apparent; Jacinta's husband in *Fortunata and Jacinta* is mad, and there are other eccentrics. This vein culminates in *Nazarín* (1895), the ironic and bitter story of a priest who tries to imitate Christ (Galdós, like Tolstoi, q.v., was much concerned with the difficulties of reconciling the spirit of Christianity with the practice of Churches and those who patronize them). In his final phase, often called 'idealistic', he is almost mystically concerned with Christian goodness. His retreat from a baldly realist position is characteristic of most Spanish writers of the period; but the work of his 'idealistic' phase mostly lacks vitality. Galdós also wrote drama and dramatic adaptations of his novels; *Reality (Realidad*, 1892), written under the influence of Ibsen (q.v.), is a stepping-stone in the Spanish realistic theatre.

The work of all Spain's other realists and naturalists, none of whom can measure up to Galdós in stature, reflects in one way or another the romantic or decadent reaction to realism. JUAN VALERA (1824–1905), who was nearly twenty years older than Galdós, was never a thoroughgoing realist; he was an elegant and remote aristocrat who adhered, in theory, to the notion of art for its own sake. But there are too many realistic elements in his highly intelligent fiction for us to take him quite at his own valuation. Valera simply wanted to be realistic in his own way. Thus, although his own first novel, *Letters of a Pretender (Cartas de un pretendiente*, 1849), was entirely autobiographical—and other of his earlier fiction incorporates autobiographical material, some of it with his apparently rather frustrated sex-life—he famously castigated Zola (q.v.) for using real-life material, and was violently anti-naturalist. Valera was a good literary critic, and his aesthetic theories are interesting. He did not really find himself as a novelist, however, until he was fifty: his earlier fiction is all either unfinished or botched. His masterpiece is his first real novel, *Pepita Jiménez* (1874; tr. 1886; 1891), which is partly in epistolary form and deals with a young student-priest torn between his weak vocation and false mysticism, and his love for a beautiful young widow, Pepita, whom he eventually marries. This ironic exposure of the dangers of the hypocrisy involved in sending unfit young men to be priests is distinguished above all by the brilliance of its characterization and the warmth of its portrait of Pepita herself. *Doña Luz*

(1879; tr. M. J. Serrano, 1893) deals with somewhat similar material, except that this time the conflict between the spiritual and the physical ends in tragedy. Valera's style is always aesthetic, but, in this demonstration of the human consequences of denying all love that is not love of God, he comes as near as he ever did to realism.

There are strong elements of realism, too, in the work of the regionalist JOSÉ MARÍA DE PEREDA (1833–1906); but he was one of the most resolutely conservative writers of his age. He began as a newspaper essayist; he then turned to plays, some of which were performed in Santander—to which his family had moved very early in his life. He first became widely known, however, for his *costumbrista* pieces, the first of which was *Montañan Scenes* (*Escenas montañesas*, 1864), sketches of life in the Montaña area, near Santander. Pereda's best novels are *Don Gonzalo González de la Gonzalera* (1879), *Sotileza* (1884) and *Up the Crag* (*Peñas arriba*, 1895). All are fervently regional and politically and religiously conservative to the point of obscurantism; but Pereda's very provincialism led him to introduce the colloquial into his fiction, and thus to make an innovation. Moreover, he was meticulously honest in his observation of people.

ARMANDO PALACIO VALDÉS (1853–1938), an Asturian, toyed with naturalism (q.v.), but none of his novels can be described as truly naturalist. Palacio Valdés is a good example of a nineteenth-century writer who, from the point of view of his reputation, survived far too long into the twentieth century. His later fiction is helplessly sentimental and clumsily and charmlessly out of tune with its epoch; there is an especially tiresome quality in his old-fashionedness, a total inability to adjust—so much so that he became an idol of some fascist critics when the Civil War broke out. His earlier work had hardly deserved this; nor, in the nineteenth century, was his patriarchal outlook—modified by a delightful and gentle disposition that he never lost—in the least out of place. His most famous book is his best: *Sister Saint Sulpice* (*La hermana San Sulpicio*, 1889; tr. N. H. Dole, 1890), the least sentimental of his warm studies of women, all of which have qualities of psychological insight. Many of his novels were translated into English. Palacio Valdés always inclined to the sentimental, but he largely compensated for this by his emphatic characterization and ability to evoke atmosphere; the books he wrote in this century are, by contrast, patriarchal fantasies.

The truest Spanish naturalist—but she, to Zola's (q.v.) amazement, was a devout Catholic, who could not finally accept determinism—was the Galician Countess EMILIA PARDO BAZÁN (1852–1921). Emilia Pardo Bazán's view of human nature was not pessimistic; but her initial approach to fiction was naturalistic in that it was 'scientific' (she went out searching for material), systematic, and concerned with the lower classes. She was the chief Spanish spokesman for naturalism. Her first wholly successful novel was *The Son of the Bondswoman* (*Los pazos de Ulloa*, 1886; tr. E. H. Hearn, 1908); this was followed by a sequel, *Mother Nature* (*La madre Naturaleza*, 1887). The first of these is the best of Emilia Pardo Bazán's novels; much of its sequel is of similar quality, but ultimately a too dutiful idealism vitiates it. The subject is the decay of Galician feudalism and the decadent morals of aristocrats (culminating in incest). Later, as the reaction against realism intensified, Emilia Pardo Bazán turned more decisively to decadent or spiritual subject-matter. In *A Christian Woman* (*Una cristiana*, 1890; tr. M. A. Springer, 1891) and its sequel *The Proof* (*La prueba*, 1890) she tried unsuccessfully to reconcile the Catholic with the scientific and liberal; *The Black Syren* (*La sirena negra*, 1908) is both decadent and symbolic in its intentions. Emilia Pardo Bazán was one of the most prolific and versatile short-story writers of her time; probably her greatest achievement is in this field.

Finally in this survey of 'pre-'98' prose writers we come to CLARÍN (ps. LEOPOLDO ALAS Y UREÑA, 1852–1901), intimate friend of his fellow-Asturian Palacio Valdés. Alas, who died too young to fulfil many of his ambitious projects, was much admired and studied by Unamuno; for this and other reasons—among them his early political and religious radicalism—he is perhaps the most important of the precursors of the Generation of '98. ('Clarín' means 'bugle'.) His first novel, *The Regentess* (*La Regenta*, 1884–5), was the most complex and sensitive social study written in nineteenth-century Spain; it is unquestionably a masterpiece, and the lack of an English translation is scandalous. Although influenced by *Madame Bovary*, *The Regentess* is by no means a plagiarism of Flaubert's novel—as was once charged. It is the story of a married woman led, by boredom, into an adultery she does not really desire. Like most of his contemporaries, Alas abandoned his naturalistic tendencies in the early Nineties to put more emphasis on morals and religion. The best of his many short stories—such as 'Benedictino'—are subtle moral studies which anticipate, in their bland irony, both Unamuno and Pirandello (qq.v.). Even at his worst in this form he is skilful and sure in his delineation of character; but he is sometimes inclined to make too harsh and melodramatic a contrast between the good and the bad. However, his technique of gradual revelation of qualities of character, often extremely satirical, was innovatory; *The Regentess* and the best stories are among the very best nineteenth-century European fiction. His essays and criticism are also superior. He is now more often known by his real name.

III

With VICENTE BLASCO IBÁÑEZ (1867–1928) we come to the Generation of '98 proper—although to an odd man out; Ibáñez was by no means one of the group described by Azorín in 1913 (this consisted of Unamuno, Baroja, Valle-Inclán, Antonio Machado, Benavente and the journalist Maeztu, qq.v.), and his unequivocally radical ideas did not coincide with theirs; nor was he concerned with style as they were; nor was he as subtle as they, or as effective a thinker. But he was their contemporary, and the title of 'the Spanish Zola', by which he is sometimes known, is somewhat misleading. And after all, Julián Marías (one of Ortega's favourite pupils, and the most distinguished of modern Spanish philosophers) has summarized 'the representative attitude of the men of 1898' as *'acceptance of reality'*. . . . This certainly applies to Ibánez. But he is in fact less a true naturalist than Emilia Pardo Bazán (q.v.), for all that he lost his Catholic faith at an early age. Ibáñez was a passionate, sincere and often crude realist; he had the fertile imagination of a Jókai (q.v.) as well as the capacity to evoke emotion; but he lacked delicacy and psychological subtlety. And he was a sentimentalist at heart. He never wrote a better book than *The Cabin* (*La barraca*, 1898; tr. F. H. Snow and B. M. Mekota, 1919), which is the high point of his first, regionalist, phase. The horrors of the First World War produced another patchily good novel, *The Four Horsemen of the Apocalypse* (*Los cuatro jinetes del Apocalipsis*, 1916; tr. C. B. Jordan, 1920); there were other effective novels, such as *Blood and Sand* (*Sangre y arena*, 1908; tr. W. A. Gillespie, 1913), a brilliant and moving study of bullfighting; but in general he increasingly tended to exploit his considerable powers to the benefit of his purse and to the detriment of his art and his capacity for psychological accuracy.

Ibáñez's regional novels are all set against a Valencian background. The best, *The Cabin*, deals with conflicts between landlords and farmers in the Huerta of Valencia, and gives incomparable insight into the nature of the peasants and their sufferings. *The Cathedral* (*La catedral*, 1903) provides a valuable example of the liberal and rational side of the Spanish character criticizing the religious and fanatical side: set in Toledo, it analyzes, with a good deal of intuitive understanding, religious fanaticism. Ibáñez's psychological novels, written between 1906 and 1909, are too sultry and melodramatic to be truly effective; but they are by no means entirely meretricious. The one exception has already been mentioned: *Blood and Sand*. Here the portrait of the Spanish bullfighting public (which is not as extensive as is normally believed by non-Spanish people) is masterly. His historical novels are not successful, though they sold well; nor are his novels of adventure, which incorporate a virulent anti-feminism. Blasco Ibáñez was exiled by Primo de Rivera, and spent his last years in Menton. He probably achieved enough to justify his reputation as a master of realism; but there is no doubt that he diffused his gifts. Even his best work, with the exception of *The Cabin*, has tended to date.

The Basque PIÓ BAROJA (1872–1956) always denied being one of the men of '98; but he was always so categorized, and with some justice. Author of more than one hundred books, he dominated Spanish fiction for over fifty years. In certain respects he may be compared to Dreiser (q.v.): his crude 'philosophy' (formed from ill-digested readings of Schopenhauer and Nietzsche, qq.v.), becomes transformed, in his creative work, to something rich and strange; he has a similar clumsy power, born out of the sort of violent obstinacy that would have ruined the creative project of a writer endowed with a superior intellect. Baroja's gloom arose from his acute disappointment at two things: his own feelings of incapacity, and his country's refusal to be what he (intelligently, and in common with the men of '98) desired it to be. He qualified as a doctor only with great difficulty; the year he spent in practice in the spa town of

Cestona, in the Basque region, discouraged him further. He went on to Madrid to manage (with his brother) a bakery. Madrid caused him more disappointment: he found it corrupt and sordid. From 1899 he had been frequenting meetings of literary men; in 1902 he borrowed enough money to set himself up as an author. From then onwards he rationalized his profound unhappiness in his fiction; he lived with his mother in Madrid or in his house, 'Itzea', in the Basque region, until her death in 1935.

In the Civil War he equivocally and unhappily lent support to Franco, but spent much of his time in France; he returned to Spain in 1940. He never married, but had a number of affairs in which he behaved in a manner reminiscent of Pavese (q.v.): as an unworthy and self-deprecating suitor. Like Unamuno, Baroja was against every system; but he was less constructive, less warm (his wistful emotional qualities are often concealed in his books by a comedy and savage irony that are reminiscent, in mood and tone if not in language, of Céline, q.v.) and more confused. His anti-clericalism—often justified in Spaniards—lacks charity; he was as opposed to the Jews as to the Catholic Church. Baroja's unhappiness and bitterness doubtless had their origin in his failure to achieve his self-appointed role as a romantic hero. Although the implications of his expressed view of human nature—cruel, selfish, incapable of justice—are pessimistic, his attitude is more aptly described as bitter. Like Dreiser, he can be exceedingly sentimental and falsely lyrical when he is describing love or passion. Baroja felt that he had failed as a doctor; he failed as a politician (during the first decade of the century); he failed as a lover (that this was deliberate is beside the point), and he felt that he had failed as a man; human beings, and Spain, had failed to live up to his over-romantic and idealistic aspirations: the surface of his fiction is anti-romantic. *Road of Perfection* (*Camino de perfección*, 1902), published in the year of his self-appointed middle-age (he was thirty), and marking the outset of his career as a full-time writer, records his defeat, finds an effective objective correlative(q.v.) for his feelings of despair. It is about the disillusion of a young idealist and his transformation into an errant and aimless wanderer.

Baroja disbelieved in 'structure'; his contribution (horrifiedly denied as such by most academic Anglo-Saxon critics) to realism is that he abandoned both 'form' and 'style' in favour of the untidiness of 'real life'. In the hands of a less gifted man this project would have been disastrous; in Baroja's it leads to some remarkable—and modernist—results. He frequently reveals the exquisite Azorín's (q.v.) elegance and grace as trivial. He lacks Dreiser's poignancy, but he does not lack human dignity or passion; and he has a comic gift Dreiser possessed in his life but not in his work.

The whole of Baroja's fiction—including nine trilogies, a tetralogy and a series of twenty-two picaresque novels about a single character, Eugenio de Aviraneta (an adventurer who actually existed, and whose biography Baroja wrote)—has by no means been fully or properly investigated outside Spain and Spanish America; it is more varied than most of its enervated and shocked Anglo-Saxon critics care to admit.

Just as Baroja wobbled, with uncomfortable violence, between Schopen-hauerean pessimism and a Nietzschean vitalism, so do his heroes. But the pessimism is transformed into a vice that Spaniards have frequently char-acterized as their own: *abulia*, paralysis of will, inability to act, inertia. Thus Fernando Osorio of the ironically entitled *The Road to Perfection* fails to make the decision that might have enabled him to effect the social reforms he believes in. On the other hand, Eugenio de Aviraneta is a man of boundless energy—a projection of the radical, idealistic Baroja, and, significantly, stripped of his fatal tendency to introversion. *Paradox, King (Paradox, Rey*, 1906; tr. N. Barbour, 1931; pt. IMSL) is a comic satire, of Swiftian proportions and high good humour, on the 'benefits of civilization' as brought to Uganda. *Laura, or the Loneliness Without Release (Laura, o la soledad sin remedio*, 1939) is probably the most moving, profound and self-revealing of all his novels. Nothing Baroja wrote is less than interesting and engaging; his influence is increasing among contemporary Spanish writers, and will eventually have its effect on those outside Spain. Many of his books were translated into English.

In the popular tradition of Blasco Ibáñez rather than in that of Baroja were FELIPE TRIGO (1865–1916), ALBERT INSÚA (1885), and ANTONIO DE HOYOS (1885–1940). None of these was entirely without merit. In their fiction, however, naturalism disintegrated into a heady eroticism. Trigo, the most important of the group, dealt with themes involving illicit love and sexual promiscuity. At his best, as in the autobiographical *The Country Doctor (El médico rural*, 1912), he has a good sense of character and an engaging humour. Insúa, born in Cuba, of a Spanish father, began as a crude imitator of Trigo, but gradually evolved an original and effective style of psychological realism. Antonio de Hoyos, Marquis of Vinent, was of a superior intellectual calibre; sometimes the preciosity of his style is reminiscent of the early Valle-Inclán (q.v.). He never grew out of his smouldering decadence; but a few of his many novels retain an authentic *fin de siècle* atmosphere.

The aggressively bohemian Galician RAMÓN MARÍA DEL VALLE-INCLÁN (1866–1936, ps. RAMÓN DEL VALLE Y PEÑA), more decisively a member of the Genera-tion of '98 than Baroja, has been unduly neglected outside Spanish-speaking countries. Valle-Inclán hid his tormented soul behind the mask of decadent adventurer in his life, and behind exquisite style in his work. Ortega admired Valle-Inclán's qualities as a writer, but accused him of deliberate and precious falsity in his style, which he claimed led him to a type of un-authenticity: instead of being at 'the height' of his own times he is a 'Renais-sance man', who indulges himself in unnecessary archaisms and even un-necessary, 'Renaissance' situations—such as incest. This is probably a just appraisal of the earlier work: Valle-Inclán's style, sometimes almost as embarrassingly 'Renaissance' as Cabell's (q.v.) is medieval, is on the whole an obstacle: Ortega's desire to open a new book by him that would tell '*human things, really human ones*', in a less elevated style, is partially justified. But under-neath this high and often irritating manner Valle-Inclán is doing all sorts of things so fascinating, original—and technically prophetic—that we cannot possibly ignore him. His devoted artistry is misleading: this is only a minor achievement; his genuine expressionism (q.v.) and versatility are different matters. Furthermore, in the last twenty years of his life he developed, and his writing became less precious. And in addition, his invention of *esperpento* (q.v.) is arguably the most intelligent—and effectively executed—manner in which the peculiar nature of the Spanish literary genius was dragged (screaming) into the twentieth century.

Valle-Inclán, who travelled much as a young man, built up a deliberately decadent, heroic and romantic legend of himself; but the writer hardly believed in the legend. Married to an actress (1907), he was himself an actor of some merit, who appeared in one of the plays of his friend Benavente (q.v.)—than whom he was a more important playwright. In 1899 he lost an arm when attacked (in a dawn raid on a café) by the journalist and critic Manuel Bueno (who became a fascist, and was killed in 1936). With his one arm, long hair, straggling beard and glasses he became a familiar sight in literary circles.

The writer behind this mask was more serious. Much of his work is based in the folk traditions of his native Galicia, of which he possessed a unique understanding. He wrote an involute, skilled poetry—his best known collection is *The Pipe of Kif* (*La pipa de Kif*, 1919). Like most of the men of '98 Valle-Inclán was stylistically susceptible to the influence of *modernismo* (q.v.), and to Darío (q.v.) in particular. Most of the poetry has dated; its *fin de siècle* medievalism and self-conscious decadence now seem laboured; yet he developed in this field, too, and his best poems are nearly all contained in his last collection, *Lyrical Chimes* (*Claves líricas*, 1930); some of these remind one of Antonio Machado. Valle-Inclán also developed his fiction. His *The Pleasant Memoirs of the Marquis de Bradomín* (*Four Sonatas*, 1902–5; tr. M. H. Broun and T. Walsh) are clearly the work of a writer of genius, as are the novels about the Carlist Wars (Valle-Inclán's Carlist sympathies never left him), *The Carlist War* (*La guerra carlista*, 1908–9); but he improved on these as he became more socially indignant (especially during the dictatorship of Rivera)—and less satisfied with the *persona* he had created for himself. The *Sonatas*, stories of an 'ugly, Catholic and sentimental' Don Juan, are clearly influenced by D'Annunzio (q.v.) and by French 'Satanism'; but for all this and their preciosity of style, they are distinctly original, and possess an authentic *frisson* not usually associated with such works. It was not until 1926, however, that Valle-Inclán wrote his best novel: *The Tyrant* (*Tirano Banderas*; tr. 1929). This is an account of a Mexican revolution, apparently 'left wing' in ideology—but in fact merely human in its outlook. Here Valle-Inclán employed his technique of *esperpento*, derived from the word meaning 'sideshow distorting mirror'. (An obvious parallel is the Italian *grottesco*, q.v., initiated by Pirandello in his novels.) In the realm of drama Valle-Inclán had evolved both a 'murderous comedy' (*comedia bárbara*) and the *esperpento*; but he applied both techniques, or attitudes, to his later fiction and poetry. In *The Tyrant Banderas* both the tyrant and his enemy, Colonel Gandarita, are presented as caricatures; the plot itself consists of grotesque parody, involving defections of the tyrant's daughters. As a whole the book anticipates the 'cruel' humour of the Sixties, and the contemporary habit of using classical or hackneyed romantic themes as ironic frameworks.

The *esperpento* has been called surrealistic (q.v.), and this makes sense inasmuch as Valle-Inclán deliberately translated the perennial Spanish concern with the absurd into modern cosmopolitan terms; but essentially it is a unique genre that transcends such categorization. In terms of the *esperpento* (one Spanish critic called it 'The negative aspect of the world, the dance witnessed by the deaf man, religion examined by the sceptic'), Spain is a grotesque caricature of Europe; by European standards she has 'failed'; her heroes suffer from *abulia* (q.v.) because they understand reality too well; consequently, trapped in their failure, they affect a haughty arrogance. Thus the Spaniard (and to some extent the Spanish-American) can be neither truly tragic nor truly comic: he must therefore be presented as grotesque, deformed, distorted—as in a fun-house mirror.

Valle-Inclán's plays anticipate the forms of modern drama, and not only the theatre of the absurd (q.v.), more remarkably than those of any other writer. *Divine Words* (*Divinas palabras*, 1920; MST), completed in 1913, but not produced until 1933, is as remarkable as any: here the beautiful is violently contrasted with its environment, to its own detriment; but although Valle-Inclán has destroyed the old image, by his play he creates, in Yeats' words, a new 'terrible beauty'. Other outstanding plays by Valle-Inclán include *The Horns of Don Friolera* (*Los cuernos de Don Friolera*, 1924) and *Bohemian Lights* (*Luces de Bohemia*, 1924).

Valle-Inclán ended, then, by evolving a whole new modernist attitude; it was the result of self-appraisal, of an examination of his own youthful role. Ortega was right about the early work; but ultimately Valle-Inclán did produce that new book that told 'human things'. The success with which he maintained coherence throughout his difficult project confers upon him, without question, the status of a major writer; that he lacks world status—and has hardly been translated—is surprising and depressing.

By comparison AZORÍN (ps. JOSÉ MARTÍNEZ RUIZ, 1873–1967), born in Monóvar, Alicante, is—for all his historical importance and charm—somewhat trivial. He represents the Generation of '98 (a term he invented) at its slightest; there is nothing of the cosmopolitan about him, and even his best work—his essays about Spain and things Spanish—can only truly appeal to Spaniards and to those who have lived in Spain. He is no interpreter: only an exquisite commentator in a minor key. He began as an anarchist and ended as a fascist. His fiction—his most notable novel is *The Choice* (*La voluntad*, 1902)—is representative of its age, but on the whole unoriginal. His delicate style is distinguished—but has been overrated by Spanish critics. He lacked real understanding of modern literature, even of the work of his friend Unamuno. His adventures in surrealistic drama, in the late Twenties and early Thirties, are contrived and lack vitality. (One of these plays, *The Outcry*, *El clamor*, was written in collaboration with Muñoz Seca, q.v.). His philosophy, a kind of modified Nietzscheanism, is conventional and lacks guts or conviction. Ortega had his measure as he had that of most of his contemporaries: conceding his genuine sensitivity, especially towards the Spanish past, he branded him as a writer who sought to petrify the trivial. In fact, Azorín was no more than an aesthete competent to capture certain aspects of the Spanish literature of the sixteenth and seventeenth centuries, and of the Spanish landscape; by the time he was fifty he was incompetent to cope with real life.

And yet his miniaturist art does have quality. The essays of *Spain* (*España*, 1912) and *An Hour of Spain* (1924; tr. A. Raleigh, 1933; pt. IMSL) do convey a lyrical and valid sense of Spain that is not to be found elsewhere. These essays, deliberately exquisite and dealing obsessively with minute detail, have inevitably dated; but with them Azorín carved a tiny and deserved niche.

GABRIEL MIRÓ (1879–1930), who was born in Alicante, was one of the most interesting novelists of his generation; his highly impressionistic, often subtle fiction well exposes the crude and vacuous rhetoric of his contemporary, the prolific Catholic traditionalist RICARDO LEÓN (1877–1943), whose pompous work—with its false and specious optimism—provides an excellent example of literary obscurantism. Miró, a frustrated painter, combined stylistic impressionism with a sensitive examination of a Spanish consciousness torn between Christianity and paganism. He himself was a convinced Christian of liberal views. *Wanderer* (*Nómada*, 1908), a study in *abulia* (q.v.), contrasts interestingly with Baroja's dynamic and deliberately crudely written *Road of Perfection* (q.v.): Miró's protagonist is trapped in contemplation; the languid style, containing much descriptive matter, reflects this. The placidity of most of his heroes is destroyed by the violence of feeling that characterizes so much of Spanish life: religious fanaticism, authoritarian politics, relentless withdrawal of compassion. His finest novels are the satirical and yet lyrical *Our Father San Daniel* (*Nuestro padre San Daniel*, 1921; tr. C. Remfry-Kidd, 1930) and its sequel *The Leprous Bishop* (*El obispo leproso*, 1926). *Figures of the Passion of our Lord* (*Figuras de la Pasión del Señor*, 1916–17) is a more uneasy book; but the exquisiteness of its descriptions of Palestine may in certain respects be compared to those of George Moore in his *The Brook Kerith* (q.v.).

Like Miró, RAMÓN PÉREZ DE AYALA (1881–1962) was much influenced by *modernismo* (q.v.), and made his debut as a poet in the *modernista* style. His best work, however, is in his fiction; this carries on the realistic tradition of Galdós and of his teacher at the University of Oviedo, Clarín (q.v.), but subjects reality to a distorting and satirical viewpoint that is reminiscent of Valle-Inclán. He is one of the most distinguished of modern Spanish novelists. Much of his fiction, all of which was written by 1926, is set in Oviedo, his birthplace, which he called Pilares. Pérez de Ayala served the Republic as an ambassador; he lived in the Argentine until 1955, when Franco allowed him to return to his own country. His first group of novels, comparatively realistic, deal with Alberto Díaz de Guzmán, a fictional equivalent of the author: *Twilight on the Peaks* (*Tinieblas en las cumbres*, 1907), *A.M.D.G.* (1912), *The Vixen's Paw* (*La pata de la raposa*, 1912; tr. T. Walsh, *The Fox's Paw*, 1924) and *Mummers and Dancers* (*Troteras y danzaderas*, 1913). The second, with its exposure of the stifling methods of Jesuit education, created a sensation; the best of the group, however, is *The Vixen's Paw*, which tells of Alberto's abandonment of his beautiful fiancée and his subsequent adventures abroad with various grotesque characters, and which most clearly anticipates his later manner. For Alberto 'thought is the obstacle to action'; he is, in essence, yet another victim of *abulia*. The last novel of this series is more diffuse, and is hardly satisfactory as fiction; but it is valuable for its portrait of bohemian Madrid and its inhabitants (such as Valle-Inclán) in the first decade of this century.

The three short 'poematic novels', *Prometheus* (*Prometeo*), *Sunday Sunlight* (*Luz de domingo*) and *The Fall of the House of Limon* (*La caída de los Limones*), all published in 1916 (tr. A. P. Hubbard and G. H. Gonkling, 1920), indicate a recovery of Pérez de Ayala's imagination. These stories are called 'poematic' because each chapter is preceded by a 'poetic' version of what is to come. They are brutal tales of misfits destroyed by a world their own ugliness mirrors: a hideous and sexually precocious idiot, criminals and their victims, grotesques and madmen.

His masterpieces, however, came in the Twenties; *Belarmino and Apolonio* (1921) and a two-part novel: *Tiger Juan* (*Tigre Juan*, 1926; tr. W. Starkie, 1933) and *The Quack* (*El curandero de su honra*, 1926). These, although not ostensibly modernistic, deserve the same treatment as has been given to Joyce or Musil or Gadda (qq.v.). They are experimental, innovatory, crammed with vitality. It is tragic that, first, his diplomatic duties in London (1932–6), and then events in Spain, silenced Pérez de Ayala: his last twenty-six years yielded only a collection of short stories (1962) and a few essays. It was in these last novels that Pérez de Ayala most successfully overcame his over-intellectual approach to life. *Belarmino and Apolonio*, about two Oviedo shoemakers, explores the difference between Belarmino's philosophical (Apollonian) character, and Apolonio's dramatic (Dionysian) character. Typically, the Dionysian is given the Apollonian name. With the punning style, which artfully mixes the colloquial with the archaic, Pérez de Ayala invented his own language. The *Tiger Juan* novels likewise invent two paradoxically opposed characters: Tiger Juan, a virile anti-Don Juan, and Vespasiano Cebón, an effeminate Don Juan. Pérez de Ayala is as important a novelist as Valle-Inclán; the lack of translations of his work is puzzling: if Gadda can be translated, then so, surely, can he. Pérez de Ayala was also an exceptionally gifted analytical critic.

The critic, biographer and novelist BENJAMÍN JARNÉS (1888–1949), born in Saragossa, has been as strangely neglected in Spain as elsewhere. Although praised by critics, his work appears to be forgotten. Jarnés was not as brilliant and penetrating as Pérez de Ayala; he failed to write a major work; but he shared Pérez de Ayala's critical abilities; these two were perhaps the most 'sentimentive' (q.v.) Spanish creative writers of this century (Ortega being, after all, only a critic). Jarnés' people are solitary, narcissistic, wholly involved in the problems of solipsism. Paul Ilie, the only critic to write pertinently on Jarnés, has singled out his *Theory of the Spinning-Top* (*Teoría del zumbel*, 1930) for special attention. This certainly has features that make the work of many novelists of the Sixties look somewhat old-fashioned: skilfully Jarnés treats his cast (of which he is a member) in the familiar realist mode, as fictional creations (his puppets) and as matter for philosophical speculation. Ilie relates Jarnés' work to surrealism (as he does that of Valle-Inclán, Lorca, Antonio Machado, Alberti, Gómez de la Serna, Aleixandre and Arderius, qq.v.). He is entitled to do this, and the results are never less than interesting; but Jarnés, although he employed certain surrealist techniques, seems to me to be more fruitfully related to recent developments in the novel. Unamuno's hope in *Mist* was to discover the real God through examining a subject that, as a novelist, he knew about: the novelist-as-God. But Jarnés' aim is to write a piece of literary criticism. He is more technical, more intellectual and less emotional in his approach. His protagonist is a small boy who spins a top (God spinning his world); this has the atheist implication that human life is the product of blind chance: 'God'-as-child, likely at any moment to abandon his game. Jarnés goes on to demonstrate, in a variety of ways, that writers of novels should not have 'intentions' rather, they should set tops in motion: the universe is the result of caprice, so, therefore, should the universe of the writer be; 'seriousness' is absurd. Jarnés, who wrote many other novels, has an approach so over-intellectual (though he warns against it) that his fiction inevitably lacks substance. Maurice Blanchot (q.v.) is a somewhat similar figure: his insights are remarkable; he is original; he possesses absolute integrity; most of his creative work fails because it is written to illustrate a philosophy. But Jarnés is none the less an important figure in modern Spanish literature; his revival seems inevitable.

More overtly surrealist, and perhaps less cunningly organized, novels were written by JOAQUÍN ARDERIU S(1890); these, especially *The Equal Princes* (1930), also impressively anticipate the techniques of the French *nouveau roman* (q.v.).

The unclassifiable RAMÓN GÓMEZ DE LA SERNA (1888–1963) is another important figure in the Spanish *avant garde*. He is usually known simply as Ramón. Gómez de la Serna, an eccentric and exhibitionistic bohemian, was the owner of many surrealistic gadgets, the chief actor in many dada-like pranks and stunts (lecturing from a circus trapeze; antics in restaurants). For all his acute awareness of modernism, he had in him something of the paradoxical type of wit of G. K. Chesterton ('If a thing's worth doing it's worth doing badly'), who was certainly no modernist. Gómez de la Serna was most famous for his *greguerías*, short semi-surrealistic aphorisms, 'graceful distortions'; with these he succeeded in making surrealistic procedures acceptable even to middle-brow audiences. And some, indeed, are meretricious and facile. Others, however, are original and disturbing rearrangements of familiar reality. The *greguerías* vary from the merely amusing or ingenious to the genuinely startling. 'The soap in the bath is the hardest fish to catch.' 'In Autumn the leaves of books should also fall.' 'Women employ tiny handkerchiefs to clear mighty sorrows and mighty catarrhs.' Ramón wrote biographies of Ruskin, Wilde, Valle-Inclán and others; critical accounts of such European movements as cubism; books of impressions such as *The Meat Market* (*El Rastro*, 1918), brilliant views of the seamy side of Madrid; plays—and many novels. Ramón's fiction is no more substantial or fundamentally serious than any of his other work, but it is intelligently entertaining and, within its limitations, genuinely innovatory. Ramón had a fertile mind; while he is too frivolous to be a major writer—in the *greguerías* (Sel. tr. H. Granville-Barker, 1944) he discovered the right, brief form in which to develop his talents—he remains important as an influence. He died in Buenos Aires, where he had lived since the Civil War.

An innovator, or at least an anticipator, of an entirely different kind was the novelist and playwright PARMENO (ps. JOSÉ LÓPEZ PINILLOS, 1875–1922), a true precursor of the *tremendismo* (q.v.) that was launched in 1942 with Cela's *The Family of Pascual Duarte* (q.v.). In both his novels and plays López Pinillos adapted naturalism to so violent an extent that he inaugurated a new type of literature—one that was not, however, to be exploited until the bitter aftermath of the Civil War. His best known play is *The Sons' Fortune (El caudal de los hijos)*. His violent and gloomy novels include *Blood of Christ*, *Eye for Eye* and *Red Tape*. He was a crude writer, but his work does have some of that sense of the overwhelming power of fate, of sheer brutality, that characterizes the best of *tremendismo*. Some of the jaundiced visions of Madrid low life in the fiction of the 'impenitent' bohemian eccentric EMILIO CARRERE (1880–1947), such as *Gardens of Night (Los jardines de la noche)*, have a similarly powerful quality.

The Basque JUAN ANTONIO DE ZUNZUNEGUI (1901) practises—with great awareness—a more straightforward realism, and a traditional kind of *costumbrismo* (q.v.), in novels that are mostly set either in the Bilbao regions or in Madrid. He is one of the most widely read of Spanish novelists. His novel *The Prize (El premio*, 1962), a satire on Spanish literary prizes, won the National Prize. . . . Some of his work, which has had in it since 1939 some elements of *tremendismo* (q.v.), has proved too strong medicine for Franco's censors, and has been banned. Zunzunegui is a powerful and gifted realistic novelist: among his best novels are *The Failure (La quiebra*, 1947), set in Bilbao, and *The Supreme Good (El supremo bien*, 1951), set in Madrid. Two other notable novels by Zunzunegui are *The Ship's Rats (Las ratas del barco*, 1950) and *Life as It Is (La vida como es*, 1953).

ARTURO BAREA (1897–1957) was not really a novelist, although his famous autobiography is sometimes classified as fiction. This is the trilogy *The Forging of a Rebel (La forja de un rebelde)*, more often known as *The Forge*, *The Track* and *The Clash*, which is how it first appeared, in the three separate volumes of an English translation by Barea's Austrian wife Ilsa, in 1944 (published in Buenos Aires in Spanish, 1952). It is Barea, an opponent of Franco who took refuge in England after 1939, who gives the finest account of the anguish of the Civil War and the tragedy of the siege of Madrid; this is ultimately worth even more than the most meticulously documented histories, for it conveys the spirit of the human—rather than the ideological—resistance to Franco's tyranny. Nothing else Barea wrote equals this, which is of classic status: it amounts to one of the most sensitive and impassioned anti-totalitarian statements of this century. The first volume tells of the author's childhood and adolescence in Madrid; the second of his military service in the African wars;

the third of Madrid during the Civil War. In *The Broken Root* (1951) he imagines the *incognito* return of an exile to Spain long after the fascist victory.

The status of RAMÓN SENDER (1902), another enemy of Franco's, and now United States citizen, is peculiar. For a few he is the greatest novelist of this century; the judgement, surely an extreme one, was originally made by Pío Baroja (q.v.), the influence of whose own fiction on Sender's is obvious. On the other hand, he is unfairly ignored in some surveys of Spanish literature. Like Baroja, Sender is fundamentally anti-literary: the novel is for him, in theory, merely an instrument of straightforward realism. But his attitude is more complicated than it appears; his true position in Spanish letters (for him, incidentally, Franco's Spain is not Spain—and so Spain is dead) is that of a bridge between Baroja and Cela (q.v.). Sender is torn between his individualism and his sense of communal needs—his belief in the continuance of the human race. One gets the sense, from his many novels, of a man punishing himself by deliberately recording every example that he can find of man's inhumanity to man. Neither Baroja nor Cela believes, of course, in brutality; but both take some imaginative relish in their descriptions of it; for both there are compensatory factors; for Sender, one feels, there is none. Most of his many novels are simply accounts of various kinds of human violence; they shock the reader because the writer himself is pained and shocked.

Sender rewrites and reissues his novels until he feels he has achieved definitive versions: what he is searching for is a compassion that he can hardly find. *Chronicle of the Dawn* (*Crónica del alba;* definitive version, 1967) is the general title of a series of novels dealing with Pepe Garcés. Garcés (in prison and condemned to die) comes to realize that he can fulfil his individuality only by recognizing its limitations; he comes to consider that love between two individual people is impossible, and so he pledges himself to work for the survival of an ideal human society. There are serious contradictions involved here, and in none of his novels does Sender show any sign of resolving them; but he is a notable realist, and the passion of his search for justice and peace has made itself felt on every page he has written. His best single novels are probably *Mr. Witt Among the Rebels* (*Mr. Witt en el Cantón*, 1935; tr. 1937), a study of the jealous anguish felt by a man as he recognizes old age encroaching, and *Requiem for a Spanish Peasant* (*Requiem por un campesino español*, definitive version, 1961; tr. E. Randall, 1960), which was originally called *Mosén Millán*. This is Sender's most dramatic and elaborately plotted novel.

MAX AUB (1903), now returned after a long exile, wrote two books on the Civil War—*Closed Field* (*Campo cerrado*, 1939) and *Field of Blood* (*Campo de sangre*, 1943)—and an amusing satire, *The True History of the Death of Francisco Franco* (*La verdadera historia de la muerte de Francisco Franco*, 1960).

The name of CAMILO JOSÉ CELA (1916) has dominated Spanish letters since the early Forties. Although a new generation of novelists has arisen, and Cela himself has been able to do little in fiction—as distinct from scholarship, travel and editorship—since 1954, it has not been forgotten that, with the publication of *The Family of Pascual Duarte* (*La familia de Pascual Duarte*, 1942), he asserted the superiority of literary over political values. He deserves his high standing. Cela was born in Galicia of a Spanish father and an Italian-English mother; as a small child he knew English, but he has now entirely forgotten that language, and even exhibits a curious fear of it. The key to the works of this odd, important writer is to be found in the fact that as a very young man he fought, with Franco, for 'order': he ended as a corporal in the victorious fascist forces. Since the time he fought for order he has found only disorder, a lack of tenderness, and injustice. In other words his quarrel, like that of almost every other Spanish writer of quality in this century, is with Spain: with the Spain that adores itself and its pride and differentness, and yet which can somehow ignore human decency. His quarrel is partly, of course, with himself—and, one may fairly add, with the Spanish government which he helped to establish. *Pascual Duarte* officially inaugurated the *tremendista* novel, so called because the reader's shock at the horror and brutality it reveals is 'tremendous'. The novel, about a man 'who had no chance in life' (his father is a drunk and his mother has no love for him), suggests new and potent possibilities for the coherent novel. The murderer Pascual Duarte's horror and terror are shared by the reader: his breaking-out into physical action is an effective metaphor for a feeling of frustration that, among intelligent and enlightened people, is general. When the censors read *Pascual Duarte* in 1943 they promptly banned it. In *Pavilion of Repose* (*Pabellón de reposo*, 1944) Cela wrote a novel that seemed less obviously violent, but was in fact even more profoundly despairing. The tubercular patients in a sanitarium find a common bond in their voided blood. In *The Hive* (*La colmena*, 1951; tr. J. M. Cohen, 1953) Cela gives an account of life in post-Civil War Madrid: hopeless, sordid, terrifying (to the sensitive) in its desolateness. Like Daniel Fuchs' *Low Company* (q.v.), *The Hive* concentrates upon one café. It is an indictment of the Franco government; but only incidentally so. Like Fuchs' novel, it accuses the society it describes; but only by telling the truth. Cela is of course more stark and more savage; he conveys the horror of poverty suffered in Madrid with great power. His indignation is not in question. Soon after writing this book—which is banned in Spain—Cela, who found himself in a politically unpleasant position on account of it (and more so because of Barea's, q.v., preface to the English translation) exiled himself to the island of Mallorca, where he has remained ever since. He has maintained, however, a house in Madrid.

In Mallorca he has edited an important literary magazine, and has developed his scholarly knowledge of Spain and all things Spanish. He has written many travel books; he has also given a short, masterly account of the modern writer he reveres above all others: *Don Pío Baroja* (1958). *La cucaña*—an untranslatable word having the sense of 'climbing a greased pole to amuse the public' and of 'anything acquired with no trouble and at other peoples' expense'—is an amusing book of memoirs published in 1959. Cela has written many short stories, collected together in numerous volumes—one of the best and fullest is *The Windmill* (*El molino de viento y otras novelas cortas*, 1956). His other novels include a modern version of the first Spanish picaresque novel, *Lazarillo de*

Tormes, *New Adventures and Mishaps of Lazarillo de Tormes* (*Nuevas andanzas y desventuras de Lazarillo de Tormes*, 1946). In this book, his third novel, Cela gives his most grotesque and distorted picture of Spain; one of its themes, that of the effects upon men of hunger (the Spanish government has done little, in its thirty-two years of power, to alleviate the lot of the Spanish poor), obsessed Cela above all others (Robert Kirsner, Cela's excellent American critic, tells us that if hunger occupies the first place in his Inferno, then academic critics are in the second). Cela's grim, gallows humour comes to the fore in the new *Lazarillo*, which presents Spain as a stage upon which a pitiless play is being presented—only occasionally interrupted by episodes of mercy or kindness. The viewpoint is throughout relentlessly amoral. Cela's least successful, but by no means his least interesting, novel is *Mrs Caldwell Talks to her Son* (*Mrs Caldwell habla con su hijo*, 1953); Kirsner claims that it is the 'most prominent paradigm of his bizarre art', and that it requires 'audience participation'. This may be true; but surrealism is not a technique suited to Cela, and this series of soliloquies, letters written in excellent Spanish by a mad English-woman to her dead son, quickly becomes monotonous. The idea is excellent; the execution leaves something to be desired. Whether it is an allegory in which Spain (Mrs Caldwell—English like Cela's mother) speaks to the dead of the Civil War, or whether it is a Freudian study of jealousy, or both, it does not come off. But it was probably a necessary experiment, and Cela by no means disgraced himself with it. *The Blond* (*La Catira*, 1955), is set in remote Venezuela, and deals with primitive people. A despondent Cela here attempted to escape both from the subject of Spain and from the possibility of being accused of disloyalty. He tried, as Kirsner points out, to do for Venezuela what he had done, in *The Hive*, for Madrid; he does not really succeed, but he does give a dramatic picture of Cela turning Venezuela into a kind of parody of his own Spain. Cela is unquestionably the finest Spanish writer of his generation; what he will now go on to do, if anything, is hard to determine. Seemingly his career as a writer of fiction came to an end in the mid-Fifties; now his spate of learned travel books—written from the viewpoint of a vagabond—seems to have come to an end. Has he, as Kirsner hints, given up the struggle with Spain and an ungrateful readership, and retreated into academicism? *San Camilo, 1936* (1969) deals with the Civil War, and is written in a highly versatile prose; it is profoundly interesting to the student of this remarkable writer—but it is too self-consciously experimental, and must be accounted a failure. But whether he writes with creative success again or not, his best novels and stories have made the most significant contribution to Spanish fiction since the days of Unamuno, Valle-Inclán, Baroja and the other men of '98.

The most intelligent and balanced novel of the Spanish Civil War to be published (after difficulties and delays and, presumably, deletions) is the massive trilogy of JOSÉ MARÍA GIRONELLA (1917). The first volume, *The Cypresses Believe in God* (*Los cipreses creen en Dios*, 1952; tr. H. de Onís, 1955), was published without difficulty because it dealt with the pre-war period. It was *A Million Dead* (*Un millón de muertos*, 1961) and *Peace Has Broken Out* (1966) that attracted the attentions of the censors. Gironella, who originally trained as a priest, both fought for Franco and lived amongst Spanish refugees in France during the Civil War. He saw both sides. Previously he had written *A Man* (*Un hombre*, 1946) and *The Tide* (1948), which criticized the Germans and considerably upset a Spain still unhappy over Hitler's defeat. The Civil War trilogy is a remarkably objective work, in which the protagonist, Ignacio Alvear, veers between left and right, and actually fights for both sides. Gironella has no bitterness against republicans; and in the concluding novel of the trilogy he leaves the reader in little doubt of his real opinion of the 'twenty-five years of peace and prosperity' promised by the fascists. This is probably not the authentically Spanish reply to all the foreign works written on the Civil War that Gironella wanted it to be, but in its unmutilated form it may have been nearer to it.

Other gifted contemporary novelists include ANA MARÍA MATUTE (1926), CARMEN LAFORET (1921) and ELENA QUIROGA (1921). Ana María Matute writes of the unhappiness of the children and young people who have been born into Franco's Spain. Her quarrel, like Cela's and that of almost every other serious contemporary novelist, is with Spain as much as with the government. Her best known novel is *Party to the Northwest* (*Fiesta al Noroeste*, 1952). She has a highly evocative and poetic style, psychological shrewdness, and acute sensitivity. Carmen Laforet's famous first novel, *Nothing* (*Nada*, 1944), came only two years after Cela's *Pascal Duarte*—and did for post-Civil War Barcelona something like what Cela was to do for Madrid in *The Hive* (q.v.). A girl comes to Barcelona full of hope; *Nothing* is the account of the relentless shattering of that hope. Barcelona is not, in this book, presented as a city regenerated by a 'new' Spain, but as a sick and squalid place. *Nothing*, which won two prizes, was however enormously successful in Spain. *The Island and the Demons* (*La isla y los demonios*, 1952), is set in the Canary Islands, where the author lived as a child. *The New Woman* (*La mujer nueva*, 1955) deals—without falseness or sentimentality—with the religious conversion of a worldly woman. Carmen Laforet has also written many short stories. She enjoys a very high reputation in Spain. Elena Quiroga has achieved equal power with her solidly realistic, but subtly written novels. The first, about a Galician aristocrat who marries his servant, was *Wind from the North* (*Viento del Norte*, 1951). Her slow-moving, analytical style owes something to Emilia Pardo-Bazán, to Pérez de Ayala and to Gabriel Miró (qq.v.).

MIGUEL DELIBES (1920), born in Valladolid, is the Spanish novelist nearest to Cela, whose grim humour and capacity for significant *esperpento* he shares; however, Delibes is closer to the spirit of realism, whereas one might call Cela a reluctant realist. His first novel, *The Cypress Tree Casts a Long Shadow* (*La sombra del ciprés es alargada*, 1947), is a moving, frightening study of a boy from Ávila who abuses his powerful instincts of love by attempting to share his bitter teacher's philosophy of indifference: to desire nothing and thus avoid loss. *The Road* (*El camino*, 1950) is more comic; once again it sees life through the eyes of a boy, this time a small one. Delibes' technically most conventional novel, finely observed and executed, is *My Beloved Son Sisí* (*Mi idolatrado hijo*

Sisí, 1954), about a son's systematic destruction of his father's dreams and ambitions for him. *Diary of a Hunter (Diario de un cazador,* 1955) is Delibes' most original book. Apart from Cela, Delibes is the most gifted of contemporary Spanish novelists.

His only rival, in fact, is JUAN GOYTISOLO (1931), born in Barcelona, and the 'angriest' of Spain's young novelists. He lives in Paris, although he makes visits to Spain. The theme that haunts him is the cruelty and injustice of war (his mother was killed in a fascist bomb attack), and what war did to the children of Spain. Like all the still active novelists discussed here, Goytisolo is obsessed —only to a greater extent—with the anguish of children and young people in a decaying and unjust society. His opposition to the government is more overt than that of any other novelist whose books are available in Spanish bookshops (not all his, of course, are). He made his reputation with *The Young Assassins (Juegos de manos,* 1954; tr. J. Rust, 1958), an intensely dramatic account of a group of politically disaffected, doomed young men who plan an assassination. *Marks of Identity (Señas de identidad,* 1966; tr. 1969) deals with the children who came to maturity in the years of Franco's rule. Most of Goytisolo's other novels—outstanding among them are *Duel in Paradise (Duelo en el Paraíso,* 1955) and *Fiestas* (1958)— deal with young people corrupted by the sickness of Spain. Some more recent novels have dealt with the fate of love, married and otherwise, in Spain—undoubtedly a microcosm of the whole corrupted West. The four novellas of *The Party's Over (Fin de fiesta,* 1962) and the novel *The Island (L'isla,* 1961) are concerned with this theme.

For a quarter of a century after the Civil War the novel of social realism or (at least implied) protest was dominant; the same applies to the drama and poetry. This was in spite of a censorship as foolish and prudish as it was rigorous. Sometimes the protest disguised itself as a kind of dreary sociological reportage —this in general produced little of value. Cela, Gironella, Ana María Matute and the other post-Civil War writers already discussed were all affected by this; but being superior imaginative writers they were also able to transcend it. However, its strength—understandable in the atmosphere of the Forties and Fifties—is aptly demonstrated by the emphasis on naturalism in the works of an unquestionably modernist writer such as Cela: it almost seems as though he cannot experiment because he cannot get away from his anguish about the real problems of the Spanish people: thus *Mrs Caldwell* (q.v.), besides possibly being an unconscious allegory of Spain, is his thinnest work, and his Venezuela is no more than a tortured Spain. But in the Sixties what was frequently called 'evasive' literature again began, as it always seems to persist in doing, to assert itself. It is not that the newer novelists either like or are indifferent to fascism (no serious Spanish writer wholeheartedly supports the regime); it is simply that they no longer have a utilitarian view of literature. It is true that, basically, their best predecessors did not, either; but their post-Civil War work did not really challenge the utilitarian conception. That of the novelists who emerged in the Sixties undoubtedly does. The major exception, in the Sixties, is Goytisolo, who cannot accept the non-utilitarian view of literature any more than, in the realm of poetry, Celaya (q.v.) can; but the conflict in his mind is a subtle one, not at all resembling the thoughts of a crude social realist. Further, it is to the dehumanizing implications of *objectismo* (the name given in Spain to the behaviouristic viewpoint of the French practitioners of the *nouveau roman*, q.v.) to which he objects most vehemently.

The new tendency is mostly clearly exemplified in *The One Day of the Week* (*El jarama*, 1956; tr. J. M. Cohen, 1962) by RAFAEL SÁNCHEZ FERLOSIO (1927), who was born in Rome. This is by no means 'the best that has come out of contemporary Spain', as its translator has rashly claimed, and a large part of what it achieves is in spite of the conscious intentions of its author, whose technique tries to be 'objective' in Robbe-Grillet's (q.v.) pseudo-scientific sense. Nevertheless, *The One Day of the Week* is in fact a humane and frequently poetic novel, describing a Sunday spent by the river by a group of young people, and the drowning of one of them. The dialogue is interesting since it is not in any way stylized but actually (like that of the English playwright Harold Pinter, q.v.) imitated from life.

Two younger men, more self-consciously modernistic than Sánchez Ferlosio, may prove important in the development of the novel in Spain. RAMÓN HERNANDEZ's (1935) grim study of prison life in *Words on the Wall* (*Palabras en el muro*, 1968) combines *tremendismo* (q.v.)—almost inevitably, since the conditions of Spanish life are in themselves peculiarly *tremendistas*—with advanced techniques. *The Immovable Tyrant* (*El tirano inmóvil*, 1971) is about disaffected Madrid adolescents. The crippled and asthmatic Bruno tries to take revenge on an underworld leader, but he eventually fails. JOSÉ MARÍA GUELBENZU (1944) has gone right back to the experimentalism of Jarnés and Arderius (qq.v.); but has also absorbed more recent European developments. His first novel, *The Mercury* (*El mercurio*) was too self-consciously a pastiche of Joyce (q.v.) and other modernist writers; but it was promising and clearly not the work of a charlatan who could not think for himself. *Mask* (*Antifaz*, 1971) confirms this judgement. It is significant that this unquestionably non-realistic novel should be a study of spiritually sick Madrid youths whose very idealism is a mask, a pretence, for boredom and nihilism. The criticism of the Spanish system is still implied, although the spirit of the natural opposition to it (decency, kindness, tolerance, flexibility) is also assailed.

IV

The existence of a truly modern theatre in Spain has not really been acknowledged. There are a number of reasons for this, the two chief ones probably being that Lorca (q.v.) has been wrongly held, outside Spain, to represent the entire genius of the Spanish theatre, and that the effect of the fascist censorship has inevitably been to weaken, if only temporarily, the impact of a powerful and unique tradition.

The Spanish theatre of the Eighties and Nineties was dominated by JOSÉ

ECHEGARAY (1832–1916), who was born in Madrid. By 1904, when he shared the Nobel Prize with the much more gifted Provençal writer Frédéric Mistral (q.v.), the tide had to some extent turned: there was an outcry from younger Spanish writers. Echegaray was a simple-minded but extremely skilful realist, whose sensational plays gained him wide success. He began as mathematician; as a liberal he was exiled to France in 1874; it was then that he began to write seriously. The genre in which he excelled was that of melodramatic tragedy. Highly effective on the stage, his drama is inevitably superficial. Thus in the famous thesis-play *The Great Galeato* (*El gran galeoto*, 1881; tr. E. Bontecou, 1917) he manages to deal with a fundamentally homosexual theme without realizing its possibilities. Don Julián invites a young man, Ernesto, to come and live with him. Slander—the horrifying consequences of which it is Echegaray's aim to demonstrate—has it that Don Julián's wife Teodora is Ernesto's lover. Falsely accused, she drops dead of a heart attack. This is now best played as high comedy; but the real interest lies in Don Julián's motives. Echegaray was an imitator of Ibsen—particularly in *The Son of Don Juan* (*El hijo de Don Juan*, 1892; tr. J. Graham, 1895), which resembles *Ghosts*—but lacked psychological subtlety and depth.

Although he (just) does not come into the scope of this book, a vastly superior playwright to Echegaray should be mentioned: Manuel Tamayo y Baus (1829–98), who gave up writing in 1870. In *Love's Madness* (*La locura de amor*, 1855) he to some extent anticipated the Pirandello of *Henry IV*; in the remarkable *A New Drama* (*Un drama nuevo*, 1867; tr. G. O. Fitzgerald and T. Guild, 1915), his greatest success, he has Yorick killing his wife's lover in a new play by Shakespeare, the audience—with the exception of Shakespeare—not knowing whether this is a part of the play-within-a-play or not. . . .

It was JACINTO BENAVENTE (1866–1954) who rescued the Spanish theatre from the crude and melodramatic sensationalist realism of Echegaray. There are two opinions of Benavente, who won the Nobel Prize in 1922. One views him as a major writer and an innovator, the other as a playwright whose innate conservatism undermines the whole of his work. It seems that the latter view will prevail. Benavente was infinitely subtler than Echegaray, and the sincerity of his critical view of high society, so far as it went, is unquestionable. But he rarely, if ever, achieved psychological or sociological profundity, and his work fails to take into account the changed circumstances of the twentieth century. His social criticism is over-sly because he depended, for his audience, on the society he wrote about. On the other hand, his style, of ironic understatement, undoubtedly made a better theatre possible; he showed up the limitations of melodrama and of over-heated, declamatory dialogue. He wrote over one hundred plays, as well as translations from Shakespeare. His *Vested Interests* (*Los intereses creados*, 1909), which mixes the traditional characters of the Italian *Commedia dell'Arte* with people from the Madrid business world, is certainly a masterpiece on the technical level. He wrote many different types of plays: children's fantasies, character drama, historical plays, social satire, symbolic tragedy and even plays based on Freudian theory. His rural dramas, of which the most famous is *The Passion Flower* (*La malquerida*, 1913), on the theme of incest, represent him at his best. He was a skilled and intelligent writer; but it was the less popular plays of his friend and contemporary Valle-Inclán, a very superior writer, that proved to be truly innovatory and prophetic. His best plays have genuine charm, and his restraint, even in the face of highly melodramatic themes, is exemplary; but his real importance lies in the realm of technique rather than in that of imaginative achievement. Many of his plays were translated in J. G. Underhill's four-volume *Plays of Jacinto Benavente* (1917–24).

The two most important followers of Benavente were MANUEL LINARES RIVAS (1878–1938), who wrote competent realistic plays of social content such as *The Claw* (*La garra*), which exposed the harshness of the divorce laws, and GREGORIO MARTÍNEZ SIERRA (1881–1947), whose best known play is *Cradle Song* (*Canción de cuna*; GMS) about an abandoned baby. Martínez Sierra, whose work is marred by a tendency to sentimentality, frequently chose women and women's problems as his subject-matter. Both he and Linares Rivas were at times more socially outspoken than Benavente; but neither had his subtlety of technique.

The extremely popular and skilful Quintero Brothers, SERAFÍN ALVAREZ QUINTERO (1871–1938) and JOAQUÍN ALVAREZ QUINTERO (1873–1944), who wrote in collaboration, had no pretensions; but they managed to entertain the Spanish public at large without producing offensive work. Their plays abound in witty if not profound portraits of typically Spanish characters. Their attitudes were nineteenth century; but they always confined their subject-matter strictly to what of the Spanish nineteenth century survived into the twentieth century. Similar to them, and with them the perpetuator of the *sainete*, or short and sparkling interlude-play, is CARLOS ARNICHES Y BARRERA (1866–1943). Both he and the Quintero Brothers wrote many of these delightful playlets. While the former usually set their plays in Andalusia, Arniches set his amongst the poor of Madrid. These dramatists are essentially a part of the tradition of *costumbrismo*.

PEDRO MUÑOZ SECA (1881–1936), who was killed by republicans in Madrid because of his support for the rebels, was an original *farceur* who evolved a type of comedy he called the *astracán*, which exposes the moral vacuity of the characters by means of ridicule. This is a kind of very poor cousin of the *esperpento* (q.v.). Muñoz Seca was none the less a skilled writer of minor comedies. Writers who carried on after him in something like the same tradition—which became an increasingly escapist one as time ran out for the Spanish people— were ENRIQUE JARDIEL PONCELA (1901–52), who was also a novelist, and MIGUEL MIHURA (1903). Mihura's work since the Civil War has been fashionable, conformist and therefore escapist. But his *Three Top Hats* (*Tres sombreros de copa*, 1932, rev. 1952; MST) is an exception. He expresses his dissatisfaction at himself by complaining of its great success—at the expense of the skilled trash he now perpetrates. *Three Top Hats*, much admired by Ionesco (q.v.), anticipates the theatre of the absurd (q.v.) in many ways; it is a satire on irresponsible pseudo-romanticism, portraying the fate of the loveless Dionisio, who cannot choose to become himself and so escape from meaningless categorization.

The tradition of verse drama in Spain was maintained, at the beginning of the period, by EDUARDO MARQUINA (1879–1946) and FRANCISCO VILLAESPESA (1877–1936), chiefly known as a *modernista* (q.v.) poet but probably more effective as a dramatist. Villaespesa had a strong personal influence on more important poets than himself, notably Jiménez; his own mellifluous verse has dated. His closet plays were never performable; but they do have rather more substance than his poetry. Marquina's plays, such as the once extremely successful *The Sun Has Set in Flanders* (*En Flandes se ha puesto el sol*, 1910), have likewise dated. Perhaps the best that can be said for either Villaespesa or Marquina is that they helped to keep a vital tradition alive. The demagogue JOSÉ MARÍA PEMÁN Y PEMARTÍN (1889), an enthusiastic fascist spokesman during the Civil War, has continued to produce verse plays that somewhat obtusely and over-grandiloquently glorify Spain's role in history. Pemán, a rank bad dramatist and apostle of cliché and false values, is only mentioned as being typical of the kind of writer wholly acceptable to the Spanish government. In the realm of verse drama only Lorca in this century achieved true success— he is unquestionably the most important Spanish dramatist of his time, and as an author of poetic tragedies is perhaps unequalled in the world since the mid-seventeenth century. Lorca is also of course the author of some excellent prose comedies. However, he was chiefly a poet, his poetry stands behind all his drama, and he has here been considered in that light.

JACINTO GRAU (1877–1959), born in Barcelona, is an odd phenomenon, a figure quite on his own. Much of his work was written away from his own country, which ignored him. He had theatrical successes in the European theatre, however, notably in Paris, Berlin and Prague. Grau was a literary eccentric, an excessively intellectual and deliberately literary writer; his characters tend to be powerful, rigid types; his style is lofty, sometimes archaic. His best plays, for all their exclusively philosophical basis, undoubtedly make an impact. Possibly he will survive as a read rather than as a produced dramatist. However unattractive his frigid rhetoric may seem, the ideas he expresses with it are neither superficial nor uninteresting; furthermore, his subject is ultimately human rather than merely abstract: he is an existentialist, and his message is similar to the existentialist playwrights': man, not God, is responsible for his own destiny and his own future. Man, as Ortega (q.v.) saw so clearly, is responsible for his own nature from one moment to the next: he must choose what to be like. Not to choose is to live without authenticity. These themes run all through Grau's work, from his early novel *Copies* (*Trasuntos*, 1900)—this was much admired by the Catalan poet Maragall (q.v.)—to his last plays of the Fifties. His most original play is perhaps the relatively early, ironic *Don Juan de Carillana* (1913), the first of his two on the Don Juan theme, in which Don Juan's anguish is caused because he cannot possess the beautiful woman he now, at fifty, desires: his own daughter, the result of an earlier passion. It is often said that the second Don Juan play, *The Hoaxer Who Did Not Hoax Himself* (*El burlador que no se burla*, 1927), is Grau's best; but *The Devil's House* (*La casa de diabolo*, 1933), in which the characters return to life in order to change their nature, is certainly as effective and is probably subtler. The writer to whom Grau is nearest in spirit—though not in style—is Unamuno (q.v.), of whom he wrote an excellent critical study. In his version of *Pygmalion* (1930) the puppets, wanting their freedom, turn upon their creator and destroy him; this is an extension of the theme of Unamuno's *Mist* (q.v.). Grau is an acquired taste, and it cannot be said that his lofty style always suits his content; but he was an original and unusual playwright, with something of his own to say.

JOAQUÍN CALVO-SOTELO (1905), born in Coruña, has written a number of honest although mostly superficial plays: farces, comedies and dramas. He has frequently been accused of plagiarism. Calvo-Sotelo, who occasionally appears embarrassed by the government of his country, writes insensitive plays on political themes—he treats fascism as a respectable and acceptable form of government, and equates support of the Republic with moral wickedness— but is much better when exposing social hypocrisy and false Catholicism. By far his best play is *The Wall* (*La muralla*, 1954), in which a set of pious and wicked people build a metaphorical wall to prevent a man from making restitution for a crime committed many years before. Generally speaking Calvo-Sotelo is a competent middlebrow playwright, too orthodox to be of much interest; but just occasionally, as in *The Wall*, he can disturb.

ALEJANDRO CASONA (ps. ALEJANDRO RODRÍGUEZ ÁLVAREZ, 1903–1965), who went into exile in Argentina during the Civil War and returned to his native Asturias only a short while before his death, is an altogether more important playwright: one of the best Spain has produced in this century. It has been said that he writes in the 'poetic and humorous' tradition of Benavente (q.v.), and certainly he owes much to the light style inaugurated by Benavente; but he is less sly and more innately critical of society than Benavente—and there is an edge to his comedy, albeit it is as charming as Benavente's, which the older playwright usually lacks. When the republican government selected Lorca (q.v.) to direct the touring company affectionately known as 'La Barraca', they chose Casona to head its twin, the 'Teatro del Pueblo'. Casona's work springs out of what in Spain is the equivalent of surrealism (to call it surrealism is misleading, and it seems in any case that Casona's 'surrealism' derives from the peculiarly Spanish obsession with the distinctions between illusion—fantasy —and reality, as in *Don Quixote*); his works of the Thirties anticipated, as Valle-Inclán's had before him, the post-Second World War theatre of the absurd. Thus his famous and ingenious *Suicide Prohibited in Springtime* (*Prohibido suicidarse en primavera*, 1937; MST) contains all the ingredients of the first phase of the theatre of the absurd—and it has a markedly higher 'human' content than, say, the plays of Ionesco. He made his reputation with *The Stranded Mermaid* (*La sirena varada*, 1934). Casona's peculiar concern is with the problem of the reality that, as Eliot (q.v.) wrote, mankind cannot stand much of: should man transform it, accept it, or retreat from it in disgust in the interests of discovering a poetic, inner vision—or make a compromise? It has been said that Casona's plays are a part of the so-called 'theatre of evasion', inasmuch as he seeks in them to establish fantastic dream-worlds; but this is an over-simplification. Actually Casona creates the 'unreal worlds' of his plays not as evasions or retreats into artistic hermeticism, but in order to demonstrate the necessity of accepting reality—of not wholly rejecting it, as a 'fiction' or as too sordid or as uninteresting. Although a modernist, Casona is fundamentally a humanist. Thus, Sirena, in *The Stranded Mermaid*, finally rejects her escapist fantasy that she is a mermaid. And the hospital of *Suicide Prohibited in Springtime*, where everything is arranged to make suicide attractive (perfumed poisoned gas, poisoned flowers and so on) is designed to reconcile its patients to life. Casona's message is that adjustment to reality requires effort of imagination. His most celebrated play is *Trees Die Upright* (*Los arboles mueren de pie*, 1949).

ANTONIO BUERO VALLEJO (1916)—born at Guadalajara, who was in prison for some time in the late Forties for 'political offences'—is, by contrast, a realist. He combines protest at human conditions with an angrily qualified optimism. For Buero Vallejo the essence of the tragedy is that man has both free will and a chance to (existentially) create for himself a noble future—a chance, however, that he is unlikely to take. And yet in this chance there also lies, always, reason for hope. Apart from his own dramatic writings, he has elaborated a detailed and valuable theory of tragedy—one in which Aristotle's *catharsis* (q.v.) functions not as 'purging' but as the 'improvement' Aristotle himself probably intended. Since Buero Vallejo lives and works in Spain, he has shown considerable courage and detachment in continuing his dramatic career with such high seriousness. He frequently writes above the censors' heads, choosing mythological and historical themes. His first success was *Story of a Staircase* (*Historia de una escalera*, 1950), a *tremendista* play written under the influence of Eugene O'Neill (q.v.) that he has since repudiated on account of its uncompromising naturalism. Among his best plays are *Madrugada* (1953), *Today Is a Holiday* (*Hoy es fiesta*, 1956), *In the Burning Dark* (*En la ardiente oscuridad*, 1950) and the cycle of historical plays which begins with *A Dreamer for the People* (*Un soñador para un pueblo*, 1958).

The concerns of ALFONSO SASTRE (1926), born in Madrid, are not dissimilar. Sastre, the leading playwright of his generation, has been active in the theatre despite government discouragement. His *Squadron Towards Death* (*Escuadra hacia la muerte*, 1953) was banned for its anti-war message (war, in the Catholic-fascist ideology of the Spanish government is 'glorious'). Sastre later (1961) founded the Realist Theatre Group—the emphasis here being less on literary realism than on the reality of conditions in Spain. Sastre, who is a 'committed' writer in the Sartrian sense, and who has been deeply influenced by Sartre's philosophy and drama, has quarrelled with Buero Vallejo's ideas about 'hope', and has nihilistically endorsed the necessity of 'unhappy endings'; but his aims remain fundamentally the same. *Everybody's Bread* (*El pan de todos*), about the disillusion of a communist who has denounced his own mother, has Sartrian power and is one of the most intelligent and effective contemporary plays on the subject of political commitment. It has true psychological depth. Sastre has convincingly attacked his 'objectivist' (q.v.) contemporaries in his interesting critical works. *In the Net* (*En la red*, 1961) is another of his best plays; this deals with Algerian revolutionaries. Plays by Sastre that have not been publicly performed in Spain include *Sad Are the Eyes of William Tell* (*Guillermo Tell tiene los ojos tristes*; NWSD) and *Death in the District* (*Muerte en el barrio*).

More recently, however, there has been a reaction in Spain to Sastre's type of overtly 'committed' drama. The very young playwrights look back to Valle-Inclán, to the French surrealism of the Twenties and Thirties, and to the contemporary *avant garde* theatre outside Spain. But they inevitably apply themselves to Spanish problems, even if they may appear not to. One of these playwrights, Fernando Arrabal (q.v.), whose flight to France and repudiation of the Spanish language represent the most extreme response, has been dealt with as a French writer. LAURO OLMO, who has remained in Spain, became well known with *The Shirt* (*La camisa*, 1962). Such short plays of his as *The News Item* (MST) are clear criticisms of the totalitarian conditions in modern Spain; this combines a strongly realistic technique with absurdism. JOSÉ-MARÍA BELLIDO (1922), born in San Sebastián, has written what is probably the most evidently anti-fascist and anti-Catholic Church play to get past the Spanish censor: *Futbol* (*Football*; MST). This amusing and skilful allegory is also equally scornful of American and Russian politics. Bellido has also written *Train to F . . .* (*Tren a F . . .*; NWSD) and *Bread and Rice*, or *Geometry in Yellow* (*El pan y el arroz o Geometría en amarillo*; NWSD). Other 'underground' playwrights include ANTONIO MARTÍNEZ BALLESTEROS (1929), from Toledo, and JOSÉ RUIBAL (both NWSD). The conformist theatre in Spain, with the occasional exception of Calvo-Sotelo (q.v.) is worthless. Censorship is still powerful (the censors' official goal remains 'purification', both social and aesthetic), and 'liberalization' has not been all it pretends. But there is a relatively new sensitivity, among the Spanish fascists, to outside opinion; the direction is undoubtedly towards more freedom in the theatre.

V

With a single exception, the Spanish poets of the nineteenth century are interesting only inasmuch as they influenced one or other, or all, of the great generation of poets who reached maturity at the very end of the century. For example, the poetry of RAMÓN DE CAMPOAMOR (1817—1901) is now unreadable; but his anti-romantic cultivation of the very short poem had a strong influence on Antonio Machado (q.v.), even though it did not lead to the creation of any worthwhile work. Again, all that is now interesting about the dated love poetry of CAROLINA CORONADO (1823–1911) is the quality of its melancholy; there is nothing else left for us to admire. SALVADOR RUEDA (1857–1933) anticipated the spirit of *modernismo*; but his own poetry has failed to stand the test of time—he is most important for his influence on Jiménez (q.v.). GASPAR NÚÑEZ DE ARCE (1834–1903) was once famous for his pompous patriotic verse; but this has proved to be no more than superficial. The pastoral poetry of JOSÉ MARÍA GABRIEL Y GALÁN (1870–1905) is superior to that of any of the above: it is more vigorous and less perfervidly rhetorical. But his attitudes are too conventional for him to have much interest for modern readers: his superiority is not more than stylistic.

The exception is Gustavo Adolfo Bécquer (1836–70), who in his seventy-six short poems (*Rimas*, 1871) lamenting the impossibility of fulfilling erotic passion achieved a complex and original poetry that makes him the only worthy nineteenth-century predecessor of the poets of '98 and '25.

The symbolist and Parnassian (qq.v.) influences were introduced into Spain by the Nicaraguan poet Ruben Darío (q.v.), the apostle of *modernismo* (q.v.), which is dealt with, in its proper place, under Latin-American literature. However, as is only occasionally pointed out, the influence of *modernismo* among the really important Spanish poets has possibly been exaggerated. Machado (q.v.) reacted against the stylistic perfection aimed at by the *modernista* poets, and at their cultivation of art for art's sake. Unamuno (q.v.), too, went to 'ordinary life' for the themes of many of his poems. *Modernismo* was of course important for its technical innovations, its almost revolutionary extension of traditional form; in the earlier part of its European phase it undoubtedly helped to widen the scope of poetry—and from this Machado himself, and others not predominantly *modernista*, certainly benefited. But the only important poet who could be said to have carried on writing in the tradition of *modernismo* is the Andalusian JUAN RAMÓN JIMÉNEZ (1881–1958). However, although all his early poetry has affinities with *modernismo*, the first influence upon him was in fact Bécquer (q.v.), from whom he justly claimed that all contemporary Spanish poetry began; and in an early book, significantly entitled *Rimas* (1902), it was to the spirit of Bécquer, as distinct from that of Darío, that he deliberately attempted to return.

When Jiménez won the Nobel Prize in 1956 it was not only for his own poetry but also, vicariously, for that of two other Spaniards, both indirect victims of the Civil War, Machado and Lorca (qq.v.). He is a poet in the tradition of Mallarmé, Valéry, Barbu, Ungaretti, his countryman Guillén (qq.v.): his poetry seeks to uncover the language of reality, to relearn the meanings of words. His first, impressionistic, decadent poetry was brilliant but over-decorative in the *modernista* manner. In his thirties he gradually abandoned this style for a more austere one, in freer verse. The poems of his last period, when he was in exile in America, are mixed: some are highly abstract, others more deliberately humanized. For all his introspection and quest for verbal purity, Jiménez is in no sense frigid; but if his faults had to be summed up in one word then that word would surely be 'preciosity'. Jiménez was a shy, retiring, delicate man who was fortunate to find a wife who shared his interests in literature and who could protect him from the outside world, some aspects of which he did not well understand. She helped him to translate the complete poetry of Tagore (q.v.), who exercised a strong influence on Jiménez. His own influence on his successors, both Spanish and Latin-American, is incalculable;

this has related most importantly to his devotion to his craft and his view of poetry as the highest form of speech. 'My interior life, my beauty, my Work' is how he expressed this: and 'Written poetry . . . continues to seem to me, to be a form of expression . . . of the ineffable, of that which can not be said. . . .' That his apparent remoteness springs from delicacy (he suffered from pathological melancholy throughout his life) and not coldness is proved by the charm and feeling of his prose classic *Platero and I* (*Platero y yo*, 1917; tr. 1946), in which Jiménez talks to his donkey, Platero, in a series of lyrical impressions of Andalusia, its places and its people. *Diary of a Recently Married Poet* (*Diario de un poeta recién casado*, 1917) is the collection in which Jiménez's poetry takes its most decisive change of direction: towards a new clarity and new purity of expression as he seeks to capture and to freeze (one might say 'detemporize') isolated moments. He records this change of direction in the poem 'Poetry':

> When first she came to me chastely,
> Dressed in her innocence only,
> As a little girl I loved her truly.
>
> Then she took to adorning herself
> With all sorts of finery
> And I hated her not knowing why.
>
> At last she became a queen,
> Gaudily hung with jewelry . . .
> What bitter contrariness and how senseless!
>
> But once more she began undressing
> And I smiled upon her.
>
> She was left in her slip,
> Her former innocence.
> And again I believed in her.
>
> And she took off her slip, too,
> And appeared quite naked . . .
> Oh naked poetry, my lifelong passion,
> Now you are mine forever!
>
> (tr. H. R. Hays, *Selected Writings*, 1957)

This of course traces Jiménez's own poetic development: the first phase, in which Bécquer was the chief influence; the period of *modernismo*, when Darío and, less obviously, Francis Jammes (q.v.)—his influence is seen most clearly in *Platero and I*—were the models; and finally, the quest for 'pure poetry'. (MEP; PI; PSV)

The poetry of ANTONIO MACHADO (1875–1939), born in Seville, probably the greatest Spanish poet since Góngora, is not less individual than that of Jiménez; it is, however, more representative of the Generation of '98—and Machado is often described as 'the' poet of the group. His elder brother MANUEL MACHADO (1874–1947), a librarian who collaborated with Antonio in the writing of several plays, was unkindly known as 'the bad Machado'. That Antonio was known as 'the good', in his own right, is an indication of the kind of man he was. Manuel's early poetry was precious and insubstantial, but where its roots were in Andalusian popular poetry it has a certain charm. Manuel became a fervent and hysterical spokesman for the fascist revolt; Antonio supported the legal government, and may be said to have died of its defeat: in January 1939 he fled over the border to Collioure, in Southern France, with his old mother: within three weeks he was dead. With this obscure death the 'official', obscurantist Spain, to which the men of '98 had so vehemently objected, gained its final revenge for over half a century of liberalism. But Machado's poetry—a poetry not political but humane in spirit—lives on. Some of its main themes are nostalgia for the innocence of childhood, romantic love (often regarded as a metaphor for other kinds of love), and—of course—Spain. Machado was as melancholy as Jiménez, but whereas the latter laboriously constructed an impersonal kind of God, a concept as philosophical as it was poetic, Machado could do little more than lament—like his friend Unamuno— his own lack of faith. Machado's poetry has its roots firmly in early Spanish literature—notably in the twelfth-century epic *Cid*, in the mystical, epigrammatic poetry of Rabí Sem Tob and in the traditional Spanish *romance* (a collection of romances: *romancero*). Machado partly anticipated Lorca (q.v.) in trying to construct a viably modern version of this medieval narrative type of poetry, which was unique in Europe. The romances, most succinctly described as Spanish ballads, reflect every phase of Spanish life. The first written romances date from the early fifteenth century, but their origin goes much further back than this. Machado's attempts to recapture the atmosphere of these poems reflect his quest for Spain's 'intrahistory' (q.v.).

Machado, who was a teacher of French literature by profession, did not have a great deal of happiness in his life. The sixteen-year-old girl he married in 1909 died in 1912, leaving him desolate. He had spent much time in Paris: around the turn of the century he had met Wilde, Moréas (qq.v.) and others; and in 1910 he studied under Bergson (q.v.), whose basically existentialist philosophy profoundly influenced his poetry. Some of his best poetry is written to a woman he calls Guiomar, whom he knew in the late Twenties and early Thirties. Like Pessoa (q.v.), he invented fictitious characters, which he used as masks for the expression of aspects of his own personality; only the often ironically stated thoughts of the critic 'Juan de Mairena' and the philosopher 'Abel Martín', on poetry and life, are all in prose. Machado's poetry concentrates upon experience rather than speculation. Its anguish is perhaps centred in the poet's sorrow that time, in passing, should precipitate such intensely sensuous imagery, and in his suspicion that there is no kind of God who ultimately concentrates that intense sweetness into himself. His friend

Jiménez has said of him that 'Even as a child' he 'sought death, the dead, and decay. . . .' He spent his life, Jiménez continues, 'preparing for death': 'When bodily death came, he died humbly, miserably, collectively, the lead animal of a persecuted human flock. . . .' Assuredly the death of Machado in exile must rest upon the conscience of every fascist—whatever the wrongs or rights of the Civil War may be.

Sometimes Machado's poetry, like that of almost all the really great European poets of his generation, has the simplicity of classical Greek, as in 'From the Road':

> The clock struck twelve . . . and that was twelve
> strokes of a spade on earth . . .
> 'My hour!' I called; but silence
> answered: 'don't be afraid,
> you'll never see the final drop
> that trembles in the water-clock.
>
> You'll sleep many hours more
> on this side of the water
> and wake one lucid morning to discover
> your boat fast anchored to the farther shore'.

At other times, as in 'Siesta', an elegy for his fictional metaphysician Abel Martín, he is sadly ironic about the nature of pure speculation. A poem which displays all his considerable powers is the famous 'Portrait'. The best English translations from Machado have been made by Willis Barnstone, and I give this poem in his excellent version:

> My childhood is memories of a patio in Seville
> and a bright orchard where lemon trees ripen;
> my youth, twenty years on the soil of Castile;
> my life, a few events as well forgotten.
>
> I've never played Lothario or Don Juan's part—
> by now you know my plain, almost monkish dress—
> yet I was struck by Cupid's intended dart
> and I loved wherever I found welcomeness.
>
> Coursing my veins are drops of Jacobinic blood,
> but my poetry springs from a quiet fountain;
> and in the good sense of the word, I am good,
> better than the upright man who holds to doctrine.

I love beauty, and true to modern aesthetics
have cut old roses from the garden of Ronsard;
but I dislike the rouge of current cosmetics,
and am no chirping bird in the latest garb.

I disdain the romances of hollow tenors
and the choir of crickets singing to the moon.
I halt among the echoes of pretenders,
and hear—amid their voices—but one tune.

Am I classic or romantic? I don't know.
I would leave my verse as a warrior his blade:
known for the manly hand that made it glow,
not for the smithy's famous mark or trade.

I chat with the man who goes with me to the end—
who speaks alone hopes to speak to God one day—
my soliloquy is talk with this good friend
who showed me the secret of philanthropic ways.

In the end I owe you nothing. You owe me what I write.
By my work I pay for the house I rent,
the clothes that cover me, my bed at night,
the plain bread that gives me nourishment.

And when the day for my last trip arrives,
and the ship, never to return, is set to leave,
you will find me on board with scant supplies,
almost naked, like the children of the sea.

> (tr. W. Barnstone, *80 Poems*, 1959;
> see also MEP; PI; PSV)

Standing between these two poets of '98 and their brilliant successors who matured in the Twenties is the unclassifiable and therefore at times unduly neglected figure of the Zamoran poet LEÓN FELIPE (ps. LEÓN CAMINO Y GALICIA, 1884–1969). Felipe, the chief influence behind whose florid free verse is Whitman, spent much of his time in Mexico and North America; he never went back to his own country after the fascist victory. Felipe, who a few years before his death voiced his dissatisfaction with much of his own poetry, has been the idealistic apostle of socialism and godless Christianity. His main inspiration has been Whitman, and he has some affinities with such declamatory Marxist, or semi-Marxist, poets as Čaks, Martinson and Becher (qq.v.); however, at his best he is perhaps nearest in spirit and style (although more overtly political) to another unclassifiable writer: Cendrars (q.v.). His poetry is usually diffuse and prosy, but it is always readable. A short poem on the Civil War well illustrates his throwaway, sardonic manner:

> God, who knows everything,
> Is cleverer than most men know.
> Now by some outlaw archbishops
> He has been kidnapped, and the crafty gang
> Has made Him broadcast on the radio:
> 'Hello, I'm here with them. Hello!'

> That doesn't mean He's on their side
> But that He's there within their prison wall.
> He tells us where He is, that's all.
> So we may go
> A rescue party for the God we know.
>
> (IMSL; see also PI)

*

The so-called Generation of '25 or '27, or of the Dictatorship (it is not as useful or justified a category as that of '98) produced as remarkable a simultaneous blossoming of poetic talents as anywhere else in Europe during this century—with the possible exception of Russia—in its first two decades. The most important and accomplished of these poets were undoubtedly Alberti, Aleixandre, Cernuda, Guillén, Lorca, and Salinas (qq.v.); but there were others such as Altolagiurre and Prados (qq.v.) who produced good poetry and criticism. These men, who knew one another, referred to themselves towards the end of the Twenties as 'The brilliant pleiad'. Some of the older of them had passed through the influences of ultraism and creationism (qq.v.), the two movements that swept over Spain in the five years immediately following the end of the First World War. Their best work reflected these influences, but rose entirely above them. However, it was ultraism that helped to produce the atmosphere that made their work possible, and an account of this Spanish and Spanish-American version of expressionism is necessary to our understanding of that work.

Vicente Huidobro (q.v.) had propounded the central theories of creationism (*creacionismo*) in Buenos Aires as early as 1916; these are discussed more fully in the section on Latin-American literature. Pierre Reverdy (q.v.) initiated it in France, where it had a short-lived vogue. Huidobro brought it into Spain himself in 1918; it was quickly taken up by JUAN LARREA (1895) and GERARDO DIEGO (1896). Both are minor poets, whose early efforts to create poems as 'natural as trees', complements to nature's own creations, really consisted of little more than light-hearted series of disparate images. Diego's most important contribution to letters has probably been his anthology of contemporary Spanish poetry (1932), which he has continually revised. (MEP)

It was the poet and critic GUILLERMO DE TORRE (1900), now in exile in Argentina, who originated the term ultraism (*ultraísmo*). His history of the post-war *avant garde* movements of Europe, *European Literatures of the Avant-Garde* (*Literaturas europeas de vanguardia*, 1925) was one of the first of its kind. Ultraism was intended as an -ism beyond all the other -isms: futurism, dadaism, simplism, advancism, and so on. Ultraism produced only fragmentary poetry; but it was a necessary development. Those who call it 'Spanish expressionism' are not fundamentally wrong. The so-called neopopularism (*neopopularismo*) of Lorca and other poets of his generation, a turning back to tradition, the people and the past (much under the influence of Machado), absorbed its revolutionary fervour and incorporated its violent metaphors. Lorca's *Poet in New York* may be described as ultraist as well as surrealist.

The oldest (except for Salinas, q.v.) and least revolutionary of the poets of the Generation of '25 is JORGE GUILLÉN (1893), who was born in Valladolid and has been in exile in the U.S.A. since the Civil War (but he returned to Spain for a visit in 1950, and in 1965 a Madrid firm issued a selection of his poetry). For the whole of his life he has been a teacher in universities. His work translates well into other languages, and Guillén enjoys the widest international reputation of any living Spanish poet. Like Jiménez, Guillén seeks a pure poetry; but in his contact with the world he finds more joy and exaltation than Jiménez or any other major poet of the century. And, even more than Jiménez, he is the Spanish disciple of Valéry. Most of his poetic life has been taken up with the composition of one book: *Cántico* (*Canticle*) which he first issued in 1928; the edition of 1950 contained 332 poems—the 1928 volume contained seventy-five. He has added two more collections to *Cántico*: *Clamor* and *Homenaje* (*Homage*). A sumptuous edition of his entire work was published in Milan in 1968: *Aire Nuestro* (*Our Air*). In his attempt to capture the essence of single moments Guillén's poetry does resemble that of Jiménez; but where the latter is deliberately misty and vague, Guillén is hard and sculptured. Like Ungaretti (q.v.), he wants to strip the poem down to its essentials.

There is some controversy over Guillén. Certain critics see him as insensitive to the particular anguish of his age, and as cold and intellectual. In *Cántico* he is by far the most optimistic of the modern European poets of his stature, and this has led critics to suspect him still further. But such a poem as 'Death, from a Distance', beautifully translated by Richard Wilbur (q.v.), demonstrates that his poems do possess emotional substance:

> When that dead-certainty appals my thought,
> My future trembles on the road ahead.
> There where the light of country fields is caught

In the blind, final precinct of the dead,
A will takes aim.
   But what is sad, stripped bare
By the sun's gaze? It does not matter now,
Not yet. What matters is the ripened pear
That even now my hand strips from the bough.

The time will come: my hand will reach, some day,
Without desire. That saddest day of all,
I shall not weep, but with a proper awe
For the great force impending, I shall say,
Lay on, just destiny. Let the white wall
Impose on me its capricious law.

Guillén's earliest poetry was often frivolous; but he soon recognized it as such. And the poems of *Clamour* and *Homage* can by no means be described as 'dehumanized', nor do they fail to consider the tragic side of life. They aptly supplement, if not equal, his achievement in *Canticle*. The best translations of his poetry are in the bilingual *Affirmation 1919–1966* (tr. J. Palley, 1968). (PSV; IMSL; PI; MEP)

PEDRO SALINAS (1892–1951) was, like Guillén, an academic by profession. He was one of the leading scholars and critics of his time; and, again like Guillén, he chose exile in 1939. As a poet he is somewhere between Jiménez and Guillén, sharing their concerns but essentially more explorative of his human situation than either. He is unusual, too, in being one of the few non-communist poets to be genuinely at home in the technological world (Hart Crane, q.v., only tried to force himself to be). Although an intellectual, he had a child-like and innocent joy in machines and gadgets. He enjoyed driving a car ('In his Fiat-4014 Pedro Salinas, every morning, eagerly seeks death, accompanied by insults, threats, angry glares of police and pedestrians' said Alberti, q.v.) in rather the same way as he enjoyed Joyce's punning in *Ulysses* (q.v.): he is a poet with a sense of fun and curiosity. But exile in the U.S.A. and ill health gradually broke this down: his later poems are more sombre than his earlier.

Salinas, the most playful of poets, has some affinities with Apollinaire (q.v.) —the casual attitude concealing a high seriousness—and more with the Swedish poet Gunnar Ekelöf (q.v.). Like Ekelöf, his chief concern is the nature of reality. His approach to this subject-matter is of course very different—as different as Spain is from Sweden. The earlier poetry of Salinas tends to construct a series of models of reality—reality as toyshop, as melodramatized trivia, as two-dimensional (he was devoted to painting), as mechanical fun-house, as geometrical (he wrote some poems that can fairly be described as cubist), and so on—and then, so to speak, contemplate them. But with the collection of love poems *My Voice Stems From You* (*La voz a ti debida*, 1933) a new note enters his work. He is still playful (one critic called these poems 'glacial psycho-technical madrigals'), but, as he says, if his beloved called to him he would

> leave it all,
> chuck it all away:
> prices, catalogues,
> maps' oceans' blue,
> days and their nights,
> old telegrams
> and a love.

In *Reason of Love* (*Razón de amor*, 1936) this note deepened, to produce such fully mature and characteristic poems as 'If Eyes Could Hear. . . .'

> If eyes could hear
> ah, how I would see you
> whose voice bathes me in light,
> in the aural light.
> When you talk
> space glows with sound: the huge dark that silence is,
> is shattered. Your word
> glows with the flush of dawning
> each day as it comes to me newly.
> When you say yes
> noon's zenith is supreme—
> and yet there is no sight.
> If you speak to me at night then is no night
> no loneliness here in my room alone
> if your voice comes bodiless and light.
> For your voice makes bodies: from your emptiness
> spring forth the myriad delicate, possible
> bodies of your voice. Lips, arms
> seeking you, are almost tricked.
> Ghost-lips, ghost-arms,
> plunge all around them seeking
> two holy creatures of your speech.
> And in the aural light,
> where no eyes see, radiantly
> and for us they kiss—
> lovers who have no more day, nor night,
> than your starry voice, your sunlight.

Salinas' last collection to appear in his lifetime, *All Most Clear* (*Todo más claro*, 1949), is shot through with gloom and horror: here Salinas condemns civilization; he no longer sees machines as harmless, but as weapons of destruction. This is reflected in his satirical novel, *The Incredible Bomb* (*La bomba increible*, 1950). But the poems of the posthumous *Confidence* (*Confianza*, 1954), while still aware of horror, suggest that before his death Salinas discovered some kind of serenity. As well as being one of the finest metaphysical love-poets of this century, Salinas was a notable critic (his book on Darío, q.v., is the best); he also wrote a dozen plays. (PI; IMSL; PSV)

Much of the life of VICENTE ALEIXANDRE (1900), born in Seville, has been plagued by serious illness, arising from kidney trouble he suffered as a young man. Unlike the other members of 'the brilliant pleiad' he did not go into exile after the Civil War: he is an invalid. But because of his loyalty to the Republic his works were banned for some years. He is now regarded as the spiritual father of the younger generation of poets in Spain. His poems were collected in 1960, and he has since issued two further volumes. His *Some Characters of the New Spanish Poetry* (1955) contains valuable, shrewd and charming reminiscences of his contemporaries. Aleixandre is nearer to surrealism (q.v.) that any of his contemporaries except Alberti (q.v.), but he is not simply a surrealist. The attitude of the earlier Aleixandre has something in common with that of Gerrit Achterberg (q.v.), another near-surrealist for whom all meaning resides in the figure of the beloved, and for whom death is love, love death. But, unlike that of Achterberg, Aleixandre's poetry has become consistently more humane and outward-looking. Nearly all of it is written in a finely cadenced free verse, of which he must be counted as one of the contemporary masters. Although so much of his poetry is difficult, anguished and 'private', it is always characterized by a glow of feeling towards others. The more overt compassion of his later work seems a natural outcome—not a sudden pang of conscience. His poetic quest, for some point at which man may make full and rich contact with the nature from which he is so mysteriously alienated, has been consistent. He has searched for this point of fusion by exploring—in succession—his erotic experience, his childhood memories, his feelings of human brotherhood. In seeking escape in poetry from pain and the proximity of death Aleixandre has—paradoxically—found meaning; his is not a poetry of evasion. His densest, least controlled work is to be found in the prose-poetry of *Passion in the Earth* (*Pasión de la tierra*, 1935); this, a necessary stage in his development, was hauled up from subconscious depths in a manner very close to the one recommended by the surrealists. Here Aleixandre roams through the exterior world and desperately, sensuously, unsuccessfully, attempts to identify himself with it.

'The Old Man and the Sun', about death, shows Aleixandre at his sweetest and best; no poem so clearly demonstrates his humanity and involvement in his human environment. It begins,

> He had lived a long time.
> He used to lean there, an old man, on a tree-trunk, on a
>   very thick tree-trunk, in the sunset evenings.
> He was old, with a wrinkled face, and eyes
>   more slaked than sad.

He leant on the tree-trunk, and the sun reached him first,
    gently biting his feet,
staying there awhile, as if huddled up.
Then it rose in the sky, submerging him, drowning him,
plucking gently at him, making him one in its sweet light. . . .

At last 'the dear old man' is 'changed into light, and . . . very slowly carried off in the sun's final rays, like so many other invisible things. . . .' Aleixandre's poetry has gradually become more intelligible (to himself as to the reader) as he has learned to place himself in the world. Life was for him once 'an instant only just long enough to say "Mary" '; now it is something in the course of which he can say 'I write for everyone' (Para todos escribo'). Aleixandre has not, perhaps, enough control or specific emotional substance to entitle him to the status of a major poet; furthermore, over the hard and difficult years of his life his exuberance and energy have diminished. But there is no doubt of the seriousness and sincerity of his project. (PSV; MEP; IMSL)

It is certainly true that the attention given outside Spain to the work of FEDERICO GARCÍA LORCA (1898–1936), born in Granada, has tended to diminish the achievements of some of his contemporaries. However, it is a moot point whether his own poetic reputation was ever actually inflated—even if his poetry was misunderstood. And while it now seems that his murder in 1936 was personal (an act of revenge) rather than pol iical—it was, however, perpetrated by fascist thugs—his role as martyr to fascism is hardly unfair to the Franco regime. There is no room for argument about what his attitude to the actual Franco regime would have been: he would have loathed it. He himself was not much interested in politics, and disliked it when people tried to make them of his participation in the government's theatrical programme. He is a major poet because he evolved an individual style that fused the naïve (q.v.) and the sentimentive (q.v.) in a unique and entirely convincing and meaningful manner. The horrified and death-haunted semi-surrealism of his *Poet in New York* (*Poeta en Nueva York*, 1940; tr. B. Belitt, 1955) is less successful than his essays in more traditional forms; but it was a stage he had to go through, and represents the isolation of a vital element in his work—as the great elegy for his friend Sánchez Mejías clearly shows. Gifted as a painter and musician, he was one of the most complete geniuses of modern times. His cruel and senseless death, at the height of his powers, is above all a comment on 'civilization'.

Lorca's work is thoroughly rooted in the popular and traditional poetry of Spain; but onto his traditionalism he grafted his fearful apprehension of the modern world, which almost from the beginning took a fragmented, semi-surrealistic form. He also took much from the seventeenth-century metaphysical poet who was suddenly 'rediscovered' (the main credit for this belongs to Dámaso Alonso) in the Twenties in Spain just as was his contemporary John Donne in Great Britain and America: Luis de Góngora y Argote (1561–1627). Lorca was as much a poet of the people as Machado, and as fundamentally apolitical. The subject of much of his poetry, again, is the 'intrahistory' (q.v.) rather than the history of Spain.

Lorca began to write plays and poetry very young; his first *Book of Poems* appeared in 1921; a book of prose impressions had appeared three years earlier. The first poems betray all the important influences, but these have not been absorbed. He reached maturity in his twenties with *Songs* (*Canciones*, 1927)—written between 1921 and 1924—and *Gipsy Ballads* (*Romancero gitano*, 1928), his finest single collection, written over the five years prior to its publication. In *Gipsy Ballads* Lorca invents an unreal, fantastically lyrical world of gipsies and their brutal and traditional oppressors, the Civil Guard. He described the book as 'an Andalusian song in which the gipsies serve as a refrain', and as a mixture of 'new themes and old suggestions'. All Lorca's love for the primitive and weak (the gipsy victims of the unweeping Civil Guard with their lead skulls and 'souls of patent leather'), all his sensuous love of nature emerge in these poems, all his awareness of death and his vision of blood as the link between it and life emerge in this collection. The poetry is lucid with folk-wisdom and directness, as in the famous lines from 'The Unfaithful Wife':

> That night I rode
> the best of all roads
> on a filly of mother-of-pearl
> without bridle or stirrups.

And yet his language is also highly sophisticated; *Gipsy Ballads* is at once spontaneous and artful.

The world of *Poet in New York*, written in 1929 but not published in its entirety until 1940, is an entirely different one, the result of a crisis in Lorca's difficult sexual life, of his painful premonitions of death and of his horror at what he saw in America (whose Negroes he saw as victims of 'civilization'). The hallucinated terror of these poems was the response Lorca found torn from him; he had gone to America (he spoke little English—or, indeed, any language but his own) in an attempt to achieve a more cosmopolitan outlook: to escape from the world of Andalusia. The shocked, horrified world of *Poet in New York*—of helpless children threatened by violence, of wounded or crippled animals ('tiny larks on crutches'; 'empty snails')—is emphatically not simply the result of the influence of French surrealism, but of a severe mental crisis. It is doubtful, in any case, if Lorca knew much more about the details of French surrealism than his close friend, the painter and exhibitionist Salvador Dali, told him.

The poems of *Poet in New York* are fascinating, painful, evocative of a great anguish at man's inhumanity to men, his materialism, his terror of death. The English-less Lorca's head is filled only with inarticulate cries of pain or coarse laughter; the poetry effectively conveys his sense of alienation. But some of it is undoubtedly either contrived or uninspired. (Lorca himself made much critical use of the concept of inspiration, *inspiración*). It reflects as much of personal neurosis, temporary dissociation, as of a sense of alienation that is available to the reader. Lorca found himself entire again in his tragic elegy for the bullfighter Ignacio Sánchez Mejías, an intellectual and literary dilettante—he wrote a play—and a friend of Lorca's contemporaries, who was killed in the ring in 1934. Into this long elegy, one of the greatest poems of its kind written in the century, Lorca concentrated all his nervous bitterness and horror of death—and perhaps his own premonitions not only of his own senseless and brutal murder but also of the holocaust that within a few months would engulf Spain itself. Lorca endowed Sánchez Mejías with the status of a tragic hero, thus giving his own elegy classical and traditional strength:

> What a fighter in the ring!
> What a climber in the mountains!
> How gentle with the wheat!
> How firm with the spurs
> and tender with the dew!
> How captivating at the fair!
> How imperious with the *banderillas*,
> final darts of darkness!
>
> But now he sleeps eternally.
> Now moss and grasses
> Open with sure fingers
> the flower of his skull.
>
> And now his blood comes singing,
> singing through the fields and marshes,
> comes sliding on frozen horns,
> wandering spiritless in the mist,
> encountering a thousand hooves,
> like a long, dark and grieving tongue—
> to gather into a pool of pain
> by the Guidalquivir of stars. . . .

Lorca's theatre contains the same mixture as his poetry. His early plays and puppet-plays were written against the grain of the fashionable theatre of the time, and were deeply influenced by the earlier plays of Valle-Inclán (q.v.). They vary from the lyrical (*Mariana Pineda*, 1927), through farce and the deliberately grotesque and fantastic to rural tragedy, in which Lorca excelled. His three most remarkable plays are all rural tragedies dealing powerfully with the frustrations produced by rigid attitudes or by the unnatural role the 'other' Spain forces upon woman. *Blood Wedding* (*Bodas de sangre*, 1933; LTT) shows sexual desire uncontained by 'honour'; *Yerma* (1934; LTT) is about a woman who murders the husband who cannot make her a mother; *The House of Bernarda Alba* (*La casa de Bernarda Alba*, 1946; LTT), which was not performed until 1945, is a tragedy of 'honour' (avoidance of scandal) leading to hideous crazy tyranny and eventual death. There is in these three plays a progression towards starkness of presentation, leading to the virtual elimination of verse in the final play. But the poetic conception remains.

Lorca's complete works were published in 1954, but much work remains to be done on the editing of his texts. Many translations into English have been made: the best is the selection by J. L. Gili (1960); Rolph Humphries has done a good version of *Romancero gitano: Gipsy Ballads* (1950). (PSV; PI; IMSL; MST; MEP)

Most of the poetry of Lorca's friend RAFAEL ALBERTI (1902), born near Cadiz, remains banned, or is at least regarded as highly suspect, in Spain; but the crude attacks on Franco's fascism and on American imperialism (etc.)—while they are understandable enough—that he has made since going into exile (he lives in Argentina) have not added to his poetic reputation. All his political poems are laboured and unoriginal, and the dogmatic—as distinct from the humane—elements of his attachment to communism must certainly be regarded as having a detrimental effect on his poetry. He became a communist in 1931, and although he was expelled from the party he remains, basically, a communist by conviction. His best poetry has not, as it happens, sprung from the conflict in him between Marxist belief and the humane impulses that adherence to it from time to time offends, but from essentially subjective experiences. The mental turbulence caused by political conversion, and then the Civil War—in which he took an active part—virtually crippled him as a poet, and he has since found his true voice only occasionally. The finest work of his exile, and an essential guide to his work, has been *The Lost Grove (La arboleda perdida*, 1959), his memoirs. His poems were collected in 1961; he has published two new collections, one in Madrid, since then. There are *Selected Poems* in English translations by L. Malan (1944) and B. Belitt (1966).

Alberti's best poetry is to be found in *Concerning the Angels (Sobre los ángeles*, 1927–8; tr. G. Connell, 1967). This is one of the seminal collections of poetry of our time: it reflects Alberti's agonized search for new values, his destroyed sexual security, his angry nostalgia for childhood. It is fascinating to contrast the 'baroque angels' of Alberti, as he searches in vain for something to believe in, with those of Rilke (q.v.). Alberti, too, felt impelled to make use of surrealistic techniques; but it is misleading, as it almost always is with Spanish writers, to call him a surrealist. In these poems he was, as he later put it in *The Lost Grove*, 'battered and betrayed', haunted by childhood fears, confused: *Concerning the Angels* is an account of a hopeless, helpless journey in the no-man's-land between the innocent belief of boyhood (Alberti was educated in a Jesuit College, and liked it) and the sophisticated faithlessness of sudden, frightened adulthood. He is haunted or hallucinated by various 'angels' dead, envious, good, revengeful—and so on. Here is 'The Envious Angel':

> Crowds on street corners
> of unreal towns and countries
> were talking.

That man is dead
but does not know it.
He wants to rob the bank,
steal clouds, stars, golden comets,
and to buy the most difficult
sky.
And that man is dead.

His brow registers quakes.
Landslides,
delirious echoes,
crash of picks and shovels
haunt his ears.
Acetylene flares,
damp corridors of gold
dazzle his sight.
His heart is filled
with explosions of stone, laughter, dynamite.
He dreams of mines.

The best of Alberti's later poetry, much of which is sadly trivial, is to be found in *Returns of the Living Distance* (*Retornos de lo vivo lejano*, 1948–56). (PSV; IMSL; MEP; PI)

The poetry of the Sevillian LUIS CERNUDA (1902–63) has not been as generally acclaimed as that of Alberti or Lorca; he has, however, a small but significant Spanish following, which regards the poetry collected in *Reality and Desire* (*La realidad y el deseo*, 1936, rev 1949, rev 1958) as the best of its time. Cernuda, who after fighting for the Republic was for a time a schoolmaster in an English public school (vile fate), died in Mexico—the most embittered of 'the brilliant pleiad'. But, a tortured homosexual who struggled, throughout his unhappy and lonely life, to persuade himself that he had chosen his destiny, Cernuda had always been embittered. A fine stylist and technician, he is one of the most thoroughgoingly negative poets of the century; his admirers are wrong in claiming him as the best—but his dogged integrity, and the unfuzzed quality of his perceptions and thought in his peculiarly solipsistic, prickly, 'deliberately personally unpleasant' (as one may put it) situation are fascinating. Cernuda hunted out the bitterness in himself on his own tough principle of 'Cultivate what others censure in you, for that is your true self'. There is no softening of attitude in Cernuda's poetry. His attitudes remain consistent: 'Public? I do not know what it is'; he hates 'friends, family, country';

Down, then, with virtue, order, poverty;
Down with everything—except defeat,
Jaw-clenching defeat. . . .

For everywhere he went (especially Scotland, which he visited presumably to recover from his experiences in the English school), he expressed loathing. But this was a general hatred of reality which sprang, essentially, from a yearning for the values of his inner dream-world (his *deseo*). In few poets is nostalgia for the naïve (q.v.) so implacably opposed to the concrete—and yet with what persistence the concrete has been approached! The whole of Cernuda's poetry may, indeed, be seen as a shuddering, hurt revulsion at it. . . . Perhaps, he suggests to the dead in a Glasgow cemetery, 'God, too, is forgetting you'. And yet, even though 'to live is to be alone with death', he finds beauty in existence, as he records in 'Spring of Long Ago':

> Now in evening's purple sunset,
> With bedewed magnolias already blossoming,
> To go along those streets while the moon swells
> Will be to dream awake.
>
> The sky will become huger with the grief
> Of flocks of swallows; water of fountains
> Will liberate the earth's pure voice.
> Sky and earth will suddenly fall silent.
>
> Alone in some choir with head on hand
> You will weep, like a ghost returned,
> Mourning how lovely earth is,
> And how futile.

Cernuda's last poems, published in Mexico in *Desolation of the Chimera* (*Desolación de la quimera*, 1962), are his most bitter of all. Some, attacks on his contemporaries and former friends (for example, Salinas), display little more than personal animus; but the best continue his bitter and lonely struggle with his pride. Cernuda, much prized by Spain's youngest poets, is a poet who will be increasingly turned to as this century draws to its bitter close: his convoluted homosexuality and his defeated dream of paradise are both relevant to the concerns of the youngest generations. (PSV; IMSL)

MANUEL ALTOLAGUIRRE (1905–59), who was born in Malaga, took part with his friend Prados (q.v.) in the defence of the Republic, and lived abroad thereafter. He was allowed to visit Spain in 1952; he died there as a result of a motor accident seven years later, after visiting the San Sebastian Film Festival. (The film director Luis Buñuel had been an associate of 'the brilliant pleiad' in the Twenties, and Altolaguirre collaborated with him on films in Mexico.) Altolaguirre lacked the energy of his contemporaries, and wrote much less; but his best poetry is finely written and evocative of his feelings of sexual loneliness and sadness. (PSV) His fellow-Malagan and friend EMILIO PRADOS (1899–1962), who died in Mexico, was the most intensely nervous and cerebral poet of this generation. Prados resembles Salinas (q.v.) in his concern for the nature of reality; but there is little in reality, it seems, for him to cling on to. Nevertheless, within his extreme limits he is a meticulous and wholly sincere poet.

*

Of a later generation, MIGUEL HERNÁNDEZ (1910–42), who was born in Alicante, was the last Spanish poet of indubitably major status. He fought for the Republic, as a soldier, and was later imprisoned by the fascists—who, in their role as proxies of God, then allowed him to die by denying him the proper food and medical care that would have enabled him to fight the tuberculosis from which he suffered. A collected edition of his works, which is incomplete, was published in the Argentine in 1961. Like Lorca, from whom however he differs considerably, Hernández fuses the popular and the modern. A peasant's son, he had little education, but was precocious and had an extraordinary intuitive grasp of such literary procedures of the past (those of Góngora, Lope de Vega, Calderón) as appealed to him in his quest to express his essentially telluric sensibility. Jiménez, among others, saluted his early promise; at least he never knew literary failure. Hernández, in his capacity as peasant poet, has affinities with Esenin (q.v.); as the popular poet of *Wind of the People* (*Viento del pueblo*, 1937), written to inspire soldiers and printed by them, he somewhat resembles the Aragon of *Heartbreak* (q.v.), although his fervent songs certainly have a more enduring value. His first collection, *Moon Connoisseur* (*Perito en lunas*, 1933), is full of promise, but somewhat over-influenced by the then fashionable neo-gongoristic manner and, particularly, by Guillén. In *The Lightning that Never Ceases* (*El rayo que no cesa*, 1936) he came nearer to his own voice. His finest poetry, however, comes in the *Song and Ballad-Book of Absences* (*Cancionero y romancero de ausencias*, 1958): these final poems of the despair and yet poetic joy of a dying man who knows that he will not see his wife or home again achieve an almost unparalleled simplicity. When his wife wrote to tell him that she had only bread and onions to feed herself and their son (Franco's 'twenty-five years of peace and prosperity'), he wrote 'The Lullaby of the Onion':

> The onion is cold
> never-ending poverty.
> Cold as your days are cold,
> Cold as my nights.
> Hunger and onions
> Black ice of hunger, and frost
> large and round.

> In a cradle of hunger
> my child lay.
> On the blood of the onion
> he sucked.

So your blood, my son
is a frosting of sugar
and onion and hunger.

A dark woman
dissolved in moonlight
pours herself drop by drop
over the cradle.
Laugh, child,
that the moon is yours to swallow
when you have need.

Laugh and laugh again,
Lark of my house!
Your laughter is to my eyes
the light of the world.
Laugh, loudly and long,
that my soul, on hearing you,
will fly free.

Your laughter frees me—it gives me
wings—it takes away
loneliness—it tears me
from my prison
Oh little mouth that flies to me!
Oh heart that on your lips bursts!

Your laughter is
a victorious sword,
conqueror of flowers
and larks.
Rival of the sun.
Future of my body
and my love.

Warm new flesh fluttering with life,
Bright questioning eyes,
A picture that had never been painted.
How many bright birds
will flutter and soar
from your body!

I awoke from innocence.
You must never wake up.
Sadness' taste is in my mouth.

You must always laugh.
Always, from your cradle, little bird.
Defend your laughter
feather by feather.

Your flight is high
my newborn son,
and so vast,
it merges with the heavens.
If only I too
could soar
to the source of your life.

On the eighth month of your life you laugh at me
With five orange blossoms in your mouth.
With five small
ferocities,
with five teeth,
with five blooming
jasmines.

They shall grow to be the guardian and strength
of tomorrow's kisses,
when you feel them
to be a weapon of love.
And someday you will feel the fire that begins there
And flows down and down, searching for
the very center of your being.

Fly my son, to the two moons
of the breast.
You will be satisfied.
It will help the sadness of the onion.
Do not crumble away.
Do not try to know what's wrong
nor what is happening.

(IMSL; see also PSV; MEP)

*

Few of the post-Civil War poets may be said to have discovered their own
voices in the way Hernández did. It has been more difficult for them to do so.
GABRIEL CELAYA (ps. RAFAEL MÚGICA, 1911), a socialist, who has proclaimed
that 'poetry is an instrument to change the world', has shown exemplary

courage; but he writes at length and in a language that is frequently too diffuse. MANUEL PINILLOS (1914), who is not at all well known outside Spain, is an over-prolific writer whose existential concerns are intelligent and interesting; unfortunately his poems possess little character.

BLAS DE OTERO (1916), born in Bilbao, regarded as the leading poet of this generation, has achieved more intensity than either of the preceding poets. Although he seldom seems able to get beyond a choked and frustrated tone, much of his poetry is extremely evocative of his anguish and inability to reconcile his political anarchism with his desire for God. His religious position recalls that of Unamuno, by whom he was influenced. He left Spain for a while, but has now returned there. An English translation, *Twenty Poems*, appeared in 1964. (PSV)

Most poets of this generation have been obsessed with similar themes; an exception is the short-lived JOSÉ LUIS HIDALGO (1919–47), a victim of tuber-culosis. Hidalgo's last book, *The Dead* (*Los muertos*, 1947), contains impassioned addresses—by a dying man—to God. These are by no means profound in content, but are remarkable for their expression of courage and for their lucid style. (PSV) VICENTE GAOS (1919) is an interesting critic; but as a poet he has tended to be intellectually and emotionally superficial and too dependent on traditional modes; he lacks linguistic resourcefulness. Some of the poems of EUGENIO DE NORA (1923), especially those in *Spain, Passion of life* (*España, pasión de vida*, 1954), are brilliantly descriptive of the Spanish landscape.

Probably more important than any of these is JOSÉ HIERRO (1922), who was clapped into jail for four years, at the age of seventeen, in 1949. He fully shares Blas de Otero's and Celaya's view of the function of poetry as social and not aesthetic; and yet he is a more personal poet. His rasping anger at aesthetes—expressed in 'For an Aesthete'—would not be likely to provoke disagreement anywhere. It begins:

> You, who scent the flower of the beautiful word,
> may not understand my words, which are odourless.
> You who seek the limpid clear water
> Should not drink of my red water.

Hierro writes evocatively and buoyantly of his own sensations of beauty; his style is the most original and clear of his time—his tone moving and unforced. (PSL; IMSL)

Ultimately CARLOS BOUSOÑO's (1923) importance will be seen to lie in his critical work. This is somewhat marred by academicism and a mania for classification; but, by virtue of his intelligence, scholarship and range, Bousoño is certainly the leading Spanish critic of his generation. His poetry, elegant and beautifully written though it is, is too mannered: it never quite bursts into life, and its attitudes often seem artificial. He has been much influenced by Aleixandre (q.v.), of whose poetry he is the leading interpreter. Bousoño's poetry is stylistically of consistently high quality; it is a pity that the strength of the impulses behind it is questionable. (PSV)

Very characteristic of the so-called 'realist', anti-lyrical generation is the poetry of ÁNGEL GONZÁLEZ (1925): anti-rhetorical, colloquial, revolutionary, disenchanted. This may represent a misguided attempt to cut out of poetry many of its natural characteristics; but there is no doubt of González's sincerity and skill. JOSÉ ÁNGEL VALENTE (1929) is usually classed with him, as a 'social realist'. His poetry, too, is compressed and restrained—but somewhat more personal. (PSV)

With the end of the Fifties and the Sixties there came a partial revolt against 'social realism'. Both CLAUDIO RODRIGUEZ (1934) (PSV) and FRANCISCO BRINES (1934), although clearly concerned with society and humane values, write a more meditative poetry. No major poet, however, has emerged since Hernández; the nearest is Hierro.

Turkish Literature

Despite the westernizing, laicist and benevolent dictatorship of Kemal Atatürk, who died in 1938, and who has never been replaced by a politician of equal calibre, Turkey remains helplessly torn between Islamic conservatism and Western ways. After the so-called Democratic Party was returned to power in the 1950 elections the clock was put back: facilities for peasant education were withdrawn, the constitution was undermined, and many writers were imprisoned. And despite the bloodless coup of 1960 and the dissolution of the Democratic party, Turkey's problems have not been solved—nor are things made easier for socially progressive (not necessarily communist) forces in the country by Russia's immediate presence, which has always been felt as a threat. All the main political parties are associated with strong feudal interests. The predicament of the modern Turkish writer is not enviable: as well as his situation in society, he has to contend with the language problem—which continues to undermine creativity in Turkey.

The 'Treasure of the Arts' (*Servet-i Fünen*) movement, named from its magazine (1891), tried to introduce French decadence into the language; but it was too literary, and failed to understand that the colloquial language was the only possible vehicle for a serious and viable modernism. The 'Young Authors' (*Genç Kalemlev*) movement (1911) represented a reaction to this. OMER SEYFEDDIN (1884–1920), short-story writer, was one of its leading members. He attained a natural style in his stories, which are however more important for their part in the history of the freeing of the language from its Arabo-Persian elements than for their content.

Two poets are important. YAHYA KEMAL BEYATLI (1884–1958), born in a part of Yugoslavia then Turkish, wrote in the traditional Ottoman manner, but his studies in Paris and his understanding of the political problems facing his country rescued his work from stultification. His was a predominantly nationalistic emotional outlook, but intellectually he appreciated the necessities of westernization. Most of his best poems were written when he was past fifty, and they were not—despite his fame—collected into a book until after his death. They represent the height to which traditional Turkish poetry can in this style be brought; their theme is really a lament for the passing of the old ways. Yahya Kemal was Turkey's ambassador to Pakistan from 1948 until within a year of his death. A selection of his poetry has been translated: *Selected Poems* (tr. S. Behlül Toygar, 1965). AHMED HAŞIM (1884–1933), who died before his full genius had had time to reveal itself, was not a language reformer; but he introduced French symbolism (q.v.) into Turkish poetry, and has exercised a strong influence.

In prose HÜSEYIN RAHMI GÜRNIPUR (1864–1944) developed a style personal to himself, and wrote his dialogues in the colloquial. He is the author of many novels and short stories, all valuable accounts of the Turkey of his time.

The most famous figure in modern Turkish literature, although no longer the most highly esteemed amongst critics, is the poet and playwright HÂMIT ABDÜLHAK TARHAN (1852–1937), who received a state funeral. He belonged to the school of the nineteenth rather than to the twentieth century, but he was energetic within that tradition. It must be stated that, for all his skill, his work has dated badly: the plays, many of them in verse and based on incidents in Moslem history, are ill-constructed and embarrassingly echo Shakespeare and other non-Turkish dramatists; his poetry is romantic, and while it helped to oust the old classical manner, put nothing adequate in its place.

The most distinguished novelist of the republican period was YAKUB KADRI KARAOSMANOĞLU (1889), who was born in Cairo. He shared Atatürk's hostility to all forms of religious fanaticism, which he revealed most clearly in his *Father Light* (1922), a story of life in a dervish convent; he also understood and absorbed more French and Russian fiction than any Turk of his period. After starting with prose-poems, he wrote short stories, novels, and memoirs. Some of his stories about important periods in modern Turkish history have been translated into German, Dutch, French and Italian: the life in Istanbul after the First World War, the corruption of reformers (*Panorama*, 1953) and stories of peasant life. HALIDE EBIB ADIVAR (1883–1964), who was educated in an American girls' school, was for a time a corporal in the Anatolian nationalist army. Out of this experience she wrote *The Daughter of Smyrna* (1922; tr. M. Y. Khan, 1933). Her earlier fiction is mostly on the theme of woman's position in society. From 1923 until 1938 she and her husband lived abroad; in 1935 she published *The Clown and his Daughter*, which she wrote in English and later translated into Turkish (1936). This is one of the most intelligent analyses of the tensions set up in Turkish society by westernization. REŞAD NURI GÜNTERKIN (1889–1956) wrote sentimental novels which are none the less valuable for their realistic portrayals of Turkish society. He achieved success with *Autobiography of a Turkish Girl* (1922; tr. W. Deedes, 1949). REFIK HALID KERAY (1888–1965) has written popular novels of little interest; but his short stories are notable for their harshness and sharp characterization. He was an opponent of Atatürk, and was exiled until 1938. His style, clear and vivid, is his highest achievement.

The only Turkish poet to gain an international reputation is NAZIM HIKMET (1902–63), an active Marxist who spent much of his life in prison. He was born in (then Turkish) Salonika, and while in Russia between 1921 and 1928 studied French, physics and chemistry at Moscow University. Sentenced in 1938, by military courts, to twenty-eight years in prison, he gained freedom in a general amnesty in 1951, after an international campaign for his release in 1949 had failed. He died in Moscow. Much of his poetry has been translated into English by Taner Baybars: *Selected Poems* (1967) and the long poem *The Moscow*

Symphony (1952; tr. 1970). Curiously enough, although Hikmet wrote in free verse and was a most original poet, his influence has, at least until very recently, been less in Turkish poetry than that of Dağlarca, Veli, Rifat and Anday (qq.v.). A few continental critics have placed him beside Lorca, and his full influence has yet to be felt in a European context. Hikmet's language was modern in a way that Turkish poetry had not before seen. The greatest influence upon him was Mayakovsky (q.v.), whose 'stepped line' he early adapted to Turkish and used ever after to great effect.

Hikmet is both a compassionate and a humane poet. As his English translator Taner Baybars has pointed out, Marxism is not fundamental to Hikmet's poetry: 'his Marxist ideology' acted 'merely as a vehicle for the expression of deep *human* emotions':

> My wife!
> My good-hearted
> golden bee
> with eyes sweeter than honey
> why ever did I write to you
> they're pressing for my hanging?
> The trial has only just begun
> and they don't really pluck your head
>   like a turnip
>
> Come, now, take no note of all that.
> Such possibilities are far-fetched.
> If you have any money
>   buy me a pair of flannel pants
> the sciatic pains have started again.
> And do not forget
>   a prisoner's wife must always think
>   beautiful thoughts.
>   (tr. Taner Baybars)

The Moscow Symphony, first published in Sofia in 1952, was originally intended as part of a long unfinished epic on modern history, *Human Landscapes from my Country*. Jedvet Bey, a rich landowner, imagines himself witnessing the Second World War from the bottom of the sea. While, later, he listens to a symphony in his orange grove, three prisoners listen to it also. Again, this eloquent poem, full of beautiful and unsentimental feeling, is effective not for its implicit Marxism but for the golden nobility of mind of which it is the embodiment. Hikmet also wrote an important autobiographical novel, *The Romantics* (1962), which was translated into French, *Les Romantiques* (1964).

FAZIL HÜSNU DAĞLARCA (1914), who was a regular army officer from 1933 until 1950, and after 1960 a bookseller in Istanbul, has for many years been regarded by the younger Turks as a major poet. However, he writes too much, and some critics have come to despise him for his copious political journalism.

But this may be somewhat unfair to his actual achievement. He is, in contrast to Hikmet, an out-and-out individualist; he writes a gnomic kind of poetry, apparently facile, and often juxtaposing modern technological man with his cave-man ancestors. 'Whenever I love a woman/I feel deep in my heart/ That before me/God loved her'; 'The night/Is a huge bird/Which drags along/ A much bigger bird': these excerpts from a sequence still in progress do not suggest that his poetry has lost any of its epigrammatic, aphoristic power. His work has appeared in the Turkish issue of *Modern Poetry in Translation* (10, 1971) and in an American selection: *Selected Poems* (tr. T. S. Halman, 1969).

However, the real modernization movement in Turkish poetry, the revolution in attitude as opposed to style, was ushered in by ORHAN VELI (1914–51), together with OTKAY RIFAT (1914) and MELIH CAVDET ANDAY (1915). (It must be remembered that Hikmet's poems were banned; they did not appear in Turkey itself until after his death, although they circulated amongst a few people.) The three published a volume, *Bizarre* (1941), which revolutionized Turkish poetry. It was unpopular, but had a strong effect on intellectuals and students. These poets' ideas were further propagated by the magazine *Varlik*. The ideas were to purge Turkish poetry of nineteenth-century (and earlier) sentiment and metrics. Veli was a mostly satirical poet; Rifat also began as such, but has gone on to more experimental writing, as in the long poem *Perçemli Sokak* (1956), whose title means (roughly) 'Wilderness of bald pate from which a ray of consciousness [hair] emanates'. This has been translated by Taner Baybars (*Modern Poetry in Translation*, 10). In it Rifat attempts a kind of surrealistic poetry—he has written 'The art of using words which is poetry . . . cannot be restricted to images which are possible in reality and therefore meaningful'—that in translation reads familiarly:

> From the fountain of grapes
> Spills the green parrot's blood
> Grass-haired, grape-eyed. . . .

Anday has moved in the opposite direction: towards social realism. Nermin Menemencioğlu's translation of his long inwards-looking meditation on social injustice is in the Turkish number of *Modern Poetry in Translation*. A later development, in the late Fifties when Turkish intellectual life was forced by repression into silence and 'deep symbolism', was the 'meaningless poetry' of CEMAL SÜREYA (1931), who published his first book in 1958. This meant a great deal to Turkish readers at the time; but Süreya's own poetry (sel. tr. N. Menemencioğlu, *Modern Poetry in Translation*, 10) resembles a compost of Twenties influences more than a man speaking in his own voice.

Some other writers, including the realist novelists YAŞAR KEMAL (1922) and ORHAN KEMAL (1914–1970), have opposed the hermeticism of this movement— but may none the less have learned from it. The best short-story writer in modern Turkish was ALI SABAHADDIN (1907–49), murdered in Thrace by policemen posing as peasants. His novel about Anatolian life in the Thirties, *Kuyucakli Yusuf*

(1937), is also outstanding. Yaşar Kemal is the most internationally famous of all Turkish writers, for *Memed, My Hawk* (1955; tr. 1961) and *The Wind from the Plain* (1961; tr. 1962); both of these memorably depict the harsh lot of the Turkish peasant. Orhan Kemal wrote vividly of the poorest and most wretched Turkish citizens.

Western Minor Literatures

I

A number of the republics of which the USSR is comprised possess distinctive literatures of their own. In this section both the oriental and western republics are dealt with.

The independent Transcaucasian republic—consisting of Armenia, Georgia and Azerbaijan—was declared in 1918; by 1922 it had become the Transcaucasian Soviet Federated Socialist Republic; in 1936 this was once again divided into its three constituent parts. The Armenian literature is very ancient: the oral literature goes back at least four thousand years. Towards the end of the last century it came under influence from Europe; the historical novel was developed by Raffi (ps. Hakob Meliq-Hakobian, 1835–88) and poetry by HOVHANNES THUMANIAN (1869–1923), whose best known work is the epic *Arush*. Such plays as *Pepo* and *The Broken Hearth*, by GABRIEL SUNDUKIAN (1825–1912), remain popular. One of the more sophisticated of the novelists is AVETIQ ISAHAKIAN (1875–1957). Since 1936 the literature has been encouraged—but also controlled—by Moscow, which means in practice a dedication to socialist realism (q.v.). The only substantial writer, the novelist YAHAN TOTOVENTS (1889–1937), died in the Stalinist purges. He was educated partly in America, and after 1922 became Armenia's leading writer. He wrote poetry and drama, but his finest work is in the realm of autobiography and fiction. *Scenes from an Armenian Childhood* (1930; tr. M. Kudian, 1962) is a classic account of the old Armenia before the Turkish massacres of 1915. His novels are of a similarly high quality.

The most important Georgian writer of the past century has been ILIA CHAVCHAVADZE (1837–1907), who was educated in Russia. A leading radical and nationalist, he was murdered by agents of the Tsar. His satirical account of Georgian life in the novel *Do You Call this a Man?* (1863) transcends the regional by virtue of its indignation and savagery. One of his poems, *The Hermit*, was translated by M. Wardrop (1895).

The only important work to appear in Mongolia since it joined the USSR in 1921 is B. RINTCHEN's novel *The Dawn on the Steppes* (1951–5).

Ossetic literature—the literature of Ossetia, or Central Caucasus (part, of course, of the USSR)—had one distinguished poet in KOSTA KHETAGUROV (1859–1906). The Ossetic language, which has affinities with Persian, is spoken by about a quarter of a million people. Since the mid-Thirties Socialist realism (q.v.) has gained ascendancy over the strong nationalist tendencies inherent in the literature.

The literature of Byelorussia, which was incorporated into the USSR in 1917, with Minsk as its centre, has been quite astonishingly lively—even if no major writer has emerged. JANKA KUPALA (1882–1942) was an important peasant poet. (LWLF)

*

The development of the literature of Estonia was abruptly checked when Soviet Russia occupied it in 1940. (The Germans subsequently entered the country; the Russians returned in 1944, and cruel mass-deportations followed over the next five years.) From 1918 Estonia had been an independent state; today it remains the fifteenth state of the USSR, although not officially recognized as such by certain countries. Its ruling communist party has been permeated by Russians; but the Estonians themselves are a Finno-Ugric people whose language is related to Finnish. They have preserved their own literature throughout a difficult history, and although the policy of the Soviet Union has hardly encouraged them to continue doing so, there is a fairly vigorous ex-patriate literature (mostly in Sweden, but also in the U.S.A., and Canada).

In Estonia, as elsewhere, mid-nineteenth-century romanticism gave way, towards the end of the century, to a more realistic approach. The first consider-able figures in modern Estonian literature were the novelist EDUARD VILDE (1865–1933) and the lyrical poet and short-story writer JUHAN LIIV (1864–1913). Vilde began as a journalist and popular light novelist; rather unusually, he graduated to serious literature, and wrote his best novels in the last years of his life. He knew German well, travelled in the U.S.A., and for a time during the First World War was the Estonian minister in Berlin. He made his first impact on Estonian literature in the Nineties, with pointedly realistic stories and novels that were almost naturalistic in mood. *A Cup Full of Poison* (1893), a description of the miseries of the poor, is typical. Just before the beginning of the First World War he refined and improved his language considerably, wholly purging it of its journalistic elements. Between 1902 and 1906 he had written a long trilogy on mid-nineteenth-century Estonian life: *The War at Mahtra, When the Peasants of Anija Visited Tallinn* and *The Prophet Maltsver*. This is sociologically valuable, but the novels and plays of his final twenty years are psychologically and artistically superior. The best is perhaps *The Dairyman of Mäeküla* (1916); this is about an aristocrat's lust for his dairyman's wife, and ranks with the best novels of social realism of its time. Vilde, who took part in the 1905 Revolution and was for a time forced to live in Finland, fiercely resisted later manifestations of modernism.

Liiv, who died of consumption, and who was mentally ill—but with periods of coherence—for the last twenty years of his life, was a pioneer realist in his earlier poetry and fiction; but in the disturbed verse of his last period he reverted to romanticism, and was influenced by symbolism (q.v.). (AMEP)

Estonia's second and more decisive modernist stage is associated with the Young Estonia (*Noor Eesti*) movement, which lasted from 1905 until the middle of the First World War. Liiv, in his last poetry, had anticipated the attachment of this group to French symbolism; now the emphasis was on Western literature and on artistic autonomy. Most of the leading writers in the group were inclined to the left in politics; but all insisted on the independence of the writer as a first requirement for successful literature. Linguistic reform, involving a new flexibility and an approximation to common speech, gave the movement impetus. The leader of the group was the poet and scholar GUSTAV SUITS (1883–1956), who went to Sweden in 1944. Suits was a scholar deeply versed in nineteenth- and early twentieth-century French literature; his poetry is emotionally somewhat insubstantial, but in his search for Parnassian (q.v.) perfection of form he has unquestionably widened the range of modern Estonian poetry. 'We want more culture!' he cried: 'Let us remain Estonians, but let us also become Europeans.' (AMEP) His schoolfellow FRIEDEBERT TUGLAS (ps. FRIEDEBERT MIHKELSON, 1886–1971), who remained in Soviet Estonia and even took over Suits's old university post for a while, combines a basic realism with a strong and occasionally irritating *fin de siècle* colouring; his short stories contain much of his best work, although his novel *Felix Ormusson* (1915), the diary of an artist who entirely rejects reality, is more than a mere period piece.

Largely independent of the Young Estonia group, with which he is nevertheless usually associated, is the poet ERNST ENNO (1875–1934), to whom symbolist techniques came more easily and naturally than to any preceding Estonian poet. Although his mystical orientalism is shallow and dated, his poetry—sometimes reminiscent of Ady's (q.v.) in its combination of modern with folklorist themes and preoccupations—remains one of the most original to come out of modern Estonia. (AMEP)

The Young Estonia group was succeeded by a new one, calling itself *Siuru* (a fabulous fire-bird in Estonian folk-lore); this wished to carry the individualism and modernism of its predecessor further than Suits and Tuglas were prepared to take them. Its most gifted member was the poet MARIE UNDER (1883). Marie Under—another of the eminent Estonian writers who fled to Sweden at the time of the second Soviet annexation—began as a lush, self-absorbed neo-romantic; the influence of the German expressionist poets (q.v.), some of whom she translated, transformed her into a much more original and interesting poet. She is now justly regarded as the leading Estonian poet of the period of independence. Her first book, *Sonnets* (1917), showed mastery of form and energy; but its eroticism was conventional, and of course it shocked conventional people. Her best collections were published in the Twenties and early Thirties. *The Bleeding Wound* (1920) and *The Heritage* (1923) represented her efforts to restore a mind suddenly shattered by conflict between personal and social preoccupations. Her poetry did not regain its intensity until her old age. Her most recent book, *On the Brink* (1963), published in her eightieth year, contains poetry that is nearer to that of her years of crisis. The magnificent title poem, translated by Ants Oras—one of the most distinguished Estonian scholars and writers of the century, now in America—sums up its grave mood:

> Times rushed. Times whirled and whirred.
> Their breath stays, rank and eerie.
> A second time, a third.
> Brief lies of soothing years.
> Time to untime all times. . . .
>
> What was the last bird's query?
> I've rhymed my answering rhymes.
> Blind silence stares and sneers.

Child of Man (1955) is a selection of Marie Under's work in an archaic English translation by W. K. Matthews that is only just better than no translation at all. Ants Oras' excellent translations have not yet been collected. Marie Under is herself a distinguished translator into Estonian—she has translated *Doctor Zhivago*, many of Rilke's poems (qq.v.) and other works. (AMEP)

A. H. TAMMSAARE (ps. ANTON HANSEN, 1878–1940) was associated with Young Estonia and then, loosely, with *Siuru*, but his vigorous and versatile art transcends the limitations of both. He is the only modern Estonian novelist whose work has the kind of epic sweep possessed by such writers as Andrić (q.v.), and, to a lesser degree, Kazantzakis (q.v.). After naturalist beginnings, he came to maturity with his drama, *Judith* (1921), an exciting retelling of the Biblical story; but his masterpiece is the mammoth novel about Estonian peasant life in the latter part of the nineteenth century and the first few years of this: *Truth and Justice* (1926–33). No single work expresses with such accuracy and pathos the nature of Estonian society in this crucial period. The chief influences upon Tammsaare were Dostoievski and Hamsun (q.v.); Shaw (q.v.), whom he translated, helped him to develop a hard-headed and quizzical manner, which became apparent in the (understandably) pessimistic work of his last years. *Old Nick of Hell Valley* (1939) is a deeply melancholy allegory which Tammsaare casts in a folkloristic framework.

Other gifted writers in the *Siuru* group included HENRIK VISNAPUU (1890–1951) and AUGUST GAILIT (1891–1960). Visnapuu's life was cut short by his sufferings in German Displaced Person Camps after he had fled from Soviet Estonia (he died in the U.S.A. soon after he arrived). His first collection, *Amores* (1917), lush and sensual love poems, is perhaps his best, although his later patriotic poetry is effective and moving. Gailit, whose family was half Latvian, wrote fantastic tales, of which the most famous is the story-sequence *Toomas Nipernaadi* (1928), about a writer who wanders about the countryside and is taken for a beggar. In exile Gailit wrote a moving and tragic novel on the theme of the flight of those Estonians who decided to escape from the Russians by crossing the Baltic Sea: *Across the Restless Sea* (1951).

In the Thirties there was a violent, mainly leftist reaction against what appeared to some—in those politically uncertain and economically disturbed times—to be a dangerously insular attitude. But few of the writers in this

Literary Orbit group—as it was called—were particularly gifted. In purely literary terms, the movement represented a reversion to the realism and naturalism of the Nineties. The many naturalistic novels of AUGUST JAKOBSON (1904–63) read like what they are: clumsy and inferior imitations of Zola (q.v.). Better writers than Jakobson supported the Literary Orbit for a time, but left it when they perceived its crude dogmatism and lack of interest in literature except as an instrument of propaganda.

The plays of AUGUST KITZBERG (1856–1927) gained a new popularity at this difficult time: these (both naturalist dramas and comedies) are well made, witty and realistic, and deserve their status as classics of the Estonian theatre. Another successful Estonian playwright is HUGO RAUDSEPP (1883–1951), whose cynical and grotesque comedies—*The Demobilized Father* (1923), *The Idler* (1935)—became exceedingly popular. Raudsepp tried to please the Soviet authorities after 1944 by writing socialist realist comedies; but they put him in prison, where he died.

MAIT METSANURK (ps. EDUARD HUBEL, 1879–1957) was a critic of society, but in a more imaginative and psychologically viable manner than Jakobson managed in his naïve fiction. Metsanurk wrote a number of vivid novels about war, the best on the subject in Estonian. KARL AUGUST HINDREY (1875–1947), who studied in Russia, Germany and Paris, stands somewhat apart. He was a brilliant writer of children's fiction and of stories about animals; but his most seriously intended novels deal with the Estonian upper middle-classes. Hindrey's point of view is undisguisedly conservative, but his portraiture is not less accurate for that. His conservatism was not of the reactionary or selfish or stupid sort: it combined eccentricity with a certain gay cynicism. He wrote excellent historical fiction. Two more leading Estonian realists who established their reputations in the period of independence are now living in Sweden: AUGUST MÄLK (1900) and KARL RISTIKIVI (1912). Mälk, like so many Estonians, was first influenced by Hamsun (q.v.); his earlier fiction deals with the lives of fishermen and dwellers by the sea; in exile he has written a more complicated and psychologically subtle kind of novel, of which *The Vernal Soil* (1963) is outstanding. Ristikivi is a realist turned magic realist (q.v.): his earlier work is in the tradition of Vilde (q.v.), but *All Soul's Night* (1953) is more in the style of Hesse (q.v.). He has written a number of successful historical novels.

One of the most gifted poets of a generation younger than that of Marie Under is BETTI ALVER (1906), wife of HEITI TALVIK (1914–45), also a poet. Talvik was removed to Siberia and there died. Betti Alver was a leading member of the 'Magicians' (*Arbujad*) circle, which sought once more to revive a lyrical and ideologically independent poetry—most of all, perhaps, in order to have something to oppose to the meaningless chaos which, with every justification, they sensed as coming. She has remained in her own country, but was silent for twenty years; then, in the mid-Sixties, she was able to publish a retrospective selection and a volume of new poetry. The Soviets disapproved, but Marie Under was 'rehabilitated' nevertheless; her books sold out overnight. (AMEP) BERNARD KANGRO (1910) lives in Sweden, and in recent years has turned to the novel. In the Thirties he wrote a distinguished nature poetry; his novel *Tartu* (1962) is a vivid and valuable account of Estonian city life in the inter-war period. (AMEP) Other important poets include ARNO VIHALEMM (1911), ALEXIS RANNIT (1914)—now in the U.S.A.—UKV MASING (1903), characterized by the Estonian poet, critic and translator IVAR IVASK as a 'Blakean mystic surrealist', KALJU LEPIK (1920) and ILMAR LAABAN (1921)—both now in exile. Vihalemm is a satirical, mocking poet; Rannit is a skilful but self-conscious heir to the symbolists. Lepik, who has been influential in the Sixties in Estonia, seems to have gained something from Enno (q.v.), and has successfully integrated folkloric elements with surrealism. Estonia's only real surrealist, however, has been Laaban, a genuinely experimental, if rather trivial, poet. Ivar Ivask is perhaps the most attractive of all the modern Estonian poets in exile: he writes a poetry of wonder and gratitude that comes from deep within him, and successfully avoids the inconsequential.

Young Estonian writers of the Sixties and Seventies have produced some of the most interesting, courageous and exciting writing in the entire Soviet Union—which has not itself done anything to encourage them. Ivask has gone so far as to claim that PAUL-EERIK RUMMO (1942) and JAAN KAPLINSKI (1941) are of the calibre of Voznesensky (q.v.). Both are anti-dogmatic, intelligent and exuberant poets, and both typify the accelerating vitality of Estonian literature both within the USSR and outside it amongst the 70,000 exiles. Another manifestation of this development is the Estonian theatre of the absurd, which flourishes.

*

The languages of Latvia and Lithuania, the other two Soviet Baltic states, are related to one another but not to Estonian and Finnish: with Old Prussian and Curonian, both extinct, they form the Baltic branch of the Indo-European languages. Modern Latvian literature begins with the first realistic portrayal of peasant life, and the first Latvian novel, *The Times of the Surveyors* (1879), by the brothers REINIS KAUDZĪTE (1839–1920) and MATĪSS KAUDZĪTE (1848–1926). This is a classic. A spate of fiction influenced by naturalism (q.v.) followed; but at the same time work was begun on a gigantic collection of Latvian folklore. The socialistic New Current (*Jaunā strāva*) combined in the Nineties with a tendency to neo-romanticism to supplant the nineteenth-century National Awakening, of which *The Times of the Surveyors* had been the finest blossom. The chief representative of this period is the poet, dramatist and translator JĀNIS RAINIS (ps. JĀNIS PLIEKŠĀNS, 1865–1929). Rainis, whose work was supplemented by that of his talented wife, the poet ASPAZIJA (ps. ELZĀ ROZENBERGA-PLIEKŠĀNE, 1868–1948), had to leave Latvia in 1905 (he had been embroiled in the affairs of that year), and did not return until after independence in 1918; thereafter he held such positions as Minister of Education, and was a leading liberal. Rainis was undoubtedly a romantic at heart; but he wore no blinkers. The main theme of his plays and poetry is hatred of oppression. He was as hated by the Tsarist Russians (who arrested him in 1897) as by the Latvian supporters of Stalin. His tragedy *Fire and Night* (1905) remains one of the most eloquent of statements of the Latvian spirit. But his best work is to be found in his more personal poetic work, as in the charmingly entitled collection *Distant Feeling in a Blue Evening* (1903) in which he explores his nostalgia and loneliness: 'Year after year your solitude will become stronger,/ For friends will quit and you must climb alone. . . .' Rainis is regarded by some as Latvia's greatest poet; this is an exaggeration, for his genuine nobility of mind too usually manifests itself in pompous and dated language. But his technique is unsurpassed; and in the drama *Jacob and His Sons* (1924) he contributed a memorable expression of his own dilemma: whether to devote himself to art or to politics. No Latvian writer has greater historical importance. Not the least important aspect of Rainis' work is his use of folkloristic themes. His political preoccupations have to some extent vitiated his achievement; but his realization that a viable literature must come to terms with its time (as well as have roots in the authentic past) gives him an immense importance. (CLP) The early poetry of his wife, Aapazija (*Crimson Flowers*, 1897), puts emphasis on social justice and the rights of women, but at heart it is as romantic as her later work (*A Soul's Journey*, 1933). She also wrote drama, but less successfully than her husband.

JĀNIS PORUKS (1871–1911) wrote introspective and melancholy lyrics, and was a symbolist and a dreamer. Yet in his novella *The Fisher of Pearls* (1895) and in other works he introduced psychological realism (as distinct from social realism) into Latvian literature. RŪDOLFS BLAUMANIS (1863–1908), originally a business man, began writing fiction in German, but at the age of thirty abandoned it for Latvian. At the time of his early death he was the leading prose author. Blaumanis, whose delicate sensibility abhorred naturalism, was a most versatile writer: his few poems are memorable, his dramas and comedies of peasant life excellent, his novellas exquisitely sensitive and psychologically shrewd. He belongs by the side of Rainis as a pioneer; his literary achievement is probably greater.

It will be noted that all the outstanding Latvian writers of the first modernist phase had their roots firmly in the past. This applies, too, to KĀRLIS SKALBE (1879–1945), a unique allegorical writer who has quite properly been compared to Hans Andersen. He wrote much poetry, some short stories and seventy-six exquisite fairy tales. Unfortunately only a few of these last have been translated into English: *Pussy's Water Mill* (tr. W. K. Matthews, 1952). Skalbe's language is limpid, lucid and delicate; he hardly puts a foot wrong. To some critics his achievement, despite his modest aims, is as great as that of any Latvian writer. To a lesser extent ANNA BRIGADERE (1869–1933) shared his gift of making ancient themes meaningful in modern contexts.

Latvia's graduation to independence after the First World War inaugurated a new phase of international modernism. JĀNIS EZERIŅŠ (1891–1924) was one of the first expressionists, although in his later and better fiction he combined realism with 'decadence' in a series of effective tales: *The Bard and the Devil*

(1920), *The Street-Organ* (1923–5). This style, although less overtly based on French models, was successfully developed in the fiction of KĀRLIS ZARIŅŠ (1899–1947).

ALEKSANDRS ČAKS (ps. ALEKSANDRS ČADARAINIS, 1902–50) certainly has some claims to be regarded as Latvia's most considerable modern poet. He was deeply influenced by Mayakovsky (q.v.), and is regarded as seminal by all his younger contemporaries. He remained in Soviet Latvia. Čaks is an impassioned, urban poet (the city of his poetry is Riga); he has enormous gifts but is sometimes prone to diffuse them into prosy chaos. However, he remains the great naïve (q.v.) Latvian poet of his generation. Outstanding among his voluminous work is the long poem 'Life', in which he sees himself as an Orpheus-figure, a priest-poet. Čaks is the first thoroughgoing Latvian modernist, and it is entirely logical that new Latvian poets in exile should claim him as their ancestor.

Freedom for Latvian writers was effectually ended by the fascist *coup d'état* of 1934. Most writers found it expedient to abandon modern techniques and concentrate on patriotic themes; such novelists as Kārlis Zariņš turned to historical fiction. Since the Soviet annexation Latvian literature has mainly flourished in exile: although there is no lack of talent in Latvia itself, the desire for free expression of such poets as OJĀRS VĀCIETIS (1933) and IMANTS ZIEDONIS (1933) is largely frustrated, although the latter's collection *I Go Into Myself* (1968) shows signs of development. ZENTA MAURINA (1897), who now lives, like a number of other Latvian writers, in West Germany, made her reputation as a critic in Latvia itself; most of her novels have appeared since she went into exile. The best of these is the autobiographical trilogy consisting of *The Far Journey* (1951), *To Venture is Beautiful* (1953) and *The Iron Bolts Break* (1957). Zenta Maurina is a conventional and Christian but meticulous writer. She has been paralysed since an attack of polio in childhood. She now writes mainly in the German language, and has been officially honoured by West Germany.

Latvia's leading living playwright, MĀRTIŅŠ ZĪVERTS (1903) now lives in Sweden. He is a skilful and over-productive author, a facile symbolist whose plays, were they more widely translated, would prove popular in almost every Western capital.

Many of the leading Latvian novelists of the generation born in the first decade of the century went to the U.S.A. There is a selection from the excellent short stories of KNUTS LASIŅŠ (1909): *The Wine of Eternity* (tr. R. Speirs, 1957); he has also written novels. ANŠLAVS EGLĪTIS (1906) is one of the most versatile and gifted of living Latvian writers of fiction; he is also a poet. His best novels sympathetically satirize the world of artists and students: *The Hunters of Brides* (1940) and *Homo Novus* (1943), set in inter-war Latvia, are picaresque novels in the manner of the early work of Iris Murdoch or John Wain (qq.v.), but are less pretentious than the former and better executed than the latter.

Poets in exile include VELTA SNIĶERE (1920), a woman poet of surrealist tendencies now living in London, and VERONIKA STĒLERTE (1912), in Sweden, whose poetry is finely written although hardly unconventional in content.

More important are LINARDS TAUNS (ps. ALFRĒDS BĒRZS, 1922–63) and GUNARS SALIŅŠ (1924), the leaders of an American school of Latvian poets calling themselves 'Hell's Kitchen' (from the district of Manhattan so named), all of whom looked back to Čaks (q.v.) as their master. Tauns is a visionary, urban poet with flashes of Baudelarian power. Saliņš possesses the same intensity of style, although so far he has confined himself to less sensational themes.

Really modern techniques have found their way into Latvian prose through the autobiographical fiction of the late GUNTIS ZARIŅŠ and BENITA VEISBERGA. Zariņš' early work was quasi-surrealist; his last, best work is simpler but absorbs the tragic lessons of modernism. *Heroism's Song of Songs* (1962) and *Exile's Song of Songs* (1967) explore the history of Pudikis: his passivity in face of Nazi evil, and then his gradual reawakening, in exile, to his human responsibilities. Zariņš, cut off from his own people, killed himself in exile. Benita Veisberga, also in exile, has from the beginning experimented with the vernacular. *I, Your Gentle Lamb* (1968) is a remarkable first novel, an exploration of the kind of alienation that led to Zariņš' suicide.

*

The Tsarist policy of 'Russification' in the latter half of the nineteenth century, which included the banning of all books in Lithuanian (1865–1904), virtually determined the strong nationalist trend of Lithuanian literature in the period. Like Estonia and Latvia, Lithuania knew a brief inter-war independence; now it, too, is one of the states of the USSR. The Roman Catholic clergy, following the example of one of their bishops, began the practice of smuggling books into the country during the period of Russian oppression; this was fortunate for the development of Lithuanian literature, although indulged in by clergy not because of any love of freedom but because of their fears for the future of their religion.

Written Lithuanian literature did not begin before the mid-eighteenth century: pressure from neighbours had given little time to develop one. One of the first important nationalistic poems was written by ANTANAS BARANAUSKAS (1835–1902), yet another Catholic priest: his charming *The Grove of Anykščiv* (1858–9) consists of variations on the subject of a pine grove.

Baranauskas virtually gave up the writing of poetry after he took orders; his fellow-priest MAIRONIS (ps. JONAS MAČIULEVIČIUS-MAČIULIS, 1862–1932), later a professor of theology at Kaunas University, dominated Lithuanian poetry for two generations: his technique (he introduced accentual verse) laid the foundations of modern Lithuanian poetry; his subject-matter—the Lithuanian past and character—played a part in creating the short-lived independent Lithuania. He wrote heroic dramas. Perhaps inevitably, his work now seems dated; but his historical importance is unquestioned.

A writer of similar historical stature but greater intrinsic importance is the scholar VINCAS KRĖVĖ-MICKIEVIČIUS (1882–1954), usually known simply as Krėvė. He began as a poet, but his best work is in drama and, more particularly, fiction. Krėvė became Foreign Minister in 1940, but went into hiding in the same year, when he learned of Stalin's duplicity. Eventually he settled in the U.S.A. His outstanding early works are *The Legends of the Old Folks of Dainava* (1912), a classic exploitation of Lithuanian folk-lore, the short-story collection *Under a Thatched Roof* (1921), and several dramas. His finest work, the epic novel *The Sons of Heaven and Earth* (1954–63), planned in the early years of this century, is unfinished; this is one of the few modern works about the life of Christ that possesses true literary quality.

Of the Baltic literatures, it was the Lithuanian and the Finnish that were most susceptible to the ultra-modernistic movements such as Russian futurism (q.v.) and German expressionism (q.v.). Nothing in Estonia or Latvia was as *avant garde* as the poet KAZYS BINKIS' (1893–1942) magazine *Four Winds*, after which a Lithuanian movement was named. Unfortunately it produced no writer of major talents. Distinct from this, and longer lasting, was the leftist 'Third Front' circle, the 'generation of independence'.

The most important members of this group were the woman poet SALOMEJA NERIS (1904–45) and the novelist PETRAS CVIRKA (1909–47), an honest social realist with a genuine satiric edge. Other writers were more loosely associated with it. BERNARDAS BRAZDŽIONIS (1907) continued the symbolist tradition developed by the mystical VYDŪNAS (ps. VILIUS STORASTA, 1868–1953), whose most popular work was the tragic drama *The World on Fire* (1928), and by JURGIS BALTRUŠAITIS (1873–1944), who began by writing in Russian but whose poems in Lithuanian, dating from 1930, attain quite an impressive technical level. Brazdžionis was an even more thoroughgoing symbolist, nominally a Christian but funadamentally a Platonist yearning for a lush world of ideals. JONAS AISTIS (ps. KOSSU ALEXANDRAVIČIUS, 1904), now living in the U.S.A., is the most original of modern Lithuanian poets: he has devoted himself to personal themes (and has signally failed when he has tried his hand at patriotic verse, as he understandably did while witnessing, from America, the assimilation of his country into the USSR), and has a style and manner entirely his own. His first book appeared in 1933; much of his best poetry is collected in *My Sister Struggle* (1951).

ANTANAS VAIČULAITIS (1906), also now in America, is the leading Lithuanian prose writer of his generation. He made his name with the novel *Valentina* (1936), a sensitive study of a girl who is too emotionally delicate to choose between the man she loves and the man to whom she is indebted. Vaičulaitis has since concentrated on delicate and evanescent short stories. Some of these are fantasies, others are about animals; in the best, nominally realistic tales of country life, an autonomous world of nature almost takes precedence over the human world.

The native Lithuanian genius has of course suffered under Soviet dictation— as any writer suffers under any dictation—but it has done so possibly less than that of any of the other recently created states of the USSR. JUOZAS GRŪSAS (1901) has been able to write plays nearer to the Western idea of the absurd (q.v.) than perhaps any other writer; and socialist realism (q.v.) has not prevented Lithuanian poets from looking back to the example of VYTAUTAS MAČERNIS (1920–45), whose attitudes were profoundly modernistic, even to the point of justifying the frequent description of him as an 'existentialist' (q.v.). The most talented poet in Soviet Lithuania is EDUARDAS MIEŽELAITIS (1919) whose communist verse is sincere but embarrassing; but his descriptive poetry is superior. Two important Lithuanian writers who went to America are the novelist and playwright ALGIRDAS LANDSBERGIS (1924) and the poet HENRIKAS RADAUSKAS (1910–70), regarded by some as Lithuania's finest poet yet. Landsbergis made his name with *The Journey* (1955), a subtle and satirical study of a Lithuanian immigrant to the United States, for which he drew upon much autobiographical material. In his plays, which have been performed throughout the U.S.A., Landsbergis has dealt with the situation of Lithuanians both in their own country and in America. Radauskas' first book was published in 1935; but it was after his exile that his poetry developed. Although indisputably a modernist, he is certainly the odd man out of modern Lithuanian poetry, since he cannot be assigned to any main trend. He tried to devote himself to that aspect of poetry that is art; but life and its anguish make themselves ironically present. Many of his poems have the quality of a series of paintings:

> In a room which has been dead for twenty years
> An old woman's shadow is yawning, turning an empty
> Coffee mill, the clock shows Sunday,
> The cuckoo fell silent, the guest was stabbed in the tavern.

It is not surprising that some of Radauskas' poems attracted Randell Jarrell (q.v.), and were translated by him.

*

Although a Ukrainian national literature—in the language known as Church Slavonic—goes back to the eleventh century, there was no writing in the Ukrainian vernacular—an East Slavic language, sometimes known as Little Russian, spoken by over forty million people, and with a dialect of its own called Ruthenian—until the late eighteenth century, when Ivan Kotliarevsky published his burlesque epic, *Eneyida*, in 1798. It was largely owing to Kotliarevsky's work that Ukrainia's national bard, still regarded as her greatest poet, Taras Shevchenko (1184–61), was able to fashion Ukrainian into a truly literary language. Shevchenko, who was not forced to deviate—either by strict imprisonment or bans on literary composition—from his commitment to freedom and justice, raised Ukrainian poetry to an international level. (UP)

Because of the Tsar Alexander II's ban on Ukrainian literature, the publication and development of realist literature—a reaction, as usual, to nineteenth-century romanticism—was seriously hindered; literary activity had to be transferred to Austrian Galicia. The most important Ukrainian realists were the poet and dramatist BORS HRINCHENKO (1863–1910), whose chief contribution was probably his compilation of a monumental Ukrainian dictionary (1907),

NECHUY (ps. IVAN LEVITSKY, 1838–1918) and, above all, IVAN FRANKO (1856–1916). Nechuy was the foremost naturalist (q.v.); influenced by Zola (q.v.), he wrote sensitively and never too dogmatically about peasants, factory-workers, fishermen and urban *literati*. The poet Ivan Franko is ranked as second only to Shevchenko—and is furthermore granted to have possessed greater learning and perhaps more purely artistic capacity; since, too, he was an important novelist and scholar, Franko is actually a more versatile writer than Shevchenko. He suffered three periods of imprisonment for his activities on behalf of his country. His rejection of Christianity did not always make his position easier with his supporters. In his fiery personality Franko combined elements of Byronic romanticism with scientific and psychological realism; the general tendency of his work, however, is in its context realistic. Although no Christian, he was undoubtedly the voice of his people—that tenth of the Ukrainian population living under the Austro-Hungarian empire. Much of his early fiction, a representative sample of which is contained in *Boa Constrictor and Other Stories* (1878; tr. F. Solasko, 1957), is naturalistic in a romantic manner: dwelling enthralledly—and with genuine power—on the corrupt capitalist system and its results. Another excellent novel that has been translated is *Zakhar Berkut* (1882; tr. T. Boresky, 1944). It is as a poet, however, that Franko excels. He is at once lyrical and realistic; in *Moses* (1905; tr. W. Semenyna, 1938; UP; tr. P. Cundy, *Selected Poems*, 1968) he presents himself as a Byronic national leader at odds with the prejudices of his own followers as well as with the tyranny of their oppressors. This remarkable poem is as memorable for its romantic egotism as for its intelligence. *Mickey the Fox* (1892), a gay animal epic loosely based on *Reynard the Fox*, is probably his crowning achievement: in it Franko comes closer to an examination of the complexities of his own nature.

After 1905 Lithuanian literature became freer to develop in its own way, and the period of symbolism and artistic self-sufficiency set in; elements in Franko's work had anticipated it. The outstanding prose writer of this period was MYKHAYLO KOTSYUBINSKY (1864–1913), who began as a realist in the manner of Nechuy (q.v.), but whose later works share the expressionism (q.v.) and semi-psychoanalytical approach of Strindberg, Hamsun and Kotsyvbinsky's own compatriot, the short-story writer VASYL STEFANYK (1871–1936), a master of compression who confined his attention to the peasantry. Kotsyubinsky's best book is his gripping and accurate portrayal of peasant life, *Fata Morgana* (1903–10). There was no outstanding poet, but LESIA UKRAYINKA (ps. LARISSA KOSACH-KVITKA, 1871–1913), who wrote competent popular verses, was the author of a number of remarkable closet-dramas on historical themes; these, which include *Cassandra*, *The Stone Guest* and *The Orgy*, are extremely original and unusual in mood and language. There is an English translation of *The Babylonian Captivity* (1903) by C. E. Bechhofer in *Five Russian Plays* (1916).

The Soviet Russians at first put no bar on Ukrainian literary self-expression; the folk element was no longer emphasized, since it was felt that Russia was no enemy but, instead, the head of a communist federation within which the

Ukraine would possess autonomy. But with Stalin and the development of socialist realism (q.v.) any attempt to foster a spirit of independence was lost. The communist but strangely nationalist organization calling itself VAPLITE, led by MYKOLA KHVYLOVYI (1893–1933), courageously resisted Stalin's dictates, as did other smaller groups. But at the beginning of the Thirties, in the now notorious purges, over one hundred writers were murdered; Khvylovyi was driven to suicide. Thus the brilliant innovatory writer PAVLO TYCHYNA (1891–1967), the most gifted since Franko, was reduced from a unique revolutionary poet to an obedient producer of conformist party verse of no literary interest whatever. (UP) Khvylovyi himself began as a poet, but his finest work is his fiction of the Twenties, which reflects his complex feelings upon realizing that Stalin was a traitor to communism as well as an enemy of Ukrainian self-expression.

MAXIM RILSKY (1895–1964) stands in complete contrast: he cultivated a Parnassian (q.v.) perfection of form and a deliberate aloofness—both from nationalism and from socialist realism. It is said that Stalin would have had him shot, but that Krushchev (who played a leading role in the Ukrainian purges) personally protected him. He was in any event imprisoned in 1931, and his works banned; he emerged a 'good communist' (of the Stalinist type), but a less good poet. Rilsky's work has been somewhat overvalued in the West, for the content of his deliberately neo-classical poetry is in fact almost negligible; but his technical resources, within the tradition, were enormous, and those who call him a master of the language—especially in his translations from Voltaire, Shakespeare, and others—do not exaggerate. (UP)

The leading futurist, a prolific poet, was MYKHAILO SEMENKO (1892–1939), who studied neurology before 1914 at St. Petersburg; a tireless experimenter, his poetry is more 'modern' in appearance than that of Tychyna (q.v.); amidst the confusion something of charm and originality emerges, although he has not the substance of his symbolist contemporary. Semenko, an anarchist, was as paranoiac as Breton (q.v.) about his futurist and constructive movement: eventually every member of his group deserted him. He was exiled to Siberia, where he died. (UP)

The Ukraine has had one dramatist of genius in this century; he was deported in 1954 by Stalin and died eight years later, at the age of fifty, in a Siberian concentration camp. MYKOLA KULISH (1892–1942) was an expressionist who gained fame with 97 (1924) and then with *Narodny Malakhiy* (1929), in which he portrayed a Don Quixote figure in modern Ukrainian society. He worked with the director Les Kurbas, who built up the modern Ukrainian theatre; Kurbas was another of Stalin's victims. Kulish's only successor worthy of note has been OLEXANDER KORNIICHUK (1910), a highly skilled dramatist but a slavish socialist realist who all too often falls into the facile and silly rhetoric that pleases only semi-literate communist bureaucrats.

The most popular of the poets in the Stalinist period was VOLODYMYR SOSYURA (1898–1965), who wrote simple but effective lyrical verse in praise of the Revolution; he managed to survive by adapting his verse to Party requirements, although during the Second World War he got himself into serious trouble for writing a too patriotic poem, 'Love Ukraine' (1942). Sosyura is a simple soul; the incautious love of country that bursts forth from time to time in his poetry suggests that the abjectness of his apologies for it was sincere: a result of his belief that the Party really does know best. He had little art, but a true lyrical gift. (UP)

MYKOLA BAZHAN (1904) started as a disciple of Semenko; severe Party criticism caused him to take up socialist realism (it has to be remembered that the alternative to this course was probably not silence but slow death in one of Stalin's arctic concentration camps). Since then he has done his best: Bazhan is— or was—an arch-intellectual, and is fundamentally a more serious poet than the unstable Semenko. His inability to develop freely has been a tragedy for Ukrainian poetry. His important futuristic poem, 'The Blind' (1930), could not be published in the USSR. (UP)

The most effective of the socialist realist prose writers is OLES HONCHAR (1918), whose short stories remain within the allowed limits without losing their tenderness, psychological accuracy and lyricism of description. The most interesting poet of the younger generation is IVAN DRACH (1936); his freedom to write in a genuinely modern style suggests that conditions in the Sixties have improved.

II

Spain has three minority literatures, Basque, Galician and Catalan. The third is, of course, by far the most substantial. Galician is a romance language, probably most properly now regarded as a dialect of Portuguese (not of Spanish, who call Galician *Gallego*). In the middle ages there was a fine body of poetry in Galician; then the literature lapsed, until revived in the universally national-istic nineteenth century. The greatest Galician writer of this time is the poet Rosalía de Castro (1837–85), who also wrote in Castilian; her epoch-making *Galician Songs* appeared in 1863. Rosalía de Castro had been anticipated in manner and technique by EDUARDO PONDAL (1835–1917), who was less gifted but nevertheless a regional poet of some distinction. Pondal's chief book of poetry (his first was mostly in Castilian) was *Complaints of the Pines* (1866). CURROS ENRIQUEZ (1851–1908) should be mentioned as an idealogue who exercised much influence. Pondal's poetic regionalism has been continued most notably by A. NORIEGA VARELA (1869–1947).

From 1906, with the foundation of a Galician academy at Galicia's chief city of Corunna, the leading Galician writers tried to create a genuinely national literature that would not be regional but truly European in scope and spirit. No major writer emerged, but some poetry and fiction of quality was written. With the advent of fascism all this was stopped, since it smacked to

Franco of 'separatism'. Now literature in Galician, building on foundations laid by the poet MANUEL ANTONIO (1901–28), is once again beginning to develop; leading figures are the poets AQUILINO IGLESIA (1909) and D'AUGUSTO MARIA CASAS (1906).

*

The Basque people live in the foothills of the Western Pyrenees, both in France and in Spain. About 800,000 people speak the language, which is Indo-European but has not convincingly been related by linguists to any other known language; more than three-quarters of the Basque people live in four provinces of Spain. The first Basque anthology was published in the late Seventies. Interest in creating a Basque literature increased only after the loss of autonomy in the Spanish civil wars of the late nineteenth century. Sabino de Arana Goiri (1865–1903) was the leader of the nationalist movement, which gave writers horizons not previously dreamed of. Before the successful fascist rebellion of 1936 the theatre had enjoyed some popularity; the most distinguished dramatist was TORIBIO ALZAGA. The best known novel was *Garoa* (1912), a portrait of a Basque village, by DOMINGO AGUIRRE (1864–1920). But the best of Basque literature lies in its poetry, as exemplified in the work of XABIER DE LIZARDI (ps. JOSÉ MARÍA AGUIRRE, 1896–1933) and ORIXE (ps. NICOLÁS ORMAECHEA, 1888–1961). Xabier de Lizardi was a gifted and highly original lyricist. Orixe, his friend, was a scholar and translator as well as poet. His greatest poetic achievement is the long poem on the Basque people, *Enskaldunak*, which he wrote in the mid-Thirties but did not publish until 1950. Both these poets repudiated modernism. Other important Basque poets are OXOBI (ps. JULES MOULIER, 1888–1958) and JON MIRANDE (1927), one of the first to exhibit modernist tendencies. The leading living novelist, who lives in exile, is the realist JUAN ANTONIO IRAZUSTA.

*

The Catalan language is intimately related to Spanish and to Provençal; it is spoken by some six million people living in Catalonia, Andorra, the province of Valencia, Rousillon (in France), the Balearics and a small part of Sardinia. The cultural centre is Barcelona. The literature, after a distinguished medieval phase, fell into decay between the sixteenth and the nineteenth centuries; the revival, called the *Renaixença* or Renaissance, was associated with romantic nationalism and political radicalism. It is usually dated from 1877, when the poem *Atlantis*, by the learned priest JACINTO VERDAGUER (1845–1902), was published; this is an energetic and technically adept epic of prehistory. Naturalism flourished in the novels of NARCÍS OLLER (1852–1930)—Zola himself drew attention to them in France—and in the successful plays of ANGEL GUIMERÀ (1849–1924); one of the most famous is *Marta of the Lowlands* (1896; tr. 1914). The *modernista* movement (q.v.) reached Catalonia at a peculiarly appropriate time: in the early years of the century the literature flourished as it has not done either before or since. That Picasso and Casals came out of this period is an indication of its nature. The leading theorist was the painter, novelist and playwright SANTIAGO RUSIÑOL (1861–1931), nearly all of whose popular works exist in Spanish versions. Rusiñol was most gifted as a painter (his paintings of Spanish gardens achieved great fame), but his often satirical novels and his many dramatic works, particularly *The Mystic* (1904), on the life of Verdaguer, have much merit.

The leading poet of this period is JOAN MARAGALL (1860–1911), born in Barcelona, who was in close touch with the Spanish 'Generation of '98' (q.v.). Maragall is the first Catalan modernist and the first to bring ideas of Nietzsche (q.v.) into Catalan poetry; he translated Goethe into Catalan. His work was much admired by his friend Unamuno (q.v.). Maragall often delivered himself of highly revolutionary remarks (he claimed to feel the presence of God more intensely in a church set on fire by revolutionaries than in a fashionable one); but at heart he was no more than a moderate. His theory of poetry is a danger-ous one: absolute spontaneity must be observed at all costs. In practice he worked harder than such a theory demands; his poetry, neo-romantic but modernist in tendency, is both direct and melodious. His 'Ode to Barcelona' remains one of the finest evocations of the city.

Meanwhile something more conservative was going on in the island of Mallorca, partly in resistance to these manifestations of modernism. The so-called Mallorcan school was started by MIQUEL COSTA I LLOBERA (1854–1922), who was born at Pollenca. Costa i Llobera became a priest at the age of thirty-four. He rejected regionalism and symbolism (q.v.) in favour of a hard, classical style that aimed at what was called 'Mediterranean clarity'. The most famous and best of his collections is his *Poems in the Style of Horace* (1906); this is one of the most skilful of the neo-classical books of poetry that appeared in Europe at this time; it has had great influence, and has been widely trans-lated.

In Catalonia itself JOSEP CARNER (1884–1969), born in Barcelona, having begun as a modernist, started during the first years of the century to concentrate on the acquirement of a classical style. His first poems were heavily symbolist (q.v.) in manner; they introduced new poetic forms into Catalan, and influenced the development of the language. Carner may be described as a conservative modernist; but his primary importance is as a stylist. He is a more interesting poet than either Maragall or Costa i Llobera: the love poems of *Useless Offering* (1924) are among his most original work. He has also written fiction and criticism. Carner was a diplomat; caught in Brussels by the fascist revolt, he never returned to Spain; he taught at universities in Mexico and Brussels. There is a selection of his poetry in English: *Poems* (tr. P. Hutchinson, 1962). For many years he represented the nerve and essence of the Catalan literary spirit. Most conspicuous among those poets who have sought to cultivate Carner's classicism are the satirist GUERAU DE LIOST (ps. JAUME BOFILL I MATES, 1878–1933), who has been compared to Jammes (q.v.), CARLES RIBA BRACONS (1893-1959)—*Poems* (tr. J. L. Gili, 1964)—and MARIANO MANENT (1898).

JOSEP SEBASTIÀ-PONS (1886–1962), a professor at Toulouse University and a native of Roussillon, was an elegant and skilled poet.

Surrealism and the other *avant garde* movements of the Twenties flourished in Catalan literature, but made relatively little impact on its conservative nature— until after the Second World War, when there has been some renewed activity. The *avant garde* writers of the Twenties and early Thirties called themselves the Sitges group (Sitges is a popular Catalonian seaside resort). JOSEP VICENS FOIX (1894) is a surrealist; his poetry has been usefully compared to the paintings of the Catalan artist Joan Miró.

All Catalan literary activity was stopped with the fascist uprising, which resulted in a period of (so far) over thirty years of tyranny for the whole of Spain. This has been most keenly felt by the Catalan and Basque peoples. Franco, the most personally vindictive of the dictators, had aged Catalan writers murdered; whole libraries of books in Catalan were burned; all teaching of Catalan was forbidden; even now the literature is not encouraged, and the Barcelona periodical *Destino*, which devotes much space to Catalan literary developments, is written in Castilian. But several established writers are again active, in Catalonia as well as in exile; and new names have come forward. Modernism is represented by the woman poet JOAN PERUCHO (1920), who writes an abstract verse that could fairly be described as 'concrete' (q.v.); SALVADOR ESPRIU (1913) is a pungent satirist. Two of Espriu's best collections are *Songs of Ariadne* (1949) and *Mrs. Death* (1945–51). He is also an important novelist; both *Doctor Rip* (1931) and *Ariadne* (1935) are innovatory in technique. JOSEP PALAU (1917), an exile, is regarded by most critics as the most gifted of living Catalan poets. *Poems of an Alchemist* (1952) collected the best of his poetry written between 1936 and 1950. PERE QUART (ps. JOAN OLIVER) is a fanciful, often charming but sometimes sinister, satirist.

Much Catalan fiction has been published, but only a small proportion of it possesses quality. Oller (q.v.), as already noted, introduced naturalism in such novels as *The Butterfly* (1882) and *Gold Fever* (1890); he was a crude but sometimes powerful writer, some of whose novels may be found in English versions. VICTOR CATALÀ (ps. CATALINA ALBERT I PARADIS, 1873–1952), born in the little fishing port of L'Escala, is a conventional but competent and sensitive realist; her first great success was *Solitude* (1905; tr. 1906). Her most distinguished follower in the well-made, pessimistic novel of peasant realism was PRUDENCIO BERTRANA (1867–1941), who began as a painter. *The Shipwrecked* (1907) was his first book to gain attention.

However, the most interesting and varied period of the Catalan novel came between the two world wars. It was in these years that the genius of JOAQUIM RUYRA (1858–1939) came to full fruition. Ruyra had published his first book, *Seascapes and Coppices* (1903), at the age of forty-five; he then remained silent for sixteen years, trying to recover from a serious illness. *Cone of Roses* (1920) and *In the Flames* are his best books. ALFONS MASERE wrote a penetrating study of neurotic people in *Zodiac*; this has not been repeated on the same scale. JOSEP PLA (1895) is the most shrewd and skilful portrayer of Catalan society: *Spring*

Nocturne (1935) is an early example. This, which embodies some interesting experiments with time-sequence, is one of the finest of all novels in Catalan. It is a satirical portrait of the life of a small market town, in the form of a series of vignettes of the guests at a banker's reception. Pla has published fiction since the advent of Franco.

Two modernists to have attracted attention in the post-war recent period are MANUEL DE PEDROLO and JORDI SARSANEDES, both of whom have been compared to Kafka. Sarsanedes achieved fame with his prose-poems collected under the title *Mites* (1954). The contemporary novel in Catalan seems at present to be influenced by Spanish *'tremendista'* (q.v.) fiction rather than by newer developments.

The Catalan theatre of this century has not been distinguished. Since Guimera and Rusiñol (qq.v.) the one outstanding name in the Catalan theatre has been JOSEP MARIA DE SAGARRA (1894). He began as a graceful and highly thought of lyric poet; he turned to poetic drama in 1918. With his verse plays —notably *Holy Thursday* (1919), *The Student and the Maid* (1921) and *Rosebush in Bloom* (1935)—Sagarra became a central figure in Catalan literature. He has also written prose plays, farces, novels—and long poems. Sagarra's theatre is conventional and superficial, but skilful and verbally delightful. He has been called the chief representative of the 'natural' as distinct from the 'intellectual' school of modern Catalan literature. He fell foul of the communists in Barcelona in 1936, and fled to France; he returned in 1941, but not as any friend of Franco's. He has been active since the end of the Second World War, but not all his writings have been published, since they have not been acceptable to the fascist censorship. He has translated the whole of Dante and of Shakespeare into Catalan.

III

The Breton language, which was brought to Brittany from the west of England (its closest affinities are with the now extinct Cornish; of living languages it is closest to Welsh), is spoken by about a million people. There are four major dialects and a number of minor ones. Like so many other small literatures that had fallen into desuetude in the seventeenth and eighteenth centuries, Breton literature enjoyed a revival during the course of the nineteenth century. This revival leaned heavily on Brittany's rich Celtic folklore (it has much in common with that of Wales); Breton authors and scholars concentrated on the establishment of a standard language. The tendency in the modern period has been to eschew folklore: to establish a literature that does not depend on the past. The fact remains that much published in Breton is, even now, based on folklore material, or imitates it. It is somewhat difficult to get away from it. Modern Welsh literature has had some influence since the beginning of the century, but not perhaps on the more important or best of the modern writers.

The great problem besetting all serious Breton writers has been one of language. All Bretons can read their own language; only a few can write it. It is very easy to fall into a lifeless artificiality; not many writers have entirely avoided this. When in 1941 a new standardized spelling was adopted, not all writers would accept it: 'there were', writes the Breton critic Pierre Trépos, 'in the mid-twentieth-century two literatures differing in spelling, vocabulary and outlook'. In 1951 Breton was given a place in the state schools, an innovation that should do much for the literature. Nevertheless, the French government, much to its discredit, has not become friendly towards the Breton language.

Undoubtedly the most famous modern Breton poet is YANN BER KALLOC'H (1888–1917), who died in the First World War. His melancholy and graceful poems were collected in 1921, with a French translation, in *Kneeling*. The dominant figure, however, in the earlier phase has been the playwright TANGUY MALMANCHE (1875–1953), who wrote in both verse and prose. Malmanche has been compared to Claudel and Synge (qq.v.), and his play *Gurvan, the Strange Knight* has been described as the greatest masterpiece of Breton literature. Many of his plays were given in French translation. The prose-writer who showed most promise, JAKEZ RIOU (1899–1937), died young. The best fiction of Riou, who also wrote *Nomenoe-oe!*, a remarkable nine-act burlesque of a history drama that contains much extravagant but none the less real poetry, is in his collection of short stories entitled *The Virgin's Herb* (1934): these stories of country life combine tenderness with a disturbing pessimism. The painter XAVIER DE LANGLAIS (1906) wrote a remarkable novel of the future, *The Island of the Wheel*. YOUENN DREZEN (1899), the exact contemporary and close friend of Riou, is among the few really distinguished modern novelists. His style and manner stand in sharp contrast to the gentle Riou's: he is harsh, earthy and uncompromisingly realistic. The best of his novels is reckoned to be *Our Lady of the Carmelites* (1942). He is also a talented playwright.

A central figure in Breton literature since the mid-Twenties has been the poet and novelist ROPARZ HÉMON (1900). Hémon, who now lives in Ireland (where he still writes, however, in the Breton language), founded in 1925 Brittany's most important and influential magazine: *North-West (Gwalarn)*. It was in the pages of this journal that the first serious effort was made to break away from folk-lore and to establish a truly international literature that would not be slavishly dependent upon French conservatism. Many translations appeared in its pages: the writers chosen (Yeats, Synge) reflect Hémon's lifelong interest in Ireland and its folklore, and his determination to give the Breton language a new flexibility. Hémon himself is distinguished as novelist and poet. His novels describe, sometimes satirically, the life of the people of his native town of Brest; his poems, some of them long, often deal with ancient Irish themes.

Other younger writers who deserve mention are MAODEZ GLANNDOUR (1909), a gently religious and meditative poet, and RONAN HUON (1922), whose verse is less traditional in form and content. These two were involved in the movement against acceptance of the 1941 standardization: they aimed at a minority audience.

A more popular writer, PIERRE HÉLIAS (1914), led the movement for acceptance of standardization; it was hoped that, through the magazine *Fame (Brud)*, the Breton public could be gradually educated in literary taste. This has not come to pass. Hélias is a skilled writer of radio plays (over 300) and stage plays as well as a novelist. JARL PRIEL (1885–1965) wrote in French for much of his life; but he finally turned to Breton, producing a stream of interesting plays, novels and autobiographical works. Breton literature is now as lively as it was before the Second World War; the writer of international stature that it has hoped for throughout the century has not appeared—Malmanche is the only one who has come near to it; but the environment is now less provincial than it has ever been before.

*

The literature that is generally known outside France as Provençal (the term in French applies to the area of the Basses-Alpes and Bouches du Rhône) is more appropriately called Occitan: this term embraces the Limousin, Languedoc and Gascon dialects, as well as the Provençal. The heyday of Occitan literature was of course in the Middle Ages, when the Troubadour poets flourished; its nineteenth-century revival was largely the work of one man of boundless energy and undoubted genius: FRÉDÉRIC MISTRAL (1830–1914), who shared the 1904 Nobel Prize with the Spanish playwright Echegaray (q.v.): this was awarded both for his own work and his efforts for a modern Occitan literature. In 1854 Mistral and six others founded the Félibrige at Avignon. This association set out to inspire a renaissance of Occitan literature (much support was given, too, to the revival of Catalan literature). It met with great success. A standard spelling and grammar were adopted; a magazine was started; a few years later a 'pan-Latinist' movement was instituted: this advocated a federation of Mediterranean countries. While some extremists wanted to separate from France, Mistral and most of his friends wanted only a federation with a virtually autonomous Provence ('We men of Provence, one flame', he wrote in his *Ode to the Catalans* of 1861, 'are frankly and loyally part of France, as you, the Catalans, are part of noble Spain. . . .'). Unfortunately the Félibrige, and to some extent Mistral himself, came for a time under the malign influence of the unhappy, deaf Charles Maurras (q.v.).

Mistral is unjustly ignored outside France. He had a noble nature, and he and his work represent Provence as no other man ever has. His poems, written in Provençal but (most of them) translated by him into French, have not all dated. He was a serene traditionalist; but in his work may be found one important element of modernism—an element that no cosmopolitanism can entirely efface: the regionalist spirit. 'Arise, Latin people!' he wrote, 'Under the canopy of the sun/The grapes are foaming in the vat:/God's wine will gush out.' Besides a considerable quantity of lyrical poetry of great vitality, Mistral wrote at least three long poems which are as successful as any epics of modern times. *Mirelle* (*Mirèio*, 1859; tr. H. Crichton, 1868; H. W. Preston, 1890; C. H. Grant, 1900) is the story of tragic love which established him: it was praised by Lamartine and made into an opera by Gounod. This is not poetry of the first order; but it is still poetry, and it is still enthralling: a story of two Provençal lovers incorporating both pastoral episodes of great charm and beauty and much Provençal folklore. With this poem Mistral refounded Provençal as a language. His two other great achievements in the difficult and defeating role of the narrative poem are *Nerto* (1878) and *Anglore* (*Lou Pouèmo dóu Rose*, 1897; tr. M. B. Jones, 1937). In addition to being the greatest Provençal poet of modern times, Mistral was a philologist of high standing: his huge dictionary of Provençal (*Tresor du Félibrige*, 1879–86) is a classic of erudition and knowledge of Provençal customs and history.

The name of ANTONIN PERBOSC (1861–1943) may yet be revived in Provençal literature. Mistral was a poet of international stature, but he was no modernist (rather, as I have mentioned, he embodies the spirit of that provincialism that is a so to speak reluctant element in modern literature); Perbosc was not of Mistral's calibre as a writer, but he was more than competent, and there was much point in his insistence upon the necessity of realism. He wrote good nature poetry, fiction and drama.

Since Mistral's time—it must be remembered that he died, an old man, on the eve of the First World War—Provençal literature has somewhat changed its aims. It can never lack a regional element; but the concerns of most of the writers are more the concerns of modern Western literature generally. Probably the most outstanding and intelligent of Mistral's successors, second only to him in reputation, was JOSEPH D'ARBAUD (1874–1950), whose mother had been an early member of the Félibrige (q.v.). D'Arbaud was regarded by Mistral himself as the best poet and novelist of his generation. For a long period he lived as a *ranchero* in the lonely and mysterious Camargue, of which he is the unchallenged laureate. His most original work is *The Beast of the Vaccares* (1924), about a strange and magical beast, half-human, half-animal, who represents the spirit of the Provençal past. D'Arbaud the novelist was regarded by most of his contemporaries as having done for Provençal prose what Mistral did for its poetry.

The poet SULI-ANDRIEU PEYRES (1890–1961) was from 1921 until his death a leading figure in Provençal literature. He founded the magazine *Marsyas*, in which he printed and encouraged young poets, in 1921; it ceased to appear with his death. Peyres was a modernist who refused to employ folklore, and, while recognizing the achievement of Mistral, rejected his (and d'Arbaud's) cultivation of the written (literary) as distinct from the oral (colloquial) language. One of the most individual of the contributors to *Marsyas* is GEORGES REBOUL (1901), rightly regarded as the first Provençal poet to employ surrealist (q.v.) techniques. Another intelligent and gifted member of the *Marsyas* group is PIERRE MILLET (1913), who has evolved the fascinating thesis that all recent Provençal poetry has originated in 'refusals': Mistral's to write of a 'real' (in the modern sense) Provence, d'Arbaud's to employ the colloquial, Peyres' to exploit folklore, Reboul's to use traditional techniques. . . . None of the latter three is or was a member of Félibrige, and all have actively opposed it; they and those of like mind—clearly they represent the modernist wing of contemporary Provençal literature—call themselves Occitan poets. It is likely that Provençal literature will benefit when a form of compromise is reached between them and the Félibrige.

IV

Those Swiss who write in the German, French or Italian language have been treated under their appropriate literature. But there are two other remarkably vigorous literatures in Switzerland: the Rhaeto-Romanic, or Rumansch (sometimes spelt Romansh), or Rhetian; and the Alamannic, or Swiss-German.

The Rumansch language is an ancient form of Latin-French, and was once spoken extensively throughout the Alps from Gotthard to Trieste. Now most of the Rumansch-speaking people, about one million, live in north-eastern Italy; there are some 55,000 people in Grisons, however, who speak a dialectical variant called Ladin. The literature of Grisons is decidedly provincial—but it is extraordinarily energetic, particularly in the realms of radio, television and theatre. The most gifted and important poet is ANDRI PEER (1921). Peer, who comes from the Engadine, is now a professor of French and Italian at the lycée in Winterthur. He has been influenced by modern French and Italian literature and by the poetry of his compatriot PEIDER LANSEL (1863–1943), who began the work—which he has continued—of purging Rumansch of clichés. The leading prose writer in Ladin is CLA BIERT (1920), whose *Only a Game* (1969), a collection of short stories, has appeared in English translation. Biert's prose reflects the Rumansch reality that can only be expressed in Rumansch language; but it is a reality that by remaining faithful to the locale, transcends it.

In Rumansch itself FLURIN CAMATHIAS (1871–1946) tried to imitate Mistral (q.v.) in creating a national epic. By far the most outstanding novelist is GIAN FONTANA (1897–1935): he wrote of urban life with true realism, and has made the most substantial cosmopolitan contribution to Rumansch literature. RETO CARATSCH (1899) is a leading satirist.

*

Some three-quarters of the Swiss people are taught the German language in their schools; but they speak various dialects of Swiss-German, which differs very considerably from what they are taught. Literature in this language has, for nationalistic and other reasons, been popular in Switzerland since the early nineteenth century. The arrival of Hitler (1933) even prompted a movement for the adoption of Alamannic as a fourth national language. The best writer in Alamannic has been RUDOLF VON TAVEL (1886–1934), historical novelist and short-story writer, who came from Bern; other writers have written effectively in other dialects, including the Basel poet and playwright DOMINIK MÜLLER (ps. PAUL SCHMITZ, 1871–1953) and the Thurgau author of comedies, ALFRED HUGGENBERGER (1875–1960).

V

In Great Britain most Welsh and Scottish writers prefer to write in English in order to reach an international audience; but a minority write in the Welsh and Gaelic languages.

Welsh literature has flourished in this century, and although no major writer has yet emerged, several deserve consideration. The poet and scholar JOHN MORRIS-JONES (1864–1929) was not creatively gifted; but through his philological work and his dictionary he has had a marked influence on the language of all writers in modern Welsh. ROBERT WILLIAMS PARRY (1884–1956) was the first to write effective free verse in the Welsh language. The chief figure in modern Welsh literature, however, and possibly the only one deserving of international attention, is undoubtedly SAUNDERS LEWIS (1893), who is poet, novelist and dramatist. Lewis, although a noted scholar and critic, is not altogether approved of by academic Welsh critics, who are as conservative as any in the entire world: he is an old-fashioned romantic, but he is also a savage satirist of contemporary Wales.

Few good novels have been written in Welsh; the best writer of short stories remains KATE ROBERTS (1891).

*

There are three writers in Gaelic, all poets, who deserve mention: SOMHAIRLE MACLEAN (1911), GEORGE CAMPBELL HAY (1915) and Ian Crichton Smith (q.v.), the best of whose work is, however, in English. Smith has written effective plays; Maclean and Hay write accomplished lyrics. Otherwise the 'Gaelic revival' consists of folk activities outside the scope of this book.

Yugoslav Literature

Yugoslavia came into being in 1918. It is one of the most heterogenous of small combinations in the world, and arose—like its literature—out of South Slav aspirations. There are two languages: Serbo-Croat and Slovenian, of which the first is the main one. The Serbs use the Cyrillic script, the Croatians and Slovenes the Roman. Important minorities speak Macedonian, Albanian, Hungarian, Rumanian, Italian, Bulgarian and Turkish. The first three of these produce literatures of some vigour. The three main religions are Orthodox (the religion of most Serbs), Catholic (Slovenes and Croats) and Mohammedan. The 'socialist realist' phase in Yugoslavia was less intense and more short-lived than in other communist countries—modernism, except for a few years immediately after Tito came to power in 1945, has flourished almost, if not quite, as it has wished.

The Croatian novel proper had been created by August Šenoa, who died in 1881, and whose social realism (laced with much Balkan romanticism) held sway over Croatian writers for some years after his death. EVGENIJ KUMIČIĆ (1850–1904) tried to outdo Zola (q.v.) and to expose the evils of society under Hungarian domination, but failed. His works have dated, and he can hardly be described as a true naturalist. *Madame Sabina* (1884), a sensational exposé of Zagreb society, is his most famous book.

The reaction against crude naturalism came in the Nineties in Yugoslavia, as elsewhere. The most distinguished Croatian writer of fiction to reflect this reaction was JANKO LESKOVAR (1861–1949), the author of two short stories and ten novellas. For the last forty-four years of his life he wrote nothing. Influenced by Turgenev, he was a sceptical pessimist—but his interest was in the psychology of man's interior struggles against fate rather than in the workings of fate, in the nature of his characters' passivity, not in the external causes of it. The best of his short novels is *The Shadows of Love* (1898): depressing, but written with sad delicacy and the psychological accuracy that he brought into Croatian fiction. Another Croatian whose work is also reminiscent of Turgenev's is KSAVER ŠANDOR DJALSKI (ps. L. BRATIĆ, 1854–1935), who began as a Balzacian realist-naturalist; later he turned to mysticism. He never bettered the early stories collected in *Under Old Roofs* (1886) and *Sad Stories* (1888).

The Serbian ŠIMO MATAVULJ (1852–1908) was a gentler and more convincing exponent of naturalism than Kumičić. He is detached, but has humour, compassion and elegance of style. *Bakonja fra Brne* (1892), about life in a Dalmatian Catholic monastery, is his masterpiece—and a Yugoslav humorous classic. He translated the French novelists from whom he had learned most: Zola, Merimée Maupassant. His contemporary STEVAN SREMAC (1855–1906) resembles him in certain respects, except that he is less literary and more provincial in style. He was a regionalist—his novels are mostly set in the town of Nis, where he taught—but not one who is only of interest to the readers of his region. The story 'Ivko Fair' (1895) is another humorous classic. In Sremac's fiction is to be found the most authoritative portrait of provincial Serbia during the years around 1900. VJENCESLAV NOVAK (1859–1905), a gifted musician, was a closer adherent of naturalism, and attributed moral decay to heredity. But his indignation at social conditions in his native Dalmatia outweighed his philosophy of life.

Svetolik Ranković, who died in 1899 at the age of thirty-six, was Leskovar's Serbian counterpart. BORISAV STANKOVIĆ (1876–1927) stands somewhat apart: born in the town of Vranje, in an area under Turkish rule until the very year of his birth, he never overcame his nostalgia for its oriental and patriarchal customs. He was undoubtedly wary of progress and 'civilization', and not without reason; but there is some truth in the accusation that he was insensitive to poverty and the social ills which accompany it. His scope is thus limited. However, he was a major writer, both in his drama *Koštana* (1907)—about a gipsy girl forced to marry a rotter—and in the novel *Sophka* (1911; tr. A. Brown, 1932), which traces the degeneration of a wealthy family, and describes the ordeal of the heroine, who is forced to marry a child and has to fight off his father's advances. It seems likely that Andrić (q.v.) learned from Stanković.

The outstanding Slovene writers of this period were Josip Jurčič (1844–81), who introduced the realistic novel into Slovene literature, and the poet JOSIP STRITAR (1836–1923), a weak poet but vigorous satirist and influential critic: he helped to educate Slovenes in foreign literatures, and popularized the work of the poet France Prešeren (1800–49), who stands to Slovene poetry as Petőfi (q.v.) does to Hungarian or Eminescu (q.v.) to Rumanian. Janko Kersnik, who died in 1897, reflected in Slovene fiction the same preoccupations as Leskovar and Ranković: his temperament may be described as 'naturalist', but his real interests lay in psychology. In the work of IVAN TAVČAR (1851–1923) we find consolidated all the advances made in fiction, together with a sensitivity to social problems. Novels such as *Ivan Savel* (1876) and *The Story of Visosko* (1919) give a memorable and accurate portrait of Slovene life from social and psychological points of view. But the finest Slovene writer of fiction was IVAN CANKAR (1876–1918), the first edition of whose volume of poetry, *Erotica* (1899), was bought up by the Bishop of Ljubljana. . . . Cankar, who drank hard and had debts, spent much of his life in Vienna. He wrote according to a 'conspiracy theory' of history that would have seemed less crude to an inhabitant of the Balkans in 1900 than it now does to us—the decent majority are pictured as exploited by an evil minority, served by coward-lackeys—but his fiction achieves great power, and his caricatures of tyrants, officials and their cringing servants are often Dickensian. His nihilistic streak, resulting in satirical stories of subversive artists, 'nuisances to society', produced even more lively work than his socialism. Some of his stories were translated in *The Bailiff Yerney and his Rights* (tr. S. Yeras and H. C. Sewell Grant, 1946). Cankar also wrote plays, some of which had great success. He died after falling down a staircase in Vienna.

*

The major Croatian poet of the nineteenth century was Petar Preradović (1818–1872); no poetry of the quality of his was seen until SILVIJE STRAHIMIR KRANJČEVIĆ (1865–1908) began publishing in the Eighties. Kranjčević had gone to Rome to train for the priesthood, but did not like what he saw there and returned to Zagreb; he became a teacher and then an inspector of schools. His poetry is fiercely radical and atheistic (the tragedy of Christ lies not in his crucifixion but in the vanity of his faith); its language is lyrical and original. Persecuted by the Church for his rejection of it, and even suspended from teaching for a time, Kranjčević represents the transition from nineteenth- to twentieth-century thinking in Croatian poetry: his rebellion is partly Nietzschean; and the intellectual depth of his nihilism is impressive. (AMYP) The Croatian VLADIMIR VIDRIĆ (1875–1909) was the first *fin de siècle* poet of Yugoslavia. He spoke much of his languid poetry, which contrasted beauty with death, aloud in salons, and was for a time a well-known literary figure in Zagreb. (AMYP)

VLADIMIR NAZOR (1876–1949), who joined Tito's partisans at the age of sixty-six, was regarded as the chief Croatian lyric poet before and immediately after the Second World War. His subject matter is Slav legend; but he interfuses the present with its spirit in a sparklingly traditional and attractive verse. His last and finest novel, *Father Loda* (1946), is set in Dalmatia, where he was born. (AMYP) AUGUSTIN UJEVIĆ (1891–1953) offers a complete contrast. He is an independent, standing outside all movements—and yet consummately Croatian in his manner. He lived in Paris during the years of the First World War, and absorbed the influences of Nerval and Verlaine. He is as effective as Nazor in his own way, which is to reject life absolutely for art. His total disillusion results in a rather thinly textured poetry; but it is often of great verbal beauty. (AMYP)

The outstanding Serbian poet, although limited in scope (like Ujević) by his deliberate rejection of life in favour of art, was the diplomat JOVAN DUČIĆ (1871–1943), who died in Indiana, whither he had emigrated. He adapted French symbolism to Serbian poetry. Undoubtedly he brought a new perfection of form into Serbian poetry, but often at the expense of a suppression of his own vitality. However, there is some release of this in his patriotic poetry and in the posthumous *Lyric Poems* (1943). (AMYP) MILAN RAKIĆ (1876–1938), also a diplomat, was equally influenced by French models—but wrote less (only about fifty poems) and has a warmer tone. Like Dučić he is essentially an 'early' modernist, and his poetry remains rooted in symbolist pessimism. (AMYP)

Where Dučić and Rakić were learned symbolists, SIMA PANDUROVIĆ (1883–1960) and VLADISLAV PETKOVIĆ-DIS (1880–1917), whose life was cut short by accidental drowning, were more shrill, more obviously modernist, and perhaps less innately so. Nevertheless, there has been an increased interest in their work since the Second World War. Petković-Dis was mostly self-taught. He was influenced by Verlaine and the French decadents, but his poetry is more personal than fundamentally pessimistic, even in his first book, *Drowned Souls* (1911). Pandurović was an altogether more strident personality, and became an over-bitter polemicist. His work was collected in *The Great Room of Youth* (1955). (Both AMYP)

MOMČILO NASTASIJEVIĆ (1894–1938), an isolated figure in his lifetime, has now become an important influence. He employed traditional forms, but experimented radically within them. To express his mystical Slav philosophy he used the language and rhythms of folk-lore and popular poetry; the poems of *The Unknown* (1927) and *The Five Musical Circles* (1932) are often so highly compressed, however, that they are impenetrable. He enjoyed one success: with his play, *Lord Malden's Daughter* (1934). ALEKSANDAR VUČO (1897) was a modernist more acceptable to the intelligentsia. A communist, he was influenced by surrealism (q.v.). Since the Second World War he has turned to writing novels, including *The Holidays* (1954; tr. A. Brown, 1959). OSKAR DAVIČO (1909) is another communist who wrote surrealist poetry between the wars and then turned to the novel after 1945. His fiction, better than his poetry, deals intelligently with the difficulties of establishing socialism—and in a way that would be unthinkable in any other European communist country. The novel *The Poem* (1952) was translated by Alec Brown in 1959.

The one outstanding Slovene poet of the pre-war period was OTON ŽUPANČIČ (1878–1949), who became director of the national theatre of Ljubljana. He achieved an international reputation despite the fact that Slovene literature is limited to a readership of less than two million people. Much of his poetry has been translated into French and German; he himself introduced Shakespeare and Molière into his country in competent translations. His first collection, *Cup of Intoxication* (1899), was over-influenced by French symbolist models; but in his later poetry he found his own voice—a voice that was to speak for the national aspirations of his people in an almost uncanny, one might in the circumstances say 'Churchillian', manner. This is explainable only in the context of the history of Yugoslavia, which between the wars was wretchedly ruled by selfish and inept governments. After the liberation he was regarded as a national hero. His poetry is more important for its linguistic clarity and lack of affectation than for its poetic content; but he was a great historical figure.

*

It was the Serbian Ivo Andrić (q.v.) who received the only Nobel Prize for Literature yet won by a Yugoslav; it might well, and perhaps with equal justice, have gone to the Croatian Marxist writer MIROSLAV KRLEŽA (1893), more versatile and not less profound than Andrić. His plays, such as the cycle on the Glembaj family, *The Glembays* (q.v.), are perhaps his most important work; but he has also written major fiction. A dedicated communist, it is significant that he has consistently attacked the narrowness of socialist realism (q.v.). His *Collected Works* needed thirty-six volumes when they were assembled in 1945; since then he has added to them. Krleža's starting-points were his love of European culture and his hatred of the decaying Austrian empire under which he was born. His savage satirical novel *The Croat God Mars* (1922), dealing with the useless slaughter of Croatians enlisted to fight for Austria, is one of the best war books. *The Return of Philip Latinovitz* (1932; tr. Z. G. Depolo, 1959) deals fictionally with his own and other Croatian writers' chief problem in the inter-war period: how to retain creative freedom in the deadly and corrupt world of a dictatorial monarchy—which was Serbian, cared nothing for Croats, and had hived off ninety-eight per cent of the country's main wealth to foreign ownership. Krleža's poetry, less original, is distinctly modernist in style. He remains the great old man of Croatian letters.

A late starter in literature, VLADAN DESNICA (1905) published nothing until he was forty-seven. He combines satire, humour and psychological insight in the tradition of Matavulj (q.v.); he has also learned from his fellow Dalmatian DINKO ŠIMUNOVIĆ (1873–1933), one of the earliest writers to apply a modern psychological attitude to regional material, and most famous for his short stories and the novel *The Vinčić Family* (1923). For sentiment towards his characters, however, Desnica substitutes an amused and gentle cynicism. He has written a play: *Jacob's Ladder* (1959). His best known novel is *The Springs of Ivan Galeb* (1957). (NWY) An interesting contrast to Desnica's treatment of modern society is to be found in the fiction of RANKO MARINKOVIĆ (1913), especially his fine study of a Dalmatian coastal town in the late Thirties, *The Cyclops* (1966). The two writers take similar attitudes, but the texture of Marinković's prose is denser—and is sometimes over-affected. His sarcasm, too, is more clearly in evidence. (NWY) MIRKO BOŽIĆ (1919) uses more conventional techniques, but is no less effective. *The Kurlans* (1952) is a highly-coloured, neo-naturalist story of a peasant family living on Božić's native Dalmatian coast. There is nothing better in post-war Yugoslav literature on its subject. He has also written plays.

The Serbian novelist IVO ANDRIĆ (1892), always a Yugoslav nationalist, was Yugoslav ambassador to Berlin in 1940. He spent the First World War in an internment camp on account of his politics. He won the Nobel Prize in 1961. He is essentially an epic novelist, and his main themes are man's isolation and feelings of insignificance before the huge panorama of history—which Andrić invests with a fabulous magnificence. Much of his fiction is set in Bosnia under the Turks. His early collections of prose poems *Ex Ponto* (1918) and *Restlessness* (1919) embody his subsequent attitude: man's is a tragic destiny: he is condemned to fear—of war, natural disaster, extinction; but Andrić simultaneously affirms the grandeur of history. His best novels are: *Bosnian Story* (1945; tr. K. Johnstone, 1958; *Bosnian Chronicle*, J. Hitrec, 1963), *The Bridge on the Drina* (1945; tr. L. Edwards, 1959) and *The Woman from Sarajevo* (1945; tr. J. Hitrec, 1965). He wrote all these during the Second World War, in occupied Belgrade. *Bosnian Story* is set in Napoleonic times. *The Bridge on the Drina*, majestically incorporating the metaphor of the bridge between past and present, and between east and west, that is to be found in his early work, is a survey of the little Bosnian town of Višegrad from the time of the building of its first bridge (1516) until the First World War. Andrić is a tough and poetic writer; one of the few who can write so intensively of a region that it attains truly universal significance. Despite his philosophical opinion of man's position in the universe, he evokes everyday things with vividness and sympathy. (AMYP)

DUSAN MATIĆ (1898) graduated from leading poetic surrealist between wars to post-war novelist. His fiction is superior to his poetry, which is, however, stylistically distinguished. *The Die is Cast* (1957) impressively demonstrates how capitalist greed made the communist victory inevitable. The Bosnian BRANKO ĆOPIĆ (1915) has achieved enormous popularity in Yugoslavia since the war. He is a prolific writer, of unusually even quality; his best book is *The Gap* (1952), a remarkably objective account of the winning-over, by Tito's partisans, of the Bosnian peasants. This could never have appeared anywhere in the Russian communist empire, for its portraits of certain partisan leaders are too un-flattering. Ćopić has written many children's books.

DOBRICA ĆOSIĆ (1921) is an important example of how much better a competent, intelligent—if not major—novelist will work under conditions of comparative political freedom. Ćosić's approach is realist and communist; but his novel of the war, *Far is the Sun* (1951), is what it is claimed to be—a classic—because of its truthfulness. The long *Divisions* (1961–3) is a remarkably sympathetic account of the Četnik movement (its leader, Mihailović, was executed after the Second World War for his cooperation with the Nazis). Ćosić is currently experimenting in more self-consciously modernist modes. (NWY)

RADOMIR KONSTANTINOVIĆ (1928) is only obliquely concerned with politics. His philosophy, expressed in *Pentagram* (1966), is akin to Camus': he sees man as trapped between the achievement of individual freedom and the necessity of political responsibility, that is, between solipsism and corruption. *Exitus* (1960) was translated by E. D. Goy in 1966. (NWY) MIODRAG BULATOVIĆ (1930) has built up an international reputation. His raw primitivism may be explained by the fact that he grew up in acute poverty, and did not read a book until he was sixteen. His theme is the increasing violence of a world in which human beings must, nevertheless, realize themselves. *The Red Cockerel* (1961; tr. E. D. Goy, 1962) revealed him as one of the most original young novelists in Europe; *Hero on a Donkey* (1965; tr. E. D. Goy, 1966) confirmed his stature. This successfully combines a savagely satirical and humorous picture of a Montenegrin town occupied by unheroic Italians, with a more symbolic theme, embodied in Gruban Malic, the hero of the title. Bulatović brilliantly justifies his theme: 'War is pornography'. (NWY)

*

Early in the century the Croatian poet and critic ANTUN GUSTAV MATOŠ (1873–1914) returned from Paris to his own country. Although not himself a very important poet, he had an important influence on Yugoslav poetry, since his ideas of symbolism were more programmatic than those of the Serbians

Dučić and Rakić (qq.v.), both of whom employed what they had absorbed from French poetry for their own purposes. (AMYP) Matoš' chief disciple was the short-lived ANTUN BRANKO ŠIMIĆ (1898–1925), who wrote in free verse— *Transfigurations* (1925)—and opened the way for new experiments. (AMYP) DRAGUTIN TADIJANOVIĆ (1905) uses a very free verse to express notions of man's essential loneliness. (AMYP) JURE KAŠTELAN (1919) is the leading younger Croatian poet. A scholar of European literature and a noted translator, he began with more or less conventional poetry on the themes of the war and the establishment of a new order. Then he turned to symbolism; his later poetry, collected in *A Few Stones and Many Dreams* (1957) and *Miracle and Death* (1964), combines tenderness with menace. (NWY)

The leading Slovene poet between the wars was EDVARD KOCBEK (1904), a Catholic expressionist to whom such post-war Slovene modernists as JOŽE UDOVIČ (1912) and KAJETAN KOVIČ (1931) looked after 1945. Contemporary Slovene poetry is the subject of an issue of *Modern Poetry in Translation* (8, 1970).

The best known post-war Yugoslav poet is the Serbian VASCO POPA (1922), a selection of whose work has appeared in English (*Selected Poems*, tr. A. Pennington, 1969). Popa's master is Nastasijevič (q.v.), whose importance is thus thrown into relief. He is surrealist and hermetic, alternating between playfulness and grim seriousness. He is not pretentious, but may sometimes seem so in English translation. His poems resemble so many menacing signals of despair in an empty universe, and can be murderous in their evocation of human cruelty:

> We danced the sun dance
> Around the lime in the midst of the heart.

He is one of the most original of European modernists, though too high claims have been made for his essentially minor poetry. (AMYP; NWY)

*

The leading Croatian dramatist of the earlier period was IVO VOJNOVIĆ (1857–1929), who was also a novelist and poet. In his early novels he learnt from Flaubert; later from Ibsen (q.v.)—and after him, from Pirandello (q.v.). He knew European literature well. *The Ragusa Trilogy* (1902), a panorama of Yugoslav history presented in three short plays, is perhaps his finest work. He dominated the Yugoslav stage for the first quarter of this century. JOSIP KOSOR (1879–1961) began as a novelist of Dalmatian peasant life, but graduated into a naturalist dramatist of some power. *Passion's Furnace* (1912; tr. F. S. Copeland, 1917) is one of the most powerful and unpatronizing of all European plays about peasantry. Other plays, including *Reconciliation* (1913; tr. J. M. Duddington) were translated and were successful outside Yugoslavia. Krleža's (q.v.) *The Glembays* (1930–2), in the tradition of Ibsen, was a brilliant trilogy on the decline of a wealthy Croatian family. MARIJAN MATKOVIĆ (1915) followed in Krleža's footsteps, but has used more modern techniques. His trilogy *The Gods Also Suffer* (1958–61) is a subtle examination of the 'personality cult'.

Select Bibliography

by the late F. Seymour-Smith

Reference books and other standard sources of literary information; with a selection of national historical and critical surveys, excluding monographs on individual authors (other than series) and anthologies.

Imprint: the place of publication other than London is stated, followed by the date of the last edition traced up to 1971. *OUP* = Oxford University Press, and includes departmental Oxford imprints such as Clarendon Press and the London OUP. But Oxford books originating outside Britain, e.g. Australia, New York, are so indicated. *CUP* = Cambridge University Press.

GENERAL AND EUROPEAN

Baker, Ernest A.: A Guide to the Best Fiction. *Routledge*, 1932.

Beer, Johannes: Der Romanführer. 14 vols. *Stuttgart, Anton Hiersemann*, 1950–69.

Benét, William Rose: The Reader's Encyclopaedia. *Harrap*, 1955.

Bompiani, Valentino: Dizionario letterario Bompiani delle opere e dei personaggi di tutti i tempi e di tutte le letterature. 9 volumes (including index volume). *Milan, Bompiani*, 1947–50. *Appendice.* 2 vols. 1964–6.

Chambers's Biographical Dictionary. *Chambers*, 1969.

Church, Margaret: Time and Reality: studies in contemporary fiction. *North Carolina;* OUP, 1963.

Contemporary Authors: an international bio-bibliographical guide. *In progress. Detroit, Gale,* 1962.

Courtney, W. F. (Editor): The Reader's Adviser. 2 vols. (Vol. 1: Literature). *New York, Bowker,* 1968–71.

Einsiedel, Wolfgang: Die Literaturen der Welt in ihrer mündlichen und schriftlichen Uberlieferung. *Zurich, Kindler,* 1964.

Ellmann, Richard and Charles Feidelson (Editors): The Modern Tradition: backgrounds of modern literature. *New York,* OUP, 1965.

Esslin, Martin: The Theatre of the Absurd. *Penguin Books,* 1968.

Fleischmann, Wolfgang B. (Editor): Encyclopaedia of World Literature in the Twentieth Century. 3 vols. *New York, Frederick Ungar,* 1967–71. (An enlarged and updated edition of Lexicon der Weltliteratur im 20 Jahrhundert. *Infra.*)

Ford, Ford Madox: The March of Literature. *Allen and Unwin,* 1939.

Frauwallner, E. and others (Editors): Die Welt Literatur. 3 vols. *Vienna,* 1951–4. *Supplement* (A–F), 1968.

Freedman, Ralph: The Lyrical Novel: studies in Hermann Hesse, André Gide and Virginia Woolf. *Princeton;* OUP, 1963.

Grigson, Geoffrey (Editor): The Concise Encyclopaedia of Modern World Literature. *Hutchinson,* 1970.

Hargreaves-Mawdsley, W. N.: Everyman's Dictionary of European Writers. *Dent,* 1968.

Harward, Timothy B. (Editor): European Patterns: contemporary patterns in European writing. *Dublin, Dolmen Press;* OUP, 1963.

Hoppé, A. J.: The Reader's Guide to Everyman's Library. *Dent,* 1971.

Josipovici, Gabriel: The World and the Book: a study of the modern novel. *Macmillan,* 1971.

Kearney, E. I. and L. S. Fitzgerald: The Continental Novel: a checklist of criticism in English, 1900–66. *New Jersey, The Scarecrow Press,* 1968.

Keller, Helen: The Reader's Digest of Books. *New York*; and *Allen and Unwin*, 1947.

Kindermann, Heinz and Margarete Dietrich: Lexikon der Weltliteratur. *Vienna, Humboldt*, 1951.

Kindlers Literatur Lexikon. 5 vols. *Zurich, Kindler*, 1965–9. (A–Ra; in progress.) Based on Bompiani *supra*.

Kronenberger, Louis and Emily Morison Beck (Editors): *Atlantic Brief Lives:* a biographical companion to the arts. *Atlantic Monthly Press Book: Boston, Little Brown*, 1971.

Kunitz, Stanley J. and Howard Haycraft: Twentieth Century Authors. *New York, the H. W. Wilson Co.*, 1942. *Supplement*, 1955.

Laird, Charlton: The World Through Literature. *New York*; and *Peter Owen*, 1959.

Lexikon der Weltliteratur im 20 Jahrhundert. 2 vols. *Freiburg, Herder*, 1960–1.

Magnus, Laurie: A Dictionary of European Literature. *Routledge*, 1926.

Melchinger, Siegfried: Drama Zwischen Shaw und Brecht. Translated by George Wellwarth as: *The Concise Encyclopaedia of Modern Drama. New York*; and *Vision Press*, 1966.

Mondadori, Alberto: Dizionario universale della Letteratura contemporanea. 4 vols. *Verona*, 1959–62.

Mukerjea, S. V.: Disjecta Membra: studies in literature and life. *Bangalore*, 1959.

Murphy, Rosalie (Editor): Contemporary Poets of the English Language. *St. James Press*, 1970.

The Penguin Companion to Literature. 4 vols. *Penguin Books*, 1969–72.

Poggioli, Renato: The Theory of the Avant Garde. *Belknap Press, Harvard University Press*, 1968.

Priestley, J. B.: Literature and Western Man. *Heinemann*, 1960.

Smith, Horatio (Editor): Columbia Dictionary of Modern European Literature. *Columbia University Press*, 1947.

Steinberg, S. H. (Editor): Cassell's Encyclopaedia of Literature. *Cassell*, 1953.

Studies in Modern European Literature and Thought Series. *Bowes and Bowes* (*The Bodley Head*) and *Yale University Press*, 1952 . . .

Van Tieghem, Philippe and Pierre Josserand: Dictionnaire des Littératures. 3 vols. *Paris, Presses Universitaires de France*, 1968.

Ward, A. C.: Longman Companion to Twentieth Century Literature. *Longman*, 1970.

Wellwarth, George E.: The Theatre of Protest and Paradox: developments in the Avant Garde drama. *New York*; and *MacGibbon and Kee*, 1965.

West, Paul: The Modern Novel. *Hutchinson*, 1965.

Writers and Critics Series (British, European and American). *Oliver and Boyd*, 1960 . . .

AFRICAN AND CARIBBEAN

Cartey, Wilfred: Whispers from a Continent: the literature of contemporary Black Africa. *Heinemann*, 1971.

Coulthard, G. R.: Race and Colour in Caribbean Literature. *OUP*, 1962.

Jahn, Janheinz: A History of Neo-African Literature. *Faber*, 1966.

James, Louis (Editor): The Islands in Between: essays in West Indian Literature. *OUP*, 1968.

King, Bruce (Editor): Introduction to Nigerian Literature. *Evans* (in association with the University of Lagos), 1971.

Moore, Gerald: Seven African Writers. *OUP*, 1962.

Ramchand, Kenneth: The West Indian Novel and its Background. *Faber*, 1970.

Ramsaran, J. A.: New approaches to African Literature: a guide to Negro-African writing, and related studies. *Ibadan University Press*, 1965.

Roscoe, Adrian A.: Mother is Gold: a study in West African Literature. *Cambridge University Press*, 1971.

Tibble, Anne: African-English Literature. *New York*; and *Peter Owen*, 1965.

Wauthier, Claude: The Literature and Thought of Modern Africa. *Pall Mall Press*, 1966.

Zell, Hans M. and Helene Silver (Editors): A Reader's Guide to African Literature. *Heinemann Educational Books*, 1971.

ALBANIAN

Mann, Stuart E.: Albanian Literature: an outline of prose, poetry and drama. *Bernard Quaritch*, 1955.

AMERICAN (*United States of America*)

Beach, J. W.: American Fiction, 1920–40. *New York, Macmillan*, 1942.

Bradbury, Malcolm and David Palmer (Editors): The American Novel in the Nineteen Twenties. (Stratford-upon-Avon Studies, 13). *Edward Arnold*, 1971.

Browning, D. C.: A Dictionary of Literary Biography: English and American. *Dent*, 1960.

Burke, W. J. and W. D. Howe: American Authors and Books, revised by Irving and Anne D. Weiss. *New York, Crown Publishers*, 1971.

Dodsworth, Martin (Editor): The Survival of Poetry: a contemporary survey by Donald Davie and others. *Faber*, 1970.

Freedman, Morris: American Drama in Social Context. *Southern Illinois University Press*, 1971.

Gerstenberger, Donna and George Hendrick: The American Novel, 1789–1959: a check list of twentieth-century criticism. *Chicago, Swallow Press*, 1961.

Gregory, Horace V. and Marya Zaturenskay: A History of American Poetry, 1900–40. *New York, Harcourt Brace*, 1967.

Guttmann, Allen: The Jewish Writer in America: assimilation and the crisis of identity. *New York; OUP*, 1971.

Handy, William J.: Modern Fiction: a formalist approach. *Southern Illinois University Press*, 1971.

Hart, James D.: The Oxford Companion to American Literature. *OUP*, 1965.

Herzberg, Max J. and others: The Reader's Encyclopaedia of American Literature. *New York, Crowell;* and *Methuen*, 1963.

Jones, Howard Mumford: Belief and Disbelief in American Literature. *University of Chicago Press*, 1969.

Lutwack, Leonard: Heroic Fiction: the epic tradition and American novels of the twentieth century. *Southern Illinois University Press*, 1971.

McCormick, John: American Literature, 1919–32: a comparative history. *New York*; and *Routledge*, 1971.

Maxwell, D. E. S.: American Fiction: the intellectual background. *Columbia University Press;* and *Routledge*, 1963.

O'Connor, William Van (Editor): Seven Modern American Novelists. *University of Minnesota; OUP*, 1964.

Pamphlets on American Writers: series. *University of Minnesota: OUP*, 1959– in progress.

Rosenthal, Macha L.: The Modern Poets: a critical introduction. *New York; OUP*, 1960.

Rosenthal, Macha L.: The New Poets: British and American poetry since World War II. *New York; OUP*, 1967.

Spender, Stephen and Donald Hall (Editors): The Concise Encyclopaedia of English and American Poets and Poetry. *Hutchinson*, 1970.

Spiller, Robert E., W. Thorp, T. H. Johnson, and H. S. Canby (Editors): Literary History of the United States. 3 vols.; Vol. 4: *Bibliography supplement. New York, Macmillan*, 1948; Vol. 4, 1959.

Tanner, Tony: American Fiction, 1950–1970. *Jonathan Cape*, 1971.

Thorp, Willard: American Writing in the Twentieth Century. *Harvard; OUP*, 1960.

Turner, Darwin T.: In a Minor Chord: three Afro-American writers and their search for identity. *Southern Illinois University Press*, 1971.

Unger, Leonard (Editor): Seven Modern American Poets: an introduction. *University of Minnesota; OUP*, 1967.

Wager, Willis: American Literature: a world view. *University of London Press*, 1961.

ARABIC

Gibbs, Sir H. A. R.: Arabic Literature. *OUP*, 1963.

Haywood, John A.: Modern Arabic Literature, 1800–1970. *Lund Humphries*, 1971.

Nicholson, R. A.: A Literary History of the Arabs. *CUP*, 1930.

Pearson, James Douglas (Editor): Index Islamicus; with Supplements: catalogue of articles on Islamic subjects in periodicals and other collective publications. *CUP*, 1906–67.

AUSTRALIAN

Argyle, Barry: An Introduction to the Australian Novel, 1830–1930. *OUP*, 1971.

Green, H. M.: A History of Australian Literature. 2 vols. *Sydney, Angus and Robertson*, 1961.

Keirnan, Brian: Images of Society and Nature; seven essays on Australian novels. *Melbourne; OUP*, 1971.

Miller, E. Morris: Australian Literature from its Beginning: a bibliography, edited by F. T. Macartney. *Angus and Robertson*, 1956.

Semmler, Clement: Twentieth Century Australian Literary Criticism. *Melbourne; OUP*, 1967.

Wilkes, G. A. and J. C. Reid: Australia and New Zealand (*The Literatures of the British Commonwealth* series). *Rider College; The Pennsylvania State University Press*, 1970.

BRITISH

(*English; Irish; Scottish and Welsh*)

Annals of English Literature, 1475–1950. *OUP*, 1961.

Boyd, Ernest A.: Ireland's Literary Renaissance; with a bibliography. *Dublin*, 1922; *Grant Richards*, 1923.

British Book News: 1940 to date. Published monthly by The British Council.

Browning, D. C.: A Dictionary of Literary Biography: English and American. *Dent*, 1960.

Burgess, Anthony: The Novel Now: a student's guide to contemporary fiction. *Faber*, 1971.

Clarke, Austin: Poetry in Modern Ireland. *Dublin, Three Candles*, 1951.

Dodsworth, Martin (Editor): The Survival of Poetry: a contemporary survey by Donald Davie and others. *Faber*, 1970.

Ellis-Fermor, Una: The Irish Dramatic Movement. *Methuen*, 1939.

Fletcher, John: New Directions in Literature: critical approaches. *Calder and Boyars*, 1968.

Ford, Boris (Editor): The Pelican Guide to English Literature: Vol. 7: The Modern Age. *Penguin Books*, 1964.

Gwynn, Stephen: Irish Literature and Drama. *Nelson*, 1936.

Harvey, Sir Paul: The Oxford Companion to English Literature, revised by Dorothy Eagle. *OUP*, 1967.

Myers, Robin: A Dictionary of Literature in the English Language: from Chaucer to 1940. 2 vols. *Pergamon Press*, 1970.

Press, John: Rule and Energy: trends in British poetry since the Second World War. *OUP*, 1963.

Rosenthal, Macha L.: The Modern Poets: a critical introduction. *New York, OUP*, 1960.

Rosenthal, Macha L.: The New Poets: British and American poetry since World War II. *New York, OUP*, 1967.

Schorer, Mark (Editor): Modern British Fiction. *New York, OUP*, 1961.

Sisson, C. H.: English Poetry, 1900–50: an assessment. *Hart-Davis*, 1971.

Spender, Stephen and Donald Hall (Editors): The Concise Encyclopaedia of English and American Poets and Poetry. *Hutchinson*, 1970.

Stewart, J. I. M.: Eight Modern Writers: Vol. 12 of *The Oxford History of English Literature. OUP*, 1963.

Watson, George (Editor): The Concise Cambridge Bibliography of English Literature 600–1950. *CUP*, 1958.

Writers and Their Work: a series of monographs in paperback on notable British writers from Chaucer to living authors of the twentieth century published as supplements to *British Book News* (*supra*) by Longman.

BULGARIAN

Hateau, Georges: Panorama de la littérature bulgare contemporaine. *Paris*, 1937.

Manning, Clarence A. and Roman Smal-Stocki: The History of Modern Bulgarian Literature. *New York, Bookman Associates*, 1960.

CANADIAN

Brown, Edward K.: On Canadian Poetry. *Toronto, The Ryerson Press*, 1944.

Brunet, Berthelot: Histoire de la littérature canadienne-française. *Montreal, Editions de l'arbre*, 1946.

Klinck, Carl F. (Editor): Literary History of Canada: Canadian literature in English. *University of Toronto Press. OUP*, 1965.

Pacey, Desmond: Creative Writing in Canada: a short history of English-Canadian Literature. *Toronto, The Ryerson Press*, 1961.

Rhodenizer, Vernon B.: Handbook of Canadian Literature. *Ottawa*, 1930.

Story, Norah: The Oxford Companion to Canadian History and Literature. *OUP*, 1967.

Tougas, Gérard: Histoire de la littérature canadienne-française. *Paris, Presses Universitaires de France*, 1960.

Watters, Reginald E.: A Check List of Canadian Literature and Background Materials, 1628–1950. *University of Toronto Press. OUP*, 1959.

CHINESE

Birch, Cyril (Editor): Chinese Communist Literature. *New York, Frederick A. Praeger*, 1963.

Ch'en Shou-yi: Chinese Literature. *New York, Ronald Press*, 1961.

Hsia, C. T.: A History of Modern Chinese Fiction. *Yale University Press*, 1971.

Scott, A. C.: Literature and the Arts in

Twentieth Century China. *Allen and Unwin*, 1965.

CZECHOSLOVAKIAN

French, Alfred: The Poets of Prague: Czech poetry between the wars. *OUP*, 1969.

Selver, Paul: Czechoslovak Literature: an outline. *Allen and Unwin*, 1942.

DUTCH

(Dutch; Flemish)

Backer, Franz de: Contemporary Flemish Literature. *Flemish PEN Centre, Bruxelles*, 1934

Ridder, André de: La Littérature flamande contemporaine: 1890–1923. *Paris, Edouard Champion*, 1923.

Tielrooy, Johannes B.: Panorama de la littérature hollandaise contemporaine. *Paris*, 1938.

Weevers, Theodor: The Poetry of the Netherlands in its European Context: 1170–1930. *OUP*, 1960.

EASTERN MINOR LITERATURES

Lang, D. M. (Editor): Guide to Eastern Literatures. *Weidenfeld and Nicolson*, 1971.

Pearson, James Douglas (Editor): Index Islamicus: catalogue of articles on Islamic subjects in periodicals and other collective publications. Supplements. *CUP*, 1906–65.

Rypka, Jan (Editor): History of Iranian Literature: Persian Literature of the twentieth century, by Vera Kubicková, pp. 353–418. *Dordrecht, Holland, D. Reidel*, 1968.

FINNISH

Havu, Ilmari: Finland's Literature. *Stockholm*, 1958.

Perret, Jean-Louis: Panorama de la littérature contemporaine de Finlande. *Paris, Éditions du Sagittaire*, 1936.

FRENCH AND BELGIAN

Adereth, Maxwell: Commitment in Modern French Literature. *Victor Gollancz*, 1967.

Alden, Douglas W. and others (Editors): Bibliography of Critical and Biographical References for the Study of Contemporary French Literature: books and articles. *New York, French Institute*, 1949–69: *in progress.*

Austin, L. J., Garnet Rees and Eugène Vinever: Studies in Modern French Literature: presented to P. Mansell Jones by pupils, colleagues and friends.

Manchester University Press, 1961.

Benn, T. V.: Current Publications on Twentieth Century French Literature. *ASLIB*, 1953.

Braun, Sydney D.: Dictionary of French Literature. *New York*; and *Peter Owen*, 1959.

Charlier, Gustave and Joseph Hanse: Histoire illustré des lettres françaises de Belgique. *Bruxelles, La Renaissance du livre*, 1958.

Clouard, Henri: Histoire de la littérature française du symbolisme à nos jours, 1885–1960. 2 vols. *Paris*, 1948–62.

Clouard, Henri and Robert Leggewie (Editors): French Writers of Today. *New York, OUP*, 1965.

Cocking, J. M.: Three Studies in Modern French Literature. *Yale University Press*, 1960.

Cruickshank, John (Editor): The Novelist as Philosopher: studies in French fiction, 1935–60. *OUP*, 1962.

Fletcher, John: New Directions in Literature: critical approaches. *Calder and Boyars*, 1968.

Girard, Marcel: Guide illustré de la littérature française moderne de 1918 à nos jours. *Paris*, 1962.

Guicharnaud, Jacques: Modern French Theatre: from Giradoux to Genet. *Yale University Press*, 1967.

Harvey, Sir Paul and J. E. Heseltine: The Oxford Companion to French Literature. *OUP*, 1959.

Lalou, René: Histoire de la littérature française contemporaine: de 1870 à nos jours, with a bibliography of representative works. 2 vols. *Paris*, 1947. (The second edition was translated into English as *Contemporary French Literature, New York*; and *Jonathan Cape*, 1925.)

Lalou, René: Le Roman français depuis 1900. Dixième edition par Georges Versini. *Paris: Que Sais-je, No. 497*, 1966.

Lalou, René: Le Théâtre en France depuis 1900. *Paris: Que Sais-je, No. 461*, 1965.

Mallinson, Vernon: Modern Belgian Literature, 1830–1960. *Heinemann*, 1966.

Peyre, Henri: Contemporary French Literature. *New York, Harper and Row*, 1964.

Peyre, Henri: French Novelists of Today. *New York, OUP*, 1967.

Peyre, Henri: Modern Literature: Vol. 1: The Literature of France. *Princeton Studies, New York, Prentice-Hall*, 1966.

Rousselot, Jean: Dictionnaire de la poésie française contemporaine. *Paris, Larousse*, 1968.

GERMAN

Bithell, Jethro: Modern German Literature, 1880–1950. *Methuen*, 1959.

Closs, August and H. M. Waidson: German Literature in the Twentieth Century (with chapters on novels by H. M. Waidson). *Introductions to German Literature*, Vol. 4. *Barrie and Jenkins*, 1969.

Flores, John: Poetry in East Germany: adjustments, visions and provocations, 1945–70. *New Haven and London, Yale University Press*, 1971.

Forster, Leonard: German Poetry, 1944–8. *Cambridge, Bowes and Bowes—now Bodley Head*, 1949.

Garten, H. F.: Modern German Drama. *Methuen*, 1959.

Hamburger, Michael: From Prophecy to Exorcism. *Longman*, 1965.

Hamburger, Michael: Reason and Energy. *Routledge*, 1957.

Hatfield, Henry: Modern German Literature: the major figures in context. *Edward Arnold*, 1968.

Keith-Smith, Brian: Essays on Contemporary German Literature. *Oswald Wolff*, 1966.

Lange, Victor: Modern German Literature, 1870–1940. *Ithaca, New York*, 1945.

Morgan, Bayard Quincy: A Critical Bibliography of German Literature in English Translation; with supplement, 1928–55. *New Jersey, The Scarecrow Press*, 1965.

Robertson, J. G.: History of German Literature. *Edinburgh, Blackwood*, 1970.

Waidson, H. M.: The Modern German Novel, 1945–65. *University of Hull; OUP*, 1971.

Waterhouse, Gilbert: A Short History of German Literature: third edition with a continuation by H. M. Waidson. *Methuen*, 1959.

GREEK

Hesseling, D. C.: Histoire de la littérature grecque moderne. Translated into French by N. Pernot. *Paris*, 1924.

Trypanis, Constantine A.: Mediaeval and Modern Greek Poetry, with an introduction. *OUP*, 1951.

HUNGARIAN

Gömöri, George: Polish and Hungarian Poetry, 1945 to 1956. *OUP*, 1966.

Jones, D. Mervyn: Five Hungarian Writers. *OUP*, 1966.

Klaniczay, Tibor, József Szander and

Miklós Szabolesi: A History of Hungarian Literature. *Collet's*, 1964.

Reményi, Joseph: Hungarian Writers and Literature. *Rutgers University Press, New Brunswick*, 1964.

Reich, Emil: Hungarian Literature: an historical and critical survey. *Jarrolds*, 1906.

Riedl, Frigyes: A History of Hungarian Literature. *Heinemann*, 1906.

Tezla, Albert: An Introductory Bibliography to the study of Hungarian Literature. *Harvard University Press*, 1964.

INDIAN AND PAKISTANI

Clark, T. W. (Editor): The Novel in India: its birth and development. *Allen and Unwin*, 1970.

Kumarappa, Bharatan (Editor): Indian Literatures of Today: a symposium. *Bombay*, 1945; and *Probsthain*, 1947.

Nagendra, Dr. (Editor): Indian Literature: short critical surveys of twelve major Indian languages and literatures. *Agra*, 1959.

Sadiq, Muhammad: A History of Urdu Literature. *OUP*, 1964.

Suhrawardy, Sháista Akhtar Bänu: A Critical Survey of the Development of the Urdu Novel and Short Story. *Longman*, 1945.

ITALIAN

Donadoni, Eugenio: A History of Italian Literature. Translated by Richard Monges. Vol. 2. *New York;* and *London University Press*, 1969.

Pacifici, Sergio (Editor): from *Verismo* to Experimentalism: essays in the modern Italian novel. *Bloomington, Indiana University Press*, 1969.

Whitfield, J. H. A Short History of Italian Literature. *Penguin Books*, 1960; and *Cassell*, 1962.

JAPANESE

Aston, W. G.: A History of Japanese Literature. *Heinemann*, 1899.

Japanese Literature in European Languages: Section IV (Modern Literature). *Japan P.E.N. Club*, 1961.

Keene, Donald: A History of Japanese Literature. *Secker and Warburg*, 1971.

Keene, Donald: Japanese Literature. *John Murray*, 1953.

Keene, Donald: Landscapes and Portraits: appreciations of Japanese culture. *Secker and Warburg*, 1971.

Keene, Donald: Modern Japanese Literature. *Thames and Hudson*, 1957.

Kokusai bunka shinkokai, Tokyo: Introduction to Contemporary Japanese Literature. *Tokyo, The Society for International Cultural Relations*, 1939.

Kunitomo, Tadao: Japanese Literature since 1868. *Tokyo, The Hokuseido Press*, 1938.

Martins Janeira, A.: Japanese and Western Literature. *Tokyo Tuttle*, 1970.

McClellan, Edwin: Two Japanese Novelists: Soseki and Toson. *University of Chicago Press*, 1969.

Miner, Earl: The Japanese Tradition in British and American Literature. *Princeton University Press*, 1958.

JEWISH

Halkin, Simon: Modern Hebrew Literature: trends and values. *New York, Schocken Books*, 1950.

Klausner, Joseph: A History of Modern Hebrew Literature, 1785–1930. Translated from the Hebrew by H. Danby, edited by L. Simon. *London*, 1932.

Roback, Abraham A.: The Story of Yiddish Literature. *New York, Yiddish Scientific Institute*, 1940.

Wallenrod, Reuben: The Literature of Modern Israel. *New York, Abelard Schumann*, 1956.

LATIN AMERICAN

Craig, G. Dundas: The Modernist Trend in Spanish American Poetry. *University of California Press*; and *CUP*, 1934.

Dos Santos Coutinho, Afrânio: Introductory Essays to *A literatura no Brasil* translated from the Portuguese by Gregory Rabassa as: *An Introduction to Literature in Brazil. New York, Institute of Latin American Studies; Columbia University Press*, 1969.

Ellison, Fred P. Brazil's New Novel: four north-eastern masters. *University of California Press*; and *CUP*, 1954.

Franco, Jean: An Introduction to Spanish-American Literature. *CUP*, 1969.

Franco, Jean: The Modern Culture of Latin America. *Penguin Books*, 1970.

Imbert, Enrique Anderson: Spanish-American Literature: a history. Translated from the Spanish by John V. Falconieri. *Detroit, Wayne State University Press*, 1963.

Putnam, Samuel: Marvelous Journey: a survey of four centuries of Brazilian writing. *New York, Alfred A. Knopf*, 1948.

Sainz de Robles, Federico Carlos: Ensayo de un Diccionario de la Literatura: Vol. 2: Escritores Espanoles e Hispano Americanos. *Madrid*, 1949.

NEW ZEALAND

McCormick, Eric Hall: New Zealand Literature. *OUP*, 1959.

Smith, Elizabeth M.: A History of New Zealand Fiction: from 1862 to the present time. *Wellington, New Zealand, A. H. and A. W. Reed*, 1939.

Wilkes, G. A. and J. C. Reid: Australia and New Zealand (*The Literatures of the British Commonwealth* series). *Rider College. The Pennsylvania State University Press*, 1970.

POLISH

Dyboski, Roman: Modern Polish Literature: a course of lectures. *Humphrey Milford*, 1924.

Gillon, Adam and Ludwik Krzyzanowski: An Introduction to Modern Polish Literature. *Rapp and Whiting*, 1964.

Gömöri, George: Polish and Hungarian Poetry, 1945–56. *OUP*, 1966.

Milosz, Czeslaw: The History of Polish Literature. *New York, Macmillan Co.; and London, Collier-Macmillan*, 1969.

Scherer-Virski, Olga: The Modern Polish Short Story. *New York, The Humanities Press*, 1955.

PORTUGUESE

Bell, Aubrey F. G.: Portuguese Literature. *OUP*, 1970.

RUMANIAN

Munteanu, Basil: Panorama de la littérature roumaine contemporaine. *Paris*, 1938. Translated as: *Modern Rumanian Literature, Bucharest*, 1939.

RUSSIAN

Field, Andrew (Editor): The Complection of Russian Literature. *Allen Lane, The Penguin Press*, 1971.

Hayward, Max and Leopold Labedz (Editors): Literature and Revolution in Soviet Russia, 1917–62: a symposium. *OUP*, 1963.

Kunitz, Joshua: Russian Literature and the Jew: a sociological enquiry into ... literary patterns. *Columbia University Press*, 1929.

Maguire, Robert A.: Red Virgin Soil: Soviet literature in the 1920's. *Princeton: OUP*, 1968.

Phelps, Gilbert: The Russian Novel in English Fiction. *Hutchinson*, 1956.

Poggioli, Renato: The Poets of Russia, 1880–1930. *Harvard Univ. Press*, 1960.

Reavey, George: Soviet Literature Today. *Lindsay Drummond*, 1946.

Simmons, Ernest: Russian Fiction and Soviet Ideology: an introduction to Fedin, Leonov and Sholokhov. *Columbia University Press*, 1958.

Slonim, Marc: Soviet Russian Literature: writers and problems. *New York; OUP*, 1964.

Struve, Glyeb P.: Soviet-Russian Literature, 1917–50. *University of Oklahoma Press*, 1951.

Swayze, Ernest Harold: Political Control of Literature in the USSR, 1946–59. *Harvard; OUP*, 1962.

SCANDINAVIAN
(*Icelandic, Danish, Norwegian, Swedish*)

Beyer, Harald: A History of Norwegian Literature. Translated by Einar Haugen. *New York, The American Scandinavian Foundation, New York University Press*, 1956.

Bredsdorff, Elias: Danish Literature in English Translation. *Copenhagen*, 1960.

Bredsdorff, Elias, Brita Mortensen and Ronald Popperwell: An Introduction to Scandinavian Literature. *CUP*, 1951.

Claudi, Jørgen: Contemporary Danish Authors: with a brief outline of Danish literature. *Det Danske Selskab, Copenhagen*, 1952.

Downs, Brian W.: Modern Norwegian Literature, 1860–1918. *CUP*, 1966.

Einarsson, Stéfan: A History of Icelandic Literature. *Johns Hopkins Press* (for the *American-Scandinavian Foundation*), *Baltimore*, 1957.

Gustafson, Alrik: A History of Swedish Literature. *University of Minnesota; OUP*, 1961.

Gustafson, Alrik: Six Scandinavian Novelists: Lie, Jacobsen, Heidenstam, Selma Lagerlof, Hamsun, Sigrid Undset. *University of Minnesota; OUP*, 1968.

Heepe, Evelyn and Niels Heltberg (Editors): Modern Danish Authors. Translated by Evelyn Heepe. *Copenhagen, Scandinavian Publishing Co.*, 1946.

Kärnell, Karl A.: Svenskt litteraturlexicon. *Lund*, 1964.

Mitchell, P. M.: A Bibliographical Guide to Danish Literature. *Copenhagen*, 1951.

Mitchell, P. M.: A History of Danish Literature. *Copenhagen, Gyldendal*, 1957.

SOUTH AFRICAN

Nathan, Manfred: South African Literature. *Cape Town*, 1925.

SPANISH

Balboutin, José Antonio: Three Spanish Poets: Rosalia de Castro; F. G. Lorca; Antonio Machado. *Alvin Redman*, 1961.

Bleiberg, Germán and Marías Julían: Diccionario de Literatura Española. *Madrid*, 1964.

Brenan, Gerald: The Literature of the Spanish People: from Roman times to the present day. *CUP*, 1953.

Eof, S. H.: The Modern Spanish Novel. *New York University Press;* and *Peter Owen*, 1961.

Fitzmaurice-Kelly, James: A New History of Spanish Literature; with a bibliography by Julia Fitzmaurice-Kelly. *Humphrey Milford*, 1926.

Morris, C. B.: A Generation of Spanish Poets. *CUP*, 1969.

Newmark, Maxim: Dictionary of Spanish Literature. *New York, Philosophical Library*, 1956.

Northup, George Tyler: An Introduction to Spanish Literature. *University of Chicago Press*, 1960.

Sainz de Robles, Federico Carlos: Ensayo de un Diccionario de la Literatura: Vol. 2: Escritores Espanolese e Hispano Americanos. *Madrid*, 1949.

Valbuena Prat, Ángel: Historia de la Literatura Española. Vol. IV. *Barcelona, Editorial* Gustavo Gili, 1953.

TURKISH

Köprülüzade, Mehmed Fuad: Ottoman Turkish Literature (in: *Encyclopaedia of Islam*). *Leyden*, 1913–38.

WESTERN MINOR LITERATURES

Manning, Clarence A.: Ukrainian Literature: studies of the leading authors. *Jersey City, the Ukrainian National Association*, 1944.

Natan, Alex. (Editor): Swiss Men of Letters: twelve literary essays. *Oswald Wolff*, 1970.

Oras, Ants and W. K. Matthews: Estonian Literature in Exile, with a bibliographical index by Bernard Kangro. *Lund, Esthonian PEN Club*, 1967.

YUGOSLAV

Barac, Antun: A History of Yugoslav Literature. Translated by Petar Mijušković: *Belgrade, Committee for Foreign Cultural Relations*, 1955.

Kadić, Ante: Contemporary Croatian Literature. *New York, The Humanities Press*, 1960.

Kadić, Ante: Contemporary Serbian Literature. *New York, The Humanities Press*, 1964.

Index

This index lists names of authors, literary and some other movements and terms, and titles of books—these are given in English only. It should be noted that where a book has been translated, the translator's title may not be an exact or even an approximate rendering of the original.
Bold type indicates a main entry. p=periodical.

Constance Ring (Skram), 1001
Constantinople (Loti), 404
Contact (p), 117
Contemplative Quarry, The (Wickham), 217
Conversation in Sicily (Vittorini), 733
Conversation with My Uncle (Sargeson), 896
Cook, George Cram, 83
Cool Million, A, or the Dismantling of Lemuel
  Pitkin (N. West), 117
Coombes, H., 203, 220
Coonardoo (Prichard), 185
Cooper, William, 202, 296–7
Copeau, Jacques, 438, 507, 511
Copić, Branko, 1132
Copies (Grau), 1072
Coppard, A. E., 276–7
Coppée, François, 413
Copper Breath (Enckell), 1028
Coral, The (Kaiser), 598
Corazzini, Sergio, 748
Cork Street, Next to the Hatter's (P. H. Johnson),
  300
Corner that Held Them, The (S. T. Warner), 283
Cornford, Frances, 225
Corps de Ballet (Guimarães Rosa), 889
Coronado, Carolina, 1075
Coronal (Claudel), 430
Coronation (Donoso), 873
Corporal Wanzi (Brownlee), 1041
Correia, Raimundo, 879
Correia, Romeu, 921
Correspondence (with Mrs. P. Campbell)
  (Shaw), 255
Corridors of Power (Snow), 287
Corruption in the Palace of Justice (Betti), 744
Cortázar, Julio, 865
Corydon (Gide), 431, 432
Cosbuc, Gheorghe, 931
Ćosić, Dobrica, 1132
Cosmicomics (Calvino), 736
Costa i Llobera, Miquel, 1118
Coster, Albert de, 419
'Costumbrismo', 1051
Cotterell, Geoffrey, 1038
Cotter's England (C. Stead), 185
Council of Egypt, The (Sciascia), 737
Count d'Orgel Opens the Ball (Radiguet), 456
Count Öderland (Frisch), 652
Count of Antwerp, The (Hallström), 1026
Count of Charolais, The (Beer-Hofmann), 560
Counter-attack (Sassoon), 243
Countess Kathleen, The (Yeats), 262
Country Doctor, The (Kafka), 621
Country Doctor, The (Trigo), 1057
Country House, The (Galsworthy), 200
Country of Origin, The (Du Perron), 368
Country of Sleep, The (Espino), 390
Country of the Pointed Firs, The (Jewett), 50
Countryman Aguilar (Amorim), 860
Countryside (de Viana), 856
Couperus, Louis, 364–5
Courteline, Georges, 426–7
Courage, James, 897–8
Coward, Noel, 261
Cowards, The (Škvorecký), 358
Cozzens, James Gould, 120
Crack-up, The (F. G. Fitzgerald), 104
Cradle and the Egg, The (Sargeson), 897

Cradle Song (Martínez Siena), 1071
Crane, Hart, 47–8, 75, 150, 152–4
Crane, Stephen, 37–40
Cranes Are Flying, The (film), (Rozov), 964
Crainic, Nichifor, 927–8
Crawford, Cheryl, 89
Crawford, F. Marion, 24
Crawford, Isabella Valancy, 331
Creangă, Ion, 927
Created Legend, The (Sologub), 967
Creation Society (China), 344–5, 346
Creation, The (Yañez), 868
'Creationism', 842, 843
Creative Effort (N. Lindsay), 178–9
Creatures That Once Were Men (Gorky), 938
Credo (Pound), 71
Creeley, Robert, 62, 64, 65, 146, 157, 168–9
Creighton, Anthony, 264
Cremona, Ninu, 381
'Crepuscular Poets', 725 f., 747
Crepuscular (Neruda), 848
Crest on the Silver, The (Grigson), 312
Cretans, The (Prevelakis), 691
Crime, A (Bernanos), 446
Crime of Honour, A (Arpino), 737
Crime of Sylvestre Bonnard, The (France), 407
Crime on Goat Island (Betti), 744
Crime Passionel (Sartre), 481
Criminals, The (Bruckner), 638
Crimson Flowers (Aspazija), 1109
Cripps, Arthur Shearly, 1038
Crises and Wreaths (Sjöberg), 1015
Critical Writings (Joyce), 273
Croat God Mars, The (Krleža), 1131
Croce, Benedetto, 715, 741
Crock of Gold, The (J. Stephens), 228
Crommelynck, Fernando, 519–20
Croquignole (Philippe), 407
Cros, Charles, 467
Crow (T. Hughes), 323
Crown of Shadow (Usigli), 875
Crucible, The (A. Miller), 94
Cruel Town (Beti), 6
Cruelty, Theatre of, 517, 657
Cruz, Eddy Dias da, see Rebelo, Marques
Cruz e Sousa, João da, 880
Cry Ararat! (Page), 334
Cry of Glory (Acevedo Díaz), 854
Cry the Beloved Country (Paton), 1042
Csokor, Theodor, 651
Cuadra, José de la, 862
Cuauhtémoc (Novo), 876
Cubism, 469
Cubist Painters, The (Apollinaire), 469
Cucaña, La (Cela), 1065
Cue for Passion (Rice), 88
Cult of the Self, The (Barrès), 405
Cults (Uppdal), 1003
Cummings, E. E., 78–80
Cunha, Euclydes da, 880
Cunningham, J. V., 155
Cup Full of Poison, A (Vilde), 1104
Cup of Intoxication (Župančič), 1130
Cure of Souls, A (M. Sinclair), 283
Cure Through Aspirin (Walschop), 375
Curnow, Allen, 895
Currey, R. N., 1039
Curtain of Green, A (Welty), 128